Department of Economic and Social Affairs
Département des affaires économiques et sociales

2003

Demographic Yearbook
Annuaire démographique

Fifty-fifth issue/Cinquante-cinquième édition

United Nations/Nations Unies
New York, 2006

The Department of Economic and Social Affairs of the United Nations Secretariat is a vital interface between global policies in the economic, social and environmental spheres and national action. The Department works in three main interlinked areas: (i) it compiles, generates and analyses a wide range of economic, social and environmental data and information on which States Members of the United Nations draw to review common problems and to take stock of policy options; (ii) it facilitates the negotiations of Member States in many intergovernmental bodies on joint courses of action to address ongoing or emerging global challenges; and (iii) it advises interested Governments on the ways and means of translating policy frameworks developed in United Nations conferences and summits into programmes at the country level and, through technical assistance, helps build national capacities.

Le Département des affaires économiques et sociales du Secrétariat de l'Organisation des Nations Unies sert de relais entre les orientations arrêtées au niveau international dans les domaines économiques, sociaux et environnementaux et les politiques exécutées à l'échelon national. Il intervient dans trois grands domaines liés les uns aux autres : i) il compile, produit et analyse une vaste gamme de données et d'éléments d'information sur des questions économiques, sociales et environnementales dont les Etats Membres de l'Organisation se servent pour examiner des problèmes communs et évaluer les options qui s'offrent à eux; ii) il facilite les négociations entre les Etats Membres dans de nombreux organes intergouvernementaux sur les orientations à suivre de façon collective afin de faire face aux problèmes mondiaux existants ou en voie d'apparition; iii) il conseille les gouvernements intéressés sur la façon de transposer les orientations politiques arrêtées à l'occasion des conférences et sommets des Nations Unies en programmes exécutables au niveau national et aide à renforcer les capacités nationales au moyen de programmes d'assistance technique.

NOTE

Symbols of United Nations documents are composed of capital letters combined with figures. Mention of such a symbol indicates a reference to a United Nations document.

The designations used in this publication have been provided by the competent authorities. Those designations and the presentation of material in this publication do not imply the expression of any opinion whatsoever on the part of the Secretariat of the United Nations concerning the legal status of any country, territory, city or area or of its authorities, or concerning the delimitation of its frontiers or boundaries.

Where the designation "country or area" appears in the headings of tables, it covers countries, territories, cities or areas.

NOTE

Les cotes des documents de l'Organisation des Nations Unies se composent de lettres majuscules et de chiffres. La simple mention d'une cote dans un texte signifie qu'il s'agit d'un document de l'Organisation.

Les appellations employées dans cette publication ont été fournies par les autorités compétentes. Ces appellations et la présentation des données qui figurent dans cette publication n'impliquent, de la part du Secrétariat de l'Organisation des Nations Unies, aucune prise de position quant au statut juridique des pays, territoires, villes ou zones, ou de leurs autorités, ni quant au tracé de leurs frontières ou limites.

L'appellation « pays ou zone » figurant dans les titres des rubriques des tableaux désigne des pays, des territoires, des villes ou des zones.

ST/ESA/STAT/SER.R/34

UNITED NATIONS PUBLICATION

Sales No. E/F.06.XIII.1

PUBLICATION DES NATIONS UNIES

Numéro de vente : E/F.06.XIII.1

ISBN 92-1-051097-6

Topics of the Demographic Yearbook series: 1948 - 2003

Sujets des diverses éditions de l'Annuaire démographique: 1948 - 2003

Year Année	Sales No. - Numéro de vente	Issue - Edition	Special topic - Sujet spécial
1948	49.XIII.1	First-Première	General demography-Démographie générale
1949-50	51.XIII.1	Second-Deuxième	Natality statistics-Statistiques de la natalité
1951	52.XIII.1	Third-Trosième	Mortality statistics-Statistiques de la mortalité
1952	53.XIII.1	Fourth-Quatrième	Population distribution-Répartition de la population
1953	54.XIII.1	Fifth-Cinquième	General demography-Démographie générale
1954	55.XIII.1	Sixth-Sixième	Natality statistics -Statistiques de la natalité
1955	56.XIII.1	Seventh-Septième	Population censuses-Recensement de population
1956	57.XIII.1	Eighth-Huitième	Ethnic and economic characteristics of population- Caractéristiques ethniques et économiques de la population
1957	58.XIII.1	Ninth-Neuvième	Mortality statistics- Statistiques de la mortalité
1958	59.XIII.1	Tenth-Dixième	Marriage and divorce statistics- Statistiques de la nuptialitè et de la divortialité
1959	60.XIII.1	Eleventh-Onzième	Natality statistics- Statistiques de la natalité
1960	61.XIII.1	Twelfth-Douzième	Population trends- l' évolution de la population
1961	62.XIII.1	Thirteenth-Treizième	Mortality Statistics- Statistiques de la mortalité
1962	63.XIII.1	Fourteenth-Quatorzième	Population census statistics I- Statistiques des recensements de population I
1963	64.XIII.1	Fifteenth-Quinzième	Population census statistics II- Statistiques des recensements de population II
1964	65.XIII.1	Sixteenth- Seizième	Population census statistics III- Statistiques des recensements de population III
1965	66.XIII.1	Seventeenth- Dix-septième	Natality statistics- Statistiques de la natalité
1966	67.XIII.1	Eighteenth- Dix-huitième	Mortality statistics I- Statistiques de la mortalité I
1967	E/F.68.XIII.1	Nineteenth- Dix-neuvième	Mortality statistics II - Statistiques de la mortalité II
1968	E/F.69.XIII.1	Twentieth-Vingtième	Marriage and divorce statistics-Statistiques de la nuptialité et de la divortialité
1969	E/F.70.XIII.1	Twenty-first- Vingt et unième	Natality statistics-Statistiques de la natalité
1970	E/F.71.XIII.1	Twenty-second- Vingt-deuxième	Population trends-l' évolution de la population
1971	E/F.72.XIII.1	Twenty-third- Vingh-troisième	Population census statistics I- Statistiques de recensements de population I
1972	E/F.73.XIII.1	Twenty-fourth- Vingt-quatrième	Population census statistics II- Statistiques des recensements de population II
1973	E/F.74.XIII.1	Twenty-fifth- Vingt-cinquième	Population census statistics III- Statistiques des recensements de population III
1974	E/F.75.XIII.1	Twenty-sixth- Vingt-sixième	Mortality statistics - Statistiques de la mortalité
1975	E/F.76.XIII.1	Twenty-seventh- Vingt-septième	Natality statistics- Statistiques de la natalité
1976	E/F.77.XIII.1	Twenty-eighth- Vingt-huitième	Marriage and divorce statistics- Statistiques de la nuptialité et de la divortialité
1977	E/F.78.XIII.1	Twenty-ninth- Vingt-neuvième	International Migration Statistics- internationales
1978	E/F.79.XIII.1	Thirtieth-Trentième	General tables- Tableaux de caractère général
1978	E/F.79.XIII.8	Special issue- Edition spéciale	Historical supplement-Supplément rétrospectif
1979	E/F.80.XIII.1	Thirty-first- Trente et unième	Population census statistics- Statistiques des recensements de population
1980	E/F.81.XIII.1	Thirty-second- Trente-deuxième	Mortality statistics- Statistiques de la mortalité
1981	E/F.82.XIII.1	Thirty-third- Trente-troisième	Natality statistics- Statistiques de la natalité
1982	E/F.83.XIII.1	Thirty-fourth-	Marriage and divorce statistics-

Topics of the Demographic Yearbook series: 1948 - 2003

Sujets des diverses éditions de l'Annuaire démographique: 1948 - 2003

Year Année	Sales No. - Numéro de vente	Issue - Edition	Special topic - Sujet spécial
1983	E/F.84.XIII.1	Trente-quatrième Thirty fifth-	Statistiques de la nuptialité et de la divortialité Population census statistics I-
1984	E/F.85.XIII.1	Trente-cinquième Thirty-sixth-	Statistiques des recensements de population I Population census statistics II-
1985	E/F.86.XIII.1	Trente-sixième Thirty-seventh-	Statistiques des recensements de population II Mortality statistics-
1986	E/F.87.XIII.1	Trente-septième Thirty-eightth-	Statistiques de la mortalité Natality statistics-
1987	E/F.88.XIII.1	Trente-Hiutième Thirty-ninth-	Statistiques de la natalité Household composition-
1988	E/F.89.XIII.1	Trente-neuvième Fortieth-	Les éléments du ménage Population census statistics-
1989	E/F.90.XIII.1	Quarantième Forty-first-	Statistiques des recensements de population International Migration Statistics-
1990	E/F.91.XIII.1	Quarante-et-unième Forty-second-	Statistiques des migration internationales Marriage and divorce statistics-
1991	E/F.92.XIII.1	Quarante-deuxième Forty-third-	Statistiques de la nuptialité et de la divortialité General tables-
1991	E/F.92.XIII.8	Quarante-troisième Special issue- Edition spéciale	Tableaux de caractère général Population ageing and the situation of elderly persons- Vieillissement de la population et situation des personnes agées
1992	E/F.94.XIII.1	Forty-forth- Quarante-quatrième	Fertility and mortality statistics- Statistiques de la fecondité et de la mortalité
1993	E/F.95.XIII.1	Forty-fifth- Quarante-cinquième	Population census statistics I- Statistiques des recensements de population I
1994	E/F.96.XIII.1	Forty-sixth- Quarante-sixième	Population census statistics II- Statistiques des recensements de population II
1995	E/F.97.XIII.1	Forty-seventh- Quarante-septième	Household composition-Les éléments du ménage
1996	E/F.98.XIII.1	Forty-eighth- Quarante-hutième	Mortality statistics- Statistiques de la mortalité
1997	E/F.99.XIII.1	Forty-ninth- Quarante-neuvième	General tables- Tableaux de caractère général
1997	E/F.99.XIII.12	Special issue- Edition spéciale (CD)	Historical supplement- Supplément rétrospectif
1998	E/F.00.XIII.1	Fiftieth- Cinquantième	General tables- Tableaux de caractère général
1999	E/F.01.XIII.1	Fifty-first- Cinquante-et-unième	General tables- Tableaux de caractère général
1999	E/F.02.XIII.6	Special issue- Edition spéciale (CD)	Natality Statistics- Statistiques de la natalité
2000	E/F.02.XIII.1	Fifty-second- Cinquante-deuxième	General tables- Tableaux de caractère général
2001	E/F.03.XIII.1	Fifty-third- Cinquante- troisième	General tables- Tableaux de caractère général
2002	E/F.05.XIII.1	Fifty-fourth- Cinquante-quatrième	General tables- Tableaux de caractère général
2003	E/F.06.XIII.1	Fifty-fifth- Cinquante-cinquième	General tables- Tableaux de caractère général

CONTENTS - TABLE DES MATIERES

Explanations of symbols ix   Explication des signes ix

TEXT

TEXTE

INTRODUCTION 1

INTRODUCTION 15

TECHNICAL NOTES ON THE STATISTICAL TABLES

NOTES TECNIQUES SUR LES TABLEAUX STATISTIQUES

1. General Remarks 2

1. Remarque d'ordre général 16

2. Geographical aspects 2

2. Considérations géographiques 16

3. Population 3

3. Population 18

4. Vital statistics 7

4. Statistiques de l'état civil 21

TABLES PUBLISHED ANNUALLY

TABLEAUX PUBLIES CHAQUE ANNEE

Table   Page   Tableaux   Page

Demographic Yearbook 2003 synoptic table 31

Tableau synoptique de l'Annuaire démographique 2003 31

WORLD SUMMARY

APERCU MONDIAL

1. Population, rate of increase, birth and
   death rates, surface area and density
   for the world, major areas and regions:
   selected years 42

1. Population, taux d'accroissement, taux de natalité et
   taux de mortalité, superficie et densité pour l'ensemble
   du monde, les grandes régions et les régions
   géographiques: diverses années 45

2. Estimates of population and its percentage
   distribution, by age and sex and sex ratio
   for all ages for the world, major areas
   and regions: 2003 49

2. Estimations de la population et pourcentage de répartition
   selon l'âge et le sexe et rapport de masculinité pour
   l'ensemble du monde, les grandes régions et
   le régions géographiques: 2003 50

3. Population by sex, rate of population
   increase, surface area and density 53

3. Population selon le sexe, taux d'accroissement de la
   population, superficie et densité 55

4. Vital statistics summary and
   expectation of life at birth: 1999 - 2003 70

4. Aperçu des statistiques de l'état civil et espérance
   de vie à la naissance: 1999 - 2003 72

POPULATION

POPULATION

5. Estimations of mid-year population:
   1994 - 2003 92

5. Estimations de la population au milieu de l'année:
   1994 - 2003 93

6. Urban and total population by sex:
   1994 - 2003 100

6. Population urbaine et population totale selon le sexe:
   1994 - 2003 105

7. Population by age, sex and urban/rural
   residence: latest available year,
   1994 - 2003 130

8. Population of capital cities and cities of
   100 000 and more inhabitants:
   latest available year 216

NATALITY

9. Live births and crude live-birth rates,
   by urban/rural residence: 1999 - 2003 301

10. Live births by age of mother, sex and
    urban/rural residence:
    latest available year , 1994 - 2003................... 316

11. Live births rates specific for age of mother,
    by urban/rural residence:
    latest available year, 1994 - 2003.................. 351

FOETAL MORTALITY

12. Late foetal deaths and late foetal death ratios,
    by urban/rural residence: 1999 - 2003 363

13. Legally induced abortions: 1994 - 2003............. 373

14. Legally induced abortions by age and
    number of previous live births of woman:
    latest available year , 1994 – 2003 379

INFANT AND MATERNAL MORTALITY

15. Infant deaths and infant mortality rates by
    urban/rural residence: 1999 - 2003 390

16. Infant deaths and infant mortality rates by
    ge and sex: latest available year,
    1994 - 2003 403

17. Maternal deaths and maternal
    mortality rates: 1995 - 2002 421

GENERAL MORTALITY

18. Deaths and crude death rates,
    by urban/rural residence: 1999 - 2003 433

19. Deaths by age, sex and urban/rural
    residence: latest available year,
    1994 - 2003 447

7. Population selon l'âge, le sexe et la résidence,
   urbaine/rurale: dernière année disponible,
   1994 - 2003 132

8. Population des capitales et des villes de 100 000
   habitants et plus: dernière année disponible 218

NATALITE

9. Naissances vivantes et taux bruts de natalité
   selon la résidence, urbaine/rural: 1999 - 2003 303

10. Naissances vivantes selon l'âge de la mère,
    le sexe et la résidence, urbaine/rurale: dernière
    année disponible 1994 -2003................................. 318

11. Naissances vivantes, taux selon l'âge de la
    mère et la résidence, urbaine/rurale:
    dernière année disponible 1994 - 2003................. 353

MORTALITE FOETALES

12. Morts fœtales tardives et rapport de mortinatalité
    selon la résidence, urbaine/rurale: 1999 - 2003 365

13. Avortements provoqués légalement: 1994 - 2003 375

14. Avortements provoqués légalement selon l'âge de la
    femme et selon le nombre des naissances vivantes
    précédentes: dernière année disponible   1994 - 2003 380

MORTALITE INFANTILE ET MORTALITE LIEE A LA MATERNITE

15. Décès d'enfants de moins d'un an et taux de mortalité
    infantile, selon la résidence, urbaine/rurale:
    1999 - 2003 392

16. Décès d'enfants de moins d'un an et taux de mortalité
    infantile selon l'âge et le sexe:
    dernière année disponible 1994 -2003................. 405

17. Mortalité liée à la maternité, nombre de décès et taux:
    1995 - 2002 424

MORTALITE GENERALE

18. Décès et taux bruts de mortalité, selon la résidence,
    urbaine/rurale: 1999 - 2003. 435

19. Décès selon l'âge, le sexe et la résidence, urbaine/rurale:
    dernière année disponible 1994 - 2003................. 449

20. Deaths rates specific for age, sex and
    urban/rural residence:
    latest available year, 1994 - 2003 505

21. Deaths by marital status, age and sex:
    latest available year, 1994 - 2003 546

22. Expectation of life at specified ages for
    each sex: latest available year ,
    1994 - 2003 605

NUPTIALITY

23. Marriages and crude marriages rates,
    by urban/rural residence: 1999 - 2003 617

24. Marriages by age of groom and age of bride:
    1999 - 2003... 629

DIVORCES

25. Divorces and crude divorce rates:
    1999 - 2003 661

ANNEX

I: UN Population Prospects 2004 - Estimates
    of mid-year population: 1994 - 2003 673

II: UN Population Prospects 2004 - Vital statistics
    summary and expectation of life at birth:
    2000 - 2005 678

INDEX

Detailed guide to the subject-matter in the
current Yearbook 683

Historical index 728

20. Taux de mortalité selon l'âge, le sexe et la résidence,
    urbaine/rurale: dernière année disponible 1994 - 2003............507

21. Décès selon l'état matrimonial, l'âge et le sexe: dernière
    année disponible, 1994 - 2003 548

22. Espérance de vie à un âge donnée pour chaque sexe:
    dernière année disponible   1994 - 2003.................................606

NUPTIALITE

23. Mariages et taux bruts de nuptialité, selon la
    résidence, urbaine/rurale: 1999 - 2003 619

24. Mariages selon l'âge de l'époux et de l'épouse:
    1999 - 2003 633

DIVORTIALITE

25. Divorces et taux bruts de divortialité: 1999 - 2003 663

ANNEX

I: Prospects de la population de l'ONU 2004 - Estimations
    de la population au milieu de l'anneé: 1994 - 2003................. 673

II: Prospects de la population de l'ONU 2004 - Aperçu des
    statistiques de l'état civil et espérance de vie à la
    naissance: 2000 - 2005 678

INDEX

Index des thèmes traités dans la présente édition de
l'Annuaire démographique... 705

Index historique 773

EXPLANATIONS OF SYMBOLS

Category not applicable	..
Data not available	...
Magnitude zero or less than half of unit employed	-
Provisional	*
Data tabulated by year of registration rather than occurrence	+
Based on less than specified minimum	◆
Relatively reliable data	Roman type
Data of lesser reliability	*Italics*

EXPLICATION DES SIGNES

Sans objet	..
Données non disponibles	...
Néant ou chiffre inférieur à la moitié de l'unité employée..	-
Données provisoires	*
Donnée exploitées selon l'année de l'enregistrement et non l'année de l'événement	+
Rapport fondé sur un nombre inférieur à celui spécifié	◆
Données relativement sûres	Charactères romains
Données dont l'exactitude est moindre	*Italiques*

INTRODUCTION

The *Demographic Yearbook* is an international compendium of national demographic statistics, provided by national statistical authorities to the Statistics Division of the United Nations Department of Economic and Social Affairs. The *Yearbook* is part of the set of coordinated and interrelated publications issued by the United Nations and its specialized agencies,[1] designed to supply basic statistical data for such users as demographers, economists, public-health workers and sociologists. Through the co-operation of national statistical services, official demographic statistics are compiled in the *Yearbook*, as available, for over 230 countries or areas throughout the world.

The *Demographic Yearbook 2003* is the fifty-fifth in a series published by the United Nations since 1948. It contains general tables including a world summary of selected demographic statistics, statistics on the size, distribution and trends in national populations, natality, foetal mortality, infant and maternal mortality, general mortality, nuptiality and divorce. Data are shown by urban/rural residence, as available. In addition, the volume provides Technical Notes, a synoptic table, a subject-matter index, a historical index and a listing of the issues of the *Yearbook* published to date.

The Technical Notes on the Statistical Tables are provided to assist the reader in using the tables. Table A, the synoptic table, provides a glance of the completeness of data coverage of the current *Yearbook*. The subject-matter index is a detailed guide to the current *Yearbook*. The cumulative historical index, located at the end of the *Yearbook*, is a guide on content and coverage of all fifty-five issues, and indicates for each of the topics that have been published, the issues in which they are presented and the years covered. A list of the *Demographic Yearbook* issues, with their corresponding sales number and the special topics featured in each issue are shown on pages iv and v.

Until the 48th issue (1996), each issue consisted of two parts, the general tables and special topic tables, published in the same volume with the regular topics.[2] Beginning with the 49th issue (1997), the special topic tables were being disseminated on CD-ROMs as supplements to the regular issues. Two CD-ROMs have so far been issued: the *Demographic Yearbook Historical Supplement*, which presents a wide panorama of basic demographic statistics for the period 1948 to 1997, and the *Demographic Yearbook: Natality Statistics*, which contains a series of detailed tables dedicated to natality and covering the period from 1980 to 1998. Three volumes of a new Demographic Yearbook Special Census Topics are now being prepared and are presented at: http://unstats.un.org/unsd/demographic/products/dyb/default.htm

Population statistics are not available for all countries or areas, for a variety of reasons. In an effort to provide estimates of mid-year population and of selected vital statistics for all countries and areas, two annexes have been introduced since the 53rd issue of the *Demographic Yearbook*. Annex 1 presents United Nations population estimates for the period 1994-2003 and the second presents the medium variant estimates of crude birth and death rates, infant mortality and total fertility rates, as well as expectation of life at birth over the period 2000-2005. These data are produced by the United Nations Population Division and are published in the *World Population Prospects - The 2004 Revision*.[3]

Demographic statistics shown in this issue of the *Yearbook* are available online at the *Demographic Yearbook* website http://unstats.un.org/unsd/demographic/products/dyb/default.htm. Information about the Statistics Division's data collection and dissemination programme is also available on the same website. Additional information can be made available by contacting the Statistics Division of the United Nations Secretariat, at demostat@un.org.

TECHNICAL NOTES ON THE STATISTICAL TABLES

1. GENERAL REMARKS

1.1 Arrangement of Technical Notes

These Technical Notes are designed to provide the reader with relevant information for using the statistical tables. Information pertaining to the *Yearbook* in general is presented in the sections dealing with geographical aspects, population and vital statistics. In addition, preceding each table are notes describing the variables, remarks on the reliability and limitation of the data, countries and areas covered, and information on the presentation of earlier data. When appropriate, details on computation of rates, ratios or percentages are presented.

1.2 Arrangement of tables

This issue contains general tables only. Since the numbering of the tables does not correspond exactly to those in previous issues, the reader is advised to use the historical index that appears at the end of this book to find the reference to data in earlier issues.

1.3 Source of data

The statistics presented in the *Demographic Yearbook* are national data provided by official statistical authorities unless otherwise indicated. The primary source of data for the *Yearbook* is a set of questionnaires sent annually by the United Nations Statistics Division to over 230 national statistical services and other appropriate government offices. Data reported on these questionnaires are supplemented, to the extent possible, with data taken from official national publications, official websites and through correspondence with national statistical services. In the interest of comparability, rates, ratios and percentages have been calculated by the Statistics Division of the United Nations, except for the life table functions, and total fertility rate, and also crude birth rate and crude death rate for some countries or areas, in table 4, as appropriately noted. The methods used by the Statistics Division to calculate these rates and ratios are described in the Technical Notes for each table. The population figures used for these computations are those pertaining to the corresponding years published in this or previous issues of the *Yearbook*.

In cases when data in this issue of the *Demographic Yearbook* differ from those published in earlier issues or related publications, statistics in this issue may be assumed to reflect revisions to these data received by October 2005.

2. GEOGRAPHICAL ASPECTS

2.1 Coverage

Data are shown for all individual countries or areas that provided the information. Table 3 is the most comprehensive in geographical coverage, presenting data on population and surface area for all countries and areas with a population of at least 50 persons. Not all of these countries or areas appear in subsequent tables. In many cases the data required for a particular table are not available. In general, the more detailed the data required for a table, the fewer the number of countries or areas that can provide them.

In addition, with one exception, rates and ratios are presented only for countries or areas reporting at least a minimum number of relevant events. The minimums are stated in the Technical Notes to individual tables. The exception, in which rates for countries or areas are shown regardless of the number of events on which they were based, is table 4, presenting a summary of vital statistics rates, crude birth rates and crude death rates respectively.

Except for summary data shown for the world and by major areas and regions in tables 1 and 2 and data shown for capital city and cities with a population of 100 000 or more in table 8, all data are presented at the national level. The number of countries shown in each table is provided in table A, the synoptic table.

2.2 Territorial composition

To the extent possible, all data, including time series data, relate to the territory within 2003 boundaries, when the data were requested from the countries or areas. Exceptions are footnoted in individual tables. Additionally, in table 3, recent changes and other relevant clarifications are specified.

Data relating to the People's Republic of China generally do not include those for Taiwan Province except in tables 1 and 2.

2.3 Nomenclature

Because of space limitations, the country or area names listed in the tables are generally the commonly employed short titles in use in the United Nations as of October 2005[4], the full titles being used only when a short form is not available. The latest version of the *Standard Country or Area Codes for Statistics Use* can be accessed at http://unstats.un.org/unsd/methods/m49/m49.htm.

2.3.1 Order of presentation

Countries or areas are listed in English alphabetical order within the following continents: Africa, North America, South America, Asia, Europe and Oceania.

The designations and presentation of the material in this publication were adopted solely for the purpose of providing a convenient geographical basis for the accompanying statistical series. The same qualification applies to all notes and explanations concerning the geographical units for which data are presented.

2.4 Surface area data

Surface area data, shown in tables 1 and 3, represent the total surface area, comprising land area and inland waters (assumed to consist of major rivers and lakes) and excluding only Polar Regions and uninhabited islands. The surface area given is the most recent estimate available. They are presented in square kilometres, a conversion factor of 2.589988 having been applied to surface areas originally reported in square miles.

2.4.1 Comparability over time

Comparability over time in surface area estimates for any given country or area may be affected by changes in the surface area estimation procedures, increases in actual land surface by reclamation, boundary changes, changes in the concept of "land surface area" used or a change in the unit of measurement used. In most cases it was possible to ascertain the reason for a revision; otherwise, the latest figures have generally been accepted as correct and substituted for those previously on file.

2.4.2 International comparability

Lack of international comparability between surface area estimates arises primarily from differences in definition. In particular, there is considerable variation in the treatment of coastal bays, inlets and gulfs, rivers and lakes. International comparability is also impaired by the variation in methods employed to estimate surface area. These range from surveys based on modern scientific methods to conjectures based on diverse types of information. Some estimates are recent while others may not be. Since neither the exact method of determining the surface area nor the precise definition of its composition and time reference is known for all countries or areas, the estimates in table 3 should not be considered strictly comparable from one country or area to another.

3. POPULATION

Population statistics, that is, those pertaining to the size, geographical distribution and demographic characteristics of the population, are presented in a number of tables of the *Demographic Yearbook*.

Data for countries or areas include population census figures, estimates based on results of sample surveys (in the absence of a census), postcensal or intercensal estimates and those derived from continuous population registers. In the present issue of the *Yearbook*, the latest available census figure of the total population of each country or area and mid-year estimates for 2000 and 2003 are presented in table 3. Mid-year estimates of total population for 10 years (1994-2003) are shown in table 5 and mid-year estimates of urban and total population by sex for 10 years (1994-2003) are shown in table 6. The latest available data on population by age, sex and urban/rural residence are given in table 7. The latest available figures on the population of capital cities and of cities or urban agglomerations of 100 000 or more inhabitants are presented in table 8.

Summary estimates of the mid-year population of the world, major areas and regions for selected years and of its age and sex distribution in 2003 are set forth in tables 1 and 2, respectively.

The statistics on total population, population by age, sex and urban/rural distribution are used in the calculation of rates in the *Yearbook*. Vital rates by age and sex were calculated using data that appear in table 7 in this issue or the corresponding tables of previous issues of the *Demographic Yearbook*.

3.1 Sources of variation of data

The comparability of data is affected by several factors, including (1) the definition of total population; (2) the definition used to classify the population into its urban/rural components; (3) the accuracy of age reporting; (4) the extent of over-enumeration or under-enumeration in the most recent census or other source of benchmark population statistics; and (5) the quality of population estimates. These five factors will be discussed in some detail in sections 3.1.1 to 3.2.2 below. Other relevant problems are discussed in the technical notes to the individual tables. Readers interested in more detail, relating in particular to the basic concepts of population size, distribution and characteristics as elaborated by the United Nations, should consult the *Principles and Recommendations for Population and Housing Censuses, Revision 1.*[5]

3.1.1 Total population

The most important impediment to comparability of total populations is the difference between the concept of a de facto and de jure population. A de facto population should include all persons physically present in the country or area at the reference date. The de jure population, by contrast, should include all usual residents of the given country or area, whether or not they were physically present in the area at the reference date. By definition, therefore, a de facto total and a de jure total are not entirely comparable.

Comparability of even two de facto or de jure totals is often affected by the fact that strict conformity to either of these concepts is rare. For example, some so-called de facto counts do not include foreign military, naval and diplomatic personnel present in the country or area on official duty, and their accompanying family members and servants; some do not include foreign visitors in transit through the country or area or transients on ships in the harbour. On the other hand, they may include such persons as merchant seamen and fishermen who are temporarily out of the country or area working at their trade.

The de jure population figure presents even greater variations in comparability, in part because it depends in the first place on the concept of "usual residence", which varies from one country or area to another and is difficult to apply consistently in a census or survey enumeration. For example, non-national civilian temporarily in a country or area as short-term workers may officially be considered residents after a stay of a specified period of time or they may be considered as non-residents throughout the duration of their stay; at the same time, these individuals may be officially considered as residents or non-residents of the country or area from which they came, depending on the duration and/or purpose of their absence. Furthermore, regardless of the official treatment, individual respondents may apply their own interpretation of residence in responding to the inquiry. In addition, there may be considerable differences in the accuracy with which countries or areas are informed about the number of their residents temporarily out of the country or area.

As far as possible, the population statistics presented in the tables of the *Yearbook* refer to the de facto population. Those reported to have been based on the de jure concept are identified as such. Figures not otherwise qualified may, therefore, be assumed to have been reported by countries or areas as being based on a de facto definition of the population. In an effort to overcome, to the extent possible, the effect of the lack of strict conformity to either the de facto or the de jure concept given above, significant exceptions with respect to inclusions and exclusions of specific population groups, are footnoted when they are known.

It should be remembered, however, that the necessary detailed information has not been available in many cases. It cannot, therefore, be assumed that figures not thus qualified reflect strict de facto or de jure definitions.

4

A possible source of variation within the statistics of a single country or area may arise from the fact that some countries or areas collect information on both the de facto and the de jure population in, for example, a census, but prepare detailed tabulations for only the de jure population. Hence, even though the total population shown in table 3 is de facto, the figures shown in the tables presenting various characteristics of the population, for example, urban/rural distribution, age and sex distribution, may be de jure. These de jure figures are footnoted when known.

3.1.2 Urban/rural classification

International comparability of urban/rural distributions is seriously impaired by the wide variation among national definitions of the concept of "urban". The definitions used by individual countries or areas and their implications are shown at the end of technical notes for table 6.

3.1.3 Age distribution

The classification of population by age is a core element of most analyses, estimation and projection of population statistics. Unfortunately, age data are subject to a number of sources of error and non-comparability. Accordingly, the reliability of age data should be of concern to users of these statistics.

3.1.3.1 Collection and compilation of age data

Age is the estimated or calculated interval of time between the date of birth and the date of the census or survey, expressed in completed solar years.[3] There are two methods of collecting information on age. The first is to obtain the date of birth for each member of the population in a census or survey and then to calculate the completed age of the individual by subtracting the date of birth from the date of enumeration.[6] The second method is to record the individual's completed age at the time of the census or survey, that is to say, age at last birthday.

The recommended method is to calculate age at last birthday by subtracting the exact date of birth from the date of the census. Some practices, however, do not use this method but instead calculate the difference between the year of birth and the year of the census. Classifications of this type are footnoted whenever possible. They can be identified to a certain extent by a smaller than expected population under one year of age. However, an irregular number of births from one year to the next or age selective omission of infants may also obscure the expected population under one year of age.

3.1.3.2 Errors in age data

Errors in age data may be due to a variety of causes, including ignorance of the correct age; reporting years of age in terms of a calendar concept other than completed solar years since birth,[7] carelessness in reporting and recording age; a general tendency to state age in figures ending in certain digits (such as zero, two, five and eight); a tendency to exaggerate length of life at advanced ages; a subconscious aversion to certain numbers; and wilful misrepresentations.

These reasons for errors in reported age data are common to most investigations of age and to most countries or areas, and they may significantly impair comparability of the data.

As a result of the above-mentioned difficulties, the age-sex distribution of population in many countries or areas shows irregularities which may be summarized as follows: (1) a deficiency in the number of infants and young children; (2) a concentration at ages ending with zero and five (that is, 5, 10, 15, 20...); (3) heaping at even ages (for example, 10, 12, 14...) relative to odd ages (for example, 11, 13, 15...); (4) unexpectedly large differences between the frequency of males and females at certain ages; and (5) unaccountably large differences between the frequencies in adjacent age groups. Comparing of identical age-sex cohorts from successive censuses, as well as studying the age-sex composition of each census, may reveal these and other inconsistencies, some of which in varying degree are characteristic of even the most modern censuses.

3.1.3.3 Evaluation of accuracy

To measure the accuracy of data by age, based on the evidence of irregularities in 5-year groups, an index was devised for presentation in the *Demographic Yearbook 1949-1950*[8]. Although this index was sensitive to various sources of inaccuracy in the data, it could also be affected considerably by real fluctuations in past demographic processes. It could not, therefore, be applied indiscriminately to all types of statistics, unless certain adjustments were made and caution used in the interpretation of results.

The publication of population statistics by single years of age in the *Demographic Yearbook 1955* made it possible to apply a simple, yet highly sensitive, index known as Whipple's Index, or the Index of Concentration,[9] the interpretation of which is relatively free from consideration of factors not connected with the accuracy of age reporting. More refined methods for the measurement of accuracy of distributions by single year of age have been devised, but this particular index was selected for presentation in the *Demographic Yearbook* for its simplicity and the wide use it has already found in other sources.

Whipple's Index is obtained by summing the age returns between 23 and 62 years inclusive and finding what percentage is borne by the sum of the returns of years ending with 5 and 0 to one-fifth of the total sum.

The results would vary between a minimum of 100, representing no concentration at all, and a maximum of 500, if no returns were recorded with any digits other than the two mentioned.[10]

The index is applicable to all age distributions for which single years are given at least to the age of 62, with the following exceptions: (1) where the data presented are the result of graduation, no irregularity is scored by Whipple's Index, even though the graduated data may still be affected by inaccuracies of a different type; and (2) where statistics on age have been derived by reference to the year of birth, and tendencies to round off the birth year would result in an excessive number of ages ending in odd numbers, the frequency of age reporting with terminal digits 5 and 0 is not an adequate measure of their accuracy.

Most recently, the index has been computed for all the single-year age distributions from censuses held between 1985 and 2003, with the exception of those excluded on the criteria set forth above. Such data are published in the special issue of the *Demographic Yearbook* special topic on population censuses, Volume 1, which is available online at http://unstats.un.org/unsd/demographic/products/dyb/dybcens.htm.

Although Whipple's Index measures only the effects of preferences for ages ending in 5 and 0, it can be assumed that such digit preference is usually connected with other sources of inaccuracy in age statements and the index can be accepted as a fair measure of the general reliability of the age distribution.

3.2 Methods used to indicate quality of published statistics

To the extent possible, efforts have been made to give the reader an indication of reliability of the statistics published in the *Demographic Yearbook*. This has been approached in several ways. Any information regarding a possible under-enumeration or over-enumeration, coming from a postcensal survey, for example, has been noted in the footnotes to table 3. Any deviation from full national coverage, as explained in section 2.1 under Geographical Aspects, has also been noted. In addition, national statistical offices have been asked to evaluate the estimates of total population they submit to the Statistics Division of the United Nations.

3.2.1 Treatment of time series of population estimates

When a series of mid-year population estimates are presented, the same indication of quality is shown for the entire series as was determined for the latest estimate. The quality is indicated by the type face employed.

No attempt has been made to split the series even though it is evident that in cases where the data are now considered reliable, in earlier years, many may have been considerably less reliable than the current classification implies. Thus it will be evident that this method overstates the probable reliability of the time series in many cases. It may also understate the reliability of estimates for years immediately preceding or following a census enumeration.

3.2.2 Treatment of estimated distributions by age and other demographic characteristics

Estimates of the age-sex distribution of population may be constructed by two major methods: (1) by applying the specific components of population change to each age-sex group of the population as enumerated at the time of the census, and (2) by distributing the total estimated for a postcensal year proportionately according to the age-sex structure at the time of the census. Estimates constructed by the latter method are not published in the *Demographic Yearbook*.

Estimated age-sex distributions are categorized as "reliable" or otherwise, according to the method of construction established for the latest estimate of total mid-year population. Hence, the quality designation of the total figure, as indicated by the code, is considered to apply also to the whole distribution by age and sex, and the data are set in *italic* or roman type, as appropriate, on this basis alone. Further evaluation of detailed age structure data has not been undertaken to date.

4. VITAL STATISTICS

For purposes of the *Demographic Yearbook*, vital statistics have been defined as statistics of live birth, death, foetal death, marriage and divorce.

This volume of the *Yearbook* presents general tables on natality, nuptiality and divorce as well as tables on mortality referring to: foetal mortality, infant and maternal mortality and general mortality.

4.1 Sources of variation of data

Most of the vital statistics data published in this *Yearbook* come from national civil registration systems. The completeness and the accuracy of the data which these systems produce vary from one country or area to another.

The provision for a national civil registration system is not universal, and in some cases, the registration system covers only certain vital events. For example, in some countries or areas only births and deaths are registered. There are also differences in the effectiveness with which national laws pertaining to civil registration operate in the various countries or areas. The manner in which the law is implemented and the degree to which the public complies with the legislation determine the reliability of the vital statistics obtained from the civil registers.

It should be noted that some statistics on marriage and divorce are obtained from sources other than civil registers. For example, in some countries or areas, the only source for data on marriages is church registers. Divorce statistics, on the other hand, are obtained from court records and/or civil registers according to national practice. The actual compilation of these statistics may be the responsibility of the civil registrar, the national statistical office or other government offices.

Other factors affecting international comparability of vital statistics are much the same as those that must be considered in evaluating the variations in other population statistics. Differences in statistical definitions of vital events, differences in geographical and ethnic coverage of the data and diverse tabulation procedures may also influence comparability.

In addition to vital statistics from civil registers, some vital statistics published in the *Yearbook* are official estimates. These estimates are frequently from sample surveys. As such, their comparability may be affected by the national completeness of reporting in household surveys, non-sampling and sampling errors and other sources of bias.

Readers interested in more detailed information on standards for vital statistics should consult the *Principles and Recommendations for a Vital Statistics System Revision 2;*[11] *Handbook of vital statistics systems and Methods Volume 1, Legal, Organizational and Technical Aspects;*[13] *Handbook of Vital Statistics Systems and Methods, Volume 2, Review of national practices;*[12] *Handbook on Civil Registration and Vital Statistics Systems: Management, Operation and Maintenance;*[13] *Handbook on Civil Registration and Vital Statistics Systems: Preparation of a Legal Framework;*[14] *Handbook on Civil Registration and Vital Statistics Systems: Developing Information, Education and Communication;*[15] *Handbook on Civil Registration and Vital Statistics Systems: Policies and Protocols for the Release and Archiving of Individual Records;*[16] and *Handbook on Civil Registration and Vital Statistics Systems: Computerization*[17]. The *Handbook of Household Surveys*[18] provides information in collection and evaluation of data on fertility, mortality and other vital events collected in household surveys. These publications are also available on the website at http://unstats.un.org/unsd/demographic/sources/civilreg/default.htm.

4.1.1 Statistical definition of events

An important source of variation lies in the statistical definition of each vital event. The *Demographic Yearbook* attempts to collect data on vital events, using the standard definitions put forth in paragraph 57 of *Principles and Recommendations for a Vital Statistics System Revision 2.*[14] These are as follows:

LIVE BIRTH is the complete expulsion or extraction from its mother of a product of conception, irrespective of the duration of pregnancy, which after such separation breathes or shows any other evidence of life such as beating of the heart, pulsation of the umbilical cord, or definite movement of voluntary muscles, whether or not the umbilical cord has been cut or the placenta is attached; each product of such a birth is considered live-born regardless of gestational age.

DEATH is the permanent disappearance of all evidence of life at any time after live birth has taken place (postnatal cessation of vital functions without capability of resuscitation). This definition therefore excludes foetal deaths.

FOETAL DEATH is death prior to the complete expulsion or extraction from its mother of a product of conception, irrespective of the duration of pregnancy; the death is indicated by the fact that after such separation the foetus does not breathe or show any other evidence of life, such as beating of the heart, pulsation of the umbilical cord, or definite movement of voluntary muscles. Late foetal deaths are those of twenty-eight or more completed weeks of gestation. These are synonymous with the events reported under the pre-1950 term stillbirth[19].

MARRIAGE is an act, ceremony or process by which the legal relationship of husband and wife is constituted. The legality of the union may be established by civil, religious or other means as recognized by the laws of each country or area.

DIVORCE is a final legal dissolution of a marriage, that is, that separation of husband and wife which confers on the parties the right to remarriage under civil, religious and/or other provisions, according to the laws of each country.

In addition to these recommended definitions, the *Demographic Yearbook* collects and presents data on abortions, defined as:

ABORTION is defined, with reference to the woman, as any interruption of pregnancy before 28 weeks of gestation with a dead foetus. There are two major categories of abortion: spontaneous and induced. Induced abortions are those initiated by deliberate action undertaken with the intention of terminating pregnancy; all other abortions are considered as spontaneous.

4.1.2 Problems relating to standard definitions

A basic problem affecting international comparability of vital statistics is deviations from the standard definitions of vital events. An example of this can be seen in the cases of live births and foetal deaths.[20] In some countries or areas, an infant must survive for at least 24 hours, to be inscribed in the live-birth register. Infants who die before the expiration of the 24-hour period are classified as late foetal deaths and, barring special tabulation procedures, they would not be counted either as live births or as deaths. Similarly, in several other countries or areas, those infants who are born alive but who die before registration of their birth, are also considered as late foetal deaths.

Unless special tabulation procedures are adopted in such cases, the live-birth and death statistics will both be deficient by the number of these infants, while the incidence of late foetal deaths will be increased by the same amount. Hence the infant mortality rate is underestimated. Although both components (infant deaths and live births) are deficient by the same absolute amount, the deficiency is proportionately greater in relation to the infant deaths, causing greater errors in the infant mortality rate than in the birth rate.

Moreover, the practice exaggerates the late foetal death ratios. Some countries or areas make provision for correcting this deficiency (at least in the total frequencies) at the tabulation stage. Data for which the correction has not been made are indicated by footnote whenever possible.

The definitions used for marriage and divorce also present problems for international comparability. Unlike birth and death, which are biological events, marriage and divorce are defined only in terms of law and custom and as such are less amenable to universally applicable statistical definitions. They have therefore been defined for statistical purposes in general terms referring to the laws of individual countries or areas. Laws pertaining to marriage and particularly to divorce, vary from one country or area to another. With respect to marriage, the most widespread requirement relates to the minimum age at which persons may marry but frequently other requirements are specified.

When known the minimum legal age of men and women at which marriage can occur with (or in some cases without) parental consent is presented in table 24-1. Laws and regulations relating to the dissolution of marriage by divorce range from total prohibition, through a wide range of grounds upon which divorces may be granted, to the granting of divorce in response to a simple statement of desire or intention by husbands.

4.1.3 Fragmentary geographical or ethnic coverage

Ideally, vital statistics for any given country or area should cover the entire geographical area and include all ethnic groups. Fragmentary coverage is, however, not uncommon. In some countries or areas, registration is compulsory for only a small part of the population, limited to certain ethnic groups, for example. In other places there is no national provision for compulsory registration, but only municipal or state ordinances that do not cover the entire geographical area. Still others have developed a registration area that comprises only a part of the country or area, the remainder being excluded because of inaccessibility or for economic and cultural considerations that make regular registration practically impossible.

4.1.4 Tabulation procedures

4.1.4.1 By place of occurrence

Vital statistics presented on the national level relate to the de facto, that is, the present-in-area population. Thus, unless otherwise noted, vital statistics for a given country or area cover all the events which occur within its present boundaries and among all segments of the population therein. They may be presumed to include events among nomadic tribes and indigenous peoples, and among nationals and foreigners. When known, deviations from the de facto concept are footnoted.

Urban/rural differentials in vital rates for some countries may vary considerably depending on whether the relevant vital events were tabulated on the basis of place of occurrence or place of usual residence. For example, if a substantial number of women residing in rural areas near major urban centres travel to hospitals or maternity homes located in a city to give birth, urban fertility and neo-natal and infant mortality rates will usually be higher (and the corresponding rural rates will usually be lower) if the events are tabulated on the basis of place of occurrence rather than on the basis of place of usual residence. A similar process will affect general mortality differentials if substantial numbers of persons residing in rural areas use urban health facilities when seriously ill.

4.1.4.2 By date of occurrence versus by date of registration

To the extent possible, the vital statistics presented in the *Demographic Yearbook* refer to events that occurred during the specified year, rather than to those that were registered during that period. However, a considerable number of countries or areas tabulate their vital statistics not by date of occurrence, but by date of registration. Because such statistics can be very misleading, the countries or areas known to tabulate vital statistics by date of registration are identified in the tables by a plus sign (+). Since information on the method of tabulating vital statistics is not available for all countries and areas, tabulation by date of registration may be more prevalent than the symbols on the vital statistics tables would indicate.

Because quality of data is inextricably related to the timeliness of registration, this must always be considered in conjunction with the quality code description in section 4.2.1 below. If registration of births is complete and timely (code C), the ill effects of tabulating by date of registration, are, for all practical purposes, nullified. Similarly, with respect to death statistics, the effect of tabulating events by date of registration may be minimized in many countries or areas in which the sanitary code requires that a death must be registered before a burial permit can be issued, and this regulation tends to make registration prompt. With respect to foetal death, registration is usually done right away or not at all. Therefore, if registration is prompt, the difference between statistics tabulated by date of occurrence and those tabulated by date of registration may be negligible. In many cases, the length of the statutory time period allowed for registering various vital events plays an important part in determining the effects of tabulation by date of registration on comparability of data.

With respect to marriage and divorce, the practice of tabulating data by date of registration does not generally pose serious problems. In many countries or areas marriage is a civil legal contract which, to establish its legality, must be celebrated before a civil officer. It follows that for these countries or areas registration would tend to be almost automatic at the time of, or immediately following, the marriage ceremony. Because the registration of a divorce in many countries or areas is the responsibility solely of the court or the authority which granted it, and since the registration record in such cases is part of the records of the court proceedings, it follows that divorces are likely to be registered soon after the decree is granted.

On the other hand, if registration is not prompt, vital statistics by date of registration will not produce internationally comparable data. Under the best circumstances, statistics by date of registration will include primarily events that occurred in the immediately preceding year; in countries or areas with less developed systems, tabulations will include some events that occurred many years in the past. Examination of available information reveals that delays of many years are not uncommon for birth registration, though the majority is recorded between two to four years after birth.

As long as registration is not prompt, statistics by date of registration will not be internationally comparable either among themselves or with statistics by date of occurrence.

It should also be mentioned that lack of international comparability is not the only limitation introduced by date-of-registration tabulation. Even within the same country or area, comparability over time may be lost by the practice of counting registrations rather than occurrences. If the number of events registered from year to year fluctuates because of ad hoc incentives to stimulate registration, or to the sudden need, for example, for proof of (unregistered) birth or death to meet certain requirements, vital statistics tabulated by date of registration are not useful in measuring and analyzing demographic levels and trends. All they can give is an indication of the fluctuations in the need for a birth, death or marriage certificate and the work-load of the registrars. Therefore statistics tabulated by date of registration may be of very limited use for either national or international studies.

4.2 Methods used to indicate quality of published vital statistics

The quality of vital statistics can be assessed in terms of a number of factors. Most fundamental is the completeness of the civil registration system on which the statistics are based. In some cases, the incompleteness of the data obtained from civil registration systems is revealed when these events are used to compute rates. However, this technique applies only where the data are markedly deficient, where they are tabulated by date of occurrence and where the population base is correctly estimated. Tabulation by date of registration will often produce rates which appear correct, simply because the numerator is artificially inflated by the inclusion of delayed registrations and, conversely, rates may be of credible magnitude because the population at risk has been underestimated. Moreover, it should be remembered that knowledge of what is credible in regard to levels of fertility, mortality and nuptiality is extremely scanty for many parts of the world, and borderline cases, which are the most difficult to appraise, are frequent.

4.2.1 Quality code for vital statistics from registers.

In the *Demographic Yearbook* annual "Questionnaire on vital statistics" national statistical offices are asked to provide their own estimates of the completeness of the births, deaths, late foetal deaths, marriages and divorces recorded in their civil registers.

On the basis of information from the questionnaires, from direct correspondence and from relevant official publications, it has been possible to classify current national statistics from civil registers of birth, death, infant death, late foetal death, marriage and divorce into three broad quality categories, as follows:

C: Data estimated to be virtually complete, that is, representing at least 90 per cent of the events occurring each year.

U: Data estimated to be incomplete, that is representing less than 90 per cent of the events occurring each year.

|: Data not derived from civil registration systems but considered reliable, such as estimates derived from projections, other estimation techniques or population and housing census.

...: Data for which no specific information is available regarding completeness.

These quality codes appear in the first column of the tables which show total frequencies and crude rates (or ratios) over a period of years for live births (table 9), late foetal deaths (table 12), infant deaths (table 15), deaths (table 18), marriages (table 23), and divorces (table 25).

The classification of countries and areas in terms of these quality codes may not be uniform. Nevertheless, it was felt that national statistical offices were in the best position to judge the quality of their data. It was considered that even the very broad categories that could be established on the basis of the available information would provide useful indicators of the quality of the vital statistics presented in this *Yearbook*.

In the past, the bases of the national estimates of completeness were usually not available. In connection with the *Demographic Yearbook 1977*, countries were asked, for the first time, to provide some indication of the basis of their completeness estimates. They were requested to indicate whether the completeness estimates reported for registered live births, deaths, and infant deaths were prepared on the basis of demographic analysis, dual record checks or some other specified method. Relatively few countries or areas have responded to this new question; therefore, no attempt has been made to revise the system of quality codes used in connection with the vital statistics data presented in the *Yearbook*. It is hoped that, in the future, more countries will be able to provide this information so that the system of quality codes used in connection with the vital statistics data presented in the *Yearbook* may be revised.

Among the countries or areas indicating that the registration of live births was estimated to be 90 per cent or more complete (and hence classified as C in table 9), the following countries or areas provided information on the basis of this completeness estimate:

(a) Demographic analysis -- Argentina, Australia, Canada, Chile, Croatia, Cuba, Czech Republic, Egypt, French Guiana, Guadeloupe, Guernsey, Iceland, Ireland, Israel, Republic of Korea, Kuwait, Latvia, Mauritius, Puerto Rico, Romania, San Marino, Singapore, Sweden, Switzerland and United States.

(b) Dual record check -- Bahamas, Barbados, Belgium, Bulgaria, Cook Islands, Cuba, Cyprus, Denmark, Estonia, Fiji, Finland, France, French Guiana, Greece, Guam, Guadeloupe, Guernsey, Hungary, Iceland, Isle of Man, Japan, Kyrgyzstan, Lithuania, Maldives, New Zealand, Peninsular Malaysia, Romania, Saint Kitts and Nevis, Saint Lucia, Singapore, Sri Lanka, Sweden, Switzerland, Tokelau, Uruguay and Venezuela.

(c) Other specified methods -- Belgium, Bermuda, Cayman Islands, China Hong Kong SAR, China Macao SAR, Germany, Greenland, Iceland, Japan, Luxembourg, Netherlands, Norway, Poland, Singapore and Slovenia.

Among the countries or areas indicating that the registration of deaths was estimated to be 90 per cent or more complete (and hence classified as C in table 18), the following countries or areas provided information on the basis of this completeness estimate:

(a) Demographic analysis -- Argentina, Australia, Canada, Chile, Cuba, Egypt, French Guiana, Guadeloupe, Guernsey, Iceland, Ireland, Israel, Kuwait, Latvia, Mauritius, Puerto Rico, Romania, San Marino, Singapore, Switzerland and United States.

(b) Dual record check -- Bahamas, Bulgaria, Cook Islands, Cuba, Denmark, Fiji, Finland, France, Greece, Greenland, Guam, Guernsey, Iceland, Isle of Man, Maldives, New Zealand, Romania, Saint Kitts and Nevis, Saint Lucia, Singapore, Sri Lanka, Sweden, Switzerland, Tokelau and Uruguay.

(c) Other specified methods -- Belgium, Bermuda, Cayman Islands, Germany, Hong Kong SAR, Iceland, Ireland, Japan, Luxembourg, Netherlands, Norway, Poland, Singapore and Slovenia.

Among the countries or areas indicating that the registration of infant deaths was estimated to be 90 per cent or more complete (and hence classified as C in table 15), the following countries or areas provided information on the basis of this completeness estimate:

(a) Demographic analysis -- Argentina, Australia, Canada, Chile, Cuba, Egypt, Iceland, Ireland, Israel, Kuwait, Latvia, Mauritius, Puerto Rico, Romania, San Marino, Singapore, Sri Lanka, Switzerland and United States.

(b) Dual record check -- Bahamas, Bulgaria, Cook Islands, Cuba, Denmark, Fiji, Finland, France, Greece, Greenland, Guam, Guernsey, Iceland, Isle of Man, Japan, Maldives, New Zealand, Romania, Saint Kitts and Nevis, Saint Lucia, Singapore, Sweden, Switzerland, Tokelau and Uruguay.

(c) Other specified methods -- Belgium, Bermuda, Cayman Islands, Germany, Hong Kong SAR, Iceland, Japan, Luxembourg, Netherlands, Norway, Poland, Singapore and Slovenia.

4.2.2 Treatment of vital statistics from registers

On the basis of the quality code described above, the vital statistics shown in all tables of the *Yearbook* are treated as either reliable or unreliable. Data coded C are considered reliable and appear in roman type. Data coded U or ... are considered unreliable and appear in *italics*. Although the quality code itself appears only in certain tables, the indication of reliability (that is, the use of *italics* to indicate unreliable data) is shown in all tables presenting vital statistics data.

In general, the quality code for deaths shown in table 18 is used to determine whether data on deaths in other tables appear in roman or *italic* type. However, for some of the maternal deaths data shown in *italics* in table 17, the known quality code differs from that ascribed on the basis of the completeness of registration of the total number of deaths. In cases where the quality code in table 18 does not correspond with the quality level implied by the typeface used in table 17, relevant information regarding the completeness of maternal mortality is given in a footnote.

The same indication of reliability used in connection with tables showing the frequencies of vital events is also used in connection with tables showing the corresponding vital rates. For example, death rates computed using deaths from a register that is incomplete or of unknown completeness are considered unreliable and appear in *italics*. Strictly speaking, to evaluate vital rates more precisely, one would have to also take into account the accuracy of population data used in the denominator of these rates. The quality of population data is discussed in section 3.2 of the Technical Notes.

It should be noted that the indications of reliability used for infant mortality rates, maternal mortality rates and late foetal death ratios (all of which are calculated using the number of live births in the denominator) are determined on the basis of the quality codes for infant deaths, deaths and late foetal deaths respectively. To evaluate these rates and ratios more precisely, one would have to take into account the quality of the live-birth data used in the denominator of these rates and ratios. The quality codes for live births are shown in table 9 and described more fully in the text of the technical notes for that table.

4.2.3 Treatment of time series of vital statistics from registers

The quality of a time series of vital statistics is more difficult to determine than the quality of data for a single year. Since a time series of vital statistics is usually generated only by a system of continuous civil registration, it was assumed that the quality of the entire series was the same as that for the latest year's data obtained from the civil register. The entire series is treated as described in section 4.2.2 above. That is, if the quality code for the latest registered data is C, the frequencies and rates for earlier years are also considered reliable and appear in roman type. Conversely, if the latest registered data are coded as U or ... then data for earlier years are considered unreliable and appear in *italics*. It is recognized that this method is not entirely satisfactory because it is known that data from earlier years in many of the series were considerably less reliable than the current code implies.

4.2.4 Treatment of estimated vital statistics

In addition to data from vital registration systems, estimated frequencies and rates of the events, usually ad hoc official estimates which have been derived either from the results of a sample survey or by demographic analyses, also appear in the *Demographic Yearbook*. Estimated frequencies and rates have been included in the tables because it is assumed that they provide information which is more accurate than that from existing civil registration systems. By implication, therefore, they are also assumed to be reliable and as such they are not set in italics. Estimated frequencies and rates continue to be treated in this manner even when they are interspersed in a time series with data from civil registers.

In tables showing the quality code, the code applies only to data from civil registers. If a series of data for a country or area contains both data from a civil register and estimated data, the code applies only to the registered data; if only estimated data are shown, the symbol (|) is shown.

4.3 Maternal mortality

According to the tenth revision of the ICD, "Maternal death" is defined as the death of a woman while pregnant or within 42 days of termination of pregnancy, irrespective of the duration and the site of the pregnancy, from any cause related to or aggravated by the pregnancy or its management but not from accidental or incidental causes.

"Maternal deaths should be subdivided into direct and indirect obstetric deaths. Direct obstetric deaths are those resulting from obstetric complications of the pregnant state (pregnancy, labour and puerperium), from interventions, omissions, incorrect treatment, or from a chain of events resulting from any of the above. Indirect obstetric deaths are those resulting from previous existing disease or disease that developed during pregnancy and which was not due to direct obstetric causes, but which was aggravated by physiologic effects of pregnancy".

While the denominator maternal rate should be the number of pregnant women, it is impossible to determine the number of pregnant women. A further recommendation by the tenth revision conference is therefore that maternal mortality rates be expressed per 100,000 live births or per 100,000 total births (live births and foetal deaths).[21] The maternal mortality rate calculated here is expressed per 100,000 live births. Although live births do not represent an unbiased estimate of pregnant women, this figure is more reliable than other estimates in particular, live births are more accurately registered than live births plus foetal deaths.

4.4 Perinatal mortality

The definition of perinatal death was recommended by the Study Group on Perinatal Mortality set up by the World Health Organization. The International Conference for the Eighth Revision of the International Classification of Diseases adopted the recommendation that the perinatal period be defined "as extending from the 28th week of gestation to the seventh day of life". Noting that several countries considered as late foetal deaths any foetal death of 20 weeks or longer gestation, the Conference agreed to accept a broader definition of perinatal death that extends from the 20th week of gestation to the 28th day of life. This alternative definition was believed to promote more complete registration of events between 28 weeks of gestation and the end of the first 6 days of life. In 1975, the Ninth Revision Conference recommended the collection of perinatal mortality statistics by use of a standard perinatal death certificate according to a definition which not only includes a minimum length of gestation but also minimum weight and length criteria.

In table 19 of the *Demographic Yearbook 1996* and previous issues of the Yearbook that included perinatal mortality statistics, the definition of perinatal deaths used is the sum of late foetal deaths (foetal deaths of 28 or more weeks of gestation) and infant deaths within the first week of life. In addition, in order to standardize the definition and eliminate differences due to national practice, the figures on perinatal death are calculated by the Statistics Division for inclusion in the *Demographic Yearbook*. Following the recommendations of the Tenth Revision Conference, the perinatal mortality rate is calculated per 1,000 live births in order to minimize the effect of limited foetal death registration on the magnitude of the denominator. [25]

NOTES

[1] The data on maternal mortality are from the World Health Organization, and are available at http://www3.who.int/whosis/menu.cfm, as on cause of death.

[2] There are two exceptions – the 1978 and 1991 issues, which were disseminated in separate volumes from the respective regular issues.

[3] *World Population Prospects: The 2004 Revision*, United Nations, New York, forthcoming. Until this is published, highlights and selected output are available by following links at www.unpopulation.org, and information about methodology and data are available in *World Population Prospects: The 2002 Revision*, Sales No. E.03.XIII.6, United Nations, New York, 2003.

[4] ST/ESA/STAT/SER.M/49/Rev.4/WWW ; http://unstats.un.org/unsd/methods/m49/m49.htm; see also Standard Country or Area Codes for Statistical Use, Sales No. M.98.XVII.9, United Nations, New York, 1999.

[5] Sales No. E.98.XVII.8, United Nations, New York, 1998.

[6] Alternatively, if a population register is used, completed ages are calculated by subtracting the date of birth of individuals listed in the register from a reference date to which the age data pertain.

[7] A source of non-comparability may result from differences in the method of reckoning age, is for example, the Western versus the Eastern or, as it is usually known, the English versus the Chinese system. By the latter, a child is considered one year old at birth and advances an additional year at each Chinese New Year. The effect of this system is most obvious at the beginning of the age span, where the frequencies in the under-one-year category are markedly understated. The effect on higher age groups is not so apparent. Distributions constructed on this basis are often adjusted before publication, but the possibility of such aberrations should not be excluded when census data by age are compared.

[8] In this index, differences were scored from expected values of ratios between numbers of either sex in the same age group, and numbers of the same sex in adjoining age group. In compounding the score, allowance had to be made for certain factors such as the effects of past fluctuations in birth rates, of heavy war casualties, and of the smallness of the population itself. A detailed description of the index, with results from its application to the data presented in the 1949-1950 and 1951 issues of the *Demographic Yearbook*, is furnished in *Population Bulletin, No. 2* (United Nations publication, Sales No. 52.XIII.4), pp. 59-79. The scores obtained from statistics presented in *Demographic Yearbook 1952* are presented in that issue, and the index has also been briefly explained in that issue, as well as those of 1953 and 1954.

[9] United States, Bureau of the Census, Thirteenth Census, Vol. I (Washington, D.C., U.S. Government Printing Office), pp. 291-292.

[10] J. T. Marten, Census of India, 1921, vol. I, part I (Calcutta, 1924), pp. 126-127.

[11] Sales No. E. 01.XVII.10, United Nations, New York, 2001; http://unstats.un.org/unsd/demographic/vital_statistics/index.htm.

[12] Sales No. E.84.XVII.11, United Nations, New York, 1985; http://unstats.un.org/unsd/demographic/vital_statistics/index.htm.

[13] *Handbook on Civil Registration and Vital Statistics Systems: Management, Operation and Maintenance*, Sales No. E.98.XVII.11, United Nations, New York, 1998. http://unstats.un.org/unsd/demographic/vital_statistics/index.htm.

[14] Sales No. E. 98.XVII.7, United Nations, New York, 1998; http://unstats.un.org/unsd/demographic/vital_statistics/index.htm.

[15] Sales No. E.98.XVII.4, United Nations, New York, 1998; http://unstats.un.org/unsd/demographic/vital_statistics/index.htm.

[16] Sales No. E.98.XVII.6, United Nations, New York, 1998; http://unstats.un.org/unsd/demographic/vital_statistics/index.htm.

[17] Sales No. E.98.XVII.10, United Nations, New York, 1998; http://unstats.un.org/unsd/demographic/vital_statistics/index.htm.

[18] *Handbook of Household Surveys*, Sales No. E.83.XVII.13, United Nations, New York, 1984.

[19] For more detailed discussion on this issue, refer to *Principles and Recommendations for a Vital Statistics System Revision 2*, Sales No. E. 01.XVII.10, United Nations, New York, 2001, para 57.

[23] For more information on historical and legal background on the use of differing definitions of live births and foetal deaths, comparisons of definitions used as of 1 January 1950, and evaluation of the effects of these differences on the calculation of various rates, see *Handbook of Vital Statistics Systems and Methods Volume 2, Review of National Practices*, Sales No. E.84.XVII.11, United Nations, New York, 1985, Chapter IV.

[21] *International Statistical Classification of Diseases and Related Health Problems*, Tenth Revision, Volume 2, World Health Organization, Geneva, 1992, pp. 129-136.

INTRODUCTION

L'Annuaire démographique est un recueil de statistiques démographiques internationales qui est établi par la Division de statistique du Département des affaires économiques et sociales de l'Organisation des Nations Unies. Il fait partie d'un ensemble de publications complémentaires publiées par l'Organisation des Nations Unies et les institutions spécialisées[1], qui ont pour objet de fournir des statistiques de base aux démographes, aux économistes, aux spécialistes de la santé publique et aux sociologues. Grâce à la coopération des services nationaux de statistique, il a été possible de faire figurer dans la présente édition des statistiques démographiques officielles pour plus de 230 pays ou zones du monde entier.

L'Annuaire démographique 2003 est le cinquante-cinquième d'une série que publie l'ONU depuis 1948. Le présent volume contient des tableaux à caractère général, y compris un aperçu mondial des statistiques démographiques de base et des tableaux qui regroupent des statistiques sur la dimension, la répartition et les tendances de la population, la natalité, la mortalité fœtale, la mortalité infantile et la mortalité liée à la maternité, la mortalité générale, la nuptialité et la divortialité. Des donnée classées selon le lieu de résidence (zone urbaine ou rurale) sont présentées dans un grand nombre de tableaux. En outre, l'*Annuaire* contient des notes techniques, un tableau synoptique, un index thématique, un index historique et une liste des éditions de l'*Annuaire* publiées jusqu'à présent.

Les notes techniques sur les tableaux statistiques sont destinées à aider le lecteur. Le tableau A, qui correspond au tableau synoptique, permet de se rendre compte en un coup d'oeil du niveau d'exhaustivité des données publiées dans le présent *Annuaire* et l'index thématique facilite le repérage des sujets abordés. À la fin de l'*Annuaire*, un index cumulatif donne des renseignements sur les matières traitées dans chacune des 55 éditions et sur les années sur lesquelles portent les données. Les numéros de vente des éditions antérieures et une liste des sujets spéciaux traités dans les différentes éditions sont indiqués aux pages iv et v.

Jusqu'à la 48ème édition (1996), chaque édition se composait de deux parties : les tableaux de caractère général et ceux sur des sujets spéciaux[2]. À partir de 49ème édition (1997), les tableaux sur les sujets spéciaux ont été publiés sur CD-ROM sous forme de suppléments à l'*Annuaire*. Deux CD-ROM ont été produits jusqu'à présent : l'*Annuaire démographique : Supplément historique*, qui présente un grand nombre de statistiques démographiques pour la période allant de 1948 à 1997, et l'*Annuaire démographique : Statistiques de la natalité*, qui contient des tableaux détaillés sur la natalité pour la période allant de 1980 à 1998. Trois volumes concernant un nouvel Annuaire démographique consacré à des thèmes de recensement spéciaux sont en cours d'établissement et sont présentés à l'adresse suivante : http://unstats.un.org/unsd/demographic/products/dyb/default.htm.

Les statistiques sur la population ne sont pas disponibles pour tous les pays et zones pour plusieurs raisons. Deux annexes ont été ajoutées à partir de la 53ème édition afin d'offrir des estimations sur la population en milieu d'année et un aperçu des statistiques de l'état civil. La première porte sur des estimations concernant la population pour chaque pays ou zone pour la période 1994-2003. La seconde présente les estimations des variantes moyennes concernant les taux bruts de natalité et de mortalité, la mortalité infantile, les indicateurs synthétiques de fécondité et l'espérance de vie à la naissance pour la période 2000-2005. Ces données ont été établies par la Division de la population de l'ONU et publiées dans *World Population Prospects - The 2004 Revision*[3].

Les statistiques démographiques figurant dans la présente édition de l'*Annuaire* sont disponibles en ligne sur les pages Web consacrées à l'Annuaire :
http://unstats.un.org/unsd/demographic/products/dyb/default.htm.
On trouvera également des renseignements sur le programme de collecte et de diffusion des données de la Division de statistique sur le même site. Il est possible de se procurer d'autres données en contactant la Division de statistique de l'Organisation des Nations Unies à l'adresse suivante : demostat@un.org.

NOTES TECHNIQUES SUR LES TABLEAUX STATISTIQUES

1. REMARQUES D'ORDRE GÉNÉRAL

1.1 Notes techniques

Les notes techniques ont pour but de donner au lecteur tous les renseignements dont il a besoin pour se servir des tableaux statistiques. Les renseignements qui concernent l'*Annuaire* en général sont présentés dans des sections portant sur diverses considérations géographiques, sur la population et sur les statistiques de natalité et de mortalité. Les tableaux sont ensuite commentés séparément et l'on trouvera pour chacun une description des variables et des observations sur la fiabilité et les lacunes des données ainsi que sur les pays et zones visés et sur les données publiées antérieurement. Des détails sont également donnés, le cas échéant, sur le mode de calcul des taux, quotients et pourcentages.

1.2 Tableaux

La présente édition contient seulement des tableaux de caractère général. Comme la numérotation des tableaux ne correspond pas exactement à celle des éditions précédentes, il est recommandé de se reporter à l'index qui figure à la fin du présent ouvrage pour trouver les données publiées dans les précédentes éditions.

1.3 Origine des données

Sauf indication contraire, les statistiques présentées dans l'*Annuaire démographique* sont des données nationales fournies par les organismes de statistique officiels. Elles sont recueillies essentiellement au moyen de questionnaires qui sont envoyés tous les ans à plus de 230 services nationaux de statistique et autres services gouvernementaux compétents. Les données communiquées en réponse à ces questionnaires sont complétées, dans toute la mesure possible, par des données tirées de publications nationales officielles et des sites Web d'organismes officiels et des renseignements communiqués par les services nationaux de statistique à la demande de l'ONU. Pour que les données soient comparables, les taux, rapports et pourcentages ont été calculés par la Division de statistique de l'ONU, à l'exception des paramètres des tables de mortalité et des indicateurs synthétiques de fécondité ainsi que des taux bruts de natalité et de mortalité pour certains pays et zones dans le tableau 4, qui ont été dûment signalés en note. Les méthodes suivies par la Division pour le calcul des taux et rapports sont décrites dans les notes techniques relatives à chaque tableau. Les chiffres de population utilisés pour ces calculs sont ceux qui figurent dans la présente édition de l'*Annuaire* ou qui ont paru dans des éditions antérieures.

Chaque fois que l'on constatera des différences entre les données du présent volume et celles des éditions antérieures de l'*Annuaire démographique*, ou de certaines publications apparentées, on pourra en conclure que les statistiques publiées cette année sont des chiffres révisés communiqués à la Division de statistique avant octobre 2005.

2. CONSIDÉRATIONS GÉOGRAPHIQUES

2.1 Portée

La portée géographique des tableaux du présent *Annuaire* est aussi complète que possible. Des données sont présentées sur tous les pays ou zones qui en ont communiquées. Le tableau 3, le plus complet, contient des données sur la population et la superficie de chaque pays ou zone ayant une population d'au moins 50 habitants. Ces pays ou zones ne figurent pas tous dans les tableaux qui suivent. Dans bien des cas, les données requises pour un tableau particulier n'étaient pas disponibles. En général, les pays ou zones qui peuvent fournir des données sont d'autant moins nombreux que les données demandées sont plus détaillées.

De plus, sauf dans un cas, les taux et rapports ne sont présentés que pour les pays ou zones ayant communiqué des chiffres correspondant à un nombre minimal de faits considérés. Les minimums sont indiqués dans les notes techniques relatives à chacun des tableaux. Le tableau faisant exception, c'est-à-dire celui où les taux pour les pays ou zones sont présentés quel que soit le nombre de faits sur lequel ils se fondent, est le tableau 4, où figurent des données récapitulatives sur les taux démographiques, les taux bruts de natalité et les taux bruts de mortalité.

À l'exception des données récapitulatives présentées dans les tableaux 1 et 2 pour l'ensemble du monde et les grandes zones et régions et des données relatives aux capitales et aux villes de 100 000 habitants ou plus dans le tableau 8, toutes les données se rapportent aux pays. Le nombre de pays sur lequel porte chacun des tableaux est indiqué dans le tableau A.

2.2 Composition territoriale

Autant que possible, toutes les données, y compris les séries chronologiques, se rapportent au territoire de 2002. Les exceptions à cette règle sont signalées en note à la fin des tableaux. On trouve dans le tableau 3 des renseignements concernant les changements intervenus récemment et d'autres précisions intéressantes.

Les données relatives à la République populaire de Chine ne comprennent généralement pas celles de la province de Taiwan ; à l'exception de celles des tableaux 1 et 2.

2.3 Nomenclature

En règle générale, pour gagner de la place, on a jugé commode de désigner dans les tableaux les pays ou zones par les noms abrégés couramment utilisés par l'Organisation des Nations Unies en octobre 2004[4], les désignations complètes n'étant utilisées que lorsqu'il n'existait pas de forme abrégée. La liste des désignations des pays ou zones est disponible à l'adresse suivante :
http://unstats.un.org/unsd/methods/m49/m49alphaf.htm.

2.3.1 Ordre de présentation

Les pays ou zones sont classés dans l'ordre alphabétique anglais et regroupés par continent comme ci-après : Afrique, Amérique du Nord, Amérique du Sud, Asie, Europe et Océanie.

Les appellations employées dans la présente édition et la présentation des données qui y figurent n'ont d'autre objet que de donner un cadre géographique commode aux séries statistiques. La même observation vaut pour toutes les notes et précisions concernant les unités géographiques pour lesquelles des données sont présentées.

2.4 Superficie

Les données relatives à la superficie qui figurent dans les tableaux 1 et 3 représentent la superficie totale, c'est-à-dire qu'elles englobent les terres émergées et les eaux intérieures (qui sont censées comprendre les principaux lacs et cours d'eau) mais excluent les régions polaires et les îles inhabitées. Les données relatives à la superficie correspondent aux chiffres estimatifs les plus récents. Les superficies sont toutes exprimées en kilomètres carrés ; les chiffres qui avaient été communiqués en miles carrés ont été convertis au moyen d'un coefficient de 2,589988.

2.4.1 Comparabilité dans le temps

La révision des estimations antérieures de la superficie, des augmentations effectives de la superficie terrestre due par exemple à des travaux d'assèchement, à des rectifications de frontières, à des changements d'interprétation du concept de « terres émergées » ou à l'utilisation de nouvelles unités de mesure peut avoir des incidences sur la comparabilité dans le temps des estimations relatives à la superficie d'un pays ou d'une zone donnés. Dans la plupart des cas, il a été possible de déterminer la raison de ces révisions; toutefois, même lorsque la raison n'était pas connue, on a remplacé les anciens chiffres par les nouveaux et on a généralement admis que ce sont ces derniers qui sont exacts.

2.4.2 Comparabilité internationale

Le manque de comparabilité internationale entre les données relatives à la superficie est dû principalement à des différences de définition. En particulier, la définition des golfes, baies et criques, lacs et cours d'eau varie sensiblement d'un pays à l'autre. La diversité des méthodes employées pour estimer les superficies nuit elle aussi à la comparabilité internationale. Certaines données proviennent de levés effectués selon des méthodes scientifiques modernes ; d'autres ne représentent que des conjectures reposant sur diverses catégories de renseignements. Certains chiffres sont récents, d'autres pas. Étant donné que ni la méthode de calcul de la superficie ni la composition du territoire et la date à laquelle se rapportent les données ne sont connues avec précision pour tous les pays ou zones, les estimations figurant dans le tableau 3 ne doivent pas être considérées comme rigoureusement comparables d'un pays ou d'une zone à une autre.

3. POPULATION

Les statistiques de la population, c'est-à-dire celles qui se rapportent à la dimension, à la répartition géographique et aux caractéristiques démographiques de la population, sont présentées dans un certain nombre de tableaux de l'*Annuaire démographique*.

Les données concernant les pays ou les zones représentent les résultats de recensements de population, des estimations fondées sur les résultats d'enquêtes par sondage (s'il n'y a pas eu recensement), des estimations postcensitaires ou intercensitaires, ou des estimations établies à partir de données provenant des registres permanents de population. Dans la présente édition, le tableau 3 indique pour chaque pays ou zone le chiffre le plus récent de la population totale issu du dernier recensement et des estimations établies au milieu de l'année 2000 et de l'année 2003. Le tableau 5 contient des estimations de la population totale au milieu de chaque année pendant 10 ans (1994-2003), et le tableau 6 des estimations de la population urbaine et de la population totale, par sexe, au milieu de chaque année pendant 10 ans (1994-2003). Les dernières données disponibles sur la répartition de la population selon l'âge, le sexe et le lieu de résidence (zone urbaine ou rurale) sont présentées dans le tableau 7. Les derniers chiffres disponibles sur la population des capitales et des villes de 100 000 habitants ou plus sont regroupés dans le tableau 8.

Les tableaux 1 et 2 présentent respectivement des estimations récapitulatives de la population du monde, des grandes zones et des régions en milieu d'année, pour certaines années, ainsi que des estimations récapitulatives, pour 2003, concernant la population répartie selon l'âge et le sexe.

On a utilisé pour le calcul des taux les statistiques de la population totale et de la population répartie selon l'âge, le sexe et le lieu de résidence (zone urbaine ou rurale). Les taux démographiques selon l'âge et le sexe ont été calculés à partir des données qui figurent dans le tableau 7 de la présente édition ou dans les tableaux correspondants d'éditions précédentes de l'*Annuaire démographique*.

3.1 Sources de variation des données

Plusieurs facteurs influent sur la comparabilité des données : 1) la définition de la population totale ; 2) les définitions utilisées pour faire la distinction entre population urbaine et population rurale ; 3) les difficultés liées aux déclarations d'âge ; 4) l'étendue du sur-dénombrement ou du sous-dénombrement dans le recensement le plus récent ou dans une autre source de statistiques de référence sur la population ; 5) la qualité des estimations relatives à la population. Ces cinq facteurs sont analysés en détail aux sections 3.1.1 à 3.2.2 ci-après. D'autres questions seront traitées dans les notes techniques relatives à chaque tableau. Pour plus de précisions concernant, notamment, les notions fondamentales de dimension, de répartition et de caractéristiques de la population qui ont été élaborées par l'Organisation des Nations Unies, le lecteur est invité à se reporter aux *Principes et recommandations concernant les recensements de la population et de l'habitat*[5].

3.1.1 Population totale

Le principal obstacle à la comparabilité des données relatives à la population totale est la différence qui existe entre population de fait et population de droit. La population de fait comprend toutes les personnes présentes dans le pays ou la zone à la date de référence, tandis que la population de droit comprend toutes celles qui résident habituellement dans le pays ou la zone, qu'elles y aient été ou non présentes à la date de référence. Par définition, la population totale de fait et la population totale de droit ne sont donc pas rigoureusement comparables entre elles.

Même lorsque l'on veut comparer deux totaux qui se rapportent à des populations de fait ou deux totaux qui se rapportent à des populations de droit, on risque souvent de faire des erreurs pour cette raison qu'il est rare que l'une et l'autre notions soient appliquées strictement. Pour citer quelques exemples, certains chiffres qui sont censés porter sur la population de fait ne tiennent pas compte du personnel militaire, naval et diplomatique étranger en fonction dans le pays ou la zone, ni des membres de leurs familles et de leurs domestiques les accompagnant; d'autres ne comprennent pas les visiteurs étrangers de passage dans le pays ou la zone ni les personnes à bord de navires ancrés dans les ports. En revanche, il arrive que l'on compte des personnes, inscrits maritimes et marins pêcheurs par exemple, qui, en raison de leur activité professionnelle, se trouvent hors du pays ou de la zone de recensement.

Les risques de disparités sont encore plus grands quand il s'agit de comparer des populations de droit, car les comparaisons dépendent au premier chef de la définition que l'on donne à l'expression « lieu de résidence habituel », qui varie d'un pays ou d'une zone à l'autre et qu'il est, de toute façon, difficile d'appliquer uniformément pour le dénombrement lors d'un recensement ou d'une enquête. Par exemple, les civils étrangers qui se trouvent temporairement dans un pays ou une zone comme travailleurs à court terme peuvent officiellement être considérés comme résidents après un séjour d'une durée déterminée, mais ils peuvent aussi être considérés comme non-résidents pendant toute la durée de leur séjour ; ailleurs, ces mêmes personnes peuvent être considérées officiellement comme résidents ou comme non-résidents du pays ou de la zone d'où elles viennent, selon la durée et, éventuellement, la raison de leur absence. Qui plus est, quel que soit son statut officiel, chacun des recensés peut, au moment de l'enquête, interpréter à sa façon la notion de résidence. De plus, les autorités nationales ou les entités responsables des zones ne savent pas toutes avec la même précision combien de leurs résidents se trouvent temporairement à l'étranger.

Les chiffres de population présentés dans les tableaux de l'*Annuaire* représentent, autant qu'il a été possible, la population de fait. Sauf indication contraire, on peut supposer que les chiffres présentés ont été communiqués par les pays ou les zones comme se rapportant à la population de fait. Les chiffres qui ont été communiqués comme se rapportant à la population de droit sont indiqués comme tels. Lorsque l'on savait que les données avaient été recueillies selon une définition de la population de fait ou de la population de droit qui s'écartait sensiblement de celle exposée plus haut, on l'a signalé en note, de manière à compenser dans toute la mesure possible les conséquences des divergences.

Il ne faut pas oublier néanmoins que l'on ne disposait pas toujours de renseignements détaillés à ce sujet. On ne peut donc partir du principe que les chiffres qui ne sont pas accompagnés d'une note signalant une divergence correspondent exactement aux définitions de la population de fait ou de la population de droit.

Il peut y avoir hétérogénéité dans les statistiques d'un même pays ou d'une même zone dans le cas des pays ou zones qui ne font une exploitation statistique détaillée des données que pour la population de droit alors qu'ils recueillent des données sur la population de droit et sur la population de fait à l'occasion d'un recensement, par exemple. Ainsi, tandis que les chiffres relatifs à la population totale qui figurent au tableau 3 se rapportent à la population de fait, ceux des tableaux qui présentent des données sur diverses caractéristiques de la population, par exemple le lieu de résidence (zone urbaine ou rurale), l'âge et le sexe, peuvent n'avoir trait qu'à la population de droit. Lorsque l'on savait que les chiffres se rapportaient à la population de droit, on l'a signalé en note.

3.1.2 Lieu de résidence (zone urbaine ou rurale)

L'hétérogénéité des définitions nationales du terme « urbain » nuit considérablement à la comparabilité internationale des données concernant la répartition selon le lieu de résidence. Les définitions utilisées par les différents pays ou zones et leurs implications sont exposées à la fin des notes techniques correspondant au tableau 6.

3.1.3 Répartition par âge

La répartition de la population selon l'âge est un paramètre fondamental de la plupart des analyses, estimations et projections relatives aux statistiques de la population. Malheureusement, ces données sont sujettes à un certain nombre d'erreurs et difficilement comparables. C'est pourquoi pratiquement tous les utilisateurs de ces statistiques doivent considérer ces répartitions avec la plus grande circonspection.

3.1.3.1 *Collecte et exploitation des données sur l'âge*

L'âge est l'intervalle de temps déterminé par calcul ou par estimation qui sépare la date de naissance de la date du recensement et qui est exprimé en années solaires révolues[3]. Les données sur l'âge peuvent être recueillies selon deux méthodes : la première consiste à obtenir la date de naissance de chaque personne à l'occasion d'un recensement ou d'un sondage, puis à calculer l'âge en années révolues en soustrayant la date de naissance de celle du dénombrement[6]. La seconde consiste à enregistrer l'âge en années révolues au moment du recensement, c'est-à-dire l'âge au dernier anniversaire.

La méthode recommandée consiste à calculer l'âge au dernier anniversaire en soustrayant la date exacte de la naissance de la date du recensement. Toutefois, on n'a pas toujours recours à cette méthode ; certains pays ou zones calculent l'âge en faisant la différence entre l'année du recensement et l'année de la naissance. Lorsque les données sur l'âge ont été établies de cette façon, on l'a signalé chaque fois que possible par une note. On peut d'ailleurs s'en rendre compte dans une certaine mesure, car les chiffres dans la catégorie des moins d'un an sont plus faibles qu'ils ne devraient l'être. Cependant, un nombre irrégulier de naissances d'une année à l'autre ou l'omission de certains âges parmi les moins d'un an peut aussi fausser les chiffres de la population de moins d'un an.

3.1.3.2 Erreurs dans les données sur l'âge

Les causes d'erreurs dans les données sur l'âge sont diverses : on peut citer notamment l'ignorance de l'âge exact, la déclaration d'années d'âge correspondant à un calendrier différent de celui des années solaires révolues depuis la naissance[7], la négligence dans les déclarations et dans la façon dont elles sont consignées, la tendance générale à déclarer des âges se terminant par certains chiffres tels que 0, 2, 5 ou 8, la tendance pour les personnes âgées à exagérer leur âge, une aversion subconsciente pour certains nombres, et les fausses déclarations faites délibérément.

Les causes d'erreurs mentionnées ci-dessus, communes à la plupart des enquêtes sur l'âge et à la plupart des pays ou zones, peuvent nuire sensiblement à la comparabilité.

À cause des difficultés indiquées ci-dessus, les répartitions par âge et par sexe de la population d'un grand nombre de pays ou de zones font apparaître les irrégularités suivantes : 1) sous-estimation des groupes d'âge correspondant aux enfants de moins d'un an et aux jeunes enfants ; 2) polarisation des déclarations sur les âges se terminant par les chiffres 0 ou 5 (c'est-à-dire 5, 10, 15, 20...) ; 3) prépondérance des âges pairs (par exemple 10, 12, 14...) au détriment des âges impairs (par exemple 11, 13, 15...) ; 4) écart considérable et surprenant entre le rapport masculin/féminin à certains âges ; 5) différences importantes et difficilement explicables entre les données concernant des groupes d'âge voisins. En comparant les statistiques provenant de recensements successifs pour des cohortes identiques sur le plan de l'âge et de la répartition par sexe et en étudiant la répartition par âge et par sexe de la population à chaque recensement, on peut déceler l'existence de ces incohérences et de quelques autres, un certain nombre d'entre elles se retrouvant à des degrés divers même dans les recensements les plus modernes.

3.1.3.3 Évaluation de l'exactitude

Pour déterminer, sur la base des anomalies relevées dans les groupes d'âge quinquennaux, le degré d'exactitude des statistiques par âge, on avait mis au point un indice spécial[8] pour l'Annuaire démographique 1949-1950. Cet indice était sensible à l'influence des différents facteurs qui limitent l'exactitude des données et il n'échappait pas non plus à celle des véritables fluctuations démographiques du passé. On ne pouvait donc l'appliquer indistinctement à tous les types de données à moins d'effectuer les ajustements nécessaires et de faire preuve de prudence dans l'interprétation des résultats.

La publication dans l'Annuaire démographique 1955 de statistiques de la population par année d'âge a permis d'utiliser un indice simple, mais très sensible, connu sous le nom d'indice de Whipple ou indice de concentration[9], dont l'interprétation échappe pratiquement à l'influence des facteurs sans rapport avec l'exactitude des déclarations d'âge. Il existe des méthodes plus perfectionnées pour évaluer l'exactitude des répartitions de population par année d'âge, mais on a décidé de se servir ici de l'indice de Whipple à cause de sa simplicité et de la large utilisation dont il a déjà fait l'objet dans d'autres publications.

L'indice de Whipple s'obtient en additionnant les déclarations d'âge comprises entre 23 et 62 ans inclusivement et en calculant le pourcentage des âges déclarés se terminant par 0 ou 5 par rapport au cinquième du nombre total de déclarations.

Les résultats varient entre un minimum de 100, s'il n'y a aucune concentration, et un maximum de 500, si aucun âge déclaré ne se termine par un chiffre autre que 0 et 5[10].

Cet indice est applicable à toutes les répartitions par âge pour lesquelles les années d'âge sont données au moins jusqu'à 62 ans, sauf dans les cas suivants : 1) lorsque les données présentées ont déjà fait l'objet d'un ajustement, l'indice de Whipple ne révèle aucune irrégularité bien que des inexactitudes d'un type différent puissent fausser ces données ; 2) lorsque les statistiques relatives à l'âge sont établies sur la base de l'année de naissance et que la tendance à arrondir l'année de naissance se traduit par une fréquence excessive des âges impairs, on ne peut utiliser la méthode reposant sur les déclarations d'âge se terminant par 5 et 0 pour évaluer l'exactitude des données recueillies.

L'indice a dernièrement été calculé pour toutes les distributions par année d'âge des recensements effectués entre 1985 et 2003, à l'exception de celles que l'on a écartées pour les motifs indiqués plus haut. Ces données sont publiées dans l 'édition spéciale de l'*Annuaire démographique* consacrée aux recensements de la population, volume I , que l'on peut consulter en ligne à l'adresse http://unstats.un.org/unsd/demographic/products/dyb/dybcens.htm .

Bien que l'indice de Whipple ne mesure que les effets de la préférence pour les âges se terminant par 5 et 0, il semble que l'on puisse admettre qu'il existe généralement certains liens entre cette préférence et d'autres sources d'inexactitudes dans les déclarations d'âge, de telle sorte que l'on peut dire qu'il donne une assez bonne idée de l'exactitude de la répartition par âge en général.

3.2 Méthodes utilisées pour indiquer la qualité des statistiques publiées

On a cherché dans toute la mesure possible à donner au lecteur une indication du degré de fiabilité des statistiques publiées dans l'*Annuaire démographique*. Pour ce faire, on a procédé de diverses façons. Chaque fois que l'on savait, grâce par exemple à une enquête post censitaire, qu'il y avait eu sous-dénombrement ou surdénombrement, on l'a signalé dans les notes qui accompagnent le tableau 3. Comme on l'a indiqué à la section 2.1 sous la rubrique « Considérations géographiques », chaque fois que les données ne portaient pas sur la totalité du pays, on l'a également signalé en note. De plus, les services nationaux de statistique ont été invités à fournir une évaluation des estimations de la population totale qu'ils communiquaient à la Division de statistique de l'ONU.

3.2.1 Traitement des séries chronologiques d'estimations de la population

En ce qui concerne les séries d'estimations de la population en milieu d'année, on considère que la qualité de la série tout entière est la même que celle de la dernière estimation. La qualité de la série est indiquée par le caractère d'imprimerie utilisé.

On n'a pas cherché à subdiviser les séries, mais il est évident que les données qui sont jugées sûres actuellement n'ont pas toutes le même degré de fiabilité et que, pour les premières années, nombre d'entre elles étaient peut-être bien moins sûres que la classification actuelle ne le laisse supposer. Ainsi, il apparaît clairement que cette méthode tend, dans bien des cas, à surestimer la fiabilité probable des séries chronologiques. Elle peut aussi inciter à sous-estimer la fiabilité des estimations pour les années qui précèdent ou qui suivent immédiatement un recensement.

3.2.2 Traitement des séries estimatives selon l'âge et d'autres caractéristiques démographiques

Des estimations de la répartition de la population par âge et par sexe peuvent être obtenues selon deux grandes méthodes : 1) en appliquant les composantes spécifiques du mouvement de la population, pour chaque groupe d'âge et pour chaque sexe, à la population dénombrée lors du recensement ; 2) en répartissant proportionnellement le chiffre total estimé pour une année postcensitaire d'après la composition par âge et par sexe au moment du recensement. Les estimations obtenues par la seconde méthode ne sont pas publiées dans l'*Annuaire démographique*.

Les séries estimatives selon l'âge et le sexe qui sont publiées sont classées en deux catégories, « sûres » ou « moins sûres », selon la méthode retenue pour le plus récent calcul estimatif de la population totale en milieu d'année. Ainsi, l'appréciation de la qualité du chiffre total, telle qu'elle ressort des signes de code, est censée s'appliquer aussi à l'ensemble de la répartition par âge et par sexe, et c'est sur cette seule base que l'on décide si les données figureront en caractères italiques ou romains. On n'a pas encore procédé à une évaluation plus poussée des données détaillées concernant la composition par âge.

4. STATISTIQUES DE L'ÉTAT CIVIL

Aux fins de l'*Annuaire démographique*, on entend par statistiques de l'état civil les statistiques des naissances vivantes.

Dans le présent volume de l'*Annuaire*, on n'a présenté que les tableaux de caractère général sur la natalité, la mortalité, la nuptialité et la divortialité. Les tableaux consacrés à la mortalité sont groupés sous les rubriques suivantes : mortalité fœtale, mortalité infantile, mortalité liée à la maternité et mortalité générale, y compris des tableaux portant sur la cause des décès.

4.1 Sources de variations des données

La plupart des statistiques de l'état civil publiées dans le présent *Annuaire* émanent des systèmes nationaux d'enregistrement des faits d'état civil. Le degré d'exhaustivité et d'exactitude de ces données varie d'un pays ou d'une zone à l'autre.

Il n'existe pas partout de système national d'enregistrement des faits d'état civil et, dans quelques cas, seuls certains faits sont enregistrés. Par exemple, dans certains pays ou zones, seuls les naissances et les décès sont enregistrés. Il existe également des différences quant au degré d'efficacité avec lequel les lois relatives à l'enregistrement des faits d'état civil sont appliquées dans les divers pays ou zones. La fiabilité des statistiques provenant des registres d'état civil dépend des modalités d'application de la loi et de la mesure dans laquelle le public s'y soumet.

Il est à signaler que dans certains cas les statistiques de la nuptialité et de la divortialité sont tirées d'autres sources que les registres d'état civil. Dans certains pays ou zones, par exemple, les seules données disponibles sur la nuptialité proviennent des registres des églises. Selon la pratique suivie par chaque pays, les statistiques de la divortialité sont tirées des actes des tribunaux et/ou des registres d'état civil. L'officier de l'état civil, le service national de statistique ou d'autres services administratifs peuvent être chargés d'établir ces statistiques.

Les autres facteurs qui influent sur la comparabilité internationale des statistiques de l'état civil sont à peu près les mêmes que ceux qu'il convient de prendre en considération pour interpréter les variations observées dans les statistiques de la population. La définition des faits d'état civil aux fins de statistique, la portée des données du point de vue géographique et ethnique ainsi que les méthodes d'exploitation des données sont autant d'éléments qui peuvent influer sur la comparabilité.

En plus des statistiques tirées des registres d'état civil, l'*Annuaire* présente des statistiques de l'état civil qui sont des estimations officielles nationales, fondées souvent sur les résultats de sondages. Aussi leur comparabilité varie-t-elle en fonction du degré d'exhaustivité des déclarations recueillies lors d'enquêtes sur les ménages, des erreurs d'échantillonnage ou autres, et des distorsions d'origines diverses.

Pour plus de détails au sujet des pratiques nationales relatives au rassemblement des statistiques d'état civil, le lecteur pourra se reporter aux : *Principes et recommandations pour un système de statistiques de l'état civil, deuxième révision*[11] ; *Manuel de statistiques de l'état civil, Volume I : aspects juridiques, organisationnels et techniques*[12] ; *Manuel des systèmes d'enregistrement des faits d'état civil et de statistiques de l'état civil : Gestion, fonctionnement et tenue*[13]; *Manuel des systèmes d'enregistrement des faits d'état civil et de statistiques de l'état civil : Élaboration d'un cadre juridique*[14] ; *Manuel des systèmes d'enregistrement des faits d'état civil et de statistiques de l'état civil : Élaboration de programmes d'information, d'éducation et de communication*[15] ; *Manuel des systèmes d'enregistrement des faits d'état civil et de statistiques de l'état civil : Principes et protocoles concernant la communication et l'archivage des documents individuels*[16]; *Manuel des systèmes d'enregistrement des faits d'état civil et de statistiques de l'état civil : Informatisation*[17]. Le *Manuel des méthodes d'enquêtes sur les ménages*[18] fournit des informations ayant trait à la collecte et à l'évaluation des données sur la fécondité, sur la mortalité et sur d'autres faits d'état civil, qui ont été recueillies au cours des enquêtes sur les ménages. Ces publications sont également disponibles sur le Web à partir de l'adresse suivante : http://unstats.un.org/unsd/demographic/sources/civilreg/default.htm.

4.1.1 Définition des faits d'état civil aux fins de la statistique

Une cause importante d'hétérogénéité dans les données est le manque d'uniformité des définitions des différents faits d'état civil. Aux fins de l'*Annuaire démographique*, il est recommandé de recueillir les données relatives aux faits d'état civil en utilisant les définitions établies au paragraphe 57 des *Principes et recommandations pour un système de statistiques de l'état civil, deuxième révision*[14]. Ces définitions sont les suivantes :

La *NAISSANCE VIVANTE* *est l'expulsion ou l'extraction complète du corps de la mère, indépendamment de la durée de la gestation, d'un produit de la conception qui, après cette séparation, respire ou manifeste tout autre signe de vie, tel que battement de cœur, pulsation du cordon ombilical ou contraction effective d'un muscle soumis à l'action de la volonté, que le cordon ombilical ait été coupé ou non et que le placenta soit ou non demeuré attaché; tout produit d'une telle naissance est considéré comme « enfant né vivant ».*

Le DÉCÈS est la disparition permanente de tout signe de vie à un moment quelconque postérieur à la naissance vivante (cessation des fonctions vitales après la naissance sans possibilité de réanimation). Cette définition ne comprend donc pas les morts fœtales.

La MORT FŒTALE est le décès d'un produit de la conception lorsque ce décès est survenu avant l'expulsion ou l'extraction complète du corps de la mère, indépendamment de la durée de la gestation; le décès est indiqué par le fait qu'après cette séparation le fœtus ne respire ni ne manifeste aucun signe de vie, tel que battement de cœur, pulsation du cordon ombilical ou contraction effective d'un muscle soumis à l'action de la volonté. Les morts fœtales tardives sont celles qui sont survenues après 28 semaines de gestation ou plus. Il n'y a aucune différence entre ces « morts fœtales tardives » et les faits désignés, avant 1950, par le terme « mortinatalité[19] ».

Le MARIAGE est l'acte, la cérémonie ou la procédure qui établit un rapport légal entre mari et femme. L'union peut être rendue légale par une procédure civile ou religieuse, ou par toute autre procédure, conformément à la législation du pays.

Le DIVORCE est la dissolution légale et définitive des liens du mariage, c'est-à-dire la séparation de l'époux et de l'épouse qui confère aux parties le droit de se remarier civilement ou religieusement, ou selon toute autre procédure, conformément à la législation du pays.

Des données concernant les avortements sont également recueillies et présentées dans l'*Annuaire démographique*, la définition retenue étant la suivante :

Par référence à la femme, l'AVORTEMENT se définit comme toute interruption de grossesse qui est survenue avant 28 semaines de gestation et dont le produit est un fœtus mort. Il existe deux grandes catégories d'avortement : l'avortement spontané et l'avortement provoqué. L'avortement provoqué a pour origine une action délibérée entreprise en vue d'interrompre une grossesse. Tout autre avortement est considéré comme spontané.

4.1.2 Problèmes posés par les définitions établies

Les variations par rapport aux définitions établies des faits d'état civil sont le principal obstacle à la comparabilité internationale des statistiques de l'état civil. Un exemple en est fourni par le cas des naissances vivantes et celui des morts fœtales[20]. Dans certains pays ou zones, il faut que le nouveau-né ait vécu 24 heures pour pouvoir être inscrit sur le registre des naissances vivantes. Les décès d'enfants qui surviennent avant l'expiration du délai de 24 heures sont classés parmi les morts fœtales tardives et, en l'absence de méthodes spéciales d'exploitation des données, ne sont comptés ni dans les naissances vivantes ni dans les décès. De même, dans plusieurs autres pays ou zones, les décès d'enfants nés vivants et décédés avant l'enregistrement de leur naissance sont également comptés parmi les morts fœtales tardives.

À moins que des méthodes spéciales n'aient été adoptées pour l'exploitation de ces données, les statistiques des naissances vivantes et des décès ne tiendront pas compte de ces cas, qui viendront en revanche accroître d'autant le nombre des morts fœtales tardives. Le taux de mortalité infantile sera donc sous-estimé. Bien que les éléments constitutifs du taux (décès d'enfants de moins d'un an et naissances vivantes) accusent exactement la même insuffisance en valeur absolue, les lacunes sont proportionnellement plus fortes pour les décès de moins d'un an, ce qui cause des erreurs plus importantes dans les taux de mortalité infantile.

De plus, cette pratique augmente les rapports de mortinatalité. Quelques pays ou zones effectuent les ajustements nécessaires pour corriger cette anomalie (du moins dans les fréquences totales) au moment de l'établissement des tableaux. Si aucun ajustement n'a été effectué, cela est indiqué dans les notes chaque fois que possible.

Les définitions du mariage et du divorce posent aussi un problème du point de vue de la comparabilité internationale. Contrairement à la naissance et au décès, qui sont des faits biologiques, le mariage et le divorce sont uniquement déterminés par la législation et la coutume et, de ce fait, il est moins facile d'en donner une définition statistique qui ait une application universelle. À des fins statistiques, ces notions ont donc été définies de manière générale par référence à la législation de chaque pays ou zone. La législation relative au mariage et plus particulièrement au divorce varie d'un pays ou d'une zone à l'autre. En ce qui concerne le mariage, l'âge de nubilité est la condition la plus fréquemment requise mais il arrive souvent que d'autres conditions soient exigées.

Lorsqu'il est connu, l'âge minimum auquel le mariage peut avoir lieu avec le consentement des parents (et dans certains cas sans le consentement des parents) est indiqué au tableau 24-1 as part of the technical notes for table 24. Les lois et règlements relatifs à la dissolution du mariage par le divorce vont de l'interdiction absolue, en passant par diverses conditions requises pour l'obtention du divorce, jusqu'à la simple déclaration, par l'époux, de son désir ou de son intention de divorcer.

4.1.3 Portée géographique ou ethnique restreinte

En principe, les statistiques de l'état civil devraient s'étendre à l'ensemble du pays ou de la zone auxquels elles se rapportent et englober tous les groupes ethniques. En fait, il n'est pas rare que les données soient fragmentaires. Dans certains pays ou zones, l'enregistrement n'est obligatoire que pour une petite partie de la population, par exemple pour certains groupes ethniques. Dans d'autres, il n'existe pas de disposition qui prescrive l'enregistrement obligatoire sur le plan national, mais seulement des règlements ou décrets des municipalités ou des États, qui ne s'appliquent pas à l'ensemble du territoire. Il en est encore autrement dans d'autres pays ou zones où les autorités ont institué une zone d'enregistrement comprenant seulement une partie du territoire, le reste étant exclu en raison des difficultés d'accès ou parce qu'il est pratiquement impossible, pour des raisons d'ordre économique ou culturel, d'y procéder à un enregistrement régulier.

4.1.4 Exploitation des données

4.1.4.1 Selon le lieu de l'événement

Les statistiques de l'état civil qui sont présentées pour l'ensemble du territoire national se rapportent à la population de fait ou population présente. En conséquence, sauf indication contraire, les statistiques de l'état civil relatives à une zone ou à un pays donné portent sur tous les faits survenus dans l'ensemble de la population, à l'intérieur des frontières actuelles de la zone ou du pays considéré. On peut donc estimer qu'elles englobent les faits d'état civil survenus dans les tribus nomades et parmi les populations autochtones ainsi que parmi les ressortissants du pays et les étrangers. Des notes signalent les exceptions lorsque celles-ci sont connues.

Pour certains pays, les écarts entre les taux démographiques pour les zones urbaines et pour les zones rurales peuvent varier notablement selon que les faits d'état civil ont été exploités sur la base du lieu de l'événement ou du lieu de résidence habituel. Par exemple, si un nombre appréciable de femmes résidant dans des zones rurales proches de grands centres urbains accouchent dans les hôpitaux ou maternités d'une ville, les taux de fécondité ainsi que les taux de mortalité néo-natale et infantile seront généralement plus élevés dans les zones urbaines (et par conséquent plus faibles dans les zones rurales) si les faits sont exploités en se fondant sur le lieu de l'événement et non sur le lieu de résidence habituel. Le phénomène sera le même dans le cas de la mortalité générale si un bon nombre de personnes résidant dans des zones rurales font appel aux services de santé des villes lorsqu'elles sont gravement malades.

4.1.4.2 Selon la date de l'événement ou la date de l'enregistrement

Autant que possible, les statistiques de l'état civil figurant dans l'*Annuaire démographique* se rapportent aux faits survenus pendant l'année considérée et non aux faits enregistrés au cours de ladite année. Bon nombre de pays ou zones, toutefois, exploitent leurs statistiques de l'état civil selon la date de l'enregistrement et non selon la date de l'événement. Comme ces statistiques risquent d'induire gravement en erreur, les pays ou zones dont on sait qu'ils établissent leurs statistiques d'après la date de l'enregistrement sont signalés dans les tableaux par un signe plus (+). On ne dispose toutefois pas pour tous les pays ou zones de renseignements complets sur la méthode d'exploitation des statistiques de l'état civil et les données sont peut-être exploitées selon la date de l'enregistrement plus souvent que ne le laisserait supposer l'emploi des signes.

Étant donné que la qualité des données est inextricablement liée aux retards dans l'enregistrement, il faudra toujours considérer en même temps le code de qualité qui est décrit à la section 4.2.1 ci-après. Évidemment, si l'enregistrement des naissances est complet et effectué en temps voulu (code 'C'), les effets perturbateurs de la méthode consistant à exploiter les données selon la date de l'enregistrement seront pratiquement annulés. De même, s'agissant des statistiques des décès, les effets pourront bien souvent être réduits au minimum dans les pays ou zones où le code sanitaire subordonne la délivrance du permis d'inhumer à l'enregistrement du décès, ce qui tend à hâter l'enregistrement. Quant aux morts fœtales, elles sont généralement déclarées immédiatement ou ne sont pas déclarées du tout. En conséquence, si l'enregistrement se fait dans un délai très court, la différence entre les statistiques établies selon la date de l'événement et celles qui sont établies selon la date de l'enregistrement peut être négligeable. Dans bien des cas, la durée des délais légaux accordés pour l'enregistrement des faits d'état civil est un facteur dont dépend dans une large mesure l'incidence sur la comparabilité de l'exploitation des données selon la date de l'enregistrement.

En ce qui concerne le mariage et le divorce, la pratique consistant à exploiter les statistiques selon la date de l'enregistrement ne pose généralement pas de graves problèmes. Le mariage étant, dans de nombreux pays ou zones, un contrat juridique civil qui, pour être légal, doit être conclu devant un officier de l'état civil, il s'ensuit que dans ces pays ou zones l'enregistrement a lieu presque systématiquement au moment de la cérémonie ou immédiatement après. De même, dans de nombreux pays ou zones, le tribunal ou l'autorité qui a prononcé le divorce est seul habilité à enregistrer cet acte, et comme l'acte d'enregistrement figure alors sur les registres du tribunal l'enregistrement suit généralement de peu le jugement.

En revanche, si l'enregistrement n'a lieu qu'avec un certain retard, les statistiques de l'état civil établies selon la date de l'enregistrement ne sont pas comparables sur le plan international. Au mieux, les statistiques par date de l'enregistrement prendront surtout en considération des faits survenus au cours de l'année précédente ; dans les pays ou zones où le système d'enregistrement n'est pas très développé, il y entrera des faits datant de plusieurs années. Il ressort des documents dont on dispose que des retards de plusieurs années dans l'enregistrement des naissances ne sont pas rares, encore que, dans la majorité des cas, les retards ne dépassent pas deux à quatre ans.

Tant que l'enregistrement se fera avec retard, les statistiques fondées sur la date d'enregistrement ne seront comparables sur le plan international ni entre elles ni avec les statistiques établies selon la date de fait d'état civil.

Il convient également de noter que l'exploitation des données selon la date de l'enregistrement ne nuit pas seulement à la comparabilité internationale des statistiques. Même à l'intérieur d'un pays ou d'une zone, le procédé qui consiste à compter les enregistrements et non les faits peut compromettre la comparabilité des chiffres sur une longue période. Si le nombre des faits d'état civil enregistrés varie d'une année à l'autre (par suite de l'application de mesures visant tout particulièrement à encourager l'enregistrement ou parce qu'il est subitement devenu nécessaire de produire le certificat d'une naissance ou d'un décès non enregistré pour l'accomplissement de certaines formalités), les statistiques de l'état civil établies d'après la date de l'enregistrement ne permettent pas de quantifier ni d'analyser l'état et l'évolution de la population. Tout au plus peuvent-elles révéler l'évolution des conditions d'exigibilité du certificat de naissance, de décès ou de mariage et les fluctuations du volume de travail des bureaux d'état civil. Les statistiques établies selon la date de l'enregistrement peuvent donc ne présenter qu'une utilité très réduite pour des études nationales ou internationales.

4.2 Méthodes utilisées pour indiquer la qualité des statistiques de l'état civil qui sont publiées

La qualité des statistiques de l'état civil peut être évaluée en se fondant sur plusieurs facteurs. Le facteur essentiel est la complétude du système d'enregistrement des faits d'état civil d'après lequel les statistiques sont établies. Dans certains cas, on constate que les données tirées de l'enregistrement ne sont pas complètes lorsque l'on les utilise pour le calcul des taux. Toutefois, cette observation est valable uniquement lorsque les statistiques présentent des lacunes évidentes, qu'elles sont exploitées d'après la date de l'événement et que l'estimation du chiffre de population pris pour base est exacte. L'exploitation des données d'après la date de l'enregistrement donne souvent des taux qui paraissent exacts, tout simplement parce que le numérateur est artificiellement gonflé par suite de l'inclusion d'un grand nombre d'enregistrements tardifs ; inversement, il arrive que des taux paraissent vraisemblables parce que l'on a sous-évalué la population étudiée. Il ne faut pas non plus oublier que les renseignements dont on dispose sur les taux de fécondité, de mortalité et de nuptialité considérés comme normaux sont extrêmement sommaires dans un grand nombre de régions du monde et que les cas limites, qui sont les plus difficiles à évaluer, sont fréquents.

4.2.1 Codage qualitatif des statistiques provenant des registres de l'état civil

Dans le questionnaire relatif au mouvement de la population qui leur est envoyé chaque année dans le cadre de l'établissement de l'*Annuaire démographique*, les services nationaux de statistique sont invités à donner leur propre évaluation du degré de complétude des données sur les naissances, les décès, les décès d'enfants de moins d'un an, les morts fœtales tardives, les mariages et les divorces figurant dans leurs registres d'état civil.

D'après les renseignements directement communiqués par les gouvernements ou extraits des questionnaires ou de publications officielles pertinentes, il a été possible de classer les statistiques de l'enregistrement des faits d'état civil (naissances, décès, décès d'enfants de moins d'un an, morts fœtales tardives, mariages et divorces) en trois grandes catégories, selon leur qualité :

C : Données jugées pratiquement complètes, c'est-à-dire représentant au moins 90 p. 100 des faits d'état civil survenant chaque année.

U : Données jugées incomplètes, c'est-à-dire représentant moins de 90 p. 100 des faits survenant chaque année.

| : Données ne provenant pas des systèmes nationaux d'enregistrement des faits d'état civil mais jugées fiables, telles que les estimations dérivées des projections, d'autres techniques d'estimation ou recensements de population ou du logement.

... : Données dont le degré de complétude ne fait pas l'objet de renseignements précis.

Ces codes de qualité figurent dans la deuxième colonne des tableaux qui présentent, pour un nombre d'années déterminé les chiffres absolus et les taux (ou rapports) bruts concernant les naissances vivantes (tableau 9), les morts fœtales tardives (tableau 12), les décès d'enfants de moins d'un an (tableau 15), les décès (tableau 18), les mariages (tableau 23) et les divorces (tableau 25).

La classification des pays ou zones selon ces codes de qualité peut ne pas être uniforme. On a estimé néanmoins que les services nationaux de statistique étaient les mieux placés pour juger de la qualité de leurs données. On a pensé que les catégories que l'on pouvait distinguer sur la base des renseignements disponibles, bien que très larges, permettaient cependant de se faire une idée de la qualité des statistiques de l'état civil publiées dans l'*Annuaire*.

Par le passé, les bases sur lesquelles les pays évaluaient l'exhaustivité de leurs données n'étaient généralement pas connues. À l'occasion de l'établissement de l'*Annuaire démographique 1977*, les pays ont été invités, pour la première fois, à donner des indications à ce sujet. On leur a demandé de préciser si leurs estimations du degré d'exhaustivité des données d'enregistrement des naissances vivantes, des décès et de la mortalité infantile reposaient sur une analyse démographique, un double contrôle des registres ou d'autres méthodes qu'ils devaient spécifier. Relativement peu de pays ou zones ont jusqu'à présent répondu à cette nouvelle question ; on n'a donc pas cherché à réviser le système de codage qualitatif utilisé pour les statistiques de l'état civil présentées dans l'*Annuaire*. Il faut espérer qu'à l'avenir davantage de pays pourront fournir ces renseignements afin que l'on puisse adapter le système de codage qualitatif.

Sur les pays ou zones qui ont estimé à 90 p. 100 ou plus le degré d'exhaustivité de leur enregistrement des naissances vivantes (classé 'C' dans le tableau 9), les pays ou zones suivants ont communiqué des renseignements concernant les bases sur lesquelles leur estimation reposait :

a) Analyse démographique : Argentine, Australie, Canada, Chili, Croatie, Cuba, Égypte, États-Unis, Guadeloupe, Guernesey, Guyane française, Irlande, Islande, Israël, Koweït, Lettonie, Maurice, Porto Rico, République de Corée, République tchèque, Roumanie, Saint-Marin, Singapour, Suède et Suisse.

b) Double contrôle des registres : Bahamas, Barbade, Belgique, Bulgarie, Chypre, Cuba, Danemark, Estonie, Fidji, Finlande, France, Guadeloupe, Guam, Guyane française, Grèce, Guernesey, Hongrie, Île de Man, Îles Cook, Islande, Kirghizistan, Lituanie, Japon, Malaisie péninsulaire, Maldives, Nouvelle-Zélande, Saint-Kitts-et-Nevis, Sainte-Lucie, Roumanie, Singapour, Sri Lanka, Suède, Suisse, Tokélaou, Uruguay et Venezuela.

c) Autre méthode : Allemagne, Belgique, Bermudes, Chine, Groenland, région administrative spéciale de Hong Kong (Chine), région administrative spéciale de Macao (Chine), Îles Caïmanes, Islande, Japon, Luxembourg, Norvège, Pays-Bas, Pologne, Singapour et Slovénie.

Sur les pays ou zones qui ont estimé à 90 p. 100 ou plus le degré d'exhaustivité de leur enregistrement des décès (classé 'C' dans le tableau 18), les pays ou zones suivants ont donné des indications touchant la base de cette estimation :

a) Analyse démographique : Argentine, Australie, Canada, Chili, Cuba, Égypte, États-Unis, Guadeloupe, Guernesey, Guyane française, Irlande, Islande, Israël, Koweït, Lettonie, Maurice, Porto Rico, Roumanie, Saint-Marin, Singapour et Suisse.

b) Double contrôle des registres : Bahamas, Bulgarie, Cuba, Danemark, Fidji, Finlande, France, Grèce, Groenland, Guam, Guernesey, Îles Cook, Île de Man, Islande, Maldives, Nouvelle-Zélande, Roumanie, Saint-Kitts-et-Nevis, Sainte-Lucie, Singapour, Sri Lanka, Suède, Suisse, Tokélaou et Uruguay.

c) Autre méthode : Allemagne, Belgique, Bermudes, région administrative spéciale de Hong Kong, Îles Caïmanes, Irlande, Islande, Japon, Luxembourg, Norvège, Pays-Bas, Pologne, Singapour et Slovénie.

Sur les pays ou zones qui ont estimé à 90 p. 100 ou plus le degré d'exhaustivité de leur enregistrement des décès à moins d'un an (classé 'C' dans le tableau 15), les pays ou zones suivants ont donné des indications touchant la base de cette estimation :

a) Analyse démographique : Argentine, Australie, Canada, Chili, Cuba, Égypte, États-Unis, Irlande, Islande, Israël, Koweït, Lettonie, Maurice, Porto Rico, Roumanie, Saint-Marin, Singapour, Sri Lanka et Suisse.

b) Double contrôle des registres : Bahamas, Bulgarie, Cuba, Danemark, Fidji, Finlande, France, Grèce, Groenland, Guam, Guernesey, Île de Man, Îles Cook, Islande, Japon, Maldives, Nouvelle-Zélande, Roumanie, Saint-Kitts-et-Nevis, Sainte-Lucie, Singapour, Suède, Suisse, Tokélaou et Uruguay.

c) Autre méthode : Allemagne, Belgique, Bermudes, région administrative spéciale de Hong Kong, Îles Caïmanes, Islande, Japon, Luxembourg, Norvège, Pays-Bas, Pologne, Singapour et Slovénie.

4.2.2 Traitement des statistiques tirées des registres d'état civil

Dans tous les tableaux de l'*Annuaire*, on a indiqué le degré de fiabilité des statistiques de l'état civil en se fondant sur le codage qualitatif décrit ci-dessus. Les statistiques codées 'C', jugées sûres, sont imprimées en caractères romains. Celles qui sont codées 'U' ou '...', jugées douteuses, sont reproduites en *italique*. Bien que le codage qualitatif proprement dit n'apparaisse que dans certains tableaux, l'indication du degré de fiabilité (c'est-à-dire l'emploi des caractères italiques pour désigner les données douteuses) se retrouve dans tous les tableaux présentant des statistiques de l'état civil.

En général, le code de qualité pour les décès utilisé au tableau 18 sert à déterminer si, dans les autres tableaux, les données relatives aux décès apparaissent en caractères romains ou en italique. Toutefois, le code associé à certaines données sur les décès liés à la maternité dans le tableau 17 diffère de celui employé dans le tableau 18 lorsque l'on sait que le degré d'exhaustivité des données diffère grandement de celui du nombre total des décès. Dans les cas où le code de qualité du tableau 18 ne correspond pas aux caractères utilisés dans le tableau 17, les renseignements concernant l'exhaustivité des statistiques des décès selon la cause sont indiqués en note à la fin du tableau.

On a utilisé la même indication de fiabilité dans les tableaux des taux démographiques et dans ceux des fréquences correspondantes. Par exemple, les taux de mortalité calculés d'après les décès figurant sur un registre incomplet ou d'exhaustivité indéterminée sont jugés douteux et apparaissent en italique. Au sens strict, pour évaluer de façon plus précise les taux démographiques, il faudrait tenir compte de la précision des données sur la population figurant au dénominateur dans les taux. La qualité des données sur la population est étudiée à la section 3.2 des notes techniques.

Il convient de noter que, pour les taux de mortalité infantile, les taux de mortalité liée à la maternité et les rapports de morts fœtales tardives (calculées en utilisant au dénominateur le nombre de naissances vivantes), les indications relatives à la fiabilité sont déterminées sur la base des codes de qualité utilisés pour les décès d'enfants de moins d'un an, les décès totaux et les morts fœtales tardives, respectivement. Pour évaluer ces taux et rapports de façon plus précise, il faudrait tenir compte de la qualité des données relatives aux naissances vivantes, utilisées au dénominateur dans leur calcul. Les codes de qualité pour les naissances vivantes figurent au tableau 9 et sont décrits plus en détail dans les notes techniques se rapportant à ce tableau.

4.2.3 Traitement des séries chronologiques de statistiques tirées des registres d'état civil

Il est plus difficile de déterminer la qualité des séries chronologiques de statistiques de l'état civil que celle des données pour une seule année. Étant donné qu'une série chronologique de statistiques de l'état civil ne peut généralement avoir pour source qu'un système permanent d'enregistrement des faits d'état civil, on a arbitrairement supposé que le degré d'exactitude de la série tout entière était le même que celui de la dernière tranche annuelle de données tirées du registre d'état civil. La série tout entière est traitée de la manière décrite à la section 4.2.2 ci-dessus : lorsque le code de qualité relatif aux données d'enregistrement les plus récentes est 'C', les fréquences et les taux relatifs aux années antérieures sont eux aussi considérés comme sûrs et figurent en caractères romains. Inversement, si les données d'enregistrement les plus récentes sont codées 'U' ou '...', les données des années antérieures sont jugées douteuses et figurent en italique. Cette méthode n'est certes pas entièrement satisfaisante, car les données des premières années de la série sont souvent beaucoup moins sûres que le code actuel ne le laisse supposer.

4.2.4 Traitement des estimations fondées sur les statistiques de l'état civil

En plus des données provenant des systèmes d'enregistrement des faits d'état civil, l'Annuaire démographique contient aussi des estimations relatives aux fréquences et aux taux. Il s'agit d'estimations officielles, généralement calculées à partir des résultats d'un sondage ou par analyse démographique. Si des estimations concernant les fréquences et les taux figurent dans les tableaux, c'est parce que l'on considère qu'elles fournissent des renseignements plus exacts que les systèmes existants d'enregistrement des faits d'état civil. En conséquence, elles sont également jugées sûres et ne sont donc pas indiquées en italique, même si elles sont entrecoupées dans une série chronologique de données tirées des registres d'état civil.

Dans les tableaux qui indiquent le code de qualité, ce code ne s'applique qu'aux données tirées des registres d'état civil. Si une série pour un pays ou une zone comprend à la fois des données tirées d'un registre d'état civil et des données estimatives, le code ne s'applique qu'aux données d'enregistrement. Si seules des données estimatives apparaissent, le symbole '|' est utilisé.

4.3 Mortalité liée à la maternité

D'après la dixième révision de la CIM, la « mortalité liée à la maternité » est définie comme le décès d'une femme survenu au cours de la grossesse ou dans un délai de 42 jours après sa terminaison, quelle qu'en soit la durée et la localisation, pour une cause quelconque déterminée ou aggravée par la grossesse ou les soins qu'elle a motivés, mais ni accidentelle ni fortuite.

Les décès liés à la maternité se répartissent en deux groupes :

1) Décès par cause obstétricale directe qui résultent de complications obstétricales (grossesse, travail et suites de couches), d'interventions, d'omissions, d'un traitement incorrect ou d'un enchaînement d'événements de l'un quelconque des facteurs ci-dessus ;

2) Décès par cause obstétricale indirecte qui résultent d'une maladie préexistante ou d'une affection apparue au cours de la grossesse, sans qu'elle soit due à des causes obstétricales directes, mais qui a été aggravée par les effets physiologiques de la grossesse.

Il est recommandé dans la dixième révision d'exprimer les taux de mortalité liée à la maternité sur la base de 100 000 naissances vivantes ou 100 000 naissances totales (naissances vivantes et morts fœtales)[21]. Le nombre de femmes enceintes aurait dû être pris comme dénominateur, mais étant donné qu'il est impossible de le déterminer, le taux de mortalité liée à la maternité est ici calculé par 100 000 naissances vivantes. Bien que les naissances vivantes ne permettent pas d'évaluer sans distorsion le nombre des femmes enceintes, leur nombre est plus fiable que d'autres estimations car le nombre des naissances vivantes est plus exactement enregistré que celui des naissances vivantes et des morts fœtales.

4.4 Mortalité périnatale

La définition de la mortalité périnatale a été recommandée par le Groupe d'étude sur la mortalité périnatale, constitué par l'Organisation mondiale de la santé. La Conférence internationale pour la huitième révision de la Classification internationale des maladies a adopté la recommandation selon laquelle la période périnatale devait être définie comme suit : « période comprise entre la vingt-huitième semaine de gestation et la septième journée de vie ». Considérant que plusieurs pays comptaient comme mort fœtale tardive toute mort fœtale intervenue 20 semaines ou plus après le début de la gestation, la Conférence a décidé d'accepter aussi une définition plus large de la mortalité périnatale qui s'étend de la vingtième semaine de la gestation à la vingt-huitième journée de vie. Cette deuxième définition devait en principe permettre un enregistrement plus complet des morts fœtales intervenues entre la vingt-huitième semaine de gestation et la fin des six premières journées de la vie. En 1975, la Conférence chargée de la neuvième révision a recommandé que les statistiques de la mortalité périnatale s'appuient sur un certificat de décès périnatal normalisé, fondé sur une définition qui prévoit non seulement une durée minimale de gestation, mais également une taille et un poids minimaux.

Dans le tableau 19 de *l'Annuaire démographique 1996* et dans les éditions antérieures de *l'Annuaire* où figuraient des statistiques sur la mortalité périnatale, la définition de mortalité périnatale s'appuie sur la somme des morts fœtales tardives (mortalité fœtale au terme de 28 semaines de gestation ou plus) et de la mortalité infantile dans la première semaine de vie. De plus, afin de normaliser la définition et d'éliminer les différences dues aux pratiques nationales, les chiffres de la mortalité périnatale cités dans *l'Annuaire démographique* sont calculés par la Division de statistique. Conformément aux recommandations de la dixième conférence de révision, le taux de mortalité périnatale a été calculé sur 1 000 naissances vivantes, afin de réduire l'effet des insuffisances d'enregistrement des morts fœtales sur le dénominateur de la fraction[25].

NOTES

[1] Les données relatives à la mortalité liée à la maternité et aux taux de mortalité selon la cause émanent de l'Organisation mondiale de la santé et sont disponibles à l'adresse suivante : http://www3.who.int/whosis/menu.cfm.

[2] Les éditions de 1978 et de 1991 font exception à la règle, puisque les tableaux sur des sujets spéciaux ont été publiés séparément.

[3] *World Population Prospects: The 2004 Revision*. Nations Unies, New York, à paraître. Dans l'intervalle, on peut consulter des extraits et certaines données sur le site www.unpopulation.org. On trouve également des éléments d'information sur les méthodes et les données dans *World Population Prospects: The 2002 Revision*, publication des Nations Unies, numéro de vente : E.03.XIII.6, New York, 2003.

[4] ST/ESA/STAT/SER.M/49/Rev.4/WWW ; http://unstats.un.org/unsd/methods/m49/m49.htm; voir également *Code standard des pays et des zones à usage statistique*, numéro de vente : M.98.XVII.9, Nations Unies, New York, 1999.

5 Publication des Nations Unies, numéro de vente : F.98.XVII.8, 1998.

[6] Lorsque l'on utilise un registre de la population, on peut également calculer l'âge en années révolues en soustrayant la date de naissance de chaque personne inscrite sur le registre de la date de référence à laquelle se rapportent les données sur l'âge.

[7] L'emploi de méthodes différentes de calcul de l'âge, par exemple la méthode occidentale et la méthode orientale, ou, comme on les désigne plus communément, la méthode anglaise et la méthode chinoise, représente une cause de non-comparabilité. Selon la méthode chinoise, on considère que l'enfant est âgé d'un an à sa naissance et qu'il avance d'un an à chaque nouvelle année chinoise. Les répercussions de cette méthode sont particulièrement apparentes dans les données pour le premier âge : les données concernant les enfants de moins d'un an sont nettement inférieures à la réalité. Les effets sur les chiffres relatifs aux groupes d'âge suivants sont moins visibles. Les séries ainsi établies sont souvent ajustées avant d'être publiées, mais il ne faut pas exclure la possibilité d'aberrations de ce genre lorsque l'on compare des données censitaires sur l'âge.

[8] Dans cet indice, on déterminait les différences à partir des rapports prévus de masculinité dans un groupe d'âge et dans les groupes d'âge adjacents. Il fallait pour cela tenir compte de l'influence de facteurs tels que les mouvements passés des taux de natalité, les pertes de guerre élevées et, le cas échéant, le faible effectif de la population. On trouvera dans le *Bulletin démographique*, no 2 (publication des Nations Unies, numéro de vente : 52.XIII.4), p. 64 à 87, un exposé détaillé sur cet indice ainsi que les résultats de son application aux données présentées dans les éditions de 1949-1950 et de 1951 de l'*Annuaire démographique*. On a fait les mêmes calculs sur les statistiques publiées dans l'*Annuaire démographique 1952* et les résultats obtenus sont indiqués dans l'édition correspondante de l'*Annuaire*, qui, comme celles de 1953 et de 1954, donne de brèves explications sur l'indice en question.

[9] United States Bureau of the Census, Thirteenth Census, vol. I (Washington, D.C., U.S. Government Printing Office), p. 291 et 292.

[10] J.T. Marten, Census of India, 1921, vol. I, partie I (Calcutta, 1924), p. 126 et 127.

[11] Numéro de vente : F.01.XVII.10, publication des Nations Unies, New York, 2003 ; http://unstats.un.org/unsd/demographic/sources/civilreg/default.htm.

[12] Numéro de vente : *E.84*.XVII.11, publication des Nations Unies, New York, 1985 ; http://unstats.un.org/unsd/demographic/sources/civilreg/default.htm.

[13] Numéro de vente : F.98.XVII.11, publication des Nations Unies, New York, 1998 ;
http://unstats.un.org/unsd/demographic/sources/civilreg/default.htm.

[14] Numéro de vente : F. 98.XVII.7, publication des Nations Unies, New York, 1998 ;
http://unstats.un.org/unsd/demographic/sources/civilreg/default.htm.

[15] Numéro de vente : F.98.XVII.4, publication des Nations Unies, New York, 1998 ;
http://unstats.un.org/unsd/demographic/sources/civilreg/default.htm.

[16] Numéro de vente : F.98.XVII.6, publication des Nations Unies, New York, 1998 ;
http://unstats.un.org/unsd/demographic/sources/civilreg/default.htm.

[17] Numéro de vente : F.98.XVII.10, publication des Nations Unies, New York, 1998 ;
http://unstats.un.org/unsd/demographic/sources/civilreg/default.htm.

[18] Numéro de vente : F.83.XVII.13, publication des Nation Unis, New York, 1984.

[19] Pour plus de précisions, voir *Principes et recommandations pour un système de statistiques de l'état civil, deuxième révision*, numéro de vente : F.01.XVII.10, publication des Nations Unies, New York, 2001, par. 57.

[20] Pour plus de précisions au sujet des considérations historiques et juridiques auxquelles se rattachent les différentes définitions correspondant aux naissances vivantes et aux morts fœtales, pour une comparaison des définitions utilisées depuis le 1er janvier 1950 et pour une évaluation des effets de ces différences de définition sur le calcul de divers taux, voir le *Manuel de statistique de l'état civil, Volume II, Étude des pratiques nationales*, numéro de vente : F.84.XVII.11, publication des Nations Unies, New York, 1985, chap. IV.

[21] Ibid., p. 129 à 136.

Table A. *Demographic Yearbook 2003* synoptic table: Availability of data by country/area, table and sex, where applicable
Tableau A. Tableau synoptique de l'*Annuaire démographique 2003:* Disponibilité des données par pays ou zone, tableau et le sexe , si disponible

General topic and table number- Suject général et numéro de tableau

Continent, country or area / Continent, pays ou zone	Table totals	Summary - Apercu 3 Total	3 M/F	4	5	Population 6 Total	6 M/F	7 Total	7 M/F	8 Total	8 M/F	Natality 9	10 Total	10 M/F	11	Foetal mortality 12	13	14
Total number of countries or areas - Total des pays ou zones	..	232	217	173	211	131	127	182	178	229	123	164	131	90	99	90	59	40

AFRICA — AFRIQUE

Continent, country or area	Table totals	3 Total	3 M/F	4	5	6 Total	6 M/F	7 Total	7 M/F	8 Total	8 M/F	9	10 Total	10 M/F	11	12	13	14
Algeria - Algérie	17	•	•	•	•	•	•	•	•	•	...	•	...	...	...	•	...	...
Angola	4	•	•	...	...	...	...	...	...	•	•	...	...	...	...	...	...	...
Benin - Bénin	13	•	•	•	•	•	•	•	•	•	•	•	...	...	...	...	...	...
Botswana	17	•	•	•	•	•	•	•	•	•	...	•	...	...	...	...	...	...
Burkina Faso	9	•	•	...	•	•	•	•	•	•	•	...	...	...	...	...	...	...
Burundi	7	•	•	•	•	•	•	•	...	•	...	...	...	...	...	...	...	...
Cameroon - Cameroun	4	•	...	...	•	•	•	...	...	•	...	...	...	...	...	...	...	...
Cape Verde - Cap-Vert	10	•	•	•	•	•	•	•	•	•	...	•	...	...	...	...	...	...
Central African Republic - République centrafricaine	6	•	•	•	•	•	...	•	...	•	...	•	...	...	...	...	...	...
Chad - Tchad	6	•	...	•	...	...	...	•	...	•	...	•	...	...	...	...	...	...
Comoros - Comores	3	•	•	...	•	...	...	•	...	•	...	•	...	...	...	...	...	...
Congo	6	•	•	•	•	...	...	•	...	•	...	•	...	...	...	...	...	...
Côte d'Ivoire	8	•	•	•	•	•	...	•	...	•	...	•	...	...	...	...	...	...
Democratic Republic of the Congo - République démocratique du Congo	3	•	•	...	...	...	...	...	...	•	...	...	...	...	...	...	...	...
Djibouti	6	•	...	...	•	...	...	...	...	•	...	...	...	...	...	...	...	...
Egypt - Égypte	30	•	•	•	•	•	•	•	•	•	•	•	•	•	•	•	...	...
Equatorial Guinea - Guinée équatoriale	2	•	...	...	...	...	...	...	...	•	...	...	...	...	...	...	...	...
Eritrea - Érythrée	3	•	•	...	...	...	...	...	...	•	...	...	...	...	...	...	...	...
Ethiopia - Éthiopie	16	•	•	•	•	•	•	•	•	•	•	...	...	...	...	...	...	...
Gabon	6	•	•	•	•	...	...	...	...	•	...	...	...	...	...	...	...	...
Gambia - Gambie	5	•	•	...	•	...	...	...	...	•	•	...	...	...	...	...	...	...
Ghana	13	•	•	•	•	•	•	•	•	•	•	•	...	...	...	...	...	...
Guinea - Guinée	5	•	•	...	...	...	...	•	•	•	...	...	...	...	...	...	...	...
Guinea-Bissau - Guinée-Bissau	4	•	•	...	•	...	...	...	...	•	...	...	...	...	...	...	...	...
Kenya	15	•	•	•	•	•	•	...	...	•	•	•	•	...	...	...	...	...
Lesotho	10	•	•	•	•	•	•	...	...	•	...	•	...	...	...	...	...	...
Liberia - Libéria	5	•	•	...	•	...	...	...	...	•	...	...	...	...	...	...	...	...
Libyan Arab Jamahiriya - Jamahiriya arabe libyenne	16	•	•	...	•	•	•	...	...	•	•	•	•	•	•	...	...	...
Madagascar	7	•	•	...	•	...	...	•	...	•	•	...	•	...	...	...	...	...
Malawi	16	•	•	•	•	•	•	•	•	•	•	•	...	...	...	...	...	...
Mali	7	•	•	...	•	...	...	...	...	•	...	•	...	...	...	...	...	...
Mauritania - Mauritanie	4	•	•	...	...	...	...	...	...	•	...	...	...	...	...	...	...	...
Mauritius - Maurice	30	•	•	•	•	•	•	•	•	•	•	•	•	•	•	•	...	...
Morocco - Maroc	18	•	...	•	•	•	•	•	•	•	...	•	•	•	...	...	...	...
Mozambique	16	•	•	•	•	•	•	...	...	•	•	•	...	...	...	...	...	...
Namibia - Namibie	17	•	•	•	•	•	•	•	•	•	•	•	...	...	...	...	...	...
Niger	4	•	•	...	...	...	...	...	...	•	•	...	...	...	...	...	...	...
Nigeria - Nigéria	6	•	•	...	...	...	...	•	...	•	...	•	...	...	...	...	•	...
Réunion	27	•	•	...	•	•	•	•	•	•	...	•	•	•	•	...	•	...
Rwanda	8	•	•	...	•	•	•	•	...	•	...	•	...	...	...	...	...	...
Saint Helena ex. dep. - Sainte-Hélène sans dép.	21	•	•	•	•	•	•	•	•	•	•	•	...	...	...	...	...	...
Saint Helena: Ascension - Sainte-Hélène: Ascension	2	•	•	...	...	...	...	...	...	...	...	...	...	...	...	...	...	...
Saint Helena: Tristan da Cunha - Sainte-Hélène: Tristan da Cunha	5	•	•	...	•	...	...	•	•	•	...	...	...	...	...	...	...	...
Sao Tome and Principe - Sao Tomé-et-Principe	4	•	•	...	•	...	...	...	...	•	...	...	...	...	...	...	...	...
Senegal - Sénégal	4	•	•	...	•	...	...	...	...	•	...	...	...	...	...	...	...	...
Seychelles	16	•	•	•	•	•	•	•	•	•	•	•	...	...	...	...	•	...
Sierra Leone	7	•	•	...	•	•	•	•	•	•	...	...	...	...	...	...	...	...
Somalia - Somalie	7	•	•	...	•	•	•	•	•	•	...	...	...	...	...	...	...	...

Table A. *Demographic Yearbook 2003* synoptic table: Availability of data by country/area, table and sex, where applicable
Tableau A. Tableau synoptique de l'*Annuaire démographique 2003:* Disponibilité des données par pays ou zone, tableau et le sexe , si disponible (continued — suite)

Continent, country or area / Continent, pays ou zone	Infant and maternal mortality - Mortalité infantile et mortalité liée à la maternité				General mortality - Mortalité générale								Nuptiality and divorces - Nuptialité et divortialité		
	15	16 Total	16 M/F	17	18	19 Total	19 M/F	20 Total	20 M/F	21 Total	21 M/F	22	23	24	25
Total number of countries or areas - Total des pays ou zones	144	108	105	100	163	135	132	86	86	75	73	119	132	91	117
AFRICA — AFRIQUE															
Algeria - Algérie	•	...	...	...	•	•	•	...	...	...	...	•	•	...	...
Angola	...	...	...	...	...	...	...	...	...	...	...	...	...	...	...
Benin - Bénin	•	...	...	...	•	...	...	...	...	...	...	...	...	...	...
Botswana	•	...	...	...	•	•	•	...	...	...	...	•	...	...	...
Burkina Faso	...	...	...	...	...	...	...	...	...	...	...	...	...	...	...
Burundi	...	...	...	...	...	...	...	...	...	...	...	...	...	...	...
Cameroon - Cameroun	...	...	...	...	...	...	...	...	...	...	...	...	...	...	...
Cape Verde - Cap-Vert	...	...	...	...	...	...	...	...	...	...	...	...	...	...	...
Central African Republic - République centrafricaine	...	...	...	...	...	...	...	...	...	...	...	...	...	...	...
Chad - Tchad	...	...	...	...	•	...	...	...	...	...	...	...	...	...	...
Comoros - Comores	...	...	...	...	...	...	...	...	...	...	...	...	...	...	...
Congo	...	...	...	...	...	...	...	...	...	...	...	...	...	...	...
Côte d'Ivoire	•	...	...	...	•	...	...	...	...	...	...	...	...	...	...
Democratic Republic of the Congo - République démocratique du Congo	...	...	...	...	...	...	...	...	...	...	...	...	...	...	...
Djibouti	...	...	...	...	...	...	...	...	...	...	...	•	•	...	•
Egypt - Égypte	•	•	•	•	•	•	•	•	•	•	•	•	•	•	•
Equatorial Guinea - Guinée équatoriale	...	...	...	...	...	...	...	...	...	...	...	...	...	...	...
Eritrea - Érythrée	...	...	...	...	...	...	...	...	...	...	...	...	...	...	...
Ethiopia - Éthiopie	•	...	...	...	•	...	...	...	...	...	...	...	•	...	•
Gabon	...	...	...	...	...	...	...	...	...	...	...	...	...	...	...
Gambia - Gambie	...	...	...	...	...	...	...	...	...	...	...	...	...	...	...
Ghana	•	...	...	...	•	...	...	...	...	...	...	...	...	...	...
Guinea - Guinée	...	...	...	...	...	...	...	...	...	...	...	...	...	...	...
Guinea-Bissau - Guinée-Bissau	...	...	...	...	...	...	...	...	...	...	...	...	...	...	...
Kenya	•	...	...	...	...	...	...	...	...	...	...	...	•	...	...
Lesotho	...	...	...	...	...	...	...	...	...	...	...	...	...	...	...
Liberia - Libéria	...	...	...	...	...	...	...	...	...	...	...	...	...	...	...
Libyan Arab Jamahiriya - Jamahiriya arabe libyenne	•	...	...	...	•	•	•	...	...	•	•	...	•	...	•
Madagascar	...	...	...	...	•	•	•	...	...	...	...	...	...	...	...
Malawi	...	...	...	...	•	•	•	•	•	...	...	...	...	...	...
Mali	...	...	...	...	•	...	...	...	...	...	...	...	...	...	...
Mauritania - Mauritanie	...	...	...	...	...	...	...	...	...	...	...	...	...	...	...
Mauritius - Maurice	•	•	•	•	•	•	•	•	•	•	•	•	•	•	•
Morocco - Maroc	•	•	•	...	•	•	•	...	...	•	•	•	•	•	•
Mozambique	•	...	...	...	•	•	•	•	•	...	...	...	...	...	...
Namibia - Namibie	...	...	...	...	•	...	...	...	...	...	...	...	...	...	...
Niger	...	...	...	...	...	...	...	...	...	...	...	...	...	...	...
Nigeria - Nigéria	...	...	...	...	...	...	...	...	...	...	...	...	...	...	...
Réunion	•	•	•	...	•	•	•	•	•	•	•	•	•	•	•
Rwanda	...	...	...	...	...	...	...	...	...	...	...	...	...	...	...
Saint Helena ex. dep. - Sainte-Hélène sans dép.	•	•	•	...	•	•	•	...	...	...	...	...	•	...	•
Saint Helena: Ascension - Sainte-Hélène: Ascension	...	...	...	...	...	...	...	...	...	...	...	...	...	...	...
Saint Helena: Tristan da Cunha - Sainte-Hélène: Tristan da Cunha	...	...	...	...	...	...	...	...	...	...	...	...	...	...	...
Sao Tome and Principe - Sao Tomé-et-Principe	...	...	...	...	...	...	...	...	...	...	...	...	...	...	...
Senegal - Sénégal	...	...	...	...	...	...	...	...	...	...	...	...	...	...	...
Seychelles	•	...	...	...	•	•	•	...	...	...	...	...	•	•	•
Sierra Leone	...	...	...	...	...	...	...	...	...	...	...	...	...	...	...
Somalia - Somalie	...	...	...	...	...	...	...	...	...	...	...	...	...	...	...

Table A. *Demographic Yearbook 2003* synoptic table: Availability of data by country/area, table and sex, where applicable
Tableau A. Tableau synoptique de l'*Annuaire démographique 2003*: Disponibilité des données par pays ou zone, tableau et le sexe , si disponible (continued — suite)

Continent, country or area / Continent, pays ou zone	Table totals	Summary - Aperçu 3 Total	3 M/F	4	5	Population 6 Total	6 M/F	7 Total	7 M/F	8 Total	8 M/F	Natality 9	10 Total	10 M/F	11	Foetal mortality 12	13	14
AFRICA — AFRIQUE																		
South Africa - Afrique du Sud	19	•	•	•	•	•	•	•	•	•	•	•	•	...	...	...	•	...
Sudan - Soudan	4	•	•	...	•	•	...	...	...	•	...	...	...	•	...	...	...	...
Swaziland	15	•	•	...	•	•	...	•	...	•	...	...	•	...	•	...	...	...
Togo	4	•	•	...	•	...	...	...	•	...	...	...	...	...	...	...	...	...
Tunisia - Tunisie	23	•	•	...	•	•	•	•	•	•	...	•	•	...	•	...	...	...
Uganda - Ouganda	9	•	•	...	•	•	•	•	•	•	...	...	...	...	...	...	...	...
United Republic of Tanzania - République Unie de Tanzanie	7	•	•	...	•	...	•	•	•	•	...	...	...	...	...	...	...	...
Western Sahara - Sahara occidental	3	•	•	...	...	...	...	...	...	...	...	...	...	...	...	...	...	...
Zambia - Zambie	9	•	•	...	•	•	•	•	•	•	...	...	...	...	...	...	...	...
Zimbabwe	8	•	...	...	•	•	•	•	•	•	...	...	...	...	...	...	...	...
AMERICA, NORTH — AMERIQUE DU NORD																		
Anguilla	19	•	•	•	•	•	•	•	...	•	•	•	•	...	•	...	•	...
Antigua and Barbuda - Antigua-et-Barbuda	16	•	•	•	•	•	•	•	•	•	...	•	•	...	•	...	...	...
Aruba	15	•	•	•	•	...	•	•	•	•	...	•	•	•	•	...	...	...
Bahamas	24	•	•	•	•	•	•	•	•	•	...	•	•	•	•	...	...	...
Barbados - Barbade	10	•	•	...	•	•	...	...	...	•	...	•	...	...	...	...	...	...
Belize	19	•	•	•	•	•	•	•	•	•	...	•	•	...	•	...	•	•
Bermuda - Bermudes	21	•	•	•	•	•	•	•	•	•	...	•	•	•	•	...	...	...
British Virgin Islands - Îles Vierges britanniques	11	•	•	•	•	...	...	...	•	...	...	•	•	...	...	...	...	•
Canada	32	•	•	•	•	•	•	•	•	•	...	•	•	•	•	•	•	•
Cayman Islands - Îles Caïmanes	15	•	...	•	•	...	•	•	•	•	...	•	•	•	•	...	...	...
Costa Rica	28	•	•	•	•	•	•	•	•	•	•	•	•	•	•	•	•	...
Cuba	30	•	•	•	•	•	•	•	•	•	•	•	•	•	•	•	•	...
Dominica - Dominique	13	•	•	•	•	...	•	•	•	•	...	•	...	...	•	...	...	...
Dominican Republic - République dominicaine	21	•	•	•	•	•	•	•	•	•	...	•	•	...	•	...	•	...
El Salvador	29	•	•	•	•	•	•	•	•	•	...	•	•	•	•	...	•	...
Greenland - Groenland	24	•	•	•	•	•	•	•	•	•	...	•	•	•	•	...	•	...
Grenada - Grenade	18	•	•	•	•	...	•	•	•	•	...	•	•	...	•	...	...	...
Guadeloupe	27	•	...	•	•	•	•	•	•	•	...	•	•	•	•	•	•	...
Guatemala	26	•	...	•	•	•	•	•	•	•	...	•	•	•	•	...	•	...
Haiti - Haïti	8	•	•	...	•	•	•	•	...	•	...	...	...	...	...	...	...	...
Honduras	9	•	•	...	•	•	•	•	...	•	...	...	...	...	...	...	...	...
Jamaica - Jamaïque	19	•	•	•	•	•	•	•	•	•	...	•	•	•	•	...	•	...
Martinique	27	•	•	•	•	•	•	•	•	•	...	•	•	•	•	•	•	...
Mexico - Mexique	29	•	•	•	•	•	•	•	•	•	...	•	•	•	•	•	•	•
Montserrat	17	•	•	•	•	•	•	•	•	•	...	•	•	...	•	...	...	...
Netherlands Antilles - Antilles néerlandaises	12	•	•	•	•	...	•	•	•	•	...	•	•	...	•	...	...	...
Nicaragua	24	•	•	•	•	•	•	•	•	•	...	•	•	•	•	...	•	...
Panama	30	•	•	•	•	•	•	•	•	•	...	•	•	•	•	•	•	•
Puerto Rico - Porto Rico	30	•	•	•	•	•	•	•	•	•	...	•	•	•	•	•	•	...
Saint Kitts and Nevis - Saint-Kitts-et-Nevis	15	•	•	•	•	•	•	•	•	•	...	•	•	...	•	...	•	...
Saint Lucia - Sainte-Lucie	26	•	•	•	•	•	•	•	•	•	...	•	•	•	•	...	•	...
Saint Pierre and Miquelon - Saint Pierre-et-Miquelon	4	•	•	...	•	...	...	...	•	...	...	...	...	...	...	...	...	...
Saint Vincent and the Grenadines - Saint Vincent-et-les Grenadines	22	•	...	•	•	•	•	•	•	•	...	•	•	...	•	...	•	...
Trinidad and Tobago - Trinité-et-Tobago	21	•	•	•	•	•	•	•	•	•	...	•	•	...	•	...	•	...
Turks Caicos Islands - Îles Turques et Caïques	21	•	•	•	•	•	•	•	•	•	...	•	•	...	•	...	•	...
United States - États-Unis	27	•	•	•	•	•	•	•	•	•	...	•	•	•	•	...	•	...
United States Virgin Islands - Îles Vierges américaines	6	•	•	...	•	...	...	...	•	...	...	...	...	...	...	...	...	...

Table A. *Demographic Yearbook 2003* synoptic table: Availability of data by country/area, table and sex, where applicable
Tableau A. Tableau synoptique de l'*Annuaire démographique 2003:* Disponibilité des données par pays ou zone, tableau et le sexe , si disponible (continued — suite)

Continent, country or area / Continent, pays ou zone	15	16 Total	16 M/F	17	18	19 Total	19 M/F	20 Total	20 M/F	21 Total	21 M/F	22	23	24	25
AFRICA — AFRIQUE															
South Africa - Afrique du Sud	...	•	•	•	...	•	...	...	...	...	...	•	...	...	...
Sudan - Soudan	...	...	...	...	...	...	...	...	...	...	...	...	...	...	...
Swaziland	...	...	...	...	•	•	•	•	...	...	...	...	...	...	...
Togo	...	...	...	...	...	•	•	...	...	...	...	...	...	...	...
Tunisia - Tunisie	•	•	•	•	•	•	•	•	...	•	•	•	•	•	•
Uganda - Ouganda	...	...	...	...	...	...	...	...	...	...	...	...	...	...	...
United Republic of Tanzania - République Unie de Tanzanie	...	...	...	...	...	...	...	...	...	...	...	...	...	...	...
Western Sahara - Sahara occidental	...	...	...	...	...	...	...	...	...	...	...	...	...	...	...
Zambia - Zambie	...	...	...	...	...	...	...	...	...	...	...	...	...	...	...
Zimbabwe	...	...	...	...	...	...	...	...	...	...	...	...	...	...	...
AMERICA, NORTH — AMERIQUE DU NORD															
Anguilla	•	...	...	•	•	•	•	...	...	...	...	...	•	•	•
Antigua and Barbuda - Antigua-et-Barbuda	...	•	•	•	•	•	•	...	...	...	...	...	•	•	...
Aruba	•	•	...	...	•	•	•	...	...	...	...	•	•	...	•
Bahamas	•	•	•	•	•	•	•	...	...	...	...	•	•	•	•
Barbados - Barbade	•	•	•	•	•	•	•	...	...	...	...	...	•	•	•
Belize	•	•	•	•	•	•	•	...	...	...	...	...	•	•	•
Bermuda - Bermudes	•	•	•	...	•	•	•	...	...	...	...	...	•	•	•
British Virgin Islands - Îles Vierges britanniques	•	...	...	...	•	•	•	...	...	...	...	...	...	...	...
Canada	•	•	•	•	•	•	•	•	•	•	•	•	•	...	...
Cayman Islands - Îles Caïmanes	...	•	•	...	•	•	•	...	...	...	...	...	•	•	...
Costa Rica	•	•	•	•	•	•	•	•	•	•	•	•	•	•	...
Cuba	•	•	•	•	•	•	•	•	•	•	•	•	•	•	•
Dominica - Dominique	•	•	•	...	•	•	•	...	...	...	...	...	•	•	•
Dominican Republic - République dominicaine	•	...	...	...	•	•	•	...	...	...	...	...	•	•	•
El Salvador	•	•	•	•	•	•	•	•	•	...	...	...	•	•	•
Greenland - Groenland	•	•	•	•	•	•	•	...	...	...	...	...	...	...	...
Grenada - Grenade	•	...	...	•	•	•	•	...	...	...	...	...	•	•	•
Guadeloupe	•	•	•	•	•	•	•	•	•	•	•	...	•	•	•
Guatemala	•	•	•	•	•	•	•	•	•	•	•	•	•	•	•
Haiti - Haïti	...	...	...	...	...	...	...	...	...	...	...	...	...	...	...
Honduras	...	...	...	...	...	...	...	...	...	...	...	...	...	...	...
Jamaica - Jamaïque	•	...	...	...	•	...	...	...	...	...	...	...	•	•	•
Martinique	•	•	•	•	•	•	•	•	•	•	•	•	•	•	•
Mexico - Mexique	•	•	•	•	•	•	•	•	•	•	•	•	•	•	...
Montserrat	...	...	•	...	•	...	...	...	...	...	...	...	•	•	•
Netherlands Antilles - Antilles néerlandaises	•	•	•	...	•	•	•	...	...	...	...	...	•	•	•
Nicaragua	•	•	•	•	•	•	•	...	...	•	•	...	•	•	•
Panama	•	•	•	•	•	•	•	•	•	•	•	...	•	•	•
Puerto Rico - Porto Rico	•	•	•	•	•	•	•	•	•	•	•	•	•	•	•
Saint Kitts and Nevis - Saint-Kitts-et-Nevis	...	...	...	...	•	...	...	...	...	...	...	...	•	•	•
Saint Lucia - Sainte-Lucie	•	•	•	•	•	•	•	...	...	...	...	...	•	•	•
Saint Pierre and Miquelon - Saint Pierre-et-Miquelon	...	...	...	...	...	...	...	...	...	...	...	...	...	...	...
Saint Vincent and the Grenadines - Saint Vincent-et-les Grenadines	•	•	•	•	•	•	•	...	...	...	...	...	•	•	•
Trinidad and Tobago - Trinité-et-Tobago	...	•	•	•	•	•	•	...	...	...	...	...	•	•	•
Turks Caicos Islands - Îles Turques et Caïques	•	...	...	•	•	•	•	...	...	...	...	•	•	•	•
United States - États-Unis	•	•	•	•	•	•	•	•	•	•	•	•	•	...	...
United States Virgin Islands - Îles Vierges américaines	...	...	...	•	...	...	...	...	...	...	...	...	...	...	...

Table A. *Demographic Yearbook 2003* synoptic table: Availability of data by country/area, table and sex, where applicable
Tableau A. Tableau synoptique de l'*Annuaire démographique 2003:* Disponibilité des données par pays ou zone, tableau et le sexe , si disponible (continued — suite)

General topic and table number- Suject général et numéro de tableau

Continent, country or area / Continent, pays ou zone	Table totals	Summary - Apercu				Population						Natality - Natalité				Foetal mortality - Mortalité foetale		
		3 Total	3 M/F	4	5	6 Total	6 M/F	7 Total	7 M/F	8 Total	8 M/F	9	10 Total	10 M/F	11	12	13	14
AMERICA, SOUTH — AMERIQUE DU SUD																		
Argentina - Argentine	23	•	•	•	•	•	•	•	•	•	•	...	•	•	•	•	•	...
Bolivia - Bolivie	14	•	•	•	•	•	•	•	•	•	...	...	•	•	•	...	•	...
Brazil - Brésil	26	•	•	•	•	•	•	•	•	•	•	...	•	•	•	...	•	...
Chile - Chili	29	•	•	•	•	•	•	•	•	•	•	...	•	•	•	...	•	...
Colombia - Colombie	23	•	•	•	•	•	•	•	•	•	•	...	•	•	•	...	•	...
Ecuador - Équateur	26	•	•	•	•	•	•	•	•	•	•	...	•	•	•	...	•	...
Falkland Islands (Malvinas) - Îles Falkland (Malvinas)	9	•	•	•	...	...	•	...	...	...	•	...	•	•	...	...	...	...
French Guiana - Guyane française	25	•	•	•	•	•	•	•	•	•	•	...	•	•	•	•	•	...
Guyana	7	•	•	•	...	...	•	...	...	...	•	...	...	...	...	...	...	...
Paraguay	15	•	•	•	...	•	•	•	•	•	•	...	•	•	...	...	...	...
Peru - Pérou	20	•	•	•	•	•	•	•	•	•	•	...	•	•	•	...	•	...
Suriname	23	•	•	•	•	•	•	•	•	•	•	•	•	•	•	•	•	...
Uruguay	29	•	•	•	•	•	•	•	•	•	•	...	•	•	•	•	•	...
Venezuela	29	•	•	•	•	•	•	•	•	•	•	...	•	•	•	•	•	...
ASIA — ASIE																		
Afghanistan	8	•	•	•	•	•	•	...	...	•	...	...	...	...	...	...	...	...
Armenia - Arménie	28	•	•	•	•	•	•	•	•	•	•	•	•	•	•	•	•	•
Azerbaijan - Azerbaïdjan	32	•	•	•	•	•	•	•	•	•	•	•	•	•	•	•	•	•
Bahrain - Bahreïn	24	•	•	•	•	•	•	•	•	•	•	•	•	•	•	•	...	...
Bangladesh	7	•	•	...	•	•	•	•	•	•	•	...	...	...	...	...	...	...
Bhutan - Bhoutan	6	•	...	...	•	•	...	•	•	•	...	...	...	...	...	...	...	...
Brunei Darussalam - Brunéi Darussalam	23	•	•	•	•	•	•	•	•	•	•	...	•	•	•	•	...	...
Cambodia - Cambodge	9	•	•	...	•	•	•	•	•	•	•	...	...	...	...	...	...	...
China - Chine[1]	17	•	•	•	•	•	•	•	•	•	•	•	•	•	...	...	...	...
China: Hong Kong SAR - Chine: Hong Kong RAS	30	•	•	•	•	...	•	•	•	•	•	•	•	•	•	•	•	•
China: Macao SAR - Chine: Macao RAS	27	•	•	•	•	...	•	•	•	•	•	•	•	•	•	•	•	...
Cyprus - Chypre	25	•	•	•	•	•	•	•	•	•	...	...	•	•	•	•	...	...
Georgia - Géorgie	31	•	•	•	•	•	•	•	•	•	•	•	•	•	•	•	•	...
India - Inde[2]	14	•	•	...	•	•	•	•	•	•	•	...	...	...	...	...	...	...
Indonesia - Indonésie	10	•	•	...	•	•	•	•	•	•	•	...	...	...	...	...	...	...
Iran (Islamic Republic of) - Iran (République islamique d')	16	•	•	•	...	•	•	•	•	•	•	...	•	•	•	...	...	...
Iraq	14	•	•	•	...	•	•	•	•	•	•	...	•	•	...	...	...	...
Israel - Israël[3]	30	•	•	•	•	•	•	•	•	•	•	•	•	•	•	•	•	•
Japan - Japon	32	•	•	•	•	•	•	•	•	•	•	•	•	•	•	•	•	•
Jordan - Jordanie	15	•	•	•	•	•	•	•	•	•	•	...	•	•	...	...	...	...
Kazakhstan	32	•	•	•	•	•	•	•	•	•	•	•	•	•	•	•	•	•
Korea (Dem. People's Republic of) - Corée (Rép. populaire dém. de)	4	•	•	...	...	...	...	...	...	•	...	...	...	...	...	...	...	...
Korea (Republic of) - Corée (République de)	27	•	•	•	•	•	•	•	•	•	•	•	•	•	...	...	...	...
Kuwait - Koweït	23	•	•	•	•	•	•	•	•	•	•	...	•	•	•	...	...	...
Kyrgyzstan - Kirghizistan	29	•	•	•	•	•	•	•	•	•	•	•	•	•	•	•	...	...
Lao People's Democratic Republic - République démocratique populaire lao	9	•	•	•	•	...	•	•	•	•	•	...	...	...	...	...	...	...
Lebanon - Liban	9	•	•	•	•	...	•	•	•	•	•	...	...	...	...	...	...	...
Malaysia - Malaisie	20	•	•	•	•	•	•	•	•	•	•	...	•	•	•	...	...	...
Maldives	26	•	•	•	•	•	•	•	•	•	•	•	•	•	•	•	...	...
Mongolia - Mongolie	25	•	•	•	•	•	•	•	•	•	•	...	•	•	•	...	•	...
Myanmar	12	•	•	...	•	•	•	•	•	•	•	...	...	...	...	...	...	...
Nepal - Népal	16	•	•	•	•	•	•	•	•	•	•	...	...	...	...	...	...	...

Table A. *Demographic Yearbook 2003* synoptic table: Availability of data by country/area, table and sex, where applicable
Tableau A. Tableau synoptique de l'*Annuaire démographique 2003:* Disponibilité des données par pays ou zone,
tableau et le sexe , si disponible (continued — suite)

Continent, country or area Continent, pays ou zone	General topic and table number- Suject général et numéro de tableau														
	Infant and maternal mortality - Mortalité infantile et mortalité liée à la maternité				General mortality - Mortalité générale								Nuptiality and divorces - Nuptialité et divortialité		
	15	16 Total	16 M/F	17	18	19 Total	19 M/F	20 Total	20 M/F	21 Total	21 M/F	22	23	24	25
AMERICA, SOUTH — AMERIQUE DU SUD															
Argentina - Argentine	•	•	•	•	•	•	•	•	•	•	...	...	•	...	
Bolivia - Bolivie	•	...	...	...	•	...	...	...	...	•	...	•	...	...	
Brazil - Brésil	•	...	...	•	•	•	...	•	...	•	•	•	•	...	
Chile - Chili	•	•	•	•	•	•	•	•	•	•	•	•	•	•	
Colombia - Colombie	•	•	•	•	•	•	...	•	...	•	•	•	...	...	
Ecuador - Équateur	•	•	•	•	•	•	...	...	...	•	•	•	•	...	
Falkland Islands (Malvinas) - Îles Falkland (Malvinas)	...	...	...	...	•	...	...	...	...	...	...	...	...	...	
French Guiana - Guyane française	•	•	•	•	•	•	...	...	...	•	•	•	•	...	
Guyana	...	...	...	•	•	•	...	...	...	•	...	...	...	...	
Paraguay	•	...	...	•	•	•	...	...	...	•	...	•	...	...	
Peru - Pérou	•	•	•	•	•	•	...	...	...	•	...	•	...	...	
Suriname	•	...	...	...	•	...	...	...	...	...	...	•	•	...	
Uruguay	•	•	•	•	•	•	•	•	•	•	...	•	•	...	
Venezuela	•	•	•	•	•	•	•	•	•	•	•	•	•	•	
ASIA — ASIE															
Afghanistan	...	...	...	...	...	...	...	...	...	•	...	...	...	...	
Armenia - Arménie	•	•	•	•	•	•	•	•	•	•	•	•	•	•	
Azerbaijan - Azerbaïdjan	•	•	•	•	•	•	•	•	•	•	•	•	•	•	
Bahrain - Bahreïn	•	•	•	•	•	•	•	•	•	•	•	•	•	•	
Bangladesh	...	...	...	...	...	...	...	...	...	...	...	•	...	...	
Bhutan - Bhoutan	...	...	...	...	...	...	...	...	...	•	...	...	...	...	
Brunei Darussalam - Brunéi Darussalam	•	...	...	•	•	•	...	...	...	•	...	•	•	...	
Cambodia - Cambodge	•	...	...	...	•	...	...	...	...	...	...	...	...	...	
China - Chine[1]	•	...	.	•	•	•	...	...	...	•	...	•	•	•	
China: Hong Kong SAR - Chine: Hong Kong RAS	•	•	•	•	•	•	•	•	•	•	•	•	•	•	
China: Macao SAR - Chine: Macao RAS	•	•	•	•	•	•	•	•	•	•	•	•	•	•	
Cyprus - Chypre	•	•	•	•	•	•	•	•	•	•	•	•	•	•	
Georgia - Géorgie	•	•	•	•	•	•	•	•	•	•	•	•	•	•	
India - Inde[2]	•	...	...	...	•	...	...	...	...	•	...	•	•	...	
Indonesia - Indonésie	...	...	...	...	...	...	...	...	...	•	...	...	...	...	
Iran (Islamic Republic of) - Iran (République islamique d')	•	...	...	...	•	...	...	...	...	•	...	•	...	•	
Iraq	...	...	...	...	...	...	...	...	...	...	...	•	...	...	
Israel - Israël[3]	•	•	•	•	•	•	•	•	•	•	...	•	•	•	
Japan - Japon	•	•	•	•	•	•	•	•	•	•	•	•	•	•	
Jordan - Jordanie	•	...	...	...	•	...	...	...	...	•	...	•	•	...	
Kazakhstan	•	•	•	•	•	•	•	•	•	•	•	•	•	•	
Korea (Dem. People's Republic of) - Corée (Rép. populaire dém. de)	...	...	...	...	...	...	...	...	...	•	...	...	...	...	
Korea (Republic of) - Corée (République de)	•	•	•	•	•	•	•	•	•	•	•	•	•	•	
Kuwait - Koweït	•	•	•	•	•	•	•	•	...	•	...	•	•	•	
Kyrgyzstan - Kirghizistan	•	•	•	•	•	•	•	•	•	•	•	•	•	•	
Lao People's Democratic Republic - République démocratique populaire lao	...	...	...	...	...	...	...	...	...	...	...	...	...	...	
Lebanon - Liban	...	...	...	...	...	...	...	...	...	...	...	•	...	...	
Malaysia - Malaisie	•	•	•	•	•	•	•	•	•	•	...	•	•	...	
Maldives	•	•	•	•	•	•	•	•	•	•	•	•	•	•	
Mongolia - Mongolie	•	...	...	•	•	•	...	...	...	•	...	•	•	•	
Myanmar	...	•	•	•	•	•	...	...	...	...	...	...	...	...	
Nepal - Népal	•	...	...	•	•	•	...	•	...	...	...	...	...	...	

Table A. *Demographic Yearbook 2003* synoptic table: Availability of data by country/area, table and sex, where applicable
Tableau A. Tableau synoptique de l'*Annuaire démographique 2003:* Disponibilité des données par pays ou zone, tableau et le sexe , si disponible (continued — suite)

General topic and table number- Suject général et numéro de tableau

Continent, country or area / Continent, pays ou zone	Table totals	Summary - Apercu 3 Total	3 M/F	4	5	Population 6 Total	6 M/F	7 Total	7 M/F	8 Total	8 M/F	Natality 9	10 Total	10 M/F	11	Foetal mortality 12	13	14
ASIA — ASIE																		
Occupied Palestinian Territory - Territoire palestinien occupé	23	•	•	•	•	•	•	•	•	•	•	•	...	...	...	•	...	...
Oman	17	•	•	•	•	•	•	•	•	•	•	•	•	...	...	•	•	...
Pakistan[4]	25	•	•	•	•	•	•	•	•	•	•	•	•	...	•	•	•	•
Philippines	26	•	•	•	•	...	•	•	•	•	•	•	•	...	•	•	•	...
Qatar	26	•	•	•	•	...	•	•	•	•	•	•	•	...	•	•	•	...
Saudi Arabia - Arabie saoudite	15	•	•	•	•	•	•	•	•	...	•	•	•	...	•	•	•	...
Singapore - Singapour	29	•	•	•	•	•	•	•	•	...	•	•	•	...	•	•	•	•
Sri Lanka	23	•	•	•	•	•	•	•	•	•	•	•	•	...	•	•	•	...
Syrian Arab Republic - République arabe syrienne	14	•	•	•	•	•	•	•	•	...	•	•	•	...	•	•	•	•
Tajikistan - Tadjikistan	23	•	•	•	•	•	•	•	•	•	•	•	•	...	•	•	•	•
Thailand - Thaïlande	21	•	•	•	•	•	•	•	•	•	•	•	•	...	•	•	•	...
Timor-Leste	3	•	•	...	•	•	•	•	•	•	•	...	...	...	...	...	...	...
Turkey - Turquie	20	•	•	•	•	•	•	•	•	•	•	•	•	...	•	•	•	...
Turkmenistan - Turkménistan	7	•	•	...	•	•	•	•	•	•	•	...	...	...	...	...	...	...
United Arab Emirates - Émirats arabes unis	9	•	•	...	•	•	•	•	•	•	•	•	...	...	...	...	...	...
Uzbekistan - Ouzbékistan	27	•	•	•	•	•	•	•	•	•	•	•	•	...	•	•	•	•
Viet Nam	10	•	•	...	•	•	•	•	•	•	•	...	...	...	...	...	...	...
Yemen - Yémen	8	•	•	...	•	•	•	•	•	•	•	...	...	...	...	...	...	...
EUROPE																		
Albania - Albanie	21	•	•	•	•	•	•	...	•	•	•	•	•	...	•	•	•	...
Andorra - Andorre	19	•	...	•	•	•	•	•	•	•	•	•	•	...	•	•	...	...
Austria - Autriche	30	•	•	•	•	•	•	•	•	•	•	•	•	...	•	•	•	...
Belarus - Bélarus	29	•	•	•	•	•	•	•	•	•	•	•	•	...	•	•	•	•
Belgium - Belgique	25	•	•	•	•	•	•	•	•	•	•	...	•	...	•	•	•	•
Bosnia and Herzegovina - Bosnie-Herzégovine	18	•	•	•	•	•	•	...	•	•	•	...	•	...	...	•	•	•
Bulgaria - Bulgarie	32	•	•	•	•	•	•	•	•	•	•	•	•	...	•	•	•	•
Channel Islands: Guernsey - Îles Anglo-Normandes: Guernesey	21	•	•	•	•	•	•	•	•	•	•	•	•	...	•	•	•	•
Channel Islands: Jersey - Îles Anglo-Normandes: Jersey	13	•	•	...	•	•	•	•	•	•	•	•	•	...	•	•	•	•
Croatia - Croatie	31	•	•	•	•	•	•	•	•	•	•	•	•	...	•	•	•	•
Czech Republic - République tchèque	32	•	•	•	•	•	•	•	•	•	•	•	•	...	•	•	•	•
Denmark - Danemark	29	•	•	•	•	...	•	•	•	•	•	•	•	...	•	•	•	•
Estonia - Estonie	32	•	•	•	•	•	•	•	•	•	•	•	•	...	•	•	•	•
Faeroe Islands - Îles Féroé	4	•	•	...	•	•	...	•	•	•	•	...	...	...	...	...	...	...
Finland - Finlande	32	•	•	•	•	•	•	•	•	•	•	•	•	...	•	•	•	•
France	30	•	•	•	•	•	•	•	•	•	•	•	•	...	•	•	•	•
Germany - Allemagne	27	...	...	•	•	•	•	•	•	•	•	•	•	...	•	•	•	•
Gibraltar	15	•	•	•	•	•	•	•	•	•	•	•	•	...	•	•	•	...
Greece - Grèce	28	•	•	•	•	•	•	...	•	•	•	•	•	...	•	•	•	•
Holy See - Saint-Siège	7	•	•	•	•	•	•	...	•	•	•	•	•	...	...	...	...	...
Hungary - Hongrie	32	•	•	•	•	•	•	•	•	•	•	•	•	...	•	•	•	•
Iceland - Islande	32	•	•	•	•	•	•	•	•	•	•	•	•	...	•	•	•	•
Ireland - Irlande	28	•	•	•	•	•	•	•	•	•	•	•	•	...	•	•	•	•
Isle of Man - Îles de Man	20	•	•	•	•	•	•	•	•	•	•	•	•	...	•	•	•	...
Italy - Italie	31	•	•	•	•	•	•	•	•	•	•	•	•	...	•	•	•	•
Latvia - Lettonie	32	•	•	•	•	•	•	•	•	•	•	•	•	...	•	•	•	•
Liechtenstein	20	•	•	•	•	•	•	•	•	•	•	•	•	...	•	•	...	...
Lithuania - Lituanie	32	•	•	•	•	•	•	•	•	•	•	•	•	...	•	•	•	•
Luxembourg	27	•	•	•	•	...	•	•	•	•	•	•	•	...	•	•	•	•
Malta - Malte	25	•	•	•	•	•	•	•	•	•	•	•	•	...	•	•	...	...

Table A. *Demographic Yearbook 2003* synoptic table: Availability of data by country/area, table and sex, where applicable
Tableau A. Tableau synoptique de l'*Annuaire démographique 2003:* Disponibilité des données par pays ou zone, tableau et le sexe , si disponible (continued — suite)

Continent, country or area / Continent, pays ou zone	Infant and maternal mortality - Mortalité infantile et mortalité liée à la maternité				General mortality - Mortalité générale								Nuptiality and divorces - Nuptialité et divortialité		
	15	16 Total	16 M/F	17	18	19 Total	19 M/F	20 Total	20 M/F	21 Total	21 M/F	22	23	24	25
ASIA — ASIE															
Occupied Palestinian Territory - Territoire palestinien occupé	•	•	•	…	•	•	•	…	…	•	•	•	•	•	•
Oman	•	…	…	…	•	•	•	…	…	…	…	•	•	…	…
Pakistan[4]	•	•	•	…	•	•	•	•	•	…	…	•	•	…	…
Philippines	•	•	•	…	•	•	•	•	•	•	…	•	•	•	…
Qatar	•	•	•	•	•	•	•	•	•	•	•	•	•	•	•
Saudi Arabia - Arabie saoudite	•	…	…	…	•	•	…	…	…	…	…	…	•	•	•
Singapore - Singapour	•	•	•	…	•	•	•	•	•	•	•	•	•	•	•
Sri Lanka	•	•	•	•	•	•	•	…	…	…	…	…	•	•	•
Syrian Arab Republic - République arabe syrienne	…	…	…	…	•	•	…	…	…	…	…	…	•	•	•
Tajikistan - Tadjikistan	…	•	•	•	•	•	…	…	…	…	…	…	•	•	•
Thailand - Thaïlande	•	•	•	•	•	•	•	…	…	…	…	…	•	•	•
Timor-Leste	…	…	…	…	…	…	…	…	…	…	…	…	…	…	…
Turkey - Turquie	•	•	…	…	•	…	…	…	…	…	…	•	•	•	•
Turkmenistan - Turkménistan	…	…	…	•	…	…	…	…	…	…	…	…	…	…	…
United Arab Emirates - Émirats arabes unis	…	…	…	…	…	…	…	…	…	…	…	…	…	…	…
Uzbekistan - Ouzbékistan	•	•	•	•	•	•	•	…	…	…	…	…	•	•	•
Viet Nam	…	…	…	…	…	…	…	…	…	…	…	…	•	…	•
Yemen - Yémen	…	…	…	…	…	…	…	…	…	…	…	…	…	…	…
EUROPE															
Albania - Albanie	•	…	…	•	•	•	…	…	…	…	…	•	•	•	•
Andorra - Andorre	•	•	•	…	•	•	•	…	…	…	…	…	•	•	•
Austria - Autriche	•	•	•	•	•	•	•	•	•	•	•	•	•	•	•
Belarus - Bélarus	•	•	•	•	•	•	•	…	…	…	…	•	•	•	•
Belgium - Belgique	•	•	•	•	•	•	•	•	•	•	•	•	•	•	•
Bosnia and Herzegovina - Bosnie-Herzégovine	•	•	•	•	•	•	…	…	…	…	…	•	•	•	•
Bulgaria - Bulgarie	•	•	…	•	•	•	…	…	…	…	…	•	•	•	•
Channel Islands: Guernsey - Îles Anglo-Normandes: Guernesey	•	•	…	…	•	•	•	…	…	…	…	…	•	•	•
Channel Islands: Jersey - Îles Anglo-Normandes: Jersey	…	•	•	•	…	…	…	…	…	…	…	…	…	…	…
Croatia - Croatie	•	•	•	•	•	•	•	•	•	•	•	•	•	•	•
Czech Republic - République tchèque	•	•	•	•	•	•	•	•	•	•	•	•	•	•	•
Denmark - Danemark	•	•	•	•	•	•	•	•	•	•	•	•	•	•	•
Estonia - Estonie	•	•	•	•	•	•	•	•	•	•	•	•	•	•	•
Faeroe Islands - Îles Féroé	…	…	…	…	…	…	…	…	…	…	…	…	…	…	…
Finland - Finlande	•	•	•	•	•	•	•	•	•	•	•	•	•	•	•
France	•	•	•	•	•	•	•	•	•	•	•	•	•	•	•
Germany - Allemagne	•	•	•	•	•	•	•	•	•	•	•	•	•	•	•
Gibraltar	•	…	…	…	•	•	…	…	…	…	…	…	•	•	•
Greece - Grèce	•	•	•	•	•	•	•	•	•	•	•	•	•	•	•
Holy See - Saint-Siège	…	…	…	…	•	…	…	…	…	…	…	…	…	…	…
Hungary - Hongrie	•	…	•	•	•	•	•	•	•	•	•	•	•	•	•
Iceland - Islande	•	•	•	•	•	•	•	•	•	•	•	•	•	•	•
Ireland - Irlande	•	•	•	•	•	•	•	•	•	•	•	•	•	•	…
Isle of Man - Îles de Man	•	•	•	•	•	•	…	…	…	…	…	•	•	•	…
Italy - Italie	•	•	•	•	•	•	•	•	•	•	•	•	•	•	•
Latvia - Lettonie	•	•	•	•	•	•	•	•	•	•	•	•	•	•	•
Liechtenstein	•	…	…	•	•	•	…	…	…	…	…	•	•	•	•
Lithuania - Lituanie	•	•	•	•	•	•	•	•	•	•	•	•	•	•	•
Luxembourg	•	•	•	•	•	•	•	•	•	•	•	•	•	•	•
Malta - Malte	•	•	•	•	•	•	•	•	•	•	•	•	•	•	…

Table A. *Demographic Yearbook 2003* synoptic table: Availability of data by country/area, table and sex, where applicable
Tableau A. Tableau synoptique de l'*Annuaire démographique 2003*: Disponibilité des données par pays ou zone, tableau et le sexe , si disponible (continued — suite)

General topic and table number- Suject général et numéro de tableau

Continent, country or area / Continent, pays ou zone	Table totals	Summary - Apercu 3 Total	M/F	4	5	Population 6 Total	M/F	7 Total	M/F	8 Total	M/F	9	Natality - Natalité 10 Total	M/F	11	Foetal mortality - Mortalité foetale 12	13	14
EUROPE																		
Monaco	11	•	•	•	•	•	...	•	•	•	...	•	...	...	...	...	...	...
Netherlands - Pays-Bas	31	•	•	•	•	•	•	•	•	•	•	•	•	•	•	•	•	•
Norway - Norvège	31	•	•	•	•	•	•	•	•	•	•	•	•	•	•	•	•	•
Poland - Pologne	31	•	•	•	•	•	•	•	•	•	•	•	•	•	•	•	•	•
Portugal	30	•	•	•	•	•	•	•	•	•	•	•	•	•	•	•	•	•
Republic of Moldova - République de Moldova	31	•	•	•	•	•	•	•	•	•	•	•	•	•	•	•	...	•
Romania - Roumanie	32	•	•	•	•	•	•	•	•	•	•	•	•	•	•	•	•	•
Russian Federation - Fédération de Russie	27	•	•	•	•	•	•	•	•	•	•	•	•	•	•	•	•	•
San Marino - Saint-Marin	28	•	•	•	•	•	•	•	•	•	•	•	•	•	•	•	•	•
Serbia and Montenegro - Serbie-et-Montenegro	32	•	•	•	•	•	•	•	•	•	•	•	•	•	•	•	•	•
Slovakia - Slovaquie	32	•	•	•	•	•	•	•	•	•	•	•	•	•	•	•	•	•
Slovenia - Slovénie	32	•	•	•	•	•	•	•	•	•	•	•	•	•	•	•	•	•
Spain - Espagne	30	•	•	•	•	•	...	•	•	•	•	•	•	•	•	•	•	•
Sweden - Suède	29	•	•	•	•	•	...	•	•	•	•	•	•	•	•	•	•	•
Switzerland - Suisse	30	•	•	•	•	•	•	•	•	•	•	•	•	•	•	•	...	...
The Former Yugoslav Rep. of Macedonia - L'ex-République yougoslave de Macédoine	31	•	•	•	•	•	•	•	•	•	•	•	•	•	•	•	•	...
Ukraine	29	•	•	•	•	•	•	•	•	•	•	•	•	•	•	•	•	•
United Kingdom - Royaume-Uni	28	•	•	•	•	...	•	•	•	•	•	•	•	•	•	•	•	•
OCEANIA — OCEANIE																		
American Samoa - Samoas américaines	10	•	•	•	•	•	...	•	•	...	...	•	...	...	...	...	...	...
Australia - Australie	28	•	•	•	•	•	•	•	•	•	•	•	•	•	•	•	...	...
Cook Islands - Îles Cook	12	•	•	•	•	•	•	•	•	•	...	•	...	...	...	...	...	...
Fiji - Fidji	14	•	•	•	•	•	•	•	•	•	...	•	...	...	...	...	...	...
French Polynesia - Polynésie française	11	•	...	•	•	•	•	•	•	•	...	•	...	...	•	...	...	...
Guam	16	•	•	•	•	•	•	•	•	•	•	•	•	...	...	...	...	...
Kiribati	5	•	•	...	•	•	•	•	...	•	...	...	•	...	...	...	...	...
Marshall Islands - Îles Marshall	15	•	•	•	•	•	•	•	•	•	...	•	...	...	...	...	...	...
Micronesia, Federated States of - Micronésie (États fédérés de)	6	•	•	•	...	...	...	•	•	...	...	•	...	...	...	...	...	...
Nauru	6	•	•	•	•	•	...	•	•	...	...	...	...	...	...	...	...	...
New Caledonia - Nouvelle-Calédonie	29	•	•	•	•	•	•	•	•	•	•	•	•	...	•	•	•	...
New Zealand - Nouvelle-Zélande	31	•	•	•	•	•	•	•	•	•	•	•	•	•	•	•	•	•
Niue - Nioué	11	•	•	•	•	•	•	•	•	•	...	•	...	...	...	...	...	...
Norfolk Island - Île Norfolk	3	•	•	...	...	...	...	•	•	...	...	...	...	...	...	...	...	...
Northern Mariana Islands - Îles Mariannes septentrionales	13	•	•	•	•	•	...	•	•	•	...	•	...	...	...	...	...	...
Palau - Palaos	14	•	...	•	•	•	•	•	•	•	...	•	...	...	•	...	...	...
Papua New Guinea - Papouasie-Nouvelle-Guinée	15	•	•	•	•	•	•	•	•	•	...	•	...	...	•	...	...	...
Pitcairn	2	•	...	...	...	...	...	•	•	...	...	...	...	...	...	...	...	...
Samoa	4	•	•	...	•	...	...	•	•	...	...	...	...	...	...	...	...	...
Solomon Islands - Îles Salomon	3	•	•	...	...	...	...	•	•	...	...	...	...	...	...	...	...	...
Tokelau - Tokélaou	4	•	•	...	...	•	•	•	•	...	...	...	...	...	...	...	...	...
Tonga	22	•	•	•	•	•	•	•	•	•	•	•	...	...	•	...	...	...
Tuvalu	3	•	•	...	...	...	...	•	•	...	...	...	...	...	...	...	...	...
Vanuatu	6	•	•	•	•	•	...	•	•	...	...	•	...	...	...	...	...	...
Wallis and Futuna Islands - Îles Wallis et Futuna	3	•	•	...	...	...	...	•	•	...	...	...	...	...	...	...	...	...

Table A. *Demographic Yearbook 2003* synoptic table: Availability of data by country/area, table and sex, where applicable
Tableau A. Tableau synoptique de l'*Annuaire démographique 2003:* Disponibilité des données par pays ou zone, tableau et le sexe , si disponible (continued — suite)

Continent, country or area / Continent, pays ou zone	Infant and maternal mortality - Mortalité infantile et mortalité liée à la maternité				General mortality - Mortalité générale								Nuptiality and divorces - Nuptialité et divortialité		
	15	16 Total	16 M/F	17	18	19 Total	19 M/F	20 Total	20 M/F	21 Total	21 M/F	22	23	24	25
EUROPE															
Monaco	...	...	...	...	•	•	•	•	•	•	•	...	•	...	•
Netherlands - Pays-Bas	•	•	•	•	•	•	•	•	•	•	•	•	•	•	•
Norway - Norvège	•	•	•	•	•	•	•	•	•	•	•	•	•	•	•
Poland - Pologne	•	•	•	•	•	•	•	•	•	•	•	•	•	•	•
Portugal	•	•	•	•	•	•	•	•	•	•	•	•	•	•	•
Republic of Moldova - République de Moldova	•	•	•	•	•	•	•	•	•	•	•	•	•	•	•
Romania - Roumanie	•	•	•	•	•	•	•	•	•	•	•	•	•	•	•
Russian Federation - Fédération de Russie	•	...	...	•	•	•	•	•	•	•	•	•	•	•	•
San Marino - Saint-Marin	•	•	•	•	•	•	•	•	•	•	•	•	•	•	•
Serbia and Montenegro - Serbie-et-Montenegro	•	•	•	•	•	•	•	•	•	•	•	•	•	•	•
Slovakia - Slovaquie	•	•	•	•	•	•	•	•	•	•	•	•	•	•	•
Slovenia - Slovénie	•	•	•	•	•	•	•	•	•	•	•	•	•	•	•
Spain - Espagne	•	•	•	•	•	•	•	•	•	•	•	•	•	•	•
Sweden - Suède	•	•	•	•	•	•	•	•	•	•	•	•	•	•	•
Switzerland - Suisse	•	•	•	•	•	•	•	•	•	•	•	•	•	•	•
The Former Yugoslav Rep. of Macedonia - L'ex-République yougoslave de Macédoine	•	•	•	•	•	•	•	•	•	•	•	•	•	•	•
Ukraine	•	•	•	•	•	•	•	•	•	...	...	•	•	•	•
United Kingdom - Royaume-Uni	•	•	•	•	•	•	•	•	•	•	•	•	•	•	•
OCEANIA — OCEANIE															
American Samoa - Samoas américaines	•	...	...	...	•	...	...	...	...	...	...	...	...	...	...
Australia - Australie	•	•	•	•	•	•	•	•	•	•	•	•	•	•	•
Cook Islands - Îles Cook	•	...	...	...	•	...	...	...	...	...	...	...	•	...	...
Fiji - Fidji	•	...	...	•	•	...	...	...	...	...	...	...	...	...	...
French Polynesia - Polynésie française	•	...	...	...	•	...	...	...	...	...	...	...	•	...	...
Guam	•	...	...	...	•	...	...	...	...	...	...	...	•	...	...
Kiribati	...	...	...	...	...	...	...	...	...	...	...	...	...	...	...
Marshall Islands - Îles Marshall	•	...	...	•	•	...	...	...	...	...	...	•	...	...	...
Micronesia, Federated States of - Micronésie (États fédérés de)	...	...	...	...	...	...	...	...	...	...	...	...	...	...	...
Nauru	...	...	...	...	...	...	...	...	...	...	...	...	•	...	...
New Caledonia - Nouvelle-Calédonie	•	•	•	•	•	•	•	•	•	•	•	•	•	•	•
New Zealand - Nouvelle-Zélande	•	•	•	•	•	•	•	•	•	•	•	•	•	•	•
Niue - Nioué	...	...	...	...	•	...	...	...	...	...	...	...	•	...	...
Norfolk Island - Île Norfolk	...	...	...	...	...	...	...	...	...	...	...	...	...	...	...
Northern Mariana Islands - Îles Mariannes septentrionales	•	...	...	...	•	•	...	...	...	...	...	...	...	...	...
Palau - Palaos	•	...	...	...	•	•	...	...	...	...	...	...	...	...	...
Papua New Guinea - Papouasie-Nouvelle-Guinée	•	...	...	...	•	...	...	...	...	...	...	...	•	...	...
Pitcairn	...	...	...	...	...	...	...	...	...	...	...	...	...	...	...
Samoa	...	...	...	...	...	...	...	...	...	...	...	...	...	...	...
Solomon Islands - Îles Salomon	...	...	...	...	...	...	...	...	...	...	...	...	...	...	...
Tokelau - Tokélaou	...	...	...	...	...	...	...	...	...	...	...	...	...	...	...
Tonga	•	•	...	•	•	...	...	...	...	...	...	...	•	•	•
Tuvalu	...	...	...	...	...	...	...	...	...	...	...	...	...	...	...
Vanuatu	...	...	...	...	...	...	...	...	...	...	...	...	...	...	...
Wallis and Futuna Islands - Îles Wallis et Futuna	...	...	...	...	...	...	...	...	...	...	...	...	...	...	...

FOOTNOTES - NOTES

• Data presented in the table - Les données présentées dans le tableau.

... Data not available - Données pas disponibles.

[1] For statistical purposes, the data for China do not include those for the Hong Kong Special Administrative Region (Hong Kong SAR), Macao special Administrative Region (Macao SAR) and Taiwan province of China. - Pour la présentation des statistiques, les données pour Chine ne comprend pas la Région Administrative Spéciale de Hong Kong (Hong Kong RAS), la Région Administrative Spéciale de Macao (Macao RAS) et Taïwan province de

Chine.

2 Including data for the Indian-held part of Jammu and Kashmir, the final status of which has not yet been determined. - Y compris les données pour la partie du Jammu et du Cachemire occupée par l'Inde dont le statut définitif n'a pas encore été déterminé.

3 Including data for East Jerusalem and Israeli residents in certain other territories under occupation by Israeli military forces since June 1967. - Y compris les données pour Jérusalem-Est et les résidents israéliens dans certains autres territoires occupés depuis 1967 par les forces armées israéliennes.

4 Excluding data for the Pakistan-held part of Jammu and Kashmir, the final status of which has not yet been determined. - Non compris les données concernant la partie du Jammu et Cachemire occupée par le Pakistan dont le statut définitif n'a pas été déterminé.

Table 1

Table 1 presents for the world, major areas and regions estimates of the order of magnitude of population size, rates of population increase, crude birth and death rates, surface area as well as population density.

Description of variables: Estimates of world population by major areas and by regions are presented for 1950, 1960, 1970, 1980, 1990, 2000 and 2003. The average annual percentage rates of population growth, the crude birth and crude death rates are shown for the period 2000 to 2005. Surface area in square kilometers and population density estimates relate to 2003.

All population estimates and rates presented in this table were prepared by the Population Division of the United Nations, Department of Economic and Social Affairs, and have been published in *World Population Prospects: The 2004 Revision*, vol. I, *Comprehensive Tables*[1].

The scheme of regionalization used for these estimates is described below. Although some continental totals are given, and all can be derived, the basic scheme presents six major areas that are so drawn as to obtain greater homogeneity in sizes of population, types of demographic circumstances and accuracy of demographic statistics. Five of the major areas are subdivided into a total of 20 regions, which are arranged within the major areas; these regions together with Northern America, which is not subdivided, make a total of 21 regions.

The major areas of Northern America and Latin America were distinguished, rather than the conventional continents of North America and South America, because population trends in the middle American mainland and the Caribbean region more closely resemble those of South America than those of America north of Mexico. Data for the traditional continents of North and South America can be obtained by adding Central America and Caribbean region to Northern America and deducting from Latin America. Latin America, as defined here, has somewhat wider limits than it would be if defined only to include the Spanish-speaking, French-speaking and Portuguese-speaking countries.

The average annual percentage rates of population growth were calculated by the Population Division, United Nations Department of Economic and Social Affairs, using an exponential rate of increase.

Crude birth and crude death rates are expressed in terms of the average annual number of births and deaths, respectively, per 1 000 mid-year population. These rates are estimated.

Surface area totals were obtained by summing the figures for individual countries or areas shown in table 3.

Computation: Density, calculated by the Statistics Division of the United Nations Department of Social and Economic Affairs, is the number of persons in the 2003 total population per square kilometer of total surface area.

Reliability of data: With the exception of surface area, all data are set in *italic* type to indicate their conjectural quality.

Limitations: The estimated orders of magnitude of population and surface area are subject to all the basic limitations set forth in connection with table 3, and to the same qualifications set forth for population and surface area statistics in sections 3 and 2.4 of the Technical Notes, respectively.

Likewise, the rates of population increase and the density index are affected by the limitations of the original figures. However, it may be noted that, in compiling data for regional and major areas totals, errors in the components may tend to compensate each other and the resulting aggregates may be more reliable than the quality of the individual components would imply.

Because of their estimated character, many of the birth and death rates shown should also be considered only as orders of magnitude, and not as measures of the true level of natality or mortality. Rates for 2002-2005 published in this Demographic Yearbook were estimated on the basis of the data available in 2004 and are, therefore, based on newer information than previously published estimates for the same years. As a result they may be different from the rates published in previous issues of the Demographic Yearbook.

Because surface area totals were obtained by summing the figures for individual countries or areas shown in table 3, they exclude places with a population of less than 50, for example, uninhabited polar areas.

In interpreting the population densities, one should consider that some of the regions include large segments of land that are uninhabitable or barely habitable, and density values calculated as described make no allowance for this, nor for differences in patterns of land settlement.

Composition of macro geographical regions and sub-regions

AFRICA

Eastern Africa
Burundi
Comoros
Djibouti
Eritrea
Ethiopia
Kenya
Madagascar
Malawi
Mauritius
Mozambique
Réunion
Rwanda
Seychelles
Somalia
Uganda
United Republic of Tanzania
Zambia
Zimbabwe

Middle Africa
Angola
Cameroon
Central African Republic
Chad
Congo
Democratic Republic of the Congo
Equatorial Guinea
Gabon
Sao Tome and Principe

Northern Africa
Algeria
Egypt
Libyan Arab Jamahiriya
Morocco
Sudan
Tunisia
Western Sahara

Southern Africa
Botswana
Lesotho
Namibia
South Africa
Swaziland

Western Africa

Benin
Burkina Faso
Cape Verde
Côte d'Ivoire
Gambia
Ghana
Guinea
Guinea-Bissau
Liberia
Mali
Mauritania
Niger
Nigeria
Saint Helena
Senegal
Sierra Leone
Togo

ASIA

Eastern Asia
China
China - Hong Kong SAR
China - Macao SAR
Japan
Korea, Democratic People's Republic of
Korea, Republic of
Mongolia

South-central Asia
Afghanistan
Bangladesh
Bhutan
India
Iran (Islamic Republic of)
Kazakhstan
Kyrgyzstan
Maldives
Nepal
Pakistan
Sri Lanka
Tajikistan
Turkmenistan
Uzbekistan

South-eastern Asia
Brunei Darussalam

Cambodia
Indonesia
Lao People's Democratic Republic
Malaysia
Myanmar
Philippines
Singapore
Thailand
Timor Leste
Viet Nam

Western Asia
Armenia
Azerbaijan
Bahrain
Cyprus
Georgia
Iraq
Israel
Jordan
Kuwait
Lebanon
Occupied Palestinian Territory
Oman
Qatar
Saudi Arabia
Syrian Arab Republic
Turkey
United Arab Emirates
Yemen

EUROPE

Eastern Europe
Belarus
Bulgaria
Czech Republic
Hungary
Poland
Republic of Moldova
Romania
Russian Federation
Slovakia
Ukraine

Northern Europe
Åland Island
Channel Islands

Denmark
Estonia
Faeroe Islands
Finland
Iceland
Ireland
Isle of Man
Latvia
Lithuania
Norway
Sweden
United Kingdom of Great Britain
   and Northern Ireland

Southern Europe
Albania
Andorra
Bosnia and Herzegovina
Croatia
Gibraltar
Greece
Holy See
Italy
Malta
Portugal
San Marino
Serbia and Montenegro
Slovenia
Spain
The Former Yugoslav Republic
   of Macedonia

Western Europe
Austria
Belgium
France
Germany
Liechtenstein
Luxembourg
Monaco
Netherlands
Switzerland

LATIN AMERICA
 + the CARIBBEAN

Caribbean
Anguilla

Antigua and Barbuda
Aruba
Bahamas
Barbados
British Virgin Islands
Cayman Islands
Cuba
Dominica
Dominican Republic
Grenada
Guadaloupe
Haiti
Jamaica
Martinique
Montserrat
Netherlands Antilles
Puerto Rico
Saint Kitts and Nevis
Saint Lucia
Saint Vincent and the
   Grenadines
Trinidad and Tobago
Turks and Caicos Islands
United States Virgin
   Islands

Central America
Belize
Costa Rica
El Salvador
Guatemala
Honduras
Mexico
Nicaragua
Panama

South America
Argentina
Bolivia
Brazil
Chile
Colombia
Ecuador
Falkland Islands (Malvinas)
French Guiana
Guyana
Paraguay
Peru

Suriname
Uruguay
Venezuela

NORTHERN AMERICA

Bermuda
Canada
Greenland
Saint Pierre and Miquelon
United States of America

OCEANIA

Australia and New Zealand
Australia
New Zealand
Norfolk Island

Melanesia
Fiji
New Caledonia
Papua New Guinea
Solomon Islands
Vanuatu

Micronesia
Guam
Kiribati
Marshall Islands
Micronesia (Federated States of)
Nauru
Northern Mariana Islands
Palau

Polynesia
American Samoa
Cook Islands
French Polynesia
Niue
Pitcairn
Samoa
Tokelau
Tonga
Tuvalu
Wallis and Futuna Islands

NOTES

[1] *World Population Prospects: The 2004 Revision*, vol. I, *Comprehensive Tables* (United Nations publication, Sales No. E.05.XIII.5), New York 2005.

Tableau 1

Le tableau 1 présente, pour l'ensemble du monde et les grandes zones et régions, des estimations concernant l'ordre de grandeur de la population, les taux d'accroissement démographique, les taux bruts de natalité et de mortalité, la superficie et la densité de peuplement.

Description des variables : Des estimations de la population mondiale par grandes zones et régions sont présentées pour 1950, 1960, 1970, 1980, 1990 et 2000 ainsi que pour 2003. Les taux annuels moyens d'accroissement de la population et les taux bruts de natalité et de mortalité portent sur la période allant de 2000 à 2005. Les indications concernant la superficie exprimée en kilomètres carrés et les estimations de la densité de population se rapportent à 2003.

Toutes les estimations de population et les taux de natalité, taux de mortalité et taux annuels d'accroissement de la population qui sont présentés dans le tableau 1 ont été établis par la Division de la population du Département des affaires économiques et sociales (Secrétariat de l'Organisation des Nations Unies), et ont été publiés dans *World Population Prospects: The 2004 Revision, Volume I: Comprehensive Tables*[1].

Bien que l'on ait donné certains totaux pour les continents (tous les autres pouvant être calculés), on a réparti le monde en huit grandes zones qui ont été découpées de manière à obtenir une plus grande homogénéité du point de vue des dimensions de population, des types de situations démographiques et de l'exactitude des statistiques démographiques.

Cinq de ces huit grandes zones ont été subdivisées en 20 régions. Avec l'Amérique septentrionale, qui n'est pas subdivisée, on arrive à un total de 21 régions.

Au lieu de faire la distinction classique entre l'Amérique du Nord et l'Amérique du Sud, on a choisi d'opérer une comparaison entre l'Amérique septentrionale et l'Amérique latine, parce que les tendances démographiques dans la partie continentale de l'Amérique centrale et dans la région des Caraïbes se rapprochent davantage de celles de l'Amérique du Sud que de celles de l'Amérique au nord du Mexique. On obtient les données pour les continents traditionnels de l'Amérique du Nord et de l'Amérique du Sud en extrayant les données concernant l'Amérique centrale et les Caraïbes de celles relatives à l'Amérique latine et en les regroupant avec celles relatives à l'Amérique septentrionale. L'Amérique latine ainsi définie a par conséquent des limites plus larges que celles des pays ou zones de langues espagnole, portugaise et française qui constituent l'Amérique latine au sens le plus strict du terme.

La Division de la population a calculé les taux annuels moyens d'accroissement de la population en appliquant un taux d'accroissement exponentiel.

Les taux bruts de natalité et de mortalité représentent respectivement le nombre annuel moyen de naissances et de décès par millier d'habitants en milieu d'année. Ces taux sont estimatifs.

La superficie totale a été obtenue en faisant la somme des superficies des pays ou zones du tableau 3.

Calculs : La densité, calculée par la Division de statistique du Département des affaires économiques et sociales, est égale au rapport entre l'effectif total de la population en 2003 et la superficie totale exprimée en kilomètres carrés.

Fiabilité des données : À l'exception des données concernant la superficie, toutes les données sont reproduites en *italique* pour en faire ressortir le caractère conjectural.

Insuffisance des données : Les estimations concernant l'ordre de grandeur de la population et la superficie reposent en partie sur les données du tableau 3 ; elles appellent donc toutes les réserves fondamentales formulées à propos de ce tableau, et celles qui ont été respectivement formulées aux sections 3 et 2.4 des Notes techniques en ce qui concerne les statistiques relatives à la population et à la superficie.

Les taux d'accroissement et les indices de densité de la population se ressentent eux aussi des insuffisances inhérentes aux données de base. Toutefois, il est à noter que, lorsque l'on additionne des données par territoire pour obtenir des totaux régionaux et par grandes zones, les erreurs qu'elles comportent arrivent parfois à s'équilibrer, de sorte que les agrégats obtenus peuvent être un peu plus exacts que chacun des éléments dont on est parti.

Vu leur caractère estimatif, nombre des taux de natalité et de mortalité du tableau 1 doivent être considérés uniquement comme des ordres de grandeur et ne sont pas censés mesurer exactement le niveau de la natalité ou de la mortalité. On s'est fondé pour établir les taux de la période 2000-2005 sur les données dont on disposait en 2004, date à laquelle les nouvelles estimations ont été établies, et beaucoup d'éléments nouveaux sont alors intervenus dans le calcul de celles-ci. C'est pourquoi il se peut qu'elles s'écartent d'estimations antérieures publiées dans d'autres éditions de l'*Annuaire* pour ces mêmes années.

Parce que les totaux des superficies ont été obtenus en additionnant les chiffres pour chaque pays ou zones, qui apparaissent dans le tableau 3, ils ne comprennent pas les lieux où la population est inférieure à 50 personnes, tels que les régions polaires inhabitées.

Pour interpréter les valeurs de la densité de population, on se souviendra qu'il existe dans certaines des régions de vastes étendues de terres inhabitables ou à peine habitables et que les chiffres calculés selon la méthode indiquée ne tiennent compte ni de ce fait ni des différences de dispersion de la population selon le mode d'habitat.

Composition des grandes zones et régions

AFRIQUE

Afrique orientale
Burundi
Comores
Djibouti
Érythrée
Éthiopie
Kenya
Madagascar
Malawi
Maurice
Mozambique
Ouganda
République-Unie de Tanzanie
Réunion
Rwanda
Seychelles
Somalie
Zambie
Zimbabwe

Afrique centrale
Angola
Cameroun
Congo
Gabon
Guinée équatoriale
République centrafricaine
République démocratique du Congo
Sao Tomé-et-Principe
Tchad

Afrique septentrionale
Algérie
Égypte
Jamahiriya arabe libyenne
Maroc
Sahara occidental
Soudan

Tunisie

Afrique australe
Afrique du Sud
Botswana
Lesotho
Namibie
Swaziland

Afrique occidentale
Bénin
Burkina Faso
Cap-Vert
Côte d'Ivoire
Gambie
Ghana
Guinée
Guinée-Bissau
Libéria
Mali
Mauritanie
Niger
Nigéria
Sainte-Hélène
Sénégal
Sierra Leone
Togo

AMÉRIQUE LATINE

Caraïbes
Anguilla
Antigua-et-Barbuda
Antilles néerlandaises
Aruba
Bahamas
Barbade
Cuba
Dominique
Grenade

Guadeloupe
Haïti
Îles Caïmanes
Îles Turques et Caïques
Îles Vierges américaines
Îles Vierges britanniques
Jamaïque
Martinique
Montserrat
Porto Rico
République dominicaine
Saint-Kitts-et-Nevis
Sainte-Lucie
Saint-Vincent-et-les Grenadines
Trinité-et-Tobago

Amérique centrale
Belize
Costa Rica
El Salvador
Guatemala
Honduras
Mexique
Nicaragua
Panama

Amérique du Sud
Argentine
Bolivie
Brésil
Chili
Colombie
Équateur
Guyana
Guyane française
Îles Falkland (Malvinas)
Paraguay
Pérou
Suriname
Uruguay

Venezuela

AMÉRIQUE SEPTENTRIONALE

Bermudes
Canada
États-Unis d'Amérique
Groenland
Saint-Pierre-et-Miquelon

ASIE

Asie orientale
Chine
Chine - Région administrative spéciale de Hong Kong
Chine - Région administrative spéciale de Macao
Japon
Mongolie
République de Corée
République populaire démocratique de Corée

Asie centrale et Asie du Sud
Afghanistan
Bangladesh
Bhoutan
Inde
Iran (République Islamique d')
Kazakhstan
Kirghizistan
Maldives
Népal
Ouzbékistan
Pakistan
Sri Lanka
Tadjikistan
Turkménistan

Asie du Sud-Est
Brunéi Darussalam
Cambodge
Indonésie
Malaisie
Myanmar
Philippines
République démocratique populaire lao
Singapour
Thaïlande
Timor-Leste
Viet Nam

Asie occidentale
Arabie saoudite
Arménie

Azerbaïdjan
Bahreïn
Chypre
Émirats arabes unis
Géorgie
Iraq
Israël
Jordanie
Koweït
Liban
Oman
Qatar
République arabe syrienne
Territoire palestinien occupé
Turquie
Yémen

EUROPE

Europe orientale
Bélarus
Bulgarie
Fédération de Russie
Hongrie
Pologne
République de Moldova
République tchèque
Roumanie
Slovaquie
Ukraine

Europe septentrionale
Danemark
Estonie
Finlande
Île de Man
Îles Anglo-Normandes
Îles Féroé
Îles Svalbard et Jan Mayen
Irlande
Islande
Lettonie
Lituanie
Norvège
Royaume-Uni de Grande-Bretagne et d'Irlande du Nord
Suède

Europe méridionale
Albanie
Andorre
Bosnie-Herzégovine
Croatie
Espagne
Ex-République yougoslave de Macédoine

Gibraltar
Grèce
Italie
Malte
Portugal
Saint-Marin
Saint-Siège
Serbie-et-Monténégro
Slovénie

Europe occidentale
Allemagne
Autriche
Belgique
France
Liechtenstein
Luxembourg
Monaco
Pays-Bas
Suisse

OCÉANIE

Australie et Nouvelle-Zélande
Australie
Île Norfolk
Nouvelle-Zélande

Mélanésie
Fidji
Îles Salomon
Nouvelle-Calédonie
Papouasie-Nouvelle-Guinée
Vanuatu

Micronésie
Guam
Îles Mariannes septentrionales
Îles Marshall
Kiribati
Micronésie (États fédérés de)
Nauru
Palaos

Polynésie
Îles Cook
Îles Wallis et Futuna
Nioué
Pitcairn
Polynésie française
Samoa
Samoa américaines
Tokélaou
Tonga
Tuvalu

---

[1] *World Population Prospects, The 2004 Revision, Volume I: Comprehensive Tables* (numéro de vente : E.05.XIII.5, publication des Nations Unies, New York, 2003).

1. Population, rate of increase, birth and death rates, surface area and density for the world, major areas and regions: selected years
Population, taux d'accroissement, taux de natalité et taux de mortalité, superficie et densité pour l'ensemble du monde, les régions macro géographiques et les composantes géographiques: diverses années

Major areas and regions Régions macro géographiques et composantes	Mid-year population estimates - Estimations de population au milieu de l'année (millions)							Annual rate of increase - Taux d'accroiss-ement annuel (%)	Crude birth rate - Taux bruts de natali-té	Crude death rate - Taux bruts de morta-lité	Surface area (km2) - Superfic-ie (km2) (000s)	Density - Densité[1]
	1950	1960	1970	1980	1990	2000	2003	2000 - 2005			2003	
WORLD TOTAL - ENSEMBLE DU MONDE	*2 520*	*3 024*	*3 697*	*4 442*	*5 280*	*6 086*	*6 314*	*1.2*	*21*	*9*	*136 056*	*46*
AFRICA - AFRIQUE	*224*	*282*	*364*	*479*	*636*	*812*	*868*	*2.2*	*38*	*15*	*30 250*	*29*
Eastern Africa - Afrique orientale	*65*	*82*	*109*	*146*	*198*	*256*	*275*	*2.4*	*41*	*17*	*6 300*	*44*
Middle Africa - Afrique centrale	*26*	*32*	*41*	*54*	*73*	*96*	*104*	*2.6*	*46*	*20*	*6 613*	*16*
Northern Africa - Afrique septentrionale	*53*	*67*	*86*	*112*	*144*	*175*	*184*	*1.7*	*26*	*7*	*8 525*	*22*
Southern Africa - Afrique méridionale	*16*	*20*	*26*	*33*	*42*	*52*	*54*	*0.7*	*24*	*17*	*2 675*	*20*
Western Africa - Afrique occidentale	*64*	*80*	*102*	*134*	*178*	*234*	*252*	*2.4*	*42*	*18*	*6 138*	*41*
LATIN AMERICA AND CARIBBEAN - AMERIQUE LATINE ET CARAIBES	*167*	*219*	*285*	*362*	*444*	*523*	*546*	*1.4*	*22*	*6*	*20 546*	*27*
Caribbean - Caraïbes	*17*	*20*	*25*	*29*	*34*	*38*	*38*	*0.9*	*20*	*8*	*234*	*165*
Central America - Amérique centrale	*37*	*50*	*68*	*91*	*113*	*136*	*143*	*1.6*	*24*	*5*	*2 480*	*58*
South America - Amérique du Sud	*113*	*148*	*192*	*242*	*297*	*349*	*365*	*1.4*	*21*	*6*	*17 832*	*20*
NORTHERN AMERICA - AMERIQUE SEPTENTRIONALE[2]	*172*	*204*	*232*	*256*	*283*	*315*	*324*	*1.0*	*14*	*8*	*21 776*	*15*
ASIA - ASIE[3]	*1 396*	*1 699*	*2 140*	*2 630*	*3 169*	*3 676*	*3 815*	*1.2*	*20*	*8*	*31 870*	*120*
Eastern Asia - Asie orientale	*671*	*792*	*987*	*1 178*	*1 350*	*1 479*	*1 507*	*0.6*	*13*	*7*	*11 763*	*128*
South Central Asia - Asie centrale méridionale	*496*	*617*	*780*	*978*	*1 226*	*1 485*	*1 560*	*1.6*	*26*	*9*	*10 791*	*145*
South Eastern Asia - Asie méridionale orientale	*178*	*223*	*286*	*358*	*440*	*519*	*541*	*1.4*	*21*	*7*	*4 495*	*120*
Western Asia - Asie occidentale[3]	*51*	*67*	*88*	*116*	*154*	*193*	*206*	*2.1*	*26*	*6*	*4 822*	*43*
EUROPE[3]	*547*	*604*	*656*	*692*	*721*	*728*	*729*	*0.0*	*10*	*12*	*22 050*	*33*
Eastern Europe - Europe orientale	*220*	*254*	*276*	*295*	*311*	*305*	*300*	*-0.5*	*10*	*14*	*18 814*	*16*
Northern Europe - Europe septentrionale	*77*	*81*	*86*	*89*	*92*	*94*	*95*	*0.3*	*11*	*10*	*1 748*	*54*
Southern Europe - Europe méridionale	*109*	*118*	*127*	*138*	*143*	*146*	*148*	*0.4*	*10*	*10*	*1 317*	*112*
Western Europe - Europe occidentale	*141*	*152*	*166*	*170*	*176*	*184*	*185*	*0.2*	*10*	*10*	*1 108*	*167*
OCEANIA - OCEANIE[2]	*12.8*	*15.9*	*19.6*	*22.9*	*26.7*	*30.9*	*32.2*	*1.3*	*17*	*7*	*8 564*	*4*
Australia and New Zealand - Australie et Nouvelle-Zélande	*10.1*	*12.6*	*15.5*	*17.8*	*20.3*	*22.9*	*23.7*	*1.1*	*13*	*7*	*8 012*	*3*
Melanesia - Melanésie	*2.3*	*2.7*	*3.4*	*4.4*	*5.5*	*6.9*	*7.4*	*2.0*	*31*	*10*	*541*	*14*
Micronesia - Micronésie	*0.1*	*0.2*	*0.2*	*0.3*	*0.4*	*0.5*	*0.5*	*1.9*	*26*	*5*	*3*	*167*
Polynesia - Polynésie	*0.2*	*0.3*	*0.4*	*0.5*	*0.5*	*0.6*	*0.6*	*1.2*	*24*	*5*	*8*	*75*

FOOTNOTES - NOTES

[1] Population per square kilometre of surface area. Figures are estimates of population divided by surface area and are not to be considered as either reflecting density in the urban sense or as indicating the supporting power of a territory's land and resources. — Habitants per kilomèter corré. Il s'agit simplement du quotient calculé en divisant la population par la superficie et n'est par considéré comme indiquant la densité au sens urbain du mot ni l'effectif de population que les terres et les ressources du territoire sont capables de nourrir.

[2] Hawaii, a state of the United States of America, is included in Northern America rather than in Oceania. — Hawaii, un Etat des Etats-Unis d'Amérique, est compris en Amérique septentrionale plutôt qu'en Océanie.

[3] The European part of Turkey is included in Western Asia rather than Europe. — La partie européenne de la Turquie est comprise en Asie Occidentale plutôt qu'en Europe.

Table 2

Table 2 presents estimates of population and the percentage distribution by age and sex as well as the sex ratio for all ages; data are presented for the world, the six major areas and the 20 regions for 2003.

Description of variables: All population estimates presented in this table were prepared by the Population Division of the United Nations Department of Economic and Social Affairs. These estimates have been published (using more detailed age groups) in the *World Population Prospects: The 2004 Revision*, vol. II, *Sex and Age Distribution of the World Population*[1].

The scheme of regionalization used for these estimates is discussed in detail in the technical notes for table 1. Age groups presented in this table are: under 15 years, 15-64 years and 65 years and over. Sex ratio refers to the number of males per 100 females of all ages.

The percentage distributions and the sex ratios that appear in this table have been calculated by the Statistics Division of the United Nations Department of Economic and Social Affairs using the Population Division estimates.

Reliability of data: All data are set in *italic* type to indicate their conjectural quality.

Limitations: The data presented in this table are from the same series of estimates, prepared by the Population Division, presented in table 1. The estimated orders of magnitude of population are subject to all the basic limitations set forth for population statistics in section 3 of the Technical Notes. In brief, because they are estimates, these distributions by broad age groups and sex should be considered only as orders of magnitude. However, in compiling data for regional and macro region totals, errors in the components tend to compensate each other and the resulting aggregates may be somewhat more reliable than the quality of the individual components would imply.

In addition, data in this table are limited by factors affecting data by age. These factors are described in the technical notes for table 7. Because the age groups presented in this table are so broad, these problems are minimized.

NOTES

[1] *World Population Prospects: The 2004 Revision*, vol. II, *Sex and Age Distribution of the World Population* (United Nations publication, Sales No. E.05.XIII.6), New York 2005.

Tableau 2

Le tableau 2 présente, pour l'ensemble du monde, les six grandes zones et les 20 régions, des estimations concernant la population en 2003 ainsi que sa répartition en pourcentage selon l'âge et le sexe, et le rapport de masculinité pour tous les âges.

Description des variables : Toutes les données figurant dans le tableau 2 ont été établies par la Division de la population du Département des affaires économiques et sociales (Secrétariat de l'Organisation des Nations Unies) et ont été publiées dans l'ouvrage intitulé *World Population Prospects: The 2004 Revision, Volume II: Sex and Age Distribution of Populations*[1].

La classification géographique utilisée pour établir ces estimations est exposée en détail dans les notes techniques relatives au tableau 1. Les groupes d'âge présentés dans ce tableau sont définis comme suit : moins de 15 ans, de 15 à 64 ans et 65 ans et plus. Le rapport de masculinité correspond au nombre d'individus de sexe masculin pour 100 individus de sexe féminin sans considération d'âge.

Les pourcentages et les rapports de masculinité qui sont présentés dans le tableau 2 ont été calculés par la Division de statistique de l'ONU à partir des estimations établies par la Division de la population.

Fiabilité des données : Toutes les données figurant dans ce tableau sont reproduites en *italique* pour en faire ressortir le caractère conjectural.

Insuffisance des données : Les données de ce tableau appartiennent à la même série d'estimations, établie par la Division de la population, que celles qui figurent au tableau 1. Les estimations concernant l'ordre de grandeur de la population appellent donc toutes les réserves fondamentales qui ont été formulées à la section 3 des Notes techniques à propos des statistiques relatives à la population. Sans entrer dans le détail, il convient de préciser que les données relatives à la répartition par grand groupe d'âge et par sexe doivent être considérées uniquement comme des ordres de grandeur en raison de leur caractère estimatif. Toutefois, il est à noter que, lorsque l'on additionne des données par territoire pour obtenir des totaux régionaux et par grandes zones, les erreurs qu'elles comportent arrivent parfois à s'équilibrer, de sorte que les agrégats obtenus peuvent être un peu plus exacts que chacun des éléments dont on est parti.

En outre, les donnés figurant dans le tableau 2 comportent certaines imprécisions en raison des facteurs influant sur les données par âge (voir à ce propos les notes techniques relatives au tableau 7). Ces imprécisions sont cependant atténuées du fait de l'étendue des groupes d'âge présentés dans le tableau 2.

NOTE

[1] *World Population Prospects, the 2004 Revision, Volume II: Comprehensive Tables* (numéro de vente E.03.XIII.6, publication des Nations Unies, New York, 2005)

2. Estimates of population and its percentage distribution, by age and sex and sex ratio for all ages for the world, major areas and regions: 2003
Estimations de la population et pourcentage de répartition selon l'âge et le sexe et rapport de masculinité pour l'ensemble du monde, les grandes regions et les régions géographiques: 2003

Major areas and regions Grandes régions et régions	Population (millions)											
	Both sexes - Les deux sexes				Male - Masculin				Female - Féminin			
	All ages - Tous âges	-15	15-64	65+	All ages - Tous âges	-15	15-64	65+	All ages - Tous âges	-15	15-64	65+
WORLD TOTAL - ENSEMBLE DU MONDE	6 314	1 824	4 035	454	3 174	936	2 040	198	3 140	888	1 995	257
AFRICA - AFRIQUE	868	363	475	29	433	184	236	13	435	180	239	16
Eastern Africa - Afrique orientale	275	123	144	8	136	62	71	4	138	61	73	4
Middle Africa - Afrique centrale	104	48	53	3	51	24	26	1	52	24	27	2
Northern Africa - Afrique septentrionale	184	63	114	8	93	32	57	4	92	31	57	5
Southern Africa - Afrique méridionale	54	18	33	2	26	9	16	1	27	9	17	1
Western Africa - Afrique occidentale	251	112	132	8	127	57	66	3	125	55	66	4
LATIN AMERICA AND CARIBBEAN -												
AMERIQUE LATINE ET CARAIBES	546	168	346	32	270	85	170	14	276	82	176	18
Caribbean - Caraïbes	38	11	25	3	19	6	12	1	19	5	12	2
Central America - Amérique centrale	143	48	87	7	70	24	42	3	73	24	45	4
South America - Amérique du Sud	365	109	234	22	181	55	116	10	184	53	118	13
NORTHERN AMERICA - AMERIQUE												
SEPTENTRIONALE[2]	324	68	217	40	160	35	108	17	165	33	109	23
ASIA - ASIE[3]	3 815	1 098	2 480	237	1 945	567	1 269	109	1 870	531	1 211	128
Eastern Asia - Asie orientale	1 507	331	1 051	125	770	174	540	57	737	157	512	69
South Central Asia - Asie centrale méridionale	1 560	531	955	75	799	273	491	35	761	258	464	40
South Eastern Asia - Asie méridionale orientale	541	165	349	28	270	84	174	12	271	81	175	15
Western Asia - Asie occidentale	206	71	126	9	106	36	65	4	100	35	60	5
EUROPE[3]	729	120	496	113	350	61	245	44	378	58	251	69
Eastern Europe - Europe orientale	300	49	210	41	141	25	102	14	159	24	108	27
Northern Europe - Europe septentrionale	95	18	63	15	46	9	31	6	49	9	31	9
Southern Europe - Europe méridionale	148	23	100	25	72	12	50	11	76	11	50	15
Western Europe - Europe occidentale	185	31	123	31	90	16	62	13	95	15	61	19
OCEANIA - OCEANIE[2]	32.23	8.20	20.84	3.18	16.07	4.22	10.43	1.42	16.15	3.98	10.41	1.76
Australia and New Zealand - Australie et Nouvelle Zélande	23.67	4.87	15.87	2.93	11.67	2.50	7.88	1.30	12.00	2.37	7.99	1.64
Melanesia - Melanésie	7.37	2.93	4.25	0.20	3.80	1.51	2.18	0.10	3.58	1.41	2.07	0.09
Micronesia - Micronésie	0.53	0.18	0.33	0.02	0.27	0.09	0.17	0.01	0.26	0.09	0.17	0.01
Polynesia - Polynésie	0.64	0.22	0.39	0.03	0.33	0.12	0.20	0.01	0.31	0.11	0.19	0.02

2. Estimates of population and its percentage distribution, by age and sex and sex ratio for all ages for the world, major areas and regions: 2003
Estimations de la population et pourcentage de répartition selon l'âge et le sexe et rapport de masculinité pour l'ensemble du monde, les grandes regions et les régions géographiques: 2003 (continued — suite)

	Percent - Pourcentage												Sex ratio - Rapport de masculinité[1]
Major areas and regions / Grandes régions et régions	Both sexes - Les deux sexes				Male - Masculin				Female - Féminin				
	All ages - Tous âges	-15	15-64	65+	All ages - Tous âges	-15	15-64	65+	All ages - Tous âges	-15	15-64	65+	
WORLD TOTAL - ENSEMBLE DU MONDE	100.0	28.9	63.9	7.2	100.0	29.5	64.3	6.2	100.0	28.3	63.5	8.2	101
AFRICA - AFRIQUE	100.0	41.9	54.8	3.3	100.0	42.4	54.6	3.0	100.0	41.3	55.0	3.7	100
Eastern Africa - Afrique orientale	100.0	44.8	52.3	3.0	100.0	45.4	52.0	2.7	100.0	44.2	52.6	3.2	98
Middle Africa - Afrique centrale	100.0	46.0	51.1	2.9	100.0	46.6	50.9	2.6	100.0	45.5	51.2	3.3	98
Northern Africa - Afrique septentrionale	100.0	33.9	61.6	4.5	100.0	34.5	61.5	4.0	100.0	33.4	61.7	4.9	101
Southern Africa - Afrique méridionale	100.0	33.8	62.2	3.9	100.0	34.8	62.0	3.2	100.0	32.9	62.4	4.7	96
Western Africa - Afrique occidentale	100.0	44.5	52.4	3.0	100.0	45.1	52.2	2.7	100.0	44.0	52.7	3.3	102
LATIN AMERICA AND CARIBBEAN - AMERIQUE LATINE ET CARAIBES	100.0	30.7	63.4	5.9	100.0	31.6	63.1	5.3	100.0	29.8	63.7	6.5	98
Caribbean - Caraïbes	100.0	28.6	64.2	7.2	100.0	29.3	64.0	6.7	100.0	27.8	64.4	7.8	98
Central America - Amérique centrale	100.0	33.8	61.3	4.9	100.0	34.9	60.5	4.6	100.0	32.7	62.0	5.3	97
South America - Amérique du Sud	100.0	29.8	64.1	6.1	100.0	30.6	64.0	5.4	100.0	28.9	64.2	6.8	98
NORTHERN AMERICA - AMERIQUE SEPTENTRIONALE[2]	100.0	20.8	66.8	12.3	100.0	21.7	67.8	10.6	100.0	20.0	65.9	14.1	97
ASIA - ASIE[3]	100.0	28.8	65.0	6.2	100.0	29.1	65.3	5.6	100.0	28.4	64.7	6.9	104
Eastern Asia - Asie orientale	100.0	21.9	69.7	8.3	100.0	22.6	70.1	7.4	100.0	21.3	69.4	9.3	104
South Central Asia - Asie centrale méridionale	100.0	34.0	61.2	4.8	100.0	34.1	61.4	4.4	100.0	33.9	60.9	5.2	105
South Eastern Asia - Asie méridionale orientale	100.0	30.5	64.4	5.1	100.0	31.1	64.3	4.6	100.0	29.9	64.5	5.6	100
Western Asia - Asie occidentale	100.0	34.5	61.0	4.5	100.0	34.4	61.7	3.9	100.0	34.7	60.2	5.0	105
EUROPE[3]	100.0	16.4	68.1	15.5	100.0	17.5	70.0	12.5	100.0	15.4	66.3	18.3	93
Eastern Europe - Europe orientale	100.0	16.4	69.9	13.8	100.0	17.8	72.1	10.1	100.0	15.1	67.9	17.0	89
Northern Europe - Europe septentrionale	100.0	18.4	65.9	15.6	100.0	19.4	67.3	13.3	100.0	17.5	64.6	17.8	95
Southern Europe - Europe méridionale	100.0	15.2	67.6	17.2	100.0	16.0	69.3	14.7	100.0	14.5	66.0	19.5	96
Western Europe - Europe occidentale	100.0	16.5	66.6	16.8	100.0	17.4	68.8	13.9	100.0	15.8	64.6	19.7	95
OCEANIA - OCEANIE[2]	100.0	25.4	64.7	9.9	100.0	26.3	64.9	8.9	100.0	24.6	64.5	10.9	99
Australia and New Zealand - Australie et Nouvelle Zélande	100.0	20.6	67.0	12.4	100.0	21.4	67.5	11.1	100.0	19.8	66.6	13.6	97
Melanesia - Melanésie	100.0	39.7	57.7	2.6	100.0	39.8	57.5	2.7	100.0	39.5	57.9	2.6	106
Micronesia - Micronésie	100.0	33.5	62.2	4.3	100.0	34.0	62.0	4.0	100.0	33.0	62.3	4.7	102
Polynesia - Polynésie	100.0	34.8	60.4	4.8	100.0	35.1	60.5	4.4	100.0	34.5	60.3	5.3	105

FOOTNOTES - NOTES

[1] Males per 100 females of all ages - Hommes pour 100 femmes de tous âges

[2] Hawaii, a state of the United States of America, is included in Northern America rather than in Oceania. — Hawaii, un Etat des Etats-Unis d'Amérique, est compris en Amérique septentrionale plutôt qu'en Océanie.

[3] The European part of Turkey is included in Western Asia rather than Europe. — La partie européenne de la Turquie est comprise en Asie Occidentale plutôt qu'en Europe.

Table 3

Table 3 presents for each country or area of the world the total, male and female population enumerated at the latest population census, estimates of the mid-year total population for 2000 and 2003, the average annual exponential rate of increase (or decrease) for the period 2000 to 2003 the surface area and the population density for 2003.

Description of variables: The total, male and female population is, unless otherwise indicated, the de facto (present-in-area) population enumerated at the most recent census for which data are available. The date of this census is given. Population census data are usually the results of a nation-wide enumeration. If, however, a nation-wide enumeration has not taken place, the results of a sample survey, essentially national in character, may be presented. Results of surveys referring to less than 50 percent of the total territory or population are not included.

Mid-year population estimates refer to the population on 1 July. Otherwise, a footnote is appended. Mid-year estimates of the total population are those provided by national statistical offices.

Surface area, expressed in square kilometres, refers to the total surface area, comprising land area and inland waters (assumed to consist of major rivers and lakes) and excluding Polar Regions as well as uninhabited islands. Exceptions to this are noted. Surface areas, originally reported in square miles by the country or area, have been converted to square kilometres using a conversion factor of 2.589988.

Computation: The annual rate of increase is the average annual percentage rate of population growth between 2000 and 2003, computed by the Statistics Division of the United Nations Department of Economic and Social Affairs using the unrounded mid-year estimates as presented in this table applying an exponential rate of increase.

Density is the number of persons in the 2003 total population per square kilometre of total surface area.

Reliability of data: Reliable mid-year population estimates are those that are based on a complete census (or a sample survey) and have been adjusted by a continuous population register or on the basis of the calculated balance of births, deaths and migration. Mid-year estimates of this type are considered reliable and appear in roman type. Mid-year estimates not calculated on this basis are considered less reliable and are shown in italics. Estimates for years prior to 2003 are considered reliable or less reliable on the basis of the 2003 quality code and appear in roman type or in *italics*, accordingly.

Census data and sample survey results are considered reliable and, therefore, appear in roman type.

Rates of population increase that were calculated using population estimates considered less reliable, as described above, are set in italics rather than roman type.

All surface area data are assumed to be reliable and therefore appear in roman type.

Population density data, however, are considered reliable or less reliable on the basis of the reliability of the 2003 population estimates used as the numerator.

Limitations: Statistics on the total population enumerated at the time of the census, estimates of the mid-year total population and surface area data are subject to the same qualifications as have been set forth for population and surface area statistics in sections 3 and 2.4 of the Technical Notes, respectively.

Regarding the limitations of census data, it should be noted that although census data are considered reliable, and therefore appear in roman type, the actual quality of census data varies widely from one country or area to another. When known, an estimate of the extent of over-enumeration or under-enumeration is given in footnotes. In the case of sample surveys, a description of the population covered is provided.

Because the reliability of the population estimates for any given country or area is based on the quality of the 2003 estimate, the reliability of estimates prior to 2003 may be overstated.

Rates of population increase are subject to all the qualifications of the population estimates mentioned above. In some cases, they simply reflect the rate calculated or assumed in constructing the estimates themselves when adequate measures of natural increase and net migration were not available. Despite their shortcomings, these rates provide a useful index for studying population change and can be useful also in evaluating the accuracy of vital and migration statistics.

Population density data as shown in this table give only an indication of actual population density as they do not take account of the dispersion or concentration of population within countries or areas nor the proportion of habitable land. They should not be interpreted as reflecting density in the urban sense or as indicating the supporting power of a territory's land and resources.

Tableau 3

Le tableau 3 indique pour chaque pays ou zone du monde la population totale selon le sexe d'après les derniers recensements effectués, les estimations concernant la population totale au milieu de l'année 2000 et de l'année 2003, le taux moyen d'accroissement annuel exponentiel positif ou négatif pour la période allant de 2000 à 2003, ainsi que la superficie et la densité de population en 2003.

Description des variables : Sauf indication contraire, la population masculine et féminine totale est la population de fait ou population présente dénombrée à l'occasion du dernier recensement dont les résultats sont disponibles. La date de ce recensement est précisée. Les données de recensement résultent généralement d'un dénombrement de population nationale. S'il n'y a jamais eu de dénombrement général, ce sont les résultats d'une enquête par sondage à caractère essentiellement national qui sont indiqués. Il n'est pas présenté de résultats d'enquêtes portant sur moins de 50 p. 100 de l'ensemble du territoire ou de la population.

Les estimations de la population en milieu d'année sont celles de la population au 1er juillet. Lorsque la date est différente, cela est signalé par une note. Les estimations de la population totale en milieu d'année sont celles qui ont été communiquées par les services nationaux de statistique.

La superficie - exprimée en kilomètres carrés - représente la superficie totale, c'est-à-dire qu'elle englobe les terres émergées et les eaux intérieures (qui sont censées comprendre les principaux lacs et cours d'eau) mais exclut les régions polaires et certaines îles inhabitées. Les exceptions à cette règle sont signalées en note. Les superficies initialement exprimées en miles carrés par les pays ou les zones ont été transformées en kilomètres carrés au moyen d'un coefficient de conversion de 2,589988.

Calculs : Le taux d'accroissement annuel est le taux annuel moyen de variation (en pourcentage) de la population entre 2000 et 2005, calculé par la Division de statistique du Département des affaires économiques et sociales (Secrétariat de l'Organisation des Nations Unies) à partir des estimations en milieu d'année non arrondies qui figurent dans le tableau après application d'un taux exponentiel d'accroissement.

La densité est égale au rapport de l'effectif total de la population en 2003 à la superficie totale, exprimée en kilomètres carrés.

Fiabilité des données : Les estimations en milieu d'année qui sont considérées sûres sont fondées sur un recensement complet (ou sur une enquête par sondage) et ont été ajustées en fonction des données provenant d'un registre permanent de population ou en fonction de la balance établie par le calcul des naissances, des décès et des migrations. Les estimations de ce type sont considérées comme sûres et apparaissent en caractères romains. Les estimations en milieu d'année dont le calcul n'a pas été effectué sur cette base sont considérées comme moins sûres et apparaissent en italique. Les estimations relatives aux années antérieures à 2003 sont jugées plus ou moins sûres en fonction du codage qualitatif de 2003 et indiquées, selon le cas, en caractères romains ou en italique.

Les données de recensements ou les résultats d'enquêtes par sondage sont considérés comme sûrs et apparaissent par conséquent en caractères romains.

Les taux d'accroissement de la population, calculés à partir d'estimations jugées moins sûres d'après les normes décrites ci-dessus, sont indiqués en italique plutôt qu'en caractères romains.

Toutes les données de superficie sont présumées sûres et apparaissent par conséquent en caractères romains. En revanche, les données relatives à la densité de la population sont considérées plus ou moins sûres en fonction de la fiabilité des estimations de la population en 2003 ayant servi de numérateur.

Insuffisance des données : Les statistiques portant sur la population totale dénombrée lors d'un recensement, les estimations de la population totale en milieu d'année et les données de superficie appellent les mêmes réserves que celles formulées aux sections 3 et 2.4 des Notes techniques à propos des statistiques relatives à la population et à la superficie.

S'agissant de l'insuffisance des données obtenues par recensement, il convient d'indiquer que, bien que ces données soient considérées comme sûres et apparaissent par conséquent en caractères romains, leur qualité réelle varie considérablement d'un pays ou d'une région à l'autre. Lorsque l'on possédait les renseignements voulus, on a donné une estimation du degré de sur-dénombrement ou de sous-dénombrement. Dans le cas des enquêtes par sondage, une description de la population considérée est fournie.

La fiabilité des estimations de la population d'un pays ou zone quelconque reposant sur la qualité des estimations de 2003, il se peut que la fiabilité des estimations antérieures à 2003 soit surévaluée.

Les taux d'accroissement appellent toutes les réserves formulées plus haut à propos des estimations concernant la population. Dans certains cas, ils représentent seulement le taux qu'il a fallu calculer ou que l'on a pris pour base pour établir les estimations elles-mêmes lorsque l'on ne disposait pas de mesures appropriées de l'accroissement naturel et des migrations nettes. Malgré leurs imperfections, ces taux fournissent des indications intéressantes pour l'étude du mouvement de la population et, utilisés avec les précautions nécessaires, ils peuvent également servir à évaluer l'exactitude des statistiques de l'état civil et des migrations.

Les données relatives à la densité de population figurant dans le tableau 3 n'ont qu'une valeur indicative en ce qui concerne la densité de population effective, car elles ne tiennent compte ni de la dispersion ou de la concentration de la population à l'intérieur des pays ou zones, ni de la proportion du territoire qui est habitable. Il ne faut donc y voir d'indication ni de la densité au sens urbain du terme ni du nombre d'habitants qui pourraient vivre sur les terres et avec les ressources naturelles du territoire considéré.

3. Population by sex, rate of population increase, surface area and density
Population selon le sexe, taux d'accroissement de la population, superficie et densité

Continent, country or area and census date / Continent, pays ou zone et date du recensement	Census type[1]	Latest available census — Dernier recensement disponible (in units — en unités) Both sexes Les deux sexes	Male Masculin	Female Feminin	Estimate type[1]	Mid-year estimates - Estimations au milieu de l'année (in thousands — en milliers) 2000	2003	Annual rate of increase Taux d'accrois sement annuel 2000-03	Surface area Superficie (km²) 2003	Density Densité 2003[2]
AFRICA — AFRIQUE										
Algeria - Algérie										
25 VI 1998	DJ	29 100 867	14 698 589	14 402 278	DJ	30 416	31 848	1.5	2 381 741	13
Angola[3]										
15 XII 1970	DF	5 646 166	2 943 974	2 702 192	...	...	...	...	1 246 700	...
Benin - Bénin										
11 II 2002	DJ	6 769 914	3 284 119	3 485 795	DF	6 169	...	...	112 622	...
Botswana										
17 VIII 2001	DF	*1 680 863	*813 488	*867 375	DF	1 653	...	...	581 730	...
Burkina Faso										
10 XII 1996	DF	10 312 609	4 970 882	5 341 727	...	...	...	...	274 000	...
Burundi										
16 VIII 1990	DF	5 139 073	2 473 599	2 665 474	...	...	...	...	27 834	...
Cameroon - Cameroun										
10 IV 1987	DF	10 493 655	...	...	...	...	...	...	475 442	...
Cape Verde - Cap-Vert										
16 VI 2000	DF	436 863	211 479	225 384	DF	435	461	2.0	4 033	114
Central African Republic - République centrafricaine										
8 XII 2003	DF	3 151 072	1 569 446	1 581 626	DF	...	3 151	...	622 984	5
Chad - Tchad[4]										
8 IV 1993	DF	6 279 931	...	...	...	...	...	...	1 284 000	...
Comoros - Comores[5]										
15 IX 1991	DF	446 817	221 152	225 665	...	...	...	...	2 235	...
Congo										
22 XII 1984	DF	1 843 421	...	...	DF	2 893	...	...	342 000	...
Côte d'Ivoire										
1 III 1988	DF	10 815 694	5 527 343	5 288 351	DF	16 402	18 001	3.1	322 463	56
Democratic Republic of the Congo - République démocratique du Congo										
1 VII 1984	DF	29 916 800	14 543 800	15 373 000	...	...	...	...	2 344 858	...
Djibouti										
11 XII 1960	DF	81 200	...	...	...	...	...	...	23 200	...
Egypt - Égypte										
19 XI 1996	DF	59 312 914	30 351 390	28 961 524	DF	63 976	67 976	2.0	1 001 449	68
Equatorial Guinea - Guinée équatoriale[6]										
4 VII 1994	DF	406 151	...	...	...	...	...	...	28 051	...
Eritrea - Érythrée										
9 V 1984	DF	2 748 304	1 374 452	1 373 852	...	...	...	...	117 600	...
Ethiopia - Éthiopie										
11 X 1994	DF	53 477 265	26 910 698	26 566 567	DF	63 495	...	...	1 104 300	...
Gabon										
31 VII 1993	DF	1 014 976	501 784	513 192	DF	1 206	...	...	267 668	...
Gambia - Gambie										
15 IV 2003	DF	*1 364 507	*676 726	*687 781	DF	1 393	...	...	11 295	...
Ghana										
26 III 2000	DF	18 912 079	9 357 382	9 554 697	DF	*18 412	...	...	238 533	...
Guinea - Guinée										
1 XII 1996	DF	*7 156 406	*3 497 979	*3 658 427	...	...	...	...	245 857	...
Guinea-Bissau - Guinée-Bissau										
1 XII 1991	DF	983 367	476 210	507 157	DF	...	1 267	...	36 125	35
Kenya										
24 VIII 1999	DF	28 686 607	14 205 589	14 481 018	DF	30 208	32 692	2.6	580 367	56
Lesotho										
14 IV 1996	DJ	1 960 069	964 346	995 723	DF	2 144	...	...	30 355	...

3. Population by sex, rate of population increase, surface area and density
Population selon le sexe, taux d'accroissement de la population, superficie et densité
(continued — suite)

| Continent, country or area and census date / Continent, pays ou zone et date du recensement | Census type[1] | Latest available census — Dernier recensement disponible (in units — en unités) | | | Estimate type[1] | Mid-year estimates - Estimations au milieu de l'année (in thousands — en milliers) | | Annual rate of increase Taux d' accrois sement annuel 2000-03 | Surface area Superficie (km²) 2003 | Density Densité 2003[2] |
		Both sexes Les deux sexes	Male Masculin	Female Feminin		2000	2003			
AFRICA — AFRIQUE										
Liberia - Libéria										
1 II 1984	DF	2 101 628	1 063 127	1 038 501	...	...	...	...	111 369	...
Libyan Arab Jamahiriya - Jamahiriya arabe libyenne[7]										
11 VIII 1995	DF	4 404 986	2 236 943	2 168 043	DF	5 125	...	...	1 759 540	...
Madagascar										
1 VIII 1993	DF	12 238 914	6 088 116	6 150 798	DF	15 085	...	...	587 041	...
Malawi[8]										
1 IX 1998	DF	9 933 868	4 867 563	5 066 305	DF	*10 475	*11 549	3.3	118 484	97
Mali										
1 IV 1998	DJ	9 790 492	4 847 436	4 943 056	DJ	10 243	...	...	1 240 192	...
Mauritania - Mauritanie										
1 XI 2000	DF	2 548 157	1 240 414	1 307 743	DF	2 645	...	...	1 025 520	...
Mauritius - Maurice										
2 VII 2000	DJ	1 178 848	583 756	595 092	DJ	1 187	1 223	1.0	2 040	599
Morocco - Maroc										
1 IX 2004	DF	*29 891 708	...	...	DF	28 705	30 088	1.6	446 550	67
Mozambique[9,10]										
1 VIII 1997	DF	16 099 246	7 714 306	8 384 940	DF	17 691	...	...	801 590	...
Namibia - Namibie[11]										
27 VIII 2001	DF	1 830 330	887 721	942 572	DF	*1 817	...	...	824 292	...
Niger										
20 V 1988	DF	7 248 100	3 590 070	3 658 030	...	...	...	...	1 267 000	...
Nigeria - Nigéria[8]										
26 XI 1991	DF	88 992 220	44 529 608	44 462 612	DF	115 224	126 153	3.0	923 768	137
Réunion										
8 III 1999	DJ	706 180	347 076	359 104	DF	722	764	1.9	2 510	304
Rwanda										
16 VIII 2002	DJ	8 128 553	3 879 448	4 249 105	...	...	...	...	26 338	...
Saint Helena ex. dep. - Sainte-Hélène sans dép.										
8 III 1998	DF	5 157	2 612	2 545	...	...	...	...	122	...
Saint Helena: Ascension - Sainte-Hélène: Ascension										
31 XII 1978	DF	849	608	241	...	...	...	...	88	...
Saint Helena: Tristan da Cunha - Sainte-Hélène: Tristan da Cunha										
31 XII 1988	DF	296	139	157	...	...	...	...	...	...
Sao Tome and Principe - Sao Tomé-et-Principe										
4 VIII 1991	DF	116 998	57 837	59 161	DF	140	...	...	964	...
Senegal - Sénégal										
27 V 1988	DJ	6 896 808	3 353 599	3 543 209	DJ	9 427	10 165	2.5	196 722	52
Seychelles										
29 VIII 1997	DF	75 876	37 589	38 287	DF	81	83	0.7	455	182
Sierra Leone										
4 XII 2004	DF	*4 963 298	*2 412 860	*2 550 438	DF	4 944	5 280	2.2	71 740	74
Somalia - Somalie										
15 II 1987	DF	7 114 431	3 741 664	3 372 767	...	...	...	...	637 657	...
South Africa - Afrique du Sud[9]										
10 X 2001	DF	*44 819 778	*21 434 041	*23 385 737	DF	43 686	46 430	2.0	1 221 037	38

3. Population by sex, rate of population increase, surface area and density
Population selon le sexe, taux d'accroissement de la population, superficie et densité
(continued — suite)

Continent, country or area and census date / Continent, pays ou zone et date du recensement	Census type[1]	Latest available census — Dernier recensement disponible (in units — en unités)			Estimate type[1]	Mid-year estimates - Estimations au milieu de l'année (in thousands — en milliers)		Annual rate of increase Taux d'accrois sement annuel 2000-03	Surface area Superficie (km²) 2003	Density Densité 2003[2]
		Both sexes Les deux sexes	Male Masculin	Female Feminin		2000	2003			
AFRICA — AFRIQUE										
Sudan - Soudan										
15 IV 1993	DF	24 940 683	12 518 638	12 422 045	DF	*31 081*	*33 334*	2.3	2 505 813	*13*
Swaziland										
11 V 1997	DF	929 718	440 154	489 564	...	...	...	...	17 364	...
Togo										
22 XI 1981	DF	2 719 567	1 325 641	1 393 926	DF	*4 629*	...	...	56 785	...
Tunisia - Tunisie										
20 IV 1994	DF	8 785 711	4 439 289	4 346 422	DF	*9 564*	*9 840	0.9	163 610	60
Uganda - Ouganda										
12 IX 2002	DF	24 442 084	11 929 803	12 512 281	DF	*22 972*	...	...	241 038	...
United Republic of Tanzania - République Unie de Tanzanie										
24 VIII 2002	DF	*34 443 603	*16 829 861	*17 613 742	...	...	...	...	945 087	...
Western Sahara - Sahara occidental[12]										
31 XII 1970	DF	76 425	43 981	32 444	...	...	...	...	266 000	...
Zambia - Zambie										
25 X 2000	DF	9 885 591	4 946 298	4 939 293	DF	*9 337*	10 744	4.7	752 618	*14*
Zimbabwe										
17 VIII 2002	DF	11 631 657	...	...	...	...	...	...	390 757	...
AMERICA, NORTH — AMERIQUE DU NORD										
Anguilla										
9 V 2001	DF	11 430	5 628	5 802	DF	11	12	2.7	91	134
Antigua and Barbuda - Antigua-et-Barbuda										
28 V 2001	DF	77 426	37 002	40 424	...	...	...	...	442	...
Aruba										
14 X 2000	DJ	90 508	43 435	47 073	DJ	91	*96	1.9	180	534
Bahamas										
1 V 2000	DF	303 611	147 715	155 896	DF	*303	*317	1.5	13 878	23
Barbados - Barbade										
1 V 2000	DF	250 010	119 926	130 084	DF	*267	...	...	430	...
Belize										
12 V 2000	DF	240 204	121 278	118 926	DF	*250*	*274	3.0	22 966	12
Bermuda - Bermudes[13]										
20 V 2000	DJ	62 059	29 802	32 257	DJ	63	62	-0.4	53	1 177
British Virgin Islands - Îles Vierges britanniques										
21 V 2001	DF	*20 647	*10 627	*10 020	DF	...	*22	...	151	144
Canada[14]										
15 V 2001	DJ	30 007 095	14 706 850	15 300 245	DJ	30 770	31 660	1.0	9 970 610	3
Cayman Islands - Îles Caïmanes										
10 X 1999	DF	39 410	...	...	DJ	40	...	...	264	...
Costa Rica										
26 VI 2000	DJ	3 810 179	1 902 614	1 907 565	DJ	3 486	4 089	5.3	51 100	80
Cuba										
6 IX 2002	DJ	11 177 743	5 597 233	5 580 510	DF	11 130	11 215	0.3	110 861	101
Dominica - Dominique[15]										
12 V 2001	DF	69 625	35 073	34 552	DF	*72*	...	...	751	...
Dominican Republic - République dominicaine										
20 X 2002	DJ	8 562 541	4 265 215	4 297 326	DF	*8 552*	8 715	0.6	48 671	*179*

3. Population by sex, rate of population increase, surface area and density
Population selon le sexe, taux d'accroissement de la population, superficie et densité
(continued — suite)

Continent, country or area and census date — Continent, pays ou zone et date du recensement	Census type[1]	Latest available census — Dernier recensement disponible (in units — en unités)			Estima-te type[1]	Mid-year estimates - Estimations au milieu de l'année (in thousands — en milliers)		Annual rate of increase Taux d' accrois sement annuel 2000-03	Surface area Superficie (km²) 2003	Density Densité 2003[2]
		Both sexes Les deux sexes	Male Masculin	Female Feminin		2000	2003			
AMERICA, NORTH — AMERIQUE DU NORD										
El Salvador										
27 IX 1992	DF	5 118 599	2 485 613	2 632 986	DF	6 276	6 638	1.9	21 041	315
Greenland - Groenland[16]										
1 VII 2000	DJ	56 124	29 989	26 135	DJ	...	57	...	2 175 600	-
Grenada - Grenade[17]										
25 V 2001	DF	102 632	50 481	52 151	DF	101	...	...	344	...
Guadeloupe[18]										
8 III 1999	DJ	422 222	203 146	219 076	DJ	428	439	0.8	1 705	257
Guatemala[9]										
24 XI 2002	DJ	11 237 196	...	...	DF	11 385	12 084	2.0	108 889	111
Haiti - Haïti										
30 VIII 1982	DJ	5 053 792	2 448 370	2 605 422	DJ	*7 959*	...	...	27 750	...
Honduras										
28 VII 2001	DF	*6 071 200	*3 000 530	*3 070 670	DF	6 369	6 861	2.5	112 088	61
Jamaica - Jamaïque										
10 IX 2001	DJ	2 607 632	1 283 547	1 324 085	DJ	2 589	2 630	0.5	10 991	239
Martinique										
8 III 1999	DJ	381 325	180 910	200 415	DJ	385	*391	0.5	1 102	354
Mexico - Mexique										
14 II 2000	DJ	97 483 412	47 592 253	49 891 159	DJ	*100 569*	*104 214*	1.2	1 958 201	*53*
Montserrat										
12 V 2001	DF	4 491	2 418	2 073	DF	*5	...	...	102	...
Netherlands Antilles - Antilles néerlandaises[19]										
29 I 2001	DJ	175 653	82 521	93 132	DJ	*179*	*179*	-0.1	800	*223*
Nicaragua										
25 IV 1995	DJ	4 357 099	2 147 105	2 209 994	DJ	*4 957*	*5 268*	2.0	130 000	*41*
Panama										
14 V 2000	DF	2 839 177	1 432 566	1 406 611	DF	*2 856*	*3 116*	2.9	75 517	*41*
Puerto Rico - Porto Rico[20]										
1 IV 2000	DJ	3 808 610	1 833 577	1 975 033	DJ	3 818	3 879	0.5	8 875	437
Saint Kitts and Nevis - Saint-Kitts-et-Nevis										
14 V 2001	DF	45 841	22 784	23 057	DF	40	...	...	261	...
Saint Lucia - Sainte-Lucie										
22 V 2001	DF	157 164	76 741	80 423	DF	156	161	1.0	539	298
Saint Pierre and Miquelon - Saint Pierre-et-Miquelon										
8 III 1999	DF	6 316	3 147	3 169	...	...	...	...	242	...
Saint Vincent and the Grenadines - Saint Vincent-et-les Grenadines[21]										
14 V 2001	DF	*109 202	...	...	DF	112	...	...	388	...
Trinidad and Tobago - Trinité-et-Tobago										
15 V 2000	DF	1 262 366	633 051	629 315	DF	1 290	1 282	-0.2	5 130	250
Turks Caicos Islands - Îles Turques et Caïques										
20 VIII 2001	DF	19 886	9 896	9 990	DJ	*18*	*22*	5.9	417	*53*
United States - États-Unis[22]										
1 IV 2000	DJ	281 421 906	138 053 563	143 368 343	DJ	275 265	*290 811	1.8	9 629 091	30

3. Population by sex, rate of population increase, surface area and density
Population selon le sexe, taux d'accroissement de la population, superficie et densité
(continued — suite)

Continent, country or area and census date / Continent, pays ou zone et date du recensement	Census type[1]	Latest available census — Dernier recensement disponible (in units — en unités)			Estimate type[1]	Mid-year estimates - Estimations au milieu de l'année (in thousands — en milliers)		Annual rate of increase Taux d' accrois sement annuel 2000-03	Surface area Superficie (km²) 2003	Density Densité 2003[2]
		Both sexes Les deux sexes	Male Masculin	Female Feminin		2000	2003			
AMERICA, NORTH — AMERIQUE DU NORD										
United States Virgin Islands - Îles Vierges américaines[20] 1 IV 2000	DJ	108 612	51 864	56 748	DJ	109	*109	0.1	347	314
AMERICA, SOUTH — AMERIQUE DU SUD										
Argentina - Argentine 18 XI 2001	DF	36 260 130	17 659 072	18 601 058	DF	37 032	37 870	0.7	2 780 400	14
Bolivia - Bolivie 5 IX 2001	DF	8 280 184	4 130 342	4 149 842	DF	8 428	9 025	2.3	1 098 581	8
Brazil - Brésil[23] 1 VIII 2000	DJ	169 799 170	83 576 015	86 223 155	DF	167 724	178 985	2.2	8 514 877	21
Chile - Chili 24 IV 2002	DF	15 116 435	7 447 695	7 668 740	DF	15 398	15 919	1.1	756 096	21
Colombia - Colombie 24 X 1993	DF	33 109 840	16 296 539	16 813 301	DF	42 299	44 531	1.7	1 138 914	39
Ecuador - Équateur[24] 25 XI 2001	DF	12 156 608	6 018 353	6 138 255	DF	12 299	12 843	1.4	283 561	45
Falkland Islands (Malvinas) - Îles Falkland (Malvinas)[25,26] 8 IV 2001	DF	2 913	1 598	1 315	...	...	...	...	12 173	...
French Guiana - Guyane française 8 III 1999	DJ	156 790	78 963	77 827	DJ	164	181	3.3	90 000	2
Guyana 12 V 1991	DF	701 704	344 928	356 776	DF	742	746	0.2	214 969	3
Paraguay 28 VIII 2002	DF	5 163 198	2 603 242	2 559 956	...	...	...	...	406 752	...
Peru - Pérou[9,27] 11 VII 1993	DF	22 048 356	10 956 375	11 091 981	DF	25 939	27 148	1.5	1 285 216	21
Suriname[28,29] 2 VIII 2004	DJ	*487 024	*244 931	*241 084	DJ	464	481	1.2	163 820	3
Uruguay[9] 22 V 1996	DF	3 163 763	1 532 288	1 631 475	DF	3 301	3 304	-	175 016	19
Venezuela[27] 30 X 2001	DF	23 054 210	11 402 869	11 651 341	DF	24 311	...	...	912 050	...
ASIA — ASIE										
Afghanistan[30] 23 VI 1979	DF	13 051 358	6 712 377	6 338 981	DF	21 770	...	...	652 090	...
Armenia - Arménie[31] 10 X 2001	DF	3 002 594	1 407 220	1 595 374	DJ	3 221	3 211	-0.1	29 800	108
Azerbaijan - Azerbaïdjan 27 I 1999	DJ	7 953 438	3 883 155	4 070 283	DF	8 049	8 234	0.8	86 600	95
Bahrain - Bahreïn 7 IV 2001	DF	650 604	373 649	276 955	DF	638	689	2.6	694	993
Bangladesh 22 I 2001	DF	*123 151 246	*62 735 988	*60 415 258	...	...	...	...	143 998	...
Bhutan - Bhoutan 11 XI 1969	DF	1 034 774	...	...	DF	678	...	...	47 000	...
Brunei Darussalam - Brunéi Darussalam 21 VIII 2001	DF	*332 844	*168 974	*163 870	DF	325	350	2.5	5 765	61

3. Population by sex, rate of population increase, surface area and density
Population selon le sexe, taux d'accroissement de la population, superficie et densité
(continued — suite)

Continent, country or area and census date / Continent, pays ou zone et date du recensement	Census type[1]	Latest available census — Dernier recensement disponible (in units — en unités)			Estimate type[1]	Mid-year estimates - Estimations au milieu de l'année (in thousands — en milliers)		Annual rate of increase Taux d'accroissement annuel 2000-03	Surface area Superficie (km²) 2003	Density Densité 2003[2]
		Both sexes Les deux sexes	Male Masculin	Female Feminin		2000	2003			
ASIA — ASIE										
Cambodia - Cambodge[32]										
3 III 1998	DF	11 437 656	5 511 408	5 926 248	DF	12 688	13 415	1.9	181 035	74
China - Chine[33,34,35,36]										
1 XI 2000	DJ	1 242 612 226	640 275 969	602 336 257	DF	1 262 645	1 288 400	0.7	9 596 961	134
China: Hong Kong SAR - Chine: Hong Kong RAS[37]										
14 III 2001	DJ	6 708 389	3 285 344	3 423 045	DJ	6 665	6 803	0.7	1 099	6 190
China: Macao SAR - Chine: Macao RAS										
23 VIII 2001	DJ	435 235	208 865	226 370	DJ	431	445	1.1	26	17 118
Cyprus - Chypre[38,39]										
1 X 2001	DJ	689 565	338 497	351 068	DJ	694	721	1.3	9 251	78
Georgia - Géorgie										
17 I 2002	DJ	4 371 535	2 061 753	2 309 782	DF	4 418	4 329	-0.7	69 700	62
India - Inde[40,41]										
1 III 2001	DF	1 028 610 328	532 156 772	496 453 556	DF	1 014 825	1 068 214	1.7	3 287 263	325
Indonesia - Indonésie[42]										
30 VI 2000	DF	206 264 595	103 417 180	102 847 415	DJ	...	214 251	...	1 904 569	112
Iran (Islamic Republic of) - Iran (République islamique d')										
23 X 1996	DJ	60 055 488	30 515 159	29 540 329	DJ	63 664	66 480	1.4	1 648 195	40
Iraq[43]										
16 X 1997	DF	19 184 543	9 536 570	9 647 973	DF	23 577	...	...	438 317	...
Israel - Israël[44]										
4 XI 1995	DJ	5 548 523	2 738 175	2 810 348	DJ	6 289	6 690	2.1	22 145	302
Japan - Japon[45]										
1 X 2000	DF	126 925 843	62 110 764	64 815 079	DF	126 843	127 649	0.2	377 873	338
Jordan - Jordanie[46]										
10 XII 1994	DF	4 139 458	2 160 725	1 978 733	DF	4 970	5 404	2.8	89 342	60
Kazakhstan										
26 II 1999	DJ	14 953 126	7 201 785	7 751 341	DF	14 884	14 909	0.1	2 724 900	5
Korea (Dem. People's Republic of) - Corée (Rép. populaire dém. de)										
31 XII 1993	DF	21 213 378	10 329 699	10 883 679	...	...	...	...	120 538	...
Korea (Republic of) - Corée (République de)[47]										
1 XI 2000	DF	46 136 101	23 158 582	22 977 519	DF	47 008	47 925	0.6	99 538	481
Kuwait - Koweït										
20 IV 1995	DF	1 575 570	913 402	662 168	DF	2 190	2 325	2.0	17 818	131
Kyrgyzstan - Kirghizistan										
24 III 1999	DJ	4 822 938	2 380 465	2 442 473	DF	4 915	5 039	0.8	199 900	25
Lao People's Democratic Republic - République démocratique populaire lao										
1 III 1995	DF	4 574 848	2 260 986	2 313 862	DF	5 218	...	...	236 800	...
Lebanon - Liban[48]										
15 XI 1970	SDF	2 126 325	1 080 015	1 046 310	...	...	...	...	10 400	...
Malaysia - Malaisie[49,50]										
5 VII 2000	DJ	23 274 690	11 853 432	11 421 258	DF	23 495	*25 048	2.1	329 847	76

3. Population by sex, rate of population increase, surface area and density
Population selon le sexe, taux d'accroissement de la population, superficie et densité
(continued — suite)

Continent, country or area and census date Continent, pays ou zone et date du recensement	Census type[1]	Latest available census — Dernier recensement disponible (in units — en unités)			Estima-te type[1]	Mid-year estimates - Estimations au milieu de l'année (in thousands — en milliers)		Annual rate of increase Taux d' accrois sement annuel 2000-03	Surface area Superficie (km²) 2003	Density Densité 2003[2]
		Both sexes Les deux sexes	Male Masculin	Female Feminin		2000	2003			
ASIA — ASIE										
Maldives										
31 III 2000	DF	270 101	137 200	132 901	DF	271	285	1.6	298	957
Mongolia - Mongolie										
5 I 2000	DF	2 373 493	1 177 981	1 195 512	DF	2 407	2 504	1.3	1 564 116	2
Myanmar										
31 III 1983	DF	35 307 913	17 518 255	17 789 658	...	...	...	...	676 578	...
Nepal - Népal[51]										
22 VI 2001	DJ	23 151 423	11 563 921	11 587 502	DJ	*22 904	...	...	147 181	...
Occupied Palestinian Territory Territoire palestinien occupé[52]										
9 XII 1997	DF	2 601 669	1 322 264	1 279 405	DF	3 149	3 515	3.7	6 020	584
Oman										
7 XII 2003	DF	2 340 815	1 313 239	1 027 576	DF	2 401	...	...	309 500	...
Pakistan[53]										
2 III 1998	DF	130 579 571	67 840 137	62 739 434	DF	137 510	147 662	2.4	796 095	185
Philippines										
1 V 2000	DJ	76 504 077	38 524 267	37 979 810	DJ	76 348	81 081	2.0	300 000	270
Qatar										
16 III 2004	DF	744 029	496 382	247 647	DF	616	719	5.1	11 000	65
Saudi Arabia - Arabie saoudite										
15 IX 2004	DF	*22 673 538	*12 557 260	*10 116 278	DF	20 474	22 019	2.4	2 149 690	10
Singapore - Singapour[54]										
30 VI 2000	DF	4 017 700	2 061 800	1 955 900	DF	4 018	4 185	1.4	683	6 128
Sri Lanka[55]										
17 VII 2001	DF	*16 864 544	*8 343 964	*8 520 580	DF	19 359	...	...	65 610	...
Syrian Arab Republic - République arabe syrienne[56]										
3 IX 1994	DF	13 782 315	7 048 906	6 733 409	DF	16 320	17 550	2.4	185 180	95
Tajikistan - Tadjikistan										
20 I 2000	DF	*6 127 000	*3 082 000	*3 045 000	DF	6 188	6 573	2.0	143 100	46
Thailand - Thaïlande										
1 IV 2000	DJ	60 617 200	29 850 100	30 767 100	DJ	61 770	...	...	513 115	...
Timor-Leste										
11 VII 2004	DF	*924 642	*467 757	*456 885	...	...	...	...	14 874	...
Turkey - Turquie										
22 X 2000	DF	67 803 927	34 346 735	33 457 192	DF	67 420	70 713	1.6	783 562	90
Turkmenistan - Turkménistan										
10 I 1995	DF	4 483 251	2 225 331	2 257 920	...	...	...	...	488 100	...
United Arab Emirates - Émirats arabes unis[57]										
17 XII 1995	DF	2 411 041	1 606 804	804 237	DF	...	4 041	...	83 600	48
Uzbekistan - Ouzbékistan										
12 I 1989	DJ	19 810 077	9 784 156	10 025 921	DF	24 650	...	...	447 400	...
Viet Nam										
1 IV 1999	DF	76 323 173	37 469 117	38 854 056	DF	77 686	80 670	1.3	331 689	243
Yemen - Yémen										
16 XII 1994	DF	14 587 807	7 473 540	7 114 267	DF	18 261	...	...	527 968	...
EUROPE										
Albania - Albanie										
1 IV 2001	DF	*3 069 275	*1 530 443	*1 538 832	DF	3 061	3 111	0.5	28 748	108

3. Population by sex, rate of population increase, surface area and density
Population selon le sexe, taux d'accroissement de la population, superficie et densité
(continued — suite)

Continent, country or area and census date / Continent, pays ou zone et date du recensement	Census type[1]	Latest available census — Dernier recensement disponible (in units — en unités)			Estima-te type[1]	Mid-year estimates - Estimations au milieu de l'année (in thousands — en milliers)		Annual rate of increase Taux d'accrois sement annuel 2000-03	Surface area Superficie (km²) 2003	Density Densité 2003[2]
		Both sexes Les deux sexes	Male Masculin	Female Feminin		2000	2003			
EUROPE										
Andorra - Andorre										
12 VII 1989	DF	46 166	...	...	DF	*66*	*70*	1.8	468	*149*
Austria - Autriche										
15 V 2001	DJ	8 032 926	3 889 189	4 143 737	DJ	8 012	8 118	0.4	83 858	97
Belarus - Bélarus										
16 II 1999	DJ	10 045 237	4 717 621	5 327 616	DF	10 005	9 874	-0.4	207 600	48
Belgium - Belgique										
1 X 2001	DJ	10 296 350	5 035 446	5 260 904	DJ	10 251	*10 376	0.4	30 528	340
Bosnia and Herzegovina - Bosnie-Herzégovine										
31 III 1991	DJ	4 377 033	2 183 795	2 193 238	DF	3 781	*3 832	0.4	51 197	75
Bulgaria - Bulgarie										
1 III 2001	DF	7 928 901	3 862 465	4 066 436	DF	8 170	7 824	-1.4	110 912	71
Channel Islands: Guernsey - Îles Anglo-Normandes: Guernesey										
29 IV 2001	DJ	59 807	29 138	30 669	DF	60	...	...	78	...
Channel Islands: Jersey - Îles Anglo-Normandes: Jersey										
11 III 2001	DJ	87 186	42 485	44 701	DF	...	88	...	116	755
Croatia - Croatie										
31 III 2001	DJ	4 437 460	2 135 900	2 301 560	DJ	4 381	4 442	0.5	56 538	79
Czech Republic - République tchèque										
1 III 2001	DJ	10 230 060	4 982 071	5 247 989	DJ	10 273	10 202	-0.2	78 866	129
Denmark - Danemark[58]										
1 I 1991	DJ	5 146 469	2 536 391	2 610 078	DJ	5 337	5 387	0.3	43 094	125
Estonia - Estonie										
31 III 2000	DJ	1 370 052	631 851	738 201	DF	1 370	1 354	-0.4	45 100	30
Faeroe Islands - Îles Féroé										
22 IX 1977	DJ	41 969	21 997	19 972	DJ	...	48	...	1 399	34
Finland - Finlande										
31 XII 2000	DJ	5 181 115	2 529 341	2 651 774	DJ	5 176	5 213	0.2	338 145	15
France[59]										
8 III 1999	DJ	58 520 688	28 419 419	30 101 269	DJ	58 896	*59 768	0.5	551 500	108
Germany - Allemagne										
....	...	...	...	...	DJ	82 183	82 534	0.1	357 022	231
Gibraltar[60]										
12 XI 2001	DF	27 495	13 644	13 851	DF	27	29	1.7	6	4 760
Greece - Grèce[61,62]										
18 III 2001	DF	10 964 020	5 431 816	5 532 204	DF	10 008	11 024	3.2	131 957	84
Holy See - Saint-Siège[16,63]										
1 VII 2000	DF	*798	*529	*269	...	...	...	...	-	...
Hungary - Hongrie										
1 II 2001	DF	10 198 315	4 850 650	5 347 665	DF	10 024	10 130	0.3	93 032	109
Iceland - Islande										
1 XII 1970	DJ	204 930	103 621	101 309	DJ	281	289	0.9	103 000	3
Ireland - Irlande										
28 IV 2002	DF	3 917 203	1 946 164	1 971 039	DF	3 787	3 996	1.8	70 273	57
Isle of Man - Îles de Man										
29 IV 2001	DJ	76 315	37 372	38 943	DJ	75	77	1.1	572	135
Italy - Italie										
21 X 2001	DF	57 110 144	27 617 335	29 492 809	DJ	57 762	57 605	-0.1	301 318	191

3. Population by sex, rate of population increase, surface area and density
Population selon le sexe, taux d'accroissement de la population, superficie et densité
(continued — suite)

Continent, country or area and census date / Continent, pays ou zone et date du recensement	Census type[1]	Latest available census — Dernier recensement disponible (in units — en unités)			Estimate type[1]	Mid-year estimates - Estimations au milieu de l'année (in thousands — en milliers)		Annual rate of increase Taux d'accrois sement annuel 2000-03	Surface area Superficie (km²) 2003	Density Densité 2003[2]
		Both sexes Les deux sexes	Male Masculin	Female Feminin		2000	2003			
EUROPE										
Latvia - Lettonie 31 III 2000	DJ	2 377 383	1 094 964	1 282 419	DF	2 373	2 325	-0.7	64 600	36
Liechtenstein 5 XII 2000	DF	33 307	16 420	16 887	DF	33	34	1.4	160	213
Lithuania - Lituanie 6 IV 2001	DJ	3 483 972	1 629 148	1 854 824	DJ	3 500	3 454	-0.4	65 300	53
Luxembourg 15 II 2001	DJ	439 539	216 541	222 998	DJ	436	450	1.0	2 586	174
Malta - Malte[64,65] 26 XI 1995	DJ	378 132	186 836	191 296	DJ	383	399	1.4	316	1 261
Monaco 23 VII 1990	DJ	29 972	14 237	15 735	DJ	*32	...	...	1	...
Netherlands - Pays-Bas[66] 1 I 2002	DJ	16 105 285	7 971 967	8 133 318	DJ	15 926	16 225	0.6	41 528	391
Norway - Norvège[67] 3 XI 2001	DJ	4 520 947	2 240 281	2 280 666	DJ	4 491	*4 565	0.5	385 155	12
Poland - Pologne[68,69,70] 20 V 2002	DF	38 230 080	18 516 403	19 713 677	DF	38 256	38 195	-0.1	312 685	122
Portugal[71] 12 III 2001	DF	*10 148 259	*4 862 699	*5 285 560	DF	10 226	10 441	0.7	91 982	114
Republic of Moldova - République de Moldova[72] 12 I 1989	DF	4 337 592	2 058 160	2 279 432	DJ	3 639	3 613	-0.2	33 851	107
Romania - Roumanie 18 III 2002	DJ	21 680 974	10 568 741	11 112 233	DJ	22 435	21 734	-1.1	238 391	91
Russian Federation - Fédération de Russie 9 X 2002	DF	*145 537 200	*67 805 700	*77 731 500	DJ	146 597	144 566	-0.5	17 098 242	8
San Marino - Saint-Marin 30 XI 1976	DF	19 149	9 654	9 495	DF	27	29	2.4	61	475
Serbia and Montenegro - Serbie-et-Montenegro[73,74,75] 31 III 2002	DJ	8 065 676	3 925 805	4 139 871	DJ	10 634	*8 153	...	102 173	...
Slovakia - Slovaquie 25 V 2001	DJ	5 379 455	2 612 515	2 766 940	DJ	5 401	5 379	-0.1	49 033	110
Slovenia - Slovénie 31 III 2002	DJ	*1 964 036	*958 576	*1 005 460	DJ	1 990	*1 997	0.1	20 256	99
Spain - Espagne[76] 1 XI 2001	DF	40 847 371	20 012 882	20 834 489	DJ	40 169	41 874	1.4	505 992	83
Svalbard and Jan Mayen Islands - Îles Svalbard et Jan Mayen[77] 1 XI 1960	DF	3 431	2 545	886	...	...	...	...	62 422	...
Sweden - Suède 1 XI 1990	DJ	8 587 353	4 242 351	4 345 002	DJ	8 872	*8 958	0.3	449 964	20
Switzerland - Suisse 5 XII 2000	DJ	7 204 055	3 519 698	3 684 357	DJ	7 184	*7 341	0.7	41 284	178
The Former Yugoslav Rep. of Macedonia - L'ex-République yougoslave de Macédoine[78] 1 XI 2002	DJ	2 022 547	1 015 377	1 007 170	DF	2 024	*2 027	-	25 713	79

3. Population by sex, rate of population increase, surface area and density
Population selon le sexe, taux d'accroissement de la population, superficie et densité
(continued — suite)

Continent, country or area and census date / Continent, pays ou zone et date du recensement	Census type[1]	Latest available census — Dernier recensement disponible (in units — en unités)			Estima-te type[1]	Mid-year estimates - Estimations au milieu de l'année (in thousands — en milliers)		Annual rate of increase Taux d' accrois sement annuel 2000-03	Surface area Superficie (km²) 2003	Density Densité 2003[2]
		Both sexes Les deux sexes	Male Masculin	Female Feminin		2000	2003			
EUROPE										
Ukraine										
5 XII 2001	DJ	48 457 102	22 441 344	26 015 758	DJ	48 889	*47 633	-0.9	603 700	79
United Kingdom - Royaume-Uni[79,80]										
29 IV 2001	DF	58 789 187	28 579 867	30 209 320	DF	58 886	59 554	0.4	242 900	245
OCEANIA — OCEANIE										
American Samoa - Samoas américaines[20]										
1 IV 2000	DJ	57 291	29 264	28 027	DJ	57	58	0.3	199	291
Australia - Australie[9]										
7 VIII 2001	DF	18 972 350	9 362 021	9 610 329	DJ	19 153	19 873	1.2	7 741 220	3
Cook Islands - Îles Cook[81]										
1 XII 2001	DF	18 027	9 303	8 724	DF	18	18	0.7	236	78
Fiji - Fidji										
25 VIII 1996	DF	775 077	393 931	381 146	...	...	...	...	18 274	...
French Polynesia - Polynésie française[82]										
7 XI 2002	DF	245 516	...	...	DF	231	247	2.2	4 000	62
Guam[20]										
1 IV 2000	DJ	154 805	79 181	75 624	DJ	...	164		549	298
Kiribati[83]										
7 XI 1995	DF	*77 658	*38 478	*39 180	...	...	...	...	726	...
Marshall Islands - Îles Marshall										
1 VI 1999	DF	50 848	26 034	24 814	DF	53	...	...	181	...
Micronesia, Federated States of - Micronésie, États Fédérés de La										
1 IV 2000	DJ	107 008	54 191	52 817	DJ	119	...	...	702	...
Nauru										
17 IV 1992	DF	9 919	5 079	4 840	DF	12	...	...	21	...
New Caledonia - Nouvelle-Calédonie[84]										
16 IV 1996	DF	196 836	100 762	96 074	DF	211	220	1.5	18 575	12
New Zealand - Nouvelle-Zélande[85]										
6 III 2001	DJ	3 820 749	1 863 309	1 957 440	DJ	3 858	4 009	1.3	270 534	15
Niue - Nioué										
7 IX 2001	DF	1 788	897	891	...	...	...	...	260	...
Norfolk Island - Île Norfolk										
7 VIII 2001	DF	2 601	1 257	1 344	...	...	...	...	36	...
Northern Mariana Islands - Îles Mariannes septentrionales										
1 IV 2000	DF	69 221	31 984	37 237	DF	72	76	1.8	464	164
Palau - Palaos										
15 IV 2000	DF	19 129	...	...	DF	19	20	1.8	459	44
Papua New Guinea - Papouasie-Nouvelle-Guinée[86]										
9 VII 2000	DF	5 190 786	2 691 744	2 499 042	DF	5 100	...	...	462 840	...
Pitcairn										
31 XII 1991	DF	66	...	...	...	...	...	...	5	...

3. Population by sex, rate of population increase, surface area and density
Population selon le sexe, taux d'accroissement de la population, superficie et densité
(continued — suite)

Continent, country or area and census date / Continent, pays ou zone et date du recensement	Census type[1]	Latest available census — Dernier recensement disponible (in units — en unités)			Estima- te type[1]	Mid-year estimates - Estimations au milieu de l'année (in thousands — en milliers)		Annual rate of increase Taux d' accrois sement annuel 2000-03	Surface area Superficie (km²) 2003	Density Densité 2003[2]
		Both sexes Les deux sexes	Male Masculin	Female Feminin		2000	2003			
OCEANIA — OCEANIE										
Samoa										
5 XI 2001	DF	176 710	92 050	84 660	DF	171	...	...	2 831	...
Solomon Islands - Îles Salomon[87]										
21 XI 1999	DF	409 042	211 381	197 661	...	...	...	...	28 896	...
Tokelau - Tokélaou										
11 X 2001	DF	1 537	761	776	...	...	...	...	12	...
Tonga[88]										
30 XI 1996	DF	97 784	49 615	48 169	DF	100	...	...	747	...
Tuvalu										
1 XI 2002	DF	9 561	4 729	4 832	...	...	...	...	26	...
Vanuatu										
16 XI 1999	DJ	186 678	95 682	90 996	...	...	...	...	12 189	...
Wallis and Futuna Islands - Îles Wallis et Futuna										
22 VII 2003	DF	14 944	7 494	7 450	...	...	...	...	200	...

FOOTNOTES - NOTES

* Provisional. — Données provisoires.

[1] 'Code' indicates the source of data, as follows:
DF - De facto
DJ - De jure
SDF - Sample survey, de facto
Le 'Code' indique la source des données, comme suit:
DF - Population de fait
DJ - Population de droit
SDF - Enquête par sondage, population de fait

[2] Population per square kilometre of surface area in 2003. Figures are estimates of population divided by surface area and are not to be considered either as reflecting density in the urban sense or as indicating the supporting power of a territory's land and resources. — Nombre d'habitants au kilomètre carré en 2003. Il s'agit simplement d'éstimations de la population divisé par celui de la superficie: il ne faut pas y voir d'indication de la densité au sens urbain du terme ni de l'effectif de population que les terres et les ressources du territoire sont capables de nourrir.
[3] Including the enclave of Cabinda. - Y compris l'enclave de Cabinda.
[4] Census results have been adjusted for underenumeration, estimated at 1.4 per cent. - Les résultat du recensement ont été ajustées pour compenser les lacunes du dénombrement, estimées à 1,4 p. 100.
[5] Census result, excluding Mayotte. - Les résultat du recensement, non compris Mayotte.
[6] Comprising Bioko (which includes Pagalu) and Rio Muni (which includes Corisco and Elobeys). - Comprend Bioko (qui comprend Pagalu) et Rio Muni (qui comprend Corisco et Elobeys).
[7] Data refer to Libyan nationals only. - Les données se raportent aux nationaux libyens seulement.
[8] Data for estimates refer to national projections. - Les estimations se referent aux projections nationales.
[9] Mid-year estimates have been adjusted for underenumeration, at latest census. - Les estimations au millieu de l'année tiennent compte d'une ajustement destiné à compenser les lacunes du dénombrement lors du dernier recensement.
[10] Census results have been adjusted for underenumeration, estimated at 5.1 per cent. - Les résultats du recensement ont été ajustées pour compenser les lacunes du dénombrement, estimées à 5,1 p. 100.

[11] The number of males and / or females excludes persons whose sex is not stated (18 urban, 19 rural). - Il n'est pas tenu compte dans le nombre d'hommes et de femmes des personnes dont le sexe n'est pas indiqué (18 en zone urbaine et 19 en zone rurale).
[12] Comprising the Northern Region (former Saguia el Hamra) and Southern Region (former Rio de Oro). - Comprend la région septentrionale (ancien Saguia-el-Hamra) et la région méridionale (ancien Rio de Oro).
[13] Excluding the institutional population. - Non compris la population dans les institutions.
[14] For 2003, updated postcensal estimates. - Pour 2003, estimations post censitaires mises à jour.
[15] Census data excluding the institutional population. - Les données de recensement non compris la population dans les institutions.
[16] Population statistics are based on administrative records. - La source de la statistique de la population sont des fichiers administratifs.
[17] Including Carriacou and other dependencies in the Grenadines. - Y compris Carriacou et les autres dépendances du groupe des îles Grenadines.
[18] Including dependencies: Marie-Galante, la Désirade, les Saintes, Petite-Terre, St. Barthélemy and French part of St. Martin. - Y compris les dépendances: Marie-Galante, la Désirade, les Saintes, Petite-Terre, Saint-Barthélemy et la partie française de Saint-Martin.
[19] Comprising Bonaire, Curaçao, Saba, St. Eustatius and Dutch part of St. Martin. - Comprend Bonaire, Curaçao, Saba, Saint-Eustache et la partie néederlandaise de Saint-Martin.
[20] Including armed forces stationed in the area. - Y compris les militaires en garnison sur le territoire.
[21] Including Bequia and other islands in the Grenadines. - Y compris Bequia et des autres îles dans les Grenadines.
[22] Excluding armed forces overseas and civilian citizens absent from country for an extended period of time. - Non compris les militaires à l'étranger, et les civils hors du pays pendant une période prolongée.
[23] Data include persons in remote areas, military personel outside the country, merchant seamen at sea, civilian seasonal workers outside the country, and other civilians outside the country, and exclude nomads, foreign military, civilian aliens temporarily in the country, transients on ships and Indian jungle population. - Y compris les personnes dans des régions éloignées, le personel militaire en dehors du pays, les marins marchands, les ouvriers saisonniers civils de couture en dehors du pays, et autres civils en dehors du pays, et non compris les nomades, les militaires étrangers, les étrangers civils temporairement dans le pays, les transiteurs sur des bateaux et les Indiens de la jungle.
[24] Excluding nomadic Indian tribes. - Non compris les tribus d'Indiens nomades.

[25] Excluding dependencies, of which South Georgia (area 3 755 km2) had an estimated population of 499 in 1964 (494 males, 5 females). The other dependencies namely, the South Sandwich group (surface area 337 km2) and a number of smaller islands, are presumed to be uninhabited. - - Non compris les dépendances, parmi lesquelles figure la Georgie du Sud (3 755 km2) avec une population estimée à 499 personnes en 1964 (494 du sexe masculin et 5 du sexe féminin). Les autres dépendances, c'est-à-dire le groupe des Sandwich de Sud (superficie: 337 km2) et certaines petites-îles, sont présumées inhabitées.

[26] A dispute exists between the governments of Argentina and the United Kingdom of Great Britain and Northern Ireland concerning sovereignty over the Falkland Islands (Malvinas). - La souveraineté sur les îles Falkland (Malvinas) fait l'objet d'un différend entre le Gouvernement argentin et le Gouvernement du Royaume-Uni de Grande-Bretagne et d'Irlande du Nord.

[27] Excluding Indian jungle population. - Non compris les Indiens de la jungle.

[28] The previous census was conducted only 16 months earlier (on 31 Mar 2003) but it was repeated because all of its data were destroyed in a fire before they could be fully processed, analyzed, and reported. - Le recensement précédent a eu lieu seulement 16 mois auparavant (le 31 mars 2003), mais a dû être refait parce que toutes les données ont été détruites dans un incendie avant que l'on n'ait pu les traiter et les analyser.

[29] Figures for male and female population do not add up to the figure for total population, because they exclude 1009 persons of unknown sex (654 urban and 355 rural). - Les chiffres relatifs à la population masculine et féminine ne correspondent pas au chiffre de la population totale, parce que l'on en a exclu 1 009 personnes de sexe inconnu (654 en zones urbaines et 355 en zones rurales).

[30] Census result, excluding nomad population. - Les résultat du recensement, non compris les nomades.

[31] The methodology used for calculating the number of the de facto and de jure population in the 2001 census data differs as follows from the methodology used in previous censuses: the duration that defines a person as being ' temporary present ' or 'temporary absent' is now 'under one year'. The previously applied definition was for '6 months'. - La méthode utilisée pour dénombrer la population présente et la population légale dans le contexte du recensement de 2001 diffère de celle qui a été appliquée lors des recensements antérieurs en ce que la durée considérée pour définir la ' présence temporaire 'ou' l'absence temporaire' était dorénavant fixée à 'moins d'un an' alors qu'elle était de '6 mois' auparavant.

[32] Excluding foreign diplomatic personnel and their dependants. - Non compris le personnel diplomatique étranger et les membres de leur famille les accompagnant.

[33] For statistical purposes, the data for China do not include those for the Hong Kong Special Administrative Region (Hong Kong SAR), Macao Special Administrative Region (Macao SAR) and Taiwan province of China. - Pour la présentation des statistiques, les données pour Chine ne comprend pas la Région Administrative Spéciale de Hong Kong (Hong Kong RAS), la Région Administrative Spéciale de Macao (Macao RAS) et Taïwan province de Chine.

[34] Census data for the civilian population of 31 provinces, municipalities and autonomous regions. - Les données du recensement pour la population civile seulement de 31 provinces, municipalités et régions autonomes.

[35] Data for 2003 have been estimated on the basis of the annual national sample surveys on Population Changes. - Les données pour 2003 ont été estimées sur la base de l'enquête annuelle "National Sample Survey on Population Changes".

[36] Estimate for 2000 have been adjusted on the basis of the Population Census of 2000. - Les estimations pour 2000 ont été ajustées à partir des résultats du recensement de la population de 2000.

[37] Data refer to Hong Kong resident population at the census moment, which covers usual residents and mobile residents. Usual residents refer to two categories of people: (1) Hong Kong permanent residents who had stayed in Hong Kong for at least three months during the six months before or for at least three months during the six months after the census moment, regardless of whether they were in Hong Kong or not at the census moment; and (2) Hong Kong non-permanent residents who were in Hong Kong at the census moment. Mobile Residents, they are Hong Kong permanent residents who had stayed in Hong Kong for at least one month but less than three months during the six months before or for at least one month but less than three months during the six months after the census moment, regardless of whether they were in Hong Kong or not at the census moment. - Les données se rapportent à la population résidente à Hong Kong au moment du recensement. Cette population est composée des résidants habituels et des résidants mobiles. La population résidente est partagée en deux catégories: (1) les résidents permanents qui ont habité à Hong Kong au moins trois mois pendant les six mois précédents ou les six mois suivants le recensement; (2) les habitants non-permanents de Hong Kong qui étaient à Hong Kong au moment du recensement. La population mobile se rapporte aux résidents permanents de Hong Kong qui

ont habité à Hong Kong pendant les six mois après le recensement pour une période comprise entre un mois et trois mois, indépendamment du fait qu'ils étaient à Hong Kong au moment du recensement au pays.

[38] Data refer to government controlled areas. - Les données se raportent aux zones contrôlées par le Gouvernement.

[39] Data include all population irrespective of citizenship, who at the time of the census have resided in the country or intended to reside for a period of at least one year. It does not distinguish between those present or absent at the time of census. - Les chiffres comprennent toute la population, quelle que soit la nationalité, qui à l'époque de recensement avait résidé dans le pays, ou avait l'intention de résider, pendant une période de au moins un an. Il n'y a pas de distinction entre les personnes présentes ou absentes au moment du recensement.

[40] Including data for the Indian-held part of Jammu and Kashmir, the final status of which has not yet been determined. - Y compris les données pour la partie du Jammu et du Cachemire occupée par l'Inde dont le statut définitif n'a pas encore été déterminé.

[41] Census data exclude Mao-Maram, Paomata and Purul sub-divisions of Senapati district of Manipur. The population of Manipur including the estimated population the three sub-divisions of Senapati district is 2,291,125 (Males 1,161,173 and females 1,129,952). - Les données de recensement non compris les subdivisions Mao-Maram Paomata et Purul du district de Senapati dans l'État du Manipur. Cet État compte 2 291 125 habitants (1 161 173 hommes et 1 129 952 femmes), y compris la population estimative des trois subdivisions du district de Senapati.

[42] Census data include an estimated population of 459 557 persons in urban and 1 857 659 persons in rural areas that were not directly enumerated, and a population of 566 403 persons in urban and 1 717 578 persons in rural areas that decline the participation. Also included are 421 399 non permanent residents (thenon permanent residents (the homeless, the crew of ships carrying nationalflag, boat/floating house people, remote located tribesmen and refugees.) - Les données du recensement y compris la population estimée a 459 557 personnes dans les zones urbaines et de 1 857 659 personnes dans les zones rurales qui n'ont pas été énumérées directement, aussi que 566 403 personnes qui non pas répondu dans les zones urbaines et de 1 717 578 personnes dans les zones rurales. Y compris 421 399 résidants non permanents (les sans abri, l'équipage des bateaux portant le drapeau national, les habitants des embarcations ou des maisons flottantes, les habitants des tribus isolées et les réfugies.)

[43] For the 1997 population census, data exclude population in three autonomous provinces in the north of the country. - Pour le recensement de 1997, la population des trois provinces autonomes dans le nord du pays est exclue.

[44] Including data for East Jerusalem and Israeli residents in certain other territories under occupation by Israeli military forces since June 1967. - Y compris les données pour Jérusalem-Est et les résidents israéliens dans certains autres territoires occupés depuis 1967 par les forces armées israéliennes.

[45] Excluding diplomatic personnel outside the country and foreign military and civilian personnel and their dependants stationed in the area. - Non compris le personnel diplomatique hors du pays ni les militaires et agents civils étrangers en poste sur le territoire et les membres de leur famille les accompagnant.

[46] Excluding data for Jordanian territory under occupation since June 1967 by Israeli military forces. Excluding foreigners, including registered Palestinian refugees. - Non compris les données pour le territoire jordanien occupé depuis juin 1967 par les forces armées israéliennes. Non compris les étrangers, mais y compris les réfugiés de Palestine enregistrés.

[47] Including diplomats and their families abroad, but excluding foreign diplomats, foreign military personnal, and their families in the country. - Y compris le personnel diplomatique et les membres de leurs familles à l'étranger, mais sans tenir compte du personnel diplomatique et militaire étranger et des membres de leurs familles.

[48] Excluding Palestinian refugees in camps. - Non compris les réfugiés de Palestine dans les camps.

[49] Excluding Malaysian citizens and permanent residents who were away or intended to be away from the country for more than six months. Excluding Malaysian military, naval and diplomatic personnel and their families outside the country, and tourists, businessman who intended to be in Malaysia for less than six months. - Non compris les citoyens malaisiens et les résidents permanents qui étaient ou qui ont prévu d'être hors du pays pour six mois ou plus. Non compris le personnel militaire Malaisien, le personnel naval ou diplomatique et leurs familles hors du pays, et les touristes et les hommes d'affaires qui avaient l'intention de rester en Malaisie moins de six mois.

[50] Census results have been adjusted for underenumeration. - Les résultats du recensement ont été ajustées pour compenser les lacunes du dénombrement

[51] Data including estimated population from household listing from Village Development Committees and Wards which could not be enumerated at the time of census. - Les données incluent la population

estimée par les listes des ménages des comités de développement des villages et des circonscriptions qui n'ont pas pu être énumérée au moment du recensement.

[52] Total population does not include Palestinian population living in those parts of Jerusalem governorate which were annexed by Israel in 1967, amounting to 210 209 persons. Likewise, the results does not include the estimates of not enumerated population based on the findings of the post enumeration study, i.e 83 805 persons. - Les données relatives à la population totale ne comprennent pas la population palestinienne -équivalent à 210 209 personnes - habitant dans les territoires du gouvernorat de Jérusalem qui ont été annexés par Israël en 1967. Egalement, les données ne tiennent pas compte des estimations de la population calculée sur la base des résultats de l'enquête postcensitaire, équivalent à 83 805 personnes.

[53] Excluding data for the Pakistan-held part of Jammu and Kashmir, the final status of which has not yet been determined. - Non compris les données concernant la partie du Jammu et Cachemire occupée par le Pakistan dont le statut définitif n'a pas été déterminé.

[54] Census result, excluding transients afloat and non-locally domiciled military and civilian services personnel and their dependants and visitors. - Les résultat du recensment, non compris les personnes de passage à bord de navires ni les militaires et agents civils non-résidents et les membres de leur famille les accompagnant et visiteurs.

[55] The Population and Housing Census 2001 did not cover the whole area of the country due to the security problems; the Census was complete in 18 districts only; in three districts it was not possible to conduct it; and in four districts it was partially conducted. - Le recensement de la population et de l'habitat en 2001 n'a pas couvert la totalité du pays pour des problèmes de sécurité ; le recensement a été complété seulement en 18 districts ; dans 3 districts ça n'a pas été possible de conduire le recensement et dans 4 districts il a été partiellement conduit.

[56] Including Palestinian refugees. - Y compris les réfugiés de Palestine.

[57] Comprising 7 sheikdoms of Abu Dhabi, Dubai, Sharjah, Ajaman, Umm al Qaiwain, Ras al Khaimah and Fujairah, and the area lying within the modified Riyadh line as announced in October 1955. - Comprend les sept cheikhats de Abou Dhabi, Dabai, Ghârdja, Adjmân, Oumm-al-Quiwaïn, Ras al Khaïma et Foudjaïra, ainsi que la zone délimitée par la ligne de Riad modifiée comme il a été annoncé en octobre 1955.

[58] Excluding Faeroe Islands and Greenland. - Non compris les Iles Féroé et Gröenland.

[50] Excluding Overseas Departments, namely French Guiana, Guadeloupe, Martinique and Reunion, shown separately. De jure population but excluding diplomatic personnel outside the country and including members of alien armed forces not living in military camps and foreign diplomatic personnel not living in embassies or consulates. - Non compris les départements d'outre-mer, c'est-à-dire la Guyane française, la Guadeloupe, la Martinique et la Réunion, qui font l'objet de rubriques distinctes. Population de droit, non compris le personnel diplomatique hors du pays et y compris les militaires étrangers ne vivant pas dans des camps militaires et le personnel diplomatique étranger ne vivant pas dans les ambassades ou les consulats.

[60] Excluding families of military personnel, visitors and transients. - Non compris les familles des militaires, ni les visiteurs et transients.

[61] Census data including armed forces stationed outside the country, but excluding alien armed forces stationed in the area. - Les données de recensement y compris les militaires hors du pays, mais non compris les militaires étrangers en garnison sur le territoire.

[62] Mid-year population excludes armed forces stationed outside the country, but includes alien armed forces stationed in the area. - Les estimations au milieu de l'année non compris les militaires en garnison hors du pays, mais y compris les militaires étrangers en garnison sur le territoire.

[63] Data refer to the Vatican City State. - Les données se rapportent aux Etat du Saint-Siè-ge.

[64] Census data including foreigners residing in Malta for 12 months before the census date and excluding foreign diplomatic personnel. - Les données de recensement y compris les les étrangers habitant à Malte pour 12 mois avant le recensement et le personnel diplomatique étrangers.

[65] Data for estimates including work and resident permit holders and foreigners residing in Malta. - Les estimations y compris les titulaires de permis de travail et de permis de séjour et les ét rangers résidant à Malte.

[66] Census result, based on compilation of continuous accounting and sample surveys. - Les résultat du recensement, d'après les résultats des dénombrements et enquêtes par sondage continue.

[67] Census data including residents temporarily outside the country. - Les données du recensement y compris les résidents se trouvant temporairement hors du pays.

[68] Excluding civilian aliens within country, but including civilian nationals temporarily outside country. - Non compris les civils étrangers dans le pays, mais y compris les civils nationaux temporairement hors du pays.

[69] Surface area includes inland waters as well as part of internal waters. - Superficie comprends les eaux intérieures et une partie des eaux situées en deçà de la ligne de base de la mer territoriale.

[70] Average year data for 2000 contain revised data according to the final results of population census 2002. - Les données annuelles moyennes pour 2000 comportent des données révisées en fonction des résultats du recensement de 2002.

[71] Including the Azores and Madeira Islands. - Y compris les Açores et Madère.

[72] Data do not include information for Transnistria and the municipality of Bender. - Les données ne tiennent pas compte de l'information sur la Transnistria et la municipalité de Bender.

[73] For 2000, estimates of Kosovo and Metohia computed on the basis of natural increases from year 1997. - Pour 2000, les estimations pour le Kosovo et la Metohia ont été calculées sur la base des incréments naturelles depuis 1997.

[74] The census figure for Serbia and Montenegro consists of the final results of the population census held in the Republic of Serbia in 2002 (which was not carried out on the territory of Kosovo and Metohia) and the final results of the 2003 Census for the Republic of Montenegro. - Le total pour la Serbie-et-Montenegro se consiste des résultats finales de recensement da la population de la République de Serbie du 2002 (qui n'a été pas conduit pour le territoire de Kosovo et Metohie) et les résultats finales de recensement de la population de la République de Montenegro du 2003.

[75] For 2003, without data for Kosovo and Metohia. - Pour 2003, sans les donées pour le Kosovo et Metohie.

[76] Including the Balearic and Canary Islands, and Alhucemas, Ceuta, Chafarinas, Melilla and Penon de Vélez de la Gomera. - Y compris les Baléares et les Canaries, Al Hoceima, Ceuta, les îles Zaffarines, Melilla et Penon de Vélez de la Gomera.

[77] Inhabited only during the winter season. Census data are for total population while estimates refer to Norwegian population only. Included also in the de jure population of Norway. - N'est habitée pendant la saison d'hiver. Les données de recensement se rapportent à la population totale, mais les estimations ne concernent que la population norvégienne, comprise également dans la population de droit de la Norvège.

[78] Figure for 2003 calculated on the base of census data 2002. - Le chiffre pour 2003 a été calculé à partir des résultats du recensement de 2002.

[79] Excluding Channel Islands and Isle of Man, shown separately. - Non compris les îles Anglo-Normandes et l'île de Man, qui font l'objet de rubriques distinctes.

[80] Population estimate for 2000 were revised in light of the local studies. - Les estimations de la population pour l'année 2000 ont été révisées en fonction d'études locales.

[81] Excluding Niue, shown separately, which is part of Cook Islands, but because of remoteness is administered separately. - Non compris Nioué, qui fait l'objet d'une rubrique distincte et qui fait partie des îles Cook, mais qui, en raison de son éloignement, est administrée séparément.

[82] Comprising Austral, Gambier, Marquesas, Rapa, Society and Tuamotu Islands. - Comprend les îles Australes, Gambier, Marquises, Rapa, de la Societé et Tuamotou.

[83] Including Christmas, Fanning, Ocean and Washington Islands. - Y compris les îles Christmas, Fanning, Océan et Washington.

[84] Including the islands of Huon, Chesterfield, Loyalty, Walpole and Belep Archipelago. - Y compris les îles Huon, Chesterfield, Loyauté et Walpole, et l'archipel Belep.

[85] Including Campbell and Kermadec Islands (population 20 in 1961, surface area 148 km2) as well as Antipodes, Auckland, Bounty, Snares, Solander and Three Kings island, all of which are uninhabited. - Y compris les îles Campbell et Kermadec (20 habitants en 1961, superficie: 148 km2) ainsi que les îles Antipodes, Auckland, Bounty, Snares, Solander et Three Kings, qui sont toutes inhabitées.

[86] Comprising eastern part of New Guinea, the Bismarck Archipelago, Bougainville and Buka of Solomon Islands group and about 600 smaller islands. - Comprend l'est de la Nouvelle-Guinée, l'archipel Bismarck, Bougainville et Buka (ces deux dernières du groupe des Salomon) et environ 600 îlots.

[87] Comprising the Solomon Islands group (except Bougainville and Buka which are included with Papua New Guinea shown separately), Ontong, Java, Rennel and Santa Cruz Islands. - Comprend les îles Salomon(à l'exception de Bougainville et de Buka dont la population est comprise dans celle de Papouasie-Nouvelle Guinée qui font l'objet d'une rubrique distincte), ainsi que les îles Ontong, Java, Rennel et Santa Cruz.

[88] Data for estimates based on the results of the 1996 population census not necessarily mid year estimated. - Les estimations d'après les résultats du recensement de la population de 1996, pas nécessairement des estimations en milieu d'année.

Table 4

Table 4 presents, for each country or area of the world, basic vital statistics including: live births, crude birth rate, deaths, crude death rate and rate of natural increase, infant deaths, infant death rate, the expectation of life at birth by sex and the total fertility rate.

Description of variables: The vital events and rates shown in this table are defined as follows[1]:

Live birth is the complete expulsion or extraction from its mother of a product of conception, irrespective of the duration of pregnancy, which after such separation breathes or shows any other evidence of life such as beating of the heart, pulsation of the umbilical cord, of definite movement of voluntary muscles, whether or not the umbilical cord has been cut or the placenta is attached; each product of such a birth is considered live-born regardless of gestational age.

Death is the permanent disappearance of all evidence of life at any time after live birth has taken place (post-natal cessation of vital functions without capability of resuscitation).

Infant deaths are deaths of live-born infants under one year of age.

Expectation of life at birth is defined as the average number of years of life for males and females if they continued to be subject to the same mortality experienced in the year(s) to which these life expectancies refer.

The total fertility rate is the average number of children that would be born alive to a hypothetical cohort of women if, throughout their reproductive years, the age-specific fertility rates for the specified year remained unchanged. The standard method of calculating the total fertility rate is the sum of the age-specific fertility rates.

Crude birth rates and crude death rates presented in this table are calculated using the number of live births and the number of deaths obtained from civil registers. These civil registration data are used only if they are considered reliable (estimated completeness of 90 per cent or more).

Similarly, infant mortality rates presented in this table are calculated using the number of live births and the number of infant deaths obtained from civil registers. If, however, the registration of births or infant deaths for any given country or area is estimated to be less than 90 per cent complete, the rates are not calculated.

The expectation-of-life values are those provided by national statistical offices.

Rate computation: The crude birth and death rates are the annual number of each of these vital events per 1 000 mid-year population.

Infant mortality rate is the annual number of deaths of infants under one year of age per 1 000 live births in the same year.

Rates of natural increase are the difference between the crude birth rate and the crude death rate. It should be noted that the rates of natural increase presented here may differ from the population growth rates presented in table 3 as rates of natural increase do not take net international migration into account while the population growth rates do.

Rates that appear in this table have been calculated by the Statistics Division of the United Nations Department of Economic and Social Affairs, unless otherwise noted. Exceptions include official estimated rates, many of which were based on sample surveys.

Rates calculated by the Statistics Division of the United Nations presented in this table have been limited to those countries or areas having a minimum number of 30 events in a given year.

Reliability of data: Rates calculated on the basis of registered vital statistics which are considered unreliable (estimated to be less than 90 per cent complete) are not calculated. Estimated rates, prepared by the individual countries or areas, are presented whenever applicable.

The designation of vital statistics as being either reliable or unreliable is discussed in general in section 4.2 of the Technical Notes. The technical notes for tables 9, 15 and 18 provide specific information on reliability of statistics on live births, infant deaths and deaths, respectively.

The values shown for life expectancy in this table come from official life tables. It is assumed that, if necessary, the basic data (population and deaths classified by age and sex) have been adjusted for deficiencies before their use in constructing the life tables.

Limitations: Statistics on births, deaths and infant deaths are subject to the same qualifications as have been set forth for vital statistics in general in section 4 of the Technical Notes and in the technical notes for individual tables presenting detailed data on these events (table 9, live births; table 15, infant deaths; table 18, deaths).

In assessing comparability it is important to take into account the reliability of the data used to calculate the rates, as discussed above.

It should be noted that crude rates are particularly affected by the age-sex structure of the population. Infant mortality rates, and to a much lesser extent crude birth rates and crude death rates, are affected by the variation in the definition of a live birth and tabulation procedures.

NOTES

[1] *Principles and Recommendations for a Vital Statistics System, Revision 2,* United Nations publication, Sales No. E.01.XVII.10, United Nations, New York, 2001.

Tableau 4

Le tableau 4 présente, pour chaque pays ou zone du monde, des statistiques de base de l'état civil comprenant, dans l'ordre, les naissances vivantes, le taux brut de natalité, les décès, le taux brut de mortalité et le taux d'accroissement naturel de la population, les décès d'enfants de moins d'un an et le taux de mortalité infantile, l'espérance de vie à la naissance par sexe et l'indice synthétique de fécondité.

Description des variables : Les faits d'état civil utilisés aux fins du calcul des taux présentés dans le tableau 4 sont définis comme suit[1] :

La naissance vivante est l'expulsion ou l'extraction complète du corps de la mère, indépendamment de la duré de la gestation, d'un produit de la conception qui après cette séparation, respire ou manifeste tout autre signe de vie, tel que battement de cœur, pulsation du cordon ombilical ou contraction effective d'un muscle soumis à l'action de la volonté, que le cordon ombilical ait été coupé ou non et que le placenta soit ou non demeuré attaché ; tout produit d'une telle naissance est considéré comme « enfant né vivant ».

Le décès est la disparition permanente de tout signe de vie à un moment quelconque postérieur à la naissance vivante (cessation des fonctions vitales après la naissance sans possibilité de réanimation).

Il convient de préciser que les chiffres relatifs aux décès d'enfants de moins d'un an se rapportent aux naissances vivantes.

L'espérance de vie à la naissance est le nombre moyen d'années que vivraient les individus de sexe masculin et de sexe féminin s'ils continuaient d'être soumis aux mêmes conditions de mortalité que celles qui existaient pendant les années auxquelles se rapportent les valeurs indiquées.

L'indice synthétique de fécondité représente le nombre moyen d'enfants que mettrait au monde une cohorte hypothétique de femmes qui seraient soumises, tout au long de leur vie, aux mêmes conditions de fécondité par âge que celles auxquelles sont soumises les femmes, dans chaque groupe d'âge, au cours d'une année ou d'une période donnée. La méthode standard pour calculer l'indice synthétique de fécondité consiste à additionner les taux de fécondité par âge simple.

Les taux bruts de natalité et de mortalité ont été établis sur la base du nombre de naissances vivantes et du nombre de décès inscrits sur les registres de l'état civil. Ces données n'ont été utilisées que lorsqu'elles étaient considérées comme sûres (degré estimatif de complétude égal ou supérieur à 90 p. 100).

De même, les taux de mortalité infantile présentés dans le tableau 4 ont été établis à partir du nombre de naissances vivantes et du nombre de décès d'enfants de moins d'un an inscrits sur les registres de l'état civil. Toutefois, lorsque les données relatives aux naissances ou aux décès d'enfants de moins d'un an pour un pays ou zone quelconque n'étaient pas considérées complètes à 90 p. 100 au moins, les indices n'ont pas été calculés.

Les chiffres concernant l'espérance de vie émanent des services nationaux de statistique.

Calcul des taux : Les taux bruts de natalité et de mortalité, représentent le nombre annuel de chacun de ces faits d'état civil pour 1 000 habitants au milieu de l'année considérée.

Les taux de mortalité infantile correspondent au nombre annuel de décès d'enfants de moins d'un an pour 1 000 naissances vivantes survenues pendant la même année.

Le taux d'accroissement naturel est égal à la différence entre le taux brut de natalité et le taux brut de mortalité. Il y a lieu de noter que les taux d'accroissement naturel indiqués dans le tableau 4 peuvent différer des taux d'accroissement de la population figurant dans le tableau 3, les taux d'accroissement naturel ne tenant pas compte des taux nets de migration internationale, alors que ceux-ci sont inclus dans les taux d'accroissement de la population.

Sauf indication contraire, les taux figurant dans le tableau 4 ont été calculés par la Division de statistique du Département des affaires économiques et sociales (Secrétariat de l'Organisation des Nations Unies). Les exceptions comprennent les taux estimatifs officiels, dont bon nombre ont été établis sur la base d'enquêtes par sondage.

Les taux calculés par la Division de statistique de l'ONU qui sont présentés dans le tableau 4 se rapportent aux seuls pays ou zones où l'on a enregistré au moins 30 événements au cours d'une année donnée.

Fiabilité des données : Les taux n'ont pas été calculés lorsque les statistiques de l'état civil issues de systèmes d'enregistrement d'état civil étaient jugées douteuses (degré estimatif de complétude inférieur à 90 p.100) et des taux estimatifs, calculés par les pays ou zones, ont été présentés lorsqu'ils étaient disponibles.

On trouve à la section 4.2 des Notes techniques des explications générales concernant la façon dont les statistiques de l'état civil ont été classées selon leur degré de fiabilité. Les notes techniques relatives aux tableaux 9, 15 et 18 ont trait respectivement à la fiabilité des statistiques des naissances vivantes, des décès d'enfants de moins d'un an et des décès.

Étant donné que les valeurs relatives à l'espérance de vie figurant dans le tableau 4 proviennent de tables officielles de mortalité, elles sont toutes présumées sûres.

Insuffisance des données : Les statistiques des naissances, décès et décès d'enfants de moins d'un an appellent toutes les réserves qui ont été formulées à propos des statistiques de l'état civil en général à la section 4 des Notes techniques et dans les notes techniques relatives aux différents tableaux présentant des données détaillées sur ces événements [tableau 9 (naissances vivantes), tableau 15 (décès d'enfants de moins d'un an) et tableau 18 (décès)].

Pour évaluer la comparabilité des divers taux, il importe de tenir compte de la fiabilité des données utilisées pour calculer ces taux, comme il a été indiqué précédemment.

Il y a lieu de noter que la structure par âge et par sexe de la population influe de façon particulière sur les taux bruts. Le manque d'uniformité dans la définition des naissances vivantes et dans les procédures de mise en tableaux a une incidence sur les taux de mortalité infantile et, à un moindre degré, sur les taux bruts de natalité et les taux bruts de mortalité.

NOTE

[1] *Principes et recommandations pour un système de statistiques de l'état civil, deuxième révision*, numéro de vente : F.01.XVII.10, publication des Nations Unies, New York, 2001.

4. Vital statistics summary and expectation of life at birth: 1999-2003
Aperçu des statistiques de l'état civil et espérance de vie à la naissance: 1999-2003

Continent, country or area and year / Continent, pays ou zone et année	Live births - Naissances vivantes			Deaths - Décès			Rate of natural increase / Taux d'accroiss-ement naturel	Infant deaths - Décès d'enfants de moins d'un an			Expectation of life at birth / Espérance de vie à la naissance		Total fertility rate / L'indice synthétique de fécondité
	Code[1]	Number Nombre	Crude birth rate Taux bruts de natalité	Code[1]	Number Nombre	Crude death rate Taux bruts de mortalité		Code[1]	Number Nombre	Rate (per 1000 births) Taux (par 1000 naissances)	Male Masculin	Female Féminin	
AFRICA — AFRIQUE													
Algeria - Algérie[2,3]													
1999	C	593 643	19.8	U	129 686	...	...	U	21 798	...	...	...	2.640
2000	C	588 628	19.4	U	127 951	...	...	U	20 291	...	72.5	74.2	2.630
2001	C	618 380	20.0	U	129 092	...	...	U	21 622	...	...	...	2.570
2002	C	616 963	19.7	U	126 557	...	...	U	19 850	...	...	...	...
Benin - Bénin[4]													
1999	I	265 980	44.4	I	71 680	12.0	32.4	...	...	...	...	...	...
2000	I	272 640	44.2	I	71 540	11.6	32.6	...	...	...	...	...	...
2001	I	263 726	41.1	I	83 417	13.0	28.1	I	25 001	94.8	...	...	...
Botswana[4,5]													
1999	I	53 407	33.2	I	16 352	10.2	23.0	...	...	...	65.7	69.0	...
2001	I	53 735	32.0	I	20 823	12.4	19.6	I	1 576	29.3	...	...	...
Cape Verde - Cap-Vert													
2000	C	12 746	29.3	...	...	...	...	...	...	...	...	...	...
2001	C	12 926	29.1	...	...	...	...	...	...	...	...	...	...
2002	C	13 123	29.0	...	...	...	...	...	...	...	...	...	...
2003	C	13 334	28.9	...	...	...	...	...	...	...	...	...	...
Chad - Tchad													
2001	...	397 896	...	...	138 025	...	...	...	...	...	...	...	...
Congo[6]													
2000	+U	38 456	...	...	...	...	...	...	...	...	...	...	...
2001	+U	41 312	...	...	...	...	...	...	...	...	...	...	...
Côte d'Ivoire[4]													
2000	I	655 904	40.0	I	201 690	12.3	27.7	I	47 000	71.7	...	...	...
Egypt - Égypte													
1999	C	1 693 025	27.0	C	401 433	6.4	20.6	C	49 765	29.4	66.3	70.5	...
2000	C	1 751 854	27.4	C	404 699	6.3	21.1	C	55 214	31.5	...	...	...
2001	C	1 741 308	26.7	C	404 531	6.2	20.5	C	49 149	28.2	65.6	67.4	...
2002	C	1 751 712	26.3	C	424 516	6.4	19.9	...	...	...	67.5	71.9	...
2003	C	1 776 000	26.1	C	440 000	6.5	19.7	...	...	...	67.9	72.3	...
Ethiopia - Éthiopie													
1999	...	2 186 023	...	...	1 062 114	...	...	...	232 660	...	...	...	...
Gabon													
2000	...	...	...	...	...	...	...	...	...	...	...	...	4.300
Ghana													
2000	...	427 215	...	...	...	...	...	...	...	...	...	...	...
2001	...	433 202	...	...	52 332	...	...	...	51 639	...	...	...	...
2002	...	...	...	...	34 682	...	...	...	34 293	...	...	...	...
Kenya													
1999	U	405 488	...	...	...	...	...	...	...	...	52.9	...	...
2000	U	470 172	...	U	214 855	...	...	...	...	...	...	...	5.040
2001	U	468 249	...	U	199 358	...	...	U	32 183	...	...	...	5.060
2002	U	494 941	...	U	206 089	...	...	U	32 459	...	...	...	4.896
2003	U	495 433	...	U	248 254	...	...	U	33 399	...	...	...	4.873
Lesotho													
2001	...	...	...	...	...	...	...	...	...	...	48.7	56.3	...
Libyan Arab Jamahiriya - Jamahiriya arabe libyenne													
2000	C	98 752	19.3	U	17 367	...	...	U	2 155	...	...	...	...
2001	C	99 187	18.7	U	18 334	...	...	U	2 568	...	...	...	...
2002	C	111 053	20.2	U	19 362	...	...	...	...	...	...	...	...
Malawi[7]													
1999	I	531 160	52.3	I	234 641	23.1	29.2	...	...	...	41.1	43.8	...
2000	I	543 654	51.9	I	228 245	21.8	30.1	...	...	...	41.7	44.3	...
2001	I	555 558	51.4	I	221 963	20.5	30.8	...	...	...	42.2	44.9	...
2002	I	567 241	50.8	I	217 205	19.4	31.3	...	...	...	42.8	45.5	...
2003	I	578 978	50.1	I	213 705	18.5	31.6	...	...	...	43.4	46.0	...
Mali													
2001	U	525 685	...	...	...	...	...	...	...	...	...	...	...

4. Vital statistics summary and expectation of life at birth: 1999-2003
Aperçu des statistiques de l'état civil et espérance de vie à la naissance: 1999-2003 (continued — suite)

Continent, country or area and year / Continent, pays ou zone et année	Live births - Naissances vivantes Co-de[1]	Live births - Naissances vivantes Number Nombre	Live births - Naissances vivantes Crude birth rate Taux bruts de natalité	Deaths - Décès Co-de[1]	Deaths - Décès Number Nombre	Deaths - Décès Crude death rate Taux bruts de mortalité	Rate of natural increase Taux d'accroiss-ement naturel	Infant deaths - Décès d'enfants de moins d'un an Co-de[1]	Infant deaths Number Nombre	Infant deaths Rate (per 1000 births) Taux (par 1000 naiss-ances)	Expectation of life at birth - Espérance de vie à la naissance Male Masculin	Expectation of life at birth Female Féminin	Total fertility rate L'indice synthétiq-ue de fécondité
FRICA — AFRIQUE													
Mauritius - Maurice													
1999	+C	20 311	17.3	+C	7 944	6.8	10.5	+C	396	19.5	^68.2	^75.3	2.050
2000	+C	20 205	17.0	+C	7 982	6.7	10.3	+C	322	15.9	...	...	1.990
2001	+C	19 696	16.4	+C	7 983	6.7	9.8	+C	282	14.3	...	...	1.910
2002	+C	19 983	16.5	+C	8 310	6.9	9.6	+C	297	14.9	^68.4	^75.3	1.940
2003	+C	19 343	15.8	+C	8 520	7.0	8.9	+C	250	12.9	68.6	75.3	1.870
Morocco - Maroc													
1999	C	529 383	18.7	U	98 304	...	...	U	8 885	...	...	...	...
2000	C	541 023	18.8	U	95 084	...	...	U	7 268	...	...	...	...
2001	C	541 298	18.6	U	95 612	...	...	U	7 970	...	...	...	...
Mozambique[4]													
2000	...	...	...	...	...	...	...	...	...	...	...	...	5.800
2001	I	753 252	42.7	I	331 162	18.8	23.9	I	99 164	131.6	...	...	5.700
2002	...	...	...	...	...	...	...	...	...	...	...	...	5.500
Namibia - Namibie[8]													
2001	I	45 157	...	I	25 061	...	...	...	...	...	...	...	...
Réunion[2]													
1999	C	14 153	19.9	C	3 825	5.4	14.5	C	84	...	...	...	2.400
2000	C	14 594	20.2	C	3 836	5.3	14.9	C	83	...	...	...	2.470
2001	C	14 541	19.8	C	3 829	5.2	14.6	C	103	7.1	71.0	79.4	2.460
2002	C	14 789	19.8	C	4 004	5.4	14.4	C	91	...	...	...	2.500
2003	C	14 427	18.9	C	4 022	5.3	13.6	C	107	7.4	71.3	79.8	2.430
Saint Helena ex. dep. - Sainte-Hélène sans dép.													
1999	C	52	...	C	45	...	...	C	-	...	...	...	...
2000	C	56	...	C	53	...	...	C	-	...	...	...	...
2001	C	36	...	C	41	...	...	C	-	...	...	...	...
Seychelles													
1999	+C	1 460	18.2	+C	560	7.0	11.2	+C	15	...	...	...	2.040
2000	+C	1 512	18.6	+C	553	6.8	11.8	+C	15	...	...	...	2.080
2001	+C	1 440	17.7	+C	554	6.8	10.9	+C	19	...	...	...	1.980
2002	+C	1 481	17.7	+C	647	7.7	10.0	+C	26	...	...	...	...
2003	+C	1 498	18.1	+C	668	8.1	10.0	+C	25	...	...	...	...
South Africa - Afrique du Sud													
1999	U	1 363 800	...	...	...	...	...	...	...	...	...	...	...
2000	U	1 407 833	...	...	...	...	...	...	...	...	...	...	2.860
2001	...	...	...	...	...	...	...	...	...	...	51.8	56.7	2.800
Tunisia - Tunisie													
1999	C	160 169	16.9	U	54 400	...	...	U	4 200	...	...	...	...
2001	C	163 300	16.9	U	53 300	...	...	...	...	...	...	...	...
AMERICA, NORTH — AMERIQUE DU NORD													
Anguilla													
1999	+C	176	16.1	+C	58	5.3	10.8	+C	1	...	...	...	...
2000	+C	193	17.1	+C	73	6.5	10.7	+C	1	...	...	...	...
2001	+C	183	15.8	+C	50	4.3	11.5	+C	-	...	...	...	...
2002	+C	169	14.2	+C	52	4.4	9.8	+C	2	...	...	...	...
2003	+C	139	11.4	+C	65	5.3	6.1	+C	2	...	...	...	...
Antigua and Barbuda - Antigua-et-Barbuda													
1999	+C	1 329	...	+C	508	...	...	...	...	...	...	...	...
2000	+C	1 528	...	+C	451	...	...	...	...	...	...	...	...
Aruba[9]													
1999	+U	1 225	...	+U	554	...	...	...	...	...	...	...	...
2000	+U	1 294	...	+U	531	...	...	...	...	...	70.0	76.0	...
2001	+U	1 266	...	+U	477	...	...	+U	4	...	...	...	...
2002	+U	1 374	...	+U	489	...	...	...	...	...	...	...	...

Continent, country or area and year / Continent, pays ou zone et année	Live births — Naissances vivantes			Deaths — Décès			Rate of natural increase — Taux d'accroiss-ement naturel	Infant deaths — Décès d'enfants de moins d'un an			Expectation of life at birth — Espérance de vie à la naissance		Total fertility rate — L'indice synthétique de fécondité
	Code[1]	Number Nombre	Crude birth rate Taux bruts de natalité	Code[1]	Number Nombre	Crude death rate Taux bruts de mortalité		Code[1]	Number Nombre	Rate (per 1000 births) Taux (par 1000 naiss-ances)	Male Masculin	Female Féminin	
AMERICA, NORTH — AMERIQUE DU NORD													
Aruba[9]													
2003	+U	1 170	...	+U	498	...	...	+U	3	...	...	...	.
Bahamas[9]													
1999	U	5 367	...	C	1 567	5.3	...	C	48	...	...	...	2.05
2000	U	5 287	...	C	1 625	5.4	...	C	52	...	...	...	1.98
2001	U	5 353	...	C	1 609	5.2	...	C	37	...	...	...	1.99
2003	U	5 054	...	C	1 649	5.2	...	C	87	...	...	...	
Barbados - Barbade													
2000	+C	3 762	14.1	+C	2 367	8.8	5.2	+C	63	...	...	...	.
2002	+C	3 812	14.1	+C	2 285	8.4	5.6	+C	54	...	...	...	.
Belize													
1999	U	6 218	...	U	1 190	...	...	U	123	...	...	...	.
2000	U	7 313	...	U	1 534	...	...	U	155	...	...	...	.
2001	U	7 082	...	U	1 261	...	...	U	120	...	...	...	.
2002	U	7 356	...	U	1 284	...	...	U	145	...	...	...	.
Bermuda - Bermudes													
1999	C	828	13.2	C	427	6.8	6.4	C	2	...	...	...	.
2000	C	838	13.3	C	473	7.5	5.8	C	-	...	...	...	1.64
2001	C	831	13.4	C	442	7.1	6.3	C	3	...	...	...	..
2002	C	830	13.4	C	404	6.5	6.9	C	-	...	...	...	..
2003	C	834	13.4	C	434	7.0	6.4	C	2	...	...	...	..
British Virgin Islands - Îles Vierges britanniques													
2000	...	...	...	...	...	...	...	+C	1	...	...	...	..
2001	+C	318	15.4	+C	101	4.9	10.5	...	...	...	...	...	..
Canada[10]													
1999	C	337 249	11.1	C	219 530	7.2	3.9	C	1 776	5.3	76.3	81.7	1.527
2000	C	327 882	10.7	C	218 062	7.1	3.6	C	1 737	5.3	77.0	82.2	1.488
2001	C	333 744	10.8	C	219 538	7.1	3.7	C	1 739	5.2	77.0	82.2	1.516
2002	C	328 802	10.5	C	223 603	7.1	3.4	C	1 762	5.4	77.2	82.1	1.501
2003	C	330 919	10.5	C	227 285	7.2	3.3	...	...	...	...	...	
Cayman Islands - Îles Caïmanes													
1999	C	604	15.5	C	128	3.3	12.2	...	...	...	...	...	..
2000	C	619	15.4	C	137	3.4	12.0	...	...	...	...	...	..
2001	C	622	15.0	C	132	3.2	11.9	...	...	...	...	...	..
Costa Rica													
1999	C	78 526	23.0	C	15 052	4.4	18.6	C	925	11.8	...	...	2.500
2000	C	78 178	22.4	C	14 944	4.3	18.1	C	798	10.2	...	...	2.000
2001	C	76 401	19.6	C	15 609	4.0	15.6	C	827	10.8	...	...	..
2002	C	71 144	17.8	C	15 004	3.8	14.0	C	793	11.1	...	...	..
2003	C	72 938	17.8	C	15 800	3.9	14.0	C	737	10.1	...	...	..
Cuba													
1999	C	150 785	13.6	C	79 499	7.2	6.4	C	977	6.5	...	...	..
2000	C	143 528	12.9	C	76 463	6.9	6.0	C	1 039	7.2	...	...	..
2001	C	138 718	12.4	C	79 395	7.1	5.3	C	861	6.2	^75.1	^79.0	..
2002	C	141 276	12.6	C	73 882	6.6	6.0	C	922	6.5	...	...	1.675
2003	C	136 795	12.2	C	78 433	7.0	5.2	C	859	6.3	...	...	1.628
Dominica - Dominique													
1999	+C	1 291	18.0	+C	631	8.8	9.2	...	...	...	...	...	..
2000	+C	1 199	16.8	+C	503	7.0	9.7	...	...	...	...	...	..
2001	+C	1 213	17.1	+C	510	7.2	9.9	+C	24	...	...	...	..
2002	+C	1 081	15.4	...	...	...	...	...	...	...	...	...	..
Dominican Republic - République dominicaine													
1999	+U	193 418	...	+U	26 956	...	...	+U	1 966	...	...	...	...
2000	+U	189 332	...	+U	23 776	...	...	+U	2 116	...	...	...	...

Continent, country or area and year / Continent, pays ou zone et née	Live births - Naissances vivantes			Deaths - Décès			Rate of natural increase Taux d'accroissement naturel	Infant deaths - Décès d'enfants de moins d'un an			Expectation of life at birth Espérance de vie à la naissance		Total fertility rate L'indice synthétique de fécondité
	Code[1]	Number Nombre	Crude birth rate Taux bruts de natalité	Code[1]	Number Nombre	Crude death rate Taux bruts de mortalité		Code[1]	Number Nombre	Rate (per 1000 births) Taux (par 1000 naissances)	Male Masculin	Female Féminin	
AMERICA, NORTH — AMERIQUE DU NORD													
El Salvador													
1999	C	153 636	25.0	C	28 056	4.6	20.4	C	1 768	11.5	...	...	...
2000	C	150 176	23.9	C	28 154	4.5	19.4	C	1 678	11.2	^67.7	^73.7	...
2001	C	138 354	21.6	C	29 559	4.6	17.0	C	1 682	12.2	...	...	...
2002	C	129 363	19.8	C	27 458	4.2	15.6	C	1 284	9.9	...	...	...
2003	C	124 476	18.8	C	29 377	4.4	14.3	C	1 322	10.6	...	...	...
Greenland - Groenland													
1999	C	947	16.9	C	482	8.6	8.3	C	16	...	^64.1	^69.5	2.340
2000	C	885	15.8	C	458	8.2	7.6	C	12	...	...	...	2.308
2001	C	937	16.6	C	438	7.8	8.8	C	10	...	...	...	2.451
2002	C	940	16.6	C	435	7.7	8.9	C	10	...	...	...	2.488
2003	C	895	15.8	C	412	7.3	8.5	C	8	...	...	...	2.361
Grenada - Grenade													
1999	+C	1 791	17.8	+C	794	7.9	9.9	+C	29	...	...	...	...
2000	+C	1 883	18.6	+C	716	7.1	11.5	+C	27	...	...	...	...
2001	+C	1 899	18.8	+C	727	7.2	11.6	+C	33	...	...	...	...
Guadeloupe[2]													
1999	C	7 341	17.3	C	2 670	6.3	11.0	C	55	...	...	...	2.200
2000	C	7 653	17.9	C	2 698	6.3	11.6	C	57	...	...	...	2.300
2001	C	7 503	17.3	C	2 765	6.4	11.0	C	49	...	...	...	2.300
2002	C	6 995	16.0	C	2 584	5.9	10.1	C	45	...	74.6	81.5	2.200
2003	C	7 047	16.1	C	2 636	6.0	10.1	C	56	...	...	...	...
Guatemala													
1999	C	360 759	32.5	C	64 563	5.8	26.7	C	13 161	36.5	...	...	...
2000	C	426 346	37.4	C	66 831	5.9	31.6	C	13 247	31.1	...	...	...
2001	C	403 532	34.6	C	69 934	6.0	28.6	...			...	...	...
2003	C	375 092	31.0	C	66 695	5.5	25.5	C	11 022	29.4	...	...	...
Jamaica - Jamaïque[11]													
1999	C	48 987	19.0	U	16 294	...	...	C	866	17.7	...	...	2.247
2000	C	48 717	18.8	U	15 251	...	...	C	863	17.7	^72.8	^76.4	2.246
2001	C	48 065	18.5	U	14 476	...	...	C	833	17.3	...	...	2.215
2002	C	44 331	16.9	U	15 876	...	...	C	809	18.2	...	...	2.044
2003	C	45 133	17.2	U	15 686	...	...	C	753	16.7	...	...	2.067
Martinique[2]													
1999	C	5 789	15.2	C	2 581	6.8	8.4	C	41	...	...	...	1.900
2000	C	6 059	15.8	C	2 692	7.0	8.8	C	40	...	...	...	2.000
2001	C	5 908	15.3	C	2 754	7.1	8.1	C	43	...	...	...	2.000
2002	C	5 446	14.0	C	2 681	6.9	7.1	C	33	...	75.4	82.2	1.900
2003	C	5 430	13.9	C	2 725	7.0	6.9	C	33	...	...	...	...
Mexico - Mexique													
1999	+U	2 769 089	...	C	443 950	4.5	...	U	40 283	...	...	...	...
2000	+U	2 798 339	...	C	437 667	4.4	...	U	38 621	...	...	...	2.651
2001	+U	2 767 610	...	C	443 127	4.4	...	U	35 911	...	...	...	2.453
2002	+U	2 699 084	...	C	459 687	4.5	...	U	36 567	...	...	...	2.285
2003	+U	2 655 894	...	C	472 140	4.5	...	U	33 355	...	...	...	...
Montserrat													
1999	+C	45	9.4	+C	59	12.4	-2.9	+C	-	...	...	...	...
Netherlands Antilles - Antilles néerlandaises													
1999	C	2 803	15.1	C	1 117	6.0	9.1	...		...	...	...	...
2000	C	2 638	14.7	C	1 196	6.7	8.0	...		...	...	...	...
2001	C	2 621	15.0	C	1 215	7.0	8.1	...		...	...	...	...
2002	C	2 382	13.7	C	1 220	7.0	6.7	...		...	...	...	...
2003	C	2 512	14.1	C	1 374	7.7	6.4	...		...	...	...	...
Nicaragua													
1999	+U	123 446	...	+U	10 818	...	...	+U	1 768	...	...	...	...
2000	+U	126 873	...	+U	13 602	...	...	+U	2 075	...	^67.2	^71.9	3.299
2001	+U	108 299	...	+U	12 789	...	...	+U	1 933	...	...	...	...

4. Vital statistics summary and expectation of life at birth: 1999-2003
Aperçu des statistiques de l'état civil et espérance de vie à la naissance: 1999-2003 (continued — suite)

Continent, country or area and year / Continent, pays ou zone et année	Code[1]	Live births - Naissances vivantes Number Nombre	Crude birth rate Taux bruts de natalité	Code[1]	Deaths - Décès Number Nombre	Crude death rate Taux bruts de mortalité	Rate of natural increase Taux d'accroiss-ement naturel	Code[1]	Infant deaths - Décès d'enfants de moins d'un an Number Nombre	Rate (per 1000 births) Taux (par 1000 naiss-ances)	Expectation of life at birth - Espérance de vie à la naissance Male Masculin	Female Féminin	Total fertility rate L'indice synthétique de fécondité
AMERICA, NORTH — AMERIQUE DU NORD													
Nicaragua													
2002	+U	120 846	...	+U	15 061	...	...	+U	2 217	...	...	...	.
2003	+U	102 676	...	+U	14 630	...	...	+U	1 989	...	...	...	..
Panama													
1999	C	64 248	22.9	U	11 938	...	...	U	1 005	...	...	...	
2000	C	64 839	22.7	U	11 841	...	...	U	1 081	...	72.2	76.8	
2001	C	63 900	22.1	U	12 442	...	...	U	1 053	...	...	...	2.49
2002	C	61 671	20.2	...	...	...	...	...	...	...	...	...	
Puerto Rico - Porto Rico													
1999	C	59 684	15.8	C	29 145	7.7	8.1	C	632	10.6	...	...	1.85
2000	C	59 460	15.6	C	28 550	7.5	8.1	C	589	9.9	...	...	2.03
2001	C	55 982	14.6	C	28 794	7.5	7.1	C	515	9.2	...	...	1.91
2002	C	52 871	13.7	C	28 098	7.3	6.4	C	516	9.8	73.2	80.9	1.81
2003	C	50 803	13.1	C	28 356	7.3	5.8	C	498	9.8	...	...	1.76
Saint Kitts and Nevis - Saint-Kitts-et-Nevis													
1999	+C	864	20.3	+C	418	9.8	10.5	...	...	...	...	...	
2000	+C	838	20.7	+C	357	8.8	11.9	...	...	...	...	...	
2001	+C	803	17.4	+C	352	7.6	9.8	...	...	...	...	...	
Saint Lucia - Sainte-Lucie[9]													
1999	C	2 997	19.5	C	981	6.4	13.1	C	42	...	69.5	73.2	2.118
2000	C	2 840	18.2	C	941	6.0	12.2	C	38	...	68.7	73.6	2.035
2001	C	2 788	17.7	C	998	6.3	11.3	C	37	...	...	...	..
2002	C	2 529	15.9	C	957	6.0	9.9	C	36	...	72.0	76.7	..
Saint Vincent and the Grenadines - Saint Vincent-et-les Grenadines													
1999	+C	2 171	19.5	+C	833	7.5	12.0	+C	47	...	...	...	..
2000	+C	2 149	19.2	+C	700	6.3	13.0	+C	35	...	...	...	..
2001	+C	2 109	19.3	+C	765	7.0	12.3	+C	39	...	...	...	..
2002	+C	1 985	18.4	+C	770	7.1	11.3	+C	36	...	...	...	..
Trinidad and Tobago - Trinité-et-Tobago													
1999	C	18 321	14.3	C	10 014	7.8	6.5	...	...	...	...	...	..
2002	C	18 026	14.1	C	9 670	7.6	6.6	...	...	...	...	...	..
Turks Caicos Islands - Îles Turques et Caïques													
1999	C	292	17.0	C	39	2.3	14.7	C	1	...	...	...	..
2000	C	290	15.7	C	67	3.6	12.1	C	-	...	...	...	..
2001	C	271	13.6	C	69	3.5	10.2	C	3	...	79.0	77.4	..
2002	C	153	7.3	C	48	2.3	5.0	C	6	...	...	...	..
2003	C	213	9.7	C	73	3.3	6.3	C	8	...	...	...	..
United States - États-Unis													
1999	C	3 959 417	14.5	C	2 391 399	8.8	5.8	C	27 937	7.1	73.9	79.4	..
2000	C	4 058 814	14.7	C	2 403 351	8.7	6.0	C	28 035	6.9	74.3	79.7	..
2001	C	4 025 933	14.1	C	2 416 425	8.5	5.7	C	27 568	6.8	74.4	79.8	..
2002	C	4 021 726	13.9	C	2 443 387	8.5	5.5	C	28 034	7.0	74.5	79.9	2.013
2003	C	4 091 063	14.1	C	2 443 908	8.4	5.7	C	28 428	6.9	...	...	..
AMERICA, SOUTH — AMERIQUE DU SUD													
Argentina - Argentine													
1999	C	686 748	18.8	C	289 543	7.9	10.9	C	12 120	17.6	...	...	...
2000	C	701 878	19.0	C	277 148	7.5	11.5	C	11 649	16.6	...	...	...
2001	C	683 495	18.2	C	285 941	7.6	10.6	C	11 111	16.3	...	...	...
2002	C	694 684	18.3	C	291 190	7.7	10.6	C	11 703	16.8	...	...	...
2003	C	697 952	18.4	C	302 064	8.0	10.5	C	11 494	16.5	...	...	...

Continent, country or area and year / Continent, pays ou zone et année	Live births Naissances vivantes			Deaths Décès			Rate of natural increase Taux d'accroissement naturel	Infant deaths Décès d'enfants de moins d'un an			Expectation of life at birth Espérance de vie à la naissance		Total fertility rate
	Code[1]	Number Nombre	Crude birth rate Taux bruts de natalité	Code[1]	Number Nombre	Crude death rate Taux bruts de mortalité		Code[1]	Number Nombre	Rate (per 1000 births) Taux (par 1000 naissances)	Male Masculin	Female Féminin	L'indice synthétique de fécondité
AMERICA, SOUTH — AMÉRIQUE DU SUD													
Bolivia - Bolivie													
1999	..	...	...	U	71 680	...	...	U	16 492	...	...	...	...
2000	U	264 941	...	U	71 742	...	...	U	16 042	...	...	...	...
Brazil - Brésil[12,13]													
1999	U	2 657 613	...	U	943 524	...	...	U	58 767	...	...	...	2.226
2000	U	2 611 422	...	U	927 783	...	...	U	53 097	...	64.8	72.6	2.200
2001	U	2 509 354	...	U	931 017	...	...	U	47 171	...	...	...	2.180
2002	U	2 581 055	...	U	958 475	...	...	U	45 243	...	67.3	74.9	2.160
2003	U	2 822 462	...	U	977 717	...	...	U	43 970	...	...	...	2.140
Chile - Chili													
1999	C	250 674	16.5	C	81 984	5.4	11.1	C	2 654	10.6	72.4	78.4	2.200
2000	C	248 893	16.2	C	78 814	5.1	11.0	C	2 336	9.4	...	...	2.100
2001	C	246 116	15.8	C	81 873	5.3	10.5	C	2 159	8.8	^74.4	^80.4	2.000
2002	C	238 981	15.2	C	81 079	5.1	10.0	C	1 964	8.2	...	...	2.000
2003	C	234 486	14.7	C	83 672	5.3	9.5	C	1 935	8.3	...	...	1.900
Colombia - Colombie[14]													
1999	U	746 194	...	U	183 551	...	...	U	14 621	...	...	...	2.730
2000	U	752 834	...	U	187 432	...	...	U	15 367	...	^69.2	^75.3	...
2001	U	724 319	...	U	191 513	...	...	U	14 430	...	^69.4	^75.5	...
2002	U	700 455	...	U	192 263	...	...	U	12 640	...	^69.6	^75.7	...
2003	U	697 029	...	U	189 072	...	...	U	11 944	...	...	...	...
Ecuador - Équateur[15]													
1999	U	218 108	...	U	55 921	...	...	U	5 372	...	...	...	...
2000	U	202 257	...	U	56 420	...	...	U	5 480	...	^71.3	^77.2	2.820
2001	U	192 786	...	U	55 214	...	...	U	4 800	...	...	...	...
2002	U	183 792	...	U	55 549	...	...	U	4 530	...	...	...	...
2003	U	178 549	...	U	53 521	...	...	U	3 985	...	...	...	...
Falkland Islands (Malvinas) - Îles Falkland (Malvinas)													
1999	+C	33	...	+C	20	...	...	...	...	...	...	...	...
2000	+C	27	...	+C	11	...	...	...	...	...	...	...	...
French Guiana - Guyane française[2]													
1999	C	4 898	30.9	C	658	4.2	26.8	C	63	...	...	...	3.900
2000	C	5 116	31.2	C	620	3.8	27.4	C	64	...	...	...	4.000
2001	C	5 114	30.1	C	668	3.9	26.2	C	70	...	...	...	3.900
2002	C	5 249	29.9	C	656	3.7	26.2	C	52	...	72.5	79.2	3.900
2003	C	5 553	30.7	C	692	3.8	26.8	C	58	...	...	...	...
Guyana													
1999	...	...	...	+C	4 197	5.4	...	...	...	...	...	...	...
Paraguay[16]													
2000	...	...	...	...	...	...	...	...	...	...	^68.6	^73.1	3.800
2001	...	...	...	I	38 514	...	...	I	3 898	...	...	...	...
Peru - Pérou[4,12,17]													
1999	I	642 874	25.2	I	162 457	6.4	18.8	I	25 098	39.0	...	...	3.090
2000	I	636 064	24.5	I	163 263	6.3	18.2	I	23 681	37.2	...	...	3.020
2001	I	630 947	23.9	I	164 296	6.2	17.7	I	22 455	35.6	...	...	2.960
2002	I	626 714	23.4	I	165 467	6.2	17.2	...	...	...	...	...	2.890
2003	I	623 521	23.0	I	166 777	6.1	16.8	...	...	...	...	...	2.830
Suriname													
1999	C	10 144	22.2	C	2 992	6.5	15.6	C	227	22.4	...	...	...
2000	C	9 804	21.1	C	3 090	6.7	14.5	C	156	15.9	...	...	...
2001	C	9 717	20.7	C	3 099	6.6	14.1	C	133	13.7	...	...	...
2002	C	10 188	21.4	C	3 125	6.6	14.8	C	148	14.5	...	...	...
Uruguay													
1999	C	54 004	16.4	C	32 430	9.9	6.6	C	776	14.4	...	...	2.260
2000	C	52 770	16.0	C	30 456	9.2	6.8	C	742	14.1	...	...	2.250

Continent, country or area and year / Continent, pays ou zone et année	Code[1]	Number Nombre	Crude birth rate Taux bruts de natalité	Code[1]	Number Nombre	Crude death rate Taux bruts de mortalité	Rate of natural increase Taux d'accroiss-ement naturel	Code[1]	Number Nombre	Rate (per 1000 births) Taux (par 1000 naiss-ances)	Male Masculin	Female Féminin	Total fertility rate L'indice synthétique de fécondité
AMERICA, SOUTH — AMERIQUE DU SUD													
Uruguay													
2001	C	51 959	15.7	C	31 228	9.4	6.3	C	721	13.9	...	...	2.23
2002	C	51 953	15.7	C	31 628	9.6	6.1	C	708	13.6	...	...	2.21
2003	C	50 631	15.3	C	32 587	9.9	5.5	C	757	15.0	71.3	79.2	
Venezuela[12]													
1999	C	527 888	22.1	C	101 907	4.3	17.8	C	9 030	17.1	...	...	
2000	C	544 416	22.4	C	103 255	4.2	18.1	C	8 524	15.7	...	...	
2001	C	529 552	21.4	C	107 867	4.4	17.0	C	8 158	15.4	...	...	
2002	C	492 678	19.5	C	105 388	4.2	15.4	C	7 645	15.5	...	...	
2003	C	555 614	...	C	118 562			...	...	...	...	...	
ASIA — ASIE													
Afghanistan													
1999	...	...	...	...	...	...	...	...	...	...	45.6	46.7	
2000	...	...	...	...	...	...	...	...	...	...	45.1	46.6	
2001	...	...	...	...	...	...	...	...	...	...	43.0	43.0	
2002	...	...	...	...	...	...	...	...	...	...	43.0	43.0	
Armenia - Arménie[18]													
1999	C	36 502	11.3	C	24 087	7.5	3.8	C	572	15.7	70.6	75.5	1.19
2000	C	34 276	10.6	C	24 025	7.5	3.2	C	540	15.8	70.6	75.5	1.10
2001	C	32 065	10.0	C	24 003	7.5	2.5	C	497	15.5	...	...	1.10
2002	C	32 229	10.0	C	25 554	8.0	2.1	C	450	14.0	...	...	1.20
2003	C	35 793	11.1	C	26 014	8.1	3.0	C	422	11.8	...	...	1.34
Azerbaijan - Azerbaïdjan[18]													
1999	+C	117 539	14.7	+C	46 295	5.8	8.9	+C	1 943	16.5	68.1	75.1	2.00
2000	+C	116 994	14.5	+C	46 701	5.8	8.7	+C	1 501	12.8	68.6	75.1	2.00
2001	+C	110 356	13.6	+C	45 284	5.6	8.0	+C	1 382	12.5	68.6	75.2	1.83
2002	+C	110 715	13.6	+C	46 522	5.7	7.9	+C	1 422	12.8	69.4	75.0	1.84
2003	+C	113 467	13.8	+C	49 001	6.0	7.8	+C	1 451	12.8	69.5	75.1	1.91
Bahrain - Bahreïn													
1999	+U	14 280	...	U	1 920	...	...	U	129	...	...	...	2.89
2000	+U	13 947	...	U	2 045	...	...	U	117	...	...	...	2.74
2001	U	13 468	...	U	1 979	...	...	U	117	...	73.2	76.2	2.57
2002	U	13 576	...	U	2 035	...	...	U	94	...	...	...	2.52
2003	U	14 560	...	U	2 114	...	...	...	...	...	...	...	
Brunei Darussalam - Brunéi Darussalam													
1999	+C	7 408	23.4	+C	905	2.9	20.5	+C	44	...	...	...	2.39
2000	+C	7 481	23.0	+C	965	3.0	20.1	+C	55	...	...	...	2.36
2001	+C	7 363	22.1	+C	1 014	3.0	19.1	+C	50	...	...	...	2.23
2002	+C	7 464	21.7	+C	1 041	3.0	18.7	+C	62	...	...	...	
2003	+C	7 047	20.2	+C	1 010	2.9	17.3	+C	67	...	...	...	
China - Chine[19,20]													
1999	I	19 090 000	15.2	...	8 100 000	6.5	8.8	...	...	...	...	...	
2000	...	...	14.0	...	...	6.4	7.6	...	...	...	69.6	73.3	
2001	...	...	13.4	...	...	6.4	7.0	...	...	...	...	...	
2002	...	...	12.9	...	...	6.4	6.4	...	...	...	...	...	
2003	...	...	12.4	...	...	6.4	6.0	...	...	...	...	...	
China: Hong Kong SAR - Chine: Hong Kong RAS[21]													
1999	C	51 281	7.8	C	33 258	5.0	2.7	C	157	3.1	77.2	82.4	0.982
2000	C	54 134	8.1	C	33 758	5.1	3.1	C	162	3.0	77.0	82.2	1.035
2001	C	48 219	7.2	C	33 378	5.0	2.2	C	124	2.6	78.4	84.6	0.932
2002	C	48 209	7.1	C	34 267	5.0	2.1	C	110	2.3	78.6	84.5	0.939
2003	C	46 965	6.9	C	36 971	5.4	1.5	C	109	2.3	78.5	84.3	0.901

Continent, country or area and year / Continent, pays ou zone et année	Live births / Naissances vivantes Code[1]	Number Nombre	Crude birth rate Taux bruts de natalité	Deaths - Décès Code[1]	Number Nombre	Crude death rate Taux bruts de mortalité	Rate of natural increase Taux d'accroiss-ement naturel	Infant deaths / Décès d'enfants de moins d'un an Code[1]	Number Nombre	Rate (per 1000 births) Taux (par 1000 naiss-ances)	Expectation of life at birth / Espérance de vie à la naissance Male Masculin	Female Féminin	Total fertility rate L'indice synthétiq-ue de fécondité
ASIA — ASIE													
China: Macao SAR - Chine: Macao RAS													
1999	C	4 148	9.7	C	1 374	3.2	6.5	C	17	...	...	...	...
2000	C	3 849	8.9	C	1 338	3.1	5.8	C	11	...	...	...	...
2001	C	3 241	7.5	C	1 327	3.1	4.4	C	14	...	...	...	...
2002	C	3 162	7.2	C	1 415	3.2	4.0	C	11	...	...	...	...
2003	C	3 212	7.2	C	1 474	3.3	3.9	C	2	...	...	...	...
Cyprus - Chypre[22]													
1999	C	8 505	12.4	C	5 070	7.4	5.0	C	51	...	...	...	1.670
2000	C	8 447	12.2	C	5 355	7.7	4.5	C	47	...	...	...	1.640
2001	C	8 167	11.6	C	4 827	6.9	4.8	C	37	...	...	...	1.570
2002	C	7 883	11.1	C	5 168	7.3	3.8	C	40	...	^77.0	^81.4	1.491
2003	C	8 088	11.2	C	5 200	7.2	4.0	C	33	...	...	...	1.498
Georgia - Géorgie[18]													
1999	C	40 778	9.2	C	47 184	10.6	-1.4	...	...	...	...	...	1.440
2000	C	40 392	9.1	C	47 410	10.7	-1.6	...	...	...	...	...	1.460
2001	C	47 589	10.8	C	46 218	10.5	0.3	C	1 098	23.1	...	...	1.440
2002	C	46 605	10.7	C	46 446	10.7	0.0	C	1 102	23.6	...	...	1.420
2003	C	46 194	10.7	C	46 055	10.6	0.0	C	1 144	24.8	69.1	74.7	1.370
India - Inde[23,24]													
1999	...	...	26.0	...	...	8.7	17.3	...	...	70.0	...	...	3.200
2000	...	...	25.8	...	...	8.5	17.3	...	...	68.0	...	...	3.200
2001	...	...	25.4	...	...	8.4	17.0	...	...	66.0	...	...	...
2002	...	...	25.0	...	...	8.1	16.9	...	...	63.0	...	...	...
2003	...	...	24.8	...	...	8.0	16.8	...	...	60.0	...	...	...
Indonesia - Indonésie													
1999	...	...	...	...	...	...	...	...	...	...	...	...	2.593
2000	...	...	...	...	...	...	...	...	...	...	...	...	2.544
Iran (Islamic Republic of) - Iran (République islamique d')													
1999	C	1 177 557	18.8	C	506 945	8.1	10.7	C	39 183	33.3	...	...	...
2000	C	1 095 165	17.2	C	382 674	6.0	11.2	...	...	...	...	...	...
2001	C	1 112 193	17.2	C	421 525	6.5	10.7	...	...	...	67.6	70.4	2.500
2002	C	1 122 104	17.1	C	337 237	5.1	12.0	...	...	...	...	...	...
2003	C	1 171 573	17.6	C	368 518	5.5	12.1	...	...	...	...	...	...
Iraq[25]													
1999	U	*532 916*	...	U	*177 483*	...	...	...	...	...	...	...	...
2000	U	*471 886*	...	U	*179 928*	...	...	...	...	...	...	...	...
Israel - Israël[26]													
1999	C	131 936	21.5	C	37 291	6.1	15.5	C	771	5.8	...	...	2.941
2000	C	136 390	21.7	C	37 688	6.0	15.7	C	748	5.5	76.5	81.1	2.954
2001	C	136 638	21.2	C	37 184	5.8	15.4	C	700	5.1	...	...	2.887
2002	C	139 535	21.2	C	38 368	5.8	15.4	C	752	5.4	77.5	81.5	2.888
2003	C	144 936	21.7	C	38 359	5.7	15.9	C	717	4.9	77.7	81.9	2.945
Japan - Japon[27]													
1999	C	1 177 669	9.3	C	982 031	7.8	1.5	C	4 010	3.4	77.1	84.0	1.340
2000	C	1 190 547	9.4	C	961 653	7.6	1.8	C	3 830	3.2	77.6	84.6	1.360
2001	C	1 170 662	9.2	C	970 331	7.6	1.6	C	3 599	3.1	78.1	84.9	1.330
2002	C	1 153 855	9.1	C	982 379	7.7	1.3	C	3 497	3.0	78.3	85.2	1.319
2003	C	1 123 610	8.8	C	1 014 951	8.0	0.9	C	3 364	3.0	78.4	85.3	1.290
Jordan - Jordanie[28]													
1999	C	135 266	27.2	C	13 936	2.8	24.4	...	...	...	...	...	...
2000	C	126 016	25.4	C	13 339	2.7	22.7	...	...	...	...	...	...
2001	C	142 956	27.2	C	16 164	3.1	24.1	...	...	...	68.8	71.1	...
2002	C	146 077	27.0	C	17 220	3.2	23.8	...	...	...	...	...	...
2003	C	148 294	27.4	C	16 937	3.1	24.3	...	...	...	...	...	...
Kazakhstan[18]													
1999	C	217 578	14.6	C	147 416	9.9	4.7	C	4 448	20.4	...	...	...

4. Vital statistics summary and expectation of life at birth: 1999-2003
Aperçu des statistiques de l'état civil et espérance de vie à la naissance: 1999-2003 (continued — suite)

Continent, country or area and year / Continent, pays ou zone et année	Code[1]	Live births Naissances vivantes		Code[1]	Deaths - Décès		Rate of natural increase Taux d'accroiss-ement naturel	Code[1]	Infant deaths Décès d'enfants de moins d'un an		Expectation of life at birth Espérance de vie à la naissance		Total fertility rate L'indice synthétique de fécondité
		Number Nombre	Crude birth rate Taux bruts de natalité		Number Nombre	Crude death rate Taux bruts de mortalité			Number Nombre	Rate (per 1000 births) Taux (par 1000 naiss-ances)	Male Masculin	Female Féminin	
ASIA — ASIE													
Kazakhstan[18]													
2000	C	222 054	14.9	C	149 778	10.1	4.9	C	4 163	18.7	...	...	
2001	C	221 487	14.9	C	147 876	10.0	5.0	C	4 239	19.1	...	...	
2002	C	227 171	15.3	C	149 381	10.1	5.2	C	3 850	16.9	...	...	
2003	C	247 946	16.6	C	155 277	10.4	6.2	C	3 824	15.4	...	...	
Korea (Republic of) - Corée (République de)[29]													
1999	C	616 322	13.2	C	246 539	5.3	7.9	C	2 776	4.5	71.7	79.2	1.42
2000	C	636 780	13.5	C	247 346	5.3	8.3	C	2 885	4.5	...	...	1.47
2001	C	557 228	11.8	C	242 730	5.1	6.6	C	3 008	5.4	72.8	80.0	1.30
2002	C	494 625	10.4	C	246 515	5.2	5.2	C	2 545	5.1	...	...	1.17
2003	C	493 471	10.3	C	245 817	5.1	5.2	C	2 470	5.0	...	...	1.19
Kuwait - Koweït													
1999	C	41 135	19.5	C	4 187	2.0	17.5	C	386	9.4	...	...	4.16
2000	C	41 843	19.1	C	4 227	1.9	17.2	C	379	9.1	...	...	4.22
2001	C	41 342	18.2	C	4 364	1.9	16.3	C	420	10.2	...	...	4.04
2002	C	43 490	19.2	C	4 342	1.9	17.3	C	418	9.6	...	...	4.14
Kyrgyzstan - Kirghizistan[18]													
1999	C	104 068	21.4	C	32 850	6.8	14.6	C	2 360	22.7	63.1	71.1	2.62
2000	C	96 770	19.7	C	34 111	6.9	12.7	C	2 225	23.0	64.9	72.4	2.40
2001	C	98 138	19.8	C	32 677	6.6	13.2	C	2 123	21.6	65.0	72.6	2.38
2002	C	101 012	20.2	C	35 235	7.1	13.2	C	2 128	21.1	64.4	72.1	2.46
2003	C	105 490	20.9	C	35 941	7.1	13.8	C	2 186	20.7	...	...	2.52
Lao People's Democratic Republic - République démocratique populaire lao													
2000	...	...	...	...	...	...	...	...	...	...	...	...	4.90
Lebanon - Liban[25]													
1999	U	85 955	...	U	19 813	...	...	...	...	...	...	...	
2000	U	87 795	...	U	19 435	...	...	...	...	...	...	...	
2001	U	85 925	...	U	18 054	...	...	...	...	...	...	...	
2002	U	85 588	...	U	18 867	...	...	...	...	...	...	...	
2003	U	81 184	...	U	18 797	...	...	...	...	...	...	...	
Malaysia - Malaisie													
1999	C	521 870	23.9	C	111 738	5.1	18.8	C	4 660	8.9	...	...	3.020
2000	C	545 096	23.2	C	104 859	4.5	18.7	C	3 578	6.6	70.4	74.9	2.961
2001	...	...	...	...	...	...	...	...	...	...	70.0	73.9	
2002	...	...	...	...	...	...	...	...	...	...	70.7	75.2	
2003	C	533 600	21.3	C	117 900	4.7	16.6	...	...	...	...	...	
Maldives													
1999	C	5 225	18.8	C	1 037	3.7	15.1	C	104	19.9	72.0	73.2	
2000	C	5 399	19.9	C	1 032	3.8	16.1	C	112	20.7	...	...	2.800
2001	C	4 897	17.7	C	1 081	3.9	13.8	C	85	...	...	...	
2002	C	5 003	17.8	C	1 113	4.0	13.9	C	89	...	70.1	71.2	
2003	C	5 154	18.1	C	1 026	3.6	14.5	C	72	...	70.4	71.3	
Mongolia - Mongolie													
1999	C	49 461	...	C	16 105	...	...	C	1 846	37.3	...	...	2.300
2000	C	48 721	20.2	C	15 472	6.4	13.8	C	1 596	32.8	...	...	2.200
2001	C	49 685	20.3	C	15 999	6.6	13.8	C	1 464	29.5	...	...	2.200
2002	C	46 922	19.0	C	15 857	6.4	12.5	C	1 390	29.6	...	...	2.100
2003	C	45 723	18.3	C	16 006	6.4	11.9	C	1 051	23.0	...	...	2.000
Nepal - Népal[30]													
2001	...	...	...	I	106 789	...	...	I	13 037				
Occupied Palestinian Territory - Territoire palestinien occupé													
1999	U	98 594	...	U	8 550	...	...	U	1 081	...	...	...	5.930
2000	U	100 626	...	U	8 781	...	...	U	1 042	...	...	...	

4. Vital statistics summary and expectation of life at birth: 1999-2003
Aperçu des statistiques de l'état civil et espérance de vie à la naissance: 1999-2003 (continued — suite)

Continent, country or area and year / Continent, pays ou zone et année	Live births - Naissances vivantes			Deaths - Décès			Rate of natural increase Taux d'accroiss-ement naturel	Infant deaths - Décès d'enfants de moins d'un an			Expectation of life at birth Espérance de vie à la naissance		Total fertility rate L'indice synthétiq-ue de fécondité
	Co-de[1]	Number Nombre	Crude birth rate Taux bruts de natalité	Co-de[1]	Number Nombre	Crude death rate Taux bruts de mortalité		Co-de[1]	Number Nombre	Rate (per 1000 births) Taux (par 1000 naiss-ances)	Male Masculin	Female Féminin	

ASIA — ASIE

Occupied Palestinian Territory - Territoire palestinien occupé
2001	U	98 190	...	U	8 910	...	...	U	1 120	...	70.4	73.6	...
2002	U	100 382	...	U	9 891	...	...	U	1 101	...	...	...	...
2003	U	99 385	...	U	9 664	...	...	U	1 101	...	...	...	...

Oman[31]
1999	U	39 922	...	U	2 440	...	...	U	386	...	72.3	74.3	...
2000	U	39 994	...	U	2 547	...	...	U	369	...	72.5	74.3	4.700
2001	U	39 297	...	U	2 550	...	...	U	335	...	72.4	75.3	4.200
2002	U	40 222	...	U	2 564	...	...	U	332	...	72.2	75.4	3.600
2003	U	40 062	...	U	2 701	...	...	U	335	...	73.1	75.4	...

Pakistan[32,33]
| 2000 | ... | ... | ... | ... | ... | ... | ... | ... | ... | ... | ... | ... | 4.300 |
| 2001 | I | 3 719 694 | 26.5 | I | 956 515 | 6.8 | 19.7 | I | 286 609 | 77.1 | 64.5 | 66.1 | 4.100 |

Philippines
1999	C	1 613 335	21.6	C	347 989	4.7	16.9	C	25 168	15.6	...	...	2.720
2000	C	1 766 440	23.1	C	366 931	4.8	18.3	C	27 714	15.7	...	...	2.965
2001	C	1 714 093	22.0	C	381 834	4.9	17.1	C	26 129	15.2	...	...	2.753
2002	C	1 666 773	21.0	C	396 297	5.0	16.0	C	23 778	14.3	...	...	2.615

Qatar
1999	C	10 846	18.5	C	1 148	2.0	16.6	C	112	10.3	...	...	...
2000	C	11 250	18.2	C	1 173	1.9	16.3	C	132	11.7	...	...	...
2001	C	12 118	18.7	C	1 210	1.9	16.8	C	111	9.2	...	...	...
2002	C	12 200	17.9	C	1 220	1.8	16.1	C	107	8.8	...	...	...
2003	C	12 856	17.9	C	1 311	1.8	16.1	C	137	10.7	...	...	...

Saudi Arabia - Arabie saoudite
| 1999 | ... | 509 352 | ... | ... | 68 521 | ... | ... | | 11 344 | ... | ... | ... | ... |
| 2000 | ... | 578 772 | ... | ... | 51 614 | ... | ... | ... | 11 071 | ... | ... | ... | 4.302 |

Singapore - Singapour[34]
1999	C	43 336	13.5	+C	15 516	4.8	8.6	+C	150	3.5	75.6	79.7	1.465
2000	C	46 997	14.4	+C	15 693	4.8	9.6	+C	137	2.9	76.0	80.0	1.598
2001	C	41 451	12.5	+C	15 367	4.6	7.9	C	100	2.4	76.4	80.3	1.406
2002	C	40 760	12.1	+C	15 820	4.7	7.4	+C	123	3.0	76.6	80.6	1.370
2003	C	37 485	10.9	+C	16 036	4.7	6.2	+C	100	2.7	77.0	80.9	1.250

Sri Lanka
1999	+C	329 121	17.3	+C	114 392	6.0	11.3	...		...	...	...	...
2001	...	...	...	...	...	...	...	+C	4 323	...	...	...	...
2002	+C	363 549	19.1	+C	110 637	5.8	13.3	...	...	...	...	...	...

Syrian Arab Republic - République arabe syrienne[2,35]
1999	C	503 473	31.3	U	56 564	...	...	...	...	...	...	...	...
2000	C	505 484	31.0	U	57 759	...	...	...	...	...	...	...	...
2001	C	524 212	31.4	U	60 814	...	...	...	...	...	...	...	...
2002	C	471 970	27.6	U	53 252	...	...	...	...	...	...	...	...
2003	C	492 639	28.1	U	53 778	...	...	...	...	...	...	...	...

Tajikistan - Tadjikistan[18]
1999	C	180 888	29.8	C	25 495	4.2	25.6	C	2 338	12.9	...	...	3.841
2000	C	167 246	27.0	C	26 492	4.3	22.7	C	2 102	12.6	...	...	3.682
2001	C	171 623	27.2	C	32 015	5.1	22.1	...	...	...	...	...	...
2002	C	175 599	27.3	C	31 142	4.8	22.4	...	...	...	...	...	...
2003	C	177 938	27.1	C	33 185	5.0	22.0	...	...	...	...	...	...

Thailand - Thaïlande
1999	+U	772 604	...	+U	362 593	...	...	+U	5 003	...	...	...	...
2000	+U	773 009	...	+U	365 741	...	...	+U	4 822	...	...	...	...
2001	+U	790 425	...	+U	369 493	...	...	+U	5 105	...	...	...	...
2002	+U	782 911	...	+U	380 364	...	...	+U	5 105	...	...	...	...

4. Vital statistics summary and expectation of life at birth: 1999-2003
Aperçu des statistiques de l'état civil et espérance de vie à la naissance: 1999-2003 (continued — suite)

Continent, country or area and year / Continent, pays ou zone et année	Live births - Naissances vivantes			Deaths - Décès			Rate of natural increase - Taux d'accroiss-ement naturel	Infant deaths - Décès d'enfants de moins d'un an			Expectation of life at birth - Espérance de vie à la naissance		Total fertility rate - L'indice synthétique de fécondité
	Code[1]	Number Nombre	Crude birth rate Taux bruts de natalité	Code[1]	Number Nombre	Crude death rate Taux bruts de mortalité		Code[1]	Number Nombre	Rate (per 1000 births) Taux (par 1000 naiss-ances)	Male Masculin	Female Féminin	
ASIA — ASIE													
Thailand - Thaïlande													
2003	+U	742 183	...	+U	384 131	...	...	+U	5 349	...	...	...	...
Turkey - Turquie[36]													
1999	I	1 501 000	22.6	I	471 000	7.1	15.5	I	64 993	43.3	...	...	2.620
2000	I	1 494 000	22.2	I	477 000	7.1	15.1	I	62 599	41.9	66.4	71.0	2.570
2001	I	1 486 000	21.7	I	485 000	7.1	14.6	I	60 332	40.6	...	...	2.520
2002	I	1 482 000	21.3	I	491 000	7.1	14.2	I	58 391	39.4	...	...	2.460
2003	I	1 479 000	20.9	I	498 000	7.0	13.9	I	56 646	38.3	...	...	2.430
Uzbekistan - Ouzbékistan[18]													
1999	C	553 745	23.1	C	140 526	5.9	17.3	C	12 358	22.3	...	...	...
2000	C	527 580	21.4	C	135 598	5.5	15.9	C	10 091	19.1	...	...	...
2001	C	512 950	20.5	C	132 542	5.3	15.2	C	9 427	18.4	...	...	...
EUROPE													
Albania - Albanie													
1999	C	57 948	19.0	C	16 720	5.5	13.5	C	708	12.2	...	...	2.100
2000	C	51 242	16.7	C	16 421	5.4	11.4	C	608	11.9	72.5	77.3	2.030
2001	C	54 283	17.7	C	15 813	5.1	12.5	C	603	11.1	...	...	2.374
2002	C	45 515	14.7	C	16 248	5.3	9.5	C	466	10.2	...	...	1.946
2003	C	47 012	15.1	C	17 967	5.8	9.3	C	395	8.4	...	...	1.980
Andorra - Andorre													
1999	C	833	12.6	C	207	3.1	9.5	C	2	...	...	...	...
2000	C	747	11.3	C	259	3.9	7.4	C	2	...	...	...	...
2001	C	777	11.8	C	237	3.6	8.2	C	2	...	...	...	...
2002	C	749	11.3	C	218	3.3	8.0	C	-	...	...	...	...
2003	C	721	10.3	C	221	3.2	7.2	C	-	...	...	...	...
Austria - Autriche													
1999	C	78 138	9.8	C	78 200	9.8	0.0	C	341	4.4	75.1	81.0	1.339
2000	C	78 268	9.8	C	76 780	9.6	0.2	C	378	4.8	75.4	81.2	1.363
2001	C	75 458	9.4	C	74 767	9.3	0.1	C	365	4.8	75.9	81.7	1.329
2002	C	78 399	9.7	C	76 131	9.4	0.3	C	318	4.1	75.8	81.7	1.393
2003	C	76 944	9.5	C	77 209	9.5	0.0	C	343	4.5	75.9	81.6	1.377
Belarus - Bélarus[18]													
1999	C	92 975	9.3	C	142 027	14.2	-4.9	C	1 064	11.4	62.2	73.9	1.300
2000	...	...	...	...	...	...	...	...	...	...	...	...	1.660
2001	...	...	...	...	...	...	...	...	...	...	...	...	1.650
2002	C	88 743	8.9	C	146 655	14.8	-5.8	C	695	7.8	62.3	74.1	1.222
2003	C	88 512	9.0	C	143 200	14.5	-5.5	C	685	7.7	62.7	74.7	1.206
Belgium - Belgique[37]													
1999	C	113 469	11.1	C	104 904	10.3	0.8	C	556	4.9	74.9	81.4	1.613
2000	C	114 883	11.2	C	104 903	10.2	1.0	C	554	4.8	74.6	80.8	...
2001	C	114 014	11.1	C	103 447	10.1	1.0	C	518	4.5	...	...	...
2002	...	...	...	C	105 642	10.2	...	C	551	...	...	...	...
Bosnia and Herzegovina - Bosnie-Herzégovine													
1999	C	42 464	11.4	C	28 637	7.7	3.7	C	431	10.1	...	...	1.360
2000	C	39 563	10.5	C	30 482	8.1	2.4	C	383	9.7	...	...	1.280
2001	C	37 717	9.9	C	30 325	8.0	1.9	C	287	7.6	71.3	76.7	1.230
2002	C	35 587	9.3	C	30 155	7.9	1.4	C	334	9.4	71.3	76.7	1.230
2003	C	36 226	9.5	C	31 757	8.3	1.2	C	268	7.4	71.3	76.7	1.530
Bulgaria - Bulgarie													
1999	C	72 291	8.8	C	111 786	13.6	-4.8	C	1 057	14.6	^68.5	^75.2	1.232
2000	C	73 679	9.0	C	115 087	14.1	-5.1	C	981	13.3	68.5	75.1	1.266
2001	C	68 180	8.6	C	112 368	14.2	-5.6	C	982	14.4	^68.7	^75.6	1.243
2002	C	66 499	8.5	C	112 617	14.3	-5.9	C	887	13.3	68.5	75.4	1.212
2003	C	67 359	8.6	C	111 927	14.3	-5.7	C	831	12.3	...	...	1.232

4. Vital statistics summary and expectation of life at birth: 1999-2003
Aperçu des statistiques de l'état civil et espérance de vie à la naissance: 1999-2003 (continued — suite)

Continent, country or area and year / Continent, pays ou zone et année	Live births / Naissances vivantes			Deaths - Décès			Rate of natural increase / Taux d'accroiss-ement naturel	Infant deaths / Décès d'enfants de moins d'un an			Expectation of life at birth / Espérance de vie à la naissance		Total fertility rate
	Code[1]	Number Nombre	Crude birth rate Taux bruts de natalité	Code[1]	Number Nombre	Crude death rate Taux bruts de mortalité	Taux d'accroiss-ement naturel	Code[1]	Number Nombre	Rate (per 1000 births) Taux (par 1000 naiss-ances)	Male Masculin	Female Féminin	L'indice synthétiq-ue de fécondité

EUROPE

Channel Islands: Guernsey - Îles Anglo-Normandes: Guernesey													
1999	C	672	11.2	C	529	8.8	2.4	C	2	...	...	...	...
2000	C	644	10.7	C	565	9.3	1.3	C	4	...	...	...	...
Croatia - Croatie													
1999	C	45 179	9.9	C	51 953	11.4	-1.5	C	350	7.7	...	...	1.380
2000	C	43 746	10.0	C	50 246	11.5	-1.5	C	324	7.4	...	...	1.390
2001	C	40 993	9.2	C	49 552	11.2	-1.9	C	315	7.7	...	...	1.380
2002	C	40 094	9.0	C	50 569	11.4	-2.4	C	282	7.0	...	...	1.340
2003	C	39 668	8.9	C	52 575	11.8	-2.9	C	251	6.3	...	...	1.327
Czech Republic - République tchèque													
1999	C	89 471	8.7	C	109 768	10.7	-2.0	C	413	4.6	71.4	78.1	1.131
2000	C	90 910	8.8	C	109 001	10.6	-1.8	C	373	4.1	71.6	78.3	1.144
2001	C	90 715	8.9	C	107 755	10.5	-1.7	C	360	4.0	72.1	78.5	1.146
2002	C	97 878	9.6	C	108 243	10.6	-1.0	C	385	3.9	72.1	78.5	1.171
2003	C	93 685	9.2	C	111 288	10.9	-1.7	C	365	3.9	72.0	78.5	1.179
Denmark - Danemark[38]													
1999	C	66 232	12.4	C	59 156	11.1	1.3	C	281	4.2	74.2	79.0	1.735
2000	C	67 084	12.6	C	57 986	10.9	1.7	C	350	5.3	74.5	79.3	1.771
2001	C	65 458	12.2	C	58 338	10.9	1.3	C	320	4.9	74.6	79.2	1.747
2002	C	64 149	11.9	C	58 610	10.9	1.0	C	284	4.4	^74.9	^79.5	1.725
2003	C	64 682	12.0	C	57 574	10.7	1.3	C	286	4.4	...	...	1.760
Estonia - Estonie[18]													
1999	C	12 545	8.7	C	18 447	12.8	-4.1	C	119	9.5	...	...	1.317
2000	C	13 089	9.6	C	18 403	13.4	-3.9	C	110	8.4	65.1	76.2	1.385
2001	C	12 632	9.3	C	18 516	13.6	-4.3	C	111	8.8	...	...	1.337
2002	C	13 001	9.6	C	18 355	13.5	-3.9	C	74	...	64.8	76.3	1.372
2003	C	13 036	9.6	C	18 152	13.4	-3.8	C	91	...	...	...	1.371
Finland - Finlande[39]													
1999	C	57 574	11.1	C	49 345	9.6	1.6	C	208	3.6	73.8	81.0	1.735
2000	C	56 742	11.0	C	49 339	9.5	1.4	C	213	3.8	...	...	1.729
2001	C	56 189	10.8	C	48 550	9.4	1.5	C	181	3.2	74.6	81.5	1.726
2002	C	55 555	10.7	C	49 418	9.5	1.2	C	168	3.0	74.8	81.5	1.718
2003	C	56 630	10.9	C	48 996	9.4	1.5	C	176	3.1	75.1	81.8	1.760
France[40]													
1999	C	744 791	12.7	C	537 661	9.2	3.5	C	3 221	4.3	...	...	1.793
2000	C	774 782	13.2	C	536 300	9.1	4.0	C	3 417	4.4	...	...	1.880
2001	C	770 945	13.0	C	531 073	9.0	4.1	C	3 438	4.5	75.5	82.9	1.888
2002	C	761 630	12.8	C	545 353	9.2	3.6	C	3 336	4.4	...	...	1.881
2003	C	760 300	12.7	C	560 077	9.4	3.4	C	3 325	4.4	...	...	1.894
Germany - Allemagne													
1999	C	770 744	9.4	C	846 330	10.3	-0.9	C	3 496	4.5	74.7	80.7	1.361
2000	C	766 999	9.3	C	838 797	10.2	-0.9	C	3 362	4.4	...	...	1.378
2001	C	734 475	8.9	C	828 541	10.1	-1.1	C	3 163	4.3	...	...	1.349
2002	C	719 250	8.7	C	841 686	10.2	-1.5	C	3 036	4.2	^75.9	^81.5	1.034
2003	C	706 721	8.6	C	853 946	10.3	-1.8	C	2 990	4.2	...	...	1.340
Gibraltar[41]													
1999	C	381	14.1	C	277	10.2	3.8	...	...	...	...	...	...
2000	C	408	15.0	C	262	9.7	5.4	...	...	...	...	...	...
2001	C	374	13.6	C	249	9.1	4.5	...	...	...	78.5	83.3	...
2002	C	371	13.0	C	242	8.5	4.5	...	...	...	...	...	...
2003	C	372	13.0	C	234	8.2	4.8	C	2	...	...	...	...
Greece - Grèce													
1999	C	116 038	11.0	C	103 304	9.8	1.2	C	619	5.3	...	...	1.300
2000	C	117 140	11.7	C	105 219	10.5	1.2	C	610	5.2	...	...	1.290
2001	C	102 282	10.2	C	102 559	10.2	0.0	C	522	5.1	...	...	1.290

4. Vital statistics summary and expectation of life at birth: 1999-2003
Aperçu des statistiques de l'état civil et espérance de vie à la naissance: 1999-2003 (continued — suite)

Continent, country or area and year / Continent, pays ou zone et année	Live births / Naissances vivantes			Deaths - Décès			Rate of natural increase / Taux d'accroiss-ement naturel	Infant deaths / Décès d'enfants de moins d'un an			Expectation of life at birth / Espérance de vie à la naissance		Total fertility rate / L'indice synthétique de fécondité
	Code[1]	Number / Nombre	Crude birth rate / Taux bruts de natalité	Code[1]	Number / Nombre	Crude death rate / Taux bruts de mortalité		Code[1]	Number / Nombre	Rate (per 1000 births) / Taux (par 1000 naiss-ances)	Male / Masculin	Female / Féminin	
EUROPE													
Greece - Grèce													
2002	C	103 838	9.5	C	103 915	9.5	0.0	C	600	5.8	...	...	1.27
2003	C	104 420	9.5	C	105 529	9.6	-0.1	C	420	4.0	76.5	81.3	1.28
Holy See - Saint-Siège													
2000	C	1	...	C	10	...	...	C	-	...	...	...	
Hungary - Hongrie													
1999	C	94 645	9.4	C	143 210	14.2	-4.8	C	798	8.4	66.3	75.1	1.28
2000	C	97 597	9.7	C	135 601	13.5	-3.8	C	900	9.2	67.1	75.6	1.33
2001	C	97 047	9.5	C	132 183	13.0	-3.4	C	789	8.1	68.2	76.5	1.31
2002	C	96 804	9.5	C	132 833	13.1	-3.5	C	693	7.2	68.3	76.6	1.30
2003	C	94 647	9.3	C	135 823	13.4	-4.1	C	690	7.3	68.3	76.5	1.27
Iceland - Islande													
1999	C	4 100	14.8	C	1 901	6.9	7.9	C	10	...	77.8	81.5	1.99
2000	C	4 315	15.3	C	1 828	6.5	8.8	C	13	...	78.0	81.4	2.07
2001	C	4 091	14.4	C	1 725	6.1	8.3	C	11	...	78.4	82.6	1.94
2002	C	4 049	14.1	C	1 821	6.3	7.7	C	9	...	^79.0	^82.4	1.93
2003	C	4 143	14.3	C	1 827	6.3	8.0	C	10	...	...	...	1.99
Ireland - Irlande[42]													
1999	+C	53 354	14.2	+C	31 683	8.5	5.8	+C	293	5.5	73.9	79.1	1.91
2000	+C	54 239	14.3	+C	31 115	8.2	6.1	+C	338	6.2	74.2	79.2	1.91
2001	+C	57 854	15.1	+C	30 212	7.9	7.2	+C	331	5.7	74.7	79.7	1.96
2002	+C	60 521	15.5	+C	29 348	7.5	8.0	+C	306	5.1	75.1	80.2	1.97
2003	+C	61 517	15.4	+C	28 823	7.2	8.2	+C	311	5.1	...	...	1.97
Isle of Man - Îles de Man													
1999	+C	894	...	+C	983	...	...	+C	6	...	...	...	...
2000	+C	831	11.1	+C	897	12.0	-0.9	+C	5	...	...	...	...
2001	+C	863	11.3	+C	855	11.2	0.1	+C	-	...	...	...	...
2002	+C	903	11.7	+C	877	11.4	0.3	+C	3	...	...	...	...
2003	+C	860	11.1	+C	852	11.0	0.1	+C	6	...	...	...	...
Italy - Italie													
1999	C	523 463	9.1	C	571 356	9.9	-0.8	C	2 723	5.2	76.0	82.1	1.22
2000	C	543 039	9.4	C	560 241	9.7	-0.3	C	2 461	4.5	76.5	82.5	1.24
2001	C	535 282	9.2	C	556 892	9.6	-0.4	C	2 482	4.6	...	...	1.25
2002	C	538 198	9.4	C	557 393	9.8	-0.3	C	2 337	4.3	...	...	1.273
2003	C	539 503	9.4	C	586 468	10.2	-0.8	C	2 482	4.6	...	...	1.295
Latvia - Lettonie[18]													
1999	C	19 396	8.1	C	32 844	13.7	-5.6	C	219	11.3	64.9	76.2	1.162
2000	C	20 248	8.5	C	32 205	13.6	-5.0	C	210	10.4	64.9	76.0	1.237
2001	C	19 664	8.3	C	32 991	14.0	-5.7	C	217	11.0	65.2	76.6	1.207
2002	C	20 044	8.6	C	32 498	13.9	-5.3	C	197	9.8	65.4	76.8	1.232
2003	C	21 006	9.0	C	32 437	13.9	-4.9	C	198	9.4	...	...	...
Liechtenstein													
1999	...	...	...	...	...	...	...	...	...	...	...	...	1.635
2000	...	...	...	...	...	...	...	...	...	...	...	...	1.582
2001	C	401	12.1	C	220	6.6	5.5	C	-	...	...	...	1.527
2002	C	395	11.7	C	215	6.4	5.3	C	1	...	...	...	1.492
2003	C	347	10.2	C	217	6.4	3.8	C	1	...	...	...	1.357
Lithuania - Lituanie[18]													
1999	C	36 415	10.3	C	40 003	11.4	-1.0	C	315	8.7	67.1	77.4	1.460
2000	C	34 149	9.8	C	38 919	11.1	-1.4	C	294	8.6	67.6	77.9	1.391
2001	C	31 546	9.1	C	40 399	11.6	-2.5	C	250	7.9	65.9	77.4	1.296
2002	C	30 014	8.7	C	41 072	11.8	-3.2	C	238	7.9	66.2	77.6	1.236
2003	C	30 598	8.9	C	40 990	11.9	-3.0	C	206	6.7	66.5	77.8	1.262
Luxembourg													
1999	C	5 582	13.0	C	3 793	8.8	4.2	C	26	...	74.7	81.2	1.710
2000	C	5 723	13.1	C	3 754	8.6	4.5	C	29	...	^74.8	^81.0	1.778
2001	C	5 459	12.4	C	3 719	8.4	3.9	C	32	...	...	...	1.654
2002	C	5 345	12.0	C	3 744	8.4	3.6	C	27	...	...	...	1.625
2003	C	5 303	11.8	C	4 053	9.0	2.8	C	26	...	...	...	1.634

4. Vital statistics summary and expectation of life at birth: 1999-2003
Aperçu des statistiques de l'état civil et espérance de vie à la naissance: 1999-2003 (continued — suite)

Continent, country or area and year / Continent, pays ou zone et année	Code[1]	Live births - Naissances vivantes Number Nombre	Crude birth rate Taux bruts de natalité	Code[1]	Deaths - Décès Number Nombre	Crude death rate Taux bruts de mortalité	Rate of natural increase Taux d'accroiss-ement naturel	Code[1]	Infant deaths - Décès d'enfants de moins d'un an Number Nombre	Rate (per 1000 births) Taux (par 1000 naiss-ances)	Expectation of life at birth Espérance de vie à la naissance Male Masculin	Female Féminin	Total fertility rate L'indice synthétiq-ue de fécondité
EUROPE													
Malta - Malte[43,44]													
1999	C	4 308	11.3	C	3 097	8.1	3.2	C	31	...	75.1	79.3	1.720
2000	C	4 255	11.1	C	2 957	7.7	3.4	C	26	...	76.4	80.4	1.720
2001	C	3 859	10.0	C	2 935	7.6	2.4	C	17	...	76.1	80.9	1.720
2002	C	3 805	9.8	C	3 031	7.8	2.0	C	23	...	75.8	80.5	1.460
2003	C	3 902	9.8	C	3 072	7.7	2.1	C	23	...	76.4	80.4	1.420
Monaco													
2000	C	771	24.1	C	564	17.6	6.5	...	...	...	...	...	...
2003	C	842	...	C	617	...	...	...	...	...	...	...	...
Netherlands - Pays-Bas[45]													
1999	C	200 445	12.7	C	140 487	8.9	3.8	C	1 048	5.2	75.3	80.5	1.650
2000	C	206 619	13.0	C	140 527	8.8	4.2	C	1 059	5.1	75.5	80.5	1.723
2001	C	202 603	12.6	C	140 377	8.7	3.9	C	1 088	5.4	75.8	80.7	1.710
2002	C	202 083	12.5	C	142 355	8.8	3.7	C	1 028	5.1	76.0	80.7	1.731
2003	C	200 297	12.3	C	141 936	8.7	3.6	C	962	4.8	...	...	1.747
Norway - Norvège[46]													
1999	C	59 298	13.3	C	45 170	10.1	3.2	C	232	3.9	75.6	81.1	1.840
2000	C	59 234	13.2	C	44 002	9.8	3.4	C	225	3.8	76.0	81.4	1.851
2001	C	56 696	12.6	C	43 981	9.7	2.8	C	223	3.9	76.2	81.5	1.784
2002	C	55 434	12.2	C	44 465	9.8	2.4	C	192	3.5	76.4	81.5	1.754
2003	C	56 458	12.4	C	42 478	9.3	3.1	C	190	3.4	77.0	81.9	1.797
Poland - Pologne													
1999	C	382 002	9.9	C	381 415	9.9	0.0	C	3 381	8.9	68.8	77.5	1.366
2000	C	378 700	9.9	C	368 028	9.6	0.3	C	3 068	8.1	69.7	77.9	1.367
2001	C	368 205	9.6	C	363 220	9.5	0.1	C	2 823	7.7	...	...	1.315
2002	C	353 765	9.3	C	359 486	9.4	-0.1	C	2 662	7.5	...	...	1.249
2003	C	351 072	9.2	C	365 230	9.6	-0.4	C	2 470	7.0	70.5	78.9	1.222
Portugal													
1999	C	116 002	11.4	C	107 871	10.6	0.8	C	671	5.8	72.0	79.1	1.489
2000	C	118 551	11.6	C	105 804	10.3	1.2	C	662	5.6	72.7	79.7	1.560
2001	C	112 774	11.0	C	105 092	10.2	0.7	C	567	5.0	...	...	1.460
2002	C	114 383	11.0	C	106 258	10.2	0.8	C	574	5.0	...	...	1.473
2003	C	112 515	10.8	C	108 795	10.4	0.4	C	465	4.1	...	...	1.444
Republic of Moldova - République de Moldova[18]													
1999	C	38 501	10.6	C	41 315	11.3	-0.8	C	714	18.5	63.7	71.0	1.369
2000	C	36 939	10.2	C	41 224	11.3	-1.2	C	681	18.4	...	...	1.286
2001	C	36 448	10.0	C	40 075	11.0	-1.0	C	597	16.4	64.5	71.8	1.249
2002	C	35 705	9.9	C	41 852	11.6	-1.7	C	528	14.8	64.4	71.7	1.211
2003	C	36 471	10.1	C	43 079	11.9	-1.8	C	522	14.3	64.5	71.6	1.219
Romania - Roumanie													
1999	C	234 600	10.4	C	265 194	11.8	-1.4	C	4 360	18.6	67.7	74.8	1.300
2000	C	234 521	10.5	C	255 820	11.4	-0.9	C	4 370	18.6	67.7	74.6	1.305
2001	C	220 368	9.8	C	259 603	11.6	-1.8	C	4 057	18.4	...	...	1.232
2002	C	210 529	9.7	C	269 666	12.4	-2.7	C	3 648	17.3	67.6	74.9	1.254
2003	C	212 459	9.8	C	266 575	12.3	-2.5	C	3 546	16.7	67.4	74.8	1.270
Russian Federation - Fédération de Russie[18]													
1999	C	1 214 689	8.3	C	2 144 316	14.6	-6.3	C	20 731	17.1	59.9	72.4	1.171
2000	C	1 266 800	8.6	C	2 225 332	15.2	-6.5	C	19 286	15.2	...	...	1.214
2001	C	1 311 604	9.0	C	2 254 856	15.4	-6.5	C	19 104	14.6	...	...	1.249
2002	C	1 396 967	9.6	C	2 332 272	16.1	-6.4	C	18 407	13.2	...	...	1.322
2003	C	1 477 301	10.2	C	2 365 826	16.4	-6.1	C	18 142	12.3	...	...	1.319
San Marino - Saint-Marin													
1999	+C	303	11.5	+C	198	7.5	4.0	+C	1	...	...	...	...
2000	+C	290	10.8	+C	188	7.0	3.8	+C	-	...	77.4	84.0	1.269
2001	+C	315	11.4	+C	195	7.1	4.3	+C	1	...	...	...	1.317
2002	+C	295	10.4	+C	203	7.1	3.2	+C	2	...	...	...	1.206
2003	+C	300	10.3	+C	216	7.5	2.9	+C	2	...	...	...	1.250

4. Vital statistics summary and expectation of life at birth: 1999-2003
Aperçu des statistiques de l'état civil et espérance de vie à la naissance: 1999-2003 (continued — suite)

Continent, country or area and year / Continent, pays ou zone et année	Live births - Naissances vivantes			Deaths - Décès			Rate of natural increase / Taux d'accroiss-ement naturel	Infant deaths - Décès d'enfants de moins d'un an			Expectation of life at birth - Espérance de vie à la naissance		Total fertility rate / L'indice synthétique de fécondité
	Code[1]	Number Nombre	Crude birth rate Taux bruts de natalité	Code[1]	Number Nombre	Crude death rate Taux bruts de mortalité		Code[1]	Number Nombre	Rate (per 1000 births) Taux (par 1000 naissances)	Male Masculin	Female Féminin	
EUROPE													
Serbia and Montenegro - Serbie-et-Montenegro[47]													
1999	C	123 970	11.7	C	115 461	10.9	0.8	C	1 691	13.6	...	...	1.625
2000	C	125 868	11.8	C	118 078	11.1	0.7	C	1 668	13.3	70.1	75.0	1.644
2001	C	130 194	12.2	C	113 063	10.6	1.6	C	1 709	13.1	...	...	1.708
2002	C	86 600	10.7	C	108 298	13.3	-2.7	C	882	10.2	69.9	75.2	1.575
2003	C	87 370	10.7	C	109 650	13.4	-2.7	C	803	9.2	...	...	...
Slovakia - Slovaquie													
1999	C	56 223	10.4	C	52 402	9.7	0.7	C	467	8.3	69.0	77.0	1.330
2000	C	55 103	10.2	C	52 703	9.8	0.4	C	473	8.6	69.2	77.4	1.297
2001	C	51 136	9.5	C	51 980	9.7	-0.2	C	319	6.2	69.5	77.5	1.205
2002	C	50 841	9.5	C	51 532	9.6	-0.1	C	388	7.6	69.9	77.6	1.190
2003	C	51 713	9.6	C	52 230	9.7	-0.1	C	406	7.9	...	...	1.205
Slovenia - Slovénie													
1999	C	17 533	8.8	C	18 885	9.5	-0.7	C	79	...	^71.9	^79.1	1.214
2000	C	18 180	9.1	C	18 588	9.3	-0.2	C	89	...	...	...	1.259
2001	C	17 477	8.8	C	18 508	9.3	-0.5	C	74	...	72.1	79.6	1.211
2002	C	17 501	8.8	C	18 701	9.4	-0.6	C	67	...	73.2	80.7	1.212
2003	C	17 321	8.7	C	19 451	9.7	-1.1	C	69	...	...	...	1.202
Spain - Espagne													
1999	C	380 130	9.5	C	371 102	9.3	0.2	C	1 700	4.5	...	...	1.197
2000	C	397 632	9.9	C	360 391	9.0	0.9	C	1 535	3.9	...	...	1.238
2001	C	406 380	10.0	C	360 131	8.9	1.1	C	1 657	4.1	76.4	83.1	1.249
2002	C	418 846	10.2	C	368 618	8.9	1.2	C	1 737	4.1	...	...	1.266
2003	C	439 863	10.5	C	383 729	9.2	1.3	C	1 733	3.9	...	...	1.303
Sweden - Suède													
1999	C	88 173	10.0	C	94 726	10.7	-0.7	C	297	3.4	77.1	81.9	1.497
2000	C	90 441	10.2	C	93 461	10.5	-0.3	C	309	3.4	...	...	1.574
2001	C	91 466	10.3	C	93 752	10.5	-0.3	C	334	3.7	77.6	82.1	1.570
2002	C	95 815	10.7	C	95 000	10.6	0.1	C	313	3.3	77.7	82.1	1.650
2003	C	99 157	11.1	C	92 961	10.4	0.7	C	308	3.1	...	...	...
Switzerland - Suisse													
1999	C	78 408	11.0	C	62 503	8.7	2.2	C	361	4.6	76.8	82.5	1.766
2000	C	78 458	10.9	C	62 528	8.7	2.2	C	386	4.9	76.9	82.6	1.496
2001	C	73 509	10.2	C	61 287	8.5	1.7	C	365	5.0	...	...	1.382
2002	C	72 372	9.9	C	61 768	8.5	1.5	C	326	4.5	...	...	1.389
2003	C	71 848	9.8	C	63 070	8.6	1.2	C	311	4.3	...	...	1.385
The Former Yugoslav Rep. of Macedonia - L'ex-République yougoslave de Macédoine													
1999	C	27 309	13.5	C	16 789	8.3	5.2	C	406	14.9	70.7	75.2	1.760
2000	C	29 308	14.5	C	17 253	8.5	6.0	C	346	11.8	...	...	1.760
2001	C	27 010	13.3	C	16 919	8.3	5.0	C	321	11.9	...	...	1.700
2002	C	27 761	13.7	C	17 962	8.8	4.8	C	283	10.2	70.8	75.7	...
2003	C	27 011	13.3	C	18 006	8.9	4.4	C	305	11.3	...	...	1.540
Ukraine[18]													
1999	...	...	...	C	739 170	14.8	...	...	...	...	...	...	1.150
2000	C	385 126	7.9	C	758 082	15.5	-7.6	C	4 606	12.0	...	...	1.100
2001	C	376 478	7.8	C	745 952	15.4	-7.6	C	4 283	11.4	...	...	1.080
2002	C	390 688	8.1	C	754 911	15.7	-7.6	C	4 023	10.3	^62.6	^74.1	1.095
2003	C	408 589	8.6	C	765 408	16.1	-7.5	C	3 882	9.5	...	...	1.147
United Kingdom - Royaume-Uni[48]													
1999	C	699 976	11.9	C	632 062	10.8	1.2	C	4 045	5.8	75.0	79.8	1.690
2000	C	679 029	11.5	C	608 366	10.3	1.2	C	3 791	5.6	75.3	80.1	1.640
2001	C	669 123	11.3	C	602 268	10.2	1.1	C	3 664	5.5	...	...	1.630
2002	C	668 777	11.3	C	606 283	10.2	1.1	C	3 499	5.2	...	...	1.640
2003	C	695 549	11.7	C	611 188	10.3	1.4	C	3 686	5.3	...	...	1.710

4. Vital statistics summary and expectation of life at birth: 1999-2003
Aperçu des statistiques de l'état civil et espérance de vie à la naissance: 1999-2003 (continued — suite)

Continent, country or area and year / Continent, pays ou zone et année	Live births - Naissances vivantes			Deaths - Décès			Rate of natural increase Taux d'accroiss-ement naturel	Infant deaths - Décès d'enfants de moins d'un an			Expectation of life at birth Espérance de vie à la naissance		Total fertility rate L'indice synthétique de fécondité
	Code[1]	Number Nombre	Crude birth rate Taux bruts de natalité	Code[1]	Number Nombre	Crude death rate Taux bruts de mortalité		Code[1]	Number Nombre	Rate (per 1000 births) Taux (par 1000 naissances)	Male Masculin	Female Féminin	
OCEANIA — OCEANIE													
American Samoa - Samoas américaines													
1999	C	1 736	30.6	C	249	4.4	26.2	C	22	...	...	...	...
2000	C	1 730	30.2	C	224	3.9	26.3	C	11	...	...	...	...
Australia - Australie													
1999	+C	248 870	13.1	+C	128 102	6.8	6.4	+C	1 408	5.7	77.0	82.4	1.757
2000	+C	249 636	13.0	+C	128 291	6.7	6.3	+C	1 290	5.2	^77.4	^82.6	1.760
2001	+C	246 394	12.7	+C	128 544	6.6	6.1	+C	1 309	5.3	^77.8	^82.8	1.733
2002	+C	250 988	12.8	+C	133 707	6.8	6.0	+C	1 264	5.0	...	...	1.761
2003	+C	251 161	12.6	+C	132 292	6.7	6.0	+C	1 199	4.8	...	...	1.755
Cook Islands - Îles Cook													
1999	+C	346	21.1	+C	96	5.9	15.2	+C	5	...	...	...	...
2000	+C	309	17.2	+C	115	6.4	10.8	+C	6	...	...	...	...
2001	+C	313	17.2	+C	88	4.8	12.4	+C	4	...	...	...	...
2002	+C	292	15.9	+C	97	5.3	10.6	+C	2	...	...	...	...
2003	+C	298	16.2	+C	86	4.7	11.5	+C	4	...	...	...	...
Fiji - Fidji													
1999	+C	16 916	21.0	+C	3 603	4.5	16.5	+C	275	16.3	...	...	...
French Polynesia - Polynésie française													
1999	C	4 580	20.1	C	1 003	4.4	15.7	C	31	...	...	...	...
2000	C	4 900	21.2	C	1 013	4.4	16.8	C	33	...	...	...	...
2001	C	4 874	20.4	C	1 170	4.9	15.5	C	36	...	...	...	...
2002	C	4 762	19.6	C	1 124	4.6	14.9	C	32	...	...	...	...
2003	C	4 503	18.2	C	1 122	4.5	13.7	C	31	...	...	...	...
Guam[49]													
1999	C	4 037	26.5	C	724	4.7	21.7	C	35	...	...	...	...
2000	C	3 790	24.5	C	667	4.3	20.2	C	23	...	...	...	...
2001	C	3 583	22.6	C	691	4.4	18.3	C	35	...	...	...	...
2002	C	3 222	20.0	C	658	4.1	15.9	C	20	...	...	...	...
2003	C	3 298	20.2	C	700	4.3	15.9	C	37	...	...	...	...
Marshall Islands - Îles Marshall													
1999	+U	1 478	...		...	...	...		...	...	65.7	69.4	5.710
2001	+U	1 511	...	+U	271	...	...	+U	40	...	...	...	...
Nauru													
1999	...	...	...	...	...	...	...	...	...	...	55.0	62.0	...
2000	...	...	...	...	...	...	...	...	...	...	57.0	64.0	...
New Caledonia - Nouvelle-Calédonie													
1999	C	4 316	20.8	C	1 095	5.3	15.5	C	27	...	69.8	75.8	2.523
2000	C	4 566	21.6	C	1 077	5.1	16.5	C	21	...	...	...	...
2001	C	4 326	20.2	C	1 131	5.3	14.9	C	24	...	70.5	76.1	...
2002	C	4 194	19.3	C	1 121	5.2	14.1	C	29	...	...	...	...
2003	C	4 102	18.6	C	1 121	5.1	13.5	C	24	...	71.3	77.3	...
New Zealand - Nouvelle-Zélande													
1999	+C	57 053	14.9	+C	28 122	7.3	7.5	+C	317	5.6	^76.0	^80.9	1.971
2000	+C	56 605	14.7	+C	26 660	6.9	7.8	+C	346	6.1	^76.3	^81.1	1.976
2001	+C	55 799	14.4	+C	27 825	7.2	7.2	+C	296	5.3	^76.7	^81.2	1.968
2002	+C	54 021	13.7	+C	28 065	7.1	6.6	+C	300	5.6	^77.0	^81.3	1.896
2003	+C	56 134	14.0	+C	28 010	7.0	7.0	+C	277	4.9	...	...	1.958
Niue - Nioué													
2002	...	24	...	...	13	...	...	...	-	...	...	...	...
Northern Mariana Islands - Îles Mariannes septentrionales													
1999	U	1 448	...	U	189	...	...	U	11	...	...	...	...

Continent, country or area and year — Continent, pays ou zone et année	Live births — Naissances vivantes			Deaths - Décès			Rate of natural increase — Taux d'accroissement naturel	Infant deaths — Décès d'enfants de moins d'un an			Expectation of life at birth — Espérance de vie à la naissance		Total fertility rate — L'indice synthétique de fécondité
	Code[1]	Number Nombre	Crude birth rate Taux bruts de natalité	Code[1]	Number Nombre	Crude death rate Taux bruts de mortalité		Code[1]	Number Nombre	Rate (per 1000 births) Taux (par 1000 naissances)	Male Masculin	Female Féminin	
OCEANIA — OCEANIE													
Palau - Palaos													
1999	C	250	13.2	C	131	6.9	6.3	C	5	...	...	...	...
2000	C	278	14.4	C	125	6.5	7.9	C	3	...	...	...	...
2001	C	300	15.3	C	138	7.0	8.3	C	5	...	...	...	...
2002	C	259	13.0	C	134	6.7	6.3	C	6	...	...	...	...
2003	C	312	15.4	C	136	6.7	8.7	C	2	...	...	...	...
Papua New Guinea - Papouasie-Nouvelle-Guinée													
2000	U	*177 629*	...	U	*7 341*	...	...	U	*2 064*	...	53.7	54.8	4.551
2001	U	*182 619*	...	U	*6 737*	...	...	U	*1 841*	...	...	...	...
2002	U	*187 645*	...	U	*7 573*	...	...	U	*2 230*	...	...	...	...
2003	U	*192 817*	...	U	*7 054*	...	...	U	*2 082*	...	...	...	...
Tonga													
1999	+C	2 599	26.0	+C	675	6.8	19.3	+C	48	...	...	...	3.523
2000	+C	2 471	24.6	+C	653	6.5	18.1	+C	28	...	...	...	3.677

FOOTNOTES - NOTES

Italics: data from civil registers which are incomplete or of unknown completeness. — *Italiques:* données incomplètes ou dont le degré d'exactitude n'est pas connu, provenant des registres de l'état civil.

^ The symbol '^' indicates that the figures for expectation of life at birth refer to more than one single year. For complete set of data on this topic, please see table 22. — Le symbole '^' indique que le chiffre pour l'expectation de vie a la naissance se réfère a une période d'années plutôt q'a un an seulement. Le tableau 22 présente l' l'information complète sur ce suject.

[1] 'Code' indicates the source of data, as follows:
C - Civil registration, estimated over 90% complete
U - Civil registration, estimated less than 90% complete
| - Other source, estimated reliable
+ - Indicates that events are counted when registered, not when they occurred.
... - Information not available

Le 'Code' indique la source des données, comme suit:
C - Registres de l'état civil considérés complèts à 90 p. 100 au moins.
U - Registres de l'état civil qui ne sont pas considérés complèts à 90 p. 100 au moins.
| - Autre source, considéré pas douteuses.
+ - Indique que les statistiques vitales sont comptées au moment de registration, pas au moment de l'évenement.
... - Information pas disponible.

[2] Excluding live-born infants who died before their birth was registered. - Non compris les enfants nés vivants décédés avant l'enregistrement de leur naissance.
[3] For Algerian population only. - Pour la population algérienne seulement.
[4] Data refer to national projections. - Les données se referent aux projections nationales.
[5] For 2001, data refer to last twelve months preceding census on August 2001. - Pour 2001, les données se rapportent pour la dernière fois à douze mois plutôt q'a le recensement août 2001.
[6] Data from civil registration centers of Brazzaville, Pointe-Noire, Dolisie, Nkayi, Mossendijo and Ouesso communes. - Données issues des centers d'enregistrement des faits d'état-civil des communes de Brazzaville, Pointe-Noire, Dolisie, Nkayi, Mossendijo et Ouesso.
[7] Data refer to national projections. Expectation on life at birth based on the 1998 Malawi Population and Housing Census. - Les données se referent aux projections nationales. Expectation de vie a la naissance basée sur les résultats du recensement de la population et de l'habitat de Malawi de 1998.
[8] Data on live births refer to last twelve months preceding census on August 2001. Deaths refer to the period January-August 2001. - Les données sur les naissances se rapportent pour la dernière fois à douze mois précédant le recensement août 2001. Décès de 2001 correspond à la période allant de janvier à août 2001.
[9] Data as reported by national statistical authorities; they may differ from data presented in other tables. - Les données comme elles ont été déclarées par l'institut national de la statistique; elles peuvent être différentes de ceux présentées dans autre tableaux.
[10] Including Canadian residents temporarily in the United States, but excluding United States residents temporarily in Canada. - Y compris les résidents canadiens se trouvant temporairement aux Etats-Unis, mais ne comprenant pas les résidents des Etats-Unis se trouvant temporairement au Canada.
[11] Including births to non-resident mothers. - Y compris les naissances chez des mères non résidentes.
[12] Excluding Indian jungle population. - Non compris les Indiens de la jungle.
[13] For 2001, data on live births include unknown sex and foreigners. - Pour 2001, les données sur les naissances compris le sexe inconnu et les étrangers.
[14] Data on live births and deaths are based on a civil registration system put in place in January 1998. - Les données sur les naissances et les décès sont basées sur un système d'enregistrement des faits d'état civil mis en place en janvier 1998.
[15] Excluding nomadic Indian tribes. - Non compris les tribus d'Indiens nomades.
[16] For 2001, data were collected from Population census held on August 2002, referring to events in calendar year 2001. - Pour 2001, les données sont tirées du recensement de la population réalisé en août 2002, concernant des événements de l'année civile 2001.
[17] Including an upward adjustment for under-registration. - Y compris un ajustement pour sous-enregistrement.
[18] Excluding infants born alive with less than 28 weeks gestation, less than 1 000 grams in weight and 35 centimeters in length, who die within seven days of birth. - Non compris les enfants nés vivants avant 28 semaines de gestation, pesant moins de 1 000 grammes, mesurant moins de 35 centimètres et décédés dans les sept jours qui ont suivi leur naissance.
[19] For statistical purposes, the data for China do not include those for the Hong Kong Special Administrative Region (Hong Kong SAR), Macao Special Administrative Region (Macao SAR) and Taiwan province of China. - Pour la présentation des statistiques, les données pour Chine ne comprend pas la Région Administrative Spéciale de Hong Kong (Hong Kong RAS), la Région Administrative Spéciale de Macao (Macao RAS) et Taïwan province de Chine.
[20] Rates for 1999 - 2003 were obtained by the Sample Survey of Population Change 2003 in China. - Les taux pour 1999 - 2003 on été obtenus par la 2003

enquête de mouvement de la population par échantillon de la Chine.

21 The fertility rates have been compiled using a population denominator which has excluded female foreign domestic helpers. - Les taux de fécondité ont été compilés pour une population (en dénominateur) ne comprenant pas les domestiques étrangères.

22 Data refer to government controlled areas. - Les données se raportent aux zones contrôlées par le Gouvernement.

23 Including data for the Indian-held part of Jammu and Kashmir, the final status of which has not yet been determined. - Y compris les données pour la partie du Jammu et du Cachemire occupée par l'Inde dont le statut définitif n'a pas encore été déterminé.

24 Rates were obtained by the Sample Registration System of India, actually a large demographic survey. - Les taux ont été obtenus par le Système de l'enregistrement par échantillon de l'Inde qui est au fait une large enquête démographique.

25 Published by the United Nations Economic and Social Commission for Western Asia. - Publié par la Commission économique et sociale des Nations Unies pour l'Asie occidentale.

26 Including data for East Jerusalem and Israeli residents in certain other territories under occupation by Israeli military forces since June 1967. - Y compris les données pour Jérusalem-Est et les résidents israéliens dans certains autres territoires occupés depuis 1967 par les forces armées israéliennes.

27 For Japanese nationals in Japan only; however, rates computed on population including foreigners except foreign military and civilian personnel and their dependants stationed in the area. - Pour les nationaux japonais au Japon seulement; toutefois, les taux sont calculés sur la base d'une population comprenant les étrangers, mais ne comprenant ni les militaires et agents civils étrangers en poste sur le territoire ni les membres de leur famille les accompagnant.

28 Excluding data for Jordanian territory under occupation since June 1967 by Israeli military forces. Excluding foreigners, including registered Palestinian refugees. - Non compris les données pour le territoire jordanien occupé depuis juin 1967 par les forces armées israéliennes. Non compris les étrangers, mais y compris les réfugiés de Palestine enregistrés.

29 Excluding alien armed forces, civilian aliens employed by armed forces, and foreign diplomatic personnel and their dependants. - Non compris les militaires étrangers, les civils étrangers employés par les forces armées ni le personnel diplomatique étranger et les membres de leur famille les accompagnant.

30 For 2001, data refer to last twelve months preceding census on June 2001. - - Pour 2001, les données se rapportent pour la dernière fois à douze mois précédant le recensement juin 2001.

31 Data refer to the recorded events in Ministry of Health hospitals and health centres only. - Les données se rapportent aux faits d'état-civil enregistrés dans les hôpitaux et les dispensaires du Ministère de la santé seulement.

32 Based on the results of the Population Growth Survey. - D'après les résultats de la 'Population Growth Survey.'

33 Excluding data for the Pakistan-held part of Jammu and Kashmir, the final status of which has not yet been determined. - Non compris les données concernant la partie du Jammu et Cachemire occupée par le Pakistan dont le statut définitif n'a pas été déterminé.

34 Excluding transients afloat and non-locally domiciled military and civilian services personnel and their dependants. - Non compris les personnes de passage à bord de navires, ni les militaires et agents civils domiciliés hors du territoire et les membres de leur famille les accompagnant.

35 Excluding nomad population and Palestinian refugees. - Non compris la population nomade et les réfugiés de Palestine.

36 Based on the results of the Population Demographic Survey. - D'après les résultats de la Population Demographic Survey.

37 Including armed forces stationed outside the country, but excluding alien armed forces stationed in the area. - Y compris les militaires nationaux hors du pays, mais non compris les militaires étrangers en garnison sur le territoire.

38 Excluding Faeroe Islands and Greenland. - Non compris les Iles Féroé et Gröenland.

39 Including nationals temporarily outside the country. - Y compris les nationaux se trouvant temporairement hors du pays.

40 Including armed forces stationed outside the country. - Y compris les militaires nationaux hors du pays.

41 Excluding armed forces. - Non compris les militaires en garnison.

42 Events registered within one year of occurrence. - Evénements enregistrés dans l'année qui suit l'événement.

43 Rates computed on population including civilian nationals temporarily outside the country. - Les taux sont calculés sur la base d'un chiffre de population qui comprend les civils nationaux temporairement hors du pays.

44 Live births to Maltese parents only. - Naissances vivantes aux parents maltais seulement.

45 Including residents outside the country if listed in a Netherlands population register. - Y compris les résidents hors du pays, s'ils sont inscrits sur un registre de population néerlandais.

46 Including residents temporarily outside the country. - Y compris les résidents se trouvant temporairement hors du pays.

47 From 2002, without data for Kosovo and Metohia. - Après 2002, sans les donées pour le Kosovo and Metohie.

48 Data revised to exclude births in Northern Ireland to non-residents of Northern Ireland. - Données révisées non compris des naissances en Irlande du Nord aux non-résidents de l'Irlande du Nord.

49 Including United States military personnel, their dependants and contract employees. - Y compris les militaires des Etats-Unis, les membres de leur famille les accompagnant et les agents contractuels des Etats-Unis.

Table 5

Table 5 presents national estimates of mid-year population for all available years between 1994 and 2003.

Description of variables: Mid-year estimates of the total population are those provided by national statistical offices. They refer to the *de facto* or *de jure* population on 1 July. In cases where the national statistical office provided data referring to the beginning or the end of a year the average was calculated by the Statistics Division. The data are presented in thousands, rounded by the Statistics Division.

For certain countries or areas, there is a discrepancy between the mid-year population estimates shown in this table and those shown in subsequent tables for the same year. Usually this discrepancy arises because the estimates for a given year are revised and the remaining tabulations are not.

Unless otherwise indicated, all estimates relate to the population within present geographical boundaries. Major exceptions to this principle are explained in footnotes.

Reliability of data: Reliable mid-year population estimates are those that are based on a complete census (or on a sample survey) and have been adjusted on a basis of a continuous population register or on the balance of births, deaths and migration. Reliable mid-year estimates appear in roman type. Mid-year estimates that are not calculated on this basis are considered less reliable and are shown in *italics*.

Limitations: Statistics on estimates of the mid-year total population are subject to the same qualifications as have been set forth for population statistics in general in section 3 of the Technical Notes.

International comparability of mid-year population estimates is also affected by the fact that some of these estimates refer to the *de jure*, and not the *de facto*, population. These are indicated in the column titled "Code". The difference between the *de facto* and the *de jure* population is discussed in section 3.1.1 of the Technical Notes.

Earlier data: Estimates of mid-year population have been shown in previous issues of the *Demographic Yearbook*. Information on the years and specific topics covered is presented in the Historical Index.

Tableau 5

Le tableau 5 présente des estimations nationales de la population en milieu d'année pour le plus grand nombre possible d'années entre 1993 et 2002.

Description des variables : Les estimations de la population totale en milieu d'année sont celles qui ont été communiquées par les services nationaux de statistique. Elles correspondent à la population de fait ou se réfèrent à la population de droit, au 1er juillet. Lorsque la date est différente, cela est signalé par une note. Sauf indication contraire, tous les chiffres sont exprimés en milliers. Les données ont été arrondies par la Division de statistique de l'ONU.

Sauf indication contraire, toutes les estimations se rapportent à la population présente sur le territoire actuel des pays ou zones considérés. Les principales exceptions à cette règle sont expliquées en note.

Fiabilité des données : Les estimations de la population en milieu d'année sont considérées sûres quand elles sont fondées sur un recensement complet (ou sur une enquête par sondage) qui a été ajusté en fonction des données provenant d'un registre permanent de population ou en fonction des naissances, décès et mouvements migratoires qui ont eu lieu pendant la période. Les estimations en milieu d'année sont considérées comme sûres et apparaissent en caractères romains. Les estimations en milieu d'année dont le calcul n'a pas été effectué sur cette base sont considérées comme moins sûres et apparaissent en italique.

Insuffisance des données : Les statistiques concernant les estimations de la population totale en milieu d'année appellent toutes les réserves qui ont été formulées à la section 3 des Notes techniques à propos des statistiques de la population en général.

Le fait que certaines des estimations concernant la population en milieu d'année se réfèrent à la population de droit et non à la population de fait influe sur la comparabilité internationale. Ces cas ont été signalés dans la colonne « Type ». La différence entre la population de fait et la population de droit est expliquée à la section 3.1.1 des Notes techniques.

Données publiées antérieurement : Des estimations de la population en milieu d'année ont été publiées dans des éditions antérieures de l'*Annuaire démographique*. Pour plus de précisions concernant les années et les sujets pour lesquels des données ont été publiées, se reporter à l'index.

5. Estimates of mid-year population: 1994 - 2003
Estimations de la population au milieu de l'anneé: 1994 - 2003

Continent and country or area / Continent et pays ou zone	Co-de[1]	Population estimates (in thousands) — Estimations (en milliers)									
		1994	1995	1996	1997	1998	1999	2000	2001	2002	2003
AFRICA — AFRIQUE											
Algeria - Algérie	DJ	27 496	28 060	28 566	29 045	29 507	29 965	30 416	30 872	31 332	31 848
Benin - Bénin	DF	5 242	5 412	5 594	5 639	5 816	5 990	6 169	*6 417	...	...
Botswana	DF	1 425	1 459	1 496	1 533	1 572	1 611	1 653	...	...	...
Burkina Faso	DF	9 889	10 200	...	11 087	10 683	...	...	...	...	...
Burundi	DF	5 875	5 982	6 088	6 194	6 300	6 483	...	...	...	...
Cameroon - Cameroun	DF	...	13 277	...	14 298	14 439	...	...	...	...	...
Cape Verde - Cap-Vert	DF	...	386	396	407	417	428	435	445	453	461
Central African Republic - République centrafricaine	DF	2 998	...	...	3 245	...	...	...	...	...	3 151
Chad - Tchad	DF	6 214	...	...	...	...	...	...	*8 322	...	...
Congo	DF	...	...	...	*2 663	*2 738	*2 815	*2 893	*2 974	...	...
Côte d'Ivoire	DF	13 695	14 230	14 781	...	15 367	15 881	16 402	16 928	17 461	18 001
Djibouti	DF	645	680	715	755	795	840	...	...	...	...
Egypt - Égypte	DF	56 344	57 510	58 755	60 080	61 341	62 652	63 976	65 292	66 628	67 976
Ethiopia - Éthiopie	DF	...	54 649	56 372	58 117	59 882	61 672	63 495	65 374	67 220	...
Gabon	DF	1 040	1 066	1 093	1 120	1 148	1 177	1 206	*1 237	...	...
Gambia - Gambie	DF	...	...	...	...	...	1 385	1 393	*1 420	...	...
Ghana	DF	*16 675	*17 198	*17 742	*18 305	*18 885	*19 484	*19 412	...	...	...
Guinea-Bissau - Guinée-Bissau	DF	...	...	...	...	...	...	...	1 211	1 238	1 267
Kenya	DF	25 478	26 227	26 999	27 793	28 611	29 453	30 208	30 970	31 807	32 692
Lesotho	DF	...	...	...	2 012	2 055	2 100	2 144	...	...	...
Liberia - Libéria	DF	2 700	2 760	2 820	2 879	...	...	...	...	...	...
Libyan Arab Jamahiriya - Jamahiriya arabe libyenne[2]	DF	4 274	4 395	4 519	4 648	4 772	4 958	5 125	5 300	5 484	...
Madagascar	DF	...	...	...	...	...	14 222	14 650	15 085	...	...
Malawi[3]	DF	9 461	9 788	10 114	10 441	...	*10 153	*10 475	*10 816	*11 175	*11 549
Mali	DJ	...	...	...	9 325	9 811	9 969	10 243	10 525	...	...
Mauritania - Mauritanie	DF	2 211	2 284	2 351	2 421	2 493	2 568	2 645	2 724	...	...
Mauritius - Maurice	DJ	1 113	1 122	1 134	1 148	1 160	1 175	1 187	1 200	1 210	1 223
Morocco - Maroc	DF	25 926	26 386	26 848	27 310	27 775	28 238	28 705	29 170	29 631	30 088
Mozambique[4]	DF	16 614	15 820	16 177	16 543	16 917	17 299	17 691	*17 656	...	...
Namibia - Namibie	DF	...	...	...	...	...	...	*1 817	...	...	...
Nigeria - Nigéria[5]	DF	...	99 210	...	...	...	...	115 224	118 801	122 444	126 153
Réunion	DF	651	663	675	686	698	710	722	735	748	764
Saint Helena ex. dep. - Sainte-Hélène sans dép.	DF	5	5	5	...	...	...	...	...	...	...
Saint Helena: Tristan da Cunha - Sainte-Hélène: Tristan da Cunha	DF	0	0	0	...	...	...	...	...	...	...
Sao Tome and Principe - Sao Tomé-et-Principe	DF	125	128	130	133	134	137	140	...	...	...
Senegal - Sénégal	DJ	8 106	8 313	8 525	8 742	8 964	9 193	9 427	9 667	9 913	10 165
Seychelles	DF	74	75	76	77	79	80	81	81	*84	83
Sierra Leone	DF	4 323	4 421	4 522	4 625	4 730	4 836	4 944	5 054	5 167	5 280
South Africa - Afrique du Sud[4]	DF	38 630	39 477	40 342	41 227	42 130	43 054	43 686	*44 328	45 454	46 430
Sudan - Soudan	DF	26 289	27 008	27 747	28 507	29 266	30 326	31 081	*31 627	32 468	33 334
Swaziland	DF	879	908	938	...	...	...	...	...	...	...
Togo	DF	3 928	4 052	4 179	4 269	4 406	4 506	4 629	4 740	4 854	...
Tunisia - Tunisie	DF	8 815	8 958	9 089	9 215	9 333	9 456	9 564	*9 674	*9 782	*9 840
Uganda - Ouganda	DF	...	19 263	19 848	20 752	21 467	22 207	22 972	*22 788	...	...
United Republic of Tanzania - République Unie de Tanzanie	DF	27 495	28 279	29 086	29 984	...	...	...	...	...	...
Zambia - Zambie	DF	8 764	9 112	9 454	9 780	10 096	10 407	9 337	10 089	10 409	10 744
Zimbabwe	DF	11 150	11 526	11 908	12 294	12 685	13 079	...	*12 960	...	...
AMERICA, NORTH — AMERIQUE DU NORD											
Anguilla	DF	10	10	10	10	11	11	11	12	12	12
Antigua and Barbuda - Antigua-et-Barbuda	DF	66	68	69	...	...	...	...	...	...	...
Aruba	DJ	78	80	83	86	88	90	91	92	*94	*96
Bahamas	DF	274	279	284	288	293	298	*303	*309	...	*317
Barbados - Barbade	DF	264	264	265	...	266	267	*267	...	*271	...

5. Estimates of mid-year population: 1994 - 2003
Estimations de la population au milieu de l'anneé: 1994 - 2003 (continued — suite)

Continent and country or area / Continent et pays ou zone	Code[1]	Population estimates (in thousands) — Estimations (en milliers)									
		1994	1995	1996	1997	1998	1999	2000	2001	2002	2003

AMERICA, NORTH — AMERIQUE DU NORD

Belize	DF	211	216	222	230	238	*243	250	*257	*265	*274
Bermuda - Bermudes[6]	DJ	61	61	62	62	62	63	63	62	62	62
British Virgin Islands - Îles Vierges britanniques	DF	...	...	...	...	...	...	...	21	...	*22
Canada[7,8,9,10]	DJ	28 999	29 302	29 611	29 907	30 157	30 493	30 770	31 021	31 373	31 660
Cayman Islands - Îles Caïmanes	DJ	31	33	34	36	38	39	40	41	*40	...
Costa Rica	DJ	3 071	3 136	3 202	3 271	3 341	3 413	3 486	3 907	3 998	4 089
Cuba	DF	10 904	10 930	10 965	11 009	11 055	11 095	11 130	11 157	11 184	11 215
Dominica - Dominique	DF	72	73	72	72	72	72	72	71	70	...
Dominican Republic - République dominicaine	DF	7 461	7 633	7 808	7 988	8 172	8 360	8 552	8 749	...	8 715
El Salvador	DF	...	5 669	5 787	5 908	6 031	6 154	6 276	6 397	6 518	6 638
Greenland - Groenland	DJ	56	56	56	56	56	56	56	56	57	57
Grenada - Grenade[11]	DF	98	98	99	100	100	101	101	101	...	...
Guadeloupe[12]	DJ	400	405	409	414	419	424	428	432	437	439
Guatemala[4]	DF	9 717	9 970	10 243	10 517	10 799	11 088	11 385	11 678	11 987	12 084
Haiti - Haïti	DJ	7 041	7 180	7 336	7 492	7 647	7 803	7 959	*8 132	...	...
Honduras	DF	5 460	5 606	5 755	5 908	6 057	6 211	6 369	6 530	6 695	6 861
Jamaica - Jamaïque	DJ	2 455	2 483	2 510	2 534	2 557	*2 574	*2 589	*2 605	*2 617	*2 630
Martinique	DJ	367	369	372	376	379	382	385	387	389	*391
Mexico - Mexique	DJ	92 051	93 613	95 110	96 541	97 921	99 266	100 569	101 826	103 040	104 214
Montserrat[13]	DF	10	10	8	6	4	5	*5	...	...	...
Netherlands Antilles - Antilles néerlandaises[14]	DJ	194	190	191	193	192	186	179	174	174	179
Nicaragua	DJ	4 299	4 427	4 549	4 674	4 803	4 936	4 957	5 059	5 162	5 268
Panama	DF	2 583	2 631	2 674	2 719	2 764	2 809	2 856	2 897	3 060	3 116
Puerto Rico - Porto Rico[15]	DJ	3 627	3 655	3 685	3 716	3 748	3 782	3 818	3 840	3 859	3 879
Saint Kitts and Nevis - Saint-Kitts-et-Nevis	DF	43	44	42	41	40	42	40	*46	...	...
Saint Lucia - Sainte-Lucie	DF	143	145	147	150	152	154	156	158	159	161
Saint Pierre and Miquelon - Saint Pierre-et-Miquelon	DF	7	7	7	...	...	...	...	...	...	...
Saint Vincent and the Grenadines - Saint Vincent-et-les Grenadines	DF	110	111	111	112	111	112	112	109	108	...
Trinidad and Tobago - Trinité-et-Tobago[16]	DF	1 250	1 260	1 264	1 275	1 278	1 284	1 290	1 267	1 276	1 282
Turks Caicos Islands - Îles Turques et Caïques	DJ	14	15	15	16	17	17	18	20	21	22
United States - États-Unis[17]	DJ	260 599	263 044	265 463	268 008	270 299	272 691	275 265	284 797	288 369	*290 811
United States Virgin Islands - Îles Vierges américaines	DJ	107	108	108	108	109	109	109	109	109	*109

AMERICA, SOUTH — AMERIQUE DU SUD

Argentina - Argentine	DF	34 318	34 768	35 220	35 672	36 125	36 578	37 032	37 487	37 944	37 870
Bolivia - Bolivie	DF	7 309	7 482	7 661	7 845	8 035	8 229	8 428	8 624	8 824	9 025
Brazil - Brésil[18]	DF	153 726	155 822	157 872	159 636	161 790	165 371	167 724	172 386	174 633	178 985
Chile - Chili	DF	14 152	14 395	14 596	14 796	14 997	15 197	15 398	15 572	15 746	15 919
Colombia - Colombie	DF	37 849	38 558	39 281	40 019	40 773	41 539	42 299	43 035	43 776	44 531
Ecuador - Équateur[19]	DF	11 187	11 397	11 591	11 773	11 948	12 121	12 299	12 480	12 661	12 843
French Guiana - Guyane française	DJ	133	137	142	148	153	158	164	170	175	181
Guyana[20,21]	DF	746	760	770	775	773	771	742	744	745	746
Paraguay	DF	4 700	4 828	4 955	5 085	5 219	*5 356	...	...	...	...
Peru - Pérou[4,22]	DF	23 421	23 837	24 258	24 681	25 104	25 525	25 939	26 347	26 749	27 148
Suriname	DJ	428	434	440	446	452	454	458	464	470	476	481
Uruguay[4]	DF	3 193	3 217	3 241	3 263	3 284	3 289	3 301	3 308	3 309	3 304
Venezuela[4,22]	DF	21 377	21 844	22 502	22 959	23 413	23 867	24 311	24 766	25 220	...

ASIA — ASIE

Afghanistan	DF	18 070	19 070	19 820	20 350	20 760	21 200	21 770	22 080	22 930	...

5. Estimates of mid-year population: 1994 - 2003
Estimations de la population au milieu de l'anneé: 1994 - 2003 (continued — suite)

Continent and country or area / Continent et pays ou zone	Code[1]	Population estimates (in thousands) — Estimations (en milliers)									
		1994	1995	1996	1997	1998	1999	2000	2001	2002	2003
ASIA — ASIE											
Armenia - Arménie	DJ	3 308	3 255	3 247	3 242	3 235	3 230	3 221	3 214	3 212	3 211
Azerbaijan - Azerbaïdjan	DF	7 597	7 685	7 763	7 838	7 913	7 983	8 049	8 111	8 141	8 234
Bahrain - Bahreïn	DF	544	559	574	589	605	621	638	655	672	689
Bangladesh	DF	117 700	119 900	122 100	124 300	126 200	*128 100	...	...	...	...
Bhutan - Bhoutan	DF	564	582	600	619	638	658	678	699	*716	...
Brunei Darussalam - Brunéi Darussalam	DF	280	287	294	302	310	317	325	333	344	350
Cambodia - Cambodge[23,24]	DF	9 869	10 200	10 340	10 368	12 242	12 462	12 688	12 922	13 164	13 415
China - Chine[25,26,27]	DF	1 191 835	1 204 855	1 217 550	1 230 075	1 241 935	1 252 735	1 262 645	1 271 850	1 280 400	1 288 400
China: Hong Kong SAR - Chine: Hong Kong RAS[28]	...	6 035	6 156	6 436	6 489	6 544	6 606	6 665	6 725	6 787	6 803
China: Macao SAR - Chine: Macao RAS	DJ	397	409	415	417	422	427	431	434	*439	445
Cyprus - Chypre[29]	DJ	639	651	661	670	679	686	694	701	710	721
Georgia - Géorgie	DF	4 862	4 734	4 616	4 532	4 487	4 452	4 418	4 386	4 357	4 329
India - Inde[30]	DF	905 449	923 459	941 579	959 792	978 081	996 430	1 014 825	1 033 248	1 050 640	1 068 214
Indonesia - Indonésie	DJ	192 216	195 294	198 320	201 353	204 392	207 437	...	208 643	211 439	214 251
Iran (Islamic Republic of) - Iran (République islamique d')	DJ	58 331	59 187	...	60 939	61 836	62 746	63 664	64 528	65 540	66 480
Iraq	DF	20 007	20 536	21 124	22 046	22 379	22 989	23 577	24 813	...	...
Israel - Israël[31]	DJ	5 399	5 545	5 685	5 829	5 971	6 125	6 289	6 439	6 570	6 690
Japan - Japon[32]	DF	125 178	125 472	125 757	126 057	126 400	126 631	126 843	127 130	127 401	127 649
Jordan - Jordanie[33]	DF	3 918	4 142	4 368	4 522	4 678	4 970	4 970	5 256	5 404	5 404
Kazakhstan	DF	16 146	15 816	15 578	15 334	15 073	14 928	14 884	14 858	14 859	14 909
Korea (Republic of) - Corée (République de)[34]	DF	44 642	45 093	45 546	45 954	46 287	46 617	47 008	47 343	47 640	47 925
Kuwait - Koweït	DF	1 620	1 802	1 894	1 980	2 027	2 107	2 190	2 275	2 262	2 325
Kyrgyzstan - Kirghizistan	DF	4 540	4 590	4 657	4 725	4 797	4 865	4 915	4 955	4 993	5 039
Lao People's Democratic Republic - République démocratique populaire lao	DF	...	4 536	...	...	...	5 091	5 218	...	*5 500	...
Malaysia - Malaisie	DF	20 112	20 689	21 169	20 996	21 475	21 852	23 495	...	...	*25 048
Maldives	DF	240	...	251	259	267	278	271	276	281	285
Mongolia - Mongolie	DF	2 207	2 243	2 276	*2 307	2 340	2 373	2 407	2 443	2 475	2 504
Myanmar	DF	43 922	...	...	*46 402	...	...	...	...	...	...
Nepal - Népal	DJ	19 862	20 341	20 832	21 331	21 843	22 367	*22 904	...	...	...
Occupied Palestinian Territory - Territoire palestinien occupé	DF	2 317	2 483	2 631	2 783	2 897	3 019	3 149	3 275	3 394	3 515
Oman	DF	2 050	2 131	2 214	2 256	2 288	2 325	2 401	2 478	2 538	...
Pakistan[35]	DF	119 390	122 360	125 380	128 420	131 510	134 510	137 510	*140 470	144 852	147 662
Philippines	DJ	68 624	70 267	69 952	71 550	73 148	74 746	76 348	77 926	79 504	81 081
Qatar	DF	480	495	511	528	557	586	616	649	683	719
Saudi Arabia - Arabie saoudite	DF	17 701	18 136	18 581	19 037	19 504	19 983	20 474	20 976	21 491	22 019
Singapore - Singapour	DF	3 421	3 526	3 670	3 794	3 922	3 951	4 018	4 131	4 171	4 185
Sri Lanka	DF	17 891	18 136	18 315	18 552	18 774	19 043	19 359	*18 700	*19 007	...
Syrian Arab Republic - République arabe syrienne[36]	DF	13 844	14 153	14 619	15 100	15 597	16 110	16 320	16 720	17 130	17 550
Tajikistan - Tadjikistan	DF	...	...	...	...	...	6 064	6 188	6 313	6 441	6 573
Thailand - Thaïlande	DJ	58 713	59 401	60 003	60 602	61 156	61 564	61 770	...	*63 482	...
Turkey - Turquie	DF	60 612	61 737	62 873	64 015	65 157	66 293	67 420	68 529	69 626	70 713
Turkmenistan - Turkménistan	DF	4 406	4 509	4 569	...	4 859	...	...	...	...	...
United Arab Emirates - Émirats arabes unis[37]	DF	...	2 314	2 443	2 624	2 776	2 938	...	...	3 754	4 041
Uzbekistan - Ouzbékistan	DF	22 282	22 690	23 130	23 560	24 051	23 954	24 650	*24 964	*25 368	...
Viet Nam	DF	72 510	73 962	75 355	74 346	75 526	76 597	77 686	...	79 727	80 670
Yemen - Yémen	DF	14 859	15 369	15 915	16 484	17 072	17 671	18 261	*18 863	*19 495	...
EUROPE											
Albania - Albanie	DF	3 035	3 050	3 076	3 075	3 055	3 054	3 061	3 074	3 093	3 111
Andorra - Andorre	DF	65	64	64	66	66	66	66	66	66	70
Austria - Autriche	DJ	7 936	7 948	7 959	7 968	7 977	7 992	8 012	8 043	8 084	8 118

5. Estimates of mid-year population: 1994 - 2003
Estimations de la population au milieu de l'anneé: 1994 - 2003 (continued — suite)

Continent and country or area / Continent et pays ou zone	Code[1]	Population estimates (in thousands) — Estimations (en milliers)									
		1994	1995	1996	1997	1998	1999	2000	2001	2002	2003
EUROPE											
Belarus - Bélarus	DF	10 308	10 281	10 250	10 220	10 191	10 035	10 005	9 971	9 925	*9 874
Belgium - Belgique	DJ	10 116	10 137	10 157	10 181	10 203	10 226	10 251	10 287	10 333	*10 376
Bosnia and Herzegovina - Bosnie-Herzégovine	DF	...	...	3 645	3 738	3 653	3 725	3 781	3 798	3 828	*3 832
Bulgaria - Bulgarie	DF	8 444	8 406	8 363	8 312	8 257	8 211	8 170	7 910	7 869	*7 824
Channel Islands: Guernsey - Îles Anglo-Normandes: Guernesey	DF	58	59	59	59	59	60	60	...	...	...
Channel Islands: Jersey - Îles Anglo-Normandes: Jersey	DF	84	84	...	...	...	...	...	...	88	88
Croatia - Croatie	DJ	4 649	4 669	4 494	4 572	4 501	4 554	4 381	...	4 443	4 442
Czech Republic - République tchèque	DJ	10 336	10 331	10 315	10 304	10 295	10 283	10 273	10 224	10 201	10 202
Denmark - Danemark[38]	DJ	5 205	5 228	5 262	5 284	5 301	5 327	5 337	5 359	5 374	5 387
Estonia - Estonie	DF	1 499	1 484	1 469	1 458	1 450	1 442	1 370	1 364	1 359	1 354
Faeroe Islands - Îles Féroé	DJ	...	...	...	...	...	...	...	...	47	48
Finland - Finlande	DJ	5 088	5 108	5 125	5 140	5 153	5 165	5 176	5 188	5 201	5 213
France[39]	DJ	57 659	57 844	58 026	58 610	58 398	58 623	58 896	59 193	*59 489	*59 768
Germany - Allemagne	DJ	81 422	81 661	81 896	82 061	82 029	82 057	82 183	82 350	82 488	82 534
Gibraltar[40]	DF	28	27	27	27	27	27	27	...	29	29
Greece - Grèce[41]	DF	10 426	10 454	10 476	10 499	10 516	10 534	10 008	*10 020	10 988	11 024
Holy See - Saint-Siège[42]	DF	...	...	...	...	1	...	...	...	...	...
Hungary - Hongrie	DF	10 261	10 229	10 193	10 155	10 114	10 068	10 024	10 188	10 159	10 130
Iceland - Islande	DJ	266	267	269	271	274	277	281	285	288	289
Ireland - Irlande	DF	3 586	3 601	3 626	3 661	3 705	3 745	3 787	3 839	3 917	3 996
Isle of Man - Îles de Man	DJ	71	72	71	72	74	...	75	76	77	77
Italy - Italie	DJ	57 204	57 301	57 380	57 523	57 588	57 646	57 762	*57 948	57 157	57 605
Latvia - Lettonie	DF	2 521	2 485	2 457	2 433	2 410	2 390	2 373	2 355	2 339	2 325
Liechtenstein	DF	30	31	31	31	32	32	33	33	34	34
Lithuania - Lituanie	DJ	3 657	3 629	3 602	3 575	3 549	3 524	3 500	3 481	3 469	3 454
Luxembourg	DJ	403	409	414	419	425	430	436	442	446	450
Malta - Malte[43]	DJ	369	371	374	377	379	380	383	385	387	399
Monaco	DJ	...	...	...	32	...	33	*32	...	...	...
Netherlands - Pays-Bas[44]	DJ	15 383	15 459	15 531	15 611	15 707	15 812	15 926	16 046	16 149	16 225
Norway - Norvège[45]	DJ	4 325	4 359	4 381	4 405	4 431	4 462	4 491	4 514	4 538	*4 565
Poland - Pologne[46,47]	DF	38 544	38 588	38 618	38 650	38 666	38 654	38 256	38 251	38 232	38 195
Portugal[48]	DF	10 004	10 030	10 058	10 091	10 129	10 172	10 226	10 293	10 368	10 441
Republic of Moldova - République de Moldova[49]	DJ	4 348	4 348	4 327	3 654	3 652	3 646	3 639	3 631	3 623	3 613
Romania - Roumanie	DJ	22 731	22 681	22 608	22 546	22 503	22 458	22 435	22 408	21 795	21 734
Russian Federation - Fédération de Russie[50]	DJ	148 408	148 376	148 160	147 915	147 671	147 215	146 597	145 976	145 306	144 566
San Marino - Saint-Marin	DF	25	25	25	26	26	26	27	28	28	29
Serbia and Montenegro - Serbie-et-Montenegro[51,52]	DJ	10 516	10 547	10 577	10 600	10 617	10 629	10 634	10 652	8 114	*8 153
Slovakia - Slovaquie	DJ	5 347	5 364	5 374	5 383	5 391	5 395	5 401	5 380	5 379	*5 379
Slovenia - Slovénie	DJ	1 989	1 988	1 991	1 987	1 983	1 986	1 990	1 992	1 996	*1 997
Spain - Espagne[53]	DJ	39 263	39 345	39 426	39 520	39 649	39 843	40 169	40 614	41 201	41 874
Sweden - Suède	DJ	8 781	8 827	8 841	8 846	8 851	8 858	8 872	8 896	8 925	*8 958
Switzerland - Suisse	DJ	6 994	7 041	7 072	7 089	7 110	7 144	7 184	7 233	7 285	*7 341
The Former Yugoslav Rep. of Macedonia - L'ex-République yougoslave de Macédoine[54]	DF	...	1 963	1 975	1 997	2 008	2 017	2 024	2 035	2 031	*2 027
Ukraine[55]	...	52 114	51 728	51 334	50 894	50 500	50 106	48 889	48 452	48 032	*47 633
United Kingdom - Royaume-Uni[56]	DF	57 862	58 025	58 164	58 314	58 475	58 684	58 886	*59 114	*59 322	59 554
OCEANIA — OCEANIE											
American Samoa - Samoas américaines[15,57]	DJ	53	53	54	55	56	57	57	58	58	58
Australia - Australie[58]	DJ	17 855	18 072	18 311	18 518	18 711	18 926	19 153	19 413	19 641	19 873
Cook Islands - Îles Cook	DF	20	19	20	18	17	16	18	*18	18	18

5. Estimates of mid-year population: 1994 - 2003
Estimations de la population au milieu de l'anneé: 1994 - 2003 (continued — suite)

Continent and country or area / Continent et pays ou zone	Co-de[1]	1994	1995	1996	1997	1998	1999	2000	2001	2002	2003
OCEANIA — OCEANIE											
Fiji - Fidji	DF	784	796	775	...	797	806	...	...	...	...
French Polynesia - Polynésie française	DF	*213*	*216*	*219*	*222*	*226*	*228*	*231*	*239*	*243*	*247*
Guam[15]	DJ	143	144	145	147	150	153	...	158	161	164
Kiribati	DF	...	*78	...	*83	...	...	...	...	...	...
Marshall Islands - Îles Marshall	DF	*54*	*56*	*57*	*61*	*63*	*51*	*53*	*55*	*57*	
Micronesia, Federated States of - Micronésie, États Fédérés de La	DJ	*104*	*107*	*110*	*110*	*112*	*113*	*119*	*117*	*120*	...
Nauru	DF	*10*	*10*	*11*	*11*	*11*	*11*	*12*	*12*	...	...
New Caledonia - Nouvelle-Calédonie	DF	*189*	*194*	*197*	*201*	*204*	*208*	*211*	*214*	*217*	*220*
New Zealand - Nouvelle-Zélande	DJ	3 620	3 673	3 732	3 781	3 815	3 835	3 858	3 880	3 939	4 009
Niue - Nioué	DF	...	...	...	...	...	...	...	...	*2	...
Northern Mariana Islands - Îles Mariannes septentrionales	DF	...	...	61	64	67	69	72	75	74	76
Palau - Palaos	DF	17	17	18	18	18	19	19	20	20	20
Papua New Guinea - Papouasie-Nouvelle-Guinée	DF	*3 997*	*4 074*	...	*4 209*	*4 600*	...	*5 100*	...	*5 462*	...
Samoa	DF	*164*	...	...	...	*168*	*169*	*171*	...	...	...
Tonga[59]	DF	...	...	...	*99*	*99*	*100*	*100*	*101*	*101*	...
Vanuatu	DF	*162*	*166*	*170*	*174*	...	...	...	...	...	...

FOOTNOTES - NOTES

Italics: estimates which are less reliable. — Italiques: estimations moins sûres.

* Provisional. — Données provisoires.

[1] 'Code' indicates the source of data, as follows:
DF Estimates of population de facto. — Population de fait
DJ Estimates of population de jure. — Population de droit

[2] Data refer to Libyan nationals only. - Les données se raportent aux nationaux libyens seulement.

[3] From 1999 data refer to national projections. - Après 1999 les données se referent aux projections nationales.

[4] Mid-year estimates have been adjusted for underenumeration, at latest census. - Les estimations au millieu de l'année tiennent compte d'une ajustement destiné à compenser les lacunes du dénombrement lors du dernier recensement.

[5] From 1995 data refer to national projections. - Après 1995 les données se referent aux projections nationales.

[6] Excluding the institutional population. - Non compris la population dans les institutions.

[7] For 1994 and 1995, revised intercensal estimates adjusted for net undercoverage. - Pour 1994 et 1995, estimations inter censitaires corrigées pour tenir en compte du sous dénombrement net.

[8] For 1996, 1997 and 1998, final intercensal estimates. - Pour 1996, 1997 et 1998, estimations inter censitaires finales.

[9] For 2001 and 2002, final postcensal estimates. - Pour 2001 et 2002, évaluations postcensal finales.

[10] For 2003, updated postcensal estimates. - Pour 2003, estimations post censitaires mises à jour.

[11] Including Carriacou and other dependencies in the Grenadines. - Y compris Carriacou et les autres dépendances du groupe des îles Grenadines.

[12] Including dependencies: Marie-Galante, la Désirade, les Saintes, Petite-Terre, St. Barthélemy and French part of St. Martin. - Y compris les dépendances: Marie-Galante, la Désirade, les Saintes, Petite-Terre, Saint-Barthélemy et la partie française de Saint-Martin.

[13] Around 1996 - 1997 volcanic activity on Montserrat escalated, forcing people to relocate. - Vers 1996 - 1997 l'activité volcanique a connu une recrudescence à Montserrat, forçant les habitants à aller ailleurs.

[14] Comprising Bonaire, Curaçao, Saba, St. Eustatius and Dutch part of St.

Martin. - Comprend Bonaire, Curaçao, Saba, Saint-Eustache et la partie néederlandaise de Saint-Martin.

[15] Including armed forces stationed in the area. - Y compris les militaires en garnison sur le territoire.

[16] Starting from 2001 data are based on 2000 census. - Chiffres basés sur les résultats du recensement de 2000.

[17] Excluding armed forces overseas and civilian citizens absent from country for an extended period of time. - Non compris les militaires à l'étranger, et les civils hors du pays pendant une période prolongée.

[18] Data include persons in remote areas, military personel outside the country, merchant seamen at sea, civilian seasonal workers outside the country, and other civilians outside the country, and exclude nomads, foreign military, civilian aliens temporarily in the country, transients on ships and Indian jungle population. - Y compris les personnes dans des régions éloignées, le personel militaire en dehors du pays, les marins marchands, les ouvriers saisonniers civils de couture en dehors du pays, et autres civils en dehors du pays, et non compris les nomades, les militaires étrangers, les étrangers civils temporairement dans le pays, les transiteurs sur des bateaux et les Indiens de la jungle.

[19] Excluding nomadic Indian tribes. - Non compris les tribus d'Indiens nomades.

[20] Data as reported by national statistical authorities. - Les données comme elles ont été déclarées par l'institut national de la statistique.

[21] Data for 1994 have been adjusted on the basis of the Population Census of 1991. - Les données pour la période 1991-1994 ont été ajustées à partir des résultats du recensement de la population de 1991.

[22] Excluding Indian jungle population. - Non compris les Indiens de la jungle.

[23] Excluding foreign diplomatic personnel and their dependants. - Non compris le personnel diplomatique étranger et les membres de leur famille les accompagnant.

[24] Starting from 1998 based on 1998 census. - Depuis 1998, à partir des résultats de recensement.

[25] For statistical purposes, the data for China do not include those for the Hong Kong Special Administrative Region (Hong Kong SAR), Macao Special Administrative Region (Macao SAR) and Taiwan province of China. - Pour la présentation des statistiques, les données pour Chine ne comprend pas la Région Administrative Spéciale de Hong Kong (Hong Kong RAS), la Région Administrative Spéciale de Macao (Macao RAS) et Taïwan province de Chine.

[26] Data from 2001 to 2003 estimated on the basis of the annual National Sample Survey on Population Changes. - Les données de 2001 à 2003 ont été estimées sur la base de l'enquête annuelle "National Sample Survey on

Population Changes".

27 Data for the period 1990 to 2000 have been adjusted on the basis of the Population Census of 2000. - Les données pour la période allant de 1990 à 2000 ont été ajustées à partir des résultats du recensement de la population de 2000.

28 Data for 1996 and before refer to defacto population and after 1996 dejure population. - Les données concernent la population de fait pour les années antérieures à 1996 et la population de droit pour les années postérieures.

29 Data refer to government controlled areas. - Les données se raportent aux zones contrôlées par le Gouvernement.

30 Including data for the Indian-held part of Jammu and Kashmir, the final status of which has not yet been determined. - Y compris les données pour la partie du Jammu et du Cachemire occupée par l'Inde dont le statut définitif n'a pas encore été déterminé.

31 Including data for East Jerusalem and Israeli residents in certain other territories under occupation by Israeli military forces since June 1967. - Y compris les données pour Jérusalem-Est et les résidents israéliens dans certains autres territoires occupés depuis 1967 par les forces armées israéliennes.

32 Excluding diplomatic personnel outside the country and foreign military and civilian personnel and their dependants stationed in the area. - Non compris le personnel diplomatique hors du pays ni les militaires et agents civils étrangers en poste sur le territoire et les membres de leur famille les accompagnant.

33 Excluding data for Jordanian territory under occupation since June 1967 by Israeli military forces. Excluding foreigners, including registered Palestinian refugees. - Non compris les données pour le territoire jordanien occupé depuis juin 1967 par les forces armées israéliennes. Non compris les étrangers, mais y compris les réfugiés de Palestine enregistrés.

34 For 1994, excluding alien armed forces, civilian aliens employed by armed forces, foreign diplomatic personnel and their dependants and Korean diplomatic personnel and their dependants outside the country. - Pour 1994, non compris les militaires étrangers, les civils étrangers employés par les forces armées, le personnel diplomatique étranger et les membres de leur famille les accompagnant et le personnel diplomatique coréen hors du pays et les membres de leurs familles les accompagnant.

35 Excluding data for the Pakistan-held part of Jammu and Kashmir, the final status of which has not yet been determined. - Non compris les données concernant la partie du Jammu et Cachemire occupée par le Pakistan dont le statut définitif n'a pas été déterminé.

36 Including Palestinian refugees. - Y compris les réfugiés de Palestine.

37 Comprising 7 sheikdoms of Abu Dhabi, Dubai, Sharjah, Ajaman, Umm al Qaiwain, Ras al Khaimah and Fujairah, and the area lying within the modified Riyadh line as announced in October 1955. - Comprend les sept cheikhats de Abou Dhabi, Dabai, Ghârdja, Adjmân, Oumm-al-Quiwaïn, Ras al Khaïma et Foudjaïra, ainsi que la zone délimitée par la ligne de Riad modifiée comme il a été annoncé en octobre 1955.

38 Excluding Faeroe Islands and Greenland. - Non compris les Iles Féroé et Grœnland.

39 Excluding Overseas Departments, namely French Guiana, Guadeloupe, Martinique and Reunion, shown separately. De jure population but excluding diplomatic personnel outside the country and including members of alien armed forces not living in military camps and foreign diplomatic personnel not living in embassies or consulates. - Non compris les départements d'outre-mer, c'est-à-dire la Guyane française, la Guadeloupe, la Martinique et la Réunion, qui font l'objet de rubriques distinctes. Population de droit, non compris le personnel diplomatique hors du pays et y compris les militaires étrangers ne vivant pas dans des camps militaires et le personnel diplomatique étranger ne vivant pas dans les ambassades ou les consulats.

40 Excluding families of military personnel, visitors and transients. - Non compris les familles des militaires, ni les visiteurs et transients.

41 Mid-year population excludes armed forces stationed outside the country, but includes alien armed forces stationed in the area. - Les estimations au millieu de l'année non compris les militaires en garnison hors du pays, mais y compris les militaires étrangers en garnison sur le territoire.

42 Data refer to the Vatican City State. - Les données se rapportent aux Etat du Saint-Siège.

43 Including work and resident permit holders and foreigners residing in Malta. - Y compris les titulaires de permis de travail et de permis de séjour et les étrangers résidant à Malte.

44 For 1994, including persons on the Central Register of Population (containing persons belonging to the Netherlands population but having no fixed municipality of residence). - Pour 1994, y compris les personnes inscrites sur le Registre central de la population (personnes appartenant à la population néerlandaise mais sans résidence fixe dans une des municipalités).

45 Including residents temporarily outside the country. - Y compris les résidents se trouvant temporairement hors du pays.

46 Average year data for 2000 and 2001 contain revised data according to the final results of population census 2002. - Les données annuelles moyennes pour 2000 et 2001 comportent des données révisées en fonction des résultats du recensement de 2002.

47 Excluding civilian aliens within country, but including civilian nationals temporarily outside country. - Non compris les civils étrangers dans le pays, mais y compris les civils nationaux temporairement hors du pays.

48 Including the Azores and Madeira Islands. - Y compris les Açores et Madère.

49 Data do not include information for Transnistria and the municipality of Bender. - Les données ne tiennent pas compte de l'information sur la Transnistria et la municipalité de Bender.

50 Figures were updated taking into acocunt the results of the 2002 All-Russian population census. - Les chiffres ont été calculés compte tenu des résultats du recensement de la population de la Fédération de Russie de 2002.

51 From 1998 to 2001, estimates of Kosovo and Metohia computed on the basis of natural increases from year 1997. - Entre 1998 et 2001, les estimations pour le Kosovo et la Metohia ont été calculées sur la base des incréments naturelles depuis 1997.

52 From 2002 without data for Kosovo and Metohia. - Après 2002 sans les donées pour le Kosovo and Metohie.

53 Including the Balearic and Canary Islands, and Alhucemas, Ceuta, Chafarinas, Melilla and Penon de Vélez de la Gomera. - Y compris les Baléares et les Canaries, Al Hoceima, Ceuta, les îles Zaffarines, Melilla et Penon de Vélez de la Gomera.

54 Figures for 2002 and 2003 were calculated on the base of census data 2002.- Les chiffres pour 2002 et 2003 ont été calculés à partir des résultats du recensement de 2002.

55 Starting from 1994 until 1999 data is de facto from 2000 and later data is de jure. - De 1994 à 1999, les données sont de fait, à partir de 2000 elles sont de jure.

56 Population estimates for 1994 to 2002 were revised in light of the local population studies. - Les estimations de la population pour les années 1994 à 2002 ont été révisées en fonction d'études locales.

57 Population estimates for the years 1991 to 1999 have been smoothed using the 1995 mid-decade household survey and the year 2000 census. - - L'estimation de la population a été lissée pour les années entre 1991 et 1999 en utilisant l'enquête des ménages de 1995 et le recensement de l'année 2000.

58 From 1994 till 2000, mid-year estimates have been adjusted for underenumeration, at latest census. - Entre 1994 et 2000, les estimations au millieu de l'année tiennent compte d'une ajustement destiné à compenser les lacunes du dénombrement lors du dernier recensement.

59 After 1996 data based on 1996 population census not necessarily mid year estimated. - À partir des résultats du recensement de la population de 1996, pas nécessairement des estimations en milieu d'année.

Table 6

Table 6 presents urban and total population by sex for as many years as possible between 1994 and 2003.

Description of variables: Data are from nation-wide population censuses or are estimates, some of which are based on sample surveys of population carried out among all segments of the population. The results of censuses are identified by a code following the date in the stub; sample surveys are further identified by footnotes; other data are generally estimates, the characteristics of which (*de jure* or *de facto)* are also indicated with a code.

Estimates of urban population presented in this table have been limited to countries or areas for which estimates have been based on the results of a sample survey or have been constructed by the component method from the results of a population census or sample survey. Distributions that result from the estimated total population being distributed by urban/rural residence according to percentages in each group at the time of a census or sample survey have not been included in this table.

Urban is defined according to the national census definition. The definition for each country is set forth at the end of the technical notes to this table.

Percentage computation: Percentages urban are the number of persons residing in an area defined as "urban" per 100 total population. They are calculated by the United Nations Statistics Division.

Reliability of data: Estimates that are believed to be less reliable are set in *italics* rather than in roman type. Classification in terms of reliability is based on the method of construction of the total population estimate as shown in table 3 and discussed in the technical notes for that table.

Limitations: Statistics on urban population by sex are subject to the same qualifications as have been set forth for population statistics in general, as discussed in section 3 of the Technical Notes.

The basic limitations imposed by variations in the definition of the total population and in the degree of under-enumeration are perhaps more important in relation to urban/rural than to any other distributions. The classification by urban and rural is affected by variations in defining usual residence for purposes of sub-national tabulations. Likewise, the geographical differentials in the degree of under-enumeration in censuses affect the comparability of these categories throughout the table. The distinction between *de facto* and *de jure* population is also very important with respect to urban/rural distributions. The difference between the *de facto* and the *de jure* population is discussed at length in section 3.1.1 of the Technical Notes.

A most important and specific limitation, however, lies in the national differences in the definition of urban. Because the distinction between urban and rural areas is made in so many different ways, the definitions have been included at the end of this table. The definitions are necessarily brief and, where the classification as urban involves administrative civil divisions, they are often given in the terminology of the particular country or area. As a result of variations in terminology, it may appear that differences between countries or areas are greater than they actually are. On the other hand, similar or identical terms (for example, town, village, district) as used in different countries or areas may have quite different meanings.

It will be seen from an examination of the definitions that they fall roughly into three major types: (1) classification of localities as urban based on size; (2) classification of administrative centres of minor civil divisions as urban and the remainder of the division as rural; and (3) classification of minor civil divisions on a set of criteria, which may include type of local government, number of inhabitants or proportion of population engaged in agriculture.

The designation of areas as urban or rural is so closely bound to historical, political, cultural, and administrative considerations that the process of developing uniform definitions and procedures moves very slowly. Not only do the definitions differ from one country or area to the other, but, they may also no longer reflect the original intention for distinguishing urban from rural. The criteria once established on the basis of administrative subdivisions (as most of these are) become fixed and resistant to change. For this reason, comparisons of time-series data may be severely affected because the definitions used become outdated. Special care must be taken in comparing data from censuses with those from sample surveys because the definitions of urban used may differ.

Despite their shortcomings, however, statistics on urban and rural population are useful in describing the diversity within the population of a country or area.

The definition of urban/rural areas is based on both qualitative and quantitative criteria that may include any combination of the following: size of population, population density, distance between built-up areas, predominant type of economic activity, conformity to legal or administrative status and urban characteristics such as specific services and facilities[1]. Although statistics classified by urban/rural areas are widely available, no international standard definition appears to be possible at this time since the meaning differs from one country or area to another. The urban/rural classification of population used here is reported according to the national definition, as indicated in a footnote to this table and described in detail in the technical notes for table 2 of the Historical Supplement[2].

Earlier data: Urban and total population by sex have been shown in previous issues of the Demographic Yearbook. For information on specific years covered, readers should consult the Historical Index.

DEFINITION OF "URBAN"

AFRICA

Botswana: Agglomeration of 5 000 or more inhabitants where 75 per cent of the economic activity is non-agricultural.
Burundi: Commune of Bujumbura.
Comoros: Administrative centres of prefectures and localities of 5 000 or more inhabitants.
Egypt: Governorates of Cairo, Alexandria, Port Said, Ismailia, Suez, frontier governorates and capitals of other governorates, as well as district capitals (Markaz).
Equatorial Guinea: District centres and localities with 300 dwellings and/or 1 500 inhabitants or more.
Ethiopia: Localities of 2 000 or more inhabitants.
Liberia: Localities of 2 000 or more inhabitants.
Malawi: All townships and town planning areas and all district centres.
Mauritius: Towns with proclaimed legal limits.
Senegal: Agglomerations of 10 000 or more inhabitants.
South Africa: Places with some form of local authority.
Sudan: Localities of administrative and/or commercial importance or with population of 5 000 or more inhabitants.
Swaziland: Localities proclaimed as urban.
Tunisia: Population living in communes.
United Republic of Tanzania: 16 gazetted townships.
Zambia: Localities of 5 000 or more inhabitants, the majority of whom all depend on non-agricultural activities.

AMERICA, NORTH

Canada: Places of 1 000 or more inhabitants, having a population density of 400 or more per square kilometre.
Costa Rica: Administrative centres of cantons.
Cuba: Population living in a nucleus of 2 000 or more inhabitants.
Dominican Republic: Administrative centres of municipalities and municipal districts, some of which include suburban zones of rural character.
El Salvador: Administrative centres of municipalities.
Greenland: Localities of 200 or more inhabitants.
Guatemala: Municipality of Guatemala Department and officially recognized centres of other departments and municipalities.
Haiti: Administrative centres of communes.
Honduras: Localities of 2 000 or more inhabitants, having essentially urban characteristics.
Mexico: Localities of 2 500 or more inhabitants.
Nicaragua: Administrative centres of municipalities and localities of 1 000 or more inhabitants with streets and electric light.
Panama: Localities of 1 500 or more inhabitants having essentially urban characteristics. Beginning 1970, localities of 1 500 or more inhabitants with such urban characteristics as streets, water supply systems, sewerage systems and electric light.
Puerto Rico: Agglomerations of 2 500 or more inhabitants, generally having population densities of 1 000 persons per square mile or more. Two types of urban areas: urbanized areas of 50 000 or more inhabitants and urban clusters of at least 2 500 and less than 50 000 inhabitants.
United States: Agglomerations of 2 500 or more inhabitants, generally having population densities of 1 000 persons per square mile or more. Two types of urban areas: urbanized areas of 50 000 or more inhabitants and urban clusters of at least 2 500 and less than 50 000 inhabitants.
U.S. Virgin Islands: Agglomerations of 2 500 or more inhabitants, generally having population densities of 1 000 persons per square mile or more. Two types of urban areas: urbanized areas of 50 000 or more inhabitants and urban clusters of at least 2 500 and less than 50 000 inhabitants. (As of Census 2000, no urbanized areas are identified in the U.S. Virgin Islands.)

AMERICA, SOUTH

Argentina: Populated centres with 2 000 or more inhabitants.
Bolivia: Localities of 2 000 or more inhabitants.
Brazil: Urban and suburban zones of administrative centres of municipalities and districts.
Chile: Populated centres which have definite urban characteristics such as certain public and municipal services.
Ecuador: Capitals of provinces and cantons.
Falkland Islands (Malvinas): Town of Stanley.
Paraguay: Cities, towns and administrative centres of departments and districts.
Peru: Populated centres with 100 or more dwellings.
Suriname: Paramaribo town.
Uruguay: Cities.
Venezuela: Centres with a population of 1 000 or more inhabitants.

ASIA

Armenia: Cities and urban-type localities, officially designated as such, usually according to the criteria of number of inhabitants and predominance of agricultural, or number of non-agricultural workers and their families.
Azerbaijan: Cities and urban-type localities, officially designated as such, usually according to the criteria of number of inhabitants and predominance of agricultural, or number of non-agricultural workers and their families.
Bahrain: Communes or villages of 2 500 or more inhabitants.
Cambodia: Towns.
China: Cities only refer to the cities proper of those designated by the State Council. In the case of cities with district establishment, the city proper refers to the whole administrative area of the district if its population density is 1 500 people per kilometre or higher; or the seat of the district government and other areas of streets under the administration of the district if the population density is less than 1 500 people per kilometre. In the case of cities without district establishment, the city proper refers to the seat of the city government and other areas of streets under the administration of the city. For the city district with the population density below 1 500 people per kilometre and the city without district establishment, if the urban construction of the district or city government seat has extended to some part of the neighboring designated town(s) or township(s), the city proper does include the whole administrative area of the town(s) or township(s).
Cyprus: Urban areas are those defined by local town plans.
Georgia: Cities and urban-type localities, officially designated as such, usually according to the criteria of number of inhabitants and predominance of agricultural, or number of non-agricultural workers and their families.
India: Towns (places with municipal corporation, municipal area committee, town committee, notified area committee or cantonment board); also, all places having 5 000 or more inhabitants, a density of not less than 1 000 persons per square mile or 400 per square kilometre, pronounced urban characteristics and at least three fourths of the adult male population employed in pursuits other than agriculture.
Indonesia: Places with urban characteristics.
Iran (Islamic Republic of): Every district with a municipality.
Israel: All settlements of more than 2 000 inhabitants, except those where at least one third of households, participating in the civilian labour force, earn their living from agriculture.
Japan: City (shi) having 50 000 or more inhabitants with 60 per cent or more of the houses located in the main built-up areas and 60 per cent or more of the population (including their dependants) engaged in manufacturing, trade or other urban type of business. Alternatively, a shi having urban facilities and conditions as defined by the prefectural order is considered as urban.
Kazakhstan: Cities and urban-type localities, officially designated as such, usually according to the criteria of number of inhabitants and predominance of agricultural, or number of non-agricultural workers and their families.
Korea, Republic of: Population living in cities irrespective of size of population.
Kyrgyzstan: Cities and urban-type localities, officially designated as such, usually according to the criteria of number of inhabitants and predominance of agricultural, or number of non-agricultural workers and their families.
Malaysia: Gazetted areas with population of 10 000 and more.
Maldives: Malé, the capital.
Mongolia: Capital and district centres.
Pakistan: Places with municipal corporation, town committee or cantonment.
Sri Lanka: Urban sector comprises of all municipal and urban council areas.
Syrian Arab Republic: Cities, Mohafaza centres and Mantika centres, and communities with 20 000 or more inhabitants.
Tajikistan: Cities and urban-type localities, officially designated as such, usually according to the criteria of number of inhabitants and predominance of agricultural, or number of non-agricultural workers and their families.
Thailand: Municipal areas.
Turkey: Population of the localities within the municipality limits of administrative centres of provinces and districts.

Turkmenistan: Cities and urban-type localities, officially designated as such, usually according to the criteria of number of inhabitants and predominance of agricultural, or number of non-agricultural workers and their families.

Uzbekistan: Cities and urban-type localities, officially designated as such, usually according to the criteria of number of inhabitants and predominance of agricultural, or number of non-agricultural workers and their families.

Viet Nam: Urban areas include inside urban districts of cities, urban quarters and towns. All other local administrative units (communes) belong to rural areas.

EUROPE

Albania: Towns and other industrial centres of more than 400 inhabitants.

Austria: Communes of more than 5 000 inhabitants.

Belarus: Cities and urban-type localities, officially designated as such, usually according to the criteria of number of inhabitants and predominance of agricultural, or number of non-agricultural workers and their families.

Bulgaria: Towns, that is, localities legally established as urban.

Czech Republic: Localities with 2 000 or more inhabitants.

Estonia: Cities and urban-type localities, officially designated as such, usually according to the criteria of number of inhabitants and predominance of agricultural, or number of non-agricultural workers and their families.

Finland: Urban communes. 1970: Localities.

France: Communes containing an agglomeration of more than 2 000 inhabitants living in contiguous houses or with not more than 200 metres between houses, also communes of which the major portion of the population is part of a multicommunal agglomeration of this nature.

Greece: Population of municipalities and communes in which the largest population centre has 10 000 or more inhabitants. Including also the population of the 18 urban agglomerations, as these were defined at the census of 1991, namely: Greater Athens, Thessaloniki, Patra, Iraklio, Volos, Chania, Irannina, Chalkida, Agrinio, Kalamata, Katerini, Kerkyra, Salamina, Chios, Egio, Rethymno, Ermoupolis, and Sparti.

Hungary: Budapest and all legally designated towns.

Iceland: Localities of 200 or more inhabitants.

Ireland: Cities and towns including suburbs of 1 500 or more inhabitants.

Latvia: Cities and urban-type localities, officially designated as such, usually according to the criteria of number of inhabitants and predominance of agricultural, or number of non-agricultural workers and their families.

Lithuania: Urban population refers to persons who live in cities and towns, i.e., the population areas with closely built permanent dwellings and with the resident population of more than 3 000 of which 2/3 of employees work in industry, social infrastructure and business. In a number of towns the population may be less than 3 000 since these areas had already the states of "town" before the law was enforced (July 1994)

Netherlands: Urban: Municipalities with a population of 2 000 and more inhabitants. Semi-urban: Municipalities with a population of less than 2 000 but with not more than 20 per cent of their economically active male population engaged in agriculture, and specific residential municipalities of commuters.

Norway: Localities of 200 or more inhabitants.

Poland: Towns and settlements of urban type, e.g. workers' settlements, fishermen's settlements, health resorts.

Portugal: Agglomeration of 10 000 or more inhabitants.

Republic of Moldova: Cities and urban-type localities, officially designated as such, usually according to the criteria of number of inhabitants and predominance of agricultural, or number of non-agricultural workers and their families.

Romania: Cities, municipalities and other towns.

Russian Federation: Cities and urban-type localities, officially designated as such, usually according to the criteria of number of inhabitants and predominance of agricultural, or number of non-agricultural workers and their families.

Slovakia: 138 cities with 5 000 inhabitants or more.

Spain: Localities of 2 000 or more inhabitants.

Switzerland: Communes of 10 000 or more inhabitants, including suburbs.

Ukraine: Cities and urban-type localities, officially designated as such, usually according to the criteria of number of inhabitants and predominance of agricultural, or number of non-agricultural workers and their families.

OCEANIA

American Samoa: Agglomerations of 2 500 or more inhabitants, generally having population densities of 1 000 persons per square mile or more. Two types of urban areas: urbanized areas of 50 000 or more inhabitants and urban clusters of at least 2 500 and less than 50 000 inhabitants. (As of Census 2000, no urbanized areas are identified in American Samoa.)

Guam: Agglomerations of 2 500 or more inhabitants, generally having population densities of 1 000 persons per square mile or more, referred to as "urban clusters".

New Caledonia: Nouméa and communes of Païta, Nouvel Dumbéa and Mont-Dore.

New Zealand: All cities, plus boroughs, town districts, townships and country towns with a population of 1 000 or more.

Northern Mariana Islands: Agglomerations of 2 500 or more inhabitants, generally having population densities of 1 000 persons per square mile or more. Two types of urban areas: urbanized areas of 50 000 or more inhabitants and urban clusters of at least 2 500 and less than 50 000 inhabitants.
Vanuatu: Luganville centre and Vila urban.

NOTES

[1] For further information, see *Social and Demographic Statistics: Classifications of Size and Type of Locality and Urban/Rural Areas.* E/CN.3/551, United Nations, New York, 1980.

[2] *Demographic Yearbook: Historical Supplement 1948-1997, CD-ROM Special Issue*, Sales No. E99.XIII.12, United Nations, 1997.

Tableau 6

Le tableau 6 présente des données sur la population urbaine et la population totale selon le sexe pour le plus grand nombre possible d'années entre 1994 et 2003.

Description des variables : Les données proviennent de recensements de la population ou sont des estimations fondées, dans certains cas, sur des enquêtes par sondage portant sur toutes les couches de la population. Le code qui figure dans la deuxième colonne du tableau indique comment les données ont été obtenues ; les enquêtes par sondage sont en outre signalées par une note en fin de tableau ; toutes les autres données sont en général des estimations et la colonne « Code » indique si elles portent sur la population de fait ou la population de droit.

Les estimations de la population urbaine qui figurent dans le tableau 6 ne concernent que les pays ou zones pour lesquels les estimations se fondent sur les résultats d'une enquête par sondage ou ont été établies par la méthode des composantes à partir des résultats d'un recensement de la population ou d'une enquête par sondage. Les répartitions selon le lieu de résidence (zone urbaine ou rurale) obtenues en appliquant à l'estimation de la population totale les pourcentages enregistrés pour chaque groupe lors d'un recensement ou d'une enquête par sondage n'ont pas été reproduites dans le tableau 6.

Le sens donné au terme « urbain » est conforme aux définitions utilisées dans les recensements nationaux. La définition pour chaque pays figure à la fin des présentes notes technique.

Calcul des pourcentages : Les pourcentages de la population urbaine sont calculés par la Division de statistique de l'Organisation des Nations Unies et représentent le nombre de personnes qui vivent dans des régions considérées comme urbaines pour 100 personnes de la population totale.

Fiabilité des données : Les estimations considérées comme moins sûres sont indiquées en italique plutôt qu'en caractères romains. Le classement du point de vue de la fiabilité est fondé sur la méthode utilisée pour établir l'estimation de la population totale qui figure au tableau 3 (voir les explications dans les notes techniques relatives à ce même tableau).

Insuffisance des données : Les statistiques de la population urbaine selon le sexe appellent toutes les réserves qui ont été formulées à la section 3 des Notes techniques à propos des statistiques de la population en général.

Les limitations fondamentales imposées par les variations de la définition de la population totale et par les lacunes du recensement se font peut-être sentir davantage dans la répartition de la population en population urbaine et population rurale que dans sa répartition suivant toute autre caractéristique. De fait, des différences dans la définition du lieu de résidence habituel utilisée pour l'exploitation des données à l'échelon sous-national influent sur la classification en population urbaine et en population rurale. De même, les différences de degré de sous-dénombrement suivant la zone, à l'occasion des recensements, ont une incidence sur la comparabilité de ces deux catégories dans l'ensemble du tableau. La distinction entre population de fait et population de droit est également très importante du point de vue de la répartition de la population en population urbaine et en population rurale. Cette distinction est expliquée en détail à la section 3.1.1 des Notes techniques.

Toutefois, la difficulté la plus importante tient au fait que les pays ou zones ne sont pas d'accord sur la définition du terme « urbain ». Les distinctions faites entre « zone urbaine » et « zone rurale » varient tellement que les définitions utilisées ont été reproduites à la fin des notes techniques du tableau 6. Les définitions sont forcément brèves et, lorsque le classement en « zone urbaine » repose sur des divisions administratives, on a souvent désigné celles-ci par le nom qu'elles portent dans la zone ou le pays considéré. Par suite des variations dans la terminologie, les différences entre pays ou zones peuvent sembler plus grandes qu'elles ne le sont réellement. Il se peut aussi que des termes similaires ou identiques, tels que ville, village ou district, aient des significations très différentes selon les pays ou zones.

On constatera, en examinant les définitions adoptées par les différents pays ou zones, qu'elles peuvent être ramenées à trois types principaux : 1) les localités dépassant certaines dimensions sont classées parmi les zones urbaines ; 2) les centres administratifs de petites circonscriptions administratives sont classées parmi les zones urbaines, le reste de la circonscription étant considéré comme zone rurale ; 3) les petites divisions administratives sont classées parmi les zones urbaines selon un critère déterminé, qui peut être soit le type d'administration locale, soit le nombre d'habitants, soit le pourcentage de la population exerçant une activité agricole.

La distinction entre régions urbaines et régions rurales est si étroitement liée à des considérations d'ordre historique, politique, culturel et administratif que l'on ne peut progresser que très lentement vers des définitions et des méthodes uniformes. Non seulement les définitions sont différentes d'une zone ou d'un pays à un autre, mais on n'y retrouve parfois même plus l'intention originale de distinguer les régions rurales des régions urbaines. Lorsque la classification est fondée, en particulier, sur le critère des circonscriptions administratives (comme la plupart le sont), elle a tendance à devenir rigide avec le temps et à décourager toute modification. Pour cette raison, la comparaison des données appartenant à des séries chronologiques risque d'être gravement faussée du fait que les définitions employées sont désormais périmées. Il faut être particulièrement prudent lorsque l'on compare des données issues de recensements avec des données provenant d'enquêtes par sondage, car il se peut que les définitions du terme « urbain » auxquelles ces données se réfèrent respectivement soient différentes.

Malgré leurs insuffisances, les statistiques sur la population urbaine et rurale permettent de mettre en évidence la diversité de la population d'un pays ou d'une zone.

La distinction entre « zone urbaine » et « zone rurale » repose sur une série de critères qualitatifs aussi bien que quantitatifs, notamment l'effectif de la population, la densité de peuplement, la distance entre îlots d'habitations, le type prédominant d'activité économique, le statut juridique ou administratif, et les caractéristiques d'une agglomération urbaine, c'est-à-dire l'existence de services publics et d'équipements collectifs[1]. Bien que les statistiques différenciant les zones urbaines des zones rurales soient très répandues, il ne paraît pas possible pour le moment d'adopter une classification internationale type de ces zones, vu la diversité des interprétations nationales. La classification de la population en population urbaine et population rurale retenue ici est celle qui correspond aux définitions nationales, comme signalé par une note à la fin du tableau 6 et dans les notes techniques relatives au tableau 2 du *Supplément historique*[2].

Données publiées antérieurement : Des statistiques concernant la population urbaine et la population totale selon le sexe ont été publiées dans des éditions antérieures de l'*Annuaire démographique*. Pour plus de précisions concernant les années pour lesquelles ces données ont été publiées, se reporter à l'index historique.

DÉFINITIONS DU TERME « URBAIN »

AFRIQUE

Afrique du Sud : Zones dotées d'une administration locale.
Botswana : Agglomération de 5 000 habitants et plus dont 75 p. 100 de l'activité économique n'est pas de type agricole.
Burundi : Commune de Bujumbura.
Comores : Chefs-lieux de préfectures et localités de 5 000 habitants et plus.
Égypte : Chefs-lieux des gouvernorats du Caire, d'Alexandrie, de Port Saïd, d'Ismaïlia, de Suez ; chefs-lieux des gouvernorats frontaliers, autres chefs-lieux de gouvernorat et chefs-lieux de district (Markaz).
Éthiopie : Localités de 2 000 habitants et plus.
Guinée équatoriale : Chefs-lieux de district et localités comprenant 300 habitations et/ou 1 500 habitants et plus.
Libéria : Localités de 2 000 habitants et plus.
Malawi : Toutes les villes et zones urbanisées et tous les chefs-lieux de district.
Maurice : Villes ayant des limites officiellement définies.
République-Unie de Tanzanie : 16 townships érigées en communes.
Sénégal : Agglomérations de 10 000 habitants et plus.
Soudan : Centres administratifs et/ou commerciaux ou localités ayant une population de 5 000 habitants et plus.
Swaziland : Localités déclarées urbaines.
Tunisie : Population vivant dans les communes.
Zambie : Localités de 5 000 habitants et plus dont l'activité économique prédominante n'est pas de type agricole.

AMÉRIQUE DU NORD

Canada : Agglomérations de 1 000 habitants ou plus ayant une densité de population d'au moins 400 habitants au kilomètre carré.

Costa Rica : Chefs-lieux de canton.

Cuba : Population vivant dans des agglomérations de 2 000 habitants ou plus.

El Salvador : Chefs-lieux de municipios.

États-Unis : Agglomérations de 2 500 habitants ou plus ayant généralement une densité de population d'au moins 1 000 habitants au mile carré. Deux types de zones urbaines : zones urbanisées de 50 000 habitants ou plus et groupements urbains comptant au moins 2 500 habitants mais moins de 50 000.

Groenland : Localités d'au moins 200 habitants.

Guatemala : Municipio du département de Guatemala et centres administratifs officiels d'autres départements et municipios.

Haïti : Chefs-lieux de communes.

Honduras : Localités d'au moins 2 000 habitants ayant des caractéristiques essentiellement urbaines.

Îles Vierges américaines : Agglomérations de 2 500 habitants ou plus ayant généralement une densité de population d'au moins 1 000 habitants au mile carré. Deux types de zones urbaines : zones urbanisées de 50 000 habitants ou plus et groupements urbains comptant au moins 2 500 habitants mais moins de 50 000. (D'après les résultats du recensement de 2000, les Îles Vierges américaines ne comptent aucune zone urbanisée.)

Mexique : Localités d'au moins 2 500 habitants.

Nicaragua : Chefs-lieux de municipios et agglomérations d'au moins 1 000 habitants dotées de rues et de l'éclairage électrique.

Panama : Localités d'au moins 1 500 habitants ayant des caractéristiques essentiellement urbaines. À partir de 1970, localités de 1 500 habitants et plus présentant des caractéristiques urbaines, telles que rues, éclairage électrique, systèmes d'approvisionnement en eau et réseaux d'égouts.

Porto Rico : Agglomérations de 2 500 habitants ou plus ayant généralement une densité de population d'au moins 1 000 habitants au mile carré. Deux types de zones urbaines : zones urbanisées de 50 000 habitants ou plus et groupements urbains comptant au moins 2 500 habitants mais moins de 50 000.

République dominicaine : Chefs-lieux de municipios et districts municipaux, dont certains comprennent des zones suburbaines ayant des caractéristiques rurales.

AMÉRIQUE DU SUD

Argentine : Centres comptant au moins 2 000 habitants.

Bolivie : Localités de 2 000 habitants et plus.

Brésil : Zones urbaines et suburbaines des chefs lieux de municipalités et de districts.

Chili : Centres de peuplement ayant des caractéristiques nettement urbaines (présence de certains services publics et municipaux).

Équateur : Capitales des provinces et chefs-lieux de canton.

Îles Falkland (Malvinas) : Ville de Stanley.

Paraguay : Grandes villes, villes et chefs-lieux des départements et des districts.

Pérou : Centres de peuplement comptant plus de 100 logements.

Suriname : Ville de Paramaribo.

Uruguay : Villes.

Venezuela : Centres de 1 000 habitants et plus.

ASIE

Arménie : Grandes villes et localités de type urbain, officiellement désignées comme telles, généralement sur la base du nombre d'habitants et de la prédominance des travailleurs agricoles ou non agricoles avec leur famille.

Azerbaïdjan : Grandes villes et localités de type urbain, officiellement désignées comme telles, généralement sur la base du nombre d'habitants et de la prédominance des travailleurs agricoles ou non agricoles avec leur famille.

Bahreïn : Communes ou villages comptant au moins 2 500 habitants.

Cambodge : Villes.

Chine : Villes désignées comme telles par le Conseil d'État. Dans le cas de villes ayant rang de district, la ville s'entend de l'ensemble de la zone administrative qui relève du district si sa densité est d'au moins 1 500 habitants au kilomètre carré ou du siège des autorités du district et d'autres zones ou rues qui relèvent du district si leur densité est inférieure à 1 500 habitants au kilomètre carré. Dans le cas des villes qui n'ont pas rang de district, la ville s'entend du siège des autorités de la commune et des autres zones ou rues qui relèvent des autorités de la commune. Dans le cas des villes ayant rang de district qui comptent moins de 1 500 habitants au kilomètre carré et des villes n'ayant pas rang de district, si l'urbanisation du siège du district ou du siège des autorités de la commune a empiété sur une partie de la ou des localités voisines, la ville inclut alors l'ensemble de la zone administrative desdites localités.

Chypre : Zones désignées comme urbaines dans les plans d'urbanisme locaux.

Géorgie : Grandes villes et localités de type urbain, officiellement désignées comme telles, généralement sur la base du nombre d'habitants et de la prédominance des travailleurs agricoles ou non agricoles avec leur famille.

Inde : Villes [localités dotées d'une charte municipale, d'un comité de zone municipale, d'un comité de zone déclarée urbaine ou d'un comité de zone de regroupement (cantonment)] ; également toutes les localités qui ont une population de 5 000 habitants au moins, une densité de population d'au moins 1 000 habitants au mile carré ou 400 au kilomètre carré, des caractéristiques urbaines prononcées et où les trois quarts au moins des adultes de sexe masculin ont une occupation non agricole.

Indonésie : Localités présentant des caractéristiques urbaines.

Iran (République islamique d') : Tous les districts comptant une municipalité.

Israël : Tous les lieux comptant au moins 2 000 habitants, à l'exception de ceux où le tiers au moins des chefs de ménage faisant partie de la population civile active vivent de l'agriculture.

Japon : Villes (shi), comptant au moins 50 000 habitants, où 60 p. 100 au moins des logements sont situés dans les principales zones bâties, et dont 60 p. 100 au moins de population (y compris les personnes à charge) exercent un métier dans l'industrie, le commerce et d'autres branches d'activités essentiellement urbaines. Tout shi possédant les équipements et présentant les caractéristiques définies comme urbaines par l'administration préfectorale est également considéré comme zone urbaine.

Kazakhstan : Grandes villes et localités de type urbain, officiellement désignées comme telles, généralement sur la base du nombre d'habitants et de la prédominance des travailleurs agricoles ou non agricoles avec leur famille.

Kirghizistan : Grandes villes et localités de type urbain, officiellement désignées comme telles, généralement sur la base du nombre d'habitants et de la prédominance des travailleurs agricoles ou non agricoles avec leur famille.

Malaisie : Zones déclarées « zones urbaines » et comptant au moins 10 000 habitants.

Maldives : Malé (capitale).

Mongolie : Capitale et chefs-lieux de district.

Ouzbékistan : Grandes villes et localités de type urbain, officiellement désignées comme telles, généralement sur la base du nombre d'habitants et de la prédominance des travailleurs agricoles ou non agricoles avec leur famille.

Pakistan : Localités dotées d'une charte municipale ou d'un comité municipal et regroupements (cantonments).

République arabe syrienne : Villes, chefs-lieux de district (Mohafaza) et chefs-lieux de sous district (Mantika), et communes d'au moins 20 000 habitants.

République de Corée : Population vivant dans des villes, quel qu'en soit le nombre d'habitants.

Sri Lanka : Secteur urbain composé de toutes les zones municipales et zones dotées d'un conseil urbain.

Tadjikistan : Grandes villes et localités de type urbain, officiellement désignées comme telles, généralement sur la base du nombre d'habitants et de la prédominance des travailleurs agricoles ou non agricoles avec leur famille.

Thaïlande : Zones municipales.

Turkménistan : Grandes villes et localités de type urbain, officiellement désignées comme telles, généralement sur la base du nombre d'habitants et de la prédominance des travailleurs agricoles ou non agricoles avec leur famille.

Turquie : Population des localités se trouvant dans les limites municipales des chefs-lieux des provinces et des districts.

Viet Nam : Zones urbaines comprises à l'intérieur des districts urbains des villes ainsi que des quartiers urbains et des localités. Toutes les autres unités administratives locales (communes) sont considérées comme zones rurales.

Yémen : Définition non communiquée.

EUROPE

Albanie : Villes et autres centres industriels de plus de 400 habitants.

Autriche : Communes de plus de 5 000 habitants.

Bélarus : Grandes villes et localités de type urbain, officiellement désignées comme telles, généralement sur la base du nombre d'habitants et de la prédominance des travailleurs agricoles ou non agricoles avec leur famille.

Bulgarie : Villes, c'est-à-dire localités reconnues comme urbaines.

Espagne : Localités de 2 000 habitants et plus.

Estonie : Grandes villes et localités de type urbain, officiellement désignées comme telles, généralement sur la base du nombre d'habitants et de la prédominance des travailleurs agricoles ou non agricoles avec leur famille.

Fédération de Russie : Grandes villes et localités de type urbain, officiellement désignées comme telles, généralement sur la base du nombre d'habitants et de la prédominance des travailleurs agricoles ou non agricoles avec leur famille.

Finlande : Communes urbaines. 1970 : Localités.

France : Communes comprenant une agglomération de plus de 2 000 habitants vivant dans des habitations contiguës ou qui ne sont pas distantes les unes des autres de plus de 200 mètres et communes où la majeure partie de la population vit dans une agglomération regroupant plusieurs communes de cette nature.

Grèce : Municipalités et communes de 10 000 habitants et plus pour l'agglomération. Y compris également 18 agglomérations urbaines, selon la définition qui en a été donnée lors du recensement de 1991, à savoir : Athènes et sa banlieue, Thessalonique, Patras, Héraklion, Volos, Chania, Ioannina, Chalkida, Agrinio, Kalamata, Katerini, Kerkyra, Salamine, Chios, Egio, Rethymno, Ermoupolis et Sparte.

Hongrie : Budapest et toutes les autres localités reconnues officiellement comme urbaines.

Irlande : Localités, y compris leur banlieues, comptant 1 500 habitants ou plus.

Islande : Localités de 200 habitants et plus.

Lettonie : Grandes villes et localités de type urbain, officiellement désignées comme telles, généralement sur la base du nombre d'habitants et de la prédominance des travailleurs agricoles ou non agricoles avec leur famille.

Lituanie : Par population urbaine, on entend les personnes qui vivent dans des villes ou des localités, à savoir les zones habitées comportant des logements permanents proches les uns des autres et dont la population est d'au moins 3 000 habitants, les deux tiers desquels sont employés dans le secteur industriel, l'infrastructure sociale ou le commerce. Un certain nombre de villes peuvent compter moins de 3 000 habitants dans la mesure où elles avaient acquis le statut de ville avant l'entrée en vigueur de la nouvelle loi en juillet 1994.

Norvège : Localités de 200 habitants et plus.

Pays Bas : Zones urbaines : municipalités comptant au moins 2 000 habitants. Zones semi-urbaines : municipalités comptant moins de 2 000 habitants, mais où 20 p. 100 au maximum de la population active de sexe masculin pratiquent l'agriculture, et certaines municipalités de caractère résidentiel dont les habitants travaillent ailleurs.

Pologne : Villes et zones de type urbain, par exemple groupements de travailleurs ou de pêcheurs et stations climatiques.

Portugal : Agglomérations d'au moins 10 000 habitants.

République de Moldova : Grandes villes et localités de type urbain, officiellement désignées comme telles, généralement sur la base du nombre d'habitants et de la prédominance des travailleurs agricoles ou non agricoles avec leur famille.

République tchèque : Localités d'au moins 2 000 habitants.

Roumanie : Grandes villes, municipalités et autres villes.

Slovaquie : 138 localités comptant 5 000 habitants et plus.

Suisse : Communes de 10 000 habitants et plus, et leurs banlieues.

Ukraine : Grandes villes et localités de type urbain, officiellement désignées comme telles, généralement sur la base du nombre d'habitants et de la prédominance des travailleurs agricoles ou non agricoles avec leur famille.

OCÉANIE

Guam : Agglomérations de 2 500 habitants ou plus ayant généralement une densité de population d'au moins 1 000 habitants au mile carré et considérées comme étant des groupements urbains.

Îles Mariannes septentrionales : Agglomérations de 2 500 habitants ou plus ayant généralement une densité de population d'au moins 1 000 habitants au mile carré. Deux types de zones urbaines : zones urbanisées de 50 000 habitants ou plus et groupements urbains comptant au moins 2 500 habitants mais moins de 50 000.

Nouvelle-Calédonie : Nouméa et communes de Païta, Dumbéa et Mont-Dore.

Nouvelle-Zélande : Grandes villes, boroughs, chefs-lieux, municipalités et chefs-lieux de comté d'au moins 1 000 habitants.

Samoa américaines : Agglomérations de 2 500 habitants ou plus ayant généralement une densité de population d'au moins 1 000 habitants au mile carré. Deux types de zones urbaines : zones urbanisées de 50 000 habitants ou plus et groupements urbains comptant au moins 2 500 habitants mais moins de 50 000. (D'après les résultats du recensement de 2000, les Samoa américaines ne comptent aucune zone urbanisée.)

Vanuatu : Centre de Luganville et Port-Vila.

NOTES

[1] Pour plus de précisions, voir *Social and Demographic Statistics: Classifications of Size and Type of Locality and Urban/Rural Areas*, E/CN.3/551, publication des Nations Unies, New York, 1980.

[2] *Annuaire démographique, Supplément historique, 1948-1997*, CD-ROM, publication des Nations Unies, numéro de vente : E/F.99.XIII.12, New York, 2000.

6. Urban and total population by sex: 1994 - 2003
Population urbaine et population totale selon le sexe: 1994 - 2003

Continent, country or area and date / Continent, pays ou zone et date	Code[1]	Both sexes - Les deux sexes			Male - Masculin			Female - Féminin		
		Total	Urban - Urbaine		Total	Urban - Urbaine		Total	Urban - Urbaine	
			Number Nombre	Percent P.100		Number Nombre	Percent P.100		Number Nombre	Percent P.100
AFRICA — AFRIQUE										
Algeria - Algérie										
25 VI 1998	CDJC	29 100 867	16 966 939	58.3	14 698 589	8 563 287	58.3	14 402 278	8 403 652	58.3
Benin - Bénin										
1 VII 1994	ESDF	5 241 843	1 917 100	36.6	2 548 310	932 172	36.6	2 693 533	984 928	36.6
1 VII 1995	ESDF	5 412 160	2 003 213	37.0	2 633 479	974 914	37.0	2 778 681	1 028 299	37.0
1 VII 1996	ESDF	5 594 499	2 098 699	37.5	2 722 854	1 019 980	37.5	2 871 645	1 078 719	37.6
1 VII 1997	ESDF	5 638 987	2 177 515	38.6	...	...	...	...	...	...
1 VII 1998	ESDF	5 816 488	2 278 190	39.2	...	...	...	...	...	...
1 VII 1999	ESDF	5 990 396	2 383 244	39.8	...	...	...	...	...	...
1 VII 2000	ESDF	6 169 084	2 492 967	40.4	3 013 705	1 220 905	40.5	3 155 379	1 272 062	40.3
11 II 2002	CDJC	6 769 914	2 630 133	38.9	3 284 119	1 280 418	39.0	3 485 795	1 349 715	38.7
Botswana[2]										
1 VII 1994	ESDF	1 424 636	672 614	47.2	684 751	...	...	739 885	...	...
1 VII 1995	ESDF	1 458 828	696 282	47.7	701 603	...	...	757 225	...	...
1 VII 1996	ESDF	1 495 993	720 783	48.2	720 207	...	...	775 786	...	...
Burkina Faso										
1 VII 1994	ESDF	9 888 789	1 469 006	14.9	4 582 412	732 887	16.0	5 306 377	736 119	13.9
1 VII 1995	ESDF	10 200 453	1 534 524	15.0	4 985 642	...	...	5 214 811	...	...
Burundi										
1 VII 1994	ESDF	5 875 413	420 826	7.2	2 857 267	221 304	7.7	3 018 146	199 522	6.6
1 VII 1995	ESDF	5 981 682	437 417	7.3	2 908 737	227 568	7.8	3 072 945	209 849	6.8
1 VII 1996	ESDF	6 087 951	454 661	7.5	2 960 208	233 221	7.9	3 127 743	221 440	7.1
1 VII 1997	ESDF	6 194 220	473 284	7.6	3 011 678	240 554	8.0	3 182 542	232 730	7.3
1 VII 1998	ESDF	6 300 489	493 297	7.8	3 064 211	...	...	3 236 278	...	...
Cameroon - Cameroun										
1 VII 1997	ESDF	14 297 617	6 748 475	47.2	...	...	...	...	...	...
1 VII 1998	ESDF	14 439 000	6 960 000	48.2	...	...	...	...	...	...
Cape Verde - Cap-Vert										
16 VI 2000	CDFC	436 863	235 470	53.9	211 479	114 928	54.3	225 384	120 542	53.5
1 VII 2001	ESDF	444 683	242 484	54.5	215 288	118 351	55.0	229 395	124 133	54.1
1 VII 2002	ESDF	452 714	249 794	55.2	219 211	121 924	55.6	233 503	127 870	54.8
1 VII 2003	ESDF	460 968	257 412	55.8	223 253	125 652	56.3	237 715	131 759	55.4
Central African Republic - République centrafricaine										
8 XII 2003	CDFC	3 151 072	1 194 851	37.9	1 569 446	598 880	38.2	1 581 626	595 969	37.7
Egypt - Égypte										
1 VII 1994	ESDF	56 343 786	24 481 023	43.4	28 874 917	12 545 982	43.4	27 468 869	11 935 041	43.4
1 VII 1995	ESDF	57 509 998	24 840 066	43.2	29 428 956	12 711 132	43.2	28 081 042	12 128 934	43.2
1 VII 1996	ESDF	58 755 211	25 019 402	42.6	30 063 860	12 801 923	42.6	28 691 351	12 217 479	42.6
19 XI 1996	CDFC	59 312 914	25 286 335	42.6	30 351 390	12 957 775	42.7	28 961 524	12 328 560	42.6
1 VII 1997	ESDF	60 080 063	25 589 396	42.6	30 736 254	13 091 232	42.6	29 343 809	12 498 164	42.6
1 VII 1998	ESDF	61 340 882	26 123 481	42.6	31 379 023	13 363 507	42.6	29 961 859	12 759 974	42.6
1 VII 1999	ESDF	62 652 065	26 641 192	42.5	32 059 065	13 632 299	42.5	30 593 000	13 008 893	42.5
1 VII 2000	ESDF	63 976 000	27 204 000	42.5	32 695 000	...	...	31 281 000	...	...
1 VII 2003	ESDF	67 976 000	28 912 000	42.5	...	...	...	...	...	...
Ethiopia - Éthiopie										
11 X 1994	CDFC	53 477 265	7 323 207	13.7	26 910 698	3 534 805	13.1	26 566 567	3 788 402	14.3
1 VII 1995	ESDF	54 649 154	7 586 700	13.9	27 498 620	3 662 625	13.3	27 150 534	3 924 075	14.5
1 VII 1996	ESDF	56 372 000	7 950 000	14.1	28 344 000	3 885 000	13.7	28 028 000	4 065 000	14.5
1 VII 1997	ESDF	58 117 000	8 315 000	14.3	29 202 000	4 094 000	14.0	28 915 000	4 221 000	14.6
1 VII 1998	ESDF	59 882 000	8 691 000	14.5	30 071 000	4 299 000	14.3	29 811 000	4 392 000	14.7
1 VII 1999	ESDF	61 672 000	9 074 000	14.7	30 956 000	4 504 000	14.5	30 716 000	4 570 000	14.9
1 VII 2000	ESDF	63 494 702	9 472 971	14.9	...	...	...	...	...	...
1 VII 2001	ESDF	65 374 320	9 883 138	15.1	32 815 082	4 938 725	15.1	32 559 238	4 944 413	15.2
1 VII 2002	ESDF	67 220 000	10 307 000	15.3	33 707 000	5 134 000	15.2	33 513 000	5 173 000	15.4
Ghana										
1 VII 1995	ESDF	17 197 816	6 779 402	39.4	...	...	...	...	...	...
27 III 2000	CDFC	18 912 079	8 274 270	43.8	9 357 382	4 043 830	43.2	9 554 697	4 230 440	44.3

6. Urban and total population by sex: 1994 - 2003
Population urbaine et population totale selon le sexe: 1994 - 2003
(continued — suite)

Continent, country or area and date / Continent, pays ou zone et date	Code[1]	Both sexes - Les deux sexes			Male - Masculin			Female - Féminin		
		Total	Urban - Urbaine		Total	Urban - Urbaine		Total	Urban - Urbaine	
			Number Nombre	Percent P.100		Number Nombre	Percent P.100		Number Nombre	Percent P.100
AFRICA — AFRIQUE										
Kenya										
1 VII 1999	ESDF	29 453 024	5 429 790	18.4	14 342 209	...	...	15 110 815	...	...
24 VIII 1999	CDFC	28 686 607	3 539 888	12.3	14 205 589	1 933 437	13.6	14 481 018	1 606 451	11.1
1 VII 2000	ESDF	30 208 400	5 830 221	19.3	14 704 400	...	...	15 504 000	...	...
1 VII 2001	ESDF	30 969 900	5 977 191	19.3	15 072 100	...	...	15 897 800	...	...
1 VII 2002	ESDF	31 807 000	6 138 751	19.3	15 477 200	...	...	16 329 800	...	...
1 VII 2003	ESDF	32 692 400	6 309 633	19.3	15 907 100	...	...	16 785 300	...	...
Lesotho[3]										
14 IV 1996	CDJC	1 960 069	312 444	15.9	964 346	...	...	995 723	...	...
1 VII 2001	SSDJ	2 157 537	288 895	13.4	1 065 484	131 861	12.4	1 092 053	157 034	14.4
Liberia - Libéria										
1 VII 1994	ESDF	2 699 888	1 194 077	44.2	...	...	...	...	...	...
1 VII 1995	ESDF	2 759 714	1 231 872	44.6	...	...	...	...	...	...
1 VII 1996	ESDF	2 819 540	1 269 668	45.0	...	...	...	...	...	...
1 VII 1997	ESDF	2 879 366	1 307 463	45.4	...	...	...	...	...	...
Madagascar[4]										
1 VII 1998	ESDF	14 222 000	3 562 000	25.0	7 091 000	1 745 000	24.6	7 132 000	1 817 000	25.5
1 VII 1999	ESDF	14 650 000	3 741 000	25.5	7 306 000	1 834 000	25.1	7 343 000	1 907 000	26.0
1 VII 2000	ESDF	15 085 000	3 927 000	26.0	7 526 000	1 926 000	25.6	7 559 000	2 001 000	26.5
Malawi[4]										
1 VII 1994	ESDF	9 461 403	1 711 200	18.1	...	...	...	...	...	...
1 VII 1995	ESDF	9 787 831	1 845 900	18.9	...	...	...	...	...	...
1 VII 1996	ESDF	10 114 257	1 980 700	19.6	...	...	...	...	...	...
1 IX 1998	CDFC	9 933 868	1 435 436	14.4	4 867 563	742 839	15.3	5 066 305	692 597	13.7
Mauritius - Maurice										
1 VII 1994	ESDJ	1 112 846	483 602	43.5	...	...	...	...	...	...
1 VII 1995	ESDJ	1 122 457	486 294	43.3	...	...	...	...	...	...
1 VII 1996	ESDJ	1 133 996	489 793	43.2	...	...	...	...	...	...
1 VII 1997	ESDJ	1 148 284	494 446	43.1	571 169	244 867	42.9	577 115	249 579	43.2
1 VII 1998	ESDJ	1 160 421	498 138	42.9	576 620	246 388	42.7	583 801	251 750	43.1
1 VII 1999	ESDJ	1 175 267	502 958	42.8	583 169	248 362	42.6	592 098	254 596	43.0
1 VII 2000	ESDJ	1 186 873	506 357	42.7	588 212	249 678	42.4	598 661	256 679	42.9
2 VII 2000	CDJC	1 178 848	503 045	42.7	583 756	247 844	42.5	595 092	255 201	42.9
1 VII 2001	ESDJ	1 199 881	510 822	42.6	594 490	251 721	42.3	605 391	259 101	42.8
1 VII 2002	ESDJ	1 210 203	513 761	42.5	599 165	252 848	42.2	611 038	260 913	42.7
1 VII 2003	ESDJ	1 222 811	518 368	42.4	605 084	255 077	42.2	617 727	263 291	42.6
Morocco - Maroc										
1 VII 1994	ESDF	25 926 000	13 270 000	51.2	...	...	...	...	...	...
2 IX 1994	CDFC	26 019 280	13 356 246	51.3	12 944 517	6 632 953	51.2	13 074 763	6 723 293	51.4
1 VII 1995	ESDF	26 386 000	13 684 000	51.9	...	...	...	...	...	...
1 VII 1996	ESDF	26 848 000	14 100 000	52.5	13 357 000	...	...	13 491 000	...	...
1 VII 1997	ESDF	27 310 000	14 524 000	53.2	13 588 000	7 173 000	52.8	13 722 000	7 351 000	53.6
1 VII 1998	ESDF	27 775 000	14 957 000	53.9	13 819 000	7 373 000	53.4	13 956 000	7 584 000	54.3
1 VII 1999	ESDF	28 238 000	15 401 000	54.5	14 049 000	7 580 000	54.0	14 189 000	7 821 000	55.1
1 VII 2000	ESDF	28 705 000	15 849 000	55.2	14 281 000	7 787 000	54.5	14 424 000	8 062 000	55.9
1 VII 2001	ESDF	29 170 000	16 307 000	55.9	14 512 000	8 000 000	55.1	14 658 000	8 307 000	56.7
1 VII 2002	ESDF	29 631 000	16 772 000	56.6	14 742 000	8 217 000	55.7	14 889 000	8 555 000	57.5
1 VII 2003	ESDF	30 088 000	17 244 000	57.3	14 972 000	8 438 000	56.4	15 116 000	8 806 000	58.3
Mozambique[5]										
1 VIII 1997	CDFC	16 099 246	4 601 132	28.6	7 714 306	2 274 116	29.5	8 384 940	2 327 016	27.8
Namibia - Namibie[6]										
27 VIII 2001	CDFC	1 830 330	603 612	33.0	887 721	300 358	33.8	942 572	303 236	32.2
Rwanda										
16 VIII 2002	CDJC	8 128 553	1 372 604	16.9	3 879 448	727 172	18.7	4 249 105	645 432	15.2
Saint Helena ex. dep. - Sainte-Hélène sans dép.										
8 III 1998	CDFC	5 157	884	17.1	2 612	452	17.3	2 545	432	17.0
Sierra Leone										
1 VII 1994	ESDF	4 322 516	1 508 234	34.9	...	...	...	...	...	...
1 VII 1995	ESDF	4 421 481	1 551 087	35.1	...	...	...	...	...	...
1 VII 1996	ESDF	4 522 314	1 594 408	35.3	...	...	...	...	...	...

6. Urban and total population by sex: 1994 - 2003
Population urbaine et population totale selon le sexe: 1994 - 2003
(continued — suite)

Continent, country or area and date / Continent, pays ou zone et date	Code[1]	Both sexes - Les deux sexes			Male - Masculin			Female - Féminin		
		Total	Urban - Urbaine		Total	Urban - Urbaine		Total	Urban - Urbaine	
			Number Nombre	Percent P.100		Number Nombre	Percent P.100		Number Nombre	Percent P.100
AFRICA — AFRIQUE										
Sierra Leone										
1 VII 1997	ESDF	4 625 013	1 638 198	35.4	...	...	...	...	...	...
1 VII 1998	ESDF	4 729 579	1 682 456	35.6	...	...	...	...	...	...
1 VII 1999	ESDF	4 836 011	1 727 184	35.7	...	...	...	...	...	...
1 VII 2000	ESDF	4 944 310	1 772 379	35.8	...	...	...	...	...	...
1 VII 2001	ESDF	5 054 476	1 818 044	36.0	...	...	...	...	...	...
1 VII 2002	ESDF	5 166 508	1 864 177	36.1	...	...	...	...	...	...
1 VII 2003	ESDF	5 280 406	1 910 779	36.2	...	...	...	...	...	...
Somalia - Somalie[7]										
1 VII 2002	SSDF	6 799 079	2 310 817	34.0	3 499 523	1 168 410	33.4	3 299 556	1 142 407	34.6
South Africa - Afrique du Sud[8,9]										
1 VII 1996	ESDF	40 342 300	21 659 400	53.7	19 394 900	10 604 600	54.7	20 947 400	11 054 800	52.8
10 X 1996	CDFC	40 583 573	21 781 807	53.7	19 520 887	10 667 927	54.6	21 062 686	11 113 880	52.8
1 VII 1997	ESDF	41 226 700	22 107 800	53.6	19 857 000	10 836 700	54.6	21 369 700	11 271 100	52.7
1 VII 1998	ESDF	42 130 500	22 565 300	53.6	20 330 100	11 073 800	54.5	21 800 400	11 491 500	52.7
1 VII 1999	ESDF	43 054 306	23 032 381	53.5	20 814 425	11 316 037	54.4	22 239 881	11 716 344	52.7
1 VII 2000	ESDF	43 685 699	23 125 194	52.9	21 016 530	11 273 108	53.6	22 669 169	11 852 086	52.3
Swaziland										
1 VII 1994	ESDF	879 081	217 309	24.7	410 924	108 790	26.5	468 157	108 519	23.2
1 VII 1995	ESDF	908 119	225 074	24.8	...	...	...	...	...	...
1 VII 1996	ESDF	937 747	237 368	25.3	438 334	118 562	27.0	499 413	118 806	23.8
11 V 1997	CDFC	929 718	214 428	23.1	440 154	106 256	24.1	489 564	108 172	22.1
Tunisia - Tunisie										
20 IV 1994	CDFC	8 785 711	5 361 927	61.0	4 439 289	2 717 168	61.2	4 346 422	2 644 759	60.8
Uganda - Ouganda										
1 VII 1995	ESDF	19 262 626	2 587 105	13.4	9 504 221	...	...	9 758 406	...	...
1 VII 1996	ESDF	19 847 689	2 764 579	13.9	9 802 558	...	...	10 045 131	...	...
1 VII 1997	ESDF	20 752 400	2 732 878	13.2	...	...	...	...	...	...
1 VII 1998	ESDF	21 467 200	2 878 135	13.4	...	...	...	...	...	...
1 VII 1999	ESDF	22 206 600	3 026 742	13.6	...	...	...	...	...	...
1 VII 2000	ESDF	22 971 500	3 178 692	13.8	...	...	...	...	...	...
12 IX 2002	CDFC	24 442 084	2 999 387	12.3	11 929 803	1 449 684	12.2	12 512 281	1 549 703	12.4
Zambia - Zambie										
1 VII 1995	ESDF	9 112 045	3 499 309	38.4	...	...	...	...	...	...
1 VII 2000	ESDF	9 337 425	3 347 069	35.8	4 594 290	1 662 739	36.2	4 743 135	1 684 330	35.5
25 X 2000	CDFC	9 885 591	3 426 862	34.7	4 946 298	1 725 359	34.9	4 939 293	1 701 503	34.4
Zimbabwe										
18 VIII 1997	SSDF	11 789 274	3 826 580	32.5	5 647 090	1 906 476	33.8	6 142 184	1 920 104	31.3
AMERICA, NORTH — AMERIQUE DU NORD										
Belize										
1 VII 1994	ESDF	211 000	106 975	50.7	104 000	52 000	50.0	107 000	54 975	51.4
1 VII 1995	ESDF	216 500	109 880	50.8	107 500	54 255	50.5	109 000	55 625	51.0
1 VII 1996	ESDF	222 000	113 640	51.2	111 000	54 440	49.0	111 000	59 200	53.3
1 VII 1997	ESDF	230 000	115 975	50.4	114 500	55 350	48.3	115 500	60 625	52.5
1 VII 1998	ESDF	238 500	120 110	50.4	118 500	57 095	48.2	120 000	63 015	52.5
1 VII 1999	ESDF	243 055	118 125	48.6	122 745	58 375	47.6	120 310	59 750	49.7
12 V 2000	CDFC	240 204	114 541	47.7	121 278	56 565	46.6	118 926	57 976	48.7
1 VII 2000	ESDF	249 800	121 455	48.6	126 080	59 985	47.6	123 720	61 470	49.7
1 VII 2001	ESDF	257 310	125 830	48.9	129 890	62 160	47.9	127 420	63 670	50.0
1 VII 2002	ESDF	265 200	130 500	49.2	133 900	64 400	48.1	131 300	66 100	50.3
1 VII 2003	ESDF	273 700	135 600	49.5	138 300	67 000	48.4	135 400	68 600	50.7
Canada[4,10,11]										
1 VII 1994	ESDJ	28 999 006	22 433 823	77.4	...	...	...	...	...	...
1 VII 1995	ESDJ	29 302 091	22 742 313	77.6	...	...	...	...	...	...
14 V 1996	CDJC	28 846 760	22 461 210	77.9	14 170 030	10 902 295	76.9	14 676 735	11 558 910	78.8
1 VII 1996	ESDJ	29 610 757	23 056 084	77.9	...	...	...	...	...	...
1 VII 1997	ESDJ	29 907 172	23 397 908	78.2	...	...	...	...	...	...
1 VII 1998	ESDJ	30 157 082	23 704 015	78.6	...	...	...	...	...	...

6. Urban and total population by sex: 1994 - 2003
Population urbaine et population totale selon le sexe: 1994 - 2003
(continued — suite)

Continent, country or area and date / Continent, pays ou zone et date	Code[1]	Both sexes - Les deux sexes			Male - Masculin			Female - Féminin		
		Total	Urban - Urbaine		Total	Urban - Urbaine		Total	Urban - Urbaine	
			Number Nombre	Percent P.100		Number Nombre	Percent P.100		Number Nombre	Percent P.100
AMERICA, NORTH — AMERIQUE DU NORD										
Canada[4,10,11]										
15 V 2001	CDJC	30 007 095	23 908 105	79.7	14 706 850	11 594 915	78.8	15 300 245	12 313 190	80.5
Costa Rica										
1 VII 1994	ESDJ	3 070 918	1 352 375	44.0	...	...	...	...	...	...
1 VII 1995	ESDJ	3 136 020	1 369 421	43.7	...	...	...	...	...	...
1 VII 1996	ESDJ	3 202 440	1 392 892	43.5	...	...	...	...	...	...
1 VII 1997	ESDJ	3 270 700	1 419 407	43.4	...	...	...	...	...	...
1 VII 1998	ESDJ	3 340 909	1 440 272	43.1	...	...	...	...	...	...
1 VII 1999	ESDJ	3 412 613	1 576 288	46.2	...	...	...	...	...	...
26 VI 2000	CDJC	3 810 179	2 249 414	59.0	1 902 614	1 096 248	57.6	1 907 565	1 153 166	60.5
1 VII 2000	ESDJ	3 486 048	1 644 638	47.2	...	...	...	...	...	...
1 VII 2001	ESDJ	3 906 742	2 305 723	59.0	...	...	...	...	...	...
1 VII 2002	ESDJ	3 997 883	2 359 158	59.0	...	...	...	...	...	...
1 VII 2003	ESDJ	4 088 773	2 412 542	59.0	2 017 467	1 167 617	57.9	2 071 306	1 244 925	60.1
Cuba										
1 VII 1994	ESDF	10 950 100	8 145 869	74.4	5 502 852	4 010 950	72.9	5 447 248	4 134 919	75.9
1 VII 1995	ESDF	10 978 148	8 151 963	74.3	5 519 755	...	...	5 458 393	...	...
1 VII 1996	ESDF	11 005 866	8 200 237	74.5	5 533 477	...	...	5 472 389	...	...
1 VII 1997	ESDF	11 065 878	8 295 762	75.0	5 541 552	4 069 554	73.4	5 524 326	4 226 208	76.5
1 VII 1998	ESDF	11 116 514	8 359 529	75.2	5 563 304	4 098 448	73.7	5 553 210	4 261 081	76.7
1 VII 1999	ESDF	11 094 972	8 363 577	75.4	5 509 823	4 059 126	73.7	5 585 149	4 304 451	77.1
1 VII 2000	ESDF	11 129 665	8 417 965	75.6	5 548 671	4 111 545	74.1	5 580 994	4 306 420	77.2
1 VII 2001	ESDF	11 157 364	8 467 052	75.9	5 586 835	4 163 395	74.5	5 570 529	4 303 657	77.3
1 VII 2002	ESDF	11 184 457	8 483 688	75.9	5 601 052	4 172 285	74.5	5 583 405	4 311 403	77.2
1 VII 2003	ESDF	11 215 229	8 501 628	75.8	5 616 275	4 181 234	74.4	5 598 954	4 320 394	77.2
Dominican Republic - République dominicaine										
1 VII 1994	ESDF	*7 461 138*	*4 212 997*	*56.5*	...	...	...	...	...	...
1 VII 1995	ESDF	*7 632 744*	*4 335 174*	*56.8*	...	...	...	...	...	...
1 VII 1996	ESDF	*7 808 297*	*4 460 894*	*57.1*	...	...	...	...	...	...
1 VII 1997	ESDF	*7 987 888*	*4 590 259*	*57.5*	...	...	...	...	...	...
1 VII 1998	ESDF	*8 171 610*	*4 723 377*	*57.8*	...	...	...	...	...	...
1 VII 1999	ESDF	*8 359 557*	*4 860 355*	*58.1*	...	...	...	...	...	...
1 VII 2000	ESDF	*8 551 826*	*5 001 305*	*58.5*	...	...	...	...	...	...
1 VII 2001	ESDF	*8 748 518*	*5 146 343*	*58.8*	...	...	...	...	...	...
1 VII 2002	ESDF	*8 562 541*	*5 446 704*	*63.6*	...	...	...	...	...	...
20 X 2002	CDJC	8 562 541	5 446 704	63.6	4 265 215	2 648 064	62.1	4 297 326	2 798 640	65.1
1 VII 2003	ESDF	*8 714 954*	*5 620 999*	*64.5*	...	...	...	...	...	...
El Salvador										
1 VII 1995	ESDF	5 668 605	3 216 533	56.7	2 776 269	1 542 163	55.5	2 892 336	1 674 370	57.9
1 VII 1996	ESDF	5 787 093	3 305 082	57.1	2 835 313	1 585 186	55.9	2 951 780	1 719 896	58.3
1 VII 1997	ESDF	5 908 460	3 394 950	57.5	2 896 114	1 629 017	56.2	3 012 346	1 765 933	58.6
1 VII 1998	ESDF	6 031 326	3 485 465	57.8	2 957 835	1 673 250	56.6	3 073 491	1 812 215	59.0
1 VII 1999	ESDF	6 154 311	3 575 956	58.1	3 019 645	1 717 489	56.9	3 134 666	1 858 467	59.3
1 VII 2000	ESDF	6 276 037	3 665 747	58.4	3 080 704	1 761 327	57.2	3 195 333	1 904 420	59.6
1 VII 2001	ESDF	6 396 890	3 754 903	58.7	3 141 208	1 804 804	57.5	3 255 682	1 950 099	59.9
1 VII 2002	ESDF	6 517 798	3 843 878	59.0	3 201 720	1 848 194	57.7	3 316 078	1 995 684	60.2
1 VII 2003	ESDF	6 638 168	3 932 569	59.2	3 261 938	1 891 429	58.0	3 376 230	2 041 140	60.5
Greenland - Groenland[12]										
1 VII 1994	ESDJ	55 576	44 902	80.8	29 665	23 767	80.1	25 911	21 135	81.6
1 VII 1995	ESDJ	55 798	45 228	81.1	29 762	23 930	80.4	26 036	21 298	81.8
1 VII 1996	ESDJ	55 917	45 330	81.1	29 828	23 993	80.4	26 089	21 337	81.8
1 VII 1997	ESDJ	56 024	45 420	81.1	29 872	24 043	80.5	26 152	21 378	81.7
1 VII 1998	ESDJ	56 076	45 489	81.1	29 904	24 092	80.6	26 172	21 397	81.8
1 VII 1999	ESDJ	56 087	45 523	81.2	29 941	24 189	80.8	26 146	21 334	81.6
1 VII 2000	CDJC	56 124	45 714	81.5	29 989	24 257	80.9	26 135	21 457	82.1
1 VII 2001	ESDJ	56 394	46 125	81.8	30 102	24 454	81.2	26 292	21 671	82.4
1 VII 2002	ESDJ	56 609	46 462	82.1	30 215	24 626	81.5	26 394	21 836	82.7

6. Urban and total population by sex: 1994 - 2003
Population urbaine et population totale selon le sexe: 1994 - 2003
(continued — suite)

Continent, country or area and date / Continent, pays ou zone et date	Code[1]	Both sexes - Les deux sexes			Male - Masculin			Female - Féminin		
		Total	Urban - Urbaine Number Nombre	Urban - Urbaine Percent P.100	Total	Urban - Urbaine Number Nombre	Urban - Urbaine Percent P.100	Total	Urban - Urbaine Number Nombre	Urban - Urbaine Percent P.100
AMERICA, NORTH — AMERIQUE DU NORD										
Greenland - Groenland[12]										
1 VII 2003	ESDJ	56 766	46 746	82.3	30 292	24 771	81.8	26 474	21 975	83.0
Haiti - Haïti										
1 VII 1994	ESDJ	7 041 445	2 251 351	32.0	...	...	...	...	...	...
1 VII 1995	ESDJ	7 180 294	2 338 842	32.6	...	...	...	...	...	...
1 VII 1996	ESDJ	7 336 028	2 433 878	33.2	...	...	...	...	...	...
1 VII 1997	ESDJ	7 491 762	2 531 060	33.8	...	...	...	...	...	...
1 VII 1998	ESDJ	7 647 496	2 630 383	34.4	...	...	...	...	...	...
1 VII 1999	ESDJ	7 803 230	2 731 843	35.0	...	...	...	...	...	...
1 VII 2000	ESDJ	7 958 964	2 835 433	35.6	...	...	...	...	...	...
Honduras										
1 VII 1994	ESDF	5 460 172	2 302 736	42.2	...	...	...	...	...	...
1 VII 1995	ESDF	5 605 581	2 393 858	42.7	...	...	...	...	...	...
1 VII 1996	ESDF	5 754 845	2 488 850	43.2	...	...	...	...	...	...
1 VII 1997	ESDF	5 908 069	2 587 337	43.8	...	...	...	...	...	...
1 VII 1998	ESDF	6 056 942	2 689 721	44.4	...	...	...	...	...	...
1 VII 1999	ESDF	6 211 412	2 796 156	45.0	...	...	...	...	...	...
1 VII 2000	ESDF	6 369 188	2 907 091	45.6	...	...	...	...	...	...
1 VII 2001	ESDF	6 530 331	3 022 150	46.3	...	...	...	...	...	...
1 VII 2002	ESDF	6 694 761	3 140 880	46.9	...	...	...	...	...	...
1 VII 2003	ESDF	6 860 842	3 260 934	47.5	3 388 874	1 555 369	45.9	3 471 968	1 705 565	49.1
Jamaica - Jamaïque[13]										
1 VII 1999	ESDJ	2 574 314	1 266 233	49.2	1 338 022	637 675	47.7	1 236 292	628 558	50.8
1 VII 2000	ESDJ	2 589 395	1 274 076	49.2	1 345 847	641 625	47.7	1 243 548	632 451	50.9
1 VII 2001	ESDJ	2 604 767	1 282 106	49.2	1 353 822	645 669	47.7	1 250 945	636 437	50.9
10 IX 2001	CDJC	2 607 632	1 353 240	51.9	1 283 547	645 374	50.3	1 324 085	707 866	53.5
1 VII 2002	ESDJ	2 617 459	1 288 981	49.2	1 360 398	649 131	47.7	1 257 061	639 850	50.9
1 VII 2003	ESDJ	2 630 368	1 295 995	49.3	1 367 086	652 663	47.7	1 263 282	643 332	50.9
Mexico - Mexique										
1 VII 1994	ESDJ	92 050 669	70 486 549	76.6	...	...	...	...	...	...
1 VII 1995	ESDJ	93 613 039	71 958 714	76.9	...	...	...	...	...	...
5 XI 1995	SSDJ	91 158 290	67 003 515	73.5	...	...	...	...	...	...
1 VII 1996	ESDJ	95 109 877	73 385 379	77.2	...	...	...	...	...	...
1 VII 1997	ESDJ	96 540 726	74 760 965	77.4	...	...	...	...	...	...
1 VII 1998	ESDJ	97 920 976	76 083 002	77.7	...	...	...	...	...	...
1 VII 1999	ESDJ	99 265 683	77 348 051	77.9	...	...	...	...	...	...
14 II 2000	CDJC	97 483 412	72 759 822	74.6	47 592 253	35 317 569	74.2	49 891 159	37 442 253	75.0
1 VII 2000	ESDJ	100 569 263	75 317 689	74.9	50 069 744	...	...	50 499 519	...	...
1 VII 2001	ESDJ	101 826 249	76 408 198	75.0	50 683 083	...	...	51 143 166	...	...
1 VII 2002	ESDJ	103 039 964	77 465 861	75.2	51 274 171	...	...	51 765 793	...	...
1 VII 2003	ESDJ	104 213 503	78 503 652	75.3	51 844 576	...	...	52 368 927	...	...
Nicaragua										
1 VII 1994	ESDJ	4 298 925	2 391 801	55.6	...	...	...	...	...	...
25 IV 1995	CDJC	4 357 099	2 370 810	54.4	2 147 105	...	...	2 209 994	...	...
1 VII 1995	ESDJ	4 426 677	2 479 178	56.0	2 199 918	1 192 131	54.2	2 226 759	1 287 047	57.8
1 VII 1996	ESDJ	4 548 755	2 535 091	55.7	2 261 141	1 221 317	54.0	2 287 614	1 313 774	57.4
1 VII 1997	ESDJ	4 674 199	2 621 328	56.1	2 324 066	1 264 550	54.4	2 350 133	1 356 778	57.7
1 VII 1998	ESDJ	4 803 102	2 710 381	56.4	2 388 742	1 309 236	54.8	2 414 360	1 401 145	58.0
1 VII 1999	ESDJ	4 935 559	2 802 340	56.8	2 455 217	1 355 417	55.2	2 480 342	1 446 923	58.3
1 VII 2000	ESDJ	4 956 964	2 835 184	57.2	2 474 984	1 361 335	55.0	2 481 980	1 473 849	59.4
1 VII 2001	ESDJ	5 058 642	2 911 746	57.6	2 526 353	1 399 561	55.4	2 532 289	1 512 185	59.7
1 VII 2002	ESDJ	5 162 274	2 990 342	57.9	2 578 680	1 438 771	55.8	2 583 594	1 551 571	60.1
1 VII 2003	ESDJ	5 267 714	3 070 843	58.3	2 631 898	1 478 922	56.2	2 635 816	1 591 921	60.4
Panama										
1 VII 1994	ESDF	2 582 566	1 413 083	54.7	1 306 173	688 653	52.7	1 276 393	724 430	56.8
1 VII 1995	ESDF	2 631 013	1 444 622	54.9	1 330 145	704 231	52.9	1 300 868	740 391	56.9
1 VII 1996	ESDF	2 674 490	1 476 665	55.2	1 351 574	719 973	53.3	1 322 916	756 692	57.2
1 VII 1997	ESDF	2 718 686	1 508 703	55.5	1 373 349	735 709	53.6	1 345 337	772 994	57.5

6. Urban and total population by sex: 1994 - 2003
Population urbaine et population totale selon le sexe: 1994 - 2003
(continued — suite)

Continent, country or area and date / Continent, pays ou zone et date	Code[1]	Both sexes - Les deux sexes			Male - Masculin			Female - Féminin		
		Total	Urban - Urbaine		Total	Urban - Urbaine		Total	Urban - Urbaine	
			Number Nombre	Percent P.100		Number Nombre	Percent P.100		Number Nombre	Percent P.100
AMERICA, NORTH — AMERIQUE DU NORD										
Panama										
1 VII 1998	ESDF	2 763 612	1 540 742	55.8	1 395 475	751 450	53.8	1 368 137	789 292	57.2
1 VII 1999	ESDF	2 809 280	1 572 780	56.0	1 417 957	767 186	54.1	1 391 323	805 594	57.9
1 VII 2000	ESDF	2 855 703	1 604 823	56.2	1 440 801	782 928	54.3	1 414 902	821 895	58.
Puerto Rico - Porto Rico[14,15]										
1 IV 2000	CDJC	3 808 610	3 594 948	94.4	1 833 577	1 723 589	94.0	1 975 033	1 871 359	94.8
1 VII 2000	ESDJ	3 817 633	3 604 039	94.4	1 837 619	...	...	1 980 014	...	...
Saint Lucia - Sainte-Lucie										
1 VII 1994	ESDF	142 689	42 193	29.6	69 327	20 500	29.6	73 362	21 693	29.6
1 VII 1995	ESDF	145 437	43 005	29.6	70 725	20 913	29.6	74 715	22 092	29.6
1 VII 1996	ESDF	147 047	43 486	29.6	71 760	21 219	29.6	75 302	22 267	29.6
1 VII 1997	ESDF	149 621	44 256	29.6	73 114	21 620	29.6	76 552	22 636	29.6
1 VII 1998	ESDF	151 972	44 932	29.6	74 320	21 976	29.6	77 632	22 956	29.6
22 V 2001	CDFC	157 164	43 316	27.6	76 741	20 711	27.0	80 423	22 605	28.1
Saint Vincent and the Grenadines - Saint Vincent-et-les Grenadines										
1 VII 1994	ESDF	109 534	47 839	43.7	...	...	...	...	...	...
1 VII 1995	ESDF	110 724	48 353	43.7	...	...	...	...	...	...
1 VII 1996	ESDF	111 105	48 522	43.7	...	...	...	...	...	...
1 VII 1997	ESDF	111 655	48 761	43.7	55 713	...	...	55 942	...	...
1 VII 1998	ESDF	111 380	48 652	43.7	55 602	...	...	55 778	...	...
1 VII 2002	ESDF	107 854	48 535	45.0	54 434	...	...	53 420	...	...
United States - États-Unis[16]										
1 IV 2000	CDJC	281 421 906	222 360 539	79.0	138 053 563	108 375 797	78.5	143 368 343	113 984 742	79.5
AMERICA, SOUTH — AMERIQUE DU SUD										
Argentina - Argentine										
1 VII 1994	ESDF	34 318 469	30 220 944	88.1	16 836 555	...	...	17 481 914	...	...
1 VII 1995	ESDF	34 768 458	30 715 258	88.3	17 055 814	14 889 186	87.3	17 712 643	15 826 072	89.3
1 VII 1996	ESDF	35 219 612	31 206 336	88.6	17 275 885	...	...	17 943 728	...	...
1 VII 1997	ESDF	35 671 894	31 697 444	88.9	17 496 945	...	...	18 174 949	...	...
1 VII 1998	ESDF	36 124 933	32 188 095	89.1	17 718 738	...	...	18 406 194	...	...
1 VII 1999	ESDF	36 578 358	32 677 810	89.3	...	...	...	...	...	...
18 XI 2001	CDFC	36 260 130	32 431 950	89.4	17 659 072	15 629 299	88.5	18 601 058	16 802 651	90.3
Bolivia - Bolivie										
1 VII 1994	ESDF	7 308 859	4 232 386	57.9	...	...	...	...	...	...
1 VII 1995	ESDF	7 481 710	4 406 129	58.9	...	...	...	...	...	...
1 VII 1996	ESDF	7 660 669	4 576 132	59.7	...	...	...	...	...	...
1 VII 1997	ESDF	7 845 341	4 751 190	60.6	...	...	...	...	...	...
1 VII 1998	ESDF	8 035 143	4 931 398	61.4	...	...	...	...	...	...
1 VII 1999	ESDF	8 229 487	5 116 850	62.2	...	...	...	...	...	...
1 VII 2000	ESDF	8 427 789	5 208 601	61.8	...	...	...	...	...	...
1 VII 2001	ESDF	8 624 268	5 375 460	62.3	...	...	...	...	...	...
5 IX 2001	CDFC	8 280 184	5 153 230	62.2	4 130 342	2 501 256	60.6	4 149 842	2 651 974	63.9
1 VII 2002	ESDF	8 823 743	5 543 908	62.8	...	...	...	...	...	...
1 VII 2003	ESDF	9 024 922	5 713 606	63.3	...	...	...	...	...	...
Brazil - Brésil[17]										
1 VIII 1996	CDJC	157 070 163	123 076 831	78.4	77 442 865	59 716 389	77.1	79 627 298	63 360 442	79.6
1 VIII 2000	CDJC	169 799 170	137 953 959	81.2	83 576 015	66 882 993	80.0	86 223 155	71 070 966	82.4
Chile - Chili										
1 VII 1994	ESDF	14 157 808	11 947 604	84.4	...	...	...	...	...	...
1 VII 1995	ESDF	14 394 940	12 184 755	84.6	...	...	...	...	...	...

6. Urban and total population by sex: 1994 - 2003
Population urbaine et population totale selon le sexe: 1994 - 2003
(continued — suite)

Continent, country or area and date / Continent, pays ou zone et date	Code[1]	Both sexes - Les deux sexes			Male - Masculin			Female - Féminin		
		Total	Urban - Urbaine		Total	Urban - Urbaine		Total	Urban - Urbaine	
			Number Nombre	Percent P.100		Number Nombre	Percent P.100		Number Nombre	Percent P.100
AMERICA, SOUTH — AMERIQUE DU SUD										
Chile - Chili										
1 VII 1996	ESDF	14 595 504	12 415 178	85.1	...	...	...	...	...	...
1 VII 1997	ESDF	14 796 076	12 645 610	85.5	...	...	...	...	...	...
1 VII 1998	E3DF	14 996 647	12 876 051	85.9	...	...	...	...	...	...
1 VII 1999	ESDF	15 197 213	13 106 477	86.2	7 520 454	6 403 647	85.1	7 676 759	6 702 830	87.3
1 VII 2000	ESDF	15 397 784	13 336 913	86.6	7 620 300	6 520 105	85.6	7 777 484	6 816 808	87.6
1 VII 2001	ESDF	15 571 679	13 494 230	86.7	7 706 752	6 598 130	85.6	7 864 927	6 896 100	87.7
24 IV 2002	CDFC	15 116 435	13 090 113	86.6	7 447 695	6 366 311	85.5	7 668 740	6 723 802	87.7
1 VII 2002	ESDF	15 745 583	13 651 558	86.7	7 793 208	6 676 157	85.7	7 952 375	6 975 401	87.7
1 VII 2003	ESDF	15 919 479	13 808 880	86.7	7 879 658	6 754 181	85.7	8 039 821	7 054 699	87.7
Colombia - Colombie										
1 VII 1995	ESDF	38 558 195	26 729 806	69.3	...	...	...	...	...	...
1 VII 1996	ESDF	39 281 340	27 390 035	69.7	...	...	...	...	...	...
1 VII 1997	ESDF	40 018 837	28 048 220	70.1	...	...	...	...	...	...
1 VII 1998	ESDF	40 772 995	28 734 719	70.5	...	...	...	...	...	...
1 VII 1999	ESDF	41 539 012	29 435 181	70.9	...	...	...	...	...	...
1 VII 2000	ESDF	42 299 300	30 125 776	71.2	...	...	...	...	...	...
1 VII 2001	ESDF	43 035 393	30 772 485	71.5	...	...	...	...	...	...
1 VII 2002	ESDF	43 775 838	31 428 374	71.8	...	...	...	...	...	...
1 VII 2003	ESDF	44 531 433	32 101 585	72.1	...	...	...	...	...	...
Ecuador - Équateur[18]										
1 VII 1994	ESDF	11 186 757	6 423 477	57.4	...	...	...	...	...	...
1 VII 1995	ESDF	11 396 692	6 596 059	57.9	...	...	...	...	...	...
1 VII 1996	ESDF	11 591 128	6 780 934	58.5	...	...	...	...	...	...
1 VII 1997	ESDF	11 772 871	6 953 116	59.1	5 914 625	3 433 722	58.1	5 858 242	3 519 394	60.1
1 VII 1998	ESDF	11 947 586	7 118 271	59.6	6 001 552	3 517 425	58.6	5 946 036	3 600 846	60.6
1 VII 1999	ESDF	12 120 981	7 282 105	60.1	6 087 690	3 600 349	59.1	6 033 294	3 681 756	61.0
1 VII 2000	ESDF	12 298 745	7 450 308	60.6	6 175 859	3 685 298	59.7	6 122 886	3 765 010	61.5
1 VII 2001	ESDF	12 479 924	7 633 850	61.2	6 265 558	3 778 158	60.3	6 214 366	3 855 692	62.0
25 XI 2001	CDFC	12 156 608	7 431 355	61.1	6 018 353	3 625 962	60.2	6 138 255	3 805 393	62.0
1 VII 2002	ESDF	12 660 728	7 817 018	61.7	6 354 906	3 870 667	60.9	6 305 821	3 946 351	62.6
1 VII 2003	ESDF	12 842 578	8 001 231	62.3	6 444 656	3 963 574	61.5	6 397 920	4 037 657	63.1
Paraguay										
28 VIII 2002	CDFC	5 163 198	2 928 437	56.7	2 603 242	1 422 339	54.6	2 559 956	1 506 098	58.8
Peru - Pérou[8,19]										
1 VII 1994	ESDF	23 421 416	16 555 123	70.7	11 786 070	...	...	11 635 346	...	...
1 VII 1995	ESDF	23 836 867	16 933 353	71.0	11 995 313	...	...	11 841 554	...	...
1 VII 1996	ESDF	24 257 671	17 294 032	71.3	12 206 832	...	...	12 050 839	...	...
1 VII 1997	ESDF	24 681 045	17 640 917	71.5	12 419 397	8 849 804	71.3	12 261 648	8 791 113	71.7
1 VII 1998	ESDF	25 104 276	17 978 819	71.6	12 631 667	9 017 356	71.4	12 472 609	8 961 463	71.8
1 VII 1999	ESDF	25 524 613	18 312 557	71.7	12 842 267	9 182 458	71.5	12 682 346	9 130 099	72.0
1 VII 2000	ESDF	25 939 329	18 647 242	71.9	13 049 847	9 348 264	71.6	12 889 482	9 298 978	72.1
1 VII 2001	ESDF	26 346 840	18 980 589	72.0	13 253 619	9 513 198	71.8	13 093 221	9 467 391	72.3
1 VII 2002	ESDF	26 748 972	19 310 309	72.2	13 454 486	9 676 260	71.9	13 294 486	9 634 049	72.5
1 VII 2003	ESDF	27 148 101	19 638 160	72.3	13 653 636	9 838 166	72.1	13 494 465	9 799 994	72.6
Uruguay[8]										
22 V 1996	CDFC	3 163 763	2 872 077	90.8	1 532 288	1 366 092	89.2	1 631 475	1 505 985	92.3
1 VII 1996	ESDF	3 241 403	2 976 727	91.8	...	...	...	...	...	...
1 VII 1997	ESDF	3 263 451	3 000 598	91.9	1 582 607	1 431 934	90.5	1 680 844	1 568 664	93.3
1 VII 1998	ESDF	3 283 971	3 023 118	92.1	1 591 876	1 443 079	90.7	1 692 095	1 580 039	93.4
1 VII 1999	ESDF	3 288 819	3 040 697	92.5	1 593 452	1 451 298	91.1	1 695 368	1 589 399	93.7
1 VII 2000	ESDF	3 300 847	3 058 437	92.7	1 598 685	1 460 013	91.3	1 702 162	1 598 424	93.9
1 VII 2001	ESDF	3 308 356	3 071 727	92.8	1 601 593	1 466 408	91.6	1 706 763	1 605 319	94.1
1 VII 2002	ESDF	3 308 527	3 077 804	93.0	1 600 814	1 469 148	91.8	1 707 713	1 608 656	94.2
1 VII 2003	ESDF	3 303 540	3 078 812	93.2	1 597 362	1 469 246	92.0	1 706 177	1 609 565	94.3
Venezuela[8,19]										
1 VII 1996	ESDF	22 501 988	19 710 481	87.6	11 333 607	9 818 511	86.6	11 168 381	9 891 970	88.6
1 VII 1997	ESDF	22 958 680	20 123 896	87.7	11 559 949	10 021 295	86.7	11 398 731	10 102 601	88.6
1 VII 1998	ESDF	23 412 742	20 534 451	87.7	11 784 967	10 222 629	86.7	11 627 775	10 311 822	88.7

6. Urban and total population by sex: 1994 - 2003
Population urbaine et population totale selon le sexe: 1994 - 2003
(continued — suite)

Continent, country or area and date / Continent, pays ou zone et date	Code[1]	Both sexes - Les deux sexes			Male - Masculin			Female - Féminin		
		Total	Urban - Urbaine		Total	Urban - Urbaine		Total	Urban - Urbaine	
			Number Nombre	Percent P.100		Number Nombre	Percent P.100		Number Nombre	Percent P.100
AMERICA, SOUTH — AMERIQUE DU SUD										
Venezuela[8,19]										
1 VII 1999	ESDF	23 867 393	20 945 043	87.8	12 010 280	10 423 959	86.8	11 857 113	10 521 084	88.7
1 VII 2000	ESDF	24 310 896	21 345 288	87.8	12 229 953	10 620 092	86.8	12 080 943	10 725 196	88.8
1 VII 2001	ESDF	24 765 581	21 754 766	87.8	12 454 204	10 820 038	86.9	12 311 377	10 934 728	88.8
1 VII 2002	ESDF	25 219 910	22 163 339	87.9	12 678 275	11 021 146	86.9	12 541 635	11 142 193	88.8
ASIA — ASIE										
Afghanistan[20,21]										
1 VII 2002	ESDF	*22 930 000*	*4 463 000*	*19.5*	*10 453 500*	*2 332 600*	*22.3*	*9 844 300*	*2 130 400*	*21.6*
Armenia - Arménie[22]										
1 VII 1994	ESDF	3 746 800	2 533 000	67.6	1 814 100	1 207 400	66.6	1 932 700	1 325 600	68.6
1 VII 1995	ESDF	3 759 950	2 534 250	67.4	1 820 165	1 207 260	66.3	1 939 785	1 326 990	68.4
1 VII 1996	ESDF	3 773 567	2 534 024	67.2	1 827 556	1 207 639	66.1	1 946 011	1 326 385	68.2
1 VII 1997	ESDF	3 785 982	2 534 076	66.9	1 835 093	1 208 745	65.9	1 950 889	1 325 331	67.9
1 VII 1998	ESDF	3 794 735	2 535 702	66.8	1 841 448	1 210 849	65.8	1 953 287	1 324 853	67.8
1 VII 1999	ESDF	3 800 817	2 535 846	66.7	1 846 592	1 212 207	65.6	1 954 225	1 323 639	67.7
1 VII 2000	ESDF	3 802 882	2 534 023	66.6	1 848 756	1 212 033	65.6	1 954 126	1 321 990	67.7
10 X 2001	CDFC	3 002 594	1 945 514	64.8	1 407 220	898 977	63.9	1 595 374	1 046 537	65.6
Azerbaijan - Azerbaïdjan										
1 VII 1994	ESDF	7 596 600	3 988 300	52.5	3 728 600	1 969 100	52.8	3 868 000	2 021 700	52.3
1 VII 1995	ESDF	7 684 900	4 020 100	52.3	3 778 700	1 977 600	52.3	3 906 200	2 042 500	52.3
1 VII 1996	ESDF	7 763 000	4 046 200	52.1	3 824 000	1 988 900	52.0	3 939 000	2 057 300	52.2
1 VII 1997	ESDF	7 838 300	4 070 200	51.9	3 864 300	2 006 500	51.9	3 974 000	2 063 700	51.9
1 VII 1998	ESDF	7 913 000	4 072 600	51.5	3 882 100	1 993 500	51.4	4 030 900	2 079 100	51.6
27 I 1999	CDJC	7 953 438	4 053 584	51.0	3 883 155	1 970 022	50.7	4 070 283	2 083 562	51.2
1 VII 1999	ESDF	7 982 800	4 074 600	51.0	3 899 600	1 981 300	50.8	4 083 200	2 093 300	51.3
1 VII 2000	ESDF	8 048 600	4 096 900	50.9	3 936 400	1 994 300	50.7	4 112 200	2 102 600	51.1
1 VII 2001	ESDF	8 111 200	4 118 800	50.8	3 971 600	2 006 800	50.5	4 139 600	2 112 000	51.0
1 VII 2002	ESDF	8 141 400	4 130 100	50.7	3 988 800	2 013 400	50.5	4 152 600	2 116 700	51.0
1 VII 2003	ESDF	8 234 100	4 242 000	51.5	4 040 800	2 070 800	51.2	4 193 300	2 171 200	51.8
Bangladesh										
22 I 2001	CDFC	123 151 246	28 808 477	23.4	62 735 988	15 360 059	24.5	60 415 258	13 448 418	22.3
Brunei Darussalam - Brunéi Darussalam										
21 VIII 2001	CDFC	332 844	238 699	71.7	168 974	120 046	71.0	163 870	118 653	72.4
Cambodia - Cambodge[23,24]										
1 III 1996	SSDF	10 702 000	1 540 000	14.4	5 119 000	738 000	14.4	5 583 000	802 000	14.4
3 III 1998	CDFC	11 437 656	1 795 575	15.7	5 511 408	878 186	15.9	5 926 248	917 389	15.5
China - Chine[25,26,27,28,29]										
1 VII 1994	ESDF	*1191835000*	*336 710 000*	*28.3*	*608 590 000*	...	...	*583 245 000*	...	...
1 VII 1995	ESDF	*1204855000*	*346 715 000*	*28.8*	*615 270 000*	...	...	*589 585 000*	...	...
1 VII 1996	ESDF	*1217550000*	*362 390 000*	*29.8*	*620 040 000*	...	...	*597 510 000*	...	...
1 VII 1997	ESDF	*1230075000*	*383 765 000*	*31.2*	*626 655 000*	...	...	*603 420 000*	...	...
1 VII 1998	ESDF	*1241935000*	*405 285 000*	*32.6*	*635 355 000*	...	...	*606 580 000*	...	...
1 VII 1999	ESDF	*1252735000*	*426 780 000*	*34.1*	*643 160 000*	...	...	*609 575 000*	...	...
1 VII 2000	ESDF	*1262645000*	*448 270 000*	*35.5*	*650 645 000*	...	...	*612 000 000*	...	...
1 XI 2000	CDJC	*1242612226*	*458 770 983*	*36.9*	*640 275 969*	*235 264 707*	*36.7*	*602 336 257*	*223 506 276*	*37.1*
1 VII 2001	ESDF	*1271850000*	*469 850 000*	*36.9*	*655 545 000*	...	...	*616 305 000*	...	...
1 VII 2002	ESDF	*1280400000*	*491 380 000*	*38.4*	*658 935 000*	...	...	*621 465 000*	...	...
1 VII 2003	ESDF	*1288400000*	*512 940 000*	*39.8*	*663 355 000*	...	...	*625 045 000*	...	...
Cyprus - Chypre[30,31]										
1 X 2001	CDJC	689 565	474 450	68.8	338 497	231 128	68.3	351 068	243 322	69.3
Georgia - Géorgie										
1 VII 1994	ESDF	4 862 100	2 635 300	54.2	...	...	...	...	...	...

6. Urban and total population by sex: 1994 - 2003
Population urbaine et population totale selon le sexe: 1994 - 2003
(continued — suite)

Continent, country or area and date / Continent, pays ou zone et date	Code[1]	Both sexes - Les deux sexes			Male - Masculin			Female - Féminin		
		Total	Urban - Urbaine		Total	Urban - Urbaine		Total	Urban - Urbaine	
			Number Nombre	Percent P.100		Number Nombre	Percent P.100		Number Nombre	Percent P.100
ASIA — ASIE										
Georgia - Géorgie										
1 VII 1995	ESDF	4 734 400	2 554 300	54.0	...	...	...	...	...	...
1 VII 1996	ESDF	4 616 500	2 479 100	53.7	...	...	...	...	...	...
1 VII 1997	ESDF	4 531 700	2 422 200	53.5	...	...	...	...	...	...
1 VII 1998	ESDF	4 487 400	2 387 300	53.2	...	...	...	...	...	...
1 VII 1999	ESDF	4 452 500	2 357 500	52.9	...	...	...	...	...	...
1 VII 2000	ESDF	4 418 300	2 328 500	52.7	...	...	...	...	...	...
1 VII 2001	ESDF	4 386 500	2 300 700	52.4	2 300 700	...	...	2 085 800	...	...
17 I 2002	CDJC	4 371 535	2 284 796	52.3	2 061 753	1 048 593	50.9	2 309 782	1 236 203	53.5
1 VII 2002	ESDF	4 357 100	2 276 600	52.3	...	...	...	...	...	...
1 VII 2003	ESDF	4 328 900	2 260 700	52.2	2 045 500	...	...	2 283 400	...	...
India - Inde[32,33]										
1 VII 1994	ESDF	*905 449 218*	*238 818 591*	*26.4*	...	...	...	...	...	...
1 VII 1995	ESDF	*923 459 258*	*245 399 484*	*26.6*	...	...	...	...	...	...
1 VII 1996	ESDF	*941 579 289*	*252 090 369*	*26.8*	487 475 000	...	...	452 065 000	...	...
1 VII 1997	ESDF	*959 792 000*	*258 905 000*	*27.0*	497 960 000	136 329 000	27.4	461 832 000	122 577 000	26.5
1 VII 1998	ESDF	*978 081 000*	*265 864 000*	*27.2*	507 167 000	139 952 000	27.6	470 914 000	125 912 000	26.7
1 VII 1999	ESDF	*996 430 000*	*272 994 000*	*27.4*	516 309 000	143 671 000	27.8	480 121 000	129 323 000	26.9
1 VII 2000	ESDF	*1014825000*	*280 330 000*	*27.6*	525 366 000	147 504 000	28.1	489 459 000	132 826 000	27.1
1 III 2001	CDFC	1028610328	286 119 689	27.8	532 156 772	150 554 098	28.3	496 453 556	135 565 591	27.3
1 VII 2001	ESDF	*1033248000*	*287 716 000*	*27.8*	534 317 000	151 355 000	28.3	498 931 000	136 357 000	27.3
1 VII 2002	ESDF	*1050640000*	*294 859 000*	*28.1*	543 188 000	155 043 000	28.5	507 452 000	139 815 000	27.6
1 VII 2003	ESDF	*1068214000*	*302 013 000*	*28.3*	552 085 000	158 728 000	28.8	516 129 000	143 287 000	27.8
Indonesia - Indonésie[34]										
31 X 1995	SSDF	194 754 808	69 937 110	35.9	96 929 931	34 722 443	35.8	97 824 877	35 214 667	36.0
30 VI 2000	CDFC	206 264 595	86 601 850	42.0	103 417 180	43 368 496	41.9	102 847 415	43 233 354	42.0
Iran (Islamic Republic of) - Iran (République islamique d')										
1 VII 1994	ESDJ	*58 331 206*	*34 738 041*	*59.6*	*29 846 228*	*17 839 668*	*59.8*	*28 484 978*	*16 898 373*	*59.3*
1 VII 1995	ESDJ	*59 187 068*	*35 762 803*	*60.4*	*30 284 145*	*18 364 139*	*60.6*	*28 902 923*	*17 398 664*	*60.2*
23 X 1996	CDJC	60 055 488	36 817 789	61.3	30 515 159	18 805 023	61.6	29 540 329	18 012 766	61.0
1 VII 1997	ESDJ	*60 938 837*	*37 826 305*	*62.1*	*31 011 770*	*19 249 804*	*62.1*	*29 927 067*	*18 576 501*	*62.1*
1 VII 1998	ESDJ	*61 835 591*	*38 839 280*	*62.8*	...	...	...	...	...	...
1 VII 1999	ESDJ	*62 745 540*	*39 856 570*	*63.5*	...	...	...	...	...	...
1 VII 2000	ESDJ	*63 663 942*	*40 873 494*	*64.2*	...	...	...	...	...	...
1 VII 2001	ESDJ	*64 528 159*	*42 173 587*	*65.4*	...	...	...	...	...	...
1 VII 2002	ESDJ	*65 540 239*	*43 054 650*	*65.7*	...	...	...	...	...	...
1 VII 2003	ESDJ	*66 480 365*	*43 892 714*	*66.0*	...	...	...	...	...	...
Iraq[35]										
16 X 1997	CDFC	19 184 543	12 945 776	67.5	9 536 570	6 466 325	67.8	9 647 973	6 479 451	67.2
Israel - Israël[8,36]										
1 VII 1994	ESDJ	5 399 300	4 843 700	89.7	2 675 800	2 390 900	89.4	2 723 500	2 453 000	90.1
1 VII 1995	ESDJ	5 544 900	4 970 500	89.6	2 746 500	2 452 000	89.3	2 798 400	2 518 200	90.0
4 XI 1995	CDJC	5 548 523	5 044 735	90.9	2 738 175	2 476 836	90.5	2 810 348	2 567 899	91.4
1 VII 1996	ESDJ	5 685 100	5 166 000	90.9	...	...	...	...	...	...
1 VII 1997	ESDJ	5 829 000	5 294 100	90.8	2 875 400	2 599 900	90.4	2 953 500	2 694 300	91.2
1 VII 1998	ESDJ	5 970 700	5 418 400	90.7	...	...	...	...	...	...
1 VII 1999	ESDJ	6 125 300	5 554 200	90.7	3 021 743	...	...	3 103 533	...	...
1 VII 2000	ESDJ	6 289 200	5 696 100	90.6	3 102 400	2 797 800	90.2	3 186 800	2 898 300	90.9
1 VII 2001	ESDJ	6 439 000	5 900 700	91.6	3 176 600	2 900 200	91.3	3 262 500	3 000 500	92.0
1 VII 2002	ESDJ	6 569 900	6 017 300	91.6	3 241 700	2 958 200	91.3	3 328 200	3 059 100	91.9
1 VII 2003	ESDJ	6 689 700	6 122 400	91.5	3 301 800	3 010 900	91.2	3 387 900	3 111 600	91.8
Japan - Japon[37]										
1 X 1995	CDFC	125 570 246	98 009 107	78.1	61 574 398	48 210 196	78.3	63 995 848	49 798 911	77.8
1 X 2000	CDFC	126 925 843	99 865 289	78.7	62 110 764	49 005 691	78.9	64 815 079	50 859 598	78.5
Jordan - Jordanie[38]										
10 XII 1994	CDFC	4 139 458	3 238 757	78.2	2 160 725	1 687 530	78.1	1 978 733	1 551 227	78.4
31 XII 1995	ESDF	*4 291 000*	*3 355 510*	*78.2*	...	...	...	...	...	...
31 XII 1996	ESDF	*4 444 000*	*3 477 800*	*78.3*	...	...	...	...	...	...

6. Urban and total population by sex: 1994 - 2003
Population urbaine et population totale selon le sexe: 1994 - 2003
(continued — suite)

Continent, country or area and date / Continent, pays ou zone et date	Code[1]	Both sexes - Les deux sexes			Male - Masculin			Female - Féminin		
		Total	Urban - Urbaine		Total	Urban - Urbaine		Total	Urban - Urbaine	
			Number Nombre	Percent P.100		Number Nombre	Percent P.100		Number Nombre	Percent P.100
ASIA — ASIE										
Jordan - Jordanie[38]										
31 XII 1997	ESDF	4 600 000	3 620 200	78.7	2 404 400	...	...	2 195 600	...	...
31 XII 1998	ESDF	4 755 750	3 743 070	78.7	2 486 800	...	...	2 268 950	...	...
31 XII 1999	ESDF	4 900 000	3 856 300	78.7	2 562 200	...	...	2 337 800	...	...
31 XII 2000	ESDF	5 039 000	3 965 695	78.7	2 635 400	2 066 126	78.4	2 403 600	1 899 567	79.0
31 XII 2001	ESDF	5 182 000	4 078 235	78.7	2 710 235	...	...	2 471 765	...	...
31 XII 2002	ESDF	5 329 000	4 193 925	78.7	2 787 115	...	...	2 541 885	...	...
31 XII 2003	ESDF	5 480 000	4 313 945	78.7	2 866 200	...	...	2 613 800	...	...
Kazakhstan										
1 VII 1994	ESDF	16 145 765	9 023 455	55.9	...	...	...	...	...	...
1 VII 1995	ESDF	15 816 243	8 807 349	55.7	...	...	...	...	...	...
1 VII 1996	ESDF	15 578 228	8 682 790	55.7	...	...	...	...	...	...
1 VII 1997	ESDF	15 334 405	8 567 329	55.9	7 393 786	4 014 495	54.3	7 940 619	4 552 834	57.3
1 VII 1998	ESDF	15 072 983	8 434 080	56.0	7 263 077	3 945 189	54.3	7 809 906	4 488 891	57.5
26 II 1999	CDJC	14 953 126	8 377 303	56.0	7 201 785	3 918 556	54.4	7 751 341	4 458 747	57.5
1 VII 1999	ESDF	14 928 373	8 406 019	56.3	7 190 238	3 933 622	54.7	7 738 135	4 472 397	57.8
1 VII 2000	ESDF	14 883 626	8 405 483	56.5	7 168 613	3 933 997	54.9	7 715 013	4 471 486	58.0
1 VII 2001	ESDF	14 858 335	8 421 366	56.7	7 156 582	3 942 353	55.1	7 701 753	4 479 013	58.2
1 VII 2002	ESDF	14 858 948	8 443 242	56.8	7 156 816	3 952 649	55.2	7 702 132	4 490 593	58.3
1 VII 2003	ESDF	14 909 018	8 487 697	56.9	7 179 583	3 971 520	55.3	7 729 435	4 516 177	58.4
Korea (Republic of) - Corée (République de)[39,40]										
1 XI 1995	CDFC	44 608 726	35 036 473	78.5	22 389 324	17 621 308	78.7	22 219 402	17 415 165	78.4
1 XI 2000	CDFC	46 136 101	36 755 144	79.7	23 158 582	18 484 139	79.8	22 977 519	18 271 005	79.5
Kyrgyzstan - Kirghizistan										
1 VII 1994	ESDF	4 540 400	1 645 200	36.2	...	...	...	...	...	...
1 VII 1995	ESDF	4 589 900	1 646 300	35.9	...	...	...	...	...	...
1 VII 1996	ESDF	4 657 400	1 660 200	35.6	...	...	...	...	...	...
1 VII 1997	ESDF	4 724 900	1 675 900	35.5	...	...	...	...	...	...
1 VII 1998	ESDF	4 797 000	1 696 900	35.4	...	...	...	...	...	...
24 III 1999	CDJC	4 822 938	1 678 623	34.8	2 380 465	802 256	33.7	2 442 473	876 367	35.9
1 VII 1999	ESDF	4 864 600	1 717 100	35.3	...	...	...	...	...	...
1 VII 2000	ESDF	4 915 300	1 738 800	35.4	...	...	...	...	...	...
1 VII 2001	ESDF	4 954 800	1 760 600	35.5	...	...	...	...	...	...
1 VII 2002	ESDF	4 993 200	1 763 600	35.3	...	...	...	...	...	...
1 VII 2003	ESDF	5 038 600	1 785 700	35.4	...	...	...	...	...	...
Lao People's Democratic Republic - République démocratique populaire lao										
1 III 1995	CDFC	4 574 848	781 753	17.1	2 260 986	...	...	2 313 862	...	...
Malaysia - Malaisie[41,42]										
1 VII 1994	ESDF	20 111 565	10 825 360	53.8	10 251 030	...	...	9 860 535	...	...
1 VII 1995	ESDF	20 689 344	11 317 218	54.7	10 563 895	...	...	10 125 449	...	...
5 VII 2000	CDJC	23 274 690	14 426 871	62.0	11 853 432	7 318 396	61.7	11 421 258	7 108 475	62.2
Maldives										
25 III 1995	CDFC	244 814	62 519	25.5	124 622	33 506	26.9	120 192	29 013	24.1
31 III 2000	CDFC	270 101	74 069	27.4	137 200	38 559	28.1	132 901	35 510	26.7
1 VII 2001	ESDF	275 975	75 680	27.4	140 184	39 398	28.1	135 791	36 282	26.7
1 VII 2002	ESDF	280 549	76 934	27.4	142 507	40 051	28.1	138 042	36 884	26.7
1 VII 2003	ESDF	285 066	78 173	27.4	144 802	40 695	28.1	140 264	37 477	26.7
Mongolia - Mongolie[43]										
1 VII 1994	ESDF	2 206 892	1 155 635	52.4	...	...	...	...	...	...
1 VII 1995	ESDF	2 242 998	1 156 249	51.5	...	...	...	...	...	...
1 VII 1996	ESDF	2 276 016	1 204 160	52.9	1 125 800	559 400	49.7	1 141 100	567 000	49.7

6. Urban and total population by sex: 1994 - 2003
Population urbaine et population totale selon le sexe: 1994 - 2003
(continued — suite)

Continent, country or area and date / Continent, pays ou zone et date	Code[1]	Both sexes - Les deux sexes Total	Urban - Urbaine Number Nombre	Urban - Urbaine Percent P.100	Male - Masculin Total	Urban - Urbaine Number Nombre	Urban - Urbaine Percent P.100	Female - Féminin Total	Urban - Urbaine Number Nombre	Urban - Urbaine Percent P.100
ASIA — ASIE										
Mongolia - Mongolie[43]										
1 VII 1997	ESDF	2 307 484	1 215 080	52.7	1 145 568	565 300	49.3	1 161 916	573 400	49.3
1 VII 1998	ESDF	2 340 134	1 242 206	53.1	1 161 666	573 100	49.3	1 178 468	581 300	49.3
5 I 2000	CDFC	2 373 493	1 344 516	56.6	1 177 981	657 081	55.8	1 195 512	687 435	57.5
1 VII 2000	ESDF	2 407 488	1 377 000	57.2	1 192 415	694 500	58.2	1 215 073	706 100	58.1
1 VII 2001	ESDF	2 442 544	1 397 100	57.2	1 209 728	...	...	1 232 816	...	...
1 VII 2002	ESDF	2 475 381	1 421 000	57.4	1 228 059	...	...	1 247 322	...	...
1 VII 2003	ESDF	2 504 023	1 464 222	58.5	1 242 269	...	...	1 261 754	...	...
Myanmar[44]										
1 VII 1994	ESDF	43 922 000	9 249 467	21.1	21 832 000	4 601 468	21.1	22 090 000	4 647 999	21.0
Nepal - Népal										
1 VII 1996	ESDJ	20 831 644	2 207 967	10.6	10 393 913	1 138 641	11.0	10 437 731	1 069 326	10.2
Occupied Palestinian Territory - Territoire palestinien occupé[45,46]										
1 VII 1997	ESDF	2 783 084	1 992 780	71.6	1 404 481	...	...	1 378 603	...	...
1 VII 1998	ESDF	2 897 113	2 074 825	71.6	1 462 532	...	...	1 434 920	...	...
1 VII 1999	ESDF	3 019 158	2 162 657	71.6	1 524 649	...	...	1 495 055	...	...
1 VII 2000	ESDF	3 149 448	2 256 470	71.6	1 590 945	...	...	1 559 111	...	...
1 VII 2001	ESDF	3 275 389	2 346 926	71.7	1 666 805	...	...	1 632 146	...	...
1 VII 2002	ESDF	3 394 046	2 432 044	71.7	1 751 271	...	...	1 713 279	...	...
1 VII 2003	ESDF	3 514 868	2 519 018	71.7	1 847 684	...	...	1 800 191	...	...
Oman										
7 XII 2003	CDFC	2 340 815	1 673 480	71.5	1 313 239	950 471	72.4	1 027 576	723 009	70.4
Pakistan[47]										
2 III 1998	CDFC	130 579 571	42 458 339	32.5	67 840 137	22 419 286	33.0	62 739 434	20 039 053	31.9
1 VII 1998	ESDF	131 510 000	42 910 000	32.6	68 290 000	22 100 000	32.4	63 220 000	20 810 000	32.9
Sri Lanka[48]										
17 VII 2001	CDFC	16 864 544	2 467 171	14.6	8 343 964	1 246 983	14.9	8 520 580	1 220 188	14.3
Syrian Arab Republic - République arabe syrienne[49]										
1 VII 1994	ESDF	13 844 000	7 112 000	51.4	7 071 000	3 702 000	52.4	6 773 000	3 410 000	50.3
3 IX 1994	CDFC	13 782 315	6 864 525	49.8	7 048 906	3 540 051	50.2	6 733 409	3 324 474	49.4
1 VII 2001	ESDF	16 720 000	8 376 000	50.1	8 552 000	...	...	8 168 000	...	...
1 VII 2002	ESDF	17 130 000	8 599 000	50.2	8 763 000	4 439 000	50.7	8 367 000	4 324 000	51.7
1 VII 2003	ESDF	17 550 000	8 806 000	50.2	8 979 000	4 541 000	50.6	8 571 000	4 265 000	49.8
Tajikistan - Tadjikistan										
1 VII 1999	ESDF	6 064 048	1 609 723	26.5	3 036 700	800 020	26.3	3 027 349	809 703	26.7
1 VII 2000	ESDF	6 188 366	1 642 401	26.5	3 099 855	817 233	26.4	3 088 512	825 168	26.7
1 VII 2001	ESDF	6 312 757	1 675 211	26.5	3 163 111	834 679	26.4	3 149 646	840 533	26.7
1 VII 2002	ESDF	6 441 009	1 705 240	26.5	3 228 657	850 898	26.4	3 212 352	854 343	26.6
1 VII 2003	ESDF	6 573 225	1 738 839	26.5	3 296 212	868 891	26.4	3 277 013	869 948	26.5
Thailand - Thaïlande[50]										
1 IV 2000	CDJC	60 617 200	18 833 700	31.1	29 850 100	9 085 400	30.4	30 767 100	9 748 300	31.7
1 VII 2002	ESDJ	63 482 287	20 731 494	32.7	31 623 509	10 072 055	31.8	31 858 778	10 659 439	33.5
Turkey - Turquie										
1 VII 1994	ESDF	60 612 000	37 316 140	61.6	...	...	...	...	...	...
1 VII 1995	ESDF	61 737 000	38 336 473	62.1	...	...	...	...	...	...
1 VII 1996	ESDF	62 873 000	39 375 130	62.6	31 789 000	...	...	31 083 000	...	...
1 VII 1997	ESDF	64 015 000	40 429 122	63.2	32 358 000	...	...	31 657 000	...	...
1 VII 1998	ESDF	65 157 000	41 494 721	63.7	32 926 000	...	...	32 230 000	...	...
1 VII 1999	ESDF	66 293 000	42 567 640	64.2	33 492 000	...	...	32 801 000	...	...
1 VII 2000	ESDF	67 420 000	43 647 130	64.7	34 053 000	...	...	33 367 000	...	...
22 X 2000	CDFC	67 803 927	44 006 274	64.9	34 346 735	22 427 603	65.3	33 457 192	21 578 671	64.5
1 VII 2001	ESDF	68 529 000	44 725 884	65.3	34 605 000	...	...	33 925 000	...	...

6. Urban and total population by sex: 1994 - 2003
Population urbaine et population totale selon le sexe: 1994 - 2003
(continued — suite)

Continent, country or area and date / Continent, pays ou zone et date	Code[1]	Both sexes - Les deux sexes			Male - Masculin			Female - Féminin		
		Total	Urban - Urbaine		Total	Urban - Urbaine		Total	Urban - Urbaine	
			Number Nombre	Percent P.100		Number Nombre	Percent P.100		Number Nombre	Percent P.100
ASIA — ASIE										
Turkey - Turquie										
1 VII 2002	ESDF	69 626 000	45 808 003	65.8	35 149 000	...	...	34 477 000	...	...
1 VII 2003	ESDF	70 712 716	46 893 963	66.3	35 687 971	...	...	35 024 745	...	...
United Arab Emirates - Émirats arabes unis[51]										
17 XII 1995	CDFC	2 411 041	1 886 708	78.3	1 606 804	...	...	804 237	...	...
Uzbekistan - Ouzbékistan										
1 VII 1994	ESDF	22 282 400	8 634 700	38.8	11 044 600	4 237 600	38.4	11 237 800	4 397 100	39.1
1 VII 1995	ESDF	22 689 700	8 711 900	38.4	11 255 900	4 278 100	38.0	11 433 800	4 433 800	38.8
1 VII 1996	ESDF	23 130 400	8 817 600	38.1	11 487 300	4 335 600	37.7	11 643 100	4 482 000	38.5
1 VII 1997	ESDF	23 560 400	8 931 400	37.9	11 710 400	4 394 700	37.5	11 850 000	4 536 700	38.3
1 VII 1998	ESDF	24 051 000	9 109 700	37.9	...	...	...	...	...	...
1 VII 1999	ESDF	23 953 922	9 037 904	37.7	11 913 994	4 450 641	37.4	12 039 928	4 587 263	38.1
1 VII 2000	ESDF	24 650 415	9 195 435	37.3	12 278 626	4 538 871	37.0	12 371 789	4 656 564	37.6
1 VII 2001	ESDF	24 964 433	9 256 101	37.1	12 442 510	4 573 055	36.8	12 521 923	4 683 046	37.4
Viet Nam										
1 VII 1994	ESDF	72 509 500	14 139 200	19.5	35 386 400	...	...	37 123 100	...	...
1 VII 1995	ESDF	73 962 400	14 575 400	19.7	36 095 400	...	...	37 867 000	...	...
1 VII 1996	ESDF	75 355 200	15 231 500	20.2	36 773 300	...	...	38 581 900	...	...
1 IV 1999	CDFC	76 323 173	18 076 823	23.7	37 469 117	8 825 112	23.6	38 854 056	9 251 711	23.8
1 VII 2002	ESDF	79 727 379	20 022 142	25.1	39 197 378	...	...	40 530 001	...	...
Yemen - Yémen										
1 VII 1994	ESDF	14 859 000	3 487 000	23.5	7 411 000	...	...	7 448 000	...	...
16 XII 1994	CDFC	14 587 807	3 423 518	23.5	7 473 540	1 856 602	24.8	7 114 267	1 566 916	22.0
1 VII 1995	ESDF	15 369 000	3 699 000	24.1	7 668 000	...	...	7 701 000	...	...
1 VII 1996	ESDF	15 915 000	3 913 000	24.6	7 943 000	...	...	7 972 000	...	...
1 VII 1997	ESDF	16 484 000	4 130 000	25.1	8 229 000	...	...	8 255 000	...	...
1 VII 2000	ESDF	18 261 000	4 802 000	26.3	9 143 000	2 587 000	28.3	9 118 000	2 215 000	24.3
EUROPE										
Albania - Albanie										
1 VII 1994	ESDF	3 035 181	1 160 615	38.2	...	...	...	...	...	...
1 VII 1995	ESDF	3 050 012	1 165 135	38.2	...	...	...	...	...	...
1 VII 1996	ESDF	3 075 545	1 186 360	38.6	...	...	...	...	...	...
1 VII 1997	ESDF	3 074 832	1 211 925	39.4	...	...	...	...	...	...
1 VII 1998	ESDF	3 055 331	1 227 208	40.2	...	...	...	...	...	...
1 VII 1999	ESDF	3 053 831	1 234 915	40.4	...	...	...	...	...	...
1 VII 2000	ESDF	3 060 908	1 249 919	40.8	...	...	...	...	...	...
1 IV 2001	CDFC	3 069 275	1 292 875	42.1	1 530 443	...	...	1 538 832	...	...
1 VII 2001	ESDF	3 073 733	1 268 370	41.3	...	...	...	...	...	...
1 VII 2002	ESDF	3 093 465	1 347 871	43.6	1 542 211	625 060	40.5	1 551 254	722 811	46.6
1 VII 2003	ESDF	3 111 163	1 375 367	44.2	1 550 728	636 985	41.1	1 560 435	738 382	47.3
Austria - Autriche										
15 V 2001	CDJC	8 032 926	5 368 693	66.8	3 889 189	2 564 828	65.9	4 143 737	2 803 865	67.7
Belarus - Bélarus										
1 VII 1994	ESDF	10 308 318	7 048 784	68.4	4 828 086	3 326 708	68.9	5 480 232	3 722 076	67.9
1 VII 1995	ESDF	10 280 805	7 066 181	68.7	4 799 416	3 319 964	69.2	5 481 389	3 746 217	68.3
1 VII 1996	ESDF	10 250 250	7 080 710	69.1	4 784 616	3 324 087	69.5	5 465 634	3 756 623	68.7
1 VII 1997	ESDF	10 219 982	7 106 247	69.5	4 769 223	3 332 777	69.9	5 450 759	3 773 470	69.2
1 VII 1998	ESDF	10 191 479	7 140 980	70.1	4 753 951	3 345 660	70.4	5 437 528	3 795 320	69.8
16 II 1999	CDJC	10 045 237	6 961 516	69.3	4 717 621	3 279 196	69.5	5 327 616	3 682 320	69.1
1 VII 1999	ESDF	10 035 210	6 971 628	69.5	4 711 689	3 282 317	69.7	5 323 521	3 689 311	69.3
1 VII 2000	ESDF	10 004 958	6 999 510	70.0	...	...	...	...	...	...
1 VII 2001	ESDF	9 970 688	7 022 386	70.4	...	...	...	...	...	...
1 VII 2002	ESDF	9 924 766	7 034 721	70.9	4 652 109	3 299 920	70.9	5 272 657	3 734 801	70.8
1 VII 2003	ESDF	9 873 826	7 040 950	71.3	4 623 963	3 297 535	71.3	5 249 863	3 743 415	71.3
Bulgaria - Bulgarie										
1 VII 1994	ESDF	8 443 591	5 718 212	67.7	4 140 802	2 792 807	67.4	4 302 789	2 925 405	68.0
1 VII 1995	ESDF	8 406 067	5 702 133	67.8	4 116 667	2 780 230	67.5	4 289 400	2 921 903	68.1

6. Urban and total population by sex: 1994 - 2003
Population urbaine et population totale selon le sexe: 1994 - 2003
(continued — suite)

Continent, country or area and date / Continent, pays ou zone et date	Code[1]	Both sexes - Les deux sexes			Male - Masculin			Female - Féminin		
		Total	Urban - Urbaine		Total	Urban - Urbaine		Total	Urban - Urbaine	
			Number Nombre	Percent P.100		Number Nombre	Percent P.100		Number Nombre	Percent P.100
EUROPE										
Bulgaria - Bulgarie										
1 VII 1996	ESDF	8 362 826	5 661 482	67.7	...	...	...	...	...	...
1 VII 1997	ESDF	8 312 068	5 623 899	67.7	4 061 233	2 734 426	67.3	4 250 835	2 889 473	68.0
1 VII 1998	ESDF	8 256 786	5 603 501	67.9	4 029 518	...	...	4 227 268	...	...
1 VII 1999	ESDF	8 210 624	5 587 165	68.0	4 002 616	...	...	4 208 008	...	...
1 VII 2000	ESDF	8 170 172	5 577 216	68.3	3 979 292	2 700 131	67.9	4 190 880	2 877 085	68.7
1 III 2001	CDFC	7 928 901	5 474 534	69.0	3 862 465	2 651 312	68.6	4 066 436	2 823 222	69.4
1 VII 2001	ESDF	7 910 430	5 477 604	69.2	3 852 034	2 652 367	68.9	4 058 397	2 825 237	69.6
1 VII 2002	ESDF	7 868 900	5 467 777	69.5	3 828 882	2 644 285	69.1	4 040 018	2 823 492	69.9
1 VII 2003	ESDF	7 823 557	5 459 344	69.8	3 803 501	2 636 908	69.3	4 020 056	2 822 436	70.2
Croatia - Croatie										
31 III 2001	CDJC	4 437 460	2 471 328	55.7	2 135 900	1 171 950	54.9	2 301 560	1 299 378	56.5
Czech Republic - République tchèque										
1 VII 1994	ESDJ	10 336 162	7 722 404	74.7	5 021 408	...	...	5 314 754	...	...
1 VII 1995	ESDJ	10 330 759	7 715 655	74.7	5 020 163	...	...	5 310 596	...	...
1 VII 1996	ESDJ	10 315 353	7 701 911	74.7	5 014 667	...	...	5 300 686	...	...
1 VII 1997	ESDJ	10 303 642	7 692 120	74.7	5 010 531	...	...	5 293 111	...	...
1 VII 1998	ESDJ	10 294 943	7 675 220	74.6	5 007 480	...	...	5 287 463	...	...
1 VII 1999	ESDJ	10 282 784	7 659 954	74.5	5 002 823	...	...	5 279 961	...	...
1 VII 2000	ESDJ	10 272 503	7 641 415	74.4	4 999 326	3 694 433	73.9	5 273 177	3 946 982	74.9
1 III 2001	CDJC	10 230 060	7 564 200	73.9	4 982 071	3 657 775	73.4	5 247 989	3 906 425	74.4
1 VII 2001	ESDJ	10 224 192	7 559 732	73.9	4 978 951	3 655 116	73.4	5 245 241	3 904 616	74.4
1 VII 2002	ESDJ	10 200 774	7 536 154	73.9	4 964 598	3 640 572	73.3	5 236 176	3 895 582	74.4
1 VII 2003	ESDJ	10 201 651	7 533 782	73.8	4 968 189	3 640 805	73.3	5 233 462	3 892 977	74.4
Estonia - Estonie										
1 VII 1994	ESDF	1 499 255	1 051 449	70.1	699 749	483 939	69.2	799 506	567 510	71.0
1 VII 1995	ESDF	1 483 942	1 037 099	69.9	691 934	476 322	68.8	792 008	560 777	70.8
1 VII 1996	ESDF	1 469 216	1 022 676	69.6	684 346	468 434	68.4	784 870	554 241	70.6
1 VII 1997	ESDF	1 457 987	1 011 012	69.3	678 674	462 004	68.1	779 313	549 008	70.4
1 VII 1998	ESDF	1 449 712	1 003 118	69.2	674 656	457 641	67.8	775 056	545 478	70.4
1 VII 1999	ESDF	1 442 389	997 188	69.1	671 130	454 363	67.7	771 259	542 825	70.4
31 III 2000	CDJC	1 370 052	923 211	67.4	631 851	415 515	65.8	738 201	507 696	68.8
1 VII 2000	ESDF	1 369 515	947 308	69.2	631 579	426 593	67.5	737 936	520 715	70.6
1 VII 2001	ESDF	1 364 101	943 944	69.2	629 020	424 985	67.6	735 081	518 959	70.6
1 VII 2002	ESDF	1 358 644	940 465	69.2	626 276	423 224	67.6	732 368	517 241	70.6
1 VII 2003	ESDF	1 353 557	937 201	69.2	623 705	421 604	67.6	729 852	515 597	70.6
Finland - Finlande										
1 VII 1994	ESDJ	5 088 333	3 266 117	64.2	2 475 923	1 560 508	63.0	2 612 410	1 705 609	65.3
1 VII 1995	ESDJ	5 107 790	3 291 480	64.4	2 486 675	1 573 544	63.3	2 621 115	1 717 936	65.5
1 VII 1996	ESDJ	5 124 573	3 323 247	64.8	2 496 148	1 589 993	63.7	2 628 425	1 733 254	65.9
1 VII 1997	ESDJ	5 139 835	3 064 503	59.6	2 504 847	1 451 773	58.0	2 634 988	1 589 177	60.3
1 VII 1998	ESDJ	5 153 498	3 089 077	59.9	2 512 587	1 476 277	58.8	2 640 911	1 612 800	61.1
1 VII 1999	ESDJ	5 165 474	3 112 147	60.2	2 519 551	1 488 063	59.1	2 645 923	1 624 084	61.4
1 VII 2000	ESDJ	5 176 208	3 157 401	61.0	...	...	...	...	...	...
31 XII 2000	CDJC	5 181 115	3 167 668	61.1	2 529 341	1 516 812	60.0	2 651 774	1 650 856	62.3
1 VII 2001	ESDJ	5 188 008	3 179 283	61.3	2 533 469	1 523 008	60.1	2 654 539	1 656 275	62.4
1 VII 2002	ESDJ	5 200 598	3 217 447	61.9	2 541 256	1 543 243	60.7	2 659 342	1 674 204	63.0
1 VII 2003	ESDJ	5 213 014	3 234 178	62.0	2 548 905	1 552 734	60.9	2 664 109	1 681 445	63.1
Hungary - Hongrie[52]										
1 VII 1994	ESDF	10 261 323	6 749 527	65.8	4 913 327	3 085 533	62.8	5 347 996	3 435 370	64.2
1 VII 1995	ESDF	10 228 989	6 670 673	65.2	4 893 810	3 038 844	62.1	5 335 179	3 401 226	63.8
1 VII 1996	ESDF	10 193 371	6 636 078	65.1	4 873 597	3 037 842	62.3	5 319 774	3 405 105	64.0
1 VII 1997	ESDF	10 154 900	6 596 923	65.0	4 852 592	3 051 927	62.9	5 302 308	3 424 289	64.6
1 VII 1998	ESDF	10 113 574	6 553 655	64.8	4 829 734	3 028 148	62.7	5 283 840	3 403 554	64.4
1 VII 1999	ESDF	10 067 507	6 508 855	64.7	4 804 690	3 016 494	62.8	5 262 817	3 395 530	64.5
1 VII 2000	ESDF	10 024 222	6 461 457	64.5	4 781 701	3 038 795	63.6	5 242 522	3 422 662	65.3
1 II 2001	CDFC	10 198 315	6 572 880	64.5	4 850 650	3 091 857	63.7	5 347 665	3 481 023	65.1
1 VII 2001	ESDF	10 187 576	6 666 009	65.4	4 843 996	3 132 262	64.7	5 343 580	3 533 747	66.1
1 VII 2002	ESDF	10 158 608	6 628 717	65.3	4 827 718	3 111 851	64.5	5 330 890	3 516 866	66.0
1 VII 2003	ESDF	10 129 552	6 595 551	65.1	4 811 285	3 092 638	64.3	5 318 268	3 502 913	65.9

6. Urban and total population by sex: 1994 - 2003
Population urbaine et population totale selon le sexe: 1994 - 2003
(continued — suite)

Continent, country or area and date / Continent, pays ou zone et date	Code[1]	Both sexes - Les deux sexes			Male - Masculin			Female - Féminin		
		Total	Urban - Urbaine		Total	Urban - Urbaine		Total	Urban - Urbaine	
			Number Nombre	Percent P.100		Number Nombre	Percent P.100		Number Nombre	Percent P.100
EUROPE										
Iceland - Islande										
1 VII 1994	ESDJ	266 006	243 261	91.4	133 332	121 133	90.9	132 519	121 952	92.0
1 VII 1995	ESDJ	267 380	245 027	91.6	134 038	122 044	91.1	133 342	122 983	92.2
1 VII 1996	ESDJ	268 927	246 983	91.8	134 779	123 025	91.3	134 148	123 958	92.4
1 VII 1997	ESDJ	270 915	249 293	92.0	135 779	124 196	91.5	135 136	125 097	92.6
1 VII 1998	ESDJ	273 794	252 356	92.2	137 092	125 634	91.6	136 702	126 722	92.7
1 VII 1999	ESDJ	277 184	255 910	92.3	138 783	127 433	91.8	138 401	128 477	92.8
1 VII 2000	ESDJ	281 154	259 661	92.4	140 718	129 258	91.9	140 436	130 403	92.9
1 VII 2001	ESDJ	285 054	263 409	92.4	142 660	131 217	92.0	142 308	132 192	92.9
1 VII 2002	ESDJ	287 559	266 010	92.5	143 860	132 371	92.0	143 699	133 639	93.0
1 VII 2003	ESDJ	289 272	267 957	92.6	144 713	133 340	92.1	144 559	134 617	93.1
Ireland - Irlande										
28 IV 1996	CDFC	3 626 087	2 107 991	58.1	1 800 232	1 018 779	56.6	1 825 855	1 089 212	59.7
1 VII 1996	ESDF	3 626 100	2 107 921	58.1	1 800 200	...	...	1 825 900	...	...
28 IV 2002	CDFC	3 917 203	2 334 300	59.6	1 946 164	1 133 500	58.2	1 971 039	1 200 800	60.9
1 VII 2002	ESDF	3 917 200	2 334 300	59.6	1 953 555	...	...	1 978 202	...	...
Italy - Italie										
1 VII 1997	ESDJ	57 522 971	17 459 276	30.4	...	...	...	...	...	...
1 VII 1998	ESDJ	57 587 985	17 419 059	30.2	27 959 131	...	...	29 628 854	...	...
1 VII 1999	ESDJ	57 646 255	17 348 485	30.1	27 985 491	...	...	29 660 764	...	...
1 VII 2000	ESDJ	57 761 956	17 329 002	30.0	...	...	...	...	...	...
Latvia - Lettonie										
1 VII 1994	ESDF	2 520 742	1 734 300	68.8	1 181 408	807 576	68.4	1 366 291	953 832	69.8
1 VII 1995	ESDF	2 485 056	1 705 665	68.6	1 165 252	794 513	68.2	1 350 350	941 802	69.7
1 VII 1996	ESDF	2 457 222	1 685 462	68.6	1 153 326	785 853	68.1	1 337 439	933 233	69.8
1 VII 1997	ESDF	2 432 851	1 668 743	68.6	1 121 142	757 156	67.5	1 311 709	911 587	69.5
1 VII 1998	ESDF	2 410 019	1 651 759	68.5	1 110 461	747 636	67.3	1 299 558	904 123	69.6
1 VII 1999	ESDF	2 390 482	1 632 603	68.3	1 101 163	736 958	66.9	1 289 319	895 645	69.5
31 III 2000	CDJC	2 377 383	1 618 144	68.1	1 094 964	729 745	66.6	1 282 419	888 399	69.3
1 VII 2000	ESDF	2 372 985	1 614 159	68.0	1 092 871	727 722	66.6	1 280 114	886 437	69.2
1 VII 2001	ESDF	2 355 011	1 599 272	67.9	1 084 485	720 359	66.4	1 270 527	878 913	69.2
1 VII 2002	ESDF	2 338 624	1 586 220	67.8	1 076 587	713 616	66.3	1 262 037	872 604	69.1
1 VII 2003	ESDF	2 325 342	1 576 965	67.8	1 070 697	709 024	66.2	1 254 645	867 941	69.2
Lithuania - Lituanie										
1 VII 1994	ESDJ	3 657 144	2 472 287	67.6	1 725 290	1 159 235	67.2	1 931 854	1 313 776	68.0
1 VII 1995	ESDJ	3 629 102	2 445 532	67.4	1 709 387	1 143 067	66.9	1 919 715	1 302 990	67.9
1 VII 1996	ESDJ	3 601 613	2 430 778	67.5	1 693 703	1 131 996	66.8	1 907 910	1 298 582	68.1
1 VII 1997	ESDJ	3 575 137	2 413 579	67.5	1 678 748	1 120 554	66.7	1 896 390	1 293 454	68.2
1 VII 1998	ESDJ	3 549 331	2 387 853	67.3	1 664 608	1 105 323	66.4	1 884 724	1 282 960	68.1
1 VII 1999	ESDJ	3 524 238	2 367 146	67.2	1 650 931	1 092 628	66.2	1 873 307	1 274 518	68.0
1 VII 2000	ESDJ	3 499 536	2 345 640	67.0	1 637 615	1 079 945	65.9	1 861 921	1 265 695	68.0
6 IV 2001	CDJC	3 483 972	2 332 098	66.9	1 629 148	1 071 986	65.8	1 854 824	1 260 112	67.9
1 VII 2001	ESDJ	3 481 292	2 330 184	66.9	1 627 704	1 070 901	65.8	1 853 588	1 259 283	67.9
1 VII 2002	ESDJ	3 469 070	2 321 713	66.9	1 620 891	1 065 912	65.8	1 848 179	1 255 801	67.9
1 VII 2003	ESDJ	3 454 205	2 307 326	66.8	1 612 996	1 058 108	65.6	1 841 209	1 249 218	67.8
Netherlands - Pays-Bas[53,54]										
1 VII 1994	ESDJ	15 382 838	9 348 881	60.8	7 606 685	4 580 054	60.2	7 776 153	4 768 827	61.3
1 VII 1995	ESDJ	15 459 006	9 424 906	61.0	7 644 886	4 619 169	60.4	7 814 120	4 805 737	61.5
1 VII 1996	ESDJ	15 530 498	9 545 330	61.5	7 679 546	4 679 415	60.9	7 850 952	4 865 915	62.0
1 VII 1997	ESDJ	15 610 650	9 678 486	62.0	7 718 439	4 745 978	61.5	7 892 211	4 932 508	62.5
1 VII 1998	ESDJ	15 707 209	9 826 124	62.6	7 766 673	4 820 259	62.1	7 940 536	5 005 865	63.0
1 VII 1999	ESDJ	15 812 088	9 974 974	63.1	7 819 794	4 895 583	62.6	7 992 294	5 079 392	63.6
1 VII 2000	ESDJ	15 925 513	10 170 596	63.9	7 878 086	4 995 169	63.4	8 047 427	5 175 427	64.3
1 VII 2001	ESDJ	16 046 180	10 388 487	64.7	7 940 911	5 106 377	64.3	8 105 269	5 282 110	65.2
1 I 2002	CDJC	16 105 285	10 447 684	64.9	7 971 967	5 137 422	64.4	8 133 318	5 310 262	65.3
1 VII 2002	ESDJ	16 148 929	10 488 796	65.0	7 993 719	5 158 261	64.5	8 155 210	5 330 535	65.4
1 VII 2003	ESDJ	16 225 302	10 598 154	65.3	8 030 693	5 212 792	64.9	8 194 610	5 385 362	65.7
Norway - Norvège[55]										
3 XI 2001	CDJC	4 520 947	3 458 699	76.5	2 240 281	1 694 153	75.6	2 280 666	1 764 546	77.4

6. Urban and total population by sex: 1994 - 2003
Population urbaine et population totale selon le sexe: 1994 - 2003
(continued — suite)

Continent, country or area and date / Continent, pays ou zone et date	Code[1]	Both sexes - Les deux sexes			Male - Masculin			Female - Féminin		
		Total	Urban - Urbaine		Total	Urban - Urbaine		Total	Urban - Urbaine	
			Number Nombre	Percent P.100		Number Nombre	Percent P.100		Number Nombre	Percent P.100
EUROPE										
Poland - Pologne[56,57]										
1 VII 1994	ESDF	38 543 577	23 858 039	61.9	18 763 139	11 339 127	60.4	19 780 438	12 350 638	62.4
1 VII 1995	ESDF	38 587 596	23 873 641	61.9	18 779 284	11 423 370	60.8	19 808 312	12 450 271	62.9
1 VII 1996	ESDF	38 618 019	23 896 823	61.9	18 789 243	11 429 857	60.8	19 828 776	12 466 966	62.9
1 VII 1997	ESDF	38 649 914	23 927 869	61.9	18 800 457	11 439 693	60.8	19 849 457	12 488 176	62.9
1 VII 1998	ESDF	38 666 145	23 931 229	61.9	18 801 934	11 436 090	60.8	19 864 211	12 495 139	62.9
1 VII 1999	ESDF	38 653 625	23 908 265	61.9	18 788 696	11 417 385	60.8	19 864 929	12 490 880	62.9
1 VII 2000	ESDF	38 255 945	23 691 220	61.9	...	...	...	...	...	...
1 VII 2001	ESDF	38 250 790	23 656 606	61.8	18 532 945	11 261 781	60.8	19 717 845	12 394 825	62.9
20 V 2002	CDFC	38 230 080	23 610 365	61.8	18 516 403	11 234 165	60.7	19 713 677	12 376 200	62.8
1 VII 2002	ESDF	38 232 301	23 607 932	61.7	18 517 179	11 232 736	60.7	19 715 122	12 375 196	62.8
1 VII 2003	ESDF	38 195 177	23 543 325	61.6	18 492 950	11 195 269	60.5	19 702 227	12 348 056	62.7
Portugal[58]										
12 III 2001	CDFC	10 148 259	5 573 842	54.9	4 862 699	2 638 617	54.3	5 285 560	2 935 225	55.5
Republic of Moldova - République de Moldova[59]										
1 VII 1997	ESDJ	3 654 208	1 525 600	41.7	1 749 374	733 792	41.9	1 904 834	791 808	41.6
1 VII 1998	ESDJ	3 652 200	1 535 200	42.0	1 748 400	739 800	42.3	1 903 800	795 400	41.8
1 VII 1999	ESDJ	3 646 400	1 530 500	42.0	1 745 550	738 850	42.3	1 900 850	791 650	41.6
1 VII 2000	ESDJ	3 639 000	1 513 300	41.6	1 742 300	730 800	41.9	1 896 700	782 500	41.3
1 VII 2001	ESDJ	3 631 462	1 485 810	40.9	1 739 081	717 661	41.3	1 892 381	768 149	40.6
1 VII 2002	ESDJ	3 623 062	1 484 676	41.0	1 735 430	716 822	41.3	1 887 632	767 854	40.7
1 VII 2003	ESDJ	3 612 874	1 481 035	41.0	1 730 861	714 970	41.3	1 882 013	766 065	40.7
Romania - Roumanie										
1 VII 1994	ESDJ	22 730 622	12 427 612	54.7	11 156 807	6 037 065	54.1	11 573 815	6 390 547	55.2
1 VII 1995	ESDJ	22 680 951	12 457 195	54.9	11 123 977	6 047 572	54.4	11 556 974	6 409 623	55.5
1 VII 1996	ESDJ	22 607 620	12 411 174	54.9	11 080 933	6 016 714	54.3	11 526 687	6 394 460	55.5
1 VII 1997	ESDJ	22 545 925	12 404 690	55.0	11 041 414	6 007 827	54.4	11 504 511	6 396 863	55.6
1 VII 1998	ESDJ	22 502 803	12 347 886	54.9	11 012 110	5 971 134	54.2	11 490 693	6 376 752	55.5
1 VII 1999	ESDJ	22 458 022	12 302 729	54.8	10 984 529	...	...	11 473 493	...	...
1 VII 2000	ESDJ	22 435 205	12 244 598	54.6	10 968 854	5 907 848	53.9	11 466 351	6 336 750	55.3
1 VII 2001	ESDJ	22 408 393	12 243 748	54.6	10 949 490	5 903 537	53.9	11 458 903	6 340 211	55.3
1 VII 2002	ESDJ	21 794 793	11 608 735	53.3	10 642 538	5 579 042	52.4	11 152 255	6 029 693	54.1
1 VII 2003	ESDJ	21 733 556	11 600 157	53.4	10 606 245	5 566 401	52.5	11 127 311	6 033 756	54.2
Russian Federation - Fédération de Russie[60]										
1 VII 1994	ESDJ	148 407 902	108 313 242	73.0	...	...	...	...	...	...
1 VII 1995	ESDJ	148 375 788	108 316 176	73.0	...	...	...	...	...	...
1 VII 1996	ESDJ	148 160 126	108 249 217	73.1	...	...	...	...	...	...
1 VII 1997	ESDJ	147 915 373	108 149 293	73.1	...	...	...	...	...	...
1 VII 1998	ESDJ	147 670 780	108 082 037	73.2	...	...	...	...	...	...
1 VII 1999	ESDJ	147 214 777	107 736 373	73.2	...	...	...	...	...	...
1 VII 2000	ESDJ	146 596 870	107 245 609	73.2	...	...	...	...	...	...
1 VII 2001	ESDJ	145 976 473	106 898 541	73.2	68 130 465	49 504 490	72.7	77 846 008	57 394 051	73.7
1 VII 2002	ESDJ	145 306 497	106 523 307	73.3	67 706 316	49 224 967	72.7	77 600 181	57 298 340	73.8
1 VII 2003	ESDJ	144 565 934	106 069 837	73.4	67 257 276	48 917 406	72.7	77 308 658	57 152 431	73.9
San Marino - Saint-Marin										
1 VII 1994	ESDF	24 889	22 505	90.4	12 382	11 194	90.4	12 507	11 311	90.4
1 VII 1995	ESDF	24 988	22 339	89.4	12 375	11 063	89.4	12 613	11 276	89.4
1 VII 1997	ESDF	25 823	23 085	89.4	12 757	11 404	89.4	13 066	11 681	89.4
1 VII 2000	ESDF	26 941	22 738	84.4	13 185	11 787	89.4	13 756	10 951	79.6
Serbia and Montenegro - Serbie-et-Montenegro[61,62]										
1 VII 1994	ESDJ	10 515 582	5 400 221	51.4	5 214 043	2 635 731	50.6	5 301 539	2 764 490	52.1

6. Urban and total population by sex: 1994 - 2003
Population urbaine et population totale selon le sexe: 1994 - 2003
(continued — suite)

Continent, country or area and date / Continent, pays ou zone et date	Code[1]	Both sexes - Les deux sexes			Male - Masculin			Female - Féminin		
		Total	Urban - Urbaine		Total	Urban - Urbaine		Total	Urban - Urbaine	
			Number Nombre	Percent P.100		Number Nombre	Percent P.100		Number Nombre	Percent P.100
EUROPE										
Serbia and Montenegro - Serbie-et-Montene-gro[61,62]										
1 VII 1995	ESDJ	10 546 983	5 420 604	51.4	5 229 817	2 646 039	50.6	5 317 166	2 774 565	52.2
1 VII 1996	ESDJ	10 577 208	5 440 835	51.4	5 245 109	2 656 349	50.6	5 332 099	2 784 486	52.2
1 VII 1997	ESDJ	10 600 067	5 456 379	51.5	5 256 354	2 664 248	50.7	5 343 713	2 792 131	52.3
1 VII 1998	ESDJ	10 616 886	5 468 037	51.5	5 264 001	2 669 658	50.7	5 352 885	2 798 379	52.3
1 VII 1999	ESDJ	10 629 358	5 477 426	51.5	5 269 974	2 674 193	50.7	5 359 384	2 803 233	52.3
1 VII 2000	ESDJ	10 633 508	5 482 862	51.6	...	...	...	...	...	...
1 VII 2001	ESDJ	10 651 650	5 495 310	51.6	5 280 896	2 683 098	50.8	5 370 754	2 812 212	52.4
1 VII 2002	ESDJ	8 113 868	4 608 767	56.8	3 948 798	2 206 353	55.9	4 165 070	2 402 414	57.7
1 VII 2003	ESDJ	8 152 676	4 654 786	57.1	3 967 478	2 227 301	56.1	4 185 198	2 427 485	58.0
Slovakia - Slovaquie										
1 VII 1994	ESDJ	5 347 413	3 045 894	57.0	2 604 937	1 472 177	56.5	2 742 476	1 573 717	57.4
1 VII 1995	ESDJ	5 363 676	3 057 117	57.0	...	...	...	...	...	...
1 VII 1996	ESDJ	5 373 793	3 062 080	57.0	...	...	...	...	...	...
1 VII 1997	ESDJ	5 383 233	3 066 450	57.0	...	...	...	...	...	...
1 VII 1998	ESDJ	5 390 866	3 066 457	56.9	...	...	...	...	...	...
1 VII 1999	ESDJ	5 395 324	3 061 062	56.7	...	...	...	...	...	...
1 VII 2000	ESDJ	5 400 679	3 059 010	56.6	...	...	...	...	...	...
25 V 2001	CDJC	5 379 455	3 022 106	56.2	2 612 515	1 453 638	55.6	2 766 940	1 568 468	56.7
1 VII 2001	ESDJ	5 379 780	3 017 527	56.1	...	...	...	...	...	...
1 VII 2002	ESDJ	5 378 809	3 011 737	56.0	2 611 452	1 447 959	55.4	2 767 357	1 563 778	56.5
1 VII 2003	ESDJ	5 378 950	3 001 776	55.8	2 610 872	1 442 174	55.2	2 768 078	1 559 602	56.3
Slovenia - Slovénie[63]										
1 VII 1994	ESDJ	1 988 850	997 916	50.2	964 113	475 551	49.3	1 024 737	522 365	51.0
31 III 2002	CDJC	1 964 036	997 772	50.8	958 576	479 356	50.0	1 005 460	518 416	51.6
1 VII 2002	ESDJ	1 995 718	975 163	48.9	976 111	462 513	47.4	1 019 607	512 650	50.3
1 VII 2003	ESDJ	1 996 773	971 513	48.7	977 436	460 811	47.1	1 019 337	510 702	50.1
Switzerland - Suisse										
1 VII 1994	ESDJ	6 993 795	4 745 834	67.9	3 416 116	...	...	3 577 679	...	...
1 VII 1995	ESDJ	7 040 687	4 768 417	67.7	3 438 605	2 304 085	67.0	3 602 082	2 464 332	68.4
1 VII 1996	ESDJ	7 071 851	4 783 434	67.6	3 453 232	2 311 082	66.9	3 618 619	2 472 352	68.3
1 VII 1997	ESDJ	7 088 906	4 789 234	67.6	3 461 432	2 314 317	66.9	3 627 474	2 474 917	68.2
1 VII 1998	ESDJ	7 110 002	4 799 607	67.5	3 471 966	2 320 098	66.8	3 638 036	2 479 509	68.2
1 VII 1999	ESDJ	7 143 991	4 823 202	67.5	3 489 699	2 333 007	66.9	3 654 292	2 490 195	68.1
1 VII 2000	ESDJ	7 184 250	4 854 390	67.6	3 510 203	2 349 347	66.9	3 674 047	2 505 043	68.2
5 XII 2000	CDJC	7 204 055	4 871 989	67.6	3 519 698	2 357 890	67.0	3 684 357	2 514 099	68.2
The Former Yugoslav Rep. of Macedonia - L'ex-République yougoslave de Macédoine										
20 VI 1994	CDJC	1 945 932	1 163 598	59.8	974 255	...	...	971 677	...	...
1 VII 1997	ESDF	1 996 869	1 189 442	59.6	999 595	590 300	59.1	997 274	599 142	60.1
Ukraine										
1 VII 1994	ESDF	52 114 400	35 400 700	67.9	...	...	...	...	...	...
1 VII 1995	ESDF	51 728 400	35 118 800	67.9	...	...	...	...	...	...
1 VII 1996	ESDF	51 334 100	34 832 500	67.9	...	...	...	...	...	...
1 VII 1997	ESDF	50 893 500	34 521 800	67.8	...	...	...	...	...	...
1 VII 1998	ESDF	50 499 900	34 271 600	67.9	...	...	...	...	...	...
1 VII 1999	ESDF	50 105 600	34 017 400	67.9	...	...	...	...	...	...
1 VII 2000	ESDJ	48 889 280	32 768 879	67.0	22 642 532	15 171 760	67.0	26 246 748	17 597 119	67.0
1 VII 2001	ESDJ	48 452 256	32 448 930	67.0	22 423 360	14 992 532	66.9	26 028 896	17 456 398	67.1
5 XII 2001	CDJC	48 457 102	32 574 371	67.2	22 441 344	15 056 675	67.1	26 015 758	17 517 696	67.3
1 VII 2002	ESDJ	48 032 005	32 181 723	67.0	22 214 426	14 843 215	66.8	25 817 580	17 338 508	67.2
1 VII 2003	ESDJ	47 632 594	31 981 796	67.1	22 019 672	14 732 101	66.9	25 612 922	17 249 695	67.3

6. Urban and total population by sex: 1994 - 2003
Population urbaine et population totale selon le sexe: 1994 - 2003
(continued — suite)

Continent, country or area and date / Continent, pays ou zone et date	Code[1]	Both sexes - Les deux sexes			Male - Masculin			Female - Féminin		
		Total	Urban - Urbaine		Total	Urban - Urbaine		Total	Urban - Urbaine	
			Number Nombre	Percent P.100		Number Nombre	Percent P.100		Number Nombre	Percent P.100
OCEANIA — OCEANIE										
Cook Islands - Îles Cook										
1 XII 1996	CDFC	19 103	11 225	58.8	9 842	5 730	58.2	9 261	5 495	59.3
Fiji - Fidji										
25 VIII 1996	CDFC	775 077	359 495	46.4	393 931	180 119	45.7	381 146	179 376	47.1
Guam[14,15]										
1 VII 1994	ESDJ	143 157	54 618	38.2	...	...	...	...	...	...
1 VII 1995	ESDJ	144 190	55 012	38.2	...	...	...	...	...	...
1 VII 1996	ESDJ	145 324	55 445	38.2	...	...	...	...	...	...
1 VII 1997	ESDJ	146 799	56 008	38.2	...	...	...	...	...	...
1 VII 1998	ESDJ	149 724	57 124	38.2	...	...	...	...	...	...
1 VII 1999	ESDJ	152 590	58 217	38.2	...	...	...	...	...	...
1 IV 2000	CDJC	154 805	144 129	93.1	79 181	...	...	75 624	...	...
1 VII 2001	ESDJ	158 330	147 411	93.1	...	...	...	...	...	...
1 VII 2002	ESDJ	161 057	149 950	93.1	...	...	...	...	...	...
1 VII 2003	ESDJ	163 593	152 311	93.1	...	...	...	...	...	...
New Caledonia - Nouvelle-Calédonie										
1 VII 1996	ESDF	*197 389*	*118 823*	*60.2*	*101 030*	...	...	*96 394*	...	...
New Zealand - Nouvelle-Zélande										
5 III 1996	CDJC	3 618 303	3 091 740	85.4	1 777 464	1 503 444	84.6	1 840 839	1 588 296	86.3
1 VII 1996	ESDJ	3 732 000	3 191 300	85.5	1 830 300	...	...	1 883 800	...	...
1 VII 1997	ESDJ	3 781 400	3 237 800	85.6	1 863 700	...	...	1 917 700	...	...
1 VII 1998	ESDJ	3 815 000	3 269 700	85.7	1 877 800	...	...	1 937 200	...	...
1 VII 1999	ESDJ	3 835 100	3 289 300	85.8	1 884 900	...	...	1 950 200	...	...
1 VII 2000	ESDJ	3 857 800	3 310 100	85.8	1 893 800	...	...	1 964 000	...	...
1 VII 2001	ESDJ	3 880 500	3 331 400	85.8	1 903 200	...	...	1 977 300	...	...
1 VII 2002	ESDJ	3 939 100	3 385 000	85.9	1 934 000	...	...	2 005 100	...	...
1 VII 2003	ESDJ	4 009 200	3 449 300	86.0	1 971 300	...	...	2 037 900	...	...
Palau - Palaos										
9 IX 1995	CDFC	17 225	12 299	71.4	9 213	...	...	8 012	...	...
15 IV 2000	CDFC	19 129	13 303	69.5	...	...	...	...	...	...
Papua New Guinea - Papouasie-Nouvelle-Guinée[64]										
9 VII 2000	CDFC	5 190 786	686 301	13.2	2 691 744	372 453	13.8	2 499 042	313 848	12.6
Tonga										
30 XI 1996	CDFC	97 784	22 400	22.9	49 615	...	...	48 169	...	...
Vanuatu										
16 XI 1999	CDJC	186 678	40 094	21.5	95 682	...	...	90 996	...	...

FOOTNOTES - NOTES

Italics: estimates which are less reliable. - Italiques: estimations moins sûres.

[1] 'Code' indicates the source of data, as follows:
CDFC - Census, de facto, complete tabulation
CDFS - Census, de facto, sample tabulation
CDJC - Census, de jure, complete tabulation
CDJS - Census, de jure, sample tabulation
SSDF - Sample survey, de facto
SSDJ - Sample survey, de jure
ESDF - Estimates, de facto
ESDJ - Estimates, de jure
Le 'Code' indique la source des données, comme suit:
CDFC - Recensement, population de fait, tabulation complète
CDFS - Recensement, population de fait, tabulation par sondage
CDJC - Recensement, population de droit, tabulation complète
CDJS - Recensement, population de droit, tabulation par sondage
SSDF - Enquête par sondage, population de fait

SSDJ - Enquête par sondage, population de droit
ESDF - Données estimatées, population de fait
ESDJ - Données estimatées, population de droit
[2] Series not strictly comparable due to differences of definitions of "urban". - - Les séries ne sont pas strictement comparables en raison de différences existant dans la définition des "regions urbaines".
[3] For 1996, data for urban and rural areas are not adjusted for under-enumeration, estimated around 5 per cent for the total country. - Pour 1996, les données pour les zones urbaines et rurales n'ont pas été adjustées pour tenir en compte de la sous-etimation de 5 p. cent approximativement.
[4] Because of rounding, totals are not in all cases the sum of the parts. - Les chiffres étant arrondis, les totaux ne correspondent pas toujours rigoureusement à la somme des chiffres partiels.
[5] Census results have been adjusted for underenumeration, estimated at 5.1 per cent. - Les résultats du recensement ont été ajustées pour compenser les lacunes du dénombrement, estimées à 5,1 p. 100.
[6] The number of males and / or females excludes persons whose sex is not stated (18 urban, 19 rural). - Il n'est pas tenu compte dans le nombre d'hommes et de femmes des personnes dont le sexe n'est pas indiqué (18 en zone urbaine et 19 en zone rurale).

[7] Based on results of a Socio Economic Survey. - Basé sur les résultats d'une enquête Socio-Economique.

[8] Mid-year estimates have been adjusted for underenumeration, at latest census. - Les estimations au milieu de l'année tiennent compte d'une ajustement destiné à compenser les lacunes du dénombrement lors du dernier recensement.

[9] Census result have been adjusted for underenumeration, estimated at 6.8 per cent. - Les résultat du recensement ont été ajustées pour compenser les lacunes du dénombrement, estimées à 6,8 p. 100.

[10] Census data have not been adjusted for underenumeration. - Les données de recensement ne tiennent pas compte de d'une ajustement destiné à compenser les lacunes du dénombrement.

[11] For 1994 and 1995, revised intercensal estimates adjusted for net undercoverage. For 1996, 1997 and 1998 final intercensal estimates. For 2001 and 2002, final postcensal estimates. For 2003 updated postcensal estimates. - - Pour 1994 et 1995, estimations inter censitaires corrigées pour tenir en compte du sous dénombrement net. Pour 1996, 1997 et 1998 estimations inter censitaires finales. Pour 2001 and 2002, évaluations postcensal finales. Pour 2003 estimations post censitaires mises à jour.

[12] For the census, population statistics are based on administrative records. - - Pour le recensement, la source de la statistique de la population sont des fichiers administratifs.

[13] For the census, including persons of unknown residence. - Pour le recensement, y compris les personnes d'état résidence inconnu.

[14] Including armed forces stationed in the area. - Y compris les militaires en garnison sur le territoire.

[15] Definition of urban and rural distribution changed from the year 2000. - La définition des régions urbaines et rurales a changée depuis 2000.

[16] Excluding armed forces overseas and civilian citizens absent from country for an extended period of time. - Non compris les militaires à l'étranger, et les civils hors du pays pendant une période prolongée.

[17] Data include persons in remote areas, military personel outside the country, merchant seamen at sea, civilian seasonal workers outside the country, and other civilians outside the country, and exclude nomads, foreign military, civilian aliens temporarily in the country, transients on ships and Indian jungle population. - Y compris les personnes dans des régions éloignées, le personel militaire en dehors du pays, les marins marchands, les ouvriers saisonniers civils de couture en dehors du pays, et autres civils en dehors du pays, et non compris les nomades, les militaires étrangers, les étrangers civils temporairement dans le pays, les transiteurs sur des bateaux et les Indiens de la jungle.

[18] Excluding nomadic Indian tribes. - Non compris les tribus d'Indiens nomades.

[19] Excluding Indian jungle population. - Non compris les Indiens de la jungle.

[20] For the urban/rural distribution, data refer to the settled population based on the 1979 Population Census; an estimated 1.5 million nomads are not included. - Pour la distribution urbaine/rurale, les données se rapportent a la population stationnaire a la base de recensement de 1979; les nomades, estimées a 1.5 million, ne sont pas inclus.

[21] For 2002 the total population was the only figure which was revised. - Pour 2002, l'effectif total de la population est le seul chiffre révisé.

[22] The methodology used for calculating the number of the de facto and de jure population in the 2001 census data differs as follows from the methodology used in previous censuses: the duration that defines a person as being 'temporary present' or 'temporary absent' is now 'under one year'. The previously applied definition was for '6 months'. - La méthode utilisée pour dénombrer la population présente et la population légale dans le contexte du recensement de 2001 diffère de celle qui a été appliquée lors des recensements antérieurs en ce que la durée considérée pour définir la 'présence temporaire' ou 'l'absence temporaire' était dorénavant fixée à 'moins d'un an' alors qu'elle était de '6 mois' auparavant.

[23] Excluding foreign diplomatic personnel and their dependants. - Non compris le personnel diplomatique étranger et les membres de leur famille les accompagnant.

[24] For 1996, based on results of a sample survey. - Pour 1996, d'après les résultats d'une enquête par sondage.

[25] For statistical purposes, the data for China do not include those for the Hong Kong Special Administrative Region (Hong Kong SAR), Macao Special Administrative Region (Macao SAR) and Taiwan province of China. - Pour la présentation des statistiques, les données pour Chine ne comprend pas la Région Administrative Spéciale de Hong Kong (Hong Kong RAS), la Région Administrative Spéciale de Macao (Macao RAS) et Taïwan province de Chine.

[26] Data for the period 1990 to 2000 have been adjusted on the basis of the Population Census of 2000. - Les données pour la période allant de 1990 à 2000 ont été ajustées à partir des résultats du recensement de la population de 2000.

[27] For estimates from 1994 to 2003, the military personnel are classified as urban population. - Le personnel militaire est classé dans la population urbaine.

[28] For 2000 census, data for the civilian population of 31 provinces, municipalities and autonomous regions. - Pour recensement de 2000, pour la population civile seulement de 31 provinces, municipalités et régions autonomes.

[29] Data from 2001 to 2003 estimated on the basis of the annual National Sample Survey on Population Changes. - Les données de 2001 à 2003 ont été estimées sur la base de l'enquête annuelle "National Sample Survey on Population Changes".

[30] Data refer to government controlled areas. - Les données se raportent aux zones contrôlées par le Gouvernement.

[31] Data include all population irrespective of citizenship, who at the time of the census have resided in the country or intended to reside for a period of at least one year. It does not distinguish between those present or absent at the time of census. - Les chiffres comprennent toute la population, quelle que soit la nationalité, qui à l'époque de recensement avait résidé dans le pays, ou avait l'intention d'y résider, pendant une période au moins un an. Il n'y a pas de distinction entre les personnes présentes ou absentes au moment du recensement.

[32] For census, data exclude Mao-Maram, Paomata and Purul sub-divisions of Senapati district of Manipur. The population of Manipur including the estimated population of the three sub-divisions of Senapati district is 2,291,125 (Males 1,161,173 and females 1,129,952). - Pour le recensement, non compris les subdivisions Mao-Maram Paomata et Purul du district de Senapati dans l'État du Manipur. Cet État compte 2 291 125 habitants (1 161 173 hommes et 1 129 952 femmes), y compris la population estimative des trois subdivisions du district de Senapati.

[33] Including data for the Indian-held part of Jammu and Kashmir, the final status of which has not yet been determined. - Y compris les données pour la partie du Jammu et du Cachemire occupée par l'Inde dont le statut définitif n'a pas encore été déterminé.

[34] For 2000, the figure includes an estimated population of 459 557 persons in urban and 1 857 659 persons in rural areas that were not directly enumerated, and a population of 566 403 persons in urban and 1 717 578 persons in rural areas that decline the participation. Also included are 421 399 non permanent residents (the homeless, the crew of ships carrying national flag, boat/floating house people, remote located tribesmen and refugees.) - Pour 2000, y compris la population estimée a 459 557 personnes dans les zones urbaines et de 1 857 659 personnes dans les zones rurales qui n'ont pas été énumérées directement, aussi que 566 403 personnes qui non pas répondu dans les zones urbaines et de 1 717 578 personnes dans les zones rurales. Y compris 421 399 résidants non permanents (les sans abri, l'équipage des bateaux portant le drapeau national, les habitants des embarcations ou des maisons flottantes, les habitants des tribus isolées et les réfugies.)

[35] For the 1997 population census, data exclude population in three autonomous provinces in the north of the country. - Pour le recensement de 1997, la population des trois provinces autonomes dans le nord du pays est exclue.

[36] Including data for East Jerusalem and Israeli residents in certain other territories under occupation by Israeli military forces since June 1967. - Y compris les données pour Jérusalem-Est et les résidents israéliens dans certains autres territoires occupés depuis 1967 par les forces armées israéliennes.

[37] Excluding diplomatic personnel outside the country and foreign military and civilian personnel and their dependants stationed in the area. - Non compris le personnel diplomatique hors du pays ni les militaires et agents civils étrangers en poste sur le territoire et les membres de leur famille les accompagnant.

[38] Excluding data for Jordanian territory under occupation since June 1967 by Israeli military forces. Excluding foreigners, including registered Palestinian refugees. - Non compris les données pour le territoire jordanien occupé depuis juin 1967 par les forces armées israéliennes. Non compris les étrangers, mais y compris les réfugiés de Palestine enregistrés.

[39] For the 1995 census, excluding alien armed forces, civilian aliens employed by armed forces, foreign diplomatic personnel and their dependants and Korean diplomatic personnel and their dependants outside the country. Also data exclude adjustment for underenumeration. - Pour le recensement de 1995, non compris les militaires étrangers, les civils étrangers employés par les forces armées, le personnel diplomatique étranger et les membres de leur famille les accompagnant et le personnel diplomatique coréen hors du pays et les membres de leurs familles les accompagnant. Les données de recensement n'ont pas été ajustées pour compenser les lacunes du dénombrement.

[40] For 2000 census, urban/rural: Places with 50 000 or more inhabitants are usually considered urban in Korea. However, the census results are composed in the basis of the minor administrative divisions such as Dongs (mostly urban areas) and Eups or Myeons (rural areas) rather than urban or rural residences. In this report, urban refers to Dongs and rural refers to Eups and Myeons. Also, including diplomats and their families abroad, but excluding foreign diplomats, foreign military personnal, and their families in the country. - Pour 2000 recensement, urbaine/rurale: les lieux avec 50,000 habitants ou plus sont habituellement considérés urbains en Corée. Cependant, les résultats du recensement ont été préparés sur la base des divisions administratives mineures comme les Dongs (principalement des zones urbaines), et les Eups ou Myeons (des zones rurales) plutôt que sur les résidences urbaines ou rurales. Dans ce rapport urbaine se rapporte aux Dongs et rural aux Eups et aux Myeons. Y compris le personnel diplomatique et les membres de leurs familles à l'étranger, mais sans tenir compte du personnel diplomatique et militaire étranger et des membres de leurs familles.

[41] For the 2000 census, excluding Malaysian citizens and permanent residents who were away or intended to be away trom the country for more than six months. Excluding Malaysian military, naval and diplomatic personnel and their families outside the country, and tourists, businessmen who intended to be in Malaysia for less than six months. - Pour le 2000 recensement, non compris les citoyens malaisiens et les résidents permanents qui étaient ou qui ont prévu

d'être hors du pays pour six mois ou plus. Non compris le personnel militaire Malaisien, le personnel naval ou diplomatique et leurs familles hors du pays, et les touristes et les hommes d'affaires qui avaient l'intention de rester en Malaisie moins de six mois.

[42] For the 2000 census results have been adjusted for underenumeration. - - Pour le 2000 recensement les résultats ont été ajustées pour compenser les lacunes du dénombrement

[43] For 2001 and before unrevised data. - Pour 2001 et avant les données n'ont pas été révisées.

[44] Data for urban refer to 170 towns out of 254 towns. Data for rural refer to 62 townships out of 158 townships. - Les données urbaines se rapportent à 170 des 254 villes. Les données rurales se rapportent à 62 des 158 municipalités.

[45] From 1998 to 2003 totals were revised but male/female distribution unrevised. - De 1998 à 2003 les totaux ont été révisés alors que la distribution masculin/féminin n'a pas été révisée.

[46] Data for urban including population in refugee camps. - Les données pour la population urbaine comprennent la population dans les camps réfugiés.

[47] Excluding data for the Pakistan-held part of Jammu and Kashmir, the final status of which has not yet been determined. - Non compris les données concernant la partie du Jammu et Cachemire occupée par le Pakistan dont le statut définitif n'a pas été déterminé.

[48] The Population and Housing Census 2001 did not cover the whole area of the country due to the security problems; the Census was complete in 18 districts only; in three districts it was not possible to conduct it; and in four districts it was partially conducted. - Le recensement de la population et de l'habitat en 2001 n'a pas couvert la totalité du pays pour des problèmes de sécurité; le recensement a été complété seulement en 18 districts; dans 3 districts ça n'a pas été possible de conduire le recensement et dans 4 districts il a été partiellement conduit.

[49] Including Palestinian refugees. - Y compris les réfugiés de Palestine

[50] For the 2000 census, data for "urban" refer to population in municipalities, data for "rural" refer to the population in non-municipal areas. - Pour le recensement de 2000, les données pour la zone urbaine se rapportent a la population des municipalités, les données pour la zone rurale se rapportent a la population au dehors des municipalités.

[51] Comprising 7 sheikdoms of Abu Dhabi, Dubai, Sharjah, Ajaman, Umm al Qaiwain, Ras al Khaimah and Fujairah, and the area lying within the modified Riyadh line as announced in October 1955. - Comprend les sept cheikhats de Abou Dhabi, Dabai, Ghârdja, Adjmân, Oumm-al-Quiwaïn, Ras al Khaïma et Foudjaïra, ainsi que la zone délimitée par la ligne de Riad modifiée comme il a été annoncé en octobre 1955.

[52] The regional grouping (urban/rural) was made from 1990 to 2000 according to the administrative division of 1 January 2000 and from 2001 according to the administrative division of 1 January 2004. - Pour les années 1990 à 2000, le découpage régional (zone urbaine/rurale) correspond au découpage administratif en vigueur au 1er janvier 2000; à partir de 2001, il correspond à celui en vigueur au 1er janvier 2004.

[53] Census result, based on compilation of continuous accounting and sample surveys. - Les résultat du recensement, d'après les résultats des dénombrements et enquêtes par sondage continue.

[54] For 1994 the total population and the male/female distribution include persons on the Central Register of Population (containing persons belonging to the Netherlands population but having no fixed municipality of residence). - Pour 1994 la population totale et le sexe masculine et féminin comprend les personnes inscrites sur le Registre central de la population (personnes appartenant à la population néerlandaise mais sans résidence fixe dans une des municipalités).

[55] Including residents temporarily outside the country. - Y compris les résidents se trouvant temporairement hors du pays.

[56] Average year data for 2000-2001 contain revised data according to the final results of population census 2002. - Les données annuelles moyennes pour 2000-2001 comportent des données révisées en fonction des résultats du recensement de 2002.

[57] Excluding civilian aliens within country, but including civilian nationals temporarily outside country. - Non compris les civils étrangers dans le pays, mais y compris les civils nationaux temporairement hors du pays.

[58] Including the Azores and Madeira Islands. - Y compris les Açores et Madère.

[59] Data do not include information for Transnistria and the municipality of Bender. - Les données ne tiennent pas compte de l'information sur la Transnistria et la municipalité de Bender.

[60] Figures were updated taking into account the results of the 2002 All-Russian population census. - Les chiffres ont été calculés compte tenu des résultats du recensement de la population de la Fédération de Russie de 2002.

[61] From 1998 - 2001, estimates of Kosovo and Metohia computed on the basis of natural increases from year 1997. - De 1998 - 2001, les estimations pour le Kosovo et la Metohia ont été calculées sur la base des incréments naturelles depuis 1997.

[62] From 2002 without data for Kosovo and Metohia. - Après 2002 sans les donées pour le Kosovo and Metohie.

[63] Urban and rural estimates do not add up to the total, as urban/ and rural data refer only to citizens. - La somme des chiffres des zones urbaines et rurales ne correspond pas au chiffre total, les données urbaines/rurales ne concernant que les ressortissants de la République de Slovénie.

[64] Comprising the eastern part of New Guinea, the Bismarck Archipelago, Bougainville and Buka of Solomon Islands group and about 600 smaller islands. - Comprend l'est de la Nouvelle-Guinée, l'archipel Bismarck, Bougainville et Buka (ces deux dernières du groupe des Salomon) et environ 600 îlots.

Table 7

Table 7 presents population by age, sex and urban/rural residence for the latest available year.

Description of variables: Data in this table are either population census figures or estimates, some of which are based on sample surveys. Data refer to the de facto population unless otherwise noted.

The reference date of the census or estimate appears in the stub of the table. In general, the estimates refer to mid-year (1 July).

Age is defined as age at last birthday, that is, the difference between the date of birth and the reference date of the age distribution expressed in completed solar years. The age classification used in this table is the following: under 1 year, 1-4 years, 5-year groups through 95-99 years, and 100 years and over.

Statistics are presented for one year, the most recent available. However, if more complete disaggregation is available for earlier years, both are displayed.

The urban/rural classification of population by age and sex is that provided by each country or area; it is presumed to be based on the national census definitions of urban population that have been set forth at the end of the technical notes to table 6.

Estimates of population by age and sex presented in this table have been limited to countries or areas for which estimates have been based on the results of a sample survey or have been constructed by the component method from the results of a population census or sample survey. Estimations derived from distributing estimated total population according to percentages in each age-sex group at the time of a census or sample survey are not included in this table.

Reliability of data: Estimates which are believed to be less reliable are set in *italics* rather than in roman type. No attempt has been made to take account of age-reporting accuracy, the evaluation of which has been described in section 3.1.3 of the Technical Notes.

Limitations: Statistics on population by age and sex are subject to the same qualifications as have been set forth for population statistics in general and age distributions in particular, as discussed in sections 3 and 3.1.3, respectively, of the Technical Notes.

Comparability of population data classified by age and sex is limited by variations in the definition of total population, discussed in detail in section 3 of the Technical Notes, and by the accuracy of the original enumeration. Both factors are more important in relation to certain age groups than to others. For example, under-enumeration is known to be more prevalent among infants and young children than among older persons. Similarly, the exclusion from the total population of certain groups that tend to be of selected ages (such as the armed forces) can markedly affect the age structure and its comparability with that for other countries or areas. Consideration should be given to the implications of these basic limitations in using the data.

In addition to these general qualifications are the special problems of comparability that arise in relation to age statistics in particular. Age distributions of population are known to suffer from certain deficiencies that have their origin in irregularities in age reporting. Although some of the irregularities tend to be obscured or eliminated when data are tabulated in five-year age groups rather than by single years, precision still continues to be affected, though the degree of distortion is not always readily seen.

Another factor limiting comparability is the age classification employed by the various countries or areas. Age may be based on the year of birth rather than the age at last birthday, in other words, calculated using the day, month and year of birth. Distributions based only on the year of birth are footnoted when known.

The absence of frequencies in the unknown age group does not necessarily indicate completely accurate reporting and tabulation of the age item. The unknowns may have been eliminated by assigning ages to them before tabulation, or by proportionately distributing the unknown category across the age groups after tabulation.

As noted in connection with table 5, intercensal estimates of total population are usually revised to accord with the results of a census of population if inexplicable discontinuities appear to exist. Postcensal age-sex distributions, however, are less likely to be revised in this way. When it is known that a total population estimate for a given year has been revised and the corresponding age distribution has not been, the age distribution is shown as provisional. Distributions of this type should be used with caution when studying trends over a period of years, though their utility for studying age structure for the specified year is probably unimpaired.

The comparability of data by urban/rural residence is affected by the national definitions of urban and rural used in tabulating these data. When known, the definitions of urban used in national population censuses are presented at the end of the technical notes for table 6. As discussed in detail in the technical notes for table 6, these definitions vary considerably from one country or area to another.

Earlier data: Population by age, sex and urban/rural residence has been shown in previous issues of the *Demographic Yearbook*. For more information on specific topics, and years for which data are reported, readers should consult the Historical Index. In addition, population by single years of age, sex and urban/rural residence are shown in the *Demographic Yearbook* Special Census Topics table 1 available online at http://unstats.un.org/unsd/demographic/products/dyb/dybcens.htm.

Tableau 7

Le tableau 7 présente les données les plus récentes dont on dispose sur la population selon l'âge, le sexe et le lieu de résidence (zone urbaine ou rurale).

Description des variables : Les données de ce tableau proviennent de recensements de la population ou correspondent à des estimations fondées, dans certains cas, sur des enquêtes par sondage. Sauf indication contraire, elles se rapportent à la population de fait.

La date du recensement ou de l'estimation figure dans la colonne de gauche du tableau. En général, les estimations se rapportent au milieu de l'année (1er juillet).

L'âge désigne l'âge au dernier anniversaire, c'est-à-dire la différence entre la date de naissance et la date de référence de la répartition par âge exprimée en années solaires révolues. La classification par âge utilisée dans ce tableau est la suivante : moins d'un an, 1 à 4 ans, groupes quinquennaux jusqu'à 95-99 ans et 100 ans et plus.

Les statistiques portent sur une année, qui correspond à celle pour laquelle on dispose des statistiques les plus récentes. Toutefois, si l'on dispose de répartitions plus complètes pour des années antérieures, les statistiques sont alors présentées pour les deux années.

La classification par zones urbaines et rurales de la population selon l'âge et le sexe est celle qui est communiquée par chaque pays ou zone ; on part du principe qu'elle repose sur les définitions de la population urbaine utilisées pour les recensements de la population nationaux telles qu'elles sont reproduites à la fin des notes techniques du tableau 6.

Les estimations de la population selon l'âge et le sexe qui figurent dans ce tableau ne concernent que les pays ou zones pour lesquels les estimations sont fondées sur les résultats d'une enquête par sondage ou ont été établies par la méthode des composantes à partir des résultats d'un recensement de la population ou d'une enquête par sondage. Les répartitions par âge et par sexe obtenues en appliquant à l'estimation de la population totale les pourcentages enregistrés pour les divers groupes d'âge pour chaque sexe lors d'un recensement ou d'une enquête par sondage n'ont pas été reproduites dans ce tableau.

Fiabilité des données : Les estimations considérées comme moins sûres sont indiquées en italique plutôt qu'en caractères romains. On n'a pas tenu compte des inexactitudes dans les déclarations d'âge, dont la méthode d'évaluation est exposée à la section 3.1.3 des Notes techniques.

Insuffisance des données : Les statistiques de la population selon l'âge et le sexe appellent les mêmes réserves que celles qui ont été formulées aux sections 3 et 3.1.3 des Notes techniques à propos des statistiques de la population en général et des répartitions par âge en particulier.

La comparabilité des statistiques de la population selon l'âge et le sexe pâtit du manque d'uniformité dans la définition de la population totale (voir la section 3 des Notes techniques) et des lacunes des dénombrements. L'influence de ces deux facteurs varie selon les groupes d'âge. Ainsi, le dénombrement des enfants de moins d'un an et des jeunes enfants comporte souvent plus de lacunes que celui des personnes plus âgées. De même, le fait que certains groupes de personnes appartenant souvent à des groupes d'âge déterminés, par exemple les militaires, ne soient pas pris en compte dans la population totale peut influer sensiblement sur la structure par âge et sur la comparabilité des données avec celles d'autres pays ou zones. Il conviendra de tenir compte de ces facteurs fondamentaux lorsque l'on utilisera les données du tableau.

Outre ces difficultés d'ordre général, la comparabilité pose des problèmes particuliers lorsqu'il s'agit des données par âge. On sait que les répartitions de la population selon l'âge présentent certaines imperfections dues à l'inexactitude des déclarations d'âge. Certaines de ces anomalies ont tendance à s'estomper ou à disparaître lorsque l'on classe les données par groupes d'âge quinquennaux et non par années d'âge, mais une certaine imprécision subsiste, même s'il n'est pas toujours facile de voir à quel point il y a distorsion.

Le degré de comparabilité dépend également de la classification par âge employée dans les divers pays ou zones. L'âge retenu peut être défini par date exacte (jour, mois et année) de naissance ou par celle du dernier anniversaire. Lorsqu'elles étaient connues, les répartitions établies seulement d'après l'année de la naissance ont été signalées en note à la fin du tableau.

Si aucun nombre ne figure dans la rangée réservée aux âges inconnus, cela ne signifie pas nécessairement que les déclarations d'âge et l'exploitation des données par âge aient été tout à fait exactes. C'est souvent une indication que l'on a attribué un âge aux personnes d'âge inconnu avant l'exploitation des données ou qu'elles ont été réparties proportionnellement entre les différents groupes après cette opération.

Comme on l'a indiqué à propos du tableau 5, les estimations intercensitaires de la population totale sont d'ordinaire rectifiées d'après les résultats des recensements de population si l'on constate des discontinuités inexplicables. Les données postcensitaires concernant la répartition de la population par âge et par sexe ont toutefois moins de chance d'être rectifiées de cette manière. Lorsque l'on savait qu'une estimation de la population totale pour une année donnée avait été rectifiée sans qu'il en soit de même pour la répartition par âge correspondante, cette dernière a été indiquée comme ayant un caractère provisoire. Les répartitions de ce type doivent être utilisées avec prudence lorsque l'on étudie les tendances sur un certain nombre d'années, quoique leur utilité pour l'étude de la structure par âge de la population pour l'année visée reste probablement entière.

La comparabilité des données selon le lieu de résidence (zone urbaine ou rurale) peut être limitée par les définitions nationales des termes « urbain » et « rural » utilisées pour la mise en tableaux de ces données. Les définitions du terme « urbain » utilisées pour les recensements nationaux de population ont été présentées à la fin des notes techniques du tableau 6 lorsqu'elles étaient connues. Comme on l'a précisé dans les notes techniques relatives au tableau 6, ces définitions varient considérablement d'un pays ou d'une zone à l'autre.

Données publiées antérieurement : Des statistiques concernant la population selon l'âge, le sexe et le lieu de résidence (zone urbaine ou rurale) ont été présentées dans des éditions antérieures de l'*Annuaire démographique*. Pour plus de précisions concernant les années et les sujets pour lesquels des données ont été publiées, se reporter à l'index historique.

Continent, country or area, date and age (in years) / Continent, pays ou zone, date et âge (en années)	Code[1]	Total			Urban - Urbaine			Rural - Rurale		
		Both sexes Les deux sexes	Male Masculin	Female Féminin	Both sexes Les deux sexes	Male Masculin	Female Féminin	Both sexes Les deux sexes	Male Masculin	Female Féminin
AFRICA — AFRIQUE										
Algeria - Algérie										
1 VII 2003										
Total	ESDJ	31 847 995	16 090 568	15 757 427	...	...	...	...	...	...
0 - 1	ESDJ	604 019	308 412	295 607	...	...	...	...	...	...
1 - 4	ESDJ	2 310 513	1 180 730	1 129 783	...	...	...	...	...	...
5 - 9	ESDJ	3 224 819	1 647 090	1 577 729	...	...	...	...	...	...
10 - 14	ESDJ	3 642 440	1 856 114	1 786 326	...	...	...	...	...	...
15 - 19	ESDJ	3 808 498	1 939 408	1 869 089	...	...	...	...	...	...
20 - 24	ESDJ	3 522 547	1 791 140	1 731 407	...	...	...	...	...	...
25 - 29	ESDJ	2 959 388	1 493 925	1 465 463	...	...	...	...	...	...
30 - 34	ESDJ	2 508 416	1 259 600	1 248 816	...	...	...	...	...	...
35 - 39	ESDJ	2 102 178	1 056 627	1 045 551	...	...	...	...	...	...
40 - 44	ESDJ	1 680 817	845 183	835 634	...	...	...	...	...	...
45 - 49	ESDJ	1 378 726	694 140	684 586	...	...	...	...	...	...
50 - 54	ESDJ	1 081 550	545 636	535 914	...	...	...	...	...	...
55 - 59	ESDJ	776 901	382 388	394 513	...	...	...	...	...	...
60 - 64	ESDJ	659 350	320 650	338 700	...	...	...	...	...	...
65 - 69	ESDJ	591 984	286 760	305 224	...	...	...	...	...	...
70 - 74	ESDJ	452 969	219 670	233 299	...	...	...	...	...	...
75 - 79	ESDJ	282 819	137 992	144 827	...	...	...	...	...	...
80+	ESDJ	260 063	125 104	134 959	...	...	...	...	...	...
Benin - Bénin										
11 II 2002										
Total	CDJC	6 769 914	3 284 119	3 485 795	2 630 133	1 280 418	1 349 715	4 139 781	2 003 701	2 136 080
0 - 1	CDJC	235 342	118 243	117 099	82 945	41 797	41 148	152 397	76 446	75 951
1 - 4	CDJC	939 907	475 297	464 610	309 993	157 189	152 804	629 914	318 108	311 806
5 - 9	CDJC	1 155 377	589 653	565 724	380 207	188 422	191 785	775 170	401 231	373 939
10 - 14	CDJC	838 749	438 376	400 373	332 753	162 989	169 764	505 996	275 387	230 609
15 - 19	CDJC	653 251	321 984	331 267	294 811	144 462	150 349	358 440	177 522	180 918
20 - 24	CDJC	563 947	243 515	320 432	262 496	123 275	139 221	301 451	120 240	181 211
25 - 29	CDJC	532 056	228 090	303 966	232 948	107 420	125 528	299 108	120 670	178 438
30 - 34	CDJC	414 166	192 429	221 737	180 416	88 668	91 748	233 750	103 761	129 989
35 - 39	CDJC	340 632	157 551	183 081	143 773	69 970	73 803	196 859	87 581	109 278
40 - 44	CDJC	264 488	125 792	138 696	109 427	54 554	54 873	155 061	71 238	83 823
45 - 49	CDJC	196 056	94 805	101 251	81 020	40 280	40 740	115 036	54 525	60 511
50 - 54	CDJC	167 901	81 461	86 440	63 992	31 615	32 377	103 909	49 846	54 063
55 - 59	CDJC	93 493	46 214	47 279	36 952	18 405	18 547	56 541	27 809	28 732
60 - 64	CDJC	116 796	53 543	63 253	38 629	17 488	21 141	78 167	36 055	42 112
65 - 69	CDJC	63 847	28 630	35 217	22 857	10 048	12 809	40 990	18 582	22 408
70 - 74	CDJC	71 231	32 523	38 708	22 048	9 550	12 498	49 183	22 973	26 210
75 - 79	CDJC	32 158	14 609	17 549	10 617	4 473	6 144	21 541	10 136	11 405
80 - 84	CDJC	41 705	18 397	23 308	11 461	4 501	6 960	30 244	13 896	16 348
85 - 89	CDJC	13 113	6 037	7 076	3 860	1 497	2 363	9 253	4 540	4 713
90 - 94	CDJC	12 256	5 945	6 311	3 413	1 457	1 956	8 843	4 488	4 355
95+	CDJC	23 098	10 753	12 345	5 317	2 201	3 116	17 781	8 552	9 229
Unk. - Inc.	CDJC	345	272	73	198	157	41	147	115	32
Botswana										
17 VIII 2001										
Total	CDFC	1 680 863	813 488	867 375	...	...	...	...	...	...
0 - 1	CDFC	42 845	21 755	21 090	...	...	...	...	...	...
1 - 4	CDFC	152 800	76 879	75 921	...	...	...	...	...	...
5 - 9	CDFC	208 296	104 129	104 167	...	...	...	...	...	...
10 - 14	CDFC	209 968	104 610	105 358	...	...	...	...	...	...
15 - 19	CDFC	203 706	99 603	104 103	...	...	...	...	...	...
20 - 24	CDFC	170 614	80 148	90 466	...	...	...	...	...	...
25 - 29	CDFC	147 766	71 877	75 889	...	...	...	...	...	...
30 - 34	CDFC	113 755	54 997	58 758	...	...	...	...	...	...
35 - 39	CDFC	95 343	44 651	50 692	...	...	...	...	...	...
40 - 44	CDFC	76 373	35 236	41 137	...	...	...	...	...	...
45 - 49	CDFC	63 480	29 573	33 907	...	...	...	...	...	...
50 - 54	CDFC	45 100	21 585	23 515	...	...	...	...	...	...
55 - 59	CDFC	33 305	15 674	17 631	...	...	...	...	...	...
60 - 64	CDFC	28 615	13 378	15 237	...	...	...	...	...	...

7. Population by age, sex and urban/rural residence: latest available year, 1994 - 2003
Population selon l'âge, le sexe et la résidence, urbaine/rurale: dernière année disponible, 1994 - 2003
(continued — suite)

Continent, country or area, date and age (in years) / Continent, pays ou zone, date et âge (en années)	Code[1]	Total			Urban - Urbaine			Rural - Rurale		
		Both sexes Les deux sexes	Male Masculin	Female Féminin	Both sexes Les deux sexes	Male Masculin	Female Féminin	Both sexes Les deux sexes	Male Masculin	Female Féminin
AFRICA — AFRIQUE										
Botswana										
17 VIII 2001										
65 - 69	CDFC	25 474	11 113	14 361	...	...	...	...	...	...
70 - 74	CDFC	21 130	8 891	12 239	...	...	...	...	...	...
75+	CDFC	36 640	14 411	22 229	...	...	...	...	...	...
Unk. - Inc.	CDFC	5 653	4 978	675	...	...	...	...	...	...
Burkina Faso										
10 XII 1996										
Total	CDFC	10 312 609	4 970 882	5 341 727	...	...	...	...	...	...
0 - 1	CDFC	346 453	173 583	172 870	...	...	...	...	...	...
1 - 4	CDFC	1 421 971	715 961	706 010	...	...	...	...	...	...
5 - 9	CDFC	1 798 242	913 006	885 236	...	...	...	...	...	...
10 - 14	CDFC	1 375 393	706 641	668 752	...	...	...	...	...	...
15 - 19	CDFC	1 082 487	534 025	548 462	...	...	...	...	...	...
20 - 24	CDFC	767 462	340 162	427 300	...	...	...	...	...	...
25 - 29	CDFC	666 645	285 292	381 353	...	...	...	...	...	...
30 - 34	CDFC	572 745	250 049	322 696	...	...	...	...	...	...
35 - 39	CDFC	467 470	205 558	261 912	...	...	...	...	...	...
40 - 44	CDFC	390 677	173 362	217 315	...	...	...	...	...	...
45 - 49	CDFC	311 624	145 091	166 533	...	...	...	...	...	...
50 - 54	CDFC	279 315	127 031	152 284	...	...	...	...	...	...
55 - 59	CDFC	208 700	102 910	105 790	...	...	...	...	...	...
60 - 64	CDFC	196 248	93 494	102 754	...	...	...	...	...	...
65 - 69	CDFC	132 659	66 895	65 764	...	...	...	...	...	...
70 - 74	CDFC	114 931	54 300	60 631	...	...	...	...	...	...
75 - 79	CDFC	62 654	31 623	31 031	...	...	...	...	...	...
80 - 84	CDFC	36 026	15 405	20 621	...	...	...	...	...	...
85 - 89	CDFC	14 151	6 253	7 898	...	...	...	...	...	...
90 - 94	CDFC	9 503	3 742	5 761	...	...	...	...	...	...
95+	CDFC	15 888	5 839	10 049	...	...	...	...	...	...
Unk. - Inc.	CDFC	41 365	20 660	20 705	...	...	...	...	...	...
Cape Verde - Cap-Vert										
1 VII 2003										
Total	ESDF	460 968	223 254	237 715	257 412	125 652	131 759	203 556	97 600	105 956
0 - 4	ESDF	58 940	30 004	28 936	30 116	15 352	14 765	28 823	14 652	14 171
5 - 9	ESDF	61 218	30 867	30 351	30 927	15 643	15 284	30 291	15 224	15 067
10 - 14	ESDF	64 803	32 445	32 358	34 166	16 918	17 248	30 636	15 526	15 110
15 - 19	ESDF	57 898	28 923	28 975	33 909	16 551	17 358	23 990	12 372	11 618
20 - 24	ESDF	42 677	21 383	21 294	26 883	13 427	13 456	15 794	7 956	7 838
25 - 29	ESDF	31 691	15 870	15 821	20 027	9 970	10 057	11 664	5 901	5 763
30 - 34	ESDF	27 198	13 321	13 877	16 627	8 322	8 306	10 570	4 999	5 571
35 - 39	ESDF	26 745	12 770	13 975	16 748	8 330	8 419	9 996	4 440	5 556
40 - 44	ESDF	22 729	10 461	12 268	13 844	6 826	7 018	8 886	3 635	5 251
45 - 49	ESDF	16 084	6 733	9 351	9 359	4 438	4 921	6 726	2 296	4 430
50 - 54	ESDF	9 378	3 674	5 704	5 496	2 386	3 110	3 882	1 288	2 594
55 - 59	ESDF	5 466	2 224	3 242	2 921	1 271	1 651	2 545	953	1 592
60 - 64	ESDF	7 569	2 919	4 650	3 580	1 404	2 176	3 989	1 515	2 474
65 - 69	ESDF	9 285	3 660	5 625	4 224	1 629	2 595	5 062	2 032	3 030
70 - 74	ESDF	7 654	3 244	4 410	3 316	1 270	2 046	4 338	1 974	2 364
75 - 79	ESDF	5 041	2 183	2 858	2 264	853	1 410	2 778	1 330	1 448
80+	ESDF	6 593	2 573	4 020	3 005	1 064	1 941	3 589	1 510	2 079
Congo										
1 VII 2001										
Total	ESDF	2 974 413	...	...	...	...	...	...	...	...
0 - 4	ESDF	501 189	...	...	...	...	...	...	...	...
5 - 9	ESDF	445 865	...	...	...	...	...	...	...	...
10 - 14	ESDF	381 915	...	...	...	...	...	...	...	...
15 - 19	ESDF	329 268	...	...	...	...	...	...	...	...
20 - 24	ESDF	268 292	...	...	...	...	...	...	...	...
25 - 29	ESDF	212 671	...	...	...	...	...	...	...	...
30 - 34	ESDF	157 941	...	...	...	...	...	...	...	...
35 - 39	ESDF	130 874	...	...	...	...	...	...	...	...

7. **Population by age, sex and urban/rural residence: latest available year, 1994 - 2003**
Population selon l'âge, le sexe et la résidence, urbaine/rurale: dernière année disponible, 1994 - 2003
(continued — suite)

Continent, country or area, date and age (in years) / Continent, pays ou zone, date et âge (en années)	Code[1]	Total			Urban - Urbaine			Rural - Rurale		
		Both sexes Les deux sexes	Male Masculin	Female Féminin	Both sexes Les deux sexes	Male Masculin	Female Féminin	Both sexes Les deux sexes	Male Masculin	Female Féminin
AFRICA — AFRIQUE										
Congo										
1 VII 2001										
40 - 44	ESDF	120 166	...	...	...	...	...	...	...	...
45 - 49	ESDF	106 781	...	...	...	...	...	...	...	...
50 - 54	ESDF	88 340	...	...	...	...	...	...	...	...
55 - 59	ESDF	74 360	...	...	...	...	...	...	...	...
60 - 64	ESDF	61 272	...	...	...	...	...	...	...	...
65 - 69	ESDF	44 914	...	...	...	...	...	...	...	...
70+	ESDF	50 565	...	...	...	...	...	...	...	...
Egypt - Égypte										
19 XI 1996										
Total	CDFC	59 312 914	30 351 390	28 961 524	25 286 335	12 957 775	12 328 560	34 026 579	17 393 615	16 632 964
0 - 1	CDFC	560 622	288 082	272 540	238 653	122 073	116 580	321 969	166 009	155 960
1 - 4	CDFC	6 294 620	3 223 694	3 070 926	2 257 688	1 152 819	1 104 869	4 036 932	2 070 875	1 966 057
5 - 9	CDFC	7 626 252	3 939 121	3 687 131	2 852 218	1 464 520	1 387 698	4 774 034	2 474 601	2 299 433
10 - 14	CDFC	7 864 002	4 076 601	3 787 401	3 116 208	1 602 009	1 514 199	4 747 794	2 474 592	2 273 202
15 - 19	CDFC	6 901 611	3 602 857	3 298 754	2 930 311	1 510 230	1 420 081	3 971 300	2 092 627	1 878 673
20 - 24	CDFC	5 075 136	2 642 620	2 432 516	2 273 551	1 167 895	1 105 656	2 801 585	1 474 725	1 326 860
25 - 29	CDFC	4 370 522	2 105 063	2 265 459	1 916 234	933 765	982 469	2 454 288	1 171 298	1 282 990
30 - 34	CDFC	3 979 720	1 993 212	1 986 508	1 847 108	917 762	929 346	2 132 612	1 075 450	1 057 162
35 - 39	CDFC	3 860 105	1 914 367	1 945 738	1 776 094	879 215	896 879	2 084 011	1 035 152	1 048 859
40 - 44	CDFC	3 173 226	1 616 449	1 556 777	1 573 960	810 931	763 029	1 599 266	805 518	793 748
45 - 49	CDFC	2 696 169	1 408 498	1 287 671	1 296 912	687 877	609 035	1 399 257	720 621	678 636
50 - 54	CDFC	2 022 136	994 936	1 027 200	984 817	503 584	481 233	1 037 319	491 352	545 967
55 - 59	CDFC	1 476 673	776 537	700 136	686 141	372 516	313 625	790 532	404 021	386 511
60 - 64	CDFC	1 398 994	706 189	692 805	665 441	349 766	315 675	733 553	356 423	377 130
65 - 69	CDFC	930 576	507 085	423 491	404 645	232 503	172 142	525 931	274 582	251 349
70 - 74	CDFC	617 669	315 767	301 902	269 065	144 153	124 912	348 604	171 614	176 990
75+	CDFC	464 858	240 302	224 556	197 282	106 154	91 128	267 576	134 148	133 428
Unk. - Inc.	CDFC	23	10	13	7	3	4	16	7	9
1 VII 2000										
Total	ESDF	63 976 000	32 695 000	31 281 000	...	...	...	...	...	...
0 - 4	ESDF	7 394 000	3 783 000	3 611 000	...	...	...	...	...	...
5 - 9	ESDF	8 225 000	4 245 000	3 980 000	...	...	...	...	...	...
10 - 14	ESDF	8 481 000	4 392 000	4 089 000	...	...	...	...	...	...
15 - 19	ESDF	7 445 000	3 882 000	3 563 000	...	...	...	...	...	...
20 - 24	ESDF	5 474 000	2 848 000	2 626 000	...	...	...	...	...	...
25 - 29	ESDF	4 714 000	2 266 000	2 448 000	...	...	...	...	...	...
30 - 34	ESDF	4 293 000	2 149 000	2 144 000	...	...	...	...	...	...
35 - 39	ESDF	4 164 000	2 064 000	2 100 000	...	...	...	...	...	...
40 - 44	ESDF	3 422 000	1 740 000	1 682 000	...	...	...	...	...	...
45 - 49	ESDF	2 909 000	1 516 000	1 393 000	...	...	...	...	...	...
50 - 54	ESDF	2 180 000	1 071 000	1 109 000	...	...	...	...	...	...
55 - 59	ESDF	1 593 000	835 000	758 000	...	...	...	...	...	...
60 - 64	ESDF	1 510 000	761 000	749 000	...	...	...	...	...	...
65 - 69	ESDF	1 003 000	546 000	457 000	...	...	...	...	...	...
70 - 74	ESDF	667 000	339 000	328 000	...	...	...	...	...	...
75+	ESDF	502 000	258 000	244 000	...	...	...	...	...	...
Ethiopia - Éthiopie										
1 VII 2002										
Total	ESDF	67 220 000	33 707 000	33 513 000	10 307 000	5 134 000	5 173 000	56 913 000	28 573 000	28 340 000
0 - 4	ESDF	11 613 528	5 858 730	5 754 798	1 295 225	675 800	619 426	10 318 302	5 182 930	5 135 372
5 - 9	ESDF	9 464 485	4 790 119	4 674 366	1 165 174	595 197	569 977	8 299 311	4 194 922	4 104 389
10 - 14	ESDF	8 134 907	4 131 454	4 003 453	1 180 977	584 705	596 272	6 953 930	3 546 749	3 407 181
15 - 19	ESDF	7 377 805	3 748 613	3 629 192	1 247 670	604 373	643 297	6 130 135	3 144 241	2 985 895
20 - 24	ESDF	6 378 061	3 230 355	3 147 705	1 186 998	579 032	607 966	5 191 062	2 651 323	2 539 739
25 - 29	ESDF	5 247 932	2 619 111	2 628 821	1 009 980	497 432	512 547	4 237 953	2 121 679	2 116 274
30 - 34	ESDF	4 259 586	2 088 116	2 171 470	809 268	405 560	403 708	3 450 318	1 682 556	1 767 762
35 - 39	ESDF	3 419 786	1 644 661	1 775 125	624 635	312 182	312 453	2 795 151	1 332 479	1 462 672
40 - 44	ESDF	2 752 267	1 309 273	1 442 994	466 806	232 349	234 457	2 285 461	1 076 924	1 208 537
45 - 49	ESDF	2 253 394	1 088 803	1 164 591	364 523	185 304	179 219	1 888 871	903 498	985 372
50 - 54	ESDF	1 829 663	902 219	927 444	284 003	144 121	139 882	1 545 660	758 098	787 562
55 - 59	ESDF	1 436 626	720 663	715 964	216 062	107 322	108 740	1 220 564	613 340	607 224

7. Population by age, sex and urban/rural residence: latest available year, 1994 - 2003
Population selon l'âge, le sexe et la résidence, urbaine/rurale: dernière année disponible, 1994 - 2003
(continued — suite)

Continent, country or area, date and age (in years) / Continent, pays ou zone, date et âge (en années)	Code[1]	Total			Urban - Urbaine			Rural - Rurale		
		Both sexes Les deux sexes	Male Masculin	Female Féminin	Both sexes Les deux sexes	Male Masculin	Female Féminin	Both sexes Les deux sexes	Male Masculin	Female Féminin
AFRICA — AFRIQUE										
Ethiopia - Éthiopie										
1 VII 2002										
60 - 64	ESDF	1 098 600	559 503	539 097	164 553	78 729	85 824	934 047	480 774	453 273
65 - 69	ESDF	813 668	417 849	395 819	122 960	56 993	65 967	690 707	360 855	329 852
70 - 74	ESDF	555 964	288 146	267 817	81 805	37 057	44 748	474 159	251 090	223 069
75+	ESDF	583 730	309 385	274 344	86 361	37 844	48 517	497 369	271 542	225 827
Ghana										
27 III 2000										
Total	CDFC	18 912 079	9 357 382	9 554 697	8 274 270	...	...	10 637 809	...	...
0 - 1	CDFC	525 258	262 041	263 217	196 042	...	...	329 216	...	...
1 - 4	CDFC	2 244 163	1 117 729	1 126 434	837 690	...	...	1 406 473	...	...
5 - 9	CDFC	2 775 206	1 390 652	1 384 554	1 053 432	...	...	1 721 774	...	...
10 - 14	CDFC	2 262 216	1 151 131	1 111 085	963 577	...	...	1 298 639	...	...
15 - 19	CDFC	1 883 753	961 162	922 591	918 094	...	...	965 659	...	...
20 - 24	CDFC	1 600 820	763 051	837 769	836 938	...	...	763 982	...	...
25 - 29	CDFC	1 487 299	695 494	791 805	747 897	...	...	739 402	...	...
30 - 34	CDFC	1 206 809	566 439	640 370	582 893	...	...	623 916	...	...
35 - 39	CDFC	1 029 765	490 864	538 901	485 638	...	...	544 127	...	...
40 - 44	CDFC	886 931	443 284	443 647	403 917	...	...	483 014	...	...
45 - 49	CDFC	720 357	377 315	343 042	318 875	...	...	401 482	...	...
50 - 54	CDFC	568 369	279 950	288 419	240 038	...	...	328 331	...	...
55 - 59	CDFC	355 842	182 843	172 999	154 952	...	...	200 890	...	...
60 - 64	CDFC	366 351	177 347	189 004	142 687	...	...	223 664	...	...
65 - 69	CDFC	258 709	129 090	129 619	103 807	...	...	154 902	...	...
70 - 74	CDFC	225 158	106 513	118 645	83 860	...	...	141 298	...	...
75 - 79	CDFC	144 830	74 268	70 562	56 031	...	...	88 799	...	...
80 - 84	CDFC	140 847	66 941	73 906	52 469	...	...	88 378	...	...
85 - 89	CDFC	107 558	58 252	49 306	46 202	...	...	61 356	...	...
90 - 94	CDFC	57 242	28 258	28 984	22 228	...	...	35 014	...	...
95+	CDFC	64 596	34 758	29 838	27 103	...	...	37 493	...	...
Guinea - Guinée										
1 XII 1996										
Total	CDFC	7 156 406	3 497 979	3 658 427	...	...	...	...	...	...
0 - 1	CDFC	249 593	126 198	123 395	...	...	...	...	...	...
1 - 4	CDFC	1 023 234	517 530	505 704	...	...	...	...	...	...
5 - 9	CDFC	1 213 159	618 249	594 910	...	...	...	...	...	...
10 - 14	CDFC	778 661	415 215	363 446	...	...	...	...	...	...
15 - 19	CDFC	662 646	315 248	347 398	...	...	...	...	...	...
20 - 24	CDFC	518 667	234 435	284 232	...	...	...	...	...	...
25 - 29	CDFC	553 395	237 650	315 745	...	...	...	...	...	...
30 - 34	CDFC	427 376	188 867	238 509	...	...	...	...	...	...
35 - 39	CDFC	372 907	173 506	199 401	...	...	...	...	...	...
40 - 44	CDFC	305 272	149 956	155 316	...	...	...	...	...	...
45 - 49	CDFC	231 669	117 477	114 192	...	...	...	...	...	...
50 - 54	CDFC	195 512	93 711	101 801	...	...	...	...	...	...
55 - 59	CDFC	142 344	75 899	66 445	...	...	...	...	...	...
60 - 64	CDFC	159 660	73 113	86 547	...	...	...	...	...	...
65 - 69	CDFC	108 893	57 077	51 816	...	...	...	...	...	...
70 - 74	CDFC	87 052	40 047	47 005	...	...	...	...	...	...
75+	CDFC	126 366	63 801	62 565	...	...	...	...	...	...
Lesotho										
1 VII 2001										
Total	SSDJ	2 157 537	1 065 484	1 092 053	288 895	131 861	157 034	1 868 642	933 623	935 019
0 - 1	SSDJ	45 867	24 441	21 426	5 590	3 177	2 413	40 277	21 264	19 013
1 - 4	SSDJ	184 467	92 420	92 047	21 097	10 832	10 265	163 370	81 588	81 782
5 - 9	SSDJ	250 417	127 720	122 697	27 655	13 408	14 247	222 762	114 312	108 450
10 - 14	SSDJ	280 429	141 486	138 943	29 492	14 094	15 398	250 937	127 392	123 545
15 - 19	SSDJ	286 404	145 591	140 813	35 686	14 075	21 611	250 719	131 517	119 202
20 - 24	SSDJ	225 779	116 163	109 616	35 176	14 235	20 941	190 603	101 928	88 675
25 - 29	SSDJ	159 700	79 705	79 995	30 051	12 477	17 574	129 648	67 227	62 421
30 - 34	SSDJ	114 507	56 175	58 332	23 915	11 542	12 373	90 592	44 633	45 959
35 - 39	SSDJ	110 264	55 375	54 889	21 547	11 162	10 385	88 717	44 213	44 504
40 - 44	SSDJ	93 645	43 925	49 720	15 044	7 468	7 576	78 602	36 457	42 145

7. Population by age, sex and urban/rural residence: latest available year, 1994 - 2003
Population selon l'âge, le sexe et la résidence, urbaine/rurale: dernière année disponible, 1994 - 2003
(continued — suite)

Continent, country or area, date and age (in years) / Continent, pays ou zone, date et âge (en années)	Code[1]	Total			Urban - Urbaine			Rural - Rurale		
		Both sexes Les deux sexes	Male Masculin	Female Féminin	Both sexes Les deux sexes	Male Masculin	Female Féminin	Both sexes Les deux sexes	Male Masculin	Female Féminin
AFRICA — AFRIQUE										
Lesotho										
1 VII 2001										
45 - 49	SSDJ	81 488	41 152	40 336	11 468	5 651	5 817	70 019	35 501	34 518
50 - 54	SSDJ	77 212	33 959	43 253	9 388	3 592	5 796	67 824	30 367	37 457
55 - 59	SSDJ	56 352	28 197	28 155	5 927	2 782	3 145	50 425	25 415	25 010
60 - 64	SSDJ	48 107	21 105	27 002	4 770	1 866	2 904	43 337	19 239	24 098
65 - 69	SSDJ	49 001	21 165	27 836	4 284	1 949	2 335	44 717	19 216	25 501
70 - 74	SSDJ	29 628	11 671	17 957	1 801	843	958	27 828	10 829	16 999
75+	SSDJ	45 242	14 815	30 427	3 208	982	2 226	42 033	13 832	28 201
Unk. - Inc.	SSDJ	19 028	10 419	8 609	2 796	1 726	1 070	16 232	8 693	7 539
Malawi										
1 IX 1998										
Total	CDFC	9 933 868	4 867 563	5 066 305	1 435 436	742 839	692 597	8 498 432	4 124 724	4 373 708
0 - 1	CDFC	368 325	182 508	185 817	49 018	24 549	24 469	319 307	157 959	161 348
1 - 4	CDFC	1 292 065	641 117	650 948	166 030	83 011	83 019	1 126 035	558 106	567 929
5 - 9	CDFC	1 440 370	714 830	725 540	183 924	90 095	93 829	1 256 446	624 735	631 711
10 - 14	CDFC	1 232 500	616 445	616 055	180 430	84 521	95 909	1 052 070	531 924	520 146
15 - 19	CDFC	1 087 936	527 865	560 071	179 240	88 044	91 196	908 696	439 821	468 875
20 - 24	CDFC	979 060	435 138	543 922	185 677	89 626	96 051	793 383	345 512	447 871
25 - 29	CDFC	792 465	393 913	398 552	152 217	85 808	66 409	640 248	308 105	332 143
30 - 34	CDFC	601 241	303 080	298 161	105 241	60 855	44 386	496 000	242 225	253 775
35 - 39	CDFC	484 827	239 043	245 784	75 067	42 734	32 333	409 760	196 309	213 451
40 - 44	CDFC	360 709	180 167	180 542	50 294	30 145	20 149	310 415	150 022	160 393
45 - 49	CDFC	332 756	166 258	166 498	38 650	23 268	15 382	294 106	142 990	151 116
50 - 54	CDFC	238 846	120 193	118 653	24 745	15 195	9 550	214 101	104 998	109 103
55 - 59	CDFC	175 226	89 909	85 317	14 921	9 171	5 750	160 305	80 738	79 567
60 - 64	CDFC	153 084	72 251	80 833	10 405	5 973	4 432	142 679	66 278	76 401
65 - 69	CDFC	139 320	65 655	73 665	7 818	4 226	3 592	131 502	61 429	70 073
70 - 74	CDFC	98 049	45 310	52 739	4 936	2 407	2 529	93 113	42 903	50 210
75 - 79	CDFC	65 485	32 151	33 334	2 936	1 489	1 447	62 549	30 662	31 887
80 - 84	CDFC	45 632	20 495	25 137	1 968	873	1 095	43 664	19 622	24 042
85 - 89	CDFC	25 214	11 540	13 674	1 042	463	579	24 172	11 077	13 095
90 - 94	CDFC	11 167	5 180	5 987	521	227	294	10 646	4 953	5 693
95+	CDFC	9 591	4 515	5 076	356	159	197	9 235	4 356	4 879
1 VII 2003										
Total	ESDF	11 548 841	5 672 569	5 876 272	...	...	...	...	...	...
0 - 4	ESDF	2 412 092	1 211 628	1 200 464	...	...	...	...	...	...
5 - 9	ESDF	1 542 049	759 066	782 983	...	...	...	...	...	...
10 - 14	ESDF	1 402 789	695 692	707 097	...	...	...	...	...	...
15 - 19	ESDF	1 206 893	602 961	603 932	...	...	...	...	...	...
20 - 24	ESDF	1 061 225	512 622	548 603	...	...	...	...	...	...
25 - 29	ESDF	950 740	420 884	529 856	...	...	...	...	...	...
30 - 34	ESDF	766 567	380 510	386 057	...	...	...	...	...	...
35 - 39	ESDF	578 190	291 635	286 555	...	...	...	...	...	...
40 - 44	ESDF	461 911	227 552	234 359	...	...	...	...	...	...
45 - 49	ESDF	339 839	169 006	170 833	...	...	...	...	...	...
50 - 54	ESDF	307 803	152 465	155 338	...	...	...	...	...	...
55+	ESDF	518 743	248 548	270 195	...	...	...	...	...	...
Mauritius - Maurice										
1 VII 2003										
Total	ESDJ	1 222 811	605 084	617 727	...	...	...	...	...	...
0 - 1	ESDJ	19 660	9 907	9 753	...	...	...	...	...	...
1 - 4	ESDJ	78 388	40 009	38 379	...	...	...	...	...	...
5 - 9	ESDJ	101 728	51 264	50 464	...	...	...	...	...	...
10 - 14	ESDJ	108 182	54 939	53 243	...	...	...	...	...	...
15 - 19	ESDJ	93 817	47 426	46 391	...	...	...	...	...	...
20 - 24	ESDJ	111 321	55 825	55 496	...	...	...	...	...	...
25 - 29	ESDJ	103 665	51 338	52 327	...	...	...	...	...	...
30 - 34	ESDJ	91 466	45 682	45 784	...	...	...	...	...	...
35 - 39	ESDJ	103 195	51 743	51 452	...	...	...	...	...	...
40 - 44	ESDJ	96 001	48 438	47 563	...	...	...	...	...	...
45 - 49	ESDJ	83 247	41 845	41 402	...	...	...	...	...	...
50 - 54	ESDJ	71 325	35 347	35 978	...	...	...	...	...	...

7. Population by age, sex and urban/rural residence: latest available year, 1994 - 2003
Population selon l'âge, le sexe et la résidence, urbaine/rurale: dernière année disponible, 1994 - 2003
(continued — suite)

Continent, country or area, date and age (in years) / Continent, pays ou zone, date et âge (en années)	Code[1]	Total			Urban - Urbaine			Rural - Rurale		
		Both sexes Les deux sexes	Male Masculin	Female Féminin	Both sexes Les deux sexes	Male Masculin	Female Féminin	Both sexes Les deux sexes	Male Masculin	Female Féminin
AFRICA — AFRIQUE										
Mauritius - Maurice										
1 VII 2003										
55 - 59	ESDJ	48 372	22 943	25 429	...	...	...	...	...	...
60 - 64	ESDJ	33 016	15 299	17 717	...	...	...	...	...	...
65 - 69	ESDJ	28 739	12 957	15 782	...	...	...	...	...	...
70 - 74	ESDJ	20 135	8 678	11 457	...	...	...	...	...	...
75 - 79	ESDJ	16 780	6 789	9 991	...	...	...	...	...	...
80 - 84	ESDJ	8 311	3 085	5 226	...	...	...	...	...	...
85+	ESDJ	5 463	1 570	3 893	...	...	...	...	...	...
Morocco - Maroc										
1 VII 2003										
Total	ESDF	30 088 000	14 972 000	15 116 000	17 244 000	8 438 000	8 806 000	12 844 000	6 534 000	6 310 000
0 - 4	ESDF	2 979 000	1 520 000	1 459 000	1 535 000	785 000	750 000	1 444 000	735 000	709 000
5 - 9	ESDF	2 942 000	1 499 000	1 443 000	1 454 000	737 000	717 000	1 488 000	762 000	726 000
10 - 14	ESDF	3 172 000	1 615 000	1 557 000	1 593 000	789 000	804 000	1 579 000	826 000	753 000
15 - 19	ESDF	3 232 000	1 642 000	1 590 000	1 669 000	811 000	858 000	1 563 000	831 000	732 000
20 - 24	ESDF	3 120 000	1 567 000	1 553 000	1 727 000	836 000	891 000	1 393 000	731 000	662 000
25 - 29	ESDF	2 746 000	1 357 000	1 389 000	1 639 000	789 000	850 000	1 107 000	568 000	539 000
30 - 34	ESDF	2 406 000	1 178 000	1 228 000	1 564 000	755 000	809 000	842 000	423 000	419 000
35 - 39	ESDF	1 972 000	937 000	1 035 000	1 349 000	630 000	719 000	623 000	307 000	316 000
40 - 44	ESDF	1 845 000	885 000	960 000	1 224 000	587 000	637 000	621 000	298 000	323 000
45 - 49	ESDF	1 474 000	754 000	720 000	975 000	505 000	470 000	499 000	249 000	250 000
50 - 54	ESDF	1 151 000	580 000	571 000	741 000	392 000	349 000	410 000	188 000	222 000
55 - 59	ESDF	756 000	357 000	399 000	471 000	228 000	243 000	285 000	129 000	156 000
60 - 64	ESDF	738 000	330 000	408 000	421 000	184 000	237 000	317 000	146 000	171 000
65 - 69	ESDF	570 000	277 000	293 000	337 000	161 000	176 000	233 000	116 000	117 000
70 - 74	ESDF	508 000	237 000	271 000	288 000	131 000	157 000	220 000	106 000	114 000
75+	ESDF	477 000	237 000	240 000	257 000	118 000	139 000	220 000	119 000	101 000
Mozambique										
1 VIII 1997										
Total	CDJC	15 278 334	7 320 948	7 957 386	4 454 859	2 201 292	2 253 567	10 823 475	5 119 656	5 703 819
0 - 1	CDJC	535 237	263 539	271 698	138 601	68 743	69 858	396 636	194 796	201 840
1 - 4	CDJC	2 206 319	1 089 667	1 116 652	558 601	277 008	281 593	1 647 718	812 659	835 059
5 - 9	CDJC	2 225 996	1 112 321	1 113 675	617 241	304 392	312 849	1 608 755	807 929	800 826
10 - 14	CDJC	1 825 665	947 236	878 429	600 911	301 921	298 990	1 224 754	645 315	579 439
15 - 19	CDJC	1 628 405	774 327	854 078	564 519	287 073	277 446	1 063 886	487 254	576 632
20 - 24	CDJC	1 464 727	637 113	827 614	461 071	217 269	243 802	1 003 656	419 844	583 812
25 - 29	CDJC	1 163 574	509 109	654 465	345 841	161 031	184 810	817 733	348 078	469 655
30 - 34	CDJC	887 710	410 148	477 562	284 119	137 905	146 214	603 591	272 243	331 348
35 - 39	CDJC	802 208	373 813	428 395	246 954	126 347	120 607	555 254	247 466	307 788
40 - 44	CDJC	573 193	270 046	303 147	173 329	90 578	82 751	399 864	179 468	220 396
45 - 49	CDJC	539 168	257 070	282 098	139 708	72 415	67 293	399 460	184 655	214 805
50 - 54	CDJC	390 962	178 902	212 060	95 508	48 098	47 410	295 454	130 804	164 650
55 - 59	CDJC	336 356	162 122	174 234	76 557	39 078	37 479	259 799	123 044	136 755
60 - 64	CDJC	239 431	114 335	125 096	57 172	27 663	29 509	182 259	86 672	95 587
65 - 69	CDJC	209 713	100 425	109 288	44 486	20 277	24 209	165 227	80 148	85 079
70 - 74	CDJC	98 014	47 407	50 607	21 390	9 542	11 848	76 624	37 865	38 759
75 - 79	CDJC	84 387	41 529	42 858	16 670	7 113	9 557	67 717	34 416	33 301
80 - 84	CDJC	32 631	15 305	17 326	6 162	2 542	3 620	26 469	12 763	13 706
85 - 89	CDJC	20 033	9 041	10 992	3 795	1 361	2 434	16 238	7 680	8 558
90 - 94	CDJC	7 179	3 537	3 642	1 114	430	684	6 065	3 107	2 958
95+	CDJC	7 426	3 956	3 470	1 110	506	604	6 316	3 450	2 866
1 VII 2000										
Total	ESDF	17 690 584	8 284 793	9 405 791	...	...	...	...	...	...
0 - 4	ESDF	3 139 293	1 514 640	1 624 653	...	...	...	...	...	...
5 - 9	ESDF	2 664 689	1 282 460	1 382 229	...	...	...	...	...	...
10 - 14	ESDF	2 208 552	1 059 016	1 149 536	...	...	...	...	...	...
15 - 19	ESDF	1 966 758	940 308	1 026 450	...	...	...	...	...	...
20 - 24	ESDF	1 540 328	743 941	796 387	...	...	...	...	...	...
25 - 29	ESDF	1 312 794	598 600	714 194	...	...	...	...	...	...
30 - 34	ESDF	1 023 631	438 932	584 699	...	...	...	...	...	...
35 - 39	ESDF	858 865	372 869	485 996	...	...	...	...	...	...
40 - 44	ESDF	745 586	341 179	404 407	...	...	...	...	...	...

7. Population by age, sex and urban/rural residence: latest available year, 1994 - 2003
Population selon l'âge, le sexe et la résidence, urbaine/rurale: dernière année disponible, 1994 - 2003
(continued — suite)

Continent, country or area, date and age (in years) / Continent, pays ou zone, date et âge (en années)	Code[1]	Total			Urban - Urbaine			Rural - Rurale		
		Both sexes Les deux sexes	Male Masculin	Female Féminin	Both sexes Les deux sexes	Male Masculin	Female Féminin	Both sexes Les deux sexes	Male Masculin	Female Féminin
AFRICA — AFRIQUE										
Mozambique										
1 VII 2000										
45 - 49	ESDF	621 564	286 675	334 889	...	...	...	...	...	...
50 - 54	ESDF	496 069	226 219	269 850	...	...	...	...	...	...
55 - 59	ESDF	388 778	173 800	214 978	...	...	...	...	...	...
60 - 64	ESDF	289 060	126 794	162 266	...	...	...	...	...	...
65 - 69	ESDF	201 364	86 207	115 157	...	...	...	...	...	...
70 - 74	ESDF	124 004	50 747	73 257	...	...	...	...	...	...
75 - 79	ESDF	66 792	26 277	40 515	...	...	...	...	...	...
80+	ESDF	42 457	16 129	26 328	...	...	...	...	...	...
Namibia - Namibie[2]										
27 VIII 2001										
Total	CDFC	1 830 330	887 721	942 572	603 612	300 358	303 236	1 226 718	587 363	639 336
0 - 1	CDFC	46 852	23 281	23 571	...	...	...	...	...	...
0 - 4	CDFC	...	...	...	67 484	33 494	33 990	173 745	86 550	87 195
1 - 4	CDFC	194 377	96 763	97 614	...	...	...	...	...	...
5 - 9	CDFC	246 964	121 785	125 179	59 123	28 683	30 440	187 841	93 102	94 739
10 - 14	CDFC	230 287	113 081	117 206	55 162	25 564	29 598	175 125	87 517	87 608
15 - 19	CDFC	202 298	99 307	102 991	55 865	25 383	30 482	146 433	73 924	72 509
20 - 24	CDFC	174 484	86 382	88 102	70 592	34 483	36 109	103 892	51 899	51 993
25 - 29	CDFC	150 783	74 304	76 479	73 635	37 316	36 319	77 148	36 988	40 160
30 - 34	CDFC	118 529	57 125	61 404	58 312	29 851	28 461	60 217	27 274	32 943
35 - 39	CDFC	96 416	45 083	51 333	46 071	23 521	22 550	50 345	21 562	28 783
40 - 44	CDFC	74 050	34 170	39 880	33 152	16 966	16 186	40 898	17 204	23 694
45 - 49	CDFC	57 749	26 942	30 807	23 576	12 615	10 961	34 173	14 327	19 846
50 - 54	CDFC	47 779	21 999	25 780	16 798	9 193	7 605	30 981	12 806	18 175
55 - 59	CDFC	35 209	16 600	18 609	10 890	5 893	4 997	24 319	10 707	13 612
60 - 64	CDFC	34 378	15 569	18 809	8 512	4 192	4 320	25 866	11 377	14 489
65 - 69	CDFC	25 262	11 399	13 863	5 458	2 596	2 862	19 804	8 803	11 001
70 - 74	CDFC	22 052	9 313	12 739	3 707	1 619	2 088	18 345	7 694	10 651
75 - 79	CDFC	16 007	6 382	9 625	2 531	1 068	1 463	13 476	5 314	8 162
80 - 84	CDFC	13 818	5 359	8 459	1 753	680	1 073	12 065	4 679	7 386
85 - 89	CDFC	5 407	2 033	3 374	973	341	632	4 434	1 692	2 742
90 - 94	CDFC	2 555	927	1 628	376	152	224	2 179	775	1 404
95+	CDFC	2 712	897	1 815	262	111	151	2 450	786	1 664
Unk. - Inc.	CDFC	32 325	19 020	13 305	9 362	6 637	2 725	22 963	12 383	10 580
Nigeria - Nigéria[3]										
1 VII 2000										
Total	ESDF	115 224 312	57 750 754	57 473 558	...	...	...	...	...	...
0 - 4	ESDF	20 294 315	10 329 530	9 964 785	...	...	...	...	...	...
5 - 9	ESDF	16 626 314	8 475 111	8 151 203	...	...	...	...	...	...
10 - 14	ESDF	14 049 846	7 040 493	7 009 353	...	...	...	...	...	...
15 - 19	ESDF	11 614 242	5 860 447	5 753 795	...	...	...	...	...	...
20 - 24	ESDF	10 607 152	5 337 280	5 269 872	...	...	...	...	...	...
25 - 29	ESDF	8 949 326	4 425 396	4 523 930	...	...	...	...	...	...
30 - 34	ESDF	7 163 277	3 354 804	3 808 473	...	...	...	...	...	...
35 - 39	ESDF	6 009 160	2 804 124	3 205 036	...	...	...	...	...	...
40 - 44	ESDF	5 162 668	2 499 916	2 662 752	...	...	...	...	...	...
45 - 49	ESDF	4 212 419	2 088 777	2 123 642	...	...	...	...	...	...
50 - 54	ESDF	3 164 357	1 636 220	1 528 137	...	...	...	...	...	...
55 - 59	ESDF	2 413 817	1 275 577	1 138 240	...	...	...	...	...	...
60 - 64	ESDF	1 715 811	921 096	794 715	...	...	...	...	...	...
65 - 69	ESDF	1 258 407	675 255	583 152	...	...	...	...	...	...
70 - 74	ESDF	928 888	480 324	448 564	...	...	...	...	...	...
75 - 79	ESDF	578 124	297 076	281 048	...	...	...	...	...	...
80+	ESDF	476 189	249 328	226 861	...	...	...	...	...	...
Réunion										
8 III 1999										
Total	CDJC	706 180	347 076	359 104	...	...	...	...	...	...
0 - 1	CDJC	2 352	1 173	1 179	...	...	...	...	...	...
1 - 4	CDJC	51 138	26 042	25 096	...	...	...	...	...	...
5 - 9	CDJC	68 635	34 964	33 671	...	...	...	...	...	...
10 - 14	CDJC	68 706	34 799	33 907	...	...	...	...	...	...

7. Population by age, sex and urban/rural residence: latest available year, 1994 - 2003
Population selon l'âge, le sexe et la résidence, urbaine/rurale: dernière année disponible, 1994 - 2003
(continued — suite)

Continent, country or area, date and age (in years) / Continent, pays ou zone, date et âge (en annèes)	Code[1]	Total			Urban - Urbaine			Rural - Rurale		
		Both sexes Les deux sexes	Male Masculin	Female Féminin	Both sexes Les deux sexes	Male Masculin	Female Féminin	Both sexes Les deux sexes	Male Masculin	Female Féminin
AFRICA — AFRIQUE										
Réunion										
8 III 1999										
15 - 19	CDJC	64 668	32 719	31 949	...	...	...	...	...	...
20 - 24	CDJC	54 528	26 932	27 596	...	...	...	...	...	...
25 - 29	CDJC	55 543	27 076	28 467	...	...	...	...	...	...
30 - 34	CDJC	63 513	30 903	32 610	...	...	...	...	...	...
35 - 39	CDJC	59 989	29 490	30 499	...	...	...	...	...	...
40 - 44	CDJC	48 666	24 039	24 627	...	...	...	...	...	...
45 - 49	CDJC	41 288	20 416	20 872	...	...	...	...	...	...
50 - 54	CDJC	30 843	15 496	15 347	...	...	...	...	...	...
55 - 59	CDJC	25 620	12 594	13 026	...	...	...	...	...	...
60 - 64	CDJC	21 632	10 232	11 400	...	...	...	...	...	...
65 - 69	CDJC	16 358	7 480	8 878	...	...	...	...	...	...
70 - 74	CDJC	13 097	5 737	7 360	...	...	...	...	...	...
75 - 79	CDJC	9 847	3 923	5 924	...	...	...	...	...	...
80 - 84	CDJC	5 252	1 775	3 477	...	...	...	...	...	...
85 - 89	CDJC	2 919	863	2 056	...	...	...	...	...	...
90 - 94	CDJC	1 187	316	871	...	...	...	...	...	...
95 - 99	CDJC	343	97	246	...	...	...	...	...	...
100+	CDJC	56	10	46	...	...	...	...	...	...
Rwanda										
16 VIII 2002										
Total	CDJC	8 128 553	3 879 448	4 249 105	1 372 604	727 172	645 432	6 755 949	3 152 276	3 603 673
0 - 1	CDJC	325 221	161 653	163 568	46 968	23 496	23 472	278 253	138 157	140 096
1 - 4	CDJC	995 010	493 437	501 573	147 083	73 621	73 462	847 927	419 816	428 111
5 - 9	CDJC	1 141 039	563 351	577 688	157 009	77 648	79 361	984 030	485 703	498 327
10 - 14	CDJC	1 095 225	536 876	558 349	149 787	71 947	77 840	945 438	464 929	480 509
15 - 19	CDJC	1 078 839	526 563	552 276	184 874	89 576	95 298	893 965	436 987	456 978
20 - 24	CDJC	810 681	382 561	428 120	177 151	98 145	79 006	633 530	284 416	349 114
25 - 29	CDJC	555 509	253 180	302 329	130 102	74 049	56 053	425 407	179 131	246 276
30 - 34	CDJC	448 439	208 742	239 697	100 840	59 871	40 969	347 599	148 871	198 728
35 - 39	CDJC	382 636	177 816	204 820	76 430	46 117	30 313	306 206	131 699	174 507
40 - 44	CDJC	363 067	168 934	194 133	63 795	38 834	24 961	299 272	130 100	169 172
45 - 49	CDJC	268 262	122 615	145 647	43 450	26 007	17 443	224 812	96 608	128 204
50 - 54	CDJC	193 382	86 925	106 457	30 845	17 673	13 172	162 537	69 252	93 285
55 - 59	CDJC	123 868	50 480	73 388	18 782	9 561	9 221	105 086	40 919	64 167
60 - 64	CDJC	111 809	45 221	66 588	15 483	7 293	8 190	96 326	37 928	58 398
65 - 69	CDJC	84 928	35 178	49 750	11 333	5 166	6 167	73 595	30 012	43 583
70 - 74	CDJC	71 020	30 970	40 050	8 790	4 025	4 765	62 230	26 945	35 285
75 - 79	CDJC	37 989	16 255	21 734	4 451	1 923	2 528	33 538	14 332	19 206
80 - 84	CDJC	26 788	12 081	14 707	3 295	1 378	1 917	23 493	10 703	12 790
85+	CDJC	14 841	6 610	8 231	2 136	842	1 294	12 705	5 768	6 937
Saint Helena ex. dep. - Sainte-Hélène sans dép.										
8 III 1998										
Total	CDJC	4 913	2 481	2 432	...	...	...	...	...	...
0 - 1	CDJC	60	33	27	...	...	...	...	...	...
1 - 4	CDJC	252	139	113	...	...	...	...	...	...
5 - 9	CDJC	369	197	172	...	...	...	...	...	...
10 - 14	CDJC	368	199	169	...	...	...	...	...	...
15 - 19	CDJC	452	217	235	...	...	...	...	...	...
20 - 24	CDJC	300	154	146	...	...	...	...	...	...
25 - 29	CDJC	370	185	185	...	...	...	...	...	...
30 - 34	CDJC	329	150	179	...	...	...	...	...	...
35 - 39	CDJC	391	181	210	...	...	...	...	...	...
40 - 44	CDJC	336	181	155	...	...	...	...	...	...
45 - 49	CDJC	340	173	167	...	...	...	...	...	...
50 - 54	CDJC	346	200	146	...	...	...	...	...	...
55 - 59	CDJC	230	124	106	...	...	...	...	...	...
60 - 64	CDJC	202	127	75	...	...	...	...	...	...
65 - 69	CDJC	190	86	104	...	...	...	...	...	...
70 - 74	CDJC	143	51	92	...	...	...	...	...	...

7. Population by age, sex and urban/rural residence: latest available year, 1994 - 2003
Population selon l'âge, le sexe et la résidence, urbaine/rurale: dernière année disponible, 1994 - 2003
(continued — suite)

Continent, country or area, date and age (in years) Continent, pays ou zone, date et âge (en années)	Code[1]	Total			Urban - Urbaine			Rural - Rurale		
		Both sexes Les deux sexes	Male Masculin	Female Féminin	Both sexes Les deux sexes	Male Masculin	Female Féminin	Both sexes Les deux sexes	Male Masculin	Female Féminin
AFRICA — AFRIQUE										
Saint Helena ex. dep. - Sainte-Hélène sans dép.										
8 III 1998										
75 - 79	CDJC	111	41	70	...	...	...	...	...	...
80 - 84	CDJC	69	25	44	...	...	...	...	...	...
85 - 89	CDJC	26	7	19	...	...	...	...	...	...
90 - 94	CDJC	18	7	11	...	...	...	...	...	...
95+	CDJC	1	-	1	...	...	...	...	...	...
Unk. - Inc.	CDJC	10	4	6	...	...	...	...	...	...
Saint Helena: Tristan da Cunha - Sainte-Hélène: Tristan da Cunha										
1 VII 1996										
Total	ESDF	286	137	149	...	...	...	...	...	...
0 - 1	ESDF	1	1	-	...	...	...	...	...	...
1 - 4	ESDF	10	7	3	...	...	...	...	...	...
5 - 9	ESDF	14	9	5	...	...	...	...	...	...
10 - 14	ESDF	17	9	8	...	...	...	...	...	...
15 - 19	ESDF	13	8	5	...	...	...	...	...	...
20 - 24	ESDF	17	3	14	...	...	...	...	...	...
25 - 29	ESDF	35	17	18	...	...	...	...	...	...
30 - 34	ESDF	12	6	6	...	...	...	...	...	...
35 - 39	ESDF	19	10	9	...	...	...	...	...	...
40 - 44	ESDF	14	4	10	...	...	...	...	...	...
45 - 49	ESDF	24	14	10	...	...	...	...	...	...
50 - 54	ESDF	18	8	10	...	...	...	...	...	...
55 - 59	ESDF	22	6	16	...	...	...	...	...	...
60 - 64	ESDF	18	11	7	...	...	...	...	...	...
65 - 69	ESDF	12	5	7	...	...	...	...	...	...
70 - 74	ESDF	22	12	10	...	...	...	...	...	...
75 - 79	ESDF	10	5	5	...	...	...	...	...	...
80 - 84	ESDF	6	1	5	...	...	...	...	...	...
85 - 89	ESDF	1	1	-	...	...	...	...	...	...
90+	ESDF	1	-	1	...	...	...	...	...	...
Seychelles										
1 VII 1998										
Total	ESDF	78 846	39 359	39 487	...	...	...	...	...	...
0 - 4	ESDF	7 515	3 899	3 616	...	...	...	...	...	...
5 - 9	ESDF	7 262	3 688	3 574	...	...	...	...	...	...
10 - 14	ESDF	7 043	3 554	3 489	...	...	...	...	...	...
15 - 19	ESDF	7 206	3 664	3 542	...	...	...	...	...	...
20 - 24	ESDF	6 831	3 452	3 379	...	...	...	...	...	...
25 - 29	ESDF	7 067	3 536	3 531	...	...	...	...	...	...
30 - 34	ESDF	7 362	3 640	3 722	...	...	...	...	...	...
35 - 39	ESDF	6 705	3 477	3 228	...	...	...	...	...	...
40 - 44	ESDF	5 155	2 793	2 362	...	...	...	...	...	...
45 - 49	ESDF	3 376	1 788	1 588	...	...	...	...	...	...
50 - 54	ESDF	2 587	1 358	1 229	...	...	...	...	...	...
55 - 59	ESDF	2 746	1 339	1 407	...	...	...	...	...	...
60 - 64	ESDF	2 217	949	1 268	...	...	...	...	...	...
65 - 69	ESDF	1 954	827	1 127	...	...	...	...	...	...
70 - 74	ESDF	1 555	655	900	...	...	...	...	...	...
75 - 79	ESDF	1 113	432	681	...	...	...	...	...	...
80+	ESDF	1 152	308	844	...	...	...	...	...	...
Sierra Leone										
1 VII 2003										
Total	ESDF	*5 280 406*	*2 606 045*	*2 674 361*	...	...	...	...	...	...
0 - 1	ESDF	*205 242*	*102 685*	*102 557*	...	...	...	...	...	...
1 - 4	ESDF	*657 985*	*331 968*	*326 016*	...	...	...	...	...	...
5 - 9	ESDF	*794 093*	*399 695*	*394 398*	...	...	...	...	...	...
10 - 14	ESDF	*516 752*	*273 918*	*242 834*	...	...	...	...	...	...

7. Population by age, sex and urban/rural residence: latest available year, 1994 - 2003
Population selon l'âge, le sexe et la résidence, urbaine/rurale: dernière année disponible, 1994 - 2003
(continued — suite)

Continent, country or area, date and age (in years) / Continent, pays ou zone, date et âge (en années)	Code[1]	Total			Urban - Urbaine			Rural - Rurale		
		Both sexes Les deux sexes	Male Masculin	Female Féminin	Both sexes Les deux sexes	Male Masculin	Female Féminin	Both sexes Les deux sexes	Male Masculin	Female Féminin
AFRICA — AFRIQUE										
Sierra Leone										
1 VII 2003										
15 - 19	ESDF	513 263	240 312	272 951	...	...	...	...	...	...
20 - 24	ESDF	408 352	182 703	225 649	...	...	...	...	...	...
25 - 29	ESDF	423 009	188 100	234 910	...	...	...	...	...	...
30 - 34	ESDF	329 828	149 713	180 116	...	...	...	...	...	...
35 - 39	ESDF	297 142	146 203	150 940	...	...	...	...	...	...
40 - 44	ESDF	220 272	108 870	111 402	...	...	...	...	...	...
45 - 49	ESDF	193 199	104 586	88 612	...	...	...	...	...	...
50 - 54	ESDF	155 484	80 832	74 652	...	...	...	...	...	...
55 - 59	ESDF	111 025	60 805	50 221	...	...	...	...	...	...
60 - 64	ESDF	116 884	59 762	57 122	...	...	...	...	...	...
65 - 69	ESDF	84 034	44 224	39 811	...	...	...	...	...	...
70 - 74	ESDF	67 884	36 953	30 932	...	...	...	...	...	...
75 - 79	ESDF	50 153	27 772	22 381	...	...	...	...	...	...
80 - 84	ESDF	38 623	19 711	18 912	...	...	...	...	...	...
85 - 89	ESDF	27 246	14 469	12 777	...	...	...	...	...	...
90+	ESDF	34 069	17 392	16 677	...	...	...	...	...	...
Unk. - Inc.	ESDF	35 894	15 402	20 492	...	...	...	...	...	...
Somalia - Somalie										
1 VII 2002										
Total	SSDF	6 799 079	3 499 523	3 299 556	2 310 817	1 168 410	1 142 407	4 488 262	2 331 113	2 157 149
0 - 4	SSDF	1 235 105	634 959	600 146	408 646	206 987	201 659	826 459	427 972	398 487
5 - 9	SSDF	1 049 189	544 431	504 758	352 471	179 293	173 178	696 718	365 138	331 580
10 - 14	SSDF	870 180	455 323	414 857	297 807	151 845	145 962	572 373	303 478	268 895
15 - 19	SSDF	725 723	373 328	352 395	250 718	125 641	125 077	475 005	247 687	227 318
20 - 24	SSDF	581 690	280 786	300 904	202 030	95 671	106 359	379 660	185 115	194 545
25 - 29	SSDF	491 651	231 254	260 397	170 250	78 983	91 267	321 401	152 271	169 130
30 - 34	SSDF	428 269	198 101	230 168	146 024	67 081	78 943	282 245	131 020	151 225
35 - 39	SSDF	366 113	175 050	191 063	123 698	58 860	64 838	242 415	116 190	126 225
40 - 44	SSDF	311 989	164 941	147 048	104 080	54 778	49 302	207 909	110 163	97 746
45 - 49	SSDF	248 939	139 351	109 588	82 971	46 198	36 773	165 968	93 153	72 815
50 - 54	SSDF	174 517	105 972	68 545	58 869	35 355	23 514	115 648	70 617	45 031
55 - 59	SSDF	124 841	79 206	45 635	42 868	26 625	16 243	81 973	52 581	29 392
60 - 64	SSDF	80 530	51 293	29 237	28 988	17 492	11 496	51 542	33 801	17 741
65 - 69	SSDF	51 554	32 843	18 711	19 396	11 603	7 793	32 158	21 240	10 918
70 - 74	SSDF	28 997	17 795	11 202	11 675	6 878	4 797	17 322	10 917	6 405
75 - 79	SSDF	12 860	6 152	6 708	5 828	3 320	2 508	7 032	2 832	4 200
80+	SSDF	16 932	8 738	8 194	4 498	1 800	2 698	12 434	6 938	5 496
South Africa - Afrique du Sud[4]										
10 X 1996										
Total	CDFC	40 583 573	19 520 887	21 062 686	21 781 807	10 667 927	11 113 880	18 801 766	8 852 960	9 948 806
0 - 1	CDFC	856 238	426 858	429 380	407 569	204 037	203 532	448 669	222 821	225 848
1 - 4	CDFC	3 587 383	1 789 905	1 797 478	1 608 627	801 912	806 715	1 978 756	987 993	990 763
5 - 9	CDFC	4 668 721	2 333 562	2 335 159	2 038 226	1 016 905	1 021 321	2 630 495	1 316 657	1 313 838
10 - 14	CDFC	4 654 098	2 308 758	2 345 340	2 061 009	1 016 787	1 044 222	2 593 089	1 291 971	1 301 118
15 - 19	CDFC	4 180 717	2 050 214	2 130 503	1 995 798	978 031	1 017 767	2 184 919	1 072 183	1 112 736
20 - 24	CDFC	3 982 354	1 917 919	2 064 435	2 271 339	1 120 919	1 150 420	1 711 015	797 000	914 015
25 - 29	CDFC	3 455 728	1 663 064	1 792 664	2 186 820	1 088 452	1 098 368	1 268 908	574 612	694 296
30 - 34	CDFC	3 074 202	1 463 499	1 610 703	1 970 405	972 890	997 515	1 103 797	490 609	613 188
35 - 39	CDFC	2 653 756	1 284 957	1 368 799	1 709 987	847 993	861 994	943 769	436 964	506 805
40 - 44	CDFC	2 138 626	1 030 597	1 108 029	1 360 825	676 387	684 438	777 801	354 210	423 591
45 - 49	CDFC	1 677 526	813 816	863 710	1 050 144	525 516	524 628	627 382	288 300	339 082
50 - 54	CDFC	1 268 895	600 476	668 419	775 141	383 915	391 226	493 754	216 561	277 193
55 - 59	CDFC	1 069 936	483 678	586 258	621 620	294 100	327 520	448 316	189 578	258 738
60 - 64	CDFC	890 537	352 053	538 484	482 701	208 117	274 584	407 836	143 936	263 900
65 - 69	CDFC	758 886	304 013	454 873	374 423	160 695	213 728	384 463	143 318	241 145
70 - 74	CDFC	482 162	195 119	287 043	254 856	105 173	149 683	227 306	89 946	137 360
75 - 79	CDFC	377 427	141 844	235 583	184 420	70 699	113 721	193 007	71 145	121 862
80 - 84	CDFC	178 903	62 072	116 831	96 886	32 757	64 129	82 017	29 315	52 702
85+	CDFC	137 284	43 230	94 054	69 901	21 596	48 305	67 383	21 634	45 749
Unk. - Inc.	CDFC	490 194	255 253	234 941	261 110	141 046	120 064	229 084	114 207	114 877

7. Population by age, sex and urban/rural residence: latest available year, 1994 - 2003
Population selon l'âge, le sexe et la résidence, urbaine/rurale: dernière année disponible, 1994 - 2003
(continued — suite)

Continent, country or area, date and age (in years) Continent, pays ou zone, date et âge (en années)	Code[1]	Total			Urban - Urbaine			Rural - Rurale		
		Both sexes Les deux sexes	Male Masculin	Female Féminin	Both sexes Les deux sexes	Male Masculin	Female Féminin	Both sexes Les deux sexes	Male Masculin	Female Féminin
AFRICA — AFRIQUE										
South Africa - Afrique du Sud[4]										
10 X 2001										
Total	CDFC	44 819 778	21 434 040	23 385 737	...	...	...	...	...	...
0 - 4	CDFC	4 449 816	2 223 731	2 226 085	...	...	...	...	...	...
5 - 9	CDFC	4 853 555	2 425 804	2 427 751	...	...	...	...	...	...
10 - 14	CDFC	5 061 917	2 518 956	2 542 961	...	...	...	...	...	...
15 - 19	CDFC	4 981 721	2 453 079	2 528 642	...	...	...	...	...	...
20 - 24	CDFC	4 294 523	2 099 293	2 195 230	...	...	...	...	...	...
25 - 29	CDFC	3 934 939	1 899 124	2 035 814	...	...	...	...	...	...
30 - 34	CDFC	3 340 901	1 594 488	1 746 412	...	...	...	...	...	...
35 - 39	CDFC	3 071 770	1 441 507	1 630 264	...	...	...	...	...	...
40 - 44	CDFC	2 619 465	1 233 632	1 385 832	...	...	...	...	...	...
45 - 49	CDFC	2 087 380	967 604	1 119 776	...	...	...	...	...	...
50 - 54	CDFC	1 638 020	769 499	868 521	...	...	...	...	...	...
55 - 59	CDFC	1 205 266	552 323	652 943	...	...	...	...	...	...
60 - 64	CDFC	1 065 294	444 510	620 784	...	...	...	...	...	...
65 - 69	CDFC	787 927	304 763	483 164	...	...	...	...	...	...
70 - 74	CDFC	631 469	232 547	398 922	...	...	...	...	...	...
75 - 79	CDFC	367 537	136 436	231 101	...	...	...	...	...	...
80 - 84	CDFC	270 945	90 835	180 111	...	...	...	...	...	...
85+	CDFC	157 333	45 909	111 425	...	...	...	...	...	...
Swaziland										
11 V 1997										
Total	CDFC	929 718	440 154	489 564	214 428	106 256	108 172	715 290	333 898	381 392
0 - 1	CDFC	24 405	12 049	12 356	5 123	2 519	2 604	19 282	9 530	9 752
1 - 4	CDFC	111 992	55 480	56 512	19 744	9 701	10 043	92 248	45 779	46 469
5 - 9	CDFC	139 245	68 976	70 269	22 232	10 663	11 569	117 013	58 313	58 700
10 - 14	CDFC	137 487	68 200	69 287	22 036	9 908	12 128	115 451	58 292	57 159
15 - 19	CDFC	112 356	54 775	57 581	24 504	10 716	13 788	87 852	44 059	43 793
20 - 24	CDFC	85 094	38 807	46 287	27 184	12 804	14 380	57 910	26 003	31 907
25 - 29	CDFC	68 043	30 147	37 896	24 731	12 610	12 121	43 312	17 537	25 775
30 - 34	CDFC	52 156	21 988	30 168	18 103	9 257	8 846	34 053	12 731	21 322
35 - 39	CDFC	45 802	19 645	26 157	15 043	7 841	7 202	30 759	11 804	18 955
40 - 44	CDFC	35 505	16 165	19 340	11 090	6 128	4 962	24 415	10 037	14 378
45 - 49	CDFC	30 371	14 461	15 910	8 627	5 068	3 559	21 744	9 393	12 351
50 - 54	CDFC	23 316	10 799	12 517	5 756	3 413	2 343	17 560	7 386	10 174
55 - 59	CDFC	17 920	8 758	9 162	3 759	2 275	1 484	14 161	6 483	7 678
60 - 64	CDFC	13 866	6 325	7 541	2 349	1 298	1 051	11 517	5 027	6 490
65 - 69	CDFC	10 152	4 645	5 507	1 340	710	630	8 812	3 935	4 877
70 - 74	CDFC	7 301	2 924	4 377	766	343	423	6 535	2 581	3 954
75 - 79	CDFC	5 269	2 175	3 094	527	256	271	4 742	1 919	2 823
80 - 84	CDFC	3 085	1 161	1 924	266	110	156	2 819	1 051	1 768
85 - 89	CDFC	1 765	707	1 058	145	64	81	1 620	643	977
90 - 94	CDFC	731	264	467	61	25	36	670	239	431
95+	CDFC	959	371	588	63	34	29	896	337	559
Unk. - Inc.	CDFC	2 898	1 332	1 566	979	513	466	1 919	819	1 100
Tunisia - Tunisie										
20 IV 1994										
Total	CDFC	8 785 711	4 439 289	4 346 422	5 361 927	2 717 168	2 644 759	3 423 784	1 722 121	1 701 663
0 - 1	CDFC	177 191	91 223	85 968	104 855	53 856	50 999	72 336	37 367	34 969
1 - 4	CDFC	791 125	405 657	385 468	447 380	229 089	218 291	343 745	176 568	167 177
5 - 9	CDFC	1 055 358	538 919	516 439	608 233	309 289	298 944	447 125	229 630	217 495
10 - 14	CDFC	1 034 646	530 178	504 468	605 460	307 625	297 835	429 186	222 553	206 633
15 - 19	CDFC	939 066	478 618	460 448	546 290	280 017	266 273	392 776	198 601	194 175
20 - 24	CDFC	818 718	412 463	406 255	497 919	254 409	243 510	320 799	158 054	162 745
25 - 29	CDFC	743 903	363 603	380 300	479 111	237 120	241 991	264 792	126 483	138 309
30 - 34	CDFC	656 615	326 172	330 443	443 690	223 004	220 686	212 925	103 168	109 757
35 - 39	CDFC	560 347	282 297	278 050	376 253	192 213	184 040	184 094	90 084	94 010
40 - 44	CDFC	437 893	219 789	218 104	291 220	150 579	140 641	146 673	69 210	77 463
45 - 49	CDFC	307 149	149 840	157 309	203 611	101 390	102 221	103 538	48 450	55 088
50 - 54	CDFC	270 357	133 005	137 352	169 597	84 240	85 357	100 760	48 765	51 995
55 - 59	CDFC	266 740	133 154	133 586	161 533	80 938	80 595	105 207	52 216	52 991

7. Population by age, sex and urban/rural residence: latest available year, 1994 - 2003
Population selon l'âge, le sexe et la résidence, urbaine/rurale: dernière année disponible, 1994 - 2003
(continued — suite)

Continent, country or area, date and age (in years) / Continent, pays ou zone, date et âge (en années)	Code[1]	Total			Urban - Urbaine			Rural - Rurale		
		Both sexes Les deux sexes	Male Masculin	Female Féminin	Both sexes Les deux sexes	Male Masculin	Female Féminin	Both sexes Les deux sexes	Male Masculin	Female Féminin
AFRICA — AFRIQUE										
Tunisia - Tunisie										
20 IV 1994										
60 - 64	CDFC	251 363	127 279	124 084	150 315	75 525	74 790	101 048	51 754	49 294
65 - 69	CDFC	173 855	91 042	82 813	102 677	52 738	49 939	71 178	38 304	32 874
70 - 74	CDFC	137 177	69 561	67 616	79 962	38 819	41 143	57 215	30 742	26 473
75 - 79	CDFC	77 202	42 546	34 656	44 044	22 951	21 093	33 158	19 595	13 563
80 - 84	CDFC	58 593	30 245	28 348	33 199	15 977	17 222	25 394	14 268	11 126
85 - 89	CDFC	16 595	8 623	7 972	9 501	4 649	4 852	7 094	3 974	3 120
90 - 94	CDFC	9 663	4 194	5 469	5 746	2 255	3 491	3 917	1 939	1 978
95 - 99	CDFC	974	410	564	572	214	358	402	196	206
100+	CDFC	1 181	471	710	759	271	488	422	200	222
1 VII 1998										
Total	ESDF	*9 333 300*	*4 709 000*	*4 624 300*	...	...	...	...	...	...
0 - 4	ESDF	*978 500*	*500 700*	*477 800*	...	...	...	...	...	...
5 - 9	ESDF	*1 015 200*	*519 500*	*495 700*	...	...	...	...	...	...
10 - 14	ESDF	*1 058 900*	*541 400*	*517 500*	...	...	...	...	...	...
15 - 19	ESDF	*1 006 100*	*514 400*	*491 700*	...	...	...	...	...	...
20 - 24	ESDF	*898 500*	*455 600*	*443 000*	...	...	...	...	...	...
25 - 29	ESDF	*795 900*	*395 900*	*399 900*	...	...	...	...	...	...
30 - 34	ESDF	*714 800*	*351 200*	*363 600*	...	...	...	...	...	...
35 - 39	ESDF	*621 900*	*310 300*	*311 600*	...	...	...	...	...	...
40 - 44	ESDF	*512 500*	*257 400*	*255 100*	...	...	...	...	...	...
45 - 49	ESDF	*384 400*	*190 800*	*193 700*	...	...	...	...	...	...
50 - 54	ESDF	*291 800*	*142 200*	*149 600*	...	...	...	...	...	...
55 - 59	ESDF	*266 800*	*131 200*	*135 600*	...	...	...	...	...	...
60 - 64	ESDF	*255 000*	*127 100*	*127 900*	...	...	...	...	...	...
65 - 69	ESDF	*208 200*	*105 500*	*102 700*	...	...	...	...	...	...
70 - 74	ESDF	*145 800*	*74 200*	*71 600*	...	...	...	...	...	...
75 - 79	ESDF	*94 700*	*48 500*	*46 200*	...	...	...	...	...	...
80+	ESDF	*84 100*	*43 000*	*41 000*	...	...	...	...	...	...
Uganda - Ouganda										
12 IX 2002										
Total	CDFC	24 442 084	11 929 803	12 512 281	2 999 387	1 449 684	1 549 703	21 442 697	10 480 119	10 962 578
0 - 1	CDFC	1 007 407	505 006	502 401	104 439	52 481	51 958	902 968	452 525	450 443
1 - 4	CDFC	3 537 016	1 767 120	1 769 896	347 233	172 444	174 789	3 189 783	1 594 676	1 595 107
5 - 9	CDFC	4 001 052	1 998 157	2 002 895	399 119	193 271	205 848	3 601 933	1 804 886	1 797 047
10 - 14	CDFC	3 509 151	1 757 111	1 752 040	391 236	180 572	210 664	3 117 915	1 576 539	1 541 376
15 - 19	CDFC	2 708 143	1 324 222	1 383 921	407 299	180 461	226 838	2 300 844	1 143 761	1 157 083
20 - 24	CDFC	2 175 580	981 994	1 193 586	392 217	180 869	211 348	1 783 363	801 125	982 238
25 - 29	CDFC	1 778 541	831 129	947 412	308 026	152 765	155 261	1 470 515	678 364	792 151
30 - 34	CDFC	1 420 073	708 138	711 935	215 168	116 304	98 864	1 204 905	591 834	613 071
35 - 39	CDFC	1 020 968	492 372	528 596	138 208	72 826	65 382	882 760	419 546	463 214
40 - 44	CDFC	828 317	400 433	427 884	96 870	50 662	46 208	731 447	349 771	381 676
45 - 49	CDFC	542 862	257 694	285 168	58 821	30 676	28 145	484 041	227 018	257 023
50 - 54	CDFC	486 060	223 345	262 715	44 728	22 839	21 889	441 332	200 506	240 826
55 - 59	CDFC	325 875	149 792	176 083	25 198	12 690	12 508	300 677	137 102	163 575
60 - 64	CDFC	363 765	173 325	190 440	24 371	11 139	13 232	339 394	162 186	177 208
65 - 69	CDFC	226 029	115 081	110 948	14 175	6 657	7 518	211 854	108 424	103 430
70 - 74	CDFC	217 160	102 858	114 302	12 538	5 157	7 381	204 622	97 701	106 921
75 - 79	CDFC	105 318	54 213	51 105	6 582	2 824	3 758	98 736	51 389	47 347
80 - 84	CDFC	112 785	52 143	60 642	7 542	2 926	4 616	105 243	49 217	56 026
85 - 89	CDFC	31 184	15 009	16 175	2 146	821	1 325	29 038	14 188	14 850
90 - 94	CDFC	27 871	13 036	14 835	2 126	786	1 340	25 745	12 250	13 495
95+	CDFC	16 927	7 625	9 302	1 345	514	831	15 582	7 111	8 471
United Republic of Tanzania - République Unie de Tanzanie										
24 VIII 2002										
Total	CDFC	34 443 603	16 829 861	17 613 742	...	...	...	...	...	...
0 - 4	CDFC	5 664 907	2 830 545	2 834 362	...	...	...	...	...	...
5 - 9	CDFC	5 130 448	2 573 993	2 556 455	...	...	...	...	...	...
10 - 14	CDFC	4 443 257	2 233 401	2 209 856	...	...	...	...	...	...

7. Population by age, sex and urban/rural residence: latest available year, 1994 - 2003
Population selon l'âge, le sexe et la résidence, urbaine/rurale: dernière année disponible, 1994 - 2003
(continued — suite)

Continent, country or area, date and age (in years) / Continent, pays ou zone, date et âge (en années)	Code[1]	Total			Urban - Urbaine			Rural - Rurale		
		Both sexes Les deux sexes	Male Masculin	Female Féminin	Both sexes Les deux sexes	Male Masculin	Female Féminin	Both sexes Les deux sexes	Male Masculin	Female Féminin
AFRICA — AFRIQUE										
United Republic of Tanzania - République Unie de Tanzanie										
24 VIII 2002										
15 - 19	CDFC	3 595 735	1 761 329	1 834 406	...	...	...	...	...	...
20 - 24	CDFC	3 148 513	1 402 077	1 746 436	...	...	...	...	...	...
25 - 29	CDFC	2 801 965	1 309 661	1 492 304	...	...	...	...	...	...
30 - 34	CDFC	2 229 046	1 087 599	1 141 447	...	...	...	...	...	...
35 - 39	CDFC	1 669 873	824 338	845 535	...	...	...	...	...	...
40 - 44	CDFC	1 348 508	669 549	678 959	...	...	...	...	...	...
45 - 49	CDFC	984 823	478 522	506 301	...	...	...	...	...	...
50 - 54	CDFC	883 820	428 501	455 319	...	...	...	...	...	...
55 - 59	CDFC	590 667	290 117	300 550	...	...	...	...	...	...
60 - 64	CDFC	604 956	287 502	317 454	...	...	...	...	...	...
65 - 69	CDFC	439 671	213 635	226 036	...	...	...	...	...	...
70 - 74	CDFC	377 852	180 246	197 606	...	...	...	...	...	...
75 - 79	CDFC	221 354	113 205	108 149	...	...	...	...	...	...
80+	CDFC	308 208	145 641	162 567	...	...	...	...	...	...
Zambia - Zambie										
1 VII 2000										
Total	ESDF	9 337 425	4 594 290	4 743 135	3 347 069	1 662 739	1 684 330	5 990 356	2 931 551	3 058 805
0 - 1	ESDF	339 228	168 841	170 387	101 775	50 699	51 076	237 453	118 142	119 311
1 - 4	ESDF	1 317 492	656 948	660 544	420 759	209 814	210 945	896 733	447 134	449 599
5 - 9	ESDF	1 461 082	729 181	731 901	500 572	247 117	253 455	960 510	482 064	478 446
10 - 14	ESDF	1 205 646	601 279	604 367	428 831	206 305	222 526	776 815	394 974	381 841
15 - 19	ESDF	1 069 996	513 320	556 676	415 197	195 518	219 679	654 799	317 802	336 997
20 - 24	ESDF	908 672	416 083	492 589	376 695	174 331	202 364	531 977	241 752	290 225
25 - 29	ESDF	741 148	361 901	379 247	308 436	155 070	153 366	432 712	206 831	225 881
30 - 34	ESDF	557 873	282 439	275 434	225 707	119 524	106 183	332 166	162 915	169 251
35 - 39	ESDF	429 987	211 356	218 631	169 148	87 763	81 385	260 839	123 593	137 246
40 - 44	ESDF	325 776	161 179	164 597	125 995	66 050	59 945	199 781	95 129	104 652
45 - 49	ESDF	245 320	122 486	122 834	91 507	50 128	41 379	153 813	72 358	81 455
50 - 54	ESDF	203 612	97 850	105 762	65 547	37 513	28 034	138 065	60 337	77 728
55 - 59	ESDF	144 838	71 905	72 933	39 418	22 860	16 558	105 420	49 045	56 375
60 - 64	ESDF	131 475	62 678	68 797	29 438	15 308	14 130	102 037	47 370	54 667
65 - 69	ESDF	100 493	52 499	47 994	20 294	10 642	9 652	80 199	41 857	38 342
70 - 74	ESDF	68 935	37 066	31 869	12 763	6 634	6 129	56 172	30 432	25 740
75 - 79	ESDF	40 649	23 301	17 348	7 217	3 793	3 424	33 432	19 508	13 924
80 - 84	ESDF	24 242	13 311	10 931	4 418	2 206	2 212	19 824	11 105	8 719
85+	ESDF	20 961	10 667	10 294	3 352	1 464	1 888	17 609	9 203	8 406
25 X 2000										
Total	CDJC	9 885 591	4 946 298	4 939 293	...	...	...	...	...	...
0 - 1	CDJC	344 302	171 621	172 681	...	...	...	...	...	...
1 - 4	CDJC	1 350 718	674 381	676 337	...	...	...	...	...	...
5 - 9	CDJC	1 516 952	758 146	758 806	...	...	...	...	...	...
10 - 14	CDJC	1 266 462	633 357	633 105	...	...	...	...	...	...
15 - 19	CDJC	1 149 583	557 197	592 386	...	...	...	...	...	...
20 - 24	CDJC	977 269	458 727	518 542	...	...	...	...	...	...
25 - 29	CDJC	797 605	400 193	397 412	...	...	...	...	...	...
30 - 34	CDJC	601 213	314 108	287 105	...	...	...	...	...	...
35 - 39	CDJC	467 166	238 292	228 874	...	...	...	...	...	...
40 - 44	CDJC	354 338	182 745	171 593	...	...	...	...	...	...
45 - 49	CDJC	268 473	140 304	128 169	...	...	...	...	...	...
50 - 54	CDJC	221 088	111 862	109 226	...	...	...	...	...	...
55 - 59	CDJC	157 193	82 263	74 930	...	...	...	...	...	...
60 - 64	CDJC	143 213	72 222	70 991	...	...	...	...	...	...
65 - 69	CDJC	107 479	58 961	48 518	...	...	...	...	...	...
70 - 74	CDJC	72 942	40 941	32 001	...	...	...	...	...	...
75 - 79	CDJC	42 678	25 347	17 331	...	...	...	...	...	...
80 - 84	CDJC	25 241	14 287	10 954	...	...	...	...	...	...
85+	CDJC	21 676	11 344	10 332	...	...	...	...	...	...

7. Population by age, sex and urban/rural residence: latest available year, 1994 - 2003
Population selon l'âge, le sexe et la résidence, urbaine/rurale: dernière année disponible, 1994 - 2003
(continued — suite)

Continent, country or area, date and age (in years) / Continent, pays ou zone, date et âge (en annèes)	Code[1]	Total			Urban - Urbaine			Rural - Rurale		
		Both sexes Les deux sexes	Male Masculin	Female Féminin	Both sexes Les deux sexes	Male Masculin	Female Féminin	Both sexes Les deux sexes	Male Masculin	Female Féminin
AFRICA — AFRIQUE										
Zimbabwe										
18 VIII 1997										
Total	SSDF	11 789 274	5 647 090	6 142 184	3 826 580	1 906 476	1 920 104	7 962 694	3 740 614	4 222 080
0 - 1	SSDF	328 913	161 914	166 999	104 258	50 698	53 560	224 655	111 216	113 439
1 - 4	SSDF	1 281 912	638 067	643 846	379 808	189 440	190 368	902 105	448 628	453 478
5 - 9	SSDF	1 646 115	797 775	848 341	417 356	197 224	220 132	1 228 760	600 552	628 209
10 - 14	SSDF	1 803 558	882 644	920 911	453 547	213 501	240 046	1 350 010	669 145	680 866
15 - 19	SSDF	1 484 654	730 379	754 274	463 901	204 411	259 491	1 020 754	525 969	494 786
20 - 24	SSDF	1 147 871	521 360	626 511	492 556	229 928	262 628	655 314	291 432	363 883
25 - 29	SSDF	888 600	427 729	460 872	415 758	223 500	192 258	472 843	204 232	268 611
30 - 34	SSDF	624 978	287 946	337 032	280 744	139 782	140 962	344 235	148 165	196 071
35 - 39	SSDF	583 724	254 357	329 366	241 206	124 241	116 966	342 519	130 119	212 399
40 - 44	SSDF	442 692	203 372	239 319	176 245	99 272	76 973	266 445	104 100	162 346
45 - 49	SSDF	366 842	179 562	187 280	131 674	80 556	51 118	235 167	99 008	136 159
50 - 54	SSDF	306 227	130 448	175 779	88 621	48 258	40 363	217 606	82 190	135 415
55 - 59	SSDF	248 868	121 506	127 362	64 434	38 289	26 144	184 435	83 217	101 218
60 - 64	SSDF	195 169	98 104	97 066	47 494	29 051	18 442	147 675	69 052	78 623
65 - 69	SSDF	179 884	93 671	86 213	32 095	19 553	12 542	147 788	74 117	73 670
70 - 74	SSDF	99 500	46 063	53 437	18 242	9 667	8 575	81 256	36 395	44 862
75+	SSDF	159 767	72 189	87 578	18 641	9 105	3 725	73 599	35 423	38 176
1 VII 1999										
Total	ESDF	*13 079 127*	*6 382 092*	*6 697 035*	...	...	...	...	...	...
0 - 4	ESDF	*2 310 243*	*1 139 151*	*1 171 092*	...	...	...	...	...	...
5 - 9	ESDF	*1 852 604*	*914 810*	*937 794*	...	...	...	...	...	...
10 - 14	ESDF	*1 546 743*	*769 315*	*777 428*	...	...	...	...	...	...
15 - 19	ESDF	*1 534 532*	*762 581*	*771 951*	...	...	...	...	...	...
20 - 24	ESDF	*1 314 285*	*651 638*	*662 647*	...	...	...	...	...	...
25 - 29	ESDF	*1 078 229*	*516 508*	*561 721*	...	...	...	...	...	...
30 - 34	ESDF	*790 666*	*370 892*	*419 774*	...	...	...	...	...	...
35 - 39	ESDF	*621 821*	*288 864*	*332 957*	...	...	...	...	...	...
40 - 44	ESDF	*521 774*	*241 733*	*280 041*	...	...	...	...	...	...
45 - 49	ESDF	*393 469*	*185 239*	*208 230*	...	...	...	...	...	...
50 - 54	ESDF	*290 602*	*142 943*	*147 659*	...	...	...	...	...	...
55 - 59	ESDF	*264 199*	*125 792*	*138 407*	...	...	...	...	...	...
60 - 64	ESDF	*190 673*	*92 081*	*98 592*	...	...	...	...	...	...
65 - 69	ESDF	*146 583*	*75 988*	*70 595*	...	...	...	...	...	...
70 - 74	ESDF	*95 959*	*47 899*	*48 060*	...	...	...	...	...	...
75+	ESDF	*126 745*	*56 658*	*70 087*	...	...	...	...	...	...
AMERICA, NORTH — AMERIQUE DU NORD										
Anguilla[5]										
9 V 2001										
Total	CDFC	11 430	5 628	5 802	...	...	...	...	...	...
0 - 1	CDFC	252	131	121	...	...	...	...	...	...
1 - 4	CDFC	821	394	427	...	...	...	...	...	...
5 - 9	CDFC	993	502	491	...	...	...	...	...	...
10 - 14	CDFC	1 136	563	573	...	...	...	...	...	...
15 - 19	CDFC	966	477	489	...	...	...	...	...	...
20 - 24	CDFC	788	375	413	...	...	...	...	...	...
25 - 29	CDFC	873	440	433	...	...	...	...	...	...
30 - 34	CDFC	999	494	505	...	...	...	...	...	...
35 - 39	CDFC	1 040	507	533	...	...	...	...	...	...
40 - 44	CDFC	881	429	452	...	...	...	...	...	...
45 - 49	CDFC	714	364	350	...	...	...	...	...	...
50 - 54	CDFC	468	236	232	...	...	...	...	...	...
55 - 59	CDFC	323	166	157	...	...	...	...	...	...
60 - 64	CDFC	304	144	160	...	...	...	...	...	...
65 - 69	CDFC	288	159	129	...	...	...	...	...	...
70 - 74	CDFC	211	82	129	...	...	...	...	...	...
75 - 79	CDFC	155	65	90	...	...	...	...	...	...
80 - 84	CDFC	102	52	50	...	...	...	...	...	...

7. Population by age, sex and urban/rural residence: latest available year, 1994 - 2003
Population selon l'âge, le sexe et la résidence, urbaine/rurale: dernière année disponible, 1994 - 2003
(continued — suite)

Continent, country or area, date and age (in years) / Continent, pays ou zone, date et âge (en années)	Code[1]	Total			Urban - Urbaine			Rural - Rurale		
		Both sexes Les deux sexes	Male Masculin	Female Féminin	Both sexes Les deux sexes	Male Masculin	Female Féminin	Both sexes Les deux sexes	Male Masculin	Female Féminin
AMERICA, NORTH — AMERIQUE DU NORD										
Anguilla[5]										
9 V 2001										
85 - 89	CDFC	79	31	48	...	...	...	...	...	...
90 - 94	CDFC	30	15	15	...	...	...	...	...	...
95+	CDFC	7	2	5	...	...	...	...	...	...
Antigua and Barbuda - Antigua-et-Barbuda										
1 VII 1996										
Total	ESDF	68 612	33 080	35 532	...	...	...	...	...	...
0 - 4	ESDF	6 259	3 193	3 066	...	...	...	...	...	...
5 - 9	ESDF	6 656	3 328	3 328	...	...	...	...	...	...
10 - 14	ESDF	6 625	3 283	3 342	...	...	...	...	...	...
15 - 19	ESDF	6 284	3 163	3 120	...	...	...	...	...	...
20 - 24	ESDF	5 687	2 842	2 845	...	...	...	...	...	...
25 - 29	ESDF	6 158	3 014	3 143	...	...	...	...	...	...
30 - 34	ESDF	5 959	2 823	3 136	...	...	...	...	...	...
35 - 39	ESDF	5 370	2 533	2 837	...	...	...	...	...	...
40 - 44	ESDF	4 246	1 980	2 266	...	...	...	...	...	...
45 - 49	ESDF	3 476	1 628	1 848	...	...	...	...	...	...
50 - 54	ESDF	2 630	1 259	1 372	...	...	...	...	...	...
55 - 59	ESDF	1 981	961	1 020	...	...	...	...	...	...
60 - 64	ESDF	1 758	804	953	...	...	...	...	...	...
65 - 69	ESDF	1 679	724	955	...	...	...	...	...	...
70 - 74	ESDF	1 511	652	859	...	...	...	...	...	...
75 - 79	ESDF	1 123	463	660	...	...	...	...	...	...
80+	ESDF	1 212	430	782	...	...	...	...	...	...
Aruba										
1 VII 2002										
Total	ESDJ	94 149	45 019	49 130	...	...	...	...	...	...
0 - 4	ESDJ	6 779	3 419	3 361	...	...	...	...	...	...
5 - 9	ESDJ	7 299	3 719	3 580	...	...	...	...	...	...
10 - 14	ESDJ	7 078	3 557	3 521	...	...	...	...	...	...
15 - 19	ESDJ	6 366	3 161	3 206	...	...	...	...	...	...
20 - 24	ESDJ	5 098	2 539	2 559	...	...	...	...	...	...
25 - 29	ESDJ	6 027	2 873	3 155	...	...	...	...	...	...
30 - 34	ESDJ	8 000	3 772	4 228	...	...	...	...	...	...
35 - 39	ESDJ	8 871	4 221	4 650	...	...	...	...	...	...
40 - 44	ESDJ	9 159	4 349	4 810	...	...	...	...	...	...
45 - 49	ESDJ	7 685	3 575	4 109	...	...	...	...	...	...
50 - 54	ESDJ	6 097	2 882	3 215	...	...	...	...	...	...
55 - 59	ESDJ	4 635	2 174	2 461	...	...	...	...	...	...
60 - 64	ESDJ	3 624	1 679	1 945	...	...	...	...	...	...
65 - 69	ESDJ	2 913	1 251	1 663	...	...	...	...	...	...
70 - 74	ESDJ	2 075	921	1 154	...	...	...	...	...	...
75 - 79	ESDJ	1 090	461	629	...	...	...	...	...	...
80 - 84	ESDJ	708	288	419	...	...	...	...	...	...
85 - 89	ESDJ	414	125	289	...	...	...	...	...	...
90 - 94	ESDJ	177	49	129	...	...	...	...	...	...
95+	ESDJ	54	6	48	...	...	...	...	...	...
Bahamas										
1 V 2000										
Total	CDFC	303 611	147 715	155 896	...	...	...	...	...	...
0 - 1	CDFC	5 908	2 929	2 979	...	...	...	...	...	...
1 - 4	CDFC	23 212	11 737	11 475	...	...	...	...	...	...
5 - 9	CDFC	31 648	16 014	15 634	...	...	...	...	...	...
10 - 14	CDFC	28 561	14 149	14 412	...	...	...	...	...	...
15 - 19	CDFC	26 439	13 355	13 084	...	...	...	...	...	...
20 - 24	CDFC	24 772	12 140	12 632	...	...	...	...	...	...
25 - 29	CDFC	26 904	13 110	13 794	...	...	...	...	...	...
30 - 34	CDFC	26 117	12 601	13 516	...	...	...	...	...	...
35 - 39	CDFC	25 887	12 438	13 449	...	...	...	...	...	...

7. Population by age, sex and urban/rural residence: latest available year, 1994 - 2003
Population selon l'âge, le sexe et la résidence, urbaine/rurale: dernière année disponible, 1994 - 2003
(continued — suite)

Continent, country or area, date and age (in years) / Continent, pays ou zone, date et âge (en années)	Code[1]	Total			Urban - Urbaine			Rural - Rurale		
		Both sexes Les deux sexes	Male Masculin	Female Féminin	Both sexes Les deux sexes	Male Masculin	Female Féminin	Both sexes Les deux sexes	Male Masculin	Female Féminin
AMERICA, NORTH — AMERIQUE DU NORD										
Bahamas										
1 V 2000										
40 - 44	CDFC	21 014	9 971	11 043	...	...	...	...	...	...
45 - 49	CDFC	15 827	7 617	8 210	...	...	...	...	...	...
50 - 54	CDFC	11 978	5 749	6 229	...	...	...	...	...	...
55 - 59	CDFC	10 142	4 768	5 374	...	...	...	...	...	...
60 - 64	CDFC	8 011	3 750	4 261	...	...	...	...	...	...
65 - 69	CDFC	5 806	2 651	3 155	...	...	...	...	...	...
70 - 74	CDFC	4 072	1 689	2 383	...	...	...	...	...	...
75 - 79	CDFC	2 615	1 039	1 576	...	...	...	...	...	...
80 - 84	CDFC	1 919	714	1 205	...	...	...	...	...	...
85 - 89	CDFC	914	293	621	...	...	...	...	...	...
90+	CDFC	451	137	314	...	...	...	...	...	...
Unk. - Inc.	CDFC	1 414	864	550	...	...	...	...	...	...
Belize										
1 VII 2003										
Total	ESDF	273 700	138 300	135 400	...	...	...	...	...	...
0 - 4	ESDF	39 470	20 015	19 455	...	...	...	...	...	...
5 - 9	ESDF	37 590	19 025	18 565	...	...	...	...	...	...
10 - 14	ESDF	35 090	17 960	17 130	...	...	...	...	...	...
15 - 19	ESDF	30 100	15 140	14 960	...	...	...	...	...	...
20 - 24	ESDF	24 380	11 920	12 460	...	...	...	...	...	...
25 - 29	ESDF	21 385	10 510	10 875	...	...	...	...	...	...
30 - 34	ESDF	18 485	9 130	9 355	...	...	...	...	...	...
35 - 39	ESDF	16 205	8 160	8 045	...	...	...	...	...	...
40 - 44	ESDF	12 855	6 660	6 195	...	...	...	...	...	...
45 - 49	ESDF	9 790	5 075	4 715	...	...	...	...	...	...
50 - 54	ESDF	7 100	3 725	3 375	...	...	...	...	...	...
55 - 59	ESDF	5 220	2 765	2 455	...	...	...	...	...	...
60 - 64	ESDF	4 540	2 505	2 035	...	...	...	...	...	...
65 - 69	ESDF	4 005	2 045	1 960	...	...	...	...	...	...
70 - 74	ESDF	3 110	1 565	1 545	...	...	...	...	...	...
75 - 79	ESDF	2 065	1 075	990	...	...	...	...	...	...
80 - 84	ESDF	1 235	560	675	...	...	...	...	...	...
85+	ESDF	1 075	465	610	...	...	...	...	...	...
Bermuda - Bermudes[6]										
20 V 2000										
Total	CDJC	62 059	29 802	32 257	...	...	...	...	...	...
0 - 1	CDJC	823	404	419	...	...	...	...	...	...
1 - 4	CDJC	3 166	1 574	1 592	...	...	...	...	...	...
5 - 9	CDJC	4 031	2 016	2 015	...	...	...	...	...	...
10 - 14	CDJC	3 827	1 907	1 920	...	...	...	...	...	...
15 - 19	CDJC	3 542	1 776	1 766	...	...	...	...	...	...
20 - 24	CDJC	3 222	1 557	1 665	...	...	...	...	...	...
25 - 29	CDJC	4 661	2 250	2 411	...	...	...	...	...	...
30 - 34	CDJC	5 461	2 707	2 754	...	...	...	...	...	...
35 - 39	CDJC	6 228	3 071	3 157	...	...	...	...	...	...
40 - 44	CDJC	5 618	2 706	2 912	...	...	...	...	...	...
45 - 49	CDJC	4 735	2 327	2 408	...	...	...	...	...	...
50 - 54	CDJC	4 146	1 994	2 152	...	...	...	...	...	...
55 - 59	CDJC	3 260	1 538	1 722	...	...	...	...	...	...
60 - 64	CDJC	2 617	1 229	1 388	...	...	...	...	...	...
65 - 69	CDJC	2 332	1 056	1 276	...	...	...	...	...	...
70 - 74	CDJC	1 845	794	1 051	...	...	...	...	...	...
75 - 79	CDJC	1 275	473	802	...	...	...	...	...	...
80 - 84	CDJC	713	249	464	...	...	...	...	...	...
85 - 89	CDJC	401	125	276	...	...	...	...	...	...
90 - 94	CDJC	122	43	79	...	...	...	...	...	...
95 - 99	CDJC	33	6	27	...	...	...	...	...	...
100+	CDJC	1	-	1	...	...	...	...	...	...

7. Population by age, sex and urban/rural residence: latest available year, 1994 - 2003
Population selon l'âge, le sexe et la résidence, urbaine/rurale: dernière année disponible, 1994 - 2003
(continued — suite)

Continent, country or area, date and age (in years) Continent, pays ou zone, date et âge (en années)	Code[1]	Total			Urban - Urbaine			Rural - Rurale		
		Both sexes Les deux sexes	Male Masculin	Female Féminin	Both sexes Les deux sexes	Male Masculin	Female Féminin	Both sexes Les deux sexes	Male Masculin	Female Féminin
AMERICA, NORTH — AMERIQUE DU NORD										
British Virgin Islands - Îles Vierges britanniques										
21 V 2001										
Total	CDJC	20 647	10 627	10 020	...	...	...	...	...	...
0 - 4	CDJC	1 787	913	874	...	...	...	...	...	...
5 - 9	CDJC	1 865	946	919	...	...	...	...	...	...
10 - 14	CDJC	1 768	880	888	...	...	...	...	...	...
15 - 19	CDJC	1 529	778	751	...	...	...	...	...	...
20 - 24	CDJC	1 465	752	713	...	...	...	...	...	...
25 - 29	CDJC	1 483	756	727	...	...	...	...	...	...
30 - 34	CDJC	1 826	913	913	...	...	...	...	...	...
35 - 39	CDJC	2 085	1 091	994	...	...	...	...	...	...
40 - 44	CDJC	1 910	991	919	...	...	...	...	...	...
45 - 49	CDJC	1 501	777	724	...	...	...	...	...	...
50 - 54	CDJC	1 128	614	514	...	...	...	...	...	...
55 - 59	CDJC	774	421	353	...	...	...	...	...	...
60 - 64	CDJC	523	267	256	...	...	...	...	...	...
65 - 69	CDJC	337	177	160	...	...	...	...	...	...
70 - 74	CDJC	282	145	137	...	...	...	...	...	...
75 - 79	CDJC	204	113	91	...	...	...	...	...	...
80+	CDJC	180	93	87	...	...	...	...	...	...
Canada[7]										
1 VII 2003										
Total	ESDJ	31 629 677	15 661 734	15 967 943	25 212 723	12 355 256	12 854 903	6 416 976	3 306 472	3 113 035
0 - 1	ESDJ	330 644	169 512	161 132	266 115	136 475	129 645	64 529	33 037	31 492
1 - 4	ESDJ	1 383 658	707 774	675 884	1 102 100	563 751	538 349	281 558	144 028	137 545
5 - 9	ESDJ	1 949 702	998 569	951 133	1 524 480	780 199	744 285	425 232	218 384	206 833
10 - 14	ESDJ	2 117 613	1 084 753	1 032 860	1 619 935	828 418	791 540	497 678	256 350	241 340
15 - 19	ESDJ	2 120 545	1 088 772	1 031 773	1 645 028	840 027	804 942	475 517	248 740	226 832
20 - 24	ESDJ	2 188 501	1 119 035	1 069 466	1 836 847	928 955	907 537	351 654	190 079	161 946
25 - 29	ESDJ	2 118 132	1 073 969	1 044 163	1 793 207	906 422	886 635	324 930	167 559	157 518
30 - 34	ESDJ	2 228 713	1 124 790	1 103 923	1 841 469	928 696	912 757	387 243	196 101	191 172
35 - 39	ESDJ	2 481 199	1 247 414	1 233 785	1 993 776	999 796	993 876	487 428	247 599	239 908
40 - 44	ESDJ	2 719 324	1 364 310	1 355 014	2 154 925	1 072 864	1 081 808	564 388	291 456	273 212
45 - 49	ESDJ	2 515 743	1 251 593	1 264 150	1 975 279	971 446	1 003 640	540 474	280 153	260 504
50 - 54	ESDJ	2 176 497	1 078 752	1 097 745	1 696 925	831 506	865 385	479 588	247 236	232 350
55 - 59	ESDJ	1 842 459	913 922	928 537	1 410 796	689 298	721 465	431 656	224 617	207 067
60 - 64	ESDJ	1 396 800	684 822	711 978	1 069 033	512 657	556 262	327 784	172 155	155 722
65 - 69	ESDJ	1 147 902	552 166	595 736	892 139	417 080	474 989	255 758	135 080	120 737
70 - 74	ESDJ	1 039 113	484 186	554 927	829 340	373 391	455 502	209 773	110 784	99 420
75 - 79	ESDJ	839 427	358 752	480 675	689 192	283 797	404 920	150 230	74 955	75 759
80 - 84	ESDJ	583 656	221 629	362 027	486 967	178 027	308 751	96 688	43 596	53 281
85 - 89	ESDJ	296 953	97 229	199 724	252 975	79 576	173 340	43 973	17 659	26 378
90+	ESDJ	153 096	39 785	113 311	132 195	32 875	99 275	20 895	6 904	14 019
Costa Rica										
1 VII 2003										
Total	ESDJ	4 088 773	2 017 467	2 071 306	2 412 542	1 167 617	1 244 925	1 676 231	849 850	826 381
0 - 1	ESDJ	60 248	30 527	29 721	32 962	14 647	18 315	27 286	15 880	11 406
1 - 4	ESDJ	279 051	141 252	137 799	148 097	74 961	73 136	130 954	66 291	64 663
5 - 9	ESDJ	402 505	204 375	198 130	217 185	112 057	105 128	185 320	92 318	93 002
10 - 14	ESDJ	442 485	227 753	214 732	239 102	125 816	113 286	203 383	101 937	101 446
15 - 19	ESDJ	440 022	224 939	215 083	252 653	128 173	124 480	187 369	96 766	90 603
20 - 24	ESDJ	389 692	196 190	193 502	244 780	123 374	121 406	144 912	72 816	72 096
25 - 29	ESDJ	299 949	148 956	150 993	181 903	91 509	90 394	118 046	57 447	60 599
30 - 34	ESDJ	290 238	141 083	149 155	168 005	79 878	88 127	122 233	61 205	61 028
35 - 39	ESDJ	310 103	144 944	165 159	180 989	81 049	99 940	129 114	63 895	65 219
40 - 44	ESDJ	286 982	133 450	153 532	174 446	78 374	96 072	112 536	55 076	57 460
45 - 49	ESDJ	223 424	105 944	117 480	144 000	63 925	80 075	79 424	42 019	37 405
50 - 54	ESDJ	188 484	94 698	93 786	122 409	60 119	62 290	66 075	34 579	31 496
55 - 59	ESDJ	115 893	53 403	62 490	72 372	31 030	41 342	43 521	22 373	21 148

7. Population by age, sex and urban/rural residence: latest available year, 1994 - 2003
Population selon l'âge, le sexe et la résidence, urbaine/rurale: dernière année disponible, 1994 - 2003
(continued — suite)

Continent, country or area, date and age (in years) / Continent, pays ou zone, date et âge (en années)	Code[1]	Total			Urban - Urbaine			Rural - Rurale		
		Both sexes Les deux sexes	Male Masculin	Female Féminin	Both sexes Les deux sexes	Male Masculin	Female Féminin	Both sexes Les deux sexes	Male Masculin	Female Féminin
AMERICA, NORTH — AMERIQUE DU NORD										
Costa Rica										
1 VII 2003										
60 - 64	ESDJ	106 094	51 800	54 294	66 729	30 719	36 010	39 365	21 081	18 284
65 - 69	ESDJ	80 418	38 330	42 088	49 558	21 979	27 579	30 860	16 351	14 509
70 - 74	ESDJ	66 915	30 475	36 440	45 599	19 369	26 230	21 316	11 106	10 210
75 - 79	ESDJ	49 986	24 345	25 641	33 147	15 502	17 645	16 839	8 843	7 996
80 - 84	ESDJ	28 734	13 082	15 652	19 773	8 212	11 561	8 961	4 870	4 091
85 - 89	ESDJ	14 983	6 075	8 908	9 781	3 049	6 732	5 202	3 026	2 176
90 - 94	ESDJ	7 113	3 237	3 876	5 403	2 092	3 311	1 710	1 145	565
95+	ESDJ	2 218	857	1 361	1 632	727	905	586	130	456
Unk. - Inc.	ESDJ	3 236	1 752	1 484	2 017	1 056	961	1 219	696	523
Cuba										
1 VII 2003										
Total	ESDF	11 215 229	5 616 275	5 598 954	8 501 628	4 181 234	4 320 394	2 713 601	1 435 041	1 278 560
0 - 1	ESDF	137 201	70 500	66 701	100 108	51 452	48 656	37 093	19 048	18 045
1 - 4	ESDF	574 173	295 249	278 924	418 274	214 921	203 353	155 899	80 328	75 571
5 - 9	ESDF	718 508	368 710	349 798	523 097	268 193	254 904	195 411	100 517	94 894
10 - 14	ESDF	847 475	436 117	411 358	625 349	320 415	304 934	222 126	115 702	106 424
15 - 19	ESDF	816 354	419 673	396 681	608 952	310 581	298 371	207 402	109 092	98 310
20 - 24	ESDF	675 989	348 583	327 406	501 046	256 818	244 228	174 943	91 765	83 178
25 - 29	ESDF	858 265	438 532	419 733	632 846	322 104	310 742	225 419	116 428	108 991
30 - 34	ESDF	1 075 398	543 866	531 532	801 785	401 345	400 440	273 613	142 521	131 092
35 - 39	ESDF	1 120 379	558 952	561 427	861 222	423 223	437 999	259 157	135 729	123 428
40 - 44	ESDF	857 620	424 403	433 217	667 990	324 518	343 472	189 630	99 885	89 745
45 - 49	ESDF	660 873	323 439	337 434	512 455	244 726	267 729	148 418	78 713	69 705
50 - 54	ESDF	639 775	314 458	325 317	501 857	240 621	261 236	137 918	73 837	64 081
55 - 59	ESDF	567 640	275 916	291 724	445 224	210 911	234 313	122 416	65 005	57 411
60 - 64	ESDF	483 982	238 748	245 234	377 367	179 659	197 708	106 615	59 089	47 526
65 - 69	ESDF	375 160	183 927	191 233	291 130	136 447	154 683	84 030	47 480	36 550
70 - 74	ESDF	295 922	143 144	152 778	230 331	105 231	125 100	65 591	37 913	27 678
75 - 79	ESDF	224 675	105 732	118 943	176 478	77 856	98 622	48 197	27 876	20 321
80 - 84	ESDF	150 526	68 344	82 182	118 828	50 020	68 808	31 698	18 324	13 374
85+	ESDF	135 314	57 982	77 332	107 289	42 193	65 096	28 025	15 789	12 236
Dominica - Dominique										
12 V 2001										
Total	CDFC	68 635	34 549	34 086	...	...	...	...	...	...
0 - 4	CDFC	6 087	3 059	3 028	...	...	...	...	...	...
5 - 9	CDFC	7 277	3 770	3 507	...	...	...	...	...	...
10 - 14	CDFC	6 847	3 395	3 452	...	...	...	...	...	...
15 - 19	CDFC	6 570	3 293	3 277	...	...	...	...	...	...
20 - 24	CDFC	4 409	2 326	2 083	...	...	...	...	...	...
25 - 29	CDFC	4 934	2 481	2 453	...	...	...	...	...	...
30 - 34	CDFC	5 456	2 753	2 703	...	...	...	...	...	...
35 - 39	CDFC	5 100	2 710	2 390	...	...	...	...	...	...
40 - 44	CDFC	4 310	2 306	2 004	...	...	...	...	...	...
45 - 49	CDFC	3 428	1 857	1 571	...	...	...	...	...	...
50 - 54	CDFC	2 717	1 400	1 317	...	...	...	...	...	...
55 - 59	CDFC	2 303	1 153	1 150	...	...	...	...	...	...
60 - 64	CDFC	2 175	975	1 200	...	...	...	...	...	...
65 - 69	CDFC	2 241	1 041	1 200	...	...	...	...	...	...
70 - 74	CDFC	1 778	831	947	...	...	...	...	...	...
75 - 79	CDFC	1 285	568	717	...	...	...	...	...	...
80 - 84	CDFC	895	347	548	...	...	...	...	...	...
85+	CDFC	823	284	539	...	...	...	...	...	...
Dominican Republic - République dominicaine										
20 X 2002										
Total	CDJC	8 562 541	4 265 215	4 297 326	5 446 704	2 648 064	2 798 640	3 115 837	1 617 151	1 498 686
0 - 1	CDJC	206 819	105 023	101 796	129 423	65 765	63 658	77 396	39 258	38 138

7. Population by age, sex and urban/rural residence: latest available year, 1994 - 2003
Population selon l'âge, le sexe et la résidence, urbaine/rurale: dernière année disponible, 1994 - 2003
(continued — suite)

Continent, country or area, date and age (in years) / Continent, pays ou zone, date et âge (en années)	Code[1]	Total			Urban - Urbaine			Rural - Rurale		
		Both sexes Les deux sexes	Male Masculin	Female Féminin	Both sexes Les deux sexes	Male Masculin	Female Féminin	Both sexes Les deux sexes	Male Masculin	Female Féminin
AMERICA, NORTH — AMERIQUE DU NORD										
Dominican Republic - République dominicaine										
20 X 2002										
1 - 4	CDJC	766 825	389 861	376 964	474 695	240 650	234 045	292 130	149 211	142 919
5 - 9	CDJC	971 881	492 845	479 036	590 809	297 879	292 930	381 072	194 966	186 106
10 - 14	CDJC	959 338	485 882	473 456	592 802	295 497	297 305	366 536	190 385	176 151
15 - 19	CDJC	838 239	418 089	420 150	534 887	260 051	274 836	303 352	158 038	145 314
20 - 24	CDJC	785 802	387 397	398 405	518 495	248 857	269 638	267 307	138 540	128 767
25 - 29	CDJC	687 785	331 527	356 258	456 484	215 653	240 831	231 301	115 874	115 427
30 - 34	CDJC	646 112	318 320	327 792	426 196	205 314	220 882	219 916	113 006	106 910
35 - 39	CDJC	590 750	287 717	303 033	389 835	185 218	204 617	200 915	102 499	98 416
40 - 44	CDJC	476 647	240 175	236 472	309 735	151 229	158 506	166 912	88 946	77 966
45 - 49	CDJC	380 028	188 288	191 740	247 776	118 243	129 533	132 252	70 045	62 207
50 - 54	CDJC	330 713	166 302	164 411	210 832	102 066	108 766	119 881	64 236	55 645
55 - 59	CDJC	233 976	115 834	118 142	146 945	69 876	77 069	87 031	45 958	41 073
60 - 64	CDJC	207 933	104 624	103 309	126 435	60 113	66 322	81 498	44 511	36 987
65 - 69	CDJC	158 365	77 400	80 965	97 293	44 811	52 482	61 072	32 589	28 483
70 - 74	CDJC	136 068	68 480	67 588	81 410	38 123	43 287	54 658	30 357	24 301
75 - 79	CDJC	77 871	37 809	40 062	47 933	21 371	26 562	29 938	16 438	13 500
80 - 84	CDJC	54 402	26 076	28 326	32 545	14 287	18 258	21 857	11 789	10 068
85 - 89	CDJC	27 303	12 772	14 531	16 966	7 230	9 736	10 337	5 542	4 795
90 - 94	CDJC	15 157	6 454	8 703	9 244	3 545	5 699	5 913	2 909	3 004
95+	CDJC	10 274	4 192	6 082	5 820	2 209	3 611	4 454	1 983	2 471
Unk. - Inc.	CDJC	253	148	105	144	77	67	109	71	38
El Salvador										
1 VII 2003										
Total	ESDF	6 638 168	3 261 938	3 376 230	3 932 569	1 891 429	2 041 140	2 705 599	1 370 509	1 335 090
0 - 1	ESDF	162 479	83 082	79 397	87 126	44 566	42 560	75 353	38 516	36 837
1 - 4	ESDF	644 889	329 352	315 537	342 656	174 855	167 801	302 233	154 497	147 736
5 - 9	ESDF	777 836	396 371	381 465	438 845	222 691	216 154	338 991	173 680	165 311
10 - 14	ESDF	720 117	365 942	354 175	404 131	203 433	200 698	315 986	162 509	153 477
15 - 19	ESDF	661 005	334 785	326 220	358 075	177 949	180 126	302 930	156 836	146 094
20 - 24	ESDF	660 518	333 143	327 375	374 723	183 684	191 039	285 795	149 459	136 336
25 - 29	ESDF	638 627	318 847	319 780	380 057	183 630	196 427	258 570	135 217	123 353
30 - 34	ESDF	509 962	246 818	263 144	324 396	152 402	171 994	185 566	94 416	91 150
35 - 39	ESDF	387 053	178 680	208 373	259 673	117 642	142 031	127 380	61 038	66 342
40 - 44	ESDF	309 588	140 553	169 035	210 767	94 677	116 090	98 821	45 876	52 945
45 - 49	ESDF	268 869	124 218	144 651	176 322	80 071	96 251	92 547	44 147	48 400
50 - 54	ESDF	225 211	105 929	119 282	143 766	66 453	77 313	81 445	39 476	41 969
55 - 59	ESDF	186 454	88 100	98 354	116 650	53 968	62 682	69 804	34 132	35 672
60 - 64	ESDF	146 201	68 603	77 598	90 734	41 238	49 496	55 467	27 365	28 102
65 - 69	ESDF	122 667	56 429	66 238	76 373	33 785	42 588	46 294	22 644	23 650
70 - 74	ESDF	97 128	43 336	53 792	61 565	26 420	35 145	35 563	16 916	18 647
75 - 79	ESDF	64 745	27 429	37 316	42 647	17 583	25 064	22 098	9 846	12 252
80+	ESDF	54 819	20 321	34 498	44 063	16 382	27 681	10 756	3 939	6 817
Greenland - Groenland										
1 VII 2000										
Total	ESDJ	56 184	30 029	26 210	45 821	24 310	21 511	10 364	5 697	4 667
0 - 1	ESDJ	843	421	422	654	325	329	190	96	94
1 - 4	ESDJ	3 966	2 022	1 944	3 097	1 603	1 497	869	420	450
5 - 9	ESDJ	5 339	2 713	2 627	4 203	2 156	2 047	1 137	558	580
10 - 14	ESDJ	5 007	2 518	2 491	4 023	2 024	1 999	984	494	492
15 - 19	ESDJ	3 982	2 064	1 921	3 313	1 684	1 629	670	380	292
20 - 24	ESDJ	3 387	1 748	1 641	2 804	1 421	1 383	584	327	258
25 - 29	ESDJ	3 432	1 854	1 579	2 745	1 485	1 263	688	370	319
30 - 34	ESDJ	5 669	3 034	2 635	4 671	2 465	2 207	1 000	570	430
35 - 39	ESDJ	5 933	3 180	2 754	4 936	2 610	2 326	998	570	429
40 - 44	ESDJ	4 775	2 723	2 052	3 975	2 238	1 737	801	488	315
45 - 49	ESDJ	3 704	2 114	1 590	3 088	1 746	1 343	617	368	249

7. Population by age, sex and urban/rural residence: latest available year, 1994 - 2003
Population selon l'âge, le sexe et la résidence, urbaine/rurale: dernière année disponible, 1994 - 2003
(continued — suite)

Continent, country or area, date and age (in years) / Continent, pays ou zone, date et âge (en années)	Code[1]	Total			Urban - Urbaine			Rural - Rurale		
		Both sexes Les deux sexes	Male Masculin	Female Féminin	Both sexes Les deux sexes	Male Masculin	Female Féminin	Both sexes Les deux sexes	Male Masculin	Female Féminin
AMERICA, NORTH — AMERIQUE DU NORD										
Greenland - Groenland										
1 VII 2000										
50 - 54	ESDJ	2 949	1 796	1 154	2 465	1 483	983	485	315	172
55 - 59	ESDJ	2 667	1 573	1 094	2 202	1 285	918	466	291	177
60 - 64	ESDJ	1 715	964	752	1 360	759	601	355	205	152
65 - 69	ESDJ	1 291	651	641	1 041	530	512	251	123	129
70 - 74	ESDJ	878	398	481	711	318	396	168	83	85
75 - 79	ESDJ	392	165	227	316	127	190	77	40	37
80 - 84	ESDJ	190	65	126	160	55	106	31	13	20
85 - 89	ESDJ	70	18	54	59	16	46	11	4	9
90 - 94	ESDJ	20	5	16	18	4	15	3	1	2
95+	ESDJ	3	3	-	2	2	-	1	1	-
Grenada - Grenade										
1 VII 2000										
Total	ESDF	101 308	50 200	51 108	...	...	...	...	...	...
0 - 4	ESDF	10 412	5 292	5 120	...	...	...	...	...	...
5 - 9	ESDF	11 547	5 798	5 749	...	...	...	...	...	...
10 - 14	ESDF	13 546	6 837	6 709	...	...	...	...	...	...
15 - 19	ESDF	11 911	6 077	5 834	...	...	...	...	...	...
20 - 24	ESDF	9 267	4 686	4 581	...	...	...	...	...	...
25 - 29	ESDF	7 290	3 883	3 407	...	...	...	...	...	...
30 - 34	ESDF	5 977	2 999	2 978	...	...	...	...	...	...
35 - 39	ESDF	6 537	3 294	3 243	...	...	...	...	...	...
40 - 44	ESDF	5 364	2 628	2 736	...	...	...	...	...	...
45 - 49	ESDF	3 780	1 955	1 825	...	...	...	...	...	...
50 - 54	ESDF	2 904	1 371	1 533	...	...	...	...	...	...
55 - 59	ESDF	2 472	1 160	1 312	...	...	...	...	...	...
60 - 64	ESDF	2 383	1 078	1 305	...	...	...	...	...	...
65 - 69	ESDF	2 356	1 010	1 346	...	...	...	...	...	...
70+	ESDF	5 562	2 132	3 430	...	...	...	...	...	...
Guadeloupe										
1 VII 2003										
Total	ESDJ	438 820	210 130	228 690	...	...	...	...	...	...
0 - 1	ESDJ	6 914	3 513	3 401	...	...	...	...	...	...
1 - 4	ESDJ	28 307	14 596	13 711	...	...	...	...	...	...
5 - 9	ESDJ	34 060	17 376	16 684	...	...	...	...	...	...
10 - 14	ESDJ	37 290	18 867	18 423	...	...	...	...	...	...
15 - 19	ESDJ	34 437	17 523	16 914	...	...	...	...	...	...
20 - 24	ESDJ	28 703	14 585	14 118	...	...	...	...	...	...
25 - 29	ESDJ	26 371	12 655	13 716	...	...	...	...	...	...
30 - 34	ESDJ	33 945	15 521	18 424	...	...	...	...	...	...
35 - 39	ESDJ	36 449	16 641	19 808	...	...	...	...	...	...
40 - 44	ESDJ	34 725	16 517	18 208	...	...	...	...	...	...
45 - 49	ESDJ	28 752	13 290	15 462	...	...	...	...	...	...
50 - 54	ESDJ	25 090	11 641	13 449	...	...	...	...	...	...
55 - 59	ESDJ	20 360	9 749	10 611	...	...	...	...	...	...
60 - 64	ESDJ	16 257	7 548	8 709	...	...	...	...	...	...
65 - 69	ESDJ	14 333	6 582	7 751	...	...	...	...	...	...
70 - 74	ESDJ	11 328	4 950	6 378	...	...	...	...	...	...
75 - 79	ESDJ	9 265	3 961	5 304	...	...	...	...	...	...
80 - 84	ESDJ	6 621	2 714	3 907	...	...	...	...	...	...
85 - 89	ESDJ	3 399	1 254	2 145	...	...	...	...	...	...
90+	ESDJ	2 214	647	1 567	...	...	...	...	...	...
Guatemala										
1 VII 2001										
Total	ESDF	11 678 411	5 888 426	5 789 985	...	...	...	...	...	...
0 - 1	ESDF	387 025	197 549	189 476	...	...	...	...	...	...
1 - 4	ESDF	1 484 040	757 626	726 414	...	...	...	...	...	...
5 - 9	ESDF	1 689 604	862 809	826 795	...	...	...	...	...	...
10 - 14	ESDF	1 495 114	763 539	731 575	...	...	...	...	...	...

7. Population by age, sex and urban/rural residence: latest available year, 1994 - 2003
Population selon l'âge, le sexe et la résidence, urbaine/rurale: dernière année disponible, 1994 - 2003
(continued — suite)

Continent, country or area, date and age (in years) / Continent, pays ou zone, date et âge (en années)	Code[1]	Total			Urban - Urbaine			Rural - Rurale		
		Both sexes Les deux sexes	Male Masculin	Female Féminin	Both sexes Les deux sexes	Male Masculin	Female Féminin	Both sexes Les deux sexes	Male Masculin	Female Féminin
AMERICA, NORTH — AMERIQUE DU NORD										
Guatemala										
1 VII 2001										
15 - 19	ESDF	1 320 329	673 506	646 823	...	...	...	...	...	...
20 - 24	ESDF	1 110 418	562 982	547 436	...	...	...	...	...	...
25 - 29	ESDF	894 268	449 807	444 461	...	...	...	...	...	...
30 - 34	ESDF	708 522	351 762	356 760	...	...	...	...	...	...
35 - 39	ESDF	571 673	281 068	290 605	...	...	...	...	...	...
40 - 44	ESDF	462 850	226 817	236 033	...	...	...	...	...	...
45 - 49	ESDF	386 977	190 123	196 854	...	...	...	...	...	...
50 - 54	ESDF	306 124	150 654	155 470	...	...	...	...	...	...
55 - 59	ESDF	244 215	121 084	123 131	...	...	...	...	...	...
60 - 64	ESDF	201 985	100 065	101 920	...	...	...	...	...	...
65 - 69	ESDF	166 701	81 453	85 248	...	...	...	...	...	...
70 - 74	ESDF	122 040	58 725	63 315	...	...	...	...	...	...
75 - 79	ESDF	74 787	35 391	39 396	...	...	...	...	...	...
80+	ESDF	51 739	23 466	28 273	...	...	...	...	...	...
Haiti - Haïti										
1 VII 1999										
Total	ESDJ	7 803 232	3 834 240	3 968 992	2 731 843	1 234 809	1 497 034	5 071 389	2 599 431	2 471 958
0 - 1	ESDJ	242 106	122 835	119 271	68 885	36 499	32 386	173 221	86 336	86 885
1 - 4	ESDJ	913 669	462 018	451 651	252 773	130 783	121 990	660 896	331 235	329 661
5 - 9	ESDJ	1 034 513	521 302	513 211	321 389	154 420	166 969	713 124	366 882	346 242
10 - 14	ESDJ	925 920	466 007	459 913	363 812	161 340	202 472	562 108	304 667	257 441
15 - 19	ESDJ	810 881	407 544	403 337	375 052	156 361	218 691	435 829	251 183	184 646
20 - 24	ESDJ	696 906	347 026	349 880	337 696	153 000	184 696	359 210	194 026	165 184
25 - 29	ESDJ	612 995	301 403	311 592	272 739	124 048	148 691	340 256	177 355	162 901
30 - 34	ESDJ	526 616	255 640	270 976	198 846	88 085	110 761	327 770	167 555	160 215
35 - 39	ESDJ	452 327	216 102	236 225	135 215	57 299	77 916	317 112	158 803	158 309
40 - 44	ESDJ	370 430	173 392	197 038	106 911	42 010	64 901	263 519	131 382	132 137
45 - 49	ESDJ	306 075	141 518	164 557	71 946	29 912	42 034	234 129	111 606	122 523
50 - 54	ESDJ	247 324	114 254	133 070	70 080	31 126	38 954	177 244	83 128	94 116
55 - 59	ESDJ	201 858	93 663	108 195	51 060	22 494	28 566	150 798	71 169	79 629
60 - 64	ESDJ	161 143	74 625	86 518	40 580	18 949	21 631	120 563	55 676	64 887
65 - 69	ESDJ	122 392	56 450	65 942	28 310	12 719	15 591	94 082	43 731	50 351
70 - 74	ESDJ	84 796	38 744	46 052	18 717	7 726	10 991	66 079	31 018	35 061
75 - 79	ESDJ	52 884	23 831	29 053	11 309	5 008	6 301	41 575	18 823	22 752
80+	ESDJ	40 397	17 886	22 511	6 523	3 030	3 493	33 874	14 856	19 018
Honduras										
1 VII 2003										
Total	ESDF	6 860 842	3 388 874	3 471 968	3 260 934	1 555 369	1 705 565	3 599 908	1 833 505	1 766 403
0 - 1	ESDF	211 122	107 546	103 576	92 446	47 136	45 310	118 676	60 410	58 266
1 - 4	ESDF	820 813	416 615	404 198	340 186	174 013	166 173	480 627	242 602	238 025
5 - 9	ESDF	949 750	480 017	469 733	389 928	198 612	191 316	559 822	281 405	278 417
10 - 14	ESDF	837 102	421 803	415 299	362 885	180 041	182 844	474 217	241 762	232 455
15 - 19	ESDF	743 031	372 741	370 290	362 858	170 460	192 398	380 173	202 281	177 892
20 - 24	ESDF	663 253	330 233	333 020	352 858	165 359	187 499	310 395	164 874	145 521
25 - 29	ESDF	559 428	276 591	282 837	299 286	142 499	156 787	260 142	134 092	126 050
30 - 34	ESDF	453 592	221 413	232 179	242 678	113 600	129 078	210 914	107 813	103 101
35 - 39	ESDF	358 774	170 994	187 780	190 971	87 412	103 559	167 803	83 582	84 221
40 - 44	ESDF	292 742	137 740	155 002	153 583	69 630	83 953	139 159	68 110	71 049
45 - 49	ESDF	244 002	114 465	129 537	124 151	56 039	68 112	119 851	58 426	61 425
50 - 54	ESDF	196 270	91 939	104 331	97 646	43 561	54 085	98 624	48 378	50 246
55 - 59	ESDF	152 017	71 521	80 496	72 441	32 030	40 411	79 576	39 491	40 085
60 - 64	ESDF	119 860	56 175	63 685	55 043	23 792	31 251	64 817	32 383	32 434
65 - 69	ESDF	95 844	44 359	51 485	44 728	18 795	25 933	51 116	25 564	25 552
70 - 74	ESDF	70 413	32 212	38 201	33 351	13 867	19 484	37 062	18 345	18 717
75 - 79	ESDF	49 736	22 968	26 768	24 076	9 963	14 113	25 660	13 005	12 655
80+	ESDF	43 093	19 542	23 551	21 819	8 560	13 259	21 274	10 982	10 292
Jamaica - Jamaïque										
1 VII 2003										
Total	ESDJ	2 630 371	1 295 999	1 334 371	1 367 088	652 665	714 422	1 263 283	643 334	619 949

7. Population by age, sex and urban/rural residence: latest available year, 1994 - 2003
Population selon l'âge, le sexe et la résidence, urbaine/rurale: dernière année disponible, 1994 - 2003
(continued — suite)

Continent, country or area, date and age (in years) Continent, pays ou zone, date et âge (en années)	Code[1]	Total			Urban - Urbaine			Rural - Rurale		
		Both sexes Les deux sexes	Male Masculin	Female Féminin	Both sexes Les deux sexes	Male Masculin	Female Féminin	Both sexes Les deux sexes	Male Masculin	Female Féminin
AMERICA, NORTH — AMERIQUE DU NORD										
Jamaica - Jamaïque 1 VII 2003										
0 - 1	ESDJ	53 407	27 219	26 188	26 940	13 750	13 189	26 467	13 469	12 998
1 - 4	ESDJ	221 798	113 041	108 757	112 401	57 371	55 031	109 397	55 670	53 727
5 - 9	ESDJ	297 448	151 106	146 342	146 184	73 777	72 407	151 264	77 329	73 935
10 - 14	ESDJ	278 290	140 722	137 568	136 812	68 778	68 034	141 478	71 944	69 533
15 - 19	ESDJ	254 180	127 689	126 491	130 142	63 922	66 220	124 039	63 767	60 271
20 - 24	ESDJ	217 768	106 007	111 762	120 930	57 004	63 926	96 838	49 003	47 835
25 - 29	ESDJ	208 735	100 074	108 661	117 790	54 250	63 541	90 945	45 825	45 120
30 - 34	ESDJ	199 252	95 037	104 215	111 713	51 130	60 583	87 540	43 908	43 632
35 - 39	ESDJ	186 532	88 473	98 059	103 690	46 901	56 789	82 842	41 572	41 270
40 - 44	ESDJ	156 799	77 040	79 759	85 323	39 643	45 680	71 476	37 397	34 079
45 - 49	ESDJ	114 662	56 400	58 262	62 638	29 168	33 471	52 024	27 232	24 792
50 - 54	ESDJ	98 124	50 154	47 970	52 104	25 206	26 898	46 021	24 948	21 072
55 - 59	ESDJ	76 299	39 021	37 278	38 486	18 653	19 832	37 813	20 368	17 445
60 - 64	ESDJ	65 860	32 133	33 727	31 868	14 744	17 125	33 992	17 389	16 602
65 - 69	ESDJ	60 398	29 185	31 212	28 118	12 851	15 267	32 279	16 334	15 945
70 - 74	ESDJ	52 553	25 096	27 457	23 906	10 782	13 124	28 647	14 314	14 333
75 - 79	ESDJ	38 914	17 879	21 035	17 113	7 218	9 895	21 801	10 660	11 140
80 - 84	ESDJ	24 764	10 403	14 361	10 523	4 079	6 444	14 241	6 324	7 917
85+	ESDJ	24 587	9 320	15 267	10 406	3 440	6 966	14 181	5 880	8 301
Martinique 1 VII 2003										
Total	ESDJ	390 552	184 084	206 468	...	...	...	...	...	...
0 - 1	ESDJ	5 308	2 689	2 619	...	...	...	...	...	...
1 - 4	ESDJ	22 005	11 111	10 894	...	...	...	...	...	...
5 - 9	ESDJ	26 660	13 396	13 264	...	...	...	...	...	...
10 - 14	ESDJ	32 269	16 238	16 031	...	...	...	...	...	...
15 - 19	ESDJ	30 959	15 604	15 355	...	...	...	...	...	...
20 - 24	ESDJ	24 445	12 443	12 002	...	...	...	...	...	...
25 - 29	ESDJ	21 449	10 056	11 393	...	...	...	...	...	...
30 - 34	ESDJ	28 639	12 979	15 660	...	...	...	...	...	...
35 - 39	ESDJ	32 946	14 796	18 150	...	...	...	...	...	...
40 - 44	ESDJ	32 070	15 115	16 955	...	...	...	...	...	...
45 - 49	ESDJ	26 675	12 304	14 371	...	...	...	...	...	...
50 - 54	ESDJ	22 706	10 400	12 306	...	...	...	...	...	...
55 - 59	ESDJ	18 643	8 646	9 997	...	...	...	...	...	...
60 - 64	ESDJ	15 718	7 223	8 495	...	...	...	...	...	...
65 - 69	ESDJ	15 531	7 080	8 451	...	...	...	...	...	...
70 - 74	ESDJ	12 103	5 326	6 777	...	...	...	...	...	...
75 - 79	ESDJ	9 775	4 087	5 688	...	...	...	...	...	...
80 - 84	ESDJ	6 751	2 615	4 136	...	...	...	...	...	...
85 - 89	ESDJ	3 600	1 299	2 301	...	...	...	...	...	...
90+	ESDJ	2 300	677	1 623	...	...	...	...	...	...
Mexico - Mexique 1 VII 2003										
Total	ESDJ	104 213 503	51 844 576	52 368 927	81 801 856	40 688 600	41 113 256	22 411 647	11 155 976	11 255 671
0 - 1	ESDJ	1 988 104	1 016 141	971 963	1 508 871	771 725	737 146	479 233	244 416	234 817
1 - 4	ESDJ	8 224 746	4 200 612	4 024 134	6 165 162	3 150 898	3 014 264	2 059 584	1 049 714	1 009 870
5 - 9	ESDJ	11 221 550	5 726 862	5 494 688	8 307 592	4 242 705	4 064 887	2 913 958	1 484 157	1 429 801
10 - 14	ESDJ	11 292 993	5 753 255	5 539 738	8 405 074	4 284 703	4 120 371	2 887 919	1 468 552	1 419 367
15 - 19	ESDJ	10 720 008	5 425 993	5 294 015	8 312 392	4 209 127	4 103 265	2 407 616	1 216 866	1 190 750
20 - 24	ESDJ	10 046 197	5 045 196	5 001 001	8 123 608	4 080 731	4 042 877	1 922 589	964 465	958 124
25 - 29	ESDJ	9 283 984	4 628 632	4 655 352	7 645 051	3 812 091	3 832 960	1 638 933	816 541	822 392
30 - 34	ESDJ	8 342 545	4 131 720	4 210 825	6 897 062	3 416 033	3 481 029	1 445 483	715 687	729 796
35 - 39	ESDJ	7 290 764	3 589 381	3 701 383	6 009 930	2 958 760	3 051 170	1 280 834	630 621	650 213
40 - 44	ESDJ	6 210 837	3 040 035	3 170 802	5 091 720	2 492 046	2 599 674	1 119 117	547 989	571 128
45 - 49	ESDJ	5 039 061	2 452 084	2 586 977	4 071 772	1 981 067	2 090 705	967 289	471 017	496 272
50 - 54	ESDJ	3 904 782	1 887 706	2 017 076	3 103 340	1 499 863	1 603 477	801 442	387 843	413 599
55 - 59	ESDJ	3 020 567	1 447 895	1 572 672	2 354 970	1 128 356	1 226 614	665 597	319 539	346 058
60 - 64	ESDJ	2 397 618	1 135 833	1 261 785	1 840 130	871 137	968 993	557 488	264 696	292 792

7. Population by age, sex and urban/rural residence: latest available year, 1994 - 2003
Population selon l'âge, le sexe et la résidence, urbaine/rurale: dernière année disponible, 1994 - 2003
(continued — suite)

Continent, country or area, date and age (in years) Continent, pays ou zone, date et âge (en années)	Code[1]	Total			Urban - Urbaine			Rural - Rurale		
		Both sexes Les deux sexes	Male Masculin	Female Féminin	Both sexes Les deux sexes	Male Masculin	Female Féminin	Both sexes Les deux sexes	Male Masculin	Female Féminin
AMERICA, NORTH — AMERIQUE DU NORD										
Mexico - Mexique										
1 VII 2003										
65 - 69	ESDJ	1 881 811	876 547	1 005 264	1 433 783	667 181	766 602	448 028	209 366	238 662
70 - 74	ESDJ	1 386 312	632 273	754 039	1 052 714	479 456	573 258	333 598	152 817	180 781
75 - 79	ESDJ	927 909	412 951	514 958	702 566	312 083	390 483	225 343	100 868	124 475
80 - 84	ESDJ	559 212	242 248	316 964	423 247	182 917	240 330	135 965	59 331	76 634
85 - 89	ESDJ	283 944	120 094	163 850	213 331	89 977	123 354	70 613	30 117	40 496
90 - 94	ESDJ	138 894	57 810	81 084	102 913	42 695	60 218	35 981	15 115	20 866
95 - 99	ESDJ	43 932	18 142	25 790	31 387	12 913	18 474	12 545	5 229	7 316
100+	ESDJ	7 733	3 166	4 567	5 241	2 136	3 105	2 492	1 030	1 462
Montserrat										
12 V 2001										
Total	CDFC	4 491	2 418	2 073	...	...	...	...	...	...
0 - 4	CDFC	311	153	158	...	...	...	...	...	...
5 - 9	CDFC	277	153	124	...	...	...	...	...	...
10 - 14	CDFC	281	148	133	...	...	...	...	...	...
15 - 19	CDFC	273	149	124	...	...	...	...	...	...
20 - 24	CDFC	206	113	93	...	...	...	...	...	...
25 - 29	CDFC	319	169	150	...	...	...	...	...	...
30 - 34	CDFC	346	176	170	...	...	...	...	...	...
35 - 39	CDFC	382	211	171	...	...	...	...	...	...
40 - 44	CDFC	325	171	154	...	...	...	...	...	...
45 - 49	CDFC	335	196	139	...	...	...	...	...	...
50 - 54	CDFC	282	170	112	...	...	...	...	...	...
55 - 59	CDFC	239	136	103	...	...	...	...	...	...
60 - 64	CDFC	203	108	95	...	...	...	...	...	...
65 - 69	CDFC	148	76	72	...	...	...	...	...	...
70 - 74	CDFC	169	94	75	...	...	...	...	...	...
75 - 79	CDFC	139	72	67	...	...	...	...	...	...
80 - 84	CDFC	107	47	60	...	...	...	...	...	...
85 - 89	CDFC	67	32	35	...	...	...	...	...	...
90 - 94	CDFC	38	14	24	...	...	...	...	...	...
95+	CDFC	21	9	12	...	...	...	...	...	...
Unk. - Inc.	CDFC	23	21	2	...	...	...	...	...	...
Netherlands Antilles - Antilles néerlandaises										
1 VII 2003										
Total	ESDJ	178 543	83 427	95 116	...	...	...	...	...	...
0 - 4	ESDJ	13 025	6 599	6 426	...	...	...	...	...	...
5 - 9	ESDJ	13 912	7 056	6 857	...	...	...	...	...	...
10 - 14	ESDJ	14 889	7 417	7 472	...	...	...	...	...	...
15 - 19	ESDJ	12 378	6 236	6 143	...	...	...	...	...	...
20 - 24	ESDJ	8 776	4 174	4 602	...	...	...	...	...	...
25 - 29	ESDJ	10 058	4 747	5 312	...	...	...	...	...	...
30 - 34	ESDJ	13 593	6 205	7 389	...	...	...	...	...	...
35 - 39	ESDJ	15 579	7 024	8 556	...	...	...	...	...	...
40 - 44	ESDJ	16 193	7 247	8 946	...	...	...	...	...	...
45 - 49	ESDJ	14 138	6 390	7 748	...	...	...	...	...	...
50 - 54	ESDJ	12 039	5 441	6 598	...	...	...	...	...	...
55 - 59	ESDJ	9 633	4 426	5 207	...	...	...	...	...	...
60 - 64	ESDJ	7 106	3 227	3 880	...	...	...	...	...	...
65 - 69	ESDJ	5 969	2 730	3 239	...	...	...	...	...	...
70 - 74	ESDJ	4 443	1 925	2 518	...	...	...	...	...	...
75 - 79	ESDJ	3 014	1 258	1 756	...	...	...	...	...	...
80 - 84	ESDJ	2 027	764	1 263	...	...	...	...	...	...
85+	ESDJ	1 775	567	1 208	...	...	...	...	...	...
Nicaragua										
1 VII 2003										
Total	ESDJ	5 267 716	2 631 898	2 635 818	3 070 843	1 478 922	1 591 921	2 196 871	1 152 976	1 043 895
0 - 4	ESDJ	729 609	372 044	357 565	385 386	196 098	189 288	344 221	175 946	168 275

7. Population by age, sex and urban/rural residence: latest available year, 1994 - 2003
Population selon l'âge, le sexe et la résidence, urbaine/rurale: dernière année disponible, 1994 - 2003
(continued — suite)

Continent, country or area, date and age (in years) — Continent, pays ou zone, date et âge (en années)	Code[1]	Total — Both sexes Les deux sexes	Total — Male Masculin	Total — Female Féminin	Urban - Urbaine — Both sexes Les deux sexes	Urban - Urbaine — Male Masculin	Urban - Urbaine — Female Féminin	Rural - Rurale — Both sexes Les deux sexes	Rural - Rurale — Male Masculin	Rural - Rurale — Female Féminin
AMERICA, NORTH — AMERIQUE DU NORD										
Nicaragua										
1 VII 2003										
5 - 9	ESDJ	711 483	362 012	349 471	389 882	196 747	193 135	321 601	165 265	156 336
10 - 14	ESDJ	675 224	342 997	332 227	381 240	190 085	191 155	293 985	152 911	141 074
15 - 19	ESDJ	624 274	316 462	307 812	357 874	175 415	182 459	266 399	141 046	125 353
20 - 24	ESDJ	543 268	274 048	269 220	317 244	152 381	164 863	226 024	121 667	104 357
25 - 29	ESDJ	438 651	219 824	218 827	272 118	130 079	142 039	166 533	89 746	76 787
30 - 34	ESDJ	350 416	173 323	177 093	227 766	107 806	119 960	122 649	65 516	57 133
35 - 39	ESDJ	278 630	135 356	143 274	178 427	82 750	95 677	100 203	52 606	47 597
40 - 44	ESDJ	229 345	111 063	118 282	144 697	66 895	77 802	84 647	44 168	40 479
45 - 49	ESDJ	188 772	91 409	97 363	114 537	52 393	62 144	74 235	39 016	35 219
50 - 54	ESDJ	145 317	70 314	75 003	87 506	39 125	48 381	57 811	31 189	26 622
55 - 59	ESDJ	103 796	50 030	53 766	62 370	27 470	34 900	41 427	22 560	18 867
60 - 64	ESDJ	81 906	39 020	42 886	49 689	21 557	28 132	32 217	17 463	14 754
65 - 69	ESDJ	64 117	29 782	34 335	39 097	16 428	22 669	25 022	13 354	11 668
70 - 74	ESDJ	47 557	21 217	26 340	28 945	11 430	17 515	18 611	9 788	8 823
75 - 79	ESDJ	32 062	13 738	18 324	19 688	7 375	12 313	12 374	6 364	6 010
80+	ESDJ	23 289	9 259	14 030	14 377	4 888	9 489	8 912	4 371	4 541
Panama										
1 VII 2000										
Total	ESDF	2 855 703	1 440 801	1 414 902	1 604 823	782 928	821 895	1 250 880	657 873	593 007
0 - 1	ESDF	59 949	30 595	29 354	30 248	15 460	14 788	29 701	15 135	14 566
1 - 4	ESDF	241 433	123 553	117 880	121 253	62 069	59 184	120 180	61 484	58 696
5 0	ESDF	300 852	153 986	146 866	150 849	77 061	73 786	150 003	76 925	73 079
10 - 14	ESDF	291 489	148 579	142 911	148 812	75 471	73 342	142 678	73 109	69 569
15 - 19	ESDF	271 684	137 805	133 878	146 537	73 631	72 906	125 147	64 174	60 974
20 - 24	ESDF	254 772	129 237	125 536	146 169	72 295	73 875	108 605	56 944	51 661
25 - 29	ESDF	250 152	125 922	124 230	150 336	71 923	78 413	99 816	53 999	45 817
30 - 34	ESDF	230 835	115 884	114 951	141 488	67 582	73 906	89 347	48 302	41 045
35 - 39	ESDF	203 446	101 421	102 025	126 268	59 890	66 378	77 178	41 531	35 647
40 - 44	ESDF	170 180	84 702	85 478	105 158	50 101	55 057	65 022	34 601	30 421
45 - 49	ESDF	140 684	70 369	70 315	86 739	41 477	45 262	53 945	28 892	25 053
50 - 54	ESDF	115 342	58 278	57 064	69 710	33 225	36 485	45 632	25 053	20 579
55 - 59	ESDF	93 684	47 379	46 305	53 771	25 760	28 011	39 913	21 619	18 294
60 - 64	ESDF	73 087	36 664	36 423	40 256	18 795	21 461	32 831	17 869	14 962
65 - 69	ESDF	55 236	27 712	27 524	30 061	13 914	16 147	25 175	13 798	11 377
70 - 74	ESDF	43 900	21 495	22 405	24 076	10 692	13 384	19 824	10 803	9 021
75 - 79	ESDF	30 250	14 158	16 092	17 010	7 216	9 794	13 240	6 942	6 298
80+	ESDF	28 727	13 063	15 664	16 083	6 367	9 716	12 644	6 696	5 948
Puerto Rico - Porto Rico[8]										
1 VII 2003										
Total	ESDJ	3 878 532	1 865 170	2 013 362	...	...	...	...	...	...
0 - 1	ESDJ	52 056	26 631	25 425	...	...	...	...	...	...
1 - 4	ESDJ	223 249	114 012	109 237	...	...	...	...	...	...
5 - 9	ESDJ	298 044	152 730	145 314	...	...	...	...	...	...
10 - 14	ESDJ	304 949	155 871	149 078	...	...	...	...	...	...
15 - 19	ESDJ	301 628	153 182	148 446	...	...	...	...	...	...
20 - 24	ESDJ	297 398	148 522	148 876	...	...	...	...	...	...
25 - 29	ESDJ	280 264	137 188	143 076	...	...	...	...	...	...
30 - 34	ESDJ	263 191	127 564	135 627	...	...	...	...	...	...
35 - 39	ESDJ	264 109	125 455	138 654	...	...	...	...	...	...
40 - 44	ESDJ	261 362	121 925	139 437	...	...	...	...	...	...
45 - 49	ESDJ	244 362	112 935	131 427	...	...	...	...	...	...
50 - 54	ESDJ	233 350	107 437	125 913	...	...	...	...	...	...
55 - 59	ESDJ	216 314	99 522	116 792	...	...	...	...	...	...
60 - 64	ESDJ	175 130	80 635	94 495	...	...	...	...	...	...
65 - 69	ESDJ	146 227	66 769	79 458	...	...	...	...	...	...
70 - 74	ESDJ	115 866	51 428	64 438	...	...	...	...	...	...
75 - 79	ESDJ	86 770	37 164	49 606	...	...	...	...	...	...
80+	ESDJ	114 263	46 200	68 063	...	...	...	...	...	...

7. Population by age, sex and urban/rural residence: latest available year, 1994 - 2003
Population selon l'âge, le sexe et la résidence, urbaine/rurale: dernière année disponible, 1994 - 2003
(continued — suite)

Continent, country or area, date and age (in years) / Continent, pays ou zone, date et âge (en années)	Code[1]	Total			Urban - Urbaine			Rural - Rurale		
		Both sexes Les deux sexes	Male Masculin	Female Féminin	Both sexes Les deux sexes	Male Masculin	Female Féminin	Both sexes Les deux sexes	Male Masculin	Female Féminin
AMERICA, NORTH — AMERIQUE DU NORD										
Saint Kitts and Nevis - Saint-Kitts-et-Nevis										
1 VII 2000										
Total	ESDF	40 410	20 400	20 010	...	...	...	...	...	...
0 - 4	ESDF	4 250	2 130	2 120	...	...	...	...	...	...
5 - 9	ESDF	4 100	2 140	1 960	...	...	...	...	...	...
10 - 14	ESDF	4 040	2 120	1 920	...	...	...	...	...	...
15 - 19	ESDF	3 870	2 000	1 870	...	...	...	...	...	...
20 - 24	ESDF	3 620	1 880	1 740	...	...	...	...	...	...
25 - 29	ESDF	3 240	1 640	1 600	...	...	...	...	...	...
30 - 34	ESDF	3 100	1 550	1 550	...	...	...	...	...	...
35 - 39	ESDF	2 910	1 430	1 480	...	...	...	...	...	...
40 - 44	ESDF	2 520	1 270	1 250	...	...	...	...	...	...
45 - 49	ESDF	1 880	900	980	...	...	...	...	...	...
50 - 54	ESDF	1 390	710	680	...	...	...	...	...	...
55 - 59	ESDF	1 100	560	540	...	...	...	...	...	...
60 - 64	ESDF	820	400	420	...	...	...	...	...	...
65 - 69	ESDF	840	410	430	...	...	...	...	...	...
70 - 74	ESDF	810	380	430	...	...	...	...	...	...
75 - 79	ESDF	700	330	370	...	...	...	...	...	...
80 - 84	ESDF	470	240	230	...	...	...	...	...	...
85+	ESDF	750	310	440	...	...	...	...	...	...
Saint Lucia - Sainte-Lucie										
1 VII 2003										
Total	ESDF	160 673	78 618	82 055	...	...	...	...	...	...
0 - 1	ESDF	2 357	1 144	1 213	...	...	...	...	...	...
1 - 4	ESDF	11 147	5 525	5 622	...	...	...	...	...	...
5 - 9	ESDF	16 466	8 289	8 177	...	...	...	...	...	...
10 - 14	ESDF	17 530	8 801	8 729	...	...	...	...	...	...
15 - 19	ESDF	17 224	8 451	8 773	...	...	...	...	...	...
20 - 24	ESDF	14 726	7 242	7 484	...	...	...	...	...	...
25 - 29	ESDF	13 110	6 354	6 756	...	...	...	...	...	...
30 - 34	ESDF	12 152	5 862	6 290	...	...	...	...	...	...
35 - 39	ESDF	11 685	5 646	6 039	...	...	...	...	...	...
40 - 44	ESDF	10 324	5 019	5 305	...	...	...	...	...	...
45 - 49	ESDF	7 750	3 900	3 850	...	...	...	...	...	...
50 - 54	ESDF	5 910	2 965	2 945	...	...	...	...	...	...
55 - 59	ESDF	4 686	2 212	2 474	...	...	...	...	...	...
60 - 64	ESDF	3 969	1 865	2 104	...	...	...	...	...	...
65 - 69	ESDF	3 637	1 734	1 903	...	...	...	...	...	...
70 - 74	ESDF	2 906	1 391	1 515	...	...	...	...	...	...
75 - 79	ESDF	1 988	929	1 059	...	...	...	...	...	...
80+	ESDF	3 106	1 289	1 817	...	...	...	...	...	...
Saint Vincent and the Grenadines - Saint Vincent-et-les Grenadines										
1 VII 2000										
Total	ESDF	111 821	55 797	56 024	...	...	...	...	...	...
0 - 1	ESDF	2 149	1 104	1 045	...	...	...	...	...	...
1 - 4	ESDF	10 539	5 371	5 168	...	...	...	...	...	...
5 - 9	ESDF	14 496	7 252	7 244	...	...	...	...	...	...
10 - 14	ESDF	14 402	7 307	7 095	...	...	...	...	...	...
15 - 19	ESDF	12 828	6 451	6 377	...	...	...	...	...	...
20 - 24	ESDF	10 224	5 244	4 980	...	...	...	...	...	...
25 - 29	ESDF	9 936	5 066	4 870	...	...	...	...	...	...
30 - 34	ESDF	8 063	4 164	3 899	...	...	...	...	...	...
35 - 39	ESDF	5 721	2 853	2 868	...	...	...	...	...	...
40 - 44	ESDF	4 254	2 182	2 072	...	...	...	...	...	...
45 - 49	ESDF	3 363	1 662	1 701	...	...	...	...	...	...

7. Population by age, sex and urban/rural residence: latest available year, 1994 - 2003
Population selon l'âge, le sexe et la résidence, urbaine/rurale: dernière année disponible, 1994 - 2003
(continued — suite)

Continent, country or area, date and age (in years) / Continent, pays ou zone, date et âge (en années)	Code[1]	Total Both sexes Les deux sexes	Total Male Masculin	Total Female Féminin	Urban - Urbaine Both sexes Les deux sexes	Urban - Urbaine Male Masculin	Urban - Urbaine Female Féminin	Rural - Rurale Both sexes Les deux sexes	Rural - Rurale Male Masculin	Rural - Rurale Female Féminin
AMERICA, NORTH — AMERIQUE DU NORD										
Saint Vincent and the Grenadines - Saint Vincent-et-les Grenadines										
1 VII 2000										
50 - 54	ESDF	3 115	1 516	1 599	...	...	...	...	...	...
55 - 59	ESDF	2 748	1 300	1 448	...	...	...	...	...	...
60 - 64	ESDF	2 702	1 283	1 419	...	...	...	...	...	...
65 - 69	ESDF	2 524	1 068	1 456	...	...	...	...	...	...
70 - 74	ESDF	1 948	862	1 086	...	...	...	...	...	...
75 - 79	ESDF	1 360	504	770	...	...	...			
80 - 84	ESDF	827	316	511	...	...	...	...	...	...
85+	ESDF	622	212	410	...	...	...	...	...	...
Trinidad and Tobago - Trinité-et-Tobago										
1 VII 1997										
Total	ESDF	1 274 799	636 340	638 459	...	...	...	...	...	...
0 - 1	ESDF	15 980	7 952	8 028	...	...	...	...	...	...
1 - 4	ESDF	76 520	38 818	37 702	...	...	...	...	...	...
5 - 9	ESDF	118 002	60 461	57 541	...	...	...	...	...	...
10 - 14	ESDF	133 509	67 766	65 743	...	...	...	...	...	...
15 - 19	ESDF	125 488	64 788	60 700	...	...	...	...	...	...
20 - 24	ESDF	113 206	57 922	55 284	...	...	...	...	...	...
25 - 29	ESDF	104 999	53 530	51 469	...	...	...	...	...	...
30 - 34	ESDF	103 806	51 190	52 616	...	...	...	...	...	...
35 - 39	ESDF	101 070	49 871	51 199	...	...	...	...	...	...
40 - 44	ESDF	89 922	45 331	44 591	...	...	...	...	...	...
45 - 49	ESDF	73 655	36 002	37 653	...	...	...	...	...	...
50 - 54	ESDF	58 076	28 693	29 383	...	...	...	...	...	...
55 - 59	ESDF	44 179	20 927	23 252	...	...	...	...	...	...
60 - 64	ESDF	34 112	16 462	17 650	...	...	...	...	...	...
65 - 69	ESDF	27 875	13 198	14 677	...	...	...	...	...	...
70 - 74	ESDF	22 245	9 516	12 729	...	...	...	...	...	...
75 - 79	ESDF	17 300	7 325	9 975	...	...	...	...	...	...
80+	ESDF	14 855	6 588	8 267	...	...	...	...	...	...
Turks Caicos Islands - Îles Turques et Caïques										
20 VIII 2001										
Total	CDJC	19 886	9 896	9 990	...	...	...	...	...	...
0 - 4	CDJC	2 324	1 053	1 271	...	...	...	...	...	...
5 - 14	CDJC	3 369	1 683	1 686	...	...	...	...	...	...
15 - 24	CDJC	2 663	1 270	1 393	...	...	...	...	...	...
25 - 49	CDJC	9 168	4 688	4 480	...	...	...	...	...	...
50 - 64	CDJC	1 605	868	737	...	...	...	...	...	...
65+	CDJC	757	334	423	...	...	...	...	...	...
United States - États-Unis[9]										
1 VII 2003										
Total	ESDJ	290 810 789	143 037 290	147 773 499	...	...	...	...	...	...
0 - 1	ESDJ	4 003 606	2 045 536	1 958 070	...	...	...	...	...	...
1 - 4	ESDJ	15 765 673	8 059 879	7 705 794	...	...	...	...	...	...
5 - 9	ESDJ	19 775 276	10 119 907	9 655 369	...	...	...	...	...	...
10 - 14	ESDJ	21 193 361	10 856 749	10 336 612	...	...	...	...	...	...
15 - 19	ESDJ	20 478 469	10 518 680	9 959 789	...	...	...	...	...	...
20 - 24	ESDJ	20 727 694	10 663 922	10 063 772	...	...	...	...	...	...
25 - 29	ESDJ	19 167 954	9 772 711	9 395 243	...	...	...	...	...	...
30 - 34	ESDJ	20 704 644	10 449 775	10 254 869	...	...	...	...	...	...
35 - 39	ESDJ	21 408 004	10 726 548	10 681 456	...	...	...	...	...	...
40 - 44	ESDJ	22 962 590	11 407 111	11 555 479	...	...	...	...	...	...
45 - 49	ESDJ	21 761 188	10 730 879	11 030 309	...	...	...	...	...	...

7. Population by age, sex and urban/rural residence: latest available year, 1994 - 2003
Population selon l'âge, le sexe et la résidence, urbaine/rurale: dernière année disponible, 1994 - 2003
(continued — suite)

Continent, country or area, date and age (in years) / Continent, pays ou zone, date et âge (en années)	Code[1]	Total Both sexes Les deux sexes	Total Male Masculin	Total Female Féminin	Urban - Urbaine Both sexes Les deux sexes	Urban - Urbaine Male Masculin	Urban - Urbaine Female Féminin	Rural - Rurale Both sexes Les deux sexes	Rural - Rurale Male Masculin	Rural - Rurale Female Féminin
AMERICA, NORTH — AMERIQUE DU NORD										
United States - États-Unis[9]										
1 VII 2003										
50 - 54	ESDJ	19 043 411	9 312 777	9 730 634	...	...	...	...	...	...
55 - 59	ESDJ	15 794 050	7 660 724	8 133 326	...	...	...	...	...	...
60 - 64	ESDJ	12 105 686	5 763 600	6 342 086	...	...	...	...	...	...
65 - 69	ESDJ	9 746 083	4 525 541	5 220 542	...	...	...	...	...	...
70 - 74	ESDJ	8 590 961	3 823 820	4 767 141	...	...	...	...	...	...
75 - 79	ESDJ	7 452 593	3 098 962	4 353 631	...	...	...	...	...	...
80 - 84	ESDJ	5 416 079	2 055 245	3 360 834	...	...	...	...	...	...
85+	ESDJ	4 713 467	1 444 924	3 268 543	...	...	...	...	...	...
United States Virgin Islands - Îles Vierges américaines[8]										
1 IV 2000										
Total	CDJC	108 612	...	...	...	...	...	...	...	...
0 - 4	CDJC	8 553	...	...	...	...	...	...	...	...
5 - 9	CDJC	10 176	...	...	...	...	...	...	...	...
10 - 14	CDJC	9 676	...	...	...	...	...	...	...	...
15 - 19	CDJC	8 688	...	...	...	...	...	...	...	...
20 - 24	CDJC	5 916	...	...	...	...	...	...	...	...
25 - 34	CDJC	13 705	...	...	...	...	...	...	...	...
35 - 44	CDJC	15 746	...	...	...	...	...	...	...	...
45 - 54	CDJC	15 521	...	...	...	...	...	...	...	...
55 - 59	CDJC	6 757	...	...	...	...	...	...	...	...
60 - 64	CDJC	4 757	...	...	...	...	...	...	...	...
65 - 74	CDJC	5 845	...	...	...	...	...	...	...	...
75 - 84	CDJC	2 505	...	...	...	...	...	...	...	...
85+	CDJC	767	...	...	...	...	...	...	...	...
AMERICA, SOUTH — AMERIQUE DU SUD										
Argentina - Argentine										
1 VII 1995										
Total	ESDF	34 768 457	16 976 701	17 609 936	30 556 905	14 820 662	15 736 243	4 029 732	2 156 039	1 873 693
0 - 4	ESDF	3 423 256	1 693 242	1 637 451	2 854 157	1 451 866	1 402 291	476 536	241 376	235 160
5 - 9	ESDF	3 339 853	1 692 161	1 638 391	2 860 036	1 452 476	1 407 560	470 516	239 685	230 831
10 - 14	ESDF	3 284 542	1 662 448	1 612 543	2 838 921	1 436 025	1 402 896	436 070	226 423	209 647
15 - 19	ESDF	3 349 962	1 683 418	1 646 642	2 943 654	1 473 952	1 469 702	386 406	209 466	176 940
20 - 24	ESDF	2 815 425	1 407 920	1 383 976	2 479 244	1 235 279	1 243 965	312 652	172 641	140 011
25 - 29	ESDF	2 470 850	1 234 773	1 220 298	2 182 440	1 085 594	1 096 846	272 631	149 179	123 452
30 - 34	ESDF	2 330 870	1 157 905	1 163 366	2 070 997	1 021 148	1 049 849	250 274	136 757	113 517
35 - 39	ESDF	2 198 005	1 072 637	1 118 988	1 960 731	946 918	1 013 813	230 894	125 719	105 175
40 - 44	ESDF	2 076 119	1 016 579	1 054 840	1 853 152	896 513	956 639	218 267	120 066	98 201
45 - 49	ESDF	1 851 125	923 726	943 144	1 669 726	813 793	855 933	197 144	109 933	87 211
50 - 54	ESDF	1 612 720	786 132	824 657	1 438 415	688 315	750 100	172 374	97 817	74 557
55 - 59	ESDF	1 431 429	683 301	746 669	1 280 730	598 896	681 834	149 240	84 405	64 835
60 - 64	ESDF	1 313 614	610 232	702 282	1 178 113	534 302	643 811	134 401	75 930	58 471
65 - 69	ESDF	1 173 708	527 186	645 792	1 055 243	462 065	593 178	117 735	65 121	52 614
70 - 74	ESDF	921 042	391 559	529 012	829 576	343 192	486 384	90 995	48 367	42 628
75 - 79	ESDF	637 312	249 995	386 978	574 790	219 340	355 450	62 183	30 655	31 528
80+	ESDF	538 624	183 487	354 907	486 980	160 988	325 992	51 414	22 499	28 915
18 XI 2001										
Total	CDFC	36 260 130	17 659 072	18 601 058	...	...	...	...	...	...
0 - 1	CDFC	677 115	344 826	332 289	...	...	...	...	...	...
1 - 4	CDFC	2 672 163	1 358 364	1 313 799	...	...	...	...	...	...
5 - 9	CDFC	3 471 217	1 760 659	1 710 558	...	...	...	...	...	...
10 - 14	CDFC	3 427 200	1 738 744	1 688 456	...	...	...	...	...	...
15 - 19	CDFC	3 188 304	1 613 030	1 575 274	...	...	...	...	...	...
20 - 24	CDFC	3 199 339	1 597 939	1 601 400	...	...	...	...	...	...

7. Population by age, sex and urban/rural residence: latest available year, 1994 - 2003
Population selon l'âge, le sexe et la résidence, urbaine/rurale: dernière année disponible, 1994 - 2003
(continued — suite)

Continent, country or area, date and age (in years) / Continent, pays ou zone, date et âge (en années)	Code[1]	Total			Urban - Urbaine			Rural - Rurale		
		Both sexes Les deux sexes	Male Masculin	Female Féminin	Both sexes Les deux sexes	Male Masculin	Female Féminin	Both sexes Les deux sexes	Male Masculin	Female Féminin
AMERICA, SOUTH — AMERIQUE DU SUD										
Argentina - Argentine										
18 XI 2001										
25 - 29	CDFC	2 695 341	1 329 493	1 365 848	...	...	...	...	...	...
30 - 34	CDFC	2 364 903	1 159 698	1 205 205	...	...	...	...	...	...
35 - 39	CDFC	2 229 617	1 086 600	1 143 017	...	...	...	...	...	...
40 - 44	CDFC	2 136 536	1 043 147	1 093 389	...	...	...	...	...	...
45 - 49	CDFC	1 971 911	959 135	1 012 776	...	...	...	...	...	...
50 - 54	CDFC	1 850 481	895 127	955 354	...	...	...	...	...	...
55 - 59	CDFC	1 504 046	718 159	785 887	...	...	...	...	...	...
60 - 64	CDFC	1 284 337	597 259	687 078	...	...	...	...	...	...
65 - 69	CDFC	1 109 788	499 544	610 244	...	...	...	...	...	...
70 - 74	CDFC	996 525	422 426	574 099	...	...	...	...	...	...
75 - 79	CDFC	727 895	289 055	438 840	...	...	...	...	...	...
80 - 84	CDFC	432 908	152 255	280 653	...	...	...	...	...	...
85 - 89	CDFC	224 463	68 423	156 040	...	...	...	...	...	...
90 - 94	CDFC	77 654	20 758	56 896	...	...	...	...	...	...
95 - 99	CDFC	16 532	4 084	12 448	...	...	...	...	...	...
100+	CDFC	1 855	347	1 508	...	...	...	...	...	...
Bolivia - Bolivie										
1 VII 2003										
Total	ESDF	9 024 922	4 495 426	4 529 495	5 713 606	2 780 802	2 932 804	3 311 316	1 714 625	1 596 692
0 - 1	ESDF	254 798	129 963	124 834	...	...	...	...	...	...
0 - 4	ESDF	...	...	...	744 336	377 941	366 395	507 820	260 704	247 117
1 - 4	ESDF	997 358	508 681	488 678	...	...	...	...	...	...
5 - 9	ESDF	1 166 265	594 608	571 657	692 312	349 521	342 790	473 953	245 087	228 866
10 - 14	ESDF	1 073 561	546 244	527 317	675 965	336 689	339 276	397 596	209 555	188 041
15 - 19	ESDF	932 510	472 358	460 151	630 783	309 369	321 414	301 727	162 989	138 737
20 - 24	ESDF	814 526	409 846	404 680	572 694	281 691	291 003	241 832	128 155	113 677
25 - 29	ESDF	721 254	359 771	361 483	494 257	239 881	254 376	226 998	119 890	107 107
30 - 34	ESDF	624 992	309 212	315 780	427 459	204 574	222 885	197 533	104 638	92 895
35 - 39	ESDF	512 151	251 779	260 373	334 677	158 910	175 767	177 474	92 868	84 606
40 - 44	ESDF	432 316	210 816	221 500	280 542	132 378	148 164	151 775	78 438	73 336
45 - 49	ESDF	366 481	176 834	189 646	229 283	107 308	121 975	137 198	69 526	67 671
50 - 54	ESDF	302 980	144 864	158 116	182 392	84 279	98 113	120 587	60 584	60 003
55 - 59	ESDF	243 463	115 925	127 538	140 577	64 747	75 830	102 886	51 178	51 708
60 - 64	ESDF	191 980	90 333	101 647	103 324	46 382	56 942	88 655	43 950	44 705
65 - 69	ESDF	155 368	71 595	83 774	82 620	36 420	46 200	72 748	35 175	37 574
70 - 74	ESDF	116 485	52 380	64 104	60 079	25 772	34 307	56 405	26 608	29 797
75 - 79	ESDF	73 314	31 963	41 351	39 546	16 287	23 258	33 768	15 676	18 092
80+	ESDF	45 120	18 254	26 866	22 759	8 652	14 107	22 361	9 602	12 759
Brazil - Brésil[10]										
1 VIII 2000										
Total	CDJC	169 799 170	83 576 015	86 223 155	137 953 959	66 882 993	71 070 966	31 845 211	16 693 022	15 152 189
0 - 1	CDJC	3 213 310	1 635 916	1 577 394	2 518 464	1 282 941	1 235 523	694 846	352 975	341 871
1 - 4	CDJC	13 162 418	6 691 010	6 471 408	10 242 356	5 207 423	5 034 933	2 920 062	1 483 587	1 436 475
5 - 9	CDJC	16 542 327	8 402 353	8 139 974	12 821 519	6 500 814	6 320 705	3 720 808	1 901 539	1 819 269
10 - 14	CDJC	17 348 067	8 777 639	8 570 428	13 530 190	6 803 898	6 726 292	3 817 877	1 973 741	1 844 136
15 - 19	CDJC	17 939 815	9 019 130	8 920 685	14 403 539	7 132 822	7 270 717	3 536 276	1 886 308	1 649 968
20 - 24	CDJC	16 141 515	8 048 218	8 093 297	13 352 132	6 549 365	6 802 767	2 789 383	1 498 853	1 290 530
25 - 29	CDJC	13 849 665	6 814 328	7 035 337	11 570 969	5 606 425	5 964 544	2 278 696	1 207 903	1 070 793
30 - 34	CDJC	13 028 944	6 363 983	6 664 961	10 918 396	5 248 443	5 669 953	2 110 548	1 115 540	995 008
35 - 39	CDJC	12 261 529	5 955 875	6 305 654	10 326 271	4 929 130	5 397 141	1 935 258	1 026 745	908 513
40 - 44	CDJC	10 546 694	5 116 439	5 430 255	8 913 019	4 249 804	4 663 215	1 633 675	866 635	767 040
45 - 49	CDJC	8 721 541	4 216 418	4 505 123	7 309 621	3 472 375	3 837 246	1 411 920	744 043	667 877
50 - 54	CDJC	7 062 601	3 415 678	3 646 923	5 833 659	2 764 708	3 068 951	1 228 942	650 970	577 972
55 - 59	CDJC	5 444 715	2 585 244	2 859 471	4 387 995	2 032 135	2 355 860	1 056 720	553 109	503 611
60 - 64	CDJC	4 600 929	2 153 209	2 447 720	3 712 213	1 676 323	2 035 890	888 716	476 886	411 830
65 - 69	CDJC	3 581 106	1 639 325	1 941 781	2 916 899	1 284 812	1 632 087	664 207	354 513	309 694
70 - 74	CDJC	2 742 302	1 229 329	1 512 973	2 249 617	966 115	1 283 502	492 685	263 214	229 471
75 - 79	CDJC	1 779 587	780 571	999 016	1 456 665	610 767	845 898	322 922	169 804	153 118
80 - 84	CDJC	1 036 034	428 501	607 533	841 798	331 002	510 796	194 236	97 499	96 737

7. **Population by age, sex and urban/rural residence: latest available year, 1994 - 2003**
Population selon l'âge, le sexe et la résidence, urbaine/rurale: dernière année disponible, 1994 - 2003
(continued — suite)

Continent, country or area, date and age (in years) / Continent, pays ou zone, date et âge (en années)	Code[1]	Total			Urban - Urbaine			Rural - Rurale		
		Both sexes Les deux sexes	Male Masculin	Female Féminin	Both sexes Les deux sexes	Male Masculin	Female Féminin	Both sexes Les deux sexes	Male Masculin	Female Féminin
AMERICA, SOUTH — AMERIQUE DU SUD										
Brazil - Brésil[10]										
1 VIII 2000										
85 - 89	CDJC	534 871	208 088	326 783	436 121	160 379	275 742	98 750	47 709	51 041
90 - 94	CDJC	180 426	65 117	115 309	147 784	50 531	97 253	32 642	14 586	18 056
95 - 99	CDJC	56 198	19 221	36 977	45 682	14 899	30 783	10 516	4 322	6 194
100+	CDJC	24 576	10 423	14 153	19 050	7 882	11 168	5 526	2 541	2 985
1 VII 2003										
Total	ESDF	178 985 306	88 047 716	90 937 590	...	...	...	...	...	...
0 - 1	ESDF	3 628 571	1 843 860	1 784 711	...	...	...	...	...	...
1 - 4	ESDF	14 002 715	7 106 729	6 895 986	...	...	...	...	...	...
5 - 9	ESDF	16 703 360	8 466 618	8 236 742	...	...	...	...	...	...
10 - 14	ESDF	16 709 416	8 451 659	8 257 757	...	...	...	...	...	...
15 - 19	ESDF	17 812 322	8 985 133	8 827 189	...	...	...	...	...	...
20 - 24	ESDF	17 166 827	8 614 650	8 552 177	...	...	...	...	...	...
25 - 29	ESDF	15 011 694	7 500 138	7 511 556	...	...	...	...	...	...
30 - 34	ESDF	13 896 692	6 885 598	7 011 094	...	...	...	...	...	...
35 - 39	ESDF	13 333 971	6 485 274	6 848 697	...	...	...	...	...	...
40 - 44	ESDF	11 983 467	5 731 523	6 251 944	...	...	...	...	...	...
45 - 49	ESDF	9 721 974	4 622 486	5 099 488	...	...	...	...	...	...
50 - 54	ESDF	7 707 919	3 646 997	4 060 922	...	...	...	...	...	...
55 - 59	ESDF	6 007 022	2 824 085	3 182 937	...	...	...	...	...	...
60 - 64	ESDF	4 838 687	2 246 661	2 592 026	...	...	...	...	...	...
65 - 69	ESDF	3 858 133	1 772 136	2 085 997	...	...	...	...	...	...
70 - 74	ESDF	2 807 165	1 248 027	1 559 138	...	...	...	...	...	...
75 - 79	ESDF	1 953 175	849 462	1 103 713	...	...	...	...	...	...
80+	ESDF	1 842 196	766 680	1 075 516	...	...	...	...	...	...
Chile - Chili										
1 VII 2003										
Total	ESDF	15 919 479	7 879 658	8 039 821	13 808 880	6 754 181	7 054 699	2 110 599	1 125 477	985 122
0 - 1	ESDF	247 907	126 270	121 637	217 203	110 607	106 596	30 704	15 663	15 041
1 - 4	ESDF	1 025 944	522 370	503 574	895 251	455 693	439 558	130 693	66 677	64 016
5 - 9	ESDF	1 392 070	708 456	683 614	1 203 957	612 201	591 756	188 113	96 255	91 858
10 - 14	ESDF	1 478 520	752 078	726 442	1 274 420	646 613	627 807	204 100	105 465	98 635
15 - 19	ESDF	1 407 078	714 910	692 168	1 220 376	615 440	604 936	186 702	99 470	87 232
20 - 24	ESDF	1 262 228	639 231	622 997	1 109 985	555 674	554 311	152 243	83 557	68 686
25 - 29	ESDF	1 199 569	604 173	595 396	1 058 385	528 387	529 998	141 184	75 786	65 398
30 - 34	ESDF	1 241 218	622 040	619 178	1 086 398	539 686	546 712	154 820	82 354	72 466
35 - 39	ESDF	1 251 219	624 487	626 732	1 086 144	535 488	550 656	165 075	88 999	76 076
40 - 44	ESDF	1 197 705	595 374	602 331	1 039 140	507 727	531 413	158 565	87 647	70 918
45 - 49	ESDF	1 003 266	496 069	507 197	872 821	423 090	449 731	130 445	72 979	57 466
50 - 54	ESDF	803 074	393 293	409 781	697 297	334 361	362 936	105 777	58 932	46 845
55 - 59	ESDF	661 985	319 094	342 891	570 348	268 756	301 592	91 637	50 338	41 299
60 - 64	ESDF	532 185	250 830	281 355	452 741	207 805	244 936	79 444	43 025	36 419
65 - 69	ESDF	415 555	189 218	226 337	348 804	153 559	195 245	66 751	35 659	31 092
70 - 74	ESDF	331 127	143 457	187 670	278 292	115 775	162 517	52 835	27 682	25 153
75 - 79	ESDF	236 136	96 046	140 090	199 783	77 503	122 280	36 353	18 543	17 810
80+	ESDF	232 693	82 262	150 431	197 535	65 816	131 719	35 158	16 446	18 712
Colombia - Colombie[11]										
1 VII 2003										
Total	ESDF	44 583 575	22 043 893	22 539 682	...	...	...	...	...	...
0 - 4	ESDF	4 791 042	2 446 010	2 345 032	...	...	...	...	...	...
5 - 9	ESDF	4 753 601	2 424 980	2 328 621	...	...	...	...	...	...
10 - 14	ESDF	4 577 069	2 331 451	2 245 618	...	...	...	...	...	...
15 - 19	ESDF	4 271 634	2 169 641	2 101 993	...	...	...	...	...	...
20 - 24	ESDF	4 035 182	2 034 755	2 000 427	...	...	...	...	...	...
25 - 29	ESDF	3 729 985	1 857 546	1 872 439	...	...	...	...	...	...
30 - 34	ESDF	3 470 520	1 703 473	1 767 047	...	...	...	...	...	...
35 - 39	ESDF	3 326 156	1 616 184	1 709 972	...	...	...	...	...	...
40 - 44	ESDF	2 849 626	1 372 289	1 477 337	...	...	...	...	...	...
45 - 49	ESDF	2 341 361	1 115 446	1 225 915	...	...	...	...	...	...

7. Population by age, sex and urban/rural residence: latest available year, 1994 - 2003
Population selon l'âge, le sexe et la résidence, urbaine/rurale: dernière année disponible, 1994 - 2003
(continued — suite)

Continent, country or area, date and age (in years) / Continent, pays ou zone, date et âge (en années)	Code[1]	Total			Urban - Urbaine			Rural - Rurale		
		Both sexes Les deux sexes	Male Masculin	Female Féminin	Both sexes Les deux sexes	Male Masculin	Female Féminin	Both sexes Les deux sexes	Male Masculin	Female Féminin
AMERICA, SOUTH — AMERIQUE DU SUD										
Colombia - Colombie[11]										
1 VII 2003										
50 - 54	ESDF	1 875 595	888 646	986 949	...	...	...	...	...	...
55 - 59	ESDF	1 384 349	657 450	726 899	...	...	...	...	...	...
60 - 64	ESDF	1 010 475	477 242	533 233	...	...	...	...	...	...
65 - 69	ESDF	772 448	354 592	417 856	...	...	...	...	...	...
70 - 74	ESDF	580 292	258 366	321 926	...	...	...	...	...	...
75 - 79	ESDF	406 562	175 828	230 734	...	...	...	...	...	...
80+	ESDF	407 678	159 994	247 684	...	...	...	...	...	...
Ecuador - Équateur[12]										
1 VII 2003										
Total	ESDF	12 842 578	6 444 656	6 397 922	8 001 231	3 963 574	4 037 657	4 841 347	2 481 082	2 360 265
0 - 1	ESDF	291 541	148 855	142 686	...	...	...	...	...	...
0 - 4	ESDF	...	...	...	839 835	433 418	406 417	613 153	307 824	305 329
1 - 4	ESDF	1 161 447	592 387	569 060	...	...	...	...	...	...
5 - 9	ESDF	1 431 703	729 463	702 240	822 130	420 356	401 774	609 573	309 107	300 466
10 - 14	ESDF	1 386 055	704 968	681 087	814 342	410 553	403 789	571 713	294 415	277 298
15 - 19	ESDF	1 325 476	672 366	653 110	833 344	411 240	422 104	492 132	261 126	231 006
20 - 24	ESDF	1 197 849	604 996	592 853	794 951	392 160	402 791	402 898	212 836	190 062
25 - 29	ESDF	1 063 799	535 221	528 578	732 221	362 384	369 837	331 578	172 837	158 741
30 - 34	ESDF	947 667	474 707	472 960	655 891	325 405	330 486	291 776	149 302	142 474
35 - 39	ESDF	832 295	415 688	416 607	557 430	276 725	280 705	274 865	138 963	135 902
40 - 44	ESDF	714 548	355 943	358 605	462 305	228 455	233 850	252 243	127 488	124 755
45 - 49	ESDF	613 640	304 293	309 347	378 906	185 709	193 197	234 734	118 584	116 150
50 - 54	ESDF	497 902	245 905	251 997	301 112	146 157	154 955	196 790	99 748	97 042
55 - 59	ESDF	374 599	184 256	190 343	221 792	105 867	115 925	152 807	78 389	74 418
60 - 64	ESDF	306 547	149 420	157 127	181 314	85 090	96 224	125 233	64 330	60 903
65 - 69	ESDF	248 066	119 289	128 777	145 624	67 065	78 559	102 442	52 224	50 218
70 - 74	ESDF	189 778	89 735	100 043	110 026	49 397	60 629	79 752	40 338	39 414
75 - 79	ESDF	134 374	62 422	71 952	77 738	34 049	43 689	56 636	28 373	28 263
80+	ESDF	125 292	54 742	70 550	72 270	29 544	42 726	53 022	25 198	27 824
Falkland Islands (Malvinas) - Îles Falkland (Malvinas)										
8 IV 2001										
Total	CDFC	2 913	1 598	1 315	...	...	...	...	...	...
0 - 4	CDFC	137	70	67	...	...	...	...	...	...
5 - 9	CDFC	146	71	75	...	...	...	...	...	...
10 - 14	CDFC	155	87	68	...	...	...	...	...	...
15 - 19	CDFC	149	69	80	...	...	...	...	...	...
20 - 24	CDFC	223	111	112	...	...	...	...	...	...
25 - 29	CDFC	271	143	128	...	...	...	...	...	...
30 - 34	CDFC	292	173	119	...	...	...	...	...	...
35 - 39	CDFC	277	159	118	...	...	...	...	...	...
40 - 44	CDFC	250	124	126	...	...	...	...	...	...
45 - 49	CDFC	241	152	89	...	...	...	...	...	...
50 - 54	CDFC	233	139	94	...	...	...	...	...	...
55 - 59	CDFC	188	117	71	...	...	...	...	...	...
60 - 64	CDFC	110	68	42	...	...	...	...	...	...
65 - 69	CDFC	90	50	40	...	...	...	...	...	...
70 - 74	CDFC	64	26	38	...	...	...	...	...	...
75 - 79	CDFC	29	15	14	...	...	...	...	...	...
80+	CDFC	58	24	34	...	...	...	...	...	...
French Guiana - Guyane française										
1 I 2003										
Total	ESDJ	178 347	88 712	89 635	...	...	...	...	...	...
0 - 1	ESDJ	5 175	2 609	2 566	...	...	...	...	...	...
1 - 4	ESDJ	18 811	9 524	9 287	...	...	...	...	...	...

7. Population by age, sex and urban/rural residence: latest available year, 1994 - 2003
Population selon l'âge, le sexe et la résidence, urbaine/rurale: dernière année disponible, 1994 - 2003
(continued — suite)

Continent, country or area, date and age (in years) / Continent, pays ou zone, date et âge (en années)	Code[1]	Total Both sexes Les deux sexes	Total Male Masculin	Total Female Féminin	Urban - Urbaine Both sexes Les deux sexes	Urban - Urbaine Male Masculin	Urban - Urbaine Female Féminin	Rural - Rurale Both sexes Les deux sexes	Rural - Rurale Male Masculin	Rural - Rurale Female Féminin
AMERICA, SOUTH — AMERIQUE DU SUD										
French Guiana - Guyane française										
1 I 2003										
5 - 9	ESDJ	20 117	10 220	9 897	...	...	...	...	...	...
10 - 14	ESDJ	18 900	9 588	9 312	...	...	...	...	...	...
15 - 19	ESDJ	16 315	8 336	7 979	...	...	...	...	...	...
20 - 24	ESDJ	12 863	6 462	6 401	...	...	...	...	...	...
25 - 29	ESDJ	11 604	5 664	5 940	...	...	...	...	...	...
30 - 34	ESDJ	14 501	6 464	8 037	...	...	...	...	...	...
35 - 39	ESDJ	14 036	6 667	7 369	...	...	...	...	...	...
40 - 44	ESDJ	12 490	6 154	6 336	...	...	...	...	...	...
45 - 49	ESDJ	9 835	5 017	4 818	...	...	...	...	...	...
50 - 54	ESDJ	7 846	4 037	3 809	...	...	...	...	...	...
55 - 59	ESDJ	5 524	3 006	2 518	...	...	...	...	...	...
60 - 64	ESDJ	3 384	1 760	1 624	...	...	...	...	...	...
65 - 69	ESDJ	2 362	1 176	1 186	...	...	...	...	...	...
70 - 74	ESDJ	1 755	880	875	...	...	...	...	...	...
75 - 79	ESDJ	1 270	541	729	...	...	...	...	...	...
80 - 84	ESDJ	864	344	520	...	...	...	...	...	...
85 - 89	ESDJ	391	145	246	...	...	...	...	...	...
90+	ESDJ	304	118	186	...	...	...	...	...	...
Paraguay										
28 VIII 2002										
Total	CDFC	5 163 198	2 603 242	2 559 956	2 928 437	1 422 339	1 506 098	2 234 761	1 180 903	1 053 858
0 - 1	CDFC	115 558	59 043	56 515	62 098	31 869	30 229	53 460	27 174	26 286
1 - 4	CDFC	491 743	250 996	240 747	256 692	130 582	126 110	235 051	120 414	114 637
5 - 9	CDFC	663 294	338 199	325 095	341 612	173 363	168 249	321 682	164 836	156 846
10 - 14	CDFC	644 714	328 120	316 594	331 808	165 636	166 172	312 906	162 484	150 422
15 - 19	CDFC	576 807	292 731	284 076	327 674	156 108	171 566	249 133	136 623	112 510
20 - 24	CDFC	472 545	238 527	234 018	294 654	139 622	155 032	177 891	98 905	78 986
25 - 29	CDFC	359 766	179 299	180 467	221 966	105 928	116 038	137 800	73 371	64 429
30 - 34	CDFC	333 192	167 025	166 167	204 138	98 568	105 570	129 054	68 457	60 597
35 - 39	CDFC	307 521	153 333	154 188	186 657	89 705	96 952	120 864	63 628	57 236
40 - 44	CDFC	284 082	145 797	138 285	170 959	84 148	86 811	113 123	61 649	51 474
45 - 49	CDFC	227 719	116 069	111 650	135 829	66 659	69 170	91 890	49 410	42 480
50 - 54	CDFC	182 317	93 396	88 921	106 049	52 006	54 043	76 268	41 390	34 878
55 - 59	CDFC	135 707	68 353	67 354	78 597	37 878	40 719	57 110	30 475	26 635
60 - 64	CDFC	114 843	56 778	58 065	64 874	29 968	34 906	49 969	26 810	23 159
65 - 69	CDFC	80 528	38 292	42 236	45 618	20 151	25 467	34 910	18 141	16 769
70 - 74	CDFC	70 708	33 286	37 422	40 227	17 320	22 907	30 481	15 966	14 515
75 - 79	CDFC	47 931	21 703	26 228	27 650	11 307	16 343	20 281	10 396	9 885
80 - 84	CDFC	29 287	12 433	16 854	16 753	6 289	10 464	12 534	6 144	6 390
85 - 89	CDFC	16 412	6 750	9 662	9 573	3 548	6 025	6 839	3 202	3 637
90+	CDFC	8 524	3 112	5 412	5 009	1 684	3 325	3 515	1 428	2 087
Peru - Pérou[13,14]										
1 VII 2003										
Total	ESDF	27 148 101	13 653 636	13 494 465	19 638 160	9 838 166	9 799 994	7 509 941	3 815 470	3 694 471
0 - 1	ESDF	609 493	311 244	298 249	396 776	202 685	194 091	212 717	108 559	104 158
1 - 4	ESDF	2 421 607	1 233 879	1 187 728	1 576 451	803 515	772 936	845 156	430 364	414 792
5 - 9	ESDF	3 035 366	1 543 434	1 491 932	1 991 380	1 014 048	977 332	1 043 986	529 386	514 600
10 - 14	ESDF	2 945 090	1 494 798	1 450 292	1 964 965	1 000 547	964 418	980 125	494 251	485 874
15 - 19	ESDF	2 741 079	1 389 378	1 351 701	1 926 252	973 987	952 265	814 827	415 391	399 436
20 - 24	ESDF	2 554 202	1 292 423	1 261 779	1 887 721	938 019	949 702	666 481	354 404	312 077
25 - 29	ESDF	2 340 315	1 181 152	1 159 163	1 797 183	894 088	903 095	543 132	287 064	256 068
30 - 34	ESDF	2 037 364	1 028 262	1 009 102	1 572 404	786 875	785 529	464 960	241 387	223 573
35 - 39	ESDF	1 788 202	900 299	887 903	1 392 115	698 578	693 537	396 087	201 721	194 366
40 - 44	ESDF	1 534 285	770 326	763 959	1 206 989	605 775	601 214	327 296	164 551	162 745
45 - 49	ESDF	1 269 376	634 416	634 960	999 588	500 722	498 866	269 788	133 694	136 094
50 - 54	ESDF	1 034 814	515 347	519 467	802 454	402 068	400 386	232 360	113 279	119 081
55 - 59	ESDF	820 794	406 579	414 215	621 212	310 045	311 167	199 582	96 534	103 048
60 - 64	ESDF	659 572	323 204	336 368	490 814	240 969	249 845	168 758	82 235	86 523

7. Population by age, sex and urban/rural residence: latest available year, 1994 - 2003
Population selon l'âge, le sexe et la résidence, urbaine/rurale: dernière année disponible, 1994 - 2003
(continued — suite)

Continent, country or area, date and age (in years) / Continent, pays ou zone, date et âge (en années)	Code[1]	Total			Urban - Urbaine			Rural - Rurale		
		Both sexes Les deux sexes	Male Masculin	Female Féminin	Both sexes Les deux sexes	Male Masculin	Female Féminin	Both sexes Les deux sexes	Male Masculin	Female Féminin
AMERICA, SOUTH — AMERIQUE DU SUD										
Peru - Pérou[13,14]										
1 VII 2003										
65 - 69	ESDF	525 381	253 070	272 311	386 020	185 194	200 826	139 361	67 876	71 485
70 - 74	ESDF	379 952	178 460	201 492	278 932	130 209	148 723	101 020	48 251	52 769
75 - 79	ESDF	243 082	110 296	132 786	181 409	81 844	99 565	61 673	28 452	33 221
80+	ESDF	208 127	87 069	121 058	165 495	68 998	96 497	42 632	18 071	24 561
Suriname[15]										
31 III 2003										
Total	CDJC	481 146	241 837	239 292	...	...	...	...	...	...
0 - 4	CDJC	50 677	25 722	24 955	...	...	...	...	...	...
5 - 9	CDJC	47 590	24 002	23 588	...	...	...	...	...	...
10 - 14	CDJC	44 498	21 643	22 855	...	...	...	...	...	...
15 - 19	CDJC	44 019	23 244	20 775	...	...	...	...	...	...
20 - 24	CDJC	40 229	20 221	20 008	...	...	...	...	...	...
25 - 29	CDJC	39 404	20 191	19 213	...	...	...	...	...	...
30 - 34	CDJC	39 743	19 400	20 343	...	...	...	...	...	...
35 - 39	CDJC	36 247	18 685	17 562	...	...	...	...	...	...
40 - 44	CDJC	31 293	16 902	14 391	...	...	...	...	...	...
45 - 49	CDJC	24 233	11 666	12 567	...	...	...	...	...	...
50 - 54	CDJC	19 790	9 454	10 336	...	...	...	...	...	...
55 - 59	CDJC	15 383	7 851	7 532	...	...	...	...	...	...
60 - 64	CDJC	11 721	5 625	6 096	...	...	...	...	...	...
65 - 69	CDJC	11 157	4 907	6 250	...	...	...	...	...	...
70 - 74	CDJC	8 007	3 874	4 133	...	...	...	...	...	...
75 - 79	CDJC	5 500	2 393	3 107	...	...	...	...	...	...
80+	CDJC	4 071	1 945	2 126	...	...	...	...	...	...
Unk. - Inc.	CDJC	2 616	1 455	1 161	...	...	...	...	...	...
Uruguay[14]										
30 VI 2003										
Total	ESDF	3 380 177	1 636 160	1 744 017	3 131 426	1 497 692	1 633 734	248 751	138 468	110 283
0 - 1	ESDF	52 982	26 951	26 031	49 355	25 106	24 249	3 627	1 845	1 782
1 - 4	ESDF	212 473	108 032	104 441	197 533	100 451	97 082	14 940	7 581	7 359
5 - 9	ESDF	281 573	143 549	138 024	260 891	133 118	127 773	20 682	10 431	10 251
10 - 14	ESDF	271 732	138 393	133 339	251 700	128 138	123 562	20 032	10 255	9 777
15 - 19	ESDF	269 566	136 966	132 600	250 458	126 857	123 601	19 108	10 109	8 999
20 - 24	ESDF	260 667	131 712	128 955	242 517	121 414	121 103	18 150	10 298	7 852
25 - 29	ESDF	241 737	120 962	120 775	225 295	111 497	113 798	16 442	9 465	6 977
30 - 34	ESDF	228 864	113 629	115 235	212 323	104 441	107 882	16 541	9 188	7 353
35 - 39	ESDF	224 305	110 277	114 028	207 499	100 847	106 652	16 806	9 430	7 376
40 - 44	ESDF	213 970	104 382	109 588	198 320	95 505	102 815	15 650	8 877	6 773
45 - 49	ESDF	195 512	94 966	100 546	180 639	86 432	94 207	14 873	8 534	6 339
50 - 54	ESDF	177 544	85 443	92 101	162 807	76 756	86 051	14 737	8 687	6 050
55 - 59	ESDF	158 221	75 149	83 072	144 840	67 048	77 792	13 381	8 101	5 280
60 - 64	ESDF	141 864	65 658	76 206	129 657	58 300	71 357	12 207	7 358	4 849
65 - 69	ESDF	131 274	58 504	72 770	120 310	51 836	68 474	10 964	6 668	4 296
70 - 74	ESDF	119 512	50 250	69 262	110 742	44 962	65 780	8 770	5 288	3 482
75 - 79	ESDF	92 239	36 295	55 944	86 334	32 924	53 410	5 905	3 371	2 534
80 - 84	ESDF	57 772	20 638	37 134	54 410	18 842	35 568	3 362	1 796	1 566
85 - 89	ESDF	30 797	9 650	21 147	29 157	8 856	20 301	1 640	794	846
90 - 94	ESDF	12 603	3 516	9 087	11 922	3 219	8 703	681	297	384
95+	ESDF	4 970	1 238	3 732	4 717	1 143	3 574	253	95	158
Venezuela[13]										
1 VII 2002										
Total	ESDF	25 219 910	12 678 275	12 541 635	22 163 339	11 021 146	11 142 193	3 056 571	1 657 129	1 399 442
0 - 1	ESDF	566 727	289 817	276 910	...	...	...	...	...	...
0 - 4	ESDF	...	...	...	2 365 585	1 212 601	1 152 984	431 255	216 828	214 427
1 - 4	ESDF	2 230 113	1 139 612	1 090 501	...	...	...	...	...	...
5 - 9	ESDF	2 731 128	1 394 224	1 336 904	2 338 027	1 195 058	1 142 969	393 101	199 166	193 935
10 - 14	ESDF	2 712 386	1 383 578	1 328 808	2 355 253	1 197 602	1 157 651	357 133	185 976	171 157
15 - 19	ESDF	2 568 391	1 306 597	1 261 794	2 258 881	1 135 863	1 123 018	309 510	170 734	138 776
20 - 24	ESDF	2 336 801	1 182 579	1 154 222	2 075 006	1 035 987	1 039 019	261 795	146 592	115 203

7. Population by age, sex and urban/rural residence: latest available year, 1994 - 2003
Population selon l'âge, le sexe et la résidence, urbaine/rurale: dernière année disponible, 1994 - 2003
(continued — suite)

Continent, country or area, date and age (in years) / Continent, pays ou zone, date et âge (en années)	Code[1]	Total			Urban - Urbaine			Rural - Rurale		
		Both sexes Les deux sexes	Male Masculin	Female Féminin	Both sexes Les deux sexes	Male Masculin	Female Féminin	Both sexes Les deux sexes	Male Masculin	Female Féminin
AMERICA, SOUTH — AMERIQUE DU SUD										
Venezuela[13]										
1 VII 2002										
25 - 29	ESDF	2 055 341	1 034 449	1 020 892	1 827 634	907 988	919 646	227 707	126 461	101 246
30 - 34	ESDF	1 871 230	938 046	933 184	1 675 269	828 977	846 292	195 961	109 069	86 892
35 - 39	ESDF	1 744 170	872 099	872 071	1 567 126	772 287	794 839	177 044	99 812	77 232
40 - 44	ESDF	1 506 179	751 648	754 531	1 358 018	667 128	690 890	148 161	84 520	63 641
45 - 49	ESDF	1 266 420	631 252	635 168	1 141 806	559 946	581 860	124 614	71 306	53 308
50 - 54	ESDF	1 044 891	520 661	524 230	935 412	457 944	477 468	109 479	62 717	46 762
55 - 59	ESDF	800 903	396 302	404 601	708 958	343 000	365 958	91 945	53 302	38 643
60 - 64	ESDF	590 879	287 629	303 250	516 207	244 396	271 811	74 672	43 233	31 439
65 - 69	ESDF	450 395	214 998	235 397	391 277	180 798	210 479	59 118	34 200	24 918
70 - 74	ESDF	344 553	160 308	184 245	299 965	135 041	164 924	44 588	25 267	19 321
75 - 79	ESDF	232 921	104 448	128 473	203 220	87 769	115 451	29 701	16 679	13 022
80+	ESDF	166 482	70 028	96 454	145 695	58 761	86 934	20 787	11 267	9 520
ASIA — ASIE										
Armenia - Arménie										
10 X 2001										
Total	CDJC	3 213 011	1 541 999	1 671 012	2 066 153	974 826	1 091 327	1 146 858	567 173	579 685
0 - 1	CDJC	34 779	18 677	16 102	20 607	10 936	9 671	14 172	7 741	6 431
1 - 4	CDJC	161 300	85 875	75 425	95 039	50 178	44 861	66 261	35 697	30 564
5 - 9	CDJC	258 524	133 667	124 857	150 469	77 722	72 747	108 055	55 945	52 110
10 - 14	CDJC	325 440	165 788	159 652	194 663	98 748	95 915	130 777	67 040	63 737
15 - 19	CDJC	313 614	157 024	156 590	200 109	98 759	101 350	113 505	58 265	55 240
20 - 24	CDJC	267 552	132 088	135 464	179 795	87 741	92 054	87 757	44 347	43 410
25 - 29	CDJC	222 596	107 554	115 042	149 304	71 583	77 721	73 292	35 971	37 321
30 - 34	CDJC	204 557	97 104	107 453	129 988	60 293	69 695	74 569	36 811	37 758
35 - 39	CDJC	244 294	114 999	129 295	151 527	68 033	83 494	92 767	46 966	45 801
40 - 44	CDJC	276 137	131 653	144 484	182 857	83 705	99 152	93 280	47 948	45 332
45 - 49	CDJC	211 525	98 992	112 533	150 655	68 574	82 081	60 870	30 418	30 452
50 - 54	CDJC	153 808	71 283	82 525	115 009	52 810	62 199	38 799	18 473	20 326
55 - 59	CDJC	80 101	35 787	44 314	58 698	26 134	32 564	21 403	9 653	11 750
60 - 64	CDJC	147 306	64 884	82 422	98 604	43 714	54 890	48 702	21 170	27 532
65 - 69	CDJC	118 666	52 763	65 903	72 931	32 227	40 704	45 735	20 536	25 199
70 - 74	CDJC	107 063	45 917	61 146	63 505	26 697	36 808	43 558	19 220	24 338
75 - 79	CDJC	55 113	19 332	35 781	34 029	11 694	22 335	21 084	7 638	13 446
80 - 84	CDJC	17 302	4 869	12 433	10 836	3 095	7 741	6 466	1 774	4 692
85+	CDJC	13 334	3 743	9 591	7 528	2 183	5 345	5 806	1 560	4 246
1 VII 2003										
Total	ESDJ	3 211 267	1 545 168	1 666 099	...	...	...	...	...	...
0 - 1	ESDJ	33 644	18 058	15 587	...	...	...	...	...	...
1 - 4	ESDJ	153 258	81 881	71 377	...	...	...	...	...	...
5 - 9	ESDJ	236 054	123 200	112 854	...	...	...	...	...	...
10 - 14	ESDJ	314 838	160 752	154 086	...	...	...	...	...	...
15 - 19	ESDJ	319 055	160 452	158 603	...	...	...	...	...	...
20 - 24	ESDJ	281 927	140 450	141 477	...	...	...	...	...	...
25 - 29	ESDJ	231 742	112 967	118 775	...	...	...	...	...	...
30 - 34	ESDJ	204 286	97 748	106 538	...	...	...	...	...	...
35 - 39	ESDJ	224 998	106 364	118 634	...	...	...	...	...	...
40 - 44	ESDJ	275 845	131 242	144 603	...	...	...	...	...	...
45 - 49	ESDJ	227 864	107 552	120 312	...	...	...	...	...	...
50 - 54	ESDJ	168 253	77 843	90 411	...	...	...	...	...	...
55 - 59	ESDJ	92 746	41 732	51 014	...	...	...	...	...	...
60 - 64	ESDJ	123 190	53 854	69 336	...	...	...	...	...	...
65 - 69	ESDJ	123 611	53 888	69 723	...	...	...	...	...	...
70 - 74	ESDJ	104 529	44 692	59 837	...	...	...	...	...	...
75 - 79	ESDJ	65 449	24 043	41 406	...	...	...	...	...	...
80 - 84	ESDJ	18 799	5 431	13 368	...	...	...	...	...	...
85+	ESDJ	11 185	3 022	8 163	...	...	...	...	...	...

7. Population by age, sex and urban/rural residence: latest available year, 1994 - 2003
Population selon l'âge, le sexe et la résidence, urbaine/rurale: dernière année disponible, 1994 - 2003
(continued — suite)

Continent, country or area, date and age (in years) / Continent, pays ou zone, date et âge (en années)	Code[1]	Total			Urban - Urbaine			Rural - Rurale		
		Both sexes Les deux sexes	Male Masculin	Female Féminin	Both sexes Les deux sexes	Male Masculin	Female Féminin	Both sexes Les deux sexes	Male Masculin	Female Féminin
ASIA — ASIE										
Azerbaijan - Azerbaïdjan										
1 VII 2003										
Total	ESDF	8 234 100	4 040 800	4 193 300	4 242 000	2 070 800	2 171 200	3 992 100	1 970 000	2 022 100
0 - 1	ESDF	112 100	60 500	51 600	50 900	27 600	23 300	61 200	32 900	28 300
1 - 4	ESDF	447 600	239 600	208 000	198 400	107 400	91 000	249 200	132 200	117 000
5 - 9	ESDF	734 600	382 800	351 800	335 500	176 300	159 200	399 100	206 500	192 600
10 - 14	ESDF	922 400	473 400	449 000	458 600	236 000	222 600	463 800	237 400	226 400
15 - 19	ESDF	886 000	452 700	433 300	459 500	235 200	224 300	426 500	217 500	209 000
20 - 24	ESDF	740 300	371 200	369 100	388 100	194 600	193 500	352 200	176 600	175 600
25 - 29	ESDF	633 300	305 000	328 300	321 200	151 400	169 800	312 100	153 600	158 500
30 - 34	ESDF	634 400	299 700	334 700	316 200	144 100	172 100	318 200	155 600	162 600
35 - 39	ESDF	676 500	319 000	357 500	349 700	160 800	188 900	326 800	158 200	168 600
40 - 44	ESDF	684 400	328 900	355 500	380 800	182 300	198 500	303 600	146 600	157 000
45 - 49	ESDF	495 900	240 500	255 400	290 500	141 100	149 400	205 400	99 400	106 000
50 - 54	ESDF	325 500	156 900	168 600	199 500	97 100	102 400	126 000	59 800	66 200
55 - 59	ESDF	174 200	82 300	91 900	108 200	51 600	56 600	66 000	30 700	35 300
60 - 64	ESDF	216 200	98 000	118 200	118 100	54 200	63 900	98 100	43 800	54 300
65 - 69	ESDF	241 500	107 300	134 200	118 200	52 500	65 700	123 300	54 800	68 500
70 - 74	ESDF	163 900	72 200	91 700	77 900	33 400	44 500	86 000	38 800	47 200
75 - 79	ESDF	84 400	33 400	51 000	43 100	16 600	26 500	41 300	16 800	24 500
80 - 84	ESDF	34 500	10 900	23 600	16 900	5 500	11 400	17 600	5 400	12 200
85 - 89	ESDF	14 100	3 700	10 400	6 300	1 800	4 500	7 800	1 900	5 900
90 - 94	ESDF	7 700	1 800	5 900	2 800	800	2 000	4 900	1 000	3 900
95 - 99	ESDF	2 800	600	2 200	1 000	300	700	1 800	300	1 500
100+	ESDF	1 800	400	1 400	600	200	400	1 200	200	1 000
Bahrain - Bahreïn[7]										
1 VII 2003										
Total	ESDF	689 418	396 278	293 140	...	...	...	...	...	...
0 - 1	ESDF	11 469	6 013	5 456	...	...	...	...	...	...
1 - 4	ESDF	50 107	25 555	24 552	...	...	...	...	...	...
5 - 9	ESDF	66 031	33 433	32 598	...	...	...	...	...	...
10 - 14	ESDF	62 501	32 203	30 297	...	...	...	...	...	...
15 - 19	ESDF	54 164	27 968	26 194	...	...	...	...	...	...
20 - 24	ESDF	62 398	34 211	28 187	...	...	...	...	...	...
25 - 29	ESDF	73 869	45 625	28 245	...	...	...	...	...	...
30 - 34	ESDF	76 990	47 699	29 293	...	...	...	...	...	...
35 - 39	ESDF	69 649	42 528	27 120	...	...	...	...	...	...
40 - 44	ESDF	58 835	37 754	21 081	...	...	...	...	...	...
45 - 49	ESDF	40 213	26 640	13 572	...	...	...	...	...	...
50 - 54	ESDF	22 696	15 004	7 691	...	...	...	...	...	...
55 - 59	ESDF	13 030	7 593	5 438	...	...	...	...	...	...
60 - 64	ESDF	10 093	5 247	4 847	...	...	...	...	...	...
65 - 69	ESDF	6 797	3 349	3 448	...	...	...	...	...	...
70 - 74	ESDF	5 181	2 650	2 531	...	...	...	...	...	...
75+	ESDF	5 397	2 803	2 594	...	...	...	...	...	...
Bhutan - Bhoutan										
31 XII 2001										
Total	ESDF	698 949	352 935	346 014	...	...	...	...	...	...
0 - 4	ESDF	107 990	54 115	53 875	...	...	...	...	...	...
5 - 9	ESDF	101 236	50 268	50 968	...	...	...	...	...	...
10 - 14	ESDF	84 687	42 889	41 798	...	...	...	...	...	...
15 - 19	ESDF	62 845	31 877	30 968	...	...	...	...	...	...
20 - 24	ESDF	55 493	27 570	27 923	...	...	...	...	...	...
25 - 29	ESDF	47 633	23 827	23 806	...	...	...	...	...	...
30 - 34	ESDF	42 745	21 569	21 176	...	...	...	...	...	...
35 - 39	ESDF	39 156	20 229	18 927	...	...	...	...	...	...
40 - 44	ESDF	33 001	17 015	15 986	...	...	...	...	...	...
45 - 49	ESDF	26 534	13 766	12 768	...	...	...	...	...	...
50 - 54	ESDF	25 170	12 955	12 215	...	...	...	...	...	...
55 - 59	ESDF	22 270	11 509	10 761	...	...	...	...	...	...
60 - 64	ESDF	20 451	10 555	9 896	...	...	...	...	...	...

7. Population by age, sex and urban/rural residence: latest available year, 1994 - 2003
Population selon l'âge, le sexe et la résidence, urbaine/rurale: dernière année disponible, 1994 - 2003
(continued — suite)

Continent, country or area, date and age (in years) / Continent, pays ou zone, date et âge (en annèes)	Code[1]	Total			Urban - Urbaine			Rural - Rurale		
		Both sexes Les deux sexes	Male Masculin	Female Féminin	Both sexes Les deux sexes	Male Masculin	Female Féminin	Both sexes Les deux sexes	Male Masculin	Female Féminin
ASIA — ASIE										
Bhutan - Bhoutan										
31 XII 2001										
65 - 69	ESDF	12 335	6 072	6 263	...	...	...	...	...	...
70 - 74	ESDF	8 388	4 201	4 187	...	...	...	...	...	...
75+	ESDF	9 015	4 518	4 497	...	...	...	...	...	...
Brunei Darussalam - Brunéi Darussalam										
21 VIII 2001										
Total	CDFC	332 844	168 974	163 870	238 699	120 046	118 653	94 145	48 928	45 217
0 - 14	CDFC	100 912	52 304	48 608	72 076	37 396	34 680	28 836	14 908	13 928
15 - 19	CDFC	27 963	14 014	13 949	20 019	10 085	9 934	7 944	3 929	4 015
20 - 24	CDFC	32 604	15 390	17 214	23 592	10 885	12 707	9 012	4 505	4 507
25 - 29	CDFC	35 773	17 884	17 889	25 856	12 573	13 283	9 917	5 311	4 606
30 - 34	CDFC	34 375	16 878	17 497	24 973	11 931	13 042	9 402	4 947	4 455
35 - 39	CDFC	28 764	14 581	14 183	21 112	10 461	10 651	7 652	4 120	3 532
40 - 44	CDFC	24 198	12 984	11 214	17 808	9 544	8 264	6 390	3 440	2 950
45 - 49	CDFC	17 149	9 150	7 999	12 402	6 637	5 765	4 747	2 513	2 234
50 - 54	CDFC	10 687	5 542	5 145	7 609	4 013	3 596	3 078	1 529	1 549
55 - 59	CDFC	6 140	3 249	2 891	4 153	2 197	1 956	1 987	1 052	935
60 - 64	CDFC	4 962	2 432	2 530	3 217	1 544	1 673	1 745	888	857
65 - 69	CDFC	3 757	1 768	1 989	2 366	1 102	1 264	1 391	666	725
70 - 74	CDFC	2 441	1 263	1 178	1 530	758	772	911	505	406
75 - 79	CDFC	1 582	793	789	1 027	492	535	555	301	254
80 - 84	CDFC	844	423	421	548	264	284	296	159	137
85 - 89	CDFC	397	188	209	252	98	154	145	90	55
90 - 94	CDFC	197	86	111	111	47	64	86	39	47
95 - 99	CDFC	66	33	33	33	14	19	33	19	14
100+	CDFC	33	12	21	15	5	10	18	7	11
Cambodia - Cambodge										
3 III 1998										
Total	CDFC	11 437 656	5 511 408	5 926 248	1 795 575	878 186	917 389	9 642 081	4 633 222	5 008 859
0 - 1	CDFC	231 609	118 075	113 534	32 869	16 851	16 018	198 740	101 224	97 516
1 - 4	CDFC	1 235 183	629 217	605 966	160 680	82 377	78 303	1 074 503	546 840	527 663
5 - 9	CDFC	1 772 820	903 976	868 844	239 934	122 652	117 282	1 532 886	781 324	751 562
10 - 14	CDFC	1 658 196	851 139	807 057	246 998	126 217	120 781	1 411 198	724 922	686 276
15 - 19	CDFC	1 344 258	664 184	680 074	233 677	113 229	120 448	1 110 581	550 955	559 626
20 - 24	CDFC	745 687	354 100	391 587	128 884	63 561	65 323	616 803	290 539	326 264
25 - 29	CDFC	888 540	426 968	461 572	157 736	79 241	78 495	730 804	347 727	383 077
30 - 34	CDFC	782 682	370 090	412 592	137 139	69 093	68 046	645 543	300 997	344 546
35 - 39	CDFC	695 868	325 331	370 537	123 310	61 255	62 055	572 558	264 076	308 482
40 - 44	CDFC	497 067	199 722	297 345	92 433	40 499	51 934	404 634	159 223	245 411
45 - 49	CDFC	415 931	175 052	240 879	72 681	32 868	39 813	343 250	142 184	201 066
50 - 54	CDFC	312 463	132 413	180 050	50 505	22 227	28 278	261 958	110 186	151 772
55 - 59	CDFC	256 930	110 189	146 741	37 186	16 284	20 902	219 744	93 905	125 839
60 - 64	CDFC	204 994	86 602	118 392	28 433	11 627	16 806	176 561	74 975	101 586
65 - 69	CDFC	166 928	70 660	96 268	21 891	8 614	13 277	145 037	62 046	82 991
70 - 74	CDFC	112 213	46 769	65 444	14 851	5 535	9 316	97 362	41 234	56 128
75 - 79	CDFC	67 528	27 838	39 690	9 135	3 337	5 798	58 393	24 501	33 892
80 - 84	CDFC	30 652	12 159	18 493	4 288	1 515	2 773	26 364	10 644	15 720
85 - 89	CDFC	13 368	5 029	8 339	1 874	592	1 282	11 494	4 437	7 057
90 - 94	CDFC	2 867	1 026	1 841	453	157	296	2 414	869	1 545
95+	CDFC	1 872	869	1 003	618	455	163	1 254	414	840
1 I 2003										
Total	ESDF	13 287 053	6 437 037	6 850 016	...	...	...	...	...	...
0 - 1	ESDF	349 751	178 370	171 381	...	...	...	...	...	...
1 - 4	ESDF	1 265 354	642 000	623 354	...	...	...	...	...	...
5 - 9	ESDF	1 869 041	951 333	917 708	...	...	...	...	...	...
10 - 14	ESDF	1 786 935	910 269	876 666	...	...	...	...	...	...
15 - 19	ESDF	1 670 707	854 965	815 742	...	...	...	...	...	...
20 - 24	ESDF	1 348 435	662 881	685 554	...	...	...	...	...	...
25 - 29	ESDF	745 213	351 746	393 467	...	...	...	...	...	...

7. Population by age, sex and urban/rural residence: latest available year, 1994 - 2003
Population selon l'âge, le sexe et la résidence, urbaine/rurale: dernière année disponible, 1994 - 2003
(continued — suite)

Continent, country or area, date and age (in years) / Continent, pays ou zone, date et âge (en années)	Code[1]	Total			Urban - Urbaine			Rural - Rurale		
		Both sexes Les deux sexes	Male Masculin	Female Féminin	Both sexes Les deux sexes	Male Masculin	Female Féminin	Both sexes Les deux sexes	Male Masculin	Female Féminin
ASIA — ASIE										
Cambodia - Cambodge										
1 I 2003										
30 - 34	ESDF	885 741	423 345	462 396	...	...	...	...	...	...
35 - 39	ESDF	777 717	365 742	411 975	...	...	...	...	...	...
40 - 44	ESDF	687 863	319 537	368 326	...	...	...	...	...	...
45 - 49	ESDF	488 421	194 369	294 052	...	...	...	...	...	...
50 - 54	ESDF	404 060	167 880	236 180	...	...	...	...	...	...
55 - 59	ESDF	298 279	124 359	173 920	...	...	...	...	...	...
60 - 64	ESDF	238 179	100 074	138 105	...	...	...	...	...	...
65 - 69	ESDF	180 654	74 343	106 311	...	...	...	...	...	...
70 - 74	ESDF	135 265	55 324	79 941	...	...	...	...	...	...
75+	ESDF	155 438	60 500	94 938	...	...	...	...	...	...
China - Chine[16]										
1 XI 2000										
Total	CDJC	1242612226	640 275 969	602 336 257	458 770 983	235 264 707	223 506 276	783 841 243	405 011 262	378 829 981
0 - 1	CDJC	13 793 799	7 460 206	6 333 593	4 449 020	2 376 585	2 072 435	9 344 779	5 083 621	4 261 158
1 - 4	CDJC	55 184 575	30 188 488	24 996 087	17 669 697	9 525 854	8 143 843	37 514 878	20 662 634	16 852 244
5 - 9	CDJC	90 152 587	48 303 208	41 849 379	26 588 363	14 180 433	12 407 930	63 564 224	34 122 775	29 441 449
10 - 14	CDJC	125 396 633	65 344 739	60 051 894	35 802 884	18 701 307	17 101 577	89 593 749	46 643 432	42 950 317
15 - 19	CDJC	103 031 165	52 878 170	50 152 995	42 231 585	21 086 911	21 144 674	60 799 580	31 791 259	29 008 321
20 - 24	CDJC	94 573 174	47 937 766	46 635 408	41 021 887	20 651 361	20 370 526	53 551 287	27 286 405	26 264 882
25 - 29	CDJC	117 602 265	60 230 758	57 371 507	48 788 516	24 820 721	23 967 795	68 813 749	35 410 037	33 403 712
30 - 34	CDJC	127 314 298	65 360 456	61 953 842	49 723 640	25 760 568	23 963 072	77 590 658	39 599 888	37 990 770
35 - 39	CDJC	109 147 295	56 141 391	53 005 904	44 518 164	23 269 889	21 248 275	64 629 131	32 871 502	31 757 629
40 - 44	CDJC	81 242 945	42 243 187	38 999 758	33 518 610	17 499 183	16 019 427	47 724 335	24 744 004	22 980 331
45 - 49	CDJC	85 521 045	43 939 603	41 581 442	31 708 706	16 245 324	15 463 382	53 812 339	27 694 279	26 118 060
50 - 54	CDJC	63 304 200	32 804 125	30 500 075	22 335 748	11 462 314	10 873 434	40 968 452	21 341 811	19 626 641
55 - 59	CDJC	46 370 375	24 061 506	22 308 869	16 004 389	8 077 159	7 927 230	30 365 986	15 984 347	14 381 639
60 - 64	CDJC	41 703 848	21 674 478	20 029 370	14 944 552	7 519 377	7 425 175	26 759 296	14 155 101	12 604 195
65 - 69	CDJC	34 780 460	17 549 348	17 231 112	12 174 470	6 128 605	6 045 865	22 605 990	11 420 743	11 185 247
70 - 74	CDJC	25 574 149	12 436 154	13 137 995	8 479 487	4 216 193	4 263 294	17 094 662	8 219 961	8 874 701
75 - 79	CDJC	15 928 330	7 175 811	8 752 519	5 000 134	2 291 543	2 708 591	10 928 196	4 884 268	6 043 928
80 - 84	CDJC	7 989 158	3 203 868	4 785 290	2 472 016	1 004 359	1 467 657	5 517 142	2 199 509	3 317 633
85 - 89	CDJC	3 030 698	1 056 941	1 973 757	994 079	347 550	646 529	2 036 619	709 391	1 327 228
90 - 94	CDJC	783 594	229 758	553 836	276 586	80 189	196 397	507 008	149 569	357 439
95 - 99	CDJC	169 756	51 373	118 383	62 255	17 827	44 428	107 501	33 546	73 955
100+	CDJC	17 877	4 635	13 242	6 195	1 455	4 740	11 682	3 180	8 502
China: Hong Kong SAR - Chine: Hong Kong RAS										
1 VII 2003										
Total	ESDJ	6 803 100	3 294 000	3 509 100	...	...	...	...	...	...
0 - 1	ESDJ	48 900	25 300	23 600	...	...	...	...	...	...
1 - 4	ESDJ	214 000	110 400	103 600	...	...	...	...	...	...
5 - 9	ESDJ	372 600	192 600	180 000	...	...	...	...	...	...
10 - 14	ESDJ	433 700	223 000	210 700	...	...	...	...	...	...
15 - 19	ESDJ	435 400	223 500	211 900	...	...	...	...	...	...
20 - 24	ESDJ	443 500	222 300	221 200	...	...	...	...	...	...
25 - 29	ESDJ	490 700	229 400	261 300	...	...	...	...	...	...
30 - 34	ESDJ	586 200	250 700	335 500	...	...	...	...	...	...
35 - 39	ESDJ	648 200	285 500	362 700	...	...	...	...	...	...
40 - 44	ESDJ	704 700	336 000	368 700	...	...	...	...	...	...
45 - 49	ESDJ	603 800	297 600	306 200	...	...	...	...	...	...
50 - 54	ESDJ	477 700	240 900	236 800	...	...	...	...	...	...
55 - 59	ESDJ	316 200	164 100	152 100	...	...	...	...	...	...
60 - 64	ESDJ	232 000	124 300	107 700	...	...	...	...	...	...
65 - 69	ESDJ	249 200	127 400	121 800	...	...	...	...	...	...
70 - 74	ESDJ	221 500	109 100	112 400	...	...	...	...	...	...
75 - 79	ESDJ	157 500	70 900	86 600	...	...	...	...	...	...
80 - 84	ESDJ	96 200	38 600	57 600	...	...	...	...	...	...
85+	ESDJ	71 100	22 400	48 700	...	...	...	...	...	...

7. Population by age, sex and urban/rural residence: latest available year, 1994 - 2003
Population selon l'âge, le sexe et la résidence, urbaine/rurale: dernière année disponible, 1994 - 2003
(continued — suite)

Continent, country or area, date and age (in years) / Continent, pays ou zone, date et âge (en années)	Code[1]	Total			Urban - Urbaine			Rural - Rurale		
		Both sexes Les deux sexes	Male Masculin	Female Féminin	Both sexes Les deux sexes	Male Masculin	Female Féminin	Both sexes Les deux sexes	Male Masculin	Female Féminin
ASIA — ASIE										
China: Macao SAR - Chine: Macao RAS										
1 VII 2003										
Total	ESDJ	445 066	213 696	231 370	...	...	...	...	...	...
0 - 4	ESDJ	17 981	9 290	8 691	...	...	...	...	...	...
5 - 9	ESDJ	29 019	15 191	13 828	...	...	...	...	...	...
10 - 14	ESDJ	38 981	20 111	18 870	...	...	...	...	...	...
15 - 19	ESDJ	40 536	20 633	19 903	...	...	...	...	...	...
20 - 24	ESDJ	30 349	13 641	16 708	...	...	...	...	...	...
25 - 29	ESDJ	29 829	13 111	16 718	...	...	...	...	...	...
30 - 34	ESDJ	35 457	14 658	20 799	...	...	...	...	...	...
35 - 39	ESDJ	39 827	16 766	23 061	...	...	...	...	...	...
40 - 44	ESDJ	47 708	22 808	24 900	...	...	...	...	...	...
45 - 49	ESDJ	43 316	22 249	21 067	...	...	...	...	...	...
50 - 54	ESDJ	28 960	15 249	13 711	...	...	...	...	...	...
55 - 59	ESDJ	17 979	9 762	8 217	...	...	...	...	...	...
60 - 64	ESDJ	10 389	5 428	4 961	...	...	...	...	...	...
65 - 69	ESDJ	10 034	4 807	5 227	...	...	...	...	...	...
70 - 74	ESDJ	9 458	4 139	5 319	...	...	...	...	...	...
75+	ESDJ	15 243	5 853	9 390	...	...	...	...	...	...
Cyprus - Chypre[17]										
1 VII 2003										
Total	ESDJ	*722 752*	*354 936*	*367 817*	...	...	...	...	...	...
0 - 1	ESDJ	*7 959*	*4 129*	*3 830*	...	...	...	...	...	...
1 - 4	ESDJ	*33 967*	*17 364*	*16 604*	...	...	...	...	...	...
5 - 9	ESDJ	*50 623*	*25 956*	*24 668*	...	...	...	...	...	...
10 - 14	ESDJ	*55 074*	*28 393*	*26 682*	...	...	...	...	...	...
15 - 19	ESDJ	*56 293*	*28 825*	*27 468*	...	...	...	...	...	...
20 - 24	ESDJ	*56 981*	*29 192*	*27 789*	...	...	...	...	...	...
25 - 29	ESDJ	*51 863*	*25 546*	*26 318*	...	...	...	...	...	...
30 - 34	ESDJ	*51 600*	*24 597*	*27 003*	...	...	...	...	...	...
35 - 39	ESDJ	*52 555*	*25 047*	*27 508*	...	...	...	...	...	...
40 - 44	ESDJ	*54 841*	*26 704*	*28 138*	...	...	...	...	...	...
45 - 49	ESDJ	*49 156*	*24 047*	*25 109*	...	...	...	...	...	...
50 - 54	ESDJ	*45 249*	*22 297*	*22 952*	...	...	...	...	...	...
55 - 59	ESDJ	*37 970*	*18 532*	*19 438*	...	...	...	...	...	...
60 - 64	ESDJ	*32 904*	*15 986*	*16 918*	...	...	...	...	...	...
65 - 69	ESDJ	*27 571*	*13 017*	*14 555*	...	...	...	...	...	...
70 - 74	ESDJ	*22 214*	*9 980*	*12 235*	...	...	...	...	...	...
75 - 79	ESDJ	*16 952*	*7 424*	*9 529*	...	...	...	...	...	...
80+	ESDJ	*18 984*	*7 906*	*11 078*	...	...	...	...	...	...
Georgia - Géorgie										
1 VII 2000										
Total	ESDF	4 945 553	2 364 247	2 581 306	2 860 786	1 348 715	1 512 071	2 084 767	1 015 532	1 069 235
0 - 1	ESDF	42 247	22 938	19 309	26 206	14 152	12 054	16 041	8 786	7 255
1 - 4	ESDF	197 055	104 267	92 788	119 229	63 120	56 109	77 826	41 147	36 679
5 - 9	ESDF	361 619	185 741	175 878	208 452	107 038	101 414	153 167	78 703	74 464
10 - 14	ESDF	409 671	209 366	200 305	229 154	116 874	112 280	180 517	92 492	88 025
15 - 19	ESDF	388 789	198 066	190 723	222 064	113 224	108 840	166 725	84 842	81 883
20 - 24	ESDF	376 407	191 927	184 480	213 454	108 613	104 841	162 953	83 314	79 639
25 - 29	ESDF	350 129	181 759	168 370	213 415	110 488	102 927	136 714	71 271	65 443
30 - 34	ESDF	363 659	175 712	187 947	214 156	100 573	113 583	149 503	75 139	74 364
35 - 39	ESDF	403 179	191 543	211 636	241 215	109 394	131 821	161 964	82 149	79 815
40 - 44	ESDF	353 366	168 218	185 148	216 428	98 958	117 470	136 938	69 260	67 678
45 - 49	ESDF	305 841	143 921	161 920	193 528	88 504	105 024	112 313	55 417	56 896
50 - 54	ESDF	216 111	100 444	115 667	137 119	62 640	74 479	78 992	37 804	41 188
55 - 59	ESDF	225 223	99 437	125 786	130 629	56 530	74 099	94 594	42 907	51 687
60 - 64	ESDF	280 405	126 438	153 967	155 346	68 463	86 883	125 059	57 975	67 084
65 - 69	ESDF	242 085	102 877	139 208	123 373	51 091	72 282	118 712	51 786	66 926
70 - 74	ESDF	218 503	85 840	132 663	111 805	41 553	70 252	106 698	44 287	62 411
75 - 79	ESDF	113 417	34 835	78 582	56 587	16 900	39 687	56 830	17 935	38 895
80 - 84	ESDF	59 039	24 600	34 439	29 156	12 606	16 550	29 883	11 994	17 889

7. Population by age, sex and urban/rural residence: latest available year, 1994 - 2003
Population selon l'âge, le sexe et la résidence, urbaine/rurale: dernière année disponible, 1994 - 2003
(continued — suite)

Continent, country or area, date and age (in years) Continent, pays ou zone, date et âge (en années)	Code[1]	Total			Urban - Urbaine			Rural - Rurale		
		Both sexes Les deux sexes	Male Masculin	Female Féminin	Both sexes Les deux sexes	Male Masculin	Female Féminin	Both sexes Les deux sexes	Male Masculin	Female Féminin
ASIA — ASIE										
Georgia - Géorgie										
1 VII 2000										
85 - 89	ESDF	27 302	11 583	15 719	13 332	5 601	7 731	13 970	5 982	7 988
90 - 94	ESDF	8 410	3 605	4 805	4 432	1 819	2 613	3 978	1 786	2 192
95 - 99	ESDF	2 730	1 020	1 710	1 510	527	983	1 220	493	727
100+	ESDF	366	110	256	196	47	149	170	63	107
1 VII 2003										
Total	ESDF	4 328 900	2 045 500	2 283 400	...	...	...	...	...	...
0 - 1	ESDF	45 100	23 900	21 200	...	...	...	...	...	...
1 - 4	ESDF	194 400	100 200	94 200	...	...	...	...	...	...
5 - 9	ESDF	272 100	139 700	132 400	...	...	...	...	...	...
10 - 14	ESDF	333 900	170 400	163 500	...	...	...	...	...	...
15 - 19	ESDF	354 300	179 100	175 200	...	...	...	...	...	...
20 - 24	ESDF	349 300	173 800	175 500	...	...	...	...	...	...
25 - 29	ESDF	325 400	160 100	165 300	...	...	...	...	...	...
30 - 34	ESDF	296 000	142 500	153 500	...	...	...	...	...	...
35 - 39	ESDF	306 000	145 400	160 600	...	...	...	...	...	...
40 - 44	ESDF	327 200	154 500	172 700	...	...	...	...	...	...
45 - 49	ESDF	308 400	144 600	163 800	...	...	...	...	...	...
50 - 54	ESDF	267 400	123 100	144 300	...	...	...	...	...	...
55 - 59	ESDF	162 200	73 100	89 100	...	...	...	...	...	...
60 - 64	ESDF	217 400	94 600	122 800	...	...	...	...	...	...
65 - 69	ESDF	202 300	86 500	115 800	...	...	...	...	...	...
70 - 74	ESDF	175 500	71 800	103 700	...	...	...	...	...	...
75 - 79	ESDF	115 700	41 600	74 100	...	...	...	...	...	...
80 - 84	ESDF	50 500	14 700	35 800	...	...	...	...	...	...
85+	ESDF	25 800	5 900	19 900	...	...	...	...	...	...
India - Inde[18,19]										
1 III 2001										
Total	CDFC	1028610328	532 156 772	496 453 556	286 119 689	150 554 098	135 565 591	742 490 639	381 602 674	360 887 965
0 - 4	CDFC	110 447 164	57 119 612	53 327 552	25 338 754	13 262 414	12 076 340	85 108 410	43 857 198	41 251 212
5 - 9	CDFC	128 316 790	66 734 833	61 581 957	29 860 545	15 640 135	14 220 410	98 456 245	51 094 698	47 361 547
10 - 14	CDFC	124 846 858	65 632 877	59 213 981	32 464 536	17 030 132	15 434 404	92 382 322	48 602 745	43 779 577
15 - 19	CDFC	100 215 890	53 939 991	46 275 899	30 154 067	16 191 573	13 962 494	70 061 823	37 748 418	32 313 405
20 - 24	CDFC	89 764 132	46 321 150	43 442 982	28 365 228	15 193 668	13 171 560	61 398 904	31 127 482	30 271 422
25 - 29	CDFC	83 422 393	41 557 546	41 864 847	25 737 253	13 180 373	12 556 880	57 685 140	28 377 173	29 307 967
30 - 34	CDFC	74 274 044	37 361 916	36 912 128	22 445 165	11 673 137	10 772 028	51 828 879	25 688 779	26 140 100
35 - 39	CDFC	70 574 085	36 038 727	34 535 358	21 615 541	11 157 103	10 458 438	48 958 544	24 881 624	24 076 920
40 - 44	CDFC	55 738 297	29 878 715	25 859 582	17 173 126	9 458 276	7 714 850	38 565 171	20 420 439	18 144 732
45 - 49	CDFC	47 408 976	24 867 886	22 541 090	14 453 974	7 844 213	6 609 761	32 955 002	17 023 673	15 931 329
50 - 54	CDFC	36 587 559	19 851 608	16 735 951	10 809 961	6 038 917	4 771 044	25 777 598	13 812 691	11 964 907
55 - 59	CDFC	27 653 347	13 583 022	14 070 325	7 682 278	4 010 268	3 672 010	19 971 069	9 572 754	10 398 315
60 - 64	CDFC	27 516 779	13 586 347	13 930 432	6 864 810	3 439 621	3 425 189	20 651 969	10 146 726	10 505 243
65 - 69	CDFC	19 806 955	9 472 103	10 334 852	4 990 199	2 401 397	2 588 802	14 816 756	7 070 706	7 746 050
70 - 74	CDFC	14 708 644	7 527 688	7 180 956	3 579 168	1 780 696	1 798 472	11 129 476	5 746 992	5 382 484
75 - 79	CDFC	6 551 225	3 263 209	3 288 016	1 721 085	851 088	869 997	4 830 140	2 412 121	2 418 019
80+	CDFC	8 038 718	3 918 980	4 119 738	2 022 345	935 920	1 086 425	6 016 373	2 983 060	3 033 313
Unk. - Inc.	CDFC	2 738 472	1 500 562	1 237 910	841 654	465 167	376 487	1 896 818	1 035 395	861 423
1 VII 2001										
Total	ESDF	1017544000	526 356 000	491 187 000	...	...	...	...	...	...
0 - 4	ESDF	109 047 000	55 987 000	53 060 000	...	...	...	...	...	...
5 - 9	ESDF	116 737 000	59 531 000	57 206 000	...	...	...	...	...	...
10 - 14	ESDF	123 531 000	63 879 000	59 653 000	...	...	...	...	...	...
15 - 19	ESDF	109 619 000	57 958 000	51 661 000	...	...	...	...	...	...
20 - 24	ESDF	90 680 000	47 966 000	42 714 000	...	...	...	...	...	...
25 - 29	ESDF	81 887 000	41 598 000	40 289 000	...	...	...	...	...	...
30 - 34	ESDF	75 555 000	37 661 000	37 894 000	...	...	...	...	...	...
35 - 39	ESDF	65 743 000	33 527 000	32 215 000	...	...	...	...	...	...
40 - 44	ESDF	56 436 000	29 644 000	26 792 000	...	...	...	...	...	...
45 - 49	ESDF	46 993 000	24 945 000	22 047 000	...	...	...	...	...	...
50 - 54	ESDF	39 099 000	20 715 000	18 384 000	...	...	...	...	...	...
55 - 59	ESDF	31 287 000	16 558 000	14 729 000	...	...	...	...	...	...

7. Population by age, sex and urban/rural residence: latest available year, 1994 - 2003
Population selon l'âge, le sexe et la résidence, urbaine/rurale: dernière année disponible, 1994 - 2003
(continued — suite)

Continent, country or area, date and age (in years) / Continent, pays ou zone, date et âge (en annèes)	Code[1]	Total			Urban - Urbaine			Rural - Rurale		
		Both sexes Les deux sexes	Male Masculin	Female Féminin	Both sexes Les deux sexes	Male Masculin	Female Féminin	Both sexes Les deux sexes	Male Masculin	Female Féminin
ASIA — ASIE										
India - Inde[18,19]										
1 VII 2001										
60 - 64	ESDF	24 184 000	12 513 000	11 671 000	...	...	...	...	...	...
65 - 69	ESDF	19 438 000	9 871 000	9 567 000	...	...	...	...	...	...
70 - 74	ESDF	13 120 000	6 647 000	6 473 000	...	...	...	...	...	...
75 - 79	ESDF	8 352 000	4 317 000	4 035 000	...	...	...	...	...	...
80+	ESDF	5 837 000	3 040 000	2 798 000	...	...	...	...	...	...
Indonesia - Indonésie[20]										
30 VI 2000										
Total	CDFC	201 241 999	100 934 962	100 307 037	85 380 627	42 759 571	42 621 056	115 861 372	58 175 391	57 685 981
0 - 1	CDFC	3 492 259	1 799 525	1 692 734	1 529 180	790 207	738 973	1 963 079	1 009 318	953 761
1 - 4	CDFC	16 810 117	8 496 176	8 313 941	6 642 545	3 361 599	3 280 946	10 167 572	5 134 577	5 032 995
5 - 9	CDFC	20 494 091	10 433 865	10 060 226	7 962 806	4 034 352	3 928 454	12 531 285	6 399 513	6 131 772
10 - 14	CDFC	20 453 732	10 460 908	9 992 824	7 951 997	4 017 276	3 934 721	12 501 735	6 443 632	6 058 103
15 - 19	CDFC	21 149 517	10 649 348	10 500 169	9 501 797	4 656 022	4 845 775	11 647 720	5 993 326	5 654 394
20 - 24	CDFC	19 258 101	9 237 464	10 020 637	9 394 813	4 528 914	4 865 899	9 863 288	4 708 550	5 154 738
25 - 29	CDFC	18 640 937	9 130 504	9 510 433	8 720 487	4 321 110	4 399 377	9 920 450	4 809 394	5 111 056
30 - 34	CDFC	16 399 720	8 204 302	8 195 418	7 499 021	3 795 282	3 703 739	8 900 699	4 409 020	4 491 679
35 - 39	CDFC	14 904 226	7 432 840	7 471 386	6 430 999	3 230 371	3 200 628	8 473 227	4 202 469	4 270 758
40 - 44	CDFC	12 467 848	6 433 438	6 034 410	5 322 075	2 767 298	2 554 777	7 145 773	3 666 140	3 479 633
45 - 49	CDFC	9 656 005	5 087 252	4 568 753	4 015 532	2 137 790	1 877 742	5 640 473	2 949 462	2 691 011
50 - 54	CDFC	7 384 968	3 791 185	3 593 783	2 905 386	1 500 733	1 404 653	4 479 582	2 290 452	2 189 130
55 - 59	CDFC	5 678 664	2 883 226	2 795 438	2 235 074	1 145 432	1 089 642	3 443 590	1 737 794	1 705 796
60 - 64	CDFC	5 321 019	2 597 076	2 723 943	1 951 238	949 193	1 002 045	3 369 781	1 647 883	1 721 898
65 - 69	CDFC	3 564 926	1 666 191	1 898 735	1 310 805	600 348	710 457	2 254 121	1 065 843	1 188 278
70 - 74	CDFC	2 837 037	1 368 190	1 468 847	1 016 304	479 243	537 061	1 820 733	888 947	931 786
75+	CDFC	2 716 985	1 257 526	1 459 459	986 136	442 204	543 932	1 730 849	815 322	915 527
Unk. - Inc.	CDFC	11 847	5 946	5 901	4 432	2 197	2 235	7 415	3 749	3 666
1 VII 2003										
Total	ESDJ	214 251 300	107 335 600	106 915 700	...	...	...	...	...	...
0 - 1	ESDJ	4 095 640	2 086 219	2 009 421	...	...	...	...	...	...
1 - 4	ESDJ	16 178 560	8 235 381	7 943 179	...	...	...	...	...	...
5 - 9	ESDJ	20 752 800	10 551 900	10 200 900	...	...	...	...	...	...
10 - 14	ESDJ	21 637 800	11 006 300	10 631 500	...	...	...	...	...	...
15 - 19	ESDJ	21 206 000	10 727 000	10 479 000	...	...	...	...	...	...
20 - 24	ESDJ	20 729 800	10 253 900	10 475 900	...	...	...	...	...	...
25 - 29	ESDJ	19 575 400	9 504 700	10 070 700	...	...	...	...	...	...
30 - 34	ESDJ	18 047 200	8 863 100	9 184 100	...	...	...	...	...	...
35 - 39	ESDJ	16 098 400	8 053 700	8 044 700	...	...	...	...	...	...
40 - 44	ESDJ	13 974 000	7 067 000	6 907 000	...	...	...	...	...	...
45 - 49	ESDJ	11 369 600	5 886 800	5 482 800	...	...	...	...	...	...
50 - 54	ESDJ	8 637 400	4 505 700	4 131 700	...	...	...	...	...	...
55 - 59	ESDJ	6 552 000	3 335 000	3 217 000	...	...	...	...	...	...
60 - 64	ESDJ	5 209 400	2 565 200	2 644 200	...	...	...	...	...	...
65 - 69	ESDJ	4 168 100	1 975 600	2 192 500	...	...	...	...	...	...
70 - 74	ESDJ	2 770 200	1 275 100	1 495 100	...	...	...	...	...	...
75+	ESDJ	3 249 000	1 443 000	1 806 000	...	...	...	...	...	...
Iran (Islamic Republic of) - Iran (République islamique d')										
23 X 1996										
Total	CDJC	60 055 488	30 515 159	29 540 329	36 817 789	18 805 023	18 012 766	23 026 293	11 604 972	11 421 321
0 - 1	CDJC	1 020 936	524 927	496 009	577 065	296 189	280 876	438 331	225 870	212 461
1 - 4	CDJC	5 142 088	2 639 181	2 502 907	2 849 490	1 460 895	1 388 595	2 265 600	1 164 225	1 101 375
5 - 9	CDJC	8 481 845	4 324 165	4 157 680	4 878 478	2 482 469	2 396 009	3 568 961	1 824 356	1 744 605
10 - 14	CDJC	9 080 676	4 622 473	4 458 203	5 519 239	2 815 729	2 703 510	3 532 506	1 792 962	1 739 544
15 - 19	CDJC	7 115 547	3 579 875	3 535 672	4 312 401	2 192 258	2 120 143	2 776 791	1 375 316	1 401 475
20 - 24	CDJC	5 221 982	2 566 453	2 655 529	3 154 588	1 552 571	1 602 017	2 049 270	1 005 536	1 043 734
25 - 29	CDJC	4 709 154	2 365 834	2 343 320	3 058 756	1 542 685	1 516 071	1 636 320	816 297	820 023
30 - 34	CDJC	3 980 066	2 012 720	1 967 346	2 709 279	1 379 337	1 329 942	1 260 670	628 651	632 019

7. Population by age, sex and urban/rural residence: latest available year, 1994 - 2003
Population selon l'âge, le sexe et la résidence, urbaine/rurale: dernière année disponible, 1994 - 2003
(continued — suite)

Continent, country or area, date and age (in years) / Continent, pays ou zone, date et âge (en années)	Code[1]	Total			Urban - Urbaine			Rural - Rurale		
		Both sexes Les deux sexes	Male Masculin	Female Féminin	Both sexes Les deux sexes	Male Masculin	Female Féminin	Both sexes Les deux sexes	Male Masculin	Female Féminin
ASIA — ASIE										
Iran (Islamic Republic of) - Iran (République islamique d')										
23 X 1996										
35 - 39	CDJC	3 571 779	1 817 609	1 754 170	2 433 263	1 253 499	1 179 764	1 128 946	559 452	569 494
40 - 44	CDJC	2 812 086	1 431 062	1 381 024	1 907 112	999 736	907 376	896 847	427 395	469 452
45 - 49	CDJC	2 013 040	990 158	1 022 882	1 326 036	679 081	646 955	680 701	308 103	372 598
50 - 54	CDJC	1 529 078	768 621	760 457	978 343	508 898	469 445	545 616	257 191	288 425
55 - 59	CDJC	1 366 728	717 251	649 477	830 201	443 453	386 748	532 070	271 309	260 761
60 - 64	CDJC	1 382 946	753 502	629 444	783 511	426 040	357 471	593 925	324 115	269 810
65 - 69	CDJC	1 076 373	577 189	499 184	601 575	313 942	287 633	470 975	260 734	210 241
70 - 74	CDJC	846 509	463 018	383 491	479 380	253 061	226 319	364 876	208 499	156 377
75 - 79	CDJC	364 118	192 898	171 220	213 209	108 117	105 092	150 168	84 342	65 826
80 - 84	CDJC	146 470	74 081	72 389	86 330	41 073	45 257	59 770	32 783	26 987
85 - 89	CDJC	76 476	35 182	41 294	43 625	18 287	25 338	32 657	16 781	15 876
90 - 94	CDJC	44 780	19 977	24 803	25 563	10 855	14 708	19 067	9 050	10 017
95+	CDJC	40 455	20 103	20 352	21 018	10 022	10 996	19 224	9 963	9 261
Unk. - Inc.	CDJC	32 356	18 880	13 476	29 327	16 826	12 501	3 002	2 042	960
1 VII 2003										
Total	ESDJ	66 480 365	33 734 989	32 745 376	...	...	...	...	...	...
0 - 4	ESDJ	4 807 794	2 445 305	2 362 489	...	...	...	...	...	...
5 - 9	ESDJ	5 637 447	2 839 161	2 798 286	...	...	...	...	...	...
10 - 14	ESDJ	7 991 789	4 091 896	3 899 893	...	...	...	...	...	...
15 - 19	ESDJ	9 382 111	4 739 781	4 642 330	...	...	...	...	...	...
20 - 24	ESDJ	8 008 983	4 050 115	3 958 868	...	...	...	...	...	...
25 - 29	ESDJ	5 689 311	2 857 406	2 831 905	...	...	...	...	...	...
30 - 34	ESDJ	4 924 984	2 479 566	2 445 418	...	...	...	...	...	...
35 - 39	ESDJ	4 135 868	2 028 609	2 107 259	...	...	...	...	...	...
40 - 44	ESDJ	3 884 570	1 978 889	1 905 681	...	...	...	...	...	...
45 - 49	ESDJ	3 162 591	1 593 668	1 568 923	...	...	...	...	...	...
50 - 54	ESDJ	2 412 315	1 208 447	1 203 868	...	...	...	...	...	...
55 - 59	ESDJ	1 634 213	814 591	819 622	...	...	...	...	...	...
60 - 64	ESDJ	1 481 234	744 120	737 114	...	...	...	...	...	...
65 - 69	ESDJ	1 236 617	677 689	558 928	...	...	...	...	...	...
70 - 74	ESDJ	1 063 275	567 944	495 331	...	...	...	...	...	...
75 - 79	ESDJ	588 524	353 746	234 778	...	...	...	...	...	...
80 - 84	ESDJ	334 730	203 613	131 117	...	...	...	...	...	...
85 - 89	ESDJ	51 085	31 754	19 331	...	...	...	...	...	...
90 - 94	ESDJ	29 181	16 573	12 608	...	...	...	...	...	...
95 - 99	ESDJ	12 147	6 824	5 323	...	...	...	...	...	...
100+	ESDJ	11 596	5 292	6 304	...	...	...	...	...	...
Iraq										
1 VII 2001										
Total	ESDF	24 813 365	12 424 655	12 388 710	16 786 216	8 435 417	8 350 799	8 027 149	3 989 238	4 037 911
0 - 4	ESDF	4 204 992	2 152 617	2 052 375	2 662 981	1 363 117	1 299 864	1 542 011	789 500	752 511
5 - 9	ESDF	3 530 274	1 792 771	1 737 503	2 271 485	1 152 236	1 119 249	1 258 789	640 535	618 254
10 - 14	ESDF	3 143 756	1 597 209	1 546 547	2 062 610	1 047 953	1 014 657	1 081 146	549 256	531 890
15 - 19	ESDF	2 704 919	1 372 868	1 332 051	1 814 193	921 904	892 289	890 726	450 964	439 762
20 - 24	ESDF	2 316 564	1 169 700	1 146 864	1 581 702	800 938	780 764	734 862	368 762	366 100
25 - 29	ESDF	1 952 402	977 701	974 701	1 359 271	684 350	674 921	593 131	293 351	299 780
30 - 34	ESDF	1 614 198	800 214	813 984	1 143 674	571 922	571 752	470 524	228 292	242 232
35 - 39	ESDF	1 279 987	623 408	656 579	927 093	458 110	468 983	352 894	165 298	187 596
40 - 44	ESDF	1 032 328	499 170	533 158	756 211	372 260	383 951	276 117	126 910	149 207
45 - 49	ESDF	807 388	388 977	418 411	595 650	293 047	302 603	211 738	95 930	115 808
50 - 54	ESDF	638 860	308 112	330 748	472 597	232 751	239 846	166 263	75 361	90 902
55 - 59	ESDF	491 447	239 599	251 848	362 238	179 763	182 475	129 209	59 836	69 373
60 - 64	ESDF	373 297	179 995	193 302	274 281	134 244	140 037	99 016	45 751	53 265
65 - 69	ESDF	267 876	125 726	142 150	195 763	92 766	102 997	72 113	32 960	39 153
70 - 74	ESDF	190 384	86 113	104 271	135 525	61 375	74 150	54 859	24 738	30 121
75 - 79	ESDF	125 816	53 516	72 300	84 924	35 403	49 521	40 892	18 113	22 779
80+	ESDF	138 877	56 959	81 918	86 018	33 278	52 740	52 859	23 681	29 178

7. **Population by age, sex and urban/rural residence: latest available year, 1994 - 2003**
Population selon l'âge, le sexe et la résidence, urbaine/rurale: dernière année disponible, 1994 - 2003
(continued — suite)

Continent, country or area, date and age (in years) / Continent, pays ou zone, date et âge (en années)	Code[1]	Total			Urban - Urbaine			Rural - Rurale		
		Both sexes Les deux sexes	Male Masculin	Female Féminin	Both sexes Les deux sexes	Male Masculin	Female Féminin	Both sexes Les deux sexes	Male Masculin	Female Féminin
ASIA — ASIE										
Israel - Israël[7,21]										
1 VII 2003										
Total	ESDJ	6 689 700	3 301 800	3 387 900	6 122 400	3 010 900	3 111 600	567 300	291 000	276 300
0 - 1	ESDJ	141 300	72 300	69 000	128 200	65 600	62 600	13 100	6 700	6 400
1 - 4	ESDJ	545 300	279 900	265 400	495 100	254 200	240 900	50 200	25 700	24 500
5 - 9	ESDJ	627 500	322 000	305 500	566 400	290 600	275 900	61 000	31 400	29 600
10 - 14	ESDJ	582 600	298 500	284 000	525 100	268 600	256 600	57 400	29 900	27 500
15 - 19	ESDJ	566 700	290 400	276 400	508 300	258 700	249 600	58 400	31 600	26 800
20 - 24	ESDJ	543 800	275 900	267 900	498 400	251 900	246 500	45 400	24 000	21 400
25 - 29	ESDJ	539 600	272 100	267 500	497 800	250 600	247 200	41 800	21 500	20 300
30 - 34	ESDJ	474 000	237 600	236 400	436 700	218 900	217 700	37 400	18 700	18 700
35 - 39	ESDJ	399 500	198 000	201 500	363 400	179 900	183 500	36 100	18 100	18 000
40 - 44	ESDJ	384 200	186 900	197 200	350 300	169 900	180 500	33 800	17 100	16 700
45 - 49	ESDJ	373 900	180 600	193 300	342 500	164 500	178 100	31 300	16 100	15 200
50 - 54	ESDJ	361 600	174 000	187 600	333 200	159 200	174 000	28 500	14 900	13 600
55 - 59	ESDJ	286 600	137 700	148 900	265 400	126 900	138 600	21 200	10 900	10 300
60 - 64	ESDJ	200 600	93 900	106 700	187 100	87 000	100 200	13 400	6 900	6 500
65 - 69	ESDJ	198 000	89 700	108 300	186 500	84 000	102 500	11 500	5 700	5 800
70 - 74	ESDJ	165 700	72 100	93 600	156 600	67 900	88 700	9 100	4 200	4 900
75 - 79	ESDJ	142 300	57 400	84 900	134 700	54 100	80 600	7 600	3 300	4 400
80 - 84	ESDJ	92 100	38 200	53 900	86 600	35 800	50 800	5 500	2 400	3 000
85 - 89	ESDJ	41 300	15 900	25 500	38 500	14 700	23 800	2 800	1 100	1 700
90+	ESDJ	23 200	8 700	14 500	21 500	8 100	13 400	1 800	600	1 100
Japan - Japon[22]										
1 X 2000										
Total	CDFC	126 925 843	62 110 764	64 815 079	99 865 289	49 005 691	50 859 598	27 060 554	13 105 073	13 955 481
0 - 1	CDFC	1 171 652	600 466	571 186	946 482	485 130	461 352	225 170	115 336	109 834
1 - 4	CDFC	4 732 446	2 422 055	2 310 391	3 771 724	1 930 430	1 841 294	960 722	491 625	469 097
5 - 9	CDFC	6 021 789	3 083 431	2 938 358	4 686 566	2 399 688	2 286 878	1 335 223	683 743	651 480
10 - 14	CDFC	6 546 612	3 353 150	3 193 462	5 000 556	2 560 796	2 439 760	1 546 056	792 354	753 702
15 - 19	CDFC	7 488 165	3 833 984	3 654 181	5 878 320	3 010 056	2 868 264	1 609 845	823 928	785 917
20 - 24	CDFC	8 421 460	4 307 242	4 114 218	6 989 577	3 582 379	3 407 198	1 431 883	724 863	707 020
25 - 29	CDFC	9 790 309	4 965 277	4 825 032	8 149 612	4 131 227	4 018 385	1 640 697	834 050	806 647
30 - 34	CDFC	8 776 610	4 436 818	4 339 792	7 301 831	3 699 586	3 602 245	1 474 779	737 232	737 547
35 - 39	CDFC	8 114 865	4 096 286	4 018 579	6 578 179	3 330 783	3 247 396	1 536 686	765 503	771 183
40 - 44	CDFC	7 800 219	3 924 171	3 876 048	6 099 826	3 068 796	3 031 030	1 700 393	855 375	845 018
45 - 49	CDFC	8 916 008	4 467 772	4 448 236	6 895 939	3 440 338	3 455 601	2 020 069	1 027 434	992 635
50 - 54	CDFC	10 441 990	5 210 038	5 231 952	8 237 639	4 085 392	4 152 247	2 204 351	1 124 646	1 079 705
55 - 59	CDFC	8 734 172	4 290 239	4 443 933	6 965 529	3 418 751	3 546 778	1 768 643	871 488	897 155
60 - 64	CDFC	7 735 833	3 749 528	3 986 305	6 039 491	2 935 344	3 104 147	1 696 342	814 184	882 158
65 - 69	CDFC	7 105 939	3 357 281	3 748 658	5 374 653	2 546 769	2 827 884	1 731 286	810 512	920 774
70 - 74	CDFC	5 900 576	2 670 270	3 230 306	4 304 854	1 951 802	2 353 052	1 595 722	718 468	877 254
75 - 79	CDFC	4 150 600	1 625 822	2 524 778	2 979 368	1 169 120	1 810 248	1 171 232	456 702	714 530
80 - 84	CDFC	2 614 689	915 268	1 699 421	1 864 830	652 632	1 212 198	749 859	262 636	487 223
85 - 89	CDFC	1 532 323	477 083	1 055 240	1 089 747	341 275	748 472	442 576	135 808	306 768
90 - 94	CDFC	570 281	149 295	420 986	401 755	105 381	296 374	168 526	43 914	124 612
95 - 99	CDFC	118 488	25 070	93 418	82 972	17 454	65 518	35 516	7 616	27 900
100+	CDFC	12 256	2 027	10 229	8 403	1 355	7 048	3 853	672	3 181
Unk. - Inc.	CDFC	228 561	148 191	80 370	217 436	141 207	76 229	11 125	6 984	4 141
1 X 2003										
Total	ESDF	127 619 000	62 304 000	65 315 000	...	...	...	...	...	...
0 - 1	ESDF	1 131 000	581 000	550 000	...	...	...	...	...	...
1 - 4	ESDF	4 669 000	2 395 000	2 274 000	...	...	...	...	...	...
5 - 9	ESDF	5 985 000	3 064 000	2 921 000	...	...	...	...	...	...
10 - 14	ESDF	6 119 000	3 135 000	2 984 000	...	...	...	...	...	...
15 - 19	ESDF	6 997 000	3 589 000	3 408 000	...	...	...	...	...	...
20 - 24	ESDF	7 859 000	4 024 000	3 835 000	...	...	...	...	...	...
25 - 29	ESDF	9 106 000	4 629 000	4 477 000	...	...	...	...	...	...
30 - 34	ESDF	9 701 000	4 896 000	4 804 000	...	...	...	...	...	...
35 - 39	ESDF	8 468 000	4 264 000	4 203 000	...	...	...	...	...	...
40 - 44	ESDF	7 859 000	3 952 000	3 907 000	...	...	...	...	...	...
45 - 49	ESDF	7 929 000	3 976 000	3 953 000	...	...	...	...	...	...

7. Population by age, sex and urban/rural residence: latest available year, 1994 - 2003
Population selon l'âge, le sexe et la résidence, urbaine/rurale: dernière année disponible, 1994 - 2003
(continued — suite)

Continent, country or area, date and age (in years) / Continent, pays ou zone, date et âge (en années)	Code[1]	Total			Urban - Urbaine			Rural - Rurale		
		Both sexes Les deux sexes	Male Masculin	Female Féminin	Both sexes Les deux sexes	Male Masculin	Female Féminin	Both sexes Les deux sexes	Male Masculin	Female Féminin
ASIA — ASIE										
Japan - Japon[22]										
1 X 2003										
50 - 54	ESDF	10 013 000	4 988 000	5 025 000	...	...	...	...	...	...
55 - 59	ESDF	9 170 000	4 523 000	4 647 000	...	...	...	...	...	...
60 - 64	ESDF	8 304 000	4 028 000	4 275 000	...	...	...	...	...	...
65 - 69	ESDF	7 405 000	3 511 000	3 894 000	...	...	...	...	...	...
70 - 74	ESDF	6 359 000	2 898 000	3 460 000	...	...	...	...	...	...
75 - 79	ESDF	4 897 000	2 062 000	2 835 000	...	...	...	...	...	...
80 - 84	ESDF	3 021 000	1 039 000	1 982 000	...	...	...	...	...	...
85 - 89	ESDF	1 699 000	522 000	1 176 000	...	...	...	...	...	...
90+	ESDF	931 000	227 000	704 000	...	...	...	...	...	...
Jordan - Jordanie[23]										
10 XII 1994										
Total	CDFC	4 139 458	2 160 725	1 978 733	3 238 757	1 687 530	1 551 227	900 701	473 195	427 506
0 - 1	CDFC	123 963	63 377	60 586	95 860	49 143	46 717	28 103	14 234	13 869
1 - 4	CDFC	492 953	252 930	240 023	377 855	193 790	184 065	115 098	59 140	55 958
5 - 9	CDFC	566 406	289 767	276 639	432 615	220 987	211 628	133 791	68 780	65 011
10 - 14	CDFC	529 059	271 179	257 880	406 464	207 860	198 604	122 595	63 319	59 276
15 - 19	CDFC	483 548	251 160	232 388	374 507	194 129	180 378	109 041	57 031	52 010
20 - 24	CDFC	453 423	243 622	209 801	357 900	191 806	166 094	95 523	51 816	43 707
25 - 29	CDFC	378 952	209 365	169 587	302 167	166 150	136 017	76 785	43 215	33 570
30 - 34	CDFC	272 376	145 584	126 792	221 111	117 967	103 144	51 265	27 617	23 648
35 - 39	CDFC	188 510	98 364	90 146	152 152	79 303	72 849	36 358	19 061	17 297
40 - 44	CDFC	141 140	73 128	68 012	111 873	57 507	54 366	29 267	15 621	13 646
45 - 49	CDFC	127 400	63 161	64 239	103 397	51 162	52 235	24 003	11 999	12 004
50 - 54	CDFC	114 318	61 149	53 169	92 506	49 729	42 777	21 812	11 420	10 392
55 - 59	CDFC	91 621	48 299	43 322	73 611	38 940	34 671	18 010	9 359	8 651
60 - 64	CDFC	68 005	35 251	32 754	53 549	27 704	25 845	14 456	7 547	6 909
65 - 69	CDFC	42 232	22 799	19 433	33 797	18 037	15 760	8 435	4 762	3 673
70 - 74	CDFC	29 618	13 621	15 997	22 472	10 222	12 250	7 146	3 399	3 747
75 - 79	CDFC	14 497	7 507	6 990	11 050	5 615	5 435	3 447	1 892	1 555
80+	CDFC	17 786	8 328	9 458	13 145	5 835	7 310	4 641	2 493	2 148
Unk. - Inc.	CDFC	3 651	2 134	1 517	2 726	1 644	1 082	925	490	435
31 XII 2003										
Total	ESDF	5 480 000	2 866 200	2 613 800	...	...	...	...	...	...
0 - 1	ESDF	128 414	65 388	63 026	...	...	...	...	...	...
1 - 4	ESDF	534 666	281 422	253 244	...	...	...	...	...	...
5 - 9	ESDF	728 840	381 206	347 634	...	...	...	...	...	...
10 - 14	ESDF	679 520	355 405	324 115	...	...	...	...	...	...
15 - 19	ESDF	674 040	358 275	315 765	...	...	...	...	...	...
20 - 24	ESDF	589 100	329 615	259 485	...	...	...	...	...	...
25 - 29	ESDF	449 360	237 895	211 465	...	...	...	...	...	...
30 - 34	ESDF	383 600	189 170	194 430	...	...	...	...	...	...
35 - 39	ESDF	301 400	151 910	149 490	...	...	...	...	...	...
40 - 44	ESDF	219 200	106 050	113 150	...	...	...	...	...	...
45 - 49	ESDF	178 100	88 850	89 250	...	...	...	...	...	...
50 - 54	ESDF	156 180	74 520	81 660	...	...	...	...	...	...
55 - 59	ESDF	145 220	74 525	70 695	...	...	...	...	...	...
60 - 64	ESDF	120 560	68 790	51 770	...	...	...	...	...	...
65 - 69	ESDF	87 861	46 331	41 530	...	...	...	...	...	...
70 - 74	ESDF	53 007	29 520	23 487	...	...	...	...	...	...
75 - 79	ESDF	28 604	15 115	13 489	...	...	...	...	...	...
80 - 84	ESDF	12 831	6 673	6 158	...	...	...	...	...	...
85 - 89	ESDF	5 553	3 182	2 371	...	...	...	...	...	...
90 - 94	ESDF	2 403	1 463	940	...	...	...	...	...	...
95+	ESDF	1 541	895	646	...	...	...	...	...	...
Kazakhstan										
1 VII 2003										
Total	ESDF	14 909 018	7 179 583	7 729 435	8 448 073	3 951 898	4 496 175	6 460 945	3 227 685	3 233 260
0 - 1	ESDF	234 335	119 950	114 385	128 679	66 069	62 610	105 656	53 881	51 775
1 - 4	ESDF	862 820	442 461	420 359	445 588	228 809	216 779	417 232	213 652	203 580
5 - 9	ESDF	1 202 166	614 170	587 996	573 383	293 417	279 966	628 783	320 753	308 030

7. Population by age, sex and urban/rural residence: latest available year, 1994 - 2003
Population selon l'âge, le sexe et la résidence, urbaine/rurale: dernière année disponible, 1994 - 2003
(continued — suite)

Continent, country or area, date and age (in years) Continent, pays ou zone, date et âge (en années)	Code[1]	Total			Urban - Urbaine			Rural - Rurale		
		Both sexes Les deux sexes	Male Masculin	Female Féminin	Both sexes Les deux sexes	Male Masculin	Female Féminin	Both sexes Les deux sexes	Male Masculin	Female Féminin
ASIA — ASIE										
Kazakhstan										
1 VII 2003										
10 - 14	ESDF	1 482 750	754 509	728 241	746 795	379 870	366 925	735 955	374 639	361 316
15 - 19	ESDF	1 554 961	789 174	765 787	813 150	410 546	402 604	741 811	378 628	363 183
20 - 24	ESDF	1 303 067	659 908	643 159	752 936	368 461	384 475	550 131	291 447	258 684
25 - 29	ESDF	1 192 176	593 951	598 225	688 105	328 256	359 849	504 071	265 695	238 376
30 - 34	ESDF	1 109 278	547 810	561 468	655 524	310 196	345 328	453 754	237 614	216 140
35 - 39	ESDF	1 067 441	520 125	547 316	632 828	297 198	335 630	434 613	222 927	211 686
40 - 44	ESDF	1 136 913	545 820	591 093	689 610	320 861	368 749	447 303	224 959	222 344
45 - 49	ESDF	941 127	441 883	499 244	580 106	264 450	315 656	361 021	177 433	183 588
50 - 54	ESDF	763 725	347 834	415 891	478 536	211 945	266 591	285 189	135 889	149 300
55 - 59	ESDF	429 798	190 729	239 069	267 395	115 324	152 071	162 403	75 405	86 998
60 - 64	ESDF	522 758	217 160	305 598	308 496	122 445	186 051	214 262	94 715	119 547
65 - 69	ESDF	449 027	184 564	264 463	273 088	106 938	166 150	175 939	77 626	98 313
70 - 74	ESDF	297 667	110 364	187 303	187 015	66 053	120 962	110 652	44 311	66 341
75 - 79	ESDF	221 723	67 380	154 343	142 260	41 459	100 801	79 463	25 921	53 542
80 - 84	ESDF	84 809	21 153	63 656	53 399	13 003	40 396	31 410	8 150	23 260
85 - 89	ESDF	35 573	7 448	28 125	22 160	4 696	17 464	13 413	2 752	10 661
90 - 94	ESDF	13 566	2 537	11 029	7 542	1 564	5 978	6 024	973	5 051
95 - 99	ESDF	2 576	488	2 088	1 209	253	956	1 367	235	1 132
100+	ESDF	762	165	597	269	85	184	493	80	413
Korea (Republic of) - Corée (République de)[24]										
1 XI 1995										
Total	CDJC	44 553 710	22 357 352	22 196 358	34 991 964	17 595 723	17 396 241	9 561 746	4 761 629	4 800 117
0 - 1	CDJC	655 707	349 050	306 657	547 347	291 276	256 071	108 360	57 774	50 586
1 - 4	CDJC	2 771 702	1 472 300	1 299 402	2 287 750	1 215 282	1 072 468	483 952	257 018	226 934
5 - 9	CDJC	3 096 115	1 626 922	1 469 193	2 514 837	1 325 013	1 189 824	581 278	301 909	279 369
10 - 14	CDJC	3 711 980	1 913 801	1 798 179	2 956 665	1 533 376	1 423 289	755 315	380 425	374 890
15 - 19	CDJC	3 863 491	1 987 044	1 876 447	3 083 565	1 589 448	1 494 117	779 926	397 596	382 330
20 - 24	CDJC	4 304 378	2 237 940	2 066 438	3 509 790	1 758 084	1 751 706	794 588	479 856	314 732
25 - 29	CDJC	4 137 913	2 078 417	2 059 496	3 473 377	1 725 122	1 748 255	664 536	353 295	311 241
30 - 34	CDJC	4 230 239	2 146 351	2 083 888	3 517 693	1 774 770	1 742 923	712 546	371 581	340 965
35 - 39	CDJC	4 133 864	2 103 016	2 030 848	3 428 662	1 731 271	1 697 391	705 202	371 745	333 457
40 - 44	CDJC	3 071 101	1 579 850	1 491 251	2 519 966	1 295 738	1 224 228	551 135	284 112	267 023
45 - 49	CDJC	2 464 295	1 261 509	1 202 786	1 951 493	1 004 316	947 177	512 802	257 193	255 609
50 - 54	CDJC	2 063 768	1 028 887	1 034 881	1 516 333	774 968	741 365	547 435	253 919	293 516
55 - 59	CDJC	1 913 461	923 625	989 836	1 264 170	626 873	637 297	649 291	296 752	352 539
60 - 64	CDJC	1 495 082	673 719	821 363	905 622	413 690	491 932	589 460	260 029	329 431
65 - 69	CDJC	1 043 979	420 873	623 106	612 437	242 461	369 976	431 542	178 412	253 130
70 - 74	CDJC	762 544	293 696	468 848	437 794	159 518	278 276	324 750	134 178	190 572
75 - 79	CDJC	455 673	160 498	295 175	255 966	83 390	172 576	199 707	77 108	122 599
80 - 84	CDJC	246 191	71 267	174 924	137 645	36 561	101 084	108 546	34 706	73 840
85+	CDJC	131 818	28 370	103 448	70 675	14 468	56 207	61 143	13 902	47 241
Unk. - Inc.	CDJC	409	217	192	177	98	79	232	119	113
1 VII 2003										
Total	ESDF	*47 925 318*	*24 126 185*	*23 799 133*	...	...	...	...	...	...
0 - 1	ESDF	*556 857*	*291 031*	*265 826*	...	...	...	...	...	...
1 - 4	ESDF	*2 400 310*	*1 259 545*	*1 140 765*	...	...	...	...	...	...
5 - 9	ESDF	*3 422 250*	*1 813 147*	*1 609 103*	...	...	...	...	...	...
10 - 14	ESDF	*3 339 316*	*1 777 385*	*1 561 931*	...	...	...	...	...	...
15 - 19	ESDF	*3 237 329*	*1 693 339*	*1 543 990*	...	...	...	...	...	...
20 - 24	ESDF	*4 040 269*	*2 084 727*	*1 955 542*	...	...	...	...	...	...
25 - 29	ESDF	*3 913 811*	*2 022 002*	*1 891 809*	...	...	...	...	...	...
30 - 34	ESDF	*4 427 739*	*2 254 709*	*2 173 030*	...	...	...	...	...	...
35 - 39	ESDF	*4 138 311*	*2 130 244*	*2 008 067*	...	...	...	...	...	...
40 - 44	ESDF	*4 307 529*	*2 175 772*	*2 131 757*	...	...	...	...	...	...
45 - 49	ESDF	*3 570 219*	*1 809 990*	*1 760 229*	...	...	...	...	...	...
50 - 54	ESDF	*2 561 026*	*1 288 091*	*1 272 935*	...	...	...	...	...	...
55 - 59	ESDF	*2 111 324*	*1 052 337*	*1 058 987*	...	...	...	...	...	...
60 - 64	ESDF	*1 929 992*	*909 838*	*1 020 154*	...	...	...	...	...	...

7. Population by age, sex and urban/rural residence: latest available year, 1994 - 2003
Population selon l'âge, le sexe et la résidence, urbaine/rurale: dernière année disponible, 1994 - 2003
(continued — suite)

Continent, country or area, date and age (in years) / Continent, pays ou zone, date et âge (en années)	Code[1]	Total			Urban - Urbaine			Rural - Rurale		
		Both sexes Les deux sexes	Male Masculin	Female Féminin	Both sexes Les deux sexes	Male Masculin	Female Féminin	Both sexes Les deux sexes	Male Masculin	Female Féminin
ASIA — ASIE										
Korea (Republic of) - Corée (République de)[24]										
1 VII 2003										
65 - 69	ESDF	1 598 342	716 174	882 168	...	...	...	...	...	...
70 - 74	ESDF	1 091 070	432 085	658 985	...	...	...	...	...	...
75 - 79	ESDF	684 988	243 712	441 276	...	...	...	...	...	...
80 - 84	ESDF	377 649	119 850	257 799	...	...	...	...	...	...
85 - 89	ESDF	162 108	41 716	120 392	...	...	...	...	...	...
90 - 94	ESDF	46 601	9 331	37 270	...	...	...	...	...	...
95+	ESDF	8 278	1 160	7 118	...	...	...	...	...	...
Kuwait - Koweït										
1 VII 1998										
Total	ESDF	2 027 103	1 226 774	800 329	...	...	...	...	...	...
0 - 1	ESDF	38 759	19 737	19 022	...	...	...	...	...	...
1 - 4	ESDF	162 578	82 913	79 665	...	...	...	...	...	...
5 - 9	ESDF	178 527	91 301	87 226	...	...	...	...	...	...
10 - 14	ESDF	162 295	82 540	79 755	...	...	...	...	...	...
15 - 19	ESDF	135 096	69 853	65 243	...	...	...	...	...	...
20 - 24	ESDF	154 165	81 411	72 754	...	...	...	...	...	...
25 - 29	ESDF	245 307	156 663	88 644	...	...	...	...	...	...
30 - 34	ESDF	273 922	186 112	87 810	...	...	...	...	...	...
35 - 39	ESDF	228 935	152 744	76 191	...	...	...	...	...	...
40 - 44	ESDF	173 732	119 508	54 224	...	...	...	...	...	...
45 - 49	ESDF	110 552	77 575	32 977	...	...	...	...	...	...
50 - 54	ESDF	66 987	46 236	20 751	...	...	...	...	...	...
55 - 59	ESDF	41 362	27 964	13 398	...	...	...	...	...	...
60 - 64	ESDF	25 882	16 652	9 230	...	...	...	...	...	...
65 - 69	ESDF	13 541	7 701	5 840	...	...	...	...	...	...
70 - 74	ESDF	7 631	4 004	3 627	...	...	...	...	...	...
75 - 79	ESDF	4 060	1 998	2 062	...	...	...	...	...	...
80 - 84	ESDF	2 111	1 073	1 038	...	...	...	...	...	...
85+	ESDF	1 661	789	872	...	...	...	...	...	...
1 VII 2002										
Total	ESDF	2 261 956	1 355 300	906 656	...	...	...	...	...	...
0 - 14	ESDF	566 285	288 632	277 653	...	...	...	...	...	...
15 - 64	ESDF	1 658 601	1 047 074	611 527	...	...	...	...	...	...
65+	ESDF	37 070	19 594	17 476	...	...	...	...	...	...
Kyrgyzstan - Kirghizistan[25]										
1 VII 2003										
Total	ESDJ	5 010 844	2 476 740	2 534 104	1 750 313	836 737	913 576	3 260 531	1 640 003	1 620 528
0 - 1	ESDJ	101 344	51 759	49 585	30 471	15 486	14 985	70 873	36 273	34 600
1 - 4	ESDJ	388 657	198 334	190 323	112 769	57 594	55 175	275 888	140 740	135 148
5 - 9	ESDJ	547 720	278 470	269 250	150 918	76 516	74 402	396 802	201 954	194 848
10 - 14	ESDJ	589 804	298 644	291 160	171 920	86 508	85 412	417 884	212 136	205 748
15 - 19	ESDJ	564 415	284 020	280 395	169 787	83 633	86 154	394 628	200 387	194 241
20 - 24	ESDJ	471 710	237 628	234 082	189 283	90 574	98 709	282 427	147 054	135 373
25 - 29	ESDJ	409 938	206 352	203 586	162 448	79 100	83 348	247 490	127 252	120 238
30 - 34	ESDJ	370 695	186 156	184 539	148 587	71 468	77 119	222 108	114 688	107 420
35 - 39	ESDJ	335 925	167 045	168 880	132 383	63 993	68 390	203 542	103 052	100 490
40 - 44	ESDJ	327 366	160 456	166 910	127 905	60 628	67 277	199 461	99 828	99 633
45 - 49	ESDJ	249 362	120 470	128 892	98 396	45 782	52 614	150 966	74 688	76 278
50 - 54	ESDJ	180 433	85 966	94 467	73 270	33 692	39 578	107 163	52 274	54 889
55 - 59	ESDJ	93 667	43 716	49 951	40 487	18 205	22 282	53 180	25 511	27 669
60 - 64	ESDJ	102 072	46 774	55 298	39 323	16 904	22 419	62 749	29 870	32 879
65 - 69	ESDJ	99 745	43 732	56 013	38 053	15 600	22 453	61 692	28 132	33 560
70 - 74	ESDJ	82 032	33 945	48 087	28 421	10 509	17 912	53 611	23 436	30 175
75 - 79	ESDJ	57 237	22 146	35 091	21 521	6 825	14 696	35 716	15 321	20 395
80 - 84	ESDJ	23 809	7 264	16 545	8 875	2 370	6 505	14 934	4 894	10 040
85 - 89	ESDJ	8 847	2 294	6 553	3 600	872	2 728	5 247	1 422	3 825
90 - 94	ESDJ	4 294	1 127	3 167	1 421	376	1 045	2 873	751	2 122

7. Population by age, sex and urban/rural residence: latest available year, 1994 - 2003
Population selon l'âge, le sexe et la résidence, urbaine/rurale: dernière année disponible, 1994 - 2003
(continued — suite)

Continent, country or area, date and age (in years) / Continent, pays ou zone, date et âge (en années)	Code[1]	Total			Urban - Urbaine			Rural - Rurale		
		Both sexes Les deux sexes	Male Masculin	Female Féminin	Both sexes Les deux sexes	Male Masculin	Female Féminin	Both sexes Les deux sexes	Male Masculin	Female Féminin
ASIA — ASIE										
Kyrgyzstan - Kirghizistan[25]										
1 VII 2003										
95 - 99	ESDJ	1 215	326	889	328	82	246	887	244	643
100+	ESDJ	557	116	441	147	20	127	410	96	314
Lao People's Democratic Republic - République démocratique populaire lao										
1 VII 2000										
Total	ESDF	5 218 300	2 579 000	2 639 300	...	...	...	...	...	...
0 - 4	ESDF	685 000	345 600	340 500	...	...	...	...	...	...
5 - 9	ESDF	807 100	407 400	398 500	...	...	...	...	...	...
10 - 14	ESDF	784 100	389 400	393 300	...	...	...	...	...	...
15 - 19	ESDF	550 600	276 000	274 500	...	...	...	...	...	...
20 - 24	ESDF	371 100	175 400	198 000	...	...	...	...	...	...
25 - 29	ESDF	357 800	165 100	192 700	...	...	...	...	...	...
30 - 34	ESDF	308 000	144 400	163 600	...	...	...	...	...	...
35 - 39	ESDF	326 900	159 900	166 300	...	...	...	...	...	...
40 - 44	ESDF	251 600	131 500	118 800	...	...	...	...	...	...
45 - 49	ESDF	205 100	110 900	95 000	...	...	...	...	...	...
50 - 54	ESDF	164 000	72 200	92 400	...	...	...	...	...	...
55 - 59	ESDF	124 700	61 900	63 300	...	...	...	...	...	...
60 - 64	ESDF	98 200	51 600	47 500	...	...	...	...	...	...
65 - 69	ESDF	73 500	36 100	37 000	...	...	...	...	...	...
70 - 74	ESDF	51 000	25 800	23 800	...	...	...	...	...	...
75+	ESDF	60 000	25 800	34 300	...	...	...	...	...	...
Malaysia - Malaisie[26,27]										
5 VII 2000										
Total	CDJC	23 274 690	11 853 432	11 421 258	14 426 871	7 318 396	7 108 475	8 847 819	4 535 036	4 312 783
0 - 4	CDJC	2 612 744	1 347 633	1 265 111	1 574 757	812 456	762 301	1 037 987	535 177	502 810
5 - 9	CDJC	2 646 527	1 364 984	1 281 543	1 534 452	792 519	741 933	1 112 075	572 465	539 610
10 - 14	CDJC	2 491 777	1 276 348	1 215 429	1 383 003	709 140	673 863	1 108 774	567 208	541 566
15 - 19	CDJC	2 367 021	1 195 803	1 171 218	1 408 673	707 968	700 705	958 348	487 835	470 513
20 - 24	CDJC	2 087 173	1 050 916	1 036 257	1 436 911	708 607	728 304	650 262	342 309	307 953
25 - 29	CDJC	1 921 052	972 668	948 384	1 315 940	653 627	662 313	605 112	319 041	286 071
30 - 34	CDJC	1 800 196	915 814	884 382	1 207 148	606 473	600 675	593 048	309 341	283 707
35 - 39	CDJC	1 705 044	866 212	838 832	1 141 371	577 947	563 424	563 673	288 265	275 408
40 - 44	CDJC	1 487 498	764 706	722 792	976 771	504 183	472 588	510 727	260 523	250 204
45 - 49	CDJC	1 168 527	604 844	563 683	743 757	389 417	354 340	424 770	215 427	209 343
50 - 54	CDJC	918 868	480 261	438 607	562 704	298 115	264 589	356 164	182 146	174 018
55 - 59	CDJC	616 598	320 119	296 479	356 078	186 312	169 766	260 520	133 807	126 713
60 - 64	CDJC	551 027	274 216	276 811	306 351	153 941	152 410	244 676	120 275	124 401
65 - 69	CDJC	346 725	164 943	181 782	189 063	89 783	99 280	157 662	75 160	82 502
70 - 74	CDJC	264 119	125 883	138 236	138 716	64 354	74 362	125 403	61 529	63 874
75+	CDJC	289 794	128 082	161 712	151 176	63 554	87 622	138 618	64 528	74 090
Maldives										
25 III 1995										
Total	CDFC	244 814	124 622	120 192	62 519	33 506	29 013	182 295	91 116	91 179
0 - 1	CDFC	7 044	3 593	3 451	1 149	592	557	5 895	3 001	2 894
1 - 4	CDFC	29 928	15 520	14 408	4 978	2 603	2 375	24 950	12 917	12 033
5 - 9	CDFC	40 759	20 840	19 919	7 203	3 671	3 532	33 556	17 169	16 387
10 - 14	CDFC	35 870	18 286	17 584	8 441	4 256	4 185	27 429	14 030	13 399
15 - 19	CDFC	24 905	12 343	12 562	9 745	5 328	4 417	15 160	7 015	8 145
20 - 24	CDFC	21 021	9 944	11 077	7 339	4 075	3 264	13 682	5 869	7 813
25 - 29	CDFC	18 191	8 802	9 389	5 854	3 229	2 625	12 337	5 573	6 764
30 - 34	CDFC	15 364	7 579	7 785	4 656	2 526	2 130	10 708	5 053	5 655
35 - 39	CDFC	12 632	6 315	6 317	3 572	1 911	1 661	9 060	4 404	4 656
40 - 44	CDFC	6 922	3 625	3 297	2 061	1 216	845	4 861	2 409	2 452
45 - 49	CDFC	6 584	3 369	3 215	1 892	1 021	871	4 692	2 348	2 344

7. Population by age, sex and urban/rural residence: latest available year, 1994 - 2003
Population selon l'âge, le sexe et la résidence, urbaine/rurale: dernière année disponible, 1994 - 2003
(continued — suite)

Continent, country or area, date and age (in years) / Continent, pays ou zone, date et âge (en années)	Code[1]	Total			Urban - Urbaine			Rural - Rurale		
		Both sexes Les deux sexes	Male Masculin	Female Féminin	Both sexes Les deux sexes	Male Masculin	Female Féminin	Both sexes Les deux sexes	Male Masculin	Female Féminin
ASIA — ASIE										
Maldives										
25 III 1995										
50 - 54	CDFC	6 247	3 205	3 042	1 643	885	758	4 604	2 320	2 284
55 - 59	CDFC	5 962	3 240	2 722	1 341	725	616	4 621	2 515	2 106
60 - 64	CDFC	5 294	3 010	2 284	1 061	563	498	4 233	2 447	1 786
65 - 69	CDFC	3 201	1 897	1 304	606	335	271	2 595	1 562	1 033
70 - 74	CDFC	2 101	1 279	822	387	222	165	1 714	1 057	657
75 - 79	CDFC	968	617	351	186	99	87	782	518	264
80 - 84	CDFC	695	394	301	102	44	58	593	350	243
85 - 89	CDFC	326	220	106	47	24	23	279	196	83
90 - 94	CDFC	163	86	77	27	12	15	136	74	62
95+	CDFC	94	67	27	17	9	8	77	58	19
Unk. - Inc.	CDFC	543	391	152	212	160	52	331	231	100
1 VII 2003										
Total	ESDF	*285 734*	*144 341*	*141 393*	...	...	...	...	...	...
0 - 1	ESDF	*6 075*	*3 106*	*2 969*	...	...	...	...	...	...
1 - 4	ESDF	*23 145*	*11 771*	*11 374*	...	...	...	...	...	...
5 - 9	ESDF	*33 674*	*17 153*	*16 521*	...	...	...	...	...	...
10 - 14	ESDF	*40 360*	*20 608*	*19 752*	...	...	...	...	...	...
15 - 19	ESDF	*39 141*	*19 800*	*19 341*	...	...	...	...	...	...
20 - 24	ESDF	*29 110*	*14 460*	*14 650*	...	...	...	...	...	...
25 - 29	ESDF	*21 553*	*10 607*	*10 946*	...	...	...	...	...	...
30 - 34	ESDF	*19 354*	*9 445*	*9 909*	...	...	...	...	...	...
35 - 39	ESDF	*17 304*	*8 535*	*8 769*	...	...	...	...	...	...
40 - 44	ESDF	*14 562*	*7 302*	*7 260*	...	...	...	...	...	...
45 - 49	ESDF	*10 336*	*5 317*	*5 019*	...	...	...	...	...	...
50 - 54	ESDF	*6 323*	*3 383*	*2 940*	...	...	...	...	...	...
55 - 59	ESDF	*6 167*	*2 927*	*3 240*	...	...	...	...	...	...
60 - 64	ESDF	*6 693*	*3 123*	*3 570*	...	...	...	...	...	...
65 - 69	ESDF	*5 325*	*2 995*	*2 330*	...	...	...	...	...	...
70 - 74	ESDF	*3 440*	*1 905*	*1 535*	...	...	...	...	...	...
75+	ESDF	*3 172*	*1 904*	*1 268*	...	...	...	...	...	...
Mongolia - Mongolie										
5 I 2000										
Total	CDFC	2 373 493	1 177 981	1 195 512	1 344 516	657 081	687 435	1 028 977	520 900	508 077
0 - 1	CDFC	49 804	25 356	24 448	23 778	12 119	11 659	26 026	13 237	12 789
1 - 4	CDFC	196 219	99 126	97 093	91 687	46 096	45 591	104 532	53 030	51 502
5 - 9	CDFC	285 664	144 315	141 349	150 401	75 700	74 701	135 263	68 615	66 648
10 - 14	CDFC	317 434	159 294	158 140	179 974	89 670	90 304	137 460	69 624	67 836
15 - 19	CDFC	263 358	133 327	130 031	154 244	75 040	79 204	109 114	58 287	50 827
20 - 24	CDFC	235 751	118 023	117 728	135 694	66 010	69 684	100 057	52 013	48 044
25 - 29	CDFC	216 652	107 962	108 690	125 644	61 274	64 370	91 008	46 688	44 320
30 - 34	CDFC	187 872	92 473	95 399	113 537	54 332	59 205	74 335	38 141	36 194
35 - 39	CDFC	172 606	84 846	87 760	108 347	52 275	56 072	64 259	32 571	31 688
40 - 44	CDFC	127 220	62 619	64 601	79 563	38 840	40 723	47 657	23 779	23 878
45 - 49	CDFC	82 888	40 562	42 326	50 873	25 089	25 784	32 015	15 473	16 542
50 - 54	CDFC	57 835	27 707	30 128	35 016	17 094	17 922	22 819	10 613	12 206
55 - 59	CDFC	55 895	27 379	28 516	30 397	15 011	15 386	25 498	12 368	13 130
60 - 64	CDFC	42 292	20 778	21 514	21 889	10 658	11 231	20 403	10 120	10 283
65 - 69	CDFC	35 415	15 982	19 433	18 480	8 145	10 335	16 935	7 837	9 098
70 - 74	CDFC	20 239	8 766	11 473	10 946	4 579	6 367	9 293	4 187	5 106
75 - 79	CDFC	14 843	5 832	9 011	7 963	3 197	4 766	6 880	2 635	4 245
80 - 84	CDFC	7 036	2 329	4 707	3 777	1 281	2 496	3 259	1 048	2 211
85 - 89	CDFC	3 376	991	2 385	1 746	519	1 227	1 630	472	1 158
90 - 94	CDFC	869	257	612	441	125	316	428	132	296
95 - 99	CDFC	196	53	143	104	24	80	92	29	63
100+	CDFC	29	4	25	15	3	12	14	1	13
1 VII 2003										
Total	ESDF	*2 504 023*	*1 242 269*	*1 261 754*	...	...	...	...	...	...
0 - 1	ESDF	*42 260*	*20 894*	*21 366*	...	...	...	...	...	...
1 - 4	ESDF	*189 282*	*94 457*	*94 825*	...	...	...	...	...	...
5 - 9	ESDF	*268 766*	*133 655*	*135 111*	...	...	...	...	...	...

7. Population by age, sex and urban/rural residence: latest available year, 1994 - 2003
Population selon l'âge, le sexe et la résidence, urbaine/rurale: dernière année disponible, 1994 - 2003
(continued — suite)

Continent, country or area, date and age (in years) / Continent, pays ou zone, date et âge (en années)	Code[1]	Total			Urban - Urbaine			Rural - Rurale		
		Both sexes Les deux sexes	Male Masculin	Female Féminin	Both sexes Les deux sexes	Male Masculin	Female Féminin	Both sexes Les deux sexes	Male Masculin	Female Féminin
ASIA — ASIE										
Mongolia - Mongolie										
1 VII 2003										
10 - 14	ESDF	316 966	158 885	158 081	...	...	...	...	...	...
15 - 19	ESDF	293 099	149 163	143 936	...	...	...	...	...	...
20 - 24	ESDF	266 079	134 032	132 047	...	...	...	...	...	...
25 - 29	ESDF	231 214	114 840	116 374	...	...	...	...	...	...
30 - 34	ESDF	198 862	98 957	99 905	...	...	...	...	...	...
35 - 39	ESDF	181 688	89 907	91 781	...	...	...	...	...	...
40 - 44	ESDF	148 692	73 336	75 356	...	...	...	...	...	...
45 - 49	ESDF	101 889	50 751	51 138	...	...	...	...	...	...
50 - 54	ESDF	69 487	33 911	35 576	...	...	...	...	...	...
55 - 59	ESDF	58 230	28 417	29 813	...	...	...	...	...	...
60 - 64	ESDF	49 501	23 106	26 395	...	...	...	...	...	...
65 - 69	ESDF	36 606	16 786	19 820	...	...	...	...	...	...
70+	ESDF	51 402	21 172	30 230	...	...	...	...	...	...
Myanmar										
1 VII 1997										
Total	ESDF	46 402 000	23 039 000	23 363 000	...	...	...	...	...	...
0 - 4	ESDF	5 786 000	2 879 000	2 907 000	...	...	...	...	...	...
5 - 9	ESDF	4 959 000	2 558 000	2 401 000	...	...	...	...	...	...
10 - 14	ESDF	4 708 000	2 440 000	2 268 000	...	...	...	...	...	...
15 - 19	ESDF	4 593 000	2 343 000	2 250 000	...	...	...	...	...	...
20 - 24	ESDF	4 299 000	2 165 000	2 134 000	...	...	...	...	...	...
25 - 29	ESDF	3 952 000	1 961 000	1 991 000	...	...	...	...	...	...
30 - 34	ESDF	3 555 000	1 745 000	1 810 000	...	...	...	...	...	...
35 - 39	ESDF	3 060 000	1 496 000	1 564 000	...	...	...	...	...	...
40 - 44	ESDF	2 594 000	1 263 000	1 331 000	...	...	...	...	...	...
45 - 49	ESDF	2 131 000	1 035 000	1 096 000	...	...	...	...	...	...
50 - 54	ESDF	1 747 000	842 000	905 000	...	...	...	...	...	...
55 - 59	ESDF	1 466 000	695 000	771 000	...	...	...	...	...	...
60 - 64	ESDF	1 202 000	561 000	641 000	...	...	...	...	...	...
65+	ESDF	2 350 000	1 056 000	1 294 000	...	...	...	...	...	...
Nepal - Népal										
1 VII 1996										
Total	ESDJ	20 831 644	10 393 913	10 437 731	2 207 967	1 138 641	1 069 326	18 623 677	9 255 272	9 368 405
0 - 4	ESDJ	3 235 783	1 658 100	1 577 683	283 174	139 204	143 970	2 952 609	1 518 896	1 433 713
5 - 9	ESDJ	2 838 712	1 447 733	1 390 979	280 407	151 796	128 611	2 558 305	1 295 937	1 262 368
10 - 14	ESDJ	2 521 943	1 275 549	1 246 394	241 904	124 110	117 794	2 280 040	1 151 439	1 128 601
15 - 19	ESDJ	2 149 812	1 041 495	1 108 317	233 403	110 195	123 208	1 916 408	931 300	985 108
20 - 24	ESDJ	1 839 716	882 635	957 081	237 790	118 604	119 186	1 601 926	764 031	837 895
25 - 29	ESDJ	1 565 942	766 431	799 511	222 983	122 864	100 119	1 342 960	643 568	699 392
30 - 34	ESDJ	1 310 586	648 320	662 266	170 140	93 500	76 640	1 140 446	554 820	585 626
35 - 39	ESDJ	1 139 089	570 183	568 906	133 684	73 273	60 411	1 005 405	496 910	508 495
40 - 44	ESDJ	983 519	494 106	489 413	105 506	56 085	49 421	878 013	438 021	439 992
45 - 49	ESDJ	839 008	423 529	415 479	81 831	44 633	37 198	757 176	378 896	378 280
50 - 54	ESDJ	698 161	351 396	346 765	62 770	32 371	30 399	635 391	319 025	316 366
55 - 59	ESDJ	566 009	283 271	282 738	49 332	24 253	25 079	516 677	259 019	257 658
60 - 64	ESDJ	438 536	216 857	221 679	38 025	17 312	20 713	400 511	199 545	200 966
65 - 69	ESDJ	318 278	154 732	163 546	28 023	13 376	14 647	290 255	141 356	148 899
70 - 74	ESDJ	208 529	98 933	109 596	19 466	8 853	10 613	189 062	90 079	98 983
75 - 79	ESDJ	115 654	53 285	62 369	12 217	4 965	7 252	103 437	48 320	55 117
80+	ESDJ	62 367	27 358	35 009	7 312	3 247	4 065	55 056	24 110	30 946
22 VI 2001										
Total	CDJC	22 736 934	11 359 378	11 377 556	...	...	...	...	...	...
0 - 1	CDJC	494 813	252 519	242 294	...	...	...	...	...	...
1 - 4	CDJC	2 260 400	1 143 196	1 117 204	...	...	...	...	...	...
5 - 9	CDJC	3 211 442	1 633 087	1 578 355	...	...	...	...	...	...
10 - 14	CDJC	2 981 932	1 533 806	1 448 126	...	...	...	...	...	...
15 - 19	CDJC	2 389 002	1 185 826	1 203 176	...	...	...	...	...	...
20 - 24	CDJC	2 016 768	946 742	1 070 026	...	...	...	...	...	...
25 - 29	CDJC	1 725 478	821 014	904 464	...	...	...	...	...	...
30 - 34	CDJC	1 489 503	726 040	763 463	...	...	...	...	...	...

7. Population by age, sex and urban/rural residence: latest available year, 1994 - 2003
Population selon l'âge, le sexe et la résidence, urbaine/rurale: dernière année disponible, 1994 - 2003
(continued — suite)

Continent, country or area, date and age (in years) Continent, pays ou zone, date et âge (en années)	Code[1]	Total			Urban - Urbaine			Rural - Rurale		
		Both sexes Les deux sexes	Male Masculin	Female Féminin	Both sexes Les deux sexes	Male Masculin	Female Féminin	Both sexes Les deux sexes	Male Masculin	Female Féminin
ASIA — ASIE										
Nepal - Népal										
22 VI 2001										
35 - 39	CDJC	1 310 653	651 351	659 302	...	...	...	...	...	...
40 - 44	CDJC	1 088 044	539 993	548 051	...	...	...	...	...	...
45 - 49	CDJC	923 373	469 695	453 678	...	...	...	...	...	...
50 - 54	CDJC	766 054	392 659	373 395	...	...	...	...	...	...
55 - 59	CDJC	602 093	318 610	283 483	...	...	...	...	...	...
60 - 64	CDJC	520 908	262 255	258 653	...	...	...	...	...	...
65 - 69	CDJC	387 223	196 053	191 170	...	...	...	...	...	...
70 - 74	CDJC	273 789	141 678	132 111	...	...	...	...	...	...
75 - 79	CDJC	165 764	82 335	83 429	...	...	...	...	...	...
80 - 84	CDJC	84 255	41 192	43 063	...	...	...	...	...	...
85 - 89	CDJC	27 947	13 630	14 317	...	...	...	...	...	...
90 - 94	CDJC	11 421	5 082	6 339	...	...	...	...	...	...
95+	CDJC	6 072	2 615	3 457	...	...	...	...	...	...
Occupied Palestinian Territory - Territoire palestinien occupé										
1 VII 2003										
Total	ESDF	3 647 875	1 847 684	1 800 191	...	...	...	...	...	...
0 - 1	ESDF	138 404	70 572	67 832	...	...	...	...	...	...
1 - 4	ESDF	511 300	260 835	250 465	...	...	...	...	...	...
5 - 9	ESDF	559 294	284 966	274 328	...	...	...	...	...	...
10 - 14	ESDF	473 972	240 721	233 251	...	...	...	...	...	...
15 - 19	ESDF	385 771	196 883	188 888	...	...	...	...	...	...
20 - 24	ESDF	321 563	164 043	157 520	...	...	...	...	...	...
25 - 29	ESDF	271 986	138 526	133 460	...	...	...	...	...	...
30 - 34	ESDF	227 459	115 831	111 628	...	...	...	...	...	...
35 - 39	ESDF	189 773	97 746	92 027	...	...	...	...	...	...
40 - 44	ESDF	153 513	79 536	73 977	...	...	...	...	...	...
45 - 49	ESDF	109 098	56 265	52 833	...	...	...	...	...	...
50 - 54	ESDF	81 213	41 128	40 085	...	...	...	...	...	...
55 - 59	ESDF	62 158	29 414	32 744	...	...	...	...	...	...
60 - 64	ESDF	48 953	21 824	27 129	...	...	...	...	...	...
65 - 69	ESDF	42 601	18 571	24 030	...	...	...	...	...	...
70 - 74	ESDF	32 449	13 965	18 484	...	...	...	...	...	...
75 - 79	ESDF	20 942	8 964	11 978	...	...	...	...	...	...
80+	ESDF	17 426	7 894	9 532	...	...	...	...	...	...
Oman										
7 XII 2003										
Total	CDFC	2 340 815	1 313 239	1 027 576	...	...	...	...	...	...
0 - 1	CDFC	48 192	24 276	23 916	...	...	...	...	...	...
1 - 4	CDFC	194 568	99 098	95 470	...	...	...	...	...	...
5 - 9	CDFC	260 928	133 360	127 568	...	...	...	...	...	...
10 - 14	CDFC	288 325	147 277	141 048	...	...	...	...	...	...
15 - 19	CDFC	266 809	136 573	130 236	...	...	...	...	...	...
20 - 24	CDFC	252 803	130 999	121 804	...	...	...	...	...	...
25 - 29	CDFC	235 363	138 181	97 182	...	...	...	...	...	...
30 - 34	CDFC	193 834	124 585	69 249	...	...	...	...	...	...
35 - 39	CDFC	160 430	104 124	56 306	...	...	...	...	...	...
40 - 44	CDFC	132 607	88 567	44 040	...	...	...	...	...	...
45 - 49	CDFC	97 690	64 232	33 458	...	...	...	...	...	...
50 - 54	CDFC	69 635	43 792	25 843	...	...	...	...	...	...
55 - 59	CDFC	41 573	24 641	16 932	...	...	...	...	...	...
60 - 64	CDFC	36 600	20 725	15 875	...	...	...	...	...	...
65 - 69	CDFC	20 068	11 462	8 606	...	...	...	...	...	...
70 - 74	CDFC	17 933	9 547	8 386	...	...	...	...	...	...
75 - 79	CDFC	7 843	4 090	3 753	...	...	...	...	...	...
80 - 84	CDFC	7 784	3 752	4 032	...	...	...	...	...	...
85+	CDFC	6 900	3 318	3 582	...	...	...	...	...	...
Unk. - Inc.	CDFC	930	640	290	...	...	...	...	...	...

7. Population by age, sex and urban/rural residence: latest available year, 1994 - 2003
Population selon l'âge, le sexe et la résidence, urbaine/rurale: dernière année disponible, 1994 - 2003
(continued — suite)

Continent, country or area, date and age (in years) Continent, pays ou zone, date et âge (en années)	Code[1]	Total			Urban - Urbaine			Rural - Rurale		
		Both sexes Les deux sexes	Male Masculin	Female Féminin	Both sexes Les deux sexes	Male Masculin	Female Féminin	Both sexes Les deux sexes	Male Masculin	Female Féminin
ASIA — ASIE										
Pakistan[28,29]										
1 VII 2001										
Total	SSDF	133 652 121	68 769 178	64 882 943	47 739 853	24 707 762	23 032 091	85 912 268	44 061 416	41 850 852
0 - 4	SSDF	18 732 802	9 375 692	9 357 110	5 912 644	2 965 946	2 946 698	12 820 158	6 409 746	6 410 412
5 - 9	SSDF	20 300 365	10 576 705	9 723 659	6 509 275	3 360 356	3 148 919	13 791 090	7 216 350	6 574 741
10 - 14	SSDF	18 116 710	9 495 592	8 621 118	6 489 101	3 368 604	3 120 497	11 627 609	6 126 988	5 500 621
15 - 19	SSDF	15 072 138	7 850 486	7 221 652	5 864 282	3 035 904	2 828 378	9 207 856	4 814 582	4 393 273
20 - 24	SSDF	12 299 567	6 226 136	6 073 430	4 814 657	2 486 396	2 328 261	7 484 910	3 739 741	3 745 169
25 - 29	SSDF	9 337 940	4 551 890	4 786 050	3 460 644	1 751 085	1 709 559	5 877 296	2 800 805	3 076 491
30 - 34	SSDF	7 575 021	3 678 187	3 896 834	2 806 216	1 405 750	1 400 466	4 768 805	2 272 437	2 496 368
35 - 39	SSDF	7 136 491	3 627 152	3 509 339	2 800 495	1 416 395	1 384 100	4 335 996	2 210 757	2 125 239
40 - 44	SSDF	5 591 207	2 876 856	2 714 351	2 125 423	1 141 692	983 730	3 465 785	1 735 164	1 730 621
45 - 49	SSDF	5 293 361	2 714 269	2 579 092	2 002 268	1 059 267	943 001	3 291 093	1 655 001	1 636 091
50 - 54	SSDF	4 091 604	2 180 843	1 910 761	1 489 897	813 492	676 405	2 601 707	1 367 350	1 234 356
55 - 59	SSDF	2 969 182	1 549 383	1 419 799	1 063 613	554 612	509 001	1 905 569	994 771	910 798
60 - 64	SSDF	2 671 393	1 487 916	1 183 477	910 139	495 767	414 372	1 761 255	992 149	769 105
65 - 69	SSDF	1 852 989	1 051 999	800 990	638 216	355 477	282 738	1 214 773	696 521	518 252
70+	SSDF	2 611 352	1 526 072	1 085 280	852 984	497 018	355 966	1 758 368	1 029 054	729 314
Philippines										
1 VII 2003										
Total	ESDJ	81 081 457	40 820 706	40 260 751	...	...	...	...	...	...
0 - 4	ESDJ	9 633 446	4 923 339	4 710 107	...	...	...	...	...	...
5 - 9	ESDJ	9 416 816	4 825 448	4 591 368	...	...	...	...	...	...
10 - 14	ESDJ	9 046 260	4 650 500	4 395 760	...	...	...	...	...	...
15 - 19	ESDJ	8 359 222	4 254 885	4 104 337	...	...	...	...	...	...
20 - 24	ESDJ	7 591 134	3 825 549	3 765 585	...	...	...	...	...	...
25 - 29	ESDJ	6 799 991	3 404 184	3 395 807	...	...	...	...	...	...
30 - 34	ESDJ	6 016 620	3 001 529	3 015 091	...	...	...	...	...	...
35 - 39	ESDJ	5 245 030	2 619 599	2 625 431	...	...	...	...	...	...
40 - 44	ESDJ	4 485 000	2 245 860	2 239 140	...	...	...	...	...	...
45 - 49	ESDJ	3 748 090	1 877 697	1 870 393	...	...	...	...	...	...
50 - 54	ESDJ	3 046 766	1 523 354	1 523 412	...	...	...	...	...	...
55 - 59	ESDJ	2 412 086	1 194 640	1 217 446	...	...	...	...	...	...
60 - 64	ESDJ	1 836 897	895 575	941 322	...	...	...	...	...	...
65 - 69	ESDJ	1 362 119	650 983	711 136	...	...	...	...	...	...
70 - 74	ESDJ	956 336	443 008	513 328	...	...	...	...	...	...
75 - 79	ESDJ	621 662	274 907	346 755	...	...	...	...	...	...
80+	ESDJ	503 982	209 649	294 333	...	...	...	...	...	...
Qatar										
1 VII 2003										
Total	ESDF	718 766	...	...	...	...	...	...	...	...
0 - 4	ESDF	56 560	...	...	...	...	...	...	...	...
5 - 9	ESDF	54 325	...	...	...	...	...	...	...	...
10 - 14	ESDF	51 042	...	...	...	...	...	...	...	...
15 - 19	ESDF	40 758	...	...	...	...	...	...	...	...
20 - 24	ESDF	57 544	...	...	...	...	...	...	...	...
25 - 29	ESDF	81 199	...	...	...	...	...	...	...	...
30 - 34	ESDF	91 590	...	...	...	...	...	...	...	...
35 - 39	ESDF	82 497	...	...	...	...	...	...	...	...
40 - 44	ESDF	73 301	...	...	...	...	...	...	...	...
45 - 49	ESDF	57 112	...	...	...	...	...	...	...	...
50 - 54	ESDF	36 085	...	...	...	...	...	...	...	...
55 - 59	ESDF	19 200	...	...	...	...	...	...	...	...
60 - 64	ESDF	8 817	...	...	...	...	...	...	...	...
65 - 69	ESDF	4 163	...	...	...	...	...	...	...	...
70+	ESDF	4 573	...	...	...	...	...	...	...	...
Saudi Arabia - Arabie saoudite										
1 VII 2003										
Total	ESDF	22 018 739	12 194 614	9 824 125	...	...	...	...	...	...
0 - 1	ESDF	598 834	312 277	286 557	...	...	...	...	...	...
1 - 4	ESDF	2 544 997	1 310 442	1 234 555	...	...	...	...	...	...

7. Population by age, sex and urban/rural residence: latest available year, 1994 - 2003
Population selon l'âge, le sexe et la résidence, urbaine/rurale: dernière année disponible, 1994 - 2003
(continued — suite)

Continent, country or area, date and age (in years) / Continent, pays ou zone, date et âge (en années)	Code[1]	Total Both sexes Les deux sexes	Total Male Masculin	Total Female Féminin	Urban - Urbaine Both sexes Les deux sexes	Urban - Urbaine Male Masculin	Urban - Urbaine Female Féminin	Rural - Rurale Both sexes Les deux sexes	Rural - Rurale Male Masculin	Rural - Rurale Female Féminin
ASIA — ASIE										
Saudi Arabia - Arabie saoudite										
1 VII 2003										
5 - 9	ESDF	3 072 006	1 578 407	1 493 599	...	...	...	...	...	...
10 - 14	ESDF	2 543 113	1 301 516	1 241 597	...	...	...	...	...	...
15 - 19	ESDF	2 060 806	1 045 332	1 015 474	...	...	...	...	...	...
20 - 24	ESDF	1 796 613	926 156	870 458	...	...	...	...	...	...
25 - 29	ESDF	1 923 745	1 144 587	779 158	...	...	...	...	...	...
30 - 34	ESDF	1 964 383	1 233 803	730 580	...	...	...	...	...	...
35 - 39	ESDF	1 651 661	1 035 949	615 712	...	...	...	...	...	...
40 - 44	ESDF	1 197 816	757 085	440 731	...	...	...	...	...	...
45 - 49	ESDF	805 314	497 511	307 803	...	...	...	...	...	...
50 - 54	ESDF	544 351	320 307	224 045	...	...	...	...	...	...
55 - 59	ESDF	388 801	214 526	174 275	...	...	...	...	...	...
60 - 64	ESDF	276 675	140 390	136 285	...	...	...	...	...	...
65 - 69	ESDF	218 541	130 554	87 987	...	...	...	...	...	...
70 - 74	ESDF	186 878	102 402	84 476	...	...	...	...	...	...
75 - 79	ESDF	100 508	60 862	39 646	...	...	...	...	...	...
80+	ESDF	143 697	82 510	61 187	...	...	...	...	...	...
Singapore - Singapour[30]										
1 VII 2003										
Total	ESDJ	3 437 300	1 710 100	1 727 200	...	...	...	...	...	...
0 - 4	ESDJ	203 800	105 300	98 500	...	...	...	...	...	...
5 - 9	ESDJ	248 100	127 800	120 300	...	...	...	...	...	...
10 - 14	ESDJ	262 200	135 000	127 300	...	...	...	...	...	...
15 - 19	ESDJ	216 300	111 300	105 000	...	...	...	...	...	...
20 - 24	ESDJ	220 200	110 700	109 600	...	...	...	...	...	...
25 - 29	ESDJ	256 300	122 500	133 800	...	...	...	...	...	...
30 - 34	ESDJ	295 900	142 100	153 800	...	...	...	...	...	...
35 - 39	ESDJ	319 400	159 000	160 400	...	...	...	...	...	...
40 - 44	ESDJ	325 600	164 300	161 300	...	...	...	...	...	...
45 - 49	ESDJ	298 000	150 400	147 600	...	...	...	...	...	...
50 - 54	ESDJ	240 100	121 000	119 100	...	...	...	...	...	...
55 - 59	ESDJ	162 300	80 800	81 400	...	...	...	...	...	...
60 - 64	ESDJ	125 500	60 900	64 500	...	...	...	...	...	...
65 - 69	ESDJ	92 900	44 500	48 400	...	...	...	...	...	...
70 - 74	ESDJ	73 400	34 300	39 100	...	...	...	...	...	...
75 - 79	ESDJ	50 100	22 700	27 400	...	...	...	...	...	...
80+	ESDJ	47 100	17 400	29 800	...	...	...	...	...	...
Sri Lanka										
1 VII 1998										
Total	ESDF	18 774 000	9 570 000	9 204 000	...	...	...	...	...	...
0 - 4	ESDF	2 345 000	1 194 000	1 151 000	...	...	...	...	...	...
5 - 9	ESDF	2 128 000	1 082 000	1 046 000	...	...	...	...	...	...
10 - 14	ESDF	2 136 000	1 090 000	1 046 000	...	...	...	...	...	...
15 - 19	ESDF	2 028 000	1 028 000	1 000 000	...	...	...	...	...	...
20 - 24	ESDF	1 931 000	969 000	962 000	...	...	...	...	...	...
25 - 29	ESDF	1 612 000	807 000	805 000	...	...	...	...	...	...
30 - 34	ESDF	1 424 000	721 000	703 000	...	...	...	...	...	...
35 - 39	ESDF	1 060 000	533 000	527 000	...	...	...	...	...	...
40 - 44	ESDF	883 000	455 000	428 000	...	...	...	...	...	...
45 - 49	ESDF	770 000	390 000	380 000	...	...	...	...	...	...
50 - 54	ESDF	682 000	360 000	322 000	...	...	...	...	...	...
55 - 59	ESDF	534 000	281 000	253 000	...	...	...	...	...	...
60 - 64	ESDF	431 000	232 000	199 000	...	...	...	...	...	...
65 - 69	ESDF	318 000	168 000	150 000	...	...	...	...	...	...
70+	ESDF	492 000	260 000	232 000	...	...	...	...	...	...

7. Population by age, sex and urban/rural residence: latest available year, 1994 - 2003
Population selon l'âge, le sexe et la résidence, urbaine/rurale: dernière année disponible, 1994 - 2003
(continued — suite)

Continent, country or area, date and age (in years) / Continent, pays ou zone, date et âge (en années)	Code[1]	Total Both sexes Les deux sexes	Total Male Masculin	Total Female Féminin	Urban - Urbaine Both sexes Les deux sexes	Urban - Urbaine Male Masculin	Urban - Urbaine Female Féminin	Rural - Rurale Both sexes Les deux sexes	Rural - Rurale Male Masculin	Rural - Rurale Female Féminin
ASIA — ASIE										
Syrian Arab Republic - République arabe syrienne[31]										
1 VII 2003										
Total	ESDF	17 550 000	8 979 000	8 571 000	8 806 000	4 541 000	4 265 000	8 744 000	4 438 000	4 306 000
0 - 1	ESDF	403 000	198 000	205 000	198 000	100 000	98 000	205 000	98 000	107 000
1 - 4	ESDF	1 736 000	893 000	843 000	812 000	423 000	389 000	924 000	470 000	454 000
5 - 9	ESDF	2 352 000	1 224 000	1 128 000	1 080 000	564 000	516 000	1 272 000	660 000	612 000
10 - 14	ESDF	2 461 000	1 274 000	1 187 000	1 171 000	605 000	566 000	1 290 000	669 000	621 000
15 - 19	ESDF	2 271 000	1 198 000	1 073 000	1 124 000	591 000	533 000	1 147 000	607 000	540 000
20 - 24	ESDF	1 639 000	859 000	780 000	845 000	451 000	394 000	794 000	408 000	386 000
25 - 29	ESDF	1 235 000	576 000	659 000	631 000	306 000	325 000	604 000	270 000	334 000
30 - 34	ESDF	1 027 000	482 000	545 000	545 000	261 000	284 000	482 000	221 000	261 000
35 - 39	ESDF	1 020 000	492 000	528 000	558 000	266 000	292 000	462 000	226 000	236 000
40 - 44	ESDF	822 000	413 000	409 000	460 000	240 000	220 000	362 000	173 000	189 000
45 - 49	ESDF	633 000	318 000	315 000	354 000	180 000	174 000	279 000	138 000	141 000
50 - 54	ESDF	563 000	282 000	281 000	301 000	153 000	148 000	262 000	129 000	133 000
55 - 59	ESDF	381 000	193 000	188 000	214 000	108 000	106 000	167 000	85 000	82 000
60 - 64	ESDF	372 000	197 000	175 000	197 000	108 000	89 000	175 000	89 000	86 000
65+	ESDF	635 000	380 000	255 000	316 000	185 000	131 000	319 000	195 000	124 000
Thailand - Thaïlande										
1 VII 2002										
Total	ESDJ	63 482 287	31 623 509	31 858 778	20 731 494	10 072 055	10 659 439	42 750 793	21 551 454	21 199 339
1 - 4	ESDJ	5 120 027	2 598 894	2 521 133	1 511 818	759 380	752 438	3 608 209	1 839 514	1 768 695
5 - 9	ESDJ	5 274 505	2 668 992	2 605 513	1 511 013	755 466	755 547	3 763 492	1 913 526	1 849 966
10 - 14	ESDJ	5 385 639	2 724 988	2 660 651	1 602 403	793 632	808 771	3 783 236	1 931 356	1 851 880
15 - 19	ESDJ	5 574 029	2 825 669	2 748 360	1 790 997	880 104	910 893	3 783 032	1 945 565	1 837 467
20 - 24	ESDJ	5 763 091	2 925 567	2 837 524	1 960 757	960 965	999 792	3 802 334	1 964 602	1 837 732
25 - 29	ESDJ	5 716 021	2 909 450	2 806 571	2 023 745	985 662	1 038 083	3 692 276	1 923 788	1 768 488
30 - 34	ESDJ	5 419 519	2 749 748	2 669 771	1 953 228	953 584	999 644	3 466 291	1 796 164	1 670 127
35 - 39	ESDJ	4 998 304	2 495 630	2 502 674	1 770 599	863 412	907 187	3 227 705	1 632 218	1 595 487
40 - 44	ESDJ	4 566 841	2 264 011	2 302 830	1 577 302	768 102	809 200	2 989 539	1 495 909	1 493 630
45 - 49	ESDJ	4 014 693	1 978 140	2 036 553	1 347 651	651 525	696 126	2 667 042	1 326 615	1 340 427
50 - 54	ESDJ	3 171 357	1 548 338	1 623 019	1 036 000	497 272	538 728	2 135 357	1 051 066	1 084 291
55 - 59	ESDJ	2 484 371	1 194 773	1 289 598	783 686	371 332	412 354	1 700 685	823 441	877 244
60 - 64	ESDJ	2 076 583	976 768	1 099 815	652 935	302 531	350 404	1 423 648	674 237	749 411
65 - 69	ESDJ	1 675 416	776 509	898 907	520 678	237 393	283 285	1 154 738	539 116	615 622
70 - 74	ESDJ	1 109 922	504 276	605 646	329 248	144 969	184 279	780 674	359 307	421 367
75+	ESDJ	1 131 969	481 756	650 213	359 434	146 726	212 708	772 535	335 030	437 505
Turkey - Turquie										
1 VII 2003										
Total	ESDF	70 712 716	35 687 971	35 024 745	...	...	...	...	...	...
0 - 1	ESDF	1 177 610	500 798	676 812	...	...	...	...	...	...
1 - 4	ESDF	5 750 978	2 931 240	2 819 738	...	...	...	...	...	...
5 - 9	ESDF	7 020 971	3 572 864	3 448 107	...	...	...	...	...	...
10 - 14	ESDF	6 555 870	3 342 678	3 213 192	...	...	...	...	...	...
15 - 19	ESDF	6 366 781	3 257 885	3 108 896	...	...	...	...	...	...
20 - 24	ESDF	6 770 363	3 461 677	3 308 686	...	...	...	...	...	...
25 - 29	ESDF	6 671 503	3 404 632	3 266 872	...	...	...	...	...	...
30 - 34	ESDF	5 869 335	2 974 812	2 894 523	...	...	...	...	...	...
35 - 39	ESDF	4 945 353	2 488 675	2 456 678	...	...	...	...	...	...
40 - 44	ESDF	4 359 525	2 208 621	2 150 905	...	...	...	...	...	...
45 - 49	ESDF	3 769 066	1 922 159	1 846 908	...	...	...	...	...	...
50 - 54	ESDF	2 990 938	1 510 227	1 480 711	...	...	...	...	...	...
55 - 59	ESDF	2 278 192	1 129 096	1 149 096	...	...	...	...	...	...
60 - 64	ESDF	1 942 541	941 771	1 000 771	...	...	...	...	...	...
65 - 69	ESDF	1 638 853	774 547	864 306	...	...	...	...	...	...
70 - 74	ESDF	1 142 618	519 806	622 812	...	...	...	...	...	...
75+	ESDF	1 462 218	746 484	715 735	...	...	...	...	...	...

7. Population by age, sex and urban/rural residence: latest available year, 1994 - 2003
Population selon l'âge, le sexe et la résidence, urbaine/rurale: dernière année disponible, 1994 - 2003
(continued — suite)

Continent, country or area, date and age (in years) / Continent, pays ou zone, date et âge (en annèes)	Code[1]	Total			Urban - Urbaine			Rural - Rurale		
		Both sexes Les deux sexes	Male Masculin	Female Féminin	Both sexes Les deux sexes	Male Masculin	Female Féminin	Both sexes Les deux sexes	Male Masculin	Female Féminin
ASIA — ASIE										
Turkmenistan - Turkménistan										
10 I 1995										
Total	CDFC	4 483 251	2 225 331	2 257 920	...	...	...	...	...	...
0 - 4	CDFC	674 693	344 429	330 264	...	...	...	...	...	...
5 - 9	CDFC	619 381	315 453	303 928	...	...	...	...	...	...
10 - 14	CDFC	516 995	263 071	253 924	...	...	...	...	...	...
15 - 19	CDFC	455 727	231 593	224 134	...	...	...	...	...	...
20 - 24	CDFC	414 632	204 256	210 376	...	...	...	...	...	...
25 - 29	CDFC	366 538	181 317	185 221	...	...	...	...	...	...
30 - 34	CDFC	351 856	173 927	177 929	...	...	...	...	...	...
35 - 39	CDFC	281 035	138 462	142 577	...	...	...	...	...	...
40 - 44	CDFC	204 313	99 575	104 738	...	...	...	...	...	...
45 - 49	CDFC	126 864	62 244	64 620	...	...	...	...	...	...
50 - 54	CDFC	97 136	48 330	48 806	...	...	...	...	...	...
55 - 59	CDFC	114 232	54 283	59 949	...	...	...	...	...	...
60 - 64	CDFC	91 473	43 379	48 094	...	...	...	...	...	...
65 - 69	CDFC	73 263	32 176	41 087	...	...	...	...	...	...
70 - 74	CDFC	43 818	15 709	28 109	...	...	...	...	...	...
75 - 79	CDFC	22 707	7 301	15 406	...	...	...	...	...	...
80 - 84	CDFC	15 942	5 060	10 882	...	...	...	...	...	...
85 - 89	CDFC	5 813	1 782	4 031	...	...	...	...	...	...
90 - 94	CDFC	2 611	737	1 874	...	...	...	...	...	...
95 - 99	CDFC	639	179	460	...	...	...	...	...	...
100+	CDFC	722	274	448	...	...	...	...	...	...
Unk. - Inc.	CDFC	2 857	1 794	1 063	...	...	...	...	...	...
United Arab Emirates - Émirats arabes unis[32]										
17 XII 1995										
Total	CDFC	2 411 041	1 606 804	804 237	...	...	...	...	...	...
0 - 4	CDFC	213 049	109 524	103 525	...	...	...	...	...	...
5 - 9	CDFC	219 291	112 984	106 307	...	...	...	...	...	...
10 - 14	CDFC	202 054	104 885	97 169	...	...	...	...	...	...
15 - 19	CDFC	158 909	83 438	75 471	...	...	...	...	...	...
20 - 24	CDFC	217 750	139 868	77 882	...	...	...	...	...	...
25 - 29	CDFC	326 513	238 104	88 409	...	...	...	...	...	...
30 - 34	CDFC	309 279	229 066	80 213	...	...	...	...	...	...
35 - 39	CDFC	288 701	219 961	68 740	...	...	...	...	...	...
40 - 44	CDFC	203 229	161 583	41 646	...	...	...	...	...	...
45 - 49	CDFC	132 016	106 166	25 850	...	...	...	...	...	...
50 - 54	CDFC	65 349	51 655	13 694	...	...	...	...	...	...
55 - 59	CDFC	33 390	25 046	8 344	...	...	...	...	...	...
60 - 64	CDFC	15 960	10 407	5 553	...	...	...	...	...	...
65 - 69	CDFC	11 089	6 492	4 597	...	...	...	...	...	...
70 - 74	CDFC	6 831	3 651	3 180	...	...	...	...	...	...
75 - 79	CDFC	3 109	1 649	1 460	...	...	...	...	...	...
80+	CDFC	4 357	2 194	2 163	...	...	...	...	...	...
Unk. - Inc.	CDFC	165	131	34	...	...	...	...	...	...
Uzbekistan - Ouzbékistan										
1 VII 2001										
Total	ESDF	24 964 433	12 442 510	12 521 923	9 256 101	4 573 055	4 683 046	15 708 332	7 869 455	7 838 877
0 - 1	ESDF	513 043	263 408	249 635	158 893	81 393	77 500	354 150	182 015	172 135
1 - 4	ESDF	2 219 863	1 138 212	1 081 651	693 448	355 999	337 449	1 526 415	782 213	744 202
5 - 9	ESDF	3 237 989	1 653 776	1 584 213	1 015 989	519 360	496 629	2 222 000	1 134 416	1 087 584
10 - 14	ESDF	3 203 022	1 627 673	1 575 349	1 049 577	533 870	515 707	2 153 445	1 093 803	1 059 642
15 - 19	ESDF	2 821 926	1 422 296	1 399 630	984 385	497 725	486 660	1 837 541	924 571	912 970
20 - 24	ESDF	2 296 834	1 157 998	1 138 836	841 326	425 348	415 978	1 455 508	732 650	722 858
25 - 29	ESDF	2 030 200	1 023 174	1 007 026	788 176	397 184	390 992	1 242 024	625 990	616 034
30 - 34	ESDF	1 749 557	861 368	888 189	726 099	372 846	353 253	1 023 458	488 522	534 936
35 - 39	ESDF	1 672 397	816 665	855 732	660 932	323 492	337 440	1 011 465	493 173	518 292

7. Population by age, sex and urban/rural residence: latest available year, 1994 - 2003
Population selon l'âge, le sexe et la résidence, urbaine/rurale: dernière année disponible, 1994 - 2003
(continued — suite)

Continent, country or area, date and age (in years) / Continent, pays ou zone, date et âge (en années)	Code[1]	Total			Urban - Urbaine			Rural - Rurale		
		Both sexes Les deux sexes	Male Masculin	Female Féminin	Both sexes Les deux sexes	Male Masculin	Female Féminin	Both sexes Les deux sexes	Male Masculin	Female Féminin
ASIA — ASIE										
Uzbekistan - Ouzbékistan										
1 VII 2001										
40 - 44	ESDF	1 479 057	728 780	750 277	612 755	297 460	315 295	866 302	431 320	434 982
45 - 49	ESDF	1 034 628	506 734	527 894	464 375	223 425	240 950	570 253	283 309	286 944
50 - 54	ESDF	696 648	337 634	359 014	340 008	161 069	178 939	356 640	176 565	180 075
55 - 59	ESDF	394 997	197 700	197 297	185 073	88 314	96 759	209 924	109 386	100 538
60 - 64	ESDF	553 697	265 428	288 269	254 409	115 715	138 694	299 288	149 713	149 575
65 - 69	ESDF	399 550	185 653	213 897	171 869	75 277	96 592	227 681	110 376	117 305
70 - 74	ESDF	325 230	143 466	181 764	146 702	57 100	89 602	178 528	86 366	92 162
75 - 79	ESDF	185 449	67 568	117 881	87 515	27 439	60 076	97 934	40 129	57 805
80 - 84	ESDF	78 794	23 459	55 335	39 138	10 729	28 409	39 656	12 730	26 926
85 - 89	ESDF	41 343	10 761	30 582	20 793	4 904	15 889	20 550	5 857	14 693
90 - 94	ESDF	19 195	6 220	12 975	9 150	2 774	6 376	10 045	3 446	6 599
95 - 99	ESDF	10 114	4 171	5 943	4 954	1 461	3 493	5 160	2 710	2 450
100+	ESDF	900	366	534	535	171	364	365	195	170
Viet Nam										
1 IV 1999										
Total	CDFC	76 323 173	37 469 117	38 854 056	18 076 823	8 825 112	9 251 711	58 246 350	28 644 005	29 602 345
0 - 1	CDFC	1 263 599	647 832	615 767	232 977	120 215	112 762	1 030 622	527 617	503 005
1 - 4	CDFC	5 908 643	3 034 911	2 873 732	1 184 870	611 659	573 211	4 723 773	2 423 252	2 300 521
5 - 9	CDFC	9 033 162	4 634 400	4 398 762	1 746 284	899 731	846 553	7 286 878	3 734 669	3 552 209
10 - 14	CDFC	9 066 562	4 654 315	4 412 247	1 775 015	913 513	861 502	7 291 547	3 740 802	3 550 745
15 - 19	CDFC	8 222 280	4 141 058	4 081 222	1 902 373	944 176	958 197	6 319 907	3 196 882	3 123 025
20 - 24	CDFC	6 925 387	3 430 084	3 495 303	1 787 592	869 997	917 595	5 137 795	2 560 087	2 577 708
25 - 29	CDFC	6 568 174	3 281 300	3 286 874	1 730 659	845 461	885 198	4 837 515	2 435 839	2 401 676
30 - 34	CDFC	6 033 706	3 003 421	3 030 285	1 582 568	776 373	806 195	4 451 138	2 227 048	2 224 090
35 - 39	CDFC	5 586 620	2 726 540	2 860 080	1 547 320	759 866	787 454	4 039 300	1 966 674	2 072 626
40 - 44	CDFC	4 550 060	2 180 363	2 369 697	1 317 660	641 149	676 511	3 232 400	1 539 214	1 693 186
45 - 49	CDFC	3 137 258	1 465 289	1 671 969	872 584	405 712	466 872	2 264 674	1 059 577	1 205 097
50 - 54	CDFC	2 104 316	964 240	1 140 076	571 834	259 517	312 317	1 532 482	704 723	827 759
55 - 59	CDFC	1 787 007	782 143	1 004 864	463 473	209 785	253 688	1 323 534	572 358	751 176
60 - 64	CDFC	1 747 308	759 708	987 600	409 484	179 982	229 502	1 337 824	579 726	758 098
65 - 69	CDFC	1 646 775	725 600	921 175	367 000	164 733	202 267	1 279 775	560 867	718 908
70 - 74	CDFC	1 211 104	500 522	710 582	262 578	111 897	150 681	948 526	388 625	559 901
75 - 79	CDFC	821 749	307 069	514 680	170 797	63 805	106 992	650 952	243 264	407 688
80 - 84	CDFC	418 244	144 203	274 041	89 323	30 036	59 287	328 921	114 167	214 754
85+	CDFC	291 219	86 119	205 100	62 432	17 505	44 927	228 787	68 614	160 173
Yemen - Yémen										
16 XII 1994										
Total	CDFC	14 587 807	7 473 540	7 114 267	3 423 518	1 856 602	1 566 916	11 164 289	5 616 938	5 547 351
0 - 1	CDFC	474 719	245 925	228 794	98 756	50 872	47 884	375 963	195 053	180 910
1 - 4	CDFC	1 920 253	969 884	950 369	372 120	189 919	182 201	1 548 133	779 965	768 168
5 - 9	CDFC	2 735 850	1 404 417	1 331 433	535 411	272 246	263 165	2 200 439	1 132 171	1 068 268
10 - 14	CDFC	2 202 884	1 186 231	1 016 653	492 788	260 979	231 809	1 710 096	925 252	784 844
15 - 19	CDFC	1 486 755	785 127	701 628	401 317	220 977	180 340	1 085 438	564 150	521 288
20 - 24	CDFC	990 006	514 157	475 849	316 136	185 604	130 532	673 870	328 553	345 317
25 - 29	CDFC	914 142	433 650	480 492	257 640	142 812	114 828	656 502	290 838	365 664
30 - 34	CDFC	780 524	370 666	409 858	219 905	123 317	96 588	560 619	247 349	313 270
35 - 39	CDFC	739 189	357 761	381 428	192 980	108 179	84 801	546 209	249 582	296 627
40 - 44	CDFC	534 930	267 057	267 873	134 608	77 669	56 939	400 322	189 388	210 934
45 - 49	CDFC	414 427	212 507	201 920	107 327	62 215	45 112	307 100	150 292	156 808
50 - 54	CDFC	383 799	193 636	190 163	88 698	49 044	39 654	295 101	144 592	150 509
55 - 59	CDFC	207 589	109 372	98 217	50 432	28 990	21 442	157 157	80 382	76 775
60 - 64	CDFC	284 731	149 934	134 797	57 530	31 440	26 090	227 201	118 494	108 707
65 - 69	CDFC	134 878	72 661	62 217	28 131	15 841	12 290	106 747	56 820	49 927
70 - 74	CDFC	171 999	89 830	82 169	30 560	15 868	14 692	141 439	73 962	67 477
75 - 79	CDFC	63 288	34 421	28 867	12 541	6 990	5 551	50 747	27 431	23 316
80 - 84	CDFC	80 755	40 421	40 334	13 648	6 582	7 066	67 107	33 839	33 268
85+	CDFC	66 040	35 095	30 945	12 457	6 596	5 861	53 583	28 499	25 084
Unk. - Inc.	CDFC	1 049	788	261	533	462	71	516	326	190

7. Population by age, sex and urban/rural residence: latest available year, 1994 - 2003
Population selon l'âge, le sexe et la résidence, urbaine/rurale: dernière année disponible, 1994 - 2003
(continued — suite)

Continent, country or area, date and age (in years) Continent, pays ou zone, date et âge (en années)	Code[1]	Total			Urban - Urbaine			Rural - Rurale		
		Both sexes Les deux sexes	Male Masculin	Female Féminin	Both sexes Les deux sexes	Male Masculin	Female Féminin	Both sexes Les deux sexes	Male Masculin	Female Féminin
ASIA — ASIE										
Yemen - Yémen										
1 VII 1997										
Total	ESDF	16 484 000	8 227 000	8 257 000	...	...	...	...	...	...
0 - 1	ESDF	712 000	363 000	349 000	...	...	...	...	...	...
1 - 4	ESDF	2 446 000	1 247 000	1 199 000	...	...	...	...	...	...
5 - 9	ESDF	2 384 000	1 213 000	1 171 000	...	...	...	...	...	...
10 - 14	ESDF	2 203 000	1 129 000	1 074 000	...	...	...	...	...	...
15 - 19	ESDF	2 024 000	1 047 000	977 000	...	...	...	...	...	...
20 - 24	ESDF	1 426 000	717 000	709 000	...	...	...	...	...	...
25 - 29	ESDF	957 000	456 000	501 000	...	...	...	...	...	...
30 - 34	ESDF	878 000	405 000	473 000	...	...	...	...	...	...
35 - 39	ESDF	821 000	377 000	444 000	...	...	...	...	...	...
40 - 44	ESDF	645 000	302 000	343 000	...	...	...	...	...	...
45 - 49	ESDF	495 000	240 000	255 000	...	...	...	...	...	...
50 - 54	ESDF	385 000	188 000	197 000	...	...	...	...	...	...
55 - 59	ESDF	297 000	146 000	151 000	...	...	...	...	...	...
60 - 64	ESDF	238 000	113 000	125 000	...	...	...	...	...	...
65 - 69	ESDF	198 000	99 000	99 000	...	...	...	...	...	...
70 - 74	ESDF	149 000	74 000	75 000	...	...	...	...	...	...
75+	ESDF	226 000	111 000	115 000	...	...	...	...	...	...
EUROPE										
Andorra - Andorre										
31 XII 1994										
Total	ESDF	64 311	34 083	30 228	...	...	...	...	...	...
0 - 4	ESDF	3 314	1 725	1 589	...	...	...	...	...	...
5 - 9	ESDF	3 243	1 697	1 546	...	...	...	...	...	...
10 - 14	ESDF	3 513	1 795	1 718	...	...	...	...	...	...
15 - 19	ESDF	3 943	2 074	1 869	...	...	...	...	...	...
20 - 24	ESDF	5 312	2 726	2 586	...	...	...	...	...	...
25 - 29	ESDF	7 000	3 608	3 392	...	...	...	...	...	...
30 - 34	ESDF	7 131	3 822	3 309	...	...	...	...	...	...
35 - 39	ESDF	6 160	3 394	2 766	...	...	...	...	...	...
40 - 44	ESDF	5 058	2 840	2 218	...	...	...	...	...	...
45 - 49	ESDF	4 296	2 389	1 907	...	...	...	...	...	...
50 - 54	ESDF	3 441	1 845	1 596	...	...	...	...	...	...
55 - 59	ESDF	2 659	1 417	1 242	...	...	...	...	...	...
60 - 64	ESDF	2 589	1 375	1 214	...	...	...	...	...	...
65 - 69	ESDF	2 267	1 181	1 086	...	...	...	...	...	...
70 - 74	ESDF	1 816	911	905	...	...	...	...	...	...
75 - 79	ESDF	1 095	565	530	...	...	...	...	...	...
80 - 84	ESDF	815	423	392	...	...	...	...	...	...
85+	ESDF	659	296	363	...	...	...	...	...	...
Austria - Autriche										
1 VII 2003										
Total	ESDJ	8 117 754	3 938 582	4 179 172	...	...	...	...	...	...
0 - 1	ESDJ	77 504	39 804	37 700	...	...	...	...	...	...
1 - 4	ESDJ	319 223	164 006	155 217	...	...	...	...	...	...
5 - 9	ESDJ	451 151	230 800	220 351	...	...	...	...	...	...
10 - 14	ESDJ	485 627	249 236	236 391	...	...	...	...	...	...
15 - 19	ESDJ	481 293	246 664	234 629	...	...	...	...	...	...
20 - 24	ESDJ	503 338	255 190	248 148	...	...	...	...	...	...
25 - 29	ESDJ	511 109	256 095	255 014	...	...	...	...	...	...
30 - 34	ESDJ	625 096	312 600	312 496	...	...	...	...	...	...
35 - 39	ESDJ	707 678	359 079	348 599	...	...	...	...	...	...
40 - 44	ESDJ	669 485	339 681	329 804	...	...	...	...	...	...
45 - 49	ESDJ	564 636	282 065	282 571	...	...	...	...	...	...
50 - 54	ESDJ	501 705	248 953	252 752	...	...	...	...	...	...
55 - 59	ESDJ	459 769	225 086	234 683	...	...	...	...	...	...
60 - 64	ESDJ	503 143	242 156	260 987	...	...	...	...	...	...
65 - 69	ESDJ	326 708	151 586	175 122	...	...	...	...	...	...

7. Population by age, sex and urban/rural residence: latest available year, 1994 - 2003
Population selon l'âge, le sexe et la résidence, urbaine/rurale: dernière année disponible, 1994 - 2003
(continued — suite)

Continent, country or area, date and age (in years) / Continent, pays ou zone, date et âge (en années)	Code[1]	Total			Urban - Urbaine			Rural - Rurale		
		Both sexes Les deux sexes	Male Masculin	Female Féminin	Both sexes Les deux sexes	Male Masculin	Female Féminin	Both sexes Les deux sexes	Male Masculin	Female Féminin
EUROPE										
Austria - Autriche										
1 VII 2003										
70 - 74	ESDJ	321 271	140 701	180 570	...	...	...	...	...	...
75 - 79	ESDJ	282 639	103 215	179 424	...	...	...	...	...	...
80 - 84	ESDJ	199 317	59 968	139 349	...	...	...	...	...	...
85 - 89	ESDJ	77 450	20 519	56 931	...	...	...	...	...	...
90 - 94	ESDJ	41 581	9 693	31 888	...	...	...	...	...	...
95+	ESDJ	8 031	1 485	6 546	...	...	...	...	...	...
Belarus - Bélarus										
1 VII 2003										
Total	ESDF	9 873 826	4 623 963	5 249 863	7 040 950	3 297 535	3 743 415	2 832 876	1 326 428	1 506 448
0 - 1	ESDF	88 100	45 321	42 779	64 734	33 303	31 431	23 366	12 018	11 348
1 - 4	ESDF	365 035	187 952	177 083	265 436	136 674	128 762	99 599	51 278	48 321
5 - 9	ESDF	491 114	252 217	238 897	340 763	175 269	165 494	150 351	76 948	73 403
10 - 14	ESDF	688 545	353 026	335 519	488 761	250 748	238 013	199 784	102 278	97 506
15 - 19	ESDF	837 038	427 302	409 736	641 015	323 128	317 887	196 023	104 174	91 849
20 - 24	ESDF	776 205	396 911	379 294	629 847	319 314	310 533	146 358	77 597	68 761
25 - 29	ESDF	701 259	352 780	348 479	546 238	271 963	274 275	155 021	80 817	74 204
30 - 34	ESDF	683 660	339 178	344 482	514 045	249 992	264 053	169 615	89 186	80 429
35 - 39	ESDF	711 794	350 349	361 445	529 625	252 382	277 243	182 169	97 967	84 202
40 - 44	ESDF	837 510	408 883	428 627	630 346	295 701	334 645	207 164	113 182	93 982
45 - 49	ESDF	765 346	365 457	399 889	581 579	267 117	314 462	183 767	98 340	85 427
50 - 54	ESDF	649 534	302 953	346 581	494 253	222 906	271 347	155 281	80 047	75 234
55 - 59	ESDF	417 710	188 064	229 646	302 067	134 822	167 245	115 643	53 242	62 401
60 - 64	ESDF	463 055	191 826	271 229	295 845	123 590	172 255	167 210	68 236	98 974
65 - 69	ESDF	474 471	182 880	291 591	266 329	103 324	163 005	208 142	79 556	128 586
70 - 74	ESDF	416 898	146 929	269 969	202 096	70 298	131 798	214 802	76 631	138 171
75 - 79	ESDF	300 411	86 027	214 384	148 496	44 179	104 317	151 915	41 848	110 067
80 - 84	ESDF	131 518	31 445	100 073	63 050	15 435	47 615	68 468	16 010	52 458
85 - 89	ESDF	48 850	9 907	38 943	23 884	5 121	18 763	24 966	4 786	20 180
90 - 94	ESDF	21 505	3 878	17 627	10 173	1 879	8 294	11 332	1 999	9 333
95 - 99	ESDF	3 741	594	3 147	2 020	316	1 704	1 721	278	1 443
100+	ESDF	527	84	443	348	74	274	179	10	169
Belgium - Belgique										
1 VII 2003										
Total	ESDJ	10 376 133	5 077 031	5 299 102	...	...	...	...	...	...
0 - 1	ESDJ	111 810	57 220	54 590	...	...	...	...	...	...
1 - 4	ESDJ	460 206	234 974	225 232	...	...	...	...	...	...
5 - 9	ESDJ	592 465	302 841	289 624	...	...	...	...	...	...
10 - 14	ESDJ	635 589	324 997	310 593	...	...	...	...	...	...
15 - 19	ESDJ	607 843	310 445	297 399	...	...	...	...	...	...
20 - 24	ESDJ	645 389	325 981	319 408	...	...	...	...	...	...
25 - 29	ESDJ	653 420	329 585	323 835	...	...	...	...	...	...
30 - 34	ESDJ	736 368	372 610	363 758	...	...	...	...	...	...
35 - 39	ESDJ	795 338	403 652	391 686	...	...	...	...	...	...
40 - 44	ESDJ	805 021	406 541	398 481	...	...	...	...	...	...
45 - 49	ESDJ	753 137	378 928	374 209	...	...	...	...	...	...
50 - 54	ESDJ	693 661	349 019	344 642	...	...	...	...	...	...
55 - 59	ESDJ	625 644	311 710	313 934	...	...	...	...	...	...
60 - 64	ESDJ	488 991	237 665	251 326	...	...	...	...	...	...
65 - 69	ESDJ	493 307	232 080	261 227	...	...	...	...	...	...
70 - 74	ESDJ	473 407	209 764	263 643	...	...	...	...	...	...
75 - 79	ESDJ	384 174	155 573	228 601	...	...	...	...	...	...
80 - 84	ESDJ	254 716	90 710	164 007	...	...	...	...	...	...
85 - 89	ESDJ	103 266	29 630	73 637	...	...	...	...	...	...
90 - 94	ESDJ	50 443	11 249	39 195	...	...	...	...	...	...
95 - 99	ESDJ	10 784	1 731	9 054	...	...	...	...	...	...
100+	ESDJ	1 159	131	1 028	...	...	...	...	...	...
Bulgaria - Bulgarie										
1 VII 2003										
Total	ESDF	7 823 557	3 803 501	4 020 056	5 459 344	2 636 908	2 822 436	2 364 214	1 166 593	1 197 621
0 - 1	ESDF	65 103	33 603	31 500	46 862	24 237	22 625	18 242	9 367	8 875

7. Population by age, sex and urban/rural residence: latest available year, 1994 - 2003
Population selon l'âge, le sexe et la résidence, urbaine/rurale: dernière année disponible, 1994 - 2003
(continued — suite)

Continent, country or area, date and age (in years) / Continent, pays ou zone, date et âge (en années)	Code[1]	Total Both sexes Les deux sexes	Total Male Masculin	Total Female Féminin	Urban - Urbaine Both sexes Les deux sexes	Urban - Urbaine Male Masculin	Urban - Urbaine Female Féminin	Rural - Rurale Both sexes Les deux sexes	Rural - Rurale Male Masculin	Rural - Rurale Female Féminin
EUROPE										
Bulgaria - Bulgarie										
1 VII 2003										
1 - 4	ESDF	265 287	136 270	129 017	187 135	96 119	91 016	78 152	40 151	38 001
5 - 9	ESDF	334 871	171 757	163 114	231 619	118 812	112 807	103 252	52 946	50 307
10 - 14	ESDF	459 339	235 913	223 426	325 601	166 593	159 008	133 738	69 320	64 418
15 - 19	ESDF	527 378	270 345	257 033	398 960	203 540	195 420	128 419	66 806	61 613
20 - 24	ESDF	555 512	285 340	270 172	425 415	214 990	210 425	130 097	70 350	59 747
25 - 29	ESDF	588 760	300 669	288 091	451 004	228 183	222 821	137 756	72 486	65 270
30 - 34	ESDF	556 793	283 284	273 509	417 741	209 012	208 729	139 052	74 273	64 780
35 - 39	ESDF	511 587	257 968	253 619	380 954	187 919	193 035	130 633	70 050	60 584
40 - 44	ESDF	538 751	269 397	269 354	403 318	196 470	206 848	135 433	72 928	62 506
45 - 49	ESDF	556 549	274 321	282 229	415 646	199 941	215 705	140 000	71 380	66 524
50 - 54	ESDF	574 816	278 608	296 209	419 578	200 150	219 428	155 238	78 458	76 781
55 - 59	ESDF	521 061	247 078	273 983	356 395	168 344	188 051	164 666	78 735	85 932
60 - 64	ESDF	432 738	198 887	233 852	263 067	121 183	141 884	169 672	77 704	91 968
65 - 69	ESDF	430 783	191 820	238 963	243 353	105 975	137 379	187 430	85 846	101 585
70 - 74	ESDF	385 906	165 878	220 028	213 620	89 017	124 603	172 286	76 861	95 425
75 - 79	ESDF	295 979	119 628	176 351	160 779	63 664	97 116	135 200	55 965	79 236
80 - 84	ESDF	160 057	60 598	99 459	85 293	31 379	53 914	74 764	29 219	45 546
85 - 89	ESDF	43 915	16 071	27 844	23 322	8 213	15 110	20 593	7 858	12 735
90 - 94	ESDF	16 006	5 337	10 669	8 454	2 779	5 676	7 552	2 558	4 994
95 - 99	ESDF	2 163	676	1 488	1 127	365	762	1 037	311	726
100+	ESDF	208	57	151	106	29	77	103	28	75
Channel Islands: Guernsey - Îles Anglo-Normandes: Guernesey										
31 III 1996										
Total	CDFC	58 681	28 244	30 437	...	...	...	...	...	...
0 - 1	CDFC	599	300	299	...	...	...	...	...	...
1 - 4	CDFC	2 781	1 436	1 345	...	...	...	...	...	...
5 - 9	CDFC	3 624	1 813	1 811	...	...	...	...	...	...
10 - 14	CDFC	3 339	1 727	1 612	...	...	...	...	...	...
15 - 19	CDFC	3 351	1 682	1 669	...	...	...	...	...	...
20 - 24	CDFC	4 075	1 935	2 140	...	...	...	...	...	...
25 - 29	CDFC	4 659	2 202	2 457	...	...	...	...	...	...
30 - 34	CDFC	4 691	2 301	2 390	...	...	...	...	...	...
35 - 39	CDFC	4 342	2 125	2 217	...	...	...	...	...	...
40 - 44	CDFC	4 044	2 057	1 987	...	...	...	...	...	...
45 - 49	CDFC	4 610	2 282	2 328	...	...	...	...	...	...
50 - 54	CDFC	3 309	1 669	1 640	...	...	...	...	...	...
55 - 59	CDFC	3 250	1 642	1 608	...	...	...	...	...	...
60 - 64	CDFC	2 798	1 360	1 438	...	...	...	...	...	...
65 - 69	CDFC	2 621	1 210	1 411	...	...	...	...	...	...
70 - 74	CDFC	2 329	1 031	1 298	...	...	...	...	...	...
75 - 79	CDFC	1 810	727	1 083	...	...	...	...	...	...
80 - 84	CDFC	1 349	468	881	...	...	...	...	...	...
85 - 89	CDFC	709	194	515	...	...	...	...	...	...
90 - 94	CDFC	316	74	242	...	...	...	...	...	...
95 - 99	CDFC	66	9	57	...	...	...	...	...	...
100+	CDFC	9	-	9	...	...	...	...	...	...
Channel Islands: Jersey - Îles Anglo-Normandes: Jersey										
10 III 1996										
Total	CDFC	85 150	41 394	43 756	...	...	...	...	...	...
0 - 1	CDFC	951	505	446	...	...	...	...	...	...
1 - 4	CDFC	3 942	2 037	1 905	...	...	...	...	...	...
5 - 9	CDFC	4 868	2 486	2 382	...	...	...	...	...	...
10 - 14	CDFC	4 356	2 231	2 125	...	...	...	...	...	...
15 - 19	CDFC	4 278	2 134	2 144	...	...	...	...	...	...

7. Population by age, sex and urban/rural residence: latest available year, 1994 - 2003
Population selon l'âge, le sexe et la résidence, urbaine/rurale: dernière année disponible, 1994 - 2003
(continued — suite)

Continent, country or area, date and age (in years) Continent, pays ou zone, date et âge (en années)	Code[1]	Total			Urban - Urbaine			Rural - Rurale		
		Both sexes Les deux sexes	Male Masculin	Female Féminin	Both sexes Les deux sexes	Male Masculin	Female Féminin	Both sexes Les deux sexes	Male Masculin	Female Féminin
EUROPE										
Channel Islands: Jersey - Îles Anglo-Normandes: Jersey										
10 III 1996										
20 - 24	CDFC	5 637	2 706	2 931	...	...	...	...	...	...
25 - 29	CDFC	7 821	3 806	4 015	...	...	...	...	...	...
30 - 34	CDFC	8 074	3 961	4 113	...	...	...	...	...	...
35 - 39	CDFC	7 109	3 527	3 582	...	...	...	...	...	...
40 - 44	CDFC	6 269	3 103	3 166	...	...	...	...	...	...
45 - 49	CDFC	6 374	3 195	3 179	...	...	...	...	...	...
50 - 54	CDFC	4 876	2 419	2 457	...	...	...	...	...	...
55 - 59	CDFC	4 654	2 377	2 277	...	...	...	...	...	...
60 - 64	CDFC	3 981	2 003	1 978	...	...	...	...	...	...
65 - 69	CDFC	3 441	1 635	1 806	...	...	...	...	...	...
70 - 74	CDFC	2 994	1 360	1 634	...	...	...	...	...	...
75 - 79	CDFC	2 209	850	1 359	...	...	...	...	...	...
80 - 84	CDFC	1 833	654	1 179	...	...	...	...	...	...
85 - 89	CDFC	1 026	301	725	...	...	...	...	...	...
90 - 94	CDFC	378	85	293	...	...	...	...	...	...
95 - 99	CDFC	73	17	56	...	...	...	...	...	...
100+	CDFC	6	2	4	...	...	...	...	...	...
Croatia - Croatie										
1 VII 2003										
Total	ESDJ	4 441 800	2 137 600	2 304 100	...	...	...	...	...	...
0 - 1	ESDJ	39 700	20 400	19 300	...	...	...	...	...	...
1 - 4	ESDJ	176 500	90 400	86 000	...	...	...	...	...	...
5 - 9	ESDJ	252 600	129 200	123 400	...	...	...	...	...	...
10 - 14	ESDJ	260 500	133 300	127 200	...	...	...	...	...	...
15 - 19	ESDJ	289 100	147 500	141 600	...	...	...	...	...	...
20 - 24	ESDJ	310 500	158 500	152 000	...	...	...	...	...	...
25 - 29	ESDJ	301 100	152 300	148 800	...	...	...	...	...	...
30 - 34	ESDJ	292 000	146 600	145 300	...	...	...	...	...	...
35 - 39	ESDJ	314 200	156 800	157 300	...	...	...	...	...	...
40 - 44	ESDJ	328 900	163 800	165 100	...	...	...	...	...	...
45 - 49	ESDJ	340 200	170 200	170 000	...	...	...	...	...	...
50 - 54	ESDJ	315 800	157 100	158 600	...	...	...	...	...	...
55 - 59	ESDJ	241 400	115 300	126 200	...	...	...	...	...	...
60 - 64	ESDJ	251 100	115 600	135 500	...	...	...	...	...	...
65 - 69	ESDJ	251 400	110 600	140 800	...	...	...	...	...	...
70 - 74	ESDJ	216 500	88 100	128 500	...	...	...	...	...	...
75 - 79	ESDJ	145 200	49 700	95 600	...	...	...	...	...	...
80 - 84	ESDJ	80 200	23 100	57 100	...	...	...	...	...	...
85+	ESDJ	34 900	9 200	25 700	...	...	...	...	...	...
Czech Republic - République tchèque										
31 XII 2003										
Total	ESDJ	10 211 455	4 974 740	5 236 715	7 535 093	3 642 897	3 892 196	2 676 362	1 331 843	1 344 519
0 - 1	ESDJ	93 692	48 099	45 593	69 004	35 485	33 519	24 688	12 614	12 074
1 - 4	ESDJ	361 971	186 180	175 791	263 001	135 243	127 758	98 970	50 937	48 033
5 - 9	ESDJ	471 435	241 968	229 467	336 880	172 562	164 318	134 555	69 406	65 149
10 - 14	ESDJ	627 377	321 600	305 777	455 361	233 067	222 294	172 016	88 533	83 483
15 - 19	ESDJ	664 041	339 746	324 295	488 087	249 702	238 385	175 954	90 044	85 910
20 - 24	ESDJ	740 059	378 523	361 536	544 170	277 378	266 792	195 889	101 145	94 744
25 - 29	ESDJ	908 216	462 235	445 981	674 117	340 856	333 261	234 099	121 379	112 720
30 - 34	ESDJ	768 638	392 656	375 982	569 233	287 921	281 312	199 405	104 735	94 670
35 - 39	ESDJ	691 477	352 534	338 943	516 218	259 971	256 247	175 259	92 563	82 696
40 - 44	ESDJ	644 474	326 823	317 651	478 579	240 082	238 497	165 895	86 741	79 154
45 - 49	ESDJ	736 388	368 086	368 302	544 875	268 212	276 663	191 513	99 874	91 639
50 - 54	ESDJ	786 882	387 933	398 949	583 886	283 636	300 250	202 996	104 297	98 699
55 - 59	ESDJ	745 580	360 330	385 250	557 813	265 261	292 552	187 767	95 069	92 698
60 - 64	ESDJ	548 033	256 226	291 807	411 005	190 596	220 409	137 028	65 630	71 398

7. Population by age, sex and urban/rural residence: latest available year, 1994 - 2003
Population selon l'âge, le sexe et la résidence, urbaine/rurale: dernière année disponible, 1994 - 2003
(continued — suite)

Continent, country or area, date and age (in years) / Continent, pays ou zone, date et âge (en années)	Code[1]	Total			Urban - Urbaine			Rural - Rurale		
		Both sexes Les deux sexes	Male Masculin	Female Féminin	Both sexes Les deux sexes	Male Masculin	Female Féminin	Both sexes Les deux sexes	Male Masculin	Female Féminin
EUROPE										
Czech Republic - République tchèque										
31 XII 2003										
65 - 69	ESDJ	411 542	182 049	229 493	302 964	133 344	169 620	108 578	48 705	59 873
70 - 74	ESDJ	398 828	164 503	234 325	291 680	119 869	171 811	107 148	44 634	62 514
75 - 79	ESDJ	320 069	116 713	203 356	234 050	85 414	148 636	86 019	31 299	54 720
80 - 84	ESDJ	202 563	64 889	137 674	148 568	47 395	101 173	53 995	17 494	36 501
85 - 89	ESDJ	56 281	15 701	40 580	41 122	11 318	29 804	15 159	4 383	10 776
90 - 94	ESDJ	29 538	7 082	22 456	21 366	4 996	16 370	8 172	2 086	6 086
95 - 99	ESDJ	4 093	819	3 274	2 910	561	2 349	1 183	258	925
100+	ESDJ	278	45	233	204	28	176	74	17	57
Denmark - Danemark[33]										
1 VII 2003										
Total	ESDJ	5 390 574	2 666 279	2 724 295	...	...	...	...	...	...
0 - 1	ESDJ	64 612	33 171	31 442	...	...	...	...	...	...
1 - 4	ESDJ	266 605	136 366	130 239	...	...	...	...	...	...
5 - 9	ESDJ	349 811	179 471	170 341	...	...	...	...	...	...
10 - 14	ESDJ	334 285	171 651	162 634	...	...	...	...	...	...
15 - 19	ESDJ	290 930	149 058	141 872	...	...	...	...	...	...
20 - 24	ESDJ	303 425	153 152	150 274	...	...	...	...	...	...
25 - 29	ESDJ	361 132	181 706	179 426	...	...	...	...	...	...
30 - 34	ESDJ	385 268	195 187	190 081	...	...	...	...	...	...
35 - 39	ESDJ	427 392	217 966	209 426	...	...	...	...	...	...
40 - 44	ESDJ	386 836	196 424	190 412	...	...	...	...	...	...
45 - 49	ESDJ	369 340	186 882	182 458	...	...	...	...	...	...
50 - 54	ESDJ	363 500	182 757	180 743	...	...	...	...	...	...
55 - 59	ESDJ	393 319	197 954	195 365	...	...	...	...	...	...
60 - 64	ESDJ	292 658	145 004	147 654	...	...	...	...	...	...
65 - 69	ESDJ	232 304	111 362	120 942	...	...	...	...	...	...
70 - 74	ESDJ	190 472	87 116	103 356	...	...	...	...	...	...
75 - 79	ESDJ	161 012	68 180	92 833	...	...	...	...	...	...
80 - 84	ESDJ	118 550	44 061	74 490	...	...	...	...	...	...
85 - 89	ESDJ	65 479	20 657	44 822	...	...	...	...	...	...
90 - 94	ESDJ	27 320	6 960	20 360	...	...	...	...	...	...
95 - 99	ESDJ	5 745	1 113	4 633	...	...	...	...	...	...
100+	ESDJ	584	88	496	...	...	...	...	...	...
Estonia - Estonie										
1 VII 2002										
Total	ESDF	1 358 644	626 276	732 368	940 465	423 224	517 241	418 179	203 052	215 127
0 - 1	ESDF	12 740	6 531	6 209	8 700	4 464	4 236	4 040	2 067	1 973
1 - 4	ESDF	49 024	25 341	23 683	32 847	16 984	15 863	16 177	8 357	7 820
5 - 9	ESDF	67 433	34 582	32 851	42 625	21 856	20 769	24 808	12 726	12 082
10 - 14	ESDF	100 098	51 355	48 743	64 339	32 967	31 372	35 759	18 388	17 371
15 - 19	ESDF	106 045	54 022	52 023	70 844	35 982	34 862	35 201	18 040	17 161
20 - 24	ESDF	97 446	49 730	47 716	72 257	35 536	36 721	25 189	14 194	10 995
25 - 29	ESDF	93 195	46 842	46 353	69 576	34 073	35 503	23 619	12 769	10 850
30 - 34	ESDF	92 972	45 936	47 036	65 889	31 993	33 896	27 083	13 943	13 140
35 - 39	ESDF	90 041	43 734	46 307	62 312	29 497	32 815	27 729	14 237	13 492
40 - 44	ESDF	99 233	47 302	51 931	69 162	31 678	37 484	30 071	15 624	14 447
45 - 49	ESDF	95 617	44 596	51 021	67 841	30 306	37 535	27 776	14 290	13 486
50 - 54	ESDF	90 783	41 319	49 464	64 454	28 106	36 348	26 329	13 213	13 116
55 - 59	ESDF	69 084	30 437	38 647	46 838	19 678	27 160	22 246	10 759	11 487
60 - 64	ESDF	81 637	34 123	47 514	56 712	22 714	33 998	24 925	11 409	13 516
65 - 69	ESDF	68 807	26 962	41 845	47 128	17 845	29 283	21 679	9 117	12 562
70 - 74	ESDF	62 624	22 332	40 292	43 899	15 373	28 526	18 725	6 959	11 766
75 - 79	ESDF	43 777	12 267	31 510	30 214	8 350	21 864	13 563	3 917	9 646
80 - 84	ESDF	21 370	5 214	16 156	14 132	3 498	10 634	7 238	1 716	5 522
85 - 89	ESDF	10 885	2 397	8 488	6 990	1 529	5 461	3 895	868	3 027
90 - 94	ESDF	4 514	852	3 662	2 798	495	2 303	1 716	357	1 359
95 - 99	ESDF	804	125	679	498	74	424	306	51	255
100+	ESDF	74	12	62	43	8	35	31	4	27

7. Population by age, sex and urban/rural residence: latest available year, 1994 - 2003
Population selon l'âge, le sexe et la résidence, urbaine/rurale: dernière année disponible, 1994 - 2003
(continued — suite)

Continent, country or area, date and age (in years) / Continent, pays ou zone, date et âge (en années)	Code[1]	Total			Urban - Urbaine			Rural - Rurale		
		Both sexes Les deux sexes	Male Masculin	Female Féminin	Both sexes Les deux sexes	Male Masculin	Female Féminin	Both sexes Les deux sexes	Male Masculin	Female Féminin
EUROPE										
Estonia - Estonie										
1 VII 2002										
Unk. - Inc.	ESDF	441	265	176	367	218	149	74	47	27
Finland - Finlande										
1 VII 2003										
Total	ESDJ	5 213 014	2 548 905	2 664 109	3 234 178	1 552 734	1 681 445	1 978 836	996 171	982 665
0 - 1	ESDJ	55 918	28 611	27 308	36 299	18 611	17 689	19 619	10 000	9 619
1 - 4	ESDJ	227 248	116 344	110 905	141 150	72 166	68 984	86 099	44 178	41 921
5 - 9	ESDJ	310 589	158 241	152 348	185 848	94 582	91 267	124 741	63 660	61 082
10 - 14	ESDJ	329 798	168 310	161 488	191 420	97 425	93 996	138 378	70 886	67 493
15 - 19	ESDJ	321 442	164 258	157 184	191 050	95 048	96 002	130 393	69 210	61 183
20 - 24	ESDJ	329 067	168 202	160 865	240 080	117 767	122 313	88 987	50 435	38 552
25 - 29	ESDJ	323 729	165 739	157 990	238 883	121 194	117 689	84 846	44 545	40 301
30 - 34	ESDJ	315 124	161 009	154 115	214 697	109 736	104 961	100 427	51 273	49 154
35 - 39	ESDJ	370 443	188 556	181 887	239 072	120 572	118 501	131 371	67 984	63 387
40 - 44	ESDJ	378 160	191 884	186 276	233 235	116 524	116 711	144 925	75 360	69 565
45 - 49	ESDJ	390 045	196 594	193 451	235 619	115 279	120 341	154 426	81 316	73 110
50 - 54	ESDJ	409 419	206 408	203 012	246 794	119 664	127 130	162 626	86 744	75 882
55 - 59	ESDJ	377 200	188 060	189 141	231 529	111 673	119 856	145 672	76 387	69 285
60 - 64	ESDJ	268 955	129 913	139 042	159 417	74 348	85 070	109 538	55 565	53 973
65 - 69	ESDJ	232 381	107 928	124 453	131 702	58 710	72 992	100 679	49 218	51 461
70 - 74	ESDJ	210 446	90 534	119 912	117 505	48 039	69 466	92 941	42 495	50 446
75 - 79	ESDJ	171 128	64 913	106 215	93 890	33 636	60 254	77 239	31 278	45 961
80 - 84	ESDJ	110 124	33 775	76 349	60 384	17 603	42 782	49 740	16 173	33 567
85 - 89	ESDJ	56 415	14 314	42 101	31 444	7 439	24 005	24 971	6 875	18 097
90 - 94	ESDJ	21 282	4 619	16 663	11 856	2 364	9 492	9 426	2 255	7 171
95+	ESDJ	4 106	697	3 410	2 309	359	1 950	1 798	338	1 460
France[34]										
1 VII 2003										
Total	ESDJ	59 767 830	29 044 220	30 723 611	...	...	...	...	...	...
0 - 1	ESDJ	757 273	387 214	370 059	...	...	...	...	...	...
1 - 4	ESDJ	3 010 841	1 540 325	1 470 516	...	...	...	...	...	...
5 - 9	ESDJ	3 587 457	1 837 315	1 750 142	...	...	...	...	...	...
10 - 14	ESDJ	3 766 679	1 928 319	1 838 360	...	...	...	...	...	...
15 - 19	ESDJ	3 870 787	1 974 435	1 896 352	...	...	...	...	...	...
20 - 24	ESDJ	3 904 719	1 975 803	1 928 916	...	...	...	...	...	...
25 - 29	ESDJ	3 764 245	1 890 675	1 873 570	...	...	...	...	...	...
30 - 34	ESDJ	4 272 714	2 137 028	2 135 687	...	...	...	...	...	...
35 - 39	ESDJ	4 326 884	2 147 908	2 178 976	...	...	...	...	...	...
40 - 44	ESDJ	4 282 316	2 112 034	2 170 282	...	...	...	...	...	...
45 - 49	ESDJ	4 175 262	2 052 284	2 122 978	...	...	...	...	...	...
50 - 54	ESDJ	4 176 891	2 065 968	2 110 923	...	...	...	...	...	...
55 - 59	ESDJ	3 506 388	1 736 986	1 769 402	...	...	...	...	...	...
60 - 64	ESDJ	2 598 248	1 265 399	1 332 849	...	...	...	...	...	...
65 - 69	ESDJ	2 596 101	1 208 902	1 387 199	...	...	...	...	...	...
70 - 74	ESDJ	2 498 238	1 095 215	1 403 023	...	...	...	...	...	...
75 - 79	ESDJ	2 102 181	848 676	1 253 506	...	...	...	...	...	...
80 - 84	ESDJ	1 480 338	541 710	938 628	...	...	...	...	...	...
85 - 89	ESDJ	608 763	184 843	423 920	...	...	...	...	...	...
90 - 94	ESDJ	377 502	93 475	284 027	...	...	...	...	...	...
95 - 99	ESDJ	90 386	17 211	73 175	...	...	...	...	...	...
100+	ESDJ	13 623	2 499	11 124	...	...	...	...	...	...
Germany - Allemagne										
1 VII 2003										
Total	ESDJ	82 534 176	40 350 447	42 183 729	...	...	...	...	...	...
0 - 1	ESDJ	712 850	365 855	346 995	...	...	...	...	...	...
1 - 4	ESDJ	3 051 571	1 565 890	1 485 681	...	...	...	...	...	...
5 - 9	ESDJ	3 995 013	2 050 191	1 944 822	...	...	...	...	...	...
10 - 14	ESDJ	4 529 412	2 323 149	2 206 263	...	...	...	...	...	...
15 - 19	ESDJ	4 707 821	2 415 686	2 292 135	...	...	...	...	...	...
20 - 24	ESDJ	4 860 247	2 467 918	2 392 330	...	...	...	...	...	...

7. Population by age, sex and urban/rural residence: latest available year, 1994 - 2003
Population selon l'âge, le sexe et la résidence, urbaine/rurale: dernière année disponible, 1994 - 2003
(continued — suite)

Continent, country or area, date and age (in years) / Continent, pays ou zone, date et âge (en annèes)	Code[1]	Total Both sexes Les deux sexes	Total Male Masculin	Total Female Féminin	Urban - Urbaine Both sexes Les deux sexes	Urban - Urbaine Male Masculin	Urban - Urbaine Female Féminin	Rural - Rurale Both sexes Les deux sexes	Rural - Rurale Male Masculin	Rural - Rurale Female Féminin
EUROPE										
Germany - Allemagne										
1 VII 2003										
25 - 29	ESDJ	4 691 671	2 388 740	2 302 932	...	...	...	...	...	...
30 - 34	ESDJ	5 864 384	3 004 344	2 860 040	...	...	...	...	...	...
35 - 39	ESDJ	7 179 404	3 694 015	3 485 389	...	...	...	...	...	...
40 - 44	ESDJ	6 876 960	3 516 180	3 360 780	...	...	...	...	...	...
45 - 49	ESDJ	5 951 201	3 015 563	2 935 638	...	...	...	...	...	...
50 - 54	ESDJ	5 465 996	2 736 279	2 729 718	...	...	...	...	...	...
55 - 59	ESDJ	4 428 231	2 208 201	2 220 030	...	...	...	...	...	...
60 - 64	ESDJ	5 570 011	2 735 524	2 834 487	...	...	...	...	...	...
65 - 69	ESDJ	4 799 739	2 281 310	2 518 429	...	...	...	...	...	...
70 - 74	ESDJ	3 545 897	1 580 812	1 965 086	...	...	...	...	...	...
75 - 79	ESDJ	2 897 586	1 069 762	1 827 824	...	...	...	...	...	...
80 - 84	ESDJ	1 992 900	591 516	1 401 384	...	...	...	...	...	...
85 - 89	ESDJ	824 914	206 189	618 726	...	...	...	...	...	...
90+	ESDJ	588 372	133 326	455 046	...	...	...	...	...	...
Gibraltar[35]										
12 XI 2001										
Total	CDFC	27 495	13 644	13 851	...	...	...	...	...	...
0 - 1	CDFC	143	74	69	...	...	...	...	...	...
1 - 4	CDFC	1 315	693	622	...	...	...	...	...	...
5 - 9	CDFC	1 773	932	841	...	...	...	...	...	...
10 - 14	CDFC	1 831	956	875	...	...	...	...	...	...
15 - 19	CDFC	1 801	917	884	...	...	...	...	...	...
20 - 24	CDFC	1 764	912	852	...	...	...	...	...	...
25 - 29	CDFC	1 770	867	903	...	...	...	...	...	...
30 - 34	CDFC	1 916	959	957	...	...	...	...	...	...
35 - 39	CDFC	2 044	1 008	1 036	...	...	...	...	...	...
40 - 44	CDFC	1 995	987	1 008	...	...	...	...	...	...
45 - 49	CDFC	1 904	988	916	...	...	...	...	...	...
50 - 54	CDFC	1 944	1 056	888	...	...	...	...	...	...
55 - 59	CDFC	1 610	844	766	...	...	...	...	...	...
60 - 64	CDFC	1 379	691	688	...	...	...	...	...	...
65 - 69	CDFC	1 247	611	636	...	...	...	...	...	...
70 - 74	CDFC	1 037	477	560	...	...	...	...	...	...
75 - 79	CDFC	895	329	566	...	...	...	...	...	...
80 - 84	CDFC	605	186	419	...	...	...	...	...	...
85 - 89	CDFC	306	100	206	...	...	...	...	...	...
90 - 94	CDFC	134	25	109	...	...	...	...	...	...
95+	CDFC	34	9	25	...	...	...	...	...	...
Unk. - Inc.	CDFC	48	23	25	...	...	...	...	...	...
Greece - Grèce[36]										
1 VII 2003										
Total	ESDF	11 023 800	5 457 207	5 566 593	...	...	...	...	...	...
0 - 1	ESDF	103 169	52 923	50 246	...	...	...	...	...	...
1 - 4	ESDF	402 494	207 262	195 233	...	...	...	...	...	...
5 - 9	ESDF	533 333	273 252	260 081	...	...	...	...	...	...
10 - 14	ESDF	573 443	296 795	276 648	...	...	...	...	...	...
15 - 19	ESDF	656 925	341 955	314 970	...	...	...	...	...	...
20 - 24	ESDF	806 603	421 261	385 342	...	...	...	...	...	...
25 - 29	ESDF	855 475	443 047	412 428	...	...	...	...	...	...
30 - 34	ESDF	869 427	445 434	423 993	...	...	...	...	...	...
35 - 39	ESDF	833 519	419 979	413 541	...	...	...	...	...	...
40 - 44	ESDF	791 932	394 472	397 459	...	...	...	...	...	...
45 - 49	ESDF	744 622	370 005	374 617	...	...	...	...	...	...
50 - 54	ESDF	686 423	338 874	347 549	...	...	...	...	...	...
55 - 59	ESDF	646 698	314 491	332 207	...	...	...	...	...	...
60 - 64	ESDF	587 968	274 171	313 797	...	...	...	...	...	...
65 - 69	ESDF	630 708	290 665	340 042	...	...	...	...	...	...
70 - 74	ESDF	559 010	253 910	305 099	...	...	...	...	...	...
75 - 79	ESDF	385 492	170 218	215 274	...	...	...	...	...	...

7. Population by age, sex and urban/rural residence: latest available year, 1994 - 2003
Population selon l'âge, le sexe et la résidence, urbaine/rurale: dernière année disponible, 1994 - 2003
(continued — suite)

Continent, country or area, date and age (in years) / Continent, pays ou zone, date et âge (en années)	Code[1]	Total			Urban - Urbaine			Rural - Rurale		
		Both sexes Les deux sexes	Male Masculin	Female Féminin	Both sexes Les deux sexes	Male Masculin	Female Féminin	Both sexes Les deux sexes	Male Masculin	Female Féminin
EUROPE										
Greece - Grèce[36]										
1 VII 2003										
80 - 84	ESDF	211 642	89 085	122 558	...	...	...	...	...	...
85 - 89	ESDF	99 201	43 932	55 268	...	...	...	...	...	...
90 - 94	ESDF	40 041	15 052	24 989	...	...	...	...	...	...
95 - 99	ESDF	4 220	107	4 112	...	...	...	...	...	...
100+	ESDF	1 454	317	1 138	...	...	...	...	...	...
Hungary - Hongrie										
1 VII 2003										
Total	ESDF	10 129 552	4 811 285	5 318 268	6 595 551	3 092 638	3 502 913	3 534 002	1 718 647	1 815 355
0 - 1	ESDF	93 985	48 359	45 626	59 399	30 500	28 899	34 586	17 860	16 727
1 - 4	ESDF	383 028	196 269	186 760	235 925	120 683	115 242	147 104	75 586	71 518
5 - 9	ESDF	531 242	272 489	258 754	319 815	163 821	155 994	211 428	108 668	102 760
10 - 14	ESDF	611 648	312 799	298 850	375 773	191 747	184 026	235 876	121 052	114 824
15 - 19	ESDF	642 047	326 778	315 269	421 982	212 076	209 906	220 065	114 702	105 363
20 - 24	ESDF	731 718	374 842	356 876	491 990	248 387	243 603	239 728	126 455	113 273
25 - 29	ESDF	850 722	433 199	417 523	582 643	293 378	289 266	268 079	139 821	128 258
30 - 34	ESDF	721 324	366 125	355 200	480 033	241 699	238 335	241 291	124 426	116 865
35 - 39	ESDF	643 283	323 242	320 041	414 151	204 994	209 158	229 132	118 249	110 884
40 - 44	ESDF	634 531	312 470	322 061	399 656	191 453	208 203	234 876	121 018	113 858
45 - 49	ESDF	806 817	391 379	415 438	525 212	246 166	279 047	281 605	145 214	136 392
50 - 54	ESDF	739 514	350 707	388 807	491 408	226 376	265 033	248 106	124 332	123 774
55 - 59	ESDF	620 889	286 278	334 611	421 777	191 252	230 526	199 112	95 026	104 086
60 - 64	ESDF	555 639	242 117	313 522	366 079	159 055	207 024	189 560	83 062	106 498
65 - 69	ESDF	475 744	193 130	282 614	304 166	123 544	180 622	171 578	69 586	101 992
70 - 74	ESDF	433 161	167 312	265 849	276 721	107 857	168 865	156 440	59 455	96 985
75 - 79	ESDF	334 221	116 513	217 708	215 050	74 890	140 160	119 172	41 623	77 549
80 - 84	ESDF	211 363	66 657	144 706	138 208	43 466	94 742	73 155	23 191	49 964
85 - 89	ESDF	67 237	19 349	47 889	46 795	13 579	33 216	20 442	5 770	14 673
90+	ESDF	41 443	11 276	30 168	28 771	7 720	21 051	12 673	3 556	9 117
Iceland - Islande										
1 VII 2003										
Total	ESDJ	289 272	144 713	144 559	267 957	133 340	134 617	21 315	11 373	9 942
0 - 1	ESDJ	4 080	2 073	2 007	3 850	1 953	1 897	230	120	110
1 - 4	ESDJ	16 862	8 588	8 274	15 816	8 053	7 763	1 046	535	511
5 - 9	ESDJ	21 798	11 113	10 685	20 290	10 337	9 953	1 508	776	732
10 - 14	ESDJ	23 033	11 779	11 254	21 126	10 794	10 332	1 907	985	922
15 - 19	ESDJ	20 627	10 504	10 123	18 896	9 593	9 303	1 731	911	820
20 - 24	ESDJ	22 335	11 353	10 982	20 654	10 454	10 200	1 681	899	782
25 - 29	ESDJ	20 616	10 438	10 178	19 428	9 786	9 642	1 188	652	536
30 - 34	ESDJ	20 456	10 353	10 103	19 273	9 740	9 533	1 183	613	570
35 - 39	ESDJ	21 348	10 625	10 723	19 900	9 881	10 019	1 448	744	704
40 - 44	ESDJ	21 400	10 761	10 639	19 806	9 924	9 882	1 594	837	757
45 - 49	ESDJ	20 078	10 196	9 882	18 584	9 364	9 220	1 494	832	662
50 - 54	ESDJ	17 526	8 934	8 592	16 230	8 220	8 010	1 296	714	582
55 - 59	ESDJ	14 540	7 392	7 148	13 401	6 771	6 630	1 139	621	518
60 - 64	ESDJ	10 638	5 282	5 356	9 713	4 790	4 923	925	492	433
65 - 69	ESDJ	9 321	4 511	4 810	8 468	4 037	4 431	853	474	379
70 - 74	ESDJ	9 019	4 279	4 740	8 223	3 817	4 406	796	462	334
75 - 79	ESDJ	7 104	3 193	3 911	6 533	2 861	3 672	571	332	239
80 - 84	ESDJ	4 823	2 045	2 778	4 447	1 831	2 616	376	214	162
85 - 89	ESDJ	2 442	900	1 542	2 208	787	1 421	234	113	121
90 - 94	ESDJ	967	322	645	884	285	599	83	37	46
95 - 99	ESDJ	233	66	167	206	57	149	27	9	18
100+	ESDJ	26	6	20	21	5	16	5	1	4
Ireland - Irlande										
28 IV 2002										
Total	CDFC	3 917 200	1 946 200	1 971 000	2 334 300	1 133 500	1 200 800	1 582 900	812 600	770 300
0 - 1	CDFC	54 500	27 800	26 700	...	...	...	...	...	...
0 - 4	CDFC	...	...	...	167 000	85 000	81 000	111 100	56 700	54 300
1 - 4	CDFC	223 100	114 200	108 900	...	...	...	...	...	...
5 - 9	CDFC	264 100	135 900	128 200	148 700	76 500	72 200	115 300	59 300	56 000

7. Population by age, sex and urban/rural residence: latest available year, 1994 - 2003
Population selon l'âge, le sexe et la résidence, urbaine/rurale: dernière année disponible, 1994 - 2003
(continued — suite)

Continent, country or area, date and age (in years) / Continent, pays ou zone, date et âge (en annèes)	Code[1]	Total Both sexes Les deux sexes	Total Male Masculin	Total Female Féminin	Urban - Urbaine Both sexes Les deux sexes	Urban - Urbaine Male Masculin	Urban - Urbaine Female Féminin	Rural - Rurale Both sexes Les deux sexes	Rural - Rurale Male Masculin	Rural - Rurale Female Féminin
EUROPE										
Ireland - Irlande										
28 IV 2002										
10 - 14	CDFC	285 700	146 100	139 600	156 500	79 800	76 700	129 200	66 300	62 900
15 - 19	CDFC	313 200	160 400	152 800	180 800	90 600	90 200	132 400	69 800	62 600
20 - 24	CDFC	328 300	165 300	163 000	229 300	110 600	118 700	99 000	54 700	44 300
25 - 29	CDFC	312 700	156 100	156 600	218 200	106 500	111 700	94 500	49 600	44 900
30 - 34	CDFC	304 700	152 400	152 300	198 500	98 200	100 300	106 100	54 100	52 000
35 - 39	CDFC	290 900	144 500	146 400	175 400	86 000	89 400	115 500	58 600	56 900
40 - 44	CDFC	272 000	135 300	136 700	156 600	76 600	80 000	115 400	58 700	56 700
45 - 49	CDFC	249 600	125 000	124 600	139 400	67 900	71 500	110 200	57 100	53 100
50 - 54	CDFC	230 800	116 600	114 200	128 100	62 600	65 500	102 700	53 900	48 800
55 - 59	CDFC	197 300	99 800	97 500	109 800	53 600	56 200	87 500	46 300	41 200
60 - 64	CDFC	154 300	77 600	76 700	87 900	42 500	45 400	66 300	35 000	31 300
65 - 69	CDFC	133 500	65 300	68 200	75 000	34 900	40 100	58 500	30 400	28 100
70 - 74	CDFC	112 100	51 700	60 400	62 000	26 800	35 200	50 100	25 000	25 100
75 - 79	CDFC	89 800	37 400	52 400	48 200	18 600	29 600	41 600	18 800	22 800
80 - 84	CDFC	58 900	22 300	36 600	31 000	10 600	20 400	27 900	11 700	16 200
85+	CDFC	41 700	12 500	29 200	22 100	5 800	16 300	19 600	6 700	12 900
1 VII 2003										
Total	ESDF	3 995 699	1 986 165	2 009 534	...	...	...	...	...	...
0 - 1	ESDF	60 243	30 858	29 385	...	...	...	...	...	...
1 - 4	ESDF	226 021	115 485	110 537	...	...	...	...	...	...
5 - 9	ESDF	270 040	138 822	131 218	...	...	...	...	...	...
10 - 14	ESDF	280 232	143 756	136 476	...	...	...	...	...	...
15 - 19	ESDF	305 363	156 358	149 005	...	...	...	...	...	...
20 - 24	ESDF	336 105	168 794	167 311	...	...	...	...	...	...
25 - 29	ESDF	322 071	161 207	160 865	...	...	...	...	...	...
30 - 34	ESDF	315 088	157 754	157 334	...	...	...	...	...	...
35 - 39	ESDF	295 872	147 630	148 242	...	...	...	...	...	...
40 - 44	ESDF	279 419	138 804	140 615	...	...	...	...	...	...
45 - 49	ESDF	254 672	127 183	127 489	...	...	...	...	...	...
50 - 54	ESDF	235 334	118 528	116 807	...	...	...	...	...	...
55 - 59	ESDF	208 438	105 658	102 781	...	...	...	...	...	...
60 - 64	ESDF	161 764	81 338	80 427	...	...	...	...	...	...
65 - 69	ESDF	136 033	66 487	69 546	...	...	...	...	...	...
70 - 74	ESDF	114 087	53 427	60 660	...	...	...	...	...	...
75 - 79	ESDF	89 852	37 589	52 264	...	...	...	...	...	...
80 - 84	ESDF	61 642	23 297	38 345	...	...	...	...	...	...
85 - 89	ESDF	29 908	9 690	20 218	...	...	...	...	...	...
90 - 94	ESDF	10 973	2 963	8 010	...	...	...	...	...	...
95+	ESDF	2 549	544	2 005	...	...	...	...	...	...
Isle of Man - Îles de Man										
1 VII 2003										
Total	ESDJ	77 464	38 019	39 444	...	...	...	...	...	...
0 - 1	ESDJ	866	443	422	...	...	...	...	...	...
1 - 4	ESDJ	3 424	1 823	1 600	...	...	...	...	...	...
5 - 9	ESDJ	4 538	2 297	2 241	...	...	...	...	...	...
10 - 14	ESDJ	4 893	2 516	2 378	...	...	...	...	...	...
15 - 19	ESDJ	4 531	2 308	2 224	...	...	...	...	...	...
20 - 24	ESDJ	4 507	2 267	2 240	...	...	...	...	...	...
25 - 29	ESDJ	4 327	2 108	2 221	...	...	...	...	...	...
30 - 34	ESDJ	5 630	2 809	2 822	...	...	...	...	...	...
35 - 39	ESDJ	5 971	2 966	3 005	...	...	...	...	...	...
40 - 44	ESDJ	5 902	2 952	2 949	...	...	...	...	...	...
45 - 49	ESDJ	5 245	2 644	2 600	...	...	...	...	...	...
50 - 54	ESDJ	5 353	2 674	2 681	...	...	...	...	...	...
55 - 59	ESDJ	5 275	2 712	2 564	...	...	...	...	...	...
60 - 64	ESDJ	4 099	2 037	2 064	...	...	...	...	...	...
65 - 69	ESDJ	3 567	1 764	1 803	...	...	...	...	...	...
70 - 74	ESDJ	3 027	1 367	1 662	...	...	...	...	...	...
75 - 79	ESDJ	2 603	1 054	1 549	...	...	...	...	...	...

7. Population by age, sex and urban/rural residence: latest available year, 1994 - 2003
Population selon l'âge, le sexe et la résidence, urbaine/rurale: dernière année disponible, 1994 - 2003
(continued — suite)

Continent, country or area, date and age (in years) Continent, pays ou zone, date et âge (en années)	Code[1]	Total			Urban - Urbaine			Rural - Rurale		
		Both sexes Les deux sexes	Male Masculin	Female Féminin	Both sexes Les deux sexes	Male Masculin	Female Féminin	Both sexes Les deux sexes	Male Masculin	Female Féminin
EUROPE										
Isle of Man - Îles de Man										
1 VII 2003										
80 - 84	ESDJ	2 023	757	1 266	...	...	...	...	...	...
85 - 89	ESDJ	1 044	359	684	...	...	...	...	...	...
90+	ESDJ	638	164	474	...	...	...	...	...	...
Italy - Italie										
1 VII 2003										
Total	ESDJ	57 604 658	27 917 416	29 687 242	...	...	...	...	...	...
0 - 1	ESDJ	539 606	276 719	262 887	...	...	...	...	...	...
1 - 4	ESDJ	2 133 286	1 094 567	1 038 720	...	...	...	...	...	...
5 - 9	ESDJ	2 657 427	1 367 088	1 290 339	...	...	...	...	...	...
10 - 14	ESDJ	2 851 424	1 463 957	1 387 467	...	...	...	...	...	...
15 - 19	ESDJ	2 893 733	1 484 384	1 409 349	...	...	...	...	...	...
20 - 24	ESDJ	3 277 697	1 667 033	1 610 664	...	...	...	...	...	...
25 - 29	ESDJ	4 087 828	2 064 211	2 023 617	...	...	...	...	...	...
30 - 34	ESDJ	4 572 543	2 308 155	2 264 388	...	...	...	...	...	...
35 - 39	ESDJ	4 754 209	2 393 611	2 360 598	...	...	...	...	...	...
40 - 44	ESDJ	4 299 552	2 149 487	2 150 066	...	...	...	...	...	...
45 - 49	ESDJ	3 854 035	1 913 745	1 940 290	...	...	...	...	...	...
50 - 54	ESDJ	3 729 580	1 837 119	1 892 461	...	...	...	...	...	...
55 - 59	ESDJ	3 542 231	1 729 921	1 812 310	...	...	...	...	...	...
60 - 64	ESDJ	3 399 827	1 625 841	1 773 986	...	...	...	...	...	...
65 - 69	ESDJ	3 140 908	1 460 937	1 679 971	...	...	...	...	...	...
70 - 74	ESDJ	2 835 048	1 249 434	1 585 614	...	...	...	...	...	...
75 - 79	ESDJ	2 327 829	940 016	1 387 813	...	...	...	...	...	...
80 - 84	ESDJ	1 528 071	546 849	981 222	...	...	...	...	...	...
85 - 89	ESDJ	724 612	227 274	497 338	...	...	...	...	...	...
90 - 94	ESDJ	373 688	100 347	273 341	...	...	...	...	...	...
95 - 99	ESDJ	73 937	15 486	58 451	...	...	...	...	...	...
100+	ESDJ	7 591	1 238	6 353	...	...	...	...	...	...
Latvia - Lettonie										
1 VII 2002										
Total	ESDF	2 338 624	1 076 587	1 262 037	1 586 220	713 616	872 604	752 404	362 971	389 433
0 - 1	ESDF	19 843	10 114	9 729	12 743	6 481	6 262	7 100	3 633	3 467
1 - 4	ESDF	75 986	38 841	37 145	47 476	24 298	23 178	28 510	14 543	13 967
5 - 9	ESDF	112 912	57 866	55 046	68 595	35 104	33 491	44 317	22 762	21 555
10 - 14	ESDF	172 819	88 306	84 513	107 772	54 998	52 774	65 047	33 308	31 739
15 - 19	ESDF	185 794	94 586	91 208	122 552	61 844	60 708	63 242	32 742	30 500
20 - 24	ESDF	163 261	83 032	80 229	111 182	55 733	55 449	52 079	27 299	24 780
25 - 29	ESDF	160 781	81 341	79 440	110 713	54 787	55 926	50 068	26 554	23 514
30 - 34	ESDF	161 156	80 119	81 037	110 675	53 612	57 063	50 481	26 507	23 974
35 - 39	ESDF	162 509	79 734	82 775	110 420	52 323	58 097	52 089	27 411	24 678
40 - 44	ESDF	178 535	86 228	92 307	123 710	57 411	66 299	54 825	28 817	26 008
45 - 49	ESDF	159 133	74 815	84 318	113 474	51 104	62 370	45 659	23 711	21 948
50 - 54	ESDF	148 488	67 754	80 734	107 237	46 791	60 446	41 251	20 963	20 288
55 - 59	ESDF	123 983	54 327	69 656	86 847	36 721	50 126	37 136	17 606	19 530
60 - 64	ESDF	146 704	61 193	85 511	102 555	41 588	60 967	44 149	19 605	24 544
65 - 69	ESDF	119 427	46 026	73 401	81 540	30 787	50 753	37 887	15 239	22 648
70 - 74	ESDF	107 312	38 112	69 200	74 333	26 304	48 029	32 979	11 808	21 171
75 - 79	ESDF	76 261	19 585	56 676	52 967	13 884	39 083	23 294	5 701	17 593
80 - 84	ESDF	36 399	8 806	27 593	24 133	6 008	18 125	12 266	2 798	9 468
85 - 89	ESDF	17 966	3 924	14 042	11 489	2 664	8 825	6 477	1 260	5 217
90 - 94	ESDF	7 743	1 568	6 175	4 804	989	3 815	2 939	579	2 360
95 - 99	ESDF	1 474	288	1 186	921	174	747	553	114	439
100+	ESDF	138	22	116	82	11	71	56	11	45
Liechtenstein										
1 VII 2003										
Total	ESDF	34 079	16 756	17 323	...	...	...	...	...	...
0 - 1	ESDF	371	192	179	...	...	...	...	...	...
1 - 4	ESDF	1 594	816	779	...	...	...	...	...	...
5 - 9	ESDF	2 103	1 052	1 051	...	...	...	...	...	...

7. Population by age, sex and urban/rural residence: latest available year, 1994 - 2003
Population selon l'âge, le sexe et la résidence, urbaine/rurale: dernière année disponible, 1994 - 2003
(continued — suite)

Continent, country or area, date and age (in years) Continent, pays ou zone, date et âge (en années)	Code[1]	Total			Urban - Urbaine			Rural - Rurale		
		Both sexes Les deux sexes	Male Masculin	Female Féminin	Both sexes Les deux sexes	Male Masculin	Female Féminin	Both sexes Les deux sexes	Male Masculin	Female Féminin
EUROPE										
Liechtenstein										
1 VII 2003										
10 - 14	ESDF	2 100	1 072	1 028	...	...	...	...	...	...
15 - 19	ESDF	2 068	1 051	1 017	...	...	...	...	...	...
20 - 24	ESDF	2 128	1 074	1 055	...	...	...	...	...	...
25 - 29	ESDF	2 297	1 144	1 153	...	...	...	...	...	...
30 - 34	ESDF	2 809	1 411	1 398	...	...	...	...	...	...
35 - 39	ESDF	3 020	1 470	1 551	...	...	...	...	...	...
40 - 44	ESDF	2 961	1 436	1 525	...	...	...	...	...	...
45 - 49	ESDF	2 674	1 350	1 324	...	...	...	...	...	...
50 - 54	ESDF	2 417	1 234	1 183	...	...	...	...	...	...
55 - 59	ESDF	2 186	1 122	1 064	...	...	...	...	...	...
60 - 64	ESDF	1 675	839	836	...	...	...	...	...	...
65 - 69	ESDF	1 148	543	605	...	...	...	...	...	...
70 - 74	ESDF	854	383	471	...	...	...	...	...	...
75 - 79	ESDF	760	266	494	...	...	...	...	...	...
80 - 84	ESDF	552	196	356	...	...	...	...	...	...
85 - 89	ESDF	246	78	168	...	...	...	...	...	...
90 - 94	ESDF	104	27	77	...	...	...	...	...	...
95 - 99	ESDF	17	4	14	...	...	...	...	...	...
100+	ESDF	1	1	...	...	...	...	...	...	...
Lithuania - Lituanie										
1 VII 2003										
Total	ESDJ	3 454 205	1 612 996	1 841 209	2 307 326	1 058 108	1 249 218	1 146 879	554 888	591 991
0 - 1	ESDJ	30 111	15 545	14 566	18 788	9 714	9 074	11 323	5 831	5 492
1 - 4	ESDJ	133 829	68 923	64 906	84 942	43 612	41 330	48 887	25 311	23 576
5 - 9	ESDJ	196 691	100 870	95 821	126 039	64 767	61 272	70 652	36 103	34 549
10 - 14	ESDJ	260 240	133 112	127 128	165 314	84 267	81 047	94 926	48 845	46 081
15 - 19	ESDJ	277 989	141 389	136 600	182 296	92 064	90 232	95 693	49 325	46 368
20 - 24	ESDJ	245 435	124 841	120 594	173 771	85 391	88 380	71 664	39 450	32 214
25 - 29	ESDJ	228 759	114 649	114 110	165 940	80 672	85 268	62 819	33 977	28 842
30 - 34	ESDJ	249 534	124 028	125 506	177 157	86 252	90 905	72 377	37 776	34 601
35 - 39	ESDJ	254 957	125 521	129 436	176 967	84 492	92 475	77 990	41 029	36 961
40 - 44	ESDJ	274 476	132 515	141 961	192 157	89 020	103 137	82 319	43 495	38 824
45 - 49	ESDJ	230 432	109 308	121 124	162 213	73 667	88 546	68 219	35 641	32 578
50 - 54	ESDJ	204 940	94 035	110 905	143 258	62 756	80 502	61 682	31 279	30 403
55 - 59	ESDJ	171 014	75 393	95 621	115 930	49 171	66 759	55 084	26 222	28 862
60 - 64	ESDJ	182 003	76 416	105 587	117 357	48 164	69 193	64 646	28 252	36 394
65 - 69	ESDJ	165 481	65 100	100 381	101 779	39 251	62 528	63 702	25 849	37 853
70 - 74	ESDJ	145 155	52 893	92 262	86 360	31 644	54 716	58 795	21 249	37 546
75 - 79	ESDJ	108 219	33 042	75 177	63 595	19 335	44 260	44 624	13 707	30 917
80 - 84	ESDJ	57 520	15 849	41 671	31 991	8 604	23 387	25 529	7 245	18 284
85 - 89	ESDJ	22 083	5 614	16 469	12 539	3 122	9 417	9 544	2 492	7 052
90 - 94	ESDJ	11 234	2 665	8 569	6 587	1 489	5 098	4 647	1 176	3 471
95 - 99	ESDJ	3 384	1 132	2 252	1 936	566	1 370	1 448	566	882
100+	ESDJ	719	156	563	410	88	322	309	68	241
Luxembourg										
1 VII 2003										
Total	ESDJ	449 950	222 015	227 936	...	...	...	...	...	...
0 - 1	ESDJ	5 302	2 766	2 536	...	...	...	...	...	...
1 - 4	ESDJ	22 607	11 628	10 979	...	...	...	...	...	...
5 - 9	ESDJ	28 983	14 826	14 157	...	...	...	...	...	...
10 - 14	ESDJ	27 728	14 221	13 507	...	...	...	...	...	...
15 - 19	ESDJ	25 491	13 016	12 475	...	...	...	...	...	...
20 - 24	ESDJ	25 930	13 174	12 756	...	...	...	...	...	...
25 - 29	ESDJ	29 957	14 997	14 960	...	...	...	...	...	...
30 - 34	ESDJ	36 328	18 151	18 177	...	...	...	...	...	...
35 - 39	ESDJ	39 920	20 259	19 662	...	...	...	...	...	...
40 - 44	ESDJ	37 156	18 871	18 285	...	...	...	...	...	...
45 - 49	ESDJ	33 217	16 811	16 406	...	...	...	...	...	...
50 - 54	ESDJ	28 835	14 832	14 004	...	...	...	...	...	...
55 - 59	ESDJ	24 365	12 495	11 871	...	...	...	...	...	...

7. Population by age, sex and urban/rural residence: latest available year, 1994 - 2003
Population selon l'âge, le sexe et la résidence, urbaine/rurale: dernière année disponible, 1994 - 2003
(continued — suite)

Continent, country or area, date and age (in years) / Continent, pays ou zone, date et âge (en années)	Code[1]	Total			Urban - Urbaine			Rural - Rurale		
		Both sexes Les deux sexes	Male Masculin	Female Féminin	Both sexes Les deux sexes	Male Masculin	Female Féminin	Both sexes Les deux sexes	Male Masculin	Female Féminin
EUROPE										
Luxembourg										
1 VII 2003										
60 - 64	ESDJ	20 863	10 200	10 664	...	...	...	...	...	...
65 - 69	ESDJ	18 440	8 697	9 743	...	...	...	...	...	...
70 - 74	ESDJ	17 632	7 940	9 693	...	...	...	...	...	...
75 - 79	ESDJ	13 250	5 129	8 121	...	...	...	...	...	...
80 - 84	ESDJ	8 068	2 526	5 543	...	...	...	...	...	...
85 - 89	ESDJ	3 886	1 074	2 812	...	...	...	...	...	...
90 - 94	ESDJ	1 677	352	1 326	...	...	...	...	...	...
95+	ESDJ	320	56	265	...	...	...	...	...	...
Malta - Malte[37]										
1 VII 2003										
Total	ESDJ	398 582	197 468	201 114	...	...	...	...	...	...
0 - 1	ESDJ	3 959	2 035	1 924	...	...	...	...	...	...
1 - 4	ESDJ	16 843	8 576	8 267	...	...	...	...	...	...
5 - 9	ESDJ	24 626	12 771	11 855	...	...	...	...	...	...
10 - 14	ESDJ	28 203	14 452	13 751	...	...	...	...	...	...
15 - 19	ESDJ	28 496	14 763	13 733	...	...	...	...	...	...
20 - 24	ESDJ	30 136	15 444	14 692	...	...	...	...	...	...
25 - 29	ESDJ	29 473	15 216	14 257	...	...	...	...	...	...
30 - 34	ESDJ	25 509	13 040	12 469	...	...	...	...	...	...
35 - 39	ESDJ	24 979	12 592	12 387	...	...	...	...	...	...
40 - 44	ESDJ	29 483	14 813	14 670	...	...	...	...	...	...
45 - 49	ESDJ	29 675	15 012	14 663	...	...	...	...	...	...
50 - 54	ESDJ	29 465	14 754	14 711	...	...	...	...	...	...
55 - 59	ESDJ	29 241	14 315	14 926	...	...	...	...	...	...
60 - 64	ESDJ	16 952	8 040	8 912	...	...	...	...	...	...
65 - 69	ESDJ	16 918	7 691	9 227	...	...	...	...	...	...
70 - 74	ESDJ	13 573	5 712	7 861	...	...	...	...	...	...
75 - 79	ESDJ	10 365	4 266	6 099	...	...	...	...	...	...
80 - 84	ESDJ	6 604	2 582	4 022	...	...	...	...	...	...
85 - 89	ESDJ	2 650	958	1 692	...	...	...	...	...	...
90+	ESDJ	1 437	438	1 000	...	...	...	...	...	...
Monaco										
21 VI 2000										
Total	CDJC	32 020	15 544	16 476	...	...	...	...	...	...
0 - 1	CDJC	145	69	76	...	...	...	...	...	...
1 - 4	CDJC	1 223	644	579	...	...	...	...	...	...
5 - 9	CDJC	1 462	747	715	...	...	...	...	...	...
10 - 14	CDJC	1 407	746	661	...	...	...	...	...	...
15 - 19	CDJC	1 337	706	631	...	...	...	...	...	...
20 - 24	CDJC	1 297	661	636	...	...	...	...	...	...
25 - 29	CDJC	1 638	830	808	...	...	...	...	...	...
30 - 34	CDJC	2 346	1 184	1 162	...	...	...	...	...	...
35 - 39	CDJC	2 386	1 205	1 181	...	...	...	...	...	...
40 - 44	CDJC	2 328	1 151	1 177	...	...	...	...	...	...
45 - 49	CDJC	2 178	1 107	1 071	...	...	...	...	...	...
50 - 54	CDJC	2 584	1 264	1 320	...	...	...	...	...	...
55 - 59	CDJC	2 405	1 163	1 242	...	...	...	...	...	...
60 - 64	CDJC	2 083	1 018	1 065	...	...	...	...	...	...
65 - 69	CDJC	1 794	854	940	...	...	...	...	...	...
70 - 74	CDJC	1 704	803	901	...	...	...	...	...	...
75 - 79	CDJC	1 598	704	894	...	...	...	...	...	...
80 - 84	CDJC	937	347	590	...	...	...	...	...	...
85 - 89	CDJC	669	216	453	...	...	...	...	...	...
90 - 94	CDJC	374	96	278	...	...	...	...	...	...
95 - 99	CDJC	96	20	76	...	...	...	...	...	...
100+	CDJC	11	2	9	...	...	...	...	...	...
Unk. - Inc.	CDJC	18	7	11	...	...	...	...	...	...

7. Population by age, sex and urban/rural residence: latest available year, 1994 - 2003
Population selon l'âge, le sexe et la résidence, urbaine/rurale: dernière année disponible, 1994 - 2003
(continued — suite)

Continent, country or area, date and age (in years) / Continent, pays ou zone, date et âge (en années)	Code[1]	Total			Urban - Urbaine			Rural - Rurale		
		Both sexes Les deux sexes	Male Masculin	Female Féminin	Both sexes Les deux sexes	Male Masculin	Female Féminin	Both sexes Les deux sexes	Male Masculin	Female Féminin
EUROPE										
Netherlands - Pays-Bas										
1 I 2003										
Total	ESDJ	16 192 572	8 015 471	8 177 101	10 529 908	5 179 099	5 350 809	5 662 664	2 836 372	2 826 292
0 - 1	ESDJ	202 386	103 818	98 568	132 720	68 208	64 512	69 666	35 610	34 056
1 - 4	ESDJ	820 227	419 480	400 747	523 999	267 883	256 116	296 228	151 597	144 631
5 - 9	ESDJ	984 718	503 582	481 136	614 030	313 763	300 267	370 688	189 819	180 869
10 - 14	ESDJ	1 002 757	512 955	489 802	623 866	318 675	305 191	378 891	194 280	184 611
15 - 19	ESDJ	958 911	491 763	467 148	611 610	310 847	300 763	347 301	180 916	166 385
20 - 24	ESDJ	972 828	491 819	481 009	688 130	339 227	348 903	284 698	152 592	132 106
25 - 29	ESDJ	1 031 179	518 928	512 251	742 632	371 082	371 550	288 547	147 846	140 701
30 - 34	ESDJ	1 295 220	656 339	638 881	888 931	452 444	436 487	406 289	203 895	202 394
35 - 39	ESDJ	1 324 943	675 781	649 162	870 709	445 586	425 123	454 234	230 195	224 039
40 - 44	ESDJ	1 275 679	645 907	629 772	823 858	417 006	406 852	451 821	228 901	222 920
45 - 49	ESDJ	1 168 260	589 999	578 261	746 303	374 569	371 734	421 957	215 430	206 527
50 - 54	ESDJ	1 123 820	569 836	553 984	709 046	357 690	351 356	414 774	212 146	202 628
55 - 59	ESDJ	1 038 381	525 879	512 502	643 424	324 128	319 296	394 957	201 751	193 206
60 - 64	ESDJ	772 807	386 143	386 664	476 182	235 201	240 981	296 625	150 942	145 683
65 - 69	ESDJ	649 864	312 394	337 470	404 190	191 342	212 848	245 674	121 052	124 622
70 - 74	ESDJ	571 857	257 288	314 569	364 836	161 117	203 719	207 021	96 171	110 850
75 - 79	ESDJ	454 765	183 786	270 979	299 622	119 201	180 421	155 143	64 585	90 558
80 - 84	ESDJ	311 084	108 826	202 258	208 276	71 512	136 764	102 808	37 314	65 494
85 - 89	ESDJ	159 983	45 327	114 656	107 992	29 661	78 331	51 991	15 666	36 325
90 - 94	ESDJ	59 433	13 274	46 159	40 338	8 472	31 866	19 095	4 802	14 293
95 - 99	ESDJ	12 250	2 167	10 083	8 366	1 375	6 991	3 884	792	3 092
100+	ESDJ	1 220	180	1 040	848	110	738	372	70	302
1 VII 2003										
Total	ESDJ	16 225 302	8 030 693	8 194 610	...	...	...	...	...	...
0 - 1	ESDJ	201 584	103 465	98 119	...	...	...	...	...	...
1 - 4	ESDJ	820 331	419 582	400 749	...	...	...	...	...	...
5 - 9	ESDJ	985 604	504 140	481 464	...	...	...	...	...	...
10 - 14	ESDJ	1 005 378	514 239	491 139	...	...	...	...	...	...
15 - 19	ESDJ	965 382	494 741	470 642	...	...	...	...	...	...
20 - 24	ESDJ	970 846	490 708	480 138	...	...	...	...	...	...
25 - 29	ESDJ	1 020 190	513 107	507 083	...	...	...	...	...	...
30 - 34	ESDJ	1 274 492	644 532	629 960	...	...	...	...	...	...
35 - 39	ESDJ	1 320 841	672 951	647 890	...	...	...	...	...	...
40 - 44	ESDJ	1 284 574	650 614	633 960	...	...	...	...	...	...
45 - 49	ESDJ	1 175 793	593 449	582 344	...	...	...	...	...	...
50 - 54	ESDJ	1 118 722	566 674	552 048	...	...	...	...	...	...
55 - 59	ESDJ	1 061 567	537 443	524 125	...	...	...	...	...	...
60 - 64	ESDJ	784 197	392 272	391 925	...	...	...	...	...	...
65 - 69	ESDJ	656 536	316 463	340 074	...	...	...	...	...	...
70 - 74	ESDJ	572 749	258 602	314 147	...	...	...	...	...	...
75 - 79	ESDJ	455 386	184 886	270 501	...	...	...	...	...	...
80 - 84	ESDJ	318 139	111 784	206 355	...	...	...	...	...	...
85 - 89	ESDJ	159 211	45 211	114 000	...	...	...	...	...	...
90 - 94	ESDJ	60 200	13 475	46 726	...	...	...	...	...	...
95+	ESDJ	13 585	2 359	11 226	...	...	...	...	...	...
Norway - Norvège[38]										
1 VII 2003										
Total	ESDJ	4 564 855	2 262 578	2 302 277	...	...	...	...	...	...
0 - 1	ESDJ	56 110	28 752	27 358	...	...	...	...	...	...
1 - 4	ESDJ	235 632	120 478	115 154	...	...	...	...	...	...
5 - 9	ESDJ	308 070	158 205	149 865	...	...	...	...	...	...
10 - 14	ESDJ	310 621	159 619	151 003	...	...	...	...	...	...
15 - 19	ESDJ	275 950	141 543	134 407	...	...	...	...	...	...
20 - 24	ESDJ	274 556	139 355	135 201	...	...	...	...	...	...
25 - 29	ESDJ	300 729	151 621	149 108	...	...	...	...	...	...
30 - 34	ESDJ	349 569	177 357	172 212	...	...	...	...	...	...
35 - 39	ESDJ	348 316	178 153	170 163	...	...	...	...	...	...
40 - 44	ESDJ	322 802	164 719	158 084	...	...	...	...	...	...

7. Population by age, sex and urban/rural residence: latest available year, 1994 - 2003
Population selon l'âge, le sexe et la résidence, urbaine/rurale: dernière année disponible, 1994 - 2003
(continued — suite)

Continent, country or area, date and age (in years) Continent, pays ou zone, date et âge (en années)	Code[1]	Total			Urban - Urbaine			Rural - Rurale		
		Both sexes Les deux sexes	Male Masculin	Female Féminin	Both sexes Les deux sexes	Male Masculin	Female Féminin	Both sexes Les deux sexes	Male Masculin	Female Féminin
EUROPE										
Norway - Norvège[38]										
1 VII 2003										
45 - 49	ESDJ	314 003	159 090	154 913	...	...	...	...	...	...
50 - 54	ESDJ	297 960	152 088	145 873	...	...	...	...	...	...
55 - 59	ESDJ	292 492	148 477	144 015	...	...	...	...	...	...
60 - 64	ESDJ	204 081	101 105	102 976	...	...	...	...	...	...
65 - 69	ESDJ	164 361	78 510	85 851	...	...	...	...	...	...
70 - 74	ESDJ	157 392	72 201	85 191	...	...	...	...	...	...
75 - 79	ESDJ	145 091	61 611	83 481	...	...	...	...	...	...
80 - 84	ESDJ	116 614	43 413	73 202	...	...	...	...	...	...
85 - 89	ESDJ	62 418	19 377	43 041	...	...	...	...	...	...
90 - 94	ESDJ	23 058	5 895	17 164	...	...	...	...	...	...
95 - 99	ESDJ	4 558	929	3 629	...	...	...	...	...	...
100+	ESDJ	477	87	390	...	...	...	...	...	...
Poland - Pologne[39]										
1 VII 2003										
Total	ESDF	38 195 177	18 492 950	19 702 227	23 543 325	11 195 269	12 348 056	14 651 852	7 297 681	7 354 171
0 - 1	ESDF	349 531	179 953	169 578	195 807	100 867	94 940	153 724	79 086	74 638
1 - 4	ESDF	1 491 882	765 235	726 647	822 374	422 415	399 959	669 508	342 820	326 688
5 - 9	ESDF	2 175 333	1 113 000	1 062 333	1 176 764	602 306	574 458	998 569	510 694	487 875
10 - 14	ESDF	2 674 129	1 368 698	1 305 431	1 484 124	759 950	724 174	1 190 005	608 748	581 257
15 - 19	ESDF	3 168 642	1 619 144	1 549 498	1 890 341	962 680	927 661	1 278 301	656 464	621 837
20 - 24	ESDF	3 232 197	1 643 019	1 589 178	2 067 635	1 035 433	1 032 202	1 164 562	607 586	556 976
25 - 29	ESDF	2 972 660	1 507 946	1 464 714	1 902 034	952 836	949 198	1 070 626	555 110	515 516
30 - 34	ESDF	2 538 101	1 286 653	1 251 448	1 566 416	785 371	781 045	971 685	501 282	470 403
35 - 39	ESDF	2 400 956	1 213 217	1 187 739	1 448 839	713 553	735 286	952 117	499 664	452 453
40 - 44	ESDF	2 762 964	1 381 664	1 381 300	1 718 228	825 389	892 839	1 044 736	556 275	488 461
45 - 49	ESDF	3 124 907	1 541 103	1 583 804	2 067 100	977 031	1 090 069	1 057 807	564 072	493 735
50 - 54	ESDF	2 855 349	1 380 685	1 474 664	1 931 067	902 088	1 028 979	924 282	478 597	445 685
55 - 59	ESDF	1 964 545	925 371	1 039 174	1 322 466	611 033	711 433	642 079	314 338	327 741
60 - 64	ESDF	1 572 114	708 322	863 792	1 015 227	448 924	566 303	556 887	259 398	297 489
65 - 69	ESDF	1 573 917	673 969	899 948	982 269	413 166	569 103	591 648	260 803	330 845
70 - 74	ESDF	1 424 249	569 882	854 367	852 397	338 465	513 932	571 852	231 417	340 435
75 - 79	ESDF	1 032 469	357 171	675 298	599 129	204 115	395 014	433 340	153 056	280 284
80 - 84	ESDF	560 780	174 682	386 098	314 621	94 509	220 112	246 159	80 173	165 986
85+	ESDF	320 452	83 236	237 216	186 487	45 138	141 349	133 965	38 098	95 867
Portugal[40]										
1 VII 2003										
Total	ESDF	10 441 075	5 048 278	5 392 798	...	...	...	...	...	...
0 - 1	ESDF	112 825	58 420	54 406	...	...	...	...	...	...
1 - 4	ESDF	441 416	226 850	214 566	...	...	...	...	...	...
5 - 9	ESDF	527 629	270 185	257 444	...	...	...	...	...	...
10 - 14	ESDF	565 506	288 625	276 881	...	...	...	...	...	...
15 - 19	ESDF	625 440	319 690	305 750	...	...	...	...	...	...
20 - 24	ESDF	750 363	380 268	370 095	...	...	...	...	...	...
25 - 29	ESDF	833 748	420 418	413 330	...	...	...	...	...	...
30 - 34	ESDF	791 216	396 008	395 208	...	...	...	...	...	...
35 - 39	ESDF	775 922	383 149	392 774	...	...	...	...	...	...
40 - 44	ESDF	758 421	372 840	385 581	...	...	...	...	...	...
45 - 49	ESDF	702 712	343 105	359 607	...	...	...	...	...	...
50 - 54	ESDF	668 185	323 499	344 686	...	...	...	...	...	...
55 - 59	ESDF	603 105	284 204	318 901	...	...	...	...	...	...
60 - 64	ESDF	536 121	250 020	286 101	...	...	...	...	...	...
65 - 69	ESDF	534 481	242 403	292 079	...	...	...	...	...	...
70 - 74	ESDF	471 754	206 005	265 749	...	...	...	...	...	...
75 - 79	ESDF	363 428	148 185	215 243	...	...	...	...	...	...
80 - 84	ESDF	227 394	86 102	141 292	...	...	...	...	...	...
85 - 89	ESDF	104 233	34 872	69 361	...	...	...	...	...	...
90 - 94	ESDF	39 934	11 840	28 094	...	...	...	...	...	...
95 - 99	ESDF	6 339	1 420	4 919	...	...	...	...	...	...
100+	ESDF	908	174	734	...	...	...	...	...	...

7. Population by age, sex and urban/rural residence: latest available year, 1994 - 2003
Population selon l'âge, le sexe et la résidence, urbaine/rurale: dernière année disponible, 1994 - 2003
(continued — suite)

Continent, country or area, date and age (in years) / Continent, pays ou zone, date et âge (en annèes)	Code[1]	Total			Urban - Urbaine			Rural - Rurale		
		Both sexes Les deux sexes	Male Masculin	Female Féminin	Both sexes Les deux sexes	Male Masculin	Female Féminin	Both sexes Les deux sexes	Male Masculin	Female Féminin
EUROPE										
Republic of Moldova - République de Moldova[41]										
1 VII 2003										
Total	ESDJ	3 612 874	1 730 861	1 882 013	1 481 035	714 970	766 065	2 131 839	1 015 891	1 115 948
0 - 1	ESDJ	35 562	18 407	17 155	12 582	6 555	6 027	22 980	11 852	11 128
1 - 4	ESDJ	147 666	76 095	71 571	50 498	26 118	24 380	97 168	49 977	47 191
5 - 9	ESDJ	236 329	121 020	115 309	78 963	40 756	38 207	157 366	80 264	77 102
10 - 14	ESDJ	312 155	159 241	152 914	117 205	59 977	57 228	194 950	99 264	95 686
15 - 19	ESDJ	366 017	185 672	180 345	140 768	71 587	69 181	225 249	114 085	111 164
20 - 24	ESDJ	326 997	165 013	161 984	128 514	66 266	62 248	198 483	98 747	99 736
25 - 29	ESDJ	295 653	149 612	146 041	121 548	59 942	61 606	174 105	89 670	84 435
30 - 34	ESDJ	229 247	113 098	116 149	120 483	62 444	58 039	108 764	50 654	58 110
35 - 39	ESDJ	231 860	111 574	120 286	107 934	51 810	56 124	123 926	59 764	64 162
40 - 44	ESDJ	286 807	136 284	150 523	132 024	61 742	70 282	154 783	74 542	80 241
45 - 49	ESDJ	271 363	128 710	142 653	125 296	58 062	67 234	146 067	70 648	75 419
50 - 54	ESDJ	249 344	115 774	133 570	114 350	53 393	60 957	134 994	62 381	72 613
55 - 59	ESDJ	123 427	54 441	68 986	56 175	26 056	30 119	67 252	28 385	38 867
60 - 64	ESDJ	146 012	62 312	83 700	56 200	25 456	30 744	89 812	36 856	52 956
65 - 69	ESDJ	130 158	53 795	76 363	46 630	19 960	26 670	83 528	33 835	49 693
70 - 74	ESDJ	103 418	39 505	63 913	32 042	12 387	19 655	71 376	27 118	44 258
75 - 79	ESDJ	71 452	24 815	46 637	23 670	7 904	15 766	47 782	16 911	30 871
80 - 84	ESDJ	34 360	11 385	22 975	10 368	3 046	7 322	23 992	8 339	15 653
85+	ESDJ	15 047	4 108	10 939	5 785	1 509	4 276	9 262	2 599	6 663
Romania - Roumanie										
1 VII 2003										
Total	ESDJ	21 733 556	10 606 245	11 127 311	11 600 157	5 566 401	6 033 756	10 133 399	5 039 844	5 093 555
0 - 1	ESDJ	208 209	106 821	101 388	98 244	50 382	47 862	109 965	56 439	53 526
1 - 4	ESDJ	868 506	446 065	422 441	387 574	199 288	188 286	480 932	246 777	234 155
5 - 9	ESDJ	1 123 607	575 934	547 673	505 752	259 264	246 488	617 855	316 670	301 185
10 - 14	ESDJ	1 432 358	731 192	701 166	739 767	376 802	362 965	692 591	354 390	338 201
15 - 19	ESDJ	1 698 393	869 193	829 200	965 741	489 500	476 241	732 652	379 693	352 959
20 - 24	ESDJ	1 689 954	864 398	825 556	993 046	497 972	495 074	696 908	366 426	330 482
25 - 29	ESDJ	1 769 396	905 828	863 568	990 630	492 219	498 411	778 766	413 609	365 157
30 - 34	ESDJ	1 766 855	897 262	869 593	974 934	469 418	505 516	791 921	427 844	364 077
35 - 39	ESDJ	1 476 606	744 426	732 180	877 131	411 572	465 559	599 475	332 854	266 621
40 - 44	ESDJ	1 347 403	672 243	675 160	839 667	391 771	447 896	507 736	280 472	227 264
45 - 49	ESDJ	1 602 456	786 790	815 666	1 033 634	492 599	541 035	568 822	294 191	274 631
50 - 54	ESDJ	1 491 874	721 861	770 013	887 763	434 097	453 666	604 111	287 764	316 347
55 - 59	ESDJ	1 082 920	513 569	569 351	555 645	266 554	289 091	527 275	247 015	280 260
60 - 64	ESDJ	1 067 237	486 648	580 589	491 651	225 736	265 915	575 586	260 912	314 674
65 - 69	ESDJ	1 087 711	478 458	609 253	459 030	201 003	258 027	628 681	277 455	351 226
70 - 74	ESDJ	905 994	384 436	521 558	362 374	150 221	212 153	543 620	234 215	309 405
75 - 79	ESDJ	643 699	257 161	386 538	250 656	97 045	153 611	393 043	160 116	232 927
80 - 84	ESDJ	324 992	115 324	209 668	125 731	41 485	84 246	199 261	73 839	125 422
85 - 89	ESDJ	95 879	32 083	63 796	40 272	12 904	27 368	55 607	19 179	36 428
90 - 94	ESDJ	42 610	14 272	28 338	18 098	5 733	12 365	24 512	8 539	15 973
95 - 99	ESDJ	6 230	2 081	4 149	2 537	757	1 780	3 693	1 324	2 369
100+	ESDJ	667	200	467	280	79	201	387	121	266
Russian Federation - Fédération de Russie										
1 VII 1999										
Total	ESDF	145 943 393	68 405 752	77 537 641	106 488 089	49 622 408	56 865 681	39 455 304	18 783 344	20 671 960
0 - 1	ESDF	1 247 988	641 652	606 336	857 488	441 150	416 338	390 500	200 502	189 998
1 - 4	ESDF	5 273 255	2 703 604	2 569 651	3 601 015	1 848 352	1 752 663	1 672 240	855 252	816 988
5 - 9	ESDF	8 624 225	4 423 897	4 200 328	5 853 019	3 003 247	2 849 772	2 771 206	1 420 650	1 350 556
10 - 14	ESDF	12 073 276	6 152 074	5 921 202	8 414 270	4 291 221	4 123 049	3 659 006	1 860 853	1 798 153
15 - 19	ESDF	11 640 353	5 903 004	5 737 349	8 427 541	4 235 850	4 191 691	3 212 812	1 667 154	1 545 658
20 - 24	ESDF	10 694 954	5 403 032	5 291 922	8 002 226	3 994 587	4 007 639	2 692 728	1 408 445	1 284 283
25 - 29	ESDF	10 132 910	5 223 463	4 909 447	7 823 180	4 033 537	3 789 643	2 309 730	1 189 926	1 119 804
30 - 34	ESDF	9 601 516	4 839 812	4 761 704	7 139 919	3 594 303	3 545 616	2 461 597	1 245 509	1 216 088
35 - 39	ESDF	12 142 415	6 036 862	6 105 553	8 979 325	4 386 590	4 592 735	3 163 090	1 650 272	1 512 818

7. Population by age, sex and urban/rural residence: latest available year, 1994 - 2003
Population selon l'âge, le sexe et la résidence, urbaine/rurale: dernière année disponible, 1994 - 2003
(continued — suite)

Continent, country or area, date and age (in years) / Continent, pays ou zone, date et âge (en années)	Code[1]	Total Both sexes Les deux sexes	Total Male Masculin	Total Female Féminin	Urban - Urbaine Both sexes Les deux sexes	Urban - Urbaine Male Masculin	Urban - Urbaine Female Féminin	Rural - Rurale Both sexes Les deux sexes	Rural - Rurale Male Masculin	Rural - Rurale Female Féminin
EUROPE										
Russian Federation - Fédération de Russie										
1 VII 1999										
40 - 44	ESDF	12 503 481	6 112 856	6 390 625	9 386 098	4 492 980	4 893 118	3 117 383	1 619 876	1 497 507
45 - 49	ESDF	11 209 888	5 366 036	5 843 852	8 637 306	4 051 810	4 585 496	2 572 582	1 314 226	1 258 356
50 - 54	ESDF	7 681 472	3 578 859	4 102 613	6 070 884	2 786 751	3 284 133	1 610 588	792 108	818 480
55 - 59	ESDF	6 440 897	2 807 088	3 633 809	4 772 163	2 063 501	2 708 662	1 668 734	743 587	925 147
60 - 64	ESDF	8 409 982	3 506 323	4 903 659	6 059 829	2 487 725	3 572 104	2 350 153	1 018 598	1 331 555
65 - 69	ESDF	6 341 925	2 423 364	3 918 561	4 335 136	1 620 168	2 714 968	2 006 789	803 196	1 203 593
70 - 74	ESDF	6 028 319	1 968 872	4 059 447	4 152 137	1 369 386	2 782 751	1 876 182	599 486	1 276 696
75 - 79	ESDF	2 941 515	713 392	2 228 123	2 034 447	501 317	1 533 130	907 068	212 075	694 993
80 - 84	ESDF	1 589 627	340 138	1 249 489	1 074 249	242 399	831 850	515 378	97 739	417 639
85 - 89	ESDF	1 000 845	192 218	808 627	642 772	132 578	510 194	358 073	59 640	298 433
90 - 94	ESDF	284 809	50 479	234 330	176 436	32 916	143 520	108 373	17 563	90 810
95 - 99	ESDF	66 543	14 515	52 028	40 569	9 526	31 043	25 974	4 989	20 985
100+	ESDF	13 198	4 212	8 986	8 080	2 514	5 566	5 118	1 698	3 420
1 I 2001										
Total	ESDF	143 954 391	67 287 019	76 667 372	...	...	...	...	...	...
0 - 1	ESDF	1 309 841	673 515	636 326	...	...	...	...	...	...
0 - 4	ESDF	4 996 000	2 566 260	2 429 740	...	...	...	...	...	...
5 - 9	ESDF	7 123 120	3 652 229	3 470 891	...	...	...	...	...	...
10 - 14	ESDF	10 825 129	5 532 869	5 292 260	...	...	...	...	...	...
15 - 19	ESDF	12 208 011	6 199 698	6 008 313	...	...	...	...	...	...
20 - 24	ESDF	10 901 116	5 494 678	5 406 438	...	...	...	...	...	...
25 - 29	ESDF	10 422 406	5 259 573	5 162 833	...	...	...	...	...	...
30 - 34	ESDF	9 534 224	4 879 484	4 654 740	...	...	...	...	...	...
35 - 39	ESDF	10 587 806	5 256 996	5 330 810	...	...	...	...	...	...
40 - 44	ESDF	12 594 636	6 146 961	6 447 675	...	...	...	...	...	...
45 - 49	ESDF	11 625 074	5 538 814	6 086 260	...	...	...	...	...	...
50 - 54	ESDF	9 832 545	4 553 051	5 279 494	...	...	...	...	...	...
55 - 59	ESDF	4 840 576	2 134 498	2 706 078	...	...	...	...	...	...
60 - 64	ESDF	8 624 902	3 525 417	5 099 485	...	...	...	...	...	...
65 - 69	ESDF	5 973 442	2 284 876	3 688 566	...	...	...	...	...	...
70 - 74	ESDF	5 966 463	2 033 884	3 932 579	...	...	...	...	...	...
75 - 79	ESDF	3 758 139	960 722	2 797 417	...	...	...	...	...	...
80 - 84	ESDF	1 533 539	338 265	1 195 274	...	...	...	...	...	...
85 - 89	ESDF	884 600	168 050	716 550	...	...	...	...	...	...
90 - 94	ESDF	299 404	59 221	240 183	...	...	...	...	...	...
95 - 99	ESDF	83 799	19 285	64 514	...	...	...	...	...	...
100+	ESDF	29 619	8 673	20 946	...	...	...	...	...	...
San Marino - Saint-Marin										
1 VII 2003										
Total	ESDF	28 992	14 207	14 785	...	...	...	...	...	...
0 - 1	ESDF	312	188	124	...	...	...	...	...	...
1 - 4	ESDF	1 248	651	597	...	...	...	...	...	...
5 - 9	ESDF	1 473	767	706	...	...	...	...	...	...
10 - 14	ESDF	1 345	709	636	...	...	...	...	...	...
15 - 19	ESDF	1 301	677	624	...	...	...	...	...	...
20 - 24	ESDF	1 546	780	766	...	...	...	...	...	...
25 - 29	ESDF	2 092	1 008	1 084	...	...	...	...	...	...
30 - 34	ESDF	2 597	1 274	1 323	...	...	...	...	...	...
35 - 39	ESDF	2 803	1 343	1 460	...	...	...	...	...	...
40 - 44	ESDF	2 479	1 254	1 225	...	...	...	...	...	...
45 - 49	ESDF	1 980	990	990	...	...	...	...	...	...
50 - 54	ESDF	1 880	941	939	...	...	...	...	...	...
55 - 59	ESDF	1 776	864	912	...	...	...	...	...	...
60 - 64	ESDF	1 489	728	761	...	...	...	...	...	...
65 - 69	ESDF	1 344	676	668	...	...	...	...	...	...
70 - 74	ESDF	1 162	513	649	...	...	...	...	...	...
75 - 79	ESDF	947	416	531	...	...	...	...	...	...
80 - 84	ESDF	700	270	430	...	...	...	...	...	...

7. Population by age, sex and urban/rural residence: latest available year, 1994 - 2003
Population selon l'âge, le sexe et la résidence, urbaine/rurale: dernière année disponible, 1994 - 2003
(continued — suite)

Continent, country or area, date and age (in years) / Continent, pays ou zone, date et âge (en années)	Code[1]	Total			Urban - Urbaine			Rural - Rurale		
		Both sexes Les deux sexes	Male Masculin	Female Féminin	Both sexes Les deux sexes	Male Masculin	Female Féminin	Both sexes Les deux sexes	Male Masculin	Female Féminin
EUROPE										
San Marino - Saint-Marin										
1 VII 2003										
85 - 89	ESDF	324	102	222	...	...	...	...	...	...
90 - 94	ESDF	160	47	113	...	...	...	...	...	...
95 - 99	ESDF	31	9	22	...	...	...	...	...	...
100+	ESDF	3	-	3	...	...	...	...	...	...
Serbia and Montenegro - Serbie-et-Monteneg-ro[42,43]										
1 VII 2000										
Total	ESDJ	10 633 508	5 271 588	5 361 920	5 482 862	2 676 715	2 806 147	5 150 646	2 594 873	2 555 773
0 - 1	ESDJ	124 833	64 923	59 910	65 403	33 965	31 438	59 430	30 958	28 472
1 - 4	ESDJ	521 569	270 305	251 264	270 429	140 097	130 332	251 140	130 208	120 932
5 - 9	ESDJ	698 840	361 765	337 075	360 042	185 150	174 892	338 798	176 615	162 183
10 - 14	ESDJ	772 963	396 370	376 593	374 454	190 369	184 085	398 509	206 001	192 508
15 - 19	ESDJ	792 267	405 080	387 187	401 854	203 968	197 886	390 413	201 112	189 301
20 - 24	ESDJ	805 115	411 765	393 350	409 656	207 424	202 232	395 459	204 341	191 118
25 - 29	ESDJ	774 329	394 880	379 449	386 468	193 832	192 636	387 861	201 048	186 813
30 - 34	ESDJ	734 554	373 161	361 393	369 752	180 931	188 821	364 802	192 230	172 572
35 - 39	ESDJ	716 009	361 759	354 250	380 637	183 347	197 290	335 372	178 412	156 960
40 - 44	ESDJ	732 707	368 944	363 763	406 042	195 635	210 407	326 665	173 309	153 356
45 - 49	ESDJ	781 354	392 557	388 797	446 557	215 265	231 292	334 797	177 292	157 505
50 - 54	ESDJ	663 329	328 278	335 051	384 676	183 940	200 736	278 653	144 338	134 315
55 - 59	ESDJ	497 729	241 182	256 547	270 006	128 641	141 365	227 723	112 541	115 182
60 - 64	ESDJ	558 705	263 403	295 302	294 935	138 591	156 344	263 770	124 812	138 958
65 - 69	ESDJ	541 997	248 176	293 821	263 183	121 354	141 829	278 814	126 822	151 992
70 - 74	ESDJ	445 900	194 017	251 883	200 298	87 149	113 149	245 602	106 868	138 734
75 - 79	ESDJ	282 116	114 811	167 305	123 548	52 195	71 353	158 568	62 616	95 952
80 - 84	ESDJ	103 019	40 326	62 693	39 501	17 023	22 478	63 518	23 303	40 215
85 - 89	ESDJ	58 616	26 299	32 317	24 532	11 474	13 058	34 084	14 825	19 259
90 - 94	ESDJ	20 981	10 131	10 850	7 973	4 553	3 420	13 008	5 578	7 430
95 - 99	ESDJ	5 758	2 991	2 767	2 548	1 557	991	3 210	1 434	1 776
100+	ESDJ	818	465	353	368	255	113	450	210	240
1 VII 2002										
Total	ESDJ	8 108 672	3 947 145	4 161 527	...	...	...	...	...	...
0 - 1	ESDJ	72 945	37 502	35 443	...	...	...	...	...	...
1 - 4	ESDJ	298 577	153 366	145 211	...	...	...	...	...	...
5 - 9	ESDJ	434 739	224 011	210 728	...	...	...	...	...	...
10 - 14	ESDJ	482 193	247 020	235 173	...	...	...	...	...	...
15 - 19	ESDJ	543 409	277 813	265 596	...	...	...	...	...	...
20 - 24	ESDJ	563 442	287 373	276 069	...	...	...	...	...	...
25 - 29	ESDJ	558 930	281 543	277 387	...	...	...	...	...	...
30 - 34	ESDJ	524 752	262 580	262 172	...	...	...	...	...	...
35 - 39	ESDJ	530 516	263 265	267 251	...	...	...	...	...	...
40 - 44	ESDJ	575 122	284 789	290 333	...	...	...	...	...	...
45 - 49	ESDJ	652 302	325 090	327 212	...	...	...	...	...	...
50 - 54	ESDJ	623 937	307 112	316 825	...	...	...	...	...	...
55 - 59	ESDJ	430 293	206 116	224 177	...	...	...	...	...	...
60 - 64	ESDJ	465 381	217 329	248 052	...	...	...	...	...	...
65 - 69	ESDJ	486 852	221 648	265 204	...	...	...	...	...	...
70 - 74	ESDJ	416 975	180 835	236 140	...	...	...	...	...	...
75 - 79	ESDJ	272 488	105 453	167 035	...	...	...	...	...	...
80 - 84	ESDJ	122 042	45 069	76 973	...	...	...	...	...	...
85 - 89	ESDJ	33 229	11 784	21 445	...	...	...	...	...	...
90 - 94	ESDJ	16 136	5 832	10 304	...	...	...	...	...	...
95 - 99	ESDJ	3 159	1 162	1 997	...	...	...	...	...	...
100+	ESDJ	1 253	453	800	...	...	...	...	...	...

7. Population by age, sex and urban/rural residence: latest available year, 1994 - 2003
Population selon l'âge, le sexe et la résidence, urbaine/rurale: dernière année disponible, 1994 - 2003
(continued — suite)

Continent, country or area, date and age (in years) / Continent, pays ou zone, date et âge (en années)	Code[1]	Total			Urban - Urbaine			Rural - Rurale		
		Both sexes Les deux sexes	Male Masculin	Female Féminin	Both sexes Les deux sexes	Male Masculin	Female Féminin	Both sexes Les deux sexes	Male Masculin	Female Féminin
EUROPE										
Slovakia - Slovaquie[44]										
1 VII 2002										
Total	ESDJ	5 378 595	2 611 362	2 767 233	...	...	...	...	...	...
0 - 1	ESDJ	50 690	26 067	24 623	...	...	...	...	...	...
1 - 4	ESDJ	219 732	112 580	107 152	...	...	...	...	...	...
5 - 9	ESDJ	322 239	165 132	157 107	...	...	...	...	...	...
10 - 14	ESDJ	391 374	199 895	191 479	...	...	...	...	...	...
15 - 19	ESDJ	435 326	222 288	213 038	...	...	...	...	...	...
20 - 24	ESDJ	464 453	236 714	227 739	...	...	...	...	...	...
25 - 29	ESDJ	452 767	230 297	222 470	...	...	...	...	...	...
30 - 34	ESDJ	370 899	187 713	183 186	...	...	...	...	...	...
35 - 39	ESDJ	379 321	190 508	188 813	...	...	...	...	...	...
40 - 44	ESDJ	392 875	197 229	195 646	...	...	...	...	...	...
45 - 49	ESDJ	416 012	205 777	210 235	...	...	...	...	...	...
50 - 54	ESDJ	366 912	178 117	188 795	...	...	...	...	...	...
55 - 59	ESDJ	267 544	123 871	143 673	...	...	...	...	...	...
60 - 64	ESDJ	227 019	100 218	126 801	...	...	...	...	...	...
65 - 69	ESDJ	196 483	82 093	114 390	...	...	...	...	...	...
70 - 74	ESDJ	177 410	68 988	108 422	...	...	...	...	...	...
75 - 79	ESDJ	135 947	48 213	87 734	...	...	...	...	...	...
80 - 84	ESDJ	70 854	23 555	47 299	...	...	...	...	...	...
85 - 89	ESDJ	27 551	8 493	19 058	...	...	...	...	...	...
90 - 94	ESDJ	11 097	3 054	8 043	...	...	...	...	...	...
95 - 99	ESDJ	1 930	503	1 427	...	...	...	...	...	...
100+	ESDJ	160	57	103	...	...	...	...	...	...
Slovenia - Slovénie[45]										
1 VII 2003										
Total	ESDJ	1 996 773	977 436	1 019 337	971 513	460 811	510 702	978 698	483 434	495 264
0 - 1	ESDJ	17 380	9 033	8 347	8 170	4 308	3 862	9 061	4 650	4 411
1 - 4	ESDJ	71 804	37 035	34 769	33 245	17 232	16 013	37 682	19 349	18 333
5 - 9	ESDJ	95 502	49 033	46 469	43 607	22 314	21 293	50 873	26 209	24 664
10 - 14	ESDJ	110 162	56 630	53 532	50 678	26 007	24 671	58 267	29 998	28 269
15 - 19	ESDJ	129 624	66 337	63 287	62 338	31 855	30 483	65 735	33 603	32 132
20 - 24	ESDJ	148 275	76 499	71 776	71 470	36 473	34 997	72 992	37 462	35 530
25 - 29	ESDJ	150 526	77 941	72 585	71 211	36 031	35 180	73 784	38 014	35 770
30 - 34	ESDJ	143 089	73 240	69 849	67 370	33 175	34 195	70 259	36 221	34 038
35 - 39	ESDJ	154 881	78 062	76 819	73 992	35 234	38 758	75 068	38 485	36 583
40 - 44	ESDJ	154 936	78 944	75 992	75 650	36 109	39 541	73 367	38 199	35 168
45 - 49	ESDJ	159 366	81 961	77 405	80 008	38 664	41 344	74 022	38 970	35 052
50 - 54	ESDJ	148 629	76 489	72 140	75 976	37 202	38 774	68 799	36 180	32 619
55 - 59	ESDJ	109 152	54 179	54 973	56 214	26 389	29 825	50 723	26 060	24 663
60 - 64	ESDJ	106 304	50 669	55 635	53 638	24 463	29 175	51 145	25 106	26 039
65 - 69	ESDJ	94 886	42 504	52 382	47 523	21 105	26 418	46 502	20 898	25 604
70 - 74	ESDJ	85 194	34 140	51 054	42 069	16 503	25 566	42 514	17 332	25 182
75 - 79	ESDJ	62 022	20 207	41 815	31 037	10 249	20 788	30 558	9 775	20 783
80 - 84	ESDJ	35 151	9 706	25 445	17 501	5 035	12 466	17 439	4 602	12 837
85 - 89	ESDJ	12 266	3 162	9 104	6 063	1 625	4 438	6 124	1 506	4 618
90 - 94	ESDJ	6 467	1 467	5 000	3 194	742	2 452	3 213	715	2 498
95 - 99	ESDJ	1 053	187	866	511	91	420	520	95	425
100+	ESDJ	104	11	93	48	5	43	51	5	46
Unk. - Inc.	ESDJ	-	-	-	-	-	-	-	-	-
Spain - Espagne										
1 VII 2003										
Total	ESDJ	41 874 277	20 554 697	21 319 580	...	...	...	...	...	...
0 - 1	ESDJ	427 019	220 339	206 680	...	...	...	...	...	...
1 - 4	ESDJ	1 621 287	832 710	788 577	...	...	...	...	...	...
5 - 9	ESDJ	1 926 445	988 351	938 094	...	...	...	...	...	...
10 - 14	ESDJ	2 094 491	1 075 982	1 018 509	...	...	...	...	...	...
15 - 19	ESDJ	2 377 707	1 219 501	1 158 206	...	...	...	...	...	...
20 - 24	ESDJ	3 065 906	1 568 396	1 497 510	...	...	...	...	...	...
25 - 29	ESDJ	3 614 427	1 853 660	1 760 767	...	...	...	...	...	...

7. Population by age, sex and urban/rural residence: latest available year, 1994 - 2003
Population selon l'âge, le sexe et la résidence, urbaine/rurale: dernière année disponible, 1994 - 2003
(continued — suite)

Continent, country or area, date and age (in years) / Continent, pays ou zone, date et âge (en années)	Code[1]	Total			Urban - Urbaine			Rural - Rurale		
		Both sexes Les deux sexes	Male Masculin	Female Féminin	Both sexes Les deux sexes	Male Masculin	Female Féminin	Both sexes Les deux sexes	Male Masculin	Female Féminin
EUROPE										
Spain - Espagne										
1 VII 2003										
30 - 34	ESDJ	3 540 486	1 809 915	1 730 571	...	...	...	...	...	...
35 - 39	ESDJ	3 421 012	1 729 329	1 691 683	...	...	...	...	...	...
40 - 44	ESDJ	3 173 281	1 589 340	1 583 941	...	...	...	...	...	...
45 - 49	ESDJ	2 784 553	1 385 761	1 398 792	...	...	...	...	...	...
50 - 54	ESDJ	2 492 321	1 232 617	1 259 704	...	...	...	...	...	...
55 - 59	ESDJ	2 329 529	1 138 057	1 191 472	...	...	...	...	...	...
60 - 64	ESDJ	1 946 778	936 299	1 010 479	...	...	...	...	...	...
65 - 69	ESDJ	1 974 113	919 472	1 054 641	...	...	...	...	...	...
70 - 74	ESDJ	1 894 107	848 686	1 045 421	...	...	...	...	...	...
75 - 79	ESDJ	1 488 352	621 786	866 566	...	...	...	...	...	...
80 - 84	ESDJ	969 295	362 356	606 939	...	...	...	...	...	...
85 - 89	ESDJ	489 806	154 623	335 183	...	...	...	...	...	...
90 - 94	ESDJ	195 848	55 298	140 550	...	...	...	...	...	...
95 - 99	ESDJ	41 879	10 702	31 177	...	...	...	...	...	...
100+	ESDJ	5 635	1 517	4 118	...	...	...	...	...	...
Sweden - Suède										
1 VII 2002										
Total	ESDJ	8 924 960	4 417 777	4 507 183	...	...	...	...	...	...
0 - 1	ESDJ	93 840	48 245	45 595	...	...	...	...	...	...
1 - 4	ESDJ	365 295	187 670	177 625	...	...	...	...	...	...
5 - 9	ESDJ	542 221	277 443	264 778	...	...	...	...	...	...
10 - 14	ESDJ	614 752	315 888	298 864	...	...	...	...	...	...
15 - 19	ESDJ	525 649	270 321	255 328	...	...	...	...	...	...
20 - 24	ESDJ	516 326	262 797	253 529	...	...	...	...	...	...
25 - 29	ESDJ	574 843	292 507	282 336	...	...	...	...	...	...
30 - 34	ESDJ	615 378	313 403	301 975	...	...	...	...	...	...
35 - 39	ESDJ	658 005	337 402	320 603	...	...	...	...	...	...
40 - 44	ESDJ	584 793	297 890	286 903	...	...	...	...	...	...
45 - 49	ESDJ	586 046	297 106	288 940	...	...	...	...	...	...
50 - 54	ESDJ	616 070	310 591	305 479	...	...	...	...	...	...
55 - 59	ESDJ	632 468	319 803	312 665	...	...	...	...	...	...
60 - 64	ESDJ	466 438	232 705	233 733	...	...	...	...	...	...
65 - 69	ESDJ	382 395	183 972	198 423	...	...	...	...	...	...
70 - 74	ESDJ	357 480	163 260	194 220	...	...	...	...	...	...
75 - 79	ESDJ	326 215	140 762	185 453	...	...	...	...	...	...
80 - 84	ESDJ	258 080	101 291	156 789	...	...	...	...	...	...
85 - 89	ESDJ	141 060	47 324	93 736	...	...	...	...	...	...
90 - 94	ESDJ	55 327	15 042	40 285	...	...	...	...	...	...
95 - 99	ESDJ	11 359	2 272	9 087	...	...	...	...	...	...
100+	ESDJ	1 088	166	922	...	...	...	...	...	...
Switzerland - Suisse										
1 VII 2002										
Total	ESDJ	7 284 753	3 559 689	3 725 064	...	...	...	...	...	...
0 - 1	ESDJ	71 903	36 992	34 911	...	...	...	...	...	...
1 - 4	ESDJ	302 164	155 186	146 979	...	...	...	...	...	...
5 - 9	ESDJ	413 583	212 072	201 512	...	...	...	...	...	...
10 - 14	ESDJ	435 510	223 421	212 089	...	...	...	...	...	...
15 - 19	ESDJ	419 608	214 781	204 828	...	...	...	...	...	...
20 - 24	ESDJ	428 802	215 680	213 123	...	...	...	...	...	...
25 - 29	ESDJ	466 805	232 227	234 578	...	...	...	...	...	...
30 - 34	ESDJ	563 550	279 918	283 632	...	...	...	...	...	...
35 - 39	ESDJ	629 980	316 954	313 026	...	...	...	...	...	...
40 - 44	ESDJ	579 983	292 525	287 459	...	...	...	...	...	...
45 - 49	ESDJ	517 705	260 779	256 927	...	...	...	...	...	...
50 - 54	ESDJ	489 939	245 626	244 313	...	...	...	...	...	...
55 - 59	ESDJ	461 853	231 061	230 792	...	...	...	...	...	...
60 - 64	ESDJ	366 559	177 982	188 577	...	...	...	...	...	...
65 - 69	ESDJ	316 879	147 527	169 353	...	...	...	...	...	...
70 - 74	ESDJ	278 440	121 583	156 857	...	...	...	...	...	...
75 - 79	ESDJ	231 920	92 956	138 964	...	...	...	...	...	...

7. Population by age, sex and urban/rural residence: latest available year, 1994 - 2003
Population selon l'âge, le sexe et la résidence, urbaine/rurale: dernière année disponible, 1994 - 2003
(continued — suite)

Continent, country or area, date and age (in years) Continent, pays ou zone, date et âge (en annèes)	Code[1]	Total			Urban - Urbaine			Rural - Rurale		
		Both sexes Les deux sexes	Male Masculin	Female Féminin	Both sexes Les deux sexes	Male Masculin	Female Féminin	Both sexes Les deux sexes	Male Masculin	Female Féminin
EUROPE										
Switzerland - Suisse										
1 VII 2002										
80 - 84	ESDJ	163 359	60 013	103 346	...	...	...	...	...	...
85 - 89	ESDJ	94 916	29 970	64 946	...	...	...	...	...	...
90 - 94	ESDJ	41 412	10 480	30 933	...	...	...	...	...	...
95+	ESDJ	9 887	1 963	7 925	...	...	...	...	...	...
The Former Yugoslav Rep. of Macedonia - L'ex-République yougoslave de Macédoine										
20 VI 1994										
Total	CDJC	1 935 034	968 931	966 103	1 156 297	574 461	581 836	778 737	394 470	384 267
0 - 1	CDJC	28 626	14 688	13 938	15 006	7 678	7 328	13 620	7 010	6 610
1 - 4	CDJC	122 661	63 281	59 380	65 521	33 772	31 749	57 140	29 509	27 631
5 - 9	CDJC	162 672	83 649	79 023	91 559	47 127	44 432	71 113	36 522	34 591
10 - 14	CDJC	166 993	85 716	81 277	97 231	49 572	47 659	69 762	36 144	33 618
15 - 19	CDJC	161 947	82 731	79 216	93 395	47 311	46 084	68 552	35 420	33 132
20 - 24	CDJC	152 720	77 984	74 736	87 496	44 132	43 364	65 224	33 852	31 372
25 - 29	CDJC	150 545	76 309	74 236	87 079	42 986	44 093	63 466	33 323	30 143
30 - 34	CDJC	147 733	74 873	72 860	89 325	44 130	45 195	58 408	30 743	27 665
35 - 39	CDJC	145 144	74 150	70 994	94 448	47 380	47 068	50 696	26 770	23 926
40 - 44	CDJC	136 590	68 684	67 906	94 134	47 158	46 976	42 456	21 526	20 930
45 - 49	CDJC	109 351	53 715	55 636	74 941	36 941	38 000	34 410	16 774	17 636
50 - 54	CDJC	99 300	48 653	50 647	64 263	31 747	32 516	35 037	16 906	18 131
55 - 59	CDJC	95 419	46 243	49 176	59 768	29 374	30 394	35 651	16 869	18 782
60 - 64	CDJC	88 511	42 203	46 308	52 236	24 720	27 516	36 275	17 483	18 792
65 - 69	CDJC	67 323	31 107	36 216	38 531	17 705	20 826	28 792	13 402	15 390
70 - 74	CDJC	50 502	22 826	27 676	27 771	12 443	15 328	22 731	10 383	12 348
75 - 79	CDJC	20 709	9 552	11 157	10 415	4 565	5 850	10 294	4 987	5 307
80 - 84	CDJC	17 372	8 030	9 342	8 587	3 792	4 795	8 785	4 238	4 547
85 - 89	CDJC	5 708	2 616	3 092	2 854	1 252	1 602	2 854	1 364	1 490
90 - 94	CDJC	1 651	671	980	844	343	501	807	328	479
95 - 99	CDJC	279	114	165	150	58	92	129	56	73
100+	CDJC	112	38	74	52	19	33	60	19	41
Unk. - Inc.	CDJC	3 166	1 098	2 068	691	256	435	2 475	842	1 633
1 VII 2003										
Total	ESDF	2 026 773	1 017 274	1 009 499	...	...	...	...	...	...
0 - 1	ESDF	23 154	11 943	11 211	...	...	...	...	...	...
1 - 4	ESDF	98 359	50 792	47 567	...	...	...	...	...	...
5 - 9	ESDF	140 097	72 227	67 870	...	...	...	...	...	...
10 - 14	ESDF	158 323	81 451	76 872	...	...	...	...	...	...
15 - 19	ESDF	165 637	84 978	80 660	...	...	...	...	...	...
20 - 24	ESDF	163 137	84 130	79 007	...	...	...	...	...	...
25 - 29	ESDF	154 594	79 090	75 504	...	...	...	...	...	...
30 - 34	ESDF	148 275	75 249	73 027	...	...	...	...	...	...
35 - 39	ESDF	150 499	76 504	73 995	...	...	...	...	...	...
40 - 44	ESDF	146 658	74 728	71 930	...	...	...	...	...	...
45 - 49	ESDF	143 320	73 291	70 029	...	...	...	...	...	...
50 - 54	ESDF	129 007	64 012	64 995	...	...	...	...	...	...
55 - 59	ESDF	99 296	48 386	50 911	...	...	...	...	...	...
60 - 64	ESDF	89 654	43 144	46 510	...	...	...	...	...	...
65 - 69	ESDF	83 415	39 146	44 270	...	...	...	...	...	...
70 - 74	ESDF	63 767	28 762	35 005	...	...	...	...	...	...
75 - 79	ESDF	40 634	17 426	23 208	...	...	...	...	...	...
80 - 84	ESDF	20 146	8 473	11 674	...	...	...	...	...	...
85 - 89	ESDF	5 312	2 292	3 021	...	...	...	...	...	...
90 - 94	ESDF	1 991	818	1 173	...	...	...	...	...	...
95+	ESDF	369	141	229	...	...	...	...	...	...
Unk. - Inc.	ESDF	1 134	296	838	...	...	...	...	...	...

7. Population by age, sex and urban/rural residence: latest available year, 1994 - 2003
Population selon l'âge, le sexe et la résidence, urbaine/rurale: dernière année disponible, 1994 - 2003
(continued — suite)

Continent, country or area, date and age (in years) / Continent, pays ou zone, date et âge (en années)	Code[1]	Total Both sexes Les deux sexes	Total Male Masculin	Total Female Féminin	Urban - Urbaine Both sexes Les deux sexes	Urban - Urbaine Male Masculin	Urban - Urbaine Female Féminin	Rural - Rurale Both sexes Les deux sexes	Rural - Rurale Male Masculin	Rural - Rurale Female Féminin
EUROPE										
Ukraine										
1 I 2000										
Total	ESDF	49 456 088	22 978 364	26 477 724	33 505 862	15 617 268	17 888 594	15 950 226	7 361 096	8 589 130
0 - 1	ESDF	384 980	198 354	186 626	236 787	122 275	114 512	148 193	76 079	72 114
1 - 4	ESDF	1 788 699	919 015	869 684	1 111 882	571 821	540 061	676 817	347 194	329 623
5 - 9	ESDF	2 916 281	1 494 369	1 421 912	1 883 784	967 011	916 773	1 032 497	527 358	505 139
10 - 14	ESDF	3 735 293	1 902 893	1 832 400	2 512 646	1 280 784	1 231 862	1 222 647	622 109	600 538
15 - 19	ESDF	3 765 026	1 911 977	1 853 049	2 658 519	1 339 952	1 318 567	1 106 507	572 025	534 482
20 - 24	ESDF	3 591 292	1 819 369	1 771 923	2 558 515	1 283 993	1 274 522	1 032 777	535 376	497 401
25 - 29	ESDF	3 572 343	1 824 781	1 747 562	2 547 820	1 295 618	1 252 202	1 024 523	529 163	495 360
30 - 34	ESDF	3 237 966	1 613 622	1 624 344	2 251 564	1 099 648	1 151 916	986 402	513 974	472 428
35 - 39	ESDF	3 764 789	1 841 151	1 923 638	2 702 737	1 294 593	1 408 144	1 062 052	546 558	515 494
40 - 44	ESDF	3 778 496	1 815 712	1 962 784	2 757 518	1 297 091	1 460 427	1 020 978	518 621	502 357
45 - 49	ESDF	3 510 913	1 651 749	1 859 164	2 601 842	1 203 492	1 398 350	909 071	448 257	460 814
50 - 54	ESDF	2 751 783	1 255 818	1 495 965	2 023 520	918 093	1 105 427	728 263	337 725	390 538
55 - 59	ESDF	2 504 490	1 088 853	1 415 637	1 628 499	713 950	914 549	875 991	374 903	501 088
60 - 64	ESDF	3 324 060	1 400 640	1 923 420	2 151 452	909 188	1 242 264	1 172 608	491 452	681 156
65 - 69	ESDF	2 105 700	833 941	1 271 759	1 221 364	490 866	730 498	884 336	343 075	541 261
70 - 74	ESDF	2 288 411	786 754	1 501 657	1 348 209	479 513	868 696	940 202	307 241	632 961
75 - 79	ESDF	1 326 381	361 585	964 796	717 931	201 080	516 851	608 450	160 505	447 945
80 - 84	ESDF	580 522	141 516	439 006	322 726	85 139	237 587	257 796	56 377	201 419
85 - 89	ESDF	387 150	86 878	300 272	198 310	48 289	150 021	188 840	38 589	150 251
90 - 94	ESDF	117 445	23 065	94 380	57 130	11 590	45 540	60 315	11 475	48 840
95 - 99	ESDF	22 689	5 518	17 171	12 130	2 765	9 365	10 559	2 753	7 806
100+	ESDF	1 379	804	575	977	517	460	402	287	115
1 I 2003										
Total	ESDJ	47 823 108	22 112 534	25 710 574	...	...	...	...	...	...
0 - 1	ESDJ	387 328	199 843	187 485	...	...	...	...	...	...
1 - 4	ESDJ	1 552 212	796 718	755 494	...	...	...	...	...	...
5 - 9	ESDJ	2 404 254	1 232 129	1 172 125	...	...	...	...	...	...
10 - 14	ESDJ	3 225 683	1 652 905	1 572 778	...	...	...	...	...	...
15 - 19	ESDJ	3 902 340	1 994 395	1 907 945	...	...	...	...	...	...
20 - 24	ESDJ	3 555 484	1 806 777	1 748 707	...	...	...	...	...	...
25 - 29	ESDJ	3 385 842	1 694 835	1 691 007	...	...	...	...	...	...
30 - 34	ESDJ	3 253 815	1 611 337	1 642 478	...	...	...	...	...	...
35 - 39	ESDJ	3 280 627	1 596 220	1 684 407	...	...	...	...	...	...
40 - 44	ESDJ	3 806 522	1 821 641	1 984 881	...	...	...	...	...	...
45 - 49	ESDJ	3 487 458	1 630 146	1 857 312	...	...	...	...	...	...
50 - 54	ESDJ	3 303 447	1 506 908	1 796 539	...	...	...	...	...	...
55 - 59	ESDJ	2 085 395	905 341	1 180 054	...	...	...	...	...	...
60 - 64	ESDJ	2 999 237	1 235 579	1 763 658	...	...	...	...	...	...
65 - 69	ESDJ	2 415 100	970 319	1 444 781	...	...	...	...	...	...
70 - 74	ESDJ	2 100 807	757 132	1 343 675	...	...	...	...	...	...
75 - 79	ESDJ	1 587 806	460 527	1 127 279	...	...	...	...	...	...
80 - 84	ESDJ	690 083	161 746	528 337	...	...	...	...	...	...
85 - 89	ESDJ	271 382	55 030	216 352	...	...	...	...	...	...
90 - 94	ESDJ	111 343	20 345	90 998	...	...	...	...	...	...
95 - 99	ESDJ	15 384	2 472	12 912	...	...	...	...	...	...
100+	ESDJ	1 559	189	1 370	...	...	...	...	...	...
United Kingdom - Royaume-Uni										
1 VII 2003										
Total	ESDF	59 553 800	29 108 000	30 445 700	...	...	...	...	...	...
0 - 1	ESDF	679 400	348 900	330 500	...	...	...	...	...	...
1 - 4	ESDF	2 703 300	1 384 200	1 319 100	...	...	...	...	...	...
5 - 9	ESDF	3 650 000	1 869 300	1 780 800	...	...	...	...	...	...
10 - 14	ESDF	3 891 400	1 995 300	1 896 200	...	...	...	...	...	...
15 - 19	ESDF	3 855 200	1 982 700	1 872 800	...	...	...	...	...	...
20 - 24	ESDF	3 719 300	1 866 900	1 852 300	...	...	...	...	...	...
25 - 29	ESDF	3 659 500	1 830 200	1 829 200	...	...	...	...	...	...
30 - 34	ESDF	4 410 800	2 187 800	2 223 000	...	...	...	...	...	...
35 - 39	ESDF	4 710 600	2 335 500	2 375 100	...	...	...	...	...	...

7. Population by age, sex and urban/rural residence: latest available year, 1994 - 2003
Population selon l'âge, le sexe et la résidence, urbaine/rurale: dernière année disponible, 1994 - 2003
(continued — suite)

Continent, country or area, date and age (in years) / Continent, pays ou zone, date et âge (en années)	Code[1]	Total			Urban - Urbaine			Rural - Rurale		
		Both sexes Les deux sexes	Male Masculin	Female Féminin	Both sexes Les deux sexes	Male Masculin	Female Féminin	Both sexes Les deux sexes	Male Masculin	Female Féminin
EUROPE										
United Kingdom - Royaume-Uni										
1 VII 2003										
40 - 44	ESDF	4 397 300	2 178 100	2 219 200	...	...	...	...	...	...
45 - 49	ESDF	3 870 800	1 916 700	1 954 100	...	...	...	...	...	...
50 - 54	ESDF	3 743 300	1 853 100	1 890 200	...	...	...	...	...	...
55 - 59	ESDF	3 810 200	1 883 100	1 927 200	...	...	...	...	...	...
60 - 64	ESDF	2 942 700	1 438 700	1 504 000	...	...	...	...	...	...
65 - 69	ESDF	2 657 100	1 278 700	1 378 400	...	...	...	...	...	...
70 - 74	ESDF	2 347 700	1 075 100	1 272 600	...	...	...	...	...	...
75 - 79	ESDF	1 932 500	820 100	1 112 400	...	...	...	...	...	...
80 - 84	ESDF	1 468 300	550 500	917 900	...	...	...	...	...	...
85 - 89	ESDF	705 800	219 400	486 200	...	...	...	...	...	...
90+	ESDF	398 500	93 700	304 900	...	...	...	...	...	...
OCEANIA — OCEANIE										
American Samoa - Samoas américaines[8]										
1 IV 2000										
Total	CDJC	57 291	29 264	28 027	...	...	...	...	...	...
0 - 4	CDJC	7 820	...	...	...	...	...	...	...	...
5 - 9	CDJC	7 788	...	...	...	...	...	...	...	...
10 - 14	CDJC	6 604	...	...	...	...	...	...	...	...
15 - 19	CDJC	5 223	...	...	...	...	...	...	...	...
20 - 24	CDJC	4 476	...	...	...	...	...	...	...	...
25 - 34	CDJC	8 707	...	...	...	...	...	...	...	...
35 - 44	CDJC	7 361	...	...	...	...	...	...	...	...
45 - 54	CDJC	4 733	...	...	...	...	...	...	...	...
55 - 59	CDJC	1 474	...	...	...	...	...	...	...	...
60 - 64	CDJC	1 204	...	...	...	...	...	...	...	...
65 - 74	CDJC	1 345	...	...	...	...	...	...	...	...
75 - 84	CDJC	465	...	...	...	...	...	...	...	...
85+	CDJC	91	...	...	...	...	...	...	...	...
Australia - Australie										
1 VII 2003										
Total	ESDJ	19 881 469	9 871 642	10 009 827	...	...	...	...	...	...
0 - 1	ESDJ	247 051	126 631	120 420	...	...	...	...	...	...
1 - 4	ESDJ	1 264 661	648 266	616 395	...	...	...	...	...	...
5 - 9	ESDJ	1 336 305	686 149	650 156	...	...	...	...	...	...
10 - 14	ESDJ	1 378 444	706 517	671 927	...	...	...	...	...	...
15 - 19	ESDJ	1 376 787	703 874	672 913	...	...	...	...	...	...
20 - 24	ESDJ	1 376 836	700 428	676 408	...	...	...	...	...	...
25 - 29	ESDJ	1 361 783	683 150	678 633	...	...	...	...	...	...
30 - 34	ESDJ	1 517 217	751 904	765 313	...	...	...	...	...	...
35 - 39	ESDJ	1 458 527	724 527	734 000	...	...	...	...	...	...
40 - 44	ESDJ	1 531 460	762 199	769 261	...	...	...	...	...	...
45 - 49	ESDJ	1 400 484	694 878	705 606	...	...	...	...	...	...
50 - 54	ESDJ	1 309 774	652 802	656 972	...	...	...	...	...	...
55 - 59	ESDJ	1 153 945	583 508	570 437	...	...	...	...	...	...
60 - 64	ESDJ	869 605	439 155	430 450	...	...	...	...	...	...
65 - 69	ESDJ	720 072	354 970	365 102	...	...	...	...	...	...
70 - 74	ESDJ	629 877	301 236	328 641	...	...	...	...	...	...
75 - 79	ESDJ	537 980	240 098	297 882	...	...	...	...	...	...
80 - 84	ESDJ	368 189	146 560	221 629	...	...	...	...	...	...
85 - 89	ESDJ	190 953	64 456	126 497	...	...	...	...	...	...
90 - 94	ESDJ	75 981	21 180	54 801	...	...	...	...	...	...
95 - 99	ESDJ	18 823	4 586	14 237	...	...	...	...	...	...
100+	ESDJ	3 766	1 199	2 567	...	...	...	...	...	...

7. Population by age, sex and urban/rural residence: latest available year, 1994 - 2003
Population selon l'âge, le sexe et la résidence, urbaine/rurale: dernière année disponible, 1994 - 2003
(continued — suite)

Continent, country or area, date and age (in years) / Continent, pays ou zone, date et âge (en années)	Code[1]	Total			Urban - Urbaine			Rural - Rurale		
		Both sexes Les deux sexes	Male Masculin	Female Féminin	Both sexes Les deux sexes	Male Masculin	Female Féminin	Both sexes Les deux sexes	Male Masculin	Female Féminin
OCEANIA — OCEANIE										
Cook Islands - Îles Cook[46,47]										
1 XII 2001										
Total	CDFC	18 027	...	...	...	...	...	...	...	...
0 - 4	CDFC	1 722	...	...	...	...	...	...	...	...
5 - 9	CDFC	1 895	...	...	...	...	...	...	...	...
10 - 14	CDFC	1 798	...	...	...	...	...	...	...	...
15 - 19	CDFC	1 460	...	...	...	...	...	...	...	...
20 - 24	CDFC	1 227	...	...	...	...	...	...	...	...
25 - 29	CDFC	1 385	...	...	...	...	...	...	...	...
30 - 34	CDFC	1 431	...	...	...	...	...	...	...	...
35 - 39	CDFC	1 367	...	...	...	...	...	...	...	...
40 - 44	CDFC	1 194	...	...	...	...	...	...	...	...
45 - 49	CDFC	925	...	...	...	...	...	...	...	...
50 - 54	CDFC	906	...	...	...	...	...	...	...	...
55 - 59	CDFC	799	...	...	...	...	...	...	...	...
60 - 64	CDFC	730	...	...	...	...	...	...	...	...
65 - 69	CDFC	538	...	...	...	...	...	...	...	...
70 - 74	CDFC	324	...	...	...	...	...	...	...	...
75 - 79	CDFC	195	...	...	...	...	...	...	...	...
80+	CDFC	131	...	...	...	...	...	...	...	...
Fiji - Fidji										
25 VIII 1996										
Total	CDFC	775 077	393 931	381 146	359 495	180 119	179 376	415 582	213 812	201 770
0 - 1	CDFC	18 239	9 282	8 957	8 136	4 213	3 923	10 103	5 069	5 034
1 - 4	CDFC	75 975	39 281	36 694	32 702	16 877	15 825	43 273	22 404	20 869
5 - 9	CDFC	87 095	44 937	42 158	35 977	18 271	17 706	51 118	26 666	24 452
10 - 14	CDFC	92 855	47 709	45 146	40 497	20 644	19 853	52 358	27 065	25 293
15 - 19	CDFC	83 682	42 829	40 853	41 404	20 748	20 656	42 278	22 081	20 197
20 - 24	CDFC	66 955	34 444	32 511	35 678	17 936	17 742	31 277	16 508	14 769
25 - 29	CDFC	61 660	31 283	30 377	30 706	15 554	15 152	30 954	15 729	15 225
30 - 34	CDFC	60 841	30 727	30 114	28 905	14 318	14 587	31 936	16 409	15 527
35 - 39	CDFC	55 779	28 525	27 254	26 975	13 523	13 452	28 804	15 002	13 802
40 - 44	CDFC	44 180	22 341	21 839	21 863	10 765	11 098	22 317	11 576	10 741
45 - 49	CDFC	37 081	18 482	18 599	18 007	8 913	9 094	19 074	9 569	9 505
50 - 54	CDFC	28 683	14 286	14 397	13 300	6 567	6 733	15 383	7 719	7 664
55 - 59	CDFC	22 245	10 857	11 388	9 562	4 560	5 002	12 683	6 297	6 386
60 - 64	CDFC	15 459	7 605	7 854	6 389	3 039	3 350	9 070	4 566	4 504
65 - 69	CDFC	10 761	5 138	5 623	4 191	1 941	2 250	6 570	3 197	3 373
70 - 74	CDFC	6 357	3 054	3 303	2 473	1 129	1 344	3 884	1 925	1 959
75 - 79	CDFC	4 152	1 881	2 271	1 558	654	904	2 594	1 227	1 367
80 - 84	CDFC	1 938	843	1 095	782	339	443	1 156	504	652
85 - 89	CDFC	772	290	482	266	97	169	506	193	313
90 - 94	CDFC	265	100	165	82	23	59	183	77	106
95+	CDFC	103	37	66	42	8	34	61	29	32
French Polynesia - Polynésie française										
1 I 1999										
Total	ESDF	227 525	117 738	109 787	...	...	...	...	...	...
0 - 1	ESDF	4 268	2 177	2 091	...	...	...	...	...	...
1 - 4	ESDF	18 470	9 604	8 866	...	...	...	...	...	...
5 - 9	ESDF	25 518	13 178	12 340	...	...	...	...	...	...
10 - 14	ESDF	25 533	13 055	12 478	...	...	...	...	...	...
15 - 19	ESDF	22 126	11 290	10 836	...	...	...	...	...	...
20 - 24	ESDF	19 077	9 884	9 193	...	...	...	...	...	...
25 - 29	ESDF	19 574	10 141	9 433	...	...	...	...	...	...
30 - 34	ESDF	19 667	10 179	9 488	...	...	...	...	...	...
35 - 39	ESDF	17 032	8 941	8 091	...	...	...	...	...	...
40 - 44	ESDF	14 421	7 640	6 781	...	...	...	...	...	...
45 - 49	ESDF	11 037	5 830	5 207	...	...	...	...	...	...
50 - 54	ESDF	9 001	4 790	4 211	...	...	...	...	...	...
55 - 59	ESDF	7 202	3 845	3 357	...	...	...	...	...	...

7. Population by age, sex and urban/rural residence: latest available year, 1994 - 2003
Population selon l'âge, le sexe et la résidence, urbaine/rurale: dernière année disponible, 1994 - 2003
(continued — suite)

Continent, country or area, date and age (in years) Continent, pays ou zone, date et âge (en années)	Code[1]	Total			Urban - Urbaine			Rural - Rurale		
		Both sexes Les deux sexes	Male Masculin	Female Féminin	Both sexes Les deux sexes	Male Masculin	Female Féminin	Both sexes Les deux sexes	Male Masculin	Female Féminin
OCEANIA — OCEANIE										
French Polynesia - Polynésie française										
1 I 1999										
60 - 64	ESDF	5 518	2 899	2 619	...	...	...	...	...	...
65 - 69	ESDF	3 998	2 042	1 956	...	...	...	...	...	...
70 - 74	ESDF	2 600	1 244	1 356	...	...	...	...	...	...
75 - 79	ESDF	1 365	585	780	...	...	...	...	...	...
80+	ESDF	1 118	414	704	...	...	...	...	...	...
Guam[8]										
1 IV 2000										
Total	CDJC	154 805	79 181	75 624	...	...	...	...	...	...
0 - 1	CDJC	3 535	1 862	1 673	...	...	...	...	...	...
1 - 4	CDJC	13 250	6 945	6 305	...	...	...	...	...	...
5 - 9	CDJC	16 090	8 270	7 820	...	...	...	...	...	...
10 - 14	CDJC	14 281	7 232	7 049	...	...	...	...	...	...
15 - 19	CDJC	12 379	6 273	6 106	...	...	...	...	...	...
20 - 24	CDJC	11 989	6 140	5 849	...	...	...	...	...	...
25 - 29	CDJC	12 944	6 584	6 360	...	...	...	...	...	...
30 - 34	CDJC	12 906	6 727	6 179	...	...	...	...	...	...
35 - 39	CDJC	12 751	6 692	6 059	...	...	...	...	...	...
40 - 44	CDJC	10 390	5 344	5 046	...	...	...	...	...	...
45 - 49	CDJC	9 042	4 608	4 434	...	...	...	...	...	...
50 - 54	CDJC	7 506	3 813	3 693	...	...	...	...	...	...
55 - 59	CDJC	4 993	2 548	2 445	...	...	...	...	...	...
60 - 64	CDJC	4 534	2 190	2 344	...	...	...	...	...	...
65 - 69	CDJC	3 399	1 628	1 771	...	...	...	...	...	...
70 - 74	CDJC	2 461	1 287	1 174	...	...	...	...	...	...
75 - 79	CDJC	1 384	681	703	...	...	...	...	...	...
80 - 84	CDJC	616	234	382	...	...	...	...	...	...
85 - 89	CDJC	248	83	165	...	...	...	...	...	...
90 - 94	CDJC	79	30	49	...	...	...	...	...	...
95 - 99	CDJC	22	9	13	...	...	...	...	...	...
100+	CDJC	6	1	5	...	...	...	...	...	...
Marshall Islands - Îles Marshall										
1 VII 2001										
Total	ESDF	54 584	27 960	26 624	...	...	...	...	...	...
0 - 4	ESDF	9 016	4 684	4 332	...	...	...	...	...	...
5 - 9	ESDF	6 653	3 391	3 262	...	...	...	...	...	...
10 - 14	ESDF	7 272	3 745	3 527	...	...	...	...	...	...
15 - 19	ESDF	6 998	3 576	3 422	...	...	...	...	...	...
20 - 24	ESDF	5 190	2 594	2 596	...	...	...	...	...	...
25 - 29	ESDF	3 982	1 991	1 991	...	...	...	...	...	...
30 - 34	ESDF	3 407	1 736	1 671	...	...	...	...	...	...
35 - 39	ESDF	2 996	· 1 538	1 458	...	...	...	...	...	...
40 - 44	ESDF	2 558	1 276	1 282	...	...	...	...	...	...
45 - 49	ESDF	2 174	1 155	1 019	...	...	...	...	...	...
50 - 54	ESDF	1 618	883	735	...	...	...	...	...	...
55 - 59	ESDF	957	514	443	...	...	...	...	...	...
60 - 64	ESDF	623	318	305	...	...	...	...	...	...
65 - 69	ESDF	478	236	242	...	...	...	...	...	...
70 - 74	ESDF	289	159	130	...	...	...	...	...	...
75+	ESDF	373	164	209	...	...	...	...	...	...
Micronesia, Federated States of - Micronésie, États Fédérés de La										
18 IX 1994										
Total	CDJC	105 506	53 923	51 583	...	...	...	...	...	...
0 - 4	CDJC	15 854	8 211	7 643	...	...	...	...	...	...
5 - 9	CDJC	15 330	8 051	7 279	...	...	...	...	...	...
10 - 14	CDJC	14 749	7 534	7 215	...	...	...	...	...	...

7. Population by age, sex and urban/rural residence: latest available year, 1994 - 2003
Population selon l'âge, le sexe et la résidence, urbaine/rurale: dernière année disponible, 1994 - 2003
(continued — suite)

Continent, country or area, date and age (in years) / Continent, pays ou zone, date et âge (en années)	Code[1]	Total			Urban - Urbaine			Rural - Rurale		
		Both sexes Les deux sexes	Male Masculin	Female Féminin	Both sexes Les deux sexes	Male Masculin	Female Féminin	Both sexes Les deux sexes	Male Masculin	Female Féminin
OCEANIA — OCEANIE										
Micronesia, Federated States of - Micronésie, États Fédérés de La										
18 IX 1994										
15 - 19	CDJC	12 251	6 431	5 820	...	...	...	...	...	...
20 - 24	CDJC	8 828	4 321	4 507	...	...	...	...	...	...
25 - 29	CDJC	7 063	3 496	3 567	...	...	...	...	...	...
30 - 34	CDJC	6 598	3 311	3 287	...	...	...	...	...	...
35 - 39	CDJC	6 079	3 077	3 002	...	...	...	...	...	...
40 - 44	CDJC	5 071	2 661	2 410	...	...	...	...	...	...
45 - 49	CDJC	3 579	1 930	1 649	...	...	...	...	...	...
50 - 54	CDJC	2 219	1 101	1 118	...	...	...	...	...	...
55 - 59	CDJC	2 105	1 033	1 072	...	...	...	...	...	...
60 - 64	CDJC	1 985	1 018	967	...	...	...	...	...	...
65 - 69	CDJC	1 395	668	727	...	...	...	...	...	...
70 - 74	CDJC	1 229	567	662	...	...	...	...	...	...
75 - 79	CDJC	581	274	307	...	...	...	...	...	...
80 - 84	CDJC	354	150	204	...	...	...	...	...	...
85+	CDJC	236	89	147	...	...	...	...	...	...
New Caledonia - Nouvelle-Calédonie 48										
16 IV 1996										
Total	CDFC	196 836	100 762	96 074	...	...	...	...	...	...
0 - 9	CDFC	41 383	21 463	19 920	...	...	...	...	...	...
10 - 19	CDFC	36 398	18 526	17 872	...	...	...	...	...	...
20 - 29	CDFC	36 027	18 335	17 692	...	...	...	...	...	...
30 - 39	CDFC	30 266	15 315	14 951	...	...	...	...	...	...
40 - 49	CDFC	22 393	11 752	10 641	...	...	...	...	...	...
50 - 59	CDFC	15 589	8 220	7 369	...	...	...	...	...	...
60 - 69	CDFC	9 022	4 592	4 430	...	...	...	...	...	...
70 - 79	CDFC	4 146	1 913	2 233	...	...	...	...	...	...
80 - 89	CDFC	1 443	593	850	...	...	...	...	...	...
90+	CDFC	169	53	116	...	...	...	...	...	...
New Zealand - Nouvelle-Zélande										
1 VII 2003										
Total	ESDJ	4 009 200	1 971 300	2 037 900	3 449 300	1 681 700	1 767 600	558 800	288 900	270 000
0 - 1	ESDJ	55 330	28 550	26 780	...	...	...	...	...	...
0 - 4	ESDJ	...	...	...	241 750	123 900	117 850	37 670	19 240	18 420
1 - 4	ESDJ	224 110	114 610	109 500	...	...	...	...	...	...
5 - 9	ESDJ	293 180	150 870	142 310	247 290	127 050	120 230	45 880	23 810	22 070
10 - 14	ESDJ	311 890	160 210	151 680	259 750	133 160	126 590	52 120	27 050	25 080
15 - 19	ESDJ	295 910	151 420	144 300	258 150	131 370	126 770	37 550	20 030	17 520
20 - 24	ESDJ	279 150	141 820	137 340	257 900	129 530	128 370	21 140	12 190	8 940
25 - 29	ESDJ	249 110	122 180	126 930	224 580	109 290	115 290	24 450	12 820	11 630
30 - 34	ESDJ	293 630	140 550	153 080	258 740	123 570	135 170	34 800	16 920	17 880
35 - 39	ESDJ	303 280	146 390	156 890	260 070	125 560	134 510	43 130	20 760	22 370
40 - 44	ESDJ	315 110	153 260	161 850	265 160	128 240	136 920	49 860	24 960	24 900
45 - 49	ESDJ	276 790	136 200	140 590	230 610	112 350	118 260	46 080	23 780	22 290
50 - 54	ESDJ	247 710	123 150	124 560	206 100	101 360	104 730	41 510	21 730	19 780
55 - 59	ESDJ	214 970	106 900	108 070	178 160	87 720	90 440	36 710	19 110	17 610
60 - 64	ESDJ	171 380	84 410	86 970	141 590	68 670	72 920	29 720	15 690	14 020
65 - 69	ESDJ	135 820	66 120	69 690	114 250	54 440	59 810	21 540	11 660	9 870
70 - 74	ESDJ	120 850	57 520	63 330	104 570	48 430	56 150	16 250	9 070	7 180
75 - 79	ESDJ	100 130	44 790	55 340	89 350	39 060	50 290	10 770	5 720	5 050
80 - 84	ESDJ	68 350	26 450	41 900	62 530	23 620	38 920	5 810	2 830	2 980
85+	ESDJ	...	...	...	48 790	14 400	34 400	3 840	1 475	2 370
85 - 89	ESDJ	35 800	11 590	24 210	...	...	...	...	...	...
90+	ESDJ	16 840	4 290	12 550	...	...	...	...	...	...

7. Population by age, sex and urban/rural residence: latest available year, 1994 - 2003
Population selon l'âge, le sexe et la résidence, urbaine/rurale: dernière année disponible, 1994 - 2003
(continued — suite)

Continent, country or area, date and age (in years) / Continent, pays ou zone, date et âge (en années)	Code[1]	Total			Urban - Urbaine			Rural - Rurale		
		Both sexes Les deux sexes	Male Masculin	Female Féminin	Both sexes Les deux sexes	Male Masculin	Female Féminin	Both sexes Les deux sexes	Male Masculin	Female Féminin
OCEANIA — OCEANIE										
Niue - Nioué										
17 VIII 1997										
Total	CDFC	2 088	1 053	1 035	...	...	...	...	...	...
0 - 4	CDFC	210	107	103	...	...	...	...	...	...
5 - 9	CDFC	229	124	105	...	...	...	...	...	...
10 - 14	CDFC	243	115	128	...	...	...	...	...	...
15 - 19	CDFC	195	105	90	...	...	...	...	...	...
20 - 24	CDFC	116	62	54	...	...	...	...	...	...
25 - 29	CDFC	126	66	60	...	...	...	...	...	...
30 - 34	CDFC	145	76	69	...	...	...	...	...	...
35 - 39	CDFC	122	68	54	...	...	...	...	...	...
40 - 44	CDFC	125	64	61	...	...	...	...	...	...
45 - 49	CDFC	94	40	54	...	...	...	...	...	...
50 - 54	CDFC	100	53	47	...	...	...	...	...	...
55 - 59	CDFC	109	52	57	...	...	...	...	...	...
60 - 64	CDFC	101	48	53	...	...	...	...	...	...
65 - 69	CDFC	51	23	28	...	...	...	...	...	...
70 - 74	CDFC	44	24	20	...	...	...	...	...	...
75+	CDFC	78	26	52	...	...	...	...	...	...
Northern Mariana Islands - Îles Mariannes septentrionales										
1 IV 2000										
Total	CDFC	69 221	31 984	37 237	...	...	...	...	...	...
0 - 4	CDFC	5 792	...	...	...	...	...	...	...	...
5 - 9	CDFC	5 420	...	...	...	...	...	...	...	...
10 - 14	CDFC	4 377	...	...	...	...	...	...	...	...
15 - 19	CDFC	3 943	...	...	...	...	...	...	...	...
20 - 24	CDFC	7 566	...	...	...	...	...	...	...	...
25 - 34	CDFC	20 181	...	...	...	...	...	...	...	...
35 - 44	CDFC	12 651	...	...	...	...	...	...	...	...
45 - 54	CDFC	6 208	...	...	...	...	...	...	...	...
55 - 59	CDFC	1 199	...	...	...	...	...	...	...	...
60 - 64	CDFC	837	...	...	...	...	...	...	...	...
65 - 74	CDFC	748	...	...	...	...	...	...	...	...
75 - 84	CDFC	233	...	...	...	...	...	...	...	...
85+	CDFC	66	...	...	...	...	...	...	...	...
Palau - Palaos										
9 IX 1995										
Total	CDFC	17 225	9 213	8 012	...	...	...	...	...	...
0 - 4	CDFC	1 762	916	846	...	...	...	...	...	...
5 - 9	CDFC	1 551	797	754	...	...	...	...	...	...
10 - 14	CDFC	1 527	798	729	...	...	...	...	...	...
15 - 19	CDFC	1 282	684	598	...	...	...	...	...	...
20 - 24	CDFC	1 427	723	704	...	...	...	...	...	...
25 - 29	CDFC	1 741	929	812	...	...	...	...	...	...
30 - 34	CDFC	1 717	1 005	712	...	...	...	...	...	...
35 - 39	CDFC	1 583	927	656	...	...	...	...	...	...
40 - 44	CDFC	1 261	727	534	...	...	...	...	...	...
45 - 49	CDFC	943	553	390	...	...	...	...	...	...
50 - 54	CDFC	603	329	274	...	...	...	...	...	...
55 - 59	CDFC	488	249	239	...	...	...	...	...	...
60 - 64	CDFC	361	174	187	...	...	...	...	...	...
65 - 69	CDFC	328	145	183	...	...	...	...	...	...
70 - 74	CDFC	278	122	156	...	...	...	...	...	...
75+	CDFC	373	135	238	...	...	...	...	...	...
15 IV 2000										
Total	CDFC	19 129	...	...	...	...	...	...	...	...
0 - 4	CDFC	1 308	...	...	...	...	...	...	...	...
5 - 9	CDFC	1 700	...	...	...	...	...	...	...	...
10 - 14	CDFC	1 555	...	...	...	...	...	...	...	...

7. Population by age, sex and urban/rural residence: latest available year, 1994 - 2003
Population selon l'âge, le sexe et la résidence, urbaine/rurale: dernière année disponible, 1994 - 2003
(continued — suite)

Continent, country or area, date and age (in years) / Continent, pays ou zone, date et âge (en années)	Code[1]	Total			Urban - Urbaine			Rural - Rurale		
		Both sexes Les deux sexes	Male Masculin	Female Féminin	Both sexes Les deux sexes	Male Masculin	Female Féminin	Both sexes Les deux sexes	Male Masculin	Female Féminin
OCEANIA — OCEANIE										
Palau - Palaos										
15 IV 2000										
15 - 19	CDFC	1 382	...	...	...	...	...	...	...	...
20 - 24	CDFC	1 342	...	...	...	...	...	...	...	...
25 - 29	CDFC	1 910	...	...	...	...	...	...	...	...
30 - 34	CDFC	2 169	...	...	...	...	...	...	...	...
35 - 39	CDFC	1 891	...	...	...	...	...	...	...	...
40 - 44	CDFC	1 651	...	...	...	...	...	...	...	...
45 - 49	CDFC	1 272	...	...	...	...	...	...	...	...
50 - 54	CDFC	886	...	...	...	...	...	...	...	...
55 - 59	CDFC	563	...	...	...	...	...	...	...	...
60 - 64	CDFC	463	...	...	...	...	...	...	...	...
65 - 69	CDFC	318	...	...	...	...	...	...	...	...
70 - 74	CDFC	274	...	...	...	...	...	...	...	...
75+	CDFC	445	...	...	...	...	...	...	...	...
Papua New Guinea - Papouasie-Nouvelle-Guinée[49]										
9 VII 2000										
Total	CDFC	5 190 786	2 691 744	2 499 042	686 301	372 453	313 848	4 504 485	2 319 291	2 185 194
0 - 1	CDFC	125 718	65 539	60 179	16 930	8 991	7 939	108 788	56 548	52 240
1 - 4	CDFC	600 962	312 237	288 725	71 219	37 178	34 041	529 743	275 059	254 684
5 - 9	CDFC	727 370	381 339	346 031	86 078	45 216	40 862	641 292	336 123	305 169
10 - 14	CDFC	620 874	330 965	289 909	75 022	39 374	35 648	545 852	291 591	254 261
15 - 19	CDFC	554 481	293 277	261 204	78 912	41 679	37 233	475 569	251 598	223 971
20 - 24	CDFC	474 801	239 863	234 938	79 915	43 166	36 749	394 886	196 697	198 189
25 - 29	CDFC	448 414	219 680	228 734	70 866	37 802	33 064	377 548	181 878	195 670
30 - 34	CDFC	384 260	191 662	192 598	57 156	30 983	26 173	327 104	160 679	166 425
35 - 39	CDFC	330 337	166 656	163 681	48 585	26 512	22 073	281 752	140 144	141 608
40 - 44	CDFC	252 368	128 910	123 458	36 195	20 956	15 239	216 173	107 954	108 219
45 - 49	CDFC	198 757	104 867	93 890	25 337	15 595	9 742	173 420	89 272	84 148
50 - 54	CDFC	151 013	79 899	71 114	16 428	10 414	6 014	134 585	69 485	65 100
55 - 59	CDFC	108 708	59 308	49 400	9 692	6 131	3 561	99 016	53 177	45 839
60 - 64	CDFC	89 503	48 530	40 973	6 723	4 247	2 476	82 780	44 283	38 497
65 - 69	CDFC	57 221	31 351	25 870	3 641	2 141	1 500	53 580	29 210	24 370
70 - 74	CDFC	35 134	19 657	15 477	1 930	1 105	825	33 204	18 552	14 652
75 - 79	CDFC	16 864	9 782	7 082	880	498	382	15 984	9 284	6 700
80 - 84	CDFC	8 669	5 041	3 628	489	295	194	8 180	4 746	3 434
85 - 89	CDFC	3 315	1 984	1 331	176	99	77	3 139	1 885	1 254
90+	CDFC	2 017	1 197	820	127	71	56	1 890	1 126	764
Tokelau - Tokélaou										
11 X 2001										
Total	CDFC	1 537	761	776	...	...	...	...	...	...
0 - 4	CDFC	218	112	106	...	...	...	...	...	...
5 - 9	CDFC	206	118	88	...	...	...	...	...	...
10 - 14	CDFC	202	102	100	...	...	...	...	...	...
15 - 19	CDFC	144	71	73	...	...	...	...	...	...
20 - 24	CDFC	85	42	43	...	...	...	...	...	...
25 - 29	CDFC	95	43	52	...	...	...	...	...	...
30 - 34	CDFC	100	50	50	...	...	...	...	...	...
35 - 39	CDFC	88	43	45	...	...	...	...	...	...
40 - 44	CDFC	84	41	43	...	...	...	...	...	...
45 - 49	CDFC	63	28	35	...	...	...	...	...	...
50 - 54	CDFC	52	20	32	...	...	...	...	...	...
55 - 59	CDFC	54	26	28	...	...	...	...	...	...
60 - 64	CDFC	49	21	28	...	...	...	...	...	...
65+	CDFC	97	44	53	...	...	...	...	...	...
Tonga										
31 XII 2002										
Total	ESDF	101 002	51 473	49 528	...	...	...	...	...	...
0 - 4	ESDF	12 179	6 295	5 884	...	...	...	...	...	...
5 - 9	ESDF	12 686	6 577	6 109	...	...	...	...	...	...

7. Population by age, sex and urban/rural residence: latest available year, 1994 - 2003
Population selon l'âge, le sexe et la résidence, urbaine/rurale: dernière année disponible, 1994 - 2003
(continued — suite)

Continent, country or area, date and age (in years) / Continent, pays ou zone, date et âge (en années)	Code[1]	Total			Urban - Urbaine			Rural - Rurale		
		Both sexes Les deux sexes	Male Masculin	Female Féminin	Both sexes Les deux sexes	Male Masculin	Female Féminin	Both sexes Les deux sexes	Male Masculin	Female Féminin
OCEANIA — OCEANIE										
Tonga										
31 XII 2002										
10 - 14	ESDF	*11 795*	*6 303*	*5 492*	...	...	...	...	...	...
15 - 19	ESDF	*11 980*	*6 241*	*5 739*	...	...	...	...	...	...
20 - 24	ESDF	*9 942*	*5 111*	*4 831*	...	...	...	...	...	...
25 - 29	ESDF	*7 057*	*3 564*	*3 493*	...	...	...	...	...	...
30 - 34	ESDF	*6 284*	*3 207*	*3 077*	...	...	...	...	...	...
35 - 39	ESDF	*5 382*	*2 723*	*2 659*	...	...	...	...	...	...
40 - 44	ESDF	*4 541*	*2 186*	*2 355*	...	...	...	...	...	...
45 - 49	ESDF	*4 029*	*1 908*	*2 121*	...	...	...	...	...	...
50 - 54	ESDF	*3 397*	*1 572*	*1 825*	...	...	...	...	...	...
55 - 59	ESDF	*3 105*	*1 467*	*1 638*	...	...	...	...	...	...
60 - 64	ESDF	*2 775*	*1 393*	*1 382*	...	...	...	...	...	...
65 - 69	ESDF	*2 277*	*1 167*	*1 110*	...	...	...	...	...	...
70 - 74	ESDF	*1 668*	*840*	*828*	...	...	...	...	...	...
75+	ESDF	*1 904*	*919*	*985*	...	...	...	...	...	...

FOOTNOTES - NOTES

Italics: estimates which are less reliable. — *Italiques:* estimations moins sûres.

[1] 'Code' indicates the source of data, as follows:
CDFC - Census, de facto, complete tabulation
CDFS - Census, de facto, sample tabulation
CDJC - Census, de jure, complete tabulation
CDJS - Census, de jure, sample tabulation
SSDF - Sample survey, de facto
SSDJ - Sample survey, de jure
ESDF - Estimates, de facto
ESDJ - Estimates, de jure
Le 'Code' indique la source des données, comme suit:
CDFC - Recensement, population de fait, tabulation complète
CDFS - Recensement, population de fait, tabulation par sondage
CDJC - Recensement, population de droit, tabulation complète
CDJS - Recensement, population de droit, tabulation par sondage
SSDF - Enquête par sondage, population de fait
SSDJ - Enquête par sondage, population de droit
ESDF - Estimations, population de fait
ESDJ - Estimations, population de droit

[2] The number of males and / or females excludes persons whose sex is not stated (18 urban, 19 rural). - Il n'est pas tenu compte dans le nombre d'hommes et de femmes des personnes dont le sexe n'est pas indiqué (18 en zone urbaine et 19 en zone rurale).

[3] Data refer to national projections. - Les données se referent aux projections nationales.

[4] For the 1996 census, data have been adjusted for underenumeration estimated at 6.8 per cent. - Pour le recensement de 1996, les données ont été ajustées pour compenser les lacunes du dénombrement estimées à 6,8 p. 100.

[5] Total population excludes persons who were not contacted at the time of the census. - La population non comprend pas les personnes qui n'ont pas été contactées à l'heure du recensement.

[6] Excluding the institutional population. - Non compris la population dans les institutions.

[7] Because of rounding, totals are not in all cases the sum of the parts. - Les chiffres étant arrondis, les totaux ne correspondent pas toujours rigoureusement à la somme des chiffres partiels.

[8] Including armed forces stationed in the area. - Y compris les militaires en garnison sur le territoire.

[9] De jure population, but excluding civilian citizens absent from country for an extended period of time. - Population de droit, mais non compris les civils hors du pays pendant une période prolongée.

[10] Data include persons in remote areas, military personel outside the country, merchant seamen at sea, civilian seasonal workers outside the country, and other civilians outside the country, and exclude nomads, foreign military, civilian aliens temporarily in the country, transients on ships and Indian jungle population. - Y compris les personnes dans des régions éloignées, le personel militaire en dehors du pays, les marins marchands, les ouvriers saisonniers civils de couture en dehors du pays, et autres civils en dehors du pays, et non compris les nomades, les militaires étrangers, les étrangers civils temporairement dans le pays, les transiteurs sur des bateaux et les Indiens de la jungle.

[11] Total in this table different from population estimates presented in other tables due to differences in methodology. - Le total figurant dans ce tableau est différent des chiffres de population présentés dans d'autres tableaux, ayant été obtenus par des méthodes différentes.

[12] Excluding nomadic Indian tribes. - Non compris les tribus d'Indiens nomades.

[13] Excluding Indian jungle population. - Non compris les Indiens de la jungle.

[14] Mid-year estimates have been adjusted for underenumeration, at latest census. - Les estimations au millieu de l'année tiennent compte d'une ajustement destiné à compenser les lacunes du dénombrement lors du dernier recensement.

[15] Figures based on census 2003 quick count and expanded post enumeration survey (PES) to census 2003. Totals do not add up to the sum because total population include, institutional population (i.e. population in institutions such as orphanage and old people's homes and special groups (e.g. vagrants, persons on ships in the harbour and diplomats) totaling 4968 (Male 2657 Female 2294 and 17 diplomats). - Les chiffres sont fondés sur le dénombrement rapide de 2003 et l'enquête postérieure au dénombrement. Les totaux ne correspondent pas à la population totale parce qu'il est tenu compte dans celle-ci de la population vivant en institutions (orphelinats, hospices) et de groupes spéciaux (vagabonds, personnes à bord de navires ancrés dans les ports et diplomates), soit 4 968 personnes (2 657 hommes et 2 294 femmes; 17 diplomates).

[16] For statistical purposes, the data for China do not include those for the Hong Kong Special Administrative Region (Hong Kong SAR), Macao Special Administrative Region (Macao SAR) and Taiwan province of China. - Pour la présentation des statistiques, les données pour Chine ne comprend pas la Région Administrative Spéciale de Hong Kong (Hong Kong RAS), la Région Administrative Spéciale de Macao (Macao RAS) et Taïwan province de Chine.

[17] Data refer to government controlled areas. - Les données se raportent aux zones contrôlées par le Gouvernement.

[18] Data exclude Mao-Maram, Paomata and Purul sub-divisions of Senapati district of Manipur. The population of Manipur including the estimated population of the three sub-divisions of Senapati district is 2,291,125 (Males 1,161,173 and females 1,129,952). - Non compris les subdivisions Mao-Maram Paomata et Purul du district de Senapati dans l'État du Manipur. Cet État compte 2 291 125 habitants (1 161 173 hommes et 1 129 952 femmes), y compris la population

estimative des trois subdivisions du district de Senapati.

[19] Including data for the Indian-held part of Jammu and Kashmir, the final status of which has not yet been determined. - Y compris les données pour la partie du Jammu et du Cachemire occupée par l'Inde dont le statut définitif n'a pas encore été déterminé.

[20] Data refer to only enumerated population with permanent residence. - Les données se rapportent à la population énumérée avec la résidence permanente.

[21] Including data for East Jerusalem and Israeli residents in certain other territories under occupation by Israeli military forces since June 1967. - Y compris les données pour Jérusalem-Est et les résidents israéliens dans certains autres territoires occupés depuis 1967 par les forces armées israéliennes.

[22] Excluding diplomatic personnel outside the country and foreign military and civilian personnel and their dependants stationed in the area. - Non compris le personnel diplomatique hors du pays ni les militaires et agents civils étrangers en poste sur le territoire et les membres de leur famille les accompagnant.

[23] Excluding data for Jordanian territory under occupation since June 1967 by Israeli military forces. Excluding foreigners, including registered Palestinian refugees. - Non compris les données pour le territoire jordanien occupé depuis juin 1967 par les forces armées israéliennes. Non compris les étrangers, mais y compris les réfugiés de Palestine enregistrés.

[24] Excluding alien armed forces, civilian aliens employed by armed forces, foreign diplomatic personnel and their dependants and Korean diplomatic personnel and their dependants outside the country. - Non compris les militaires étrangers, les civils étrangers employés par les forces armées, le personnel diplomatique étranger et les membres de leur famille les accompagnant et le personnel diplomatique coréen hors du pays et les membres de leurs familles les accompagnant.

[25] Data refer to constant population as reported by national statistical authorities, meaning that it does not include migrant population. - Les données se rapportent à la population constante déclarée par les autorités statistiques nationales; la population migrante n'est donc pas comprise.

[26] Excluding Malaysian citizens and permanent residents who were away or intended to be away from the country for more than six months. Excluding Malaysian military, naval and diplomatic personnel and their families outside the country, and tourists, businessman who intended to be in Malaysia for less than six months. - Non compris les citoyens malaisiens et les résidents permanents qui étaient ou qui ont prévu d'être hors du pays pour six mois ou plus. Non compris le personnel militaire Malaisien, le personnel naval ou diplomatique et leurs familles hors du pays, et les touristes et les hommes d'affaires qui avaient l'intention de rester en Malaisie moins de six mois.

[27] Census results have been adjusted for underenumeration. - Les résultats du recensement ont été ajustées pour compenser les lacunes du dénombrement

[28] Excluding data for the Pakistan-held part of Jammu and Kashmir, the final status of which has not yet been determined. - Non compris les données concernant la partie du Jammu et Cachemire occupée par le Pakistan dont le statut définitif n'a pas été déterminé.

[29] Data based on Population Demographic Survey. These estimates do not reflect completely accurately the actual population and vital events of the country. - D'après les résultats de l'Enquête démographique par sondage. Ces estimations ne dénotent pas d'une manière complètement ponctuelle la population actuelle et les statistiques de l'état civil du pays.

[30] Excluding transients afloat and military and civilian services personnel and their dependants abroad. - Non compris les personnes de passage à bord de navires ni les militaires et agents civils et les membres de leur famille les accompagnant à l'étranger.

[31] Including Palestinian refugees. - Y compris les réfugiés de Palestine.

[32] Comprising 7 sheikdoms of Abu Dhabi, Dubai, Sharjah, Ajaman, Umm al Qaiwain, Ras al Khaimah and Fujairah, and the area lying within the modified Riyadh line as announced in October 1955. - Comprend les sept cheikhats de Abou Dhabi, Dabai, Ghârdja, Adjmân, Oumm-al-Quiwaïn, Ras al Khaïma et Foudjaïra, ainsi que la zone délimitée par la ligne de Riad modifiée comme il a été annoncé en octobre 1955.

[33] Excluding Faeroe Islands and Greenland. - Non compris les Iles Féroé et Gröenland.

[34] Excluding Overseas Departments, namely French Guiana, Guadeloupe, Martinique and Reunion, shown separately. De jure population but excluding diplomatic personnel outside the country and including members of alien armed forces not living in military camps and foreign diplomatic personnel not living in embassies or consulates. - Non compris les départements d'outre-mer, c'est-à-dire la Guyane française, la Guadeloupe, la Martinique et la Réunion, qui font l'objet de rubriques distinctes. Population de droit, non compris le personnel diplomatique hors du pays et y compris les militaires étrangers ne vivant pas dans des camps militaires et le personnel diplomatique étranger ne vivant pas dans les ambassades ou les consulats.

[35] Excluding families of military personnel, visitors and transients. - Non compris les familles des militaires, ni les visiteurs et transients.

[36] Mid-year population excludes armed forces stationed outside the country, but includes alien armed forces stationed in the area. - Les estimations au millieu de l'année non compris les militaires en garnison hors du pays, mais y compris les militaires étrangers en garnison sur le territoire.

[37] Maltese population only. - Population Maltaise seulement.

[38] Including residents temporarily outside the country. - Y compris les résidents se trouvant temporairement hors du pays.

[39] Excluding civilian aliens within country, but including civilian nationals temporarily outside country. - Non compris les civils étrangers dans le pays, mais y compris les civils nationaux temporairement hors du pays.

[40] Including the Azores and Madeira Islands. - Y compris les Açores et Madère.

[41] Data do not include information for Transnistria and the municipality of Bender. - Les données ne tiennent pas compte de l'information sur la Transnistria et la municipalité de Bender.

[42] For 2000 estimates of Kosovo and Metohia computed on the basis of natural increases from year 1997. - Pour 2000 les estimations pour le Kosovo et la Metohia ont été calculées sur la base des incréments naturelles depuis 1997.

[43] For 2002 without data for Kosovo and Metohia. - Pour 2002 sans les donées pour le Kosovo and Metohie.

[44] Includes all population with permanent residence on the territory of the Slovak Republic. - Y compris la population de résidence permanente dans le territoire.

[45] Figures for urban and rural areas do not add up to the total, as urban/ and rural data refer only to citizens of the Republic of Slovenia. - La somme des chiffres des zones urbaines et rurales ne correspond pas au chiffre total, les données urbaines/rurales ne concernant que les ressortissants de la République de Slovénie.

[46] Excluding Niue, shown separately, which is part of Cook Islands, but because of remoteness is administered separately. - Non compris Nioué, qui fait l'objet d'une rubrique distincte et qui fait partie des îles Cook, mais qui, en raison de son éloignement, est administrée séparément.

[47] The resident population consisted of 14,990 (7,738 males and 7,252 females). - Population résidente de 14 990 (7 738 hommes et 7 252 femmes).

[48] Including the islands of Huon, Chesterfield, Loyalty, Walpole and Belep Archipelago. - Y compris les îles Huon, Chesterfield, Loyauté et Walpole, et l'archipel Belep.

[49] Comprising eastern part of New Guinea, the Bismarck Archipelago, Bougainville and Buka of Solomon Islands group and about 600 smaller islands. - Comprend l'est de la Nouvelle-Guinée, l'archipel Bismarck, Bougainville et Buka (ces deux dernières du groupe des Salomon) et environ 600 îlots.

Table 8

Table 8 presents population of capital cities and cities of 100 000 or more inhabitants for the latest available year.

Description of variables: Since the way in which cities are delimited differs from one country or area to another, the table not only presents data for the so-called city proper, but also for the urban agglomeration, if available.

City proper is defined as a locality with legally fixed boundaries and an administratively recognized urban status, usually characterized by some form of local government.

Urban agglomeration has been defined as comprising the city or town proper and also the suburban fringe or densely settled territory lying outside of, but adjacent to, the city boundaries.

For some countries or areas, however, the data relate to entire administrative divisions known, for example, as shi or municipalities (municipios) which are composed of a populated centre and adjoining territory, some of which may contain other, often separate urban localities or may be distinctively rural in character. For this group of countries or areas the type of civil division is given in a footnote.

The surface area of the city or urban agglomeration is presented, when available.

City names are presented in the original language of the country or area in which the cities are located. In cases where the original names are not in the Roman alphabet, they have been Romanized. Cities are listed in English alphabetical order.

Capital cities are shown in the table regardless of their population size. The names of the capital cities are printed in capital letters. The designation of any specific city as a capital city is as reported by the country or area.

The table also covers cities whose urban agglomeration's population exceeds 100 000; that is, while the urban agglomeration should have a population of 100 000 or more to be included in the table, the city proper may be of a smaller population size.

The reference date of each population figure appears in the stub of the table. Estimates based on results of sample surveys and city censuses as well as those derived from other sources are noted in the "code" column.

Reliability of data: Specific information is generally not available on the reliability of the estimates of the population of cities or urban agglomerations presented in this table.

In the absence of such quality assessment, data from population censuses, sample surveys and city censuses are considered to be reliable and, therefore, set in roman type. Other estimates are considered to be reliable if they are based on a complete census (or a sample survey), and have been adjusted by a continuous population register or adjusted on the basis of the calculated balance of births, deaths, and migration.

Limitations: Statistics on the population of capital cities and cities of 100 000 or more inhabitants are subject to the same qualifications as have been set forth for population statistics in general as discussed in section 3 of the Technical Notes.

International comparability of data on city population is limited to a great extent by variations in national concepts and definitions. Although an effort is made to reduce the sources of non-comparability somewhat by presenting the data for both city proper and urban agglomeration, many serious problems of comparability remain.

Data presented in the "city proper" column for some countries represent an urban administrative area legally distinguished from surrounding rural territory, while for other countries these data represent a commune or an equally small administrative unit. In still other countries, the administrative units may be relatively extensive and thereby include considerable territories beyond the urban centre itself.

City data are also especially affected by whether the data refer to de facto or de jure population, as well as variations among countries in how each of these concepts is applied. With reference to the total population, the difference between the de facto and de jure population is discussed at length in section 3.1.1 of the Technical Notes.

Data on city populations based on intercensal estimates present additional problems: comparability is impaired by the different methods used in making the estimates and by the loss of precision in applying to selected segments of the population, methods best suited for the whole population. For example, it is far more difficult to apply the component method of estimating population growth to cities than it is to the entire country.

Births and deaths occurring in the cities do not all originate in the population present in or resident of that area. Therefore, the use of natural increase to estimate the probable size of the city population is a potential source of error. Internal migration is another component of population change that cannot be measured with accuracy in many areas. Because of these factors, estimates in this table may be less valuable in general and in particular limited for purposes of international comparison.

City data, even when set in roman type, are often not as reliable as estimates for the total population of the country or area. Furthermore, because the sources of these data include censuses (national or city), surveys and estimates, the years to which they refer vary widely. In addition, because city boundaries may alter over time, comparisons covering different years should be carried out with caution.

Earlier data: Population of capital cities and cities with a population of 100 000 or more have been shown in previous issues of the *Demographic Yearbook*. For more information on specific topics and years for which data are reported, readers should consult the Historical Index.

Tableau 8

Le tableau 8 présente les données les plus récentes dont on dispose sur la population des capitales et des villes de 100 000 habitants et plus.

Description des variables : Étant donné que les villes ne sont pas délimitées de la même manière dans tous les pays ou zones, on s'est efforcé de donner, dans ce tableau, des chiffres correspondant non seulement aux villes proprement dites, mais aussi, le cas échéant, aux agglomérations urbaines.

On entend par villes proprement dites les localités qui ont des limites juridiquement définies et sont administrativement considérées comme villes, ce qui se caractérise généralement par l'existence d'une autorité locale.

L'agglomération urbaine comprend, par définition, la ville proprement dite ainsi que la proche banlieue, c'est-à-dire la zone fortement peuplée qui est extérieure, mais contiguë aux limites de la ville.

En outre, dans certains pays ou zones, les données se rapportent à des divisions administratives entières, connues par exemple sous le nom de shi ou de municipios, qui comportent une agglomération et le territoire avoisinant, lequel peut englober d'autres agglomérations urbaines tout à fait distinctes ou être à caractère essentiellement rural. Pour ce groupe de pays ou zones, le type de division administrative est indiqué en note.

On trouvera à la fin du tableau la superficie de la ville ou agglomération urbaine chaque fois que possible.

Les noms des villes sont indiqués dans la langue du pays ou zone où ces villes sont situées. Les noms de villes qui ne sont pas à l'origine libellés en caractères latins ont été romanisés. Les villes sont énumérées dans l'ordre alphabétique anglais.

Les capitales figurent dans le tableau quel que soit le chiffre de leur population et leur nom a été imprimé en lettres majuscules. Ne sont indiquées comme capitales que les villes ainsi désignées par le pays ou zone intéressé.

En ce qui concerne les autres villes, le tableau indique celles dont la population est égale ou supérieure à 100 000 habitants. Ce chiffre limite s'applique à l'agglomération urbaine et non à la ville proprement dite, dont la population peut être moindre.

L'année à laquelle se réfère le chiffre correspondant à chaque population figure dans la colonne de gauche du tableau. La colonne « Code » permet de savoir si les estimations sont fondées sur les résultats d'enquêtes par sondage ou de recensements municipaux ou sont tirées d'autres sources.

Fiabilité des données : On ne possède généralement pas de renseignements précis sur la fiabilité des estimations de la population des villes ou agglomérations urbaines présentées dans ce tableau.

Les données provenant de recensements de la population, d'enquêtes par sondage ou de recensements municipaux sont jugées sûres et figurent par conséquent en caractères romains. D'autres estimations sont considérées comme sûres si elles sont fondées sur un recensement complet (ou une enquête par sondage) et ont été ajustées en fonction des données provenant d'un registre permanent de population ou en fonction de la balance, établie par le calcul des naissances, des décès et des migrations.

Insuffisance des données : Les statistiques portant sur la population des capitales et des villes de 100 000 habitants et plus appellent toutes les réserves qui ont été formulées à la section 3 des Notes techniques à propos des statistiques de la population en général.

La comparabilité internationale des données portant sur la population des villes est compromise dans une large mesure par la diversité des définitions nationales. Bien que l'on se soit efforcé de réduire les facteurs de non-comparabilité en présentant à la fois dans le tableau les données relatives aux villes proprement dites et celles concernant les agglomérations urbaines, de graves problèmes de comparabilité n'en subsistent pas moins.

Pour certains pays, les données figurant dans la colonne intitulée « Ville proprement dite » correspondent à une zone administrative urbaine juridiquement distincte du territoire rural environnant, tandis que pour d'autres pays ces données correspondent à une commune ou petite unité administrative analogue. Pour d'autres encore, les unités administratives en cause peuvent être relativement étendues et englober par conséquent un vaste territoire au-delà du centre urbain lui-même.

L'emploi de données se rapportant tantôt à la population de fait, tantôt à la population de droit, ainsi que les différences de traitement de ces deux notions d'un pays à l'autre influent particulièrement sur les statistiques urbaines. En ce qui concerne la population totale, la différence entre population de fait et population de droit est expliquée en détail à la section 3.1.1 des Notes techniques.

Les statistiques relatives à la population urbaine qui sont fondées sur des estimations intercensitaires posent encore plus de problèmes que les données issues de recensement. Leur comparabilité est compromise par la diversité des méthodes employées pour établir les estimations et par l'imprécision qui résulte de l'application de certaines méthodes à telles ou telles composantes de la population alors qu'elles sont conçues pour être appliquées à l'ensemble de la population. La méthode des composantes, par exemple, est beaucoup plus difficile à appliquer en vue de l'estimation de l'accroissement de la population lorsqu'il s'agit de villes que lorsqu'il s'agit d'un pays tout entier.

Les naissances et décès qui surviennent dans les villes ne correspondent pas tous à la population présente ou résidente. En conséquence, des erreurs peuvent se produire si l'on établit pour les villes des estimations fondées sur l'accroissement naturel de la population. Les migrations intérieures constituent un second élément d'estimation que, dans bien des régions, on ne peut pas toujours mesurer avec exactitude. Pour ces raisons, les estimations présentées dans ce tableau risquent dans l'ensemble d'être peu fiables et leur valeur est particulièrement limitée du point de vue des comparaisons internationales.

Même lorsqu'elles figurent en caractères romains, il arrive souvent que les statistiques urbaines ne soient pas aussi fiables que les estimations concernant la population totale de la zone ou du pays considéré. De surcroît, comme ces statistiques proviennent aussi bien de recensements (nationaux ou municipaux) que d'enquêtes ou d'estimations, les années auxquelles elles se rapportent sont extrêmement variables. Enfin, comme les limites urbaines varient parfois d'une époque à une autre, il y a lieu d'être prudent lorsque l'on compare des données se rapportant à des années différentes.

Données publiées antérieurement : Des statistiques concernant la population des capitales et des villes de 100 000 habitants ou plus ont été présentées dans des éditions antérieures de l'*Annuaire démographique*. Pour plus de précisions concernant les années et les sujets pour lesquels des données ont été publiées, se reporter à l'index.

8. Population of capital cities and cities of 100 000 and more inhabitants: latest available year
Population des capitales et des villes de 100 000 habitants et plus: dernière année disponible

(See notes at end of table. — Voir notes à la fin du tableau.)

Continent, country or area, date and city — Continent, pays ou zone, date et ville	Code[1]	City proper — Ville proprement dite Population				Urban agglomeration — Agglomération urbaine Population			
		Both sexes Les deux sexes	Male Masculin	Female Féminin	Surface area Superficie (km²)	Both sexes Les deux sexes	Male Masculin	Female Féminin	Surface area Superficie (km²)
AFRICA — AFRIQUE									
Algeria — Algérie									
25 VI 1998									
ALGER (EL DJAZAIR)	CDJC	1 569 897	...	...	...	...	...	...	...
Annaba	CDJC	352 523	...	...	...	...	...	...	...
Batna	CDJC	246 800	...	...	...	...	...	...	...
Béchar	CDJC	134 523	...	...	...	...	...	...	...
Bejaïa	CDJC	144 405	...	...	...	...	...	...	...
Biskra	CDJC	177 060	...	...	...	...	...	...	...
Blida (El Boulaïda)	CDJC	229 788	...	...	...	...	...	...	...
Bordj Bou Arreridj	CDJC	129 004	...	...	...	...	...	...	...
Bordj el Kiffan	CDJC	103 690	...	...	...	...	...	...	...
Chlef (Ech Cheliff)	CDJC	174 314	...	...	...	...	...	...	...
Constantine (Qacentina)	CDJC	465 021	...	...	...	...	...	...	...
El Djelfa	CDJC	158 679	...	...	...	...	...	...	...
El Eulma	CDJC	104 758	...	...	...	...	...	...	...
El Oued (El Wad)	CDJC	105 151	...	...	...	...	...	...	...
Ghardaïa	CDJC	127 959	...	...	...	...	...	...	...
Guelma	CDJC	108 682	...	...	...	...	...	...	...
Jijel	CDJC	106 306	...	...	...	...	...	...	...
Medea (Lemdiyya)	CDJC	128 427	...	...	...	...	...	...	...
Mostaganem	CDJC	125 911	...	...	...	...	...	...	...
M'Sila	CDJC	102 151	...	...	...	...	...	...	...
Oran (Wahran)	CDJC	705 335	...	...	...	...	...	...	...
Ouargla (Wargla)	CDJC	139 381	...	...	...	...	...	...	...
Relizane	CDJC	104 644	...	...	...	...	...	...	...
Saïda	CDJC	113 533	...	...	...	...	...	...	...
Sétif (Stif)	CDJC	214 842	...	...	...	...	...	...	...
Sidi-bel-Abbès	CDJC	183 931	...	...	...	...	...	...	...
Skikda	CDJC	153 531	...	...	...	...	...	...	...
Souk Ahras	CDJC	114 512	...	...	...	...	...	...	...
Tebessa	CDJC	154 335	...	...	...	...	...	...	...
Tiaert	CDJC	148 850	...	...	...	...	...	...	...
Tlemcen (Tilimsen)	CDJC	156 258	...	...	...	...	...	...	...
Tougourt	CDJC	114 183	...	...	...	...	...	...	...
Angola									
1 VII 1993									
Huambo	ESDF	...	...	...	...	400 000	...	...	...
LUANDA	ESDF	...	...	...	...	1 822 407	855 676	936 731	...
Benin — Bénin									
1 VII 2000									
Cotonou	ESDF	650 660	318 752	331 908	79	...	...	...	...
Parakou	ESDF	144 627	73 603	71 024	441	...	...	...	...
PORTO-NOVO	ESDF	232 756	113 737	119 019	50	...	...	...	...
Botswana									
17 VIII 2001									
Francistown	CDFC	83 023	...	...	79	113 315	...	...	...
GABORONE	CDFC	186 007	...	...	169	282 150	...	...	...
Burkina Faso									
10 XII 1996									
Bobo Dioulasso	CDFC	309 771	157 021	152 750	...	...	...	...	...
OUAGADOUGOU	CDFC	709 736	364 674	345 062	...	750 398	384 807	365 591	...
Burundi									
16 VIII 1990									
BUJUMBURA	CDFC	235 440	129 195	106 245	...	...	...	...	...
Cameroon — Cameroun									
1 VII 1998									
Bafoussam	ESDF	205 620	...	...	...	...	...	...	...
Bamenda	ESDF	252 083	...	...	...	...	...	...	...
Bertoua	ESDF	129 067	...	...	...	...	...	...	...
Douala	ESDF	1 382 900	...	...	...	...	...	...	...
Edéa	ESDF	101 200	...	...	...	...	...	...	...
Garoua	ESDF	293 081	...	...	...	...	...	...	...

8. Population of capital cities and cities of 100 000 and more inhabitants: latest available year
Population des capitales et des villes de 100 000 habitants et plus: dernière année disponible (continued — suite)

(See notes at end of table. — Voir notes à la fin du tableau.)

Continent, country or area, date and city Continent, pays ou zone, date et ville	Code[1]	City proper — Ville proprement dite Population				Urban agglomeration — Agglomération urbaine Population			
		Both sexes Les deux sexes	Male Masculin	Female Féminin	Surface area Superficie (km²)	Both sexes Les deux sexes	Male Masculin	Female Féminin	Surface area Superficie (km²)
AFRICA — AFRIQUE									
Cameroon — Cameroun									
1 VII 1998									
Kousséri	ESDF	233 280	...	...	...	...	...	...	...
Kumba	ESDF	110 860	...	...	...	...	...	...	...
Loum	ESDF	115 781	...	...	...	...	...	...	...
Maroua	ESDF	225 469	...	...	...	...	...	...	...
Ngaoundéré	ESDF	156 804	...	...	...	...	...	...	...
Nkongsamba	ESDF	104 908	...	...	...	...	...	...	...
YAOUNDE	ESDF	1 293 000	...	...	...	...	...	...	...
Cape Verde — Cap-Vert									
1 VII 1990									
PRAIA	CDFC	61 644	...	...	...	...	...	...	...
Central African Republic — République centrafricaine									
8 XII 1988									
BANGUI	CDFC	451 690	...	...	...	...	...	...	...
Chad — Tchad									
8 IV 1993									
N'DJAMENA	CDFC	530 965	...	...	...	...	...	...	...
Comoros — Comores									
15 IX 1991									
MORONI	CDFC	30 365	...	...	...	...	...	...	...
Congo									
1 VII 1984									
BRAZZAVILLE	CDFC	596 200	...	...	...	...	...	...	...
Pointe-Noire	CDFC	298 014	...	...	...	...	...	...	...
Côte d'Ivoire									
1 III 1988									
Abidjan	CDFC	1 929 079	...	...	...	...	...	...	...
Bouake	CDFC	329 850	...	...	...	362 192	...	...	...
Daloa	CDFC	121 842	...	...	...	127 923	...	...	...
Korhogo	CDFC	109 445	...	...	...	112 888	...	...	...
YAMOUSSOUKRO	CDFC	106 786	...	...	...	126 191	...	...	...
Democratic Republic of the Congo — République démocratique du Congo									
1 VII 1984									
Boma	ESDF	197 617	...	...	...	...	...	...	...
Bukavu	ESDF	167 950	...	...	...	...	...	...	...
Kananga	ESDF	298 693	...	...	...	...	...	...	...
Kikwit	ESDF	149 296	...	...	...	...	...	...	...
KINSHASA	ESDF	2 664 309	...	...	...	...	...	...	...
Kisangani	ESDF	317 581	...	...	...	...	...	...	...
Kolwezi	ESDF	416 122	...	...	...	...	...	...	...
Likasi (Jadotville)	ESDF	213 862	...	...	...	...	...	...	...
Lubumbashi	ESDF	564 830	...	...	...	...	...	...	...
Matadi	ESDF	138 798	...	...	...	...	...	...	...
Mbandaka	ESDF	137 291	...	...	...	...	...	...	...
Mbuji-Mayi	ESDF	486 235	...	...	...	...	...	...	...
Djibouti									
1 VII 1995									
DJIBOUTI	ESDF	383 000	...	...	...	...	...	...	...
Egypt — Égypte									
19 XI 1996									
Alexandria	CDFC	3 339 076	1 707 477	1 631 599	...	...	...	...	...
Al Orizah	CDFC	100 482	53 081	47 401	...	...	...	...	...
Assyût	CDFC	343 662	182 151	161 511	...	...	...	...	...
Aswan	CDFC	219 541	111 640	107 901	...	...	...	...	...
Banha	CDFC	135 892	69 154	66 738	...	...	...	...	...
Beni-Suef	CDFC	171 734	87 105	84 629	...	...	...	...	...
CAIRO	CDFC	6 800 992	3 486 260	3 314 732	...	...	...	...	...
Damanhûr	CDFC	209 423	107 965	101 458	...	...	...	...	...
El-Mahalla El-Kubra	CDFC	394 924	199 100	195 824	...	...	...	...	...

8. Population of capital cities and cities of 100 000 and more inhabitants: latest available year
Population des capitales et des villes de 100 000 habitants et plus: dernière année disponible (continued — suite)

(See notes at end of table. — Voir notes à la fin du tableau.)

Continent, country or area, date and city / Continent, pays ou zone, date et ville	Code[1]	City proper — Ville proprement dite Population				Urban agglomeration — Agglomération urbaine Population			
		Both sexes Les deux sexes	Male Masculin	Female Féminin	Surface area Superficie (km²)	Both sexes Les deux sexes	Male Masculin	Female Féminin	Surface area Superficie (km²)
AFRICA — AFRIQUE									
Egypt — Égypte									
19 XI 1996									
Faiyûm	CDFC	260 830	134 462	126 368	...	...	...	...	...
Giza	CDFC	2 221 817	1 139 665	1 082 152	...	...	...	...	...
Imbaba	CDFC	523 265	266 793	256 472	...	...	...	...	...
Ismailia	CDFC	255 134	129 004	126 130	...	...	...	...	...
Kafr-El-Dwar	CDFC	101 056	51 491	49 565	...	...	...	...	...
Kena	CDFC	155 382	79 038	76 344	...	...	...	...	...
Luxer	CDFC	153 758	79 753	74 005	...	...	...	...	...
Mansûra	CDFC	369 409	187 622	181 787	...	...	...	...	...
Menia	CDFC	201 440	103 428	98 012	...	...	...	...	...
Port Said	CDFC	472 335	242 502	229 833	...	...	...	...	...
Shebin-El-Kom	CDFC	156 794	79 868	76 926	...	...	...	...	...
Shubra-El-Khema	CDFC	870 776	449 271	421 505	...	...	...	...	...
Sohag	CDFC	170 417	85 918	84 499	...	...	...	...	...
Suez	CDFC	417 527	214 133	203 394	...	...	...	...	...
Tanta	CDFC	372 893	188 594	184 299	...	...	...	...	...
Zagazig	CDFC	267 469	136 094	131 375	...	...	...	...	...
Equatorial Guinea — Guinée équatoriale									
1 VII 1983									
MALABO	CDFC	30 418	...	...	...	...	...	...	...
Eritrea — Érythrée									
1 VII 1990									
ASMARA	ESDF	358 100	...	...	...	...	...	...	...
Ethiopia — Ethiopie									
1 VII 2002									
ADDIS ABABA	ESDF	2 646 000	1 273 000	1 373 000	...	...	...	...	...
Awassa	ESDF	103 725	52 308	51 417	...	...	...	...	...
Bahir Dar	ESDF	140 084	72 736	67 348	2 800	...	...	...	...
Debre Zeit	ESDF	108 632	53 648	54 984	...	...	...	...	...
Dessie	ESDF	141 616	72 578	69 038	1 508	...	...	...	...
Dire Dawa	ESDF	237 012	118 880	118 132	1 768	...	...	...	...
Gondar	ESDF	163 097	82 229	80 868	4 027	...	...	...	...
Harar	ESDF	105 000	53 000	52 000	...	...	...	...	...
Jimma	ESDF	131 708	67 138	64 570	...	...	...	...	...
Mekele	ESDF	141 433	71 990	69 443	2 444	...	...	...	...
Nazareth	ESDF	189 362	94 822	94 540	...	...	...	...	...
Gabon									
1 VII 1993									
LIBREVILLE	CDFC	362 386	184 192	178 194	...	418 616	212 383	206 233	...
Gambia — Gambie									
1 VII 1993									
BANJUL	CDFC	42 326	22 268	20 058	12	...	...	...	...
Ghana									
26 III 2000									
ACCRA	CDFC	1 658 937	817 404	841 533	...	...	...	...	...
Kumasi	CDFC	1 170 270	587 012	583 258	...	...	...	...	...
Sekondi-Takoradi	CDFC	202 317	100 854	101 463	...	...	...	...	...
Tamale	CDFC	175 436	86 794	88 642	...	...	...	...	...
Tema	CDFC	141 479	68 467	73 012	...	...	...	...	...
Guinea — Guinée									
1 XII 1996									
CONAKRY	CDFC	1 091 500	...	...	...	...	...	...	...
Kankan	CDFC	...	...	...	...	261 341	...	...	...
Kindia	CDFC	...	...	...	...	287 607	...	...	...
Labé	CDFC	...	...	...	...	249 515	...	...	...
Nzérékoré	CDFC	...	...	...	...	282 772	...	...	...
Guinea-Bissau — Guinée-Bissau									
1 XII 1991									
BISSAU	CDFC	197 600	...	...	...	...	...	...	...

8. Population of capital cities and cities of 100 000 and more inhabitants: latest available year
Population des capitales et des villes de 100 000 habitants et plus: dernière année disponible (continued — suite)

(See notes at end of table. — Voir notes à la fin du tableau.)

Continent, country or area, date and city / Continent, pays ou zone, date et ville	Code[1]	City proper — Ville proprement dite Population				Urban agglomeration — Agglomération urbaine Population			
		Both sexes Les deux sexes	Male Masculin	Female Féminin	Surface area Superficie (km²)	Both sexes Les deux sexes	Male Masculin	Female Féminin	Surface area Superficie (km²)
AFRICA — AFRIQUE									
Kenya									
1 VII 2003									
Eldoret	ESDF	194 456	101 117	93 339	151	...	...	...	...
Kisumu	ESDF	226 088	113 044	113 044	475	...	...	...	...
Mombasa	ESDF	767 454	403 923	363 531	230	...	...	...	...
NAIROBI	ESDF	2 656 997	1 347 255	1 309 742	696	...	...	...	...
Nakuru	ESDF	255 645	130 379	125 266	290	...	...	...	...
Lesotho									
12 IV 1986									
MASERU	CDFC	109 382	...	...	...	...	...	...	...
Liberia — Libéria									
1 VII 1984									
MONROVIA	CDFC	421 053	...	...	...	...	...	...	...
Libyan Arab Jamahiriya — Jamahiriya arabe libyenne									
1 VII 1990									
Al Khums	ESDJ	200 000	...	...	...	...	...	...	...
BENGHAZI[2]	ESDJ	800 000	...	...	...	...	...	...	...
Misurata	ESDJ	360 000	...	...	...	...	...	...	...
Sebha	ESDJ	150 000	...	...	...	...	...	...	...
TRIPOLI[2]	ESDJ	1 500 000	...	...	...	...	...	...	...
Zuwarah	ESDJ	280 000	...	...	...	...	...	...	...
Madagascar									
1 VIII 1993									
ANTANANARIVO[3]	CDJC	710 236	346 073	364 163	72	...	...	...	...
Antsirabe	CDJC	126 062	62 288	63 774	112	...	...	...	...
Fianarantsoa	CDJC	109 260	52 757	56 504	85	...	...	...	...
Mahajanga	CDJC	106 780	52 711	54 068	14	...	...	...	...
Toamasina	CDJC	137 782	66 844	70 938	20	...	...	...	...
Malawi									
1 VII 2003									
Blantyre City	ESDF	646 235	...	...	...	...	...	...	...
LILONGWE	ESDF	597 619	...	...	328	...	...	...	...
Mzuzu	ESDF	119 592	...	...	...	...	...	...	...
Mali									
1 IV 1998									
BAMAKO	CDJC	1 016 167	520 688	495 479	252	...	...	...	...
Mauritania — Mauritanie									
1 XI 2000									
NOUAKCHOTT	CDFC	558 195	...	...	...	...	...	...	...
Mauritius — Maurice									
1 VII 2003									
Beau Bassin-Rose Hill	ESDJ	106 978	52 235	54 743	20	...	...	...	...
PORT LOUIS	ESDJ	147 688	73 273	74 415	46	...	...	...	...
Vacoas - Phoenix	ESDJ	103 564	51 125	52 439	54	...	...	...	...
Morocco — Maroc[4]									
1 VII 2003									
Agadir	ESDF	494 000	...	...	...	...	...	...	...
Béni-Mellal	ESDF	998 000	...	...	...	...	...	...	...
Casablanca (Dar-el-Beida)[5]	ESDF	3 389 000	...	...	...	...	...	...	...
El-Jadida	ESDF	1 102 000	...	...	...	...	...	...	...
Fès	ESDF	1 185 000	...	...	...	...	...	...	...
Kénitra	ESDF	598 000	...	...	...	...	...	...	...
Khouribga	ESDF	336 000	...	...	...	...	...	...	...
Marrakech[5]	ESDF	1 068 000	...	...	...	...	...	...	...
Meknès[5]	ESDF	680 000	...	...	...	...	...	...	...
Mohammedia	ESDF	223 000	...	...	...	...	...	...	...
Oujda	ESDF	486 000	...	...	...	...	...	...	...
RABAT	ESDF	673 000	...	...	...	...	...	...	...
Safi	ESDF	906 000	...	...	...	...	...	...	...
Salé	ESDF	880 000	...	...	...	...	...	...	...
Tanger	ESDF	782 000	...	...	...	...	...	...	...

8. Population of capital cities and cities of 100 000 and more inhabitants: latest available year
Population des capitales et des villes de 100 000 habitants et plus: dernière année disponible (continued — suite)

(See notes at end of table. — Voir notes à la fin du tableau.)

Continent, country or area, date and city / Continent, pays ou zone, date et ville	Code[1]	City proper — Ville proprement dite Population				Urban agglomeration — Agglomération urbaine Population			
		Both sexes Les deux sexes	Male Masculin	Female Féminin	Surface area Superficie (km²)	Both sexes Les deux sexes	Male Masculin	Female Féminin	Surface area Superficie (km²)
AFRICA — AFRIQUE									
Morocco — Maroc[4]									
1 VII 2003									
Tétouan	ESDF	*652 000*	...	...	...	...	...	...	...
Mozambique									
1 VIII 1997									
Beira	CDFC	397 368	...	...	...	...	...	...	...
Chimoio	CDFC	171 056	...	...	...	...	...	...	...
MAPUTO	CDFC	966 837	...	...	...	1 391 499	...	...	...
Matola	CDFC	424 662	...	...	...	...	...	...	...
Mocuba	CDFC	124 650	...	...	...	...	...	...	...
Nacala	CDFC	158 248	...	...	...	...	...	...	...
Nampula	CDFC	303 346	...	...	...	...	...	...	...
Quelimane	CDFC	150 116	...	...	...	...	...	...	...
Tete	CDFC	101 984	...	...	...	...	...	...	...
Namibia — Namibie									
27 VIII 2001									
WINDHOEK	CDFC	...	...	...	...	233 529	117 306	116 222	...
Niger[6]									
1 VII 1988									
Maradi	CDJC	110 739	54 355	56 384	...	...	...	...	...
NIAMEY	CDJC	397 437	203 172	194 265	...	...	...	...	...
Zinder	CDJC	120 160	60 936	59 224	...	...	...	...	...
Nigeria — Nigéria									
26 XI 1991									
Aba	CDFC	500 183	...	...	...	...	...	...	...
Abeokuta	CDFC	352 735	...	...	...	...	...	...	...
ABUJA	CDFC	107 069	...	...	...	378 671	...	...	...
Ado-Ekiti	CDFC	156 122	...	...	...	...	...	...	...
Akure	CDFC	239 124	...	...	...	...	...	...	...
Awka	CDFC	104 682	...	...	...	...	...	...	...
Bauchi	CDFC	206 537	...	...	...	...	...	...	...
Benin City	CDFC	762 719	...	...	...	...	...	...	...
Bida	CDFC	111 245	...	...	...	...	...	...	...
Calabar	CDFC	310 839	...	...	...	...	...	...	...
Damaturu	CDFC	141 897	...	...	...	...	...	...	...
Ede	CDFC	142 363	...	...	...	...	...	...	...
Effon-Alaiye	CDFC	158 977	...	...	...	...	...	...	...
Enugu	CDFC	407 756	...	...	...	...	...	...	...
Gboko	CDFC	101 281	...	...	...	...	...	...	...
Gombe	CDFC	163 604	...	...	...	...	...	...	...
Gusau	CDFC	132 393	...	...	...	...	...	...	...
Ibadan	CDFC	1 835 300	...	...	...	...	...	...	...
Ife	CDFC	186 856	...	...	...	...	...	...	...
Ijebu-Ode	CDFC	124 313	...	...	...	...	...	...	...
Ikare	CDFC	103 843	...	...	...	...	...	...	...
Ikire	CDFC	111 435	...	...	...	...	...	...	...
Ikorodu	CDFC	184 674	...	...	...	...	...	...	...
Ikot Ekpene	CDFC	119 402	...	...	...	...	...	...	...
Ilawe-Ekiti	CDFC	104 049	...	...	...	...	...	...	...
Ilesha	CDFC	139 445	...	...	...	...	...	...	...
Ilorin	CDFC	532 089	...	...	...	...	...	...	...
Ise	CDFC	108 136	...	...	...	...	...	...	...
Iseyin	CDFC	170 936	...	...	...	...	...	...	...
Iwo	CDFC	125 645	...	...	...	...	...	...	...
Jimeta	CDFC	141 724	...	...	...	...	...	...	...
Jos	CDFC	510 300	...	...	...	...	...	...	...
Kaduna	CDFC	993 642	...	...	...	...	...	...	...
Kano	CDFC	2 166 554	...	...	...	...	...	...	...
Katsina	CDFC	259 315	...	...	...	...	...	...	...
Lagos	CDFC	5 195 247	...	...	...	...	...	...	...
Maiduguri	CDFC	618 278	...	...	...	...	...	...	...
Makurdi	CDFC	151 515	...	...	...	...	...	...	...

8. Population of capital cities and cities of 100 000 and more inhabitants: latest available year
Population des capitales et des villes de 100 000 habitants et plus: dernière année disponible (continued — suite)

(See notes at end of table. — Voir notes à la fin du tableau.)

Continent, country or area, date and city / Continent, pays ou zone, date et ville	Code[1]	City proper — Ville proprement dite Population				Urban agglomeration — Agglomération urbaine Population			
		Both sexes Les deux sexes	Male Masculin	Female Féminin	Surface area Superficie (km²)	Both sexes Les deux sexes	Male Masculin	Female Féminin	Surface area Superficie (km²)
AFRICA — AFRIQUE									
Nigeria — Nigéria									
26 XI 1991									
Minna	CDFC	189 191	...	...	...	...	...	...	...
Mubi	CDFC	128 900	...	...	...	...	...	...	...
Nnewi	CDFC	121 065	...	...	...	...	...	...	...
Ogbomosho	CDFC	433 030	...	...	...	...	...	...	...
Okene	CDFC	312 775	...	...	...	...	...	...	...
Okpogho	CDFC	105 127	...	...	...	...	...	...	...
Ondo	CDFC	146 051	...	...	...	...	...	...	...
Onitsha	CDFC	350 280	...	...	...	...	...	...	...
Oshogbo	CDFC	250 951	...	...	...	...	...	...	...
Owerri	CDFC	119 711	...	...	...	...	...	...	...
Owo	CDFC	157 181	...	...	...	...	...	...	...
Oyo	CDFC	369 894	...	...	...	...	...	...	...
Port Harcourt	CDFC	703 421	...	...	...	...	...	...	...
Sagamu	CDFC	127 513	...	...	...	...	...	...	...
Sango Otta	CDFC	103 332	...	...	...	...	...	...	...
Sapele	CDFC	109 576	...	...	...	...	...	...	...
Sokoto	CDFC	329 639	...	...	...	...	...	...	...
Suleja	CDFC	105 075	...	...	...	...	...	...	...
Ugep	CDFC	134 773	...	...	...	...	...	...	...
Umuahia	CDFC	147 167	...	...	...	...	...	...	...
Warri	CDFC	363 382	...	...	...	...	...	...	...
Zaria	CDFC	612 257	...	...	...	...	...	...	...
Réunion									
1 VII 2002									
SAINT-DENIS[7]	ESDF	134 042	63 922	70 120	143	...	...	...	...
Rwanda									
1 VII 1991									
KIGALI	CDJC	233 640	125 550	108 090	...	...	...	...	...
St. Helena ex. dep. — Sainte-Hélène sans dép.									
8 III 1998									
JAMESTOWN	CDFC	884	452	432	4	...	...	...	...
Sao Tome and Principe — Sao Tomé-et-Principe									
4 VIII 1991									
SAO TOME	CDJC	43 400	...	...	...	...	...	...	...
Senegal — Sénégal									
1 VII 1999									
DAKAR	ESDF	879 703	...	...	500	1 976 533	...	...	...
Kaolack	ESDF	227 915	...	...	...	...	...	...	...
Mbour	ESDF	135 619	...	...	...	...	...	...	...
Pikine-Guediawaye[8]	ESDF	1 096 830	...	...	...	...	...	...	...
Saint Louis	ESDF	147 961	...	...	...	...	...	...	...
Thiès	ESDF	256 113	...	...	...	...	...	...	...
Ziguinchor	ESDF	199 871	...	...	...	...	...	...	...
Seychelles									
29 VIII 1997									
VICTORIA	CDFC	...	...	...	...	24 701	...	...	...
Sierra Leone									
1 VII 1985									
FREETOWN	CDFC	469 776	...	...	...	...	...	...	...
Somalia — Somalie									
1 VII 2001									
MOGADISHU	ESDF	*1 212 000*	...	...	...	...	...	...	...
South Africa — Afrique du Sud									
10 X 1996									
Alexandra	CDFC	171 284	...	...	...	...	...	...	...
Benoni	CDFC	366 343	...	...	...	...	...	...	...
Bloemfontein	CDFC	350 504	...	...	...	...	...	...	...
Boksburg	CDFC	263 179	...	...	...	...	...	...	...

8. Population of capital cities and cities of 100 000 and more inhabitants: latest available year
Population des capitales et des villes de 100 000 habitants et plus: dernière année disponible (continued — suite)

(See notes at end of table. — Voir notes à la fin du tableau.)

Continent, country or area, date and city / Continent, pays ou zone, date et ville	Code[1]	City proper — Ville proprement dite Population				Urban agglomeration — Agglomération urbaine Population			
		Both sexes Les deux sexes	Male Masculin	Female Féminin	Surface area Superficie (km²)	Both sexes Les deux sexes	Male Masculin	Female Féminin	Surface area Superficie (km²)
AFRICA — AFRIQUE									
South Africa — Afrique du Sud									
10 X 1996									
Botshabelo	CDFC	177 971	...	...	...	...	...	...	...
CAPE TOWN[9]	CDFC	987 007	...	...	...	...	...	...	...
Durban	CDFC	669 242	...	...	...	...	...	...	...
Germiston	CDFC	164 252	...	...	...	...	...	...	...
Johannesburg	CDFC	752 349	...	...	...	...	...	...	...
Kathiehong	CDFC	344 803	...	...	...	...	...	...	...
Kempton Park	CDFC	344 426	...	...	...	...	...	...	...
Khayelitsa	CDFC	314 239	...	...	...	...	...	...	...
Kimberley	CDFC	206 070	...	...	...	...	...	...	...
Mangaung	CDFC	176 525	...	...	...	...	...	...	...
Pietermaritzburg	CDFC	405 385	...	...	...	...	...	...	...
Port Elizabeth	CDFC	775 255	...	...	...	...	...	...	...
PRETORIA[9]	CDFC	692 348	340 363	351 985	...	...	...	...	...
Roodepoort	CDFC	279 340	...	...	...	...	...	...	...
Soweto	CDFC	904 165	...	...	...	...	...	...	...
Springs	CDFC	163 304	...	...	...	...	...	...	...
Tembisa	CDFC	237 676	...	...	...	...	...	...	...
Umlazi	CDFC	339 715	...	...	...	...	...	...	...
Vereeniging	CDFC	379 638	...	...	...	...	...	...	...
Sudan — Soudan									
15 IV 1993									
Al-Fasher	CDFC	141 884	...	...	...	...	...	...	...
Al-Gadarif	CDFC	191 164	...	...	...	...	...	...	...
Al-Gezira	CDFC	211 362	...	...	...	...	...	...	...
Al-Obeid	CDFC	229 425	...	...	...	...	...	...	...
Juba	CDFC	114 980	...	...	...	...	...	...	...
Kassala	CDFC	234 622	...	...	...	...	...	...	...
KHARTOUM	CDFC	947 483	...	...	...	2 919 773	...	...	...
Khartoum North	CDFC	700 887	...	...	...	...	...	...	...
Kosti	CDFC	173 599	...	...	...	...	...	...	...
Nyala	CDFC	227 183	...	...	...	...	...	...	...
Omdurman	CDFC	1 271 403	...	...	...	...	...	...	...
Port Sudan	CDFC	308 195	...	...	...	...	...	...	...
Swaziland									
1 VII 1986									
MBABANE	CDFC	38 290	...	...	...	...	...	...	...
Togo									
1 VII 1990									
LOME	ESDF	450 000	...	...	...	...	...	...	...
Tunisia — Tunisie									
1 VII 1998									
Bizerte	ESDF	105 520	...	...	...	...	...	...	...
Gabes	ESDF	104 950	...	...	...	...	...	...	...
Kairouan	ESDF	110 280	...	...	...	...	...	...	...
Sfax	ESDF	248 800	...	...	...	...	...	...	...
TUNIS	ESDF	702 330	...	...	...	...	...	...	...
Uganda — Ouganda									
12 IX 2002									
Gulu	CDFC	113 144	...	...	...	...	...	...	...
KAMPALA	CDFC	1 208 544	588 433	620 111	...	...	...	...	...
United Republic of Tanzania — République Unie de Tanzanie									
28 VIII 1988									
Arusha	CDFC	134 708	69 875	64 833	...	...	...	...	...
Dar es Salaam	CDFC	1 360 850	715 925	644 925	...	...	...	...	...
DODOMA	CDFC	203 833	101 437	102 396	...	...	...	...	...
Mbeya	CDFC	152 844	74 259	78 585	...	...	...	...	...
Morogoro	CDFC	117 760	59 144	58 616	...	...	...	...	...
Mwanza	CDFC	223 013	113 779	109 234	...	...	...	...	...
Shinyanga	CDFC	100 724	50 117	50 607	...	...	...	...	...

8. Population of capital cities and cities of 100 000 and more inhabitants: latest available year
Population des capitales et des villes de 100 000 habitants et plus: dernière année disponible (continued — suite)

(See notes at end of table. — Voir notes à la fin du tableau.)

Continent, country or area, date and city / Continent, pays ou zone, date et ville	Code[1]	City proper — Ville proprement dite Population				Urban agglomeration — Agglomération urbaine Population			
		Both sexes Les deux sexes	Male Masculin	Female Féminin	Surface area Superficie (km²)	Both sexes Les deux sexes	Male Masculin	Female Féminin	Surface area Superficie (km²)
AFRICA — AFRIQUE									
United Republic of Tanzania — République Unie de Tanzanie 28 VIII 1988									
Tanga	CDFC	187 455	96 259	91 196	...	...	...	...	...
Zanzibar	CDFC	157 634	77 787	79 847	...	...	...	...	...
Western Sahara — Sahara occidental 1 VII 1999									
EL AAIUN	ESDF	169 000	...	...	...	...	...	...	...
Zambia — Zambie 1 VII 2000									
Chingola	E3DF	164 964	82 643	82 321	1 678	...	...	...	...
Kabwe	ESDF	170 387	84 041	86 346	1 572	...	...	...	...
Kitwe	ESDF	362 423	180 865	181 558	777	...	...	...	...
Luanshya	ESDF	144 009	72 449	71 560	811	...	...	...	...
LUSAKA	ESDF	1 057 212	528 891	528 321	360	...	...	...	...
Mufulira	ESDF	137 272	68 253	69 019	1 637	...	...	...	...
Ndola	ESDF	371 221	185 043	186 178	1 103	...	...	...	...
Zimbabwe 18 VIII 1992									
Bulawayo	CDFC	621 742	309 864	311 878	479	...	...	...	...
Chitungwiza	CDFC	274 912	137 890	137 022	...	...	...	...	...
Gweru	CDFC	128 037	64 472	63 565	...	...	...	...	...
HARARE	CDFC	1 189 103	623 345	565 758	872	...	...	...	...
Mutare	CDFC	131 367	68 413	62 954	...	...	...	...	...
AMERICA, NORTH — AMERIQUE DU NORD									
Anguilla 1 VII 2001									
THE VALLEY	CDJC	4 904	...	...	...	...	...	...	...
Antigua and Barbuda — Antigua-et-Barbuda 1 VII 1991									
ST. JOHN	CDFC	22 342	...	...	...	...	...	...	...
Aruba 6 X 1991									
ORANJESTAD	CDFC	20 045	9 441	10 604	...	...	...	...	...
Bahamas 1 V 2000									
NASSAU	CDFC	...	...	...	...	210 832	...	...	...
Barbados — Barbade 1 VII 1980									
BRIDGETOWN	CDFC	7 466	...	...	...	...	...	...	...
Belize 1 VII 2000									
BELMOPAN	ESDF	8 305	4 050	4 255	...	...	...	...	...
Bermuda — Bermudes[10] 20 V 2000									
HAMILTON	CDJC	969	508	461	0	...	...	...	...
British Virgin Islands — Iles Vierges britanniques 1 VII 1992									
ROAD TOWN	ESDF	3 500	...	...	...	...	...	...	...
Canada 1 VII 2003									
Abbotsford	ESDJ	...	...	...	...	158 174	79 472	78 702	626
Calgary	ESDJ	...	...	...	...	1 016 616	513 080	503 536	5 083
Edmonton	ESDJ	...	...	...	...	990 525	496 273	494 252	9 419
Halifax	ESDJ	...	...	...	...	377 932	184 861	193 071	5 496
Hamilton	ESDJ	...	...	...	...	702 917	346 553	356 364	1 372
Kingston	ESDJ	...	...	...	...	155 471	77 108	78 363	1 907

8. Population of capital cities and cities of 100 000 and more inhabitants: latest available year
Population des capitales et des villes de 100 000 habitants et plus: dernière année disponible (continued — suite)

(See notes at end of table. — Voir notes à la fin du tableau.)

Continent, country or area, date and city Continent, pays ou zone, date et ville	Code[1]	City proper — Ville proprement dite Population				Urban agglomeration — Agglomération urbaine Population			
		Both sexes Les deux sexes	Male Masculin	Female Féminin	Surface area Superficie (km²)	Both sexes Les deux sexes	Male Masculin	Female Féminin	Surface area Superficie (km²)
AMERICA, NORTH — AMERIQUE DU NORD									
Canada									
1 VII 2003									
Kitchener	ESDJ	...	...	...	...	444 094	221 031	223 063	827
London	ESDJ	...	...	...	...	457 233	224 004	233 229	2 333
Montréal	ESDJ	...	...	...	...	3 574 516	1 749 159	1 825 357	4 047
Oshawa	ESDJ	...	...	...	...	319 322	159 751	159 571	903
OTTAWA	ESDJ	...	...	...	...	1 132 181	556 384	575 797	5 318
Québec	ESDJ	...	...	...	...	705 898	343 632	362 266	3 154
Regina	ESDJ	...	...	...	...	197 016	96 209	100 807	3 408
St. Catharines	ESDJ	...	...	...	...	393 639	193 149	200 490	1 406
St. John's	ESDJ	...	...	...	...	179 709	86 784	92 925	805
Saint John	ESDJ	...	...	...	...	126 180	61 132	65 048	3 360
Saskatoon	ESDJ	...	...	...	...	233 939	114 818	119 121	5 192
Sherbrooke	ESDJ	...	...	...	...	160 876	78 538	82 338	1 108
Sudbury	ESDJ	...	...	...	...	160 324	78 542	81 782	3 536
Thunder Bay	ESDJ	...	...	...	...	125 488	61 926	63 562	2 548
Toronto	ESDJ	...	...	...	...	5 101 610	2 513 767	2 587 843	5 903
Trois-Rivières	ESDJ	...	...	...	...	140 558	67 941	72 617	880
Vancouver	ESDJ	...	...	...	...	2 134 286	1 054 437	1 079 849	2 879
Victoria	ESDJ	...	...	...	...	326 668	157 106	169 562	695
Windsor	ESDJ	...	...	...	...	328 966	163 467	165 499	1 023
Winnipeg	ESDJ	...	...	...	...	698 210	342 729	355 481	4 151
Cayman Islands — Iles Caïmanes									
1 X 1999									
GEORGE TOWN	CDFC	20 626	...	...	...	...	...	...	...
Costa Rica									
1 VII 2003									
Alajuela	ESDJ	241 177	122 986	118 191	388	...	...	...	...
Cartago	ESDJ	142 442	71 889	70 553	288	...	...	...	...
Heredia	ESDJ	112 461	55 422	57 039	283	...	...	...	...
Puntarenas	ESDJ	111 458	57 716	53 742	1 842	...	...	...	...
SAN JOSE	ESDJ	334 780	165 046	169 734	45	...	...	...	...
Cuba									
1 VII 2003									
Bayamo	ESDF	144 067	...	...	...	...	...	...	...
Camagüey	ESDF	302 054	...	...	...	...	...	...	...
Ciego de Avila	ESDF	106 975	...	...	...	...	...	...	...
Cienfuegos	ESDF	141 258	...	...	...	...	...	...	...
Guantánamo	ESDF	207 788	...	...	...	...	...	...	...
Holguín	ESDF	270 060	...	...	...	...	...	...	...
LA HABANA	ESDF	2 202 239	...	...	727	...	...	...	...
Las Tunas	ESDF	144 152	...	...	...	...	...	...	...
Matanzas	ESDF	127 758	...	...	...	...	...	...	...
Pinar del Río	ESDF	139 484	...	...	...	...	...	...	...
Sancti Spíritus	ESDF	98 552	...	...	...	...	...	...	...
Santa Clara	ESDF	210 358	...	...	...	...	...	...	...
Santiago de Cuba	ESDF	423 930	...	...	...	...	...	...	...
Dominica — Dominique									
1 VII 1991									
ROSEAU	CDFC	16 243	...	...	...	...	...	...	...
Dominican Republic — République dominicaine									
1 VII 2001									
San Pedro de Macoris	ESDF	*266 629*	...	...	...	...	...	...	...
Santiago de los Caballeros	ESDF	*836 614*	...	...	...	...	...	...	...
SANTO DOMINGO	ESDF	*2 677 056*	...	...	...	...	...	...	...
El Salvador[11]									
1 VII 2003									
Ahuachapan	ESDF	115 521	57 593	57 928	245	...	...	...	...
Apopa	ESDF	192 728	91 699	100 830	52	...	...	...	...

(See notes at end of table. — Voir notes à la fin du tableau.)

Continent, country or area, date and city / Continent, pays ou zone, date et ville	Code[1]	City proper — Ville proprement dite Population				Urban agglomeration — Agglomération urbaine Population			
		Both sexes Les deux sexes	Male Masculin	Female Féminin	Surface area Superficie (km²)	Both sexes Les deux sexes	Male Masculin	Female Féminin	Surface area Superficie (km²)
AMERICA, NORTH — AMERIQUE DU NORD									
El Salvador[11]									
1 VII 2003									
Ciudad Delgado	ESDF	164 069	78 063	85 837	33	...	...	...	...
Cuscatancingo	ESDF	104 640	49 787	54 745	5	...	...	...	...
Ilopango	ESDF	144 985	68 983	75 852	35	...	...	...	...
Mejicanos	ESDF	200 917	95 596	105 114	22	...	...	...	...
Nueva San Salvador	ESDF	175 286	86 161	89 097	112	...	...	...	...
SAN SALVADOR	ESDF	497 844	236 873	261 836	886	...	...	...	...
San Martin	ESDF	123 663	58 838	64 697	56	...	...	...	...
San Miguel	ESDF	259 197	128 026	131 171	594	...	...	...	...
Santa Ana	ESDF	261 568	129 155	132 413	400	...	...	...	...
Sonsonate	ESDF	103 490	51 402	52 088	233	...	...	...	...
Soyapango	ESDF	290 412	138 177	152 739	30	...	...	...	...
Greenland — Groenland									
1 VII 2000									
NUUK (GODTHAB)	ESDJ	13 552	7 265	6 287	...	...	...	...	...
Grenada — Grenade									
1 VII 1981									
ST. GEORGE'S	CDFC	4 788	...	...	...	...	...	...	...
Guadeloupe									
8 III 1999									
BASSE-TERRE	CDJC	12 377	5 687	6 690	...	44 747	21 252	23 495	...
Pointe-à-Pitre	CDJC	...	...	...	...	171 773	...	...	...
Guatemala									
1 VII 2001									
GUATEMALA	ESDF	_1 022 001_	_491 891_	_530 110_	228	...	...	...	...
Escuintla	ESDF	_114 626_	_57 893_	_56 733_	332	...	...	...	...
Mixco	ESDF	_452 134_	_221 928_	_230 206_	99	...	...	...	...
Quetzaltenango	ESDF	_152 223_	_76 272_	_75 951_	120	...	...	...	...
Villa Nueva	ESDF	_390 329_	_192 238_	_198 091_	114	...	...	...	...
Haiti — Haïti									
1 VII 1999									
Cap-Haitien	ESDJ	_113 555_	_50 064_	_63 491_	10	...	...	...	...
Carrefour	ESDJ	_336 222_	_146 838_	_189 384_	23	...	...	...	...
Delmas	ESDJ	_284 079_	_124 774_	_159 305_	26	...	...	...	...
PORT-AU-PRINCE	ESDJ	_990 558_	_436 170_	_554 388_	21	...	...	...	...
Honduras									
1 VII 2003									
La Ceiba	ESDF	137 815	67 691	70 124	...	...	...	...	...
San Pedro Sula	ESDF	518 736	251 514	267 222	...	...	...	...	...
TEGUCIGALPA	ESDF	858 437	411 687	446 749	...	...	...	...	...
Jamaica — Jamaïque									
1 VII 1991									
KINGSTON	CDFC	103 962	...	...	22	538 144	250 369	287 775	...
Martinique									
8 III 1999									
FORT-DE-FRANCE	CDJC	94 152	42 812	51 340	...	134 796	61 705	73 091	...
Mexico — Mexique[12,13]									
1 VII 2003									
Acapulco (de Juárez)	ESDJ	...	...	...	...	_819 517_	...	...	...
Acayucan	ESDJ	...	...	...	...	_106 713_	...	...	...
Aguascalientes	ESDJ	...	...	...	...	_766 312_	...	...	...
Apizaco	ESDJ	...	...	...	...	_174 619_	...	...	...
Campeche	ESDJ	_206 337_	...	...	...	...	...	...	...
Cancun	ESDJ	...	...	...	...	_510 950_	...	...	...
Celaya	ESDJ	_299 398_	...	...	...	...	...	...	...
Chetumal	ESDJ	_130 952_	...	...	...	...	...	...	...
Chihuahua	ESDJ	...	...	...	...	_738 855_	...	...	...
Chilpacingo (de los Bravo)	ESDJ	_154 030_	...	...	...	...	...	...	...
Ciudad Acuña	ESDJ	_129 834_	...	...	...	...	...	...	...

8. Population of capital cities and cities of 100 000 and more inhabitants: latest available year
Population des capitales et des villes de 100 000 habitants et plus: dernière année disponible (continued — suite)

(See notes at end of table. — Voir notes à la fin du tableau.)

Continent, country or area, date and city Continent, pays ou zone, date et ville	Code[1]	City proper — Ville proprement dite Population				Urban agglomeration — Agglomération urbaine Population			
		Both sexes Les deux sexes	Male Masculin	Female Féminin	Surface area Superficie (km²)	Both sexes Les deux sexes	Male Masculin	Female Féminin	Surface area Superficie (km²)
AMERICA, NORTH — AMERIQUE DU NORD									
Mexico — Mexique[12,13]									
1 VII 2003									
Ciudad Del Carmen	ESDJ	139 352	...	...	...	...	...	...	...
Ciudad Obregón	ESDJ	264 166	...	...	...	...	...	...	...
Ciudad Valles	ESDJ	109 420	...	...	...	...	...	...	...
Ciudad Victoria	ESDJ	271 873	...	...	...	...	...	...	...
Coatzacoalcos	ESDJ	...	...	...	...	323 509	...	...	...
Colimas	ESDJ	...	...	...	...	226 495	...	...	...
Córdoba	ESDJ	...	...	...	...	289 122	...	...	...
Cuautla	ESDJ	...	...	...	...	387 840	...	...	...
Cuernavaca	ESDJ	...	...	...	...	804 140	...	...	...
Culiacán Rosales	ESDJ	584 280	...	...	...	...	...	...	...
Delicias	ESDJ	103 886	...	...	...	...	...	...	...
Durango (Victoria de Durango) ...	ESDJ	454 565	...	...	...	...	...	...	...
Ensenada	ESDJ	...	...	...	...	261 128	...	...	...
Fresnillo	ESDJ	103 013	...	...	...	...	...	...	...
Guadalajara	ESDJ	...	...	...	...	3 944 094	...	...	...
Guanajuato	ESDJ	...	...	...	...	102 195	...	...	...
Guaynas	ESDJ	...	...	...	...	191 201	...	...	...
Hermosillo	ESDJ	594 299	...	...	...	...	...	...	...
Hidalgo del Parral	ESDJ	103 716	...	...	...	...	...	...	...
Iguala (de la Independencia)	ESDJ	111 043	...	...	...	...	...	...	...
Irapuato	ESDJ	344 194	...	...	...	...	...	...	...
Juárez	ESDJ	...	...	...	...	1 379 589	...	...	...
La Paz	ESDJ	...	...	...	...	178 101	...	...	...
La Piedad	ESDJ	...	...	...	...	243 555	...	...	...
Lázaro Cárdenas	ESDJ	...	...	...	...	137 065	...	...	...
León (de los Aldama)	ESDJ	...	...	...	...	1 379 851	...	...	...
Los Mochis	ESDJ	213 964	...	...	...	...	...	...	...
Manzanillo	ESDJ	101 536	...	...	...	...	...	...	...
Matamoros	ESDJ	...	...	...	...	474 667	...	...	...
Mazatlán	ESDJ	352 409	...	...	...	...	...	...	...
Mérida	ESDJ	...	...	...	...	863 756	...	...	...
Mexicali	ESDJ	...	...	...	...	609 714	...	...	...
MEXICO, CIUDAD DE	ESDJ	...	...	...	...	19 493 539	...	...	...
Minatitlán	ESDJ	...	...	...	...	336 240	...	...	...
Monclova	ESDJ	...	...	...	...	299 265	...	...	...
Monterrey	ESDJ	...	...	...	...	3 542 979	...	...	...
Morelia	ESDJ	...	...	...	...	709 941	...	...	...
Moroleón - Uriangato	ESDJ	...	...	...	...	107 767	...	...	...
Navojoa	ESDJ	104 947	...	...	...	...	...	...	...
Nogales	ESDJ	179 415	...	...	...	...	...	...	...
Nuevo Laredo	ESDJ	...	...	...	...	354 372	...	...	...
Oaxaca de Juárez	ESDJ	...	...	...	...	495 241	...	...	...
Ocotlán	ESDJ	...	...	...	...	133 569	...	...	...
Orizaba	ESDJ	...	...	...	...	391 620	...	...	...
Pachuca (de Soto)	ESDJ	...	...	...	...	404 861	...	...	...
Piedras Negras	ESDJ	...	...	...	...	167 994	...	...	...
Poza Rica de Hidalgo	ESDJ	...	...	...	...	460 733	...	...	...
Puebla de Zaragoza	ESDJ	...	...	...	...	2 016 956	...	...	...
Puerto Vallarta	ESDJ	...	...	...	...	276 378	...	...	...
Querétaro	ESDJ	...	...	...	...	877 837	...	...	...
Reynosa	ESDJ	...	...	...	...	603 335	...	...	...
Rioverde - Ciudad Fernández	ESDJ	...	...	...	...	131 505	...	...	...
Salamanca	ESDJ	146 432	...	...	...	...	...	...	...
Saltillo	ESDJ	...	...	...	...	697 652	...	...	...
San Cristobal de las Casas	ESDJ	124 404	...	...	...	...	...	...	...
San Francisco del Rincón	ESDJ	...	...	...	...	159 788	...	...	...
San Juan del Río	ESDJ	112 166	...	...	...	...	...	...	...
San Luis Potosí	ESDJ	...	...	...	...	895 602	...	...	...

8. Population of capital cities and cities of 100 000 and more inhabitants: latest available year
Population des capitales et des villes de 100 000 habitants et plus: dernière année disponible (continued — suite)

(See notes at end of table. — Voir notes à la fin du tableau.)

Continent, country or area, date and city / Continent, pays ou zone, date et ville	Code[1]	City proper — Ville proprement dite Population				Urban agglomeration — Agglomération urbaine Population			
		Both sexes Les deux sexes	Male Masculin	Female Féminin	Surface area Superficie (km²)	Both sexes Les deux sexes	Male Masculin	Female Féminin	Surface area Superficie (km²)
AMERICA, NORTH — AMERIQUE DU NORD									
Mexico — Mexique[12,13]									
1 VII 2003									
San Luis Rio Colorado	ESDJ	144 593	...	...	...	...	...	...	...
San Martín Texmelucan	ESDJ	...	...	...	...	155 376	...	...	...
Tampico	ESDJ	...	...	...	...	806 919	...	...	...
Tapachula (de Cordova y Ordoñez)	ESDJ	196 951	...	...	...	...	...	...	...
Tecomán	ESDJ	...	...	...	...	134 285	...	...	...
Tehuacán	ESDJ	223 497	...	...	...	...	...	...	...
Tepic	ESDJ	...	...	...	...	369 582	...	...	...
Tijuana	ESDJ	...	...	...	...	1 437 729	...	...	...
Tlaxcala	ESDJ	...	...	...	...	269 457	...	...	...
Toluca (de Lerdo)	ESDJ	...	...	...	...	1 567 750	...	...	...
Torreón	ESDJ	...	...	...	...	1 082 616	...	...	...
Tula	ESDJ	...	...	...	...	179 635	...	...	...
Tulancingo	ESDJ	...	...	...	...	204 684	...	...	...
Tuxtla Gutiérrez	ESDJ	...	...	...	...	545 105	...	...	...
Uruapan	ESDJ	...	...	...	...	245 080	...	...	...
Veracruz	ESDJ	...	...	...	...	656 100	...	...	...
Villahermosa	ESDJ	...	...	...	...	648 819	...	...	...
Xalapa-Enriquez	ESDJ	...	...	...	...	545 706	...	...	...
Zacatecas	ESDJ	...	...	...	...	245 244	...	...	...
Zamora de Hidalgo	ESDJ	...	...	...	...	228 914	...	...	...
Montserrat									
1 VII 1980									
PLYMOUTH	CDFC	1 478	...	...	...	...	...	...	...
Netherlands Antilles — Antilles néerlandaises									
1 VII 1992									
WILLEMSTAD	CDJC	2 345	...	...	...	...	...	...	...
Nicaragua									
1 VII 2003									
Chinandega	ESDJ	...	...	...	...	125 699	...	...	...
Leon	ESDJ	...	...	...	...	148 362	...	...	...
MANAGUA	ESDJ	...	...	...	...	1 008 903	...	...	...
Masaya	ESDJ	...	...	...	...	120 945	...	...	...
Tipitapa	ESDJ	...	...	...	...	118 507	...	...	...
Panama									
1 VII 2000									
PANAMA[14]	ESDF	484 261	230 747	253 514	107	...	...	...	...
San Miguelito	ESDF	331 692	161 901	169 791	50	...	...	...	...
Puerto Rico — Porto Rico[15]									
1 VII 2003									
Arecibo	ESDJ	101 735	...	...	326	...	...	...	...
Bayamón	ESDJ	224 915	...	...	115	...	...	...	...
Caguas	ESDJ	142 161	...	...	152	...	...	...	...
Carolina	ESDJ	187 337	...	...	117	...	...	...	...
Guaynabo	ESDJ	101 762	...	...	70	...	...	...	...
Ponce	ESDJ	185 930	...	...	297	...	...	...	...
SAN JUAN	ESDJ	433 733	...	...	124	...	...	...	...
Saint Kitts-Nevis — Saint-Kitts-et-Nevis									
1 VII 1980									
BASSETERRE	CDFC	14 161	...	...	...	...	...	...	...
Saint Lucia — Sainte-Lucie									
22 V 2001									
CASTRIES	CDFC	11 092	5 238	5 854	...	...	...	...	...

8. Population of capital cities and cities of 100 000 and more inhabitants: latest available year
Population des capitales et des villes de 100 000 habitants et plus: dernière année disponible (continued — suite)

(See notes at end of table. — Voir notes à la fin du tableau.)

Continent, country or area, date and city — Continent, pays ou zone, date et ville	Code[1]	City proper — Ville proprement dite Population				Urban agglomeration — Agglomération urbaine Population			
		Both sexes Les deux sexes	Male Masculin	Female Féminin	Surface area Superficie (km²)	Both sexes Les deux sexes	Male Masculin	Female Féminin	Surface area Superficie (km²)
AMERICA, NORTH — AMERIQUE DU NORD									
Saint Pierre and Miquelon — Saint Pierre-et-Miquelon									
8 III 1999									
SAINT-PIERRE	CDFC	5 618	...	...	...	...	...	...	...
Saint Vincent and the Grenadines — Saint Vincent-et-les Grenadines									
12 V 1991									
KINGSTOWN	CDFC	15 466	...	...	...	...	...	...	...
Trinidad and Tobago — Trinité-et-Tobago									
1 VII 1996									
PORT-OF-SPAIN	ESDF	43 396	20 739	22 657	12	...	...	...	...
Turks and Caicos Islands — Iles Turques et Caïques									
1 VII 1990									
GRAND TURK	CDFC	3 691	...	...	...	...	...	...	...
United States — Etats-Unis[16,17]									
1 IV 2000									
Abilene (TX)	CDJC	115 930	58 529	57 401	...	...	...	...	
Akron (OH)	CDJC	217 074	103 670	113 404	...	570 215	273 779	296 436	...
Albuquerque (NM)	CDJC	448 607	217 887	230 720	...	598 191	291 380	306 811	...
Alexandria (VA)[18]	CDJC	128 283	61 974	66 309					
Allentown (PA)	CDJC	106 632	51 037	55 595	...	576 408	277 504	298 904	...
Amarillo (TX)	CDJC	173 627	83 370	90 257	...	179 312	88 361	90 951	...
Anaheim (CA)[19]	CDJC	328 014	164 058	163 956	...	...	...	...	...
Anchorage (AK)	CDJC	260 283	131 668	128 615	...	...	...	...	
Ann Arbor (MI)	CDJC	114 024	56 352	57 672	...	283 904	140 009	143 895	
Arlington (TX)[20]	CDJC	332 969	166 465	166 504					
Arlington (VA)[18]	CDJC	189 453	95 443	94 010	...	...	...	...	...
Arvada (CO)[21]	CDJC	102 153	50 021	52 132	...	...			
Athens (GA)	CDJC	101 489	49 532	51 957	...	106 482	51 880	54 602	
Atlanta (GA)	CDJC	416 474	206 725	209 749	...	3 499 840	1 726 532	1 773 308	
Augusta-Richmond (GA)	CDJC	199 775	96 375	103 400	...	335 630	161 488	174 142	
Aurora (CO)[21]	CDJC	276 393	136 901	139 492	...	...	...	...	...
Aurora (IL)[22]	CDJC	142 990	72 020	70 970	...	...	...	...	...
Austin (TX)	CDJC	656 562	337 569	318 993	...	901 920	459 585	442 335	
Bakersfield (CA)	CDJC	247 057	120 105	126 952	...	396 125	193 835	202 290	
Baltimore (MD)	CDJC	651 154	303 687	347 467	...	2 076 354	992 299	1 084 055	
Baton Rouge (LA)	CDJC	227 818	108 255	119 563	...	479 019	229 835	249 184	
Beaumont (TX)	CDJC	113 866	54 142	59 724	...	139 304	66 185	73 119	
Bellevue (WA)[23]	CDJC	109 569	54 347	55 222					
Berkeley (CA)[24]	CDJC	102 743	50 456	52 287	...	...	...	...	
Birmingham (AL)	CDJC	242 820	112 046	130 774	...	663 615	311 940	351 675	
Boise City (ID)	CDJC	185 787	92 014	93 773	...	272 625	135 444	137 181	
Boston (MA)	CDJC	589 141	283 588	305 553	...	4 032 484	1 943 524	2 088 960	
Bridgeport (CT)	CDJC	139 529	66 554	72 975	...	888 890	427 957	460 933	
Brownsville (TX)	CDJC	139 722	65 783	73 939	...	165 776	78 553	87 223	
Buffalo (NY)	CDJC	292 648	137 443	155 205	...	976 703	462 511	514 192	
Burbank (CA)[19]	CDJC	100 316	48 635	51 681	...	...	...	...	...
Cambridge (MA)[25]	CDJC	101 355	49 674	51 681	...	...	...	...	...
Cape Coral (FL)	CDJC	102 286	49 584	52 702	...	329 757	160 034	169 723	
Carrollton (TX)[20]	CDJC	109 576	54 275	55 301	...	...			
Cedar Rapids (IA)	CDJC	120 758	58 833	61 925	...	155 334	75 686	79 648	
Chandler (AZ)[26]	CDJC	176 581	88 140	88 441	...	...	...	...	
Charlotte (NC)	CDJC	540 828	264 978	275 850	...	758 927	372 894	386 033	
Chattanooga (TN)	CDJC	155 554	73 370	82 184	...	343 509	163 502	180 007	
Chesapeake (VA)[27]	CDJC	199 184	96 728	102 456	...				
Chicago (IL)	CDJC	2 896 016	1 405 107	1 490 909	...	8 307 904	4 055 013	4 252 891	
Chula Vista (CA)[28]	CDJC	173 556	84 237	89 319	...	...	...	...	...
Cincinnati (OH)	CDJC	331 285	156 357	174 928	...	1 503 262	725 248	778 014	...

8. Population of capital cities and cities of 100 000 and more inhabitants: latest available year
Population des capitales et des villes de 100 000 habitants et plus: dernière année disponible (continued — suite)

(See notes at end of table. — Voir notes à la fin du tableau.)

Continent, country or area, date and city / Continent, pays ou zone, date et ville	Code[1]	City proper — Ville proprement dite Population				Urban agglomeration — Agglomération urbaine Population			
		Both sexes Les deux sexes	Male Masculin	Female Féminin	Surface area Superficie (km²)	Both sexes Les deux sexes	Male Masculin	Female Féminin	Surface area Superficie (km²)

AMERICA, NORTH — AMERIQUE DU NORD

United States — Etats-Unis[16,17]
  1 IV 2000

Clarksville (TN)	CDJC	103 455	51 950	51 505	...	121 775	63 266	58 509	...
Clearwater (FL)[29]	CDJC	108 787	52 065	56 722	...	...	...	...	...
Cleveland (OH)	CDJC	478 403	226 550	251 853	...	1 786 647	849 505	937 142	...
Colorado Springs (CO)	CDJC	360 890	178 469	182 421	...	466 122	233 696	232 426	...
Columbia (SC)	CDJC	116 278	56 999	59 279	...	420 537	202 432	218 105	...
Columbus (GA)	CDJC	186 291	90 617	95 674	...	242 324	119 409	122 915	...
Columbus (OH)	CDJC	711 470	345 878	365 592	...	1 133 193	551 065	582 128	...
Concord (CA)	CDJC	121 780	60 147	61 633	...	552 624	270 187	282 437	...
Coral Springs (FL)[30]	CDJC	117 549	57 251	60 298	...	...	...	...	...
Corona (CA)[31]	CDJC	124 966	61 849	63 117	...	...	...	...	...
Corpus Christi (TX)	CDJC	277 454	135 572	141 882	...	293 925	143 704	150 221	...
Costa Mesa (CA)[19]	CDJC	108 724	55 694	53 030	...	...	...	...	...
Dallas (TX)	CDJC	1 188 580	598 991	589 589	...	4 145 659	2 063 116	2 082 543	...
Daly City (CA)[24]	CDJC	103 621	50 971	52 650	...	...	...	...	...
Dayton (OH)	CDJC	166 179	80 142	86 037	...	703 444	338 473	364 971	...
Denver (CO)	CDJC	554 636	280 207	274 429	...	1 984 887	991 426	993 461	...
Des Moines (IA)	CDJC	198 682	96 157	102 525	...	370 505	179 494	191 011	...
Detroit (MI)	CDJC	951 270	448 319	502 951	...	3 903 377	1 889 137	2 014 240	...
Downey (CA)[19]	CDJC	107 323	52 176	55 147	...	...	...	...	...
Durham (NC)	CDJC	187 035	89 884	97 151	...	287 796	137 048	150 748	...
El Monte (CA)[19]	CDJC	115 965	58 584	57 381	...	...	...	...	...
El Paso (TX)	CDJC	563 662	267 651	296 011	...	674 801	325 037	349 764	...
Elizabeth (NJ)[32]	CDJC	120 568	59 674	60 894	...	...	...	...	...
Erie (PA)	CDJC	103 717	49 355	54 362	...	194 804	93 306	101 498	...
Escondido (CA)[28]	CDJC	133 559	66 233	67 326	...	...	...	...	...
Eugene (OR)	CDJC	137 893	67 540	70 353	...	224 049	109 745	114 304	...
Evansville (IN)	CDJC	121 582	57 170	64 412	...	211 989	100 474	111 515	...
Fayetteville (NC)	CDJC	121 015	57 967	63 048	...	172 585	85 786	86 799	...
Flint (MI)	CDJC	124 943	58 704	66 239	...	365 096	173 954	191 142	...
Fontana (CA)[31]	CDJC	128 929	63 982	64 947	...	...	...	...	...
Fort Collins (CO)	CDJC	118 652	59 593	59 059	...	206 633	103 085	103 548	...
Fort Lauderdale (FL)[30]	CDJC	152 397	79 826	72 571	...	...	...	...	...
Fort Wayne (IN)	CDJC	205 727	99 659	106 068	...	287 759	140 309	147 450	...
Fort Worth (TX)[20]	CDJC	534 694	263 720	270 974	...	...	...	...	...
Fremont (CA)[24]	CDJC	203 413	102 273	101 140	...	...	...	...	...
Fresno (CA)	CDJC	427 652	210 107	217 545	...	554 923	271 889	283 034	...
Fullerton (CA)[19]	CDJC	126 003	62 276	63 727	...	...	...	...	...
Garden Grove (CA)[19]	CDJC	165 196	82 688	82 508	...	...	...	...	...
Garland (TX)[20]	CDJC	215 768	106 937	108 831	...	...	...	...	...
Gary (IN)[22]	CDJC	102 746	47 088	55 658	...	...	...	...	...
Gilbert (AZ)[26]	CDJC	109 697	54 531	55 166	...	...	...	...	...
Glendale (AZ)[26]	CDJC	218 812	109 168	109 644	...	...	...	...	...
Glendale (CA)[19]	CDJC	194 973	93 074	101 899	...	...	...	...	...
Grand Prairie (TX)[20]	CDJC	127 427	63 058	64 369	...	...	...	...	...
Grand Rapids (MI)	CDJC	197 800	96 761	101 039	...	539 080	263 464	275 616	...
Green Bay (WI)	CDJC	102 313	50 433	51 880	...	187 316	92 661	94 655	...
Greensboro (NC)	CDJC	223 891	105 573	118 318	...	267 884	127 184	140 700	...
Hampton (VA)[27]	CDJC	146 437	72 579	73 858	...	...	...	...	...
Hartford (CT)	CDJC	121 578	58 071	63 507	...	851 535	406 302	445 233	...
Hayward (CA)[24]	CDJC	140 030	69 490	70 540	...	...	...	...	...
Henderson (NV)[33]	CDJC	175 381	87 001	88 380	...	...	...	...	...
Hialeah (FL)[30]	CDJC	226 419	108 893	117 526	...	...	...	...	...
Hollywood (FL)[30]	CDJC	139 357	67 577	71 780	...	...	...	...	...
Honolulu (HI)	CDJC	371 657	182 628	189 029	...	718 182	359 930	358 252	...
Houston (TX)	CDJC	1 953 631	975 551	978 080	...	3 822 509	1 903 082	1 919 427	...
Huntington Beach (CA)[19]	CDJC	189 594	95 004	94 590	...	...	...	...	...
Huntsville (AL)	CDJC	158 216	76 174	82 042	...	213 253	104 854	108 399	...
Independence (MO)[34]	CDJC	113 288	54 173	59 115	...	...	...	...	...

8. Population of capital cities and cities of 100 000 and more inhabitants: latest available year
Population des capitales et des villes de 100 000 habitants et plus: dernière année disponible (continued — suite)

(See notes at end of table. — Voir notes à la fin du tableau.)

Continent, country or area, date and city / Continent, pays ou zone, date et ville	Code[1]	City proper — Ville proprement dite Population				Urban agglomeration — Agglomération urbaine Population			
		Both sexes Les deux sexes	Male Masculin	Female Féminin	Surface area Superficie (km²)	Both sexes Les deux sexes	Male Masculin	Female Féminin	Surface area Superficie (km²)
AMERICA, NORTH — AMERIQUE DU NORD									
United States — Etats-Unis[16,17]									
1 IV 2000									
Indianapolis (IN)	CDJC	791 926	383 035	408 891	...	1 218 919	592 172	626 747	...
Inglewood (CA)[19]	CDJC	112 580	53 423	59 157	...	...	...	...	...
Irvine (CA)[19]	CDJC	143 072	69 235	73 837	...	...	...	...	...
Irving (TX)[20]	CDJC	191 615	97 687	93 928	...	...	...	...	...
Jackson (MS)	CDJC	184 256	85 656	98 600	...	292 637	137 618	155 019	...
Jacksonville (FL)	CDJC	735 617	356 284	379 333	...	882 295	427 937	454 358	...
Jersey City (NJ)[32]	CDJC	240 055	117 144	122 911	...	...	...	...	...
Joliet (IL)[22]	CDJC	106 221	52 623	53 598	...	...	...	...	...
Kansas City (KS)[34]	CDJC	146 866	71 769	75 097	...	...	...	...	...
Kansas City (MO)	CDJC	441 545	213 141	228 404	...	1 361 744	659 663	702 081	...
Knoxville (TN)	CDJC	173 890	82 390	91 500	...	419 830	201 687	218 143	...
Lafayette (LA)	CDJC	110 257	53 158	57 099	...	178 079	86 129	91 950	...
Lakewood (CO)[21]	CDJC	144 126	71 141	72 985	...	...	...	...	...
Lancaster (CA)	CDJC	118 718	60 257	58 461	...	263 532	131 583	131 949	...
Lansing (MI)	CDJC	119 128	57 186	61 942	...	300 032	143 861	156 171	...
Laredo (TX)	CDJC	176 576	84 704	91 872	...	...	...	...	...
Las Vegas (NV)	CDJC	478 434	243 077	235 357	...	1 314 357	666 831	647 526	...
Lexington-Fayette (KY)	CDJC	260 512	127 905	132 607	...	...	...	...	...
Lincoln (NE)	CDJC	225 581	112 361	113 220	...	226 582	112 952	113 630	...
Little Rock (AR)	CDJC	183 133	86 322	96 811	...	360 331	171 576	188 755	...
Livonia (MI)[35]	CDJC	100 545	48 718	51 827	...	...	...	...	...
Long Beach (CA)[19]	CDJC	461 522	226 718	234 804	...	...	...	...	...
Los Angeles (CA)	CDJC	3 694 820	1 841 805	1 853 015	...	11 789 487	5 834 856	5 954 631	...
Louisville (KY)	CDJC	256 231	121 153	135 078	...	863 582	413 482	450 100	...
Lowell (MA)[25]	CDJC	105 167	51 807	53 360	...	...	...	...	...
Lubbock (TX)	CDJC	199 564	97 023	102 541	...	202 225	98 607	103 618	...
Madison (WI)	CDJC	208 054	102 248	105 806	...	329 533	161 918	167 615	...
Manchester (NH)	CDJC	107 006	52 394	54 612	...	143 549	70 246	73 303	...
McAllen (TX)	CDJC	106 414	50 438	55 976	...	523 144	253 443	269 701	...
Memphis (TN)	CDJC	650 100	307 643	342 457	...	972 091	464 365	507 726	...
Mesa (AZ)[26]	CDJC	396 375	196 378	199 997	...	...	...	...	...
Mesquite (TX)[20]	CDJC	124 523	59 987	64 536	...	...	...	...	...
Miami (FL)	CDJC	362 470	180 194	182 276	...	4 919 036	2 371 683	2 547 353	...
Milwaukee (WI)	CDJC	596 974	285 363	311 611	...	1 308 913	631 147	677 766	...
Minneapolis (MN)	CDJC	382 618	192 232	190 386	...	2 388 593	1 172 421	1 216 172	...
Mobile (AL)	CDJC	198 915	93 015	105 900	...	317 605	150 166	167 439	...
Modesto (CA)	CDJC	188 856	91 572	97 284	...	310 945	152 392	158 553	...
Montgomery (AL)	CDJC	201 568	94 573	106 995	...	...	...	...	...
Moreno Valley (CA)[31]	CDJC	142 381	69 645	72 736	...	...	...	...	...
Naperville (IL)[22]	CDJC	128 358	62 831	65 527	...	...	...	...	...
Nashville-Davidson (TN)	CDJC	569 891	275 865	294 026	...	749 935	363 237	386 698	...
New Haven (CT)	CDJC	123 626	59 185	64 441	...	531 314	255 062	276 252	...
New Orleans (LA)	CDJC	484 674	227 094	257 580	...	1 009 283	478 904	530 379	...
New York (NY)	CDJC	8 008 278	3 794 204	4 214 074	...	17 799 861	8 531 001	9 268 860	...
Newark (NJ)[32]	CDJC	273 546	132 701	140 845	...	...	...	...	...
Newport News (VA)[27]	CDJC	180 150	87 178	92 972	...	...	...	...	...
Norfolk (VA)[27]	CDJC	234 403	119 830	114 573	...	...	...	...	...
North Las Vegas (NV)[33]	CDJC	115 488	58 947	56 541	...	...	...	...	...
Norwalk (CA)[19]	CDJC	103 298	51 109	52 189	...	...	...	...	...
Oakland (CA)[24]	CDJC	399 484	192 757	206 727	...	...	...	...	...
Oceanside (CA)[28]	CDJC	161 029	79 719	81 310	...	...	...	...	...
Oklahoma City (OK)	CDJC	506 132	247 313	258 819	...	747 003	361 768	385 235	...
Omaha (NE)	CDJC	390 007	190 032	199 975	...	626 623	306 737	319 886	...
Ontario (CA)[19]	CDJC	158 007	79 225	78 782	...	...	...	...	...
Orange (CA)[19]	CDJC	128 821	64 665	64 156	...	...	...	...	...
Orlando (FL)	CDJC	185 951	90 080	95 871	...	1 157 431	569 693	587 738	...
Overland Park (KS)[34]	CDJC	149 080	72 170	76 910	...	...	...	...	...
Oxnard (CA)	CDJC	170 358	87 090	83 268	...	337 591	170 338	167 253	...

(See notes at end of table. — Voir notes à la fin du tableau.)

Continent, country or area, date and city / Continent, pays ou zone, date et ville	Code[1]	City proper — Ville proprement dite Population				Urban agglomeration — Agglomération urbaine Population			
		Both sexes Les deux sexes	Male Masculin	Female Féminin	Surface area Superficie (km²)	Both sexes Les deux sexes	Male Masculin	Female Féminin	Surface area Superficie (km²)
AMERICA, NORTH — AMERIQUE DU NORD									
United States — Etats-Unis[16,17]									
1 IV 2000									
Palmdale (CA)[36]	CDJC	116 670	57 338	59 332	...	...	...	...	...
Pasadena (CA)[19]	CDJC	133 936	65 495	68 441	...	...	...	...	...
Pasadena (TX)[37]	CDJC	141 674	70 767	70 907	...	...	...	...	...
Paterson (NJ)[32]	CDJC	149 222	72 473	76 749	...	...	...	...	...
Pembroke Pines (FL)[30]	CDJC	137 427	64 044	73 383	...	...	...	...	...
Peoria (AZ)[26]	CDJC	108 364	52 058	56 306	...	...	...	...	...
Peoria (IL)	CDJC	112 936	53 471	59 465	...	247 172	118 965	128 207	...
Philadelphia (PA)	CDJC	1 517 550	705 107	812 443	...	5 149 079	2 458 575	2 690 504	...
Phoenix (AZ)	CDJC	1 321 045	671 760	649 285	...	2 907 049	1 451 459	1 455 590	...
Pittsburgh (PA)	CDJC	334 563	159 119	175 444	...	1 753 136	830 794	922 342	...
Plano (TX)[20]	CDJC	222 030	110 619	111 411	...	...	...	...	...
Pomona (CA)[19]	CDJC	149 473	75 630	73 843	...	...	...	...	...
Portland (OR)	CDJC	529 121	261 565	267 556	...	1 583 138	782 186	800 952	...
Portsmouth (VA)[27]	CDJC	100 565	48 583	51 982	...	...	...	...	...
Providence (RI)	CDJC	173 618	83 035	90 583	...	1 174 548	562 552	611 996	...
Provo (UT)	CDJC	105 166	50 572	54 594	...	303 680	149 740	153 940	...
Pueblo (CO)	CDJC	102 121	49 442	52 679	...	123 351	60 082	63 269	...
Raleigh (NC)	CDJC	276 093	136 648	139 445	...	541 527	268 248	273 279	...
Rancho Cucamonga (CA)[19]	CDJC	127 743	63 895	63 848	...	...	...	...	...
Reno (NV)	CDJC	180 480	92 254	88 226	...	303 689	153 751	149 938	...
Richmond (VA)	CDJC	197 790	92 068	105 722	...	818 836	388 082	430 754	...
Riverside (CA)	CDJC	255 166	125 705	129 461	...	1 506 816	744 245	762 571	...
Rochester (NY)	CDJC	219 773	105 083	114 690	...	694 396	333 601	360 795	...
Rockford (IL)	CDJC	150 115	72 384	77 731	...	270 414	132 078	138 336	...
Sacramento (CA)	CDJC	407 018	197 784	209 234	...	1 393 498	679 713	713 785	...
St. Louis (MO)	CDJC	348 189	163 567	184 622	...	2 077 662	989 609	1 088 053	...
St. Paul (MN)[38]	CDJC	287 151	138 863	148 288	...	...	...	...	...
St. Petersburg (FL)[29]	CDJC	248 232	118 411	129 821	...	...	...	...	...
Salem (OR)	CDJC	136 924	68 752	68 172	...	207 229	103 225	104 004	...
Salinas (CA)	CDJC	151 060	80 361	70 699	...	179 173	94 641	84 532	...
Salt Lake City (UT)	CDJC	181 743	92 045	89 698	...	887 650	447 308	440 342	...
San Antonio (TX)	CDJC	1 144 646	553 245	591 401	...	1 327 554	644 527	683 027	...
San Bernardino (CA)[31]	CDJC	185 401	91 150	94 251	...	...	...	...	...
San Buenaventura (CA)[39]	CDJC	100 916	49 654	51 262	...	...	...	...	...
San Diego (CA)	CDJC	1 223 400	616 884	606 516	...	2 674 436	1 340 333	1 334 103	...
San Francisco (CA)	CDJC	776 733	394 828	381 905	...	2 995 769	1 483 586	1 512 183	...
San Jose (CA)	CDJC	894 943	454 798	440 145	...	1 538 312	780 426	757 886	...
Santa Ana (CA)[19]	CDJC	337 977	175 219	162 758	...	...	...	...	...
Santa Clara (CA)[40]	CDJC	102 361	52 086	50 275	...	...	...	...	...
Santa Clarita (CA)	CDJC	151 088	74 764	76 324	...	170 481	84 389	86 092	...
Santa Rosa (CA)	CDJC	147 595	72 078	75 517	...	285 408	139 279	146 129	...
Savannah (GA)	CDJC	131 510	62 039	69 471	...	208 886	100 295	108 591	...
Scottsdale (AZ)[26]	CDJC	202 705	97 785	104 920	...	...	...	...	...
Seattle (WA)	CDJC	563 374	280 973	282 401	...	2 712 205	1 348 157	1 364 048	...
Shreveport (LA)	CDJC	200 145	93 333	106 812	...	275 213	129 928	145 285	...
Simi Valley (CA)	CDJC	111 351	55 098	56 253	...	112 345	55 613	56 732	...
Sioux Falls (SD)	CDJC	123 975	61 120	62 855	...	124 269	61 294	62 975	...
South Bend (IN)	CDJC	107 789	51 383	56 406	...	276 498	133 001	143 497	...
Spokane (WA)	CDJC	195 629	94 267	101 362	...	334 858	162 346	172 512	...
Springfield (IL)	CDJC	111 454	52 370	59 084	...	153 516	72 705	80 811	...
Springfield (MA)	CDJC	152 082	71 802	80 280	...	573 610	275 874	297 736	...
Springfield (MO)	CDJC	151 580	73 016	78 564	...	215 004	103 722	111 282	...
Stamford (CT)[41]	CDJC	117 083	56 622	60 461	...	...	...	...	...
Sterling Heights (MI)[35]	CDJC	124 471	60 970	63 501	...	...	...	...	...
Stockton (CA)	CDJC	243 771	118 751	125 020	...	313 392	154 676	158 716	...
Sunnyvale (CA)[40]	CDJC	131 760	67 783	63 977	...	...	...	...	...
Syracuse (NY)	CDJC	147 306	69 308	77 998	...	402 267	191 058	211 209	...
Tacoma (WA)[23]	CDJC	193 556	94 419	99 137	...	...	...	...	...

8. Population of capital cities and cities of 100 000 and more inhabitants: latest available year
Population des capitales et des villes de 100 000 habitants et plus: dernière année disponible (continued — suite)

(See notes at end of table. — Voir notes à la fin du tableau.)

Continent, country or area, date and city / Continent, pays ou zone, date et ville	Code[1]	City proper — Ville proprement dite Population				Urban agglomeration — Agglomération urbaine Population			
		Both sexes Les deux sexes	Male Masculin	Female Féminin	Surface area Superficie (km²)	Both sexes Les deux sexes	Male Masculin	Female Féminin	Surface area Superficie (km²)
AMERICA, NORTH — AMERIQUE DU NORD									
United States — Etats-Unis[16,17]									
1 IV 2000									
Tallahassee (FL)	CDJC	150 624	71 137	79 487	...	204 260	96 906	107 354	...
Tampa (FL)	CDJC	303 447	148 050	155 397	...	2 062 339	993 534	1 068 805	...
Tempe (AZ)[26]	CDJC	158 625	81 942	76 683	...	...	...	...	...
Thousand Oaks (CA)	CDJC	117 005	57 440	59 565	...	210 990	103 703	107 287	...
Toledo (OH)	CDJC	313 619	150 204	163 415	...	503 008	241 733	261 275	...
Topeka (KS)	CDJC	122 377	58 759	63 618	...	142 411	68 617	73 794	...
Torrance (CA)[19]	CDJC	137 946	67 087	70 859	...	...	...	...	...
Tucson (AZ)	CDJC	486 699	238 408	248 291	...	720 425	349 836	370 589	...
Tulsa (OK)	CDJC	393 049	189 937	203 112	...	558 329	270 413	287 916	...
Vallejo (CA)	CDJC	116 760	56 553	60 207	...	158 967	77 207	81 760	...
Vancouver (WA)[42]	CDJC	143 560	70 644	72 916	...	...	...	...	...
Virginia Beach (VA)	CDJC	425 257	210 524	214 733	...	1 394 439	686 732	707 707	...
Waco (TX)	CDJC	113 726	54 295	59 431	...	153 198	73 707	79 491	...
Warren (MI)[35]	CDJC	138 247	67 560	70 687	...	...	...	...	...
WASHINGTON (DC)	CDJC	572 059	269 366	302 693	...	3 933 920	1 909 345	2 024 575	...
Waterbury (CT)	CDJC	107 271	50 781	56 490	...	189 026	90 406	98 620	...
West Covina (CA)[19]	CDJC	105 080	51 019	54 061	...	...	...	...	...
West Valley City (UT)[43]	CDJC	108 896	55 078	53 818	...	...	...	...	...
Westminster (CO)[21]	CDJC	100 940	50 509	50 431	...	...	...	...	...
Wichita (KS)	CDJC	344 284	169 604	174 680	...	422 301	208 080	214 221	...
Wichita Falls (TX)	CDJC	104 197	53 657	50 540	...	...	...	...	...
Winston-Salem (NC)	CDJC	185 776	87 345	98 431	...	299 290	142 748	156 542	...
Worcester (MA)	CDJC	172 648	82 914	89 734	...	429 882	207 809	222 073	...
Yonkers (NY)[32]	CDJC	196 086	92 132	103 954	...	...	...	...	...
United States Virgin Islands — Iles Vierges américaines[15]									
1 IV 2000									
CHARLOTTE AMALIE	CDFC	11 004	...	...	...	18 914	...	...	...
AMERICA, SOUTH — AMERIQUE DU SUD									
Argentina — Argentine									
1 VII 1991									
Avellaneda	CDFC	344 024	...	...	...	...	...	...	...
Bahía Blanca	CDFC	260 096	...	...	...	...	...	...	...
BUENOS AIRES	CDFC	2 965 403	...	...	...	11 298 030	...	...	...
Catamarca	CDFC	109 882	...	...	...	132 626	...	...	...
Comodoro Rivadavia	CDFC	124 104	...	...	...	...	...	...	...
Concordia	CDFC	116 485	...	...	...	...	...	...	...
Córdoba	CDFC	1 157 507	...	...	...	1 208 554	...	...	...
Corrientes	CDFC	258 103	...	...	...	...	...	...	...
Formosa	CDFC	147 636	...	...	...	...	...	...	...
General San Martín	CDFC	406 809	...	...	...	...	...	...	...
La Matanza	CDFC	1 120 088	...	...	...	...	...	...	...
Lanus	CDFC	468 561	...	...	...	...	...	...	...
La Plata	CDFC	521 936	...	...	...	642 979	...	...	...
Lomas de Zamora	CDFC	574 330	...	...	...	...	...	...	...
Mar del Plata	CDFC	512 880	...	...	...	...	...	...	...
Mendoza	CDFC	121 620	...	...	...	773 113	...	...	...
Morón	CDFC	643 553	...	...	...	...	...	...	...
Neuquén	CDFC	167 296	...	...	...	183 579	...	...	...
Paraná	CDFC	207 041	...	...	...	211 936	...	...	...
Posadas	CDFC	201 273	...	...	...	210 755	...	...	...
Quilmes	CDFC	511 234	...	...	...	...	...	...	...
Resistencia	CDFC	229 212	...	...	...	292 287	...	...	...
Río Cuarto	CDFC	134 355	...	...	...	138 853	...	...	...
Rosario	CDFC	907 718	...	...	...	1 118 905	...	...	...

8. Population of capital cities and cities of 100 000 and more inhabitants: latest available year
Population des capitales et des villes de 100 000 habitants et plus: dernière année disponible (continued — suite)

(See notes at end of table. — Voir notes à la fin du tableau.)

Continent, country or area, date and city Continent, pays ou zone, date et ville	Code[1]	City proper — Ville proprement dite Population				Urban agglomeration — Agglomération urbaine Population			
		Both sexes Les deux sexes	Male Masculin	Female Féminin	Surface area Superficie (km²)	Both sexes Les deux sexes	Male Masculin	Female Féminin	Surface area Superficie (km²)
AMERICA, SOUTH — AMERIQUE DU SUD									
Argentina — Argentine									
1 VII 1991									
Salta	CDFC	367 550	...	...	...	370 904	...	...	...
San Fernando	CDFC	141 063	...	...	...	...	...	...	...
San Isidro	CDFC	299 023	...	...	...	...	...	...	...
San Juan	CDFC	119 423	...	...	...	352 691	...	...	...
San Miguel de Tucumán	CDFC	470 809	...	...	...	622 324	...	...	...
San Nicolás	CDFC	119 302	...	...	...	...	...	...	...
San Salvador de Jujuy	CDFC	178 748	...	...	...	180 102	...	...	...
Santa Fé	CDFC	353 063	...	...	...	406 388	...	...	...
Santiago del Estero	CDFC	189 947	...	...	...	263 471	...	...	...
Vicente López	CDFC	289 505	...	...	...	...	...	...	...
Bolivia — Bolivie									
1 VII 2003									
Cochabamba	ESDF	559 872	267 544	292 328	...	...	...	...	...
El Alto	ESDF	733 987	361 326	372 661	...	...	...	...	...
LA PAZ[44]	ESDF	832 730	397 072	435 658	...	...	...	...	...
Oruro	ESDF	215 898	104 271	111 627	...	...	...	...	...
Potosí	ESDF	144 225	69 163	75 063	...	...	...	...	...
Santa Cruz	ESDF	1 240 111	603 635	636 476	...	...	...	...	...
SUCRE[44]	ESDF	220 925	105 736	115 189	...	...	...	...	...
Tarija	ESDF	153 415	73 752	79 662	...	...	...	...	...
Brazil — Brésil[11]									
1 VII 2003									
Abaeteluba	ESDF	...	...	...	...	129 300	...	...	1 090
Açailândia	ESDF	...	...	...	...	100 841	...	...	...
Aguas Lindas de Goiás	ESDF	...	...	...	...	149 598	...	...	...
Alagoinhas	ESDF	...	...	...	...	136 868	...	...	761
Almirante Tamandaré	ESDF	...	...	...	...	105 848	...	...	...
Alvorada	ESDF	...	...	...	...	205 476	...	...	...
Americana	ESDF	...	...	...	...	197 345	...	...	...
Ananindeua	ESDF	...	...	...	...	468 463	...	...	485
Anápolis	ESDF	...	...	...	...	307 977	...	...	...
Angra dos Reis	ESDF	...	...	...	...	136 525	...	...	...
Aparecida de Goiania	ESDF	...	...	...	...	417 409	...	...	...
Apucarana	ESDF	...	...	...	...	114 375	...	...	556
Aracaju	ESDF	...	...	...	...	491 898	...	...	151
Araçatuba	ESDF	...	...	...	...	177 823	...	...	2 668
Araguaina	ESDF	...	...	...	...	123 353	...	...	...
Araguario	ESDF	...	...	...	...	107 459	...	...	...
Arapiraca	ESDF	...	...	...	...	197 520	...	...	...
Araraquara	ESDF	...	...	...	...	194 401	...	...	...
Araras	ESDF	...	...	...	...	112 783	...	...	...
Araucária	ESDF	...	...	...	...	110 956	...	...	...
Atibaia	ESDF	...	...	...	...	124 108	...	...	...
Bagé	ESDF	...	...	...	...	120 129	...	...	7 185
Barbacena	ESDF	...	...	...	...	121 397	...	...	...
Barueri	ESDF	...	...	...	...	248 034	...	...	...
Barra Mansa	ESDF	...	...	...	...	174 500	...	...	830
Barreiras	ESDF	...	...	...	...	130 512	...	...	...
Barretos	ESDF	...	...	...	...	108 273	...	...	...
Bauru	ESDF	...	...	...	...	344 258	...	...	702
Belém	ESDF	...	...	...	...	1 386 482	...	...	736
Belford Roxo	ESDF	...	...	...	...	472 325	...	...	...
Belo Horizonte	ESDF	...	...	...	...	2 350 564	...	...	335
Bento Gonçalves	ESDF	...	...	...	...	100 467	...	...	...
Betim	ESDF	...	...	...	...	376 318	...	...	376
Birigui	ESDF	...	...	...	...	104 138	...	...	...
Blumenou	ESDF	...	...	...	...	287 350	...	...	509
Boa Vista	ESDF	...	...	...	...	236 319	...	...	...

(See notes at end of table. — Voir notes à la fin du tableau.)

Continent, country or area, date and city Continent, pays ou zone, date et ville	Code[1]	City proper — Ville proprement dite Population				Urban agglomeration — Agglomération urbaine Population			
		Both sexes Les deux sexes	Male Masculin	Female Féminin	Surface area Superficie (km²)	Both sexes Les deux sexes	Male Masculin	Female Féminin	Surface area Superficie (km²)

AMERICA, SOUTH — AMERIQUE DU SUD

Brazil — Brésil[11]
  1 VII 2003

Botucatu	ESDF	...	...	...	...	117 308	...	...	...
Bragança	ESDF	...	...	...	...	100 924	...	...	...
Bragança Paulista	ESDF	...	...	...	...	137 935	...	...	770
BRASILIA	ESDF	...	...	...	...	2 282 049	...	...	5 794
Cabo de Santo Agostinho	ESDF	...	...	...	...	166 286	...	...	...
Cabo Frio	ESDF	...	...	...	...	153 735	...	...	...
Cachoeirinha	ESDF	...	...	...	...	117 501	...	...	...
Cachoeiro de Itapemirim	ESDF	...	...	...	...	191 033	...	...	892
Camacari	ESDF	...	...	...	...	186 399	...	...	718
Camaragibe	ESDF	...	...	...	...	143 732	...	...	...
Cametá	ESDF	...	...	...	...	104 210	...	...	...
Campina Grande	ESDF	...	...	...	...	372 366	...	...	970
Campinas	ESDF	...	...	...	...	1 031 887	...	...	781
Campo Grande	ESDF	...	...	...	...	734 164	...	...	8 091
Campo Largo	ESDF	...	...	...	...	103 176	...	...	...
Campos dos Goytacazes	ESDF	...	...	...	...	422 731	...	...	4 536
Canoas	ESDF	...	...	...	...	324 994	...	...	...
Carapicuíba	ESDF	...	...	...	...	375 859	...	...	...
Cariacica	ESDF	...	...	...	...	349 811	...	...	279
Caruaru	ESDF	...	...	...	...	274 124	...	...	936
Cascavel	ESDF	...	...	...	...	272 243	...	...	2 074
Castanhal	ESDF	...	...	...	...	151 668	...	...	1 003
Catanduva	ESDF	...	...	...	...	113 578	...	...	...
Caucaia	ESDF	...	...	...	...	294 284	...	...	1 293
Caxias	ESDF	...	...	...	...	142 971	...	...	6 724
Caxias do Sul	ESDF	...	...	...	...	396 261	...	...	1 601
Chapecó	ESDF	...	...	...	...	165 220	...	...	...
Codo	ESDF	...	...	...	...	113 889	...	...	4 923
Colatina	ESDF	...	...	...	...	109 226	...	...	2 094
Colombo	ESDF	...	...	...	...	216 966	...	...	...
Conselheiro Lafaiete	ESDF	...	...	...	...	109 904	...	...	...
Contagem	ESDF	...	...	...	...	583 386	...	...	167
Coronel Fabriciano	ESDF	...	...	...	...	102 588	...	...	...
Cotia	ESDF	...	...	...	...	170 296	...	...	...
Crato	ESDF	...	...	...	...	111 894	...	...	...
Criciúma	ESDF	...	...	...	...	182 785	...	...	...
Cubatao	ESDF	...	...	...	...	117 120	...	...	...
Cuiabá	ESDF	...	...	...	...	524 666	...	...	3 922
Curitiba	ESDF	...	...	...	...	1 727 010	...	...	427
Diadema	ESDF	...	...	...	...	383 629	...	...	...
Divinópolis	ESDF	...	...	...	...	200 636	...	...	716
Dourados	ESDF	...	...	...	...	179 810	...	...	4 082
Duque de Caxias	ESDF	...	...	...	...	830 679	...	...	463
Embu	ESDF	...	...	...	...	234 174	...	...	...
Feira de Santana	ESDF	...	...	...	...	519 173	...	...	1 344
Ferraz de Vasconcelos	ESDF	...	...	...	...	166 086	...	...	...
Florianópolis	ESDF	...	...	...	...	386 913	...	...	440
Fortaleza	ESDF	...	...	...	...	2 332 657	...	...	336
Foz do Iguaçu	ESDF	...	...	...	...	293 646	...	...	596
Franca	ESDF	...	...	...	...	315 770	...	...	...
Francisco Morato	ESDF	...	...	...	...	159 316	...	...	...
Franco da Rocha	ESDF	...	...	...	...	119 710	...	...	...
Garanhuns	ESDF	...	...	...	...	125 141	...	...	456
Goiânia	ESDF	...	...	...	...	1 181 438	...	...	788
Governador Valadares	ESDF	...	...	...	...	255 651	...	...	2 447
Gravatai	ESDF	...	...	...	...	259 100	...	...	...
Guaratinguetá	ESDF	...	...	...	...	110 323	...	...	...
Guaíba	ESDF	...	...	...	...	102 290	...	...	...

8. Population of capital cities and cities of 100 000 and more inhabitants: latest available year
Population des capitales et des villes de 100 000 habitants et plus: dernière année disponible (continued — suite)

(See notes at end of table. — Voir notes à la fin du tableau.)

Continent, country or area, date and city / Continent, pays ou zone, date et ville	Code[1]	City proper — Ville proprement dite Population				Urban agglomeration — Agglomération urbaine Population			
		Both sexes Les deux sexes	Male Masculin	Female Féminin	Surface area Superficie (km²)	Both sexes Les deux sexes	Male Masculin	Female Féminin	Surface area Superficie (km²)
AMERICA, SOUTH — AMERIQUE DU SUD									
Brazil — Brésil[11]									
1 VII 2003									
Guarapari	ESDF	...	...	...	...	102 089	...	...	...
Guarapuava	ESDF	...	...	...	...	164 772	...	...	5 365
Guarujá	ESDF	...	...	...	...	292 828	...	...	...
Guarulhos	ESDF	...	...	...	...	1 218 862	...	...	...
Hortolandia	ESDF	...	...	...	...	186 726	...	...	...
Ibirité	ESDF	...	...	...	...	161 208	...	...	...
Ilhéus	ESDF	...	...	...	...	221 294	...	...	1 712
Imperatriz	ESDF	...	...	...	...	231 950	...	...	6 014
Indaiatuba	ESDF	...	...	...	...	170 703	...	...	...
Ipatinga	ESDF	...	...	...	...	229 133	...	...	231
Itabiraí	ESDF	...	...	...	...	104 846	...	...	...
Itaboraí	ESDF	...	...	...	...	210 735	...	...	569
Itabuna	ESDF	...	...	...	...	202 523	...	...	...
Itajaí	ESDF	...	...	...	...	161 789	...	...	...
Itapetininga	ESDF	...	...	...	...	137 733	...	...	2 035
Itapecerica da Serra	ESDF	...	...	...	...	152 283	...	...	...
Itapevi	ESDF	...	...	...	...	190 373	...	...	...
Itapipoca	ESDF	...	...	...	...	103 145	...	...	...
Itaquaquecetuba	ESDF	...	...	...	...	328 345	...	...	...
Itu	ESDF	...	...	...	...	149 758	...	...	640
Jaboatao dos Guarapes	ESDF	...	...	...	...	630 008	...	...	...
Jacareí	ESDF	...	...	...	...	205 360	...	...	...
Jandira	ESDF	...	...	...	...	106 742	...	...	...
Jaraguá do Sul	ESDF	...	...	...	...	124 661	...	...	...
Jaú	ESDF	...	...	...	...	121 333	...	...	...
Jequié	ESDF	...	...	...	...	148 449	...	...	3 113
Ji-Paraná	ESDF	...	...	...	...	113 441	...	...	...
Joao Pessoa	ESDF	...	...	...	...	649 410	...	...	...
Joinville	ESDF	...	...	...	...	477 971	...	...	1 080
Juazeiro	ESDF	...	...	...	...	198 065	...	...	5 615
Juàzeiro do Norte	ESDF	...	...	...	...	231 920	...	...	...
Juiz de Fora	ESDF	...	...	...	...	493 121	...	...	1 424
Jundiaí	ESDF	...	...	...	...	340 907	...	...	432
Lages	ESDF	...	...	...	...	165 068	...	...	5 287
Lauro de Freitas	ESDF	...	...	...	...	136 258	...	...	...
Limeira	ESDF	...	...	...	...	270 223	...	...	...
Linhares	ESDF	...	...	...	...	119 824	...	...	4 388
Londrina	ESDF	...	...	...	...	480 822	...	...	2 129
Luziânia	ESDF	...	...	...	...	173 138	...	...	4 653
Macae	ESDF	...	...	...	...	152 063	...	...	...
Macapá	ESDF	...	...	...	...	326 466	...	...	...
Maceió	ESDF	...	...	...	...	884 320	...	...	517
Magé	ESDF	...	...	...	...	227 467	...	...	744
Manaus	ESDF	...	...	...	...	1 592 555	...	...	11 349
Maraba	ESDF	...	...	...	...	191 508	...	...	14 320
Maracanau	ESDF	...	...	...	...	191 317	...	...	...
Marília	ESDF	...	...	...	...	215 911	...	...	1 194
Maringá	ESDF	...	...	...	...	313 465	...	...	490
Mauá	ESDF	...	...	...	...	398 482	...	...	...
Mesquita	ESDF	...	...	...	...	179 517	...	...	...
Moji das Cruzes	ESDF	...	...	...	...	359 519	...	...	749
Moji-Guaçu	ESDF	...	...	...	...	136 258	...	...	960
Montes Claros	ESDF	...	...	...	...	336 132	...	...	4 135
Mossoró	ESDF	...	...	...	...	224 910	...	...	2 108
Natal	ESDF	...	...	...	...	766 081	...	...	...
Nilópolis	ESDF	...	...	...	...	151 465	...	...	...
Niterói	ESDF	...	...	...	...	471 403	...	...	131
Nossa Senhora do Socorro	ESDF	...	...	...	...	164 569	...	...	...

8. Population of capital cities and cities of 100 000 and more inhabitants: latest available year
Population des capitales et des villes de 100 000 habitants et plus: dernière année disponible (continued — suite)

(See notes at end of table. — Voir notes à la fin du tableau.)

Continent, country or area, date and city Continent, pays ou zone, date et ville	Code[1]	City proper — Ville proprement dite Population				Urban agglomeration — Agglomération urbaine Population			
		Both sexes Les deux sexes	Male Masculin	Female Féminin	Surface area Superficie (km²)	Both sexes Les deux sexes	Male Masculin	Female Féminin	Surface area Superficie (km²)
AMERICA, SOUTH — AMERIQUE DU SUD									
Brazil — Brésil[11]									
1 VII 2003									
Nova Friburgo	ESDF	...	...	...	...	176 669	...	...	930
Nova Iguaçu	ESDF	...	...	...	...	817 117	...	...	795
Nôvo Hamburgo	ESDF	...	...	...	...	251 854	...	...	...
Olinda	ESDF	...	...	...	...	381 502	...	...	...
Ourinhos	ESDF	...	...	...	...	102 533	...	...	...
Osasco	ESDF	...	...	...	...	695 879	...	...	...
Palhoça	ESDF	...	...	...	...	120 346	...	...	...
Palmas	ESDF	...	...	...	...	187 639	...	...	...
Paranaguá	ESDF	...	...	...	...	141 635	...	...	1 015
Parintins	ESDF	...	...	...	...	105 002	...	...	...
Parnaíba	ESDF	...	...	...	...	140 190	...	...	1 053
Parnamirim	ESDF	...	...	...	...	156 181	...	...	...
Passo Fundo	ESDF	...	...	...	...	182 233	...	...	1 596
Paulo Afonso	ESDF	...	...	...	...	101 568	...	...	...
Passos	ESDF	...	...	...	...	103 670	...	...	...
Patos de Minas	ESDF	...	...	...	...	134 622	...	...	3 336
Paulista	ESDF	...	...	...	...	288 273	...	...	...
Pelotas	ESDF	...	...	...	...	338 544	...	...	1 924
Petrolina	ESDF	...	...	...	...	247 322	...	...	6 116
Petrópolis	ESDF	...	...	...	...	302 477	...	...	771
Pindamonhangaba	ESDF	...	...	...	...	138 320	...	...	719
Pinhais	ESDF	...	...	...	...	117 078	...	...	...
Piracicaba	ESDF	...	...	...	...	355 039	...	...	1 426
Poços de Caldas	ESDF	...	...	...	...	148 712	...	...	533
Poà	ESDF	...	...	...	...	105 805	...	...	...
Ponta Grossa	ESDF	...	...	...	...	295 383	...	...	2 212
Porto Alegre	ESDF	...	...	...	...	1 416 363	...	...	...
Porto Seguro	ESDF	...	...	...	...	127 048	...	...	...
Porto Velho	ESDF	...	...	...	...	380 884	...	...	...
Pouso Alegre	ESDF	...	...	...	...	119 572	...	...	...
Praia Grande	ESDF	...	...	...	...	229 542	...	...	...
Presidente Prudente	ESDF	...	...	...	...	201 347	...	...	554
Queimados	ESDF	...	...	...	...	133 881	...	...	...
Recife	ESDF	...	...	...	...	1 486 869	...	...	...
Resende	ESDF	...	...	...	...	115 086	...	...	...
Ribeirao das Neves	ESDF	...	...	...	...	299 687	...	...	...
Ribeirao Prêto	ESDF	...	...	...	...	542 912	...	...	...
Ribeirao Pires	ESDF	...	...	...	...	114 473	...	...	...
Rio Branco	ESDF	...	...	...	...	286 082	...	...	...
Rio Claro	ESDF	...	...	...	...	183 597	...	...	503
Rio de Janeiro	ESDF	...	...	...	...	6 051 399	...	...	1 256
Rio Grande	ESDF	...	...	...	...	193 789	...	...	2 825
Rio Verde	ESDF	...	...	...	...	130 211	...	...	9 136
Rondonópolis	ESDF	...	...	...	...	163 824	...	...	4 594
Sabára	ESDF	...	...	...	...	128 492	...	...	...
Salvador	ESDF	...	...	...	...	2 631 831	...	...	313
Santa Bárbara D'Oeste	ESDF	...	...	...	...	182 808	...	...	...
Santa Cruz do Sul	ESDF	...	...	...	...	116 081	...	...	...
Santa Luzia (Minas Gerais)	ESDF	...	...	...	...	209 057	...	...	...
Santa Maria	ESDF	...	...	...	...	261 980	...	...	3 279
Salto	ESDF	...	...	...	...	103 844	...	...	...
Santa Rita	ESDF	...	...	...	...	126 839	...	...	...
Santarém	ESDF	...	...	...	...	272 237	...	...	...
Santo André	ESDF	...	...	...	...	665 923	...	...	...
Santos	ESDF	...	...	...	...	418 255	...	...	725
Sao Bernardo do Campo	ESDF	...	...	...	...	773 099	...	...	319
Sao Caetano do Sul	ESDF	...	...	...	...	135 357	...	...	...
Sao Carlo	ESDF	...	...	...	...	210 841	...	...	1 120

8. Population of capital cities and cities of 100 000 and more inhabitants: latest available year
Population des capitales et des villes de 100 000 habitants et plus: dernière année disponible (continued — suite)

(See notes at end of table. — Voir notes à la fin du tableau.)

Continent, country or area, date and city / Continent, pays ou zone, date et ville	Code[1]	City proper — Ville proprement dite Population				Urban agglomeration — Agglomération urbaine Population			
		Both sexes Les deux sexes	Male Masculin	Female Féminin	Surface area Superficie (km²)	Both sexes Les deux sexes	Male Masculin	Female Féminin	Surface area Superficie (km²)
AMERICA, SOUTH — AMERIQUE DU SUD									
Brazil — Brésil[11]									
1 VII 2003									
Sao Gonçalo	ESDF	...	...	...	...	948 216	...	...	...
Sao Joao de Meriti	ESDF	...	...	...	...	461 638	...	...	...
Sao José	ESDF	...	...	...	...	192 679	...	...	...
Sao José de Ribamar	ESDF	...	...	...	...	126 271	...	...	...
Sao José do Rio Prêto	ESDF	...	...	...	...	398 079	...	...	586
Sao José dos Campos	ESDF	...	...	...	...	589 050	...	...	1 186
Sao José dos Pinhais	ESDF	...	...	...	...	243 750	...	...	923
Sao Leopoldo	ESDF	...	...	...	...	206 702	...	...	...
Sao Luís	ESDF	...	...	...	...	959 124	...	...	822
Sao Paulo	ESDF	...	...	...	...	10 838 581	...	...	1 493
Sao Vicente	ESDF	...	...	...	...	321 474	...	...	...
Sapucaia do Sul	ESDF	...	...	...	...	131 917	...	...	...
Serra	ESDF	...	...	...	...	371 986	...	...	549
Sertaozinho	ESDF	...	...	...	...	102 815	...	...	...
Sete Lagoas	ESDF	...	...	...	...	205 833	...	...	...
Simoes Filho	ESDF	...	...	...	...	105 117	...	...	...
Sobral	ESDF	...	...	...	...	169 532	...	...	1 646
Sorocaba	ESDF	...	...	...	...	552 194	...	...	...
Sumaré	ESDF	...	...	...	...	225 307	...	...	208
Susano	ESDF	...	...	...	...	264 528	...	...	...
Taboao da Serra	ESDF	...	...	...	...	216 914	...	...	...
Taubaté	ESDF	...	...	...	...	263 251	...	...	...
Tatuí	ESDF	...	...	...	...	102 930	...	...	...
Teixeira de Freitas	ESDF	...	...	...	...	118 681	...	...	...
Teófilo Otoni	ESDF	...	...	...	...	128 109	...	...	...
Teresina	ESDF	...	...	...	...	775 477	...	...	1 356
Teresópolis	ESDF	...	...	...	...	146 994	...	...	768
Timon	ESDF	...	...	...	...	141 109	...	...	1 702
Toledo	ESDF	...	...	...	...	104 332	...	...	...
Uberaba	ESDF	...	...	...	...	274 988	...	...	4 524
Uberlândia	ESDF	...	...	...	...	570 042	...	...	4 040
Uruguaiana	ESDF	...	...	...	...	133 481	...	...	6 763
Valparaiso de Goiás	ESDF	...	...	...	...	115 032	...	...	...
Varginha	ESDF	...	...	...	...	119 760	...	...	...
Várzea Grande	ESDF	...	...	...	...	242 674	...	...	900
Várzea Paulista	ESDF	...	...	...	...	105 051	...	...	...
Viamao	ESDF	...	...	...	...	251 407	...	...	...
Vila Velha	ESDF	...	...	...	...	387 204	...	...	...
Vitória	ESDF	...	...	...	...	309 507	...	...	...
Vitória da Conquista	ESDF	...	...	...	...	281 684	...	...	3 743
Vitória de Santo Antao	ESDF	...	...	...	...	123 130	...	...	344
Volta Redonda	ESDF	...	...	...	...	253 226	...	...	...
Chile — Chili									
1 VII 2002									
Antofagasta	ESDF	257 207	126 807	130 400	...	...	...	...	...
Arica	ESDF	189 743	94 142	95 601	...	...	...	...	...
Calama	ESDF	132 669	67 037	65 632	...	...	...	...	...
Chillán	ESDF	176 863	84 145	92 718	...	...	...	...	...
Concepción	ESDF	391 733	191 631	200 102	...	...	...	...	...
Copiapó	ESDF	127 504	64 719	62 785	...	...	...	...	...
Coquimbo	ESDF	141 796	69 022	72 774	...	...	...	...	...
Iquique	ESDF	175 677	89 698	85 979	...	...	...	...	...
La Serena	ESDF	135 526	65 476	70 050	...	...	...	...	...
Los Angeles	ESDF	121 649	59 268	62 381	...	...	...	...	...
Osorno	ESDF	135 204	65 076	70 128	...	...	...	...	...
Puente Alto	ESDF	458 906	224 970	233 936	...	...	...	...	...
Puerto Montt	ESDF	144 880	71 064	73 816	...	...	...	...	...
Punta Arenas	ESDF	126 586	65 204	61 382	...	...	...	...	...

(See notes at end of table. — Voir notes à la fin du tableau.)

Continent, country or area, date and city / Continent, pays ou zone, date et ville	Code[1]	City proper — Ville proprement dite Population				Urban agglomeration — Agglomération urbaine Population			
		Both sexes Les deux sexes	Male Masculin	Female Féminin	Surface area Superficie (km²)	Both sexes Les deux sexes	Male Masculin	Female Féminin	Surface area Superficie (km²)
AMERICA, SOUTH — AMERIQUE DU SUD									
Chile — Chili									
1 VII 2002									
Quilpué	ESDF	124 586	58 601	65 985	...	...	...	...	...
Rancagua	ESDF	221 881	107 635	114 246	...	...	...	...	...
San Bernardo	ESDF	262 623	131 378	131 245	...	...	...	...	...
SANTIAGO[45]	ESDF	4 886 629	2 350 058	2 536 571	...	...	...	...	...
Talca	ESDF	187 513	89 436	98 077	...	...	...	...	...
Talcahuano	ESDF	288 666	141 793	146 873	...	...	...	...	...
Temuco	ESDF	287 326	137 389	149 937	...	...	...	...	...
Valdivia	ESDF	128 533	62 578	65 955	...	...	...	...	...
Valparaíso	ESDF	285 389	139 970	145 419	...	...	...	...	...
Viña del Mar	ESDF	350 221	167 602	182 619	...	...	...	...	...
Colombia — Colombie[46]									
1 VII 2003									
Apartadó	ESDF	...	...	...	...	100 773	...	...	607
Armenia	ESDF	...	...	...	...	316 301	...	...	115
Barrancabermeja	ESDF	...	...	...	...	206 486	...	...	1 274
Barranquilla	ESDF	...	...	...	...	1 359 700	...	...	166
Bello	ESDF	...	...	...	...	390 012	...	...	151
Bucaramanga	ESDF	...	...	...	...	568 136	...	...	154
Buenaventura	ESDF	...	...	...	...	276 517	...	...	6 785
Buga	ESDF	...	...	...	...	131 229	...	...	873
Cali	ESDF	...	...	...	...	2 369 696	...	...	552
Cartagena	ESDF	...	...	...	...	1 004 074	...	...	570
Cartago	ESDF	...	...	...	...	138 120	...	...	260
Ciénaga	ESDF	...	...	...	...	122 981	...	...	1 366
Facatativa	ESDF	...	...	...	...	100 083	...	...	160
Cúcuta	ESDF	...	...	...	...	722 485	...	...	1 098
Dos Quebradas	ESDF	...	...	...	...	188 547	...	...	80
Duitama	ESDF	...	...	...	...	120 589	...	...	229
Envigado	ESDF	...	...	...	...	170 065	...	...	51
Florencia (Caquetá)	ESDF	...	...	...	...	146 987	...	...	2 292
Floridablanca	ESDF	...	...	...	...	253 568	...	...	101
Fusagasuga	ESDF	...	...	...	...	110 603	...	...	206
Girardot	ESDF	...	...	...	...	130 743	...	...	130
Girón	ESDF	...	...	...	...	117 661	...	...	681
Ibagué	ESDF	...	...	...	...	444 460	...	...	1 439
Itagüi	ESDF	...	...	...	...	278 726	...	...	17
Lorica	ESDF	...	...	...	...	126 487	...	...	890
Magangué	ESDF	...	...	...	...	169 176	...	...	1 102
Maicao	ESDF	...	...	...	...	134 842	...	...	2 229
Malambo	ESDF	...	...	...	...	102 661	...	...	108
Manizales	ESDF	...	...	...	...	378 965	...	...	477
Medellín	ESDF	...	...	...	...	2 071 391	...	...	387
Montería	ESDF	...	...	...	...	343 607	...	...	3 043
Neiva	ESDF	...	...	...	...	367 811	...	...	1 468
Ocaña	ESDF	...	...	...	...	102 633	...	...	463
Palmira	ESDF	...	...	...	...	291 053	...	...	1 044
Pasto	ESDF	...	...	...	...	415 629	...	...	1 181
Popayán	ESDF	...	...	...	...	236 090	...	...	464
Pereira	ESDF	...	...	...	...	510 739	...	...	702
Piedecuesta	ESDF	...	...	...	...	103 014	...	...	481
Sahagún	ESDF	...	...	...	...	134 613	...	...	993
SANTA FE DE BOGOTA	ESDF	...	...	...	...	7 029 928	...	...	1 635
Santa Marta	ESDF	...	...	...	...	434 937	...	...	2 369
Sincelejo	ESDF	...	...	...	...	262 003	...	...	292
Soacha	ESDF	...	...	...	...	310 038	...	...	187
Sogamoso	ESDF	...	...	...	...	162 543	...	...	214
Soledad	ESDF	...	...	...	...	336 190	...	...	67
Tuluá	ESDF	...	...	...	...	189 008	...	...	818

(See notes at end of table. — Voir notes à la fin du tableau.)

Continent, country or area, date and city Continent, pays ou zone, date et ville	Code[1]	City proper — Ville proprement dite Population				Urban agglomeration — Agglomération urbaine Population			
		Both sexes Les deux sexes	Male Masculin	Female Féminin	Surface area Superficie (km²)	Both sexes Les deux sexes	Male Masculin	Female Féminin	Surface area Superficie (km²)
AMERICA, SOUTH — AMERIQUE DU SUD									
Colombia — Colombie[46]									
1 VII 2003									
Tumaco	ESDF	...	...	...	...	166 030	...	...	3 778
Tunja	ESDF	...	...	...	...	125 373	...	...	118
Turbo	ESDF	...	...	...	...	123 604	...	...	3 090
Valledupar	ESDF	...	...	...	...	356 818	...	...	4 225
Villavicencio	ESDF	...	...	...	...	358 621	...	...	1 328
Zipaquira	ESDF	...	...	...	...	100 966	...	...	194
Ecuador — Equateur									
1 VII 2003									
Ambato	ESDF	169 103	...	...	27	...	...	...	...
Cuenca	ESDF	303 994	...	...	47	...	...	...	...
Durán	ESDF	183 731	...	...	...	...	...	...	...
Esmeraldas	ESDF	103 063	...	...	8	...	...	...	...
Guayaquil	ESDF	2 090 039	...	...	193	...	...	...	...
Ibarra	ESDF	118 116	...	...	39	...	...	...	...
Loja	ESDF	129 429	...	...	21	...	...	...	...
Machala	ESDF	217 266	...	...	23	...	...	...	...
Manta	ESDF	193 232	...	...	38	...	...	...	...
Milagro	ESDF	119 420	...	...	17	...	...	...	...
Portoviejo	ESDF	194 916	...	...	38	...	...	...	...
Quevedo	ESDF	128 068	...	...	20	...	...	...	...
QUITO	ESDF	1 482 447	...	...	170	...	...	...	...
Riobamba	ESDF	140 558	...	...	24	...	...	...	...
Santo Domingo de los Colorados	ESDF	211 689	...	...	43	...	...	...	...
Falkland Islands (Malvinas) — Iles Falkland (Malvinas)									
8 IV 2001									
STANLEY	CDFC	1 989	1 009	980	...	...	...	...	...
French Guiana — Guyane Française									
8 III 1999									
CAYENNE[7]	CDJC	50 395	24 496	25 899	24	65 933	32 394	33 539	70
Guyana									
1 VII 2001									
GEORGETOWN	ESDF	...	...	...	...	280 000	...	...	...
Paraguay									
28 VIII 2002									
ASUNCION[47]	CDFC	513 399	...	...	117	1 620 483	...	...	...
Capiatá	CDFC	154 469	...	...	...	...	...	...	...
Ciudad del Este	CDFC	223 350	...	...	57	333 535	...	...	...
Fernando de la Mora	CDFC	114 332	...	...	...	...	...	...	...
Lambaré	CDFC	119 984	...	...	...	...	...	...	...
Luque	CDFC	170 433	...	...	...	...	...	...	...
San Lorenzo	CDFC	202 745	...	...	91	...	...	...	...
Peru — Pérou[48]									
1 VII 2003									
Arequipa	ESDF	770 659	...	...	...	...	...	...	...
Ayacucho	ESDF	134 612	...	...	...	...	...	...	...
Cajamarca	ESDF	119 615	...	...	...	...	...	...	...
Callao	ESDF	798 875	...	...	...	...	...	...	...
Chiclayo	ESDF	494 702	...	...	...	...	...	...	...
Chimbote	ESDF	342 030	...	...	...	...	...	...	...
Chincha Alta	ESDF	133 189	...	...	...	...	...	...	...
Cuzco	ESDF	305 039	...	...	...	...	...	...	...
Huancayo	ESDF	323 246	...	...	...	...	...	...	...
Huánuco	ESDF	159 220	...	...	...	...	...	...	...
Ica	ESDF	252 012	...	...	...	...	...	...	...
Iquitos	ESDF	323 688	...	...	...	...	...	...	...
Juliaca	ESDF	189 265	...	...	...	...	...	...	...
LIMA	ESDF	7 075 339	...	...	...	...	...	...	...

(See notes at end of table. — Voir notes à la fin du tableau.)

Continent, country or area, date and city — Continent, pays ou zone, date et ville	Code[1]	City proper — Ville proprement dite Population				Urban agglomeration — Agglomération urbaine Population			
		Both sexes Les deux sexes	Male Masculin	Female Féminin	Surface area Superficie (km²)	Both sexes Les deux sexes	Male Masculin	Female Féminin	Surface area Superficie (km²)
AMERICA, SOUTH — AMERIQUE DU SUD									
Peru — Pérou[48]									
1 VII 2003									
Pisco	ESDF	*105 301*	...	...	...	...	...	...	...
Piura	ESDF	*354 109*	...	...	...	...	...	...	...
Pucallpa	ESDF	*232 565*	...	...	...	...	...	...	...
Puno	ESDF	*108 176*	...	...	...	...	...	...	...
Sullana	ESDF	*172 879*	...	...	...	...	...	...	...
Tacna	ESDF	*250 036*	...	...	...	...	...	...	...
Tarapoto	ESDF	*109 301*	...	...	...	...	...	...	...
Trujillo	ESDF	*620 410*	...	...	...	...	...	...	...
Suriname									
31 III 2003									
PARAMARIBO	CDJC	243 556	120 759	122 780	182	...	...	...	...
Uruguay									
30 VI 2003									
MONTEVIDEO	ESDF	1 382 778	647 427	735 351	530	...	...	...	...
Venezuela									
1 VII 1998									
Acarigua-Araure	ESDF	227 684	...	...	1 065	...	...	...	...
Barcelona	ESDF	301 595	...	...	463	...	...	...	...
Barcelona-Puerto La Cruz	ESDF	484 149	...	...	707	...	...	...	...
Barinas	ESDF	221 558	...	...	848	...	...	...	...
Barquisimeto	ESDF	810 809	...	...	2 645	...	...	...	...
Cabimas	ESDF	213 290	...	...	175	...	...	...	...
CARACAS	ESDF	1 975 294	...	...	433	...	...	...	...
Carúpano	ESDF	116 107	...	...	203	...	...	...	...
Catia la Mar	ESDF	117 013	...	...	76	...	...	...	...
Ciudad Bolívar	ESDF	278 525	...	...	5 851	...	...	...	...
Ciudad Guayana	ESDF	641 998	...	...	1 612	...	...	...	...
Coro	ESDF	167 048	...	...	438	...	...	...	...
Cumaná	ESDF	265 621	...	...	405	...	...	...	...
Guarenas	ESDF	169 202	...	...	180	...	...	...	...
Los Teques	ESDF	176 292	...	...	98	...	...	...	...
Maracaibo	ESDF	1 706 547	...	...	604	...	...	...	...
Maracay	ESDF	458 761	...	...	169	...	...	...	...
Maturín	ESDF	262 167	...	...	...	...	...	...	...
Mérida	ESDF	272 437	...	...	482	...	...	...	...
Puerto Cabello	ESDF	176 347	...	...	309	...	...	...	...
Punto Fijo	ESDF	118 126	...	...	31	...	...	...	...
San Cristóbal	ESDF	272 374	...	...	248	...	...	...	...
San Fernando de Apure	ESDF	121 949	...	...	...	...	...	...	...
Turmero	ESDF	203 434	...	...	208	...	...	...	...
Valencia	ESDF	1 263 888	...	...	1 212	...	...	...	...
Valera	ESDF	121 090	...	...	55	...	...	...	...
ASIA — ASIE									
Afghanistan									
1 VII 1988									
Herat	ESDF	*177 300*	...	...	...	...	...	...	...
KABUL	ESDF	*1 424 400*	...	...	...	...	...	...	...
Kandahar (Quandahar)	ESDF	*225 500*	...	...	...	...	...	...	...
Mazar-i-Sharif	ESDF	*130 600*	...	...	...	...	...	...	...
Armenia — Arménie									
10 X 2001									
Gyumri (Leninakan)	CDJC	107 394	50 284	57 110	50	...	...	...	...
Vanadzor (Kirovakan)	CDJC	150 917	70 846	80 071	25	...	...	...	...
YEREVAN	CDJC	1 103 488	513 546	589 942	227	...	...	...	...

(See notes at end of table. — Voir notes à la fin du tableau.)

Continent, country or area, date and city / Continent, pays ou zone, date et ville	Code[1]	City proper — Ville proprement dite Population				Urban agglomeration — Agglomération urbaine Population			
		Both sexes Les deux sexes	Male Masculin	Female Féminin	Surface area Superficie (km²)	Both sexes Les deux sexes	Male Masculin	Female Féminin	Surface area Superficie (km²)
ASIA — ASIE									
Azerbaijan — Azerbaïdjan									
1 VII 2003									
BAKU	ESDF	1 834 300	895 000	939 300	2 130	...	...	...	...
Ganja	ESDF	302 700	145 800	156 900	110	...	...	...	...
Sumgayit	ESDF	290 200	142 700	147 500	80	...	...	...	...
Bahrain — Bahreïn									
7 IV 2001									
MANAMA	CDFC	153 395	98 320	55 075	27	...	...	...	...
Bangladesh									
1 VII 1991									
Barisal	CDFC	...	...	...	...	163 481	...	...	...
Chittagong	CDFC	...	...	...	...	1 363 998	...	...	...
Comilla	CDFC	...	...	...	...	143 282	...	...	...
DHAKA	CDFC	...	...	...	...	3 397 187	...	...	...
Dinajpur	CDFC	...	...	...	...	126 189	...	...	...
Jamalpur	CDFC	...	...	...	...	101 242	...	...	...
Jessore	CDFC	...	...	...	...	160 198	...	...	...
Khulna	CDFC	...	...	...	...	545 849	...	...	...
Mymensingh	CDFC	...	...	...	...	185 517	...	...	...
Narayanganj	CDFC	...	...	...	...	268 952	...	...	...
Nawabganj	CDFC	...	...	...	...	121 205	...	...	...
Pabna	CDFC	...	...	...	...	104 479	...	...	...
Rajshahi	CDFC	...	...	...	...	299 671	...	...	...
Rangpur	CDFC	...	...	...	...	203 931	...	...	...
Saidpur	CDFC	...	...	...	...	102 030	...	...	...
Tangail	CDFC	...	...	...	...	104 387	...	...	...
Tongi	CDFC	...	...	...	...	154 175	...	...	...
Bhutan — Bhoutan									
1 VII 2001									
THIMPHU	ESDF	32 000	...	...	...	...	...	...	...
Brunei Darussalam — Brunéi Darussalam									
21 VIII 2001									
BANDAR SERI BEGAWAN	CDFC	27 285	13 639	13 646	...	...	...	...	...
Cambodia — Cambodge									
1 VII 2002									
Bat Dambang	ESDF	171 382	82 785	88 597	114	...	...	...	...
PHNOM PENH	ESDF	703 963	339 763	364 200	21	1 234 444	...	...	...
Seam Reab	ESDF	140 966	69 052	71 914	292	...	...	...	...
China — Chine									
1 VII 1999									
Chiayi	ESDF	264 286	133 270	131 016	...	...	...	...	...
Hsinchu	ESDF	359 087	183 682	175 405	...	...	...	...	...
Kaohsiung[49]	ESDF	1 468 586	744 243	724 343	...	...	...	...	...
Keelung	ESDF	383 272	196 952	186 320	...	...	...	...	...
Taichung	ESDF	930 175	461 069	469 106	...	...	...	...	...
Tainan	ESDF	725 445	366 061	359 384	...	...	...	...	...
Taipei[49]	ESDF	2 640 322	1 310 368	1 329 954	...	...	...	...	...
1 XI 2000									
Acheng	CDJC	638 894	327 774	311 120	...	...	...	...	...
Akesu	CDJC	561 822	295 811	266 011	...	...	...	...	...
Aletai	CDJC	178 510	91 207	87 303	...	...	...	...	...
Anda	CDJC	473 091	243 349	229 742	...	...	...	...	...
An'guo	CDJC	378 830	189 944	188 886	...	...	...	...	...
Ankang	CDJC	843 426	443 270	400 156	...	...	...	...	...
Anlu	CDJC	611 990	314 089	297 901	...	...	...	...	...
Anning	CDJC	295 173	161 481	133 692	...	...	...	...	...
Anqing	CDJC	582 751	293 884	288 867	...	...	...	...	...
Anqiu	CDJC	1 096 782	554 403	542 379	...	...	...	...	...
Anshan	CDJC	1 556 285	787 838	768 447	...	...	...	...	...
Anshun	CDJC	767 307	395 894	371 413	...	...	...	...	...

8. Population of capital cities and cities of 100 000 and more inhabitants: latest available year
Population des capitales et des villes de 100 000 habitants et plus: dernière année disponible (continued — suite)

(See notes at end of table. — Voir notes à la fin du tableau.)

Continent, country or area, date and city / Continent, pays ou zone, date et ville	Code[1]	City proper — Ville proprement dite Population				Urban agglomeration — Agglomération urbaine Population			
		Both sexes Les deux sexes	Male Masculin	Female Féminin	Surface area Superficie (km²)	Both sexes Les deux sexes	Male Masculin	Female Féminin	Surface area Superficie (km²)
ASIA — ASIE									
China — Chine									
1 XI 2000									
Anyang	CDJC	768 992	390 120	378 872	...	...	...	...	...
Atushi	CDJC	200 345	101 867	98 478	...	...	...	...	...
Baicheng	CDJC	484 979	244 453	240 526	...	...	...	...	...
Baise	CDJC	340 483	177 310	163 173	...	...	...	...	...
Baishan	CDJC	335 400	172 109	163 291	...	...	...	...	...
Baiyin	CDJC	460 982	243 672	217 310	...	...	...	...	...
Baoding	CDJC	902 496	455 625	446 871	...	...	...	...	...
Baoji	CDJC	600 377	308 493	291 884	...	...	...	...	...
Baoshan	CDJC	846 865	430 076	416 789	...	...	...	...	...
Baotou	CDJC	1 671 181	862 495	808 686	...	...	...	...	...
Bazhong	CDJC	1 185 862	616 323	569 539	...	...	...	...	...
Bazhou	CDJC	557 901	285 321	272 580	...	...	...	...	...
Beian	CDJC	442 474	226 743	215 731	...	...	...	...	...
Beihai	CDJC	558 635	290 544	268 091	...	...	...	...	...
BEIJING (PEKING)	CDJC	11 509 595	6 020 903	5 488 692	...	...	...	...	...
Beiliu	CDJC	1 049 035	557 967	491 068	...	...	...	...	...
Beining	CDJC	527 217	270 153	257 064	...	...	...	...	...
Beipiao	CDJC	573 836	291 584	282 252	...	...	...	...	...
Bengbu	CDJC	809 399	413 444	395 955	...	...	...	...	...
Benxi	CDJC	980 069	495 102	484 967	...	...	...	...	...
Bijie	CDJC	1 128 230	589 537	538 693	...	...	...	...	...
Binzhou	CDJC	600 883	299 952	300 931	...	...	...	...	...
Bole	CDJC	224 869	116 506	108 363	...	...	...	...	...
Botou	CDJC	550 888	280 209	270 679	...	...	...	...	...
Bozhou	CDJC	1 351 939	697 126	654 813	...	...	...	...	...
Cangzhou	CDJC	443 561	223 648	219 913	...	...	...	...	...
Cenxi	CDJC	731 623	384 212	347 411	...	...	...	...	...
Changchun	CDJC	3 225 557	1 647 216	1 578 341	...	...	...	...	...
Changde	CDJC	1 346 739	686 467	660 272	...	...	...	...	...
Changge	CDJC	646 306	332 022	314 284	...	...	...	...	...
Changji	CDJC	387 169	202 275	184 894	...	...	...	...	...
Changle	CDJC	689 815	358 963	330 852	...	...	...	...	...
Changning	CDJC	795 223	428 332	366 891	...	...	...	...	...
Changsha	CDJC	2 122 873	1 099 304	1 023 569	...	...	...	...	...
Changshu	CDJC	1 239 637	598 034	641 603	...	...	...	...	...
Changyi	CDJC	683 182	340 763	342 419	...	...	...	...	...
Changzhi	CDJC	648 981	332 246	316 735	...	...	...	...	...
Changzhou	CDJC	1 081 845	552 850	528 995	...	...	...	...	...
Chaohu	CDJC	778 864	396 961	381 903	...	...	...	...	...
Chaoyang (Guangdong)	CDJC	2 470 812	1 256 428	1 214 384	...	...	...	...	...
Chaoyang (Liaoning)	CDJC	475 038	238 128	236 910	...	...	...	...	...
Chaozhou	CDJC	363 582	181 260	182 322	...	...	...	...	...
Chengde	CDJC	437 251	221 221	216 030	...	...	...	...	...
Chengdu	CDJC	4 333 541	2 258 996	2 074 545	...	...	...	...	...
Chenghai	CDJC	860 003	428 157	431 846	...	...	...	...	...
Chenzhou	CDJC	655 014	340 799	314 215	...	...	...	...	...
Chibi	CDJC	510 926	267 233	243 693	...	...	...	...	...
Chifeng	CDJC	1 153 723	589 450	564 273	...	...	...	...	...
Chishui	CDJC	251 780	130 227	121 553	...	...	...	...	...
Chizhou	CDJC	555 489	280 395	275 094	...	...	...	...	...
Chongqing	CDJC	9 691 901	5 013 398	4 678 503	...	...	...	...	...
Chongzhou	CDJC	650 698	330 345	320 353	...	...	...	...	...
Chuxiong	CDJC	503 682	261 315	242 367	...	...	...	...	...
Chuzhou	CDJC	493 735	251 117	242 618	...	...	...	...	...
Cixi	CDJC	1 214 537	615 279	599 258	...	...	...	...	...
Conghua	CDJC	517 552	264 150	253 402	...	...	...	...	...
Daan	CDJC	430 512	219 682	210 830	...	...	...	...	...
Dafeng	CDJC	756 766	383 391	373 375	...	...	...	...	...
Dali	CDJC	521 169	262 564	258 605	...	...	...	...	...

(See notes at end of table. — Voir notes à la fin du tableau.)

Continent, country or area, date and city — Continent, pays ou zone, date et ville	Code[1]	City proper — Ville proprement dite Population				Urban agglomeration — Agglomération urbaine Population			
		Both sexes Les deux sexes	Male Masculin	Female Féminin	Surface area Superficie (km²)	Both sexes Les deux sexes	Male Masculin	Female Féminin	Surface area Superficie (km²)
ASIA — ASIE									
China — Chine									
1 XI 2000									
Dalian	CDJC	3 245 191	1 641 485	1 603 706	...	...	...	...	...
Dandong	CDJC	780 414	389 277	391 137	...	...	...	...	...
Dangyang	CDJC	495 946	253 125	242 821	...	...	...	...	...
Danjiangkou	CDJC	501 126	262 922	238 204	...	...	...	...	...
Danyang	CDJC	877 232	442 296	434 936	...	...	...	...	...
Danzhou	CDJC	835 465	442 636	392 829	...	...	...	...	...
Daqing	CDJC	1 380 051	704 765	675 286	...	...	...	...	...
Dashiqiao	CDJC	714 670	370 713	343 957	...	...	...	...	...
Datong	CDJC	1 526 744	785 754	740 990	...	...	...	...	...
Daye	CDJC	873 859	460 417	413 442	...	...	...	...	...
Dazhou	CDJC	384 525	192 819	191 706	...	...	...	...	...
Dehui	CDJC	878 349	448 146	430 203	...	...	...	...	...
Dengfeng	CDJC	609 085	321 081	288 004	...	...	...	...	...
Dengta	CDJC	502 149	259 895	242 254	...	...	...	...	...
Dengzhou	CDJC	1 290 656	677 791	612 865	...	...	...	...	...
Dexing	CDJC	297 784	155 178	142 606	...	...	...	...	...
Deyang	CDJC	628 876	324 823	304 053	...	...	...	...	...
Dezhou	CDJC	552 445	277 994	274 451	...	...	...	...	...
Dingzhou	CDJC	1 107 903	559 214	548 689	...	...	...	...	...
Dongfang	CDJC	358 318	188 840	169 478	...	...	...	...	...
Donggang	CDJC	640 340	324 344	315 996	...	...	...	...	...
Dongguan	CDJC	6 445 777	3 035 742	3 410 035	...	...	...	...	...
Dongsheng	CDJC	252 566	129 512	123 054	...	...	...	...	...
Dongtai	CDJC	1 164 653	583 122	581 531	...	...	...	...	...
Dongxing	CDJC	108 131	58 939	49 192	...	...	...	...	...
Dongyang	CDJC	753 094	375 565	377 529	...	...	...	...	...
Dongying	CDJC	788 844	407 241	381 603	...	...	...	...	...
Dujiangyan	CDJC	621 980	314 845	307 135	...	...	...	...	...
Dunhua	CDJC	480 834	247 966	232 868	...	...	...	...	...
Dunhuang	CDJC	187 578	96 679	90 899	...	...	...	...	...
Duyun	CDJC	463 426	241 421	222 005	...	...	...	...	...
Enping	CDJC	464 898	240 765	224 133	...	...	...	...	...
Enshi	CDJC	755 725	397 284	358 441	...	...	...	...	...
Emeishan	CDJC	423 070	217 201	205 869	...	...	...	...	...
Ezhou	CDJC	1 023 285	533 940	489 345	...	...	...	...	...
Fangchenggang	CDJC	422 514	233 979	188 535	...	...	...	...	...
Feicheng	CDJC	948 602	476 032	472 570	...	...	...	...	...
Fengcheng (Jiangxi)	CDJC	1 216 412	644 029	572 383	...	...	...	...	...
Fengcheng (Liaoning)	CDJC	560 384	288 402	271 982	...	...	...	...	...
Fenghua	CDJC	471 558	239 252	232 306	...	...	...	...	...
Fengnan	CDJC	550 872	285 442	265 430	...	...	...	...	...
Fengzhen	CDJC	264 204	137 562	126 642	...	...	...	...	...
Fenyang	CDJC	387 046	199 129	187 917	...	...	...	...	...
Foshan	CDJC	768 656	398 973	369 683	...	...	...	...	...
Fuan	CDJC	554 057	296 379	257 678	...	...	...	...	...
Fuding	CDJC	521 070	276 419	244 651	...	...	...	...	...
Fujin	CDJC	420 579	215 650	204 929	...	...	...	...	...
Fukang	CDJC	152 965	80 372	72 593	...	...	...	...	...
Fuqing	CDJC	1 174 540	597 890	576 650	...	...	...	...	...
Fuquan	CDJC	292 720	155 972	136 748	...	...	...	...	...
Fushun	CDJC	1 434 447	722 549	711 898	...	...	...	...	...
Fuxin	CDJC	627 855	311 912	315 943	...	...	...	...	...
Fuyang (Anhui)	CDJC	628 633	324 172	304 461	...	...	...	...	...
Fuyang (Zhejiang)	CDJC	1 719 057	878 560	840 497	...	...	...	...	...
Fuzhou (Fujian)	CDJC	2 124 435	1 086 638	1 037 797	...	...	...	...	...
Fuzhou (Jiangxi)	CDJC	1 007 391	533 936	473 455	...	...	...	...	...
Gaizhou	CDJC	883 811	455 641	428 170	...	...	...	...	...
Ganzhou	CDJC	494 600	254 272	240 328	...	...	...	...	...
Gaoan	CDJC	788 329	416 678	371 651	...	...	...	...	...

(See notes at end of table. — Voir notes à la fin du tableau.)

Continent, country or area, date and city / Continent, pays ou zone, date et ville	Code[1]	City proper — Ville proprement dite Population				Urban agglomeration — Agglomération urbaine Population			
		Both sexes Les deux sexes	Male Masculin	Female Féminin	Surface area Superficie (km²)	Both sexes Les deux sexes	Male Masculin	Female Féminin	Surface area Superficie (km²)
ASIA — ASIE									
China — Chine									
1 XI 2000									
Gaobeidian	CDJC	538 582	268 027	270 555					
Gaocheng	CDJC	758 269	380 317	377 952	...	...	...	...	...
Gaomi	CDJC	842 403	420 956	421 447	...	...	...	...	...
Gaoming	CDJC	301 041	159 746	141 295	...	...	...	...	...
Gaoping	CDJC	471 671	236 439	235 232	...	...	...	...	...
Gaoyao	CDJC	625 125	314 474	310 651	...	...	...	...	...
Gaoyou	CDJC	797 752	392 863	404 889	...	...	...	...	...
Gaozhou	CDJC	1 219 132	639 497	579 635	...	...	...	...	...
Geermu	CDJC	135 897	73 572	62 325	...	...	...	...	...
Gejiu	CDJC	453 311	243 377	209 934	...	...	...	...	...
Genhe	CDJC	157 337	80 485	76 852	...	...	...	...	...
Gongyi	CDJC	777 202	395 784	381 418	...	...	...	...	...
Gongzhuling	CDJC	1 041 735	532 134	509 601	...	...	...	...	...
Guang'an	CDJC	1 093 103	561 454	531 649	...	...	...	...	...
Guanghan	CDJC	577 298	289 596	287 702	...	...	...	...	...
Guangshui	CDJC	885 936	458 607	427 329	...	...	...	...	...
Guangyuan	CDJC	905 057	467 422	437 635	...	...	...	...	...
Guangzhou	CDJC	8 524 826	4 445 052	4 079 774	...	...	...	...	...
Guigang	CDJC	1 413 128	731 298	681 830	...	...	...	...	...
Guilin	CDJC	804 571	414 004	390 567	...	...	...	...	...
Guiping	CDJC	1 359 035	716 617	642 418	...	...	...	...	...
Guixi	CDJC	535 517	282 662	252 855	...	...	...	...	...
Guiyang	CDJC	2 985 105	1 568 544	1 416 561	...	...	...	...	...
Gujiao	CDJC	205 702	110 105	95 597	...	...	...	...	...
Haerbin	CDJC	3 481 504	1 759 609	1 721 895	...	...	...	...	...
Haicheng	CDJC	1 181 130	606 805	574 325	...	...	...	...	...
Haikou	CDJC	830 192	431 774	398 418	...	...	...	...	...
Hailaer	CDJC	262 184	132 849	129 335	...	...	...	...	...
Hailin	CDJC	435 677	222 525	213 152	...	...	...	...	...
Hailun	CDJC	720 008	368 751	351 257	...	...	...	...	...
Haimen	CDJC	942 952	431 066	511 886	...	...	...	...	...
Haining	CDJC	666 080	331 349	334 731	...	...	...	...	...
Haiyang	CDJC	654 594	329 202	325 392	...	...	...	...	...
Hami	CDJC	388 714	201 005	187 709	...	...	...	...	...
Hancheng	CDJC	387 041	201 881	185 160	...	...	...	...	...
Hanchuan	CDJC	1 057 396	552 093	505 303	...	...	...	...	...
Handan	CDJC	1 329 734	693 882	635 852	...	...	...	...	...
Hangzhou	CDJC	2 451 319	1 301 103	1 150 216	...	...	...	...	...
Hanzhong	CDJC	503 871	258 142	245 729	...	...	...	...	...
Hebi	CDJC	495 336	260 212	235 124	...	...	...	...	...
Hechi	CDJC	318 348	167 526	150 822	...	...	...	...	...
Hechuan	CDJC	1 420 520	732 503	688 017	...	...	...	...	...
Hefei	CDJC	1 659 075	879 749	779 326	...	...	...	...	...
Hegang	CDJC	694 640	354 262	340 378	...	...	...	...	...
Heihe	CDJC	192 764	97 488	95 276	...	...	...	...	...
Hejian	CDJC	757 581	383 621	373 960	...	...	...	...	...
Hejin	CDJC	368 572	195 677	172 895	...	...	...	...	...
Helong	CDJC	215 266	110 051	105 215	...	...	...	...	...
Hengshui	CDJC	422 761	212 417	210 344	...	...	...	...	...
Hengyang	CDJC	879 051	450 222	428 829	...	...	...	...	...
Heshan (Guangdong)	CDJC	405 779	202 461	203 318	...	...	...	...	...
Heshan (Guangxi)	CDJC	131 249	69 205	62 044	...	...	...	...	...
Hetian	CDJC	186 127	94 034	92 093	...	...	...	...	...
Heyuan	CDJC	227 773	115 330	112 443	...	...	...	...	...
Heze	CDJC	1 280 031	656 790	623 241	...	...	...	...	...
Hezhou	CDJC	850 023	446 208	403 815	...	...	...	...	...
Honghu	CDJC	877 775	459 997	417 778	...	...	...	...	...
Hongjiang	CDJC	485 061	250 434	234 627	...	...	...	...	...
Houma	CDJC	225 123	113 997	111 126	...	...	...	...	...

(See notes at end of table. — Voir notes à la fin du tableau.)

Continent, country or area, date and city — Continent, pays ou zone, date et ville	Code[1]	City proper — Ville proprement dite Population				Urban agglomeration — Agglomération urbaine Population			
		Both sexes Les deux sexes	Male Masculin	Female Féminin	Surface area Superficie (km²)	Both sexes Les deux sexes	Male Masculin	Female Féminin	Surface area Superficie (km²)

ASIA — ASIE

China — Chine
1 XI 2000

Huadian	CDJC	444 415	228 624	215 791	...	...	...	...	...
Huaian	CDJC	1 200 679	619 541	581 138	...	...	...	...	...
Huaibei	CDJC	741 195	382 444	358 751	...	...	...	...	...
Huaihua	CDJC	346 522	178 221	168 301	...	...	...	...	...
Huainan	CDJC	1 357 228	701 205	656 023	...	...	...	...	...
Huaiyin	CDJC	555 052	282 186	272 866	...	...	...	...	...
Huanggang	CDJC	373 568	194 607	178 961	...	...	...	...	...
Huanghua	CDJC	483 273	251 128	232 145	...	...	...	...	...
Huangshan	CDJC	406 200	208 004	198 196	...	...	...	...	...
Huangshi (Hubei)	CDJC	653 722	334 712	319 010	...	...	...	...	...
Huayin	CDJC	242 488	125 006	117 482	...	...	...	...	...
Huaying	CDJC	352 257	183 962	168 295	...	...	...	...	...
Huazhou	CDJC	1 007 796	529 550	478 246	...	...	...	...	...
Huhehaote	CDJC	1 406 955	724 328	682 627	...	...	...	...	...
Huixian	CDJC	776 326	394 763	381 563	...	...	...	...	...
Huiyang	CDJC	862 822	429 006	433 816	...	...	...	...	...
Huizhou	CDJC	591 686	292 216	299 470	...	...	...	...	...
Hulin	CDJC	311 509	160 842	150 667	...	...	...	...	...
Huludao	CDJC	900 936	456 211	444 725	...	...	...	...	...
Hunchun	CDJC	211 091	108 873	102 218	...	...	...	...	...
Huozhou	CDJC	274 955	142 316	132 639	...	...	...	...	...
Huzhou	CDJC	1 145 414	573 421	571 993	...	...	...	...	...
Jiamusi	CDJC	859 944	433 369	426 575	...	...	...	...	...
Jian (Jiangxi)	CDJC	473 113	244 476	228 637	...	...	...	...	...
Jian (Jilin)	CDJC	239 849	124 475	115 374	...	...	...	...	...
Jiande	CDJC	473 062	242 606	230 456	...	...	...	...	...
Jiangdu	CDJC	1 053 023	512 151	540 872	...	...	...	...	...
Jiangjin	CDJC	1 322 890	686 106	636 784	...	...	...	...	...
Jiangmen	CDJC	536 317	271 693	264 624	...	...	...	...	...
Jiangshan	CDJC	473 222	241 301	231 921	...	...	...	...	...
Jiangyan	CDJC	861 321	419 333	441 988	...	...	...	...	...
Jiangyin	CDJC	1 315 472	665 719	649 753	...	...	...	...	...
Jiangyou	CDJC	849 761	436 112	413 649	...	...	...	...	...
Jian'ou	CDJC	478 651	249 624	229 027	...	...	...	...	...
Jianyang (Sichuan)	CDJC	1 412 523	728 353	684 170	...	...	...	...	...
Jianyang (Fujian)	CDJC	317 848	167 066	150 782	...	...	...	...	...
Jiaohe	CDJC	474 109	243 510	230 599	...	...	...	...	...
Jiaonan	CDJC	827 771	419 331	408 440	...	...	...	...	...
Jiaozhou	CDJC	783 478	388 207	395 271	...	...	...	...	...
Jiaozuo	CDJC	747 299	384 395	362 904	...	...	...	...	...
Jiaxing	CDJC	881 923	445 646	436 277	...	...	...	...	...
Jiayuguan	CDJC	159 541	85 959	73 582	...	...	...	...	...
Jieshou	CDJC	640 878	327 384	313 494	...	...	...	...	...
Jiexiu	CDJC	372 993	190 675	182 318	...	...	...	...	...
Jieyang	CDJC	633 570	324 831	308 739	...	...	...	...	...
Jilin	CDJC	1 953 134	984 762	968 372	...	...	...	...	...
Jimo	CDJC	1 111 202	553 261	557 941	...	...	...	...	...
Ji'nan	CDJC	2 999 934	1 539 067	1 460 867	...	...	...	...	...
Jinchang	CDJC	204 902	106 725	98 177	...	...	...	...	...
Jincheng	CDJC	304 221	157 663	146 558	...	...	...	...	...
Jingdezhen	CDJC	444 720	228 747	215 973	...	...	...	...	...
Jinggangshan	CDJC	145 769	74 722	71 047	...	...	...	...	...
Jinghong	CDJC	443 672	229 846	213 826	...	...	...	...	...
Jingjiang	CDJC	639 665	316 885	322 780	...	...	...	...	...
Jingmen	CDJC	583 373	300 284	283 089	...	...	...	...	...
Jingzhou	CDJC	1 177 150	598 951	578 199	...	...	...	...	...
Jinhua	CDJC	424 859	216 773	208 086	...	...	...	...	...
Jining (Shandong)	CDJC	1 050 522	530 322	520 200	...	...	..	...	...
Jining (Inner Mongolia)	CDJC	272 448	136 913	135 535	...	...	...	...	...

8. Population of capital cities and cities of 100 000 and more inhabitants: latest available year
Population des capitales et des villes de 100 000 habitants et plus: dernière année disponible (continued — suite)

(See notes at end of table. — Voir notes à la fin du tableau.)

Continent, country or area, date and city — Continent, pays ou zone, date et ville	Code[1]	City proper — Ville proprement dite Population				Urban agglomeration — Agglomération urbaine Population			
		Both sexes Les deux sexes	Male Masculin	Female Féminin	Surface area Superficie (km²)	Both sexes Les deux sexes	Male Masculin	Female Féminin	Surface area Superficie (km²)
ASIA — ASIE									
China — Chine									
1 XI 2000									
Jinjiang	CDJC	1 479 259	772 066	707 193	...	...	...	...	...
Jinshi	CDJC	243 242	126 619	116 623	...	...	...	...	...
Jintan	CDJC	533 350	256 798	276 552	...	...	...	...	...
Jinzhong	CDJC	534 357	274 957	259 400	...	...	...	...	...
Jinzhou (Liaoning)	CDJC	861 991	430 777	431 214	...	...	...	...	...
Jinzhou (Hebei)	CDJC	520 942	265 012	255 930	...	...	...	...	...
Jishou	CDJC	294 297	151 422	142 875	...	...	...	...	...
Jiujiang	CDJC	551 329	280 126	271 203	...	...	...	...	...
Jiuquan	CDJC	346 258	177 943	168 315	...	...	...	...	...
Jiutai	CDJC	799 729	411 067	388 662	...	...	...	...	...
Jixi	CDJC	910 782	467 547	443 235	...	...	...	...	...
Jiyuan	CDJC	626 478	323 554	302 924	...	...	...	...	...
Jizhou	CDJC	373 825	187 005	186 820	...	...	...	...	...
Jurong	CDJC	594 316	302 713	291 603	...	...	...	...	...
Kaifeng	CDJC	796 171	398 133	398 038	...	...	...	...	...
Kaili	CDJC	433 236	230 692	202 544	...	...	...	...	...
Kaiping	CDJC	668 692	326 560	342 132	...	...	...	...	...
Kaiyuan (Liaoning)	CDJC	529 736	271 422	258 314	...	...	...	...	...
Kaiyuan (Yunnan)	CDJC	292 039	152 771	139 268	...	...	...	...	...
Kashi (Xinjiang)	CDJC	340 640	172 136	168 504	...	...	...	...	...
Kelamayi	CDJC	270 232	143 500	126 732	...	...	...	...	...
Kuerle	CDJC	381 943	199 344	182 599	...	...	...	...	...
Kuitun	CDJC	285 299	148 740	136 559	...	...	...	...	...
Kunming	CDJC	3 035 406	1 615 096	1 420 310	...	...	...	...	...
Kunshan	CDJC	750 074	377 433	372 641	...	...	...	...	...
Laiwu	CDJC	1 233 525	626 549	606 976	...	...	...	...	...
Laixi	CDJC	728 796	366 400	362 396	...	...	...	...	...
Laiyang	CDJC	897 681	453 293	444 388	...	...	...	...	...
Laizhou	CDJC	889 361	450 192	439 169	...	...	...	...	...
Langfang	CDJC	715 388	363 094	352 294	...	...	...	...	...
Langzhong	CDJC	787 809	400 390	387 419	...	...	...	...	...
Lanxi	CDJC	607 196	314 090	293 106	...	...	...	...	...
Lanzhou	CDJC	2 087 759	1 092 661	995 098	...	...	...	...	...
Laohekou	CDJC	509 468	257 204	252 264	...	...	...	...	...
Lasa	CDJC	223 001	117 004	105 997	...	...	...	...	...
Lechang	CDJC	423 444	223 788	199 656	...	...	...	...	...
Leiyang	CDJC	1 180 235	631 431	548 804	...	...	...	...	...
Leizhou	CDJC	1 268 298	674 213	594 085	...	...	...	...	...
Leling	CDJC	615 833	313 642	302 191	...	...	...	...	...
Lengshuijiang	CDJC	339 701	175 071	164 630	...	...	...	...	...
Leping	CDJC	729 639	381 937	347 702	...	...	...	...	...
Leqing	CDJC	1 162 765	605 494	557 271	...	...	...	...	...
Leshan	CDJC	1 120 158	567 028	553 130	...	...	...	...	...
Lianjiang	CDJC	1 205 764	642 214	563 550	...	...	...	...	...
Lianyuan	CDJC	996 893	521 941	474 952	...	...	...	...	...
Lianyungang	CDJC	687 242	354 350	332 892	...	...	...	...	...
Lianzhou	CDJC	409 360	212 292	197 068	...	...	...	...	...
Liaocheng	CDJC	950 319	474 976	475 343	...	...	...	...	...
Liaoyang	CDJC	728 492	365 833	362 659	...	...	...	...	...
Liaoyuan	CDJC	462 233	234 701	227 532	...	...	...	...	...
Lichuan	CDJC	786 984	417 988	368 996	...	...	...	...	...
Liling	CDJC	934 396	484 127	450 269	...	...	...	...	...
Lin'an	CDJC	514 238	261 852	252 386	...	...	...	...	...
Linfen	CDJC	724 403	367 377	357 026	...	...	...	...	...
Lingbao	CDJC	722 890	377 872	345 018	...	...	...	...	...
Linghai	CDJC	647 310	332 906	314 404	...	...	...	...	...
Lingwu	CDJC	249 890	128 364	121 526	...	...	...	...	...
Lingyuan	CDJC	620 121	324 554	295 567	...	...	...	...	...
Linhai	CDJC	948 618	479 625	468 993	...	...	...	...	...

(See notes at end of table. — Voir notes à la fin du tableau.)

Continent, country or area, date and city Continent, pays ou zone, date et ville	Code[1]	City proper — Ville proprement dite Population				Urban agglomeration — Agglomération urbaine Population			
		Both sexes Les deux sexes	Male Masculin	Female Féminin	Surface area Superficie (km²)	Both sexes Les deux sexes	Male Masculin	Female Féminin	Surface area Superficie (km²)
ASIA — ASIE									
China — Chine									
1 XI 2000									
Linhe	CDJC	510 965	260 835	250 130	...	...	...	...	...
Linjiang	CDJC	184 901	94 904	89 997	...	...	...	...	...
Linqing	CDJC	694 247	348 411	345 836	...	...	...	...	...
Linxia	CDJC	202 498	104 017	98 481	...	...	...	...	...
Linxiang	CDJC	448 452	235 723	212 729	...	...	...	...	...
Linyi	CDJC	1 938 510	988 940	949 570	...	...	...	...	...
Linzhou	CDJC	982 254	501 659	480 595	...	...	...	...	...
Lishi	CDJC	235 678	121 253	114 425	...	...	...	...	...
Lishui	CDJC	348 241	178 908	169 333	...	...	...	...	...
Liuan	CDJC	1 559 037	807 902	751 135	...	...	...	...	...
Liupanshui	CDJC	995 055	523 692	471 363	...	...	...	...	...
Liuyang	CDJC	1 307 572	680 610	626 962	...	...	...	...	...
Liuzhou	CDJC	1 220 392	634 909	585 483	...	...	...	...	...
Liyang	CDJC	740 871	375 694	365 177	...	...	...	...	...
Longhai	CDJC	816 318	415 936	400 382	...	...	...	...	...
Longjing	CDJC	261 551	132 150	129 401	...	...	...	...	...
Longkou	CDJC	671 335	337 507	333 828	...	...	...	...	...
Longquan	CDJC	250 398	131 534	118 864	...	...	...	...	...
Longyan	CDJC	543 731	298 481	245 250	...	...	...	...	...
Loudi	CDJC	398 577	205 172	193 405	...	...	...	...	...
Lucheng	CDJC	213 944	111 293	102 651	...	...	...	...	...
Lufeng	CDJC	1 164 767	600 959	563 808	...	...	...	...	...
Luoding	CDJC	866 190	449 131	417 059	...	...	...	...	...
Luohe	CDJC	304 105	150 273	153 832	...	...	...	...	...
Luoyang	CDJC	1 491 680	759 425	732 255	...	...	...	...	...
Luquan	CDJC	397 449	202 340	195 109	...	...	...	...	...
Luxi (Yunnan)	CDJC	337 406	172 038	165 368	...	...	...	...	...
Luzhou	CDJC	1 252 884	636 652	616 232	...	...	...	...	...
Maanshan	CDJC	567 576	292 994	274 582	...	...	...	...	...
Macheng	CDJC	1 129 047	595 391	533 656	...	...	...	...	...
Manzhouli	CDJC	181 112	92 853	88 259	...	...	...	...	...
Maoming	CDJC	644 301	335 713	308 588	...	...	...	...	...
Meihekou	CDJC	617 674	317 226	300 448	...	...	...	...	...
Meishan	CDJC	799 309	402 889	396 420	...	...	...	...	...
Meixian	CDJC	313 821	160 925	152 896	...	...	...	...	...
Meizhou	CDJC	354 302	178 658	175 644	...	...	...	...	...
Mianyang	CDJC	1 162 962	604 414	558 548	...	...	...	...	...
Mianzhu	CDJC	515 830	263 098	252 732	...	...	...	...	...
Miluo	CDJC	658 867	342 113	316 754	...	...	...	...	...
Mingguang	CDJC	569 585	290 126	279 459	...	...	...	...	...
Miquan	CDJC	180 952	95 368	85 584	...	...	...	...	...
Mishan	CDJC	438 277	224 565	213 712	...	...	...	...	...
Mudanjiang	CDJC	1 014 206	512 000	502 206	...	...	...	...	...
Muling	CDJC	310 096	158 623	151 473	...	...	...	...	...
Nan'an	CDJC	1 385 276	700 218	685 058	...	...	...	...	...
Nanchang	CDJC	1 844 253	952 504	891 749	...	...	...	...	...
Nanchong	CDJC	1 771 920	922 452	849 468	...	...	...	...	...
Nanchuan	CDJC	631 853	326 307	305 546	...	...	...	...	...
Nan'gong	CDJC	467 356	234 978	232 378	...	...	...	...	...
Nanhai	CDJC	2 133 741	1 111 731	1 022 010	...	...	...	...	...
Nanjing	CDJC	3 624 234	1 935 931	1 688 303	...	...	...	...	...
Nankang	CDJC	694 987	338 836	356 151	...	...	...	...	...
Nanning	CDJC	1 766 701	924 916	841 785	...	...	...	...	...
Nanping	CDJC	488 818	257 352	231 466	...	...	...	...	...
Nantong	CDJC	771 386	386 206	385 180	...	...	...	...	...
Nanxiong	CDJC	372 844	185 330	187 514	...	...	...	...	...
Nanyang	CDJC	1 584 715	814 822	769 893	...	...	...	...	...
Nehe	CDJC	672 295	343 873	328 422	...	...	...	...	...
Neijiang	CDJC	1 391 931	709 053	682 878	...	...	...	...	...

(See notes at end of table. — Voir notes à la fin du tableau.)

Continent, country or area, date and city / Continent, pays ou zone, date et ville	Code[1]	City proper — Ville proprement dite Population				Urban agglomeration — Agglomération urbaine Population			
		Both sexes Les deux sexes	Male Masculin	Female Féminin	Surface area Superficie (km²)	Both sexes Les deux sexes	Male Masculin	Female Féminin	Surface area Superficie (km²)

ASIA — ASIE

China — Chine
1 XI 2000

Ning'an	CDJC	437 328	223 201	214 127	...	...	...	...	...
Ningbo	CDJC	1 567 499	804 850	762 649	...	...	...	...	...
Ningde	CDJC	400 293	213 131	187 162	...	...	...	...	...
Ningguo	CDJC	381 842	199 915	181 927	...	...	...	...	...
Panjin	CDJC	602 541	309 377	293 164	...	...	...	...	...
Panshi	CDJC	530 470	273 219	257 251	...	...	...	...	...
Panzhihua	CDJC	690 739	363 585	327 154	...	...	...	...	...
Penglai	CDJC	500 408	252 726	247 682	...	...	...	...	...
Pengzhou	CDJC	770 749	389 697	381 052	...	...	...	...	...
Pingdingshan	CDJC	900 903	470 362	430 541	...	...	...	...	...
Pingdu	CDJC	1 321 975	670 685	651 290	...	...	...	...	...
Pinghu	CDJC	507 899	249 848	258 051	...	...	...	...	...
Pingliang	CDJC	454 996	236 426	218 570	...	...	...	...	...
Pingxiang (Jiangxi)	CDJC	783 445	402 198	381 247	...	...	...	...	...
Pingxiang (Guangxi)	CDJC	107 046	57 445	49 601	...	...	...	...	...
Pizhou	CDJC	1 539 922	791 332	748 590	...	...	...	...	...
Pulandian	CDJC	757 844	385 636	372 208	...	...	...	...	...
Puning	CDJC	1 856 402	954 242	902 160	...	...	...	...	...
Putian	CDJC	443 926	216 578	227 348	...	...	...	...	...
Puyang	CDJC	448 290	229 387	218 903	...	...	...	...	...
Qian'an	CDJC	632 704	323 330	309 374	...	...	...	...	...
Qianjiang	CDJC	992 438	506 290	486 148	...	...	...	...	...
Qidong	CDJC	1 057 073	495 819	561 254	...	...	...	...	...
Qingdao	CDJC	2 720 972	1 359 527	1 361 445	...	...	...	...	...
Qingtongxia	CDJC	248 640	129 121	119 519	...	...	...	...	...
Qingyuan	CDJC	506 680	258 819	247 861	...	...	...	...	...
Qingzhen	CDJC	471 305	248 079	223 226	...	...	...	...	...
Qingzhou	CDJC	894 468	450 090	444 378	...	...	...	...	...
Qinhuangdao	CDJC	817 487	411 355	406 132	...	...	...	...	...
Qinyang	CDJC	446 404	224 725	221 679	...	...	...	...	...
Qinzhou	CDJC	1 035 504	578 428	457 076	...	...	...	...	...
Qionghai	CDJC	449 845	236 560	213 285	...	...	...	...	...
Qionglai	CDJC	631 577	321 382	310 195	...	...	...	...	...
Qiongshan	CDJC	678 149	355 557	322 592	...	...	...	...	...
Qiqihaer	CDJC	1 540 089	776 191	763 898	...	...	...	...	...
Qitaihe	CDJC	486 704	254 500	232 204	...	...	...	...	...
Qixia	CDJC	651 357	331 148	320 209	...	...	...	...	...
Quanzhou	CDJC	1 192 286	616 826	575 460	...	...	...	...	...
Qufu	CDJC	625 313	317 685	307 628	...	...	...	...	...
Qujing	CDJC	648 956	333 756	315 200	...	...	...	...	...
Quzhou	CDJC	286 271	148 054	138 217	...	...	...	...	...
Renhuai	CDJC	520 759	270 091	250 668	...	...	...	...	...
Renqiu	CDJC	768 900	390 649	378 251	...	...	...	...	...
Rizhao	CDJC	1 148 190	576 050	572 140	...	...	...	...	...
Rongcheng	CDJC	732 147	368 156	363 991	...	...	...	...	...
Rugao	CDJC	1 362 533	659 720	702 813	...	...	...	...	...
Ruian	CDJC	1 207 788	627 593	580 195	...	...	...	...	...
Ruichang	CDJC	398 844	209 755	189 089	...	...	...	...	...
Ruijin	CDJC	535 499	280 328	255 171	...	...	...	...	...
Ruili	CDJC	155 210	80 532	74 678	...	...	...	...	...
Rushan	CDJC	580 326	291 047	289 279	...	...	...	...	...
Ruzhou	CDJC	923 245	474 090	449 155	...	...	...	...	...
Sanhe	CDJC	456 882	229 788	227 094	...	...	...	...	...
Sanmenxia	CDJC	288 746	149 846	138 900	...	...	...	...	...
Sanming	CDJC	337 105	178 031	159 074	...	...	...	...	...
Sanshui	CDJC	440 119	230 835	209 284	...	...	...	...	...
Sanya	CDJC	482 296	254 293	228 003	...	...	...	...	...
Shahe	CDJC	474 260	243 171	231 089	...	...	...	...	...
Shanghai	CDJC	14 348 535	7 414 274	6 934 261	...	...	...	...	...

(See notes at end of table. — Voir notes à la fin du tableau.)

Continent, country or area, date and city / Continent, pays ou zone, date et ville	Code[1]	City proper — Ville proprement dite Population				Urban agglomeration — Agglomération urbaine Population			
		Both sexes Les deux sexes	Male Masculin	Female Féminin	Surface area Superficie (km²)	Both sexes Les deux sexes	Male Masculin	Female Féminin	Surface area Superficie (km²)
ASIA — ASIE									
China — Chine									
1 XI 2000									
Shangqiu	CDJC	1 428 983	729 319	699 664	...	...	...	...	...
Shangrao	CDJC	327 703	164 698	163 005	...	...	...	...	...
Shangyu	CDJC	722 523	354 917	367 606	...	...	...	...	...
Shangzhi	CDJC	582 764	298 966	283 798	...	...	...	...	...
Shangzhou	CDJC	530 883	279 160	251 723	...	...	...	...	...
Shantou	CDJC	1 270 112	636 189	633 923	...	...	...	...	...
Shanwei	CDJC	409 677	211 746	197 931	...	...	...	...	...
Shaoguan	CDJC	535 070	282 616	252 454	...	...	...	...	...
Shaowu	CDJC	288 401	151 117	137 284	...	...	...	...	...
Shaoxing	CDJC	633 118	310 860	322 258	...	...	...	...	...
Shaoyang	CDJC	607 868	309 563	298 305	...	...	...	...	...
Shengzhou	CDJC	671 221	345 614	325 607	...	...	...	...	...
Shenyang	CDJC	5 303 053	2 700 380	2 602 673	...	...	...	...	...
Shenzhen	CDJC	7 008 831	3 454 392	3 554 439	...	...	...	...	...
Shenzhou	CDJC	568 558	289 086	279 472	...	...	...	...	...
Shifang	CDJC	432 579	218 447	214 132	...	...	...	...	...
Shihezi	CDJC	590 115	305 253	284 862	...	...	...	...	...
Shijiazhuang	CDJC	1 969 975	1 005 476	964 499	...	...	...	...	...
Shishi	CDJC	498 786	264 700	234 086	...	...	...	...	...
Shishou	CDJC	602 649	310 486	292 163	...	...	...	...	...
Shiyan	CDJC	589 824	309 552	280 272	...	...	...	...	...
Shizuishan	CDJC	314 296	163 261	151 035	...	...	...	...	...
Shouguang	CDJC	1 081 991	548 020	533 971	...	...	...	...	...
Shuangcheng	CDJC	749 182	382 673	366 509	...	...	...	...	...
Shuangliao	CDJC	404 499	206 071	198 428	...	...	...	...	...
Shuangyashan	CDJC	487 294	248 542	238 752	...	...	...	...	...
Shulan	CDJC	660 065	340 293	319 772	...	...	...	...	...
Shunde	CDJC	1 694 152	893 580	800 572	...	...	...	...	...
Shuozhou	CDJC	563 896	290 621	273 275	...	...	...	...	...
Sihui	CDJC	409 804	209 936	199 868	...	...	...	...	...
Simao	CDJC	230 834	120 071	110 763	...	...	...	...	...
Siping	CDJC	492 841	247 416	245 425	...	...	...	...	...
Songyuan	CDJC	538 469	273 101	265 368	...	...	...	...	...
Songzi	CDJC	859 941	437 980	421 961	...	...	...	...	...
Suihua	CDJC	800 207	405 382	394 825	...	...	...	...	...
Suining	CDJC	1 355 388	696 590	658 798	...	...	...	...	...
Suizhou	CDJC	1 598 752	818 936	779 816	...	...	...	...	...
Suqian	CDJC	244 651	124 719	119 932	...	...	...	...	...
Suzhou (Anhui)	CDJC	1 601 181	819 067	782 114	...	...	...	...	...
Suzhou (Jiangsu)	CDJC	1 344 709	686 919	657 790	...	...	...	...	...
Tacheng	CDJC	149 210	76 056	73 154	...	...	...	...	...
Taian	CDJC	1 538 211	775 346	762 865	...	...	...	...	...
Taicang	CDJC	515 063	250 788	264 275	...	...	...	...	...
Taishan	CDJC	948 716	478 773	469 943	...	...	...	...	...
Taixing	CDJC	1 235 454	618 158	617 296	...	...	...	...	...
Taiyuan	CDJC	2 558 382	1 321 216	1 237 166	...	...	...	...	...
Taizhou (Zhejiang)	CDJC	1 491 963	766 497	725 466	...	...	...	...	...
Taizhou (Jiangsu)	CDJC	607 660	303 078	304 582	...	...	...	...	...
Tangshan	CDJC	1 711 311	863 091	848 220	...	...	...	...	...
Taonan	CDJC	441 096	224 878	216 218	...	...	...	...	...
Tengzhou	CDJC	1 548 817	811 999	736 818	...	...	...	...	...
Tianchang	CDJC	590 745	297 550	293 195	...	...	...	...	...
Tianjin	CDJC	7 499 181	3 825 069	3 674 112	...	...	...	...	...
Tianmen	CDJC	1 613 739	849 283	764 456	...	...	...	...	...
Tianshui	CDJC	1 146 986	594 508	552 478	...	...	...	...	...
Tiefa	CDJC	239 636	121 471	118 165	...	...	...	...	...
Tieli	CDJC	354 601	181 024	173 577	...	...	...	...	...
Tieling	CDJC	433 799	217 795	216 004	...	...	...	...	...
Tongcheng	CDJC	660 772	321 098	339 674	...	...	...	...	...

(See notes at end of table. — Voir notes à la fin du tableau.)

Continent, country or area, date and city — Continent, pays ou zone, date et ville	Code[1]	City proper — Ville proprement dite Population				Urban agglomeration — Agglomération urbaine Population			
		Both sexes Les deux sexes	Male Masculin	Female Féminin	Surface area Superficie (km²)	Both sexes Les deux sexes	Male Masculin	Female Féminin	Surface area Superficie (km²)
ASIA — ASIE									
China — Chine									
1 XI 2000									
Tongchuan	CDJC	404 257	211 294	192 963	...	...	...	...	...
Tonghua	CDJC	460 148	231 960	228 188	...	...	...	...	...
Tongjiang	CDJC	164 595	85 426	79 169	...	...	...	...	...
Tongliao	CDJC	793 913	400 930	392 983	...	...	...	...	...
Tongling	CDJC	362 477	188 130	174 347	...	...	...	...	...
Tongren	CDJC	308 583	163 632	144 951	...	...	...	...	...
Tongshi	CDJC	100 836	53 146	47 690	...	...	...	...	...
Tongxiang	CDJC	713 399	360 567	352 832	...	...	...	...	...
Tongzhou	CDJC	1 371 498	652 777	718 721	...	...	...	...	...
Tulufan	CDJC	251 652	129 183	122 469	...	...	...	...	...
Tumen	CDJC	132 368	67 067	65 301	...	...	...	...	...
Urumqi	CDJC	1 753 298	911 328	841 970	...	...	...	...	...
Wafangdian	CDJC	956 063	489 377	466 686	...	...	...	...	...
Wanning	CDJC	513 604	272 751	240 853	...	...	...	...	...
Wanyuan	CDJC	536 685	278 918	257 767	...	...	...	...	...
Weifang	CDJC	1 380 300	696 720	683 580	...	...	...	...	...
Weihai	CDJC	609 219	307 867	301 352	...	...	...	...	...
Weihui	CDJC	464 371	233 151	231 220	...	...	...	...	...
Weinan	CDJC	888 866	451 028	437 838	...	...	...	...	...
Wenchang	CDJC	509 271	260 432	248 839	...	...	...	...	...
Wendeng	CDJC	675 061	335 330	339 731	...	...	...	...	...
Wenling	CDJC	1 162 783	604 031	558 752	...	...	...	...	...
Wenzhou	CDJC	1 915 548	1 028 001	887 547	...	...	...	...	...
Wuan	CDJC	720 196	373 108	347 088	...	...	...	...	...
Wuchang	CDJC	888 782	454 587	434 195	...	...	...	...	...
Wuchuan	CDJC	822 482	429 336	393 146	...	...	...	...	...
Wudalianchi	CDJC	338 689	176 002	162 687	...	...	...	...	...
Wugang (Hunan)	CDJC	694 847	363 904	330 943	...	...	...	...	...
Wugang (Henan)	CDJC	313 089	164 347	148 742	...	...	...	...	...
Wuhai	CDJC	427 553	223 947	203 606	...	...	...	...	...
Wuhan	CDJC	8 312 700	4 306 729	4 005 971	...	...	...	...	...
Wuhu	CDJC	697 197	359 560	337 637	...	...	...	...	...
Wujiang	CDJC	857 104	426 423	430 681	...	...	...	...	...
Wujin	CDJC	1 420 204	719 200	701 004	...	...	...	...	...
Wulanhaote	CDJC	269 162	135 406	133 756	...	...	...	...	...
Wusu	CDJC	190 359	100 288	90 071	...	...	...	...	...
Wuwei	CDJC	946 506	488 872	457 634	...	...	...	...	...
Wuxi	CDJC	1 425 766	732 231	693 535	...	...	...	...	...
Wuxian	CDJC	1 128 429	557 717	570 712	...	...	...	...	...
Wuxue	CDJC	719 426	381 959	337 467	...	...	...	...	...
Wuyishan	CDJC	212 156	112 006	100 150	...	...	...	...	...
Wuzhong	CDJC	355 442	181 909	173 533	...	...	...	...	...
Wuzhou	CDJC	381 043	193 424	187 619	...	...	...	...	...
Xiamen	CDJC	2 053 070	1 061 697	991 373	...	...	...	...	...
Xi'an	CDJC	4 481 508	2 320 642	2 160 866	...	...	...	...	...
Xiangcheng	CDJC	1 052 468	546 760	505 708	...	...	...	...	...
Xiangfan	CDJC	871 388	443 899	427 489	...	...	...	...	...
Xiangtan	CDJC	707 783	363 619	344 164	...	...	...	...	...
Xiangxiang	CDJC	807 718	413 489	394 229	...	...	...	...	...
Xianning	CDJC	567 598	295 836	271 762	...	...	...	...	...
Xiantao	CDJC	1 474 078	774 487	699 591	...	...	...	...	...
Xianyang	CDJC	953 860	493 153	460 707	...	...	...	...	...
Xiaogan	CDJC	883 123	454 917	428 206	...	...	...	...	...
Xiaoshan	CDJC	1 233 348	613 229	620 119	...	...	...	...	...
Xiaoyi	CDJC	414 154	215 941	198 213	...	...	...	...	...
Xichang	CDJC	615 212	318 658	296 554	...	...	...	...	...
Xifeng	CDJC	317 669	163 228	154 441	...	...	...	...	...
Xilin'haote	CDJC	173 796	89 527	84 269	...	...	...	...	...
Xingcheng	CDJC	524 527	269 567	254 960	...	...	...	...	...

(See notes at end of table. — Voir notes à la fin du tableau.)

Continent, country or area, date and city / Continent, pays ou zone, date et ville	Code[1]	City proper — Ville proprement dite Population				Urban agglomeration — Agglomération urbaine Population			
		Both sexes Les deux sexes	Male Masculin	Female Féminin	Surface area Superficie (km²)	Both sexes Les deux sexes	Male Masculin	Female Féminin	Surface area Superficie (km²)

ASIA — ASIE

China — Chine
  1 XI 2000

Xinghua	CDJC	1 441 659	745 856	695 803	...	...	...	...	...
Xingning	CDJC	871 507	436 749	434 758	...	...	...	...	...
Xingping	CDJC	551 523	284 879	266 644	...	...	...	...	...
Xingtai	CDJC	536 282	272 661	263 621	...	...	...	...	...
Xingyang	CDJC	619 840	316 049	303 791	...	...	...	...	...
Xingyi	CDJC	719 605	375 079	344 526	...	...	...	...	...
Xinhui	CDJC	932 425	467 557	464 868	...	...	...	...	...
Xi'ning	CDJC	854 466	440 359	414 107	...	...	...	...	...
Xinji	CDJC	623 219	314 536	308 683	...	...	...	...	...
Xinle	CDJC	439 644	220 811	218 833	...	...	...	...	...
Xinmi	CDJC	779 014	406 291	372 723	...	...	...	...	...
Xinmin	CDJC	653 719	333 683	320 036	...	...	...	...	...
Xintai	CDJC	1 344 395	687 569	656 826	...	...	...	...	...
Xinxiang	CDJC	775 941	394 224	381 717	...	...	...	...	...
Xinyang	CDJC	1 255 750	644 031	611 719	...	...	...	...	...
Xinyi (Guangdong)	CDJC	907 978	464 088	443 890	...	...	...	...	...
Xinyi (Jiangsu)	CDJC	962 656	491 509	471 147	...	...	...	...	...
Xinyu	CDJC	778 391	408 940	369 451	...	...	...	...	...
Xinzheng	CDJC	609 173	315 462	293 711	...	...	...	...	...
Xinzhou	CDJC	496 608	251 708	244 900	...	...	...	...	...
Xishan	CDJC	1 181 073	599 540	581 533	...	...	...	...	...
Xuancheng	CDJC	822 707	428 470	394 237	...	...	...	...	...
Xuanwei	CDJC	1 292 825	691 846	600 979	...	...	...	...	...
Xuchang	CDJC	373 387	188 476	184 911	...	...	...	...	...
Xuzhou	CDJC	1 679 626	866 686	812 940	...	...	...	...	...
Yaan	CDJC	334 475	171 237	163 238	...	...	...	...	...
Yakeshi	CDJC	405 806	207 451	198 355	...	...	...	...	...
Yan'an	CDJC	403 868	209 240	194 628	...	...	...	...	...
Yancheng	CDJC	683 663	347 576	336 087	...	...	...	...	...
Yangchun	CDJC	840 581	440 930	399 651	...	...	...	...	...
Yangjiang	CDJC	538 069	276 769	261 300	...	...	...	...	...
Yangquan	CDJC	655 317	346 209	309 108	...	...	...	...	...
Yangzhong	CDJC	301 672	150 538	151 134	...	...	...	...	...
Yangzhou	CDJC	711 993	362 425	349 568	...	...	...	...	...
Yanji	CDJC	432 339	223 342	208 997	...	...	...	...	...
Yanshi	CDJC	816 026	414 890	401 136	...	...	...	...	...
Yantai	CDJC	1 724 404	871 452	852 952	...	...	...	...	...
Yibin	CDJC	809 099	419 397	389 702	...	...	...	...	...
Yichang	CDJC	712 738	371 510	341 228	...	...	...	...	...
Yicheng	CDJC	522 835	266 340	256 495	...	...	...	...	...
Yichun (Jiangxi)	CDJC	920 357	480 945	439 412	...	...	...	...	...
Yichun (Heilongjiang)	CDJC	814 016	413 071	400 945	...	...	...	...	...
Yidu	CDJC	385 779	196 716	189 063	...	...	...	...	...
Yima	CDJC	136 543	73 411	63 132	...	...	...	...	...
Yinchuan	CDJC	807 487	415 203	392 284	...	...	...	...	...
Yingcheng	CDJC	650 485	340 907	309 578	...	...	...	...	...
Yingde	CDJC	810 446	421 964	388 482	...	...	...	...	...
Yingkou	CDJC	698 059	353 751	344 308	...	...	...	...	...
Yingtan	CDJC	178 406	92 050	86 356	...	...	...	...	...
Yi'ning	CDJC	357 519	179 862	177 657	...	...	...	...	...
Yiwu	CDJC	912 670	461 103	451 567	...	...	...	...	...
Yixing	CDJC	1 164 275	592 095	572 180	...	...	...	...	...
Yiyang	CDJC	1 228 881	629 842	599 039	...	...	...	...	...
Yizheng	CDJC	610 356	311 144	299 212	...	...	...	...	...
Yizhou	CDJC	549 434	288 084	261 350	...	...	...	...	...
Yong'an	CDJC	334 852	180 109	154 743	...	...	...	...	...
Yongcheng	CDJC	1 264 607	654 047	610 560	...	...	...	...	...
Yongchuan	CDJC	984 730	507 848	476 882	...	...	...	...	...
Yongkang	CDJC	557 067	290 946	266 121	...	...	...	...	...

(See notes at end of table. — Voir notes à la fin du tableau.)

Continent, country or area, date and city / Continent, pays ou zone, date et ville	Code[1]	City proper — Ville proprement dite Population				Urban agglomeration — Agglomération urbaine Population			
		Both sexes Les deux sexes	Male Masculin	Female Féminin	Surface area Superficie (km²)	Both sexes Les deux sexes	Male Masculin	Female Féminin	Surface area Superficie (km²)
ASIA — ASIE									
China — Chine									
1 XI 2000									
Yongji	CDJC	421 244	214 446	206 798		...	...	...	...
Yongzhou	CDJC	976 539	508 021	468 518	...	...	...	...	...
Yuanjiang	CDJC	700 236	363 730	336 506	...	...	...	...	...
Yuanping	CDJC	471 853	244 751	227 102	...	...	...	...	...
Yucheng	CDJC	494 301	248 103	246 198	...	...	...	...	...
Yueyang	CDJC	912 993	471 170	441 823	...	...	...	...	...
Yuhang	CDJC	817 715	419 877	397 838	...	...	...	...	...
Yulin (Shaanxi)	CDJC	451 337	232 951	218 386	...	...	...	...	...
Yulin (Guangxi)	CDJC	918 229	491 729	426 500	...	...	...	...	...
Yumen	CDJC	188 931	99 832	89 099	...	...	...	...	...
Yuncheng	CDJC	604 381	304 489	299 892	...	...	...	...	...
Yunfu	CDJC	261 636	136 789	124 847	...	...	...	...	...
Yunzhou	CDJC	598 387	303 581	294 806	...	...	...	...	...
Yushu	CDJC	1 155 670	592 213	563 457	...	...	...	...	...
Yuxi	CDJC	409 044	206 139	202 905	...	...	...	...	...
Yuyao	CDJC	852 719	429 835	422 884	...	...	...	...	...
Yuzhou	CDJC	1 122 669	587 728	534 941	...	...	...	...	...
Zaoyang	CDJC	1 054 374	538 588	515 786	...	...	...	...	...
Zaozhuang	CDJC	1 996 798	1 025 190	971 608	...	...	...	...	...
Zengcheng	CDJC	899 644	466 540	433 104	...	...	...	...	...
Zhalantun	CDJC	409 051	211 922	197 129	...	...	...	...	...
Zhangjiagang	CDJC	957 223	466 771	490 452	...	...	...	...	...
Zhangjiajie	CDJC	453 723	234 454	219 269	...	...	...	...	...
Zhangjiakou	CDJC	903 348	455 048	448 300	...	...	...	...	...
Zhangping	CDJC	264 757	140 779	123 978	...	...	...	...	...
Zhangqiu	CDJC	977 324	485 925	491 399	...	...	...	...	...
Zhangshu	CDJC	527 823	273 691	254 132	...	...	...	...	...
Zhangye	CDJC	486 688	248 469	238 219	...	...	...	...	...
Zhangzhou	CDJC	567 884	291 597	276 287	...	...	...	...	...
Zhanjiang	CDJC	1 350 665	707 187	643 478	...	...	...	...	...
Zhaodong	CDJC	832 657	424 694	407 963	...	...	...	...	...
Zhaoqing	CDJC	507 834	254 086	253 748	...	...	...	...	...
Zhaotong	CDJC	727 959	377 931	350 028	...	...	...	...	...
Zhaoyuan	CDJC	593 705	297 504	296 201	...	...	...	...	...
Zhengzhou	CDJC	2 589 387	1 347 037	1 242 350	...	...	...	...	...
Zhenjiang	CDJC	695 663	364 429	331 234	...	...	...	...	...
Zhijiang	CDJC	508 835	257 013	251 822	...	...	...	...	...
Zhongshan	CDJC	2 363 322	1 175 587	1 187 735	...	...	...	...	...
Zhongxiang	CDJC	1 021 998	516 758	505 240	...	...	...	...	...
Zhoukou	CDJC	323 738	162 443	161 295	...	...	...	...	...
Zhoushan	CDJC	715 685	362 426	353 259	...	...	...	...	...
Zhuanghe	CDJC	835 062	422 677	412 385	...	...	...	...	...
Zhucheng	CDJC	1 053 695	531 390	522 305	...	...	...	...	...
Zhuhai	CDJC	833 908	414 067	419 841	...	...	...	...	...
Zhuji	CDJC	1 070 675	535 820	534 855	...	...	...	...	...
Zhumadian	CDJC	338 036	170 485	167 551	...	...	...	...	...
Zhuozhou	CDJC	546 754	275 834	270 920	...	...	...	...	...
Zhuzhou	CDJC	879 996	454 057	425 939	...	...	...	...	...
Zibo	CDJC	2 817 479	1 429 838	1 387 641	...	...	...	...	...
Zigong	CDJC	1 051 384	532 479	518 905	...	...	...	...	...
Zixing	CDJC	351 581	181 632	169 949	...	...	...	...	...
Ziyang	CDJC	1 016 034	527 326	488 708	...	...	...	...	...
Zoucheng	CDJC	1 101 003	571 761	529 242	...	...	...	...	...
Zunhua	CDJC	683 662	348 121	335 541	...	...	...	...	...
Zunyi	CDJC	691 694	358 839	332 855	...	...	...	...	...
China - HongKong SAR — Chine - HongKong RAS									
14 III 2001									
HONG KONG	CDJC	6 708 389	3 285 344	3 423 045	1 099	...	...	...	...

8. Population of capital cities and cities of 100 000 and more inhabitants: latest available year
Population des capitales et des villes de 100 000 habitants et plus: dernière année disponible (continued — suite)

(See notes at end of table. — Voir notes à la fin du tableau.)

Continent, country or area, date and city / Continent, pays ou zone, date et ville	Code[1]	City proper — Ville proprement dite Population				Urban agglomeration — Agglomération urbaine Population			
		Both sexes Les deux sexes	Male Masculin	Female Féminin	Surface area Superficie (km²)	Both sexes Les deux sexes	Male Masculin	Female Féminin	Surface area Superficie (km²)
ASIA — ASIE									
China - Macao SAR — Chine - Macao RAS									
1 VII 2003									
MACAO	ESDJ	445 066	213 696	231 370	26	...	...	...	...
Cyprus — Chypre									
31 XII 2003									
LEFKOSIA[50]	ESDJ	...	...	...	...	*213 500*	...	...	...
Lemesos[51]	ESDJ	...	...	...	...	*167 800*	...	...	...
Georgia — Géorgie									
1 VII 2003									
Batumi	ESDF	120 200	...	...	...	...	...	...	...
Kutaisi	ESDF	183 800	...	...	...	...	...	...	...
Rustavi	ESDF	115 000	...	...	...	...	...	...	...
TBILISI	ESDF	1 059 600	...	...	...	...	...	...	...
India — Inde[52]									
1 III 2001									
Abohar	CDFC	124 303	66 434	57 869	23	...	...	...	...
Achalpur	CDFC	107 304	55 678	51 626	...	...	...	...	...
Adilabad	CDFC	108 233	55 023	53 210	...	128 196	64 883	63 313	...
Adityapur	CDFC	119 221	63 855	55 366	...	...	...	...	...
Adoni	CDFC	155 969	78 908	77 061	30	161 125	81 577	79 548	...
Agartala	CDFC	189 327	94 398	94 929	16	...	...	...	...
Agra	CDFC	1 259 979	674 902	585 077	121	1 321 410	708 622	612 788	141
Ahmedabad	CDFC	3 515 361	1 863 886	1 651 475	...	4 519 278	2 397 728	2 121 550	...
Ahmednagar	CDFC	307 455	159 409	148 046	18	347 396	184 604	162 792	30
Aizawl	CDFC	229 714	116 983	112 731	110	...	...	...	...
Ajmer	CDFC	485 197	253 854	231 343	242	490 138	256 379	233 759	...
Akola	CDFC	399 978	206 433	193 545	23	...	...	...	...
Alandur	CDFC	146 154	74 784	71 370	...	...	...	...	...
Alappuzha	CDFC	177 079	85 708	91 371	70	282 727	137 232	145 495	84
Aligarh	CDFC	667 732	357 152	310 580	34	...	...	...	...
Alipurduar	CDFC	...	...	...	...	114 069	58 527	55 542	26
Allahabad	CDFC	990 298	549 754	440 544	...	1 049 579	581 876	467 703	...
Alwal	CDFC	106 424	56 562	49 862	...	...	...	...	...
Alwar	CDFC	260 245	139 141	121 104	...	265 850	143 238	122 612	58
Ambala	CDFC	139 222	73 956	65 266	17	168 003	92 610	75 393	38
Ambala Sadar	CDFC	106 378	55 461	50 917	...	...	...	...	...
Ambarnath	CDFC	203 795	107 378	96 417	...	...	...	...	...
Ambattur	CDFC	302 492	156 237	146 255	...	...	...	...	...
Amravati	CDFC	549 370	283 789	265 581	122	...	...	...	...
Amritsar	CDFC	975 695	524 127	451 568	...	1 011 327	543 638	467 689	...
Amroha	CDFC	164 890	86 836	78 054	6	...	...	...	...
Anand	CDFC	130 462	68 032	62 430	...	218 064	115 183	102 881	...
Anantapur	CDFC	220 951	112 273	108 678	...	243 359	123 976	119 383	...
Anklesvar	CDFC	...	...	...	...	112 648	60 265	52 383	...
Arcot	CDFC	...	...	...	...	126 975	62 938	64 037	19
Arrah	CDFC	203 395	109 876	93 519	31	...	...	...	...
Asansol	CDFC	486 304	256 551	229 753	25	1 090 171	576 813	513 358	223
Ashoknagar Kalyangarh	CDFC	111 475	56 340	55 135	...	...	...	...	...
Aurangabad	CDFC	872 667	458 869	413 798	139	891 841	468 815	423 026	148
Avadi	CDFC	230 913	119 187	111 726	...	...	...	...	...
Azamgarh	CDFC	104 943	51 284	53 659	...	...	...	...	...
Bahadurgarh	CDFC	119 839	65 835	54 004	...	131 924	72 851	59 073	...
Baharampur	CDFC	160 168	81 795	78 373	17	170 343	87 038	83 305	19
Bahraich	CDFC	168 376	89 532	78 844	13	...	...	...	...
Baidyabati	CDFC	108 231	56 429	51 802	...	...	...	...	...
Baleshwar	CDFC	106 032	55 637	50 395	...	156 274	82 034	74 240	42
Ballia	CDFC	102 226	55 123	47 103	...	...	...	...	...
Bally	CDFC	261 575	149 810	111 765	12	...	...	...	...
Balurghat	CDFC	135 516	68 822	66 694	...	143 095	72 687	70 408	8
Banda	CDFC	134 822	72 663	62 159	...	139 387	75 172	64 215	...

(See notes at end of table. — Voir notes à la fin du tableau.)

Continent, country or area, date and city / Continent, pays ou zone, date et ville	Code[1]	City proper — Ville proprement dite Population				Urban agglomeration — Agglomération urbaine Population			
		Both sexes Les deux sexes	Male Masculin	Female Féminin	Surface area Superficie (km²)	Both sexes Les deux sexes	Male Masculin	Female Féminin	Surface area Superficie (km²)
ASIA — ASIE									
India — Inde[52]									
1 III 2001									
Bangalore	CDFC	4 292 223	2 240 956	2 051 267	...	5 686 844	2 983 926	2 702 918	446
Bangaon	CDFC	102 115	52 489	49 626	...	...	...	...	...
Bankura	CDFC	128 811	66 333	62 478	19	...	...	...	...
Bansberia	CDFC	104 453	55 403	49 050	...	...	...	...	...
Baranagar	CDFC	250 615	132 701	117 914	7	...	...	...	...
Barasat	CDFC	231 515	118 367	113 148	...	...	...	...	...
Barddhaman	CDFC	285 871	148 824	137 047	23	...	...	...	...
Bareilly	CDFC	699 839	368 022	331 817	107	729 800	386 418	343 382	124
Baripada	CDFC	...	...	...	...	100 593	53 610	46 983	...
Barrackpur	CDFC	144 331	76 268	68 063	14	...	...	...	...
Barshi	CDFC	104 786	53 894	50 892	...	...	...	...	...
Basirhat	CDFC	113 120	57 876	55 244	22	...	...	...	...
Basti	CDFC	106 985	56 813	50 172	...	...	...	...	...
Batala	CDFC	126 646	67 026	59 620	...	147 753	78 342	69 411	...
Bathinda	CDFC	217 389	117 359	100 030	97	...	...	...	...
Beawar	CDFC	123 701	64 394	59 307	...	125 923	65 569	60 354	18
Begusarai	CDFC	...	...	...	...	107 203	57 349	49 854	...
Belgaum	CDFC	399 600	204 846	194 754	142	506 235	261 862	244 373	155
Bellary	CDFC	317 000	163 082	153 918	66	...	...	...	...
Bettiah	CDFC	116 692	61 803	54 889	...	...	...	...	...
Bhadravati	CDFC	160 392	81 260	79 132	...	...	...	...	...
Bhadreswar	CDFC	105 944	57 991	47 953	...	...	...	...	...
Bhagalpur	CDFC	340 349	182 704	157 645	30	349 709	187 627	162 082	31
Bhalswa Jahangir Pur	CDFC	151 427	83 289	68 138	...	...	...	...	...
Bharatpur	CDFC	204 456	109 809	94 647	41	205 104	110 148	94 956	51
Bharuch	CDFC	148 391	76 568	71 823	...	176 531	91 273	85 258	...
Bhatpara	CDFC	441 956	243 065	198 891	16	...	...	...	...
Bhavani	CDFC	...	...	...	...	104 285	52 804	51 481	...
Bhavnagar	CDFC	510 958	267 019	243 939	...	517 578	270 458	247 120	...
Bheemavaram	CDFC	137 327	69 487	67 840	26	141 975	71 938	70 037	...
Bhilai Nagar	CDFC	553 837	289 853	263 984	89	...	...	...	...
Bhilwara	CDFC	280 185	148 642	131 543	118	...	...	...	...
Bhind	CDFC	153 768	83 009	70 759	17	...	...	...	...
Bhiwandi	CDFC	598 703	367 858	230 845	26	621 390	382 493	238 897	28
Bhiwani	CDFC	169 424	91 726	77 698	28	...	...	...	...
Bhopal	CDFC	1 433 875	755 685	678 190	285	1 454 830	766 602	688 228	...
Bhubaneswar	CDFC	647 302	360 476	286 826	125	657 477	365 848	291 629	...
Bhusawal	CDFC	172 366	89 187	83 179	13	187 524	97 192	90 332	25
Bid	CDFC	138 091	71 790	66 301	8	...	...	...	...
Bidar	CDFC	172 298	89 715	82 583	...	173 678	90 449	83 229	47
Bidhan Nagar	CDFC	167 848	85 215	82 633	...	...	...	...	...
Bihar	CDFC	231 972	121 813	110 159	24	...	...	...	...
Bijapur	CDFC	245 946	126 554	119 392	...	253 307	130 237	123 070	75
Bikaner	CDFC	529 007	282 450	246 557	166	...	...	...	...
Bilaspur	CDFC	265 178	137 273	127 905	36	330 291	170 898	159 393	46
Birnagar	CDFC	...	...	...	...	115 104	59 179	55 925	...
Bokaro Steel City	CDFC	394 173	213 044	181 129	163	497 855	268 668	229 187	183
Bommanahalli	CDFC	201 220	108 040	93 180	...	...	...	...	...
Botad	CDFC	100 059	52 668	47 391	...	...	...	...	...
Brahmapur	CDFC	289 724	150 089	139 635	80	...	...	...	...
Budaun	CDFC	148 138	78 294	69 844	4	...	...	...	...
Bulandshahr	CDFC	176 256	93 066	83 190	12	...	...	...	...
Burhanpur	CDFC	194 360	100 031	94 329	13	...	...	...	...
Byatarayanapura	CDFC	180 931	94 683	86 248	...	...	...	...	...
Chakdaha	CDFC	...	...	...	...	101 278	51 321	49 957	...
Champdani	CDFC	103 232	57 874	45 358	...	...	...	...	...
Chandan Nagar	CDFC	162 166	84 222	77 944	10	...	...	...	...
Chandausi	CDFC	103 757	55 167	48 590	...	...	...	...	...
Chandigarh	CDFC	808 796	451 387	357 409	70	...	...	...	...

8. Population of capital cities and cities of 100 000 and more inhabitants: latest available year
Population des capitales et des villes de 100 000 habitants et plus: dernière année disponible (continued — suite)

(See notes at end of table. — Voir notes à la fin du tableau.)

Continent, country or area, date and city / Continent, pays ou zone, date et ville	Code[1]	City proper — Ville proprement dite Population				Urban agglomeration — Agglomération urbaine Population			
		Both sexes Les deux sexes	Male Masculin	Female Féminin	Surface area Superficie (km²)	Both sexes Les deux sexes	Male Masculin	Female Féminin	Surface area Superficie (km²)
ASIA — ASIE									
India — Inde[52]									
1 III 2001									
Chandrapur	CDFC	297 612	148 499	149 113	56	...	...	...	...
Chapra	CDFC	178 835	96 077	82 758	17	...	...	...	...
Chennai (Madras)	CDFC	4 216 268	2 161 605	2 054 663	174	6 424 624	3 294 328	3 130 296	612
Cherthala	CDFC	...	...	...	...	141 512	68 740	72 772	93
Chhatarpur	CDFC	...	...	...	...	109 021	58 393	50 628	...
Chhindwara	CDFC	122 309	63 583	58 726	...	153 635	79 889	73 746	...
Chikmagalur	CDFC	101 022	51 611	49 411	...	...	...	...	...
Chirala	CDFC	...	...	...	...	166 877	83 262	83 615	48
Chirkunda	CDFC	...	...	...	...	106 200	56 528	49 672	...
Chitradurga	CDFC	122 594	62 811	59 783	...	125 060	64 075	60 985	16
Chittoor	CDFC	152 966	77 044	75 922	33	...	...	...	...
Churu	CDFC	...	...	...	...	101 853	53 099	48 754	...
Coimbatore	CDFC	923 085	476 056	447 029	106	1 446 034	743 161	702 873	317
Coonoor	CDFC	...	...	...	...	101 234	51 089	50 145	...
Cuddalore	CDFC	158 569	80 113	78 456	28	...	...	...	...
Cuddapah	CDFC	125 725	63 165	62 560	42	260 899	132 297	128 602	78
Cuttack	CDFC	535 139	286 192	248 947	122	587 637	314 435	273 202	153
Dallo Pura	CDFC	132 628	71 349	61 279	...	...	...	...	...
Damoh	CDFC	112 160	58 898	53 262	...	127 939	67 244	60 695	36
Darbhanga	CDFC	266 834	142 042	124 792	19	...	...	...	...
Darjiling	CDFC	107 530	53 325	54 205	...	109 163	54 131	55 032	...
Dasarahalli	CDFC	263 636	143 225	120 411	...	...	...	...	...
Davangere	CDFC	363 780	187 603	176 177	...	...	...	...	...
Dehradun	CDFC	447 808	236 852	210 956	37	527 859	279 653	248 206	86
Dehri	CDFC	119 007	63 552	55 455	...	...	...	...	...
Delhi[53]	CDFC	9 817 439	5 378 658	4 438 781	431	12 791 458	7 021 896	5 769 562	624
Delhi Cantonment	CDFC	124 452	75 700	48 752	...	...	...	...	...
Deoghar	CDFC	...	...	...	...	112 501	61 405	51 096	...
Deoli	CDFC	119 432	66 575	52 857	...	...	...	...	...
Deoria	CDFC	104 222	54 737	49 485	...	...	...	...	...
Dewas	CDFC	230 658	120 610	110 048	100	...	...	...	...
Dhanbad	CDFC	198 963	108 400	90 563	23	1 064 357	578 602	485 755	201
Dharmavaram	CDFC	103 400	52 799	50 601	...	...	...	...	...
Dhule	CDFC	341 473	177 631	163 842	46	...	...	...	...
Dibrugarh	CDFC	122 523	65 736	56 787	15	137 879	74 239	63 640	16
Dimapur	CDFC	107 382	61 595	45 787	...	...	...	...	...
Dinapur Nizamat	CDFC	130 339	69 024	61 315	...	...	...	...	...
Dindigul	CDFC	196 619	98 969	97 650	14	...	...	...	...
Dohad	CDFC	...	...	...	...	112 087	57 765	54 322	...
Dumdum	CDFC	101 319	52 868	48 451	...	...	...	...	...
Durg	CDFC	231 182	118 896	112 286	51	...	...	...	...
Durgapur	CDFC	492 996	263 426	229 570	154	...	...	...	...
Durg-Bhilai Nagar	CDFC	...	...	...	...	923 559	480 432	443 127	183
Eluru	CDFC	189 772	92 405	97 367	15	215 343	104 987	110 356	...
English Bazar	CDFC	161 448	82 932	78 516	...	224 392	115 454	108 938	19
Erode	CDFC	151 184	76 726	74 458	8	391 169	199 306	191 863	132
Etah	CDFC	107 098	56 960	50 138	...	...	...	...	...
Etawah	CDFC	211 460	112 833	98 627	9	...	...	...	...
Faizabad	CDFC	144 924	76 078	68 846	33	208 164	114 252	93 912	63
Faridabad	CDFC	1 054 981	580 548	474 433	178	...	...	...	...
Farrukhabad-cum-Fategarh	CDFC	227 876	120 783	107 093	17	242 558	129 608	112 950	21
Fatehpur	CDFC	151 757	79 836	71 921	57	...	...	...	...
Firozabad	CDFC	278 801	147 980	130 821	9	432 213	230 477	201 736	12
Gadag-Betgeri	CDFC	154 849	78 672	76 177	35	...	...	...	...
Gajuwaka	CDFC	258 944	133 461	125 483	...	...	...	...	...
Gandhinagar	CDFC	195 891	103 814	92 077	57	...	...	...	...
Ganganagar	CDFC	210 788	115 412	95 376	21	222 833	121 877	100 956	...
Gangawati	CDFC	...	...	...	...	101 397	51 253	50 144	...
Gaya	CDFC	383 197	203 252	179 945	29	394 185	209 926	184 259	32

(See notes at end of table. — Voir notes à la fin du tableau.)

Continent, country or area, date and city Continent, pays ou zone, date et ville	Code[1]	City proper — Ville proprement dite Population				Urban agglomeration — Agglomération urbaine Population			
		Both sexes Les deux sexes	Male Masculin	Female Féminin	Surface area Superficie (km²)	Both sexes Les deux sexes	Male Masculin	Female Féminin	Surface area Superficie (km²)
ASIA — ASIE									
India — Inde[52] 1 III 2001									
Ghatlodiya	CDFC	106 259	56 040	50 219	...	...	...	...	...
Ghaziabad	CDFC	968 521	521 408	447 113	64	...	...	...	...
Ghazipur	CDFC	...	...	...	...	103 283	54 321	48 962	...
Giridih	CDFC	...	...	...	...	105 212	55 154	50 058	...
Godhra	CDFC	121 852	63 143	58 709	...	131 144	67 933	63 211	...
Gonda	CDFC	122 164	67 400	54 764	...	...	...	...	...
Gondiya	CDFC	120 878	61 435	59 443	18	...	...	...	...
Gorakhpur	CDFC	624 570	330 450	294 120	137	...	...	...	...
Gudivada	CDFC	112 245	55 439	56 806	13	...	...	...	...
Gudiyatham	CDFC	...	...	...	...	100 021	49 822	50 199	...
Gulbarga	CDFC	427 929	222 623	205 306	...	435 631	226 848	208 783	43
Guna	CDFC	137 132	72 462	64 670	46	...	...	...	...
Guntakul	CDFC	117 403	59 364	58 039	52	...	...	...	...
Guntur	CDFC	514 707	257 939	256 768	30	...	...	...	...
Gurgaon	CDFC	173 542	92 985	80 557	15	229 243	123 370	105 873	24
Guruvayur	CDFC	...	...	...	...	138 676	64 550	74 126	50
Guwahati	CDFC	808 021	441 347	366 674	217	814 575	445 649	368 926	...
Gwalior	CDFC	826 919	442 484	384 435	290	865 800	465 388	400 412	303
Habra	CDFC	127 695	65 263	62 432	18	239 170	121 603	117 567	37
Hajipur	CDFC	119 276	63 762	55 514	...	...	...	...	...
Haldia	CDFC	170 695	89 886	80 809	69	...	...	...	...
Haldwani-cum-Kathgodam	CDFC	129 140	68 826	60 314	11	159 020	84 611	74 409	...
Halisahar	CDFC	124 479	67 124	57 355	...	...	...	...	...
Hanumangarh	CDFC	129 654	69 583	60 071	...	...	...	...	...
Haora (Howrah)	CDFC	1 008 704	547 969	460 735	52	...	...	...	...
Hapur	CDFC	211 987	112 962	99 025	14	...	...	...	...
Hardoi	CDFC	112 474	59 877	52 597	...	...	...	...	...
Hardwar	CDFC	175 010	94 650	80 360	15	220 433	119 159	101 274	42
Hassan	CDFC	117 386	60 225	57 161	...	133 317	68 337	64 980	27
Hathras	CDFC	123 243	65 908	57 335	8	126 352	67 568	58 784	...
Hazaribag	CDFC	127 243	67 905	59 338	...	135 446	72 296	63 150	...
Hindupur	CDFC	125 056	64 159	60 897	38	...	...	...	...
Hisar	CDFC	256 810	140 240	116 570	45	263 070	143 816	119 254	49
Hoshiarpur	CDFC	148 243	78 946	69 297	28	...	...	...	...
Hospet	CDFC	163 284	83 430	79 854	28	...	...	...	...
Hubli-Dharwad	CDFC	786 018	403 270	382 748	191	...	...	...	...
Hugli-Chinsurah	CDFC	170 201	86 728	83 473	17	...	...	...	...
Hyderabad	CDFC	3 449 878	1 773 899	1 675 979	...	5 533 640	2 854 938	2 678 702	...
Ichalakaranji	CDFC	257 572	135 988	121 584	30	285 795	150 934	134 861	38
Imphal	CDFC	217 275	107 593	109 682	33	245 967	121 588	124 379	37
Indore	CDFC	1 597 441	839 843	757 598	...	1 639 044	861 758	777 286	165
Itarsi	CDFC	...	...	...	...	109 288	57 118	52 170	...
Jabalpur	CDFC	951 469	496 829	454 640	154	1 117 200	588 556	528 644	224
Jagadhri	CDFC	101 300	55 910	45 390	...	...	...	...	...
Jagdalpur	CDFC	...	...	...	...	103 216	53 048	50 168	...
Jaipur	CDFC	2 324 319	1 239 711	1 084 608	200	...	...	...	...
Jalandhar	CDFC	701 223	376 925	324 298	80	709 255	381 116	328 139	...
Jalgaon	CDFC	368 579	193 464	175 115	62	...	...	...	...
Jalna	CDFC	235 529	121 728	113 801	82	...	...	...	...
Jalpaiguri	CDFC	100 212	50 570	49 642	...	...	...	...	...
Jammu	CDFC	378 431	206 061	172 370	...	607 642	330 769	276 873	...
Jamnagar	CDFC	447 734	235 093	212 641	...	558 462	292 954	265 508	...
Jamshedpur	CDFC	570 349	300 081	270 268	60	1 101 804	580 336	521 468	160
Jamuria	CDFC	129 456	68 741	60 715	...	...	...	...	...
Jaunpur	CDFC	159 996	84 179	75 817	25	...	...	...	...
Jetpur Navagadh	CDFC	104 311	54 772	49 539	...	...	...	...	...
Jhansi	CDFC	383 248	203 003	180 245	48	463 281	246 495	216 786	83
Jhunjhunun	CDFC	100 476	52 814	47 662	...	...	...	...	...
Jind	CDFC	136 089	73 557	62 532	...	...	...	...	...

(See notes at end of table. — Voir notes à la fin du tableau.)

Continent, country or area, date and city / Continent, pays ou zone, date et ville	Code[1]	City proper — Ville proprement dite Population				Urban agglomeration — Agglomération urbaine Population			
		Both sexes Les deux sexes	Male Masculin	Female Féminin	Surface area Superficie (km²)	Both sexes Les deux sexes	Male Masculin	Female Féminin	Surface area Superficie (km²)
ASIA — ASIE									
India — Inde[52]									
1 III 2001									
Jodhpur	CDFC	846 408	450 816	395 592	79	856 034	455 860	400 174	...
Jorhat	CDFC	...	...	...	60	135 091	71 837	63 254	69
Junagadh	CDFC	168 686	86 935	81 751	...	252 138	130 318	121 820	...
Kaithal	CDFC	117 226	63 090	54 136	...	...	...	...	...
Kakinada	CDFC	289 920	143 905	146 015	39	368 672	183 619	185 053	58
Kalol	CDFC	100 021	53 098	46 923	...	112 025	59 532	52 493	...
Kalyan	CDFC	1 193 266	633 395	559 871	225	...	...	...	...
Kamarhati	CDFC	314 334	168 633	145 701	11	...	...	...	...
Kamptee	CDFC	...	...	...	...	137 056	71 633	65 423	36
Kancheepuram	CDFC	152 984	77 058	75 926	12	188 349	94 942	93 407	40
Kanchrapara	CDFC	126 118	65 197	60 921	13	...	...	...	...
Kanhangad	CDFC	...	...	...	...	129 364	61 954	67 410	84
Kannur	CDFC	...	...	...	...	498 175	237 101	261 074	145
Kanpur	CDFC	2 532 138	1 354 581	1 177 557	267	2 690 486	1 440 140	1 250 346	299
Kapra	CDFC	159 176	82 914	76 262	...	...	...	...	...
Karaikkudi	CDFC	...	...	...	...	125 185	62 230	62 955	79
Karawal Nagar	CDFC	148 549	80 364	68 185	...	...	...	...	...
Karimnagar	CDFC	203 819	104 514	99 305	24	215 782	110 479	105 303	...
Karnal	CDFC	210 476	112 263	98 213	22	222 017	118 428	103 589	24
Karur	CDFC	...	...	...	...	153 123	77 130	75 993	19
Katihar	CDFC	175 169	93 567	81 602	25	190 862	102 126	88 736	...
Khammam	CDFC	158 022	80 072	77 950	...	196 763	100 255	96 508	26
Khandwa	CDFC	171 976	88 859	83 117	36	...	...	...	...
Khanna	CDFC	103 059	55 290	47 769	...	...	...	...	...
Kharagpur	CDFC	207 984	107 506	100 478	91	296 323	152 700	143 623	125
Khardaha	CDFC	116 252	61 254	54 998	...	...	...	...	...
Khargone	CDFC	...	...	...	...	103 980	54 236	49 744	...
Kirari Suleman Nagar	CDFC	153 874	84 908	68 966	...	...	...	...	...
Kishangarh	CDFC	116 156	61 025	55 131	...	...	...	...	...
Koch Bihar	CDFC	...	...	...	...	102 922	52 186	50 736	...
Kochi	CDFC	596 473	295 351	301 122	109	1 355 406	670 462	684 944	373
Kolar	CDFC	113 299	57 773	55 526	...	...	...	...	...
Kolhapur	CDFC	485 183	251 958	233 225	67	497 554	258 400	239 154	67
Kolkata (Calcutta)[54]	CDFC	4 580 544	2 506 029	2 074 515	185	13 216 546	7 072 114	6 144 432	897
Kollam	CDFC	361 441	177 586	183 855	41	379 975	186 842	193 133	68
Korba	CDFC	315 695	165 028	150 667	35	...	...	...	...
Kota	CDFC	695 899	369 897	326 002	221	704 731	374 570	330 161	...
Kothagudem	CDFC	...	...	...	...	105 265	52 377	52 888	35
Kottayam	CDFC	...	...	...	...	172 867	84 915	87 952	64
Kozhikode	CDFC	436 527	211 785	224 742	96	880 168	428 984	451 184	233
Krishnanagar	CDFC	139 070	70 512	68 558	16	148 645	75 381	73 264	...
Krishnarajapura	CDFC	187 453	98 107	89 346	...	...	...	...	...
Kukatpalle	CDFC	290 591	152 159	138 432	...	...	...	...	...
Kulti	CDFC	290 057	152 947	137 110	...	...	...	...	...
Kumbakonam	CDFC	140 021	69 607	70 414	13	160 827	80 012	80 815	15
Kurnool	CDFC	267 739	135 859	131 880	15	320 619	163 071	157 548	46
L.B. Nagar	CDFC	261 987	135 636	126 351	...	...	...	...	...
Lakhimpur	CDFC	120 566	64 804	55 762	...	...	...	...	...
Lalitpur	CDFC	111 810	58 901	52 909	...	...	...	...	...
Latur	CDFC	299 828	156 477	143 351	21	...	...	...	...
Loni	CDFC	120 659	64 976	55 683	...	...	...	...	...
Lucknow	CDFC	2 207 340	1 165 932	1 041 408	310	2 266 933	1 199 273	1 067 660	338
Ludhiana	CDFC	1 395 053	789 868	605 185	135	...	...	...	...
Machilipatnam	CDFC	183 370	91 400	91 970	27	...	...	...	...
Madanapalle	CDFC	...	...	...	...	107 262	54 507	52 755	...
Madhyamgram	CDFC	155 503	79 716	75 787	...	...	...	...	...
Madurai	CDFC	922 913	466 909	456 004	47	1 194 665	604 728	589 937	115
Mahadevapura	CDFC	135 597	72 803	62 794	...	...	...	...	...
Mahbubnagar	CDFC	130 849	67 019	63 830	14	139 483	71 508	67 975	...

8. Population of capital cities and cities of 100 000 and more inhabitants: latest available year
Population des capitales et des villes de 100 000 habitants et plus: dernière année disponible (continued — suite)

(See notes at end of table. — Voir notes à la fin du tableau.)

Continent, country or area, date and city / Continent, pays ou zone, date et ville	Code[1]	City proper — Ville proprement dite Population				Urban agglomeration — Agglomération urbaine Population			
		Both sexes Les deux sexes	Male Masculin	Female Féminin	Surface area Superficie (km²)	Both sexes Les deux sexes	Male Masculin	Female Féminin	Surface area Superficie (km²)
ASIA — ASIE									
India — Inde[52]									
1 III 2001									
Mahesana	CDFC	...	...	...	...	141 367	74 928	66 439	...
Maheshtala	CDFC	389 214	204 734	184 480	...				
Mainpuri	CDFC	...	...	...	...	102 007	54 043	47 964	...
Malappuram	CDFC	...	...	...	...	170 364	83 669	86 695	111
Malegaon	CDFC	409 190	208 744	200 446	13	...	...	...	...
Malerkotla	CDFC	106 802	56 872	49 930	...	...	...	...	...
Malkajgiri	CDFC	175 000	90 000	85 000	...	...	...	...	...
Mancherial	CDFC	...	...	...	...	118 047	60 371	57 676	...
Mandsaur	CDFC	116 483	60 269	56 214	...	117 532	60 860	56 672	...
Mandya	CDFC	131 211	66 630	64 581	17	...	...	...	...
Mangalore	CDFC	398 745	200 234	198 511	75	538 560	269 176	269 384	155
Mango	CDFC	166 091	87 322	78 769	...	...	...	...	...
Mathura	CDFC	298 827	159 249	139 578	9	319 235	171 516	147 719	22
Maunath Bhanjan	CDFC	210 071	108 696	101 375	9	...	...	...	...
Medinipur	CDFC	153 349	78 365	74 984	15	...	...	...	...
Meerut	CDFC	1 074 229	571 074	503 155	142	1 167 399	624 904	542 495	178
Mira-Bhayandar	CDFC	520 301	286 458	233 843	...	...	...	...	...
Mirzapur-cum-Vindhyachal	CDFC	205 264	109 872	95 392	39	...	...	...	...
Modinagar	CDFC	112 918	60 260	52 658	10	139 642	74 570	65 072	17
Moga	CDFC	124 624	66 843	57 781	...	134 242	71 996	62 246	...
Moradabad	CDFC	641 240	340 217	301 023	34	...	...	...	...
Morena	CDFC	150 890	82 281	68 609	96	...	...	...	...
Mormugoa	CDFC	...	...	...	...	104 689	55 927	48 762	...
Motihari	CDFC	101 506	54 629	46 877	...	109 250	59 517	49 733	...
Mughalsarai	CDFC	...	...	...	...	116 246	61 572	54 674	...
Mumbai (Bombay)	CDFC	11 914 398	6 577 902	5 336 496	466	16 368 084	8 979 172	7 388 912	1 041
Munger	CDFC	187 311	100 374	86 937	18	...	...	...	...
Murwara (Katni)	CDFC	186 738	97 666	89 072	107	...	...	...	...
Muzaffarnagar	CDFC	316 452	166 998	149 454	...	331 403	174 877	156 526	12
Muzaffarpur	CDFC	305 465	163 907	141 558	26	...	...	...	...
Mysore	CDFC	742 261	377 132	365 129	103	785 800	399 904	385 896	129
Nabadwip	CDFC	115 036	58 268	56 768	...	125 346	63 544	61 802	...
Nadiad	CDFC	192 799	100 452	92 347	...	196 679	102 469	94 210	...
Nagaon	CDFC	107 471	56 888	50 583	...	123 054	64 976	58 078	...
Nagercoil	CDFC	208 149	103 075	105 074	24	...	...	...	...
Nagpur	CDFC	2 051 320	1 058 692	992 628	217	2 122 965	1 097 723	1 025 242	229
Naihati	CDFC	215 432	113 706	101 726	4	...	...	...	...
Nala Sopara	CDFC	184 664	99 629	85 035	...	...	...	...	...
Nalgonda	CDFC	110 651	56 495	54 156	...	111 745	57 042	54 703	...
Nanded	CDFC	430 598	224 766	205 832	21	...	...	...	...
Nandyal	CDFC	151 771	76 914	74 857	15	156 216	79 145	77 071	...
Nangloi Jat	CDFC	150 371	82 358	68 013	...	...	...	...	...
Nashik	CDFC	1 076 967	579 638	497 329	259	1 152 048	619 962	532 086	322
Navghar-Manikpur	CDFC	116 700	61 806	54 894	...	...	...	...	...
Navi Mumbai (New Bombay)	CDFC	703 947	395 891	308 056	...	...	...	...	...
Navsari	CDFC	134 009	69 766	64 243	...	229 323	122 335	106 988	...
Neemuch	CDFC	107 496	56 509	50 987	...	112 691	59 250	53 441	...
Nellore	CDFC	378 947	191 283	187 664	48	404 922	204 269	200 653	...
NEW DELHI[55,56]	CDFC	294 783	161 596	133 187	...	...	...	...	...
Neyveli	CDFC	128 133	65 632	62 501	97	138 387	70 920	67 467	116
Nizamabad	CDFC	286 956	145 457	141 499	37	...	...	...	...
Noida	CDFC	293 908	162 306	131 602	90	...	...	...	...
North Barrackpur	CDFC	123 523	63 827	59 696	...	...	...	...	...
North Dumdum	CDFC	220 032	112 868	107 164	...	...	...	...	...
Ongole	CDFC	149 589	76 134	73 455	8	152 945	77 862	75 083	20
Orai	CDFC	139 444	74 974	64 470	...	...	...	...	...
Ozhukarai	CDFC	217 623	110 038	107 585	...	...	...	...	...
Palakkad	CDFC	130 736	64 293	66 443	30	197 281	96 790	100 491	59
Palanpur	CDFC	110 383	58 019	52 364	...	122 279	64 343	57 936	...

8. Population of capital cities and cities of 100 000 and more inhabitants: latest available year
Population des capitales et des villes de 100 000 habitants et plus: dernière année disponible (continued — suite)

(See notes at end of table. — Voir notes à la fin du tableau.)

Continent, country or area, date and city / Continent, pays ou zone, date et ville	Code[1]	City proper — Ville proprement dite Population				Urban agglomeration — Agglomération urbaine Population			
		Both sexes Les deux sexes	Male Masculin	Female Féminin	Surface area Superficie (km²)	Both sexes Les deux sexes	Male Masculin	Female Féminin	Surface area Superficie (km²)
ASIA — ASIE									
India — Inde[52]									
1 III 2001									
Pali	CDFC	187 571	99 258	88 313	84	...	...	...	...
Pallavaram	CDFC	143 984	73 152	70 832	...	...	...	...	...
Palwal	CDFC	100 528	53 577	46 951	...	...	...	...	...
Panchkula Urban Estate	CDFC	140 992	75 925	65 067	...	...	...	...	...
Panihati	CDFC	348 379	180 068	168 311	19	...	...	...	...
Panipat	CDFC	261 665	143 565	118 100	21	353 983	194 697	159 286	...
Panvel	CDFC	104 031	54 967	49 064	...	...	...	...	...
Parbhani	CDFC	259 170	133 892	125 278	58	...	...	...	...
Patan	CDFC	112 038	59 031	53 007	...	113 568	59 889	53 679	...
Pathankot	CDFC	159 559	87 505	72 054	...	168 275	91 998	76 277	...
Patiala	CDFC	302 870	162 465	140 405	...	323 309	173 412	149 897	...
Patna	CDFC	1 376 950	749 868	627 082	107	1 707 429	925 857	781 572	129
Phagwara	CDFC	...	...	...	...	102 111	55 224	46 887	...
Phusro	CDFC	...	...	...	...	174 367	93 656	80 711	84
Pilibhit	CDFC	124 082	65 824	58 258	10	...	...	...	...
Pimpri Chinchwad	CDFC	1 006 417	543 436	462 981	...	...	...	...	...
Pollachi	CDFC	...	...	...	...	127 993	64 417	63 576	43
Pondicherry	CDFC	220 749	109 386	111 363	20	505 715	253 336	252 379	67
Porbandar	CDFC	133 083	68 261	64 822	...	197 414	101 882	95 532	...
Port Blair	CDFC	100 186	55 507	44 679	...	...	...	...	...
Proddatur	CDFC	164 932	82 826	82 106	7	...	...	...	...
Pudukkottai	CDFC	108 947	54 537	54 410	...	...	...	...	...
Pune	CDFC	2 540 069	1 325 694	1 214 375	146	3 755 525	1 980 941	1 774 584	423
Puri	CDFC	157 610	82 229	75 381	17	...	...	...	...
Purnia	CDFC	171 235	92 573	78 662	45	196 757	106 051	90 706	60
Puruliya	CDFC	113 766	59 171	54 595	...	...	...	...	...
Quthbullapur	CDFC	225 816	118 463	107 353	...	...	...	...	...
Rae Bareli	CDFC	169 285	88 961	80 324	50	...	...	...	...
Raichur	CDFC	205 634	105 714	99 920	...	...	...	...	...
Raiganj	CDFC	165 222	87 489	77 733	11	175 064	92 742	82 322	15
Raigarh	CDFC	110 987	57 465	53 522	...	115 740	59 916	55 824	...
Raipur	CDFC	605 131	314 369	290 762	...	699 264	364 034	335 230	64
Rajahmundry	CDFC	313 347	158 027	155 320	52	408 341	205 655	202 686	64
Rajapalayam	CDFC	121 982	61 080	60 902	11	...	...	...	...
Rajarhat Gopalpur	CDFC	271 781	140 179	131 602	...	...	...	...	...
Rajkot	CDFC	966 642	506 915	459 727	...	1 002 160	525 797	476 363	...
Rajnandgaon	CDFC	143 727	72 964	70 763	93	...	...	...	...
Rajpur Sonarpur	CDFC	336 390	173 591	162 799	...	...	...	...	...
Ramagundam	CDFC	235 540	120 307	115 233	28	236 623	120 871	115 752	...
Rampur	CDFC	281 549	146 621	134 928	20	...	...	...	...
Ranaghat	CDFC	...	...	...	...	145 172	73 804	71 368	25
Ranchi	CDFC	846 454	450 514	395 940	177	862 850	459 251	403 599	182
Raniganj	CDFC	122 891	65 360	57 531	...	...	...	...	...
Ratlam	CDFC	221 267	113 982	107 285	39	233 480	120 473	113 007	41
Raurkela	CDFC	224 601	121 028	103 573	133	484 292	258 466	225 826	157
Rewa	CDFC	183 232	98 476	84 756	55	...	...	...	...
Rewari	CDFC	100 946	54 111	46 835	...	...	...	...	...
Rishra	CDFC	113 259	62 602	50 657	...	...	...	...	...
Robertson Pet	CDFC	141 294	70 568	70 726	...	156 961	78 574	78 387	...
Rohtak	CDFC	286 773	154 153	132 620	28	294 537	158 299	136 238	...
Roorkee	CDFC	...	...	...	...	114 811	63 861	50 950	...
S.A.S. Nagar (Mohali)	CDFC	123 284	65 570	57 714	...	...	...	...	...
Sagar	CDFC	232 321	122 491	109 830	36	309 164	163 018	146 146	52
Saharanpur	CDFC	452 925	239 456	213 469	25	...	...	...	...
Saharsa	CDFC	124 015	67 010	57 005	...	...	...	...	...
Salem	CDFC	693 236	352 770	340 466	20	748 513	381 042	367 471	93
Sambalpur	CDFC	154 164	79 914	74 250	50	226 966	117 954	109 012	90
Sambhal	CDFC	182 930	97 264	85 666	16	...	...	...	...
Sangli-Miraj-Kupwad	CDFC	436 639	224 195	212 444	...	447 632	229 852	217 780	...

(See notes at end of table. — Voir notes à la fin du tableau.)

Continent, country or area, date and city / Continent, pays ou zone, date et ville	Code[1]	City proper — Ville proprement dite Population				Urban agglomeration — Agglomération urbaine Population			
		Both sexes Les deux sexes	Male Masculin	Female Féminin	Surface area Superficie (km²)	Both sexes Les deux sexes	Male Masculin	Female Féminin	Surface area Superficie (km²)

ASIA — ASIE

India — Inde[52]
1 III 2001

Santipur	CDFC	138 195	70 084	68 111	25	...	...	...	...
Sasaram	CDFC	131 042	69 665	61 377	...	...	...	...	...
Satara	CDFC	108 043	55 935	52 108	...	...	...	...	...
Satna	CDFC	225 468	120 203	105 265	...	229 323	122 335	106 988	...
Sawai Madhopur	CDFC	...	...	...	...	101 994	53 942	48 052	...
Secunderabad	CDFC	204 182	103 274	100 908	...	...	...	...	...
Serampore	CDFC	197 955	105 613	92 342	6	...	...	...	...
Serilingampalle	CDFC	150 525	75 462	75 063	...	...	...	...	...
Shahjahanpur	CDFC	297 932	162 796	135 136	13	323 166	176 910	146 256	23
Shillong	CDFC	132 876	66 129	66 747	10	267 881	134 416	133 465	25
Shimla	CDFC	142 161	80 772	61 389	32	144 578	82 424	62 154	35
Shimoga	CDFC	274 105	140 107	133 998	...	...	...	...	...
Shivapuri	CDFC	146 859	78 395	68 464	81	...	...	...	...
Sikar	CDFC	184 904	96 327	88 577	23	185 506	96 646	88 860	...
Silchar	CDFC	142 393	72 727	69 666	16	184 285	94 321	89 964	...
Siliguri	CDFC	470 275	249 942	220 333	16	...	...	...	...
Singrauli	CDFC	185 580	100 342	85 238	...	...	...	...	...
Sirsa	CDFC	160 129	85 802	74 327	19	...	...	...	...
Sitapur	CDFC	151 827	79 682	72 145	26	...	...	...	...
Sivakasi	CDFC	...	...	...	...	121 312	60 923	60 389	13
Siwan	CDFC	108 172	57 223	50 949	...	...	...	...	...
Solapur	CDFC	873 037	444 885	428 152	...	...	...	...	...
Sonipat	CDFC	216 213	117 654	98 559	28	225 151	122 488	102 663	...
South Dum Dum	CDFC	392 150	200 182	191 968	11	...	...	...	...
Srikakulam	CDFC	109 666	54 788	54 878	...	117 066	58 613	58 453	...
Srinagar	CDFC	894 940	481 750	413 190	...	971 357	523 017	448 340	...
Sultan Pur Majra	CDFC	163 716	88 313	75 403	...	...	...	...	...
Sultanpur	CDFC	100 085	53 163	46 922	...	...	...	...	...
Surat	CDFC	2 433 787	1 372 307	1 061 480	...	2 811 466	1 597 093	1 214 373	...
Surendranagar Dudhrej	CDFC	156 417	81 430	74 987	...	...	...	...	...
Tadepalligudem	CDFC	102 303	50 476	51 827	...	...	...	...	...
Tambaram	CDFC	137 609	70 181	67 428	...	...	...	...	...
Tenali	CDFC	149 839	74 868	74 971	15	...	...	...	...
Thane	CDFC	1 261 517	674 660	586 857	144	...	...	...	...
Thanesar	CDFC	120 072	65 786	54 286	...	122 704	67 239	55 465	...
Thanjavur	CDFC	215 725	106 950	108 775	15	...	...	...	...
Thiruvananthapuram	CDFC	744 739	365 899	378 840	142	889 191	437 009	452 182	178
Thoothukkudi (Tuticorin)	CDFC	216 058	107 781	108 277	13	242 860	121 205	121 655	140
Thrissur	CDFC	317 474	154 188	163 286	...	330 067	160 386	169 681	88
Tinsukia	CDFC	...	...	...	...	108 102	59 515	48 587	...
Tiruchchirappalli	CDFC	746 062	373 541	372 521	23	847 131	424 541	422 590	166
Tirunelveli	CDFC	411 298	203 173	208 125	15	431 603	213 399	218 204	87
Tirupati	CDFC	227 657	117 786	109 871	16	302 678	154 845	147 833	20
Tiruppur	CDFC	346 551	180 629	165 922	44	542 787	282 872	259 915	91
Tiruvannamalai	CDFC	130 301	66 026	64 275	14	...	...	...	...
Tiruvottiyur	CDFC	211 768	108 938	102 830	...	...	...	...	...
Titagarh	CDFC	124 198	70 608	53 590	3	...	...	...	...
Tonk	CDFC	135 663	70 135	65 528	...	...	...	...	...
Tumkur	CDFC	248 592	129 215	119 377	...	...	...	...	...
Udaipur	CDFC	389 317	205 319	183 998	64	...	...	...	...
Udupi	CDFC	113 039	55 933	57 106	...	127 060	62 644	64 416	73
Ujjain	CDFC	429 933	223 745	206 188	...	430 669	224 223	206 446	92
Ulhasnagar	CDFC	472 943	251 610	221 333	22	...	...	...	...
Uluberia	CDFC	202 095	105 735	96 360	...	...	...	...	...
Unnao	CDFC	144 917	76 474	68 443	16	...	...	...	...
Uppal Kalan	CDFC	118 259	61 299	56 960	...	...	...	...	...
Uttarpara Kotrung	CDFC	150 204	78 661	71 543	...	...	...	...	...
Vadakara	CDFC	...	...	...	...	123 965	59 743	64 222	39
Vadodara	CDFC	1 306 035	684 130	621 905	...	1 492 398	783 237	709 161	...

(See notes at end of table. — Voir notes à la fin du tableau.)

Continent, country or area, date and city / Continent, pays ou zone, date et ville	Code[1]	City proper — Ville proprement dite Population				Urban agglomeration — Agglomération urbaine Population			
		Both sexes Les deux sexes	Male Masculin	Female Féminin	Surface area Superficie (km²)	Both sexes Les deux sexes	Male Masculin	Female Féminin	Surface area Superficie (km²)
ASIA — ASIE									
India — Inde[52]									
1 III 2001									
Valsad	CDFC	...	...	...	...	145 650	75 322	70 328	...
Vaniyambadi	CDFC	...	...	...	...	103 841	51 668	52 173	...
Varanasi	CDFC	1 100 748	584 514	516 234	83	1 211 749	644 922	566 827	105
Vasai	CDFC	...	...	...	...	174 382	91 121	83 261	...
Vejalpur	CDFC	113 304	58 828	54 476	...	...	...	...	...
Vellore	CDFC	177 413	88 048	89 365	12	388 211	193 779	194 432	62
Veraval	CDFC	141 207	72 074	69 133	...	157 869	80 813	77 056	...
Vidisha	CDFC	125 457	66 579	58 878	...	...	...	...	...
Vijayawada	CDFC	825 436	436 366	389 070	...	1 011 152	531 084	480 068	105
Virar	CDFC	118 945	63 762	55 183	...	...	...	...	...
Visakhapatnam	CDFC	969 608	489 038	480 570	78	1 329 472	674 080	655 392	318
Vizianagarm	CDFC	174 324	86 111	88 213	21	195 462	96 771	98 691	30
Wadhwan	CDFC	...	...	...	...	219 828	114 217	105 611	...
Warangal	CDFC	528 570	267 820	260 750	57	577 190	292 709	284 481	67
Wardha	CDFC	111 070	57 447	53 623	8	...	...	...	...
Yamunanagar	CDFC	189 587	101 888	87 699	16	306 640	166 324	140 316	42
Yavatmal	CDFC	122 906	62 838	60 068	10	141 970	72 883	69 087	13
Indonesia — Indonésie									
1 VII 2003									
Ambon	ESDF	224 160	...	...	359	...	...	...	...
Balikpapan	ESDF	429 568	...	...	503	...	...	...	...
Banda Aceh	ESDF	269 943	...	...	61	...	...	...	...
Bandar Lampung	ESDF	789 755	...	...	193	...	...	...	...
Bandjarmasin	ESDF	567 345	...	...	72	...	...	...	...
Bandung	ESDF	2 231 139	...	...	1 670	...	...	...	...
Batam	ESDF	547 550	...	...	969	...	...	...	...
Bengkulu	ESDF	254 693	...	...	145	...	...	...	...
Binjai	ESDF	226 468	...	...	9	...	...	...	...
Bitung	ESDF	163 074	...	...	304	...	...	...	...
Blitar	ESDF	123 327	...	...	33	...	...	...	...
Bogor	ESDF	816 911	...	...	119	...	...	...	...
Cirebon	ESDF	273 311	...	...	37	...	...	...	...
Denpasar	ESDF	502 873	...	...	124	...	...	...	...
Gorontalo	ESDF	145 828	...	...	65	...	...	...	...
JAKARTA	ESDF	8 640 184	...	...	740	...	...	...	...
Jambi	ESDF	444 551	...	...	205	...	...	...	...
Jayapura	ESDF	192 961	...	...	740	...	...	...	...
Kediri	ESDF	252 126	...	...	63	...	...	...	...
Madiun	ESDF	170 408	...	...	34	...	...	...	...
Magelang	ESDF	121 079	...	...	18	...	...	...	...
Makasar (Ujung Pandang)	ESDF	1 151 245	...	...	199	...	...	...	...
Malang	ESDF	770 483	...	...	145	...	...	...	...
Manado	ESDF	412 425	...	...	157	...	...	...	...
Mataram	ESDF	341 770	...	...	61	...	...	...	...
Medan	ESDF	1 983 659	...	...	265	...	...	...	...
Mojokerto	ESDF	112 137	...	...	16	...	...	...	...
Padang	ESDF	770 451	...	...	694	...	...	...	...
Pekalongan	ESDF	272 208	...	...	45	...	...	...	...
Pakanbaru	ESDF	672 480	...	...	632	...	...	...	...
Palangkaraya	ESDF	166 017	...	...	2 400	...	...	...	...
Palembang	ESDF	1 290 599	...	...	369	...	...	...	...
Pangkal Pinang	ESDF	158 163	...	...	89	...	...	...	...
Pare Pare	ESDF	113 290	...	...	99	...	...	...	...
Pasuruan	ESDF	176 987	...	...	35	...	...	...	...
Pematang Siantar	ESDF	224 446	...	...	80	...	...	...	...
Pontianak	ESDF	483 224	...	...	108	...	...	...	...
Probolinggo	ESDF	200 465	...	...	57	...	...	...	...
Salatiga	ESDF	160 592	...	...	57	...	...	...	...
Samarinda	ESDF	563 570	...	...	781	...	...	...	...

8. Population of capital cities and cities of 100 000 and more inhabitants: latest available year
Population des capitales et des villes de 100 000 habitants et plus: dernière année disponible (continued — suite)

(See notes at end of table. — Voir notes à la fin du tableau.)

Continent, country or area, date and city / Continent, pays ou zone, date et ville	Code[1]	City proper — Ville proprement dite Population				Urban agglomeration — Agglomération urbaine Population			
		Both sexes Les deux sexes	Male Masculin	Female Féminin	Surface area Superficie (km²)	Both sexes Les deux sexes	Male Masculin	Female Féminin	Surface area Superficie (km²)
ASIA — ASIE									
Indonesia — Indonésie									
1 VII 2003									
Semarang	ESDF	1 396 059	...	...	374	...	...	...	...
Sukabumi	ESDF	269 987	...	...	48	...	...	...	...
Surabaya	ESDF	2 689 728	...	...	351	...	...	...	...
Surakarta	ESDF	492 325	...	...	44	...	...	...	...
Tangerang	ESDF	1 471 396	...	...	187	...	...	...	...
Tanjung Balai	ESDF	145 572	...	...	68	...	...	...	...
Tebing Tinggi	ESDF	132 982	...	...	32	...	...	...	...
Tegal	ESDF	242 423	...	...	35	...	...	...	...
Yogyakarta	ESDF	392 239	...	...	33	...	...	...	...
Iran (Islamic Republic of) — Iran (République islamique d')									
1 VII 2003									
Abadan	ESDJ	277 998	...	...	...	...	...	...	...
Ahwaz	ESDJ	949 054	...	...	...	...	...	...	...
Amol	ESDJ	195 588	...	...	...	...	...	...	...
Andimeshk	ESDJ	133 932	...	...	...	...	...	...	...
Arak	ESDJ	476 568	...	...	...	...	...	...	...
Ardabil	ESDJ	390 682	...	...	...	...	...	...	...
Babol	ESDJ	196 569	...	...	...	...	...	...	...
Bandar-e-Abbas	ESDJ	315 075	...	...	...	...	...	...	...
Birjand	ESDJ	186 893	...	...	...	...	...	...	...
Bojnurd	ESDJ	182 465	...	...	...	...	...	...	...
Borujerd	ESDJ	244 205	...	...	...	...	...	...	...
Bukand	ESDJ	173 005	...	...	...	...	...	...	...
Bushehr	ESDJ	150 411	...	...	...	...	...	...	...
Dezful	ESDJ	241 544	...	...	...	...	...	...	...
Esfahan	ESDJ	1 523 006	...	...	...	...	...	...	...
Gonbad-e-Kavus	ESDJ	125 215	...	...	...	...	...	...	...
Gorgan	ESDJ	241 085	...	...	...	...	...	...	...
Hamadan	ESDJ	494 378	...	...	...	...	...	...	...
Ilam	ESDJ	141 915	...	...	...	...	...	...	...
Islam Shahr (Qasemabad)	ESDJ	273 520	...	...	...	...	...	...	...
Karaj	ESDJ	1 212 220	...	...	...	...	...	...	...
Kashan	ESDJ	244 877	...	...	...	...	...	...	...
Kerman	ESDJ	529 748	...	...	...	...	...	...	...
Kermanshah	ESDJ	816 428	...	...	...	...	...	...	...
Khomeini shahr	ESDJ	181 110	...	...	...	...	...	...	...
Khoramabad	ESDJ	313 177	...	...	...	...	...	...	...
Khoramshahr	ESDJ	142 506	...	...	...	...	...	...	...
Khoy	ESDJ	166 974	...	...	...	...	...	...	...
Mahabad	ESDJ	137 173	...	...	...	...	...	...	...
Malayer	ESDJ	169 060	...	...	...	...	...	...	...
Marvadsht	ESDJ	125 072	...	...	...	...	...	...	...
Maraqeh	ESDJ	155 350	...	...	...	...	...	...	...
Mashhad	ESDJ	2 070 604	...	...	...	...	...	...	...
Masjed Soleyman	ESDJ	132 496	...	...	...	...	...	...	...
Najafabad	ESDJ	204 637	...	...	...	...	...	...	...
Neyshabur	ESDJ	205 842	...	...	...	...	...	...	...
Orumiyeh	ESDJ	601 478	...	...	...	...	...	...	...
Qaem shahr	ESDJ	168 359	...	...	...	...	...	...	...
Qazvin	ESDJ	306 984	...	...	...	...	...	...	...
Qarchak	ESDJ	165 462	...	...	...	...	...	...	...
Qods	ESDJ	236 463	...	...	...	...	...	...	...
Qom	ESDJ	986 922	...	...	...	...	...	...	...
Rasht	ESDJ	519 481	...	...	...	...	...	...	...
Sabzewar	ESDJ	215 278	...	...	...	...	...	...	...
Sanandaj	ESDJ	327 969	...	...	...	...	...	...	...
Saqez	ESDJ	148 445	...	...	...	...	...	...	...
Sari	ESDJ	253 052	...	...	...	...	...	...	...

(See notes at end of table. — Voir notes à la fin du tableau.)

Continent, country or area, date and city / Continent, pays ou zone, date et ville	Code[1]	City proper — Ville proprement dite Population				Urban agglomeration — Agglomération urbaine Population			
		Both sexes Les deux sexes	Male Masculin	Female Féminin	Surface area Superficie (km²)	Both sexes Les deux sexes	Male Masculin	Female Féminin	Surface area Superficie (km²)
ASIA — ASIE									
Iran (Islamic Republic of) — Iran (République islamique d')									
1 VII 2003									
Shahr Kord	ESDJ	121 337	...	...	...	...	...	...	...
Shahrud	ESDJ	128 642	...	...	...	...	...	...	...
Shiraz	ESDJ	1 197 847	...	...	...	...	...	...	...
Sirjan	ESDJ	197 303	...	...	...	...	...	...	...
Tabriz	ESDJ	1 365 476	...	...	...	...	...	...	...
TEHRAN	CODJ	7 188 938	...	...	...	...	...	...	...
Varamin	ESDJ	187 178	...	...	...	...	...	...	...
Yazd	ESDJ	432 233	...	...	...	...	...	...	...
Zabol	ESDJ	118 424	...	...	...	...	...	...	...
Zahedan	ESDJ	534 771	...	...	...	...	...	...	...
Zanjan	ESDJ	346 253	...	...	...	...	...	...	...
Iraq									
1 VII 1987									
Adhamiyah	CDFC	464 151	...	...	...	...	...	...	...
Amara	CDFC	208 797	...	...	...	...	...	...	...
BAGHDAD[57]	CDFC	3 841 268	...	...	...	...	...	...	...
Basra	CDFC	406 296	...	...	...	...	...	...	...
Diwaniya	CDFC	196 519	...	...	...	...	...	...	...
Erbil	CDFC	485 968	...	...	...	...	...	...	...
Hilla	CDFC	268 834	...	...	...	...	...	...	...
Kadhimain	CDFC	521 444	...	...	...	...	...	...	...
Karradah Sharqiyah	CDFC	235 554	...	...	...	...	...	...	...
Kerbala	CDFC	296 705	...	...	...	...	...	...	...
Kirkuk	CDFC	418 624	...	...	...	...	...	...	...
Kut	CDFC	183 183	...	...	...	...	...	...	...
Majnoon	CDFC	244 545	...	...	...	...	...	...	...
Mosul	CDFC	664 221	...	...	...	...	...	...	...
Najaf	CDFC	309 010	...	...	...	...	...	...	...
Nasariya	CDFC	265 937	...	...	...	...	...	...	...
Ramadi	CDFC	192 556	...	...	...	...	...	...	...
Sulamaniya	CDFC	364 096	...	...	...	...	...	...	...
Israel — Israël									
1 VII 2003									
Ashdod	ESDJ	189 800	93 000	96 800	47	...	...	...	...
Ashqelon	ESDJ	103 900	50 600	53 200	48	...	...	...	...
Bat Yam	ESDJ	132 900	63 000	69 900	8	...	...	...	...
Be'er Sheva	ESDJ	182 200	88 700	93 600	53	...	...	...	...
Bene Beraq	ESDJ	139 300	69 500	69 700	7	...	...	...	...
Haifa	ESDJ	270 100	129 600	140 500	64	...	...	...	...
Holon	ESDJ	165 800	79 800	86 000	19	...	...	...	...
JERUSALEM[58,59]	ESDJ	686 800	341 200	345 600	125	...	...	...	...
Netanya	ESDJ	165 900	79 900	86 000	29	...	...	...	...
Petah Tiqwa	ESDJ	173 200	83 800	89 400	36	...	...	...	...
Ramat Gan	ESDJ	126 600	59 400	67 100	13	...	...	...	...
Rishon Leziyyon	ESDJ	213 100	103 800	109 300	59	...	...	...	...
Tel Aviv-Yafo	ESDJ	361 900	172 900	189 000	52	...	...	...	...
Japan — Japon[60,61,62]									
1 VII 2003									
Abiko	ESDF	129 628	64 424	65 204	43	...	...	...	...
Ageo	ESDF	217 131	108 678	108 453	46	...	...	...	...
Aizuwakamatsu	ESDF	116 835	55 702	61 133	315	...	...	...	...
Akashi	ESDF	291 743	142 174	149 569	49	...	...	...	...
Akishima	ESDF	109 596	55 309	54 287	17	...	...	...	...
Akita	ESDF	318 068	151 569	166 499	460	...	...	...	...
Amagasaki	ESDF	462 890	225 836	237 054	50	...	...	...	...
Anjo	ESDF	164 305	83 331	80 974	86	...	...	...	...
Aomori	ESDF	296 208	139 503	156 705	692	...	...	...	...
Asahikawa	ESDF	362 496	171 333	191 163	748	...	...	...	...

8. Population of capital cities and cities of 100 000 and more inhabitants: latest available year
Population des capitales et des villes de 100 000 habitants et plus: dernière année disponible (continued — suite)

(See notes at end of table. — Voir notes à la fin du tableau.)

Continent, country or area, date and city / Continent, pays ou zone, date et ville	Code[1]	City proper — Ville proprement dite Population				Urban agglomeration — Agglomération urbaine Population			
		Both sexes Les deux sexes	Male Masculin	Female Féminin	Surface area Superficie (km²)	Both sexes Les deux sexes	Male Masculin	Female Féminin	Surface area Superficie (km²)
ASIA — ASIE									
Japan — Japon[60,61,62]									
1 VII 2003									
Asaka	ESDF	124 633	65 173	59 460	18	...	...	...	...
Ashikaga	ESDF	161 105	78 878	82 227	178	...	...	...	...
Atsugi	ESDF	221 038	115 092	105 946	94	...	...	...	...
Beppu	ESDF	126 804	57 180	69 624	125	...	...	...	...
Chiba	ESDF	910 550	457 874	452 676	272	...	...	...	...
Chigasaki	ESDF	225 657	111 445	114 212	36	...	...	...	...
Chofu	ESDF	210 700	106 567	104 133	22	...	...	...	...
Daito	ESDF	128 934	64 544	64 390	18	...	...	...	...
Ebetsu	ESDF	123 749	59 814	63 935	188	...	...	...	...
Ebina	ESDF	120 458	61 355	59 103	26	...	...	...	...
Fuchu	ESDF	236 679	123 896	112 783	29	...	...	...	...
Fuji	ESDF	236 896	117 614	119 282	214	...	...	...	...
Fujieda	ESDF	129 266	63 264	66 002	141	...	...	...	...
Fujimi	ESDF	104 967	52 746	52 221	20	...	...	...	...
Fujinomiya	ESDF	122 069	60 127	61 942	315	...	...	...	...
Fujisawa	ESDF	389 813	195 598	194 215	70	...	...	...	...
Fukaya	ESDF	103 698	51 791	51 907	69	...	...	...	...
Fukui	ESDF	252 250	122 949	129 301	341	...	...	...	...
Fukuoka	ESDF	1 378 400	663 414	714 986	339	...	...	...	...
Fukushima	ESDF	290 879	140 563	150 316	746	...	...	...	...
Fukuyama	ESDF	405 759	196 297	209 462	364	...	...	...	...
Funabashi	ESDF	564 264	286 672	277 592	86	...	...	...	...
Gifu	ESDF	404 390	191 560	212 830	195	...	...	...	...
Habikino	ESDF	119 890	57 389	62 501	26	...	...	...	...
Hachinohe	ESDF	241 652	116 513	125 139	214	...	...	...	...
Hachioji	ESDF	546 559	278 317	268 242	186	...	...	...	...
Hadano	ESDF	168 252	86 866	81 386	104	...	...	...	...
Hakodate	ESDF	284 651	131 128	153 523	347	...	...	...	...
Hamamatsu	ESDF	594 146	295 973	298 173	257	...	...	...	...
Handa	ESDF	113 037	55 982	57 055	47	...	...	...	...
Higashihiroshima	ESDF	128 172	65 773	62 399	288	...	...	...	...
Higashikurume	ESDF	113 779	56 469	57 310	13	...	...	...	...
Higashimurayama	ESDF	144 137	71 337	72 800	17	...	...	...	...
Higashiosaka	ESDF	513 185	252 419	260 766	62	...	...	...	...
Hikone	ESDF	108 664	53 533	55 131	98	...	...	...	...
Himeji	ESDF	480 619	231 444	249 175	276	...	...	...	...
Hino	ESDF	171 591	88 407	83 184	28	...	...	...	...
Hirakata	ESDF	404 895	195 846	209 049	65	...	...	...	...
Hiratsuka	ESDF	255 924	129 771	126 153	68	...	...	...	...
Hirosaki	ESDF	174 649	80 266	94 383	274	...	...	...	...
Hiroshima	ESDF	1 137 610	551 830	585 780	742	...	...	...	...
Hitachi	ESDF	190 495	95 363	95 132	153	...	...	...	...
Hitachinaka	ESDF	152 595	76 851	75 744	99	...	...	...	...
Hofu	ESDF	118 561	57 281	61 280	189	...	...	...	...
Ibaraki	ESDF	262 779	129 514	133 265	77	...	...	...	...
Ichihara	ESDF	279 642	143 659	135 983	368	...	...	...	...
Ichikawa	ESDF	462 959	239 192	223 767	57	...	...	...	...
Ichinomiya	ESDF	277 628	135 799	141 829	82	...	...	...	...
Iida	ESDF	107 006	51 029	55 977	325	...	...	...	...
Ikeda	ESDF	100 949	49 391	51 558	22	...	...	...	...
Ikoma	ESDF	112 905	53 835	59 070	53	...	...	...	...
Imabari	ESDF	117 388	54 404	62 984	75	...	...	...	...
Inazawa	ESDF	101 136	50 439	50 697	48	...	...	...	...
Iruma	ESDF	150 302	74 719	75 583	45	...	...	...	...
Isehara	ESDF	100 225	51 331	48 894	56	...	...	...	...
Isesaki	ESDF	129 331	64 521	64 810	65	...	...	...	...
Ishinomaki	ESDF	118 228	57 159	61 069	137	...	...	...	...
Itami	ESDF	192 388	94 951	97 437	25	...	...	...	...
Iwaki	ESDF	357 575	174 229	183 346	1 231	...	...	...	...

(See notes at end of table. — Voir notes à la fin du tableau.)

Continent, country or area, date and city / Continent, pays ou zone, date et ville	Code[1]	City proper — Ville proprement dite Population				Urban agglomeration — Agglomération urbaine Population			
		Both sexes Les deux sexes	Male Masculin	Female Féminin	Surface area Superficie (km²)	Both sexes Les deux sexes	Male Masculin	Female Féminin	Surface area Superficie (km²)
ASIA — ASIE									
Japan — Japon[60,61,62]									
1 VII 2003									
Iwakuni	ESDF	104 595	49 795	54 800	221	...	...	...	...
Iwatsuki	ESDF	109 696	55 067	54 629	49	...	...	...	...
Izumi (Osaka)	ESDF	176 280	85 771	90 509	85	...	...	...	...
Joetsu	ESDF	134 940	65 772	69 168	249	...	...	...	...
Kadoma	ESDF	133 957	66 647	67 310	12	...	...	...	...
Kagoshima	ESDF	554 472	258 803	295 669	290	...	...	...	...
Kakamigahara	ESDF	133 418	65 456	67 962	80	...	...	...	...
Kakogawa	ESDF	266 392	130 342	136 050	139	...	...	...	...
Kamagaya	ESDF	102 924	51 138	51 786	21	...	...	...	...
Kamakura	ESDF	168 227	80 448	87 779	40	...	...	...	...
Kanazawa	ESDF	456 842	222 454	234 388	468	...	...	...	...
Kariya	ESDF	137 145	71 612	65 533	50	...	...	...	...
Kashihara	ESDF	125 601	60 380	65 221	40	...	...	...	...
Kashiwa	ESDF	332 781	166 345	166 436	73	...	...	...	...
Kasuga	ESDF	108 140	53 144	54 996	14	...	...	...	...
Kasugai	ESDF	293 809	146 968	146 841	93	...	...	...	...
Kasukabe	ESDF	204 102	101 792	102 310	38	...	...	...	...
Kawachinagano	ESDF	119 579	56 887	62 692	110	...	...	...	...
Kawagoe	ESDF	333 784	168 885	164 899	109	...	...	...	...
Kawaguchi	ESDF	474 740	242 537	232 203	56	...	...	...	...
Kawanishi	ESDF	156 687	74 734	81 953	53	...	...	...	...
Kawasaki	ESDF	1 292 705	670 118	622 587	143	...	...	...	...
Kiryu	ESDF	112 586	54 439	58 147	137	...	...	...	...
Kisarazu	ESDF	122 641	61 308	61 333	139	...	...	...	...
Kishiwada	ESDF	202 078	97 604	104 474	72	...	...	...	...
Kitakyushu[63]	ESDF	1 003 860	473 936	529 924	485	...	...	...	...
Kitami	ESDF	111 473	54 001	57 472	421	...	...	...	...
Kobe	ESDF	1 514 833	721 052	793 781	550	...	...	...	...
Kochi	ESDF	332 568	155 396	177 172	145	...	...	...	...
Kodaira	ESDF	182 664	91 411	91 253	20	...	...	...	...
Kofu	ESDF	194 603	95 750	98 853	172	...	...	...	...
Koganei	ESDF	113 931	57 722	56 209	11	...	...	...	...
Kokubunji	ESDF	115 346	58 121	57 225	11	...	...	...	...
Komaki	ESDF	146 111	74 056	72 055	63	...	...	...	...
Komatsu	ESDF	108 730	52 635	56 095	371	...	...	...	...
Koriyama	ESDF	337 804	167 282	170 522	757	...	...	...	...
Koshigaya	ESDF	314 423	157 849	156 574	60	...	...	...	...
Kumagaya	ESDF	156 364	78 555	77 809	85	...	...	...	...
Kumamoto	ESDF	669 412	317 176	352 236	267	...	...	...	...
Kurashiki	ESDF	433 904	209 403	224 501	299	...	...	...	...
Kure	ESDF	203 089	98 030	105 059	146	...	...	...	...
Kurume	ESDF	238 330	113 212	125 118	125	...	...	...	...
Kusatsu	ESDF	117 625	60 679	56 946	48	...	...	...	...
Kushiro	ESDF	189 240	90 681	98 559	222	...	...	...	...
Kuwana	ESDF	109 317	53 538	55 779	57	...	...	...	...
Kyoto	ESDF	1 466 321	701 091	765 230	610	...	...	...	...
Machida	ESDF	399 274	197 966	201 308	72	...	...	...	...
Maebashi	ESDF	284 994	139 173	145 821	147	...	...	...	...
Matsubara	ESDF	130 573	63 524	67 049	17	...	...	...	...
Matsudo	ESDF	472 351	237 293	235 058	61	...	...	...	...
Matsue	ESDF	152 596	73 845	78 751	221	...	...	...	...
Matsumoto	ESDF	209 202	103 545	105 657	266	...	...	...	...
Matsusaka	ESDF	125 543	60 522	65 021	210	...	...	...	...
Matsuyama	ESDF	477 518	225 108	252 410	289	...	...	...	...
Minoh	ESDF	125 352	60 634	64 718	48	...	...	...	...
Misato	ESDF	129 843	66 201	63 642	30	...	...	...	...
Mishima	ESDF	111 606	54 718	56 888	62	...	...	...	...
Mitaka	ESDF	176 335	88 374	87 961	17	...	...	...	...
Mito	ESDF	248 762	121 066	127 696	176	...	...	...	...

(See notes at end of table. — Voir notes à la fin du tableau.)

Continent, country or area, date and city / Continent, pays ou zone, date et ville	Code[1]	City proper — Ville proprement dite Population				Urban agglomeration — Agglomération urbaine Population			
		Both sexes Les deux sexes	Male Masculin	Female Féminin	Surface area Superficie (km²)	Both sexes Les deux sexes	Male Masculin	Female Féminin	Surface area Superficie (km²)
ASIA — ASIE									
Japan — Japon[60,61,62]									
1 VII 2003									
Miyakonojo	ESDF	132 369	62 173	70 196	306	...	...	...	...
Miyazaki	ESDF	308 122	144 525	163 597	287	...	...	...	...
Moriguchi	ESDF	148 917	72 879	76 038	13	...	...	...	...
Morioka	ESDF	287 885	137 754	150 131	489	...	...	...	...
Muroran	ESDF	101 584	49 008	52 576	81	...	...	...	...
Musashino	ESDF	136 313	66 105	70 208	11	...	...	...	...
Nagano	ESDF	361 345	175 673	185 672	404	...	...	...	...
Nagaoka	ESDF	194 419	95 446	98 973	262	...	...	...	...
Nagareyama	ESDF	151 966	75 352	76 614	35	...	...	...	...
Nagasaki	ESDF	418 773	193 903	224 870	241	...	...	...	...
Nagoya	ESDF	2 191 869	1 088 681	1 103 188	326	...	...	...	...
Naha	ESDF	307 405	147 903	159 502	39	...	...	...	...
Nara	ESDF	365 144	173 001	192 143	212	...	...	...	...
Narashino	ESDF	157 598	79 924	77 674	21	...	...	...	...
Neyagawa	ESDF	246 800	121 411	125 389	25	...	...	...	...
Niigata	ESDF	529 724	256 557	273 167	206	...	...	...	...
Niihama	ESDF	124 872	59 595	65 277	161	...	...	...	...
Niiza	ESDF	150 729	76 007	74 722	23	...	...	...	...
Nishio	ESDF	102 080	51 291	50 789	76	...	...	...	...
Nishinomiya	ESDF	454 949	216 586	238 363	99	...	...	...	...
Nishitokyo	ESDF	185 279	92 230	93 049	16	...	...	...	...
Nobeoka	ESDF	123 107	57 619	65 488	284	...	...	...	...
Noda	ESDF	150 711	75 559	75 152	74	...	...	...	...
Numazu	ESDF	206 695	102 150	104 545	152	...	...	...	...
Obihiro	ESDF	173 510	83 908	89 602	619	...	...	...	...
Odawara	ESDF	199 396	98 123	101 273	114	...	...	...	...
Ogaki	ESDF	150 443	72 948	77 495	80	...	...	...	...
Oita	ESDF	441 460	212 590	228 870	361	...	...	...	...
Okayama	ESDF	634 528	305 162	329 366	513	...	...	...	...
Okazaki	ESDF	345 985	173 526	172 459	227	...	...	...	...
Okinawa	ESDF	123 790	59 563	64 227	49	...	...	...	...
Ome	ESDF	141 933	71 414	70 519	103	...	...	...	...
Omuta	ESDF	134 668	61 278	73 390	82	...	...	...	...
Osaka	ESDF	2 625 360	1 283 299	1 342 061	222	...	...	...	...
Ota	ESDF	150 113	75 936	74 177	98	...	...	...	...
Otaru	ESDF	147 459	67 586	79 873	243	...	...	...	...
Otsu	ESDF	296 726	144 083	152 643	302	...	...	...	...
Oyama	ESDF	157 402	79 181	78 221	172	...	...	...	...
Saga	ESDF	167 085	79 208	87 877	104	...	...	...	...
Sagamihara	ESDF	619 348	314 379	304 969	90	...	...	...	...
Saitama	ESDF	1 054 623	531 406	523 217	168	...	...	...	...
Sakai	ESDF	792 553	382 758	409 795	137	...	...	...	...
Sakata	ESDF	100 063	47 907	52 156	176	...	...	...	...
Sakura	ESDF	172 380	84 642	87 738	104	...	...	...	...
Sanda	ESDF	113 883	55 461	58 422	210	...	...	...	...
Sapporo	ESDF	1 848 859	882 264	966 595	1 121	...	...	...	...
Sasebo	ESDF	240 016	112 959	127 057	248	...	...	...	...
Sayama	ESDF	160 989	81 449	79 540	49	...	...	...	...
Sendai	ESDF	1 021 837	499 845	521 992	784	...	...	...	...
Seto	ESDF	132 099	65 371	66 728	112	...	...	...	...
Shimonoseki	ESDF	248 933	116 540	132 393	224	...	...	...	...
Shizuoka	ESDF	702 793	342 498	360 295	1 374	...	...	...	...
Shunan	ESDF	155 069	74 831	80 238	656	...	...	...	...
Soka	ESDF	231 559	118 725	112 834	27	...	...	...	...
Suita	ESDF	352 334	172 966	179 368	36	...	...	...	...
Suzuka	ESDF	190 043	94 438	95 605	195	...	...	...	...
Tachikawa	ESDF	168 475	84 441	84 034	24	...	...	...	...
Tajimi	ESDF	103 784	50 415	53 369	78	...	...	...	...
Takamatsu	ESDF	334 694	161 667	173 027	194	...	...	...	...

8. Population of capital cities and cities of 100 000 and more inhabitants: latest available year
Population des capitales et des villes de 100 000 habitants et plus: dernière année disponible (continued — suite)

(See notes at end of table. — Voir notes à la fin du tableau.)

Continent, country or area, date and city / Continent, pays ou zone, date et ville	Code[1]	City proper — Ville proprement dite Population				Urban agglomeration — Agglomération urbaine Population			
		Both sexes Les deux sexes	Male Masculin	Female Féminin	Surface area Superficie (km²)	Both sexes Les deux sexes	Male Masculin	Female Féminin	Surface area Superficie (km²)
ASIA — ASIE									
Japan — Japon[60,61,62]									
1 VII 2003									
Takaoka	ESDF	170 041	81 519	88 522	151	...	...	...	...
Takarazuka	ESDF	218 411	102 835	115 576	102	...	...	...	...
Takasaki	ESDF	241 589	118 829	122 760	111	...	...	...	...
Takatsuki	ESDF	353 782	172 010	181 772	105	...	...	...	...
Tama	ESDF	145 788	73 477	72 311	21	...	...	...	...
Toda	ESDF	112 031	58 728	53 303	18	...	...	...	...
Tokai	ESDF	101 449	52 714	48 735	43	...	...	...	...
Tokorozawa	ESDF	330 229	100 000	107 500	72	...	...		...
Tokushima	ESDF	267 437	126 895	140 542	191	...	...	...	...
TOKYO[64]	ESDF	8 333 923	4 137 940	4 195 983	621	...	...	...	...
Tomakomai	ESDF	172 678	84 409	88 269	561	...	...	...	...
Tondabayashi	ESDF	126 428	60 463	65 965	40	...	...	...	...
Tottori	ESDF	151 889	74 241	77 648	237	...	...	...	...
Toyama	ESDF	325 341	157 512	167 829	209	...	...	...	...
Toyota	ESDF	358 319	188 921	169 398	290	...	...	...	...
Toyohashi	ESDF	369 743	183 611	186 132	261	...	...	...	...
Toyokawa	ESDF	119 322	59 263	60 059	65	...	...	...	...
Toyonaka	ESDF	388 987	188 038	200 949	36	...	...	...	...
Tsu	ESDF	164 349	79 890	84 459	102	...	...	...	...
Tsuchiura	ESDF	135 190	67 008	68 182	82	...	...	...	...
Tsukuba	E3DF	195 831	100 652	95 179	260	...	...	...	...
Ube	ESDF	172 698	82 470	90 228	210	...	...	...	...
Ueda	ESDF	125 333	61 630	63 703	177	...	...	...	...
Uji	ESDF	188 807	92 245	96 562	68	...	...	...	...
Urasoe	ESDF	104 382	51 260	53 122	19	...	...	...	...
Urayasu	ESDF	145 632	74 920	70 712	17	...	...	...	...
Utsunomiya	ESDF	448 973	224 430	224 543	312	...	...	...	...
Wakayama	ESDF	382 061	180 532	201 529	209	...	...	...	...
Yachiyo	ESDF	177 016	87 869	89 147	51	...	...	...	...
Yaizu	ESDF	120 091	58 421	61 670	46	...	...	...	...
Yamagata	ESDF	255 453	123 041	132 412	381	...	...	...	...
Yamaguchi	ESDF	142 379	67 948	74 431	357	...	...	...	...
Yamato	ESDF	218 590	110 873	107 717	27	...	...	...	...
Yao	ESDF	273 651	133 021	140 630	42	...	...	...	...
Yatsushiro	ESDF	104 809	49 003	55 806	147	...	...	...	...
Yokkaichi	ESDF	294 423	144 886	149 537	197	...	...	...	...
Yokohama	ESDF	3 523 065	1 779 123	1 743 942	437	...	...	...	...
Yokosuka	ESDF	430 793	216 904	213 889	101	...	...	...	...
Yonago	ESDF	140 287	66 755	73 532	106	...	...	...	...
Zama	ESDF	128 723	66 322	62 401	18	...	...	...	...
Jordan — Jordanie									
31 XII 2003									
AMMAN	ESDF	*1 254 284*	...	...	...	...	...	...	...
Irbid	ESDF	*272 681*	...	...	...	...	...	...	...
Russiefa	ESDF	*240 630*	...	...	...	...	...	...	...
Zarqa	ESDF	*472 830*	...	...	...	...	...	...	...
Kazakhstan									
1 I 2003									
Aktau	ESDF	150 594	73 109	77 485	...	168 371	82 173	86 198	...
Aktobe	ESDF	247 006	114 387	132 619	...	276 660	128 963	147 697	...
Almaty	ESDF	1 149 641	521 543	628 098	...	1 149 641	521 543	628 098	...
ASTANA	ESDF	501 998	243 833	258 165	...	501 998	243 833	258 165	...
Atirau	ESDF	143 693	67 492	76 201	...	194 989	92 435	102 554	...
Ekibastuz	ESDF	119 766	56 334	63 432	...	141 617	66 969	74 648	...
Karaganda	ESDF	423 512	193 233	230 279	...	423 697	193 319	230 378	...
Koktshetau	ESDF	121 661	55 426	66 235	...	133 124	60 796	72 328	...
Kustanai	ESDF	203 446	92 354	111 092	...	203 446	92 354	111 092	...
Kyzylorda	ESDF	156 335	74 176	82 159	...	194 427	93 774	100 653	...
Pavlodar	ESDF	283 356	129 422	153 934	...	300 942	137 890	163 052	...

(See notes at end of table. — Voir notes à la fin du tableau.)

Continent, country or area, date and city / Continent, pays ou zone, date et ville	Code[1]	City proper — Ville proprement dite Population				Urban agglomeration — Agglomération urbaine Population			
		Both sexes Les deux sexes	Male Masculin	Female Féminin	Surface area Superficie (km²)	Both sexes Les deux sexes	Male Masculin	Female Féminin	Surface area Superficie (km²)
ASIA — ASIE									
Kazakhstan									
1 I 2003									
Petropavlovsk (Severo-Kazakhstanskaya oblast)	ESDF	192 820	86 719	106 101	...	193 693	87 180	106 513	...
Rudni	ESDF	102 803	47 320	55 483	...	114 609	52 951	61 658	...
Semipalatinsk	ESDF	266 620	120 918	145 702	...	294 889	134 910	159 979	...
Shimkent	ESDF	506 663	241 324	265 339	...	506 663	241 324	265 339	...
Taldykorgan	ESDF	97 574	43 574	54 000	...	118 416	53 921	64 495	...
Taraz	ESDF	323 301	149 143	174 158	...	323 301	149 143	174 158	...
Temirtau	ESDF	159 413	73 390	86 023	...	168 972	78 024	90 948	...
Uralsk	ESDF	193 041	87 388	105 653	...	220 958	100 739	120 219	...
Ust-Kamenogorsk	ESDF	296 880	134 246	162 634	...	307 100	139 247	167 853	...
Korea (Dem. People's Republic of) — Corée (Rép. populaire dém. de)									
1 VII 1993									
Chongjin	CDFC	582 480	...	...	...	...	...	...	...
Haeju	CDFC	229 172	...	...	...	...	...	...	...
Hamhung	CDFC	709 730	...	...	...	...	...	...	...
Hyesan	CDFC	178 020	...	...	...	...	...	...	...
Kaesong	CDFC	334 433	...	...	...	...	...	...	...
Kanggye	CDFC	223 410	...	...	...	...	...	...	...
Nampho	CDFC	731 448	...	...	...	...	...	...	...
Phyongsong	CDFC	272 934	...	...	...	...	...	...	...
PYONGYANG	CDFC	2 741 260	...	...	...	...	...	...	...
Sariwon	CDFC	254 146	...	...	...	...	...	...	...
Sinuiji	CDFC	326 011	...	...	...	...	...	...	...
Wonsan	CDFC	300 148	...	...	...	...	...	...	...
Korea (Republic of) — Corée (République de)									
1 VII 2003									
Busan (Pusan)	ESDF	3 685 290	1 842 597	1 842 693	748	...	...	...	...
Daegu (Taegu)	ESDF	2 547 231	1 284 324	1 262 907	885	...	...	...	...
Daejeon (Taejon)	ESDF	1 463 009	740 406	722 603	539	...	...	...	...
Gwangju (Kwangchu)	ESDF	1 428 929	714 734	714 195	501	...	...	...	...
Incheon	ESDF	2 615 133	1 324 700	1 290 433	955	...	...	...	...
Jeju (Cheju)	ESDF	534 647	266 649	267 998	255	...	...	...	...
SEOUL	ESDF	10 024 308	5 044 617	4 979 691	605	...	...	...	...
Ulsan	ESDF	1 066 271	549 669	516 602	1 055	...	...	...	...
Kuwait — Koweït									
20 IV 1995									
Jaleeb Al-Shuykh	CDFC	102 169	78 748	23 421	...	...	...	...	...
KUWAIT CITY	CDFC	28 747	23 601	5 146	...	...	...	...	...
Salmiya	CDFC	129 775	77 672	52 103	...	...	...	...	...
Kyrgyzstan — Kirghizistan									
1 VII 2003									
BISHKEK	ESDJ	805 491	385 423	420 068	127	...	...	...	...
Osh	ESDJ	227 250	108 299	118 951	24	...	...	...	...
Lao People's Democratic Republic — République démocratique populaire lao									
1 III 1995									
VIENTIANE	CDFC	...	...	...	...	528 100	...	...	...
Lebanon — Liban									
15 XI 1970									
BEIRUT	SSDF	474 870	239 130	235 740	...	938 940	...	...	...
Tripoli	SSDF	127 611	...	...	...	...	...	...	...
Malaysia — Malaisie									
1 VII 1991									
Alor Setar	CDFC	124 412	...	...	...	164 444	...	...	...
George Town	CDFC	219 603	...	...	...	...	...	...	...
Ipoh	CDFC	382 853	...	...	...	468 841	...	...	...

(See notes at end of table. — Voir notes à la fin du tableau.)

Continent, country or area, date and city / Continent, pays ou zone, date et ville	Code[1]	City proper — Ville proprement dite Population				Urban agglomeration — Agglomération urbaine Population			
		Both sexes Les deux sexes	Male Masculin	Female Féminin	Surface area Superficie (km²)	Both sexes Les deux sexes	Male Masculin	Female Féminin	Surface area Superficie (km²)
ASIA — ASIE									
Malaysia — Malaisie									
1 VII 1991									
Johore Bharu	CDFC	328 436	...	...	...	441 703	...	...	...
Klang	CDFC	243 355	...	...	...	368 379	...	...	...
Kota Bahru	CDFC	219 582	...	...	...	234 581	...	...	...
KUALA LUMPUR	CDFC	1 145 342	...	...	...	...	...	...	...
Kuala Terengganu	CDFC	228 119	...	...	...	...	...	...	...
Kuantan	CDFC	199 484	...	...	...	202 445	...	...	...
Petaling Jaya	CDFC	254 350	...	...	...	350 995	...	...	...
Seleyang Baru	CDFC	124 228	...	...	...	134 197	...	...	...
Seremban	CDFC	182 869	...	...	...	193 237	...	...	...
Shah Alam	CDFC	102 019	...	...	...	117 027	...	...	...
Sungai Petani	CDFC	114 763	...	...	...	116 977	...	...	...
Taiping	CDFC	183 261	...	...	...	200 324	...	...	...
Kota Kinabalu	CDFC	76 120	...	...	...	160 184	...	...	...
Sandakan	CDFC	125 841	...	...	...	156 675	...	...	...
Kuching	CDFC	148 059	...	...	...	277 905	...	...	...
Sibu	CDFC	126 381	...	...	...	133 479	...	...	...
Maldives									
31 III 2000									
MALE	CDFC	74 069	38 559	35 510	...	...	...	...	...
Mongolia — Mongolie									
1 VII 2003									
ULAANBAATAR	ESDF	*893 437*	*433 737*	*459 700*	*190*	...	...	...	...
Myanmar									
1 VII 1983									
Bassein	CDFC	144 096	...	...	...	...	...	...	...
Mandalay	CDFC	532 949	...	...	...	...	...	...	...
Monywa	CDFC	106 843	...	...	...	...	...	...	...
Moulmein	CDFC	219 961	...	...	...	...	...	...	...
Pegu	CDFC	150 528	...	...	...	...	...	...	...
Sittwe	CDFC	107 621	...	...	...	...	...	...	...
Taunggyi	CDFC	108 231	...	...	...	...	...	...	...
YANGON	CDFC	2 513 023	...	...	...	...	...	...	...
Nepal — Népal									
22 VI 2001									
Biratnagar	CDJC	166 674	87 664	79 010	58	...	...	...	...
Birgunj	CDJC	112 484	60 956	51 528	21	...	...	...	...
KATHMANDU	CDJC	671 846	360 103	311 743	49	...	...	...	...
Lalitpur	CDJC	162 991	84 502	78 489	15	...	...	...	...
Pokhara	CDJC	156 312	79 563	76 749	55	...	...	...	...
Occupied Palestinian Territory — Territoire palestinien occupé									
1 VII 2003									
Gaza	ESDF	*381 360*	*194 235*	*187 125*	*38*	...	...	...	...
Hebron	ESDF	*155 303*	*80 638*	*74 665*	*49*	...	...	...	...
Khan Yunis	ESDF	*116 880*	*59 558*	*57 322*	*...*	...	...	...	...
Nablus	ESDF	*127 367*	*64 809*	*62 557*	*26*	...	...	...	...
Oman									
7 VII 2003									
MUSCAT	CDFC	24 893	13 695	11 198	...	...	...	...	...
Salalah	CDFC	156 530	92 489	64 041	...	...	...	...	...
Pakistan[65]									
1 VII 1998									
Abbotabad	CDFC	106 101	61 698	44 403	...	...	...	...	...
Bahawalnagar	CDFC	111 313	57 779	53 534	...	...	...	...	...
Bahawalpur	CDFC	408 395	222 228	186 167	...	...	...	...	...
Burewala	CDFC	152 097	78 726	73 371	...	...	...	...	...
Chiniot	CDFC	172 522	90 474	82 048	...	...	...	...	...
Chishtian	CDFC	102 287	52 427	49 860	...	...	...	...	...
Dadu	CDFC	102 550	53 508	49 042	...	...	...	...	...

(See notes at end of table. — Voir notes à la fin du tableau.)

Continent, country or area, date and city Continent, pays ou zone, date et ville	Code[1]	City proper — Ville proprement dite Population				Urban agglomeration — Agglomération urbaine Population			
		Both sexes Les deux sexes	Male Masculin	Female Féminin	Surface area Superficie (km²)	Both sexes Les deux sexes	Male Masculin	Female Féminin	Surface area Superficie (km²)
ASIA — ASIE									
Pakistan[65]									
1 VII 1998									
Daska	CDFC	102 883	52 359	50 524	...	...	...	...	...
Dera Ghazi Khan	CDFC	190 542	98 738	91 804	...	...	...	...	...
Faisalabad (Lyallpur)	CDFC	2 008 861	1 053 085	955 776	...	...	...	...	...
Gojra	CDFC	117 872	60 598	57 294	...	...	...	...	...
Gujranwala	CDFC	1 132 509	588 512	543 997	...	...	...	...	...
Gujrat	CDFC	251 792	128 524	123 268	...	...	...	...	...
Hafizabad	CDFC	133 678	69 231	64 447	...	...	...	...	...
Hyderabad	CDFC	1 166 894	612 283	554 611	...	...	...	...	...
ISLAMABAD	CDFC	529 180	290 717	238 463	...	...	...	...	...
Jacobabad	CDFC	138 780	71 854	66 926	...	...	...	...	...
Jaranwala	CDFC	106 785	55 819	51 166	...	...	...	...	...
Jhang	CDFC	293 366	153 123	140 243	...	...	...	...	...
Jhelum	CDFC	147 392	79 169	68 223	...	...	...	...	...
Kamoke	CDFC	152 288	78 848	73 440	...	...	...	...	...
Karachi	CDFC	9 339 023	5 029 900	4 309 123	...	...	...	...	...
Kasur	CDFC	245 321	129 553	115 768	...	...	...	...	...
Khairpur	CDFC	105 637	55 358	50 279	...	...	...	...	...
Khanewal	CDFC	133 986	69 145	64 841	...	...	...	...	...
Khanpur	CDFC	120 382	62 371	58 011	...	...	...	...	...
Kohat	CDFC	126 627	71 505	55 122	...	...	...	...	...
Lahore	CDFC	5 143 495	2 707 220	2 436 275	...	...	...	...	...
Larkana	CDFC	270 283	140 622	129 661	...	...	...	...	...
Mangora	CDFC	173 868	91 742	82 126	...	...	...	...	...
Mardan	CDFC	245 926	129 247	116 679	...	...	...	...	...
Mirpur Khas	CDFC	189 671	97 940	91 731	...	...	...	...	...
Multan	CDFC	1 197 384	637 911	559 473	...	...	...	...	...
Muridke	CDFC	111 951	58 210	53 741	...	...	...	...	...
Muzaffargharh	CDFC	123 404	66 556	56 848	...	...	...	...	...
Nawabshah	CDFC	189 244	98 116	91 128	...	...	...	...	...
Okara	CDFC	201 815	104 245	97 570	...	...	...	...	...
Pakpattan	CDFC	109 033	56 676	52 357	...	...	...	...	...
Peshawar	CDFC	982 816	521 901	460 915	...	...	...	...	...
Quetta	CDFC	565 137	307 759	257 378	...	...	...	...	...
Rahimyar Khan	CDFC	233 537	121 446	112 091	...	...	...	...	...
Rawalpindi	CDFC	1 409 768	750 530	659 238	...	...	...	...	...
Sadiqabad	CDFC	144 391	75 217	69 174	...	...	...	...	...
Sahiwal	CDFC	208 778	108 992	99 786	...	...	...	...	...
Sargodha	CDFC	458 440	239 837	218 603	...	...	...	...	...
Shakkarpur	CDFC	134 883	69 713	65 170	...	...	...	...	...
Sheikhu Pura	CDFC	280 263	146 739	133 524	...	...	...	...	...
Sialkote	CDFC	421 502	227 398	194 104	...	...	...	...	...
Sukkur	CDFC	335 551	175 679	159 872	...	...	...	...	...
Tandoadam	CDFC	104 907	54 670	50 237	...	...	...	...	...
Wah Cantonment	CDFC	198 891	104 230	94 661	...	...	...	...	...
Philippines									
1 V 2000									
Angeles	CDJC	267 788	132 972	134 816	60	...	...	...	...
Bacolod	CDJC	429 076	209 729	219 347	156	...	...	...	...
Baguio	CDJC	252 386	124 208	128 178	49	...	...	...	...
Batangas	CDJC	247 588	123 740	123 848	283	...	...	...	...
Butuan	CDJC	267 279	135 735	131 544	345	...	...	...	...
Cagayan de Oro	CDJC	461 877	228 524	233 353	373	...	...	...	...
Cebu	CDJC	718 821	351 640	367 181	281	...	...	...	...
Cotabato	CDJC	163 849	79 853	83 996	144	...	...	...	...
Dagupan	CDJC	130 328	64 468	65 860	37	...	...	...	...
Davao	CDJC	1 147 116	573 242	573 874	1 211	...	...	...	...
Digos	CDJC	125 171	63 107	62 064	...	...	...	...	...
Dumaguete	CDJC	102 265	49 378	52 887	...	...	...	...	...
General Santos	CDJC	411 822	207 496	204 326	402	...	...	...	...

(See notes at end of table. — Voir notes à la fin du tableau.)

Continent, country or area, date and city Continent, pays ou zone, date et ville	Code[1]	City proper — Ville proprement dite Population				Urban agglomeration — Agglomération urbaine Population			
		Both sexes Les deux sexes	Male Masculin	Female Féminin	Surface area Superficie (km²)	Both sexes Les deux sexes	Male Masculin	Female Féminin	Surface area Superficie (km²)
ASIA — ASIE									
Philippines									
1 V 2000									
Iligan	CDJC	285 061	141 641	143 420	673	...	...	...	...
Iloilo	CDJC	366 391	177 620	188 771	56	...	...	...	...
Kalookan (Caloocan)	CDJC	1 177 604	587 890	589 714	56	...	...	...	...
Kidapawan	CDJC	101 205	51 278	49 927	...	...	...	...	...
Koronadal	CDJC	133 786	67 493	66 293	...	...	...	...	...
Las Piñas	CDJC	472 780	229 776	243 004	...	...	...	...	...
Legasp	CDJC	157 010	78 141	78 869	154	...	...	...	...
Lucena City	CDJC	196 075	97 380	98 695	80	...	...	...	...
Makati	CDJC	471 379	226 422	244 957	...	...	...	...	...
Malabalay	CDJC	123 672	63 381	60 291	...	...	...	...	...
Mandaue	CDJC	259 728	128 501	131 227	12	...	...	...	...
Mandaluyong	CDJC	278 474	135 287	143 187	...	...	...	...	...
MANILA	CDJC	1 581 082	770 491	810 591	614	...	...	...	...
Marawi	CDJC	131 090	63 110	67 980	23	...	...	...	...
Marikina	CDJC	391 170	191 585	199 585	...	...	...	...	...
Muntinlupa	CDJC	379 310	187 381	191 929	47	...	...	...	...
Olongapo	CDJC	194 260	95 585	98 675	103	...	...	...	...
Pagadian	CDJC	142 585	71 009	71 576	332	...	...	...	...
Paranaque	CDJC	449 811	217 828	231 983	...	...	...	...	...
Pasay	CDJC	354 908	175 041	179 867	14	...	...	...	...
Pasig	CDJC	505 058	246 047	259 011	...	...	...	...	...
Puerto Princesa	CDJC	161 912	83 045	78 867	2	...	...	...	...
Quezon City	CDJC	2 173 831	1 064 780	1 109 051	166	...	...	...	...
Roxas	CDJC	126 352	62 542	63 810	95	...	...	...	...
San Fernando City	CDJC	102 082	50 792	51 290	...	...	...	...	...
Surigao	CDJC	118 534	59 253	59 281	225	...	...	...	...
Taguig	CDJC	467 375	233 712	233 663	...	...	...	...	...
Tagum	CDJC	179 531	90 004	89 527	...	...	...	...	...
Tarlac	CDJC	262 481	132 532	129 949	...	...	...	...	...
Valenzuela	CDJC	485 433	244 373	241 060	...	...	...	...	...
Zamboanga	CDJC	601 794	302 089	299 705	464	...	...	...	...
Qatar									
1 III 1997									
Al-Rayyan	CDJC	169 774	110 588	59 186	893	...	...	...	...
DOHA	CDJC	264 009	171 791	92 218	159	...	...	...	...
Saudi Arabia — Arabie saoudite									
27 IX 1992									
Abha	CDFC	112 148	62 676	49 472	...	...	...	...	...
Ad-Dammam	CDFC	482 117	297 284	184 833	...	...	...	...	...
Al-Hufuf	CDFC	225 840	121 231	104 609	...	...	...	...	...
Al-Kharj	CDFC	148 687	83 339	65 348	...	...	...	...	...
Al-Khubar	CDFC	142 981	92 632	50 349	...	...	...	...	...
Al-Madinah	CDFC	609 318	333 229	276 089	...	...	...	...	...
Al-Mubarraz	CDFC	219 097	116 469	102 628	...	...	...	...	...
Ar'ar	CDFC	105 752	57 563	48 189	...	...	...	...	...
Ath-Thuqbah	CDFC	126 014	77 513	48 501	...	...	...	...	...
At-Ta'if	CDFC	408 129	217 879	190 250	...	...	...	...	...
Buraydah	CDFC	240 091	133 957	106 134	...	...	...	...	...
Hafar al-Batin	CDFC	138 401	73 863	64 538	...	...	...	...	...
Ha'il	CDFC	175 518	95 915	79 603	...	...	...	...	...
Jiddah	CDFC	2 021 095	1 196 740	824 355	...	...	...	...	...
Khamis Mushayt	CDFC	217 990	121 245	96 745	...	...	...	...	...
Makkah	CDFC	952 429	514 298	438 131	...	...	...	...	...
RIYADH	CDFC	2 723 222	1 594 407	1 128 819	...	...	...	...	...
Tabuk	CDFC	286 384	162 789	123 595	...	...	...	...	...
Singapore — Singapour									
1 VII 1999									
SINGAPORE	ESDF	3 894 000	...	...	...	...	...	...	...

8. Population of capital cities and cities of 100 000 and more inhabitants: latest available year
Population des capitales et des villes de 100 000 habitants et plus: dernière année disponible (continued — suite)

(See notes at end of table. — Voir notes à la fin du tableau.)

Continent, country or area, date and city Continent, pays ou zone, date et ville	Code[1]	City proper — Ville proprement dite Population				Urban agglomeration — Agglomération urbaine Population			
		Both sexes Les deux sexes	Male Masculin	Female Féminin	Surface area Superficie (km²)	Both sexes Les deux sexes	Male Masculin	Female Féminin	Surface area Superficie (km²)
ASIA — ASIE									
Sri Lanka									
1 VII 1990									
COLOMBO	ESDF	615 000	...	...	...	...	...	...	...
Dehiwala-Mount Lavinia	ESDF	196 000	...	...	...	...	...	...	...
Jaffna	ESDF	129 000	...	...	...	...	...	...	...
Kandy	ESDF	104 000	...	...	...	...	...	...	...
Moratuwa	ESDF	170 000	...	...	...	...	...	...	...
Syrian Arab Republic — République arabe syrienne									
1 VII 2000									
Aleppo	ESDF	3 818 000	1 968 000	1 850 000	...	...	...	...	...
Al-Hasakeh	ESDF	1 295 000	657 000	638 000	...	...	...	...	...
Al-Kamishli	ESDF	467 120	229 542	237 578	...	...	...	...	...
Al-Rakka	ESDF	708 000	360 000	348 000	...	...	...	...	...
DAMASCUS	ESDF	1 675 000	865 000	810 000	...	...	...	...	...
Deir El-Zor	ESDF	803 000	404 000	399 000	...	...	...	...	...
Hama	ESDF	1 525 000	780 000	745 000	...	...	...	...	...
Homs	ESDF	1 365 000	698 000	667 000	...	...	...	...	...
Lattakia	ESDF	890 000	455 000	435 000	...	...	...	...	...
Tajikistan — Tadjikistan									
1 VII 1993									
DUSHANBE	ESDJ	528 600	...	...	...	...	...	...	...
Thailand — Thaïlande									
1 VII 2002									
BANGKOK	ESDJ	...	...	...	...	7 917 000	3 777 000	4 140 000	1 569
Buri Ram	ESDJ	...	...	...	...	209 422	103 236	106 186	10 323
Chachoengsao	ESDJ	...	...	...	...	136 757	66 900	69 857	5 351
Chaiyaphum	ESDJ	...	...	...	...	183 160	91 174	91 986	12 778
Chanthaburi	ESDJ	...	...	...	...	151 738	75 128	76 610	6 338
Chiang Mai	ESDJ	...	...	...	...	390 445	194 072	196 373	20 107
Chiang Rai	ESDJ	...	...	...	...	197 793	99 969	97 824	11 678
Chon Buri	ESDJ	...	...	...	...	556 545	275 351	281 194	4 363
Kalasin	ESDJ	...	...	...	...	191 744	96 148	95 596	6 947
Kanchanaburi	ESDJ	...	...	...	...	164 353	80 691	83 662	19 483
Khon Kaen	ESDJ	...	...	...	...	398 533	197 778	200 755	10 886
Lampang	ESDJ	...	...	...	...	226 503	112 418	114 085	12 534
Loei	ESDJ	...	...	...	...	101 540	51 723	49 817	11 425
Lop Buri	ESDJ	...	...	...	...	122 123	60 891	61 232	6 200
Lumphun	ESDJ	...	...	...	...	106 226	53 335	52 891	4 506
Maha Sarakham	ESDJ	...	...	...	...	120 926	58 649	62 277	5 292
Nakhon Pathom	ESDJ	...	...	...	...	243 813	117 596	126 217	2 168
Nakhon Ratchasima	ESDJ	...	...	...	...	566 104	276 925	289 179	20 494
Nakhon Sawan	ESDJ	...	...	...	...	236 163	113 951	122 212	9 598
Nakhon Si Thammarat	ESDJ	...	...	...	...	287 761	139 923	147 838	9 943
Narathiwat	ESDJ	...	...	...	...	166 081	83 082	82 999	4 475
Nong Bua Lam Phu	ESDJ	...	...	...	...	111 176	55 872	55 304	3 859
Nong Khai	ESDJ	...	...	...	...	185 556	93 325	92 231	7 332
Nonthaburi	ESDJ	...	...	...	...	564 835	273 604	291 231	622
Pathum Thani	ESDJ	...	...	...	...	280 365	136 072	144 293	1 526
Pattani	ESDJ	...	...	...	...	123 675	61 406	62 269	1 940
Phayao	ESDJ	...	...	...	...	111 195	56 311	54 884	6 335
Phetchabun	ESDJ	...	...	...	...	152 980	74 615	78 365	12 668
Phetchaburi	ESDJ	...	...	...	...	163 340	79 317	84 023	6 225
Phichit	ESDJ	...	...	...	...	120 795	57 339	63 456	4 531
Phitsanulok	ESDJ	...	...	...	...	158 628	76 015	82 613	10 816
Phra Nakhon Si Ayutthaya	ESDJ	...	...	...	...	243 518	116 101	127 417	2 557
Phrae	ESDJ	...	...	...	...	113 542	56 168	57 374	6 539
Prachuap Khiri Khan	ESDJ	...	...	...	...	163 070	79 845	83 225	6 368
Ratchaburi	ESDJ	...	...	...	...	250 650	120 854	129 796	5 197
Rayong	ESDJ	...	...	...	...	212 129	106 858	105 271	3 552
Roi Et	ESDJ	...	...	...	...	154 162	77 163	76 999	8 299

(See notes at end of table. — Voir notes à la fin du tableau.)

Continent, country or area, date and city / Continent, pays ou zone, date et ville	Code[1]	City proper — Ville proprement dite Population				Urban agglomeration — Agglomération urbaine Population			
		Both sexes Les deux sexes	Male Masculin	Female Féminin	Surface area Superficie (km²)	Both sexes Les deux sexes	Male Masculin	Female Féminin	Surface area Superficie (km²)
ASIA — ASIE									
Thailand — Thaïlande									
1 VII 2002									
Sakon Nakhon	ESDJ	...	...	...	...	146 795	72 790	74 005	9 606
Samut Prakan	ESDJ	...	...	...	...	680 363	332 881	347 482	1 004
Samut Sakhon	ESDJ	...	...	...	...	190 595	91 375	99 220	872
Saraburi	ESDJ	...	...	...	...	209 274	104 501	104 773	3 577
Si Sa Ket	ESDJ	...	...	...	...	151 251	74 862	76 389	8 840
Songkhla	ESDJ	...	...	...	...	437 747	213 072	224 675	7 394
Sukhothai	ESDJ	...	...	...	...	116 026	55 681	60 345	6 596
Suphan Buri	ESDJ	...	...	...	...	154 249	73 024	81 225	5 358
Surat Thani	ESDJ	...	...	...	...	281 161	137 869	143 292	12 892
Surin	ESDJ	...	...	...	...	106 835	51 563	55 272	8 124
Trang	ESDJ	...	...	...	...	127 194	61 557	65 637	4 918
Ubon Ratchathani	ESDJ	...	...	...	...	274 120	135 579	138 541	15 745
Udon Thani	ESDJ	...	...	...	...	403 467	202 154	201 313	11 730
Yala	ESDJ	...	...	...	...	117 076	58 502	58 574	4 521
Timor-Leste									
1 VII 2001									
DILI	ESDF	56 000	...	...	...	...	...	...	...
Turkey — Turquie									
1 VII 2003									
Adana[66]	ESDF	...	...	...	...	1 187 098	...	...	...
Adiyaman	ESDF	203 880	...	...	...	...	...	...	...
Afyon	ESDF	137 411	...	...	...	...	...	...	...
Aksaray	ESDF	141 521	...	...	...	...	...	...	...
ANKARA[67]	ESDF	...	...	...	...	3 729 453	...	...	...
Antalya	ESDF	670 229	...	...	...	...	...	...	...
Aydin	ESDF	152 918	...	...	...	...	...	...	...
Balikesir	ESDF	227 428	...	...	...	...	...	...	...
Bandirma	ESDF	102 733	...	...	...	...	...	...	...
Batman	ESDF	277 349	...	...	...	...	...	...	...
Bursa[68]	ESDF	...	...	...	...	1 305 059	...	...	...
Ceyhan	ESDF	114 956	...	...	...	...	...	...	...
Corlu	ESDF	164 431	...	...	...	...	...	...	...
Corum	ESDF	173 960	...	...	...	...	...	...	...
Denizli	ESDF	295 319	...	...	...	...	...	...	...
Derince[69]	ESDF	101 744	...	...	...	...	...	...	...
Diyarbakir	ESDF	595 951	...	...	...	...	...	...	...
Edirne	ESDF	122 932	...	...	...	...	...	...	...
Elazig	ESDF	281 560	...	...	...	...	...	...	...
Erzincan	ESDF	110 196	...	...	...	...	...	...	...
Erzurum	ESDF	396 092	...	...	...	...	...	...	...
Eskisehir	ESDF	498 836	...	...	...	...	...	...	...
Gaziantep[70]	ESDF	...	...	...	...	926 458	...	...	...
Gebze	ESDF	282 938	...	...	...	...	...	...	...
Hatay	ESDF	149 607	...	...	...	...	...	...	...
Içel	ESDF	568 388	...	...	...	...	...	...	...
Inegol	ESDF	115 096	...	...	...	...	...	...	...
Iskenderun	ESDF	158 695	...	...	...	...	...	...	...
Isparta	ESDF	157 913	...	...	...	...	...	...	...
Istanbul[71]	ESDF	...	...	...	...	9 555 719	...	...	...
Izmir[72]	ESDF	...	...	...	...	2 299 584	...	...	...
Kahramanmaras	ESDF	354 891	...	...	...	...	...	...	...
Karaman	ESDF	113 687	...	...	...	...	...	...	...
Kayseri[73]	ESDF	...	...	...	...	566 162	...	...	...
Kirikkale	ESDF	208 086	...	...	...	...	...	...	...
Kiziltepe	ESDF	130 904	...	...	...	...	...	...	...
Kocaeli	ESDF	194 055	...	...	...	...	...	...	...
Konya[74]	ESDF	...	...	...	...	810 957	...	...	...
Kütahya	ESDF	175 905	...	...	...	...	...	...	...
Malatya	ESDF	412 724	...	...	...	...	...	...	...

8. Population of capital cities and cities of 100 000 and more inhabitants: latest available year
Population des capitales et des villes de 100 000 habitants et plus: dernière année disponible (continued — suite)

(See notes at end of table. — Voir notes à la fin du tableau.)

Continent, country or area, date and city / Continent, pays ou zone, date et ville	Code[1]	City proper — Ville proprement dite Population				Urban agglomeration — Agglomération urbaine Population			
		Both sexes Les deux sexes	Male Masculin	Female Féminin	Surface area Superficie (km²)	Both sexes Les deux sexes	Male Masculin	Female Féminin	Surface area Superficie (km²)
ASIA — ASIE									
Turkey — Turquie									
1 VII 2003									
Manisa	ESDF	230 223	...	...	...	...	...	...	...
Nazilli	ESDF	112 269	...	...	...	...	...	...	...
Ordu	ESDF	113 756	...	...	...	...	...	...	...
Osmaniye	ESDF	189 238	...	...	...	...	...	...	...
Sakarya	ESDF	283 516	...	...	...	...	...	...	...
Samsun	ESDF	377 927	...	...	...	...	...	...	...
Sanliurfa	ESDF	411 159	...	...	...	...	...	...	...
Siirt	ESDF	106 966	...	...	...	...	...	...	...
Sivas	ESDF	256 914	...	...	...	...	...	...	...
Siverek	ESDF	149 236	...	...	...	...	...	...	...
Tarsus	ESDF	222 693	...	...	...	...	...	...	...
Tekirdag	ESDF	113 285	...	...	...	...	...	...	...
Tokat	ESDF	121 694	...	...	...	...	...	...	...
Trabzon	ESDF	228 013	...	...	...	...	...	...	...
Turhal	ESDF	103 225	...	...	...	...	...	...	...
Usak	ESDF	145 758	...	...	...	...	...	...	...
Van	ESDF	324 352	...	...	...	...	...	...	...
Viransehir	ESDF	144 731	...	...	...	...	...	...	...
Turkmenistan — Turkménistan									
1 VII 1990									
ASHKHABAD	ESDF	407 000	...	...	...	...	...	...	...
Chardzhou	ESDF	164 000	...	...	...	...	...	...	...
Tashauz	ESDF	114 000	...	...	...	...	...	...	...
United Arab Emirates — Emirats Arabes Unis									
1 VII 2002									
ABU DHABI	ESDF	527 000	359 000	168 000	...	...	...	...	...
Ajman	ESDF	205 000	122 000	83 000	...	...	...	...	...
Al-Ayn	ESDF	328 000	215 000	113 000	...	...	...	...	...
Al-Sharjah	ESDF	488 000	317 000	171 000	...	...	...	...	...
Dubai	ESDF	1 089 000	759 000	330 000	...	...	...	...	...
Uzbekistan — Ouzbékistan									
1 VII 2001									
Almalyk	ESDF	113 114	56 317	56 797	...	...	...	...	...
Andizhan	ESDF	338 366	165 159	173 207	...	...	...	...	...
Angren	ESDF	128 757	64 060	64 697	...	...	...	...	...
Bukhara	ESDF	237 361	118 613	118 748	...	...	...	...	...
Chirchik	ESDF	141 742	70 203	71 539	...	...	...	...	...
Banjzak	ESDF	131 512	68 441	63 071	...	...	...	...	...
Fergana	ESDF	183 037	87 142	95 895	...	...	...	...	...
Karshi	ESDF	204 690	104 159	100 531	...	...	...	...	...
Kokand	ESDF	197 450	95 872	101 578	...	...	...	...	...
Margilan	ESDF	149 646	73 899	75 747	...	...	...	...	...
Namangan	ESDF	391 297	197 962	193 335	...	...	...	...	...
Navoi	ESDF	138 082	70 577	67 505	...	...	...	...	...
Nukus	ESDF	212 012	103 918	108 094	...	...	...	...	...
Samarkand	ESDF	361 339	178 608	182 731	...	...	...	...	...
TASHKENT	ESDF	2 137 218	1 043 213	1 094 005	...	...	...	...	...
Termez	ESDF	116 467	60 031	56 436	...	...	...	...	...
Urgentch	ESDF	138 609	67 667	70 942	...	...	...	...	...
Viet Nam									
1 VII 1992									
Buonmathuot	ESDF	282 095	...	...	...	...	...	...	...
Campha	ESDF	209 086	...	...	...	...	...	...	...
Cantho	ESDF	215 587	...	...	...	...	...	...	...
Dalat	ESDF	106 409	...	...	...	...	...	...	...
Da Nang	ESDF	382 674	...	...	...	...	...	...	...
Haiphong	ESDF	783 133	...	...	22	...	...	...	...
HANOI	ESDF	1 073 760	...	...	46	...	...	...	...

8. Population of capital cities and cities of 100 000 and more inhabitants: latest available year
Population des capitales et des villes de 100 000 habitants et plus: dernière année disponible (continued — suite)

(See notes at end of table. — Voir notes à la fin du tableau.)

Continent, country or area, date and city Continent, pays ou zone, date et ville	Code[1]	City proper — Ville proprement dite Population				Urban agglomeration — Agglomération urbaine Population			
		Both sexes Les deux sexes	Male Masculin	Female Féminin	Surface area Superficie (km²)	Both sexes Les deux sexes	Male Masculin	Female Féminin	Surface area Superficie (km²)
ASIA — ASIE									
Viet Nam									
1 VII 1992									
Ho Chi Minh[75]	ESDF	*3 015 743*	...	...	140	...	...	...	...
Hon Gai	ESDF	*127 484*	...	...	...	...	...	...	...
Hué	ESDF	*219 149*	...	...	...	...	...	...	...
Longxuyen	ESDF	*132 681*	...	...	...	...	...	...	...
Mytho	ESDF	*108 404*	...	...	...	...	...	...	...
Namdinh	ESDF	*171 699*	...	...	...	...	...	...	...
Nhatrang	ESDF	*221 331*	...	...	...	...	...	...	...
Qui Nhon	ESDF	*163 385*	...	...	...	...	...	...	...
Rach Gia	ESDF	*141 132*	...	...	...	...	...	...	...
Thai Nguyen	ESDF	*127 643*	...	...	...	...	...	...	...
Vinh	ESDF	*112 455*	...	...	...	...	...	...	...
Vungtau	ESDF	*145 145*	...	...	...	...	...	...	...
Yemen — Yémen									
16 XII 1994									
Adan	CDFC	398 294	...	...	...	...	...	...	...
Al-Hudaydah (Hodeidah)	CDFC	298 452	...	...	...	...	...	...	...
Al-Mukalla	CDFC	122 359	...	...	...	...	...	...	...
Ibb	CDFC	103 312	...	...	...	...	...	...	...
SANA'A	CDFC	954 448	...	...	...	...	...	...	...
Ta'izz	CDFC	317 571	...	...	...	...	...	...	...
EUROPE									
Albania — Albanie[76]									
1 VII 2003									
TIRANA	ESDF	392 863	194 006	198 857	31	...	...	...	...
Andorra — Andorre									
1 VII 2003									
ANDORRA LA VELLA	ESDJ	...	...	...	...	*21 245*	*10 702*	*10 543*	...
Austria — Autriche[77,78]									
15 V 2001									
Bregenz	CDJC	...	...	...	...	180 737	88 695	92 042	334
Graz	CDJC	226 244	106 228	120 016	128	287 135	135 966	151 169	349
Innsbruck	CDJC	113 392	53 141	60 251	105	183 120	86 949	96 171	348
Klagenfurt	CDJC	90 141	41 396	48 745	120	100 416	46 365	54 051	187
Linz	CDJC	183 504	86 686	96 818	96	270 770	129 560	141 210	249
Salzburg	CDJC	142 662	66 231	76 431	66	210 276	99 004	111 272	259
WIEN	CDJC	1 550 123	731 344	818 779	415	1 825 287	863 717	961 570	1 160
Belarus — Bélarus									
1 VII 2003									
Baranovichi	ESDF	168 765	78 689	90 076	55	...	...	...	...
Bobruisk	ESDF	220 972	103 431	117 541	90	...	...	...	...
Borisov	ESDF	150 474	71 162	79 312	47	...	...	...	...
Brest	ESDF	297 301	137 283	160 018	74	...	...	...	...
Gomel	ESDF	...	...	...	...	491 826	224 758	267 068	118
Grodno	ESDF	313 584	145 357	168 227	93	...	...	...	...
Lida	...	...	...	...	38	...	...	...	...
MINSK	ESDF	1 733 854	806 830	927 024	305	...	...	...	...
Mogilev	ESDF	364 587	169 081	195 506	108	...	...	...	...
Mozir	ESDF	111 591	53 778	57 813	38	...	...	...	...
Novopolotsk	ESDF	...	...	...	...	107 117	51 024	56 093	52
Orsha	ESDF	...	...	...	...	140 643	67 139	73 504	51
Pinsk	ESDF	130 711	61 477	69 234	42	...	...	...	...
Soligorsk	ESDF	101 534	48 007	53 527	9	...	...	...	...
Vitebsk	ESDF	...	...	...	...	350 693	157 864	192 829	89
Belgium — Belgique[79]									
1 VII 2000									
Antwerpen (Anvers)	ESDJ	445 570	216 319	229 251	205	...	...	...	...
Brugge	ESDJ	116 559	56 436	60 123	138	...	...	...	...

8. Population of capital cities and cities of 100 000 and more inhabitants: latest available year
Population des capitales et des villes de 100 000 habitants et plus: dernière année disponible (continued — suite)

(See notes at end of table. — Voir notes à la fin du tableau.)

Continent, country or area, date and city Continent, pays ou zone, date et ville	Code[1]	City proper — Ville proprement dite Population				Urban agglomeration — Agglomération urbaine Population			
		Both sexes Les deux sexes	Male Masculin	Female Féminin	Surface area Superficie (km²)	Both sexes Les deux sexes	Male Masculin	Female Féminin	Surface area Superficie (km²)
EUROPE									
Belgium — Belgique[79]									
1 VII 2000									
BRUXELLES (BRUSSEL)	ESDJ	964 405	461 065	503 340	161	...	...	...	...
Charleroi	ESDJ	200 233	96 214	104 019	102	...	...	...	...
Gent (Gand)	ESDJ	224 685	109 142	115 543	156	...	...	...	...
Liège (Luik)	ESDJ	184 550	89 176	95 374	69	...	...	...	...
Namur	ESDJ	105 248	50 251	54 997	176	...	...	...	...
Bosnia and Herzegovina — Bosnie-Herzégovine									
1 VII 1991									
Banja Luka	ESDJ	195 994	...	...	1 239	...	...	...	...
Doboj	ESDJ	102 624	...	...	697	...	...	...	...
Mostar	ESDJ	127 034	...	...	1 227	...	...	...	...
Prijedor	ESDJ	112 635	...	...	834	...	...	...	...
SARAJEVO	ESDJ	529 021	...	...	2 095	...	...	...	...
Tuzla	ESDJ	131 866	...	...	303	...	...	...	...
Zenica	ESDJ	145 837	...	...	505	...	...	...	...
Bulgaria — Bulgarie[46,80]									
1 VII 2003									
Bourgas	ESDF	191 537	92 654	98 883	...	193 603	93 666	99 937	481
Pleven	ESDF	118 186	57 334	60 853	...	122 888	59 670	63 218	817
Plovdiv	ESDF	340 398	162 312	178 086	...	340 398	162 312	178 086	74
Rousse	ESDF	159 441	76 874	82 567	...	159 441	76 874	82 567	437
SOFIA	ESDF	1 120 649	529 458	591 192	...	1 145 963	541 823	604 140	1 311
Stara Zagora	ESDF	142 797	69 704	73 093	...	142 797	69 704	73 093	1 005
Varna	ESDF	312 778	151 860	160 918	...	312 778	151 860	160 918	210
Channel Islands: Guernsey — Iles Anglo-Normandes: Guernesey									
29 IV 2001									
ST. PETER PORT	CDJC	16 488	...	...	...	...	...	...	...
Channel Islands — Iles Anglo-Normandes: Jersey									
11 III 2001									
ST. HELIER	CDJC	28 310	13 669	14 641	9	...	...	...	...
Croatia — Croatie									
1 VII 2001									
Osijek	ESDJ	90 411	41 592	48 819	...	114 616	59 437	61 119	...
Rijeka	ESDJ	143 800	68 382	75 418	...	144 043	68 511	75 532	...
Split	ESDJ	175 140	83 720	91 420	...	188 694	90 484	98 210	...
ZAGREB	ESDJ	691 724	321 507	370 217	1 405	779 145	363 992	415 153	...
Czech Republic — République tchéque									
31 XII 2003									
Brno	ESDJ	369 559	175 255	194 304	230	...	...	...	...
Hradec Králové	ESDJ	95 195	45 440	49 755	106	...	...	...	...
Liberec	ESDJ	97 770	46 634	51 136	106	...	...	...	...
Olomouc	ESDJ	101 268	47 806	53 462	103	...	...	...	...
Ostrava	ESDJ	313 088	151 086	162 002	214	...	...	...	...
Plzen	ESDJ	164 180	78 966	85 214	138	...	...	...	...
PRAHA	ESDJ	1 165 581	555 482	610 099	496	...	...	...	...
Östí nad Labem	ESDJ	94 105	45 289	48 816	94	...	...	...	...
Denmark — Danemark									
1 VII 2001									
Ålborg	ESDJ	161 661	79 829	81 832	560	...	...	...	...
Århus	ESDJ	286 668	140 451	146 217	469	...	...	...	...
KOBENHAVN	ESDJ	499 148	244 025	255 123	123	...	...	...	...
Odense	ESDJ	183 691	89 341	94 350	364	...	...	...	...
Estonia — Estonie									
1 VII 2002									
TALLINN	ESDF	397 792	179 167	218 625	158	...	...	...	...
Tartu	ESDF	101 165	44 982	56 183	39	...	...	...	...

8. Population of capital cities and cities of 100 000 and more inhabitants: latest available year
Population des capitales et des villes de 100 000 habitants et plus: dernière année disponible (continued — suite)

(See notes at end of table. — Voir notes à la fin du tableau.)

Continent, country or area, date and city / Continent, pays ou zone, date et ville	Code[1]	City proper — Ville proprement dite Population				Urban agglomeration — Agglomération urbaine Population			
		Both sexes Les deux sexes	Male Masculin	Female Féminin	Surface area Superficie (km²)	Both sexes Les deux sexes	Male Masculin	Female Féminin	Surface area Superficie (km²)
EUROPE									
Faeroe Islands — Iles Féroé									
1 VII 1992									
THORSHAVN	ESDJ	14 671	...	...	63	16 218	...	...	79
Finland — Finlande									
1 VII 2003									
Espoo	ESDJ	222 914	108 901	114 014	312	...	...	...	...
HELSINKI	ESDJ	559 523	260 339	299 185	185	...	...	...	...
Oulu	ESDJ	125 258	60 948	64 310	328	...	...	...	...
Tampere	ESDJ	200 395	95 634	104 761	523	...	...	...	...
Turku	ESDJ	174 839	81 548	93 291	243	...	...	...	...
Vantaa	ESDJ	182 965	89 389	93 576	241	...	...	...	...
France[81,82]									
8 III 1999									
Aix-en-Provence	CDJC	134 280	62 220	72 060	186	...	...	...	...
Amiens	CDJC	135 406	63 513	71 893	49	...	...	...	...
Angers	CDJC	151 406	69 235	82 171	43	...	...	...	...
Besançon	CDJC	117 693	54 692	63 001	65	...	...	...	...
Bordeaux	CDJC	215 277	99 637	115 640	49	...	...	...	...
Boulogne-Billancourt	CDJC	106 384	49 840	56 544	6	...	...	...	...
Brest	CDJC	149 495	71 431	78 064	50	...	...	...	...
Caen	CDJC	114 079	52 605	61 474	26	...	...	...	...
Clermont-Ferrand	CDJC	136 968	63 702	73 266	43	...	...	...	...
Dijon	CDJC	150 144	69 331	80 813	40	...	...	...	...
Grenoble	CDJC	153 531	73 311	80 220	18	...	...	...	...
Le Havre	CDJC	190 806	90 882	99 924	47	...	...	...	...
Le Mans	CDJC	145 994	68 982	77 012	53	...	...	...	...
Lille[83]	CDJC	184 445	86 196	98 249	30	...	...	...	...
Limoges	CDJC	134 055	62 106	71 949	77	...	...	...	...
Lyon[84]	CDJC	444 852	206 422	238 430	48	...	...	...	...
Marseille	CDJC	796 525	376 082	420 443	241	...	...	...	...
Metz	CDJC	123 720	59 670	64 050	42	...	...	...	...
Montpellier	CDJC	225 748	103 437	122 311	57	...	...	...	...
Mulhouse	CDJC	110 129	53 963	56 166	22	...	...	...	...
Nantes	CDJC	270 474	126 599	143 875	65	...	...	...	...
Nancy	CDJC	103 533	47 345	56 188	15	...	...	...	...
Nice	CDJC	343 166	157 148	186 018	72	...	...	...	...
Nîmes	CDJC	133 391	62 451	70 940	162	...	...	...	...
Orléans	CDJC	113 077	53 728	59 349	27	...	...	...	...
PARIS	CDJC	2 125 017	995 844	1 129 173	105	...	...	...	...
Perpignan	CDJC	105 027	47 870	57 157	68	...	...	...	...
Reims	CDJC	187 183	88 707	98 476	47	...	...	...	...
Rennes	CDJC	206 221	95 224	110 997	50	...	...	...	...
Rouen	CDJC	106 356	49 432	56 924	21	...	...	...	...
Saint-Étienne	CDJC	180 393	84 135	96 258	80	...	...	...	...
Strasbourg[83]	CDJC	263 682	124 926	138 756	78	...	...	...	...
Toulon	CDJC	160 549	74 964	85 585	43	...	...	...	...
Toulouse	CDJC	390 174	185 107	205 067	118	...	...	...	...
Tours	CDJC	132 637	60 117	72 520	34	...	...	...	...
Villeurbanne	CDJC	124 451	59 519	64 932	15	...	...	...	...
Germany — Allemagne									
1 VII 1999									
Aachen	ESDJ	243 825	121 671	122 154	161	...	...	...	...
Augsburg	ESDJ	254 867	121 846	133 021	147	...	...	...	...
Bergisch Gladbach	ESDJ	106 150	50 723	55 427	83	...	...	...	...
BERLIN	ESDJ	3 386 667	1 644 575	1 742 092	891	...	...	...	...
Bielefeld	ESDJ	321 125	152 701	168 424	258	...	...	...	...
Bochum	ESDJ	392 830	190 433	202 397	145	...	...	...	...
Bonn	ESDJ	301 048	143 416	157 632	141	...	...	...	...
Bottrop	ESDJ	121 097	58 490	62 607	101	...	...	...	...
Braunschweig	ESDJ	246 322	119 350	126 972	192	...	...	...	...
Bremen	ESDJ	540 330	259 439	280 891	327	...	...	...	...

8. Population of capital cities and cities of 100 000 and more inhabitants: latest available year
Population des capitales et des villes de 100 000 habitants et plus: dernière année disponible (continued — suite)

(See notes at end of table. — Voir notes à la fin du tableau.)

Continent, country or area, date and city / Continent, pays ou zone, date et ville	Code[1]	City proper — Ville proprement dite Population				Urban agglomeration — Agglomération urbaine Population			
		Both sexes Les deux sexes	Male Masculin	Female Féminin	Surface area Superficie (km²)	Both sexes Les deux sexes	Male Masculin	Female Féminin	Surface area Superficie (km²)
EUROPE									
Germany — Allemagne									
1 VII 1999									
Bremerhaven	ESDJ	122 735	59 991	62 744	78	...	...	...	...
Chemnitz	ESDJ	263 222	125 123	138 099	176	...	...	...	...
Cottbus	ESDJ	110 894	53 712	57 182	150	...	...	...	...
Darmstadt	ESDJ	137 776	67 680	70 096	122	...	...	...	...
Dortmund	ESDJ	590 213	286 880	303 333	280	...	...	...	...
Dresden	ESDJ	476 668	229 565	247 103	237	...	...	...	...
Duisburg	ESDJ	519 793	252 735	267 058	233	...	...	...	...
Düsseldorf	ESDJ	568 855	268 630	300 225	217	...	...	...	...
Erfurt	ESDJ	201 267	96 937	104 330	269	...	...	...	...
Erlangen	ESDJ	100 750	48 939	51 811	77	...	...	...	...
Essen	ESDJ	599 515	286 350	313 165	210	...	...	...	...
Frankfurt am Main	ESDJ	643 821	314 431	329 390	248	...	...	...	...
Freiburg im Breisgau	ESDJ	202 455	96 025	106 430	153	...	...	...	...
Fürth	ESDJ	109 771	52 773	56 998	63	...	...	...	...
Gelsenkirchen	ESDJ	281 979	135 781	146 198	105	...	...	...	...
Gera	ESDJ	114 718	55 211	59 507	152	...	...	...	...
Göttingen	ESDJ	124 775	60 334	64 441	117	...	...	...	...
Hagen	ESDJ	205 201	98 338	106 863	160	...	...	...	...
Halle	ESDJ	254 360	121 314	133 046	135	...	...	...	...
Hamburg	ESDJ	1 704 735	824 686	880 049	755	...	...	...	...
Hamm	ESDJ	181 804	89 307	92 497	226	...	...	...	...
Hannover	ESDJ	514 718	245 017	269 701	204	...	...	...	...
Heidelberg	ESDJ	139 672	65 694	73 978	109	...	...	...	...
Heilbronn	ESDJ	119 526	58 400	61 126	100	...	...	...	...
Herne	ESDJ	175 661	85 577	90 084	51	...	...	...	...
Hildesheim	ESDJ	104 013	48 910	55 103	93	...	...	...	...
Ingolstadt	ESDJ	114 826	56 417	58 409	133	...	...	...	...
Kaiserslautern	ESDJ	100 025	49 247	50 778	140	...	...	...	...
Karlsruhe	ESDJ	277 204	134 775	142 429	173	...	...	...	...
Kassel	ESDJ	196 211	93 058	103 153	107	...	...	...	...
Kiel	ESDJ	233 795	113 274	120 521	117	...	...	...	...
Koblenz	ESDJ	108 003	51 340	56 663	105	...	...	...	...
Köln	ESDJ	962 507	466 543	495 964	405	...	...	...	...
Krefeld	ESDJ	241 769	117 087	124 682	138	...	...	...	...
Leipzig	ESDJ	489 532	235 789	253 743	176	...	...	...	...
Leverkusen	ESDJ	160 841	78 116	82 725	79	...	...	...	...
Lübeck	ESDJ	213 326	101 024	112 302	214	...	...	...	...
Lüdwigshafen am Rhein	ESDJ	163 771	81 257	82 514	78	...	...	...	...
Magdeburg	ESDJ	235 073	112 839	122 234	193	...	...	...	...
Mainz	ESDJ	183 134	89 093	94 041	98	...	...	...	...
Mannheim	ESDJ	307 730	151 145	156 585	145	...	...	...	...
Moers	ESDJ	106 837	51 824	55 013	68	...	...	...	...
Mönchengladbach	ESDJ	263 697	126 721	136 976	170	...	...	...	...
Mülheim an der Ruhr	ESDJ	173 895	82 677	91 218	91	...	...	...	...
München	ESDJ	1 194 560	571 363	623 197	311	...	...	...	...
Münster (Westf.)	ESDJ	264 670	123 825	140 845	303	...	...	...	...
Neuss	ESDJ	149 702	72 522	77 180	99	...	...	...	...
Nürnberg	ESDJ	486 628	233 415	253 213	186	...	...	...	...
Oberhausen	ESDJ	222 349	107 562	114 787	77	...	...	...	...
Offenbach am Main	ESDJ	116 627	57 539	59 088	45	...	...	...	...
Oldenburg	ESDJ	154 125	73 572	80 553	103	...	...	...	...
Osnabrück	ESDJ	164 539	77 981	86 558	120	...	...	...	...
Paderborn	ESDJ	137 647	67 010	70 637	179	...	...	...	...
Pforzheim	ESDJ	117 227	55 738	61 489	98	...	...	...	...
Potsdam	ESDJ	128 983	62 651	66 332	109	...	...	...	...
Recklinghausen	ESDJ	125 022	60 456	64 566	66	...	...	...	...
Regensburg	ESDJ	125 236	59 600	65 636	81	...	...	...	...
Remscheid	ESDJ	120 125	57 923	62 202	75	...	...	...	...
Reutlingen	ESDJ	110 343	53 564	56 779	87	...	...	...	...

8. Population of capital cities and cities of 100 000 and more inhabitants: latest available year
Population des capitales et des villes de 100 000 habitants et plus: dernière année disponible (continued — suite)

(See notes at end of table. — Voir notes à la fin du tableau.)

Continent, country or area, date and city / Continent, pays ou zone, date et ville	Code[1]	City proper — Ville proprement dite Population				Urban agglomeration — Agglomération urbaine Population			
		Both sexes Les deux sexes	Male Masculin	Female Féminin	Surface area Superficie (km²)	Both sexes Les deux sexes	Male Masculin	Female Féminin	Surface area Superficie (km²)
EUROPE									
Germany — Allemagne									
1 VII 1999									
Rostock	ESDJ	203 279	99 627	103 652	181	...	...	...	...
Saarbrücken	ESDJ	183 836	87 875	95 961	167	...	...	...	...
Salzgitter	ESDJ	112 934	54 808	58 126	224	...	...	...	...
Schwerin	ESDJ	102 878	49 428	53 450	130	...	...	...	...
Siegen	ESDJ	109 225	53 585	55 640	115	...	...	...	...
Solingen	ESDJ	165 583	79 712	85 871	89	...	...	...	...
Stuttgart	ESDJ	582 443	284 977	297 466	207	...	...	...	...
Ulm	ESDJ	116 103	56 511	59 592	119	...	...	...	...
Wiesbaden	ESDJ	268 716	129 032	139 684	204	...	...	...	...
Witten	ESDJ	103 384	49 545	53 839	72	...	...	...	...
Wolfsburg	ESDJ	121 954	59 761	62 193	204	...	...	...	...
Wuppertal	ESDJ	368 993	176 350	192 643	168	...	...	...	...
Würzburg	ESDJ	127 350	58 801	68 549	88	...	...	...	...
Zwickau	ESDJ	104 146	49 513	54 633	73	...	...	...	...
Gibraltar									
1 VII 1991									
GIBRALTAR	CDFC	28 074	...	...	...	...	...	...	...
Greece — Grèce[85]									
18 III 2001									
ATHINAI	CDJC	789 166	374 900	414 266	39	...	...	...	...
Calithèa	CDJC	115 150	54 137	61 013	5	...	...	...	...
Iraclion	CDJC	135 761	66 956	68 805	52	...	...	...	...
Larissa	CDJC	131 095	64 000	67 095	88	...	...	...	...
Patrai	CDJC	168 530	82 981	85 549	57	...	...	...	...
Pésterion	CDJC	146 743	72 391	74 352	10	...	...	...	...
Pireas	CDJC	181 933	87 362	94 571	...	...	...	...	...
Thessaloniki	CDJC	385 406	180 122	205 284	...	...	...	...	...
Holy See — Saint-Siège[86]									
1 VII 1988									
VATICAN CITY	ESDF	766	...	...	...	...	...	...	...
Hungary — Hongrie									
1 VII 2003									
BUDAPEST	ESDF	1 712 326	780 722	931 604	525	...	...	...	...
Debrecen	ESDF	205 302	95 445	109 857	462	...	...	...	...
Györ	ESDF	128 742	60 615	68 128	175	...	...	...	...
Kecskemét	ESDF	107 635	50 121	57 514	321	...	...	...	...
Miskolc	ESDF	179 046	83 084	95 962	237	...	...	...	...
Nyiregyhaza	ESDF	116 720	54 342	62 378	274	...	...	...	...
Pécs	ESDF	158 301	73 026	85 275	163	...	...	...	...
Szeged	ESDF	162 723	74 890	87 833	281	...	...	...	...
Székesfehérvar	ESDF	102 224	48 335	53 889	171	...	...	...	...
Iceland — Islande[87,88]									
1 VII 2003									
REYKJAVIK	ESDJ	112 960	55 389	57 571	100	180 823	89 154	91 669	...
Ireland — Irlande									
28 IV 2002									
Cork	CDFC	123 062	59 263	63 799	40	186 239	90 348	95 891	...
DUBLIN	CDFC	495 781	237 813	257 968	118	1 004 614	485 209	519 405	...
Isle of Man — Ile de Man									
30 IV 2001									
DOUGLAS	CDJC	25 347	12 460	12 887	...	...	...	...	...
Italy — Italie									
31 XII 2003									
Ancona	ESDJ	101 545	48 335	53 210	124	...	...	...	...
Bari	ESDJ	314 166	150 861	163 305	116	...	...	...	...
Bergamo	ESDJ	114 190	53 392	60 798	40	...	...	...	...
Bologna	ESDJ	373 539	174 107	199 432	141	...	...	...	...
Brescia	ESDJ	191 114	90 381	100 733	91	...	...	...	...
Cagliari	ESDJ	162 560	75 925	86 635	86	...	...	...	...

(See notes at end of table. — Voir notes à la fin du tableau.)

Continent, country or area, date and city / Continent, pays ou zone, date et ville	Code[1]	City proper — Ville proprement dite Population				Urban agglomeration — Agglomération urbaine Population			
		Both sexes Les deux sexes	Male Masculin	Female Féminin	Surface area Superficie (km²)	Both sexes Les deux sexes	Male Masculin	Female Féminin	Surface area Superficie (km²)
EUROPE									
Italy — Italie									
31 XII 2003									
Catania	ESDJ	307 774	145 424	162 350	181	...	...	...	...
Ferrara	ESDJ	131 135	61 295	69 840	404	...	...	...	...
Firenze	ESDJ	367 259	170 866	196 393	102	...	...	...	...
Foggia	ESDJ	154 792	74 957	79 835	508	...	...	...	...
Forli	ESDJ	110 209	52 885	57 324	228	...	...	...	...
Genova	ESDJ	601 338	280 436	320 902	244	...	...	...	...
Giugliano in Campania	ESDJ	103 735	51 089	52 646	94	...	...	...	...
Latina	ESDJ	110 025	53 021	57 004	278	...	...	...	...
Livorno	ESDJ	155 880	74 079	81 801	104	...	...	...	...
Messina	ESDJ	248 616	118 772	129 844	211	...	...	...	...
Milano	ESDJ	1 271 898	597 010	674 888	182	...	...	...	...
Modena	ESDJ	178 874	85 924	92 950	183	...	...	...	...
Napoli	ESDJ	1 000 449	478 459	521 990	117	...	...	...	...
Novara	ESDJ	102 260	49 146	53 114	103	...	...	...	...
Padova	ESDJ	208 938	98 232	110 706	93	...	...	...	...
Palermo	ESDJ	679 730	324 754	354 976	159	...	...	...	...
Parma	ESDJ	164 528	77 646	86 882	261	...	...	...	...
Perugia	ESDJ	153 857	73 017	80 840	450	...	...	...	...
Pescara	ESDJ	122 083	57 603	64 480	33	...	...	...	...
Prato	ESDJ	176 013	85 376	90 637	98	...	...	...	...
Ravenna	ESDJ	139 021	67 071	71 950	653	...	...	...	...
Reggio di Calabria	ESDJ	181 440	87 339	94 101	236	...	...	...	...
Reggio nell'Emilia	ESDJ	146 705	70 809	75 896	232	...	...	...	...
Rimini	ESDJ	131 785	63 444	68 341	134	...	...	...	...
ROMA	ESDJ	2 542 003	1 192 349	1 349 654	1 308	...	...	...	...
Salerno	ESDJ	136 678	64 588	72 090	59	...	...	...	...
Sassari	ESDJ	121 849	58 370	63 479	546	...	...	...	...
Siracusa	ESDJ	123 022	59 956	63 066	204	...	...	...	...
Taranto	ESDJ	199 131	95 083	104 048	210	...	...	...	...
Terni	ESDJ	108 403	51 397	57 006	212	...	...	...	...
Torino	ESDJ	867 857	410 925	456 932	130	...	...	...	...
Trento	ESDJ	108 577	51 895	56 682	158	...	...	...	...
Trieste	ESDJ	208 309	97 044	111 265	84	...	...	...	...
Venezia	ESDJ	271 663	128 662	143 001	416	...	...	...	...
Verona	ESDJ	258 115	122 671	135 444	207	...	...	...	...
Vicenza	ESDJ	111 409	52 967	58 442	81	...	...	...	...
Latvia — Lettonie[89]									
1 VII 2002									
Daugavpils	ESDF	113 009	50 936	62 073	73	...	...	...	...
RIGA	ESDF	743 195	331 152	412 043	307	...	...	...	...
Liechtenstein[90]									
30 VI 2003									
VADUZ	ESDF	5 000	2 382	2 618	17	...	...	...	...
Lithuania — Lituanie									
1 VII 2003									
Kaunas	ESDJ	371 292	167 308	203 984	157	...	...	...	...
Klaipeda	ESDJ	190 906	88 308	102 598	98	...	...	...	...
Panevezhis	ESDJ	118 208	53 913	64 295	50	...	...	...	...
Shauliai	ESDJ	131 948	60 221	71 727	81	...	...	...	...
VILNIUS	ESDJ	541 330	246 412	294 918	394	...	...	...	...
Luxembourg									
1 VII 2003									
LUXEMBOURG-VILLE	ESDJ	77 827	...	...	51	...	...	...	...
Malta — Malte[91]									
1 VII 2003									
VALLETTA	ESDF	7 137	3 399	3 738	...	...	...	...	...
Monaco									
1 VII 1999									
MONACO	ESDJ	33 268	...	...	...	...	...	...	...

8. Population of capital cities and cities of 100 000 and more inhabitants: latest available year
Population des capitales et des villes de 100 000 habitants et plus: dernière année disponible (continued — suite)

(See notes at end of table. — Voir notes à la fin du tableau.)

Continent, country or area, date and city Continent, pays ou zone, date et ville	Code[1]	City proper — Ville proprement dite Population				Urban agglomeration — Agglomération urbaine Population			
		Both sexes Les deux sexes	Male Masculin	Female Féminin	Surface area Superficie (km²)	Both sexes Les deux sexes	Male Masculin	Female Féminin	Surface area Superficie (km²)
EUROPE									
Netherlands — Pays-Bas[92]									
1 I 2003									
Almere	ESDJ	165 106	82 389	82 717	130	...	...	...	...
Amersfoort	ESDJ	131 221	64 086	67 135	63	160 219	78 366	81 853	120
AMSTERDAM	ESDJ	736 562	363 330	373 232	165	1 013 147	498 272	514 875	366
Apeldoorn	ESDJ	155 741	76 515	79 226	340	...	...	...	...
Arnhem	ESDJ	141 528	69 773	71 755	98	143 055	70 527	72 528	126
Breda	ESDJ	164 397	79 788	84 609	127	...	...	...	...
Dordrecht	ESDJ	120 043	58 966	61 077	80	246 187	121 027	125 160	158
Ede	ESDJ	104 771	51 466	53 305	318	...	...	...	...
Eindhoven	ESDJ	206 118	103 631	102 487	87	308 213	154 522	153 691	181
Emmen	ESDJ	108 198	53 537	54 661	337	...	...	...	...
Enschede	ESDJ	152 321	77 559	74 762	141	...	...	...	...
Geleen-Sittard	ESDJ	97 806	48 225	49 581	80	141 467	69 925	71 542	122
Groningen	ESDJ	177 172	87 548	89 624	80	196 180	96 462	99 718	121
Haarlem	ESDJ	147 097	71 484	75 613	29	189 902	91 554	98 348	76
Haarlemmermeer	ESDJ	122 902	61 429	61 473	180	...	...	...	...
Heerlen-Kerkrade	ESDJ	93 969	46 102	47 867	45	214 261	105 319	108 942	109
Leiden	ESDJ	117 689	57 547	60 142	22	253 106	123 838	129 268	93
Maastricht	ESDJ	121 982	58 742	63 240	57	...	...	...	...
Nijmegen	ESDJ	156 198	75 123	81 075	54	...	...	...	...
Rotterdam	ESDJ	599 651	294 665	304 986	206	1 008 390	495 373	513 017	352
s-Gravenhage	ESDJ	463 826	226 622	237 204	83	627 645	304 782	322 863	189
s-Hertogenbosch	ESDJ	132 501	65 226	67 275	85	157 774	77 653	80 121	118
Tilburg	ESDJ	197 917	97 773	100 144	116	220 427	108 926	111 501	158
Utrecht	ESDJ	265 151	127 863	137 288	96	400 559	194 706	205 853	170
Zaanstad	ESDJ	139 464	68 817	70 647	74	...	...	...	...
Zoetermeer	ESDJ	112 594	55 152	57 442	35	...	...	...	...
Zwolle	ESDJ	109 955	53 410	56 545	112	...	...	...	...
Norway — Norvège									
1 VII 2003									
Bergen	ESDJ	236 427	116 277	120 150	445	...	...	...	...
OSLO	ESDJ	519 644	253 163	266 481	427	...	...	...	...
Stavanger	ESDJ	111 706	55 052	56 655	66	...	...	...	...
Trondheim	ESDJ	153 525	75 521	78 004	321	...	...	...	...
Poland — Pologne[93]									
1 VII 2003									
Bialystok	ESDF	291 465	137 204	154 261	94	...	...	...	...
Bielsko-Biala	ESDF	177 538	83 972	93 566	125	...	...	...	...
Bydgoszcz	ESDF	371 237	174 329	196 908	174	...	...	...	...
Bytom	ESDF	191 890	93 123	98 767	69	...	...	...	...
Chorzów	ESDF	116 018	55 454	60 564	34	...	...	...	...
Czestochowa	ESDF	250 241	118 116	132 125	160	...	...	...	...
Dabrowa Górnicza	ESDF	131 652	63 653	67 999	188	...	...	...	...
Elblag	ESDF	127 899	61 351	66 548	80	...	...	...	...
Gdansk	ESDF	461 482	219 500	241 982	262	...	...	...	...
Gdynia	ESDF	253 587	121 478	132 109	136	...	...	...	...
Gliwice	ESDF	202 057	97 660	104 397	134	...	...	...	...
Grudziadz	ESDF	100 032	47 547	52 485	59	...	...	...	...
Gorzów Wielkopolski	ESDF	125 394	59 875	65 519	86	...	...	...	...
Jastrzebie-Zdrój	ESDF	96 648	48 068	48 580	85	...	...	...	...
Kalisz	ESDF	109 211	51 204	58 007	70	...	...	...	...
Katowice	ESDF	323 710	153 254	170 456	164	...	...	...	...
Kielce	ESDF	211 085	100 296	110 789	109	...	...	...	...
Koszalin	ESDF	108 254	51 676	56 578	83	...	...	...	...
Kraków	ESDF	757 427	354 813	402 614	327	...	...	...	...
Legnica	ESDF	106 735	50 722	56 013	56	...	...	...	...
Lódz	ESDF	781 932	357 077	424 855	294	...	...	...	...
Lublin	ESDF	358 079	165 725	192 354	148	...	...	...	...
Olsztyn	ESDF	172 672	80 020	92 652	88	...	...	...	...
Opole	ESDF	129 073	60 565	68 508	96	...	...	...	...

8. Population of capital cities and cities of 100 000 and more inhabitants: latest available year
Population des capitales et des villes de 100 000 habitants et plus: dernière année disponible (continued — suite)

(See notes at end of table. — Voir notes à la fin du tableau.)

Continent, country or area, date and city / Continent, pays ou zone, date et ville	Code[1]	City proper — Ville proprement dite Population				Urban agglomeration — Agglomération urbaine Population			
		Both sexes Les deux sexes	Male Masculin	Female Féminin	Surface area Superficie (km²)	Both sexes Les deux sexes	Male Masculin	Female Féminin	Surface area Superficie (km²)
EUROPE									
Poland — Pologne[93]									
1 VII 2003									
Plock	ESDF	128 066	61 483	66 583	88	...	...	...	...
Poznan	ESDF	575 742	268 261	307 481	261	...	...	...	...
Radom	ESDF	228 710	109 587	119 123	112	...	...	...	...
Ruda Slaska	ESDF	148 936	72 780	76 156	78	...	...	...	...
Rybnik	ESDF	142 626	70 068	72 558	148	...	...	...	...
Rzeszów	ESDF	159 649	75 388	84 261	54	...	...	...	...
Slupsk	ESDF	99 492	47 097	52 395	43	...	...	...	...
Sosnowiec	ESDF	230 720	110 024	120 696	91	...	...	...	...
Szczecin	ESDF	414 685	197 486	217 199	301	...	...	...	...
Tarnów	ESDF	119 193	56 794	62 399	72	...	...	...	...
Torun	ESDF	210 357	97 800	112 557	116	...	...	...	...
Tychy	ESDF	132 415	64 510	67 905	82	...	...	...	...
Walbrzych	ESDF	129 252	61 018	68 234	85	...	...	...	...
WARSZAWA	ESDF	1 688 300	780 414	907 886	517	...	...	...	...
Wloclawek	ESDF	120 933	57 254	63 679	85	...	...	...	...
Wroclaw	ESDF	638 459	299 622	338 837	293	...	...	...	...
Zabrze	ESDF	194 148	93 978	100 170	80	...	...	...	...
Zielona Góra	ESDF	118 319	55 641	62 678	58	...	...	...	...
Portugal									
1 VII 2003									
Amadora	ESDF	176 670	84 744	91 926	24	...	...	...	...
Funchal	ESDF	101 256	47 164	54 092	34	...	...	...	...
LISBOA	ESDF	540 022	246 366	293 656	85	...	...	...	...
Porto	ESDF	244 998	11 213	133 785	40	...	...	...	...
Setubal	ESDF	118 696	57 936	60 760	...	...	...	...	...
Republic of Moldova — République de Moldova									
1 VII 2001									
Beltsy	ESDF	144 371	71 171	73 200	41	...	...	...	...
KISHINEV	ESDF	654 927	316 591	338 336	121	...	...	...	...
Romania — Roumanie									
1 VII 2003									
Arad	ESDJ	170 944	80 109	90 835	267	...	...	...	...
Bacau	ESDJ	182 446	88 098	94 348	43	...	...	...	...
Baia Mare	ESDJ	142 291	68 611	73 680	233	...	...	...	...
Botosani	ESDJ	117 011	56 325	60 686	41	...	...	...	...
Braila	ESDJ	220 933	105 978	114 955	33	...	...	...	...
Brasov	ESDJ	286 327	137 461	148 866	267	...	...	...	...
BUCURESTI	ESDJ	1 930 335	898 564	1 031 771	238	...	...	...	...
Buzau	ESDJ	138 286	66 552	71 734	81	...	...	...	...
Cluj-Napoca	ESDJ	297 461	140 466	156 995	180	...	...	...	...
Constanta	ESDJ	308 910	146 811	162 099	127	...	...	...	...
Craiova	ESDJ	299 641	144 359	155 282	81	...	...	...	...
Drobeta Turnu-Severin	ESDJ	110 727	53 659	57 068	55	...	...	...	...
Focsani	ESDJ	101 891	48 941	52 950	...	...	...	...	...
Galati	ESDJ	299 451	146 069	153 382	246	...	...	...	...
Iasi	ESDJ	319 075	151 082	167 993	94	...	...	...	...
Oradea	ESDJ	207 270	98 279	108 991	111	...	...	...	...
Piatra Neamt	ESDJ	111 063	53 148	57 915	77	...	...	...	...
Pitesti	ESDJ	172 627	83 063	89 564	41	...	...	...	...
Ploiesti	ESDJ	236 836	111 909	124 927	58	...	...	...	...
Rimnicu Vilcea	ESDJ	112 804	54 546	58 258	90	...	...	...	...
Satu-Mare	ESDJ	117 477	55 774	61 703	150	...	...	...	...
Sibiu	ESDJ	155 950	73 152	82 798	122	...	...	...	...
Suceava	ESDJ	108 076	52 066	56 010	52	...	...	...	...
Timisoara	ESDJ	305 977	143 966	162 011	49	...	...	...	...
Tirgu-Mures	ESDJ	149 047	70 938	78 109	130	...	...	...	...

(See notes at end of table. — Voir notes à la fin du tableau.)

Continent, country or area, date and city / Continent, pays ou zone, date et ville	Code[1]	City proper — Ville proprement dite Population				Urban agglomeration — Agglomération urbaine Population			
		Both sexes Les deux sexes	Male Masculin	Female Féminin	Surface area Superficie (km²)	Both sexes Les deux sexes	Male Masculin	Female Féminin	Surface area Superficie (km²)
EUROPE									
Russian Federation — Fédération de Russie[94,95]									
1 VII 1999									
Abakan	ESDF	168 047	77 027	91 020	...	...	...	...	...
Achinsk	ESDF	121 419	57 161	64 258	...	122 800	...	...	...
Almetievsk	ESDF	141 764	68 085	73 679	...	151 850	...	...	...
Angarsk	ESDF	265 410	130 419	134 991	...	270 750	...	...	...
Arkhangelsk	ESDF	364 985	169 342	195 643	...	372 200	...	...	...
Armavir	ESDF	163 832	75 976	87 856	...	180 700	...	...	...
Arzamas	ESDF	110 465	51 174	59 291	...	...	...	...	...
Astrakhan	ESDF	482 402	224 336	258 066	...	...	...	...	...
Balakovo	ESDF	208 030	97 808	110 222	...	208 650	...	...	...
Balashikha	ESDF	132 559	59 927	72 632	...	...	...	...	...
Barnaul	ESDF	579 900	268 946	310 954	...	647 600	...	...	...
Belgorod	ESDF	338 308	156 067	182 241	...	...	...	...	...
Berezniki	ESDF	182 900	92 307	90 593	...	185 150	...	...	...
Biisk	ESDF	224 493	103 772	120 721	...	236 250	...	...	...
Blagoveshchensk (Amurskaya oblast)	ESDF	220 102	106 277	113 825	...	223 500	...	...	...
Bratsk	ESDF	279 664	134 389	145 275	...	...	...	...	...
Bryansk	ESDF	455 158	213 605	241 553	...	477 450	...	...	...
Cheboksary	ESDF	459 156	216 659	242 497	...	471 650	...	...	...
Chelyabinsk	ESDF	1 084 208	501 602	582 606	...	1 111 100	...	...	...
Cherepovets	ESDF	323 545	153 635	169 910	...	...	...	...	...
Cherkessk	ESDF	121 032	56 199	64 833	...	...	...	...	...
Chita	ESDF	308 863	146 756	162 107	...	309 300	...	...	...
Dimitrovgrad	ESDF	136 605	65 234	71 371	...	...	...	...	...
Dzerzhinsk (Novgorodskaya oblast)	ESDF	278 246	129 783	148 463	...	289 100	...	...	...
Ekaterinoburg	ESDF	1 267 393	578 680	688 713	...	1 313 750	...	...	...
Elektrostal	ESDF	147 159	67 416	79 743	...	...	...	...	...
Elets	ESDF	118 987	55 033	63 954	...	...	...	...	...
Elista	ESDF	102 189	47 480	54 709	...	106 150	...	...	...
Engels	ESDF	189 826	88 715	101 111	...	224 800	...	...	...
Glazov	ESDF	106 473	49 720	56 753	...	...	...	...	...
Ioshkap-Ola	ESDF	249 550	114 431	135 119	...	278 500	...	...	...
Irkutsk	ESDF	591 047	264 536	326 511	...	...	...	...	...
Ivanovo	ESDF	458 531	206 380	252 151	...	...	...	...	...
Izhevsk	ESDF	653 691	302 203	351 488	...	...	...	...	...
Kaliningrad (Kaliningradskaya oblast)	ESDF	425 089	204 456	220 633	...	...	...	...	...
Kaluga	ESDF	339 703	155 720	183 983	...	357 100	...	...	...
Kamensk-Uralsky	ESDF	190 352	88 328	102 024	...	192 000	...	...	...
Kamyshin	ESDF	125 901	58 968	66 933	...	...	...	...	...
Kansk	ESDF	108 063	51 654	56 409	...	...	...	...	...
Kazan	ESDF	1 091 656	499 838	591 818	...	1 092 150	...	...	...
Kemerovo	ESDF	492 240	222 475	269 765	...	532 200	...	...	...
Khabarovsk	ESDF	608 853	296 436	312 417	...	...	...	...	...
Khimki	ESDF	134 962	60 229	74 733	...	136 300	...	...	...
Kirov (Azerbaidzhanskaya SSR)	ESDF	465 628	213 653	251 975	...	508 150	...	...	...
Kiselevsk	ESDF	110 005	51 798	58 207	...	115 900	...	...	...
Kislovodsk	ESDF	112 481	51 301	61 180	...	117 100	...	...	...
Kolomna	ESDF	150 905	69 344	81 561	...	...	...	...	...
Komsomolsk-na-Amure	ESDF	294 268	140 015	154 253	...	...	...	...	...
Korolev	ESDF	133 789	60 577	73 212	...	161 600	...	...	...
Kostroma	ESDF	287 818	132 062	155 756	...	...	...	...	...
Kovrov	ESDF	161 298	73 154	88 144	...	...	...	...	...
Krasnodar	ESDF	639 917	298 694	341 223	...	757 150	...	...	...
Krasnoyarsk	ESDF	876 418	394 992	481 426	...	...	...	...	...
Kurgan	ESDF	364 211	168 153	196 058	...	...	...	...	...
Kursk	ESDF	440 208	200 923	239 285	...	...	...	...	...

8. Population of capital cities and cities of 100 000 and more inhabitants: latest available year
Population des capitales et des villes de 100 000 habitants et plus: dernière année disponible (continued — suite)

(See notes at end of table. — Voir notes à la fin du tableau.)

Continent, country or area, date and city / Continent, pays ou zone, date et ville	Code[1]	City proper — Ville proprement dite Population				Urban agglomeration — Agglomération urbaine Population			
		Both sexes Les deux sexes	Male Masculin	Female Féminin	Surface area Superficie (km²)	Both sexes Les deux sexes	Male Masculin	Female Féminin	Surface area Superficie (km²)
EUROPE									
Russian Federation — Fédération de Russie[94,95]									
1 VII 1999									
Leninsk-Kuznetsky	ESDF	114 079	54 109	59 970	...	153 800	...	...	...
Lipetsk	ESDF	518 926	243 479	275 447	...	...	...	...	...
Lyubertsy	ESDF	164 210	73 397	90 813	...	...	...	...	...
Magadan	ESDF	121 330	59 226	62 104	...	130 450	...	...	...
Magnitogorsk	ESDF	426 866	199 646	227 220	...	427 300	...	...	...
Maikop	ESDF	166 860	75 470	91 390	...	178 550	...	...	...
Makhachkala	ESDF	330 942	163 560	167 382	...	378 650	...	...	...
Mezhdurechensk	ESDF	104 551	50 729	53 822	...	...	...	...	...
Miass	ESDF	165 811	77 932	87 879	...	179 400	...	...	...
Michurinsk	ESDF	118 610	53 026	65 584	...	...	...	...	...
MOSKVA	ESDF	8 297 056	3 724 694	4 572 362	...	8 537 700	...	...	...
Murmansk	ESDF	378 552	187 960	190 592	...	...	...	...	...
Murom	ESDF	140 993	65 615	75 378	...	...	...	...	...
Mytishchi	ESDF	156 631	69 397	87 234	...	...	...	...	...
Naberezhnye Tchelny	ESDF	521 282	250 577	270 705	...	524 400	...	...	...
Nakhodka	ESDF	158 559	80 172	78 387	...	188 150	...	...	...
Naltchik	ESDF	230 131	108 218	121 913	...	250 600	...	...	...
Neftekamsk	ESDF	117 352	55 296	62 056	...	124 650	...	...	...
Nevinnomyssk	ESDF	132 111	62 335	69 776	...	...	...	...	...
Nizhnekamsk	ESDF	224 426	105 993	118 433	...	...	...	...	...
Nizhenvartovsk	ESDF	238 071	118 840	119 231	...	...	...	...	...
Nizhny Tagil	ESDF	392 942	184 439	208 503	...	...	...	...	...
Nizhny Novgorod	ESDF	1 357 555	619 859	737 696	...	1 366 100	...	...	...
Noginsk	ESDF	117 446	52 784	64 662	...	...	...	...	...
Norilsk	ESDF	148 797	75 009	73 788	...	244 450	...	...	...
Novocheboksarsk	ESDF	124 628	58 624	66 004	...	124 900	...	...	...
Novocherkassk	ESDF	184 306	92 582	91 724	...	198 950	...	...	...
Novokuybishevsk	ESDF	115 758	51 706	64 052	...	117 900	...	...	...
Novokuznetsk	ESDF	564 353	262 313	302 040	...	579 250	...	...	...
Novomoskovsk (Tulskaya oblast)	ESDF	138 220	61 797	76 423	...	...	...	...	...
Novorossiysk	ESDF	204 652	97 198	107 454	...	248 850	...	...	...
Novoshakhtinsk	ESDF	101 566	48 083	53 483	...	118 450	...	...	...
Novosibirsk	ESDF	1 400 328	636 563	763 765	...	...	...	...	...
Novotroitsk	ESDF	109 681	53 577	56 104	...	117 400	...	...	...
Obninsk	ESDF	108 029	52 965	55 064	...	...	...	...	...
Odintsovo	ESDF	128 227	58 345	69 882	...	...	...	...	...
Oktyabrsky	ESDF	111 423	53 153	58 270	...	...	...	...	...
Omsk	ESDF	1 153 314	536 759	616 555	...	1 177 000	...	...	...
Orekhovo-Zuevo	ESDF	125 399	55 394	70 005	...	...	...	...	...
Orel	ESDF	341 854	155 373	186 481	...	...	...	...	...
Orenburg	ESDF	522 643	238 134	284 509	...	541 500	...	...	...
Orsk	ESDF	274 849	130 618	144 231	...	280 000	...	...	...
Penza	ESDF	528 140	243 904	284 236	...	528 500	...	...	...
Perm	ESDF	1 014 360	472 602	541 758	...	1 024 250	...	...	...
Pervouralsk	ESDF	135 588	64 826	70 762	...	163 850	...	...	...
Petropavlovsk-Kamchatsky	ESDF	198 424	102 034	96 390	...	209 650	...	...	...
Petrozavodsk	ESDF	282 401	130 133	152 268	...	282 650	...	...	...
Podolsk	ESDF	193 735	86 646	107 089	...	...	...	...	...
Prokopyevsk	ESDF	236 174	111 692	124 482	...	236 350	...	...	...
Pskov	ESDF	201 846	91 042	110 804	...	...	...	...	...
Pyatigorsk	ESDF	128 257	56 836	71 421	...	184 600	...	...	...
Rostov-na-Donu	ESDF	1 003 482	461 383	542 099	...	...	...	...	...
Rubtsovsk	ESDF	163 252	77 811	85 441	...	...	...	...	...
Ryazan	ESDF	528 116	241 727	286 389	...	531 200	...	...	...
Rybinsk	ESDF	241 450	111 568	129 882	...	...	...	...	...
Salavat	ESDF	157 847	74 820	83 027	...	...	...	...	...
Samara (Samarskaya oblast)	ESDF	1 164 859	522 584	642 275	...	1 183 350	...	...	...
Saransk	ESDF	316 086	143 809	172 277	...	344 700	...	...	...

(See notes at end of table. — Voir notes à la fin du tableau.)

Continent, country or area, date and city Continent, pays ou zone, date et ville	Code[1]	City proper — Ville proprement dite Population				Urban agglomeration — Agglomération urbaine Population			
		Both sexes Les deux sexes	Male Masculin	Female Féminin	Surface area Superficie (km²)	Both sexes Les deux sexes	Male Masculin	Female Féminin	Surface area Superficie (km²)
EUROPE									
Russian Federation — Fédération de Russie[94,95]									
1 VII 1999									
Sarapyul	ESDF	105 623	48 418	57 205	...	106 350	...	...	...
Saratov	ESDF	875 256	404 967	470 289	...	...	...	...	...
Sergiev Posad	ESDF	111 256	49 010	62 246	...	...	...	...	...
Serpukhov	ESDF	133 685	62 466	71 219	...	...	...	...	...
Severodvinsk	ESDF	235 799	120 852	114 947	...	238 250	...	...	...
Seversk	ESDF	119 146	56 316	62 830	...	...	...	...	...
Shakhty	ESDF	221 538	101 638	119 900	...	250 900	...	...	...
Shchelkovo	ESDF	104 847	46 819	58 028	...	...	...	...	...
Smolensk	ESDF	351 498	161 833	189 665	...	...	...	...	...
Sochi	ESDF	334 009	153 852	180 157	...	395 800	...	...	...
Solikamsk	ESDF	106 164	52 534	53 630	...	...	...	...	...
St. Petersburg	ESDF	4 678 102	2 110 381	2 567 721	...	...	...	...	...
Starsy Oskol	ESDF	212 182	100 715	111 467	...	...	...	...	...
Stavropol	ESDF	342 642	157 317	185 325	...	342 700	...	...	...
Sterlitamak	ESDF	264 729	125 804	138 925	...	...	...	...	...
Surgut	ESDF	277 781	138 507	139 274	...	...	...	...	...
Syktivkar	ESDF	229 879	108 010	121 869	...	246 800	...	...	...
Syzran	ESDF	186 367	83 947	102 420	...	...	...	...	...
Taganrog	ESDF	284 850	131 569	153 281	...	...	...	...	...
Tambov	ESDF	312 453	141 980	170 473	...	...	...	...	...
Tolyatti	ESDF	720 430	350 308	370 122	...	734 300	...	...	...
Tomsk	ESDF	481 462	231 737	249 725	...	...	...	...	...
Tula	ESDF	506 147	230 960	275 187	...	554 650	...	...	...
Tver	ESDF	450 795	208 622	242 173	...	455 150	...	...	...
Tyumen	ESDF	502 214	235 033	267 181	...	556 200	...	...	...
Ufa	ESDF	1 087 788	510 451	577 337	...	1 093 700	...	...	...
Uhta	ESDF	101 192	48 564	52 628	...	129 200	...	...	...
Ulan-Ude	ESDF	370 175	174 278	195 897	...	394 400	...	...	...
Ulyanovsk	ESDF	668 030	314 674	353 356	...	690 300	...	...	...
Usolie Sibirskoye	ESDF	103 831	51 374	52 457	...	...	...	...	...
Ussuriisk	ESDF	157 095	74 155	82 940	...	...	...	...	...
Ust-Ulimsk	ESDF	106 502	52 501	54 001	...	...	...	...	...
Uzno-Sakhalinsk	ESDF	176 515	83 990	92 525	...	184 500	...	...	...
Velikie Luky	ESDF	116 275	53 704	62 571	...	...	...	...	...
Velikiy Novgorod	ESDF	229 461	108 308	121 153	...	238 000	...	...	...
Vladikavkaz (Osetinskaya ASSR)	ESDF	308 810	142 412	166 398	...	322 500	...	...	...
Vladimir	ESDF	335 083	157 803	177 280	...	356 850	...	...	...
Vladivostok	ESDF	606 895	291 561	315 334	...	636 600	...	...	...
Volgodonsk	ESDF	179 712	88 832	90 880	...	187 000	...	...	...
Volgograd	ESDF	992 341	459 366	532 975	...	1 024 900	...	...	...
Vologda	ESDF	300 449	137 301	163 148	...	309 750	...	...	...
Volzhsky	ESDF	285 920	134 010	151 910	...	294 850	...	...	...
Voronezh	ESDF	903 224	416 952	486 272	...	978 100	...	...	...
Votkinsk	ESDF	102 102	47 727	54 375	...	...	...	...	...
Yakutsk	ESDF	196 417	93 210	103 207	...	228 350	...	...	...
Yaroslave	ESDF	614 095	278 692	335 403	...	...	...	...	...
Zelenodolsk	ESDF	101 300	45 749	55 551	...	...	...	...	...
Zelenograd	ESDF	207 501	97 718	109 783	...	...	...	...	...
Zlatoust	ESDF	197 928	91 663	106 265	...	200 350	...	...	...
San Marino — Saint-Marin									
1 VII 2003									
SAN MARINO	ESDF	...	...	...	...	4 479	2 176	2 303	...
Serbia and Montenegro — Serbie-et-Montenegro									
31 III 2002									
BEOGRAD	CDJC	1 281 801	601 088	680 713	...	1 576 124	747 854	828 270	3 224
Cacak	CDJC	73 217	35 250	37 967	...	117 072	56 894	60 178	636
Kragujevac	CDJC	146 373	71 005	75 368	...	175 802	85 630	90 172	835

(See notes at end of table. — Voir notes à la fin du tableau.)

Continent, country or area, date and city / Continent, pays ou zone, date et ville	Code[1]	City proper — Ville proprement dite Population				Urban agglomeration — Agglomération urbaine Population			
		Both sexes Les deux sexes	Male Masculin	Female Féminin	Surface area Superficie (km²)	Both sexes Les deux sexes	Male Masculin	Female Féminin	Surface area Superficie (km²)
EUROPE									
Serbia and Montenegro — Serbie-et-Monténegro									
31 III 2002									
Kraljevo	CDJC	62 922	30 349	32 573	...	121 707	59 670	62 037	1 529
Krusevac	CDJC	57 347	27 306	30 041	...	131 368	63 757	67 611	854
Leskovac	CDJC	68 826	33 548	35 278	...	156 252	77 641	78 611	1 024
Nis	CDJC	178 161	85 709	92 452	...	250 518	122 339	128 179	597
Novi Sad	CDJC	235 165	110 317	124 848	...	299 294	142 033	157 261	699
Pancevo	CDJC	92 326	44 404	47 922	...	127 162	61 769	65 393	755
Podgorica	CDJC	140 262	...	...	...	169 132	...	...	1 441
Sabac	CDJC	55 163	26 125	29 038	...	122 893	59 971	62 922	775
Smederevo	CDJC	62 805	30 535	32 270	...	109 809	54 099	55 710	163
Subotica	CDJC	107 726	51 012	56 714	...	148 401	71 080	77 321	1 007
Zrenjanin	CDJC	79 773	37 915	41 858	...	132 051	63 788	68 263	1 326
Slovakia — Slovaquie									
1 VII 2002									
BRATISLAVA	ESDJ	427 425	199 960	227 465	368	...	...	...	...
Kosice	ESDJ	235 832	112 642	123 190	244	...	...	...	...
Slovenia — Slovénie									
1 VII 2003									
LJUBLJANA	ESDJ	248 956	115 431	133 525	164	250 603	116 244	134 359	171
Maribor	ESDJ	92 951	43 721	49 230	38	107 538	50 882	56 656	99
Spain — Espagne[96]									
1 VII 2001									
Albacete	ESDJ	149 434	73 118	76 316	12 431	...	...	...	...
Alicante	ESDJ	279 535	133 842	145 693	2 008	...	...	...	...
Almería	ESDJ	172 055	83 580	88 475	2 962	...	...	...	...
Badajoz	ESDJ	127 736	61 724	66 012	15 302	...	...	...	...
Barcelona	ESDJ	1 392 641	645 778	746 863	991	...	...	...	...
Bilbao	ESDJ	346 683	163 657	183 026	413	...	...	...	...
Burgos	ESDJ	161 520	77 752	83 768	1 084	...	...	...	...
Cádiz	ESDJ	132 872	63 267	69 605	112	...	...	...	...
Castellón de la Plana	ESDJ	139 009	67 626	71 383	1 075	...	...	...	...
Córdoba	ESDJ	303 874	145 870	158 004	12 533	...	...	...	...
Donostia - San Sebastián	ESDJ	177 831	83 418	94 413	615	...	...	...	...
Granada	ESDJ	231 577	107 066	124 511	882	...	...	...	...
Huelva	ESDJ	138 605	66 712	71 893	1 513	...	...	...	...
Jaén	ESDJ	106 449	51 274	55 175	4 243	...	...	...	...
La Coruña	ESDJ	235 847	109 402	126 445	376	...	...	...	...
Las Palmas de Gran Canaria	ESDJ	357 601	175 390	182 211	1 005	...	...	...	...
León	ESDJ	140 638	65 374	75 264	392	...	...	...	...
Lleida	ESDJ	110 770	53 629	57 141	2 120	...	...	...	...
Logroño	ESDJ	130 024	62 371	67 653	796	...	...	...	...
MADRID	ESDJ	2 912 705	1 353 349	1 559 356	6 058	...	...	...	...
Málaga	ESDJ	545 966	261 923	284 043	3 930	...	...	...	...
Murcia	ESDJ	353 943	171 763	182 180	8 865	...	...	...	...
Ourense	ESDJ	102 896	47 855	55 041	845	...	...	...	...
Oviedo	ESDJ	198 989	92 363	106 626	1 866	...	...	...	...
Palma de Mallorca	ESDJ	313 766	152 241	161 525	2 008	...	...	...	...
Pamplona	ESDJ	164 054	77 561	86 493	238	...	...	...	...
Salamanca	ESDJ	153 943	71 790	82 153	386	...	...	...	...
Santa Cruz de Tenerife	ESDJ	200 015	95 764	104 251	1 506	...	...	...	...
Santander	ESDJ	177 180	82 556	94 624	348	...	...	...	...
Sevilla	ESDJ	686 853	327 131	359 722	1 413	...	...	...	...
Tarragona	ESDJ	115 756	56 117	59 639	624	...	...	...	...
Valencia	ESDJ	745 216	354 340	390 876	1 346	...	...	...	...
Valladolid	ESDJ	309 116	147 960	161 156	1 975	...	...	...	...
Vitoria-Gasteiz	ESDJ	218 746	107 514	111 232	2 768	...	...	...	...
Zaragoza	ESDJ	593 204	284 834	308 370	10 631	...	...	...	...

8. Population of capital cities and cities of 100 000 and more inhabitants: latest available year
Population des capitales et des villes de 100 000 habitants et plus: dernière année disponible (continued — suite)

(See notes at end of table. — Voir notes à la fin du tableau.)

Continent, country or area, date and city / Continent, pays ou zone, date et ville	Code[1]	City proper — Ville proprement dite Population				Urban agglomeration — Agglomération urbaine Population			
		Both sexes Les deux sexes	Male Masculin	Female Féminin	Surface area Superficie (km²)	Both sexes Les deux sexes	Male Masculin	Female Féminin	Surface area Superficie (km²)
EUROPE									
Sweden — Suède									
1 VII 1999									
Göteborg	ESDJ	462 470	226 323	236 147	449	788 970	389 432	399 538	...
Helsingborg	ESDJ	116 870	56 377	60 493	346	...	...	...	...
Jönköping	ESDJ	116 344	56 809	59 535	1 485	...	...	...	...
Linköping	ESDJ	132 500	66 412	66 088	1 431	...	...	...	...
Malmö	ESDJ	257 574	123 610	133 964	154	518 506	252 814	265 692	...
Norrköping	ESDJ	122 212	60 089	62 123	1 491	...	...	...	...
Orebro	ESDJ	123 503	59 759	63 744	1 371	...	...	...	...
STOCKHOLM	ESDJ	743 703	356 604	387 099	187	1 643 366	800 874	842 492	...
Umeå	ESDJ	103 970	51 325	52 645	2 316	...	...	...	...
Uppsala	ESDJ	188 478	91 600	96 878	2 465	...	...	...	...
Västerås	ESDJ	125 433	62 033	63 400	956	...	...	...	...
Switzerland — Suisse									
1 VII 2001									
Bâle	ESDJ	165 356	78 073	87 283	24	401 610	192 661	208 949	271
BERNE	ESDJ	122 427	56 721	65 706	52	320 058	152 617	167 441	410
Genève	ESDJ	175 403	82 201	93 202	16	467 040	223 324	243 716	436
Lausanne	ESDJ	115 208	53 701	61 507	41	290 881	139 072	151 809	275
Zürich	ESDJ	339 234	162 164	177 070	88	960 310	468 595	491 715	847
The Former Yougoslav Rep. of Macedonia — L'ex-République yougoslave de Macédoine									
1 XI 2002									
SKOPLJE	CDJC	467 257	229 485	237 772	...	...	...	...	...
Ukraine									
5 XII 2001									
Alchevsk	CDFC	118 611	54 646	63 965	...	...	...	...	...
Berdyansk	CDFC	121 759	54 878	66 881	...	...	...	...	...
Bila Tserkva (Belaya Tserkov)	CDFC	196 023	92 100	103 923	...	...	...	...	...
Cherkasy	CDFC	292 761	135 539	157 222	...	...	...	...	...
Chernlhiv	CDFC	299 038	139 444	159 594	...	...	...	...	...
Chernivtsy	CDFC	236 691	109 675	127 016	...	...	...	...	...
Dnieprodzerzhynsk	CDFC	254 869	115 539	139 330	...	...	...	...	...
Dnipropetrovsk	CDFC	1 053 951	482 903	571 048	...	...	...	...	...
Donetsk (Donestskaya oblast)	CDFC	1 007 440	451 820	555 620	...	...	...	...	...
Enakievo (Yenakievo)	CDFC	104 266	46 894	57 372	...	...	...	...	...
Evpotoriya	CDFC	103 244	46 118	57 126	...	...	...	...	...
Horlivka	CDFC	289 872	131 508	158 364	...	...	...	...	...
Ivano-Frankivsk	CDFC	215 288	102 331	112 957	...	...	...	...	...
Kerch	CDFC	158 165	71 826	86 339	...	...	...	...	...
Kharkiv	CDFC	1 449 871	664 252	785 619	...	...	...	...	...
Kherson	CDFC	324 424	147 359	177 065	...	...	...	...	...
Khmelnytskiy (Hmilnyk)	CDFC	251 077	117 544	133 533	...	...	...	...	...
KYIV (KIEV)	CDFC	2 566 953	1 193 356	1 373 597	...	...	...	...	...
Kirovohrad	CDFC	250 629	114 460	136 169	...	...	...	...	...
Kramatorsk	CDFC	180 487	80 895	99 592	...	...	...	...	...
Kremenchuh	CDFC	232 960	107 642	125 318	...	...	...	...	...
Kryviy Rig	CDFC	666 812	304 784	362 028	...	...	...	...	...
Lysychansk	CDFC	114 905	52 218	62 687	...	...	...	...	...
Luhansk	CDFC	459 294	206 624	252 670	...	...	...	...	...
Lutsk	CDFC	205 585	93 911	111 674	...	...	...	...	...
Lviv	CDFC	725 202	341 779	383 423	...	...	...	...	...
Makyivka	CDFC	387 609	177 325	210 284	...	...	...	...	...
Mariupol	CDFC	488 462	224 232	264 230	...	...	...	...	...
Melitopol	CDFC	160 352	73 195	87 157	...	...	...	...	...
Mykolayiv (Nikolaevskaya oblast)	CDFC	509 102	232 823	276 279	...	...	...	...	...
Nikopol	CDFC	138 218	62 531	75 687	...	...	...	...	...
Odessa	CDFC	1 010 298	470 353	539 945	...	...	...	...	...
Pavlohrad	CDFC	119 672	56 077	63 595	...	...	...	...	...
Poltava	CDFC	310 755	143 567	167 188	...	...	...	...	...

8. Population of capital cities and cities of 100 000 and more inhabitants: latest available year
Population des capitales et des villes de 100 000 habitants et plus: dernière année disponible (continued — suite)

(See notes at end of table. — Voir notes à la fin du tableau.)

Continent, country or area, date and city — Continent, pays ou zone, date et ville	Code[1]	City proper — Ville proprement dite Population				Urban agglomeration — Agglomération urbaine Population			
		Both sexes Les deux sexes	Male Masculin	Female Féminin	Surface area Superficie (km²)	Both sexes Les deux sexes	Male Masculin	Female Féminin	Surface area Superficie (km²)
EUROPE									
Ukraine									
5 XII 2001									
Rivne	CDFC	245 323	113 525	131 798	...	...	...	...	...
Sevastopol	CDFC	340 190	154 896	185 294	...	...	...	...	...
Simpheropol	CDFC	338 038	150 159	187 879	...	...	...	...	...
Siverodonetsk	CDFC	120 225	54 272	65 953	...	...	...	...	...
Slovyansk	CDFC	122 575	54 068	68 507	...	...	...	...	...
Sumy	CDFC	292 139	133 927	158 212	...	...	...	...	...
Ternopil	CDFC	226 029	106 095	119 934	...	...	...	...	...
Uzhhorod	CDFC	115 568	54 078	61 490	...	...	...	...	...
Vinnytsya	CDFC	354 639	164 682	189 957	...	...	...	...	...
Zaporizhya	CDFC	810 620	369 432	441 188	...	...	...	...	...
Zhytomyr	CDFC	282 823	131 602	151 221	...	...	...	...	...
United Kingdom — Royaume-Uni[97]									
1 VII 1996									
Aberdeen	ESDF	217 260	106 198	111 062	186	...	...	...	...
Aberdeenshire	ESDF	227 430	113 042	114 388	6 318	...	...	...	...
Amber Valley	ESDF	115 224	57 285	57 939	265	...	...	...	...
Angus	ESDF	110 780	54 044	56 736	2 181	...	...	...	...
Arun	ESDF	137 978	65 564	72 414	221	...	...	...	...
Ashfield	ESDF	108 558	53 753	54 805	110	...	...	...	...
Aylesbury Vale	ESDF	154 927	77 051	77 876	903	...	...	...	...
Barking & Dagenham[98]	ESDF	153 715	75 092	78 623	34	...	...	...	...
Barnet[98]	ESDF	319 353	155 895	163 458	89	...	...	...	...
Barnsley	ESDF	227 213	111 642	115 571	328	...	...	...	...
Basildon	ESDF	163 280	80 407	82 873	110	...	...	...	...
Basingstoke & Deane	ESDF	147 914	73 469	74 445	634	...	...	...	...
Bassetlaw	ESDF	106 303	52 748	53 555	637	...	...	...	...
Bath & North East Somerset	ESDF	164 725	80 342	84 383	351	...	...	...	...
Bedford	ESDF	137 451	68 477	68 974	477	...	...	...	...
Belfast[99]	ESDF	297 300	...	...	110	...	...	...	...
Bexley[98]	ESDF	219 311	107 360	111 951	61	...	...	...	...
Birmingham	ESDF	1 020 589	504 342	516 247	265	...	...	...	...
Blackburn	ESDF	139 491	68 701	70 790	137	...	...	...	...
Blackpool	ESDF	152 459	73 875	78 584	35	...	...	...	...
Bolton	ESDF	265 449	130 861	134 588	140	...	...	...	...
Bournemouth	ESDF	160 749	76 297	84 452	46	...	...	...	...
Bracknell Forest	ESDF	110 092	55 725	54 367	109	...	...	...	...
Bradford	ESDF	483 422	238 407	245 015	366	...	...	...	...
Braintree	ESDF	126 236	62 500	63 736	612	...	...	...	...
Breckland	ESDF	113 654	55 573	58 081	1 305	...	...	...	...
Brent[98]	ESDF	247 525	123 645	123 880	44	...	...	...	...
Bridgend	ESDF	130 080	63 056	67 024	246	...	...	...	...
Brighton	ESDF	156 124	76 842	79 282	58	...	...	...	...
Bristol	ESDF	399 633	198 167	201 466	110	...	...	...	...
Broadland	ESDF	113 896	55 984	57 912	552	...	...	...	...
Bromley[98]	ESDF	295 584	143 424	152 160	152	...	...	...	...
Broxtowe	ESDF	111 429	55 215	56 214	81	...	...	...	...
Bury	ESDF	181 873	90 104	91 769	99	...	...	...	...
Caerphilly	ESDF	169 125	83 049	86 076	278	...	...	...	...
Calderdale	ESDF	192 844	94 093	98 751	363	...	...	...	...
Cambridge	ESDF	116 701	58 498	58 203	41	...	...	...	...
Camden[98]	ESDF	189 119	92 370	96 749	22	...	...	...	...
Canterbury	ESDF	136 481	66 429	70 052	309	...	...	...	...
Cardiff[100]	ESDF	315 040	154 656	160 384	140	...	...	...	...
Carlisle	ESDF	103 102	50 308	52 794	1 040	...	...	...	...
Carmarthenshire	ESDF	169 108	82 270	86 838	2 395	...	...	...	...
Charnwood	ESDF	155 724	77 740	77 984	279	...	...	...	...
Chelmsford	ESDF	156 601	77 147	79 454	342	...	...	...	...
Cheltenham	ESDF	106 692	52 428	54 264	47	...	...	...	...
Cherwell	ESDF	132 687	65 387	67 300	589	...	...	...	...

8. Population of capital cities and cities of 100 000 and more inhabitants: latest available year
Population des capitales et des villes de 100 000 habitants et plus: dernière année disponible (continued — suite)

(See notes at end of table. — Voir notes à la fin du tableau.)

Continent, country or area, date and city / Continent, pays ou zone, date et ville	Code[1]	City proper — Ville proprement dite Population				Urban agglomeration — Agglomération urbaine Population			
		Both sexes Les deux sexes	Male Masculin	Female Féminin	Surface area Superficie (km²)	Both sexes Les deux sexes	Male Masculin	Female Féminin	Surface area Superficie (km²)
EUROPE									
United Kingdom — Royaume-Uni[97]									
1 VII 1996									
Chester	ESDF	119 221	58 314	60 907	448	...	...	...	...
Chesterfield	ESDF	100 673	49 514	51 159	66	...	...	...	...
Chichester	ESDF	104 112	47 863	56 249	786	...	...	...	...
Colchester	ESDF	154 176	76 091	78 085	334	...	...	...	...
Conwy	ESDF	110 596	52 510	58 086	1 130	...	...	...	...
Coventry	ESDF	306 503	151 502	155 001	97	...	...	...	...
Crewe & Nantwich	ESDF	113 670	56 612	57 058	430	...	...	...	...
Croydon[98]	ESDF	333 787	163 998	169 789	87	...	...	...	...
Dacorum	ESDF	134 733	66 410	68 323	212	...	...	...	...
Darlington	ESDF	101 257	49 307	51 950	197	...	...	...	...
Derby	ESDF	233 708	115 901	117 807	78	...	...	...	...
Derry	ESDF	104 400	...	...	380	...	...	...	...
Doncaster	ESDF	291 804	143 806	147 998	581	...	...	...	...
Dover	ESDF	107 398	52 359	55 039	315	...	...	...	...
Dudley	ESDF	312 194	154 918	157 276	98	...	...	...	...
Dumfries & Galloway	ESDF	147 600	71 703	75 897	6 439	...	...	...	...
Dundee	ESDF	150 250	71 740	78 510	65	...	...	...	...
Ealing[98]	ESDF	297 033	148 140	148 893	55	...	...	...	...
East Ayrshire	ESDF	122 350	59 110	63 240	1 252	...	...	...	...
East Devon	ESDF	123 105	57 740	65 365	814	...	...	...	...
East Dunbartonshire	ESDF	110 750	54 125	56 625	172	...	...	...	...
East Hampshire	ESDF	110 761	53 872	56 889	515	...	...	...	...
East Hertfordshire	ESDF	123 553	61 771	61 782	477	...	...	...	...
East Lindsey	ESDF	123 058	59 401	63 657	1 760	...	...	...	...
East Riding of Yorkshire	ESDF	308 689	150 842	157 847	2 415	...	...	...	...
East Staffordshire	ESDF	100 421	49 951	50 470	390	...	...	...	...
Eastleigh	ESDF	111 732	55 310	56 422	80	...	...	...	...
Edinburgh[101]	ESDF	448 850	216 730	232 120	262	...	...	...	...
Elmbridge	ESDF	124 539	60 298	64 241	97	...	...	...	...
Enfield[98]	ESDF	262 613	129 236	133 377	81	...	...	...	...
Epping Forest	ESDF	119 512	58 424	61 088	340	...	...	...	...
Erewash	ESDF	106 818	53 033	53 785	109	...	...	...	...
Exeter	ESDF	107 729	53 152	54 577	47	...	...	...	...
Falkirk	ESDF	143 040	69 469	73 571	299	...	...	...	...
Fareham	ESDF	103 748	50 413	53 335	74	...	...	...	...
Fife	ESDF	349 300	169 204	180 096	1 323	...	...	...	...
Flintshire	ESDF	144 918	71 443	73 475	438	...	...	...	...
Gateshead	ESDF	200 968	98 242	102 726	143	...	...	...	...
Gedling	ESDF	112 194	54 985	57 209	120	...	...	...	...
Glasgow	ESDF	616 430	294 237	322 193	175	...	...	...	...
Gloucester	ESDF	106 834	53 328	53 506	41	...	...	...	...
Greenwich[98]	ESDF	212 073	103 156	108 917	48	...	...	...	...
Guildford	ESDF	124 567	61 520	63 047	271	...	...	...	...
Gwynedd	ESDF	117 775	57 195	60 580	2 548	...	...	...	...
Hackney[98]	ESDF	193 843	95 559	98 284	20	...	...	...	...
Halton	ESDF	123 038	60 479	62 559	74	...	...	...	...
Hammersmith & Fulham[98]	ESDF	156 718	74 635	82 083	16	...	...	...	...
Haringey[98]	ESDF	216 111	107 188	108 923	30	...	...	...	...
Harrogate	ESDF	147 635	70 360	77 275	1 333	...	...	...	...
Harrow[98]	ESDF	210 670	103 517	107 153	51	...	...	...	...
Havant & Waterloo	ESDF	117 341	56 816	60 525	55	...	...	...	...
Havering[98]	ESDF	230 909	113 300	117 609	118	...	...	...	...
Highland	ESDF	208 700	102 383	106 317	25 784	...	...	...	...
Hillingdon[98]	ESDF	247 718	122 684	125 034	110	...	...	...	...
Horsham	ESDF	118 569	58 198	60 371	530	...	...	...	...
Hounslow[98]	ESDF	205 798	102 875	102 923	58	...	...	...	...
Huntingdonshire	ESDF	152 742	75 372	77 370	923	...	...	...	...
Ipswich	ESDF	113 642	55 641	58 001	39	...	...	...	...
Isle of Wight	ESDF	125 466	60 464	65 002	380	...	...	...	...

8. Population of capital cities and cities of 100 000 and more inhabitants: latest available year
Population des capitales et des villes de 100 000 habitants et plus: dernière année disponible (continued — suite)

(See notes at end of table. — Voir notes à la fin du tableau.)

Continent, country or area, date and city / Continent, pays ou zone, date et ville	Code[1]	City proper — Ville proprement dite Population				Urban agglomeration — Agglomération urbaine Population			
		Both sexes Les deux sexes	Male Masculin	Female Féminin	Surface area Superficie (km²)	Both sexes Les deux sexes	Male Masculin	Female Féminin	Surface area Superficie (km²)
EUROPE									
United Kingdom — Royaume-Uni[97]									
1 VII 1996									
Islington[98]	ESDF	175 990	85 525	90 465	15	...	...	...	...
Kensington & Chelsea[98]	ESDF	159 039	77 469	81 570	12	...	...	...	...
Kings Lynn & West Norfolk	ESDF	131 214	64 551	66 663	1 429	...	...	...	...
Kingston-upon-Hull	ESDF	266 775	132 393	134 382	71	...	...	...	...
Kingston-upon-Thames[98]	ESDF	141 837	69 980	71 857	38	...	...	...	...
Kirklees	ESDF	388 807	191 176	197 631	410	...	...	...	...
Knowsley	ESDF	154 053	74 838	79 215	97	...	...	...	...
Lambeth[98]	ESDF	264 727	129 763	134 964	27	...	...	...	...
Lancaster	ESDF	136 948	66 569	70 379	576	...	...	...	...
Leeds	ESDF	726 939	359 351	367 588	562	...	...	...	...
Leicester	ESDF	294 830	146 359	148 471	73	...	...	...	...
Lewisham[98]	ESDF	241 495	116 451	125 044	35	...	...	...	...
Lisburn	ESDF	108 400	...	...	447	...	...	...	...
Liverpool	ESDF	467 995	228 398	239 597	113	...	...	...	...
LONDON[102]	ESDF	7 074 265	3 474 931	3 599 334	1 578	...	...	...	...
Luton	ESDF	181 468	91 012	90 456	43	...	...	...	...
Macclesfield	ESDF	152 604	74 565	78 039	525	...	...	...	...
Maidstone	ESDF	140 664	69 243	71 421	393	...	...	...	...
Manchester	ESDF	430 818	212 530	218 288	116	...	...	...	...
Mansfield	ESDF	101 355	50 288	51 067	77	...	...	...	...
Merton[98]	ESDF	182 291	89 704	92 587	38	...	...	...	...
Mid Bedfordshire	ESDF	118 945	58 957	59 988	503	...	...	...	...
Mid Sussex	ESDF	125 329	61 787	63 542	333	...	...	...	...
Middlesborough	ESDF	146 778	71 871	74 907	54	...	...	...	...
Milton Keynes	ESDF	197 131	98 274	98 857	309	...	...	...	...
Neath Port Talbot	ESDF	139 459	68 064	71 395	442	...	...	...	...
Newark & Sherwood	ESDF	104 464	51 558	52 906	651	...	...	...	...
Newbury	ESDF	143 727	71 390	72 337	704	...	...	...	...
Newcastle-under-Lyme	ESDF	122 314	60 137	62 177	211	...	...	...	...
Newcastle-upon-Tyne	ESDF	282 338	138 883	143 455	112	...	...	...	...
Newham[98]	ESDF	228 857	114 740	114 117	36	...	...	...	...
New Forest	ESDF	169 513	82 041	87 472	753	...	...	...	...
Newport	ESDF	136 789	66 839	69 950	190	...	...	...	...
North Ayrshire	ESDF	139 520	67 163	72 357	884	...	...	...	...
North East Lincolnshire	ESDF	158 503	77 615	80 888	192	...	...	...	...
North Hertfordshire	ESDF	114 941	56 925	58 016	375	...	...	...	...
North Lanarkshire	ESDF	325 940	158 347	167 593	474	...	...	...	...
North Lincolnshire	ESDF	152 767	75 457	77 310	838	...	...	...	...
North Somerset	ESDF	185 340	90 218	95 122	375	...	...	...	...
North Tyneside	ESDF	193 619	92 875	100 744	84	...	...	...	...
North Wiltshire	ESDF	121 747	60 947	60 800	768	...	...	...	...
Northampton	ESDF	192 382	94 840	97 542	81	...	...	...	...
Norwich	ESDF	126 221	61 878	64 343	39	...	...	...	...
Nottingham	ESDF	283 969	140 237	143 732	75	...	...	...	...
Nuneaton & Bedworth	ESDF	118 340	59 060	59 280	79	...	...	...	...
Oldham	ESDF	220 172	107 764	112 408	141	...	...	...	...
Oxford	ESDF	137 343	69 220	68 123	46	...	...	...	...
Pembrokeshire	ESDF	113 597	55 413	58 184	1 590	...	...	...	...
Perth & Kinross	ESDF	132 570	63 937	68 633	5 311	...	...	...	...
Peterborough	ESDF	158 674	79 264	79 410	333	...	...	...	...
Plymouth	ESDF	255 826	125 854	129 972	80	...	...	...	...
Poole	ESDF	139 226	67 391	71 835	65	...	...	...	...
Portsmouth	ESDF	190 370	97 010	93 360	40	...	...	...	...
Powys	ESDF	124 418	61 771	62 647	5 196	...	...	...	...
Preston	ESDF	134 818	67 195	67 623	142	...	...	...	...
Reading	ESDF	142 851	72 310	70 541	40	...	...	...	...
Redbridge[98]	ESDF	230 578	113 277	117 301	56	...	...	...	...
Redcar & Cleveland	ESDF	139 785	68 465	71 320	245	...	...	...	...
Reigate & Banstead	ESDF	119 307	58 576	60 731	129	...	...	...	...

(See notes at end of table. — Voir notes à la fin du tableau.)

Continent, country or area, date and city / Continent, pays ou zone, date et ville	Code[1]	City proper — Ville proprement dite Population				Urban agglomeration — Agglomération urbaine Population			
		Both sexes Les deux sexes	Male Masculin	Female Féminin	Surface area Superficie (km²)	Both sexes Les deux sexes	Male Masculin	Female Féminin	Surface area Superficie (km²)
EUROPE									
United Kingdom — Royaume-Uni[97]									
1 VII 1996									
Renfrewshire	ESDF	178 550	86 208	92 342	261	...	...	...	...
Rhondda, Cynon, Taff	ESDF	240 117	118 610	121 507	424	...	...	...	...
Richmond-upon-Thames[98]	ESDF	179 877	87 176	92 701	55	...	...	...	...
Rochdale	ESDF	207 563	101 884	105 679	160	...	...	...	...
Rochester-upon-Medway	ESDF	144 478	71 379	73 099	160	...	...	...	...
Rotherham	ESDF	255 342	126 360	128 982	283	...	...	...	...
Rushcliffe	ESDF	103 500	51 092	52 408	409	...	...	...	...
St. Albans	ESDF	130 267	64 373	65 894	161	...	...	...	...
St. Helens	ESDF	179 483	88 293	91 190	133	...	...	...	...
Salford	ESDF	229 179	113 589	115 590	97	...	...	...	...
Salisbury	ESDF	112 534	54 503	58 031	1 004	...	...	...	...
Sandwell	ESDF	292 196	143 434	148 762	86	...	...	...	...
Scarborough	ESDF	108 258	51 709	56 549	817	...	...	...	...
Scottish Borders	ESDF	106 100	51 101	54 999	4 734	...	...	...	...
Sedgemoor	ESDF	101 866	50 178	51 688	564	...	...	...	...
Sefton	ESDF	289 739	138 360	151 379	153	...	...	...	...
Sevenoaks	ESDF	110 476	53 984	56 492	368	...	...	...	...
Sheffield	ESDF	530 375	263 775	266 600	367	...	...	...	...
Slough	ESDF	110 482	54 004	55 790	27	...	...	...	...
Solihull	ESDF	203 922	99 688	104 234	179	...	...	...	...
South Ayrshire	ESDF	114 630	54 802	59 828	1 202	...	...	...	...
South Bedfordshire	ESDF	110 949	55 159	55 790	213	...	...	...	...
South Cambridgeshire	ESDF	128 422	63 498	64 924	902	...	...	...	...
South Gloucestershire	ESDF	235 129	117 579	117 550	497	...	...	...	...
South Lakeland	ESDF	100 889	48 658	52 231	1 554	...	...	...	...
South Lanarkshire	ESDF	307 450	148 701	158 749	1 771	...	...	...	...
South Kesteven	ESDF	119 951	58 374	61 577	943	...	...	...	...
South Norfolk	ESDF	105 778	52 113	53 665	908	...	...	...	...
South Oxfordshire	ESDF	124 637	61 467	63 170	679	...	...	...	...
South Ribble	ESDF	103 020	50 250	52 770	113	...	...	...	...
South Somerset	ESDF	150 710	73 645	77 065	959	...	...	...	...
South Staffordshire	ESDF	103 284	51 022	52 262	408	...	...	...	...
South Tyneside	ESDF	156 078	75 999	80 079	64	...	...	...	...
Southampton	ESDF	214 859	108 325	106 534	50	...	...	...	...
Southend-on-Sea	ESDF	172 266	82 911	89 355	42	...	...	...	...
Southwark[98]	ESDF	229 871	113 282	116 589	29	...	...	...	...
Stafford	ESDF	124 531	61 660	62 871	599	...	...	...	...
Stockport	ESDF	291 080	141 315	149 765	126	...	...	...	...
Stockton-on-Tees	ESDF	179 009	88 068	90 941	204	...	...	...	...
Stoke-on-Trent	ESDF	254 438	126 133	128 305	93	...	...	...	...
Stratford-on-Avon	ESDF	111 211	54 170	57 041	977	...	...	...	...
Stroud	ESDF	108 022	53 091	54 931	461	...	...	...	...
Suffolk Coastal	ESDF	118 681	58 278	60 403	892	...	...	...	...
Sunderland	ESDF	294 261	143 574	150 687	138	...	...	...	...
Sutton[98]	ESDF	175 527	85 353	90 174	43	...	...	...	...
Swale	ESDF	117 562	58 744	58 818	373	...	...	...	...
Swansea	ESDF	230 180	112 876	117 304	378	...	...	...	...
Tameside	ESDF	220 722	109 005	111 717	103	...	...	...	...
Teignbridge	ESDF	116 743	56 289	60 454	674	...	...	...	...
Tendring	ESDF	132 265	62 860	69 405	337	...	...	...	...
Test Valley	ESDF	107 182	53 019	54 163	637	...	...	...	...
Thamesdown	ESDF	174 598	87 176	87 422	230	...	...	...	...
Thanet	ESDF	125 543	59 567	65 976	103	...	...	...	...
The Wrekin	ESDF	144 154	71 507	72 647	290	...	...	...	...
Thurrock	ESDF	132 283	65 807	66 476	164	...	...	...	...
Tonbridge & Malling	ESDF	104 991	52 141	52 850	240	...	...	...	...
Torbay	ESDF	123 413	57 936	65 477	63	...	...	...	...
Tower Hamlets[98]	ESDF	176 635	88 852	87 783	20	...	...	...	...
Trafford	ESDF	218 893	107 360	111 533	106	...	...	...	...

8. Population of capital cities and cities of 100 000 and more inhabitants: latest available year
Population des capitales et des villes de 100 000 habitants et plus: dernière année disponible (continued — suite)

(See notes at end of table. — Voir notes à la fin du tableau.)

Continent, country or area, date and city / Continent, pays ou zone, date et ville	Code[1]	City proper — Ville proprement dite Population				Urban agglomeration — Agglomération urbaine Population			
		Both sexes Les deux sexes	Male Masculin	Female Féminin	Surface area Superficie (km²)	Both sexes Les deux sexes	Male Masculin	Female Féminin	Surface area Superficie (km²)
EUROPE									
United Kingdom — Royaume-Uni[97]									
1 VII 1996									
Tunbridge Wells	ESDF	102 616	49 544	53 072	332	...	...	...	...
Vale of Glamorgan	ESDF	119 358	58 142	61 216	335	...	...	...	...
Vale of White Horse	ESDF	112 545	56 987	55 558	579	...	...	...	...
Vale Royal	ESDF	115 233	56 748	58 485	380	...	...	...	...
Wakefield	ESDF	317 342	157 184	160 158	333	...	...	...	...
Walsall	ESDF	262 593	130 111	132 482	106	...	...	...	...
Waltham Forest[98]	ESDF	220 249	108 187	112 062	40	...	...	...	...
Wandsworth[98]	ESDF	266 169	129 106	137 063	35	...	...	...	...
Warrington	ESDF	189 012	93 732	95 280	176	...	...	...	...
Warwick	ESDF	122 506	60 228	62 278	282	...	...	...	...
Waveney	ESDF	107 731	52 025	55 706	370	...	...	...	...
Waverley	ESDF	114 133	55 348	58 785	345	...	...	...	...
Wealden	ESDF	138 030	65 888	72 142	836	...	...	...	...
West Lancashire	ESDF	109 763	54 031	55 732	338	...	...	...	...
West Lothian	ESDF	150 770	74 178	76 592	425	...	...	...	...
West Wiltshire	ESDF	108 889	53 732	55 157	517	...	...	...	...
Westminster[98]	ESDF	204 063	101 174	102 889	22	...	...	...	...
Wigan	ESDF	309 786	153 353	156 433	199	...	...	...	...
Winchester	ESDF	106 007	51 653	54 354	661	...	...	...	...
Windsor & Maidenhead	ESDF	141 548	70 387	71 161	198	...	...	...	...
Wirral	ESDF	329 179	157 640	171 539	159	...	...	...	...
Wokingham	ESDF	142 361	71 935	70 426	179	...	...	...	...
Wolverhampton	ESDF	244 453	120 455	123 998	69	...	...	...	...
Wrexham Maelor	ESDF	123 308	59 817	63 491	498	...	...	...	...
Wychavon	ESDF	108 009	52 849	55 160	664	...	...	...	...
Wycombe	ESDF	164 045	81 812	82 233	325	...	...	...	...
Wyre	ESDF	104 348	49 847	54 501	284	...	...	...	...
York	ESDF	175 095	85 359	89 736	271	...	...	...	...
OCEANIA — OCEANIE									
American Samoa — Samoa américaines[15]									
1 IV 2000									
PAGO PAGO	CDFC	4 278	...	...	...	...	...	...	...
Australia — Australie[103]									
1 VII 2003									
Adelaide[104]	ESDJ	1 119 097	548 959	570 138	1 827	...	...	...	...
Albury-Wodonga[105]	ESDJ	100 182	49 526	50 656	4 562	...	...	...	...
Brisbane[104]	ESDJ	1 735 181	857 660	877 521	4 673	...	...	...	...
Cairns[105]	ESDJ	117 531	59 173	58 358	488	...	...	...	...
CANBERRA[104]	ESDJ	323 004	159 546	163 458	806	...	...	...	...
Canberra-Queanbeyan[105]	ESDJ	368 136	182 321	185 815	3 239	...	...	...	...
Darwin[104]	ESDJ	108 039	57 366	50 673	3 122	...	...	...	...
Geelong[105]	ESDJ	162 637	79 281	83 356	388	...	...	...	...
Gold Coast-Tweed[105]	ESDJ	456 908	225 122	231 786	1 238	...	...	...	...
Wollongong[105]	ESDJ	273 234	136 639	136 595	1 089	...	...	...	...
Greater Hobart[104]	ESDJ	199 926	97 615	102 311	1 357	...	...	...	...
Launceston[105]	ESDJ	100 664	49 057	51 607	803	...	...	...	...
Melbourne[104]	ESDJ	3 555 321	1 749 997	1 805 324	7 694	...	...	...	...
Newcastle[105]	ESDJ	501 335	247 922	253 413	4 042	...	...	...	...
Perth[104]	ESDJ	1 431 498	708 844	722 654	5 386	...	...	...	...
Sunshine Coast[105]	ESDJ	200 366	97 777	102 589	457	...	...	...	...
Sydney[104]	ESDJ	4 198 543	2 083 134	2 115 409	12 145	...	...	...	...
Toowoomba[105]	ESDJ	113 815	54 944	58 871	554	...	...	...	...
Townsville[105]	ESDJ	140 761	71 328	69 433	454	...	...	...	...
Cook Islands — Iles Cook									
1 XII 2001									
RAROTONGA	CDFC	12 188	...	...	...	...	...	...	...

8. Population of capital cities and cities of 100 000 and more inhabitants: latest available year
Population des capitales et des villes de 100 000 habitants et plus: dernière année disponible (continued — suite)

(See notes at end of table. — Voir notes à la fin du tableau.)

Continent, country or area, date and city / Continent, pays ou zone, date et ville	Code[1]	City proper — Ville proprement dite Population				Urban agglomeration — Agglomération urbaine Population			
		Both sexes Les deux sexes	Male Masculin	Female Féminin	Surface area Superficie (km²)	Both sexes Les deux sexes	Male Masculin	Female Féminin	Surface area Superficie (km²)
OCEANIA — OCEANIE									
Fiji — Fidji									
31 VIII 1996									
SUVA	CDFC	77 366	38 518	38 848	...	167 975	83 910	84 065	...
French Polynesia — Polynésie francaise									
7 XI 2002									
PAPEETE	CDFC	26 181	...	...	...	124 864	...	...	...
Guam[15]									
1 IV 2000									
AGANA	CDJC	1 100	672	428	3	...	...	...	...
Kiribati									
7 XI 2000									
TARAWA	CDFC	...	...	...	...	36 717	...	...	...
Marshall Islands — Iles Marshall									
1 VI 1999									
MAJURO	CDFC	23 676	12 075	11 601	...	...	...	...	...
Micronesia, Federated States of — Micronésie, États fédérés de									
1 IV 2000									
PALIKIR	CDJC	6 227	...	...	...	...	...	...	...
Nauru									
17 IV 1992									
YAREN	CDFC	672	...	...	...	...	...	...	...
New Caledonia — Nouvelle-Calédonie									
16 IV 1996									
NOUMEA	CDFC	76 293	38 443	37 850	46	118 823	60 327	58 496	1 643
New Zealand — Nouvelle-Zélande[106,107,108]									
1 VII 2003									
Auckland	ESDJ	415 100	...	...	633	1 199 300	...	...	1 086
Christchurch	ESDJ	338 800	...	...	452	358 000	...	...	608
Dunedin[109]	ESDJ	121 100	...	...	3 342	113 600	...	...	255
Hamilton	ESDJ	126 500	...	...	94	178 900	...	...	1 100
Manukau	ESDJ	317 500	...	...	683	...	...	...	...
Napier-Hastings	ESDJ	...	...	...	...	118 400	...	...	375
Northshore	ESDJ	205 000	...	...	130	...	...	...	...
Tauranga	ESDJ	98 500	...	...	168	103 600	...	...	178
Waitakere	ESDJ	185 600	...	...	367	...	...	...	...
WELLINGTON	ESDJ	179 000	...	...	290	363 400	...	...	444
Niue — Nioué									
13 IX 2001									
ALOFI	CDFC	615	...	...	...	...	...	...	...
Norfolk Island — Ile Norfolk									
1 VII 1997									
KINGSTON	ESDF	*800*	...	...	...	...	...	...	...
Northern Mariana Islands — Iles Mariannes du Nord									
1 IV 2000									
GARAPAN	CDFC	3 588	...	...	...	...	...	...	...
Palau — Palaos									
15 IV 2000									
KOROR	CDFC	10 600	...	...	...	...	...	...	...
Papua New Guinea — Papouasie-Nouvelle-Guinée									
9 VII 2000									
PORT MORESBY	CDFC	254 158	138 974	115 184	...	...	...	...	...
Pitcairn									
1 VII 1993									
ADAMSTOWN	CDFC	53	...	...	5	...	...	...	...

8. Population of capital cities and cities of 100 000 and more inhabitants: latest available year
Population des capitales et des villes de 100 000 habitants et plus: dernière année disponible (continued — suite)

(See notes at end of table. — Voir notes à la fin du tableau.)

Continent, country or area, date and city / Continent, pays ou zone, date et ville	Code[1]	City proper — Ville proprement dite Population				Urban agglomeration — Agglomération urbaine Population			
		Both sexes Les deux sexes	Male Masculin	Female Féminin	Surface area Superficie (km²)	Both sexes Les deux sexes	Male Masculin	Female Féminin	Surface area Superficie (km²)
OCEANIA — OCEANIE									
Samoa									
1 XI 2001									
APIA	CDFC	38 836	...	...	...	...	...	...	...
Solomon Islands — Iles Salomon									
21 XI 1999									
HONIARA	CDFC	49 107	...	...	...	...	...	...	...
Tonga									
1 VII 2000									
NUKU'ALOFA	ESDF	21 538	10 625	10 913	...	30 336	15 115	15 221	...
Tuvalu									
17 XI 1991									
FUNAFUTI	CDFC	3 839	...	...	...	...	...	...	...
Vanuatu									
16 XI 1999									
PORT VILA	CDFC	29 356	...	...	...	...	...	...	...
Wallis and Futuna Islands — Iles Wallis et Futuna									
3 X 1996									
META-UTU	CDFC	1 137	...	...	...	...	...	...	...

GENERAL NOTES - NOTES GENERALES

The capital city of each country is shown in capital letters. Figures in italics are estimates of questionable reliability. For definition of city proper and urban agglomeration, method of evaluation and limitations of data see Technical Notes for this table. — Le nom de la capitale de chaque pays est imprimé en majuscules. Les chiffres en italiques snot des estimations de quality duteous. Pour la definition de la vile procurement diet et de l'agglomération urbaine, et pour les méthodes d'évaluation et les insuffisances des données voir Notes techniques pour ce tableau.

FOOTNOTES - NOTES

[1] 'Code' indicates the source of data, as follows:
CDFC - Census, de facto, complete tabulation
CDFS - Census, de facto, sample tabulation
CDJC - Census, de jure, complete tabulation
CDJS - Census, de jure, sample tabulation
SSDF - Sample survey, de facto
SSDJ - Sample survey, de jure
ESDF - Estimates, de facto
ESDJ - Estimates, de jure
Le 'Code' indique la source des données, comme suit:
CDFC - Recensement, population de fait, tabulation complète
CDFS - Recensement, population de fait, tabulation par sondage
CDJC - Recensement, population de droit, tabulation complète
CDJS - Recensement, population de droit, tabulation par sondage
SSDF - Enquête par sondage, population de fait
SSDJ - Enquête par sondage, population de droit
ESDF - Données estimatées, population de fait
ESDJ - Données estimatées, population de droit
[2] Dual capitals. — Le pays a deux capitales.
[3] For the urban commune of Antananarivo. — Pour la commune urbaine de Antananarivo.
[4] Data for city proper refer to population in municipalities. - Les données concernant la ville proprement dite se rapportent a la population des municipalités.
[5] Data include those for two or more cities. - Les données présentées concernent deux villes ou plus.

[6] Data for cities proper refer to communes. — Les données pour les villes se réfèrent aux communes.
[7] For communes which may contain rural areas as well as urban centre. — Commune(s) pouvant comprendre un centre urbain et une zone rurale.
[8] Included in urban agglomeration of Dakar. — Comprise dans l'agglomération urbaine de Dakar.
[9] Pretoria is the administrative capital, Cape Town the legislative capital. — Pretoria est la capital administrative, Le Cap la capitale législative.
[10] Excluding persons residing in institutions. — Non compris les personnes dans les institutions.
[11] For municipalities which may contain an urban centre as well as a rural area. — Pour municipios qui peuvent comprendre un centre urbain et aussi une zone rurale.
[12] The definition of locality is based on the 2000 Population census. - La localité est définie survant le recensement general de la population de 2000.
[13] Urban agglomeration (Metropolitan area) refers to 2 or more municipalities where there is only one urban concentration. - L'agglomération urbaine (zone métropolitaine) se rapporte à 2 municipalités ou plus où il y a seulement une concentration urbaine.
[14] Including municipalities of Bella Vista, Betania, Calidonia, Curundu, El Chorillo, Juan Diaz, Parque Lefevre, Pedregal, Pueblo Nuevo, Rio Abajo, San Felipe, San Francisco and Santa Ana. — Y compris les corregimientos de Bella Vista, Betania, Calidonia, Curundu, El Chorillo, Juan Diaz, Parque Lefevre, Pedregal, Pueblo Nuevo, Rio Abajo, San Felipe, San Francisco et Santa Ana.
[15] Including armed forces stationed in the area. — Y compris les militaires en garnison sur le territoire.
[16] Excluding armed forces overseas and civilian citizens absent from country for extended period of time. — Non compris les militaires à l'étranger et les civils hors du pays pendant une période prolongée.
[17] City refers to a type of incorporated place in 49 states and the District of Columbia, that has an elected government and provides a range of government functions and services. Also included are Honolulu, Hawaii Census Designated Place (CDP), for which the Census Bureau reports data under agreement with the State of Hawaii (instead of the combined city and county of Honolulu), and Arlington, VA CDP (which is coextensive with Arlington County - an entirely urban county that provides the same levels of services and functions as a municipality. - Par ville, on entend un lieu doté de la personnalité morale dans 49 États et dans le district de Columbia, qui a un gouvernement élu et fournit tout un ensemble de fonctions et de services publics. Sont également inclus Honolulu, lieu chargé du recensement pour Hawaii, pour lequel le Census Bureau établit les données en accord avec

l'État de Hawaii (au lieu de la ville et du comté d'Honolulu), et Arlington, lieu chargé du recensement pour la Virginie, qui est de même étendue que le comté d'Arlington, lequel est un comté entièrement urbain qui offre les mêmes niveaux de services et de fonctions qu'une municipalité.

[18] Included in urban agglomeration of Washington, DC--VA--MD. — Comprise dans l'agglomération urbaine de Washington, DC--VA--MD

[19] Included in urban agglomeration of Los Angeles--Long Beach--Santa Ana, CA. — Comprise dans l'agglomération urbaine de Los Angeles--Long Beach--Santa Ana, CA.

[20] Included in urban agglomeration of Dallas--Fort Worth--Arlington, TX. — Comprise dans l'agglomération urbaine de Dallas--Fort Worth--Arlington, TX.

[21] Included in urban agglomeration of Denver--Aurora, CO. — Comprise dans l'agglomération urbaine de Denver--Aurora, CO.

[22] Included in urban agglomeration of Chicago, IL--IN. — Comprise dans l'agglomération urbaine de Chicago, IL--IN.

[23] Included in urban agglomeration of Seattle, WA. — Comprise dans l'agglomération urbaine de Seattle, WA.

[24] Included in urban agglomeration of San Francisco--Oakland, CA. — Comprise dans l'agglomération urbaine de San Francisco--Oakland, CA.

[25] Included in urban agglomeration of Boston, MA--NH--RI. — Comprise dans l'agglomération urbaine de Boston, MA--NH--RI.

[26] Included in urban agglomeration of Phoenix--Mesa, AZ. — Comprise dans l'agglomération urbaine de Phoenix--Mesa, AZ.

[27] Included in urban agglomeration of Virginia Beach, VA. — Comprise dans l'agglomération urbaine de Virginia Beach, VA.

[28] Included in urban agglomeration of San Diego, CA. — Comprise dans l'agglomération urbaine de San Diego, CA.

[29] Included in urban agglomeration of Tampa--St. Petersburg, FL. — Comprise dans l'agglomération urbaine de Tampa--St. Petersburg, FL.

[30] Included in urban agglomeration of Miami, FL. — Comprise dans l'agglomération urbaine de Miami, FL.

[31] Included in urban agglomeration of Riverside--San Bernardino, CA. — Comprise dans l'agglomération urbaine de Riverside--San Bernardino, CA.

[32] Included in urban agglomeration of New York--Newark, NY--NJ--CT. — Comprise dans l'agglomération urbaine de New York--Newark, NY--NJ--CT.

[33] Included in urban agglomeration of Las Vegas, NV. — Comprise dans l'agglomération urbaine de Las Vegas, NV.

[34] Included in urban agglomeration of Kansas City, MO--KS. — Comprise dans l'agglomération urbaine de Kansas City, MO--KS.

[35] Included in urban agglomeration of Detroit, MI. — Comprise dans l'agglomération urbaine de Detroit, MI.

[36] Included in urban agglomeration of Lancaster--Palmdale, CA. — Comprise dans l'agglomération urbaine de Lancaster--Palmdale, CA.

[37] Included in urban agglomeration of Houston, TX. — Comprise dans l'agglomération urbaine de Houston, TX.

[38] Included in urban agglomeration of Minneapolis--St. Paul, MN. — Comprise dans l'agglomération urbaine de Minneapolis--St. Paul, MN.

[39] Included in urban agglomeration of Oxnard, CA. Comprise dans l'agglomération urbaine de Oxnard, CA.

[40] Included in urban agglomeration of San Jose, CA. — Comprise dans l'agglomération urbaine de San Jose, CA.

[41] Included in urban agglomeration of Bridgeport--Stamford, CT--NY. — Comprise dans l'agglomération urbaine de Bridgeport--Stamford, CT--NY.

[42] Included in urban agglomeration of Portland, OR--WA. — Comprise dans l'agglomération urbaine de Portland, OR--WA.

[43] Included in urban agglomeration of Salt Lake City, UT. — Comprise dans l'agglomération urbaine de Salt Lake City, UT.

[44] La Paz is the actual capital and the seat of the Government but Sucre is the legal capital and the seat of the judiciary. — La Paz est la capitale effective et le siège du gouvernement, mais Sucre est la capitale constitutionnelle et la siège du pouvoir judiciaire.

[45] 'Metropolitan area' Grand Santiago. — 'Zone métropolitaine' Grand Santiago.

[46] Urban agglomeration refers to the urban part of the municipality with a proper city center. - L'agglomération urbaine se rapporte à la partie urbaine de la municipalité avec un centre de la ville.

[47] Data for urban agglomeration refer to 'metropolitan area', comprising Asuncion proper and localities of Trinidad, Zeballos Cué, Campo Grande and Lamboré. — Les données pour l'agglomération urbaine se rapportent à la 'zone métropolitaine' comprenant la ville d'Asuncion proprement dite et les localités de Trinidad, Zeballos Cué, Campo Grande et Lamboré.

[48] City population refers to urban population of districts within the city. - La population des villes se rapporte à la population urbaine des districts compris dans la ville.

[49] For municipalities which may contain rural area as well as urban centre. — Pour les municipalités qui peuvent comprendre un centre urbaine et une zone rurale.

[50] Lefkosia urban agglomeration is composed of Lefkosia municipality, Agios Dometios, Egkomi, Strovolos, Aglangia, Lakatameia, Anthoupoli, Latsia and Geri. — L'agglomération urbaine de Lefkosia se comprend de la municipalité de Lefkosia et Agios Dometios, Egkomi, Strovolos, Aglangia, Lakatameia, Anthoupoli, Latsia et Geri.

[51] Lemesos urban agglomeration is composed of Lemesos municipality, Mesa Geitonia, Agios Athanasios, Germasogeia, Pano Polemidia, Ypsonas, Kato Polemidia, and parts of Mouttagiaka, Agios Tychon, Parekklisia,

Monagrouli, Moni, Pyrgos and Tserkezoi. — L'agglomération urbaine de Lemesos se comprend de la municipalité de Lemesos et Mesa Geitonia, Agios Athanasios, Germasogeia, Pano Polemidia, Ypsonas, Kato Polemidia, et certaines parties des Mouttagiaka, Agios Tychon, Parekklisia, Monagrouli, Moni, Pyrgos et Tserkezoi.

[52] Including data for the India-held part of Jammu and Kashmir, the final status of which has not yet been determined. Excluding cities for Assam state. — Y compris les données concernant la partie de Jammu-et-Cachemire occupée par l'Inde, dont le statut définitif n'a pas encore été déterminé. Non compris les villes de l'état d'Assam.

[53] Data for urban agglomeration includes New Delhi. — Les données pour l'agglomération urbaine y compris New Delhi.

[54] Data for urban agglomeration include Bally, Baranagar, Barrackpur, Bhatpara, Calcutta Municipal Corporation, Chandan Nagar, Garden Reach, Houghly-Chinsura, Howrah, Jadarpur, Kamarhati, Naihati, Panihati, Serampore, South Dum Dum, South Suburban, and Titagarh. — Les données pour l'agglomération urbaine y compris Bally, Baranagar, Barrackpur, Bhatpara, Calcutta Municipal Corporation, Chandan Nagar, Garden Reach, Houghly Chinsura, Howrah, Jadarpur, Kamarhati, Naihati, Panihati, Serampopre, South Dum Dum, South Suburban et Titagarh.

[55] Included in urban agglomeration of Delhi. — Comprise dans l'agglomération urbaine de Delhi.

[56] Data refer to the New Delhi Municipal Council. — Les données se rapportent au New Delhi Municipal Council.

[57] Including Karkh, Rassaiah, Adhamiya and Kadhimain Qadha Centres and Maamoon, Mansour and Karradah-Sharqiyah Nahlyas. — Y compris les cazas de Karkh, Adhamiya et Kadhimain ainsi que les nahiyas de Maamoon, Mansour et Karradah-Sharqiyah.

[58] Designation and data provided by Israel. The position of the United Nations on the question of Jerusalem is contained in General Assembly resolution 181 (II) and subsequent resolutions of the General Assembly and the Security Council concerning this question. — Appelation de données fournies par Israel. La position des Nations Unies concernant la question de Jérusalem est décrite dans la résolution 181 (II) de l'Assemblée générale et résolutions ultérieures de l'Assemblée générale et du Conseil de sécurité sur cette question.

[59] Including East Jerusalem. — Y compris Jérusalem-Est.

[60] Excluding diplomatic personnel outside country and foreign military and civilian personnel and their dependants stationed in the area. — Non compris le personnel diplomatique hors du territoire, les militaires et agents civils étrangers en poste sur le territoire et les membres de leur famille les accompagnant.

[61] Except for Tokyo, all data refer to shi, a minor division which may include some scattered or rural population as well as an urban centre. — Sauf pour Tokyo, toutes les données se rapportent à des shi, petites divisions administratives qui peuvent comprendre des peuplements dispersés ou ruraux en plus d'un centre urbain.

[62] Data excluding Hokkaido region. — Non compris la région de Hokkaido.

[63] Including Kokura, Moji, Tobata, Wakamatsu and Yahata (Yawata). — Y compris Kokura, Moji, Tobata, Wakamatsu et Yahata (Yawata).

[64] Data for city proper refer to 23 wards (ku) of the old city. The urban agglomeration figures refer to Tokyo-to (Tokyo Prefecture), comprising the 23 wards plus 14 urban counties (shi), 18 towns (machi) and 8 villages (mura). The 'Tokyo Metropolitan Area' comprises the 23 wards of Tokyo-to plus 21 cities, 20 towns and 2 villages. The 'Keihin Metropolitan Area' (Tokyo-Yokohama Metropolitan Area) plus 9 cities (one of which is Yokohama City) and two towns, with a total population of 20 485 542 on 1 October 1965. — Les données concernant la ville proprement dite se rapportent aux 23 circonscriptions de la vieille ville. Les chiffres pour l'agglomération urbaine se rapportent à Tokyo-to (préfecture de Tokyo), comprenant les 23 circonscriptions plus 14 cantons urbains (Shi), 18 villes (machi) et 8 villages (mura). La 'zone métropolitaine de Tokyo' comprend les 23 circonscriptions de Tokyo-to plus 21 municipalités, 20 villes et 2 villages. La 'zone métropolitaine de Keihin' (zone métropolitaine de Tokyo-Yokohama) comprend la zone métropolitaine de Tokyo, plus 9 municipalités, dont l'une est Yokohama et 2 villes, elle comptait 20 485 542 habitants au 1er octobre 1965.

[65] Excluding data for the Pakistan-held part of Jammu and Kashmir, the final status of which has not yet been determined, and for Junagardh, Manavadar, Gilgit and Baltistan. — Non compris les données pour la partie de Jammu-Cachemire occupée par le Pakistan dont le status definitif n'a pas encore été déterminé, et le Junagardh, le Manavadar, le Gilgit et le Baltistan.

[66] Covers Seyhan and Yuregir districts in Adana. - Y compris la population des districts de Seyhan et de Yuregir.

[67] Covers Altindag, Cankaya, Etimesgut, Golbasi, Kecioren, Mamak, Sincan, and Yenimahalle districts in Ankara. - Y compris la population des districts de Altindag, de Cankaya, de Etimesgut, de Golbasi, de Kecioren, de Mamak, de Sincan, et de Yenimahalle.

[68] Covers Nilufer, Osmangazi and Yildirim districts in Bursa. - Y compris la population des districts de Nilufer, de Osmangazi et de Yildirim.

[69] District centre. — Le centre du district.

[70] Covers Sahinbey and Sehitkamil districts in Gaziantep. - Y compris la population des districts de Sahinbey et de Sehitkamil.

[71] Covers Adalar, Avcilar, Bagcilar, Bahcelievler, Bakirkoy, Bayrampasa,

Besiktas, Beykoz, Beyoglu, Eminonu, Esenler, Eyup, Fatih, Gaziosmanpasa, Gungoren, Kadikoy, Kagithane, Kartal, Kucukcekmece, Maltepe, Pendik, Sariyer, Sisli, Sultanbeyli, Tuzla, Umraniye, Uskudar, Zentinburnu districts in Istanbul. - Y compris la population des districts de Adalar, de Avcilar, de Bagcilar, de Bahcelievler, de Bakirkoy, de Bayrampasa, de Besiktas, de Beykoz, de Beyoglu, de Eminonu, de Esenler, de Eyup, de Fatih, de Gaziosmanpasa, de Gungoren, de Kadikoy, de Kagithane, de Kartal, de Kucukcekmece, de Maltepe, de Pendik, de Sariyer, de Sisli, de Sultanbeyli, de Tuzla, de Umraniye, de Uskudar, et de Zentinburnu.

[72] Covers Bolcova, Bornova, Buca, Cigli, Gaziemir, Guzelbahce, Karsiyaka, Konak and Narlidere districts in Izmir. - Y compris la population des districts de Bolcova, de Bornova, de Buca, de Cigli, de Gaziemir, de Guzelbahce, de Karsiyaka, de Konak et de Narlidere.

[73] Covers Kocasinan and Melikgazi districts in Kayseri. - Y compris la population des districts de Kocasinan et de Melikgazi.

[74] Covers Karatay, Meram and Selcuklu districts Konya. - Y compris la population des districts de Karatay, de Meram et de Selcuklu.

[75] Including Cholon. - Y compris Cholon.

[76] City is defined as a residential center that has a zoning and urbanisation plan approved by law. - Une ville est définie comme centre résidentiel soumis à un règlement de zonage et à un plan d'urbanisation approuvés par voie législative.

[77] City proper refers to commune or municipality. - La ville proprement dite se rapporte à la commune ou à la municipalité

[78] Urban agglomeration refers to core area of an urban region. The core area consists of a densely inhabited area and of urban localities in short distance as well as of next situated urban localities, agglomerated in case of mutual commuting to work (at least 35 index points). - Par agglomération urbaine, on entend la zone centrale d'une région urbaine, qui est constituée d'une zone de peuplement dense et des localités urbaines avoisinantes, ainsi que des localités urbaines situées un peu plus loin, les habitants des unes allant travailler dans les autres (35 points d'indice au minimum).

[79] Data for cities proper refer to communes which may contain an urban centre and a rural area. — Les données concernant les villes proprement dites se rapportent à des communes qui peuvent comprendre un centre urbain et une zone rurale.

[80] City is a settlement with a status of city according to the administrative-territorial division of the country at the end of the respective year. - La ville est une agglomération avec un statut de ville selon la division administratif-territoriale du pays à la fin de l'année respective.

[81] Data for cities proper refer to communes which are centres for urban agglomeration. — Les données concernant les villes proprement dites se rapportent à des communes qui sont des centres d'agglomérations urbaines.

[82] De jure population, but excluding diplomatic personnel outside the country and including foreign diplomatic personnel not living in embassies or consulates. — Population de droit, mais non compris le personnel diplomatique hors du pays et y compris le personnel diplomatique étranger qui ne vit pas dans les ambassades ou les consulats.

[83] Data refer to French territory of this international agglomeration. — Les données se rapportent aux habitants de cette agglomération internationale qui vivent en territoire francais.

[84] Including Villeurbanne. — Y compris Villeurbanne.

[85] Including armed forces stationed outside the country but excluding alien armed forces stationed in the area. — Y compris les militaires en garnison hors du pays, mais non compris les militaires étrangers en garnison sur le territoire.

[86] Data refer to the Vatican City State. — Les données se rapportent aux Etat du Saint-Siège.

[87] The boundaries of a city are related to the boundaries of a commune. - Les limites d'une ville correspondent aux limites d'une commune.

[88] The urban agglomeration of the capital area is much bigger and includes the following communes: Bessastaðahreppur, Garðabær, Hafnarfjörður, Kjósarhreppur, Kópavogur, Mosfellsbær ,Reykjavík, Seltjarnarnes. - L'agglomération urbaine de la capitale est beaucoup plus étendue et comprend les communes suivantes : Bessastaðahreppur, Garðabær, Hafnarfjörður, Kjósarhreppur, Kópavogur, Mosfellsbær ,Reykjavík, Seltjarnarnes.

[89] City is populated area with no less than 2 000 resident population, which is approved by the Cabinet of Ministers'. - Une ville est une zone de peuplement comptant au moins 2 000 habitants, selon une réglementation approuvée par le Cabinet ministériel.

[90] Population is not classified as 'urban' or 'rural'. About 95% of the population in Liechtenstein are living in a community with a population of 2000 and more. - La population n'est pas classée en 'urbaine' et 'rurale'. Environ 95 % de la population du Liechtenstein vit en agglomération comptant plus de 2 000 habitants.

[91] Including civilian nationals temporarily outside the country. — Y compris les civils nationaux temporairement hors du pays.

[92] Data for cities proper refer to administrative units (municipalities). — Les données concernant les villes proprement dites se rapportent à des unités administratives (municipalités).

[93] City is defined as administratively separated area entitled to civil (municipal) rights. Urban agglomeration is not defined. - Une ville est définie comme une zone administrativement distincte dotée de droits municipaux. Il n'y a pas de définition de l'agglomération urbaine.

[94] City is defined as industrial and cultural centers according to the legislation. - Une ville est définie comme centre culturel et industriel, conformément à la législation.

[95] Urban agglomeration includes the city and its populated localities subordinated to its authority. - Une agglomération urbaine comprend la ville et les localités peuplées qui relèvent de la même autorité.

[96] 2001 data refer to municipals with 100 000 + population. - Les données de 2001 font référence aux municipalités de plus de 100 000 habitants.

[97] For county districts, unitary authorities and London boroughs. — Pour les districts de province, autorités d'unité et cartiers de Londres.

[98] Greater London Borough included in figure for 'Greater London' conurbation. — Le chiffre relatif à l'ensemble urbain du 'Grand Londres' comprend le Greater London Borough.

[99] Capital of Northern Ireland. — Capitale de l'Irlande du Nord.

[100] Capital of Wales for certain purposes. — Considérée à certains égards comme la capitale du pays de Galles.

[101] Capital of Scotland. — Capitale de l'Ecosse.

[102] 'Greater London' conurbation as reconstituted in 1965 and comprising 32 new Greater London Boroughs. — Ensemble urbain du 'Grand Londres', tel qu'il a été reconstitué en 1965, comprenant 32 nouveaux Greater London Boroughs.

[103] For all regions it is not possible to distinguish between 'city proper' and 'urban agglomeration' areas, therefore data has been include under 'city proper'. - Il n'est pas possible de distinguer pour toutes les régions entre 'ville proprement dite' et 'agglomération urbaine', et les données sont donc présentées sous 'ville proprement dite'.

[104] Statistical division, which is a relatively stable area that includes a large buffer around each city to reduce the need to change boundaries as the city grows. - Division statistique, définie comme zone relativement stable comprenant une zone-tampon assez étendue autour de chaque ville, ce qui permet de ne pas avoir à en modifier aussi souvent les limites à mesure que la ville s'étend.

[105] Statistical district, which includes a much smaller buffer and basically just represent the urban area of that city. - District statistique, comprenant une zone-tampon beaucoup plus restreinte, et représentant pour l'essentiel la seule zone urbaine de la ville considérée.

[106] Excludes inland water and oceanic areas. - Exclut les eaux intérieures et les zones océaniques.

[107] A city is a territorial authority which is a distinct entity, is predominantly urban in character, has a minimum population of 50,000 and is a major centre of activity within its parent region. - Une ville est une collectivité territoriale qui constitue une entité distincte, est à prédominance urbaine, compte au moins 50 000 habitants et est un grand centre d'activité dans la région où elle est située.

[108] Urban agglomerations refer to main urban areas that are centres with populations of 30,000 or more. - Les agglomérations urbaines désignent les principales zones urbaines qui sont des centres de population comptant au moins 30 000 habitants.

[109] The Territorial Authority of Dunedin City (3341.53 sq km) includes a large hinterland of rural area. The Dunedin 'Urban Area' (255.13 sq km) is the area of Dunedin City that is urban. - La collectivité territoriale de Dunedin (3 341,53 kilomètres carrés) comprend de vastes étendues rurales. La 'zone urbaine' de Dunedin (255,13 kilomètres carrés) correspond à la zone urbanisée de la ville de Dunedin.

Table 9

Table 9 presents live births and live-birth rates by urban/rural residence for as many years as possible between 1999 and 2003.

Description of variables: Live birth is defined as the complete expulsion or extraction from its mother of a product of conception, irrespective of the duration of pregnancy, which after such separation, breathes or shows any other evidence of life such as beating of the heart, pulsation of the umbilical cord, or definite movements of voluntary muscles, whether or not the umbilical cord has been cut or the placenta is attached; each product of such a birth is considered live-born[1].

Statistics on the number of live births are obtained from civil registers unless otherwise noted. For those countries or areas where civil registration statistics on live births are considered reliable (estimated completeness of 90 per cent or more) the birth rates shown have been calculated on the basis of registered live births. However, for countries or areas where civil registration of live births is non-existent or considered unreliable (estimated completeness of less than 90 per cent or of unknown completeness), estimates provided by national statistical authorities are presented and are identified by the code "|" in the first column.

Rate computation: Crude live-birth rates are the annual number of live births per 1 000 mid-year population.

Rates by urban/rural residence are the annual number of live births, in the appropriate urban or rural category, per 1 000 corresponding mid-year population. Rates are calculated only for data considered complete, that is, coded with a "C" and for estimates, coded "|". These rates have been calculated by the Statistics Division of the United Nations Department for Economic and Social Affairs.

Rates presented in this table are limited to those countries or areas having a minimum number of 30 live births in a given year.

In addition, some rates were obtained from sample surveys, using different methods[2]; to distinguish them from civil registration data, estimated rates are identified by a footnote.

Reliability of data: Each country or area has been asked to indicate the estimated completeness of the live births recorded in its civil register. These national assessments are indicated by the quality codes (C) and (U) that appear in the first column of this table.

"C" indicates that the data are estimated to be virtually complete, that is, representing at least 90 per cent of the live births occurring each year, while "U" indicates that data are estimated to be incomplete, that is, representing less than 90 per cent of the live births occurring each year. A third code (...) indicates that no information was provided regarding completeness.

Data from civil registers that are reported as incomplete or of unknown completeness (coded "U" or "...") are considered unreliable. They appear in italics in this table and rates are not calculated for these data.

These quality codes apply only to data from civil registers. If data from other sources are presented, the symbol (|) is shown instead of the quality code. For more information about the quality of vital statistics data in general, and the information available on the basis of the completeness estimates in particular, see section 4.2 of the Technical Notes.

Limitations: Statistics on live births are subject to the same qualifications as have been set forth for vital statistics in general and birth statistics in particular as discussed in section 4 of the Technical Notes.

The reliability of data, an indication of which is described above, is an important factor in considering the limitations. In addition, some live births are tabulated by date of registration and not by date of occurrence; these have been indicated by a plus sign "+". Whenever the lag between the date of occurrence and date of registration is prolonged and, therefore, a large proportion of the live-birth registrations are delayed, birth statistics for any given year may be seriously affected.

Another factor that limits international comparability is the practice of some countries or areas not to include in live-birth statistics infants who were born alive but died before the registration of the birth or within the first 24 hours of life, thus underestimating the total number of life births. Statistics of this type are footnoted.

In addition, it should be noted that rates are affected also by the quality and limitations of the population estimates that are used in their computation. The problems of under-enumeration or over-enumeration and, to some extent, the differences in definition of total population have been discussed in section 3 of the Technical Notes dealing with population data in general, and specific information pertaining to individual countries or areas is given in the footnotes to table 3.

The rates estimated from the results of sample surveys are subject to possibilities of considerable error as a result of omissions in reporting of births, or as a result of erroneous reporting of births that occurred outside the reference period. However, rates estimated from sample surveys have the advantage of the availability of a built-in and strictly corresponding population base.

It should be emphasized that crude birth rates - like crude death, marriage and divorce rates - may be seriously affected by the age-sex structure of the populations to which they relate. Nevertheless, they do provide a simple measure of the level of and changes in natality.

The urban/rural classification of birth may refer to the residence of mother or the place of delivery, as the national practices vary and is provided by each country or area. In addition, the comparability of data by urban/rural residence is affected by the national definition of urban and rural used in tabulating these data. It is assumed, in the absence of specific information to the contrary, that the definitions of urban and rural used in connection with the national population census were also used in the compilation of the vital statistics for each country or area. However, it cannot be excluded that, for a given country or area, different definitions of urban and rural are used for the vital statistics data and the population census data respectively. When known, the definitions of urban used in national population census are presented at the end of the technical notes to table 6. As discussed in detail in the technical notes to table 6, these definitions vary considerably from one area or country to another. Urban/rural differentials in vital rates may also be affected by whether the vital events have been tabulated in terms of place of occurrence or place of usual residence. This problem is discussed in more detail in section 4.1.4.1 of the Technical notes.

Earlier data: Live births have been shown in each issue of the *Demographic Yearbook*. Data included in this table update the series covering a period of years as follows:

Issue	Years Covered
Special Edition on Natality, CD, 1999	
- Numbers	1980 - 1999
- Rates	1985 - 1999
Historical Supplement, CD, 1997	1948 – 1997
1992	1983 – 1992
1986	1967 – 1986
1981	1962 – 1981
Historical Supplement, 1979	1948 - 1977

For further information on years covered prior to 1948, readers should consult the Historical Index.

NOTES

[1] *Principles and Recommendations for a Vital Statistics System Revision 2,* Sales No. E. 01.XVII.10, United Nations, New York, 2001.
[2] *Manual X: Indirect Techniques for Demographic Estimation,* United Nations publication, Sales No. E.83.XIII.2, United Nations, New York, 1983.

Tableau 9

Le tableau 9 présente des données sur les naissances vivantes et les taux bruts de natalité selon le lieu de résidence (zone urbaine ou rurale) pour le plus grand nombre d'années possible entre 1999 et 2003.

Description des variables : La naissance vivante est l'expulsion ou l'extraction complète du corps de la mère, indépendamment de la durée de gestation, d'un produit de la conception qui, après cette séparation, respire ou manifeste tout autre signe de vie, tel que battement de cœur, pulsation du cordon ombilical ou contraction effective d'un muscle soumis à l'action de la volonté, que le cordon ombilical ait été coupé ou non et que le placenta soit ou non demeuré attaché ; tout produit d'une telle naissance est considéré comme « enfant né vivant »[1].

Sauf indication contraire, les statistiques relatives au nombre de naissances vivantes sont établies sur la base des registres de l'état civil. Pour les pays ou zones où les statistiques obtenues auprès des services de l'état civil sont jugées sûres (complétude estimée à 90 p. 100 ou plus), les taux de natalité indiqués ont été calculés par la Division de statistique de l'ONU d'après les naissances vivantes enregistrées. En revanche, pour les pays ou zones où les services de l'état civil n'enregistrent pas les naissances vivantes et ceux où l'enregistrement des naissances vivantes est de qualité douteuse (complétude estimée à moins de 90 p. 100 ou degré de complétude inconnu), on a présenté, autant que possible, des taux estimatifs nationaux signalés par le code '|'.

Calcul des taux : Les taux bruts de natalité représentent le nombre annuel de naissances vivantes pour 1 000 habitants au milieu de l'année.

Les taux selon le lieu de résidence (zone urbaine ou rurale) représentent le nombre annuel de naissances vivantes, classées selon la catégorie urbaine ou rurale appropriée pour 1 000 habitants au milieu de l'année. Les taux ont été calculés seulement pour les données considérées complètes, c'est-à-dire celles associées au code 'C'. Ces taux ont été calculés par la Division de statistique du Département des affaires économiques et sociales.

Les taux présentés dans ce tableau se rapportent seulement aux pays ou zones où l'on a enregistré un nombre minimal de 30 naissances vivantes au cours d'une année donnée.

Dans certains cas, les données ont été calculées à partir d'enquêtes par sondage, en utilisant différentes techniques indirectes d'estimation démographique[2]. Pour les distinguer des données qui proviennent des registres de l'état civil, les taux estimatifs ont été signalés par une note.

Fiabilité des données : Il a été demandé à chaque pays ou zone d'indiquer le degré estimatif de complétude des données sur les naissances vivantes figurant dans ses registres d'état civil. Ces évaluations nationales sont signalées par les codes de qualité 'C' et 'U' qui apparaissent dans la deuxième colonne du tableau.

La lettre 'C' indique que les données sont jugées à peu près complètes, c'est-à-dire qu'elles représentent au moins 90 p. 100 des naissances vivantes survenues chaque année ; la lettre 'U' signifie que les données sont jugées incomplètes, c'est-à-dire qu'elles représentent moins de 90 p. 100 des naissances vivantes survenues chaque année. Un troisième code, '...', indique qu'aucun renseignement n'a été communiqué quant à la complétude des données.

Les données provenant des registres de l'état civil qui sont déclarées incomplètes ou dont le degré de complétude n'est pas connu (code 'U' ou '...') sont jugées douteuses. Elles apparaissent en italique dans le tableau. Les taux pour ces données ne sont pas calculés.

Les codes de qualité ne s'appliquent qu'aux données provenant des registres de l'état civil. Si l'on présente des données autres que celles de l'état civil, le signe '|' est utilisé à la place du code de qualité. Pour plus de précisions sur la qualité des données reposant sur les statistiques de l'état civil en général et les estimations de complétude en particulier, voir la section 4.2 des Notes techniques.

Insuffisance des données : Les statistiques concernant les naissances vivantes appellent toutes les réserves qui ont été formulées à propos des statistiques de l'état civil en général et des statistiques des naissances en particulier (voir la section 4 des Notes techniques).

La fiabilité des données, au sujet de laquelle des indications ont été fournies plus haut, est un facteur important. Il faut également tenir compte du fait que, dans certains cas, les données relatives aux naissances vivantes sont exploitées selon la date de l'enregistrement et non selon la date de l'événement ; ces cas ont été signalés par le signe '+'. Chaque fois que le décalage entre l'événement et son enregistrement est grand et qu'une forte proportion des naissances vivantes fait l'objet d'un enregistrement tardif, les statistiques des naissances vivantes pour une année donnée peuvent être considérablement faussées.

Un autre facteur qui nuit à la comparabilité internationale est la pratique de certains pays ou zones qui consiste à ne pas inclure dans les statistiques des naissances vivantes les enfants nés vivants mais décédés avant l'enregistrement de leur naissance ou dans les 24 heures qui ont suivi la naissance, pratique qui conduit à sous-estimer le nombre total de naissances vivantes. Lorsque ce facteur a joué, cela a été signalé en note à la fin du tableau.

La qualité et les limitations des estimations concernant la population ont également une incidence sur le calcul des taux. Les problèmes liés au sur-dénombrement ou au sous-dénombrement et, dans une certaine mesure, aux différences dans la définition de la population totale ont été abordés à la section 3 des Notes techniques relative aux données sur la population en général et des précisions sur certains pays ou zones sont données dans les notes se rapportant au tableau 3.

Les taux estimatifs fondés sur les résultats d'enquêtes par sondage comportent des possibilités d'erreurs considérables dues soit à des omissions dans les déclarations, soit au fait que l'on a déclaré à tort des naissances survenues en réalité hors de la période considérée. Toutefois, les taux estimatifs fondés sur les résultats d'enquêtes par sondage présentent un gros avantage : le chiffre de population utilisé comme base est, par définition, rigoureusement correspondant.

Il faut souligner que les taux bruts de natalité, de même que les taux bruts de mortalité, de nuptialité et de divortialité, peuvent varier très sensiblement selon la structure par âge et par sexe de la population à laquelle ils se rapportent. Ils offrent néanmoins un moyen simple de mesurer le niveau et l'évolution de la natalité.

La classification des naissances selon le lieu de résidence (zone urbaine ou rurale) peut se rapporter au lieu de résidence de la mère ou au lieu d'occurrence et correspond à celle indiquée par chaque pays ou zone. En outre, la comparabilité des données selon le lieu de résidence (zone urbaine ou rurale) peut être limitée par les définitions nationales des termes « urbain » et « rural » utilisées pour la mise en tableaux de ces données. En l'absence d'indications contraires, on a supposé que les mêmes définitions avaient servi pour le recensement national de la population et pour l'établissement des statistiques de l'état civil pour chaque pays ou zone. Toutefois, il n'est pas exclu que, pour une zone ou un pays donné, des définitions différentes aient été retenues. Les définitions du terme « urbain » utilisées pour les recensements nationaux de population ont été présentées à la fin des notes techniques du tableau 6 lorsqu'elles étaient connues. Comme on l'a précisé dans les notes techniques relatives au tableau 6, ces définitions varient considérablement d'un pays ou d'une zone à l'autre. La différence entre ces taux pour les zones urbaines et rurales pourra aussi être faussée selon que les faits d'état civil auront été classés d'après le lieu de l'événement ou le lieu de résidence habituel. Ce problème est examiné plus en détail à la section 4.1.4.1 des Notes techniques.

Données publiées antérieurement : Les différentes éditions de l'*Annuaire démographique* contiennent des données sur les naissances vivantes. Les données qui figurent dans le tableau 9 actualisent les données qui portaient sur les périodes suivantes :

Éditions	Années considérées
Édition spéciale sur les statistiques de la natalité (CD-ROM), 1999	
- Nombre	1980 - 1999
- Taux	1985 - 1999
Supplément historique (CD-ROM), 1997	1948 – 1997

1992	1983 – 1992
1986	1967 – 1986
1981	1962 – 1981
Supplément rétrospectif, 1979	1948 - 1977

Pour plus de détails concernant les années antérieures à 1948, se reporter à l'index historique.

NOTES

[1] *Principes et recommandations pour un système de statistique de l'état civil, deuxième révision,* numéro de vente : F.01.XVII.10, publication des Nations Unies, New York, 2003.
[2] *Manuel X, techniques indirectes d'estimation démographique,* numéro de vente : F.83.XIII.2, publication des Nations Unies, New York, 1984.

9. Live births and crude birth rates, by urban/rural residence: 1999 - 2003
Naissances vivantes et taux bruts de natalité selon la résidence, urbaine/rurale: 1999 - 2003

Continent, country or area and urban/rural residence / Continent, pays ou zone et résidence urbaine/rurale	Code[1]	Number - Nombre					Rate - Taux				
		1999	2000	2001	2002	2003	1999	2000	2001	2002	2003
AFRICA — AFRIQUE											
Algeria - Algérie[2,3]	C										
Total		593 643	588 628	618 380	616 963	...	19.8	19.4	20.0	19.7	...
Benin - Bénin[4]	I										
Total		265 980	272 640	263 726	...	...	44.4	44.2	41.1	...	...
Botswana[4]	I										
Total		53 407	...	53 735	...	...	33.2	...	32.0	...	...
Cape Verde - Cap-Vert	C										
Total		...	12 746	12 926	13 123	13 334	...	29.3	29.1	29.0	28.9
Chad - Tchad	...										
Total[5]		...	...	397 896	...	...	...	...	...	...	...
Congo[5]	+U										
Total		...	38 456	41 312	...	...	...	...	...	...	...
Côte d'Ivoire[4]	I										
Total		...	655 904	...	...	...	...	40.0	...	...	...
Egypt - Égypte	C										
Total		1 693 025	1 751 854	1 741 308	1 751 712	*1 776 000	27.0	27.4	26.7	26.3	*26.1
Urban-Urbaine	C	657 902	...	...	...	...	24.7	...	...	...	...
Rural-Rurale	C	1 035 123	...	...	...	...	28.7	...	...	...	...
Ethiopia - Éthiopie	...										
Total		2 186 023	...	...	...	...	...	...	...	...	...
Urban-Urbaine	...	171 698	...	...	...	...	...	...	...	...	...
Rural-Rurale	...	2 014 325	...	...	...	...	...	...	...	...	...
Ghana	...										
Total		...	427 215	433 202	...	...	...	...	...	...	...
Kenya	U										
Total		405 488	470 712	468 249	494 941	495 433	...	...	...	...	...
Libyan Arab Jamahiriya - Jamahiriya arabe libyenne	C										
Total		...	98 752	99 187	111 053	...	...	19.3	18.7	20.2	...
Malawi[4]	I										
Total		531 160	543 654	555 558	567 241	578 978	52.3	51.9	51.4	50.8	50.1
Mali	U										
Total		...	...	525 685	...	...	...	...	...	...	...
Mauritius - Maurice	+C										
Total		20 311	20 205	19 696	19 983	19 343	17.3	17.0	16.4	16.5	15.8
Urban-Urbaine	+C	8 140	7 994	7 768	7 930	7 580	16.2	15.8	15.2	15.4	14.6
Rural-Rurale	+C	12 171	12 211	11 928	12 053	11 763	18.1	17.9	17.3	17.3	16.7
Morocco - Maroc[6]	C										
Total		529 383	541 023	541 298	...	...	18.7	18.8	18.6	...	...
Urban-Urbaine	C	256 501	274 945	282 380	...	...	16.7	17.3	17.3	...	...
Rural-Rurale	C	272 069	265 343	258 297	...	...	21.2	20.6	20.1	...	...
Mozambique[4]	I										
Total		...	...	753 252	...	...	...	...	42.7	...	...
Namibia - Namibie[7]	I										
Total		...	...	45 157	...	...	...	...	24.7	...	...
Urban-Urbaine	I	...	...	15 352	...	...	...	...	25.4	...	...
Rural-Rurale	I	...	...	29 805	...	...	...	...	24.3	...	...
Réunion[2]	C										
Total		14 153	14 594	14 541	14 789	*14 427	19.9	20.2	19.8	19.8	*18.9
Saint Helena ex. dep. - Sainte-Hélène sans dép.	C										
Total		52	56	36	...	...	...	...	...	...	...
Seychelles	+C										
Total		1 460	1 512	1 440	1 481	1 498	18.2	18.6	17.7	17.7	18.1
South Africa - Afrique du Sud	U										
Total		1 363 800	1 407 833	...	...	...	...	...	...	...	...
Tunisia - Tunisie	C										
Total		160 169	...	*163 300	...	...	16.9	...	*16.9	...	...
AMERICA, NORTH — AMERIQUE DU NORD											
Anguilla	+C										
Total		176	193	183	169	139	16.1	17.1	15.8	14.2	11.4

9. Live births and crude birth rates, by urban/rural residence: 1999 - 2003
Naissances vivantes et taux bruts de natalité selon la résidence, urbaine/rurale: 1999 - 2003
(continued — suite)

Continent, country or area and urban/rural residence — Continent, pays ou zone et résidence urbaine/rurale	Code[1]	Number - Nombre					Rate - Taux				
		1999	2000	2001	2002	2003	1999	2000	2001	2002	2003
AMERICA, NORTH — AMERIQUE DU NORD											
Antigua and Barbuda - Antigua-et-Barbuda											
Total	+C	1 329	1 528	...	...	...	...	...	...	...	...
Aruba[8]											
Total	+U	*1 225*	*1 294*	*1 266*	**1 374*	**1 170*	...	...	...	...	...
Bahamas[8]											
Total	U	*5 367*	*5 287*	*5 353*	...	*5 054*	...	...	...	...	...
Barbados - Barbade											
Total	+C	...	3 762	...	*3 812	...	...	14.1	...	*14.1	...
Belize											
Total	U	*6 218*	*7 313*	*7 082*	*7 356*	...	...	...	...	...	...
Bermuda - Bermudes											
Total	C	828	838	831	830	834	13.2	13.3	13.4	13.4	13.4
British Virgin Islands - Îles Vierges britanniques											
Total	+C	...	...	*318	...	...	...	...	*15.4	...	...
Canada[9]											
Total	C	337 249	327 882	333 744	328 802	*330 919	11.1	10.7	10.8	10.5	*10.5
Cayman Islands - Îles Caïmanes											
Total	C	604	619	*622	...	...	15.5	15.4	*15.0	...	...
Costa Rica											
Total	C	78 526	78 178	76 401	71 144	72 938	23.0	22.4	19.6	17.8	17.8
Urban-Urbaine	C	35 326	34 958	...	...	...	22.4	21.3	...	...	...
Rural-Rurale	C	43 200	43 219	...	...	...	23.5	23.5	...	...	...
Cuba											
Total	C	150 785	143 528	138 718	141 276	136 795	13.6	12.9	12.4	12.6	12.2
Urban-Urbaine	C	109 028	104 521	102 285	103 994	100 429	13.0	12.4	12.1	12.3	11.8
Rural-Rurale	C	41 757	39 007	36 433	37 282	36 366	15.3	14.4	13.5	13.8	13.4
Dominica - Dominique											
Total	+C	1 291	1 199	1 213	1 081	...	18.0	16.8	17.1	15.4	...
Dominican Republic - République dominicaine											
Total	+U	*193 418*	*189 332*	...	...	...	...	...	...	...	...
El Salvador											
Total	C	153 636	150 176	138 354	129 363	124 476	25.0	23.9	21.6	19.8	18.8
Urban-Urbaine	C	100 458	92 959	83 478	77 779	73 311	28.1	25.4	22.2	20.2	18.6
Rural-Rurale	C	53 178	57 217	54 876	51 584	51 165	20.6	21.9	20.8	19.3	18.9
Greenland - Groenland											
Total	C	947	885	937	940	895	16.9	...	16.6	16.6	15.8
Urban-Urbaine	C	734	698	780	745	717	16.1	...	16.9	16.0	15.3
Rural-Rurale	C	213	187	157	195	178	20.2	...	15.3	19.2	17.8
Grenada - Grenade											
Total	+C	1 791	1 883	1 899	...	...	17.8	18.6	18.8	...	...
Guadeloupe											
Total	C	7 341	7 653	7 503	6 995	7 047	17.3	17.9	17.3	16.0	16.1
Guatemala											
Total	C	360 759	426 346	403 532	...	375 092	32.5	37.4	34.6	...	31.0
Urban-Urbaine	C	140 491	...	...	...	...	...	...	...	...	...
Rural-Rurale	C	220 268	...	...	...	...	...	...	...	...	...
Jamaica - Jamaïque[10]											
Total	C	48 987	48 717	48 065	44 331	*45 133	19.0	18.8	18.5	16.9	*17.2
Martinique[2]											
Total	C	5 789	6 059	5 908	5 446	5 430	15.2	15.8	15.3	14.0	13.9
Mexico - Mexique[6]											
Total	+U	*2 769 089*	*2 798 339*	*2 767 610*	*2 699 084*	*2 655 894*	...	...	...	...	...
Urban-Urbaine	+U	*1 804 415*	*1 806 199*	*1 749 126*	*1 762 883*	*1 684 413*	...	...	...	...	...
Rural-Rurale	+U	*786 089*	*762 200*	*748 772*	*718 257*	*721 339*	...	...	...	...	...
Montserrat											
Total	+C	45	...	...	...	...	9.4	...	...	...	...
Netherlands Antilles - Antilles néerlandaises											
Total	C	2 803	2 638	2 621	2 382	2 512	15.1	14.7	15.0	13.7	14.1

9. Live births and crude birth rates, by urban/rural residence: 1999 - 2003
Naissances vivantes et taux bruts de natalité selon la résidence, urbaine/rurale: 1999 - 2003
(continued — suite)

Continent, country or area and urban/rural residence / Continent, pays ou zone et résidence urbaine/rurale	Code[1]	Number - Nombre					Rate - Taux				
		1999	2000	2001	2002	2003	1999	2000	2001	2002	2003
AMERICA, NORTH — AMERIQUE DU NORD											
Nicaragua											
Total	+U	123 446	126 873	108 299	120 846	102 676	...	...	...	...	...
Urban-Urbaine	+U	74 851	76 786	65 209	65 387	57 846	...	...	...	...	...
Rural-Rurale	+U	48 595	50 087	43 090	55 459	44 830	...	...	...	...	...
Panama											
Total	C	64 248	64 839	63 900	61 671	...	22.9	22.7	22.1	20.2	...
Urban-Urbaine	C	32 724	32 510	...	...	...	20.8	20.3	...	...	...
Rural-Rurale	C	31 524	32 329	...	...	...	25.5	25.8	...	...	...
Puerto Rico - Porto Rico[6]											
Total	C	59 684	59 460	55 982	52 871	50 803	15.8	15.6	14.6	13.7	13.1
Urban-Urbaine	C	30 561	30 464	29 323	...	26 642	...	...	...	...	...
Rural-Rurale	C	29 096	28 967	26 635	...	24 151	...	...	...	...	...
Saint Kitts and Nevis - Saint-Kitts-et-Nevis											
Total	+C	864	838	*803	...	...	20.3	20.7	*17.4	...	...
Saint Lucia - Sainte-Lucie											
Total	C	2 997	2 840	2 788	2 529		19.5	18.2	17.7	15.9	...
Saint Vincent and the Grenadines - Saint Vincent-et-les Grenadines											
Total	+C	2 171	2 149	2 109	1 985	...	19.5	19.2	19.3	18.4	...
Trinidad and Tobago - Trinité-et-Tobago											
Total	C	18 321	...	...	*18 026		14.3	...	...	*14.1	
Turks Caicos Islands - Îles Turques et Caïques											
Total	C	292	290	271	153	213	17.0	15.7	13.6	7.3	9.7
United States - États-Unis											
Total	C	3 959 417	4 058 814	4 025 933	4 021 726	*4 091 063	14.5	14.7	14.1	13.9	*14.1
AMERICA, SOUTH — AMERIQUE DU SUD											
Argentina - Argentine											
Total	C	686 748	701 878	683 495	694 684	697 952	18.8	19.0	18.2	18.3	18.4
Bolivia - Bolivie											
Total	U	...	264 941				...	...	...	...	...
Brazil - Brésil[11,12]											
Total	U	2 657 613	2 611 422	2 509 354	2 581 055	2 822 462	...	...	...	...	...
Chile - Chili											
Total	C	250 674	248 893	246 116	238 981	234 486	16.5	16.2	15.8	15.2	14.7
Urban-Urbaine	C	218 607	218 395	216 015	213 171	209 572	16.7	16.4	16.0	15.6	15.2
Rural-Rurale	C	32 067	30 498	30 101	25 810	24 914	15.3	14.8	14.5	12.3	11.8
Colombia - Colombie[6,13]											
Total	U	746 194	752 834	724 319	700 455	*697 029	...	...	...	...	...
Urban-Urbaine	U	570 263	574 208	552 445	539 729	*537 679	...	...	...	...	...
Rural-Rurale	U	153 039	153 865	154 404	148 599	*145 132	...	...	...	...	...
Ecuador - Équateur[14]											
Total	U	218 108	202 257	192 786	183 792	178 549	...	...	...	...	...
Urban-Urbaine	U	162 276	151 570	148 551	143 377	137 189	...	...	...	...	...
Rural-Rurale	U	55 832	50 687	44 235	40 415	41 360	...	...	...	...	...
Falkland Islands (Malvinas) - Îles Falkland (Malvinas)											
Total	+C	33	27	...	...	...	...	...	...	...	...
French Guiana - Guyane française[2]											
Total	C	4 898	5 116	5 114	5 249	5 553	30.9	31.2	30.1	29.9	30.7
Peru - Pérou[4,11,15]											
Total	I	642 874	636 064	630 947	626 714	623 521	25.2	24.5	23.9	23.4	23.0
Suriname[6,16]											
Total	C	10 144	9 804	9 717	10 188	...	22.2	21.1	20.7	21.4	...
Urban-Urbaine	C	6 875	6 018	6 016	6 298	...	...	...	...	...	...

9. **Live births and crude birth rates, by urban/rural residence: 1999 - 2003**
Naissances vivantes et taux bruts de natalité selon la résidence, urbaine/rurale: 1999 - 2003
(continued — suite)

Continent, country or area and urban/rural residence — Continent, pays ou zone et résidence urbaine/rurale	Code[1]	Number - Nombre					Rate - Taux				
		1999	2000	2001	2002	2003	1999	2000	2001	2002	2003
AMERICA, SOUTH — AMERIQUE DU SUD											
Suriname[6,16]											
Rural-Rurale	C	3 269	3 786	3 490	3 670	...	...	...	...	...	...
Uruguay											
Total	C	54 004	52 770	51 959	51 953	*50 631	16.4	16.0	15.7	15.7	*15.3
Venezuela[11]											
Total	C	527 888	544 416	529 552	492 678	555 614	22.1	22.4	21.4	19.5	...
ASIA — ASIE											
Armenia - Arménie[17]											
Total	C	36 502	34 276	32 065	32 229	35 793	11.3	10.6	10.0	10.0	11.1
Urban-Urbaine	C	22 458	21 390	...	20 804	22 629	10.7	10.3	...	10.1	11.0
Rural-Rurale	C	14 044	12 886	...	11 425	13 164	12.5	11.4	...	10.0	11.5
Azerbaijan - Azerbaïdjan[17]											
Total	+C	117 539	116 994	110 356	110 715	113 467	14.7	14.5	13.6	13.6	13.8
Urban-Urbaine	+C	50 083	49 631	49 676	49 733	51 057	12.3	12.1	12.1	12.0	12.0
Rural-Rurale	+C	67 456	67 363	60 680	60 982	62 410	17.3	17.0	15.2	15.2	15.6
Bahrain - Bahreïn[18]											
Total	+U	14 280	13 947	13 468	13 576	*14 560	...	...	...	...	...
Brunei Darussalam - Brunéi Darussalam											
Total	+C	7 408	7 481	7 363	7 464	7 047	23.4	23.0	22.1	21.7	20.2
China - Chine[19,20]											
Total	I	19 090 000	...	...	...	...	15.2	14.0	13.4	12.9	12.4
China: Hong Kong SAR - Chine: Hong Kong RAS											
Total	C	51 281	54 134	48 219	48 209	46 965	7.8	8.1	7.2	7.1	6.9
China: Macao SAR - Chine: Macao RAS											
Total	C	4 148	3 849	3 241	3 162	3 212	9.7	8.9	7.5	7.2	7.2
Cyprus - Chypre[6,21]											
Total	C	8 505	8 447	8 167	7 883	8 088	12.4	12.2	11.6	11.1	11.2
Urban-Urbalne	C	5 640	5 732	4 760	4 806	4 854	...	...	...	...	...
Rural-Rurale	C	2 789	2 648	2 926	2 637	2 692	...	...	...	...	...
Georgia - Géorgie[17]											
Total	C	40 778	40 392	47 589	46 605	46 194	9.2	9.1	10.8	10.7	10.7
Urban-Urbaine	C	25 862	25 520	25 078	...	34 589	11.0	11.0	10.9	...	15.3
Rural-Rurale	C	14 916	14 872	15 338	...	11 605	7.1	7.1	7.4	...	5.6
India - Inde[22,23]											
Total	I	...	...	...	...	...	26.0	25.8	25.4	25.0	24.8
Urban-Urbaine	I	...	...	...	...	...	20.8	20.7	20.3	20.0	19.8
Rural-Rurale	I	...	...	...	...	...	27.6	27.6	27.1	26.6	26.4
Iran (Islamic Republic of) - Iran (République islamique d')											
Total	C	1 177 557	1 095 165	1 112 193	1 122 104	1 171 573	18.8	17.2	17.2	17.1	17.6
Urban-Urbaine	C	744 839	709 638	724 072	734 332	768 845	18.7	17.4	17.2	17.1	17.5
Rural-Rurale	C	432 718	385 527	388 121	387 772	402 728	18.9	16.9	17.4	17.2	17.8
Iraq[24]											
Total	U	532 916	471 886	...	...	...	...	...	...	...	...
Israel - Israël[6,25]											
Total	C	131 936	136 390	136 638	139 535	144 936	21.5	21.7	21.2	21.2	21.7
Urban-Urbaine	C	118 003	121 700	124 640	126 795	131 658	21.2	21.4	21.1	21.1	21.5
Rural-Rurale	C	13 933	14 690	11 998	12 738	13 272	24.4	24.8	22.3	23.1	23.4
Japan - Japon[6,26]											
Total	C	1 177 669	1 190 547	1 170 662	1 153 855	1 123 610	9.3	9.4	9.2	9.1	8.8
Urban-Urbaine	C	951 533	962 392	947 755	939 091	917 627	...	...	...	...	...
Rural-Rurale	C	225 894	227 945	222 709	214 569	205 813	...	...	...	...	...
Jordan - Jordanie[27]											
Total	C	135 266	126 016	142 956	146 077	148 294	27.2	25.4	27.2	27.0	27.4
Kazakhstan[17]											
Total	C	217 578	222 054	221 487	227 171	247 946	14.6	14.9	14.9	15.3	16.6
Urban-Urbaine	C	110 167	114 505	115 316	122 151	138 680	13.1	13.6	13.7	14.5	16.3

9. Live births and crude birth rates, by urban/rural residence: 1999 - 2003
Naissances vivantes et taux bruts de natalité selon la résidence, urbaine/rurale: 1999 - 2003
(continued — suite)

Continent, country or area and urban/rural residence / Continent, pays ou zone et résidence urbaine/rurale	Code[1]	Number - Nombre					Rate - Taux				
		1999	2000	2001	2002	2003	1999	2000	2001	2002	2003
ASIA — ASIE											
Kazakhstan[17]											
Rural-Rurale	C	107 411	107 549	106 171	105 020	109 266	16.5	16.6	16.5	16.4	17.0
Korea (Republic of) - Corée (République de)[28]											
Total	C	616 322	636 780	557 228	494 625	*493 471	13.2	13.5	11.8	10.4	*10.3
Urban-Urbaine	C	500 744	519 767	453 431	404 409	...	...	...	...	...	...
Rural-Rurale	C	115 578	117 013	103 797	90 216	...	...	...	...	...	...
Kuwait - Koweït											
Total	C	41 135	41 843	41 342	43 490	...	19.5	19.1	18.2	19.2	...
Kyrgyzstan - Kirghizistan[17]											
Total	C	104 068	96 770	98 138	101 012	105 490	21.4	19.7	19.8	20.2	20.9
Urban-Urbaine	C	28 328	28 193	28 491	30 195	31 866	16.5	16.2	16.2	17.1	17.8
Rural-Rurale	C	75 740	68 577	69 647	70 817	73 624	24.1	21.6	21.8	21.9	22.6
Lebanon - Liban[24]											
Total	U	85 955	87 795	85 925	85 588	81 184	...	...	...	...	...
Malaysia - Malaisie[2]											
Total	C	521 870	545 096	...	...	*533 600	23.9	23.2	...	...	*21.3
Maldives											
Total	C	5 225	5 399	4 897	5 003	5 154	18.8	19.9	17.7	17.8	18.1
Urban-Urbaine	C	1 489	1 568	1 636	1 877	1 965	...	...	21.6	24.4	25.1
Rural-Rurale	C	3 736	3 831	3 261	3 125	3 189	...	...	16.3	15.3	15.4
Mongolia - Mongolie											
Total	C	49 461	48 721	49 685	46 922	45 723	...	20.2	20.3	19.0	18.3
Urban-Urbaine	C	24 219	23 828	24 691	24 067	24 315	...	17.3	17.7	16.9	16.6
Rural-Rurale	C	25 242	24 893	24 994	22 855	21 408	...	24.2	23.9	21.7	20.6
Occupied Palestinian Territory - Territoire palestinien occupé											
Total	U	98 594	100 626	98 190	100 382	99 385	...	...	...	...	...
Oman[29]											
Total	U	39 922	39 994	39 297	40 222	40 062	...	...	...	...	...
Pakistan[30,31]											
Total	I	...	...	3 719 694	...	...	...	...	26.5	...	...
Urban-Urbaine	I	...	...	1 192 190	...	...	...	...	...	...	...
Rural-Rurale	I	...	...	2 527 504	...	...	...	...	...	...	...
Philippines											
Total	C	1 613 335	1 766 440	1 714 093	1 666 773	...	21.6	23.1	22.0	21.0	...
Qatar											
Total	C	10 846	11 250	12 118	12 200	12 856	18.5	18.2	18.7	17.9	17.9
Saudi Arabia - Arabie saoudite											
Total	...	509 352	578 772	...	...	...	...	...	...	...	...
Singapore - Singapour[32]											
Total	C	43 336	46 997	41 451	40 760	37 485	11.0	11.7	10.0	9.8	9.0
Sri Lanka											
Total	+C	329 121	...	...	*363 549	...	17.3	...	...	*19.1	...
Syrian Arab Republic - République arabe syrienne[2,33]											
Total	C	503 473	505 484	524 212	471 970	492 639	31.3	31.0	31.4	27.6	28.1
Tajikistan - Tadjikistan[15,17]											
Total	I	180 888	167 246	171 623	175 599	177 938	29.8	27.0	27.2	27.3	27.1
Urban-Urbaine	I	40 579	42 382	45 454	42 823	45 182	25.2	25.8	27.1	25.1	26.0
Rural-Rurale	I	140 309	124 864	126 169	132 776	132 756	31.5	27.5	27.2	28.0	27.5
Thailand - Thaïlande											
Total	+U	772 604	773 009	790 425	782 911	742 183	...	...	...	...	...
Urban-Urbaine	+U	116 268	119 794	...	...	...	...	...	...	...	...
Rural-Rurale	+U	656 336	653 215	...	...	...	...	...	...	...	...
Turkey - Turquie[34]											
Total	I	1 501 000	1 494 000	1 486 000	1 482 000	1 479 000	22.6	22.2	21.7	21.3	20.9
Uzbekistan - Ouzbékistan[17]											
Total	C	553 745	527 580	512 950	...	...	23.1	21.4	20.5	...	...

9. Live births and crude birth rates, by urban/rural residence: 1999 - 2003
Naissances vivantes et taux bruts de natalité selon la résidence, urbaine/rurale: 1999 - 2003
(continued — suite)

Continent, country or area and urban/rural residence Continent, pays ou zone et résidence urbaine/rurale	Code[1]	Number - Nombre					Rate - Taux				
		1999	2000	2001	2002	2003	1999	2000	2001	2002	2003
ASIA — ASIE											
Uzbekistan - Ouzbékistan[17]											
Urban-Urbaine	C	173 209	163 834	159 492	...	...	19.2	17.8	17.2	...	...
Rural-Rurale	C	380 536	363 746	353 458	...	...	25.5	23.5	22.5	...	...
EUROPE											
Albania - Albanie											
Total	C	57 948	51 242	54 283	45 515	47 012	19.0	16.7	17.7	14.7	15.1
Andorra - Andorre											
Total	C	833	747	777	749	721	12.6	11.3	11.8	11.3	10.3
Austria - Autriche											
Total	C	78 138	78 268	75 458	78 399	76 944	9.8	9.8	9.4	9.7	9.5
Belarus - Bélarus[17]											
Total	C	92 975	...	...	88 743	88 512	9.3	...	...	8.9	9.0
Urban-Urbaine	C	66 380	...	...	65 091	64 814	9.5	...	...	9.3	9.2
Rural-Rurale	C	26 595	...	...	23 652	23 698	8.7	...	...	8.2	8.4
Belgium - Belgique[35]											
Total	C	113 469	114 883	*114 014	...	...	11.1	11.2	*11.1	...	...
Bosnia and Herzegovina - Bosnie-Herzégovine											
Total	C	42 464	39 563	37 717	35 587	35 234	11.4	10.5	9.9	9.3	9.2
Bulgaria - Bulgarie											
Total	C	72 291	73 679	68 180	66 499	67 359	8.8	9.0	8.6	8.5	8.6
Urban-Urbaine	C	...	52 789	48 567	47 779	48 597	...	9.5	8.9	8.7	8.9
Rural-Rurale	C	...	20 890	19 613	18 720	18 762	...	8.1	8.1	7.8	7.9
Channel Islands: Guernsey - Îles Anglo-Normandes: Guernesey											
Total	C	672	644	...	...	...	11.2	10.7	...	...	...
Croatia - Croatie											
Total	C	45 179	43 746	40 993	40 094	39 668	9.9	10.0	9.2	9.0	8.9
Urban-Urbaine	C	...	24 768	22 938	22 539	21 837	...	...	9.3	...	...
Rural-Rurale	C	...	18 978	18 055	17 555	17 831	...	...	9.2	...	...
Czech Republic - République tchèque											
Total	C	89 471	90 910	90 715	97 878	93 685	8.7	8.8	8.9	9.6	9.2
Urban-Urbaine	C	65 460	66 868	67 081	73 482	69 120	8.5	8.8	8.9	9.8	9.2
Rural-Rurale	C	24 011	24 042	23 634	24 396	24 565	9.2	9.1	8.9	9.2	9.2
Denmark - Danemark[36]											
Total	C	66 232	67 084	65 458	64 149	64 682	12.4	12.6	12.2	11.9	12.0
Estonia - Estonie[6,17]											
Total	C	12 545	13 089	12 632	13 001	13 036	8.7	9.6	9.3	9.6	9.6
Urban-Urbaine	C	...	8 684	8 645	8 840	9 049	...	9.2	9.2	9.4	9.7
Rural-Rurale	C	...	4 402	3 987	4 161	3 987	...	10.4	9.5	10.0	9.6
Finland - Finlande[37]											
Total	C	57 574	56 742	56 189	55 555	56 630	11.1	11.0	10.8	10.7	10.9
Urban-Urbaine	C	36 621	...	36 191	36 263	37 303	11.8	...	11.4	11.3	11.5
Rural-Rurale	C	20 953	...	19 998	19 292	19 327	10.2	...	10.0	9.7	9.8
France[38,39]											
Total	C	744 791	774 782	770 945	761 630	*760 300	12.7	13.2	13.0	12.8	*12.7
Urban-Urbaine	C	570 503	589 608	585 317	577 724	...	...	...	...	...	...
Rural-Rurale	C	172 966	183 787	184 112	182 454	...	...	...	...	...	...
Germany - Allemagne											
Total	C	770 744	766 999	734 475	719 250	706 721	9.4	9.3	8.9	8.7	8.6
Gibraltar[40]											
Total	+C	381	408	374	371	372	14.1	15.0	...	13.0	13.0
Greece - Grèce											
Total	C	116 038	117 140	102 282	103 838	104 420	11.0	11.7	10.2	9.5	9.5
Holy See - Saint-Siège											
Total	C	...	1	...	...	...	...	...	...	...	...
Hungary - Hongrie[6]											
Total	C	94 645	97 597	97 047	96 804	94 647	9.4	9.7	9.5	9.5	9.3

9. Live births and crude birth rates, by urban/rural residence: 1999 - 2003
Naissances vivantes et taux bruts de natalité selon la résidence, urbaine/rurale: 1999 - 2003
(continued — suite)

Continent, country or area and urban/rural residence Continent, pays ou zone et résidence urbaine/rurale	Code[1]	Number - Nombre					Rate - Taux				
		1999	2000	2001	2002	2003	1999	2000	2001	2002	2003
EUROPE											
Hungary - Hongrie[6]											
Urban-Urbaine	C	57 113	59 029	59 119	60 753	59 280	8.8	9.1	8.9	9.2	9.0
Rural-Rurale	C	36 836	37 781	37 019	35 248	34 465	10.4	10.6	10.5	10.0	9.8
Iceland - Islande											
Total	C	4 100	4 315	4 091	4 049	4 143	14.8	15.3	14.4	14.1	14.3
Urban-Urbaine	C	3 833	4 025	3 849	3 823	3 906	15.0	15.5	14.6	14.4	14.6
Rural-Rurale	C	267	290	242	226	237	12.6	13.5	11.2	10.5	11.1
Ireland - Irlande[41]											
Total	+C	53 354	54 239	57 854	60 521	61 517	14.2	14.3	15.1	15.5	15.4
Urban-Urbaine	+C	30 827	...	...	...	...	...	...	...	...	...
Rural-Rurale	+C	22 527	...	...	...	...	...	...	...	...	...
Isle of Man - Îles de Man											
Total	+C	894	831	863	903	860	...	11.1	11.3	11.7	11.1
Italy - Italie[8]											
Total	C	523 463	543 039	535 282	538 198	539 503	9.1	9.4	9.2	9.4	9.4
Latvia - Lettonie[17]											
Total	C	19 396	20 248	19 664	20 044	21 006	8.1	8.5	8.3	8.6	9.0
Urban-Urbaine	C	12 072	12 737	12 531	12 938	13 891	7.4	7.9	7.8	8.2	8.8
Rural-Rurale	C	7 324	7 511	7 133	7 106	7 115	9.7	9.9	9.4	9.4	9.5
Liechtenstein											
Total	C	...	...	401	395	347	...	...	12.1	11.7	10.2
Lithuania - Lituanie[17]											
Total	C	36 415	34 149	31 546	30 014	30 598	10.3	9.8	9.1	8.7	8.9
Urban-Urbaine	C	...	21 008	19 672	18 697	19 140	...	9.0	8.4	8.1	8.3
Rural-Rurale	C	...	13 141	11 874	11 317	11 458	...	11.4	10.3	9.9	10.0
Luxembourg											
Total	C	5 582	5 723	5 459	5 345	5 303	13.0	13.1	12.4	12.0	11.8
Malta - Malte[42,43]											
Total	C	4 308	4 255	3 859	3 805	3 902	11.3	11.1	10.0	9.8	9.8
Monaco											
Total	C	...	771	...	...	842	...	24.1	...	...	...
Netherlands - Pays-Bas[44]											
Total	C	200 445	206 619	202 603	202 083	200 297	12.7	13.0	12.6	12.5	12.3
Urban-Urbaine	C	...	132 318	132 295	132 825	132 805	...	13.0	12.7	12.7	12.5
Rural-Rurale	C	...	74 301	70 308	69 258	67 492	...	12.9	12.4	12.2	12.0
Norway - Norvège											
Total	C	59 298	59 234	56 696	55 434	56 458	13.3	13.2	12.6	12.2	12.4
Poland - Pologne											
Total	C	382 002	378 700	368 205	353 765	351 072	9.9	9.9	9.6	9.3	9.2
Urban-Urbaine	C	208 173	...	205 708	197 434	199 583	8.7	...	8.7	8.4	8.5
Rural-Rurale	C	173 829	...	162 497	156 331	151 489	11.8	...	11.1	10.7	10.3
Portugal											
Total	C	116 002	118 551	112 774	114 383	112 515	11.4	11.6	11.0	11.0	10.8
Republic of Moldova - République de Moldova[17]											
Total	C	38 501	36 939	36 448	35 705	36 471	10.6	10.2	10.0	9.9	10.1
Urban-Urbaine	C	13 238	12 722	12 542	12 747	12 788	8.6	8.4	8.4	8.6	8.6
Rural-Rurale	C	25 263	24 217	23 906	22 958	23 683	11.9	11.4	11.1	10.7	11.1
Romania - Roumanie											
Total	C	234 600	234 521	220 368	210 529	212 459	10.4	10.5	9.8	9.7	9.8
Urban-Urbaine	C	...	108 254	102 432	98 190	100 915	...	8.8	8.4	8.5	8.7
Rural-Rurale	C	...	126 267	117 936	112 339	111 544	...	12.4	11.6	11.0	11.0
Russian Federation - Fédération de Russie[17]											
Total	C	1 214 689	1 266 800	1 311 604	1 396 967	1 477 301	8.3	8.6	9.0	9.6	10.2
Urban-Urbaine	C	842 640	...	928 642	998 056	1 050 565	7.8	...	8.7	9.4	9.9
Rural-Rurale	C	372 049	...	382 962	398 911	426 736	9.4	...	9.8	10.3	11.1
San Marino - Saint-Marin											
Total	+C	303	290	315	295	300	11.5	10.8	11.4	10.4	10.3
Urban-Urbaine	+C	...	259	...	...	...	...	11.4	...	...	...
Rural-Rurale	+C	...	31	...	...	...	...	7.4	...	...	...
Serbia and Montenegro - Serbie-et-Montenegro[45]											
Total	C	123 970	125 868	130 194	86 600	87 370	11.7	11.8	12.2	10.7	10.7

9. Live births and crude birth rates, by urban/rural residence: 1999 - 2003
Naissances vivantes et taux bruts de natalité selon la résidence, urbaine/rurale: 1999 - 2003
(continued — suite)

Continent, country or area and urban/rural residence / Continent, pays ou zone et résidence urbaine/rurale	Code[1]	Number - Nombre					Rate - Taux				
		1999	2000	2001	2002	2003	1999	2000	2001	2002	2003
EUROPE											
Serbia and Montenegro - Serbie-et-Montenegro[45]											
Urban-Urbaine	C	64 489	66 409	69 491	54 356	54 296	11.8	12.1	12.6	11.8	11.7
Rural-Rurale	C	59 481	59 459	60 703	32 244	33 074	11.5	11.5	11.8	9.2	9.5
Slovakia - Slovaquie											
Total	C	56 223	55 103	51 136	50 841	51 713	10.4	10.2	9.5	9.5	9.6
Urban-Urbaine	C	28 693	...	26 106	26 321	26 798	9.4	...	8.7	8.7	8.9
Rural-Rurale	C	27 530	...	25 030	24 520	24 915	11.8	...	10.6	10.4	10.5
Slovenia - Slovénie											
Total	C	17 533	18 180	17 477	17 501	17 321	8.8	9.1	8.8	8.8	8.7
Urban-Urbaine	C	8 017	8 306	8 039	8 400	8 425	...	...	...	8.6	8.7
Rural-Rurale	C	9 516	9 874	9 438	9 101	8 896	...	...	...	9.3	9.1
Spain - Espagne											
Total	C	380 130	397 632	406 390	418 846	*420 963	9.6	9.9	10.0	10.2	*10.5
Sweden - Suède											
Total	C	88 173	90 441	91 466	95 815	99 157	10.0	10.2	10.3	10.7	11.1
Switzerland - Suisse											
Total	C	78 408	78 458	73 509	72 372	71 848	11.0	10.9	10.2	9.9	9.8
Urban-Urbaine	C	51 771	52 393	49 292	52 869	52 727	10.7	10.8	...	...	...
Rural-Rurale	C	26 637	26 065	24 217	19 503	19 121	11.5	11.2	...	...	...
The Former Yugoslav Rep. of Macedonia - L'ex-République yougoslave de Macédoine											
Total	C	27 309	29 308	27 010	27 761	*27 011	13.5	14.5	13.3	13.7	*13.3
Urban-Urbaine	C	14 375	15 579	14 761	14 909	...	...	...	...	...	...
Rural-Rurale	C	12 934	13 729	12 249	12 852	...	...	...	...	...	...
Ukraine[17]											
Total	C	...	385 126	376 478	390 688	408 589	...	7.9	7.8	8.1	8.6
Urban-Urbaine	C	...	...	237 228	248 877	266 415	...	...	7.3	7.7	8.3
Rural-Rurale	C	...	...	139 250	141 811	142 174	...	...	8.7	8.9	9.1
United Kingdom - Royaume-Uni[46,47]											
Total	C	699 976	679 029	669 123	668 777	695 549	11.9	11.5	11.3	11.3	11.7
OCEANIA — OCEANIE											
American Samoa - Samoas américaines											
Total	C	1 736	1 730	...	...	...	30.6	30.2	...	...	...
Australia - Australie											
Total	+C	248 870	249 636	246 394	250 988	251 161	13.1	13.0	12.7	12.8	12.6
Cook Islands - Îles Cook											
Total	+C	346	309	313	292	298	21.1	17.2	17.2	15.9	16.2
Fiji - Fidji											
Total	+C	16 916	...	...	...	...	21.0	...	...	...	...
French Polynesia - Polynésie française											
Total	C	4 580	4 900	4 874	4 762	4 503	20.1	21.2	20.4	19.6	18.2
Guam[48]											
Total	C	4 037	3 790	3 583	3 222	3 298	26.5	...	22.6	20.0	20.2
Marshall Islands - Îles Marshall[49]											
Total	+U	1 478	...	*1 511	...	...	...	...	...	...	...
New Caledonia - Nouvelle-Calédonie											
Total	C	4 316	4 566	4 326	4 194	4 102	20.8	21.6	20.2	19.3	18.6
New Zealand - Nouvelle-Zélande[6]											
Total	+C	57 053	56 605	55 799	54 021	56 134	14.9	14.7	14.4	13.7	14.0
Urban-Urbaine	+C	49 536	49 374	48 745	47 068	49 166	15.1	14.9	14.6	13.9	14.3
Rural-Rurale	+C	7 293	7 126	6 986	6 896	6 878	13.4	13.0	12.7	12.5	12.3
Niue - Nioué											
Total	...	...	...	...	24	...	...	...	...	...	...

9. Live births and crude birth rates, by urban/rural residence: 1999 - 2003
Naissances vivantes et taux bruts de natalité selon la résidence, urbaine/rurale: 1999 - 2003
(continued — suite)

Continent, country or area and urban/rural residence / Continent, pays ou zone et résidence urbaine/rurale	Code[1]	Number - Nombre					Rate - Taux				
		1999	2000	2001	2002	2003	1999	2000	2001	2002	2003
OCEANIA — OCEANIE											
Northern Mariana Islands - Îles Mariannes septentrionales											
Total	U	*1 448*	...	...	...	...	...	...	...	...	...
Palau - Palaos											
Total	C	250	278	300	259	312	13.2	14.4	15.3	13.0	15.4
Papua New Guinea - Papouasie-Nouvelle-Guinée											
Total	U	...	*177 629*	*182 619*	*187 645*	*192 817*	...	...	...	...	...
Tonga											
Total	+C	2 599	2 471	...	...	...	26.0	24.6	...	...	...

FOOTNOTES - NOTES

*Italics:*data from civil registers which are incomplete or of unknown completeness. — Italiques: données incomplètes ou dont le degré de complétude n'est pas connu provenant des registres de l'état civil.

* Provisional. — Données provisoires.

[1] 'Code' indicates the source of data, as follows:
C - Civil registration, estimated over 90% complete
U - Civil registration, estimated less than 90% complete
| - Other source, estimated reliable
+ - Data tabulated by date of registration rather than occurence.
... - Information not available

Le 'Code' indique la source des données, comme suit:
C - Registres de l'état civil considérés complèts à 90 p. 100 au moins.
U - Registres de l'état civil qui ne sont pas considérés complèts à 90 p. 100 au moins.
| - Autre source, considérée pas douteuses.
+ - Données exploitées selon la date de l'enregistrement et non la date de l'événement.
... - Information pas disponible.

[2] Excluding live-born infants who died before their birth was registered. - Non compris les enfants nés vivants décédés avant l'enregistrement de leur naissance.
[3] For Algerian population only. - Pour la population algérienne seulement.
[4] Data refer to national projections. - Les données se referent aux projections nationales.
[5] Data from civil registration centers of Brazzaville, Pointe-Noire, Dolisie, Nkayi, Mossendijo and Ouesso communes. - Données issues des centers d'enregistrement des faits d'état-civil des communes de Brazzaville, Pointe-Noire, Dolisie, Nkayi, Mossendijo et Ouesso.
[6] Figures for urban and rural areas do not add up to the total, since they do not include the category 'Unknown residence'. - La somme des donées pour la residence urbaine et rurale n'est pas égale au total parce qu'elle n'inclue pas la catégorie 'Residence inconnue'.
[7] For 2001, data refer to last twelve months preceding census on August 2001. - Pour 2001, les données se rapportent pour la dernière fois à douze mois précédant le recensement août 2001.
[8] Data as reported by national statistical authorities; they may differ from data presented in other tables. - Les données comme elles ont été déclarées par l'institut national de la statistique; elles peuvent être différentes de ceux présentées dans autre tableaux.
[9] Including Canadian residents temporarily in the United States, but excluding United States residents temporarily in Canada. - Y compris les résidents canadiens se trouvant temporairement aux Etats-Unis, mais ne comprenant pas les résidents des Etats-Unis se trouvant temporairement au Canada.
[10] Including births to non-resident mothers. - Y compris les naissances chez des mères non résidentes.

[11] Excluding Indian jungle population. - Non compris les Indiens de la jungle.
[12] Total includes unknown sex and foreigners. - Le total compris le sexe inconnu et les étrangers.
[13] Data on live births and deaths are based on a civil registration system put in place in January 1998. - Les données sur les naissances et les décès sont basées sur un système d'enregistrement des faits d'état civil mis en place en janvier 1998.
[14] Excluding nomadic Indian tribes. - Non compris les tribus d'Indiens nomades.
[15] Including an upward adjustment for under-registration. - Y compris un ajustement pour sous-enregistrement.
[16] Data for urban refer to the total of the district of Paramaribo (capital) and Wanica district. - Les données relatives aux zones urbaines correspondent au total pour le district de Paramaribo (capitale) et le district de Wanica.
[17] Excluding infants born alive with less than 28 weeks gestation, less than 1 000 grams in weight and 35 centimeters in length, who die within seven days of birth. - Non compris les enfants nés vivants avant 28 semaines de gestation, pesant moins de 1 000 grammes, mesurant moins de 35 centimètres et décédés dans les sept jours qui ont suivi leur naissance.
[18] For 1999 and 2000 by registration, starting from 2001 by occurence. - Pour 1999 et 2000 les données sont presentées selon la date d'enregistrement; pour 2001 et après les données sont présentées selon la date de l'evénement.
[19] For statistical purposes, the data for China do not include those for the Hong Kong Special Administrative Region (Hong Kong SAR), Macao Special Administrative Region (Macao SAR) and Taiwan province of China. - Pour la présentation des statistiques, les données pour Chine ne comprend pas la Région Administrative Spéciale de Hong Kong (Hong Kong RAS), la Région Administrative Spéciale de Macao (Macao RAS) et Taïwan province de Chine.
[20] Rates for 2000 - 2003 were obtained by the Sample Survey of Population Change 2003 in China. - Les taux pour 2000 - 2003 on été obtenus par la 2003 enquête de mouvement de la population par échantillon de la Chine.
[21] Data refer to government controlled areas. - Les données se raportent aux zones contrôlées par le Gouvernement.
[22] Including data for the Indian-held part of Jammu and Kashmir, the final status of which has not yet been determined. - Y compris les données pour la partie du Jammu et du Cachemire occupée par l'Inde dont le statut définitif n'a pas encore été déterminé.
[23] Rates were obtained by the Sample Registration System of India, actually a large demographic survey. - Les taux ont été obtenus par le Système de l'enregistrement par échantillon de l'Inde qui est au fait une large enquête démographique.
[24] Published by the United Nations Economic and Social Commission for Western Asia. - Publié par la Commission économique et sociale des Nations Unies pour l'Asie occidentale.
[25] Including data for East Jerusalem and Israeli residents in certain other territories under occupation by Israeli military forces since June 1967. - Y compris les données pour Jérusalem-Est et les résidents israéliens dans certains autres territoires occupés depuis 1967 par les forces armées israéliennes.
[26] For Japanese nationals in Japan only; however, rates computed on population including foreigners except foreign military and civilian personnel and their dependants stationed in the area. - Pour les nationaux japonais au Japon seulement; toutefois, les taux sont calculés sur la base d'une population

comprenant les étrangers, mais ne comprenant ni les militaires et agents civils étrangers en poste sur le territoire ni les membres de leur famille les accompagnant.

[27] Excluding data for Jordanian territory under occupation since June 1967 by Israeli military forces. Excluding foreigners, including registered Palestinian refugees. - Non compris les données pour le territoire jordanien occupé depuis juin 1967 par les forces armées israéliennes. Non compris les étrangers, mais y compris les réfugiés de Palestine enregistrés.

[28] Excluding alien armed forces, civilian aliens employed by armed forces, and foreign diplomatic personnel and their dependants. - Non compris les militaires étrangers, les civils étrangers employés par les forces armées ni le personnel diplomatique étranger et les membres de leur famille les accompagnant.

[29] Data refer to the recorded events in Ministry of Health hospitals and health centres only. - Les données se rapportent aux faits d'état-civil enregistrés dans les hôpitaux et les dispensaires du Ministère de la santé seulement.

[30] Based on the results of the Population Growth Survey. - D'après les résultats de la 'Population Growth Survey.'

[31] Excluding data for the Pakistan-held part of Jammu and Kashmir, the final status of which has not yet been determined. - Non compris les données concernant la partie du Jammu et Cachemire occupée par le Pakistan dont le statut définitif n'a pas été déterminé.

[32] Excluding transients afloat and military and civilian services personnel and their dependants abroad. - Non compris les personnes de passage à bord de navires ni les militaires et agents civils et les membres de leur famille les accompagnant à l'étranger.

[33] Excluding nomad population and Palestinian refugees. - Non compris la population nomade et les réfugiés de Palestine.

[34] Based on the results of the Population Demographic Survey. - D'après les résultats de la Population Demographic Survey.

[35] Including armed forces stationed outside the country, but excluding alien armed forces stationed in the area. - Y compris les militaires nationaux hors du pays, mais non compris les militaires étrangers en garnison sur le territoire.

[36] Excluding Faeroe Islands and Greenland. - Non compris les Iles Féroé et Gröenland.

[37] Including nationals temporarily outside the country. - Y compris les nationaux se trouvant temporairement hors du pays.

[38] Including armed forces stationed outside the country. - Y compris les militaires nationaux hors du pays.

[39] Urban/rural figures, excluding nationals outside the country. - Les chiffres urbaine/rurale, non compris les nationaux hors du pays.

[40] For 1999 and 2000, excluding armed forces. - Pour 1999 et 2000, non compris les militaires en garnison.

[41] Events registered within one year of occurrence. - Evénements enregistrés dans l'année qui suit l'événement.

[42] Live births to Maltese parents only. - Naissances vivantes aux parents maltais seulement.

[43] Rates computed on population including civilian nationals temporarily outside the country. - Les taux sont calculés sur la base d'un chiffre de population qui comprend les civils nationaux temporairement hors du pays.

[44] Including residents outside the country if listed in a Netherlands population register. - Y compris les résidents hors du pays, s'ils sont inscrits sur un registre de population néerlandais.

[45] From 2002, without data for Kosovo and Metohia. - Après 2002, sans les données pour le Kosovo and Metohie.

[46] Data revised to exclude births in Northern Ireland to non-residents of Northern Ireland. - Données révisées non compris des naissances en Irlande du Nord aux non-résidents de l'Irlande du Nord.

[47] Data tabulated by date of occurrence for England and Wales, and by date of registration for Northern Ireland and Scotland. - Données exploitées selon la date de l'événement pour l'Angleterre et le pays de Galles, et selon la date de l'enregistrement pour l'Irlande du Nord et l'Ecosse.

[48] Including United States military personnel, their dependants and contract employees. - Y compris les militaires des Etats-Unis, les membres de leur famille les accompagnant et les agents contractuels des Etats-Unis.

[49] Excluding United States military personnel, their dependants and contract employees. - Non compris les militaires des Etats-Unis, les membres de leur famille les accompagnant et les agents contractuels des Etats-Unis.

Table 10

Table 10 presents live births by age of mother, sex of the child and urban/rural residence for the latest available year.

Description of variables: Age is defined as age at last birthday, that is, the difference between the date of birth and the date of the occurrence of the event, expressed in completed solar years. The age classification used in this table is the following: under 15 years, 5-year age groups through 45-49 years, and 50 years and over.

Reliability of data: Data from civil registers of live births which are reported as incomplete (less than 90 per cent completeness) or of unknown completeness are considered unreliable and are set in *italics* rather than in roman type. Table 9 and the technical notes for that table provide more detailed information on the completeness of live-birth registration. For more information about the quality of vital statistics data in general, see section 4.2 of the Technical Notes.

Limitations: Statistics on live births by age of mother are subject to the same qualifications as have been set forth for vital statistics in general and birth statistics in particular as discussed in section 4 of the Technical Notes.

The reliability of the data described above, is an important factor in considering the limitations. In addition, some live births are tabulated by date of registration and not by date of occurrence; these are indicated in the table by a plus sign "+". Whenever the lag between the date of occurrence and date of registration is prolonged and, therefore, a large proportion of the live-birth registrations are delayed, birth statistics for any given year may be seriously affected. For example, the age of the mother will almost always refer to the date of registration rather than to the date of birth of the child. Hence, in those countries or areas where registration of births is delayed, possibly for years, statistics on births by age of mother should be used with caution.

Another factor which limits international comparability is the practice of some countries or areas of not including in live-birth statistics infants who were born alive but died before the registration of the birth or within the first 24 hours of life, thus underestimating the total number of live births. Statistics of this type are footnoted.

Because these statistics are classified according to age, they are subject to the limitations with respect to accuracy of age reporting similar to those already discussed in connection with section 3.1.3 of the Technical Notes. The factors influencing the accuracy of reporting may be somewhat dissimilar in vital statistics (because of the differences in the method of taking a census and registering a birth) but, in general, the same errors can be observed. The absence of frequencies in the unknown age group does not necessarily indicate completely accurate reporting and tabulation of the age item. It is often an indication that the unknowns have been eliminated by assigning ages to them before tabulation, or by proportionate distribution after tabulation.

On the other hand, large frequencies in the unknown age category may indicate that a large proportion of the births are born outside of wedlock, the records for which tend to be incomplete in so far as characteristics of the parents are concerned.

Another limitation of age reporting may result from calculating age of mother at birth of child (or at time of registration) from year of birth rather than from day, month and year of birth. Information on this factor is given in footnotes when known.

In few countries, data by age refer to deliveries rather than to live births causing under-enumeration in the event of a multiple birth. This practice leads to lack of strict comparability, both among countries or areas relying on this practice and between data shown in this table and table 9.

The comparability of data by urban/rural residence is affected by the national definitions of urban and rural used in tabulating these data. It is assumed, in the absence of specific information to the contrary, that the definitions of urban and rural used in connection with the national population census were also used in the compilation of the vital statistics for each country or area. However, the possibility cannot be excluded that, for a given country or area, the same definitions of urban and rural are not used for both the vital statistics data and the population census data. When known, the definitions of urban used in national population censuses are presented at the end of table 6. As discussed in detail in the technical notes for table 6, these definitions vary considerably from one country or area to another.

Earlier data: Live births by age of mother have been shown for the latest available year in each issue of the Yearbook. Data included in this table update the series covering period of years as follows:

Issue	Years Covered
Special Edition on Natality, CD, 1999	1990 – 1998
Historical Supplement CD, 1997	1948 – 1997
1992	1983 – 1992
1986	1977 – 1988
1981	1972 – 1980
Historical Supplement, 1979	1948 - 1977

For further information on years covered prior to 1948, readers should consult the Historical Index.

Tableau 10

Le tableau 10 présente les données les plus récentes dont on dispose sur les naissances vivantes selon l'âge de la mère, le sexe de l'enfant et le lieu de résidence (zone urbaine ou rurale).

Description des variables : L'âge désigne l'âge au dernier anniversaire, c'est-à-dire la différence entre la date de naissance et la date de l'événement exprimée en années solaires révolues. La classification par âge utilisée dans ce tableau comprend les catégories suivantes : moins de 15 ans, groupes quinquennaux jusqu'à 45-49 ans, 50 ans et plus, et âge inconnu.

Fiabilité des données : Les données sur les naissances vivantes provenant des registres de l'état civil qui sont déclarées incomplètes (degré de complétude inférieur à 90 p. 100) ou dont le degré de complétude n'est pas connu sont jugées douteuses et apparaissent en italique et non en caractères romains. Le tableau 9 et les notes techniques qui s'y rapportent présentent des renseignements plus détaillés sur le degré de complétude de l'enregistrement des naissances vivantes. Pour plus de précisions sur la qualité des statistiques de l'état civil en général, voir la section 4.2 des Notes techniques.

Insuffisance des données : Les statistiques relatives aux naissances vivantes selon l'âge de la mère appellent toutes les réserves qui ont été formulées à propos des statistiques de l'état civil en général et des statistiques de naissances en particulier (voir la section 4 des Notes techniques).

La fiabilité des données, au sujet de laquelle des indications ont été données plus haut, est un facteur important. Il faut également tenir compte du fait que, dans certains cas, les données relatives aux naissances vivantes sont exploitées selon la date de l'enregistrement et non la date de l'événement ; ces cas ont été signalés dans le tableau par le signe '+'. Chaque fois que le décalage entre l'événement et son enregistrement est grand et qu'une forte proportion des naissances vivantes fait l'objet d'un enregistrement tardif, les statistiques des naissances vivantes pour une année donnée peuvent être considérablement faussées. Par exemple, l'âge de la mère représente presque toujours son âge à la date de l'enregistrement et non à la date de la naissance de l'enfant. Ainsi, dans les pays ou zones où l'enregistrement des naissances est tardif, le retard atteignant parfois plusieurs années, il faut utiliser avec prudence les statistiques concernant les naissances selon l'âge de la mère.

Un autre facteur qui nuit à la comparabilité internationale est la pratique de certains pays ou zones qui consiste à ne pas inclure dans les statistiques des naissances vivantes les enfants nés vivants mais décédés avant l'enregistrement de leur naissance ou dans les 24 heures qui ont suivi la naissance, pratique qui conduit à sous-estimer le nombre total de naissances vivantes. Quand pareil facteur a joué, cela a été signalé en note à la fin du tableau.

Étant donné que les statistiques du tableau 10 sont classées selon l'âge, elles appellent les mêmes réserves concernant l'exactitude des déclarations d'âge que celles formulées à la section 3.1.3 des Notes techniques. Dans le cas des statistiques de l'état civil, les facteurs qui interviennent à cet égard sont parfois différents, étant donné que le recensement de la population et l'enregistrement des naissances se font par des méthodes différentes, mais, d'une manière générale, les erreurs observées seront les mêmes. Si aucun nombre ne figure dans la rangée réservée aux âges inconnus, cela ne signifie pas nécessairement que les déclarations d'âge et l'exploitation des données par âge ont été tout à fait exactes. C'est souvent une indication que l'on a attribué un âge aux personnes d'âge inconnu avant l'exploitation des données ou qu'elles ont été réparties proportionnellement entre les différents groupes après cette opération.

À l'inverse, lorsque le nombre des personnes d'âge inconnu est important, cela peut signifier que la proportion de naissances parmi les mères célibataires est élevée, étant donné qu'en pareil cas l'acte de naissance ne contient pas tous les renseignements concernant les parents.

Les déclarations par âge peuvent comporter des distorsions, du fait que l'âge de la mère au moment de la naissance d'un enfant (ou de la déclaration de naissance) est donné par année de naissance et non par date exacte (jour, mois et année).

Dans quelques pays, la classification par âges se réfère aux accouchements, et non aux naissances vivantes, ce qui conduit à un sous-dénombrement en cas de naissances gémellaires. Cette pratique nuit à la comparabilité des données, à la fois entre pays ou zones qui recourent à cette méthode et entre les données présentées dans le tableau 10 et celles du tableau 9.

La comparabilité des données selon le lieu de résidence (zone urbaine ou rurale) peut être limitée par les définitions nationales des termes « urbain » et « rural » utilisées pour la mise en tableaux de ces données. En l'absence d'indications contraires, on a supposé que les mêmes définitions avaient servi pour le recensement national de la population et pour l'établissement des statistiques de l'état civil pour chaque pays ou zone. Toutefois, il n'est pas exclu que, pour une zone ou un pays donné, des définitions différentes aient été retenues. Les définitions du terme « urbain » utilisées pour les recensements nationaux de population ont été présentées à la fin des notes techniques du tableau 6 lorsqu'elles étaient connues. Comme on l'a précisé dans les notes techniques relatives au tableau 6, ces définitions varient considérablement d'un pays ou d'une zone à l'autre.

Données publiées antérieurement : Les différentes éditions de l'*Annuaire démographique* regroupent les dernières statistiques dont on disposait à l'époque sur les naissances vivantes selon l'âge de la mère. Les données qui figurent dans le tableau 10 actualisent les données qui portaient sur les périodes suivantes :

Éditions	Années considérées
Édition spéciale sur les statistiques de la natalité (CD-ROM), 1999	1990 – 1998
Supplément historique (CD-ROM), 1997	1948 – 1997
1992	1983 – 1992
1986	1977 – 1988
1981	1972 – 1980
Supplément rétrospectif, 1979	1948 – 1977

Pour plus de détails concernant les années antérieures à 1948, se reporter à l'index historique.

10. Live births by age of mother, sex of the child and urban/rural residence: latest available year, 1994 - 2003
Naissances vivantes selon l'âge de la mère, le sexe de l'enfant et la résidence, urbaine/rurale: dernière année disponible, 1994 - 2003

Continent, country or area, year and age (in years) / Continent, pays ou zone, année et âge (en années)	Code[1]	Total			Urban - Urbaine			Rural - Rurale		
		Both sexes - Les deux sexes	Male - Masculin	Female - Féminin	Both sexes - Les deux sexes	Male - Masculin	Female - Féminin	Both sexes - Les deux sexes	Male - Masculin	Female - Féminin
AFRICA — AFRIQUE										
Egypt - Égypte										
1999										
Total	C	1 693 025	870 195	822 830	657 902	338 638	319 264	1 035 123	531 557	503 566
0 - 19	C	58 512	29 955	28 557	20 778	10 785	9 993	37 734	19 170	18 564
20 - 24	C	449 584	231 642	217 942	169 931	87 629	82 302	279 653	144 013	135 640
25 - 29	C	491 555	252 991	238 564	187 184	96 644	90 540	304 371	156 347	148 024
30 - 34	C	309 972	159 186	150 786	124 244	63 653	60 591	185 728	95 533	90 195
35 - 39	C	163 663	83 988	79 675	61 243	31 423	29 820	102 420	52 565	49 855
40 - 44	C	38 298	19 828	18 470	13 614	7 005	6 609	24 684	12 823	11 861
45+	C	8 219	4 201	4 018	2 341	1 193	1 148	5 878	3 008	2 870
Unk.- Inc.	C	173 222	88 404	84 818	78 567	40 306	38 261	94 655	48 098	46 557
Kenya										
2000										
Total	U	470 712	...	...	...	...	...	...	...	...
0 - 14	U	1 033	...	...	...	...	...	...	...	...
15 - 19	U	72 510	...	...	...	...	...	...	...	...
20 - 24	U	151 037	...	...	...	...	...	...	...	...
25 - 29	U	117 804	...	...	...	...	...	...	...	...
30 - 34	U	76 286	...	...	...	...	...	...	...	...
35 - 39	U	33 301	...	...	...	...	...	...	...	...
40 - 44	U	9 096	...	...	...	...	...	...	...	...
45 - 49	U	1 571	...	...	...	...	...	...	...	...
50+	U	218	...	...	...	...	...	...	...	...
Unk.- Inc.	U	7 856	...	...	...	...	...	...	...	...
Libyan Arab Jamahiriya - Jamahiriya arabe libyenne										
2002										
Total	C	111 053	57 722	53 331	...	...	...	...	...	...
0 - 19	C	1 196	592	604	...	...	...	...	...	...
20 - 24	C	15 018	7 845	7 173	...	...	...	...	...	...
25 - 29	C	32 713	16 877	15 836	...	...	...	...	...	...
30 - 34	C	33 325	17 384	15 941	...	...	...	...	...	...
35 - 39	C	18 702	9 777	8 925	...	...	...	...	...	...
40 - 44	C	6 422	3 296	3 126	...	...	...	...	...	...
45+	C	676	364	312	...	...	...	...	...	...
Unk.- Inc.	C	3 001	1 587	1 414	...	...	...	...	...	...
Mauritius - Maurice										
2003										
Total	C	19 165	9 802	9 363	...	...	...	...	...	...
0 - 14	C	28	15	13	...	...	...	...	...	...
15 - 19	C	1 692	886	806	...	...	...	...	...	...
20 - 24	C	6 077	3 143	2 934	...	...	...	...	...	...
25 - 29	C	5 776	2 947	2 829	...	...	...	...	...	...
30 - 34	C	3 281	1 637	1 644	...	...	...	...	...	...
35 - 39	C	1 837	933	904	...	...	...	...	...	...
40 - 44	C	411	207	204	...	...	...	...	...	...
45 - 49	C	26	15	11	...	...	...	...	...	...
50+	C	-	-	-	...	...	...	...	...	...
Unk.- Inc.	C	37	19	18	...	...	...	...	...	...
Morocco - Maroc[2]										
2001										
Total	C	541 298	277 242	264 056	282 380	144 818	137 562	258 297	132 082	126 215
0 - 14	C	1 016	525	491	457	234	223	559	291	268
15 - 19	C	45 049	23 151	21 898	19 695	10 164	9 531	25 327	12 973	12 354
20 - 24	C	131 163	67 353	63 810	62 623	32 254	30 369	68 480	35 068	33 412
25 - 29	C	136 599	69 989	66 610	73 246	37 596	35 650	63 288	32 360	30 928
30 - 34	C	117 851	60 300	57 551	66 841	34 234	32 607	50 954	26 040	24 914
35 - 39	C	75 484	38 586	36 898	43 396	22 230	21 166	32 054	16 336	15 718
40 - 44	C	27 453	13 958	13 495	13 819	6 959	6 860	13 624	6 991	6 633
45 - 49	C	3 974	1 998	1 976	1 445	713	732	2 528	1 284	1 244

10. Live births by age of mother, sex of the child and urban/rural residence: latest available year, 1994 - 2003

Naissances vivantes selon l'âge de la mère, le sexe de l'enfant et la résidence, urbaine/rurale: dernière année disponible, 1994 - 2003 (continued — suite)

Continent, country or area, year and age (in years) / Continent, pays ou zone, année et âge (en années)	Code[1]	Total Both sexes - Les deux sexes	Total Male - Masculin	Total Female - Féminin	Urban - Urbaine Both sexes - Les deux sexes	Urban - Urbaine Male - Masculin	Urban - Urbaine Female - Féminin	Rural - Rurale Both sexes - Les deux sexes	Rural - Rurale Male - Masculin	Rural - Rurale Female - Féminin
AFRICA — AFRIQUE										
Morocco - Maroc[2]										
2001										
50+	C	1 105	556	549	313	157	156	791	399	392
Unk.- Inc.	C	1 604	826	778	545	277	268	692	340	352
Namibia - Namibie[3]										
2001										
Total	I	45 157	22 643	22 514	15 352	7 678	7 674	29 805	14 965	14 840
12 - 14	I	74	37	37	16	4	12	58	33	25
15 - 19	I	5 278	2 638	2 640	1 377	665	712	3 901	1 973	1 928
20 - 24	I	11 964	5 997	5 967	3 827	1 930	1 897	8 137	4 067	4 070
25 - 29	I	11 056	5 563	5 493	4 389	2 231	2 158	6 667	3 332	3 335
30 - 34	I	8 429	4 259	4 170	3 217	1 621	1 596	5 212	2 638	2 574
35 - 39	I	5 292	2 636	2 656	1 793	882	911	3 499	1 754	1 745
40 - 44	I	2 383	1 187	1 196	613	297	316	1 770	890	880
45+	I	681	326	355	120	48	72	561	278	283
Réunion[4]										
2003										
Total	C	14 427	7 412	7 015	...	...	...	...	...	...
0 - 19	C	1 241	596	645	...	...	...	...	...	...
20 - 24	C	3 054	1 596	1 458	...	...	...	...	...	...
25 - 29	C	3 925	2 046	1 879	...	...	...	...	...	...
30 - 34	C	3 478	1 788	1 690	...	...	...	...	...	...
35 - 39	C	2 110	1 064	1 046	...	...	...	...	...	...
40 - 44	C	596	309	287	...	...	...	...	...	...
45+	C	23	13	10	...	...	...	...	...	...
Saint Helena ex. dep. - Sainte-Hélène sans dép.										
2000										
Total	C	56	32	24	...	...	...	...	...	...
15 - 19	C	7	3	4	...	...	...	...	...	...
20 - 24	C	16	10	6	...	...	...	...	...	...
25 - 29	C	12	5	7	...	...	...	...	...	...
30 - 34	C	13	9	4	...	...	...	...	...	...
35 - 39	C	7	4	3	...	...	...	...	...	...
40 - 44	C	1	1	-	...	...	...	...	...	...
South Africa - Afrique du Sud										
1999										
Total	U	1 363 800	...	...	...	...	...	...	...	...
15 - 19	U	195 560	...	...	...	...	...	...	...	...
20 - 24	U	362 872	...	...	...	...	...	...	...	...
25 - 29	U	339 586	...	...	...	...	...	...	...	...
30 - 34	U	246 119	...	...	...	...	...	...	...	...
35 - 39	U	140 344	...	...	...	...	...	...	...	...
40 - 44	U	52 428	...	...	...	...	...	...	...	...
45 - 49	U	13 437	...	...	...	...	...	...	...	...
50+	U	4 439	...	...	...	...	...	...	...	...
Unk.- Inc.	U	9 015	...	...	...	...	...	...	...	...
Swaziland[5]										
1997										
Total	I	31 087	...	...	6 915	...	...	24 172	...	...
15 - 19	I	4 192	...	...	897	...	...	3 295	...	...
20 - 24	I	8 927	...	...	2 107	...	...	6 820	...	...
25 - 29	I	7 537	...	...	1 895	...	...	5 642	...	...
30 - 34	I	4 893	...	...	1 021	...	...	3 872	...	...
35 - 39	I	3 413	...	...	664	...	...	2 749	...	...
40 - 44	I	1 247	...	...	194	...	...	1 053	...	...
45 - 49	I	564	...	...	78	...	...	486	...	...
50+	I	230	...	...	32	...	...	198	...	...
Unk.- Inc.	I	84	...	...	27	...	...	57	...	...

10. Live births by age of mother, sex of the child and urban/rural residence: latest available year, 1994 - 2003

Naissances vivantes selon l'âge de la mère, le sexe de l'enfant et la résidence, urbaine/rurale: dernière année disponible, 1994 - 2003 (continued — suite)

Continent, country or area, year and age (in years) / Continent, pays ou zone, année et âge (en années)	Code[1]	Total			Urban - Urbaine			Rural - Rurale		
		Both sexes - Les deux sexes	Male - Masculin	Female - Féminin	Both sexes - Les deux sexes	Male - Masculin	Female - Féminin	Both sexes - Les deux sexes	Male - Masculin	Female - Féminin
AFRICA — AFRIQUE										
Tunisia - Tunisie										
1998										
Total	C	166 718	...	...	...	...	...	...	...	...
15 - 19	C	3 650	...	...	...	...	...	...	...	...
20 - 24	C	28 802	...	...	...	...	...	...	...	...
25 - 29	C	44 260	...	...	...	...	...	...	...	...
30 - 34	C	39 518	...	...	...	...	...	...	...	...
35 - 39	C	19 869	...	...	...	...	...	...	...	...
40 - 44	C	5 327	...	...	...	...	...	...	...	...
45+	C	650	...	...	...	...	...	...	...	...
Unk.- Inc.	C	2 446	...	...	...	...	...	...	...	...
AMERICA, NORTH — AMERIQUE DU NORD										
Anguilla										
2003										
Total	+C	139	...	...	...	...	...	...	...	...
15 - 19	+C	25	...	...	...	...	...	...	...	...
20 - 24	+C	41	...	...	...	...	...	...	...	...
25 - 29	+C	32	...	...	...	...	...	...	...	...
30 - 34	+C	28	...	...	...	...	...	...	...	...
35 - 39	+C	9	...	...	...	...	...	...	...	...
40+	+C	4	...	...	...	...	...	...	...	...
Antigua and Barbuda - Antigua-et-Barbuda										
1995										
Total	+C	1 347	...	...	...	...	...	...	...	...
0 - 14	+C	4	...	...	...	...	...	...	...	...
15 - 19	+C	209	...	...	...	...	...	...	...	...
20 - 24	+C	377	...	...	...	...	...	...	...	...
25 - 29	+C	350	...	...	...	...	...	...	...	...
30 - 34	+C	246	...	...	...	...	...	...	...	...
35 - 39	+C	128	...	...	...	...	...	...	...	...
40 - 44	+C	23	...	...	...	...	...	...	...	...
45+	+C	2	...	...	...	...	...	...	...	...
Unk.- Inc.	+C	8	...	...	...	...	...	...	...	...
Aruba[6]										
2002										
Total	+U	1 315	...	...	...	...	...	...	...	...
15 - 19	+U	126	...	...	...	...	...	...	...	...
20 - 24	+U	309	...	...	...	...	...	...	...	...
25 - 29	+U	321	...	...	...	...	...	...	...	...
30 - 34	+U	327	...	...	...	...	...	...	...	...
35 - 39	+U	198	...	...	...	...	...	...	...	...
40 - 44	+U	29	...	...	...	...	...	...	...	...
45 - 49	+U	5	...	...	...	...	...	...	...	...
Bahamas[6]										
2001										
Total	U	4 495	2 305	2 190	...	...	...	...	...	...
0 - 14	U	5	3	2	...	...	...	...	...	...
15 - 19	U	568	282	286	...	...	...	...	...	...
20 - 24	U	1 120	567	553	...	...	...	...	...	...
25 - 29	U	1 154	602	552	...	...	...	...	...	...
30 - 34	U	904	460	444	...	...	...	...	...	...
35 - 39	U	601	319	282	...	...	...	...	...	...
40 - 44	U	125	63	62	...	...	...	...	...	...
45 - 49	U	10	5	5	...	...	...	...	...	...
Unk.- Inc.	U	8	4	4	...	...	...	...	...	...
Belize										
2002										
Total	U	7 356	...	...	...	...	...	...	...	...

10. Live births by age of mother, sex of the child and urban/rural residence: latest available year, 1994 - 2003
Naissances vivantes selon l'âge de la mère, le sexe de l'enfant et la résidence, urbaine/rurale: dernière année disponible, 1994 - 2003 (continued — suite)

Continent, country or area, year and age (in years) / Continent, pays ou zone, année et âge (en années)	Code[1]	Total Both sexes - Les deux sexes	Total Male - Masculin	Total Female - Féminin	Urban - Urbaine Both sexes - Les deux sexes	Urban - Urbaine Male - Masculin	Urban - Urbaine Female - Féminin	Rural - Rurale Both sexes - Les deux sexes	Rural - Rurale Male - Masculin	Rural - Rurale Female - Féminin
AMERICA, NORTH — AMERIQUE DU NORD										
Belize										
2002										
0 - 14	U	22	...	...	...	...	...	...	...	...
15 - 19	U	1 237	...	...	...	...	...	...	...	...
20 - 24	U	2 233	...	...	...	...	...	...	...	...
25 - 29	U	1 712	...	...	...	...	...	...	...	...
30 - 34	U	1 106	...	...	...	...	...	...	...	...
35 - 39	U	566	...	...	...	...	...	...	...	...
40 - 44	U	165	...	...	...	...	...	...	...	...
45+	U	17	...	...	...	...	...	...	...	...
Unk.- Inc.	U	298	...	...	...	...	...	...	...	...
Bermuda - Bermudes										
2003										
Total	C	834	...	...	...	...	...	...	...	...
15 - 19	C	79	...	...	...	...	...	...	...	...
20 - 24	C	116	...	...	...	...	...	...	...	...
25 - 29	C	203	...	...	...	...	...	...	...	...
30 - 34	C	250	...	...	...	...	...	...	...	...
35 - 39	C	148	...	...	...	...	...	...	...	...
40+	C	38	...	...	...	...	...	...	...	...
Canada[7]										
2002										
Total	C	328 802	168 842	159 960	...	...	...	...	...	...
0 - 14	C	120	63	57	...	...	...	...	...	...
15 - 19	C	15 413	7 856	7 557	...	...	...	...	...	...
20 - 24	C	56 729	29 096	27 633	...	...	...	...	...	...
25 - 29	C	100 646	51 666	48 980	...	...	...	...	...	...
30 - 34	C	100 768	51 676	49 092	...	...	...	...	...	...
35 - 39	C	46 468	23 970	22 498	...	...	...	...	...	...
40 - 44	C	8 354	4 353	4 001	...	...	...	...	...	...
45 - 49	C	286	154	132	...	...	...	...	...	...
50+	C	7	2	5	...	...	...	...	...	...
Unk.- Inc.	C	11	6	5	...	...	...	...	...	...
Cayman Islands - Îles Caïmanes										
1994										
Total	+C	531	246	285	...	...	...	...	...	...
0 - 14	+C	2	1	1	...	...	...	...	...	...
15 - 19	+C	62	31	31	...	...	...	...	...	...
20 - 24	+C	136	69	67	...	...	...	...	...	...
25 - 29	+C	139	55	84	...	...	...	...	...	...
30 - 34	+C	142	64	78	...	...	...	...	...	...
35 - 39	+C	37	20	17	...	...	...	...	...	...
40+	+C	13	6	7	...	...	...	...	...	...
Costa Rica										
2003										
Total	C	72 938	...	...	...	...	...	...	...	...
0 - 14	C	479	...	...	...	...	...	...	...	...
15 - 19	C	14 356	...	...	...	...	...	...	...	...
20 - 24	C	21 974	...	...	...	...	...	...	...	...
25 - 29	C	16 796	...	...	...	...	...	...	...	...
30 - 34	C	11 461	...	...	...	...	...	...	...	...
35 - 39	C	5 891	...	...	...	...	...	...	...	...
40 - 44	C	1 476	...	...	...	...	...	...	...	...
45+	C	100	...	...	...	...	...	...	...	...
Unk.- Inc.	C	405	...	...	...	...	...	...	...	...
Cuba										
2003										
Total	C	136 795	70 500	66 295	100 429	51 855	48 574	36 366	18 645	17 721
0 - 14	C	491	250	241	282	154	128	209	96	113

323

10. Live births by age of mother, sex of the child and urban/rural residence: latest available year, 1994 - 2003
Naissances vivantes selon l'âge de la mère, le sexe de l'enfant et la résidence, urbaine/rurale: dernière année disponible, 1994 - 2003 (continued — suite)

Continent, country or area, year and age (in years) Continent, pays ou zone, année et âge (en années)	Code[1]	Total			Urban - Urbaine			Rural - Rurale		
		Both sexes - Les deux sexes	Male - Masculin	Female - Féminin	Both sexes - Les deux sexes	Male - Masculin	Female - Féminin	Both sexes - Les deux sexes	Male - Masculin	Female - Féminin
AMERICA, NORTH — AMERIQUE DU NORD										
Cuba										
2003										
15 - 19	C	18 661	9 644	9 017	12 167	6 309	5 858	6 494	3 335	3 159
20 - 24	C	32 034	16 506	15 528	23 019	11 870	11 149	9 015	4 636	4 379
25 - 29	C	37 807	19 443	18 364	28 039	14 451	13 588	9 768	4 992	4 776
30 - 34	C	31 879	16 489	15 390	24 431	12 624	11 807	7 448	3 865	3 583
35 - 39	C	13 780	7 056	6 724	10 844	5 585	5 259	2 936	1 471	1 465
40 - 44	C	2 045	1 063	982	1 576	825	751	469	238	231
45 - 49	C	61	35	26	40	25	15	21	10	11
50+	C	23	10	13	17	8	9	6	2	4
Unk.- Inc.	C	14	4	10	14	4	10	-	-	-
Dominican Republic - République dominicaine										
1999										
Total	+U	*193 418*	*99 127*	*94 291*	...	...	...	...	...	...
0 - 14	+U	*1 665*	*909*	*756*	...	...	...	...	...	...
15 - 19	+U	*23 353*	*11 880*	*11 473*	...	...	...	...	...	...
20 - 24	+U	*53 145*	*27 213*	*25 932*	...	...	...	...	...	...
25 - 29	+U	*51 520*	*26 568*	*24 952*	...	...	...	...	...	...
30 - 34	+U	*32 644*	*16 649*	*15 995*	...	...	...	...	...	...
35 - 39	+U	*15 335*	*7 867*	*7 468*	...	...	...	...	...	...
40 - 44	+U	*6 015*	*3 124*	*2 891*	...	...	...	...	...	...
45 - 49	+U	*2 624*	*1 388*	*1 236*	...	...	...	...	...	...
50+	+U	*2 558*	*1 238*	*1 320*	...	...	...	...	...	...
Unk.- Inc.	+U	*4 559*	*2 291*	*2 268*	...	...	...	...	...	...
El Salvador										
2003										
Total	C	124 476	64 988	59 488	73 311	38 272	35 039	51 165	26 716	24 449
0 - 14	C	1 161	595	566	646	316	330	515	279	236
15 - 19	C	24 405	12 797	11 608	13 289	6 951	6 338	11 116	5 846	5 270
20 - 24	C	38 372	20 075	18 297	23 252	12 114	11 138	15 120	7 961	7 159
25 - 29	C	30 333	15 914	14 419	18 882	9 909	8 973	11 451	6 005	5 446
30 - 34	C	17 680	9 087	8 593	10 737	5 570	5 167	6 943	3 517	3 426
35 - 39	C	9 033	4 740	4 293	4 979	2 613	2 366	4 054	2 127	1 927
40 - 44	C	2 797	1 426	1 371	1 236	654	582	1 561	772	789
45 - 49	C	299	145	154	116	59	57	183	86	97
50+	C	49	31	18	19	12	7	30	19	11
Unk.- Inc.	C	347	178	169	155	74	81	192	104	88
Greenland - Groenland										
2003										
Total	C	895	480	415	717	386	331	178	94	84
0 - 14	C	1	1	-	-	-	-	1	1	-
15 - 19	C	100	52	48	83	40	43	17	12	5
20 - 24	C	262	144	118	208	123	85	54	21	33
25 - 29	C	203	104	99	158	77	81	45	27	18
30 - 34	C	179	93	86	142	75	67	37	18	19
35 - 39	C	128	72	56	107	57	50	21	15	6
40 - 44	C	20	13	7	18	13	5	2	-	2
45 - 49	C	2	1	1	1	1	-	1	-	1
Grenada - Grenade										
2000										
Total	+C	1 883	...	...	...	...	...	...	...	...
0 - 14	+C	9	...	...	...	...	...	...	...	...
15 - 19	+C	310	...	...	...	...	...	...	...	...
20 - 24	+C	490	...	...	...	...	...	...	...	...
25 - 29	+C	452	...	...	...	...	...	...	...	...
30 - 34	+C	339	...	...	...	...	...	...	...	...
35 - 39	+C	208	...	...	...	...	...	...	...	...

10. Live births by age of mother, sex of the child and urban/rural residence: latest available year, 1994 - 2003
Naissances vivantes selon l'âge de la mère, le sexe de l'enfant et la résidence, urbaine/rurale: dernière année disponible, 1994 - 2003 (continued — suite)

Continent, country or area, year and age (in years) / Continent, pays ou zone, année et âge (en années)	Code[1]	Total			Urban - Urbaine			Rural - Rurale		
		Both sexes - Les deux sexes	Male - Masculin	Female - Féminin	Both sexes - Les deux sexes	Male - Masculin	Female - Féminin	Both sexes - Les deux sexes	Male - Masculin	Female - Féminin
AMERICA, NORTH — AMERIQUE DU NORD										
Grenada - Grenade										
2000										
40 - 44	+C	73	...	...	...	...	...	...	...	...
45+	+C	2	...	...	...	...	...	...	...	...
Guadeloupe										
2003										
Total	C	7 047	3 543	3 504	...	...	...	...	...	...
0 - 14	C	7	2	5	...	...	...	...	...	...
15 - 19	C	431	215	216	...	...	...	...	...	...
20 - 24	C	1 140	500	560	...	...	...	...	...	...
25 - 29	C	1 815	912	903	...	...	...	...	...	...
30 - 34	C	2 001	1 005	996	...	...	...	...	...	...
35 - 39	C	1 280	637	643	...	...	...	...	...	...
40 - 44	C	352	177	175	...	...	...	...	...	...
45+	C	13	7	6	...	...	...	...	...	...
Guatemala										
1999										
Total	C	360 759	183 621	177 138	140 491	...	...	220 268	...	...
0 - 14	C	1 776	892	884	677	...	...	1 099	...	...
15 - 19	C	65 999	33 808	32 191	25 674	...	...	40 325	...	...
20 - 24	C	108 223	54 947	53 276	44 487	...	...	63 736	...	...
25 - 29	C	79 683	40 608	39 075	32 492	...	...	47 191	...	...
30 - 34	C	53 921	27 473	26 448	20 520	...	...	33 401	...	...
35 - 39	C	34 730	17 623	17 107	11 694	...	...	23 036	...	...
40 - 44	C	13 305	6 722	6 583	3 955	...	...	9 350	...	...
45 - 49	C	1 981	973	1 008	502	...	...	1 479	...	...
50+	C	557	288	269	119	...	...	438	...	...
Unk.- Inc.	C	584	287	297	371	...	...	213	...	...
Jamaica - Jamaïque[8]										
2003										
Total	C	45 133	...	...	...	...	...	...	...	...
0 - 14	C	319	...	...	...	...	...	...	...	...
15 - 19	C	8 480	...	...	...	...	...	...	...	...
20 - 24	C	12 411	...	...	...	...	...	...	...	...
25 - 29	C	9 802	...	...	...	...	...	...	...	...
30 - 34	C	7 968	...	...	...	...	...	...	...	...
35 - 39	C	4 677	...	...	...	...	...	...	...	...
40 - 44	C	1 351	...	...	...	...	...	...	...	...
45 - 49	C	54	...	...	...	...	...	...	...	...
50+	C	-	...	...	...	...	...	...	...	...
Unk.- Inc.	C	71	...	...	...	...	...	...	...	...
Martinique[4,9]										
2003										
Total	C	5 430	2 774	2 656	...	...	...	...	...	...
0 - 14	C	6	3	3	...	...	...	...	...	...
15 - 19	C	397	217	180	...	...	...	...	...	...
20 - 24	C	812	397	415	...	...	...	...	...	...
25 - 29	C	1 330	698	632	...	...	...	...	...	...
30 - 34	C	1 554	759	795	...	...	...	...	...	...
35 - 39	C	1 038	541	497	...	...	...	...	...	...
40 - 44	C	283	155	128	...	...	...	...	...	...
45+	C	10	4	6	...	...	...	...	...	...
Mexico - Mexique[2]										
2003										
Total	+U	2 655 894	1 307 080	1 348 354	1 684 413	853 189	831 064	721 339	359 268	361 939
0 - 14	+U	9 933	4 654	5 277	5 032	2 481	2 551	4 310	1 903	2 405
15 - 19	+U	403 436	204 345	199 046	264 997	134 890	130 083	126 229	63 241	62 969
20 - 24	+U	737 283	372 705	364 488	501 381	254 514	246 824	216 652	108 493	108 116
25 - 29	+U	641 611	324 539	316 995	452 043	229 758	222 238	173 592	86 738	86 827
30 - 34	+U	414 762	209 113	205 598	292 383	148 248	144 109	112 038	55 608	56 406

10. Live births by age of mother, sex of the child and urban/rural residence: latest available year, 1994 - 2003
Naissances vivantes selon l'âge de la mère, le sexe de l'enfant et la résidence, urbaine/rurale: dernière année disponible, 1994 - 2003 (continued — suite)

Continent, country or area, year and age (in years) / Continent, pays ou zone, année et âge (en années)	Code[1]	Total			Urban - Urbaine			Rural - Rurale		
		Both sexes - Les deux sexes	Male - Masculin	Female - Féminin	Both sexes - Les deux sexes	Male - Masculin	Female - Féminin	Both sexes - Les deux sexes	Male - Masculin	Female - Féminin
AMERICA, NORTH — AMERIQUE DU NORD										
Mexico - Mexique[2]										
2003										
35 - 39	+U	187 927	94 106	93 791	123 863	62 445	61 404	59 315	29 317	29 982
40 - 44	+U	51 731	25 857	25 871	29 509	14 780	14 726	20 877	10 407	10 470
45 - 49	+U	6 718	3 298	3 419	3 263	1 629	1 633	3 251	1 568	1 683
50+	+U	2 056	964	1 092	852	407	445	1 118	517	601
Unk.- Inc.	+U	200 437	67 499	132 777	11 090	4 037	7 051	3 957	1 476	2 480
Montserrat										
1999										
Total	+C	45	19	26	...	...	...	...	...	...
0 - 14	+C	-	-	-	...	...	...	...	...	...
15 - 19	+C	7	5	2	...	...	...	...	...	...
20 - 24	+C	10	4	6	...	...	...	...	...	...
25 - 29	+C	11	4	7	...	...	...	...	...	...
30 - 34	+C	12	4	8	...	...	...	...	...	...
35 - 39	+C	5	2	3	...	...	...	...	...	...
40 - 44	+C	-	-	-	...	...	...	...	...	...
45 - 49	+C	-	-	-	...	...	...	...	...	...
50+	+C	-	-	-	...	...	...	...	...	...
Unk.- Inc.	+C	-	-	-	...	...	...	...	...	...
Nicaragua										
2003										
Total	+U	102 676	52 949	49 727	57 846	29 735	28 111	44 830	23 214	21 616
0 - 14	+U	968	502	466	525	285	240	443	217	226
15 - 19	+U	27 493	14 198	13 295	15 139	7 769	7 370	12 354	6 429	5 925
20 - 24	+U	34 602	17 975	16 627	19 981	10 349	9 632	14 621	7 626	6 995
25 - 29	+U	20 707	10 632	10 075	11 945	6 129	5 816	8 762	4 503	4 259
30 - 34	+U	11 347	5 806	5 541	6 559	3 313	3 246	4 788	2 493	2 295
35 - 39	+U	5 871	2 991	2 880	2 991	1 532	1 459	2 880	1 459	1 421
40 - 44	+U	1 478	744	734	643	331	312	835	413	422
45 - 49	+U	170	80	90	53	21	32	117	59	58
50+	+U	40	21	19	10	6	4	30	15	15
Panama										
1999										
Total	C	64 248	33 077	31 171	32 724	16 894	15 830	31 524	16 183	15 341
0 - 14	C	537	290	247	205	114	91	332	176	156
15 - 19	C	12 126	6 288	5 838	5 594	2 893	2 701	6 532	3 395	3 137
20 - 24	C	18 281	9 435	8 846	9 344	4 846	4 498	8 937	4 589	4 348
25 - 29	C	15 488	7 964	7 524	8 369	4 321	4 048	7 119	3 643	3 476
30 - 34	C	10 451	5 314	5 137	5 822	2 989	2 833	4 629	2 325	2 304
35 - 39	C	4 925	2 581	2 344	2 553	1 309	1 244	2 372	1 272	1 100
40 - 44	C	1 076	528	548	448	226	222	628	302	326
45 - 49	C	95	46	49	14	9	5	81	37	44
50+	C	23	9	14	1	-	1	22	9	13
Unk.- Inc.	C	1 246	622	624	374	187	187	872	435	437
2002										
Total	C	61 671	...	...	...	...	...	...	...	...
0 - 14	C	476	...	...	...	...	...	...	...	...
15 - 19	C	11 265	...	...	...	...	...	...	...	...
20 - 24	C	17 578	...	...	...	...	...	...	...	...
25 - 29	C	14 636	...	...	...	...	...	...	...	...
30 - 34	C	10 711	...	...	...	...	...	...	...	...
35 - 39	C	4 927	...	...	...	...	...	...	...	...
40 - 44	C	1 202	...	...	...	...	...	...	...	...
45 - 49	C	85	...	...	...	...	...	...	...	...
50+	C	22	...	...	...	...	...	...	...	...
Unk.- Inc.	C	769	...	...	...	...	...	...	...	...

10. Live births by age of mother, sex of the child and urban/rural residence: latest available year, 1994 - 2003

Naissances vivantes selon l'âge de la mère, le sexe de l'enfant et la résidence, urbaine/rurale: dernière année disponible, 1994 - 2003 (continued — suite)

Continent, country or area, year and age (in years) / Continent, pays ou zone, année et âge (en années)	Code[1]	Total			Urban - Urbaine			Rural - Rurale		
		Both sexes - Les deux sexes	Male - Masculin	Female - Féminin	Both sexes - Les deux sexes	Male - Masculin	Female - Féminin	Both sexes - Les deux sexes	Male - Masculin	Female - Féminin
AMERICA, NORTH — AMERIQUE DU NORD										
Puerto Rico - Porto Rico[2]										
2000										
Total	C	59 460	30 593	28 867	30 464	15 589	14 875	28 967	14 991	13 976
0 - 14	C	272	155	117	115	62	53	156	93	63
15 - 19	C	11 118	5 735	5 383	4 972	2 552	2 420	6 140	3 181	2 959
20 - 24	C	19 423	10 005	9 418	9 360	4 804	4 556	10 057	5 197	4 860
25 - 29	C	15 152	7 806	7 346	8 167	4 169	3 998	6 983	3 637	3 346
30 - 34	C	8 902	4 515	4 387	5 123	2 586	2 537	3 779	1 929	1 850
35 - 39	C	3 762	1 974	1 788	2 243	1 176	1 067	1 518	797	721
40 - 44	C	748	362	386	437	218	219	311	144	167
45 - 49	C	29	14	15	18	7	11	10	7	3
Unk.- Inc.	C	54	27	27	29	15	14	13	6	7
2003										
Total	C	50 803	26 191	24 612	...	...	...	...	...	...
0 - 14	C	182	89	93	...	...	...	...	...	...
15 - 19	C	8 817	4 536	4 281	...	...	...	...	...	...
20 - 24	C	16 767	8 591	8 176	...	...	...	...	...	...
25 - 29	C	13 056	6 764	6 292	...	...	...	...	...	...
30 - 34	C	7 904	4 107	3 797	...	...	...	...	...	...
35 - 39	C	3 376	1 761	1 615	...	...	...	...	...	...
40 - 44	C	651	313	338	...	...	...	...	...	...
45 - 49	C	31	21	10	...	...	...	...	...	...
50+	C	1	1	-	...	...	...	...	...	...
Unk.- Inc.	C	18	8	10	...	...	...	...	...	...
Saint Kitts and Nevis - Saint-Kitts-et-Nevis										
2001										
Total	+C	803	...	...	...	...	...	...	...	...
10 - 14	+C	3	...	...	...	...	...	...	...	...
15 - 19	+C	164	...	...	...	...	...	...	...	...
20 - 24	+C	241	...	...	...	...	...	...	...	...
25 - 29	+C	166	...	...	...	...	...	...	...	...
30 - 34	+C	148	...	...	...	...	...	...	...	...
35 - 39	+C	67	...	...	...	...	...	...	...	...
40+	+C	14	...	...	...	...	...	...	...	...
Saint Lucia - Sainte-Lucie										
2002										
Total	C	2 529	1 299	1 230	...	...	...	...	...	...
0 - 14	C	8	5	3	...	...	...	...	...	...
15 - 19	C	447	223	224	...	...	...	...	...	...
20 - 24	C	686	356	330	...	...	...	...	...	...
25 - 29	C	569	284	285	...	...	...	...	...	...
30 - 34	C	469	238	231	...	...	...	...	...	...
35 - 39	C	277	156	121	...	...	...	...	...	...
40 - 44	C	71	36	35	...	...	...	...	...	...
45 - 49	C	2	1	1	...	...	...	...	...	...
Saint Vincent and the Grenadines - Saint Vincent-et-les Grenadines										
2002										
Total	+C	1 985	1 002	983	...	...	...	...	...	...
0 - 14	+C	13	1	12	...	...	...	...	...	...
15 - 19	+C	412	203	209	...	...	...	...	...	...
20 - 24	+C	551	301	250	...	...	...	...	...	...
25 - 29	+C	466	230	236	...	...	...	...	...	...
30 - 34	+C	319	147	172	...	...	...	...	...	...
35 - 39	+C	175	88	87	...	...	...	...	...	...

10. Live births by age of mother, sex of the child and urban/rural residence: latest available year, 1994 - 2003
Naissances vivantes selon l'âge de la mère, le sexe de l'enfant et la résidence, urbaine/rurale: dernière année disponible, 1994 - 2003 (continued — suite)

Continent, country or area, year and age (in years) Continent, pays ou zone, année et âge (en années)	Code[1]	Total			Urban - Urbaine			Rural - Rurale		
		Both sexes - Les deux sexes	Male - Masculin	Female - Féminin	Both sexes - Les deux sexes	Male - Masculin	Female - Féminin	Both sexes - Les deux sexes	Male - Masculin	Female - Féminin
AMERICA, NORTH — AMERIQUE DU NORD										
Saint Vincent and the Grenadines - Saint Vincent-et-les Grenadines										
2002										
40 - 44	+C	37	26	11	...	...	...	...	...	...
45 - 49	+C	4	1	3	...	...	...	...	...	...
Unk.- Inc.	+C	8	5	3	...	...	...	...	...	...
Trinidad and Tobago - Trinité-et-Tobago										
1997										
Total	C	18 452	9 343	9 109	...	...	...	...	...	...
0 - 14	C	37	20	17	...	...	...	...	...	...
15 - 19	C	2 588	1 323	1 265	...	...	...	...	...	...
20 - 24	C	5 353	2 721	2 632	...	...	...	...	...	...
25 - 29	C	4 519	2 297	2 222	...	...	...	...	...	...
30 - 34	C	3 678	1 877	1 801	...	...	...	...	...	...
35 - 39	C	1 804	879	925	...	...	...	...	...	...
40 - 44	C	417	198	219	...	...	...	...	...	...
45+	C	24	11	13	...	...	...	...	...	...
Unk.- Inc.	C	32	17	15	...	...	...	...	...	...
Turks Caicos Islands - Îles Turques et Caïques										
2003										
Total	C	213	107	106	...	...	...	...	...	...
0 - 14	C	-	-	-	...	...	...	...	...	...
15 - 19	C	23	13	10	...	...	...	...	...	...
20 - 24	C	47	24	23	...	...	...	...	...	...
25 - 29	C	57	32	25	...	...	...	...	...	...
30 - 34	C	59	29	30	...	...	...	...	...	...
35 - 39	C	17	7	10	...	...	...	...	...	...
40 - 44	C	4	1	3	...	...	...	...	...	...
45+	C	-	-	-	...	...	...	...	...	...
Unk.- Inc.	C	6	1	5	...	...	...	...	...	...
United States - États-Unis										
2002										
Total	C	4 021 726	...	...	...	...	...	...	...	...
0 - 14	C	7 315	...	...	...	...	...	...	...	...
15 - 19	C	425 493	...	...	...	...	...	...	...	...
20 - 24	C	1 022 106	...	...	...	...	...	...	...	...
25 - 29	C	1 060 391	...	...	...	...	...	...	...	...
30 - 34	C	951 219	...	...	...	...	...	...	...	...
35 - 39	C	453 927	...	...	...	...	...	...	...	...
40 - 44	C	95 788	...	...	...	...	...	...	...	...
45 - 49	C	5 224	...	...	...	...	...	...	...	...
50+	C	263	...	...	...	...	...	...	...	...
AMERICA, SOUTH — AMERIQUE DU SUD										
Argentina - Argentine										
2000										
Total	C	701 878	...	...	...	...	...	...	...	...
0 - 14	C	3 208	...	...	...	...	...	...	...	...
15 - 19	C	103 129	...	...	...	...	...	...	...	...
20 - 24	C	192 871	...	...	...	...	...	...	...	...
25 - 29	C	176 768	...	...	...	...	...	...	...	...
30 - 34	C	129 374	...	...	...	...	...	...	...	...

10. Live births by age of mother, sex of the child and urban/rural residence: latest available year, 1994 - 2003
Naissances vivantes selon l'âge de la mère, le sexe de l'enfant et la résidence, urbaine/rurale: dernière année disponible, 1994 - 2003 (continued — suite)

Continent, country or area, year and age (in years) / Continent, pays ou zone, année et âge (en années)	Code[1]	Total			Urban - Urbaine			Rural - Rurale		
		Both sexes - Les deux sexes	Male - Masculin	Female - Féminin	Both sexes - Les deux sexes	Male - Masculin	Female - Féminin	Both sexes - Les deux sexes	Male - Masculin	Female - Féminin
AMERICA, SOUTH — AMERIQUE DU SUD										
Argentina - Argentine										
2000										
35 - 39	C	69 733	...	...	...	...	...	...	...	...
40 - 44	C	19 767	...	...	...	...	...	...	...	...
45 - 49	C	1 575	...	...	...	...	...	...	...	...
50+	C	163	...	...	...	...	...	...	...	...
Unk.- Inc.	C	5 290	...	...	...	...	...	...	...	...
Brazil - Brésil[10]										
2003										
Total	U	2 822 462	1 445 825	1 376 039	...	...	...	...	...	...
0 - 14	U	20 861	10 690	10 171	...	...	...	...	...	...
15 - 19	U	563 454	289 357	274 097	...	...	...	...	...	...
20 - 24	U	871 916	447 973	423 943	...	...	...	...	...	...
25 - 29	U	675 905	345 069	330 836	...	...	...	...	...	...
30 - 34	U	408 699	209 203	199 496	...	...	...	...	...	...
35 - 39	U	201 033	102 804	98 229	...	...	...	...	...	...
40 - 44	U	53 005	26 887	26 118	...	...	...	...	...	...
45 - 49	U	4 386	2 176	2 210	...	...	...	...	...	...
50+	U	579	283	296	...	...	...	...	...	...
Unk.- Inc.	U	22 624	11 383	10 643	...	...	...	...	...	...
Chile - Chili										
2003										
Total	C	234 480	119 963	114 523	...	...	...	...	...	...
0 - 14	C	994	502	492	...	...	...	...	...	...
15 - 19	C	33 838	17 390	16 448	...	...	...	...	...	...
20 - 24	C	54 536	27 926	26 610	...	...	...	...	...	...
25 - 29	C	56 443	28 775	27 668	...	...	...	...	...	...
30 - 34	C	50 557	25 945	24 612	...	...	...	...	...	...
35 - 39	C	29 662	15 211	14 451	...	...	...	...	...	...
40 - 44	C	8 087	4 026	4 061	...	...	...	...	...	...
45 - 49	C	362	185	177	...	...	...	...	...	...
50+	C	7	3	4	...	...	...	...	...	...
Colombia - Colombie[2,11]										
2003										
Total	U	697 029	357 987	339 042	537 679	275 894	261 785	145 132	74 711	70 421
0 - 14	U	5 821	2 984	2 837	3 898	1 965	1 933	1 731	924	807
15 - 19	U	148 269	76 603	71 666	108 840	56 176	52 664	36 023	18 643	17 380
20 - 24	U	208 532	106 965	101 567	161 092	82 596	78 496	43 579	22 336	21 243
25 - 29	U	151 502	77 692	73 810	120 289	61 580	58 709	28 554	14 707	13 847
30 - 34	U	104 377	53 614	50 763	83 791	43 027	40 764	18 851	9 713	9 138
35 - 39	U	56 710	29 034	27 676	44 837	22 963	21 874	10 900	5 594	5 306
40 - 44	U	15 244	7 727	7 517	11 232	5 682	5 550	3 717	1 888	1 829
45 - 49	U	1 141	597	544	789	403	386	321	173	148
50+	U	81	47	34	52	31	21	24	13	11
Unk.- Inc.	U	5 352	2 724	2 628	2 859	1 471	1 388	1 432	720	712
Ecuador - Équateur[12]										
2003										
Total	U	178 549	90 710	87 839	137 189	69 697	67 492	41 360	21 013	20 347
0 - 14	U	701	355	346	534	263	271	167	92	75
15 - 19	U	30 756	15 686	15 070	23 125	11 819	11 306	7 631	3 867	3 764
20 - 24	U	54 245	27 688	26 557	41 622	21 201	20 421	12 623	6 487	6 136
25 - 29	U	40 175	20 431	19 744	31 603	16 088	15 515	8 572	4 343	4 229
30 - 34	U	27 303	13 857	13 446	21 281	10 834	10 447	6 022	3 023	2 999
35 - 39	U	14 981	7 509	7 472	11 225	5 596	5 629	3 756	1 913	1 843
40 - 44	U	5 214	2 578	2 636	3 393	1 668	1 725	1 821	910	911
45 - 49	U	772	384	388	433	218	215	339	166	173
50+	U	-	-	-	-	-	-	-	-	-
Unk.- Inc.	U	4 402	2 222	2 180	3 973	2 010	1 963	429	212	217

10. Live births by age of mother, sex of the child and urban/rural residence: latest available year, 1994 - 2003
Naissances vivantes selon l'âge de la mère, le sexe de l'enfant et la résidence, urbaine/rurale: dernière année disponible, 1994 - 2003 (continued — suite)

Continent, country or area, year and age (in years) / Continent, pays ou zone, année et âge (en années)	Code[1]	Total			Urban - Urbaine			Rural - Rurale		
		Both sexes - Les deux sexes	Male - Masculin	Female - Féminin	Both sexes - Les deux sexes	Male - Masculin	Female - Féminin	Both sexes - Les deux sexes	Male - Masculin	Female - Féminin
AMERICA, SOUTH — AMERIQUE DU SUD										
French Guiana - Guyane française[4]										
2003										
Total	C	5 553	2 842	2 711	...	...	...	...	...	...
0 - 14	C	62	32	30	...	...	...	...	...	...
15 - 19	C	830	431	399	...	...	...	...	...	...
20 - 24	C	1 292	695	597	...	...	...	...	...	...
25 - 29	C	1 405	705	700	...	...	...	...	...	...
30 - 34	C	1 157	596	561	...	...	...	...	...	...
35 - 39	C	624	299	325	...	...	...	...	...	...
40 - 44	C	173	78	95	...	...	...	...	...	...
45 - 49	C	10	6	4	...	...	...	...	...	...
50+	C	-	-	-	...	...	...	...	...	...
Peru - Pérou[10,13]										
2002										
Total	+U	*355 870*	*183 326*	*172 544*	...	...	...	...	...	...
0 - 14	+U	*986*	...	...	...	...	...	...	...	...
15 - 19	+U	*48 340*	...	...	...	...	...	...	...	...
20 - 24	+U	*95 905*	...	...	...	...	...	...	...	...
25 - 29	+U	*88 304*	...	...	...	...	...	...	...	...
30 - 34	+U	*65 196*	...	...	...	...	...	...	...	...
35 - 39	+U	*39 100*	...	...	...	...	...	...	...	...
40 - 44	+U	*12 899*	...	...	...	...	...	...	...	...
45 - 49	+U	*1 441*	...	...	...	...	...	...	...	...
50+	+U	*210*	...	...	...	...	...	...	...	...
Unk.- Inc.	+U	*3 489*	...	...	...	...	...	...	...	...
Suriname[14]										
2002										
Total	C	10 188	...	...	6 298	...	...	3 670	...	...
0 - 14	C	64	...	...	26	...	...	38	...	...
15 - 19	C	1 665	...	...	956	...	...	686	...	...
20 - 24	C	2 787	...	...	1 770	...	...	953	...	...
25 - 29	C	2 486	...	...	1 650	...	...	776	...	...
30 - 34	C	1 795	...	...	1 146	...	...	606	...	...
35 - 39	C	924	...	...	576	...	...	329	...	...
40 - 44	C	238	...	...	147	...	...	87	...	...
45+	C	22	...	...	8	...	...	14	...	...
Unk.- Inc.	C	207	...	...	17	...	...	184	...	...
Uruguay										
2002										
Total	C	51 997	...	...	...	...	...	...	...	...
0 - 14	C	207	...	...	...	...	...	...	...	...
15 - 19	C	8 226	...	...	...	...	...	...	...	...
20 - 24	C	13 117	...	...	...	...	...	...	...	...
25 - 29	C	13 033	...	...	...	...	...	...	...	...
30 - 34	C	9 954	...	...	...	...	...	...	...	...
35 - 39	C	5 395	...	...	...	...	...	...	...	...
40 - 44	C	1 473	...	...	...	...	...	...	...	...
45 - 49	C	79	...	...	...	...	...	...	...	...
50+	C	4	...	...	...	...	...	...	...	...
Unk.- Inc.	C	508	...	...	...	...	...	...	...	...
Venezuela[10]										
2002										
Total	C	492 678	254 969	237 709	...	...	...	...	...	...
0 - 14	C	5 148	2 660	2 488	...	...	...	...	...	...
15 - 19	C	100 062	51 874	48 188	...	...	...	...	...	...
20 - 24	C	146 417	75 965	70 452	...	...	...	...	...	...
25 - 29	C	110 318	56 888	53 430	...	...	...	...	...	...
30 - 34	C	73 522	38 081	35 441	...	...	...	...	...	...
35 - 39	C	36 756	18 951	17 805	...	...	...	...	...	...

10. Live births by age of mother, sex of the child and urban/rural residence: latest available year, 1994 - 2003

Naissances vivantes selon l'âge de la mère, le sexe de l'enfant et la résidence, urbaine/rurale: dernière année disponible, 1994 - 2003 (continued — suite)

Continent, country or area, year and age (in years) / Continent, pays ou zone, année et âge (en années)	Code[1]	Total			Urban - Urbaine			Rural - Rurale		
		Both sexes - Les deux sexes	Male - Masculin	Female - Féminin	Both sexes - Les deux sexes	Male - Masculin	Female - Féminin	Both sexes - Les deux sexes	Male - Masculin	Female - Féminin
AMERICA, SOUTH — AMERIQUE DU SUD										
Venezuela[10]										
2002										
40 - 44	C	10 443	5 408	5 035	...	...	...	...	...	...
45 - 49	C	1 376	685	691	...	...	...	...	...	...
50+	C	412	186	226	...	...	...	...	...	...
Unk.- Inc.	C	8 224	4 271	3 953	...	...	...	...	...	...
ASIA — ASIE										
Armenia - Arménie[15]										
2000										
Total	C	34 276	...	...	21 390	...	...	12 886	...	...
15 - 19	C	4 937	...	...	2 673	...	...	2 264	...	...
20 - 24	C	16 183	...	...	10 067	...	...	6 116	...	...
25 - 29	C	7 562	...	...	5 029	...	...	2 533	...	...
30 - 34	C	3 292	...	...	2 100	...	...	1 192	...	...
35 - 39	C	1 765	...	...	1 154	...	...	611	...	...
40 - 44	C	501	...	...	343	...	...	158	...	...
45 - 49	C	21	...	...	13	...	...	8	...	...
50+	C	15	...	...	11	...	...	4	...	...
2003										
Total	C	35 793	...	...	...	...	...	...	...	...
15 - 19	C	4 652	...	...	...	...	...	...	...	...
20 - 24	C	17 914	...	...	...	...	...	...	...	...
25 - 29	C	8 490	...	...	...	...	...	...	...	...
30 - 34	C	3 151	...	...	...	...	...	...	...	...
35 - 39	C	1 212	...	...	...	...	...	...	...	...
40 - 44	C	347	...	...	...	...	...	...	...	...
45 - 49	C	25	...	...	...	...	...	...	...	...
50+	C	2	...	...	...	...	...	...	...	...
Azerbaijan - Azerbaïdjan[15]										
2003										
Total	+C	113 467	61 299	52 168	51 057	27 803	23 254	62 410	33 496	28 914
15 - 19	+C	11 993	6 259	5 734	4 422	2 343	2 079	7 571	3 916	3 655
20 - 24	+C	46 646	24 665	21 981	20 341	10 805	9 536	26 305	13 860	12 445
25 - 29	+C	31 283	17 000	14 283	15 225	8 312	6 913	16 058	8 688	7 370
30 - 34	+C	15 034	8 492	6 542	7 209	4 105	3 104	7 825	4 387	3 438
35 - 39	+C	6 683	3 882	2 801	3 038	1 778	1 260	3 645	2 104	1 541
40 - 44	+C	1 725	958	767	781	447	334	944	511	433
45 - 49	+C	91	34	57	36	8	28	55	26	29
50+	+C	12	9	3	5	5	-	7	4	3
Bahrain - Bahreïn										
2002										
Total	U	13 576	6 953	6 623	...	...	...	...	...	...
15 - 19	U	349	185	164	...	...	...	...	...	...
20 - 24	U	2 645	1 359	1 286	...	...	...	...	...	...
25 - 29	U	4 147	2 098	2 049	...	...	...	...	...	...
30 - 34	U	3 413	1 779	1 634	...	...	...	...	...	...
35 - 39	U	2 299	1 175	1 124	...	...	...	...	...	...
40 - 44	U	655	322	333	...	...	...	...	...	...
45 - 49	U	51	27	24	...	...	...	...	...	...
50+	U	9	5	4	...	...	...	...	...	...
Unk.- Inc.	U	8	3	5	...	...	...	...	...	...
Brunei Darussalam - Brunéi Darussalam										
2002										
Total	+C	7 464	3 818	3 646	...	...	...	...	...	...
0 - 14	+C	7	4	3	...	...	...	...	...	...
15 - 19	+C	387	187	200	...	...	...	...	...	...

10. Live births by age of mother, sex of the child and urban/rural residence: latest available year, 1994 - 2003
Naissances vivantes selon l'âge de la mère, le sexe de l'enfant et la résidence, urbaine/rurale: dernière année disponible, 1994 - 2003 (continued — suite)

Continent, country or area, year and age (in years) / Continent, pays ou zone, année et âge (en années)	Code[1]	Total			Urban - Urbaine			Rural - Rurale		
		Both sexes - Les deux sexes	Male - Masculin	Female - Féminin	Both sexes - Les deux sexes	Male - Masculin	Female - Féminin	Both sexes - Les deux sexes	Male - Masculin	Female - Féminin
ASIA — ASIE										
Brunei Darussalam - Brunéi Darussalam										
2002										
20 - 24	+C	1 585	819	766	...	...	...	...	...	...
25 - 29	+C	2 125	1 072	1 053	...	...	...	...	...	...
30 - 34	+C	1 967	994	973	...	...	...	...	...	...
35 - 39	+C	1 052	560	492	...	...	...	...	...	...
40 - 44	+C	317	169	148	...	...	...	...	...	...
45 - 49	+C	21	12	9	...	...	...	...	...	...
50+	+C	-	-	-	...	...	...	...	...	...
Unk.- Inc.	+C	3	1	2	...	...	...	...	...	...
China: Hong Kong SAR - Chine: Hong Kong RAS[16]										
2003										
Total	C	46 965	24 406	22 559	...	...	...	...	...	...
0 - 14	C	14	10	4	...	...	...	...	...	...
15 - 19	C	748	393	355	...	...	...	...	...	...
20 - 24	C	6 197	3 271	2 926	...	...	...	...	...	...
25 - 29	C	13 390	6 826	6 564	...	...	...	...	...	...
30 - 34	C	16 575	8 648	7 927	...	...	...	...	...	...
35 - 39	C	8 461	4 417	4 044	...	...	...	...	...	...
40 - 44	C	1 516	804	712	...	...	...	...	...	...
45 - 49	C	58	33	25	...	...	...	...	...	...
50+	C	3	2	1	...	...	...	...	...	...
Unk.- Inc.	C	3	2	1	...	...	...	...	...	...
China: Macao SAR - Chine: Macao RAS										
2003										
Total	C	3 212	1 701	1 511	...	...	...	...	...	...
0 - 14	C	-	-	-	...	...	...	...	...	...
15 - 19	C	87	51	36	...	...	...	...	...	...
20 - 24	C	463	252	211	...	...	...	...	...	...
25 - 29	C	901	465	436	...	...	...	...	...	...
30 - 34	C	1 123	597	526	...	...	...	...	...	...
35 - 39	C	527	271	256	...	...	...	...	...	...
40 - 44	C	109	63	46	...	...	...	...	...	...
45 - 49	C	2	2	-	...	...	...	...	...	...
50+	C	-	-	-	...	...	...	...	...	...
Cyprus - Chypre[2,17]										
2003										
Total	C	8 088	4 166	3 922	4 854	2 538	2 316	2 692	1 343	1 349
15 - 19	C	156	77	79	70	41	29	83	35	48
20 - 24	C	1 342	683	659	696	356	340	612	311	301
25 - 29	C	2 413	1 249	1 164	1 481	764	717	891	459	432
30 - 34	C	1 886	971	915	1 278	679	599	568	276	292
35 - 39	C	765	406	359	508	273	235	244	125	119
40 - 44	C	179	99	80	115	66	49	58	31	27
45 - 49	C	11	9	2	8	6	2	3	3	-
50+	C	5	1	4	5	1	4	-	-	-
Unk.- Inc.	C	1 331	671	660	693	352	341	233	103	130
Georgia - Géorgie[15]										
2003										
Total	C	46 194	24 469	21 725	...	...	...	...	...	...
0 - 14	C	65	34	31	...	...	...	...	...	...
15 - 19	C	5 842	3 003	2 839	...	...	...	...	...	...
20 - 24	C	16 463	8 677	7 786	...	...	...	...	...	...
25 - 29	C	12 449	6 633	5 816	...	...	...	...	...	...
30 - 34	C	7 269	3 864	3 405	...	...	...	...	...	...
35 - 39	C	3 040	1 698	1 342	...	...	...	...	...	...
40 - 44	C	929	494	435	...	...	...	...	...	...

10. Live births by age of mother, sex of the child and urban/rural residence: latest available year, 1994 - 2003

Naissances vivantes selon l'âge de la mère, le sexe de l'enfant et la résidence, urbaine/rurale: dernière année disponible, 1994 - 2003 (continued — suite)

Continent, country or area, year and age (in years) / Continent, pays ou zone, année et âge (en années)	Code[1]	Total Both sexes - Les deux sexes	Total Male - Masculin	Total Female - Féminin	Urban - Urbaine Both sexes - Les deux sexes	Urban - Urbaine Male - Masculin	Urban - Urbaine Female - Féminin	Rural - Rurale Both sexes - Les deux sexes	Rural - Rurale Male - Masculin	Rural - Rurale Female - Féminin
ASIA — ASIE										
Georgia - Géorgie[15]										
2003										
45 - 49	C	47	18	29	...	...	...	...	...	...
50+	C	14	9	5	...	...	...	...	...	...
Unk.- Inc.	C	76	39	37	...	...	...	...	...	...
Iran (Islamic Republic of) - Iran (République islamique d')										
1994										
Total	U	1 304 255	...	...	657 275	...	...	646 980	...	...
0 - 14	U	2 059	...	...	1 047	...	...	112	...	...
15 - 19	U	150 317	...	...	70 834	...	...	79 483	...	...
20 - 24	U	411 003	...	...	216 621	...	...	194 382	...	...
25 - 29	U	338 933	...	...	177 085	...	...	161 848	...	...
30 - 34	U	212 503	...	...	102 545	...	...	109 958	...	...
35 - 39	U	126 843	...	...	66 304	...	...	60 539	...	...
40 - 44	U	45 713	...	...	17 297	...	...	28 416	...	...
45 - 49	U	12 355	...	...	2 883	...	...	9 472	...	...
50+	U	4 529	...	...	2 059	...	...	2 470	...	...
Iraq[18]										
2000										
Total	U	471 886	...	...	...	...	...	...	...	...
15 - 19	U	21 367	...	...	...	...	...	...	...	...
20 - 24	U	115 973	...	...	...	...	...	...	...	...
25 - 29	U	149 287	...	...	...	...	...	...	...	...
30 - 34	U	110 981	...	...	...	...	...	...	...	...
35 - 39	U	52 196	...	...	...	...	...	...	...	...
40 - 44	U	16 717	...	...	...	...	...	...	...	...
45+	U	5 365	...	...	...	...	...	...	...	...
Israel - Israël[2,19]										
2003										
Total	C	144 936	74 271	70 665	131 658	67 421	64 237	13 272	6 848	6 424
0 - 14	C	6	5	1	6	5	1	-	-	-
15 - 19	C	4 271	2 170	2 101	3 975	2 013	1 962	295	157	138
20 - 24	C	30 339	15 568	14 771	28 160	14 467	13 693	2 179	1 101	1 078
25 - 29	C	48 263	24 567	23 696	44 061	22 383	21 678	4 202	2 184	2 018
30 - 34	C	38 599	19 875	18 724	34 468	17 737	16 731	4 129	2 137	1 992
35 - 39	C	18 244	9 441	8 803	16 282	8 429	7 853	1 961	1 011	950
40 - 44	C	4 447	2 260	2 187	3 998	2 023	1 975	449	237	212
45 - 49	C	329	160	169	297	150	147	32	10	22
50+	C	42	20	22	37	18	19	5	2	3
Unk.- Inc.	C	396	205	191	374	196	178	20	9	11
Japan - Japon[2,20]										
2003										
Total	C	1 123 610	576 736	546 874	917 627	470 994	446 633	205 813	105 648	100 165
0 - 14	C	49	25	24	39	22	17	10	3	7
15 - 19	C	19 532	10 021	9 511	15 178	7 781	7 397	4 354	2 240	2 114
20 - 24	C	142 068	72 855	69 213	109 886	56 326	53 560	32 177	16 526	15 651
25 - 29	C	395 975	203 414	192 561	319 296	164 062	155 234	76 649	39 339	37 310
30 - 34	C	408 585	209 726	198 859	341 256	175 147	166 109	67 232	34 523	32 709
35 - 39	C	139 489	71 506	67 983	117 027	60 011	57 016	22 427	11 474	10 953
40 - 44	C	17 478	8 950	8 528	14 588	7 453	7 135	2 887	1 496	1 391
45 - 49	C	402	217	185	327	171	156	75	46	29
50+	C	19	13	6	18	13	5	1	-	1
Unk.- Inc.	C	13	9	4	12	8	4	1	1	-
Kazakhstan[15]										
2003										
Total	C	247 946	127 610	120 336	138 680	71 549	67 131	109 266	56 061	53 205
0 - 14	C	52	27	25	32	18	14	20	9	11
15 - 19	C	19 689	10 071	9 618	10 878	5 520	5 358	8 811	4 551	4 260
20 - 24	C	87 393	44 820	42 573	47 812	24 612	23 200	39 581	20 208	19 373

10. Live births by age of mother, sex of the child and urban/rural residence: latest available year, 1994 - 2003
Naissances vivantes selon l'âge de la mère, le sexe de l'enfant et la résidence, urbaine/rurale: dernière année disponible, 1994 - 2003 (continued — suite)

Continent, country or area, year and age (in years) / Continent, pays ou zone, année et âge (en années)	Code[1]	Total			Urban - Urbaine			Rural - Rurale		
		Both sexes - Les deux sexes	Male - Masculin	Female - Féminin	Both sexes - Les deux sexes	Male - Masculin	Female - Féminin	Both sexes - Les deux sexes	Male - Masculin	Female - Féminin
ASIA — ASIE										
Kazakhstan[15]										
2003										
25 - 29	C	71 827	37 140	34 687	40 921	21 293	19 628	30 906	15 847	15 059
30 - 34	C	42 848	22 078	20 770	24 359	12 557	11 802	18 489	9 521	8 968
35 - 39	C	20 810	10 767	10 043	11 674	6 024	5 650	9 136	4 743	4 393
40 - 44	C	4 739	2 405	2 334	2 589	1 321	1 268	2 150	1 084	1 066
45 - 49	C	228	126	102	109	60	49	119	66	53
50+	C	17	10	7	9	4	5	8	6	2
Unk.- Inc.	C	343	166	177	297	140	157	46	26	20
Korea (Republic of) - Corée (République de)[21]										
2002										
Total	C	494 625	259 123	235 502	...	...	...	...	...	...
0 - 14	C	54	24	30	...	...	...	...	...	...
15 - 19	C	4 323	2 474	1 849	...	...	...	...	...	...
20 - 24	C	52 150	27 094	25 056	...	...	...	...	...	...
25 - 29	C	227 172	117 622	109 550	...	...	...	...	...	...
30 - 34	C	170 489	90 306	80 183	...	...	...	...	...	...
35 - 39	C	34 265	18 364	15 901	...	...	...	...	...	...
40 - 44	C	5 177	2 732	2 445	...	...	...	...	...	...
45 - 49	C	353	165	188	...	...	...	...	...	...
50+	C	36	16	20	...	...	...	...	...	...
Unk.- Inc.	C	606	326	280	...	...	...	...	...	...
Kyrgyzstan - Kirghizistan[15]										
2003										
Total	C	105 490	54 243	51 247	31 866	16 350	15 516	73 624	37 893	35 731
0 - 14	C	5	1	4	2	-	2	3	1	2
15 - 19	C	7 977	4 144	3 833	2 101	1 120	981	5 876	3 024	2 852
20 - 24	C	38 566	19 869	18 697	10 989	5 715	5 274	27 577	14 154	13 423
25 - 29	C	29 409	15 138	14 271	9 192	4 673	4 519	20 217	10 465	9 752
30 - 34	C	17 680	9 018	8 662	5 747	2 883	2 864	11 933	6 135	5 798
35 - 39	C	8 614	4 410	4 204	2 776	1 429	1 347	5 838	2 981	2 857
40 - 44	C	2 587	1 330	1 257	782	403	379	1 805	927	878
45 - 49	C	326	164	162	100	40	60	226	124	102
50+	C	119	64	55	26	13	13	93	51	42
Unk.- Inc.	C	207	105	102	151	74	77	56	31	25
Malaysia - Malaisie[4,22]										
2000										
Total	U	442 502	227 833	214 669	288 681	148 872	139 809	153 821	78 961	74 860
0 - 14	U	89	47	42	41	24	17	48	23	25
15 - 19	U	10 816	5 444	5 372	6 023	3 011	3 012	4 793	2 433	2 360
20 - 24	U	76 980	39 595	37 385	46 425	23 962	22 463	30 555	15 633	14 922
25 - 29	U	145 378	74 917	70 461	97 627	50 283	47 344	47 751	24 634	23 117
30 - 34	U	120 993	62 746	58 247	83 106	43 051	40 055	37 887	19 695	18 192
35 - 39	U	66 180	33 916	32 264	43 270	22 313	20 957	22 910	11 603	11 307
40 - 44	U	19 668	9 960	9 708	10 850	5 536	5 314	8 818	4 424	4 394
45 - 49	U	1 628	809	819	761	390	371	867	419	448
50+	U	91	47	44	51	26	25	40	21	19
Unk.- Inc.	U	679	352	327	527	276	251	152	76	76
Maldives										
2003										
Total	C	5 154	2 686	2 468	1 965	1 037	928	3 189	1 649	1 540
0 - 14	C	2	2	-	-	-	-	2	2	-
15 - 19	C	278	130	148	86	45	41	192	85	107
20 - 24	C	1 704	906	798	698	375	323	1 006	531	475
25 - 29	C	1 460	753	707	632	337	295	828	416	412
30 - 34	C	1 023	529	494	375	191	184	648	338	310
35 - 39	C	556	301	255	146	78	68	410	223	187

10. Live births by age of mother, sex of the child and urban/rural residence: latest available year, 1994 - 2003
Naissances vivantes selon l'âge de la mère, le sexe de l'enfant et la résidence, urbaine/rurale: dernière année disponible, 1994 - 2003 (continued — suite)

Continent, country or area, year and age (in years) / Continent, pays ou zone, année et âge (en années)	Code[1]	Total			Urban - Urbaine			Rural - Rurale		
		Both sexes - Les deux sexes	Male - Masculin	Female - Féminin	Both sexes - Les deux sexes	Male - Masculin	Female - Féminin	Both sexes - Les deux sexes	Male - Masculin	Female - Féminin
ASIA — ASIE										
Maldives										
2003										
40 - 44	C	112	57	55	25	11	14	87	46	41
45 - 49	C	11	4	7	2	-	2	9	4	5
50+	C	3	1	2	1	-	1	2	1	1
Mongolia - Mongolie										
2003										
Total	C	45 723	23 092	22 631	24 315	...	...	21 408	...	...
0 - 14	C	21	12	9	7	...	...	14	...	...
15 - 19	C	2 659	1 334	1 325	1 206	...	...	1 453	...	...
20 - 24	C	16 251	8 288	7 963	8 471	...	...	7 780	...	...
25 - 29	C	13 912	6 930	6 982	7 361	...	...	6 551	...	...
30 - 34	C	8 067	4 085	3 982	4 537	...	...	3 530	...	...
35 - 39	C	3 507	1 769	1 738	1 938	...	...	1 569	...	...
40 - 44	C	1 079	565	514	616	...	...	463	...	...
45 - 49	C	108	54	54	70	...	...	38	...	...
50+	C	119	55	64	109	...	...	10	...	...
Myanmar[23]										
1994										
Total	U	...	...	...	261 213	...	...	267 591	...	...
15 - 19	U	...	...	...	21 193	...	...	16 097	...	...
20 - 24	U	...	...	...	75 330	...	...	78 045	...	...
25 - 29	U	...	...	...	75 164	...	...	76 801	...	...
30 - 34	U	...	...	...	52 092	...	...	46 736	...	...
35 - 39	U	...	...	...	27 289	...	...	34 690	...	...
40 - 44	U	...	...	...	8 379	...	...	11 596	...	...
45 - 49	U	...	...	...	961	...	...	1 014	...	...
Oman[18]										
1999										
Total	...	44 067	...	...	...	...	...	...	...	...
15 - 19	...	4 096	...	...	...	...	...	...	...	...
20 - 24	...	13 224	...	...	...	...	...	...	...	...
25 - 29	...	11 504	...	...	...	...	...	...	...	...
30 - 34	...	7 759	...	...	...	...	...	...	...	...
35 - 39	...	5 563	...	...	...	...	...	...	...	...
40 - 44	...	1 739	...	...	...	...	...	...	...	...
45+	...	182	...	...	...	...	...	...	...	...
Pakistan[24,25]										
2001										
Total	I	3 719 694	1 942 845	1 776 849	1 192 190	610 755	581 435	2 527 504	1 332 090	1 195 414
15 - 19	I	174 701	98 230	76 471	52 677	26 339	26 338	122 024	71 891	50 133
20 - 24	I	984 168	520 993	463 175	316 062	163 001	153 061	668 106	357 992	310 114
25 - 29	I	1 162 599	613 628	548 971	389 611	202 757	186 854	772 988	410 871	362 117
30 - 34	I	768 434	405 355	363 079	247 483	129 705	117 778	520 951	275 650	245 301
35 - 39	I	415 924	205 786	210 138	133 183	61 622	71 561	282 741	144 164	138 577
40 - 44	I	157 293	69 010	88 283	41 247	20 872	20 375	116 046	48 138	67 908
45 - 49	I	56 576	29 842	26 734	11 927	6 460	5 467	44 649	23 382	21 267
Philippines										
2002										
Total	C	1 666 773	866 521	800 252	...	...	...	...	...	...
0 - 14	C	762	408	354	...	...	...	...	...	...
15 - 19	C	122 242	63 321	58 921	...	...	...	...	...	...
20 - 24	C	472 408	245 836	226 572	...	...	...	...	...	...
25 - 29	C	457 535	238 988	218 547	...	...	...	...	...	...
30 - 34	C	342 236	177 775	164 461	...	...	...	...	...	...
35 - 39	C	192 176	99 479	92 697	...	...	...	...	...	...
40 - 44	C	67 470	34 661	32 809	...	...	...	...	...	...
45 - 49	C	8 148	4 119	4 029	...	...	...	...	...	...
50+	C	610	304	306	...	...	...	...	...	...
Unk.- Inc.	C	3 186	1 630	1 556	...	...	...	...	...	...

10. Live births by age of mother, sex of the child and urban/rural residence: latest available year, 1994 - 2003

Naissances vivantes selon l'âge de la mère, le sexe de l'enfant et la résidence, urbaine/rurale: dernière année disponible, 1994 - 2003 (continued — suite)

Continent, country or area, year and age (in years) / Continent, pays ou zone, année et âge (en années)	Code[1]	Total			Urban - Urbaine			Rural - Rurale		
		Both sexes - Les deux sexes	Male - Masculin	Female - Féminin	Both sexes - Les deux sexes	Male - Masculin	Female - Féminin	Both sexes - Les deux sexes	Male - Masculin	Female - Féminin
ASIA — ASIE										
Qatar										
2003										
Total	C	12 856	6 564	6 292	...	...	...	...	...	...
15 - 19	C	360	177	183	...	...	...	...	...	...
20 - 24	C	2 690	1 353	1 337	...	...	...	...	...	...
25 - 29	C	3 912	2 024	1 888	...	...	...	...	...	...
30 - 34	C	3 314	1 698	1 616	...	...	...	...	...	...
35 - 39	C	1 870	952	918	...	...	...	...	...	...
40 - 44	C	619	311	308	...	...	...	...	...	...
45 - 49	C	83	43	40	...	...	...	...	...	...
50+	C	8	6	2	...	...	...	...	...	...
Saudi Arabia - Arabie saoudite										
2000										
Total	...	578 772	296 617	282 155	...	...	...	...	...	...
0 - 19	...	27 317	15 093	12 224	...	...	...	...	...	...
20 - 24	...	109 111	54 997	54 114	...	...	...	...	...	...
25 - 29	...	148 705	71 437	77 268	...	...	...	...	...	...
30 - 34	...	129 008	70 830	58 178	...	...	...	...	...	...
35 - 39	...	106 755	54 235	52 520	...	...	...	...	...	...
40 - 44	...	48 231	25 075	23 156	...	...	...	...	...	...
45+	...	9 645	4 950	4 695	...	...	...	...	...	...
Singapore - Singapour[26]										
2003										
Total	C	37 485	19 268	18 217	...	...	...	...	...	...
0 - 14	C	17	10	7	...	...	...	...	...	...
15 - 19	C	714	358	356	...	...	...	...	...	...
20 - 24	C	3 692	1 874	1 818	...	...	...	...	...	...
25 - 29	C	11 421	5 913	5 508	...	...	...	...	...	...
30 - 34	C	14 528	7 478	7 050	...	...	...	...	...	...
35 - 39	C	6 069	3 086	2 983	...	...	...	...	...	...
40 - 44	C	1 017	537	480	...	...	...	...	...	...
45 - 49	C	23	10	13	...	...	...	...	...	...
50+	C	1	-	1	...	...	...	...	...	...
Unk.- Inc.	C	3	2	1	...	...	...	...	...	...
Sri Lanka										
1996										
Total	+C	340 649	173 603	167 046	234 715	119 540	115 175	105 934	54 063	51 871
0 - 14	+C	139	73	66	109	59	50	30	14	16
15 - 19	+C	28 271	14 483	13 788	18 849	9 594	9 255	9 422	4 889	4 533
20 - 24	+C	83 244	42 548	40 696	54 727	27 881	26 846	28 517	14 667	13 850
25 - 29	+C	101 510	51 840	49 670	70 277	35 933	34 344	31 233	15 907	15 326
30 - 34	+C	76 096	38 601	37 495	55 159	27 969	27 190	20 937	10 632	10 305
35 - 39	+C	42 130	21 467	20 663	28 886	14 765	14 121	13 244	6 702	6 542
40 - 44	+C	8 378	4 168	4 210	6 143	3 076	3 067	2 235	1 092	1 143
45 - 49	+C	804	386	418	534	250	284	270	136	134
50+	+C	77	37	40	31	13	18	46	24	22
Tajikistan - Tadjikistan[15]										
1999										
Total	U	114 015	60 552	53 463	23 602	12 650	10 952	90 413	47 902	42 511
15 - 19	U	10 026	5 239	4 787	2 207	1 156	1 051	7 819	4 083	3 736
20 - 24	U	38 400	20 275	18 125	8 093	4 355	3 738	30 307	15 920	14 387
25 - 29	U	30 752	16 431	14 321	6 394	3 414	2 980	24 358	13 017	11 341
30 - 34	U	20 245	10 744	9 501	4 144	2 223	1 921	16 101	8 521	7 580
35 - 39	U	10 957	5 873	5 084	2 116	1 153	963	8 841	4 720	4 121
40 - 44	U	2 819	1 532	1 287	441	226	215	2 378	1 306	1 072
45 - 49	U	234	128	106	31	17	14	203	111	92
50+	U	37	25	12	5	4	1	32	21	11
Unk.- Inc.	U	545	305	240	171	102	69	374	203	171

Continent, country or area, year and age (in years) / Continent, pays ou zone, année et âge (en années)	Code[1]	Total			Urban - Urbaine			Rural - Rurale		
		Both sexes - Les deux sexes	Male - Masculin	Female - Féminin	Both sexes - Les deux sexes	Male - Masculin	Female - Féminin	Both sexes - Les deux sexes	Male - Masculin	Female - Féminin
ASIA — ASIE										
Thailand - Thaïlande										
2000										
Total	+U	773 009	397 523	375 486	...	...	...	...	...	...
0 - 14	+U	1 478	779	699	...	...	...	...	...	...
15 - 19	+U	86 675	44 787	41 888	...	...	...	...	...	...
20 - 24	+U	207 225	106 314	100 911	...	...	...	...	...	...
25 - 29	+U	218 767	112 516	106 251	...	...	...	...	...	...
30 - 34	+U	154 337	79 321	75 016	...	...	...	...	...	...
35 - 39	+U	68 568	35 298	33 270	...	...	...	...	...	...
40 - 44	+U	16 339	8 497	7 842	...	...	...	...	...	...
45 - 49	+U	1 850	932	918	...	...	...	...	...	...
50+	+U	421	212	209	...	...	...	...	...	...
Unk.- Inc.	+U	17 349	8 867	8 482	...	...	...	...	...	...
Turkey - Turquie[24]										
1997										
Total	I	1 377 000	...	...	...	...	...	...	...	...
0 - 14	I	-	...	...	...	...	...	...	...	...
15 - 19	I	165 000	...	...	...	...	...	...	...	...
20 - 24	I	531 000	...	...	...	...	...	...	...	...
25 - 29	I	387 000	...	...	...	...	...	...	...	...
30 - 34	I	182 000	...	...	...	...	...	...	...	...
35 - 39	I	79 000	...	...	...	...	...	...	...	...
40 - 44	I	28 000	...	...	...	...	...	...	...	...
45+	I	5 000	...	...	...	...	...	...	...	...
Uzbekistan - Ouzbékistan[15]										
2000										
Total	C	527 580	...	...	163 834	...	...	363 746	...	...
15 - 19	C	28 179	...	...	10 217	...	...	17 962	...	...
20 - 24	C	228 743	...	...	69 369	...	...	159 374	...	...
25 - 29	C	160 082	...	...	48 315	...	...	111 767	...	...
30 - 34	C	78 316	...	...	25 084	...	...	53 232	...	...
35 - 39	C	26 866	...	...	9 095	...	...	17 771	...	...
40 - 44	C	4 979	...	...	1 639	...	...	3 340	...	...
45 - 49	C	348	...	...	96	...	...	252	...	...
50+	C	67	...	...	19	...	...	48	...	...
EUROPE										
Albania - Albanie										
2003										
Total	C	47 012	24 894	22 118	19 481	10 357	9 124	27 531	14 537	12 994
15 - 19	C	2 534	1 300	1 234	1 054	542	512	1 480	758	722
20 - 24	C	14 617	7 558	7 059	5 520	2 815	2 705	9 097	4 743	4 354
25 - 29	C	15 837	8 445	7 392	6 535	3 495	3 040	9 302	4 950	4 352
30 - 34	C	9 421	5 065	4 356	4 243	2 304	1 939	5 178	2 761	2 417
35 - 39	C	3 477	1 911	1 566	1 576	893	683	1 901	1 018	883
40 - 44	C	799	449	350	358	214	144	441	235	206
45 - 49	C	74	38	36	31	14	17	43	24	19
50+	C	23	14	9	10	7	3	13	7	6
Unk.- Inc.	C	230	114	116	154	73	81	76	41	35
Andorra - Andorre										
2003										
Total	C	721	380	341	...	...	...	...	...	...
15 - 19	C	13	10	3	...	...	...	...	...	...
20 - 24	C	95	48	47	...	...	...	...	...	...
25 - 29	C	201	108	93	...	...	...	...	...	...
30 - 34	C	265	133	132	...	...	...	...	...	...
35 - 39	C	127	70	57	...	...	...	...	...	...
40 - 44	C	19	10	9	...	...	...	...	...	...
45 - 49	C	1	1	-	...	...	...	...	...	...

10. Live births by age of mother, sex of the child and urban/rural residence: latest available year, 1994 - 2003

Naissances vivantes selon l'âge de la mère, le sexe de l'enfant et la résidence, urbaine/rurale: dernière année disponible, 1994 - 2003 (continued — suite)

Continent, country or area, year and age (in years) / Continent, pays ou zone, année et âge (en années)	Code[1]	Total			Urban - Urbaine			Rural - Rurale		
		Both sexes - Les deux sexes	Male - Masculin	Female - Féminin	Both sexes - Les deux sexes	Male - Masculin	Female - Féminin	Both sexes - Les deux sexes	Male - Masculin	Female - Féminin
EUROPE										
Austria - Autriche										
2003										
Total	C	76 944	39 542	37 402	...	...	...	...	...	...
0 - 14	C	16	11	5	...	...	...	...	...	...
15 - 19	C	3 090	1 572	1 518	...	...	...	...	...	...
20 - 24	C	14 178	7 173	7 005	...	...	...	...	...	...
25 - 29	C	24 091	12 356	11 735	...	...	...	...	...	...
30 - 34	C	22 971	11 884	11 087	...	...	...	...	...	...
35 - 39	C	10 585	5 512	5 073	...	...	...	...	...	...
40 - 44	C	1 941	984	957	...	...	...	...	...	...
45 - 49	C	71	49	22	...	...	...	...	...	...
50+	C	1	1	-	...	...	...	...	...	...
Belarus - Bélarus[15]										
2003										
Total	C	88 512	45 627	42 885	64 814	33 379	31 435	23 698	12 248	11 450
0 - 14	C	17	9	8	11	7	4	6	2	4
15 - 19	C	9 503	4 863	4 640	6 084	3 087	2 997	3 419	1 776	1 643
20 - 24	C	35 336	18 224	17 112	25 735	13 224	12 511	9 601	5 000	4 601
25 - 29	C	25 457	13 067	12 390	19 333	9 963	9 370	6 124	3 104	3 020
30 - 34	C	12 724	6 629	6 095	9 723	5 043	4 680	3 001	1 586	1 415
35 - 39	C	4 396	2 265	2 131	3 159	1 641	1 518	1 237	624	613
40 - 44	C	956	514	442	670	367	303	286	147	139
45+	C	43	23	20	25	14	11	18	9	9
Unk.- Inc.	C	80	33	47	74	33	41	6	-	6
Bosnia and Herzegovina - Bosnie-Herzégovine										
2003										
Total	C	35 234	...	...	...	...	...	...	...	...
10 - 14	C	11	...	...	...	...	...	...	...	...
15 - 19	C	1 957	...	...	...	...	...	...	...	...
20 - 24	C	10 842	...	...	...	...	...	...	...	...
25 - 29	C	11 460	...	...	...	...	...	...	...	...
30 - 34	C	6 763	...	...	...	...	...	...	...	...
35 - 39	C	2 867	...	...	...	...	...	...	...	...
40 - 44	C	587	...	...	...	...	...	...	...	...
45 - 49	C	31	...	...	...	...	...	...	...	...
Unk.- Inc.	C	716	...	...	...	...	...	...	...	...
Bulgaria - Bulgarie										
2003										
Total	C	67 359	34 670	32 689	48 597	25 157	23 440	18 762	9 513	9 249
0 - 14	C	330	147	183	203	94	109	127	53	74
15 - 19	C	10 059	5 141	4 918	5 853	3 021	2 832	4 206	2 120	2 086
20 - 24	C	21 730	11 164	10 566	14 594	7 575	7 019	7 136	3 589	3 547
25 - 29	C	21 685	11 127	10 558	17 000	8 755	8 245	4 685	2 372	2 313
30 - 34	C	10 167	5 309	4 858	8 247	4 298	3 949	1 920	1 011	909
35 - 39	C	2 853	1 502	1 351	2 286	1 191	1 095	567	311	256
40 - 44	C	482	250	232	367	197	170	115	53	62
45 - 49	C	19	15	4	13	11	2	6	4	2
50+	C	1	1	-	1	1	-	-	-	-
Unk.- Inc.	C	33	14	19	33	14	19	-	-	-
Channel Islands: Guernsey - Îles Anglo-Normandes: Guernesey										
2000										
Total	C	644	336	308	...	...	...	...	...	...
15 - 19	C	42	15	27	...	...	...	...	...	...
20 - 24	C	84	49	35	...	...	...	...	...	...
25 - 29	C	192	101	91	...	...	...	...	...	...
30 - 34	C	200	102	98	...	...	...	...	...	...

10. Live births by age of mother, sex of the child and urban/rural residence: latest available year, 1994 - 2003

Naissances vivantes selon l'âge de la mère, le sexe de l'enfant et la résidence, urbaine/rurale: dernière année disponible, 1994 - 2003 (continued — suite)

Continent, country or area, year and age (in years) / Continent, pays ou zone, année et âge (en années)	Code[1]	Total Both sexes - Les deux sexes	Total Male - Masculin	Total Female - Féminin	Urban - Urbaine Both sexes - Les deux sexes	Urban - Urbaine Male - Masculin	Urban - Urbaine Female - Féminin	Rural - Rurale Both sexes - Les deux sexes	Rural - Rurale Male - Masculin	Rural - Rurale Female - Féminin
EUROPE										
Channel Islands: Guernsey - Îles Anglo-Normandes: Guernesey										
2000										
35 - 39	C	106	60	46	...	...	...	...	...	...
40 - 44	C	20	9	11	...	...	...	...	...	...
Channel Islands: Jersey - Îles Anglo-Normandes: Jersey										
1994										
Total	+C	1 142	589	553	...	...	...	...	...	...
0 - 14	+C	1	1	-	...	...	...	...	...	...
15 - 19	+C	31	17	14	...	...	...	...	...	...
20 - 24	+C	161	86	75	...	...	...	...	...	...
25 - 29	+C	390	201	189	...	...	...	...	...	...
30 - 34	+C	398	198	200	...	...	...	...	...	...
35 - 39	+C	140	77	63	...	...	...	...	...	...
40+	+C	21	9	12	...	...	...	...	...	...
Croatia - Croatie										
2003										
Total	C	39 668	20 381	19 287	21 837	11 276	10 561	17 831	9 105	8 726
0 - 14	C	5	2	3	1	1	-	4	1	3
15 - 19	C	1 972	1 012	960	727	378	349	1 245	634	611
20 - 24	C	10 158	5 171	4 987	4 506	2 355	2 151	5 652	2 816	2 836
25 - 29	C	13 843	7 069	6 774	7 848	4 022	3 826	5 995	3 047	2 948
30 - 34	C	9 318	4 865	4 453	6 006	3 127	2 879	3 312	1 738	1 574
35 - 39	C	3 617	1 854	1 763	2 279	1 154	1 125	1 338	700	638
40 - 44	C	692	378	314	428	221	207	264	157	107
45 - 49	C	27	12	15	19	8	11	8	4	4
50+	C	1	1	-	-	-	-	1	1	-
Unk.- Inc.	C	35	17	18	23	10	13	12	7	5
Czech Republic - République tchèque										
2003										
Total	C	93 685	48 131	45 554	69 120	35 581	33 539	24 565	12 550	12 015
0 - 14	C	26	13	13	24	12	12	2	1	1
15 - 19	C	3 687	1 834	1 853	2 730	1 363	1 367	957	471	486
20 - 24	C	19 919	10 188	9 731	13 735	7 094	6 641	6 184	3 094	3 090
25 - 29	C	42 048	21 691	20 357	30 825	15 887	14 938	11 223	5 804	5 419
30 - 34	C	20 964	10 812	10 152	16 336	8 433	7 903	4 628	2 379	2 249
35 - 39	C	6 008	3 076	2 932	4 651	2 388	2 263	1 357	688	669
40 - 44	C	991	493	498	786	383	403	205	110	95
45 - 49	C	41	24	17	32	21	11	9	3	6
50+	C	1	-	1	1	-	1	-	-	-
Unk.- Inc.	C	-	-	-	-	-	-	-	-	-
Denmark - Danemark[27]										
2003										
Total	C	64 682	...	...	...	...	...	...	...	...
15 - 19	C	851	...	...	...	...	...	...	...	...
20 - 24	C	6 967	...	...	...	...	...	...	...	...
25 - 29	C	22 540	...	...	...	...	...	...	...	...
30 - 34	C	23 039	...	...	...	...	...	...	...	...
35 - 39	C	9 766	...	...	...	...	...	...	...	...
40 - 44	C	1 460	...	...	...	...	...	...	...	...
45 - 49	C	54	...	...	...	...	...	...	...	...
50 - 50	C	2	...	...	...	...	...	...	...	...

10. Live births by age of mother, sex of the child and urban/rural residence: latest available year, 1994 - 2003
Naissances vivantes selon l'âge de la mère, le sexe de l'enfant et la résidence, urbaine/rurale: dernière année disponible, 1994 - 2003 (continued — suite)

Continent, country or area, year and age (in years) / Continent, pays ou zone, année et âge (en années)	Code[1]	Total			Urban - Urbaine			Rural - Rurale		
		Both sexes - Les deux sexes	Male - Masculin	Female - Féminin	Both sexes - Les deux sexes	Male - Masculin	Female - Féminin	Both sexes - Les deux sexes	Male - Masculin	Female - Féminin
EUROPE										
Estonia - Estonie[15]										
2002										
Total	C	13 001	6 619	6 382	8 840	4 505	4 335	4 161	2 114	2 047
0 - 14	C	2	-	2	1	-	1	1	-	1
15 - 19	C	1 137	545	592	668	327	341	469	218	251
20 - 24	C	3 644	1 854	1 790	2 407	1 220	1 187	1 237	634	603
25 - 29	C	4 105	2 089	2 016	2 948	1 507	1 441	1 157	582	575
30 - 34	C	2 729	1 416	1 313	1 887	973	914	842	443	399
35 - 39	C	1 125	578	547	761	386	375	364	192	172
40 - 44	C	252	136	116	162	91	71	90	45	45
45 - 49	C	5	1	4	4	1	3	1	-	1
50+	C	1	-	1	1	-	1	-	-	-
Unk.- Inc.	C	1	-	1	1	-	1	-	-	-
Finland - Finlande[28]										
2003										
Total	C	56 630	28 839	27 791	37 303	19 031	18 272	19 327	9 808	9 519
0 - 14	C	4	3	1	1	1	-	3	2	1
15 - 19	C	1 626	795	831	1 064	539	525	562	256	306
20 - 24	C	9 165	4 739	4 426	6 053	3 127	2 926	3 112	1 612	1 500
25 - 29	C	18 254	9 232	9 022	12 184	6 163	6 021	6 070	3 069	3 001
30 - 34	C	16 482	8 341	8 141	10 875	5 507	5 368	5 607	2 834	2 773
35 - 39	C	8 992	4 651	4 341	5 826	3 016	2 810	3 166	1 635	1 531
40 - 44	C	2 006	1 030	976	1 239	645	594	767	385	382
45 - 49	C	98	47	51	59	32	27	39	15	24
50+	C	3	1	2	2	1	1	1	-	1
France[9,29,30]										
2002										
Total	C	761 630	389 981	371 649	577 724	295 785	281 939	182 454	93 428	89 026
0 - 14	C	43	20	23	34	17	17	9	3	6
15 - 19	C	15 218	7 781	7 437	13 013	6 672	6 341	2 189	1 100	1 089
20 - 24	C	106 917	54 649	52 268	86 380	44 127	42 253	20 415	10 457	9 958
25 - 29	C	249 785	127 943	121 842	186 192	95 481	90 711	63 211	32 267	30 944
30 - 34	C	250 567	128 391	122 176	184 603	94 572	90 031	65 421	33 525	31 896
35 - 39	C	113 302	58 036	55 266	86 706	44 378	42 328	26 274	13 485	12 789
40 - 44	C	24 603	12 548	12 055	19 796	10 027	9 769	4 747	2 494	2 253
45 - 49	C	1 155	592	563	962	491	471	186	96	90
50+	C	40	21	19	38	20	18	2	1	1
Germany - Allemagne										
2003										
Total	C	706 721	362 709	344 012	...	...	...	...	...	...
0 - 14	C	182	98	84	...	...	...	...	...	...
15 - 19	C	26 546	13 642	12 904	...	...	...	...	...	...
20 - 24	C	120 894	61 930	58 964	...	...	...	...	...	...
25 - 29	C	198 749	101 949	96 800	...	...	...	...	...	...
30 - 34	C	224 356	115 388	108 968	...	...	...	...	...	...
35 - 39	C	116 917	59 847	57 070	...	...	...	...	...	...
40 - 44	C	18 446	9 511	8 935	...	...	...	...	...	...
45 - 49	C	614	336	278	...	...	...	...	...	...
50+	C	17	8	9	...	...	...	...	...	...
Gibraltar										
2002										
Total	C	375	...	...	...	...	...	...	...	...
15 - 19	C	25	...	...	...	...	...	...	...	...
20 - 24	C	59	...	...	...	...	...	...	...	...
25 - 29	C	120	...	...	...	...	...	...	...	...
30 - 34	C	115	...	...	...	...	...	...	...	...
35 - 39	C	46	...	...	...	...	...	...	...	...
40 - 44	C	10	...	...	...	...	...	...	...	...
Greece - Grèce										
2003										
Total	C	104 420	...	...	...	...	...	...	...	...

10. Live births by age of mother, sex of the child and urban/rural residence: latest available year, 1994 - 2003
Naissances vivantes selon l'âge de la mère, le sexe de l'enfant et la résidence, urbaine/rurale: dernière année disponible, 1994 - 2003 (continued — suite)

Continent, country or area, year and age (in years) / Continent, pays ou zone, année et âge (en années)	Code[1]	Total			Urban - Urbaine			Rural - Rurale		
		Both sexes - Les deux sexes	Male - Masculin	Female - Féminin	Both sexes - Les deux sexes	Male - Masculin	Female - Féminin	Both sexes - Les deux sexes	Male - Masculin	Female - Féminin
EUROPE										
Greece - Grèce										
2003										
10 - 14	C	92	...	...	...	...	...	...	...	...
15 - 19	C	3 416	...	...	...	...	...	...	...	...
20 - 24	C	16 840	...	...	...	...	...	...	...	...
25 - 29	C	33 953	...	...	...	...	...	...	...	...
30 - 34	C	32 926	...	...	...	...	...	...	...	...
35 - 39	C	14 430	...	...	...	...	...	...	...	...
40 - 44	C	2 495	...	...	...	...	...	...	...	...
45 - 49	C	235	...	...	...	...	...	...	...	...
50+	C	33	...	...	...	...	...	...	...	...
Hungary - Hongrie[2]										
2003										
Total	C	94 647	48 863	45 784	59 280	30 589	28 691	34 465	17 785	16 680
0 - 14	C	118	70	48	55	30	25	63	40	23
15 - 19	C	6 483	3 370	3 113	3 092	1 578	1 514	3 326	1 755	1 571
20 - 24	C	20 143	10 385	9 758	10 802	5 592	5 210	9 057	4 635	4 422
25 - 29	C	37 089	19 136	17 953	24 126	12 394	11 732	12 680	6 584	6 096
30 - 34	C	22 022	11 363	10 659	15 246	7 906	7 340	6 591	3 359	3 232
35 - 39	C	7 452	3 866	3 586	5 072	2 634	2 438	2 309	1 201	1 108
40 - 44	C	1 289	644	645	855	435	420	422	203	219
45 - 49	C	50	28	22	31	19	12	17	8	9
50+	C	1	1	-	1	1	-	-	-	-
Iceland - Islande										
2003										
Total	C	4 143	2 102	2 041	3 906	1 988	1 918	237	114	123
15 - 19	C	164	75	89	155	72	83	9	3	6
20 - 24	C	834	423	411	790	403	387	44	20	24
25 - 29	C	1 326	674	652	1 267	645	622	59	29	30
30 - 34	C	1 169	602	567	1 087	558	529	82	44	38
35 - 39	C	520	265	255	484	251	233	36	14	22
40 - 44	C	126	61	65	120	58	62	6	3	3
45 - 49	C	4	2	2	3	1	2	1	1	-
Ireland - Irlande[31]										
2003										
Total	+C	61 485	...	...	...	...	...	...	...	...
15 - 19	+C	2 791	...	...	...	...	...	...	...	...
20 - 24	+C	8 469	...	...	...	...	...	...	...	...
25 - 29	+C	14 806	...	...	...	...	...	...	...	...
30 - 34	+C	20 881	...	...	...	...	...	...	...	...
35 - 39	+C	11 978	...	...	...	...	...	...	...	...
40 - 44	+C	2 173	...	...	...	...	...	...	...	...
45 - 49	+C	50	...	...	...	...	...	...	...	...
Unk.- Inc.	+C	325	...	...	...	...	...	...	...	...
Italy - Italie										
2003										
Total	C	535 282	...	...	...	...	...	...	...	...
10 - 14	C	3	...	...	...	...	...	...	...	...
15 - 19	C	9 445	...	...	...	...	...	...	...	...
20 - 24	C	54 441	...	...	...	...	...	...	...	...
25 - 29	C	149 513	...	...	...	...	...	...	...	...
30 - 34	C	181 317	...	...	...	...	...	...	...	...
35 - 39	C	93 580	...	...	...	...	...	...	...	...
40 - 44	C	15 643	...	...	...	...	...	...	...	...
45 - 49	C	703	...	...	...	...	...	...	...	...
50 - 50	C	73	...	...	...	...	...	...	...	...
Unk.- Inc.	C	30 564	...	...	...	...	...	...	...	...
Latvia - Lettonie[15]										
2002										
Total	C	20 044	10 273	9 771	12 938	6 627	6 311	7 106	3 646	3 460
0 - 14	C	1	1	-	1	1	-	-	-	-

10. Live births by age of mother, sex of the child and urban/rural residence: latest available year, 1994 - 2003
Naissances vivantes selon l'âge de la mère, le sexe de l'enfant et la résidence, urbaine/rurale: dernière année disponible, 1994 - 2003 (continued — suite)

Continent, country or area, year and age (in years) / Continent, pays ou zone, année et âge (en années)	Code[1]	Total			Urban - Urbaine			Rural - Rurale		
		Both sexes - Les deux sexes	Male - Masculin	Female - Féminin	Both sexes - Les deux sexes	Male - Masculin	Female - Féminin	Both sexes - Les deux sexes	Male - Masculin	Female - Féminin
EUROPE										
Latvia - Lettonie[15]										
2002										
15 - 19	C	1 456	768	688	802	410	392	654	358	296
20 - 24	C	5 821	2 985	2 836	3 509	1 820	1 689	2 312	1 165	1 147
25 - 29	C	6 381	3 271	3 110	4 288	2 169	2 119	2 093	1 102	991
30 - 34	C	4 147	2 119	2 028	2 858	1 491	1 367	1 289	628	661
35 - 39	C	1 746	889	857	1 176	579	597	570	310	260
40 - 44	C	455	227	228	282	148	134	173	79	94
45 - 49	C	30	9	21	17	5	12	13	4	9
50+	C	1	1	-	1	1	-	-	-	-
Unk.- Inc.	C	6	3	3	4	3	1	2	-	2
Liechtenstein										
2003										
Total	C	347	183	164	...	...	...	...	...	...
15 - 19	C	9	5	4	...	...	...	...	...	...
20 - 24	C	34	16	18	...	...	...	...	...	...
25 - 29	C	106	57	49	...	...	...	...	...	...
30 - 34	C	126	67	59	...	...	...	...	...	...
35 - 39	C	62	35	27	...	...	...	...	...	...
40 - 44	C	9	3	6	...	...	...	...	...	...
45+	C	1	-	1	...	...	...	...	...	...
Lithuania - Lituanie[15]										
2003										
Total	C	30 598	15 821	14 777	19 140	9 951	9 189	11 458	5 870	5 588
0 - 14	C	7	5	2	3	1	2	4	4	...
15 - 19	C	2 794	1 483	1 311	1 459	770	689	1 335	713	622
20 - 24	C	9 161	4 771	4 390	5 358	2 815	2 543	3 803	1 956	1 847
25 - 29	C	9 715	4 970	4 745	6 475	3 354	3 121	3 240	1 616	1 624
30 - 34	C	5 826	3 017	2 809	3 895	2 029	1 866	1 931	988	943
35 - 39	C	2 469	1 262	1 207	1 582	810	772	887	452	435
40 - 44	C	597	298	299	348	162	186	249	136	113
45 - 49	C	21	11	10	13	7	6	8	4	4
Unk.- Inc.	C	8	4	4	7	3	4	1	1	-
Luxembourg										
2003										
Total	C	5 303	2 814	2 489	...	...	...	...	...	...
0 - 14	C	-	-	-	...	...	...	...	...	...
15 - 19	C	138	79	59	...	...	...	...	...	...
20 - 24	C	733	381	352	...	...	...	...	...	...
25 - 29	C	1 546	797	749	...	...	...	...	...	...
30 - 34	C	1 863	1 007	856	...	...	...	...	...	...
35 - 39	C	863	468	395	...	...	...	...	...	...
40 - 44	C	151	75	76	...	...	...	...	...	...
45+	C	7	6	1	...	...	...	...	...	...
Unk.- Inc.	C	2	1	1	...	...	...	...	...	...
Malta - Malte[32]										
2003										
Total	C	3 902	...	...	...	...	...	...	...	...
15 - 19	C	219	...	...	...	...	...	...	...	...
20 - 24	C	784	...	...	...	...	...	...	...	...
25 - 29	C	1 441	...	...	...	...	...	...	...	...
30 - 34	C	1 018	...	...	...	...	...	...	...	...
35 - 39	C	361	...	...	...	...	...	...	...	...
40 - 44	C	77	...	...	...	...	...	...	...	...
45 - 49	C	2	...	...	...	...	...	...	...	...
50+	C	-	...	...	...	...	...	...	...	...
Unk.- Inc.	C	-	...	...	...	...	...	...	...	...
Netherlands - Pays-Bas[33]										
2002										
Total	C	202 083	103 734	98 349	132 825	68 325	64 500	69 258	35 409	33 849

10. Live births by age of mother, sex of the child and urban/rural residence: latest available year, 1994 - 2003

Naissances vivantes selon l'âge de la mère, le sexe de l'enfant et la résidence, urbaine/rurale: dernière année disponible, 1994 - 2003 (continued — suite)

Continent, country or area, year and age (in years) / Continent, pays ou zone, année et âge (en années)	Code[1]	Total			Urban - Urbaine			Rural - Rurale		
		Both sexes - Les deux sexes	Male - Masculin	Female - Féminin	Both sexes - Les deux sexes	Male - Masculin	Female - Féminin	Both sexes - Les deux sexes	Male - Masculin	Female - Féminin
EUROPE										
Netherlands - Pays-Bas[33]										
2002										
0 - 14	C	17	10	7	16	9	7	1	1	-
15 - 19	C	2 632	1 358	1 274	2 141	1 100	1 041	491	258	233
20 - 24	C	17 667	9 018	8 649	13 355	6 840	6 515	4 312	2 178	2 134
25 - 29	C	51 907	26 519	25 388	33 612	17 205	16 407	18 295	9 314	8 981
30 - 34	C	86 077	44 322	41 755	54 218	28 014	26 204	31 859	16 308	15 551
35 - 39	C	37 859	19 477	18 382	25 198	12 977	12 221	12 661	6 500	6 161
40 - 44	C	5 701	2 910	2 791	4 118	2 092	2 026	1 583	818	765
45 - 49	C	213	116	97	102	00	70	51	30	21
50+	C	10	4	6	5	2	3	5	2	3
2003										
Total	C	200 297	...	...	...	...	...	...	...	...
15 - 19	C	3 324	...	...	...	...	...	...	...	...
20 - 24	C	19 828	...	...	...	...	...	...	...	...
25 - 29	C	55 568	...	...	...	...	...	...	...	...
30 - 34	C	82 699	...	...	...	...	...	...	...	...
35 - 39	C	34 282	...	...	...	...	...	...	...	...
40 - 44	C	4 441	...	...	...	...	...	...	...	...
45 - 49	C	150	...	...	...	...	...	...	...	...
50+	C	5	...	...	...	...	...	...	...	...
Norway - Norvège[9]										
2002										
Total	C	55 434	...	...	...	...	...	...	...	...
12 - 14	C	4	...	...	...	...	...	...	...	...
15 - 19	C	1 322	...	...	...	...	...	...	...	...
20 - 24	C	8 032	...	...	...	...	...	...	...	...
25 - 29	C	18 556	...	...	...	...	...	...	...	...
30 - 34	C	18 907	...	...	...	...	...	...	...	...
35 - 39	C	7 365	...	...	...	...	...	...	...	...
40 - 44	C	1 211	...	...	...	...	...	...	...	...
45 - 49	C	37	...	...	...	...	...	...	...	...
Poland - Pologne										
2003										
Total	C	351 072	180 634	170 438	199 583	102 546	97 037	151 489	78 088	73 401
0 - 14	C	45	23	22	32	19	13	13	4	9
15 - 19	C	22 469	11 595	10 874	12 009	6 183	5 826	10 460	5 412	5 048
20 - 24	C	101 915	52 486	49 429	52 884	27 230	25 654	49 031	25 256	23 775
25 - 29	C	128 978	66 460	62 518	76 995	39 519	37 476	51 983	26 941	25 042
30 - 34	C	66 158	33 895	32 263	40 246	20 664	19 582	25 912	13 231	12 681
35 - 39	C	24 782	12 752	12 030	13 801	7 094	6 707	10 981	5 658	5 323
40 - 44	C	6 406	3 275	3 131	3 444	1 761	1 683	2 962	1 514	1 448
45 - 49	C	316	145	171	171	75	96	145	70	75
50+	C	3	3	-	1	1	-	2	2	-
Portugal										
2003										
Total	C	112 515	58 210	54 305	...	...	...	...	...	...
0 - 14	C	76	37	39	...	...	...	...	...	...
15 - 19	C	6 067	3 146	2 921	...	...	...	...	...	...
20 - 24	C	18 953	9 797	9 156	...	...	...	...	...	...
25 - 29	C	37 063	19 214	17 849	...	...	...	...	...	...
30 - 34	C	33 417	17 253	16 164	...	...	...	...	...	...
35 - 39	C	14 039	7 201	6 838	...	...	...	...	...	...
40 - 44	C	2 749	1 482	1 267	...	...	...	...	...	...
45 - 49	C	145	77	68	...	...	...	...	...	...
50+	C	4	3	1	...	...	...	...	...	...
Unk.- Inc.	C	2	-	2	...	...	...	...	...	...

10. Live births by age of mother, sex of the child and urban/rural residence: latest available year, 1994 - 2003
Naissances vivantes selon l'âge de la mère, le sexe de l'enfant et la résidence, urbaine/rurale: dernière année disponible, 1994 - 2003 (continued — suite)

Continent, country or area, year and age (in years) Continent, pays ou zone, année et âge (en années)	Code[1]	Total			Urban - Urbaine			Rural - Rurale		
		Both sexes - Les deux sexes	Male - Masculin	Female - Féminin	Both sexes - Les deux sexes	Male - Masculin	Female - Féminin	Both sexes - Les deux sexes	Male - Masculin	Female - Féminin
EUROPE										
Republic of Moldova - République de Moldova[15]										
2003										
Total	C	36 471	18 932	17 539	12 788	6 679	6 109	23 683	12 253	11 430
0 - 14	C	16	10	6	3	3	-	13	7	6
15 - 19	C	5 242	2 763	2 479	1 303	702	601	3 939	2 061	1 878
20 - 24	C	14 529	7 499	7 030	4 780	2 465	2 315	9 749	5 034	4 715
25 - 29	C	9 872	5 120	4 752	3 852	2 012	1 840	6 020	3 108	2 912
30 - 34	C	4 728	2 468	2 260	1 994	1 072	922	2 734	1 396	1 338
35 - 39	C	1 659	856	803	687	348	339	972	508	464
40 - 44	C	398	202	196	153	69	84	245	133	112
45 - 49	C	13	7	6	5	3	2	8	4	4
50+	C	4	2	2	2	-	2	2	2	-
Unk.- Inc.	C	10	5	5	9	5	4	1	-	1
Romania - Roumanie										
2003										
Total	C	212 459	109 497	102 962	100 915	52 074	48 841	111 544	57 423	54 121
0 - 14	C	518	276	242	176	93	83	342	183	159
15 - 19	C	27 706	14 377	13 329	8 931	4 664	4 267	18 775	9 713	9 062
20 - 24	C	65 756	33 778	31 978	27 005	13 847	13 158	38 751	19 931	18 820
25 - 29	C	68 187	35 023	33 164	36 763	18 938	17 825	31 424	16 085	15 339
30 - 34	C	36 293	18 759	17 534	20 357	10 535	9 822	15 936	8 224	7 712
35 - 39	C	11 772	6 124	5 648	6 640	3 462	3 178	5 132	2 662	2 470
40 - 44	C	2 086	1 076	1 010	981	493	488	1 105	583	522
45 - 49	C	138	82	56	60	41	19	78	41	37
50+	C	3	2	1	2	1	1	1	1	-
Russian Federation - Fédération de Russie[15]										
2003										
Total	C	1 477 301	...	...	1 050 565	...	...	426 736	...	...
0 - 14	C	445	...	...	280	...	...	165	...	...
15 - 19	C	169 863	...	...	108 013	...	...	61 850	...	...
20 - 24	C	546 779	...	...	386 246	...	...	160 533	...	...
25 - 29	C	415 211	...	...	311 620	...	...	103 591	...	...
30 - 34	C	217 696	...	...	163 310	...	...	54 386	...	...
35 - 39	C	79 474	...	...	57 055	...	...	22 419	...	...
40 - 44	C	17 093	...	...	11 782	...	...	5 311	...	...
45 - 49	C	774	...	...	510	...	...	264	...	...
50+	C	23	...	...	19	...	...	4	...	...
Unk.- Inc.	C	29 943	...	...	11 730	...	...	18 213	...	...
San Marino - Saint-Marin										
2003										
Total	+C	300	161	139	...	...	...	...	...	...
0 - 14	+C	1	-	1	...	...	...	...	...	...
15 - 19	+C	4	1	3	...	...	...	...	...	...
20 - 24	+C	17	10	7	...	...	...	...	...	...
25 - 29	+C	72	40	32	...	...	...	...	...	...
30 - 34	+C	121	66	55	...	...	...	...	...	...
35 - 39	+C	73	36	37	...	...	...	...	...	...
40 - 44	+C	11	8	3	...	...	...	...	...	...
45+	+C	1	-	1	...	...	...	...	...	...
Serbia and Montenegro - Serbie-et-Montenegro[34]										
2002										
Total	C	86 600	44 678	41 922	54 356	28 102	26 254	32 244	16 576	15 668
0 - 14	C	61	27	34	27	13	14	34	14	20

10. Live births by age of mother, sex of the child and urban/rural residence: latest available year, 1994 - 2003

Naissances vivantes selon l'âge de la mère, le sexe de l'enfant et la résidence, urbaine/rurale: dernière année disponible, 1994 - 2003 (continued — suite)

Continent, country or area, year and age (in years) / Continent, pays ou zone, année et âge (en années)	Code[1]	Total			Urban - Urbaine			Rural - Rurale		
		Both sexes - Les deux sexes	Male - Masculin	Female - Féminin	Both sexes - Les deux sexes	Male - Masculin	Female - Féminin	Both sexes - Les deux sexes	Male - Masculin	Female - Féminin
EUROPE										
Serbia and Montenegro - Serbie-et-Montenegro[34]										
2002										
15 - 19	C	6 575	3 366	3 209	3 110	1 602	1 508	3 465	1 764	1 701
20 - 24	C	26 273	13 546	12 727	14 776	7 637	7 139	11 497	5 909	5 588
25 - 29	C	29 054	14 998	14 056	18 801	9 718	9 083	10 253	5 280	4 973
30 - 34	C	16 743	8 639	8 104	11 922	6 153	5 769	4 821	2 486	2 335
35 - 39	C	6 020	3 119	2 901	4 395	2 284	2 111	1 625	835	790
40 - 44	C	1 288	678	610	940	497	443	348	181	107
45 - 49	C	76	40	36	56	35	21	20	5	15
50+	C	10	6	4	5	3	2	5	3	2
Unk.- Inc.	C	500	259	241	324	160	164	176	99	77
Slovakia - Slovaquie										
2002										
Total	C	50 841	26 015	24 826	26 321	13 449	12 872	24 520	12 566	11 954
0 - 14	C	37	13	24	22	7	15	15	6	9
15 - 19	C	4 543	2 284	2 259	1 890	916	974	2 653	1 368	1 285
20 - 24	C	15 619	8 039	7 580	7 214	3 661	3 553	8 405	4 378	4 027
25 - 29	C	18 557	9 472	9 085	10 207	5 275	4 932	8 350	4 197	4 153
30 - 34	C	8 434	4 350	4 084	4 910	2 529	2 381	3 524	1 821	1 703
35 - 39	C	3 050	1 556	1 494	1 733	887	846	1 317	669	648
40 - 44	C	577	291	286	330	167	163	247	124	123
45 - 49	C	24	10	14	15	7	8	9	3	6
Slovenia - Slovénie										
2003										
Total	C	17 321	8 930	8 391	8 425	4 344	4 081	8 896	4 586	4 310
0 - 14	C	2	1	1	1	-	1	1	1	-
15 - 19	C	366	204	162	160	90	70	206	114	92
20 - 24	C	3 177	1 662	1 515	1 300	701	599	1 877	961	916
25 - 29	C	6 881	3 568	3 313	3 186	1 632	1 554	3 695	1 936	1 759
30 - 34	C	4 939	2 510	2 429	2 671	1 351	1 320	2 268	1 159	1 109
35 - 39	C	1 678	840	838	937	476	461	741	364	377
40 - 44	C	268	136	132	162	87	75	106	49	57
45 - 49	C	10	9	1	8	7	1	2	2	-
Spain - Espagne										
2002										
Total	C	418 846	215 995	202 851	...	...	...	...	...	...
0 - 14	C	121	62	59	...	...	...	...	...	...
15 - 19	C	11 745	6 148	5 597	...	...	...	...	...	...
20 - 24	C	43 027	22 121	20 906	...	...	...	...	...	...
25 - 29	C	111 537	57 462	54 075	...	...	...	...	...	...
30 - 34	C	162 267	83 663	78 604	...	...	...	...	...	...
35 - 39	C	77 838	40 134	37 704	...	...	...	...	...	...
40 - 44	C	11 751	6 118	5 633	...	...	...	...	...	...
45 - 49	C	525	267	258	...	...	...	...	...	...
50+	C	35	20	15	...	...	...	...	...	...
Sweden - Suède										
2002										
Total	C	95 815	...	...	...	...	...	...	...	...
12 - 14	C	5	...	...	...	...	...	...	...	...
15 - 19	C	1 691	...	...	...	...	...	...	...	...
20 - 24	C	12 081	...	...	...	...	...	...	...	...
25 - 29	C	30 818	...	...	...	...	...	...	...	...
30 - 34	C	33 423	...	...	...	...	...	...	...	...
35 - 39	C	15 151	...	...	...	...	...	...	...	...
40 - 44	C	2 545	...	...	...	...	...	...	...	...
45 - 49	C	96	...	...	...	...	...	...	...	...
50+	C	5	...	...	...	...	...	...	...	...

10. Live births by age of mother, sex of the child and urban/rural residence: latest available year, 1994 - 2003

Naissances vivantes selon l'âge de la mère, le sexe de l'enfant et la résidence, urbaine/rurale: dernière année disponible, 1994 - 2003 (continued — suite)

Continent, country or area, year and age (in years) / Continent, pays ou zone, année et âge (en années)	Code[1]	Total Both sexes - Les deux sexes	Total Male - Masculin	Total Female - Féminin	Urban - Urbaine Both sexes - Les deux sexes	Urban - Urbaine Male - Masculin	Urban - Urbaine Female - Féminin	Rural - Rurale Both sexes - Les deux sexes	Rural - Rurale Male - Masculin	Rural - Rurale Female - Féminin
EUROPE										
Switzerland - Suisse										
2001										
Total	C	73 509	37 739	35 770	49 292	25 221	24 071	24 217	12 518	11 699
0 - 14	C	2	2	-	2	2	-	-	-	-
15 - 19	C	1 144	588	556	825	427	398	319	161	158
20 - 24	C	8 919	4 578	4 341	6 131	3 098	3 033	2 788	1 480	1 308
25 - 29	C	22 003	11 362	10 641	14 119	7 276	6 843	7 884	4 086	3 798
30 - 34	C	27 327	14 025	13 302	18 207	9 356	8 851	9 120	4 669	4 451
35 - 39	C	12 187	6 193	5 994	8 587	4 347	4 240	3 600	1 846	1 754
40 - 44	C	1 856	947	909	1 367	683	684	489	264	225
45 - 49	C	60	37	23	43	25	18	17	12	5
50+	C	11	7	4	11	7	4	-	-	-
2002										
Total	C	72 372	...	...	...	...	...	...	...	...
12 - 14	C	1	...	...	...	...	...	...	...	...
15 - 19	C	1 105	...	...	...	...	...	...	...	...
20 - 24	C	8 680	...	...	...	...	...	...	...	...
25 - 29	C	21 080	...	...	...	...	...	...	...	...
30 - 34	C	26 795	...	...	...	...	...	...	...	...
35 - 39	C	12 656	...	...	...	...	...	...	...	...
40 - 44	C	1 963	...	...	...	...	...	...	...	...
45 - 49	C	83	...	...	...	...	...	...	...	...
50+	C	9	...	...	...	...	...	...	...	...
The Former Yugoslav Rep. of Macedonia - L'ex-République yougoslave de Macédoine										
2002										
Total	C	27 761	14 312	13 449	14 909	7 706	7 203	12 852	6 606	6 246
0 - 14	C	35	16	19	27	10	17	8	6	2
15 - 19	C	2 062	1 067	995	1 046	558	488	1 016	509	507
20 - 24	C	9 338	4 916	4 422	4 711	2 480	2 231	4 627	2 436	2 191
25 - 29	C	9 764	5 006	4 758	5 337	2 750	2 587	4 427	2 256	2 171
30 - 34	C	4 828	2 434	2 394	2 793	1 391	1 402	2 035	1 043	992
35 - 39	C	1 417	703	714	807	413	394	610	290	320
40 - 44	C	287	152	135	172	96	76	115	56	59
45 - 49	C	11	8	3	7	4	3	4	4	-
Unk.- Inc.	C	19	10	9	9	4	5	10	6	4
2003										
Total	C	27 011	...	...	...	...	...	...	...	...
12 - 14	C	20	...	...	...	...	...	...	...	...
15 - 19	C	2 050	...	...	...	...	...	...	...	...
20 - 24	C	8 843	...	...	...	...	...	...	...	...
25 - 29	C	9 648	...	...	...	...	...	...	...	...
30 - 34	C	4 700	...	...	...	...	...	...	...	...
35 - 39	C	1 456	...	...	...	...	...	...	...	...
40 - 44	C	245	...	...	...	...	...	...	...	...
45 - 49	C	13	...	...	...	...	...	...	...	...
50 - 50	C	4	...	...	...	...	...	...	...	...
Unk.- Inc.	C	32	...	...	...	...	...	...	...	...
Ukraine[15]										
2003										
Total	C	408 589	...	...	266 415	...	...	142 174	...	...
0 - 14	C	138	...	...	67	...	...	71	...	...
15 - 19	C	54 290	...	...	30 068	...	...	24 222	...	...
20 - 24	C	163 197	...	...	105 040	...	...	58 157	...	...
25 - 29	C	113 417	...	...	77 600	...	...	35 817	...	...
30 - 34	C	54 269	...	...	37 746	...	...	16 523	...	...
35 - 39	C	18 051	...	...	12 294	...	...	5 757	...	...
40 - 44	C	3 924	...	...	2 501	...	...	1 423	...	...

10. Live births by age of mother, sex of the child and urban/rural residence: latest available year, 1994 - 2003

Naissances vivantes selon l'âge de la mère, le sexe de l'enfant et la résidence, urbaine/rurale: dernière année disponible, 1994 - 2003 (continued — suite)

Continent, country or area, year and age (in years) / Continent, pays ou zone, année et âge (en années)	Code[1]	Total			Urban - Urbaine			Rural - Rurale		
		Both sexes - Les deux sexes	Male - Masculin	Female - Féminin	Both sexes - Les deux sexes	Male - Masculin	Female - Féminin	Both sexes - Les deux sexes	Male - Masculin	Female - Féminin
EUROPE										
Ukraine[15]										
2003										
45 - 49	C	162	...	...	103	...	...	59	...	...
50+	C	5	...	...	5	...	...	-	...	...
Unk.- Inc.	C	1 136	...	...	991	...	...	145	...	...
United Kingdom - Royaume-Uni[35,36]										
2003										
Total	C	695 549	356 578	338 971	...	...	...	...	...	...
0 - 14	C	242	127	115	...	...	...	...	...	...
15 - 19	C	49 633	25 604	24 029	...	...	...	...	...	...
20 - 24	C	259 733	66 658	63 208	...	...	...	...	...	...
25 - 29	C	175 473	89 709	85 764	...	...	...	...	...	...
30 - 34	C	210 071	107 737	102 334	...	...	...	...	...	...
35 - 39	C	109 038	55 976	53 062	...	...	...	...	...	...
40 - 44	C	20 233	10 272	9 961	...	...	...	...	...	...
45 - 49	C	853	433	420	...	...	...	...	...	...
50+	C	80	34	46	...	...	...	...	...	...
Unk.- Inc.	C	60	28	32	...	...	...	...	...	...
OCEANIA — OCEANIE										
Australia - Australie										
2003										
Total	+C	251 161	129 193	121 968	...	...	...	...	...	...
0 - 14	+C	79	43	36	...	...	...	...	...	...
15 - 19	+C	10 732	5 525	5 207	...	...	...	...	...	...
20 - 24	+C	36 302	18 656	17 646	...	...	...	...	...	...
25 - 29	+C	69 604	35 768	33 836	...	...	...	...	...	...
30 - 34	+C	86 077	44 285	41 792	...	...	...	...	...	...
35 - 39	+C	39 876	20 478	19 398	...	...	...	...	...	...
40 - 44	+C	7 706	3 992	3 714	...	...	...	...	...	...
45 - 49	+C	318	192	126	...	...	...	...	...	...
50+	+C	12	10	2	...	...	...	...	...	...
Unk.- Inc.	+C	455	244	211	...	...	...	...	...	...
Guam[37]										
2003										
Total	C	3 298	1 682	1 616	...	...	...	...	...	...
0 - 14	C	3	2	1	...	...	...	...	...	...
15 - 19	C	355	179	176	...	...	...	...	...	...
20 - 24	C	883	462	421	...	...	...	...	...	...
25 - 29	C	854	450	404	...	...	...	...	...	...
30 - 34	C	717	347	370	...	...	...	...	...	...
35 - 39	C	389	184	205	...	...	...	...	...	...
40 - 44	C	87	53	34	...	...	...	...	...	...
45 - 49	C	6	2	4	...	...	...	...	...	...
50+	C	1	1	-	...	...	...	...	...	...
Unk.- Inc.	C	3	2	1	...	...	...	...	...	...
Kiribati										
1996										
Total	U	2 299	...	...	...	...	...	...	...	...
0 - 14	U	1	...	...	...	...	...	...	...	...
15 - 19	U	131	...	...	...	...	...	...	...	...
20 - 24	U	469	...	...	...	...	...	...	...	...
25 - 29	U	631	...	...	...	...	...	...	...	...
30 - 34	U	616	...	...	...	...	...	...	...	...
35 - 39	U	363	...	...	...	...	...	...	...	...
40 - 44	U	74	...	...	...	...	...	...	...	...
45 - 49	U	14	...	...	...	...	...	...	...	...

10. Live births by age of mother, sex of the child and urban/rural residence: latest available year, 1994 - 2003

Naissances vivantes selon l'âge de la mère, le sexe de l'enfant et la résidence, urbaine/rurale: dernière année disponible, 1994 - 2003 (continued — suite)

Continent, country or area, year and age (in years) / Continent, pays ou zone, année et âge (en années)	Code[1]	Total — Both sexes - Les deux sexes	Total — Male - Masculin	Total — Female - Féminin	Urban - Urbaine — Both sexes - Les deux sexes	Urban - Urbaine — Male - Masculin	Urban - Urbaine — Female - Féminin	Rural - Rurale — Both sexes - Les deux sexes	Rural - Rurale — Male - Masculin	Rural - Rurale — Female - Féminin
OCEANIA — OCEANIE										
Marshall Islands - Îles Marshall[38]										
1999										
Total	+U	1 478	...	...	...	...	...	...	...	...
0 - 14	+U	3	...	...	...	...	...	...	...	...
15 - 19	+U	279	...	...	...	...	...	...	...	...
20 - 24	+U	482	...	...	...	...	...	...	...	...
25 - 29	+U	373	...	...	...	...	...	...	...	...
30 - 34	+U	211	...	...	...	...	...	...	...	...
35 - 39	+U	108	...	...	...	...	...	...	...	...
40 - 44	+U	19	...	...	...	...	...	...	...	...
50+	+U	1	...	...	...	...	...	...	...	...
New Caledonia - Nouvelle-Calédonie										
2003										
Total	C	4 102	...	...	...	...	...	...	...	...
0 - 14	C	-	...	...	...	...	...	...	...	...
15 - 19	C	190	...	...	...	...	...	...	...	...
20 - 24	C	1 017	...	...	...	...	...	...	...	...
25 - 29	C	1 215	...	...	...	...	...	...	...	...
30 - 34	C	1 030	...	...	...	...	...	...	...	...
35 - 39	C	518	...	...	...	...	...	...	...	...
40 - 44	C	130	...	...	...	...	...	...	...	...
45 - 49	C	2	...	...	...	...	...	...	...	...
New Zealand - Nouvelle-Zélande[2]										
2003										
Total	+C	56 134	28 820	27 314	49 166	25 215	23 951	6 878	3 558	3 320
0 - 14	+C	29	12	17	28	11	17	1	1	-
15 - 19	+C	3 755	1 903	1 852	3 347	1 684	1 663	398	212	186
20 - 24	+C	9 467	4 863	4 604	8 488	4 344	4 144	947	505	442
25 - 29	+C	13 990	7 243	6 747	12 258	6 342	5 916	1 715	890	825
30 - 34	+C	17 523	8 989	8 534	15 245	7 811	7 434	2 259	1 170	1 089
35 - 39	+C	9 304	4 744	4 560	8 060	4 126	3 934	1 236	612	624
40 - 44	+C	1 975	1 015	960	1 665	855	810	307	159	148
45 - 49	+C	86	49	37	70	40	30	15	9	6
50+	+C	5	2	3	5	2	3	-	-	-
Northern Mariana Islands - Îles Mariannes septentrionales										
1999										
Total	U	1 448	...	...	...	...	...	...	...	...
0 - 14	U	2	...	...	...	...	...	...	...	...
15 - 19	U	157	...	...	...	...	...	...	...	...
20 - 24	U	313	...	...	...	...	...	...	...	...
25 - 29	U	385	...	...	...	...	...	...	...	...
30 - 34	U	360	...	...	...	...	...	...	...	...
35 - 39	U	145	...	...	...	...	...	...	...	...
40 - 44	U	34	...	...	...	...	...	...	...	...
45 - 49	U	1	...	...	...	...	...	...	...	...
50+	U	51	...	...	...	...	...	...	...	...
Palau - Palaos										
1999										
Total	C	250	...	...	...	...	...	...	...	...
15 - 19	C	20	...	...	...	...	...	...	...	...
20 - 24	C	40	...	...	...	...	...	...	...	...
25 - 29	C	70	...	...	...	...	...	...	...	...
30 - 34	C	77	...	...	...	...	...	...	...	...
35 - 39	C	33	...	...	...	...	...	...	...	...
40 - 44	C	10	...	...	...	...	...	...	...	...

10. Live births by age of mother, sex of the child and urban/rural residence: latest available year, 1994 - 2003

Naissances vivantes selon l'âge de la mère, le sexe de l'enfant et la résidence, urbaine/rurale: dernière année disponible, 1994 - 2003 (continued — suite)

Continent, country or area, year and age (in years) / Continent, pays ou zone, année et âge (en années)	Code[1]	Total			Urban - Urbaine			Rural - Rurale		
		Both sexes - Les deux sexes	Male - Masculin	Female - Féminin	Both sexes - Les deux sexes	Male - Masculin	Female - Féminin	Both sexes - Les deux sexes	Male - Masculin	Female - Féminin
OCEANIA — OCEANIE										
Tonga										
2000										
Total	+C	2 471	...	...	...	...	...	...	...	...
0 - 14	+C	2	...	...	...	...	...	...	...	...
15 - 19	+C	101	...	...	...	...	...	...	...	...
20 - 24	+C	528	...	...	...	...	...	...	...	...
25 - 29	+C	695	...	...	...	...	...	...	...	...
30 - 34	+C	688	...	...	...	...	...	...	...	...
35 - 39	+C	314	...	...	...	...	...	...	...	...
40 - 44	+C	122	...	...	...	...	...	...	...	...
45 - 49	+C	14	...	...	...	...	...	...	...	...
Unk.- Inc.	+C	7	...	...	...	...	...	...	...	...

FOOTNOTES - NOTES

Italics: data from civil registers which are incomplete or of unknown completeness. — *Italiques:* données incomplètes ou dont le degré d'exactitude n'est pas connu provenant des registres de l'état civil.

[1] 'Code' indicates the source of data, as follows:
C - Civil registration, estimated over 90% complete
U - Civil registration, estimated less than 90% complete
| - Other source, estimated reliable
+ - Data tabulated by date of registration rather than occurence.
... - Information not available

Le 'Code' indique la source des données, comme suit:
C - Registres de l'état civil considérés complèts à 90 p. 100 au moins.
U - Registres de l'état civil qui ne sont pas considérés complèts à 90 p. 100 au moins.
| - Autre source, considérée pas douteuses.
+ - Données exploitées selon la date de l'enregistrement et non la date de l'événement.
... - Information pas disponible.

[2] Figures for urban and rural areas do not add up to the total, since they do not include the category 'Unknown residence'. - La somme des donées pour la residence urbaine et rurale n'est pas égale au total parce qu'elle n'inclue pas la catégorie 'Residence inconnue'.
[3] For 2001, data refer to last twelve months preceding census on August 2001. - Pour 2001, les données se rapportent pour la dernière fois à douze mois précédant le recensement août 2001.
[4] Excluding live-born infants who died before their birth was registered. - Non compris les enfants nés vivants décédés avant l'enregistrement de leur naissance.
[5] Data for 1997 refer to last twelve months preceding population and housing census of 1997. - Les données pour 1997 se réfèrent au douze mois précédant le recensement de population et de l'habitat de 1997.
[6] Data as reported by national statistical authorities; they may differ from data presented in other tables. - Les données comme elles ont été déclarées par l'institut national de la statistique; elles peuvent être différentes de ceux présentées dans autre tableaux.
[7] Including Canadian residents temporarily in the United States, but excluding United States residents temporarily in Canada. - Y compris les résidents canadiens se trouvant temporairement aux Etats-Unis, mais ne comprenant pas les résidents des Etats-Unis se trouvant temporairement au Canada.
[8] Including births to non-resident mothers. - Y compris les naissances chez des mères non résidentes.

[9] Age classification is based on year of birth of mother rather than the exact age of mother at birth of child. - Le classement selon l'âge est basé sur l'année de naissance de la mère et non sur l'age exacte de la mère au moment de naissance de l'enfant.
[10] Excluding Indian jungle population. - Non compris les Indiens de la jungle.
[11] Data on live births and deaths are based on a civil registration system put in place in January 1998. - Les données sur les naissances et les décès sont basées sur un système d'enregistrement des faits d'état clvll mls en place en janvier 1998.
[12] Excluding nomadic Indian tribes. - Non compris les tribus d'Indiens nomades.
[13] Data refer to registered live births only. - Les données concernent les naissances vivantes enregistrées seulement.
[14] Data for urban refer to the total of the district of Paramaribo (capital) and Wanica district. - Les données relatives aux zones urbaines correspondent au total pour le district de Paramaribo (capitale) et le district de Wanica.
[15] Excluding infants born alive with less than 28 weeks gestation, less than 1 000 grams in weight and 35 centimeters in length, who die within seven days of birth. - Non compris les enfants nés vivants avant 28 semaines de gestation, pesant moins de 1 000 grammes, mesurant moins de 35 centimètres et décédés dans les sept jours qui ont suivi leur naissance.
[16] Including unknown sex. - Y compris le sexe inconnu.
[17] Data refer to government controlled areas. - Les données se raportent aux zones contrôlées par le Gouvernement.
[18] Published by the United Nations Economic and Social Commission for Western Asia. - Publié par la Commission économique et sociale des Nations Unies pour l'Asie occidentale.
[19] Beginning 1970, including data for East Jerusalem and Israeli residents in certain other territories under occupation by Israeli military forces since 1967. - A partir de 1970, y compris les données pour Jérusalem-Est et les résidents israéliens dans certains autres territoires occupés depuis juin 1967 par les forces armées israéliennes.
[20] Data refer to Japanese nationals in Japan only. - Les données se raportent aux nationaux japonais au Japon seulement.
[21] Excluding alien armed forces, civilian aliens employed by armed forces, and foreign diplomatic personnel and their dependants. - Non compris les militaires étrangers, les civils étrangers employés par les forces armées ni le personnel diplomatique étranger et les membres de leur famille les accompagnant.
[22] Data refer to Peninsular Malaysia only. - Les données ne concernent que la partie péninsulaire de la Malaisie.
[23] Data for urban refer to 170 towns out of 254 towns and data for rural refer to 62 townships out of 158 townships. - Les données urbaines se rapportent à 170 des 254 villes et les données rurales se rapportent à 62 des 158 municipalités.
[24] Based on the results of the Population Growth Survey. - D'après

les résultats de la 'Population Growth Survey.'

[25] Excluding data for the Pakistan-held part of Jammu and Kashmir, the final status of which has not yet been determined. - Non compris les données concernant la partie du Jammu et Cachemire occupée par le Pakistan dont le statut définitif n'a pas été déterminé.

[26] Excluding transients afloat and military and civilian services personnel and their dependants abroad. - Non compris les personnes de passage à bord de navires ni les militaires et agents civils et les membres de leur famille les accompagnant à l'étranger.

[27] Excluding Faeroe Islands and Greenland. - Non compris les Iles Féroé et Gröenland.

[28] Including nationals temporarily outside the country. - Y compris les nationaux se trouvant temporairement hors du pays.

[29] Including armed forces stationed outside the country. - Y compris les militaires nationaux hors du pays.

[30] Urban/rural figures, excluding nationals outside the country. - Les chiffres urbaine/rurale, non compris les nationaux hors du pays.

[31] Births registered within one year of occurrence. - Naissances enregistrées dans l'année qui suit l'événement.

[32] Live births to Maltese parents only. - Naissances vivantes aux parents maltais seulement.

[33] Including residents outside the country if listed in a Netherlands population register. - Y compris les résidents hors du pays, s'ils sont inscrits sur un registre de population néerlandais.

[34] From 2002, without data for Kosovo and Metohia. - Après 2002, sans les donées pour le Kosovo and Metohie.

[35] Data revised to exclude births in Northern Ireland to non-residents of Northern Ireland. - Données révisées non compris des naissances en Irlande du Nord aux non-résidents de l'Irlande du Nord.

[36] Data tabulated by date of occurrence for England and Wales, and by date of registration for Northern Ireland and Scotland. - Données exploitées selon la date de l'événement pour l'Angleterre et le pays de Galles, et selon la date de l'enregistrement pour l'Irlande du Nord et l'Ecosse.

[37] Including United States military personnel, their dependants and contract employees. - Y compris les militaires des Etats-Unis, les membres de leur famille les accompagnant et les agents contractuels des Etats-Unis.

[38] Excluding United States military personnel, their dependants and contract employees. - Non compris les militaires des Etats-Unis, les membres de leur famille les accompagnant et les agents contractuels des Etats-Unis.

Table 11

Table 11 presents live-birth rates by age of mother and urban/rural residence for the latest available year.

Description of variables: Age is defined as age at last birthday preceding the live birth, that is, the difference between the date of birth and the date of the occurrence of the event, expressed in completed solar years. The age classification used in this table is the following: under 20 years, 5-year age groups through 40-44 years, and 45 years or over.

Rate computation: Live-birth rates specific to age of mother are the annual number of births to women in each age group (as shown in table 10) per 1 000 female population in the same age group.

Birth rates by age of mother and urban/rural residence are the annual number of live births that occurred to a specific age-urban/rural group (as shown in table 10) per 1 000 females in the corresponding age-urban/rural group. These rates have been calculated by the Statistics Division of the United Nations.

Since relatively few births occur to women below 15 or above 50 years of age, birth rates for women under 20 years of age and for those 45 years of age or over are computed on the female population aged 15-19 and 45-49, respectively. Similarly, the rate for women of "All ages" is based on all live births irrespective of age of mother, and is computed on the female population aged 15-49 years. This rate for "All ages" is known as the general fertility rate.

Births to mothers of unknown age are distributed proportionately across the age groups, by the Statistics Division of the United Nations, in accordance with the distribution of births by age of mother prior to the calculation of the rates.

The population used in computing the rates is the estimated or enumerated distribution of females by age. First priority is given to an estimate for the mid-point of the same year (as shown in table 7), second priority to census returns of the year to which the births referred, and third priority to an estimate for some other point of time in the year.

Rates presented in this table are limited to those for countries or areas having at least a total of 100 live births in a given year.

Reliability of data: Rates are not computed if the data on live births from civil registers are reported as incomplete (less than 90 per cent completeness) or of unknown completeness. Table 9 and the technical notes for that table provide more detailed information on the completeness of live-birth registration. For more information about the quality of vital statistics data in general, and the information available on the basis of the completeness of estimates in particular, see section 4.2 of the Technical Notes.

Limitations: Rates shown in this table are subject to the same limitations that affect the corresponding frequencies and are set forth in the technical notes for table 10. These include differences in the completeness of registration, the treatment of infants who were born alive but died before the registration of the birth or within the first 24 hours of life, the method used to determine age of mother and the quality of the reported information relating to age of mother. In addition, some rates are based on births tabulated by date of registration and not by date of occurrence; these have been indicated by a plus sign "+".

The effect of including delayed registration on the distribution of births by age of mother may be noted in the age-specific fertility rates for women at older ages. In some cases, high age-specific rates for women aged 45 years and over may reflect age of mother at registration of birth and not fertility at these older ages.

The comparability of data by urban/rural residence is affected by the national definitions of urban and rural used in tabulating these data. It is assumed, in the absence of specific information to the contrary, that the definitions of urban and rural used in connection with the national population census were also used in the compilation of the vital statistics for each country or area. However, it is possible that, for a given country or area, the definitions of urban and rural used for both the vital statistics data and the population census data are not the same. When known, the definitions of urban used in national population censuses are presented at the end of the technical notes for table 6. As discussed in detail in the technical notes for table 6, these definitions vary considerably from one country or area to another.

In addition to problems of comparability, vital rates classified by urban/rural residence are also subject to certain special types of bias. If, when calculating vital rates, different definitions of urban are used in connection with the vital events and the population data and if this results in a net difference between the numerator and denominator of the rate in the population at risk, then the vital rates would be biased. Urban/rural differentials in vital rates may also be affected by whether the vital events have been tabulated in terms of place of occurrence or place of usual residence. This problem is discussed in more detail in section 4.1.4.1 of the Technical Notes.

Earlier data: Live-birth rates specific for age of mother have been shown for the latest available year in each issue of the Yearbook. Data included in this table update the series covering a period of years as follows:

Issue	Years Covered
Special Topic on Natality, CD, 1999	1990 – 1998
Historical Supplement CD, 1997	1948 – 1997
1992	1983 – 1992
1986	1977 – 1985
1981	1972 – 1980
Historical Supplement, 1979	1948 - 1977

Tableau 11

Le tableau 11 présente les taux des naissances vivantes selon l'âge de la mère et selon le lieu de résidence (zone urbaine ou rurale) correspondant aux données les plus récentes dont on dispose.

Description des variables : L'âge désigne l'âge au dernier anniversaire précédant la naissance, c'est-à-dire la différence entre la date de naissance et la date de l'événement, exprimée en années solaires révolues. La classification par âge utilisée dans le tableau 11 comprend les catégories suivantes : moins de 20 ans, groupes quinquennaux jusqu'à 40-44 ans, et 45 et plus.

Calcul des taux : Les taux des naissances vivantes selon l'âge de la mère représentent le nombre annuel de naissances dans chaque groupe d'âge (voir tableau 10) pour 1 000 femmes des mêmes groupes d'âge.

Les taux de natalité selon l'âge de la mère et le lieu de résidence (zone urbaine ou rurale) représentent le nombre annuel de naissances vivantes intervenues dans un groupe d'âge donné parmi la population urbaine ou rurale (comme il est indiqué au tableau 10) pour 1 000 femmes du groupe d'âge correspondant parmi la population urbaine ou rurale. Ces taux ont été calculés par la Division de statistique de l'ONU.

Étant donné que le nombre de naissances parmi les femmes de moins de 15 ans ou de plus de 50 ans est relativement peu élevé, les taux de natalité parmi les femmes âgées de moins de 20 ans et celles de 45 ans et plus ont été calculés sur la base des populations féminines âgées de 15 à 19 ans et de 45 à 49 ans, respectivement. De même, le taux pour les femmes de « tous âges » est fondé sur la totalité des naissances vivantes, indépendamment de l'âge de la mère et ce chiffre est rapporté à l'effectif de la population féminine âgée de 15 à 49 ans. Ce taux « tous âges » est le taux global de fécondité.

Les naissances pour lesquelles l'âge de la mère était inconnu ont été réparties par la Division de statistique de l'ONU, avant le calcul des taux, suivant les proportions observées pour celles où l'âge de la mère était connu.

Les chiffres de population utilisés pour le calcul des taux proviennent de dénombrements ou de répartitions estimatives de la population féminine selon l'âge. On a utilisé de préférence les estimations de la population au milieu de l'année considérée selon les chiffres du tableau 7 ; à défaut, on s'est contenté des données censitaires se rapportant à l'année des naissances et, si ces données manquaient également, d'estimations établies à un autre moment de l'année.

Les taux présentés dans ce tableau ne concernent que les pays ou zones où l'on a enregistré un total d'au moins 100 naissances vivantes dans une année donnée.

Fiabilité des données : On a choisi de ne pas faire figurer dans le tableau 11 des taux calculés à partir de données sur les naissances vivantes issues de registres de l'état civil qui sont déclarées incomplètes (degré de complétude inférieur à 90 p. 100) ou dont le degré de complétude n'est pas connu. Le tableau 9 et les notes techniques qui s'y rapportent présentent des renseignements plus détaillés sur le degré de complétude de l'enregistrement des naissances vivantes. Pour plus de précisions sur la qualité des données reposant sur les statistiques de l'état civil en général et les estimations de complétude en particulier, voir la section 4.2 des Notes techniques.

Insuffisance des données : Les taux du tableau 11 appellent les mêmes réserves que celles concernant les fréquences correspondantes (voir à ce sujet les notes techniques relatives au tableau 10). Leurs imperfections tiennent notamment au degré de complétude de l'enregistrement, au classement des enfants nés vivants décédés avant l'enregistrement de leur naissance ou dans les 24 heures qui ont suivi la naissance, à la méthode utilisée pour déterminer l'âge de la mère et à l'exactitude des renseignements concernant l'âge de la mère. En outre, dans certains cas, les données relatives aux naissances sont exploitées selon la date de l'enregistrement et non selon la date de l'événement ; ces cas ont été signalés par le signe '+'.

On peut se rendre compte, d'après les taux relatifs aux groupes d'âge les plus avancés, des conséquences que peut avoir l'inclusion, dans les statistiques des naissances selon l'âge de la mère, des naissances enregistrées tardivement. Dans certains cas, il se peut que des taux élevés pour le groupe d'âge 45 ans et plus ne traduisent pas le niveau de fécondité de ce groupe d'âge, mais l'âge de la mère au moment où la naissance a été enregistrée.

La comparabilité des données selon le lieu de résidence (zone urbaine ou rurale) peut être limitée par les définitions nationales des termes « urbain » et « rural » utilisées pour le classement de ces données. En l'absence d'indications contraires, on a supposé que les mêmes définitions avaient servi pour le recensement national de la population et pour l'établissement des statistiques de l'état civil pour chaque pays ou zone. Toutefois, il n'est pas exclu que, pour une zone ou un pays donné, des définitions différentes aient été retenues. Les définitions du terme « urbain » utilisées pour les recensements nationaux de population ont été présentées à la fin du tableau 6 lorsqu'elles étaient connues. Comme on l'a précisé dans les notes techniques relatives au tableau 6, ces définitions varient considérablement d'un pays ou d'une zone à l'autre.

Outre les problèmes de comparabilité, les taux démographiques classés selon le lieu de résidence (zone urbaine ou rurale) sont également sujets à des distorsions particulières. Si l'on utilise des définitions différentes du terme « urbain » pour classer les faits d'état civil et les données relatives à la population lors du calcul des taux et qu'il en résulte une différence nette entre le numérateur et le dénominateur pour le taux de la population exposée au risque, les taux démographiques s'en trouveront faussés. La différence entre ces taux pour les zones urbaines et rurales pourra aussi être faussée selon que les faits d'état civil auront été classés d'après le lieu de l'événement ou d'après le lieu de résidence habituel. Ce problème est examiné plus en détail à la section 4.1.4.1 des Notes techniques.

Données publiées antérieurement : Les différentes éditions de l'*Annuaire démographique* regroupent les statistiques les plus récentes dont on disposait à l'époque sur les taux de naissances vivantes selon l'âge de la mère. Les données qui figurent dans le tableau 11 actualisent les données qui portaient sur les périodes suivantes :

Éditions	**Années considérées**
Édition spéciale sur les statistiques de la natalité (CD-ROM), 1999	1990 – 1998
Supplément historique (CD-ROM), 1997	1948 – 1997
1992	1983 – 1992
1986	1977 – 1985
1981	1972 – 1980
Supplément rétrospectif, 1979	1948 - 1977

11. Live-birth rates by age of mother and urban/rural residence: latest available year, 1994 - 2003
Naissances vivantes, taux selon l'âge de la mère et la résidence, urbaine/rurale: dernière année
disponible, 1994 - 2003

Continent, country or area, year and urban/rural residence — Continent, pays ou zone,année, et résidence urbaine/rurale	Age of mother (in years) - Age de la mère (en années)							
	All ages Tous âges[1]	-20[2]	20-24	25-29	30-34	35-39	40-44	45+[3]
AFRICA — AFRIQUE								
Egypt - Égypte								
1999								
Total	108.4	18.5	192.8	226.3	162.8	87.7	25.7	6.7
Mauritius - Maurice								
2003								
Total	56.3	37.1	109.7	110.6	71.8	35.8	8.7	0.6
Morocco - Maroc								
2001								
Total	66.7	28.9	88.3	102.3	104.4	73.6	32.1	7.6
Urban - Urbaine	57.5	23.8	74.5	90.2	89.9	63.4	24.9	4.2
Rural - Rurale	80.5	34.7	106.0	120.9	132.0	93.7	45.4	13.1
Namibia - Namibie[4]								
2001								
Total	100.1	51.2	135.8	144.6	137.3	103.1	59.8	22.1
Urban - Urbaine	84.8	45.2	106.0	120.8	113.0	79.5	37.9	10.9
Rural - Rurale	110.4	53.8	156.5	166.0	158.2	121.6	74.7	28.3
Réunion[5]								
1999								
Total	72.0	35.1	115.9	143.0	107.1	61.3	15.1	1.3
Swaziland[6]								
1997								
Total	133.2	73.0	193.4	199.4	162.6	130.8	64.7	50.0
Urban - Urbaine	106.6	65.3	147.1	157.0	115.9	92.6	39.2	31.0
Rural - Rurale	143.5	75.4	214.3	219.4	182.0	145.4	73.4	55.5
Tunisia - Tunisie								
1998								
Total	67.8	7.5	66.0	112.3	110.3	64.7	21.2	3.4
AMERICA, NORTH — AMERIQUE DU NORD								
Anguilla[+]								
2001								
Total	57.6	61.7	136.3	102.2	49.8	37.7	15.6	...
Antigua and Barbuda - Antigua-et-Barbuda[+]								
1995								
Total	73.2	71.6	114.7	106.6	82.8	53.8	11.8	1.4
Bermuda - Bermudes								
2000								
Total	49.1	25.5	81.1	83.4	97.3	51.3	5.1	...
Canada[7]								
2002								
Total	40.5	15.2	54.0	95.4	89.4	36.1	6.2	0.2
Costa Rica								
2003								
Total	63.7	69.4	114.2	111.9	77.3	35.9	9.7	0.9
Cuba								
2003								
Total	45.5	48.3	97.9	90.1	60.0	24.5	4.7	0.2
Urban - Urbaine	43.6	41.7	94.3	90.2	61.0	24.8	4.6	0.2
Rural - Rurale	51.6	68.2	108.4	89.6	56.8	23.8	5.2	0.4
El Salvador								
2003								
Total	70.8	78.6	117.5	95.1	67.4	43.5	16.6	2.4
Urban - Urbaine	67.0	77.5	122.0	96.3	62.6	35.1	10.7	1.4
Rural - Rurale	77.0	79.9	111.3	93.2	76.5	61.3	29.6	4.4
Greenland - Groenland								
2000								
Total	62.4	60.9	154.8	126.0	75.9	35.9	7.3	0.6
Urban - Urbaine	58.7	52.8	153.3	118.8	72.5	33.1	6.9	0.7
Rural - Rurale	81.6	106.2	162.8	153.6	93.0	51.3	9.5	0.0

11. Live-birth rates by age of mother and urban/rural residence: latest available year, 1994 - 2003
Naissances vivantes, taux selon l'âge de la mère et la résidence, urbaine/rurale: dernière année disponible, 1994 - 2003 (continued — suite)

Continent, country or area, year and urban/rural residence / Continent, pays ou zone,année, et résidence urbaine/rurale	All ages Tous âges[1]	-20[2]	20-24	25-29	30-34	35-39	40-44	45+[3]
			Age of mother (in years) - Age de la mère (en années)					

AMERICA, NORTH — AMERIQUE DU NORD

	All ages Tous âges[1]	-20[2]	20-24	25-29	30-34	35-39	40-44	45+[3]
Grenada - Grenade+								
2000								
Total	76.5	54.7	107.0	132.7	113.8	64.1	26.7	1.1
Guadeloupe								
2003								
Total	60.4	25.9	81.3	132.3	108.6	64.6	19.3	0.8
Guatemala								
1999								
Total	141.4	110.3	211.2	193.4	162.6	128.3	60.1	13.8
Jamaica - Jamaïque[8]								
2003								
Total	65.7	69.7	111.2	90.3	76.6	47.8	17.0	0.9
Martinique[5,9]								
2003								
Total	52.3	26.2	67.7	116.7	99.2	57.2	16.7	0.7
Panama								
1999								
Total	86.6	97.4	148.3	128.8	95.0	51.0	13.3	1.8
Urban - Urbaine	71.7	81.1	127.1	109.7	81.7	40.3	8.5	0.3
Rural - Rurale	110.6	117.3	179.0	161.1	118.7	70.7	22.0	4.4
2000								
Total	85.7	95.8	148.7	128.2	94.8	50.8	14.2	1.8
Puerto Rico - Porto Rico								
2003								
Total	51.5	60.6	112.7	91.3	58.3	24.4	4.7	0.2
Saint Kitts and Nevis - Saint-Kitts-et-Nevis+								
2000								
Total	80.0	86.6	140.2	123.1	80.0	57.4	20.0	1.0
Saint Lucia - Sainte-Lucie								
2002								
Total	72.8	...	96.1	83.9	76.4	45.9	14.1	0.6
Saint Vincent and the Grenadines - Saint Vincent-et-les Grenadines+								
2000								
Total	80.3	73.0	128.5	100.1	80.0	72.8	16.5	0.6
Trinidad and Tobago - Trinité-et-Tobago								
1997								
Total	52.2	43.3	97.0	88.0	70.0	35.3	9.4	0.6
United States - États-Unis								
2002								
Total	55.2	43.7	103.6	113.6	91.5	41.4	8.3	0.5

AMERICA, SOUTH — AMERIQUE DU SUD

	All ages Tous âges[1]	-20[2]	20-24	25-29	30-34	35-39	40-44	45+[3]
Argentina - Argentine								
2003								
Total	73.8	59.1	115.1	117.6	107.7	61.6	18.5	1.4
Chile - Chili								
2003								
Total	55.0	50.3	87.5	94.8	81.7	47.3	13.4	0.7
French Guiana - Guyane française[5]								
2003								
Total	118.5	111.8	201.8	236.5	144.0	84.7	27.3	2.1
Suriname								
2000								
Total	85.4	68.3	150.1	148.2	104.3	56.2	16.0	1.8

11. Live-birth rates by age of mother and urban/rural residence: latest available year, 1994 - 2003
Naissances vivantes, taux selon l'âge de la mère et la résidence, urbaine/rurale: dernière année disponible, 1994 - 2003 (continued — suite)

Continent, country or area, year and urban/rural residence Continent, pays ou zone,année, et résidence urbaine/rurale	All ages Tous âges[1]	-20[2]	20-24	25-29	30-34	35-39	40-44	45+[3]
AMERICA, SOUTH — **AMERIQUE DU SUD**								
Uruguay								
2002								
Total	64.4	65.5	103.2	107.0	90.0	49.7	13.9	0.9
Venezuela[10]								
2002								
Total	74.3	84.8	129.0	109.9	80.1	42.9	14.1	2.9
ASIA — ASIE								
Armenia - Arménie[11]								
2000								
Total	31.7	27.3	103.2	53.7	23.5	10.6	3.0	0.3
Urban - Urbaine	20.0	22.1	92.3	53.5	22.7	10.2	2.8	0.3
Rural - Rurale	38.7	37.9	128.0	54.0	25.1	11.3	3.4	0.4
2003								
Total	39.4	29.3	126.6	71.5	29.6	10.2	2.4	0.2
Azerbaijan - Azerbaïdjan+,[11]								
2003								
Total	46.6	27.7	126.4	95.3	44.9	18.7	4.9	0.4
Urban - Urbaine	39.4	19.7	105.1	89.7	41.9	16.1	3.9	0.3
Rural - Rurale	54.9	36.2	149.8	101.3	48.1	21.6	6.0	0.6
Brunel Darussalam - Brunéi Darussalam+								
2001								
Total	73.7	29.9	90.9	125.0	108.1	68.0	24.5	1.8
China: Hong Kong SAR - Chine: Hong Kong RAS[12]								
2003								
Total	22.7	3.6	28.0	51.2	49.4	23.3	4.1	0.2
China: Macao SAR - Chine: Macao RAS								
2003								
Total	22.4	4.4	27.7	53.9	54.0	22.9	4.4	0.1
Cyprus - Chypre[13]								
2003								
Total	42.7	6.6	56.2	106.8	81.3	32.4	7.4	0.7
Georgia - Géorgie[11]								
2000								
Total	31.3	30.9	82.5	59.5	30.2	12.9	3.9	0.7
Urban - Urbaine	32.5	31.6	86.7	64.2	34.2	14.4	4.4	0.8
Rural - Rurale	29.4	30.0	77.0	52.1	24.1	10.5	3.1	0.6
2003								
Total	39.6	33.8	94.0	75.4	47.4	19.0	5.4	0.4
Israel - Israël[14]								
2003								
Total	88.4	15.5	113.6	180.9	163.7	90.8	22.6	1.9
Urban - Urbaine	87.6	16.0	114.6	178.7	158.8	89.0	22.2	1.9
Rural - Rurale	96.8	11.0	102.0	207.3	221.1	109.1	26.9	2.4
Japan - Japon[15]								
2003								
Total	39.3	5.7	37.0	88.4	85.1	33.2	4.5	0.1
Kazakhstan[11]								
2003								
Total	58.9	25.8	136.1	120.2	76.4	38.1	8.0	0.5
Urban - Urbaine	55.2	27.2	124.6	114.0	70.7	34.9	7.0	0.4
Rural - Rurale	64.5	24.3	153.1	129.7	85.6	43.2	9.7	0.7
Korea (Republic of) - Corée (République de)[16]								
2002								
Total	36.7	2.7	26.8	116.2	79.2	16.9	2.5	0.2

11. Live-birth rates by age of mother and urban/rural residence: latest available year, 1994 - 2003
Naissances vivantes, taux selon l'âge de la mère et la résidence, urbaine/rurale: dernière année disponible, 1994 - 2003 (continued — suite)

Continent, country or area, year and urban/rural residence / Continent, pays ou zone, année, et résidence urbaine/rurale	Age of mother (in years) - Age de la mère (en années)							
	All ages Tous âges[1]	-20[2]	20-24	25-29	30-34	35-39	40-44	45+[3]
ASIA — ASIE								
Kuwait - Koweït								
1998								
Total	86.7	20.8	131.5	147.3	113.7	71.0	31.2	6.4
Kyrgyzstan - Kirghizistan[11]								
2003								
Total	77.2	28.5	165.1	144.7	96.0	51.1	15.5	3.5
Urban - Urbaine	59.7	24.5	111.9	110.8	74.9	40.8	11.7	2.4
Rural - Rurale	88.3	30.3	203.9	168.3	111.2	58.1	18.1	4.2
Maldives								
2003								
Total	67.9	14.5	116.3	133.4	103.2	63.4	15.4	2.8
Mongolia - Mongolie								
2003								
Total	64.3	18.6	123.1	119.5	80.7	38.2	14.3	4.4
Pakistan[17,18]								
2001								
Total	120.8	24.2	162.0	242.9	197.2	118.5	57.9	21.9
Urban - Urbaine	103.0	18.6	135.8	227.9	176.7	96.2	41.9	12.6
Rural - Rurale	131.6	27.8	178.4	251.3	208.7	133.0	67.1	27.3
Philippines								
2000								
Total	91.1	31.6	139.2	163.1	132.4	86.3	36.1	6.2
Qatar								
1997								
Total	103.4	23.6	165.7	229.5	136.1	78.6	38.2	10.8
Singapore - Singapour[19]								
2003								
Total	38.6	7.0	33.7	85.4	94.5	37.8	6.3	0.2
Sri Lanka+								
1996								
Total	72.6	29.1	88.7	129.1	110.9	81.8	20.0	2.4
Turkey - Turquie[17]								
1997								
Total	81.1	50.0	173.6	144.9	73.3	36.1	15.5	3.4
Uzbekistan - Ouzbékistan[11]								
2000								
Total	82.7	21.1	205.4	161.4	89.7	31.5	7.0	0.8
Urban - Urbaine	65.7	21.8	167.9	123.6	73.0	26.6	5.4	0.5
Rural - Rurale	93.6	20.7	227.5	185.9	100.6	34.7	8.2	1.1
EUROPE								
Austria - Autriche								
2003								
Total	38.3	13.2	57.1	94.5	73.5	30.4	5.9	0.3
Belarus - Bélarus[11]								
2003								
Total	33.1	23.3	93.2	73.1	37.0	12.2	2.2	0.1
Urban - Urbaine	31.0	19.2	83.0	70.6	36.9	11.4	2.0	0.1
Rural - Rurale	40.9	37.3	139.7	82.6	37.3	14.7	3.0	0.2
Bulgaria - Bulgarie								
2003								
Total	35.6	40.4	80.5	75.3	37.2	11.3	1.8	0.1
Urban - Urbaine	33.4	31.0	69.4	76.3	39.5	11.9	1.8	0.1
Rural - Rurale	42.5	70.3	119.4	71.8	29.6	9.4	1.8	0.1
Channel Islands: Guernsey - Îles Anglo-Normandes: Guernesey								
1996								
Total	43.5	24.0	37.4	91.6	89.1	41.0	5.5	...
Croatia - Croatie								
2003								
Total	36.7	14.0	66.9	93.1	64.2	23.0	4.2	0.2

11. Live-birth rates by age of mother and urban/rural residence: latest available year, 1994 - 2003
Naissances vivantes, taux selon l'âge de la mère et la résidence, urbaine/rurale: dernière année disponible, 1994 - 2003 (continued — suite)

Continent, country or area, year and urban/rural residence / Continent, pays ou zone,année, et résidence urbaine/rurale	All ages Tous âges[1]	-20[2]	20-24	25-29	30-34	35-39	40-44	45+[3]
EUROPE								
Czech Republic - République tchèque								
2002								
Total	38.5	13.7	64.5	96.2	53.9	17.7	3.0	0.1
Urban - Urbaine	38.7	14.5	61.8	96.2	56.8	18.5	3.1	0.1
Rural - Rurale	38.1	11.7	72.2	96.3	45.2	15.0	2.6	0.1
2003								
Total	36.9	11.4	53.8	94.4	57.4	17.6	3.1	0.1
Denmark - Danemark[20]								
2003								
Total	52.0	6.0	46.4	125.6	121.2	46.6	7.7	0.3
Estonia - Estonie[11]								
2002								
Total	38.0	21.9	76.4	88.6	58.0	24.3	4.9	0.1
Urban - Urbaine	35.5	19.2	65.6	83.0	55.7	23.2	4.3	0.1
Rural - Rurale	44.5	27.4	112.5	106.6	64.1	27.0	6.2	0.1
Finland - Finlande[21]								
2003								
Total	47.5	10.4	57.0	115.5	106.9	49.4	10.8	0.5
Urban - Urbaine	46.8	11.1	49.5	103.5	103.6	49.2	10.6	0.5
Rural - Rurale	48.9	9.2	80.7	150.6	114.1	49.9	11.0	0.5
France[9,22]								
2002								
Total	53.1	8.1	55.9	129.4	117.7	51.7	11.4	0.6
Germany - Allemagne								
2003								
Total	36.0	11.7	50.5	86.3	78.4	33.5	5.5	0.2
Gibraltar								
2001								
Total	60.9	24.9	77.5	168.3	110.8	43.4	7.9	...
Greece - Grèce								
2003								
Total	38.4	11.1	43.7	82.3	77.7	34.9	6.3	0.7
Hungary - Hongrie								
2003								
Total	37.8	20.9	56.4	88.8	62.0	23.3	4.0	0.1
Urban - Urbaine	35.3	15.0	44.3	83.4	64.0	24.2	4.1	0.1
Rural - Rurale	41.8	32.2	80.0	98.9	56.4	20.8	3.7	0.1
Iceland - Islande								
2003								
Total	57.0	16.2	75.9	130.3	115.7	48.5	11.8	0.4
Urban - Urbaine	57.6	16.7	77.5	131.4	114.0	48.3	12.1	0.3
Rural - Rurale	49.1	11.0	56.3	110.1	143.9	51.1	7.9	1.5
Ireland - Irlande[+,23]								
2003								
Total	58.5	18.8	50.9	92.5	133.4	81.2	15.5	0.4
Italy - Italie								
2003								
Total	38.9	7.1	35.7	78.1	84.6	41.9	7.7	0.4
Latvia - Lettonie[11]								
2002								
Total	33.9	16.0	72.6	80.3	51.2	21.1	4.9	0.4
Urban - Urbaine	31.1	13.2	63.3	76.7	50.1	20.2	4.3	0.3
Rural - Rurale	40.5	21.4	93.3	89.0	53.8	23.1	6.7	0.6
Liechtenstein								
2003								
Total	38.5	8.8	32.2	91.9	90.1	40.0	5.9	0.8
Lithuania - Lituanie[11]								
2003								
Total	34.4	20.5	76.0	85.2	46.4	19.1	4.2	0.2
Urban - Urbaine	30.0	16.2	60.6	76.0	42.9	17.1	3.4	0.1
Rural - Rurale	45.8	28.9	118.1	112.3	55.8	24.0	6.4	0.2

11. Live-birth rates by age of mother and urban/rural residence: latest available year, 1994 - 2003
Naissances vivantes, taux selon l'âge de la mère et la résidence, urbaine/rurale: dernière année disponible, 1994 - 2003 (continued — suite)

Continent, country or area, year and urban/rural residence Continent, pays ou zone,année, et résidence urbaine/rurale	All ages Tous âges[1]	-20[2]	20-24	25-29	30-34	35-39	40-44	45+[3]
				Age of mother (in years) - Age de la mère (en années)				
EUROPE								
Luxembourg								
2003								
Total	47.0	11.1	57.5	103.4	102.5	43.9	8.3	0.4
Malta - Malte[24]								
2003								
Total	40.3	15.9	53.4	101.1	81.6	29.1	5.2	0.1
Netherlands - Pays-Bas[25]								
2002								
Total	51.0	5.8	36.8	97.6	133.4	58.2	9.2	0.4
Urban - Urbaine	50.1	7.3	38.5	88.0	123.9	59.2	10.3	0.5
Rural - Rurale	53.0	3.0	32.3	122.0	153.3	56.2	7.2	0.3
2003								
Total	50.7	7.1	41.3	109.6	131.3	52.9	7.0	0.3
Norway - Norvège[9]								
2002								
Total	51.8	10.1	59.5	121.0	109.3	44.1	7.7	0.2
Poland - Pologne								
2003								
Total	35.1	14.5	64.1	88.1	52.9	20.9	4.6	0.2
Urban - Urbaine	31.1	13.0	51.2	81.1	51.5	18.8	3.9	0.2
Rural - Rurale	42.1	16.8	88.0	100.8	55.1	24.3	6.1	0.3
Portugal								
2003								
Total	42.9	20.1	51.2	89.7	84.6	35.7	7.1	0.4
Republic of Moldova - République de Moldova[11]								
2003								
Total	35.8	29.2	89.7	67.6	40.7	13.8	2.6	0.1
Urban - Urbaine	28.8	18.9	76.8	62.6	34.4	12.2	2.2	0.1
Rural - Rurale	41.3	35.6	97.8	71.3	47.1	15.1	3.1	0.1
Romania - Roumanie								
2003								
Total	37.9	34.0	79.7	79.0	41.7	16.1	3.1	0.2
Urban - Urbaine	29.4	19.1	54.5	73.8	40.3	14.3	2.2	0.1
Rural - Rurale	51.1	54.2	117.3	86.1	43.8	19.2	4.9	0.3
Russian Federation - Fédération de Russie[11]								
1999								
Total	31.1	29.3	92.6	64.9	32.5	11.2	2.2	0.1
Urban - Urbaine	28.5	25.2	85.6	60.4	30.7	10.1	1.8	0.1
Rural - Rurale	39.4	40.4	114.4	79.8	37.8	14.4	3.5	0.2
2001								
Total	33.5	27.6	94.6	70.6	39.0	13.4	2.4	0.1
San Marino - Saint-Marin+								
2003								
Total	40.1	8.0	22.2	66.4	91.5	50.0	9.0	1.0
Serbia and Montenegro - Serbie-et-Montenegro[26]								
2000								
Total	47.9	25.2	105.5	108.9	62.6	24.5	4.9	0.5
Urban - Urbaine	46.7	21.7	98.2	116.1	70.6	27.2	5.2	0.4
Rural - Rurale	49.2	28.8	113.1	101.5	53.8	21.2	4.6	0.6
2001								
Total	49.5	25.3	105.7	113.6	66.3	25.9	5.1	0.4
Slovakia - Slovaquie								
2002								
Total	35.3	21.5	68.6	83.4	46.0	16.2	2.9	0.1
Slovenia - Slovénie								
2003								
Total	34.1	5.8	44.3	94.8	70.7	21.8	3.5	0.1
Urban - Urbaine	33.1	5.3	37.1	90.6	78.1	24.2	4.1	0.2
Rural - Rurale	36.4	6.4	52.8	103.3	66.6	20.3	3.0	0.1

11. Live-birth rates by age of mother and urban/rural residence: latest available year, 1994 - 2003
Naissances vivantes, taux selon l'âge de la mère et la résidence, urbaine/rurale: dernière année disponible, 1994 - 2003 (continued — suite)

Continent, pays ou zone, année, et résidence urbaine/rurale	All ages Tous âges[1]	-20[2]	20-24	25-29	30-34	35-39	40-44	45+[3]
EUROPE								
Spain - Espagne								
2001								
Total	39.1	10.0	27.4	65.5	95.1	45.8	7.4	0.4
Sweden - Suède								
2002								
Total	48.2	6.6	47.7	109.2	110.7	47.3	8.9	0.3
Switzerland - Suisse								
2002								
Total	40.4	5.4	40.7	89.9	94.5	40.4	6.8	0.4
The Former Yugoslav Rep. of Macedonia - L'ex-République yougoslave de Macédoine								
2003								
Total	51.5	25.4	112.1	127.9	64.4	19.7	3.4	0.2
Ukraine[11]								
2003								
Total	32.6	28.6	93.6	67.3	33.1	10.7	2.0	0.1
United Kingdom - Royaume-Uni[27,28]								
2003								
Total	48.6	26.6	70.1	95.9	94.5	45.9	9.1	0.5
OCEANIA — OCEANIE								
Australia - Australie[+]								
2003								
Total	50.2	16.1	53.8	102.8	112.7	54.4	10.0	0.5
New Caledonia - Nouvelle-Calédonie								
2003								
Total	71.2	20.3	109.2	129.5	118.9	64.8	18.3	0.3
New Zealand - Nouvelle-Zélande[+]								
2003								
Total	55.0	26.2	68.9	110.2	114.5	59.3	12.2	0.6
Urban - Urbaine	54.9	26.6	66.1	106.3	112.8	59.9	12.2	0.6
Rural - Rurale	54.8	22.8	105.9	147.5	126.3	55.3	12.3	0.7
Tonga[+]								
1999								
Total	110.2	28.3	128.3	220.2	201.6	128.2	49.3	3.2

FOOTNOTES - NOTES

[+] Data tabulated by date of registration rather than occurrence. — Données exploitées selon la date de l'enregistrement et non la date de l'événement.

[1] Rates computed on female population aged 15-49. — Taux calculés sur la base de la population féminine de 15 à 49 ans.

[2] Rates computed on female population aged 15-19. — Taux calculés sur la base de la population féminine de 15 à 19 ans.

[3] Rates computed on female population aged 45-49. — Taux calculés sur la base de la population féminine de 45 à 49 ans.

[4] For 2001, data refer to last twelve months preceding census on August 2001. - Pour 2001, les données se rapportent pour la dernière fois à douze mois précédant le recensement août 2001.

[5] Excluding live-born infants who died before their birth was registered. - Non compris les enfants nés vivants décédés avant l'enregistrement de leur naissance.

[6] Data for 1997 refer to last twelve months preceding population and housing census of 1997. - Les données pour 1997 se réfèrent au douze mois précédant le recensement de population et de l'habitat de 1997.

[7] Including Canadian residents temporarily in the United States, but excluding United States residents temporarily in Canada. - Y compris les résidents canadiens se trouvant temporairement aux Etats-Unis, mais ne comprenant pas les résidents des Etats-Unis se trouvant temporairement au Canada.

[8] Including births to non-resident mothers. - Y compris les naissances chez des mères non résidentes.

[9] Age classification is based on year of birth of mother rather than the exact age of mother at birth of child. - Le classement selon l'âge est basé sur l'année de naissance de la mère et non sur l'age exacte de la mère au moment de naissance de l'enfant.

[10] Excluding Indian jungle population. - Non compris les Indiens de la jungle.

[11] Excluding infants born alive with less than 28 weeks gestation, less than 1 000 grams in weight and 35 centimeters in length, who die within seven days of birth. - Non compris les enfants nés vivants avant 28 semaines de gestation, pesant moins de 1 000 grammes, mesurant moins de 35 centimètres et décédés dans les sept jours qui ont suivi leur naissance.

[12] Including unknown sex. - Y compris le sexe inconnu.

[13] Data refer to government controlled areas. - Les données se raportent aux zones contrôlées par le Gouvernement.

[14] Beginning 1970, including data for East Jerusalem and Israeli residents in certain other territories under occupation by Israeli military forces since 1967. - A partir de 1970, y compris les données pour Jérusalem-Est et les résidents israéliens dans certains autres territoires occupés depuis juin 1967 par les forces armées israéliennes.

[15] Data refer to Japanese nationals in Japan only. - Les données se raportent aux nationaux japonais au Japon seulement.

[16] Excluding alien armed forces, civilian aliens employed by armed forces, and foreign diplomatic personnel and their dependants. - Non compris les militaires étrangers, les civils étrangers employés par les forces armées ni le personnel diplomatique étranger et les membres de leur famille les accompagnant.

[17] Based on the results of the Population Growth Survey. - D'après les résultats de la 'Population Growth Survey.'

[18] Excluding data for the Pakistan-held part of Jammu and Kashmir, the final status of which has not yet been determined. - Non compris les données concernant la partie du Jammu et Cachemire occupée par le Pakistan dont le statut définitif n'a pas été déterminé.

[19] Excluding transients afloat and military and civilian services personnel and their dependants abroad. - Non compris les personnes de passage à bord de navires ni les militaires et agents civils et les membres de leur famille les accompagnant à l'étranger.

[20] Excluding Faeroe Islands and Greenland. - Non compris les Iles Féroé et Gröenland.

[21] Including nationals temporarily outside the country. - Y compris les nationaux se trouvant temporairement hors du pays.

[22] Including armed forces stationed outside the country. - Y compris les militaires nationaux hors du pays.

[23] Births registered within one year of occurrence. - Naissances enregistrées dans l'année qui suit l'événement.

[24] Live births to Maltese parents only. - Naissances vivantes aux parents maltais seulement.

[25] Including residents outside the country if listed in a Netherlands population register. - Y compris les résidents hors du pays, s'ils sont inscrits sur un registre de population néerlandais.

[26] From 2002, without data for Kosovo and Metohia. - Après 2002, sans les donées pour le Kosovo and Metohie.

[27] Data revised to exclude births in Northern Ireland to non-residents of Northern Ireland. - Données révisées non compris des naissances en Irlande du Nord aux non-résidents de l'Irlande du Nord.

[28] Data tabulated by date of occurrence for England and Wales, and by date of registration for Northern Ireland and Scotland. - Données exploitées selon la date de l'événement pour l'Angleterre et le pays de Galles, et selon la date de l'enregistrement pour l'Irlande du Nord et l'Ecosse.

Table 12

Table 12 presents late foetal deaths and late foetal-death ratios by urban/rural residence for as many years as possible between 1999 and 2003.

Description of variables: Late foetal deaths are foetal deaths[i] of 28 or more completed weeks of gestation. Foetal deaths of unknown gestational age are included with those 28 or more weeks.

Statistics on the number of late foetal deaths are obtained from civil registers unless otherwise noted.

The urban/rural classification of late foetal deaths is as provided by each country or area; it is presumed to be based on the national census definitions of urban population that have been set forth at the end of the technical notes for table 6.

Ratio computation: Late foetal-death ratios are the annual number of late foetal deaths per 1 000 live births (as shown in table 9) in the same year. The live-birth base was adopted because it is assumed to be more comparable from one country or area to another than the sum of live births and foetal deaths.

Ratios by urban/rural residence are the annual number of late foetal deaths, in the appropriate urban or rural category, per 1 000 corresponding live births (as shown in table 9). These ratios have been calculated by the Statistics Division of the United Nations.

Ratios presented in this table have been limited to those for countries or areas and urban/rural areas having at least a total of 30 late foetal deaths in a given year.

Reliability of data: Each country or area has been asked to indicate the estimated completeness of the late foetal deaths recorded in its civil register. These national assessments are indicated by the quality codes, C and U that appear in the first column of this table.

C indicates that the data are estimated to be virtually complete, that is, representing at least 90 per cent of the late foetal deaths occurring each year, while U indicates that data are estimated to be incomplete, that is, representing less than 90 per cent of the late foetal deaths occurring each year. The code ... indicates that no information was provided regarding completeness.

Data from civil registers which are reported as incomplete or of unknown completeness (coded U or ...) are considered unreliable. They appear in italics in this table. Ratios are not computed for data so coded.

For more information about the quality of vital statistics data in general, see section 4.2 of the Technical Notes.

Limitations: Statistics on late foetal deaths are subject to the same qualifications as have been set forth for vital statistics in general and foetal-death statistics in particular as discussed in section 4 of the Technical Notes.

The reliability of the data is a very important factor. Of all vital statistics, the registration of foetal deaths is probably the most incomplete.

Variation in the definition of foetal deaths, and in particular late foetal deaths, also limits international comparability. The criterion of 28 or more completed weeks of gestation to distinguish late foetal deaths is not universally used; some countries or areas use different durations of gestation or other criteria such as size of the foetus. In addition, the difficulty of accurately determining gestational age further reduces comparability. However, to promote comparability, late foetal deaths shown in this table are restricted to those of at least 28 or more completed weeks of gestation. Wherever this is not possible a footnote is provided.

Another factor introducing variation in the definition of late foetal deaths is the practice by some countries or areas of including in late foetal-death statistics infants who were born alive but died before the registration of the birth or within the first 24 hours of life, thus overestimating the total number of late foetal deaths. This has also the effect of inflating the late foetal-death ratios unduly by decreasing the birth denominator and increasing the foetal-death numerator. Statistics of this type are footnoted.

In addition, late foetal-death ratios are subject to the limitations of the data on live births with which they have been calculated. These have been set forth in the technical notes for table 9.

Regarding the computation of the ratios, it must be pointed out that when late foetal deaths and live births are both under registered, the resulting ratios may be of reasonable magnitude. For the countries or areas where live-birth registration is poorest, the late foetal-death ratios may be the largest, effectively masking the completeness of the base data. For this reason, possible variations in birth-registration completeness as well as the reported completeness of late foetal deaths must always be borne in mind in evaluating late foetal-death ratios.

In addition to the indirect effect of live-birth under-registration, late foetal-death ratios may be seriously affected by date-of-registration tabulation of live births. When the annual number of live births registered and reported fluctuates over a wide range due to changes in legislation or to special needs for proof of birth on the part of large segments of the population, then the late foetal-death ratios will also fluctuate, but inversely. Because of these effects, data for countries or areas known to tabulate live births by date of registration should be used with caution.

Finally, it may be noted that the counting of live-born infants as late foetal deaths, because they died before the registration of the birth or within the first 24 hours of life, has the effect of inflating the late foetal-death ratios unduly by decreasing the birth denominator and increasing the foetal-death numerator. This factor should not be overlooked in using data from this table.

The comparability of data by urban/rural residence is affected by the national definitions of urban and rural used in tabulating these data. It is assumed, in the absence of specific information to the contrary, that the definitions of urban and rural used in connection with the national population census were also used in the compilation of the vital statistics for each country or area. However, it cannot be excluded that, for a given country or area, different definitions of urban and rural are used for the vital statistics data and the population census data respectively. When known, the definitions of urban used in national population censuses are presented at the end of the technical notes for table 6. As discussed in detail in the technical notes for table 6, these definitions vary considerably from one country or area to another.

Urban/rural differentials in late foetal death ratios may also be affected by whether the late foetal deaths and live births have been tabulated in terms of place of occurrence or place of usual residence. This problem is discussed in more detail in section 4.1.4.1 of the Technical Notes.

Earlier data: Late foetal deaths and late foetal-death ratios have been shown in each issue of the Demographic Yearbook beginning with the 1951 issue. A special topic CD on natality published in 2001 presents the data for all available years from 1990 to 1998. For more information on specific topics, and years for which data are reported, readers should consult the Historical Index.

NOTES

[i] For definition, see section 4.1.1.3 of the Technical Notes.

Tableau 12

Le tableau 12 présente des données sur les morts fœtales tardives et les rapports de mortinatalité selon le lieu de résidence (zone urbaine ou rurale) pour le plus grand nombre d'années possible entre 1999 et 2003.

Description des variables : Par mort fœtale tardive, on entend le décès d'un fœtus[1] survenu après 28 semaines complètes de gestation au moins. Les morts fœtales pour lesquelles la durée de la période de gestation n'est pas connue sont comprises dans cette catégorie.

Sauf indication contraire, les statistiques du nombre de morts fœtales tardives sont établies sur la base des registres de l'état civil.

La classification des morts fœtales tardives selon le lieu de résidence (zone urbaine ou rurale) est celle qui a été communiquée par chaque pays ou zone ; on part du principe qu'elle repose sur les définitions de la population urbaine utilisées pour les recensements nationaux, telles qu'elles sont reproduites à la fin des notes techniques du tableau 6.

Calcul des rapports : Les rapports de mortinatalité représentent le nombre annuel de morts fœtales tardives pour 1 000 naissances vivantes (telles qu'elles sont présentées au tableau 9) survenues pendant la même année. On a pris pour base de calcul les naissances vivantes parce que l'on pense qu'elle sont plus facilement comparables d'un pays ou d'une zone à l'autre que la somme des naissances vivantes et des morts fœtales.

Les rapports selon le lieu de résidence (zone urbaine ou rurale) représentent le nombre annuel de morts fœtales tardives, classées selon la catégorie urbaine ou rurale appropriée pour 1 000 naissances vivantes (telles qu'elles sont présentées au tableau 9) survenues parmi la population correspondante. Ces rapports ont été calculés par la Division de statistique de l'ONU.

Les rapports présentés dans le tableau 12 ne concernent que les pays ou zones où l'on a enregistré un total d'au moins 1 000 morts fœtales tardives pendant une année donnée.

Fiabilité des données : Il a été demandé à chaque pays ou zone d'indiquer le degré estimatif de complétude des données sur les morts fœtales tardives figurant dans ses registres d'état civil. Ces évaluations nationales sont signalées par les codes de qualité 'C', 'U' et '...' qui apparaissent dans la deuxième colonne du tableau.

La lettre 'C' indique que les données sont jugées à peu près complètes, c'est-à-dire qu'elles représentent au moins 90 p. 100 des morts fœtales tardives survenues chaque année ; la lettre 'U' signifie que les données sont jugées incomplètes, c'est-à-dire qu'elles représentent moins de 90 p.100 des morts fœtales tardives survenues chaque année. Le code '...' indique qu'aucun renseignement n'a été communiqué quant à la complétude des données.

Les données provenant des registres de l'état civil qui sont déclarées incomplètes ou dont le degré de complétude n'est pas connu (code 'U' ou '...') sont jugées douteuses. Elles apparaissent en italique dans le tableau ; les rapports, dans ces cas, n'ont pas été calculés.

Pour plus de précisions sur la qualité des données reposant sur les statistiques de l'état civil en général, voir la section 4.2 des Notes techniques.

Insuffisance des données : Les statistiques des morts fœtales tardives appellent toutes les réserves qui ont été formulées à propos des statistiques de l'état civil en général et des statistiques concernant les morts fœtales en particulier (voir la section 4 des Notes techniques).

La fiabilité des données est un facteur très important. Les statistiques concernant les morts fœtales sont probablement les moins complètes de toutes les statistiques de l'état civil.

L'hétérogénéité des définitions de la mort fœtale et, en particulier, de la mort fœtale tardive nuit aussi à la comparabilité internationale des données. Le critère des 28 semaines complètes de gestation au moins n'est pas universellement utilisé ; certains pays ou zones retiennent des critères différents pour la durée de la période de gestation ou d'autres critères tels que la taille du fœtus. De surcroît, la comparabilité est rendue malaisée par le fait qu'il est difficile d'établir avec précision l'âge gestationnel. Pour faciliter les comparaisons, les morts fœtales tardives considérées ici sont exclusivement celles qui sont survenues au terme de 28 semaines de gestation au moins. Les exceptions sont signalées en note.

Un autre facteur d'hétérogénéité dans la définition de la mort fœtale tardive est la pratique de certains pays ou zones qui consiste à inclure dans les statistiques des morts fœtales tardives les enfants nés vivants mais décédés avant l'enregistrement de leur naissance ou dans les 24 heures qui ont suivi la naissance, pratique qui conduit à surestimer le nombre total des morts fœtales tardives. Cela donne aussi des rapports de mortinatalité exagérés parce que le dénominateur (nombre de naissances) se trouve alors diminué et le numérateur (morts fœtales) augmenté. Quand pareil facteur a joué, cela a été signalé en note.

Les rapports de mortinatalité appellent en outre toutes les réserves qui ont été formulées à propos des statistiques des naissances vivantes qui ont servi à leur calcul (voir à ce sujet les notes techniques relatives au tableau 9).

En ce qui concerne le calcul des rapports, il convient de noter que, si l'enregistrement des morts fœtales tardives et celui des naissances vivantes sont loin d'être exhaustifs, les rapports de mortinatalité peuvent être raisonnables. C'est parfois pour les pays ou zones où l'enregistrement des naissances vivantes laisse le plus à désirer que les rapports de mortinatalité sont les plus élevés, ce qui masque le caractère incomplet des données de base. Aussi, pour porter un jugement sur la qualité des rapports de mortinatalité, il ne faut jamais oublier que la complétude de l'enregistrement des naissances comme celle de l'enregistrement des morts fœtales tardives peuvent varier sensiblement.

Hormis les effets indirects des lacunes de l'enregistrement des naissances vivantes, il arrive que les rapports de mortinatalité soient considérablement faussés lorsque l'exploitation des données relatives aux naissances se fait d'après la date de l'enregistrement. Si le nombre des naissances vivantes enregistrées vient à varier notablement d'une année à l'autre par suite de modifications de la législation ou parce que de très nombreuses personnes ont besoin de se procurer une attestation de naissance, les rapports de mortinatalité varient également, mais en sens inverse. Il convient donc d'utiliser avec prudence le données des pays ou zones où les statistiques sont établies d'après la date de l'enregistrement.

Enfin, on notera que l'inclusion parmi les morts fœtales tardives des décès d'enfants nés vivants qui sont décédés avant l'enregistrement de leur naissance ou dans les 24 heures qui ont suivi la naissance conduit à des rapports de mortinatalité exagérés parce que le dénominateur (nombre de naissances) se trouve alors diminué et le numérateur (morts fœtales) augmenté. Il importe de ne pas négliger ce facteur lorsque l'on utilise les données du tableau 12.

La comparabilité des données selon le lieu de résidence (zone urbaine ou rurale) peut être limitée par les définitions nationales des termes « urbain » et « rural » utilisées pour la mise en tableaux de ces données. En l'absence d'indications contraires, on a supposé que les mêmes définitions avaient servi pour le recensement national de la population et pour l'établissement des statistiques de l'état civil pour chaque pays ou zone. Toutefois, il n'est pas exclu que, pour une zone ou un pays donné, des définitions différentes aient été retenues. Les définitions du terme « urbain » utilisées pour les recensements nationaux de population ont été présentées à la fin des notes techniques du tableau 6 lorsqu'elles étaient connues. Comme on l'a précisé dans les notes techniques relatives au tableau 6, ces définitions varient considérablement d'un pays ou d'une zone à l'autre.

La différence entre les rapports de mortinatalité pour les zones urbaines et rurales pourra aussi être faussée selon que les morts fœtales tardives et les naissances vivantes auront été classées d'après le lieu de l'événement ou le lieu de résidence habituel. Ce problème est examiné plus en détail à la section 4.1.4.1 des Notes techniques.

Données publiées antérieurement : Les éditions de l'*Annuaire démographique* parues à partir de 1951 contiennent des statistiques concernant les morts fœtales tardives et les rapports de mortinatalité. Un CD-ROM sur la natalité paru en 2001 présente les données pour toutes les années disponibles de 1990 à 1998. Pour plus de précisions concernant les années et les sujets pour lesquels des données ont été publiées, se reporter à l'index.

---

[1] Pour la définition, voir la section 4.1.1.3 des Notes techniques.

12. Late foetal deaths and late foetal death ratios, by urban/rural residence; 1999 - 2003
Morts foetales tardives et rapports de mortinatalité, selon la résidence, urbaine/rurale: 1999 - 2003

Continent, country or area and urban/rural residence / Continent, pays ou zone et résidence, urbaine/rurale	Code[1]	Number - Nombre					Ratio - Rapport				
		1999	2000	2001	2002	2003	1999	2000	2001	2002	2003
AFRICA — AFRIQUE											
Algeria - Algérie											
Total	+C	14 420	14 891	15 654	17 135	...	24.3	25.3	25.3	27.8	...
Egypt - Égypte[2]											
Total	+U	5 782	...	...	...	...	...	...	...	...	...
Urban - Urbaine	+U	4 630	...	...	...	...	...	...	...	...	...
Rural - Rurale	+U	1 152	...	...	...	...	...	...	...	...	...
Mauritius - Maurice											
Total	+C	226	266	244	203	220	11.1	13.2	12.4	10.2	11.4
Urban - Urbaine	+C	90	115	83	86	79	11.1	14.4	10.7	10.8	10.4
Rural - Rurale	+C	136	151	161	117	141	11.2	12.4	13.5	9.7	12.0
AMERICA, NORTH — AMERIQUE DU NORD											
Bermuda - Bermudes											
Total	C	2	...	...	...	...	...	...	...	...	...
Canada[3]											
Total	C	1 087	1 060	1 097	1 028	...	3.2	3.2	3.3	3.1	...
Costa Rica											
Total	C	...	528	510	...	471	...	6.8	6.7	...	6.5
Cuba[4]											
Total	C	1 643	1 629	1 982	1 983	1 868	10.9	11.3	14.3	14.0	13.7
Urban - Urbaine	C	1 202	...	...	...	...	11.0	...	...	...	...
Rural - Rurale	C	441	...	...	...	...	10.6	...	...	...	...
El Salvador											
Total	C	621	766	706	617	535	4.0	5.1	5.1	4.8	4.3
Urban - Urbaine	C	491	557	611	550	461	4.9	6.0	7.3	7.1	6.3
Rural - Rurale	C	130	209	95	67	74	2.4	3.7	1.7	1.3	1.4
Guadeloupe											
Total	C	101	90	77	118	151	13.8	11.8	10.3	16.9	21.4
Guatemala											
Total	C	6 253	...	...	...	...	17.3	...	...	...	...
Urban - Urbaine	C	4 124	...	...	...	...	29.4	...	...	...	...
Rural - Rurale	C	2 129	...	...	...	...	9.7	...	...	...	...
Martinique											
Total	C	42	62	60	89	118	7.3	10.2	10.2	16.3	21.7
Mexico - Mexique[5]											
Total	+U	16 916	16 487	15 270	14 971	14 513	...	...	...	...	...
Urban - Urbaine	+U	12 377	12 347	11 398	10 951	10 734	...	...	...	...	...
Rural - Rurale	+U	4 461	4 064	3 795	3 696	3 556	...	...	...	...	...
Panama[6]											
Total	U	428	...	394	...	...	...	...	...	...	...
Urban - Urbaine	U	217	...	...	...	...	...	...	...	...	...
Rural - Rurale	U	211	...	...	...	...	...	...	...	...	...
Puerto Rico - Porto Rico[5]											
Total	C	684	651	584	234	206	11.5	10.9	10.4	4.4	4.1
Urban - Urbaine	C	...	360	361	138	...	...	11.8	12.3	...	...
Rural - Rurale	C	...	290	220	90	...	...	10.0	8.3	...	...
Saint Lucia - Sainte-Lucie											
Total	...	46	49	...	...	...	...	...	...	...	...
Saint Vincent and the Grenadines - Saint Vincent-et-les Grenadines											
Total	+C	18	20	18	16	...	...	...	...	...	...
Trinidad and Tobago - Trinité-et-Tobago											
Total	C	228	...	...	...	...	12.4	...	...	...	...
Turks Caicos Islands - Îles Turques et Caïques											
Total	C	3	2	1	1	1	...	...	...	...	...
United States - États-Unis											
Total	C	13 887	13 948	13 704	13 285	...	3.5	3.4	3.4	3.3	...

12. Late foetal deaths and late foetal death ratios, by urban/rural residence; 1999 - 2003
Morts foetales tardives et rapports de mortinatalité, selon la résidence, urbaine/rurale: 1999 - 2003
(continued — suite)

Continent, country or area and urban/rural residence — Continent, pays ou zone et résidence, urbaine/rurale	Code[1]	Number - Nombre					Ratio - Rapport				
		1999	2000	2001	2002	2003	1999	2000	2001	2002	2003
AMERICA, SOUTH — AMERIQUE DU SUD											
Argentina - Argentine											
Total	...	4 296	...	5 314	...	...	...	...	...	...	...
Brazil - Brésil[7]											
Total	...	19 849	19 298	18 341	...	30 201	...	...	...	...	...
Chile - Chili											
Total	C	1 080	1 116	1 278	1 197	1 404	4.3	4.5	5.2	5.0	6.0
Urban - Urbaine	C	915	672	1 095	1 044	1 220	4.2	3.1	5.1	4.9	5.8
Rural - Rurale	C	165	444	183	153	184	5.1	14.6	6.1	5.9	7.4
Colombia - Colombie[5,8]											
Total	...	5 260	5 284	6 104	6 086	8 482	...	...	...	...	...
Urban - Urbaine	...	3 397	3 343	3 956	3 931	6 072	...	...	...	...	...
Rural - Rurale	...	1 384	1 473	1 618	1 693	1 875	...	...	...	...	...
Ecuador - Équateur[9]											
Total	...	3 173	2 824	2 751	2 685	2 298	...	...	...	...	...
Urban - Urbaine	...	2 801	2 412	2 384	2 372	1 992	...	...	...	...	...
Rural - Rurale	...	372	412	367	313	306	...	...	...	...	...
French Guiana - Guyane française											
Total	C	61	61	51	72	69	12.5	11.9	10.0	13.7	12.4
Suriname											
Total	...	108	...	...	...	...	...	...	...	...	...
Uruguay											
Total	C	535	436	...	...	...	9.9	8.3	...	...	...
Venezuela[7]											
Total	...	4 664	4 529	4 149	3 852	...	...	...	...	...	...
ASIA — ASIE											
Armenia - Arménie											
Total	C	292	289	269	236	289	8.0	8.4	8.4	7.3	8.1
Urban - Urbaine	C	234	215	...	196	227	10.4	10.1	...	9.4	10.0
Rural - Rurale	C	58	74	...	40	62	4.1	5.7	...	3.5	4.7
Azerbaijan - Azerbaïdjan											
Total	+C	425	418	425	443	431	3.6	3.6	3.9	4.0	3.8
Bahrain - Bahreïn											
Total	...	26	20	17	19	...	...	...	...	...	...
China: Hong Kong SAR - Chine: Hong Kong RAS											
Total	...	228	301	221	308	189	...	...	...	...	...
China: Macao SAR - Chine: Macao RAS											
Total	C	10	12	8	8	8	...	...	...	...	...
Georgia - Géorgie											
Total	C	794	693	746	726	811	19.5	17.2	15.7	15.6	17.6
Urban - Urbaine	C	790	690	...	...	791	30.5	27.0	...	...	22.9
Rural - Rurale	C	4	3	...	...	20	...	...	...	...	...
Israel - Israël[5,10,11]											
Total	C	557	573	595	549	...	4.2	4.2	4.4	3.9	...
Urban - Urbaine	C	506	507	532	498	...	4.3	4.2	4.3	3.9	...
Rural - Rurale	C	43	55	43	46	...	3.1	3.7	3.6	3.6	...
Japan - Japon[5,12]											
Total	C	3 139	3 050	2 882	2 851	2 692	2.7	2.6	2.5	2.5	2.4
Urban - Urbaine	C	2 509	2 424	2 345	2 288	2 161	2.6	2.5	2.5	2.4	2.4
Rural - Rurale	C	625	624	534	562	529	2.8	2.7	2.4	2.6	2.6
Kazakhstan											
Total	C	1 899	1 812	1 719	1 748	1 768	8.7	8.2	7.8	7.7	7.1
Urban - Urbaine	C	1 194	1 147	1 059	1 050	1 169	10.8	10.0	9.2	8.6	8.4
Rural - Rurale	C	705	665	660	698	599	6.6	6.2	6.2	6.6	5.5
Kuwait - Koweït											
Total	C	255	269	286	325	...	6.2	6.4	6.9	7.5	...
Kyrgyzstan - Kirghizistan											
Total	C	660	608	617	759	879	6.3	6.3	6.3	7.5	8.3
Urban - Urbaine	C	...	361	335	395	470	...	12.8	11.8	13.1	14.7

12. Late foetal deaths and late foetal death ratios, by urban/rural residence; 1999 - 2003
Morts foetales tardives et rapports de mortinatalité, selon la résidence, urbaine/rurale: 1999 - 2003
(continued — suite)

Continent, country or area and urban/rural residence / Continent, pays ou zone et résidence, urbaine/rurale	Code[1]	Number - Nombre					Ratio - Rapport				
		1999	2000	2001	2002	2003	1999	2000	2001	2002	2003
ASIA — ASIE											
Kyrgyzstan - Kirghizistan											
Rural - Rurale	C	...	247	282	364	409	...	3.6	4.0	5.1	5.6
Malaysia - Malaisie[13]											
Total	...	...	2 003	...	...	...	...	...	...	...	...
Maldives[14]											
Total	...	61	71	53	61	71	...	...	...	...	...
Urban - Urbaine	...	16	25	20	27	28	...	...	...	...	...
Rural - Rurale	...	45	46	33	34	43	...	...	...	...	...
Oman[15]											
Total	U	425	388	365	376	381	...	...	...	...	...
Philippines											
Total	...	4 721	5 127	4 765	4 645	...	...	...	...	...	...
Qatar											
Total	C	77	76	75	62	81	7.1	6.8	6.2	5.1	6.3
Singapore - Singapour											
Total	+C	125	143	107	114	95	2.9	3.0	2.6	2.8	2.5
Tajikistan - Tadjikistan											
Total	C	972	...	1 057	1 096	1 043	5.4	...	6.2	6.2	5.9
Urban - Urbaine	C	578	...	915	940	899	14.2	...	20.1	22.0	19.9
Rural - Rurale	C	394	...	142	156	144	2.8	...	1.1	1.2	1.1
Uzbekistan - Ouzbékistan											
Total	C	3 600	3 062	2 902	...	...	6.5	5.8	5.7	...	...
Urban - Urbaine	C	1 441	1 148	1 138	...	...	8.3	7.0	7.1	...	...
Rural - Rurale	C	2 159	1 914	1 764	...	...	5.7	5.3	5.0	...	...
EUROPE											
Andorra - Andorre											
Total	C	...	...	1	-	3	...	...	...	...	...
Austria - Autriche											
Total	C	316	331	278	338	307	4.0	4.2	3.7	4.3	4.0
Belgium - Belgique[16]											
Total	C	556	554	583	...	...	4.9	4.8	5.1	...	...
Bosnia and Herzegovina - Bosnie-Herzégovine											
Total	C	224	159	193	138	150	5.3	4.0	5.1	3.9	4.1
Bulgaria - Bulgarie											
Total	C	540	555	500	539	549	7.5	7.5	7.3	8.1	8.2
Urban - Urbaine	C	...	365	246	323	348	...	6.9	5.1	6.8	7.2
Rural - Rurale	C	...	190	254	216	201	...	9.1	13.0	11.5	10.7
Channel Islands: Guernsey - Îles Anglo-Normandes: Guernesey											
Total	C	1	4	...	...	...	...	...	...	...	...
Croatia - Croatie											
Total	C	205	229	216	189	180	4.5	5.2	5.3	4.7	4.5
Urban - Urbaine	C	...	127	111	108	94	...	5.1	4.8	4.8	4.3
Rural - Rurale	C	...	102	105	81	86	...	5.4	5.8	4.6	4.8
Czech Republic - République tchèque											
Total	C	303	259	263	261	272	3.4	2.8	2.9	2.7	2.9
Urban - Urbaine	C	215	197	200	207	209	3.3	2.9	3.0	2.8	3.0
Rural - Rurale	C	88	62	63	54	63	3.7	2.6	2.7	2.2	2.6
Denmark - Danemark											
Total	C	...	248	277	224	239	...	3.7	4.2	3.5	3.7
Estonia - Estonie											
Total	C	82	67	63	74	63	6.5	5.1	5.0	5.7	4.8
Urban - Urbaine	C	...	41	42	45	45	...	4.7	4.9	5.1	5.0
Rural - Rurale	C	...	24	21	29	18	...	...	...	...	...
Finland - Finlande[17]											
Total	C	...	...	185	134	133	...	...	3.3	2.4	2.3
Urban - Urbaine	C	...	...	94	82	84	...	...	2.6	2.3	2.3
Rural - Rurale	C	...	...	91	52	49	...	...	4.6	2.7	2.5

12. Late foetal deaths and late foetal death ratios, by urban/rural residence; 1999 - 2003
Morts foetales tardives et rapports de mortinatalité, selon la résidence, urbaine/rurale: 1999 - 2003
(continued — suite)

Continent, country or area and urban/rural residence / Continent, pays ou zone et résidence, urbaine/rurale	Code[1]	Number - Nombre					Ratio - Rapport				
		1999	2000	2001	2002	2003	1999	2000	2001	2002	2003
EUROPE											
France[2,18,19]											
Total	C	3 442	...	3 741	6 682	7 368	4.6	...	4.9	8.8	9.7
Urban - Urbaine	C	2 674	...	2 959	5 231	5 774	4.7	...	5.1	9.1	...
Rural - Rurale	C	719	...	754	1 401	1 511	4.2	...	4.1	7.7	...
Germany - Allemagne											
Total	C	3 118	...	2 881	2 700	2 699	4.0	...	3.9	3.8	3.8
Greece - Grèce											
Total	C	550	...	588	...	504	4.7	...	5.7	...	4.8
Hungary - Hongrie[5,20]											
Total	C	471	538	550	523	530	5.0	5.5	5.7	5.4	5.6
Urban - Urbaine	C	241	313	304	306	291	4.2	5.3	5.1	5.0	4.9
Rural - Rurale	C	225	225	244	208	237	6.1	6.0	6.6	5.9	6.9
Iceland - Islande											
Total	C	19	15	10	7	4	...	...	...	...	...
Urban - Urbaine	C	...	13	9	7	4	...	...	...	...	...
Rural - Rurale	C	...	2	1	-	-	...	...	...	...	...
Ireland - Irlande											
Total	+C	311	...	259	274	...	5.8	...	4.5	4.5	...
Isle of Man - Îles de Man											
Total	+C	4	3	...	...	...	...	...	...	...	...
Italy - Italie											
Total	C	...	...	...	1 721	...	...	...	...	3.2	...
Latvia - Lettonie											
Total	C	165	158	138	130	130	8.5	7.8	7.0	6.5	6.2
Urban - Urbaine	C	93	99	88	108	76	7.7	7.8	7.0	8.3	5.5
Rural - Rurale	C	72	59	50	68	54	9.8	7.9	7.0	9.6	7.6
Lithuania - Lituanie											
Total	C	207	221	167	193	168	5.7	6.5	5.3	6.4	5.5
Urban - Urbaine	C	...	120	90	125	106	...	5.7	4.6	6.7	5.5
Rural - Rurale	C	...	101	77	68	62	...	7.7	6.5	6.0	5.4
Luxembourg											
Total	C	14	...	23	20	17	...	...	...	...	...
Netherlands - Pays-Bas[21]											
Total	C	944	...	...	945	928	4.7	...	...	4.7	4.6
Urban - Urbaine	C	...	...	...	617	631	...	...	...	4.6	4.8
Rural - Rurale	C	...	...	...	328	297	...	...	...	4.7	4.4
Norway - Norvège											
Total	C	241	225	241	197	213	4.1	3.8	4.3	3.6	3.8
Poland - Pologne											
Total	C	1 882	...	1 574	1 372	1 322	4.9	...	4.3	3.9	3.8
Urban - Urbaine	C	983	...	797	703	687	4.7	...	3.9	3.6	3.4
Rural - Rurale	C	899	...	777	669	635	5.2	...	4.8	4.3	4.2
Portugal											
Total	C	...	...	390	388	349	...	...	3.5	3.4	3.1
Romania - Roumanie											
Total	C	1 459	1 393	1 282	1 319	1 290	6.2	5.9	5.8	6.3	6.1
Urban - Urbaine	C	...	612	567	602	569	...	5.7	5.5	6.1	5.6
Rural - Rurale	C	...	781	715	717	721	...	6.2	6.1	6.4	6.5
Russian Federation - Fédération de Russie											
Total	C	8 864	...	8 711	8 998	9 043	7.3	...	6.6	6.4	6.1
Urban - Urbaine	C	6 472	...	6 416	6 687	6 624	7.7	...	6.9	6.7	6.3
Rural - Rurale	C	2 392	...	2 295	2 311	2 419	6.4	...	6.0	5.8	5.7
San Marino - Saint-Marin											
Total	+C	1	2	1	...	2	...	...	...	...	...
Urban - Urbaine	+C	...	2	...	...	...	...	...	...	...	...
Rural - Rurale	+C	...	-	...	...	...	...	...	...	...	...
Serbia and Montenegro - Serbie-et-Montenegro[22]											
Total	C	722	715	741	479	453	5.8	5.7	5.7	5.5	5.2
Urban - Urbaine	C	...	...	415	308	286	...	...	6.0	5.7	5.3
Rural - Rurale	C	...	...	356	171	167	...	...	5.9	5.3	5.0
Slovakia - Slovaquie											
Total	C	259	...	207	194	217	4.6	...	4.0	3.8	4.2

12. Late foetal deaths and late foetal death ratios, by urban/rural residence; 1999 - 2003
Morts foetales tardives et rapports de mortinatalité, selon la résidence, urbaine/rurale: 1999 - 2003
(continued — suite)

Continent, country or area and urban/rural residence / Continent, pays ou zone et résidence, urbaine/rurale	Code[1]	Number - Nombre					Ratio - Rapport				
		1999	2000	2001	2002	2003	1999	2000	2001	2002	2003
EUROPE											
Slovakia - Slovaquie											
Urban - Urbaine	C	117	...	100	95	114	4.1	...	3.8	3.6	4.3
Rural - Rurale	C	142	...	107	99	103	5.2	...	4.3	4.0	4.1
Slovenia - Slovénie											
Total	C	66	68	85	93	94	3.8	3.7	4.9	5.3	5.4
Urban - Urbaine	C	...	32	38	43	45	...	3.9	4.7	5.1	5.3
Rural - Rurale	C	...	36	46	50	49	...	3.6	4.9	5.5	5.5
Spain - Espagne											
Total	C	1 275	...	1 541	1 470	1 494	3.4	...	3.8	3.5	3.4
Sweden - Suède											
Total	C	321	355	349	352	359	3.6	3.9	3.8	3.7	3.6
Switzerland - Suisse											
Total	C	277	283	279	255	306	3.5	3.6	3.8	3.5	4.3
Urban - Urbaine ,,,,,,,,,,,,,,,,,,,	C	165	170	176	186	232	0.2	3.2	3.6	3.5	4.4
Rural - Rurale	C	112	113	103	69	74	4.2	4.3	4.3	3.5	3.9
The Former Yugoslav Rep. of Macedonia - L'ex-République yougoslave de Macédoine											
Total	C	...	266	284	291	232	...	9.1	10.5	10.5	8.6
Urban - Urbaine	C	...	150	182	187	...	...	9.6	12.3	12.5	...
Rural - Rurale	C	...	116	102	104	...	...	8.4	8.3	8.1	...
Ukraine											
Total	C	...	...	1 830	1 837	1 969	...	...	4.9	4.7	4.8
Urban - Urbaine	C	...	...	1 214	1 270	1 361	...	...	5.1	5.1	5.1
Rural - Rurale	C	...	...	616	567	608	...	...	4.4	4.0	4.3
United Kingdom - Royaume-Uni											
Total	C	3 723	3 594	3 572	3 772	3 989	5.3	5.3	5.3	5.6	5.7
OCEANIA — OCEANIE											
Australia - Australie											
Total	+C	770	802	751	714	759	3.1	3.2	3.0	2.8	3.0
French Polynesia - Polynésie française											
Total	C	26	23	31	17	35	...	...	6.4	...	7.8
New Caledonia - Nouvelle-Calédonie											
Total	+C	28	33	36	30	25	...	7.2	8.3	7.2	...
New Zealand - Nouvelle-Zélande											
Total	+C	172	168	157	167	169	3.0	3.0	2.8	3.1	3.0
Urban - Urbaine	+C	147	137	138	150	150	3.0	2.8	2.8	3.2	3.1
Rural - Rurale	+C	25	31	19	17	19	...	4.4	...	...	...
Papua New Guinea - Papouasie-Nouvelle-Guinée											
Total	U	...	1 003	922	1 080	991	...	...	...	...	...

FOOTNOTES - NOTES

Italics: data from civil registers which are incomplete or of unknown completeness. — *Italiques:* données incomplètes ou dont le degré d'exactitude n'est pas connu, provenant des registres de l'état civil.

[1] 'Code' indicates the source of data, as follows:
C - Civil registration, estimated over 90% complete
U - Civil registration, estimated less than 90% complete
| - Other source, estimated reliable
+ - Data tabulated by date of registration rather than occurence.
... - Information not available

Le 'Code' indique la source des données, comme suit:
C - Registres de l'état civil considérés complèts à 90 p. 100 au moins.
U - Registres de l'état civil qui ne sont pas considérés complèts à 90 p. 100 au moins.
| - Autre source, considérée pas douteuses.
+ - Données exploitées selon la date de l'enregistrement et non la date de l'événement.
... - Information pas disponible.

[2] Foetal deaths after at least 180 days (6 calendar months or 26 weeks) of gestation. - Morts foetales survenues après 180 jours (6 mois civils ou 26 semaines) au moins de gestation.
[3] Including Canadian residents temporarily in the United States, but excluding United States residents temporarily in Canada. - Y compris les résidents canadiens se trouvant temporairement aux Etats-Unis, mais ne comprenant pas les résidents des Etats-Unis se trouvant temporairement au Canada.
[4] Late foetal death is indicated by the fact that the foetus is at least 500 grams or more in weight. - Les décès foetaux tardifs sont caractérisés par le fait que le foetus pèse au moins 500 grammes.

[5] Figures for urban and rural areas do not add up to the total, since they do not include the category 'Unknown residence'. - La somme des donées pour la residence urbaine et rurale n'est pas égale au total parce qu'elle n'inclue pas la catégorie 'Residence inconnue'.

[6] Excluding tribal Indian population. - Non compris les Indiens vivant en tribus.

[7] Excluding Indian jungle population. - Non compris les Indiens de la jungle.

[8] Data include unknown gestational weeks. - Les données comprennnent les cas où le nombre de semaines de gestation n'est pas connu.

[9] Excluding nomadic Indian tribes. - Non compris les tribus d'Indiens nomades.

[10] Including data for East Jerusalem and Israeli residents in certain other territories under occupation by Israeli military forces since June 1967. - Y compris les données pour Jérusalem-Est et les résidents israéliens dans certains autres territoires occupés depuis 1967 par les forces armées israéliennes.

[11] Data for 1999 and 2000 include 8 and 9 foetal deaths of unknown gestational age and weight over 1000 grams respectively. - Les données pour 1999 et 2000 comprennent huit et neuf décès intra-utérins, respectivement, pour lesquels l'âge gestationnel est inconnu et le poids est supérieur à 1 000 grammes.

[12] Data refer to Japanese nationals in Japan only. - Les données se raportent aux nationaux japonais au Japon seulement.

[13] Data refer to Peninsular Malaysia only. - Les données ne concernent que la partie péninsulaire de la Malaisie.

[14] Data refer to total foetal deaths. - Y compris toutes les morts foetales.

[15] Data refer to the recorded events in Ministry of Health hospitals and health centres only. - Les données se rapportent aux faits d'état-civil enregistrés dans les hôpitaux et les dispensaires du Ministère de la santé seulement.

[16] Including armed forces stationed outside the country, but excluding alien armed forces stationed in the area. - Y compris les militaires nationaux hors du pays, mais non compris les militaires étrangers en garnison sur le territoire.

[17] Including nationals temporarily outside the country. - Y compris les nationaux se trouvant temporairement hors du pays.

[18] Urban/rural figures, excluding nationals outside the country. - Les chiffres urbaine/rurale, non compris les nationaux hors du pays.

[19] The strong increase in still births number is due to a legislative change: according to a circular of november 2001, a still birth bulletin is now drawn up after 22 weeks of amenorrhea or for a 500 g weight. These new criteria take the place of the 180 days of gestation, existing in the registry declaration. - La forte évolution du nombre d'enfants sans vie est liée à un changement législatif : selon une circulaire de novembre 2001, un acte d'enfant sans vie correspond désormais au terme de vingt-deux semaines d'aménorrhée ou à un poids de 500 grammes. Ces critères se substituent au délai de 180 jours de gestation prévu dans l'état civil.

[20] Late foetal death is indicated by the fact that the foetus is at least 24 completed weeks of gestational and does not show any sign of life after the separation from its mother; the foetus has to be 30 cm or more in length or 500 grams or more in weight if its gestational age cannot be determined. - Pour qu'il y ait mort foetale tardive, il faut que le décès d'un foetus survienne après 24 semaines complètes de gestation au moins,que le foetus n'ait pas donné signe de vie après avoir été séparé de la mère, qu'il mesure 30 centimètres au moins ou pèse 500 grammes si la durée de la période de gestation n'est pas connue.

[21] Including residents outside the country if listed in a Netherlands population register. - Y compris les résidents hors du pays, s'ils sont inscrits sur un registre de population néerlandais.

[22] Starting from 2002, without data for Kosovo and Metohia. - Pour 2002 et après, sans les donées pour le Kosovo and Metohie.

Table 13

Table 13 presents legally induced abortions for as many years as possible between 1994 and 2003.

Description of variables: There are two major categories of abortion: spontaneous and induced. Induced abortions are those initiated by deliberate action undertaken with the intention of terminating pregnancy; all other abortions are considered as spontaneous.

The induction of abortion is subject to governmental regulation in most, if not all, countries or areas. This regulation varies from complete prohibition in some countries or areas to abortion on request, with services provided by governmental health authorities, in others. More generally, governments have attempted to define the conditions under which a pregnancy may lawfully be terminated and have established procedures for authorizing abortion in individual cases.

In an effort to provide more complete interpretation of these statistics, countries or areas providing data on legally induced abortions have been requested to communicate grounds for legally induced abortions in their country or area. This information is presented in table 13-1 below.

Reliability of data: Unlike data on live births and foetal deaths, which are generally collected through systems of vital registration, data on abortion are collected from a variety of sources. Because of this, the quality specification, showing the completeness of civil registers, which is presented for other tables, does not appear here.

Limitations: With regard to the collection of information on abortions, a variety of sources are used, but hospital records are the most common source of information. This implies that most cases that have no contact with hospitals are missed. Data from other sources are probably also incomplete. The data in the present table are limited to legally induced abortions, which, by their nature, might be assumed to be more complete than data on all induced abortions.

Earlier data: Legally induced abortions have been shown previously in all issues of the *Demographic Yearbook* since the 1971 issue.

13-1 Grounds for legally induced abortions

Country/area	Grounds for abortion					
	(a) Continuation of pregnancy would involve risk to the life of the pregnant woman greater than if the pregnancy were terminated.	(b) Continuation of pregnancy would involve risk of injury to the physical health of the pregnant woman greater than if the pregnancy were terminated.	(c) Continuation of pregnancy would involve risk of injury to the mental health of the pregnant woman greater than if the pregnancy were terminated.	(d) Continuation of pregnancy would involve risk of injury to the mental or physical health of any existing children of the family greater than if the pregnancy were terminated.	(e) There is a substantial risk that if the child were born it would suffer from such physical or mental abnormalities as to be seriously handicapped.	(f) Other
Canada	x	x	x			
Mexico		x				
China Hong Kong SAR	x	x	x	x	x	x
Israel	x	x	x		x	x
Japan	x	x				x
Singapore	x	x	x	x	x	x
Czech Rep.	x	x	x		x	x
Denmark	x	x	x	x	x	
Estonia	x	x	x	x	x	
Finland	x	x	x		x	x
France	x	x	x	x	x	
Greece	x	x	x	x	x	
Hungary	x	x	x	x	x	

Country/area	Grounds for abortion					
	(a) Continuation of pregnancy would involve risk to the life of the pregnant woman greater than if the pregnancy were terminated.	(b) Continuation of pregnancy would involve risk of injury to the physical health of the pregnant woman greater than if the pregnancy were terminated.	(c) Continuation of pregnancy would involve risk of injury to the mental health of the pregnant woman greater than if the pregnancy were terminated.	(d) Continuation of pregnancy would involve risk of injury to the mental or physical health of any existing children of the family greater than if the pregnancy were terminated.	(e) There is a substantial risk that if the child were born it would suffer from such physical or mental abnormalities as to be seriously handicapped.	(f) Other
Iceland	x	x	x	x	x	x
Italy	x	x	x		x	x
Latvia	x	x	x		x	
Lithuania						x
Netherlands	x	x	x		x	
Norway	x	x	x	x	x	x
Poland	x	x			x	x
Republic of Moldova	x	x	x	x	x	
Romania	x	x	x		x	
United Kingdom	x	x	x	x	x	

Tableau 13

Ce tableau présente des données relatives aux avortements provoqués légalement, pour le plus grand nombre d'années possible entre 1994 et 2003.

Description des variables : L'avortement peut être spontané ou provoqué. L'avortement provoqué est celui qui résulte de manœuvres délibérées, entreprises afin d'interrompre la grossesse ; tous les autres avortements sont considérés comme spontanés.

L'interruption délibérée de la grossesse fait l'objet d'une réglementation officielle dans la plupart des pays ou zones, sinon dans tous. Cette réglementation va de l'interdiction totale à l'autorisation de l'avortement sur demande, pratiqué par des services de santé publique. Le plus souvent, les gouvernements se sont efforcés de définir les circonstances dans lesquelles la grossesse peut être interrompue licitement et de fixer une procédure d'autorisation.

Dans un effort de fournir une interprétation plus complète de ces statistiques, les pays ou les zones fournissant des données sur des avortements légalement induits ont été demandés pour communiquer des raisons pour des avortements légalement induits dans leur pays ou zone. Cette information est présentée dans le tableau 13-1 ci-dessous.

Fiabilité des données : À la différence des données sur les naissances vivantes et les morts fœtales, qui proviennent généralement des registres d'état civil, les données sur l'avortement sont tirées de sources diverses. Aussi ne trouve-t-on pas ici une évaluation de la qualité des données semblable à celle qui indique, pour les autres tableaux, le degré d'exhaustivité des données de l'état civil.

Insuffisance des données : En ce qui concerne les renseignements sur l'avortement, un grand nombre de sources sont utilisées, les relevés hospitaliers restant cependant la source la plus commune. Il s'ensuit que la plupart des cas qui ne passent pas par les hôpitaux sont ignorés. Il faut aussi tenir compte du fait que les données provenant d'autres sources sont probablement incomplètes. Les données du tableau 13 se limitent aux avortements provoqués pour raisons légales dont on peut supposer, en raison de leur nature même, que les statistiques sont plus complètes que les données concernant l'ensemble des avortements provoqués.

Données publiées antérieurement : Des statistiques concernant les avortements provoqués pour raisons légales sont publiées dans *l'Annuaire démographique* depuis 1971.

13-1 Motifs d'autorisation pour avortements provoqués légalement

Pays ou zone	Motifs d'autorisation					
	(a) La non-interruption de la grossesse comporterait, pour la vie de la femme enceinte, un risque plus grave que celui de l'avortement.	(b) La non-interruption de la grossesse comporterait, pour la santé physique de la femme enceinte, un risque plus grave que celui de l'avortement.	(c) La non-interruption de la grossesse comporterait, pour la santé mentale de la femme, un risque plus grave que celui de l'avortement.	(d) La non-interruption de la grossesse comporterait, pour la santé mentale ou physique d'un enfant déjà né dans la famille, un risque plus grave que celui de l'avortement.	(e) L'enfant né à terme courrait un risque important de souffrir d'anomalies physiques ou mentales entraînant pour lui un grave handicap.	(f) Autres motifs.
Canada	x	x	x			
Mexique		x				
Chine: Hong Kong RAS	x	x	x	x	x	x
Israël	x	x	x		x	x
Japon	x	x				x
Singapour	x	x	x	x	x	x
République tchèque	x	x	x		x	x
Danemark	x	x	x	x	x	

Pays ou zone	Motifs d'autorisation					
	(a) La non-interruption de la grossesse comporterait, pour la vie de la femme enceinte, un risque plus grave que celui de l'avortement.	(b) La non-interruption de la grossesse comporterait, pour la santé physique de la femme enceinte, un risque plus grave que celui de l'avortement.	(c) La non-interruption de la grossesse comporterait, pour la santé mentale de la femme, un risque plus grave que celui de l'avortement.	(d) La non-interruption de la grossesse comporterait, pour la santé mentale ou physique d'un enfant déjà né dans la famille, un risque plus grave que celui de l'avortement.	(e) L'enfant né à terme courrait un risque important de souffrir d'anomalies physiques ou mentales entraînant pour lui un grave handicap.	(f) Autres motifs.
Estonie	x	x	x	x	x	
Finlande	x	x	x		x	x
France	x	x	x	x	x	
Grèce	x	x	x	x	x	
Hongrie	x	x	x	x	x	
Islande	x	x	x	x	x	x
Italie	x	x	x		x	x
Lettonie	x	x	x		x	
Lituanie						x
Pays-Bas	x	x	x		x	
Norvège	x	x	x	x	x	x
Pologne	x	x			x	x
République de Moldova	x	x	x	x	x	
Roumanie	x	x	x		x	
Royaume-Uni	x	x	x	x	x	

13. Legally induced abortions: 1994 - 2003
Avortements provoqués légalement: 1994 - 2003

Continent and country or area Continent et pays ou zone	Number - Nombre									
	1994	1995	1996	1997	1998	1999	2000	2001	2002	2003
AFRICA — AFRIQUE										
Réunion	...	...	4 567	4 729	4 652	4 522	4 404	4 339	4 385	...
Seychelles	...	...	...	...	...	536	495	461	460	440
South Africa - Afrique du Sud[1]	...	...	...	...	28 978	...	...	...	...	...
AMERICA, NORTH — AMERIQUE DU NORD										
Anguilla	...	...	...	...	...	...	...	...	...	24
Canada	106 255	108 248	111 659	111 709	110 331	105 666	105 427	106 418	105 154	...
Cuba	89 421	83 963	...	80 097	75 109	80 037	76 293	69 563	70 823	65 628
Dominican Republic - République dominicaine	...	18 377	20 852	22 911	31 068	...	...	...	...	...
Greenland - Groenland	1 000	879	862	843	915	842	944	809	821	869
Mexico - Mexique	...	...	2 724	2 938	3 189	3 359	3 281	3 120	3 223	3 486
Panama[2]	...	...	...	...	...	...	11	...	...	...
Puerto Rico - Porto Rico	...	...	...	...	...	...	...	1 229	...	...
Turks Caicos Islands - Îles Turques et Caïques[3]	...	...	...	...	...	...	...	...	39	32
ASIA — ASIE										
Armenia - Arménie	30 571	30 726	31 323	25 266	18 286	14 403	11 769	10 419	9 372	10 290
Azerbaijan - Azerbaïdjan	33 280	28 610	28 375	25 182	24 914	20 878	17 501	18 332	16 606	16 903
Bahrain - Bahreïn	...	...	...	1 592	1 680	1 658	1 655	1 747	1 749	...
China: Hong Kong SAR - Chine: Hong Kong RAS	26 049	25 363	25 041	23 939	22 086	20 891	21 375	20 235	18 649	17 419
Georgia - Géorgie	48 953	43 549	...	...	...	...	...	...	...	...
Israel - Israël[4,5]	16 903	17 627	17 447	19 210	18 500	18 372	18 689	19 131	19 126	...
Japan - Japon[6]	364 350	343 024	338 867	337 799	333 220	337 288	341 146	341 588	329 326	319 831
Kazakhstan	260 200	224 100	193 462	156 222	148 799	137 808	...	...	...	...
Kyrgyzstan - Kirghizistan	49 325	27 111	...	31 598	28 090	25 790	22 044	23 390	18 690	19 225
Mongolia - Mongolie	...	...	15 588	12 870	...	...	...	...	...	...
Singapore - Singapour	15 690	14 504	14 362	13 827	13 838	13 753	13 734	13 140	12 749	12 272
Tajikistan - Tadjikistan	35 709	...	...	...	...	21 234	22 066	19 087	21 104	18 822
Uzbekistan - Ouzbékistan	120 434	104 400	104 620	...	...	...	...	...	...	...
EUROPE										
Albania - Albanie	31 622	31 874	32 538	22 103	18 944	19 930	21 004	17 125	17 500	12 087
Belarus - Bélarus	207 658	193 280	174 098	152 660	145 339	135 824	121 895	101 402	89 895	80 174
Belgium - Belgique	...	...	...	...	11 999	12 734	13 762	14 775	14 791	15 595
Bulgaria - Bulgarie	97 567	97 092	...	87 896	...	...	61 378	51 165	50 824	48 035
Channel Islands: Guernsey - Îles Anglo-Normandes: Guernesey ..	...	...	...	57	104	92	89	...	...	...
Croatia - Croatie	19 673	14 282	12 339	10 036	8 907	8 064	7 534	6 574	6 191	5 923
Czech Republic - République tchèque	54 836	49 531	48 086	45 022	42 959	39 382	34 623	32 528	31 142	29 298
Denmark - Danemark[7]	17 598	17 720	18 135	17 152	16 592	16 271	15 681	15 315	14 991	15 622
Estonia - Estonie	19 784	17 671	16 887	16 615	...	14 503	12 743	...	10 834	10 619
Finland - Finlande	10 013	9 884	10 437	10 238	10 744	10 819	10 930	10 696	10 902	10 709
France	189 193	179 648	187 114	188 796	195 960	196 885	...	202 128	*205 593	...
Germany - Allemagne	103 586	97 937	...	130 890	...	130 471	134 609	134 964	130 387	128 030
Greece - Grèce	12 608	...	12 542	...	...	...	...	...	...	...
Hungary - Hongrie	74 491	76 957	76 600	74 564	68 971	65 981	59 249	56 404	56 075	53 789
Iceland - Islande	775	807	854	921	...	945	987	984	926	...
Italy - Italie	135 956	134 137	138 925	140 166	138 354	138 708	...	132 073	131 039	124 118
Latvia - Lettonie	26 795	25 933	24 227	21 768	19 964	18 031	17 240	15 647	14 685	...
Lithuania - Lituanie[8]	30 326	31 278	27 832	22 680	21 022	18 846	16 259	13 677	12 495	11 513
Netherlands - Pays-Bas	20 811	20 932	22 441	...	24 141	...	...	...	...	...
Norway - Norvège	...	13 672	...	...	14 028	14 251	14 635	13 887	13 557	13 888
Poland - Pologne[9]	874	559	491	3 171	312	151	138	123	159	174
Republic of Moldova - République de Moldova	...	44 252	46 010	...	31 293	27 908	20 395	16 028	15 739	17 551
Romania - Roumanie	530 191	502 840	456 221	347 126	259 888	...	257 865	198 086	247 608	224 807
Russian Federation - Fédération de Russie	2 481 493	2 766 362	...	...	...	...	...	...	...	...
Serbia and Montenegro - Serbie-et-Montenegro	98 942	96 854	83 577	64 099	58 739	...	...	...	...	...

Continent and country or area Continent et pays ou zone	Number - Nombre									
	1994	1995	1996	1997	1998	1999	2000	2001	2002	2003
EUROPE										
Slovakia - Slovaquie	34 883	35 879	...	...	21 109	19 949	...	18 026	17 382	16 222
Slovenia - Slovénie	11 324	10 791	10 218	...	9 116	8 707	8 429	7 799	7 327	6 873
Spain - Espagne	47 832	...	51 002	46 902	53 847	58 399	63 756	69 857	77 125	79 788
Sweden - Suède	32 293	31 441	32 117	31 433	31 008	...	30 980	31 772	33 365	34 473
The Former Yugoslav Rep. of Macedonia - L'ex-République yougoslave de Macédoine	...	...	...	12 028	...	...	...	...	...	...
Ukraine	...	...	...	...	...	...	...	369 750	345 367	315 835
United Kingdom - Royaume-Uni[10] ..	169 964	167 297	189 473	191 855	199 887	195 394	197 366	197 913	...	...
OCEANIA — OCEANIE										
New Caledonia - Nouvelle-Calédonie	...	...	...	1 528	1 466	...	...	...	...	...
New Zealand - Nouvelle-Zélande	12 835	13 652	14 805	15 208	15 029	15 501	16 103	16 410	17 380	18 511

FOOTNOTES - NOTES

* Provisional. — Données provisoires.

[1] Data refer to both 1997 and 1998. - Les données se rapportent à 1997 et à 1998.

[2] Data refer to abortions granted for medical reasons by the Comision Multidisciplinaria Nacional de Aborto Terapéutico. - Les données se réfèrent aux avortements autorisés pour des raisons médicales par la Comision Multidisciplinaria Nacional de Aborto Terapéutico.

[3] For abortions performed in hospitals at Grand Turk and Providenciales. - Pour des avortements exécutés dans les hôpitaux dans Grand Turk et Providenciales.

[4] Including data for East Jerusalem and Israeli residents in certain other territories under occupation by Israeli military forces since June 1967. - Y compris les données pour Jérusalem-Est et les résidents israéliens dans certains autres territoires occupés depuis 1967 par les forces armées israéliennes.

[5] Data refer to authorization to interrupt pregancy. - Les données se rapportent à l'autorisation d'interrompre le pregancy.

[6] Data refer to Japanese nationals in Japan only. - Les données se raportent aux nationaux japonais au Japon seulement.

[7] Excluding Faeroe Islands and Greenland. - Non compris les Iles Féroé et Gröenland.

[8] Data refer to requested abortions only and exclude a abortions due to therapeutic reasons. - Les données se rapportent seulement aux interruptions volontaires de grossesse et excluent les avortements effectués pour des rasions thérapeutiques.

[9] Based on hospital and polyclinic records. - D'après les registres des hôpitaux et des polycliniques.

[10] For residents only. - Pour les résidents seulement.

Table 14

Table 14 presents legally induced abortions by age and number of previous live births of women for the latest available year.

Description of variables: Age is defined as age at last birthday, that is, the difference between the date of birth and the date of the occurrence of the event, expressed in complete solar years. The age classification used in this table is the following: under 15 years, 5-year age groups through 45-49 years and 50 years and over.

Except where otherwise indicated, eight categories are used in classifying the number of previous live births: 0 through 5, 6 or more live births, and, if required, number of live births unknown.

In an effort to provide more complete interpretation of these statistics, countries or areas providing data on legally induced abortions have been requested to communicate grounds for legally induced abortions in their country or area. This information is presented in table 13-1 below.

Reliability of data: Unlike data on live births and foetal deaths, which are generally collected through systems of vital registration, data on abortion are collected from a variety of sources. Because of this, the quality specification, showing the completeness of civil registers, which is presented for other tables, does not appear here.

Limitations: With regard to the collection of information on abortions, a variety of sources are used, but hospital records are the most common source of information. This implies that most cases that have no contact with hospitals are missed. Data from other sources are probably also incomplete. The data in the present table are limited to legally induced abortions, which, by their nature, might be assumed to be more complete than data on all induced abortions.

In addition, deficiencies in the reporting of age and number of previous live births of the woman, differences in the method used for obtaining the age of the woman, and the proportion of abortions for which age or previous live births of the woman are unknown must all be taken into account in using these data.

Earlier data: Legally induced abortions by age and previous live births of women have been shown previously in most issues of the *Demographic Yearbook* since the 1971 issue. For more information on specific topics and years for which data are reported, readers should consult the Index.

Tableau 14

Le tableau 14 présente les données les plus récentes dont on dispose sur les avortements provoqués pour des raisons légales, selon l'âge de la mère et le nombre de naissances vivantes précédentes.

Description des variables : Les notes techniques du tableau 13 contiennent une classification des avortements provoqués légalement.

L'âge considéré est l'âge au dernier anniversaire, c'est-à-dire la différence entre la date de naissance et la date de l'avortement, exprimée en années solaires révolues. La classification par âge utilisée dans le tableau 14 est la suivante : moins de 15 ans, groupes quinquennaux jusqu'à 45-49 ans, 50 ans et plus, et âge inconnu.

Sauf indication contraire, les naissances vivantes antérieures sont classées dans les huit catégories suivantes: 0 à 5 naissances vivantes, 6 naissances vivantes ou plus et, le cas échéant, nombre de naissances vivantes inconnu.

Dans un effort de fournir une interprétation plus complète de ces statistiques, les pays ou les zones fournissant des données sur des avortements légalement induits ont été demandés pour communiquer des raisons pour des avortements légalement induits dans leur pays ou zone. Cette information est présentée dans le tableau 13-1.

Fiabilité des données : À la différence des données sur les naissances vivantes et les morts fœtales, qui proviennent généralement des registres d'état civil, les données sur l'avortement sont tirées de sources diverses. Aussi ne trouve-t-on pas ici une évaluation de la qualité des données semblable à celle qui indique, pour les autres tableaux, le degré d'exhaustivité des données de l'état civil.

Insuffisance des données : En ce qui concerne les renseignements sur l'avortement, un grand nombre de sources sont utilisées, les relevés hospitaliers restant cependant la source la plus commune. Il s'ensuit que la plupart des cas qui ne passent pas par les hôpitaux sont ignorés. Il faut aussi tenir compte du fait que les données provenant d'autres sources sont probablement incomplètes. Les données du tableau 14 se limitent aux avortements provoqués pour raisons légales dont on peut supposer, en raison de leur nature même, que les statistiques sont plus complètes que les données concernant l'ensemble des avortements provoqués.

En outre, on doit tenir compte, lorsque l'on utilise ces données, des erreurs de déclaration de l'âge de la mère et du nombre des naissances vivantes précédentes, de l'hétérogénéité des méthodes de calcul de l'âge de la mère et de la proportion d'avortements pour lesquels l'âge de la mère ou le nombre des naissances vivantes ne sont pas connus.

Données publiées antérieurement : Depuis 1971, la plupart des éditions de l'*Annuaire démographique* contiennent des statistiques concernant les avortements provoqués pour raisons légales, selon l'âge de la mère et le nombre de naissances vivantes antérieures. Pour plus de précisions concernant les années et les sujets pour lesquels des données ont été publiées, se reporter à l'index.

14. Legally induced abortions by age and number of previous live births of women: latest available year, 1994 - 2003
Avortments provoqués légalement selon l'âge de la femme et selon le nombre des naissances vivantes précédentes: dernière année disponible, 1994 - 2003

Continent, country or area, year and age Continent, pays ou zone, année et âge	Total	0	1	2	3	4	5	6+	Unknown Inconnu
		\multicolumn{8}{c}{Number of previous live births - Nombre des naissances vivantes précédentes}							

Continent, country or area, year and age	Total	0	1	2	3	4	5	6+	Unknown Inconnu
AMERICA, NORTH — AMERIQUE DU NORD									
Canada									
2001									
Total	106 418	...	...	...	...	...	...	...	...
0 - 14	412	...	...	...	...	...	...	...	...
15 - 19	19 968	...	...	...	...	...	...	...	...
20 - 24	32 730	...	...	...	...	...	...	...	...
25 - 29	22 012	...	...	...	...	...	...	...	...
30 - 34	16 243	...	...	...	...	...	...	...	...
35 - 39	10 977	...	...	...	...	...	...	...	...
40+	4 043	...	...	...	...	...	...	...	...
Unknown	33	...	...	...	...	...	...	...	...
Mexico - Mexique									
2003									
Total	3 486	843	1 108	690	280	89	46	36	394
0 - 14	13	10	-	-	-	-	-	-	3
15 - 19	468	208	143	20	3	-	-	-	94
20 - 24	974	276	385	170	29	2	1	1	110
25 - 29	887	172	305	223	75	16	7	4	85
30 - 34	580	73	160	158	97	26	23	8	35
35 - 39	308	34	64	82	52	35	12	15	14
40 - 44	82	11	16	23	13	8	3	6	2
45 - 49	5	-	-	1	1	-	-	2	1
50+	1	-	1	-	-	-	-	-	-
Unknown	168	59	34	13	10	2	-	-	50
Panama[1]									
2000									
Total	11	7	3	-	-	-	-	1	-
15 - 19	2	2	-	-	-	-	-	-	-
20 - 24	4	3	1	-	-	-	-	-	-
25 - 29	2	1	1	-	-	-	-	-	-
30 - 34	2	-	1	-	-	-	-	1	-
35+	1	1	-	-	-	-	-	-	-
ASIA — ASIE									
Azerbaijan - Azerbaïdjan									
2003									
Total	16 903	...	...	...	...	...	...	...	...
15 - 19	809	...	...	...	...	...	...	...	...
20 - 24	4 119	...	...	...	...	...	...	...	...
25 - 29	5 115	...	...	...	...	...	...	...	...
30 - 34	4 131	...	...	...	...	...	...	...	...
35+	2 729	...	...	...	...	...	...	...	...
China: Hong Kong SAR - Chine: Hong Kong RAS[2]									
2003									
Total	17 419	9 582	3 392	3 618	677	150	...	...	...
0 - 14	31	31	-	-	-	-	...	...	...
15 - 19	1 498	1 453	41	4	-	-	...	...	...
20 - 24	3 901	3 460	354	81	6	-	...	...	...
25 - 29	3 747	2 563	740	376	55	13	...	...	...
30 - 34	3 346	1 324	966	895	135	26	...	...	...
35 - 39	3 184	586	872	1 389	277	60	...	...	...
40 - 44	1 559	152	382	799	184	42	...	...	...
45+	153	13	37	74	20	9	...	...	...
Georgia - Géorgie[3]									
1995									
Total	32 016	...	...	...	...	...	...	...	...
0 - 14	177	...	...	...	...	...	...	...	...
15 - 19	2 508	...	...	...	...	...	...	...	...
20 - 34	25 510	...	...	...	...	...	...	...	...

14. Legally induced abortions by age and number of previous live births of women: latest available year, 1994 - 2003
Avortments provoqués légalement selon l'âge de la femme et selon le nombre des naissances vivantes précédentes: dernière année disponible, 1994 - 2003 (continued — suite)

Continent, country or area, year and age / Continent, pays ou zone, année et âge	Total	\multicolumn{9}{c}{Number of previous live births - Nombre des naissances vivantes précédentes}
		0	1	2	3	4	5	6+	Unknown Inconnu

Continent, country or area, year and age	Total	0	1	2	3	4	5	6+	Unknown Inconnu
ASIA — ASIE									
Georgia - Géorgie[3]									
1995									
35+	3 821	...	...	...	...	...	...	...	...
Israel - Israël[4]									
2002									
Total	19 126	8 087	3 206	3 725	2 344	1 027	374	336	27
0 - 14	95	92	2	2	-	-	-	-	-
15 - 19	2 796	2 687	91	12	1	-	-	-	5
20 - 24	4 060	3 008	705	266	66	10	-	-	4
25 - 29	3 994	1 569	1 078	905	286	102	38	9	7
30 - 34	3 625	511	821	1 237	642	254	91	62	7
35 - 39	2 853	162	351	857	850	360	139	132	2
40 - 44	1 528	41	140	409	445	275	100	117	1
45 - 49	152	8	14	35	53	23	5	13	1
50+	4	-	-	-	-	1	1	2	-
Unknown	19	9	4	3	1	2	-	`	-
Japan - Japon[5]									
2003									
Total	319 831	...	...	...	...	...	...	...	...
0 - 14	483	...	...	...	...	...	...	...	...
15 - 19	39 992	...	...	...	...	...	...	...	...
20 - 24	77 469	...	...	...	...	...	...	...	...
25 - 29	66 297	...	...	...	...	...	...	...	...
30 - 34	63 923	...	...	...	...	...	...	...	...
35 - 39	48 687	...	...	...	...	...	...	...	...
40 - 44	20 950	...	...	...	...	...	...	...	...
45 - 49	1 853	...	...	...	...	...	...	...	...
50+	28	...	...	...	...	...	...	...	...
Unknown	149	...	...	...	...	...	...	...	...
Kazakhstan									
1999									
Total	137 808	...	...	...	...	...	...	...	...
0 - 14	177	...	...	...	...	...	...	...	...
15 - 18	8 971	...	...	...	...	...	...	...	...
19 - 35	105 204	...	...	...	...	...	...	...	...
36+	23 456	...	...	...	...	...	...	...	...
Singapore - Singapour[2]									
2000									
Total	13 734	6 529	1 983	3 116	1 607	499	...	...	...
0 - 14	37	37	-	-	-	-	...	...	...
15 - 19	1 693	1 571	101	21	-	-	...	...	...
20 - 24	3 302	2 668	399	181	46	8	...	...	...
25 - 29	3 053	1 498	601	666	224	64	...	...	...
30 - 34	2 506	497	480	919	487	123	...	...	...
35 - 39	2 169	200	290	918	569	192	...	...	...
40 - 44	901	56	107	376	263	99	...	...	...
45+	73	2	5	35	18	13	...	...	...
Tajikistan - Tadjikistan									
2003									
Total	18 822	...	...	...	...	...	...	...	...
0 - 14	2	...	...	...	...	...	...	...	...
15 - 19	1 493	...	...	...	...	...	...	...	...
20 - 34	11 830	...	...	...	...	...	...	...	...
35+	5 497	...	...	...	...	...	...	...	...
EUROPE									
Belarus - Bélarus									
2003									
Total	80 174	...	...	...	...	...	...	...	...
0 - 14	38	...	...	...	...	...	...	...	...
15 - 19	7 583	...	...	...	...	...	...	...	...

14. Legally induced abortions by age and number of previous live births of women: latest available year, 1994 - 2003
Avortments provoqués légalement selon l'âge de la femme et selon le nombre des naissances vivantes précédentes: dernière année disponible, 1994 - 2003 (continued — suite)

Continent, country or area, year and age / Continent, pays ou zone, année et âge	Total	0	1	2	3	4	5	6+	Unknown Inconnu
EUROPE									
Belarus - Bélarus									
2003									
20 - 24	20 601	...	...	...	...	...	...	...	...
25 - 29	19 740	...	...	...	...	...	...	...	...
30 - 34	15 800	...	...	...	...	...	...	...	...
35 - 39	10 905	...	...	...	...	...	...	...	...
40 - 44	4 999	...	...	...	...	...	...	...	...
45+	508	...	...	...	...	...	...	...	...
Belgium - Belgique									
2003									
Total	15 595	...	...	...	...	...	...	...	...
0 - 14	65	...	...	...	...	...	...	...	...
15 - 19	2 097	...	...	...	...	...	...	...	...
20 - 24	4 032	...	...	...	...	...	...	...	...
25 - 29	3 411	...	...	...	...	...	...	...	...
30 - 34	3 001	...	...	...	...	...	...	...	...
35 - 39	2 107	...	...	...	...	...	...	...	...
40 - 44	810	...	...	...	...	...	...	...	...
45 - 49	67	...	...	...	...	...	...	...	...
50+	1	...	...	...	...	...	...	...	...
Unknown	4	...	...	...	...	...	...	...	...
Bulgaria - Bulgarie									
2003									
Total	48 035	...	...	...	...	...	...	...	...
0 - 14	159	...	...	...	...	...	...	...	...
15 - 19	4 686	...	...	...	...	...	...	...	...
20 - 24	12 278	...	...	...	...	...	...	...	...
25 - 29	13 250	...	...	...	...	...	...	...	...
30 - 34	9 868	...	...	...	...	...	...	...	...
35 - 39	5 790	...	...	...	...	...	...	...	...
40 - 44	1 839	...	...	...	...	...	...	...	...
45 - 49	153	...	...	...	...	...	...	...	...
50+	12	...	...	...	...	...	...	...	...
Channel Islands: Guernsey - Îles Anglo-Normandes: Guernesey									
2000									
Total	89	46	21	11	9	1	1	-	-
0 - 14	1	1	-	-	-	-	-	-	-
15 - 19	12	11	1	-	-	-	-	-	-
20 - 24	30	17	13	-	-	-	-	-	-
25 - 29	18	11	3	3	1	-	-	-	-
30 - 34	15	4	3	4	2	1	1	-	-
35 - 39	10	1	1	4	4	-	-	-	-
40 - 44	3	1	-	-	2	-	-	-	-
Croatia - Croatie									
2003									
Total	5 923	1 586	1 175	2 066	723	210	56	49	58
0 - 14	1	1	-	-	-	-	-	-	-
15 - 19	493	439	45	1	1	-	-	-	7
20 - 24	1 021	626	217	125	35	5	3	-	10
25 - 29	1 136	273	335	377	98	30	7	6	10
30 - 34	1 255	122	247	587	198	56	18	16	11
35 - 39	1 273	64	203	635	250	78	15	15	13
40 - 44	569	18	89	286	115	34	12	10	5
45 - 49	32	-	9	14	7	1	1	-	-
50+	2	1	-	1	-	-	-	-	-
Unknown	141	42	30	40	19	6	-	2	2
Czech Republic - République tchèque									
2003									
Total	29 298	7 637	7 453	10 493	2 784	617	218	96	-

14. Legally induced abortions by age and number of previous live births of women: latest available year, 1994 - 2003
Avortments provoqués légalement selon l'âge de la femme et selon le nombre des naissances vivantes précédentes: dernière année disponible, 1994 - 2003 (continued — suite)

Continent, country or area, year and age / Continent, pays ou zone, année et âge	Total	\multicolumn{9}{c}{Number of previous live births - Nombre des naissances vivantes précédentes}
		0	1	2	3	4	5	6+	Unknown Inconnu

Continent, country or area, year and age	Total	0	1	2	3	4	5	6+	Unknown Inconnu
EUROPE									
Czech Republic - République tchèque									
2003									
0 - 14	43	43	-	-	-	-	-	-	-
15 - 19	2 640	2 324	280	33	3	-	-	-	-
20 - 24	5 712	3 118	1 812	625	130	17	6	4	-
25 - 29	7 498	1 613	2 620	2 597	477	136	44	11	-
30 - 34	6 509	368	1 591	3 356	895	192	79	28	-
35 - 39	4 675	143	832	2 613	821	174	60	32	-
40 - 44	1 993	25	290	1 135	412	83	29	19	-
45 - 49	223	3	28	130	46	14	-	2	-
50+	5	-	-	4	-	1	-	-	-
Unknown	-	-	-	-	-	-	-	-	-
Denmark - Danemark[6]									
2002									
Total	14 991	...	...	...	...	...	...	...	...
0 - 14	-	...	...	...	...	...	...	...	...
15 - 19	1 915	...	...	...	...	...	...	...	...
20 - 24	3 102	...	...	...	...	...	...	...	...
25 - 29	3 156	...	...	...	...	...	...	...	...
30 - 34	3 159	...	...	...	...	...	...	...	...
35 - 39	2 753	...	...	...	...	...	...	...	...
40 - 44	837	...	...	...	...	...	...	...	...
45 - 49	69	...	...	...	...	...	...	...	...
50+	-	...	...	...	...	...	...	...	...
Unknown	-	...	...	...	...	...	...	...	...
Estonia - Estonie									
2003									
Total	10 619	2 881	3 800	2 835	776	217	58	28	24
0 - 14	22	22	-	-	-	-	-	-	-
15 - 19	1 460	1 255	193	10	-	-	-	-	2
20 - 24	2 562	1 133	1 130	250	34	9	-	-	6
25 - 29	2 361	330	1 206	661	134	19	5	3	3
30 - 34	2 049	90	726	892	237	74	14	10	6
35 - 39	1 464	41	399	678	237	75	22	9	3
40 - 44	646	10	137	319	120	35	16	5	4
45 - 49	55	-	9	25	14	5	1	1	-
50+	-	-	-	-	-	-	-	-	-
Unknown	-	-	-	-	-	-	-	-	-
Finland - Finlande									
2003									
Total	10 749	5 678	1 890	1 919	899	255	81	27	-
0 - 14	61	61	-	-	-	-	-	-	-
15 - 19	2 342	2 192	139	10	1	-	-	-	-
20 - 24	2 725	1 925	544	220	32	4	-	-	-
25 - 29	1 935	818	466	436	163	47	5	-	-
30 - 34	1 643	381	353	527	278	72	26	6	-
35 - 39	1 454	214	282	521	296	92	35	14	-
40 - 44	539	83	99	183	116	37	14	7	-
45 - 49	50	4	7	22	13	3	1	-	-
France									
2001									
Total	198 700	...	...	...	...	...	...	...	...
0 - 14	-	...	...	...	...	...	...	...	...
15 - 19	27 033	...	...	...	...	...	...	...	...
20 - 24	48 649	...	...	...	...	...	...	...	...
25 - 29	43 382	...	...	...	...	...	...	...	...
30 - 34	38 068	...	...	...	...	...	...	...	...
35 - 39	28 834	...	...	...	...	...	...	...	...
40 - 44	11 536	...	...	...	...	...	...	...	...
45 - 49	1 198	...	...	...	...	...	...	...	...
50+	-	...	...	...	...	...	...	...	...

14. Legally induced abortions by age and number of previous live births of women: latest available year, 1994 - 2003
Avortments provoqués légalement selon l'âge de la femme et selon le nombre des naissances vivantes précédentes: dernière année disponible, 1994 - 2003 (continued — suite)

Continent, country or area, year and age Continent, pays ou zone, année et âge	Total	0	1	2	3	4	5	6+	Unknown Inconnu
EUROPE									
Germany - Allemagne									
2001									
Total	134 964	53 352	34 413	32 277	10 705	2 883	830	504	-
0 - 14	696	685	7	4	-	-	-	-	-
15 - 19	16 453	14 835	1 440	150	27	-	-	1	-
20 - 24	30 120	18 444	8 012	2 942	592	110	13	7	-
25 - 29	27 897	9 651	8 917	6 854	1 844	487	106	38	-
30 - 34	29 053	6 036	8 539	9 979	3 242	853	262	142	-
35 - 39	22 091	2 879	5 658	8 745	3 391	955	278	185	-
40 - 44	8 025	779	1 732	3 315	1 481	443	155	120	-
45 - 49	629	43	108	288	128	35	16	11	-
2002									
Total	130 387	...	...	...	...	...	...	...	...
0 - 14	761	...	...	...	...	...	...	...	...
15 - 19	15 948	...	...	...	...	...	...	...	...
20 - 24	29 923	...	...	...	...	...	...	...	...
25 - 29	26 550	...	...	...	...	...	...	...	...
30 - 34	27 068	...	...	...	...	...	...	...	...
35 - 39	21 405	...	...	...	...	...	...	...	...
40 - 44	8 045	...	...	...	...	...	...	...	...
45 - 49	687	...	...	...	...	...	...	...	...
Greece - Grèce									
1996									
Total	12 542	...	...	...	...	...	...	...	...
0 - 14	17	...	...	...	...	...	...	...	...
15 - 19	468	...	...	...	...	...	...	...	...
20 - 29	5 460	...	...	...	...	...	...	...	...
30 - 39	5 313	...	...	...	...	...	...	...	...
40 - 49	1 007	...	...	...	...	...	...	...	...
50+	41	...	...	...	...	...	...	...	...
Unknown	236	...	...	...	...	...	...	...	...
Hungary - Hongrie									
2003									
Total	53 789	14 402	12 752	14 117	7 912	2 748	1 049	809	-
0 - 14	189	179	8	2	-	-	-	-	-
15 - 19	6 139	4 777	1 090	223	47	2	-	9	-
20 - 24	11 600	5 100	3 380	1 823	958	269	61	9	-
25 - 29	13 744	3 001	3 848	3 505	2 182	823	267	118	-
30 - 34	11 097	889	2 554	3 975	2 256	777	332	314	-
35 - 39	7 681	237	1 363	3 103	1 772	646	291	269	-
40 - 44	2 876	74	448	1 321	640	214	90	89	-
45 - 49	233	3	36	134	36	13	6	5	-
50+	8	-	1	3	2	1	1	-	-
Unknown	222	142	24	28	19	3	1	5	-
Iceland - Islande									
2000									
Total	987	...	...	...	...	...	...	...	...
0 - 14	8	...	...	...	...	...	...	...	...
15 - 19	257	...	...	...	...	...	...	...	...
20 - 24	241	...	...	...	...	...	...	...	...
25 - 29	209	...	...	...	...	...	...	...	...
30 - 34	132	...	...	...	...	...	...	...	...
35 - 39	93	...	...	...	...	...	...	...	...
40 - 44	46	...	...	...	...	...	...	...	...
45 - 49	1	...	...	...	...	...	...	...	...
Italy - Italie									
2002									
Total	131 039	56 495	28 595	32 744	9 846	2 173	620	257	309
0 - 14	245	234	9	2	-	-	-	-	-
15 - 19	10 359	9 434	782	95	9	-	-	1	38
20 - 24	25 605	18 484	4 859	1 844	266	50	14	4	84
25 - 29	30 252	14 753	7 831	5 999	1 299	221	50	19	80

14. Legally induced abortions by age and number of previous live births of women: latest available year, 1994 - 2003

Avortments provoqués légalement selon l'âge de la femme et selon le nombre des naissances vivantes précédentes: dernière année disponible, 1994 - 2003 (continued — suite)

Continent, country or area, year and age / Continent, pays ou zone, année et âge	Total	Number of previous live births - Nombre des naissances vivantes précédentes							
		0	1	2	3	4	5	6+	Unknown Inconnu
EUROPE									
Italy - Italie									
2002									
30 - 34	29 117	8 223	7 553	9 860	2 725	528	143	38	47
35 - 39	24 138	3 945	5 385	10 114	3 519	807	219	113	36
40 - 44	10 009	1 178	1 951	4 326	1 797	501	169	72	15
45 - 49	841	59	144	363	187	55	23	9	1
50+	41	9	5	14	9	2	1	-	1
Unknown	432	176	76	127	35	9	1	1	7
Latvia - Lettonie									
2002									
Total	14 685	...	...	...	...	...	...	...	...
0 - 14	8	...	...	...	...	...	...	...	...
15 - 19	1 518	...	...	...	...	...	...	...	...
20 - 24	3 529	...	...	...	...	...	...	...	...
25 - 29	3 459	...	...	...	...	...	...	...	...
30 - 34	2 985	...	...	...	...	...	...	...	...
35 - 39	2 078	...	...	...	...	...	...	...	...
40 - 44	988	...	...	...	...	...	...	...	...
45 - 49	107	...	...	...	...	...	...	...	...
50+	13	...	...	...	...	...	...	...	...
Lithuania - Lituanie[7]									
2003									
Total	11 513	1 420	...	...	...	...	...	...	10 093
0 - 14	3	3	...	...	...	...	...	...	-
15 - 19	872	462	...	...	...	...	...	...	410
20 - 24	2 472	561	...	...	...	...	...	...	1 911
25 - 29	2 622	229	...	...	...	...	...	...	2 393
30 - 34	2 639	110	...	...	...	...	...	...	2 529
35 - 39	1 930	44	...	...	...	...	...	...	1 886
40 - 44	879	9	...	...	...	...	...	...	870
45 - 49	96	2	...	...	...	...	...	...	94
Norway - Norvège									
2003									
Total	13 888	...	...	...	...	...	...	...	...
0 - 14	49	...	...	...	...	...	...	...	...
15 - 19	2 153	...	...	...	...	...	...	...	...
20 - 24	3 637	...	...	...	...	...	...	...	...
25 - 29	2 905	...	...	...	...	...	...	...	...
30 - 34	2 620	...	...	...	...	...	...	...	...
35 - 39	1 844	...	...	...	...	...	...	...	...
40 - 44	635	...	...	...	...	...	...	...	...
45+	44	...	...	...	...	...	...	...	...
Unknown	1	...	...	...	...	...	...	...	...
Republic of Moldova - République de Moldova									
2003									
Total	17 551	...	...	...	...	...	...	...	...
0 - 14	16	...	...	...	...	...	...	...	...
15 - 19	1 859	...	...	...	...	...	...	...	...
20 - 29	12 383	...	...	...	...	...	...	...	...
30+	3 293	...	...	...	...	...	...	...	...
Romania - Roumanie									
2003									
Total	224 807	...	...	...	...	...	...	...	...
0 - 14	868	...	...	...	...	...	...	...	...
15 - 19	19 489	...	...	...	...	...	...	...	...
20 - 24	50 508	...	...	...	...	...	...	...	...
25 - 29	58 781	...	...	...	...	...	...	...	...
30 - 34	52 343	...	...	...	...	...	...	...	...
35 - 39	32 749	...	...	...	...	...	...	...	...
40 - 44	9 044	...	...	...	...	...	...	...	...
45 - 49	1 000	...	...	...	...	...	...	...	...

14. Legally induced abortions by age and number of previous live births of women: latest available year, 1994 - 2003
Avortments provoqués légalement selon l'âge de la femme et selon le nombre des naissances vivantes précédentes: dernière année disponible, 1994 - 2003 (continued — suite)

Continent, country or area, year and age / Continent, pays ou zone, année et âge	Number of previous live births - Nombre des naissances vivantes précédentes								
	Total	0	1	2	3	4	5	6+	Unknown Inconnu
EUROPE									
Romania - Roumanie									
2003									
50+	25	...	...	...	...	...	...	...	...
Russian Federation - Fédération de Russie[3]									
1995									
Total	2 255 797	...	...	...	...	...	...	...	...
0 - 14	2 217	...	...	...	...	...	...	...	...
15 - 19	233 166	...	...	...	...	...	...	...	...
20 - 34	1 551 440	...	...	...	...	...	...	...	...
35+	468 974	...	...	...	...	...	...	...	...
Serbia and Montenegro - Serbie-et-Montenegro[2]									
1998									
Total	58 739	6 941	10 691	31 998	7 022	2 085	...	...	2
0 - 14	10	...	...	...	...	...	...	...	...
15 - 19	9 725	...	...	...	...	...	...	...	...
20 - 24	28 223	...	...	...	...	...	...	...	...
25 - 29	19 649	...	...	...	...	...	...	...	...
30 - 34	1 121	...	...	...	...	...	...	...	...
35 - 39	4	...	...	...	...	...	...	...	...
40+	7	...	...	...	...	...	...	...	...
Slovakia - Slovaquie									
2002									
Total	17 382	4 539	4 204	5 786	1 905	606	201	141	-
0 - 14	10	10	-	-	-	-	-	-	-
15 - 19	1 622	1 346	222	44	10	-	-	-	-
20 - 24	3 762	1 868	1 184	553	113	34	9	1	-
25 - 29	4 489	915	1 433	1 549	395	120	50	27	-
30 - 34	3 555	241	777	1 692	569	181	55	40	-
35 - 39	2 716	114	454	1 340	525	186	59	38	-
40 - 44	1 140	38	125	562	271	84	27	33	-
45 - 49	86	6	9	45	22	1	1	2	-
50+	2	1	-	1	-	-	-	-	-
Slovenia - Slovénie									
2003									
Total	6 873	2 113	1 593	2 352	644	127	27	14	3
0 - 14	8	8	-	-	-	-	-	-	-
15 - 19	544	516	26	2	-	-	-	-	-
20 - 24	1 306	905	312	75	10	4	-	-	-
25 - 29	1 494	448	492	462	77	10	4	-	1
30 - 34	1 435	156	362	686	179	38	5	8	1
35 - 39	1 418	63	287	748	254	51	12	2	1
40 - 44	604	16	105	343	110	20	6	4	-
45 - 49	57	...	6	33	14	4	-	-	-
50+	2	-	1	1	-	-	-	-	-
Unknown	5	1	2	2	-	-	-	-	-
Spain - Espagne[8]									
2002									
Total	77 125	40 172	17 159	13 506	4 329	1 228	718	...	13
0 - 14	274	273	1	-	-	-	-	...	-
15 - 19	10 385	9 288	965	119	9	2	-	...	2
20 - 24	21 056	15 066	4 303	1 376	246	53	9	...	3
25 - 29	18 205	9 404	4 655	2 990	854	216	84	...	2
30 - 34	13 620	4 128	3 810	3 884	1 273	340	183	...	2
35 - 39	9 507	1 598	2 541	3 456	1 253	394	263	...	2
40 - 44	3 756	392	831	1 545	633	190	163	...	2
45 - 49	322	23	53	136	61	33	16	...	-
Sweden - Suède[9]									
2002									
Total	33 365	16 730	5 271	6 757	2 859	875	250	130	493
0 - 14	263	258	-	-	-	-	-	-	5

Avortments provoqués légalement selon l'âge de la femme et selon le nombre des naissances vivantes précédentes: dernière année disponible, 1994 - 2003 (continued — suite)

Continent, country or area, year and age / Continent, pays ou zone, année et âge	Total	\multicolumn{8}{c}{Number of previous live births - Nombre des naissances vivantes précédentes}							
	Total	0	1	2	3	4	5	6+	Unknown Inconnu
EUROPE									
Sweden - Suède[9]									
2002									
15 - 19	6 240	5 888	191	7	3	-	-	-	151
20 - 24	7 614	5 781	1 253	386	56	2	-	1	135
25 - 29	6 416	2 978	1 504	1 369	384	71	18	5	87
30 - 34	5 895	1 221	1 208	2 207	872	260	55	17	55
35 - 39	4 973	473	826	2 030	1 075	374	99	56	40
40 - 44	1 771	116	268	696	414	149	68	43	17
45 - 49	187	10	21	62	55	19	10	8	2
50+	1	1	-	-	-	-	-	-	-
Unknown	5	4	-	-	-	-	-	-	1
Ukraine									
2003									
Total	315 835	...	...	...	...	...	...	...	...
0 - 14	162	...	...	...	...	...	...	...	...
15 - 17	7 842	...	...	...	...	...	...	...	...
18 - 34	255 033	...	...	...	...	...	...	...	...
35+	52 798	...	...	...	...	...	...	...	...
United Kingdom - Royaume-Uni[10]									
2000									
Total	197 366	105 328	37 645	33 532	13 982	4 683	1 414	753	29
0 - 14	1 170	1 165	4	1	-	-	-	-	-
15 - 19	40 225	35 254	4 393	528	40	4	-	-	6
20 - 24	53 590	35 263	11 732	5 183	1 150	222	25	9	6
25 - 29	42 680	20 273	9 640	8 295	3 212	953	231	71	5
30 - 34	31 928	8 925	7 004	9 504	4 339	1 491	455	205	5
35 - 39	20 684	3 562	3 711	7 438	3 771	1 433	485	279	5
40 - 44	6 526	794	1 081	2 375	1 359	542	203	171	1
45 - 49	490	62	66	189	108	36	14	15	-
50+	25	4	4	9	2	2	1	3	-
Unknown	48	26	10	10	1	-	-	-	1
2001									
Total	197 913	...	...	...	...	...	...	...	...
0 - 14	1 157	...	...	...	...	...	...	...	...
15 - 19	40 387	...	...	...	...	...	...	...	...
20 - 24	54 878	...	...	...	...	...	...	...	...
25 - 29	41 126	...	...	...	...	...	...	...	...
30 - 34	31 921	...	...	...	...	...	...	...	...
35 - 39	21 096	...	...	...	...	...	...	...	...
40 - 44	6 833	...	...	...	...	...	...	...	...
45 - 49	513	...	...	...	...	...	...	...	...
Unknown	2	...	...	...	...	...	...	...	...
OCEANIA — OCEANIE									
New Zealand - Nouvelle-Zélande									
2003									
Total	18 511	9 451	3 312	3 206	1 526	634	233	149	...
0 - 14	89	88	1	-	-	-	-	-	...
15 - 19	3 757	3 316	386	52	3	-	-	-	...
20 - 24	5 670	3 614	1 160	639	195	49	11	2	...
25 - 29	3 619	1 388	761	821	419	169	45	16	...
30 - 34	2 800	705	567	811	423	168	73	53	...
35 - 39	1 846	263	329	646	314	166	76	52	...
40 - 44	692	70	106	225	166	78	24	23	...
45+	38	7	2	12	6	4	4	3	...

FOOTNOTES - NOTES

[1] Data refer to abortions granted for medical reasons by the Comision Multidisciplinaria Nacional de Aborto Terapéutico. - Les données se réfèrent aux avortements autorisés pour des raisons médicales par la Comision Multidisciplinaria Nacional de Aborto Terapéutico.

[2] Column '4' includes '5' and over. - Colonne '4' compris '5' plus.

3 Data as reported by national statistical authorities; they may differ from data presented in other tables. - Les données comme elles ont été déclarées par l'institut national de la statistique; elles peuvent être différentes de ceux présentées dans autre tableaux.

4 Including data for East Jerusalem and Israeli residents in certain other territories under occupation by Israeli military forces since June 1967. - Y compris les données pour Jérusalem-Est et les résidents israéliens dans certains autres territoires occupés depuis 1967 par les forces armées israéliennes.

5 Data refer to Japanese nationals in Japan only. - Les données se raportent aux nationaux japonais au Japon seulement.

6 Excluding Faeroe Islands and Greenland. - Non compris les Iles Féroé et Gröenland.

7 Data refer to requested abortions only and exclude a abortions due to therapeutic reasons. - Les données se rapportent seulement aux interruptions volontaires de grossesse et excluent les avortements effectués pour des rasions thérapeutiques.

8 Column '5' includes '6' and over. - Colonne '5' compris '6' plus.

9 Abortion by previous deliveries of mother rather than previous live births of mother. - Avortements selon les accouchements précédents de la mère plutôt que selon les naissances vivantes de la mère.

10 For residents only. - Pour les résidents seulement.

Table 15

Table 15 presents infant deaths and infant mortality rates by urban/rural residence for as many years as possible between 1999 and 2003.

Description of variables: Infant deaths are deaths of live-born infants under one year of age.

Statistics on the number of infant deaths are obtained from civil registers unless otherwise noted. Infant mortality rates are, in most instances, calculated from data on registered infant deaths and registered live births for a country or area where civil registration is considered reliable (that is, with an estimated completeness of 90 per cent or more).

The urban/rural classification of infant deaths is that provided by each country or area; it is presumed to be based on the national census definitions of urban population that have been set forth at the end of the technical notes of table 6.

Rate computation: Infant mortality rates are the annual number of deaths of infants under one year of age per 1 000 live births (as shown in table 9) in the same year.

Rates by urban/rural residence are the annual number of infant deaths, in the appropriate urban or rural category, per 1 000 corresponding live births (as shown in table 9). These rates have been calculated by the Statistics Division of the United Nations.

Rates presented in this table have been limited to those for countries or areas having at least a total of 100 infant deaths in a given year and for which the quality code is represented by a C or a symbol |.

Reliability of data: Each country or area has been asked to indicate the estimated completeness of the infant deaths recorded in its civil register. These national assessments are indicated by the quality codes C, U and | that appear in the first column of this table.

C indicates that the data are estimated to be virtually complete, that is, representing at least 90 per cent of the infant deaths occurring each year, while U indicates that data are estimated to be incomplete that is, representing less than 90 per cent of the infant deaths occurring each year. The code I indicates that the source of data is not civil registration, but is still considered reliable. The code ... indicates that no information was provided regarding completeness.

Data from civil registers that are reported as incomplete or of unknown completeness (coded U or ...) are considered unreliable. They appear in italics in this table; rates are not computed for data so coded.

Limitations: Statistics on infant deaths are subject to the same qualifications as have been set forth for vital statistics in general and death statistics in particular as discussed in section 4 of the Technical Notes.

The reliability of the data, an indication of which is described above, is an important factor in considering the limitations. In addition, some infant deaths are tabulated by date of registration and not by date of occurrence; these have been indicated by a plus sign (+). Whenever the lag between the date of occurrence and date of registration is prolonged and, therefore, a large proportion of the infant-death registrations are delayed, infant-death statistics for any given year may be seriously affected.

Another factor that limits international comparability is the practice of some countries or areas not to include in infant-death statistics infants who were born alive but died before the registration of the birth or within the first 24 hours of life, thus underestimating the total number of infant deaths. Statistics of this type are footnoted.

The method of reckoning age at death for infants may also introduce non-comparability. If year alone, rather than completed minutes, hours, days and months elapsed since birth, is used to calculate age at time of death, many of the infants who died during the eleventh month of life and some of those who died at younger ages will be classified as having completed one year of age and thus be excluded. The effect would be to underestimate the number of infant deaths. Information on this factor is given in footnotes when known. Reckoning of infant age is further discussed in the technical notes for table 16.

In addition, infant mortality rates are subject to the limitations of the data on live births with which they have been calculated. These have been set forth in the technical notes for table 9.

Because the two components of the infant mortality rate, infant deaths in the numerator and live births in the denominator, are both obtained from systems of civil registration, the limitations which affect live-birth statistics are very similar to those which have been mentioned above in connection with the infant-death statistics. It is important to consider the reliability of the data (the completeness of registration) and the method of tabulation (by date of occurrence or by date of registration) of live-birth statistics as well as infant-death statistics, both of which are used to calculate infant mortality rates. The quality code and use of italics to indicate unreliable data presented in this table refer only to infant deaths. Similarly, the indication of the basis of tabulation (the use of the symbol (+) to indicate data tabulated by date of registration) presented in this table also refers only to infant deaths. Table 9 provides the corresponding information for live births.

If the registration of infant deaths is more complete than the registration of live births, then infant mortality rates would be biased upwards. If, however, the registration of live births is more complete than registration of infant deaths, infant mortality rates would be biased downwards. If both infant deaths and live births are tabulated by registration, it should be noted that deaths tend to be more promptly reported than births.

Infant mortality rates may be seriously affected by the practice of some countries or areas of not considering infants that were born alive but died before the registration of the birth or within the first 24 hours of life as live-birth and subsequently infant death. Although this practice results in both the number of infant deaths in the numerator and the number of live births in the denominator being underestimated, its impact is greater on the numerator of the infant mortality rate. As a result this practice causes infant mortality rates to be biased downwards.

Infant mortality rates will also be underestimated if the method of reckoning age at death results in an underestimation of the number of infant deaths. This point has been discussed above.

Because of all these factors care should be taken in comparing and rank ordering infant mortality rates.

With respect to the method of calculating infant mortality rates used in this table, it should be noted that no adjustment was made to take account of the fact that a proportion of the infant deaths that occur during a given year are deaths of infants that were born during the preceding year and hence are not taken from the universe of births used to compute the rates. However, unless the number of live births or infant deaths is changing rapidly, the error involved is insignificant.

Estimated rates based directly on the results of sample surveys are subject to considerable error as a result of omissions in reporting infant deaths or as a result of erroneous reporting of those infant deaths that occurred outside the period of reference. However, such rates do have the advantage of having a "built-in" and corresponding base.

The comparability of data by urban/rural residence is affected by the national definitions of urban and rural used in tabulating these data. It is assumed, in the absence of specific information to the contrary, that the definitions of urban and rural used in connection with the national population census were also used in the compilation of the vital statistics for each country or area. However, it cannot be excluded that, for a given country or area, different definitions of urban and rural are used for the vital statistics data and the population census data respectively. When known, the definitions of urban used in national population censuses are presented at the end of the technical notes for table 6. As discussed in detail in the technical notes for table 6, these definitions vary considerably from one country or area to another.

Urban/rural differentials in infant mortality rates may also be affected by whether the infant deaths and live births have been tabulated in terms of place of occurrence or place of usual residence. This problem is discussed in more detail in section 4.1.4.1 of the Technical Notes.

Earlier data: Infant deaths and infant mortality rates have been shown in previous issues of the *Demographic Yearbook*. For more information on specific topics and years for which data are reported, readers should consult the Historical Index.

Tableau 15

Le tableau 15 présente des données sur les décès d'enfants de moins d'un an et les taux de mortalité infantile selon le lieu de résidence (zone urbaine ou rurale) pour le plus grand nombre d'années possible entre 1999 et 2003.

Description des variables : Les chiffres se rapportent aux décès d'enfants de moins d'un an.

Sauf indication contraire, les statistiques concernant le nombre de décès d'enfants de moins d'un an sont établies à partir des registres de l'état civil. Dans la plupart des cas, les taux de mortalité infantile sont calculés à partir des données relatives aux décès enregistrés d'enfants de moins d'un an et aux naissances vivantes enregistrées dans un pays ou une zone lorsque les registres de l'état civil sont jugés fiables (exhaustivité estimée à 90 p. 100 ou plus).

La classification des décès d'enfants de moins d'un an selon le lieu de résidence (zone urbaine ou rurale) est celle qui a été communiquée par chaque pays ou zone ; on part du principe qu'elle repose sur les définitions de la population urbaine utilisées pour les recensements nationaux, telles qu'elles sont reproduites à la fin des notes techniques du tableau 6.

Calcul des taux : Les taux de mortalité infantile représentent le nombre annuel de décès d'enfants de moins d'un an pour 1 000 naissances vivantes (fréquences du tableau 9) survenues pendant la même année.

Les taux selon le lieu de résidence (zone urbaine ou rurale) représentent le nombre annuel de décès d'enfants de moins d'un an, classés selon la catégorie urbaine ou rurale appropriée pour 1 000 naissances vivantes survenues parmi la population correspondante (fréquences du tableau 9). Ces taux ont été calculés par la Division de statistique de l'ONU.

Les taux présentés dans ce tableau se rapportent seulement aux pays ou zones où l'on a enregistré au moins un total de 100 décès d'enfants de moins d'un an au cours d'une année donnée et pour lesquels le code de qualité est soit 'C', soit '|'.

Fiabilité des données : Il a été demandé à chaque pays ou zone d'indiquer le degré estimatif de complétude des données sur les décès d'enfants de moins d'un an figurant dans ses registres d'état civil. Ces évaluations nationales sont signalées par les codes de qualité 'C', 'U' et '|' qui apparaissent dans la deuxième colonne du tableau.

La lettre 'C' indique que les données sont jugées à peu près complètes, c'est-à-dire qu'elles représentent au moins 90 p. 100 des décès d'enfants de moins d'un an survenus chaque année ; la lettre 'U' signifie que les données sont jugées incomplètes, c'est-à-dire qu'elles représentent moins de 90 p.100 des décès d'enfants de moins d'un an survenus chaque année. Le symbole 'I' indique que la source des données n'est pas un registre de l'état civil, mais est quand même considérée fiable. Le code '...' dénote qu'aucun renseignement n'a été communiqué quant à la complétude des données.

Les données provenant des registres de l'état civil qui sont déclarées incomplètes ou dont le degré de complétude n'est pas connu (code 'U' ou '...') sont jugées douteuses. Elles apparaissent en italique dans le tableau ; les taux, dans ces cas là, n'ont pas été calculés.

Insuffisance des données : Les statistiques des décès d'enfants de moins d'un an appellent toutes les réserves qui ont été formulées à propos des statistiques de l'état civil en général et des statistiques concernant les décès en particulier (voir la section 4 des Notes techniques).

La fiabilité des données, au sujet de laquelle des indications ont été fournies plus haut, est un facteur important. Il faut également tenir compte du fait que, dans certains cas, les données relatives aux décès d'enfants de moins d'un an sont exploitées selon la date de l'enregistrement et non la date de l'événement ; ces cas ont été signalés par le signe '+'. Chaque fois que le décalage entre l'événement et son enregistrement est grand et qu'une forte proportion des décès d'enfants de moins d'un an fait l'objet d'un enregistrement tardif, les statistiques des décès d'enfants de moins d'un an pour une année donnée peuvent être considérablement faussées.

Un autre facteur qui nuit à la comparabilité internationale est la pratique de certains pays ou zones qui consiste à ne pas inclure dans les statistiques des décès d'enfants de moins d'un an les enfants nés vivants mais décédés avant l'enregistrement de leur naissance ou dans les 24 heures qui ont suivi la naissance, pratique qui conduit à sous-estimer le nombre total de décès d'enfants de moins d'un an. Quand pareil facteur a joué, cela a été signalé en note.

Les méthodes appliquées pour calculer l'âge au moment du décès peuvent également nuire à la comparabilité des données. Si l'on utilise à cet effet l'année seulement, et non pas les minutes, heures, jours et mois qui se sont écoulés depuis la naissance, de nombreux enfants décédés au cours du onzième mois qui a suivi leur naissance et certains enfants décédés encore plus jeunes seront classés comme décédés à un an révolu et donc exclus des données. Cette pratique conduit à sous-estimer le nombre de décès d'enfants de moins d'un an. Les renseignements dont on dispose sur ce facteur apparaissent en note à la fin du tableau. La question du calcul de l'âge au moment du décès est examinée plus en détail dans les notes techniques se rapportant au tableau 16.

Les taux de mortalité infantile appellent en outre toutes les réserves qui ont été formulées à propos des statistiques des naissances vivantes qui ont servi à leur calcul (voir à ce sujet les notes techniques relatives au tableau 9).

Les deux composantes du taux de mortalité infantile - décès d'enfants de moins d'un an au numérateur et naissances vivantes au dénominateur - étant obtenues à partir des registres de l'état civil, les statistiques des naissances vivantes appellent des réserves presque identiques à celles qui ont été formulées plus haut à propos des statistiques des décès d'enfants de moins d'un an. Il importe de prendre en considération la fiabilité des données (complétude de l'enregistrement) et le mode d'exploitation (selon la date de l'événement ou selon la date de l'enregistrement) dans le cas des statistiques des naissances vivantes tout comme dans le cas de celles des décès d'enfants de moins d'un an, puisque les unes et les autres servent au calcul des taux de mortalité infantile. Dans le tableau 15, le code de qualité et l'emploi de caractères italiques pour signaler les données moins sûres ne concernent que les décès d'enfants de moins d'un an. L'indication du mode d'exploitation des données (emploi du signe '+' pour signaler les données exploitées selon la date de l'enregistrement) ne porte là aussi que sur les décès d'enfants de moins d'un an. Le tableau 9 contient les renseignements correspondants pour les naissances vivantes.

Si l'enregistrement des décès d'enfants de moins d'un an est plus complet que l'enregistrement des naissances vivantes, les taux de mortalité infantile seront entachés d'une erreur par excès. En revanche, si l'enregistrement des naissances vivantes est plus complet que l'enregistrement des décès d'enfants de moins d'un an, les taux de mortalité infantile seront entachés d'une erreur par défaut. Si les décès d'enfants de moins d'un an et les naissances vivantes sont exploitées selon la date de l'enregistrement, il convient de ne pas perdre de vue que les décès sont, en règle générale, déclarés plus rapidement que les naissances.

Les taux de mortalité infantile peuvent être gravement faussés par la pratique de certains pays ou zones qui consiste à ne pas classer dans les naissances vivantes et ensuite dans les décès d'enfants de moins d'un an les enfants nés vivants mais décédés soit avant l'enregistrement de leur naissance, soit dans les 24 heures qui ont suivi la naissance. Cette pratique conduit à sous-estimer aussi bien le nombre des décès d'enfants de moins d'un an, qui constitue le numérateur, que le nombre des naissances vivantes, qui constitue le dénominateur, mais c'est pour le numérateur du taux de mortalité infantile que la distorsion est la plus marquée. Ce système a pour effet d'introduire une erreur par défaut dans les taux de mortalité infantile.

Les taux de mortalité infantile seront également sous-estimés si la méthode utilisée pour calculer l'âge au moment du décès conduit à sous-estimer le nombre de décès d'enfants de moins d'un an. Cette question a été examinée plus haut.

Tous ces facteurs sont importants et il faut donc en tenir compte lorsque l'on compare et classe les taux de mortalité infantile.

En ce qui concerne la méthode de calcul des taux de mortalité infantile utilisée dans le tableau, il convient de noter qu'il n'a pas été tenu compte du fait qu'une partie des décès survenus pendant une année donnée sont des décès d'enfants nés l'année précédente et ne correspondent donc pas à l'ensemble des naissances utilisé pour le calcul des taux. Toutefois, l'erreur n'est pas grave, à moins que le nombre des naissances vivantes ou des décès d'enfants de moins d'un an ne varie rapidement.

Les taux estimatifs fondés directement sur les résultats d'enquêtes par sondage comportent des possibilités d'erreurs considérables dues soit à des omissions dans les déclarations de décès d'enfants de moins d'un an, soit au fait que l'on a déclaré à tort des décès survenus en réalité hors de la période considérée. Ils présentent aussi un avantage puisque le chiffre des naissances vivantes utilisé comme base est connu par définition et rigoureusement correspondant.

La comparabilité des données selon le lieu de résidence (zone urbaine ou rurale) peut être limitée par les définitions nationales des termes « urbain » et « rural » utilisées pour la mise en tableaux de ces données. En l'absence d'indications contraires, on a supposé que les mêmes définitions avaient servi pour le recensement national de la population et pour l'établissement des statistiques de l'état civil pour chaque pays ou zone. Toutefois, il n'est pas exclu que, pour une zone ou un pays donné, des définitions différentes aient été retenues. Les définitions du terme « urbain » utilisées pour les recensements nationaux de population ont été présentées à la fin des notes techniques du tableau 6 lorsqu'elles étaient connues. Comme on l'a précisé dans les notes techniques relatives au tableau 6, ces définitions varient considérablement d'un pays ou d'une zone à l'autre.

La différence entre les taux de mortalité infantile pour les zones urbaines et rurales pourra aussi être faussée selon que les décès d'enfants de moins d'un an et les naissances vivantes auront été classés d'après le lieu de l'événement ou le lieu de résidence habituel. Ce problème est examiné plus en détail à la section 4.1.4.1 des Notes techniques.

Données publiées antérieurement : Des statistiques concernant les décès d'enfants de moins d'un an et les taux de mortalité infantile ont déjà été présentées dans des éditions antérieures de l'*Annuaire démographique*. Pour plus de précisions concernant les années et les sujets pour lesquels des données ont été publiées, se reporter à l'index historique.

15. Infant deaths and infant mortality rates, by urban/rural residence: 1999 - 2003
Décès d'enfants de moins d'un an et taux de mortalité infantile, selon la résidence, urbaine/rurale: 1999 - 2003

Continent, country or area and urban/rural residence Continent, pays ou zone et résidence, urbaine/rurale	Code[1]	Number - Nombre					Rate - Taux				
		1999	2000	2001	2002	2003	1999	2000	2001	2002	2003
AFRICA — AFRIQUE											
Algeria - Algérie[2,3]											
Total	U	*21 798*	*20 291*	*21 622*	*19 850*	...	...	...	...	...	...
Benin - Bénin[4]											
Total	I	...	...	25 001	...	...	...	...	94.8	...	...
Botswana[5]											
Total	I	...	...	1 576	...	...	...	...	29.3	...	...
Côte d'Ivoire[4]											
Total	I	...	47 000	...	...	...	...	71.7	...	...	...
Egypt - Égypte											
Total	C	49 765	55 214	49 149	...	...	29.4	31.5	28.2	...	...
Urban-Urbaine	C	19 265	...	...	...	...	29.3	...	...	...	...
Rural-Rurale	C	30 500	...	...	...	...	29.5	...	...	...	...
Ethiopia - Éthiopie											
Total	...	*232 660*	...	...	...	...	...	...	...	...	...
Ghana											
Total	...	...	...	*51 639*	*34 293*	...	...	...	...	...	...
Kenya											
Total	U	...	...	*32 183*	*32 459*	*33 399*	...	...	...	...	...
Libyan Arab Jamahiriya - Jamahiriya arabe libyenne											
Total	U	...	*2 155*	*2 568*	...	...	...	...	...	...	...
Mauritius - Maurice											
Total	+C	396	322	282	297	250	19.5	15.9	14.3	14.9	12.9
Urban-Urbaine	+C	149	127	114	102	93	18.3	15.9	14.7	12.9	...
Rural-Rurale	+C	247	195	168	195	157	20.3	16.0	14.1	16.2	13.3
Morocco - Maroc[6]											
Total	U	*8 885*	*7 268*	*7 379*	...	...	...	...	...	...	...
Urban-Urbaine	U	*2 867*	*2 875*	*2 804*	...	...	...	...	...	...	...
Rural-Rurale	U	*5 998*	*4 384*	*4 569*	...	...	...	...	...	...	...
Mozambique[4]											
Total	I	...	...	99 164	...	...	...	...	131.6	...	...
Réunion											
Total	C	84	83	103	91	*107	...	...	7.1	...	*7.4
Saint Helena ex. dep. - Sainte-Hélène sans dép.											
Total	C	-	-	-	...	...	...	...	...	...	...
Seychelles											
Total	+C	15	15	19	26	25	...	...	...	...	...
Tunisia - Tunisie											
Total	U	*4 200*	...	...	...	...	...	...	...	...	...
AMERICA, NORTH — AMERIQUE DU NORD											
Anguilla											
Total	+C	1	1	-	2	2	...	...	...	...	...
Aruba											
Total	+U	...	...	4	...	*3	...	...	...	...	...
Bahamas											
Total	C	48	52	37	...	87	...	...	...	...	...
Barbados - Barbade											
Total	+C	...	63	...	*54	...	...	...	...	...	...
Belize											
Total	U	*123*	*155*	*120*	*145*	...	...	...	...	...	...
Bermuda - Bermudes											
Total	C	2	-	3	-	2	...	...	...	...	...
British Virgin Islands - Îles Vierges britanniques											
Total	+C	...	1	...	...	...	...	...	...	...	...
Canada[7]											
Total	C	1 776	1 737	1 739	1 762	...	5.3	5.3	5.2	5.4	...
Costa Rica											
Total	C	925	798	827	793	737	11.8	10.2	10.8	11.1	10.1
Cuba[6]											
Total	C	977	1 039	861	922	*859	6.5	7.2	6.2	6.5	*6.3

15. Infant deaths and infant mortality rates, by urban/rural residence: 1999 - 2003
Décès d'enfants de moins d'un an et taux de mortalité infantile, selon la résidence, urbaine/rurale: 1999 - 2003
(continued — suite)

Continent, country or area and urban/rural residence Continent, pays ou zone et résidence, urbaine/rurale	Code[1]	Number - Nombre					Rate - Taux				
		1999	2000	2001	2002	2003	1999	2000	2001	2002	2003
AMERICA, NORTH — **AMERIQUE DU NORD**											
Cuba[6]											
Urban-Urbaine	C	747	769	649	719	...	6.9	7.4	6.3	6.9	...
Rural-Rurale	C	230	269	212	203	...	5.5	6.9	5.8	5.4	...
Dominica - Dominique											
Total	+C	...	...	24	...	...	...	...	...	...	...
Dominican Republic - République dominicaine											
Total	+U	1 966	2 116	...	...	...	...	...	...	...	...
El Salvador											
Total	C	1 768	1 678	1 682	1 284	1 322	11.5	11.2	12.2	9.9	10.6
Urban-Urbaine	C	1 114	1 079	1 091	821	847	11.1	11.6	13.1	10.6	11.6
Rural-Rurale	C	654	599	591	463	475	12.3	10.5	10.8	9.0	9.3
Greenland - Groenland											
Total	C	16	12	10	10	8	...	...	...	...	...
Urban-Urbaine	C	16	11	10	7	8	...	...	...	...	...
Rural-Rurale	C	-	1	-	3	-	...	...	...	...	...
Grenada - Grenade											
Total	+C	29	27	33	...	...	...	...	...	...	...
Guadeloupe											
Total	C	55	57	49	45	56	...	...	...	...	...
Guatemala											
Total	C	13 161	13 247	...	...	11 022	36.5	31.1	...	...	29.4
Jamaica - Jamaïque											
Total	C	866	863	833	809	*753	17.7	17.7	17.3	18.2	*16.7
Martinique											
Total	C	41	40	43	33	33	...	...	...	...	...
Mexico - Mexique[6]											
Total	U	40 283	38 621	35 911	36 567	33 355	...	...	...	...	...
Urban-Urbaine	U	29 940	29 135	27 056	27 207	25 073	...	...	...	...	...
Rural-Rurale	U	10 054	9 163	8 503	8 498	7 714	...	...	...	...	...
Nicaragua											
Total	+U	1 768	2 075	1 933	2 217	1 989	...	...	...	...	...
Urban-Urbaine	+U	1 004	1 140	1 114	1 309	1 086	...	...	...	...	...
Rural-Rurale	+U	764	935	819	908	903	...	...	...	...	...
Panama											
Total	U	1 005	1 081	1 053	...	...	...	...	...	...	...
Urban-Urbaine	U	490	...	...	...	...	...	...	...	...	...
Rural-Rurale	U	515	...	...	...	...	...	...	...	...	...
Puerto Rico - Porto Rico[6]											
Total	C	632	589	515	516	498	10.6	9.9	9.2	9.8	9.8
Urban-Urbaine	C	357	327	311	...	297	11.7	10.7	10.6	...	11.1
Rural-Rurale	C	274	262	204	...	199	9.4	9.0	7.7	...	8.2
Saint Lucia - Sainte-Lucie											
Total	C	42	38	37	36	...	...	...	...	...	...
Saint Vincent and the Grenadines - Saint Vincent-et-les Grenadines											
Total	+C	47	35	39	36	...	...	...	...	...	...
Turks Caicos Islands - Îles Turques et Caïques											
Total	C	1	-	3	6	8	...	...	...	...	...
United States - États-Unis											
Total	C	27 937	28 035	27 568	28 034	28 428	7.1	6.9	6.8	7.0	6.9
AMERICA, SOUTH — **AMERIQUE DU SUD**											
Argentina - Argentine											
Total	C	12 120	11 649	11 111	11 703	11 494	17.6	16.6	16.3	16.8	16.5
Bolivia - Bolivie											
Total	U	16 492	16 042	...	...	...	...	...	...	...	...
Brazil - Brésil[8]											
Total	U	58 767	53 097	47 171	45 243	48 039	...	...	...	...	...

15. Infant deaths and infant mortality rates, by urban/rural residence: 1999 - 2003
Décès d'enfants de moins d'un an et taux de mortalité infantile, selon la résidence, urbaine/rurale: 1999 - 2003
(continued — suite)

Continent, country or area and urban/rural residence / Continent, pays ou zone et résidence, urbaine/rurale	Code[1]	Number - Nombre					Rate - Taux				
		1999	2000	2001	2002	2003	1999	2000	2001	2002	2003
AMERICA, SOUTH — AMERIQUE DU SUD											
Chile - Chili											
Total	C	2 654	2 336	2 159	1 964	1 935	10.6	9.4	8.8	8.2	8.3
Urban-Urbaine	C	2 252	1 991	1 855	1 715	1 691	10.3	9.1	8.6	8.0	8.1
Rural-Rurale	C	402	345	304	249	244	12.5	11.3	10.1	9.6	9.8
Colombia - Colombie[6,9]											
Total	U	14 621	15 367	14 430	12 640	*11 944	...	...	...	...	...
Urban-Urbaine	U	10 234	11 014	10 458	8 970	*8 621	...	...	...	...	...
Rural-Rurale	U	3 299	3 354	3 163	2 922	*2 661	...	...	...	...	...
Ecuador - Équateur[10]											
Total	U	5 372	5 480	4 800	4 530	3 985	...	...	...	...	...
Urban-Urbaine	U	3 885	4 020	3 544	3 420	3 085	...	...	...	...	...
Rural-Rurale	U	1 487	1 460	1 256	1 110	900	...	...	...	...	...
French Guiana - Guyane française[2]											
Total	C	63	64	70	52	58	...	...	...	...	...
Paraguay[11]											
Total	I	...	...	3 898	...	...	...	...	...	...	...
Urban-Urbaine	I	...	...	2 076	...	...	...	...	...	...	...
Rural-Rurale	I	...	...	1 822	...	...	...	...	...	...	...
Peru - Pérou[4,8,12]											
Total	I	25 098	23 681	22 455	...	...	39.0	37.2	35.6	...	...
Suriname											
Total	C	227	156	133	148	...	22.4	15.9	13.7	14.5	...
Uruguay											
Total	C	776	742	721	708	*757	14.4	14.1	13.9	13.6	*15.0
Venezuela[8]											
Total	C	9 030	8 524	8 158	7 645	...	17.1	15.7	15.4	15.5	...
ASIA — ASIE											
Armenia - Arménie[13]											
Total	C	572	540	497	450	422	15.7	15.8	15.5	14.0	11.8
Urban-Urbaine	C	373	357	...	300	311	16.6	16.7	...	14.4	13.7
Rural-Rurale	C	199	183	...	150	111	14.2	14.2	...	13.1	8.4
Azerbaijan - Azerbaïdjan[13]											
Total	+C	1 943	1 501	1 382	1 422	1 451	16.5	12.8	12.5	12.8	12.8
Urban-Urbaine	+C	780	642	558	554	633	15.6	12.9	11.2	11.1	12.4
Rural-Rurale	+C	1 163	859	824	868	818	17.2	12.8	13.6	14.2	13.1
Bahrain - Bahreïn											
Total	U	129	117	117	94	...	...	...	...	...	...
Brunei Darussalam - Brunéi Darussalam											
Total	+C	44	55	50	62	67	...	...	...	...	...
China: Hong Kong SAR - Chine: Hong Kong RAS											
Total	C	157	162	124	110	109	3.1	3.0	2.6	2.3	2.3
China: Macao SAR - Chine: Macao RAS											
Total	C	17	11	14	11	2	...	...	...	...	...
Cyprus - Chypre[14]											
Total	C	51	47	37	40	33	...	...	...	...	...
Georgia - Géorgie[13]											
Total	C	...	...	1 098	1 102	1 144	...	...	23.1	23.6	24.8
Urban-Urbaine	C	...	...	...	...	1 057	...	...	...	...	30.6
Rural-Rurale	C	...	...	...	...	87	...	...	...	...	...
India - Inde[15]											
Total	...	...	...	...	...	...	70.0	68.0	66.0	63.0	60.0
Urban-Urbaine	...	...	...	...	...	...	44.0	44.0	42.0	40.0	38.0
Rural-Rurale	...	...	...	...	...	...	75.0	74.0	72.0	69.0	66.0
Iran (Islamic Republic of) - Iran (République islamique d')											
Total	C	39 183	...	...	...	...	33.3	...	...	...	...

15. Infant deaths and infant mortality rates, by urban/rural residence: 1999 - 2003
Décès d'enfants de moins d'un an et taux de mortalité infantile, selon la résidence, urbaine/rurale: 1999 - 2003
(continued — suite)

Continent, country or area and urban/rural residence / Continent, pays ou zone et résidence, urbaine/rurale	Code[1]	Number - Nombre					Rate - Taux				
		1999	2000	2001	2002	2003	1999	2000	2001	2002	2003
ASIA — ASIE											
Israel - Israël[6,16]											
Total	C	771	748	*700	*752	*717	5.8	5.5	*5.1	*5.4	*4.9
Urban-Urbaine	C	676	675	*632	*678	*641	5.7	5.5	*5.1	*5.3	*4.9
Rural-Rurale	C	93	73	*67	*73	*75	...	...	...	...	...
Japan - Japon[6,17]											
Total	C	4 010	3 830	3 599	3 497	3 364	3.4	3.2	3.1	3.0	3.0
Urban-Urbaine	C	3 144	3 075	2 896	2 815	2 728	3.3	3.2	3.1	3.0	3.0
Rural-Rurale	C	857	747	698	672	631	3.8	3.3	3.1	3.1	3.1
Kazakhstan[13]											
Total	C	4 448	4 163	4 239	3 850	3 824	20.4	18.7	19.1	16.9	15.4
Urban-Urbaine	C	2 461	2 314	2 371	2 203	2 349	22.3	20.2	20.6	18.0	16.9
Rural-Rurale	C	1 987	1 849	1 868	1 647	1 475	18.5	17.2	17.6	15.7	13.5
Korea (Republic of) - Corée (République de)[18]											
Total	C	2 776	2 885	3 008	2 545	*2 470	4.5	4.5	5.4	5.1	*5.0
Kuwait - Koweït											
Total	C	386	379	420	418	...	9.4	9.1	10.2	9.6	...
Kyrgyzstan - Kirghizistan[13]											
Total	C	2 360	2 225	2 123	2 128	2 186	22.7	23.0	21.6	21.1	20.7
Urban-Urbaine	C	756	836	785	852	880	26.7	29.7	27.6	28.2	27.6
Rural-Rurale	C	1 604	1 389	1 338	1 276	1 306	21.2	20.3	19.2	18.0	17.7
Malaysia - Malaisie											
Total	C	4 660	3 578	...	...	...	8.9	6.6	...	...	...
Maldives											
Total	C	104	112	85	89	72	19.9	20.7	...	...	...
Urban-Urbaine	C	19	27	22	28	16	...	...	...	...	...
Rural-Rurale	C	85	85	63	61	56	...	...	...	...	...
Mongolia - Mongolie											
Total	C	1 846	1 596	1 464	1 390	1 051	37.3	32.8	29.5	29.6	23.0
Urban-Urbaine	C	903	808	710	626	520	37.3	33.9	28.8	26.0	21.4
Rural-Rurale	C	943	788	754	764	531	37.4	31.7	30.2	33.4	24.8
Nepal - Népal[19]											
Total	I	...	...	13 037	...	...	...	...	...	...	...
Occupied Palestinian Territory - Territoire palestinien occupé											
Total	U	*1 081*	*1 042*	*1 120*	*1 101*	*1 101*	...	...	...	...	...
Oman[20]											
Total	U	*386*	*369*	*335*	*332*	*335*	...	...	...	...	...
Pakistan[21,22]											
Total	I	...	...	286 609	...	...	...	...	77.1	...	...
Urban-Urbaine	I	...	...	82 185	...	...	...	...	68.9	...	...
Rural-Rurale	I	...	...	204 424	...	...	...	...	80.9	...	...
Philippines											
Total	C	25 168	27 714	26 129	23 778	...	15.6	15.7	15.2	14.3	...
Qatar											
Total	C	112	*132	111	107	137	10.3	*11.7	9.2	8.8	10.7
Saudi Arabia - Arabie saoudite											
Total	...	*11 344*	*11 071*	...	...	...	...	...	...	...	...
Singapore - Singapour[23]											
Total	+C	150	137	100	123	100	3.5	2.9	2.4	3.0	2.7
Sri Lanka											
Total	+C	...	...	*4 323	...	...	...	...	...	...	...
Tajikistan - Tadjikistan[13]											
Total	C	2 338	2 102	...	...	...	12.9	12.6	...	...	...
Urban-Urbaine	C	681	713	...	...	...	16.8	16.8	...	...	...
Rural-Rurale	C	1 657	1 389	...	...	...	11.8	11.1	...	...	...
Thailand - Thaïlande											
Total	+U	*5 003*	*4 822*	*5 105*	*5 105*	*5 349*	...	...	...	...	...
Urban-Urbaine	+U	*711*	*801*	...	...	...	...	...	...	...	...
Rural-Rurale	+U	*4 292*	*4 021*	...	...	...	...	...	...	...	...
Turkey - Turquie[24]											
Total	I	64 993	62 599	60 332	58 391	56 646	43.3	41.9	40.6	39.4	38.3
Urban-Urbaine	I	15 870	15 543	14 947	...	...	...	...	...	...	...
Rural-Rurale	I	49 123	47 056	45 385	...	...	...	...	...	...	...

15. Infant deaths and infant mortality rates, by urban/rural residence: 1999 - 2003
Décès d'enfants de moins d'un an et taux de mortalité infantile, selon la résidence, urbaine/rurale: 1999 - 2003
(continued — suite)

Continent, country or area and urban/rural residence / Continent, pays ou zone et résidence, urbaine/rurale	Code[1]	Number - Nombre					Rate - Taux				
		1999	2000	2001	2002	2003	1999	2000	2001	2002	2003
ASIA — ASIE											
Uzbekistan - Ouzbékistan[13]											
Total	C	12 358	10 091	9 427	...	...	22.3	19.1	18.4	...	...
Urban-Urbaine	C	4 293	3 703	3 399	...	...	24.8	22.6	21.3	...	...
Rural-Rurale	C	8 065	6 388	6 028	...	...	21.2	17.6	17.1	...	...
EUROPE											
Albania - Albanie											
Total	C	708	608	603	466	395	12.2	11.9	11.1	10.2	8.4
Andorra - Andorre											
Total	C	2	2	2	-	-	...	...	...	...	...
Austria - Autriche											
Total	C	341	378	365	318	343	4.4	4.8	4.8	4.1	4.5
Belarus - Bélarus[10]											
Total	C	1 064	...	...	695	685	11.4	...	...	7.8	7.7
Urban-Urbaine	C	651	...	...	454	440	9.8	...	...	7.0	6.8
Rural-Rurale	C	413	...	...	241	245	15.5	...	...	10.2	10.3
Belgium - Belgique[25]											
Total	C	556	554	518	551	...	4.9	4.8	4.5	...	...
Bosnia and Herzegovina - Bosnie-Herzégovine											
Total	C	431	383	287	334	268	10.1	9.7	7.6	9.4	7.4
Bulgaria - Bulgarie											
Total	C	1 057	981	982	887	831	14.6	13.3	14.4	13.3	12.3
Urban-Urbaine	C	...	657	625	571	522	...	12.4	12.9	12.0	10.7
Rural-Rurale	C	...	324	357	316	309	...	15.5	18.2	16.9	16.5
Channel Islands: Guernsey - Îles Anglo-Normandes: Guernesey											
Total	C	2	4	...	...	...	...	...	...	...	...
Croatia - Croatie											
Total	C	350	324	315	282	251	7.7	7.4	7.7	7.0	6.3
Urban-Urbaine	C	...	194	179	144	135	...	7.8	7.8	6.4	6.2
Rural-Rurale	C	...	130	136	138	116	...	6.9	7.5	7.9	6.5
Czech Republic - République tchèque											
Total	C	413	373	360	385	365	4.6	4.1	4.0	3.9	3.9
Urban-Urbaine	C	307	272	266	288	266	4.7	4.1	4.0	3.9	3.8
Rural-Rurale	C	106	101	94	97	99	4.4	4.2	...	...	...
Denmark - Danemark[26]											
Total	C	281	358	320	284	286	4.2	5.3	4.9	4.4	4.4
Estonia - Estonie[6,13]											
Total	C	119	110	111	74	91	9.5	8.4	8.8	...	...
Urban-Urbaine	C	...	73	81	53	59	...	...	...	...	...
Rural-Rurale	C	...	36	30	21	32	...	...	...	...	...
Finland - Finlande[27]											
Total	C	208	213	181	168	176	3.6	3.8	3.2	3.0	3.1
Urban-Urbaine	C	...	...	112	109	107	...	...	3.1	3.0	2.9
Rural-Rurale	C	...	...	69	59	69	...	...	...	...	...
France[28,29]											
Total	C	3 221	3 417	3 438	3 336	*3 325	4.3	4.4	4.5	4.4	*4.4
Urban-Urbaine	C	2 551	...	2 694	2 634	*2 640	4.5	...	4.6	4.6	...
Rural-Rurale	C	644	...	725	674	*660	3.7	...	3.9	3.7	...
Germany - Allemagne											
Total	C	3 496	3 362	3 163	3 036	2 990	4.5	4.4	4.3	4.2	4.2
Gibraltar											
Total	C	...	...	...	...	2	...	...	...	...	...
Greece - Grèce											
Total	C	619	610	522	600	420	5.3	5.2	5.1	5.8	4.0
Hungary - Hongrie[6]											
Total	C	798	900	789	693	690	8.4	9.2	8.1	7.2	7.3
Urban-Urbaine	C	480	532	471	421	375	8.4	9.0	8.0	6.9	6.3
Rural-Rurale	C	312	359	311	269	308	8.5	9.5	8.4	7.6	8.9

15. Infant deaths and infant mortality rates, by urban/rural residence: 1999 - 2003
Décès d'enfants de moins d'un an et taux de mortalité infantile, selon la résidence, urbaine/rurale: 1999 - 2003
(continued — suite)

Continent, country or area and urban/rural residence / Continent, pays ou zone et résidence, urbaine/rurale	Code[1]	Number - Nombre					Rate - Taux				
		1999	2000	2001	2002	2003	1999	2000	2001	2002	2003
EUROPE											
Iceland - Islande											
Total	C	10	13	11	9	10	...	...	...	...	...
Ireland - Irlande[6,30]											
Total	+C	293	338	331	306	311	5.5	6.2	5.7	5.1	5.1
Urban-Urbaine	+C	195	...	...	...	...	6.3	...	...	...	...
Rural-Rurale	+C	98	...	...	...	...	...	...	...	...	...
Isle of Man - Îles de Man											
Total	+C	6	5	-	3	6	...	...	...	...	...
Italy - Italie											
Total	C	2 723	2 461	2 482	2 337	2 482	5.2	4.5	4.6	4.3	4.6
Latvia - Lettonie[13]											
Total	C	219	210	217	197	198	11.3	10.4	11.0	9.8	9.4
Urban-Urbaine	C	144	124	139	105	129	11.9	9.7	11.1	8.1	9.3
Rural-Rurale	C	75	86	78	92	69	...	...	...	...	...
Liechtenstein											
Total	C	...	...	-	1	1	...	...	...	...	...
Lithuania - Lituanie[13]											
Total	C	315	294	250	238	206	8.7	8.6	7.9	7.9	6.7
Urban-Urbaine	C	174	172	148	128	108	...	8.2	7.5	6.8	5.6
Rural-Rurale	C	141	122	102	110	98	...	9.3	8.6	9.7	...
Luxembourg											
Total	C	26	29	32	27	26	...	...	...	...	...
Malta - Malte											
Total	C	31	26	17	23	23	...	...	...	...	...
Netherlands - Pays-Bas[31]											
Total	C	1 048	1 059	1 088	1 028	962	5.2	5.1	5.4	5.1	4.8
Norway - Norvège[32]											
Total	C	232	225	223	192	190	3.9	3.8	3.9	3.5	3.4
Poland - Pologne											
Total	C	3 381	3 068	2 823	2 662	2 470	8.9	8.1	7.7	7.5	7.0
Urban-Urbaine	C	1 908	...	1 575	1 551	1 446	9.2	...	7.7	7.9	7.2
Rural-Rurale	C	1 473	...	1 248	1 111	1 024	8.5	...	7.7	7.1	6.8
Portugal											
Total	C	671	662	567	574	465	5.8	5.6	5.0	5.0	4.1
Republic of Moldova - République de Moldova[13]											
Total	C	714	681	597	528	522	18.5	18.4	16.4	14.8	14.3
Urban-Urbaine	C	277	236	212	192	178	20.9	18.6	16.9	15.1	13.9
Rural-Rurale	C	437	445	385	336	344	17.3	18.4	16.1	14.6	14.5
Romania - Roumanie											
Total	C	4 360	4 370	4 057	3 648	3 546	18.6	18.6	18.4	17.3	16.7
Urban-Urbaine	C	...	1 744	1 594	1 426	1 381	...	16.1	15.6	14.5	13.7
Rural-Rurale	C	...	2 626	2 463	2 222	2 165	...	20.8	20.9	19.8	19.4
Russian Federation - Fédération de Russie[13]											
Total	C	20 731	19 286	19 104	18 407	18 142	17.1	15.2	14.6	13.2	12.3
Urban-Urbaine	C	13 657	...	12 899	12 511	12 235	16.2	...	13.9	12.5	11.6
Rural-Rurale	C	7 074	...	6 205	5 896	5 907	19.0	...	16.2	14.8	13.8
San Marino - Saint-Marin											
Total	+C	1	-	1	2	2	...	...	...	...	...
Serbia and Montenegro - Serbie-et-Montenegro[33]											
Total	C	1 691	1 668	1 709	882	803	13.6	13.3	13.1	10.2	9.2
Urban-Urbaine	C	939	962	1 006	616	537	14.6	14.5	14.5	11.3	9.9
Rural-Rurale	C	752	706	703	266	266	12.6	11.9	11.6	8.2	8.0
Slovakia - Slovaquie											
Total	C	467	473	319	388	406	8.3	8.6	6.2	7.6	7.9
Urban-Urbaine	C	235	...	147	191	176	8.2	...	5.6	7.3	6.6
Rural-Rurale	C	232	...	172	197	230	8.4	...	6.9	8.0	9.2
Slovenia - Slovénie											
Total	C	79	89	74	67	69	...	...	...	...	...
Urban-Urbaine	C	31	34	33	37	37	...	...	...	...	...
Rural-Rurale	C	48	55	41	30	32	...	...	...	...	...

15. Infant deaths and infant mortality rates, by urban/rural residence: 1999 - 2003
Décès d'enfants de moins d'un an et taux de mortalité infantile, selon la résidence, urbaine/rurale: 1999 - 2003
(continued — suite)

Continent, country or area and urban/rural residence / Continent, pays ou zone et résidence, urbaine/rurale	Code[1]	Number - Nombre					Rate - Taux				
		1999	2000	2001	2002	2003	1999	2000	2001	2002	2003
EUROPE											
Spain - Espagne											
Total	C	1 700	1 535	1 657	1 737	1 733	4.5	3.9	4.1	4.1	3.9
Sweden - Suède											
Total	C	297	309	334	313	308	3.4	3.4	3.7	3.3	3.1
Switzerland - Suisse											
Total	C	361	386	365	326	311	4.6	4.9	5.0	4.5	4.3
Urban-Urbaine	C	237	262	248	242	225	4.6	5.0	5.0	4.6	4.3
Rural-Rurale	C	124	124	117	84	86	4.7	4.8	4.8	...	...
The Former Yugoslav Rep. of Macedonia - L'ex-République yougoslave de Macédoine											
Total	C	406	346	321	283	*305	14.9	11.8	11.9	10.2	*11.3
Urban-Urbaine	C	201	185	182	157	...	14.0	11.9	12.3	10.5	...
Rural-Rurale	C	205	161	139	126	...	15.8	11.7	11.3	9.8	...
Ukraine[13]											
Total	C	...	4 606	4 283	4 023	3 882	...	12.0	11.4	10.3	9.5
Urban-Urbaine	C	...	...	2 690	2 543	2 531	...	...	11.3	10.2	9.5
Rural-Rurale	C	...	...	1 593	1 480	1 351	...	...	11.4	10.4	9.5
United Kingdom - Royaume-Uni											
Total	C	4 045	3 791	3 664	3 499	*3 686	5.8	5.6	5.5	5.2	*5.3
OCEANIA — OCEANIE											
American Samoa - Samoas américaines											
Total	C	22	11	...	...	...	...	...	...	...	...
Australia - Australie											
Total	+C	1 408	1 290	1 309	1 264	1 199	5.7	5.2	5.3	5.0	4.8
Cook Islands - Îles Cook											
Total	+C	5	6	4	2	4	...	...	...	...	...
Fiji - Fidji											
Total	+C	275	...	...	...	...	16.3	...	...	...	...
French Polynesia - Polynésie française											
Total	C	31	33	36	32	31	...	...	...	...	...
Guam[34]											
Total	C	35	23	35	20	37	...	...	...	...	...
Marshall Islands - Îles Marshall											
Total	+U	...	...	40	...	...	...	...	...	...	...
New Caledonia - Nouvelle-Calédonie											
Total	C	27	21	24	29	24	...	...	...	...	...
New Zealand - Nouvelle-Zélande[6]											
Total	+C	317	346	296	300	277	5.6	6.1	5.3	5.6	4.9
Urban-Urbaine	+C	261	289	253	255	231	5.3	5.9	5.2	5.4	4.7
Rural-Rurale	+C	33	32	26	24	27	...	...	...	...	...
Northern Mariana Islands - Îles Mariannes septentrionales											
Total	U	11	...	...	...	...	...	...	...	...	...
Palau - Palaos											
Total	C	5	3	5	6	2	...	...	...	...	...
Papua New Guinea - Papouasie-Nouvelle-Guinée											
Total	U	...	2 064	1 841	2 230	2 082	...	...	...	...	...
Tonga											
Total	+C	48	28	...	...	...	...	...	...	...	...

FOOTNOTES - NOTES

Italics: data from civil registers which are incomplete or of unknown completeness. — *Italiques:* données incomplètes ou dont le degré d'exactitude n'est pas connu provenant des registres de l'état civil.

* Provisional. — Données provisoires.

[1] 'Code' indicates the source of data, as follows:
C - Civil registration, estimated over 90% complete

U - Civil registration, estimated less than 90% complete
| - Other source, estimated reliable
+ - Data tabulated by date of registration rather than occurence.
... - Information not available

Le 'Code' indique la source des données, comme suit:
C - Registres de l'état civil considérés complèts à 90 p. 100 au moins.
U - Registres de l'état civil qui ne sont pas considérés complèts à 90 p. 100 au moins.
| - Autre source, considérée pas douteuses.
+ - Données exploitées selon la date de l'enregistrement et non la date de l'événement.
... - Information pas disponible.

[2] Excluding live-born infants who died before their birth was registered. - Non compris les enfants nés vivants décédés avant l'enregistrement de leur naissance.

[3] For Algerian population only. - Pour la population algérienne seulement.

[4] Data refer to national projections. - Les données se referent aux projections nationales.

[5] For 2001, data refer to last twelve months preceding census on August 2001. - Pour 2001, les données se rapportent pour la dernière fois à douze mois précédant le recensement août 2001.

[6] Figures for urban and rural areas do not add up to the total, since they do not include the category 'Unknown residence'. - La somme des données pour la residence urbaine et rurale n'est pas égale au total parce qu'elle n'inclue pas la catégorie 'Residence inconnue'.

[7] Including Canadian residents temporarily in the United States, but excluding United States residents temporarily in Canada. - Y compris les résidents canadiens se trouvant temporairement aux Etats-Unis, mais ne comprenant pas les résidents des Etats-Unis se trouvant temporairement au Canada.

[8] Excluding Indian jungle population. - Non compris les Indiens de la jungle.

[9] Data on live births and deaths are based on a civil registration system put in place in January 1998. - Les données sur les naissances et les décès sont basées sur un système d'enregistrement des faits d'état civil mis en place en janvier 1998.

[10] Excluding nomadic Indian tribes. - Non compris les tribus d'Indiens nomades.

[11] For 2001, data were collected from Population census held on August 2002, referring to events in calendar year 2001. - Pour 2001, les données sont tirées du recensement de la population réalisé en août 2002, concernant des événements de l'année civile 2001.

[12] Including an upward adjustment for under-registration. - Y compris un ajustement pour sous-enregistrement.

[13] Excluding infants born alive with less than 28 weeks gestation, less than 1 000 grams in weight and 35 centimeters in length, who die within seven days of birth. - Non compris les enfants nés vivants avant 28 semaines de gestation, pesant moins de 1 000 grammes, mesurant moins de 35 centimètres et décédés dans les sept jours qui ont suivi leur naissance.

[14] Data refer to government controlled areas. - Les données se raportent aux zones contrôlées par le Gouvernement.

[15] Rates were obtained by the Sample Registration System of India, a large demographic survey. - Les taux ont été obtenus par le Système de l'enregistrement par échantillon de l'Inde qui est au fait une large enquête démographique.

[16] Including data for East Jerusalem and Israeli residents in certain other territories under occupation by Israeli military forces since June 1967. - Y compris les données pour Jérusalem-Est et les résidents israéliens dans certains autres territoires occupés depuis 1967 par les forces armées israéliennes.

[17] Data refer to Japanese nationals in Japan only. - Les données se raportent aux nationaux japonais au Japon seulement.

[18] Excluding alien armed forces, civilian aliens employed by armed forces, and foreign diplomatic personnel and their dependants. - Non compris les militaires étrangers, les civils étrangers employés par les forces armées ni le personnel diplomatique étranger et les membres de leur famille les accompagnant.

[19] For 2001, data refer to last twelve months preceding census on June 2001. - Pour 2001, les données se rapportent pour la dernière fois à douze mois précédant le recensement juin 2001.

[20] Data refer to the recorded events in Ministry of Health hospitals and health centres only. - Les données se rapportent aux faits d'état-civil enregistrés dans les hôpitaux et les dispensaires du Ministère de la santé seulement.

[21] Excluding data for the Pakistan-held part of Jammu and Kashmir, the final status of which has not yet been determined. - Non compris les données concernant la partie du Jammu et Cachemire occupée par le Pakistan dont le statut définitif n'a pas été déterminé.

[22] Based on the results of the Population Growth Survey. - D'après les résultats de la 'Population Growth Survey.'

[23] Excluding transients afloat and non-locally domiciled military and civilian services personnel and their dependants. - Non compris les personnes de passage à bord de navires, ni les militaires et agents civils domiciliés hors du territoire et les membres de leur famille les accompagnant.

[24] Based on the results of the Population Demographic Survey. - - D'après les résultats de la Population Demographic Survey.

[25] Including armed forces stationed outside the country, but excluding alien armed forces stationed in the area. - Y compris les militaires nationaux hors du pays, mais non compris les militaires étrangers en garnison sur le territoire.

[26] Excluding Faeroe Islands and Greenland. - Non compris les Iles Féroé et Gröenland.

[27] Including nationals temporarily outside the country. - Y compris les nationaux se trouvant temporairement hors du pays.

[28] Including armed forces stationed outside the country. - Y compris les militaires nationaux hors du pays.

[29] Urban/rural figures, excluding nationals outside the country. - Les chiffres urbaine/rurale, non compris les nationaux hors du pays.

[30] Events registered within one year of occurrence. - Evénements enregistrés dans l'année qui suit l'événement.

[31] Including residents outside the country if listed in a Netherlands population register. - Y compris les résidents hors du pays, s'ils sont inscrits sur un registre de population néerlandais.

[32] Including residents temporarily outside the country. - Y compris les résidents se trouvant temporairement hors du pays.

[33] From 2002, without data for Kosovo and Metohia. - Après 2002, sans les données pour le Kosovo and Metohie.-

[34] Including United States military personnel, their dependants and contract employees. - Y compris les militaires des Etats-Unis, les membres de leur famille les accompagnant et les agents contractuels des Etats-Unis.

Table 16

Table 16 presents infant deaths and infant mortality rates by age and sex for latest available year.

Description of variables: Age is defined as hours, days and months of life completed, based on the difference between the hour, day, month and year of birth and the hour, day, month and year of death. The age classification used in this table is the following: under 1 day, 1-6 days, 7-27 days and 28-364 days. For some countries or areas the statistics presented are for several years, and include those years for which data only recently become available and were therefore not published in previous issues of the *Demographic Yearbook*.

Rate computation: Infant mortality rates are the annual number of deaths of infants under one year of age per 1 000 live births (as shown in table 9) in the same year.

Infant mortality rates by age and sex are the annual number of infant deaths that occurred in a specific age-sex group per 1 000 live births in the corresponding sex group (as shown in table 9). These rates have been calculated by the Statistics Division of the United Nations. The denominator for all these rates, regardless of age of infant at death, is the number of live births by sex.

Infant deaths of unknown age are included only in the rate for under one year of age. Deaths under the category of sex "unknown" are included in the rate for the total and, hence, these rates, shown in the first column of the table, should agree with the infant mortality rates shown in table 15. Discrepancies are explained in footnotes.

Rates presented in this table have been limited to those for countries or areas having at least a total of 1 000 deaths in a given year. Moreover, rates specific for individual sub-categories based on 30 or fewer infant deaths are identified by the symbol (♦).

Reliability of data: Data from civil registers of infant deaths which are reported as incomplete (less than 90 percent completeness) or of unknown completeness are considered unreliable and are set in italics rather than in roman type. Rates on these data are not computed. Tables 9 and 15 and the technical notes for these tables provide more detailed information on the completeness of infant death registration. For more information about the quality of vital statistics data in general, and the information available on the basis of the completeness of estimates in particular, see section 4.2 of the Technical Notes.

Limitations: Statistics on infant deaths by age and sex are subject to the same qualifications as have been set forth for vital statistics in general and death statistics in particular as discussed in section 4 of the Technical Notes.

The reliability of the data, an indication of which is described above, is an important factor in considering the limitations. In addition, some infant deaths are tabulated by date of registration and not by date of occurrence; these have been indicated by a plus sign (+). Whenever the lag between the date of occurrence and date of registration is prolonged and, therefore, a large proportion of the infant-death registrations are delayed, infant-death statistics for any given year may be seriously affected.

Another factor that limits international comparability is the practice of some countries or areas of not including in infant-death statistics infants who were born alive but died before the registration of the birth or within the first 24 hours of life, thus underestimating the total number of infant deaths. Statistics of this type are footnoted. In this table in particular, this practice may contribute to the lack of comparability among deaths under one year, under 28 days, under one week and under one day.

Variation in the method of reckoning age at the time of death may also introduce non-comparability. Although it is to some degree a limiting factor throughout the age span, it is an especially important consideration with respect to deaths at ages under one day and under one week (early neonatal deaths) and under 28 days (neonatal deaths). As noted above, the recommended method of reckoning infant age at death is to calculate duration of life in minutes, hours and days, as appropriate. This gives age in completed units of time. In some countries or areas, however, infant age is calculated to the nearest day only, that is, age at death for an infant is the difference between the day, month and year of birth and the day, month and year of death. The result of this procedure is to classify as deaths at age one day, many deaths of infants that occurred before the infants had completed 24 hours of life. The under-one-day class is thus understated while the frequency in the 1-6-day age group is inflated.

403

A special limitation on comparability of neonatal (under 28 days) deaths is the variation in the classification of infant age used. It is evident from the footnotes that some countries or areas continue to report infant age in calendar, rather than lunar month (4-week or 28- day) periods. This failure to tabulate infant deaths under 4 weeks of age in terms of completed days introduces another source of variation between countries or areas. Deaths classified as occurring under one month usually connote deaths within any one calendar month; these frequencies are not strictly comparable with those referring to deaths within 4 weeks or 27 completed days.

In addition, infant mortality rates by age and sex are subject to the limitations of the data on live births with which they have been calculated. These have been set forth in the technical notes for table 9. These limitations have also been discussed in the technical notes for table 15.

In addition, it should be noted that infant mortality rates by age are affected by the problems related to the practice of excluding infants who were born alive but died before the registration of the birth or within the first 24 hours of life from both infant-death and live-birth statistics and the problems related to the reckoning of infant age at death. These factors, which have been described above, may affect certain age groups more than others. In so far as the numbers of infant deaths for the various age groups are underestimated or overestimated, the corresponding rates for the various age groups will also be underestimated or overestimated. The youngest age groups are more likely to be underestimated than other age groups; the youngest age group (under one day) is likely to be the most seriously affected.

Earlier data: Infant deaths and infant mortality rates by age and sex have been shown in previous issues of the *Demographic Yearbook*. For information on specific years covered, readers should consult the Historical Index.

Tableau 16

Le tableau 16 présente les données les plus récentes dont on dispose sur les décès d'enfants de moins d'un an et les taux de mortalité infantile selon l'âge et le sexe.

Description des variables : L'âge est exprimé en heures, jours et mois révolus et est calculé en retranchant la date de la naissance (heure, jour, mois et année) de celle du décès (heure, jour, mois et année). La classification par âge utilisée dans le tableau est la suivante : moins d'un jour, 1 à 6 jours, 7 à 27 jours et 28 à 364 jours. Pour certains pays et zones, les statistiques portent sur plusieurs années. Cela s'explique par le fait qu'elles ne sont disponibles que depuis peu et n'ont donc pas pu être publiées dans les éditions précédentes de l'*Annuaire démographique*.

Calcul des taux : Les taux de mortalité infantile selon l'âge et le sexe représentent le nombre annuel de décès d'enfants de moins d'un an selon l'âge et le sexe pour 1 000 naissances vivantes d'enfants du même sexe (fréquences du tableau 9) survenues au cours de l'année considérée.

Les taux de mortalité infantile selon l'âge et le sexe représentent le nombre annuel de décès d'enfants de moins d'un an intervenu dans un groupe d'âge donné parmi la population de sexe masculin ou féminin (fréquences du tableau 9) pour 1 000 naissances vivantes survenues parmi la population du même sexe. Ces taux ont été calculés par la Division de statistique de l'ONU.

Le dénominateur de tous ces taux, quel que soit l'âge de l'enfant au moment du décès, est le nombre de naissances vivantes selon le sexe.

Il n'est tenu compte des décès d'enfants d'âge « inconnu » que pour le calcul du taux relatif à l'ensemble des décès de moins d'un an. Étant donné que les décès d'enfants de sexe inconnu sont compris dans le numérateur des taux concernant le total qui figurent dans la deuxième colonne du tableau 16, les chiffres obtenus devraient concorder avec les taux de mortalité infantile du tableau 15. Les divergences sont expliquées en note.

Les taux présentés dans le tableau 16 ne concernent que les pays ou zones où l'on a enregistré un total d'au moins 1 000 décès au cours d'une année donnée. Les taux relatifs à des sous-catégories qui sont fondées sur un nombre égal ou inférieur à 30 décès d'enfants âgés de moins d'un an sont signalés par le signe '♦'.

Fiabilité des données : Les données relatives aux décès d'enfants de moins d'un an provenant de registres de l'état civil qui sont déclarées incomplètes (degré de complétude inférieur à 90 p.100) ou dont le degré de complétude n'est pas connu sont jugées douteuses et apparaissent en italique et non en caractères romains. Les taux à partir de ces données n'ont pas été calculés. Les tableaux 9 et 15 et les notes techniques se rapportant à ces tableaux comportent des renseignements plus détaillés sur le degré de complétude de l'enregistrement des décès d'enfants de moins d'un an. Pour plus de précisions sur la qualité des données reposant sur les statistiques de l'état civil en général et les estimations de complétude en particulier, voir la section 4.2 des Notes techniques.

Insuffisance des données : Les statistiques des décès d'enfants de moins d'un an selon l'âge et le sexe appellent toutes les réserves qui ont été formulées à propos des statistiques de l'état civil en général et des statistiques concernant les décès en particulier (voir la section 4 des Notes techniques).

La fiabilité des données, au sujet de laquelle des indications ont été fournies plus haut, est un facteur important. Il faut également tenir compte du fait que, dans certains cas, les données relatives aux décès d'enfants de moins d'un an sont exploitées selon la date de l'enregistrement et non la date de l'événement ; ces cas ont été signalés par le signe '+'. Chaque fois que le décalage entre l'événement et son enregistrement est grand et qu'une forte proportion des décès d'enfants de moins d'un an fait l'objet d'un enregistrement tardif, les statistiques des décès d'enfants de moins d'un an pour une année donnée peuvent être considérablement faussées.

Un autre facteur qui nuit à la comparabilité internationale est la pratique de certains pays ou zones qui consiste à ne pas inclure dans les statistiques des décès d'enfants de moins d'un an les enfants nés vivants mais décédés soit avant l'enregistrement de leur naissance, soit dans les 24 heures qui ont suivi la naissance, pratique qui conduit à sous-estimer le nombre total de décès d'enfants de moins d'un an. Quand pareil facteur a joué, cela a été signalé en note. Dans le tableau 16 en particulier, ce système peut limiter la comparabilité des données concernant les décès d'enfants de moins d'un an, de moins de 28 jours, de moins d'une semaine et de moins d'un jour.

Le manque d'uniformité des méthodes suivies pour calculer l'âge au moment du décès nuit également à la comparabilité des données. Ce facteur influe dans une certaine mesure sur les données relatives à la mortalité à tous les âges, mais il a des répercussions particulièrement marquées sur les statistiques des décès de moins d'un jour et de moins d'une semaine (mortalité néo-natale précoce) et de moins de 28 jours (mortalité néo-natale). Comme on l'a dit, l'âge d'un enfant de moins d'un an à son décès est calculé, selon la méthode recommandée, en évaluant la durée de vie en minutes, heures et jours, selon le cas. L'âge est ainsi exprimé en unités de temps révolues. Toutefois, dans certains pays ou zones, l'âge de ces enfants est ramené au jour le plus proche en retranchant la date de la naissance (jour, mois et année) de celle du décès (jour, mois et année). Il s'ensuit que de nombreux décès survenus dans les vingt-quatre heures qui suivent la naissance sont classés comme décès d'un jour. Dans ces conditions, les données concernant les décès de moins d'un jour sont entachées d'une erreur par défaut et celles qui se rapportent aux décès de 1 à 6 jours d'une erreur par excès.

La comparabilité des données relatives à la mortalité néo-natale (moins de 28 jours) est influencée par un facteur spécial : l'hétérogénéité de la classification par âge utilisée pour les enfants de moins d'un an. Les notes figurant à la fin des tableaux montrent que, dans un certain nombre de pays ou zones, on continue d'utiliser le mois civil au lieu du mois lunaire (4 semaines ou 28 jours).

Lorsque les données relatives aux décès de moins de 4 semaines ne sont pas exploitées sur la base de l'âge en jours révolus, il existe une nouvelle cause de non-comparabilité internationale. Les décès de moins d'un mois sont généralement ceux qui se produisent au cours d'un mois civil ; les taux calculés sur la base de ces données ne sont pas strictement comparables à ceux qui sont établis à partir des données concernant les décès survenus dans les 4 semaines ou 27 jours révolus qui suivent la naissance.

Les taux de mortalité infantile selon l'âge et le sexe appellent en outre toutes les réserves qui ont été formulées à propos des statistiques des naissances vivantes qui ont servi à leur calcul (voir à ce sujet les notes techniques relatives au tableau 9). Ces insuffisances ont également été examinées dans les notes techniques relatives au tableau 15.

Il convient de signaler aussi que les taux de mortalité infantile selon l'âge peuvent être gravement faussés par la pratique qui consiste à ne pas classer dans les naissances vivantes et ensuite dans les décès d'enfants de moins d'un an les enfants nés vivants mais décédés soit avant l'enregistrement de leur naissance, soit dans les 24 heures qui ont suivi la naissance, et par les problèmes que pose le calcul de l'âge de l'enfant au moment du décès. Ces facteurs, qui ont été décrits plus haut, peuvent fausser les statistiques concernant certains groupes d'âge plus que d'autres. Si le nombre des décès d'enfants de moins d'un an pour chaque groupe d'âge est sous-estimé ou surestimé, les taux correspondants pour chacun de ces groupes d'âge seront eux aussi sous-estimés ou surestimés. Les risques de sous-estimation sont plus grands pour les groupes les plus jeunes ; c'est pour le groupe d'âge le plus jeune de tous (moins d'un jour) que les données risquent de comporter les plus grosses erreurs.

Données publiées antérieurement : Des statistiques des décès d'enfants de moins d'un an et des taux de mortalité infantile selon l'âge et le sexe ont déjà été présentées dans des éditions antérieures de l'*Annuaire démographique*. Pour plus de précisions concernant les années pour lesquelles ces données ont été publiées, se reporter à l'index.

16. Infant deaths and infant mortality rates by age and sex: latest available year, 1994 - 2003
Décčs d'enfants de moins d'un an et taux de mortalité infantile selon l'âge et le sexe: derničre année disponible, 1994 - 2003

Continent, country or area, year, age (in days) and urban/rural residence Continent, pays ou zone, année, âge (en jours) et résidence,urbaine/rurale	Number - Nombre			Rate - Taux		
	Both sexes Les deux sexes	Male Masculin	Female Féminin	Both sexes Les deux sexes	Male Masculin	Female Féminin
AFRICA — AFRIQUE						
Egypt - Égypte						
1999						
Total	49 765	26 263	23 502	29.4	30.2	28.6
Under 1 day - Moins d'un jour	7 992	4 418	3 574	4.7	5.1	4.3
1-6	8 352	5 127	3 225	4.9	5.9	3.9
7-27	6 028	3 488	2 540	3.6	4.0	3.1
28-364	27 393	13 230	14 163	16.2	15.2	17.2
Mauritius - Maurice+						
2003						
Total	250	133	117	...	...	...
Under 1 day - Moins d'un jour	44	25	19	...	...	...
1-6	88	48	40	...	...	...
7-27	45	21	24	...	...	...
28-364	73	39	34	...	...	...
Morocco - Maroc						
2001						
Total	7 379	4 022	3 357	...	...	...
0-27	1 638	912	726	...	...	...
28-364	5 729	3 103	2 626	...	...	...
Unknown - Inconnu	12	7	5	...	...	...
Réunion						
2003						
Total	107	59	48	...	...	...
Under 1 day - Moins d'un jour	43	26	17	...	...	...
1-6	19	12	7	...	...	...
7-27	16	7	9	...	...	...
28-364	29	14	15	...	...	...
Saint Helena ex. dep. - Sainte-Hélčne sans dép.						
1998						
Total	1	1	-	...	...	...
Under 1 day - Moins d'un jour	1	1	-	...	...	...
1-6	-	-	-	...	...	...
7-27	-	-	-	...	...	...
28-364	-	-	-	...	...	...
South Africa - Afrique du Sud						
1996						
Total	24 560	12 979	11 581	...	...	...
Under 1 day - Moins d'un jour	3 795	2 098	1 697	...	...	...
1-6	4 542	2 427	2 115	...	...	...
7-27	2 415	1 288	1 127	...	...	...
28-364	13 808	7 166	6 642	...	...	...
Tunisia - Tunisie						
1998						
Total	3 098	1 775	1 323	...	...	...
Under 1 day - Moins d'un jour	464	281	183	...	...	...
1-6	847	485	362	...	...	...
7-27	559	332	227	...	...	...
28-364	1 227	677	550	...	...	...
Unknown - Inconnu	1	-	1	...	...	...
AMERICA, NORTH — AMERIQUE DU NORD						
Antigua and Barbuda - Antigua-et-Barbuda+						
1995						
Total	23	12	11	...	...	...
Under 1 day - Moins d'un jour	6	3	3	...	...	...
1-6	10	5	5	...	...	...
7-27	3	2	1	...	...	...
28-364	4	2	2	...	...	...
Bahamas						
2001						
Total	37	23	14	...	...	...
0-6	8	7	1	...	...	...
7-27	15	8	7	...	...	...
28-364	14	8	6	...	...	...

16. Infant deaths and infant mortality rates by age and sex: latest available year, 1994 - 2003
Décčs d'enfants de moins d'un an et taux de mortalité infantile selon l'âge et le sexe: dernièvre année disponible, 1994 - 2003 (continued — suite)

Continent, country or area, year, age (in days) and urban/rural residence Continent, pays ou zone, année, âge (en jours) et résidence,urbaine/rurale	Number - Nombre			Rate - Taux		
	Both sexes Les deux sexes	Male Masculin	Female Féminin	Both sexes Les deux sexes	Male Masculin	Female Féminin
AMERICA, NORTH — AMERIQUE DU NORD						
Bermuda - Bermudes						
1996						
Total	3	1	2	...	...	...
Under 1 day - Moins d'un jour	1	1	-	...	...	...
1-6	1	-	1	...	...	...
7-27	-	-	-	...	...	...
28-364	1	-	1	...	...	...
Canada[1]						
2002						
Total	1 762	980	782	5.4	5.8	4.9
Under 1 day - Moins d'un jour	812	451	361	2.5	2.7	2.3
1-6	254	142	112	0.8	0.8	0.7
7-27	211	116	95	0.6	0.7	0.6
28-364	485	271	214	1.5	1.6	1.3
Cayman Islands - Îles Cadmanes						
1996						
Total	6	3	3	...	...	...
Under 1 day - Moins d'un jour	4	1	3	...	...	...
1-6	-	-	-	...	...	...
7-27	-	-	-	...	...	...
28-364	2	2	-	...	...	...
Costa Rica						
2003						
Total	737	409	328	...	...	...
Under 1 day - Moins d'un jour	202	117	85	...	...	...
1-6	200	120	80	...	...	...
7-27	107	57	50	...	...	...
28-364	228	115	113	...	...	...
Cuba						
2002						
Total	922	555	367	...	...	...
Under 1 day - Moins d'un jour	111	53	58	...	...	...·
1-6	277	180	97	...	...	...
7-27	203	125	78	...	...	...
28-364	331	197	134	...	...	...
El Salvador						
2003						
Total	1 322	747	575	10.6	11.5	9.7
Under 1 day - Moins d'un jour	147	83	64	1.2	1.3	1.1
1-6	193	110	83	1.6	1.7	1.4
7-27	184	99	85	1.5	1.5	1.4
28-364	798	455	343	6.4	7.0	5.8
Greenland - Groenland						
2003						
Total	8	6	2	...	...	...
Under 1 day - Moins d'un jour	3	3	-	...	...	...
1-6	2	1	1	...	...	...
28-364	3	2	1	...	...	...
Guadeloupe						
2003						
Total	56	34	22	...	...	...
Under 1 day - Moins d'un jour	13	5	8	...	...	...
1-6	8	4	4	...	...	...
7-27	19	12	7	...	...	...
28-364	16	13	3	...	...	...
Guatemala						
1999						
Total	13 161	7 349	5 812	36.5	40.0	32.8
Under 1 day - Moins d'un jour	999	570	429	2.8	3.1	2.4
1-6	2 180	1 286	894	6.0	7.0	5.0
7-27	1 741	949	792	4.8	5.2	4.5
28-364	8 241	4 544	3 697	22.8	24.7	20.9

16. Infant deaths and infant mortality rates by age and sex: latest available year, 1994 - 2003
Décčs d'enfants de moins d'un an et taux de mortalité infantile selon l'âge et le sexe: derničre année disponible, 1994 - 2003 (continued — suite)

Continent, country or area, year, age (in days) and urban/rural residence Continent, pays ou zone, année, âge (en jours) et résidence,urbaine/rurale	Number - Nombre			Rate - Taux		
	Both sexes Les deux sexes	Male Masculin	Female Féminin	Both sexes Les deux sexes	Male Masculin	Female Féminin
AMERICA, NORTH — AMERIQUE DU NORD						
Martinique						
2003						
Total	33	14	19	...	...	...
Under 1 day - Moins d'un jour	9	4	5	...	...	...
1-6	11	5	6	...	...	...
7-27	4	1	3	...	...	...
28-364	9	4	5	...	...	...
Mexico - Mexique[2]						
2003						
Total	33 355	19 008	14 236	...	...	...
Under 1 day - Moins d'un jour	7 081	3 949	3 084	...	...	...
1-6	8 298	4 995	3 283	...	...	...
7-27	5 427	3 030	2 389	...	...	...
28-364	12 548	7 033	5 480	...	...	...
Unknown - Inconnu	1	1	-	...	...	...
Montserrat						
1996						
Total	1	1	-	...	...	...
Under 1 day - Moins d'un jour	1	1	-	...	...	...
0-6	-	-	-	...	...	...
7-27	-	-	-	...	...	...
28-364	-	-	-	...	...	...
Nicaragua[+]						
2003						
Total	1 989	1 119	870	...	...	...
Under 1 day - Moins d'un jour	324	188	136	...	...	...
1-6	701	382	319	...	...	...
7-27	254	155	99	...	...	...
28-364	710	394	316	...	...	...
Panama						
1999						
Total	1 005	571	434	...	...	...
Under 1 day - Moins d'un jour	147	78	69	...	...	...
1-6	253	145	108	...	...	...
7-27	207	127	80	...	...	...
28-364	398	221	177	...	...	...
Puerto Rico - Porto Rico[3]						
2002						
Total	515	292	223	...	...	...
Under 1 day - Moins d'un jour	128	72	56	...	...	...
1-6	133	78	55	...	...	...
7-27	116	62	54	...	...	...
28-364	138	80	58	...	...	...
2003						
Total	498	...	...	...	...	...
Under 1 day - Moins d'un jour	110	...	...	...	...	...
1-6	134	...	...	...	...	...
7-27	119	...	...	...	...	...
28-364	131	...	...	...	...	...
Unknown - Inconnu	4	...	...	...	...	...
Saint Lucia - Sainte-Lucie						
2002						
Total	36	17	19	...	...	...
Under 1 day - Moins d'un jour	11	5	6	...	...	...
1-6	16	6	10	...	...	...
7-27	2	1	1	...	...	...
28-364	7	5	2	...	...	...
Saint Vincent and the Grenadines - Saint Vincent-et-les Grenadines[+]						
2000						
Total	35	24	11	...	...	...
Under 1 day - Moins d'un jour	13	9	4	...	...	...
1-6	7	4	3	...	...	...
7-27	2	2	-	...	...	...

16. Infant deaths and infant mortality rates by age and sex: latest available year, 1994 - 2003
Décčs d'enfants de moins d'un an et taux de mortalité infantile selon l'âge et le sexe: derničre année disponible, 1994 - 2003 (continued — suite)

Continent, country or area, year, age (in days) and urban/rural residence Continent, pays ou zone, année, âge (en jours) et résidence,urbaine/rurale	Number - Nombre			Rate - Taux		
	Both sexes Les deux sexes	Male Masculin	Female Féminin	Both sexes Les deux sexes	Male Masculin	Female Féminin
AMERICA, NORTH — AMERIQUE DU NORD						
Saint Vincent and the Grenadines - Saint Vincent-et-les Grenadines[+]						
2000						
28-364	13	9	4	...	...	...
Trinidad and Tobago - Trinité-et-Tobago						
1997						
Total	316	170	146	...	...	...
Under 1 day - Moins d'un jour	76	45	31	...	...	...
1-6	118	62	56	...	...	...
7-27	48	22	26	...	...	...
28-364	74	41	33	...	...	...
United States - États-Unis						
2001						
Total	27 568	15 477	12 091	6.8	7.5	6.1
Under 1 day - Moins d'un jour	10 898	6 122	4 776	2.7	3.0	2.4
1-6	3 713	2 139	1 574	0.9	1.0	0.8
7-27	3 654	1 976	1 678	0.9	1.0	0.9
28-364	9 303	5 240	4 063	2.3	2.5	2.1
AMERICA, SOUTH — AMERIQUE DU SUD						
Argentina - Argentine[2]						
1998						
Total	13 082	7 472	5 576	19.1	21.2	16.8
0-6	6 084	3 531	2 546	8.9	10.0	7.7
7-27	1 881	1 073	807	2.8	3.0	2.4
28-364	5 117	2 868	2 223	7.5	8.2	6.7
Brazil - Brésil[4]						
2003						
Total	48 039	28 189	19 850	...	...	...
Under 1 day - Moins d'un jour	10 565	5 969	4 596	...	...	...
1-6	10 997	6 403	4 594	...	...	...
7-27	6 909	3 858	3 051	...	...	...
28-364	15 526	8 702	6 824	...	...	...
Unknown - Inconnu	4 042	3 257	785	...	...	...
Chile - Chili						
2003						
Total	1 935	1 061	874	8.3	8.8	7.6
Under 1 day - Moins d'un jour	605	315	290	2.6	2.6	2.5
1-6	332	187	145	1.4	1.6	1.3
7-27	275	168	107	1.2	1.4	0.9
28-364	723	391	332	3.1	3.3	2.9
Colombia - Colombie[2,5]						
2003						
Total	11 944	6 758	5 179	...	...	...
Under 1 day - Moins d'un jour	2 802	1 595	1 203	...	...	...
1-6	2 582	1 543	1 037	...	...	...
7-27	1 909	1 024	885	...	...	...
28-364	4 636	2 588	2 047	...	...	...
Unknown - Inconnu	15	8	7	...	...	...
Ecuador - Équateur[6]						
2003						
Total	3 985	2 195	1 790	...	...	...
Under 1 day - Moins d'un jour	676	367	309	...	...	...
1-6	785	463	322	...	...	...
7-27	602	331	271	...	...	...
28-364	1 922	1 034	888	...	...	...
French Guiana - Guyane française[7]						
2003						
Total	58	32	26	...	...	...
Under 1 day - Moins d'un jour	10	3	7	...	...	...
1-6	15	10	5	...	...	...
7-27	16	12	4	...	...	...
28-364	17	7	10	...	...	...

16. Infant deaths and infant mortality rates by age and sex: latest available year, 1994 - 2003
Décčs d'enfants de moins d'un an et taux de mortalité infantile selon l'âge et le sexe: derničre année disponible, 1994 - 2003 (continued — suite)

Continent, country or area, year, age (in days) and urban/rural residence Continent, pays ou zone, année, âge (en jours) et résidence,urbaine/rurale	Number - Nombre			Rate - Taux		
	Both sexes Les deux sexes	Male Masculin	Female Féminin	Both sexes Les deux sexes	Male Masculin	Female Féminin
AMERICA, SOUTH — AMERIQUE DU SUD						
Peru - Pérou[4,8]						
2001						
Total	6 604	3 658	2 933	...	...	...
Under 1 day - Moins d'un jour	1 130	641	484	...	...	...
1-6	1 250	708	536	...	...	...
7-27	1 053	585	467	...	...	...
28-364	3 171	1 724	1 446	...	...	...
Suriname						
1994						
Total	211	...	...	...	...	...
Under 1 day - Moins d'un jour	16	...	...	...	...	...
1-6	85	...	...	...	...	...
7-27	28	...	...	...	...	...
28-364	82	...	...	...	...	...
Uruguay[2]						
2000						
Total	742	434	304	...	...	...
Under 1 day - Moins d'un jour	152	87	61	...	...	...
1-6	124	74	50	...	...	...
7-27	142	90	52	...	...	...
28-364	324	183	141	...	...	...
Venezuela[4]						
2001						
Total	8 158	4 710	3 448	15.4	17.1	13.5
0-27	5 657	3 288	2 369	10.7	12.0	9.3
28-364	2 501	1 422	1 079	4.7	5.2	4.2
ASIA — ASIE						
Armenia - Arménie[9]						
2003						
Total	422	256	166	...	...	...
Under 1 day - Moins d'un jour	73	53	20	...	...	...
1-6	172	101	71	...	...	...
7-27	44	25	19	...	...	...
28-364	133	77	56	...	...	...
Azerbaijan - Azerbaddjan[+,9]						
2003						
Total	1 451	818	633	12.8	13.3	12.1
Under 1 day - Moins d'un jour	112	70	42	1.0	1.1	0.8
1-6	221	154	67	1.9	2.5	1.3
7-27	36	26	10	0.3	♦0.4	♦0.2
28-364	1 082	568	514	9.5	9.3	9.9
Bahrain - Bahređn						
2002						
Total	94	48	46	...	...	...
0-6	29	14	15	...	...	...
7-27	22	9	13	...	...	...
28-364	43	25	18	...	...	...
China: Hong Kong SAR - Chine: Hong Kong RAS						
2003						
Total	109	57	52	...	...	...
Under 1 day - Moins d'un jour	12	7	5	...	...	...
1-6	22	10	12	...	...	...
7-27	20	13	7	...	...	...
28-364	55	27	28	...	...	...
China: Macao SAR - Chine: Macao RAS						
2003						
Total	2	1	1	...	...	...
Under 1 day - Moins d'un jour	-	-	-	...	...	...
1-6	1	-	1	...	...	...
7-27	-	-	-	...	...	...
28-364	1	1	-	...	...	...

16. Infant deaths and infant mortality rates by age and sex: latest available year, 1994 - 2003
Décčs d'enfants de moins d'un an et taux de mortalité infantile selon l'âge et le sexe: dernière année disponible, 1994 - 2003 (continued — suite)

Continent, country or area, year, age (in days) and urban/rural residence / Continent, pays ou zone, année, âge (en jours) et résidence,urbaine/rurale	Number - Nombre			Rate - Taux		
	Both sexes Les deux sexes	Male Masculin	Female Féminin	Both sexes Les deux sexes	Male Masculin	Female Féminin
ASIA — ASIE						
Cyprus - Chypre[10]						
2003						
Total	33	20	13	...	...	...
Under 1 day - Moins d'un jour	6	4	2	...	...	...
1-6	8	5	3	...	...	...
7-27	4	3	1	...	...	...
28-364	9	6	3	...	...	...
Unknown - Inconnu	6	2	4	...	...	...
Georgia - Géorgie[9]						
2003						
Total	1 144	657	487	24.8	26.9	22.4
Under 1 day - Moins d'un jour	342	171	171	7.4	7.0	7.9
1-6	508	298	210	11.0	12.2	9.7
7-27	96	73	23	2.1	3.0	◆1.1
28-364	198	115	83	4.3	4.7	3.8
Israel - Israël[11]						
2003						
Total	717	384	333	...	...	...
Under 1 day - Moins d'un jour	154	91	63	...	...	...
1-6	175	90	85	...	...	...
7-27	122	74	48	...	...	...
28-364	266	129	137	...	...	...
Japan - Japon[12]						
2003						
Total	3 364	1 787	1 577	3.0	3.1	2.9
Under 1 day - Moins d'un jour	821	403	418	0.7	0.7	0.8
1-6	482	272	420	0.4	0.5	0.8
7-27	576	301	275	0.5	0.5	0.5
28-364	1 485	811	674	1.3	1.4	1.2
Kazakhstan[9]						
2003						
Total	3 824	2 234	1 590	15.4	17.5	13.2
Under 1 day - Moins d'un jour	332	175	157	1.3	1.4	1.3
1-6	1 438	882	556	5.8	6.9	4.6
7-27	523	323	200	2.1	2.5	1.7
28-364	1 531	854	677	6.2	6.7	5.6
Kuwait - Koweďt						
2002						
Total	418	225	193	...	...	...
Under 1 day - Moins d'un jour	114	72	42	...	...	...
1-6	82	45	37	...	...	...
7-27	89	47	42	...	...	...
28-364	133	61	72	...	...	...
Kyrgyzstan - Kirghizistan[9]						
2002						
Total	2 128	1 288	840	21.1	25.0	17.0
Under 1 day - Moins d'un jour	274	157	117	2.7	3.0	2.4
1-6	628	396	232	6.2	7.7	4.7
7-27	229	130	99	2.3	2.5	2.0
28-364	997	605	392	9.9	11.7	7.9
Malaysia - Malaisie						
2000						
Total	3 578	2 026	1 552	6.6	7.2	5.9
Under 1 day - Moins d'un jour	115	69	46	0.2	0.2	0.2
1-6	1 353	777	576	2.5	2.8	2.2
7-27	584	319	265	1.1	1.1	1.0
28-364	1 526	861	665	2.8	3.1	2.5
Maldives[13]						
2003						
Total	74	41	33	...	...	...
Under 1 day - Moins d'un jour	18	9	9	...	...	...
1-6	28	16	12	...	...	...
7-27	5	3	2	...	...	...
28-364	23	13	10	...	...	...

16. Infant deaths and infant mortality rates by age and sex: latest available year, 1994 - 2003
Décès d'enfants de moins d'un an et taux de mortalité infantile selon l'âge et le sexe: dernière année disponible, 1994 - 2003 (continued — suite)

Continent, country or area, year, age (in days) and urban/rural residence Continent, pays ou zone, année, âge (en jours) et résidence,urbaine/rurale	Number - Nombre			Rate - Taux		
	Both sexes Les deux sexes	Male Masculin	Female Féminin	Both sexes Les deux sexes	Male Masculin	Female Féminin
ASIA — ASIE						
Myanmar[14]						
1994						
Urban - Urbaine						
Total	12 395	6 685	5 710	...	...	...
Under 1 day - Moins d'un jour	419	228	191	...	...	...
1-6	3 492	1 862	1 630	...	...	...
7-27	2 548	1 308	1 240	...	...	...
28-364	5 764	3 184	2 580	...	...	...
Unknown - Inconnu	172	103	69	...	...	...
Occupied Palestinian Territory - Territoire palestinien occupé						
2003						
Total	1 101	564	537	...	...	...
Under 1 day - Moins d'un jour	52	24	28	...	...	...
1-6	281	156	125	...	...	...
7-27	248	132	116	...	...	...
28-364	520	252	268	...	...	...
Pakistan[15,16]						
2001						
Total	286 609	149 832	136 777	77.1	77.1	77.0
Under 1 day - Moins d'un jour	14 921	10 569	4 352	4.0	5.4	2.4
1-6	106 313	58 441	47 873	28.6	30.1	26.9
7-27	52 846	25 491	27 355	14.2	13.1	15.4
28-364	112 531	55 332	57 198	30.3	28.5	32.2
Philippines						
2002						
Total	23 778	13 925	9 853	14.3	16.1	12.3
Under 1 day - Moins d'un jour	4 541	2 646	1 895	2.7	3.1	2.4
1-6	6 091	3 725	2 366	3.7	4.3	3.0
7-27	2 689	1 591	1 098	1.6	1.8	1.4
28-364	10 457	5 963	4 494	6.3	6.9	5.6
Qatar						
2003						
Total	137	75	62	...	...	...
Under 1 day - Moins d'un jour	-	-	-	...	...	...
1-6	52	31	21	...	...	...
7-27	39	22	17	...	...	...
28-364	46	22	24	...	...	...
Singapore - Singapour+,[17]						
2003						
Total	100	56	44	...	...	...
Under 1 day - Moins d'un jour	15	12	3	...	...	...
1-6	25	16	9	...	...	...
7-27	20	10	10	...	...	...
28-364	40	18	22	...	...	...
Sri Lanka+						
1996						
Total	5 879	3 271	2 608	17.3	18.8	15.6
Under 1 day - Moins d'un jour	1 630	899	731	4.8	5.2	4.4
1-6	1 818	1 072	746	5.3	6.2	4.5
7-27	952	526	426	2.8	3.0	2.6
28-364	1 479	774	705	4.3	4.5	4.2
Tajikistan - Tadjikistan[9]						
1994						
Total	6 880	3 896	2 984	42.4	46.4	38.2
Under 1 day - Moins d'un jour	251	153	98	1.5	1.8	1.3
1-6	1 006	617	389	6.2	7.3	5.0
7-27	526	293	233	3.2	3.5	3.0
28-364	5 099	2 827	2 272	31.4	33.6	29.1
Unknown - Inconnu	13	6	7	♦0.1	♦0.1	♦0.1
Thailand - Thaïlande+						
1999						
Total	5 003	2 765	2 238	...	...	...
Under 1 day - Moins d'un jour	287	135	152	...	...	...

16. Infant deaths and infant mortality rates by age and sex: latest available year, 1994 - 2003
Décčs d'enfants de moins d'un an et taux de mortalité infantile selon l'âge et le sexe: derničre année disponible, 1994 - 2003 (continued — suite)

Continent, country or area, year, age (in days) and urban/rural residence Continent, pays ou zone, année, âge (en jours) et résidence,urbaine/rurale	Number - Nombre			Rate - Taux		
	Both sexes Les deux sexes	Male Masculin	Female Féminin	Both sexes Les deux sexes	Male Masculin	Female Féminin
ASIA — ASIE						
Thailand - Thadlande[+]						
1999						
1-6	764	439	325	...	...	...
7-27	760	434	326	...	...	...
28-364	3 192	1 757	1 435	...	...	...
Turkey - Turquie[18,19]						
1999						
Urban - Urbaine						
Total	15 870	8 931	6 939	...	...	...
1-6	8 483	4 876	3 607	...	...	...
7-27	1 978	1 093	885	...	...	...
28-364	5 409	2 962	2 447	...	...	...
Uzbekistan - Ouzbékistan[9]						
2000						
Total	10 091	5 805	4 286	19.1	21.4	16.7
Under 1 day - Moins d'un jour	607	355	252	1.2	1.3	1.0
1-6	2 179	1 352	827	4.1	5.0	3.2
7-27	1 279	731	548	2.4	2.7	2.1
28-364	6 026	3 367	2 659	11.4	12.4	10.4
EUROPE						
Andorra - Andorre						
2001						
Total	2	-	2	...	...	...
Under 1 day - Moins d'un jour	1	-	1	...	...	...
1-6	-	-	-	...	...	...
7-27	-	-	-	...	...	...
28-364	1	-	1	...	...	...
Austria - Autriche						
2003						
Total	343	192	151	...	...	...
Under 1 day - Moins d'un jour	131	68	63	...	...	...
1-6	54	33	21	...	...	...
7-27	53	35	18	...	...	...
28-364	105	56	49	...	...	...
Belarus - Bélarus[9]						
2002						
Total	695	397	298	...	...	...
Under 1 day - Moins d'un jour	82	46	36	...	...	...
1-6	134	84	50	...	...	...
7-27	123	82	41	...	...	...
28-364	356	185	171	...	...	...
Belgium - Belgique[20]						
2000						
Total	554	305	249	...	...	...
Under 1 day - Moins d'un jour	91	46	45	...	...	...
1-6	153	85	68	...	...	...
7-27	90	56	34	...	...	...
28-364	220	118	102	...	...	...
Bosnia and Herzegovina - Bosnie-Herzégovine						
2003						
Total	268	154	114	...	...	...
Under 1 day - Moins d'un jour	76	45	31	...	...	...
1-6	93	58	35	...	...	...
7-27	35	20	15	...	...	...
28-364	64	31	33	...	...	...
Bulgaria - Bulgarie						
2003						
Total	831	488	343	...	...	...
Under 1 day - Moins d'un jour	142	95	47	...	...	...
1-6	155	90	65	...	...	...
7-27	163	89	74	...	...	...
28-364	371	214	157	...	...	...

16. Infant deaths and infant mortality rates by age and sex: latest available year, 1994 - 2003
Décčs d'enfants de moins d'un an et taux de mortalité infantile selon l'âge et le sexe: derničre année disponible, 1994 - 2003 (continued — suite)

Continent, country or area, year, age (in days) and urban/rural residence / Continent, pays ou zone, année, âge (en jours) et résidence,urbaine/rurale	Number - Nombre			Rate - Taux		
	Both sexes Les deux sexes	Male Masculin	Female Féminin	Both sexes Les deux sexes	Male Masculin	Female Féminin
EUROPE						
Channel Islands: Guernsey - Îles Anglo-Normandes: Guernesey						
1995						
Total	2	...	...	...	...	...
Under 1 day - Moins d'un jour	-	...	...	...	...	...
1-6	-	...	...	...	...	...
7-27	1	...	...	...	...	...
28-364	1	...	...	...	...	...
Channel Islands: Jersey - Îles Anglo-Normandes: Jersey+						
1994						
Total	2	-	2	...	...	...
Under 1 day - Moins d'un jour	-	-	-	...	...	...
1-6	1	-	1	...	...	...
7-27	-	-	-	...	...	...
28-364	1	-	1	...	...	...
Croatia - Croatie						
2003						
Total	251	148	103	...	...	...
Under 1 day - Moins d'un jour	78	47	31	...	...	...
1-6	79	46	33	...	...	...
7-27	39	23	16	...	...	...
28-364	55	32	23	...	...	...
Czech Republic - République tchčque						
2003						
Total	365	207	158	...	...	...
Under 1 day - Moins d'un jour	48	21	27	...	...	...
1-6	81	50	31	...	...	...
7-27	92	53	39	...	...	...
28-364	144	83	61	...	...	...
Denmark - Danemark[21]						
2003						
Total	286	165	121	...	...	...
Under 1 day - Moins d'un jour	101	56	45	...	...	...
1-6	78	46	32	...	...	...
7-27	25	19	6	...	...	...
28-364	82	44	38	...	...	...
Estonia - Estonie[9]						
2003						
Total	91	56	35	...	...	...
Under 1 day - Moins d'un jour	26	14	12	...	...	...
1-6	13	8	5	...	...	...
7-27	13	8	5	...	...	...
28-364	39	26	13	...	...	...
Finland - Finlande[22]						
2003						
Total	176	93	83	...	...	...
Under 1 day - Moins d'un jour	52	26	26	...	...	...
1-6	41	21	20	...	...	...
7-27	23	12	11	...	...	...
28-364	60	34	26	...	...	...
France[23]						
2003						
Total	3 325	1 904	1 421	4.4	4.9	3.8
Under 1 day - Moins d'un jour	779	452	327	1.0	1.2	0.9
1-6	748	432	316	1.0	1.1	0.9
7-27	679	370	309	0.9	1.0	0.8
28-364	1 119	650	469	1.5	1.7	1.3
Germany - Allemagne						
2003						
Total	2 990	1 700	1 290	4.2	4.7	3.7
Under 1 day - Moins d'un jour	828	463	365	1.2	1.3	1.1
1-6	666	410	256	0.9	1.1	0.7
7-27	449	245	204	0.6	0.7	0.6

16. Infant deaths and infant mortality rates by age and sex: latest available year, 1994 - 2003
Décčs d'enfants de moins d'un an et taux de mortalité infantile selon l'âge et le sexe: derničre année disponible, 1994 - 2003 (continued — suite)

Continent, country or area, year, age (in days) and urban/rural residence Continent, pays ou zone, année, âge (en jours) et résidence,urbaine/rurale	Number - Nombre			Rate - Taux		
	Both sexes Les deux sexes	Male Masculin	Female Féminin	Both sexes Les deux sexes	Male Masculin	Female Féminin
EUROPE						
Germany - Allemagne						
2003						
28-364	1 047	582	465	1.5	1.6	1.4
Greece - Grčce						
2003						
Total	420	236	184	...	...	...
Under 1 day - Moins d'un jour	74	38	36	...	...	...
1-6	112	61	51	...	...	...
7-27	95	58	37	...	...	...
28-364	139	79	60	...	...	...
Hungary - Hongrie						
2003						
Total	690	389	301	...	...	...
Under 1 day - Moins d'un jour	158	93	65	...	...	...
1-6	178	98	80	...	...	...
7-27	113	63	50	...	...	...
28-364	241	135	106	...	...	...
Iceland - Islande						
2003						
Total	10	6	4	...	...	...
Under 1 day - Moins d'un jour	4	3	1	...	...	...
1-6	3	-	3	...	...	...
7-27	1	1	-	...	...	...
28-364	2	2	-	...	...	...
Ireland - Irlande[+,24]						
2003						
Total	311	182	129	...	...	...
Under 1 day - Moins d'un jour	128	75	53	...	...	...
1-6	59	36	23	...	...	...
7-27	44	24	20	...	...	...
28-364	80	47	33	...	...	...
Isle of Man - Îles de Man						
1996						
Total	2	1	1	...	...	...
Under 1 day - Moins d'un jour	1	-	1	...	...	...
1-6	1	1	-	...	...	...
7-27	-	-	-	...	...	...
28-364	-	-	-	...	...	...
Italy - Italie						
2003						
Total	2 482	1 370	1 112	4.6	4.9	4.2
Under 1 day - Moins d'un jour	660	378	282	1.2	1.4	1.1
1-6	663	363	300	1.2	1.3	1.1
7-27	493	277	216	0.9	1.0	0.8
28-364	666	352	314	1.2	1.3	1.2
Latvia - Lettonie[9]						
2002						
Total	197	111	86	...	...	...
Under 1 day - Moins d'un jour	20	13	7	...	...	...
1-6	58	30	28	...	...	...
7-27	37	20	17	...	...	...
28-364	82	48	34	...	...	...
Lithuania - Lituanie[9]						
2003						
Total	206	119	87	...	...	...
Under 1 day - Moins d'un jour	32	21	11	...	...	...
1-6	47	26	21	...	...	...
7-27	34	21	13	...	...	...
28-364	93	51	42	...	...	...
Luxembourg						
2003						
Total	26	16	10	...	...	...
Under 1 day - Moins d'un jour	7	5	2	...	...	...
1-6	4	2	2	...	...	...

16. Infant deaths and infant mortality rates by age and sex: latest available year, 1994 - 2003
Décčs d'enfants de moins d'un an et taux de mortalité infantile selon l'âge et le sexe: dernicre année disponible, 1994 - 2003 (continued — suite)

Continent, country or area, year, age (in days) and urban/rural residence Continent, pays ou zone, année, âge (en jours) et résidence,urbaine/rurale	Number - Nombre			Rate - Taux		
	Both sexes Les deux sexes	Male Masculin	Female Féminin	Both sexes Les deux sexes	Male Masculin	Female Féminin
EUROPE						
Luxembourg						
2003						
7-27	3	3	1	...	...	...
28-364	12	7	5	...	...	...
Malta - Malte						
2001						
Total	17	12	5	...	...	...
0-6	10	7	3	...	...	...
7-27	2	1	1	...	...	...
28-364	5	4	1	...	...	...
Netherlands - Pays-Bas[25]						
2003						
Total	962	562	400	...	...	...
Under 1 day - Moins d'un jour	320	192	128	...	...	...
1-6	235	145	90	...	...	...
7-27	170	83	87	...	...	...
28-364	237	142	95	...	...	...
Norway - Norvčge[26]						
2003						
Total	190	106	84	...	...	...
Under 1 day - Moins d'un jour	52	27	25	...	...	...
1-6	51	31	20	...	...	...
7-27	13	6	7	...	...	...
28-364	42	25	17	...	...	...
Unknown - Inconnu	32	17	15	...	...	...
Poland - Pologne						
2003						
Total	2 470	1 383	1 087	7.0	7.7	6.4
Under 1 day - Moins d'un jour	718	376	342	2.0	2.1	2.0
1-6	593	350	243	1.7	1.9	1.4
7-27	449	256	193	1.3	1.4	1.1
28-364	710	401	309	2.0	2.2	1.8
Portugal						
2003						
Total	465	234	231	...	...	...
Under 1 day - Moins d'un jour	113	56	57	...	...	...
1-6	119	77	42	...	...	...
7-27	72	35	37	...	...	...
28-364	161	66	95	...	...	...
Republic of Moldova - République de Moldova[9]						
2003						
Total	522	309	213	...	...	...
Under 1 day - Moins d'un jour	48	29	19	...	...	...
1-6	154	101	53	...	...	...
7-27	70	43	27	...	...	...
28-364	250	136	114	...	...	...
Romania - Roumanie						
2003						
Total	3 546	2 060	1 486	16.7	18.8	14.4
Under 1 day - Moins d'un jour	255	147	108	1.2	1.3	1.0
1-6	1 006	608	398	4.7	5.6	3.9
7-27	604	362	242	2.8	3.3	2.4
28-364	1 681	943	738	7.9	8.6	7.2
San Marino - Saint-Marin+						
2003						
Total	2	1	1	...	...	...
Under 1 day - Moins d'un jour	1	1	1	...	...	...
7-27	1	1	1	...	...	...
Serbia and Montenegro - Serbie-et-Montenegro[27]						
2003						
Total	803	442	361	...	...	...
Under 1 day - Moins d'un jour	170	104	66	...	...	...
1-6	281	152	129	...	...	...

16. Infant deaths and infant mortality rates by age and sex: latest available year, 1994 - 2003
Décčs d'enfants de moins d'un an et taux de mortalité infantile selon l'âge et le sexe: derničre année disponible, 1994 - 2003 (continued — suite)

Continent, country or area, year, age (in days) and urban/rural residence Continent, pays ou zone, année, âge (en jours) et résidence,urbaine/rurale	Number - Nombre			Rate - Taux		
	Both sexes Les deux sexes	Male Masculin	Female Féminin	Both sexes Les deux sexes	Male Masculin	Female Féminin
EUROPE						
Serbia and Montenegro - Serbie-et-Montenegro[27]						
2003						
7-27	128	66	62	...	...	...
28-364	224	120	104	...	...	...
Slovakia - Slovaquie						
2003						
Total	406	230	176	...	...	...
Under 1 day - Moins d'un jour	74	43	31	...	...	...
1-6	105	61	44	...	...	...
7-27	55	31	24	...	...	...
28-364	172	95	77	...	...	...
Slovenia - Slovénie						
2003						
Total	69	37	32	...	...	...
Under 1 day - Moins d'un jour	23	13	10	...	...	...
1-6	17	8	9	...	...	...
7-27	13	6	7	...	...	...
28-364	16	10	6	...	...	...
Spain - Espagne						
2003						
Total	1 733	964	769	3.9	4.3	3.6
Under 1 day - Moins d'un jour	322	180	142	0.7	0.8	0.7
1-6	368	211	157	0.8	0.9	0.7
7-27	416	234	182	0.9	1.0	0.9
28-364	627	339	288	1.4	1.5	1.4
Sweden - Sučde						
2002						
Total	313	172	141	...	...	...
Under 1 day - Moins d'un jour	62	32	30	...	...	...
1-6	98	49	49	...	...	...
7-27	51	30	21	...	...	...
28-364	101	60	41	...	...	...
Switzerland - Suisse						
2003						
Total	311	167	144	...	...	...
Under 1 day - Moins d'un jour	133	69	64	...	...	...
1-6	66	35	31	...	...	...
7-27	40	25	15	...	...	...
28-364	72	38	34	...	...	...
The Former Yugoslav Rep. of Macedonia - L'ex-République yougoslave de Macédoine						
2003						
Total	305	181	124	...	...	...
Under 1 day - Moins d'un jour	91	53	38	...	...	...
1-6	90	57	33	...	...	...
7-27	46	22	24	...	...	...
28-364	78	49	29	...	...	...
Ukraine[9]						
2003						
Total	3 882	2 296	1 586	9.5	10.9	8.0
Under 1 day - Moins d'un jour	332	194	138	0.8	0.9	0.7
1-6	1 129	666	463	2.8	3.2	2.3
7-27	693	412	281	1.7	2.0	1.4
28-364	1 724	1 022	702	4.2	4.9	3.5
Unknown - Inconnu	4	2	2	0.0	0.0	0.0
United Kingdom - Royaume-Uni						
2003						
Total	3 686	2 029	1 657	5.3	5.7	4.9
Under 1 day - Moins d'un jour	1 073	593	480	1.5	1.7	1.4
1-6	873	483	390	1.3	1.4	1.2
7-27	583	300	283	0.8	0.8	0.8
28-364	1 157	653	504	1.7	1.8	1.5

16. Infant deaths and infant mortality rates by age and sex: latest available year, 1994 - 2003
Décčs d'enfants de moins d'un an et taux de mortalité infantile selon l'âge et le sexe: derničre année disponible, 1994 - 2003 (continued — suite)

Continent, country or area, year, age (in days) and urban/rural residence Continent, pays ou zone, année, âge (en jours) et résidence,urbaine/rurale	Number - Nombre			Rate - Taux		
	Both sexes Les deux sexes	Male Masculin	Female Féminin	Both sexes Les deux sexes	Male Masculin	Female Féminin
OCEANIA — OCEANIE						
Australia - Australie+						
2003						
Total	1 199	677	522	4.8	5.2	4.3
Under 1 day - Moins d'un jour	499	267	232	2.0	2.1	1.9
1-6	185	108	77	0.7	0.8	0.6
7-27	149	86	63	0.6	0.7	0.5
28-364	366	216	150	1.5	1.7	1.2
New Caledonia - Nouvelle-Calédonie						
2003						
Total	24	14	10	...	...	...
Under 1 day - Moins d'un jour	5	2	3	...	...	...
1-6	4	3	1	...	...	...
7-27	3	2	1	...	...	...
28-364	12	7	5	...	...	...
New Zealand - Nouvelle-Zélande+						
2003						
Total	277	164	113	...	...	...
Under 1 day - Moins d'un jour	80	47	33	...	...	...
1-6	50	27	23	...	...	...
7-27	33	19	14	...	...	...
28-364	114	71	43	...	...	...
Tonga+						
1997						
Total	20	...	...	...	...	...
Under 1 day - Moins d'un jour	4	...	...	...	...	...
1-6	2	...	...	...	...	...
7-27	2	...	...	...	...	...
28-364	12	...	...	...	...	...

FOOTNOTES - NOTES

Italics: data from civil registers which are incomplete or of unknown completeness. — *Italiques:* données incomplčtes ou dont le degré d'exactitude n'est pas connu provenant des registres de l'état civil.

+ Data tabulated by date of registration rather than occurrence. — Données exploitées selon la date de l'enregistrement et non la date de l'événement.

♦ Rates based on 30 or fewer infant deaths. — Taux basés sur 30 dčcčs d'enfants ou moins.

1 Including Canadian residents temporarily in the United States, but excluding United States residents temporarily in Canada. - Y compris les résidents canadiens se trouvant temporairement aux Etats-Unis, mais ne comprenant pas les résidents des Etats-Unis se trouvant temporairement au Canada.

2 The category "Both sexes" includes infant deaths of unknown sex. - La catégorie "Les deux sexes" comprenne les décčs d'enfants de moins d'un an dont on ignore le sexe.

3 For 2002 data as reported by national statistical authorities; they may differ from data presented in other tables. - Pour 2002 les données comme elles ont été déclarées par l'institut national de la statistique; elles peuvent ętre différentes de ceux présentées dans autre tableaux.

4 Excluding Indian jungle population. - Non compris les Indiens de la jungle.

5 Data on live births and deaths are based on a civil registration system put in place in January 1998. - Les données sur les naissances et les décčs sont basées sur un systčme d'enregistrement des faits d'état civil mis en place en janvier 1998.

6 Excluding nomadic Indian tribes. - Non compris les tribus d'Indiens nomades.

7 Excluding live-born infants who died before their birth was registered. - Non compris les enfants nés vivants décédés avant l'enregistrement de leur naissance.

8 Data refer to registered infant deaths only. - Les données se rapportent aux décčs enregistrés d'enfants de moins de 1 an seulement.

9 Excluding infants born alive with less than 28 weeks gestation, less than 1 000 grams in weight and 35 centimeters in length, who die within seven days of birth. - Non compris les enfants nés vivants avant 28 semaines de gestation, pesant moins de 1 000 grammes, mesurant moins de 35 centimčtres et décédés dans les sept jours qui ont suivi leur naissance.

10 Data refer to government controlled areas. - Les données se raportent aux zones contrôlées par le Gouvernement.

11 Including data for East Jerusalem and Israeli residents in certain other territories under occupation by Israeli military forces since June 1967. - Y compris les données pour Jérusalem-Est et les résidents israéliens dans certains autres territoires occupés depuis 1967 par les forces armées israéliennes.

12 Data refer to Japanese nationals in Japan only. - Les données se raportent aux nationaux japonais au Japon seulement.

13 For 2003 data as reported by national statistical authorities; they may differ from data presented in other tables. - Pour 2003 les données comme elles ont été déclarées par l'institut national de la statistique; elles peuvent ętre différentes de ceux présentées dans autre tableaux.

14 Data for urban refer to 170 towns out of 254 towns. - Les données urbaines se rapportent f 170 des 254 villes.

15 Based on the results of the Population Growth Survey. - D'aprčs les résultats de la 'Population Growth Survey.'

16 Excluding data for the Pakistan-held part of Jammu and Kashmir, the final status of which has not yet been determined. - Non compris les données concernant la partie du Jammu et Cachemire occupée par le Pakistan dont le statut définitif n'a pas été déterminé.

17 Excluding transients afloat and non-locally domiciled military and

civilian services personnel and their dependants. - Non compris les personnes de passage f bord de navires, ni les militaires et agents civils domiciliés hors du territoire et les membres de leur famille les accompagnant.

[18] Based on the results of the Population Demographic Survey. - - D'aprčs les résultats de la Population Demographic Survey.

[19] Deaths in province and district centers. - Les décčs aux centres des provinces et des zones seulement.

[20] Including armed forces stationed outside the country, but excluding alien armed forces stationed in the area. - Y compris les militaires nationaux hors du pays, mais non compris les militaires étrangers en garnison sur le territoire.

[21] Excluding Faeroe Islands and Greenland. - Non compris les Iles Féroé et Gröenland.

[22] Including nationals temporarily outside the country. - Y compris les nationaux se trouvant temporairement hors du pays.

[23] Including armed forces stationed outside the country. - Y compris les militaires nationaux hors du pays.

[24] Events registered within one year of occurrence. - Evénements enregistrés dans l'année qui suit l'événement.

[25] Including residents outside the country if listed in a Netherlands population register. - Y compris les résidents hors du pays, s'ils sont inscrits sur un registre de population néerlandais.

[26] Including residents temporarily outside the country. - Y compris les résidents se trouvant temporairement hors du pays.

[27] From 2002, without data for Kosovo and Metohia. - Aprčs 2002, sans les donées pour le Kosovo and Metohie.

Table 17

Table 17 presents maternal deaths and maternal mortality rates for as many years as possible between 1995 and 2002. The table is a replicate of Table 17 in the *Demographic Yearbook* 2002.

Description of variables: Maternal deaths are defined for the purposes of the Demographic Yearbook as those caused by deliveries and complications of pregnancy, childbirth and the puerperium, within 42 days of termination of pregnancy. They are usually defined as deaths coded "38-41" for ICD-9 Basic Tabulation List or as deaths coded "A34", "O00-O95", "O98-O99" for ICD-10, respectively. However, data for ICD-10 shown in this table include deaths due to "O96" and "O97" which refer to deaths from any obstetric cause occurring more than 42 days but less than one year after delivery and death from sequelae of direct obstetric causes occurring one year or more after delivery. For details on causes and corresponding ICD codes, see Table 17-1 below.

For further information on the definition of maternal mortality from the tenth revisions of the *International Statistical Classification of Diseases and Related Health Problems*[1], see also section 4.3 of the Technical Notes.

Statistics on maternal death presented in this table are provided by the World Health Organisation. They are limited to countries or areas that meet the criterion that cause-of-death statistics are either classified by or convertible to the ninth or tenth revisions mentioned above. Data that are classified by the tenth revision are set in bold in the table.

Rate computation: Maternal mortality rates are the annual number of maternal deaths per 100 000 live births (table 9) in the same year. These rates have been calculated by the Statistics Division of the United Nations. Rates based on 30 or fewer maternal deaths are identified by the symbol (♦).

Reliability of data: In general the quality code for deaths shown in table 18 is used to determine whether data on deaths in other tables appear in roman or *italic* type. However, the reliability of data for the completeness of cause of death data is provided by the World Health Organisation it may differ from the reliability of data for the total number of deaths. Therefore, there are cases when the quality code in table 18 does not correspond with the typeface used in this table.

Countries and areas that have incomplete (less than 90 per cent completeness) or of unknown completeness of cause of deaths data coverage are considered unreliable and are set in italics rather than in roman type. Rates on these data are not computed.

In addition, when it is known that registration of cause of death does not cover certain areas of a country, rates are not computed. Those countries are Georgia, Republic of Moldova and Russian Federation, as indicated in the footnote 7, 19 and 20, respectively. All other footnotes pertaining to the inclusion or exclusion of certain population of a country refer only to the live births in the denominator.

Limitations: Statistics on maternal deaths are subject to the same qualifications that have been set forth for vital statistics in general and death statistics in particular as discussed in section 4 of the Technical Notes. The reliability of the data, an indication of which is described above, is an important factor in considering the limitations. In addition, maternal-death statistics are subject to all the qualifications relating to cause-of-death statistics. These have been set forth in section 4 of the Technical Notes.

Maternal mortality rates are subject to the limitations of the data on live births with which they have been calculated. These have been set forth in the technical notes for table 9.

The calculation of the maternal mortality rates based on the total number of live births approximates the risk of dying from complications of pregnancy, childbirth or puerperium. Ideally this rate should be based on the number of women exposed to the risk of pregnancy, in other words, the number of women conceiving. Since it is impossible to know how many women have conceived, the total number of live births is used in calculating this rate.

NOTES

[1] *International Statistical Classification of Diseases and Related Health Problems*, Tenth Revision, Volume 2, World Health Organization, Geneva, 1992.

Earlier data: Maternal deaths and maternal mortality rates have been shown in previous issues of the *Demographic Yearbook*. For information on specific years covered, the reader should consult the Index.

It should however be noted that in issues prior to 1975, maternal mortality rates were calculated using the female population rather than live births. Therefore, maternal mortality rates published since 1975 are not comparable to the earlier maternal death rates.

Table 17-1. Tabulation list for ICD-9 and ICD-10 data for presentation in the Demographic Yearbook

Disease	ICD-10	ICD-9 Basic Tabulation List
All causes	**A00-Y89**	**01-56**
Certain infectious and parasitic diseases	**A00-B99**	**01-07, 184**
Intestinal infectious diseases	A00-A09	01
Tuberculosis	A15-A19	02
Tetanus[i]	A33, A35	037
Diphtheria	A36	033
Whooping cough	A37	034
Meningococcal infection	A39	036
Septicaemia	A40-A41	038
Acute poliomyelitis	A80	040
Measles	B05	042
Viral hepatitis	B15-B19	046
Human immunodeficiency virus [HIV] disease	B20-B24	184
Malaria	B50-B54	052
Neoplasms	**C00-D48**	**08-17**
Malignant neoplasms	**C00-C97**	**08-14**
Malignant neoplasm of lip, oral cavity and pharynx	C00-C14	08
Malignant neoplasm of oesophagus	C15	090
Malignant neoplasm of stomach	C16	091
Malignant neoplasm of colon, rectosigmoid junction, rectum, anus and anal canal	C18-C21	093-094
Malignant neoplasm of liver and intrahepatic bile ducts	C22	095
Malignant neoplasm of pancreas	C25	096
Malignant neoplasm of trachea, bronchus and lung	C33-C34	101
Malignant neoplasm of **female** breast	C50	113
Malignant neoplasm of cervix uteri	C53	120
Malignant neoplasm of prostate	C61	124
Malignant neoplasm of lymphoid, haematopoietic and related tissue	C81-C96	14
Disorders of the blood and blood-forming organs and certain disorders involving the immune mechanism	**D50-D89**	**20**
Anaemias	D50-D64	200
Endocrine, nutritional and metabolic diseases	**E00-E88**	**18-19, minus 184**
Diabetes mellitus	E10-E14	181
Malnutrition	E40-E46	190-192
Mental and behavioural disorders	**F01-F99**	**21**
Diseases of the nervous system	**G00-G98**	**22**
Diseases of the circulatory system	**I00-I99**	**25-30**

Table 17-1. Tabulation list for ICD-9 and ICD-10 data for presentation in the Demographic Yearbook

Disease	ICD-10	ICD-9 Basic Tabulation List
Acute rheumatic fever and chronic rheumatic heart diseases	I01-I09	25
Hypertensive diseases	I10-I13	26
Ischaemic heart diseases	I20-I25	27
Cerebrovascular diseases	I60-I69	29
Diseases of arteries, arterioles and capillaries	I70-I79	300-302
Diseases of the respiratory system	**J00-J98**	**31-32**
Influenza	J10-J11	322
Pneumonia	J12-J18	321
Chronic lower respiratory diseases	J40-J47	323-325
Diseases of the digestive system	**K00-K92**	**33-34**
Gastric and duodenal ulcer	K25-K27	341
Diseases of the liver	K70-K76	347
Diseases of the musculoskeletal system and connective tissue	**M00-M99**	**43**
Diseases of the genitourinary system	**N00-N98**	**35-37**
Disorders of kidney and ureter	N00-N28	350-351
Hyperplasia of prostate	N40	360
Pregnancy, childbirth and the puerperium	**O00-O99**	**38-41**
Pregnancy with abortive outcome	O00-O07	38
Other direct obstetric causes[i]	O10-092, O95, A34	39
Indirect obstetric causes	O98-O99	40
Certain conditions originating in the perinatal period	**P00-P96**	**45**
Congenital malformations, deformations and chromosomal abnormalities	**Q00-Q99**	**44**
Symptoms, signs and abnormal clinical and laboratory findings, not elsewhere classified	**R00-R99**	**46**
All other diseases	**H00-H95, L00-L98**	**23-24, 42**
External causes	**V01-Y89**	**E47-E56**
Accidents	**V01-X59**	**E47-E53**
Transport accidents	V01-V99	E47
Falls	W00-W19	E50
Accidental drowning and submersion	W65-W74	E521
Exposure to smoke, fire and flames	X00-X09	E51
Accidental poisoning by and exposure to noxious substances	X40-X49	E48
Intentional self-harm	**X60-X84**	**E54**
Assault	**X85-Y09**	**E55**
All other external causes	Y10-Y89	E56

---

[i] In ICD-10 obstetrical tetanus is classified to A34 but in this table it is included with the "Other direct obstetric causes".

Tableau 17

Ce tableau présente des statistiques et des taux de mortalité liée à la maternité pour le plus grand nombre d'années possible entre 1995 et 2002.

Description des variables : Aux fins de *l'Annuaire démographique*, les décès liés à la maternité sont ceux entraînés par l'accouchement ou les complications de la grossesse, de l'accouchement et des suites de couches dans un délai de 42 jours après la terminaison de la grossesse. Ils sont généralement associés aux codes 38 à 41 dans le cas de la liste de base pour la mise en tableaux de la CIM-9 et aux codes A34, O00 à O95 et O98 et O99 dans le cas de la CIM-10. Les statistiques associées à des codes correspondant à la CIM-10 englobent des décès de type O96 et O97, qui désignent les décès liés à des causes obstétriques se produisant après 42 jours mais moins d'un an après l'accouchement et les décès entraînés par les séquelles de complications obstétriques directes qui se produisent un an ou plus après l'accouchement. Pour plus de précisions sur les causes des décès et les codes correspondants de la CIM, voir le tableau 17-1.

Pour plus de précisions concernant les définitions de la mortalité liée à la maternité dans la dixième révision de la *Classification statistique internationale des maladies et des problèmes de santé connexes*[1], se reporter également à la section 4.3 des Notes techniques.

Les statistiques de mortalité liée à la maternité présentées dans le tableau 17 émanent de l'Organisation mondiale de la santé. Elles ne se rapportent qu'aux pays ou zones qui répondent aux critères selon lesquels les statistiques relatives à la cause des décès sont conformes à la liste de la neuvième ou de la dixième révision de la CIM ou peuvent être aisément comparées aux catégories de cette liste. Les données conformes à la dixième révision sont indiquées en gras dans le tableau.

Calcul des taux : Les taux de mortalité liée à la maternité représentent le nombre annuel de décès dus à la maternité pour 100 000 naissances vivantes (fréquences du tableau 9) de la même année. Ces taux ont été calculés par la Division de statistique de l'ONU. Les taux fondés sur 30 décès liés à la maternité ou moins sont signalés par le signe '♦'.

Fiabilité des données : En général, les code de qualité associés aux données sur les décès indiqués au tableau 18 servent à déterminer si, dans les autres tableaux, les données relatives à la mortalité apparaissent en caractères romains ou italiques. Toutefois, les renseignements relatifs à la fiabilité des données concernant l'exhaustivité des données classées en fonction de la cause des décès émanent de l'Organisation mondiale de la santé et il est possible qu'ils ne correspondent pas avec le degré de fiabilité des données portant sur le nombre total des décès. Il y a donc des cas où les codes de qualité figurant dans le tableau 18 ne coïncident pas avec les caractères utilisés dans le présent tableau.

Les statistiques relatives aux pays et aux zones pour lesquels la couverture des données concernant les causes des décès est incomplète (degré de complétude inférieur à 90 p. 100) ou dont le degré de complétude n'est pas connu sont jugées douteuses et apparaissent en italique et non en caractères romains. Les taux correspondants ne sont pas calculés.

En outre, lorsque l'on sait que l'enregistrement des causes des décès ne couvre pas certaines zones d'un pays, les taux ne sont pas non plus calculés. Cela est le cas de la Géorgie, de la République de Moldova et de la Fédération de Russie, comme indiqué dans les notes 7, 19 et 20 respectivement. En ce qui concerne toutes les autres notes qui portent sur l'inclusion ou l'exclusion de certaines populations dans un pays, ce sont les naissances vivantes qui figurent au dénominateur.

Insuffisance des données : Les statistiques de la mortalité liée à la maternité appellent toutes les réserves qui ont été formulées à propos des statistiques de l'état civil en général et des statistiques relatives à la mortalité en particulier (voir la section 4 des Notes techniques). La fiabilité des données, au sujet de laquelle des indications ont été fournies plus haut, est un facteur important. En outre, les statistiques de la mortalité liée à la maternité appellent les mêmes réserves que celles exposées à la section 4 des Notes techniques en ce qui concerne les statistiques des causes de décès.

Les taux de mortalité liée à la maternité appellent également toutes les réserves formulées à propos des statistiques des naissances vivantes qui ont servi à leur calcul (voir à ce sujet les notes techniques relatives au tableau 9).

En prenant le nombre total des naissances vivantes comme base pour le calcul des taux de mortalité liée à la maternité, on obtient une mesure approximative de la probabilité de décès dus aux complications de la grossesse, de l'accouchement et des suites de couches. Idéalement, ces taux devraient être calculés sur la base du nombre de femmes exposées aux risques liés à la grossesse, c'est-à-dire sur la base du nombre de femmes qui conçoivent. Étant donné qu'il est impossible de connaître le nombre de femmes ayant conçu, c'est le nombre total de naissances vivantes que l'on utilise pour calculer ces taux.

Données publiées antérieurement : Des statistiques concernant les décès liés à la maternité (nombre de décès et taux) ont déjà été présentées dans des éditions antérieures de *l'Annuaire démographique*. Pour plus de précisions concernant les années pour lesquelles ces données ont été publiées, se reporter à l'index.

Il faut souligner que, avant 1975, les taux de mortalité liée à la maternité étaient calculés sur la base de la population féminine et non sur celle du nombre de naissances vivantes. Ils ne sont donc pas comparables à ceux qui figurent dans les éditions de l'*Annuaire démographique* parues après 1975.

Tableau 17-1. Liste de tabulation pour les données ICD-9 et ICD-10 pour la présentation dans l'annuaire démographique

Maladie	ICD-10	ICD-9 Basic Tabulation List
Toutes externes	**A00-Y89**	**01-56**
Certaines maladies infectieuses et parasitaires	**A00-B99**	**01-07, 184**
Maladies infectieuses intestinales	A00-A09	01
Tuberculose	A15-A19	02
Tétanos[2]	A33, A35	037
Diphtérie	A36	033
Coqueluche	A37	034
Infection à méningocoques	A39	036
Septicémie	A40-A41	038
Poliomyélite aiguë	A80	040
Rougeole	B05	042
Hépatite virale	B15-B19	046
Maladies dues au virus de l'immunodéficience humaine (VIH)	B20-B24	184
Malaria	B50-B54	052
Tumeurs	**C00-D48**	**08-17**
Tumeurs malignes	**C00-C97**	**08-14**
Tumeur maligne de la lèvre, de la cavité buccale et du pharynx	C00-C14	08
Tumeur maligne de l'oesophage	C15	090
Tumeur maligne de l'estomac	C16	091
sigmoïdienne, du rectum, de l'anus et du canal anal	C18-C21	093-094
Tumeur maligne du foie et des voies bilaires intrahépatiques	C22	095
Tumeur maligne du pancréas	C25	096
Tumeur maligne de la trachée, des bronches et du poumon	C33-C34	101
Tumeur maligne du sein chez la femme	C50	113
Tumeur maligne du col de l'utérus	C53	120
Tumeur maligne de la prostate	C61	124
Tumeurs malignes primitives ou présumées primitives des tissus lymphoïde, hématopoïétique et apparentés	C81-C96	14
Maladies du sang et des organes hématopoïétiques et certains troubles du système immunitaire	**D50-D89**	**20**

Tableau 17-1. Liste de tabulation pour les données ICD-9 et ICD-10 pour la présentation dans l'annuaire démographique

Maladie	ICD-10	ICD-9 Basic Tabulation List
Anémies	D50-D64	200
Maladies endocriniennes, nutritionnelles et métaboliques	**E00-E88**	**18-19, minus 184**
Diabète sucré	E10-E14	181
Malnutrition	E40-E46	190-192
Troubles mentaux et du comportement	**F01-F99**	**21**
Maladies du système nerveux	**G00-G98**	**22**
Maladies de l'appareil circulatoire	**I00-I99**	**25-30**
Rhumatisme articularie aigu et cardiopathies rhumatismales chroniques	I01-I09	25
Maladies hypertensives	I10-I13	26
Cardiopathies ischémiques	I20-I25	27
Maladies cérébrovasculaires	I60-I69	29
Maladies des artères, artérioles et capillaires	I70-I79	300-302
Maladies de l'appareil respiratoire	**J00-J98**	**31-32**
Grippe	J10-J11	322
Pneumopathies	J12-J18	321
Maladies chroniques des voies respiratoires inférieures	J40-J47	323-325
Maladies de l'appareil digestif	**K00-K92**	**33-34**
Ulcère de l'estomac et du duodénum	K25-K27	341
Maladies du foie	K70-K76	347
Maladies du système ostéo-articularie, des muscles et du tissu conjonctif	**M00-M99**	**43**
Maladies de l'appareil génito-urinaire	**N00-N98**	**35-37**
Affections du rein et de l'uretère	N00-N28	350-351
Hyperplasie de la prostate	N40	360
Grossesse, accouchement et puerpéralité	**O00-O99**	**38-41**
Grossesse se terminant par un avortement	O00-O07	38
Autres décès maternels directs^{Error! Bookmark not defined.}	O10-092, O95, A34	39
Décès maternels indirects	O98-O99	40
Certaines affections dont l'origine se situe dans la période périnatale	**P00-P96**	**45**
Malformations congénitales et anomalies chromosomiques	**Q00-Q99**	**44**
Symptômes, signes et résultats anormaux d'examens cliniques et de laboratoire, non classés ailleurs	**R00-R99**	**46**
Toutes autres maladies	**H00-H95, L00-L98**	**23-24, 42**
Causes externes	**V01-Y89**	**E47-E56**
Accidents	**V01-X59**	**E47-E53**
Accidents de transport	V01-V99	E47
Chutes	W00-W19	E50
Noyade et submersion accidentelles	W65-W74	E521
Exposition à la fumée, au feu et aux flammes	X00-X09	E51
Intoxication accidentelle par des substances nocives et exposition à ces substances	X40-X49	E48
Lésions auto-infligées	**X60-X84**	**E54**
Agresssions	**X85-Y09**	**E55**
Toutes autres causes externes	Y10-Y89	E56

NOTE

[1] *Classification statistique internationale des maladies et des problèmes de santé connexes*, dixième révision, volume 2. Genève, Organisation mondiale de la santé, 1992.

[2] In ICD-10 obstetrical tetanus is classified to A34 but in this table it is included with the "Other direct obstetric causes".

17. Maternal deaths and maternal death rates: 1995 - 2002
Mortalité liée à la maternité nombre de décès et taux: 1995 - 2002

Continent and country or area Continent et pays ou zone	1995	1996	1997	1998	1999	2000	2001	2002
AFRICA — AFRIQUE								
Egypt - Égypte								
Number - Nombre	...	...	...	...	...	*492*	...	...
Mauritius - Maurice								
Number - Nombre	12	6	10	4	7	3	...	...
Rate — Taux	◆58.2	◆29.3	◆50.0	◆20.6	◆34.5	◆14.8	...	...
South Africa - Afrique du Sud								
Number - Nombre	*499*	*606*	...	...	...	...	...	...
AMERICA, NORTH — AMERIQUE DU NORD								
Anguilla								
Number - Nombre	-	...	...	...	...	-	...	...
Antigua and Barbuda - Antigua-et-Barbuda								
Number - Nombre	*2*	...	...	...	...	...	...	...
Bahamas								
Number - Nombre	*4*	-	-	*1*	*1*	*2*	...	...
Barbados - Barbade								
Number - Nombre	-	...	...	...	...	1	...	...
Rate — Taux	-	...	...	...	...	◆26.6	...	...
Belize								
Number - Nombre	1	-	3	9	3	5	...	...
Rate — Taux	◆15.1	-	◆40.8	◆150.4	◆48.2	◆68.4	...	...
Bermuda - Bermudes								
Number - Nombre	...	...	...	...	...	-	...	...
British Virgin Islands - Îles Vierges britanniques								
Number - Nombre	-				...	...	...	...
Canada[1]								
Number - Nombre	17	18	19	13	8	11	...	...
Rate — Taux	◆4.5	◆4.9	◆5.5	◆3.8	◆2.4	◆3.4	...	...
Cayman Islands - Îles Caïmanes								
Number - Nombre	-	-	-	-	-	*1*	...	...
Costa Rica								
Number - Nombre	*16*	*23*	*29*	*14*	*15*	*28*	*24*	*27*
Cuba								
Number - Nombre	70	51	59	59	66	58	57	...
Rate — Taux	47.6	36.4	38.6	39.1	43.8	40.4	41.1	...
Dominica - Dominique								
Number - Nombre	1	-	-	1	-	...	...	...
Rate — Taux	◆66.6	-	-	◆81.3	-	...	...	...
Dominican Republic - République dominicaine								
Number - Nombre	*77*	*43*	*74*	*64*	...	...	...	...
El Salvador								
Number - Nombre	*55*	*42*	*42*	*42*	*23*	...	...	...
Grenada - Grenade								
Number - Nombre	-	-	...	...	...	...	...	...
Guatemala								
Number - Nombre	*360*	*335*	*342*	*324*	*316*	...	...	...
Mexico - Mexique								
Number - Nombre	1 454	1 291	1 266	1 430	1 411	1 325	1 268	...
Rate — Taux	52.9	47.7	46.9	53.6	51.0	47.3	45.8	...
Nicaragua								
Number - Nombre	...	*123*	*127*	*113*	*138*	*97*	...	...
Panama								
Number - Nombre	...	*35*	*28*	*30*	*31*	*30*	...	...
Puerto Rico - Porto Rico								
Number - Nombre	*9*	*11*	*13*	*8*	*10*	*14*	...	...
Saint Kitts and Nevis - Saint-Kitts-et-Nevis								
Number - Nombre	1	...	...	...	...	...	...	...
Rate — Taux	◆125.5	...	...	...	...	...	...	...
Saint Lucia - Sainte-Lucie								
Number - Nombre	-	1	-	-	1	3	1	...
Rate — Taux	-	◆31.8	-	-	◆33.4	◆105.6	◆35.9	...
Saint Vincent and the Grenadines - Saint Vincent-et-les Grenadines								
Number - Nombre	4	2	1	-	1	...	...	...

428

17. Maternal deaths and maternal death rates: 1995 - 2002
Mortalité liée à la maternité nombre de décès et taux: 1995 - 2002 (continued — suite)

Continent and country or area Continent et pays ou zone	1995	1996	1997	1998	1999	2000	2001	2002
AMERICA, NORTH — AMERIQUE DU NORD								
Saint Vincent and the Grenadines - Saint Vincent-et-les Grenadines								
Rate — Taux	♦153.0	♦85.5	♦43.3	-	♦46.1	...	...	...
Trinidad and Tobago - Trinité-et-Tobago								
Number - Nombre	13	...	...	8	...	...	...	...
Rate — Taux	♦67.5	...	...	...	...	...	...	...
Turks Caicos Islands - Îles Turques et Caïques								
Number - Nombre	-	-	-	-	-	...	...	...
United States - États-Unis								
Number - Nombre	277	294	327	281	**406**	**404**	...	...
Rate — Taux	7.1	7.6	8.4	7.1	**10.3**	**10.0**	...	...
United States Virgin Islands - Îles Vierges américaines								
Number - Nombre	...	...	1	-	-	1	...	...
AMERICA, SOUTH — AMERIQUE DU SUD								
Argentina - Argentine								
Number - Nombre	290	317	**265**	**260**	**287**	**245**	**309**	...
Rate — Taux	44.0	46.9	**38.3**	**38.1**	**41.8**	**34.9**	**45.2**	...
Brazil - Brésil[2]								
Number - Nombre	*1 632*	*1 465*	*1 791*	*1 937*	*1 823*	*1 648*	...	...
Chile - Chili								
Number - Nombre	86	63	**61**	**55**	**60**	**49**	**45**	...
Rate — Taux	30.7	23.8	**23.5**	**21.4**	**23.9**	**19.7**	**18.3**	...
Colombia - Colombie[3]								
Number - Nombre	*411*	*430*	*420*	*721*	*676*	...	...	...
Ecuador - Équateur[4]								
Number - Nombre	*170*	*194*	*162*	*153*	*209*	*232*	...	...
Guyana								
Number - Nombre	35	26	...	...	...	...	...	...
Paraguay								
Number - Nombre	104	*109*	*89*	*96*	*103*	*140*	...	...
Peru - Pérou[2,5]								
Number - Nombre	*301*	*337*	*246*	*279*	*261*	*263*	...	...
Uruguay								
Number - Nombre	14	11	*17*	*11*	6	9	...	...
Rate — Taux	♦24.7	♦18.7	♦*29.3*	♦*20.1*	♦11.1	♦17.1	...	...
Venezuela[2]								
Number - Nombre	...	297	308	256	313	327	...	...
Rate — Taux	...	59.6	59.6	51.0	59.3	60.1	...	...
ASIA — ASIE								
Armenia - Arménie[6]								
Number - Nombre	17	10	17	10	12	18	7	3
Rate — Taux	♦34.7	♦20.8	♦38.7	♦25.4	♦32.9	♦52.5	♦21.8	...
Azerbaijan - Azerbaïdjan[6]								
Number - Nombre	*53*	*56*	*41*	*51*	*51*	*44*	*27*	*22*
Bahrain - Bahreïn								
Number - Nombre	...	...	**2**	**2**	**3**	**2**	...	...
Rate — Taux	...	...	♦**14.9**	♦**14.9**	♦**21.0**	♦**14.3**	...	...
China: Hong Kong SAR - Chine: Hong Kong RAS								
Number - Nombre	5	2	1	1	1	3	...	...
Georgia - Géorgie[7]								
Number - Nombre	17	9	13	15	9	4	4	...
Israel - Israël[8]								
Number - Nombre	7	9	12	11	9	...	...	...
Rate — Taux	♦6.0	♦7.4	♦9.6	♦8.5	♦6.8	...	...	...
Japan - Japon[9]								
Number - Nombre	**90**	**80**	**81**	**89**	**79**	**84**	...	...
Rate — Taux	**7.6**	**6.6**	**6.8**	**7.4**	**6.7**	**7.1**	...	...
Kazakhstan[6]								
Number - Nombre	*159*	*134*	*137*	*122*	*98*	*94*	*87*	*80*

Continent and country or area Continent et pays ou zone	1995	1996	1997	1998	1999	2000	2001	2002
ASIA — ASIE								
Korea (Republic of) - Corée (République de)[10]								
Number - Nombre	*88*	*75*	*66*	*63*	*77*	*62*	*70*	...
Kuwait - Koweït								
Number - Nombre	*1*	*3*	*7*	*3*	*3*	*2*	*1*	*3*
Kyrgyzstan - Kirghizistan[6]								
Number - Nombre	*52*	*27*	*64*	*35*	*44*	*44*	*43*	*54*
Philippines								
Number - Nombre	*1 485*	*1 549*	*1 513*	*1 579*	...	...	...	...
Qatar								
Number - Nombre	-	...	...	...	...	...	...	...
Singapore - Singapour								
Number - Nombre	*2*	*2*	*1*	*5*	*2*	*8*	*4*	...
Sri Lanka								
Number - Nombre	*81*	...	...	...	...	...	...	...
Tajikistan - Tadjikistan[6]								
Number - Nombre	*95*	*58*	*38*	...	*45*	*36*	*40*	...
Thailand - Thaïlande								
Number - Nombre	*96*	*120*	*87*	*63*	*93*	*102*	...	*114*
Turkmenistan - Turkménistan[6]								
Number - Nombre	*63*	*49*	*21*	*16*	...	...	...	...
Uzbekistan - Ouzbékistan[6]								
Number - Nombre	*128*	*76*	*62*	*48*	*80*	*182*	...	...
EUROPE								
Albania - Albanie								
Number - Nombre	*9*	*8*	*5*	*8*	*2*	*8*	*2*	...
Austria - Autriche								
Number - Nombre	1	4	2	4	1	2	5	**2**
Rate — Taux	♦1.1	♦4.5	♦2.4	♦4.9	♦1.3	♦2.6	♦6.6	♦**2.6**
Belarus - Bélarus[6]								
Number - Nombre	14	21	23	26	19	20	13	...
Rate — Taux	♦13.8	♦21.9	♦25.7	♦28.1	♦20.4	...	...	...
Belgium - Belgique[11]								
Number - Nombre	11	6	10	...	...	...	...	...
Rate — Taux	♦9.5	♦5.3	♦8.6	...	...	...	...	...
Bulgaria - Bulgarie								
Number - Nombre	10	14	12	10	16	13	13	11
Rate — Taux	♦13.9	♦19.4	♦18.7	♦15.3	♦22.1	♦17.6	♦19.1	♦16.5
Croatia - Croatie								
Number - Nombre	**6**	**1**	**6**	**3**	**5**	**3**	**1**	**4**
Rate — Taux	♦**12.0**	♦**1.9**	♦**10.8**	♦**6.4**	♦**11.1**	♦**6.9**	♦**2.4**	♦**10.0**
Czech Republic - République tchèque								
Number - Nombre	2	5	2	5	6	5	3	**3**
Rate — Taux	♦2.1	♦5.5	♦2.2	♦5.5	♦6.7	♦5.5	♦3.3	♦**3.1**
Denmark - Danemark[12]								
Number - Nombre	7	4	5	2	4	-	...	...
Rate — Taux	♦10.0	♦5.9	♦7.4	♦3.0	♦6.0	-	...	...
Estonia - Estonie[6]								
Number - Nombre	7	-	2	2	2	5	1	1
Rate — Taux	♦51.6	-	♦15.8	♦16.4	♦15.9	♦38.2	♦7.9	♦7.7
Finland - Finlande[13]								
Number - Nombre	1	2	3	3	2	3	3	3
Rate — Taux	♦1.6	♦3.3	♦5.1	♦5.3	♦3.5	♦5.3	♦5.3	♦5.4
France[14]								
Number - Nombre	70	97	70	75	55	50	...	...
Rate — Taux	9.6	13.2	9.6	10.2	7.4	6.5	...	...
Germany - Allemagne								
Number - Nombre	41	51	49	44	37	43	27	...
Rate — Taux	5.4	6.4	6.0	5.5	4.8	5.6	♦3.7	...
Greece - Grèce								
Number - Nombre	-	4	-	7	6	-	4	...
Rate — Taux	-	♦4.0	-	♦6.9	♦5.2	-	♦3.9	...
Hungary - Hongrie								
Number - Nombre	17	12	21	6	4	10	5	8
Rate — Taux	♦15.2	♦11.4	♦20.9	♦6.2	♦4.2	♦10.2	♦5.2	♦8.3

17. Maternal deaths and maternal death rates: 1995 - 2002
Mortalité liée à la maternité nombre de décès et taux: 1995 - 2002 (continued — suite)

Continent and country or area / Continent et pays ou zone	1995	1996	1997	1998	1999	2000	2001	2002
EUROPE								
Iceland - Islande								
Number - Nombre	-	-	-	-	-	-	1	...
Rate — Taux	-	-	-	-	-	-	♦24.4	...
Ireland - Irlande[15]								
Number - Nombre	-	3	3	2	1	1	3	...
Rate — Taux	-	♦6.0	♦5.7	♦3.7	♦1.9	♦1.8	♦5.2	...
Italy - Italie								
Number - Nombre	17	20	23	18	14	16	11	...
Rate — Taux	♦3.2	♦3.8	♦4.3	♦3.5	♦2.7	♦2.9	♦2.1	...
Latvia - Lettonie[6]								
Number - Nombre	5	4	8	9	8	5	5	1
Rate — Taux	♦23.2	♦20.2	♦42.5	♦48.9	♦41.2	♦24.7	♦25.4	♦5.0
Lithuania - Lituanie[6]								
Number - Nombre	7	5	6	5	5	3	4	6
Rate — Taux	♦17.0	♦12.8	♦15.9	♦13.5	♦13.7	♦8.8	♦12.7	♦20.0
Luxembourg								
Number - Nombre	1	-	-	1	-	1	-	-
Rate — Taux	♦18.4	-	-	♦18.6	-	♦17.5	-	-
Malta - Malte[16]								
Number - Nombre	1	1	-	1	1	-	2	-
Rate — Taux	♦21.7	♦20.2	-	♦22.3	♦23.2	-	♦51.8	-
Netherlands - Pays-Bas[17]								
Number - Nombre	14	23	15	23	19	18	...	...
Rate — Taux	♦7.3	♦12.1	♦7.8	♦11.5	♦9.5	♦8.7	...	...
Norway - Norvège[18]								
Number - Nombre	4	1	1	4	5	2	3	...
Rate — Taux	♦6.6	♦1.6	♦1.7	♦6.9	♦8.4	♦3.4	♦5.3	...
Poland - Pologne								
Number - Nombre	43	21	...	...	20	30	13	19
Rate — Taux	9.9	♦4.9	...	...	♦5.2	♦7.9	♦3.5	♦5.4
Portugal								
Number - Nombre	9	6	6	9	6	3	6	8
Rate — Taux	♦8.4	♦5.4	♦5.3	♦7.9	♦5.2	♦2.5	♦5.3	♦7.0
Republic of Moldova - République de Moldova[19]								
Number - Nombre	23	22	23	15	11	10	16	11
Romania - Roumanie								
Number - Nombre	113	95	98	96	98	75	75	47
Rate — Taux	47.8	41.1	41.4	40.5	41.8	32.0	34.0	22.3
Russian Federation - Fédération de Russie[20]								
Number - Nombre	727	636	633	565	537	503	479	469
San Marino - Saint-Marin								
Number - Nombre	-	-	-	-	-	-	...	...
Serbia and Montenegro - Serbie-et-Monténégro								
Number - Nombre	...	...	...	...	...	7	...	...
Rate — Taux	...	...	...	...	...	♦5.6	...	...
Slovakia - Slovaquie								
Number - Nombre	5	3	1	5	5	1	7	...
Rate — Taux	♦8.1	♦5.0	♦1.7	♦8.7	♦8.9	♦1.8	♦13.7	...
Slovenia - Slovénie								
Number - Nombre	1	3	2	-	2	2	3	-
Rate — Taux	♦5.3	♦16.0	♦11.0	-	♦11.4	♦11.0	♦17.2	-
Spain - Espagne								
Number - Nombre	11	11	8	10	14	14	17	...
Rate — Taux	♦3.0	♦3.0	♦2.2	♦2.7	♦3.7	♦3.6	♦4.2	...
Sweden - Suède								
Number - Nombre	4	5	3	7	1	4	3	...
Rate — Taux	♦3.9	♦5.3	♦3.3	♦7.9	♦1.1	♦4.4	♦3.3	...
Switzerland - Suisse								
Number - Nombre	7	3	3	3	6	5	1	...
Rate — Taux	♦8.5	♦3.6	♦3.7	♦3.8	♦7.7	♦6.4	♦1.4	...
The Former Yugoslav Rep. of Macedonia - L'ex-République yougoslave de Macédoine								
Number - Nombre	7	-	1	1	2	4	...	...
Rate — Taux	♦21.8	-	♦3.4	♦3.4	♦7.3	♦13.6	...	...

Continent and country or area Continent et pays ou zone	1995	1996	1997	1998	1999	2000	2001	2002
EUROPE								
Ukraine[6]								
Number - Nombre	159	142	111	114	98	95	90	85
Rate — Taux	32.3	30.4	25.1	27.2	...	24.7	23.9	21.8
United Kingdom - Royaume-Uni[21]								
Number - Nombre	51	48	39	49	37	46	**50**	**40**
Rate — Taux	7.0	6.5	5.4	6.8	5.3	6.8	**7.5**	**6.0**
OCEANIA — OCEANIE								
Australia - Australie								
Number - Nombre	21	13	12	**5**	**13**	**13**	**12**	...
Rate — Taux	♦8.2	♦5.1	♦4.8	♦**2.0**	♦**5.2**	♦**5.2**	♦**4.9**	...
Fiji - Fidji								
Number - Nombre	...	...	...	...	*1*	...	...	...
New Zealand - Nouvelle-Zélande								
Number - Nombre	2	4	3	3	4	5	...	...
Rate — Taux	♦3.5	♦7.0	♦5.2	♦5.4	♦7.0	♦8.8	...	...

FOOTNOTES - NOTES

Data in bold refer to maternal deaths based on ICD-10 Classification, otherwise data refer to maternal deaths based on ICD-9 Classification. - Les données en typographie gras se rapportent aux décès maternelles basées sur la classification CIM-10, autrement les données se rapportent aux décès maternelles basées sur la classification CIM-9.

Italics: data from civil registers that are incomplete or of unknown completeness. — *Italiques:* données incomplètes ou dont le degré d'exactitude n'est pas connu, provenant des registres de l'état civil.

♦ Rates based on 30 or fewer deaths. — Taux basés sur 30 décès ou moins.

[1] Including Canadian residents temporarily in the United States, but excluding United States residents temporarily in Canada. - Y compris les résidents canadiens se trouvant temporairement aux Etats-Unis, mais ne comprenant pas les résidents des Etats-Unis se trouvant temporairement au Canada.
[2] Excluding Indian jungle population. - Non compris les Indiens de la jungle.
[3] Data on live births and deaths are based on a civil registration system put in place in January 1998. - Les données sur les naissances et les décès sont basées sur un système d'enregistrement des faits d'état civil mis en place en janvier 1998.
[4] Excluding nomadic Indian tribes. - Non compris les tribus d'Indiens nomades.
[5] Denominator refer to national projections. - Le dénominateur se referent aux projections nationales.
[6] The denominator excluded infants born alive with less than 28 weeks gestation, less than 1 000 grams in weight and 35 centimeters in length, who die within seven days of birth. - Le dénominateur ne compris pas des enfants nés vivants avant 28 semaines de gestation, pesant moins de 1 000 grammes, mesurant moins de 35 centimètres et décédés dans les sept jours qui ont suivi leur naissance.
[7] Data on maternal deaths do not include those in the Abkhazia and South Osetia region; therefore rates are not computed. - Les données sur le mortalité liée a la maternité ne comprennent pas ceux de la région de Abkhazia et South Osetia, en conséquence, les taux n'ont pas étés calcules.
[8] Including data for East Jerusalem and Israeli residents in certain other territories under occupation by Israeli military forces since June 1967. - Y compris les données pour Jérusalem-Est et les résidents israéliens dans certains autres territoires occupés depuis 1967 par les forces armées israéliennes.
[9] Data refer to Japanese nationals in Japan only. - Les données se raportent aux nationaux japonais au Japon seulement.
[10] Excluding alien armed forces, civilian aliens employed by armed forces, and foreign diplomatic personnel and their dependants. - Non compris les militaires étrangers, les civils étrangers employés par les forces armées ni le personnel diplomatique étranger et les membres de leur famille les accompagnant.
[11] Including armed forces stationed outside the country, but excluding alien armed forces stationed in the area. - Y compris les militaires nationaux hors du pays, mais non compris les militaires étrangers en garnison sur le territoire.
[12] Excluding Faeroe Islands and Greenland. - Non compris les îles Féroé et Gröenland.
[13] Including nationals temporarily outside the country. - Y compris les nationaux se trouvant temporairement hors du pays.
[14] Including armed forces stationed outside the country. - Y compris les militaires nationaux hors du pays.
[15] Denominator refers to live births registered within one year of occurrence. - Le dénominateur se referrer aux Evénements enregistrés dans l'année qui suit l'événement.
[16] Denominator refers to live births to Maltese parents only. - Le dénominateur se referrer aux naissances vivantes aux parents maltais seulement.
[17] Including residents outside the country if listed in a Netherlands population register. - Y compris les résidents hors du pays, s'ils sont inscrits sur un registre de population néerlandais.
[18] Including residents temporarily outside the country. - Y compris les résidents se trouvant temporairement hors du pays.
[19] Data on maternal deaths do not include those in the Transnistria region; therefore rates are not computed. - Les données sur le mortalité liée a la maternité ne comprennent pas ceux de la région de Transnistria,en conséquence, les taux n'ont pas étés calcules.
[20] Data on maternal deaths do not include those in the Chechnya region; therefore rates are not computed. - Les données sur la mortalité liée a la maternité ne comprennent pas ceux de la région de Chechnya,en conséquence, les taux n'ont pas étés calcules.
[21] Denominator excludes births in Northern Ireland to non-residents of Northern Ireland. - Le dénominateur n'inclure pas des naissances en Irlande du Nord aux non-résidents de l'Irlande du Nord.

Table 18

Table 18 presents deaths and crude death rates by urban/rural residence for as many years as possible between 1999 and 2003.

Description of variables: Death is defined as the permanent disappearance of all evidence of life at any time after live birth has taken place (post-natal cessation of vital functions without capability of resuscitation).

Statistics on the number of deaths are obtained from civil registers unless otherwise noted. For those countries or areas where civil registration statistics on deaths are considered reliable (estimated completeness of 90 per cent or more), the death rates shown have been calculated on the basis of registered deaths.

The urban/rural classification of deaths is that provided by each country or area; it is presumed to be based on the national census definitions of urban population that have been set forth at the end of the technical notes for table 6.

For certain countries, there is a discrepancy between the total number of deaths shown in this table and those shown in subsequent tables for the same year. Usually this discrepancy arises because the total number of deaths occurring in a given year is revised although the remaining tabulations are not.

Rate computation: Crude death rates are the annual number of deaths per 1 000 mid-year population.

Rates by urban/rural residence are the annual number of deaths, in the appropriate urban or rural category, per 1 000 corresponding mid-year population. These rates are calculated by the Statistics Division of the United Nations.

Rates presented in this table are limited to those countries or areas with a minimum number of 30 deaths in a given year.

Reliability of data: Each country or area has been asked to indicate the estimated completeness of the infant deaths recorded in its civil register. These national assessments are indicated by the quality codes (C), (U) and (I) that appear in the first column of this table. C indicates that the data are estimated to be virtually complete, that is, representing at least 90 per cent of the deaths occurring each year, while U indicates that data are estimated to be incomplete that is, representing less than 90 per cent of the deaths occurring each year. The code (I) indicates that the source of data is different than civil registration, but still considered reliable and explained by footnote. The code (...) indicates that no information was provided regarding completeness.

Data from civil registers that are reported as incomplete or of unknown completeness (code U or ...) are considered unreliable. They appear in italics in this table; rates based on these data are not computed.

Limitations: Statistics on deaths are subject to the same qualifications as have been set forth for vital statistics in general and death statistics in particular as discussed in section 4 of the Technical Notes.

The reliability of the data, an indication of which is described above, is an important factor in considering the limitations. In addition, some deaths are tabulated by date of registration and not by date of occurrence; these have been indicated with a plus sign (+). Whenever the lag between the date of occurrence and date of registration is prolonged and, therefore, a large proportion of the death registrations are delayed, death statistics for any given year may be seriously affected. However, delays in the registration of deaths are less common and shorter than in the registration of live births.

International comparability in mortality statistics may also be affected by the exclusion of deaths of infants who were born alive but died before the registration of the birth or within the first 24 hours of life. Statistics of this type are footnoted.

In addition, it should be noted that rates are affected also by the quality and limitations of the population estimates that are used in their computation. The problems of under-enumeration or over-enumeration and, to some extent, the differences in definition of total population have been discussed in section 3 of the Technical Notes dealing with population data in general, and specific information pertaining to individual countries or areas is given in the footnotes to table 3.

Estimated rates based directly on the results of sample surveys are subject to considerable error as a result of omissions in reporting deaths or as a result of erroneous reporting of those that occurred outside the period of reference. However, such rates do have the advantage of having a "built-in" and corresponding base.

It should be emphasized that crude death rates -- like other crude rates, such as of birth, marriage and divorce -- may be seriously affected by the age-sex structure of the populations to which they relate. Nevertheless, they do provide a simple measure of the level and changes in mortality.

The comparability of data by urban/rural residence is affected by the national definitions of urban and rural used in tabulating these data. It is assumed, in the absence of specific information to the contrary, that the definitions of urban and rural used in connection with the national population census were also used in the compilation of the vital statistics for each country or area. However, it cannot be excluded that, for a given country or area, different definitions of urban and rural are used for the vital statistics data and the population census data respectively. When known, the definitions of urban used in national population censuses are presented at the end of the technical notes for table 6. As discussed in detail in the technical notes for table 6, these definitions vary considerably from one country or area to another.

In addition to problems of comparability, vital rates classified by urban/rural residence are also subject to certain types of bias. If, when calculating vital rates, different definitions of urban are used in connection with the vital events and the population data and if this results in a net difference between the numerator and denominator of the rate in the population at risk, then the vital rates would be biased. Urban/rural differentials in vital rates may also be affected by whether the vital events have been tabulated in terms of place of occurrence or place of usual residence. This problem is discussed in more detail in section 4.1.4.1 of the Technical Notes.

Earlier data: Deaths and crude death rates have been shown in each issue of the Demographic Yearbook. Data included in this table update the series covering a period of years as follows :

Issue	Years Covered
Historical Supplement CD, 1997	1948 – 1997
1992	1983 – 1992
1985	1976 – 1985
1980	1971 – 1980
Historical Supplement, 1979	1948 – 1977

Tableau 18

Le tableau 18 présente le nombre des décès et les taux bruts de mortalité selon le lieu de résidence (zone urbaine ou rurale) pour le plus grand nombre d'années possible entre 1999 et 2003.

Description des variables : Le décès est défini comme la disparition permanente de tout signe de vie à un moment quelconque postérieur à la naissance vivante (cessation des fonctions vitales après la naissance sans possibilité de réanimation).

Sauf indication contraire, les statistiques relatives au nombre de décès sont établies sur la base des registres d'état civil. Pour les pays ou zones où les données concernant l'enregistrement des décès par les services de l'état civil sont jugées sûres (complétude estimée à 90 p. 100 ou plus), les taux de mortalité ont été calculés d'après les décès enregistrés.

La répartition des décès entre zones urbaines et zones rurales est celle qui a été communiquée par chaque pays ou zone ; on part du principe qu'elle repose sur les définitions de la population urbaine utilisées pour les recensements nationaux, qui sont reproduites à la fin des notes techniques du tableau 6.

Pour quelques pays il y a une discordance entre le nombre total des décès vivantes présenté dans ce tableau et ceux présentés après pour la même année. Habituellement ces différences apparaissent lorsque le nombre total des décès pour une certaine année a été révisé alors que les autres tabulations ne l'ont pas été.

Calcul des taux : Les taux bruts de mortalité représentent le nombre annuel de décès pour 1 000 habitants en milieu d'année.

Les taux selon le lieu de résidence (zone urbaine ou rurale) représentent le nombre annuel de décès, classés selon la catégorie urbaine ou rurale appropriée, pour 1 000 habitants en milieu d'année. Ces taux ont été calculés par la Division de statistique de l'ONU.

Les taux présentés dans ce tableau se rapportent seulement aux pays ou zones où l'on a enregistré un nombre minimal de 30 décès au cours d'une année donnée.

Fiabilité des données : Il a été demandé à chaque pays ou zone d'indiquer le degré estimatif de complétude des données sur les décès d'enfants de moins d'un an figurant dans ses registres d'état civil. Ces évaluations nationales sont signalées par les codes de qualité 'C', 'U' et 'I' qui apparaissent dans la deuxième colonne du tableau.

La lettre 'C' indique que les données sont jugées à peu près complètes, c'est-à-dire qu'elles représentent au moins 90 p. 100 des décès d'enfants de moins d'un an survenus chaque année ; la lettre 'U' signifie que les données sont jugées incomplètes, c'est-à-dire qu'elles représentent moins de 90 p.100 des décès d'enfants de moins d'un an survenus chaque année. Le symbole 'I' indique que la source des données est fiable mais n'est pas un registre de l'état civil ; le symbole, dans ce cas, est accompagné par une note explicative. Le code '...' dénote qu'aucun renseignement n'a été communiqué quant à la complétude des données.

Les données provenant des registres de l'état civil qui sont déclarées incomplètes ou dont le degré de complétude n'est pas connu (code 'U' ou '...') sont jugées douteuses. Elles apparaissent en italique dans le présent tableau et les taux correspondants n'ont pas été calculés.

Insuffisance des données : Les statistiques relatives à la mortalité appellent les mêmes réserves que celles qui ont été formulées à propos des statistiques de l'état civil en général et des statistiques relatives aux décès en particulier (voir la section 4 des Notes techniques).

La fiabilité des données, au sujet de laquelle des indications ont été fournies plus haut, est un facteur important. Il faut également tenir compte du fait que, dans certains cas, les décès sont classés par date d'enregistrement et non par date d'occurrence ; ces cas ont été signalés par le signe '+'. Chaque fois que le décalage entre le décès et son enregistrement est grand et qu'une forte proportion des décès fait l'objet d'un enregistrement tardif, les statistiques relatives aux décès survenus pendant l'année peuvent être considérablement faussées.

En règle générale, toutefois, les décès sont enregistrés beaucoup plus rapidement que les naissances vivantes, et les retards prolongés sont rares.

Un autre facteur qui nuit à la comparabilité internationale est la pratique qui consiste à ne pas inclure dans les statistiques de la mortalité les enfants nés vivants mais décédés avant l'enregistrement de leur naissance ou dans les 24 heures qui ont suivi la naissance. Quand pareil facteur a joué, cela a été signalé en note à la fin du tableau.

Il convient de noter par ailleurs que l'exactitude des taux dépend également de la qualité et des limitations des estimations de la population qui sont utilisées pour leur calcul. Le problème des erreurs par excès ou par défaut commises lors du dénombrement et, dans une certaine mesure, le problème de l'hétérogénéité des définitions de la population totale ont été examinés à la section 3 des Notes techniques, relative à la population en général ; des indications concernant certains pays ou zones sont données en note à la fin du tableau 3.

Les taux estimatifs fondés directement sur les résultats d'enquêtes par sondage comportent des possibilités d'erreurs considérables dues soit à des omissions dans les déclarations des décès, soit au fait que l'on a déclaré à tort des décès survenus en réalité hors de la période considérée. Toutefois, ces taux présentent un avantage : le chiffre de population utilisé comme base est connu par définition et rigoureusement correspondant.

Il faut souligner que les taux bruts de mortalité, de même que les taux bruts de natalité, de nuptialité et de divortialité, peuvent varier très sensiblement selon la composition par âge et par sexe de la population à laquelle ils se rapportent. Ils offrent néanmoins un moyen simple de mesurer le niveau et l'évolution de la mortalité.

La comparabilité des données selon le lieu de résidence (zone urbaine ou rurale) peut être limitée par les définitions nationales des termes « urbain » et « rural » utilisées pour le classement de ces données. En l'absence d'indications contraires, on a supposé que les mêmes définitions avaient servi pour le recensement national de la population et pour l'établissement des statistiques de l'état civil pour chaque pays ou zone. Toutefois, il n'est pas exclu que, pour une zone ou un pays donné, des définitions différentes aient été retenues. Les définitions du terme « urbain » utilisées pour les recensements nationaux de population ont été présentées à la fin du tableau 6 lorsqu'elles étaient connues. Comme on l'a précisé dans les notes techniques relatives au tableau 6, ces définitions varient considérablement d'un pays ou d'une zone à l'autre.

Outre les problèmes de comparabilité, les taux démographiques classés selon le lieu de résidence « urbaine » ou « rurale » sont également sujets à des distorsions particulières. Si l'on utilise des définitions différentes du terme « urbain » pour classer les faits d'état civil et les données relatives à la population lors du calcul des taux et qu'il en résulte une différence nette entre le numérateur et le dénominateur pour le taux de la population exposée au risque, les taux démographiques s'en trouveront faussés. La différence entre ces taux pour les zones urbaines et rurales pourra aussi être faussée selon que les faits d'état civil auront été classés d'après le lieu où ils se sont produits ou d'après le lieu de résidence habituel. Ce problème est examiné plus en détail à la section 4.1.4.1 des Notes techniques.

Données publiées antérieurement : Les différentes éditions de l'*Annuaire démographique* contiennent des statistiques des décès et des taux bruts de mortalité. Les données qui figurent dans le tableau 18 actualisent les données qui portaient sur les périodes suivantes :

Éditions	Années considérées
Supplément historique (CD-ROM), 1997	1948 – 1997
1992	1983 – 1992
1985	1976 – 1985
1980	1971 – 1980
Supplément rétrospectif, 1979	1948 – 1977

18. Deaths and crude death rates, by urban/rural residence: 1999 - 2003
Décès et taux bruts de mortalité, selon la résidence, urbaine/rurale: 1999 - 2003

Continent, country or area, and urban/rural residence / Continent, pays ou zone et résidence, urbaine/rurale	Co-de[1]	Number - Nombre					Rate - Taux				
		1999	2000	2001	2002	2003	1999	2000	2001	2002	2003
AFRICA — AFRIQUE											
Algeria - Algérie[2,3]											
Total	U	129 686	127 951	129 092	126 557	...	...	...	...	...	...
Benin - Bénin[4]											
Total	I	71 680	71 540	83 417	...	...	12.0	11.6	13.0	...	...
Botswana[4,5]											
Total	I	16 352	...	20 823	...	...	10.2	...	12.4	...	...
Urban - Urbaine	I	...	...	10 041	...	...	...	...	...	...	...
Rural - Rurale	I	...	...	10 782	...	...	...	...	...	...	...
Chad - Tchad											
Total	...	...	...	138 025	...	...	...	...	...	...	...
Côte d'Ivoire[4]											
Total	I	...	201 690	...	...	...	...	12.3	...	...	...
Egypt - Égypte											
Total	C	401 133	404 600	404 531	*424 516	*440 000	6.4	6.3	6.2	*6.4	*6.5
Urban - Urbaine	C	181 665	...	...	...	...	6.8	...	...	...	...
Rural - Rurale	C	219 768	...	...	...	...	6.1	...	...	...	...
Ethiopia - Éthiopie											
Total	...	1 062 114	...	...	...	...	...	...	...	...	...
Urban - Urbaine	...	110 929	...	...	...	...	...	...	...	...	...
Rural - Rurale	...	951 185	...	...	...	...	...	...	...	...	...
Ghana											
Total	...	...	...	52 332	34 682	...	...	...	...	...	...
Kenya											
Total	U	...	214 855	199 358	206 089	248 254	...	...	...	...	...
Libyan Arab Jamahiriya - Jamahiriya arabe libyenne											
Total	U	...	17 367	18 334	19 362	...	...	...	...	...	...
Malawi[4]											
Total	I	234 641	228 245	221 963	217 205	213 705	23.1	21.8	20.5	19.4	18.5
Mauritius - Maurice											
Total	+C	7 944	7 982	7 983	8 310	8 520	6.8	6.7	6.7	6.9	7.0
Urban - Urbaine	+C	3 711	3 685	3 634	3 702	3 942	7.4	7.3	7.1	7.2	7.6
Rural - Rurale	+C	4 233	4 297	4 349	4 608	4 578	6.3	6.3	6.3	6.6	6.5
Morocco - Maroc[6]											
Total	U	98 304	95 084	95 612	...	...	...	...	...	...	...
Urban - Urbaine	U	53 935	55 092	55 745	...	...	...	...	...	...	...
Rural - Rurale	U	44 121	39 768	39 787	...	...	...	...	...	...	...
Mozambique[4]											
Total	I	...	...	331 162	...	...	...	...	18.8	...	...
Namibia - Namibie[7]											
Total	I	...	...	25 061	...	...	...	...	...	...	...
Urban - Urbaine	I	...	...	6 529	...	...	...	...	...	...	...
Rural - Rurale	I	...	...	18 532	...	...	...	...	...	...	...
Réunion[2]											
Total	C	3 825	3 836	3 829	4 004	*4 022	5.4	5.3	5.2	5.4	*5.3
Saint Helena ex. dep. - Sainte-Hélène sans dép.											
Total	C	45	53	41	...	...	...	...	...	...	...
Seychelles											
Total	+C	560	553	554	647	668	7.0	6.8	6.8	7.7	8.1
Tunisia - Tunisie											
Total	U	54 400	...	*53 300	...	...	...	...	...	...	...
AMERICA, NORTH — AMERIQUE DU NORD											
Anguilla											
Total	+C	58	73	50	52	65	5.3	6.5	4.3	4.4	5.3
Antigua and Barbuda - Antigua-et-Barbuda											
Total	+C	508	451	...	...	...	...	...	...	...	...

18. Deaths and crude death rates, by urban/rural residence: 1999 - 2003
Décès et taux bruts de mortalité, selon la résidence, urbaine/rurale: 1999 - 2003 (continued — suite)

Continent, country or area, and urban/rural residence — Continent, pays ou zone et résidence, urbaine/rurale	Co-de[1]	Number - Nombre					Rate - Taux				
		1999	2000	2001	2002	2003	1999	2000	2001	2002	2003

AMERICA, NORTH — AMERIQUE DU NORD

Aruba											
Total	+U	*554*	*531*	*477*	*°489*	*°498*	...	...	...	...	...
Bahamas											
Total	C	1 567	1 625	1 609	...	1 649	5.3	5.4	5.2	...	5.2
Barbados - Barbade											
Total	+C	...	2 367	...	°2 285	...	...	8.8	...	°8.4	...
Belize											
Total	U	*1 190*	*1 534*	*1 261*	*1 284*	...	...	...	...	...	...
Bermuda - Bermudes											
Total	C	427	473	442	404	434	6.8	7.5	7.1	6.5	7.0
British Virgin Islands - Îles Vierges britanniques											
Total	+C	...	...	°101	...	...	...	...	°4.9	...	...
Canada[8]											
Total	C	219 530	218 062	219 538	223 603	227 285	7.2	7.1	7.1	7.1	7.2
Cayman Islands - Îles Caïmanes											
Total	C	128	137	132	...	...	3.3	3.4	3.2	...	...
Costa Rica											
Total	C	15 052	14 944	15 609	15 004	15 800	4.4	4.3	4.0	3.8	3.9
Cuba[6]											
Total	C	79 499	76 463	79 395	73 882	°78 433	7.2	6.9	7.1	6.6	°7.0
Urban - Urbaine	C	64 362	61 950	64 579	60 167	...	7.7	7.4	7.6	7.1	...
Rural - Rurale	C	15 072	14 513	14 794	13 697	...	5.5	5.4	5.5	5.1	...
Dominica - Dominique											
Total	+C	631	503	510	...	...	8.8	7.0	7.2	...	...
Dominican Republic - République dominicaine											
Total	+U	*26 956*	*23 776*	...	...	...	...	...	...	...	...
El Salvador											
Total	C	28 056	28 154	29 559	27 458	29 377	4.6	4.5	4.6	4.2	4.4
Urban - Urbaine	C	18 770	19 276	20 921	19 595	20 856	5.2	5.3	5.6	5.1	5.3
Rural - Rurale	C	9 286	8 878	8 638	7 863	8 521	3.6	3.4	3.3	2.9	3.1
Greenland - Groenland											
Total	C	482	458	438	435	412	8.6	8.2	7.8	7.7	7.3
Urban - Urbaine	C	372	378	361	344	340	8.2	8.3	7.8	7.4	7.3
Rural - Rurale	C	110	80	77	91	72	10.4	7.7	7.5	9.0	7.2
Grenada - Grenade											
Total	+C	794	716	727	...	...	7.9	7.1	7.2	...	...
Guadeloupe[2]											
Total	C	2 670	2 698	2 765	2 584	2 636	6.3	6.3	6.4	5.9	6.0
Guatemala											
Total	C	64 563	66 831	69 934	...	66 695	5.8	5.9	6.0	...	5.5
Jamaica - Jamaïque											
Total	U	*16 294*	*15 251*	*14 476*	*15 876*	*°15 686*	...	...	...	...	...
Martinique[2]											
Total	C	2 581	2 692	2 754	2 681	2 725	6.8	7.0	7.1	6.9	7.0
Mexico - Mexique[6]											
Total	C	443 950	437 667	443 127	459 687	472 140	4.5	4.4	4.4	4.5	4.5
Urban - Urbaine	C	332 434	333 980	336 551	342 331	354 633	4.3	4.4	4.4	4.4	4.5
Rural - Rurale	C	105 664	97 870	100 670	107 345	109 167	4.8	3.9	4.0	4.2	4.2
Montserrat											
Total	+C	59	...	...	...	...	12.4	...	...	...	...
Netherlands Antilles - Antilles néerlandaises											
Total	C	1 117	1 196	1 215	1 220	1 374	6.0	6.7	7.0	7.0	7.7
Nicaragua											
Total	+U	*10 818*	*13 602*	*12 789*	*15 061*	*14 630*	...	...	...	...	...
Urban - Urbaine	+U	*7 173*	*8 851*	*8 240*	*9 801*	*9 753*	...	...	...	...	...
Rural - Rurale	+U	*3 645*	*4 751*	*4 549*	*5 260*	*4 877*	...	...	...	...	...

18. Deaths and crude death rates, by urban/rural residence: 1999 - 2003
Décès et taux bruts de mortalité, selon la résidence, urbaine/rurale: 1999 - 2003 (continued — suite)

Continent, country or area, and urban/rural residence / Continent, pays ou zone et résidence, urbaine/rurale	Co-de[1]	Number - Nombre					Rate - Taux				
		1999	2000	2001	2002	2003	1999	2000	2001	2002	2003
AMERICA, NORTH — AMERIQUE DU NORD											
Panama											
Total	U	11 938	11 841	12 442	...	...	...	...	...	...	...
Urban - Urbaine	U	7 108	...	...	...	...	...	...	...	...	...
Rural - Rurale	U	4 830	...	...	...	...	...	...	...	...	...
Puerto Rico - Porto Rico[6]											
Total	C	29 145	28 550	28 794	28 098	28 356	7.7	7.5	7.5	7.3	7.3
Urban - Urbaine	C	15 595	15 516	15 406	15 026	15 038	...	...	...	...	...
Rural - Rurale	C	13 542	12 991	13 367	13 009	13 283	...	...	...	...	...
Saint Kitts and Nevis - Saint-Kitts-et-Nevis											
Total	+C	418	357	352	...	...	9.8	8.8	7.6	...	...
Saint Lucia - Sainte-Lucie											
Total	C	981	941	998	957	...	6.4	6.0	6.3	6.0	...
Saint Vincent and the Grenadines - Saint Vincent-et-les Grenadines											
Total	+C	833	700	765	770	...	7.5	6.3	7.0	7.1	...
Trinidad and Tobago - Trinité-et-Tobago											
Total	C	10 014	...	...	*9 670	...	7.8	...	...	*7.6	...
Turks Caicos Islands - Îles Turques et Caïques											
Total	C	39	67	69	48	73	2.3	3.6	3.5	2.3	3.3
United States - États-Unis											
Total	C	2 391 399	2 403 351	2 416 425	2 443 387	2 443 908	8.8	8.7	8.5	8.5	8.4
AMERICA, SOUTH — AMERIQUE DU SUD											
Argentina - Argentine											
Total	C	289 543	277 148	285 941	291 190	302 064	7.9	7.5	7.6	7.7	8.0
Bolivia - Bolivie											
Total	U	71 680	71 742	...	...	...	...	...	...	...	...
Brazil - Brésil[9]											
Total	U	943 524	927 783	931 017	958 475	977 717	...	...	...	...	...
Chile - Chili											
Total	C	81 984	78 814	81 873	81 079	83 672	5.4	5.1	5.3	5.1	5.3
Urban - Urbaine	C	68 715	66 422	68 884	69 209	72 647	5.2	5.0	5.1	5.1	5.3
Rural - Rurale	C	13 269	12 392	12 989	11 870	11 025	6.3	6.0	6.3	5.7	5.2
Colombia - Colombie[6,10]											
Total	U	183 551	187 432	191 513	192 263	*189 072	...	...	...	...	...
Urban - Urbaine	U	135 788	138 935	143 333	143 237	*142 575	...	...	...	...	...
Rural - Rurale	U	36 772	38 316	38 610	38 095	*37 138	...	...	...	...	...
Ecuador - Équateur[11]											
Total	U	55 921	56 420	55 214	55 549	53 521	...	...	...	...	...
Urban - Urbaine	U	38 834	41 278	40 423	42 236	40 585	...	...	...	...	...
Rural - Rurale	U	17 087	15 142	14 791	13 313	12 936	...	...	...	...	...
Falkland Islands (Malvinas) - Îles Falkland (Malvinas)											
Total	+C	20	11	...	...	...	...	...	...	...	...
French Guiana - Guyane française[2]											
Total	C	658	620	668	656	692	4.2	3.8	3.9	3.7	3.8
Guyana											
Total	+C	4 197	...	...	...	...	5.4	...	...	...	...

Continent, country or area, and urban/rural residence / Continent, pays ou zone et résidence, urbaine/rurale	Co-de[1]	Number - Nombre					Rate - Taux				
		1999	2000	2001	2002	2003	1999	2000	2001	2002	2003
AMERICA, SOUTH — AMERIQUE DU SUD											
Paraguay[12]											
Total	I	...	...	38 514	...	...	...	...	...	...	...
Urban - Urbaine	I	...	...	23 907	...	...	...	...	...	...	...
Rural - Rurale	I	...	...	14 607	...	...	...	...	...	...	...
Peru - Pérou[4,9,13]											
Total	I	162 457	163 263	164 296	165 467	166 777	6.4	6.3	6.2	6.2	6.1
Suriname[6,14]											
Total	C	2 992	3 090	3 099	3 125	...	6.5	6.7	6.6	6.6	...
Urban - Urbaine	C	2 171	2 249	...	2 218	...	...	...	...	...	...
Rural - Rurale	C	821	841	...	871	...	...	...	...	...	...
Uruguay											
Total	C	32 430	30 456	31 228	31 628	32 587	9.9	9.2	9.4	9.6	9.9
Venezuela[9]											
Total	C	101 907	103 255	107 867	105 388	118 562	4.3	4.2	4.4	4.2	...
ASIA — ASIE											
Armenia - Arménie[15]											
Total	C	24 087	24 025	24 003	25 554	26 014	7.5	7.5	7.5	8.0	8.1
Urban - Urbaine	C	15 834	15 682	...	16 737	16 870	7.5	7.5	...	8.1	8.2
Rural - Rurale	C	8 253	8 343	...	8 817	9 144	7.3	7.4	...	7.7	8.0
Azerbaijan - Azerbaïdjan[15]											
Total	+C	46 295	46 701	45 284	46 522	49 001	5.8	5.8	5.6	5.7	6.0
Urban - Urbaine	+C	22 828	23 530	23 382	23 605	24 999	5.6	5.7	5.7	5.7	5.9
Rural - Rurale	+C	23 467	23 171	21 902	22 917	24 002	6.0	5.9	5.5	5.7	6.0
Bahrain - Bahreïn											
Total	U	1 920	2 045	1 979	2 035	*2 114	...	...	...	...	...
Brunei Darussalam - Brunéi Darussalam											
Total	+C	905	965	1 014	1 041	1 010	2.9	3.0	3.0	3.0	2.9
China - Chine[16,17]											
Total	...	8 100 000	...	...	...	...	6.5	6.4	6.4	6.4	6.4
China: Hong Kong SAR - Chine: Hong Kong RAS											
Total	C	33 258	33 758	33 378	34 267	36 971	5.0	5.1	5.0	5.0	5.4
China: Macao SAR - Chine: Macao RAS											
Total	C	1 374	1 338	1 327	1 415	1 474	3.2	3.1	3.1	3.2	3.3
Cyprus - Chypre[18]											
Total	C	5 070	5 355	4 827	5 168	5 200	7.4	7.7	6.9	7.3	7.2
Georgia - Géorgie[15]											
Total	C	47 184	47 410	46 218	46 446	46 055	10.6	10.7	10.5	10.7	10.6
Urban - Urbaine	C	...	...	...	...	28 887	...	...	...	...	12.8
Rural - Rurale	C	...	...	...	...	17 168	...	...	...	...	8.3
India - Inde[19,20]											
Total		...	...	...	...	...	8.7	8.5	8.4	8.1	8.0
Urban - Urbaine		...	...	...	...	...	6.3	6.3	6.3	6.1	6.0
Rural - Rurale		...	...	...	...	...	9.4	9.3	9.1	8.7	8.7
Iran (Islamic Republic of) - Iran (République islamique d')											
Total	C	506 945	382 674	421 525	337 237	368 518	8.1	6.0	6.5	5.1	5.5
Iraq[21]											
Total	U	177 483	179 928	...	...	...	...	...	...	...	...
Israel - Israël[6,22]											
Total	C	37 291	37 688	*37 184	*38 368	*38 359	6.1	6.0	*5.8	*5.8	*5.7
Urban - Urbaine	C	34 834	35 307	*34 751	*35 922	*35 941	6.3	6.2	*5.9	*6.0	*5.9
Rural - Rurale	C	2 452	2 376	*2 429	*2 442	*2 416	4.3	4.0	*4.5	*4.4	*4.3
Japan - Japon[6,23]											
Total	C	982 031	961 653	970 331	982 379	1 014 951	7.8	7.6	7.6	7.7	8.0

18. Deaths and crude death rates, by urban/rural residence: 1999 - 2003
Décès et taux bruts de mortalité, selon la résidence, urbaine/rurale: 1999 - 2003 (continued — suite)

Continent, country or area, and urban/rural residence / Continent, pays ou zone et résidence, urbaine/rurale	Co-de[1]	Number - Nombre					Rate - Taux				
		1999	2000	2001	2002	2003	1999	2000	2001	2002	2003
ASIA — ASIE											
Japan - Japon[6,23]											
Urban - Urbaine	C	717 456	704 610	712 639	724 274	750 810	...	...	...	...	...
Rural - Rurale	C	262 171	254 767	255 462	256 004	261 979	...	...	...	...	...
Jordan - Jordanie[24]											
Total	C	13 936	13 339	16 164	17 220	16 937	2.8	2.7	3.1	3.2	3.1
Kazakhstan[15]											
Total	C	147 416	149 778	147 876	149 381	155 277	9.9	10.1	10.0	10.1	10.4
Urban - Urbaine	C	92 526	94 594	94 166	95 470	99 595	11.0	11.3	11.2	11.3	11.7
Rural - Rurale	C	54 890	55 184	53 710	53 911	55 682	8.4	8.5	8.3	8.4	8.7
Korea (Republic of) - Corée (République de)[25]											
Total	C	246 539	247 346	242 730	246 515	*245 817	5.3	5.3	5.1	5.2	*5.1
Urban - Urbaine	C	152 121	155 754	154 230	157 755		...	...	...	...	...
Rural - Rurale	C	94 418	91 592	88 500	88 760		...	...	...	...	...
Kuwait - Koweït											
Total	C	4 187	4 227	4 364	4 342	...	2.0	1.9	1.9	1.9	...
Kyrgyzstan - Kirghizistan[15]											
Total	C	32 850	34 111	32 677	35 235	35 941	6.8	6.9	6.6	7.1	7.1
Urban - Urbaine	C	12 628	13 595	12 783	13 583	13 943	7.4	7.8	7.3	7.7	7.8
Rural - Rurale	C	20 222	20 516	19 894	21 652	21 998	6.4	6.5	6.2	6.7	6.8
Lebanon - Liban[21]											
Total	U	19 813	19 435	18 054	18 867	18 797	...	...	...	...	...
Malaysia - Malaisie											
Total	C	111 738	104 859	...	...	*117 900	5.1	4.5	...	...	*4.7
Maldives											
Total	C	1 037	1 032	1 081	1 113	1 026	3.7	3.8	3.9	4.0	3.6
Urban - Urbaine	C	301	298	288	347	297	...	4.0	3.8	4.5	3.8
Rural - Rurale	C	736	734	793	766	729	...	3.7	4.0	3.8	3.5
Mongolia - Mongolie											
Total	C	16 105	15 472	15 999	15 857	16 006	...	6.4	6.6	6.4	6.4
Urban - Urbaine	C	8 726	8 888	9 215	8 981	9 480	...	6.5	6.6	6.3	6.5
Rural - Rurale	C	7 379	6 584	6 784	6 876	6 526	...	6.4	6.5	6.5	6.3
Nepal - Népal[26]											
Total	I	...	...	106 789			...	...	4.6	...	...
Occupied Palestinian Territory - Territoire palestinien occupé											
Total	U	8 550	8 781	8 910	9 891	9 664	...	...	...	...	...
Oman[27]											
Total	U	2 440	2 547	2 550	2 564	2 701	...	...	...	...	...
Pakistan[28,29]											
Total	I	...	...	956 515	...	...	...	...	6.8	...	...
Urban - Urbaine	I	...	...	302 482	...	...	...	...	...	...	...
Rural - Rurale	I	...	...	654 033	...	...	...	...	...	...	...
Philippines											
Total	C	347 989	366 931	381 834	396 297	...	4.7	4.8	4.9	5.0	...
Qatar											
Total	C	1 148	1 173	1 210	1 220	1 311	2.0	1.9	1.9	1.8	1.8
Saudi Arabia - Arabie saoudite											
Total	...	68 521	51 614	...			...	...	...	...	...
Singapore - Singapour[30]											
Total	+C	15 516	15 693	15 367	15 820	16 036	4.8	4.8	4.6	4.7	4.7
Sri Lanka											
Total	+C	*114 392	...	...	*110 637	...	*6.0	...	...	*5.8	...
Syrian Arab Republic - République arabe syrienne[2,31]											
Total	U	56 564	57 759	60 814	53 252	53 778	...	...	...	...	...

Continent, country or area, and urban/rural residence / Continent, pays ou zone et résidence, urbaine/rurale	Code[1]	Number - Nombre					Rate - Taux				
		1999	2000	2001	2002	2003	1999	2000	2001	2002	2003
ASIA — ASIE											
Tajikistan - Tadjikistan[15]											
Total	C	25 495	26 492	32 015	31 142	33 185	4.2	4.3	5.1	4.8	5.0
Urban - Urbaine	C	7 633	8 715	9 452	9 274	9 722	4.7	5.3	5.6	5.4	5.6
Rural - Rurale	C	17 862	17 777	22 563	21 868	23 463	4.0	3.9	4.9	4.6	4.9
Thailand - Thaïlande											
Total	+U	362 593	365 741	369 493	380 364	384 131	...	...	...	...	...
Urban - Urbaine	+U	36 796	37 257	...	...	...	...	...	...	...	...
Rural - Rurale	+U	325 797	328 484	...	...	...	...	...	...	...	...
Turkey - Turquie[32]											
Total	I	471 000	477 000	485 000	491 000	498 000	7.1	7.1	7.1	7.1	7.0
Urban - Urbaine	I	185 141	174 315	175 137	...	...	4.3	4.0	3.9	...	...
Rural - Rurale	I	285 859	302 685	309 863	...	...	12.0	12.7	13.0	...	...
Uzbekistan - Ouzbékistan[15]											
Total	C	140 526	135 598	132 542	...	...	5.9	5.5	5.3	...	...
Urban - Urbaine	C	61 167	61 130	59 743	...	...	6.8	6.6	6.5	...	...
Rural - Rurale	C	79 359	74 468	72 799	...	...	5.3	4.8	4.6	...	...
EUROPE											
Albania - Albanie											
Total	C	16 720	16 421	15 813	16 248	17 967	5.5	5.4	5.1	5.3	5.8
Urban - Urbaine	C	...	...	...	8 560	8 923	...	...	...	6.4	6.5
Rural - Rurale	C	...	...	...	7 688	9 044	...	...	...	4.4	5.2
Andorra - Andorre											
Total	C	207	259	237	218	221	3.1	3.9	3.6	3.3	3.2
Austria - Autriche											
Total	C	78 200	76 780	74 767	76 131	77 209	9.8	9.6	9.3	9.4	9.5
Urban - Urbaine	C	46 752	...	...	...	...	...	...	...	...	...
Rural - Rurale	C	31 448	...	...	...	...	...	...	...	...	...
Belarus - Bélarus[15]											
Total	C	142 027	...	...	146 655	143 200	14.2	...	...	14.8	14.5
Urban - Urbaine	C	73 654	...	...	77 020	75 420	10.6	...	...	10.9	10.7
Rural - Rurale	C	68 373	...	...	69 635	67 780	22.3	...	...	24.1	23.9
Belgium - Belgique[33]											
Total	C	104 904	104 903	103 447	105 642	...	10.3	10.2	10.1	10.2	...
Bosnia and Herzegovina - Bosnie-Herzégovine											
Total	C	28 637	30 482	30 325	30 155	31 757	7.7	8.1	8.0	7.9	8.3
Bulgaria - Bulgarie											
Total	C	111 786	115 087	112 368	112 617	111 927	13.6	14.1	14.2	14.3	14.3
Urban - Urbaine	C	...	64 184	62 778	63 765	64 495	...	11.5	11.5	11.7	11.8
Rural - Rurale	C	...	50 903	49 590	48 852	47 432	...	19.6	20.4	20.3	20.1
Channel Islands: Guernsey - Îles Anglo-Normandes: Guernesey											
Total	C	529	565	...	...	...	8.8	9.3	...	...	...
Croatia - Croatie											
Total	C	51 953	50 246	49 552	50 569	52 575	11.4	11.5	11.2	11.4	11.8
Urban - Urbaine	C	...	25 130	24 838	24 984	25 976	...	...	10.1	...	...
Rural - Rurale	C	...	25 116	24 714	25 585	26 599	...	...	12.6	...	...
Czech Republic - République tchèque											
Total	C	109 768	109 001	107 755	108 243	111 288	10.7	10.6	10.5	10.6	10.9
Urban - Urbaine	C	78 518	78 276	77 649	78 023	80 561	10.3	10.2	10.3	10.4	10.7
Rural - Rurale	C	31 250	30 725	30 106	30 220	30 727	11.9	11.7	11.3	11.3	11.5
Denmark - Danemark[34]											
Total	C	59 156	57 986	58 338	58 610	57 574	11.1	10.9	10.9	10.9	10.7

18. Deaths and crude death rates, by urban/rural residence: 1999 - 2003
Décès et taux bruts de mortalité, selon la résidence, urbaine/rurale: 1999 - 2003 (continued — suite)

Continent, country or area, and urban/rural residence / Continent, pays ou zone et résidence, urbaine/rurale	Co-de[1]	Number - Nombre					Rate - Taux				
		1999	2000	2001	2002	2003	1999	2000	2001	2002	2003
EUROPE											
Estonia - Estonie[6,15]											
Total	C	18 447	18 403	18 516	18 355	18 152	12.8	13.4	13.6	13.5	13.4
Urban - Urbaine	C	12 087	11 665	12 119	12 309	12 106	12.1	12.3	12.8	13.1	12.9
Rural - Rurale	C	6 185	6 518	6 240	5 920	6 037	13.9	15.4	14.9	14.2	14.5
Finland - Finlande[35]											
Total	C	49 345	49 339	48 550	49 418	48 996	9.6	9.5	9.4	9.5	9.4
Urban - Urbaine	C	...	...	26 928	27 591	27 156	...	...	8.5	8.6	8.4
Rural - Rurale	C	...	...	21 622	21 827	21 840	...	...	10.8	11.0	11.0
France[36,37]											
Total	C	537 661	536 300	531 073	545 353	*560 077	9.2	9.1	9.0	9.2	*9.4
Urban - Urbaine	C	378 644	...	375 209	388 762	*401 468	...	...	...	...	...
Rural - Rurale	C	157 115	...	153 959	154 433	*156 627	...	...	...	...	...
Germany - Allemagne											
Total	C	846 330	838 797	828 541	841 686	853 946	10.3	10.2	10.1	10.2	10.3
Gibraltar[38]											
Total	C	277	262	249	242	234	10.2	9.7	9.1	8.5	8.2
Greece - Grèce											
Total	C	103 304	105 219	102 559	103 915	105 529	9.8	10.5	10.2	9.5	9.6
Urban - Urbaine	C	...	...	...	57 288	58 197	...	...	...	...	...
Rural - Rurale	C	...	...	...	46 627	47 332	...	...	...	...	...
Holy See - Saint-Siège											
Total	C	...	10	...	...	...	...	...	...	...	...
Hungary - Hongrie[39]											
Total	C	143 210	135 601	132 183	132 833	135 823	14.2	13.5	13.0	13.1	13.4
Urban - Urbaine	C	86 726	82 209	81 673	83 112	84 106	13.3	12.7	12.3	12.5	12.8
Rural - Rurale	C	55 646	52 614	49 857	49 128	51 086	15.6	14.8	14.2	13.9	14.5
Iceland - Islande											
Total	C	1 901	1 828	1 725	1 821	1 827	6.9	6.5	6.1	6.3	6.3
Urban - Urbaine	C	1 729	1 683	1 555	1 658	1 676	6.8	6.5	5.9	6.2	6.3
Rural - Rurale	C	172	145	170	163	151	8.1	6.7	7.9	7.6	7.1
Ireland - Irlande[40]											
Total	+C	31 683	31 115	30 212	29 348	28 823	8.5	8.2	7.9	7.5	7.2
Urban - Urbaine	+C	17 288	...	...	...	...	...	...	...	...	...
Rural - Rurale	+C	14 395	...	...	...	...	...	...	...	...	...
Isle of Man - Îles de Man											
Total	+C	983	897	855	877	852	...	12.0	11.2	11.4	11.0
Italy - Italie											
Total	C	571 356	560 241	556 892	557 393	*586 468	9.9	9.7	9.6	9.8	*10.2
Latvia - Lettonie[15]											
Total	C	32 844	32 205	32 991	32 498	32 437	13.7	13.6	14.0	13.9	13.9
Urban - Urbaine	C	21 246	20 921	21 460	21 059	21 038	13.0	13.0	13.4	13.3	13.3
Rural - Rurale	C	11 598	11 284	11 531	11 439	11 399	15.3	14.9	15.3	15.2	15.2
Liechtenstein											
Total	C	...	...	220	215	217	...	...	6.6	6.4	6.4
Lithuania - Lituanie[15]											
Total	C	40 003	38 919	40 399	41 072	40 990	11.4	11.1	11.6	11.8	11.9
Urban - Urbaine	C	...	21 932	22 962	23 175	23 082	...	9.4	9.9	10.0	10.0
Rural - Rurale	C	...	16 987	17 437	17 897	17 908	...	14.7	15.1	15.6	15.6
Luxembourg											
Total	C	3 793	3 754	3 719	3 744	4 053	8.8	8.6	8.4	8.4	9.0
Malta - Malte[41]											
Total	C	3 097	2 957	2 935	3 031	3 072	8.1	7.7	7.6	7.8	7.7
Monaco											
Total	C	...	564	...	...	617	...	17.6	...	...	...
Netherlands - Pays-Bas[42]											
Total	C	140 487	140 527	140 377	142 355	141 936	8.9	8.8	8.7	8.8	8.7
Urban - Urbaine	C	...	92 934	93 616	94 926	94 744	...	9.1	9.0	9.1	8.9
Rural - Rurale	C	...	47 593	46 761	47 429	47 192	...	8.3	8.3	8.4	8.4
Norway - Norvège[43]											
Total	C	45 170	44 002	43 981	44 465	42 478	10.1	9.8	9.7	9.8	9.3

18. Deaths and crude death rates, by urban/rural residence: 1999 - 2003
Décès et taux bruts de mortalité, selon la résidence, urbaine/rurale: 1999 - 2003 (continued — suite)

Continent, country or area, and urban/rural residence / Continent, pays ou zone et résidence, urbaine/rurale	Co-de[1]	Number - Nombre					Rate - Taux				
		1999	2000	2001	2002	2003	1999	2000	2001	2002	2003
EUROPE											
Poland - Pologne											
Total	C	381 415	368 028	363 220	359 486	365 230	9.9	9.6	9.5	9.4	9.6
Urban - Urbaine	C	223 630	...	215 615	213 629	216 349	9.4	...	9.1	9.0	9.2
Rural - Rurale	C	157 785	...	147 605	145 857	148 881	10.7	...	10.1	10.0	10.2
Portugal											
Total	C	107 871	105 804	105 092	106 258	108 795	10.6	10.3	10.2	10.2	10.4
Urban - Urbaine		...	...	...	...	...	...	...	...	...	...
Rural - Rurale		...	...	...	...	...	...	...	...	...	...
Republic of Moldova - République de Moldova[15]											
Total	C	41 315	41 224	40 075	41 852	43 079	11.3	11.3	11.0	11.6	11.9
Urban - Urbaine	C	13 512	13 266	12 844	13 229	13 650	8.8	8.8	8.6	8.9	9.2
Rural - Rurale	C	27 803	27 958	27 231	28 623	29 429	13.1	13.2	12.7	13.4	13.8
Romania - Roumanie											
Total	C	265 194	255 820	259 603	269 666	266 575	11.8	11.4	11.6	12.4	12.3
Urban - Urbaine	C	...	108 436	110 063	113 225	112 283	...	8.9	9.0	9.8	9.7
Rural - Rurale	C	...	147 384	149 540	156 441	154 292	...	14.5	14.7	15.4	15.2
Russian Federation - Fédération de Russie[15]											
Total	C	2 144 316	2 225 332	2 254 856	2 332 272	2 365 826	14.6	15.2	15.4	16.1	16.4
Urban - Urbaine	C	1 499 466	...	1 592 254	1 638 822	1 657 569	13.9	...	14.9	15.4	15.6
Rural - Rurale	C	644 850	...	662 602	693 450	708 257	16.3	...	17.0	17.9	18.4
San Marino - Saint-Marin											
Total	+C	198	188	195	203	216	7.5	7.0	7.1	7.1	7.5
Urban - Urbaine	+C	...	168	...	...	...	...	7.4	...	...	...
Rural - Rurale	+C	...	20	...	...	...	...	...	...	...	...
Serbia and Montenegro - Serbie-et-Montenegro[44]											
Total	C	115 461	118 078	113 063	108 298	109 650	10.9	11.1	10.6	13.3	13.4
Urban - Urbaine	C	57 007	59 324	57 280	55 129	55 615	10.4	10.8	10.4	12.0	11.9
Rural - Rurale	C	58 454	58 754	55 783	53 169	54 035	11.3	11.4	10.8	15.2	15.4
Slovakia - Slovaquie											
Total	C	52 402	52 703	51 980	51 532	52 230	9.7	9.8	9.7	9.6	9.7
Urban - Urbaine	C	24 492	...	24 520	24 737	25 272	8.0	...	8.1	8.2	8.4
Rural - Rurale	C	27 910	...	27 460	26 795	26 958	12.0	...	11.6	11.3	11.3
Slovenia - Slovénie											
Total	C	18 885	18 588	18 508	18 701	19 451	9.5	9.3	9.3	9.4	9.7
Urban - Urbaine	C	8 409	8 345	8 277	8 684	8 983	...	...	...	8.9	9.2
Rural - Rurale	C	10 476	10 243	10 231	10 017	10 468	...	...	...	10.3	10.7
Spain - Espagne											
Total	C	371 102	360 391	360 131	368 618	*383 729	9.3	9.0	8.9	8.9	*9.2
Sweden - Suède											
Total	C	94 726	93 461	93 752	95 009	92 961	10.7	10.5	10.5	10.6	10.4
Switzerland - Suisse											
Total	C	62 503	62 528	61 287	61 768	63 070	8.7	8.7	8.5	8.5	8.6
Urban - Urbaine	C	42 693	42 868	42 157	45 108	46 062	8.9	8.8	...	...	...
Rural - Rurale	C	19 810	19 660	19 130	16 660	17 008	8.5	8.4	...	...	...
The Former Yugoslav Rep. of Macedonia - L'ex-République yougoslave de Macédoine											
Total	C	16 789	17 253	16 919	17 962	18 006	8.3	8.5	8.3	8.8	8.9
Urban - Urbaine	C	9 539	10 013	9 939	10 452	10 597	...	...	...	...	...
Rural - Rurale	C	7 250	7 240	6 980	7 510	7 409	...	...	...	...	...
Ukraine[15]											
Total	C	739 170	758 082	745 952	754 911	765 408	14.8	15.5	15.4	15.7	16.1
Urban - Urbaine	C	...	...	450 329	454 406	459 965	...	...	13.9	14.1	14.4
Rural - Rurale	C	...	...	295 623	300 505	305 443	...	...	18.5	19.0	19.5

18. Deaths and crude death rates, by urban/rural residence: 1999 - 2003
Décès et taux bruts de mortalité, selon la résidence, urbaine/rurale: 1999 - 2003 (continued — suite)

Continent, country or area, and urban/rural residence Continent, pays ou zone et résidence, urbaine/rurale	Co-de[1]	Number - Nombre					Rate - Taux				
		1999	2000	2001	2002	2003	1999	2000	2001	2002	2003
EUROPE											
United Kingdom - Royaume-Uni											
Total	C	632 062	608 366	602 268	606 283	*611 188	10.8	10.3	10.2	10.2	*10.3
OCEANIA — OCEANIE											
American Samoa - Samoas américaines											
Total	C	249	224	...	...	...	4.4	3.9	...	...	...
Australia - Australie											
Total	+C	128 102	128 291	128 544	133 707	132 292	6.8	6.7	6.6	6.8	6.7
Cook Islands - Îles Cook											
Total	+C	96	115	88	97	86	5.9	6.4	4.8	5.3	4.7
Fiji - Fidji											
Total	+C	3 603	...	...	...	...	4.5	...	...	...	...
French Polynesia - Polynésie française											
Total	C	1 003	1 013	1 170	1 124	1 122	4.4	4.4	4.9	4.6	4.5
Guam[45]											
Total	C	724	667	691	658	700	4.7	4.3	4.4	4.1	4.3
Marshall Islands - Îles Marshall											
Total	+U	...	...	271	...	...	...	...	...	...	...
New Caledonia - Nouvelle-Calédonie											
Total	C	1 095	1 077	1 131	1 121	1 121	5.3	5.1	5.3	5.2	5.1
New Zealand - Nouvelle-Zélande[6]											
Total	+C	28 122	26 660	27 825	28 065	28 010	7.3	6.9	7.2	7.1	7.0
Urban - Urbaine	+C	25 385	24 014	25 093	25 390	25 279	7.7	7.3	7.5	7.5	7.3
Rural - Rurale	+C	2 620	2 563	2 677	2 611	2 654	4.8	4.7	4.9	4.7	4.7
Niue - Nioué											
Total	...	...	...	...	13	...	...	...	...	...	...
Northern Mariana Islands - Îles Mariannes septentrionales											
Total	U	189	...	...	...	...	...	...	...	...	...
Palau - Palaos											
Total	C	131	125	138	134	136	6.9	6.5	7.0	6.7	6.7
Papua New Guinea - Papouasie-Nouvelle-Guinée											
Total	U	...	7 341	6 737	7 573	7 054	...	...	...	...	...
Tonga											
Total	+C	675	653	...	...	...	6.8	6.5	...	...	...

FOOTNOTES - NOTES

Italics: data from civil registers which are incomplete or of unknown completeness. — *Italiques:* données incomplètes ou dont le degré d'exactitude n'est pas connu, provenant des registres de l'état civil.

* Provisional. — Données provisoires.

[1] 'Code' indicates the source of data, as follows:
C - Civil registration, estimated over 90% complete
U - Civil registration, estimated less than 90% complete
| - Other source, estimated reliable
+ - Data tabulated by date of registration rather than occurence.
... - Information not available

Le 'Code' indique la source des données, comme suit:
C - Registres de l'état civil considérés complèts à 90 p. 100 au moins.
U - Registres de l'état civil qui ne sont pas considérés complèts à 90 p. 100 au moins.
| - Autre source, considérée pas douteuses.
+ - Données exploitées selon la date de l'enregistrement et non la date de l'événement.
... - Information pas disponible.

[2] Excluding live-born infants who died before their birth was registered. - Non compris les enfants nés vivants décédés avant l'enregistrement de leur naissance.
[3] For Algerian population only. - Pour la population algérienne seulement.
[4] Data refer to national projections. - Les données se referent aux projections nationales.

[5] For 2001, data refer to last twelve months preceding census on August 2001. - Pour 2001, les données se rapportent pour la dernière fois à douze mois précédant le recensement août 2001.

[6] Figures for urban and rural areas do not add up to the total, since they do not include the category 'Unknown residence'. - La somme des données pour la residence urbaine et rurale n'est pas égale au total parce qu'elle n'inclue pas la catégorie 'Residence inconnue'.

[7] Deaths for 2001 refer to the period January-August 2001 - Le chiffer des décès de 2001 correspond à la période allant de janvier à août 2001.

[8] Including Canadian residents temporarily in the United States, but excluding United States residents temporarily in Canada. - Y compris les résidents canadiens se trouvant temporairement aux Etats-Unis, mais ne comprenant pas les résidents des Etats-Unis se trouvant temporairement au Canada.

[9] Excluding Indian jungle population. - Non compris les Indiens de la jungle.

[10] Data on live births and deaths are based on a civil registration system put in place in January 1998. - Les données sur les naissances et les décès sont basées sur un système d'enregistrement des faits d'état civil mis en place en janvier 1998.

[11] Excluding nomadic Indian tribes. - Non compris les tribus d'Indiens nomades.

[12] For 2001, data were collected from Population census held on August 2002, referring to events in calendar year 2001. - Pour 2001, les données sont tirées du recensement de la population réalisé en août 2002, concernant des événements de l'année civile 2001.

[13] Including an upward adjustment for under-registration. - Y compris un ajustement pour sous-enregistrement.

[14] Data for urban refer to the total of the district of Paramaribo (capital) and Wanica district. - Les données relatives aux zones urbaines correspondent au total pour le district de Paramaribo (capitale) et le district de Wanica.

[15] Excluding infants born alive with less than 28 weeks gestation, less than 1 000 grams in weight and 35 centimeters in length, who die within seven days of birth. - Non compris les enfants nés vivants avant 28 semaines de gestation, pesant moins de 1 000 grammes, mesurant moins de 35 centimètres et décédés dans les sept jours qui ont suivi leur naissance.

[16] For statistical purposes, the data for China do not include those for the Hong Kong Special Administrative Region (Hong Kong SAR), Macao Special Administrative Region (Macao SAR) and Taiwan province of China. - Pour la présentation des statistiques, les données pour Chine ne comprend pas la Région Administrative Spéciale de Hong Kong (Hong Kong RAS), la Région Administrative Spéciale de Macao (Macao RAS) et Taïwan province de Chine.

[17] Rates for 1999 - 2003 were obtained by the Sample Survey of Population Change 2003 in China. - Les taux pour 1999 - 2003 on été obtenus par la 2003 enquête de mouvement de la population par échantillon de la Chine.

[18] Data refer to government controlled areas. - Les données se raportent aux zones contrôlées par le Gouvernement.

[19] Including data for the Indian-held part of Jammu and Kashmir, the final status of which has not yet been determined. - Y compris les données pour la partie du Jammu et du Cachemire occupée par l'Inde dont le statut définitif n'a pas encore été déterminé.

[20] Rates were obtained by the Sample Registration System of India, actually a large demographic survey. - Les taux ont été obtenus par le Système de l'enregistrement par échantillon de l'Inde qui est au fait une large enquête démographique.

[21] Published by the United Nations Economic and Social Commission for Western Asia. - Publié par la Commission économique et sociale des Nations Unies pour l'Asie occidentale.

[22] Including data for East Jerusalem and Israeli residents in certain other territories under occupation by Israeli military forces since June 1967. - Y compris les données pour Jérusalem-Est et les résidents israéliens dans certains autres territoires occupés depuis 1967 par les forces armées israéliennes.

[23] For Japanese nationals in Japan only; however, rates computed on population including foreigners except foreign military and civilian personnel and their dependants stationed in the area. - Pour les nationaux japonais au Japon seulement; toutefois, les taux sont calculés sur la base d'une population comprenant les étrangers, mais ne comprenant ni les militaires et agents civils étrangers en poste sur le territoire ni les membres de leur famille les accompagnant.

[24] Excluding data for Jordanian territory under occupation since June 1967 by Israeli military forces. Excluding foreigners, including registered Palestinian refugees. - Non compris les données pour le territoire jordanien occupé depuis juin 1967 par les forces armées israéliennes. Non compris les étrangers, mais y compris les réfugiés de Palestine enregistrés.

[25] Excluding alien armed forces, civilian aliens employed by armed forces, and foreign diplomatic personnel and their dependants. - Non compris les militaires étrangers, les civils étrangers employés par les forces armées ni le personnel diplomatique étranger et les membres de leur famille les accompagnant.

[26] For 2001, data refer to last twelve months preceding census on June 2001. - Pour 2001, les données se rapportent pour la dernière fois à douze mois précédant le recensement juin 2001.

[27] Data refer to the recorded events in Ministry of Health hospitals and health centres only. - Les données se rapportent aux faits d'état-civil enregistrés dans les hôpitaux et les dispensaires du Ministère de la santé seulement.

[28] Based on the results of the Population Growth Survey. - D'après les résultats de la 'Population Growth Survey.'

[29] Excluding data for the Pakistan-held part of Jammu and Kashmir, the final status of which has not yet been determined. - Non compris les données concernant la partie du Jammu et Cachemire occupée par le Pakistan dont le statut définitif n'a pas été déterminé.

[30] Excluding transients afloat and non-locally domiciled military and civilian services personnel and their dependants. - Non compris les personnes de passage þ bord de navires, ni les militaires et agents civils domiciliés hors du territoire et les membres de leur famille les accompagnant.

[31] Excluding nomad population and Palestinian refugees. - Non compris la population nomade et les réfugiés de Palestine.

[32] Based on the results of the Population Demographic Survey. - - D'après les résultats de la Population Demographic Survey.

[33] Including armed forces stationed outside the country, but excluding alien armed forces stationed in the area. - Y compris les militaires nationaux hors du pays, mais non compris les militaires étrangers en garnison sur le territoire.

[34] Excluding Faeroe Islands and Greenland. - Non compris les Iles Féroé et Gröenland.

[35] Including nationals temporarily outside the country. - Y compris les nationaux se trouvant temporairement hors du pays.

[36] Including armed forces stationed outside the country. - Y compris les militaires nationaux hors du pays.

[37] Data for urban/rural, excluding nationals outside the country. - Les données selon la résidence urbaine/rurale, non compris les nationaux hors du pays.

[38] Excluding armed forces. - Non compris les militaires en garnison.

[39] Data for urban/rural residence, for the de jure population. - Les données selon la résidence urbaine/rurale, pour la population de droit.

[40] Events registered within one year of occurrence. - Evénements enregistrés dans l'année qui suit l'événement.

[41] Rates computed on population including civilian nationals temporarily outside the country. - Les taux sont calculés sur la base d'un chiffre de population qui comprend les civils nationaux temporairement hors du pays.

[42] Including residents outside the country if listed in a Netherlands population register. - Y compris les résidents hors du pays, s'ils sont inscrits sur un registre de population néerlandais.

[43] Including residents temporarily outside the country. - Y compris les résidents se trouvant temporairement hors du pays.

[44] From 2002, without data for Kosovo and Metohia. - Après 2002, sans les donées pour le Kosovo et Metohie.

[45] Including United States military personnel, their dependants and contract employees. - Y compris les militaires des Etats-Unis, les membres de leur famille les accompagnant et les agents contractuels des Etats-Unis.

Table 19

Table 19 presents deaths by age, sex and urban/rural residence for latest available year.

Description of variables: Age is defined as age at last birthday, that is, the difference between the date of birth and the date of the occurrence of the event, expressed in completed solar years. The age classification used in this table is the following: under 1 year, 1-4 years, 5-year age groups through 95-99 years, and 100 years or over.

The urban/rural classification of deaths is that provided by each country or area; it is presumed to be based on the national census definitions of urban population that have been set forth at the end of the technical notes for table 6.

Reliability of data: Data from civil registers of deaths that are reported as incomplete (less than 90 per cent completeness) or of unknown completeness are considered unreliable and are set in italics rather than in roman type. Table 18 and the technical notes for that table provide more detailed information on the completeness of death registration. For more information about the quality of vital statistics data in general and the information available on the basis of the completeness estimates in particular, see section 4.2 of the Technical Notes.

Limitations: Statistics on deaths by age and sex are subject to the same qualifications as have been set forth for vital statistics in general and death statistics in particular as discussed in section 4 of the Technical Notes.

The reliability of the data is an important factor in considering the limitations. In addition, some deaths are tabulated by date of registration and not by date of occurrence; these have been indicated by a plus sign (+). Whenever the lag between the date of occurrence and date of registration is prolonged and, therefore, a large proportion of the death registrations are delayed, death statistics for any given year may be seriously affected. However, delays in the registration of deaths are less common and shorter than in the registration of live births.

International comparability in mortality statistics may also be affected by the exclusion of deaths of infants who were born alive but died before the registration of the birth or within the first 24 hours of life. Statistics of this type are footnoted.

Because these statistics are classified according to age, they are subject to the limitations with respect to accuracy of age reporting similar to those already discussed in connection with section 3.1.3 of the Technical Notes. The factors influencing the accuracy of reporting may be somewhat dissimilar in vital statistics (because of the differences in the method of taking a census and registering a death) but, in general, the same errors can be observed.

The absence of frequencies in the unknown age group does not necessarily indicate completely accurate reporting and tabulation of the age item. It is often an indication that the unknowns have been eliminated by assigning ages to them before tabulation, or by proportionate distribution after tabulation.

International comparability of statistics on deaths by age is also affected by the use of different methods to determine age at death. If age is obtained from an item that simply requests age at death in completed years or is derived from information on year of birth and death rather than from information on complete date (day, month and year) of birth and death, the number of deaths classified in the under-one-year age group will tend to be reduced and the number of deaths in the next age group will tend to be somewhat increased. A similar bias may affect other age groups but its impact is usually negligible. Information on this factor is given in the footnotes when known.

The comparability of data by urban/rural residence is affected by the national definitions of urban and rural used in tabulating these data. It is assumed, in the absence of specific information to the contrary, that the definitions of urban and rural used in connection with the national population census were also used in the compilation of the vital statistics for each country or area. However, it cannot be excluded that, for a given country or area, different definitions of urban and rural are used for the vital statistics data and the population census data respectively. When known, the definitions of urban used in national population censuses are presented at the end of the technical notes for table 6. As discussed in detail in the technical notes for table 6, these definitions vary considerably from one country or area to another.

Earlier data: Deaths by age and sex have been shown for the latest available year in each issue of the Yearbook since the 1955 issue. Data included in this table update the series covering a period of years as follows:

Issue	Years Covered
Historical Supplement CD, 1997	1948 – 1997
1996	1987 – 1995
1992	1983 – 1992
1985	1976 – 1984
1980	1971 – 1979
Historical Supplement, 1979	1948 - 1977

Data have been presented by urban/rural residence in each regular issue of the Yearbook since the 1967 issue.

Tableau 19

Le tableau 19 présente les données les plus récentes dont on dispose sur les décès selon l'âge, le sexe et le lieu de résidence (zone urbaine ou rurale).

Description des variables : L'âge considéré est l'âge au dernier anniversaire, c'est-à-dire la différence entre la date de naissance et la date du décès, exprimée en années solaires révolues. La classification par âge est la suivante : moins d'un an, 1 à 4 ans, groupes quinquennaux jusqu'à 95-99 ans et 100 ans et plus.

La classification des décès selon le lieu de résidence (zone urbaine ou rurale) est celle qui a été communiquée par chaque pays ou zone ; on part du principe qu'elle repose sur les définitions de la population urbaine utilisées pour les recensements nationaux, qui sont reproduites à la fin des notes techniques du tableau 6.

Fiabilité des données : Les données sur les décès issues des registres d'état civil qui sont déclarées incomplètes (degré d'exhaustivité inférieur à 90 p.100) ou dont le degré d'exhaustivité n'est pas connu sont jugées douteuses et apparaissent en italique et non en caractères romains. Le tableau 18 et les notes techniques s'y rapportant présentent des renseignements plus détaillés sur le degré d'exhaustivité de l'enregistrement des décès. Pour plus de précisions sur la qualité des statistiques de l'état civil en général et le degré de complétude en particulier, voir la section 4.2 des Notes techniques.

Insuffisance des données : Les statistiques des décès selon l'âge et le sexe appellent les mêmes réserves que les statistiques de l'état civil en général et les statistiques relatives à la mortalité en particulier (voir la section 4 des Notes techniques).

La fiabilité des données est un facteur important. Il faut également tenir compte du fait que, dans certains cas, les données relatives aux décès sont classées par date d'enregistrement et non par date d'occurrence ; ces cas ont été signalés par le signe '+'. Chaque fois que le décalage entre le décès et son enregistrement est grand et qu'une forte proportion des décès fait l'objet d'un enregistrement tardif, les statistiques des décès de l'année peuvent être considérablement faussées.

En règle générale, toutefois, les décès sont enregistrés beaucoup plus rapidement que les naissances vivantes, et les retards prolongés sont rares.

Un autre facteur qui nuit à la comparabilité internationale est la pratique de certains pays ou zones qui consiste à ne pas inclure dans les statistiques des décès les enfants nés vivants mais décédés avant l'enregistrement de leur naissance ou dans les 24 heures qui ont suivi la naissance, pratique qui conduit à sous-évaluer le nombre de décès à moins d'un an. Quand pareil facteur a joué, cela a été signalé en note à la fin du tableau.

Étant donné que les statistiques relatives à la mortalité sont classées selon l'âge, elles appellent les mêmes réserves concernant l'exactitude des déclarations d'âge que celles qui ont été formulées à la section 3.1.3 des Notes techniques. Dans le cas des données d'état civil, les facteurs qui interviennent à cet égard sont parfois un peu différents, du fait que le recensement et l'enregistrement des décès se font par des méthodes différentes, mais, d'une manière générale, les erreurs observées sont les mêmes.

Si aucun nombre ne figure dans la rangée réservée aux âges inconnus, cela ne signifie pas nécessairement que les déclarations d'âge et le classement par âge sont tout à fait exacts. C'est souvent une indication que l'on a attribué un âge aux personnes d'âge inconnu avant l'exploitation des données ou qu'elles ont été réparties proportionnellement entre les différents groupes après cette opération.

Le manque d'uniformité des méthodes suivies pour obtenir l'âge au moment du décès nuit également à la comparabilité internationale des données. Si l'âge est connu, soit d'après la réponse à une simple question sur l'âge du décès en années révolues, soit d'après l'année de la naissance et l'année du décès, et non d'après des renseignements concernant la date exacte (jour, mois et année) de la naissance et du décès, le nombre de décès classés dans la catégorie « moins d'un an » sera entaché d'une erreur par défaut et le chiffre figurant dans la catégorie suivante d'une erreur par excès.

Les données pour les autres groupes d'âge pourront être entachées d'une distorsion analogue, mais les répercussions seront généralement négligeables. Les imperfections, lorsqu'elles étaient connues, ont été signalées en note à la fin du tableau.

La comparabilité des données selon le lieu de résidence (zone urbaine ou rurale) peut être limitée par les définitions nationales des termes « urbain » et « rural » utilisées pour le classement de ces données. En l'absence d'indications contraires, on a supposé que les mêmes définitions avaient servi pour le recensement national de la population et pour l'établissement des statistiques de l'état civil pour chaque pays ou zone. Toutefois, il n'est pas exclu que, pour une zone ou un pays donné, des définitions différentes aient été retenues. Les définitions du terme « urbain » utilisées pour les recensements nationaux de population ont été présentées à la fin du tableau 6 lorsqu'elles étaient connues. Comme on l'a précisé dans les notes techniques relatives au tableau 6, ces définitions varient considérablement d'un pays ou d'une zone à l'autre.

Données publiées antérieurement : Les éditions de l'*Annuaire démographique* parues depuis 1955 présentent les statistiques les plus récentes dont on disposait à l'époque sur les décès selon l'âge et le sexe. Les données qui figurent dans le tableau 19 actualisent les données qui portaient sur les périodes suivantes :

Éditions	Années considérées
Supplément historique (CD-ROM), 1997	1948 – 1997
1996	1987 – 1995
1992	1983 – 1992
1985	1976 – 1984
1980	1971 – 1979
Supplément rétrospectif, 1979	1948 - 1977

Des données selon le lieu de résidence (zone urbaine ou rurale) ont été présentées dans toutes les éditions de l'*Annuaire* depuis celle de 1967, exception faite des éditions spéciales.

19. Deaths by age, sex and urban/rural residence: latest available year, 1994 - 2003
Décès selon l'âge, le sexe et la résidence, urbaine/rurale: dernière année disponible, 1994 - 2003

Continent, country or area, year and age (in years) / Continent, pays ou zone, année et âge (en années)	Code[1]	Total Both sexes - Les deux sexes	Total Male - Masculin	Total Female - Féminin	Urban - Urbaine Both sexes - Les deux sexes	Urban - Urbaine Male - Masculin	Urban - Urbaine Female - Féminin	Rural - Rurale Both sexes - Les deux sexes	Rural - Rurale Male - Masculin	Rural - Rurale Female - Féminin
AFRICA — AFRIQUE										
Algeria - Algérie[2,3]										
1998										
Total	+U	131 708	73 352	58 356	...	...	...	...	...	...
0 - 1	+U	21 169	12 009	9 160	...	...	...	...	...	...
1 - 4	+U	4 475	2 378	2 097	...	...	...	...	...	...
5 - 9	+U	2 759	1 592	1 167	...	...	...	...	...	...
10 - 14	+U	2 272	1 373	899	...	...	...	...	...	...
15 - 19	+U	3 017	1 947	1 070	...	...	...	...	...	...
20 - 24	+U	3 425	2 335	1 090	...	...	...	...	...	...
25 - 29	+U	3 508	2 355	1 153	...	...	...	...	...	...
30 - 34	+U	3 216	1 958	1 258	...	...	...	...	...	...
35 - 39	+U	3 195	1 770	1 425	...	...	...	...	...	...
40 - 44	+U	3 468	1 959	1 509	...	...	...	...	...	...
45 - 49	+U	3 771	2 135	1 636	...	...	...	...	...	...
50 - 54	+U	3 777	2 184	1 593	...	...	...	...	...	...
55 - 59	+U	5 113	2 908	2 205	...	...	...	...	...	...
60 - 64	+U	7 616	4 227	3 389	...	...	...	...	...	...
65 - 69	+U	8 962	4 937	4 025	...	...	...	...	...	...
70 - 74	+U	10 320	5 732	4 588	...	...	...	...	...	...
75 - 79	+U	11 346	6 241	5 105	...	...	...	...	...	...
80+	+U	30 299	15 312	14 987	...	...	...	...	...	...
Botswana[4]										
2001										
Total	I	20 823	10 800	10 023	10 041	5 204	4 837	10 782	5 596	5 186
0 - 1	I	1 576	815	761	718	364	354	858	451	407
1 - 4	I	1 187	637	550	551	294	257	636	343	293
5 - 9	I	484	251	233	210	118	92	274	133	141
10 - 14	I	249	114	135	112	51	61	137	63	74
15 - 19	I	386	179	207	192	88	104	194	91	103
20 - 24	I	1 090	388	702	520	197	323	570	191	379
25 - 29	I	2 091	848	1 243	1 056	443	613	1 035	405	630
30 - 34	I	2 376	1 235	1 141	1 208	631	577	1 168	604	564
35 - 39	I	2 039	1 132	907	997	550	447	1 042	582	460
40 - 44	I	1 595	910	685	842	483	359	753	427	326
45 - 49	I	1 334	814	520	702	422	280	632	392	240
50 - 54	I	858	529	329	418	253	165	440	276	164
55 - 59	I	669	416	253	333	208	125	336	208	128
60 - 64	I	638	386	252	316	197	119	322	189	133
65 - 69	I	673	374	299	308	154	154	365	220	145
70 - 74	I	601	322	279	261	131	130	340	191	149
75 - 79	I	569	315	254	256	144	112	313	171	142
80+	I	1 634	740	894	762	329	433	872	411	461
Unknown - Inconnu	I	774	395	379	279	147	132	495	248	247
Egypt - Égypte										
1999										
Total	C	401 433	218 195	183 238	181 665	103 100	78 565	219 768	115 095	104 673
0 - 1	C	49 765	26 263	23 502	19 265	10 846	8 419	30 500	15 417	15 083
1 - 4	C	13 891	7 032	6 859	4 047	2 254	1 793	9 844	4 778	5 066
5 - 9	C	5 502	3 213	2 289	2 232	1 367	865	3 270	1 846	1 424
10 - 14	C	5 222	3 008	2 214	2 354	1 429	925	2 868	1 579	1 289
15 - 19	C	6 150	3 830	2 320	3 275	2 151	1 124	2 875	1 679	1 196
20 - 24	C	6 219	3 978	2 241	3 449	2 362	1 087	2 770	1 616	1 154
25 - 29	C	5 738	3 532	2 206	3 104	2 062	1 042	2 634	1 470	1 164
30 - 34	C	6 060	3 744	2 316	3 090	1 990	1 100	2 970	1 754	1 216
35 - 39	C	8 567	5 239	3 328	4 281	2 705	1 576	4 286	2 534	1 752
40 - 44	C	10 907	7 090	3 817	5 595	3 611	1 984	5 312	3 479	1 833
45 - 49	C	16 651	10 812	5 839	8 632	5 570	3 062	8 019	5 242	2 777
50 - 54	C	22 002	13 557	8 445	11 596	7 229	4 367	10 406	6 328	4 078
55 - 59	C	24 114	14 682	9 432	12 154	7 548	4 606	11 960	7 134	4 826
60 - 64	C	33 825	19 470	14 355	16 736	9 696	7 040	17 089	9 774	7 315
65 - 69	C	42 332	23 770	18 562	19 916	11 497	8 419	22 416	12 273	10 143
70 - 74	C	46 533	24 287	22 246	21 071	11 253	9 818	25 462	13 034	12 428
75+	C	97 955	44 688	53 267	40 868	19 530	21 338	57 087	25 158	31 929

19. Deaths by age, sex and urban/rural residence: latest available year, 1994 - 2003
Décès selon l'âge, le sexe et la résidence, urbaine/rurale: dernière année disponible, 1994 - 2003 (continued — suite)

Continent, country or area, year and age (in years) / Continent, pays ou zone, année et âge (en années)	Code[1]	Total			Urban - Urbaine			Rural - Rurale		
		Both sexes - Les deux sexes	Male - Masculin	Female - Féminin	Both sexes - Les deux sexes	Male - Masculin	Female - Féminin	Both sexes - Les deux sexes	Male - Masculin	Female - Féminin
AFRICA — AFRIQUE										
Kenya										
2002										
Total	U	206 089	107 108	98 981	...	...	...	...	...	...
0 - 1	U	32 459	16 735	15 724	...	...	...	...	...	...
1 - 4	U	22 623	12 166	10 457	...	...	...	...	...	...
5 - 14	U	11 035	5 889	5 146	...	...	...	...	...	...
15 - 24	U	15 157	6 083	9 074	...	...	...	...	...	...
25 - 34	U	29 921	13 485	16 436	...	...	...	...	...	...
35 - 44	U	27 720	14 714	13 006	...	...	...	...	...	...
45 - 54	U	19 896	11 770	8 126	...	...	...	...	...	...
55 - 74	U	26 196	15 183	11 013	...	...	...	...	...	...
75+	U	21 082	11 083	9 999	...	...	...	...	...	...
Libyan Arab Jamahiriya - Jamahiriya arabe libyenne										
2002										
Total	U	19 362	11 278	8 084	...	...	...	...	...	...
0 - 1	U	2 194	1 190	1 004	...	...	...	...	...	...
1 - 4	U	891	546	345	...	...	...	...	...	...
5 - 9	U	267	142	125	...	...	...	...	...	...
10 - 19	U	670	432	238	...	...	...	...	...	...
20 - 29	U	1 100	824	276	...	...	...	...	...	...
30 - 39	U	1 287	820	467	...	...	...	...	...	...
40 - 49	U	1 118	621	497	...	...	...	...	...	...
50 - 59	U	1 492	860	632	...	...	...	...	...	...
60 - 69	U	2 936	1 754	1 182	...	...	...	...	...	...
70 - 79	U	3 812	2 254	1 558	...	...	...	...	...	...
80+	U	3 595	1 835	1 760	...	...	...	...	...	...
Malawi[5]										
1998										
Total	I	208 040	113 856	94 184	22 186	12 404	9 782	185 854	101 452	84 402
0 - 1	I	44 928	24 977	19 951	5 241	2 968	2 273	39 687	22 009	17 678
1 - 4	I	59 930	32 821	27 109	6 180	3 435	2 745	53 750	29 386	24 364
5 - 9	I	16 717	9 200	7 517	1 628	926	702	15 089	8 274	6 815
10 - 14	I	9 638	4 849	4 789	801	440	361	8 837	4 409	4 428
15 - 19	I	7 130	3 427	3 703	672	336	336	6 458	3 091	3 367
20 - 24	I	11 710	6 947	4 763	1 240	629	611	10 470	6 318	4 152
25 - 29	I	9 290	4 853	4 437	1 168	548	620	8 122	4 305	3 817
30 - 34	I	8 797	4 481	4 316	1 168	621	547	7 629	3 860	3 769
35 - 39	I	7 036	3 678	3 358	969	553	416	6 067	3 125	2 942
40 - 44	I	6 338	3 713	2 625	822	527	295	5 516	3 186	2 330
45 - 49	I	5 639	3 705	1 934	587	388	199	5 052	3 317	1 735
50 - 54	I	3 677	2 160	1 517	461	310	151	3 216	1 850	1 366
55 - 59	I	3 872	1 739	2 133	335	200	135	3 537	1 539	1 998
60 - 64	I	2 921	1 620	1 301	259	152	107	2 662	1 468	1 194
65 - 69	I	2 695	1 257	1 438	156	90	66	2 539	1 167	1 372
70 - 74	I	2 228	1 358	870	131	76	55	2 097	1 282	815
75 - 79	I	1 599	942	657	104	64	40	1 495	878	617
80 - 84	I	1 516	842	674	92	52	40	1 424	790	634
85+	I	2 379	1 287	1 092	172	89	83	2 207	1 198	1 009
Mauritius - Maurice										
2003										
Total	+C	8 520	4 754	3 766	...	...	...	...	...	...
0 - 1	+C	250	133	117	...	...	...	...	...	...
1 - 4	+C	59	30	29	...	...	...	...	...	...
5 - 9	+C	25	13	12	...	...	...	...	...	...
10 - 14	+C	40	20	20	...	...	...	...	...	...
15 - 19	+C	48	30	18	...	...	...	...	...	...
20 - 24	+C	82	55	27	...	...	...	...	...	...
25 - 29	+C	97	58	39	...	...	...	...	...	...
30 - 34	+C	140	101	39	...	...	...	...	...	...
35 - 39	+C	231	162	69	...	...	...	...	...	...
40 - 44	+C	334	235	99	...	...	...	...	...	...
45 - 49	+C	472	324	148	...	...	...	...	...	...
50 - 54	+C	627	414	213	...	...	...	...	...	...
55 - 59	+C	605	374	231	...	...	...	...	...	...

Continent, country or area, year and age (in years) / Continent, pays ou zone, année et âge (en années)	Code[1]	Total			Urban - Urbaine			Rural - Rurale		
		Both sexes - Les deux sexes	Male - Masculin	Female - Féminin	Both sexes - Les deux sexes	Male - Masculin	Female - Féminin	Both sexes - Les deux sexes	Male - Masculin	Female - Féminin
AFRICA — AFRIQUE										
Mauritius - Maurice										
2003										
60 - 64	+C	715	420	295	...	...	...	...	...	...
65 - 69	+C	920	540	380	...	...	...	...	...	...
70 - 74	+C	930	527	403	...	...	...	...	...	...
75 - 79	+C	1 096	561	535	...	...	...	...	...	...
80 - 84	+C	881	396	485	...	...	...	...	...	...
85+	+C	967	360	607	...	...	...	...	...	...
Unknown - Inconnu	+C	1	1	-	...	...	...	...	...	...
Morocco - Maroc[6]										
2001										
Total	U	95 612	62 023	33 589	55 745	34 330	21 415	39 787	27 639	12 148
0 - 1	U	7 379	4 022	3 357	2 804	1 566	1 238	4 569	2 453	2 116
1 - 4	U	3 066	1 590	1 476	965	521	444	2 100	1 068	1 032
5 - 9	U	1 300	787	513	518	323	195	782	464	318
10 - 14	U	1 346	805	541	617	381	236	727	423	304
15 - 19	U	1 954	1 174	780	1 064	664	400	889	509	380
20 - 24	U	2 721	1 734	987	1 522	991	531	1 195	740	455
25 - 29	U	2 685	1 679	1 006	1 491	959	532	1 189	716	473
30 - 34	U	2 784	1 685	1 099	1 689	1 051	638	1 093	632	461
35 - 39	U	2 884	1 716	1 168	1 821	1 094	727	1 058	619	439
40 - 44	U	3 683	2 272	1 411	2 400	1 479	921	1 279	791	488
45 - 49	U	3 798	2 476	1 322	2 538	1 635	903	1 255	837	418
50 - 54	U	4 385	2 925	1 460	2 899	1 899	1 000	1 484	1 024	460
55 - 59	U	4 949	3 229	1 720	3 244	1 998	1 246	1 698	1 228	470
60 - 64	U	8 122	5 290	2 832	5 114	3 093	2 021	3 003	2 194	809
65 - 69	U	9 255	6 243	3 012	5 926	3 671	2 255	3 322	2 568	754
70 - 74	U	11 272	7 590	3 682	6 932	4 182	2 750	4 337	3 406	931
75 - 79	U	9 110	6 417	2 693	5 560	3 552	2 008	3 543	2 859	684
80+	U	14 063	9 896	4 167	8 111	5 022	3 089	5 942	4 868	1 074
Unknown - Inconnu	U	856	493	363	530	249	281	322	240	82
Mozambique[7]										
1997										
Total	I	385 754	206 737	179 017	70 750	39 060	31 690	315 004	167 677	147 327
0 - 1	I	99 947	54 065	45 882	16 506	9 132	7 374	83 441	44 933	38 508
1 - 4	I	123 644	66 656	56 988	16 230	8 766	7 464	107 414	57 890	49 524
5 - 9	I	31 778	17 034	14 744	4 267	2 367	1 900	27 511	14 667	12 844
10 - 14	I	14 914	8 144	6 770	2 407	1 337	1 070	12 507	6 807	5 700
15 - 19	I	12 169	5 896	6 273	2 624	1 379	1 245	9 545	4 517	5 028
20 - 24	I	10 633	4 883	5 750	2 691	1 328	1 363	7 942	3 555	4 387
25 - 29	I	9 556	4 643	4 913	2 606	1 378	1 228	6 950	3 265	3 685
30 - 34	I	8 691	4 610	4 081	2 490	1 454	1 036	6 201	3 156	3 045
35 - 39	I	8 180	4 411	3 769	2 340	1 350	990	5 840	3 061	2 779
40 - 44	I	7 276	4 092	3 184	2 158	1 289	869	5 118	2 803	2 315
45 - 49	I	7 208	4 194	3 014	2 130	1 307	823	5 078	2 887	2 191
50 - 54	I	7 386	4 227	3 159	2 191	1 299	892	5 195	2 928	2 267
55 - 59	I	5 300	3 090	2 210	1 484	890	594	3 816	2 200	1 616
60 - 64	I	7 853	4 380	3 473	2 309	1 293	1 016	5 544	3 087	2 457
65 - 69	I	5 348	2 962	2 386	1 608	911	697	3 740	2 051	1 689
70 - 74	I	5 008	2 897	2 111	1 536	855	681	3 472	2 042	1 430
75 - 79	I	3 440	1 918	1 522	1 054	589	465	2 386	1 329	1 057
80+	I	6 610	3 512	3 098	1 751	894	857	4 859	2 618	2 241
Unknown - Inconnu	I	10 813	5 123	5 690	2 368	1 242	1 126	8 445	3 881	4 564
Namibia - Namibie[8,9]										
2001										
Total	I	25 061	12 338	12 137	6 529	3 354	3 175	18 532	9 063	8 962
0 - 4	I	4 631	2 180	2 343	1 084	487	582	3 547	1 693	1 761
5 - 9	I	938	461	447	174	90	83	764	371	364
10 - 14	I	508	246	256	110	48	60	398	198	196
15 - 19	I	658	317	330	173	81	88	485	236	242
20 - 24	I	1 240	492	740	334	149	184	906	343	556
25 - 29	I	1 791	799	989	502	228	274	1 289	571	715
30 - 34	I	2 032	1 029	988	545	278	264	1 487	751	724
35 - 39	I	1 845	1 003	837	532	290	241	1 313	713	596
40 - 44	I	1 370	753	615	406	220	186	964	533	429

19. Deaths by age, sex and urban/rural residence: latest available year, 1994 - 2003
Décès selon l'âge, le sexe et la résidence, urbaine/rurale: dernière année disponible, 1994 - 2003 (continued — suite)

Continent, country or area, year and age (in years) Continent, pays ou zone, année et âge (en années)	Code[1]	Total			Urban - Urbaine			Rural - Rurale		
		Both sexes - Les deux sexes	Male - Masculin	Female - Féminin	Both sexes - Les deux sexes	Male - Masculin	Female - Féminin	Both sexes - Les deux sexes	Male - Masculin	Female - Féminin
AFRICA — AFRIQUE										
Namibia - Namibie[8,9]										
2001										
45 - 49	I	1 099	609	485	323	181	142	776	428	343
50 - 54	I	866	547	317	289	182	107	577	365	210
55 - 59	I	699	419	279	208	121	87	491	298	192
60 - 64	I	761	431	315	244	137	105	517	294	210
65 - 69	I	576	310	260	160	89	69	416	221	191
70 - 74	I	729	405	322	203	100	101	526	305	221
75 - 79	I	571	266	291	147	71	73	424	195	218
80 - 84	I	539	228	299	139	54	84	400	174	215
85 - 89	I	361	162	189	92	40	50	269	122	139
90 - 94	I	246	102	138	50	22	28	196	80	110
95+	I	373	131	242	52	23	29	321	108	213
Unknown - Inconnu	I	3 228	1 448	1 455	762	384	338	2 466	1 064	1 117
Réunion[2]										
2003										
Total	C	4 022	2 311	1 711	...	...	...	...	...	...
0 - 1	C	107	59	48	...	...	...	...	...	...
1 - 4	C	19	11	8	...	...	...	...	...	...
5 - 9	C	9	4	5	...	...	...	...	...	...
10 - 14	C	14	8	6	...	...	...	...	...	...
15 - 19	C	38	30	8	...	...	...	...	...	...
20 - 24	C	44	34	10	...	...	...	...	...	...
25 - 29	C	36	26	10	...	...	...	...	...	...
30 - 34	C	81	52	29	...	...	...	...	...	...
35 - 39	C	126	93	33	...	...	...	...	...	...
40 - 44	C	159	118	41	...	...	...	...	...	...
45 - 49	C	196	144	52	...	...	...	...	...	...
50 - 54	C	222	162	60	...	...	...	...	...	...
55 - 59	C	234	165	69	...	...	...	...	...	...
60 - 64	C	267	178	89	...	...	...	...	...	...
65 - 69	C	396	258	138	...	...	...	...	...	...
70 - 74	C	425	264	161	...	...	...	...	...	...
75 - 79	C	478	268	210	...	...	...	...	...	...
80 - 84	C	482	220	262	...	...	...	...	...	...
85+	C	689	217	472	...	...	...	...	...	...
Saint Helena ex. dep. - Sainte-Hélène sans dép.										
1999										
Total	C	45	24	21	...	...	...	...	...	...
50 - 54	C	2	1	1	...	...	...	...	...	...
55 - 59	C	3	3	-	...	...	...	...	...	...
60 - 64	C	5	3	2	...	...	...	...	...	...
65 - 69	C	2	1	1	...	...	...	...	...	...
70 - 74	C	7	3	4	...	...	...	...	...	...
75 - 79	C	9	5	4	...	...	...	...	...	...
80 - 84	C	8	5	3	...	...	...	...	...	...
85 - 89	C	5	2	3	...	...	...	...	...	...
90 - 94	C	3	-	3	...	...	...	...	...	...
95+	C	1	1	-	...	...	...	...	...	...
Seychelles										
2001										
Total	+C	554	330	224	...	...	...	...	...	...
0 - 1	+C	19	8	11	...	...	...	...	...	...
1 - 4	+C	3	2	1	...	...	...	...	...	...
5 - 9	+C	1	-	1	...	...	...	...	...	...
10 - 14	+C	1	1	-	...	...	...	...	...	...
15 - 19	+C	2	1	1	...	...	...	...	...	...
20 - 24	+C	8	8	-	...	...	...	...	...	...
25 - 29	+C	10	10	-	...	...	...	...	...	...
30 - 34	+C	13	11	2	...	...	...	...	...	...
35 - 39	+C	17	11	6	...	...	...	...	...	...
40 - 44	+C	32	25	7	...	...	...	...	...	...
45 - 49	+C	27	21	6	...	...	...	...	...	...
50 - 54	+C	26	20	6	...	...	...	...	...	...

19. Deaths by age, sex and urban/rural residence: latest available year, 1994 - 2003
Décès selon l'âge, le sexe et la résidence, urbaine/rurale: dernière année disponible, 1994 - 2003 (continued — suite)

Continent, country or area, year and age (in years) / Continent, pays ou zone, année et âge (en années)	Code[1]	Total			Urban - Urbaine			Rural - Rurale		
		Both sexes - Les deux sexes	Male - Masculin	Female - Féminin	Both sexes - Les deux sexes	Male - Masculin	Female - Féminin	Both sexes - Les deux sexes	Male - Masculin	Female - Féminin
AFRICA — AFRIQUE										
Seychelles										
2001										
55 - 59	+C	28	22	6	...	...	...	...	...	...
60 - 64	+C	44	29	15	...	...	...	...	...	...
65 - 69	+C	59	33	26	...	...	...	...	...	...
70 - 74	+C	57	35	22	...	...	...	...	...	...
75 - 79	+C	61	35	26	...	...	...	...	...	...
80 - 84	+C	68	36	32	...	...	...	...	...	...
85+	+C	78	22	56	...	...	...	...	...	...
South Africa - Afrique du Sud										
1996										
Total	...	327 068	186 538	140 530	...	...	...	...	...	...
0 - 1	...	24 560	12 979	11 581	...	...	...	...	...	...
1 - 4	...	8 052	4 313	3 739	...	...	...	...	...	...
5 - 9	...	3 098	1 816	1 282	...	...	...	...	...	...
10 - 14	...	2 758	1 602	1 156	...	...	...	...	...	...
15 - 19	...	6 789	4 334	2 455	...	...	...	...	...	...
20 - 24	...	14 257	9 347	4 910	...	...	...	...	...	...
25 - 29	...	17 690	11 477	6 213	...	...	...	...	...	...
30 - 34	...	19 258	12 709	6 549	...	...	...	...	...	...
35 - 39	...	18 249	11 953	6 296	...	...	...	...	...	...
40 - 44	...	18 562	12 328	6 234	...	...	...	...	...	...
45 - 49	...	19 259	12 895	6 364	...	...	...	...	...	...
50 - 54	...	18 817	12 366	6 451	...	...	...	...	...	...
55 - 59	...	22 238	13 715	8 523	...	...	...	...	...	...
60 - 64	...	21 975	12 084	9 891	...	...	...	...	...	...
65 - 69	...	25 965	13 942	12 023	...	...	...	...	...	...
70 - 74	...	22 817	12 274	10 543	...	...	...	...	...	...
75 - 79	...	25 202	11 837	13 365	...	...	...	...	...	...
80 - 84	...	17 137	7 376	9 761	...	...	...	...	...	...
85+	...	19 193	6 443	12 750	...	...	...	...	...	...
Unknown - Inconnu	...	1 192	748	444	...	...	...	...	...	...
Swaziland[7]										
1997										
Total	I	8 480	4 714	3 766	1 370	753	617	7 110	3 961	3 149
0 - 4	I	2 043	1 068	975	301	165	136	1 742	903	839
5 - 9	I	191	104	87	29	15	14	162	89	73
10 - 14	I	143	74	69	23	12	11	120	62	58
15 - 19	I	258	123	135	42	20	22	216	103	113
20 - 24	I	455	199	256	86	39	47	369	160	209
25 - 29	I	603	317	286	112	62	50	491	255	236
30 - 34	I	577	321	256	97	54	43	480	267	213
35 - 39	I	529	315	214	95	49	46	434	266	168
40 - 44	I	489	309	180	86	54	32	403	255	148
45 - 49	I	434	287	147	81	49	32	353	238	115
50 - 54	I	439	274	165	78	48	30	361	226	135
55 - 59	I	358	235	123	64	40	24	294	195	99
60 - 64	I	365	237	128	50	25	25	315	212	103
65 - 69	I	305	195	110	43	31	12	262	164	98
70 - 74	I	315	189	126	41	22	19	274	167	107
75+	I	745	341	404	97	41	56	648	300	348
Unknown - Inconnu	I	231	126	105	45	27	18	186	99	87
Tunisia - Tunisie										
1995										
Total	U	42 601	25 213	17 388	32 359	19 003	13 356	10 242	6 210	4 032
0 - 1	U	4 248	2 434	1 814	3 538	2 063	1 475	710	371	339
1 - 4	U	1 055	574	481	718	398	320	337	176	161
5 - 9	U	533	301	232	410	227	183	123	74	49
10 - 14	U	398	238	160	319	189	130	79	49	30
15 - 19	U	529	345	184	408	261	147	121	84	37
20 - 24	U	684	457	227	555	371	184	129	86	43
25 - 29	U	698	479	219	564	397	167	134	82	52
30 - 34	U	805	511	294	646	424	222	159	87	72
35 - 39	U	797	480	317	639	386	253	158	94	64
40 - 44	U	887	520	367	726	434	292	161	86	75

Continent, country or area, year and age (in years) / Continent, pays ou zone, année et âge (en années)	Code[1]	Total			Urban - Urbaine			Rural - Rurale		
		Both sexes - Les deux sexes	Male - Masculin	Female - Féminin	Both sexes - Les deux sexes	Male - Masculin	Female - Féminin	Both sexes - Les deux sexes	Male - Masculin	Female - Féminin
AFRICA — AFRIQUE										
Tunisia - Tunisie										
1995										
45 - 49	U	991	598	393	815	498	317	176	100	76
50 - 54	U	1 154	748	406	959	636	323	195	112	83
55 - 59	U	2 093	1 341	752	1 714	1 105	609	379	236	143
60 - 64	U	3 012	1 847	1 165	2 420	1 490	930	592	357	235
65 - 69	U	3 883	2 394	1 489	3 045	1 890	1 155	838	504	334
70 - 74	U	4 227	2 503	1 724	3 243	1 923	1 320	984	580	404
75 - 79	U	5 002	2 966	2 036	3 619	2 071	1 548	1 383	895	488
80 - 84	U	4 854	2 885	1 969	3 308	1 863	1 445	1 546	1 022	524
85+	U	4 815	2 501	2 314	3 303	1 585	1 718	1 512	916	596
Unknown - Inconnu	U	1 936	1 091	845	1 410	792	618	526	299	227
1998										
Total	U	42 571	25 319	17 252	...	...	...	...	...	...
0 - 1	U	3 098	1 775	1 323	...	...	...	...	...	...
1 - 4	U	2 096	1 196	900	...	...	...	...	...	...
5 - 9	U	412	252	160	...	...	...	...	...	...
10 - 14	U	382	236	146	...	...	...	...	...	...
15 - 19	U	578	408	170	...	...	...	...	...	...
20 - 24	U	653	459	194	...	...	...	...	...	...
25 - 29	U	612	425	187	...	...	...	...	...	...
30 - 34	U	801	528	273	...	...	...	...	...	...
35 - 39	U	812	519	293	...	...	...	...	...	...
40 - 44	U	998	631	367	...	...	...	...	...	...
45 - 49	U	1 161	737	424	...	...	...	...	...	...
50 - 54	U	1 267	805	462	...	...	...	...	...	...
55 - 59	U	1 833	1 152	681	...	...	...	...	...	...
60 - 64	U	2 920	1 843	1 077	...	...	...	...	...	...
65 - 69	U	4 337	2 673	1 664	...	...	...	...	...	...
70 - 74	U	4 918	2 943	1 975	...	...	...	...	...	...
75 - 79	U	5 201	2 930	2 271	...	...	...	...	...	...
80+	U	10 199	5 681	4 518	...	...	...	...	...	...
Unknown - Inconnu	U	293	126	167	...	...	...	...	...	...
AMERICA, NORTH — AMERIQUE DU NORD										
Anguilla										
2003										
Total	+C	65	39	26	...	...	...	...	...	...
0 - 4	+C	2	1	1	...	...	...	...	...	...
5 - 9	+C	1	-	1	...	...	...	...	...	...
15 - 19	+C	2	-	2	...	...	...	...	...	...
30 - 34	+C	6	4	2	...	...	...	...	...	...
45 - 49	+C	6	4	2	...	...	...	...	...	...
60 - 64	+C	4	2	2	...	...	...	...	...	...
65 - 69	+C	2	1	1	...	...	...	...	...	...
70 - 74	+C	5	2	3	...	...	...	...	...	...
75 - 79	+C	7	4	3	...	...	...	...	...	...
80 - 84	+C	11	8	3	...	...	...	...	...	...
85+	+C	19	13	6	...	...	...	...	...	...
Antigua and Barbuda - Antigua-et-Barbuda										
1995										
Total	+C	454	233	221	...	...	...	...	...	...
0 - 1	+C	23	11	12	...	...	...	...	...	...
1 - 4	+C	4	3	1	...	...	...	...	...	...
10 - 14	+C	1	1	-	...	...	...	...	...	...
15 - 19	+C	2	1	1	...	...	...	...	...	...
20 - 24	+C	5	2	3	...	...	...	...	...	...
25 - 29	+C	3	2	1	...	...	...	...	...	...
30 - 34	+C	8	6	2	...	...	...	...	...	...
35 - 39	+C	10	5	5	...	...	...	...	...	...
40 - 44	+C	12	5	7	...	...	...	...	...	...
45 - 49	+C	7	5	2	...	...	...	...	...	...

19. Deaths by age, sex and urban/rural residence: latest available year, 1994 - 2003
Décès selon l'âge, le sexe et la résidence, urbaine/rurale: dernière année disponible, 1994 - 2003 (continued — suite)

Continent, country or area, year and age (in years) / Continent, pays ou zone, année et âge (en années)	Code[1]	Total			Urban - Urbaine			Rural - Rurale		
		Both sexes - Les deux sexes	Male - Masculin	Female - Féminin	Both sexes - Les deux sexes	Male - Masculin	Female - Féminin	Both sexes - Les deux sexes	Male - Masculin	Female - Féminin
AMERICA, NORTH — AMERIQUE DU NORD										
Antigua and Barbuda - Antigua-et-Barbuda										
1995										
50 - 54	+C	22	14	8	...	...	...	...	...	...
55 - 59	+C	27	22	5	...	...	...	...	...	...
60 - 64	+C	31	21	10	...	...	...	...	...	...
65 - 69	+C	46	25	21	...	...	...	...	...	...
70 - 74	+C	47	25	22	...	...	...	...	...	...
75 - 79	+C	62	24	38	...	...	...	...	...	...
80 - 84	+C	62	28	34	...	...	...	...	...	...
85+	+C	79	31	48	...	...	...	...	...	...
Unknown - Inconnu	+C	3	2	1	...	...	...	...	...	...
Bahamas										
2001										
Total	C	1 609	879	730	...	...	...	...	...	...
0 - 1	C	37	23	14	...	...	...	...	...	...
1 - 4	C	14	6	8	...	...	...	...	...	...
5 - 9	C	7	5	2	...	...	...	...	...	...
10 - 14	C	7	3	4	...	...	...	...	...	...
15 - 19	C	22	17	5	...	...	...	...	...	...
20 - 24	C	25	17	8	...	...	...	...	...	...
25 - 29	C	62	40	22	...	...	...	...	...	...
30 - 34	C	86	55	31	...	...	...	...	...	...
35 - 39	C	97	58	39	...	...	...	...	...	...
40 - 44	C	118	78	40	...	...	...	...	...	...
45 - 49	C	106	64	42	...	...	...	...	...	...
50 - 54	C	91	53	38	...	...	...	...	...	...
55 - 59	C	108	63	45	...	...	...	...	...	...
60 - 64	C	111	71	40	...	...	...	...	...	...
65 - 69	C	145	80	65	...	...	...	...	...	...
70 - 74	C	126	64	62	...	...	...	...	...	...
75 - 79	C	120	60	60	...	...	...	...	...	...
80 - 84	C	141	72	69	...	...	...	...	...	...
85 - 89	C	108	37	71	...	...	...	...	...	...
90 - 94	C	52	7	45	...	...	...	...	...	...
95 - 99	C	19	6	13	...	...	...	...	...	...
100+	C	7	-	7	...	...	...	...	...	...
Belize										
2001										
Total	U	1 261	762	499	...	...	...	...	...	...
0 - 1	U	120	...	...	...	...	...	...	...	...
1 - 4	U	32	...	...	...	...	...	...	...	...
5 - 9	U	15	...	...	...	...	...	...	...	...
10 - 14	U	12	...	...	...	...	...	...	...	...
15 - 19	U	35	...	...	...	...	...	...	...	...
20 - 24	U	41	...	...	...	...	...	...	...	...
25 - 29	U	54	...	...	...	...	...	...	...	...
30 - 34	U	51	...	...	...	...	...	...	...	...
35 - 39	U	56	...	...	...	...	...	...	...	...
40 - 44	U	53	...	...	...	...	...	...	...	...
45 - 49	U	62	...	...	...	...	...	...	...	...
50 - 54	U	53	...	...	...	...	...	...	...	...
55 - 59	U	57	...	...	...	...	...	...	...	...
60 - 64	U	68	...	...	...	...	...	...	...	...
65 - 69	U	98	...	...	...	...	...	...	...	...
70 - 74	U	122	...	...	...	...	...	...	...	...
75 - 79	U	87	...	...	...	...	...	...	...	...
80+	U	239	...	...	...	...	...	...	...	...
Unknown - Inconnu	U	6	...	...	...	...	...	...	...	...
Bermuda - Bermudes										
2003										
Total	C	434	...	...	...	...	...	...	...	...
0 - 14	C	2	...	...	...	...	...	...	...	...

19. Deaths by age, sex and urban/rural residence: latest available year, 1994 - 2003
Décès selon l'âge, le sexe et la résidence, urbaine/rurale: dernière année disponible, 1994 - 2003 (continued — suite)

Continent, country or area, year and age (in years) / Continent, pays ou zone, année et âge (en années)	Code[1]	Total			Urban - Urbaine			Rural - Rurale		
		Both sexes - Les deux sexes	Male - Masculin	Female - Féminin	Both sexes - Les deux sexes	Male - Masculin	Female - Féminin	Both sexes - Les deux sexes	Male - Masculin	Female - Féminin
AMERICA, NORTH — AMERIQUE DU NORD										
Bermuda - Bermudes										
2003										
15 - 24	C	2	...	...	...	...	...	...	...	...
25 - 44	C	31	...	...	...	...	...	...	...	...
45 - 64	C	81	...	...	...	...	...	...	...	...
65 - 84	C	197	...	...	...	...	...	...	...	...
85+	C	121	...	...	...	...	...	...	...	...
Canada[10]										
2002										
Total	C	223 603	113 266	110 337	...	...	...	...	...	...
0 - 1	C	1 762	980	782	...	...	...	...	...	...
1 - 4	C	319	168	151	...	...	...	...	...	...
5 - 9	C	231	137	94	...	...	...	...	...	...
10 - 14	C	332	194	138	...	...	...	...	...	...
15 - 19	C	978	673	305	...	...	...	...	...	...
20 - 24	C	1 238	886	352	...	...	...	...	...	...
25 - 29	C	1 144	819	325	...	...	...	...	...	...
30 - 34	C	1 565	1 049	516	...	...	...	...	...	...
35 - 39	C	2 528	1 569	959	...	...	...	...	...	...
40 - 44	C	3 822	2 382	1 440	...	...	...	...	...	...
45 - 49	C	5 573	3 369	2 204	...	...	...	...	...	...
50 - 54	C	7 566	4 641	2 925	...	...	...	...	...	...
55 - 59	C	10 035	6 120	3 915	...	...	...	...	...	...
60 - 64	C	12 536	7 665	4 871	...	...	...	...	...	...
65 - 69	C	17 248	10 571	6 677	...	...	...	...	...	...
70 - 74	C	24 657	14 614	10 043	...	...	...	...	...	...
75 - 79	C	32 659	17 750	14 909	...	...	...	...	...	...
80 - 84	C	35 959	17 326	18 633	...	...	...	...	...	...
85 - 89	C	33 031	13 453	19 578	...	...	...	...	...	...
90+	C	30 417	8 899	21 518	...	...	...	...	...	...
Unknown - Inconnu	C	3	1	2	...	...	...	...	...	...
Cayman Islands - Îles Caïmanes										
1994										
Total	C	149	81	68	...	...	...	...	...	...
0 - 1	C	7	1	6	...	...	...	...	...	...
15 - 24	C	5	5	-	...	...	...	...	...	...
25 - 44	C	11	7	4	...	...	...	...	...	...
45 - 64	C	30	24	6	...	...	...	...	...	...
65+	C	96	44	52	...	...	...	...	...	...
Costa Rica										
2003										
Total	C	15 800	8 949	6 851	...	...	...	...	...	...
0 - 1	C	737	409	328	...	...	...	...	...	...
1 - 4	C	96	50	46	...	...	...	...	...	...
5 - 9	C	129	76	53	...	...	...	...	...	...
10 - 14	C	86	38	48	...	...	...	...	...	...
15 - 19	C	280	199	81	...	...	...	...	...	...
20 - 24	C	343	257	86	...	...	...	...	...	...
25 - 29	C	287	223	64	...	...	...	...	...	...
30 - 34	C	329	221	108	...	...	...	...	...	...
35 - 39	C	390	283	107	...	...	...	...	...	...
40 - 44	C	497	323	174	...	...	...	...	...	...
45 - 49	C	656	409	247	...	...	...	...	...	...
50 - 54	C	712	452	260	...	...	...	...	...	...
55 - 59	C	825	510	315	...	...	...	...	...	...
60 - 64	C	968	561	407	...	...	...	...	...	...
65 - 69	C	1 232	732	500	...	...	...	...	...	...
70 - 74	C	1 555	891	664	...	...	...	...	...	...
75 - 79	C	1 772	953	819	...	...	...	...	...	...
80 - 84	C	1 790	928	862	...	...	...	...	...	...
85+	C	3 077	1 404	1 673	...	...	...	...	...	...
Unknown - Inconnu	C	39	30	9	...	...	...	...	...	...

19. Deaths by age, sex and urban/rural residence: latest available year, 1994 - 2003
Décès selon l'âge, le sexe et la résidence, urbaine/rurale: dernière année disponible, 1994 - 2003 (continued — suite)

Continent, country or area, year and age (in years) / Continent, pays ou zone, année et âge (en années)	Code[1]	Total			Urban - Urbaine			Rural - Rurale		
		Both sexes - Les deux sexes	Male - Masculin	Female - Féminin	Both sexes - Les deux sexes	Male - Masculin	Female - Féminin	Both sexes - Les deux sexes	Male - Masculin	Female - Féminin
AMERICA, NORTH — AMERIQUE DU NORD										
Cuba[6]										
2002										
Total	C	73 882	40 477	33 405	60 167	32 173	27 994	13 697	8 292	5 405
0 - 1	C	922	555	367	719	421	298	203	134	69
1 - 4	C	223	127	96	175	101	74	48	26	22
5 - 9	C	187	115	72	131	80	51	55	35	20
10 - 14	C	211	136	75	157	106	51	54	30	24
15 - 19	C	401	283	118	303	212	91	98	71	27
20 - 24	C	444	301	143	329	222	107	114	79	35
25 - 29	C	809	549	260	591	400	191	218	149	69
30 - 34	C	1 103	700	403	843	532	311	259	167	92
35 - 39	C	1 567	945	622	1 242	748	494	323	196	127
40 - 44	C	1 748	1 062	686	1 350	813	537	396	247	149
45 - 49	C	2 226	1 316	910	1 775	1 035	740	450	281	169
50 - 54	C	3 254	1 933	1 321	2 652	1 583	1 069	602	350	252
55 - 59	C	4 402	2 615	1 787	3 655	2 177	1 478	746	437	309
60 - 64	C	5 482	3 263	2 219	4 504	2 684	1 820	977	578	399
65 - 69	C	6 480	3 676	2 804	5 363	3 050	2 313	1 115	624	491
70 - 74	C	8 131	4 702	3 429	6 689	3 781	2 908	1 440	919	521
75 - 79	C	9 305	5 095	4 210	7 697	4 121	3 576	1 608	974	634
80 - 84	C	10 338	5 362	4 976	8 501	4 244	4 257	1 836	1 117	719
85+	C	16 639	7 734	8 905	13 482	5 855	7 627	3 154	1 878	1 276
Unknown - Inconnu	C	10	8	2	9	8	1	1	-	1
2003										
Total	C	78 433	42 302	36 131	...	...	...	...	...	...
0 - 4	C	1 101	595	506	...	...	...	...	...	...
5 - 9	C	144	103	41	...	...	...	...	...	...
10 - 14	C	195	119	76	...	...	...	...	...	...
15 - 19	C	401	272	129	...	...	...	...	...	...
20 - 24	C	470	319	151	...	...	...	...	...	...
25 - 29	C	719	497	222	...	...	...	...	...	...
30 - 34	C	1 087	713	374	...	...	...	...	...	...
35 - 39	C	1 464	888	576	...	...	...	...	...	...
40 - 44	C	1 801	1 097	704	...	...	...	...	...	...
45 - 49	C	2 247	1 300	947	...	...	...	...	...	...
50 - 54	C	3 358	2 011	1 347	...	...	...	...	...	...
55 - 59	C	4 499	2 599	1 900	...	...	...	...	...	...
60 - 64	C	5 795	3 455	2 340	...	...	...	...	...	...
65 - 69	C	6 754	3 798	2 956	...	...	...	...	...	...
70+	C	48 398	24 536	23 862	...	...	...	...	...	...
Dominican Republic - République dominicaine										
1999										
Total	+U	26 956	15 624	11 332	...	...	...	...	...	...
0 - 1	+U	2 250	1 218	1 032	...	...	...	...	...	...
1 - 4	+U	477	273	204	...	...	...	...	...	...
5 - 9	+U	276	143	133	...	...	...	...	...	...
10 - 14	+U	259	138	121	...	...	...	...	...	...
15 - 19	+U	495	330	165	...	...	...	...	...	...
20 - 24	+U	823	570	253	...	...	...	...	...	...
25 - 29	+U	945	600	345	...	...	...	...	...	...
30 - 34	+U	981	651	330	...	...	...	...	...	...
35 - 39	+U	955	619	336	...	...	...	...	...	...
40 - 44	+U	954	615	339	...	...	...	...	...	...
45 - 49	+U	994	600	394	...	...	...	...	...	...
50 - 54	+U	1 175	719	456	...	...	...	...	...	...
55 - 59	+U	1 246	765	481	...	...	...	...	...	...
60 - 64	+U	1 644	985	659	...	...	...	...	...	...
65 - 69	+U	2 065	1 192	873	...	...	...	...	...	...
70 - 74	+U	2 090	1 233	857	...	...	...	...	...	...
75 - 79	+U	2 050	1 185	865	...	...	...	...	...	...
80 - 84	+U	1 726	956	770	...	...	...	...	...	...
85+	+U	2 944	1 440	1 504	...	...	...	...	...	...

19. Deaths by age, sex and urban/rural residence: latest available year, 1994 - 2003
Décès selon l'âge, le sexe et la résidence, urbaine/rurale: dernière année disponible, 1994 - 2003 (continued —
suite)

Continent, country or area, year and age (in years) / Continent, pays ou zone, année et âge (en années)	Code[1]	Total			Urban - Urbaine			Rural - Rurale		
		Both sexes - Les deux sexes	Male - Masculin	Female - Féminin	Both sexes - Les deux sexes	Male - Masculin	Female - Féminin	Both sexes - Les deux sexes	Male - Masculin	Female - Féminin
AMERICA, NORTH — AMERIQUE DU NORD										
Dominican Republic - République dominicaine										
1999										
Unknown - Inconnu	+U	2 607	1 392	1 215	...	...	...	...	...	...
El Salvador										
2003										
Total	C	29 377	17 040	12 337	20 856	11 916	8 940	8 521	5 124	3 397
0 - 1	C	1 322	747	575	847	475	372	475	272	203
1 - 4	C	477	263	214	282	160	122	195	103	92
5 - 9	C	218	126	92	135	73	62	83	53	30
10 - 14	C	265	163	102	181	107	74	84	56	28
15 - 19	C	756	562	194	538	408	130	218	154	64
20 - 24	C	1 194	957	237	866	698	168	328	259	69
25 - 29	C	1 252	1 012	240	907	740	167	345	272	73
30 - 34	C	1 056	827	229	754	592	162	302	235	67
35 - 39	C	1 155	845	310	839	606	233	316	239	77
40 - 44	C	1 109	766	343	798	565	233	311	201	110
45 - 49	C	1 215	814	401	849	578	271	366	236	130
50 - 54	C	1 329	817	512	958	583	375	371	234	137
55 - 59	C	1 512	950	562	1 061	656	405	451	294	157
60 - 64	C	1 867	1 025	842	1 348	738	610	519	287	232
65 - 69	C	2 156	1 173	983	1 509	792	717	647	381	266
70 - 74	C	2 475	1 298	1 177	1 740	896	844	735	402	333
75 - 79	C	2 735	1 384	1 351	1 980	991	989	755	393	362
80 - 84	C	2 792	1 321	1 471	1 977	895	1 082	815	426	389
85+	C	4 492	1 990	2 502	3 287	1 363	1 924	1 205	627	578
Greenland - Groenland										
2003										
Total	C	412	235	177	340	197	143	72	38	34
0 - 1	C	8	6	2	8	6	2	-	-	-
1 - 4	C	4	2	2	3	2	1	1	-	1
5 - 9	C	1	-	1	1	-	1	-	-	-
10 - 14	C	2	2	-	2	2	-	-	-	-
15 - 19	C	12	7	5	11	7	4	1	-	1
20 - 24	C	17	13	4	15	11	4	2	2	-
25 - 29	C	5	3	2	5	3	2	-	-	-
30 - 34	C	10	5	5	5	2	3	5	3	2
35 - 39	C	16	12	4	13	10	3	3	2	1
40 - 44	C	15	11	4	13	10	3	2	1	1
45 - 49	C	21	13	8	17	9	8	4	4	-
50 - 54	C	23	13	10	18	10	8	5	3	2
55 - 59	C	36	25	11	31	21	10	5	4	1
60 - 64	C	32	18	14	26	16	10	6	2	4
65 - 69	C	61	40	21	48	34	14	13	6	7
70 - 74	C	64	29	35	50	23	27	14	6	8
75 - 79	C	38	19	19	34	17	17	4	2	2
80 - 84	C	32	13	19	27	11	16	5	2	3
85+	C	15	4	11	13	3	10	2	1	1
Grenada - Grenade										
2000										
Total	+C	716	365	351	...	...	...	...	...	...
0 - 1	+C	27	10	17	...	...	...	...	...	...
1 - 4	+C	1	1	-	...	...	...	...	...	...
5 - 9	+C	1	1	-	...	...	...	...	...	...
10 - 14	+C	4	4	-	...	...	...	...	...	...
15 - 19	+C	8	2	6	...	...	...	...	...	...
20 - 24	+C	11	9	2	...	...	...	...	...	...
25 - 29	+C	17	13	4	...	...	...	...	...	...
30 - 34	+C	21	11	10	...	...	...	...	...	...
35 - 39	+C	17	7	10	...	...	...	...	...	...
40 - 44	+C	14	9	5	...	...	...	...	...	...
45 - 49	+C	21	13	8	...	...	...	...	...	...
50 - 54	+C	27	15	12	...	...	...	...	...	...

19. Deaths by age, sex and urban/rural residence: latest available year, 1994 - 2003
Décès selon l'âge, le sexe et la résidence, urbaine/rurale: dernière année disponible, 1994 - 2003 (continued — suite)

Continent, country or area, year and age (in years) / Continent, pays ou zone, année et âge (en années)	Code[1]	Total			Urban - Urbaine			Rural - Rurale		
		Both sexes - Les deux sexes	Male - Masculin	Female - Féminin	Both sexes - Les deux sexes	Male - Masculin	Female - Féminin	Both sexes - Les deux sexes	Male - Masculin	Female - Féminin
AMERICA, NORTH — AMERIQUE DU NORD										
Grenada - Grenade										
2000										
55 - 59	+C	24	17	7	...	...	...	...	...	...
60 - 64	+C	50	30	20	...	...	...	...	...	...
65 - 69	+C	61	35	26	...	...	...	...	...	...
70 - 74	+C	81	52	29	...	...	...	...	...	...
75 - 79	+C	96	50	46	...	...	...	...	...	...
80 - 84	+C	69	27	42	...	...	...	...	...	...
85 - 89	+C	84	34	50	...	...	...	...	...	...
90 - 94	+C	52	16	36	...	...	...	...	...	...
95 - 99	+C	24	8	16	...	...	...	...	...	...
100+	+C	6	1	5	...	...	...	...	...	...
Guadeloupe										
2003										
Total	C	2 636	1 405	1 231	...	...	...	...	...	...
0 - 1	C	56	34	22	...	...	...	...	...	...
1 - 4	C	9	5	4	...	...	...	...	...	...
5 - 9	C	5	4	1	...	...	...	...	...	...
10 - 14	C	5	3	2	...	...	...	...	...	...
15 - 19	C	21	18	3	...	...	...	...	...	...
20 - 24	C	23	19	4	...	...	...	...	...	...
25 - 29	C	23	17	6	...	...	...	...	...	...
30 - 34	C	39	31	8	...	...	...	...	...	...
35 - 39	C	60	40	20	...	...	...	...	...	...
40 - 44	C	76	47	29	...	...	...	...	...	...
45 - 49	C	102	71	31	...	...	...	...	...	...
50 - 54	C	112	87	25	...	...	...	...	...	...
55 - 59	C	128	85	43	...	...	...	...	...	...
60 - 64	C	177	96	81	...	...	...	...	...	...
65 - 69	C	213	126	87	...	...	...	...	...	...
70 - 74	C	257	141	116	...	...	...	...	...	...
75 - 79	C	316	180	136	...	...	...	...	...	...
80 - 84	C	356	185	171	...	...	...	...	...	...
85 - 89	C	329	124	205	...	...	...	...	...	...
90 - 94	C	205	65	140	...	...	...	...	...	...
95 - 99	C	96	19	77	...	...	...	...	...	...
100+	C	28	8	20	...	...	...	...	...	...
Guatemala										
1999										
Total	C	64 563	37 062	27 501	...	...	...	...	...	...
0 - 1	C	13 161	7 349	5 812	...	...	...	...	...	...
1 - 4	C	5 113	2 670	2 443	...	...	...	...	...	...
5 - 9	C	1 179	611	568	...	...	...	...	...	...
10 - 14	C	935	564	371	...	...	...	...	...	...
15 - 19	C	1 712	1 091	621	...	...	...	...	...	...
20 - 24	C	2 229	1 544	685	...	...	...	...	...	...
25 - 29	C	2 190	1 563	627	...	...	...	...	...	...
30 - 34	C	2 272	1 565	707	...	...	...	...	...	...
35 - 39	C	2 372	1 631	741	...	...	...	...	...	...
40 - 44	C	2 344	1 514	830	...	...	...	...	...	...
45 - 49	C	2 503	1 609	894	...	...	...	...	...	...
50 - 54	C	2 521	1 545	976	...	...	...	...	...	...
55 - 59	C	2 508	1 421	1 087	...	...	...	...	...	...
60 - 64	C	2 978	1 702	1 276	...	...	...	...	...	...
65 - 69	C	3 793	2 062	1 731	...	...	...	...	...	...
70 - 74	C	4 140	2 231	1 909	...	...	...	...	...	...
75 - 79	C	4 260	2 276	1 984	...	...	...	...	...	...
80 - 84	C	3 590	1 887	1 703	...	...	...	...	...	...
85 - 89	C	2 784	1 320	1 464	...	...	...	...	...	...
90 - 94	C	1 219	537	682	...	...	...	...	...	...
95+	C	541	213	328	...	...	...	...	...	...
Unknown - Inconnu	C	219	157	62	...	...	...	...	...	...

19. Deaths by age, sex and urban/rural residence: latest available year, 1994 - 2003
Décès selon l'âge, le sexe et la résidence, urbaine/rurale: dernière année disponible, 1994 - 2003 (continued — suite)

Continent, country or area, year and age (in years) / Continent, pays ou zone, année et âge (en années)	Code[1]	Total			Urban - Urbaine			Rural - Rurale		
		Both sexes - Les deux sexes	Male - Masculin	Female - Féminin	Both sexes - Les deux sexes	Male - Masculin	Female - Féminin	Both sexes - Les deux sexes	Male - Masculin	Female - Féminin
AMERICA, NORTH — AMERIQUE DU NORD										
Martinique[2]										
2003										
Total	C	2 725	1 421	1 304	...	...	...	...	...	...
0 - 1	C	33	14	19	...	...	...	...	...	...
1 - 4	C	8	3	5	...	...	...	...	...	...
5 - 9	C	6	3	3	...	...	...	...	...	...
10 - 14	C	5	4	1	...	...	...	...	...	...
15 - 19	C	20	16	4	...	...	...	...	...	...
20 - 24	C	20	14	6	...	...	...	...	...	...
25 - 29	C	21	16	5	...	...	...	...	...	...
30 - 34	C	40	29	11	...	...	...	...	...	...
35 - 39	C	42	27	15	...	...	...	...	...	...
40 - 44	C	53	36	17	...	...	...	...	...	...
45 - 49	C	81	50	31	...	...	...	...	...	...
50 - 54	C	91	55	36	...	...	...	...	...	...
55 - 59	C	97	58	39	...	...	...	...	...	...
60 - 64	C	137	84	53	...	...	...	...	...	...
65 - 69	C	189	118	71	...	...	...	...	...	...
70 - 74	C	267	156	111	...	...	...	...	...	...
75 - 79	C	360	213	147	...	...	...	...	...	...
80 - 84	C	439	221	218	...	...	...	...	...	...
85 - 89	C	386	178	208	...	...	...	...	...	...
90 - 94	C	273	85	188	...	...	...	...	...	...
95 - 99	C	129	35	94	...	...	...	...	...	...
100+	C	28	6	22	...	...	...	...	...	...
Mexico - Mexique[6,8]										
2003										
Total	C	472 140	261 680	210 096	354 633	192 724	161 689	109 167	63 064	46 032
0 - 1	C	33 355	19 008	14 236	25 073	14 246	10 737	7 714	4 440	3 257
1 - 4	C	6 700	3 655	3 036	4 317	2 382	1 930	2 279	1 217	1 058
5 - 9	C	3 149	1 819	1 328	2 140	1 227	911	943	561	382
10 - 14	C	3 808	2 263	1 541	2 563	1 532	1 030	1 180	692	485
15 - 19	C	7 332	5 023	2 304	5 117	3 503	1 611	2 007	1 380	625
20 - 24	C	9 562	6 959	2 597	6 900	5 018	1 876	2 344	1 706	638
25 - 29	C	11 173	8 234	2 929	8 221	6 027	2 192	2 536	1 889	644
30 - 34	C	12 400	8 946	3 449	9 077	6 535	2 539	2 818	2 004	814
35 - 39	C	13 915	9 770	4 139	10 222	7 131	3 085	3 134	2 177	957
40 - 44	C	16 515	10 940	5 571	12 315	8 073	4 239	3 666	2 447	1 219
45 - 49	C	19 804	12 585	7 213	15 095	9 456	5 635	4 242	2 763	1 477
50 - 54	C	23 425	13 947	9 467	18 147	10 679	7 460	4 804	2 907	1 894
55 - 59	C	27 949	16 219	11 714	21 614	12 429	9 175	5 889	3 457	2 429
60 - 64	C	33 642	18 700	14 930	25 776	14 137	11 630	7 345	4 194	3 149
65 - 69	C	39 536	21 496	18 021	30 509	16 349	14 146	8 545	4 843	3 697
70 - 74	C	44 905	23 919	20 963	34 333	17 911	16 407	10 100	5 696	4 396
75 - 79	C	45 753	23 572	22 165	35 062	17 563	17 488	10 269	5 749	4 515
80 - 84	C	44 176	21 851	22 312	33 312	15 921	17 383	10 508	5 729	4 775
85 - 89	C	33 454	15 193	18 248	25 288	10 934	14 345	7 927	4 130	3 794
90 - 94	C	24 640	10 414	14 225	18 179	7 309	10 870	6 292	3 029	3 262
95 - 99	C	10 709	4 110	6 595	7 765	2 829	4 936	2 873	1 250	1 619
100+	C	4 042	1 493	2 548	2 681	939	1 741	1 332	539	793
Unknown - Inconnu	C	2 196	1 564	565	927	594	323	420	265	153
Montserrat										
1999										
Total	+C	59	39	20	...	...	...	...	...	...
0 - 1	+C	-	-	-	...	...	...	...	...	...
1 - 4	+C	-	-	-	...	...	...	...	...	...
5 - 9	+C	-	-	-	...	...	...	...	...	...
10 - 14	+C	-	-	-	...	...	...	...	...	...
15 - 19	+C	1	-	1	...	...	...	...	...	...
20 - 24	+C	-	-	-	...	...	...	...	...	...
25 - 29	+C	-	-	-	...	...	...	...	...	...
30 - 34	+C	-	-	-	...	...	...	...	...	...
35 - 39	+C	-	-	-	...	...	...	...	...	...

Continent, country or area, year and age (in years) / Continent, pays ou zone, année et âge (en années)	Code[1]	Total			Urban - Urbaine			Rural - Rurale		
		Both sexes - Les deux sexes	Male - Masculin	Female - Féminin	Both sexes - Les deux sexes	Male - Masculin	Female - Féminin	Both sexes - Les deux sexes	Male - Masculin	Female - Féminin
AMERICA, NORTH — AMERIQUE DU NORD										
Montserrat										
1999										
40 - 44	+C	-	-	-	...	...	...	...	...	...
45 - 49	+C	1	1	-	...	...	...	...	...	...
50 - 54	+C	1	1	-	...	...	...	...	...	...
55 - 59	+C	2	2	-	...	...	...	...	...	...
60 - 64	+C	3	2	1	...	...	...	...	...	...
65 - 69	+C	3	2	1	...	...	...	...	...	...
70 - 74	+C	7	6	1	...	...	...	...	...	...
75 - 79	+C	5	4	1	...	...	...	...	...	...
80 - 84	+C	15	8	7	...	...	...	...	...	...
85 - 89	+C	11	5	6	...	...	...	...	...	...
90+	+C	9	7	2	...	...	...	...	...	...
Unknown - Inconnu	+C	1	1	-	...	...	...	...	...	...
Nicaragua										
2003										
Total	+U	14 630	8 291	6 339	9 753	5 347	4 406	4 877	2 944	1 933
0 - 1	+U	1 989	1 119	870	1 086	593	493	903	526	377
1 - 4	+U	413	237	176	183	100	83	230	137	93
5 - 9	+U	167	99	68	83	55	28	84	44	40
10 - 14	+U	178	113	65	100	65	35	78	48	30
15 - 19	+U	399	267	132	228	161	67	171	106	65
20 - 24	+U	488	347	141	303	220	83	185	127	58
25 - 29	+U	420	297	123	267	194	73	153	103	50
30 - 34	+U	405	286	119	258	178	80	147	108	39
35 - 30	+U	485	311	174	317	205	112	168	106	62
40 - 44	+U	531	367	164	360	247	113	171	120	51
45 - 49	+U	680	430	250	491	303	188	189	127	62
50 - 54	+U	660	407	253	458	271	187	202	136	66
55 - 59	+U	755	445	310	547	317	230	208	128	80
60 - 64	+U	816	441	375	552	300	252	264	141	123
65 - 69	+U	905	484	421	632	318	314	273	166	107
70 - 74	+U	1 140	623	517	825	437	388	315	186	129
75 - 79	+U	1 186	640	546	874	440	434	312	200	112
80 - 84	+U	1 113	540	573	812	375	437	301	165	136
85 - 89	+U	917	445	472	649	296	353	268	149	119
90 - 94	+U	570	233	337	435	165	270	135	68	67
95+	+U	413	160	253	293	107	186	120	53	67
Panama										
1999										
Total	U	11 938	6 978	4 960	7 108	4 042	3 066	4 830	2 936	1 894
0 - 1	U	1 005	571	434	490	284	206	515	287	228
1 - 4	U	302	157	145	81	42	39	221	115	106
5 - 9	U	122	76	46	49	25	24	73	51	22
10 - 14	U	95	58	37	30	17	13	65	41	24
15 - 19	U	222	154	68	117	84	33	105	70	35
20 - 24	U	302	224	78	159	119	40	143	105	38
25 - 29	U	332	246	86	190	139	51	142	107	35
30 - 34	U	369	261	108	225	163	62	144	98	46
35 - 39	U	329	222	107	197	128	69	132	94	38
40 - 44	U	396	260	136	239	158	81	157	102	55
45 - 49	U	411	272	139	265	178	87	146	94	52
50 - 54	U	496	329	167	301	210	91	195	119	76
55 - 59	U	514	322	192	319	198	121	195	124	71
60 - 64	U	663	405	258	413	251	162	250	154	96
65 - 69	U	817	489	328	468	268	200	349	221	128
70 - 74	U	1 012	594	418	620	360	260	392	234	158
75 - 79	U	1 255	693	562	796	415	381	459	278	181
80 - 84	U	1 324	704	620	860	449	411	464	255	209
85 - 89	U	1 066	548	518	690	328	362	376	220	156
90 - 94	U	553	241	312	376	142	234	177	99	78
95 - 99	U	210	75	135	141	45	96	69	30	39
100+	U	49	24	25	38	17	21	11	7	4

Continent, country or area, year and age (in years) — Continent, pays ou zone, année et âge (en années)	Code[1]	Total			Urban - Urbaine			Rural - Rurale		
		Both sexes - Les deux sexes	Male - Masculin	Female - Féminin	Both sexes - Les deux sexes	Male - Masculin	Female - Féminin	Both sexes - Les deux sexes	Male - Masculin	Female - Féminin
AMERICA, NORTH — AMERIQUE DU NORD										
Panama										
1999										
Unknown - Inconnu	U	*94*	*53*	*41*	*44*	*22*	*22*	*50*	*31*	*19*
Puerto Rico - Porto Rico[6]										
2003										
Total	C	28 356	15 758	12 598	15 038	8 095	6 943	13 283	7 633	5 650
0 - 1	C	498	288	210	294	168	126	198	114	84
1 - 4	C	47	26	21	27	15	12	19	10	9
5 - 9	C	32	16	16	13	6	7	19	10	9
10 - 14	C	47	31	16	16	11	5	31	20	11
15 - 19	C	201	161	40	106	89	17	95	72	23
20 - 24	C	419	359	60	238	204	34	179	153	26
25 - 29	C	414	345	69	228	188	40	185	156	29
30 - 34	C	404	304	100	217	163	54	187	141	46
35 - 39	C	526	382	144	275	191	84	249	189	60
40 - 44	C	661	453	208	341	232	109	320	221	99
45 - 49	C	898	580	318	471	302	169	426	277	149
50 - 54	C	1 221	781	440	613	378	235	608	403	205
55 - 59	C	1 627	1 035	592	807	518	289	819	517	302
60 - 64	C	2 006	1 206	800	1 027	614	413	979	592	387
65 - 69	C	2 311	1 410	901	1 165	703	462	1 145	706	439
70 - 74	C	2 869	1 589	1 280	1 507	833	674	1 360	754	606
75 - 79	C	3 450	1 894	1 556	1 846	975	871	1 602	917	685
80 - 84	C	3 882	1 956	1 926	2 120	1 016	1 104	1 761	939	822
85+	C	6 822	2 924	3 898	3 720	1 482	2 238	3 099	1 440	1 659
Unknown - Inconnu	C	21	18	3	7	7	-	2	2	-
Saint Kitts and Nevis - Saint-Kitts-et-Nevis										
2001										
Total	+C	352	181	171	...	...	...	...	...	...
0 - 1	+C	10	3	7	...	...	...	...	...	...
1 - 4	+C	6	1	5	...	...	...	...	...	...
5 - 9	+C	3	3	-	...	...	...	...	...	...
10 - 14	+C	2	1	1	...	...	...	...	...	...
15 - 19	+C	2	1	1	...	...	...	...	...	...
20 - 24	+C	2	1	1	...	...	...	...	...	...
25 - 29	+C	6	4	2	...	...	...	...	...	...
30 - 34	+C	5	3	2	...	...	...	...	...	...
35 - 39	+C	8	6	2	...	...	...	...	...	...
40 - 44	+C	9	6	3	...	...	...	...	...	...
45 - 49	+C	22	16	6	...	...	...	...	...	...
50 - 54	+C	9	4	5	...	...	...	...	...	...
55 - 59	+C	12	8	4	...	...	...	...	...	...
60 - 64	+C	13	9	4	...	...	...	...	...	...
65 - 69	C	19	9	10	...	...	...	...	...	...
70 - 74	+C	29	17	12	...	...	...	...	...	...
75 - 79	+C	63	31	32	...	...	...	...	...	...
80 - 84	+C	56	25	31	...	...	...	...	...	...
85+	+C	76	33	43	...	...	...	...	...	...
Saint Lucia - Sainte-Lucie										
2002										
Total	C	957	511	446	...	...	...	...	...	...
0 - 1	C	36	17	19	...	...	...	...	...	...
1 - 4	C	6	2	4	...	...	...	...	...	...
5 - 9	C	3	2	1	...	...	...	...	...	...
10 - 14	C	8	4	4	...	...	...	...	...	...
15 - 19	C	7	6	1	...	...	...	...	...	...
20 - 24	C	22	12	10	...	...	...	...	...	...
25 - 29	C	23	17	6	...	...	...	...	...	...
30 - 34	C	22	17	5	...	...	...	...	...	...
35 - 39	C	27	17	10	...	...	...	...	...	...
40 - 44	C	30	17	13	...	...	...	...	...	...
45 - 49	C	46	30	16	...	...	...	...	...	...

Continent, country or area, year and age (in years) / Continent, pays ou zone, année et âge (en années)	Code[1]	Total			Urban - Urbaine			Rural - Rurale		
		Both sexes - Les deux sexes	Male - Masculin	Female - Féminin	Both sexes - Les deux sexes	Male - Masculin	Female - Féminin	Both sexes - Les deux sexes	Male - Masculin	Female - Féminin
AMERICA, NORTH — AMERIQUE DU NORD										
Saint Lucia - Sainte-Lucie										
2002										
50 - 54	C	44	30	14	...	...	...	...	...	...
55 - 59	C	53	34	19	...	...	...	...	...	...
60 - 64	C	55	27	28	...	...	...	...	...	...
65 - 69	C	61	30	31	...	...	...	...	...	...
70 - 74	C	101	59	42	...	...	...	...	...	...
75 - 79	C	117	65	52	...	...	...	...	...	...
80 - 84	C	110	55	55	...	...	...	...	...	...
85+	C	168	65	103	...	...	...	...	...	...
Unknown - Inconnu	C	18	5	13	...	...	...	...	...	...
Saint Vincent and the Grenadines - Saint Vincent-et-les Grenadines										
2002										
Total	+C	770	377	393	...	...	...	...	...	...
0 - 1	+C	36	22	14	...	...	...	...	...	...
1 - 4	+C	4	1	3	...	...	...	...	...	...
5 - 9	+C	6	3	3	...	...	...	...	...	...
10 - 14	+C	7	4	3	...	...	...	...	...	...
15 - 19	+C	8	6	2	...	...	...	...	...	...
20 - 24	+C	16	11	5	...	...	...	...	...	...
25 - 29	+C	13	7	6	...	...	...	...	...	...
30 - 34	+C	23	12	11	...	...	...	...	...	...
35 - 39	+C	32	20	12	...	...	...	...	...	...
40 - 44	+C	19	15	4	...	...	...	...	...	...
45 - 49	+C	28	16	12	...	...	...	...	...	...
50 - 54	+C	41	23	18	...	...	...	...	...	...
55 - 59	+C	39	20	19	...	...	...	...	...	...
60 - 64	+C	49	23	26	...	...	...	...	...	...
65 - 69	+C	50	22	28	...	...	...	...	...	...
70 - 74	+C	74	43	31	...	...	...	...	...	...
75 - 79	+C	98	47	51	...	...	...	...	...	...
80 - 84	+C	90	35	55	...	...	...	...	...	...
85+	+C	132	46	86	...	...	...	...	...	...
Unknown - Inconnu	+C	5	1	4	...	...	...	...	...	...
Trinidad and Tobago - Trinité-et-Tobago										
1997										
Total	C	9 157	5 034	4 123	...	...	...	...	...	...
0 - 1	C	316	170	146	...	...	...	...	...	...
1 - 4	C	58	32	26	...	...	...	...	...	...
5 - 9	C	38	24	14	...	...	...	...	...	...
10 - 14	C	48	25	23	...	...	...	...	...	...
15 - 19	C	92	53	39	...	...	...	...	...	...
20 - 24	C	157	105	52	...	...	...	...	...	...
25 - 29	C	165	103	62	...	...	...	...	...	...
30 - 34	C	261	163	98	...	...	...	...	...	...
35 - 39	C	303	184	119	...	...	...	...	...	...
40 - 44	C	350	219	131	...	...	...	...	...	...
45 - 49	C	399	236	163	...	...	...	...	...	...
50 - 54	C	480	296	184	...	...	...	...	...	...
55 - 59	C	600	347	253	...	...	...	...	...	...
60 - 64	C	755	398	357	...	...	...	...	...	...
65 - 69	C	883	475	408	...	...	...	...	...	...
70 - 74	C	995	577	418	...	...	...	...	...	...
75 - 79	C	1 083	606	477	...	...	...	...	...	...
80 - 84	C	971	510	461	...	...	...	...	...	...
85 - 89	C	727	326	401	...	...	...	...	...	...
90 - 94	C	323	134	109	...	...	...	...	...	...
95 - 99	C	126	45	81	...	...	...	...	...	...
100+	C	25	5	20	...	...	...	...	...	...
Unknown - Inconnu	C	2	1	1	...	...	...	...	...	...

19. Deaths by age, sex and urban/rural residence: latest available year, 1994 - 2003
Décès selon l'âge, le sexe et la résidence, urbaine/rurale: dernière année disponible, 1994 - 2003 (continued — suite)

Continent, country or area, year and age (in years) / Continent, pays ou zone, année et âge (en années)	Code[1]	Total			Urban - Urbaine			Rural - Rurale		
		Both sexes - Les deux sexes	Male - Masculin	Female - Féminin	Both sexes - Les deux sexes	Male - Masculin	Female - Féminin	Both sexes - Les deux sexes	Male - Masculin	Female - Féminin
AMERICA, NORTH — AMERIQUE DU NORD										
Trinidad and Tobago - Trinité-et-Tobago										
1999										
Total	C	10 014	...	...	...	...	...	...	...	...
0 - 1	C	322	...	...	...	...	...	...	...	...
1 - 14	C	150	...	...	...	...	...	...	...	...
15 - 24	C	267	...	...	...	...	...	...	...	...
25 - 49	C	1 632	...	...	...	...	...	...	...	...
50 - 64	C	2 113	...	...	...	...	...	...	...	...
65+	C	5 530	...	...	...	...	...	...	...	...
Turks Caicos Islands - Îles Turques et Caïques										
2003										
Total	C	73	34	39	...	...	...	...	...	...
0 - 1	C	9	5	4	...	...	...	...	...	...
1 - 4	C	-	-	-	...	...	...	...	...	...
5 - 9	C	2	1	1	...	...	...	...	...	...
10 - 14	C	-	-	-	...	...	...	...	...	...
15 - 19	C	-	-	-	...	...	...	...	...	...
20 - 24	C	1	-	1	...	...	...	...	...	...
25 - 29	C	2	2	-	...	...	...	...	...	...
30 - 34	C	3	-	3	...	...	...	...	...	...
35 - 39	C	5	3	2	...	...	...	...	...	...
40 - 44	C	4	-	4	...	...	...	...	...	...
45 - 49	C	6	4	2	...	...	...	...	...	...
50 - 54	C	2	1	1	...	...	...	...	...	...
55 - 59	C	3	2	1	...	...	...	...	...	...
60 - 64	C	5	4	1	...	...	...	...	...	...
65 - 69	C	5	3	2	...	...	...	...	...	...
70 - 74	C	3	-	3	...	...	...	...	...	...
75 - 79	C	3	-	3	...	...	...	...	...	...
80 - 84	C	5	2	3	...	...	...	...	...	...
85+	C	14	6	8	...	...	...	...	...	...
Unknown - Inconnu	C	1	1	-	...	...	...	...	...	...
United States - États-Unis										
2003										
Total	C	2 443 908	1 198 454	1 245 454	...	...	...	...	...	...
0 - 1	C	28 428	16 131	12 297	...	...	...	...	...	...
1 - 4	C	4 905	2 807	2 098	...	...	...	...	...	...
5 - 14	C	6 903	4 116	2 787	...	...	...	...	...	...
15 - 24	C	33 050	24 232	8 818	...	...	...	...	...	...
25 - 34	C	40 731	28 216	12 515	...	...	...	...	...	...
35 - 44	C	88 433	55 839	32 594	...	...	...	...	...	...
45 - 54	C	175 591	109 830	65 761	...	...	...	...	...	...
55 - 64	C	261 505	155 748	105 757	...	...	...	...	...	...
65 - 74	C	413 227	231 375	181 852	...	...	...	...	...	...
75 - 84	C	702 641	341 875	360 766	...	...	...	...	...	...
85+	C	687 959	227 932	460 027	...	...	...	...	...	...
Unknown - Inconnu	C	535	353	182	...	...	...	...	...	...
AMERICA, SOUTH — AMERIQUE DU SUD										
Argentina - Argentine[8]										
1998										
Total	C	280 180	153 747	126 319	...	...	...	...	...	...
0 - 1	C	13 082	7 472	5 576	...	...	...	...	...	...
1 - 4	C	2 285	1 287	996	...	...	...	...	...	...
5 - 9	C	1 002	604	395	...	...	...	...	...	...
10 - 14	C	1 045	627	418	...	...	...	...	...	...
15 - 19	C	2 639	1 814	823	...	...	...	...	...	...
20 - 24	C	3 225	2 344	879	...	...	...	...	...	...
25 - 29	C	3 300	2 340	959	...	...	...	...	...	...

19. Deaths by age, sex and urban/rural residence: latest available year, 1994 - 2003
Décès selon l'âge, le sexe et la résidence, urbaine/rurale: dernière année disponible, 1994 - 2003 (continued — suite)

Continent, country or area, year and age (in years) / Continent, pays ou zone, année et âge (en années)	Code[1]	Total			Urban - Urbaine			Rural - Rurale		
		Both sexes - Les deux sexes	Male - Masculin	Female - Féminin	Both sexes - Les deux sexes	Male - Masculin	Female - Féminin	Both sexes - Les deux sexes	Male - Masculin	Female - Féminin
AMERICA, SOUTH — AMERIQUE DU SUD										
Argentina - Argentine[8]										
1998										
30 - 34	C	3 479	2 349	1 129	...	...	...	...	...	...
35 - 39	C	4 053	2 609	1 442	...	...	...	...	...	...
40 - 44	C	5 719	3 703	2 013	...	...	...	...	...	...
45 - 49	C	8 581	5 504	3 076	...	...	...	...	...	...
50 - 54	C	11 692	7 710	3 976	...	...	...	...	...	...
55 - 59	C	15 084	10 079	5 002	...	...	...	...	...	...
60 - 64	C	19 791	13 010	6 773	...	...	...	...	...	...
65 - 69	C	27 471	17 604	9 862	...	...	...	...	...	...
70 - 74	C	33 324	20 030	13 287	...	...	...	...	...	...
75 - 79	C	36 600	19 638	16 957	...	...	...	...	...	...
80 - 84	C	36 107	16 553	19 552	...	...	...	...	...	...
85+	C	50 913	17 914	32 993	...	...	...	...	...	...
Unknown - Inconnu	C	788	556	211	...	...	...	...	...	...
Brazil - Brésil[11]										
2003										
Total	U	977 717	572 622	405 095	...	...	...	...	...	...
0 - 1	U	43 970	24 932	19 038	...	...	...	...	...	...
1 - 4	U	8 965	4 989	3 976	...	...	...	...	...	...
5 - 9	U	4 852	2 873	1 979	...	...	...	...	...	...
10 - 14	U	5 679	3 539	2 140	...	...	...	...	...	...
15 - 19	U	18 674	14 583	4 091	...	...	...	...	...	...
20 - 24	U	27 452	22 444	5 008	...	...	...	...	...	...
25 - 29	U	26 166	20 344	5 822	...	...	...	...	...	...
30 - 34	U	27 258	20 264	6 994	...	...	...	...	...	...
35 - 39	U	32 474	23 023	9 451	...	...	...	...	...	...
40 - 44	U	39 862	26 945	12 917	...	...	...	...	...	...
45 - 49	U	48 366	31 664	16 702	...	...	...	...	...	...
50 - 54	U	54 928	35 257	19 671	...	...	...	...	...	...
55 - 59	U	61 892	38 610	23 282	...	...	...	...	...	...
60 - 64	U	73 022	44 591	28 431	...	...	...	...	...	...
65 - 69	U	85 519	50 282	35 237	...	...	...	...	...	...
70 - 74	U	98 426	55 595	42 831	...	...	...	...	...	...
75 - 79	U	102 236	54 575	47 661	...	...	...	...	...	...
80 - 84	U	89 219	43 768	45 451	...	...	...	...	...	...
85 - 89	U	69 606	30 252	39 354	...	...	...	...	...	...
90 - 94	U	38 440	15 082	23 358	...	...	...	...	...	...
95 - 99	U	14 312	5 020	9 292	...	...	...	...	...	...
100+	U	2 357	733	1 624	...	...	...	...	...	...
Unknown - Inconnu	U	4 042	3 257	785	...	...	...	...	...	...
Chile - Chili										
2003										
Total	C	83 672	45 482	38 190	72 647	38 782	33 865	11 025	6 700	4 325
0 - 1	C	1 935	1 061	874	1 691	936	755	244	125	119
1 - 4	C	396	218	178	329	179	150	67	39	28
5 - 9	C	250	147	103	207	120	87	43	27	16
10 - 14	C	318	205	113	265	170	95	53	35	18
15 - 19	C	616	460	156	502	373	129	114	87	27
20 - 24	C	999	790	209	838	661	177	161	129	32
25 - 29	C	1 051	827	224	903	713	190	148	114	34
30 - 34	C	1 300	981	319	1 114	837	277	186	144	42
35 - 39	C	1 690	1 223	467	1 418	1 012	406	272	211	61
40 - 44	C	2 233	1 489	744	1 901	1 241	660	332	248	84
45 - 49	C	2 845	1 833	1 012	2 491	1 582	909	354	251	103
50 - 54	C	3 631	2 287	1 344	3 187	1 992	1 195	444	295	149
55 - 59	C	4 812	3 038	1 774	4 224	2 644	1 580	588	394	194
60 - 64	C	6 177	3 783	2 394	5 420	3 289	2 131	757	494	263
65 - 69	C	7 299	4 410	2 889	6 324	3 775	2 549	975	635	340
70 - 74	C	10 073	5 816	4 257	8 768	4 968	3 800	1 305	848	457
75 - 79	C	10 875	5 884	4 991	9 418	5 003	4 415	1 457	881	576
80 - 84	C	10 676	5 049	5 627	9 255	4 259	4 996	1 421	790	631
85 - 89	C	9 082	3 713	5 369	7 887	3 123	4 764	1 195	590	605

19. Deaths by age, sex and urban/rural residence: latest available year, 1994 - 2003
Décès selon l'âge, le sexe et la résidence, urbaine/rurale: dernière année disponible, 1994 - 2003 (continued — suite)

Continent, country or area, year and age (in years) Continent, pays ou zone, année et âge (en années)	Code[1]	Total			Urban - Urbaine			Rural - Rurale		
		Both sexes - Les deux sexes	Male - Masculin	Female - Féminin	Both sexes - Les deux sexes	Male - Masculin	Female - Féminin	Both sexes - Les deux sexes	Male - Masculin	Female - Féminin
AMERICA, SOUTH — AMERIQUE DU SUD										
Chile - Chili										
2003										
90 - 94	C	5 383	1 756	3 627	4 691	1 466	3 225	692	290	402
95 - 99	C	1 720	446	1 274	1 538	385	1 153	182	61	121
100+	C	284	63	221	253	51	202	31	12	19
Unknown - Inconnu	C	27	3	24	23	3	20	4	-	4
Colombia - Colombie[6,8]										
2003										
Total	U	189 072	111 366	77 652	142 575	80 922	61 643	37 138	23 404	13 723
0 - 1	U	11 944	6 758	5 179	8 621	4 876	3 741	2 661	1 520	1 140
1 - 4	U	2 775	1 505	1 270	1 773	958	815	906	493	413
5 - 9	U	1 351	766	585	869	505	364	408	216	192
10 - 14	U	1 539	941	597	1 006	619	387	457	276	181
15 - 19	U	5 386	4 142	1 243	3 648	2 835	813	1 195	878	317
20 - 24	U	8 621	7 219	1 395	5 751	4 795	956	1 822	1 508	313
25 - 29	U	7 457	6 132	1 320	4 825	3 905	918	1 595	1 311	283
30 - 34	U	6 824	5 421	1 397	4 567	3 530	1 036	1 495	1 202	291
35 - 39	U	6 750	5 061	1 688	4 637	3 358	1 279	1 493	1 152	340
40 - 44	U	6 845	4 651	2 190	5 004	3 267	1 736	1 401	1 013	386
45 - 49	U	7 209	4 540	2 667	5 467	3 308	2 158	1 372	941	431
50 - 54	U	8 002	4 797	3 204	6 086	3 511	2 574	1 573	1 034	539
55 - 59	U	8 779	5 073	3 706	6 890	3 857	3 033	1 596	1 012	584
60 - 64	U	11 435	6 396	5 038	8 936	4 880	4 056	2 170	1 312	858
65 - 69	U	14 214	7 863	6 351	11 150	6 065	5 085	2 710	1 568	1 142
70 - 74	U	18 434	9 971	8 463	14 529	7 668	6 861	3 435	2 015	1 420
75 - 79	U	18 583	9 830	8 753	14 735	7 609	7 126	3 416	1 971	1 445
80 - 84	U	17 762	8 683	9 079	14 214	6 732	7 482	3 217	1 767	1 450
85 - 89	U	13 297	6 161	7 136	10 760	4 831	5 929	2 285	1 206	1 079
90 - 94	U	7 060	3 011	4 049	5 829	2 414	3 415	1 133	557	576
95 - 99	U	1 777	714	1 063	1 481	565	916	271	136	135
100+	U	1 094	371	723	933	308	625	149	56	93
Unknown - Inconnu	U	1 934	1 360	556	864	526	338	378	260	115
Ecuador - Équateur[12]										
2003										
Total	U	53 521	30 366	23 155	40 585	23 172	17 413	12 936	7 194	5 742
0 - 1	U	3 985	2 195	1 790	3 085	1 717	1 368	900	478	422
1 - 4	U	1 800	996	804	1 144	645	499	656	351	305
5 - 14	U	1 364	787	577	987	560	427	377	227	150
15 - 49	U	12 089	8 213	3 876	9 266	6 417	2 849	2 823	1 796	1 027
50 - 64	U	8 053	4 821	3 232	6 241	3 737	2 504	1 812	1 084	728
65+	U	26 173	13 317	12 856	19 825	10 071	9 754	6 348	3 246	3 102
Unknown - Inconnu	U	57	37	20	37	25	12	20	12	8
French Guiana - Guyane française[2]										
2003										
Total	C	692	435	257	...	...	...	...	...	...
0 - 1	C	58	32	26	...	...	...	...	...	...
1 - 4	C	17	10	7	...	...	...	...	...	...
5 - 9	C	3	1	2	...	...	...	...	...	...
10 - 14	C	6	5	1	...	...	...	...	...	...
15 - 19	C	15	10	5	...	...	...	...	...	...
20 - 24	C	17	11	6	...	...	...	...	...	...
25 - 29	C	31	25	6	...	...	...	...	...	...
30 - 34	C	26	18	8	...	...	...	...	...	...
35 - 39	C	38	28	10	...	...	...	...	...	...
40 - 44	C	34	24	10	...	...	...	...	...	...
45 - 49	C	38	26	12	...	...	...	...	...	...
50 - 54	C	44	33	11	...	...	...	...	...	...
55 - 59	C	36	25	11	...	...	...	...	...	...
60 - 64	C	45	29	16	...	...	...	...	...	...
65 - 69	C	43	28	15	...	...	...	...	...	...
70 - 74	C	47	36	11	...	...	...	...	...	...
75 - 79	C	50	37	13	...	...	...	...	...	...

Continent, country or area, year and age (in years) / Continent, pays ou zone, année et âge (en années)	Code[1]	Total			Urban - Urbaine			Rural - Rurale		
		Both sexes - Les deux sexes	Male - Masculin	Female - Féminin	Both sexes - Les deux sexes	Male - Masculin	Female - Féminin	Both sexes - Les deux sexes	Male - Masculin	Female - Féminin
AMERICA, SOUTH — AMERIQUE DU SUD										
French Guiana - Guyane française[2]										
2003										
80 - 84	C	49	19	30	...	...	...	...	...	...
85 - 89	C	53	24	29	...	...	...	...	...	...
90 - 94	C	23	8	15	...	...	...	...	...	...
95 - 99	C	15	4	11	...	...	...	...	...	...
100+	C	4	2	2	...	...	...	...	...	...
Paraguay[8,13]										
2001										
Total	I	38 514	20 073	15 948	23 907	12 238	10 148	14 607	7 835	5 800
0 - 1	I	3 898	2 219	1 662	2 076	1 156	911	1 822	1 063	751
1 - 4	I	1 666	939	720	745	419	322	921	520	398
5 - 9	I	554	308	242	289	163	123	265	145	119
10 - 14	I	446	255	189	213	104	108	233	151	81
15 - 19	I	1 019	640	379	582	380	202	437	260	177
20 - 24	I	1 208	863	340	675	488	183	533	375	157
25 - 29	I	1 061	754	302	641	461	177	420	293	125
30 - 34	I	927	626	297	581	401	177	346	225	120
35 - 39	I	1 115	664	449	681	405	275	434	259	174
40 - 44	I	1 222	730	489	781	465	314	441	265	175
45 - 49	I	1 550	929	619	1 035	632	402	515	297	217
50 - 54	I	1 765	999	763	1 176	658	516	589	341	247
55 - 59	I	1 703	997	702	1 134	668	463	569	329	239
60 - 64	I	2 378	1 333	1 039	1 560	882	674	818	451	365
65 - 69	I	2 373	1 278	1 093	1 622	848	774	751	430	319
70 - 74	I	2 996	1 744	1 246	2 026	1 162	860	970	582	386
75 - 79	I	2 793	1 483	1 300	1 740	877	860	1 053	606	440
80 - 84	I	2 846	1 377	1 465	1 889	876	1 010	957	501	455
85 - 89	I	2 220	1 006	1 209	1 485	652	831	735	354	378
90+	I	1 912	670	1 227	1 236	394	835	676	276	392
Unknown - Inconnu	I	2 862	259	216	1 740	147	131	1 122	112	85
Peru - Pérou[11]										
2001										
Total	+U	79 871	42 702	37 169	...	...	...	...	...	...
0 - 1	+U	6 559	3 632	2 927	...	...	...	...	...	...
1 - 4	+U	2 241	1 182	1 059	...	...	...	...	...	...
5 - 9	+U	997	582	415	...	...	...	...	...	...
10 - 14	+U	849	495	354	...	...	...	...	...	...
15 - 19	+U	1 491	883	608	...	...	...	...	...	...
20 - 24	+U	1 980	1 210	770	...	...	...	...	...	...
25 - 29	+U	2 107	1 372	735	...	...	...	...	...	...
30 - 34	+U	2 157	1 394	763	...	...	...	...	...	...
35 - 39	+U	2 371	1 457	914	...	...	...	...	...	...
40 - 44	+U	2 542	1 487	1 055	...	...	...	...	...	...
45 - 49	+U	2 817	1 561	1 256	...	...	...	...	...	...
50 - 54	+U	3 372	1 850	1 522	...	...	...	...	...	...
55 - 59	+U	3 626	2 016	1 610	...	...	...	...	...	...
60 - 64	+U	4 783	2 643	2 140	...	...	...	...	...	...
65 - 69	+U	5 827	3 220	2 607	...	...	...	...	...	...
70 - 74	+U	7 185	3 923	3 262	...	...	...	...	...	...
75 - 79	+U	7 690	4 157	3 533	...	...	...	...	...	...
80 - 84	+U	7 722	3 888	3 834	...	...	...	...	...	...
85 - 89	+U	6 464	2 971	3 493	...	...	...	...	...	...
90 - 94	+U	3 999	1 655	2 344	...	...	...	...	...	...
95+	+U	2 677	906	1 771	...	...	...	...	...	...
Unknown - Inconnu	+U	415	218	197	...	...	...	...	...	...
Suriname[6,14]										
2002										
Total	C	3 125	1 783	1 342	2 218	1 266	952	871	493	378
0 - 1	C	148	84	64	112	68	44	34	14	20
1 - 4	C	53	27	26	31	17	14	22	10	12
5 - 9	C	10	5	5	7	2	5	3	3	-

Continent, country or area, year and age (in years) / Continent, pays ou zone, année et âge (en années)	Code[1]	Total			Urban - Urbaine			Rural - Rurale		
		Both sexes - Les deux sexes	Male - Masculin	Female - Féminin	Both sexes - Les deux sexes	Male - Masculin	Female - Féminin	Both sexes - Les deux sexes	Male - Masculin	Female - Féminin
AMERICA, SOUTH — AMERIQUE DU SUD										
Suriname[6,14]										
2002										
10 - 14	C	23	12	11	17	10	7	6	2	4
15 - 19	C	37	23	14	23	12	11	14	11	3
20 - 24	C	74	44	30	44	27	17	29	17	12
25 - 29	C	70	49	21	52	38	14	16	10	6
30 - 34	C	105	73	32	68	50	18	37	23	14
35 - 39	C	127	88	39	94	66	28	29	20	9
40 - 44	C	171	106	65	125	79	46	42	23	19
45 - 49	C	143	78	65	112	61	51	31	17	14
50 - 54	C	153	87	66	121	66	55	31	20	11
55 - 59	C	199	127	72	141	87	54	56	38	18
60 - 64	C	256	151	105	182	110	72	69	38	31
65 - 69	C	359	195	164	257	143	114	99	50	49
70 - 74	C	334	197	137	221	134	87	108	60	48
75 - 79	C	304	170	134	211	112	99	90	55	35
80 - 84	C	233	107	126	158	74	84	74	33	41
85 - 89	C	184	97	87	133	64	69	49	32	17
90 - 94	C	104	54	50	78	39	39	26	15	11
95 - 99	C	27	8	19	21	7	14	5	1	4
100+	C	11	1	10	10	-	10	1	1	-
Uruguay[8]										
2002										
Total	C	31 628	16 796	14 819	...	...	...	...	...	...
0 - 1	C	708	401	304	...	...	...	...	...	...
1 - 4	C	104	69	35	...	...	...	...	...	...
5 - 9	C	63	31	32	...	...	...	...	...	...
10 - 14	C	67	42	25	...	...	...	...	...	...
15 - 19	C	182	139	43	...	...	...	...	...	...
20 - 24	C	249	199	50	...	...	...	...	...	...
25 - 29	C	260	196	64	...	...	...	...	...	...
30 - 34	C	301	200	101	...	...	...	...	...	...
35 - 39	C	339	218	120	...	...	...	...	...	...
40 - 44	C	494	273	221	...	...	...	...	...	...
45 - 49	C	754	467	287	...	...	...	...	...	...
50 - 54	C	1 108	724	384	...	...	...	...	...	...
55 - 59	C	1 501	990	511	...	...	...	...	...	...
60 - 64	C	2 095	1 422	673	...	...	...	...	...	...
65 - 69	C	2 842	1 818	1 024	...	...	...	...	...	...
70 - 74	C	3 938	2 395	1 542	...	...	...	...	...	...
75+	C	16 534	7 149	9 381	...	...	...	...	...	...
Unknown - Inconnu	C	89	63	22	...	...	...	...	...	...
Venezuela[11]										
2002										
Total	C	105 388	64 917	40 471	...	...	...	...	...	...
0 - 1	C	7 645	4 406	3 239	...	...	...	...	...	...
1 - 4	C	1 937	1 077	860	...	...	...	...	...	...
5 - 9	C	829	493	336	...	...	...	...	...	...
10 - 14	C	1 061	668	393	...	...	...	...	...	...
15 - 19	C	3 540	2 929	611	...	...	...	...	...	...
20 - 24	C	5 301	4 579	722	...	...	...	...	...	...
25 - 29	C	4 293	3 578	715	...	...	...	...	...	...
30 - 34	C	3 957	3 002	955	...	...	...	...	...	...
35 - 39	C	3 621	2 586	1 035	...	...	...	...	...	...
40 - 44	C	4 168	2 795	1 373	...	...	...	...	...	...
45 - 49	C	4 878	3 164	1 714	...	...	...	...	...	...
50 - 54	C	5 518	3 549	1 969	...	...	...	...	...	...
55 - 59	C	5 802	3 719	2 083	...	...	...	...	...	...
60 - 64	C	6 494	4 032	2 462	...	...	...	...	...	...
65 - 69	C	7 964	4 746	3 218	...	...	...	...	...	...
70 - 74	C	9 145	5 339	3 806	...	...	...	...	...	...
75 - 79	C	9 369	5 076	4 293	...	...	...	...	...	...
80 - 84	C	8 247	4 164	4 083	...	...	...	...	...	...

19. Deaths by age, sex and urban/rural residence: latest available year, 1994 - 2003
Décès selon l'âge, le sexe et la résidence, urbaine/rurale: dernière année disponible, 1994 - 2003 (continued — suite)

Continent, country or area, year and age (in years) / Continent, pays ou zone, année et âge (en années)	Code[1]	Total			Urban - Urbaine			Rural - Rurale		
		Both sexes - Les deux sexes	Male - Masculin	Female - Féminin	Both sexes - Les deux sexes	Male - Masculin	Female - Féminin	Both sexes - Les deux sexes	Male - Masculin	Female - Féminin
AMERICA, SOUTH — AMERIQUE DU SUD										
Venezuela[11]										
2002										
85 - 89	C	6 270	2 793	3 477	...	...	...	...	...	...
90 - 94	C	3 518	1 463	2 055	...	...	...	...	...	...
95 - 99	C	1 201	420	781	...	...	...	...	...	...
100+	C	364	133	231	...	...	...	...	...	...
Unknown - Inconnu	C	266	206	60	...	...	...	...	...	...
ASIA — ASIE										
Armenia - Arménie[15]										
2000										
Total	C	24 025	12 277	11 748	15 682	8 115	7 567	8 343	4 162	4 181
0 - 1	C	540	348	192	357	234	123	183	114	69
1 - 4	C	143	80	63	81	45	36	62	35	27
5 - 9	C	60	27	33	39	18	21	21	9	12
10 - 14	C	68	51	17	45	35	10	23	16	7
15 - 19	C	136	108	28	78	57	21	58	51	7
20 - 24	C	155	113	42	109	82	27	46	31	15
25 - 29	C	169	108	61	122	77	45	47	31	16
30 - 34	C	253	175	78	166	117	49	87	58	29
35 - 39	C	456	303	153	305	198	107	151	105	46
40 - 44	C	662	437	225	458	310	148	204	127	77
45 - 49	C	806	541	265	633	423	210	173	118	55
50 - 54	C	898	576	322	697	443	254	201	133	68
55 - 59	C	874	570	304	666	443	223	208	127	81
60 - 64	C	2 689	1 639	1 050	1 900	1 186	714	789	453	336
65 - 69	C	3 332	1 952	1 380	2 117	1 234	883	1 215	718	497
70 - 74	C	4 898	2 510	2 388	3 098	1 548	1 550	1 800	962	838
75 - 79	C	3 018	1 255	1 763	1 954	769	1 185	1 064	486	578
80 - 84	C	1 860	602	1 258	1 197	385	812	663	217	446
85+	C	3 008	882	2 126	1 660	511	1 149	1 348	371	977
2003										
Total	C	26 014	13 442	12 636	...	...	...	...	...	...
0 - 1	C	422	256	166	...	...	...	...	...	...
1 - 4	C	63	32	31	...	...	...	...	...	...
5 - 9	C	53	35	18	...	...	...	...	...	...
10 - 14	C	51	28	23	...	...	...	...	...	...
15 - 19	C	98	74	24	...	...	...	...	...	...
20 - 24	C	128	95	33	...	...	...	...	...	...
25 - 29	C	152	101	51	...	...	...	...	...	...
30 - 34	C	214	154	60	...	...	...	...	...	...
35 - 39	C	359	248	111	...	...	...	...	...	...
40 - 44	C	696	464	232	...	...	...	...	...	...
45 - 49	C	940	634	306	...	...	...	...	...	...
50 - 54	C	1 106	726	380	...	...	...	...	...	...
55 - 59	C	977	625	352	...	...	...	...	...	...
60 - 64	C	2 027	1 249	778	...	...	...	...	...	...
65 - 69	C	3 548	2 082	1 466	...	...	...	...	...	...
70 - 74	C	4 987	2 708	2 279	...	...	...	...	...	...
75 - 79	C	4 993	2 265	2 728	...	...	...	...	...	...
80 - 84	C	2 320	768	1 552	...	...	...	...	...	...
85 - 89	C	1 535	469	1 066	...	...	...	...	...	...
90 - 94	C	1 005	293	712	...	...	...	...	...	...
95 - 99	C	261	57	204	...	...	...	...	...	...
100+	C	79	79	64	...	...	...	...	...	...
Azerbaijan - Azerbaïdjan[15]										
2003										
Total	+C	49 001	25 563	23 438	24 999	13 280	11 719	24 002	12 283	11 719
0 - 1	+C	1 451	819	632	633	382	251	818	437	381
1 - 4	+C	803	423	380	112	64	48	691	359	332
5 - 9	+C	431	240	191	155	85	70	276	155	121
10 - 14	+C	338	191	147	147	86	61	191	105	86

19. Deaths by age, sex and urban/rural residence: latest available year, 1994 - 2003
Décès selon l'âge, le sexe et la résidence, urbaine/rurale: dernière année disponible, 1994 - 2003 (continued — suite)

Continent, country or area, year and age (in years) / Continent, pays ou zone, année et âge (en années)	Code[1]	Total			Urban - Urbaine			Rural - Rurale		
		Both sexes - Les deux sexes	Male - Masculin	Female - Féminin	Both sexes - Les deux sexes	Male - Masculin	Female - Féminin	Both sexes - Les deux sexes	Male - Masculin	Female - Féminin
ASIA — ASIE										
Azerbaijan - Azerbaïdjan[15]										
2003										
15 - 19	+C	461	299	162	212	140	72	249	159	90
20 - 24	+C	573	379	194	295	203	92	278	176	102
25 - 29	+C	671	465	206	337	242	95	334	223	111
30 - 34	+C	838	555	283	435	288	147	403	267	136
35 - 39	+C	1 235	808	427	660	445	215	575	363	212
40 - 44	+C	1 828	1 194	634	1 055	721	334	773	473	300
45 - 49	+C	2 127	1 411	716	1 292	875	417	835	536	299
50 - 54	+C	2 342	1 557	785	1 467	976	491	875	581	294
55 - 59	+C	1 960	1 240	720	1 230	779	451	730	461	269
60 - 64	+C	4 351	2 554	1 797	2 392	1 431	961	1 959	1 123	836
65 - 69	+C	7 409	4 116	3 293	3 757	2 122	1 635	3 652	1 994	1 658
70 - 74	+C	8 164	4 290	3 874	3 972	2 036	1 936	4 192	2 254	1 938
75 - 79	+C	6 003	2 792	3 211	3 175	1 401	1 774	2 828	1 391	1 437
80 - 84	+C	3 391	1 125	2 266	1 730	546	1 184	1 661	579	1 082
85 - 89	+C	2 068	560	1 508	1 070	263	807	998	297	701
90 - 94	+C	1 450	356	1 094	593	144	449	857	212	645
95 - 99	+C	559	107	452	163	33	130	396	74	322
100+	+C	548	82	466	117	18	99	431	64	367
Bahrain - Bahreïn										
2002										
Total	U	2 035	1 239	796	...	...	...	...	...	...
0 - 1	U	94	48	46	...	...	...	...	...	...
1 - 4	U	27	15	12	...	...	...	...	...	...
5 - 9	U	21	9	12	...	...	...	...	...	...
10 - 14	U	18	14	4	...	...	...	...	...	...
15 - 19	U	24	15	9	...	...	...	...	...	...
20 - 24	U	43	31	12	...	...	...	...	...	...
25 - 29	U	46	32	14	...	...	...	...	...	...
30 - 34	U	62	47	15	...	...	...	...	...	...
35 - 39	U	81	48	33	...	...	...	...	...	...
40 - 44	U	105	72	33	...	...	...	...	...	...
45 - 49	U	97	69	28	...	...	...	...	...	...
50 - 54	U	99	74	25	...	...	...	...	...	...
55 - 59	U	119	85	34	...	...	...	...	...	...
60 - 64	U	174	100	74	...	...	...	...	...	...
65 - 69	U	199	107	92	...	...	...	...	...	...
70 - 74	U	269	142	127	...	...	...	...	...	...
75+	U	557	331	226	...	...	...	...	...	...
Brunei Darussalam - Brunéi Darussalam										
2003										
Total	+C	1 010	555	455	...	...	...	...	...	...
0 - 4	+C	83	40	43	...	...	...	...	...	...
5 - 9	+C	8	2	6	...	...	...	...	...	...
10 - 14	+C	12	6	6	...	...	...	...	...	...
15 - 19	+C	19	11	8	...	...	...	...	...	...
20 - 24	+C	22	17	5	...	...	...	...	...	...
25 - 29	+C	19	14	5	...	...	...	...	...	...
30 - 34	+C	39	26	13	...	...	...	...	...	...
35 - 39	+C	37	24	13	...	...	...	...	...	...
40 - 44	+C	48	29	19	...	...	...	...	...	...
45 - 49	+C	47	29	18	...	...	...	...	...	...
50 - 54	+C	58	31	27	...	...	...	...	...	...
55 - 59	+C	48	34	14	...	...	...	...	...	...
60 - 64	+C	67	35	32	...	...	...	...	...	...
65 - 69	+C	77	44	33	...	...	...	...	...	...
70+	+C	426	213	213	...	...	...	...	...	...
China - Chine[16]										
1999										
Total	...	7 420 000	4 140 000	3 280 000	...	...	...	...	...	...
0 - 4	...	474 000	237 000	237 000	...	...	...	...	...	...
5 - 9	...	40 000	22 000	18 000	...	...	...	...	...	...

19. Deaths by age, sex and urban/rural residence: latest available year, 1994 - 2003
Décès selon l'âge, le sexe et la résidence, urbaine/rurale: dernière année disponible, 1994 - 2003 (continued — suite)

Continent, country or area, year and age (in years) Continent, pays ou zone, année et âge (en années)	Code[1]	Total			Urban - Urbaine			Rural - Rurale		
		Both sexes - Les deux sexes	Male - Masculin	Female - Féminin	Both sexes - Les deux sexes	Male - Masculin	Female - Féminin	Both sexes - Les deux sexes	Male - Masculin	Female - Féminin
ASIA — ASIE										
China - Chine[16]										
1999										
10 - 14	...	33 000	20 000	13 000	...	...	...	...	...	...
15 - 19	...	72 000	38 000	34 000	...	...	...	...	...	...
20 - 24	...	104 000	59 000	45 000	...	...	...	...	...	...
25 - 29	...	165 000	87 000	78 000	...	...	...	...	...	...
30 - 34	...	180 000	112 000	68 000	...	...	...	...	...	...
35 - 39	...	147 000	93 000	54 000	...	...	...	...	...	...
40 - 44	...	229 000	150 000	79 000	...	...	...	...	...	...
45 - 49	...	306 000	199 000	107 000	...	...	...	...	...	...
50 - 54	...	286 000	177 000	109 000	...	...	...	...	...	...
55 - 59	...	414 000	242 000	172 000	...	...	...	...	...	...
60 - 64	...	673 000	432 000	241 000	...	...	...	...	...	...
65 - 69	...	906 000	540 000	366 000	...	...	...	...	...	...
70 - 74	...	1 028 000	594 000	434 000	...	...	...	...	...	...
75 - 79	...	947 000	528 000	419 000	...	...	...	...	...	...
80 - 84	...	799 000	381 000	418 000	...	...	...	...	...	...
85 - 89	...	423 000	174 000	249 000	...	...	...	...	...	...
90+	...	193 000	54 000	139 000	...	...	...	...	...	...
China: Hong Kong SAR - Chine: Hong Kong RAS[8]										
2003										
Total	C	36 971	20 821	16 149	...	...	...	...	...	...
0 - 1	C	109	57	52	...	...	...	...	...	...
1 - 4	C	43	23	20	...	...	...	...	...	...
5 - 9	C	31	20	11	...	...	...	...	...	...
10 - 14	C	44	23	21	...	...	...	...	...	...
15 - 19	C	87	56	31	...	...	...	...	...	...
20 - 24	C	177	120	57	...	...	...	...	...	...
25 - 29	C	262	174	88	...	...	...	...	...	...
30 - 34	C	313	178	135	...	...	...	...	...	...
35 - 39	C	493	316	177	...	...	...	...	...	...
40 - 44	C	811	517	294	...	...	...	...	...	...
45 - 49	C	1 220	789	431	...	...	...	...	...	...
50 - 54	C	1 451	995	456	...	...	...	...	...	...
55 - 59	C	1 519	1 072	447	...	...	...	...	...	...
60 - 64	C	1 951	1 450	501	...	...	...	...	...	...
65 - 69	C	3 126	2 110	1 016	...	...	...	...	...	...
70 - 74	C	4 838	3 205	1 633	...	...	...	...	...	...
75 - 79	C	5 984	3 589	2 395	...	...	...	...	...	...
80 - 84	C	5 894	3 019	2 875	...	...	...	...	...	...
85+	C	8 571	3 069	5 502	...	...	...	...	...	...
Unknown - Inconnu	C	47	39	7	...	...	...	...	...	...
China: Macao SAR - Chine: Macao RAS										
2003										
Total	C	1 474	771	703	...	...	...	...	...	...
0 - 1	C	2	1	1	...	...	...	...	...	...
1 - 4	C	3	1	2	...	...	...	...	...	...
5 - 9	C	2	1	1	...	...	...	...	...	...
10 - 14	C	1	-	1	...	...	...	...	...	...
15 - 19	C	11	7	4	...	...	...	...	...	...
20 - 24	C	10	6	4	...	...	...	...	...	...
25 - 29	C	15	12	3	...	...	...	...	...	...
30 - 34	C	15	11	4	...	...	...	...	...	...
35 - 39	C	38	17	21	...	...	...	...	...	...
40 - 44	C	63	39	24	...	...	...	...	...	...
45 - 49	C	81	57	24	...	...	...	...	...	...
50 - 54	C	54	34	20	...	...	...	...	...	...
55 - 59	C	60	35	25	...	...	...	...	...	...
60 - 64	C	62	41	21	...	...	...	...	...	...
65 - 69	C	111	70	41	...	...	...	...	...	...
70 - 74	C	195	120	75	...	...	...	...	...	...
75 - 79	C	220	116	104	...	...	...	...	...	...

19. Deaths by age, sex and urban/rural residence: latest available year, 1994 - 2003
Décès selon l'âge, le sexe et la résidence, urbaine/rurale: dernière année disponible, 1994 - 2003 (continued — suite)

Continent, country or area, year and age (in years) / Continent, pays ou zone, année et âge (en années)	Code[1]	Total			Urban - Urbaine			Rural - Rurale		
		Both sexes - Les deux sexes	Male - Masculin	Female - Féminin	Both sexes - Les deux sexes	Male - Masculin	Female - Féminin	Both sexes - Les deux sexes	Male - Masculin	Female - Féminin
ASIA — ASIE										
China: Macao SAR - Chine: Macao RAS										
2003										
80 - 84	C	227	107	120	...	...	...	...	...	...
85+	C	301	94	207	...	...	...	...	...	...
Unknown - Inconnu	C	3	2	1	...	...	...	...	...	...
Cyprus - Chypre[17]										
2003										
Total	C	5 200	2 764	2 436	...	...	...	...	...	...
0 - 1	C	33	19	14	...	...	...	...	...	...
1 - 4	C	8	2	6	...	...	...	...	...	...
5 - 9	C	8	5	3	...	...	...	...	...	...
10 - 14	C	8	6	2	...	...	...	...	...	...
15 - 19	C	32	21	11	...	...	...	...	...	...
20 - 24	C	33	28	5	...	...	...	...	...	...
25 - 29	C	27	17	10	...	...	...	...	...	...
30 - 34	C	34	24	10	...	...	...	...	...	...
35 - 39	C	41	23	18	...	...	...	...	...	...
40 - 44	C	45	30	15	...	...	...	...	...	...
45 - 49	C	86	59	27	...	...	...	...	...	...
50 - 54	C	145	80	65	...	...	...	...	...	...
55 - 59	C	183	123	60	...	...	...	...	...	...
60 - 64	C	273	177	96	...	...	...	...	...	...
65 - 69	C	416	250	166	...	...	...	...	...	...
70 - 74	C	542	277	265	...	...	...	...	...	...
75 - 79	C	754	400	354	...	...	...	...	...	...
80 - 84	C	818	415	403	...	...	...	...	...	...
85+	C	1 519	691	828	...	...	...	...	...	...
Unknown - Inconnu	C	195	117	78	...	...	...	...	...	...
Georgia - Géorgie[15]										
2003										
Total	C	46 055	22 829	23 226	...	...	...	...	...	...
0 - 1	C	1 144	657	487	...	...	...	...	...	...
1 - 4	C	131	79	52	...	...	...	...	...	...
5 - 9	C	35	20	15	...	...	...	...	...	...
10 - 14	C	66	28	38	...	...	...	...	...	...
15 - 19	C	107	70	37	...	...	...	...	...	...
20 - 24	C	212	141	71	...	...	...	...	...	...
25 - 29	C	319	195	124	...	...	...	...	...	...
30 - 34	C	415	326	89	...	...	...	...	...	...
35 - 39	C	551	358	193	...	...	...	...	...	...
40 - 44	C	885	558	327	...	...	...	...	...	...
45 - 49	C	1 246	886	360	...	...	...	...	...	...
50 - 54	C	1 970	1 337	633	...	...	...	...	...	...
55 - 59	C	1 899	1 188	711	...	...	...	...	...	...
60 - 64	C	3 188	1 891	1 297	...	...	...	...	...	...
65 - 69	C	5 393	3 204	2 189	...	...	...	...	...	...
70 - 74	C	7 115	3 720	3 395	...	...	...	...	...	...
75 - 79	C	8 841	3 988	4 853	...	...	...	...	...	...
80 - 84	C	5 716	2 146	3 570	...	...	...	...	...	...
85+	C	6 822	2 037	4 785	...	...	...	...	...	...
Israel - Israël[6,18]										
2003										
Total	C	38 359	19 332	19 027	35 941	18 077	17 864	2 416	1 254	1 162
0 - 1	C	717	384	333	641	349	292	75	35	40
1 - 4	C	173	106	67	155	95	60	18	11	7
5 - 9	C	85	42	43	78	37	41	7	5	2
10 - 14	C	87	59	28	75	49	26	12	10	2
15 - 19	C	216	153	63	188	130	58	28	23	5
20 - 24	C	334	273	61	299	244	55	35	29	6
25 - 29	C	271	198	73	249	182	67	22	16	6
30 - 34	C	293	194	99	273	181	92	20	13	7
35 - 39	C	371	243	128	355	233	122	16	10	6
40 - 44	C	519	330	189	493	316	177	26	14	12

Continent, country or area, year and age (in years) / Continent, pays ou zone, année et âge (en années)	Code[1]	Total			Urban - Urbaine			Rural - Rurale		
		Both sexes - Les deux sexes	Male - Masculin	Female - Féminin	Both sexes - Les deux sexes	Male - Masculin	Female - Féminin	Both sexes - Les deux sexes	Male - Masculin	Female - Féminin
ASIA — ASIE										
Israel - Israël[6,18]										
2003										
45 - 49	C	755	482	273	705	446	259	50	36	14
50 - 54	C	1 136	690	446	1 069	648	421	67	42	25
55 - 59	C	1 509	920	589	1 425	874	551	84	46	38
60 - 64	C	1 732	1 041	691	1 646	987	659	86	54	32
65 - 69	C	2 859	1 677	1 182	2 740	1 613	1 127	118	63	55
70 - 74	C	4 111	2 243	1 868	3 888	2 118	1 770	223	125	98
75 - 79	C	5 984	2 960	3 024	5 640	2 768	2 872	344	192	152
80 - 84	C	6 500	3 071	3 429	6 118	2 874	3 244	382	197	185
85+	C	10 705	4 266	6 439	9 902	3 933	5 969	803	333	470
Unknown - Inconnu	C	2	-	2	2	-	2	-	-	-
Japan - Japon[19]										
2003										
Total	C	1 014 951	551 746	463 205	...	...	...	...	...	...
0 - 1	C	3 364	1 787	1 577	...	...	...	...	...	...
1 - 4	C	1 154	615	539	...	...	...	...	...	...
5 - 9	C	663	370	293	...	...	...	...	...	...
10 - 14	C	662	377	285	...	...	...	...	...	...
15 - 19	C	2 132	1 460	672	...	...	...	...	...	...
20 - 24	C	3 284	2 319	965	...	...	...	...	...	...
25 - 29	C	4 581	3 186	1 395	...	...	...	...	...	...
30 - 34	C	6 022	4 072	1 950	...	...	...	...	...	...
35 - 39	C	7 199	4 752	2 447	...	...	...	...	...	...
40 - 44	C	10 386	7 034	3 352	...	...	...	...	...	...
45 - 49	C	16 574	11 227	5 347	...	...	...	...	...	...
50 - 54	C	34 522	23 609	10 913	...	...	...	...	...	...
55 - 59	C	45 325	31 535	13 790	...	...	...	...	...	...
60 - 64	C	59 459	41 343	18 116	...	...	...	...	...	...
65 - 69	C	84 109	57 644	26 465	...	...	...	...	...	...
70 - 74	C	118 835	78 884	39 951	...	...	...	...	...	...
75 - 79	C	147 462	89 520	57 942	...	...	...	...	...	...
80 - 84	C	154 129	76 401	77 728	...	...	...	...	...	...
85 - 89	C	156 568	66 350	90 218	...	...	...	...	...	...
90 - 94	C	111 400	37 235	74 165	...	...	...	...	...	...
95 - 99	C	39 096	10 010	29 086	...	...	...	...	...	...
100+	C	7 323	1 416	5 907	...	...	...	...	...	...
Unknown - Inconnu	C	702	600	102	...	...	...	...	...	...
Kazakhstan[15]										
2003										
Total	C	155 277	87 216	68 061	99 595	56 357	43 238	55 682	30 859	24 823
0 - 1	C	3 824	2 234	1 590	2 349	1 409	940	1 475	825	650
1 - 4	C	1 022	564	458	414	223	191	608	341	267
5 - 9	C	544	328	216	281	172	109	263	156	107
10 - 14	C	679	410	269	347	210	137	332	200	132
15 - 19	C	1 688	1 155	533	973	643	330	715	512	203
20 - 24	C	2 737	2 010	727	1 606	1 192	414	1 131	818	313
25 - 29	C	3 609	2 718	891	2 317	1 742	575	1 292	976	316
30 - 34	C	4 337	3 312	1 025	2 817	2 165	652	1 520	1 147	373
35 - 39	C	5 232	3 895	1 337	3 462	2 586	876	1 770	1 309	461
40 - 44	C	8 082	5 973	2 109	5 443	4 032	1 411	2 639	1 941	698
45 - 49	C	9 576	6 898	2 678	6 593	4 775	1 818	2 983	2 123	860
50 - 54	C	10 981	7 651	3 330	7 512	5 329	2 183	3 469	2 322	1 147
55 - 59	C	8 618	5 807	2 811	5 752	3 926	1 826	2 866	1 881	985
60 - 64	C	15 291	9 592	5 699	9 534	6 014	3 520	5 757	3 578	2 179
65 - 69	C	18 206	10 922	7 284	11 265	6 772	4 493	6 941	4 150	2 791
70 - 74	C	17 766	9 251	8 515	11 258	5 740	5 518	6 508	3 511	2 997
75 - 79	C	18 518	7 409	11 109	12 002	4 655	7 347	6 516	2 754	3 762
80 - 84	C	10 584	3 204	7 380	6 688	1 997	4 691	3 896	1 207	2 689
85+	C	12 649	2 793	9 856	7 667	1 701	5 966	4 982	1 092	3 890
Unknown - Inconnu	C	1 334	1 090	244	1 315	1 074	241	19	16	3

Continent, country or area, year and age (in years) / Continent, pays ou zone, année et âge (en années)	Code[1]	Total			Urban - Urbaine			Rural - Rurale		
		Both sexes - Les deux sexes	Male - Masculin	Female - Féminin	Both sexes - Les deux sexes	Male - Masculin	Female - Féminin	Both sexes - Les deux sexes	Male - Masculin	Female - Féminin
ASIA — ASIE										
Korea (Republic of) - Corée (République de)[20]										
2002										
Total	C	246 515	135 510	111 005	...	...	...	...	...	...
0 - 1	C	2 545	1 416	1 129	...	...	...	...	...	...
1 - 4	C	1 080	608	472	...	...	...	...	...	...
5 - 9	C	802	481	321	...	...	...	...	...	...
10 - 14	C	566	343	223	...	...	...	...	...	...
15 - 19	C	1 229	831	398	...	...	...	...	...	...
20 - 24	C	2 006	1 322	684	...	...	...	...	...	...
25 - 29	C	2 527	1 725	802	...	...	...	...	...	...
30 - 34	C	3 902	2 674	1 228	...	...	...	...	...	...
35 - 39	C	5 656	4 069	1 587	...	...	...	...	...	...
40 - 44	C	9 363	7 007	2 356	...	...	...	...	...	...
45 - 49	C	11 303	8 559	2 744	...	...	...	...	...	...
50 - 54	C	12 071	9 053	3 018	...	...	...	...	...	...
55 - 59	C	14 950	10 905	4 045	...	...	...	...	...	...
60 - 64	C	22 047	15 389	6 658	...	...	...	...	...	...
65 - 69	C	26 236	16 826	9 410	...	...	...	...	...	...
70 - 74	C	29 232	15 929	13 303	...	...	...	...	...	...
75 - 79	C	33 455	15 798	17 657	...	...	...	...	...	...
80 - 84	C	31 314	12 519	18 795	...	...	...	...	...	...
85 - 89	C	22 262	6 958	15 304	...	...	...	...	...	...
90 - 94	C	10 674	2 605	8 069	...	...	...	...	...	...
95+	C	3 273	487	2 786	...	...	...	...	...	...
Unknown - Inconnu	C	22	6	16	...	...	...	...	...	...
Kuwait - Koweït										
2002										
Total	C	4 342	2 755	1 587	...	...	...	...	...	...
0 - 1	C	418	225	193	...	...	...	...	...	...
1 - 4	C	74	43	31	...	...	...	...	...	...
5 - 9	C	56	33	23	...	...	...	...	...	...
10 - 14	C	48	28	20	...	...	...	...	...	...
15 - 19	C	76	61	15	...	...	...	...	...	...
20 - 24	C	135	103	32	...	...	...	...	...	...
25 - 29	C	150	120	30	...	...	...	...	...	...
30 - 34	C	163	123	40	...	...	...	...	...	...
35 - 39	C	163	130	33	...	...	...	...	...	...
40 - 44	C	247	197	50	...	...	...	...	...	...
45 - 49	C	239	165	74	...	...	...	...	...	...
50 - 54	C	266	181	85	...	...	...	...	...	...
55 - 59	C	280	186	94	...	...	...	...	...	...
60 - 64	C	365	221	144	...	...	...	...	...	...
65 - 69	C	348	222	126	...	...	...	...	...	...
70 - 74	C	392	227	165	...	...	...	...	...	...
75 - 79	C	309	170	139	...	...	...	...	...	...
80 - 84	C	250	132	118	...	...	...	...	...	...
85+	C	239	118	121	...	...	...	...	...	...
Unknown - Inconnu	C	124	70	54	...	...	...	...	...	...
Kyrgyzstan - Kirghizistan[15]										
2003										
Total	C	35 941	19 701	16 240	13 943	7 700	6 243	21 998	12 001	9 997
0 - 1	C	2 186	1 278	908	880	518	362	1 306	760	546
1 - 4	C	675	354	321	102	51	51	573	303	270
5 - 9	C	229	134	95	47	24	23	182	110	72
10 - 14	C	222	147	75	62	38	24	160	109	51
15 - 19	C	399	256	143	103	57	46	296	199	97
20 - 24	C	562	385	177	176	127	49	386	258	128
25 - 29	C	796	555	241	285	211	74	511	344	167
30 - 34	C	984	724	260	365	260	105	619	464	155
35 - 39	C	1 245	894	351	515	379	136	730	515	215
40 - 44	C	1 737	1 230	507	729	531	198	1 008	699	309
45 - 49	C	1 898	1 339	559	854	618	236	1 044	721	323
50 - 54	C	2 087	1 426	661	954	659	295	1 133	767	366

19. Deaths by age, sex and urban/rural residence: latest available year, 1994 - 2003
Décès selon l'âge, le sexe et la résidence, urbaine/rurale: dernière année disponible, 1994 - 2003 (continued — suite)

Continent, country or area, year and age (in years) / Continent, pays ou zone, année et âge (en années)	Code[1]	Total			Urban - Urbaine			Rural - Rurale		
		Both sexes - Les deux sexes	Male - Masculin	Female - Féminin	Both sexes - Les deux sexes	Male - Masculin	Female - Féminin	Both sexes - Les deux sexes	Male - Masculin	Female - Féminin
ASIA — ASIE										
Kyrgyzstan - Kirghizistan[15]										
2003										
55 - 59	C	1 476	937	539	687	462	225	789	475	314
60 - 64	C	2 866	1 763	1 103	1 167	729	438	1 699	1 034	665
65 - 69	C	3 714	2 210	1 504	1 467	871	596	2 247	1 339	908
70 - 74	C	4 546	2 363	2 183	1 650	829	821	2 896	1 534	1 362
75 - 79	C	4 357	1 877	2 480	1 751	699	1 052	2 606	1 178	1 428
80 - 84	C	2 823	955	1 868	1 074	324	750	1 749	631	1 118
85 - 89	C	1 518	449	1 069	634	172	462	884	277	607
90 - 94	C	931	262	669	300	81	219	631	181	450
95 - 99	C	347	75	272	66	12	54	281	63	218
100+	C	290	44	246	26	7	19	264	37	227
Unknown - Inconnu	C	53	44	9	49	41	8	4	3	1
Malaysia - Malaisie[21]										
2000										
Total	C	104 859	60 793	44 066	53 723	31 170	22 553	35 457	20 347	15 110
0 - 1	C	3 578	2 026	1 552	1 678	953	725	1 265	721	544
1 - 4	C	1 282	694	588	555	301	254	540	294	246
5 - 9	C	836	500	336	336	194	142	343	214	129
10 - 14	C	961	597	364	402	256	146	377	242	135
15 - 19	C	1 966	1 480	486	984	748	236	741	562	179
20 - 24	C	2 229	1 677	552	1 072	799	273	813	623	190
25 - 29	C	2 281	1 746	535	1 166	909	257	768	600	168
30 - 34	C	2 669	2 000	669	1 418	1 085	333	863	651	212
35 - 39	C	3 249	2 337	912	1 772	1 325	447	968	681	287
40 - 44	C	4 078	2 793	1 285	2 274	1 621	653	1 191	790	401
45 - 49	C	4 728	3 090	1 638	2 636	1 793	843	1 327	827	500
50 - 54	C	6 106	3 901	2 205	3 273	2 130	1 143	1 912	1 212	700
55 - 59	C	7 070	4 485	2 585	3 719	2 401	1 318	2 179	1 358	821
60 - 64	C	9 943	6 103	3 840	5 144	3 158	1 986	3 396	2 094	1 302
65 - 69	C	11 029	6 257	4 772	5 618	3 198	2 420	3 640	2 020	1 620
70 - 74	C	12 160	6 622	5 538	6 047	3 269	2 778	4 384	2 339	2 045
75 - 79	C	11 807	5 874	5 933	5 761	2 765	2 996	4 315	2 125	2 190
80 - 84	C	9 179	4 272	4 907	4 662	2 083	2 579	3 263	1 508	1 755
85+	C	9 571	4 276	5 295	5 132	2 140	2 992	3 167	1 484	1 683
Unknown - Inconnu	C	137	63	74	74	42	32	5	2	3
Maldives										
2003										
Total	C	1 026	591	435	297	181	116	729	410	319
0 - 1	C	72	41	31	16	13	3	56	28	28
1 - 4	C	23	18	5	3	2	1	20	16	4
5 - 9	C	14	10	4	3	2	1	11	8	3
10 - 14	C	13	8	5	7	5	2	6	3	3
15 - 19	C	12	11	1	7	6	1	5	5	-
20 - 24	C	10	6	4	5	4	1	5	2	3
25 - 29	C	14	8	6	1	1	-	13	7	6
30 - 34	C	12	5	7	6	2	4	6	3	3
35 - 39	C	24	14	10	12	7	5	12	7	5
40 - 44	C	30	18	12	13	6	7	17	12	5
45 - 49	C	26	11	15	11	6	5	15	5	10
50 - 54	C	31	21	10	15	9	6	16	12	4
55 - 59	C	48	29	19	26	16	10	22	13	9
60 - 64	C	114	56	58	42	24	18	72	32	40
65 - 69	C	141	81	60	38	25	13	103	56	47
70 - 74	C	165	96	69	35	20	15	130	76	54
75 - 79	C	124	71	53	19	10	9	105	61	44
80 - 84	C	79	45	34	19	13	6	60	32	28
85 - 89	C	42	25	17	10	6	4	32	19	13
90 - 94	C	21	13	8	6	3	3	15	10	5
95 - 99	C	5	-	5	-	-	-	5	-	5
100+	C	6	4	2	3	1	2	3	3	-
Mongolia - Mongolie										
2003										
Total	C	16 006	9 499	6 507	9 480	...	...	6 526	...	...

19. Deaths by age, sex and urban/rural residence: latest available year, 1994 - 2003
Décès selon l'âge, le sexe et la résidence, urbaine/rurale: dernière année disponible, 1994 - 2003 (continued — suite)

Continent, country or area, year and age (in years) — Continent, pays ou zone, année et âge (en années)	Code[1]	Total			Urban - Urbaine			Rural - Rurale		
		Both sexes - Les deux sexes	Male - Masculin	Female - Féminin	Both sexes - Les deux sexes	Male - Masculin	Female - Féminin	Both sexes - Les deux sexes	Male - Masculin	Female - Féminin
ASIA — ASIE										
Mongolia - Mongolie										
2003										
0 - 1	C	1 051	602	449	520	...	...	531	...	...
1 - 4	C	356	202	154	138	...	...	218	...	...
5 - 9	C	116	66	50	61	...	...	55	...	...
10 - 14	C	112	69	43	61	...	...	51	...	...
15 - 19	C	210	139	71	135	...	...	75	...	...
20 - 24	C	327	235	92	174	...	...	153	...	...
25 - 29	C	455	321	134	275	...	...	180	...	...
30 - 34	C	552	385	167	351	...	...	201	...	...
35 - 39	C	716	515	201	499	...	...	217	...	...
40 - 44	C	989	676	313	663	...	...	326	...	...
45 - 49	C	1 076	693	383	701	...	...	375	...	...
50 - 54	C	1 044	664	380	645	...	...	399	...	...
55 - 59	C	1 123	699	424	704	...	...	419	...	...
60 - 64	C	1 513	927	586	867	...	...	646	...	...
65 - 69	C	1 530	940	590	882	...	...	648	...	...
70 - 74	C	1 589	879	710	904	...	...	685	...	...
75 - 79	C	1 200	620	580	722	...	...	478	...	...
80 - 84	C	1 042	504	538	605	...	...	437	...	...
85 - 89	C	641	242	399	376	...	...	265	...	...
90 - 94	C	275	89	186	139	...	...	136	...	...
95 - 99	C	72	29	43	49	...	...	23	...	...
100+	C	17	3	14	9	...	...	8	...	...
Myanmar[22]										
1994										
Total	U	...	...	...	80 421	...	...	86 579	...	...
0 - 1	U	...	...	...	12 168	...	...	13 177	...	...
1 - 4	U	...	...	...	6 543	...	...	7 399	...	...
5 - 14	U	...	...	...	5 333	...	...	5 118	...	...
15 - 24	U	...	...	...	4 812	...	...	4 978	...	...
25 - 34	U	...	...	...	5 288	...	...	6 030	...	...
35 - 44	U	...	...	...	6 202	...	...	5 701	...	...
45 - 54	U	...	...	...	8 173	...	...	6 927	...	...
55 - 64	U	...	...	...	10 256	...	...	10 187	...	...
65 - 74	U	...	...	...	10 633	...	...	12 403	...	...
75 - 84	U	...	...	...	7 846	...	...	10 713	...	...
85+	U	...	...	...	2 531	...	...	3 810	...	...
Unknown - Inconnu	U	...	...	...	636	...	...	136	...	...
Nepal - Népal[23]										
2001										
Total	I	106 789	59 544	47 245	...	...	...	...	...	...
0 - 1	I	13 037	6 956	6 081	...	...	...	...	...	...
1 - 4	I	9 790	5 590	4 200	...	...	...	...	...	...
5 - 9	I	3 320	1 726	1 594	...	...	...	...	...	...
10 - 14	I	2 304	1 332	972	...	...	...	...	...	...
15 - 19	I	2 523	1 293	1 230	...	...	...	...	...	...
20 - 24	I	2 747	1 449	1 298	...	...	...	...	...	...
25 - 29	I	2 688	1 429	1 259	...	...	...	...	...	...
30 - 34	I	2 474	1 303	1 172	...	...	...	...	...	...
35 - 39	I	2 839	1 594	1 244	...	...	...	...	...	...
40 - 44	I	2 970	1 828	1 142	...	...	...	...	...	...
45 - 49	I	3 553	2 027	1 526	...	...	...	...	...	...
50 - 54	I	4 662	2 771	1 891	...	...	...	...	...	...
55 - 59	I	6 115	3 612	2 503	...	...	...	...	...	...
60 - 64	I	8 337	4 710	3 626	...	...	...	...	...	...
65 - 69	I	8 667	4 764	3 903	...	...	...	...	...	...
70 - 74	I	9 606	5 512	4 093	...	...	...	...	...	...
75 - 79	I	8 113	4 657	3 456	...	...	...	...	...	...
80+	I	13 042	6 990	6 052	...	...	...	...	...	...
Occupied Palestinian Territory - Territoire palestinien occupé										
2003										
Total	U	9 664	5 474	4 190	...	...	...	...	...	...

19. Deaths by age, sex and urban/rural residence: latest available year, 1994 - 2003
Décès selon l'âge, le sexe et la résidence, urbaine/rurale: dernière année disponible, 1994 - 2003 (continued — suite)

Continent, country or area, year and age (in years) / Continent, pays ou zone, année et âge (en années)	Code[1]	Total			Urban - Urbaine			Rural - Rurale		
		Both sexes - Les deux sexes	Male - Masculin	Female - Féminin	Both sexes - Les deux sexes	Male - Masculin	Female - Féminin	Both sexes - Les deux sexes	Male - Masculin	Female - Féminin
ASIA — ASIE										
Occupied Palestinian Territory - Territoire palestinien occupé										
2003										
0 - 1	U	1 101	564	537	...	...	...	...	...	...
1 - 4	U	373	204	169	...	...	...	...	...	...
5 - 9	U	175	113	62	...	...	...	...	...	...
10 - 14	U	136	103	33	...	...	...	...	...	...
15 - 19	U	290	249	41	...	...	...	...	...	...
20 - 24	U	246	212	34	...	...	...	...	...	...
25 - 29	U	206	170	36	...	...	...	...	...	...
30 - 34	U	166	130	36	...	...	...	...	...	...
35 - 39	U	164	105	59	...	...	...	...	...	...
40 - 44	U	212	133	79	...	...	...	...	...	...
45 - 49	U	244	169	75	...	...	...	...	...	...
50 - 54	U	334	219	115	...	...	...	...	...	...
55 - 59	U	462	271	191	...	...	...	...	...	...
60 - 64	U	644	322	322	...	...	...	...	...	...
65 - 69	U	896	445	451	...	...	...	...	...	...
70 - 74	U	1 090	544	546	...	...	...	...	...	...
75 - 79	U	1 080	534	546	...	...	...	...	...	...
80 - 84	U	769	405	364	...	...	...	...	...	...
85 - 89	U	528	282	246	...	...	...	...	...	...
90 - 94	U	268	145	123	...	...	...	...	...	...
95 - 99	U	192	104	88	...	...	...	...	...	...
100+	U	88	51	37	...	...	...	...	...	...
Oman[24]										
2003										
Total	U	2 701	...	...	...	...	...	...	...	...
0 - 1	U	335	...	...	...	...	...	...	...	...
1 - 4	U	51	...	...	...	...	...	...	...	...
5 - 14	U	71	...	...	...	...	...	...	...	...
15 - 44	U	339	...	...	...	...	...	...	...	...
45+	U	1 905	...	...	...	...	...	...	...	...
Pakistan[25,26]										
2001										
Total	I	956 515	511 841	444 674	302 482	163 260	139 222	654 033	348 581	305 452
0 - 4	I	371 909	193 418	178 491	107 672	56 590	51 081	264 237	136 827	127 410
5 - 9	I	32 340	16 170	16 170	9 515	5 509	4 006	22 825	10 661	12 164
10 - 14	I	22 389	7 463	14 926	9 014	3 506	5 509	13 375	3 957	9 417
15 - 19	I	21 145	11 817	9 329	7 011	4 006	3 005	14 134	7 810	6 324
20 - 24	I	23 011	9 329	13 682	6 510	3 506	3 005	16 501	5 823	10 677
25 - 29	I	19 280	9 951	9 329	6 510	3 005	3 506	12 769	6 946	5 823
30 - 34	I	19 280	12 438	6 841	7 011	4 006	3 005	12 268	8 432	3 836
35 - 39	I	29 852	17 414	12 438	11 018	7 011	4 006	18 835	10 403	8 432
40 - 44	I	22 389	11 195	11 195	8 514	3 005	5 509	13 876	8 190	5 686
45 - 49	I	28 608	17 414	11 195	12 019	8 514	3 506	16 589	8 900	7 689
50 - 54	I	35 450	19 901	15 548	13 522	9 515	4 006	21 928	10 386	11 542
55 - 59	I	39 181	20 523	18 658	13 021	6 010	7 011	26 160	14 514	11 646
60 - 64	I	54 107	27 365	26 743	13 522	7 011	6 510	40 586	20 353	20 232
65 - 69	I	53 485	25 499	27 986	17 027	6 510	10 517	36 458	18 988	17 470
70+	I	184 089	111 946	72 143	60 597	35 557	25 040	123 492	76 389	47 103
Philippines										
2002										
Total	C	396 297	232 530	163 767	...	...	...	...	...	...
0 - 1	C	23 778	13 925	9 853	...	...	...	...	...	...
1 - 4	C	10 976	6 028	4 948	...	...	...	...	...	...
5 - 9	C	5 332	3 060	2 272	...	...	...	...	...	...
10 - 14	C	4 772	2 796	1 976	...	...	...	...	...	...
15 - 19	C	6 614	4 331	2 283	...	...	...	...	...	...
20 - 24	C	9 704	6 749	2 955	...	...	...	...	...	...
25 - 29	C	10 668	7 522	3 146	...	...	...	...	...	...
30 - 34	C	12 557	8 553	4 004	...	...	...	...	...	...
35 - 39	C	14 663	9 839	4 824	...	...	...	...	...	...
40 - 44	C	17 455	11 594	5 861	...	...	...	...	...	...

Continent, country or area, year and age (in years) / Continent, pays ou zone, année et âge (en années)	Code[1]	Total			Urban - Urbaine			Rural - Rurale		
		Both sexes - Les deux sexes	Male - Masculin	Female - Féminin	Both sexes - Les deux sexes	Male - Masculin	Female - Féminin	Both sexes - Les deux sexes	Male - Masculin	Female - Féminin
ASIA — ASIE										
Philippines										
2002										
45 - 49	C	20 997	14 142	6 855	...	...	...	...	...	...
50 - 54	C	25 009	16 846	8 163	...	...	...	...	...	...
55 - 59	C	26 261	17 583	8 678	...	...	...	...	...	...
60 - 64	C	31 463	20 281	11 182	...	...	...	...	...	...
65 - 69	C	34 866	21 153	13 713	...	...	...	...	...	...
70 - 74	C	34 989	20 035	14 954	...	...	...	...	...	...
75 - 79	C	34 113	17 778	16 335	...	...	...	...	...	...
80 - 84	C	31 387	14 354	17 033	...	...	...	...	...	...
85 - 89	C	23 159	9 413	13 746	...	...	...	...	...	...
90 - 94	C	12 011	4 464	7 547	...	...	...	...	...	...
95+	C	5 099	1 837	3 262	...	...	...	...	...	...
Unknown - Inconnu	C	424	247	177	...	...	...	...	...	...
Qatar										
2003										
Total	C	1 311	896	415	...	...	...	...	...	...
0 - 1	C	137	75	62	...	...	...	...	...	...
1 - 4	C	23	18	5	...	...	...	...	...	...
5 - 9	C	12	6	6	...	...	...	...	...	...
10 - 14	C	20	11	9	...	...	...	...	...	...
15 - 19	C	47	42	5	...	...	...	...	...	...
20 - 24	C	55	50	5	...	...	...	...	...	...
25 - 29	C	45	37	8	...	...	...	...	...	...
30 - 34	C	61	50	11	...	...	...	...	...	...
35 - 39	C	60	46	14	...	...	...	...	...	...
40 - 44	C	72	61	11	...	...	...	...	...	...
45 - 49	C	84	68	16	...	...	...	...	...	...
50 - 54	C	83	66	17	...	...	...	...	...	...
55 - 59	C	95	65	30	...	...	...	...	...	...
60 - 64	C	103	62	41	...	...	...	...	...	...
65 - 69	C	122	76	46	...	...	...	...	...	...
70 - 74	C	102	59	43	...	...	...	...	...	...
75 - 79	C	75	42	33	...	...	...	...	...	...
80 - 84	C	50	32	18	...	...	...	...	...	...
85 - 89	C	32	17	15	...	...	...	...	...	...
90 - 94	C	17	6	11	...	...	...	...	...	...
95+	C	16	7	9	...	...	...	...	...	...
Singapore - Singapour[8,27]										
2003										
Total	+C	16 036	8 908	7 126	...	...	...	...	...	...
0 - 1	+C	100	56	44	...	...	...	...	...	...
1 - 4	+C	41	24	17	...	...	...	...	...	...
5 - 9	+C	32	22	10	...	...	...	...	...	...
10 - 14	+C	39	24	15	...	...	...	...	...	...
15 - 19	+C	88	58	30	...	...	...	...	...	...
20 - 24	+C	169	106	63	...	...	...	...	...	...
25 - 29	+C	161	115	46	...	...	...	...	...	...
30 - 34	+C	213	156	57	...	...	...	...	...	...
35 - 39	+C	284	186	98	...	...	...	...	...	...
40 - 44	+C	431	290	141	...	...	...	...	...	...
45 - 49	+C	656	427	229	...	...	...	...	...	...
50 - 54	+C	854	533	321	...	...	...	...	...	...
55 - 59	+C	974	643	331	...	...	...	...	...	...
60 - 64	+C	1 299	825	474	...	...	...	...	...	...
65 - 69	+C	1 646	1 032	614	...	...	...	...	...	...
70 - 74	+C	2 023	1 233	790	...	...	...	...	...	...
75 - 79	+C	2 267	1 215	1 052	...	...	...	...	...	...
80 - 84	+C	1 992	920	1 072	...	...	...	...	...	...
85 - 89	+C	1 493	580	913	...	...	...	...	...	...
90 - 94	+C	917	351	566	...	...	...	...	...	...
95 - 99	+C	283	83	200	...	...	...	...	...	...
100+	+C	57	17	40	...	...	...	...	...	...
Unknown - Inconnu	+C	17	12	3	...	...	...	...	...	...

Continent, country or area, year and age (in years) / Continent, pays ou zone, année et âge (en années)	Code[1]	Total			Urban - Urbaine			Rural - Rurale		
		Both sexes - Les deux sexes	Male - Masculin	Female - Féminin	Both sexes - Les deux sexes	Male - Masculin	Female - Féminin	Both sexes - Les deux sexes	Male - Masculin	Female - Féminin
ASIA — ASIE										
Sri Lanka										
1996										
Total	+C	122 161	79 784	42 377	60 131	39 546	20 585	62 030	40 238	21 792
0 - 1	+C	5 879	3 271	2 608	5 062	2 816	2 246	817	455	362
1 - 4	+C	1 237	667	570	805	432	373	432	235	197
5 - 9	+C	924	514	410	551	301	250	373	213	160
10 - 14	+C	990	550	440	562	292	270	428	258	170
15 - 19	+C	3 320	2 487	833	1 512	1 015	497	1 808	1 472	336
20 - 24	+C	6 180	5 241	939	2 828	2 279	549	3 352	2 962	390
25 - 29	+C	5 875	4 966	909	2 557	2 041	516	3 318	2 925	393
30 - 34	+C	4 712	3 875	837	2 177	1 673	504	2 535	2 202	333
35 - 39	+C	4 838	3 793	1 045	2 467	1 853	614	2 371	1 940	431
40 - 44	+C	4 607	3 585	1 022	2 650	2 048	602	1 957	1 537	420
45 - 49	+C	5 819	4 309	1 510	3 514	2 649	865	2 305	1 660	645
50 - 54	+C	6 387	4 511	1 876	3 883	2 806	1 077	2 504	1 705	799
55 - 59	+C	6 904	4 867	2 037	4 015	2 896	1 119	2 889	1 971	918
60 - 64	+C	8 431	5 529	2 902	4 598	3 143	1 455	3 833	2 386	1 447
65 - 69	+C	10 699	6 751	3 948	5 491	3 530	1 961	5 208	3 221	1 987
70 - 74	+C	12 549	7 424	5 125	5 884	3 538	2 346	6 665	3 886	2 779
75 - 79	+C	10 704	6 080	4 624	4 489	2 569	1 920	6 215	3 511	2 704
80 - 84	+C	10 071	5 404	4 667	3 609	1 950	1 659	6 462	3 454	3 008
85+	+C	12 035	5 960	6 075	3 477	1 715	1 762	8 558	4 245	4 313
Tajikistan - Tadjikistan[15]										
1994										
Total	C	39 943	21 339	18 604	13 068	7 083	5 985	26 875	14 256	12 619
0 - 1	C	6 880	3 896	2 984	1 930	1 136	794	4 950	2 760	2 190
1 - 4	C	5 267	2 742	2 525	745	402	343	4 522	2 340	2 182
5 - 9	C	753	416	337	145	88	57	608	328	280
10 - 14	C	522	315	207	120	82	38	402	233	169
15 - 19	C	671	440	231	204	142	62	467	298	169
20 - 24	C	902	574	328	302	203	99	600	371	229
25 - 29	C	984	626	358	310	220	90	674	406	268
30 - 34	C	1 106	668	438	381	260	121	725	408	317
35 - 39	C	983	594	389	378	264	114	605	330	275
40 - 44	C	1 035	646	389	489	327	162	546	319	227
45 - 49	C	890	546	344	405	271	134	485	275	210
50 - 54	C	1 219	795	424	556	383	173	663	412	251
55 - 59	C	2 154	1 283	871	934	612	322	1 220	671	549
60 - 64	C	2 783	1 541	1 242	1 009	578	431	1 774	963	811
65 - 69	C	3 108	1 695	1 413	1 232	660	572	1 876	1 035	841
70 - 74	C	2 803	1 254	1 549	1 038	438	600	1 765	816	949
75 - 79	C	2 264	983	1 281	917	351	566	1 347	632	715
80 - 84	C	2 380	1 013	1 367	1 013	344	669	1 367	669	698
85+	C	3 219	1 299	1 920	949	315	634	2 270	984	1 286
Unknown - Inconnu	C	20	13	7	11	7	4	9	6	3
Thailand - Thaïlande										
1999										
Total	+U	362 593	213 427	149 166	36 796	21 674	15 122	325 797	191 753	134 044
0 - 1	+U	5 003	2 765	2 238	711	359	352	4 292	2 406	1 886
1 - 4	+U	5 948	3 193	2 755	451	246	205	5 497	2 947	2 550
5 - 9	+U	3 040	1 804	1 236	184	106	78	2 856	1 698	1 158
10 - 14	+U	2 162	1 300	862	181	112	69	1 981	1 188	793
15 - 19	+U	6 504	4 861	1 643	553	408	145	5 951	4 453	1 498
20 - 24	+U	11 727	8 192	3 535	1 280	972	308	10 447	7 220	3 227
25 - 29	+U	22 108	16 139	5 969	1 860	1 447	413	20 248	14 692	5 556
30 - 34	+U	23 928	18 116	5 812	2 242	1 715	527	21 686	16 401	5 285
35 - 39	+U	20 640	15 414	5 226	2 120	1 607	513	18 520	13 807	4 713
40 - 44	+U	18 982	13 089	5 893	2 120	1 480	640	16 862	11 609	5 253
45 - 49	+U	18 489	12 071	6 418	2 107	1 380	727	16 382	10 691	5 691
50 - 54	+U	18 660	11 727	6 933	2 017	1 267	750	16 643	10 460	6 183
55 - 59	+U	21 563	13 072	8 491	2 322	1 419	903	19 241	11 653	7 588
60 - 64	+U	27 435	16 057	11 378	3 029	1 810	1 219	24 406	14 247	10 159
65 - 69	+U	31 442	17 504	13 938	3 299	1 895	1 404	28 143	15 609	12 534
70 - 74	+U	32 171	17 261	14 910	3 202	1 660	1 542	28 969	15 601	13 368

Continent, country or area, year and age (in years) — Continent, pays ou zone, année et âge (en années)	Code[1]	Total			Urban - Urbaine			Rural - Rurale		
		Both sexes - Les deux sexes	Male - Masculin	Female - Féminin	Both sexes - Les deux sexes	Male - Masculin	Female - Féminin	Both sexes - Les deux sexes	Male - Masculin	Female - Féminin
ASIA — ASIE										
Thailand - Thaïlande										
1999										
75 - 79	+U	30 537	15 485	15 052	2 971	1 449	1 522	27 566	14 036	13 530
80 - 84	+U	26 406	11 901	14 505	2 803	1 203	1 600	23 603	10 698	12 905
85+	+U	32 613	12 063	20 550	3 292	1 118	2 174	29 321	10 945	18 376
Unknown - Inconnu	+U	3 235	1 413	1 822	52	21	31	3 183	1 392	1 791
Uzbekistan - Ouzbékistan[15]										
2000										
Total	C	135 598	70 794	64 804	61 130	32 195	28 935	74 468	38 599	35 869
0 - 1	C	10 091	5 805	4 286	3 703	2 136	1 567	6 388	3 669	2 719
1 - 4	C	5 417	2 925	2 492	1 177	645	532	4 240	2 280	1 960
5 - 9	C	1 474	886	588	423	251	172	1 051	635	416
10 - 14	C	1 436	852	584	442	260	182	994	592	402
15 - 19	C	2 001	1 289	712	709	475	234	1 292	814	478
20 - 24	C	2 849	1 758	1 091	1 155	789	366	1 694	969	725
25 - 29	C	3 427	2 177	1 250	1 501	1 023	478	1 926	1 154	772
30 - 34	C	3 660	2 403	1 257	1 657	1 185	472	2 003	1 218	785
35 - 39	C	4 181	2 759	1 422	1 993	1 407	586	2 188	1 352	836
40 - 44	C	5 086	3 277	1 809	2 584	1 789	795	2 502	1 488	1 014
45 - 49	C	5 290	3 445	1 845	2 797	1 924	873	2 493	1 521	972
50 - 54	C	5 765	3 647	2 118	3 140	2 052	1 088	2 625	1 595	1 030
55 - 59	C	6 104	3 794	2 310	3 056	1 990	1 066	3 048	1 804	1 244
60 - 64	C	12 287	7 257	5 030	5 897	3 603	2 294	6 390	3 654	2 736
65 - 69	C	14 077	7 757	6 320	6 312	3 601	2 711	7 765	4 156	3 609
70 - 74	C	17 094	8 713	8 381	8 142	4 010	4 132	8 952	4 703	4 249
75 - 79	C	12 547	4 824	7 723	6 043	2 111	3 932	6 504	2 713	3 791
80 - 84	C	8 807	2 836	5 971	4 430	1 285	3 145	4 377	1 551	2 826
85 - 89	C	7 198	2 312	4 886	3 747	1 011	2 736	3 451	1 301	2 150
90 - 94	C	3 782	1 295	2 487	1 515	421	1 094	2 267	874	1 393
95 - 99	C	1 963	579	1 384	511	167	344	1 452	412	1 040
100+	C	1 062	204	858	196	60	136	866	144	722
EUROPE										
Albania - Albanie										
2003										
Total	C	17 967	10 038	7 929	8 923	5 095	3 828	9 044	4 943	4 101
0 - 1	C	395	200	195	157	82	75	238	118	120
1 - 4	C	302	168	134	89	55	34	213	113	100
5 - 9	C	139	84	55	55	34	21	84	50	34
10 - 14	C	130	85	45	48	33	15	82	52	30
15 - 19	C	171	119	52	74	56	18	97	63	34
20 - 24	C	211	144	67	76	54	22	135	90	45
25 - 29	C	195	134	61	76	57	19	119	77	42
30 - 34	C	218	156	62	98	71	27	120	85	35
35 - 39	C	236	146	90	111	69	42	125	77	48
40 - 44	C	402	268	134	218	152	66	184	116	68
45 - 49	C	433	278	155	243	162	81	190	116	74
50 - 54	C	586	388	198	372	236	136	214	152	62
55 - 59	C	706	483	223	387	270	117	319	213	106
60 - 64	C	1 210	805	405	649	435	214	561	370	191
65 - 69	C	1 760	1 180	580	1 016	679	337	744	501	243
70 - 74	C	2 400	1 522	878	1 230	778	452	1 170	744	426
75 - 79	C	2 497	1 314	1 183	1 310	687	623	1 187	627	560
80 - 84	C	2 802	1 369	1 433	1 374	679	695	1 428	690	738
85 - 89	C	1 761	745	1 016	752	309	443	1 009	436	573
90 - 94	C	963	309	654	419	146	273	544	163	381
95 - 99	C	329	99	230	132	37	95	197	62	135
100+	C	121	42	79	37	14	23	84	28	56
Andorra - Andorre										
2003										
Total	C	221	136	85	...	...	...	...	...	...
1 - 4	C	2	1	1	...	...	...	...	...	...
5 - 9	C	1	-	1	...	...	...	...	...	...

19. Deaths by age, sex and urban/rural residence: latest available year, 1994 - 2003
Décès selon l'âge, le sexe et la résidence, urbaine/rurale: dernière année disponible, 1994 - 2003 (continued — suite)

Continent, country or area, year and age (in years) / Continent, pays ou zone, année et âge (en années)	Code[1]	Total			Urban - Urbaine			Rural - Rurale		
		Both sexes - Les deux sexes	Male - Masculin	Female - Féminin	Both sexes - Les deux sexes	Male - Masculin	Female - Féminin	Both sexes - Les deux sexes	Male - Masculin	Female - Féminin
EUROPE										
Andorra - Andorre										
2003										
15 - 19	C	2	2	-	...	...	...	...	...	...
25 - 29	C	3	2	1	...	...	...	...	...	...
30 - 34	C	2	2	-	...	...	...	...	...	...
35 - 39	C	4	4	-	...	...	...	...	...	...
40 - 44	C	1	1	-	...	...	...	...	...	...
45 - 49	C	7	6	1	...	...	...	...	...	...
50 - 54	C	10	9	1	...	...	...	...	...	...
55 - 59	C	8	4	4	...	...	...	...	...	...
60 - 64	C	11	9	2	...	...	...	...	...	...
65 - 69	C	17	13	4	...	...	...	...	...	...
70 - 74	C	24	11	13	...	...	...	...	...	...
75 - 79	C	00	20	10	...	...	...	...	...	...
80 - 84	C	34	20	14	...	...	...	...	...	...
85 - 89	C	29	12	17	...	...	...	...	...	...
90 - 94	C	25	17	8	...	...	...	...	...	...
95 - 99	C	8	2	6	...	...	...	...	...	...
100+	C	3	1	2	...	...	...	...	...	...
Austria - Autriche										
1999										
Total	C	78 200	35 880	42 320	46 752	20 596	26 156	31 448	15 284	16 164
0 - 1	C	341	176	165	191	100	91	150	76	74
1 - 4	C	98	67	31	51	37	14	47	30	17
5 - 9	C	51	28	23	25	11	14	26	17	9
10 - 14	C	72	36	36	38	17	21	34	19	15
15 - 19	C	276	197	79	110	78	30	160	119	41
20 - 24	C	330	257	73	177	136	41	153	121	32
25 - 29	C	348	251	97	183	132	51	165	119	46
30 - 34	C	512	352	160	313	201	112	199	151	48
35 - 39	C	806	550	256	472	324	148	334	226	108
40 - 44	C	1 075	714	361	621	406	215	454	308	146
45 - 49	C	1 433	922	511	848	523	325	585	399	186
50 - 54	C	2 251	1 468	783	1 425	916	509	826	552	274
55 - 59	C	3 554	2 373	1 181	2 238	1 464	774	1 316	909	407
60 - 64	C	3 939	2 654	1 285	2 194	1 461	733	1 745	1 193	552
65 - 69	C	6 004	3 939	2 065	3 267	2 091	1 176	2 737	1 848	889
70 - 74	C	8 963	5 084	3 879	5 131	2 793	2 338	3 832	2 291	1 541
75 - 79	C	12 409	5 726	6 683	7 297	3 256	4 041	5 112	2 470	2 642
80 - 84	C	10 218	3 965	6 253	6 134	2 373	3 761	4 084	1 592	2 492
85+	C	25 520	7 121	18 399	16 031	4 277	11 754	9 489	2 844	6 645
2003										
Total	C	77 209	35 448	41 761	...	...	...	...	...	...
0 - 1	C	343	192	151	...	...	...	...	...	...
1 - 4	C	90	48	42	...	...	...	...	...	...
5 - 9	C	40	27	13	...	...	...	...	...	...
10 - 14	C	64	32	32	...	...	...	...	...	...
15 - 19	C	253	169	84	...	...	...	...	...	...
20 - 24	C	335	258	77	...	...	...	...	...	...
25 - 29	C	276	211	65	...	...	...	...	...	...
30 - 34	C	424	285	139	...	...	...	...	...	...
35 - 39	C	670	447	223	...	...	...	...	...	...
40 - 44	C	1 014	662	352	...	...	...	...	...	...
45 - 49	C	1 488	971	517	...	...	...	...	...	...
50 - 54	C	2 123	1 434	689	...	...	...	...	...	...
55 - 59	C	3 031	1 953	1 078	...	...	...	...	...	...
60 - 64	C	4 891	3 219	1 672	...	...	...	...	...	...
65 - 69	C	4 746	3 120	1 626	...	...	...	...	...	...
70 - 74	C	7 975	4 802	3 173	...	...	...	...	...	...
75 - 79	C	11 596	5 719	5 877	...	...	...	...	...	...
80 - 84	C	14 360	5 506	8 854	...	...	...	...	...	...
85 - 89	C	11 003	3 383	7 620	...	...	...	...	...	...
90 - 94	C	9 490	2 437	7 053	...	...	...	...	...	...
95 - 99	C	2 664	526	2 138	...	...	...	...	...	...

19. Deaths by age, sex and urban/rural residence: latest available year, 1994 - 2003
Décès selon l'âge, le sexe et la résidence, urbaine/rurale: dernière année disponible, 1994 - 2003 (continued — suite)

Continent, country or area, year and age (in years) / Continent, pays ou zone, année et âge (en années)	Code[1]	Total			Urban - Urbaine			Rural - Rurale		
		Both sexes - Les deux sexes	Male - Masculin	Female - Féminin	Both sexes - Les deux sexes	Male - Masculin	Female - Féminin	Both sexes - Les deux sexes	Male - Masculin	Female - Féminin
EUROPE										
Austria - Autriche										
2003										
100+	C	333	47	286	...	...	...	...	...	...
Belarus - Bélarus[15]										
2003										
Total	C	143 200	76 023	67 177	75 420	42 090	33 330	67 780	33 933	33 847
0 - 1	C	685	409	276	440	273	167	245	136	109
1 - 4	C	198	116	82	89	49	40	109	67	42
5 - 9	C	136	89	47	71	50	21	65	39	26
10 - 14	C	159	103	56	95	54	41	64	49	15
15 - 19	C	607	459	148	367	260	107	240	199	41
20 - 24	C	1 132	915	217	731	578	153	401	337	64
25 - 29	C	1 575	1 303	272	956	781	175	619	522	97
30 - 34	C	2 174	1 734	440	1 314	1 025	289	860	709	151
35 - 39	C	3 072	2 421	651	1 891	1 442	449	1 181	979	202
40 - 44	C	4 895	3 809	1 086	3 093	2 321	772	1 802	1 488	314
45 - 49	C	6 786	5 202	1 584	4 370	3 271	1 099	2 416	1 931	485
50 - 54	C	8 448	6 283	2 165	5 644	4 130	1 514	2 804	2 153	651
55 - 59	C	7 749	5 394	2 355	5 013	3 474	1 539	2 736	1 920	816
60 - 64	C	12 551	8 522	4 029	7 372	5 037	2 335	5 179	3 485	1 694
65 - 69	C	16 635	10 159	6 476	8 786	5 350	3 436	7 849	4 809	3 040
70 - 74	C	21 513	11 458	10 055	10 256	5 449	4 807	11 257	6 009	5 248
75 - 79	C	22 256	8 952	13 304	10 709	4 493	6 216	11 547	4 459	7 088
80 - 84	C	15 309	4 672	10 637	7 032	2 177	4 855	8 277	2 495	5 782
85 - 89	C	9 006	2 196	6 810	3 946	1 035	2 911	5 060	1 161	3 899
90 - 94	C	5 972	1 219	4 753	2 318	500	1 818	3 654	719	2 935
95 - 99	C	1 660	359	1 301	601	153	448	1 059	206	853
100+	C	484	90	394	140	35	105	344	55	289
Unknown - Inconnu	C	198	159	39	186	153	33	12	6	6
Belgium - Belgique[28]										
2002										
Total	C	105 642	52 436	53 206	...	...	...	...	...	...
0 - 1	C	492	288	204	...	...	...	...	...	...
1 - 4	C	127	74	53	...	...	...	...	...	...
5 - 9	C	87	53	34	...	...	...	...	...	...
10 - 14	C	88	46	42	...	...	...	...	...	...
15 - 19	C	282	200	82	...	...	...	...	...	...
20 - 24	C	450	348	102	...	...	...	...	...	...
25 - 29	C	498	361	137	...	...	...	...	...	...
30 - 34	C	595	406	189	...	...	...	...	...	...
35 - 39	C	921	610	311	...	...	...	...	...	...
40 - 44	C	1 400	905	495	...	...	...	...	...	...
45 - 49	C	2 239	1 462	777	...	...	...	...	...	...
50 - 54	C	3 232	2 062	1 170	...	...	...	...	...	...
55 - 59	C	4 095	2 683	1 412	...	...	...	...	...	...
60 - 64	C	5 057	3 291	1 766	...	...	...	...	...	...
65 - 69	C	7 919	5 125	2 794	...	...	...	...	...	...
70 - 74	C	12 038	7 409	4 629	...	...	...	...	...	...
75 - 79	C	17 080	9 516	7 564	...	...	...	...	...	...
80 - 84	C	17 439	8 112	9 327	...	...	...	...	...	...
85 - 89	C	15 974	5 672	10 302	...	...	...	...	...	...
90 - 94	C	11 457	3 021	8 436	...	...	...	...	...	...
95 - 99	C	3 645	718	2 927	...	...	...	...	...	...
100+	C	527	74	453	...	...	...	...	...	...
Bosnia and Herzegovina - Bosnie-Herzégovine[29]										
2003										
Total	C	31 757	16 590	15 167	...	...	...	...	...	...
0 - 1	C	270	155	115	...	...	...	...	...	...
1 - 4	C	55	32	23	...	...	...	...	...	...
5 - 9	C	26	16	10	...	...	...	...	...	...
10 - 14	C	38	24	14	...	...	...	...	...	...
15 - 19	C	116	83	33	...	...	...	...	...	...
20 - 24	C	139	96	43	...	...	...	...	...	...

Continent, country or area, year and age (in years) / Continent, pays ou zone, année et âge (en années)	Code[1]	Total			Urban - Urbaine			Rural - Rurale		
		Both sexes - Les deux sexes	Male - Masculin	Female - Féminin	Both sexes - Les deux sexes	Male - Masculin	Female - Féminin	Both sexes - Les deux sexes	Male - Masculin	Female - Féminin

EUROPE

Bosnia and Herzegovina -
Bosnie-Herzégovine[29]
2003

25 - 29	C	168	118	50	...	...	...	...	...	...
30 - 34	C	194	131	63	...	...	...	...	...	...
35 - 39	C	317	227	90	...	...	...	...	...	...
40 - 44	C	579	394	185	...	...	...	...	...	...
45 - 49	C	1 018	676	342	...	...	...	...	...	...
50 - 54	C	1 456	993	463	...	...	...	...	...	...
55 - 59	C	1 662	1 083	579	...	...	...	...	...	...
60 - 64	C	2 982	1 805	1 177	...	...	...	...	...	...
65 - 69	C	5 027	2 912	2 115	...	...	...	...	...	...
70 - 74	C	6 279	3 421	2 858	...	...	...	...	...	...
75 - 79	C	5 313	2 259	3 054	...	...	...	...	...	...
80 - 84	C	3 581	1 280	2 301	...	...	...	...	...	...
85 - 89	C	1 429	500	929	...	...	...	...	...	...
90 - 94	C	847	285	562	...	...	...	...	...	...
95 - 99	C	198	75	123	...	...	...	...	...	...
100+	C	22	7	15	...	...	...	...	...	...
Unknown - Inconnu	C	40	17	23	...	...	...	...	...	...

Bulgaria - Bulgarie
2003

Total	C	111 927	59 992	51 935	64 495	34 703	29 792	47 432	25 289	22 143
0 - 1	C	831	488	343	522	306	216	309	182	127
1 - 4	C	158	83	75	86	48	38	72	35	37
5 - 9	C	79	54	25	51	35	16	28	19	9
10 - 14	C	144	89	55	82	53	29	62	36	26
15 - 19	C	260	181	79	193	135	58	67	46	21
20 - 24	C	443	332	111	313	242	71	130	90	40
25 - 29	C	566	406	160	414	297	117	152	109	43
30 - 34	C	642	438	204	450	299	151	192	139	53
35 - 39	C	927	630	297	647	430	217	280	200	80
40 - 44	C	1 617	1 105	512	1 096	729	367	521	376	145
45 - 49	C	2 755	1 937	818	1 945	1 330	615	810	607	203
50 - 54	C	4 735	3 412	1 323	3 302	2 349	953	1 433	1 063	370
55 - 59	C	6 314	4 478	1 836	4 142	2 876	1 266	2 172	1 602	570
60 - 64	C	7 783	5 215	2 568	4 737	3 157	1 580	3 046	2 058	988
65 - 69	C	11 999	7 441	4 558	6 853	4 184	2 669	5 146	3 257	1 889
70 - 74	C	16 560	9 201	7 359	9 308	5 141	4 167	7 252	4 060	3 192
75 - 79	C	21 679	10 611	11 068	11 967	5 827	6 140	9 712	4 784	4 928
80 - 84	C	19 427	8 326	11 101	10 303	4 393	5 910	9 124	3 933	5 191
85 - 89	C	9 000	3 508	5 492	4 766	1 758	3 008	4 234	1 750	2 484
90 - 94	C	5 018	1 743	3 275	2 761	919	1 842	2 257	824	1 433
95 - 99	C	910	297	613	516	185	331	394	112	282
100+	C	80	17	63	41	10	31	39	7	32

Channel Islands: Guernsey -
Îles Anglo-Normandes:
Guernesey
2000

Total	C	565	264	301	...	...	...	...	...	...
0 - 1	C	4	3	1	...	...	...	...	...	...
1 - 4	C	1	-	1	...	...	...	...	...	...
15 - 19	C	4	3	1	...	...	...	...	...	...
20 - 24	C	1	-	1	...	...	...	...	...	...
25 - 29	C	1	1	-	...	...	...	...	...	...
30 - 34	C	2	1	1	...	...	...	...	...	...
35 - 39	C	2	2	-	...	...	...	...	...	...
40 - 44	C	4	4	-	...	...	...	...	...	...
45 - 49	C	7	5	2	...	...	...	...	...	...
50 - 54	C	13	9	4	...	...	...	...	...	...
55 - 59	C	13	7	6	...	...	...	...	...	...
60 - 64	C	30	15	15	...	...	...	...	...	...
65 - 69	C	45	29	16	...	...	...	...	...	...
70 - 74	C	57	27	30	...	...	...	...	...	...

Continent, country or area, year and age (in years) Continent, pays ou zone, année et âge (en années)	Code[1]	Total			Urban - Urbaine			Rural - Rurale		
		Both sexes - Les deux sexes	Male - Masculin	Female - Féminin	Both sexes - Les deux sexes	Male - Masculin	Female - Féminin	Both sexes - Les deux sexes	Male - Masculin	Female - Féminin
EUROPE										
Channel Islands: Guernsey - Îles Anglo-Normandes: Guernesey										
2000										
75 - 79	C	71	38	33	...	...	...	...	...	...
80 - 84	C	103	55	48	...	...	...	...	...	...
85 - 89	C	108	45	63	...	...	...	...	...	...
90 - 94	C	68	14	54	...	...	...	...	...	...
95 - 99	C	24	3	21	...	...	...	...	...	...
100+	C	5	2	3	...	...	...	...	...	...
Unknown - Inconnu	C	2	1	1	...	...	...	...	...	...
Channel Islands: Jersey - Îles Anglo-Normandes: Jersey										
1994										
Total	+C	803	368	435	...	...	...	...	...	...
0 - 1	+C	2	-	2	...	...	...	...	...	...
5 - 9	+C	3	2	1	...	...	...	...	...	...
15 - 19	+C	5	3	2	...	...	...	...	...	...
20 - 24	+C	1	-	1	...	...	...	...	...	...
25 - 29	+C	2	1	1	...	...	...	...	...	...
30 - 34	+C	5	4	1	...	...	...	...	...	...
35 - 39	+C	5	3	2	...	...	...	...	...	...
40 - 44	+C	9	7	2	...	...	...	...	...	...
45 - 49	+C	23	11	12	...	...	...	...	...	...
50 - 54	+C	17	8	9	...	...	...	...	...	...
55 - 59	+C	30	24	6	...	...	...	...	...	...
60 - 64	+C	48	36	12	...	...	...	...	...	...
65 - 69	+C	55	34	21	...	...	...	...	...	...
70 - 74	+C	101	47	54	...	...	...	...	...	...
75+	+C	497	188	309	...	...	...	...	...	...
Croatia - Croatie										
2003										
Total	C	52 575	26 519	26 056	25 976	13 085	12 891	26 599	13 434	13 165
0 - 1	C	251	148	103	135	82	53	116	66	50
1 - 4	C	42	25	17	18	13	5	24	12	12
5 - 9	C	38	22	16	17	11	6	21	11	10
10 - 14	C	49	35	14	22	15	7	27	20	7
15 - 19	C	150	102	48	86	58	28	64	44	20
20 - 24	C	223	184	39	129	103	26	94	81	13
25 - 29	C	210	164	46	114	84	30	96	80	16
30 - 34	C	283	214	69	165	124	41	118	90	28
35 - 39	C	368	259	109	165	111	54	203	148	55
40 - 44	C	736	528	208	359	250	109	377	278	99
45 - 49	C	1 310	927	383	692	460	232	618	467	151
50 - 54	C	1 945	1 388	557	1 014	678	336	931	710	221
55 - 59	C	2 326	1 650	676	1 255	844	411	1 071	806	265
60 - 64	C	3 699	2 489	1 210	1 944	1 279	665	1 755	1 210	545
65 - 69	C	6 032	3 893	2 139	3 008	1 935	1 073	3 024	1 958	1 066
70 - 74	C	8 540	4 846	3 694	4 043	2 250	1 793	4 497	2 596	1 901
75 - 79	C	9 422	4 184	5 238	4 555	2 073	2 482	4 867	2 111	2 756
80 - 84	C	8 767	3 057	5 710	4 205	1 493	2 712	4 562	1 564	2 998
85 - 89	C	4 232	1 328	2 904	2 042	662	1 380	2 190	666	1 524
90 - 94	C	3 158	871	2 287	1 584	463	1 121	1 574	408	1 166
95 - 99	C	717	182	535	380	89	291	337	93	244
100+	C	65	17	48	38	6	32	27	11	16
Unknown - Inconnu	C	12	6	6	6	2	4	6	4	2
Czech Republic - République tchèque										
2003										
Total	C	111 288	55 880	55 408	80 561	40 062	40 499	30 727	15 818	14 909
0 - 1	C	365	207	158	266	163	103	99	44	55
1 - 4	C	89	49	40	63	37	26	26	12	14
5 - 9	C	67	42	25	43	29	14	24	13	11
10 - 14	C	102	64	38	72	45	27	30	19	11

19. Deaths by age, sex and urban/rural residence: latest available year, 1994 - 2003
Décès selon l'âge, le sexe et la résidence, urbaine/rurale: dernière année disponible, 1994 - 2003 (continued — suite)

Continent, country or area, year and age (in years) Continent, pays ou zone, année et âge (en années)	Code[1]	Total			Urban - Urbaine			Rural - Rurale		
		Both sexes - Les deux sexes	Male - Masculin	Female - Féminin	Both sexes - Les deux sexes	Male - Masculin	Female - Féminin	Both sexes - Les deux sexes	Male - Masculin	Female - Féminin
EUROPE										
Czech Republic - République tchèque										
2003										
15 - 19	C	288	206	82	209	140	69	79	66	13
20 - 24	C	509	394	115	349	269	80	160	125	35
25 - 29	C	594	459	135	433	327	106	161	132	29
30 - 34	C	662	487	175	484	356	128	178	131	47
35 - 39	C	897	634	263	653	457	196	244	177	67
40 - 44	C	1 311	903	408	946	637	309	365	266	99
45 - 49	C	2 797	1 945	852	2 096	1 424	672	701	521	180
50 - 54	C	4 899	3 424	1 475	3 627	2 479	1 148	1 272	945	327
55 - 59	C	7 224	4 937	2 287	5 276	3 556	1 720	1 948	1 381	567
60 - 64	C	7 764	5 155	2 609	5 714	3 727	1 987	2 050	1 428	622
65 - 69	C	9 355	5 894	3 461	6 734	4 190	2 544	2 621	1 704	917
70 - 74	C	14 421	8 104	6 317	10 381	5 787	4 594	4 040	2 317	1 723
75 - 79	C	19 413	9 185	10 228	14 002	6 616	7 386	5 411	2 569	2 842
80 - 84	C	19 332	7 597	11 735	13 934	5 444	8 490	5 398	2 153	3 245
85 - 89	C	11 233	3 565	7 668	8 077	2 523	5 554	3 156	1 042	2 114
90 - 94	C	8 186	2 255	5 931	5 904	1 592	4 312	2 282	663	1 619
95 - 99	C	1 641	353	1 288	1 205	252	953	436	101	335
100+	C	139	21	118	93	12	81	46	9	37
Denmark - Danemark[30]										
2003										
Total	C	57 574	28 146	29 428	...	...	...	...	...	...
0 - 1	C	286	165	121	...	...	...	...	...	...
1 - 4	C	67	42	25	...	...	...	...	...	...
5 - 9	C	34	19	15	...	...	...	...	...	...
10 - 14	C	48	29	19	...	...	...	...	...	...
15 - 19	C	96	76	20	...	...	...	...	...	...
20 - 24	C	156	109	47	...	...	...	...	...	...
25 - 29	C	191	135	56	...	...	...	...	...	...
30 - 34	C	273	182	91	...	...	...	...	...	...
35 - 39	C	456	304	152	...	...	...	...	...	...
40 - 44	C	695	461	234	...	...	...	...	...	...
45 - 49	C	1 214	749	465	...	...	...	...	...	...
50 - 54	C	1 772	1 097	675	...	...	...	...	...	...
55 - 59	C	2 938	1 808	1 130	...	...	...	...	...	...
60 - 64	C	3 411	2 090	1 321	...	...	...	...	...	...
65 - 69	C	4 445	2 587	1 858	...	...	...	...	...	...
70 - 74	C	6 150	3 390	2 760	...	...	...	...	...	...
75 - 79	C	8 182	4 410	3 772	...	...	...	...	...	...
80 - 84	C	9 852	4 617	5 235	...	...	...	...	...	...
85 - 89	C	8 895	3 530	5 365	...	...	...	...	...	...
90 - 94	C	6 164	1 890	4 274	...	...	...	...	...	...
95 - 99	C	1 936	408	1 528	...	...	...	...	...	...
100+	C	313	48	265	...	...	...	...	...	...
Estonia - Estonie[6,15]										
2002										
Total	C	18 355	9 369	8 986	11 953	6 078	5 875	6 276	3 189	3 087
0 - 1	C	74	46	28	53	35	18	21	11	10
1 - 4	C	24	18	6	9	7	2	15	11	4
5 - 9	C	24	15	9	16	10	6	8	5	3
10 - 14	C	19	13	6	12	8	4	7	5	2
15 - 19	C	95	78	17	71	57	14	22	19	3
20 - 24	C	172	143	29	127	106	21	44	36	8
25 - 29	C	162	139	23	114	98	16	47	40	7
30 - 34	C	225	179	46	156	118	38	69	61	8
35 - 39	C	293	235	58	205	161	44	85	72	13
40 - 44	C	518	377	141	374	270	104	135	101	34
45 - 49	C	773	575	198	550	408	142	212	158	54
50 - 54	C	997	716	281	678	474	204	309	236	73
55 - 59	C	980	679	301	614	425	189	355	245	110
60 - 64	C	1 616	1 117	499	1 074	717	357	538	396	142
65 - 69	C	1 885	1 220	665	1 214	773	441	667	443	224

Continent, country or area, year and age (in years) / Continent, pays ou zone, année et âge (en années)	Code[1]	Total			Urban - Urbaine			Rural - Rurale		
		Both sexes - Les deux sexes	Male - Masculin	Female - Féminin	Both sexes - Les deux sexes	Male - Masculin	Female - Féminin	Both sexes - Les deux sexes	Male - Masculin	Female - Féminin
EUROPE										
Estonia - Estonie[6,15]										
2002										
70 - 74	C	2 536	1 376	1 160	1 724	923	801	811	452	359
75 - 79	C	2 524	994	1 530	1 673	647	1 026	849	346	503
80 - 84	C	2 100	665	1 435	1 288	396	892	812	269	543
85 - 89	C	1 748	436	1 312	1 071	273	798	677	163	514
90 - 94	C	1 159	215	944	708	124	584	450	91	359
95 - 99	C	304	58	246	174	30	144	130	28	102
100+	C	42	3	39	29	2	27	13	1	12
Unknown - Inconnu	C	85	72	13	19	16	3	-	-	-
Finland - Finlande[31]										
2003										
Total	C	48 996	23 922	25 074	27 156	12 848	14 308	21 840	11 074	10 766
0 - 1	C	176	93	83	107	54	53	69	39	30
1 - 4	C	48	34	14	35	24	11	13	10	3
5 - 9	C	29	16	13	10	6	4	19	10	9
10 - 14	C	51	38	13	25	15	10	26	23	3
15 - 19	C	138	103	35	63	46	17	75	57	18
20 - 24	C	238	177	61	158	114	44	80	63	17
25 - 29	C	239	182	57	148	112	36	91	70	21
30 - 34	C	247	182	65	155	111	44	92	71	21
35 - 39	C	431	316	115	252	179	73	179	137	42
40 - 44	C	725	508	217	424	294	130	301	214	87
45 - 49	C	1 239	877	362	750	520	230	489	357	132
50 - 54	C	1 947	1 377	570	1 140	771	369	807	606	201
55 - 59	C	2 539	1 790	749	1 473	999	474	1 066	791	275
60 - 64	C	2 648	1 826	822	1 546	1 043	503	1 102	783	319
65 - 69	C	3 381	2 214	1 167	1 841	1 168	673	1 540	1 046	494
70 - 74	C	5 201	3 198	2 003	2 833	1 693	1 140	2 368	1 505	863
75 - 79	C	7 384	3 833	3 551	3 983	2 000	1 983	3 401	1 833	1 568
80 - 84	C	8 170	3 268	4 902	4 395	1 697	2 698	3 775	1 571	2 204
85 - 89	C	7 677	2 362	5 315	4 166	1 214	2 952	3 511	1 148	2 363
90 - 94	C	4 984	1 222	3 762	2 807	631	2 176	2 177	591	1 586
95 - 99	C	1 349	285	1 064	761	144	617	588	141	447
100+	C	155	21	134	84	13	71	71	8	63
France[32,33,34]										
2002										
Total	C	534 183	272 371	261 812	378 495	188 711	189 784	153 746	82 352	71 394
0 - 1	C	3 138	1 766	1 372	2 452	1 387	1 065	666	371	295
1 - 4	C	695	400	295	499	279	220	175	106	69
5 - 9	C	455	260	195	314	182	132	128	71	57
10 - 14	C	538	308	230	334	196	138	180	101	79
15 - 19	C	1 737	1 234	503	1 090	770	320	618	448	170
20 - 24	C	2 637	1 989	648	1 801	1 334	467	784	616	168
25 - 29	C	2 849	2 123	726	2 100	1 558	542	688	525	163
30 - 34	C	3 623	2 599	1 024	2 700	1 893	807	860	656	204
35 - 39	C	5 629	3 835	1 794	4 178	2 810	1 368	1 368	958	410
40 - 44	C	9 017	5 987	3 030	6 668	4 373	2 295	2 257	1 544	713
45 - 49	C	14 018	9 554	4 464	10 378	7 018	3 360	3 504	2 434	1 070
50 - 54	C	20 167	14 096	6 071	14 907	10 346	4 561	5 092	3 625	1 467
55 - 59	C	21 500	15 082	6 418	15 795	10 993	4 802	5 542	3 969	1 573
60 - 64	C	23 788	16 576	7 212	16 933	11 698	5 235	6 670	4 747	1 923
65 - 69	C	36 468	24 556	11 912	25 697	16 944	8 753	10 585	7 481	3 104
70 - 74	C	53 783	34 172	19 611	37 350	23 115	14 235	16 233	10 919	5 314
75 - 79	C	74 097	41 850	32 247	51 155	28 092	23 063	22 761	13 643	9 118
80 - 84	C	79 610	39 114	40 496	56 014	26 778	29 236	23 461	12 263	11 198
85 - 89	C	78 411	29 924	48 487	55 346	20 484	34 862	22 995	9 412	13 583
90 - 94	C	71 381	20 946	50 435	50 630	14 300	36 330	20 708	6 633	14 075
95 - 99	C	26 016	5 390	20 626	18 705	3 715	14 990	7 297	1 666	5 631
100+	C	4 626	610	4 016	3 449	446	3 003	1 174	164	1 010
Germany - Allemagne										
2003										
Total	C	853 946	396 270	457 676	...	...	...	...	...	...
0 - 1	C	2 990	1 700	1 290	...	...	...	...	...	...

19. Deaths by age, sex and urban/rural residence: latest available year, 1994 - 2003
Décès selon l'âge, le sexe et la résidence, urbaine/rurale: dernière année disponible, 1994 - 2003 (continued — suite)

Continent, country or area, year and age (in years) / Continent, pays ou zone, année et âge (en années)	Code[1]	Total			Urban - Urbaine			Rural - Rurale		
		Both sexes - Les deux sexes	Male - Masculin	Female - Féminin	Both sexes - Les deux sexes	Male - Masculin	Female - Féminin	Both sexes - Les deux sexes	Male - Masculin	Female - Féminin
EUROPE										
Germany - Allemagne										
2003										
1 - 4	C	680	381	299	...	...	...	...	...	...
5 - 9	C	477	275	202	...	...	...	...	...	...
10 - 14	C	570	346	224	...	...	...	...	...	...
15 - 19	C	1 819	1 287	532	...	...	...	...	...	...
20 - 24	C	2 516	1 880	636	...	...	...	...	...	...
25 - 29	C	2 469	1 815	654	...	...	...	...	...	...
30 - 34	C	3 700	2 573	1 127	...	...	...	...	...	...
35 - 39	C	7 004	4 713	2 291	...	...	...	...	...	...
40 - 44	C	11 560	7 694	3 866	...	...	...	...	...	...
45 - 49	C	17 195	11 497	5 698	...	...	...	...	...	...
50 - 54	C	24 319	16 045	8 274	...	...	...	...	...	...
55 - 59	C	29 669	19 768	9 901	...	...	...	...	...	...
60 - 64	C	55 446	37 333	18 113	...	...	...	...	...	...
65 - 69	C	75 575	49 663	25 912	...	...	...	...	...	...
70 - 74	C	94 809	57 650	37 159	...	...	...	...	...	...
75 - 79	C	123 398	60 833	62 565	...	...	...	...	...	...
80 - 84	C	147 937	56 291	91 646	...	...	...	...	...	...
85 - 89	C	114 473	34 073	80 400	...	...	...	...	...	...
90 - 94	C	102 857	24 423	78 434	...	...	...	...	...	...
95 - 99	C	30 602	5 516	25 086	...	...	...	...	...	...
100+	C	3 881	514	3 367	...	...	...	...	...	...
Greece - Grèce										
2003										
Total	C	105 529	54 942	50 587	58 197	29 891	28 306	47 332	25 051	22 281
0 - 1	C	420	236	184	308	174	134	112	62	50
1 - 4	C	74	39	35	48	24	24	26	15	11
5 - 9	C	51	29	22	27	15	12	24	14	10
10 - 14	C	79	47	32	46	26	20	33	21	12
15 - 19	C	317	237	80	179	131	48	138	106	32
20 - 24	C	504	421	83	327	278	49	177	143	34
25 - 29	C	518	404	114	349	266	83	169	138	31
30 - 34	C	619	454	165	410	297	113	209	157	52
35 - 39	C	791	563	228	521	362	159	270	201	69
40 - 44	C	1 188	828	360	749	505	244	439	323	116
45 - 49	C	1 730	1 182	548	1 132	743	389	598	439	159
50 - 54	C	2 482	1 719	763	1 591	1 089	502	891	630	261
55 - 59	C	3 706	2 596	1 110	2 365	1 644	721	1 341	952	389
60 - 64	C	4 702	3 216	1 486	2 804	1 887	917	1 898	1 329	569
65 - 69	C	8 424	5 478	2 946	4 773	3 051	1 722	3 651	2 427	1 224
70 - 74	C	12 963	7 812	5 151	7 302	4 318	2 984	5 661	3 494	2 167
75 - 79	C	17 809	9 455	8 354	9 835	5 053	4 782	7 974	4 402	3 572
80 - 84	C	17 660	8 074	9 586	9 583	4 158	5 425	8 077	3 916	4 161
85 - 89	C	16 567	6 606	9 961	8 673	3 313	5 360	7 894	3 293	4 601
90 - 94	C	10 980	4 171	6 809	5 359	1 943	3 416	5 621	2 228	3 393
95 - 99	C	3 315	1 202	2 113	1 523	532	991	1 792	670	1 122
100+	C	630	173	457	293	82	211	337	91	246
Hungary - Hongrie[35]										
2003										
Total	C	135 192	69 565	65 627	84 106	42 032	42 074	51 086	27 533	23 553
0 - 1	C	683	385	298	375	225	150	308	160	148
1 - 4	C	120	67	53	58	33	25	62	34	28
5 - 9	C	92	47	45	50	27	23	42	20	22
10 - 14	C	114	69	45	71	44	27	43	25	18
15 - 19	C	232	158	74	141	97	44	91	61	30
20 - 24	C	408	309	99	265	195	70	143	114	29
25 - 29	C	582	439	143	371	277	94	211	162	49
30 - 34	C	799	572	227	468	334	134	331	238	93
35 - 39	C	1 236	877	359	700	494	206	536	383	153
40 - 44	C	2 682	1 866	816	1 526	1 028	498	1 156	838	318
45 - 49	C	5 793	4 090	1 703	3 412	2 311	1 101	2 381	1 779	602
50 - 54	C	7 406	5 121	2 285	4 518	3 003	1 515	2 888	2 118	770
55 - 59	C	8 770	6 027	2 743	5 509	3 670	1 839	3 261	2 357	904

Continent, country or area, year and age (in years) / Continent, pays ou zone, année et âge (en années)	Code[1]	Total			Urban - Urbaine			Rural - Rurale		
		Both sexes - Les deux sexes	Male - Masculin	Female - Féminin	Both sexes - Les deux sexes	Male - Masculin	Female - Féminin	Both sexes - Les deux sexes	Male - Masculin	Female - Féminin
EUROPE										
Hungary - Hongrie[35]										
2003										
60 - 64	C	10 556	6 981	3 575	6 430	4 176	2 254	4 126	2 805	1 321
65 - 69	C	12 883	7 897	4 986	7 738	4 632	3 106	5 145	3 265	1 880
70 - 74	C	17 886	9 790	8 096	10 796	5 826	4 970	7 090	3 964	3 126
75 - 79	C	21 464	9 961	11 503	13 194	5 995	7 199	8 270	3 966	4 304
80 - 84	C	21 626	8 331	13 295	13 694	5 194	8 500	7 932	3 137	4 795
85 - 89	C	11 489	3 750	7 739	7 758	2 555	5 203	3 731	1 195	2 536
90 - 94	C	8 373	2 415	5 958	5 634	1 634	4 000	2 739	781	1 958
95 - 99	C	1 798	371	1 427	1 258	256	1 002	540	115	425
100+	C	198	41	157	139	26	113	59	15	44
Unknown - Inconnu	C	2	1	1	1	-	1	1	1	-
Iceland - Islande										
2003										
Total	C	1 827	901	926	1 676	810	866	151	91	60
0 - 1	C	10	6	4	10	6	4	-	-	-
1 - 4	C	2	-	2	2	-	2	-	-	-
5 - 9	C	4	3	1	4	3	1	-	-	-
10 - 14	C	2	2	-	2	2	-	-	-	-
15 - 19	C	5	2	3	4	2	2	1	-	1
20 - 24	C	10	7	3	9	6	3	1	1	-
25 - 29	C	9	7	2	8	6	2	1	1	-
30 - 34	C	9	5	4	8	4	4	1	1	-
35 - 39	C	11	4	7	10	3	7	1	1	-
40 - 44	C	22	9	13	22	9	13	-	-	-
45 - 49	C	28	20	8	26	20	6	2	-	2
50 - 54	C	46	26	20	41	23	18	5	3	2
55 - 59	C	73	42	31	70	39	31	3	3	-
60 - 64	C	80	51	29	71	45	26	9	6	3
65 - 69	C	107	59	48	102	57	45	5	2	3
70 - 74	C	208	114	94	193	105	88	15	9	6
75 - 79	C	237	136	101	218	121	97	19	15	4
80 - 84	C	333	164	169	303	149	154	30	15	15
85 - 89	C	322	132	190	289	111	178	33	21	12
90 - 94	C	217	84	133	203	75	128	14	9	5
95 - 99	C	75	25	50	66	22	44	9	3	6
100+	C	17	3	14	15	2	13	2	1	1
Ireland - Irlande[36]										
1999										
Total	+C	31 683	16 480	15 203	17 288	8 599	8 689	14 395	7 881	6 514
0 - 1	+C	293	160	133	195	108	87	98	52	46
1 - 4	+C	68	39	29	37	25	12	31	14	17
5 - 9	+C	41	28	13	20	14	6	21	14	7
10 - 14	+C	56	37	19	31	19	12	25	18	7
15 - 19	+C	171	123	48	90	64	26	81	59	22
20 - 24	+C	233	179	54	130	103	27	103	76	27
25 - 29	+C	196	149	47	109	83	26	87	66	21
30 - 34	+C	222	153	69	141	94	47	81	59	22
35 - 39	+C	279	174	105	178	111	67	101	63	38
40 - 44	+C	406	243	163	232	143	89	174	100	74
45 - 49	+C	637	392	245	409	249	160	228	143	85
50 - 54	+C	888	553	335	514	301	213	374	252	122
55 - 59	+C	1 226	777	449	747	460	287	479	317	162
60 - 64	+C	1 675	1 065	610	1 003	626	377	672	439	233
65 - 69	+C	2 606	1 630	976	1 485	897	588	1 121	733	388
70 - 74	+C	3 961	2 375	1 586	2 224	1 300	924	1 737	1 075	662
75 - 79	+C	5 492	3 005	2 487	2 877	1 499	1 378	2 615	1 506	1 109
80 - 84	+C	5 601	2 666	2 935	2 823	1 221	1 602	2 778	1 445	1 333
85+	+C	7 632	2 732	4 900	4 043	1 282	2 761	3 589	1 450	2 139
2003										
Total	+C	28 823	14 735	14 088	...	...	...	...	...	...
0 - 1	+C	311	182	129	...	...	...	...	...	...
1 - 4	+C	45	27	18	...	...	...	...	...	...
5 - 9	+C	29	17	12	...	...	...	...	...	...

Continent, country or area, year and age (in years) / Continent, pays ou zone, année et âge (en années)	Code[1]	Total			Urban - Urbaine			Rural - Rurale		
		Both sexes - Les deux sexes	Male - Masculin	Female - Féminin	Both sexes - Les deux sexes	Male - Masculin	Female - Féminin	Both sexes - Les deux sexes	Male - Masculin	Female - Féminin
EUROPE										
Ireland - Irlande[36]										
2003										
10 - 14	+C	44	25	19	...	...	...	...	...	...
15 - 19	+C	146	102	44	...	...	...	...	...	...
20 - 24	+C	230	180	50	...	...	...	...	...	...
25 - 29	+C	215	158	57	...	...	...	...	...	...
30 - 34	+C	204	151	53	...	...	...	...	...	...
35 - 39	+C	275	174	101	...	...	...	...	...	...
40 - 44	+C	372	233	139	...	...	...	...	...	...
45 - 49	+C	531	325	206	...	...	...	...	...	...
50 - 54	+C	844	522	322	...	...	...	...	...	...
55 - 59	+C	1 300	794	506	...	...	...	...	...	...
60 - 64	+C	1 678	1 034	644	...	...	...	...	...	...
65 - 69	+C	2 255	1 417	838	...	...	...	...	...	...
70 - 74	+C	3 166	1 886	1 280	...	...	...	...	...	...
75 - 79	+C	4 550	2 426	2 124	...	...	...	...	...	...
80 - 84	+C	5 225	2 476	2 749	...	...	...	...	...	...
85 - 89	+C	4 262	1 714	2 548	...	...	...	...	...	...
90 - 94	+C	2 373	731	1 642	...	...	...	...	...	...
95 - 99	+C	667	144	523	...	...	...	...	...	...
100+	+C	101	17	84	...	...	...	...	...	...
Isle of Man - Îles de Man										
1999										
Total	+C	983	471	512	...	...	...	...	...	...
0 - 1	+C	6	3	3	...	...	...	...	...	...
1 - 4	+C	3	3	-	...	...	...	...	...	...
5 - 9	+C	1	-	1	...	...	...	...	...	...
10 - 14	+C	2	1	1	...	...	...	...	...	...
15 - 19	+C	2	1	1	...	...	...	...	...	...
20 - 24	+C	1	1	-	...	...	...	...	...	...
25 - 29	+C	3	1	2	...	...	...	...	...	...
30 - 34	+C	6	4	2	...	...	...	...	...	...
35 - 39	+C	10	7	3	...	...	...	...	...	...
40 - 44	+C	6	5	1	...	...	...	...	...	...
45 - 49	+C	12	7	5	...	...	...	...	...	...
50 - 54	+C	16	6	10	...	...	...	...	...	...
55 - 59	+C	27	19	8	...	...	...	...	...	...
60 - 64	+C	42	23	19	...	...	...	...	...	...
65 - 69	+C	68	33	35	...	...	...	...	...	...
70 - 74	+C	96	60	36	...	...	...	...	...	...
75 - 79	+C	166	82	84	...	...	...	...	...	...
80 - 84	+C	184	85	99	...	...	...	...	...	...
85+	+C	332	130	202	...	...	...	...	...	...
Italy - Italie										
2001										
Total	C	556 892	279 032	277 860	...	...	...	...	...	...
0 - 1	C	2 482	1 370	1 112	...	...	...	...	...	...
1 - 4	C	443	245	198	...	...	...	...	...	...
5 - 9	C	293	175	118	...	...	...	...	...	...
10 - 14	C	395	247	148	...	...	...	...	...	...
15 - 19	C	1 241	932	309	...	...	...	...	...	...
20 - 24	C	2 037	1 568	469	...	...	...	...	...	...
25 - 29	C	2 629	2 001	628	...	...	...	...	...	...
30 - 34	C	3 210	2 340	870	...	...	...	...	...	...
35 - 39	C	4 353	2 915	1 438	...	...	...	...	...	...
40 - 44	C	5 532	3 615	1 917	...	...	...	...	...	...
45 - 49	C	7 713	4 908	2 805	...	...	...	...	...	...
50 - 54	C	13 067	8 412	4 655	...	...	...	...	...	...
55 - 59	C	17 866	11 795	6 071	...	...	...	...	...	...
60 - 64	C	29 093	19 170	9 923	...	...	...	...	...	...
65 - 69	C	43 037	27 795	15 242	...	...	...	...	...	...
70 - 74	C	64 659	39 757	24 902	...	...	...	...	...	...
75 - 79	C	90 091	49 329	40 762	...	...	...	...	...	...
80 - 84	C	79 202	37 204	41 998	...	...	...	...	...	...

19. Deaths by age, sex and urban/rural residence: latest available year, 1994 - 2003
Décès selon l'âge, le sexe et la résidence, urbaine/rurale: dernière année disponible, 1994 - 2003 (continued — suite)

Continent, country or area, year and age (in years) / Continent, pays ou zone, année et âge (en années)	Code[1]	Total			Urban - Urbaine			Rural - Rurale		
		Both sexes - Les deux sexes	Male - Masculin	Female - Féminin	Both sexes - Les deux sexes	Male - Masculin	Female - Féminin	Both sexes - Les deux sexes	Male - Masculin	Female - Féminin
EUROPE										
Italy - Italie										
2001										
85 - 89	C	102 076	39 958	62 118	...	...	...	...	...	...
90 - 94	C	65 367	20 402	44 965	...	...	...	...	...	...
95 - 99	C	19 190	4 386	14 804	...	...	...	...	...	...
100+	C	2 916	508	2 408	...	...	...	...	...	...
Latvia - Lettonie[15]										
2002										
Total	C	32 498	16 423	16 075	21 059	10 645	10 414	11 439	5 778	5 661
0 - 1	C	197	111	86	105	58	47	92	53	39
1 - 4	C	54	31	23	26	18	8	28	13	15
5 - 9	C	55	34	21	33	21	12	22	13	9
10 - 14	C	37	22	15	22	13	9	15	9	6
15 - 19	C	134	89	45	85	55	30	49	34	15
20 - 24	C	238	196	42	156	121	35	82	75	7
25 - 29	C	269	233	36	169	149	20	100	84	16
30 - 34	C	417	335	82	281	221	60	136	114	22
35 - 39	C	558	430	128	370	288	82	188	142	46
40 - 44	C	883	671	212	585	444	141	298	227	71
45 - 49	C	1 194	885	309	825	604	221	369	281	88
50 - 54	C	1 644	1 187	457	1 106	769	337	538	418	120
55 - 59	C	1 901	1 306	595	1 282	865	417	619	441	178
60 - 64	C	3 028	2 069	959	1 961	1 302	659	1 067	767	300
65 - 69	C	3 431	2 126	1 305	2 226	1 358	868	1 205	768	437
70 - 74	C	4 341	2 380	1 961	2 828	1 537	1 291	1 513	843	670
75 - 79	C	4 643	1 788	2 855	3 079	1 202	1 877	1 564	586	978
80 - 84	C	3 908	1 231	2 677	2 477	782	1 695	1 431	449	982
85 - 89	C	2 885	723	2 162	1 808	471	1 337	1 077	252	825
90 - 94	C	2 058	445	1 613	1 233	282	951	825	163	662
95 - 99	C	542	116	426	347	75	272	195	41	154
100+	C	74	9	65	52	7	45	22	2	20
Unknown - Inconnu	C	7	6	1	3	3	-	4	3	1
Liechtenstein										
2003										
Total	C	217	103	114	...	...	...	...	...	...
0 - 1	C	1	-	1	...	...	...	...	...	...
1 - 4	C	-	-	-	...	...	...	...	...	...
5 - 9	C	1	-	1	...	...	...	...	...	...
10 - 14	C	1	1	-	...	...	...	...	...	...
15 - 19	C	1	-	1	...	...	...	...	...	...
20 - 24	C	1	1	-	...	...	...	...	...	...
25 - 29	C	1	1	-	...	...	...	...	...	...
30 - 34	C	1	-	1	...	...	...	...	...	...
35 - 39	C	3	3	-	...	...	...	...	...	...
45 - 49	C	7	2	5	...	...	...	...	...	...
50 - 54	C	9	4	5	...	...	...	...	...	...
55 - 59	C	7	4	3	...	...	...	...	...	...
60 - 64	C	17	11	6	...	...	...	...	...	...
65 - 69	C	15	11	4	...	...	...	...	...	...
70 - 74	C	15	9	6	...	...	...	...	...	...
75 - 79	C	36	17	19	...	...	...	...	...	...
80 - 84	C	43	25	18	...	...	...	...	...	...
85 - 89	C	29	8	21	...	...	...	...	...	...
90 - 94	C	22	3	19	...	...	...	...	...	...
95 - 99	C	6	2	4	...	...	...	...	...	...
100+	C	1	1	-	...	...	...	...	...	...
Lithuania - Lituanie[15]										
2003										
Total	C	40 990	21 859	19 131	23 082	12 249	10 833	17 908	9 610	8 298
0 - 1	C	206	119	87	108	65	43	98	54	44
1 - 4	C	60	35	25	33	19	14	27	16	11
5 - 9	C	39	24	15	22	14	8	17	10	7
10 - 14	C	60	34	26	29	13	16	31	21	10
15 - 19	C	226	162	64	129	95	34	97	67	30

Continent, country or area, year and age (in years) Continent, pays ou zone, année et âge (en années)	Code[1]	Total			Urban - Urbaine			Rural - Rurale		
		Both sexes - Les deux sexes	Male - Masculin	Female - Féminin	Both sexes - Les deux sexes	Male - Masculin	Female - Féminin	Both sexes - Les deux sexes	Male - Masculin	Female - Féminin
EUROPE										
Lithuania - Lituanie[15]										
2003										
20 - 24	C	334	287	47	193	162	31	141	125	16
25 - 29	C	414	335	79	220	170	50	194	165	29
30 - 34	C	617	498	119	360	283	77	257	215	42
35 - 39	C	765	594	171	432	324	108	333	270	63
40 - 44	C	1 314	985	329	811	585	226	503	400	103
45 - 49	C	1 667	1 224	443	1 028	734	294	639	490	149
50 - 54	C	2 112	1 529	583	1 297	906	391	815	623	192
55 - 59	C	2 353	1 655	698	1 503	1 039	464	850	616	234
60 - 64	C	3 327	2 240	1 087	1 956	1 286	670	1 371	954	417
65 - 69	C	4 168	2 667	1 501	2 403	1 500	903	1 765	1 167	598
70 - 74	C	5 260	2 952	2 308	2 981	1 679	1 302	2 279	1 273	1 006
75 - 79	C	5 990	2 612	3 378	3 340	1 446	1 894	2 650	1 166	1 484
80 - 84	C	5 132	1 856	3 276	2 644	909	1 735	2 488	947	1 541
85 - 89	C	3 439	1 063	2 376	1 783	531	1 252	1 656	532	1 124
90 - 94	C	2 413	608	1 805	1 288	324	964	1 125	284	841
95 - 99	C	896	315	581	432	138	294	464	177	287
100+	C	195	63	132	87	25	62	108	38	70
Unknown - Inconnu	C	3	2	1	3	2	1	-	-	-
Luxembourg										
2003										
Total	C	4 053	2 005	2 048	...	...	...	...	...	...
0 - 1	C	26	16	10	...	...	...	...	...	...
1 - 4	C	3	2	1	...	...	...	...	...	...
5 - 9	C	3	2	1	...	...	...	...	...	...
10 - 14	C	5	2	3	...	...	...	...	...	...
15 - 19	C	7	4	3	...	...	...	...	...	...
20 - 24	C	18	17	1	...	...	...	...	...	...
25 - 29	C	21	16	5	...	...	...	...	...	...
30 - 34	C	29	21	8	...	...	...	...	...	...
35 - 39	C	41	26	15	...	...	...	...	...	...
40 - 44	C	61	43	18	...	...	...	...	...	...
45 - 49	C	88	60	28	...	...	...	...	...	...
50 - 54	C	117	85	32	...	...	...	...	...	...
55 - 59	C	165	117	48	...	...	...	...	...	...
60 - 64	C	226	140	86	...	...	...	...	...	...
65 - 69	C	349	218	131	...	...	...	...	...	...
70 - 74	C	512	306	206	...	...	...	...	...	...
75 - 79	C	598	301	297	...	...	...	...	...	...
80 - 84	C	637	267	370	...	...	...	...	...	...
85 - 89	C	614	222	392	...	...	...	...	...	...
90 - 94	C	389	114	275	...	...	...	...	...	...
95 - 99	C	129	26	103	...	...	...	...	...	...
100+	C	15	-	15	...	...	...	...	...	...
Malta - Malte										
2003										
Total	C	3 072	1 541	1 531	...	...	...	...	...	...
0 - 1	C	23	16	7	...	...	...	...	...	...
1 - 4	C	2	1	1	...	...	...	...	...	...
5 - 9	C	2	1	1	...	...	...	...	...	...
10 - 14	C	2	1	1	...	...	...	...	...	...
15 - 19	C	8	7	1	...	...	...	...	...	...
20 - 24	C	16	10	6	...	...	...	...	...	...
25 - 29	C	17	11	6	...	...	...	...	...	...
30 - 34	C	14	8	6	...	...	...	...	...	...
35 - 39	C	24	12	12	...	...	...	...	...	...
40 - 44	C	34	24	10	...	...	...	...	...	...
45 - 49	C	58	41	17	...	...	...	...	...	...
50 - 54	C	82	49	33	...	...	...	...	...	...
55 - 59	C	137	82	55	...	...	...	...	...	...
60 - 64	C	152	86	66	...	...	...	...	...	...
65 - 69	C	262	156	106	...	...	...	...	...	...
70 - 74	C	393	230	163	...	...	...	...	...	...

19. Deaths by age, sex and urban/rural residence: latest available year, 1994 - 2003
Décès selon l'âge, le sexe et la résidence, urbaine/rurale: dernière année disponible, 1994 - 2003 (continued — suite)

Continent, country or area, year and age (in years) / Continent, pays ou zone, année et âge (en années)	Code[1]	Total			Urban - Urbaine			Rural - Rurale		
		Both sexes - Les deux sexes	Male - Masculin	Female - Féminin	Both sexes - Les deux sexes	Male - Masculin	Female - Féminin	Both sexes - Les deux sexes	Male - Masculin	Female - Féminin
EUROPE										
Malta - Malte										
2003										
75 - 79	C	504	257	247	...	...	...	...	...	...
80 - 84	C	615	283	332	...	...	...	...	...	...
85 - 89	C	398	154	244	...	...	...	...	...	...
90+	C	329	112	217	...	...	...	...	...	...
Netherlands - Pays-Bas[37]										
2003										
Total	C	141 936	69 012	72 924	94 744	44 958	49 786	47 192	24 054	23 138
0 - 1	C	872	511	361	569	336	233	303	175	128
1 - 4	C	267	155	112	171	103	68	96	52	44
5 - 9	C	159	98	61	100	63	37	59	35	24
10 - 14	C	143	83	60	91	54	37	52	29	23
15 - 19	C	282	176	106	176	114	62	106	62	44
20 - 24	C	386	269	117	226	151	75	160	118	42
25 - 29	C	475	309	166	338	214	124	137	95	42
30 - 34	C	704	452	252	495	317	178	209	135	74
35 - 39	C	1 048	619	429	709	414	295	339	205	134
40 - 44	C	1 845	1 064	781	1 255	732	523	590	332	258
45 - 49	C	2 777	1 538	1 239	1 912	1 060	852	865	478	387
50 - 54	C	4 249	2 454	1 795	2 881	1 651	1 230	1 368	803	565
55 - 59	C	6 334	3 865	2 469	4 108	2 449	1 659	2 226	1 416	810
60 - 64	C	7 322	4 572	2 750	4 705	2 919	1 786	2 617	1 653	964
65 - 69	C	10 079	6 366	3 713	6 608	4 102	2 506	3 471	2 264	1 207
70 - 74	C	15 000	9 088	5 912	9 777	5 744	4 033	5 223	3 344	1 879
75 - 79	C	20 384	11 277	9 107	13 643	7 416	6 227	6 741	3 861	2 880
80 - 84	C	25 282	12 183	13 099	17 066	8 066	9 000	8 216	4 117	4 099
85 - 89	C	22 781	8 412	14 369	15 319	5 521	9 798	7 462	2 891	4 571
90 - 94	C	15 362	4 293	11 069	10 389	2 759	7 630	4 973	1 534	3 439
95 - 99	C	5 329	1 076	4 253	3 607	683	2 924	1 722	393	1 329
100+	C	856	152	704	599	90	509	257	62	195
Norway - Norvège[38]										
2003										
Total	C	42 478	20 565	21 913	...	...	...	...	...	...
0 - 1	C	187	105	82	...	...	...	...	...	...
1 - 4	C	61	30	31	...	...	...	...	...	...
5 - 9	C	36	23	13	...	...	...	...	...	...
10 - 14	C	50	30	20	...	...	...	...	...	...
15 - 19	C	126	91	35	...	...	...	...	...	...
20 - 24	C	169	122	47	...	...	...	...	...	...
25 - 29	C	200	144	56	...	...	...	...	...	...
30 - 34	C	261	188	73	...	...	...	...	...	...
35 - 39	C	320	219	101	...	...	...	...	...	...
40 - 44	C	464	286	178	...	...	...	...	...	...
45 - 49	C	653	407	246	...	...	...	...	...	...
50 - 54	C	985	611	374	...	...	...	...	...	...
55 - 59	C	1 610	978	632	...	...	...	...	...	...
60 - 64	C	1 743	1 069	674	...	...	...	...	...	...
65 - 69	C	2 369	1 499	870	...	...	...	...	...	...
70 - 74	C	3 752	2 235	1 517	...	...	...	...	...	...
75 - 79	C	5 892	3 222	2 670	...	...	...	...	...	...
80 - 84	C	8 361	4 097	4 264	...	...	...	...	...	...
85 - 89	C	8 215	3 172	5 043	...	...	...	...	...	...
90 - 94	C	5 117	1 595	3 522	...	...	...	...	...	...
95 - 99	C	1 581	344	1 237	...	...	...	...	...	...
100+	C	224	45	179	...	...	...	...	...	...
Unknown - Inconnu	C	102	53	49	...	...	...	...	...	...
Poland - Pologne										
2003										
Total	C	365 230	193 919	171 311	216 349	113 213	103 136	148 881	80 706	68 175
0 - 1	C	2 470	1 383	1 087	1 446	791	655	1 024	592	432
1 - 4	C	390	237	153	188	113	75	202	124	78
5 - 9	C	363	221	142	178	102	76	185	119	66
10 - 14	C	504	309	195	249	144	105	255	165	90

494

Continent, country or area, year and age (in years) Continent, pays ou zone, année et âge (en années)	Code[1]	Total			Urban - Urbaine			Rural - Rurale		
		Both sexes - Les deux sexes	Male - Masculin	Female - Féminin	Both sexes - Les deux sexes	Male - Masculin	Female - Féminin	Both sexes - Les deux sexes	Male - Masculin	Female - Féminin
EUROPE										
Poland - Pologne										
2003										
15 - 19	C	1 456	1 047	409	767	539	228	689	508	181
20 - 24	C	2 304	1 842	462	1 354	1 058	296	950	784	166
25 - 29	C	2 356	1 860	496	1 463	1 110	353	893	750	143
30 - 34	C	2 771	2 174	597	1 640	1 250	390	1 131	924	207
35 - 39	C	4 194	3 220	974	2 463	1 841	622	1 731	1 379	352
40 - 44	C	8 193	6 106	2 087	4 929	3 479	1 450	3 264	2 627	637
45 - 49	C	14 886	10 842	4 044	9 623	6 685	2 938	5 263	4 157	1 106
50 - 54	C	21 179	15 005	6 174	13 894	9 539	4 355	7 285	5 466	1 819
55 - 59	C	21 157	14 709	6 448	14 070	9 485	4 585	7 087	5 224	1 863
60 - 64	C	24 709	16 867	7 842	16 065	10 664	5 401	8 644	6 203	2 441
65 - 69	C	36 498	23 552	12 946	22 576	14 156	8 420	13 922	9 396	4 526
70 - 74	C	50 543	29 001	21 542	30 034	16 855	13 179	20 509	12 146	8 363
75 - 79	C	57 641	27 337	30 304	33 087	15 365	17 722	24 554	11 972	12 582
80 - 84	C	51 038	19 986	31 052	27 684	10 545	17 139	23 354	9 441	13 913
85 - 89	C	32 898	10 579	22 319	18 013	5 505	12 508	14 885	5 074	9 811
90 - 94	C	23 213	6 169	17 044	12 836	3 177	9 659	10 377	2 992	7 385
95 - 99	C	5 783	1 339	4 444	3 387	737	2 650	2 396	602	1 794
100+	C	684	134	550	403	73	330	281	61	220
Portugal										
2003										
Total	C	108 795	55 968	52 827	...	...	...	...	...	...
0 - 1	C	465	234	231	...	...	...	...	...	...
1 - 4	C	126	68	58	...	...	...	...	...	...
5 - 9	C	103	61	42	...	...	...	...	...	...
10 - 14	C	121	68	53	...	...	...	...	...	...
15 - 19	C	298	213	85	...	...	...	...	...	...
20 - 24	C	553	414	139	...	...	...	...	...	...
25 - 29	C	762	551	211	...	...	...	...	...	...
30 - 34	C	993	752	241	...	...	...	...	...	...
35 - 39	C	1 272	923	349	...	...	...	...	...	...
40 - 44	C	1 751	1 265	486	...	...	...	...	...	...
45 - 49	C	2 387	1 677	710	...	...	...	...	...	...
50 - 54	C	3 044	2 077	967	...	...	...	...	...	...
55 - 59	C	3 883	2 568	1 315	...	...	...	...	...	...
60 - 64	C	5 223	3 445	1 778	...	...	...	...	...	...
65 - 69	C	8 378	5 391	2 987	...	...	...	...	...	...
70 - 74	C	12 641	7 492	5 149	...	...	...	...	...	...
75 - 79	C	17 635	9 400	8 235	...	...	...	...	...	...
80 - 84	C	19 343	9 028	10 315	...	...	...	...	...	...
85 - 89	C	16 604	6 489	10 115	...	...	...	...	...	...
90 - 94	C	10 108	3 161	6 947	...	...	...	...	...	...
95 - 99	C	2 684	624	2 060	...	...	...	...	...	...
100+	C	421	67	354	...	...	...	...	...	...
Republic of Moldova - République de Moldova[15]										
2003										
Total	C	43 079	21 913	21 166	13 650	7 205	6 445	29 429	14 708	14 721
0 - 1	C	522	309	213	178	104	74	344	205	139
1 - 4	C	129	69	60	28	14	14	101	55	46
5 - 9	C	83	51	32	27	15	12	56	36	20
10 - 14	C	109	70	39	38	23	15	71	47	24
15 - 19	C	181	127	54	64	48	16	117	79	38
20 - 24	C	321	248	73	126	100	26	195	148	47
25 - 29	C	383	293	90	152	119	33	231	174	57
30 - 34	C	467	341	126	196	144	52	271	197	74
35 - 39	C	833	579	254	324	226	98	509	353	156
40 - 44	C	1 481	1 049	432	592	411	181	889	638	251
45 - 49	C	2 198	1 517	681	890	601	289	1 308	916	392
50 - 54	C	3 093	2 019	1 074	1 207	805	402	1 886	1 214	672
55 - 59	C	2 122	1 251	871	851	527	324	1 271	724	547
60 - 64	C	4 080	2 332	1 748	1 383	842	541	2 697	1 490	1 207
65 - 69	C	5 256	2 802	2 454	1 578	865	713	3 678	1 937	1 741

19. Deaths by age, sex and urban/rural residence: latest available year, 1994 - 2003
Décès selon l'âge, le sexe et la résidence, urbaine/rurale: dernière année disponible, 1994 - 2003 (continued — suite)

Continent, country or area, year and age (in years) Continent, pays ou zone, année et âge (en années)	Code[1]	Total			Urban - Urbaine			Rural - Rurale		
		Both sexes - Les deux sexes	Male - Masculin	Female - Féminin	Both sexes - Les deux sexes	Male - Masculin	Female - Féminin	Both sexes - Les deux sexes	Male - Masculin	Female - Féminin
EUROPE										
Republic of Moldova - République de Moldova[15]										
2003										
70 - 74	C	6 393	3 095	3 298	1 726	842	884	4 667	2 253	2 414
75 - 79	C	6 428	2 621	3 807	1 915	773	1 142	4 513	1 848	2 665
80 - 84	C	5 168	1 919	3 249	1 350	459	891	3 818	1 460	2 358
85 - 89	C	2 351	793	1 558	634	186	448	1 717	607	1 110
90 - 94	C	1 211	363	848	324	87	237	887	276	611
95 - 99	C	232	56	176	57	9	48	175	47	128
100+	C	38	9	29	10	5	5	28	4	24
Romania - Roumanie										
2003										
Total	C	266 575	142 710	123 865	112 283	60 965	51 318	154 292	81 745	72 547
0 - 1	C	3 546	2 060	1 486	1 381	809	572	2 165	1 251	914
1 - 4	C	641	379	262	240	138	102	401	241	160
5 - 9	C	383	226	157	153	93	60	230	133	97
10 - 14	C	616	380	236	279	162	117	337	218	119
15 - 19	C	886	592	294	434	278	156	452	314	138
20 - 24	C	1 246	896	350	610	441	169	636	455	181
25 - 29	C	1 538	1 145	393	709	505	204	829	640	189
30 - 34	C	2 358	1 726	632	1 061	740	321	1 297	986	311
35 - 39	C	3 167	2 248	919	1 468	981	487	1 699	1 267	432
40 - 44	C	5 391	3 881	1 510	2 748	1 852	896	2 643	2 029	614
45 - 49	C	10 253	7 360	2 893	5 811	4 023	1 788	4 442	3 337	1 105
50 - 54	C	13 517	9 447	4 070	7 488	5 199	2 289	6 029	4 248	1 781
55 - 59	C	14 463	9 793	4 670	7 335	4 956	2 379	7 128	4 837	2 291
60 - 64	C	20 461	13 454	7 007	9 554	6 344	3 210	10 907	7 110	3 797
65 - 69	C	30 913	18 795	12 118	13 166	8 030	5 136	17 747	10 765	6 982
70 - 74	C	39 598	21 659	17 939	15 805	8 628	7 177	23 793	13 031	10 762
75 - 79	C	46 031	21 977	24 054	17 309	8 141	9 168	28 722	13 836	14 886
80 - 84	C	37 595	14 800	22 795	13 675	5 227	8 448	23 920	9 573	14 347
85 - 89	C	19 236	6 831	12 405	7 316	2 514	4 802	11 920	4 317	7 603
90 - 94	C	12 220	4 258	7 962	4 735	1 604	3 131	7 485	2 654	4 831
95 - 99	C	2 320	753	1 567	924	284	640	1 396	469	927
100+	C	196	50	146	82	16	66	114	34	80
Russian Federation - Fédération de Russie[15]										
2003										
Total	C	2 365 826	1 272 543	1 093 283	1 657 569	897 121	760 448	708 257	375 422	332 835
0 - 1	C	18 142	10 429	7 713	12 235	7 021	5 214	5 907	3 408	2 499
1 - 4	C	4 297	2 509	1 788	2 449	1 433	1 016	1 848	1 076	772
5 - 9	C	2 898	1 804	1 094	1 739	1 085	654	1 159	719	440
10 - 14	C	4 270	2 785	1 485	2 650	1 700	950	1 620	1 085	535
15 - 19	C	15 360	11 073	4 287	10 020	7 168	2 852	5 340	3 905	1 435
20 - 24	C	28 968	22 901	6 067	19 996	15 656	4 340	8 972	7 245	1 727
25 - 29	C	39 416	31 335	8 081	28 563	22 607	5 956	10 853	8 728	2 125
30 - 34	C	47 106	36 893	10 213	34 281	26 675	7 606	12 825	10 218	2 607
35 - 39	C	62 987	48 972	14 015	44 819	34 521	10 298	18 168	14 451	3 717
40 - 44	C	110 330	85 277	25 053	79 268	60 791	18 477	31 062	24 486	6 576
45 - 49	C	145 809	110 292	35 517	105 970	79 616	26 354	39 839	30 676	9 163
50 - 54	C	178 480	130 527	47 953	132 638	96 588	36 050	45 842	33 939	11 903
55 - 59	C	131 161	90 971	40 190	98 910	68 684	30 226	32 251	22 287	9 964
60 - 64	C	212 204	140 169	72 035	148 044	97 569	50 475	64 160	42 600	21 560
65 - 69	C	257 102	153 787	103 315	176 243	104 328	71 915	80 859	49 459	31 400
70 - 74	C	311 529	158 640	152 889	207 909	103 636	104 273	103 620	55 004	48 616
75 - 79	C	333 176	125 242	207 934	231 076	87 120	143 956	102 100	38 122	63 978
80 - 84	C	197 469	49 802	147 667	138 582	35 506	103 076	58 887	14 296	44 591
85 - 89	C	145 831	28 902	116 929	99 933	20 942	78 991	45 898	7 960	37 938
90 - 94	C	82 455	13 489	68 966	54 330	9 686	44 644	28 125	3 803	24 322
95 - 99	C	16 864	2 167	14 697	10 632	1 510	9 122	6 232	657	5 575
100+	C	2 388	281	2 107	1 200	166	1 034	1 188	115	1 073
Unknown - Inconnu	C	17 584	14 296	3 288	16 082	13 113	2 969	1 502	1 183	319

Continent, country or area, year and age (in years) Continent, pays ou zone, année et âge (en années)	Code[1]	Total			Urban - Urbaine			Rural - Rurale		
		Both sexes - Les deux sexes	Male - Masculin	Female - Féminin	Both sexes - Les deux sexes	Male - Masculin	Female - Féminin	Both sexes - Les deux sexes	Male - Masculin	Female - Féminin
EUROPE										
San Marino - Saint-Marin										
2003										
Total	+C	216	111	105	...	...	...	...	...	...
0 - 1	+C	2	1	1	...	...	...	...	...	...
1 - 4	+C	-	-	-	...	...	...	...	...	...
5 - 9	+C	-	-	-	...	...	...	...	...	...
10 - 14	+C	-	-	-	...	...	...	...	...	...
15 - 19	+C	-	-	-	...	...	...	...	...	...
20 - 24	+C	1	1	-	...	...	...	...	...	...
25 - 29	+C	1	-	1	...	...	...	...	...	...
30 - 34	+C	1	-	1	...	...	...	...	...	...
35 - 39	+C	1	-	1	...	...	...	...	...	...
40 - 44	+C	1	-	1	...	...	...	...	...	...
45 - 49	+C	1	-	1	...	...	...	...	...	...
50 - 54	+C	7	4	3	...	...	...	...	...	...
55 - 59	+C	4	3	1	...	...	...	...	...	...
60 - 64	+C	9	5	4	...	...	...	...	...	...
65 - 69	+C	12	9	3	...	...	...	...	...	...
70 - 74	+C	26	19	7	...	...	...	...	...	...
75 - 79	+C	26	20	6	...	...	...	...	...	...
80 - 84	+C	37	17	20	...	...	...	...	...	...
85 - 89	+C	36	18	18	...	...	...	...	...	...
90 - 94	+C	34	11	23	...	...	...	...	...	...
95 - 99	+C	12	3	9	...	...	...	...	...	...
100+	+C	5	-	5	...	...	...	...	...	...
Serbia and Montenegro - Serbie-et-Montenegro[39]										
2002										
Total	C	108 298	55 601	52 697	55 129	28 479	26 650	53 169	27 122	26 047
0 - 1	C	882	521	361	616	371	245	266	150	116
1 - 4	C	116	62	54	71	41	30	45	21	24
5 - 9	C	89	51	38	56	30	26	33	21	12
10 - 14	C	121	77	44	74	46	28	47	31	16
15 - 19	C	239	162	77	150	99	51	89	63	26
20 - 24	C	368	275	93	230	166	64	138	109	29
25 - 29	C	474	339	135	320	233	87	154	106	48
30 - 34	C	539	359	180	312	208	104	227	151	76
35 - 39	C	803	491	312	475	275	200	328	216	112
40 - 44	C	1 522	988	534	883	544	339	639	444	195
45 - 49	C	3 174	2 083	1 091	1 897	1 195	702	1 277	888	389
50 - 54	C	4 828	3 260	1 568	3 025	1 991	1 034	1 803	1 269	534
55 - 59	C	5 198	3 452	1 746	3 063	1 974	1 089	2 135	1 478	657
60 - 64	C	8 684	5 402	3 282	4 825	2 951	1 874	3 859	2 451	1 408
65 - 69	C	14 374	8 410	5 964	7 720	4 567	3 153	6 654	3 843	2 811
70 - 74	C	19 948	10 405	9 543	9 663	5 019	4 644	10 285	5 386	4 899
75 - 79	C	21 091	9 424	11 667	10 072	4 470	5 602	11 019	4 954	6 065
80 - 84	C	13 957	5 539	8 418	6 204	2 407	3 797	7 753	3 132	4 621
85 - 89	C	6 806	2 495	4 311	3 176	1 094	2 082	3 630	1 401	2 229
90 - 94	C	4 097	1 451	2 646	1 844	636	1 208	2 253	815	1 438
95 - 99	C	821	285	536	366	117	249	455	168	287
100+	C	98	23	75	36	8	28	62	15	47
Unknown - Inconnu	C	69	47	22	51	37	14	18	10	8
Slovakia - Slovaquie										
2002										
Total	C	51 532	27 415	24 117	24 737	13 002	11 735	26 795	14 413	12 382
0 - 1	C	388	189	199	191	94	97	197	95	102
1 - 4	C	74	38	36	33	18	15	41	20	21
5 - 9	C	78	50	28	35	22	13	43	28	15
10 - 14	C	71	39	32	37	18	19	34	21	13
15 - 19	C	197	136	61	106	76	30	91	60	31
20 - 24	C	312	246	66	181	150	31	131	96	35
25 - 29	C	348	267	81	192	146	46	156	121	35
30 - 34	C	376	287	89	177	137	40	199	150	49
35 - 39	C	598	457	141	300	227	73	298	230	68

Continent, country or area, year and age (in years) Continent, pays ou zone, année et âge (en années)	Code[1]	Total			Urban - Urbaine			Rural - Rurale		
		Both sexes - Les deux sexes	Male - Masculin	Female - Féminin	Both sexes - Les deux sexes	Male - Masculin	Female - Féminin	Both sexes - Les deux sexes	Male - Masculin	Female - Féminin
EUROPE										
Slovakia - Slovaquie										
2002										
40 - 44	C	1 140	856	284	612	440	172	528	416	112
45 - 49	C	2 017	1 494	523	1 043	727	316	974	767	207
50 - 54	C	2 761	2 056	705	1 466	1 046	420	1 295	1 010	285
55 - 59	C	3 074	2 150	924	1 602	1 094	508	1 472	1 056	416
60 - 64	C	3 822	2 570	1 252	1 849	1 229	620	1 973	1 341	632
65 - 69	C	5 092	3 137	1 955	2 464	1 481	983	2 628	1 656	972
70 - 74	C	6 969	3 805	3 164	3 260	1 718	1 542	3 709	2 087	1 622
75 - 79	C	8 695	4 038	4 657	4 068	1 843	2 225	4 627	2 195	2 432
80 - 84	C	7 129	2 889	4 240	3 224	1 314	1 910	3 905	1 575	2 330
85 - 89	C	4 840	1 660	3 180	2 254	751	1 503	2 586	909	1 677
90 - 94	C	2 835	869	1 966	1 300	390	910	1 535	479	1 056
95 - 99	C	654	166	488	316	72	244	338	94	244
100+	C	62	16	46	27	9	18	35	7	28
Slovenia - Slovénie										
2003										
Total	C	19 451	10 074	9 377	8 983	4 611	4 372	10 468	5 463	5 005
0 - 1	C	69	37	32	32	16	16	37	21	16
1 - 4	C	15	10	5	9	7	2	6	3	3
5 - 9	C	13	6	7	6	4	2	7	2	5
10 - 14	C	11	7	4	4	3	1	7	4	3
15 - 19	C	70	47	23	29	16	13	41	31	10
20 - 24	C	110	87	23	49	38	11	61	49	12
25 - 29	C	107	87	20	52	43	9	55	44	11
30 - 34	C	122	90	32	54	41	13	68	49	19
35 - 39	C	212	159	53	101	71	30	111	88	23
40 - 44	C	360	249	111	169	112	57	191	137	54
45 - 49	C	613	457	156	293	205	88	320	252	68
50 - 54	C	900	653	247	424	297	127	476	356	120
55 - 59	C	971	684	287	461	313	148	510	371	139
60 - 64	C	1 322	931	391	601	428	173	721	503	218
65 - 69	C	1 908	1 268	640	863	550	313	1 045	718	327
70 - 74	C	2 728	1 602	1 126	1 282	724	558	1 446	878	568
75 - 79	C	3 066	1 420	1 646	1 395	666	729	1 671	754	917
80 - 84	C	2 951	1 163	1 788	1 336	567	769	1 615	596	1 019
85 - 89	C	1 943	626	1 317	919	287	632	1 024	339	685
90 - 94	C	1 514	405	1 109	691	183	508	823	222	601
95 - 99	C	403	82	321	190	40	150	213	42	171
100+	C	43	4	39	23	-	23	20	4	16
Spain - Espagne										
2002										
Total	C	368 618	193 269	175 349	...	...	...	...	...	...
0 - 1	C	1 737	991	746	...	...	...	...	...	...
1 - 4	C	396	222	174	...	...	...	...	...	...
5 - 9	C	278	156	122	...	...	...	...	...	...
10 - 14	C	320	198	122	...	...	...	...	...	...
15 - 19	C	972	704	268	...	...	...	...	...	...
20 - 24	C	1 816	1 391	425	...	...	...	...	...	...
25 - 29	C	2 180	1 648	532	...	...	...	...	...	...
30 - 34	C	2 848	2 102	746	...	...	...	...	...	...
35 - 39	C	3 963	2 821	1 142	...	...	...	...	...	...
40 - 44	C	5 276	3 735	1 541	...	...	...	...	...	...
45 - 49	C	6 950	4 847	2 103	...	...	...	...	...	...
50 - 54	C	9 381	6 673	2 708	...	...	...	...	...	...
55 - 59	C	12 664	9 106	3 558	...	...	...	...	...	...
60 - 64	C	15 761	11 193	4 568	...	...	...	...	...	...
65 - 69	C	27 619	19 015	8 604	...	...	...	...	...	...
70 - 74	C	41 042	26 298	14 744	...	...	...	...	...	...
75 - 79	C	56 332	32 489	23 843	...	...	...	...	...	...
80 - 84	C	63 052	30 174	32 878	...	...	...	...	...	...
85 - 89	C	60 360	23 051	37 309	...	...	...	...	...	...
90 - 94	C	40 554	12 663	27 891	...	...	...	...	...	...
95 - 99	C	13 035	3 369	9 666	...	...	...	...	...	...

Continent, country or area, year and age (in years) Continent, pays ou zone, année et âge (en années)	Code[1]	Total			Urban - Urbaine			Rural - Rurale		
		Both sexes - Les deux sexes	Male - Masculin	Female - Féminin	Both sexes - Les deux sexes	Male - Masculin	Female - Féminin	Both sexes - Les deux sexes	Male - Masculin	Female - Féminin
EUROPE										
Spain - Espagne										
2002										
100+	C	2 082	423	1 659	...	...	...	...	...	...
Sweden - Suède										
2002										
Total	C	95 009	45 780	49 229	...	...	...	...	...	...
0 - 1	C	313	172	141	...	...	...	...	...	...
1 - 4	C	69	46	23	...	...	...	...	...	...
5 - 9	C	36	16	20	...	...	...	...	...	...
10 - 14	C	67	41	26	...	...	...	...	...	...
15 - 19	C	173	109	64	...	...	...	...	...	...
20 - 24	C	274	210	64	...	...	...	...	...	...
25 - 29	C	258	180	78	...	...	...	...	...	...
30 - 34	C	341	231	110	...	...	...	...	...	...
35 - 39	C	477	308	169	...	...	...	...	...	...
40 - 44	C	708	458	250	...	...	...	...	...	...
45 - 49	C	1 143	675	468	...	...	...	...	...	...
50 - 54	C	1 973	1 214	759	...	...	...	...	...	...
55 - 59	C	3 411	2 067	1 344	...	...	...	...	...	...
60 - 64	C	3 876	2 412	1 464	...	...	...	...	...	...
65 - 69	C	5 370	3 279	2 091	...	...	...	...	...	...
70 - 74	C	8 390	4 934	3 456	...	...	...	...	...	...
75 - 79	C	13 237	7 375	5 862	...	...	...	...	...	...
80 - 84	C	18 669	9 208	9 461	...	...	...	...	...	...
85 - 89	C	18 840	7 730	11 110	...	...	...	...	...	...
90 - 94	C	12 735	4 057	8 678	...	...	...	...	...	...
95 - 99	C	4 091	963	3 128	...	...	...	...	...	...
100+	C	558	95	463	...	...	...	...	...	...
Switzerland - Suisse										
2001										
Total	C	61 287	29 915	31 372	42 157	19 952	22 205	19 130	9 963	9 167
0 - 1	C	365	209	156	248	145	103	117	64	53
1 - 4	C	90	52	38	52	26	26	38	26	12
5 - 9	C	41	23	18	26	16	10	15	7	8
10 - 14	C	59	36	23	32	14	18	27	22	5
15 - 19	C	177	128	49	92	61	31	85	67	18
20 - 24	C	245	192	53	167	126	41	78	66	12
25 - 29	C	269	185	84	185	121	64	84	64	20
30 - 34	C	408	277	131	302	201	101	106	76	30
35 - 39	C	579	377	202	393	254	139	186	123	63
40 - 44	C	757	491	266	533	337	196	224	154	70
45 - 49	C	1 104	722	382	752	476	276	352	246	106
50 - 54	C	1 651	1 064	587	1 158	731	427	493	333	160
55 - 59	C	2 331	1 475	856	1 670	1 024	646	661	451	210
60 - 64	C	2 832	1 829	1 003	1 966	1 237	729	866	592	274
65 - 69	C	4 096	2 642	1 454	2 800	1 760	1 040	1 296	882	414
70 - 74	C	5 724	3 518	2 206	3 902	2 327	1 575	1 822	1 191	631
75 - 79	C	8 189	4 517	3 672	5 544	2 991	2 553	2 645	1 526	1 119
80 - 84	C	9 968	4 819	5 149	6 718	3 157	3 561	3 250	1 662	1 588
85 - 89	C	11 270	4 298	6 972	7 684	2 851	4 833	3 586	1 447	2 139
90 - 94	C	8 207	2 428	5 779	5 818	1 658	4 160	2 389	770	1 619
95 - 99	C	2 554	582	1 972	1 834	404	1 430	720	178	542
100+	C	371	51	320	281	35	246	90	16	74
2002										
Total	C	61 228	29 875	31 353	...	...	...	...	...	...
0 - 1	C	363	209	154	...	...	...	...	...	...
1 - 4	C	90	52	38	...	...	...	...	...	...
5 - 9	C	40	23	17	...	...	...	...	...	...
10 - 14	C	58	35	23	...	...	...	...	...	...
15 - 19	C	176	127	49	...	...	...	...	...	...
20 - 24	C	241	190	51	...	...	...	...	...	...
25 - 29	C	266	182	84	...	...	...	...	...	...
30 - 34	C	401	271	130	...	...	...	...	...	...
35 - 39	C	572	371	201	...	...	...	...	...	...

19. Deaths by age, sex and urban/rural residence: latest available year, 1994 - 2003
Décès selon l'âge, le sexe et la résidence, urbaine/rurale: dernière année disponible, 1994 - 2003 (continued — suite)

Continent, country or area, year and age (in years) / Continent, pays ou zone, année et âge (en années)	Code[1]	Total			Urban - Urbaine			Rural - Rurale		
		Both sexes - Les deux sexes	Male - Masculin	Female - Féminin	Both sexes - Les deux sexes	Male - Masculin	Female - Féminin	Both sexes - Les deux sexes	Male - Masculin	Female - Féminin

EUROPE

Switzerland - Suisse
2002

40 - 44	C	752	486	266	...	...	...	...	...	...
45 - 49	C	1 102	721	381	...	...	...	...	...	...
50 - 54	C	1 650	1 063	587	...	...	...	...	...	...
55 - 59	C	2 329	1 473	856	...	...	...	...	...	...
60 - 64	C	2 828	1 826	1 002	...	...	...	...	...	...
65 - 69	C	4 091	2 640	1 451	...	...	...	...	...	...
70 - 74	C	5 722	3 517	2 205	...	...	...	...	...	...
75 - 79	C	8 182	4 512	3 670	...	...	...	...	...	...
80 - 84	C	9 965	4 819	5 146	...	...	...	...	...	...
85 - 89	C	11 268	4 297	6 971	...	...	...	...	...	...
90 - 94	C	8 207	2 428	5 779	...	...	...	...	...	...
95 - 99	C	2 554	582	1 972	...	...	...	...	...	...
100+	C	371	51	320	...	...	...	...	...	...

The Former Yugoslav Rep. of Macedonia - L'ex-République yougoslave de Macédoine
2003

Total	C	18 006	9 832	8 174	10 597	5 846	4 751	7 409	3 986	3 423
0 - 1	C	305	181	124	199	117	82	106	64	42
1 - 4	C	43	26	17	19	11	8	24	15	9
5 - 9	C	21	13	8	11	7	4	10	6	4
10 - 14	C	39	27	12	24	16	8	15	11	4
15 - 19	C	76	47	29	51	30	21	25	17	8
20 - 24	C	95	75	20	53	41	12	42	34	8
25 - 29	C	106	73	33	58	41	17	48	32	16
30 - 34	C	119	92	27	64	52	12	55	40	15
35 - 39	C	175	113	62	95	63	32	80	50	30
40 - 44	C	321	224	97	217	150	67	104	74	30
45 - 49	C	564	407	157	373	263	110	191	144	47
50 - 54	C	837	556	281	580	379	201	257	177	80
55 - 59	C	1 006	651	355	653	436	217	353	215	138
60 - 64	C	1 400	852	548	873	547	326	527	305	222
65 - 69	C	2 220	1 311	909	1 357	809	548	863	502	361
70 - 74	C	2 820	1 486	1 334	1 641	865	776	1 179	621	558
75 - 79	C	3 221	1 535	1 686	1 857	889	968	1 364	646	718
80 - 84	C	2 666	1 240	1 426	1 474	676	798	1 192	564	628
85+	C	1 969	921	1 048	996	453	543	973	468	505
Unknown - Inconnu	C	3	2	1	2	1	1	1	1	-

Ukraine[15]
2003

Total	C	765 408	387 131	378 277	459 965	240 475	219 490	305 443	146 656	158 787
0 - 1	C	3 882	2 296	1 586	2 531	1 506	1 025	1 351	790	561
1 - 4	C	1 279	734	545	663	380	283	616	354	262
5 - 9	C	841	523	318	459	283	176	382	240	142
10 - 14	C	972	634	338	556	365	191	416	269	147
15 - 19	C	3 113	2 204	909	1 940	1 373	567	1 173	831	342
20 - 24	C	5 712	4 390	1 322	3 765	2 847	918	1 947	1 543	404
25 - 29	C	8 739	6 762	1 977	6 027	4 569	1 458	2 712	2 193	519
30 - 34	C	11 650	8 899	2 751	8 048	6 022	2 026	3 602	2 877	725
35 - 39	C	15 780	12 096	3 684	10 757	8 081	2 676	5 023	4 015	1 008
40 - 44	C	25 309	19 611	5 698	17 444	13 314	4 130	7 865	6 297	1 568
45 - 49	C	33 552	25 302	8 250	23 053	17 140	5 913	10 499	8 162	2 337
50 - 54	C	44 770	32 352	12 418	30 860	22 062	8 798	13 910	10 290	3 620
55 - 59	C	38 472	26 126	12 346	25 873	17 609	8 264	12 599	8 517	4 082
60 - 64	C	70 868	45 940	24 928	44 183	28 540	15 643	26 685	17 400	9 285
65 - 69	C	87 894	52 231	35 663	53 850	31 784	22 066	34 044	20 447	13 597
70 - 74	C	103 423	52 979	50 444	59 501	30 422	29 079	43 922	22 557	21 365
75 - 79	C	126 011	49 055	76 956	73 127	28 932	44 195	52 884	20 123	32 761
80 - 84	C	87 149	24 510	62 639	46 628	13 569	33 059	40 521	10 941	29 580
85 - 89	C	54 377	12 283	42 094	29 887	7 227	22 660	24 490	5 056	19 434
90 - 94	C	33 855	6 803	27 052	17 110	3 677	13 433	16 745	3 126	13 619
95 - 99	C	6 786	1 141	5 645	3 214	586	2 628	3 572	555	3 017

19. Deaths by age, sex and urban/rural residence: latest available year, 1994 - 2003
Décès selon l'âge, le sexe et la résidence, urbaine/rurale: dernière année disponible, 1994 - 2003 (continued — suite)

Continent, country or area, year and age (in years) / Continent, pays ou zone, année et âge (en années)	Code[1]	Total			Urban - Urbaine			Rural - Rurale		
		Both sexes - Les deux sexes	Male - Masculin	Female - Féminin	Both sexes - Les deux sexes	Male - Masculin	Female - Féminin	Both sexes - Les deux sexes	Male - Masculin	Female - Féminin
EUROPE										
Ukraine[15]										
2003										
100+	C	793	114	679	325	56	269	468	58	410
Unknown - Inconnu	C	181	146	35	164	131	33	17	15	2
United Kingdom - Royaume-Uni										
2003										
Total	C	611 188	288 604	322 584	...	...	...	...	...	...
0 - 1	C	3 686	2 029	1 657	...	...	...	...	...	...
1 - 4	C	663	351	312	...	...	...	...	...	...
5 - 9	C	390	214	176	...	...	...	...	...	...
10 - 14	C	510	289	221	...	...	...	...	...	...
15 - 19	C	1 393	969	424	...	...	...	...	...	...
20 - 24	C	2 006	1 467	539	...	...	...	...	...	...
25 - 29	C	2 222	1 556	666	...	...	...	...	...	...
30 - 34	C	3 403	2 267	1 136	...	...	...	...	...	...
35 - 39	C	4 923	3 156	1 767	...	...	...	...	...	...
40 - 44	C	6 967	4 252	2 715	...	...	...	...	...	...
45 - 49	C	9 689	5 783	3 906	...	...	...	...	...	...
50 - 54	C	14 830	8 906	5 924	...	...	...	...	...	...
55 - 59	C	23 399	14 181	9 218	...	...	...	...	...	...
60 - 64	C	30 388	18 644	11 744	...	...	...	...	...	...
65 - 69	C	43 916	26 366	17 550	...	...	...	...	...	...
70 - 74	C	65 022	37 208	27 814	...	...	...	...	...	...
75 - 79	C	91 979	48 365	43 614	...	...	...	...	...	...
80 - 84	C	114 112	52 568	61 544	...	...	...	...	...	...
85 - 89	C	95 959	35 532	60 427	...	...	...	...	...	...
90 - 94	C	68 030	19 423	48 607	...	...	...	...	...	...
95 - 99	C	23 708	4 600	19 108	...	...	...	...	...	...
100+	C	3 990	476	3 514	...	...	...	...	...	...
Unknown - Inconnu	C	3	2	1	...	...	...	...	...	...
OCEANIA — OCEANIE										
Australia - Australie										
2003										
Total	+C	132 292	68 330	63 962	...	...	...	...	...	...
0 - 1	+C	1 199	677	522	...	...	...	...	...	...
1 - 4	+C	270	150	120	...	...	...	...	...	...
5 - 9	+C	149	90	59	...	...	...	...	...	...
10 - 14	+C	157	83	74	...	...	...	...	...	...
15 - 19	+C	630	447	183	...	...	...	...	...	...
20 - 24	+C	837	621	216	...	...	...	...	...	...
25 - 29	+C	945	695	250	...	...	...	...	...	...
30 - 34	+C	1 180	800	380	...	...	...	...	...	...
35 - 39	+C	1 479	967	512	...	...	...	...	...	...
40 - 44	+C	2 106	1 341	765	...	...	...	...	...	...
45 - 49	+C	2 884	1 792	1 092	...	...	...	...	...	...
50 - 54	+C	3 646	2 251	1 395	...	...	...	...	...	...
55 - 59	+C	5 356	3 404	1 952	...	...	...	...	...	...
60 - 64	+C	6 780	4 231	2 549	...	...	...	...	...	...
65 - 69	+C	9 031	5 712	3 319	...	...	...	...	...	...
70 - 74	+C	13 302	8 326	4 976	...	...	...	...	...	...
75 - 79	+C	19 328	11 054	8 274	...	...	...	...	...	...
80 - 84	+C	22 607	11 337	11 270	...	...	...	...	...	...
85 - 89	+C	21 097	8 670	12 427	...	...	...	...	...	...
90 - 94	+C	13 812	4 421	9 391	...	...	...	...	...	...
95 - 99	+C	4 689	1 138	3 551	...	...	...	...	...	...
100+	+C	794	110	684	...	...	...	...	...	...
Unknown - Inconnu	+C	14	13	1	...	...	...	...	...	...
Marshall Islands - Îles Marshall										
1997										
Total	+U	243	135	108	...	...	...	...	...	...
0 - 1	+U	49	17	32	...	...	...	...	...	...

Continent, country or area, year and age (in years) / Continent, pays ou zone, année et âge (en années)	Code[1]	Total			Urban - Urbaine			Rural - Rurale		
		Both sexes - Les deux sexes	Male - Masculin	Female - Féminin	Both sexes - Les deux sexes	Male - Masculin	Female - Féminin	Both sexes - Les deux sexes	Male - Masculin,	Female - Féminin
OCEANIA — OCEANIE										
Marshall Islands - Îles Marshall										
1997										
1 - 4	+U	7	1	6	...	...	...	...	...	...
5 - 9	+U	2	1	1	...	...	...	...	...	...
10 - 14	+U	2	1	1	...	...	...	...	...	...
15 - 19	+U	8	6	2	...	...	...	...	...	...
20 - 24	+U	10	9	1	...	...	...	...	...	...
25 - 29	+U	9	6	3	...	...	...	...	...	...
30 - 34	+U	8	2	6	...	...	...	...	...	...
35 - 39	+U	6	5	1	...	...	...	...	...	...
40 - 44	+U	10	5	5	...	...	...	...	...	...
45 - 49	+U	18	12	6	...	...	...	...	...	...
50 - 54	+U	13	9	4	...	...	...	...	...	...
55 - 59	+U	17	10	7	...	...	...	...	...	...
60 - 64	+U	17	13	4	...	...	...	...	...	...
65 - 69	+U	19	12	7	...	...	...	...	...	...
70 - 74	+U	13	6	7	...	...	...	...	...	...
75+	+U	35	20	15	...	...	...	...	...	...
New Caledonia - Nouvelle-Calédonie										
2003										
Total	C	1 121	666	455	...	...	...	...	...	...
0 - 1	C	24	14	10	...	...	...	...	...	...
1 - 4	C	10	9	1	...	...	...	...	...	...
5 - 9	C	8	4	4	...	...	...	...	...	...
10 - 14	C	5	2	3	...	...	...	...	...	...
15 - 19	C	12	7	5	...	...	...	...	...	...
20 - 24	C	30	22	8	...	...	...	...	...	...
25 - 29	C	22	13	9	...	...	...	...	...	...
30 - 34	C	28	22	6	...	...	...	...	...	...
35 - 39	C	27	16	11	...	...	...	...	...	...
40 - 44	C	36	26	10	...	...	...	...	...	...
45 - 49	C	47	29	18	...	...	...	...	...	...
50 - 54	C	56	32	24	...	...	...	...	...	...
55 - 59	C	101	65	36	...	...	...	...	...	...
60 - 64	C	89	60	29	...	...	...	...	...	...
65 - 69	C	136	82	54	...	...	...	...	...	...
70 - 74	C	142	92	50	...	...	...	...	...	...
75 - 79	C	134	74	60	...	...	...	...	...	...
80 - 84	C	91	42	49	...	...	...	...	...	...
85 - 89	C	72	32	40	...	...	...	...	...	...
90 - 94	C	35	21	14	...	...	...	...	...	...
95+	C	16	2	14	...	...	...	...	...	...
New Zealand - Nouvelle-Zélande[6]										
2003										
Total	+C	28 010	14 020	13 990	25 279	12 351	12 928	2 654	1 621	1 033
0 - 1	+C	277	164	113	231	132	99	27	20	7
1 - 4	+C	79	39	40	68	33	35	10	5	5
5 - 9	+C	38	22	16	35	21	14	3	1	2
10 - 14	+C	57	38	19	45	32	13	12	6	6
15 - 19	+C	214	139	75	178	113	65	34	24	10
20 - 24	+C	186	132	54	157	105	52	27	25	2
25 - 29	+C	184	130	54	159	110	49	24	19	5
30 - 34	+C	259	172	87	216	138	78	41	32	9
35 - 39	+C	325	199	126	272	171	101	52	27	25
40 - 44	+C	467	281	186	395	245	150	71	35	36
45 - 49	+C	633	365	268	540	317	223	91	46	45
50 - 54	+C	892	516	376	767	439	328	123	76	47
55 - 59	+C	1 185	693	492	1 015	580	435	167	111	56
60 - 64	+C	1 539	917	622	1 297	770	527	238	145	93
65 - 69	+C	2 014	1 185	829	1 729	998	731	283	185	98
70 - 74	+C	2 975	1 756	1 219	2 656	1 542	1 114	315	211	104
75 - 79	+C	3 957	2 234	1 723	3 584	1 980	1 604	366	249	117

Continent, country or area, year and age (in years) Continent, pays ou zone, année et âge (en années)	Code[1]	Total			Urban - Urbaine			Rural - Rurale		
		Both sexes - Les deux sexes	Male - Masculin	Female - Féminin	Both sexes - Les deux sexes	Male - Masculin	Female - Féminin	Both sexes - Les deux sexes	Male - Masculin	Female - Féminin
OCEANIA — OCEANIE										
New Zealand - Nouvelle-Zélande[6]										
2003										
80 - 84	+C	4 641	2 296	2 345	4 300	2 093	2 207	337	202	135
85 - 89	+C	4 264	1 675	2 589	3 992	1 535	2 457	260	135	125
90 - 94	+C	2 772	852	1 920	2 626	789	1 837	139	61	78
95 - 99	+C	901	196	705	868	189	679	32	6	26
100+	+C	151	19	132	149	19	130	2	-	2
Northern Mariana Islands - Îles Mariannes septentrionales[40]										
1999										
Total	U	*189*	*99*	*91*	...	...	...	...	...	...
0 - 4	U	*16*	*8*	*8*	...	...	...	...	...	...
5 - 9	U	*1*	*.*	*1*	...	...	...	...	...	...
15 - 19	U	*6*	*4*	*3*	...	...	...	...	...	...
20 - 24	U	*9*	*6*	*3*	...	...	...	...	...	...
25 - 29	U	*7*	*6*	*1*	...	...	...	...	...	...
30 - 34	U	*5*	*4*	*1*	...	...	...	...	...	...
35 - 39	U	*10*	*4*	*6*	...	...	...	...	...	...
40 - 44	U	*7*	*6*	*1*	...	...	...	...	...	...
45 - 49	U	*16*	*4*	*12*	...	...	...	...	...	...
50 - 54	U	*16*	*8*	*8*	...	...	...	...	...	...
55 - 59	U	*9*	*3*	*6*	...	...	...	...	...	...
60 - 64	U	*15*	*8*	*7*	...	...	...	...	...	...
65 - 69	U	*15*	*9*	*6*	...	...	...	...	...	...
70 - 74	U	*20*	*13*	*7*	...	...	...	...	...	...
75 - 79	U	*12*	*5*	*7*	...	...	...	...	...	...
80 - 84	U	*13*	*7*	*6*	...	...	...	...	...	...
85+	U	*12*	*4*	*8*	...	...	...	...	...	...
Palau - Palaos										
1999										
Total	C	131	78	53	...	...	...	...	...	...
0 - 1	C	5	3	2	...	...	...	...	...	...
1 - 14	C	4	2	2	...	...	...	...	...	...
15 - 24	C	3	3	-	...	...	...	...	...	...
25 - 44	C	22	16	6	...	...	...	...	...	...
45 - 64	C	41	27	14	...	...	...	...	...	...
65+	C	56	27	29	...	...	...	...	...	...
Tonga										
2000										
Total	+C	653	334	319	...	...	...	...	...	...
0 - 1	+C	28	12	16	...	...	...	...	...	...
1 - 9	+C	23	10	13	...	...	...	...	...	...
10 - 19	+C	14	10	4	...	...	...	...	...	...
20 - 29	+C	21	10	11	...	...	...	...	...	...
30 - 39	+C	16	5	11	...	...	...	...	...	...
40 - 49	+C	33	20	13	...	...	...	...	...	...
50 - 59	+C	78	37	41	...	...	...	...	...	...
60 - 69	+C	116	67	49	...	...	...	...	...	...
70+	+C	299	151	148	...	...	...	...	...	...
Unknown - Inconnu	+C	25	12	13	...	...	...	...	...	...

FOOTNOTES - NOTES

Italics: data from civil registers which are incomplete or of unknown completeness. — Italiques: données incomplètes ou dont le degré d'exactitude n'est pas connu provenant des registres de l'état civil.

[1] 'Code' indicates the source of data, as follows:
C - Civil registration, estimated over 90% complete
U - Civil registration, estimated less than 90% complete
| - Other source, estimated reliable
+ - Data tabulated by date of registration rather than occurence.
... - Information not available

Le 'Code' indique la source des données, comme suit:
C - Registres de l'état civil considérés complèts à 90 p. 100 au moins.
U - Registres de l'état civil qui ne sont pas considérés complèts à 90 p. 100 au moins.
| - Autre source, considérée pas douteuses.
+ - Données exploitées selon la date de l'enregistrement et non la date de l'événement.
... - Information pas disponible.

[2] Excluding live-born infants who died before their birth was registered. - - Non compris les enfants nés vivants décédés avant l'enregistrement de leur naissance.

[3] For Algerian population only. - Pour la population algérienne seulement.

[4] For 2001, data refer to last twelve months preceding census on August 2001. - Pour 2001, les données se rapportent pour la dernière fois à douze mois précédant le recensement août 2001.

[5] Based on the results of the population census. - D'après les résultats du recensement de la population.

[6] Figures for urban and rural areas do not add up to the total, since they do not include the category 'Unknown residence'. - La somme des données pour la residence urbaine et rurale n'est pas égale au total parce qu'elle n'inclue pas la catégorie 'Residence inconnue'.

[7] Data for 1997 refer to last twelve months preceding population and housing census of 1997. - Les données pour 1997 se réfèrent au douze mois précédant le recensement de population et de l'habitat de 1997.

[8] Data for male and female categories exclude deaths of unknown sex. - - Les données pour le sexe masculin et féminin ne comprennent pas les décès ou on ignore le sexe.

[9] Deaths for 2001 refer to the period January-August 2001. - Le chiffer des décès de 2001 correspond à la période allant de janvier à août 2001.

[10] Including Canadian residents temporarily in the United States, but excluding United States residents temporarily in Canada. - Y compris les résidents canadiens se trouvant temporairement aux Etats-Unis, mais ne comprenant pas les résidents des Etats-Unis se trouvant temporairement au Canada.

[11] Excluding Indian jungle population. - Non compris les Indiens de la jungle.

[12] Excluding nomadic Indian tribes. - Non compris les tribus d'Indiens nomades.

[13] For 2001, data were collected from Population census held on August 2002, referring to events in calendar year 2001. - Pour 2001, les données sont tirées du recensement de la population réalisé en août 2002, concernant des événements de l'année civile 2001.

[14] Data for urban refer to the total of the district of Paramaribo (capital) and Wanica district. - Les données relatives aux zones urbaines correspondent au total pour le district de Paramaribo (capitale) et le district de Wanica.

[15] Excluding infants born alive with less than 28 weeks gestation, less than 1 000 grams in weight and 35 centimeters in length, who die within seven days of birth. - Non compris les enfants nés vivants avant 28 semaines de gestation, pesant moins de 1 000 grammes, mesurant moins de 35 centimètres et décédés dans les sept jours qui ont suivi leur naissance.

[16] For statistical purposes, the data for China do not include those for the Hong Kong Special Administrative Region (Hong Kong SAR), Macao Special Administrative Region (Macao SAR) and Taiwan province of China. - Pour la présentation des statistiques, les données pour Chine ne comprend pas la Région Administrative Spéciale de Hong Kong (Hong Kong RAS), la Région Administrative Spéciale de Macao (Macao RAS) et Taïwan province de Chine.

[17] Data refer to government controlled areas. - Les données se raportent aux zones contrôlées par le Gouvernement.

[18] Including data for East Jerusalem and Israeli residents in certain other territories under occupation by Israeli military forces since June 1967. - Y compris les données pour Jérusalem-Est et les résidents israéliens dans certains autres territoires occupés depuis 1967 par les forces armées israéliennes.

[19] Data refer to Japanese nationals in Japan only. - Les données se raportent aux nationaux japonais au Japon seulement.

[20] Excluding alien armed forces, civilian aliens employed by armed forces, and foreign diplomatic personnel and their dependants. - Non compris les militaires étrangers, les civils étrangers employés par les forces armées ni le personnel diplomatique étranger et les membres de leur famille les accompagnant.

[21] Data for urban/rural refer to Peninsular Malaysia only. - Les données ventilées par lieu de résidence (urbain/rural) concernent la Malaisie péninsulaire seulement.

[22] Data for urban refer to 170 towns out of 254 towns. Data for rural refer to 62 townships out of 158 townships. - Les données urbaines se rapportent à 170 des 254 villes.Les données rurales se rapportent à 62 des 158 municipalités.

[23] For 2001, data refer to last twelve months preceding census on June 2001. - Pour 2001, les données se rapportent pour la dernière fois à douze mois précédant le recensement juin 2001.

[24] Data refer to the recorded events in Ministry of Health hospitals and health centres only. - Les données se rapportent aux faits d'état-civil enregistrés dans les hôpitaux et les dispensaires du Ministère de la santé seulement.

[25] Excluding data for the Pakistan-held part of Jammu and Kashmir, the final status of which has not yet been determined. - Non compris les données concernant la partie du Jammu et Cachemire occupée par le Pakistan dont le statut définitif n'a pas été déterminé.

[26] Based on the results of the Population Growth Survey. - D'après les résultats de la 'Population Growth Survey.'

[27] Excluding transients afloat and non-locally domiciled military and civilian services personnel and their dependants. - Non compris les personnes de passage þ bord de navires, ni les militaires et agents civils domiciliés hors du territoire et les membres de leur famille les accompagnant.

[28] Including armed forces stationed outside the country, but excluding alien armed forces stationed in the area. - Y compris les militaires nationaux hors du pays, mais non compris les militaires étrangers en garnison sur le territoire.

[29] Age classification based on year of birth rather than exact date of birth. - - Le classement selon l'âge est basé sur l'année de naissances et non sur la date exacte de naissance.

[30] Excluding Faeroe Islands and Greenland. - Non compris les Iles Féroé et Gröenland.

[31] Including nationals temporarily outside the country. - Y compris les nationaux se trouvant temporairement hors du pays.

[32] Including armed forces stationed outside the country. - Y compris les militaires nationaux hors du pays.

[33] For ages five years and over, age classification based on year of birth rather than exact date of birth. - A partir de cinq ans, le classement selon l'âge est basé sur l'année de naissances et non sur la date exacte de naissance.

[34] Data for urban/rural, excluding nationals outside the country. - Les données selon la résidence urbaine/rurale, non compris les nationaux hors du pays.

[35] Data for urban/rural residence, for the de jure population. - Les données selon la résidence urbaine/rurale, pour la population de droit.

[36] Events registered within one year of occurrence. - Evénements enregistrés dans l'année qui suit l'événement.

[37] Including residents outside the country if listed in a Netherlands population register. - Y compris les résidents hors du pays, s'ils sont inscrits sur un registre de population néerlandais.

[38] Including residents temporarily outside the country. - Y compris les résidents se trouvant temporairement hors du pays.

[39] From 2002, without data for Kosovo and Metohia. - Après 2002, sans les donées pour le Kosovo and Metohie .

[40] Figures for male and female do not add up to total since they were compiled from different sources. - La somme des données par sexe n'est pas identique au total car les données pour les hommes et les femmes proviennent de sources différentes.

Table 20

Table 20 presents death rates by age, sex and urban/rural residence for the latest available year.

Description of variables: Age is defined as age at last birthday, that is, the difference between the date of birth and the date of the occurrence of the event, expressed in completed solar years. The age classification used in this table is the following: under 1 year, 1-4 years, 5-year age groups through 95-99, and 100 years or over.

The urban/rural classification of deaths is that provided by each country or area; it is presumed to be based on the national census definition of urban population that have been set forth at the end of the technical notes for table 6.

Rate computation: Death rates specific for age and sex are the annual number of deaths in each age-sex group (as shown in table 19) per 1 000 population in the same age-sex group.

Death rates by age, sex and urban/rural residence are the annual number of deaths that occurred in a specific age-sex-urban/rural group (as shown in table 19) per 1 000 population in the corresponding age-sex-urban/rural group (as shown in table 7). These rates are calculated by the Statistics Division of the United Nations.

Deaths at unknown age and the population of unknown age are excluded from age-specific rate calculations but are part of the death rate for all ages combined.

Death rates for infants under one year of age in this table differ from the infant mortality rates shown elsewhere, because the latter are computed per 1 000 live births rather than per 1 000 population.

The population used in computing the rates is estimated or enumerated distributions by age and sex. First priority was given to an estimate for the mid-point of the same year (as shown in table 7), second priority to census returns of the year to which the deaths referred and third priority to an estimate for some other point of time in the year.

Rates presented in this table have been limited to those for countries or areas having at least a total of 1 000 deaths in a given year. Moreover, rates specific for individual sub-categories that are based on 30 or fewer deaths are identified by the symbol (♦).

Reliability of data: Rates are not computed if data from civil registers of deaths are reported as incomplete (less than 90 per cent completeness) or of unknown completeness, and therefore deemed unreliable. Table 18 and the technical notes for that table provide more detailed information on the completeness of death registration. For more information about the quality of vital statistics, see section 4.2 of the Technical Notes.

Limitations: Rates shown in this table are subject to all the same limitations that affect the corresponding frequencies and are set forth in the technical notes for table 19.

These include differences in the completeness of registration, the treatment of infants who were born alive but died before the registration of their birth or within the first 24 hours of life, the method used to determine age at death and the quality of the reported information relating to age at death. In addition, some rates are based on deaths tabulated by date of registration and not by date of occurrence; these have been indicated with a plus sign (+).

The problem of obtaining precise correspondence between deaths (numerator) and population (denominator) as regards the inclusion or exclusion of armed forces, refugees, displaced persons and other special groups is particularly difficult where age-specific death rates are concerned. In cases where it was not possible to achieve strict correspondence, the differences in coverage are noted. Male rates in the age range 20 to 40 years may be especially affected by this non-correspondence, and care should be exercised in using these rates for comparative purposes. Even when deaths and population do correspond conceptually, comparability of the rates may be affected by abnormal conditions such as absence from the country or area of large numbers of young men in the military forces or working abroad as temporary workers. Death rates may appear high in the younger ages, simply because a large section of the able-bodied members of the age group, whose death rates under normal conditions might be less than the average for persons of their age, is not included.

Also, in a number of cases the rates shown here for all ages combined differ from crude death rates shown elsewhere, because in this table they are computed on the population for which an appropriate age-sex distribution was available, while the crude death rates shown elsewhere may utilize a different total population. The population by age and sex might refer to a census date within the year rather than to the mid-point, or it might be more or less inclusive as regards ethnic groups, armed forces and so forth. In a few instances, the difference is attributable to the fact that the rates in this table were computed on the mean population whereas the corresponding rates in other tables were computed on an estimate for 1 July.

The comparability of data by urban/rural residence is affected by the national definitions of urban and rural used in tabulating these data. It is assumed, in the absence of specific information to the contrary, that the definitions of urban and rural used in connection with the national population census were also used in the compilation of the vital statistics for each country or area. However, it cannot be excluded that, for a given country or area, different definitions of urban and rural are used for the vital statistics data and the population census data respectively. When known, the definitions of urban used in national population censuses are presented at the end of the technical notes for table 6. As discussed in detail in the technical notes for table 6, these definitions vary considerably from one country or area to another.

In addition to problems of comparability, vital rates classified by urban/rural residence are also subject to certain special types of bias. If, when calculating vital rates, different definitions of urban are used in connection with the vital events and the population data and if this results in a net difference between the numerator and denominator of the rate in the population at risk, then the vital rates would be biased. Urban/rural differentials in vital rates may also be affected by whether the vital events have been tabulated in terms of place of occurrence or place of usual residence. This problem is discussed in more detail in section 4.1.4.1 of the Technical Notes.

Earlier data: Death rates specific for age and sex have been shown for the latest available year in many of the issues of the Yearbook since the 1955 issue. Data included in this table update the series shown in the Yearbook and in the Special Supplements covering a period of years as follows:

Issue	Years Covered
Historical Supplement CD, 1997	1948 – 1997
1996	1987 - 1995
1992	1983 – 1992
1985	1976 – 1984
1980	1971 – 1979
Historical Supplement, 1979	1948 - 1977

Tableau 20

Le tableau 20 présente les taux de mortalité selon l'âge et le sexe et selon le lieu de résidence (zone urbaine ou rurale) correspondant à la dernière année pour laquelle on disposait de données.

Description des variables : L'âge considéré est l'âge au dernier anniversaire, c'est-à-dire la différence entre la date de naissance et la date du décès, exprimée en années solaires révolues. La classification par âge est la suivante : moins d'un an, 1 à 4 ans, groupes quinquennaux jusqu'à 95-99 ans et 100 ans et plus.

La classification des décès selon le lieu de résidence (zone urbaine ou rurale) est celle qui a été communiquée par chaque pays ou zone ; on part du principe qu'elle repose sur les définitions de la population urbaine utilisées pour les recensements nationaux, qui sont reproduites à la fin des notes techniques du tableau 6.

Calcul des taux : Les taux de mortalité selon l'âge et le sexe représentent le nombre annuel de décès survenus pour chaque sexe et chaque groupe d'âge (fréquences du tableau 19) pour 1 000 personnes du même groupe.

Les taux de mortalité selon l'âge, le sexe et le lieu de résidence (zone urbaine ou rurale) représentent le nombre annuel de décès survenus dans un groupe d'âge et de sexe donnés parmi la population urbaine ou rurale (fréquences du tableau 19) pour 1 000 personnes du même groupe parmi la population urbaine ou rurale. Ces taux ont été calculés par la Division de statistique de l'ONU.

On n'a pas tenu compte des décès à un âge inconnu ni de la population d'âge inconnu, sauf dans les taux de mortalité pour tous les âges combinés.

Il convient de noter que, dans ce tableau, les taux de mortalité des groupes de moins d'un an sont différents des taux de mortalité infantile qui figurent dans d'autres tableaux, ces derniers ayant été établis pour 1 000 naissances vivantes et non pour 1 000 habitants.

Les chiffres de population utilisés pour le calcul des taux proviennent de dénombrements ou de répartitions estimatives de la population selon l'âge et le sexe. On a utilisé de préférence les estimations de la population au milieu de l'année considérée selon les chiffres du tableau 7 ; à défaut, on s'est contenté des données censitaires se rapportant à l'année des décès et, si ces données manquaient également, d'estimations établies à un autre moment de l'année.

Les taux présentés dans le tableau 20 ne se rapportent qu'aux pays ou zones où l'on a enregistré un total d'au moins 1 000 décès pendant l'année. Les taux relatifs à des sous-catégories, qui sont fondés sur 30 décès ou moins, sont signalés par le signe '♦'.

Fiabilité des données : On a choisi de ne pas faire figurer dans le tableau 20 des taux calculés à partir de données sur les décès issues de registres d'état civil qui sont déclarées incomplètes (degré d'exhaustivité inférieur à 90 p. 100) ou dont le degré d'exhaustivité n'est pas connu. Le tableau 18 et les notes techniques s'y rapportant présentent des renseignements plus détaillés sur le degré d'exhaustivité de l'enregistrement des décès. Pour plus de précisions sur la qualité des statistiques de l'état civil, voir la section 4.2 des Notes techniques.

Insuffisance des données : Les taux présentés dans le tableau 20 appellent les mêmes réserves que celles formulées à propos des fréquences correspondantes (voir à ce sujet les notes techniques se rapportant au tableau 19).

Leurs imperfections tiennent notamment aux différences d'exhaustivité de l'enregistrement, au classement des enfants nés vivants mais décédés avant l'enregistrement de leur naissance ou dans les 24 heures qui ont suivi la naissance, à la méthode utilisée pour obtenir l'âge au moment du décès, et à la qualité des déclarations concernant l'âge au moment du décès. En outre, dans certains cas, les données relatives aux décès sont classées par date d'enregistrement et non par date de l'événement ; ces cas ont été signalés par le signe '+'.

S'agissant des taux de mortalité par âge, il est particulièrement difficile d'établir une correspondance exacte entre les décès (numérateur) et la population (dénominateur) du fait de l'inclusion ou de l'exclusion des militaires, des réfugiés, des personnes déplacées et d'autres groupes spéciaux. Dans les cas où il n'a pas été possible de parvenir à une correspondance exacte, des notes signalent les différences de portée peuvent être tout particulièrement influencés par ce manque de correspondance, et il importe d'être prudent quand on les utilise dans des comparaisons. Il convient d'ajouter que, même lorsque population et décès correspondent, la comparabilité des taux peut être compromise par des conditions anormales telles que l'absence du pays ou de la zone d'un grand nombre de jeunes gens qui sont sous les drapeaux ou qui travaillent à l'étranger comme travailleurs temporaires. Il arrive ainsi que les taux de mortalité paraissent élevés parmi les groupes les plus jeunes simplement parce que l'on en a exclu un grand nombre d'individus en bonne santé pour lesquels le taux de mortalité pourrait être, dans des conditions normales, inférieur à la moyenne observée pour les personnes du même âge.

De même, les taux indiqués pour tous les âges combinés diffèrent dans plusieurs cas des taux bruts de mortalité qui figurent dans d'autres tableaux, parce qu'ils se rapportent à une population pour laquelle on disposait d'une répartition par âge et par sexe appropriée, tandis que les taux bruts de mortalité indiqués ailleurs peuvent avoir été calculés sur la base d'un chiffre de population totale différent. Ainsi, il est possible que les chiffres de population par âge et par sexe proviennent d'un recensement effectué dans le courant de l'année et non au milieu de l'année, et qu'ils se différencient des autres chiffres de population en excluant ou en incluant certains groupes ethniques, les militaires, etc. Quelquefois, la différence tient à ce que les taux du tableau 20 ont été calculés sur la base de la population moyenne, alors que les taux correspondants des autres tableaux reposent sur une estimation au 1er juillet. Les écarts de cet ordre sont insignifiants, mais il n'en a pas été tenu compte dans le tableau.

La comparabilité des données selon le lieu de résidence (zone urbaine ou rurale) peut être limitée par les définitions nationales des termes « urbain » et « rural » utilisées pour le classement de ces données. En l'absence d'indications contraires, on a supposé que les mêmes définitions avaient servi pour le recensement national de la population et pour l'établissement des statistiques de l'état civil pour chaque pays ou zone. Toutefois, il n'est pas exclu que, pour une zone ou un pays donné, des définitions différentes aient été retenues. Les définitions du terme « urbain » utilisées pour les recensements nationaux de population ont été présentées à la fin du tableau 6 lorsqu'elles étaient connues. Comme on l'a précisé dans les notes techniques relatives au tableau 6, ces définitions varient considérablement d'un pays ou d'une zone à l'autre.

Outre les problèmes de comparabilité, les taux démographiques classés selon le lieu de résidence (zone urbaine ou rurale) sont également sujets à des distorsions particulières. Si l'on utilise des définitions différentes du terme « urbain » pour classer les faits d'état civil et les données relatives à la population lors du calcul des taux et qu'il en résulte une différence nette entre le numérateur et le dénominateur pour le taux de la population exposée au risque, les taux démographiques s'en trouveront faussés. La différence entre ces taux pour les zones urbaines et rurales pourra aussi être faussée selon que les faits d'état civil auront été classés d'après le lieu où ils se sont produits ou d'après le lieu de résidence habituel.

Ce problème est examiné plus en détail à la section 4.1.4.1 des Notes techniques.

Données publiées antérieurement : Un certain nombre d'éditions de l'*Annuaire* parues depuis 1955 présentent les statistiques les plus récentes dont on disposait à l'époque sur les taux de mortalité selon l'âge et le sexe. Les données du tableau 20 actualisent celles qui figuraient dans les éditions de l'*Annuaire démographique* et dans les *Suppléments spéciaux* qui portaient sur les périodes suivantes :

Éditions	Années considérées
Supplément historique (CD-ROM), 1997	1948 – 1997
1996	1987 - 1995
1992	1983 – 1992
1985	1976 – 1984
1980	1971 – 1979
Supplément rétrospectif, 1979	1948 - 1977

20. Death rates specific for age, sex and urban/rural residence: latest available year, 1994 - 2003
Taux de mortalité selon l'âge, le sexe et la résidence, urbaine/rurale: dernière année disponible, 1994 - 2003

Continent, country or area, year and age (in years) Continent, pays ou zone, année et âge (en années)	Total			Urban - Urbaine			Rural - Rurale		
	Both sexes Les deux sexes	Male Masculin	Female Féminin	Both sexes Les deux sexes	Male Masculin	Female Féminin	Both sexes Les deux sexes	Male Masculin	Female Féminin
AFRICA — AFRIQUE									
Botswana[1]									
2001									
Total	12.4	13.3	11.6	...	...	...	...	...	...
0-1	36.8	37.5	36.1	...	...	...	...	...	...
1-4	7.8	8.3	7.2	...	...	...	...	...	...
5-9	2.3	2.4	2.2	...	...	...	...	...	...
10-14	1.2	1.1	1.3	...	...	...	...	...	...
15-19	1.9	1.8	2.0	...	...	...	...	...	...
20-24	6.4	4.8	7.8	...	...	...	...	...	...
25-29	14.2	11.8	16.4	...	...	...	...	...	...
30-34	20.9	22.5	19.4	...	...	...	...	...	...
35-39	21.4	25.4	17.9	...	...	...	...	...	...
40-44	20.9	25.8	16.7	...	...	...	...	...	...
45-49	21.0	27.5	15.3	...	...	...	...	...	...
50-54	19.0	24.5	14.0	...	...	...	...	...	...
55-59	20.1	26.5	14.3	...	...	...	...	...	...
60-64	22.3	28.9	16.5	...	...	...	...	...	...
65-69	26.4	33.7	20.8	...	...	...	...	...	...
70-74	28.4	36.2	22.8	...	...	...	...	...	...
75+	15.5	21.9	11.4	...	...	...	...	...	...
Egypt - Égypte									
1996									
Total	6.3	6.6	5.9	6.9	7.7	6.2	6.0	6.0	6.0
0-1	26.6	26.4	26.7	79.3	85.2	73.1	89.3	83.7	95.2
1-4	2.6	2.5	2.7	2.3	2.4	2.2	3.0	2.8	3.2
5-9	0.8	0.9	0.8	0.9	1.1	0.8	0.8	0.9	0.8
10-14	0.7	0.8	0.6	0.8	1.0	0.6	0.6	0.7	0.6
15-19	1.1	1.2	0.9	1.2	1.5	0.9	0.8	0.8	0.7
20-24	1.0	1.2	0.8	1.5	1.9	1.0	0.8	0.9	0.8
25-29	1.2	1.4	1.1	1.7	2.2	1.3	1.0	1.1	0.9
30-34	1.6	2.0	1.3	2.0	2.6	1.4	1.4	1.7	1.2
35-39	2.4	2.8	1.9	2.4	3.0	1.9	1.9	2.3	1.6
40-44	3.6	4.6	2.5	3.7	4.7	2.7	3.1	4.0	2.1
45-49	5.9	7.4	4.3	6.2	7.5	4.8	4.9	6.1	3.7
50-54	8.8	10.6	7.0	10.3	12.3	8.2	8.4	10.5	6.5
55-59	13.7	17.2	10.4	17.9	20.5	14.9	14.2	16.9	11.4
60-64	24.8	29.8	20.3	25.6	28.4	22.6	22.1	25.4	18.9
65-69	39.1	46.9	32.1	45.9	46.3	45.3	38.9	40.6	37.0
70-74	64.0	72.5	56.8	72.7	73.2	72.0	66.6	69.0	64.3
75+	148.5	143.9	152.4	185.3	163.6	210.5	187.5	159.2	216.0
1999									
Total	6.4	6.8	6.0	...	...	...	...	...	...
0-1	34.3	35.4	33.2	...	...	...	...	...	...
1-4	2.4	2.4	2.4	...	...	...	...	...	...
5-9	0.7	0.8	0.6	...	...	...	...	...	...
10-14	0.6	0.7	0.6	...	...	...	...	...	...
15-19	0.8	1.0	0.7	...	...	...	...	...	...
20-24	1.2	1.4	0.9	...	...	...	...	...	...
25-29	1.2	1.6	0.9	...	...	...	...	...	...
30-34	1.4	1.8	1.1	...	...	...	...	...	...
35-39	2.1	2.6	1.6	...	...	...	...	...	...
40-44	3.3	4.2	2.3	...	...	...	...	...	...
45-49	5.8	7.3	4.3	...	...	...	...	...	...
50-54	10.3	12.9	7.8	...	...	...	...	...	...
55-59	15.5	17.9	12.7	...	...	...	...	...	...
60-64	22.9	26.1	19.6	...	...	...	...	...	...
65-69	43.1	44.4	41.5	...	...	...	...	...	...
70-74	71.3	72.7	69.7	...	...	...	...	...	...
75+	199.5	175.9	224.8	...	...	...	...	...	...
Malawi[2]									
1998									
Total	20.9	23.4	18.6	15.5	16.7	14.1	21.9	24.6	19.3
0-1	122.0	136.9	107.4	106.9	120.9	92.9	124.3	139.3	109.6
1-4	46.4	51.2	41.6	37.2	41.4	33.1	47.7	52.7	42.9

509

20. Death rates specific for age, sex and urban/rural residence: latest available year, 1994 - 2003
Taux de mortalité selon l'âge, le sexe et la résidence, urbaine/rurale: dernière année disponible, 1994 - 2003 (continued — suite)

Continent, country or area, year and age (in years) Continent, pays ou zone, année et âge (en années)	Total			Urban - Urbaine			Rural - Rurale		
	Both sexes Les deux sexes	Male Masculin	Female Féminin	Both sexes Les deux sexes	Male Masculin	Female Féminin	Both sexes Les deux sexes	Male Masculin	Female Féminin
AFRICA — AFRIQUE									
Malawi[2]									
1998									
5-9	11.6	12.9	10.4	8.9	10.3	7.5	12.0	13.2	10.8
10-14	7.8	7.9	7.8	4.4	5.2	3.8	8.4	8.3	8.5
15-19	6.6	6.5	6.6	3.7	3.8	3.7	7.1	7.0	7.2
20-24	12.0	16.0	8.8	6.7	7.0	6.4	13.2	18.3	9.3
25-29	11.7	12.3	11.1	7.7	6.4	9.3	12.7	14.0	11.5
30-34	14.6	14.8	14.5	11.1	10.2	12.3	15.4	15.9	14.9
35-39	14.5	15.4	13.7	12.9	12.9	12.9	14.8	15.9	13.8
40-44	17.6	20.6	14.5	16.3	17.5	14.6	17.8	21.2	14.5
45-49	16.9	22.3	11.6	15.2	16.7	12.9	17.2	23.2	11.5
50-54	15.4	18.0	12.8	18.6	20.4	15.8	15.0	17.6	12.5
55-59	22.1	19.3	25.0	22.5	21.8	23.5	22.1	19.1	25.1
60-64	19.1	22.4	16.1	24.9	25.4	24.1	18.7	22.1	15.6
65-69	19.3	19.1	19.5	20.0	21.3	18.4	19.3	19.0	19.6
70-74	22.7	30.0	16.5	26.5	31.6	21.7	22.5	29.9	16.2
75-79	24.4	29.3	19.7	35.4	43.0	27.6	23.9	28.6	19.3
80-84	33.2	41.1	26.8	46.7	59.6	36.5	32.6	40.3	26.4
85+	51.7	60.6	44.1	89.6	104.8	77.6	50.1	58.8	42.6
Mauritius - Maurice+									
2003									
Total	7.0	7.9	6.1	...	...	...	...	...	...
0-1	12.7	13.4	12.0	...	...	...	...	...	...
1-4	0.8	◆0.7	◆0.8	...	...	...	...	...	...
5-9	◆0.2	◆0.3	◆0.2	...	...	...	...	...	...
10-14	0.4	◆0.4	◆0.4	...	...	...	...	...	...
15-19	0.5	◆0.6	◆0.4	...	...	...	...	...	...
20-24	0.7	1.0	◆0.5	...	...	...	...	...	...
25-29	0.9	1.1	0.7	...	...	...	...	...	...
30-34	1.5	2.2	0.9	...	...	...	...	...	...
35-39	2.2	3.1	1.3	...	...	...	...	...	...
40-44	3.5	4.9	2.1	...	...	...	...	...	...
45-49	5.7	7.7	3.6	...	...	...	...	...	...
50-54	8.8	11.7	5.9	...	...	...	...	...	...
55-59	12.5	16.3	9.1	...	...	...	...	...	...
60-64	21.7	27.5	16.7	...	...	...	...	...	...
65-69	32.0	41.7	24.1	...	...	...	...	...	...
70-74	46.2	60.7	35.2	...	...	...	...	...	...
75-79	65.3	82.6	53.5	...	...	...	...	...	...
80-84	106.0	128.4	92.8	...	...	...	...	...	...
85+	177.0	229.3	155.9	...	...	...	...	...	...
Mozambique[3]									
1997									
Total	25.2	28.2	22.5	15.9	17.7	14.1	29.1	32.8	25.8
0-1	186.7	205.1	168.9	119.1	132.8	105.6	210.4	230.7	190.8
1-4	56.0	61.2	51.0	29.1	31.6	26.5	65.2	71.2	59.3
5-9	14.3	15.3	13.2	6.9	7.8	6.1	17.1	18.2	16.0
10-14	8.2	8.6	7.7	4.0	4.4	3.6	10.2	10.5	9.8
15-19	7.5	7.6	7.3	4.6	4.8	4.5	9.0	9.3	8.7
20-24	7.3	7.7	6.9	5.8	6.1	5.6	7.9	8.5	7.5
25-29	8.2	9.1	7.5	7.5	8.6	6.6	8.5	9.4	7.8
30-34	9.8	11.2	8.5	8.8	10.5	7.1	10.3	11.6	9.2
35-39	10.2	11.8	8.8	9.5	10.7	8.2	10.5	12.4	9.0
40-44	12.7	15.2	10.5	12.5	14.2	10.5	12.8	15.6	10.5
45-49	13.4	16.3	10.7	15.2	18.0	12.2	12.7	15.6	10.2
50-54	18.9	23.6	14.9	22.9	27.0	18.8	17.6	22.4	13.8
55-59	15.8	19.1	12.7	19.4	22.8	15.8	14.7	17.9	11.8
60-64	32.8	38.3	27.8	40.4	46.7	34.4	30.4	35.6	25.7
65-69	25.5	29.5	21.8	36.1	44.9	28.8	22.6	25.6	19.9
70-74	51.1	61.1	41.7	71.8	89.6	57.5	45.3	53.9	36.9
75-79	40.8	46.2	35.5	63.2	82.8	48.7	35.2	38.6	31.7
80+	202.6	229.5	178.8	284.2	351.7	236.7	183.6	205.1	163.5

20. Death rates specific for age, sex and urban/rural residence: latest available year, 1994 - 2003
Taux de mortalité selon l'âge, le sexe et la résidence, urbaine/rurale: dernière année disponible, 1994 - 2003 (continued — suite)

Continent, country or area, year and age (in years) / Continent, pays ou zone, année et âge (en années)	Total			Urban - Urbaine			Rural - Rurale		
	Both sexes Les deux sexes	Male Masculin	Female Féminin	Both sexes Les deux sexes	Male Masculin	Female Féminin	Both sexes Les deux sexes	Male Masculin	Female Féminin
AFRICA — AFRIQUE									
Réunion[4]									
1999									
Total	5.4	6.5	4.4	...	...	...	...	...	...
0-1	35.7	40.1	31.4	...	...	...	...	...	...
1-4	◆0.5	◆0.6	◆0.4	...	...	...	...	...	...
5-9	◆0.2	◆0.2	◆0.1	...	...	...	...	...	...
10-14	◆0.3	◆0.3	◆0.3	...	...	...	...	...	...
15-19	0.5	◆0.9	◆0.2	...	...	...	...	...	...
20-24	0.9	1.6	◆0.3	...	...	...	...	...	...
25-29	1.0	1.3	◆0.6	...	...	...	...	...	...
30-34	1.6	2.3	◆0.9	...	...	...	...	...	...
35-39	1.5	2.4	◆0.7	...	...	...	...	...	...
40-44	3.2	4.8	1.5	...	...	...	...	...	...
45-49	4.7	6.7	2.7	...	...	...	...	...	...
50-54	7.3	11.1	3.4	...	...	...	...	...	...
55-59	9.9	14.6	5.3	...	...	...	...	...	...
60-64	14.8	20.5	9.6	...	...	...	...	...	...
65-69	21.0	29.1	14.1	...	...	...	...	...	...
70-74	31.5	45.8	20.4	...	...	...	...	...	...
75-79	46.6	64.2	34.9	...	...	...	...	...	...
80-84	77.9	106.5	63.3	...	...	...	...	...	...
85-89	108.9	134.4	98.2	...	...	...	...	...	...
90-94	160.1	183.5	151.5	...	...	...	...	...	...
95-99	180.8	◆123.7	203.3	...	...	...	...	...	...
100+	◆321.4	◆400.0	◆304.3	...	...	...	...	...	...
Swaziland[3]									
1997									
Total	9.1	10.7	7.7	6.4	7.1	5.7	9.9	11.9	8.3
0-4	15.0	15.8	14.2	12.1	13.5	10.8	15.6	16.3	14.9
5-9	1.4	1.5	1.2	◆1.3	◆1.4	◆1.2	1.4	1.5	1.2
10-14	1.0	1.1	1.0	◆1.0	◆1.2	◆0.9	1.0	1.1	1.0
15-19	2.3	2.2	2.3	1.7	◆1.9	◆1.6	2.5	2.3	2.6
20-24	5.3	5.1	5.5	3.2	3.0	3.3	6.4	6.2	6.6
25-29	8.9	10.5	7.5	4.5	4.9	4.1	11.3	14.5	9.2
30-34	11.1	14.6	8.5	5.4	5.8	4.9	14.1	21.0	10.0
35-39	11.5	16.0	8.2	6.3	6.2	6.4	14.1	22.5	8.9
40-44	13.8	19.1	9.3	7.8	8.8	6.4	16.5	25.4	10.3
45-49	14.3	19.8	9.2	9.4	9.7	9.0	16.2	25.3	9.3
50-54	18.8	25.4	13.2	13.6	14.1	◆12.8	20.6	30.6	13.3
55-59	20.0	26.8	13.4	17.0	17.6	◆16.2	20.8	30.1	12.9
60-64	26.3	37.5	17.0	21.3	◆19.3	◆23.8	27.4	42.2	15.9
65-69	30.0	42.0	20.0	32.1	43.7	◆19.0	29.7	41.7	20.1
70-74	43.1	64.6	28.8	53.5	◆64.1	◆44.9	41.9	64.7	27.1
75+	68.7	79.2	61.7	97.1	90.1	102.9	65.8	77.9	58.0
AMERICA, NORTH — AMERIQUE DU NORD									
Bahamas									
2000									
Total	5.4	6.1	4.7	...	...	...	...	...	...
0-1	8.8	◆8.9	◆8.7	...	...	...	...	...	...
1-4	◆0.8	◆0.9	◆0.8	...	...	...	...	...	...
5-9	◆0.4	◆0.6	◆0.3	...	...	...	...	...	...
10-14	◆0.4	◆0.4	◆0.4	...	...	...	...	...	...
15-19	◆0.6	◆0.9	◆0.3	...	...	...	...	...	...
20-24	1.6	◆2.1	◆1.1	...	...	...	...	...	...
25-29	2.9	3.3	2.5	...	...	...	...	...	...
30-34	2.9	3.7	◆2.2	...	...	...	...	...	...
35-39	4.1	5.5	2.8	...	...	...	...	...	...
40-44	5.1	7.2	3.3	...	...	...	...	...	...
45-49	6.3	8.1	4.5	...	...	...	...	...	...
50-54	8.4	11.3	5.8	...	...	...	...	...	...
55-59	10.5	14.3	7.1	...	...	...	...	...	...

20. Death rates specific for age, sex and urban/rural residence: latest available year, 1994 - 2003
Taux de mortalité selon l'âge, le sexe et la résidence, urbaine/rurale: dernière année disponible, 1994 - 2003 (continued — suite)

Continent, country or area, year and age (in years) / Continent, pays ou zone, année et âge (en années)	Total			Urban - Urbaine			Rural - Rurale		
	Both sexes Les deux sexes	Male Masculin	Female Féminin	Both sexes Les deux sexes	Male Masculin	Female Féminin	Both sexes Les deux sexes	Male Masculin	Female Féminin
AMERICA, NORTH — AMERIQUE DU NORD									
Bahamas									
2000									
60-64	14.2	18.1	10.8	...	...	...	...	...	...
65-69	22.2	27.2	18.1	...	...	...	...	...	...
70-74	29.2	33.7	26.0	...	...	...	...	...	...
75-79	43.6	50.0	39.3	...	...	...	...	...	...
80-84	71.4	72.8	70.5	...	...	...	...	...	...
85-89	102.8	146.8	82.1	...	...	...	...	...	...
90+	184.0	248.2	156.1	...	...	...	...	...	...
Canada[5]									
2002									
Total	7.1	7.3	7.0	...	...	...	...	...	...
0-1	5.4	5.9	4.9	...	...	...	...	...	...
1-4	0.2	0.2	0.2	...	...	...	...	...	...
5-9	0.1	0.1	0.1	...	...	...	...	...	...
10-14	0.2	0.2	0.1	...	...	...	...	...	...
15-19	0.5	0.6	0.3	...	...	...	...	...	...
20-24	0.6	0.8	0.3	...	...	...	...	...	...
25-29	0.5	0.8	0.3	...	...	...	...	...	...
30-34	0.7	0.9	0.5	...	...	...	...	...	...
35-39	1.0	1.2	0.7	...	...	...	...	...	...
40-44	1.4	1.8	1.1	...	...	...	...	...	...
45-49	2.3	2.7	1.8	...	...	...	...	...	...
50-54	3.5	4.4	2.7	...	...	...	...	...	...
55-59	5.8	7.1	4.4	...	...	...	...	...	...
60-64	9.4	11.7	7.1	...	...	...	...	...	...
65-69	15.1	19.3	11.3	...	...	...	...	...	...
70-74	24.0	30.9	18.2	...	...	...	...	...	...
75-79	39.7	51.4	31.2	...	...	...	...	...	...
80-84	64.7	82.9	53.8	...	...	...	...	...	...
85-89	111.7	139.8	98.2	...	...	...	...	...	...
90+	201.7	223.6	193.8	...	...	...	...	...	...
Costa Rica									
2003									
Total	3.9	4.4	3.3	...	...	...	...	...	...
0-1	12.2	13.4	11.0	...	...	...	...	...	...
1-4	0.3	0.4	0.3	...	...	...	...	...	...
5-9	0.3	0.4	0.3	...	...	...	...	...	...
10-14	0.2	0.2	0.2	...	...	...	...	...	...
15-19	0.6	0.9	0.4	...	...	...	...	...	...
20-24	0.9	1.3	0.4	...	...	...	...	...	...
25-29	1.0	1.5	0.4	...	...	...	...	...	...
30-34	1.1	1.6	0.7	...	...	...	...	...	...
35-39	1.3	2.0	0.6	...	...	...	...	...	...
40-44	1.7	2.4	1.1	...	...	...	...	...	...
45-49	2.9	3.9	2.1	...	...	...	...	...	...
50-54	3.8	4.8	2.8	...	...	...	...	...	...
55-59	7.1	9.6	5.0	...	...	...	...	...	...
60-64	9.1	10.8	7.5	...	...	...	...	...	...
65-69	15.3	19.1	11.9	...	...	...	...	...	...
70-74	23.2	29.2	18.2	...	...	...	...	...	...
75-79	35.4	39.1	31.9	...	...	...	...	...	...
80-84	62.3	70.9	55.1	...	...	...	...	...	...
85+	126.6	138.1	118.3	...	...	...	...	...	...
Cuba									
2002									
Total	6.6	7.2	5.9	7.1	7.8	6.5	4.9	5.6	4.1
0-1	6.7	7.8	5.5	7.1	8.1	6.0	5.6	7.2	3.9
1-4	0.4	0.4	0.3	0.4	0.4	0.3	0.3	◆0.3	◆0.3
5-9	0.3	0.3	0.2	0.2	0.3	0.2	0.3	0.3	◆0.2
10-14	0.2	0.3	0.2	0.2	0.3	0.2	0.2	◆0.2	◆0.2
15-19	0.5	0.7	0.3	0.5	0.7	0.3	0.5	0.7	◆0.3

20. Death rates specific for age, sex and urban/rural residence: latest available year, 1994 - 2003
Taux de mortalité selon l'âge, le sexe et la résidence, urbaine/rurale: dernière année disponible, 1994 - 2003 (continued — suite)

Continent, country or area, year and age (in years) Continent, pays ou zone, année et âge (en années)	Total			Urban - Urbaine			Rural - Rurale		
	Both sexes Les deux sexes	Male Masculin	Female Féminin	Both sexes Les deux sexes	Male Masculin	Female Féminin	Both sexes Les deux sexes	Male Masculin	Female Féminin
AMERICA, NORTH —									
AMERIQUE DU NORD									
Cuba									
2002									
20-24	0.7	0.9	0.4	0.7	0.9	0.4	0.6	0.8	0.4
25-29	0.8	1.1	0.5	0.9	1.2	0.5	0.8	1.1	0.6
30-34	1.0	1.3	0.7	1.1	1.4	0.8	0.9	1.1	0.7
35-39	1.4	1.7	1.1	1.5	1.8	1.1	1.3	1.4	1.1
40-44	2.3	2.8	1.8	2.3	2.8	1.7	2.2	2.6	1.8
45-49	3.3	4.0	2.7	3.4	4.2	2.7	2.9	3.4	2.4
50-54	5.1	6.1	4.0	5.3	6.6	4.1	4.3	4.7	3.8
55-59	7.9	9.6	6.2	8.3	10.4	6.4	6.2	6.8	5.5
00-04	11.7	14.0	9.4	12.4	15.3	9.6	9.2	9.9	8.4
65-74	22.1	26.0	18.5	23.7	28.8	19.2	17.0	18.0	15.6
75-84	74.8	87.4	63.8	79.0	96.0	65.9	59.9	64.1	54.2
85+	128.3	137.9	121.0	134.0	147.4	125.3	108.5	114.9	100.2
2003									
Total	7.0	7.5	6.5	...	...	...	...	...	...
0-4	1.5	1.6	1.5	...	...	...	...	...	...
5-9	0.2	0.3	0.1	...	...	...	...	...	...
10-14	0.2	0.3	0.2	...	...	...	...	...	...
15-19	0.5	0.6	0.3	...	...	...	...	...	...
20-24	0.7	0.9	0.5	...	...	...	...	...	...
25-29	0.8	1.1	0.5	...	...	...	...	...	...
30-34	1.0	1.3	0.7	...	...	...	...	...	...
35-39	1.3	1.6	1.0	...	...	...	...	...	...
40-44	2.1	2.6	1.6	...	...	...	...	...	...
45-49	3.4	4.0	2.8	...	...	...	...	...	...
50-54	5.2	6.4	4.1	...	...	...	...	...	...
55-59	7.9	9.4	6.5	...	...	...	...	...	...
60-64	12.0	14.5	9.5	...	...	...	...	...	...
65-69	18.0	20.6	15.5	...	...	...	...	...	...
70+	60.0	65.4	55.3	...	...	...	...	...	...
El Salvador									
2003									
Total	4.4	5.2	3.7	5.3	6.3	4.4	3.1	3.7	2.5
0-1	8.1	9.0	7.2	9.7	10.7	8.7	6.3	7.1	5.5
1-4	0.7	0.8	0.7	0.8	0.9	0.7	0.6	0.7	0.6
5-9	0.3	0.3	0.2	0.3	0.3	0.3	0.2	0.3	♦0.2
10-14	0.4	0.4	0.3	0.4	0.5	0.4	0.3	0.3	♦0.2
15-19	1.1	1.7	0.6	1.5	2.3	0.7	0.7	1.0	0.4
20-24	1.8	2.9	0.7	2.3	3.8	0.9	1.1	1.7	0.5
25-29	2.0	3.2	0.8	2.4	4.0	0.9	1.3	2.0	0.6
30-34	2.1	3.4	0.9	2.3	3.9	0.9	1.6	2.5	0.7
35-39	3.0	4.7	1.5	3.2	5.2	1.6	2.5	3.9	1.2
40-44	3.6	5.4	2.0	3.8	6.0	2.0	3.1	4.4	2.1
45-49	4.5	6.6	2.8	4.8	7.2	2.8	4.0	5.3	2.7
50-54	5.9	7.7	4.3	6.7	8.8	4.9	4.6	5.9	3.3
55-59	8.1	10.8	5.7	9.1	12.2	6.5	6.5	8.6	4.4
60-64	12.8	14.9	10.9	14.9	17.9	12.3	9.4	10.5	8.3
65-69	17.6	20.8	14.8	19.8	23.4	16.8	14.0	16.8	11.2
70-74	25.5	30.0	21.9	28.3	33.9	24.0	20.7	23.8	17.9
75-79	42.2	50.5	36.2	46.4	56.4	39.5	34.2	39.9	29.5
80+	132.9	162.9	115.2	119.5	137.8	108.6	187.8	267.3	141.9
Guadeloupe									
2003									
Total	6.0	6.7	5.4	...	...	...	...	...	...
0-1	8.1	9.7	♦6.5	...	...	...	...	...	...
1-4	♦0.3	♦0.3	♦0.3	...	...	...	...	...	...
5-9	♦0.1	♦0.2	♦0.1	...	...	...	...	...	...
10-14	♦0.1	♦0.2	♦0.1	...	...	...	...	...	...
15-19	♦0.6	♦1.0	♦0.2	...	...	...	...	...	...
20-24	♦0.8	♦1.3	♦0.3	...	...	...	...	...	...
25-29	♦0.9	♦1.3	♦0.4	...	...	...	...	...	...

20. Death rates specific for age, sex and urban/rural residence: latest available year, 1994 - 2003
Taux de mortalité selon l'âge, le sexe et la résidence, urbaine/rurale: dernière année disponible, 1994 - 2003 (continued — suite)

Continent, country or area, year and age (in years) / Continent, pays ou zone, année et âge (en années)	Total			Urban - Urbaine			Rural - Rurale		
	Both sexes Les deux sexes	Male Masculin	Female Féminin	Both sexes Les deux sexes	Male Masculin	Female Féminin	Both sexes Les deux sexes	Male Masculin	Female Féminin
AMERICA, NORTH — AMERIQUE DU NORD									
Guadeloupe									
2003									
30-34	1.1	2.0	◆0.4	...	...	...	...	...	...
35-39	1.6	2.4	◆1.0	...	...	...	...	...	...
40-44	2.2	2.8	◆1.6	...	...	...	...	...	...
45-49	3.5	5.3	2.0	...	...	...	...	...	...
50-54	4.5	7.5	◆1.9	...	...	...	...	...	...
55-59	6.3	8.7	4.1	...	...	...	...	...	...
60-64	10.9	12.7	9.3	...	...	...	...	...	...
65-69	14.9	19.1	11.2	...	...	...	...	...	...
70-74	22.7	28.5	18.2	...	...	...	...	...	...
75-79	34.1	45.4	25.6	...	...	...	...	...	...
80-84	53.8	68.2	43.8	...	...	...	...	...	...
85-89	96.8	98.9	95.6	...	...	...	...	...	...
90+	148.6	142.2	151.2	...	...	...	...	...	...
Guatemala									
1999									
Total	5.8	6.6	5.0	...	...	...	...	...	...
0-1	34.9	38.1	31.4	...	...	...	...	...	...
1-4	3.6	3.6	3.5	...	...	...	...	...	...
5-9	0.7	0.7	0.7	...	...	...	...	...	...
10-14	0.7	0.8	0.5	...	...	...	...	...	...
15-19	1.4	1.7	1.0	...	...	...	...	...	...
20-24	2.1	2.9	1.3	...	...	...	...	...	...
25-29	2.6	3.8	1.5	...	...	...	...	...	...
30-34	3.4	4.8	2.1	...	...	...	...	...	...
35-39	4.4	6.2	2.7	...	...	...	...	...	...
40-44	5.4	7.1	3.7	...	...	...	...	...	...
45-49	6.9	9.0	4.9	...	...	...	...	...	...
50-54	8.8	10.9	6.8	...	...	...	...	...	...
55-59	10.8	12.2	9.3	...	...	...	...	...	...
60-64	15.2	17.5	12.9	...	...	...	...	...	...
65+	9.8	11.1	8.6	...	...	...	...	...	...
Martinique[4]									
2003									
Total	7.0	7.7	6.3	...	...	...	...	...	...
0-1	6.2	◆5.2	◆7.3	...	...	...	...	...	...
1-4	◆0.4	◆0.3	◆0.5	...	...	...	...	...	...
5-9	◆0.2	◆0.2	◆0.2	...	...	...	...	...	...
10-14	◆0.2	◆0.2	◆0.1	...	...	...	...	...	...
15-19	◆0.6	◆1.0	◆0.3	...	...	...	...	...	...
20-24	◆0.8	◆1.1	◆0.5	...	...	...	...	...	...
25-29	◆1.0	◆1.6	◆0.4	...	...	...	...	...	...
30-34	1.4	◆2.2	◆0.7	...	...	...	...	...	...
35-39	1.3	◆1.8	◆0.8	...	...	...	...	...	...
40-44	1.7	2.4	◆1.0	...	...	...	...	...	...
45-49	3.0	4.1	2.2	...	...	...	...	...	...
50-54	4.0	5.3	2.9	...	...	...	...	...	...
55-59	5.2	6.7	3.9	...	...	...	...	...	...
60-64	8.7	11.6	6.2	...	...	...	...	...	...
65-69	12.2	16.7	8.4	...	...	...	...	...	...
70-74	22.1	29.3	16.4	...	...	...	...	...	...
75-79	36.8	52.1	25.8	...	...	...	...	...	...
80-84	65.0	84.5	52.7	...	...	...	...	...	...
85-89	107.2	137.0	90.4	...	...	...	...	...	...
90+	187.0	186.1	187.3	...	...	...	...	...	...
Mexico - Mexique									
2003									
Total	4.5	5.0	4.0	4.3	4.7	3.9	4.9	5.7	4.1
0-1	16.8	18.7	14.6	16.6	18.5	14.6	16.1	18.2	13.9
1-4	0.8	0.9	0.8	0.7	0.8	0.6	1.1	1.2	1.0
5-9	0.3	0.3	0.2	0.3	0.3	0.2	0.3	0.4	0.3

20. Death rates specific for age, sex and urban/rural residence: latest available year, 1994 - 2003
Taux de mortalité selon l'âge, le sexe et la résidence, urbaine/rurale: dernière année disponible, 1994 - 2003 (continued — suite)

Continent, country or area, year and age (in years) — Continent, pays ou zone, année et âge (en années)	Total			Urban - Urbaine			Rural - Rurale		
	Both sexes Les deux sexes	Male Masculin	Female Féminin	Both sexes Les deux sexes	Male Masculin	Female Féminin	Both sexes Les deux sexes	Male Masculin	Female Féminin
AMERICA, NORTH — AMERIQUE DU NORD									
Mexico - Mexique									
2003									
10-14	0.3	0.4	0.3	0.3	0.4	0.2	0.4	0.5	0.3
15-19	0.7	0.9	0.4	0.6	0.8	0.4	0.8	1.1	0.5
20-24	1.0	1.4	0.5	0.8	1.2	0.5	1.2	1.8	0.7
25-29	1.2	1.8	0.6	1.1	1.6	0.6	1.5	2.3	0.8
30-34	1.5	2.2	0.8	1.3	1.9	0.7	1.9	2.8	1.1
35-39	1.9	2.7	1.1	1.7	2.4	1.0	2.4	3.5	1.5
40-44	2.7	3.6	1.8	2.4	3.2	1.6	3.3	4.5	2.1
45-49	3.9	5.1	2.8	3.7	4.8	2.7	4.4	5.9	3.0
50-54	6.0	7.4	4.7	5.8	7.1	4.7	6.0	7.5	4.6
55-59	9.3	11.2	7.4	9.2	11.0	7.5	8.8	10.8	7.0
60-64	14.0	16.5	11.8	14.0	16.2	12.0	13.2	15.8	10.8
65-69	21.0	24.5	17.9	21.3	24.5	18.5	19.1	23.1	15.5
70-74	32.4	37.8	27.8	32.6	37.4	28.6	30.3	37.3	24.3
75-79	49.3	57.1	43.0	49.9	56.3	44.8	45.6	57.0	36.3
80-84	79.0	90.2	70.4	78.7	87.0	72.3	77.3	96.6	62.3
85-89	117.8	126.5	111.4	118.5	121.5	116.3	112.3	137.1	93.7
90-94	177.4	180.1	175.4	176.6	171.2	180.5	174.9	200.4	156.3
95-99	243.8	226.5	255.7	247.4	219.1	267.2	229.0	239.1	221.3
100+	522.7	471.6	557.9	511.5	439.6	560.7	534.5	523.3	542.4
Puerto Rico - Porto Rico									
2003									
Total	7.3	8.4	6.3	...	...	...	...	...	...
0-1	9.6	10.8	8.3	...	...	...	...	...	...
1-4	0.2	♦0.2	♦0.2	...	...	...	...	...	...
5-9	0.1	♦0.1	♦0.1	...	...	...	...	...	...
10-14	0.2	0.2	♦0.1	...	...	...	...	...	...
15-19	0.7	1.1	0.3	...	...	...	...	...	...
20-24	1.4	2.4	0.4	...	...	...	...	...	...
25-29	1.5	2.5	0.5	...	...	...	...	...	...
30-34	1.5	2.4	0.7	...	...	...	...	...	...
35-39	2.0	3.0	1.0	...	...	...	...	...	...
40-44	2.5	3.7	1.5	...	...	...	...	...	...
45-49	3.7	5.1	2.4	...	...	...	...	...	...
50-54	5.2	7.3	3.5	...	...	...	...	...	...
55-59	7.5	10.4	5.1	...	...	...	...	...	...
60-64	11.5	15.0	8.5	...	...	...	...	...	...
65-69	15.8	21.1	11.3	...	...	...	...	...	...
70-74	24.8	30.9	19.9	...	...	...	...	...	...
75-79	39.8	51.0	31.4	...	...	...	...	...	...
80+	93.7	105.6	85.6	...	...	...	...	...	...
Trinidad and Tobago - Trinité-et-Tobago									
1997									
Total	7.2	7.9	6.5	...	...	...	...	...	...
0-1	19.8	21.4	18.2	...	...	...	...	...	...
1-4	0.8	0.8	♦0.7	...	...	...	...	...	...
5-9	0.3	♦0.4	♦0.2	...	...	...	...	...	...
10-14	0.4	♦0.4	♦0.3	...	...	...	...	...	...
15-19	0.7	0.8	0.6	...	...	...	...	...	...
20-24	1.4	1.8	0.9	...	...	...	...	...	...
25-29	1.6	1.9	1.2	...	...	...	...	...	...
30-34	2.5	3.2	1.9	...	...	...	...	...	...
35-39	3.0	3.7	2.3	...	...	...	...	...	...
40-44	3.9	4.8	2.9	...	...	...	...	...	...
45-49	5.4	6.6	4.3	...	...	...	...	...	...
50-54	8.3	10.3	6.3	...	...	...	...	...	...
55-59	13.6	16.6	10.9	...	...	...	...	...	...
60-64	22.1	24.2	20.2	...	...	...	...	...	...
65-69	31.7	36.0	27.8	...	...	...	...	...	...
70-74	44.7	60.6	32.8	...	...	...	...	...	...

20. Death rates specific for age, sex and urban/rural residence: latest available year, 1994 - 2003
Taux de mortalité selon l'âge, le sexe et la résidence, urbaine/rurale: dernière année disponible, 1994 - 2003 (continued — suite)

Continent, country or area, year and age (in years) Continent, pays ou zone, année et âge (en années)	Total			Urban - Urbaine			Rural - Rurale		
	Both sexes Les deux sexes	Male Masculin	Female Féminin	Both sexes Les deux sexes	Male Masculin	Female Féminin	Both sexes Les deux sexes	Male Masculin	Female Féminin
AMERICA, NORTH — **AMERIQUE DU NORD**									
Trinidad and Tobago - Trinité-et-Tobago 1997									
75-79	62.6	82.7	47.8	...	...	...	...	...	...
80+	146.2	154.8	139.3	...	...	...	...	...	...
United States - États-Unis 2003									
Total	8.4	8.4	8.4	...	...	...	...	...	...
0-1	7.1	7.9	6.3	...	...	...	...	...	...
1-4	0.3	0.3	0.3	...	...	...	...	...	...
5-14	0.2	0.2	0.1	...	...	...	...	...	...
15-24	0.8	1.1	0.4	...	...	...	...	...	...
25-34	1.0	1.4	0.6	...	...	...	...	...	...
35-44	2.0	2.5	1.5	...	...	...	...	...	...
45-54	4.3	5.5	3.2	...	...	...	...	...	...
55-64	9.4	11.6	7.3	...	...	...	...	...	...
65-74	22.5	27.7	18.2	...	...	...	...	...	...
75-84	54.6	66.3	46.8	...	...	...	...	...	...
85+	146.0	157.7	140.7	...	...	...	...	...	...
AMERICA, SOUTH — **AMERIQUE DU SUD**									
Argentina - Argentine 1995									
Total	7.7	8.7	6.8	...	...	...	...	...	...
0-4	4.9	5.5	4.5	...	...	...	...	...	...
5-9	0.3	0.3	0.2	...	...	...	...	...	...
10-14	0.3	0.4	0.3	...	...	...	...	...	...
15-19	0.7	1.0	0.5	...	...	...	...	...	...
20-24	1.1	1.5	0.6	...	...	...	...	...	...
25-29	1.3	1.8	0.8	...	...	...	...	...	...
30-34	1.4	1.9	1.0	...	...	...	...	...	...
35-39	1.9	2.5	1.3	...	...	...	...	...	...
40-44	2.8	3.6	2.0	...	...	...	...	...	...
45-49	4.5	5.8	3.1	...	...	...	...	...	...
50-54	6.9	9.3	4.5	...	...	...	...	...	...
55-59	10.3	14.4	6.3	...	...	...	...	...	...
60-64	15.6	22.4	9.4	...	...	...	...	...	...
65-69	23.0	32.5	14.9	...	...	...	...	...	...
70-74	35.0	48.3	24.5	...	...	...	...	...	...
75-79	52.8	70.3	40.7	...	...	...	...	...	...
80+	146.1	170.7	131.4	...	...	...	...	...	...
Chile - Chili 2003									
Total	5.3	5.8	4.8	5.3	5.7	4.8	5.2	6.0	4.4
0-1	7.8	8.4	7.2	7.8	8.5	7.1	7.9	8.0	7.9
1-4	0.4	0.4	0.4	0.4	0.4	0.3	0.5	0.6	◆0.4
5-9	0.2	0.2	0.2	0.2	0.2	0.1	0.2	◆0.3	◆0.2
10-14	0.2	0.3	0.2	0.2	0.3	0.2	0.3	0.3	◆0.2
15-19	0.4	0.6	0.2	0.4	0.6	0.2	0.6	0.9	◆0.3
20-24	0.8	1.2	0.3	0.8	1.2	0.3	1.1	1.5	0.5
25-29	0.9	1.4	0.4	0.9	1.3	0.4	1.0	1.5	0.5
30-34	1.0	1.6	0.5	1.0	1.6	0.5	1.2	1.7	0.6
35-39	1.4	2.0	0.7	1.3	1.9	0.7	1.6	2.4	0.8
40-44	1.9	2.5	1.2	1.8	2.4	1.2	2.1	2.8	1.2
45-49	2.8	3.7	2.0	2.9	3.7	2.0	2.7	3.4	1.8
50-54	4.5	5.8	3.3	4.6	6.0	3.3	4.2	5.0	3.2
55-59	7.3	9.5	5.2	7.4	9.8	5.2	6.4	7.8	4.7
60-64	11.6	15.1	8.5	12.0	15.8	8.7	9.5	11.5	7.2
65-69	17.6	23.3	12.8	18.1	24.6	13.1	14.6	17.8	10.9
70-74	30.4	40.5	22.7	31.5	42.9	23.4	24.7	30.6	18.2

20. Death rates specific for age, sex and urban/rural residence: latest available year, 1994 - 2003
Taux de mortalité selon l'âge, le sexe et la résidence, urbaine/rurale: dernière année disponible, 1994 - 2003 (continued — suite)

Continent, country or area, year and age (in years) / Continent, pays ou zone, année et âge (en années)	Total			Urban - Urbaine			Rural - Rurale		
	Both sexes Les deux sexes	Male Masculin	Female Féminin	Both sexes Les deux sexes	Male Masculin	Female Féminin	Both sexes Les deux sexes	Male Masculin	Female Féminin
AMERICA, SOUTH — AMERIQUE DU SUD									
Chile - Chili									
2003									
75-79	46.1	61.3	35.6	47.1	64.6	36.1	40.1	47.5	32.3
80+	116.7	134.0	107.1	119.6	141.1	108.9	100.1	106.0	95.0
Suriname									
2000									
Total	7.1	8.0	6.1	...	...	...	...	...	...
0-4	4.3	4.2	4.5	...	...	...	...	...	...
5-9	♦0.4	♦0.5	♦0.3	...	...	...	...	...	...
10-14	♦0.5	♦0.7	♦0.3	...	...	...	...	...	...
15-19	1.2	1.5	♦0.9	...	...	...	...	...	...
20-24	1.9	2.8	♦1.0	...	...	...	...	...	...
25-29	2.9	3.5	2.4	...	...	...	...	...	...
30-34	3.4	4.4	2.5	...	...	...	...	...	...
35-39	4.1	5.4	2.8	...	...	...	...	...	...
40-44	5.1	6.8	3.4	...	...	...	...	...	...
45-49	8.1	9.9	6.5	...	...	...	...	...	...
50-54	11.6	14.3	8.9	...	...	...	...	...	...
55-59	15.4	20.1	11.6	...	...	...	...	...	...
60-64	22.3	26.4	18.6	...	...	...	...	...	...
65-69	30.0	36.8	23.9	...	...	...	...	...	...
70-74	45.5	50.4	40.4	...	...	...	...	...	...
75-79	72.7	93.3	56.4	...	...	...	...	...	...
80+	149.8	160.5	141.8	...	...	...	...	...	...
Uruguay									
2002									
Total	9.6	10.5	8.7	...	...	...	...	...	...
0-1	14.0	15.4	12.3	...	...	...	...	...	...
1-4	0.5	0.6	0.3	...	...	...	...	...	...
5-9	0.2	0.2	0.2	...	...	...	...	...	...
10-14	0.2	0.3	♦0.2	...	...	...	...	...	...
15-19	0.7	1.0	0.3	...	...	...	...	...	...
20-24	1.0	1.5	0.4	...	...	...	...	...	...
25-29	1.1	1.6	0.5	...	...	...	...	...	...
30-34	1.4	1.8	0.9	...	...	...	...	...	...
35-39	1.6	2.1	1.1	...	...	...	...	...	...
40-44	2.4	2.7	2.1	...	...	...	...	...	...
45-49	4.0	5.1	2.9	...	...	...	...	...	...
50-54	6.5	8.8	4.3	...	...	...	...	...	...
55-59	9.9	13.8	6.4	...	...	...	...	...	...
60-64	15.0	22.0	9.0	...	...	...	...	...	...
65-69	22.0	31.8	14.3	...	...	...	...	...	...
70-74	33.3	47.7	22.7	...	...	...	...	...	...
75+	90.1	106.6	80.6	...	...	...	...	...	...
Venezuela[6]									
2002									
Total	4.2	5.1	3.2	...	...	...	...	...	...
0-1	13.5	15.2	11.7	...	...	...	...	...	...
1-4	0.9	0.9	0.8	...	...	...	...	...	...
5-9	0.3	0.4	0.3	...	...	...	...	...	...
10-14	0.4	0.5	0.3	...	...	...	...	...	...
15-19	1.4	2.2	0.5	...	...	...	...	...	...
20-24	2.3	3.9	0.6	...	...	...	...	...	...
25-29	2.1	3.5	0.7	...	...	...	...	...	...
30-34	2.1	3.2	1.0	...	...	...	...	...	...
35-39	2.1	3.0	1.2	...	...	...	...	...	...
40-44	2.8	3.7	1.8	...	...	...	...	...	...
45-49	3.9	5.0	2.7	...	...	...	...	...	...
50-54	5.3	6.8	3.8	...	...	...	...	...	...
55-59	7.2	9.4	5.1	...	...	...	...	...	...
60-64	11.0	14.0	8.1	...	...	...	...	...	...
65-69	17.7	22.1	13.7	...	...	...	...	...	...

20. Death rates specific for age, sex and urban/rural residence: latest available year, 1994 - 2003
Taux de mortalité selon l'âge, le sexe et la résidence, urbaine/rurale: dernière année disponible, 1994 - 2003 (continued — suite)

Continent, country or area, year and age (in years) Continent, pays ou zone, année et âge (en années)	Total			Urban - Urbaine			Rural - Rurale		
	Both sexes Les deux sexes	Male Masculin	Female Féminin	Both sexes Les deux sexes	Male Masculin	Female Féminin	Both sexes Les deux sexes	Male Masculin	Female Féminin
AMERICA, SOUTH —									
AMERIQUE DU SUD									
Venezuela[6]									
2002									
70-74	26.5	33.3	20.7	...	...	...	...	...	...
75-79	40.2	48.6	33.4	...	...	...	...	...	...
80+	117.7	128.1	110.2	...	...	...	...	...	...
ASIA — ASIE									
Armenia - Arménie[7]									
2000									
Total	6.3	6.6	6.0	6.2	6.7	5.7	6.6	6.5	6.6
0-1	15.5	18.4	12.0	16.5	20.1	12.3	13.8	15.6	11.5
1-4	0.8	0.9	0.8	0.8	0.8	0.7	0.9	1.0	♦0.9
5-9	0.2	♦0.2	0.2	0.2	♦0.2	♦0.2	♦0.2	♦0.1	♦0.2
10-14	0.2	0.3	♦0.1	0.2	0.3	♦0.1	♦0.2	♦0.2	♦0.1
15-19	0.4	0.6	♦0.2	0.3	0.5	♦0.2	0.5	0.8	♦0.1
20-24	0.5	0.7	0.3	0.5	0.7	♦0.2	0.5	0.6	♦0.3
25-29	0.6	0.7	0.4	0.6	0.8	0.5	0.5	0.6	♦0.3
30-34	0.9	1.3	0.6	0.9	1.4	0.5	0.9	1.1	♦0.6
35-39	1.4	2.0	0.9	1.5	2.1	0.9	1.4	1.9	0.8
40-44	2.1	2.9	1.3	2.1	3.1	1.2	2.1	2.6	1.7
45-49	3.4	5.0	2.1	3.7	5.5	2.2	2.8	3.7	1.8
50-54	5.7	8.1	3.8	5.9	8.3	3.9	5.2	7.3	3.4
55-59	8.1	11.8	5.1	8.5	12.5	5.2	7.1	9.7	5.0
60-64	15.6	21.2	11.1	16.4	23.0	11.0	14.1	17.7	11.1
65-69	26.0	34.2	19.4	26.4	35.5	19.5	25.3	32.3	19.3
70-74	41.0	48.3	35.4	40.8	46.5	36.3	41.5	51.6	33.9
75-79	58.9	66.4	54.5	55.6	57.7	54.4	66.0	87.2	54.8
80-84	78.1	76.9	78.6	69.0	65.7	70.7	102.3	110.4	98.8
85+	125.8	95.4	144.9	96.9	76.6	109.9	198.6	144.1	231.9
2003									
Total	8.1	8.7	7.6	...	...	...	...	...	...
0-1	12.5	14.2	10.6	...	...	...	...	...	...
1-4	0.4	0.4	0.4	...	...	...	...	...	...
5-9	0.2	0.3	♦0.2	...	...	...	...	...	...
10-14	0.2	♦0.2	♦0.1	...	...	...	...	...	...
15-19	0.3	0.5	♦0.2	...	...	...	...	...	...
20-24	0.5	0.7	0.2	...	...	...	...	...	...
25-29	0.7	0.9	0.4	...	...	...	...	...	...
30-34	1.0	1.6	0.6	...	...	...	...	...	...
35-39	1.6	2.3	0.9	...	...	...	...	...	...
40-44	2.5	3.5	1.6	...	...	...	...	...	...
45-49	4.1	5.9	2.5	...	...	...	...	...	...
50-54	6.6	9.3	4.2	...	...	...	...	...	...
55-59	10.5	15.0	6.9	...	...	...	...	...	...
60-64	16.5	23.2	11.2	...	...	...	...	...	...
65-69	28.7	38.6	21.0	...	...	...	...	...	...
70-74	47.7	60.6	38.1	...	...	...	...	...	...
75-79	76.3	94.2	65.9	...	...	...	...	...	...
80-84	123.4	141.4	116.1	...	...	...	...	...	...
85+	257.5	297.2	250.6	...	...	...	...	...	...
Azerbaijan - Azerbaïdjan+,[7]									
2003									
Total	6.0	6.3	5.6	5.9	6.4	5.4	6.0	6.2	5.8
0-1	12.9	13.5	12.2	12.4	13.8	10.8	13.4	13.3	13.5
1-4	1.8	1.8	1.8	0.6	0.6	0.5	2.8	2.7	2.8
5-9	0.6	0.6	0.5	0.5	0.5	0.4	0.7	0.8	0.6
10-14	0.4	0.4	0.3	0.3	0.4	0.3	0.4	0.4	0.4
15-19	0.5	0.7	0.4	0.5	0.6	0.3	0.6	0.7	0.4
20-24	0.8	1.0	0.5	0.8	1.0	0.5	0.8	1.0	0.6
25-29	1.1	1.5	0.6	1.0	1.6	0.6	1.1	1.5	0.7
30-34	1.3	1.9	0.8	1.4	2.0	0.9	1.3	1.7	0.8

20. Death rates specific for age, sex and urban/rural residence: latest available year, 1994 - 2003
Taux de mortalité selon l'âge, le sexe et la résidence, urbaine/rurale: dernière année disponible, 1994 - 2003 (continued — suite)

Continent, country or area, year and age (in years) / Continent, pays ou zone, année et âge (en années)	Total			Urban - Urbaine			Rural - Rurale		
	Both sexes Les deux sexes	Male Masculin	Female Féminin	Both sexes Les deux sexes	Male Masculin	Female Féminin	Both sexes Les deux sexes	Male Masculin	Female Féminin
ASIA — ASIE									
Azerbaijan - Azerbaïdjan[+,7]									
2003									
35-39	1.8	2.5	1.2	1.9	2.8	1.1	1.8	2.3	1.3
40-44	2.7	3.6	1.8	2.8	4.0	1.7	2.5	3.2	1.9
45-49	4.3	5.9	2.8	4.4	6.2	2.8	4.1	5.4	2.8
50-54	7.2	9.9	4.7	7.4	10.1	4.8	6.9	9.7	4.4
55-59	11.3	15.1	7.8	11.4	15.1	8.0	11.1	15.0	7.6
60-64	20.1	26.1	15.2	20.3	26.4	15.0	20.0	25.6	15.4
65-69	30.7	38.4	24.5	31.8	40.4	24.9	29.6	36.4	24.2
70-74	49.8	59.4	42.2	51.0	61.0	43.5	48.7	58.1	41.1
75-79	71.1	83.6	63.0	73.7	84.4	66.9	68.5	82.8	58.7
80-84	98.3	103.2	96.0	102.4	99.3	103.9	94.4	107.2	88.7
85-89	146.7	151.4	145.0	169.8	146.1	179.3	127.9	156.3	118.8
90-94	188.3	197.8	185.4	211.8	180.0	224.5	174.9	212.0	165.4
95-99	199.6	178.3	205.5	163.0	110.0	185.7	220.0	246.7	214.7
100+	304.4	205.0	332.9	195.0	♦90.0	247.5	359.2	320.0	367.0
Brunei Darussalam - Brunéi Darussalam[+]									
2001									
Total	3.0	3.4	2.7	...	...	...	...	...	...
0-14	♦0.2	♦0.2	♦0.1	...	...	...	...	...	...
15-19	♦0.6	♦0.7	♦0.5	...	...	...	...	...	...
20-24	♦0.7	♦1.1	♦0.4	...	...	...	...	...	...
25-29	♦0.8	♦1.2	♦0.4	...	...	...	...	...	...
30-34	♦0.7	♦0.9	♦0.5	...	...	...	...	...	...
35-39	1.4	♦1.6	♦1.2	...	...	...	...	...	...
40-44	1.6	♦1.8	♦1.3	...	...	...	...	...	...
45-49	3.4	4.8	♦1.9	...	...	...	...	...	...
50-54	5.6	7.4	♦3.7	...	...	...	...	...	...
55-59	9.6	11.1	♦8.0	...	...	...	...	...	...
60-64	13.1	15.2	♦11.1	...	...	...	...	...	...
65-69	29.5	32.2	27.1	...	...	...	...	...	...
70+	72.8	74.0	71.7	...	...	...	...	...	...
China: Hong Kong SAR - Chine: Hong Kong RAS									
2003									
Total	5.4	6.3	4.6	...	...	...	...	...	...
0-1	2.2	2.3	2.2	...	...	...	...	...	...
1-4	0.2	♦0.2	♦0.2	...	...	...	...	...	...
5-9	0.1	♦0.1	♦0.1	...	...	...	...	...	...
10-14	0.1	♦0.1	♦0.1	...	...	...	...	...	...
15-19	0.2	0.3	0.1	...	...	...	...	...	...
20-24	0.4	0.5	0.3	...	...	...	...	...	...
25-29	0.5	0.8	0.3	...	...	...	...	...	...
30-34	0.5	0.7	0.4	...	...	...	...	...	...
35-39	0.8	1.1	0.5	...	...	...	...	...	...
40-44	1.2	1.5	0.8	...	...	...	...	...	...
45-49	2.0	2.7	1.4	...	...	...	...	...	...
50-54	3.0	4.1	1.9	...	...	...	...	...	...
55-59	4.8	6.5	2.9	...	...	...	...	...	...
60-64	8.4	11.7	4.7	...	...	...	...	...	...
65-69	12.5	16.6	8.3	...	...	...	...	...	...
70-74	21.8	29.4	14.5	...	...	...	...	...	...
75-79	38.0	50.6	27.7	...	...	...	...	...	...
80-84	61.3	78.2	49.9	...	...	...	...	...	...
85+	120.5	137.0	113.0	...	...	...	...	...	...
China: Macao SAR - Chine: Macao RAS									
2003									
Total	3.3	3.6	3.0	...	...	...	...	...	...
0-4	♦0.3	♦0.2	♦0.3	...	...	...	...	...	...
5-9	♦0.1	♦0.1	♦0.1	...	...	...	...	...	...
10-14	-	-	♦0.1	...	...	...	...	...	...

20. Death rates specific for age, sex and urban/rural residence: latest available year, 1994 - 2003
Taux de mortalité selon l'âge, le sexe et la résidence, urbaine/rurale: dernière année disponible, 1994 - 2003 (continued — suite)

Continent, country or area, year and age (in years) Continent, pays ou zone, année et âge (en années)	Total			Urban - Urbaine			Rural - Rurale		
	Both sexes Les deux sexes	Male Masculin	Female Féminin	Both sexes Les deux sexes	Male Masculin	Female Féminin	Both sexes Les deux sexes	Male Masculin	Female Féminin
ASIA — ASIE									
China: Macao SAR - Chine: Macao RAS									
2003									
15-19	◆0.3	◆0.3	◆0.2	...	...	...	...	...	...
20-24	◆0.3	◆0.4	◆0.2	...	...	...	...	...	...
25-29	◆0.5	◆0.9	◆0.2	...	...	...	...	...	...
30-34	◆0.4	◆0.8	◆0.2	...	...	...	...	...	...
35-39	1.0	◆1.0	◆0.9	...	...	...	...	...	...
40-44	1.3	1.7	◆1.0	...	...	...	...	...	...
45-49	1.9	2.6	◆1.1	...	...	...	...	...	...
50-54	1.9	2.2	◆1.5	...	...	...	...	...	...
55-59	3.3	3.6	◆3.0	...	...	...	...	...	...
60-64	6.0	7.6	◆4.2	...	...	...	...	...	...
65-69	11.1	14.6	7.8	...	...	...	...	...	...
70-74	20.6	29.0	14.1	...	...	...	...	...	...
75+	49.1	54.2	45.9	...	...	...	...	...	...
Cyprus - Chypre[8]									
2003									
Total	7.2	7.8	6.6	...	...	...	...	...	...
0-1	4.1	◆4.6	◆3.7	...	...	...	...	...	...
1-4	◆0.2	◆0.1	◆0.4	...	...	...	...	...	...
5-9	◆0.2	◆0.2	◆0.1	...	...	...	...	...	...
10-14	◆0.1	◆0.2	◆0.1	...	...	...	...	...	...
15-19	0.6	◆0.7	◆0.4	...	...	...	...	...	...
20-24	0.6	◆1.0	◆0.2	...	...	...	...	...	...
25-29	◆0.5	◆0.7	◆0.4	...	...	...	...	...	...
30-34	0.7	◆1.0	◆0.4	...	...	...	...	...	...
35-39	0.8	◆0.9	◆0.7	...	...	...	...	...	...
40-44	0.8	◆1.1	◆0.5	...	...	...	...	...	...
45-49	1.7	2.5	◆1.1	...	...	...	...	...	...
50-54	3.2	3.6	2.8	...	...	...	...	...	...
55-59	4.8	6.6	3.1	...	...	...	...	...	...
60-64	8.3	11.1	5.7	...	...	...	...	...	...
65-69	15.1	19.2	11.4	...	...	...	...	...	...
70-74	24.4	27.8	21.7	...	...	...	...	...	...
75-79	44.5	53.9	37.1	...	...	...	...	...	...
80+	123.1	139.9	111.1	...	...	...	...	...	...
Georgia - Géorgie[7]									
2003									
Total	10.6	11.2	10.2	...	...	...	...	...	...
0-1	25.4	27.5	23.0	...	...	...	...	...	...
1-4	0.7	0.8	0.6	...	...	...	...	...	...
5-9	0.1	◆0.1	◆0.1	...	...	...	...	...	...
10-14	0.2	◆0.2	0.2	...	...	...	...	...	...
15-19	0.3	0.4	0.2	...	...	...	...	...	...
20-24	0.6	0.8	0.4	...	...	...	...	...	...
25-29	1.0	1.2	0.8	...	...	...	...	...	...
30-34	1.4	2.3	0.6	...	...	...	...	...	...
35-39	1.8	2.5	1.2	...	...	...	...	...	...
40-44	2.7	3.6	1.9	...	...	...	...	...	...
45-49	4.0	6.1	2.2	...	...	...	...	...	...
50-54	7.4	10.9	4.4	...	...	...	...	...	...
55-59	11.7	16.3	8.0	...	...	...	...	...	...
60-64	14.7	20.0	10.6	...	...	...	...	...	...
65-69	26.7	37.0	18.9	...	...	...	...	...	...
70-74	40.5	51.8	32.7	...	...	...	...	...	...
75-79	76.4	95.9	65.5	...	...	...	...	...	...
80-84	113.2	146.0	99.7	...	...	...	...	...	...
85+	264.4	345.3	240.5	...	...	...	...	...	...
Israel - Israël[9]									
2003									
Total	5.7	5.9	5.6	5.9	6.0	5.7	4.3	4.3	4.2
0-1	5.1	5.3	4.8	5.0	5.3	4.7	5.7	5.2	6.2

20. Death rates specific for age, sex and urban/rural residence: latest available year, 1994 - 2003
Taux de mortalité selon l'âge, le sexe et la résidence, urbaine/rurale: dernière année disponible, 1994 - 2003 (continued — suite)

Continent, country or area, year and age (in years) / Continent, pays ou zone, année et âge (en années)	Total			Urban - Urbaine			Rural - Rurale		
	Both sexes Les deux sexes	Male Masculin	Female Féminin	Both sexes Les deux sexes	Male Masculin	Female Féminin	Both sexes Les deux sexes	Male Masculin	Female Féminin
ASIA — ASIE									
Israel - Israël[9]									
2003									
1-4	0.3	0.4	0.3	0.3	0.4	0.2	♦0.4	♦0.4	♦0.3
5-9	0.1	0.1	0.1	0.1	0.1	0.1	♦0.1	♦0.2	♦0.1
10-14	0.1	0.2	♦0.1	0.1	0.2	♦0.1	♦0.2	♦0.3	♦0.1
15-19	0.4	0.5	0.2	0.4	0.5	0.2	♦0.5	♦0.7	♦0.2
20-24	0.6	1.0	0.2	0.6	1.0	0.2	0.8	♦1.2	♦0.3
25-29	0.5	0.7	0.3	0.5	0.7	0.3	♦0.5	♦0.7	♦0.3
30-34	0.6	0.8	0.4	0.6	0.8	0.4	♦0.5	♦0.7	♦0.4
35-39	0.9	1.2	0.6	1.0	1.3	0.7	♦0.4	♦0.6	♦0.3
40-44	1.4	1.8	1.0	1.4	1.9	1.0	♦0.8	♦0.8	♦0.7
45-49	2.0	2.7	1.4	2.1	2.7	1.5	1.6	2.2	♦0.9
50-54	3.1	4.0	2.4	3.2	4.1	2.4	2.4	2.8	♦1.8
55-59	5.3	6.7	4.0	5.4	6.9	4.0	4.0	4.2	3.7
60-64	8.6	11.1	6.5	8.8	11.3	6.6	6.4	7.8	4.9
65-69	14.4	18.7	10.9	14.7	19.2	11.0	10.3	11.1	9.5
70-74	24.8	31.1	20.0	24.8	31.2	20.0	24.5	29.8	20.0
75-79	42.1	51.6	35.6	41.9	51.2	35.6	45.3	58.2	34.5
80-84	70.6	80.4	63.6	70.6	80.3	63.9	69.5	82.1	61.7
85+	166.0	173.4	161.0	165.0	172.5	160.5	174.6	195.9	167.9
Japan - Japon[10]									
2003									
Total	8.0	8.9	7.1	...	...	...	...	...	...
0-1	3.0	3.1	2.9	...	...	...	...	...	...
1-4	0.2	0.3	0.2	...	...	...	...	...	...
5-9	0.1	0.1	0.1	...	...	...	...	...	...
10-14	0.1	0.1	0.1	...	...	...	...	...	...
15-19	0.3	0.4	0.2	...	...	...	...	...	...
20-24	0.4	0.6	0.3	...	...	...	...	...	...
25-29	0.5	0.7	0.3	...	...	...	...	...	...
30-34	0.6	0.8	0.4	...	...	...	...	...	...
35-39	0.9	1.1	0.6	...	...	...	...	...	...
40-44	1.3	1.8	0.9	...	...	...	...	...	...
45-49	2.1	2.8	1.4	...	...	...	...	...	...
50-54	3.4	4.7	2.2	...	...	...	...	...	...
55-59	4.9	7.0	3.0	...	...	...	...	...	...
60-64	7.2	10.3	4.2	...	...	...	...	...	...
65-69	11.4	16.4	6.8	...	...	...	...	...	...
70-74	18.7	27.2	11.5	...	...	...	...	...	...
75-79	30.1	43.4	20.4	...	...	...	...	...	...
80-84	51.0	73.5	39.2	...	...	...	...	...	...
85-89	92.2	127.1	76.7	...	...	...	...	...	...
90+	169.5	214.4	155.1	...	...	...	...	...	...
Kazakhstan[7]									
2003									
Total	10.4	12.1	8.8	11.8	14.3	9.6	8.6	9.6	7.7
0-1	16.3	18.6	13.9	18.3	21.3	15.0	14.0	15.3	12.6
1-4	1.2	1.3	1.1	0.9	1.0	0.9	1.5	1.6	1.3
5-9	0.5	0.5	0.4	0.5	0.6	0.4	0.4	0.5	0.3
10-14	0.5	0.5	0.4	0.5	0.6	0.4	0.5	0.5	0.4
15-19	1.1	1.5	0.7	1.2	1.6	0.8	1.0	1.4	0.6
20-24	2.1	3.0	1.1	2.1	3.2	1.1	2.1	2.8	1.2
25-29	3.0	4.6	1.5	3.4	5.3	1.6	2.6	3.7	1.3
30-34	3.9	6.0	1.8	4.3	7.0	1.9	3.3	4.8	1.7
35-39	4.9	7.5	2.4	5.5	8.7	2.6	4.1	5.9	2.2
40-44	7.1	10.9	3.6	7.9	12.6	3.8	5.9	8.6	3.1
45-49	10.2	15.6	5.4	11.4	18.1	5.8	8.3	12.0	4.7
50-54	14.4	22.0	8.0	15.7	25.1	8.2	12.2	17.1	7.7
55-59	20.1	30.4	11.8	21.5	34.0	12.0	17.6	24.9	11.3
60-64	29.3	44.2	18.6	30.9	49.1	18.9	26.9	37.8	18.2
65-69	40.5	59.2	27.5	41.3	63.3	27.0	39.5	53.5	28.4
70-74	59.7	83.8	45.5	60.2	86.9	45.6	58.8	79.2	45.2
75-79	83.5	110.0	72.0	84.4	112.3	72.9	82.0	106.2	70.3

20. Death rates specific for age, sex and urban/rural residence: latest available year, 1994 - 2003
Taux de mortalité selon l'âge, le sexe et la résidence, urbaine/rurale: dernière année disponible, 1994 - 2003 (continued — suite)

Continent, country or area, year and age (in years) / Continent, pays ou zone, année et âge (en années)	Total			Urban - Urbaine			Rural - Rurale		
	Both sexes Les deux sexes	Male Masculin	Female Féminin	Both sexes Les deux sexes	Male Masculin	Female Féminin	Both sexes Les deux sexes	Male Masculin	Female Féminin
ASIA — ASIE									
Kazakhstan[7]									
2003									
80-84	124.8	151.5	115.9	125.2	153.6	116.1	124.0	148.1	115.6
85+	241.0	262.5	235.6	245.9	257.8	242.7	233.9	270.3	225.4
Korea (Republic of) - Corée (République de)[11]									
2002									
Total	5.2	5.7	4.7	...	...	...	...	...	...
0-1	4.5	4.8	4.2	...	...	...	...	...	...
1-4	0.4	0.5	0.4	...	...	...	...	...	...
5-9	0.2	0.3	0.2	...	...	...	...	...	...
10-14	0.2	0.2	0.1	...	...	...	...	...	...
15-19	0.4	0.5	0.2	...	...	...	...	...	...
20-24	0.5	0.6	0.4	...	...	...	...	...	...
25-29	0.6	0.8	0.4	...	...	...	...	...	...
30-34	0.9	1.2	0.6	...	...	...	...	...	...
35-39	1.4	1.9	0.8	...	...	...	...	...	...
40-44	2.2	3.3	1.1	...	...	...	...	...	...
45-49	3.4	5.0	1.7	...	...	...	...	...	...
50-54	4.8	7.2	2.4	...	...	...	...	...	...
55-59	7.3	10.8	3.9	...	...	...	...	...	...
60-64	11.6	17.2	6.6	...	...	...	...	...	...
65-69	17.1	24.7	11.0	...	...	...	...	...	...
70-74	28.4	39.8	21.2	...	...	...	...	...	...
75-79	50.9	67.6	41.7	...	...	...	...	...	...
80-84	89.3	113.3	78.2	...	...	...	...	...	...
85-89	146.3	181.8	134.4	...	...	...	...	...	...
90-94	251.4	311.5	236.7	...	...	...	...	...	...
95+	420.0	465.6	412.9	...	...	...	...	...	...
Kuwait - Koweït									
1998									
Total	2.1	2.2	1.9	...	...	...	...	...	...
0-1	11.6	12.6	10.6	...	...	...	...	...	...
1-4	0.6	0.6	0.5	...	...	...	...	...	...
5-9	0.3	♦0.3	♦0.3	...	...	...	...	...	...
10-14	0.2	♦0.3	♦0.2	...	...	...	...	...	...
15-19	0.6	0.9	♦0.3	...	...	...	...	...	...
20-24	0.7	1.0	0.4	...	...	...	...	...	...
25-29	0.5	0.6	0.4	...	...	...	...	...	...
30-34	0.6	0.7	0.4	...	...	...	...	...	...
35-39	0.8	0.9	0.7	...	...	...	...	...	...
40-44	1.3	1.5	0.8	...	...	...	...	...	...
45-49	2.0	2.1	1.5	...	...	...	...	...	...
50-54	3.9	4.3	3.1	...	...	...	...	...	...
55-59	7.0	7.0	6.9	...	...	...	...	...	...
60-64	13.5	12.8	14.7	...	...	...	...	...	...
65-69	25.9	27.3	24.1	...	...	...	...	...	...
70-74	46.3	47.0	45.5	...	...	...	...	...	...
75-79	69.7	77.6	62.1	...	...	...	...	...	...
80-84	120.8	119.3	122.4	...	...	...	...	...	...
85+	172.8	181.2	165.1	...	...	...	...	...	...
2002									
Total	1.9	2.0	1.8	...	...	...	...	...	...
0-14	1.1	1.1	1.0	...	...	...	...	...	...
15-64	1.3	1.4	1.0	...	...	...	...	...	...
65+	41.5	44.4	38.3	...	...	...	...	...	...
Kyrgyzstan - Kirghizistan[7]									
2003									
Total	7.2	8.0	6.4	8.0	9.2	6.8	6.7	7.3	6.2
0-1	21.6	24.7	18.3	28.9	33.4	24.2	18.4	21.0	15.8
1-4	1.7	1.8	1.7	0.9	0.9	0.9	2.1	2.2	2.0
5-9	0.4	0.5	0.4	0.3	♦0.3	♦0.3	0.5	0.5	0.4
10-14	0.4	0.5	0.3	0.4	0.4	♦0.3	0.4	0.5	0.2

20. Death rates specific for age, sex and urban/rural residence: latest available year, 1994 - 2003
Taux de mortalité selon l'âge, le sexe et la résidence, urbaine/rurale: dernière année disponible, 1994 - 2003 (continued — suite)

Continent, country or area, year and age (in years) Continent, pays ou zone, année et âge (en années)	Total			Urban - Urbaine			Rural - Rurale		
	Both sexes Les deux sexes	Male Masculin	Female Féminin	Both sexes Les deux sexes	Male Masculin	Female Féminin	Both sexes Les deux sexes	Male Masculin	Female Féminin
ASIA — ASIE									
Kyrgyzstan - Kirghizistan[7]									
2003									
15-19	0.7	0.9	0.5	0.6	0.7	0.5	0.8	1.0	0.5
20-24	1.2	1.6	0.8	0.9	1.4	0.5	1.4	1.8	0.9
25-29	1.9	2.7	1.2	1.8	2.7	0.9	2.1	2.7	1.4
30-34	2.7	3.9	1.4	2.5	3.6	1.4	2.8	4.0	1.4
35-39	3.7	5.4	2.1	3.9	5.9	2.0	3.6	5.0	2.1
40-44	5.3	7.7	3.0	5.7	8.8	2.9	5.1	7.0	3.1
45-49	7.6	11.1	4.3	8.7	13.5	4.5	6.9	9.7	4.2
50-54	11.6	16.6	7.0	13.0	19.6	7.5	10.6	14.7	6.7
55-59	15.8	21.4	10.8	17.0	25.4	10.1	14.8	18.6	11.3
60-64	20.1	37.7	19.9	29.7	43.1	19.5	27.1	34.0	20.2
65-69	37.2	50.5	26.9	38.6	55.8	26.5	36.4	47.6	27.1
70-74	55.4	69.6	45.4	58.1	78.9	45.8	54.0	65.5	45.1
75-79	76.1	84.8	70.7	81.4	102.4	71.6	73.0	76.9	70.0
80-84	118.6	131.5	112.9	121.0	136.7	115.3	117.1	128.9	111.4
85-89	171.6	195.7	163.1	176.1	197.2	169.4	168.5	194.8	158.7
90-94	216.8	232.5	211.2	211.1	215.4	209.6	219.6	241.0	212.1
95+	359.5	269.2	389.5	193.7	◆186.3	195.7	420.2	294.1	465.0
Malaysia - Malaisie									
2000									
Total	4.7	5.4	4.0	...	...	...	...	...	...
0-4	1.8	2.0	1.7	...	...	...	...	...	...
5-9	0.3	0.4	0.3	...	...	...	...	...	...
10-14	0.4	0.5	0.3	...	...	...	...	...	...
15-19	0.9	1.3	0.4	...	...	...	...	...	...
20-24	1.1	1.7	0.6	...	...	...	...	...	...
25-29	1.3	1.9	0.6	...	...	...	...	...	...
30-34	1.6	2.4	0.8	...	...	...	...	...	...
35-39	2.0	2.9	1.1	...	...	...	...	...	...
40-44	3.0	4.0	1.9	...	...	...	...	...	...
45-49	4.1	5.3	2.9	...	...	...	...	...	...
50-54	7.0	8.8	5.2	...	...	...	...	...	...
55-59	10.9	13.6	8.1	...	...	...	...	...	...
60-64	18.5	22.7	14.3	...	...	...	...	...	...
65-69	28.9	34.7	23.7	...	...	...	...	...	...
70-74	47.8	55.4	41.1	...	...	...	...	...	...
75-79	75.0	85.0	67.2	...	...	...	...	...	...
80+	145.2	161.9	133.7	...	...	...	...	...	...
Maldives									
2003									
Total	3.6	4.1	3.1	...	...	...	...	...	...
0-1	11.9	13.2	10.4	...	...	...	...	...	...
1-4	◆1.0	◆1.5	◆0.4	...	...	...	...	...	...
5-9	◆0.4	◆0.6	◆0.2	...	...	...	...	...	...
10-14	◆0.3	◆0.4	◆0.3	...	...	...	...	...	...
15-19	◆0.3	◆0.6	◆0.1	...	...	...	...	...	...
20-24	◆0.3	◆0.4	◆0.3	...	...	...	...	...	...
25-29	◆0.6	◆0.8	◆0.5	...	...	...	...	...	...
30-34	◆0.6	◆0.5	◆0.7	...	...	...	...	...	...
35-39	◆1.4	◆1.6	◆1.1	...	...	...	...	...	...
40-44	◆2.1	◆2.5	◆1.7	...	...	...	...	...	...
45-49	◆2.5	◆2.1	◆3.0	...	...	...	...	...	...
50-54	4.9	◆6.2	◆3.4	...	...	...	...	...	...
55-59	7.8	◆9.9	◆5.9	...	...	...	...	...	...
60-64	17.0	17.9	16.2	...	...	...	...	...	...
65-69	26.5	27.0	25.8	...	...	...	...	...	...
70-74	48.0	50.4	45.0	...	...	...	...	...	...
75+	77.2	74.1	82.0	...	...	...	...	...	...
Mongolia - Mongolie									
2003									
Total	6.4	7.6	5.2	...	...	...	...	...	...
0-1	24.9	28.8	21.0	...	...	...	...	...	...

20. Death rates specific for age, sex and urban/rural residence: latest available year, 1994 - 2003
Taux de mortalité selon l'âge, le sexe et la résidence, urbaine/rurale: dernière année disponible, 1994 - 2003 (continued — suite)

Continent, country or area, year and age (in years) / Continent, pays ou zone, année et âge (en années)	Total			Urban - Urbaine			Rural - Rurale		
	Both sexes Les deux sexes	Male Masculin	Female Féminin	Both sexes Les deux sexes	Male Masculin	Female Féminin	Both sexes Les deux sexes	Male Masculin	Female Féminin
ASIA — ASIE									
Mongolia - Mongolie									
2003									
1-4	1.9	2.1	1.6	...	...	...	...	...	...
5-9	0.4	0.5	0.4	...	...	...	...	...	...
10-14	0.4	0.4	0.3	...	...	...	...	...	...
15-19	0.7	0.9	0.5	...	...	...	...	...	...
20-24	1.2	1.8	0.7	...	...	...	...	...	...
25-29	2.0	2.8	1.2	...	...	...	...	...	...
30-34	2.8	3.9	1.7	...	...	...	...	...	...
35-39	3.9	5.7	2.2	...	...	...	...	...	...
40-44	6.7	9.2	4.2	...	...	...	...	...	...
45-49	10.6	13.7	7.5	...	...	...	...	...	...
50-54	15.0	19.6	10.7	...	...	...	...	...	...
55-59	19.3	24.6	14.2	...	...	...	...	...	...
60-64	30.6	40.1	22.2	...	...	...	...	...	...
65-69	41.8	56.0	29.8	...	...	...	...	...	...
70+	74.5	94.6	60.5	...	...	...	...	...	...
Nepal - Népal[12]									
2001									
Total	4.7	5.2	4.2	...	...	...	...	...	...
0-1	26.3	27.5	25.1	...	...	...	...	...	...
1-4	4.3	4.9	3.8	...	...	...	...	...	...
5-9	1.0	1.1	1.0	...	...	...	...	...	...
10-14	0.8	0.9	0.7	...	...	...	...	...	...
15-19	1.1	1.1	1.0	...	...	...	...	...	...
20-24	1.4	1.5	1.2	...	...	...	...	...	...
25-29	1.6	1.7	1.4	...	...	...	...	...	...
30-34	1.7	1.8	1.5	...	...	...	...	...	...
35-39	2.2	2.4	1.9	...	...	...	...	...	...
40-44	2.7	3.4	2.1	...	...	...	...	...	...
45-49	3.8	4.3	3.4	...	...	...	...	...	...
50-54	6.1	7.1	5.1	...	...	...	...	...	...
55-59	10.2	11.3	8.8	...	...	...	...	...	...
60-64	16.0	18.0	14.0	...	...	...	...	...	...
65-69	22.4	24.3	20.4	...	...	...	...	...	...
70-74	35.1	38.9	31.0	...	...	...	...	...	...
75-79	48.9	56.6	41.4	...	...	...	...	...	...
80+	154.8	169.7	140.5	...	...	...	...	...	...
Pakistan[13,14]									
2001									
Total	7.2	7.4	6.9	6.3	6.6	6.0	7.6	7.9	7.3
0-4	19.9	20.6	19.1	18.2	19.1	17.3	20.6	21.3	19.9
5-9	1.6	1.5	1.7	1.5	1.6	1.3	1.7	1.5	1.9
10-14	1.2	0.8	1.7	1.4	1.0	1.8	1.2	0.6	1.7
15-19	1.4	1.5	1.3	1.2	1.3	1.1	1.5	1.6	1.4
20-24	1.9	1.5	2.3	1.4	1.4	1.3	2.2	1.6	2.9
25-29	2.1	2.2	1.9	1.9	1.7	2.1	2.2	2.5	1.9
30-34	2.5	3.4	1.8	2.5	2.8	2.1	2.6	3.7	1.5
35-39	4.2	4.8	3.5	3.9	4.9	2.9	4.3	4.7	4.0
40-44	4.0	3.9	4.1	4.0	2.6	5.6	4.0	4.7	3.3
45-49	5.4	6.4	4.3	6.0	8.0	3.7	5.0	5.4	4.7
50-54	8.7	9.1	8.1	9.1	11.7	5.9	8.4	7.6	9.4
55-59	13.2	13.2	13.1	12.2	10.8	13.8	13.7	14.6	12.8
60-64	20.3	18.4	22.6	14.9	14.1	15.7	23.0	20.5	26.3
65-69	28.9	24.2	34.9	26.7	18.3	37.2	30.0	27.3	33.7
70+	70.5	73.4	66.5	71.0	71.5	70.3	70.2	74.2	64.6
Philippines									
2000									
Total	4.8	5.6	3.9	...	...	...	...	...	...
0-1	14.5	16.5	12.3	...	...	...	...	...	...
1-4	1.5	1.6	1.4	...	...	...	...	...	...
5-9	0.6	0.7	0.5	...	...	...	...	...	...
10-14	0.5	0.6	0.4	...	...	...	...	...	...

20. Death rates specific for age, sex and urban/rural residence: latest available year, 1994 - 2003
Taux de mortalité selon l'âge, le sexe et la résidence, urbaine/rurale: dernière année disponible, 1994 - 2003 (continued — suite)

Continent, country or area, year and age (in years) Continent, pays ou zone, année et âge (en années)	Total			Urban - Urbaine			Rural - Rurale		
	Both sexes Les deux sexes	Male Masculin	Female Féminin	Both sexes Les deux sexes	Male Masculin	Female Féminin	Both sexes Les deux sexes	Male Masculin	Female Féminin
ASIA — ASIE									
Philippines									
2000									
15-19	0.8	1.1	0.5	...	...	...	...	...	...
20-24	1.3	1.9	0.8	...	...	...	...	...	...
25-29	1.7	2.4	1.1	...	...	...	...	...	...
30-34	2.1	2.9	1.4	...	...	...	...	...	...
35-39	2.8	3.8	1.9	...	...	...	...	...	...
40-44	3.8	5.1	2.6	...	...	...	...	...	...
45-49	5.7	7.5	3.8	...	...	...	...	...	...
50-54	8.5	11.3	5.6	...	...	...	...	...	...
55-59	12.3	16.8	8.0	...	...	...	...	...	...
60-64	17.9	23.9	12.3	...	...	...	...	...	...
65-69	26.5	34.6	19.3	...	...	...	...	...	...
70-74	39.1	49.6	30.5	...	...	...	...	...	...
75-79	60.4	73.8	50.3	...	...	...	...	...	...
80-84	94.7	109.4	84.6	...	...	...	...	...	...
85-89	157.7	166.8	151.8	...	...	...	...	...	...
90-94	206.4	229.6	194.2	...	...	...	...	...	...
95+	212.5	189.9	228.2	...	...	...	...	...	...
Qatar									
1997									
Total	2.0	2.1	1.8	...	...	...	...	...	...
0-1	16.4	15.1	17.9	...	...	...	...	...	...
1-4	◆0.6	◆0.9	◆0.3	...	...	...	...	...	...
5-9	◆0.4	◆0.4	◆0.3	...	...	...	...	...	...
10-14	◆0.3	◆0.4	◆0.2	...	...	...	...	...	...
15-19	◆0.5	◆1.0	◆0.1	...	...	...	...	...	...
20-24	0.9	◆1.2	◆0.3	...	...	...	...	...	...
25-29	0.8	0.9	◆0.4	...	...	...	...	...	...
30-34	0.7	0.9	◆0.5	...	...	...	...	...	...
35-39	0.8	0.9	◆0.6	...	...	...	...	...	...
40-44	1.0	1.1	◆0.8	...	...	...	...	...	...
45-49	1.9	1.9	◆1.9	...	...	...	...	...	...
50-54	3.1	2.8	◆4.2	...	...	...	...	...	...
55-59	7.3	7.7	◆6.3	...	...	...	...	...	...
60-64	14.9	14.5	◆15.8	...	...	...	...	...	...
65-69	28.7	32.2	◆22.2	...	...	...	...	...	...
70-74	39.3	41.3	◆35.7	...	...	...	...	...	...
75-79	84.0	89.9	◆74.3	...	...	...	...	...	...
80+	133.1	126.4	142.9	...	...	...	...	...	...
2003									
Total	1.8	...	...	...	...	...	...	...	...
0-4	2.8	...	...	...	...	...	...	...	...
5-9	◆0.2	...	...	...	...	...	...	...	...
10-14	◆0.4	...	...	...	...	...	...	...	...
15-19	1.2	...	...	...	...	...	...	...	...
20-24	1.0	...	...	...	...	...	...	...	...
25-29	0.6	...	...	...	...	...	...	...	...
30-34	0.7	...	...	...	...	...	...	...	...
35-39	0.7	...	...	...	...	...	...	...	...
40-44	1.0	...	...	...	...	...	...	...	...
45-49	1.5	...	...	...	...	...	...	...	...
50-54	2.3	...	...	...	...	...	...	...	...
55-59	4.9	...	...	...	...	...	...	...	...
60-64	11.7	...	...	...	...	...	...	...	...
65-69	29.3	...	...	...	...	...	...	...	...
70+	49.6	...	...	...	...	...	...	...	...
Singapore - Singapour+,15									
2003									
Total	4.7	5.2	4.1	...	...	...	...	...	...
0-4	0.7	0.8	0.6	...	...	...	...	...	...
5-9	0.1	◆0.2	◆0.1	...	...	...	...	...	...
10-14	0.1	◆0.2	◆0.1	...	...	...	...	...	...

20. Death rates specific for age, sex and urban/rural residence: latest available year, 1994 - 2003
Taux de mortalité selon l'âge, le sexe et la résidence, urbaine/rurale: dernière année disponible, 1994 - 2003 (continued — suite)

Continent, country or area, year and age (in years) / Continent, pays ou zone, année et âge (en années)	Total			Urban - Urbaine			Rural - Rurale		
	Both sexes Les deux sexes	Male Masculin	Female Féminin	Both sexes Les deux sexes	Male Masculin	Female Féminin	Both sexes Les deux sexes	Male Masculin	Female Féminin
ASIA — ASIE									
Singapore - Singapour[+,15]									
2003									
15-19	0.4	0.5	♦0.3	...	...	...	...	...	...
20-24	0.8	1.0	0.6	...	...	...	...	...	...
25-29	0.6	0.9	0.3	...	...	...	...	...	...
30-34	0.7	1.1	0.4	...	...	...	...	...	...
35-39	0.9	1.2	0.6	...	...	...	...	...	...
40-44	1.3	1.8	0.9	...	...	...	...	...	...
45-49	2.2	2.8	1.6	...	...	...	...	...	...
50-54	3.6	4.4	2.7	...	...	...	...	...	...
55-59	6.0	8.0	4.1	...	...	...	...	...	...
60-64	10.4	13.5	7.3	...	...	...	...	...	...
65-69	17.7	23.2	12.7	...	...	...	...	...	...
70-74	27.6	35.9	20.2	...	...	...	...	...	...
75-79	45.2	53.5	38.4	...	...	...	...	...	...
80+	100.7	112.1	93.7	...	...	...	...	...	...
Sri Lanka[+]									
1996									
Total	6.7	8.5	4.7	...	...	...	...	...	...
0-4	3.1	3.4	2.8	...	...	...	...	...	...
5-9	0.4	0.5	0.4	...	...	...	...	...	...
10-14	0.5	0.5	0.4	...	...	...	...	...	...
15-19	1.7	2.5	0.9	...	...	...	...	...	...
20-24	3.3	5.5	1.0	...	...	...	...	...	...
25-29	3.7	6.3	1.2	...	...	...	...	...	...
30-34	3.4	5.5	1.2	...	...	...	...	...	...
35-39	4.7	7.3	2.0	...	...	...	...	...	...
40-44	5.3	8.1	2.4	...	...	...	...	...	...
45-49	7.7	11.3	4.1	...	...	...	...	...	...
50-54	9.6	12.9	6.0	...	...	...	...	...	...
55-59	13.2	17.7	8.2	...	...	...	...	...	...
60-64	20.1	24.5	15.0	...	...	...	...	...	...
65-69	34.5	41.2	27.0	...	...	...	...	...	...
70-74	56.3	61.9	49.8	...	...	...	...	...	...
75-79	81.7	88.1	74.6	...	...	...	...	...	...
80+	176.8	177.6	176.1	...	...	...	...	...	...
Uzbekistan - Ouzbékistan[7]									
2000									
Total	5.5	5.8	5.2	6.6	7.1	6.2	4.8	5.0	4.6
0-1	19.1	21.4	16.6	22.6	25.4	19.6	17.5	19.6	15.3
1-4	2.3	2.4	2.2	1.6	1.7	1.5	2.6	2.8	2.5
5-9	0.4	0.5	0.4	0.4	0.5	0.3	0.5	0.6	0.4
10-14	0.5	0.5	0.4	0.4	0.5	0.4	0.5	0.6	0.4
15-19	0.7	0.9	0.5	0.7	1.0	0.5	0.7	0.9	0.5
20-24	1.3	1.6	1.0	1.4	1.9	0.9	1.2	1.4	1.0
25-29	1.7	2.2	1.3	1.9	2.5	1.2	1.6	1.9	1.3
30-34	2.1	2.9	1.4	2.4	3.3	1.4	2.0	2.5	1.5
35-39	2.5	3.4	1.7	3.0	4.3	1.7	2.2	2.7	1.6
40-44	3.6	4.8	2.6	4.4	6.3	2.6	3.1	3.7	2.5
45-49	5.4	7.2	3.7	6.2	8.9	3.7	4.7	5.8	3.6
50-54	9.4	12.2	6.7	10.2	14.1	6.7	8.5	10.4	6.6
55-59	14.2	17.6	10.8	15.3	20.9	10.2	13.2	15.0	11.3
60-64	22.3	27.5	17.5	23.3	31.4	16.5	21.5	24.5	18.4
65-69	35.9	43.2	29.7	37.2	49.2	28.2	34.8	39.0	30.9
70-74	52.7	61.0	46.2	54.6	69.8	45.0	51.2	55.1	47.4
75-79	72.9	80.3	68.9	73.8	84.7	69.0	72.1	77.2	68.8
80-84	114.2	129.9	108.1	115.6	127.9	111.3	112.9	131.6	104.7
85-89	164.0	194.7	152.6	166.2	183.1	160.8	161.7	204.8	143.4
90-94	195.5	192.3	197.2	171.3	152.4	179.9	215.8	219.9	213.3
95+	316.6	202.4	394.2	156.3	168.0	151.3	460.7	220.9	700.6

20. Death rates specific for age, sex and urban/rural residence: latest available year, 1994 - 2003
Taux de mortalité selon l'âge, le sexe et la résidence, urbaine/rurale: dernière année disponible, 1994 - 2003 (continued — suite)

Continent, country or area, year and age (in years) / Continent, pays ou zone, année et âge (en années)	Total			Urban - Urbaine			Rural - Rurale		
	Both sexes Les deux sexes	Male Masculin	Female Féminin	Both sexes Les deux sexes	Male Masculin	Female Féminin	Both sexes Les deux sexes	Male Masculin	Female Féminin
EUROPE									
Austria - Autriche									
2003									
Total	9.5	9.0	10.0	...	...	...	...	...	...
0-1	4.4	4.8	4.0	...	...	...	...	...	...
1-4	0.3	0.3	0.3	...	...	...	...	...	...
5-9	0.1	♦0.1	♦0.1	...	...	...	...	...	...
10-14	0.1	0.1	0.1	...	...	...	...	...	...
15-19	0.5	0.7	0.4	...	...	...	...	...	...
20-24	0.7	1.0	0.3	...	...	...	...	...	...
25-29	0.5	0.8	0.3	...	...	...	...	...	...
30-34	0.7	0.9	0.4	...	...	...	...	...	...
35-39	0.9	1.2	0.6	...	...	...	...	...	...
40-44	1.5	1.9	1.1	...	...	...	...	...	...
45-49	2.6	3.4	1.8	...	...	...	...	...	...
50-54	4.2	5.8	2.7	...	...	...	...	...	...
55-59	6.6	8.7	4.6	...	...	...	...	...	...
60-64	9.7	13.3	6.4	...	...	...	...	...	...
65-69	14.5	20.6	9.3	...	...	...	...	...	...
70-74	24.8	34.1	17.6	...	...	...	...	...	...
75-79	41.0	55.4	32.8	...	...	...	...	...	...
80-84	72.0	91.8	63.5	...	...	...	...	...	...
85-89	142.1	164.9	133.8	...	...	...	...	...	...
90-94	228.2	251.4	221.2	...	...	...	...	...	...
95+	373.2	385.9	370.3	...	...	...	...	...	...
Belarus - Bélarus[7]									
2003									
Total	14.5	16.4	12.8	10.7	12.8	8.9	23.9	25.6	22.5
0-1	7.8	9.0	6.5	6.8	8.2	5.3	10.5	11.3	9.6
1-4	0.5	0.6	0.5	0.3	0.4	0.3	1.1	1.3	0.9
5-9	0.3	0.4	0.2	0.2	0.3	♦0.1	0.4	0.5	♦0.4
10-14	0.2	0.3	0.2	0.2	0.2	0.2	0.3	0.5	♦0.2
15-19	0.7	1.1	0.4	0.6	0.8	0.3	1.2	1.9	0.4
20-24	1.5	2.3	0.6	1.2	1.8	0.5	2.7	4.3	0.9
25-29	2.2	3.7	0.8	1.8	2.9	0.6	4.0	6.5	1.3
30-34	3.2	5.1	1.3	2.6	4.1	1.1	5.1	7.9	1.9
35-39	4.3	6.9	1.8	3.6	5.7	1.6	6.5	10.0	2.4
40-44	5.8	9.3	2.5	4.9	7.8	2.3	8.7	13.1	3.3
45-49	8.9	14.2	4.0	7.5	12.2	3.5	13.1	19.6	5.7
50-54	13.0	20.7	6.2	11.4	18.5	5.6	18.1	26.9	8.7
55-59	18.6	28.7	10.3	16.6	25.8	9.2	23.7	36.1	13.1
60-64	27.1	44.4	14.9	24.9	40.8	13.6	31.0	51.1	17.1
65-69	35.1	55.6	22.2	33.0	51.8	21.1	37.7	60.4	23.6
70-74	51.6	78.0	37.2	50.7	77.5	36.5	52.4	78.4	38.0
75-79	74.1	104.1	62.1	72.1	101.7	59.6	76.0	106.6	64.4
80-84	116.4	148.6	106.3	111.5	141.0	102.0	120.9	155.8	110.2
85-89	184.4	221.7	174.9	165.2	202.1	155.1	202.7	242.6	193.2
90-94	277.7	314.3	269.6	227.9	266.1	219.2	322.4	359.7	314.5
95+	502.3	662.2	472.1	312.9	482.1	279.6	738.4	906.2	708.4
Belgium - Belgique[16]									
2002									
Total	10.2	10.4	10.1	...	...	...	...	...	...
0-4	1.1	1.2	0.9	...	...	...	...	...	...
5-9	0.1	0.2	0.1	...	...	...	...	...	...
10-14	0.1	0.1	0.1	...	...	...	...	...	...
15-19	0.5	0.6	0.3	...	...	...	...	...	...
20-24	0.7	1.1	0.3	...	...	...	...	...	...
25-29	0.8	1.1	0.4	...	...	...	...	...	...
30-34	0.8	1.1	0.5	...	...	...	...	...	...
35-39	1.1	1.5	0.8	...	...	...	...	...	...
40-44	1.8	2.2	1.3	...	...	...	...	...	...
45-49	3.0	3.9	2.1	...	...	...	...	...	...
50-54	4.7	5.9	3.4	...	...	...	...	...	...
55-59	6.9	9.1	4.7	...	...	...	...	...	...

20. Death rates specific for age, sex and urban/rural residence: latest available year, 1994 - 2003
Taux de mortalité selon l'âge, le sexe et la résidence, urbaine/rurale: dernière année disponible, 1994 - 2003 (continued — suite)

Continent, country or area, year and age (in years) Continent, pays ou zone, année et âge (en années)	Total			Urban - Urbaine			Rural - Rurale		
	Both sexes Les deux sexes	Male Masculin	Female Féminin	Both sexes Les deux sexes	Male Masculin	Female Féminin	Both sexes Les deux sexes	Male Masculin	Female Féminin
EUROPE									
Belgium - Belgique[16]									
2002									
60-64	10.2	13.7	6.9	...	...	...	...	...	...
65-69	16.0	22.0	10.6	...	...	...	...	...	...
70-74	25.6	35.7	17.6	...	...	...	...	...	...
75-79	44.5	61.6	33.0	...	...	...	...	...	...
80-84	76.0	99.9	63.0	...	...	...	...	...	...
85+	181.3	210.9	171.0	...	...	...	...	...	...
Bulgaria - Bulgarie									
2003									
Total	14.3	15.8	12.9	11.8	13.2	10.6	20.1	21.7	18.5
0-1	12.8	14.5	10.9	11.1	12.6	9.5	16.9	19.4	14.3
1-4	0.6	0.6	0.6	0.5	0.5	0.4	0.9	0.9	1.0
5-9	0.2	0.3	◆0.2	0.2	0.3	◆0.1	◆0.3	◆0.4	◆0.2
10-14	0.3	0.4	0.2	0.3	0.3	◆0.2	0.5	0.5	◆0.4
15-19	0.5	0.7	0.3	0.5	0.7	0.3	0.5	0.7	◆0.3
20-24	0.8	1.2	0.4	0.7	1.1	0.3	1.0	1.3	0.7
25-29	1.0	1.4	0.6	0.9	1.3	0.5	1.1	1.5	0.7
30-34	1.2	1.5	0.7	1.1	1.4	0.7	1.4	1.9	0.8
35-39	1.8	2.4	1.2	1.7	2.3	1.1	2.1	2.9	1.3
40-44	3.0	4.1	1.9	2.7	3.7	1.8	3.8	5.2	2.3
45-49	5.0	7.1	2.9	4.7	6.7	2.9	5.7	8.2	3.1
50-54	8.2	12.2	4.5	7.9	11.7	4.3	9.2	13.5	4.8
55-59	12.1	18.1	6.7	11.6	17.1	6.7	13.2	20.3	6.6
60-64	18.0	26.2	11.0	18.0	26.1	11.1	18.0	26.5	10.7
65-69	27.9	38.8	19.1	28.2	39.5	19.4	27.5	37.9	18.6
70-74	42.9	55.5	33.4	43.6	57.8	33.4	42.1	52.8	33.5
75-79	73.2	88.7	62.8	74.4	91.5	63.2	71.8	85.5	62.2
80-84	121.4	137.4	111.6	120.8	140.0	109.6	122.0	134.6	114.0
85-89	204.9	218.3	197.2	204.4	214.1	199.1	205.6	222.7	195.1
90-94	313.5	326.6	307.0	326.6	330.7	324.5	298.9	322.1	286.9
95-99	420.7	439.3	412.0	457.9	506.8	434.4	379.9	360.1	388.4
100+	384.6	◆298.2	417.2	386.8	◆344.8	402.6	378.6	◆250.0	426.7
Croatia - Croatie									
2001									
Total	11.2	11.7	10.6	10.1	10.8	9.4	12.6	12.9	12.3
0-1	7.3	7.6	7.1	7.6	7.8	7.4	7.0	7.2	6.7
1-4	0.3	0.4	◆0.2	◆0.3	◆0.3	◆0.2	0.4	◆0.5	◆0.2
5-9	0.2	◆0.2	◆0.1	◆0.1	◆0.2	◆0.1	◆0.2	◆0.2	◆0.2
10-14	0.2	◆0.2	◆0.1	◆0.1	◆0.2	◆0.1	◆0.2	◆0.3	◆0.1
15-19	0.5	0.8	0.3	0.5	0.7	◆0.3	0.5	0.9	◆0.2
20-24	0.8	1.2	0.3	0.8	1.3	◆0.3	0.7	1.1	◆0.3
25-29	0.7	1.1	0.3	0.7	1.0	◆0.3	0.7	1.2	◆0.2
30-34	0.9	1.2	0.5	0.9	1.2	0.6	0.9	1.2	◆0.5
35-39	1.4	2.1	0.8	1.3	1.9	0.8	1.5	2.2	0.7
40-44	2.4	3.5	1.3	2.1	3.0	1.2	2.9	4.2	1.5
45-49	4.0	5.9	2.1	3.6	5.5	1.9	4.7	6.6	2.4
50-54	6.5	9.4	3.7	5.9	8.5	3.7	7.4	10.6	3.9
55-59	9.8	14.4	5.6	9.5	13.9	5.6	10.2	15.0	5.6
60-64	15.2	22.4	9.1	14.5	21.0	8.8	16.1	24.1	9.4
65-69	24.2	34.9	16.0	23.3	33.0	15.5	25.2	37.0	16.4
70-74	39.4	54.0	29.5	38.9	53.7	28.9	39.8	54.3	30.2
75-79	62.9	80.2	54.7	60.9	75.0	54.0	65.1	85.7	55.5
80-84	106.1	126.4	97.4	100.2	122.5	90.3	112.4	130.7	104.8
85-89	168.2	191.2	159.2	155.3	182.5	144.5	182.5	201.1	175.3
90-94	275.0	318.6	260.5	254.2	322.9	232.1	298.2	314.8	292.4
95+	406.9	427.2	401.1	360.6	396.4	351.1	459.9	448.1	463.6
2003									
Total	11.8	12.4	11.3	...	...	...	...	...	...
0-1	6.3	7.3	5.3	...	...	...	...	...	...
1-4	0.2	◆0.3	◆0.2	...	...	...	...	...	...
5-9	0.2	◆0.2	◆0.1	...	...	...	...	...	...
10-14	0.2	0.3	◆0.1	...	...	...	...	...	...

20. Death rates specific for age, sex and urban/rural residence: latest available year, 1994 - 2003
Taux de mortalité selon l'âge, le sexe et la résidence, urbaine/rurale: dernière année disponible, 1994 - 2003 (continued — suite)

Continent, country or area, year and age (in years) / Continent, pays ou zone, année et âge (en années)	Total			Urban - Urbaine			Rural - Rurale		
	Both sexes Les deux sexes	Male Masculin	Female Féminin	Both sexes Les deux sexes	Male Masculin	Female Féminin	Both sexes Les deux sexes	Male Masculin	Female Féminin
EUROPE									
Croatia - Croatie									
2003									
15-19	0.5	0.7	0.3	...	...	...	...	...	...
20-24	0.7	1.2	0.3	...	...	...	...	...	...
25-29	0.7	1.1	0.3	...	...	...	...	...	...
30-34	1.0	1.5	0.5	...	...	...	...	...	...
35-39	1.2	1.7	0.7	...	...	...	...	...	...
40-44	2.2	3.2	1.3	...	...	...	...	...	...
45-49	3.9	5.4	2.3	...	...	...	...	...	...
50-54	6.2	8.8	3.5	...	...	...	...	...	...
55-59	9.6	14.3	5.4	...	...	...	...	...	...
60-64	14.7	21.5	8.9	...	...	...	...	...	...
65-69	24.0	35.2	15.2	...	...	...	...	...	...
70-74	39.4	55.0	28.7	...	...	...	...	...	...
75-79	64.9	84.2	54.8	...	...	...	...	...	...
80-84	109.3	132.3	100.0	...	...	...	...	...	...
85+	234.2	260.7	224.7	...	...	...	...	...	...
Czech Republic - République tchèque									
2003									
Total	10.9	11.2	10.6	10.7	11.0	10.4	11.5	11.9	11.1
0-1	3.9	4.3	3.5	3.9	4.6	3.1	4.0	3.5	4.6
1-4	0.2	0.3	0.2	0.2	0.3	◆0.2	◆0.3	◆0.2	◆0.3
5-9	0.1	0.2	◆0.1	0.1	◆0.2	◆0.1	◆0.2	◆0.2	◆0.2
10-14	0.2	0.2	0.1	0.2	0.2	◆0.1	◆0.2	◆0.2	◆0.1
15-19	0.4	0.6	0.3	0.4	0.6	0.3	0.4	0.7	◆0.2
20-24	0.7	1.0	0.3	0.6	1.0	0.3	0.8	1.2	0.4
25-29	0.7	1.0	0.3	0.6	1.0	0.3	0.7	1.1	◆0.3
30-34	0.9	1.3	0.5	0.9	1.2	0.5	0.9	1.3	0.5
35-39	1.3	1.8	0.8	1.3	1.8	0.8	1.4	1.9	0.8
40-44	2.0	2.8	1.3	2.0	2.7	1.3	2.2	3.1	1.3
45-49	3.7	5.2	2.3	3.8	5.3	2.4	3.7	5.2	2.0
50-54	6.2	8.8	3.7	6.2	8.7	3.8	6.3	9.1	3.3
55-59	9.8	13.9	6.0	9.5	13.4	5.9	10.4	14.5	6.1
60-64	14.6	20.8	9.2	13.9	19.6	9.0	15.0	21.8	8.7
65-69	22.7	32.3	15.0	22.2	31.4	15.0	24.1	35.0	15.3
70-74	35.9	49.1	26.7	35.6	48.3	26.7	37.7	51.9	27.6
75-79	60.5	78.8	50.0	59.8	77.5	49.7	62.9	82.1	51.9
80-84	101.3	124.2	90.5	93.8	114.9	83.9	100.0	123.1	88.9
85-89	184.7	210.4	174.8	196.4	222.9	186.4	208.2	237.7	196.2
90-94	280.7	321.8	267.7	276.3	318.7	263.4	279.2	317.8	266.0
95-99	415.1	449.7	406.4	414.1	449.2	405.7	368.6	391.5	362.2
100+	538.8	◆525.0	541.3	455.9	◆428.6	460.2	621.6	◆529.4	649.1
Denmark - Danemark[17]									
2003									
Total	10.7	10.6	10.8	...	...	...	...	...	...
0-1	4.4	5.0	3.8	...	...	...	...	...	...
1-4	0.3	0.3	◆0.2	...	...	...	...	...	...
5-9	0.1	◆0.1	◆0.1	...	...	...	...	...	...
10-14	0.1	◆0.2	◆0.1	...	...	...	...	...	...
15-19	0.3	0.5	◆0.1	...	...	...	...	...	...
20-24	0.5	0.7	0.3	...	...	...	...	...	...
25-29	0.5	0.7	0.3	...	...	...	...	...	...
30-34	0.7	0.9	0.5	...	...	...	...	...	...
35-39	1.1	1.4	0.7	...	...	...	...	...	...
40-44	1.8	2.3	1.2	...	...	...	...	...	...
45-49	3.3	4.0	2.5	...	...	...	...	...	...
50-54	4.9	6.0	3.7	...	...	...	...	...	...
55-59	7.5	9.1	5.8	...	...	...	...	...	...
60-64	11.7	14.4	8.9	...	...	...	...	...	...
65-69	19.1	23.2	15.4	...	...	...	...	...	...
70-74	32.3	38.9	26.7	...	...	...	...	...	...
75-79	50.8	64.7	40.6	...	...	...	...	...	...

20. Death rates specific for age, sex and urban/rural residence: latest available year, 1994 - 2003
Taux de mortalité selon l'âge, le sexe et la résidence, urbaine/rurale: dernière année disponible, 1994 - 2003 (continued — suite)

Continent, country or area, year and age (in years) / Continent, pays ou zone, année et âge (en années)	Total			Urban - Urbaine			Rural - Rurale		
	Both sexes Les deux sexes	Male Masculin	Female Féminin	Both sexes Les deux sexes	Male Masculin	Female Féminin	Both sexes Les deux sexes	Male Masculin	Female Féminin
EUROPE									
Denmark - Danemark[17]									
2003									
80-84	83.1	104.8	70.3	...	...	...	...	...	...
85-89	135.8	170.9	119.7	...	...	...	...	...	...
90-94	225.6	271.6	209.9	...	...	...	...	...	...
95-99	337.0	366.6	329.8	...	...	...	...	...	...
100+	536.0	545.5	534.3	...	...	...	...	...	...
Estonia - Estonie[7]									
2002									
Total	13.5	15.0	12.3	12.7	14.4	11.4	15.0	15.7	14.3
0-1	5.8	7.0	♦4.5	6.1	7.8	♦4.2	♦5.2	♦5.3	♦5.1
1-4	♦0.5	♦0.7	♦0.3	♦0.3	♦0.4	♦0.1	♦0.9	♦1.3	♦0.5
5-9	♦0.4	♦0.4	♦0.3	♦0.4	♦0.5	♦0.3	♦0.3	♦0.4	♦0.2
10-14	♦0.2	♦0.3	♦0.1	♦0.2	♦0.2	♦0.1	♦0.2	♦0.3	♦0.1
15-19	0.9	1.4	♦0.3	1.0	1.6	♦0.4	♦0.6	♦1.1	♦0.2
20-24	1.8	2.9	♦0.6	1.8	3.0	♦0.6	1.7	2.5	♦0.7
25-29	1.7	3.0	♦0.5	1.6	2.9	♦0.5	2.0	3.1	♦0.6
30-34	2.4	3.9	1.0	2.4	3.7	1.1	2.5	4.4	♦0.6
35-39	3.3	5.4	1.3	3.3	5.5	1.3	3.1	5.1	♦1.0
40-44	5.2	8.0	2.7	5.4	8.5	2.8	4.5	6.5	2.4
45-49	8.1	12.9	3.9	8.1	13.5	3.8	7.6	11.1	4.0
50-54	11.0	17.3	5.7	10.5	16.9	5.6	11.7	17.9	5.6
55-59	14.2	22.3	7.8	13.1	21.6	7.0	16.0	22.8	9.6
60-64	19.8	32.7	10.5	18.9	31.6	10.5	21.6	34.7	10.5
65-69	27.4	45.2	15.9	25.8	43.3	15.1	30.8	48.6	17.8
70-74	40.5	61.6	28.8	39.3	60.0	28.1	43.3	65.0	30.5
75-79	57.7	81.0	48.6	55.4	77.5	46.9	62.6	88.3	52.1
80-84	98.3	127.5	88.8	91.1	113.2	83.9	112.2	156.8	98.3
85-89	160.6	181.9	154.6	153.2	178.5	146.1	173.8	187.8	169.8
90-94	256.8	252.3	257.8	253.0	250.5	253.6	262.2	254.9	264.2
95+	394.1	445.3	384.6	375.2	390.2	372.5	424.3	♦527.3	404.3
Finland - Finlande[18]									
2003									
Total	9.4	9.4	9.4	8.4	8.3	8.5	11.0	11.1	11.0
0-1	3.1	3.3	3.0	2.9	2.9	3.0	3.5	3.9	♦3.1
1-4	0.2	0.3	♦0.1	0.2	♦0.3	♦0.2	♦0.2	♦0.2	♦0.1
5-9	♦0.1	♦0.1	♦0.1	♦0.1	♦0.1	-	♦0.2	♦0.2	♦0.1
10-14	0.2	0.2	♦0.1	♦0.1	♦0.2	♦0.1	♦0.2	♦0.3	-
15-19	0.4	0.6	0.2	0.3	0.5	♦0.2	0.6	0.8	♦0.3
20-24	0.7	1.1	0.4	0.7	1.0	0.4	0.9	1.2	♦0.4
25-29	0.7	1.1	0.4	0.6	0.9	0.3	1.1	1.6	♦0.5
30-34	0.8	1.1	0.4	0.7	1.0	0.4	0.9	1.4	♦0.4
35-39	1.2	1.7	0.6	1.1	1.5	0.6	1.4	2.0	0.7
40-44	1.9	2.6	1.2	1.8	2.5	1.1	2.1	2.8	1.3
45-49	3.2	4.5	1.9	3.2	4.5	1.9	3.2	4.4	1.8
50-54	4.8	6.7	2.8	4.6	6.4	2.9	5.0	7.0	2.6
55-59	6.7	9.5	4.0	6.4	8.9	4.0	7.3	10.4	4.0
60-64	9.8	14.1	5.9	9.7	14.0	5.9	10.1	14.1	5.9
65-69	14.5	20.5	9.4	14.0	19.9	9.2	15.3	21.3	9.6
70-74	24.7	35.3	16.7	24.1	35.2	16.4	25.5	35.4	17.1
75-79	43.1	59.0	33.4	42.4	59.5	32.9	44.0	58.6	34.1
80-84	74.2	96.8	64.2	72.8	96.4	63.1	75.9	97.1	65.7
85-89	136.1	165.0	126.2	132.5	163.2	123.0	140.6	167.0	130.6
90-94	234.2	264.6	225.8	236.8	266.9	229.2	231.0	262.1	221.2
95+	366.3	439.0	351.3	366.0	437.3	352.8	366.5	440.8	349.3
France[19,20]									
2002									
Total	9.0	9.4	8.6	...	...	...	...	...	...
0-1	4.1	4.5	3.7	...	...	...	...	...	...
1-4	0.2	0.3	0.2	...	...	...	...	...	...
5-9	0.1	0.1	0.1	...	...	...	...	...	...
10-14	0.1	0.2	0.1	...	...	...	...	...	...
15-19	0.4	0.6	0.3	...	...	...	...	...	...

20. Death rates specific for age, sex and urban/rural residence: latest available year, 1994 - 2003
Taux de mortalité selon l'âge, le sexe et la résidence, urbaine/rurale: dernière année disponible, 1994 - 2003 (continued — suite)

Continent, country or area, year and age (in years) Continent, pays ou zone, année et âge (en années)	Total			Urban - Urbaine			Rural - Rurale		
	Both sexes Les deux sexes	Male Masculin	Female Féminin	Both sexes Les deux sexes	Male Masculin	Female Féminin	Both sexes Les deux sexes	Male Masculin	Female Féminin
EUROPE									
France[19,20]									
2002									
20-24	0.7	1.0	0.3	...	...	...	...	...	...
25-29	0.7	1.1	0.4	...	...	...	...	...	...
30-34	0.9	1.2	0.5	...	...	...	...	...	...
35-39	1.3	1.8	0.8	...	...	...	...	...	...
40-44	2.1	2.8	1.4	...	...	...	...	...	...
45-49	3.4	4.6	2.1	...	...	...	...	...	...
50-54	4.8	6.8	2.9	...	...	...	...	...	...
55-59	6.6	9.4	3.9	...	...	...	...	...	...
60-64	9.2	13.2	5.4	...	...	...	...	...	...
65-69	13.9	20.2	8.5	...	...	...	...	...	...
70-74	21.6	31.4	14.0	...	...	...	...	...	...
75-79	35.4	49.7	25.8	...	...	...	...	...	...
80-84	59.9	80.4	48.0	...	...	...	...	...	...
85-89	117.1	148.0	103.7	...	...	...	...	...	...
90-94	195.2	234.4	182.6	...	...	...	...	...	...
95-99	296.3	325.1	289.6	...	...	...	...	...	...
100+	375.9	281.6	396.0	...	...	...	...	...	...
Germany - Allemagne									
2003									
Total	10.3	9.8	10.8	...	...	...	...	...	...
0-1	4.2	4.6	3.7	...	...	...	...	...	...
1-4	0.2	0.2	0.2	...	...	...	...	...	...
5-9	0.1	0.1	0.1	...	...	...	...	...	...
10-14	0.1	0.1	0.1	...	...	...	...	...	...
15-19	0.4	0.5	0.2	...	...	...	...	...	...
20-24	0.5	0.8	0.3	...	...	...	...	...	...
25-29	0.5	0.8	0.3	...	...	...	...	...	...
30-34	0.6	0.9	0.4	...	...	...	...	...	...
35-39	1.0	1.3	0.7	...	...	...	...	...	...
40-44	1.7	2.2	1.2	...	...	...	...	...	...
45-49	2.9	3.8	1.9	...	...	...	...	...	...
50-54	4.4	5.9	3.0	...	...	...	...	...	...
55-59	6.7	9.0	4.5	...	...	...	...	...	...
60-64	10.0	13.6	6.4	...	...	...	...	...	...
65-69	15.7	21.8	10.3	...	...	...	...	...	...
70-74	26.7	36.5	18.9	...	...	...	...	...	...
75-79	42.6	56.9	34.2	...	...	...	...	...	...
80-84	74.2	95.2	65.4	...	...	...	...	...	...
85-89	138.8	165.3	129.9	...	...	...	...	...	...
90+	233.4	228.4	234.9	...	...	...	...	...	...
Greece - Grèce									
2003									
Total	9.6	10.1	9.1	...	...	...	...	...	...
0-1	4.1	4.5	3.7	...	...	...	...	...	...
1-4	0.2	0.2	0.2	...	...	...	...	...	...
5-9	0.1	◆0.1	◆0.1	...	...	...	...	...	...
10-14	0.1	0.2	0.1	...	...	...	...	...	...
15-19	0.5	0.7	0.3	...	...	...	...	...	...
20-24	0.6	1.0	0.2	...	...	...	...	...	...
25-29	0.6	0.9	0.3	...	...	...	...	...	...
30-34	0.7	1.0	0.4	...	...	...	...	...	...
35-39	0.9	1.3	0.6	...	...	...	...	...	...
40-44	1.5	2.1	0.9	...	...	...	...	...	...
45-49	2.3	3.2	1.5	...	...	...	...	...	...
50-54	3.6	5.1	2.2	...	...	...	...	...	...
55-59	5.7	8.3	3.3	...	...	...	...	...	...
60-64	8.0	11.7	4.7	...	...	...	...	...	...
65-69	13.4	18.8	8.7	...	...	...	...	...	...
70-74	23.2	30.8	16.9	...	...	...	...	...	...
75-79	46.2	55.5	38.8	...	...	...	...	...	...
80-84	83.4	90.6	78.2	...	...	...	...	...	...

20. Death rates specific for age, sex and urban/rural residence: latest available year, 1994 - 2003
Taux de mortalité selon l'âge, le sexe et la résidence, urbaine/rurale: dernière année disponible, 1994 - 2003 (continued — suite)

Continent, country or area, year and age (in years) / Continent, pays ou zone, année et âge (en années)	Total			Urban - Urbaine			Rural - Rurale		
	Both sexes Les deux sexes	Male Masculin	Female Féminin	Both sexes Les deux sexes	Male Masculin	Female Féminin	Both sexes Les deux sexes	Male Masculin	Female Féminin
EUROPE									
Greece - Grèce									
2003									
85-89	167.0	150.4	180.2	...	...	...	...	...	...
90+	326.5	358.4	310.2	...	...	...	...	...	...
Hungary - Hongrie[21]									
2003									
Total	13.3	14.5	12.3	12.8	13.6	12.0	14.5	16.0	13.0
0-1	7.3	8.0	6.5	6.3	7.4	5.2	8.9	9.0	8.8
1-4	0.3	0.3	0.3	0.2	0.3	♦0.2	0.4	0.4	♦0.4
5-9	0.2	0.2	0.2	0.2	♦0.2	♦0.1	0.2	♦0.2	♦0.2
10-14	0.2	0.2	0.2	0.2	0.2	♦0.1	0.2	♦0.2	♦0.2
15-19	0.4	0.5	0.2	0.3	0.5	0.2	0.4	0.5	♦0.3
20-24	0.6	0.8	0.3	0.5	0.8	0.3	0.6	0.9	♦0.3
25-29	0.7	1.0	0.3	0.6	0.9	0.3	0.8	1.2	0.4
30-34	1.1	1.6	0.6	1.0	1.4	0.6	1.4	1.9	0.8
35-39	1.9	2.7	1.1	1.7	2.4	1.0	2.3	3.2	1.4
40-44	4.2	6.0	2.5	3.8	5.4	2.4	4.9	6.9	2.8
45-49	7.2	10.5	4.1	6.5	9.4	3.9	8.5	12.3	4.4
50-54	10.0	14.6	5.9	9.2	13.3	5.7	11.6	17.0	6.2
55-59	14.1	21.1	8.2	13.1	19.2	8.0	16.4	24.8	8.7
60-64	19.0	28.8	11.4	17.6	26.3	10.9	21.8	33.8	12.4
65-69	27.1	40.9	17.6	25.4	37.5	17.2	30.0	46.9	18.4
70-74	41.3	58.5	30.5	39.0	54.0	29.4	45.3	66.7	32.2
75-79	64.2	85.5	52.8	61.4	80.1	51.4	69.4	95.3	55.5
80-84	102.3	125.0	91.9	99.1	119.5	89.7	108.4	135.3	96.0
85-89	170.9	193.8	161.6	165.8	188.2	156.6	182.5	207.1	172.8
90+	250.2	250.7	250.0	244.4	248.2	243.0	263.4	256.2	266.2
Iceland - Islande									
2003									
Total	6.3	6.2	6.4	6.3	6.1	6.4	7.1	8.0	6.0
0-1	♦2.5	♦2.9	♦2.0	♦2.6	♦3.1	♦2.1	-	-	-
1-4	♦0.1	-	♦0.2	♦0.1	-	♦0.3	-	-	-
5-9	♦0.2	♦0.3	♦0.1	♦0.2	♦0.3	♦0.1	-	-	-
10-14	♦0.1	♦0.2	-	♦0.1	♦0.2		-	-	-
15-19	♦0.2	♦0.2	♦0.3	♦0.2	♦0.2	♦0.2	♦0.6	-	♦1.2
20-24	♦0.4	♦0.6	♦0.3	♦0.4	♦0.6	♦0.3	♦0.6	♦1.1	-
25-29	♦0.4	♦0.7	♦0.2	♦0.4	♦0.6	♦0.2	♦0.8	♦1.5	-
30-34	♦0.4	♦0.5	♦0.4	♦0.4	♦0.4	♦0.4	♦0.8	♦1.6	-
35-39	♦0.5	♦0.4	♦0.7	♦0.5	♦0.3	♦0.7	♦0.7	♦1.3	-
40-44	♦1.0	♦0.8	♦1.2	♦1.1	♦0.9	♦1.3	-	-	-
45-49	♦1.4	♦2.0	♦0.8	♦1.4	♦2.1	♦0.7	♦1.3	-	♦3.0
50-54	2.6	♦2.9	♦2.3	2.5	♦2.8	♦2.2	♦3.9	♦4.2	♦3.4
55-59	5.0	5.7	4.3	5.2	5.8	4.7	2.6	♦4.8	-
60-64	7.5	9.7	♦5.4	7.3	9.4	♦5.3	♦9.7	♦12.2	♦6.9
65-69	11.5	13.1	10.0	12.0	14.1	10.2	♦5.9	♦4.2	♦7.9
70-74	23.1	26.6	19.8	23.5	27.5	20.0	♦18.8	♦19.5	♦18.0
75-79	33.4	42.6	25.8	33.4	42.3	26.4	♦33.3	♦45.2	♦16.7
80-84	69.0	80.2	60.8	68.1	81.4	58.9	♦79.8	♦70.1	♦92.6
85-89	131.9	146.7	123.2	130.9	141.0	125.3	141.0	♦185.8	♦99.2
90-94	224.4	260.9	206.2	229.6	263.2	213.7	♦168.7	♦243.2	♦108.7
95-99	321.9	♦378.8	299.4	320.4	♦386.0	295.3	♦333.3	♦333.3	♦333.3
100+	♦653.8	♦500.0	♦700.0	♦714.3	♦400.0	♦812.5	♦400.0	♦1000.0	♦250.0
Ireland - Irlande[+,22]									
1996									
Total	8.8	9.2	8.3	8.1	8.4	7.8	9.7	10.4	9.0
0-1	5.7	6.2	5.2	6.1	6.6	5.5	5.2	5.6	4.9
1-4	0.3	0.3	0.3	0.3	♦0.3	♦0.3	0.4	♦0.4	♦0.4
5-9	0.1	♦0.2	♦0.1	♦0.1	♦0.2	♦0.1	♦0.1	♦0.2	-
10-14	0.2	0.2	♦0.1	0.2	♦0.2	♦0.1	♦0.2	♦0.2	♦0.1
15-19	0.5	0.6	0.3	0.4	0.5	♦0.2	0.6	0.8	♦0.4
20-24	0.8	1.3	0.3	0.6	1.0	♦0.2	1.3	1.9	♦0.5
25-29	0.8	1.2	0.4	0.7	1.1	♦0.3	1.0	1.5	♦0.6
30-34	0.8	1.1	0.5	0.8	1.1	0.5	0.8	1.2	♦0.5

20. Death rates specific for age, sex and urban/rural residence: latest available year, 1994 - 2003
Taux de mortalité selon l'âge, le sexe et la résidence, urbaine/rurale: dernière année disponible, 1994 - 2003 (continued — suite)

Continent, country or area, year and age (in years) / Continent, pays ou zone, année et âge (en années)	Total			Urban - Urbaine			Rural - Rurale		
	Both sexes Les deux sexes	Male Masculin	Female Féminin	Both sexes Les deux sexes	Male Masculin	Female Féminin	Both sexes Les deux sexes	Male Masculin	Female Féminin
EUROPE									
Ireland - Irlande[+,22]									
1996									
35-39	1.0	1.4	0.6	1.0	1.3	0.7	1.1	1.5	0.6
40-44	1.6	2.0	1.2	1.5	2.0	1.1	1.7	2.0	1.4
45-49	2.5	3.0	1.9	2.8	3.5	2.1	2.1	2.5	1.6
50-54	4.6	5.5	3.6	4.6	5.7	3.5	4.5	5.2	3.7
55-59	7.4	9.5	5.3	8.1	10.7	5.6	6.5	8.0	4.8
60-64	13.2	17.1	9.3	14.0	18.6	9.8	12.2	15.3	8.7
65-69	23.1	30.9	16.1	24.1	32.9	17.0	21.9	28.8	14.8
70-74	38.2	49.6	29.0	40.6	54.6	30.8	35.5	45.0	26.8
75-79	63.2	81.2	50.3	66.1	89.6	52.0	60.3	74.4	48.3
80-84	106.1	135.3	88.3	103.3	140.5	85.2	108.8	131.3	92.0
85+	202.3	239.5	185.9	196.8	247.4	179.4	208.6	233.2	194.7
2003									
Total	7.2	7.4	7.0	...	...	...	...	...	...
0-1	5.2	5.9	4.4	...	...	...	...	...	...
1-4	0.2	♦0.2	♦0.2	...	...	...	...	...	...
5-9	♦0.1	♦0.1	♦0.1	...	...	...	...	...	...
10-14	0.2	♦0.2	♦0.1	...	...	...	...	...	...
15-19	0.5	0.7	0.3	...	...	...	...	...	...
20-24	0.7	1.1	0.3	...	...	...	...	...	...
25-29	0.7	1.0	0.4	...	...	...	...	...	...
30-34	0.6	1.0	0.3	...	...	...	...	...	...
35-39	0.9	1.2	0.7	...	...	...	...	...	...
40-44	1.3	1.7	1.0	...	...	...	...	...	...
45-49	2.1	2.6	1.6	...	...	...	...	...	...
50-54	3.6	4.4	2.8	...	...	...	...	...	...
55-59	6.2	7.5	4.9	...	...	...	...	...	...
60-64	10.4	12.7	8.0	...	...	...	...	...	...
65-69	16.6	21.3	12.0	...	...	...	...	...	...
70-74	27.8	35.3	21.1	...	...	...	...	...	...
75-79	50.6	64.5	40.6	...	...	...	...	...	...
80-84	84.8	106.3	71.7	...	...	...	...	...	...
85-89	142.5	176.9	126.0	...	...	...	...	...	...
90-94	216.3	246.7	205.0	...	...	...	...	...	...
95+	301.3	296.0	302.7	...	...	...	...	...	...
Italy - Italie									
2001									
Total	9.8	10.1	9.4	...	...	...	...	...	...
0-1	4.7	5.0	4.3	...	...	...	...	...	...
1-4	0.2	0.2	0.2	...	...	...	...	...	...
5-9	0.1	0.1	0.1	...	...	...	...	...	...
10-14	0.1	0.2	0.1	...	...	...	...	...	...
15-19	0.4	0.6	0.2	...	...	...	...	...	...
20-24	0.6	0.9	0.3	...	...	...	...	...	...
25-29	0.6	0.9	0.3	...	...	...	...	...	...
30-34	0.7	1.0	0.4	...	...	...	...	...	...
35-39	0.9	1.3	0.6	...	...	...	...	...	...
40-44	1.4	1.8	0.9	...	...	...	...	...	...
45-49	2.1	2.7	1.5	...	...	...	...	...	...
50-54	3.4	4.4	2.4	...	...	...	...	...	...
55-59	5.4	7.3	3.6	...	...	...	...	...	...
60-64	8.4	11.6	5.5	...	...	...	...	...	...
65-69	14.0	19.5	9.2	...	...	...	...	...	...
70-74	23.1	32.3	15.8	...	...	...	...	...	...
75-79	39.4	54.0	29.7	...	...	...	...	...	...
80-84	64.1	83.5	53.2	...	...	...	...	...	...
85-89	121.2	149.1	108.2	...	...	...	...	...	...
90-94	198.6	231.1	186.6	...	...	...	...	...	...
95-99	305.4	325.7	299.8	...	...	...	...	...	...
100+	461.9	470.4	460.2	...	...	...	...	...	...

Continent, country or area, year and age (in years) Continent, pays ou zone, année et âge (en années)	Total			Urban - Urbaine			Rural - Rurale		
	Both sexes Les deux sexes	Male Masculin	Female Féminin	Both sexes Les deux sexes	Male Masculin	Female Féminin	Both sexes Les deux sexes	Male Masculin	Female Féminin
EUROPE									
Latvia - Lettonie[7]									
2002									
Total	13.9	15.3	12.7	13.3	14.9	11.9	15.2	15.9	14.5
0-1	9.9	11.0	8.8	8.2	8.9	7.5	13.0	14.6	11.2
1-4	0.7	0.8	◆0.6	◆0.5	◆0.7	◆0.3	◆1.0	◆0.9	◆1.1
5-9	0.5	0.6	◆0.4	0.5	◆0.6	◆0.4	◆0.5	◆0.6	◆0.4
10-14	0.2	◆0.2	◆0.2	◆0.2	◆0.2	◆0.2	◆0.2	◆0.3	◆0.2
15-19	0.7	0.9	0.5	0.7	0.9	◆0.5	0.8	1.0	◆0.5
20-24	1.5	2.4	0.5	1.4	2.2	0.6	1.6	2.7	◆0.3
25-29	1.7	2.9	0.5	1.5	2.7	◆0.4	2.0	3.2	◆0.7
30-34	2.6	4.2	1.0	2.5	4.1	1.1	2.7	4.3	◆0.9
35-39	3.4	5.4	1.5	3.4	5.5	1.4	3.6	5.2	1.9
40-44	4.9	7.8	2.3	4.7	7.7	2.1	5.4	7.9	2.7
45-49	7.5	11.8	3.7	7.3	11.8	3.5	8.1	11.9	4.0
50-54	11.1	17.5	5.7	10.3	16.4	5.6	13.0	19.9	5.9
55-59	15.3	24.0	8.5	14.8	23.6	8.3	16.7	25.0	9.1
60-64	20.6	33.8	11.2	19.1	31.3	10.8	24.2	39.1	12.2
65-69	28.7	46.2	17.8	27.3	44.1	17.1	31.8	50.4	19.3
70-74	40.5	62.4	28.3	38.0	58.4	26.9	45.9	71.4	31.6
75-79	60.9	91.3	50.4	58.1	86.6	48.0	67.1	102.8	55.6
80-84	107.4	139.8	97.0	102.6	130.2	93.5	116.7	160.5	103.7
85-89	160.6	184.3	154.0	157.4	176.8	151.5	166.3	200.0	158.1
90-94	265.8	283.8	261.2	256.7	285.1	249.3	280.7	281.5	280.5
95-99	367.7	402.8	359.2	376.8	431.0	364.1	352.6	359.6	350.8
100+	536.2	◆409.1	560.3	634.1	◆636.4	633.8	◆392.9	◆181.8	◆444.4
Lithuania - Lituanie[7]									
2003									
Total	11.9	13.6	10.4	10.0	11.6	8.7	15.6	17.3	14.0
0-1	6.8	7.7	6.0	5.7	6.7	4.7	8.7	9.3	8.0
1-4	0.4	0.5	◆0.4	0.4	◆0.4	◆0.3	◆0.6	◆0.6	◆0.5
5-9	0.2	◆0.2	◆0.2	◆0.2	◆0.2	◆0.1	◆0.2	◆0.3	◆0.2
10-14	0.2	0.3	◆0.2	◆0.2	◆0.2	◆0.2	0.3	◆0.4	◆0.2
15-19	0.8	1.1	0.5	0.7	1.0	0.4	1.0	1.4	◆0.6
20-24	1.4	2.3	0.4	1.1	1.9	0.4	2.0	3.2	◆0.5
25-29	1.8	2.9	0.7	1.3	2.1	0.6	3.1	4.9	◆1.0
30-34	2.5	4.0	0.9	2.0	3.3	0.8	3.6	5.7	1.2
35-39	3.0	4.7	1.3	2.4	3.8	1.2	4.3	6.6	1.7
40-44	4.8	7.4	2.3	4.2	6.6	2.2	6.1	9.2	2.7
45-49	7.2	11.2	3.7	6.3	10.0	3.3	9.4	13.7	4.6
50-54	10.3	16.3	5.3	9.1	14.4	4.9	13.2	19.9	6.3
55-59	13.8	22.0	7.3	13.0	21.1	7.0	15.4	23.5	8.1
60-64	18.3	29.3	10.3	16.7	26.7	9.7	21.2	33.8	11.5
65-69	25.2	41.0	15.0	23.6	38.2	14.4	27.7	45.1	15.8
70-74	36.2	55.8	25.0	34.5	53.1	23.8	38.8	59.9	26.8
75-79	55.4	79.1	44.9	52.5	74.8	42.8	59.4	85.1	48.0
80-84	89.2	117.1	78.6	82.6	105.6	74.2	97.5	130.7	84.3
85-89	155.7	189.3	144.3	142.2	170.1	133.0	173.5	213.5	159.4
90-94	214.8	228.1	210.6	195.5	217.6	189.1	242.1	241.5	242.3
95-99	264.8	278.3	258.0	223.1	243.8	214.6	320.4	312.7	325.4
100+	271.2	403.8	234.5	212.2	◆284.1	192.5	349.5	558.8	290.5
Luxembourg									
2003									
Total	9.0	9.0	9.0	...	...	...	...	...	...
0-1	◆4.9	◆5.8	◆3.9	...	...	...	...	...	...
1-4	◆0.1	◆0.2	◆0.1	...	...	...	...	...	...
5-9	◆0.1	◆0.1	◆0.1	...	...	...	...	...	...
10-14	◆0.2	◆0.1	◆0.2	...	...	...	...	...	...
15-19	◆0.3	◆0.3	◆0.2	...	...	...	...	...	...
20-24	◆0.7	◆1.3	◆0.1	...	...	...	...	...	...
25-29	◆0.7	◆1.1	◆0.3	...	...	...	...	...	...
30-34	◆0.8	◆1.2	◆0.4	...	...	...	...	...	...
35-39	1.0	◆1.3	◆0.8	...	...	...	...	...	...
40-44	1.6	2.3	◆1.0	...	...	...	...	...	...

20. Death rates specific for age, sex and urban/rural residence: latest available year, 1994 - 2003
Taux de mortalité selon l'âge, le sexe et la résidence, urbaine/rurale: dernière année disponible, 1994 - 2003 (continued — suite)

Continent, country or area, year and age (in years) / Continent, pays ou zone, année et âge (en années)	Total			Urban - Urbaine			Rural - Rurale		
	Both sexes Les deux sexes	Male Masculin	Female Féminin	Both sexes Les deux sexes	Male Masculin	Female Féminin	Both sexes Les deux sexes	Male Masculin	Female Féminin
EUROPE									
Luxembourg									
2003									
45-49	2.6	3.6	♦1.7	...	...	...	...	...	...
50-54	4.1	5.7	2.3	...	...	...	...	...	...
55-59	6.8	9.4	4.0	...	...	...	...	...	...
60-64	10.8	13.7	8.1	...	...	...	...	...	...
65-69	18.9	25.1	13.4	...	...	...	...	...	...
70-74	29.0	38.5	21.3	...	...	...	...	...	...
75-79	45.1	58.7	36.6	...	...	...	...	...	...
80-84	79.0	105.7	66.8	...	...	...	...	...	...
85-89	158.0	206.7	139.4	...	...	...	...	...	...
90-94	232.0	323.9	207.4	...	...	...	...	...	...
95+	450.0	♦464.3	445.3	...	...	...	...	...	...
Malta - Malte									
2003									
Total	7.7	7.8	7.6	...	...	...	...	...	...
0-1	♦5.8	♦7.9	♦3.6	...	...	...	...	...	...
1-4	♦0.1	♦0.1	♦0.1	...	...	...	...	...	...
5-9	♦0.1	♦0.1	♦0.1	...	...	...	...	...	...
10-14	♦0.1	♦0.1	♦0.1	...	...	...	...	...	...
15-19	♦0.3	♦0.5	♦0.1	...	...	...	...	...	...
20-24	♦0.5	♦0.6	♦0.4	...	...	...	...	...	...
25-29	♦0.6	♦0.7	♦0.4	...	...	...	...	...	...
30-34	♦0.5	♦0.6	♦0.5	...	...	...	...	...	...
35-39	♦1.0	♦1.0	♦1.0	...	...	...	...	...	...
40-44	1.2	♦1.6	♦0.7	...	...	...	...	...	...
45-49	2.0	2.7	♦1.2	...	...	...	...	...	...
50-54	2.8	3.3	2.2	...	...	...	...	...	...
55-59	4.7	5.7	3.7	...	...	...	...	...	...
60-64	9.0	10.7	7.4	...	...	...	...	...	...
65-69	15.5	20.3	11.5	...	...	...	...	...	...
70-74	29.0	40.3	20.7	...	...	...	...	...	...
75-79	48.6	60.2	40.5	...	...	...	...	...	...
80-84	93.1	109.6	82.5	...	...	...	...	...	...
85-89	150.2	160.8	144.2	...	...	...	...	...	...
90+	228.9	255.7	217.0	...	...	...	...	...	...
Netherlands - Pays-Bas[23]									
2003									
Total	8.7	8.6	8.9	9.0	8.7	9.3	8.3	8.5	8.2
0-1	4.3	4.9	3.7	4.3	4.9	3.6	4.3	4.9	3.8
1-4	0.3	0.4	0.3	0.3	0.4	0.3	0.3	0.3	0.3
5-9	0.2	0.2	0.1	0.2	0.2	0.1	0.2	0.2	♦0.1
10-14	0.1	0.2	0.1	0.1	0.2	0.1	0.1	♦0.1	♦0.1
15-19	0.3	0.4	0.2	0.3	0.4	0.2	0.3	0.3	0.3
20-24	0.4	0.5	0.2	0.3	0.4	0.2	0.6	0.8	0.3
25-29	0.5	0.6	0.3	0.5	0.6	0.3	0.5	0.6	0.3
30-34	0.6	0.7	0.4	0.6	0.7	0.4	0.5	0.7	0.4
35-39	0.8	0.9	0.7	0.8	0.9	0.7	0.7	0.9	0.6
40-44	1.4	1.6	1.2	1.5	1.8	1.3	1.3	1.5	1.2
45-49	2.4	2.6	2.1	2.6	2.8	2.3	2.0	2.2	1.9
50-54	3.8	4.3	3.3	4.1	4.6	3.5	3.3	3.8	2.8
55-59	6.0	7.2	4.7	6.4	7.6	5.2	5.6	7.0	4.2
60-64	9.3	11.7	7.0	9.9	12.4	7.4	8.8	11.0	6.6
65-69	15.4	20.1	10.9	16.3	21.4	11.8	14.1	18.7	9.7
70-74	26.2	35.1	18.8	26.8	35.7	19.8	25.2	34.8	17.0
75-79	44.8	61.0	33.7	45.5	62.2	34.5	43.5	59.8	31.8
80-84	79.5	109.0	63.5	81.9	112.8	65.8	79.9	110.3	62.6
85-89	143.1	186.1	126.0	141.9	186.1	125.1	143.5	184.5	125.8
90-94	255.2	318.6	236.9	257.5	325.7	239.4	260.4	319.5	240.6
95+	455.3	520.6	441.6	...	...	...	...	...	...
95-99	...	...	...	431.1	496.7	418.3	443.4	496.2	429.8
100+	...	...	...	706.4	818.2	689.7	690.9	885.7	645.7

20. Death rates specific for age, sex and urban/rural residence: latest available year, 1994 - 2003
Taux de mortalité selon l'âge, le sexe et la résidence, urbaine/rurale: dernière année disponible, 1994 - 2003 (continued — suite)

Continent, country or area, year and age (in years) / Continent, pays ou zone, année et âge (en années)	Total			Urban - Urbaine			Rural - Rurale		
	Both sexes Les deux sexes	Male Masculin	Female Féminin	Both sexes Les deux sexes	Male Masculin	Female Féminin	Both sexes Les deux sexes	Male Masculin	Female Féminin
EUROPE									
Norway - Norvège[24]									
2003									
Total	9.3	9.1	9.5	...	...	...	...	...	...
0-1	3.3	3.7	3.0	...	...	...	...	...	...
1-4	0.3	◆0.2	0.3	...	...	...	...	...	...
5-9	0.1	◆0.1	◆0.1	...	...	...	...	...	...
10-14	0.2	◆0.2	◆0.1	...	...	...	...	...	...
15-19	0.5	0.6	0.3	...	...	...	...	...	...
20-24	0.6	0.9	0.3	...	...	...	...	...	...
25-29	0.7	0.9	0.4	...	...	...	...	...	...
30-34	0.7	1.1	0.4	...	...	...	...	...	...
35-39	0.9	1.2	0.6	...	...	...	...	...	...
40-44	1.4	1.7	1.1	...	...	...	...	...	...
45-49	2.1	2.6	1.6	...	...	...	...	...	...
50-54	3.3	4.0	2.6	...	...	...	...	...	...
55-59	5.5	6.6	4.4	...	...	...	...	...	...
60-64	8.5	10.6	6.5	...	...	...	...	...	...
65-69	14.4	19.1	10.1	...	...	...	...	...	...
70-74	23.8	31.0	17.8	...	...	...	...	...	...
75-79	40.6	52.3	32.0	...	...	...	...	...	...
80-84	71.7	94.4	58.2	...	...	...	...	...	...
85-89	131.6	163.7	117.2	...	...	...	...	...	...
90-94	221.9	270.6	205.2	...	...	...	...	...	...
95-99	346.9	370.3	340.9	...	...	...	...	...	...
100+	469.6	517.2	459.0	...	...	...	...	...	...
Poland - Pologne									
2003									
Total	9.6	10.5	8.7	9.2	10.1	8.4	10.2	11.1	9.3
0-1	7.1	7.7	6.4	7.4	7.8	6.9	6.7	7.5	5.8
1-4	0.3	0.3	0.2	0.2	0.3	0.2	0.3	0.4	0.2
5-9	0.2	0.2	0.1	0.2	0.2	0.1	0.2	0.2	0.1
10-14	0.2	0.2	0.1	0.2	0.2	0.1	0.2	0.3	0.2
15-19	0.5	0.6	0.3	0.4	0.6	0.2	0.5	0.8	0.3
20-24	0.7	1.1	0.3	0.7	1.0	0.3	0.8	1.3	0.3
25-29	0.8	1.2	0.3	0.8	1.2	0.4	0.8	1.4	0.3
30-34	1.1	1.7	0.5	1.0	1.6	0.5	1.2	1.8	0.4
35-39	1.7	2.7	0.8	1.7	2.6	0.8	1.8	2.8	0.8
40-44	3.0	4.4	1.5	2.9	4.2	1.6	3.1	4.7	1.3
45-49	4.8	7.0	2.6	4.7	6.8	2.7	5.0	7.4	2.2
50-54	7.4	10.9	4.2	7.2	10.6	4.2	7.9	11.4	4.1
55-59	10.8	15.9	6.2	10.6	15.5	6.4	11.0	16.6	5.7
60-64	15.7	23.8	9.1	15.8	23.8	9.5	15.5	23.9	8.2
65-69	23.2	34.9	14.4	23.0	34.3	14.8	23.5	36.0	13.7
70-74	35.5	50.9	25.2	35.2	49.8	25.6	35.9	52.5	24.6
75-79	55.8	76.5	44.9	55.2	75.3	44.9	56.7	78.2	44.9
80-84	91.0	114.4	80.4	88.0	111.6	77.9	94.9	117.8	83.8
85+	195.3	218.9	187.0	185.7	210.3	177.9	208.6	229.1	200.4
Portugal									
2003									
Total	10.4	11.1	9.8	...	...	...	...	...	...
0-1	4.1	4.0	4.2	...	...	...	...	...	...
1-4	0.3	0.3	0.3	...	...	...	...	...	...
5-9	0.2	0.2	0.2	...	...	...	...	...	...
10-14	0.2	0.2	0.2	...	...	...	...	...	...
15-19	0.5	0.7	0.3	...	...	...	...	...	...
20-24	0.7	1.1	0.4	...	...	...	...	...	...
25-29	0.9	1.3	0.5	...	...	...	...	...	...
30-34	1.3	1.9	0.6	...	...	...	...	...	...
35-39	1.6	2.4	0.9	...	...	...	...	...	...
40-44	2.3	3.4	1.3	...	...	...	...	...	...
45-49	3.4	4.9	2.0	...	...	...	...	...	...
50-54	4.6	6.4	2.8	...	...	...	...	...	...
55-59	6.4	9.0	4.1	...	...	...	...	...	...

20. Death rates specific for age, sex and urban/rural residence: latest available year, 1994 - 2003
Taux de mortalité selon l'âge, le sexe et la résidence, urbaine/rurale: dernière année disponible, 1994 - 2003 (continued — suite)

Continent, country or area, year and age (in years) Continent, pays ou zone, année et âge (en années)	Total			Urban - Urbaine			Rural - Rurale		
	Both sexes Les deux sexes	Male Masculin	Female Féminin	Both sexes Les deux sexes	Male Masculin	Female Féminin	Both sexes Les deux sexes	Male Masculin	Female Féminin
EUROPE									
Portugal									
2003									
60-64	9.7	13.8	6.2	...	...	...	...	...	...
65-69	15.7	22.2	10.2	...	...	...	...	...	...
70-74	26.8	36.4	19.4	...	...	...	...	...	...
75-79	48.5	63.4	38.3	...	...	...	...	...	...
80-84	85.1	104.9	73.0	...	...	...	...	...	...
85-89	159.3	186.1	145.8	...	...	...	...	...	...
90-94	253.1	267.0	247.3	...	...	...	...	...	...
95-99	423.4	439.4	418.8	...	...	...	...	...	...
100+	463.7	385.1	482.3	...	...	...	...	...	...
Republic of Moldova - République de Moldova[7]									
2003									
Total	11.9	12.7	11.2	9.2	10.1	8.4	13.8	14.5	13.2
0-1	14.7	16.8	12.4	14.1	15.9	12.3	15.0	17.3	12.5
1-4	0.9	0.9	0.8	♦0.6	♦0.5	♦0.6	1.0	1.1	1.0
5-9	0.4	0.4	0.3	♦0.3	♦0.4	♦0.3	0.4	0.4	♦0.3
10-14	0.3	0.4	0.3	0.3	♦0.4	♦0.3	0.4	0.5	♦0.3
15-19	0.5	0.7	0.3	0.5	0.7	♦0.2	0.5	0.7	0.3
20-24	1.0	1.5	0.5	1.0	1.5	♦0.4	1.0	1.5	0.5
25-29	1.3	2.0	0.6	1.3	2.0	0.5	1.3	1.9	0.7
30-34	2.0	3.0	1.1	1.6	2.3	0.9	2.5	3.9	1.3
35-39	3.6	5.2	2.1	3.0	4.4	1.7	4.1	5.9	2.4
40-44	5.2	7.7	2.9	4.5	6.7	2.6	5.7	8.6	3.1
45-49	8.1	11.8	4.8	7.1	10.4	4.3	9.0	13.0	5.2
50-54	12.4	17.4	8.0	10.6	15.1	6.6	14.0	19.5	9.3
55-59	17.2	23.0	12.6	15.1	20.2	10.8	18.9	25.5	14.1
60-64	27.9	37.4	20.9	24.6	33.1	17.6	30.0	40.4	22.8
65-69	40.4	52.1	32.1	33.8	43.3	26.7	44.0	57.2	35.0
70-74	61.8	78.3	51.6	53.9	68.0	45.0	65.4	83.1	54.5
75-79	90.0	105.6	81.6	80.9	97.8	72.4	94.4	109.3	86.3
80-84	150.4	168.6	141.4	130.2	150.7	121.7	159.1	175.1	150.6
85+	254.7	297.2	238.7	177.2	190.2	172.6	303.1	359.4	281.1
Romania - Roumanie									
2003									
Total	12.3	13.5	11.1	9.7	11.0	8.5	15.2	16.2	14.2
0-1	17.0	19.3	14.7	14.1	16.1	12.0	19.7	22.2	17.1
1-4	0.7	0.8	0.6	0.6	0.7	0.5	0.8	1.0	0.7
5-9	0.3	0.4	0.3	0.3	0.4	0.2	0.4	0.4	0.3
10-14	0.4	0.5	0.3	0.4	0.4	0.3	0.5	0.6	0.4
15-19	0.5	0.7	0.4	0.4	0.6	0.3	0.6	0.8	0.4
20-24	0.7	1.0	0.4	0.6	0.9	0.3	0.9	1.2	0.5
25-29	0.9	1.3	0.5	0.7	1.0	0.4	1.1	1.5	0.5
30-34	1.3	1.9	0.7	1.1	1.6	0.6	1.6	2.3	0.9
35-39	2.1	3.0	1.3	1.7	2.4	1.0	2.8	3.8	1.6
40-44	4.0	5.8	2.2	3.3	4.7	2.0	5.2	7.2	2.7
45-49	6.4	9.4	3.5	5.6	8.2	3.3	7.8	11.3	4.0
50-54	9.1	13.1	5.3	8.4	12.0	5.0	10.0	14.8	5.6
55-59	13.4	19.1	8.2	13.2	18.6	8.2	13.5	19.6	8.2
60-64	19.2	27.6	12.1	19.4	28.1	12.1	18.9	27.3	12.1
65-69	28.4	39.3	19.9	28.7	39.9	19.9	28.2	38.8	19.9
70-74	43.7	56.3	34.4	43.6	57.4	33.8	43.8	55.6	34.8
75-79	71.5	85.5	62.2	69.1	83.9	59.7	73.1	86.4	63.9
80-84	115.7	128.3	108.7	108.8	126.0	100.3	120.0	129.6	114.4
85-89	200.6	212.9	194.4	181.7	194.8	175.5	214.4	225.1	208.7
90-94	286.8	298.3	281.0	261.6	279.8	253.2	305.4	310.8	302.4
95-99	372.4	361.8	377.7	364.2	375.2	359.6	378.0	354.2	391.3
100+	293.9	250.0	312.6	292.9	♦202.5	328.4	294.6	281.0	300.8
Russian Federation - Fédération de Russie[7]									
1999									
Total	14.7	16.3	13.3	14.1	15.8	12.6	16.3	17.4	15.3

20. Death rates specific for age, sex and urban/rural residence: latest available year, 1994 - 2003
Taux de mortalité selon l'âge, le sexe et la résidence, urbaine/rurale: dernière année disponible, 1994 - 2003 (continued — suite)

Continent, country or area, year and age (in years) / Continent, pays ou zone, année et âge (en années)	Total			Urban - Urbaine			Rural - Rurale		
	Both sexes Les deux sexes	Male Masculin	Female Féminin	Both sexes Les deux sexes	Male Masculin	Female Féminin	Both sexes Les deux sexes	Male Masculin	Female Féminin
EUROPE									
Russian Federation - Fédération de Russie[7]									
1999									
0-1	16.6	18.7	14.4	15.9	18.0	13.7	18.1	20.3	15.8
1-4	1.0	1.1	0.9	0.8	0.9	0.7	1.4	1.6	1.3
5-9	0.5	0.6	0.4	0.4	0.5	0.3	0.6	0.7	0.5
10-14	0.5	0.6	0.3	0.4	0.5	0.3	0.6	0.7	0.4
15-19	1.4	2.0	0.8	1.4	1.9	0.8	1.6	2.2	0.9
20-24	2.8	4.5	1.1	2.7	4.4	1.1	3.1	4.8	1.2
25-29	3.3	5.2	1.3	3.1	4.8	1.2	3.9	6.3	1.4
30-34	4.1	6.5	1.6	3.9	6.1	1.6	4.6	7.4	1.7
35-39	5.2	8.3	2.2	5.0	8.1	2.2	5.8	9.0	2.4
40-44	7.2	11.4	3.2	6.9	11.1	3.1	8.0	12.2	3.4
45-49	10.2	16.1	4.8	9.9	15.8	4.6	11.3	17.0	5.4
50-54	14.1	22.1	7.1	13.6	21.6	6.9	15.8	23.7	8.2
55-59	19.6	31.2	10.7	19.1	30.6	10.3	21.1	32.9	11.7
60-64	26.5	42.0	15.3	25.6	41.1	14.9	28.6	44.3	16.5
65-69	37.9	58.4	25.2	37.3	57.8	25.1	39.2	59.6	25.5
70-74	52.7	77.7	40.5	53.2	77.3	41.3	51.6	78.7	38.9
75-79	74.8	100.4	66.6	75.7	99.3	68.0	72.7	103.0	63.5
80-84	122.7	148.6	115.6	126.0	149.4	119.2	115.7	146.8	108.5
85+	206.3	200.1	207.8	214.3	207.2	216.2	192.3	185.0	193.8
2001									
Total	15.7	17.9	13.7	...	...	...	...	...	...
0-1	14.6	16.7	12.3	...	...	...	...	...	...
0-4	4.8	5.5	4.0	...	...	...	...	...	...
5-9	0.5	0.6	0.4	...	...	...	...	...	...
10-14	0.5	0.6	0.3	...	...	...	...	...	...
15-19	1.4	1.9	0.8	...	...	...	...	...	...
20-24	2.8	4.4	1.1	...	...	...	...	...	...
25-29	3.6	5.8	1.4	...	...	...	...	...	...
30-34	4.4	6.9	1.9	...	...	...	...	...	...
35-39	6.0	9.6	2.5	...	...	...	...	...	...
40-44	8.1	12.9	3.5	...	...	...	...	...	...
45-49	11.4	18.1	5.2	...	...	...	...	...	...
50-54	15.7	24.8	7.8	...	...	...	...	...	...
55-59	21.6	34.0	11.9	...	...	...	...	...	...
60-64	29.1	47.1	16.6	...	...	...	...	...	...
65-69	38.3	59.4	25.2	...	...	...	...	...	...
70-74	55.8	82.9	41.9	...	...	...	...	...	...
75-79	71.6	95.3	63.5	...	...	...	...	...	...
80-84	115.3	137.2	109.1	...	...	...	...	...	...
85-89	194.3	203.8	192.1	...	...	...	...	...	...
90-94	256.4	208.2	268.3	...	...	...	...	...	...
95-99	185.5	101.9	210.5	...	...	...	...	...	...
100+	76.6	28.8	96.3	...	...	...	...	...	...
Serbia and Montenegro - Serbie-et-Montenegro[25]									
2000									
Total	11.1	11.7	10.5	10.8	11.6	10.1	11.4	11.8	11.0
0-1	13.4	15.3	11.3	14.7	16.8	12.4	11.9	13.6	10.0
1-4	0.6	0.6	0.6	0.6	0.6	0.5	0.7	0.7	0.6
5-9	0.2	0.3	0.2	0.1	0.2	◆0.1	0.3	0.4	0.2
10-14	0.2	0.3	0.2	0.2	0.3	0.2	0.2	0.3	0.2
15-19	0.5	0.6	0.3	0.5	0.6	0.3	0.4	0.6	0.3
20-24	0.7	1.0	0.4	0.8	1.2	0.4	0.6	0.8	0.4
25-29	0.7	1.0	0.4	0.8	1.2	0.4	0.7	0.9	0.4
30-34	1.0	1.2	0.7	1.1	1.3	0.8	0.9	1.1	0.6
35-39	1.5	2.0	1.1	1.6	2.2	1.1	1.4	1.9	0.9
40-44	2.7	3.6	1.7	2.9	3.9	1.9	2.4	3.2	1.5
45-49	4.7	6.2	3.2	5.0	6.6	3.4	4.3	5.6	2.9
50-54	7.4	10.1	4.8	7.8	10.9	5.0	6.9	9.2	4.4
55-59	12.2	16.2	8.4	12.8	17.0	9.0	11.5	15.4	7.6

20. Death rates specific for age, sex and urban/rural residence: latest available year, 1994 - 2003
Taux de mortalité selon l'âge, le sexe et la résidence, urbaine/rurale: dernière année disponible, 1994 - 2003 (continued — suite)

Continent, country or area, year and age (in years) / Continent, pays ou zone, année et âge (en années)	Total			Urban - Urbaine			Rural - Rurale		
	Both sexes Les deux sexes	Male Masculin	Female Féminin	Both sexes Les deux sexes	Male Masculin	Female Féminin	Both sexes Les deux sexes	Male Masculin	Female Féminin
EUROPE									
Serbia and Montenegro - Serbie-et-Monténégro[25]									
2000									
60-64	18.9	24.9	13.6	19.8	25.8	14.5	17.9	23.8	12.6
65-69	31.3	40.2	23.7	33.0	41.9	25.5	29.6	38.6	22.1
70-74	47.2	56.3	40.1	51.5	60.8	44.3	43.7	52.7	36.8
75-79	75.1	81.9	70.4	81.0	83.9	78.8	70.5	80.2	64.2
80-84	104.7	108.7	102.2	120.0	107.8	129.3	95.2	109.3	87.0
85+	176.2	143.6	204.3	188.8	132.3	246.2	167.4	152.8	178.7
2002									
Total	13.4	14.1	12.7	...	...	...	...	...	...
0-1	12.1	13.9	10.2	...	...	...	...	...	...
1-4	0.4	0.4	0.4	...	...	...	...	...	...
5-9	0.2	0.2	0.2	...	...	...	...	...	...
10-14	0.3	0.3	0.2	...	...	...	...	...	...
15-19	0.4	0.6	0.3	...	...	...	...	...	...
20-24	0.7	1.0	0.3	...	...	...	...	...	...
25-29	0.8	1.2	0.5	...	...	...	...	...	...
30-34	1.0	1.4	0.7	...	...	...	...	...	...
35-39	1.5	1.9	1.2	...	...	...	...	...	...
40-44	2.6	3.5	1.8	...	...	...	...	...	...
45-49	4.9	6.4	3.3	...	...	...	...	...	...
50-54	7.7	10.6	4.9	...	...	...	...	...	...
55-59	12.1	16.7	7.8	...	...	...	...	...	...
60-64	18.7	24.9	13.2	...	...	...	...	...	...
65-69	29.5	37.9	22.5	...	...	...	...	...	...
70-74	47.8	57.5	40.4	...	...	...	...	...	...
75-79	77.4	89.4	69.8	...	...	...	...	...	...
80-84	114.4	122.9	109.4	...	...	...	...	...	...
85-89	204.8	211.7	201.0	...	...	...	...	...	...
90-94	253.9	248.8	256.8	...	...	...	...	...	...
95-99	259.9	245.3	268.4	...	...	...	...	...	...
100+	78.2	♦50.8	93.8	...	...	...	...	...	...
Slovakia - Slovaquie									
2001									
Total	9.7	10.6	8.8	8.1	8.9	7.4	11.6	12.8	10.6
0-1	6.1	6.9	5.3	5.6	6.0	5.1	6.6	7.7	5.4
1-4	0.4	0.5	0.3	0.4	♦0.4	♦0.4	0.4	0.7	♦0.2
5-9	0.2	0.3	♦0.1	0.2	♦0.3	♦0.1	0.2	♦0.3	♦0.1
10-14	0.2	0.3	♦0.1	0.2	0.3	♦0.1	0.2	♦0.3	♦0.2
15-19	0.4	0.6	0.3	0.4	0.5	0.3	0.5	0.6	0.3
20-24	0.6	0.9	0.2	0.5	0.8	♦0.2	0.7	1.1	♦0.3
25-29	0.8	1.2	0.4	0.8	1.1	0.4	0.9	1.4	0.4
30-34	1.1	1.7	0.5	1.0	1.5	0.5	1.3	1.9	0.6
35-39	1.7	2.5	0.8	1.4	2.1	0.9	2.0	3.0	0.8
40-44	2.9	4.3	1.6	2.4	3.5	1.5	3.7	5.4	1.8
45-49	4.9	7.2	2.7	4.3	6.1	2.7	5.9	8.8	2.7
50-54	7.7	11.5	4.1	6.8	10.2	3.7	9.0	13.5	4.6
55-59	11.6	17.6	6.6	10.5	15.5	6.3	13.1	20.1	6.9
60-64	18.3	28.3	10.4	16.8	25.2	10.2	19.8	31.6	10.5
65-69	27.0	40.5	17.2	25.9	37.8	17.3	28.0	43.3	17.2
70-74	41.7	59.7	30.3	40.5	55.5	30.8	42.8	63.7	29.9
75-79	65.1	83.4	55.1	63.3	79.9	54.0	66.7	86.6	56.0
80-84	106.5	131.3	94.1	103.4	126.3	91.4	109.3	135.9	96.3
85-89	174.9	198.7	164.3	170.7	196.1	159.3	178.5	200.9	168.5
90-94	274.0	293.2	266.7	266.7	278.1	262.6	279.9	304.7	270.1
95-99	339.0	318.9	345.9	326.0	262.0	349.0	351.0	375.0	343.2
100+	259.6	♦125.0	330.9	275.9	♦90.9	♦388.9	♦239.1	♦178.6	♦265.6
2002									
Total	9.6	10.5	8.7	...	...	...	...	...	...
0-1	7.7	7.3	8.1	...	...	...	...	...	...
1-4	0.3	0.3	0.3	...	...	...	...	...	...
5-9	0.2	0.3	♦0.2	...	...	...	...	...	...

20. Death rates specific for age, sex and urban/rural residence: latest available year, 1994 - 2003
Taux de mortalité selon l'âge, le sexe et la résidence, urbaine/rurale: dernière année disponible, 1994 - 2003 (continued — suite)

Continent, country or area, year and age (in years) Continent, pays ou zone, année et âge (en années)	Total			Urban - Urbaine			Rural - Rurale		
	Both sexes Les deux sexes	Male Masculin	Female Féminin	Both sexes Les deux sexes	Male Masculin	Female Féminin	Both sexes Les deux sexes	Male Masculin	Female Féminin
EUROPE									
Slovakia - Slovaquie									
2002									
10-14	0.2	0.2	0.2	...	...	...	...	...	...
15-19	0.5	0.6	0.3	...	...	...	...	...	...
20-24	0.7	1.0	0.3	...	...	...	...	...	...
25-29	0.8	1.2	0.4	...	...	...	...	...	...
30-34	1.0	1.5	0.5	...	...	...	...	...	...
35-39	1.6	2.4	0.7	...	...	...	...	...	...
40-44	2.9	4.3	1.5	...	...	...	...	...	...
45-49	4.8	7.3	2.5	...	...	...	...	...	...
50-54	7.5	11.5	3.7	...	...	...	...	...	...
55-59	11.5	17.4	6.4	...	...	...	...	...	...
60-64	16.8	25.6	9.9	...	...	...	...	...	...
65-69	25.9	38.2	17.1	...	...	...	...	...	...
70-74	39.3	55.2	29.2	...	...	...	...	...	...
75-79	64.0	83.8	53.1	...	...	...	...	...	...
80-84	100.6	122.6	89.6	...	...	...	...	...	...
85-89	175.7	195.5	166.9	...	...	...	...	...	...
90-94	255.5	284.5	244.4	...	...	...	...	...	...
95-99	338.9	330.0	342.0	...	...	...	...	...	...
100+	387.5	♦280.7	446.6	...	...	...	...	...	...
Slovenia - Slovénie									
2003									
Total	9.7	10.3	9.2	9.2	10.0	8.6	10.7	11.3	10.1
0-1	4.0	4.1	3.8	3.9	♦3.7	♦4.1	4.1	♦4.5	♦3.6
1-4	♦0.2	♦0.3	♦0.1	♦0.3	♦0.4	♦0.1	♦0.2	♦0.2	♦0.2
5-9	♦0.1	♦0.1	♦0.2	♦0.1	♦0.2	♦0.1	♦0.1	♦0.1	♦0.2
10-14	♦0.1	♦0.1	♦0.1	♦0.1	♦0.1	-	♦0.1	♦0.1	♦0.1
15-19	0.5	0.7	♦0.4	♦0.5	♦0.5	♦0.4	0.6	0.9	♦0.3
20-24	0.7	1.1	♦0.3	0.7	1.0	♦0.3	0.8	1.3	♦0.3
25-29	0.7	1.1	♦0.3	0.7	1.2	♦0.3	0.7	1.2	♦0.3
30-34	0.9	1.2	0.5	0.8	1.2	♦0.4	1.0	1.4	0.6
35-39	1.4	2.0	0.7	1.4	2.0	♦0.8	1.5	2.3	♦0.6
40-44	2.3	3.2	1.5	2.2	3.1	1.4	2.6	3.6	1.5
45-49	3.8	5.6	2.0	3.7	5.3	2.1	4.3	6.5	1.9
50-54	6.1	8.5	3.4	5.6	8.0	3.3	6.9	9.8	3.7
55-59	8.9	12.6	5.2	8.2	11.9	5.0	10.1	14.2	5.6
60-64	12.4	18.4	7.0	11.2	17.5	5.9	14.1	20.0	8.4
65-69	20.1	29.8	12.2	18.2	26.1	11.8	22.5	34.4	12.8
70-74	32.0	46.9	22.1	30.5	43.9	21.8	34.0	50.7	22.6
75-79	49.4	70.3	39.4	44.9	65.0	35.1	54.7	77.1	44.1
80-84	84.0	119.8	70.3	76.3	112.6	61.7	92.6	129.5	79.4
85-89	158.4	198.0	144.7	151.6	176.6	142.4	167.2	225.1	148.3
90-94	234.1	276.1	221.8	216.3	246.6	207.2	256.1	310.5	240.6
95-99	382.7	438.5	370.7	371.8	439.6	357.1	409.6	442.1	402.4
100+	413.5	♦363.6	419.4	♦479.2	-	♦534.9	♦392.2	♦800.0	♦347.8
Spain - Espagne									
2000									
Total	9.0	9.7	8.4	...	...	...	...	...	...
0-1	4.5	4.8	4.2	...	...	...	...	...	...
1-4	0.3	0.3	0.2	...	...	...	...	...	...
5-9	0.2	0.2	0.1	...	...	...	...	...	...
10-14	0.2	0.2	0.1	...	...	...	...	...	...
15-19	0.5	0.7	0.3	...	...	...	...	...	...
20-24	0.6	0.9	0.3	...	...	...	...	...	...
25-29	0.7	1.0	0.3	...	...	...	...	...	...
30-34	0.9	1.3	0.5	...	...	...	...	...	...
35-39	1.3	1.9	0.7	...	...	...	...	...	...
40-44	1.9	2.6	1.1	...	...	...	...	...	...
45-49	2.6	3.7	1.5	...	...	...	...	...	...
50-54	3.9	5.7	2.2	...	...	...	...	...	...
55-59	5.8	8.5	3.2	...	...	...	...	...	...
60-64	9.0	13.4	5.0	...	...	...	...	...	...

20. Death rates specific for age, sex and urban/rural residence: latest available year, 1994 - 2003
Taux de mortalité selon l'âge, le sexe et la résidence, urbaine/rurale: dernière année disponible, 1994 - 2003 (continued — suite)

Continent, country or area, year and age (in years) Continent, pays ou zone, année et âge (en années)	Total			Urban - Urbaine			Rural - Rurale		
	Both sexes Les deux sexes	Male Masculin	Female Féminin	Both sexes Les deux sexes	Male Masculin	Female Féminin	Both sexes Les deux sexes	Male Masculin	Female Féminin
EUROPE									
Spain - Espagne									
2000									
65-69	14.3	21.0	8.5	...	...	...	...	...	...
70-74	23.1	33.2	15.1	...	...	...	...	...	...
75-79	40.0	55.6	29.2	...	...	...	...	...	...
80-84	69.5	89.0	58.6	...	...	...	...	...	...
85-89	129.0	155.8	116.7	...	...	...	...	...	...
90-94	229.7	252.9	220.4	...	...	...	...	...	...
95+	448.6	441.9	451.1	...	...	...	...	...	...
Sweden - Suède									
2002									
Total	10.6	10.4	10.9	...	...	...	...	...	...
0-1	3.3	3.6	3.1	...	...	...	...	...	...
1-4	0.2	0.2	◆0.1	...	...	...	...	...	...
5-9	0.1	◆0.1	◆0.1	...	...	...	...	...	...
10-14	0.1	0.1	◆0.1	...	...	...	...	...	...
15-19	0.3	0.4	0.3	...	...	...	...	...	...
20-24	0.5	0.8	0.3	...	...	...	...	...	...
25-29	0.4	0.6	0.3	...	...	...	...	...	...
30-34	0.6	0.7	0.4	...	...	...	...	...	...
35-39	0.7	0.9	0.5	...	...	...	...	...	...
40-44	1.2	1.5	0.9	...	...	...	...	...	...
45-49	2.0	2.3	1.6	...	...	...	...	...	...
50-54	3.2	3.9	2.5	...	...	...	...	...	...
55-59	5.4	6.5	4.3	...	...	...	...	...	...
60-64	8.3	10.4	6.3	...	...	...	...	...	...
65-69	14.0	17.8	10.5	...	...	...	...	...	...
70-74	23.5	30.2	17.8	...	...	...	...	...	...
75-79	40.6	52.4	31.6	...	...	...	...	...	...
80-84	72.3	90.9	60.3	...	...	...	...	...	...
85-89	133.6	163.3	118.5	...	...	...	...	...	...
90-94	230.2	269.7	215.4	...	...	...	...	...	...
95-99	360.2	423.9	344.2	...	...	...	...	...	...
100+	512.9	572.3	502.2	...	...	...	...	...	...
Switzerland - Suisse									
2002									
Total	8.4	8.4	8.4	...	...	...	...	...	...
0-1	5.0	5.6	4.4	...	...	...	...	...	...
1-4	0.3	0.3	0.3	...	...	...	...	...	...
5-9	0.1	◆0.1	◆0.1	...	...	...	...	...	...
10-14	0.1	0.2	◆0.1	...	...	...	...	...	...
15-19	0.4	0.6	0.2	...	...	...	...	...	...
20-24	0.6	0.9	0.2	...	...	...	...	...	...
25-29	0.6	0.8	0.4	...	...	...	...	...	...
30-34	0.7	1.0	0.5	...	...	...	...	...	...
35-39	0.9	1.2	0.6	...	...	...	...	...	...
40-44	1.3	1.7	0.9	...	...	...	...	...	...
45-49	2.1	2.8	1.5	...	...	...	...	...	...
50-54	3.4	4.3	2.4	...	...	...	...	...	...
55-59	5.0	6.4	3.7	...	...	...	...	...	...
60-64	7.7	10.3	5.3	...	...	...	...	...	...
65-69	12.9	17.9	8.6	...	...	...	...	...	...
70-74	20.6	28.9	14.1	...	...	...	...	...	...
75-79	35.3	48.5	26.4	...	...	...	...	...	...
80-84	61.0	80.3	49.8	...	...	...	...	...	...
85-89	118.7	143.4	107.3	...	...	...	...	...	...
90-94	198.2	231.7	186.8	...	...	...	...	...	...
95+	295.8	322.5	289.2	...	...	...	...	...	...
The Former Yugoslav Rep. of Macedonia - L'ex-République yougoslave de Macédoine									
2003									
Total	8.9	9.7	8.1	...	...	...	...	...	...

20. Death rates specific for age, sex and urban/rural residence: latest available year, 1994 - 2003
Taux de mortalité selon l'âge, le sexe et la résidence, urbaine/rurale: dernière année disponible, 1994 - 2003 (continued — suite)

Continent, country or area, year and age (in years) Continent, pays ou zone, année et âge (en années)	Total			Urban - Urbaine			Rural - Rurale		
	Both sexes Les deux sexes	Male Masculin	Female Féminin	Both sexes Les deux sexes	Male Masculin	Female Féminin	Both sexes Les deux sexes	Male Masculin	Female Féminin
EUROPE									
The Former Yugoslav Rep. of Macedonia - L'ex-République yougoslave de Macédoine									
2003									
0-1	13.2	15.2	11.1	...	...	...	...	...	...
1-4	0.4	◆0.5	◆0.4	...	...	...	...	...	...
5-9	◆0.1	◆0.2	◆0.1	...	...	...	...	...	...
10-14	0.2	◆0.3	◆0.2	...	...	...	...	...	...
15-19	0.5	0.6	◆0.4	...	...	...	...	...	...
20-24	0.6	0.9	◆0.3	...	...	...	...	...	...
25-29	0.7	0.9	0.4	...	...	...	...	...	...
30-34	0.8	1.2	◆0.4	...	...	...	...	...	...
35-39	1.2	1.5	0.8	...	...	...	...	...	...
40-44	2.2	3.0	1.3	...	...	...	...	...	...
45-49	3.9	5.6	2.2	...	...	...	...	...	...
50-54	6.5	8.7	4.3	...	...	...	...	...	...
55-59	10.1	13.5	7.0	...	...	...	...	...	...
60-64	15.6	19.7	11.8	...	...	...	...	...	...
65-69	26.6	33.5	20.5	...	...	...	...	...	...
70-74	44.2	51.7	38.1	...	...	...	...	...	...
75-79	79.3	88.1	72.6	...	...	...	...	...	...
80-84	132.3	146.3	122.2	...	...	...	...	...	...
85+	256.6	283.3	236.9	...	...	...	...	...	...
Ukraine[7]									
1998									
Total	14.3	15.2	13.6	12.5	13.8	11.4	18.1	18.3	18.0
0-1	12.4	14.5	10.2	12.4	14.5	10.1	12.4	14.5	10.3
1-4	0.9	1.0	0.8	0.7	0.8	0.6	1.3	1.4	1.2
5-9	0.4	0.5	0.3	0.3	0.4	0.3	0.5	0.6	0.4
10-14	0.4	0.5	0.3	0.4	0.5	0.3	0.4	0.5	0.3
15-19	0.9	1.2	0.6	0.8	1.1	0.5	1.1	1.4	0.7
20-24	1.6	2.5	0.7	1.5	2.3	0.7	1.8	2.8	0.7
25-29	2.1	3.3	1.0	2.0	3.1	1.0	2.4	3.7	0.9
30-34	2.9	4.5	1.2	2.7	4.4	1.2	3.1	4.8	1.3
35-39	4.0	6.3	1.7	3.7	6.0	1.7	4.6	7.2	1.8
40-44	5.8	9.3	2.6	5.4	8.8	2.4	6.9	10.6	3.1
45-49	8.5	13.5	4.1	8.0	12.6	4.0	10.1	15.9	4.6
50-54	12.3	19.4	6.4	11.9	18.7	6.2	13.2	21.0	6.8
55-59	15.9	24.9	9.0	15.6	24.1	8.8	16.6	26.2	9.3
60-64	24.8	37.5	15.2	24.8	37.1	15.4	24.9	38.2	14.9
65-69	32.7	48.6	22.4	33.4	48.6	23.3	31.7	48.5	21.2
70-74	50.1	71.5	39.8	51.6	72.0	41.4	48.0	70.8	37.7
75-79	77.4	99.6	69.1	79.3	98.6	71.6	75.3	100.9	66.6
80-84	118.3	138.9	111.9	120.3	136.4	114.7	115.9	142.6	108.7
85-89	189.9	206.2	185.3	195.8	206.6	192.4	184.2	205.6	178.6
90-94	271.9	270.4	272.3	265.5	269.3	264.5	278.2	271.6	280.0
95+	389.6	267.6	430.8	334.4	247.7	364.0	450.0	289.8	503.4
2003									
Total	16.0	17.5	14.7	...	...	...	...	...	...
0-1	10.0	11.5	8.5	...	...	...	...	...	...
1-4	0.8	0.9	0.7	...	...	...	...	...	...
5-9	0.3	0.4	0.3	...	...	...	...	...	...
10-14	0.3	0.4	0.2	...	...	...	...	...	...
15-19	0.8	1.1	0.5	...	...	...	...	...	...
20-24	1.6	2.4	0.8	...	...	...	...	...	...
25-29	2.6	4.0	1.2	...	...	...	...	...	...
30-34	3.6	5.5	1.7	...	...	...	...	...	...
35-39	4.8	7.6	2.2	...	...	...	...	...	...
40-44	6.6	10.8	2.9	...	...	...	...	...	...
45-49	9.6	15.5	4.4	...	...	...	...	...	...
50-54	13.6	21.5	6.9	...	...	...	...	...	...
55-59	18.4	28.9	10.5	...	...	...	...	...	...
60-64	23.6	37.2	14.1	...	...	...	...	...	...

20. Death rates specific for age, sex and urban/rural residence: latest available year, 1994 - 2003
Taux de mortalité selon l'âge, le sexe et la résidence, urbaine/rurale: dernière année disponible, 1994 - 2003 (continued — suite)

Continent, country or area, year and age (in years) / Continent, pays ou zone, année et âge (en années)	Total			Urban - Urbaine			Rural - Rurale		
	Both sexes Les deux sexes	Male Masculin	Female Féminin	Both sexes Les deux sexes	Male Masculin	Female Féminin	Both sexes Les deux sexes	Male Masculin	Female Féminin
EUROPE									
Ukraine[7]									
2003									
65-69	36.4	53.8	24.7	...	...	...	...	...	...
70-74	49.2	70.0	37.5	...	...	...	...	...	...
75-79	79.4	106.5	68.3	...	...	...	...	...	...
80-84	126.3	151.5	118.6	...	...	...	...	...	...
85-89	200.4	223.2	194.6	...	...	...	...	...	...
90-94	304.1	334.4	297.3	...	...	...	...	...	...
95+	447.3	471.6	442.8	...	...	...	...	...	...
United Kingdom - Royaume-Uni									
2003									
Total	10.3	9.9	10.6	...	...	...	...	...	...
0-1	5.4	5.8	5.0	...	...	...	...	...	...
1-4	0.2	0.3	0.2	...	...	...	...	...	...
5-9	0.1	0.1	0.1	...	...	...	...	...	...
10-14	0.1	0.1	0.1	...	...	...	...	...	...
15-19	0.4	0.5	0.2	...	...	...	...	...	...
20-24	0.5	0.8	0.3	...	...	...	...	...	...
25-29	0.6	0.9	0.4	...	...	...	...	...	...
30-34	0.8	1.0	0.5	...	...	...	...	...	...
35-39	1.0	1.4	0.7	...	...	...	...	...	...
40-44	1.6	2.0	1.2	...	...	...	...	...	...
45-49	2.5	3.0	2.0	...	...	...	...	...	...
50-54	4.0	4.8	3.1	...	...	...	...	...	...
55-59	6.1	7.5	4.8	...	...	...	...	...	...
60-64	10.3	13.0	7.8	...	...	...	...	...	...
65-69	16.5	20.6	12.7	...	...	...	...	...	...
70-74	27.7	34.6	21.9	...	...	...	...	...	...
75-79	47.6	59.0	39.2	...	...	...	...	...	...
80-84	77.7	95.5	67.0	...	...	...	...	...	...
85-89	136.0	162.0	124.3	...	...	...	...	...	...
90+	240.2	261.5	233.6	...	...	...	...	...	...
OCEANIA — OCEANIE									
Australia - Australie+									
2003									
Total	6.7	6.9	6.4	...	...	...	...	...	...
0-1	4.9	5.3	4.3	...	...	...	...	...	...
1-4	0.2	0.2	0.2	...	...	...	...	...	...
5-9	0.1	0.1	0.1	...	...	...	...	...	...
10-14	0.1	0.1	0.1	...	...	...	...	...	...
15-19	0.5	0.6	0.3	...	...	...	...	...	...
20-24	0.6	0.9	0.3	...	...	...	...	...	...
25-29	0.7	1.0	0.4	...	...	...	...	...	...
30-34	0.8	1.1	0.5	...	...	...	...	...	...
35-39	1.0	1.3	0.7	...	...	...	...	...	...
40-44	1.4	1.8	1.0	...	...	...	...	...	...
45-49	2.1	2.6	1.5	...	...	...	...	...	...
50-54	2.8	3.4	2.1	...	...	...	...	...	...
55-59	4.6	5.8	3.4	...	...	...	...	...	...
60-64	7.8	9.6	5.9	...	...	...	...	...	...
65-69	12.5	16.1	9.1	...	...	...	...	...	...
70-74	21.1	27.6	15.1	...	...	...	...	...	...
75-79	35.9	46.0	27.8	...	...	...	...	...	...
80-84	61.4	77.4	50.9	...	...	...	...	...	...
85-89	110.5	134.5	98.2	...	...	...	...	...	...
90-94	181.8	208.7	171.4	...	...	...	...	...	...
95-99	249.1	248.1	249.4	...	...	...	...	...	...
100+	210.8	91.7	266.5	...	...	...	...	...	...

20. Death rates specific for age, sex and urban/rural residence: latest available year, 1994 - 2003
Taux de mortalité selon l'âge, le sexe et la résidence, urbaine/rurale: dernière année disponible, 1994 - 2003 (continued — suite)

Continent, country or area, year and age (in years) / Continent, pays ou zone, année et âge (en années)	Total			Urban - Urbaine			Rural - Rurale		
	Both sexes Les deux sexes	Male Masculin	Female Féminin	Both sexes Les deux sexes	Male Masculin	Female Féminin	Both sexes Les deux sexes	Male Masculin	Female Féminin
OCEANIA — OCEANIE									
New Caledonia - Nouvelle-Calédonie 1994									
Total	5.8	6.6	4.9	...	...	...	...	...	...
0-1	9.8	♦10.4	♦9.2	...	...	...	...	...	...
1-4	♦1.4	♦1.3	♦1.4	...	...	...	...	...	...
5-9	♦0.8	♦1.1	♦0.4	...	...	...	...	...	...
10-14	♦0.2	♦0.2	♦0.2	...	...	...	...	...	...
15-19	♦1.1	♦1.8	♦0.3	...	...	...	...	...	...
20-24	2.2	3.4	♦1.0	...	...	...	...	...	...
25-29	♦1.1	♦1.4	♦0.7	...	...	...	...	...	...
30-34	♦1.9	♦3.3	♦0.6	...	...	...	...	...	...
35-39	2.8	♦3.6	♦2.0	...	...	...	...	...	...
40-44	3.7	♦4.2	♦3.1	...	...	...	...	...	...
45-49	4.7	6.0	♦3.3	...	...	...	...	...	...
50-54	7.9	8.1	♦7.6	...	...	...	...	...	...
55-59	12.2	14.1	10.1	...	...	...	...	...	...
60-64	22.0	25.8	18.1	...	...	...	...	...	...
65-69	26.2	36.5	16.2	...	...	...	...	...	...
75-84	77.2	87.8	67.6	...	...	...	...	...	...
80+	108.8	118.7	101.9	...	...	...	...	...	...
New Zealand - Nouvelle-Zélande+ 2003									
Total	7.0	7.1	6.9	7.3	7.3	7.3	4.7	5.6	3.8
0-1	5.0	5.7	4.2	...	...	...	...	...	...
0-4	...	...	...	1.2	1.3	1.1	1.0	♦1.3	♦0.7
1-4	0.4	0.3	0.4	...	...	...	...	...	...
5-9	0.1	♦0.1	♦0.1	0.1	♦0.2	♦0.1	♦0.1	-	♦0.1
10-14	0.2	0.2	♦0.1	0.2	0.2	♦0.1	♦0.2	♦0.2	♦0.2
15-19	0.7	0.9	0.5	0.7	0.9	0.5	0.9	♦1.2	♦0.6
20-24	0.7	0.9	0.4	0.6	0.8	0.4	♦1.3	♦2.1	♦0.2
25-29	0.7	1.1	0.4	0.7	1.0	0.4	♦1.0	♦1.5	♦0.4
30-34	0.9	1.2	0.6	0.8	1.1	0.6	1.2	1.9	♦0.5
35-39	1.1	1.4	0.8	1.0	1.4	0.8	1.2	♦1.3	♦1.1
40-44	1.5	1.8	1.1	1.5	1.9	1.1	1.4	1.4	1.4
45-49	2.3	2.7	1.9	2.3	2.8	1.9	2.0	1.9	2.0
50-54	3.6	4.2	3.0	3.7	4.3	3.1	3.0	3.5	2.4
55-59	5.5	6.5	4.6	5.7	6.6	4.8	4.5	5.8	3.2
60-64	9.0	10.9	7.2	9.2	11.2	7.2	8.0	9.2	6.6
65-69	14.8	17.9	11.9	15.1	18.3	12.2	13.1	15.9	9.9
70-74	24.6	30.5	19.2	25.4	31.8	19.8	19.4	23.3	14.5
75-79	39.5	49.9	31.1	40.1	50.7	31.9	34.0	43.5	23.2
80-84	67.9	86.8	56.0	68.8	88.6	56.7	58.0	71.4	45.3
85+	...	...	...	156.5	175.8	148.3	112.8	136.9	97.5
85-89	119.1	144.5	106.9	...	...	...	...	...	...
90+	227.1	248.7	219.7	...	...	...	...	...	...

FOOTNOTES - NOTES

♦ Rates based on 30 or fewer deaths. — Taux basés sur 30 décès ou moins.

+ Data tabulated by year of registration rather than occurrence. — Données exploitées selon l'année de l'enregistrement et non l'année de l'événement.

[1] For 2001, data refer to last twelve months preceding census on August 2001. - Pour 2001, les données se rapportent pour la dernière fois à douze mois précédant le recensement août 2001.

[2] Based on the results of the population census. - D'après les résultats du recensement de la population.

[3] Data for 1997 refer to last twelve months preceding population and housing census of 1997. - Les données pour 1997 se réfèrent au douze mois précédant le recensement de population et de l'habitat de 1997.

[4] Excluding live-born infants who died before their birth was registered. - Non compris les enfants nés vivants décédés avant l'enregistrement de leur naissance.

[5] Including Canadian residents temporarily in the United States, but excluding United States residents temporarily in Canada. - Y compris les résidents canadiens se trouvant temporairement aux Etats-Unis, mais ne comprenant pas les résidents des Etats-Unis se trouvant temporairement au Canada.

[6] Excluding Indian jungle population. - Non compris les Indiens de la jungle.

[7] Excluding infants born alive with less than 28 weeks gestation, less than 1 000 grams in weight and 35 centimeters in length, who die within seven days of birth. - Non compris les enfants nés vivants avant 28 semaines de gestation, pesant moins de 1 000 grammes, mesurant

moins de 35 centimètres et décédés dans les sept jours qui ont suivi leur naissance.

[8] Data refer to government controlled areas. - Les données se raportent aux zones contrôlées par le Gouvernement.

[9] Including data for East Jerusalem and Israeli residents in certain other territories under occupation by Israeli military forces since June 1967. - Y compris les données pour Jérusalem-Est et les résidents israéliens dans certains autres territoires occupés depuis 1967 par les forces armées israéliennes.

[10] For Japanese nationals in Japan only; however, rates computed on population including foreigners except foreign military and civilian personnel and their dependants stationed in the area. - Pour les nationaux japonais au Japon seulement; toutefois, les taux sont calculés sur la base d'une population comprenant les étrangers, mais ne comprenant ni les militaires et agents civils étrangers en poste sur le territoire ni les membres de leur famille les accompagnant.

[11] Excluding alien armed forces, civilian aliens employed by armed forces, and foreign diplomatic personnel and their dependants. - Non compris les militaires étrangers, les civils étrangers employés par les forces armées ni le personnel diplomatique étranger et les membres de leur famille les accompagnant.

[12] For 2001, data refer to last twelve months preceding census on June 2001. - Pour 2001, les données se rapportent pour la dernière fois à douze mois précédant le recensement juin 2001.

[13] Excluding data for the Pakistan-held part of Jammu and Kashmir, the final status of which has not yet been determined. - Non compris les données concernant la partie du Jammu et Cachemire occupée par le Pakistan dont le statut définitif n'a pas été déterminé.

[14] Based on the results of the Population Growth Survey. - D'après les résultats de la 'Population Growth Survey.'

[15] Excluding transients afloat and non-locally domiciled military and civilian services personnel and their dependants. - Non compris les personnes de passage þ bord de navires, ni les militaires et agents civils domiciliés hors du territoire et les membres de leur famille les accompagnant.

[16] Including armed forces stationed outside the country, but excluding alien armed forces stationed in the area. - Y compris les militaires nationaux hors du pays, mais non compris les militaires étrangers en garnison sur le territoire.

[17] Excluding Faeroe Islands and Greenland. - Non compris les Iles Féroé et Gröenland.

[18] Including nationals temporarily outside the country. - Y compris les nationaux se trouvant temporairement hors du pays.

[19] Including armed forces stationed outside the country. - Y compris les militaires nationaux hors du pays.

[20] For ages five years and over, age classification based on year of birth rather than exact date of birth. - A partir de cinq ans, le classement selon l'âge est basé sur l'année de naissances et non sur la date exacte de naissance.

[21] Data for urban/rural residence, for the de jure population. - Les données selon la résidence urbaine/rurale, pour la population de droit.

[22] Events registered within one year of occurrence. - Evénements enregistrés dans l'année qui suit l'événement.

[23] Including residents outside the country if listed in a Netherlands population register. - Y compris les résidents hors du pays, s'ils sont inscrits sur un registre de population néerlandais.

[24] Including residents temporarily outside the country. - Y compris les résidents se trouvant temporairement hors du pays.

[25] For 2002, without data for Kosovo and Metohia. - Pour 2002, sans les donées pour le Kosovo and Metohie .

Table 21

Table 21 presents deaths by marital status, age and sex for the latest available year.

Description of variables: Marital status is defined as the personal status of each individual in relation to the marriage laws and customs of the country.

The marital status classifications used in this table is the following: single (never married), married, in consensual union, married but separated, divorced and not remarried, widowed and not remarried as well as unknown marital status. Unless otherwise specified, when the category of "married but separated" is not shown separately, it can be assumed that persons in this category are shown as "married".

Age is defined as age at last birthday, that is, the difference between the date of birth and the reference date of the age distribution expressed in completed solar years. The age classification used in this table is the following: under 15 years, 5-year age groups through 99, 100 years and over and age unknown. Data for some countries or areas deviate from this standard age classification.

Reliability of data: Data from civil registers of deaths that are reported as incomplete (less than 90 per cent completeness) or of unknown completeness are considered unreliable and are set in italics rather than in roman type.

Table 18 and the Technical Notes for that table provide more detailed information on the completeness of death registration. For more information about the quality of vital statistics data in general, and the information available on the basis of the completeness estimates in particular, see section 4.2 of the Technical Notes.

Limitations: Statistics on deaths by marital status, age and sex are subject to the same qualifications as have been set forth for vital statistics in general as discussed in section 4 of the Technical Notes.

Comparability is also affected by the accuracy of the response to the questions on marital status. Divorced or separated persons may erroneously be reported as single, while those in consensual unions may be reported as married. Also, persons who are divorced may report themselves as single, married or widowed.

Because these statistics are classified according to age, they are subject to the limitations with respect to accuracy of age reporting similar to those already discussed in connection with section 3.1.3 of the Technical Notes.

The reliability of the data, an indication of which is described above, is an important factor in considering the limitations. In addition, some deaths are tabulated by date of registration and not by date of occurrence; these have been indicated by a (+). Whenever the lag between the date of occurrence and date of registration is prolonged and, therefore, a large proportion of the death registrations are delayed, death statistics for any given year are seriously affected.

As a rule, however, delays in the registration of deaths are less common and shorter than in the registration of live births.

Another factor that limits international comparability is the practice of some countries or areas to not include in infant-death statistics, infants who were born alive but died before the registration of the birth or within the first 24 hours of life, thus underestimating the number of deaths under one year of age. Statistics of this type are footnoted.

The absence of frequencies in the unknown age group does not necessarily indicate completely accurate reporting and tabulation of the age item. It is often an indication that the unknowns have been eliminated by assigning ages to them before tabulation, or by proportionate distribution after tabulation.

International comparability of statistics on deaths by age is also affected by the use of different methods to determine age at death. If age is obtained from an item that simply requests age at death in completed years or is derived from information on year of birth and death rather than from information on complete date (day, month and year) of birth and death, the number of deaths classified in the under-one-year age group will tend to be reduced and the number of deaths in the next age group will tend to be somewhat increased.

A similar bias may affect other age groups but its impact is usually negligible. Information on this factor is given in the footnotes when known.

Earlier data: Deaths by marital status, age and sex have been shown for the latest available year in previous issues of the Demographic Yearbook featuring mortality as the special topic. For information on specific years covered, readers should consult the Index.

Tableau 21

Le tableau 21 indique le nombre de décès selon l'état matrimonial, l'âge et le sexe pour la dernière année sur laquelle on soit renseigné.

Description des variables: L'état matrimonial d'une personne est sa situation vis-à-vis des lois ou coutumes de son pays concernant le mariage.

La classification selon l'état matrimonial utilisée dans ce tableau est la suivante: célibataires (n'ayant jamais été mariés), mariés, en union consensuelle, mariés mais séparées, divorcés non remariés, veufs non remariés et personnes d'état matrimonial inconnu. Sauf indication contraire, on peut supposer que les "séparés", lorsqu'ils n'apparaissent pas séparément, sont comptés parmi les "mariés".

L'âge est l'âge au dernier anniversaire, c'est-à-dire la différence entre la date de naissance et la date de référence de la répartition par âge, exprimée en années solaires révolues. La classification par âge utilisée dans le tableau est la suivante: moins de 15 ans, groupes quinquennaux jusqu'a 99 ans, 100 ans et plus, age inconnu. Les données concernant certains pays ou zones s'écartent de cette classification.

On constatera qua la signe "... " figure parfois au regard de la catégorie des moins de 15 ans. Il signifie que la répartition des décès selon l'état matrimonial n'est pas effectuée pour les moins de 15 ans. La même classification a été utilisée pour les deux sexes.

Fiabilité des données: Les données extraites des registres d'état civil qui sont déclarées incomplètes (degré d'exhaustivité inférieur a 90 p. 100) ou dont le degré d'exhaustivité n'est pas connu sont jugées douteuses et apparaissent en italiques et non en caractères romains.

Le tableau 18 et les Notes techniques y relatives présentent des renseignements plus détaillés sur le degré d'exhaustivité de l'enregistrement des décès. Pour plus de précisions sur la qualité des statistiques de l'état civil en général, et sur les estimations de l'exhaustivité en particulier, voir la section 4.2 des Notes techniques.

Insuffisance des données: Les statistiques de la mortalité selon 1'état matrimonial, l'âge et le sexe appellent les mêmes réserves que les statistiques de l'état civil en général (voir la section 4 des Notes techniques).

Leur comparabilité est également influencée par le degré d'exactitude des réponses aux questions concernant l'état matrimonial. Il arrive que les divorcés et séparés soient inexactement déclarés comme célibataires et les personnes en union consensuelle comme mariés. Il arrive aussi que des divorces se déclarent célibataires, mariés ou veufs.

Comme ces statistiques sont classées selon l'âge, elles appellent les mêmes réserves concernant l'exactitude des déclarations d'âge que celles dont il a été fait mention dans la section 3.1.3 des Notes techniques.

La fiabilité des données, au sujet de laquelle des indications ont été fournies plus haut, est un facteur important en l'occurrence. Il faut également tenir compte du fait que, dans certains cas, les décès sont classés par date d'enregistrement et non par date effective; ces cas on été identifiés par le signe "+". Lorsque le décalage entre les décès et leur enregistrement est grand, c'est-à-dire qu'une forte proportion des décès fait l'objet d'un enregistrement tardif, les statistiques des décès de l'année peuvent être sérieusement faussées.

En règle générale toutefois, les décès sont enregistrés beaucoup plus rapidement que les naissances vivantes, et les longs retards sont rares.

Un autre facteur qui nuit à la comparabilité internationale est la pratique de certains pays ou zones qui consiste à ne pas inclure dans les statistiques des décès les enfants nés vivants mais décédés avant l'enregistrement de leur naissance ou dans les 24 heures qui ont suivi la naissance, pratique qui conduit à sous-évaluer le nombre des décès à moins d'un an. Quand tel était le cas, on l'a signalé en note au bas du tableau.

Si aucun nombre ne figure dans la colonne réservée aux âges inconnus, cela ne signifie pas nécessairement que les déclarations d'âge et le classement par âge sont tout à fait exacts. C'est souvent une indication que les personnes d'âge inconnu se sont vu attribuer une âge avant la répartition, ou été reparties proportionnellement aux effectifs connus après cette opération.

Le manque d'uniformité des méthodes suivies pour obtenir l'âge au moment du décès nuit également à la comparabilité internationale des données de mortalité. Si l'âge est connu soit d'après la réponse à une simple question sur l'âge du décès en années révolues, soit d'après l'année de la naissance et l'année du décès, et not d'après des renseignements concernant la date exacte (année, mois et jour) de la naissance et du décès, le nombre de décès classés dans la catégorie "moins d'un an" sera entaché d'une erreur par défaut et le chiffre figurant dans la catégorie suivante d'une erreur par excès. Les données pour les autres groupes d'âge pourront être entachées d'une distorsion analogue, mais ses répercusions seront généralement négligeables. Ces imperfections, quand elles étaient connues, ont été signalées on note au bas du tableau.

Données publiées antérieurement: Des statistiques des décès salon l'état matrimonial, l'âge et le sexe figurent déjà, considérées dans des éditions antérieures de l'Annuaire démographique présentant la mortalité comme sujet spécial. Pour plus de précisions concernant les années considérées, se reporter à l'Index.

21. Deaths by marital status, age and sex: latest available year, 1994 - 2003
Décès selon l'état matrimonial, l'âge et le sexe: dernière année disponible, 1994 - 2003

Continent, country or area, date and age (in years) Continent, pays ou zone, date et âge (en années)	Code[1]	Total	Single (never married) - Célibataires	Married - Mariés	In consensual union - En union consensuelle	Married but separated - Mariés mais séparées	Divorced and not remarried - Divorcées non remariés	Widowed and not remarried - Veufs non remariés	Unknown - Inconnu
AFRICA — AFRIQUE									
Egypt - Égypte									
1999									
Male									
15+	C	178 679	12 347	135 064	...	...	1 118	23 946	6 204
15 - 19	C	3 830	1 345	106	...	...	3	28	2 348
20 - 24	C	3 978	3 007	652	...	...	17	78	224
25 - 29	C	3 532	1 729	1 547	...	...	21	70	165
30 - 34	C	3 744	858	2 650	...	...	55	45	136
35 - 39	C	5 239	603	4 375	...	...	57	63	141
40 - 44	C	7 090	451	6 313	...	...	82	68	176
45 - 49	C	10 812	489	9 864	...	...	89	166	204
50 - 54	C	13 557	505	12 382	...	...	117	326	227
55 - 59	C	14 682	400	13 393	...	...	102	536	251
60 - 64	C	19 470	510	17 089	...	...	129	1 412	330
65 - 69	C	23 770	656	19 943	...	...	146	2 554	471
70 - 74	C	24 287	626	18 857	...	...	136	4 213	455
75+	C	44 688	1 168	27 893	...	...	164	14 387	1 076
Female									
15+	C	148 374	6 674	49 935	...	...	1 847	85 980	3 938
15 - 19	C	2 320	1 240	264	...	...	12	91	713
20 - 24	C	2 241	938	1 026	...	...	38	124	115
25 - 29	C	2 206	443	1 459	...	...	58	164	82
30 - 34	C	2 316	311	1 716	...	...	66	147	76
35 - 39	C	3 328	319	2 573	...	...	117	234	85
40 - 44	C	3 817	253	2 982	...	...	108	367	107
45 - 49	C	5 839	319	4 384	...	...	202	811	123
50 - 54	C	8 445	341	5 814	...	...	209	1 904	177
55 - 59	C	9 432	285	5 672	...	...	181	3 082	212
60 - 64	C	14 355	398	6 727	...	...	236	6 712	282
65 - 69	C	18 562	460	6 498	...	...	195	11 063	346
70 - 74	C	22 246	457	5 070	...	...	186	16 111	422
75+	C	53 267	910	5 750	...	...	239	45 170	1 198
Libyan Arab Jamahiriya - Jamahiriya arabe libyenne									
2002									
Male									
Total	U	11 278	3 044	7 577	...	...	45	385	227
0 - 19	U	2 310	1 841	324	...	...	3	14	128
20 - 29	U	824	647	168	...	...	-	3	6
30 - 39	U	820	252	543	...	...	3	4	18
40 - 49	U	621	55	545	...	...	9	8	4
50 - 59	U	860	31	805	...	...	7	7	10
60 - 69	U	1 754	59	1 619	...	...	8	49	19
70 - 79	U	2 254	76	2 046	...	...	5	105	22
80+	U	1 835	83	1 527	...	...	10	195	20
Female									
Total	U	8 084	1 800	3 677	...	...	145	2 321	141
0 - 19	U	1 712	1 411	161	...	...	2	73	65
20 - 29	U	276	148	115	...	...	3	7	3
30 - 39	U	467	87	328	...	...	7	34	11
40 - 49	U	497	25	394	...	...	19	46	13
50 - 59	U	632	18	459	...	...	30	119	6
60 - 69	U	1 182	30	771	...	...	28	343	10
70 - 79	U	1 558	33	797	...	...	23	688	17
80+	U	1 760	48	652	...	...	33	1 011	16

21. Deaths by marital status, age and sex: latest available year, 1994 - 2003
Décès selon l'état matrimonial, l'âge et le sexe: dernière année disponible, 1994 - 2003
(continued — suite)

Continent, country or area, date and age (in years) / Continent, pays ou zone, date et âge (en annèes)	Code[1]	Total	Single (never married) - Célibataires	Married - Mariés	In consensual union - En union consensuelle	Married but separated - Mariés mais séparées	Divorced and not remarried - Divorcées non remariés	Widowed and not remarried - Veufs non remariés	Unknown - Inconnu
AFRICA — AFRIQUE									
Mauritius - Maurice									
2003									
Male									
Total	+C	4 754	843	2 346	...	...	27	373	1 165
0 - 14	+C	196	159	2	...	...	-	1	34
15 - 19	+C	30	29	-	...	...	-	-	1
20 - 24	+C	55	44	4	...	...	-	-	7
25 - 29	+C	58	35	16	...	...	-	1	6
30 - 34	+C	101	41	41	...	...	-	-	19
35 - 39	+C	162	51	69	...	...	3	-	39
40 - 44	+C	235	70	108	...	...	2	1	54
45 - 49	+C	324	73	169	...	...	3	3	76
50 - 54	+C	414	70	243	...	...	4	6	91
55 - 59	+C	374	36	244	...	...	2	6	86
60 - 64	+C	420	34	267	...	...	1	19	99
65 - 69	+C	540	48	303	...	...	5	37	147
70 - 74	+C	527	52	291	...	...	2	51	131
75 - 79	+C	561	37	288	...	...	4	91	141
80 - 84	+C	396	36	182	...	...	1	58	119
85 - 89	+C	232	21	86	...	...	-	58	67
90+	+C	128	7	32	...	...	-	41	48
Unk. - Inc. ...	+C	1	-	1	...	...	-	-	-
Female									
Total	+C	3 766	657	983	...	...	12	1 349	765
0 - 14	+C	178	146	1	...	...	-	-	31
15 - 19	+C	18	16	-	...	...	-	-	2
20 - 24	+C	27	15	9	...	...	-	1	2
25 - 29	+C	39	17	13	...	...	-	1	8
30 - 34	+C	39	5	27	...	...	-	1	6
35 - 39	+C	69	13	40	...	...	-	4	12
40 - 44	+C	99	19	58	...	...	-	6	16
45 - 49	+C	148	28	86	...	...	2	15	17
50 - 54	+C	213	29	107	...	...	1	30	46
55 - 59	+C	231	33	115	...	...	1	41	41
60 - 64	+C	295	28	125	...	...	1	88	53
65 - 69	+C	380	40	129	...	...	1	148	62
70 - 74	+C	403	49	102	...	...	2	174	76
75 - 79	+C	535	65	86	...	...	1	268	115
80 - 84	+C	485	63	57	...	...	3	246	116
85 - 89	+C	351	48	17	...	...	-	192	94
90+	+C	256	43	11	...	...	-	134	68
Unk. - Inc. ...	+C	-	-	-	...	...	-	-	-
Réunion[2]									
2002									
Male									
Total	C	2 315	658	1 168	...	...	180	309	-
0 - 14	C	69	69	-	...	...	-	-	-
15 - 19	C	27	27	-	...	...	-	-	-
20 - 24	C	36	34	2	...	...	-	-	-
25 - 29	C	43	41	2	...	...	-	-	-
30 - 34	C	56	36	17	...	...	3	-	-
35 - 39	C	85	60	16	...	...	9	-	-
40 - 44	C	102	55	41	...	...	6	-	-
45 - 49	C	135	60	53	...	...	19	3	-
50 - 54	C	172	59	79	...	...	27	7	-
55 - 59	C	181	49	93	...	...	26	13	-
60 - 64	C	221	42	141	...	...	22	16	-
65 - 69	C	244	48	151	...	...	29	16	-
70 - 74	C	268	30	173	...	...	22	43	-
75 - 79	C	252	28	170	...	...	3	51	-

21. Deaths by marital status, age and sex: latest available year, 1994 - 2003
Décès selon l'état matrimonial, l'âge et le sexe: dernière année disponible, 1994 - 2003
(continued — suite)

Continent, country or area, date and age (in years) / Continent, pays ou zone, date et âge (en années)	Code[1]	Total	Single (never married) - Célibataires	Married - Mariés	In consensual union - En union consensuelle	Married but separated - Mariés mais séparées	Divorced and not remarried - Divorcées non remariés	Widowed and not remarried - Veufs non remariés	Unknown - Inconnu
AFRICA — AFRIQUE									
Réunion[2]									
2002									
Male									
80 - 84	C	214	12	131	...	...	10	61	-
85 - 89	C	130	4	74	...	...	3	49	-
90 - 94	C	64	3	21	...	...	1	39	-
95 - 99	C	13	-	4	...	...	-	9	-
100+	C	3	1	-	...	...	-	2	-
Female									
Total	C	1 689	392	396	...	...	74	827	-
0 - 14	C	50	50	-	...	...	-	-	-
15 - 19	C	6	5	-	...	...	-	1	-
20 - 24	C	10	10	-	...	...	-	-	-
25 - 29	C	9	6	3	...	...	-	-	-
30 - 34	C	27	18	6	...	...	1	2	-
35 - 39	C	24	16	6	...	...	1	1	-
40 - 44	C	33	12	16	...	...	4	1	-
45 - 49	C	56	22	19	...	...	9	6	-
50 - 54	C	73	20	35	...	...	8	10	-
55 - 59	C	68	14	35	...	...	8	11	-
60 - 64	C	109	15	54	...	...	6	34	-
65 - 69	C	119	14	56	...	...	7	42	-
70 - 74	C	171	27	63	...	...	10	71	-
75 - 79	C	211	32	46	...	...	9	124	-
80 - 84	C	236	38	36	...	...	5	157	-
85 - 89	C	232	39	13	...	...	4	176	-
90 - 94	C	179	32	8	...	...	2	137	-
95 - 99	C	60	17	-	...	...	-	43	-
100+	C	16	5	-	...	...	-	11	-
Tunisia - Tunisie									
1998									
Male									
Total	U	25 319	5 297	16 306	...	...	315	2 625	776
0 - 14	U	2 663	2 663	-	...	...	-	-	-
15 - 19	U	408	404	3	...	...	1	-	-
20 - 24	U	459	440	14	...	...	-	2	3
25 - 29	U	425	339	71	...	...	4	1	10
30 - 34	U	528	273	226	...	...	10	8	11
35 - 39	U	519	125	367	...	...	13	3	11
40 - 44	U	631	93	498	...	...	13	5	22
45 - 49	U	737	65	604	...	...	32	9	27
50 - 54	U	805	72	687	...	...	19	10	17
55 - 59	U	1 152	66	1 010	...	...	19	20	37
60 - 64	U	1 843	107	1 579	...	...	32	61	64
65 - 69	U	2 673	103	2 328	...	...	36	151	55
70 - 74	U	2 943	136	2 421	...	...	25	288	73
75 - 79	U	2 930	105	2 285	...	...	35	439	66
80+	U	5 807	168	3 867	...	...	71	1 569	132
Unk. - Inc. ...	U	796	138	346	...	...	5	59	248
Female									
Total	U	17 252	3 019	5 132	...	...	334	8 310	457
0 - 14	U	1 952	1 952	-	...	...	-	-	-
15 - 19	U	170	156	12	...	...	-	-	2
20 - 24	U	194	136	47	...	...	1	5	5
25 - 29	U	187	96	82	...	...	6	1	2
30 - 34	U	273	82	169	...	...	10	5	7
35 - 39	U	293	73	184	...	...	18	10	8
40 - 44	U	367	49	279	...	...	18	18	3
45 - 49	U	424	40	312	...	...	20	40	12
50 - 54	U	462	32	354	...	...	12	57	7
55 - 59	U	681	32	481	...	...	19	132	17

21. Deaths by marital status, age and sex: latest available year, 1994 - 2003
Décès selon l'état matrimonial, l'âge et le sexe: dernière année disponible, 1994 - 2003
(continued — suite)

Continent, country or area, date and age (in years) / Continent, pays ou zone, date et âge (en années)	Code[1]	Total	Single (never married) - Célibataires	Married - Mariés	In consensual union - En union consensuelle	Married but separated - Mariés mais séparées	Divorced and not remarried - Divorcées non remariés	Widowed and not remarried - Veufs non remariés	Unknown - Inconnu
AFRICA — AFRIQUE									
Tunisia - Tunisie									
1998									
Female									
60 - 64	U	1 077	43	639	...	...	34	333	28
65 - 69	U	1 664	51	790	...	...	40	745	38
70 - 74	U	1 975	53	673	...	...	45	1 172	32
75 - 79	U	2 271	48	482	...	...	44	1 645	52
80+	U	4 685	86	489	...	...	58	3 973	79
Unk. - Inc. ...	U	577	90	139	...	...	9	174	165
AMERICA, NORTH — AMERIQUE DU NORD									
Bahamas									
2001									
Male									
Total	C	879	380	361	...	...	31	101	6
0 - 14	C	37	37	-	...	...	-	-	-
15 - 19	C	17	17	-	...	...	-	-	-
20 - 24	C	17	17	-	...	...	-	-	-
25 - 29	C	40	34	6	...	...	-	-	-
30 - 34	C	55	40	14	...	...	-	1	-
35 - 39	C	58	42	14	...	...	1	1	-
40 - 44	C	78	47	26	...	...	3	2	-
45 - 49	C	64	25	31	...	...	6	2	-
50 - 54	C	53	22	28	...	...	2	1	-
55 - 59	C	63	18	36	...	...	4	5	-
60 - 64	C	71	30	27	...	...	4	8	2
65 - 69	C	80	14	54	...	...	-	11	1
70 - 74	C	64	11	33	...	...	4	14	2
75 - 79	C	60	11	33	...	...	2	13	1
80 - 84	C	72	8	38	...	...	5	21	-
85 - 89	C	37	5	17	...	...	-	15	-
90 - 94	C	7	1	3	...	...	-	3	-
95 - 99	C	6	1	1	...	...	-	4	-
100+	C	-	-	-	...	...	-	-	-
Female									
Total	C	730	262	196	...	...	22	249	1
0 - 14	C	28	28	-	...	...	-	-	-
15 - 19	C	5	5	-	...	...	-	-	-
20 - 24	C	8	7	1	...	...	-	-	-
25 - 29	C	22	18	3	...	...	-	1	-
30 - 34	C	31	18	12	...	...	-	1	-
35 - 39	C	39	21	14	...	...	-	4	-
40 - 44	C	40	18	18	...	...	2	2	-
45 - 49	C	42	15	19	...	...	3	5	-
50 - 54	C	38	13	11	...	...	5	9	-
55 - 59	C	45	17	16	...	...	3	9	-
60 - 64	C	40	16	13	...	...	3	8	-
65 - 69	C	65	22	21	...	...	2	20	-
70 - 74	C	62	15	22	...	...	1	24	-
75 - 79	C	60	16	19	...	...	-	25	-
80 - 84	C	69	9	12	...	...	-	47	1
85 - 89	C	71	15	12	...	...	2	42	-
90 - 94	C	45	6	2	...	...	1	36	-
95 - 99	C	13	2	1	...	...	-	10	-
100+	C	7	1	-	...	...	-	6	-

21. Deaths by marital status, age and sex: latest available year, 1994 - 2003
Décès selon l'état matrimonial, l'âge et le sexe: dernière année disponible, 1994 - 2003
(continued — suite)

Continent, country or area, date and age (in years) / Continent, pays ou zone, date et âge (en années)	Code[1]	Total	Single (never married) - Célibataires	Married - Mariés	In consensual union - En union consensuelle	Married but separated - Mariés mais séparées	Divorced and not remarried - Divorcées non remariés	Widowed and not remarried - Veufs non remariés	Unknown - Inconnu
AMERICA, NORTH — AMERIQUE DU NORD									
Canada[3]									
2002									
Male									
Total	C	113 266	16 924	63 074	...	1 045	7 928	20 158	4 137
0 - 14	C	1 479	1 479	-	...	-	-	-	-
15 - 19	C	673	654	1	...	-	-	-	18
20 - 24	C	886	789	22	...	2	2	-	71
25 - 29	C	819	607	112	...	7	10	1	82
30 - 34	C	1 049	630	262	...	15	45	5	92
35 - 39	C	1 569	766	516	...	35	110	5	137
40 - 44	C	2 382	980	877	...	39	272	14	200
45 - 49	C	3 369	996	1 519	...	66	505	40	243
50 - 54	C	4 641	984	2 405	...	79	754	91	328
55 - 59	C	6 120	950	3 630	...	107	890	169	374
60 - 64	C	7 665	996	4 807	...	91	989	375	407
65 - 69	C	10 571	1 191	6 791	...	125	1 213	832	419
70 - 74	C	14 614	1 523	9 592	...	147	1 142	1 737	473
75 - 79	C	17 750	1 590	11 401	...	141	930	3 195	493
80 - 84	C	17 326	1 284	10 637	...	103	607	4 280	415
85 - 89	C	13 453	886	7 136	...	65	309	4 824	233
90+	C	8 899	619	3 366	...	23	150	4 590	151
Unk. - Inc. ...	C	1	-	-	...	-	-	-	1
Female									
Total	C	110 337	11 951	29 316	...	653	6 279	59 308	2 830
0 - 14	C	1 165	1 165	-	...	-	-	-	-
15 - 19	C	305	296	2	...	-	-	-	7
20 - 24	C	352	304	22	...	2	1	1	22
25 - 29	C	325	223	80	...	4	5	-	13
30 - 34	C	516	223	190	...	5	43	4	51
35 - 39	C	959	333	417	...	23	105	10	71
40 - 44	C	1 440	384	712	...	27	179	33	105
45 - 49	C	2 204	455	1 178	...	43	326	59	143
50 - 54	C	2 925	436	1 657	...	58	459	146	169
55 - 59	C	3 915	466	2 208	...	56	649	389	147
60 - 64	C	4 871	439	2 672	...	61	663	855	181
65 - 69	C	6 677	543	3 360	...	78	696	1 811	189
70 - 74	C	10 043	690	4 328	...	77	868	3 820	260
75 - 79	C	14 909	990	4 896	...	80	834	7 745	364
80 - 84	C	18 633	1 342	4 103	...	61	656	12 083	388
85 - 89	C	19 578	1 657	2 428	...	49	445	14 615	384
90+	C	21 518	2 005	1 063	...	29	350	17 737	334
Unk. - Inc. ...	C	2	-	-	...	-	-	-	2
Costa Rica									
1995									
Male									
15+	C	7 195	1 866	3 630	281	...	175	975	268
15 - 19	C	156	144	2	2	...	-	-	8
20 - 24	C	209	166	14	22	...	-	-	7
25 - 29	C	243	152	56	21	...	4	-	10
30 - 34	C	257	146	71	25	...	2	-	13
35 - 39	C	277	116	124	15	...	9	1	12
40 - 44	C	299	104	131	22	...	17	5	20
45 - 49	C	280	87	152	14	...	11	3	13
50 - 54	C	359	97	206	21	...	13	8	14
55 - 59	C	423	80	265	21	...	23	15	19
60 - 64	C	548	102	363	23	...	19	30	11
65 - 69	C	653	130	420	13	...	18	53	19
70 - 74	C	773	124	483	21	...	20	90	35
75 - 79	C	790	147	437	22	...	11	146	27

21. Deaths by marital status, age and sex: latest available year, 1994 - 2003
Décès selon l'état matrimonial, l'âge et le sexe: dernière année disponible, 1994 - 2003
(continued — suite)

Continent, country or area, date and age (in years) Continent, pays ou zone, date et âge (en annèes)	Code[1]	Total	Single (never married) - Célibataires	Married - Mariés	In consensual union - En union consensuelle	Married but separated - Mariés mais séparées	Divorced and not remarried - Divorcées non remariés	Widowed and not remarried - Veufs non remariés	Unknown - Inconnu
AMERICA, NORTH — AMERIQUE DU NORD									
Costa Rica									
1995									
Male									
80 - 84	C	766	115	419	24	...	12	183	13
85+	C	1 135	151	483	13	...	16	440	32
Unk. - Inc. ...	C	27	5	4	2	...	-	1	15
Female									
15+	C	5 386	1 254	1 825	164	...	129	1 908	106
15 - 19	C	72	61	5	4	...	-	-	2
20 - 24	C	64	37	16	9	...	2	-	-
25 - 29	C	67	31	25	8	...	2	1	-
30 - 34	C	111	38	52	12	...	2	5	2
35 - 39	C	115	29	61	14	...	5	1	5
40 - 44	C	157	43	88	16	...	3	3	4
45 - 49	C	177	48	102	12	...	8	4	3
50 - 54	C	213	52	122	14	...	9	12	4
55 - 59	C	297	60	177	17	...	14	25	4
60 - 64	C	341	76	188	10	...	14	48	5
65 - 69	C	470	94	235	14	...	7	112	8
70 - 74	C	604	105	264	12	...	22	188	13
75 - 79	C	666	141	199	10	...	16	290	10
80 - 84	C	790	155	163	5	...	13	441	13
85+	C	1 232	281	126	7	...	12	778	28
Unk. - Inc. ...	C	10	3	2	-	...	-	-	5
Cuba[4]									
1999									
Male									
15+	C	42 784	15 429	21 431	...	...	...	...	5 924
15 - 19	C	262	186	12	...	...	...	...	64
20 - 24	C	467	261	94	...	...	...	...	112
25 - 29	C	795	332	289	...	...	...	...	174
30 - 34	C	957	345	402	...	...	...	...	210
35 - 39	C	1 078	373	500	...	...	...	...	205
40 - 44	C	1 087	393	541	...	...	...	...	153
45 - 49	C	1 549	541	774	...	...	...	...	234
50 - 54	C	2 004	593	1 146	...	...	...	...	265
55 - 59	C	2 649	824	1 500	...	...	...	...	325
60 - 64	C	3 100	936	1 768	...	...	...	...	396
65 - 69	C	3 981	1 148	2 355	...	...	...	...	478
70 - 74	C	4 945	1 621	2 723	...	...	...	...	601
75 - 79	C	5 732	2 002	2 985	...	...	...	...	745
80 - 84	C	5 859	2 199	2 894	...	...	...	...	766
85+	C	8 311	3 674	3 446	...	...	...	...	1 191
Unk. - Inc. ...	C	8	1	2	...	...	...	...	5
Female									
15+	C	34 921	16 945	12 492	...	...	...	...	5 484
15 - 19	C	184	112	34	...	...	...	...	38
20 - 24	C	193	67	104	...	...	...	...	22
25 - 29	C	387	113	237	...	...	...	...	37
30 - 34	C	472	148	262	...	...	...	...	62
35 - 39	C	576	145	371	...	...	...	...	60
40 - 44	C	685	179	432	...	...	...	...	74
45 - 49	C	1 024	320	574	...	...	...	...	130
50 - 54	C	1 422	450	790	...	...	...	...	182
55 - 59	C	1 753	622	927	...	...	...	...	204
60 - 64	C	2 302	851	1 128	...	...	...	...	323
65 - 69	C	3 037	1 230	1 328	...	...	...	...	479
70 - 74	C	3 905	1 734	1 601	...	...	...	...	570
75 - 79	C	4 637	2 371	1 539	...	...	...	...	727

21. Deaths by marital status, age and sex: latest available year, 1994 - 2003
Décès selon l'état matrimonial, l'âge et le sexe: dernière année disponible, 1994 - 2003
(continued — suite)

Continent, country or area, date and age (in years) Continent, pays ou zone, date et âge (en années)	Code[1]	Total	Single (never married) - Célibataires	Married - Mariés	In consensual union - En union consensuelle	Married but separated - Mariés mais séparées	Divorced and not remarried - Divorcées non remariés	Widowed and not remarried - Veufs non remariés	Unknown - Inconnu
AMERICA, NORTH — AMERIQUE DU NORD									
Cuba[4]									
1999									
Female									
80 - 84	C	5 297	2 970	1 438	...	...	...	...	889
85+	C	9 045	5 633	1 727	...	...	...	...	1 685
Unk. - Inc. ...	C	2	-	-	...	...	...	...	2
El Salvador[5]									
1999									
Both sexes									
Total	C	25 283	15 099	6 952	604	...	229	2 166	233
0 - 14	C	120	120	-	-	...	-	-	-
15 - 19	C	847	814	12	16	...	-	-	5
20 - 24	C	1 230	1 104	65	45	...	1	3	12
25 - 29	C	1 184	946	171	48	...	4	3	12
30 - 34	C	1 099	830	192	61	...	7	4	5
35 - 39	C	1 086	774	247	43	...	6	6	10
40 - 44	C	1 032	677	278	32	...	15	16	14
45 - 49	C	1 276	777	380	64	...	16	22	17
50 - 54	C	1 258	711	435	50	...	21	27	14
55 - 59	C	1 528	846	541	49	...	24	51	17
60 - 64	C	1 692	932	592	44	...	19	84	21
65 - 69	C	2 085	1 093	766	36	...	30	135	25
70 - 74	C	2 257	1 170	795	37	...	33	210	12
75 - 79	C	2 490	1 252	850	24	...	18	324	22
80 - 84	C	2 276	1 137	715	21	...	13	365	25
85+	C	3 823	1 916	913	34	...	22	916	22
Greenland - Groenland[6]									
1996									
Male									
Total	C	256	89	95	...	...	20	38	14
0 - 14	C	20	9	-	...	...	-	-	11
15 - 19	C	12	12	-	...	...	-	-	-
20 - 24	C	14	13	1	...	...	-	-	-
25 - 29	C	13	12	1	...	...	-	-	-
30 - 34	C	11	7	2	...	...	1	-	1
35 - 39	C	10	7	2	...	...	1	-	-
40 - 44	C	14	10	1	...	...	3	-	-
45 - 49	C	4	2	2	...	...	-	-	-
50 - 54	C	19	1	13	...	...	3	2	-
55 - 59	C	22	4	11	...	...	6	1	-
60 - 64	C	30	8	16	...	...	3	2	1
65 - 69	C	27	-	18	...	...	1	8	-
70 - 74	C	20	2	9	...	...	-	8	1
75 - 79	C	24	2	11	...	...	1	10	-
80 - 84	C	10	-	5	...	...	-	5	-
85 - 89	C	3	-	-	...	...	1	2	-
90 - 94	C	1	-	1	...	...	-	-	-
95 - 99	C	2	-	2	...	...	-	-	-
100+	C	-	-	-	...	...	-	-	-
Guadeloupe									
2003									
Male									
Total	C	1 405	491	600	...	...	148	166	-
0 - 14	C	46	46	-	...	...	-	-	-
15 - 19	C	18	18	-	...	...	-	-	-
20 - 24	C	19	19	-	...	...	-	-	-
25 - 29	C	17	14	2	...	...	1	-	-
30 - 34	C	31	24	5	...	...	1	1	-

21. Deaths by marital status, age and sex: latest available year, 1994 - 2003
Décès selon l'état matrimonial, l'âge et le sexe: dernière année disponible, 1994 - 2003
(continued — suite)

Continent, country or area, date and age (in years) / Continent, pays ou zone, date et âge (en années)	Code[1]	Total	Single (never married) - Célibataires	Married - Mariés	In consensual union - En union consensuelle	Married but separated - Mariés mais séparées	Divorced and not remarried - Divorcées non remariés	Widowed and not remarried - Veufs non remariés	Unknown - Inconnu
AMERICA, NORTH — AMERIQUE DU NORD									
Guadeloupe									
2003									
Male									
35 - 39	C	40	32	7	...	...	1	-	-
40 - 44	C	47	33	10	...	...	4	-	-
45 - 49	C	71	42	23	...	...	5	1	-
50 - 54	C	87	34	35	...	...	17	1	-
55 - 59	C	85	30	38	...	...	16	1	-
60 - 64	C	96	24	55	...	...	15	2	-
65 - 69	C	126	43	61	...	...	16	6	-
70 - 74	C	141	33	75	...	...	23	10	-
75 - 79	C	180	34	112	...	...	15	19	-
80 - 84	C	185	37	97	...	...	17	34	-
85 - 89	C	124	17	57	...	...	10	40	-
90 - 94	C	65	10	19	...	...	4	32	-
95 - 99	C	19	-	3	...	...	2	14	-
100+	C	8	1	1	...	...	1	5	-
Female									
Total	C	1 231	371	297	...	...	71	492	-
0 - 14	C	29	29	-	...	...	-	-	-
15 - 19	C	3	3	-	...	...	-	-	-
20 - 24	C	4	4	-	...	...	-	-	-
25 - 29	C	6	4	2	...	...	-	-	-
30 - 34	C	8	5	3	...	...	-	-	-
35 - 39	C	20	12	6	...	...	2	-	-
40 - 44	C	29	11	13	...	...	4	1	-
45 - 49	C	31	14	11	...	...	5	1	-
50 - 54	C	25	8	12	...	...	4	1	-
55 - 59	C	43	12	21	...	...	9	1	-
60 - 64	C	81	23	37	...	...	9	12	-
65 - 69	C	87	25	41	...	...	6	15	-
70 - 74	C	116	38	43	...	...	3	32	-
75 - 79	C	136	35	36	...	...	11	54	-
80 - 84	C	171	36	37	...	...	8	90	-
85 - 89	C	205	49	21	...	...	7	128	-
90 - 94	C	140	40	11	...	...	2	87	-
95 - 99	C	77	18	3	...	...	1	55	-
100+	C	20	5	-	...	...	-	15	-
Guatemala									
1999									
Male									
Total	C	37 062	23 687	10 191	1 433	...	19	473	1 259
0 - 14	C	11 194	10 644	86	10	...	1	10	443
15 - 24	C	2 635	2 268	227	66	...	1	1	72
25 - 44	C	6 273	3 545	2 049	382	...	6	20	271
45 - 64	C	6 277	2 728	2 899	402	...	5	51	192
65+	C	10 526	4 448	4 912	570	...	6	391	199
Unk. - Inc. ...	C	157	54	18	3	...	-	-	82
Female									
Total	C	27 501	17 961	6 955	1 024	...	18	920	623
0 - 14	C	9 194	8 748	63	10	...	1	20	352
20 - 24	C	1 306	925	253	103	...	-	3	22
25 - 44	C	2 905	1 315	1 237	256	...	3	33	61
45 - 64	C	4 233	1 913	1 934	246	...	4	85	51
65+	C	9 801	5 027	3 460	407	...	10	775	122
Unk. - Inc. ...	C	62	33	8	2	...	-	4	15

21. Deaths by marital status, age and sex: latest available year, 1994 - 2003
Décès selon l'état matrimonial, l'âge et le sexe: dernière année disponible, 1994 - 2003
(continued — suite)

Continent, country or area, date and age (in years) / Continent, pays ou zone, date et âge (en années)	Code[1]	Total	Single (never married) - Célibataires	Married - Mariés	In consensual union - En union consensuelle	Married but separated - Mariés mais séparées	Divorced and not remarried - Divorcées non remariés	Widowed and not remarried - Veufs non remariés	Unknown - Inconnu
AMERICA, NORTH — AMERIQUE DU NORD									
Martinique[2]									
2003									
Male									
Total	C	1 421	451	613	...	....	126	231	-
0 - 14	C	24	24	-	...	....			-
15 - 19	C	16	16	-	...	....	-	-	-
20 - 24	C	14	14	-	...	...	-	-	-
25 - 29	C	16	15	1	...	...	-	-	-
30 - 34	C	29	27	1	...	...	-	1	-
35 - 39	C	27	19	8	...	...	-	-	-
40 - 44	C	36	23	10	...	...	2	1	-
45 - 49	C	50	28	16	...	...	6	-	-
50 - 54	C	55	26	21	...	...	8	-	-
55 - 59	C	58	17	22	...	...	18	1	-
60 - 64	C	84	35	36	...	...	11	2	-
65 - 69	C	118	26	68	...	...	18	6	-
70 - 74	C	156	44	85	...	...	14	13	-
75 - 79	C	213	53	110	...	...	18	32	-
80 - 84	C	221	42	113	...	...	14	52	-
85 - 89	C	178	27	88	...	...	7	56	-
90 - 94	C	85	10	26	...	...	8	41	-
95 - 99	C	35	4	8	...	...	2	21	-
100+	C	6	1	-	...	...	-	5	-
Female									
Total	C	1 304	420	291	...	...	84	509	-
0 - 14	C	28	28	-	...	...	-	-	-
15 - 19	C	4	4	-	...	...	-	-	-
20 - 24	C	6	6	-	...	...	-	-	-
25 - 29	C	5	5	-	...	...	-	-	-
30 - 34	C	11	8	2	...	...	1	-	-
35 - 39	C	15	8	6	...	...	1	-	-
40 - 44	C	17	14	2	...	...	1	-	-
45 - 49	C	31	13	10	...	...	7	1	-
50 - 54	C	36	13	18	...	...	5	-	-
55 - 59	C	39	16	13	...	...	8	2	-
60 - 64	C	53	13	28	...	...	4	8	-
65 - 69	C	71	12	36	...	...	11	12	-
70 - 74	C	111	25	48	...	...	7	31	-
75 - 79	C	147	38	45	...	...	12	52	-
80 - 84	C	218	72	43	...	...	9	94	-
85 - 89	C	208	57	24	...	...	10	117	-
90 - 94	C	188	51	14	...	...	4	119	-
95 - 99	C	94	33	2	...	...	3	56	-
100+	C	22	4	-	...	...	1	17	-
Mexico - Mexique[7]									
2003									
Male									
Total	C	261 680	43 814	124 552	18 704	4 225	3 068	36 239	25 204
0 - 14	C	26 745	1 407	4	1	-	-	2	25 204
15 - 19	C	5 023	4 554	130	221	6	1	5	-
20 - 24	C	6 959	4 733	1 132	873	36	15	8	-
25 - 29	C	8 234	4 038	2 521	1 227	83	59	27	-
30 - 34	C	8 946	3 519	3 467	1 287	168	91	44	-
35 - 39	C	9 770	3 380	4 262	1 216	258	147	78	-
40 - 44	C	10 940	2 912	5 538	1 323	376	239	157	-
45 - 49	C	12 585	2 722	7 112	1 414	435	309	255	-
50 - 54	C	13 947	2 249	8 730	1 367	427	315	498	-
55 - 59	C	16 219	2 093	10 774	1 447	424	348	838	-

21. Deaths by marital status, age and sex: latest available year, 1994 - 2003
Décès selon l'état matrimonial, l'âge et le sexe: dernière année disponible, 1994 - 2003
(continued — suite)

Continent, country or area, date and age (in years) / Continent, pays ou zone, date et âge (en années)	Code[1]	Total	Single (never married) - Célibataires	Married - Mariés	In consensual union - En union consensuelle	Married but separated - Mariés mais séparées	Divorced and not remarried - Divorcées non remariés	Widowed and not remarried - Veufs non remariés	Unknown - Inconnu
AMERICA, NORTH — AMERIQUE DU NORD									
Mexico - Mexique[7]									
2003									
Male									
60 - 64	C	18 700	2 090	12 588	1 498	406	336	1 423	-
65 - 69	C	21 496	2 129	14 383	1 442	390	301	2 516	-
70 - 74	C	23 919	2 162	15 132	1 558	383	278	4 045	-
75 - 79	C	23 572	1 991	14 020	1 303	299	250	5 415	-
80 - 84	C	21 851	1 663	11 762	1 132	252	168	6 572	-
85 - 89	C	15 193	1 020	7 213	663	139	111	5 864	-
90 - 94	C	10 414	580	3 982	439	86	66	5 142	-
95 - 99	C	4 110	254	1 257	153	21	17	2 362	-
100+	C	1 493	92	386	69	8	8	900	-
Unk. - Inc. ...	C	1 564	226	159	71	28	9	88	-
Female									
Total	C	210 096	26 517	65 568	11 521	3 702	2 589	78 641	19 168
0 - 14	C	20 141	849	7	7	-	-	3	19 168
15 - 19	C	2 304	1 842	149	249	7	1	6	-
20 - 24	C	2 597	1 451	614	413	35	14	18	-
25 - 29	C	2 929	1 072	1 168	494	62	27	44	-
30 - 34	C	3 449	953	1 621	596	94	50	80	-
35 - 39	C	4 139	970	2 113	640	127	75	151	-
40 - 44	C	5 571	1 028	3 060	800	208	136	264	-
45 - 49	C	7 213	1 107	4 198	814	279	185	544	-
50 - 54	C	9 467	1 272	5 510	878	335	237	1 110	-
55 - 59	C	11 714	1 322	6 791	930	358	280	1 914	-
60 - 64	C	14 930	1 602	7 991	1 066	450	259	3 405	-
65 - 69	C	18 021	1 799	8 614	958	437	258	5 789	-
70 - 74	C	20 963	2 119	8 154	967	461	293	8 787	-
75 - 79	C	22 165	2 272	6 528	823	311	267	11 728	-
80 - 84	C	22 312	2 389	4 560	762	242	210	13 906	-
85 - 89	C	18 248	1 953	2 522	509	164	145	12 779	-
90 - 94	C	14 225	1 466	1 247	332	90	102	10 829	-
95 - 99	C	6 595	702	446	166	26	31	5 135	-
100+	C	2 548	265	159	82	10	16	1 968	-
Unk. - Inc. ...	C	565	84	116	35	6	3	181	-
Nicaragua									
2003									
Male									
15+	+U	6 723	1 799	2 689	1 506	...	75	622	32
15 - 19	+U	267	234	3	25	...	-	1	4
20 - 24	+U	347	239	24	84	...	-	-	-
25 - 29	+U	297	156	44	86	...	3	2	6
30 - 34	+U	286	110	78	94	...	-	1	3
35 - 39	+U	311	113	83	106	...	3	2	4
40 - 44	+U	367	108	141	107	...	1	6	4
45 - 49	+U	430	115	178	128	...	2	3	4
50 - 54	+U	407	87	180	118	...	12	7	3
55 - 59	+U	445	93	220	107	...	11	14	-
60 - 64	+U	441	71	218	115	...	10	27	-
65 - 69	+U	484	85	254	103	...	7	34	1
70 - 74	+U	623	112	317	125	...	8	60	1
75 - 79	+U	640	101	323	109	...	5	100	2
80 - 84	+U	540	88	241	86	...	8	117	-
85 - 89	+U	445	48	223	61	...	3	110	-
90 - 94	+U	233	20	102	35	...	-	76	-
95+	+U	160	19	60	17	...	2	62	-
Female									
15+	+U	5 160	1 352	1 544	860	...	68	1 328	8

21. Deaths by marital status, age and sex: latest available year, 1994 - 2003
Décès selon l'état matrimonial, l'âge et le sexe: dernière année disponible, 1994 - 2003
(continued — suite)

Continent, country or area, date and age (in years) / Continent, pays ou zone, date et âge (en années)	Code[1]	Total	Single (never married) - Célibataires	Married - Mariés	In consensual union - En union consensuelle	Married but separated - Mariés mais séparées	Divorced and not remarried - Divorcées non remariés	Widowed and not remarried - Veufs non remariés	Unknown - Inconnu
AMERICA, NORTH — AMERIQUE DU NORD									
Nicaragua									
2003									
Female									
15 - 19	+U	132	88	5	36	...	1	-	2
20 - 24	+U	141	69	22	50	...	-	-	-
25 - 29	+U	123	44	26	49	...	1	3	-
30 - 34	+U	119	47	31	40	...	1	-	-
35 - 39	+U	174	60	68	41	...	2	3	-
40 - 44	+U	164	46	63	49	...	-	6	-
45 - 49	+U	250	69	101	61	...	3	16	-
50 - 54	+U	253	64	117	44	...	1	27	-
55 - 59	+U	310	81	116	67	...	8	38	-
60 - 64	+U	375	83	142	72	...	6	71	1
65 - 69	+U	421	86	155	74	...	7	98	1
70 - 74	+U	517	106	192	79	...	4	136	-
75 - 79	+U	546	123	164	54	...	7	197	1
80 - 84	+U	573	127	142	54	...	7	242	1
85 - 89	+U	472	111	94	51	...	13	202	1
90 - 94	+U	337	85	58	24	...	5	165	-
95+	+U	253	63	48	15	...	2	124	1
Panama[8]									
1999									
Male									
15+	U	6 116	1 889	1 939	963	...	73	431	821
15 - 19	U	154	125	1	9	...	-	-	19
20 - 24	U	224	152	6	46	...	-	-	20
25 - 29	U	246	132	22	62	...	1	1	28
30 - 34	U	261	123	33	71	...	4	-	30
35 - 39	U	222	97	51	46	...	3	-	25
40 - 44	U	260	108	64	54	...	5	3	26
45 - 49	U	272	102	88	47	...	5	2	28
50 - 54	U	329	98	115	54	...	5	7	50
55 - 59	U	322	82	123	69	...	10	3	35
60 - 64	U	405	110	152	61	...	12	7	63
65 - 69	U	489	113	183	99	...	4	25	65
70 - 74	U	594	148	236	76	...	5	45	84
75 - 79	U	693	153	284	91	...	5	62	98
80 - 84	U	704	162	287	80	...	5	98	72
85+	U	888	172	293	93	...	9	176	145
Unk. - Inc. ...	U	53	12	1	5	...	-	2	33
Female									
15+	U	4 298	1 056	1 281	582	...	79	822	478
15 - 19	U	68	46	1	17	...	-	-	4
20 - 24	U	78	32	8	32	...	-	-	6
25 - 29	U	86	24	24	30	...	1	1	6
30 - 34	U	108	29	18	46	...	1	1	13
35 - 39	U	107	31	31	33	...	-	1	11
40 - 44	U	136	33	54	30	...	6	2	11
45 - 49	U	139	32	57	30	...	3	6	11
50 - 54	U	167	41	70	35	...	4	2	15
55 - 59	U	192	42	80	36	...	7	8	19
60 - 64	U	258	65	103	44	...	7	19	20
65 - 69	U	328	69	110	54	...	9	45	41
70 - 74	U	418	101	143	48	...	7	67	52
75 - 79	U	562	129	176	49	...	15	129	64
80 - 84	U	620	145	180	45	...	8	164	78
85+	U	990	232	225	48	...	11	374	100
Unk. - Inc. ...	U	41	5	1	5	...	-	3	27

21. Deaths by marital status, age and sex: latest available year, 1994 - 2003
Décès selon l'état matrimonial, l'âge et le sexe: dernière année disponible, 1994 - 2003
(continued — suite)

Continent, country or area, date and age (in years) / Continent, pays ou zone, date et âge (en années)	Code[1]	Total	Single (never married) - Célibataires	Married - Mariés	In consensual union - En union consensuelle	Married but separated - Mariés mais séparées	Divorced and not remarried - Divorcées non remariés	Widowed and not remarried - Veufs non remariés	Unknown - Inconnu
AMERICA, NORTH — AMERIQUE DU NORD									
Puerto Rico - Porto Rico									
2003									
Male									
Total	C	15 758	3 984	7 391	...	...	1 741	2 612	30
0 - 14	C	357	357	-	...	...	-	-	-
15 - 19	C	161	157	2	...	...	1	-	1
20 - 24	C	359	315	40	...	...	4	-	-
25 - 29	C	345	269	64	...	...	12	-	-
30 - 34	C	304	178	88	...	...	34	2	2
35 - 39	C	382	223	95	...	...	61	3	-
40 - 44	C	453	240	124	...	...	81	8	-
45 - 49	C	580	233	210	...	...	127	10	-
50 - 54	C	781	255	353	...	...	146	26	1
55 - 59	C	1 035	260	532	...	...	205	37	1
60 - 64	C	1 206	272	660	...	...	204	68	2
65 - 69	C	1 410	243	839	...	...	217	109	2
70 - 74	C	1 589	250	978	...	...	175	183	3
75 - 79	C	1 894	238	1 124	...	...	182	349	1
80 - 84	C	1 956	216	1 055	...	...	138	546	1
85+	C	2 924	269	1 227	...	...	154	1 271	3
Unk. - Inc. ...	C	22	9	-	...	...	-	-	13
Female									
Total	C	12 598	1 874	3 315	...	...	1 319	6 079	11
0 - 14	C	263	263	-	...	...	-	-	-
15 - 19	C	40	39	1	...	...	-	-	-
20 - 24	C	60	49	10	...	...	1	-	-
25 - 29	C	69	40	24	...	...	5	-	-
30 - 34	C	100	45	36	...	...	15	4	-
35 - 39	C	144	61	53	...	...	25	5	-
40 - 44	C	208	59	84	...	...	51	14	-
45 - 49	C	318	82	151	...	...	59	25	1
50 - 54	C	440	103	216	...	...	87	34	-
55 - 59	C	592	104	291	...	...	118	79	-
60 - 64	C	800	107	390	...	...	136	167	-
65 - 69	C	901	118	377	...	...	113	291	2
70 - 74	C	1 280	128	462	...	...	160	530	-
75 - 79	C	1 556	131	517	...	...	150	757	1
80 - 84	C	1 926	205	356	...	...	147	1 217	1
85+	C	3 898	340	347	...	...	252	2 956	3
Unk. - Inc. ...	C	3	-	-	...	...	-	-	3
United States - États-Unis									
1999									
Male									
15+	C	1 152 070	139 330	650 342	...	...	133 019	222 545	6 834
15 - 24	C	22 414	20 694	1 431	...	...	191	36	62
25 - 34	C	28 276	16 591	8 445	...	...	2 861	149	230
35 - 44	C	57 118	21 589	21 928	...	...	12 295	583	723
45 - 54	C	95 659	18 740	48 137	...	...	25 565	2 021	1 196
55 - 64	C	142 724	14 690	88 588	...	...	30 737	7 324	1 385
65 - 74	C	254 920	18 649	169 815	...	...	32 591	32 373	1 492
75+	C	550 959	28 377	311 998	...	...	28 779	180 059	1 746
Female									
15+	C	1 198 192	94 837	297 639	...	...	111 720	691 367	2 629
15 - 24	C	8 242	7 134	909	...	...	154	34	11
25 - 34	C	12 790	5 800	5 057	...	...	1 702	173	58
35 - 44	C	32 138	8 471	15 296	...	...	7 124	1 078	169
45 - 54	C	57 315	8 256	30 328	...	...	14 177	4 318	236

21. Deaths by marital status, age and sex: latest available year, 1994 - 2003
Décès selon l'état matrimonial, l'âge et le sexe: dernière année disponible, 1994 - 2003
(continued — suite)

Continent, country or area, date and age (in years) Continent, pays ou zone, date et âge (en années)	Code[1]	Total	Single (never married) - Célibataires	Married - Mariés	In consensual union - En union consensuelle	Married but separated - Mariés mais séparées	Divorced and not remarried - Divorcées non remariés	Widowed and not remarried - Veufs non remariés	Unknown - Inconnu
AMERICA, NORTH — AMERIQUE DU NORD									
United States - États-Unis									
1999									
Female									
55 - 64	C	96 255	7 669	49 790	...	...	20 089	18 396	311
65 - 74	C	197 680	10 748	81 217	...	...	25 920	79 314	481
75+	C	793 772	46 759	115 042	...	...	42 554	588 054	1 363
AMERICA, SOUTH — AMERIQUE DU SUD									
Brazil - Brésil[9]									
2003									
Male									
Total	U	572 622	224 420	251 385	...	15 667	7 647	63 513	9 990
0 - 14	U	36 333	36 329	4	...	-	-	-	-
15 - 19	U	14 583	14 300	101	...	14	2	12	154
20 - 24	U	22 444	21 157	902	...	38	8	27	312
25 - 29	U	20 344	17 059	2 618	...	151	41	46	429
30 - 34	U	20 264	14 538	4 644	...	351	157	83	491
35 - 39	U	23 023	13 940	7 323	...	707	326	171	556
40 - 44	U	26 945	13 124	10 942	...	1 311	611	322	635
45 - 49	U	31 664	11 738	15 907	...	1 895	819	713	592
50 - 54	U	35 257	10 527	19 932	...	2 082	988	1 156	572
55 - 59	U	38 610	9 665	23 411	...	2 085	1 027	1 890	532
60 - 64	U	44 591	10 224	27 559	...	1 942	1 003	3 324	539
65 - 69	U	50 282	10 425	31 334	...	1 684	934	5 413	492
70 - 74	U	55 595	11 084	33 668	...	1 417	766	8 195	465
75 - 79	U	54 575	10 071	31 617	...	982	476	11 043	386
80 - 84	U	43 768	8 544	22 334	...	588	280	11 755	267
85 - 89	U	30 252	6 416	12 839	...	275	140	10 403	179
90 - 94	U	15 082	3 425	4 942	...	118	54	6 459	84
95 - 99	U	5 020	1 469	1 185	...	26	15	2 118	207
100+	U	733	221	112	...	1	-	381	18
Unk. - Inc. ...	U	3 257	164	11	...	-	-	2	3 080
Female									
Total	U	405 095	143 645	104 554	...	7 575	3 920	141 849	3 552
0 - 14	U	27 133	27 130	3	...	-	-	-	-
15 - 19	U	4 091	3 897	140	...	4	-	9	41
20 - 24	U	5 008	4 229	651	...	19	6	38	65
25 - 29	U	5 822	4 412	1 214	...	56	32	46	62
30 - 34	U	6 994	4 465	2 069	...	136	83	136	105
35 - 39	U	9 451	4 955	3 530	...	354	179	307	126
40 - 44	U	12 917	5 689	5 557	...	578	291	665	137
45 - 49	U	16 702	6 076	7 809	...	851	420	1 375	171
50 - 54	U	19 671	6 151	9 752	...	870	434	2 279	185
55 - 59	U	23 282	6 710	11 196	...	889	456	3 846	185
60 - 64	U	28 431	7 473	12 634	...	892	497	6 750	185
65 - 69	U	35 237	8 733	13 634	...	846	463	11 325	236
70 - 74	U	42 831	10 174	13 446	...	778	419	17 732	282
75 - 79	U	47 661	11 191	11 188	...	561	303	24 123	295
80 - 84	U	45 451	11 271	6 739	...	376	213	26 598	254
85 - 89	U	39 354	10 354	3 469	...	235	92	24 966	238
90 - 94	U	23 358	6 661	1 187	...	100	23	15 241	146
95 - 99	U	9 292	3 447	296	...	27	9	5 427	86
100+	U	1 624	592	36	...	3	-	977	16
Unk. - Inc. ...	U	785	35	4	...	-	-	9	737

21. Deaths by marital status, age and sex: latest available year, 1994 - 2003
Décès selon l'état matrimonial, l'âge et le sexe: dernière année disponible, 1994 - 2003
(continued — suite)

Continent, country or area, date and age (in years) / Continent, pays ou zone, date et âge (en années)	Code[1]	Total	Single (never married) - Célibataires	Married - Mariés	In consensual union - En union consensuelle	Married but separated - Mariés mais séparées	Divorced and not remarried - Divorcées non remariés	Widowed and not remarried - Veufs non remariés	Unknown - Inconnu
AMERICA, SOUTH — AMERIQUE DU SUD									
Chile - Chili									
2003									
Male									
12+	C	43 992	27 760	15 813	...	...	...	419	-
12 - 14	C	141	141	-	...	...	...	-	-
15 - 19	C	460	458	2	...	...	...	-	-
20 - 24	C	790	742	48	...	...	...	-	-
25 - 29	C	827	649	177	...	...	...	1	-
30 - 34	C	981	631	346	...	...	...	4	"
35 - 39	C	1 223	700	520	...	...	...	3	-
40 - 44	C	1 489	743	732	...	...	...	14	-
45 - 49	C	1 833	940	885	...	...	...	8	-
50 - 54	C	2 287	1 439	839	...	...	...	9	-
55 - 59	C	3 038	2 132	889	...	...	...	17	-
60 - 64	C	3 783	2 703	1 051	...	...	...	29	-
65+	C	27 140	16 482	10 324	...	...	...	334	-
Female									
12+	C	37 000	21 388	14 692	...	...	...	920	-
12 - 14	C	78	78	-	...	...	...	-	-
15 - 19	C	156	154	2	...	...	...	-	-
20 - 24	C	209	181	26	...	...	...	2	-
25 - 29	C	224	157	63	...	...	...	4	-
30 - 34	C	319	149	166	...	...	...	4	-
35 - 39	C	467	192	266	...	...	...	9	-
40 - 44	C	744	303	431	...	...	...	10	-
45 - 49	C	1 012	626	376	...	...	...	10	-
50 - 54	C	1 344	943	382	...	...	...	19	-
55 - 59	C	1 774	1 369	383	...	...	...	22	-
60 - 64	C	2 394	1 848	514	...	...	...	32	-
65+	C	28 279	15 388	12 083	...	...	...	808	-
Colombia - Colombie[8]									
2003									
Male									
Total	U	111 366	31 184	36 100	15 200	...	2 476	9 835	16 571
0 - 14	U	9 970	9 807	2	1	...	1	3	156
15 - 19	U	4 142	3 061	32	230	...	5	10	804
20 - 24	U	7 219	3 913	212	1 291	...	29	16	1 758
25 - 29	U	6 132	2 322	483	1 614	...	45	13	1 655
30 - 34	U	5 421	1 569	884	1 570	...	73	20	1 305
35 - 39	U	5 061	1 213	1 212	1 413	...	77	20	1 126
40 - 44	U	4 651	1 096	1 339	1 178	...	162	43	833
45 - 49	U	4 540	992	1 594	972	...	183	54	745
50 - 54	U	4 797	855	1 996	889	...	218	98	741
55 - 59	U	5 073	722	2 427	888	...	232	146	658
60 - 64	U	6 396	851	3 223	949	...	267	280	826
65 - 69	U	7 863	942	4 107	983	...	295	592	944
70 - 74	U	9 971	1 128	5 186	986	...	281	1 225	1 165
75 - 79	U	9 830	1 017	4 947	878	...	268	1 622	1 098
80 - 84	U	8 683	820	4 110	646	...	173	2 010	924
85 - 89	U	6 161	464	2 657	404	...	105	1 908	623
90 - 94	U	3 011	211	1 152	171	...	33	1 190	254
95 - 99	U	714	38	243	30	...	12	327	64
100+	U	371	29	103	18	...	2	188	31
Unk. - Inc. ...	U	1 360	134	191	89	...	15	70	861
Female									
Total	U	77 652	19 653	18 329	6 394	...	2 211	24 078	6 987
0 - 14	U	7 631	7 505	1	9	...	-	1	115
15 - 19	U	1 243	863	17	162	...	6	6	189

21. Deaths by marital status, age and sex: latest available year, 1994 - 2003
Décès selon l'état matrimonial, l'âge et le sexe: dernière année disponible, 1994 - 2003
(continued — suite)

Continent, country or area, date and age (in years) Continent, pays ou zone, date et âge (en annèes)	Code[1]	Total	Single (never married) - Célibataires	Married - Mariés	In consensual union - En union consensuelle	Married but separated - Mariés mais séparées	Divorced and not remarried - Divorcées non remariés	Widowed and not remarried - Veufs non remariés	Unknown - Inconnu
AMERICA, SOUTH — AMERIQUE DU SUD									
Colombia - Colombie[8]									
2003									
Female									
20 - 24	U	1 395	672	114	350	...	13	10	236
25 - 29	U	1 320	468	214	361	...	24	18	235
30 - 34	U	1 397	372	345	417	...	46	31	186
35 - 39	U	1 688	406	504	434	...	76	55	213
40 - 44	U	2 190	497	718	516	...	118	90	251
45 - 49	U	2 667	475	957	601	...	191	182	261
50 - 54	U	3 204	549	1 252	553	...	220	280	350
55 - 59	U	3 706	626	1 520	477	...	235	459	389
60 - 64	U	5 038	772	2 038	481	...	280	978	489
65 - 69	U	6 351	892	2 304	487	...	261	1 764	643
70 - 74	U	8 463	1 119	2 753	486	...	267	3 045	793
75 - 79	U	8 753	1 217	2 173	370	...	189	4 025	779
80 - 84	U	9 079	1 285	1 677	312	...	143	4 900	762
85 - 89	U	7 136	1 018	1 053	185	...	82	4 232	566
90 - 94	U	4 049	568	419	109	...	35	2 652	266
95 - 99	U	1 063	166	101	22	...	10	705	59
100+	U	723	103	64	12	...	7	501	36
Unk. - Inc. ...	U	556	80	105	50	...	8	144	169
Ecuador - Équateur[10]									
2003									
Male									
12+	U	26 673	8 625	11 628	2 153	...	470	3 173	624
12 - 14	U	285	268	-	-	...	-	-	17
15 - 19	U	807	746	19	22	...	-	1	19
20 - 24	U	1 285	985	149	122	...	6	1	22
25 - 29	U	1 221	736	268	169	...	10	7	31
30 - 34	U	1 135	544	354	193	...	13	10	21
35 - 39	U	1 119	488	441	145	...	12	10	23
40 - 44	U	1 285	473	594	141	...	20	21	36
45 - 49	U	1 361	463	632	166	...	44	29	27
50 - 54	U	1 485	410	818	132	...	34	55	36
55 - 59	U	1 576	441	848	144	...	42	68	33
60 - 64	U	1 760	454	988	127	...	43	117	31
65 - 69	U	2 036	502	1 144	144	...	44	164	38
70 - 74	U	2 437	499	1 332	201	...	48	306	51
75 - 79	U	2 557	520	1 349	140	...	61	433	54
80 - 84	U	2 368	445	1 171	114	...	38	532	68
85+	U	3 919	643	1 516	192	...	55	1 410	103
Unk. - Inc. ...	U	37	8	5	1	...	-	9	14
Female									
12+	U	20 185	5 798	6 107	1 362	...	466	5 970	482
12 - 14	U	201	176	4	-	...	-	-	21
15 - 19	U	475	375	34	55	...	4	1	6
20 - 24	U	450	252	102	75	...	6	7	8
25 - 29	U	454	191	161	90	...	1	3	8
30 - 34	U	466	186	183	76	...	7	6	8
35 - 39	U	515	170	225	74	...	19	11	16
40 - 44	U	693	215	332	81	...	23	28	14
45 - 49	U	823	245	393	98	...	32	40	15
50 - 54	U	918	248	448	95	...	38	63	26
55 - 59	U	1 092	267	543	99	...	41	126	16
60 - 64	U	1 222	336	527	122	...	45	170	22
65 - 69	U	1 489	365	666	89	...	42	294	33
70 - 74	U	1 889	487	683	103	...	46	530	40

21. Deaths by marital status, age and sex: latest available year, 1994 - 2003
Décès selon l'état matrimonial, l'âge et le sexe: dernière année disponible, 1994 - 2003
(continued — suite)

Continent, country or area, date and age (in years) — Continent, pays ou zone, date et âge (en années)	Code[1]	Total	Single (never married) - Célibataires	Married - Mariés	In consensual union - En union consensuelle	Married but separated - Mariés mais séparées	Divorced and not remarried - Divorcées non remariés	Widowed and not remarried - Veufs non remariés	Unknown - Inconnu
AMERICA, SOUTH — AMERIQUE DU SUD									
Ecuador - Équateur[10]									
2003									
Female									
75 - 79	U	2 098	503	644	86	...	37	780	48
80 - 84	U	2 305	546	553	78	...	50	1 018	60
85+	U	5 075	1 234	603	141	...	75	2 888	134
Unk. - Inc. ...	U	20	2	6	-	...	-	5	7
French Guiana - Guyane française[2]									
2003									
Male									
Total	C	435	278	124	...	...	13	20	-
0 - 14	C	48	48	-	...	...	-	-	-
15 - 19	C	10	10	-	...	...	-	-	-
20 - 24	C	11	9	1	...	...	-	1	-
25 - 29	C	25	24	1	...	...	-	-	-
30 - 34	C	18	17	1	...	...	-	-	-
35 - 39	C	28	25	2	...	...	1	-	-
40 - 44	C	24	15	9	...	...	-	-	-
45 - 49	C	26	18	7	...	...	1	-	-
50 - 54	C	33	20	10	...	...	3	-	-
55 - 59	C	25	14	7	...	...	3	1	-
60 - 64	C	29	11	17	...	...	1	-	-
65 - 69	C	28	14	11	...	...	1	2	-
70 - 74	C	36	14	18	...	...	2	2	-
75 - 79	C	37	16	17	...	...	1	3	-
80 - 84	C	19	9	8	...	...	-	2	-
85 - 89	C	24	7	13	...	...	-	4	-
90 - 94	C	8	5	1	...	...	-	2	-
95 - 99	C	4	1	1	...	...	-	2	-
100+	C	2	1	-	...	...	-	1	-
Female									
Total	C	257	146	41	...	...	15	55	-
0 - 14	C	36	36	-	...	...	-	-	-
15 - 19	C	5	5	-	...	...	-	-	-
20 - 24	C	6	5	1	...	...	-	-	-
25 - 29	C	6	4	1	...	...	-	1	-
30 - 34	C	8	6	2	...	...	-	-	-
35 - 39	C	10	9	-	...	...	1	-	-
40 - 44	C	10	6	2	...	...	2	-	-
45 - 49	C	12	6	4	...	...	2	-	-
50 - 54	C	11	6	3	...	...	1	1	-
55 - 59	C	11	7	2	...	...	2	-	-
60 - 64	C	16	7	6	...	...	2	1	-
65 - 69	C	15	5	5	...	...	1	4	-
70 - 74	C	11	5	2	...	...	1	3	-
75 - 79	C	13	8	2	...	...	1	2	-
80 - 84	C	30	10	5	...	...	1	14	-
85 - 89	C	29	9	4	...	...	-	16	-
90 - 94	C	15	7	1	...	...	-	7	-
95 - 99	C	11	4	1	...	...	1	5	-
100+	C	2	1	-	...	...	-	1	-
Suriname									
1996									
Both sexes									
Total	C	2 894	1 598	884	...	...	82	330	-
0 - 14	C	555	555	-	...	...	-	-	-

21. Deaths by marital status, age and sex: latest available year, 1994 - 2003
Décès selon l'état matrimonial, l'âge et le sexe: dernière année disponible, 1994 - 2003
(continued — suite)

Continent, country or area, date and age (in years) / Continent, pays ou zone, date et âge (en annèes)	Code[1]	Total	Single (never married) - Célibataires	Married - Mariés	In consensual union - En union consensuelle	Married but separated - Mariés mais séparées	Divorced and not remarried - Divorcées non remariés	Widowed and not remarried - Veufs non remariés	Unknown - Inconnu
AMERICA, SOUTH — AMERIQUE DU SUD									
Suriname									
1996									
Both sexes									
15 - 19	C	45	44	1	...	...	-	-	-
20 - 24	C	77	71	4	...	...	-	2	-
25 - 29	C	80	66	12	...	...	2	-	-
30 - 34	C	102	80	17	...	...	-	5	-
35 - 39	C	92	48	38	...	...	4	2	-
40 - 44	C	87	57	25	...	...	4	1	-
45 - 49	C	119	47	61	...	...	5	6	-
50 - 54	C	120	48	56	...	...	6	10	-
55 - 59	C	197	76	98	...	...	7	16	-
60 - 64	C	244	72	126	...	...	10	36	-
65 - 69	C	261	77	118	...	...	14	52	-
70 - 74	C	239	81	110	...	...	13	35	-
75 - 79	C	221	92	90	...	...	5	34	-
80 - 84	C	201	83	62	...	...	6	50	-
85 - 89	C	139	59	37	...	...	3	40	-
90 - 94	C	72	23	22	...	...	2	25	-
95 - 99	C	32	14	5	...	...	1	12	-
100+	C	11	5	2	...	...	-	4	-
2002									
Both sexes									
Total	C	3 125	1 454	1 179	...	...	156	336	-
Uruguay									
2000									
Male									
Total	C	16 407	3 877	8 530	1 016	2 505	385	6	88
0 - 14	C	579	579	-	-	-	-	-	-
15 - 19	C	118	117	1	-	-	-	-	-
20 - 24	C	213	198	12	-	-	3	-	-
25 - 29	C	172	125	38	6	-	3	-	-
30 - 34	C	182	98	65	10	1	8	-	-
35 - 39	C	252	102	121	19	2	8	-	-
40 - 44	C	289	92	149	35	1	11	1	-
45 - 49	C	491	145	265	55	13	13	-	-
50 - 54	C	731	205	388	92	27	17	2	-
55 - 59	C	1 031	243	615	105	34	32	2	-
60 - 64	C	1 396	321	803	150	80	42	-	-
65 - 69	C	1 967	366	1 209	154	178	59	-	1
70 - 74	C	2 293	393	1 401	151	297	51	-	-
75 - 79	C	2 316	354	1 390	107	411	54	-	-
80 - 84	C	1 950	264	1 066	74	502	43	1	-
85+	C	2 340	275	1 007	58	959	41	-	-
Unk. - Inc. ...	C	87	-	-	-	-	-	-	87
Female									
Total	C	14 043	2 600	3 167	744	7 265	231	5	31
0 - 14	C	398	398	-	-	-	-	-	-
15 - 19	C	52	50	2	-	-	-	-	-
20 - 24	C	62	50	11	-	-	1	-	-
25 - 29	C	67	32	25	3	3	3	1	-
30 - 34	C	84	30	46	6	1	1	-	-
35 - 39	C	116	44	64	4	3	1	-	-
40 - 44	C	218	53	122	30	7	6	-	-
45 - 49	C	275	61	168	29	13	4	-	-
50 - 54	C	374	67	206	58	38	4	1	-
55 - 59	C	512	85	271	62	86	7	1	-
60 - 64	C	664	120	316	66	147	15	-	-
65 - 69	+U	1 056	140	428	91	377	20	-	-

21. Deaths by marital status, age and sex: latest available year, 1994 - 2003
Décès selon l'état matrimonial, l'âge et le sexe: dernière année disponible, 1994 - 2003
(continued — suite)

Continent, country or area, date and age (in years) Continent, pays ou zone, date et âge (en années)	Code[1]	Total	Single (never married) - Célibataires	Married - Mariés	In consensual union - En union consensuelle	Married but separated - Mariés mais séparées	Divorced and not remarried - Divorcées non remariés	Widowed and not remarried - Veufs non remariés	Unknown - Inconnu
AMERICA, SOUTH — AMERIQUE DU SUD									
Uruguay									
2000									
Female									
70 - 74	C	1 457	200	473	95	666	23	-	-
75 - 79	C	1 965	274	470	117	1 078	25	1	-
80 - 84	C	2 235	309	327	86	1 478	34	1	-
85+	C	4 477	687	238	97	3 368	87	-	-
Unk. - Inc. ...	C	31	-	-	-	-	-	-	31
Venezuela[9]									
2002									
Male									
12+	C	58 726	37 098	17 240	513	82	1 067	2 726	-
12 - 14	C	453	448	3	-	-	1	1	-
15 - 19	C	2 929	2 894	20	3	2	5	5	-
20 - 24	C	4 579	4 362	159	29	7	5	17	-
25 - 29	C	3 578	3 128	360	54	9	10	17	-
30 - 34	C	3 002	2 454	465	42	9	17	15	-
35 - 39	C	2 586	1 958	548	31	5	30	14	-
40 - 44	C	2 795	1 962	702	41	7	63	20	-
45 - 49	C	3 164	2 034	968	41	3	89	29	-
50 - 54	C	3 549	2 145	1 214	26	8	106	50	-
55 - 60	C	3 719	2 116	1 345	16	6	122	84	-
60 - 64	C	4 032	2 144	1 602	45	4	126	111	-
65 - 69	C	4 746	2 434	1 950	29	6	144	183	-
70 - 74	C	5 339	2 577	2 279	35	4	128	316	-
75 - 79	C	5 076	2 328	2 150	32	6	97	463	-
80 - 84	C	4 164	1 887	1 703	24	2	60	488	-
85 - 89	C	2 793	1 133	1 120	21	2	42	475	-
90 - 94	C	1 463	647	480	9	2	12	313	-
95 - 99	C	420	198	117	1	-	8	96	-
100+	C	133	72	31	1	-	-	29	-
Unk. - Inc. ...	C	206	177	24	3	-	2	-	-
Female									
12+	C	35 904	20 126	8 888	297	126	876	5 591	-
12 - 14	C	261	257	3	-	-	1	-	-
15 - 19	C	611	579	22	3	1	2	4	-
20 - 24	C	722	641	61	8	6	2	4	-
25 - 29	C	715	588	99	11	1	6	10	-
30 - 34	C	955	731	184	15	3	12	10	-
35 - 39	C	1 035	714	254	24	2	29	12	-
40 - 44	C	1 373	911	369	18	9	42	24	-
45 - 49	C	1 714	1 029	546	22	12	63	42	-
50 - 54	C	1 969	1 103	664	22	14	85	81	-
55 - 59	C	2 083	1 120	707	21	15	94	126	-
60 - 64	C	2 462	1 342	824	15	10	96	175	-
65 - 69	C	3 218	1 675	1 033	25	14	82	389	-
70 - 74	C	3 806	1 856	1 075	37	11	95	732	-
75 - 79	C	4 293	2 147	1 068	20	8	111	939	-
80 - 84	C	4 083	2 031	873	16	12	72	1 079	-
85 - 89	C	3 477	1 733	640	24	6	45	1 029	-
90 - 94	C	2 055	1 067	319	8	2	30	629	-
95 - 99	C	781	427	105	3	-	7	239	-
100+	C	231	145	21	2	-	2	61	-
Unk. - Inc. ...	C	60	30	21	3	-	-	6	-

21. Deaths by marital status, age and sex: latest available year, 1994 - 2003
Décès selon l'état matrimonial, l'âge et le sexe: dernière année disponible, 1994 - 2003
(continued — suite)

Continent, country or area, date and age (in years) Continent, pays ou zone, date et âge (en années)	Code[1]	Total	Single (never married) - Célibataires	Married - Mariés	In consensual union - En union consensuelle	Married but separated - Mariés mais séparées	Divorced and not remarried - Divorcées non remariés	Widowed and not remarried - Veufs non remariés	Unknown - Inconnu
ASIA — ASIE									
Azerbaijan - Azerbaïdjan[11]									
2003									
Male									
Total	+C	25 563	2 646	19 567	...	...	383	2 967	-
0 - 14	+C	1 673	1 101	571	...	...	-	1	-
15 - 19	+C	299	258	40	...	...	-	1	-
20 - 24	+C	379	281	94	...	...	-	4	-
25 - 29	+C	465	265	195	...	...	1	4	-
30 - 34	+C	555	175	367	...	...	5	8	-
35 - 39	+C	808	124	657	...	...	20	7	-
40 - 44	+C	1 194	97	1 051	...	...	26	20	-
45 - 49	+C	1 411	57	1 299	...	...	31	24	-
50 - 54	+C	1 557	58	1 420	...	...	43	36	-
55 - 59	+C	1 240	31	1 142	...	...	28	39	-
60 - 64	+C	2 554	44	2 294	...	...	46	170	-
65 - 69	+C	4 116	54	3 596	...	...	45	421	-
70 - 74	+C	4 290	58	3 484	...	...	54	694	-
75 - 79	+C	2 792	31	1 996	...	...	47	718	-
80 - 84	+C	1 125	10	754	...	...	15	346	-
85 - 89	+C	560	1	320	...	...	9	230	-
90 - 94	+C	356	-	190	...	...	11	155	-
95 - 99	+C	107	-	52	...	...	-	55	-
100+	+C	82	1	45	...	...	2	34	-
Female									
Total	+C	23 438	2 027	11 782	...	...	509	9 120	-
0 - 14	+C	1 350	903	446	...	...	1	-	-
15 - 19	+C	162	141	21	...	...	-	-	-
20 - 24	+C	194	120	70	...	...	1	3	-
25 - 29	+C	206	74	124	...	...	2	6	-
30 - 34	+C	283	63	186	...	...	13	21	-
35 - 39	+C	427	79	323	...	...	14	11	-
40 - 44	+C	634	89	487	...	...	22	36	-
45 - 49	+C	716	77	541	...	...	24	74	-
50 - 54	+C	785	49	571	...	...	34	131	-
55 - 59	+C	720	36	509	...	...	34	141	-
60 - 64	+C	1 797	61	1 185	...	...	63	488	-
65 - 69	+C	3 293	82	2 094	...	...	41	1 076	-
70 - 74	+C	3 874	67	2 043	...	...	68	1 696	-
75 - 79	+C	3 211	81	1 345	...	...	76	1 709	-
80 - 84	+C	2 266	36	780	...	...	36	1 414	-
85 - 89	+C	1 508	34	426	...	...	31	1 017	-
90 - 94	+C	1 094	18	311	...	...	23	742	-
95 - 99	+C	452	5	174	...	...	8	265	-
100+	+C	466	12	146	...	...	18	290	-
China: Hong Kong SAR - Chine: Hong Kong RAS[8]									
2003									
Male									
Total	C	20 821	1 960	13 101	...	...	495	2 929	2 336
0 - 14	C	123	123	-	...	...	-	-	-
15 - 19	C	56	50	3	...	...	-	-	3
20 - 24	C	120	103	8	...	...	-	-	9
25 - 29	C	174	133	34	...	...	3	-	4
30 - 34	C	178	98	63	...	...	9	-	8
35 - 39	C	316	123	148	...	...	23	3	19
40 - 44	C	517	122	315	...	...	37	7	36
45 - 49	C	789	129	523	...	...	61	11	65
50 - 54	C	995	124	679	...	...	72	20	100

21. Deaths by marital status, age and sex: latest available year, 1994 - 2003
Décès selon l'état matrimonial, l'âge et le sexe: dernière année disponible, 1994 - 2003
(continued — suite)

Continent, country or area, date and age (in years) / Continent, pays ou zone, date et âge (en années)	Code[1]	Total	Single (never married) - Célibataires	Married - Mariés	In consensual union - En union consensuelle	Married but separated - Mariés mais séparées	Divorced and not remarried - Divorcées non remariés	Widowed and not remarried - Veufs non remariés	Unknown - Inconnu
ASIA — ASIE									
China: Hong Kong SAR - Chine: Hong Kong RAS[8]									
2003									
Male									
55 - 59	C	1 072	114	739	...	...	54	44	121
60 - 64	C	1 450	102	1 039	...	...	50	63	196
65 - 69	C	2 110	141	1 503	...	...	52	132	282
70 - 74	C	3 205	204	2 208	...	...	54	358	381
75 - 79	C	3 589	200	2 380	...	...	40	560	409
80 - 84	C	3 019	125	1 896	...	...	18	645	335
85+	C	3 069	69	1 563	...	...	22	1 086	329
Unk. - Inc. ...	C	39	-	-	...	...	-	-	39
Female									
Total	C	16 149	1 037	5 466	...	...	219	7 939	1 488
0 - 14	C	104	104	-	...	...	-	-	-
15 - 19	C	31	29	1	...	...	-	-	1
20 - 24	C	57	49	4	...	...	1	-	3
25 - 29	C	88	57	24	...	...	4	-	3
30 - 34	C	135	52	61	...	...	10	2	10
35 - 39	C	177	44	88	...	...	21	4	20
40 - 44	C	294	52	194	...	...	21	4	23
45 - 49	C	431	56	295	...	...	34	16	30
50 - 54	C	456	47	312	...	...	26	32	39
55 - 59	C	447	23	307	...	...	19	63	35
60 - 64	C	501	8	344	...	...	14	87	48
65 - 69	C	1 016	21	630	...	...	8	284	73
70 - 74	C	1 633	35	817	...	...	20	607	154
75 - 79	C	2 395	67	886	...	...	13	1 227	202
80 - 84	C	2 875	89	728	...	...	11	1 767	280
85+	C	5 502	303	775	...	...	17	3 846	561
Unk. - Inc. ...	C	7	1	-	...	...	-	-	6
China: Macao SAR - Chine: Macao RAS[4]									
2002									
Male									
Total	C	786	160	311	...	...	7	18	290
0 - 14	C	10	10	-	...	...	-	-	-
15 - 19	C	6	6	-	...	...	-	-	-
20 - 24	C	8	5	2	...	...	-	-	1
25 - 29	C	10	7	-	...	...	-	-	3
30 - 34	C	11	5	2	...	...	1	-	3
35 - 39	C	27	11	16	...	...	-	-	-
40 - 44	C	36	7	28	...	...	-	-	1
45 - 49	C	43	11	27	...	...	2	1	2
50 - 54	C	51	16	31	...	...	2	-	2
55 - 59	C	51	11	35	...	...	1	-	4
60 - 64	C	38	7	19	...	...	-	1	11
65 - 69	C	77	11	44	...	...	1	1	20
70 - 74	C	97	21	37	...	...	-	1	38
75 - 79	C	109	21	26	...	...	-	5	57
80 - 84	C	103	8	29	...	...	-	5	61
85+	C	104	3	15	...	...	-	4	82
Unk. - Inc. ...	C	5	-	-	...	...	-	-	5
Female									
Total	C	629	65	136	...	...	4	65	359
0 - 14	C	8	8	-	...	...	-	-	-
15 - 19	C	7	6	-	...	...	-	-	1
20 - 24	C	1	-	1	...	...	-	-	-

21. Deaths by marital status, age and sex: latest available year, 1994 - 2003
Décès selon l'état matrimonial, l'âge et le sexe: dernière année disponible, 1994 - 2003
(continued — suite)

Continent, country or area, date and age (in years) / Continent, pays ou zone, date et âge (en années)	Code[1]	Total	Single (never married) - Célibataires	Married - Mariés	In consensual union - En union consensuelle	Married but separated - Mariés mais séparées	Divorced and not remarried - Divorcées non remariés	Widowed and not remarried - Veufs non remariés	Unknown - Inconnu
ASIA — ASIE									
China: Macao SAR - Chine: Macao RAS[4]									
2002									
Female									
25 - 29	C	6	4	2	...	...	-	-	-
30 - 34	C	9	5	3	...	...	1	-	-
35 - 39	C	12	8	4	...	...	-	-	-
40 - 44	C	20	6	14	...	...	-	-	-
45 - 49	C	17	4	9	...	...	2	1	1
50 - 54	C	15	3	11	...	...	-	-	1
55 - 59	C	22	2	16	...	...	1	-	3
60 - 64	C	20	-	12	...	...	-	-	8
65 - 69	C	42	-	21	...	...	-	2	19
70 - 74	C	63	3	11	...	...	-	7	42
75 - 79	C	115	7	14	...	...	-	14	80
80 - 84	C	99	4	10	...	...	-	15	70
85+	C	172	5	8	...	...	-	26	133
Unk. - Inc.	C	1	-	-	...	...	-	-	1
Georgia - Géorgie[11]									
2001									
Male									
Total	C	19 569	2 102	15 218	...	-	216	2 031	2
0 - 15	C	428	419	9	...	-	-	-	-
16 - 19	C	95	30	65	...	-	-	-	-
20 - 24	C	137	54	82	...	-	-	1	-
25 - 29	C	271	45	219	...	-	3	4	-
30 - 34	C	350	68	273	...	-	5	3	1
35 - 39	C	506	80	410	...	-	8	8	-
40 - 44	C	711	97	582	...	-	17	15	-
45 - 49	C	857	132	702	...	-	11	12	-
50 - 54	C	924	116	762	...	-	20	26	-
55 - 59	C	877	105	731	...	-	14	27	-
60 - 64	C	1 980	136	1 732	...	-	32	80	-
65 - 69	C	2 936	218	2 469	...	-	33	216	-
70 - 74	C	3 787	257	3 062	...	-	36	432	-
75 - 79	C	2 713	150	2 087	...	-	17	459	-
80 - 84	C	1 361	87	964	...	-	5	305	-
85+	C	1 582	88	1 038	...	-	14	442	-
Unk. - Inc.	C	54	20	31	...	-	1	1	1
Female									
Total	C	19 770	2 025	11 512	...	7	285	5 941	-
0 - 15	C	247	243	3	...	-	-	1	-
16 - 19	C	63	12	40	...	-	2	9	-
20 - 24	C	71	14	49	...	-	1	7	-
25 - 29	C	99	21	72	...	-	1	5	-
30 - 34	C	113	17	85	...	-	4	7	-
35 - 39	C	162	28	117	...	-	4	13	-
40 - 44	C	242	42	175	...	-	6	19	-
45 - 49	C	299	54	210	...	-	11	24	-
50 - 54	C	370	62	271	...	-	10	27	-
55 - 59	C	434	51	331	...	-	8	44	-
60 - 64	C	1 460	139	1 052	...	-	34	235	-
65 - 69	C	2 110	189	1 507	...	2	33	379	-
70 - 74	C	3 268	308	2 015	...	-	46	899	-
75 - 79	C	3 648	320	2 064	...	-	51	1 213	-
80 - 84	C	2 888	255	1 445	...	1	35	1 152	-
85+	C	4 262	259	2 058	...	2	39	1 904	-
Unk. - Inc.	C	34	11	18	...	2	-	3	-

21. Deaths by marital status, age and sex: latest available year, 1994 - 2003
Décès selon l'état matrimonial, l'âge et le sexe: dernière année disponible, 1994 - 2003
(continued — suite)

Continent, country or area, date and age (in years) / Continent, pays ou zone, date et âge (en années)	Code[1]	Total	Single (never married) - Célibataires	Married - Mariés	In consensual union - En union consensuelle	Married but separated - Mariés mais séparées	Divorced and not remarried - Divorcées non remariés	Widowed and not remarried - Veufs non remariés	Unknown - Inconnu
ASIA — ASIE									
Japan - Japon[12,13]									
2003									
Male									
Total	C	551 746	48 830	371 579	...	...	35 426	94 284	1 627
0 - 14	C	3 149	3 149	-	...	...	-	-	-
15 - 19	C	1 460	1 450	5	...	...	2	-	3
20 - 24	C	2 319	2 176	94	...	...	41	2	6
25 - 29	C	3 186	2 499	488	...	...	190	3	6
30 - 34	C	4 072	2 488	1 080	...	...	466	28	10
35 - 39	C	4 752	2 279	1 693	...	...	727	37	16
40 - 44	C	7 034	2 604	3 189	...	...	1 152	61	28
45 - 49	C	11 227	3 544	5 597	...	...	1 929	114	43
50 - 54	C	23 609	5 882	13 120	...	...	4 093	419	95
55 - 59	C	31 535	5 414	19 807	...	...	5 258	935	121
60 - 64	C	41 343	4 783	28 885	...	...	5 602	1 900	173
65 - 69	C	57 644	4 186	43 906	...	...	5 376	4 026	150
70 - 74	C	78 884	3 399	62 343	...	...	4 430	8 573	139
75 - 79	C	89 520	2 355	70 118	...	...	2 941	14 011	95
80 - 84	C	76 401	1 367	56 355	...	...	1 658	16 968	53
85 - 89	C	66 350	775	43 177	...	...	986	21 365	47
90 - 94	C	37 235	367	18 278	...	...	450	18 105	35
95 - 99	C	10 010	96	3 204	...	...	111	6 592	7
100+	C	1 416	17	240	...	...	14	1 145	-
Unk. - Inc. ...	C	600	...	...	...	...	...	...	600
Female									
Total	C	463 205	32 668	120 303	...	...	23 914	285 572	748
0 - 14	C	2 694	2 694	-	...	...	-	-	-
15 - 19	C	672	664	6	...	...	2	-	-
20 - 24	C	965	875	56	...	...	30	2	2
25 - 29	C	1 395	980	287	...	...	119	4	5
30 - 34	C	1 950	872	787	...	...	255	29	7
35 - 39	C	2 447	715	1 296	...	...	365	66	5
40 - 44	C	3 352	702	2 119	...	...	451	71	9
45 - 49	C	5 347	785	3 663	...	...	736	157	6
50 - 54	C	10 913	1 324	7 583	...	...	1 457	533	16
55 - 59	C	13 790	1 352	9 409	...	...	1 774	1 232	23
60 - 64	C	18 116	1 527	11 763	...	...	1 987	2 799	40
65 - 69	C	26 465	2 014	15 687	...	...	2 223	6 502	39
70 - 74	C	39 951	3 084	20 139	...	...	2 505	14 177	46
75 - 79	C	57 942	4 154	21 230	...	...	3 267	29 211	80
80 - 84	C	77 728	4 312	15 697	...	...	3 484	54 129	106
85 - 89	C	90 218	3 509	8 190	...	...	2 813	75 605	101
90 - 94	C	74 165	2 126	2 190	...	...	1 748	67 989	112
95 - 99	C	29 086	820	189	...	...	591	27 446	40
100+	C	5 907	159	12	...	...	107	5 620	9
Unk. - Inc. ...	C	102	...	...	...	...	...	...	102
Kazakhstan[11]									
2003									
Male									
Total	C	87 216	24 577	37 426	...	...	7 152	12 266	5 795
0 - 14	C	3 535	1 876	1 279	...	...	6	19	355
15 - 19	C	1 155	736	360	...	...	-	22	37
20 - 24	C	2 002	1 160	691	...	...	18	60	73
25 - 29	C	2 711	1 311	1 114	...	...	110	48	128
30 - 34	C	3 291	1 273	1 395	...	...	328	65	230
35 - 39	C	3 880	1 144	1 680	...	...	609	82	365
40 - 44	C	5 963	1 680	2 573	...	...	967	167	576
45 - 49	C	6 882	1 793	3 008	...	...	1 184	234	663
50 - 54	C	7 656	1 927	3 470	...	...	1 100	410	749
55 - 59	C	5 838	1 404	2 849	...	...	693	416	476

21. Deaths by marital status, age and sex: latest available year, 1994 - 2003
Décès selon l'état matrimonial, l'âge et le sexe: dernière année disponible, 1994 - 2003
(continued — suite)

Continent, country or area, date and age (in years) / Continent, pays ou zone, date et âge (en annèes)	Code[1]	Total	Single (never married) - Célibataires	Married - Mariés	In consensual union - En union consensuelle	Married but separated - Mariés mais séparées	Divorced and not remarried - Divorcées non remariés	Widowed and not remarried - Veufs non remariés	Unknown - Inconnu
ASIA — ASIE									
Kazakhstan[11]									
2003									
Male									
60 - 64	C	9 601	2 578	4 458	...	...	823	1 268	474
65 - 69	C	10 945	2 657	5 287	...	...	707	1 953	341
70 - 74	C	9 255	2 289	4 104	...	...	334	2 395	133
75 - 79	C	7 414	1 648	3 163	...	...	182	2 347	74
80 - 84	C	3 204	648	1 205	...	...	62	1 265	24
85 - 89	C	1 700	274	555	...	...	24	833	14
90 - 94	C	839	130	182	...	...	3	521	3
95 - 99	C	196	34	38	...	...	1	123	-
100+	C	59	10	12	...	...	1	36	-
Unk. - Inc. ...	C	1 090	5	3	...	...	-	2	1 080
Female									
Total	C	68 061	11 441	16 706	...	...	4 099	33 829	1 986
0 - 14	C	2 532	1 315	934	...	...	11	15	257
15 - 19	C	533	330	176	...	...	1	14	12
20 - 24	C	723	397	272	...	...	12	20	22
25 - 29	C	888	371	357	...	...	79	30	51
30 - 34	C	1 024	332	418	...	...	136	71	67
35 - 39	C	1 327	382	548	...	...	196	100	101
40 - 44	C	2 107	529	887	...	...	339	203	149
45 - 49	C	2 676	627	1 135	...	...	399	340	175
50 - 54	C	3 336	732	1 409	...	...	410	581	204
55 - 59	C	2 816	576	1 139	...	...	283	701	117
60 - 64	C	5 698	1 112	1 865	...	...	491	2 095	135
65 - 69	C	7 291	1 193	2 194	...	...	478	3 301	125
70 - 74	C	8 507	1 173	1 856	...	...	474	4 899	105
75 - 79	C	11 107	1 217	1 894	...	...	450	7 466	80
80 - 84	C	7 385	595	878	...	...	194	5 653	65
85 - 89	C	5 352	306	429	...	...	100	4 459	58
90 - 94	C	3 197	158	202	...	...	36	2 778	23
95 - 99	C	903	61	76	...	...	7	755	4
100+	C	415	33	35	...	...	3	344	-
Unk. - Inc. ...	C	244	2	2	...	...	-	4	236
Korea (Republic of) - Corée (République de)[14]									
2002									
Male									
Total	C	135 510	13 787	94 267	...	...	6 786	19 927	743
0 - 14	C	2 848	2 848	-	...	...	-	-	-
15 - 19	C	831	828	-	...	...	-	-	3
20 - 24	C	1 322	1 261	53	...	...	4	3	1
25 - 29	C	1 725	1 411	250	...	...	47	14	3
30 - 34	C	2 674	1 441	1 032	...	...	176	17	8
35 - 39	C	4 069	1 477	2 056	...	...	460	57	19
40 - 44	C	7 007	1 598	4 263	...	...	989	131	26
45 - 49	C	8 559	1 045	5 911	...	...	1 273	281	49
50 - 54	C	9 053	613	6 929	...	...	1 094	373	44
55 - 59	C	10 905	391	8 963	...	...	936	574	41
60 - 64	C	15 389	310	13 155	...	...	703	1 146	75
65 - 69	C	16 826	178	14 333	...	...	427	1 802	86
70 - 74	C	15 929	156	12 955	...	...	280	2 441	97
75 - 79	C	15 798	114	11 627	...	...	197	3 760	100
80 - 84	C	12 519	66	8 027	...	...	134	4 193	99
85 - 89	C	6 958	34	3 515	...	...	48	3 293	68
90 - 94	C	2 605	13	1 083	...	...	16	1 474	19
95+	C	487	2	114	...	...	2	366	3
Unk. - Inc. ...	C	6	1	1	...	...	-	2	2

21. Deaths by marital status, age and sex: latest available year, 1994 - 2003
Décès selon l'état matrimonial, l'âge et le sexe: dernière année disponible, 1994 - 2003
(continued — suite)

Continent, country or area, date and age (in years) / Continent, pays ou zone, date et âge (en années)	Code[1]	Total	Single (never married) - Célibataires	Married - Mariés	In consensual union - En union consensuelle	Married but separated - Mariés mais séparées	Divorced and not remarried - Divorcées non remariés	Widowed and not remarried - Veufs non remariés	Unknown - Inconnu
ASIA — ASIE									
Korea (Republic of) - Corée (République de)[14]									
2002									
Female									
Total	C	111 005	6 101	26 718	...	...	2 901	74 395	890
0 - 14	C	2 145	2 145	-	...	...	-	-	-
15 - 19	C	398	393	1	...	...	-	-	4
20 - 24	C	684	621	49	...	...	9	4	1
25 - 29	C	802	452	294	...	...	43	13	-
30 - 34	C	1 228	313	742	...	...	142	26	5
35 - 39	C	1 587	182	1 126	...	...	213	55	11
40 - 44	C	2 356	185	1 708	...	...	316	140	7
45 - 49	C	2 744	166	2 001	...	...	302	266	9
50 - 54	C	3 018	135	2 139	...	...	257	473	14
55 - 59	C	4 045	128	2 593	...	...	234	1 063	27
60 - 64	C	6 658	157	3 620	...	...	275	2 563	43
65 - 69	C	9 410	205	3 914	...	...	243	4 994	54
70 - 74	C	13 303	272	3 432	...	...	254	9 210	135
75 - 79	C	17 657	269	2 688	...	...	224	14 321	155
80 - 84	C	18 795	239	1 585	...	...	215	16 570	186
85 - 89	C	15 304	149	636	...	...	96	14 282	141
90 - 94	C	8 069	62	160	...	...	60	7 710	77
95+	C	2 786	26	28	...	...	18	2 693	21
Unk. - Inc.	C	16	2	2	...	...	-	12	-
Occupied Palestinian Territory - Territoire palestinien occupé									
2003									
Male									
Total	U	5 474	1 570	3 392	...	...	25	487	-
0 - 14	U	984	984	-	...	...	-	-	-
15 - 19	U	249	249	-	...	...	-	-	-
20 - 24	U	212	188	24	...	...	-	-	-
25 - 29	U	170	68	102	...	...	-	-	-
30 - 34	U	130	16	111	...	...	2	1	-
35 - 39	U	105	7	95	...	...	3	-	-
40 - 44	U	133	8	122	...	...	3	-	-
45 - 49	U	169	5	161	...	...	1	2	-
50 - 54	U	219	8	208	...	...	2	1	-
55 - 59	U	271	5	259	...	...	1	6	-
60 - 64	U	322	7	305	...	...	1	9	-
65 - 69	U	445	5	405	...	...	1	34	-
70 - 74	U	544	3	481	...	...	3	57	-
75 - 79	U	534	10	432	...	...	1	91	-
80 - 84	U	405	4	303	...	...	3	95	-
85 - 89	U	282	-	200	...	...	2	80	-
90 - 94	U	145	2	93	...	...	1	49	-
95 - 99	U	104	1	65	...	...	1	37	-
100+	U	51	-	26	...	...	-	25	-
Female									
Total	U	4 190	1 075	1 422	...	...	43	1 649	1
0 - 14	U	801	801	-	...	...	-	-	-
15 - 19	U	41	38	3	...	...	-	-	-
20 - 24	U	34	24	10	...	...	-	-	-
25 - 29	U	36	19	15	...	...	2	-	-
30 - 34	U	36	8	25	...	...	-	3	-

21. Deaths by marital status, age and sex: latest available year, 1994 - 2003
Décès selon l'état matrimonial, l'âge et le sexe: dernière année disponible, 1994 - 2003
(continued — suite)

Continent, country or area, date and age (in years) Continent, pays ou zone, date et âge (en années)	Code[1]	Total	Single (never married) - Célibataires	Married - Mariés	In consensual union - En union consensuelle	Married but separated - Mariés mais séparées	Divorced and not remarried - Divorcées non remariés	Widowed and not remarried - Veufs non remariés	Unknown - Inconnu
ASIA — ASIE									
Occupied Palestinian Territory - Territoire palestinien occupé									
2003									
Female									
35 - 39	U	59	18	39	...	...	-	2	-
40 - 44	U	79	18	60	...	...	1	-	-
45 - 49	U	75	5	62	...	...	1	7	-
50 - 54	U	115	27	65	...	...	5	18	-
55 - 59	U	191	17	130	...	...	5	39	-
60 - 64	U	322	20	188	...	...	6	108	-
65 - 69	U	451	21	224	...	...	7	198	1
70 - 74	U	546	23	220	...	...	6	297	-
75 - 79	U	546	16	179	...	...	2	349	-
80 - 84	U	364	5	107	...	...	2	250	-
85 - 89	U	246	8	46	...	...	2	190	-
90 - 94	U	123	3	32	...	...	1	87	-
95 - 99	U	88	3	13	...	...	2	70	-
100+	U	37	1	4	...	...	1	31	-
Pakistan[15,16]									
2001									
Male									
10+	I	302 255	42 291	212 697	...	...	1 244	46 022	-
10 - 14	I	7 463	7 463	-	...	...	-	-	-
15 - 19	I	11 817	11 817	-	...	...	-	-	-
20 - 24	I	9 329	6 841	2 488	...	...	-	-	-
25 - 29	I	9 951	4 975	4 975	...	...	-	-	-
30 - 34	I	12 438	1 866	10 573	...	...	-	-	-
35 - 39	I	17 414	3 110	13 682	...	...	622	-	-
40 - 44	I	11 195	-	11 195	...	...	-	-	-
45 - 49	I	17 414	-	16 792	...	...	-	622	-
50 - 54	I	19 901	-	16 792	...	...	622	2 488	-
55 - 59	I	20 523	-	19 280	...	...	-	1 244	-
60 - 64	I	27 365	622	24 255	...	...	-	2 488	-
65 - 69	I	25 499	1 244	19 280	...	...	-	4 975	-
70+	I	111 946	4 353	73 387	...	...	-	34 206	-
Female									
10+	I	250 012	34 206	129 360	...	...	2 488	83 959	-
10 - 14	I	14 926	14 304	622	...	...	-	-	-
15 - 19	I	9 329	9 329	-	...	...	-	-	-
20 - 24	I	13 682	5 597	6 219	...	...	1 244	622	-
25 - 29	I	9 329	1 244	8 085	...	...	-	-	-
30 - 34	I	6 841	622	5 597	...	...	-	622	-
35 - 39	I	12 438	-	11 195	...	...	-	1 244	-
40 - 44	I	11 195	622	9 951	...	...	622	-	-
45 - 49	I	11 195	-	8 707	...	...	-	2 488	-
50 - 54	I	15 548	-	12 438	...	...	-	3 110	-
55 - 59	I	18 658	622	13 682	...	...	622	3 732	-
60 - 64	I	26 743	622	13 682	...	...	-	12 438	-
65 - 69	I	27 986	622	14 926	...	...	-	12 438	-
70+	I	72 143	622	24 255	...	...	-	47 266	-
Philippines[4,8]									
2000									
Male									
10+	C	191 429	39 579	122 834	...	...	1 132	27 244	640
Female									
10+	C	130 447	20 725	55 621	...	...	1 054	52 598	449

21. Deaths by marital status, age and sex: latest available year, 1994 - 2003
Décès selon l'état matrimonial, l'âge et le sexe: dernière année disponible, 1994 - 2003
(continued — suite)

Continent, country or area, date and age (in years) / Continent, pays ou zone, date et âge (en annèes)	Code[1]	Total	Single (never married) - Célibataires	Married - Mariés	In consensual union - En union consensuelle	Married but separated - Mariés mais séparées	Divorced and not remarried - Divorcées non remariés	Widowed and not remarried - Veufs non remariés	Unknown - Inconnu
ASIA — ASIE									
Qatar									
2003									
Male									
15+	C	785	127	641	...	...	10	7	-
15 - 19	C	42	40	2	...	...	-	-	-
20 - 24	C	50	35	15	...	...	-	-	-
25 - 29	C	37	20	17	...	...	-	-	-
30 - 34	C	50	7	43	...	...	-	-	-
35 - 39	C	45	3	41	...	...	-	1	-
40 - 44	C	61	5	54	...	...	-	2	-
45 - 49	C	68	2	66	...	...	-	-	-
50 - 54	C	66	3	62	...	...	-	1	-
55 - 59	C	65	3	62	...	...	-	-	-
60 - 64	C	62	2	59	...	...	1	-	-
65 - 69	C	76	3	73	...	...	-	-	-
70 - 74	C	59	1	57	...	...	1	-	-
75 - 79	C	42	-	38	...	...	4	-	-
80 - 84	C	32	1	29	...	...	1	1	-
85 - 89	C	17	1	14	...	...	1	1	-
90 - 94	C	6	-	4	...	...	1	1	-
95+	C	7	1	5	...	...	1	-	-
Female									
15+	C	333	21	238	...	...	62	12	-
15 - 19	C	5	4	1	...	...	-	-	-
20 - 24	C	5	5	-	...	...	-	-	-
25 - 29	C	8	3	5	...	...	-	-	-
30 - 34	C	11	1	10	...	...	-	-	-
35 - 39	C	14	1	13	...	...	-	-	-
40 - 44	C	11	1	9	...	...	1	-	-
45 - 49	C	16	1	13	...	...	1	1	-
50 - 54	C	17	-	16	...	...	1	-	-
55 - 59	C	30	2	25	...	...	3	-	-
60 - 64	C	41	1	29	...	...	10	1	-
65 - 69	C	46	-	33	...	...	10	3	-
70 - 74	C	43	-	29	...	...	12	2	-
75 - 79	C	33	2	21	...	...	9	1	-
80 - 84	C	18	-	11	...	...	5	2	-
85 - 89	C	15	-	12	...	...	3	-	-
90 - 94	C	11	-	4	...	...	6	1	-
95+	C	9	-	7	...	...	1	1	-
Singapore - Singapour[17]									
2003									
Male									
Total	+C	8 903	1 253	6 775	...	...	172	581	122
0 - 14	+C	125	125	-	...	...	-	-	-
15 - 19	+C	58	57	-	...	...	-	-	1
20 - 24	+C	106	98	5	...	...	1	-	2
25 - 29	+C	115	82	26	...	...	-	-	7
30 - 34	+C	157	72	66	...	...	7	-	12
35 - 39	+C	186	77	95	...	...	5	-	9
40 - 44	+C	289	88	181	...	...	10	-	10
45 - 49	+C	427	108	291	...	...	19	2	7
50 - 54	+C	532	96	395	...	...	28	4	9
55 - 59	+C	640	81	524	...	...	23	6	6
60 - 64	+C	825	80	708	...	...	18	16	3
65 - 69	+C	1 032	81	882	...	...	19	42	8
70 - 74	+C	1 233	72	1 063	...	...	20	68	10
75 - 79	+C	1 214	65	1 034	...	...	11	94	10
80 - 84	+C	920	40	744	...	...	7	126	3
85 - 89	+C	580	20	451	...	...	2	101	6

21. Deaths by marital status, age and sex: latest available year, 1994 - 2003
Décès selon l'état matrimonial, l'âge et le sexe: dernière année disponible, 1994 - 2003
(continued — suite)

Continent, country or area, date and age (in years) / Continent, pays ou zone, date et âge (en années)	Code[1]	Total	Single (never married) - Célibataires	Married - Mariés	In consensual union - En union consensuelle	Married but separated - Mariés mais séparées	Divorced and not remarried - Divorcées non remariés	Widowed and not remarried - Veufs non remariés	Unknown - Inconnu
ASIA — ASIE									
Singapore - Singapour[17]									
2003									
Male									
90 - 94	+C	351	7	248	...	...	2	89	5
95 - 99	+C	83	2	51	...	...	-	28	2
100+	+C	17	1	11	...	...	-	5	-
Unk. - Inc.	+C	...	1	-	...	...	-	-	12
Female									
Total	+C	7 124	573	4 458	...	...	98	1 949	46
0 - 14	+C	85	85	-	...	...			
15 - 19	+C	30	26	2	...	...	-	-	2
20 - 24	+C	63	57	5	...	...			1
25 - 29	+C	46	19	24	...	...	3		
30 - 34	+C	56	18	34	...	...	3		1
35 - 39	+C	98	25	62	...	...	10	-	1
40 - 44	+C	141	25	106	...	...	8	1	1
45 - 49	+C	229	51	161	...	...	12	4	1
50 - 54	+C	320	50	249	...	...	10	11	-
55 - 59	+C	331	36	257	...	...	12	25	1
60 - 64	+C	473	27	377	...	...	11	58	-
65 - 69	+C	614	18	476	...	...	7	110	3
70 - 74	+C	790	22	542	...	...	9	209	8
75 - 79	+C	1 052	31	684	...	...	12	320	5
80 - 84	+C	1 072	21	634	...	...	-	406	11
85 - 89	+C	912	30	474	...	...	1	404	3
90 - 94	+C	567	23	278	...	...	-	265	1
95 - 99	+C	199	5	81	...	...	-	112	1
100+	+C	40	3	12	...	...	-	24	1
Unk. - Inc.	+C	6	1	-	...	...	-	-	5
EUROPE									
Austria - Autriche									
2003									
Male									
Total	C	35 448	4 628	20 900	...	...	2 884	7 036	-
0 - 14	C	299	299	-	...	...	-	-	-
15 - 19	C	169	169	-	...	...	-	-	-
20 - 24	C	258	250	5	...	...	2	1	-
25 - 29	C	211	177	24	...	...	10	-	-
30 - 34	C	285	177	79	...	...	29	-	-
35 - 39	C	447	218	159	...	...	69	1	-
40 - 44	C	662	244	272	...	...	141	5	-
45 - 49	C	971	273	475	...	...	208	15	-
50 - 54	C	1 434	302	767	...	...	330	35	-
55 - 59	C	1 953	327	1 135	...	...	417	74	-
60 - 64	C	3 219	434	2 118	...	...	491	176	-
65 - 69	C	3 120	353	2 171	...	...	301	295	-
70 - 74	C	4 802	433	3 432	...	...	277	660	-
75 - 79	C	5 719	354	3 950	...	...	246	1 169	-
80 - 84	C	5 506	283	3 509	...	...	200	1 514	-
85 - 89	C	3 383	182	1 730	...	...	98	1 373	-
90 - 94	C	2 437	127	934	...	...	56	1 320	-
95 - 99	C	526	25	134	...	...	8	359	-
100+	C	47	1	6	...	...	1	39	-
Female									
Total	C	41 761	5 090	7 819	...	...	3 169	25 683	-
0 - 14	C	238	238	-	...	...	-	-	-
15 - 19	C	84	84	-	...	...	-	-	-
20 - 24	C	77	72	3	...	...	1	1	-

21. Deaths by marital status, age and sex: latest available year, 1994 - 2003
Décès selon l'état matrimonial, l'âge et le sexe: dernière année disponible, 1994 - 2003
(continued — suite)

Continent, country or area, date and age (in years) Continent, pays ou zone, date et âge (en années)	Code[1]	Total	Single (never married) - Célibataires	Married - Mariés	In consensual union - En union consensuelle	Married but separated - Mariés mais séparées	Divorced and not remarried - Divorcées non remariés	Widowed and not remarried - Veufs non remariés	Unknown - Inconnu
EUROPE									
Austria - Autriche									
2003									
Female									
25 - 29	C	65	41	20	...	...	3	1	-
30 - 34	C	139	65	53	...	...	20	1	-
35 - 39	C	223	62	119	...	...	40	2	-
40 - 44	C	352	83	181	...	...	83	5	-
45 - 49	C	517	78	288	...	...	124	27	-
50 - 54	C	689	94	411	...	...	127	57	-
55 - 59	C	1 078	131	576	...	...	244	127	-
60 - 64	C	1 672	174	883	...	...	258	357	-
65 - 69	C	1 626	167	733	...	...	188	538	-
70 - 74	C	3 173	328	1 148	...	...	258	1 439	-
75 - 79	C	5 877	661	1 468	...	...	447	3 301	-
80 - 84	C	8 854	982	1 278	...	...	560	6 034	-
85 - 89	C	7 620	797	438	...	...	397	5 988	-
90 - 94	C	7 053	737	196	...	...	334	5 786	-
95 - 99	C	2 138	257	22	...	...	77	1 782	-
100+	C	286	39	2	...	...	8	237	-
Bulgaria - Bulgarie									
2003									
Male									
Total	C	59 992	4 705	39 366	...	...	3 061	12 751	109
0 - 14	C	714	714	-	...	...	-	-	-
15 - 19	C	181	181	-	...	...	-	-	-
20 - 24	C	332	313	19	...	...	-	-	-
25 - 29	C	406	325	72	...	...	7	1	1
30 - 34	C	438	229	186	...	...	22	1	-
35 - 39	C	630	211	352	...	...	65	1	1
40 - 44	C	1 105	307	626	...	...	158	12	2
45 - 49	C	1 937	359	1 243	...	...	285	42	8
50 - 54	C	3 412	461	2 377	...	...	475	93	6
55 - 59	C	4 478	425	3 338	...	...	522	186	7
60 - 64	C	5 215	333	4 066	...	...	406	397	13
65 - 69	C	7 441	265	5 905	...	...	378	875	18
70 - 74	C	9 201	237	7 006	...	...	296	1 648	14
75 - 79	C	10 611	204	7 224	...	...	250	2 915	18
80 - 84	C	8 326	86	4 874	...	...	127	3 223	16
85 - 89	C	3 508	32	1 519	...	...	42	1 912	3
90 - 94	C	1 743	18	508	...	...	22	1 193	2
95 - 99	C	297	2	51	...	...	6	238	-
100+	C	17	3	-	...	...	-	14	-
Female									
Total	C	51 935	2 243	17 752	...	...	2 304	29 560	76
0 - 14	C	498	498	-	...	...	-	-	-
15 - 19	C	79	78	1	...	...	-	-	-
20 - 24	C	111	94	17	...	...	-	-	-
25 - 29	C	160	101	54	...	...	3	2	-
30 - 34	C	204	61	125	...	...	16	2	-
35 - 39	C	297	63	185	...	...	43	6	-
40 - 44	C	512	83	324	...	...	68	37	-
45 - 49	C	818	87	570	...	...	109	51	1
50 - 54	C	1 323	79	935	...	...	152	153	4
55 - 59	C	1 836	90	1 226	...	...	196	318	6
60 - 64	C	2 568	99	1 579	...	...	190	692	8
65 - 69	C	4 558	114	2 470	...	...	253	1 710	11
70 - 74	C	7 359	192	3 221	...	...	327	3 614	5
75 - 79	C	11 068	243	3 641	...	...	407	6 764	13
80 - 84	C	11 101	206	2 440	...	...	318	8 122	15
85 - 89	C	5 492	86	688	...	...	142	4 571	5

21. Deaths by marital status, age and sex: latest available year, 1994 - 2003
Décès selon l'état matrimonial, l'âge et le sexe: dernière année disponible, 1994 - 2003
(continued — suite)

Continent, country or area, date and age (in years) / Continent, pays ou zone, date et âge (en années)	Code[1]	Total	Single (never married) - Célibataires	Married - Mariés	In consensual union - En union consensuelle	Married but separated - Mariés mais séparées	Divorced and not remarried - Divorcées non remariés	Widowed and not remarried - Veufs non remariés	Unknown - Inconnu
EUROPE									
Bulgaria - Bulgarie									
2003									
Female									
90 - 94	C	3 275	65	251	...	...	60	2 893	6
95 - 99	C	613	4	24	...	...	20	563	2
100+	C	63	-	1	...	...	-	62	-
Croatia - Croatie									
2003									
Male									
Total	C	26 519	2 679	16 865	...	...	1 221	5 313	441
0 - 14	C	230	230	-	...	...	-	-	-
15 - 19	C	102	98	-	...	...	-	-	4
20 - 24	C	184	166	15	...	...	1	1	1
25 - 29	C	164	120	37	...	...	3	1	3
30 - 34	C	214	110	87	...	...	11	-	6
35 - 39	C	259	112	127	...	...	9	2	9
40 - 44	C	528	172	283	...	...	52	8	13
45 - 49	C	927	241	553	...	...	86	24	23
50 - 54	C	1 388	272	918	...	...	144	35	19
55 - 59	C	1 650	218	1 157	...	...	153	91	31
60 - 64	C	2 489	196	1 863	...	...	168	216	46
65 - 69	C	3 893	233	2 890	...	...	211	500	59
70 - 74	C	4 846	191	3 492	...	...	174	904	85
75 - 79	C	4 184	135	2 723	...	...	114	1 149	63
80 - 84	C	3 057	94	1 778	...	...	67	1 073	45
85 - 89	C	1 328	52	629	...	...	24	606	17
90 - 94	C	871	28	273	...	...	2	556	12
95 - 99	C	182	9	39	...	...	-	132	2
100+	C	17	-	1	...	...	1	15	-
Unk. - Inc.	C	6	2	-	...	...	1	-	3
Female									
Total	C	26 056	2 230	6 000	...	...	1 284	16 089	453
0 - 14	C	150	150	-	...	...	-	-	-
15 - 19	C	48	47	-	...	...	-	-	1
20 - 24	C	39	35	2	...	...	1	-	1
25 - 29	C	46	22	21	...	...	2	-	1
30 - 34	C	69	32	28	...	...	3	2	4
35 - 39	C	109	23	73	...	...	10	1	2
40 - 44	C	208	32	143	...	...	20	10	3
45 - 49	C	383	45	259	...	...	45	24	10
50 - 54	C	557	59	358	...	...	54	71	15
55 - 59	C	676	64	408	...	...	48	136	20
60 - 64	C	1 210	87	636	...	...	113	349	25
65 - 69	C	2 139	134	958	...	...	125	880	42
70 - 74	C	3 694	256	1 176	...	...	221	1 968	73
75 - 79	C	5 238	421	1 070	...	...	261	3 391	95
80 - 84	C	5 710	425	656	...	...	231	4 316	82
85 - 89	C	2 904	205	135	...	...	76	2 442	46
90 - 94	C	2 287	147	63	...	...	57	1 994	26
95 - 99	C	535	40	11	...	...	16	465	3
100+	C	48	6	2	...	...	1	38	1
Unk. - Inc.	C	6	-	1	...	...	-	2	3
Czech Republic - République tchèque									
2003									
Male									
Total	C	55 880	5 724	31 426	...	...	6 853	11 877	-
0 - 14	C	362	362	-	...	...	-	-	-
15 - 19	C	206	205	-	...	...	1	-	-

21. Deaths by marital status, age and sex: latest available year, 1994 - 2003
Décès selon l'état matrimonial, l'âge et le sexe: dernière année disponible, 1994 - 2003
(continued — suite)

Continent, country or area, date and age (in years) — Continent, pays ou zone, date et âge (en annèes)	Code[1]	Total	Single (never married) - Célibataires	Married - Mariés	In consensual union - En union consensuelle	Married but separated - Mariés mais séparées	Divorced and not remarried - Divorcées non remariés	Widowed and not remarried - Veufs non remariés	Unknown - Inconnu
EUROPE									
Czech Republic - République tchèque									
2003									
Male									
20 - 24	C	394	371	17	...	...	5	1	-
25 - 29	C	459	336	85	...	...	38	-	-
30 - 34	C	487	226	166	...	...	95	-	-
35 - 39	C	634	222	261	...	...	146	5	-
40 - 44	C	903	257	358	...	...	279	9	-
45 - 49	C	1 945	400	914	...	...	502	00	-
50 - 54	C	3 424	592	1 808	...	...	924	100	-
55 - 59	C	4 937	581	2 954	...	...	1 170	232	-
60 - 64	C	5 155	446	3 404	...	...	937	368	-
65 - 69	C	5 894	389	3 993	...	...	793	719	-
70 - 74	C	8 104	432	5 483	...	...	743	1 446	-
75 - 79	C	9 185	401	5 724	...	...	552	2 508	-
80 - 84	C	7 597	293	4 103	...	...	371	2 830	-
85 - 89	C	3 565	131	1 449	...	...	132	1 853	-
90 - 94	C	2 255	66	656	...	...	66	1 467	-
95 - 99	C	353	13	48	...	...	9	283	-
100+	C	21	1	3	...	...	-	17	-
Female									
Total	C	55 408	2 987	11 541	...	...	5 099	35 781	-
0 - 14	C	261	261	-	...	...	-	-	-
15 - 19	C	82	82	-	...	...	-	-	-
20 - 24	C	115	97	17	...	...	1	-	-
25 - 29	C	135	73	43	...	...	16	3	-
30 - 34	C	175	35	96	...	...	41	3	-
35 - 39	C	263	47	157	...	...	55	4	-
40 - 44	C	408	61	227	...	...	104	16	-
45 - 49	C	852	72	502	...	...	218	60	-
50 - 54	C	1 475	102	877	...	...	352	144	-
55 - 59	C	2 287	136	1 280	...	...	450	421	-
60 - 64	C	2 609	121	1 336	...	...	432	720	-
65 - 69	C	3 461	138	1 457	...	...	457	1 409	-
70 - 74	C	6 317	229	2 026	...	...	679	3 383	-
75 - 79	C	10 228	403	2 017	...	...	874	6 934	-
80 - 84	C	11 735	475	1 141	...	...	745	9 374	-
85 - 89	C	7 668	324	284	...	...	377	6 683	-
90 - 94	C	5 931	260	74	...	...	251	5 346	-
95 - 99	C	1 288	65	7	...	...	45	1 171	-
100+	C	118	6	2	...	...	-	110	-
Denmark - Danemark[18]									
2003									
Male									
Total	C	28 146	4 038	14 071	...	...	3 604	6 433	-
0 - 14	C	255	255	-	...	...	-	-	-
15 - 19	C	76	76	-	...	...	-	-	-
20 - 24	C	109	103	6	...	...	-	-	-
25 - 29	C	135	114	17	...	...	4	-	-
30 - 34	C	182	124	45	...	...	13	-	-
35 - 39	C	304	167	90	...	...	46	1	-
40 - 44	C	461	220	147	...	...	91	3	-
45 - 49	C	749	308	267	...	...	165	9	-
50 - 54	C	1 097	310	481	...	...	289	17	-
55 - 59	C	1 808	314	914	...	...	509	71	-
60 - 64	C	2 090	287	1 181	...	...	509	113	-
65 - 69	C	2 587	283	1 588	...	...	493	223	-
70 - 74	C	3 390	338	2 069	...	...	428	555	-

21. Deaths by marital status, age and sex: latest available year, 1994 - 2003
Décès selon l'état matrimonial, l'âge et le sexe: dernière année disponible, 1994 - 2003
(continued — suite)

Continent, country or area, date and age (in years) / Continent, pays ou zone, date et âge (en années)	Code[1]	Total	Single (never married) - Célibataires	Married - Mariés	In consensual union - En union consensuelle	Married but separated - Mariés mais séparées	Divorced and not remarried - Divorcées non remariés	Widowed and not remarried - Veufs non remariés	Unknown - Inconnu
EUROPE									
Denmark - Danemark[18]									
2003									
Male									
75 - 79	C	4 410	399	2 573	...	...	424	1 014	-
80 - 84	C	4 617	358	2 392	...	...	353	1 514	-
85 - 89	C	3 530	236	1 592	...	...	191	1 511	-
90 - 94	C	1 890	120	610	...	...	75	1 085	-
95 - 99	C	408	22	94	...	...	12	280	-
100+	C	48	4	5	...	...	2	37	-
Female									
Total	C	29 428	2 705	6 670	...	...	3 308	16 745	-
0 - 14	C	180	180	-	...	...	-	-	-
15 - 19	C	20	20	-	...	...	-	-	-
20 - 24	C	47	42	5	...	...	-	-	-
25 - 29	C	56	38	13	...	...	4	1	-
30 - 34	C	91	45	36	...	...	9	1	-
35 - 39	C	152	58	72	...	...	19	3	-
40 - 44	C	234	71	108	...	...	52	3	-
45 - 49	C	465	122	218	...	...	108	17	-
50 - 54	C	675	97	351	...	...	198	29	-
55 - 59	C	1 130	104	651	...	...	281	94	-
60 - 64	C	1 321	89	743	...	...	308	181	-
65 - 69	C	1 858	109	877	...	...	332	540	-
70 - 74	C	2 760	176	1 078	...	...	371	1 135	-
75 - 79	C	3 772	249	966	...	...	418	2 139	-
80 - 84	C	5 235	352	874	...	...	472	3 537	-
85 - 89	C	5 365	364	481	...	...	402	4 118	-
90 - 94	C	4 274	380	167	...	...	249	3 478	-
95 - 99	C	1 528	171	29	...	...	71	1 257	-
100+	C	265	38	1	...	...	14	212	-
Estonia - Estonie[11]									
2002									
Male									
Total	C	9 369	1 507	4 519	271	...	1 343	1 465	264
0 - 14	C	92	92	-	-	...	-	-	-
15 - 19	C	78	78	-	-	...	-	-	-
20 - 24	C	143	130	3	5	...	2	-	3
25 - 29	C	139	97	16	12	...	8	-	6
30 - 34	C	179	78	47	19	...	28	-	7
35 - 39	C	235	71	74	21	...	58	1	10
40 - 44	C	377	99	128	12	...	116	6	16
45 - 49	C	575	115	227	30	...	168	11	24
50 - 54	C	716	129	322	26	...	184	27	28
55 - 59	C	679	110	335	27	...	145	34	28
60 - 64	C	1 117	143	594	30	...	217	105	28
65 - 69	C	1 220	124	716	24	...	170	169	17
70 - 74	C	1 376	94	819	28	...	136	288	11
75 - 79	C	994	61	578	15	...	59	271	10
80 - 84	C	665	46	375	11	...	28	205	-
85 - 89	C	436	24	199	10	...	16	185	2
90 - 94	C	215	10	72	1	...	7	123	2
95 - 99	C	58	6	13	-	...	1	38	-
100+	C	3	-	1	-	...	-	2	-
Unk. - Inc. ...	C	72	-	-	-	...	-	-	72
Female									
Total	C	8 986	1 099	1 665	90	...	949	5 097	86
0 - 14	C	49	49	-	-	...	-	-	-
15 - 19	C	17	16	-	-	...	-	-	1
20 - 24	C	29	26	1	1	...	1	-	-

21. Deaths by marital status, age and sex: latest available year, 1994 - 2003
Décès selon l'état matrimonial, l'âge et le sexe: dernière année disponible, 1994 - 2003
(continued — suite)

Continent, country or area, date and age (in years) / Continent, pays ou zone, date et âge (en années)	Code[1]	Total	Single (never married) - Célibataires	Married - Mariés	In consensual union - En union consensuelle	Married but separated - Mariés mais séparées	Divorced and not remarried - Divorcées non remariés	Widowed and not remarried - Veufs non remariés	Unknown - Inconnu
EUROPE									
Estonia - Estonie[11]									
2002									
Female									
25 - 29	C	23	13	4	2	...	3	-	1
30 - 34	C	46	16	18	4	...	7	1	-
35 - 39	C	58	8	27	-	...	17	4	2
40 - 44	C	141	26	54	7	...	43	5	6
45 - 49	C	198	37	80	2	...	55	16	8
50 - 54	C	281	34	123	8	...	72	36	8
55 - 59	C	301	34	119	5	...	71	68	4
60 - 64	C	499	49	185	13	...	87	159	6
65 - 69	C	665	72	239	3	...	102	243	6
70 - 74	C	1 160	119	303	14	...	136	582	6
75 - 79	C	1 530	163	289	12	...	152	906	8
80 - 84	C	1 435	147	129	6	...	99	1 050	4
85 - 89	C	1 312	149	66	8	...	55	1 030	4
90 - 94	C	944	100	27	5	...	36	771	5
95 - 99	C	246	35	1	-	...	11	195	4
100+	C	39	6	-	-	...	2	31	-
Unk. - Inc. ...	C	13	-	-	-	...	-	-	13
Finland - Finlande[19,20]									
2003									
Male									
Total	C	23 922	4 714	11 640	...	...	3 433	4 132	3
0 - 14	C	181	181	-	...	...	-	-	-
15 - 19	C	103	103	-	...	...	-	-	-
20 - 24	C	177	172	4	...	...	1	-	-
25 - 29	C	182	152	24	...	...	6	-	-
30 - 34	C	182	138	33	...	...	11	-	-
35 - 39	C	316	208	53	...	...	55	-	-
40 - 44	C	508	268	133	...	...	105	2	-
45 - 49	C	877	361	255	...	...	246	15	-
50 - 54	C	1 377	465	451	...	...	438	23	1
55 - 59	C	1 790	460	765	...	...	523	41	1
60 - 64	C	1 826	371	932	...	...	450	72	-
65 - 69	C	2 214	420	1 215	...	...	442	137	1
70 - 74	C	3 198	484	1 947	...	...	436	330	-
75 - 79	C	3 833	445	2 342	...	...	363	683	-
80 - 84	C	3 268	253	1 902	...	...	197	916	-
85 - 89	C	2 362	132	1 132	...	...	94	1 004	-
90 - 94	C	1 222	84	394	...	...	59	685	-
95 - 99	C	285	15	53	...	...	6	211	-
100+	C	21	2	5	...	...	1	13	-
Female									
Total	C	25 074	3 634	4 784	...	...	2 659	13 995	2
0 - 14	C	123	123	-	...	...	-	-	-
15 - 19	C	35	35	-	...	...	-	-	-
20 - 24	C	61	58	2	...	...	1	-	-
25 - 29	C	57	38	15	...	...	4	-	-
30 - 34	C	65	37	18	...	...	10	-	-
35 - 39	C	115	49	47	...	...	17	2	-
40 - 44	C	217	83	90	...	...	42	2	-
45 - 49	C	362	96	143	...	...	113	10	-
50 - 54	C	570	131	256	...	...	148	35	-
55 - 59	C	749	131	372	...	...	179	67	-
60 - 64	C	822	96	425	...	...	193	107	1
65 - 69	C	1 167	169	522	...	...	212	263	1
70 - 74	C	2 003	214	742	...	...	305	742	-
75 - 79	C	3 551	443	922	...	...	415	1 771	-

21. Deaths by marital status, age and sex: latest available year, 1994 - 2003
Décès selon l'état matrimonial, l'âge et le sexe: dernière année disponible, 1994 - 2003
(continued — suite)

Continent, country or area, date and age (in years) — Continent, pays ou zone, date et âge (en années)	Code[1]	Total	Single (never married) - Célibataires	Married - Mariés	In consensual union - En union consensuelle	Married but separated - Mariés mais séparées	Divorced and not remarried - Divorcées non remariés	Widowed and not remarried - Veufs non remariés	Unknown - Inconnu
EUROPE									
Finland - Finlande[19,20]									
2003									
Female									
80 - 84	C	4 902	596	726	...	...	408	3 172	-
85 - 89	C	5 315	617	373	...	...	366	3 959	-
90 - 94	C	3 762	515	117	...	...	191	2 939	-
95 - 99	C	1 064	178	14	...	...	49	823	-
100+	C	134	25	-	...	...	6	103	-
France[21,22]									
2001									
Male									
Total	C	272 274	42 910	159 956	...	...	19 273	50 135	-
0 - 14	C	2 958	2 958	-	...	...	-	-	-
15 - 19	C	1 257	1 244	8	...	...	2	3	-
20 - 24	C	2 052	1 994	47	...	...	2	9	-
25 - 29	C	2 147	1 835	273	...	...	22	17	-
30 - 34	C	2 631	1 802	702	...	...	112	15	-
35 - 39	C	3 876	2 198	1 310	...	...	332	36	-
40 - 44	C	5 904	2 329	2 483	...	...	1 004	88	-
45 - 49	C	9 588	2 646	4 675	...	...	2 080	187	-
50 - 54	C	13 560	2 808	7 508	...	...	2 896	348	-
55 - 59	C	13 870	2 141	8 652	...	...	2 527	550	-
60 - 64	C	16 547	2 430	10 945	...	...	2 225	947	-
65 - 69	C	24 610	3 501	16 962	...	...	2 173	1 974	-
70 - 74	C	33 658	4 048	23 712	...	...	2 038	3 860	-
75 - 79	C	41 551	4 131	29 075	...	...	1 617	6 728	-
80 - 84	C	36 855	2 790	24 467	...	...	1 083	8 515	-
85 - 89	C	32 459	2 300	18 169	...	...	688	11 302	-
90 - 94	C	21 866	1 378	9 184	...	...	371	10 933	-
95 - 99	C	6 143	342	1 676	...	...	89	4 036	-
100+	C	742	35	108	...	...	12	587	-
Female									
Total	C	258 799	28 280	57 662	...	...	14 227	158 630	-
0 - 14	C	2 178	2 178	-	...	...	-	-	-
15 - 19	C	542	512	12	...	...	4	14	-
20 - 24	C	661	611	37	...	...	2	11	-
25 - 29	C	741	559	156	...	...	12	14	-
30 - 34	C	1 060	588	375	...	...	71	26	-
35 - 39	C	1 815	746	833	...	...	200	36	-
40 - 44	C	2 857	750	1 472	...	...	519	116	-
45 - 49	C	4 305	810	2 381	...	...	888	226	-
50 - 54	C	5 742	866	3 326	...	...	1 086	464	-
55 - 59	C	5 926	727	3 607	...	...	865	727	-
60 - 64	C	7 246	738	4 278	...	...	821	1 409	-
65 - 69	C	11 599	1 061	6 100	...	...	989	3 449	-
70 - 74	C	19 096	1 733	8 293	...	...	1 204	7 866	-
75 - 79	C	30 742	2 864	10 082	...	...	1 515	16 281	-
80 - 84	C	36 121	3 067	7 719	...	...	1 659	23 676	-
85 - 89	C	50 032	3 946	5 663	...	...	1 847	38 576	-
90 - 94	C	51 061	4 035	2 767	...	...	1 779	42 480	-
95 - 99	C	22 432	2 024	519	...	...	651	19 238	-
100+	C	4 643	465	42	...	...	115	4 021	-
Germany - Allemagne									
2003									
Male									
Total	C	396 270	41 698	244 071	...	...	31 155	79 346	-
0 - 14	C	2 702	2 702	-	...	...	-	-	-
15 - 19	C	1 287	1 285	2	...	...	-	-	-
20 - 24	C	1 880	1 810	66	...	...	3	1	-

21. **Deaths by marital status, age and sex: latest available year, 1994 - 2003**
Décès selon l'état matrimonial, l'âge et le sexe: dernière année disponible, 1994 - 2003
(continued — suite)

Continent, country or area, date and age (in years) Continent, pays ou zone, date et âge (en années)	Code[1]	Total	Single (never married) - Célibataires	Married - Mariés	In consensual union - En union consensuelle	Married but separated - Mariés mais séparées	Divorced and not remarried - Divorcées non remariés	Widowed and not remarried - Veufs non remariés	Unknown - Inconnu
EUROPE									
Germany - Allemagne									
2003									
Male									
25 - 29	C	1 815	1 480	287	...	...	47	1	-
30 - 34	C	2 573	1 631	743	...	...	188	11	-
35 - 39	C	4 713	2 390	1 685	...	...	619	19	-
40 - 44	C	7 694	2 788	3 284	...	...	1 569	53	-
45 - 49	C	11 497	3 113	5 681	...	...	2 536	167	-
50 - 54	C	16 045	3 113	9 137	...	...	3 399	396	-
55 - 59	C	19 768	3 013	12 351	...	...	3 704	700	-
60 - 64	C	37 333	4 852	24 851	...	...	5 367	2 263	-
65 - 69	C	49 663	4 506	35 501	...	...	4 970	4 686	-
70 - 74	C	57 650	3 337	42 166	...	...	3 492	8 655	-
75 - 79	C	60 833	2 305	42 967	...	...	2 432	13 129	-
80 - 84	C	56 291	1 588	36 476	...	...	1 538	16 689	-
85 - 89	C	34 073	896	18 036	...	...	721	14 420	-
90 - 94	C	24 423	686	9 459	...	...	488	13 790	-
95 - 99	C	5 516	176	1 307	...	...	76	3 957	-
100+	C	514	27	72	...	...	6	409	-
Female									
Total	C	457 676	43 216	98 657	...	...	31 559	284 244	-
0 - 14	C	2 015	2 015	-	...	...	-	-	-
15 - 19	C	532	528	4	...	...	-	-	-
20 - 24	C	636	578	54	...	...	2	2	-
25 - 29	C	654	444	178	...	...	28	4	-
30 - 34	C	1 127	455	540	...	...	119	13	-
35 - 39	C	2 291	655	1 222	...	...	365	49	-
40 - 44	C	3 866	715	2 289	...	...	741	121	-
45 - 49	C	5 698	733	3 579	...	...	1 104	282	-
50 - 54	C	8 274	780	5 271	...	...	1 498	725	-
55 - 59	C	9 901	839	6 139	...	...	1 615	1 308	-
60 - 64	C	18 113	1 288	10 664	...	...	2 539	3 622	-
65 - 69	C	25 912	1 973	13 511	...	...	2 669	7 759	-
70 - 74	C	37 159	2 950	15 079	...	...	2 977	16 153	-
75 - 79	C	62 565	5 923	17 239	...	...	4 099	35 304	-
80 - 84	C	91 646	8 252	14 062	...	...	5 281	64 051	-
85 - 89	C	80 400	6 258	5 479	...	...	4 069	64 594	-
90 - 94	C	78 434	5 996	2 873	...	...	3 402	66 163	-
95 - 99	C	25 086	2 410	444	...	...	922	21 310	-
100+	C	3 367	424	30	...	...	129	2 784	-
Greece - Grèce									
2003									
Male									
Total	C	54 942	5 131	37 494	...	194	1 115	11 008	-
0 - 14	C	351	157	-	...	194	-	-	-
15 - 19	C	237	237	-	...	-	-	-	-
20 - 24	C	421	408	11	...	-	-	2	-
25 - 29	C	404	345	53	...	-	4	2	-
30 - 34	C	454	307	133	...	-	9	5	-
35 - 39	C	563	267	265	...	-	24	7	-
40 - 44	C	828	293	471	...	-	49	15	-
45 - 49	C	1 182	288	802	...	-	78	14	-
50 - 54	C	1 719	289	1 266	...	-	126	38	-
55 - 59	C	2 596	301	2 056	...	-	143	96	-
60 - 64	C	3 216	272	2 661	...	-	128	155	-
65 - 69	C	5 478	344	4 560	...	-	151	423	-
70 - 74	C	7 812	443	6 308	...	-	140	921	-
75 - 79	C	9 455	446	7 228	...	-	127	1 654	-
80 - 84	C	8 074	346	5 589	...	-	74	2 065	-
85 - 89	C	6 606	236	3 839	...	-	39	2 492	-

21. Deaths by marital status, age and sex: latest available year, 1994 - 2003
Décès selon l'état matrimonial, l'âge et le sexe: dernière année disponible, 1994 - 2003
(continued — suite)

Continent, country or area, date and age (in years) / Continent, pays ou zone, date et âge (en années)	Code[1]	Total	Single (never married) - Célibataires	Married - Mariés	In consensual union - En union consensuelle	Married but separated - Mariés mais séparées	Divorced and not remarried - Divorcées non remariés	Widowed and not remarried - Veufs non remariés	Unknown - Inconnu
EUROPE									
Greece - Grèce									
2003									
Male									
90 - 94	C	4 171	130	1 815	...	-	15	2 211	-
95 - 99	C	1 202	16	394	...	-	7	785	-
100+	C	173	6	43	...	-	1	123	-
Female									
Total	C	50 587	4 120	13 201	...	156	1 056	32 054	-
0 - 14	C	273	117	-	...	156	-	-	-
15 - 19	C	80	80	-	...	-	-	-	-
20 - 24	C	83	73	7	...	-	-	3	-
25 - 29	C	114	84	22	...	-	1	7	-
30 - 34	C	165	69	82	...	-	4	10	-
35 - 39	C	228	79	126	...	-	14	9	-
40 - 44	C	360	73	233	...	-	35	19	-
45 - 49	C	548	110	366	...	-	38	34	-
50 - 54	C	763	124	514	...	-	54	71	-
55 - 59	C	1 110	150	731	...	-	73	156	-
60 - 64	C	1 486	162	951	...	-	71	302	-
65 - 69	C	2 946	275	1 671	...	-	98	902	-
70 - 74	C	5 151	453	2 329	...	-	136	2 233	-
75 - 79	C	8 354	662	2 566	...	-	159	4 967	-
80 - 84	C	9 586	666	1 820	...	-	166	6 934	-
85 - 89	C	9 961	569	1 175	...	-	111	8 106	-
90 - 94	C	6 809	289	504	...	-	70	5 946	-
95 - 99	C	2 113	72	93	...	-	21	1 927	-
100+	C	457	13	11	...	-	5	428	-
Hungary - Hongrie									
2003									
Male									
Total	C	70 016	7 201	39 834	...	...	8 395	14 585	1
0 - 14	C	573	573	-	...	...	-	-	-
15 - 19	C	162	162	-	...	...	-	-	-
20 - 24	C	314	297	15	...	...	2	-	-
25 - 29	C	449	356	77	...	...	16	-	-
30 - 34	C	594	325	195	...	...	71	3	-
35 - 39	C	898	363	339	...	...	182	14	-
40 - 44	C	1 901	593	757	...	...	504	47	-
45 - 49	C	4 142	982	1 872	...	...	1 127	161	-
50 - 54	C	5 181	799	2 721	...	...	1 341	320	-
55 - 59	C	6 081	645	3 533	...	...	1 386	517	-
60 - 64	C	7 039	558	4 584	...	...	1 156	741	-
65 - 69	C	7 940	436	5 455	...	...	832	1 217	-
70 - 74	C	9 814	394	6 672	...	...	745	2 003	-
75 - 79	C	9 986	314	6 392	...	...	531	2 749	-
80 - 84	C	8 341	224	4 693	...	...	316	3 108	-
85 - 89	C	3 756	94	1 679	...	...	112	1 871	-
90 - 94	C	2 421	67	767	...	...	65	1 522	-
95 - 99	C	373	10	80	...	...	6	277	-
100+	C	41	1	3	...	...	2	35	-
Unk. - Inc.	C	10	8	-	...	...	1	-	1
Female									
Total	C	65 807	4 226	14 272	...	...	5 958	41 351	-
0 - 14	C	445	445	-	...	...	-	-	-
15 - 19	C	76	76	-	...	...	-	-	-
20 - 24	C	104	99	2	...	...	2	1	-
25 - 29	C	146	92	43	...	...	11	...	-
30 - 34	C	234	94	109	...	...	24	7	-
35 - 39	C	365	64	199	...	...	83	19	-
40 - 44	C	824	110	467	...	...	187	60	-

21. Deaths by marital status, age and sex: latest available year, 1994 - 2003
Décès selon l'état matrimonial, l'âge et le sexe: dernière année disponible, 1994 - 2003
(continued — suite)

Continent, country or area, date and age (in years) / Continent, pays ou zone, date et âge (en années)	Code[1]	Total	Single (never married) - Célibataires	Married - Mariés	In consensual union - En union consensuelle	Married but separated - Mariés mais séparées	Divorced and not remarried - Divorcées non remariés	Widowed and not remarried - Veufs non remariés	Unknown - Inconnu
EUROPE									
Hungary - Hongrie									
2003									
Female									
45 - 49	C	1 722	139	971	...	...	393	219	-
50 - 54	C	2 298	182	1 226	...	...	488	402	-
55 - 59	C	2 754	175	1 380	...	...	499	700	-
60 - 64	C	3 593	193	1 615	...	...	526	1 259	-
65 - 69	C	5 006	224	1 934	...	...	539	2 309	-
70 - 74	C	8 106	359	2 308	...	...	734	4 705	-
75 - 79	C	11 517	516	2 217	...	...	907	7 077	-
80 - 84	C	13 315	647	1 319	...	...	801	10 548	-
85 - 89	C	7 750	400	358	...	...	440	6 552	-
90 - 94	C	5 967	317	111	...	...	266	5 273	-
95 - 99	C	1 427	86	13	...	...	54	1 274	-
100+	C	157	7	-	...	...	4	146	-
Unk. - Inc. ...	C	1	1	-	...	...	-	-	-
Iceland - Islande									
2003									
Male									
Total	C	901	186	421	21	7	73	191	2
0 - 14	C	11	11	-	-	-	-	-	-
15 - 19	C	2	2	-	-	-	-	-	-
20 - 24	C	7	7	-	-	-	-	-	-
25 - 29	C	7	4	1	1	-	-	-	1
30 - 34	C	5	1	2	-	-	1	-	1
35 - 39	C	4	2	1	-	-	1	-	-
40 - 44	C	9	5	2	-	1	1	-	-
45 - 49	C	20	4	9	2	-	5	-	-
50 - 54	C	26	8	12	-	-	5	1	-
55 - 59	C	42	9	21	2	-	9	1	-
60 - 64	C	51	11	29	2	1	7	1	-
65 - 69	C	59	7	33	3	2	6	8	-
70 - 74	C	114	14	71	-	-	12	17	-
75 - 79	C	136	21	73	4	-	11	27	-
80 - 84	C	164	35	74	4	2	8	41	-
85 - 89	C	132	23	47	2	1	7	52	-
90 - 94	C	84	16	39	1	-	-	28	-
95 - 99	C	25	4	7	-	-	-	14	-
100+	C	3	2	-	-	-	-	1	-
Female									
Total	C	926	140	234	8	8	76	460	-
0 - 14	C	7	7	-	-	-	-	-	-
15 - 19	C	3	3	-	-	-	-	-	-
20 - 24	C	3	3	-	-	-	-	-	-
25 - 29	C	2	1	-	1	-	-	-	-
30 - 34	C	4	1	1	1	-	1	-	-
35 - 39	C	7	3	3	-	-	1	-	-
40 - 44	C	13	4	4	1	-	3	1	-
45 - 49	C	8	2	4	-	-	2	-	-
50 - 54	C	20	1	13	1	-	3	2	-
55 - 59	C	31	1	22	-	-	5	3	-
60 - 64	C	29	5	16	1	1	5	1	-
65 - 69	C	48	5	31	-	1	6	5	-
70 - 74	C	94	5	45	-	3	12	29	-
75 - 79	C	101	9	33	1	1	10	47	-
80 - 84	C	169	18	35	1	1	15	99	-
85 - 89	C	190	31	23	1	1	7	127	-
90 - 94	C	133	26	4	-	-	4	99	-
95 - 99	C	50	10	-	-	-	2	38	-
100+	C	14	5	-	-	-	-	9	-

21. Deaths by marital status, age and sex: latest available year, 1994 - 2003
Décès selon l'état matrimonial, l'âge et le sexe: dernière année disponible, 1994 - 2003
(continued — suite)

Continent, country or area, date and age (in years) — Continent, pays ou zone, date et âge (en années)	Code[1]	Total	Single (never married) - Célibataires	Married - Mariés	In consensual union - En union consensuelle	Married but separated - Mariés mais séparées	Divorced and not remarried - Divorcées non remariés	Widowed and not remarried - Veufs non remariés	Unknown - Inconnu
EUROPE									
Ireland - Irlande[23]									
2003									
Male									
Total	+C	14 735	4 817	6 905	...	228	104	2 681	-
0 - 14	+C	251	251	-	...	-	-	-	-
15 - 19	+C	102	102	-	...	-	-	-	-
20 - 24	+C	180	179	1	...	-	-	-	-
25 - 29	+C	158	143	15	...	-	-	-	-
30 - 34	+C	151	105	40	...	3	3	-	-
35 - 39	+C	174	95	76	...	1	2	-	-
40 - 44	+C	233	110	109	...	9	3	2	-
45 - 49	+C	325	118	174	...	22	8	3	-
50 - 54	+C	522	176	292	...	29	14	11	-
55 - 59	+C	794	253	489	...	27	9	16	-
60 - 64	+C	1 034	326	591	...	35	19	63	-
65 - 69	+C	1 417	426	798	...	31	17	145	-
70 - 74	+C	1 886	569	1 065	...	19	9	224	-
75 - 79	+C	2 426	688	1 250	...	22	10	456	-
80 - 84	+C	2 476	641	1 117	...	19	5	694	-
85 - 89	+C	1 714	426	653	...	9	5	621	-
90 - 94	+C	731	169	198	...	1	-	363	-
95 - 99	+C	144	35	31	...	1	-	77	-
100+	+C	17	5	6	...	-	-	6	-
Female									
Total	+C	14 088	3 160	3 273	...	125	55	7 475	-
0 - 14	+C	178	178	-	...	-	-	-	-
15 - 19	+C	44	44	-	...	-	-	-	-
20 - 24	+C	50	47	3	...	-	-	-	-
25 - 29	+C	57	46	10	...	-	-	1	-
30 - 34	+C	53	35	16	...	2	-	-	-
35 - 39	+C	101	48	51	...	1	1	-	-
40 - 44	+C	139	44	85	...	6	3	1	-
45 - 49	+C	206	41	138	...	6	8	13	-
50 - 54	+C	322	71	211	...	14	4	22	-
55 - 59	+C	506	83	345	...	15	8	55	-
60 - 64	+C	644	115	378	...	23	11	117	-
65 - 69	+C	838	145	418	...	19	4	252	-
70 - 74	+C	1 280	236	475	...	15	1	553	-
75 - 79	+C	2 124	417	498	...	13	8	1 188	-
80 - 84	+C	2 749	573	375	...	4	4	1 793	-
85 - 89	+C	2 548	554	181	...	7	-	1 806	-
90 - 94	+C	1 642	355	69	...	-	1	1 217	-
95 - 99	+C	523	105	19	...	-	2	397	-
100+	+C	84	23	1	...	-	-	60	-
Italy - Italie									
2001									
Male									
Total	C	278 999	34 519	182 778	...	278	3 121	56 041	2 262
0 - 14	C	2 037	2 037	-	...	-	-	-	-
15 - 19	C	932	917	3	...	-	-	-	12
20 - 24	C	1 568	1 492	46	...	-	-	1	29
25 - 29	C	2 001	1 662	271	...	1	4	1	62
30 - 34	C	2 339	1 496	745	...	4	20	8	66
35 - 39	C	2 915	1 297	1 443	...	11	73	21	70
40 - 44	C	3 615	1 235	2 135	...	15	130	32	68
45 - 49	C	4 908	1 227	3 376	...	12	173	53	67
50 - 54	C	8 412	1 501	6 287	...	32	341	165	86
55 - 59	C	11 795	1 817	9 134	...	40	339	369	96
60 - 64	C	19 169	2 482	15 244	...	34	390	893	126
65 - 69	C	27 791	3 120	21 974	...	30	416	2 048	203

21. Deaths by marital status, age and sex: latest available year, 1994 - 2003
Décès selon l'état matrimonial, l'âge et le sexe: dernière année disponible, 1994 - 2003
(continued — suite)

Continent, country or area, date and age (in years) / Continent, pays ou zone, date et âge (en années)	Code[1]	Total	Single (never married) - Célibataires	Married - Mariés	In consensual union - En union consensuelle	Married but separated - Mariés mais séparées	Divorced and not remarried - Divorcées non remariés	Widowed and not remarried - Veufs non remariés	Unknown - Inconnu
EUROPE									
Italy - Italie									
2001									
Male									
70 - 74	C	39 750	3 890	30 621	...	36	423	4 503	277
75 - 79	C	49 324	4 011	35 835	...	26	382	8 695	375
80 - 84	C	37 198	2 454	24 885	...	16	219	9 356	268
85 - 89	C	39 953	2 544	21 644	...	16	149	15 317	283
90 - 94	C	20 399	1 089	8 003	...	3	56	11 112	136
95 - 99	C	4 385	229	1 069	...	2	6	3 048	31
100+	C	508	19	63	...	-	-	419	7
Female									
Total	C	277 811	36 941	64 569	...	151	2 706	171 170	2 274
0 - 14	C	1 576	1 576	-	...	-	-	-	-
15 - 19	C	309	303	3	...	-	-	-	3
20 - 24	C	469	409	41	...	-	-	1	18
25 - 29	C	628	413	184	...	-	3	2	26
30 - 34	C	870	384	443	...	3	16	9	15
35 - 39	C	1 438	428	890	...	3	45	49	23
40 - 44	C	1 917	423	1 300	...	10	97	61	26
45 - 49	C	2 805	500	2 005	...	10	131	138	21
50 - 54	C	4 654	644	3 449	...	15	185	326	35
55 - 59	C	6 068	738	4 335	...	7	174	766	48
60 - 64	C	9 922	1 179	6 496	...	14	230	1 923	80
65 - 69	C	15 241	1 765	8 302	...	14	261	4 785	114
70 - 74	C	24 901	3 031	10 392	...	20	339	10 915	204
75 - 79	C	40 752	5 153	11 794	...	23	424	23 021	337
80 - 84	C	41 992	4 944	7 474	...	14	333	28 865	362
85 - 89	C	62 106	7 406	5 430	...	7	305	48 472	486
90 - 94	C	44 952	5 401	1 782	...	10	123	37 281	355
95 - 99	C	14 803	1 911	232	...	-	37	12 524	99
100+	C	2 408	333	17	...	1	3	2 032	22
Latvia - Lettonie[11]									
2002									
Male									
Total	C	16 423	2 246	8 273	...	...	2 284	2 683	937
0 - 14	C	198	160	-	...	...	-	-	38
15 - 19	C	89	87	-	...	...	-	-	2
20 - 24	C	196	179	11	...	...	1	-	5
25 - 29	C	233	168	47	...	...	5	-	13
30 - 34	C	335	154	111	...	...	42	-	28
35 - 39	C	430	122	181	...	...	84	9	34
40 - 44	C	671	145	278	...	...	171	14	63
45 - 49	C	885	168	363	...	...	252	14	88
50 - 54	C	1 187	174	518	...	...	305	49	141
55 - 59	C	1 306	175	644	...	...	287	83	117
60 - 64	C	2 069	229	1 114	...	...	380	213	133
65 - 69	C	2 126	150	1 283	...	...	292	311	90
70 - 74	C	2 380	127	1 485	...	...	237	455	76
75 - 79	C	1 788	87	1 072	...	...	126	455	48
80 - 84	C	1 231	60	662	...	...	58	421	30
85 - 89	C	723	42	310	...	...	24	330	17
90 - 94	C	445	12	161	...	...	16	249	7
95 - 99	C	116	7	32	...	...	4	72	1
100+	C	9	-	1	...	...	-	8	-
Unk. - Inc. ...	C	6	-	-	...	...	-	-	6
Female									
Total	C	16 075	1 870	3 027	...	...	1 513	9 070	595
0 - 14	C	145	107	-	...	...	-	-	38
15 - 19	C	45	44	1	...	...	-	-	-
20 - 24	C	42	36	5	...	...	-	-	1

21. Deaths by marital status, age and sex: latest available year, 1994 - 2003
Décès selon l'état matrimonial, l'âge et le sexe: dernière année disponible, 1994 - 2003
(continued — suite)

Continent, country or area, date and age (in years) / Continent, pays ou zone, date et âge (en années)	Code[1]	Total	Single (never married) - Célibataires	Married - Mariés	In consensual union - En union consensuelle	Married but separated - Mariés mais séparées	Divorced and not remarried - Divorcées non remariés	Widowed and not remarried - Veufs non remariés	Unknown - Inconnu
EUROPE									
Latvia - Lettonie[11]									
2002									
Female									
25 - 29	C	36	21	9	...	...	3	-	3
30 - 34	C	82	28	36	...	...	13	2	3
35 - 39	C	128	27	44	...	...	37	7	13
40 - 44	C	212	34	96	...	...	50	19	13
45 - 49	C	309	39	136	...	...	78	32	24
50 - 54	C	457	39	211	...	...	98	70	39
55 - 59	C	595	49	245	...	...	114	147	40
60 - 64	C	959	76	370	...	...	185	274	54
65 - 69	C	1 305	128	422	...	...	194	520	41
70 - 74	C	1 961	213	570	...	...	207	912	59
75 - 79	C	2 855	348	506	...	...	249	1 670	82
80 - 84	C	2 677	277	248	...	...	143	1 929	80
85 - 89	C	2 162	206	81	...	...	75	1 747	53
90 - 94	C	1 613	166	41	...	...	56	1 314	36
95 - 99	C	426	27	5	...	...	10	371	13
100+	C	65	5	1	...	...	1	56	2
Unk. - Inc. ...	C	1	-	-	...	...	-	-	1
Liechtenstein									
2003									
Male									
Total	C	103	15	68	...	-	9	11	-
Female									
Total	C	114	19	23	...	1	7	64	-
Lithuania - Lituanie[11]									
2003									
Male									
Total	C	21 859	2 725	13 093	...	...	2 372	3 512	157
0 - 14	C	212	196	-	...	...	-	-	16
15 - 19	C	162	161	1	...	...	-	-	-
20 - 24	C	287	260	18	...	...	6	1	2
25 - 29	C	335	211	107	...	...	14	1	2
30 - 34	C	498	206	218	...	...	68	2	4
35 - 39	C	594	149	298	...	...	133	4	10
40 - 44	C	985	203	524	...	...	223	18	17
45 - 49	C	1 224	210	669	...	...	299	28	18
50 - 54	C	1 529	210	874	...	...	364	56	25
55 - 59	C	1 655	172	1 014	...	...	321	120	28
60 - 64	C	2 240	218	1 458	...	...	328	220	16
65 - 69	C	2 667	176	1 881	...	...	274	329	7
70 - 74	C	2 952	132	2 126	...	...	166	523	5
75 - 79	C	2 612	96	1 785	...	...	84	646	1
80 - 84	C	1 856	59	1 153	...	...	60	582	2
85 - 89	C	1 063	32	550	...	...	22	458	1
90 - 94	C	608	19	289	...	...	6	293	1
95 - 99	C	315	14	111	...	...	4	186	-
100+	C	63	1	17	...	...	-	45	-
Unk. - Inc. ...	C	2	-	-	...	...	-	-	2
Female									
Total	C	19 131	2 182	4 658	...	...	1 285	10 947	59
0 - 14	C	153	140	-	...	...	-	-	13
15 - 19	C	64	61	3	...	...	-	-	-
20 - 24	C	47	37	7	...	...	1	-	2
25 - 29	C	79	38	31	...	...	8	2	-
30 - 34	C	119	26	64	...	...	24	3	2
35 - 39	C	171	31	84	...	...	47	6	3
40 - 44	C	329	41	175	...	...	87	25	1

21. Deaths by marital status, age and sex: latest available year, 1994 - 2003
Décès selon l'état matrimonial, l'âge et le sexe: dernière année disponible, 1994 - 2003
(continued — suite)

Continent, country or area, date and age (in years) / Continent, pays ou zone, date et âge (en années)	Code[1]	Total	Single (never married) - Célibataires	Married - Mariés	In consensual union - En union consensuelle	Married but separated - Mariés mais séparées	Divorced and not remarried - Divorcées non remariés	Widowed and not remarried - Veufs non remariés	Unknown - Inconnu
EUROPE									
Lithuania - Lituanie[11]									
2003									
Female									
45 - 49	C	443	39	238	...	...	106	56	4
50 - 54	C	583	63	290	...	...	138	90	2
55 - 59	C	698	55	344	...	...	131	164	4
60 - 64	C	1 087	100	518	...	...	135	329	5
65 - 69	C	1 501	156	597	...	...	143	601	4
70 - 74	C	2 308	208	782	...	...	149	1 167	2
75 - 79	C	3 378	403	740	...	...	165	2 066	4
80 - 84	C	3 276	338	456	...	...	80	2 397	5
85 - 89	C	2 376	229	204	...	...	42	1 897	4
90 - 94	C	1 805	154	97	...	...	26	1 527	1
95 - 99	C	581	55	25	...	...	3	497	1
100+	C	132	8	3	...	...	-	120	1
Unk. - Inc. ...	C	1	-	-	...	...	-	-	1
Luxembourg									
2003									
Male									
Total	C	2 005	275	1 149	...	18	137	426	-
0 - 14	C	22	22	-	...	-	-	-	-
15 - 19	C	4	4	-	...	-	-	-	-
20 - 24	C	17	16	1	...	-	-	-	-
25 - 29	C	16	14	2	...	-	-	-	-
30 - 34	C	21	16	3	...	1	1	-	-
35 - 39	C	26	15	9	...	-	2	-	-
40 - 44	C	43	18	15	...	3	7	-	-
45 - 49	C	60	18	27	...	2	12	1	-
50 - 54	C	85	16	53	...	1	12	3	-
55 - 59	C	117	17	69	...	1	25	5	-
60 - 64	C	140	15	102	...	2	16	5	-
65 - 69	C	218	24	147	...	3	22	22	-
70 - 74	C	306	16	221	...	2	18	49	-
75 - 79	C	301	23	197	...	1	15	65	-
80 - 84	C	267	18	159	...	1	5	84	-
85 - 89	C	222	17	100	...	1	1	103	-
90 - 94	C	114	5	41	...	-	-	68	-
95 - 99	C	26	1	3	...	-	1	21	-
100+	C	-	-	-	...	-	-	-	-
Female									
Total	C	2 048	224	468	...	3	81	1 272	-
0 - 14	C	15	15	-	...	-	-	-	-
15 - 19	C	3	3	-	...	-	-	-	-
20 - 24	C	1	-	1	...	-	-	-	-
25 - 29	C	5	1	4	...	-	-	-	-
30 - 34	C	8	2	4	...	1	-	1	-
35 - 39	C	15	5	7	...	-	2	1	-
40 - 44	C	18	4	9	...	-	1	4	-
45 - 49	C	28	7	16	...	-	4	1	-
50 - 54	C	32	2	22	...	-	4	4	-
55 - 59	C	48	2	35	...	1	6	4	-
60 - 64	C	86	7	44	...	1	11	23	-
65 - 69	C	131	14	62	...	-	13	42	-
70 - 74	C	206	19	85	...	-	9	93	-
75 - 79	C	297	27	93	...	-	9	168	-
80 - 84	C	370	31	52	...	-	14	273	-
85 - 89	C	392	45	25	...	-	7	315	-
90 - 94	C	275	27	7	...	-	1	240	-
95 - 99	C	103	11	2	...	-	-	90	-
100+	C	15	2	-	...	-	-	13	-

589

21. Deaths by marital status, age and sex: latest available year, 1994 - 2003
Décès selon l'état matrimonial, l'âge et le sexe: dernière année disponible, 1994 - 2003
(continued — suite)

Continent, country or area, date and age (in years) / Continent, pays ou zone, date et âge (en années)	Code[1]	Total	Single (never married) - Célibataires	Married - Mariés	In consensual union - En union consensuelle	Married but separated - Mariés mais séparées	Divorced and not remarried - Divorcées non remariés	Widowed and not remarried - Veufs non remariés	Unknown - Inconnu
EUROPE									
Malta - Malte									
2002									
Male									
Total	C	1 604	282	884	...	...	24	324	90
0 - 14	C	18	18	-	...	...	-	-	-
15 - 19	C	8	7	-	...	...	-	-	1
20 - 24	C	10	9	-	...	...	-	-	1
25 - 29	C	16	9	5	...	...	-	-	2
30 - 34	C	7	7	-	...	...	-	-	-
35 - 39	C	9	2	6	...	...	1	-	-
40 - 44	C	17	6	8	...	...	1	-	2
45 - 49	C	34	7	22	...	...	2	1	2
50 - 54	C	64	14	44	...	...	2	1	3
55 - 59	C	83	12	60	...	...	5	4	2
60 - 64	C	84	18	58	...	...	1	2	5
65 - 69	C	182	29	123	...	...	3	12	15
70 - 74	C	223	37	145	...	...	2	32	7
75 - 79	C	265	43	143	...	...	3	55	21
80 - 84	C	301	38	159	...	...	3	89	12
85 - 89	C	182	18	78	...	...	1	74	11
90 - 94	C	101	15	26	...	...	-	54	6
95 - 99	C	-	-	-	...	...	-	-	-
100+	C	-	-	-	...	...	-	-	-
Female									
Total	C	1 427	330	404	...	...	6	628	59
0 - 14	C	16	14	-	...	...	-	-	2
15 - 19	C	1	1	-	...	...	-	-	-
20 - 24	C	3	3	-	...	...	-	-	-
25 - 29	C	5	2	3	...	...	-	-	-
30 - 34	C	6	1	3	...	...	1	1	-
35 - 39	C	8	1	5	...	...	-	2	-
40 - 44	C	9	1	8	...	...	-	-	-
45 - 49	C	25	6	17	...	...	-	2	-
50 - 54	C	32	8	20	...	...	-	3	1
55 - 59	C	53	14	32	...	...	1	4	2
60 - 64	C	66	12	40	...	...	1	8	5
65 - 69	C	99	26	50	...	...	2	20	1
70 - 74	C	181	44	62	...	...	-	65	10
75 - 79	C	243	52	79	...	...	1	103	8
80 - 84	C	260	39	44	...	...	-	162	15
85 - 89	C	225	48	23	...	...	-	143	11
90 - 94	C	195	56	18	...	...	-	115	6
95 - 99	C	-	-	-	...	...	-	-	-
100+	C	-	-	-	...	...	-	-	-
Netherlands - Pays-Bas[24]									
2002									
Male									
Total	C	68 998	8 733	40 467	...	...	5 489	14 309	-
0 - 14	C	838	838	-	...	...	-	-	-
15 - 19	C	211	211	-	...	...	-	-	-
20 - 24	C	319	304	13	...	...	2	-	-
25 - 29	C	286	250	31	...	...	5	-	-
30 - 34	C	493	369	106	...	...	18	-	-
35 - 39	C	694	360	241	...	...	93	-	-
40 - 44	C	979	373	448	...	...	153	5	-
45 - 49	C	1 558	472	790	...	...	281	15	-
50 - 54	C	2 397	481	1 359	...	...	505	52	-
55 - 59	C	3 720	553	2 396	...	...	675	96	-
60 - 64	C	4 641	577	3 177	...	...	646	241	-
65 - 69	C	6 475	698	4 567	...	...	740	470	-

21. Deaths by marital status, age and sex: latest available year, 1994 - 2003
Décès selon l'état matrimonial, l'âge et le sexe: dernière année disponible, 1994 - 2003
(continued — suite)

Continent, country or area, date and age (in years) / Continent, pays ou zone, date et âge (en années)	Code[1]	Total	Single (never married) - Célibataires	Married - Mariés	In consensual union - En union consensuelle	Married but separated - Mariés mais séparées	Divorced and not remarried - Divorcées non remariés	Widowed and not remarried - Veufs non remariés	Unknown - Inconnu
EUROPE									
Netherlands - Pays-Bas[24]									
2002									
Male									
70 - 74	C	9 423	859	6 676	...	...	783	1 105	-
75 - 79	C	11 620	856	7 796	...	...	681	2 287	-
80 - 84	C	11 723	732	7 169	...	...	520	3 302	-
85 - 89	C	8 504	482	4 163	...	...	265	3 594	-
90 - 94	C	3 947	249	1 316	...	...	105	2 277	-
95 - 99	C	1 041	59	201	...	...	16	765	-
100+	C	129	10	18	...	...	1	100	-
Female									
Total	C	73 357	8 162	18 058	...	...	5 149	41 988	-
0 - 14	C	629	629	-	...	...	-	-	-
15 - 19	C	110	110	-	...	...	-	-	-
20 - 24	C	115	100	14	...	...	1	-	-
25 - 29	C	182	134	42	...	...	6	-	-
30 - 34	C	293	138	134	...	...	18	3	-
35 - 39	C	458	156	253	...	...	46	3	-
40 - 44	C	734	187	411	...	...	123	13	-
45 - 49	C	1 279	221	758	...	...	253	47	-
50 - 54	C	1 811	211	1 137	...	...	362	101	-
55 - 59	C	2 383	225	1 498	...	...	439	221	-
60 - 64	C	2 770	213	1 680	...	...	431	446	-
65 - 69	C	3 770	276	2 077	...	...	464	953	-
70 - 74	C	6 127	511	2 608	...	...	558	2 450	-
75 - 79	C	9 385	812	2 879	...	...	649	5 045	-
80 - 84	C	13 174	1 069	2 689	...	...	674	8 742	-
85 - 89	C	14 393	1 408	1 387	...	...	613	10 985	-
90 - 94	C	11 032	1 182	436	...	...	357	9 057	-
95 - 99	C	4 022	486	52	...	...	138	3 346	-
100+	C	690	94	3	...	...	17	576	-
Norway - Norvège[25]									
2003									
Male									
Total	C	20 565	3 363	10 327	...	278	1 794	4 792	11
0 - 14	C	189	189	-	...	-	-	-	-
15 - 19	C	92	92	-	...	-	-	-	-
20 - 24	C	124	122	1	...	1	-	-	-
25 - 29	C	145	127	13	...	2	2	1	-
30 - 34	C	190	145	25	...	11	8	1	-
35 - 39	C	220	132	47	...	16	24	1	-
40 - 44	C	286	146	78	...	17	44	1	-
45 - 49	C	408	134	137	...	21	108	5	3
50 - 54	C	613	151	274	...	27	146	14	1
55 - 59	C	982	168	523	...	40	213	35	3
60 - 64	C	1 072	175	588	...	30	235	43	1
65 - 69	C	1 502	209	886	...	26	254	126	1
70 - 74	C	2 241	297	1 361	...	29	264	290	-
75 - 79	C	3 226	406	1 962	...	30	229	598	1
80 - 84	C	4 109	414	2 366	...	17	163	1 148	1
85 - 89	C	3 177	278	1 459	...	7	79	1 354	-
90 - 94	C	1 597	137	534	...	4	22	900	-
95 - 99	C	344	35	68	...	-	3	238	-
100+	C	48	6	5	...	-	-	37	-
Female									
Total	C	21 913	2 534	4 599	...	115	1 506	13 158	1
0 - 14	C	148	148	-	...	-	-	-	-
15 - 19	C	36	36	-	...	-	-	-	-
20 - 24	C	47	42	3	...	2	-	-	-

21. Deaths by marital status, age and sex: latest available year, 1994 - 2003
Décès selon l'état matrimonial, l'âge et le sexe: dernière année disponible, 1994 - 2003
(continued — suite)

Continent, country or area, date and age (in years) — Continent, pays ou zone, date et âge (en annèes)	Code[1]	Total	Single (never married) - Célibataires	Married - Mariés	In consensual union - En union consensuelle	Married but separated - Mariés mais séparées	Divorced and not remarried - Divorcées non remariés	Widowed and not remarried - Veufs non remariés	Unknown - Inconnu
EUROPE									
Norway - Norvège[25]									
2003									
Female									
25 - 29	C	57	42	9	...	2	4	-	-
30 - 34	C	74	50	15	...	1	8	-	-
35 - 39	C	102	36	47	...	5	13	1	-
40 - 44	C	178	60	70	...	5	42	1	-
45 - 49	C	246	51	111	...	17	62	5	-
50 - 54	C	374	53	196	...	10	91	24	-
55 - 59	C	633	65	351	...	17	142	57	1
60 - 64	C	675	55	364	...	14	129	113	-
65 - 69	C	871	61	422	...	9	128	251	-
70 - 74	C	1 521	108	642	...	9	151	611	-
75 - 79	C	2 675	211	855	...	11	187	1 411	-
80 - 84	C	4 272	403	861	...	10	220	2 778	-
85 - 89	C	5 046	477	514	...	3	189	3 863	-
90 - 94	C	3 525	422	128	...	-	102	2 873	-
95 - 99	C	1 239	190	10	...	-	35	1 004	-
100+	C	194	24	1	...	-	3	166	-
Poland - Pologne									
2003									
Male									
Total	C	193 919	24 836	120 197	...	472	13 183	35 231	-
0 - 14	C	2 150	2 150	-	...	-	-	-	-
15 - 19	C	1 047	1 045	2	...	-	-	-	-
20 - 24	C	1 842	1 718	117	...	-	5	2	-
25 - 29	C	1 860	1 253	549	...	3	50	5	-
30 - 34	C	2 174	1 043	938	...	8	161	24	-
35 - 39	C	3 220	1 316	1 457	...	16	379	52	-
40 - 44	C	6 106	2 058	3 041	...	34	828	145	-
45 - 49	C	10 842	2 968	5 850	...	63	1 626	335	-
50 - 54	C	15 005	2 752	9 246	...	83	2 225	699	-
55 - 59	C	14 709	1 864	9 897	...	71	1 932	945	-
60 - 64	C	16 867	1 676	12 050	...	57	1 550	1 534	-
65 - 69	C	23 552	1 684	17 399	...	39	1 504	2 926	-
70 - 74	C	29 001	1 390	21 228	...	42	1 277	5 064	-
75 - 79	C	27 337	891	18 746	...	34	849	6 817	-
80 - 84	C	19 986	572	12 140	...	18	444	6 812	-
85+	C	18 221	456	7 537	...	4	353	9 871	-
Female									
Total	C	171 311	15 999	41 864	...	321	8 212	104 915	-
0 - 14	C	1 577	1 577	-	...	-	-	-	-
15 - 19	C	409	405	4	...	-	-	-	-
20 - 24	C	462	390	66	...	-	1	5	-
25 - 29	C	496	243	231	...	1	17	4	-
30 - 34	C	597	166	364	...	1	50	16	-
35 - 39	C	974	161	685	...	-	87	41	-
40 - 44	C	2 087	280	1 388	...	15	275	129	-
45 - 49	C	4 044	451	2 750	...	19	479	345	-
50 - 54	C	6 174	603	3 971	...	27	706	867	-
55 - 59	C	6 448	583	3 895	...	21	649	1 300	-
60 - 64	C	7 842	542	4 233	...	24	660	2 383	-
65 - 69	C	12 946	871	5 698	...	30	986	5 361	-
70 - 74	C	21 542	1 495	7 077	...	54	1 206	11 710	-
75 - 79	C	30 304	2 367	6 417	...	48	1 248	20 224	-
80 - 84	C	31 052	2 404	3 628	...	37	978	24 005	-
85+	C	44 357	3 461	1 457	...	44	870	38 525	-

21. Deaths by marital status, age and sex: latest available year, 1994 - 2003
Décès selon l'état matrimonial, l'âge et le sexe: dernière année disponible, 1994 - 2003
(continued — suite)

Continent, country or area, date and age (in years) / Continent, pays ou zone, date et âge (en années)	Code[1]	Total	Single (never married) - Célibataires	Married - Mariés	In consensual union - En union consensuelle	Married but separated - Mariés mais séparées	Divorced and not remarried - Divorcées non remariés	Widowed and not remarried - Veufs non remariés	Unknown - Inconnu
EUROPE									
Portugal									
2003									
Male									
Total	C	55 968	7 365	33 394	...	...	1 973	13 003	233
0 - 14	C	431	431	-	...	...	-	-	-
15 - 19	C	213	212	1	...	...	-	-	-
20 - 24	C	414	380	21	...	...	3	4	6
25 - 29	C	551	420	101	...	...	16	8	6
30 - 34	C	752	478	229	...	...	30	5	10
35 - 39	C	923	478	344	...	...	81	11	9
40 - 44	C	1 265	434	612	...	...	178	15	26
45 - 49	C	1 677	420	995	...	...	208	33	21
50 - 54	C	2 077	367	1 424	...	...	204	67	15
55 - 59	C	2 568	336	1 853	...	...	235	128	16
60 - 64	C	3 445	375	2 599	...	...	196	262	13
65 - 69	C	5 391	507	4 021	...	...	213	627	23
70 - 74	C	7 492	631	5 436	...	...	202	1 207	16
75 - 79	C	9 400	704	6 312	...	...	184	2 176	24
80 - 84	C	9 028	579	5 413	...	...	120	2 893	23
85 - 89	C	6 489	416	2 923	...	...	69	3 066	15
90 - 94	C	3 161	169	990	...	...	29	1 967	6
95 - 99	C	624	28	111	...	...	5	478	2
100+	C	67	-	9	...	...	-	56	2
Female									
Total	C	52 827	7 461	13 508	...	...	1 455	30 242	161
0 - 14	C	384	384	-	...	...	-	-	-
15 - 19	C	85	83	2	...	...	-	-	-
20 - 24	C	139	119	15	...	...	3	2	-
25 - 29	C	211	126	55	...	...	10	19	1
30 - 34	C	241	111	103	...	...	15	11	1
35 - 39	C	349	109	198	...	...	32	9	1
40 - 44	C	486	98	295	...	...	57	33	3
45 - 49	C	710	138	432	...	...	84	55	1
50 - 54	C	967	161	616	...	...	88	98	4
55 - 59	C	1 315	194	809	...	...	101	202	9
60 - 64	C	1 778	238	1 078	...	...	97	362	3
65 - 69	C	2 987	355	1 636	...	...	124	864	8
70 - 74	C	5 149	587	2 191	...	...	164	2 190	17
75 - 79	C	8 235	990	2 584	...	...	199	4 443	19
80 - 84	C	10 315	1 246	2 082	...	...	197	6 768	22
85 - 89	C	10 115	1 294	1 015	...	...	164	7 617	25
90 - 94	C	6 947	894	359	...	...	93	5 572	29
95 - 99	C	2 060	275	34	...	...	26	1 709	16
100+	C	354	59	4	...	...	1	288	2
Republic of Moldova - République de Moldova[11]									
2003									
Male									
Total	C	21 913	1 891	12 811	...	...	1 179	360	5 672
0 - 15	C	511	507	4	...	...	-	-	-
16 - 19	C	115	114	-	...	...	-	-	1
20 - 24	C	248	212	31	...	...	3	-	2
25 - 29	C	293	156	113	...	...	13	1	10
30 - 34	C	341	112	176	...	...	40	2	11
35 - 39	C	579	127	336	...	...	79	12	25
40 - 44	C	1 049	150	686	...	...	134	16	63
45 - 49	C	1 517	130	1 052	...	...	214	22	99
50 - 54	C	2 019	92	1 509	...	...	204	36	178
55 - 59	C	1 251	54	892	...	...	114	29	162

21. Deaths by marital status, age and sex: latest available year, 1994 - 2003
Décès selon l'état matrimonial, l'âge et le sexe: dernière année disponible, 1994 - 2003
(continued — suite)

Continent, country or area, date and age (in years) / Continent, pays ou zone, date et âge (en années)	Code[1]	Total	Single (never married) - Célibataires	Married - Mariés	In consensual union - En union consensuelle	Married but separated - Mariés mais séparées	Divorced and not remarried - Divorcées non remariés	Widowed and not remarried - Veufs non remariés	Unknown - Inconnu
EUROPE									
Republic of Moldova - République de Moldova[11]									
2003									
Male									
60 - 64	C	2 332	64	1 676	...	...	140	42	410
65 - 69	C	2 802	55	1 885	...	...	96	52	714
70 - 74	C	3 095	49	1 903	...	...	69	58	1 016
75 - 79	C	2 621	32	1 375	...	...	48	35	1 131
80 - 84	C	1 919	20	823	...	...	17	37	1 022
85+	C	1 221	17	350	...	...	8	18	828
Female									
Total	C	21 166	1 666	6 234	...	...	765	156	12 345
0 - 15	C	350	348	2	...	...	-	-	-
16 - 19	C	48	46	2	...	...	-	-	-
20 - 24	C	73	56	15	...	...	-	-	2
25 - 29	C	90	31	49	...	...	7	-	3
30 - 34	C	126	21	74	...	...	15	4	12
35 - 39	C	254	43	154	...	...	32	4	21
40 - 44	C	432	49	282	...	...	41	3	57
45 - 49	C	681	46	442	...	...	80	7	106
50 - 54	C	1 074	77	645	...	...	109	14	229
55 - 59	C	871	74	458	...	...	70	6	263
60 - 64	C	1 748	115	802	...	...	103	15	713
65 - 69	C	2 454	158	921	...	...	101	16	1 258
70 - 74	C	3 298	203	1 007	...	...	74	29	1 985
75 - 79	C	3 807	209	792	...	...	65	25	2 716
80 - 84	C	3 249	125	429	...	...	45	18	2 632
85+	C	2 611	65	160	...	...	23	15	2 348
Romania - Roumanie									
2003									
Male									
Total	C	142 710	16 674	75 890	...	...	8 049	42 097	-
0 - 14	C	3 045	3 045	-	...	...	-	-	-
15 - 19	C	592	589	1	...	...	-	2	-
20 - 24	C	896	860	33	...	...	-	3	-
25 - 29	C	1 145	871	240	...	...	27	7	-
30 - 34	C	1 726	907	666	...	...	133	20	-
35 - 39	C	2 248	909	1 016	...	...	283	40	-
40 - 44	C	3 881	1 280	1 847	...	...	629	125	-
45 - 49	C	7 360	1 793	4 009	...	...	1 222	336	-
50 - 54	C	9 447	1 643	5 737	...	...	1 364	703	-
55 - 59	C	9 793	1 071	6 487	...	...	1 114	1 121	-
60 - 64	C	13 454	1 066	8 930	...	...	1 076	2 382	-
65 - 69	C	18 795	913	12 405	...	...	927	4 550	-
70 - 74	C	21 659	704	13 245	...	...	645	7 065	-
75 - 79	C	21 977	561	11 627	...	...	389	9 400	-
80 - 84	C	14 800	282	6 467	...	...	183	7 868	-
85+	C	11 892	180	3 180	...	...	57	8 475	-
Female									
Total	C	123 865	10 673	30 917	...	...	4 419	77 856	-
0 - 14	C	2 141	2 141	-	...	...	-	-	-
15 - 19	C	294	288	5	...	...	1	-	-
20 - 24	C	350	282	61	...	...	5	2	-
25 - 29	C	393	213	156	...	...	19	5	-
30 - 34	C	632	231	326	...	...	49	26	-
35 - 39	C	919	206	561	...	...	101	51	-
40 - 44	C	1 510	249	958	...	...	185	118	-
45 - 49	C	2 893	387	1 778	...	...	380	348	-

21. Deaths by marital status, age and sex: latest available year, 1994 - 2003
Décès selon l'état matrimonial, l'âge et le sexe: dernière année disponible, 1994 - 2003
(continued — suite)

Continent, country or area, date and age (in years) / Continent, pays ou zone, date et âge (en annèes)	Code[1]	Total	Single (never married) - Célibataires	Married - Mariés	In consensual union - En union consensuelle	Married but separated - Mariés mais séparées	Divorced and not remarried - Divorcées non remariés	Widowed and not remarried - Veufs non remariés	Unknown - Inconnu
EUROPE									
Romania - Roumanie									
2003									
Female									
50 - 54	C	4 070	459	2 437	...	...	438	736	-
55 - 59	C	4 670	385	2 636	...	...	375	1 274	-
60 - 64	C	7 007	536	3 401	...	...	416	2 654	-
65 - 69	C	12 118	788	5 003	...	...	531	5 796	-
70 - 74	C	17 939	1 082	5 535	...	...	562	10 760	-
75 - 79	C	24 054	1 349	4 791	...	...	619	17 295	-
80 - 84	C	22 795	1 165	2 562	...	...	437	18 601	-
85+	C	22 080	912	707	...	...	301	20 160	-
San Marino - Saint-Marin									
2003									
Male									
Total	+C	111	14	75	...	...	1	21	-
0 - 14	+C	1	1	-	...	...	-	-	-
15 - 19	+C	-	-	-	...	...	-	-	-
20 - 24	+C	1	1	-	...	...	-	-	-
25 - 29	+C	-	-	-	...	...	-	-	-
30 - 34	+C	-	-	-	...	...	-	-	-
35 - 39	+C	-	-	-	...	...	-	-	-
40 - 44	+C	-	-	-	...	...	-	-	-
45 - 49	+C	-	-	-	...	...	-	-	-
50 - 54	+C	4	2	2	...	...	-	-	-
55 - 59	+C	3	1	2	...	...	-	-	-
60 - 64	+C	5	-	5	...	...	-	-	-
65 - 69	+C	9	3	5	...	...	1	-	-
70 - 74	+C	19	3	14	...	...	-	2	-
75 - 79	+C	20	1	17	...	...	-	2	-
80 - 84	+C	17	1	12	...	...	-	4	-
85 - 89	+C	18	-	11	...	...	-	7	-
90 - 94	+C	11	1	6	...	...	-	4	-
95 - 99	+C	3	-	1	...	...	-	2	-
100+	+C	-	-	-	...	...	-	-	-
Female									
Total	+C	105	16	29	...	...	1	59	-
0 - 14	+C	1	1	-	...	...	-	-	-
15 - 19	+C	-	-	-	...	...	-	-	-
20 - 24	+C	-	-	-	...	...	-	-	-
25 - 29	+C	1	-	1	...	...	-	-	-
30 - 34	+C	1	1	-	...	...	-	-	-
35 - 39	+C	1	-	1	...	...	-	-	-
40 - 44	+C	1	1	-	...	...	-	-	-
45 - 49	+C	1	-	1	...	...	-	-	-
50 - 54	+C	3	-	3	...	...	-	-	-
55 - 59	+C	1	-	1	...	...	-	-	-
60 - 64	+C	4	-	4	...	...	-	-	-
65 - 69	+C	3	-	3	...	...	-	-	-
70 - 74	+C	7	-	2	...	...	-	5	-
75 - 79	+C	6	1	2	...	...	-	3	-
80 - 84	+C	20	1	8	...	...	-	11	-
85 - 89	+C	18	6	1	...	...	1	10	-
90 - 94	+C	23	4	2	...	...	-	17	-
95 - 99	+C	9	-	-	...	...	-	9	-
100+	+C	5	1	-	...	...	-	4	-

21. Deaths by marital status, age and sex: latest available year, 1994 - 2003
Décès selon l'état matrimonial, l'âge et le sexe: dernière année disponible, 1994 - 2003
(continued — suite)

Continent, country or area, date and age (in years) / Continent, pays ou zone, date et âge (en années)	Code[1]	Total	Single (never married) - Célibataires	Married - Mariés	In consensual union - En union consensuelle	Married but separated - Mariés mais séparées	Divorced and not remarried - Divorcées non remariés	Widowed and not remarried - Veufs non remariés	Unknown - Inconnu
EUROPE									
Serbia and Montenegro - Serbie-et-Monte-negro[26]									
2002									
Male									
Total	C	55 601	4 315	35 611	-	...	...	2 564	12 632	479
0 - 14	C	711	711	-	...	...	-	-	-
15 - 19	C	162	153	4	...	...	-	-	5
20 - 24	C	275	251	15	...	...	-	-	9
25 - 29	C	339	235	77	...	...	10	2	15
30 - 34	C	359	170	152	...	...	21	4	12
35 - 39	C	491	184	255	...	...	35	5	12
40 - 44	C	988	292	556	...	...	105	14	21
45 - 49	C	2 083	366	1 368	...	...	260	63	26
50 - 54	C	3 260	355	2 361	...	...	385	119	40
55 - 59	C	3 452	246	2 665	...	...	299	201	41
60 - 64	C	5 402	303	4 268	...	...	307	470	54
65 - 69	C	8 410	365	6 459	...	...	362	1 169	55
70 - 74	C	10 405	306	7 382	...	...	359	2 306	52
75 - 79	C	9 424	207	5 894	...	...	258	3 001	64
80 - 84	C	5 539	110	2 832	...	...	105	2 469	23
85+	C	4 254	55	1 321	...	...	58	2 807	13
Unk. - Inc. ...	C	47	6	2	...	...	-	2	37
Female									
Total	C	52 697	3 467	16 535	...	...	2 778	29 650	267
0 - 14	C	497	497	-	...	...	-	-	-
15 - 19	C	77	73	3	...	...	-	1	-
20 - 24	C	93	76	15	...	...	-	1	1
25 - 29	C	135	73	50	...	...	5	1	6
30 - 34	C	180	58	93	...	...	17	8	4
35 - 39	C	312	75	193	...	...	26	11	7
40 - 44	C	534	83	349	...	...	71	24	7
45 - 49	C	1 091	136	728	...	...	119	100	8
50 - 54	C	1 568	143	1 044	...	...	150	215	16
55 - 59	C	1 746	155	1 084	...	...	143	351	13
60 - 64	C	3 282	200	1 849	...	...	230	983	20
65 - 69	C	5 964	363	2 830	...	...	418	2 319	34
70 - 74	C	9 543	472	3 540	...	...	572	4 921	38
75 - 79	C	11 667	510	3 036	...	...	569	7 503	49
80 - 84	C	8 418	332	1 306	...	...	268	6 489	23
85+	C	7 568	217	411	...	...	189	6 721	30
Unk. - Inc. ...	C	22	4	4	...	...	1	2	11
Slovakia - Slovaquie									
2002									
Male									
Total	C	27 415	3 649	14 320	...	...	2 487	6 959	-
0 - 14	C	316	316	-	...	...	-	-	-
15 - 19	C	136	127	-	...	...	4	5	-
20 - 24	C	246	222	10	...	...	5	9	-
25 - 29	C	267	192	51	...	...	12	12	-
30 - 34	C	287	144	98	...	...	27	18	-
35 - 39	C	457	183	187	...	...	66	21	-
40 - 44	C	856	280	377	...	...	159	40	-
45 - 49	C	1 494	433	675	...	...	297	89	-
50 - 54	C	2 056	408	1 074	...	...	383	191	-
55 - 59	C	2 150	294	1 290	...	...	363	203	-
60 - 64	C	2 570	260	1 607	...	...	312	391	-
65 - 69	C	3 137	252	2 035	...	...	254	596	-
70 - 74	C	3 805	197	2 377	...	...	234	997	-

21. Deaths by marital status, age and sex: latest available year, 1994 - 2003
Décès selon l'état matrimonial, l'âge et le sexe: dernière année disponible, 1994 - 2003
(continued — suite)

Continent, country or area, date and age (in years) / Continent, pays ou zone, date et âge (en années)	Code[1]	Total	Single (never married) - Célibataires	Married - Mariés	In consensual union - En union consensuelle	Married but separated - Mariés mais séparées	Divorced and not remarried - Divorcées non remariés	Widowed and not remarried - Veufs non remariés	Unknown - Inconnu
EUROPE									
Slovakia - Slovaquie									
2002									
Male									
75 - 79	C	4 038	155	2 298	...	...	180	1 405	-
80 - 84	C	2 889	85	1 378	...	...	127	1 299	-
85 - 89	C	1 660	61	630	...	...	47	922	-
90 - 94	C	869	32	206	...	...	12	619	-
95 - 99	C	166	6	25	...	...	5	130	-
100+	C	16	2	2	...	...	-	12	-
Female									
Total	C	24 117	1 810	4 860	...	...	1 420	16 027	-
0 - 14	C	295	295	-	...	...	-	-	-
15 - 19	C	61	59	-	...	...	-	2	-
20 - 24	C	66	50	11	...	...	2	3	-
25 - 29	C	81	45	28	...	...	3	5	-
30 - 34	C	89	26	45	...	...	15	3	-
35 - 39	C	141	33	75	...	...	22	11	-
40 - 44	C	284	47	157	...	...	57	23	-
45 - 49	C	523	67	298	...	...	87	71	-
50 - 54	C	705	72	395	...	...	105	133	-
55 - 59	C	924	84	486	...	...	114	240	-
60 - 64	C	1 252	64	579	...	...	128	481	-
65 - 69	C	1 955	86	700	...	...	168	1 001	-
70 - 74	C	3 164	168	831	...	...	189	1 976	-
75 - 79	C	4 657	242	764	...	...	212	3 439	-
80 - 84	C	4 240	205	355	...	...	166	3 514	-
85 - 89	C	3 180	152	99	...	...	86	2 843	-
90 - 94	C	1 966	88	32	...	...	55	1 791	-
95 - 99	C	488	23	5	...	...	10	450	-
100+	C	46	4	-	...	...	1	41	-
Slovenia - Slovénie									
2003									
Male									
Total	C	10 074	1 599	6 098	...	...	686	1 691	-
0 - 14	C	60	60	-	...	...	-	-	-
15 - 19	C	47	47	-	...	...	-	-	-
20 - 24	C	87	84	3	...	...	-	-	-
25 - 29	C	87	81	5	...	...	1	-	-
30 - 34	C	90	69	18	...	...	3	-	-
35 - 39	C	159	92	51	...	...	16	-	-
40 - 44	C	249	124	90	...	...	35	-	-
45 - 49	C	457	187	201	...	...	64	5	-
50 - 54	C	653	161	376	...	...	100	16	-
55 - 59	C	684	140	433	...	...	79	32	-
60 - 64	C	931	136	639	...	...	86	70	-
65 - 69	C	1 268	114	929	...	...	101	124	-
70 - 74	C	1 602	120	1 158	...	...	70	254	-
75 - 79	C	1 420	86	965	...	...	58	311	-
80 - 84	C	1 163	56	726	...	...	47	334	-
85 - 89	C	626	22	333	...	...	12	259	-
90 - 94	C	405	17	154	...	...	12	222	-
95 - 99	C	82	3	16	...	...	2	61	-
100+	C	4	-	1	...	...	-	3	-
Female									
Total	C	9 377	1 353	2 143	...	...	588	5 293	-
0 - 14	C	48	48	-	...	...	-	-	-
15 - 19	C	23	23	-	...	...	-	-	-
20 - 24	C	23	21	2	...	...	-	-	-
25 - 29	C	20	17	3	...	...	-	-	-

21. Deaths by marital status, age and sex: latest available year, 1994 - 2003
Décès selon l'état matrimonial, l'âge et le sexe: dernière année disponible, 1994 - 2003
(continued — suite)

Continent, country or area, date and age (in years) / Continent, pays ou zone, date et âge (en années)	Code[1]	Total	Single (never married) - Célibataires	Married - Mariés	In consensual union - En union consensuelle	Married but separated - Mariés mais séparées	Divorced and not remarried - Divorcées non remariés	Widowed and not remarried - Veufs non remariés	Unknown - Inconnu
EUROPE									
Slovenia - Slovénie									
2003									
Female									
30 - 34	C	32	17	14	...	...	1	-	-
35 - 39	C	53	22	25	...	...	4	2	-
40 - 44	C	111	25	70	...	...	14	2	-
45 - 49	C	156	23	92	...	...	26	15	-
50 - 54	C	247	30	157	...	...	34	26	-
55 - 59	C	287	30	171	...	...	34	52	-
60 - 64	C	391	43	193	...	...	39	116	-
65 - 69	C	640	71	288	...	...	64	217	-
70 - 74	C	1 126	116	409	...	...	81	520	-
75 - 79	C	1 646	209	374	...	...	97	966	-
80 - 84	C	1 788	239	215	...	...	90	1 244	-
85 - 89	C	1 317	171	82	...	...	54	1 010	-
90 - 94	C	1 109	188	38	...	...	41	842	-
95 - 99	C	321	53	10	...	...	8	250	-
100+	C	39	7	-	...	...	1	31	-
Spain - Espagne									
2002									
Male									
Total	C	193 269	27 442	121 502	...	...	4 721	39 604	-
0 - 14	C	1 567	1 564	1	...	...	-	2	-
15 - 19	C	704	673	20	...	...	2	9	-
20 - 24	C	1 391	1 249	96	...	...	9	37	-
25 - 29	C	1 648	1 254	320	...	...	23	51	-
30 - 34	C	2 102	1 270	668	...	...	95	69	-
35 - 39	C	2 821	1 310	1 172	...	...	238	101	-
40 - 44	C	3 735	1 302	1 909	...	...	389	135	-
45 - 49	C	4 847	1 199	2 958	...	...	537	153	-
50 - 54	C	6 673	1 352	4 530	...	...	578	213	-
55 - 59	C	9 106	1 558	6 562	...	...	590	396	-
60 - 64	C	11 193	1 618	8 405	...	...	539	631	-
65 - 69	C	19 015	2 428	14 460	...	...	570	1 557	-
70 - 74	C	26 298	2 911	19 768	...	...	475	3 144	-
75 - 79	C	32 489	2 933	23 252	...	...	352	5 952	-
80 - 84	C	30 174	2 235	19 487	...	...	195	8 257	-
85 - 89	C	23 051	1 537	12 336	...	...	92	9 086	-
90 - 94	C	12 663	818	4 731	...	...	29	7 085	-
95 - 99	C	3 369	204	757	...	...	8	2 400	-
100+	C	423	27	70	...	...	-	326	-
Female									
Total	C	175 349	24 418	44 303	...	...	1 894	104 734	-
0 - 14	C	1 164	1 159	4	...	...	-	1	-
15 - 19	C	268	255	8	...	...	-	5	-
20 - 24	C	425	369	39	...	...	2	15	-
25 - 29	C	532	347	147	...	...	12	26	-
30 - 34	C	746	331	317	...	...	52	46	-
35 - 39	C	1 142	356	612	...	...	109	65	-
40 - 44	C	1 541	364	947	...	...	148	82	-
45 - 49	C	2 103	366	1 402	...	...	194	141	-
50 - 54	C	2 708	395	1 864	...	...	209	240	-
55 - 59	C	3 558	464	2 430	...	...	200	464	-
60 - 64	C	4 568	538	2 962	...	...	150	918	-
65 - 69	C	8 604	915	5 183	...	...	183	2 323	-
70 - 74	C	14 744	1 673	7 144	...	...	189	5 738	-
75 - 79	C	23 843	2 869	8 380	...	...	187	12 407	-
80 - 84	C	32 878	4 147	7 065	...	...	122	21 544	-
85 - 89	C	37 309	4 795	4 184	...	...	82	28 248	-
90 - 94	C	27 891	3 611	1 367	...	...	39	22 874	-

21. Deaths by marital status, age and sex: latest available year, 1994 - 2003
Décès selon l'état matrimonial, l'âge et le sexe: dernière année disponible, 1994 - 2003
(continued — suite)

Continent, country or area, date and age (in years) / Continent, pays ou zone, date et âge (en années)	Code[1]	Total	Single (never married) - Célibataires	Married - Mariés	In consensual union - En union cohsensuelle	Married but separated - Mariés mais séparées	Divorced and not remarried - Divorcées non remariés	Widowed and not remarried - Veufs non remariés	Unknown - Inconnu
EUROPE									
Spain - Espagne									
2002									
Female									
95 - 99	C	9 666	1 247	214	...	...	14	8 191	-
100+	C	1 659	217	34	...	...	2	1 406	-
Sweden - Suède									
2002									
Male									
Total	C	45 780	7 836	21 901	...	...	5 857	10 186	-
0 - 14	C	275	275	-	...	...	-	-	-
15 - 19	C	109	109	-	...	...	-	-	-
20 - 24	C	210	207	2	...	...	1	-	-
25 - 29	C	180	165	12	...	...	3	-	-
30 - 34	C	231	179	34	...	...	16	2	-
35 - 39	C	308	199	71	...	...	36	2	-
40 - 44	C	458	264	114	...	...	77	3	-
45 - 49	C	675	304	217	...	...	148	6	-
50 - 54	C	1 214	443	435	...	...	327	9	-
55 - 59	C	2 067	559	883	...	...	583	42	-
60 - 64	C	2 412	521	1 146	...	...	662	83	-
65 - 69	C	3 279	518	1 791	...	...	757	213	-
70 - 74	C	4 934	692	2 819	...	...	898	525	-
75 - 79	C	7 375	1 019	4 177	...	...	937	1 242	-
80 - 84	C	9 208	1 081	5 052	...	...	777	2 298	-
85 - 89	C	7 730	809	3 556	...	...	455	2 910	-
90 - 94	C	4 057	400	1 401	...	...	156	2 100	-
95 - 99	C	963	81	180	...	...	23	679	-
100+	C	95	11	11	...	...	1	72	-
Female									
Total	C	49 229	5 300	10 097	...	...	5 449	28 383	-
0 - 14	C	210	210	-	...	...	-	-	-
15 - 19	C	64	64	-	...	...	-	-	-
20 - 24	C	64	58	4	...	...	2	-	-
25 - 29	C	78	71	6	...	...	-	1	-
30 - 34	C	110	68	33	...	...	9	-	-
35 - 39	C	169	81	73	...	...	15	-	-
40 - 44	C	250	97	92	...	...	58	3	-
45 - 49	C	468	132	206	...	...	118	12	-
50 - 54	C	759	172	345	...	...	217	25	-
55 - 59	C	1 344	227	669	...	...	363	85	-
60 - 64	C	1 464	172	743	...	...	390	159	-
65 - 69	C	2 091	190	1 026	...	...	445	430	-
70 - 74	C	3 456	321	1 452	...	...	612	1 071	-
75 - 79	C	5 862	438	1 938	...	...	753	2 733	-
80 - 84	C	9 461	720	1 943	...	...	960	5 838	-
85 - 89	C	11 110	975	1 124	...	...	867	8 144	-
90 - 94	C	8 678	856	392	...	...	470	6 960	-
95 - 99	C	3 128	372	47	...	...	154	2 555	-
100+	C	463	76	4	...	...	16	367	-
Switzerland - Suisse									
2001									
Male									
Total	C	29 915	4 274	17 518	...	...	2 120	5 990	13
0 - 14	C	320	320	-	...	...	-	-	-
15 - 19	C	128	128	-	...	...	-	-	-
20 - 24	C	192	184	8	...	...	-	-	-
25 - 29	C	185	152	27	...	...	6	-	-
30 - 34	C	277	181	70	...	...	23	2	1
35 - 39	C	377	173	156	...	...	46	2	-
40 - 44	C	491	157	256	...	...	74	4	-

21. Deaths by marital status, age and sex: latest available year, 1994 - 2003
Décès selon l'état matrimonial, l'âge et le sexe: dernière année disponible, 1994 - 2003
(continued — suite)

Continent, country or area, date and age (in years) Continent, pays ou zone, date et âge (en années)	Code[1]	Total	Single (never married) - Célibataires	Married - Mariés	In consensual union - En union consensuelle	Married but separated - Mariés mais séparées	Divorced and not remarried - Divorcées non remariés	Widowed and not remarried - Veufs non remariés	Unknown - Inconnu
EUROPE									
Switzerland - Suisse									
2001									
Male									
45 - 49	C	722	197	398	...	...	120	6	1
50 - 54	C	1 064	209	652	...	...	184	18	1
55 - 59	C	1 475	201	935	...	...	291	47	1
60 - 64	C	1 829	264	1 245	...	...	236	82	2
65 - 69	C	2 642	316	1 860	...	...	262	203	1
70 - 74	C	3 518	393	2 505	...	...	254	364	2
75 - 79	C	4 517	421	3 048	...	...	243	804	1
80 - 84	C	4 819	431	3 003	...	...	206	1 178	1
85 - 89	C	4 298	330	2 243	...	...	113	1 611	1
90 - 94	C	2 428	185	946	...	...	52	1 245	-
95 - 99	C	582	29	157	...	...	9	386	1
100+	C	51	3	9	...	...	1	38	-
Female									
Total	C	31 372	4 651	6 801	...	...	2 193	17 704	23
0 - 14	C	235	235	-	...	...	-	-	-
15 - 19	C	49	47	2	...	...	-	-	-
20 - 24	C	53	44	7	...	...	-	1	1
25 - 29	C	84	57	25	...	...	2	-	-
30 - 34	C	131	60	61	...	...	8	2	-
35 - 39	C	202	63	95	...	...	38	6	-
40 - 44	C	266	57	148	...	...	55	6	-
45 - 49	C	382	74	218	...	...	75	15	-
50 - 54	C	587	89	357	...	...	107	34	-
55 - 59	C	856	99	534	...	...	157	64	2
60 - 64	C	1 003	135	537	...	...	155	175	1
65 - 69	C	1 454	158	752	...	...	176	367	1
70 - 74	C	2 206	249	951	...	...	208	797	1
75 - 79	C	3 672	439	1 062	...	...	287	1 881	3
80 - 84	C	5 149	700	991	...	...	286	3 171	1
85 - 89	C	6 972	918	754	...	...	313	4 982	5
90 - 94	C	5 779	848	278	...	...	245	4 401	7
95 - 99	C	1 972	316	25	...	...	70	1 560	1
100+	C	320	63	4	...	...	11	242	-
The Former Yugoslav Rep. of Macedonia - L'ex-République yougoslave de Macédoine									
2003									
Male									
Total	C	9 832	748	6 477	...	...	133	2 445	29
0 - 14	C	247	247	-	...	...	-	-	-
15 - 19	C	47	43	3	...	...	-	-	1
20 - 24	C	75	59	11	...	...	-	4	1
25 - 29	C	73	42	30	...	...	-	1	-
30 - 34	C	92	34	54	...	...	3	-	1
35 - 39	C	113	29	77	...	...	5	1	1
40 - 44	C	224	34	181	...	...	7	2	-
45 - 49	C	407	46	337	...	...	14	10	-
50 - 54	C	556	38	491	...	...	12	11	4
55 - 59	C	651	36	556	...	...	17	37	5
60 - 64	C	852	14	746	...	...	14	70	8
65 - 69	C	1 311	29	1 046	...	...	14	219	3
70 - 74	C	1 486	36	1 093	...	...	18	338	1
75 - 79	C	1 535	30	933	...	...	16	554	2
80 - 84	C	1 240	24	645	...	...	9	560	2

21. Deaths by marital status, age and sex: latest available year, 1994 - 2003
Décès selon l'état matrimonial, l'âge et le sexe: dernière année disponible, 1994 - 2003
(continued — suite)

Continent, country or area, date and age (in years) / Continent, pays ou zone, date et âge (en années)	Code[1]	Total	Single (never married) - Célibataires	Married - Mariés	In consensual union - En union consensuelle	Married but separated - Mariés mais séparées	Divorced and not remarried - Divorcées non remariés	Widowed and not remarried - Veufs non remariés	Unknown - Inconnu
EUROPE									
The Former Yugoslav Rep. of Macedonia - L'ex-République yougoslave de Macédoine									
2003									
Male									
85+	C	921	5	274	...	...	4	638	-
Unk. - Inc. ...	C	2	2	-	...	...	-	-	-
Female									
Total	C	8 174	468	3 271	...	...	189	4 220	26
0 - 14	C	161	161	-	...	...	-	-	-
15 - 19	C	29	27	1	...	...	-	1	-
20 - 24	C	20	14	4	...	...	-	2	-
25 - 29	C	33	16	15	...	...	1	1	-
30 - 34	C	27	7	17	...	...	2	1	-
35 - 39	C	62	10	46	...	...	3	3	-
40 - 44	C	97	11	79	...	...	3	4	-
45 - 49	C	157	11	123	...	...	5	16	2
50 - 54	C	281	25	204	...	...	16	36	-
55 - 59	C	355	25	247	...	...	20	61	2
60 - 64	C	548	26	356	...	...	21	144	1
65 - 69	C	909	27	521	...	...	31	328	2
70 - 74	C	1 334	41	621	...	...	30	637	5
75 - 79	C	1 686	32	559	...	...	35	1 053	7
80 - 84	C	1 426	23	354	...	...	18	1 028	3
85+	C	1 048	12	124	...	...	4	904	4
Unk. - Inc. ...	C	1	-	-	...	...	-	1	
OCEANIA — OCEANIE									
Australia - Australie									
2003									
Male									
Total	+C	68 330	10 490	37 443	640	...	5 496	13 072	1 189
0 - 14	+C	1 000	999	-	-	...	-	-	3
15 - 19	+C	447	398	3	-	...	-	-	45
20 - 24	+C	621	574	21	7	...	-	-	18
25 - 29	+C	695	557	86	23	...	11	-	18
30 - 34	+C	800	521	175	38	...	38	-	27
35 - 39	+C	967	486	336	32	...	82	4	27
40 - 44	+C	1 341	533	507	52	...	201	7	41
45 - 49	+C	1 792	552	833	50	...	281	25	51
50 - 54	+C	2 251	506	1 177	55	...	415	35	63
55 - 59	+C	3 404	549	2 016	57	...	622	66	94
60 - 64	+C	4 231	593	2 642	66	...	684	152	94
65 - 69	+C	5 712	691	3 755	72	...	712	365	117
70 - 74	+C	8 326	891	5 449	57	...	803	954	172
75 - 79	+C	11 054	1 026	7 105	56	...	726	1 980	161
80 - 84	+C	11 337	793	6 840	44	...	519	3 003	138
85 - 89	+C	8 670	515	4 455	21	...	275	3 331	73
90 - 94	+C	4 421	261	1 698	8	...	98	2 326	30
95 - 99	+C	1 138	35	320	3	...	26	746	10
100+	+C	110	6	25	-	...	3	77	-
Unk. - Inc. ...	+C	13	4	-	-	...	-	-	9
Female									
Total	+C	63 962	5 957	16 795	314	...	3 965	36 443	488
0 - 14	+C	775	774	-	-	...	-	-	-

21. Deaths by marital status, age and sex: latest available year, 1994 - 2003
Décès selon l'état matrimonial, l'âge et le sexe: dernière année disponible, 1994 - 2003
(continued — suite)

Continent, country or area, date and age (in years) / Continent, pays ou zone, date et âge (en années)	Code[1]	Total	Single (never married) - Célibataires	Married - Mariés	In consensual union - En union consensuelle	Married but separated - Mariés mais séparées	Divorced and not remarried - Divorcées non remariés	Widowed and not remarried - Veufs non remariés	Unknown - Inconnu
OCEANIA — OCEANIE									
Australia - Australie									
2003									
Female									
15 - 19	+C	183	162	3	-	...	-	-	18
20 - 24	+C	216	188	17	5	...	-	-	5
25 - 29	+C	250	169	54	10	...	8	-	8
30 - 34	+C	380	196	133	13	...	31	-	7
35 - 39	+C	512	176	239	12	...	68	7	10
40 - 44	+C	765	207	394	16	...	108	20	20
45 - 49	+C	1 092	222	600	33	...	184	31	22
50 - 54	+C	1 395	167	861	24	...	251	68	24
55 - 59	+C	1 952	210	1 192	22	...	340	171	17
60 - 64	+C	2 549	203	1 519	30	...	404	355	38
65 - 69	+C	3 319	243	1 815	25	...	415	783	38
70 - 74	+C	4 976	288	2 288	27	...	432	1 892	49
75 - 79	+C	8 274	424	2 957	36	...	521	4 289	47
80 - 84	+C	11 270	607	2 522	29	...	538	7 514	60
85 - 89	+C	12 427	728	1 547	18	...	411	9 667	56
90 - 94	+C	9 391	638	567	10	...	177	7 953	46
95 - 99	+C	3 551	285	82	3	...	69	3 095	17
100+	+C	684	70	5	-	...	7	597	4
Unk. - Inc. ...	+C	-	-	-	-	...	-	-	-
New Caledonia - Nouvelle-Calédonie[27]									
2003									
Male									
Total	C	666	357	309	...	...	...	...	-
0 - 14	C	29	29	-	...	...	...	...	-
15 - 19	C	7	7	-	...	...	...	...	-
20 - 24	C	22	22	-	...	...	...	...	-
25 - 29	C	13	13	-	...	...	...	...	-
30 - 34	C	22	18	4	...	...	...	...	-
35 - 39	C	16	14	2	...	...	...	...	-
40 - 44	C	26	17	9	...	...	...	...	-
45 - 49	C	29	15	14	...	...	...	...	-
50 - 54	C	32	15	17	...	...	...	...	-
55 - 59	C	65	30	35	...	...	...	...	-
60 - 64	C	60	31	29	...	...	...	...	-
65 - 69	C	82	34	48	...	...	...	...	-
70 - 74	C	92	35	57	...	...	...	...	-
75 - 79	C	74	26	48	...	...	...	...	-
80 - 84	C	42	17	25	...	...	...	...	-
85 - 89	C	32	22	10	...	...	...	...	-
90 - 94	C	21	10	11	...	...	...	...	-
95+	C	2	2	-	...	...	...	...	-
Female									
Total	C	455	323	132	...	...	...	...	-
0 - 14	C	18	18	-	...	...	...	...	-
15 - 19	C	5	5	-	...	...	...	...	-
20 - 24	C	8	8	-	...	...	...	...	-
25 - 29	C	9	8	1	...	...	...	...	-
30 - 34	C	6	4	2	...	...	...	...	-
35 - 39	C	11	6	5	...	...	...	...	-
40 - 44	C	10	3	7	...	...	...	...	-
45 - 49	C	18	6	12	...	...	...	...	-
50 - 54	C	24	11	13	...	...	...	...	-
55 - 59	C	36	21	15	...	...	...	...	-
60 - 64	C	29	14	15	...	...	...	...	-

21. Deaths by marital status, age and sex: latest available year, 1994 - 2003
Décès selon l'état matrimonial, l'âge et le sexe: dernière année disponible, 1994 - 2003
(continued — suite)

Continent, country or area, date and age (in years) / Continent, pays ou zone, date et âge (en années)	Code[1]	Total	Single (never married) - Célibataires	Married - Mariés	In consensual union - En union consensuelle	Married but separated - Mariés mais séparées	Divorced and not remarried - Divorcées non remariés	Widowed and not remarried - Veufs non remariés	Unknown - Inconnu
OCEANIA — OCEANIE									
New Caledonia - Nouvelle-Calédonie[27]									
2003									
Female									
65 - 69	C	54	30	24	...	...	...	...	-
70 - 74	C	50	40	10	...	...	...	...	-
75 - 79	C	60	45	15	...	...	...	...	-
80 - 84	C	49	42	7	...	...	...	...	-
85 - 89	C	40	34	6	...	...	...	...	-
90 - 94	C	14	14	-	...	...	...	...	-
95+	C	14	14	-	...	...	...	...	-
New Zealand - Nouvelle-Zélande									
2003									
Male									
Total	+C	14 020	2 160	7 435	...	361	1 067	2 982	15
0 - 14	+C	263	263	-	...	-	-	-	-
15 - 19	+C	139	139	-	...	-	-	-	-
20 - 24	+C	132	129	2	...	1	-	-	-
25 - 29	+C	130	108	15	...	5	-	-	2
30 - 34	+C	172	124	36	...	5	6	-	1
35 - 39	+C	199	110	66	...	10	12	1	-
40 - 44	+C	281	115	106	...	24	29	5	2
45 - 49	+C	365	96	189	...	23	52	4	1
50 - 54	+C	516	96	289	...	37	81	11	2
55 - 59	+C	693	117	401	...	45	104	26	-
60 - 64	+C	917	116	594	...	35	135	36	1
65 - 69	+C	1 185	113	761	...	48	153	110	-
70 - 74	+C	1 756	149	1 129	...	49	189	240	-
75 - 79	+C	2 234	185	1 391	...	36	137	482	3
80 - 84	+C	2 296	160	1 315	...	26	98	695	2
85 - 89	+C	1 675	90	791	...	14	47	732	1
90 - 94	+C	852	38	305	...	2	21	486	-
95 - 99	+C	196	10	43	...	-	3	140	-
100+	+C	19	2	2	...	1	-	14	-
Female									
Total	+C	13 990	1 483	3 648	...	194	752	7 907	6
0 - 14	+C	188	188	-	...	-	-	-	-
15 - 19	+C	75	74	1	...	-	-	-	-
20 - 24	+C	54	48	6	...	-	-	-	-
25 - 29	+C	54	39	13	...	-	1	1	-
30 - 34	+C	87	49	27	...	4	6	-	1
35 - 39	+C	126	45	55	...	15	10	1	-
40 - 44	+C	186	47	96	...	13	23	7	-
45 - 49	+C	268	52	139	...	16	49	12	-
50 - 54	+C	376	44	224	...	20	63	24	1
55 - 59	+C	492	49	290	...	18	84	51	-
60 - 64	+C	622	49	347	...	22	78	126	-
65 - 69	+C	829	54	429	...	18	84	243	1
70 - 74	+C	1 219	70	528	...	22	94	505	-
75 - 79	+C	1 723	115	555	...	16	93	944	-
80 - 84	+C	2 345	136	502	...	22	74	1 610	1
85 - 89	+C	2 589	179	298	...	6	63	2 042	1
90 - 94	+C	1 920	176	122	...	-	24	1 597	1
95 - 99	+C	705	60	14	...	2	5	624	-
100+	+C	132	9	2	...	-	1	120	-

FOOTNOTES - NOTES

Italics: data from civil registers which are incomplete or of unknown completeness. — Italiques: données incomplètes ou dont le degré d'exactitude n'est pas connu provenant des registres de l'état civil.

[1] 'Code' indicates the source of data, as follows:
C - Civil registration, estimated over 90% complete
U - Civil registration, estimated less than 90% complete
| - Other source, estimated reliable
+ - Data tabulated by date of registration rather than occurence.
... - Information not available

Le 'Code' indique la source des données, comme suit:
C - Registres de l'état civil considérés complèts à 90 p. 100 au moins.
U - Registres de l'état civil qui ne sont pas considérés complèts à 90 p. 100 au moins.
| - Autre source, considérée pas douteuses.
+ - Données exploitées selon la date de l'enregistrement et non la date de l'événement.
... - Information pas disponible.

[2] Excluding live-born infants who died before their birth was registered. - Non compris les enfants nés vivants décédés avant l'enregistrement de leur naissance.

[3] Including Canadian residents temporarily in the United States, but excluding United States residents temporarily in Canada. - Y compris les résidents canadiens se trouvant temporairement aux Etats-Unis, mais ne comprenant pas les résidents des Etats-Unis se trouvant temporairement au Canada.

[4] Data are for married, and in consensual union. - Les données mariés et en union consensuelle.

[5] Excluding persons who have not reached the age of puberty. - - Non compris les personnes n'ayant pas atteint l'âge de la puberté.

[6] Data for single including in consensual union. - Les données célibataires incluent et en union consensuelle.

[7] Data as reported by national statistical authorities. - Les données comme elles ont été déclarées par l'institut national de la statistique.

[8] Data for divorced including separated. - Les données divorcées incluent et séparées.

[9] Excluding Indian jungle population. - Non compris les Indiens de la jungle.

[10] Excluding nomadic Indian tribes. - Non compris les tribus d'Indiens nomades.

[11] Excluding infants born alive with less than 28 weeks gestation, less than 1 000 grams in weight and 35 centimeters in length, who die within seven days of birth. - Non compris les enfants nés vivants avant 28 semaines de gestation, pesant moins de 1 000 grammes, mesurant moins de 35 centimètres et décédés dans les sept jours qui ont suivi leur naissance.

[12] Data refer to Japanese nationals in Japan only. - Les données se raportent aux nationaux japonais au Japon seulement.

[13] Figures for the category "unknown" adjusted by United Nations Statistics Division. - Les chiffres pour la categorie par la Division de statistique de l'ONU.

[14] Excluding alien armed forces, civilian aliens employed by armed forces, and foreign diplomatic personnel and their dependants. - Non compris les militaires étrangers, les civils étrangers employés par les forces armées ni le personnel diplomatique étranger et les membres de leur famille les accompagnant.

[15] Based on the results of the Population Growth Survey. - D'après les résultats de la 'Population Growth Survey.'

[16] Excluding data for the Pakistan-held part of Jammu and Kashmir, the final status of which has not yet been determined. - Non compris les données concernant la partie du Jammu et Cachemire occupée par le Pakistan dont le statut définitif n'a pas été déterminé.

[17] Excluding transients afloat and non-locally domiciled military and civilian services personnel and their dependants. - Non compris les personnes de passage à bord de navires, ni les militaires et agents civils domiciliés hors du territoire et les membres de leur famille les accompagnant.

[18] Excluding Faeroe Islands and Greenland. - Non compris les Iles Féroé et Gröenland.

[19] Partner in a registered partnership is classified under unknown marital status category. - Les partenaires d'un pacte civil enregistrés ont classés dans la rubrique état matrimonial inconnu.

[20] Including nationals temporarily outside the country. - Y compris les nationaux se trouvant temporairement hors du pays.

[21] For ages five years and over, age classification based on year of birth rather than exact date of birth. - A partir de cinq ans, le classement selon l'âge est basé sur l'année de naissances et non sur la date exacte de naissance.

[22] Including armed forces stationed outside the country. - Y compris les militaires nationaux hors du pays.

[23] Events registered within one year of occurrence. - Evénements enregistrés dans l'année qui suit l'événement.

[24] Including residents outside the country if listed in a Netherlands population register. - Y compris les résidents hors du pays, s'ils sont inscrits sur un registre de population néerlandais.

[25] Including residents temporarily outside the country. - Y compris les résidents se trouvant temporairement hors du pays.

[26] From 2002, without data for Kosovo and Metohia. - Après 2002, sans les donées pour le Kosovo and Metohie.

[27] Data for single including widowed and divorced. - Les données célibataires incluent veufs et divorcées.

Table 22

Table 22 presents expectation of life at specified ages for each sex for the latest available year.

Description of variables: Expectation of life, e_x is defined as the average number of years of life remaining to persons reaching age x if they continued to be subject to the mortality conditions of the period indicated in the table.

Male and female expectations are shown separately for selected ages beginning at birth (age 0) and proceeding with ages 5, 10, 15, 20, 25, 30, 35, 40, 45, 50, 55, 60, 65, 70, 75, 85, 90, 95 and 100 years.

The table shows life expectancy derived from an abridged or full life table as reported by the country or area.

Data are shown with one decimal regardless of the number of digits provided in the original computation.

Life table computation: From the demographic point of view, a life table is regarded as a theoretical model of a population that is continuously replenished by births and depleted by deaths. The model gives a complete picture of the mortality experience of a population based on the assumption that the theoretical cohort is subject, throughout its existence, to the age-specific mortality rates observed at a particular time. Thus levels of mortality prevailing at the time a life table is constructed are assumed to remain unchanged into the future until all members of the cohort have died.

Reliability of data: The values shown in this table come from official life tables. It is assumed that, if necessary, the basic data (population and deaths classified by age and sex) have been adjusted for deficiencies before their use in constructing the life tables.

Limitations: Expectation-of-life values are subject to the same qualifications as have been set forth for population statistics in general and death statistics in particular, as discussed in sections 3 and 4, respectively, of the Technical Notes. They must be interpreted strictly using the underlying assumption that surviving cohorts are subjected to the same age-specific mortality rates of the period to which the life table refers.

Earlier data: Expectation of life at specified ages for each sex has been shown in previous issues of the *Demographic Yearbook*. Data included in this table update the series covering a period of years as follows:

Issue	Years Covered
Historical Supplement CD, 1997	1948 – 1997
Special Issue on Population Ageing and the Situation of Elderly Persons, 1991	1950 – 1990
Historical Supplement, 1979	1948 – 1977
1948	1896 – 1947

Tableau 22

Le tableau 22 présente les espérances de vie à des âges déterminés, pour chaque sexe, qui correspondent à la dernière année pour laquelle on dispose de données.

Description des variables : L'espérance de vie, e_x, se définit comme le nombre moyen d'années restant à vivre aux hommes et aux femmes qui ont atteint les âges indiqués, à supposer qu'ils continuent de connaître les mêmes conditions de mortalité observées pendant la période sur laquelle porte le tableau.

Les chiffres sont présentés séparément pour chaque sexe à partir de la naissance (âge 0) et pour les âges suivants : 5,10, 15, 20, 25, 30, 35, 40, 45, 50, 55, 60, 65, 70, 75, 80, 85, 90, 95 et 100 ans.

Dans le tableau figurent les espérances de vie calculées selon les tables de mortalité abrégées ou complètes communiquées par les pays et les zones.

Les données sont arrondies à la première décimale, indépendamment du nombre de décimales qui figurent dans le calcul initial.

Calcul des tables de mortalité : Du point de vue démographique, les tables de mortalité sont considérées comme des modèles théoriques représentant une population constamment reconstituée par les naissances et réduite par les décès. Ces modèles donnent un aperçu complet de la mortalité d'une population et reposent sur l'hypothèse que chaque cohorte théoriquement distinguée connaît, pendant toute son existence, le taux de mortalité par âge observé à un moment donné. Les mortalités correspondant à l'époque à laquelle sont calculées les tables de mortalité sont ainsi censées demeurer inchangées dans l'avenir jusqu'au décès de tous les membres de la cohorte.

Fiabilité des donnés : Étant donné que les chiffres figurant dans ce tableau proviennent de tables officielles de mortalité, elles sont toutes présumées sûres. En ce qui concerne les chiffres extraits de tables officielles de mortalité, on part du principe que les données de base (effectif de la population et nombre de décès selon l'âge et le sexe) ont été ajustées, en tant que de besoin, avant de servir à l'établissement de la table de mortalité.

Insuffisance des données : Les espérances de vie appellent les mêmes réserves que celles qui ont été formulées à propos des statistiques de la population en général et des statistiques de mortalité en particulier (voir les sections 3 et 4 des Notes techniques). Lorsque l'on interprète les données, il ne faut jamais perdre de vue que, par hypothèse, les cohortes de survivants sont soumises, pour chaque âge, aux conditions de mortalité de la période visée par la table de mortalité.

Données publiées antérieurement : Les espérances de vie à des âges déterminés pour chaque sexe figuraient déjà dans des éditions antérieures de l'*Annuaire démographique*. Les données présentées dans le tableau 22 actualisent les données qui portaient sur les périodes suivantes :

Éditions	Années considérées
Supplément historique (CD-ROM), 1997	1948 – 1997
Édition spéciale sur le vieillissement de la population et la situation des personnes âgées, 1991	1950 – 1990
Supplément rétrospectif, 1979	1948 – 1977
1948	1896 – 1947

22. Expectation of life at specified ages for each sex: latest available year, 1994 - 2003
Espérance de vie à un âge donné pour chaque sexe: dernière année disponible, 1994 - 2003

Continent, country or area and date / Continent, pays ou zone et date	Age (in years) - Age (en années)																				
	0	5	10	15	20	25	30	35	40	45	50	55	60	65	70	75	80	85	90	95	100
AFRICA — AFRIQUE																					
Algeria - Algérie[1]																					
2000																					
Male	72.5	70.6	65.8	61.0	56.3	51.6	46.9	42.2	37.6	33.0	28.5	24.1	19.9	16.1	12.4	9.0	5.9	...	...	...	...
Female	74.2	72.1	67.3	62.5	57.7	52.9	48.1	43.3	38.6	34.0	29.5	25.1	20.7	16.6	12.8	9.3	6.1	...	...	...	...
Botswana[2]																					
1999																					
Male	65.7	...	...	...	...	...	...	...	...	...	...	...	...	...	...	...	...	...	...	...	...
Female	69.0	...	...	...	...	...	...	...	...	...	...	...	...	...	...	...	...	...	...	...	...
Djibouti																					
1998																					
Male	49.0	...	...	...	...	...	...	...	...	...	...	...	...	...	...	...	...	...	...	...	...
Female	52.0	...	...	...	...	...	...	...	...	...	...	...	...	...	...	...	...	...	...	...	...
Egypt - Égypte																					
2003																					
Male	67.9	...	...	...	...	...	...	...	...	...	...	...	...	...	...	...	...	...	...	...	...
Female	72.3	...	...	...	...	...	...	...	...	...	...	...	...	...	...	...	...	...	...	...	...
Ethiopia - Éthiopie																					
1994																					
Male	49.8	55.2	51.2	46.8	42.7	38.9	35.0	31.1	27.4	23.7	20.2	16.9	13.8	11.0	8.6	6.5	5.0	...	...	...	...
Female	51.8	56.9	53.0	48.8	44.8	40.9	37.1	33.4	29.6	25.9	22.1	18.6	15.2	12.1	9.4	7.1	5.4	...	...	...	...
Kenya																					
1999																					
Male	52.9	54.8	51.1	46.6	42.3	38.3	34.5	21.0	27.7	24.4	21.0	17.7	14.5	11.6	8.9	6.7	5.0	3.8	3.1	2.5	...
Lesotho																					
2001																					
Male	48.7	...	...	...	...	...	...	...	...	...	...	...	...	...	...	...	...	...	...	...	...
Female	56.3	...	...	...	...	...	...	...	...	...	...	...	...	...	...	...	...	...	...	...	...
Malawi[3]																					
1992 - 1997																					
Male	43.5	52.1	49.5	45.7	41.9	38.4	34.8	31.2	27.6	24.0	20.6	17.3	14.1	11.2	8.6	6.3	4.4	...	...	...	...
Female	46.8	54.5	52.0	48.2	44.4	40.6	36.9	33.2	29.6	25.9	22.2	18.6	15.1	11.9	9.2	6.8	4.6	...	...	...	...
2003																					
Male	43.4	...	...	...	...	...	...	...	...	...	...	...	...	...	...	...	...	...	...	...	...
Female	46.0	...	...	...	...	...	...	...	...	...	...	...	...	...	...	...	...	...	...	...	...
Mauritius - Maurice																					
2003																					
Male	68.6	64.8	59.8	55.0	50.1	45.4	40.7	36.0	31.6	27.3	23.2	19.5	16.1	13.2	10.5	8.4	6.4	5.0	...	...	...
Female	75.3	71.4	66.5	61.6	56.7	51.8	47.0	42.2	37.5	32.8	27.3	24.1	20.1	16.7	13.4	10.6	8.1	6.3	...	...	...
Réunion																					
2003																					
Male	71.3	...	...	...	...	...	...	...	...	...	...	...	...	...	...	...	...	...	...	...	...
Female	79.8	...	...	...	...	...	...	...	...	...	...	...	...	...	...	...	...	...	...	...	...
South Africa - Afrique du Sud																					
2001																					
Male	51.8	...	...	...	...	...	...	...	...	...	...	...	...	...	...	...	...	...	...	...	...
Female	56.7	...	...	...	...	...	...	...	...	...	...	...	...	...	...	...	...	...	...	...	...
Swaziland[4]																					
1997																					
Male	58.0	...	...	...	...	...	...	...	...	...	...	...	...	...	...	...	...	...	...	...	...
Female	63.0	...	...	...	...	...	...	...	...	...	...	...	...	...	...	...	...	...	...	...	...
Tunisia - Tunisie																					
1995																					
Male	69.6	67.5	62.7	57.9	53.1	48.4	43.8	39.2	34.6	30.1	25.8	21.6	17.7	14.1	10.8	7.9	5.2	3.5	...	...	...
Female	73.1	70.7	65.9	61.0	56.2	51.3	46.5	41.7	37.0	32.4	27.8	23.3	19.1	15.0	11.3	7.8	4.8	2.9	...	...	...
AMERICA, NORTH — AMERIQUE DU NORD																					
Aruba																					
2000																					
Male	70.0	65.4	60.5	55.6	50.9	46.7	42.3	37.7	33.0	28.5	24.2	20.1	16.3	13.1	10.4	8.1	5.7	3.9	...	...	...
Female	76.0	71.9	67.0	62.0	57.2	52.5	47.7	43.0	38.3	33.6	28.9	24.4	20.5	16.7	13.1	10.4	7.5	5.5	...	...	...

22. Expectation of life at specified ages for each sex: latest available year, 1994 - 2003
Espérance de vie à un âge donné pour chaque sexe: dernière année disponible, 1994 - 2003 (continued — suite)

Continent, country or area and date / Continent, pays ou zone et date	0	5	10	15	20	25	30	35	40	45	50	55	60	65	70	75	80	85	90	95	100
AMERICA, NORTH — AMERIQUE DU NORD																					
Canada																					
2002																					
Male	77.2	72.8	67.8	62.9	58.0	53.3	48.5	43.7	38.9	34.3	29.7	25.3	21.1	17.2	13.7	10.5	7.9	5.6	4.1	...	...
Female	82.1	77.6	72.6	67.7	62.8	57.9	53.0	48.1	43.2	38.5	33.8	29.2	24.8	20.6	16.7	13.0	9.8	7.0	5.0	...	...
Costa Rica																					
1990 - 1995																					
Male	72.9	69.5	64.6	59.8	54.9	50.3	45.6	40.8	36.2	31.6	27.1	22.8	18.8	15.1	11.8	9.1	6.9	...	...	...	...
Female	77.6	73.9	69.0	64.1	59.2	54.3	49.4	44.6	39.9	35.2	30.6	26.2	21.9	17.9	14.1	10.7	7.8	...	...	...	...
Cuba																					
2001 - 2003																					
Male	75.1	70.8	65.9	61.0	56.2	51.4	46.7	42.0	37.4	32.8	28.5	24.3	20.4	16.7	13.3	10.3	7.7	5.3	...	...	...
Female	79.0	74.5	69.6	64.7	59.8	54.9	50.0	45.2	40.5	35.8	31.2	26.8	22.6	18.6	14.9	11.5	8.6	5.8	...	...	...
Dominican Republic - République dominicaine																					
1995 - 2000																					
Male	69.8	67.7	62.9	58.1	53.4	48.8	44.2	39.7	35.2	30.8	26.5	22.4	18.5	15.0	11.8	9.1	7.1	...	...	...	...
Female	73.1	71.2	66.4	61.6	56.8	52.0	47.3	42.7	38.1	33.5	29.1	24.8	20.7	16.9	13.3	10.3	7.9	...	...	...	...
El Salvador																					
1995 - 2000																					
Male	66.5	64.6	59.9	55.1	50.5	46.2	42.0	37.8	33.8	29.7	25.8	22.0	18.3	14.9	11.7	8.9	6.6	...	...	...	...
Female	72.5	70.3	65.5	60.7	56.0	51.4	46.8	42.3	37.9	33.6	29.3	25.2	21.2	17.4	13.9	10.8	8.1	...	...	...	...
2000 - 2005																					
Male	67.7	...	...	...	...	...	...	...	...	...	...	...	...	...	...	...	...	...	...	...	...
Female	73.7	...	...	...	...	...	...	...	...	...	...	...	...	...	...	...	...	...	...	...	...
Greenland - Groenland																					
1999 - 2003																					
Male	64.1	60.7	55.9	51.3	47.5	43.7	39.5	35.2	30.7	26.4	22.3	18.1	14.7	11.5	9.1	7.1	5.9	5.2	...	...	...
Female	69.5	65.5	60.6	55.9	51.4	46.9	42.4	37.8	33.1	28.6	24.4	20.4	16.4	13.4	10.5	7.8	6.2	5.3	...	...	...
Guadeloupe																					
2002																					
Male	74.6	70.2	65.3	60.4	55.7	51.2	46.8	42.2	37.7	33.2	29.0	24.8	20.9	17.3	13.8	10.6	7.9	5.1	2.0	0.5	...
Female	81.5	77.0	72.1	67.1	62.1	57.3	52.4	47.6	42.9	38.2	33.5	28.8	24.4	20.3	16.4	12.7	9.0	5.7	2.3	0.5	...
Guatemala																					
1995 - 2000																					
Male	61.4	60.6	56.0	51.2	46.8	42.7	38.8	34.9	31.2	27.4	23.7	20.1	16.8	13.6	10.7	8.2	6.1	...	...	...	...
Female	67.2	66.2	62.6	56.9	52.2	47.7	43.3	38.9	34.6	30.4	26.3	22.3	18.6	15.2	12.0	9.2	6.9	...	...	...	...
Jamaica - Jamaïque																					
2000 - 2002																					
Male	72.8	69.3	64.4	59.5	54.7	50.1	45.7	41.4	37.1	32.8	28.6	24.6	20.8	17.4	14.3	11.7	9.5	7.9	...	...	...
Female	76.4	73.0	68.0	63.1	58.2	53.4	48.7	44.1	39.6	35.1	30.7	26.5	22.6	18.9	15.6	12.7	10.2	8.1	...	...	...
Martinique																					
2002																					
Male	75.4	71.0	66.0	61.1	56.3	51.7	47.1	42.5	37.9	33.4	28.9	24.7	20.4	16.5	13.0	10.0	7.5	4.8	2.0	0.5	...
Female	82.2	77.7	72.8	67.9	62.9	58.0	53.0	48.1	43.3	38.6	34.0	29.3	24.8	20.3	16.3	12.3	8.9	5.5	2.3	0.5	...
Netherlands Antilles - Antilles néerlandaises																					
1998 - 2002																					
Male	72.1	67.8	63.0	58.0	53.3	48.7	44.2	39.5	34.9	30.4	26.2	22.3	18.5	15.0	12.1	9.4	7.0	5.3	4.4	3.2	2.3
Female	78.7	74.5	69.5	64.6	59.7	54.9	50.1	45.3	40.6	35.9	31.3	27.0	22.8	18.7	15.0	11.7	8.7	6.5	4.7	3.0	2.1
Nicaragua																					
2000 - 2005																					
Male	67.2	65.3	60.6	55.7	51.2	46.8	42.4	38.2	34.0	29.9	25.9	22.1	18.5	15.2	12.1	9.4	6.9	...	...	...	...
Female	71.9	69.5	64.8	60.0	55.3	50.6	45.9	41.3	36.8	32.4	28.1	24.0	20.2	16.6	13.3	10.3	7.5	...	...	...	...
Panama[5]																					
2000																					
Male	72.2	69.2	64.4	59.5	54.8	50.2	45.6	41.0	36.4	31.9	27.5	23.3	19.3	15.6	12.4	9.5	7.1	...	...	...	...
Female	76.8	73.7	68.9	64.0	59.2	54.3	49.5	44.8	40.1	35.4	30.9	26.4	22.2	18.1	14.3	10.9	7.9	...	...	...	...

22. Expectation of life at specified ages for each sex: latest available year, 1994 - 2003
Espérance de vie à un âge donné pour chaque sexe: dernière année disponible, 1994 - 2003 (continued — suite)

Continent, country or area and date / Continent, pays ou zone et date	Age (in years) - Age (en années)																				
	0	5	10	15	20	25	30	35	40	45	50	55	60	65	70	75	80	85	90	95	100
AMERICA, NORTH — AMERIQUE DU NORD																					
Puerto Rico - Porto Rico																					
2002																					
Male	73.2	69.1	64.1	59.2	54.5	50.2	45.8	41.3	37.0	32.7	28.5	24.5	20.8	17.2	13.9	10.9	8.4	6.3	4.7	3.4	2.4
Female	80.9	76.6	71.6	66.7	61.8	56.9	52.0	47.2	42.5	37.8	33.2	28.7	24.4	20.3	16.4	12.9	9.8	7.2	5.0	3.4	2.3
Saint Kitts and Nevis - Saint-Kitts-et-Nevis																					
1998																					
Male	68.2	65.0	60.1	55.3	50.5	45.8	41.1	36.5	32.7	28.5	24.3	20.6	16.6	13.3	11.0	9.1	6.6	4.7	3.4	2.2	0.4
Female	70.7	67.5	62.5	57.6	52.7	48.0	43.4	38.8	34.4	29.8	25.4	21.2	17.6	14.2	11.3	8.9	6.3	4.6	3.3	2.2	0.4
Saint Lucia - Sainte-Lucie																					
2002																					
Male	72.0	68.0	63.2	58.3	53.6	49.2	44.7	40.2	35.8	31.5	27.4	23.7	20.4	16.9	13.6	11.3	9.3	7.2	...	...	...
Female	76.7	73.0	68.1	63.2	58.3	53.5	48.6	43.8	39.0	34.5	30.2	26.0	21.9	18.5	15.0	12.1	9.9	6.9	...	...	...
Turks Caicos Islands - Îles Turques et Caïques																					
2001																					
Male	79.0	75.3	70.3	65.3	60.3	55.8	50.8	46.0	41.2	37.1	33.0	28.4	24.3	20.8	17.5	12.5	7.5	4.1	...	...	...
Female	77.4	72.5	67.5	62.5	57.5	52.9	48.2	43.4	38.6	33.8	29.6	25.0	20.0	17.0	13.2	11.7	10.3	8.8	...	...	...
United States - États-Unis																					
2002																					
Male	74.5	70.2	65.3	60.3	55.6	51.0	46.3	41.6	37.0	32.6	28.3	24.1	20.2	16.6	13.2	10.3	7.8	5.7	4.2	3.2	2.5
Female	79.9	75.4	70.5	65.5	60.7	55.8	51.0	46.1	41.4	36.7	32.2	27.7	23.5	19.5	15.8	12.4	9.4	6.9	5.0	3.7	2.8
AMERICA, SOUTH — AMERIQUE DU SUD																					
Bolivia - Bolivie																					
1995 - 2000																					
Male	59.8	60.8	56.7	52.2	48.0	43.7	39.5	35.3	31.2	27.1	23.2	19.5	15.9	12.7	9.8	7.5	5.9	...	...	...	...
Female	63.2	63.8	59.7	55.2	50.8	46.5	42.1	37.8	33.6	29.4	25.3	21.4	17.6	14.0	10.8	8.3	6.5	...	...	...	...
Brazil - Brésil[6]																					
2002																					
Male	67.3	65.0	60.2	55.3	50.8	46.6	42.3	38.1	34.0	29.9	26.1	22.4	19.0	15.8	13.0	10.6	8.8	...	...	...	...
Female	74.9	72.2	67.3	62.4	57.6	52.8	48.1	43.4	38.8	34.3	30.0	25.9	21.9	18.3	15.0	12.0	9.6	...	...	...	...
Chile - Chili																					
2001 - 2002																					
Male	74.4	70.3	65.4	60.4	55.7	51.0	46.4	41.8	37.2	32.6	28.2	24.1	20.1	16.5	13.3	10.5	8.1	6.2	4.8	4.5	8.5
Female	80.4	76.2	71.2	66.3	61.4	56.5	51.6	46.8	41.9	37.2	32.5	28.0	23.7	19.7	15.9	12.5	9.5	7.1	5.2	3.9	2.9
Colombia - Colombie																					
2002 - 2007																					
Male	69.6	67.0	62.2	57.3	52.8	48.5	44.2	39.8	35.5	31.1	26.8	22.7	18.8	15.3	12.2	9.6	7.5	...	...	...	...
Female	75.7	72.9	68.0	63.2	58.3	53.6	48.8	44.0	39.3	34.7	30.2	25.8	21.8	17.9	14.5	11.5	9.2	...	...	...	...
Ecuador - Équateur[7]																					
2000 - 2005																					
Male	71.3	68.8	64.1	59.3	54.8	50.5	46.3	42.0	37.8	33.6	29.6	25.5	21.6	17.9	14.4	11.2	8.1	...	...	...	...
Female	77.2	74.2	69.4	64.5	59.8	55.1	50.4	45.7	41.1	36.6	32.2	27.8	23.7	19.6	15.8	12.2	8.8	...	...	...	...
French Guiana - Guyane française																					
2002																					
Male	72.5	68.7	63.8	58.9	54.2	49.7	45.0	40.7	36.3	32.1	27.9	23.8	19.8	16.4	12.8	9.7	7.3	4.8	2.0	0.5	...
Female	79.2	75.3	70.6	65.7	60.8	55.9	51.1	46.4	41.8	37.1	32.7	28.1	23.8	19.8	15.6	12.1	8.4	4.9	2.3	0.5	...
Paraguay																					
1990 - 1995																					
Male	66.3	65.5	60.8	56.0	51.3	46.7	42.1	37.5	32.9	28.5	24.2	20.2	16.5	13.2	10.2	7.7	5.6	...	...	...	...
Female	70.8	69.3	64.5	59.7	54.9	50.1	45.4	40.7	36.0	31.5	27.0	22.8	18.7	14.9	11.5	8.5	6.2	...	...	...	...

22. Expectation of life at specified ages for each sex: latest available year, 1994 - 2003
Espérance de vie à un âge donné pour chaque sexe: dernière année disponible, 1994 - 2003 (continued — suite)

Continent, country or area and date / Continent, pays ou zone et date	Age (in years) - Age (en années)																				
	0	5	10	15	20	25	30	35	40	45	50	55	60	65	70	75	80	85	90	95	100
AMERICA, SOUTH — AMERIQUE DU SUD																					
Paraguay																					
2000 - 2005																					
Male	68.6	...	...	...	...	...	...	...	...	...	...	...	...	...	...	...	...	...	...	...	...
Female	73.1	...	...	...	...	...	...	...	...	...	...	...	...	...	...	...	...	...	...	...	...
Peru - Pérou[6]																					
1995 - 2000																					
Male	65.9	65.9	61.4	56.6	52.0	47.4	42.9	38.5	34.1	29.8	25.6	21.7	18.1	14.7	11.7	9.2	7.0	...	...	...	...
Female	70.8	70.2	65.6	60.7	55.9	51.2	46.5	41.9	37.3	32.9	28.5	24.3	20.3	16.5	13.3	10.4	7.8	...	...	...	...
Uruguay																					
2003																					
Male	71.3	67.7	62.8	57.8	53.1	48.5	43.8	39.1	34.5	30.0	25.7	21.7	18.0	14.7	11.8	9.3	7.2	5.5	4.6	4.1	...
Female	79.2	75.3	70.4	65.4	60.6	55.7	50.8	46.0	41.2	36.5	32.0	27.6	23.3	19.3	15.5	12.1	9.1	6.7	5.4	4.9	...
Venezuela[6]																					
1995 - 2000																					
Male	68.6	66.6	61.8	56.9	52.3	47.8	43.3	38.8	34.3	29.9	25.6	21.6	17.9	14.5	11.4	8.6	5.9	...	...	...	...
Female	74.4	72.1	67.2	62.3	57.4	52.6	47.8	43.1	38.4	33.7	29.2	24.9	20.8	16.9	13.3	9.9	6.9	...	...	...	...
ASIA — ASIE																					
Afghanistan																					
2002																					
Male	43.0	...	...	...	...	...	...	...	...	...	...	...	...	...	...	...	...	...	...	...	...
Female	43.0	...	...	...	...	...	...	...	...	...	...	...	...	...	...	...	...	...	...	...	...
Armenia - Arménie																					
2000																					
Male	70.6	67.0	62.1	57.2	52.4	47.6	42.8	38.1	33.4	29.0	23.9	20.6	16.8	13.5	10.5	7.8	5.0	1.0	...	...	...
Female	75.5	71.7	66.8	61.8	56.9	52.0	47.1	42.2	37.4	32.6	28.0	23.4	19.1	15.1	11.4	8.0	5.0	1.0	...	...	...
Azerbaijan - Azerbaïdjan																					
2003																					
Male	69.5	65.9	61.1	56.3	51.4	46.7	42.0	37.4	32.8	28.4	24.1	20.2	16.5	13.6	10.9	9.0	7.2	5.4	3.9	3.7	0.9
Female	75.1	70.7	65.9	61.0	56.1	51.2	46.4	41.6	36.8	32.1	27.5	23.1	18.9	15.3	11.9	9.2	6.6	4.8	2.5	3.1	0.8
Bahrain - Bahreïn																					
2001																					
Male	73.2	...	64.4	59.5	54.7	49.9	45.2	40.4	35.6	30.9	26.4	22.0	17.8	14.1	11.3	9.5	...	...	...	...	...
Female	76.2	...	67.1	62.1	57.2	52.3	47.4	42.5	37.7	32.9	28.2	23.7	19.6	15.9	12.9	10.9	...	...	...	...	...
Bangladesh																					
1994																					
Male	58.6	61.4	57.3	53.0	48.6	44.0	40.1	34.8	30.8	26.0	22.0	18.6	15.1	12.1	9.0	6.4	4.6	...	...	...	...
Female	58.2	60.4	56.6	51.4	47.1	42.6	38.4	34.1	30.0	26.2	22.3	18.5	15.0	11.9	8.6	5.9	4.0	...	...	...	...
1998																					
Male	60.7	...	...	...	...	...	...	...	...	...	...	...	...	...	...	...	...	...	...	...	...
Female	60.9	...	...	...	...	...	...	...	...	...	...	...	...	...	...	...	...	...	...	...	...
Bhutan - Bhoutan[8]																					
1994																					
Male	66.0	...	...	...	...	...	...	...	...	...	...	...	...	...	...	...	...	...	...	...	...
Female	66.2	...	...	...	...	...	...	...	...	...	...	...	...	...	...	...	...	...	...	...	...
China - Chine[9]																					
2000																					
Male	69.6	...	...	...	...	...	...	...	...	...	...	...	...	...	...	...	...	...	...	...	...
Female	73.3	...	...	...	...	...	...	...	...	...	...	...	...	...	...	...	...	...	...	...	...
China: Hong Kong SAR - Chine: Hong Kong RAS																					
2003																					
Male	78.5	73.8	68.9	63.9	59.0	54.2	49.3	44.5	39.7	35.0	30.5	26.0	21.9	18.0	14.3	11.2	8.8	6.8	5.2	4.0	3.0
Female	84.3	79.6	74.6	69.6	64.7	59.7	54.8	49.9	45.1	40.2	35.5	30.8	26.2	21.8	17.6	13.7	10.4	7.7	5.5	3.9	2.7
China: Macao SAR - Chine: Macao RAS																					
1993 - 1996																					
Male	75.1	70.8	65.8	61.0	56.1	51.3	46.6	41.8	37.1	32.4	27.8	23.3	19.2	15.3	11.9	8.9	6.3	4.5	3.1	...	...
Female	80.0	75.6	70.7	65.7	60.8	55.9	51.0	46.2	41.3	36.5	31.8	27.2	22.7	18.6	14.7	11.3	8.4	6.0	4.2	...	...

22. Expectation of life at specified ages for each sex: latest available year, 1994 - 2003
Espérance de vie à un âge donné pour chaque sexe: dernière année disponible, 1994 - 2003 (continued — suite)

Continent, country or area and date / Continent, pays ou zone et date	0	5	10	15	20	25	30	35	40	45	50	55	60	65	70	75	80	85	90	95	100
Age (in years) - Age (en années)																					

ASIA — ASIE

	0	5	10	15	20	25	30	35	40	45	50	55	60	65	70	75	80	85	90	95	100
Cyprus - Chypre[10]																					
2002 - 2003																					
Male	77.0	72.4	67.5	62.6	57.8	53.1	48.4	43.6	38.8	34.0	29.4	24.9	20.7	16.6	13.0	9.8	7.2	5.1	...	...	...
Female	81.4	76.9	71.9	67.0	62.1	57.2	52.3	47.4	42.5	37.6	32.8	28.2	23.6	19.2	15.1	11.4	8.3	5.9	...	...	...
Georgia - Géorgie[11]																					
2003																					
Male	69.1	66.2	61.2	56.3	51.4	46.6	41.9	37.3	32.8	28.3	24.1	20.3	16.8	13.4	10.6	8.0	6.5	5.9	...	...	...
Female	74.7	71.6	66.6	61.7	56.8	51.8	47.0	42.2	37.4	32.7	28.1	23.6	19.5	15.4	11.7	8.4	5.6	2.8	...	...	...
India - Inde[12]																					
1993 - 1997																					
Male	60.4	62.2	57.8	53.1	48.5	44.0	39.5	35.1	30.7	26.5	22.5	18.9	15.5	12.6	10.1	...	...	...	...	...	...
Female	61.8	64.6	60.4	55.8	51.3	47.0	42.7	38.2	33.8	29.4	25.1	21.2	17.5	14.2	11.4	...	...	...	...	...	...
1995 - 1999																					
Male	60.8	...	...	...	...	...	...	...	...	...	...	...	...	...	...	...	...	...	...	...	...
Female	62.5	...	...	...	...	...	...	...	...	...	...	...	...	...	...	...	...	...	...	...	...
Indonesia - Indonésie																					
1990 - 1995																					
Male	61.0	...	...	...	...	...	...	...	...	...	...	...	...	...	...	...	...	...	...	...	...
Female	64.5	...	...	...	...	...	...	...	...	...	...	...	...	...	...	...	...	...	...	...	...
Iran (Islamic Republic of) - Iran (République islamique d')																					
2001																					
Male	67.6	...	...	...	...	...	...	...	...	...	...	...	...	...	...	...	...	...	...	...	...
Female	70.4	...	...	...	...	...	...	...	...	...	...	...	...	...	...	...	...	...	...	...	...
Iraq																					
1997																					
Male	58.0	...	...	...	...	...	...	...	...	...	...	...	...	...	...	...	...	...	...	...	...
Female	59.0	...	...	...	...	...	...	...	...	...	...	...	...	...	...	...	...	...	...	...	...
Israel - Israël[13]																					
2003																					
Male	77.7	73.2	68.3	63.3	58.5	53.8	48.9	44.1	39.4	34.7	30.2	25.7	21.5	17.6	14.0	10.9	8.4	6.4	4.0	3.2	3.3
Female	81.9	77.3	72.4	67.4	62.5	57.6	52.7	47.8	42.9	38.1	33.3	28.7	24.2	19.9	15.9	12.3	9.2	6.7	4.1	3.2	3.3
Japan - Japon[14]																					
2003																					
Male	78.4	73.7	68.7	63.8	58.9	54.0	49.2	44.4	39.7	35.0	30.5	26.1	22.0	18.0	14.4	11.1	8.3	6.0	4.3	3.1	2.3
Female	85.3	80.6	75.7	70.7	65.8	60.9	56.0	51.1	46.2	41.4	36.7	32.0	27.5	23.0	18.8	14.7	11.0	8.0	5.6	3.9	2.8
Jordan - Jordanie[15]																					
2001																					
Male	68.8	...	...	...	...	...	...	...	...	...	...	...	...	...	...	...	...	...	...	...	...
Female	71.1	...	...	...	...	...	...	...	...	...	...	...	...	...	...	...	...	...	...	...	...
Kazakhstan																					
1997																					
Male	59.0	56.3	51.4	46.6	42.0	37.7	33.5	29.5	25.6	22.0	18.6	15.7	13.0	10.8	8.7	6.9	5.4	4.2	3.2	2.4	1.8
Female	70.2	67.2	62.3	57.4	52.6	48.0	43.3	38.7	34.2	29.8	25.6	21.8	18.0	14.7	11.7	9.0	6.8	5.0	3.6	2.6	1.8
Korea (Dem. People's Republic of) - Corée (Rép. populaire dém. de)																					
1990 - 1995																					
Male	67.7	...	...	...	...	...	...	...	...	...	...	...	...	...	...	...	...	...	...	...	...
Female	73.9	...	...	...	...	...	...	...	...	...	...	...	...	...	...	...	...	...	...	...	...
Korea (Republic of) - Corée (République de)[16]																					
2001																					
Male	72.8	68.4	63.5	58.6	53.7	48.9	44.1	39.4	34.7	30.3	26.0	22.0	18.1	14.6	11.4	8.6	6.4	4.8	3.5	2.6	2.0
Female	80.0	75.6	70.7	65.7	60.8	55.9	51.0	46.2	41.3	36.6	31.9	27.2	22.7	18.4	14.4	10.9	7.9	5.7	4.2	3.2	2.6

22. Expectation of life at specified ages for each sex: latest available year, 1994 - 2003
Espérance de vie à un âge donné pour chaque sexe: dernière année disponible, 1994 - 2003 (continued — suite)

Continent, country or area and date / Continent, pays ou zone et date	Age (in years) - Age (en années)																				
	0	5	10	15	20	25	30	35	40	45	50	55	60	65	70	75	80	85	90	95	100
ASIA — ASIE																					
Kyrgyzstan - Kirghizistan 2002																					
Male	64.4	61.5	56.7	51.8	47.0	42.4	37.9	33.6	29.4	25.5	21.6	18.2	15.0	12.2	9.9	7.5	5.3	3.5	2.2	1.2	0.6
Female	72.1	68.9	64.0	59.1	54.2	49.4	44.7	40.0	35.4	30.9	26.5	22.2	18.3	14.6	11.2	8.1	5.6	3.6	2.1	1.2	0.6
Malaysia - Malaisie 2002																					
Male	70.7	66.5	61.7	56.8	52.2	47.6	43.1	38.5	34.0	29.6	25.2	21.0	17.1	13.7	10.7	8.0	5.8	...	...	...	...
Female	75.2	71.0	66.1	61.2	56.3	51.5	46.6	41.8	37.0	32.3	27.7	23.2	19.1	15.3	11.9	8.8	6.4	...	...	...	...
Maldives 2003																					
Male	70.4	66.8	62.0	57.1	52.2	47.4	42.6	37.7	32.9	28.3	23.6	19.3	15.4	11.7	8.0	...	...	...	...	...	...
Female	71.3	67.5	62.6	57.7	52.8	47.9	43.0	38.2	33.4	28.7	24.0	19.6	15.3	11.7	7.7	...	...	...	...	...	...
Mongolia - Mongolie 1996 - 2000																					
Male	61.1	60.0	55.3	50.5	45.8	41.2	38.8	32.5	28.2	24.0	20.2	16.9	13.6	10.9	8.5	...	...	...	...	...	...
Female	66.6	65.3	60.5	55.6	50.8	46.2	41.5	36.9	32.9	28.0	23.9	20.3	16.8	14.0	11.3	...	...	...	...	...	...
Occupied Palestinian Territory - Territoire palestinien occupé 2001																					
Male	70.4	67.5	62.7	57.8	53.1	48.4	43.6	38.9	34.2	29.6	25.2	21.1	17.2	13.8	10.7	8.1	6.1	...	...	...	...
Female	73.6	70.3	65.4	60.5	55.7	50.9	46.1	41.3	36.6	32.0	27.5	23.2	19.0	15.2	11.7	8.8	6.4	...	...	...	...
Oman 2003																					
Male	73.1	...	...	...	...	...	...	...	...	...	...	...	...	...	...	...	...	...	...	...	...
Female	75.4	...	...	...	...	...	...	...	...	...	...	...	...	...	...	...	...	...	...	...	...
Pakistan[17] 2001																					
Male	64.5	66.2	61.6	56.9	52.2	47.6	43.2	38.8	34.6	30.4	26.3	22.4	18.8	15.4	12.4	9.9	7.9	5.8	...	...	...
Female	66.1	67.7	63.3	58.8	54.2	49.8	45.2	40.6	36.3	32.0	27.6	23.7	20.1	17.2	14.4	11.3	9.1	6.6	...	...	...
Singapore - Singapour[18] 2003																					
Male	77.0	72.3	67.3	62.4	57.5	52.6	47.8	42.9	38.1	33.4	28.8	24.4	20.2	16.3	12.9	9.9	7.0	4.5	...	...	...
Female	80.9	76.2	71.2	66.2	61.3	56.4	51.5	46.5	41.7	36.8	32.1	27.5	23.0	18.7	14.8	11.1	7.7	4.7	...	...	...
Turkey - Turquie[19] 2000																					
Male	66.4	...	...	...	...	...	...	...	...	...	...	...	...	...	...	...	...	...	...	...	...
Female	71.0	...	...	...	...	...	...	...	...	...	...	...	...	...	...	...	...	...	...	...	...
EUROPE																					
Albania - Albanie 2000																					
Male	72.5	69.5	64.8	59.9	55.1	50.4	45.8	41.1	36.4	31.8	27.3	22.9	18.6	14.8	11.3	8.4	6.0	3.8	...	...	...
Female	77.3	74.4	69.5	64.7	59.8	54.9	50.0	45.2	40.3	35.5	30.8	26.1	21.6	17.3	13.2	9.6	6.4	3.8	...	...	...
Austria - Autriche 2003																					
Male	75.9	71.4	66.4	61.5	56.7	52.0	47.2	42.4	37.6	33.0	28.5	24.2	20.2	16.4	12.9	9.8	7.2	5.1	3.6	2.6	...
Female	81.6	77.0	72.0	67.0	62.2	57.3	52.3	47.4	42.6	37.8	33.1	28.5	24.1	19.8	15.7	11.8	8.5	5.8	3.9	2.7	...
Belarus - Bélarus 2003																					
Male	62.7	58.4	53.5	48.6	43.8	39.3	35.0	30.8	26.8	23.0	19.5	16.3	13.5	11.2	9.0	7.1	5.5	4.1	2.9	2.1	1.4
Female	74.7	70.3	65.4	60.4	55.5	50.7	45.9	41.2	36.5	31.9	27.5	23.3	19.4	15.7	12.2	9.2	6.7	4.8	3.3	2.2	1.4
Belgium - Belgique[20] 2000																					
Male	74.6	70.1	65.1	60.2	55.4	50.7	46.0	41.3	36.6	32.0	27.5	23.3	19.3	15.5	12.1	9.1	6.7	4.7	3.2	2.1	...
Female	80.8	76.3	71.3	66.3	61.4	56.6	51.7	46.8	42.0	37.3	32.7	28.2	23.8	19.5	15.4	11.7	8.4	5.8	3.7	2.3	...

22. Expectation of life at specified ages for each sex: latest available year, 1994 - 2003
Espérance de vie à un âge donné pour chaque sexe: dernière année disponible, 1994 - 2003 (continued — suite)

Continent, country or area and date / Continent, pays ou zone et date	0	5	10	15	20	25	30	35	40	45	50	55	60	65	70	75	80	85	90	95	100
EUROPE																					
Bosnia and Herzegovina - Bosnie-Herzégovine																					
2003																					
Male	71.3	...	...	...	...	...	...	...	...	...	...	...	...	...	...	...	...	...	...	...	...
Female	76.7	...	...	...	...	...	...	...	...	...	...	...	...	...	...	...	...	...	...	...	...
Bulgaria - Bulgarie																					
2002																					
Male	68.5	64.8	59.9	55.0	50.2	45.5	40.8	36.1	31.5	27.2	23.2	19.5	16.0	13.0	10.2	7.8	5.8	3.6	3.0	2.2	0.5
Female	75.4	71.6	66.7	61.7	56.8	52.0	47.1	42.3	37.5	32.9	28.4	24.0	19.7	15.7	12.1	8.9	6.4	4.0	3.2	2.3	0.5
Czech Republic - République tchèque																					
2003																					
Male	72.0	67.4	62.5	57.5	52.7	47.9	43.2	38.4	33.8	29.2	24.9	20.9	17.2	13.8	10.8	8.1	5.9	4.1	2.8	1.8	1.2
Female	78.5	73.8	68.9	63.9	59.0	54.1	49.2	44.3	39.4	34.7	30.0	25.6	21.3	17.1	13.3	9.8	6.9	4.5	2.8	1.6	1.0
Denmark - Danemark																					
2002 - 2003																					
Male	74.9	70.3	65.4	60.4	55.6	50.8	46.0	41.2	36.5	31.9	27.5	23.2	19.2	15.5	12.1	9.2	6.8	4.9	3.4	2.5	1.9
Female	79.5	74.9	69.9	65.0	60.0	55.1	50.2	45.3	40.5	35.7	31.1	26.7	22.4	18.3	14.7	11.4	8.5	6.0	4.1	2.8	1.9
Estonia - Estonie																					
2002																					
Male	64.8	60.5	55.7	50.8	46.0	41.6	37.1	32.7	28.6	24.8	21.4	18.2	15.3	12.6	10.2	8.1	6.2	4.6	3.5	2.5	1.8
Female	76.3	72.1	67.2	62.3	57.4	52.5	47.7	42.9	38.2	33.6	29.3	25.2	21.3	17.2	13.6	10.3	7.4	5.3	3.3	2.1	1.3
Finland - Finlande[21]																					
2003																					
Male	75.1	70.4	65.5	60.6	55.7	51.0	46.3	41.5	36.9	32.3	28.0	23.8	19.9	16.1	12.6	9.6	7.0	4.9	3.4	2.2	1.4
Female	81.8	77.1	72.1	67.2	62.2	57.3	52.4	47.6	42.7	37.9	33.2	28.7	24.2	19.9	15.7	11.8	8.5	5.8	3.9	2.7	1.7
France[21]																					
2001																					
Male	75.5	70.9	66.0	61.0	56.2	51.5	46.8	42.1	37.4	33.0	28.7	24.6	20.6	16.9	13.5	10.4	7.6	5.5	3.9	3.0	2.6
Female	82.9	78.3	73.3	68.4	63.5	58.6	53.7	48.8	44.0	39.3	34.7	30.2	25.7	21.4	17.2	13.2	9.7	6.8	4.6	3.2	2.3
Germany - Allemagne																					
2002 - 2004																					
Male	75.9	71.3	66.4	61.4	56.6	51.8	46.9	42.1	37.4	32.8	28.3	24.1	20.0	16.3	12.8	9.8	7.2	5.2	3.6	2.6	1.9
Female	81.5	76.9	72.0	67.0	62.1	57.2	52.2	47.3	42.5	37.7	33.0	28.5	24.1	19.8	15.7	11.9	8.6	6.0	4.0	2.8	2.0
Gibraltar																					
2001																					
Male	78.5	73.5	68.5	63.5	58.5	53.5	...	43.5	...	33.9	...	25.8	...	17.9	...	11.3	...	...	...	...	...
Female	83.3	79.5	75.0	70.0	65.0	60.0	...	50.3	...	40.3	...	30.3	...	20.6	...	13.7	...	...	...	...	...
Greece - Grèce																					
2003																					
Male	76.5	71.9	66.9	62.0	57.2	52.5	47.7	42.9	38.2	33.6	29.1	24.8	20.7	16.8	13.2	10.1	7.5	5.5	4.2	3.1	2.3
Female	81.3	76.6	71.7	66.7	61.8	56.9	51.9	47.0	42.2	37.4	32.6	27.9	23.4	18.9	14.6	10.8	7.5	5.3	4.0	3.0	2.2
Hungary - Hongrie																					
2003																					
Male	68.3	63.9	59.0	54.0	49.2	44.4	39.6	34.9	30.3	26.2	22.4	19.0	15.8	12.9	10.2	7.9	5.9	4.1	2.5	1.4	0.6
Female	76.5	72.1	67.2	62.2	57.3	52.4	47.5	42.6	37.8	33.3	28.9	24.7	20.6	16.7	13.0	9.7	6.9	4.6	2.8	1.6	0.6
Iceland - Islande																					
2002 - 2003																					
Male	79.0	74.3	69.3	64.4	59.4	54.6	49.8	45.0	40.1	35.3	30.7	26.1	21.9	17.8	13.9	10.6	7.7	5.5	3.8	2.6	...
Female	82.4	77.6	72.7	67.7	62.8	57.9	53.0	48.1	43.3	38.5	33.7	29.1	24.7	20.4	16.2	12.5	8.8	6.2	4.4	3.1	...
Ireland - Irlande																					
2002																					
Male	75.1	70.6	65.7	60.8	56.0	51.2	46.5	41.8	37.0	32.3	27.8	23.4	19.2	15.4	11.9	8.9	6.4	4.6	3.3	2.4	1.7
Female	80.2	75.7	70.8	65.8	60.9	56.0	51.1	46.2	41.4	36.6	31.9	27.4	22.9	18.7	14.8	11.2	8.2	5.8	4.1	2.9	2.1
Isle of Man - Îles de Man																					
1996																					
Male	73.7	68.7	65.7	58.7	53.7	49.2	44.8	40.3	35.9	31.3	26.7	22.4	18.4	15.2	12.1	9.4	7.5	5.6	...	...	...
Female	79.8	75.0	70.0	65.0	60.0	55.0	50.0	45.0	40.1	35.2	30.6	26.0	21.9	18.3	14.4	11.3	8.6	6.1	...	...	...

22. Expectation of life at specified ages for each sex: latest available year, 1994 - 2003
Espérance de vie à un âge donné pour chaque sexe: dernière année disponible, 1994 - 2003 (continued — suite)

Continent, country or area and date / Continent, pays ou zone et date	0	5	10	15	20	25	30	35	40	45	50	55	60	65	70	75	80	85	90	95	100
EUROPE																					
Italy - Italie 2000																					
Male	76.5	72.0	67.0	62.1	57.3	52.6	47.8	43.0	38.3	33.6	29.0	24.6	20.4	16.5	13.0	9.9	7.3	5.2	3.8	2.6	1.8
Female	82.5	77.9	73.0	68.0	63.1	58.2	53.3	48.4	43.5	38.7	34.0	29.4	24.9	20.5	16.4	12.5	9.2	6.5	4.5	3.0	2.0
Latvia - Lettonie 2002																					
Male	65.4	61.4	56.5	51.6	46.7	42.1	37.6	33.4	29.4	25.6	21.9	18.4	15.1	12.1	9.3	7.0	5.1	3.6	2.5	...	...
Female	76.8	72.8	67.9	63.0	58.1	53.3	48.5	43.7	39.0	35.4	30.0	25.8	21.8	18.1	14.7	11.7	9.1	7.0	5.2	...	...
Lithuania - Lituanie 2003																					
Male	66.5	62.1	57.2	52.3	47.5	43.0	38.6	34.4	30.1	26.2	22.5	19.2	16.2	13.3	10.8	8.5	6.5	4.9	4.0	3.3	2.5
Female	77.8	73.4	68.5	63.6	58.7	53.8	49.0	44.2	39.5	34.9	30.5	26.2	22.1	18.1	14.3	10.9	8.0	5.8	4.5	4.1	4.3
Luxembourg 2000 - 2002																					
Male	74.8	70.4	65.4	60.5	55.7	51.0	46.3	41.6	36.9	32.3	27.8	23.6	19.5	15.8	12.5	9.5	7.0	5.0	3.4	2.1	1.5
Female	81.0	76.5	71.5	66.6	61.6	56.7	51.9	47.0	42.2	37.4	32.8	28.2	23.8	19.7	15.8	12.2	9.1	6.5	4.3	2.6	1.5
Malta - Malte 2003																					
Male	76.4	72.0	67.1	62.1	57.2	52.4	47.6	42.8	37.9	33.2	28.7	24.1	19.7	15.7	12.1	9.3	6.8	5.1	...	...	...
Female	80.4	76.1	71.1	66.1	61.2	56.3	51.4	46.5	41.7	36.9	32.1	27.4	22.9	18.7	14.6	11.0	7.9	5.7	...	...	...
Netherlands - Pays-Bas[22] 2002																					
Male	76.0	71.0	66.0	61.1	56.3	51.4	46.6	41.7	37.0	32.2	27.7	23.3	19.1	15.2	11.8	8.8	6.4	4.6	3.3	2.4	...
Female	80.7	75.6	70.7	65.7	60.8	55.9	51.0	46.1	41.2	36.5	31.9	27.4	23.1	18.9	14.9	11.3	8.2	5.6	3.8	2.6	...
Norway - Norvège[23] 2003																					
Male	77.0	72.4	67.4	62.5	57.7	53.0	48.2	43.4	38.7	34.0	29.4	25.0	20.7	16.7	13.1	9.9	7.1	4.9	3.4	2.6	...
Female	81.9	77.3	72.3	67.4	62.4	57.5	52.6	47.8	42.9	38.1	33.4	28.8	24.4	20.1	16.0	12.3	8.9	6.1	4.1	2.8	...
Poland - Pologne 2003																					
Male	70.5	66.2	61.2	56.3	51.4	46.7	42.0	37.3	32.8	28.5	24.4	20.6	17.1	14.0	11.2	8.7	6.6	5.0	3.6	2.6	1.9
Female	78.9	74.5	69.5	64.6	59.7	54.7	49.8	44.9	40.1	35.4	30.8	26.4	22.2	18.1	14.2	10.8	7.9	5.6	3.9	2.7	1.8
Portugal 2000																					
Male	72.7	68.3	63.4	58.5	53.7	49.1	44.5	39.9	35.4	31.0	26.7	22.5	18.5	14.7	11.4	8.3	5.8	3.6	2.4	1.4	...
Female	79.7	75.2	70.3	65.3	60.4	55.5	50.6	45.8	41.0	36.3	31.6	27.1	22.6	18.3	14.2	10.5	7.2	4.5	2.8	1.6	...
Republic of Moldova - République de Moldova 2003																					
Male	64.5	60.8	55.9	51.0	46.2	41.5	36.9	32.4	28.2	24.2	20.5	17.2	14.0	11.3	8.9	7.0	5.2	3.9	2.5	2.5	...
Female	71.6	67.8	62.9	57.9	53.0	48.1	43.3	38.5	33.9	29.3	25.0	20.9	17.1	13.7	10.7	8.1	5.9	4.5	2.7	2.3	...
Romania - Roumanie 2003																					
Male	67.4	64.0	59.1	54.3	49.5	44.7	40.0	35.4	30.9	26.8	22.9	19.4	16.0	13.0	10.4	7.9	6.0	4.4	3.3	2.5	1.8
Female	74.8	71.2	66.3	61.4	56.5	51.6	46.8	41.9	37.2	32.6	28.1	23.8	19.7	15.8	12.2	9.1	6.5	4.7	3.3	2.4	1.8
Russian Federation - Fédération de Russie 1999																					
Male	59.9	56.4	51.5	46.7	42.2	38.0	34.0	30.0	26.2	22.6	19.3	16.3	13.5	11.1	9.0	7.3	5.8	4.7	3.8	3.2	3.5
Female	72.4	68.7	63.8	59.0	54.2	49.5	44.8	40.1	35.5	31.0	26.7	22.6	18.6	15.0	11.8	9.0	6.8	5.0	3.7	2.9	3.1
San Marino - Saint-Marin 2000																					
Male	77.4	73.0	68.0	63.1	58.5	53.8	49.1	44.3	39.5	34.7	30.0	25.6	21.4	17.2	13.5	10.5	7.7	5.7	3.8	2.3	0.5
Female	84.0	79.6	74.6	69.6	64.7	59.7	54.8	49.9	45.0	40.2	35.4	30.7	26.0	21.6	17.1	13.1	9.2	6.3	4.2	2.7	0.5

22. Expectation of life at specified ages for each sex: latest available year, 1994 - 2003
Espérance de vie à un âge donné pour chaque sexe: dernière année disponible, 1994 - 2003 (continued — suite)

Continent, country or area and date / Continent, pays ou zone et date	0	5	10	15	20	25	30	35	40	45	50	55	60	65	70	75	80	85	90	95	100
EUROPE																					
Serbia and Montenegro - Serbie-et-Montenegro[24]																					
2002																					
Male	69.9	65.8	60.9	56.0	51.1	46.4	41.6	36.9	32.2	27.8	23.6	19.7	16.2	13.1	10.3	7.9	6.0	4.2	...	...	...
Female	75.2	71.0	66.0	61.1	56.2	51.3	46.4	41.6	36.8	32.1	27.6	23.2	19.0	15.2	11.7	8.8	6.4	4.4	...	...	...
Slovakia - Slovaquie																					
2002																					
Male	69.9	65.5	60.4	55.5	50.6	45.7	40.9	36.1	31.4	26.8	22.4	18.3	14.5	11.0	8.0	5.3	3.2	2.0	3.1	2.1	0.8
Female	77.6	73.4	68.3	63.4	58.4	53.5	48.6	43.7	38.8	33.9	29.2	24.5	20.0	15.7	11.7	8.0	4.9	2.0	3.0	1.8	0.7
Slovenia - Slovénie																					
2002																					
Male	73.2	68.6	63.6	58.6	53.8	49.1	44.3	39.6	34.9	30.4	26.1	22.1	18.4	14.9	11.8	9.2	6.9	4.5	3.9	3.0	1.0
Female	80.7	76.0	71.0	66.0	61.2	56.3	51.3	46.4	41.6	36.9	32.2	27.7	23.4	19.2	15.2	11.6	8.5	5.6	4.2	2.9	1.0
Spain - Espagne																					
2001																					
Male	76.4	71.8	66.8	61.9	57.1	52.3	47.5	42.8	38.1	33.6	29.1	24.8	20.8	16.9	13.4	10.3	7.6	5.5	3.9	2.8	1.9
Female	83.1	78.5	73.6	68.6	63.7	58.8	53.8	49.0	44.1	39.3	34.6	29.9	25.4	20.9	16.7	12.7	9.2	6.5	4.4	2.9	1.7
Sweden - Suède																					
2002																					
Male	77.7	73.1	68.1	63.1	58.3	53.5	48.6	43.8	39.0	34.3	29.6	25.2	20.9	16.9	13.2	10.0	7.2	5.0	3.4	2.5	...
Female	82.1	77.4	72.4	67.5	62.5	57.6	52.7	47.8	42.9	38.1	33.4	28.8	24.3	20.0	16.0	12.2	8.8	6.1	4.1	2.9	...
Switzerland - Suisse																					
2000																					
Male	76.9	72.4	67.5	62.5	57.7	53.0	48.2	43.5	38.7	34.0	29.5	25.1	20.9	16.9	13.3	10.1	7.4	5.2	3.5	2.3	...
Female	82.6	78.0	73.0	68.1	63.1	58.2	53.3	48.4	43.6	38.8	34.1	29.4	25.0	20.7	16.5	12.6	9.1	6.2	4.0	2.4	...
The Former Yugoslav Rep. of Macedonia - L'ex-République yougoslave de Macédoine																					
2002																					
Male	70.8	66.9	62.0	57.1	52.3	47.5	42.7	38.0	33.3	28.7	24.5	20.5	16.7	13.3	10.3	7.6	5.5	4.0	2.9	2.9	1.3
Female	75.7	71.7	66.8	61.8	56.9	52.0	47.1	42.2	37.4	32.6	28.0	23.5	19.3	15.2	11.6	8.5	6.2	4.5	3.5	2.8	0.4
Ukraine																					
2002 - 2003																					
Male	62.6	58.6	53.8	48.9	44.1	39.6	35.3	31.2	27.3	23.6	20.2	17.2	14.3	11.8	9.4	7.4	5.6	4.2	3.0	2.1	0.8
Female	74.1	69.9	65.0	60.1	55.2	50.4	45.7	41.0	36.4	31.9	27.5	23.4	19.4	15.6	12.2	9.1	6.6	4.7	3.2	2.2	0.8
United Kingdom - Royaume-Uni																					
2000																					
Male	75.3	70.9	65.9	61.0	56.1	51.4	46.6	41.9	37.1	32.5	27.9	23.6	19.5	15.7	12.2	9.4	7.0	5.0	3.7	2.6	2.0
Female	80.1	75.6	70.6	65.7	60.8	55.8	51.0	46.1	41.2	36.5	31.8	27.3	23.0	18.8	15.0	11.5	8.6	6.1	4.2	3.0	2.2
OCEANIA — OCEANIE																					
Australia - Australie																					
2001 - 2003																					
Male	77.8	73.3	68.3	63.4	58.6	53.8	49.1	44.4	39.6	35.0	30.4	25.9	21.6	17.6	13.9	10.6	7.9	5.6	4.1	3.1	2.5
Female	82.8	78.3	73.3	68.4	63.4	58.5	53.6	48.8	43.9	39.1	34.4	29.8	25.3	21.0	16.9	13.1	9.7	6.9	4.8	3.6	2.9
Marshall Islands - Îles Marshall																					
1999																					
Male	65.7	...	...	...	...	...	...	...	...	...	...	...	...	...	...	...	...	...	...	...	...
Female	69.4	...	...	...	...	...	...	...	...	...	...	...	...	...	...	...	...	...	...	...	...
Nauru																					
2000																					
Male	57.0	...	...	...	...	...	...	...	...	...	...	...	...	...	...	...	...	...	...	...	...
Female	64.0	...	...	...	...	...	...	...	...	...	...	...	...	...	...	...	...	...	...	...	...

22. Expectation of life at specified ages for each sex: latest available year, 1994 - 2003
Espérance de vie à un âge donné pour chaque sexe: dernière année disponible, 1994 - 2003 (continued — suite)

Continent, country or area and date / Continent, pays ou zone et date	0	5	10	15	20	25	30	35	40	45	50	55	60	65	70	75	80	85	90	95	100
OCEANIA — OCEANIE																					
New Caledonia - Nouvelle-Calédonie																					
2003																					
Male	71.3	67.0	62.1	57.2	52.4	48.0	43.3	38.8	34.2	29.7	25.4	21.2	17.4	13.8	11.0	9.0	7.1	5.1	3.8	9.8	...
Female	77.3	72.7	67.8	62.9	58.1	53.3	48.5	43.8	39.0	34.3	29.8	25.4	21.5	17.4	14.3	10.9	8.5	6.4	5.0	2.7	...
New Zealand - Nouvelle-Zélande																					
2002 - 2004																					
Male	77.0	72.6	67.6	62.7	58.0	53.2	48.5	43.7	39.0	34.4	29.8	25.4	21.1	17.1	13.5	10.3	7.6	5.4	3.9	...	...
Female	81.3	76.8	71.9	66.9	62.1	57.2	52.3	47.5	42.6	37.9	33.2	28.7	24.3	20.1	16.1	12.5	9.3	6.5	4.5	...	...
Papua New Guinea - Papouasie-Nouvel-le-Guinée																					
2000																					
Male	53.7	54.1	50.2	45.7	41.6	37.7	33.7	29.8	25.9	22.1	18.5	15.0	11.9	9.2	6.8	5.0	3.6	2.6	1.7	0.6	...
Female	54.8	54.7	50.8	46.3	42.1	38.1	34.1	30.1	26.2	22.3	18.6	15.2	12.0	9.2	6.8	5.0	3.6	2.5	1.6	0.6	...
Tonga																					
1998																					
Male	69.8	66.5	61.6	56.7	52.0	47.2	42.5	37.8	33.1	28.5	24.1	20.0	16.2	13.0	10.4	7.2	5.5	...	...	...	...
Female	71.8	68.3	63.4	58.6	53.7	48.9	44.2	39.4	34.8	30.2	25.8	21.6	17.7	14.1	11.2	7.8	5.9	...	...	...	...

FOOTNOTES - NOTES

1 For Algerian population only. Pour la population algérienne seulement. - Pour la population algérienne seulement.

2 Data refer to national projections. - Les données se referent aux projections nationales.

3 Projections based on the 1998 Malawi Population and Housing Census. - Les projections sont basées sur les résultats du recensement de la population et de l'habitat de Malawi de 1998.

4 Data for 1997 refer to last twelve months preceding population and housing census of 1997. - Les données pour 1997 se réfèrent au douze mois précédant le recensement de population et de l'habitat de 1997.

5 Excluding tribal Indian population. - Non compris les Indiens vivant en tribus.

6 Excluding Indian jungle population. - Non compris les Indiens de la jungle.

7 Excluding nomadic Indian tribes. - Non compris les tribus d'Indiens nomades.

8 Based on 1994 national health survey. - Basé sur l'enquête par sondage de santé pour 1994.

9 For statistical purposes, the data for China do not include those for the Hong Kong Special Administrative Region (Hong Kong SAR), Macao Special Administrative Region (Macao SAR) and Taiwan province of China. - Pour la présentation des statistiques, les données pour Chine ne comprend pas la Région Administrative Spéciale de Hong Kong (Hong Kong RAS), la Région Administrative Spéciale de Macao (Macao RAS) et Taïwan province de Chine.

10 Data refer to government controlled areas. - Les données se raportent aux zones contrôlées par le Gouvernement.

11 Data as reported by national statistical authorities. - Les données comme elles ont été déclarées par l'institut national de la statistique.

12 Including data for the Indian-held part of Jammu and Kashmir, the final status of which has not yet been determined. - Y compris les données pour la partie du Jammu et du Cachemire occupée par l'Inde dont le statut définitif n'a pas encore été déterminé.

13 Including data for East Jerusalem and Israeli residents in certain other territories under occupation by Israeli military forces since June 1967. - Y compris les données pour Jérusalem-Est et les résidents israéliens dans certains autres territoires occupés depuis 1967 par les forces armées israéliennes.

14 Data refer to Japanese nationals in Japan only. - Les données se raportent aux nationaux japonais au Japon seulement.

15 Excluding data for Jordanian territory under occupation since June 1967 by Israeli military forces. Excluding foreigners, including registered Palestinian refugees. - Non compris les données pour le territoire jordanien occupé depuis juin 1967 par les forces armées israéliennes. Non compris les étrangers, mais y compris les réfugiés de Palestine enregistrés.

16 Excluding alien armed forces stationed in the area. - Non compris les militaires étrangers en garnison sur le territoire.

17 Excluding data for the Pakistan-held part of Jammu and Kashmir, the final status of which has not yet been determined. - Non compris les données concernant la partie du Jammu et Cachemire occupée par le Pakistan dont le statut définitif n'a pas été déterminé.

18 Excluding transients afloat and non-locally domiciled military and civilian services personnel and their dependants. - Non compris les personnes de passage à bord de navires, ni les militaires et agents civils domiciliés hors du territoire et les membres de leur famille les accompagnant.

19 Based on the results of the Population Demographic Survey. - D'après les résultats de la Population Demographic Survey.

20 Including armed forces stationed outside the country, but excluding alien armed forces stationed in the area. - Y compris les militaires nationaux hors du pays, mais non compris les militaires étrangers en garnison sur le territoire.

21 Including nationals temporarily outside the country. - Y compris les nationaux se trouvant temporairement hors du pays.

22 Including residents outside the country if listed in a Netherlands population register. - Y compris les résidents hors du pays, s'ils sont inscrits sur un registre de population néerlandais.

23 Including residents temporarily outside the country.. - Y compris les résidents se trouvant temporairement hors du pays.

24 Without data for Kosovo and Metohia. - Sans les donées pour le Kosovo and Metohie.

Table 23

Table 23 presents number of marriages and crude marriage rates by urban/rural residence for as many years as possible between 1999 and 2003.

Description of variables: Marriage is defined as the act, ceremony or process by which the legal relationship of husband and wife is constituted. The legality of the union may be established by civil, religious or other means as recognized by the laws of each country. [i]

Marriage statistics in this table, therefore, include both first marriages and remarriages after divorce, widowhood or annulment. They do not, unless otherwise noted, include resumption of marriage ties after legal separation. These statistics refer to the number of marriages performed, and not to the number of persons marrying.

Statistics shown are obtained from civil registers of marriage. Exceptions, such as data from church registers, are identified in the footnotes.

The urban/rural classification of marriages is that provided by each country or area; it is presumed to be based on the national census definitions of urban population which have been set forth at the end of the technical notes for table 6.

For certain countries, there is a discrepancy between the total number of marriages shown in this table and those shown in subsequent tables for the same year. Usually this discrepancy arises because the total number of marriages occurring in a given year is revised although the remaining tabulations are not.

Rate computation: Crude marriage rates are the annual number of marriages per 1 000 mid-year population. Rates by urban/rural residence are the annual number of marriages, in the appropriate urban or rural category, per 1 000 corresponding mid-year population. These rates are calculated by the Statistics Division of the United Nations. Rates presented in this table have been limited to those for countries or areas having at least a total of 30 marriages in a given year.

Reliability of data: Each country or area has been asked to indicate the estimated completeness of the number of marriages recorded in its civil register. These national assessments are indicated by the quality codes C and U that appear in the first column of this table.

C indicates that the data are estimated to be virtually complete, that is, representing at least 90 per cent of the marriages occurring each year, while U indicates that data are estimated to be incomplete, that is, representing less than 90 per cent of the marriages occurring each year. The code ... indicates that no information was provided regarding completeness.

Data from civil registers which are reported as incomplete or of unknown completeness (coded U or ...) are considered unreliable. They appear in italics in this table; rates are not computed for these data.

These quality codes apply only to data from civil registers. For more information about the quality of vital statistics data in general, see section 4.2 of the Technical Notes.

Limitations: Statistics on marriages are subject to the same qualifications that have been set forth for vital statistics in general and marriage statistics in particular as discussed in section 4 of the Technical Notes.

The fact that marriage is a legal event, unlike birth and death that are biological events, has implications for international comparability of data. Marriage has been defined, for statistical purposes, in terms of the laws of individual countries or areas. These laws vary throughout the world. In addition, comparability is further limited because some countries or areas compile statistics only for civil marriages although religious marriages may also be legally recognized; in other countries or areas, the only available records are church registers and, therefore, the statistics may not reflect marriages that are civil marriages only.

Because in many countries or areas marriage is a civil legal contract which, to establish its legality, must be celebrated before a civil officer, it follows that for these countries or areas registration would tend to be almost automatic at the time of, or immediately following, the marriage ceremony. This factor should be kept in mind when considering the reliability of data, described above. For this reason the practice of tabulating data by date of registration does not generally pose serious problems of comparability as it does in the case of birth and death statistics.

As indicators of family formation, the statistics on the number of marriages presented in this table are bound to be deficient to the extent that they do not include either customary unions, which are not registered even though they are considered legal and binding under customary law, or consensual unions (also known as extra-legal or de facto unions). In general, lower marriage rates over a period of years are an indication of higher incidence of customary or consensual unions.

In addition, rates are affected also by the quality and limitations of the population estimates that are used in their computation. The problems of under-enumeration or over-enumeration and, to some extent, the differences in definition of total population have been discussed in section 3 of the Technical Notes dealing with population data in general, and specific information pertaining to individual countries or areas is given in the footnotes to table 3.

Strict correspondence between the numerator of the rate and the denominator is not always obtained; for example, marriages among civilian and military segments of the population may be related to civilian population. The effect of this may be to increase the rates, but, in most cases, this effect is negligible.

It should be emphasized that crude marriage rates like crude birth, death and divorce rates, may be seriously affected by the age-sex-marital structure of the population to which they relate. Crude marriage rates do, however, provide a simple measure of the level and changes in marriage.

The comparability of data by urban/rural residence is affected by the national definitions of urban and rural used in tabulating these data. It is assumed, in the absence of specific information to the contrary, that the definitions of urban and rural used in connection with the national population census were also used in the compilation of the vital statistics for each country or area. However, it cannot be excluded that, for a given country or area, different definitions of urban and rural are used for the vital statistics data and the population census data respectively. When known, the definitions of urban in national population censuses are presented at the end of the technical notes for table 6. As discussed in detail in the notes, these definitions vary considerably from one country or area to another.

In addition to problems of comparability, marriage rates classified by urban/rural residence are also subject to certain special types of bias. If, when calculating marriage rates, different definitions of urban are used in connection with the vital events and the population data, and if this results in a net difference between the numerator and denominator of the rate in the population at risk, then the marriage rates would be biased. Urban/rural differentials in marriage rates may also be affected by whether the vital events have been tabulated in terms of place of occurrence or place of usual residence. This problem is discussed in more detail in section 4.1.4.1. of the Technical Notes.

Earlier data: Marriages and crude marriage rates have been shown in each issue of the *Demographic Yearbook*. For more information on specific topics, and years for which data are reported, readers should consult the Historical Index.

NOTES

[i] *Principles and Recommendations for a Vital Statistics System Revision 2*, Sales No. E. 01.XVII.10, United Nations, New York, 2001

618

Tableau 23

Le tableau 23 présente des données sur les mariages et les taux bruts de nuptialité selon le lieu de résidence (zone urbaine ou rurale) pour le plus grand nombre possible d'années entre 1999 et 2003.

Description des variables : Le mariage désigne l'acte, la cérémonie ou la procédure qui établit un rapport légal entre mari et femme. L'union peut être rendue légale par une procédure civile ou religieuse, ou par toute autre procédure, conformément à la législation du pays[1].

Les statistiques de la nuptialité présentées dans ce tableau comprennent donc les premiers mariages et les remariages faisant suite à un divorce, un veuvage ou une annulation. Toutefois, sauf indication contraire, elles ne comprennent pas les unions reconstituées après une séparation légale. Ces statistiques se rapportent au nombre de mariages célébrés, non au nombre de personnes qui se marient.

Les statistiques présentées reposent sur l'enregistrement des mariages par les services de l'état civil. Les exceptions (données provenant des registres des églises, par exemple) font l'objet d'une note à la fin du tableau.

La classification des mariages selon le lieu de résidence (zone urbaine ou rurale) est celle qui a été communiquée par chaque pays ou zone ; on part du principe qu'elle repose sur les définitions de la population urbaine utilisées pour les recensements nationaux telles qu'elles sont reproduites à la fin des notes techniques se rapportant au tableau 6.

Pour quelques pays il y a une discordance entre le nombre total des décès vivantes présenté dans ce tableau et ceux présentés après pour la même année. Habituellement ces différences apparaissent lorsque le nombre total des décès pour une certaine année a été révisé alors que les autres tabulations ne l'ont pas été.

Calcul des taux : Les taux bruts de nuptialité représentent le nombre annuel de mariages pour 1 000 habitants au milieu de l'année. Les taux selon le lieu de résidence (zone urbaine ou rurale) représentent le nombre annuel de mariages, classés selon la catégorie urbaine ou rurale appropriée, pour 1 000 habitants au milieu de l'année. Ces taux ont été calculés par la Division de statistique de l'ONU. Les taux du tableau 23 ne se rapportent qu'aux pays ou zones où l'on a enregistré un total d'au moins 30 mariages pendant une année donnée.

Fiabilité des données : Il a été demandé à chaque pays ou zone d'indiquer le degré estimatif de complétude des données sur les mariages figurant dans ses registres d'état civil. Ces évaluations nationales sont signalées par les codes de qualité 'C' et 'U' qui apparaissent dans la deuxième colonne du tableau.

La lettre 'C' indique que les données sont jugées à peu près complètes, c'est-à-dire qu'elles représentent au moins 90 p. 100 des mariages survenus chaque année ; la lettre 'U' signale que les données sont jugées incomplètes, c'est-à-dire qu'elles représentent moins de 90 p. 100 des mariages survenus chaque année. Le code '...' indique qu'aucun renseignement n'a été communiqué quant à la complétude des données.

Les données issues des registres de l'état civil qui sont déclarées incomplètes ou dont le degré de complétude n'est pas connu (code 'U' ou '...') sont jugées douteuses. Elles apparaissent en italique dans le tableau et les taux correspondants n'ont pas été calculés.

Les codes de qualité ne s'appliquent qu'aux données provenant des registres de l'état civil. Pour plus de précisions sur la qualité des données reposant sur les statistiques de l'état civil en général, voir la section 4.2 des Notes techniques.

Insuffisance des données : Les statistiques relatives aux mariages appellent les mêmes réserves que celles qui ont été formulées à propos des statistiques de l'état civil en général et des statistiques concernant la nuptialité en particulier (voir la section 4 des Notes techniques).

Le fait que le mariage soit un acte juridique, à la différence de la naissance et du décès, qui sont des faits biologiques, a des répercussions sur la comparabilité internationale des données. Aux fins de la statistique, le mariage est défini par la législation de chaque pays ou zone. Cette législation varie d'un pays à l'autre. La comparabilité est limitée en outre du fait que certains pays ou zones ne réunissent des statistiques que pour les mariages civils, bien que les mariages religieux y soient également reconnus par la loi ; dans d'autres, les seuls relevés disponibles sont les registres des églises et, en conséquence, les statistiques peuvent ne pas rendre compte des mariages exclusivement civils.

Étant donné que, dans de nombreux pays ou zones, le mariage est un contrat juridique civil qui, pour être légal, doit être conclu devant un officier d'état civil, il s'ensuit que dans ces pays ou zones l'enregistrement se fait à peu près systématiquement au moment de la cérémonie ou immédiatement après. Il faut tenir compte de cet élément lorsque l'on évalue la fiabilité des données, dont il est question plus haut. C'est pourquoi la pratique consistant à exploiter les données selon la date de l'enregistrement ne pose généralement pas les graves problèmes de comparabilité auxquels on se heurte dans le cas des statistiques concernant les naissances et les décès.

Les statistiques relatives au nombre des mariages présentées dans ce tableau donnent une idée forcément trompeuse de la formation des familles, dans la mesure où elles ne tiennent compte ni des mariages coutumiers, qui ne sont pas enregistrés bien qu'ils soient considérés comme légaux et créateurs d'obligations en vertu du droit coutumier, ni des unions consensuelles (appelées également unions non légalisées ou unions de fait). En général, une diminution du taux de nuptialité pendant un certain nombre d'années indique une augmentation des mariages coutumiers ou des unions consensuelles.

L'exactitude des taux dépend également de la qualité et des insuffisances des estimations de population qui sont utilisées pour leur calcul. Le problème des erreurs par excès ou par défaut commises lors du dénombrement et, dans une certaine mesure, le problème de l'hétérogénéité des définitions de la population totale ont été examinés à la section 3 des Notes techniques relative à la population en général ; des indications concernant les différents pays ou zones sont données en note à la fin du tableau 3.

Il n'a pas toujours été possible d'obtenir une correspondance rigoureuse entre le numérateur et le dénominateur pour le calcul des taux. Par exemple, les mariages parmi la population civile et les militaires sont parfois rapportés à la population civile. Cela peut avoir pour effet d'accroître les taux, mais, dans la plupart des cas, il est probable que la différence sera négligeable.

Il faut souligner que les taux bruts de nuptialité, de même que les taux bruts de natalité, de mortalité et de divortialité, peuvent varier sensiblement selon la structure par âge et par sexe de la population à laquelle ils se rapportent. Les taux bruts de nuptialité offrent néanmoins un moyen simple de mesurer la fréquence et l'évolution des mariages.

La comparabilité des données selon le lieu de résidence (zone urbaine ou rurale) peut être limitée par les définitions nationales des termes « urbain » et « rural » utilisées pour le classement de ces données. En l'absence d'indications contraires, on a supposé que les mêmes définitions avaient servi pour le recensement national de la population et pour l'établissement des statistiques de l'état civil pour chaque pays ou zone. Toutefois, il n'est pas exclu que, pour une zone ou un pays donné, des définitions différentes aient été retenues. Les définitions du terme « urbain » utilisées pour les recensements nationaux de population ont été présentées à la fin des notes techniques du tableau 6 lorsqu'elles étaient connues. Comme on l'a précisé dans les notes techniques relatives au tableau 6, ces définitions varient considérablement d'un pays ou d'une zone à l'autre.

Outre les problèmes de comparabilité, les taux de nuptialité classés selon le lieu de résidence (zone urbaine ou rurale) sont également sujets à des distorsions particulières. Si l'on utilise des définitions différentes du terme « urbain » pour classer les faits d'état civil et les données relatives à la population lors du calcul des taux et qu'il en résulte une différence nette entre le numérateur et le dénominateur pour le taux de la population exposée au risque, les taux de nuptialité s'en trouveront faussés. La différence entre ces taux pour les zones urbaines et rurales pourra aussi être faussée selon que les faits d'état civil auront été classés d'après le lieu où ils se sont produits ou d'après le lieu de résidence habituel. Ce problème est examiné plus en détail à la section 4.1.4.1 des Notes techniques.

Données publiées antérieurement : Les différentes éditions de l'Annuaire démographique regroupent des données sur le nombre des mariages. Pour plus de précisions concernant les années et les sujets pour lesquels des données ont été publiées, se reporter à l'index historique.

NOTE

[1] Principes et recommandations pour un système de statistiques de l'état civil, deuxième révision, numéro de vente : F.01.XVII.10, publication des Nations Unies, New York, 2003.

23. Marriages and crude marriage rates, by urban/rural residence: 1999 - 2003
Mariages et taux bruts de nuptialité, selon la résidence, urbaine/rurale: 1999 - 2003

Continent, country or area and urban/rural residence / Continent, pays ou zone et résidence, urbaine/rurale	Code[1]	Marriages - Mariages					Rate - Taux				
		1999	2000	2001	2002	2003	1999	2000	2001	2002	2003
AFRICA — AFRIQUE											
Algeria - Algérie[2]											
Total	...	163 126	177 548	194 273	218 620	...	...	...	...	...	...
Djibouti[3]											
Total	...	3 808	...	...	...	...	...	...	...	...	...
Egypt - Égypte[4]											
Total	+...	525 412	592 381	457 534	490 770	491 000	...	...	...	...	...
Urban-Urbaine	+...	191 224	...	...	...	...	...	...	...	...	...
Rural-Rurale	+...	334 188	...	...	...	...	...	...	...	...	...
Ethiopia - Éthiopie											
Total	...	630 290	...	...	...	...	...	...	...	...	...
Urban-Urbaine	...	24 093	...	...	...	...	...	...	...	...	...
Rural-Rurale	...	606 197	...	...	...	...	...	...	...	...	...
Libyan Arab Jamahiriya - Jamahiriya arabe libyenne[5]											
Total	U	19 348	27 655	28 661	33 323	...	...	...	...	...	...
Mauritius - Maurice											
Total	+C	11 295	10 963	10 635	10 484	10 812	9.6	9.2	8.9	8.7	8.8
Urban-Urbaine	+C	3 537	3 542	3 423	3 295	3 298	7.0	7.0	6.7	6.4	6.4
Rural-Rurale	+C	7 758	7 421	7 212	7 189	7 514	11.5	10.9	10.5	10.3	10.7
Réunion											
Total	C	3 446	3 444	3 508	3 284	*3 212	4.9	4.8	4.8	4.4	*4.2
Saint Helena ex. dep. - Sainte-Hélène sans dép.											
Total	C	25	17	20	...	...	...	...	...	...	...
Seychelles											
Total	+C	883	949	790	865	823	11.0	11.7	9.7	10.3	9.9
Tunisia - Tunisie											
Total	...	60 082	...	61 800	...	...	...	...	...	...	...
AMERICA, NORTH — AMERIQUE DU NORD											
Anguilla[6]											
Total	C	73	68	51	53	75	6.7	6.0	4.4	4.4	6.1
Aruba											
Total	C	578	616	546	649	...	6.4	6.8	5.9	6.9	...
Bahamas											
Total	C	2 204	2 366	1 787	...	...	7.4	7.8	5.8	...	...
Barbados - Barbade											
Total	C	...	*3 516	...	...	...	...	*13.1	...	...	...
Belize											
Total	+C	1 517	1 546	1 558	1 622	...	6.2	6.2	6.1	6.1	...
Bermuda - Bermudes											
Total	C	1 093	1 023	923	937	861	17.4	16.2	14.9	15.2	13.8
Canada											
Total	C	155 742	157 395	146 618	146 738	...	5.1	5.1	4.7	4.7	...
Cayman Islands - Îles Caïmanes											
Total	+C	375	...	...	...	...	9.6	...	...	...	...
Costa Rica											
Total	C	25 613	24 436	23 790	...	24 448	7.5	7.0	6.1	...	6.0
Cuba											
Total	C	57 252	57 001	54 345	56 876	54 739	5.2	5.1	4.9	5.1	4.9
Urban-Urbaine	C	51 645	51 762	49 429	51 728	50 103	6.2	6.1	5.8	6.1	5.9
Rural-Rurale	C	5 607	5 239	4 916	5 148	4 636	2.1	1.9	1.8	1.9	1.7
Dominica - Dominique											
Total	+C	*339	...	...	...	...	*4.7	...	...	...	...
Dominican Republic - République dominicaine											
Total	+C	36 446	33 904	24 470	...	...	4.4	4.0	2.8	...	...
El Salvador											
Total	+C	34 306	28 231	29 216	25 998	24 972	5.6	4.5	4.6	4.0	3.8
Urban-Urbaine	+C	27 071	22 525	23 668	22 102	20 836	7.6	6.1	6.3	5.7	5.3
Rural-Rurale	+C	7 235	5 706	5 548	3 896	4 136	2.8	2.2	2.1	1.5	1.5
Grenada - Grenade											
Total	+C	570	616	*509	...	...	5.7	6.1	*5.0	...	...

23. Marriages and crude marriage rates, by urban/rural residence: 1999 - 2003
Mariages et taux bruts de nuptialité, selon la résidence, urbaine/rurale: 1999 - 2003 (continued — suite)

Continent, country or area and urban/rural residence / Continent, pays ou zone et résidence, urbaine/rurale	Code[1]	Marriages - Mariages					Rate - Taux				
		1999	2000	2001	2002	2003	1999	2000	2001	2002	2003
AMERICA, NORTH — AMERIQUE DU NORD											
Guadeloupe											
Total	C	1 892	1 935	1 929	1 809	1 701	4.5	4.5	4.5	4.1	3.9
Guatemala											
Total	C	60 922	...	...	...	...	5.5	...	...	...	...
Jamaica - Jamaïque											
Total	+C	29 155	27 028	22 308	23 070	22 476	11.3	10.4	8.6	8.8	8.5
Martinique											
Total	C	1 591	1 591	1 572	1 524	1 414	4.2	4.1	4.1	3.9	3.6
Mexico - Mexique[7]											
Total	+C	743 856	707 422	665 434	616 654	584 142	7.5	7.0	6.5	6.0	5.6
Urban-Urbaine	+C	556 723	530 888	501 426	469 962	436 860	7.2	7.0	6.6	6.1	5.6
Rural-Rurale	+C	176 747	160 037	145 362	134 326	132 873	8.1	6.3	5.7	5.3	5.2
Montserrat											
Total	+...	19	...	...	...	...	...	...	...	...	...
Netherlands Antilles - Antilles néerlandaises											
Total	C	956	1 595	1 447	1 177	748	5.1	8.9	8.3	6.7	4.2
Nicaragua											
Total	+C	28 005	24 268	21 140	21 039	20 411	5.7	4.9	4.2	4.1	3.9
Panama[8]											
Total	C	10 388	10 430	9 767	*9 392	...	3.7	3.7	3.4	*3.1	...
Urban-Urbaine	C	7 506	7 499	7 416	*7 687	...	4.8	4.7	...	...	...
Rural-Rurale	C	2 882	2 931	2 351	*1 705	...	2.3	2.3	...	...	...
Puerto Rico - Porto Rico											
Total	C	27 255	25 980	28 598	25 645	25 236	7.2	6.8	7.4	6.6	6.5
Saint Lucia - Sainte-Lucie											
Total	C	732	655	513	472	...	4.8	4.2	3.2	3.0	...
Saint Vincent and the Grenadines - Saint Vincent-et-les Grenadines											
Total	+C	630	673	506	509	...	5.6	6.0	4.6	4.7	...
Turks Caicos Islands - Îles Turques et Caïques											
Total	C	402	543	520	593	491	23.4	29.4	26.1	28.4	22.3
United States - États-Unis											
Total	C	2 358 000	2 329 000	2 345 000	*2 254 000	*2 187 000	8.6	8.5	8.2	*7.8	*7.5
AMERICA, SOUTH — AMERIQUE DU SUD											
Argentina - Argentine											
Total	C	147 649	141 027	130 533	122 343	...	4.0	3.8	3.5	3.2	...
Brazil - Brésil[9]											
Total	U	788 744	732 721	710 121	...	748 981	...	...	...	...	...
Chile - Chili											
Total	+C	69 765	66 607	64 088	60 971	56 659	4.6	4.3	4.1	3.9	3.6
Urban-Urbaine	+C	60 772	58 531	56 427	54 730	51 807	4.6	4.4	4.2	4.0	3.8
Rural-Rurale	+C	8 993	8 076	7 661	6 241	4 852	4.3	3.9	3.7	3.0	2.3
Ecuador - Équateur[10]											
Total	U	77 593	74 875	67 741	66 208	65 393	...	...	...	...	...
French Guiana - Guyane française											
Total	C	548	518	547	522	524	3.5	3.2	3.2	3.0	2.9
Suriname											
Total	C	2 257	2 267	2 006	2 005	...	4.9	4.9	4.3	4.2	...
Uruguay											
Total	C	15 488	13 888	13 988	14 073	14 147	4.7	4.2	4.2	4.3	4.3
Venezuela[9]											
Total	C	90 220	91 088	81 516	73 163	...	3.8	3.7	3.3	2.9	...
ASIA — ASIE											
Armenia - Arménie											
Total	C	12 459	10 986	12 302	13 682	...	3.9	3.4	3.8	4.3	...

23. Marriages and crude marriage rates, by urban/rural residence: 1999 - 2003
Mariages et taux bruts de nuptialité, selon la résidence, urbaine/rurale: 1999 - 2003 (continued — suite)

Continent, country or area and urban/rural residence / Continent, pays ou zone et résidence, urbaine/rurale	Code[1]	Marriages - Mariages					Rate - Taux				
		1999	2000	2001	2002	2003	1999	2000	2001	2002	2003
ASIA — ASIE											
Armenia - Arménie											
Urban-Urbaine	C	8 560	7 626	...	...	...	4.1	3.7	...	...	...
Rural-Rurale	C	3 899	3 360	...	...	...	3.5	3.0	...	...	...
Azerbaijan - Azerbaïdjan											
Total	+C	37 382	39 611	41 861	41 661	56 091	4.7	4.9	5.2	5.1	6.8
Urban-Urbaine	+C	18 799	19 994	22 927	22 438	26 935	4.6	4.9	5.6	5.4	6.3
Rural-Rurale	+C	18 583	19 617	18 934	19 223	29 156	4.8	5.0	4.7	4.8	7.3
Bahrain - Bahreïn											
Total	...	3 673	3 963	4 504	4 909	5 373	...	...	...	...	...
Brunei Darussalam - Brunéi Darussalam											
Total	...	2 318	2 184	2 091	2 288	2 262	...	...	...	...	...
China - Chine[11]											
Total	+C	8 853 000	8 485 000	8 050 000	7 860 000	8 114 000	7.1	6.7	6.3	6.1	6.3
China: Hong Kong SAR - Chine: Hong Kong RAS											
Total	C	31 287	30 879	32 825	32 070	35 439	4.7	4.6	4.9	4.7	5.2
China: Macao SAR - Chine: Macao RAS											
Total	+C	1 367	1 222	1 222	1 209	1 309	3.2	2.8	2.8	2.8	2.9
Cyprus - Chypre[12]											
Total	C	9 080	9 282	10 574	10 284	10 810	13.2	13.4	15.1	14.5	15.0
Urban-Urbaine	C	...	...	...	6 641	...	...	...	...	...	...
Rural-Rurale	C	...	...	...	3 643	...	...	...	...	...	...
Georgia - Géorgie											
Total	C	13 845	12 870	13 336	12 535	12 696	3.1	2.9	3.0	2.9	2.9
Urban-Urbaine	C	...	7 977	8 027	...	8 161	...	3.4	3.5	...	3.6
Rural-Rurale	C	...	4 893	5 309	...	4 535	...	2.3	2.5	...	2.2
Iran (Islamic Republic of) - Iran (République islamique d')											
Total	C	611 519	646 498	641 940	650 960	681 034	9.7	10.2	9.9	9.9	10.2
Urban-Urbaine	C	476 723	499 143	496 229	513 772	522 160	12.0	12.2	11.8	11.9	11.9
Rural-Rurale	C	134 796	147 355	145 711	137 188	158 874	5.9	6.5	6.5	6.1	7.0
Iraq[13]											
Total	C	148 963	171 134	...	...	...	6.5	7.3	...	...	...
Israel - Israël[14]											
Total	C	40 236	38 894	38 924	39 718		6.6	6.2	6.0	6.0	...
Japan - Japon[15]											
Total	+C	762 028	798 138	799 999	757 331	740 191	6.0	6.3	6.3	5.9	5.8
Urban-Urbaine	+C	630 726	661 245	663 506	629 906	617 978	...	...	...	...	...
Rural-Rurale	+C	131 302	136 893	136 493	127 425	122 213	...	...	...	...	...
Jordan - Jordanie[16]											
Total	+C	39 443	45 618	49 794	46 873	48 784	7.9	9.2	9.5	8.7	9.0
Kazakhstan											
Total	C	85 872	90 873	92 852	98 986	110 414	5.8	6.1	6.2	6.7	7.4
Urban-Urbaine	C	50 178	52 006	54 395	58 529	66 794	6.0	6.2	6.5	6.9	7.9
Rural-Rurale	C	35 694	38 867	38 457	40 457	43 620	5.5	6.0	6.0	6.3	6.8
Korea (Republic of) - Corée (République de)											
Total	+C	362 673	334 030	320 063	306 573	304 932	7.8	3.6	6.8	6.4	6.4
Urban-Urbaine	+C	294 612	273 040	261 575	252 808	251 873	...	7.4	...	...	...
Rural-Rurale	+C	68 061	60 990	58 488	53 765	53 059	...	6.5	...	...	...
Kuwait - Koweït											
Total	C	10 847	10 785	11 830	11 973		5.1	4.9	5.2	5.3	...
Kyrgyzstan - Kirghizistan											
Total	C	26 033	24 294	27 455	31 240	34 266	5.4	4.9	5.5	6.3	6.8
Urban-Urbaine	C	7 926	7 528	8 258	9 065	9 953	4.6	4.3	4.7	5.1	5.6
Rural-Rurale	C	18 107	16 766	19 197	22 175	24 313	5.8	5.3	6.0	6.9	7.5
Lebanon - Liban[13]											
Total	C	32 673	32 564	33 704	35 392	35 841	...	...	...	...	...
Maldives											
Total	...	4 767	5 151	3 202	2 594	3 088	...	...	...	...	...
Urban-Urbaine	...	2 412	2 705	1 159	1 121	1 376	...	...	...	...	...
Rural-Rurale	...	2 355	2 446	2 043	1 473	1 712	...	...	...	...	...

23. Marriages and crude marriage rates, by urban/rural residence: 1999 - 2003
Mariages et taux bruts de nuptialité, selon la résidence, urbaine/rurale: 1999 - 2003 (continued — suite)

Continent, country or area and urban/rural residence / Continent, pays ou zone et résidence, urbaine/rurale	Code[1]	Marriages - Mariages					Rate - Taux				
		1999	2000	2001	2002	2003	1999	2000	2001	2002	2003
ASIA — ASIE											
Mongolia - Mongolie											
Total	C	13 722	12 601	12 393	13 514	14 572	...	5.2	5.1	5.5	5.8
Urban-Urbaine	C	7 383	6 096	6 091	7 206	8 374	...	4.4	4.4	5.1	5.7
Rural-Rurale	C	6 339	6 505	6 302	6 308	6 198	...	6.3	6.0	6.0	6.0
Occupied Palestinian Territory - Territoire palestinien occupé											
Total	C	24 874	23 890	24 635	22 611	26 267	8.2	7.6	7.5	6.7	7.5
Philippines											
Total	U	551 445	577 387	559 162	583 167	...	...	...	...	...	...
Qatar											
Total	C	1 905	2 096	2 194	2 351	2 550	3.3	3.4	3.4	3.4	3.5
Saudi Arabia - Arabie saoudite											
Total	...	74 938	79 595	81 576	90 982		...	...	...	...	...
Singapore - Singapour[17,18,19]											
Total	+C	25 648	22 561	22 280	23 198	21 962	6.5	5.6	5.4	5.6	5.2
Sri Lanka											
Total	+U	169 634	186 548	186 698	190 618		...	...	...	...	...
Syrian Arab Republic - République arabe syrienne[20]											
Total	+U	136 157	139 843	153 842	174 449		...	...	...	...	...
Tajikistan - Tadjikistan											
Total	C	22 736	26 597	28 827	32 262	39 143	3.7	4.3	4.6	5.0	6.0
Urban-Urbaine	C	6 938	8 510	8 587	9 721	11 190	4.3	5.2	5.1	5.7	6.4
Rural-Rurale	C	15 798	18 087	20 240	22 541	27 953	3.5	4.0	4.4	4.8	5.8
Thailand - Thaïlande											
Total	C	*354 198	...	...	...	...	*5.8	...	...	...	...
Turkey - Turquie[21]											
Total	+U	475 613	461 417	453 213	447 820		...	...	...	...	...
Urban-Urbaine	+U	294 248	301 280	296 295	299 930		...	...	...	...	...
Rural-Rurale	+U	181 365	160 137	156 918	147 890		...	...	...	...	...
Uzbekistan - Ouzbékistan											
Total	C	170 525	168 908	170 101	...	...	7.1	6.9	6.8	...	...
Urban-Urbaine	C	64 685	65 104	64 302	...	...	7.2	7.1	6.9	...	...
Rural-Rurale	C	105 840	103 804	105 799	...	...	7.1	6.7	6.7	...	...
Viet Nam											
Total	C	...	...	...	*964 701		...	...	...	*12.1	...
Urban-Urbaine	C	...	...	...	*254 281		...	...	...	*12.7	...
Rural-Rurale	C	...	...	...	*710 420		...	...	...	*11.9	...
EUROPE											
Albania - Albanie											
Total	C	27 254	25 820	25 717	26 202	27 342	8.9	8.4	8.4	8.5	8.8
Urban-Urbaine	C	...	...	...	12 171	11 785	...	...	...	9.0	8.6
Rural-Rurale	C	...	...	...	14 031	15 557	...	...	...	8.0	9.0
Andorra - Andorre											
Total	C	178	226	213	186	197	2.7	3.4	3.2	2.8	2.8
Austria - Autriche[22]											
Total	C	39 485	39 228	34 213	36 570	37 195	4.9	4.9	4.3	4.5	4.6
Belarus - Bélarus											
Total	C	72 994	...	...	66 652	69 905	7.3	...	...	6.7	7.1
Urban-Urbaine	C	57 648	...	...	53 838	57 028	8.3	...	...	7.7	8.1
Rural-Rurale	C	15 346	...	...	12 814	12 877	5.0	...	...	4.4	4.5
Belgium - Belgique[23]											
Total	C	44 171	45 123	42 110	40 434	*41 777	4.3	4.4	4.1	3.9	*4.0
Bosnia and Herzegovina - Bosnie-Herzégovine											
Total	C	22 472	21 897	20 302	20 766	20 733	6.0	5.8	5.3	5.4	5.4
Bulgaria - Bulgarie[24]											
Total	C	35 540	35 164	31 974	29 218	30 645	4.3	4.3	4.0	3.7	3.9
Urban-Urbaine	C	...	26 576	24 466	23 085	24 543	...	4.8	4.5	4.2	4.5
Rural-Rurale	C	...	8 588	7 508	6 133	6 102	...	3.3	3.1	2.6	2.6

Continent, country or area and urban/rural residence / Continent, pays ou zone et résidence, urbaine/rurale	Code[1]	Marriages - Mariages					Rate - Taux				
		1999	2000	2001	2002	2003	1999	2000	2001	2002	2003
EUROPE											
Channel Islands: Guernsey - Îles Anglo-Normandes: Guernesey											
Total	C	385	343	...	...	...	6.4	5.7	...	...	...
Croatia - Croatie											
Total	C	23 778	22 017	22 076	22 806	22 337	5.2	5.0	...	5.1	5.0
Urban-Urbaine	C	...	12 439	12 380	12 918	12 375	...	...	...	...	...
Rural-Rurale	C	...	9 578	9 696	9 888	9 962	...	...	...	...	...
Czech Republic - République tchèque											
Total	C	53 523	55 321	52 374	52 732	48 943	5.2	5.4	5.1	5.2	4.8
Urban-Urbaine	C	40 370	41 763	39 666	40 014	37 134	5.3	5.5	5.2	5.3	4.9
Rural-Rurale	C	13 153	13 558	12 708	12 718	11 809	5.0	5.2	4.8	4.8	4.4
Denmark - Danemark[25]											
Total	C	35 439	38 388	36 567	37 210	35 041	6.7	7.2	6.8	6.9	6.5
Estonia - Estonie[26]											
Total	C	5 590	5 485	5 647	5 853	...	3.9	4.0	4.1	4.3	...
Urban-Urbaine	C	...	3 929	...	4 020	...	...	4.1	...	4.3	...
Rural-Rurale	C	...	1 304	...	1 491	...	...	3.1	...	3.6	...
Finland - Finlande[27]											
Total	C	24 271	26 150	24 830	26 969	25 815	4.7	5.1	4.8	5.2	5.0
Urban-Urbaine	C	...	...	17 843	19 398	18 534	...	...	5.6	6.0	5.7
Rural-Rurale	C	...	...	6 987	7 571	7 281	...	...	3.5	3.8	3.7
France[28,29]											
Total	C	286 191	297 922	288 255	279 087	*275 963	4.9	5.1	4.9	4.7	*4.6
Urban-Urbaine	C	222 831	...	222 689	214 125	*210 905	...	...	...	...	...
Rural-Rurale	C	59 000	...	61 111	60 099	*59 503	...	...	...	...	...
Germany - Allemagne											
Total	C	430 674	418 550	389 591	391 967	382 911	5.2	5.1	4.7	4.8	4.6
Gibraltar											
Total	C	161	149	164	166	179	5.9	5.5	...	5.8	6.3
Greece - Grèce											
Total	C	61 165	61 848	58 491	...	61 081	5.8	6.2	5.8	...	5.5
Hungary - Hongrie[28]											
Total	C	45 465	48 110	43 583	46 008	45 398	4.5	4.8	4.3	4.5	4.5
Urban-Urbaine	C	29 345	31 314	28 876	31 207	30 703	4.5	4.8	4.3	4.7	4.7
Rural-Rurale	C	15 138	15 890	13 769	13 912	13 702	4.3	4.5	3.9	3.9	3.9
Iceland - Islande[30]											
Total	C	1 560	1 777	1 484	1 652	*1 473	5.6	6.3	5.2	5.7	*5.1
Urban-Urbaine	C	1 471	1 668	1 406	1 581	*1 400	5.7	6.4	5.3	5.9	*5.2
Rural-Rurale	C	89	109	78	71	*73	4.2	5.1	3.6	3.3	*3.4
Ireland - Irlande											
Total	+C	18 526	19 168	19 246	20 047	20 302	4.9	5.1	5.0	5.1	5.1
Isle of Man - Îles de Man											
Total	C	377	417	392	430	413	...	5.6	5.1	5.6	5.3
Italy - Italie											
Total	C	280 330	284 410	264 026	270 013	*257 880	4.9	4.9	4.6	4.7	*4.5
Latvia - Lettonie											
Total	C	9 399	9 211	9 258	9 738	9 989	3.9	3.9	3.9	4.2	4.3
Urban-Urbaine	C	6 955	...	6 755	7 115	7 373	4.3	...	4.2	4.5	4.7
Rural-Rurale	C	2 444	...	2 503	2 623	2 616	3.2	...	3.3	3.5	3.5
Liechtenstein											
Total	C	...	...	199	175	149	...	...	6.0	5.2	4.4
Lithuania - Lituanie											
Total	C	17 868	16 906	15 764	16 151	16 975	5.1	4.8	4.5	4.7	4.9
Urban-Urbaine	C	12 150	11 705	11 036	11 637	12 066	5.1	5.0	4.7	5.0	5.2
Rural-Rurale	C	5 718	5 201	4 728	4 514	4 909	4.9	4.5	4.1	3.9	4.3
Luxembourg[30]											
Total	C	2 090	2 148	1 983	2 020	2 001	4.9	4.9	4.5	4.5	4.4
Malta - Malte[31]											
Total	C	2 409	2 545	2 194	2 240	2 350	6.3	6.7	5.7	5.8	5.9
Monaco											
Total	C	...	160	...	175	183	...	5.0	...	...	...

23. Marriages and crude marriage rates, by urban/rural residence: 1999 - 2003
Mariages et taux bruts de nuptialité, selon la résidence, urbaine/rurale: 1999 - 2003 (continued — suite)

Continent, country or area and urban/rural residence / Continent, pays ou zone et résidence, urbaine/rurale	Code[1]	Marriages - Mariages					Rate - Taux				
		1999	2000	2001	2002	2003	1999	2000	2001	2002	2003
EUROPE											
Netherlands - Pays-Bas[32,33,34]											
Total	C	89 428	88 074	82 091	85 808	80 427	5.7	5.5	5.1	5.3	5.0
Urban-Urbaine	C	48 708	47 515	45 261	47 645	45 295	4.9	4.7	4.4	4.5	4.3
Rural-Rurale	C	33 024	31 923	27 847	28 671	26 897	5.7	5.5	4.9	5.1	4.8
Norway - Norvège[35]											
Total	C	23 456	25 356	22 967	24 069	22 361	5.3	5.6	5.1	5.3	4.9
Poland - Pologne											
Total	C	219 398	211 150	195 122	191 935	195 446	5.7	5.5	5.1	5.0	5.1
Urban-Urbaine	C	131 990	...	118 210	115 816	118 709	5.5	...	5.0	4.9	5.0
Rural-Rurale	C	87 408	...	76 912	76 119	76 737	5.9	...	5.3	5.2	5.2
Portugal											
Total	C	68 710	63 752	58 390	56 457	53 735	6.8	6.2	5.7	5.4	5.1
Republic of Moldova - République de Moldova											
Total	C	23 524	21 684	21 065	21 685	24 961	6.5	6.0	5.8	6.0	6.9
Urban-Urbaine	C	9 886	9 514	9 727	10 194	11 520	6.5	6.3	6.5	6.9	7.8
Rural-Rurale	C	13 638	12 170	11 338	11 491	13 441	6.4	5.7	5.3	5.4	6.3
Romania - Roumanie											
Total	C	140 014	135 808	129 930	129 018	133 953	6.2	6.1	5.8	5.9	6.2
Urban-Urbaine	C	...	79 128	77 231	76 547	81 483	...	6.5	6.3	6.6	7.0
Rural-Rurale	C	...	56 680	52 699	52 471	52 470	...	5.6	5.2	5.2	5.2
Russian Federation - Fédération de Russie											
Total	C	911 162	1 266 800	1 001 589	1 019 762	1 091 778	6.2	8.6	6.9	7.0	7.6
San Marino - Saint-Marin											
Total	C	231	193	174	208	200	8.8	7.2	6.3	7.3	6.9
Serbia and Montenegro - Serbie-et-Montenegro[36]											
Total	C	53 034	58 318	57 165	45 741	45 964	5.0	5.5	5.4	5.6	5.6
Urban-Urbaine	C	29 921	33 251	32 572	28 262	28 866	5.5	6.1	5.9	6.1	6.2
Rural-Rurale	C	23 113	25 067	24 593	17 479	17 098	4.5	4.9	4.8	5.0	4.9
Slovakia - Slovaquie											
Total	C	27 340	25 903	23 795	25 062	26 002	5.1	4.8	4.4	4.7	4.8
Urban-Urbaine	C	14 320	...	13 591	14 370	15 068	4.7	...	4.5	4.8	5.0
Rural-Rurale	C	13 020	...	10 204	10 692	10 934	5.6	...	4.3	4.5	4.6
Slovenia - Slovénie											
Total	C	7 716	7 201	6 935	7 064	6 756	3.9	3.6	3.5	3.5	3.4
Urban-Urbaine	C	...	3 571	3 569	3 768	3 624	...	...	...	3.9	3.7
Rural-Rurale	C	...	3 630	3 366	3 296	3 132	...	...	...	3.4	3.2
Spain - Espagne											
Total	C	208 129	216 451	208 057	211 522	*210 155	5.2	5.4	5.1	5.1	*5.0
Sweden - Suède											
Total	C	35 682	39 895	35 778	38 012	39 041	4.0	4.5	4.0	4.3	4.4
Switzerland - Suisse											
Total	C	40 646	39 758	35 987	40 213	40 056	5.7	5.5	5.0	5.5	5.5
Urban-Urbaine	C	28 427	28 031	25 668	31 057	30 869	5.9	5.8	...	...	...
Rural-Rurale	C	12 219	11 727	10 319	9 156	9 187	5.3	5.0	...	...	...
The Former Yugoslav Rep. of Macedonia - L'ex-République yougoslave de Macédoine											
Total	C	14 172	14 255	13 267	14 522	*14 402	7.0	7.0	6.5	7.1	*7.1
Urban-Urbaine	C	...	7 530	7 584	7 905	...	...	...	...	...	...
Rural-Rurale	C	...	6 725	5 683	6 617	...	...	...	...	...	...
Ukraine											
Total	C	...	...	309 602	317 228	370 966	...	...	6.4	6.6	7.8
Urban-Urbaine	C	...	...	223 638	231 532	277 014	...	...	6.9	7.2	8.7
Rural-Rurale	C	...	...	85 964	85 696	93 952	...	...	5.4	5.4	6.0
United Kingdom - Royaume-Uni											
Total	C	301 083	305 912	286 129	293 021	306 214	5.1	5.2	4.8	4.9	5.1

23. Marriages and crude marriage rates, by urban/rural residence: 1999 - 2003
Mariages et taux bruts de nuptialité, selon la résidence, urbaine/rurale: 1999 - 2003 (continued — suite)

Continent, country or area and urban/rural residence Continent, pays ou zone et résidence, urbaine/rurale	Code[1]	Marriages - Mariages					Rate - Taux				
		1999	2000	2001	2002	2003	1999	2000	2001	2002	2003
OCEANIA — OCEANIE											
Australia - Australie											
Total	+C	114 316	113 429	103 130	105 435	106 394	6.0	5.9	5.3	5.4	5.4
Cook Islands - Îles Cook											
Total	+C	387	715	578	604	623	23.6	39.7	31.8	32.8	33.9
French Polynesia - Polynésie française											
Total	C	1 107	1 091	964	1 042	1 047	4.9	4.7	4.0	4.3	4.2
Guam[37]											
Total	C	1 456	1 499	1 418	1 288	1 334	9.5	...	9.0	8.0	8.2
New Caledonia - Nouvelle-Calédonie											
Total	C	943	995	925	905	873	4.5	4.7	4.3	4.2	4.0
New Zealand - Nouvelle-Zélande											
Total	+C	21 085	20 655	19 972	20 690	21 419	5.5	5.4	5.1	5.3	5.3
Niue - Nioué											
Total	...	*15*	*12*	*8*	*15*	*3*	...	...	...	...	...
Tonga											
Total	+C	770	747	...	...	...	7.7	7.4	...	...	...

FOOTNOTES - NOTES

Italics: data from civil registers which are incomplete or of unknown completeness.
-Italiques: données incomplètes ou dont le degré d'exactitude n'est pas connu, provenant des registres de l'état civil.

* Provisional. — Données provisoires.

[1] 'Code' indicates the source of data, as follows:
C - Civil registration, estimated over 90% complete
U - Civil registration, estimated less than 90% complete
+ - Data tabulated by date of registration rather than occurence.
... - Information not available

Le 'Code' indique la source des données, comme suit:
C - Registres de l'état civil considérés complets à 90 p. 100 au moins.
U - Registres de l'état civil qui ne sont pas considérés complets à 90 p. 100 au moins.
+ - Données exploitées selon la date de l'enregistrement et non la date de l'événement.
... - Information pas disponible.

[2] For Algerian population only. - Pour la population algérienne seulement.
[3] Data refer to the district of Djibouti only - Les données portent uniquement sur le district de Djibouti.
[4] Including marriages resumed after 'revocable divorce' (among Moslem population), which approximates legal separation. - Y compris les unions reconstituées après un 'divorce révocable' (parmi la population musulmane), qui est à peu près l'équivalent d'une séparation légale.
[5] Data refer to Libyan nationals only. - Les données se raportent aux nationaux libyens seulement.
[6] Data exclude visitors. - Les données non compris des visiteurs.
[7] Urban and rural distribution of marriages are displayed by place of residence of bride. The difference between 'Total' and the sum of urban and rural is due to the unknown place of residence of the bride. - La distribution des mariages entre zones urbaines et rurales est montrée selon le lieu de résidence de la mariée. La différence entre le 'Total' et la somme des chiffres pour les zones urbaines et rurales est due aux cas où le lieu de résidence de la mariée n'est pas connu.
[8] Excluding tribal Indian population. - Non compris les Indiens vivant en tribus.
[9] Excluding Indian jungle population. - Non compris les Indiens de la jungle.
[10] Excluding nomadic Indian tribes. - Non compris les tribus d'Indiens nomades.
[11] For statistical purposes, the data for China do not include those for the Hong Kong Special Administrative Region (Hong Kong SAR), Macao Special Administrative Region (Macao SAR) and Taiwan province of China. - Pour la présentation des statistiques, les données pour Chine ne comprend pas la Région Administrative Spéciale de Hong Kong (Hong Kong RAS), la Région Administrative Spéciale de Macao (Macao RAS) et Taïwan province de Chine.
[12] Data refer to government controlled areas. - Les données se raportent aux zones contrôlées par le Gouvernement.
[13] Published by the United Nations Economic and Social Commission for Western Asia. - Publié par la Commission économique et sociale des Nations Unies pour l'Asie occidentale.
[14] Including data for East Jerusalem and Israeli residents in certain other territories under occupation by Israeli military forces since June 1967. - Y compris les données pour Jérusalem-Est et les résidents israéliens dans certains autres territoires occupés depuis 1967 par les forces armées israéliennes.
[15] For Japanese nationals in Japan only; however, rates computed using total population. - Pour les nationaux japonais au Japon seulement; toutefois, les taux sont calculés sur la base de la population totale.
[16] Excluding data for Jordanian territory under occupation since June 1967 by Israeli military forces. Excluding foreigners, including registered Palestinian refugees. - Non compris les données pour le territoire jordanien occupé depuis juin 1967 par les forces armées israéliennes. Non compris les étrangers, mais y compris les réfugiés de Palestine enregistrés.
[17] Registration of Kandyan marriages is complete; registration of Moslem and general marriages is incomplete. - Tous les mariages des Kandyens sont enregistrés; l'enregistrement des mariages musulmans et des autres mariages est incomplet.
[18] Rates computed on population excluding transients afloat and non-locally domiciled military and civilian services personnel and their dependants. - Taux calculés sur la base d'un chiffre de population qui ne comprend pas les personnes de passage à bord de navires, ni les militaires et agents civils domiciliés hors du territoire et les membres de leur famille les accompagnant.
[19] Figures exclude marriages previously officiated outside Singapore or under religious and customary rites. - Les figures excluent les mariages célébrés précédemment au dehors de Singapoure ou sous les rites réligieuse ou accoutumés.
[20] Excluding nomads. - Non compris les nomades.
[21] Data refer to provincial capitals and district centres only. - Les données se rapportent aux capitales des provinces et les chefs-lieux de districts seulement.
[22] Excluding aliens temporarily in the area. - Non compris les étrangers se trouvant temporairement le territoire.
[23] Including armed forces stationed outside the country, but excluding alien armed forces in the area unless marriage performed by local foreign authority. - Y compris les militaires nationaux hors du pays et les militaires étrangers en garnison sur le territoire, sauf si le mariage a été célébré pour l'autorité locale.
[24] Including Bulgarian nationals outside the country, but excluding aliens in the area. - Y compris les nationaux bulgares à l'étranger, mais non compris les étrangers sur le territoire.
[25] Excluding Faeroe Islands and Greenland. - Non compris les Iles Féroé et Gröenland.

[26] Urban and rural distribution of marriages and divorces is displayed by place of residence of groom/husband. The difference between 'Total' and the sum of urban and rural is due to the unknown place of residence of grooms/husbands and to grooms/husbands living outside Estonia. - Les mariages et divorces sont classés par rapport à la résidence urbaine/rurale de l'époux. La somme des mariages et divorces par résidence urbaine/rurale est différente du 'total' car elle ne tient pas compte ni des résidences inconnues de l'époux ni des mariages et divorces d'époux vivant à l'étranger.

[27] Marriages in which the bride was resident in Finland only. - Mariages où l'épouse a la résidence en Finlande seulement.

[28] The difference between 'Total' and the sum of 'urban' and 'rural' is due to the cases of unknown place of residence or residence abroad. - La différence entre le 'Total' et la somme des données selon la résidence urbaine/rurale se rapporte à la situation ou on ignore la résidence ou si la résidence est à l'étranger.

[29] Including armed forces stationed outside the country. - Y compris les militaires nationaux hors du pays.

[30] Data refer to de jure population. - Les données se raportent a la population de droit

[31] Rates computed on population including civilian nationals temporarily outside the country. - Les taux sont calculés sur la base d'un chiffre de population qui comprend les civils nationaux temporairement hors du pays.

[32] From 2001, including same sex marriages. - Après 2001, y compris les mariages entre personnes du même sexe.

[33] Marriages of couples of which at least one partner is recorded in a Dutch municipal register, irrespective of the country where the marriage was performed. - Mariages où un des conjoints au moins est inscrit dans un registre municipal néerlandais, quel que soit le pays où le mariage a été contracté.

[34] The difference between 'Total' and the sum of 'urban' and 'rural' is due to marriages (of which at least one partner recorded in a Dutch municipal register) contracted abroad. - La différence entre le Total et la somme des zones urbaines et des zones rurales est due aux mariages contractés à l'étranger (dont un des conjoints au moins est inscrit dans un registre municipal néerlandais).

[35] Marriages in which the groom was resident in Norway only. - Mariages où l'époux a la résidence en Norvège seulement.

[36] From 2002, without data for Kosovo and Metohia. - Après 2002, sans les donées pour le Kosovo and Metohie.

[37] Including United States military personnel, their dependants and contract employees. - Y compris les militaires des Etats-Unis, les membres de leur famille les accompagnant et les agents contractuels des Etats-Unis.

Table 24

Table 24 presents the marriages by age of groom and age of bride for as many years as possible between 1999 and 2003.

Description of variables: Marriage is defined as the act, ceremony or process by which the legal relationship of husband and wife is constituted. The legality of the union may be established by civil, religious or other means as recognized by the laws of each country.[i]

Marriage statistics in this table, therefore, include both first marriages and remarriages after divorce, widowhood or annulment. They do not, unless otherwise noted, include resumption of marriage ties after legal separation. These statistics refer to the number of marriages performed, and not to the number of persons marrying.

Age is defined as age at last birthday, that is, the difference between the date of birth and the date of the occurrence of the event, expressed in completed solar years. The age classification generally used in this table is the following: under 15 years, 5-year age groups through 90-94, and 100 years and over. The same classification is used for both grooms and brides.

In an effort to provide interpretation of these statistics, countries or areas providing data on marriages by age of bride and groom have been requested to specify "the minimum legal age at which marriage can take place with and without parental consent". This information is presented in the table 24-1 below.

Reliability of data: Data from civil registers of marriages that are reported as incomplete (less than 90 per cent completeness) or of unknown completeness are considered unreliable and are set in *italics* rather than in roman type. Table 23 and the technical notes for that table provide more detailed information on the completeness of marriage registration. For more information about the quality of vital statistics data in general, see section 4.2 of the Technical Notes.

Limitations: Statistics on marriages by age of groom and age of bride are subject to the same qualifications as have been set forth for vital statistics in general and marriage statistics in particular as discussed in Section 4 of the Technical Notes.

The fact that marriage is a legal event, unlike birth and death that are biological events, has implications for international comparability of data. Marriage has been defined, for statistical purposes, in terms of the laws of individual countries or areas. These laws vary throughout the world. In addition, comparability is further limited because some countries or areas compile statistics only for civil marriages although religious marriages may also be legally recognized; in other countries or areas, the only available records are church registers and, therefore, the statistics may not reflect to marriages that are civil marriages only.

Because in many countries or areas marriage is a civil legal contract which, to establish its legality, must be celebrated before a civil officer, it follows that for these countries or areas registration would tend to be almost automatic at the time of, or immediately following, the marriage ceremony. This factor should be kept in mind when considering the reliability of data, described above. For this reason the practice of tabulating data by date of registration does not generally pose serious problems of comparability as it does in the case of birth and death statistics.

Because these statistics are classified according to age, they are subject to the limitations with respect to accuracy of age reporting similar to those already discussed in connection with Section 3.1.3 of the Technical Notes. It is probable that biases are less pronounced in marriage statistics, because information is obtained from the persons concerned and since marriage is a legal act, the participants are likely to give correct information. However, in some countries or areas, there appears to be a concentration of marriages at the legal minimum age for marriage and at the age at which valid marriage may be contracted without parental consent, indicating perhaps an overstatement in some cases to comply with the law.

Aside from the possibility of age misreporting, it should be noted that marriage patterns at younger ages, that is, for ages up to 24 years, are influenced to a large extent by laws regarding the minimum age for marriage

Factors that may influence age reporting, particularly at older ages include an inclination to understate the age of the bride in order that it may be equal to or less than that of the groom.

The absence of frequencies in the unknown age group does not necessarily indicate completely accurate reporting and tabulation of the age item. It is sometimes an indication that the unknowns have been eliminated by assigning ages to them before tabulation, or by proportionate distribution after tabulation.

Another age-reporting factor that must be kept in mind in using these data is the variation that may result from calculating age at marriage from year of birth rather than from day, month and year of birth. Information on this factor is given in footnotes when known.

Earlier data: Marriages by age of groom and age of bride have been shown for the latest available year in most issues of the *Demographic Yearbook*. In addition, issues, including those featuring marriage and divorce statistics, have presented data covering a period of years. For information on the specific topics and the years covered, readers should consult the Historical Index.

24-1 Minimum legal age at which marriage can take place

Country or area	With parental consent		Without parental consent	
	Groom	Bride	Groom	Bride
Africa				
Egypt	18	16	...	...
Mauritius	16	16	18	18
America, North				
Anguilla	...	...	18	18
Bahamas	..	..	..	..
Bermuda	16	16	18	18
Canada	16	16	16	16
Costa Rica	16	16	18	18
Cuba	14	14	16	16
El Salvador	15	14	15	14
Mexico	16	14	18	18
Panama	16	14	18	18
Puerto Rico	16	14	18	16
America, South				
Brazil	15	12	...	...
Chile	14	12	18	18
Ecuador	14	12	...	...
Uruguay	14	12	18	18
Venezuela	21	18	...	...
Asia				
Armenia	18	17	...	...
Azerbaijan	18	17	...	...
Bahrain	15	...	...	...
China: Hong Kong SAR	16	16	21	21

Country or area	With parental consent		Without parental consent	
	Groom	Bride	Groom	Bride
China: Macao SAR	16	16	18	18
Israel	...	17	...	17
Japan	18	16	20	20
Kazakhstan	16	16	18	17
Korea (Republic of)	18	16	20	20
Kyrgyzstan	18	18	18	18
Occupied Palestinian Territory	14	14	...	...
Philippines	18-20	18-20	21	21
Singapore	16 (Muslim marriages) 18 (Civil marriages)	16 (Muslim marriages) 18 (Civil marriages)	21 (Muslim marriages) 21 (Civil marriages)	.. (Muslim marriages) 21 (Civil marriage) 18 if person has previously been married
Tajikistan	17	17	16	16
Turkey	17	17	18	18
Uzbekistan	17	17	17	17
Europe				
Albania	18	16	...	...
Austria	18	16	18	16
Belarus	18	18	18	18
Belgium	17	15	18	18
Bosnia and Herzegovina	18	18	18	18
Bulgaria	16	16	18	18
Croatia	16	16	18	18
Czech Republic	16	16	18	18
Denmark	18	15	18	18
Estonia	15	15	18	18
Finland	Consent of Ministry of Justice necessary	Consent of Ministry of Justice necessary	18	18
France	16	14	18	18
Hungary	16	16	18	18
Iceland	18	18	18	18
Italy	16	16	...	...
Latvia	16	16	18	18

Country or area	With parental consent		Without parental consent	
	Groom	Bride	Groom	Bride
Lithuania	15 (by judgment)	15 (by judgment)	18	18
Luxembourg	…	…	18	18
Malta	16	16	18	18
Netherlands	16	16	18	18
Norway	16	16	18	18
Poland	..	16, 17	18	18
Portugal	16	16	18	18
Republic of Moldova	16	14	18	16
Romania	17	16	18	18
Russian Federation	16	16	18	18
Serbia and Montenegro	16	16	18	18
Slovakia	16	16	18	18
Slovenia	15	15	18	18
Spain	…	…	18	18
Sweden	18	18	18	18
Switzerland	…	…	18	18
The Former Yugoslav Rep. of Macedonia	16	16	18	18
Ukraine	14	14	18	17
United Kingdom	16	16	18	18
Oceania				
Australia	16	16	18	16
New Zealand	16	16	16	16

NOTES

[i] *Principles and Recommendations for a Vital Statistics System Revision 2,* Sales No. E. 01.XVII.10, United Nations, New York, 2001

Tableau 24

Le tableau 24 présente des statistiques concernant les mariages classés selon l'âge de l'époux et selon l'âge de l'épouse pour le plus grand nombre possible d'années entre 1999 et 2003.

Description des variables : Le mariage désigne l'acte, la cérémonie ou la procédure qui établit un rapport légal entre mari et femme. L'union peut être rendue légale par une procédure civile ou religieuse, ou par toute autre procédure, conformément à la législation du pays[1].

Les statistiques de la nuptialité présentées dans ce tableau comprennent donc les premiers mariages et les remariages faisant suite à un divorce, un veuvage ou une annulation. Toutefois, sauf indication contraire, elles ne comprennent pas les unions reconstituées après une séparation légale. Ces statistiques se rapportent au nombre de mariages célébrés, non au nombre de personnes qui se marient.

L'âge désigne l'âge au dernier anniversaire, c'est-à-dire la différence entre la date de naissance et la date de l'événement, exprimée en années solaires révolues. Le classement par âge utilisé dans le tableau 24 comprend les groupes suivants : moins de 15 ans, groupes quinquennaux jusqu'à 90-94 ans, 100 ans et plus. On a adopté la même classification pour les deux sexes.

Dans un effort de fournir l'interprétation de ces statistiques, les pays ou les zones fournissant des données sur les mariages par l'âge de l'épouse et de par l'âge de mari ont été demandés d'indiquer "l'âge légal minimum avec auquel le mariage peut avoir lieu avec et sans consentement parental". Cette information est présentée dans le tableau 24-1 ci-dessous.

Fiabilité des données : Les données sur les mariages issues des registres de l'état civil qui sont déclarées incomplètes (degré de complétude inférieur à 90 p. 100) ou dont le degré de complétude n'est pas connu sont jugées douteuses et apparaissent en italique et non en caractères romains. Le tableau 23 et les notes techniques s'y rapportant présentent des renseignements plus détaillés sur le degré de complétude de l'enregistrement des mariages. Pour plus de précisions sur la qualité des données reposant sur les statistiques de l'état civil en général, voir la section 4.2 des notes techniques.

Insuffisance des données : Les statistiques des mariages selon l'âge de l'époux et selon l'âge de l'épouse appellent les mêmes réserves que celles formulées à propos des statistiques de l'état civil en général et des statistiques de la nuptialité en particulier (voir la section 4 des Notes techniques).

Le fait que le mariage soit un acte juridique, à la différence de la naissance et du décès, qui sont des faits biologiques, a des répercussions sur la comparabilité internationale des données. Aux fins de la statistique, le mariage est défini par la législation de chaque pays ou zone. Cette législation varie d'un pays à l'autre. La comparabilité est limitée en outre du fait que certains pays et zones ne réunissent des statistiques que pour les mariages civils, bien que les mariages religieux y soient également reconnus par la loi ; dans d'autres, les seuls relevés disponibles sont les registres des églises et, en conséquence, les statistiques peuvent ne pas rendre compte des mariages exclusivement civils.

Le mariage étant, dans de nombreux pays ou zones, un contrat juridique civil qui, pour être légal, doit être conclu devant un officier d'état civil, il s'ensuit que, dans ces pays ou zones, l'enregistrement se fait à peu près systématiquement au moment de la cérémonie ou immédiatement après. Il faut tenir compte de cet élément lorsque l'on évalue la fiabilité des données, dont il est question plus haut. C'est pourquoi la pratique consistant à exploiter les données selon la date de l'enregistrement ne pose généralement pas les graves problèmes de comparabilité auxquels on se heurte dans le cas des statistiques des naissances et des décès.

Étant donné que ces statistiques sont classées selon l'âge, elles appellent les mêmes réserves concernant l'exactitude des déclarations d'âge que celles dont il a déjà été question à la section 3.1.3 des Notes techniques. Il est probable que les statistiques de la nuptialité sont moins faussées par ce genre d'erreur, car les renseignements sont donnés par les intéressés eux-mêmes, et, comme le mariage est un acte juridique, il y a toutes chances que leurs déclarations soient exactes. Toutefois, dans certains pays ou zones, il semble y avoir une concentration de mariages à l'âge minimal légal de nubilité ainsi qu'à l'âge auquel le mariage peut être valablement contracté sans le consentement des parents, ce qui peut indiquer que certains déclarants se vieillissent pour se conformer à la loi.

Outre la possibilité d'erreurs dans les déclarations d'âge, il convient de noter que la législation fixant l'âge minimal de nubilité influe notablement sur les caractéristiques de la nuptialité pour les premiers âges, c'est-à-dire jusqu'à 24 ans.

Parmi les facteurs pouvant exercer une influence sur les déclarations d'âge, en particulier celles qui sont faites par des personnes plus âgées, il faut citer la tendance à diminuer l'âge de l'épouse de façon qu'il soit égal ou inférieur à celui de l'époux.

Si aucun nombre ne figure dans la rangée réservée aux âges inconnus, cela ne signifie pas nécessairement que les déclarations d'âge et l'exploitation des données par âge aient été tout à fait exactes. C'est parfois une indication que l'on a attribué un âge aux personnes d'âge inconnu avant l'exploitation des données ou qu'elles ont été réparties proportionnellement entre les différents groupes après cette opération.

Il importe de ne pas oublier non plus, lorsque l'on utilisera ces données, que l'on calcule parfois l'âge des conjoints au moment du mariage sur la base de l'année de naissance seulement et non d'après la date exacte (jour, mois et année) de naissance. Des renseignements à ce sujet sont donnés en note chaque fois que possible.

Donnés publiées antérieurement : On trouve dans la plupart des éditions de l'*Annuaire démographique* des statistiques concernant les mariages selon l'âge de l'époux et selon l'âge de l'épouse qui ont été établies à partir des données les plus récentes dont on disposait à l'époque. En outre, certaines éditions, y compris celles qui étaient plus particulièrement consacrées aux statistiques de la nuptialité et de la divortialité, présentaient des séries chronologiques. Pour plus de précisions concernant les années et les sujets pour lesquels des données ont été publiées, se reporter à l'index historique.

24-1 L'âge légal minimum avec auquel le mariage peut avoir lieu

Pays ou zone	Avec consentement parental		Sans consentement parental	
	Epoux	Epouse	Epoux	Epouse
Afrique				
Egypte	18	16	…	…
Maurice	16	16	18	18
Amérique du Nord				
Anguilla	…	…	18	18
Bahamas	..	..	..	..
Bermudes	16	16	18	18
Canada	16	16	16	16
Costa Rica	16	16	18	18
Cuba	14	14	16	16
El Salvador	15	14	15	14
Mexique	16	14	18	18
Panama	16	14	18	18
Porto Rico	16	14	18	16
Amérique du Sud				
Brésil	15	12	…	…
Chili	14	12	18	18
Equateur	14	12	…	…
Uruguay	14	12	18	18

Pays ou zone	Avec consentement parental		Sans consentement parental	
	Epoux	Epouse	Epoux	Epouse
Venezuela	21	18	...	...
Asie				
Arménie	18	17	...	...
Azerbaïdjan	18	17	...	...
Bahreïn	15	...	...	...
Chine: Hong Kong RAS	16	16	21	21
Chine: Macao RAS	16	16	18	18
Israël	...	17	...	17
Japon	18	16	20	20
Kazakhstan	16	16	18	17
Corée (République de)	18	16	20	20
Kirghizistan	18	18	18	18
Territoire palestinien occupé	14	14	...	...
Philippines	18-20	18-20	21	21
Singapour	16 (mariages musulmans) 18 (mariages civils)	16 (mariages musulmans) 18 (mariages civils)	21 (mariages musulmans) 21 (mariages civils)	.. (mariages musulmans) 21 (mariages civils) 18 si le mariage n'est pas le premier
Tadjikistan	17	17	16	16
Turquie	17	17	18	18
Ouzbékistan	17	17	17	17
Europe				
Albanie	18	16	...	...
Autriche	18	16	18	16
Bélarus	18	18	18	18
Belgique	17	15	18	18
Bosnie-Herzégovine	18	18	18	18
Bulgarie	16	16	18	18
Croatie	16	16	18	18
République tchèque	16	16	18	18
Danemark	18	15	18	18
Estonie	15	15	18	18

Pays ou zone	Avec consentement parental		Sans consentement parental	
	Epoux	Epouse	Epoux	Epouse
Finlande	Agrément du Ministère de la justice requis	Agrément du Ministère de la justice requis	18	18
France	16	14	18	18
Hongrie	16	16	18	18
Islande	18	18	18	18
Italie	16	16	…	…
Lettonie	16	16	18	18
Lituanie	15 (en vertu d'une décision de justice)	15 (en vertu d'une décision de justice)	18	18
Luxembourg	…	…	18	18
Malte	16	16	18	18
Pays-Bas	16	16	18	18
Norvège	16	16	18	18
Pologne	..	16, 17	18	18
Portugal	16	16	18	18
République de Moldova	16	14	18	16
Roumanie	17	16	18	18
Fédération de Russie	16	16	18	18
Serbie-et-Montenegro	16	16	18	18
Slovaque	16	16	18	18
Slovénie	15	15	18	18
Espagne	…	…	18	18
Suede	18	18	18	18
Suisse	…	…	18	18
L'ex-République yougoslave de Macédoine	16	16	18	18
Ukraine	14	14	18	17
Royaume-Uni	16	16	18	18
Océanie				
Australie	16	16	18	16
Nouvelle-Zélande	16	16	16	16

NOTE

[1] *Principes et recommandations pour un système de statistiques de l'état civil, deuxième révision*, numéro de vente F.01.XVII.10, publication des Nations Unies, New York, 2003.

Continent, country or area and age / Continent, pays ou zone et âge	1999 Groom Epoux	1999 Bride Epouse	2000 Groom Epoux	2000 Bride Epouse	2001 Groom Epoux	2001 Bride Epouse	2002 Groom Epoux	2002 Bride Epouse	2003 Groom Epoux	2003 Bride Epouse
AFRICA — AFRIQUE										
Egypt - Égypte+,1										
All ages - Tous âges	525 412	525 412	...	...	...	...	...	...	...	...
0-19	14 982	64 422	...	...	...	...	...	...	...	...
20-24	115 939	152 234	...	...	...	...	...	...	...	...
25-29	192 784	143 382	...	...	...	...	...	...	...	...
30-34	111 874	134 280	...	...	...	...	...	...	...	...
35-39	42 038	14 515	...	...	...	...	...	...	...	...
40-44	16 707	7 500	...	...	...	...	...	...	...	...
45-49	11 422	4 447	...	...	...	...	...	...	...	...
50-54	6 527	2 185	...	...	...	...	...	...	...	...
55-59	4 296	987	...	...	...	...	...	...	...	...
60-64	3 514	617	...	...	...	...	...	...	...	...
65-69	2 549	333	...	...	...	...	...	...	...	...
70-74	1 555	178	...	...	...	...	...	...	...	...
75+	1 045	329	...	...	...	...	...	...	...	...
Unknown - Inconnu	180	3	...	...	...	...	...	...	...	...
Mauritius - Maurice+										
All ages - Tous âges	11 295	11 295	10 963	10 963	10 635	10 635	10 484	10 484	10 812	10 812
0-14	-	-	-	-	-	1	-	-	-	-
15-19	172	2 442	163	2 054	167	1 819	134	1 666	147	1 531
20-24	2 402	4 356	2 243	4 132	2 131	4 025	2 130	4 078	2 111	4 040
25-29	3 879	2 009	3 663	2 180	3 587	2 152	3 599	2 162	3 717	2 416
30-34	2 405	1 142	2 297	1 148	2 206	1 184	2 109	1 156	2 141	1 230
35-39	1 115	673	1 152	689	1 148	675	1 129	687	1 221	726
40-44	573	318	631	362	548	352	579	338	587	435
45-49	342	195	381	208	345	227	357	210	378	228
50-54	174	98	172	99	246	108	201	97	253	126
55-59	115	25	136	44	119	50	123	46	129	51
60-64	54	19	66	23	58	22	59	27	67	15
65-69	39	11	26	12	35	9	41	11	35	5
70-74	13	3	17	9	23	7	15	3	14	4
75+	12	4	16	3	22	4	8	3	12	4
Unknown - Inconnu	-	-	-	-	-	-	-	-	-	1
Réunion										
All ages - Tous âges	3 446	3 446	...	...	...	...	3 284	3 284	...	...
15-19	...	214	...	...	...	...	...	148	...	...
18-19	19	...	...	...	...	...	16	...	...	...
20-24	461	985	...	...	...	...	402	823	...	...
25-29	1 113	954	...	...	...	...	908	921	...	...
30-34	835	629	...	...	...	...	761	551	...	...
35-39	409	315	...	...	...	...	428	372	...	...
40-44	237	146	...	...	...	...	294	229	...	...
45-49	142	93	...	...	...	...	192	99	...	...
50-54	94	49	...	...	...	...	120	65	...	...
55-59	49	26	...	...	...	...	62	38	...	...
60+	87	35	...	...	...	...	101	38	...	...
Seychelles+										
All ages - Tous âges	...	...	...	...	790	790	...	...	...	...
15-19	...	...	...	...	7	26	...	...	...	...
20-24	...	...	...	...	66	136	...	...	...	...
25-29	...	...	...	...	149	198	...	...	...	...
30-34	...	...	...	...	210	196	...	...	...	...
35-39	...	...	...	...	156	103	...	...	...	...
40-44	...	...	...	...	92	62	...	...	...	...
45-49	...	...	...	...	43	35	...	...	...	...
50-54	...	...	...	...	27	19	...	...	...	...
55+	...	...	...	...	40	15	...	...	...	...
AMERICA, NORTH — AMERIQUE DU NORD										
Anguilla										
All ages - Tous âges	...	...	...	...	...	...	...	...	75	75
18-23	...	...	...	...	...	...	...	...	9	13
24-29	...	...	...	...	...	...	...	...	24	24
30-35	...	...	...	...	...	...	...	...	17	17
36-41	...	...	...	...	...	...	...	...	9	9

24. Marriages by age of bridegroom and by age of bride: 1999 - 2003
Mariages selon l'âge de l'époux et selon l'âge de l'épouse: 1999 - 2003 (continued — suite)

Continent, country or area and age / Continent, pays ou zone et âge	1999 Groom Epoux	1999 Bride Epouse	2000 Groom Epoux	2000 Bride Epouse	2001 Groom Epoux	2001 Bride Epouse	2002 Groom Epoux	2002 Bride Epouse	2003 Groom Epoux	2003 Bride Epouse
AMERICA, NORTH — AMERIQUE DU NORD										
Anguilla										
42-47	...	...	...	...	...	...	...	...	10	6
48-53	...	...	...	...	...	...	...	...	1	3
54-58	...	...	...	...	...	...	...	...	1	1
59-64	...	...	...	...	...	...	...	...	2	1
65+	...	...	...	...	...	...	...	...	2	1
Unknown - Inconnu	...	...	...	...	...	...	...	...	-	-
Bahamas										
All ages - Tous âges	...	...	...	...	1 787	1 787	...	...	...	...
15-19	...	...	...	...	11	82	...	...	...	...
20-24	...	...	...	...	254	430	...	...	...	...
25-29	...	...	...	...	490	474	...	...	...	...
30-34	...	...	...	...	406	333	...	...	...	...
35-39	...	...	...	...	247	197	...	...	...	...
40-44	...	...	...	...	120	132	...	...	...	...
45-49	...	...	...	...	97	61	...	...	...	...
50-54	...	...	...	...	64	41	...	...	...	...
55-59	...	...	...	...	36	12	...	...	...	...
60+	...	...	...	...	51	14	...	...	...	...
Unknown - Inconnu	...	...	...	...	11	11	...	...	...	...
Bermuda - Bermudes										
All ages - Tous âges	...	...	...	...	...	...	937	937	861	861
0-19	...	...	...	...	...	...	2	8	-	9
20-29	...	...	...	...	...	...	206	302	191	256
30-39	...	...	...	...	...	...	423	397	386	380
40-49	...	...	...	...	...	...	165	146	162	152
50-59	...	...	...	...	...	...	97	65	91	52
60+	...	...	...	...	...	...	44	19	31	12
Canada										
All ages - Tous âges	...	...	...	...	146 618	146 618	146 738	146 738	...	...
15-19	...	...	...	...	976	3 674	919	3 504	...	...
20-24	...	...	...	...	19 912	32 479	19 421	31 526	...	...
25-29	...	...	...	...	43 787	45 073	43 355	45 377	...	...
30-34	...	...	...	...	30 309	25 056	30 788	25 579	...	...
35-39	...	...	...	...	18 172	14 550	18 266	14 675	...	...
40-44	...	...	...	...	11 308	9 481	11 497	9 526	...	...
45-49	...	...	...	...	7 580	6 728	7 711	6 827	...	...
50-54	...	...	...	...	5 670	4 345	5 667	4 349	...	...
55-59	...	...	...	...	3 466	2 295	3 686	2 372	...	...
60-64	...	...	...	...	2 053	1 190	2 101	1 254	...	...
65-69	...	...	...	...	1 386	791	1 362	807	...	...
70-74	...	...	...	...	965	501	910	481	...	...
75+	...	...	...	...	970	426	974	431	...	...
Unknown - Inconnu	...	...	...	...	64	29	81	30	...	...
Costa Rica										
All ages - Tous âges	...	...	24 436	24 436	23 790	23 790	...	...	24 448	24 448
0-14	...	...	-	155	-	81	...	...	-	30
15-19	...	...	1 419	5 209	1 328	4 907	...	...	1 110	4 335
20-24	...	...	7 094	7 722	6 934	7 629	...	...	6 642	7 642
25-29	...	...	6 413	4 852	6 101	4 669	...	...	6 362	5 105
30-34	...	...	3 797	2 525	3 667	2 444	...	...	3 809	2 609
35-39	...	...	2 046	1 394	2 015	1 394	...	...	2 227	1 607
40-44	...	...	1 209	870	1 184	923	...	...	1 420	1 013
45-49	...	...	763	547	807	530	...	...	825	668
50+	...	...	...	...	...	...	...	...	1 524	837
50-54	...	...	478	294	444	294	...	...	...	...
55-59	...	...	270	179	300	162	...	...	...	...
60-64	...	...	207	94	227	105	...	...	...	...
65+	...	...	333	117	562	127	...	...	...	...
Unknown - Inconnu	...	...	407	478	441	525	...	...	529	602
Cuba										
All ages - Tous âges	57 252	57 252	57 001	57 001	...	...	...	...	...	...
0-14	2	318	5	282	...	...	...	...	...	...
15-19	1 608	7 629	1 509	7 141	...	...	...	...	...	...
20-24	10 239	13 212	9 384	12 143	...	...	...	...	...	...

24. Marriages by age of bridegroom and by age of bride: 1999 - 2003
Mariages selon l'âge de l'époux et selon l'âge de l'épouse: 1999 - 2003 (continued — suite)

Continent, country or area and age / Continent, pays ou zone et âge	1999 Groom Epoux	1999 Bride Epouse	2000 Groom Epoux	2000 Bride Epouse	2001 Groom Epoux	2001 Bride Epouse	2002 Groom Epoux	2002 Bride Epouse	2003 Groom Epoux	2003 Bride Epouse
AMERICA, NORTH — AMERIQUE DU NORD										
Cuba										
25-29	13 724	12 174	13 332	11 956	...	...	...	...	...	...
30-34	10 420	8 552	10 127	8 527	...	...	...	...	...	...
35-39	6 955	5 802	7 587	6 409	...	...	...	...	...	...
40-44	4 021	3 080	4 158	3 398	...	...	...	...	...	...
45-49	3 100	2 379	3 139	2 566	...	...	...	...	...	...
50-54	2 367	1 653	2 515	1 861	...	...	...	...	...	...
55-59	1 738	1 040	1 918	1 159	...	...	...	...	...	...
60-64	1 250	648	1 362	721	...	...	...	...	...	...
65-69	785	320	798	360	...	...	...	...	...	...
70-74	484	213	539	222	...	...	...	...	...	...
75+	507	176	572	202	...	...	...	...	...	...
Unknown - Inconnu	52	56	56	54	...	...	...	...	...	...
El Salvador+										
All ages - Tous âges	34 346	34 346	28 275	28 275	29 287	29 287	26 077	26 077	25 071	25 071
0-14	-	105	-	80	-	85	-	42	-	45
15-19	1 717	5 613	1 366	4 343	1 272	4 262	1 026	3 446	928	3 283
20-24	9 792	10 981	7 831	8 997	7 999	9 207	6 609	7 790	6 394	7 568
25-29	8 849	7 383	6 999	6 005	7 211	6 369	6 601	6 012	6 451	5 900
30-34	5 099	4 126	4 287	3 327	4 547	3 628	4 048	3 247	3 923	3 195
35-39	3 001	2 344	2 544	2 034	2 712	2 113	2 539	2 040	2 415	1 818
40-44	1 918	1 384	1 583	1 273	1 742	1 322	1 626	1 302	1 516	1 157
45-49	1 293	972	1 126	890	1 225	935	1 043	820	1 028	833
50-54	897	625	838	526	806	570	845	588	750	516
55-59	660	325	581	361	599	358	612	331	576	328
60-64	456	239	471	207	512	206	478	231	413	199
65+	664	249	649	232	662	232	650	228	677	229
Grenada - Grenade+										
All ages - Tous âges	570	570	616	616	...	...	...	...	...	...
15-19	2	10	2	16	...	...	...	...	...	...
20-24	34	92	44	91	...	...	...	...	...	...
25-29	131	160	132	163	...	...	...	...	...	...
30-34	143	114	149	122	...	...	...	...	...	...
35-39	102	88	112	93	...	...	...	...	...	...
40-44	51	37	70	58	...	...	...	...	...	...
45-49	40	23	50	38	...	...	...	...	...	...
50-54	20	21	18	13	...	...	...	...	...	...
55-59	18	5	14	9	...	...	...	...	...	...
60-64	13	9	13	8	...	...	...	...	...	...
65+	13	8	11	4	...	...	...	...	...	...
Unknown - Inconnu	-	3	1	1	...	...	...	...	...	...
Guadeloupe										
All ages - Tous âges	...	...	...	...	...	...	1 809	1 809	1 701	1 701
0-14	...	...	...	...	...	...	-	-	-	-
15-19	...	...	...	...	...	...	-	35	3	28
20-24	...	...	...	...	...	...	91	223	49	226
25-29	...	...	...	...	...	...	377	523	320	423
30-34	...	...	...	...	...	...	503	401	437	412
35-39	...	...	...	...	...	...	369	255	328	238
40-44	...	...	...	...	...	...	204	165	197	122
45-49	...	...	...	...	...	...	99	89	121	94
50-54	...	...	...	...	...	...	68	45	74	61
55-59	...	...	...	...	...	...	44	29	63	35
60-64	...	...	...	...	...	...	19	23	41	29
65-69	...	...	...	...	...	...	34	10	30	11
70+	...	...	...	...	...	...	1	11	38	22
Jamaica - Jamaïque+										
All ages - Tous âges	...	...	...	...	...	...	...	...	22 476	22 476
15-19	...	...	...	...	...	...	...	...	58	363
20-24	...	...	...	...	...	...	...	...	2 159	3 873
25-29	...	...	...	...	...	...	...	...	5 278	5 978
30-34	...	...	...	...	...	...	...	...	5 264	4 771
35-39	...	...	...	...	...	...	...	...	3 631	3 090
40-44	...	...	...	...	...	...	...	...	2 399	2 054
45-49	...	...	...	...	...	...	...	...	1 543	1 173

24. Marriages by age of bridegroom and by age of bride: 1999 - 2003
Mariages selon l'âge de l'époux et selon l'âge de l'épouse: 1999 - 2003 (continued — suite)

Continent, country or area and age / Continent, pays ou zone et âge	1999 Groom Epoux	1999 Bride Epouse	2000 Groom Epoux	2000 Bride Epouse	2001 Groom Epoux	2001 Bride Epouse	2002 Groom Epoux	2002 Bride Epouse	2003 Groom Epoux	2003 Bride Epouse
AMERICA, NORTH — AMERIQUE DU NORD										
Jamaica - Jamaïque[+]										
50-54	...	...	...	...	...	...	...	...	874	622
55-59	...	...	...	...	...	...	...	...	536	266
60-64	...	...	...	...	...	...	...	...	316	139
65+	...	...	...	...	...	...	...	...	418	147
Martinique										
All ages - Tous âges	...	...	...	...	...	...	1 524	1 524	1 414	1 414
15-19	...	...	...	...	...	...	1	6	1	11
20-24	...	...	...	...	...	...	42	140	46	144
25-29	...	...	...	...	...	...	321	432	235	328
30-34	...	...	...	...	...	...	366	340	340	353
35-39	...	...	...	...	...	...	281	236	273	203
40-44	...	...	...	...	...	...	176	142	185	144
45-49	...	...	...	...	...	...	95	88	114	83
50-54	...	...	...	...	...	...	92	65	83	60
55-59	...	...	...	...	...	...	55	25	48	38
60-64	...	...	...	...	...	...	41	26	31	17
65-69	...	...	...	...	...	...	23	13	24	17
70+	...	...	...	...	...	...	31	11	...	16
70-74	...	...	...	...	...	...	...	...	29	...
75-79	...	...	...	...	...	...	...	...	4	...
80+	...	...	...	...	...	...	...	...	1	...
Unknown - Inconnu	...	...	...	...	...	...	...	...	-	-
Mexico - Mexique[+]										
All ages - Tous âges	743 856	743 856	707 422	707 422	...	...	...	...	584 142	584 142
0-14	432	9 005	684	8 345	...	...	...	...	651	5 767
15-19	100 317	221 571	95 878	208 090	...	...	...	...	72 248	159 789
20-24	279 710	262 171	257 844	243 353	...	...	...	...	204 677	198 599
25-29	194 658	142 456	186 990	140 046	...	...	...	...	156 597	120 060
30-34	79 061	51 580	77 951	51 131	...	...	...	...	71 657	48 765
35-39	35 831	23 587	34 904	23 276	...	...	...	...	30 433	20 718
40-44	18 654	12 724	18 056	12 392	...	...	...	...	16 217	11 282
45-49	10 605	7 475	11 030	7 740	...	...	...	...	9 716	7 144
50+	24 588	13 287	24 085	13 049	...	...	...	...	...	...
50-54	...	...	...	...	...	...	...	...	6 274	4 483
55-59	...	...	...	...	...	...	...	...	4 707	3 046
60-64	...	...	...	...	...	...	...	...	4 412	2 094
65-69	...	...	...	...	...	...	...	...	2 892	1 260
70-74	...	...	...	...	...	...	...	...	1 788	696
75-79	...	...	...	...	...	...	...	...	1 088	305
80-84	...	...	...	...	...	...	...	...	520	106
85-89	...	...	...	...	...	...	...	...	174	19
90-94	...	...	...	...	...	...	...	...	74	5
95+	...	...	...	...	...	...	...	...	17	4
Unknown - Inconnu	...	...	...	...	...	...	...	...	-	-
Panama[2]										
All ages - Tous âges	10 388	10 388	...	...	...	...	...	...	...	...
0-14	-	20	...	...	...	...	...	...	...	...
15-19	192	832	...	...	...	...	...	...	...	...
20-24	1 828	2 626	...	...	...	...	...	...	...	...
25-29	3 000	2 904	...	...	...	...	...	...	...	...
30-34	2 015	1 551	...	...	...	...	...	...	...	...
35-39	1 146	817	...	...	...	...	...	...	...	...
40-49	1 099	866	...	...	...	...	...	...	...	...
50-59	520	383	...	...	...	...	...	...	...	...
60-69	316	131	...	...	...	...	...	...	...	...
70+	129	34	...	...	...	...	...	...	...	...
Unknown - Inconnu	143	224	...	...	...	...	...	...	...	...
Puerto Rico - Porto Rico										
All ages - Tous âges	27 255	27 255	25 980	25 980	...	...	25 645	25 645	25 236	25 236
0-14	-	133	-	117	...	...	-	74	...	53
15-19	2 115	4 721	1 921	4 281	...	...	1 445	3 401	1 275	3 256
20-24	8 298	8 420	7 705	8 016	...	...	6 861	7 500	6 572	7 149
25-29	6 538	5 547	6 190	5 378	...	...	6 209	5 508	6 071	5 481
30-34	3 370	2 929	3 298	2 759	...	...	3 590	3 073	3 585	3 067

Continent, country or area and age / Continent, pays ou zone et âge	1999 Groom Epoux	1999 Bride Epouse	2000 Groom Epoux	2000 Bride Epouse	2001 Groom Epoux	2001 Bride Epouse	2002 Groom Epoux	2002 Bride Epouse	2003 Groom Epoux	2003 Bride Epouse
AMERICA, NORTH — AMERIQUE DU NORD										
Puerto Rico - Porto Rico										
35-39	2 090	1 897	2 044	1 771	...	...	2 162	1 987	2 240	1 985
40-44	1 416	1 247	1 360	1 245	...	...	1 545	1 383	1 590	1 415
45-49	988	851	1 022	874	...	...	1 158	1 022	1 130	1 078
50-54	808	600	812	621	...	...	860	672	903	714
55+	1 632	910	1 628	917	...	...	1 815	1 025	1 869	1 038
Unknown - Inconnu	-	-	-	1	...	...	-	-	1	-
Saint Lucia - Sainte-Lucie										
All ages - Tous âges	...	...	...	...	...	...	472	472	...	...
0-14	...	...	...	...	...	...	-	-	...	...
15-19	...	...	...	...	...	...	1	12	...	...
20-24	...	...	...	...	...	...	34	74	...	...
25-29	...	...	...	...	...	...	104	121	...	...
30-34	...	...	...	...	...	...	107	90	...	...
35-39	...	...	...	...	...	...	74	76	...	...
40-44	...	...	...	...	...	...	58	44	...	...
45-49	...	...	...	...	...	...	30	20	...	...
50-54	...	...	...	...	...	...	21	12	...	...
55 59	...	...	...	...	...	...	13	12	...	...
60-64	...	...	...	...	...	...	8	5	...	...
65+	...	...	...	...	...	...	22	6	...	...
Unknown - Inconnu	...	...	...	...	...	...	-	-	...	...
Turks Caicos Islands - Îles Turques et Caïques										
All ages - Tous âges	...	...	...	...	...	...	593	593	491	491
0-14	...	...	...	...	...	...	-	-	-	-
15-19	...	...	...	...	...	...	1	2	-	3
20-24	...	...	...	...	...	...	20	52	19	48
25-29	...	...	...	...	...	...	130	148	123	163
30-34	...	...	...	...	...	...	164	193	130	131
35-39	...	...	...	...	...	...	116	93	96	59
40-44	...	...	...	...	...	...	80	56	52	47
45-49	...	...	...	...	...	...	47	30	30	24
50-54	...	...	...	...	...	...	19	15	23	9
55-59	...	...	...	...	...	...	10	2	14	5
60+	...	...	...	...	...	...	4	-	2	1
Unknown - Inconnu	...	...	...	...	...	...	2	2	2	1
AMERICA, SOUTH — AMERIQUE DU SUD										
Brazil - Brésil[3]										
All ages - Tous âges	788 744	788 744	732 721	732 721	710 121	710 121	...	...	748 981	748 981
0-14	33	2 029	44	1 685	68	1 270	...	...	41	884
15-19	42 959	204 117	38 702	181 666	29 709	150 034	...	...	26 963	127 944
20-24	265 970	264 658	242 980	245 478	219 990	238 056	...	...	207 172	244 922
25-29	229 418	158 292	212 531	149 788	208 510	154 755	...	...	221 444	176 401
30-34	117 125	73 913	109 911	70 890	114 045	75 584	...	...	130 217	91 134
35-39	54 337	36 382	52 524	35 456	55 806	38 510	...	...	65 892	45 887
40-44	26 571	18 968	25 876	18 483	28 223	20 246	...	...	34 914	25 050
45-49	15 655	11 660	14 766	10 978	16 104	12 624	...	...	19 764	15 014
50-54	10 198	7 099	9 851	6 960	11 121	7 971	...	...	12 881	9 420
55-59	7 738	4 768	7 190	4 281	7 659	4 688	...	...	8 899	5 675
60-64	6 125	2 746	5 824	2 630	6 132	2 803	...	...	6 895	3 163
65+	11 521	2 931	11 035	2 756	12 294	3 051	...	...	13 798	3 365
Unknown - Inconnu	1 094	1 181	1 487	1 670	460	529	...	...	101	122
Chile - Chili[+]										
All ages - Tous âges	69 765	69 765	...	...	...	...	60 971	60 971	56 659	56 659
0-14	2	178	...	...	...	...	-	91	-	66
15-19	2 687	10 607	...	...	...	...	1 757	7 169	1 445	5 905
20-24	20 200	23 817	...	...	...	...	14 876	19 574	13 323	18 150
25-29	24 430	19 675	...	...	...	...	21 636	18 399	19 540	17 082
30-34	11 648	7 712	...	...	...	...	11 669	7 767	11 520	7 735
35-39	4 748	3 493	...	...	...	...	4 797	3 365	4 615	3 191
40-44	2 165	1 670	...	...	...	...	2 209	1 806	2 199	1 723

24. Marriages by age of bridegroom and by age of bride: 1999 - 2003
Mariages selon l'âge de l'époux et selon l'âge de l'épouse: 1999 - 2003 (continued — suite)

Continent, country or area and age / Continent, pays ou zone et âge	1999 Groom Epoux	1999 Bride Epouse	2000 Groom Epoux	2000 Bride Epouse	2001 Groom Epoux	2001 Bride Epouse	2002 Groom Epoux	2002 Bride Epouse	2003 Groom Epoux	2003 Bride Epouse
AMERICA, SOUTH — AMERIQUE DU SUD										
Chile - Chili[+]										
45-49	1 067	905	...	...	...	...	1 151	972	1 210	1 037
50-54	743	603	...	...	...	...	758	671	717	590
55-59	547	414	...	...	...	...	550	441	543	455
60-64	443	291	...	...	...	...	442	297	463	308
65-69	417	184	...	...	...	...	375	193	361	188
70-74	288	118	...	...	...	...	318	138	305	131
75+	380	98	...	...	...	...	433	88	418	98
Ecuador - Équateur[4]										
All ages - Tous âges	...	...	...	...	...	...	66 208	66 208	65 393	65 393
0-14	...	...	...	...	...	...	41	676	30	626
15-19	...	...	...	...	...	...	7 701	18 148	7 147	17 214
20-24	...	...	...	...	...	...	23 466	23 091	22 867	22 924
25-29	...	...	...	...	...	...	16 284	12 147	16 072	12 073
30-34	...	...	...	...	...	...	8 059	5 285	8 242	5 514
35-39	...	...	...	...	...	...	4 162	2 903	4 310	2 792
40-44	...	...	...	...	...	...	2 314	1 592	2 432	1 728
45-49	...	...	...	...	...	...	1 523	999	1 529	1 058
50-54	...	...	...	...	...	...	942	563	960	605
55-59	...	...	...	...	...	...	605	333	611	336
60-64	...	...	...	...	...	...	409	178	414	211
65-69	...	...	...	...	...	...	263	141	320	160
70+	...	...	...	...	...	...	439	152	459	152
French Guiana - Guyane française										
All ages - Tous âges	...	...	...	...	...	...	522	522	524	524
15-19	...	...	...	...	...	...	3	22	4	25
20-24	...	...	...	...	...	...	39	101	34	90
25-29	...	...	...	...	...	...	101	118	100	128
30-34	...	...	...	...	...	...	113	97	131	117
35-39	...	...	...	...	...	...	90	68	86	64
40-44	...	...	...	...	...	...	55	54	54	30
45-49	...	...	...	...	...	...	50	24	38	34
50-54	...	...	...	...	...	...	28	15	25	22
55-59	...	...	...	...	...	...	15	16	29	7
60-64	...	...	...	...	...	...	14	3	8	3
65-69	...	...	...	...	...	...	7	3	4	3
70-74	...	...	...	...	...	...	7	1	6	1
75-79	...	...	...	...	...	...	-	-	1	-
80+	...	...	...	...	...	...	-	-	4	-
Suriname										
All ages - Tous âges	2 257	2 257	2 267	2 267	2 006	2 006	2 005	2 005	...	...
0-14	-	11	-	2	-	7	-	6	...	...
15-19	32	415	34	378	24	377	23	382	...	...
20-24	441	635	409	586	393	535	421	596	...	...
25-29	642	455	618	459	520	383	542	333	...	...
30-34	412	286	386	327	390	277	367	233	...	...
35-39	246	190	269	207	215	168	208	187	...	...
40-44	150	113	181	130	151	110	142	113	...	...
45-49	118	78	141	63	105	70	101	72	...	...
50-54	75	35	77	55	80	38	65	36	...	...
55+	141	39	152	60	128	41	136	47	...	...
Uruguay										
All ages - Tous âges	...	...	13 888	13 888	...	...	...	...	...	...
0-19	...	...	360	1 536	...	...	...	...	...	...
20-24	...	...	2 856	3 752	...	...	...	...	...	...
25-29	...	...	4 292	3 940	...	...	...	...	...	...
30-34	...	...	2 524	1 860	...	...	...	...	...	...
35-39	...	...	1 260	920	...	...	...	...	...	...
40-49	...	...	1 144	932	...	...	...	...	...	...
50+	...	...	1 444	940	...	...	...	...	...	...
Unknown - Inconnu	...	...	8	8	...	...	...	...	...	...
Venezuela[3]										
All ages - Tous âges	...	...	91 088	91 088	81 516	81 516	73 163	73 163	...	...
0-14	...	...	54	1 061	38	886	38	673	...	...

Continent, country or area and age / Continent, pays ou zone et âge	1999		2000		2001		2002		2003	
	Groom Epoux	Bride Epouse	Groom Epoux	Bride Epouse	Groom Epoux	Bride Epouse	Groom Epoux	Bride Epouse	Groom Epoux	Bride Epouse
AMERICA, SOUTH — AMERIQUE DU SUD										
Venezuela[3]										
15-19	...	...	6 282	18 749	4 977	15 993	4 233	13 452	...	...
20-24	...	...	26 750	28 925	23 441	25 634	20 114	22 819	...	...
25-29	...	...	25 569	20 833	22 958	18 632	21 009	17 730	...	...
30-34	...	...	14 152	10 016	13 084	9 450	12 435	8 786	...	...
35-39	...	...	7 488	5 160	6 904	4 827	6 253	4 277	...	...
40-44	...	...	4 195	2 781	3 992	2 655	3 569	2 344	...	...
45-49	...	...	2 618	1 617	2 491	1 585	2 168	1 380	...	...
50-54	...	...	1 597	862	1 449	833	1 292	789	...	...
55-59	...	...	844	440	786	406	750	368	...	...
60+	...	...	1 539	644	1 396	615	1 302	545	...	...
ASIA — ASIE										
Armenia - Arménie										
All âges - Tous âges	12 459	12 459	10 986	10 986	...	...	...	...	...	...
15-19	202	3 088	104	1 865	...	...	...	...	...	...
20-24	4 460	6 548	3 603	6 349	...	...	...	...	...	...
25-29	4 528	1 625	4 342	1 709	...	...	...	...	...	...
30-34	1 845	473	1 607	404	...	...	...	...	...	...
35-39	710	264	624	222	...	...	...	...	...	...
40-44	257	199	272	177	...	...	...	...	...	...
45-49	130	114	137	112	...	...	...	...	...	...
50-54	99	60	83	63	...	...	...	...	...	...
55-59	67	29	43	21	...	...	...	...	...	...
60+	161	59	171	64	...	...	...	...	...	...
Azerbaijan - Azerbaïdjan[+]										
All ages - Tous âges	37 382	37 382	39 611	39 611	41 861	41 861	41 661	41 661	56 091	56 091
0-17	22	2 649	11	2 473	15	2 348	12	2 140	21	2 556
18-19	802	7 417	539	7 331	470	7 661	405	7 024	461	9 704
20-24	10 172	16 523	10 393	18 010	11 123	19 299	10 507	19 338	14 363	26 394
25-29	15 015	5 977	16 361	6 741	17 230	7 334	17 081	7 779	23 063	10 422
30-34	6 986	2 339	7 721	2 399	8 162	2 656	8 425	2 627	11 126	3 458
35-39	2 144	1 260	2 245	1 378	2 525	1 306	2 706	1 312	3 710	1 738
40-44	766	674	907	728	952	727	1 023	805	1 361	997
45-49	387	252	413	283	404	281	461	324	648	474
50-54	235	108	284	119	276	112	299	142	377	183
55-59	199	47	155	43	136	54	146	64	217	69
60+	654	136	582	106	568	83	596	106	744	96
Bahrain - Bahreïn										
All ages - Tous âges	3 673	3 673	...	...	...	...	4 909	4 909	...	...
0-14	-	32	...	...	...	...	-	23	...	...
15-19	99	897	...	...	...	...	78	972	...	...
20-24	1 176	1 509	...	...	...	...	1 476	2 191	...	...
25-29	1 198	603	...	...	...	...	1 809	968	...	...
30-34	543	340	...	...	...	...	724	366	...	...
35-39	278	165	...	...	...	...	355	214	...	...
40-44	162	86	...	...	...	...	194	115	...	...
45-49	83	28	...	...	...	...	112	41	...	...
50+	133	12	...	...	...	...	158	17	...	...
Unknown - Inconnu	1	1	...	...	...	...	3	2	...	...
Brunei Darussalam - Brunéi Darussalam										
All ages - Tous âges	...	...	2 184	2 184	...	...	...	...	2 262	2 262
0-14	...	...	11	15	...	...	...	...	-	13
15-19	...	...	125	412	...	...	...	...	82	314
20-24	...	...	688	834	...	...	...	...	658	844
25-29	...	...	733	551	...	...	...	...	828	713
30-34	...	...	313	192	...	...	...	...	351	216
35-39	...	...	137	87	...	...	...	...	164	87
40-44	...	...	70	48	...	...	...	...	67	36
45-49	...	...	44	22	...	...	...	...	46	22
50-54	...	...	31	13	...	...	...	...	26	13
55-59	...	...	10	5	...	...	...	...	19	2
60-64	...	...	10	5	...	...	...	...	12	2

24. Marriages by age of bridegroom and by age of bride: 1999 - 2003
Mariages selon l'âge de l'époux et selon l'âge de l'épouse: 1999 - 2003 (continued — suite)

Continent, country or area and age / Continent, pays ou zone et âge	1999 Groom Epoux	1999 Bride Epouse	2000 Groom Epoux	2000 Bride Epouse	2001 Groom Epoux	2001 Bride Epouse	2002 Groom Epoux	2002 Bride Epouse	2003 Groom Epoux	2003 Bride Epouse
ASIA — ASIE										
Brunei Darussalam - Brunéi Darussalam										
65-69	...	...	7	-	...	...	...	...	3	-
70+	...	...	5	-	...	...	...	...	6	-
China: Hong Kong SAR - Chine: Hong Kong RAS										
All ages - Tous âges	31 287	31 287	30 879	30 879	32 825	32 825	32 070	32 070	35 439	35 439
15-19	250	1 061	232	966	208	947	211	865	178	858
20-24	3 519	7 578	3 091	6 728	3 169	7 164	2 930	6 898	2 832	7 364
25-29	10 078	12 379	9 997	12 566	10 373	13 143	9 275	12 105	9 855	13 331
30-34	8 242	5 965	8 027	6 101	8 546	6 773	8 124	6 895	9 502	8 120
35-39	4 534	2 328	4 609	2 489	4 891	2 664	4 784	2 881	5 172	3 207
40-44	2 029	802	2 047	923	2 300	1 027	2 690	1 195	3 080	1 334
45-49	903	374	1 077	439	1 256	486	1 511	577	1 809	630
50-54	506	223	593	206	721	211	907	285	1 138	302
55-59	308	150	333	116	377	99	522	132	607	126
60-64	324	165	299	121	330	110	336	88	438	57
65-69	264	146	257	117	281	104	333	74	349	51
70-74	194	87	185	71	208	61	235	51	264	37
75+	136	29	132	36	165	36	212	24	215	22
China: Macao SAR - Chine: Macao RAS+										
All ages - Tous âges	1 367	1 367	1 222	1 222	1 222	1 222	1 209	1 209	1 309	1 309
15-19	11	54	7	43	10	52	9	45	20	53
20-24	140	267	142	223	129	233	126	247	121	305
25-29	484	613	411	509	392	480	388	462	444	511
30-34	357	224	271	227	298	200	290	243	366	265
35-39	200	110	175	102	156	109	165	88	160	97
40-44	73	43	99	54	88	55	79	54	77	41
45-49	28	18	42	20	48	28	77	34	72	21
50-54	26	10	24	11	28	26	30	16	15	5
55-59	8	4	13	9	21	16	14	8	10	3
60-64	13	10	9	8	16	5	8	1	5	2
65-69	8	9	11	10	16	9	8	6	9	2
70+	...	...	...	...	20	9	15	5	10	4
70-74	12	4	13	6	...	...	...	...	...	...
75+	7	1	5	-	...	...	...	...	...	...
Cyprus - Chypre[5]										
All ages - Tous âges	9 080	9 080	9 282	9 282	...	...	10 284	10 284	10 810	10 810
15-19	69	630	84	572	...	...	73	477	41	392
20-24	1 632	2 883	1 479	2 627	...	...	1 497	2 742	1 352	2 642
25-29	3 150	2 844	3 087	2 974	...	...	3 187	3 306	3 362	3 626
30-34	1 924	1 328	2 091	1 505	...	...	2 467	1 845	2 691	2 107
35-39	1 013	637	1 033	696	...	...	1 275	833	1 443	933
40-44	477	324	541	390	...	...	658	457	743	529
45-49	316	194	372	250	...	...	395	273	464	252
50-54	221	139	260	148	...	...	281	180	283	164
55-59	109	48	133	62	...	...	183	80	175	89
60+	166	53	194	50	...	...	226	48	243	61
Unknown - Inconnu	3	-	8	8	...	...	42	43	13	15
Georgia - Géorgie										
All ages - Tous âges	...	...	12 870	12 870	...	...	...	...	...	...
0-15	...	...	3	233	...	...	...	...	...	...
16-19	...	...	747	2 582	...	...	...	...	...	...
20-24	...	...	4 055	5 200	...	...	...	...	...	...
25-29	...	...	3 459	2 505	...	...	...	...	...	...
30-34	...	...	2 152	1 059	...	...	...	...	...	...
35-39	...	...	1 141	580	...	...	...	...	...	...
40-44	...	...	551	291	...	...	...	...	...	...
45-49	...	...	272	165	...	...	...	...	...	...
50-54	...	...	173	99	...	...	...	...	...	...
55-59	...	...	71	41	...	...	...	...	...	...
60+	...	...	241	108	...	...	...	...	...	...
Unknown - Inconnu	...	...	5	7	...	...	...	...	...	...
Israel - Israël[6]										
All ages - Tous âges	40 236	40 236	...	...	38 924	38 924	39 718	39 718	...	...

24. Marriages by age of bridegroom and by age of bride: 1999 - 2003
Mariages selon l'âge de l'époux et selon l'âge de l'épouse: 1999 - 2003 (continued — suite)

Continent, country or area and age — Continent, pays ou zone et âge	1999 Groom Epoux	1999 Bride Epouse	2000 Groom Epoux	2000 Bride Epouse	2001 Groom Epoux	2001 Bride Epouse	2002 Groom Epoux	2002 Bride Epouse	2003 Groom Epoux	2003 Bride Epouse
ASIA — ASIE										
Israel - Israël[6]										
0-19	1 305	7 337	...	...	1 284	7 014	1 347	7 271	...	...
20-24	12 066	17 335	...	...	11 008	15 716	10 977	15 596	...	...
25-29	16 469	10 556	...	...	16 273	11 135	16 533	11 497	...	...
30-34	5 873	2 542	...	...	6 106	2 870	6 572	3 177	...	...
35-39	1 994	960	...	...	1 940	956	1 998	979	...	...
40-44	895	480	...	...	897	463	926	477	...	...
45-49	502	299	...	...	542	291	479	268	...	...
50-54	306	139	...	...	295	217	313	189	...	...
55-59	188	85	...	...	185	73	188	84	...	...
60-64	139	65	...	...	144	71	144	58	...	...
65-69	101	58	...	...	108	46	108	38	...	...
70-74	96	38	...	...	71	20	63	30	...	...
75+	80	19	...	...	71	20	58	14	...	...
Unknown - Inconnu	222	323	...	...	-	32	12	40	...	...
Japan - Japon[+,7]										
All ages - Tous âges	685 626	685 626	708 159	708 159	709 864	709 864	671 602	671 602	651 544	651 544
0-19	9 836	20 075	10 772	21 607	10 894	22 216	9 946	20 818	8 821	19 126
20-24	120 702	184 703	119 706	179 410	113 415	169 807	102 377	151 931	93 122	138 832
25-29	290 946	318 464	296 363	326 418	290 929	322 253	268 111	298 966	249 134	281 696
30-34	148 177	102 291	155 381	113 693	163 873	124 609	163 467	127 802	166 485	134 448
35-39	57 572	30 029	62 382	34 542	63 731	37 556	63 537	38 848	67 240	42 337
40-44	23 290	10 785	24 912	11 800	25 989	12 848	25 743	13 138	27 081	14 385
45-49	14 587	7 907	15 031	7 858	15 241	7 573	14 130	7 187	14 241	7 227
50-54	9 394	5 760	11 179	6 564	12 530	6 750	11 232	6 376	10 919	6 321
55-59	5 576	3 150	6 221	3 430	6 457	3 214	6 109	3 361	6 937	3 695
60-64	2 889	1 462	3 229	1 669	3 545	1 700	3 660	1 842	4 063	1 987
65-69	1 471	631	1 608	743	1 831	778	1 780	789	1 886	924
70-74	712	251	828	286	876	289	866	367	947	367
75+	468	114	541	137	547	184	639	177	664	193
Unknown - Inconnu	6	4	6	2	6	-	5	-	4	6
Jordan - Jordanie[+,8]										
All ages - Tous âges	39 443	39 443	...	...	...	...	...	...	...	...
0-14	5	36	...	...	...	...	...	...	...	...
15-19	1 095	12 991	...	...	...	...	...	...	...	...
20-24	10 920	15 789	...	...	...	...	...	...	...	...
25-29	15 384	6 517	...	...	...	...	...	...	...	...
30-34	6 781	2 414	...	...	...	...	...	...	...	...
35-39	2 378	990	...	...	...	...	...	...	...	...
40-44	1 017	414	...	...	...	...	...	...	...	...
45-49	621	163	...	...	...	...	...	...	...	...
50+	...	129	...	...	...	...	...	...	...	...
50-54	361	...	...	...	...	...	...	...	...	...
55-59	345	...	...	...	...	...	...	...	...	...
60-64	231	...	...	...	...	...	...	...	...	...
65+	305	...	...	...	...	...	...	...	...	...
Kazakhstan										
All ages - Tous âges	85 872	85 872	...	...	...	...	...	...	110 414	110 414
0-14	1	1	...	...	...	...	...	...	-	-
15-19	4 214	18 629	...	...	...	...	...	...	3 769	17 568
20-24	36 288	40 975	...	...	...	...	...	...	39 569	53 270
25-29	25 026	13 429	...	...	...	...	...	...	36 302	21 459
30-34	9 047	4 960	...	...	...	...	...	...	15 021	8 367
35-39	4 372	2 849	...	...	...	...	...	...	6 483	3 795
40-44	2 391	1 641	...	...	...	...	...	...	3 659	2 256
45-49	1 409	1 136	...	...	...	...	...	...	2 021	1 363
50-54	854	751	...	...	...	...	...	...	1 320	964
55-59	590	467	...	...	...	...	...	...	639	453
60-64	...	...	...	...	...	...	...	...	668	420
60+	1 660	1 015	...	...	...	...	...	...	...	...
65-69	...	...	...	...	...	...	...	...	503	298
70-74	...	...	...	...	...	...	...	...	237	120
75-79	...	...	...	...	...	...	...	...	165	52
80-84	...	...	...	...	...	...	...	...	42	10
85-89	...	...	...	...	...	...	...	...	14	3
90-94	...	...	...	...	...	...	...	...	1	3

24. Marriages by age of bridegroom and by age of bride: 1999 - 2003
Mariages selon l'âge de l'époux et selon l'âge de l'épouse: 1999 - 2003 (continued — suite)

Continent, country or area and age / Continent, pays ou zone et âge	1999 Groom Epoux	1999 Bride Epouse	2000 Groom Epoux	2000 Bride Epouse	2001 Groom Epoux	2001 Bride Epouse	2002 Groom Epoux	2002 Bride Epouse	2003 Groom Epoux	2003 Bride Epouse
ASIA — ASIE										
Kazakhstan										
Unknown - Inconnu	20	19	...	...	...	...	...	...	1	13
Korea (Republic of) - Corée (République de)+										
All ages - Tous âges	362 673	362 673	334 030	334 030	320 063	320 063	...	...	...	...
0-14	11	83	1	65	6	41	...	...	...	...
15-19	2 340	9 301	2 096	8 255	1 899	6 895	...	...	...	...
20-24	28 989	99 688	25 062	86 319	21 914	74 009	...	...	...	...
25-29	182 337	178 029	163 203	164 887	147 192	158 129	...	...	...	...
30-34	91 889	36 928	89 551	38 294	91 070	41 655	...	...	...	...
35-39	26 929	18 206	25 481	16 924	26 123	17 687	...	...	...	...
40-44	13 272	10 602	12 791	10 131	14 404	11 577	...	...	...	...
45-49	6 835	4 960	6 731	4 921	7 615	5 579	...	...	...	...
50-54	4 332	2 566	4 155	2 303	4 611	2 523	...	...	...	...
55+	5 590	2 247	4 959	1 931	5 223	1 963	...	...	...	...
Unknown - Inconnu	149	63	-	-	6	5	...	...	...	...
Kuwait - Koweït										
All ages - Tous âges	...	...	10 785	10 785	...	...	...	...	...	...
15-19	...	...	416	2 832	...	...	...	...	...	...
20-24	...	...	3 806	3 941	...	...	...	...	...	...
25-29	...	...	3 096	1 931	...	...	...	...	...	...
30-34	...	...	1 596	1 021	...	...	...	...	...	...
35-44	...	...	1 320	894	...	...	...	...	...	...
45+	...	...	551	166	...	...	...	...	...	...
Kyrgyzstan - Kirghizistan										
All ages - Tous âges	26 033	26 033	24 294	24 294	27 455	27 455	31 240	31 240	34 266	34 266
15-19	833	7 010	760	6 417	830	6 666	768	6 953	815	7 015
20-24	11 019	12 585	9 966	11 863	10 746	13 596	11 206	15 498	11 942	17 470
25-29	8 950	3 565	8 587	3 353	9 753	4 050	11 657	5 106	13 164	5 751
30-34	2 603	1 144	2 543	1 149	3 196	1 407	4 294	1 728	4 743	2 036
35-39	1 033	682	963	585	1 179	646	1 422	793	1 595	866
40-44	522	384	560	349	669	403	727	452	803	461
45-49	351	241	265	188	358	273	401	268	457	245
50-54	204	158	209	146	251	171	262	170	256	170
55-59	150	66	93	65	91	57	107	70	111	75
60-64	167	111	150	94	163	96	166	95	142	68
65-69	94	43	86	37	90	44	101	48	111	65
70-74	72	28	77	31	73	30	57	39	60	23
75+	32	15	35	17	56	16	72	20	-	21
Unknown - Inconnu	3	1	-	-	-	-	-	-	67	-
Mongolia - Mongolie										
All ages - Tous âges	13 722	13 722	12 601	12 601	12 393	12 393	...	...	...	...
18-19	780	1 506	417	1 323	473	1 177	...	...	...	...
20-24	5 771	6 778	5 173	5 989	4 917	5 813	...	...	...	...
25-29	4 477	3 567	4 342	3 433	4 135	3 335	...	...	...	...
30-34	1 634	1 165	1 689	1 212	1 580	1 196	...	...	...	...
35-39	644	411	611	434	839	620	...	...	...	...
40-44	244	176	208	211	302	175	...	...	...	...
45-49	94	72	85	47	78	54	...	...	...	...
50+	78	47	76	42	69	23	...	...	...	...
Occupied Palestinian Territory - Territoire palestinien occupé										
All ages - Tous âges	24 874	24 874	23 890	23 890	24 635	24 635	22 611	22 611	26 267	26 267
0-14	5	743	1	682	3	926	3	810	3	920
15-19	2 363	13 817	2 332	13 163	2 396	13 168	2 093	11 893	2 099	13 470
20-24	10 705	6 816	9 961	6 641	10 255	6 963	9 505	6 640	10 628	8 085
25-29	7 280	1 965	7 190	1 991	7 426	2 046	6 982	1 930	8 655	2 278
30-34	2 234	818	2 207	757	2 222	804	1 942	685	2 532	817
35-39	850	426	799	401	841	481	769	381	892	406
40-44	400	175	443	165	427	145	413	183	485	201
45-49	293	69	264	54	304	60	270	58	286	57
50-54	216	19	206	22	235	30	200	20	225	20
55+	526	23	...	...	...	...	...	...	...	...
55-59	...	...	176	10	191	7	132	7	154	9
60-64	...	...	119	3	126	3	107	1	105	3
65-69	...	...	91	1	104	1	97	3	95	1

Continent, country or area and age / Continent, pays ou zone et âge	1999 Groom Epoux	1999 Bride Epouse	2000 Groom Epoux	2000 Bride Epouse	2001 Groom Epoux	2001 Bride Epouse	2002 Groom Epoux	2002 Bride Epouse	2003 Groom Epoux	2003 Bride Epouse
ASIA — ASIE										
Occupied Palestinian Territory - Territoire palestinien occupé										
70-74	...	...	55	-	57	1	63	-	62	-
75+	...	...	45	-	48	-	35	-	46	-
Unknown - Inconnu	2	3	1	-	-	-	-	-	-	-
Philippines										
All ages - Tous âges	551 445	551 445	577 387	577 387	...	...	583 167	583 167	...	...
0-19	23 275	85 779	23 069	85 632	...	...	20 425	80 800	...	...
20-24	178 891	216 999	185 502	227 738	...	...	185 224	232 790	...	...
25-29	176 196	136 689	182 176	142 420	...	...	185 828	146 876	...	...
30-34	85 613	56 920	91 555	61 519	...	...	94 770	62 664	...	...
35-39	38 969	26 063	41 495	28 141	...	...	42 505	28 343	...	...
40-44	19 244	12 768	21 624	14 513	...	...	22 041	14 589	...	...
45-49	11 047	7 083	12 541	7 795	...	...	12 584	7 906	...	...
50+	17 936	8 803	19 176	9 365	...	...	19 655	9 036	...	...
Unknown - Inconnu	274	341	249	264	...	...	135	163	...	...
Qatar										
All ages - Tous âges	1 905	1 905	...	...	2 194	2 194	2 351	2 351	2 550	2 550
0-14	...	...	...	...	...	9	...	8	...	5
0-19	54	382	...	...	34	...	36	...	35	...
15-19	...	...	...	...	...	374	...	374	...	346
20-24	514	815	...	...	563	970	610	1 037	611	1 096
25-29	726	419	...	...	858	494	882	582	966	653
30-34	315	179	...	...	420	173	469	197	515	259
35-39	162	67	...	...	145	101	171	89	200	97
40-44	51	30	...	...	81	56	94	42	105	62
45-49	38	5	...	...	46	9	44	17	64	24
50-54	12	5	...	...	22	7	17	2	27	6
55-59	14	3	...	...	9	1	9	-	11	1
60-64	11	-	...	...	10	-	11	...	10	-
60+	...	...	...	...	...	...	...	1	...	-
65-69	4	-	...	...	2	-	5	...	1	...
70-74	3	-	...	...	3	-	2	...	4	...
75+	1	-	...	...	-	-	1	...	1	...
Unknown - Inconnu	-	-	...	...	1	-	-	2	-	1
Singapore - Singapour+,9,10										
All ages - Tous âges	25 648	25 648	22 561	22 561	22 280	22 280	23 198	23 198	21 962	21 962
0-14	-					1				-
15-19	160	879	188	883	194	821	157	747	139	620
20-24	3 163	7 828	2 577	6 486	2 464	6 450	2 371	6 399	2 103	5 639
25-29	11 146	10 910	9 504	9 648	9 235	9 420	9 830	10 270	8 923	9 798
30-34	5 725	3 428	5 144	3 125	5 185	3 223	5 595	3 470	5 613	3 539
35-39	2 787	1 465	2 563	1 330	2 535	1 342	2 629	1 243	2 476	1 254
40-44	1 383	657	1 367	645	1 352	587	1 297	592	1 323	616
45-49	668	303	641	270	669	260	693	295	714	318
50-54	325	110	295	109	341	107	306	112	373	114
55-59	143	38	132	33	145	35	175	51	179	49
60+	148	30	150	32	159	35	145	19	119	15
Tajikistan - Tadjikistan										
All ages - Tous âges	...	...	26 597	26 597	...	...	...	...	...	...
15-19	...	...	2 278	10 431	...	...	...	...	...	...
20-24	...	...	13 733	12 345	...	...	...	...	...	...
25-29	...	...	7 534	2 575	...	...	...	...	...	...
30-34	...	...	1 741	654	...	...	...	...	...	...
35-39	...	...	560	264	...	...	...	...	...	...
40-44	...	...	293	122	...	...	...	...	...	...
45-49	...	...	122	66	...	...	...	...	...	...
50-54	...	...	77	65	...	...	...	...	...	...
55-59	...	...	60	16	...	...	...	...	...	...
60-64	...	...	87	19	...	...	...	...	...	...
65-69	...	...	42	9	...	...	...	...	...	...
70-74	...	...	25	11	...	...	...	...	...	...
75+	...	...	17	1	...	...	...	...	...	...
Unknown - Inconnu	...	...	28	19	...	...	...	...	...	...
Turkey - Turquie+,11										
All ages - Tous âges	475 613	475 613	461 417	461 417	...	...	447 820	447 820	...	...

24. Marriages by age of bridegroom and by age of bride: 1999 - 2003
Mariages selon l'âge de l'époux et selon l'âge de l'épouse: 1999 - 2003 (continued — suite)

Continent, country or area and age / Continent, pays ou zone et âge	1999 Groom Epoux	1999 Bride Epouse	2000 Groom Epoux	2000 Bride Epouse	2001 Groom Epoux	2001 Bride Epouse	2002 Groom Epoux	2002 Bride Epouse	2003 Groom Epoux	2003 Bride Epouse
ASIA — ASIE										
Turkey - Turquie+,11										
0-14	-	1 044	-	794	...	...	-	56	...	...
15-19	23 958	134 599	20 557	122 116	...	...	12 791	89 528	...	...
20-24	166 893	202 235	159 922	199 168	...	...	146 045	215 165	...	...
25-29	190 673	89 314	188 516	91 997	...	...	196 070	95 032	...	...
30-34	53 441	25 684	52 057	25 011	...	...	51 744	24 599	...	...
35-39	18 481	11 481	18 300	10 859	...	...	17 915	10 906	...	...
40-44	7 733	4 833	7 738	4 853	...	...	7 998	5 479	...	...
45-49	4 406	2 680	4 309	2 708	...	...	4 802	2 992	...	...
50-54	2 737	1 384	2 932	1 591	...	...	3 171	1 876	...	...
55-59	2 165	939	2 117	886	...	...	2 049	871	...	...
60-64	...	...	...	...	...	...	1 840	614	...	...
60+	5 126	1 420	4 969	1 434	...	...	...	...	...	...
65-69	...	...	...	...	...	...	1 635	391	...	...
70-74	...	...	...	...	...	...	1 210	211	...	...
75+	...	...	...	...	...	...	550	100	...	...
Uzbekistan - Ouzbékistan										
All ages - Tous âges	170 525	170 525	168 908	168 908	...	...	...	...	...	...
0-17	183	10 847	158	9 606	...	...	...	...	...	...
18-19	12 058	61 917	8 625	52 422	...	...	...	...	...	...
20-24	106 637	77 044	102 113	84 289	...	...	...	...	...	...
25-29	36 733	12 092	41 332	13 386	...	...	...	...	...	...
30-34	7 074	4 026	8 139	4 351	...	...	...	...	...	...
35-39	3 114	2 077	3 369	2 103	...	...	...	...	...	...
40-44	1 645	932	1 911	1 134	...	...	...	...	...	...
45-49	1 101	556	1 118	626	...	...	...	...	...	...
50-54	536	363	684	440	...	...	...	...	...	...
55-59	581	278	454	194	...	...	...	...	...	...
60+	863	393	1 005	354	...	...	...	...	...	...
Unknown - Inconnu	-	-	-	3	...	...	...	...	...	...
EUROPE										
Albania - Albanie										
All ages - Tous âges	...	...	20 949	20 949	...	...	...	...	...	...
15-19	...	...	186	4 696	...	...	...	...	...	...
20-24	...	...	4 326	10 275	...	...	...	...	...	...
25-29	...	...	9 011	3 863	...	...	...	...	...	...
30-34	...	...	4 864	1 283	...	...	...	...	...	...
35-39	...	...	1 520	468	...	...	...	...	...	...
40-44	...	...	540	199	...	...	...	...	...	...
45-49	...	...	240	99	...	...	...	...	...	...
50+	...	...	262	66	...	...	...	...	...	...
Unknown - Inconnu	...	...	-	-	...	...	...	...	...	...
Austria - Autriche12										
All ages - Tous âges	39 485	39 485	39 228	39 228	34 213	34 213	36 570	36 570	37 195	37 195
15-19	398	1 469	360	1 507	389	1 334	449	1 420	447	1 396
20-24	4 597	8 840	4 386	8 227	3 852	7 261	4 020	7 565	4 080	7 373
25-29	11 600	12 528	11 118	12 369	9 019	10 063	9 182	10 528	8 904	10 564
30-34	10 388	7 857	10 346	8 071	8 795	7 063	9 343	7 368	9 358	7 625
35-39	5 239	3 870	5 579	4 103	5 118	3 740	5 662	4 290	5 874	4 399
40-44	2 628	2 068	2 872	2 248	2 704	2 151	3 143	2 423	3 417	2 641
45-49	1 534	1 284	1 610	1 234	1 527	1 233	1 767	1 369	1 935	1 504
50-54	1 238	795	1 191	785	1 148	740	1 213	830	1 211	902
55-59	1 014	524	951	424	823	365	859	490	953	485
60-64	414	127	446	157	478	165	581	190	637	192
65-69	194	70	176	55	169	46	160	48	178	69
70-74	127	34	100	30	94	30	101	28	98	29
75+	114	19	93	18	97	22	...	...	...	...
75-79	...	...	...	...	...	...	55	13	59	12
80-84	...	...	...	...	...	...	27	7	33	2
85-89	...	...	...	...	...	...	5	-	11	1
90-94	...	...	...	...	...	...	2	1	-	1
95+	...	...	...	...	...	...	1	-	-	-
Belarus - Bélarus										
All ages - Tous âges	72 994	72 994	...	...	...	...	66 652	66 652	69 905	69 905

Continent, country or area and age / Continent, pays ou zone et âge	1999 Groom Epoux	1999 Bride Epouse	2000 Groom Epoux	2000 Bride Epouse	2001 Groom Epoux	2001 Bride Epouse	2002 Groom Epoux	2002 Bride Epouse	2003 Groom Epoux	2003 Bride Epouse
EUROPE										
Belarus - Bélarus										
0-17	207	2 234	...	...	...	...	174	1 473	112	1 368
18-19	2 821	13 130	...	...	...	...	2 205	10 378	2 229	9 977
20-24	32 986	31 399	...	...	...	...	28 696	29 986	29 274	32 120
25-29	17 337	11 159	...	...	...	...	17 032	10 687	18 453	11 695
30-34	7 097	5 164	...	...	...	...	6 658	4 851	7 349	5 288
35-39	4 611	3 527	...	...	...	...	3 779	2 901	3 941	2 857
40-44	2 837	2 325	...	...	...	...	2 820	2 205	2 915	2 222
45-49	1 768	1 496	...	...	...	...	1 853	1 572	2 018	1 667
50-54	1 114	942	...	...	...	...	1 317	1 074	1 362	1 133
55-59	694	560	...	...	...	...	638	502	779	575
60+	1 522	1 058	...	...	...	...	1 480	1 023	1 473	1 003
Belgium - Belgique[13]										
All ages - Tous âges	...	...	45 123	45 123	...	...	...	...	...	...
15-19	...	...	217	1 410	...	...	...	...	...	...
20-24	...	...	6 944	13 112	...	...	...	...	...	...
25-29	...	...	16 216	14 485	...	...	...	...	...	...
30-34	...	...	8 374	6 169	...	...	...	...	...	...
35-39	...	...	4 795	3 702	...	...	...	...	...	...
40-44	...	...	2 963	2 556	...	...	...	...	...	...
45-49	...	...	2 138	1 805	...	...	...	...	...	...
50-54	...	...	1 599	1 065	...	...	...	...	...	...
55-59	...	...	831	437	...	...	...	...	...	...
60-64	...	...	494	195	...	...	...	...	...	...
65-69	...	...	255	106	...	...	...	...	...	...
70-74	...	...	159	45	...	...	...	...	...	...
75+	...	...	138	36	...	...	...	...	...	...
Bosnia and Herzegovina - Bosnic Horzógovino										
All ages - Tous âges	22 472	22 472	21 897	21 897	20 302	20 302	20 766	20 766	20 733	20 733
0-14	-	1	-	2	-	1	-	1	-	1
15-19	277	3 970	284	3 748	277	3 571	283	3 465	275	3 260
20-24	6 255	8 934	6 238	8 925	5 877	8 316	5 848	8 422	5 694	8 541
25-29	7 302	4 666	7 165	4 704	6 704	4 211	6 944	4 539	7 111	4 587
30-34	4 082	2 199	3 877	1 983	3 361	1 800	3 535	1 899	3 446	1 865
35-39	2 025	1 096	1 958	996	1 741	949	1 822	911	1 778	958
40-44	...	...	...	...	...	...	...	...	927	578
40-49	1 431	936	1 389	964	1 399	861	1 329	930	...	...
45-49	...	...	...	...	...	...	...	...	536	382
50+	993	586	981	561	935	573	989	544	...	...
50-54	...	...	...	...	...	...	...	...	281	231
55-59	...	...	...	...	...	...	...	...	194	113
60-64	...	...	...	...	...	...	...	...	159	93
65-69	...	...	...	...	...	...	...	...	151	68
70-74	...	...	...	...	...	...	...	...	94	19
75+	...	...	...	...	...	...	...	...	68	12
Unknown - Inconnu	107	84	5	14	8	20	16	55	19	25
Bulgaria - Bulgarie[14]										
All ages - Tous âges	...	...	35 164	35 164	31 974	31 974	29 218	29 218	30 645	30 645
15-19	...	...	...	...	...	...	401	3 579	358	3 077
16-17	...	...	15	745	...	...	...	...	...	...
16-19	...	...	...	...	473	3 523	...	...	...	...
18-19	...	...	518	4 312	...	...	...	...	...	...
20-24	...	...	9 941	14 706	8 292	13 287	7 033	11 713	6 614	11 719
25-29	...	...	12 931	8 896	12 363	8 848	11 817	8 854	12 355	9 970
30-34	...	...	5 431	2 733	5 387	2 654	5 347	2 624	5 940	3 070
35-39	...	...	2 330	1 296	2 128	1 068	1 944	957	2 238	1 121
40-44	...	...	1 286	835	1 147	690	1 013	569	1 198	655
45-49	...	...	929	595	748	469	584	359	709	415
50-54	...	...	603	383	528	360	419	266	487	309
55-59	...	...	330	212	320	194	263	139	303	160
60-64	...	...	297	173	209	134	149	72	147	62
65-69	...	...	229	129	180	87	107	52	130	47
70-74	...	...	176	100	98	33	73	17	79	26
75+	...	...	148	49	101	31	68	17	87	14

Continent, country or area and age / Continent, pays ou zone et âge	1999		2000		2001		2002		2003	
	Groom Epoux	Bride Epouse	Groom Epoux	Bride Epouse	Groom Epoux	Bride Epouse	Groom Epoux	Bride Epouse	Groom Epoux	Bride Epouse
EUROPE										
Croatia - Croatie										
All ages - Tous âges	...	...	22 017	22 017	22 076	22 076	22 806	22 806	22 337	22 337
15-19	...	...	205	2 438	224	2 456	211	2 263	223	2 017
20-24	...	...	5 289	8 667	5 251	8 414	5 160	8 661	4 728	8 212
25-29	...	...	8 475	6 355	8 529	6 558	8 789	6 895	8 638	7 061
30-34	...	...	4 150	2 205	4 117	2 230	4 394	2 446	4 502	2 563
35-39	...	...	1 717	906	1 677	907	1 838	933	1 894	956
40-44	...	...	774	492	781	478	835	523	831	498
45-49	...	...	465	346	459	329	505	400	490	366
50-54	...	...	278	217	309	265	361	276	324	269
55-59	...	...	190	135	196	170	190	154	195	147
60-64	...	...	154	108	157	136	168	119	156	103
65-69	...	...	137	76	145	79	139	71	148	86
70-74	...	...	103	41	127	28	103	37	104	39
75+	...	...	72	10	94	14	104	16	...	...
75-79	...	...	...	...	...	...	...	...	66	13
80-84	...	...	...	...	...	...	...	...	24	2
85-89	...	...	...	...	...	...	...	...	5	-
90-94	...	...	...	...	...	...	...	...	1	-
Unknown - Inconnu	...	...	8	21	10	12	9	12	8	5
Czech Republic - République tchèque										
All ages - Tous âges	53 523	53 523	55 321	55 321	52 374	52 374	52 732	52 732	48 943	48 943
15-19	913	4 037	701	3 014	482	2 404	414	1 960	274	1 504
20-24	16 183	24 214	14 462	23 523	11 569	19 971	9 629	17 782	7 380	14 570
25-29	17 987	13 484	20 368	16 164	20 343	17 486	21 160	19 285	19 674	19 069
30-34	7 041	4 061	7 732	4 497	8 195	4 717	8 941	5 495	9 414	5 729
35-39	3 443	2 125	3 834	2 375	4 053	2 356	4 389	2 573	4 250	2 538
40-44	2 355	1 810	2 356	1 845	2 234	1 699	2 436	1 707	2 275	1 697
45-49	2 038	1 713	2 220	1 786	1 973	1 662	2 058	1 720	1 946	1 610
50-54	1 675	1 162	1 668	1 145	1 651	1 144	1 669	1 165	1 666	1 117
55-59	901	474	1 014	563	929	560	1 081	638	1 073	669
60-64	430	212	443	206	444	189	457	229	486	243
65-69	285	125	266	116	227	85	237	95	231	114
70-74	142	67	142	55	129	61	153	53	142	53
75+	130	39	115	32	145	40	...	...	...	...
75-79	...	...	...	...	...	...	75	22	86	25
80-84	...	...	...	...	...	...	26	5	40	5
85-89	...	...	...	...	...	...	3	1	4	-
90-94	...	...	...	...	...	...	3	2	2	-
95+	...	...	...	...	...	...	1	-	-	-
Denmark - Danemark[15]										
All ages - Tous âges	...	...	38 388	38 388	...	...	37 210	37 210	35 041	35 041
0-14	...	...	-	-	...	...	-	2	-	5
15-19	...	...	203	753	...	...	207	845	95	438
20-24	...	...	2 195	4 458	...	...	2 026	3 941	1 503	3 170
25-29	...	...	9 821	12 002	...	...	9 034	11 196	8 195	10 348
30-34	...	...	9 214	7 922	...	...	8 844	7 788	8 782	7 893
35-39	...	...	5 988	4 593	...	...	6 143	4 639	5 786	4 608
40-44	...	...	3 326	2 749	...	...	3 389	2 761	3 324	2 599
45-49	...	...	2 360	1 810	...	...	2 317	1 910	2 318	1 846
50-54	...	...	1 825	1 363	...	...	1 745	1 294	1 605	1 317
55-59	...	...	1 203	732	...	...	1 367	793	1 388	855
60-64	...	...	582	328	...	...	603	384	696	417
65-69	...	...	272	171	...	...	309	180	272	190
70-74	...	...	131	72	...	...	142	72	152	76
75+	...	...	117	54	...	...	...	...	...	...
75-79	...	...	...	...	...	...	62	42	73	39
80-84	...	...	...	...	...	...	38	12	31	11
85-89	...	...	...	...	...	...	3	7	12	11
90-94	...	...	...	...	...	...	2	-	4	-
95-99	...	...	...	...	...	...	-	-	-	-
100+	...	...	...	...	...	...	-	-	-	-
Unknown - Inconnu	...	...	1 151	1 381	...	...	979	1 344	805	1 218
Estonia - Estonie										
All ages - Tous âges	...	...	5 485	5 485	...	...	5 853	5 853	...	...

24. Marriages by age of bridegroom and by age of bride: 1999 - 2003
Mariages selon l'âge de l'époux et selon l'âge de l'épouse: 1999 - 2003 (continued — suite)

Continent, country or area and age / Continent, pays ou zone et âge	1999 Groom Epoux	1999 Bride Epouse	2000 Groom Epoux	2000 Bride Epouse	2001 Groom Epoux	2001 Bride Epouse	2002 Groom Epoux	2002 Bride Epouse	2003 Groom Epoux	2003 Bride Epouse
EUROPE										
Estonia - Estonie										
15-19	...	...	110	492	...	...	78	414	...	...
20-24	...	...	1 293	1 773	...	...	1 151	1 751	...	...
25-29	...	...	1 569	1 327	...	...	1 762	1 604	...	...
30-34	...	...	898	672	...	...	1 132	864	...	...
35-39	...	...	472	375	...	...	590	414	...	...
40-44	...	...	382	264	...	...	388	274	...	...
45-49	...	...	255	233	...	...	292	237	...	...
50-54	...	...	191	155	...	...	197	151	...	...
55-59	...	...	116	67	...	...	114	65	...	...
60-64	...	...	88	66	...	...	86	43	...	...
65-69	...	...	53	34	...	...	30	21	...	...
70-74	...	...	39	19	...	...	20	11	...	...
75+	...	...	19	8	...	...	...	...	...	...
75-79	...	...	...	...	...	...	9	3	...	...
80-84	...	...	...	...	...	...	3	1	...	...
90-94	...	...	...	...	...	...	1	-	...	...
Finland - Finlande[16]										
All ages - Tous âges	...	...	...	...	24 830	24 830	26 969	26 969	25 815	25 815
15-19	...	...	...	...	275	813	237	779	224	704
20-24	...	...	...	...	3 130	5 100	3 144	5 047	2 859	4 663
25-29	...	...	...	...	7 088	7 340	7 646	8 262	7 393	8 110
30-34	...	...	...	...	5 382	4 518	5 852	4 756	5 587	4 587
35-39	...	...	...	...	3 356	2 614	3 635	2 956	3 646	2 878
40-44	...	...	...	...	2 027	1 673	2 263	1 851	2 153	1 798
45-49	...	...	...	...	1 437	1 308	1 738	1 597	1 593	1 420
50-54	...	...	...	...	1 027	791	1 172	876	1 072	825
55-59	...	...	...	...	548	361	676	469	695	489
60-64	...	...	...	...	298	178	340	209	329	191
65-69	...	...	...	...	136	71	116	89	134	78
70-74	...	...	...	...	72	38	95	42	65	49
75+	...	...	...	...	54	25	...	...	...	...
75-79	...	...	...	...	...	...	29	23	42	18
80-84	...	...	...	...	...	...	21	11	17	5
85-89	...	...	...	...	...	...	4	2	6	-
90-94	...	...	...	...	...	...	1	-	-	-
France[17,18]										
All ages - Tous âges	286 191	286 191	...	...	...	...	279 087	279 087	...	...
0-14		3	...	...	...	...	-	2	...	...
15-19	407	3 509	...	...	...	...	439	4 086	...	...
20-24	22 455	53 482	...	...	...	...	21 762	50 412	...	...
25-29	106 040	110 711	...	...	...	...	90 060	96 470	...	...
30-34	67 503	51 868	...	...	...	...	70 534	55 112	...	...
35-39	35 368	27 928	...	...	...	...	36 562	29 272	...	...
40-44	20 575	16 302	...	...	...	...	21 989	17 721	...	...
45-49	13 420	10 429	...	...	...	...	14 186	11 532	...	...
50-54	9 861	6 818	...	...	...	...	10 757	7 866	...	...
55-59	4 689	2 633	...	...	...	...	6 289	3 740	...	...
60-64	2 722	1 210	...	...	...	...	3 102	1 421	...	...
65-69	1 473	691	...	...	...	...	1 526	787	...	...
70-74	828	344	...	...	...	...	968	397	...	...
75+	850	263	...	...	...	...	...	...	...	...
75-79	...	...	...	...	...	...	540	171	...	...
80-84	...	...	...	...	...	...	248	76	...	...
85-89	...	...	...	...	...	...	100	17	...	...
90-94	...	...	...	...	...	...	21	4	...	...
95-99	...	...	...	...	...	...	4	1	...	...
100+	...	...	...	...	...	...	-	-	...	...
Unknown - Inconnu	...	...	...	...	...	...	-	-	...	...
Hungary - Hongrie										
All ages - Tous âges	45 465	45 465	48 110	48 110	43 583	43 583	46 008	46 008	45 398	45 398
15-19	887	4 495	769	3 821	667	2 978	559	2 631	441	2 160
20-24	14 143	19 910	12 651	19 345	9 409	15 230	8 253	14 639	6 942	12 974
25-29	15 301	11 426	17 853	14 203	16 383	14 216	18 422	16 561	18 553	17 643
30-34	6 408	3 793	7 662	4 746	7 629	4 959	8 770	5 708	9 475	6 139
35-39	2 690	1 772	2 906	1 922	3 158	2 074	3 437	2 177	3 609	2 246

Continent, country or area and age / Continent, pays ou zone et âge	1999 Groom Epoux	1999 Bride Epouse	2000 Groom Epoux	2000 Bride Epouse	2001 Groom Epoux	2001 Bride Epouse	2002 Groom Epoux	2002 Bride Epouse	2003 Groom Epoux	2003 Bride Epouse
EUROPE										
Hungary - Hongrie										
40-44	1 969	1 434	2 040	1 335	2 028	1 337	1 975	1 361	1 843	1 304
45-49	1 521	1 171	1 633	1 254	1 663	1 236	1 763	1 260	1 705	1 261
50-54	977	689	1 046	723	1 089	769	1 161	869	1 131	868
55-59	658	375	657	365	663	392	718	402	751	431
60-64	371	191	357	202	371	216	416	197	465	173
65-69	242	116	228	111	233	102	233	111	170	109
70-74	161	59	168	57	153	49	163	59	153	57
75+	137	34	140	26	137	25	...	...	...	...
75-79	...	...	...	...	...	...	71	24	96	27
80-84	...	...	...	...	...	...	48	8	53	6
85-89	...	...	...	...	...	...	15	-	7	
90-94	...	...	...	...	...	...	3	1	2	
95-99	...	...	...	...	...	...	1		2	
Iceland - Islande[19]										
All ages - Tous âges	1 560	1 560	1 777	1 777	...	...	1 619	1 619	1 473	1 473
15-19	4	31	5	30	...	...	3	28	3	11
20-24	115	226	117	259	...	...	118	224	108	205
25-29	433	501	477	590	...	...	433	495	344	456
30-34	388	330	459	361	...	...	399	363	386	338
35-39	260	223	300	244	...	...	259	220	258	217
40-44	140	112	167	136	...	...	161	133	161	109
45-49	109	68	108	79	...	...	102	70	81	59
50-54	56	37	77	37	...	...	56	36	57	32
55-59	27	20	29	23	...	...	49	28	32	22
60-64	14	2	18	13	...	...	15	13	25	16
65-69	4	5	14	3	...	...	14	6	10	4
70-74	6	4	3	1	...	...	4	1	5	1
75+	4	-	2	1	...	...	...	2	...	...
75-79	...	...	...	...	...	...	3	...	2	1
80-84	...	...	...	...	...	...	1	...	1	1
85+	...	...	...	...	...	...	2	...	-	1
Unknown - Inconnu	-	1	1	-	...	...	-	-	-	-
Isle of Man - Îles de Man										
All ages - Tous âges	403	403	...	...	...	...	...	...	...	...
15-19	1	7	...	...	...	...	...	...	...	...
20-24	37	64	...	...	...	...	...	...	...	...
25-29	99	119	...	...	...	...	...	...	...	...
30-34	103	79	...	...	...	...	...	...	...	...
35-39	59	47	...	...	...	...	...	...	...	...
40-44	30	34	...	...	...	...	...	...	...	...
45-49	22	23	...	...	...	...	...	...	...	...
50-54	21	16	...	...	...	...	...	...	...	...
55-59	12	5	...	...	...	...	...	...	...	...
60-64	8	3	...	...	...	...	...	...	...	...
65-69	2	5	...	...	...	...	...	...	...	...
70-74	6	1	...	...	...	...	...	...	...	...
75+	3	-	...	...	...	...	...	...	...	...
Italy - Italie										
All ages - Tous âges	280 330	280 330	...	...	264 026	264 026	...	...	...	...
15-19	1 180	9 520	...	...	1 021	7 962	...	...	...	...
20-24	26 384	68 763	...	...	21 476	55 768	...	...	...	...
25-29	107 180	115 570	...	...	92 579	107 362	...	...	...	...
30-34	87 563	54 787	...	...	84 554	56 763	...	...	...	...
35-39	31 034	17 270	...	...	34 221	19 808	...	...	...	...
40-44	11 210	6 277	...	...	12 620	7 649	...	...	...	...
45-49	5 606	3 317	...	...	6 382	3 703	...	...	...	...
50-54	3 758	2 192	...	...	4 314	2 349	...	...	...	...
55-59	2 514	1 239	...	...	2 572	1 285	...	...	...	...
60-64	1 656	703	...	...	1 887	727	...	...	...	...
65-69	1 021	371	...	...	1 087	339	...	...	...	...
70-74	655	215	...	...	705	193	...	...	...	...
75+	569	106	...	...	...	...	...	...	...	...
75-79	...	...	...	...	386	91	...	...	...	...
80-84	...	...	...	...	135	20	...	...	...	...
85-89	...	...	...	...	69	7	...	...	...	...

24. Marriages by age of bridegroom and by age of bride: 1999 - 2003
Mariages selon l'âge de l'époux et selon l'âge de l'épouse: 1999 - 2003 (continued — suite)

Continent, country or area and age / Continent, pays ou zone et âge	1999 Groom Epoux	1999 Bride Epouse	2000 Groom Epoux	2000 Bride Epouse	2001 Groom Epoux	2001 Bride Epouse	2002 Groom Epoux	2002 Bride Epouse	2003 Groom Epoux	2003 Bride Epouse
EUROPE										
Italy - Italie										
90-94	...	...	...	...	17	-	...	...	...	...
95-99	...	...	...	...	1	-	...	...	...	...
Latvia - Lettonie										
All ages - Tous âges	9 399	9 399	9 211	9 211	9 258	9 258	9 738	9 738	...	...
15-19	222	859	217	787	174	719	158	655	...	...
20-24	2 758	3 503	2 588	3 351	2 585	3 407	2 465	3 366	...	...
25-29	2 673	2 114	2 719	2 171	2 843	2 326	3 044	2 618	...	...
30-34	1 215	940	1 272	1 049	1 387	1 069	1 664	1 286	...	...
35-39	743	572	679	541	689	558	743	593	...	...
40-44	526	401	520	394	504	394	509	380	...	...
45-49	317	285	342	279	327	275	362	302	...	...
50-54	269	251	301	237	268	210	277	207	...	...
55-59	210	165	177	134	161	103	154	120	...	...
60-64	184	166	148	136	149	103	138	111	...	...
65-69	142	71	119	58	66	47	97	66	...	...
70-74	82	50	79	53	67	32	63	31	...	...
75+	58	22	50	21	38	15	...	...	...	...
75-79	...	...	...	...	...	...	43	12	...	...
80-84	...	...	...	...	...	...	13	2	...	...
85+	...	...	...	...	...	...	8		...	...
Lithuania - Lituanie										
All ages - Tous âges	...	...	16 906	16 906	15 764	15 764	16 151	16 151	16 975	16 975
0-14	...	...	-	1	-	2	-	1	-	4
15-19	...	...	667	2 455	459	1 976	391	1 786	390	1 718
20-24	...	...	6 251	7 279	5 460	6 759	5 352	6 901	5 334	7 037
25-29	...	...	4 750	3 466	4 694	3 472	5 011	3 754	5 367	4 283
30-34	...	...	2 035	1 405	1 991	1 396	2 110	1 478	2 399	1 633
35-39	...	...	1 064	765	1 060	744	1 119	768	1 144	797
40-44	...	...	689	525	682	470	758	533	828	534
45-49	...	...	447	363	455	350	433	340	482	395
50-54	...	...	328	253	335	254	332	245	382	233
55-59	...	...	226	167	247	134	222	150	222	138
60-64	...	...	203	110	147	96	212	94	205	101
65-69	...	...	116	72	117	58	98	61	104	62
70-74	...	...	70	31	61	38	49	29	59	26
75+	...	...	60	14	56	15	64	11	59	14
Luxembourg[19]										
All ages - Tous âges	...	...	...	...	1 983	1 983	2 022	2 022	2 001	2 001
15-19	...	...	...	...	6	59	7	62	9	50
20-24	...	...	...	...	206	346	191	389	163	371
25-29	...	...	...	...	521	660	562	592	532	569
30-34	...	...	...	...	541	452	521	479	502	496
35-39	...	...	...	...	284	203	302	229	335	240
40-44	...	...	...	...	161	115	183	124	170	125
45-49	...	...	...	...	130	81	120	75	117	74
50-54	...	...	...	...	69	39	65	39	75	44
55-59	...	...	...	...	36	13	28	18	49	20
60-64	...	...	...	...	11	10	19	7	24	8
65-69	...	...	...	...	10	2	14	4	15	1
70-74	...	...	...	...	5	1	5	2	5	2
75+	...	...	...	...	3	1	...	...	...	...
75-79	...	...	...	...	...	...	3	-	4	...
80-84	...	...	...	...	...	...	2	1	1	-
85-89	...	...	...	...	...	...	1	1	-	-
Malta - Malte										
All ages - Tous âges	...	...	2 545	2 545	...	...	2 240	2 240	...	...
16-19	...	...	41	169	...	...	22	120	...	...
20-24	...	...	724	1 230	...	...	478	193	...	...
25-29	...	...	1 123	776	...	...	1 007	766	...	...
30-34	...	...	379	210	...	...	381	223	...	...
35-39	...	...	132	67	...	...	169	116	...	...
40-44	...	...	61	43	...	...	83	42	...	...
45-49	...	...	30	27	...	...	36	32	...	...
50-54	...	...	28	10	...	...	29	10	...	...
55-59	...	...	15	5	...	...	15	15	...	...

24. Marriages by age of bridegroom and by age of bride: 1999 - 2003
Mariages selon l'âge de l'époux et selon l'âge de l'épouse: 1999 - 2003 (continued — suite)

Continent, country or area and age / Continent, pays ou zone et âge	1999 Groom Epoux	1999 Bride Epouse	2000 Groom Epoux	2000 Bride Epouse	2001 Groom Epoux	2001 Bride Epouse	2002 Groom Epoux	2002 Bride Epouse	2003 Groom Epoux	2003 Bride Epouse
EUROPE										
Malta - Malte										
60-64	...	...	5	2	...	...	11	3	...	...
65+	...	...	7	6	...	...	9	6	...	...
Netherlands - Pays-Bas[20]										
All ages - Tous âges	...	...	88 074	88 074	79 677	79 677	83 970	83 970	...	...
0-19	...	...	492	2 788	321	2 073	320	2 192	...	...
20-24	...	...	7 607	16 663	6 351	13 982	6 629	14 193	...	...
25-29	...	...	26 834	30 821	21 217	25 922	20 914	26 550	...	...
30-34	...	...	25 122	18 739	24 441	18 785	25 985	20 328	...	...
35-39	...	...	11 759	7 911	11 410	7 840	12 769	8 907	...	...
40-44	...	...	5 805	4 195	5 789	4 280	6 414	4 669	...	...
45-49	...	...	3 681	2 855	3 523	2 759	3 782	2 836	...	...
50-54	...	...	3 011	2 115	2 736	1 983	2 866	2 053	...	...
55-59	...	...	1 657	1 027	1 744	1 031	1 995	1 166	...	...
60-64	...	...	1 113	529	1 001	513	1 170	567	...	...
65+	...	...	993	431	...	...	...	...	...	...
65-69	...	...	...	...	606	297	638	317	...	...
70-74	...	...	...	...	305	122	295	116	...	...
75+	...	...	...	...	233	90	...	...	...	...
75-79	...	...	...	...	...	...	124	53	...	...
80-84	...	...	...	...	...	...	53	18	...	...
85-89	...	...	...	...	...	...	15	5	...	...
95-99	...	...	...	...	...	...	1	-	...	...
Norway - Norvège[18,21]										
All ages - Tous âges	23 456	23 456	25 356	25 356	22 967	22 967	...	...	22 361	22 361
0-14	...	...	...	...	...	...	...	...	-	1
15-19	90	516	110	501	114	551	...	...	81	484
20-24	1 796	4 004	1 800	4 101	1 641	3 706	...	...	1 518	3 478
25-29	6 754	8 145	7 010	8 666	5 932	7 459	...	...	5 294	6 898
30-34	6 105	5 014	6 845	5 696	6 114	5 149	...	...	5 926	5 173
35-39	3 414	2 504	3 827	2 793	3 565	2 622	...	...	3 718	2 786
40-44	1 953	1 385	2 115	1 526	2 028	1 413	...	...	2 094	1 462
45-49	1 331	893	1 466	993	1 417	1 025	...	...	1 424	1 003
50-54	1 024	570	1 121	661	1 087	574	...	...	1 090	565
55-59	547	255	583	265	578	282	...	...	676	318
60-64	244	84	281	82	309	97	...	...	326	122
65-69	106	44	111	37	99	52	...	...	127	44
70-74	57	20	45	20	42	22	...	...	52	11
75+	35	21	42	14	41	15	...	...	...	...
75-79	...	...	...	...	...	...	...	...	25	9
80-84	...	...	...	...	...	...	...	...	10	6
85+	...	...	...	...	...	...	...	...	-	1
Unknown - Inconnu	-	1	-	1	...	...	...	...	-	-
Poland - Pologne										
All ages - Tous âges	219 398	219 398	...	...	...	...	...	...	195 446	195 446
15-19	6 746	29 583	...	...	...	...	...	...	...	...
16-19	...	...	...	...	...	...	...	...	...	16 821
18-19	...	...	...	...	...	...	...	...	3 263	...
20-24	95 243	118 358	...	...	...	...	...	...	63 180	92 635
25-29	71 636	42 483	...	...	...	...	...	...	81 258	57 236
30-34	19 143	9 708	...	...	...	...	...	...	23 048	12 220
35-39	8 100	4 762	...	...	...	...	...	...	7 977	4 304
40-44	5 206	4 094	...	...	...	...	...	...	4 509	2 953
45-49	3 815	3 416	...	...	...	...	...	...	3 405	2 923
50-54	2 639	2 530	...	...	...	...	...	...	2 748	2 545
55-59	1 677	1 492	...	...	...	...	...	...	1 700	1 495
60-64	1 693	1 410	...	...	...	...	...	...	1 336	984
65-69	1 532	928	...	...	...	...	...	...	1 171	720
70-74	1 081	438	...	...	...	...	...	...	927	415
75+	887	196	...	...	...	...	...	...	...	...
75-79	...	...	...	...	...	...	...	...	589	151
80-84	...	...	...	...	...	...	...	...	250	39
85+	...	...	...	...	...	...	...	...	85	5
Portugal										
All ages - Tous âges	...	...	...	...	58 390	58 390	56 457	56 457	53 735	53 735
0-16	...	...	...	...	24	492	10	396	9	305

Continent, country or area and age	1999		2000		2001		2002		2003	
Continent, pays ou zone et âge	Groom Epoux	Bride Epouse	Groom Epoux	Bride Epouse	Groom Epoux	Bride Epouse	Groom Epoux	Bride Epouse	Groom Epoux	Bride Epouse
EUROPE										
Portugal										
17-19	...	...	...	...	1 256	5 234	1 058	4 520	888	3 679
20-24	...	...	...	...	15 079	19 551	13 087	17 580	11 252	15 705
25-29	...	...	...	...	23 394	20 079	23 541	20 663	22 041	19 889
30-34	...	...	...	...	9 488	6 519	9 979	7 007	10 291	7 378
35-39	...	...	...	...	3 495	2 559	3 469	2 610	3 644	2 761
40-44	...	...	...	...	1 797	1 378	1 770	1 362	1 866	1 540
45-49	...	...	...	...	1 140	956	1 093	842	1 193	940
50-54	...	...	...	...	806	591	740	612	833	641
55-59	...	...	...	...	609	400	580	352	567	377
60-64	...	...	...	...	437	282	406	240	368	219
65-69	...	...	...	...	399	175	329	146	336	153
70-74	...	...	...	...	235	108	175	79	220	79
75-79	...	...	...	...	132	49	129	38	141	52
80-84	...	...	...	...	65	13	60	9	60	13
85-89					25	3	28	-	20	3
90-94	...	...	...	...	8	1	2	1	4	1
95-99	...	...	...	...	1	-	1	-	2	-
100+	...	...	...	...	-	-	-	-	-	-
Unknown - Inconnu	...	...	...	...	-	-	-	-	-	-
Republic of Moldova - République de Moldova[22]										
All ages - Tous âges	18 221	18 221	16 554	16 554	16 076	16 076	16 663	16 663	18 970	18 970
0-15	-	67	-	53	-	28	-	13	-	9
16-19	1 058	7 170	1 026	6 118	838	5 572	863	5 183	905	5 444
20-24	11 199	8 883	9 669	8 302	9 176	8 344	9 145	8 961	10 065	10 455
25-29	4 639	1 553	4 480	1 500	4 676	1 619	5 148	1 915	6 142	2 401
30-34	849	281	844	285	887	267	984	299	1 286	430
35-39	245	94	251	76	251	80	233	85	317	102
40-44	71	41	76	33	90	38	93	40	133	42
45-49	42	29	29	29	26	13	28	20	36	16
50-54	22	11	13	11	19	9	27	11	21	16
55-59	10	7	16	8	8	9	5	6	10	6
60-64	14	18	13	12	14	10	11	12	4	2
65-69	12	16	16	18	9	13	9	8	9	8
70-74	16	24	20	40	7	15	12	30	6	11
75+	39	19	101	69	72	56	105	80	35	27
Unknown - Inconnu	5	8	-	-	3	3	-	-	1	1
Romania - Roumanie										
All ages - Tous âges	...	...	135 808	135 808	129 930	129 930	129 018	129 018	133 953	133 953
15-19	...	...	1 993	24 646	1 604	21 434	1 566	20 325	1 515	20 460
20-24	...	...	47 311	60 585	41 940	56 394	38 798	54 046	36 495	52 913
25-29	...	...	47 973	27 792	47 305	28 671	48 987	30 400	52 997	34 460
30-34	...	...	19 580	11 571	20 085	12 196	20 420	12 549	21 152	12 685
35-39	...	...	6 494	3 692	6 179	3 485	6 734	4 102	8 687	5 523
40-44	...	...	4 530	2 865	4 561	2 781	4 345	2 556	4 467	2 745
45-49	...	...	3 156	2 015	3 191	2 168	3 259	2 179	3 351	2 331
50-54	...	...	1 831	1 204	1 990	1 273	2 016	1 368	2 290	1 442
55-59	...	...	1 029	619	1 143	616	1 051	645	1 140	627
60-64	...	...	943	409	...	...	...	...	...	...
60+	...	...	...	...	1 932	912	1 842	848	1 859	767
65-69	...	...	485	257	...	...	...	...	...	...
70-74	...	...	288	107	...	...	...	...	...	...
75+	...	...	195	46	...	...	...	...	...	...
Russian Federation - Fédération de Russie										
All ages - Tous âges	911 162	911 162	...	...	...	...	...	...	...	...
0-17	3 773	32 945	...	...	...	...	...	...	...	...
18-24	425 864	530 779	...	...	...	...	...	...	...	...
25-34	297 276	202 142	...	...	...	...	...	...	...	...
35+	184 148	145 226	...	...	...	...	...	...	...	...
Unknown - Inconnu	101	70	...	...	...	...	...	...	...	...
San Marino - Saint-Marin										
All ages - Tous âges	...	...	193	193	...	...	...	...	200	200
15-19	...	...	1	2	...	...	...	...	1	1
20-24	...	...	14	41	...	...	...	...	8	20

24. Marriages by age of bridegroom and by age of bride: 1999 - 2003
Mariages selon l'âge de l'époux et selon l'âge de l'épouse: 1999 - 2003 (continued — suite)

Continent, country or area and age / Continent, pays ou zone et âge	1999 Groom Epoux	1999 Bride Epouse	2000 Groom Epoux	2000 Bride Epouse	2001 Groom Epoux	2001 Bride Epouse	2002 Groom Epoux	2002 Bride Epouse	2003 Groom Epoux	2003 Bride Epouse
EUROPE										
San Marino - Saint-Marin										
25-29	...	...	70	90	...	...	...	...	58	52
30-34	...	...	59	34	...	...	...	...	56	31
35-39	...	...	20	15	...	...	...	...	35	17
40-44	...	...	14	5	...	...	...	...	15	5
45-49	...	...	4	2	...	...	...	...	3	1
50-54	...	...	3	3	...	...	...	...	4	1
55-59	...	...	1	1	...	...	...	...	2	2
60-64	...	...	3	-	...	...	...	...	2	1
65-69	...	...	1	-	...	...	...	...	2	-
70-74	...	...	1	-	...	...	...	...	-	-
75+	...	...	1	-	...	...	...	...	1	-
Unknown - Inconnu	...	...	1	-	...	...	...	...	13	69
Serbia and Montenegro - Serbie-et-Montenegro[23]										
All ages - Tous âges	...	...	58 318	58 318	...	...	45 741	45 741	...	...
15-19	...	...	1 060	8 356	...	...	560	5 238	...	...
20-24	...	...	14 740	22 784	...	...	9 372	16 223	...	...
25-29	...	...	20 743	14 859	...	...	15 982	12 604	...	...
30-34	...	...	10 463	5 389	...	...	9 046	5 217	...	...
35-39	...	...	4 332	2 288	...	...	3 985	2 125	...	...
40-44	...	...	2 176	1 411	...	...	2 176	1 322	...	...
45-49	...	...	1 417	1 112	...	...	1 346	1 030	...	...
50-54	...	...	929	759	...	...	991	725	...	...
55-59	...	...	586	402	...	...	529	410	...	...
60-64	...	...	528	314	...	...	483	279	...	...
65-69	...	...	456	215	...	...	402	183	...	...
70-74	...	...	320	113	...	...	286	98	...	...
75+	...	...	291	114	...	...	283	63	...	...
Unknown - Inconnu	...	...	277	202	...	...	300	224	...	...
Slovakia - Slovaquie										
All ages - Tous âges	27 340	27 340	...	...	23 795	23 795	25 062	25 062	...	...
15-19	933	4 368	...	...	614	2 830	565	2 606	...	...
20-24	11 285	14 035	...	...	7 949	11 251	7 258	10 975	...	...
25-29	9 013	5 580	...	...	9 078	6 331	10 020	7 577	...	...
30-34	2 776	1 487	...	...	2 950	1 545	3 510	1 872	...	...
35-39	1 317	712	...	...	1 282	666	1 521	759	...	...
40-44	762	431	...	...	668	438	783	472	...	...
45-49	517	366	...	...	469	368	559	381	...	...
50-54	328	191	...	...	343	179	357	218	...	...
55-59	176	81	...	...	171	87	198	104	...	...
60-64	86	49	...	...	124	51	131	52	...	...
65-69	79	22	...	...	81	35	83	32	...	...
70-74	39	15	...	...	38	11	36	8	...	...
75+	29	3	...	...	28	3	...	...	...	...
75-79	...	...	...	...	...	...	30	4	...	...
80-84	...	...	...	...	...	...	9	2	...	...
85-89	...	...	...	...	...	...	1	-	...	...
90-94	...	...	...	...	...	...	1	-	...	...
Slovenia - Slovénie										
All ages - Tous âges	7 716	7 716	7 201	7 201	6 935	6 935	7 064	7 064	6 756	6 756
0-14	-	1	-	-	-	1	-	1	-	-
15-19	42	334	32	226	34	225	29	189	36	194
20-24	1 318	2 656	1 076	2 279	976	1 988	865	1 874	839	1 695
25-29	3 092	2 768	2 894	2 820	2 770	2 799	2 666	2 790	2 503	2 725
30-34	1 693	995	1 724	976	1 646	997	1 756	1 162	1 733	1 176
35-39	695	384	633	392	683	380	793	422	752	401
40-44	314	216	316	171	281	194	354	249	331	218
45-49	184	166	205	165	200	127	227	159	200	141
50-54	140	85	118	71	129	97	136	111	150	106
55-59	80	44	70	42	78	53	87	47	81	52
60-64	51	29	46	33	42	33	59	29	57	24
65-69	52	23	40	16	38	25	39	18	28	13
70-74	22	10	33	8	30	11	24	5	20	5
75+	33	5	14	2	28	5	...	...	...	...
75-79	...	...	...	...	...	...	18	7	12	2

Continent, country or area and age / Continent, pays ou zone et âge	1999 Groom Epoux	1999 Bride Epouse	2000 Groom Epoux	2000 Bride Epouse	2001 Groom Epoux	2001 Bride Epouse	2002 Groom Epoux	2002 Bride Epouse	2003 Groom Epoux	2003 Bride Epouse
EUROPE										
Slovenia - Slovénie										
80-84	...	...	...	...	...	...	9	1	8	3
85-89	...	...	...	...	...	...	1	-	5	-
90-94	...	...	...	...	...	...	1	-	1	-
95+	...	...	...	...	...	...	-	-	-	-
Spain - Espagne										
All ages - Tous âges	...	...	...	...	...	...	211 522	211 522	...	...
0-14	...	...	...	...	...	...	1	13	...	...
15-19	...	...	...	...	...	...	836	3 244	...	...
20-24	...	...	...	...	...	...	17 400	36 913	...	...
25-29	...	...	...	...	...	...	88 281	99 837	...	...
30-34	...	...	...	...	...	...	64 248	45 707	...	...
35-39	...	...	...	...	...	...	21 289	13 922	...	...
40-44	...	...	...	...	...	...	8 334	5 567	...	...
45-49	...	...	...	...	...	...	4 180	2 912	...	...
50-54	...	...	...	...	...	...	2 640	1 606	...	...
55-59	...	...	...	...	...	...	1 696	852	...	...
60-64	...	...	...	...	...	...	981	419	...	...
65-69	...	...	...	...	...	...	754	291	...	...
70-74	...	...	...	...	...	...	458	120	...	...
75-79	...	...	...	...	...	...	218	72	...	...
80-84	...	...	...	...	...	...	125	34	...	...
85-89	...	...	...	...	...	...	61	9	...	...
90-94	...	...	...	...	...	...	15	4	...	...
95+	...	...	...	...	...	...	5	-	...	...
Sweden - Suède										
All ages - Tous âges	...	...	...	...	33 077	33 077	38 012	38 012	...	...
15-19	...	...	...	...	70	359	421	328	...	...
20-24	...	...	...	...	1 519	3 118	2 268	3 120	...	...
25-29	...	...	...	...	7 699	10 240	8 061	10 264	...	...
30-34	...	...	...	...	9 267	8 314	10 300	8 760	...	...
35-39	...	...	...	...	5 595	4 468	6 524	5 023	...	...
40-44	...	...	...	...	3 050	2 345	3 596	2 645	...	...
45-49	...	...	...	...	2 095	1 763	2 393	1 902	...	...
50-54	...	...	...	...	1 694	1 309	1 892	1 443	...	...
55-59	...	...	...	...	1 183	698	1 474	868	...	...
60-64	...	...	...	...	514	250	603	300	...	...
65-69	...	...	...	...	186	113	239	131	...	...
70-74	...	...	...	...	111	58	132	55	...	...
75+	...	...	...	...	94	42	...	...	...	...
75-79	...	...	...	...	...	...	67	34	...	...
80-84	...	...	...	...	...	...	32	13	...	...
85-89	...	...	...	...	...	...	10	2	...	...
90-94	...	...	...	...	...	...	-	1	...	...
Unknown - Inconnu	...	...	...	...	...	...	-	3 123	...	...
Switzerland - Suisse										
All ages - Tous âges	...	...	39 758	39 758	35 987	35 987	...	...	...	...
0-14	...	...	-	3	-	1	...	...	...	...
15-19	...	...	229	1 112	189	950	...	...	...	...
20-24	...	...	3 628	7 357	3 040	6 486	...	...	...	...
25-29	...	...	10 574	13 047	8 939	11 398	...	...	...	...
30-34	...	...	10 962	9 051	10 100	8 476	...	...	...	...
35-39	...	...	5 756	4 059	5 641	4 035	...	...	...	...
40-44	...	...	3 071	2 039	2 905	1 883	...	...	...	...
45-49	...	...	1 962	1 413	1 812	1 208	...	...	...	...
50-54	...	...	1 605	938	1 425	851	...	...	...	...
55-59	...	...	1 045	470	1 041	457	...	...	...	...
60-64	...	...	501	158	479	149	...	...	...	...
65-69	...	...	218	59	230	47	...	...	...	...
70-74	...	...	97	31	102	26	...	...	...	...
75+	...	...	110	21	84	20	...	...	...	...
The Former Yugoslav Rep. of Macedonia - L'ex-République yougoslave de Macédoine										
All ages - Tous âges	14 172	14 172	14 255	14 255	13 267	13 267	14 522	14 522	...	...
15-19	539	3 314	551	3 151	458	2 759	472	2 869	...	...

Continent, country or area and age / Continent, pays ou zone et âge	1999 Groom Epoux	1999 Bride Epouse	2000 Groom Epoux	2000 Bride Epouse	2001 Groom Epoux	2001 Bride Epouse	2002 Groom Epoux	2002 Bride Epouse	2003 Groom Epoux	2003 Bride Epouse
EUROPE										
The Former Yugoslav Rep. of Macedonia - L'ex-République yougoslave de Macédoine										
20-24	5 258	6 292	5 059	6 241	4 397	5 719	4 955	6 398	...	...
25-29	5 214	3 057	5 205	3 166	5 109	3 152	5 516	3 459	...	...
30-34	1 877	772	2 032	848	1 946	869	2 111	908	...	...
35-39	666	331	715	376	674	319	774	380	...	...
40-44	274	153	307	179	270	172	296	194	...	...
45-49	117	99	131	107	153	114	134	137	...	...
50-54	74	47	75	65	84	71	89	74	...	...
55-59	44	35	56	29	45	23	37	29	...	...
60-64	39	20	47	19	42	33	40	30	...	...
65-69	33	12	29	14	33	16	46	20	...	...
70-74	17	6	24	6	32	6	29	5	...	...
75+	20	5	24	5	24	4	23	19	...	...
Unknown - Inconnu	-	29	-	49	-	10	-	-	...	...
Ukraine										
All ages - Tous âges	...	...	...	...	309 602	309 602	...	...	370 966	370 966
0-15	...	...	...	...	14	807	...	...	9	684
16-19	...	...	...	...	13 624	71 888	...	...	14 358	77 711
20-24	...	...	...	...	127 627	124 256	...	...	148 115	156 493
25-29	...	...	...	...	76 809	45 768	...	...	99 431	59 132
30-34	...	...	...	...	31 069	20 755	...	...	40 198	26 153
35-39	...	...	...	...	17 747	12 487	...	...	20 264	14 112
40-44	...	...	...	...	12 662	9 876	...	...	15 203	11 153
45-49	...	...	...	...	8 662	7 514	...	...	10 515	8 711
50-54	...	...	...	...	6 798	5 820	...	...	7 823	6 626
55-59	...	...	...	...	3 486	2 811	...	...	4 413	3 211
60+	...	...	...	...	11 104	7 620	...	...	10 637	6 980
United Kingdom - Royaume-Uni										
All ages - Tous âges	301 083	301 083	305 912	305 912	...	...	293 021	293 021	...	...
15-19	2 528	9 250	2 390	8 870	...	...	2 023	7 505	...	...
20-24	32 096	57 182	31 096	55 646	...	...	28 666	51 478	...	...
25-29	90 412	94 703	85 870	92 753	...	...	74 858	82 892	...	...
30-34	72 129	60 446	73 809	62 478	...	...	72 592	62 279	...	...
35-39	40 244	31 981	43 653	34 891	...	...	44 189	35 978	...	...
40-44	21 870	18 155	24 366	19 806	...	...	25 558	21 019	...	...
45-49	14 753	12 176	15 919	13 230	...	...	15 910	13 232	...	...
50-54	11 828	8 646	12 872	9 391	...	...	11 891	8 955	...	...
55-59	6 463	3 781	6 939	4 121	...	...	8 055	4 903	...	...
60-64	3 822	2 302	4 075	2 321	...	...	4 324	2 366	...	...
65-69	2 406	1 249	2 410	1 247	...	...	2 451	1 251	...	...
70-74	1 312	670	1 319	683	...	...	1 328	662	...	...
75+	1 220	542	1 194	475	...	...	...	...	...	...
75-79	...	...	...	...	...	...	746	328	...	...
80-84	...	...	...	...	...	...	316	128	...	...
85-89	...	...	...	...	...	...	113	44	...	...
90-94	...	...	...	...	...	...	1	1	...	...
Unknown - Inconnu	...	...	...	...	...	...	-	-	...	...
OCEANIA — OCEANIE										
Australia - Australie+										
All ages - Tous âges	114 316	114 316	113 429	113 429	103 130	103 130	105 435	105 435	106 394	106 394
15-19	756	3 291	702	3 221	609	2 778	573	2 654	562	2 523
20-24	17 966	29 220	16 752	27 332	14 440	23 853	14 190	23 369	13 401	22 712
25-29	38 122	38 375	37 293	37 723	33 091	33 938	31 875	33 425	31 761	33 333
30-34	23 233	18 584	23 818	19 438	22 390	18 845	24 136	20 546	25 210	21 467
35-39	13 155	9 787	12 923	9 953	12 067	9 038	12 518	9 671	12 682	9 949
40-44	7 145	5 720	7 562	5 901	7 136	5 462	7 554	5 807	7 865	6 101
45-49	5 076	4 026	5 080	4 194	4 693	3 881	5 062	4 124	5 128	4 177
50-54	3 708	2 469	3 944	2 727	3 680	2 535	3 853	2 734	3 813	2 785
55-59	2 096	1 227	2 242	1 347	2 115	1 262	2 522	1 439	2 703	1 563
60-64	1 231	677	1 341	725	1 224	688	1 289	718	1 407	766
65-69	770	424	787	424	741	393	817	422	760	463

Continent, country or area and age / Continent, pays ou zone et âge	1999 Groom Epoux	1999 Bride Epouse	2000 Groom Epoux	2000 Bride Epouse	2001 Groom Epoux	2001 Bride Epouse	2002 Groom Epoux	2002 Bride Epouse	2003 Groom Epoux	2003 Bride Epouse
OCEANIA — OCEANIE										
Australia - Australie+										
70-74	560	309	513	257	447	241	511	296	517	300
75+	498	207	472	187	497	216	...	...	...	...
75-79	...	...	...	...	...	...	326	153	361	170
80-84	...	...	...	...	...	...	159	59	171	62
85-89	...	...	...	...	...	...	41	14	46	18
90-94	...	...	...	...	...	...	8	4	7	5
95-99	...	...	...	...	...	...	-	-	-	-
New Caledonia - Nouvelle-Calédonie										
All ages - Tous âges	943	943	...	...	...	...	...	...	873	873
0-19	4	27	...	...	...	...	...	...	1	24
20-24	78	230	...	...	...	...	...	...	65	146
25-29	300	289	...	...	...	...	...	...	199	255
30-34	213	182	...	...	...	...	...	...	228	184
35-39	142	104	...	...	...	...	...	...	139	105
40-49	136	79	...	...	...	...	...	...	125	109
50-59	52	27	...	...	...	...	...	...	85	35
60+	18	5	...	...	...	...	...	...	31	15
New Zealand - Nouvelle-Zélande+										
All ages - Tous âges	21 085	21 085	...	...	...	...	20 690	20 690	21 419	21 419
15-19	199	665	...	...	...	...	225	639	212	599
20-24	3 033	4 692	...	...	...	...	2 776	4 178	2 890	4 417
25-29	6 200	6 585	...	...	...	...	5 417	5 849	5 487	5 932
30-34	4 539	3 820	...	...	...	...	4 583	4 199	4 810	4 372
35-39	2 637	2 095	...	...	...	...	2 651	2 256	2 740	2 270
40-44	1 580	1 291	...	...	...	...	1 760	1 377	1 775	1 486
45-49	1 019	821	...	...	...	...	1 182	929	1 246	1 012
50-54	783	542	...	...	...	...	845	614	870	630
55-59	465	255	...	...	...	...	539	283	649	348
60-64	261	141	...	...	...	...	307	169	355	172
65-69	168	91	...	...	...	...	182	91	188	84
70-74	106	42	...	...	...	...	119	50	107	55
75+	95	45	...	...	...	...	104	56	90	42
Tonga+										
All ages - Tous âges	...	...	747	747	...	...	...	...	...	...
15-19	...	...	62	169	...	...	...	...	...	...
20-24	...	...	257	278	...	...	...	...	...	...
25-29	...	...	217	163	...	...	...	...	...	...
30-34	...	...	106	82	...	...	...	...	...	...
35-39	...	...	36	27	...	...	...	...	...	...
40-44	...	...	28	9	...	...	...	...	...	...
45-49	...	...	12	10	...	...	...	...	...	...
50+	...	...	29	9	...	...	...	...	...	...

FOOTNOTES - NOTES

Italics: data from civil registers which are incomplete or of unknown completeness. — *Italiques:* données incomplètes ou dont le degré d'exactitude n'est pas connu, provenant des registres de l'état civil.

+ Data tabulated by date of registration rather than occurrence. — Données exploitées selon la date de l'enregistrement et non la date de l'événement.

1 Including marriages resumed after 'revocable divorce' (among Moslem population), which approximates legal separation. - Y compris les unions reconstituées après un 'divorce révocable' (parmi la population musulmane), qui est à peu près l'équivalent d'une séparation légale.
2 Excluding tribal Indian population. - Non compris les Indiens vivant en tribus.
3 Excluding Indian jungle population. - Non compris les Indiens de la jungle.
4 Excluding nomadic Indian tribes. - Non compris les tribus d'Indiens nomades.
5 Data refer to government controlled areas. - Les données se raportent aux zones contrôlées par le Gouvernement.
6 Including data for East Jerusalem and Israeli residents in certain other territories under occupation by Israeli military forces since June 1967. - Y compris les données pour Jérusalem-Est et les résidents israéliens dans certains autres territoires occupés depuis 1967 par les forces armées israéliennes.
7 Data refer to Japanese nationals in Japan only; and to grooms and brides married for the first time whose marriages occurred and were registered in the same year. - Les données se raportent aux nationaux japonais au Japon seulement; et aux époux et épouses mariés pour la première fois, dont le mariage a été célébré et enregistré la même année.
8 Excluding data for Jordanian territory under occupation since June 1967 by Israeli military forces. Excluding foreigners, including registered Palestinian refugees. - Non compris les données pour le territoire jordanien occupé depuis juin 1967 par les forces armées israéliennes. Non compris les étrangers, mais y compris les réfugiés de Palestine enregistrés.
9 Registration of Kandyan marriages is complete; registration of Moslem and general marriages is incomplete. - Tous les mariages des Kandyens sont enregistrés; l'enregistrement des mariages musulmans et des autres mariages est incomplet.
10 Figures exclude marriages previously officiated outside Singapore or under religious and customary rites. - Les figures excluent les mariages célébrés

précédemment au dehors de Singapoure ou sous les rites réligieuse ou accoutumés.

[11] Data refer to provincial capitals and district centres only. - Les données se rapportent aux capitales des provinces et les chefs-lieux de districts seulement.

[12] Excluding aliens temporarily in the area. - Non compris les étrangers se trouvant temporairement le territoire.

[13] Including armed forces stationed outside the country, but excluding alien armed forces in the area unless marriage performed by local foreign authority. - Y compris les militaires nationaux hors du pays et les militaires étrangers en garnison sur le territoire, sauf si le mariage a été célébré pour l'autorité locale.

[14] Including Bulgarian nationals outside the country, but excluding aliens in the area. - Y compris les nationaux bulgares à l'étranger, mais non compris les étrangers sur le territoire.

[15] Excluding Faeroe Islands and Greenland. - Non compris les Iles Féroé et Gröenland.

[16] Marriages in which the bride was resident in Finland only. - Mariages où l'épouse a la résidence en Finlande seulement.

[17] Including armed forces stationed outside the country. - Y compris les militaires nationaux hors du pays.

[18] Age classification based on year of birth rather than exact date of birth. - Le classement selon l'âge est basé sur l'année de naissances et non sur la date exacte de naissance.

[19] Data refer to de jure population. - Les données se raportent a la population de droit

[20] Including residents outside the country if listed in a Netherlands population register. - Y compris les résidents hors du pays, s'ils sont inscrits sur un registre de population néerlandais.

[21] Marriages in which the groom was resident in Norway only. - Mariages où l'époux a la résidence en Norvège seulement.

[22] Data refer to first marriages only. - Données se rapportent aux premiers mariages seulement.

[23] Starting from 2002, without data for Kosovo and Metohia. - Pour 2002 et après, sans les donées pour le Kosovo and Metohie.

Table 25

Table 25 presents number of divorces and crude divorce rates for as many years as possible between 1999 and 2003.

Description of variables: Divorce is defined as a final legal dissolution of a marriage, that is, that separation of husband and wife which confers on the parties the right to remarriage under civil, religious and/or other provisions, according to the laws of each country[j].

Unless otherwise noted, divorce statistics exclude legal separations that do not allow remarriage. These statistics refer to the number of divorces granted, and not to the number of persons divorcing.

Divorce statistics are obtained from court records and/or civil registers according to national practice. The actual compilation of these statistics may be the responsibility of the civil registrar, the national statistical office or other government offices.

The urban/rural classification of divorces is that provided by each country or area; it is presumed to be based on the national census definitions of urban population which have been set forth at the end of the technical notes for table 6.

Rate computation: Crude divorce rates by urban/rural residence are the annual number of divorces per 1 000 mid-year population. Rates presented in this table have been limited to those countries or areas having at least a total of 30 divorces in a given year. These rates have been calculated by the Statistics Division of the United Nations.

Reliability of data: Each country or area has been asked to indicate the estimated completeness of the divorces recorded in its civil register. These national assessments are indicated by the quality codes C and U that appear in the first column of this table.

C indicates that the data are estimated to be virtually complete, that is, representing at least 90 per cent of the divorces that occur each year, while U indicates that data are estimated to be incomplete, that is, representing less than 90 per cent of the divorces occurring each year. The code ... indicates that no information was provided regarding completeness.

Data from civil registers which are reported as incomplete or of unknown completeness (coded U or ...) are considered unreliable. They appear in *italics* in this table and the rates were not computed on data so coded. These quality codes apply only to data from civil registers. For more information about the quality of vital statistics data in general, see section 4.2 of the Technical Notes.

Limitations: Statistics on divorces are subject to the same qualifications as have been set forth for vital statistics in general and divorce statistics in particular as discussed in section 4 of the Technical Notes.

Divorce, like marriage, is a legal event, and this has implications for international comparability of data. Divorce has been defined, for statistical purposes, in terms of the laws of individual countries or areas. The laws pertaining to divorce vary considerably from one country or area to another. This variation in the legal provision for divorce also affects the incidence of divorce, which is relatively low in countries or areas where divorce decrees are difficult to obtain.

Since divorces are granted by courts and statistics on divorce refer to the actual divorce decree, effective as of the date of the decree, marked year-to-year fluctuations may reflect court delays and clearances rather than trends in the incidence of divorce. The comparability of divorce statistics may also be affected by tabulation procedures. In some countries or areas annulments and/or legal separations may be included. This practice is more common for countries or areas in which the number of divorces is small. Information on this practice is given in the footnotes when known.

Because the registration of a divorce in many countries or areas is the responsibility solely of the court or the authority which granted it, and since the registration recording such cases is part of the records of the court proceedings, it follows that divorces are likely to be registered soon after the decree is granted. For this reason the practice of tabulating data by date of registration does not generally pose serious problems of comparability as it does in the case of birth and death statistics.

As noted briefly above, the incidence of divorce is affected by the relative ease or difficulty of obtaining a divorce according to the laws of individual countries or areas. The incidence of divorce is also affected by the ability of individuals to meet financial and other costs of the court procedures. Connected with this aspect is the influence of certain religious faiths on the incidence of divorce. For all these reasons, divorce statistics are not strictly comparable as measures of family dissolution by legal means. Furthermore, family dissolution by other than legal means, such as separation, is not measured in statistics for divorce.

For certain countries or areas there is or was no legal provision for divorce in the sense used here, and therefore no data for these countries or areas appear in this table.

In addition, it should be noted that rates are affected also by the quality and limitations of the population estimates that are used in their computation. The problems of under-enumeration or over-enumeration, and to some extent, the differences in definition of total population, have been discussed in section 3 of the Technical Notes dealing with population data in general, and specific information pertaining to individual countries or areas is given in the footnotes to table 3.

As will be seen from the footnotes, strict correspondence between the numerator of the rate and the denominator is not always obtained; for example, divorces among civilian plus military segments of the population may be related to civilian population only. The effect of this may be to increase the rates but, in most cases, the effect is negligible.

As mentioned above, data for some countries or areas may include annulments and/or legal separations. This practice affects the comparability of the crude divorce rates. For example, inclusion of annulments in the numerator of the rates produces a negligible effect on the rates, but inclusion of legal separations may have a measurable effect on the level.

It should be emphasized that crude divorce rates like crude birth, death and marriage rates may be seriously affected by age-sex structure of the populations to which they relate. Like crude marriage rates, they are also affected by the existing distribution of the population by marital status. Nevertheless, crude divorce rates provide a simple measure of the level and changes in divorce.

The comparability of data by urban/rural residence is affected by the national definitions of urban and rural used in tabulating these data. It is assumed, in the absence of specific information to the contrary, that the definitions of urban and rural used in connection with the national population census were also used in the compilation of the vital statistics for each country or area. However, it cannot be excluded that, for a given country or area, different definitions of urban and rural are used for the vital statistics data and the population census data respectively. When known, the definitions of urban in national population censuses are presented at the end of the technical notes for table 6. As discussed in detail in the notes, these definitions vary considerably from one country or area to another.

In addition to problems of comparability, divorce rates classified by urban/rural residence are also subject to certain special types of bias. If, when calculating divorce rates, different definitions of urban are used in connection with the vital events and the population data, and if this results in a net difference between the numerator and denominator of the rate in the population at risk, then the divorce rates would be biased. Urban/rural differentials in divorce rates may also be affected by whether the vital events have been tabulated in terms of place of occurrence or place of usual residence. This problem is discussed in more detail in section 4.1.4.1. of the Technical Notes.

Earlier data: Divorces have been shown in previous issues of the Demographic Yearbook. The earliest data, which were for 1935, appeared in the 1951 issue. For more information on specific topics and years for which data are reported, readers should consult the Historical Index.

NOTES

[i] For definition, please see section 4.1.1.4 of the Technical Notes.

Tableau 25

Le tableau 25 présente des statistiques concernant les divorces et les taux bruts de divortialité pour le plus grand nombre d'années possible entre 1999 et 2003.

Description des variables : Le divorce est la dissolution légale et définitive des liens du mariage, c'est-à-dire la séparation de l'époux et de l'épouse qui confère aux parties le droit de se remarier civilement ou religieusement, ou selon toute autre procédure, conformément à la législation du pays[1].

Sauf indication contraire, les statistiques de la divortialité n'englobent pas les séparations légales qui excluent un remariage. Ces statistiques se rapportent aux jugements de divorce prononcés, non aux personnes divorcées.

Les statistiques de la divortialité proviennent, selon la pratique suivie par chaque pays, des actes des tribunaux et/ou des registres de l'état civil. L'officier d'état civil, les services nationaux de statistique ou d'autres services gouvernementaux peuvent être chargés d'établir ces statistiques.

La classification des divorces selon le lieu de résidence (zone urbaine ou rurale) est celle qui a été communiquée par chaque pays ou zone ; on part du principe qu'elle repose sur les définitions de la population urbaine utilisées pour les recensements nationaux, qui sont reproduites à la fin des notes techniques du tableau 6.

Calcul des taux : Les taux bruts de divortialité selon le lieu de résidence (zone urbaine ou rurale) représentent le nombre annuel de divorces enregistrés pour 1 000 habitants au milieu de l'année. Les taux du tableau 25 ne se rapportent qu'aux pays ou zones où l'on a enregistré un total d'au moins 30 divorces pendant une année donnée. Ces taux ont été calculés par la Division de statistique de l'ONU.

Fiabilité des données : Il a été demandé à chaque pays ou zone d'indiquer le degré estimatif de complétude des données sur les divorces figurant dans ses registres d'état civil. Ces évaluations nationales sont désignées par les codes de qualité 'C' et 'U' qui apparaissent dans la deuxième colonne du tableau.

La lettre 'C' indique que les données sont jugées à peu près complètes, c'est-à-dire qu'elles représentent au moins 90 p. 100 des divorces survenus chaque année ; la lettre 'U' signale que les données sont jugées incomplètes, c'est-à-dire qu'elles représentent moins de 90 p. 100 des divorces survenus chaque année. Le code '...' indique qu'aucun renseignement n'a été communiqué quant à la complétude des données.

Les données issues des registres de l'état civil qui sont déclarées incomplètes ou dont le degré de complétude n'est pas connu (code 'U' ou '...') sont jugées douteuses. Elles apparaissent en italique dans le tableau et les taux correspondants n'ont pas été calculés. Les codes de qualité ne s'appliquent qu'aux données extraites des registres de l'état civil. Pour plus de précisions sur la qualité des données reposant sur les statistiques de l'état civil en général, voir la section 4.2 des Notes techniques.

Insuffisance des données : Les statistiques des divorces appellent les mêmes réserves que celles formulées à propos des statistiques de l'état civil en général et des statistiques de divortialité en particulier (voir la section 4 des Notes techniques).

Le divorce est, comme le mariage, un acte juridique, et ce fait influe sur la comparabilité internationale des données. Aux fins de la statistique, le divorce est défini par la législation de chaque pays ou zone. La législation sur le divorce varie considérablement d'un pays ou d'une zone à l'autre, ce qui influe aussi sur la fréquence des divorces, laquelle est relativement faible dans les pays ou zones où le jugement de divorce est difficile à obtenir.

Du fait que les divorces sont prononcés par les tribunaux et que les statistiques de la divortialité se rapportent aux jugements de divorce proprement dits, qui prennent effet à la date où ces jugements sont rendus, il se peut que des fluctuations annuelles accusées traduisent le rythme plus ou moins rapide auquel les affaires sont jugées plutôt que l'évolution de la fréquence des divorces. Les méthodes d'exploitation des données peuvent aussi influer sur la comparabilité des statistiques de la divortialité. Dans certains pays ou zones, ces statistiques peuvent comprendre les annulations et/ou les séparations légales. C'est notamment le cas dans les pays ou zones où les divorces sont peu nombreux. Lorsqu'ils sont connus, des renseignements à ce propos sont donnés en note à la fin du tableau.

Étant donné que dans de nombreux pays ou zones, le tribunal ou l'autorité qui a prononcé le divorce est seul habilité à enregistrer cet acte, et, comme l'acte d'enregistrement figure alors sur les registres du tribunal, l'enregistrement suit généralement de peu le jugement. C'est pourquoi la pratique consistant à exploiter les données selon la date de l'enregistrement ne pose généralement pas les graves problèmes de comparabilité auxquels on se heurte dans le cas des statistiques des naissances et des décès.

Comme on l'a brièvement mentionné ci-dessus, la fréquence des divorces est fonction notamment de la facilité relative avec laquelle la législation de chaque pays ou zone permet d'obtenir le divorce. Elle dépend également de la capacité des intéressés à supporter les frais de procédure. Il faut aussi citer l'influence de certaines religions sur la fréquence des divorces. Pour toutes ces raisons, les statistiques de divortialité ne sont pas rigoureusement comparables et ne permettent pas de mesurer exactement la fréquence des dissolutions légales des mariages. De plus, elles ne rendent pas compte des cas de dissolution extrajudiciaire du mariage, comme la séparation.

Dans certains pays ou zones, il n'existe ou il n'existait pas de législation sur le divorce selon l'acception retenue aux fins du tableau 25, si bien que l'on ne dispose pas de données les concernant.

De surcroît, il convient de noter que l'exactitude des taux dépend également de la qualité et des insuffisances des estimations de population qui sont utilisées pour leur calcul. Le problème des erreurs par excès ou par défaut commises lors du dénombrement et, dans une certaine mesure, le problème de l'hétérogénéité des définitions de la population totale ont été examinés à la section 3 des Notes techniques, relative à la population en général ; des explications concernant les différents pays ou zones sont données en note à la fin du tableau 3.

Comme on le verra dans les notes, il n'a pas toujours été possible d'obtenir une correspondance rigoureuse entre le numérateur et le dénominateur pour le calcul des taux. Par exemple, les divorces parmi la population civile et les militaires sont parfois rapportés à la population civile seulement. Cela peut avoir pour effet d'accroître les taux, mais, dans la plupart des cas, il est probable que la différence sera négligeable.

Comme indiqué plus haut, les données concernant certains pays ou zones peuvent comprendre les annulations et/ou les séparations légales. Cette pratique influe sur la comparabilité des taux bruts de divortialité. Par exemple, l'inclusion des annulations dans le numérateur a une influence négligeable, mais l'inclusion des séparations légales peut avoir un effet appréciable.

Il faut souligner que les taux bruts de divortialité, de même que les taux bruts de natalité, de mortalité et de nuptialité, peuvent varier sensiblement selon la structure par âge et par sexe. Comme les taux bruts de nuptialité, ils peuvent également varier en raison de la répartition de la population selon l'état matrimonial. Les taux bruts de divortialité offrent néanmoins un moyen simple de mesurer la fréquence et l'évolution des divorces.

La comparabilité des données selon le lieu de résidence (zone urbaine ou rurale) peut être limitée par les définitions nationales des termes « urbain » et « rural » utilisées pour la mise en tableaux de ces données. En l'absence d'indications contraires, on a supposé que les mêmes définitions avaient servi pour le recensement national de la population et pour l'établissement des statistiques de l'état civil pour chaque pays ou zone. Toutefois, il n'est pas exclu que, pour une zone ou un pays donné, des définitions différentes aient été retenues. Les définitions du terme « urbain » utilisées pour les recensements nationaux de population ont été présentées à la fin des notes techniques du tableau 6 lorsqu'elles étaient connues. Comme on l'a précisé dans les notes techniques relatives au tableau 6, ces définitions varient considérablement d'un pays ou d'une zone à l'autre.

Outre les problèmes de comparabilité, les taux de divortialité classés selon le lieu de résidence (zone urbaine ou rurale) sont également sujets à des distorsions particulières. Si l'on utilise des définitions différentes du terme « urbain » pour classer les faits d'état civil et les données relatives à la population lors du calcul des taux et qu'il en résulte une différence nette entre le numérateur et le dénominateur pour le taux de la population exposée au risque, les taux de divortialité s'en trouveront faussés. La différence entre ces taux pour les zones urbaines et rurales pourra aussi être faussée selon que les faits d'état civil auront été classés d'après le lieu de l'événement ou d'après le lieu de résidence habituel. Ce problème est examiné plus en détail à la section 4.1.4.1 des Notes techniques.

Données publiées antérieurement : Des statistiques concernant les divorces ont déjà été présentées dans des éditions antérieures de l'*Annuaire démographique*. Les plus anciennes, qui portaient sur 1935, ont été publiées dans l'édition de 1951. Pour plus de précisions concernant les années et les sujets pour lesquels des données ont été publiées, se reporter à l'index historique.

NOTE

[1] Pour la définition, voir la section 4.1.1.4 des Notes techniques.

25. Divorces and crude divorce rates by urban/rural residence: 1999 - 2003
Divorces et taux bruts de divortialité selon la résidence, urbaine/rurale: 1999 - 2003

Continent and country or area and urban/rural residence / Continent et pays ou zone et résidence urbaine/rurale	Code[1]	Divorces					Rate - Taux				
		1999	2000	2001	2002	2003	1999	2000	2001	2002	2003
AFRICA — AFRIQUE											
Djibouti[2]											
Total	...	1 207	...	...	...	...	...	...	...	...	...
Egypt - Égypte[3]											
Total	U	73 414	68 991	70 279	68 505	61 000	...	...	...	...	...
Urban	U	39 829	...	...	...	...	...	...	...	...	...
Rural	U	33 585	...	...	...	...	...	...	...	...	...
Ethiopia - Éthiopie											
Total	...	161 390	...	...	...	...	...	...	...	...	...
Urban	...	3 770	...	...	...	...	...	...	...	...	...
Rural	...	157 620	...	...	...	...	...	...	...	...	...
Libyan Arab Jamahiriya - Jamahiriya arabe libyenne[4]											
Total	C	1 095	1 444	1 662	1 740	...	0.22	0.28	0.31	0.32	...
Mauritius - Maurice											
Total	+C	1 150	1 191	1 512	1 291	1 190	0.98	1.00	1.26	1.07	0.97
Réunion											
Total	C	1 057	934	904	940	*844	1.49	1.29	1.23	1.26	*1.10
Saint Helena ex. dep. - Sainte-Hélène sans dép.											
Total	C	-	9	-	...	...	...	...	...	...	...
Seychelles											
Total	+C	102	88	109	112	126	1.27	1.08	1.34	1.34	1.52
Tunisia - Tunisie											
Total	...	8 915	...	...	...	...	...	...	...	...	...
AMERICA, NORTH — AMERIQUE DU NORD											
Anguilla											
Total	+C	...	10	2	8	6	...	...	...	...	...
Aruba											
Total	C	292	329	332	493	...	3.26	3.63	3.61	5.27	...
Bahamas[5]											
Total	C	452	503	...	...	...	1.52	1.66	...	...	...
Belize											
Total	+C	72	43	36	45	...	0.30	0.17	0.14	0.17	...
Bermuda - Bermudes											
Total	C	223	260	150	230	185	3.56	4.13	2.42	3.72	2.97
Canada											
Total	C	70 910	71 144	71 110	70 155	...	2.33	2.31	2.29	2.24	...
Cayman Islands - Îles Caïmanes											
Total	C	64	...	...	...	...	1.64	...	...	...	...
Cuba											
Total	C	40 068	37 937	37 260	35 590	33 851	3.61	3.41	3.34	3.18	3.02
Urban	C	...	...	35 069	32 966	31 130	...	...	4.14	3.89	3.66
Rural	C	...	...	2 191	2 624	2 721	...	...	0.81	0.97	1.00
Dominica - Dominique											
Total	...	61	...	...	...	...	...	...	...	...	...
Dominican Republic - République dominicaine											
Total	C	9 639	...	8 358	...	...	1.15	...	0.96	...	...
El Salvador											
Total	C	3 146	3 430	2 662	4 253	4 220	0.51	0.55	0.42	0.65	0.64
Grenada - Grenade											
Total	C	120	102	*114	...	...	1.19	1.01	*1.13	...	...
Guadeloupe											
Total	C	861	695	904	...	...	2.03	1.62	2.09	...	...
Guatemala											
Total	...	1 373	...	...	...	...	...	...	...	...	...
Jamaica - Jamaïque											
Total	C	1 131	1 106	1 691	1 745	1 600	0.44	0.43	0.65	0.67	0.61
Martinique											
Total	C	670	553	*453	...	...	1.75	1.44	*1.17	...	...
Mexico - Mexique[6]											
Total	+C	49 271	52 358	57 370	60 641	64 248	0.50	0.52	0.56	0.59	0.62

25. Divorces and crude divorce rates by urban/rural residence: 1999 - 2003
Divorces et taux bruts de divortialité selon la résidence, urbaine/rurale: 1999 - 2003 (continued — suite)

Continent and country or area and urban/rural residence / Continent et pays ou zone et résidence urbaine/rurale	Code[1]	Divorces					Rate - Taux				
		1999	2000	2001	2002	2003	1999	2000	2001	2002	2003
AMERICA, NORTH — AMERIQUE DU NORD											
Mexico - Mexique[6]											
Urban	+C	43 498	44 676	50 221	52 589	55 272	0.56	0.59	0.66	0.68	0.70
Rural	+C	2 222	2 413	2 448	2 626	2 908	0.10	0.10	0.10	0.10	0.11
Montserrat											
Total	+...	5	...	...	...	...	...	...	...	...	...
Netherlands Antilles - Antilles néerlandaises											
Total	+C	532	412	420	160	540	2.86	2.30	2.41	0.92	3.02
Nicaragua[7]											
Total	C	2 903	...	...	...	...	0.59	...	...	...	...
Panama[7]											
Total	C	2 135	2 189	2 309	*2 224	...	0.76	0.77	0.80	*0.73	...
Urban	C	1 838	1 856	1 987	*1 944	...	1.17	1.16	...	...	...
Rural	C	297	333	322	*233	...	0.24	0.27	...	...	...
Puerto Rico - Porto Rico											
Total	C	15 550	17 829	13 870	14 578	14 225	4.11	4.67	3.61	3.78	3.67
Saint Lucia - Sainte-Lucie											
Total	C	63	49	76	40	...	0.41	0.31	0.48	0.25	...
Saint Vincent and the Grenadines - Saint Vincent-et-les Grenadines											
Total	C	64	57	61	46	...	0.57	0.51	0.56	0.43	...
Turks Caicos Islands - Îles Turques et Caïques											
Total	C	15	22	24	46	9	...	...	...	2.20	...
AMERICA, SOUTH — AMERIQUE DU SUD											
Brazil - Brésil[8]											
Total	...	121 333	121 417	122 791	...	135 564	...	...	...	...	...
Ecuador - Équateur[9]											
Total	+...	8 968	10 796	11 068	10 987	10 912	...	...	...	...	...
French Guiana - Guyane française											
Total	C	142	147	120	...	...	0.90	0.90	0.71	...	...
Suriname											
Total	C	384	392	567	797	...	0.84	0.85	1.21	1.67	...
Uruguay											
Total	+C	7 002	6 822	7 409	6 761	*14 003	2.13	2.07	2.24	2.04	*4.24
Venezuela[8]											
Total	...	20 544	19 062	16 939	16 627	...	...	...	...	...	...
ASIA — ASIE											
Armenia - Arménie											
Total	C	1 253	1 343	1 776	1 684	*1 820	0.39	0.42	0.55	0.52	*0.57
Urban	C	1 091	1 166	...	...	...	0.52	0.56	...	...	...
Rural	C	162	177	...	...	...	0.14	0.16	...	...	...
Azerbaijan - Azerbaïdjan											
Total	+C	5 013	5 478	5 382	5 738	6 671	0.63	0.68	0.66	0.70	0.81
Urban	+C	4 028	4 332	4 341	4 726	5 555	0.99	1.06	1.05	1.14	1.31
Rural	+C	985	1 146	1 041	1 012	1 116	0.25	0.29	0.26	0.25	0.28
Bahrain - Bahreïn											
Total	...	834	769	801	838	923	...	...	...	...	...
Brunei Darussalam - Brunéi Darussalam											
Total	...	389	369	332	328	349	...	...	...	...	...
China - Chine											
Total	+C	1 202 000	1 213 000	1 250 000	1 177 000	1 330 000	0.96	0.96	0.98	0.92	1.03
China: Hong Kong SAR - Chine: Hong Kong RAS											
Total	...	13 408	13 247	13 425	12 943	13 829	...	...	...	...	...

Continent and country or area and urban/rural residence / Continent et pays ou zone et résidence urbaine/rurale	Code[1]	Divorces					Rate - Taux				
		1999	2000	2001	2002	2003	1999	2000	2001	2002	2003
ASIA — ASIE											
China: Macao SAR - Chine: Macao RAS											
Total	C	283	369	348	385	440	0.66	0.86	0.80	0.88	0.99
Cyprus - Chypre[6,10]											
Total	C	1 193	1 182	1 197	1 320	1 472	1.74	1.70	1.71	1.86	2.04
Urban	C	929	898	...	1 023	1 162	...	...	...	...	...
Rural	C	172	234	...	247	267	...	...	...	...	...
Georgia - Géorgie											
Total	C	1 622	1 854	1 987	1 836	1 825	0.36	0.42	0.45	0.42	0.42
Urban	C	...	1 820	1 964	...	1 802	...	0.78	0.85	...	0.80
Rural	C	...	34	23	...	23	...	0.02	...	...	...
Iran (Islamic Republic of) - Iran (République islamique d')											
Total	C	51 044	53 797	60 559	67 256	72 359	0.81	0.85	0.94	1.03	1.09
Urban	C	45 274	47 936	54 603	61 074	64 213	1.14	1.17	1.29	1.42	1.46
Rural	C	5 770	5 861	5 956	6 182	8 146	0.25	0.26	0.27	0.27	0.36
Israel - Israël[11]											
Total	C	10 683	10 723	11 164	10 939	...	1.74	1.70	1.73	1.67	...
Japan - Japon[12]											
Total	+C	250 529	264 246	285 911	289 836	283 854	1.98	2.08	2.25	2.27	2.22
Urban	+C	208 522	218 935	235 968	238 811	234 304	...	...	...	...	...
Rural	+C	42 007	45 311	49 943	51 025	49 550	...	...	...	...	...
Jordan - Jordanie[13]											
Total	+C	7 885	8 241	9 017	9 032	9 022	1.59	1.66	1.72	1.67	1.67
Kazakhstan											
Total	C	25 583	27 391	29 599	31 236	31 717	1.71	1.84	1.99	2.10	2.13
Urban	C	21 226	22 753	24 227	25 563	26 451	2.53	2.71	2.88	3.03	3.12
Rural	C	4 357	4 638	5 372	5 673	5 266	0.67	0.72	0.83	0.88	0.82
Korea (Republic of) - Corée (République de)[14]											
Total	+C	118 014	119 982	135 014	145 324	167 096	2.53	2.55	2.85	3.05	3.49
Urban	+C	97 577	98 864	110 825	119 788	138 207	...	...	...	...	...
Rural	+C	20 437	21 118	24 189	25 536	28 889	...	...	...	...	...
Kuwait - Koweït											
Total	C	3 412	3 649	3 851	3 891	...	1.62	1.67	1.69	1.72	...
Kyrgyzstan - Kirghizistan											
Total	C	6 287	5 348	5 861	6 104	5 367	1.29	1.09	1.18	1.22	1.07
Urban	C	3 914	3 392	3 756	3 780	3 280	2.28	1.95	2.13	2.14	1.84
Rural	C	2 373	1 956	2 105	2 324	2 087	0.75	0.62	0.66	0.72	0.64
Lebanon - Liban[15]											
Total	+C	3 654	4 282	4 617	4 536	4 793	...	...	...	...	...
Maldives											
Total	...	2 742	2 674	1 529	836	1 135	...	...	...	...	...
Urban	...	1 576	1 492	641	431	530	...	...	...	...	...
Rural	...	1 166	1 182	888	405	605	...	...	...	...	...
Mongolia - Mongolie											
Total	C	941	815	650	688	884	...	0.34	0.27	0.28	0.35
Urban	C	836	748	577	583	813	...	0.54	0.41	0.41	0.56
Rural	C	105	67	73	105	71	...	0.07	0.07	0.10	0.07
Occupied Palestinian Territory - Territoire palestinien occupé											
Total	C	3 761	3 546	3 687	3 045	3 909	1.25	1.13	1.13	0.90	1.11
Qatar											
Total	C	496	615	566	732	790	0.85	1.00	0.87	1.07	1.10
Saudi Arabia - Arabie saoudite											
Total	...	17 528	18 583	16 425	18 765	...	...	...	...	...	...
Singapore - Singapour											
Total	+C	5 084	4 943	4 838	5 538	6 293	0.71	0.68	0.65	0.73	0.83
Syrian Arab Republic - République arabe syrienne[16]											
Total	U	12 453	11 863	13 077	14 314	...	...	...	...	...	...
Tajikistan - Tadjikistan											
Total	C	2 285	2 373	2 266	2 283	2 390	0.38	0.38	0.36	0.35	0.36

25. Divorces and crude divorce rates by urban/rural residence: 1999 - 2003
Divorces et taux bruts de divortialité selon la résidence, urbaine/rurale: 1999 - 2003 (continued — suite)

Continent and country or area and urban/rural residence / Continent et pays ou zone et résidence urbaine/rurale	Code[1]	Divorces					Rate - Taux				
		1999	2000	2001	2002	2003	1999	2000	2001	2002	2003
ASIA — ASIE											
Tajikistan - Tadjikistan											
Urban	C	1 789	1 789	1 820	1 822	1 860	1.11	1.09	1.09	1.07	1.07
Rural	C	496	584	446	461	530	0.11	0.13	0.10	0.10	0.11
Turkey - Turquie											
Total	U	31 540	34 862	50 402	51 096	...	...	...	...	...	...
Urban	U	27 405	29 891	...	...	...	...	...	...	...	...
Rural	U	4 135	4 971	...	...	...	...	...	...	...	...
Uzbekistan - Ouzbékistan											
Total	C	14 608	19 903	15 646	...	...	0.61	0.81	0.63	...	...
Urban	C	10 503	12 169	...	...	...	1.16	1.32	...	...	...
Rural	C	4 105	7 734	...	...	...	0.28	0.50	...	...	...
Viet Nam											
Total	C	...	...	...	*39 829	...	...	...	...	*0.50	...
Urban	C	...	...	...	*14 542	...	...	...	...	*0.73	...
Rural	C	...	...	...	*25 287	...	...	...	...	*0.42	...
EUROPE											
Albania - Albanie											
Total	C	2 114	2 168	2 462	3 494	3 634	0.69	0.71	0.80	1.13	1.17
Austria - Autriche[17]											
Total	C	18 512	19 552	20 582	19 918	19 066	2.32	2.44	2.56	2.46	2.35
Belarus - Bélarus											
Total	C	47 254	43 512	...	37 386	31 679	4.71	4.35	...	3.77	3.21
Urban	C	38 823	...	...	31 066	26 453	5.57	...	...	4.42	3.76
Rural	C	8 431	...	...	6 320	5 226	2.75	...	...	2.19	1.84
Belgium - Belgique[18]											
Total	C	26 423	27 002	29 314	30 020	*31 055	2.58	2.63	2.85	2.96	*3.02
Bosnia and Herzegovina - Bosnie-Herzégovine											
Total	C	1 995	1 929	2 126	2 272	1 918	0.54	0.51	0.56	0.59	0.50
Bulgaria - Bulgarie[19,20]											
Total	C	9 781	10 578	10 275	10 197	12 000	1.19	1.29	1.30	1.30	1.53
Urban	C	...	9 021	8 765	8 613	9 973	...	1.62	1.60	1.58	1.83
Rural	C	...	1 554	1 503	1 584	2 027	...	0.60	0.62	0.66	0.86
Channel Islands: Guernsey - Îles Anglo-Normandes: Guernesey											
Total	C	142	173	...	...	...	2.36	2.86	...	...	...
Croatia - Croatie											
Total	C	3 721	4 419	4 670	4 496	4 935	0.82	1.01	1.05	1.01	1.11
Urban	C	...	3 255	3 445	3 241	3 554	...	...	1.39	...	...
Rural	C	...	1 164	1 225	1 255	1 381	...	...	0.62	...	...
Czech Republic - République tchèque											
Total	C	23 657	29 704	31 586	31 758	32 824	2.30	2.89	3.09	3.11	3.22
Urban	C	19 376	24 454	26 044	26 070	26 569	2.53	3.20	3.45	3.46	3.53
Rural	C	4 281	5 250	5 542	5 688	6 255	1.63	2.00	2.08	2.13	2.34
Denmark - Danemark[21]											
Total	C	13 537	14 381	14 597	15 304	15 763	2.54	2.69	2.72	2.85	2.93
Estonia - Estonie[22]											
Total	C	4 561	4 230	4 312	4 074	3 973	3.16	3.09	3.16	3.00	2.94
Urban	C	...	3 169	...	3 030	2 865	...	3.35	...	3.22	3.06
Rural	C	...	935	...	907	970	...	2.21	...	2.17	2.33
Finland - Finlande[23]											
Total	C	14 030	13 913	13 568	13 336	13 475	2.72	2.69	2.62	2.56	2.58
Urban	C	...	...	9 624	9 561	9 613	...	...	3.03	2.97	2.97
Rural	C	...	...	3 944	3 775	3 862	...	...	1.96	1.90	1.95
France[24]											
Total	C	116 813	114 005	112 631	118 686	127 966	1.99	1.94	1.90	2.00	2.14
Germany - Allemagne											
Total	C	190 590	194 408	197 498	204 214	213 975	2.32	2.37	2.40	2.48	2.59
Gibraltar											
Total	C	89	96	129	150	159	3.28	3.54	...	5.26	5.57

25. Divorces and crude divorce rates by urban/rural residence: 1999 - 2003
Divorces et taux bruts de divortialité selon la résidence, urbaine/rurale: 1999 - 2003 (continued — suite)

Continent and country or area and urban/rural residence / Continent et pays ou zone et résidence urbaine/rurale	Code[1]	Divorces					Rate - Taux				
		1999	2000	2001	2002	2003	1999	2000	2001	2002	2003
EUROPE											
Greece - Grèce											
Total	C	9 629	11 119	*9 500	...	...	0.91	1.11	*0.95	...	...
Hungary - Hongrie[6]											
Total	C	25 605	23 968	24 376	25 493	25 040	2.54	2.39	2.39	2.51	2.47
Urban	C	18 457	17 265	17 547	18 528	18 135	2.84	2.67	2.63	2.80	2.75
Rural	C	6 990	6 564	6 653	6 797	6 770	1.96	1.84	1.89	1.93	1.92
Iceland - Islande[25]											
Total	C	473	545	551	529	*531	1.71	1.94	1.93	1.84	*1.84
Urban	C	440	519	522	504	*508	1.72	2.00	1.98	1.89	*1.90
Rural	C	33	26	29	25	*23	1.55	...	...	...	...
Ireland - Irlande											
Total	C	...	2 623	2 838	2 591	2 970	...	0.69	0.74	0.66	0.74
Isle of Man - Îles de Man											
Total	+C	388	394	353	402	338	...	5.26	4.62	5.21	4.36
Italy - Italie											
Total	C	34 341	37 573	40 051	41 835	41 835	0.60	0.65	0.69	0.73	0.73
Latvia - Lettonie											
Total	C	6 010	6 134	5 740	5 952	4 828	2.51	2.58	2.44	2.55	2.08
Urban	C	4 824	...	4 639	4 769	3 774	2.95	...	2.90	3.01	2.39
Rural	C	1 186	...	1 101	1 183	1 054	1.56	...	1.46	1.57	1.41
Liechtenstein											
Total	C	...	...	82	99	84	...	...	2.47	2.94	2.46
Lithuania - Lituanie											
Total	C	11 390	10 882	11 024	10 579	10 599	3.23	3.11	3.17	3.05	3.07
Urban	C	8 806	8 503	8 598	8 398	8 377	3.72	3.63	3.69	3.62	3.63
Rural	C	2 584	2 379	2 426	2 181	2 222	2.23	2.06	2.11	1.90	1.94
Luxembourg											
Total	C	1 043	1 030	1 028	1 092	1 026	2.42	2.36	2.33	2.45	2.28
Monaco											
Total	C	...	82	...	69	73	...	2.56	...	...	...
Netherlands - Pays-Bas[20]											
Total	C	33 571	34 650	37 104	33 179	31 479	2.12	2.18	2.31	2.05	1.94
Urban	C	...	24 507	...	23 582	22 700	...	2.41	...	2.25	2.14
Rural	C	...	9 708	...	8 999	8 245	...	1.69	...	1.59	1.47
Norway - Norvège											
Total	C	9 124	10 053	10 308	10 450	10 757	2.04	2.24	2.28	2.30	2.36
Poland - Pologne[6]											
Total	C	42 020	42 770	45 243	45 414	48 632	1.09	1.12	1.18	1.19	1.27
Urban	C	35 523	...	38 209	38 254	40 876	1.49	...	1.62	1.62	1.74
Rural	C	6 425	...	7 034	7 072	7 669	0.44	...	0.48	0.48	0.52
Portugal											
Total	C	17 676	19 104	18 851	27 960	22 818	1.74	1.87	1.83	2.70	2.19
Republic of Moldova - République de Moldova											
Total	C	8 913	9 707	10 808	12 698	14 672	2.44	2.67	2.98	3.50	4.06
Urban	C	6 526	6 652	7 309	8 947	10 565	4.26	4.40	4.92	6.03	7.13
Rural	C	2 387	3 055	3 499	3 751	4 107	1.13	1.44	1.63	1.75	1.93
Romania - Roumanie											
Total	C	34 408	30 725	31 135	31 790	33 073	1.53	1.37	1.39	1.46	1.52
Urban	C	...	22 486	22 362	22 675	23 542	...	1.84	1.83	1.95	2.03
Rural	C	...	8 239	8 773	9 115	9 531	...	0.81	0.86	0.89	0.94
Russian Federation - Fédération de Russie											
Total	C	532 533	627 703	763 493	853 647	798 824	3.62	4.28	5.23	5.87	5.53
San Marino - Saint-Marin											
Total	+C	51	38	49	45	45	1.93	1.41	1.77	1.58	1.55
Serbia and Montenegro - Serbie-et-Montenegro[26]											
Total	C	7 211	8 520	8 723	10 488	8 432	0.68	0.80	0.82	1.29	1.03
Urban	C	4 999	5 817	5 949	7 312	5 750	0.91	1.06	1.08	1.59	1.24
Rural	C	2 212	2 703	2 774	3 176	2 682	0.43	0.52	0.54	0.91	0.77
Slovakia - Slovaquie											
Total	C	9 664	9 273	9 817	10 960	10 716	1.79	1.72	1.82	2.04	1.99
Urban	C	7 150	...	7 172	7 782	7 720	2.34	...	2.38	2.58	2.57
Rural	C	2 514	...	2 645	3 178	2 996	1.08	...	1.12	1.34	1.26

Continent and country or area and urban/rural residence / Continent et pays ou zone et résidence urbaine/rurale	Code[1]	Divorces					Rate - Taux				
		1999	2000	2001	2002	2003	1999	2000	2001	2002	2003
EUROPE											
Slovenia - Slovénie											
Total	C	2 074	2 125	2 274	2 457	2 461	1.04	1.07	1.14	1.23	1.23
Urban	C	...	1 392	1 433	1 533	1 533	...	...	...	1.57	1.58
Rural	C	...	733	841	924	928	...	...	...	0.95	0.95
Spain - Espagne											
Total	C	36 900	38 973	28 451	30 104	31 419	0.93	0.97	0.70	0.73	0.75
Sweden - Suède											
Total	C	21 000	21 502	21 022	21 322	21 130	2.37	2.42	2.36	2.39	2.36
Switzerland - Suisse[20]											
Total	C	20 768	10 511	15 778	16 363	16 799	2.91	1.46	2.18	2.25	2.29
Urban	C	15 513	7 841	11 707	12 953	13 177	3.22	1.62	2.39	...	...
Rural	C	5 296	2 670	4 071	3 410	3 622	2.28	1.15	1.74	...	...
The Former Yugoslav Rep. of Macedonia - L'ex-République yougoslave de Macédoine											
Total	C	1 045	1 325	1 448	1 310	*1 405	0.52	0.65	0.71	0.64	*0.69
Ukraine											
Total	C	...	...	181 334	183 538	177 183	...	...	3.74	3.82	3.72
Urban	C	...	...	147 877	145 457	138 053	...	...	4.56	4.52	4.32
Rural	C	...	...	33 457	38 081	39 130	...	...	2.09	2.40	2.50
United Kingdom - Royaume-Uni											
Total	C	158 418	154 273	156 562	160 528	166 536	2.70	2.62	2.65	2.71	2.80
OCEANIA — OCEANIE											
Australia - Australie											
Total	+C	52 566	49 906	55 330	54 004	53 145	2.78	2.61	2.85	2.75	2.67
New Caledonia - Nouvelle-Calédonie											
Total	C	161	159	230	219	246	0.78	0.75	1.07	1.01	1.12
New Zealand - Nouvelle-Zélande											
Total	+C	9 931	9 699	9 683	10 292	*10 491	2.59	2.51	2.50	2.61	*2.62
Niue - Nioué											
Total	...	...	...	...	-	...	...	...	...	...	...
Tonga[27]											
Total	+C	91	113	...	...	...	0.91	1.13	...	...	...

FOOTNOTES - NOTES

Italics: data from civil registers which are incomplete or of unknown completeness. — *Italiques:* données incomplètes ou dont le degré d'exactitude n'est pas connu, provenant des registres de l'état civil.

* Provisional. — Données provisoires.

[1] 'Code' indicates the source of data, as follows:
C - Civil registration, estimated over 90% complete
U - Civil registration, estimated less than 90% complete
+ - Data tabulated by date of registration rather than occurence.
... - Information not available

Le 'Code' indique la source des données, comme suit:
C - Registres de l'état civil considérés complèts à 90 p. 100 au moins.
U - Registres de l'état civil qui ne sont pas considérés complèts à 90 p. 100 au moins.
+ - Données exploitées selon la date de l'enregistrement et non la date de l'événement.
... - Information pas disponible.

[2] Data refer to the district of Djibouti only - Les données portent uniquement sur le district de Djibouti.
[3] Including 'revocable divorces' (among Moslem population), which approximate legal separations. - Y compris les 'divorces révocables' (parmi la population musulmane), qui sont à peu près l'équivalent des séparations légales.
[4] Data refer to Libyan nationals only. - Les données se raportent aux nationaux libyens seulement.
[5] Petitions for divorce entered in court. - Demandes de divorce en instance devant les tribunaux.
[6] Figures for urban and rural areas do not add up to the total, since they do not include the category 'Unknown residence'. - La somme des donées pour la residence urbaine et rurale n'est pas égale au total parce qu'elle n'inclue pas la catégorie 'Residence inconnue'.
[7] Excluding tribal Indian population. - Non compris les Indiens vivant en tribus.
[8] Excluding Indian jungle population. - Non compris les Indiens de la jungle.
[9] Excluding nomadic Indian tribes. - Non compris les tribus d'Indiens nomades.
[10] Data refer to government controlled areas. - Les données se raportent aux zones contrôlées par le Gouvernement.
[11] Including data for East Jerusalem and Israeli residents in certain other territories under occupation by Israeli military forces since June 1967. - Y compris les données pour Jérusalem-Est et les résidents israéliens dans certains autres territoires occupés depuis 1967 par les forces armées israéliennes.
[12] Data refer to Japanese nationals in Japan only. - Les données se raportent aux nationaux japonais au Japon seulement.
[13] Excluding data for Jordanian territory under occupation since June 1967 by Israeli military forces. Excluding foreigners, including registered Palestinian

refugees. - Non compris les données pour le territoire jordanien occupé depuis juin 1967 par les forces armées israéliennes. Non compris les étrangers, mais y compris les réfugiés de Palestine enregistrés.

[14] Excluding alien armed forces, civilian aliens employed by armed forces, and foreign diplomatic personnel and their dependants. - Non compris les militaires étrangers, les civils étrangers employés par les forces armées ni le personnel diplomatique étranger et les membres de leur famille les accompagnant.

[15] Published by the United Nations Economic and Social Commission for Western Asia. - Publié par la Commission économique et sociale des Nations Unies pour l'Asie occidentale.

[16] Excluding nomads. - Non compris les nomades.

[17] Excluding aliens temporarily in the area. - Non compris les étrangers se trouvant temporairement le territoire.

[18] Including divorces among armed forces stationed outside the country and alien armed forces in the area. - Y compris les divorces de militaires nationaux hors du pays et les militaires étrangers en garnison sur le territoire.

[19] Including Bulgarian nationals outside the country, but excluding foreigners in the country. - Y compris les nationaux bulgares à l'étranger, mais non compris les étrangers sur le territoire.

[20] Data for urban and rural areas were not revised, as opposed to data for the whole. - Les données selon la résidence urbaine/rurale n'ont pas été révisées, ce qui a été le cas avec les données pour l'ensemble du pays.

[21] Excluding Faeroe Islands and Greenland. - Non compris les Iles Féroé et Gröenland.

[22] Urban and rural distribution of marriages and divorces is displayed by place of residence of groom/husband. The difference between 'Total' and the sum of urban and rural is due to the unknown place of residence of grooms/husbands and to grooms/husbands living outside Estonia. - Les mariages et divorces sont classés par rapport à la résidence urbaine/rurale de l'époux. La somme des mariages et divorces par résidence urbaine/rurale est différente du 'total' car elle ne tient pas compte ni des résidences inconnues de l'époux ni des mariages et divorces d'époux vivant à l'étranger.

[23] Including nationals temporarily outside the country. - Y compris les nationaux se trouvant temporairement hors du pays.

[24] Rates computed on population including armed forces stationed outside the country, but excluding alien armed forces living in military camps within the country. - Taux calculés sur la base de la population qui comprend les militaires nationaux hors du pays, mais pas les militaires étrangers en garnison sur le territoire.

[25] Data refer to de jure population. - Les données se raportent a la population de droit.

[26] From 2002, without data for Kosovo and Metohia. - Après 2002, sans les donées pour le Kosovo and Metohie.

[27] Including annulments. - Y compris les annulations.

Continent and country or area Continent et pays ou zone	Population estimates (in thousands) - Estimations (en milliers)[1]									
	1994	1995	1996	1997	1998	1999	2000	2001	2002	2003
AFRICA — AFRIQUE										
Algeria - Algérie	27 736	28 271	28 756	29 200	29 617	30 033	30 463	30 914	31 383	31 866
Angola	11 936	12 280	12 597	12 897	13 191	13 501	13 841	14 215	14 619	15 047
Benin - Bénin	5 995	6 201	6 398	6 591	6 783	6 983	7 197	7 425	7 667	7 919
Botswana	1 580	1 616	1 650	1 682	1 711	1 736	1 754	1 766	1 771	1 772
Burkina Faso	9 563	9 832	10 103	10 378	10 662	10 965	11 292	11 645	12 022	12 418
Burundi	6 089	6 159	6 215	6 260	6 308	6 379	6 486	6 633	6 818	7 037
Cameroon - Cameroun	12 977	13 302	13 623	13 937	14 247	14 553	14 856	15 157	15 455	15 748
Cape Verde - Cap-Vert	392	401	411	420	430	440	451	461	472	484
Central African Republic - République centrafricaine ...	3 331	3 414	3 494	3 572	3 645	3 714	3 777	3 835	3 887	3 937
Chad - Tchad	6 825	7 034	7 248	7 469	7 701	7 948	8 216	8 505	8 814	9 133
Comoros - Comores	590	607	625	643	661	680	699	718	738	757
Congo	2 822	2 916	3 014	3 116	3 222	3 329	3 438	3 547	3 657	3 769
Côte d'Ivoire	14 339	14 755	15 174	15 591	15 999	16 383	16 735	17 051	17 336	17 604
Democratic Republic of the Congo - République démocratique du Congo	43 686	44 999	46 123	47 097	48 003	48 959	50 052	51 308	52 706	54 231
Djibouti	597	609	626	647	670	693	715	733	750	765
Egypt - Égypte	60 101	61 225	62 379	63 562	64 774	66 016	67 285	68 585	69 913	71 267
Equatorial Guinea - Guinée équatoriale	388	398	408	418	428	438	449	459	470	481
Eritrea - Érythrée	3 070	3 097	3 148	3 220	3 313	3 426	3 557	3 707	3 875	4 053
Ethiopia - Éthiopie	58 220	60 007	61 748	63 452	65 133	66 818	68 525	70 259	72 015	73 795
Gabon	1 086	1 119	1 151	1 183	1 215	1 245	1 272	1 297	1 320	1 341
Gambia - Gambie	1 078	1 115	1 154	1 194	1 234	1 275	1 316	1 357	1 397	1 438
Ghana	17 280	17 725	18 160	18 586	19 009	19 434	19 867	20 309	20 758	21 212
Guinea - Guinée	7 280	7 525	7 738	7 925	8 095	8 261	8 434	8 617	8 807	9 003
Guinea-Bissau - Guinée-Bissau	1 154	1 189	1 224	1 258	1 292	1 328	1 366	1 406	1 449	1 494
Kenya	26 401	27 226	27 942	28 643	29 331	30 011	30 689	31 364	32 040	32 734
Lesotho	1 672	1 692	1 714	1 735	1 756	1 774	1 788	1 796	1 800	1 800
Liberia - Libéria	2 067	2 141	2 283	2 480	2 704	2 909	3 065	3 161	3 206	3 222
Libyan Arab Jamahiriya - Jamahiriya arabe libyenne	4 713	4 808	4 904	5 001	5 101	5 203	5 306	5 412	5 519	5 629
Madagascar	13 536	13 946	14 371	14 812	15 266	15 727	16 195	16 667	17 144	17 626
Malawi	9 971	10 111	10 322	10 590	10 897	11 212	11 512	11 796	12 070	12 339
Mali	9 878	10 147	10 424	10 710	11 007	11 318	11 647	11 994	12 358	12 736
Mauritania - Mauritanie	2 241	2 300	2 362	2 428	2 496	2 569	2 645	2 724	2 807	2 893
Mauritius - Maurice[2]	1 111	1 125	1 138	1 150	1 162	1 174	1 186	1 198	1 210	1 221
Morocco - Maroc	26 553	27 004	27 452	27 898	28 343	28 787	29 231	29 675	30 120	30 568
Mozambique	15 333	15 854	16 321	16 747	17 143	17 526	17 911	18 296	18 676	19 052
Namibia - Namibie	1 601	1 652	1 703	1 755	1 806	1 853	1 894	1 930	1 960	1 986
Niger	9 609	9 929	10 268	10 624	10 997	11 384	11 782	12 193	12 617	13 052
Nigeria - Nigéria	101 196	103 914	106 639	109 371	112 109	114 854	117 608	120 368	123 134	125 912
Réunion	652	664	676	688	700	712	724	737	749	761
Rwanda	5 530	5 439	5 674	6 180	6 845	7 500	8 025	8 383	8 614	8 758
Saint Helena - Sainte-Hélène[3]	5	5	5	5	5	5	5	5	5	5
Sao Tome and Principe - Sao Tomé-et-Principe	125	128	130	132	134	137	140	143	146	149
Senegal - Sénégal	8 886	9 120	9 357	9 598	9 843	10 091	10 343	10 598	10 856	11 119
Seychelles	75	75	76	76	76	77	77	78	78	79
Sierra Leone	4 123	4 137	4 167	4 212	4 279	4 376	4 509	4 683	4 892	5 119
Somalia - Somalie	6 332	6 312	6 359	6 466	6 623	6 809	7 012	7 228	7 461	7 708
South Africa - Afrique du Sud	40 923	41 894	42 787	43 607	44 350	45 017	45 610	46 126	46 561	46 919
Sudan - Soudan	28 657	29 352	30 058	30 778	31 499	32 210	32 902	33 568	34 213	34 856
Swaziland	938	953	969	985	1 000	1 013	1 023	1 030	1 033	1 035
Togo	4 382	4 512	4 663	4 832	5 011	5 191	5 364	5 527	5 684	5 836
Tunisia - Tunisie	8 840	8 977	9 105	9 227	9 342	9 453	9 563	9 673	9 781	9 888
Uganda - Ouganda	20 257	20 892	21 533	22 183	22 853	23 558	24 309	25 111	25 965	26 869
United Republic of Tanzania - République Unie de Tanzanie	30 029	30 930	31 771	32 560	33 309	34 038	34 763	35 486	36 205	36 919
Western Sahara - Sahara occidental	251	259	268	276	284	292	300	307	313	321
Zambia - Zambie	9 325	9 559	9 795	10 030	10 262	10 487	10 702	10 906	11 102	11 291

Annex I: United Nations Projections - Annual interpolated mid-year population, estimates 1994-2003
Annexe I: Projections de la population - Population au milieu de l'année interpolée, estimations 1994 - 2003
(continued — suite)

Continent and country or area Continent et pays ou zone	Population estimates (in thousands) - Estimations (en milliers)[1]									
	1994	1995	1996	1997	1998	1999	2000	2001	2002	2003
AFRICA — AFRIQUE										
Zimbabwe	11 609	11 820	12 012	12 185	12 339	12 476	12 595	12 698	12 786	12 863
AMERICA, NORTH — AMERIQUE DU NORD										
Anguilla	10	10	11	11	11	11	11	11	12	12
Antigua and Barbuda - Antigua-et-Barbuda	68	70	71	72	74	75	76	78	79	80
Aruba	81	84	87	88	90	91	92	94	95	97
Bahamas	274	279	284	288	293	297	301	306	310	314
Barbados - Barbade	261	262	263	264	265	265	266	267	268	268
Belize	208	214	220	225	231	237	242	248	253	259
Bermuda - Bermudes	61	61	62	62	62	63	63	63	63	64
British Virgin Islands - Îles Vierges britanniques	18	18	19	19	20	20	21	21	21	21
Canada	29 007	29 302	29 586	29 858	30 127	30 401	30 689	30 993	31 312	31 636
Cayman Islands - Îles Caïmanes	31	33	34	36	37	38	40	41	42	43
Costa Rica	3 390	3 475	3 563	3 655	3 748	3 840	3 929	4 014	4 097	4 176
Cuba	10 809	10 867	10 924	10 980	11 033	11 082	11 125	11 161	11 193	11 220
Dominica - Dominique	74	75	76	76	77	77	78	78	78	78
Dominican Republic - République dominicaine	7 557	7 672	7 788	7 905	8 024	8 143	8 265	8 388	8 514	8 641
El Salvador	5 548	5 669	5 790	5 912	6 035	6 158	6 280	6 402	6 523	6 643
Greenland - Groenland	56	56	56	56	56	56	56	56	56	57
Grenada - Grenade	99	99	100	100	101	101	102	102	102	102
Guadeloupe	406	409	413	417	421	426	430	434	438	441
Guatemala	9 747	9 970	10 197	10 428	10 665	10 910	11 166	11 434	11 711	11 998
Haiti - Haïti	7 291	7 391	7 496	7 603	7 713	7 826	7 939	8 053	8 170	8 287
Honduras	5 469	5 625	5 783	5 944	6 105	6 265	6 424	6 582	6 738	6 893
Jamaica - Jamaïque	2 460	2 484	2 507	2 528	2 548	2 567	2 585	2 600	2 614	2 627
Martinique	373	375	378	380	382	384	386	388	390	392
Mexico - Mexique	90 915	92 523	94 096	95 636	97 144	98 627	100 088	101 528	102 946	104 337
Montserrat	11	10	9	8	6	5	4	3	4	4
Netherlands Antilles - Antilles néerlandaises	189	187	184	182	179	177	176	176	177	179
Nicaragua	4 374	4 477	4 576	4 671	4 766	4 861	4 959	5 059	5 162	5 268
Panama	2 617	2 670	2 725	2 781	2 837	2 893	2 950	3 006	3 063	3 119
Puerto Rico - Porto Rico	3 664	3 696	3 727	3 756	3 783	3 809	3 835	3 860	3 885	3 909
Saint Kitts and Nevis - Saint-Kitts-et-Nevis	40	40	40	40	40	40	40	41	41	42
Saint Lucia - Sainte-Lucie	146	148	149	151	152	153	154	156	157	158
Saint Pierre and Miquelon - Saint Pierre-et-Miquelon	6	6	6	6	6	6	6	6	6	6
Saint Vincent and the Grenadines - Saint Vincent-et-les Grenadines ..	112	113	114	114	115	115	116	117	117	118
Trinidad and Tobago - Trinité-et-Tobago	1 251	1 259	1 266	1 271	1 276	1 280	1 285	1 289	1 293	1 297
Turks Caicos Islands - Îles Turques et Caïques	15	15	16	17	17	18	19	21	22	24
United States - États-Unis	266 711	269 603	272 511	275 434	278 358	281 269	284 154	287 004	289 821	292 617
United States Virgin Islands - Îles Vierges américaines	106	107	108	109	110	110	111	111	112	112
AMERICA, SOUTH — AMERIQUE DU SUD										
Argentina - Argentine	34 396	34 835	35 266	35 689	36 102	36 504	36 896	37 274	37 642	38 005
Bolivia - Bolivie	7 315	7 482	7 648	7 813	7 980	8 147	8 317	8 488	8 661	8 835
Brazil - Brésil	158 978	161 376	163 819	166 301	168 812	171 335	173 858	176 377	178 895	181 408
Chile - Chili	14 161	14 395	14 617	14 828	15 029	15 223	15 412	15 596	15 776	15 951
Colombia - Colombie	37 819	38 542	39 262	39 981	40 697	41 410	42 120	42 826	43 528	44 224
Ecuador - Équateur	11 188	11 396	11 592	11 777	11 954	12 129	12 306	12 486	12 668	12 853
Falkland Islands (Malvinas) - Îles Falkland (Malvinas)	2	2	3	3	3	3	3	3	3	3

Annex I: United Nations Projections - Annual interpolated mid-year population, estimates 1994-2003
Annexe I: Projections de la population - Population au milieu de l'année interpolée, estimations 1994 - 2003
(continued — suite)

Continent and country or area Continent et pays ou zone	Population estimates (in thousands) - Estimations (en milliers)[1]									
	1994	1995	1996	1997	1998	1999	2000	2001	2002	2003
AMERICA, SOUTH — AMERIQUE DU SUD										
French Guiana - Guyane française	134	139	143	149	154	159	164	169	174	178
Guyana	730	732	734	737	739	741	744	746	747	749
Paraguay	4 705	4 829	4 954	5 080	5 208	5 338	5 470	5 604	5 740	5 878
Peru - Pérou	23 421	23 837	24 259	24 685	25 112	25 536	25 952	26 361	26 763	27 162
Suriname	412	415	418	422	426	430	434	437	441	444
Uruguay	3 195	3 218	3 242	3 267	3 292	3 317	3 342	3 366	3 391	3 415
Venezuela	21 620	22 087	22 554	23 020	23 486	23 952	24 418	24 884	25 350	25 816
ASIA — ASIE										
Afghanistan	19 566	20 669	21 471	22 031	22 476	22 999	23 735	24 724	25 912	27 231
Armenia - Arménie	3 293	3 227	3 178	3 143	3 119	3 100	3 082	3 065	3 050	3 037
Azerbaijan - Azerbaïdjan	7 689	7 791	7 880	7 957	8 024	8 085	8 143	8 198	8 250	8 302
Bahrain - Bahreïn	566	584	603	622	640	657	672	685	696	706
Bangladesh	113 946	116 455	118 946	121 426	123 905	126 398	128 916	131 461	134 029	136 615
Bhutan - Bhoutan	1 710	1 733	1 765	1 803	1 847	1 893	1 938	1 982	2 026	2 071
Brunei Darussalam - Brunéi Darussalam	287	295	303	310	318	326	333	341	349	358
Cambodia - Cambodge	11 059	11 368	11 662	11 943	12 215	12 481	12 744	13 007	13 268	13 531
China - Chine[4]	1 207 601	1 219 331	1 230 978	1 242 413	1 253 510	1 264 075	1 273 979	1 283 202	1 291 841	1 300 039
China - Hong Kong SAR - Chine - Hong Kong RAS[5]	6 085	6 187	6 283	6 375	6 464	6 551	6 637	6 721	6 803	6 884
China - Macao SAR - Chine - Macao RAS[6]	406	413	420	426	433	439	444	448	451	454
Cyprus - Chypre	720	731	742	753	765	776	786	797	807	816
Timor-Leste	846	848	830	797	758	730	722	738	775	827
Georgia - Géorgie	5 126	5 033	4 954	4 886	4 828	4 774	4 720	4 666	4 614	4 565
India - Inde	918 292	935 572	952 828	970 041	987 177	1 004 200	1 021 084	1 037 809	1 054 373	1 070 800
Indonesia - Indonésie	192 875	195 649	198 388	201 094	203 783	206 472	209 174	211 893	214 622	217 354
Iran (Islamic Republic of) - Iran (République islamique d')	61 359	62 324	63 239	64 105	64 918	65 671	66 365	66 998	67 587	68 172
Iraq	20 967	21 632	22 301	22 977	23 662	24 360	25 075	25 806	26 550	27 303
Israel - Israël	5 200	5 374	5 533	5 680	5 818	5 951	6 084	6 216	6 346	6 474
Japan - Japon	125 121	125 472	125 812	126 142	126 458	126 756	127 034	127 290	127 525	127 736
Jordan - Jordanie	4 094	4 288	4 453	4 594	4 718	4 841	4 972	5 113	5 261	5 412
Kazakhstan	16 048	15 866	15 682	15 495	15 317	15 161	15 033	14 942	14 885	14 855
Korea (Dem. People's Republic of) - Corée (Rép. populaire dém. de)	20 689	20 918	21 134	21 336	21 525	21 700	21 862	22 011	22 147	22 271
Korea (Republic of) - Corée (République de)	44 592	45 007	45 405	45 788	46 149	46 481	46 779	47 040	47 265	47 463
Kuwait - Koweït	1 739	1 696	1 727	1 820	1 955	2 099	2 230	2 340	2 438	2 525
Kyrgyzstan - Kirghizistan	4 542	4 588	4 648	4 720	4 799	4 878	4 952	5 020	5 084	5 144
Lao People's Democratic Republic - République démocratique populaire lao	4 572	4 686	4 801	4 917	5 036	5 156	5 279	5 404	5 531	5 661
Lebanon - Liban	3 091	3 177	3 243	3 292	3 330	3 364	3 398	3 434	3 469	3 504
Malaysia - Malaisie	19 839	20 362	20 892	21 427	21 961	22 486	22 997	23 492	23 971	24 437
Maldives	244	252	259	267	275	282	290	298	306	313
Mongolia - Mongolie	2 363	2 389	2 413	2 434	2 454	2 474	2 497	2 523	2 552	2 582
Myanmar	43 775	44 500	45 193	45 857	46 496	47 117	47 724	48 319	48 900	49 463
Nepal - Népal	21 145	21 682	22 226	22 776	23 329	23 881	24 431	24 975	25 515	26 053
Oman	2 113	2 177	2 239	2 299	2 354	2 402	2 442	2 471	2 493	2 511
Pakistan	123 105	126 075	129 247	132 581	135 998	139 381	142 648	145 772	148 791	151 768
Philippines	66 921	68 396	69 871	71 346	72 820	74 293	75 766	77 237	78 705	80 166
Qatar	515	526	536	547	560	579	606	642	686	733
Saudi Arabia - Arabie saoudite	18 222	18 682	19 187	19 728	20 299	20 888	21 484	22 088	22 704	23 326
Singapore - Singapour	3 374	3 478	3 588	3 703	3 817	3 923	4 017	4 097	4 163	4 220
Sri Lanka	18 669	18 872	19 074	19 272	19 467	19 659	19 848	20 033	20 215	20 394
Syrian Arab Republic - République arabe syrienne	14 367	14 755	15 151	15 556	15 968	16 387	16 813	17 245	17 683	18 129

Annex I: United Nations Projections - Annual interpolated mid-year population, estimates 1994-2003
Annexe I: Projections de la population - Population au milieu de l'année interpolée, estimations 1994 - 2003
(continued — suite)

Continent and country or area / Continent et pays ou zone	Population estimates (in thousands) - Estimations (en milliers)[1]									
	1994	1995	1996	1997	1998	1999	2000	2001	2002	2003
ASIA — ASIE										
Tajikistan - Tadjikistan	5 688	5 770	5 851	5 932	6 011	6 087	6 159	6 227	6 293	6 360
Thailand - Thaïlande	57 642	58 336	59 001	59 638	60 252	60 851	61 438	62 017	62 586	63 145
Turkey - Turquie	61 522	62 620	63 742	64 883	66 026	67 149	68 234	69 275	70 277	71 252
Turkmenistan - Turkménistan	4 101	4 193	4 270	4 334	4 390	4 445	4 502	4 564	4 630	4 698
United Arab Emirates - Émirats arabes unis	2 307	2 435	2 569	2 709	2 863	3 040	3 247	3 488	3 756	4 031
Uzbekistan - Ouzbékistan	22 478	22 918	23 320	23 688	24 034	24 375	24 724	25 083	25 452	25 828
Viet Nam	71 878	73 163	74 362	75 481	76 548	77 602	78 671	79 765	80 877	82 000
Occupied Palestinian Territory - Territoire palestinien occupé	2 511	2 610	2 713	2 820	2 930	3 040	3 150	3 259	3 367	3 476
Yemen - Yémen	14 600	15 219	15 796	16 339	16 863	17 390	17 937	18 506	19 094	19 702
EUROPE										
Albania - Albanie	3 173	3 133	3 104	3 083	3 070	3 063	3 062	3 066	3 078	3 094
Andorra - Andorre	62	64	65	66	66	66	66	66	66	67
Austria - Autriche	7 998	8 047	8 076	8 088	8 090	8 090	8 096	8 110	8 128	8 150
Belarus - Bélarus	10 273	10 249	10 217	10 177	10 131	10 081	10 029	9 975	9 921	9 866
Belgium - Belgique	10 101	10 137	10 172	10 207	10 241	10 274	10 304	10 331	10 356	10 379
Bosnia and Herzegovina - Bosnie-Herzégovine	3 531	3 420	3 412	3 489	3 618	3 750	3 847	3 900	3 921	3 918
Bulgaria - Bulgarie	8 377	8 297	8 225	8 162	8 105	8 051	7 997	7 942	7 888	7 834
Channel Islands - Îles Anglo-Normandes	144	144	144	145	146	146	147	147	148	148
Croatia - Croatie	4 660	4 669	4 654	4 618	4 572	4 531	4 505	4 498	4 506	4 522
Czech Republic - République tchèque	10 331	10 331	10 324	10 312	10 297	10 281	10 267	10 256	10 246	10 238
Denmark - Danemark	5 207	5 228	5 250	5 273	5 295	5 318	5 340	5 360	5 379	5 397
Estonia - Estonie	1 476	1 447	1 424	1 405	1 390	1 378	1 367	1 357	1 348	1 341
Faeroe Islands - Îles Féroé ..	45	44	44	44	45	45	46	46	46	46
Finland - Finlande	5 086	5 108	5 125	5 140	5 152	5 164	5 177	5 191	5 205	5 220
France	57 937	58 203	58 441	58 655	58 857	59 061	59 278	59 511	59 756	60 008
Germany - Allemagne	81 312	81 661	81 917	82 086	82 191	82 268	82 344	82 427	82 507	82 583
Gibraltar	27	27	27	27	28	28	28	28	28	28
Greece - Grèce	10 561	10 657	10 741	10 813	10 875	10 928	10 975	11 015	11 048	11 075
Holy See - Saint-Siège[7]	1	1	1	1	1	1	1	1	1	1
Hungary - Hongrie	10 336	10 329	10 316	10 297	10 275	10 250	10 226	10 201	10 176	10 150
Iceland - Islande	265	267	270	273	276	279	281	284	287	289
Ireland - Irlande	3 582	3 609	3 638	3 670	3 706	3 749	3 801	3 863	3 933	4 007
Isle of Man - Îles de Man	72	72	73	74	75	76	77	77	77	77
Italy - Italie	57 184	57 301	57 401	57 486	57 562	57 637	57 715	57 797	57 880	57 961
Latvia - Lettonie	2 544	2 498	2 461	2 432	2 410	2 391	2 373	2 357	2 343	2 330
Liechtenstein	31	31	31	32	32	32	33	33	34	34
Lithuania - Lituanie	3 653	3 628	3 602	3 575	3 548	3 522	3 500	3 481	3 467	3 455
Luxembourg	399	405	411	417	423	429	435	441	447	453
Malta - Malte	374	378	381	384	387	389	392	394	396	398
Monaco	31	32	32	32	33	33	33	34	34	34
Netherlands - Pays-Bas	15 361	15 459	15 553	15 642	15 728	15 813	15 898	15 982	16 066	16 148
Norway - Norvège	4 333	4 359	4 387	4 416	4 446	4 475	4 502	4 528	4 552	4 575
Poland - Pologne	38 535	38 595	38 635	38 656	38 663	38 660	38 649	38 633	38 612	38 587
Portugal	10 009	10 030	10 058	10 092	10 132	10 177	10 225	10 277	10 331	10 386
Republic of Moldova - République de Moldova	4 351	4 339	4 327	4 314	4 302	4 289	4 275	4 260	4 246	4 231
Romania - Roumanie	22 816	22 681	22 555	22 435	22 323	22 217	22 117	22 025	21 942	21 866
Russian Federation - Fédération de Russie	148 440	148 189	147 947	147 691	147 398	147 030	146 560	145 985	145 327	144 618
San Marino - Saint-Marin	25	26	26	26	26	27	27	27	27	28
Serbia and Montenegro - Serbie-et-Montenegro	10 494	10 548	10 577	10 583	10 574	10 559	10 545	10 534	10 525	10 517
Slovakia - Slovaquie	5 347	5 364	5 377	5 386	5 393	5 397	5 400	5 402	5 402	5 402
Slovenia - Slovénie	1 959	1 964	1 967	1 968	1 968	1 967	1 967	1 967	1 967	1 967
Spain - Espagne	39 808	39 921	40 021	40 117	40 238	40 430	40 717	41 117	41 610	42 144
Sweden - Suède	8 789	8 827	8 850	8 859	8 861	8 865	8 877	8 901	8 933	8 970
Switzerland - Suisse	6 972	7 003	7 037	7 072	7 107	7 139	7 167	7 191	7 210	7 226

Annex I: United Nations Projections - Annual interpolated mid-year population, estimates 1994-2003
Annexe I: Projections de la population - Population au milieu de l'année interpolée, estimations 1994 - 2003
(continued — suite)

Continent and country or area / Continent et pays ou zone	Population estimates (in thousands) - Estimations (en milliers)[1]									
	1994	1995	1996	1997	1998	1999	2000	2001	2002	2003
EUROPE										
The Former Yugoslav Rep. of Macedonia - L'ex-République yougoslave de Macédoine ..	1 954	1 963	1 973	1 983	1 993	2 002	2 010	2 016	2 022	2 026
Ukraine	51 776	51 531	51 180	50 733	50 215	49 667	49 116	48 573	48 036	47 508
United Kingdom - Royaume-Uni	57 479	57 670	57 865	58 064	58 264	58 466	58 670	58 874	59 080	59 282
OCEANIA — OCEANIE										
American Samoa - Samoas américaines	52	53	54	55	56	57	58	59	60	62
Australia - Australie[8]	17 726	17 941	18 162	18 388	18 618	18 846	19 071	19 293	19 512	19 728
Cook Islands - Îles Cook	20	20	20	20	19	19	19	19	18	18
Fiji - Fidji	758	768	777	786	794	803	811	819	826	834
French Polynesia - Polynésie française	212	216	220	224	228	232	236	240	244	249
Guam	143	146	148	149	151	153	155	158	161	164
Kiribati	79	80	82	84	86	88	90	92	94	95
Marshall Islands - Îles Marshall	51	51	51	51	51	51	52	53	55	57
Micronesia, Federated States of - Micronésie, États Fédérés de La	106	107	108	108	108	107	107	107	108	109
Nauru	10	11	11	11	12	12	12	13	13	13
New Caledonia - Nouvelle-Calédonie	189	193	198	202	206	211	215	220	224	228
New Zealand - Nouvelle-Zélande	3 613	3 658	3 695	3 727	3 755	3 784	3 818	3 857	3 901	3 946
Niue - Nioué	2	2	2	2	2	2	2	2	2	1
Northern Mariana Islands - Îles Mariannes septentrionales	55	57	60	62	65	67	70	72	74	77
Palau - Palaos	17	17	18	18	19	19	19	20	20	20
Papua New Guinea - Papouasie-Nouvelle-Guin- ée	4 567	4 687	4 809	4 931	5 055	5 177	5 299	5 419	5 538	5 656
Pitcairn	-	-	-	-	-	-	-	-	-	-
Samoa	167	168	170	172	174	176	177	179	181	182
Solomon Islands - Îles Salomon	354	364	374	385	396	407	419	430	442	454
Tokelau - Tokélaou	1	1	1	1	1	1	1	1	1	1
Tonga	96	97	98	98	99	100	100	101	101	102
Tuvalu	10	10	10	10	10	10	10	10	10	10
Vanuatu	168	172	176	180	184	188	191	195	199	203
Wallis and Futuna Islands - Îles Wallis et Futuna	14	14	14	15	15	15	15	15	15	15

FOOTNOTES - NOTES

[1] For 1994-2003 all data refer to annual interpolated estimates of mid-year population. Both the estimates and the projections are produced by the Population Division of the Department for Economic and Social Affairs of the UN Secretariat and published in *World Population Prospects - The 2004 Revision,* United Nations publication, ST/ESA/SER.A/244, Volume I, New York, 2005. — Les données pour 1994-2003 sont des estimations de population au milieu de l'année interpolée et ceux pour 2001 sont des projections de la population au milieu de l'année de variante moyenne. Toutes ces données sont produites par la Division pour la population de Département des affaires économiques et sociales du Secrétariat de l'Organisation des Nations Unies et ont été publiées dans *World Population Prospects - The 2004 Revision,* United Nations publication, ST/ESA/SER.A/244, Volume I, New York, 2005.

[2] Including Agalega, Rodrigues and Saint Brandon. — Y compris Agalega, Rodrigues et Saint Brandon.

[3] Including Ascension and Tristan da Cunha. — Y compris Ascension et Tristan da Cunha.

[4] For statistical purposes, the data for China do not include Hong Kong and Macao Special Administrative Regions (SAR) of China. — A des fins statistiques, les données pour la Chine ne comprennent pas les Régions Administratives Spéciales (SAR) de Hong Kong et Macao.

[5] As of 1 July 1997, Hong Kong became a Special Administrative Region (SAR) of China. — A partir du 1 juillet 1997, Hong Kong est devenue une Région Administrative Spéciale (SAR) de la Chine.

[6] As of 20 December 1999, Macao became a Special Administrative Region (SAR) of China. — A partir du 20 décembre 1999, Macao est devenue une Région Administrative Spéciale (SAR) de la Chine.

[7] Refers to the Vatican City State. — Ce rapport à l'état du Vatican.

[8] Including Christmas Island, Cocos (Keeling) Islands and Norfolk Island. — Y compris Christmas Island, Cocos (Keeling) Islands et Norfolk Island.

Annex II: United Nations Medium Variant Population Projections - Vital statistics summary and expectation of life at birth: 2000 - 2005

Annexe II: Projections de la population de variante moyenne de l'ONU - Aperçu des statistiques de l'état civil et espérance de vie à la naissance: 2000 - 2005

Continent, country or area Continent, pays ou zone	Crude birth rate — Taux bruts de natalité[1]	Crude death rate — Taux bruts de mortalité[1]	Infant mortality rate — Décès d'enfants de moins d'un an[1]	Expectation of life at birth — Espérance de vie à la naissance[1]		Total fertilty rate— Indice synthétique de fécondité[1]	Natural increase — Accroissement naturel[1]
				Male — Masculin	Female — Féminin		
AFRICA — AFRIQUE							
Algeria - Algérie	20.8	5.0	37.4	69.7	72.2	2.53	1.57
Angola	48.5	22.3	138.8	39.2	42.2	6.75	2.63
Benin - Bénin	42.1	12.9	105.1	53.0	54.5	5.87	2.92
Botswana	26.9	25.0	51.0	36.0	37.1	3.20	0.19
Burkina Faso	47.1	17.2	121.4	46.7	48.1	6.67	3.00
Burundi	43.7	18.9	105.9	42.5	44.4	6.80	2.48
Cameroon - Cameroun	35.9	17.2	94.3	45.1	46.5	4.65	1.86
Cape Verde - Cap-Vert	30.9	5.3	29.8	66.8	73.0	3.77	2.56
Central African Republic - République centrafricaine	37.8	22.1	98.2	38.5	40.3	4.96	1.56
Chad - Tchad	48.2	20.1	116.0	42.5	44.8	6.65	2.81
Comoros - Comores	36.5	7.4	57.7	60.9	65.1	4.89	2.91
Congo	44.1	13.2	72.3	50.6	53.1	6.29	3.09
Côte d'Ivoire	37.5	17.0	118.3	45.2	46.8	5.06	2.05
Democratic Republic of the Congo - République démocratique du Congo	49.5	20.4	118.5	42.1	44.1	6.70	2.91
Djibouti	36.2	12.7	93.2	51.4	53.9	5.09	2.34
Egypt - Égypte	26.3	6.0	36.7	67.5	71.8	3.29	2.04
Equatorial Guinea - Guinée équatoriale	42.9	20.0	102.0	42.8	44.2	5.89	2.30
Eritrea - Érythrée	39.9	11.6	64.6	51.5	55.4	5.53	2.84
Ethiopia - Éthiopie	41.1	16.3	99.5	46.5	48.6	5.87	2.48
Gabon	31.6	12.5	57.9	53.8	55.4	4.02	1.91
Gambia - Gambie	36.0	12.0	77.0	54.0	56.9	4.75	2.40
Ghana	32.1	10.8	62.3	56.2	57.2	4.39	2.13
Guinea - Guinée	42.2	13.8	105.5	53.2	54.0	5.92	2.84
Guinea-Bissau - Guinée-Bissau	49.8	20.0	119.7	43.1	46.2	7.10	2.97
Kenya	38.8	15.5	67.8	47.9	46.2	5.00	2.33
Lesotho	28.5	23.6	66.5	34.9	38.1	3.65	0.48
Liberia - Libéria	49.8	20.7	141.9	41.4	43.5	6.80	2.91
Libyan Arab Jamahiriya - Jamahiriya arabe libyenne	23.3	4.0	19.2	71.4	76.1	3.03	1.93
Madagascar	39.7	12.0	78.8	54.0	56.7	5.40	2.77
Malawi	44.6	21.8	110.8	39.7	39.6	6.10	2.28
Mali	49.7	17.8	133.5	47.1	48.4	6.92	3.19
Mauritania - Mauritanie	41.8	14.2	96.7	50.9	54.1	5.79	2.76
Mauritius - Maurice[2]	16.4	6.7	15.0	68.7	75.6	1.97	0.97
Morocco - Maroc	23.3	5.8	38.1	67.4	71.7	2.76	1.74
Mozambique	40.4	20.2	100.9	41.0	42.8	5.51	2.02
Namibia - Namibie	29.1	14.6	43.8	47.7	49.4	3.95	1.45
Niger	55.1	21.2	152.7	44.2	44.3	7.91	3.40
Nigeria - Nigéria	42.0	19.4	114.4	43.1	43.5	5.85	2.26
Réunion	20.1	5.4	7.7	71.3	79.6	2.49	1.48
Rwanda	41.0	18.3	115.5	41.9	45.3	5.70	2.27
Sao Tome and Principe - Sao Tomé-et-Principe	34.2	8.8	82.4	61.9	63.8	4.06	2.55
Senegal - Sénégal	37.4	11.7	83.5	54.4	56.8	5.05	2.57
Sierra Leone	46.7	23.7	165.1	39.3	42.0	6.50	2.31
Somalia - Somalie	45.8	18.4	126.1	45.0	47.3	6.43	2.75
South Africa - Afrique du Sud	23.8	16.2	42.7	47.1	51.0	2.80	0.76
Sudan - Soudan	33.5	11.2	72.2	54.9	57.9	4.45	2.23
Swaziland	29.6	26.7	73.1	32.5	33.4	3.95	0.30
Togo	39.5	12.3	92.5	52.3	56.2	5.37	2.73
Tunisia - Tunisie	16.8	5.4	22.2	71.1	75.3	2.00	1.14
Uganda - Ouganda	50.2	16.1	81.2	46.5	47.1	7.10	3.41
United Republic of Tanzania - République Unie de Tanzanie	38.1	16.7	104.4	45.6	46.4	5.04	2.14
Western Sahara - Sahara occidental	27.5	7.7	53.3	62.2	65.7	3.90	1.99
Zambia - Zambie	41.3	22.8	95.1	37.9	36.9	5.65	1.84
Zimbabwe	30.0	22.7	62.3	37.5	36.9	3.56	0.73

Annex II: United Nations Medium Variant Population Projections - Vital statistics summary and expectation of life at birth:
2000 - 2005
Annexe II: Projections de la population de variante moyenne de l'ONU - Aperçu des statistiques de l'état civil et espérance
de vie à la naissance: 2000 - 2005

(continued — suite)

Continent, country or area / Continent, pays ou zone	Crude birth rate — Taux bruts de natalité[1]	Crude death rate — Taux bruts de mortalité[1]	Infant mortality rate — Décès d'enfants de moins d'un an[1]	Expectation of life at birth — Espérance de vie à la naissance[1]		Total fertilty rate— Indice synthétique de fécondité[1]	Natural increase — Accroissement naturel[1]
				Male — Masculin	Female — Féminin		
AMERICA, NORTH — AMERIQUE DU NORD							
Bahamas	19.8	7.2	13.8	66.2	72.7	2.30	1.26
Barbados - Barbade	12.2	8.7	10.8	71.1	78.3	1.50	0.35
Belize	27.3	5.1	30.5	69.5	74.5	3.20	2.22
Canada	10.5	7.2	5.1	77.3	82.4	1.51	0.34
Costa Rica	19.1	3.9	10.5	75.8	80.6	2.28	1.52
Cuba	12.4	7.0	6.1	75.3	79.1	1.61	0.54
Dominican Republic - République dominicaine	24.5	6.5	34.6	63.7	70.9	2.73	1.79
El Salvador	25.3	5.8	26.4	67.7	73.7	2.88	1.94
Guadeloupe	16.3	6.1	7.3	74.9	81.7	2.06	1.02
Guatemala	35.8	6.6	38.9	63.4	70.8	4.60	2.92
Haiti - Haïti	30.4	13.6	61.6	50.6	52.3	3.98	1.69
Honduras	29.9	6.2	31.9	65.6	69.7	3.72	2.38
Jamaica - Jamaïque	20.3	7.6	14.9	68.9	72.5	2.44	1.27
Martinique	14.3	7.2	7.1	75.5	81.6	1.98	0.71
Mexico - Mexique	21.7	4.5	20.5	72.4	77.4	2.40	1.73
Netherlands Antilles - Antilles néerlandaises	14.8	7.0	13.2	72.9	79.1	2.12	0.78
Nicaragua	29.1	5.0	30.1	67.2	71.9	3.30	2.41
Panama	22.7	5.0	20.6	72.3	77.4	2.70	1.77
Puerto Rico - Porto Rico	14.4	8.1	9.9	71.6	80.5	1.92	0.63
Saint Lucia - Sainte-Lucie	18.8	7.0	14.9	70.8	73.9	2.24	1.18
Saint Vincent and the Grenadines - Saint Vincent-et-les Grenadines	20.5	6.8	25.6	68.2	73.8	2.27	1.38
Trinidad and Tobago - Trinité-et-Tobago	14.2	7.9	13.7	66.9	73.0	1.61	0.63
United States - États-Unis	14.0	8.4	6.9	74.6	80.0	2.04	0.57
United States Virgin Islands - Îles Vierges américaines	14.6	5.7	9.5	74.6	82.6	2.22	0.88
AMERICA, SOUTH — AMERIQUE DU SUD							
Argentina - Argentine	18.0	7.7	15.0	70.6	78.1	2.35	1.03
Bolivia - Bolivie	30.2	8.2	55.6	61.8	66.0	3.96	2.21
Brazil - Brésil	20.7	6.6	27.4	66.4	74.4	2.35	1.41
Chile - Chili	15.7	5.0	8.0	74.8	80.8	2.00	1.08
Colombia - Colombie	22.2	5.4	25.6	69.2	75.3	2.62	1.68
Ecuador - Équateur	23.3	4.9	24.9	71.3	77.2	2.82	1.84
French Guiana - Guyane française	25.0	3.7	14.1	72.5	78.4	3.41	2.13
Guyana	21.9	9.1	49.1	59.8	65.9	2.29	1.27
Paraguay	29.6	5.0	37.0	68.6	73.1	3.87	2.45
Peru - Pérou	23.3	6.1	33.4	67.3	72.4	2.86	1.72
Suriname	21.3	7.1	25.6	65.8	72.5	2.60	1.41
Uruguay	16.8	9.1	13.1	71.6	78.9	2.30	0.77
Venezuela	22.9	4.9	17.5	69.9	75.8	2.72	1.79
ASIA — ASIE							
Afghanistan	49.3	19.6	149.0	45.8	46.3	7.48	2.98
Armenia - Arménie	11.1	8.8	30.2	67.9	74.6	1.33	0.23
Azerbaijan - Azerbaïdjan	15.8	7.0	75.5	63.2	70.5	1.85	0.89
Bahrain - Bahreïn	18.8	3.2	13.8	72.9	75.8	2.47	1.56
Bangladesh	27.6	8.0	58.8	61.8	63.4	3.25	1.96
Bhutan - Bhoutan	30.6	8.7	55.7	61.5	63.9	4.40	2.19
Brunei Darussalam - Brunéi Darussalam ...	23.6	2.8	6.1	74.2	78.9	2.50	2.08
Cambodia - Cambodge	30.8	10.8	94.8	52.1	59.6	4.14	1.99
China - Chine[3]	13.6	6.8	34.7	69.8	73.3	1.70	0.68
China - Hong Kong SAR - Chine - Hong Kong RAS[4]	8.3	5.3	3.8	78.6	84.6	0.94	0.30
China - Macao SAR - Chine - Macao RAS[5]	7.3	4.3	7.7	77.8	82.0	0.84	0.29

Annex II: United Nations Medium Variant Population Projections - Vital statistics summary and expectation of life at birth: 2000 - 2005
Annexe II: Projections de la population de variante moyenne de l'ONU - Aperçu des statistiques de l'état civil et espérance de vie à la naissance: 2000 - 2005

(continued — suite)

Continent, country or area Continent, pays ou zone	Crude birth rate — Taux bruts de natalité[1]	Crude death rate — Taux bruts de mortalité[1]	Infant mortality rate — Décès d'enfants de moins d'un an[1]	Expectation of life at birth — Espérance de vie à la naissance[1]		Total fertilty rate — Indice synthétique de fécondité[1]	Natural increase — Accroissement naturel[1]
				Male — Masculin	Female — Féminin		
ASIA — ASIE							
Cyprus - Chypre	12.1	7.2	6.2	76.0	81.0	1.63	0.49
Timor-Leste	47.4	12.6	93.7	54.1	56.3	7.79	3.47
Georgia - Géorgie	11.2	11.1	40.5	66.5	74.3	1.48	0.01
India - Inde	24.6	8.8	67.6	61.7	64.7	3.07	1.58
Indonesia - Indonésie	21.0	7.5	42.7	64.6	68.6	2.37	1.35
Iran (Islamic Republic of) - Iran (République islamique d')	18.6	5.3	33.7	68.8	71.7	2.12	1.33
Iraq	35.7	9.7	94.3	57.3	60.4	4.83	2.59
Israel - Israël	20.7	5.7	5.1	77.5	81.6	2.85	1.51
Japan - Japon	9.2	8.0	3.2	78.3	85.3	1.33	0.12
Jordan - Jordanie	27.8	4.2	23.3	69.8	72.8	3.53	2.36
Kazakhstan	16.1	10.8	61.2	57.8	68.9	1.95	0.52
Korea (Dem. People's Republic of) - Corée (Rép. populaire dém. de)	16.4	10.7	45.7	60.1	66.1	2.00	0.56
Korea (Republic of) - Corée (République de)	10.3	5.5	3.8	73.2	80.5	1.23	0.47
Kuwait - Koweït	19.5	1.8	10.3	75.1	79.4	2.38	1.77
Kyrgyzstan - Kirghizistan	22.6	7.5	55.1	62.6	71.1	2.71	1.51
Lao People's Democratic Republic - République démocratique populaire lao	35.9	12.6	88.0	53.3	55.8	4.83	2.33
Lebanon - Liban	19.0	6.7	22.5	69.7	74.0	2.32	1.23
Malaysia - Malaisie	22.9	4.6	10.1	70.8	75.5	2.93	1.82
Maldives	31.5	6.3	42.6	66.9	65.8	4.33	2.52
Mongolia - Mongolie	22.8	7.3	58.2	61.9	65.9	2.45	1.55
Myanmar	20.8	9.7	74.7	57.4	62.9	2.46	1.11
Nepal - Népal	30.4	8.7	64.4	60.9	61.7	3.71	2.17
Oman	25.6	2.8	15.6	72.7	75.6	3.78	2.28
Pakistan	31.1	8.3	78.6	62.7	63.1	4.27	2.28
Philippines	25.7	5.1	28.1	68.1	72.4	3.22	2.06
Qatar	19.1	3.2	11.6	71.1	75.9	3.03	1.59
Saudi Arabia - Arabie saoudite	28.5	3.9	22.5	69.9	73.8	4.09	2.47
Singapore - Singapour	10.1	4.9	3.0	76.7	80.5	1.35	0.52
Sri Lanka	16.4	6.0	17.2	71.3	76.7	1.97	1.04
Syrian Arab Republic - République arabe syrienne	28.7	3.5	18.2	71.4	74.9	3.47	2.52
Tajikistan - Tadjikistan	29.5	7.6	89.2	61.0	66.3	3.81	2.19
Thailand - Thaïlande	16.3	7.3	19.6	66.0	73.7	1.93	0.91
Turkey - Turquie	21.4	6.6	41.6	66.3	70.9	2.46	1.47
Turkmenistan - Turkménistan	22.9	8.3	78.3	58.2	66.7	2.76	1.46
United Arab Emirates - Émirats arabes unis	16.3	1.3	8.9	76.3	80.6	2.53	1.49
Uzbekistan - Ouzbékistan	23.7	6.8	58.0	63.3	69.7	2.74	1.69
Viet Nam	20.2	6.1	29.9	68.4	72.4	2.32	1.42
Occupied Palestinian Territory - Territoire palestinien occupé	38.8	4.2	20.9	70.8	73.9	5.57	3.46
Yemen - Yémen	41.0	8.7	69.0	59.1	61.7	6.20	3.23
EUROPE							
Albania - Albanie	17.2	6.4	25.0	70.9	76.7	2.29	1.08
Austria - Autriche	9.4	9.6	4.6	75.9	81.7	1.39	...
Belarus - Bélarus	9.2	14.5	14.9	62.4	74.0	1.24	...
Belgium - Belgique	10.9	10.0	4.2	75.7	81.9	1.66	0.09
Bosnia and Herzegovina - Bosnie-Herzégovine	9.7	8.6	13.5	71.3	76.7	1.32	0.10
Bulgaria - Bulgarie	8.7	14.3	13.2	68.8	75.6	1.24	...
Channel Islands - Îles Anglo-Normandes	10.3	9.9	5.5	75.9	80.8	1.40	0.04
Croatia - Croatie	9.1	11.5	6.9	71.3	78.4	1.35	...
Czech Republic - République tchèque	8.9	10.8	5.6	72.2	78.7	1.17	...
Denmark - Danemark	11.9	10.8	4.8	74.8	79.4	1.75	0.11

Annex II: United Nations Medium Variant Population Projections - Vital statistics summary and expectation of life at birth: 2000 - 2005
Annexe II: Projections de la population de variante moyenne de l'ONU - Aperçu des statistiques de l'état civil et espérance de vie à la naissance: 2000 - 2005

(continued — suite)

Continent, country or area Continent, pays ou zone	Crude birth rate — Taux bruts de natalité[1]	Crude death rate — Taux bruts de mortalité[1]	Infant mortality rate — Décès d'enfants de moins d'un an[1]	Expectation of life at birth — Espérance de vie à la naissance[1]		Total fertility rate— Indice synthétique de fécondité[1]	Natural increase — Accroissement naturel[1]
				Male — Masculin	Female — Féminin		
EUROPE							
Estonia - Estonie	9.7	13.7	9.8	65.4	76.9	1.37	...
Finland - Finlande	10.7	9.5	3.9	75.0	81.7	1.72	0.12
France	12.5	9.4	4.5	75.8	83.0	1.87	0.31
Germany - Allemagne	8.5	10.3	4.5	75.6	81.4	1.32	...
Greece - Grèce	9.3	9.9	6.5	75.6	80.8	1.25	...
Hungary - Hongrie	9.5	13.0	8.3	68.4	76.7	1.30	...
Iceland - Islande	14.4	6.3	3.2	78.7	82.5	1.97	0.80
Ireland - Irlande	15.3	7.6	5.5	75.1	80.3	1.94	0.77
Italy - Italie	9.2	10.0	5.2	76.8	83.0	1.28	...
Latvia - Lettonie	0.0	10.4	10.2	65.6	76.9	1.26	...
Lithuania - Lituanie	9.0	11.8	9.1	66.5	77.8	1.28	...
Luxembourg	12.6	8.2	5.4	75.1	81.4	1.73	0.45
Malta - Malte	10.1	7.9	7.1	75.8	80.7	1.50	0.22
Netherlands - Pays-Bas	12.1	9.0	4.5	75.6	81.0	1.72	0.31
Norway - Norvège	12.2	9.6	3.8	76.7	81.8	1.79	0.26
Poland - Pologne	9.5	9.7	8.8	70.2	78.4	1.26	...
Portugal	10.9	10.5	5.6	73.8	80.5	1.47	0.04
Republic of Moldova - République de Moldova	10.1	11.5	25.8	63.7	71.1	1.23	...
Romania - Roumanie	9.9	12.2	18.1	67.7	75.0	1.26	...
Russian Federation - Fédération de Russie	10.1	15.3	16.9	59.1	72.2	1.33	...
Serbia and Montenegro - Serbie-et-Montenegro	11.8	10.7	13.0	70.9	75.6	1.65	0.11
Slovakia - Slovaquie	9.5	9.7	7.8	70.0	77.9	1.20	...
Slovenia - Slovénie	8.8	9.8	5.5	72.6	79.9	1.22	...
Spain - Espagne	10.4	8.8	4.6	75.8	83.1	1.27	0.15
Sweden - Suède	10.6	10.4	3.3	77.8	82.3	1.64	0.02
Switzerland - Suisse	9.7	8.5	4.4	77.6	83.1	1.41	0.12

The Former Yugoslav Rep. of Macedonia -
  L'ex-République yougoslave de
  Macédoine ....
	11.8	8.4	16.0	71.2	76.2	1.53	0.34

Ukraine	8.2	16.3	15.6	60.1	72.5	1.12	...
United Kingdom - Royaume-Uni	11.4	10.3	5.3	75.9	80.6	1.66	0.11
OCEANIA — OCEANIE							
Australia - Australie[6]	12.7	6.7	4.9	77.6	82.8	1.75	0.60
Fiji - Fidji	23.6	6.2	21.8	65.7	70.0	2.92	1.73
French Polynesia - Polynésie française	19.3	4.8	8.8	70.6	75.8	2.39	1.45
Guam	22.3	4.7	9.8	72.4	77.0	2.95	1.75
Micronesia, Federated States of - Micronésie, États Fédérés de La	30.9	6.2	38.0	66.9	68.2	4.35	2.46
New Caledonia - Nouvelle-Calédonie	19.2	4.9	6.6	72.6	77.8	2.43	1.43
New Zealand - Nouvelle-Zélande	14.0	7.3	5.4	76.7	81.3	1.96	0.67
Papua New Guinea - Papouasie-Nouvelle-Guinée	31.7	10.7	70.6	54.7	55.8	4.10	2.10
Samoa	29.4	5.7	25.7	67.1	73.5	4.42	2.37
Solomon Islands - Îles Salomon	33.6	7.2	34.3	61.6	62.9	4.33	2.63
Tonga	24.2	5.9	21.0	70.9	73.4	3.54	1.83
Vanuatu	31.4	5.7	34.3	66.8	70.4	4.15	2.57

FOOTNOTES - NOTES

[1] All data are medium variant projections, produced by the Population Division of the Department for Economic and Social Affairs of the UN Secretariat and published in *World Population Prospects - The 2004 Revision,* United Nations publication, ST/ESA/SER.A/244, Volume I, New York, 2005. — Toutes ces données sont des projections de la population au milieu de l'année de variante moyenne; elles sont produites par la Division pour la population de Département des affaires économiques et sociales du Secrétariat de l'Organisation des Nations Unies et ont été publiées dans *World Population Prospects - The 2004 Revision,* United Nations publication, ST/ESA/SER.A/244, Volume I, New York, 2005.

[2] Including Agalega, Rodrigues and Saint Brandon. — Y compris Agalega, Rodrigues et Saint Brandon.

[3] For statistical purposes, the data for China do not include Hong Kong and Macao Special Administrative Regions (SAR) of China. — A des fins statistiques, les données pour la Chine ne comprennent pas les Régions Administratives Spéciales (SAR) de Hong Kong et Macao.

[4] As of 1 July 1997, Hong Kong became a Special Administrative Region

(SAR) of China. — A partir du 1 juillet 1997, Hong Kong est devenue une Région Administrative Spéciale (SAR) de la Chine.

[5] As of 20 December 1999, Macao became a Special Administrative Region (SAR) of China. — A partir du 20 décembre 1999, Macao est devenue une Région Administrative Spéciale (SAR) de la Chine.

[6] Including Christmas Island, Cocos (Keeling) Islands and Norfolk Island. — Y compris Christmas Island, Cocos (Keeling) Islands et Norfolk Island.

ABORIGINES
    See INDIGENOUS PEOPLES
ABORTION
    defined...8, 373
    grounds for, in different countries (table)...373
    types, spontaneous and induced...373
ABORTIONS, LEGALLY INDUCED, NUMBER OF
    collection of data...379
    tabulation of
        Legally induced abortions...Table 13
        Legally induced abortions by age and number of previous live
            births of woman...Table 14
AFGHANISTAN...43-44; Tables 3, 4, 5, 6, 8, 22
AFRICA (MAJOR AREA)...43-44; Tables 1, 2
AGE
    at last birthday...5, 130, 447
    ending with zero or certain other digits...5
    errors in data, causes of...5
    misreporting and misrepresentations of...5
    reckoning of, English vs. Chinese systems...14n7
    reliability of data...5-6
    tabulation by
        abortions
            Legally induced abortions by age and number of previous
                live births of woman...Table 14
        birth rate and births
            Live birth rates specific for age of mother, by
                urban/rural residence...Table 11
            Live births by age of mother, sex and urban/rural
                residence...Table 10
        death rate and deaths
            Death rates specific for age, sex and urban/rural
                residence...Table 20
            Deaths by age, sex and urban/rural residence...Table 19

            Deaths by marital status, age and sex...Table 21
            Infant deaths and infant mortality rates by age and
                sex...Table 16
        expectation of life
            Expectation of life at specified ages for each sex...Table
                22
        marriages
            Marriages by age of groom and age of bride...Table 24
        population

Estimates of population and its percentage distribution, by age and sex and sex ratio for all ages for the world, major areas and regions...Table 2

Population by age, sex and urban/rural residence...Table 7

AGE DISTRIBUTION
   defined...5

AGE GROUPS
   defined...49

AGE-SEX DISTRIBUTION
   estimates of...6-7

ÅLAND ISLAND...43

ALBANIA...44; Tables 3, 4, 5, 6, 8, 9, 10, 13, 15, 17, 18, 19, 22, 23, 24, 25

ALGERIA...43-44; Tables 3, 4, 5, 6, 7, 8, 9, 12, 15, 18, 19, 22, 23

ALIENS
   See FOREIGNERS

AMERICAN SAMOA...44; Tables 3, 4, 5, 7, 8, 9, 15, 18

ANDORRA...44; Tables 3, 4, 5, 7, 8, 9, 10, 11, 12, 15, 16, 18, 19, 23

ANGOLA...43-44; Tables 3, 8

ANGUILLA...44; Tables 3, 4, 5, 7, 8, 9, 10, 11, 13, 15, 17, 18, 19, 23, 24, 25

ANTIGUA AND BARBUDA...44; Tables 3, 4, 5, 7, 8, 9, 10, 11, 16, 17, 18, 19

AREAS, MAJOR
   availability of data for, in present Demographic Yearbook...Table A

   countries that compose...43-44

   defined...42

   names of...3

   tabulation by
      Estimates of population and its percentage distribution, by age and sex and sex ratio for all ages for the world, major areas and regions...Table 2
      Population, rate of increase, birth and death rates, surface area and density for the world, major areas and regions...Table 1

ARGENTINA...11, 44; Tables 3, 4, 5, 6, 7, 8, 9, 10, 11, 12, 15, 16, 17, 18, 19, 20, 23

ARMENIA...43-44; Tables 3, 4, 5, 6, 7, 8, 9, 10, 11, 12, 13, 15, 16, 17, 18, 19, 20, 22, 23, 24, 25

ARUBA...44; Tables 3, 4, 5, 7, 8, 9, 10, 15, 18, 22, 23, 25

ASCENSION
   See SAINT HELENA

ASIA (MAJOR AREA)...43-44; Tables 1, 2

AUSTRALIA...11, 44; Tables 3, 4, 5, 7, 8, 9, 10, 11, 12, 15, 16, 17, 18, 19, 20, 21, 22, 23, 24, 25

AUSTRALIA AND NEW ZEALAND (MAJOR REGION)...44; Tables 1, 2

AUSTRIA...44; Tables 3, 4, 5, 6, 7, 8, 9, 10, 11, 12, 15, 16, 17, 18,
          19, 20, 21, 22, 23, 24, 25

AZERBAIJAN...43-44; Tables 3, 4, 5, 6, 7, 8, 9, 10, 11, 12, 13, 14,
          15, 16, 17, 18, 19, 20, 21, 22, 23, 24, 25

BAHAMAS...11, 12, 44; Tables 3, 4, 5, 7, 8, 9, 10, 15, 16, 17, 18, 19,
          20, 21, 23, 24, 25

BAHRAIN...43-44; Tables 3, 4, 5, 7, 8, 9, 10, 12, 13, 15, 16, 17, 18,
          19, 22, 23, 24, 25

BANGLADESH...43-44; Tables 3, 5, 6, 8, 22

BARBADOS...11, 44; Tables 3, 4, 5, 8, 9, 15, 17, 18, 23

BELARUS...43; Tables 3, 4, 5, 6, 7, 8, 9, 10, 11, 13, 14, 15, 16, 17,
          18, 19, 20, 22, 23, 24, 25

BELGIUM...11, 12, 44; Tables 3, 4, 5, 7, 8, 9, 12, 13, 14, 15, 16, 17,
          18, 19, 20, 22, 23, 24, 25

BELIZE...44; Tables 3, 4, 5, 6, 7, 8, 9, 10, 15, 17, 18, 19, 23, 25

BENIN...43-44; Tables 3, 4, 5, 6, 7, 8, 9, 15, 18

BERMUDA...11, 12, 44; Tables 3, 4, 5, 7, 8, 9, 10, 11, 12, 15, 17, 18,
          19, 23, 25

BHUTAN...43-44; Tables 3, 5, 7, 8, 22

BIRTH, AT
    tabulation by
        Vital statistics summary and expectation of life at
                birth...Table 4
BIRTH, LIVE
    defined...8, 70, 301
    sources of data...8, 9
BIRTH RATE
    defined...70
    method of calculating series...42, 301, 351
    tabulation of
        Live birth rates specific for age of mother, by urban/rural
                residence...Table 11
        Live births and crude live-birth rates, by urban/rural
                residence...Table 9
        Population, rate of increase, birth and death rates, surface
                area and density for the world, major areas and
                regions...Table 1
        Vital statistics summary and expectation of life at
                birth...Table 4; Annex II
BIRTHS, LIVE, NUMBER OF
    method of calculating series...316
    registration of, delayed...10, 316, 351, 364, 390
    sources of data...7
    tabulation of

        Legally induced abortions by age and number of previous live
                births of woman...Table 14
        Live births and crude live-birth rates, by urban/rural
                residence...Table 9
        Live births by age of mother, sex and urban/rural
                residence...Table 10
        Vital statistics summary and expectation of life at
                birth...Table 4
BOLIVIA...44; Tables 3, 4, 5, 6, 7, 8, 9, 15, 18, 22
BOSNIA AND HERZEGOVINA...44; Tables 3, 4, 5, 8, 9, 10, 15, 16, 18, 19,
                22, 23, 24, 25
BOTSWANA...43-44; Tables 3, 4, 5, 6, 7, 8, 9, 15, 18, 19, 20, 22
BRAZIL...44; Tables 3, 4, 5, 6, 7, 8, 9, 10, 12, 15, 16, 17, 18, 19,
                21, 22, 23, 24, 25
BRITISH VIRGIN ISLANDS...44; Tables 3, 4, 5, 7, 8, 9, 15, 17, 18
BRUNEI DARUSSALAM...43-44; Tables 3, 4, 5, 6, 7, 8, 9, 10, 11, 15, 18,
                19, 20, 23, 24, 25
BULGARIA...11, 12, 43; Tables 3, 4, 5, 6, 7, 8, 9, 10, 11, 12, 13, 14,
                15, 16, 17, 18, 19, 20, 21, 22, 23, 24, 25
BURIAL PERMIT...9
BURKINA FASO...43-44; Tables 3, 5, 6, 7, 8
BURUNDI...43-44; Tables 3, 5, 6, 8

CAMBODIA...43-44; Tables 3, 5, 6, 7, 8
CAMEROON...43-44; Tables 3, 5, 6, 8
CANADA...11, 44; Tables 3, 4, 5, 6, 7, 8, 9, 10, 11, 12, 13, 14, 15,
                16, 17, 18, 19, 20, 21, 22, 23, 24, 25
CAPE VERDE...43-44; Tables 3, 4, 5, 6, 7, 8, 9
CAPITAL CITIES
    tabulation of
        Population of capital cities and cities of 100,000 and more
                inhabitants...Table 8
CARIBBEAN (MAJOR REGION)...42, 44; Tables 1, 2
CAYMAN ISLANDS...11, 12, 44; Tables 3, 4, 5, 8, 9, 10, 16, 17, 18, 19,
                23, 25
CENSUS FIGURES...3-4
    reliability of...53
CENTRAL AFRICAN REPUBLIC...43-44; Tables 3, 5, 6, 8
CENTRAL AMERICA (MAJOR REGION)...42, 44; Tables 1, 2
CHAD...43-44; Tables 3, 4, 5, 8, 9, 18
CHANNEL ISLANDS...43
    Guernsey...11, 12; Tables 3, 4, 5, 7, 8, 9, 10, 11, 12, 13, 14,
                15, 16, 18, 19, 23, 25
    Jersey...Tables 3, 5, 7, 8, 10, 16, 19
CHILE...11, 44; Tables 3, 4, 5, 6, 7, 8, 9, 10, 11, 12, 15, 16, 17,
                18, 19, 20, 21, 22, 23, 24

CHINA...43-44; Tables 3, 4, 5, 6, 7, 8, 9, 18, 19, 22, 23, 25
   Hong Kong, SAR...11, 12, 43-44; Tables 3, 4, 5, 7, 8, 9, 10, 11,
           12, 13, 14, 15, 16, 17, 18, 19, 20, 21, 22, 23, 24, 25
   Macao, SAR...11, 43-44; Tables 3, 4, 5, 7, 8, 9, 10, 11, 12, 15,
           16, 18, 19, 20, 21, 22, 23, 24, 25
CHINA, PEOPLE'S REPUBLIC OF...3
CHRISTMAS ISLANDS
   See also KIRIBATI
CITIES
   capital...216
   defined...216
   tabulation of
       Population of capital cities and cities of 100,000 and more
           inhabitants...Table 8
   See also URBAN/RURAL RESIDENCE
CIVIL REGISTRATION
   data from...7, 70, 301, 433
       incomplete...9, 10
       quality of...10-11, 12, 433, 617, 661
   date of, tabulation by...9
   delay in...9, 447
COLOMBIA...44; Tables 3, 4, 5, 6, 7, 8, 9, 10, 12, 15, 16, 17, 18, 19,
           21, 22
COMOROS...43-44; Tables 3, 8
COMPARABILITY OF STATISTICS...4
   international...3, 10
   over time...3
CONGO, DEMOCRATIC REPUBLIC OF THE...43-44; Tables 3, 4, 5, 7, 8, 9
CONGO, REPUBLIC OF THE...43-44; Tables 3, 8
CONTINENTS
   statistical treatment of...42
COOK ISLANDS...11, 12, 44; Tables 3, 4, 5, 6, 7, 8, 9, 15, 18, 23
COSTA RICA...44; Tables 3, 4, 5, 6, 7, 8, 9, 10, 11, 12, 15, 16, 17,
           18, 19, 20, 21, 22, 23, 24
CÔTE D'IVOIRE...43-44; Tables 3, 4, 5, 8, 9, 15, 18
COUNTRIES
   availability of data for, in present Demographic Yearbook...Table
           A
   names of...3
   regionalization of, into continents, major areas and regions...43-
           44
CROATIA...11, 44; Tables 3, 4, 5, 6, 7, 8, 9, 10, 11, 12, 13, 14, 15,
           16, 17, 18, 19, 20, 21, 23, 24, 25
CUBA...11, 12, 44; Tables 3, 4, 5, 6, 7, 8, 9, 10, 11, 12, 13, 15, 16,
           17, 18, 19, 20, 21, 22, 23, 24, 25

CYPRUS...11, 43-44; Tables 3, 4, 5, 6, 7, 8, 9, 10, 11, 15, 16, 18, 19, 20, 22, 23, 24, 25

CZECH REPUBLIC...11, 43; Tables 3, 4, 5, 6, 7, 8, 9, 10, 11, 12, 13, 14, 15, 16, 17, 18, 19, 20, 21, 22, 23, 24, 25

DATA
   availability of, in present Demographic Yearbook...Table A
   comparability of
      international and within a country...10
   quality of
      affected by delay in registration...9
      codes used for...42, 53
DATE OF OCCURRENCE...9
DEATH
   age at...546
   cause of...421
   defined...8, 70
   sources of data...8, 9
DEATH RATE
   defined...70
   method of calculating series...42, 433, 505
   tabulation of
      Death rates specific for age, sex and urban/rural
            residence...Table 20
      Deaths and crude death rates, by urban/rural residence...Table
            18
      Population, rate of increase, birth and death rates, surface
            area and density for the world, major areas and
            regions...Table 1
      Vital statistics summary and expectation of life at
            birth...Table 4; Annex II
DEATHS, NUMBER OF
   delay in registration of...447
   sources of data...7, 433
   statistics on...9
   tabulation of
      age
         Death rates specific for age, sex and urban/rural
               residence...Table 20
         Deaths by age, sex and urban/rural residence...Table 19
         Deaths by marital status, age and sex...Table 21
         Infant deaths and infant mortality rates by age and
               sex...Table 16
      marital status
         Deaths by marital status, age and sex...Table 21
      sex

Death rates specific for age, sex and urban/rural
    residence…Tables 20, 21
Deaths by age, sex and urban/rural residence…Table 19
Infant deaths and infant mortality rates by age and
    sex…Table 16
summary
    Vital statistics summary and expectation of life at
        birth…Table 4
urban/rural residence
    Deaths and crude death rates, by urban/rural
        residence…Table 18
    Deaths by age, sex and urban/rural residence…Table 19
See also FOETAL DEATHS, LATE; INFANT DEATHS; MATERNAL DEATHS
DE FACTO POPULATION…4, 9, 53
DE JURE POPULATION…4
DEMOGRAPHIC ANALYSIS
    used to assess vital statistics…11
DEMOGRAPHIC YEARBOOK
    history and contents of…1
DENMARK…11, 12, 44; Tables 3, 4, 5, 7, 8, 9, 10, 11, 12, 13, 14, 15,
            16, 17, 18, 19, 20, 21, 22, 23, 24, 25
DENOMINATOR
    accuracy of, in computing rates…12
    correspondence of population with that of numerator…505
DIVORCE
    defined…8, 9, 661
DIVORCE RATE
    method of calculating series…661
    tabulation of
        Divorces and crude divorce rates…Table 25
DIVORCES, NUMBER OF
    registration of…9, 661
    statistics on…7
    tabulation of
        Divorces and crude divorce rates…Table 25
DJIBOUTI…43-44; Tables 3, 5, 8, 22, 23, 25
DOMINICA…44; Tables 3, 4, 5, 7, 8, 9, 15, 17, 18, 23, 25
DOMINICAN REPUBLIC…44; Tables 3, 4, 5, 6, 7, 8, 9, 10, 13, 15, 17,
            18, 19, 22, 23, 25
DUAL RECORD CHECKS
    used to assess vital statistics…11

EASTERN AFRICA (MAJOR REGION)…43-44; Tables 1, 2
EASTERN ASIA (MAJOR REGION)…43-44; Tables 1, 2
EASTERN EUROPE (MAJOR REGION)…43; Tables 1, 2

ECUADOR...44; Tables 3, 4, 5, 6, 7, 8, 9, 10, 12, 15, 16, 17, 18, 19, 21, 22, 23, 24, 25

EGYPT...11, 43-44; Tables 3, 4, 5, 6, 7, 8, 9, 10, 11, 12, 15, 16, 17, 18, 19, 20, 21, 22, 23, 24, 25

EL SALVADOR...44; Tables 3, 4, 5, 6, 7, 8, 9, 10, 11, 12, 15, 16, 17, 18, 19, 20, 21, 22, 23, 24, 25

ENUMERATION
   nation-wide...53

EQUATORIAL GUINEA...43-44; Tables 3, 8

ERITREA...43-44; Tables 3, 8

ESTIMATES
   data from...301
   quality of...6-7
   Tables of
      Estimates of population and its percentage distribution, by age and sex and sex ratio for all ages for the world, major areas and regions...Table 2
      Estimations of mid-year population...Table 5; Annex I

ESTONIA...11, 44; Tables 3, 4, 5, 6, 7, 8, 9, 10, 11, 12, 13, 14, 15, 16, 17, 18, 19, 20, 21, 22, 23, 24, 25

ETHIOPIA...43-44; Tables 3, 4, 5, 6, 7, 8, 9, 15, 18, 22, 23, 25

ETHNIC COVERAGE
   fragmentary...9

EUROPE (MAJOR AREA)...43-44; Tables 1, 2

EXPECTATION OF LIFE
   defined...70, 605
   tabulation of
      Expectation of life at specified ages for each sex...Table 22
      Vital statistics summary and expectation of life at birth...Table 4; Annex II

FAEROE ISLANDS...44; Tables 3, 5, 8

FALKLAND ISLANDS (MALVINAS)...44; Tables 3, 4, 7, 8, 9, 18

FERTILITY RATE
   defined...70
   tabulation of
      Vital statistics summary and expectation of life at birth...Table 4; Annex II
   See also BIRTH RATE

FIJI...11, 12, 44; Tables 3, 4, 5, 6, 7, 8, 9, 15, 17, 18

FINLAND...11, 12, 44; Tables 3, 4, 5, 6, 7, 8, 9, 10, 11, 12, 13, 14, 15, 16, 17, 18, 19, 20, 21, 22, 23, 24, 25

FOETAL DEATH
   defined...8

FOETAL DEATH, LATE
   defined...8, 9, 13, 363

FOETAL DEATH, LATE, RATIO
  method of calculating series...363
  tabulation of
    Late foetal deaths and late foetal death ratios, by
        urban/rural residence...Table 12
FOETAL DEATHS, LATE, NUMBER OF
  registration of...9
  tabulation of
    Late foetal deaths and late foetal death ratios, by
        urban/rural residence...Table 12
FOETAL MORTALITY
  Tables of...Tables 12-14
FOREIGNERS
  tabulation of...9
FOREIGN MILITARY, NAVAL AND DIPLOMATIC PERSONNEL...4
  deaths among...505
FOREIGN VISITORS IN TRANSIT...4
FRANCE...11, 12, 44; Tables 3, 4, 5, 7, 8, 9, 10, 11, 12, 13, 14, 15,
        16, 17, 18, 19, 20, 21, 22, 23, 24, 25
FRENCH GUIANA...11, 44; Tables 3, 4, 5, 7, 8, 9, 10, 11, 12, 15, 16,
        18, 19, 21, 22, 23, 24, 25
FRENCH POLYNESIA...44; Tables 3, 4, 5, 7, 8, 9, 12, 15, 18, 23

GABON...43-44; Tables 3, 4, 5, 8
GAMBIA...43-44; Tables 3, 5, 8
GEOGRAPHICAL COVERAGE
  fragmentary...9
GEORGIA...43-44; Tables 3, 4, 5, 6, 7, 8, 9, 10, 11, 12, 13, 14, 15,
        16, 17, 18, 19, 20, 21, 22, 23, 24, 25
GERMANY...11, 12, 44; Tables 4, 5, 7, 8, 9, 10, 11, 12, 13, 14, 15,
        16, 17, 18, 19, 20, 21, 22, 23, 25
GHANA...43-44; Tables 3, 4, 5, 6, 7, 8, 9, 15, 18
GIBRALTAR...44; Tables 3, 4, 5, 7, 8, 9, 10, 11, 15, 18, 23, 25
GREECE...11, 12, 44; Tables 3, 4, 5, 7, 8, 9, 10, 11, 12, 13, 14, 15,
        16, 17, 18, 19, 20, 21, 22, 23, 25
GREENLAND...11, 12, 44; Tables 3, 4, 5, 6, 7, 8, 9, 10, 11, 13, 15,
        16, 18, 19, 21, 22
GRENADA...44; Tables 3, 4, 5, 7, 8, 9, 10, 11, 15, 17, 18, 19, 20, 23,
        24, 25
GUADELOUPE...11, 44; Tables 3, 4, 5, 7, 8, 9, 10, 11, 12, 15, 16, 18,
        19, 20, 21, 22, 23, 24, 25
GUAM...11, 12, 44; Tables 3, 4, 5, 6, 7, 8, 9, 10, 15, 18, 23
GUATEMALA...44; Tables 3, 4, 5, 7, 8, 9, 10, 11, 12, 15, 16, 17, 18,
        19, 20, 21, 22, 23, 25
GUINEA...43-44; Tables 3, 7, 8
GUINEA-BISSAU...43-44; Tables 3, 5, 8

GUYANA...44; Tables 3, 4, 5, 8, 17, 18

HAITI...44; Tables 3, 5, 6, 7, 8
HOLY SEE...44; Tables 3, 4, 5, 8, 9, 18
HONDURAS...44; Tables 3, 5, 6, 7, 8
HONG KONG
    See CHINA, HONG KONG, SAR
HOUSEHOLD SURVEYS...7
HUNGARY...11, 43; Tables 3, 4, 5, 6, 7, 8, 9, 10, 11, 12, 13, 14, 15,
            16, 17, 18, 19, 20, 21, 22, 23, 24, 25

ICELAND...11, 12, 44; Tables 3, 4, 5, 6, 7, 8, 9, 10, 11, 12, 13, 14,
            15, 16, 17, 18, 19, 20, 21, 22, 23, 24, 25
INDIA...43-44; Tables 3, 4, 5, 6, 7, 8, 9, 15, 18, 22
INDIGENOUS PEOPLES
    tabulation of...9
INDONESIA...43-44; Tables 3, 4, 5, 6, 7, 8, 22
INFANT DEATH
    defined...13, 70, 390
INFANT DEATH RATE
    defined...8, 9
    method of calculating series...70, 390, 403
    tabulation of
        Infant deaths and infant mortality rates by age and sex...Table
            16
        Infant deaths and infant mortality rates by urban/rural
            residence...Table 15
        Vital statistics summary and expectation of life at
            birth...Table 4; Annex II
INFANT DEATHS, NUMBER OF
    exclusions of, in calculating total deaths, in some cases...447
    reliability of data...403
    tabulation of
        Infant deaths and infant mortality rates by age and sex...Table
            16
        Infant deaths and infant mortality rates by urban/rural
            residence...Table 15
        Vital statistics summary and expectation of life at
            birth...Table 4
INFANT MORTALITY
    Tables of...Tables 15-17
IRAN...43-44; Tables 3, 4, 5, 6, 7, 8, 9, 10, 15, 18, 22, 23, 25
IRAQ...43-44; Tables 3, 4, 5, 6, 7, 8, 9, 10, 18, 22, 23
IRELAND...11, 44; Tables 3, 4, 5, 6, 7, 8, 9, 10, 11, 12, 15, 16, 17,
            18, 19, 20, 21, 22, 23, 25

ISLE OF MAN...11, 12, 44; Tables 3, 4, 5, 7, 8, 9, 12, 15, 16, 18, 19,
             22, 23, 24, 25
ISRAEL...11, 43-44; Tables 3, 4, 5, 6, 7, 8, 9, 10, 11, 12, 13, 14,
             15, 16, 17, 18, 19, 20, 22, 23, 24, 25
ITALY...44; Tables 3, 4, 5, 6, 7, 8, 9, 10, 11, 12, 13, 14, 15, 16,
             17, 18, 19, 20, 21, 22, 23, 24, 25

JAMAICA...44; Tables 3, 4, 5, 6, 7, 8, 9, 10, 11, 15, 18, 22, 23, 24,
             25
JAPAN...11, 12, 43-44; Tables 3, 4, 5, 6, 7, 8, 9, 10, 11, 12, 13, 14,
             15, 16, 17, 18, 19, 20, 21, 22, 23, 24, 25
JORDAN...43-44; Tables 3, 4, 5, 6, 7, 8, 9, 18, 22, 23, 24, 25

KAZAKHSTAN...43-44; Tables 3, 4, 5, 6, 7, 8, 9, 10, 11, 12, 13, 14,
             15, 16, 17, 18, 19, 20, 21, 22, 23, 24, 25
KENYA...43-44; Tables 3, 4, 5, 6, 8, 9, 10, 15, 18, 19, 22
KIRIBATI...44; Tables 3, 5, 8, 10
KOREA, DEMOCRATIC PEOPLE'S REPUBLIC OF...43-44; Tables 3, 8, 22
KOREA, REPUBLIC OF...11, 43-44; Tables 3, 4, 5, 6, 7, 8, 9, 10, 11,
             15, 17, 18, 19, 20, 21, 22, 23, 24, 25
KUWAIT...11, 43-44; Tables 3, 4, 5, 7, 8, 9, 11, 12, 15, 16, 17, 18,
             19, 20, 23, 24, 25
KYRGYZSTAN...11, 43-44; Tables 3, 4, 5, 6, 7, 8, 9, 10, 11, 12, 13,
             15, 16, 17, 18, 19, 20, 22, 23, 24, 25

LAO PEOPLE'S DEMOCRATIC REPUBLIC...43-44; Tables 3, 4, 5, 6, 7, 8
LATE FOETAL DEATHS
    See FOETAL DEATHS, LATE
LATIN AMERICA (MAJOR AREA)...42, 44; Tables 1, 2
LATVIA...11, 44; Tables 3, 4, 5, 6, 7, 8, 9, 10, 11, 12, 13, 14, 15,
             16, 17, 18, 19, 20, 21, 22, 23, 24, 25
LEBANON...43-44; Tables 3, 4, 8, 9, 18, 23, 25
LEGALLY INDUCED ABORTIONS
    See ABORTIONS, LEGALLY INDUCED
LESOTHO...43-44; Tables 3, 4, 5, 6, 7, 8, 22
LIBERIA...43-44; Tables 3, 5, 6, 8
LIBYAN ARAB JAMAHIRIYA...43-44; Tables 3, 4, 5, 8, 9, 10, 15, 18, 19,
             21, 23, 25
LIECHTENSTEIN...44; Tables 3, 4, 5, 7, 8, 9, 10, 11, 15, 18, 19, 21,
             23, 25
LIFE TABLES
    method of calculating series...605
    See also EXPECTATION OF LIFE
LITHUANIA...11, 44; Tables 3, 4, 5, 6, 7, 8, 9, 10, 11, 12, 13, 14,
             15, 16, 17, 18, 19, 20, 21, 22, 23, 24, 25
LIVE BIRTHS

See BIRTHS, LIVE

LUXEMBOURG...11, 12, 44; Tables 3, 4, 5, 7, 8, 9, 10, 11, 12, 15, 16,
          17, 18, 19, 20, 21, 22, 23, 24, 25

MACAO

    See CHINA, MACAO, SAR

MACEDONIA, FORMER YUGOSLAV REPUBLIC OF...44; Tables 3, 4, 5, 6, 7, 8,
          9, 10, 11, 12, 13, 15, 16, 17, 18, 19, 20, 21, 22, 23,
          24, 25

MADAGASCAR...43-44; Tables 3, 5, 6, 8

MALAWI...43-44; Tables 3, 4, 5, 6, 7, 8, 9, 15, 18, 19, 20, 22

MALAYSIA...43-44; Tables 3, 4, 5, 6, 7, 8, 9, 12, 15, 16, 18, 19, 20,
          22

    Peninsular...11

MALDIVES...11, 12, 43-44; Tables 3, 4, 5, 6, 7, 8, 9, 10, 11, 12, 15,
          16, 18, 19, 20, 22, 23, 25

MALI...43-44; Tables 3, 4, 5, 8, 9

MALTA...44; Tables 3, 4, 5, 7, 8, 9, 10, 11, 15, 16, 17, 18, 19, 20,
          21, 22, 23, 24

MARITAL STATUS

    defined...546

    misreporting and misrepresentations of...546

    reliability of data...546

    tabulation by

        deaths

            Deaths by marital status, age and sex...Table 21

MARRIAGE

    defined...8, 9, 617, 629

    minimum legal age of...9, 629

MARRIAGE RATE

    method of calculating series...617

    tabulation of

        Marriages and crude marriage rates, by urban/rural
            residence...Table 23

MARRIAGES, NUMBER OF

    registration of...9, 617, 629

    statistics on...7

    tabulation of

        Marriages and crude marriage rates, by urban/rural
            residence...Table 23

        Marriages by age of groom and age of bride...Table 24

MARSHALL ISLANDS...44; Tables 3, 4, 5, 7, 8, 9, 10, 15, 18, 19, 22

MARTINIQUE...44; Tables 3, 4, 5, 7, 8, 9, 10, 11, 12, 15, 16, 18, 19,
          20, 21, 22, 23, 24, 25

MATERNAL DEATH...13

    defined...13, 421

MATERNAL DEATH RATE
    method of calculating series...13, 421
    tabulation of
        Maternal deaths and maternal mortality rates...Table 17
MATERNAL DEATHS, NUMBER OF
    method of calculating series...421
    tabulation of
        Maternal deaths and maternal mortality rates...Table 17
MAURITANIA...43-44; Tables 3, 5, 8
MAURITIUS...11, 43-44; Tables 3, 4, 5, 6, 7, 8, 9, 10, 11, 12, 15, 16,
            17, 18, 19, 20, 21, 22, 23, 24, 25
MELANESIA (MAJOR REGION)...44; Tables 1, 2
MEN
    tabulation by
        Marriages by age of groom and age of bride...Table 24
        Vital statistics summary and expectation of life at
            birth...Table 4; Annex II
MEXICO...44; Tables 3, 4, 5, 6, 7, 8, 9, 10, 12, 13, 14, 15, 16, 17,
            18, 19, 20, 21, 23, 24, 25
MICRONESIA, FEDERATED STATES OF...44; Tables 3, 5, 7, 8
MICRONESIA (MAJOR REGION)...44; Tables 1, 2
MIDDLE AFRICA (MAJOR REGION)...43-44; Tables 1, 2
MID-YEAR POPULATION
    estimates...92
    method of calculating series...53
    reliability of...92
    tabulation of
        Estimations of mid-year population...Table 5; Annex I
MOLDOVA, REPUBLIC OF...43; Tables 3, 4, 5, 6, 7, 8, 9, 10, 11, 13, 14,
            15, 16, 17, 18, 19, 20, 21, 22, 23, 24, 25
MONACO...44; Tables 3, 4, 5, 7, 8, 9, 18, 23, 25
MONGOLIA...43-44; Tables 3, 4, 5, 6, 7, 8, 9, 10, 11, 13, 15, 18, 19,
            20, 22, 23, 24, 25
MONTSERRAT...44; Tables 3, 4, 5, 7, 8, 9, 10, 15, 16, 18, 19, 23, 25
MOROCCO...43-44; Tables 3, 4, 5, 6, 7, 8, 9, 10, 11, 15, 16, 18, 19
MORTALITY
    tables of...Tables 12-22
MOTHER
    See "MATERNAL" ENTRIES; WOMEN
MOZAMBIQUE...43-44; Tables 3, 4, 5, 6, 7, 8, 9, 15, 18, 19, 20
MYANMAR...43-44; Tables 3, 5, 6, 7, 8, 10, 16, 19

NAMIBIA...43-44; Tables 3, 4, 5, 6, 7, 8, 9, 10, 11, 18, 19
NATALITY
    Tables of...Tables 9-11
NATIONAL STATISTICAL OFFICES

own estimates of completeness of statistics...11

NAURU...44; Tables 3, 4, 5, 8, 22

NEPAL...43-44; Tables 3, 4, 5, 6, 7, 8, 15, 18, 19, 20

NETHERLANDS...11, 12, 44; Tables 3, 4, 5, 6, 7, 8, 9, 10, 11, 12, 13, 15, 16, 17, 18, 19, 20, 21, 22, 23, 24, 25

NETHERLANDS ANTILLES...44; Tables 3, 4, 5, 7, 8, 9, 18, 22, 23, 25

NEW CALEDONIA...44; Tables 3, 4, 5, 6, 7, 8, 9, 10, 11, 12, 13, 15, 16, 18, 19, 20, 21, 22, 23, 24, 25

NEW ZEALAND...11, 12, 44; Tables 3, 4, 5, 6, 7, 8, 9, 10, 11, 12, 13, 14, 15, 16, 17, 18, 19, 20, 21, 22, 23, 24, 25

NICARAGUA...44; Tables 3, 4, 5, 6, 7, 8, 9, 10, 15, 16, 17, 18, 19, 21, 22, 23, 25

NIGER...43-44; Tables 3, 8

NIGERIA...43-44; Tables 3, 5, 7, 8

NIUE...44; Tables 3, 4, 5, 7, 8, 9, 18, 23, 25

NOMADIC TRIBES
    tabulation of...9

NORFOLK ISLAND...44; Tables 3, 8

NORTH AMERICA (CONTINENT)...42

NORTHERN AFRICA (MAJOR REGION)...43-44; Tables 1, 2

NORTHERN AMERICA (MAJOR AREA)...42, 44; Tables 1, 2

NORTHERN EUROPE (MAJOR REGION)...43-44; Tables 1, 2

NORTHERN MARIANA ISLANDS...44; Tables 3, 4, 5, 7, 8, 9, 10, 15, 18, 19

NORWAY...11, 12, 44; Tables 3, 4, 5, 6, 7, 8, 9, 10, 11, 12, 13, 14, 15, 16, 17, 18, 19, 20, 21, 22, 23, 24, 25

NUPTIALITY
    Tables of...Tables 23-25
    See also DIVORCE; MARRIAGE

OBSTETRIC DEATHS
    direct and indirect...13

OCCURRENCE
    date of, tabulation by...9-10
    place of, tabulation by...9

OCEANIA (MAJOR AREA)...44; Tables 1, 2

OMAN...43-44; Tables 3, 4, 5, 6, 7, 8, 9, 10, 12, 15, 18, 19, 22

PAKISTAN...43-44; Tables 3, 4, 5, 6, 7, 8, 9, 10, 11, 15, 16, 18, 19, 20, 21, 22

PALAU...44; Tables 3, 4, 5, 6, 7, 8, 9, 10, 15, 18, 19

PALESTINIAN TERRITORY, OCCUPIED...43-44; Tables 3, 4, 5, 6, 7, 8, 9, 15, 16, 18, 19, 21, 22, 23, 24, 25

PANAMA...44; Tables 3, 4, 5, 6, 7, 8, 9, 10, 11, 12, 13, 14, 15, 16, 17, 18, 19, 21, 22, 23, 24, 25

PAPUA NEW GUINEA...44; Tables 3, 4, 5, 6, 7, 8, 9, 12, 15, 18, 22

PARAGUAY...44; Tables 3, 4, 5, 6, 7, 8, 15, 17, 18, 19, 22

PERINATAL MORTALITY...13
   defined...13
PERU...44; Tables 3, 4, 5, 6, 7, 8, 9, 10, 15, 16, 17, 18, 19, 22
PHILIPPINES...43-44; Tables 3, 4, 5, 7, 8, 9, 10, 11, 12, 15, 16, 17,
            18, 19, 20, 21, 23, 24
PITCAIRN...44; Tables 3, 8
PLACE OF OCCURRENCE...9
PLACE OF USUAL RESIDENCE...9
POLAND...11, 12, 43; Tables 3, 4, 5, 6, 7, 8, 9, 10, 11, 12, 13, 15,
            16, 17, 18, 19, 20, 21, 22, 23, 24, 25
POLYNESIA (MAJOR REGION)...44; Tables 1, 2
POPULATION
   defined...53
   estimates
      quality of...6
   statistics on...4-7
   tabulation of...Tables 5-8
      age
         Estimates of population and its percentage distribution,
            by age and sex and sex ratio for all ages for the
            world, major areas and regions...Table 2
         Population by age, sex and urban/rural residence...Table 7
      cities
         Population of capital cities and cities of 100,000 and
            more inhabitants...Table 8
      estimates
         Estimates of population and its percentage distribution,
            by age and sex and sex ratio for all ages for the
            world, major areas and regions...Table 2
         Estimations of mid-year population...Table 5; Annex I
      sex
         Estimates of population and its percentage distribution,
            by age and sex and sex ratio for all ages for the
            world, major areas and regions...Table 2
         Population by age, sex and urban/rural residence...Table 7
         Population by sex, rate of population increase, surface
            area and density...Table 3
      urban/rural residence
         Population by age, sex and urban/rural residence...Table 7
         Urban and total population by sex...Tables 5, 6
      world
         Population, rate of increase, birth and death rates,
            surface area and density for the world, major areas
            and regions...Table 1
POPULATION DENSITY
   defined...53

method of calculating series...42
tabulation of
    Population, rate of increase, birth and death rates, surface
        area and density for the world, major areas and
        regions...Table 1
    Population by sex, rate of population increase, surface area
        and density...Table 3
POPULATION INCREASE
method of calculating series...42, 53, 70
tabulation of
    Population, rate of increase, birth and death rates, surface
        area and density for the world, major areas and
        regions...Table 1
    Population by sex, rate of population increase, surface area
        and density...Table 3
    Vital statistics summary and expectation of life at
        birth...Table 4; Annex II
PORTUGAL...44; Tables 3, 4, 5, 6, 7, 8, 9, 10, 11, 12, 15, 16, 17, 18,
        19, 20, 21, 22, 23, 24, 25
PREGNANCY
termination of, defined...8
PUERTO RICO...11, 44; Tables 3, 4, 5, 6, 7, 8, 9, 10, 11, 12, 13, 15,
        16, 17, 18, 19, 20, 21, 22, 23, 24, 25

QATAR...43-44; Tables 3, 4, 5, 7, 8, 9, 10, 11, 12, 15, 16, 17, 18,
        19, 20, 21, 23, 24, 25

RATES AND RATIOS
calculation of...4, 70
quality of, depending on quality of denominator...12
REGIONS, MAJOR
countries that compose...43-44
defined...42
tabulation by
    Estimates of population and its percentage distribution, by
        age and sex and sex ratio for all ages for the world,
        major areas and regions...Table 2
    Population, rate of increase, birth and death rates, surface
        area and density for the world, major areas and
        regions...Table 1
REGISTRATION
See CIVIL REGISTRATION
RESIDENT
usual...4, 9
RÉUNION...43-44; Tables 3, 4, 5, 7, 8, 9, 10, 11, 13, 15, 16, 18, 19,
        20, 21, 22, 23, 24, 25

ROMANIA...11, 12, 43; Tables 3, 4, 5, 6, 7, 8, 9, 10, 11, 12, 13, 14,
            15, 16, 17, 18, 19, 20, 21, 22, 23, 24, 25
RUSSIAN FEDERATION...43; Tables 3, 4, 5, 6, 7, 8, 9, 10, 11, 12, 13,
            14, 15, 17, 18, 19, 20, 22, 23, 24, 25
RWANDA...43-44; Tables 3, 6, 7, 8

SAINT HELENA...43-44; Tables 3, 4, 5, 6, 7, 8, 9, 10, 15, 16, 18, 19,
            23, 25
    Ascension...Table 3
    Tristan da Cunha...Tables 3, 5, 7
SAINT KITTS-NEVIS...11, 12, 44; Tables 3, 4, 5, 7, 8, 9, 10, 11, 17,
            18, 19, 22
SAINT LUCIA...11, 12, 44; Tables 3, 4, 5, 6, 7, 8, 9, 10, 11, 12, 15,
            16, 17, 18, 19, 22, 23, 24, 25
SAINT PIERRE AND MIQUELON...44; Tables 3, 5, 8
SAINT VINCENT AND THE GRENADINES...44; Tables 3, 4, 5, 6, 7, 8, 9, 10,
            11, 12, 15, 16, 17, 18, 19, 23, 25
SAMOA...44; Tables 3, 5, 8
SAMPLE SURVEYS...7, 53
SAN MARINO...11, 44; Tables 3, 4, 5, 6, 7, 8, 9, 10, 11, 12, 15, 16,
            17, 18, 19, 21, 22, 23, 24, 25
SAO TOME AND PRINCIPE...43-44; Tables 3, 5, 8
SAUDI ARABIA...43-44; Tables 3, 4, 5, 7, 8, 9, 10, 15, 18, 23, 25
SENEGAL...43-44; Tables 3, 5, 8
SEPARATION, LEGAL...661
SERBIA AND MONTENEGRO...44; Tables 3, 4, 5, 6, 7, 8, 9, 10, 11, 12,
            13, 14, 15, 16, 17, 18, 19, 20, 21, 22, 23, 24, 25
SEX
    tabulation by
        births
            Live births by age of mother, sex and urban/rural
                residence...Table 10
        death rate and deaths
            Death rates specific for age, sex and urban/rural
                residence...Table 20
            Deaths by age, sex and urban/rural residence...Table 19
            Deaths by marital status, age and sex...Table 21
            Infant deaths and infant mortality rates by age and
                sex...Table 16
        expectation of life
            Expectation of life at specified ages for each sex...Table
                22
        population
            Estimates of population and its percentage distribution,
                by age and sex and sex ratio for all ages for the
                world, major areas and regions...Table 2

Population by age, sex and urban/rural residence...Table 7

Population by sex, rate of population increase, surface
area and density...Table 3

Urban and total population by sex...Tables 5, 6

SEX RATIO
defined...49

SEYCHELLES...43-44; Tables 3, 4, 5, 7, 8, 9, 13, 15, 18, 19, 23, 24, 25

SIERRA LEONE...43-44; Tables 3, 5, 6, 7, 8

SINGAPORE...11, 12, 43-44; Tables 3, 4, 5, 7, 8, 9, 10, 11, 12, 13, 14, 15, 16, 17, 18, 19, 21, 22, 23, 24, 25

SLOVAKIA...43; Tables 3, 4, 5, 6, 7, 8, 9, 10, 11, 12, 13, 14, 15, 16, 17, 18, 19, 20, 21, 22, 23, 24, 25

SLOVENIA...11, 12, 44; Tables 3, 4, 5, 6, 7, 8, 9, 10, 11, 12, 13, 14, 15, 16, 17, 18, 19, 20, 21, 22, 23, 24, 25

SOLOMON ISLANDS...44; Tables 3, 8

SOMALIA...43-44; Tables 3, 6, 7, 8

SOUTH AFRICA...43-44; Tables 3, 4, 5, 6, 7, 8, 9, 10, 13, 16, 17, 19, 23

SOUTH AMERICA (CONTINENT)...42

SOUTH AMERICA (MAJOR REGION)...44; Tables 1, 2

SOUTH CENTRAL ASIA (MAJOR REGION)...43-44; Tables 1, 2

SOUTH EASTERN ASIA (MAJOR REGION)...43-44; Tables 1, 2

SOUTHERN AFRICA (MAJOR REGION)...43-44; Tables 1, 2

SOUTHERN EUROPE (MAJOR REGION)...44; Tables 1, 2

SPAIN...44; Tables 3, 4, 5, 7, 8, 9, 10, 11, 12, 13, 14, 15, 16, 17, 18, 19, 20, 21, 22, 23, 24, 25

SRI LANKA...11, 43-44; Tables 3, 4, 5, 6, 7, 8, 9, 10, 11, 15, 16, 17, 18, 19, 20, 23

STATISTICS
on CD and online...1
See also COMPARABILITY OF STATISTICS; VITAL STATISTICS

SUDAN...43-44; Tables 3, 5, 8

SUMMARIES
Tables of
Vital statistics summary and expectation of life at
birth...Table 4; Annex II
World summary...Tables 1-4

SUMMARY DATA...2

SURFACE AREA
data on...3
defined...53
method of calculating series...42
tabulation by

        Population, rate of increase, birth and death rates, surface
            area and density for the world, major areas and
            regions...Table 1
        Population by sex, rate of population increase, surface area
            and density...Table 3

SURINAME...44; Tables 3, 4, 5, 7, 8, 9, 10, 11, 12, 15, 16, 18, 19,
            20, 21, 23, 24, 25

SURVEYS
    See HOUSEHOLD SURVEYS; SAMPLE SURVEYS

SVALBARD AND JAN MAYEN ISLANDS...Table 3

SWAZILAND...43-44; Tables 3, 5, 6, 7, 8, 10, 11, 19, 20, 22

SWEDEN...11, 12, 44; Tables 3, 4, 5, 7, 8, 9, 10, 11, 12, 13, 14, 15,
            16, 17, 18, 19, 20, 21, 22, 23, 24, 25

SWITZERLAND...11, 12, 44; Tables 3, 4, 5, 6, 7, 8, 9, 10, 11, 12, 15,
            16, 17, 18, 19, 20, 21, 22, 23, 24, 25

SYRIAN ARAB REPUBLIC...43-44; Tables 3, 4, 5, 6, 7, 8, 9, 18, 23, 25

TABLES
    codes and symbols used in...9
    synoptic table of...30-40; Table A

TABULATION
    by date of occurrence...9-10
    by place of occurrence...9

TAIWAN PROVINCE...3

TAJIKISTAN...43-44; Tables 3, 4, 5, 6, 8, 9, 10, 12, 13, 14, 15, 16,
            17, 18, 19, 23, 24, 25

TANZANIA, UNITED REPUBLIC OF...43-44; Tables 3, 5, 7, 8

THAILAND...43-44; Tables 3, 4, 5, 6, 7, 8, 9, 10, 15, 16, 17, 18, 19,
            23

TIME SERIES
    quality of, derived from systems of continuous civil
            registration...12

TIMOR, EAST (TIMOR LESTE)...43-44; Tables 3, 8

TOGO...43-44; Tables 3, 5, 8

TOKELAU...11, 12, 44; Tables 3, 7

TONGA...44; Tables 3, 4, 5, 6, 7, 8, 9, 10, 11, 15, 16, 18, 19, 22,
            23, 24, 25

TRINIDAD AND TOBAGO...44; Tables 3, 4, 5, 7, 8, 9, 10, 11, 12, 16, 17,
            18, 19, 20

TRISTAN DA CUNHA
    See SAINT HELENA

TUNISIA...43-44; Tables 3, 4, 5, 6, 7, 8, 9, 10, 11, 15, 16, 18, 19,
            21, 22, 23, 25

TURKEY...43-44; Tables 3, 4, 5, 6, 7, 8, 9, 10, 11, 15, 16, 18, 22,
            23, 24, 25

TURKMENISTAN...43-44; Tables 3, 5, 7, 8, 17

TURKS AND CAICOS ISLANDS...44; Tables 3, 4, 5, 7, 8, 9, 10, 12, 13, 15, 17, 18, 19, 22, 23, 24, 25

TUVALU...44; Tables 3, 8

UGANDA...43-44; Tables 3, 5, 6, 7, 8

UKRAINE...43; Tables 3, 4, 5, 6, 7, 8, 9, 10, 11, 12, 13, 14, 15, 16, 17, 18, 19, 20, 22, 23, 24, 25

UNITED ARAB EMIRATES...43-44; Tables 3, 5, 6, 7, 8

UNITED KINGDOM...44; Tables 3, 4, 5, 7, 8, 9, 10, 11, 12, 13, 14, 15, 16, 17, 18, 19, 20, 22, 23, 24, 25

UNITED NATIONS POPULATION DIVISION...42, 49

UNITED NATIONS STATISTICS DIVISION...2

UNITED STATES...11, 44; Tables 3, 4, 5, 6, 7, 8, 9, 10, 11, 12, 15, 16, 17, 18, 19, 20, 21, 22, 23

UNITED STATES VIRGIN ISLANDS...44; Tables 3, 5, 7, 8, 17

URBAN AGGLOMERATION
    defined...216

URBAN POPULATION
    method of calculating series...100
    tabulation of
        Urban and total population by sex...Tables 5, 6
    See also CITIES

URBAN/RURAL RESIDENCE
    availability of data for, in present Demographic Yearbook...Table
            A
    defined...5, 100
    national differences in definition of...100-104
    tabulation by
        birth rate and births
            Live birth rates specific for age of mother, by
                urban/rural residence...Table 11
            Live births and crude live-birth rates, by urban/rural
                residence...Table 9
            Live births by age of mother, sex and urban/rural
                residence...Table 10
        death rate and deaths
            Death rates specific for age, sex and urban/rural
                residence...Table 20
            Deaths and crude death rates, by urban/rural
                residence...Table 18
            Deaths by age, sex and urban/rural residence...Table 19
        foetal deaths
            Late foetal deaths and late foetal death ratios, by
                urban/rural residence...Table 12
        infant deaths

Infant deaths and infant mortality rates by urban/rural
residence...Table 15
marriages
Marriages and crude marriage rates, by urban/rural
residence...Table 23
population
Population by age, sex and urban/rural residence...Table 7
See also CITIES
URUGUAY...11, 12, 44; Tables 3, 4, 5, 6, 7, 8, 9, 10, 11, 12, 15, 16,
17, 18, 19, 20, 21, 22, 23, 24, 25
UZBEKISTAN...43-44; Tables 3, 4, 5, 6, 7, 8, 9, 10, 11, 12, 13, 15,
16, 17, 18, 19, 20, 23, 24, 25

VANUATU...44; Tables 3, 5, 6, 8
VENEZUELA...11, 44; Tables 3, 4, 5, 6, 7, 8, 9, 10, 11, 12, 15, 16,
17, 18, 19, 20, 21, 22, 23, 24, 25
VIET NAM...43-44; Tables 3, 5, 6, 7, 8, 23, 25
VITAL STATISTICS...7-13
comparability of...7
definition of components of...70
estimated, reliability of...12, 70
events, defined...7-8
fragmentary...9
method of calculating series...9-10
nonstandard definitions of events...8-9
published standards for...7
quality of
methods and codes used to indicate...6-7, 10-11
variability in, due to tabulation procedures...9
sources of data...7-10
Table of
Vital statistics summary and expectation of life at
birth...Table 4; Annex II
typographic codes used to indicate reliability of...12

WALLIS AND FUTUNA ISLANDS...44; Tables 3, 8
WESTERN AFRICA (MAJOR REGION)...43-44; Tables 1, 2
WESTERN ASIA (MAJOR REGION)...43-44; Tables 1, 2
WESTERN EUROPE (MAJOR REGION)...44; Tables 1, 2
WESTERN SAHARA...43-44; Tables 3, 8
WHIPPLE'S INDEX...6
WOMEN
tabulation by
Legally induced abortions by age and number of previous live
births of woman...Table 14

Live birth rates specific for age of mother, by urban/rural
    residence...Table 11
Live births by age of mother, sex and urban/rural
    residence...Table 10
Marriages by age of groom and age of bride...Table 24
Vital statistics summary and expectation of life at
    birth...Table 4; Annex II
WORKERS
  short-term...4
  temporary, living abroad
  deaths among...505
WORLD, THE
  tabulation by
    Estimates of population and its percentage distribution, by
      age and sex and sex ratio for all ages for the world,
      major areas and regions...Table 2
    Population, rate of increase, birth and death rates, surface
      area and density for the world, major areas and
      regions...Table 1
    World summary...Tables 1-4
WORLD POPULATION PROSPECTS...49

YEMEN...43-44; Tables 3, 5, 6, 7, 8

ZAMBIA...43-44; Tables 3, 5, 6, 7, 8
ZIMBABWE...43-44; Tables 3, 5, 6, 7, 8

ABORIGÈNES

    Voir POPULATIONS AUTOCHTONES

ACCROISSEMENT DE LA POPULATION

    exploitation des données

        aperçu des statistiques de l'état civil et espérance de vie à la naissance...tableau 4; annexe II

        population, taux d'accroissement, de natalité et de mortalité, superficie et densité pour l'ensemble du monde, les grandes régions et les régions géographiques...tableau 1

        population selon le sexe, taux d'accroissement de la population, superficie et densité...tableau 3

    méthode de calcul...45, 55, 72

AFGHANISTAN...47; tableaux 3, 4, 5, 6, 8, 22

AFRIQUE (GRANDE ZONE)...46; tableaux 1, 2

AFRIQUE AUSTRALE (RÉGION)...46; tableaux 1, 2

AFRIQUE CENTRALE (RÉGION)...46; tableaux 1, 2

AFRIQUE DU SUD...46; tableaux 3, 4, 5, 6, 7, 8, 9, 10, 13, 16, 17, 19, 23

AFRIQUE OCCIDENTALE (RÉGION)...46; tableaux 1, 2

AFRIQUE ORIENTALE (RÉGION)...46; tableaux 1, 2

AFRIQUE SEPTENTRIONALE (RÉGION)...46; tableaux 1, 2

ÂGE

    au dernier anniversaire...20, 132, 449

    causes d'erreurs dans les données...20

    exploitation des données

        avortements

            avortements provoqués légalement selon l'âge de la femme et selon le nombre des naissances vivantes précédentes...tableau 14

        décès et taux de mortalité

            décès d'enfants de moins d'un an et taux de mortalité infantile selon l'âge et le sexe...tableau 16

            décès selon l'âge, le sexe et la résidence, urbaine/rurale...tableau 19

            décès selon l'état matrimonial, l'âge et le sexe...tableau 21

            taux de mortalité selon l'âge, le sexe et la résidence, urbaine/rurale...tableau 20

        espérance de vie

            espérance de vie à un âge donné pour chaque sexe...tableau 22

        mariages

            mariages selon l'âge de l'époux et de l'épouse...tableau 24

        naissances

            naissances vivantes, taux selon l'âge de la mère et la résidence, urbaine/rurale...tableau 11

naissances vivantes selon l'âge de la mère, le sexe de
l'enfant et la résidence, urbaine/rurale...tableau 10

population

estimations de la population et pourcentage de répartition
selon l'âge et le sexe et rapport de masculinité pour
l'ensemble du monde, les grandes régions et les
régions géographiques...tableau 2

population selon l'âge, le sexe et la résidence,
urbaine/rurale...tableau 7

fiabilité des données...20-21

méthodes de calcul (méthodes anglaise et chinoise)...29n7

négligences dans les déclarations et fausses déclarations...20

se terminant par zéro ou certains autres chiffres...20

AGGLOMÉRATION URBAINE

définition...218

ALBANIE...44; tableaux 3, 4, 5, 6, 8, 9, 10, 13, 15, 17, 18, 19, 22,
23, 24, 25

ALGÉRIE...46; tableaux 3, 4, 5, 6, 7, 8, 9, 12, 15, 18, 19, 22, 23

ALLEMAGNE...12, 26-27, 44; tableaux 4, 5, 7, 8, 9, 10, 11, 12, 13, 14,
15, 16, 17, 18, 19, 20, 21, 22, 23, 25

AMÉRIQUE CENTRALE (RÉGION)...45, 46; tableaux 1, 2

AMÉRIQUE DU NORD (CONTINENT)...45

AMÉRIQUE DU SUD (CONTINENT)...45

AMÉRIQUE DU SUD (RÉGION)...46; tableaux 1, 2

AMÉRIQUE LATINE (GRANDE ZONE)...45, 46; tableaux 1, 2

AMÉRIQUE SEPTENTRIONALE (GRANDE ZONE)...45, 47; tableaux 1, 2

ANALYSE DÉMOGRAPHIQUE

évaluation des statistiques de l'état civil...26

ANDORRE...44; tableaux 3, 4, 5, 7, 8, 9, 10, 11, 12, 15, 16, 18, 19,
23

ANGOLA...46; tableaux 3, 8

ANGUILLA...46; tableaux 3, 4, 5, 7, 8, 9, 10, 11, 13, 15, 17, 18, 19,
23, 24, 25

ANNUAIRE DÉMOGRAPHIQUE

historique et teneur...15

ANTIGUA-ET-BARBUDA...46; tableaux 3, 4, 5, 7, 8, 9, 10, 11, 16, 17,
18, 19

ANTILLES NÉERLANDAISES...46; tableaux 3, 4, 5, 7, 8, 9, 18, 22, 23, 25

ARABIE SAOUDITE...47; tableaux 3, 4, 5, 7, 8, 9, 10, 15, 18, 23, 25

ARGENTINE...26-27, 46; tableaux 3, 4, 5, 6, 7, 8, 9, 10, 11, 12, 15,
16, 17, 18, 19, 20, 23

ARMÉNIE...47; tableaux 3, 4, 5, 6, 7, 8, 9, 10, 11, 12, 13, 15, 16,
17, 18, 19, 20, 22, 23, 24, 25

ARUBA...46; tableaux 3, 4, 5, 7, 8, 9, 10, 15, 18, 22, 23, 25

ASCENSION

Voir SAINTE-HÉLÈNE

ASIE (GRANDE ZONE)...47; tableaux 1, 2

ASIE CENTRALE ET DU SUD (RÉGION), 40...47; tableaux 1, 2

ASIE DU SUD-EST (RÉGION), 40...47; tableaux 1, 2

ASIE OCCIDENTALE (RÉGION)...47; tableaux 1, 2

ASIE ORIENTALE (RÉGION)...47; tableaux 1, 2

AUSTRALIE...26-27, 44; tableaux 3, 4, 5, 7, 8, 9, 10, 11, 12, 15, 16,
            17, 18, 19, 20, 21, 22, 23, 24, 25

AUSTRALIE ET NOUVELLE-ZÉLANDE (RÉGION)...44; tableaux 1, 2

AUTRICHE...44; tableaux 3, 4, 5, 6, 7, 8, 9, 10, 11, 12, 15, 16, 17,
            18, 19, 20, 21, 22, 23, 24, 25

AVORTEMENT

    définition...23, 375

    motifs d'autorisation, selon les pays...375

    types...375

AVORTEMENTS LÉGAUX, NOMBRE

    collecte des données...380

    exploitation des données

        avortements provoqués légalement...tableau 13

        avortements provoqués légalement selon l'âge de la femme et
            selon le nombre des naissances vivantes
            précédentes...tableau 14

AZERBAÏDJAN...47; tableaux 3, 4, 5, 6, 7, 8, 9, 10, 11, 12, 13, 14,
            15, 16, 17, 18, 19, 20, 21, 22, 23, 24, 25

BAHAMAS...12, 26-27, 46; tableaux 3, 4, 5, 7, 8, 9, 10, 15, 16, 17,
            18, 19, 20, 21, 23, 24, 25

BAHREÏN...47; tableaux 3, 4, 5, 7, 8, 9, 10, 12, 13, 15, 16, 17, 18,
            19, 22, 23, 24, 25

BANGLADESH...47; tableaux 3, 5, 6, 8, 22

BARBADE...26-27, 46; tableaux 3, 4, 5, 8, 9, 15, 17, 18, 23

BÉLARUS...47; tableaux 3, 4, 5, 6, 7, 8, 9, 10, 11, 13, 14, 15, 16,
            17, 18, 19, 20, 22, 23, 24, 25

BELGIQUE...12, 26-27, 44; tableaux 3, 4, 5, 7, 8, 9, 12, 13, 14, 15,
            16, 17, 18, 19, 20, 22, 23, 24, 25

BELIZE...46; tableaux 3, 4, 5, 6, 7, 8, 9, 10, 15, 17, 18, 19, 23, 25

BÉNIN...46; tableaux 3, 4, 5, 6, 7, 8, 9, 15, 18

BERMUDES...12, 26-27, 47; tableaux 3, 4, 5, 7, 8, 9, 10, 11, 12, 15,
            17, 18, 19, 23, 25

BHOUTAN...47; tableaux 3, 5, 7, 8, 22

BOLIVIE...46; tableaux 3, 4, 5, 6, 7, 8, 9, 15, 18, 22

BOSNIE-HERZÉGOVINE...44; tableaux 3, 4, 5, 8, 9, 10, 15, 16, 18, 19,
            22, 23, 24, 25

BOTSWANA...46; tableaux 3, 4, 5, 6, 7, 8, 9, 15, 18, 19, 20, 22

BRÉSIL...46; tableaux 3, 4, 5, 6, 7, 8, 9, 10, 12, 15, 16, 17, 18, 19,
            21, 22, 23, 24, 25

BRUNÉI DARUSSALAM...47; tableaux 3, 4, 5, 6, 7, 8, 9, 10, 11, 15, 18,
            19, 20, 23, 24, 25

BULGARIE...12, 26-27, 47; tableaux 3, 4, 5, 6, 7, 8, 9, 10, 11, 12,
          13, 14, 15, 16, 17, 18, 19, 20, 21, 22, 23, 24, 25
BURKINA FASO...46; tableaux 3, 5, 6, 7, 8
BURUNDI...46; tableaux 3, 5, 6, 8

CAMBODGE...47; tableaux 3, 5, 6, 7, 8
CAMEROUN...46; tableaux 3, 5, 6, 8
CANADA...26-27, 47; tableaux 3, 4, 5, 6, 7, 8, 9, 10, 11, 12, 13, 14,
          15, 16, 17, 18, 19, 20, 21, 22, 23, 24, 25
CAPITALES
    exploitation des données
        population des capitales et des villes de 100 000 habitants
            et plus...tableau 8
CAP-VERT...46; tableaux 3, 4, 5, 6, 7, 8, 9
CARAÏBES (RÉGION)...45, 46; tableaux 1, 2
CHILI...26-27, 46; tableaux 3, 4, 5, 6, 7, 8, 9, 10, 11, 12, 15, 16,
          17, 18, 19, 20, 21, 22, 23, 24
CHINE (RÉPUBLIQUE POPULAIRE DE)...17, 43-44; tableaux 3, 4, 5, 6, 7,
          8, 9, 18, 19, 22, 23, 25
    région administrative spéciale de Hong Kong...12, 26-27, 47;
            tableaux 3, 4, 5, 7, 8, 9, 10, 11, 12, 13, 14, 15, 16,
            17, 18, 19, 20, 21, 22, 23, 24, 25
    région administrative spéciale de Macao...26-27, 47; tableaux 3,
            4, 5, 7, 8, 9, 10, 11, 12, 15, 16, 18, 19, 20, 21, 22,
            23, 24, 25
CHRISTMAS ISLANDS
    voir KIRIBATI
CHYPRE...26-27, 47; tableaux 3, 4, 5, 6, 7, 8, 9, 10, 11, 15, 16, 18,
          19, 20, 22, 23, 24, 25
COLOMBIE...46; tableaux 3, 4, 5, 6, 7, 8, 9, 10, 12, 15, 16, 17, 18,
          19, 21, 22
COMORES...46; tableaux 3, 8
COMPARABILITÉ DES STATISTIQUES...18
    au fil du temps...17
    sur le plan international...17, 25
CONGO (RÉPUBLIQUE DÉMOCRATIQUE DU)...46; tableaux 3, 4, 5, 7, 8, 9
CONGO (RÉPUBLIQUE DU)...46; tableaux 3, 8
CONTINENTS
    traitement statistique...45
CORÉE (RÉPUBLIQUE DE)...26-27, 47; tableaux 3, 4, 5, 6, 7, 8, 9, 10,
          11, 15, 17, 18, 19, 20, 21, 22, 23, 24, 25
CORÉE (RÉPUBLIQUE POPULAIRE DÉMOCRATIQUE DE)...47; tableaux 3, 8, 22
COSTA RICA...46; tableaux 3, 4, 5, 6, 7, 8, 9, 10, 11, 12, 15, 16, 17,
          18, 19, 20, 21, 22, 23, 24
CÔTE D'IVOIRE...46; tableaux 3, 4, 5, 8, 9, 15, 18
CROATIE...26-27, 44; tableaux 3, 4, 5, 6, 7, 8, 9, 10, 11, 12, 13, 14,
          15, 16, 17, 18, 19, 20, 21, 23, 24, 25

CUBA...12, 26–27, 46; tableaux 3, 4, 5, 6, 7, 8, 9, 10, 11, 12, 13,
        15, 16, 17, 18, 19, 20, 21, 22, 23, 24, 25

DANEMARK...12, 26–27, 44; tableaux 3, 4, 5, 7, 8, 9, 10, 11, 12, 13,
        14, 15, 16, 17, 18, 19, 20, 21, 22, 23, 24, 25
DATE DE L'ÉVÉNEMENT...24–25
DÉCÈS
    âge de...548
    cause...424
    définition...23, 72
    sources de données...23
DÉCÈS, NOMBRE
    exploitation des données
        âge
            décès d'enfants de moins d'un an et taux de mortalité
                infantile selon l'âge et le sexe...tableau 16
            décès selon l'âge, le sexe et la résidence,
                urbaine/rurale...tableau 19
            décès selon l'état matrimonial, l'âge et le sexe...tableau
                21
            taux de mortalité selon l'âge, le sexe et la résidence,
                urbaine/rurale...tableau 20
        aperçu
            aperçu des statistiques de l'état civil et espérance de
                vie à la naissance...tableau 4
        état matrimonial
            décès selon l'état matrimonial, l'âge et le sexe...tableau
                21
        lieu de résidence (zone urbaine ou rurale)
            décès et taux bruts de mortalité, selon la résidence,
                urbaine/rurale...tableau 18
            décès selon l'âge, le sexe et la résidence,
                urbaine/rurale...tableau 19
        sexe
            décès d'enfants de moins d'un an et taux de mortalité
                infantile selon l'âge et le sexe...tableau 16
            décès selon l'âge, le sexe et la résidence,
                urbaine/rurale...tableau 19
            décès selon l'état matrimonial, l'âge et le sexe...tableau
                21
            taux de mortalité selon l'âge, le sexe et la résidence,
                urbaine/rurale...tableau 20
    retards dans l'enregistrement...449
    sources de données...22, 435
    statistiques...25
    Voir aussi DÉCÈS D'ENFANTS DE MOINS D'UN AN; MORTALITÉ LIÉE À LA
            MATERNITÉ; MORT FOETALE, TARDIVE

DÉCÈS D'ENFANTS DE MOINS D'UN AN
    définition...29, 72, 392
DÉCÈS D'ENFANTS DE MOINS D'UN AN, NOMBRE
    exclusions de, pour calculer décès, dans certains cas...449
    exploitation des données
        aperçu des statistiques de l'état civil et espérance de vie à
            la naissance...tableau 4
        décès d'enfants de moins d'un an et taux de mortalité
            infantile selon l'âge et le sexe...tableau 16
        décès d'enfants de moins d'un an et taux de mortalité
            infantile selon la résidence, urbaine/rurale...tableau
            15
    fiabilité des données...405
DÉCÈS PAR CAUSE OBSTÉTRICALE
    directes et indirectes...28
DÉNOMBREMENTS GÉNÉRALES
    au niveau national...55
DÉNOMINATEUR
    calcul des taux, fiabilité...27
    correspondance du dénominateur et du numérateur...507
DENSITÉ DE POPULATION
    définition...55
    exploitation des données
        population, taux d'accroissement, de natalité et de
            mortalité, superficie et densité pour l'ensemble du
            monde, les grandes régions et les régions
            géographiques...tableau 1
        population selon le sexe, taux d'accroissement de la
            population, superficie et densité...tableau 3
    méthode de calcul...45
DIVISION DE LA POPULATION, ONU...45, 50
DIVISION DE STATISTIQUE, ONU...16
DIVORCE
    définition...23, 24, 663
DIVORCES, NOMBRE
    enregistrement...25, 663
    exploitation des données
        Divorces et taux bruts de divortialité...tableau 25
    statistiques...22
DJIBOUTI...46; tableaux 3, 5, 8, 22, 23, 25
DOMINIQUE...46; tableaux 3, 4, 5, 7, 8, 9, 15, 17, 18, 23, 25
DONNÉES
    comparabilité
        sur le plan international et au niveau national...25
    figurant dans L'Annuaire demographique...tableau A
    qualité
        codes...45, 55

influence des retards d'enregistrement…25
DOUBLE CONTRÔLE DES REGISTRES
    évaluation des statistiques de l'état civil…26

ÉGYPTE…26-27, 46; tableaux 3, 4, 5, 6, 7, 8, 9, 10, 11, 12, 15, 16, 17, 18, 19, 20, 21, 22, 23, 24, 25
EL SALVADOR…46; tableaux 3, 4, 5, 6, 7, 8, 9, 10, 11, 12, 15, 16, 17, 18, 19, 20, 21, 22, 23, 24, 25
ÉMIRATS ARABES UNIS…47; tableaux 3, 5, 6, 7, 8
ENQUÊTE PAR SONDAGE…22, 55
ENQUÊTE SUR LES MÉNAGES…22
ENREGISTREMENT DES FAITS D'ÉTAT CIVIL
    données…22, 72, 303, 435
        incomplètes…24, 25
        qualité…25-26, 28, 135, 619, 663
    exploitation des données selon la date de l'événement…24-25
    retard…25, 449
ÉQUATEUR…46; tableaux 3, 4, 5, 6, 7, 8, 9, 10, 12, 15, 16, 17, 18, 19, 21, 22, 23, 24, 25
ÉRYTHRÉE…46; tableaux 3, 8
ESPAGNE…44; tableaux 3, 4, 5, 7, 8, 9, 10, 11, 12, 13, 14, 15, 16, 17, 18, 19, 20, 21, 22, 23, 24, 25
ESPÉRANCE DE VIE
    définition…72, 606
    exploitation des données
        aperçu des statistiques de l'état civil et espérance de vie à la naissance…tableau 4; annexe II
        espérance de vie à un âge donné pour chaque sexe…tableau 22
ESTIMATIONS
    données…303
    qualité…21
    tableaux
        estimations de la population au milieu de l'année…tableau 5; annexe I
        estimations de la population et pourcentage de répartition selon l'âge et le sexe et rapport de masculinité pour l'ensemble du monde, les grandes régions et les régions géographiques…tableau 2
ESTONIE…26-27, 44; tableaux 3, 4, 5, 6, 7, 8, 9, 10, 11, 12, 13, 14, 15, 16, 17, 18, 19, 20, 21, 22, 23, 24, 25
ÉTAT CIVIL
    Voir aussi ENREGISTREMENT DES FAITS D'ÉTAT CIVIL
ÉTAT MATRIMONIAL
    définition…548
    exploitation des données
        décès

décès selon l'état matrimonial, l'âge et le sexe...tableau 21

fiabilité des données...548

négligences dans les déclarations et fausses déclarations...548

ÉTATS-UNIS D'AMÉRIQUE...26–27, 47; tableaux 3, 4, 5, 6, 7, 8, 9, 10, 11, 12, 15, 16, 17, 18, 19, 20, 21, 22, 23

ÉTHIOPIE...46; tableaux 3, 4, 5, 6, 7, 8, 9, 15, 18, 22, 23, 25

ÉTRANGERS

exploitation des données...24

EUROPE (GRANDE ZONE)...47; tableaux 1, 2

EUROPE MÉRIDIONALE (RÉGION)...44; tableaux 1, 2

EUROPE OCCIDENTALE (RÉGION)...44; tableaux 1, 2

EUROPE ORIENTALE (RÉGION)...47; tableaux 1, 2

EUROPE SEPTENTRIONALE (RÉGION)...43–44; tableaux 1, 2

ÉVÉNEMENT

exploitation des données

selon la date de l'événement...24–25

selon le lieu de l'événement...24

FEMMES

exploitation des données

aperçu des statistiques de l'état civil et espérance de vie à la naissance...tableau 4; annexe II

avortements provoqués légalement selon l'âge de la femme et selon le nombre des naissances vivantes précédentes...tableau 14

mariages selon l'âge de l'époux et de l'épouse...tableau 24

naissances vivantes, taux selon l'âge de la mère et la résidence, urbaine/rurale...tableau 11

naissances vivantes selon l'âge de la mère, le sexe de l'enfant et la résidence, urbaine/rurale...tableau 10

FIDJI...12, 26–27, 44; tableaux 3, 4, 5, 6, 7, 8, 9, 15, 17, 18

FINLANDE...12, 26–27, 44; tableaux 3, 4, 5, 6, 7, 8, 9, 10, 11, 12, 13, 14, 15, 16, 17, 18, 19, 20, 21, 22, 23, 24, 25

FRANCE...12, 26–27, 44; tableaux 3, 4, 5, 7, 8, 9, 10, 11, 12, 13, 14, 15, 16, 17, 18, 19, 20, 21, 22, 23, 24, 25

GABON...46; tableaux 3, 4, 5, 8

GAMBIE...46; tableaux 3, 5, 8

GÉORGIE...47; tableaux 3, 4, 5, 6, 7, 8, 9, 10, 11, 12, 13, 14, 15, 16, 17, 18, 19, 20, 21, 22, 23, 24, 25

GHANA...46; tableaux 3, 4, 5, 6, 7, 8, 9, 15, 18

GIBRALTAR...44; tableaux 3, 4, 5, 7, 8, 9, 10, 11, 15, 18, 23, 25

GRANDES ZONES

définition...45

exploitation des données

estimations de la population et pourcentage de répartition
selon l'âge et le sexe et rapport de masculinité pour
l'ensemble du monde, les grandes régions et les
régions géographiques…tableau 2

population, taux d'accroissement, de natalité et de
mortalité, superficie et densité pour l'ensemble du
monde, les grandes régions et les régions
géographiques…tableau 1

figurant dans L'Annuaire demographique…tableau A

noms…17

pays qui composent…45-47

GRÈCE…12, 26-27, 44; tableaux 3, 4, 5, 7, 8, 9, 10, 11, 12, 13, 14,
15, 16, 17, 18, 19, 20, 21, 22, 23, 25

GRENADE…46; tableaux 3, 4, 5, 7, 8, 9, 10, 11, 15, 17, 18, 19, 20,
23, 24, 25

GROENLAND…12, 26-27, 47; tableaux 3, 4, 5, 6, 7, 8, 9, 10, 11, 13,
15, 16, 18, 19, 21, 22

GROSSESSE
interruption…23

GROUPES D'ÂGE
définition…50

GUADELOUPE…26-27, 46; tableaux 3, 4, 5, 7, 8, 9, 10, 11, 12, 15, 16,
18, 19, 20, 21, 22, 23, 24, 25

GUAM…12, 26-27, 44; tableaux 3, 4, 5, 6, 7, 8, 9, 10, 15, 18, 23

GUATEMALA…46; tableaux 3, 4, 5, 7, 8, 9, 10, 11, 12, 15, 16, 17, 18,
19, 20, 21, 22, 23, 25

GUINÉE…46; tableaux 3, 7, 8

GUINÉE-BISSAU…46; tableaux 3, 5, 8

GUINÉE ÉQUATORIALE…46; tableaux 3, 8

GUYANA…46; tableaux 3, 4, 5, 8, 17, 18

GUYANE FRANÇAISE…26-27, 46; tableaux 3, 4, 5, 7, 8, 9, 10, 11, 12,
15, 16, 18, 19, 21, 22, 23, 24, 25

HAÏTI…46; tableaux 3, 5, 6, 7, 8

HOMMES
exploitation des données
aperçu des statistiques de l'état civil et espérance de vie à
la naissance…tableau 4; annexe II
mariages selon l'âge de l'époux et de l'épouse…tableau 24

HONDURAS…46; tableaux 3, 5, 6, 7, 8

HONG KONG
Voir CHINE, RÉGION ADMINISTRATIVE SPÉCIALE DE HONG KONG

HONGRIE…26-27, 47; tableaux 3, 4, 5, 6, 7, 8, 9, 10, 11, 12, 13, 14,
15, 16, 17, 18, 19, 20, 21, 22, 23, 24, 25

ÎLE DE MAN…12, 26-27, 44; tableaux 3, 4, 5, 7, 8, 9, 12, 15, 16, 18,
19, 22, 23, 24, 25

ÎLE NORFOLK...44; tableaux 3, 8

ÎLES ANGLO-NORMANDES...43

    Guernesey...12, 26-27; tableaux 3, 4, 5, 7, 8, 9, 10, 11, 12, 13, 14, 15, 16, 18, 19, 23, 25

    Jersey...tableaux 3, 5, 7, 8, 10, 16, 19

ÎLES CAÏMANES...12, 26-27, 46; tableaux 3, 4, 5, 8, 9, 10, 16, 17, 18, 19, 23, 25

ÎLES COOK...12, 26-27, 44; tableaux 3, 4, 5, 6, 7, 8, 9, 15, 18, 23

ÎLES FALKLAND (MALVINAS)...46; tableaux 3, 4, 7, 8, 9, 18

ÎLES FÉROÉ...44; tableaux 3, 5, 8

ÎLES MARIANNES SEPTENTRIONALES...44; tableaux 3, 4, 5, 7, 8, 9, 10, 15, 18, 19

ÎLES MARSHALL...44; tableaux 3, 4, 5, 7, 8, 9, 10, 15, 18, 19, 22

ÎLES SALOMON...44; tableaux 3, 8

ÎLES SVALBARD ET JAN MAYEN...43; tableau 3

ÎLES TURQUES ET CAÏQUES...46; tableaux 3, 4, 5, 7, 8, 9, 10, 12, 13, 15, 17, 18, 19, 22, 23, 24, 25

ÎLES VIERGES AMÉRICAINES...46; tableaux 3, 5, 7, 8, 17

ÎLES VIERGES BRITANNIQUES...46; tableaux 3, 4, 5, 7, 8, 9, 15, 17, 18

ÎLES WALLIS ET FUTUNA...44; tableaux 3, 8

INDE...47; tableaux 3, 4, 5, 6, 7, 8, 9, 15, 18, 22

INDONÉSIE...47; tableaux 3, 4, 5, 6, 7, 8, 22

IRAN...47; tableaux 3, 4, 5, 6, 7, 8, 9, 10, 15, 18, 22, 23, 25

IRAQ...47; tableaux 3, 4, 5, 6, 7, 8, 9, 10, 18, 22, 23

IRLANDE...26-27, 44; tableaux 3, 4, 5, 6, 7, 8, 9, 10, 11, 12, 15, 16, 17, 18, 19, 20, 21, 22, 23, 25

ISLANDE...12, 26-27, 44; tableaux 3, 4, 5, 6, 7, 8, 9, 10, 11, 12, 13, 14, 15, 16, 17, 18, 19, 20, 21, 22, 23, 24, 25

ISRAËL...26-27, 47; tableaux 3, 4, 5, 6, 7, 8, 9, 10, 11, 12, 13, 14, 15, 16, 17, 18, 19, 20, 22, 23, 24, 25

ITALIE...44; tableaux 3, 4, 5, 6, 7, 8, 9, 10, 11, 12, 13, 14, 15, 16, 17, 18, 19, 20, 21, 22, 23, 24, 25

JAMAÏQUE...46; tableaux 3, 4, 5, 6, 7, 8, 9, 10, 11, 15, 18, 22, 23, 24, 25

JAPON...12, 26-27, 47; tableaux 3, 4, 5, 6, 7, 8, 9, 10, 11, 12, 13, 14, 15, 16, 17, 18, 19, 20, 21, 22, 23, 24, 25

JORDANIE...47; tableaux 3, 4, 5, 6, 7, 8, 9, 18, 22, 23, 24, 25

KAZAKHSTAN...47; tableaux 3, 4, 5, 6, 7, 8, 9, 10, 11, 12, 13, 14, 15, 16, 17, 18, 19, 20, 21, 22, 23, 24, 25

KENYA...46; tableaux 3, 4, 5, 6, 8, 9, 10, 15, 18, 19, 22

KIRGHIZISTAN...26-27, 47; tableaux 3, 4, 5, 6, 7, 8, 9, 10, 11, 12, 13, 15, 16, 17, 18, 19, 20, 22, 23, 24, 25

KIRIBATI...44; tableaux 3, 5, 8, 10

KOWEÏT...26-27, 47; tableaux 3, 4, 5, 7, 8, 9, 11, 12, 15, 16, 17, 18, 19, 20, 23, 24, 25

LAO, RÉPUBLIQUE DÉMOCRATIQUE POPULAIRE...47; tableaux 3, 4, 5, 6, 7, 8
LESOTHO...46; tableaux 3, 4, 5, 6, 7, 8, 22
LETTONIE...26-27, 44; tableaux 3, 4, 5, 6, 7, 8, 9, 10, 11, 12, 13,
        14, 15, 16, 17, 18, 19, 20, 21, 22, 23, 24, 25
LIBAN...47; tableaux 3, 4, 8, 9, 18, 23, 25
LIBÉRIA...46; tableaux 3, 5, 6, 8
LIBYENNE, JAMAHIRIYA ARABE...46; tableaux 3, 4, 5, 8, 9, 10, 15, 18,
        19, 21, 23, 25
LIECHTENSTEIN...44; tableaux 3, 4, 5, 7, 8, 9, 10, 11, 15, 18, 19, 21,
        23, 25
LIEU DE L'ÉVÉNEMENT...24
LIEU DE RÉSIDENCE (ZONE URBAINE OU RURALE)
    définition...19, 105
    exploitation des données
        décès d'enfants de moins d'un an
            décès d'enfants de moins d'un an et taux de mortalité
                infantile selon le lieu de résidence (zone...tableau 15
        mariages
            mariages et taux bruts de nuptialité, selon la résidence,
                urbaine/rurale...tableau 23
        morts foetales
            morts foetales tardives et rapports de mortinatalité selon
                la résidence, urbaine/rurale...tableau 12
        naissances
            naissances vivantes, taux selon l'âge de la mère et la
                résidence, urbaine/rurale...tableau 11
            naissances vivantes et taux bruts de natalité selon la
                résidence, urbaine/rurale...tableau 9
            naissances vivantes selon l'âge de la mère, le sexe de
                l'enfant et la résidence, urbaine/rurale...tableau 10
        population
            population selon l'âge, le sexe et la résidence,
                urbaine/rurale...tableau 7
        taux de mortalité et décès
            décès et taux bruts de mortalité, selon la résidence,
                urbaine/rurale...tableau 18
            décès selon l'âge, le sexe et la résidence,
                urbaine/rurale...tableau 19
            taux de mortalité selon l'âge, le sexe et la résidence,
                urbaine/rurale...tableau 20
    figurant dans L'Annuaire demographique...tableau A
    hétérogénéité des définitions nationales...105-109
    Voir aussi VILLES
LIEU DE RÉSIDENCE HABITUEL...24
LITUANIE...26-27, 44; tableaux 3, 4, 5, 6, 7, 8, 9, 10, 11, 12, 13,
        14, 15, 16, 17, 18, 19, 20, 21, 22, 23, 24, 25

LUXEMBOURG...12, 26-27, 44; tableaux 3, 4, 5, 7, 8, 9, 10, 11, 12, 15, 16, 17, 18, 19, 20, 21, 22, 23, 24, 25

MACAO
    Voir CHINE, RÉGION ADMINISTRATIVE SPÉCIALE DE MACAO
MACÉDOINE (EX-RÉPUBLIQUE YOUGOSLAVE DE)...44; tableaux 3, 4, 5, 6, 7, 8, 9, 10, 11, 12, 13, 15, 16, 17, 18, 19, 20, 21, 22, 23, 24, 25
MADAGASCAR...46; tableaux 3, 5, 6, 8
MALAISIE...47; tableaux 3, 4, 5, 6, 7, 8, 9, 12, 15, 16, 18, 19, 20, 22
    péninsulaire...26-27
MALAWI...46; tableaux 3, 4, 5, 6, 7, 8, 9, 15, 18, 19, 20, 22
MALDIVES...12, 26-27, 47; tableaux 3, 4, 5, 6, 7, 8, 9, 10, 11, 12, 15, 16, 18, 19, 20, 22, 23, 25
MALI...46; tableaux 3, 4, 5, 8, 9
MALTE...44; tableaux 3, 4, 5, 7, 8, 9, 10, 11, 15, 16, 17, 18, 19, 20, 21, 22, 23, 24
MARIAGE
    âge de nubilité...24, 633
    définition...23, 24, 619, 633
MARIAGES, NOMBRE
    enregistrement...25, 619, 633
    exploitation des données
        mariages et taux bruts de nuptialité, selon la résidence, urbaine/rurale...tableau 23
        mariages selon l'âge de l'époux et de l'épouse...tableau 24
    statistiques...22
MAROC...46; tableaux 3, 4, 5, 6, 7, 8, 9, 10, 11, 15, 16, 18, 19
MARTINIQUE...46; tableaux 3, 4, 5, 7, 8, 9, 10, 11, 12, 15, 16, 18, 19, 20, 21, 22, 23, 24, 25
MASCULINITÉ, RAPPORT DE
    définition...50
MAURICE...26-27, 46; tableaux 3, 4, 5, 6, 7, 8, 9, 10, 11, 12, 15, 16, 17, 18, 19, 20, 21, 22, 23, 24, 25
MAURITANIE...46; tableaux 3, 5, 8
MÉLANÉSIE (RÉGION)...44; tableaux 1, 2
MÉNAGES
    Voir ENQUÊTE SUR LES MÉNAGES
MÈRE
    Voir FEMMES; LES ENTRÉES CONCERNANT MATERNITÉ
MEXIQUE...46; tableaux 3, 4, 5, 6, 7, 8, 9, 10, 12, 13, 14, 15, 16, 17, 18, 19, 20, 21, 23, 24, 25
MICRONÉSIE (ÉTATS FÉDÉRÉS DE)...44; tableaux 3, 5, 7, 8
MICRONÉSIE (RÉGION)...44; tableaux 1, 2
MOLDOVA (RÉPUBLIQUE DE)...47; tableaux 3, 4, 5, 6, 7, 8, 9, 10, 11, 13, 14, 15, 16, 17, 18, 19, 20, 21, 22, 23, 24, 25

MONACO…44; tableaux 3, 4, 5, 7, 8, 9, 18, 23, 25
MONDE
    aperçu…tableaux 1-4
    exploitation des données
        estimations de la population et pourcentage de répartition
                selon l'âge et le sexe et rapport de masculinité pour
                l'ensemble du monde, les grandes régions et les
                régions géographiques…tableau 2
        population, taux d'accroissement, de natalité et de
                mortalité, superficie et densité pour l'ensemble du
                monde, les grandes régions et les régions
                géographiques…tableau 1
MONGOLIE…47; tableaux 3, 4, 5, 6, 7, 8, 9, 10, 11, 13, 15, 18, 19,
                20, 22, 23, 24, 25
MONTSERRAT…46; tableaux 3, 4, 5, 7, 8, 9, 10, 15, 16, 18, 19, 23, 25
MORTALITÉ…tableaux 12-22
MORTALITÉ INFANTILE…tableaux 15-17
MORTALITÉ LIÉE À LA MATERNITÉ…28
    définition…28, 424
MORTALITÉ LIÉE À LA MATERNITÉ, NOMBRE
    exploitation des données
        mortalité liée à la maternité, nombre de décès et
                taux…tableau 17
    méthode de calcul…424
MORTALITÉ PÉRINATALE…28
    définition…28
MORT FOETALE…tableaux 12-14
    définition…23
MORT FOETALE TARDIVE
    définition…23, 29, 365
MORT FOETALE TARDIVE, NOMBRE
    enregistrement…25
    exploitation des données
        morts foetales tardives et rapports de mortinatalité selon la
                résidence, urbaine/rurale…tableau 12
MORT FOETALE TARDIVE, RAPPORTS
    exploitation des données
        morts foetales tardives et rapports de mortinatalité selon la
                résidence, urbaine/rurale…tableau 12
    méthode de calcul…365
MOZAMBIQUE…46; tableaux 3, 4, 5, 6, 7, 8, 9, 15, 18, 19, 20
MYANMAR…47; tableaux 3, 5, 6, 7, 8, 10, 16, 19

NAISSANCE, À
    exploitation des données
        aperçu des statistiques de l'état civil et espérance de vie à
                la naissance…tableau 4

NAISSANCE VIVANTE
    définition...23, 72, 303
    sources de données...23
NAISSANCE VIVANTE, NOMBRE
    enregistrement tardif...25, 318, 353, 366, 392
    exploitation des données
        aperçu des statistiques de l'état civil et espérance de vie à
                la naissance...tableau 4
        avortements provoqués légalement selon l'âge de la femme et
                selon le nombre des naissances vivantes
                précédentes...tableau 14
        naissances vivantes et taux bruts de natalité selon la
                résidence, urbaine/rurale...tableau 9
        naissances vivantes selon l'âge de la mère, le sexe de
                l'enfant et la résidence, urbaine/rurale...tableau 10
    méthode de calcul...318
    sources de données...22
NAMIBIE...46; tableaux 3, 4, 5, 6, 7, 8, 9, 10, 11, 18, 19
NATALITÉ...tableaux 9-11
NAURU...44; tableaux 3, 4, 5, 8, 22
NÉPAL...47; tableaux 3, 4, 5, 6, 7, 8, 15, 18, 19, 20
NICARAGUA...46; tableaux 3, 4, 5, 6, 7, 8, 9, 10, 15, 16, 17, 18, 19,
                21, 22, 23, 25
NIGER...46; tableaux 3, 8
NIGÉRIA...46; tableaux 3, 5, 7, 8
NIOUÉ...44; tableaux 3, 4, 5, 7, 8, 9, 18, 23, 25
NORVÈGE...12, 26-27, 44; tableaux 3, 4, 5, 6, 7, 8, 9, 10, 11, 12, 13,
                14, 15, 16, 17, 18, 19, 20, 21, 22, 23, 24, 25
NOUVELLE-CALÉDONIE...44; tableaux 3, 4, 5, 6, 7, 8, 9, 10, 11, 12, 13,
                15, 16, 18, 19, 20, 21, 22, 23, 24, 25
NOUVELLE-ZÉLANDE...12, 26-27, 44; tableaux 3, 4, 5, 6, 7, 8, 9, 10,
                11, 12, 13, 14, 15, 16, 17, 18, 19, 20, 21, 22, 23,
                24, 25
NUPTIALITÉ...tableaux 23-25
    Voir aussi DIVORCE; MARIAGE

OCÉANIE (GRANDE ZONE)...44; tableaux 1, 2
OMAN...47; tableaux 3, 4, 5, 6, 7, 8, 9, 10, 12, 15, 18, 19, 22
OUGANDA...46; tableaux 3, 5, 6, 7, 8
OUZBÉKISTAN...47; tableaux 3, 4, 5, 6, 7, 8, 9, 10, 11, 12, 13, 15,
                16, 17, 18, 19, 20, 23, 24, 25

PAKISTAN...47; tableaux 3, 4, 5, 6, 7, 8, 9, 10, 11, 15, 16, 18, 19,
                20, 21, 22
PALAOS...44; tableaux 3, 4, 5, 6, 7, 8, 9, 10, 15, 18, 19
PALESTINIEN, TERRITOIRE OCCUPÉ...47; tableaux 3, 4, 5, 6, 7, 8, 9, 15,
                16, 18, 19, 21, 22, 23, 24, 25

PANAMA...46; tableaux 3, 4, 5, 6, 7, 8, 9, 10, 11, 12, 13, 14, 15, 16,
        17, 18, 19, 21, 22, 23, 24, 25
PAPOUASIE-NOUVELLE-GUINÉE...44; tableaux 3, 4, 5, 6, 7, 8, 9, 12, 15,
        18, 22
PARAGUAY...46; tableaux 3, 4, 5, 6, 7, 8, 15, 17, 18, 19, 22
PAYS
    figurant dans L'Annuaire demographique...tableau A
    noms...17
    régionalization de, par continents, grandes zones et régions...45-
        47
PAYS-BAS...12, 26-27, 44; tableaux 3, 4, 5, 6, 7, 8, 9, 10, 11, 12,
        13, 15, 16, 17, 18, 19, 20, 21, 22, 23, 24, 25
PERMIS D'INHUMER...25
PÉROU...46; tableaux 3, 4, 5, 6, 7, 8, 9, 10, 15, 16, 17, 18, 19, 22
PERSONNEL MILITAIRE, NAVAL ET DIPLOMATIQUE ÉTRANGER...18
    décès...507
PHILIPPINES...47; tableaux 3, 4, 5, 7, 8, 9, 10, 11, 12, 15, 16, 17,
        18, 19, 20, 21, 23, 24
PITCAIRN...44; tableaux 3, 8
POLOGNE...12, 26-27, 47; tableaux 3, 4, 5, 6, 7, 8, 9, 10, 11, 12, 13,
        15, 16, 17, 18, 19, 20, 21, 22, 23, 24, 25
POLYNÉSIE (RÉGION)...44; tableaux 1, 2
POLYNÉSIE FRANÇAISE...44; tableaux 3, 4, 5, 7, 8, 9, 12, 15, 18, 23
POPULATION
    définition...55
    estimations
        qualité...21
    exploitation des données...tableaux 5-8
        âge
            estimations de la population et pourcentage de répartition
                selon l'âge et le sexe et rapport de masculinité pour
                l'ensemble du monde, les grandes régions et les
                régions géographiques...tableau 2
            population selon l'âge, le sexe et la résidence,
                urbaine/rurale...tableau 7
        estimations
            estimations de la population au milieu de l'année...tableau
                5; annexe I
            estimations de la population et pourcentage de répartition
                selon l'âge et le sexe et rapport de masculinité pour
                l'ensemble du monde, les grandes régions et les
                régions géographiques...tableau 2
        lieu de résidence (zone urbaine ou rurale)
            population selon l'âge, le sexe et la résidence,
                urbaine/rurale...tableau 7
            population urbaine et population rurale selon le
                sexe...tableau 5

    population urbaine et population totale selon le sexe...tableau 6

  monde
    population, taux d'accroissement, de natalité et de mortalité, superficie et densité pour l'ensemble du monde, les grandes régions et les régions géographiques...tableau 1

  sexe
    estimations de la population et pourcentage de répartition selon l'âge et le sexe et rapport de masculinité pour l'ensemble du monde, les grandes régions et les régions géographiques...tableau 2
    population selon l'âge, le sexe et la résidence, urbaine/rurale...tableau 7
    population selon le sexe, taux d'accroissement de la population, superficie et densité...tableau 3

  villes
    population des capitales et des villes de 100 000 habitants et plus...tableau 8

  statistiques...18-21

POPULATION AU MILIEU DE L'ANNÉE
  estimations...93
  exploitation des données
    estimations de la population au milieu de l'année...tableau 5; annexe I
  fiabilité...93
  méthode de calcul...55

POPULATION DE DROIT...18

POPULATION DE FAIT...18, 24, 55

POPULATION RURALE
  Voir LIEU DE RÉSIDENCE (ZONE URBAINE OU RURALE)

POPULATIONS AUTOCHTONES
  exploitation des données...24

POPULATION URBAINE
  exploitation des données
    population urbaine et population rurale selon le sexe...tableau 5
    population urbaine et population totale selon le sexe...tableau 6
  méthode de calcul...105
  Voir aussi LIEU DE RÉSIDENCE (ZONE URBAINE OU RURALE); VILLES

PORTÉE ETHNIQUE
  portée...24

PORTÉE GÉOGRAPHIQUE...24

PORTO RICO...26-27, 46; tableaux 3, 4, 5, 6, 7, 8, 9, 10, 11, 12, 13, 15, 16, 17, 18, 19, 20, 21, 22, 23, 24, 25

PORTUGAL...44; tableaux 3, 4, 5, 6, 7, 8, 9, 10, 11, 12, 15, 16, 17,
            18, 19, 20, 21, 22, 23, 24, 25

QATAR...47; tableaux 3, 4, 5, 7, 8, 9, 10, 11, 12, 15, 16, 17, 18, 19,
            20, 21, 23, 24, 25

RAPPORT DE MASCULINITÉ
    définition...50
RÉCAPITULATIFS...16
    aperçu des statistiques de l'état civil et espérance de vie à la
            naissance...tableau 4; annexe II
    monde...tableaux 1-4
RECENSEMENTS...17-18, 19-20
    fiabilité...55
RÉGIONS
    définition...45
    exploitation des données
        estimations de la population et pourcentage de répartition
            selon l'âge et le sexe et rapport de masculinité pour
            l'ensemble du monde, les grandes régions et les
            régions géographiques...tableau 2
        population, taux d'accroissement, de natalité et de
            mortalité, superficie et densité pour l'ensemble du
            monde, les grandes régions et les régions
            géographiques...tableau 1
    figurant dans L'Annuaire demographique...tableau A
    noms...17
    pays qui composent...45-47
RÉPARTITION PAR ÂGE
    définition...19
RÉPARTITION PAR ÂGE ET PAR SEXE
    estimations...21
RÉPUBLIQUE CENTRAFRICAINE...46; tableaux 3, 5, 6, 8
RÉPUBLIQUE DOMINICAINE...46; tableaux 3, 4, 5, 6, 7, 8, 9, 10, 13, 15,
            17, 18, 19, 22, 23, 25
RÉSIDENCE
    Voir LIEU DE RÉSIDENCE (ZONE URBAINE OU RURALE)
RÉSIDENCE HABITUELLE...19, 24
RÉUNION...46; tableaux 3, 4, 5, 7, 8, 9, 10, 11, 13, 15, 16, 18, 19,
            20, 21, 22, 23, 24, 25
ROUMANIE...12, 26-27, 47; tableaux 3, 4, 5, 6, 7, 8, 9, 10, 11, 12,
            13, 14, 15, 16, 17, 18, 19, 20, 21, 22, 23, 24, 25
ROYAUME-UNI DE GRANDE-BRETAGNE ET D'IRLANDE DU NORD...44; tableaux 3,
            4, 5, 7, 8, 9, 10, 11, 12, 13, 14, 15, 16, 17, 18, 19,
            20, 22, 23, 24, 25
RUSSIE (FÉDÉRATION DE)...47; tableaux 3, 4, 5, 6, 7, 8, 9, 10, 11, 12,
            13, 14, 15, 17, 18, 19, 20, 22, 23, 24, 25

RWANDA...46; tableaux 3, 6, 7, 8

SAHARA OCCIDENTAL...46; tableaux 3, 8
SAINTE-HÉLÈNE...46; tableaux 3, 4, 5, 6, 7, 8, 9, 10, 15, 16, 18, 19,
          23, 25
    Ascension...tableau 3
    Tristan da Cunha...tableaux 3, 5, 7
SAINTE-LUCIE...12, 26-27, 46; tableaux 3, 4, 5, 6, 7, 8, 9, 10, 11,
          12, 15, 16, 17, 18, 19, 22, 23, 24, 25
SAINT-KITTS-ET-NEVIS...12, 26-27, 46; tableaux 3, 4, 5, 7, 8, 9, 10,
          11, 17, 18, 19, 22
SAINT-MARIN...26-27, 44; tableaux 3, 4, 5, 6, 7, 8, 9, 10, 11, 12, 15,
          16, 17, 18, 19, 21, 22, 23, 24, 25
SAINT-PIERRE-ET-MIQUELON...47; tableaux 3, 5, 8
SAINT-SIÈGE...44; tableaux 3, 4, 5, 8, 9, 18
SAINT-VINCENT-ET-LES GRENADINES...46; tableaux 3, 4, 5, 6, 7, 8, 9,
          10, 11, 12, 15, 16, 17, 18, 19, 23, 25
SAMOA...44; tableaux 3, 5, 8
SAMOA AMÉRICAINES...44; tableaux 3, 4, 5, 7, 8, 9, 15, 18
SAO TOMÉ-ET-PRINCIPE...46; tableaux 3, 5, 8
SÉNÉGAL...46; tableaux 3, 5, 8
SÉPARATION LÉGALE...663
SERBIE-ET-MONTÉNÉGRO...44; tableaux 3, 4, 5, 6, 7, 8, 9, 10, 11, 12,
          13, 14, 15, 16, 17, 18, 19, 20, 21, 22, 23, 24, 25
SÉRIES CHRONOLOGIQUES
    qualité des données provenant de systèmes permanents
          d'enregistrement des faits d'état civil...28
SERVICES NATIONAUX DE STATISTIQUE
    estimations concernant la complétude des statistiques par soi-
          même...26
SEXE
    exploitation des données
        espérance de vie
            espérance de vie à un âge donné pour chaque sexe...tableau
            22
        naissances
            naissances vivantes selon l'âge de la mère, le sexe de
                l'enfant et la résidence, urbaine/rurale...tableau 10
        population
            estimations de la population et pourcentage de répartition
                selon l'âge et le sexe et rapport de masculinité pour
                l'ensemble du monde, les grandes régions et les
                régions géographiques...tableau 2
            population selon l'âge, le sexe et la résidence,
                urbaine/rurale...tableau 7
            population selon le sexe, taux d'accroissement de la
                population, superficie et densité...tableau 3

population urbaine et population rurale selon le
sexe...tableau 5

population urbaine et population totale selon le
sexe...tableau 6

taux de mortalité et décès

décès d'enfants de moins d'un an et taux de mortalité
infantile selon l'âge et le sexe...tableau 16

décès selon l'âge, le sexe et la résidence,
urbaine/rurale...tableau 19

décès selon l'état matrimonial, l'âge et le sexe...tableau
21

taux de mortalité selon l'âge, le sexe et la résidence,
urbaine/rurale...tableau 20

SEYCHELLES...46; tableaux 3, 4, 5, 7, 8, 9, 13, 15, 18, 19, 23, 24, 25

SIERRA LEONE...46; tableaux 3, 5, 6, 7, 8

SINGAPOUR...12, 26–27, 47; tableaux 3, 4, 5, 7, 8, 9, 10, 11, 12, 13,
14, 15, 16, 17, 18, 19, 21, 22, 23, 24, 25

SLOVAQUIE...47; tableaux 3, 4, 5, 6, 7, 8, 9, 10, 11, 12, 13, 14, 15,
16, 17, 18, 19, 20, 21, 22, 23, 24, 25

SLOVÉNIE...12, 26–27, 44; tableaux 3, 4, 5, 6, 7, 8, 9, 10, 11, 12,
13, 14, 15, 16, 17, 18, 19, 20, 21, 22, 23, 24, 25

SOMALIE...46; tableaux 3, 6, 7, 8

SONDAGE

Voir ENQUÊTE PAR SONDAGE

SOUDAN...46; tableaux 3, 5, 8

SRI LANKA...26–27, 47; tableaux 3, 4, 5, 6, 7, 8, 9, 10, 11, 15, 16,
17, 18, 19, 20, 23

STATISTIQUES

sur CD-ROM et en ligne...15

Voir aussi COMPARABILITÉ DES STATISTIQUES; STATISTIQUES DE
L'ÉTAT CIVIL

STATISTIQUES DE L'ÉTAT CIVIL...21–27

aperçu des statistiques de l'état civil et espérance de vie à la
naissance...tableau 4; annexe II

comparabilité...22

conventions typographiques...27

définition des faits d'état civil...22–23

définitions établies et non établies...23–24

éléments pris en compte...72

évaluation de la fiabilité...28, 72

méthode de calcul...24–25

portée...24

publications...22

qualité

méthodes et codes...21, 25–26

variations dues aux méthodes utilisées...24

sources de données...22–25

SUÈDE...12, 26–27, 44; tableaux 3, 4, 5, 7, 8, 9, 10, 11, 12, 13, 14,
                15, 16, 17, 18, 19, 20, 21, 22, 23, 24, 25
SUISSE...12, 26–27, 44; tableaux 3, 4, 5, 6, 7, 8, 9, 10, 11, 12, 15,
                16, 17, 18, 19, 20, 21, 22, 23, 24, 25
SUPERFICIE
    définition...55
    données...17
    exploitation des données
        population, taux d'accroissement, de natalité et de
                mortalité, superficie et densité pour l'ensemble du
                monde, les grandes régions et les régions
                géographiques...tableau 1
        population selon le sexe, taux d'accroissement de la
                population, superficie et densité...tableau 3
    méthode de calcul...45
SURINAME...46; tableaux 3, 4, 5, 7, 8, 9, 10, 11, 12, 15, 16, 18, 19,
                20, 21, 23, 24, 25
SWAZILAND...46; tableaux 3, 5, 6, 7, 8, 10, 11, 19, 20, 22
SYRIENNE, RÉPUBLIQUE ARABE...47; tableaux 3, 4, 5, 6, 7, 8, 9, 18, 23,
                25

TABLEAUX
    codes et symboles...25
    par date de l'évènement...24–25
    par lieu de l'évènement...24
    table synoptique, des tableaux...30–40; tableau A
TABLES DE MORTALITÉ
    méthode de calcul...606
    Voir aussi ESPÉRANCE DE VIE
TADJIKISTAN...47; tableaux 3, 4, 5, 6, 8, 9, 10, 12, 13, 14, 15, 16,
                17, 18, 19, 23, 24, 25
TAIWAN (PROVINCE)...17
TANZANIE (RÉPUBLIQUE-UNIE DE)...46; tableaux 3, 5, 7, 8
TAUX DE DIVORTIALITÉ
    exploitation des données
        Divorces et taux bruts de divortialité...tableau 25
    méthode de calcul...663
TAUX DE FÉCONDITÉ
    définition...72
    exploitation des données
        aperçu des statistiques de l'état civil et espérance de vie à
                la naissance...tableau 4; annexe II
    Voir aussi TAUX DE NATALITÉ
TAUX DE MORTALITÉ
    définition...72
    exploitation des données

aperçu des statistiques de l'état civil et espérance de vie à
la naissance...tableau 4; annexe II

décès et taux bruts de mortalité, selon la résidence,
urbaine/rurale...tableau 18

population, taux d'accroissement, de natalité et de
mortalité, superficie et densité pour l'ensemble du
monde, les grandes régions et les régions
géographiques...tableau 1

taux de mortalité selon l'âge, le sexe et la résidence,
urbaine/rurale...tableau 20

méthode de calcul...45, 435, 507

TAUX DE MORTALITÉ INFANTILE

définition...23

exploitation des données

aperçu des statistiques de l'état civil et espérance de vie à
la naissance...tableau 4; annexe II

décès d'enfants de moins d'un an et taux de mortalité
infantile selon l'âge et le sexe...tableau 16

décès d'enfants de moins d'un an et taux de mortalité
infantile selon la résidence, urbaine/rurale...tableau
15

méthode de calcul...72, 392, 405

TAUX DE MORTALITÉ LIÉE À LA MATERNITÉ

exploitation des données

mortalité liée à la maternité, nombre de décès et taux...28,
424; tableau 17

TAUX DE NATALITÉ

définition...72

exploitation des données

aperçu des statistiques de l'état civil et espérance de vie à
la naissance...tableau 4; annexe II

naissances vivantes, taux selon l'âge de la mère et la
résidence, urbaine/rurale...tableau 11

naissances vivantes et taux bruts de natalité selon la
résidence, urbaine/rurale...tableau 9

population, taux d'accroissement, de natalité et de
mortalité, superficie et densité pour l'ensemble du
monde, les grandes régions et les régions
géographiques...tableau 1

méthode de calcul...45, 303, 353

TAUX DE NUPTIALITÉ

exploitation des données

mariages et taux bruts de nuptialité, selon la résidence,
urbaine/rurale...tableau 23

méthode de calcul...619

TAUX ET RAPPORTS

calcul...18, 72

qualité (en fonction du dénominateur)...27
TCHAD...46; tableaux 3, 4, 5, 8, 9, 18
TCHÈQUE, RÉPUBLIQUE...26-27, 47; tableaux 3, 4, 5, 6, 7, 8, 9, 10, 11,
        12, 13, 14, 15, 16, 17, 18, 19, 20, 21, 22, 23, 24, 25
THAÏLANDE...47; tableaux 3, 4, 5, 6, 7, 8, 9, 10, 15, 16, 17, 18, 19,
        23
TIMOR-LESTE...47; tableaux 3, 8
TOGO...46; tableaux 3, 5, 8
TOKÉLAOU...12, 26-27, 44; tableaux 3, 7
TONGA...44; tableaux 3, 4, 5, 6, 7, 8, 9, 10, 11, 15, 16, 18, 19, 22,
        23, 24, 25
TRAVAILLEURS
    à court terme...19
    temporaires vivant à l'étranger
        décès...507
TRIBUS NOMADES
    exploitation des données...24
TRINITÉ-ET-TOBAGO...46; tableaux 3, 4, 5, 7, 8, 9, 10, 11, 12, 16, 17,
        18, 19, 20
TRISTAN DA CUNHA
    Voir SAINTE-HÉLÈNE
TUNISIE...46; tableaux 3, 4, 5, 6, 7, 8, 9, 10, 11, 15, 16, 18, 19,
        21, 22, 23, 25
TURKMÉNISTAN...47; tableaux 3, 5, 7, 8, 17
TURQUIE...47; tableaux 3, 4, 5, 6, 7, 8, 9, 10, 11, 15, 16, 18, 22,
        23, 24, 25
TUVALU...44; tableaux 3, 8

UKRAINE...47; tableaux 3, 4, 5, 6, 7, 8, 9, 10, 11, 12, 13, 14, 15,
        16, 17, 18, 19, 20, 22, 23, 24, 25
URUGUAY...12, 26-27, 46; tableaux 3, 4, 5, 6, 7, 8, 9, 10, 11, 12, 15,
        16, 17, 18, 19, 20, 21, 22, 23, 24, 25

VANUATU...44; tableaux 3, 5, 6, 8
VENEZUELA...26-27, 46; tableaux 3, 4, 5, 6, 7, 8, 9, 10, 11, 12, 15,
        16, 17, 18, 19, 20, 21, 22, 23, 24, 25
VIET NAM...47; tableaux 3, 5, 6, 7, 8, 23, 25
VILLES
    capitales...218
    définition...218
    exploitation des données
        population des capitales et des villes de 100 000 habitants
            et plus...tableau 8
    Voir aussi LIEU DE RÉSIDENCE (ZONE URBAINE OU RURALE)
VISITEURS ÉTRANGERS DE PASSAGE...19

WHIPPLE (INDICE)...20

WORLD POPULATION PROSPECTS...50

YÉMEN...47; tableaux 3, 5, 6, 7, 8

ZAMBIE...46; tableaux 3, 5, 6, 7, 8
ZIMBABWE...46; tableaux 3, 5, 6, 7, 8
ZONES (GRANDES)
    Voir GRANDES ZONES
ZONE URBAINE OU RURALE
    Voir LIEU DE RÉSIDENCE

Subject-matter	Year of issue	Time coverage	Subject-matter	Year of issue	Time coverage
A				1953	1900-53
				1954	1900-54[i]
				1955	1900-55[i]
Abortions, Legal	1971	Latest			
	1972	1964-72			
	1973	1965-73	**Births**	1948	1932-47
	1974	1965-74		1949/50	1934-49
	1975	1965-74		1951	1935-50
	1976	1966-75		1952	1936-51
	1977	1967-76		1953	1950-52
	1978	1968-77		1954	1938-53
	1979	1969-78		1955	1946-54
	1980	1971-79		1956	1947-55
	1981	1972-80		1957	1948-56
	1982	1973-81		1958	1948-57
	1983	1974-82		1959	1949-58
	1984	1975-83		1960	1950-59
	1985	1976-84		1961	1952-61
	1986	1977-85		1962	1953-62
	1987	1978-86		1963	1954-63
	1988	1979-87		1964	1960-64
	1989	1980-88		1965	1946-65
	1990	1981-89		1966	1957-66
	1991	1982-90		1967	1963-67
	1992	1983-91		1968	1964-68
	1993	1984-92		1969	1950-69
	1994	1985-93		1970	1966-70
	1995	1986-94		1971	1967-71
	1996	1987-95		1972	1968-72
	1997	1988-96		1973	1969-73
	1998	1989-97		1974	1970-74
	1999	1990-98		1975	1956-75
	2000	1991-99		1976	1972-76
	2001	1993-01		1977	1973-77
	2002	1993-02		1978	1974-78
	2003	1994-03		1978HS[ii]	1948-78
- by age of mother and number of previous live births of mother	1971-1975	Latest		1979	1975-79
	1977-1981	Latest		1980	1976-80
	1983-2003	Latest		1981	1962-81
Ageing (see: Population)				1982	1978-82
Annulments	1958	1948-57		1983	1979-83
	1968	1958-67		1984	1980-84
	1976	1966-75		1985	1981-85
				1986	1967-86
				1987	1983-87
Annulment rates	1958	1948-57		1988	1984-88
	1968	1958-67		1989	1985-89
	1976	1966-75		1990	1986-90
				1991	1987-91
B				1992	1983-92
				1993	1989-93
				1994	1990-94
				1995	1991-95
Bibliography	1948	1930-48		1996	1992-96
	1949/50	1930-50		1997	1993-97
	1951-1952	1930-51[i]			

Subject-matter	Year of issue	Time coverage	Subject-matter	Year of issue	Time coverage
	1997HS[iii]	1948-97		1959	1949-58
	1998	1994-98		1965	1955-64
	1999	1995-99		1969	1963-68
	1999CD[iv]	1980-99		1975	1966-74
	2000	1996-00		1981	1972-80
	2001	1997-01		1986	1977-85
	2002	1998-02		1999CD[iv]	1990-98
	2003	1999-03	- by age of mother and sex		
- by age of father	1949/50	1942-49		1965-1968	Latest
	1954	1936-53		1969	1963-68
	1959	1949-58		1970-1974	Latest
	1965	1955-64		1975	1966-74
	1969	1963-68		1976-1978	Latest
	1975	1966-74		1978HS[ii]	1948-77
	1981	1972-80		1979-1980	Latest
	1999CD[iv]	1990-98		1981	1972-80
- by age of mother	1948	1936-47		1982-1985	Latest
	1949/50	1936-49		1986	1977-85
	1954	1936-53		1987-1991	Latest
	1955-1956	Latest		1992	1983-92
	1958	Latest		1993-1997	Latest
	1959	1949-58		1997HS[iii]	1948-96
	1960-1964	Latest		1998-99	Latest
	1965	1955-64		1999CD[iv]	1990-98
	1966-1968	Latest		2000-2003	Latest
	1969	1963-68	- by age of mother and urban/rural residence (see: by urban/rural residence, below)		
	1970-1974	Latest			
	1975	1966-74			
	1976-1978	Latest	- by birth order	1948	1936-47
	1978HS[ii]	1948-77		1949/50	1936-49
	1979-1980	Latest		1954	1936-53
	1981	1972-80		1955	Latest
	1982-1985	Latest		1959	1949-58
	1986	1977-85		1965	1955-64
	1987-1991	Latest		1969	1963-68
	1992	1983-92		1975	1966-74
	1993-1997	Latest		1981	1972-80
	1997HS[iii] [3]	1948-96		1986	1977-85
	1998-99	Latest		1999CD[iv]	1990-98
	1999CD[iv]	1990-98			
	2000-2003	Latest	- by birth weight	1975	Latest
- by age of mother and birth order	1949/50	1936-47		1981	1972-80
	1954	Latest		1986	1977-85
				1999CD[iv]	1990-98

Subject-matter	Year of issue	Time coverage	Subject-matter	Year of issue	Time coverage
- by gestational age	1975	Latest		1971	1967-71
	1981	1972-80		1972	1968-72
	1986	1977-85		1973	1969-73
	1999CD[iv]	1990-98		1974	1970-74
				1975	1956-75
- by legitimacy status				1976	1972-76
	1959	1949-58		1977	1973-77
	1965	1955-64		1978	1974-78
	1969	1963-68		1979	1975-79
	1975	1966-74		1980	1976-80
	1981	1972-80		1981	1962-81
	1986	1977-85		1982	1978-82
	1999CD[iv]	1990-98		1983	1979-83
- by month	2002	1980-02		1984	1980-84
				1985	1981-85
- by occupation of father	1965	Latest		1986	1967-86
	1969	Latest		1987	1983-87
				1988	1984-88
- by sex	1959	1949-58		1989	1985-89
	1965	1955-64		1990	1986-90
	1967-1968	Latest		1991	1987-91
	1969	1963-68		1992	1983-92
	1970-1974	Latest		1993	1989-93
	1975	1956-75		1994	1990-94
	1976-1980	Latest		1995	1991-95
	1981	1962-81		1996	1992-96
	1982-1985	Latest		1997	1993-97
	1986	1967-86		1998	1994-98
	1987-1991	Latest		1999	1995-99
	1992	1983-92		1999CD[iv]	1980-99
	1993-1999	Latest		2000	1996-00
	1999CD[iv]	1990-98		2001	1997-01
	2000-2003	Latest		2002	1998-02
				2003	1999-03
- by plurality	1965	Latest	- by urban/rural residence and age of mother		
	1969	Latest		1965	Latest
	1975	Latest		1969-1974	Latest
	1981	1972-80		1975	1966-74
	1986	1977-85		1976-1980	Latest
	1999CD[iv]	1990-98		1981	1972-80
- by urban/rural residence	1965	Latest		1982-1985	Latest
	1967	Latest		1986	1977-85
	1968	1964-68		1987-1991	Latest
	1969	1964-68		1992	1983-92
	1970	1966-70		1993-1997	Latest
				1997HS[iii]	1948-96
				1998-1999	Latest
				1999CD[iv]	1990-98
				2000-2003	Latest

Subject-matter	Year of issue	Time coverage	Subject-matter	Year of issue	Time coverage
				1951	1905-30^v
- illegitimate	1959	1949-58			1930-50
	1965	1955-64		1952	1920-34^v
	1969	1963-68			1934-51
	1975	1966-74		1953	1920-39^v
	1981	1972-80			1940-52
	1986	1977-85		1954	1920-39^v
	1999CD^{iv}	1990-98			1939-53
- legitimate	1948	1936-47		1955	1920-34^v
	1949/50	1936-49			1946-54
	1954	1936-53		1956	1947-55
	1959	1949-58		1957	1948-56
	1965	1955-64		1958	1948-57
	1969	1963-68		1959	1920-54^v
	1975	1966-74			1953-58
	1981	1972-80		1960	1950-59
	1986	1977-85		1961	1945-59^v
	1999CD^{iv}	1990-98			1952-61
- legitimate, by age of father	1959	1949-58		1962	1945-54^v
	1965	1955-64			1952-62
	1969	1963-68		1963	1945-59^v
	1975	1966-74			1954-63
	1981	1972-80		1964	1960-64
	1986	1977-85		1965	1920-64^v
- legitimate, by age of mother	1954	1936-53			1950-65
	1959	1949-58		1966	1950-64^v
	1965	1955-64			1957-66
	1969	1963-68		1967	1963-67
	1975	1966-74		1968	1964-68
	1981	1972-80		1969	1925-69^v
	1986	1977-85			1954-69
- legitimate, by duration of marriage	1948	1936-47		1970	1966-70
	1949/50	1936-49		1971	1967-71
	1954	1936-53		1972	1968-72
	1959	1949-58		1973	1969-73
	1965	1955-64		1974	1970-74
	1969	1963-68		1975	1956-75
	1975	1966-74		1976	1972-76
	1981	1972-80		1977	1973-77
	1986	1977-85		1978	1974-78
	1999CD^{iv}	1990-98		1978HS^{ii}	1948-78
				1979	1975-79
				1980	1976-80
Birth rates.............................	1948	1932-47		1981	1962-81
	1949/50	1932-49		1982	1978-82
				1983	1979-83
				1984	1980-84
				1985	1981-85
				1986	1967-86
				1987	1983-87
				1988	1984-88
				1989	1985-89
				1990	1986-90
				1991	1987-91

Subject-matter	Year of issue	Time coverage	Subject-matter	Year of issue	Time coverage
	1992	1983-92		2000-2003	Latest
	1993	1989-93	- by age of mother and birth order	1954	1948 and 1951
	1994	1990-94		1959	1949-58
	1995	1991-95		1965	1955-64
	1996	1992-96		1969	1963-68
	1997	1993-97		1975	1966-74
	1997HS[iii]	1948-97		1981	1972-80
	1998	1994-98		1986	1977-85
	1999	1995-99		1999CD[iv]	1990-98
	1999CD[iv]	1985-99	- by age of mother and urban/rural residence (see: by urban/rural residence, below)		
	2000	1996-00			
	2001	1997-01			
	2002	1998-02			
	2003	1999-03	- by birth order	1951	1936-49
- by age of father	1949/50	1942-49		1952	1936-50
	1954	1936-53		1953	1936-52
	1959	1949-58		1954	1936-53
	1965	1955-64		1955	Latest
	1969	1963-68		1959	1949-58
	1975	1966-74		1965	1955-64
	1981	1972-80		1969	1963-68
	1986	1977-85		1975	1966-74
	1999CD[iv]	1990-98		1981	1972-80
- by age of mother	1948	1936-47		1986	1977-85
	1949/50	1936-49		1999CD[iv]	1990-98
	1951	1936-50	- by urban/rural residence	1965	Latest
	1952	1936-50		1967	Latest
	1953	1936-52		1968	1964-68
	1954	1936-53		1969	1964-68
	1955-1956	Latest		1970	1966-70
	1959	1949-58		1971	1967-71
	1965	1955-64		1972	1968-72
	1969	1963-68		1973	1969-73
	1975	1966-74		1974	1970-74
	1976-1978	Latest		1975	1956-75
	1978HS[ii]	1948-77		1976	1972-76
	1979-1980	Latest		1977	1973-77
	1981	1972-80		1978	1974-78
	1982-1985	Latest		1979	1975-79
	1986	1977-85		1980	1976-80
	1987-1991	Latest		1981	1962-81
	1992	1983-92		1982	1978-82
	1993-1997	Latest		1983	1979-83
	1997HS[iii]	1948-96		1984	1980-84
	1998-1999	Latest		1985	1981-85
	1999CD[iv]	1990-98			

Subject-matter	Year of issue	Time coverage	Subject-matter	Year of issue	Time coverage
	1986	1967-86		1987-1992	1985-90
	1987	1983-87		1993-1997	1990-95
	1988	1984-88		1998-2000	1995-00
	1989	1985-89		2001-2003	2000-05
	1990	1986-90			
	1991	1987-91	for regions	1949/1950	1947
	1992	1983-92		1956-1977	Latest
	1993	1989-93		1978-1979	1970-75
	1994	1990-94		1980-1983	1975-80
	1995	1991-95		1984-1986	1980-85
	1996	1992-96		1987-1992	1985-90
	1997	1993-97		1993-1997	1990-95
	1998	1994-98		1998-2000	1995-00
	1999	1995-99		2001-2003	2000-05
	1999CD[iv]	1985-99			
	2000	1996-00	for the world	1949/50	1947
	2001	1997-01		1956-1977	Latest
	2002	1998-02		1978-1979	1970-75
	2003	1999-03		1980-1983	1975-80
- by urban/rural residence and age of mother	1965	Latest		1984-1986	1980-85
	1969	Latest		1987-1992	1985-90
	1975	1966-74		1993-1997	1990-95
	1976-1980	Latest		1998-2000	1995-00
	1981	1972-80		2001-2003	2000-05
	1982-1985	Latest			
	1986	1977-85	- illegitimate	1959	1949-58
	1987-1991	Latest			
	1992	1983-92	- legitimate	1954	1936-53
	1993-1997	Latest		1959	1949-58
	1997HS[iii]	1948-96		1965	Latest
	1998-1999	Latest		1969	Latest
	1999CD[iv]	1990-98		1975	Latest
	2000-2003	Latest		1981	Latest
- estimated:				1986	Latest
for continents	1949/50	1947	- legitimate by age of father	1959	1949-58
	1956-1977	Latest		1965	Latest
	1978-1979	1970-75		1969	Latest
	1980-1983	1975-80		1975	Latest
	1984-1986	1980-85		1981	Latest
	1987-1992	1985-90		1986	Latest
	1993-1997	1990-95	- legitimate by age of mother	1954	1936-53
	1998-2000	1995-00		1959	1949-58
	2001-2003	2000-05		1965	Latest
for macro regions	1964-1977	Latest		1969	Latest
	1978-1979	1970-75		1975	Latest
	1980-1983	1975-80		1981	Latest
	1984-1986	1980-85		1986	Latest
			- legitimate by duration of marriage	1959	1950-57
				1965	Latest
				1969	Latest
				1975	Latest

Subject-matter	Year of issue	Time coverage	Subject-matter	Year of issue	Time coverage
Birth Ratios				1955	1945-54
- fertility	1949/1950	Latest		1959	1949-58
	1954	Latest		1963	1955-63
	1959	1949-58		1965	1955-65
	1965	1955-65		1969	Latest
	1969	1963-68		1978HS[ii]	1948-77
	1975	1965-74		1997HS[iii]	1948-96
	1978HS[ii]	1948-77	- ever born, by age of mother and urban/rural residence		
	1981	1972-80		1971	1962-71
	1986	1977-85		1973	1965-73
	1997HS[iii]	1948-96		1975	1965-74
	1999CD[iv]	1980-99		1981	1972-80
				1986	1977-85
- illegitimate	1959	1949-58		1997HS[iii]	1948-96
	1965	1955-64			
	1969	1963-68	- involved in divorces	1958	1949-57
	1975	1965-74		1968	1958-67
	1981	1972-80		1976	1966-75
	1986	1977-85		1982	1972-81
				1990	1980-89
Birth to women under 20 by single years of age of mother			- living, by age of mother	1949/50	Latest
- by urban/rural residence	1986	1970-85		1954	1930-53
				1955	1945-54
C				1959	1949-58
				1963	1955-63
Child-woman ratios	1949/50	1900-50		1965	1955-65
	1954	1900-52		1968	1955-67
	1955	1945-54		1969	Latest
	1959	1935-59		1978HS[ii]	1948-77
	1963	1955-63		1997HS[iii]	1948-96
	1965	1945-65	- living, by age of mother and urban/rural residence		
	1969	Latest		1971	1962-71
	1975	1966-74		1973	1965-73
	1978HS[ii]	1948-77		1975	1965-74
	1981	1962-80		1981	1972-80
	1986	1967-85		1986	1977-85
	1997HS[iii]	1948-96		1997HS[iii]	1948-96
	1999CD[iv]	1980-99			
- by urban/rural residence	1965	Latest	**Cities (see: Population)**		
	1969	Latest			
			D		
Children					
- ever born, by age of mother	1949/50	Latest	**Deaths**	1948	1932-47
	1954	1930-53		1949/50	1934-49
				1951	1935-50
				1952	1936-51
				1953	1950-52
				1954	1946-53
				1955	1946-54
				1956	1947-55

Subject-matter	Year of issue	Time coverage	Subject-matter	Year of issue	Time coverage
	1957	1940-56		1961	1955-60
	1958	1948-57		1962-1965	Latest
	1959	1949-58		1966	1961-65
	1960	1950-59		1967-1973	Latest
	1961	1952-61		1974	1965-73
	1962	1953-62		1975-1979	Latest
	1963	1954-63		1978HS[ii]	1948-77
	1964	1960-64		1980	1971-79
	1966	1947-66		1981-1984	Latest
	1967	1963-67		1985	1976-84
	1968	1964-68		1986-1991	Latest
	1969	1965-69		1992	1983-92
	1970	1966-70		1993-1995	Latest
	1971	1967-71		1996	1987-95
	1972	1968-72		1997	Latest
	1973	1969-73		1997HS[iii]	1948-96
	1974	1965-74		1998-2003	Latest
	1975	1971-75	- by age and sex and urban/rural residence		
	1976	1972-76		1967-1973	Latest
	1977	1973-77		1974	1965-73
	1978	1974-78		1975-1979	Latest
	1978HS[ii]	1948-78		1980	1971-79
	1979	1975-79		1981-1984	Latest
	1980	1971-80		1985	1976-84
	1981	1977-81		1986-1991	Latest
	1982	1978-82		1992	1983-92
	1983	1979-83		1993-1995	Latest
	1984	1980-84		1996	1987-95
	1985	1976-85		1997	Latest
	1986	1982-86		1997HS[iii]	1948-96
	1987	1983-87		1998-2003	Latest
	1988	1984-88	- by cause	1951	1947-50
	1989	1985-89		1952	1947-51[vi]
	1990	1986-90		1953	Latest
	1991	1987-91		1954	1945-53
	1992	1983-92		1955-1956	Latest
	1993	1989-93		1957	1952-56
	1994	1990-94		1958-1960	Latest
	1995	1991-95		1961	1955-60
	1996	1987-96		1962-1965	Latest
	1997	1993-97		1966	1960-65
	1997HS[iii]	1948-97		1967-1973	Latest
	1998	1994-98		1974	1965-73
	1999	1995-99		1975-1979	Latest
	2000	1996-00		1980	1971-79
	2001	1997-01		1981-1984	Latest
	2002	1998-02		1985	1976-84
	2003	1999-03		1986-1991	Latest
- by age and sex	1948	1936-47		1991PA[vii]	1960-90
	1951	1936-50		1992-1995	Latest
	1955-1956	Latest		1996	1987-95
	1957	1948-56		1997-2000	Latest
	1958-1960	Latest		2002	1995-02

Subject-matter	Year of issue	Time coverage	Subject-matter	Year of issue	Time coverage
- by cause, age and sex	1951	Latest	- by urban/rural residence	1967	Latest
	1952	Latest		1968	1964-68
	1957	Latest		1969	1965-69
	1961	Latest		1970	1966-70
	1967	Latest		1971	1967-71
	1974	Latest		1972	1968-72
	1980	Latest		1973	1969-73
	1985	Latest		1974	1965-74
	1991PA[vii]	1960-90		1975	1971-75
	1996	Latest		1976	1972-76
- by cause, age and sex and urban/rural residence	1967	Latest		1977	1973-77
				1978	1974-78
				1979	1975-79
				1980	1971-80
				1981	1977-81
- by cause and sex	1967	Latest		1982	1978-82
	1974	Latest		1983	1979-83
	1980	Latest		1984	1980-84
	1985	Latest		1985	1976-85
	1996	Latest		1986	1982-86
				1987	1983-87
- by marital status, age and sex	1958	Latest		1988	1984-88
	1961	Latest		1989	1985-89
	1967	Latest		1990	1986-90
	1974	Latest		1991	1987-91
	1980	Latest		1992	1983-92
	1985	Latest		1993	1989-93
	1991PA[vii]	1950-90		1994	1990-94
	1996	Latest		1995	1991-95
	2003	Latest		1996	1987-96
- by month	1951	1946-50		1997	1993-97
	1967	1962-66		1998	1994-98
	1974	1965-73		1999	1995-99
	1980	1971-79		2000	1996-00
	1985	1976-84		2001	1997-01
	2001	1985-00		2002	1998-02
- by occupation and age, males	1957	Latest		2003	1999-03
	1961	1957-60	- of infants (see infant deaths)		
	1967	1962-66			
	1957	Latest	**Death rates**	1948	1932-47
- by type of certification and cause:				1949/50	1932-49
numbers	1957	Latest		1951	1905-30[v]
	1974	1965-73			1930-50
	1980	1971-79		1952	1920-34[v]
	1985	1976-84			1934-51
percent	1957	Latest		1953	1920-39[v]
	1961	1955-60			1940-52
	1966	1960-65		1954	1920-39[v]
	1974	1965-73			1946-53
	1980	1971-79		1955	1920-34[v]
	1985	1976-84			1946-54
				1956	1947-55
				1957	1930-56

Subject-matter	Year of issue	Time coverage	Subject-matter	Year of issue	Time coverage
	1958	1948-57		1949/50	1936-49
	1959	1949-58		1951	1936-50
	1960	1950-59		1952	1936-51
	1961	1945-59[v]		1953	1940-52
		1952-61		1954	1946-53
	1962	1945-54[v]		1955-1956	Latest
		1952-62		1957	1948-56
	1963	1945-59[v]		1961	1952-60
		1954-63		1966	1950-65
	1964	1960-64		1972	Latest
	1965	1961-65		1974	1965-73
	1966	1920-64[v]		1975-1979	Latest
		1951-66		1978HS[ii]	1948-77
	1967	1963-67		1980	1971-79
	1968	1964-68		1981-1984	Latest
	1969	1965-69		1985	1976-84
	1970	1966-70		1986-1991	Latest
	1971	1967-71		1991PA[vii]	1950-1990
	1972	1968-72		1992	1983-1992
	1973	1969-73		1993-1995	Latest
	1974	1965-74		1996	1987-95
	1975	1971-75		1997	Latest
	1976	1972-76		1997HS[iii]	1948-96
	1977	1973-77		1998-2003	Latest
	1978	1974-78				
	1978HS[ii]	1948-78	- by age and sex and urban/rural residence		
	1979	1975-79		1967	Latest
	1980	1971-80		1972	Latest
	1981	1977-81		1974	1965-73
	1982	1978-82		1975-1979	Latest
	1983	1979-83		1980	1971-79
	1984	1980-84		1981-1984	Latest
	1985	1976-85		1985	1976-84
	1986	1982-86		1986-1991	Latest
	1987	1983-87		1991PA[vii]	1950-1990
	1988	1984-88		1992	1983-1992
	1989	1985-89		1993-1995	Latest
	1990	1986-90		1996	1987-95
	1991	1987-91		1997	Latest
	1992	1983-92		1997HS[iii]	1948-96
	1993	1989-93		1998-2003	Latest
	1994	1990-94				
	1995	1991-95	- by cause	1951	1947-49
	1996	1987-96		1952	1947-51[vi]
	1997	1993-97		1953	1947-52
	1997HS[iii]	1948-97		1954	1945-53
	1998	1994-98		1955-1956	Latest
	1999	1995-99		1957	1952-56
	2000	1996-00		1958-1960	Latest
	2001	1997-01		1961	1955-60
	2002	1998-02		1962-1965	Latest
	2003	1999-03		1966	1960-65
- by age and sex	1948	1935-47		1967-1973	Latest
				1974	1965-73

Index
Historical index
(See notes at end of index)

Subject-matter	Year of issue	Time coverage	Subject-matter	Year of issue	Time coverage
	1975-1979	Latest		1988	1984-88
	1980	1971-79		1989	1985-89
	1981-1984	Latest		1990	1986-90
	1985	1976-84		1991	1987-91
	1986-1991	Latest		1992	1983-92
	1991PA[vii]	1960-90		1993	1989-93
	1992-1995	Latest		1994	1990-94
	1996	1987-95		1995	1991-95
	1997-2000	Latest		1996	1987-96
	2002	1995-02		1997	1993-97
				1998	1994-98
- by cause, age and sex	1957	Latest		1999	1995-99
	1961	Latest		1987	1983-87
	1991PA[vii]	1960-90		1988	1984-88
				1989	1985-89
- by cause and sex	1967	Latest		1990	1986-90
	1974	Latest		1991	1987-91
	1980	Latest		1992	1983-92
	1985	Latest		1993	1989-93
	1996	Latest		1994	1990-94
- by marital status, age and sex	1961	Latest		1995	1991-95
	1967	Latest		1996	1987-96
	1974	Latest		1997	1993-97
	1980	Latest		1998	1994-98
	1985	Latest		1999	1995-99
	1996	Latest		2000	1996-00
- by occupation, age and sex	1957	Latest		2001	1997-01
				2002	1998-02
- by occupation and age, males	1961	Latest		2003	1999-03
	1967	Latest	- estimated		
- by urban/rural residence	1967	Latest	for continents	1949/50	1947
	1968	1964-68		1956-1977	Latest
	1969	1965-69		1978-1979	1970-75
	1970	1966-70		1980-1983	1975-80
	1971	1967-71		1984-1986	1980-85
	1972	1968-72		1984-1986	1980-85
	1973	1969-73		1987-1992	1985-90
	1974	1965-74		1993-1997	1990-95
	1975	1971-75		1998-2000	1995-00
	1976	1972-76		2001-2003	2000-05
	1977	1973-77	for macro regions	1964-1977	Latest
	1978	1974-78		1978-1979	1970-75
	1979	1975-79		1980-1983	1975-80
	1980	1971-80		1984-1986	1980-85
	1981	1977-81		1987-1992	1985-90
	1982	1978-82		1993-1997	1990-95
	1983	1979-83		1998-2000	1995-00
	1984	1980-84		2001-2003	2000-05
	1985	1976-85	for regions	1949/50	1947
	1986	1982-86		1956-1977	Latest
	1987	1983-87		1978-1979	1970-75
				1980-1983	1975-80
				1984-1986	1980-85

Subject-matter	Year of issue	Time coverage	Subject-matter	Year of issue	Time coverage
	1987-1992	1985-90		1953	1950-52
	1993-1997	1990-95		1954	1946-53
	1998-2000	1995-00		1955	1946-54
	2001-2003	2000-05		1956	1947-55
				1957	1948-56
for the world	1949/50	1947		1958	1940-57
	1956-1977	Latest		1959	1949-58
	1978-1979	1970-75		1960	1950-59
	1980-1983	1975-80		1961	1952-61
	1984-1986	1980-85		1962	1953-62
	1987-1992	1985-90		1963	1954-63
	1993-1997	1990-95		1964	1960-64
	1998-2000	1995-00		1965	1961-65
	2001-2003	2000-05		1966	1962-66
- of infants (see: Infant deaths)				1967	1963-67
				1968	1949-68
				1969	1965-69
Density of population:				1970	1966-70
- of continents	1949/50	1920-49		1971	1967-71
	1951-1999	Latest		1972	1968-72
	2000	2000		1973	1969-73
	2001	2001		1974	1970-74
	2002	2002		1975	1971-75
	2003	2003		1976	1957-76
				1977	1973-77
- of countries	1948-1999	Latest		1978	1974-78
	2000	2000		1979	1975-79
	2001	2001		1980	1976-80
	2002	2002		1981	1977-81
	2003	2003		1982	1963-82
				1983	1979-83
- of major areas	1964-1999	Latest		1984	1980-84
	2000	2000		1985	1981-85
	2001	2001		1986	1982-86
	2002	2002		1987	1983-87
	2003	2003		1988	1984-88
				1989	1985-89
- of regions	1949/50	1920-49		1990	1971-90
	1952-1999	Latest		1991	1987-91
	2000	2000		1992	1988-92
	2001	2001		1993	1989-93
	2002	2002		1994	1990-94
	2003	2003		1995	1991-95
				1996	1992-96
- of the world	1949/50	1920-49		1997	1993-97
	1952-1999	Latest		1998	1994-98
	2000	2000		1999	1995-99
	2001	2001		2000	1996-00
	2002	2002		2001	1997-01
	2003	2003		2002	1998-02
				2003	1999-03
Disability (see: Population)					
			- by age of husband	1968	1958-67
Divorces	1951	1935-50		1976	1966-75
	1952	1936-51			

Subject-matter	Year of issue	Time coverage	Subject-matter	Year of issue	Time coverage
	1982	1972-81		1970	1966-70
	1987	1975-86		1971	1967-71
	1990	1980-89		1972	1968-72
				1973	1969-73
- by age of wife	1968	1958-67		1974	1970-74
	1976	1966-75		1975	1971-75
	1982	1972-81		1976	1957-76
	1987	1975-86		1977	1973-77
	1990	1980-89		1978	1974-78
- by age of wife classified by age of husband				1979	1975-79
	1958	1946-57		1980	1976-80
	1968	Latest		1969	1965-69
	1976	Latest		1970	1966-70
	1982	Latest		1971	1967-71
	1982	Latest		1972	1968-72
	1990	Latest		1973	1969-73
- by duration of marriage				1974	1970-74
	1958	1948-57		1975	1971-75
	1968	1958-67		1976	1957-76
	1976	1966-75		1977	1973-77
	1982	1972-81		1978	1974-78
	1990	1980-89		1979	1975-79
- by duration of marriage and age of husband, wife				1980	1976-80
	1958	1946-57		1969	1965-69
	1968	Latest		1970	1966-70
	1976	Latest		1971	1967-71
	1982	Latest		1972	1968-72
	1990	Latest		1973	1969-73
- by number of children involved				1974	1970-74
	1958	1948-57		1975	1971-75
	1968	1958-67		1976	1957-76
	1976	1966-75		1977	1973-77
	1982	1972-81		1978	1974-78
	1990	1980-89		1979	1975-79
				1980	1976-80
Divorce rates	1952	1935-51		1981	1977-81
	1953	1936-52		1982	1963-82
	1954	1946-53		1983	1979-83
	1955	1946-54		1984	1980-84
	1956	1947-55		1985	1981-85
	1957	1948-56		1986	1982-86
	1958	1930-57		1987	1983-87
	1959	1949-58		1988	1984-88
	1960	1950-59		1989	1985-89
	1961	1952-61		1990	1971-90
	1962	1953-62		1991	1987-91
	1963	1954-63		1992	1988-92
	1964	1960-64		1993	1989-93
	1965	1961-65		1994	1990-94
	1966	1962-66		1995	1991-95
	1967	1963-67		1996	1992-96
	1968	1920-64[v]		1997	1993-97
		1953-68		1998	1994-98
	1969	1965-69		1999	1995-99

Subject-matter	Year of issue	Time coverage	Subject-matter	Year of issue	Time coverage
	2000	1996-00		1953	1936-52
	2001	1997-01		1954	1936-53
	2002	1998-02		1955-1956	Latest
	2003	1999-03		1959	1949-58
				1960-1964	Latest
- by age of husband	1968	Latest		1965	1955-64
	1976	Latest		1966-1974	Latest
	1982	Latest		1975	1966-74
	1987	1975-86		1976-1978	Latest
	1990	Latest		1978HS[ii]	1948-77
				1979-1980	Latest
- by age of wife	1968	Latest		1981	1962-80
	1976	Latest		1982-1985	Latest
	1982	Latest		1986	1977-85
	1987	1975-86		1987-1991	Latest
	1990	Latest		1992	1983-92
- for married couples	1953	1935-52		1993-1997	Latest
	1954	1935-53		1997HS[iii]	1948-96
	1958	1935-56		1998	Latest
	1968	1935-67	- total	1986	1967-85
	1976	1966-75		1987-1997	Latest
	1978HS[ii]	1948-77		1997HS[iii]	1948-96
	1982	1972-81		1998	1995-98
	1990	1980-89		1999	1996-99
				1999CD[iv]	1980-99
				2000	1995-00
				2001	1997-01
				2002	1998-02
				2003	1999-03

E

Economically active population (see: Population)

Economically inactive population (see: Population)

Emigrants (see: Migration)

Ethnic composition (see: Population)

Expectation of life (see: Life tables)

F

Fertility rates

Subject-matter	Year of issue	Time coverage
- general	1948	1936-47
	1949/50	1936-49
	1951	1936-50
	1952	1936-50

Subject-matter	Year of issue	Time coverage
Fertility ratios	1949/50	1900-50
	1954	1900-52
	1955	1945-54
	1959	1935-59
	1963	1955-63
	1965	1955-65
	1969	Latest
	1975	1966-74
	1978HS[ii]	1948-77
	1981	1962-80
	1986	1967-85
	1997HS[iii]	1948-96
	1999CD[iv]	1980-99
Foetal deaths		
- by period of gestation	1957	1950-56
	1959	1949-58

Subject-matter	Year of issue	Time coverage	Subject-matter	Year of issue	Time coverage
	1961	1952-60		1987	1982-86
	1965	5-Latest		1988	1983-87
	1966	1956-65		1989	1984-88
	1967-1968	Latest		1990	1985-89
	1969	1963-68		1991	1986-90
	1974	1965-73		1992	1987-91
	1975	1966-74		1993	1988-92
	1980	1971-79		1994	1989-93
	1981	1972-80		1995	1990-94
	1985	1976-84		1996	1987-95
	1986	1977-85		1997	1992-96
	1996	1987-95		1998	1993-97
	1999CD[iv]	1990-98		1999	1994-98
				1999CD[iv]	1990-98
Foetal deaths, late	1951	1935-50		2000	1995-99
	1952	1936-51		2001	1997-01
	1953	1936-52		2002	1998-02
	1954	1938-53		2003	1999-03
	1955	1946-54			
	1956	1947-55	- by age of mother	1954	1936-53
	1957	1948-56		1959	1949-58
	1958	1948-57		1965	1955-64
	1959	1949-58		1969	1963-68
	1960	1950-59		1975	1966-74
	1961	1952-60		1981	1972-80
	1962	1953-61		1986	1977-85
	1963	1953-62	- by age of mother		
	1964	1959-63	and birth order	1954	Latest
	1965	1955-64		1959	1949-58
	1966	1947-65		1965	3-Latest
	1967	1962-66		1969	1963-68
	1968	1963-67		1975	1966-74
	1969	1959-68		1981	1972-80
	1970	1965-69		1986	1977-85
	1971	1966-70	- by period of		
	1972	1967-71	gestation	1957	1950-56
	1973	1968-72		1959	1949-58
	1974	1965-73		1961	1952-60
	1975	1966-74		1965	5-Latest
	1976	1971-75		1966	1956-65
	1977	1972-76		1967-1968	Latest
	1978	1973-77		1969	1963-68
	1979	1974-78		1974	1965-73
	1980	1971-79		1975	1966-74
	1981	1972-80		1980	1971-79
	1982	1977-81		1981	1972-80
	1983	1978-82		1985	1976-84
	1984	1979-83		1986	1977-85
	1985	1975-84		1996	1987-95
	1986	1977-85	- by sex	1961	1952-60

Subject-matter	Year of issue	Time coverage	Subject-matter	Year of issue	Time coverage
	1965	5 Latest		1969	1963-68
	1969	1963-68		1975	1966-74
	1975	1966-74		1981	1972-80
	1981	1972-80		1986	1977-85
	1986	1977-85			
- by urban/rural residence			- legitimate	1959	1949-58
	1971	1966-70		1965	1955-64
	1972	1967-71		1969	1963-68
	1973	1968-72		1975	1966-74
	1974	1965-73		1981	1972-80
	1975	1966-74		1986	1977-85
	1976	1971-75	- legitimate by age of mother	1959	1949-58
	1977	1972-76		1965	1955-64
	1978	1973-77		1969	1963-68
	1979	1974-78		1975	1966-74
	1980	1971-79		1981	1972-80
	1981	1972-80		1986	1977-85
	1982	1977-81		1996	1987-95
	1983	1978-82			
	1984	1979-83	**Foetal Death Ratios**		
	1985	1975-84	- by period of gestation	1957	1950-56
	1986	1977-85		1959	1949-58
	1987	1982-86		1961	1952-60
	1988	1983-87		1965	5-Latest
	1989	1984-88		1966	1956-65
	1990	1985-89		1967-1968	Latest
	1991	1986-90		1969	1963-68
	1992	1987-91		1974	1965-73
	1993	1988-92		1975	1966-74
	1994	1989-93		1980	1971-79
	1995	1990-94		1981	1972-80
	1996	1987-95		1985	1976-84
	1997	1992-96		1986	1977-85
	1998	1993-97		1996	1987-95
	1999	1994-98		1999CD[iv]	1990-98
	1999CD[iv]	1990-98			
	2000	1995-99			
	2001	1997-01	**Foetal death ratios, late**	1951	1935-50
	2002	1998-02		1952	1935-51
	2003	1999-03		1953	1936-52
- illegitimate	1961	1952-60		1954	1938-53
	1965	5-Latest		1955	1946-54
	1969	1963-68		1956	1947-55
	1975	1966-74		1957	1948-56
	1981	1972-80		1958	1948-57
	1986	1977-85		1959	1920-54[v]
					1953-58
- illegitimate, percent				1960	1950-59
	1961	1952-60		1961	1945-49[v]
	1965	5-Latest			1952-60

Subject-matter	Year of issue	Time coverage	Subject-matter	Year of issue	Time coverage
	1962	1945-54[v]		1959	1949-58
		1952-61		1965	1955-64
	1963	1945-59[v]		1969	1963-68
		1953-62		1975	1966-74
	1964	1959-63		1981	1972-80
	1965	1950-64[v]		1986	1977-85
		1955-64		1996	1987-95
	1966	1950-64[v]		1999CD[iv]	1990-98
		1956-65	- by age of mother and birth order		
	1967	1962-66		1954	Latest
	1968	1963-67		1959	1949-58
	1969	1950-64[v]		1965	3-Latest
		1959-68		1969	1963-68
	1970	1965-69		1975	1966-74
	1971	1966-70		1981	1972-80
	1972	1967-71		1986	1977-85
	1973	1968-72		1999CD[iv]	1990-98
	1974	1965-73	- by period of gestation		
	1975	1966-74		1957	1950-56
	1976	1971-75		1959	1949-58
	1977	1972-76		1961	1952-60
	1978	1973-77		1965	5-Latest
	1979	1974-78		1966	1956-65
	1980	1971-79		1967-1968	Latest
	1981	1972-80		1969	1963-68
	1982	1977-81		1974	1965-73
	1983	1978-82		1975	1966-74
	1984	1979-83		1980	1971-79
	1985	1975-84		1981	1972-80
	1986	1977-85		1985	1976-84
	1987	1982-86		1986	1977-85
	1988	1983-87	- by urban/rural residence		
	1989	1984-88		1971	1966-70
	1990	1985-89		1972	1967-71
	1991	1986-90		1973	1968-72
	1992	1987-91		1974	1965-73
	1993	1988-92		1975	1966-74
	1994	1989-93		1976	1971-75
	1995	1990-94		1977	1972-76
	1996	1987-95		1978	1973-77
	1997	1992-96		1979	1974-78
	1998	1993-97		1980	1971-79
	1999	1994-98		1981	1972-80
	1999CD[iv]	1990-98		1982	1977-81
	2000	1995-99		1983	1978-82
	2001	1997-01		1984	1979-83
	2002	1998-02		1985	1975-84
	2003	1999-03		1986	1977-85
- by age of mother	1954	1936-53		1987	1982-86
				1988	1983-87

Subject-matter	Year of issue	Time coverage	Subject-matter	Year of issue	Time coverage
	1989	1984-88		1968	Latest
	1990	1985-89		1971	1962-71
	1991	1986-90		1973	1965-73[vi]
	1992	1987-91		1976	Latest
	1993	1988-92		1982	Latest
	1994	1989-93		1987	1975-86
	1995	1990-94		1990	1980-89
	1996	1987-95	- by age, sex of householder, size and urban/rural residence	1987	1975-86
	1997	1992-96			
	1998	1993-97			
	1999	1994-98			
	1999CD[iv]	1990-98	- by family type and urban/rural residence	1987	1975-86
	2000	1995-99			
	2001	1997-01			
	2002	1998-02	- by marital status of householder and urban/rural residence	1987	1975-86
	2003	1999-03		1995	1985-95
- illegitimate	1961	1952-60	- by relationship to householder and urban/rural residence		
	1965	5-Latest		1987	1975-86
- legitimate	1959	1949-58		1995	1985-95
	1965	1955-64			
	1969	1963-68	- by size	1955	1945-54
	1975	1966-74		1962	1955-62
	1981	1972-80		1963	1955-63[vi]
	1986	1977-85		1971	1962-71
				1973	1965-73[vi]
- legitimate by age of mother	1959	1949-58		1976	Latest
	1965	1955-64		1982	Latest
	1969	1963-68		1987	1975-86
	1975	1966-74		1990	1980-89
	1981	1972-80		1995	1985-95
	1986	1977-85	- and number of persons 60+	1991PA[vii]	Latest
			- by urban/rural residence	1968	Latest
G				1971	1962-71
				1973	1965-73[vi]
Gestational age of foetal deaths (see: Foetal deaths)				1976	Latest
				1982	Latest
				1987	1975-86
Gross reproduction rates (see: Reproduction rates)				1990	1980-89
				1995	1985-95
H			- headship rates by age and sex of householder and urban/rural residence		
				1987	1975-86
Homeless (see: Population)				1995	1985-95
Households			- number of	1955	1945-54
- average size of	1962	1955-62		1962	1955-62
	1963	1955-63[vi]		1963	1955-63[vi]
				1968	Latest
				1971	1962-71

Subject-matter	Year of issue	Time coverage	Subject-matter	Year of issue	Time coverage
	1973	1965-73[vi]	- birth(s)	1959	1949-58
	1976	Latest		1965	1955-64
	1982	Latest		1969	1963-68
	1987	1975-86		1975	1966-74
	1990	1980-89		1981	1972-80
	1995	1985-95		1986	1977-85
- and number of persons 60+	1991PA[vii]	Latest		1999CD[iv]	1990-98
- number of family nuclei by size of	1973	1965-73	- birth ratios	1959	1949-58
	1976	Latest		1965	1955-64
	1982	Latest		1969	1963-68
	1987	1975-86		1975	1966-74
	1990	1980-90		1981	1972-80
- population by relationship	1987	1975-86		1986	1977-85
	1991PA[vii]	Latest		1999CD[iv]	1990-98
- by sex and persons 60+	1991PA[vii]	Latest	- foetal death(s),	1961	1952-60
- population in each type of	1955	1945-54		1965	5-Latest
	1962	1955-62		1969	1963-68
	1963	1955-63[vi]		1975	1966-74
	1968	Latest		1981	1972-80
	1971	1962-71		1986	1977-85
	1973	1965-73[vi]	- foetal death ratios, late	1961	1952-60
	1976	Latest		1965	5-Latest
	1982	Latest		1969	1963-68
	1987	1975-86		1975	1966-74
	1990	1980-89		1981	1972-80
	1995	1985-95		1986	1977-85

Illiteracy rates(see: Population)

Immigrants (see: Migration)

Illegitimacy rates and ratios

Subject-matter	Year of issue	Time coverage
- of births	1959	1949-58
	1965	1955-64
	1969	1963-68
	1975	1966-74
	1981	1972-80
	1986	1977-85
	1999CD[iv]	1990-98
- of foetal deaths, late	1961	1952-60
	1965	5-Latest
	1969	1963-68
	1975	1966-74
	1981	1972-80
	1986	1977-85

Illegitimate (see also: Births and Foetal deaths, late)

Subject-matter	Year of issue	Time coverage
Infant deaths	1948	1932-47
	1949/50	1934-49
	1951	1935-50
	1952	1936-51
	1953	1950-52
	1954	1946-53
	1955	1946-54
	1956	1947-55
	1957	1948-56
	1958	1948-57
	1959	1949-58
	1960	1950-59
	1961	1952-61
	1962	1953-62
	1963	1954-63
	1964	1960-64

Subject-matter	Year of issue	Time coverage	Subject-matter	Year of issue	Time coverage
	1965	1961-65		1986-1991	Latest
	1966	1947-66		1992	1983-92
	1967	1963-67		1993-1995	Latest
	1968	1964-68		1996	1987-95
	1969	1965-69		1997-2003	Latest
	1970	1966-70	- by age and sex and urban/rural residence		
	1971	1967-71		1967-1973	Latest
	1972	1968-72		1974	1965-73
	1973	1969-73		1975-1979	Latest
	1974	1965-74		1980	1971-79
	1975	1971-75		1981-1984	Latest
	1976	1972-76		1985	1976-84
	1977	1973-77		1986-1991	Latest
	1978	1974-78		1992	1983-92
	1978HS[ii]	1948-78		1993-1995	Latest
	1979	1975-79		1996	1987-95
	1980	1971-80		1997-1999	Latest
	1981	1977-81			
	1982	1978-82	- by month	1967	1962-66
	1983	1979-83		1974	1965-73
	1984	1980-84		1980	1971-79
	1985	1976-85		1985	1976-84
	1986	1982-86			
	1987	1983-87	- by urban/rural residence	1967	Latest
	1988	1984-88		1968	1964-68
	1989	1985-89		1969	1965-69
	1990	1986-90		1970	1966-70
	1991	1987-91		1971	1967-71
	1992	1983-92		1972	1968-72
	1993	1989-93		1973	1969-73
	1994	1990-94		1974	1965-74
	1995	1991-95		1975	1971-75
	1996	1987-96		1976	1972-76
	1997	1993-97		1977	1973-77
	1997HS[iii]	1948-97		1978	1974-78
	1998	1994-98		1979	1975-79
	1999	1995-99		1980	1971-80
	2000	1996-00		1981	1977-81
	2001	1997-01		1982	1978-82
	2002	1998-02		1983	1979-83
	2003	1999-03		1984	1980-84
- by age and sex	1948	1936-47		1985	1976-85
	1951	1936-49		1986	1982-86
	1957	1948-56		1987	1983-87
	1961	1952-60		1988	1984-88
	1962-1965	Latest		1989	1985-89
	1966	1956-65		1990	1986-90
	1967-1973	Latest		1991	1987-91
	1974	1965-73		1992	1983-92
	1975-1979	Latest		1993	1989-93
	1980	1971-79		1994	1990-94
	1981-1984	Latest		1995	1991-95
	1985	1976-84		1996	1987-96
				1997	1993-97

Subject-matter	Year of issue	Time coverage	Subject-matter	Year of issue	Time coverage
	1998	1994-98		1987	1983-87
	1999	1995-99		1988	1984-88
	2000	1996-00		1989	1985-89
	2001	1997-01		1990	1986-90
	2002	1998-02		1991	1987-91
	2003	1999-03		1992	1983-92
				1993	1989-93
Infant mortality rates	1948	1932-47		1994	1990-94
	1949/50	1932-49		1995	1991-95
	1951	1930-50		1996	1987-96
	1952	1920-34[v]		1997	1993-97
		1934-51		1997HS[iii]	1948-97
	1953	1920-39[v]		1998	1994-98
		1940-52		1999	1995-99
	1954	1920-39[v]		2000	1996-00
		1946-53		2001	1997-01
	1955	1920-34[v]		2002	1998-02
		1946-54		2003	1999-03
	1956	1947-55			
	1957	1948-56	- by age and sex	1948	1936-47
	1958	1948-57		1951	1936-49
	1959	1949-58		1957	1948-56
	1960	1950-59		1961	1952-60
	1961	1945-59[v]		1966	1956-65
		1952-61		1967	1962-66
	1962	1945-54[v]		1971-1973	Latest
		1952-62		1974	1965-73
	1963	1945-59[v]		1975-1979	Latest
	1963	1954-63		1980	1971-79
	1964	1960-64		1981-1984	Latest
	1965	1961-65		1985	1976-84
	1966	1920-64[v]		1986-1991	Latest
		1951-66		1992	1983-92
	1967	1963-67		1993-1995	Latest
	1968	1964-68		1996	1987-95
	1969	1965-69		1997-2003	Latest
	1970	1966-70	- by age and sex and urban/rural residence		
	1971	1967-71		1971-1973	Latest
	1972	1968-72		1974	1965-73
	1973	1969-73		1975-1979	Latest
	1974	1965-74		1980	1971-79
	1975	1971-75		1981-1984	Latest
	1976	1972-76		1985	1976-84
	1977	1973-77		1986-1991	Latest
	1978	1974-78		1992	1983-92
	1978HS[ii]	1948-78		1993-1995	Latest
	1979	1975-79		1996	1987-95
	1980	1971-80		1997-1999	Latest
	1981	1977-81	- by urban/rural residence		
	1982	1978-82		1967	Latest
	1983	1979-83		1968	1964-68
	1984	1980-84		1969	1965-69
	1985	1976-85		1970	1966-70
	1986	1982-86		1971	1967-71

Subject-matter	Year of issue	Time coverage	Subject-matter	Year of issue	Time coverage
	1972	1968-72	**Life tables**		
	1973	1969-73	- expectation of life		
	1974	1965-74	at birth, by sex	1959-1973	Latest
	1975	1971-75		1974	2-Latest
	1976	1972-76		1975-1978	Latest
	1977	1973-77		1978HS[ii]	1948-77
	1978	1974-78		1979	Latest
	1979	1975-79		1980	2-Latest
	1980	1971-80		1981-1984	Latest
	1981	1977-81		1985	2-Latest
	1982	1978-82		1986-1991	Latest
	1983	1979-83		1991PA[vii]	1950-90
	1984	1980-84		1992-1995	Latest
	1985	1976-85		1996	2-Latest
	1986	1982-00		1997	Latest
	1987	1983-87		1997HS[iii]	1948-96
	1988	1984-88		1998-2003	Latest
	1989	1985-89	- expectation of life		
	1990	1986-90	at specified ages,		
	1991	1987-91	by sex	1948	1891 -1945
	1992	1983-92		1951	1891 -1950
	1993	1989-93		1952	1891 -1951[vi]
	1994	1990-94		1953	1891 -1952
	1995	1991-95		1954	1891 -1953[vi]
	1996	1987-96		1955-1956	Latest
	1997	1993-97		1957	1900-56
	1998	1994-98		1958-1960	Latest
	1999	1995-99		1961	1940-60
	2000	1996-00		1962-1964	Latest
	2001	1997-01		1966	2-Latest
	2002	1998-02		1967	1900-66
	2003	1999-03		1968-1973	Latest
Intercensal rates of population increase	1948	1900-48		1974	2-Latest
	1949/50	1900-50		1975-1978	Latest
	1951	1900-51		1978HS[ii]	1948-77
	1952	1850-1952		1979	Latest
	1953	1850-1953		1980	2-Latest
	1955	1850-1954		1981-1984	Latest
	1960	1900-61		1985	2-Latest
	1962	1900-62		1986-1991	Latest
	1964	1955-64		1991PA[vii]	1950-90
	1970	1900-70		1992-1995	Latest
	1978HS[ii]	1948-78		1996	2-Latest
	1997HS[iii]	1948-97		1997	Latest
				1997HS[iii]	1948-96
International migration (see: Migration)				1998-2003	Latest
L			- mortality rates at specified ages, by sex	1948	1891-1945
Late foetal deaths(see: Foetal deaths, late)				1951	1891-1950

Subject-matter	Year of issue	Time coverage		Subject-matter	Year of issue	Time coverage
	1952	1891-1951[vi]			1970	1966-70
	1953	1891-1952			1971	1967-71
	1954	1891-1953[vi]			1972	1968-72
	1957	1900-56			1973	1969-73
	1961	1940-60			1974	1970-74
	1966	2-Latest			1975	1971-75
	1974	2-Latest			1976	1957-76
	1980	2-Latest			1977	1973-77
	1985	2-Latest			1978	1974-78
	1996	2-Latest			1979	1975-79
- survivors at specified ages, by sex					1980	1976-80
	1948	1891-1945			1981	1977-81
	1951	1891-1950			1982	1963-82
	1952	1891-1951[vi]			1983	1979-83
	1953	1891-1952			1984	1980-84
	1954	1891-1953[vi]			1985	1981-85
	1957	1900-56			1986	1982-86
	1961	1940-60			1987	1983-87
	1966	2-Latest			1988	1984-88
	1974	2-Latest			1989	1985-89
	1980	2-Latest			1990	1971-90
	1985	2-Latest			1991	1987-91
	1996	2-Latest			1992	1988-92
					1993	1989-93
Literacy (see: Population)					1994	1990-94
					1995	1991-95
Localities (see: Population)					1996	1992-96
					1997	1993-97
M					1998	1994-98
					1999	1995-99
Major civil divisions (see: Population)					2000	1996-00
					2001	1997-01
					2002	1998-02
					2003	1999-03
Marriages	1948	1932-47		- by age of bride	1948	1936-47
	1949/50	1934-49			1949/50	1936-49
	1951	1935-50			1958	1948-57
	1952	1936-51			1959-1967	Latest
	1953	1950-52			1968	1958-67
	1954	1946-53			1969-1975	Latest
	1955	1946-54			1976	1966-75
	1956	1947-55			1977-1981	Latest
	1957	1948-56			1982	1972-81
	1958	1940-57			1983-1986	Latest
	1959	1949-58			1987	1975-86
	1960	1950-59			1988-1989	Latest
	1961	1952-61			1990	1980-1989
	1962	1953-62			1991-1997	Latest
	1963	1954-63			1998	1993-97
	1964	1960-64			1999	1994-98
	1965	1956-65			2000	1995-99
	1966	1962-66			2001	1997-01
	1967	1963-67			2002	1998-02
	1968	1949-68			2003	1999-03
	1969	1965-69				

Subject-matter	Year of issue	Time coverage	Subject-matter	Year of issue	Time coverage
- by age of bride classified by age of groom	1958	1948-57	and age	1958	1946-57
	1968	Latest		1968	Latest
	1976	Latest		1976	Latest
	1982	Latest		1982	Latest
	1990	Latest		1990	Latest
- by age of bride and previous marital status	1958	1948-57	and previous marital status of groom	1949/50	Latest
	1968	Latest		1958	1948-57
	1976	Latest		1968	1958-67
	1982	Latest		1976	1966-75
	1990	Latest		1982	1972-81
- by age of groom	1948	1936-47		1990	1980-89
	1949/50	1936-49	- by previous marital status of groom:		
	1958	1948-57	and age	1958	1946-57
	1959-1967	Latest		1968	Latest
	1968	1958-67		1976	Latest
	1969-1975	Latest		1982	Latest
	1976	1966-75		1990	Latest
	1977-1981	Latest	and previous marital status of bride	1949/50	Latest
	1982	1972-81		1958	1948-57
	1983-1986	Latest		1968	1958-67
	1987	1975-86		1976	1966-75
	1988-1989	Latest		1982	1972-81
	1990	1980-1989		1990	1980-89
	1990-1997	Latest	-by urban/rural residence	1968	Latest
	1998	1993-97		1969	1965-69
	1999	1994-98		1970	1966-70
	2000	1995-99		1971	1967-71
	2001	1997-01		1972	1968-72
	2002	1998-02		1973	1969-73
	2003	1999-03		1974	1970-74
- by age of groom classified by age of bride	1958	1948-57		1975	1971-75
	1968	Latest		1976	1957-76
	1976	Latest		1977	1973-77
	1982	Latest		1978	1974-78
	1990	Latest		1979	1975-79
- by age of groom and previous marital status	1958	1948-57		1980	1976-80
				1981	1977-81
	1968	Latest		1982	1963-82
	1976	Latest		1983	1979-83
	1982	Latest		1984	1980-84
	1990	Latest		1985	1981-85
				1986	1982-86
				1987	1983-87
				1988	1984-88
- by month	1968	1963-67		1989	1985-89
				1990	1971-90
- by previous marital status of bride:				1991	1987-91
				1992	1988-92
				1993	1989-93

751

Subject-matter	Year of issue	Time coverage	Subject-matter	Year of issue	Time coverage
	1994	1990-94		1981	1977-81
	1995	1991-95		1982	1963-82
	1996	1992-96		1983	1979-83
	1997	1993-97		1984	1980-84
	1998	1994-98		1985	1981-85
	1999	1995-99		1986	1982-86
	2000	1996-00		1987	1983-87
	2001	1997-01		1988	1984-88
	2002	1998-02		1989	1985-89
	2003	1999-03		1990	1971-90
				1991	1987-91
Marriage, first				1992	1988-92
- by detailed age of groom and bride	1976	Latest		1993	1989-93
				1994	1990-94
	1982	1972-81		1995	1991-95
	1990	1980-89		1996	1992-96
				1997	1993-97
Marriage rates	1948	1932-47		1998	1994-98
	1949/50	1932-49		1999	1995-99
	1951	1930-50		2000	1996-00
	1952	1920-34[v]		2001	1997-01
		1934-51		2002	1998-02
	1953	1920-39[v]		2003	1999-03
		1940-52			
	1954	1920-39[v]	- by age and sex	1948	1936-46
		1946-53		1949/50	1936-49
	1955	1920-34[v]		1953	1936-51
		1946-54		1954	1936-52
	1956	1947-55		1958	1935-56
	1957	1948-56		1968	1955-67
	1958	1930-57		1976	1966-75
	1959	1949-58		1982	1972-81
	1960	1950-59		1987	1975-86
	1961	1952-61		1990	1980-89
	1962	1953-62	- by sex among marriageable population		
	1963	1954-63		1958	1935-56
	1964	1960-64		1968	1935-67
	1965	1956-65		1976	1966-75
	1966	1962-66		1982	1972-81
	1967	1963-67		1990	1980-89
	1968	1920-64[v]	- by urban/rural residence		
		1953-68		1968	Latest
	1969	1965-69		1969	1965-69
	1970	1966-70		1970	1966-70
	1971	1967-71		1971	1967-71
	1972	1968-72		1972	1968-72
	1973	1969-73		1973	1969-73
	1974	1970-74		1974	1970-74
	1975	1971-75		1975	1971-75
	1976	1957-76		1976	1957-76
	1977	1973-77		1977	1973-77
	1978	1974-78		1978	1974-78
	1979	1975-79		1979	1975-79
	1980	1976-80		1980	1976-80

Subject-matter	Year of issue	Time coverage	Subject-matter	Year of issue	Time coverage
	1981	1977-81		1989	1979-88
	1982	1963-82		1990	1980-89
	1983	1979-83		1991	1981-90
	1984	1980-84		1992	1982-91
	1985	1981-85		1993	1983-92
	1986	1982-86		1994	1984-93
	1987	1983-87		1995	1985-94
	1988	1984-88		1996	1986-95
	1989	1985-89		1997	1987-96
	1990	1971-90		1998	1988-97
	1991	1987-91		1999	1989-98
	1992	1988-92		2000	1991-00
	1993	1989-93		2001	1991-00
	1994	1990-94		2002	1995-02
	1995	1991-95		2003	1995-02
	1996	1992-96			
	1997	1993-97	- by age	1951	Latest
	1998	1994-98		1952	Latest[vi]
	1999	1995-99		1957	Latest
	2000	1996-00		1961	Latest
	2001	1997-01		1967	Latest
	2002	1998-02		1974	Latest
	2003	1999-03		1980	Latest
				1985	Latest
Marriage rates, first					
-by detailed age of groom and bride	1982	1972-81	**Maternal mortality rates**..........	1951	1947-50
	1990	1980-89		1952	1947-51
				1953	Latest
				1954	1945-53
Married population by age and sex (see: Population by marital status)				1955-1956	Latest
				1957	1952-62
				1958-1960	Latest
				1961	1955-60
Maternal death	1951	1947-50		1962-1965	Latest
	1952	1947-51		1966	1960-65
	1953	Latest		1967-1973	Latest
	1954	1945-53		1974	1965-73
	1955-1956	Latest		1975	1966-74
	1957	1952-56		1976	1966-75
	1958-1960	Latest		1977	1967-76
	1961	1955-60		1978	1968-77
	1962-1965	Latest		1979	1969-78
	1966	1960-65		1980	1971-79
	1967-1973	Latest		1981	1972-80
	1974	1965-73		1982	1972-81
	1975-1979	Latest		1983	1973-82
	1980	1971-79		1984	1974-83
	1981	1972-80		1985	1975-84
	1982	1972-81		1986	1976-85
	1983	1973-82		1987	1977-86
	1984	1974-83		1988	1978-87
	1985	1975-84		1989	1979-88
	1986	1976-85		1990	1980-89
	1987	1977-86		1991	1981-90
	1988	1978-87			

Subject-matter	Year of issue	Time coverage	Subject-matter	Year of issue	Time coverage
	1992	1982-91		1954	1948-53
	1993	1983-92		1957	1951-56
	1994	1984-93		1959	1953-58
	1995	1985-94		1962	1956-61
	1996	1986-95		1966	1960-65
	1997	1987-96		1968	1966-67
	1998	1988-97		1977	1967-76
	1999	1989-98		1985	1975-84
	2000	1991-00		1989	1979-88
	2001	1991-00		1996	1986-95
	2002	1995-02			
	2003	1995-02	- emigrants, long term:		
Migration (international):			by age and sex	1948	1945-47
- arrivals	1970	1963-69		1949/50	1946-48
	1972	1965-71		1951	1948-50
	1974	1967-73		1952	1949-51
	1976	1969-75		1954	1950-53
	1977	1967-76		1957	1953-56
	1985	1975-84		1959	1955-58
	1989	1979-88		1962	1958-61
	1996	1986-95		1966	1960-65
	1972	1965-71		1970	1962-69
	1974	1967-73		1977	1967-76
	1976	1969-75		1989	1975-88
- arrivals, by major categories	1949/50	1945-49	by country or area of intended residence	1948	1945-47
	1951	1946-50		1949/50	1945-48
	1952	1947-51		1951	1948-50
	1954	1948-53		1952	1949-51
	1957	1951-56		1954	1950-53
	1959	1953-58		1957	1953-56
	1962	1956-61		1959	1956-58
	1966	1960-65		1977	1958-76
	1968	1966-67		1989	1975-88
	1977	1967-76			
	1985	1975-84	- immigrants, long term		
	1989	1979-88	by age and sex	1948	1945-47
	1996	1986-95		1949/50	1946-48
- continental and inter-continental	1948	1936-47		1951	1948-50
	1977	1967-76		1952	1949-51
				1954	1950-53
- departures	1970	1963-69		1957	1953-56
	1972	1965-71		1959	1955-58
	1974	1967-73		1962	1958-61
	1976	1969-75		1966	1960-65
	1977	1967-76		1970	1962-69
	1985	1975-84		1977	1967-76
	1989	1979-88		1989	1975-88
	1996	1986-95	by country or area of last	1948	1945-47
- departures, by major categories	1949/50	1945-49			
	1951	1946-50			
	1952	1947-51			

Subject-matter	Year of issue	Time coverage
residence		
	1949/50	1945-48
	1951	1948-50
	1952	1949-51
	1954	1950-53
	1957	1953-56
	1959	1956-58
	1977	1958-76
	1989	1975-88
	1948	1945-47
	1949/50	1945-48
- refugees, by country or area of destination:		
repatriated by the International Refugee Organization	1952	1947-51
resettled by the International Refugee Organization	1952	1947-51

Mortality [see: Death(s), Death rates, infant deaths, infant mortality rates, Foetal death(s), Foetal death ratios, Life tables, Maternal deaths, Maternal mortality rates, Neonatal deaths, Neo-natal mortality rates, Perinatal mortality, Post-neo-natal deaths, Post-neo-natal mortality rates]

N

Natality (see: Births and Birthrates)

Subject-matter	Year of issue	Time coverage
Natural increase rates	1958-1978	Latest
	1978HS[ii]	1948-78
	1979-1997	Latest
	1998	1995-98
	1999	1996-99
	2000	1995-00
	2001-2003	2000-05

Neo-natal mortality

	Year of issue	Time coverage
- by sex	1948	1936-47
	1951	1936-50
	1957	1948-56
	1961	1952-60
	1963-1965	Latest
	1966	1961-65

Subject-matter	Year of issue	Time coverage
	1967	1962-66
	2000-2003	Latest
- by sex and urban/rural residence	1968-1973	Latest
	1974	1965-73
	1975-1979	Latest
	1980	1971-79
	1981-1984	Latest
	1985	1976-84
	1986-1991	Latest
	1992	1983-92
	1993-1995	Latest
	1996	1087-05
	1997	Latest
	1997HS[iii]	1948-96
	1998-1999	Latest

Neo-natal mortality rates

	Year of issue	Time coverage
- by sex	1948	1936-47
	1951	1936-50
	1957	1948-56
	1961	1952-60
	1966	1956-65
	1967	1962-66
	2000-2003	Latest
- by sex and urban/rural residence	1971-1973	Latest
	1974	1965-73
	1975-1979	Latest
	1980	1971-79
	1981-1984	Latest
	1985	1976-84
	1986-1991	Latest
	1992	1983-92
	1993-1995	Latest
	1996	1987-95
	1997	Latest
	1997HS[iii]	1948-96
	1998-1999	Latest

Net reproduction rates (see: Reproduction rates)

Nuptiality (see: Marriages)

P

Subject-matter	Year of issue	Time coverage
Perinatal deaths	1961	1952-60
	1966	1956-65
	1971	1966-70
	1974	1965-73

Subject-matter	Year of issue	Time coverage	Subject-matter	Year of issue	Time coverage
	1980	1971-79		1960	1940-60
	1985	1976-84		1961-1969	Latest
	1996	1987-95		1970	1950-70
- by urban/rural residence	1971	1966-70		1971-1997	Latest
	1974	1965-73		1997HS[iii]	1948-97
	1980	1971-79		1998-2003	Latest
	1985	1976-84			
	1996	1987-95	percentage distribution	1948-1949/50	1945 and Latest[vi]
				1951-1952	Latest
Perinatal death ratios	1961	1952-60	- by country or area of birth and sex (see also: foreign-born, below)		
	1966	1956-65			
	1971	1966-70		1956	1945-55
	1974	1965-73		1963	1955-63
	1980	1971-79		1964	1955-64[vi]
	1985	1976-84		1971	1962-71
	1996	1987-95		1973	1965-73[vi]
- by urban/rural residence	1971	1966-70	- by country or area of birth and sex and age (see also: foreign-born, below)		
	1974	1965-73			
	1980	1971-79			
	1985	1976-84		1977	Latest
	1996	1987-95		1983	1974-83
				1989	1980-88[vi]
Population					
- Ageing selected indicators	1991PA[vii]	1950-90	- by citizenship	1956	1945-55
				1963	1955-63
- by age groups and sex:				1964	1955-64[vi]
				1971	1962-71
				1973	1965-73[vi]
enumerated	1948-1952	Latest	- by citizenship, sex and age		
	1953	1950-52		1977	Latest
	1954-1959	Latest[vi]		1983	1974-83
	1960	1940-60		1989	Latest
	1961	Latest	- by ethnic composition and sex		
	1962	1955-62			
	1963	1955-63		1956	1945-55
	1964	1955-64[vi]		1963	1955-63
	1965-1969	Latest		1964	1955-64[vi]
	1970	1950-70		1971	1962-71
	1971	1962-71		1973	1965-73[vi]
	1972	Latest		1979	1970-79[vi]
	1973	1965-73		1983	1974-83
	1974-1978	Latest		1993	1985-93
	1978HS[ii]	1948-77	- by households, number and size (see also: Households)		
	1979-1991	Latest			
	1991PA[vii]	1950-90		1955	1945-54
	1992-1997	Latest		1962	1955-62
	1997HS[iii]	1948-97		1963	1955-63[vi]
	1998-2003	Latest		1968	Latest
estimated	1948-	1945		1971	1962-71
	1949/50	and Latest[vi]		1973	1965-73[vi]
	1951-1959	Latest		1976	Latest
				1982	Latest
				1987	1975-86

Subject-matter	Year of issue	Time coverage	Subject-matter	Year of issue	Time coverage
	1990	1980-89		1960	1920-61
	1995	1985-95		1962	1955-62
- by language and sex	1956	1945-55		1963	1955-63[vi]
	1963	1955-63		1970	1950-70
	1964	1955-64[vi]		1971	1962-71
	1971	1962-71		1973	1965-73[vi]
	1973	1965-73[vi]		1979	1970-79[vi]
	1979	1970-79[vi]		1983	1974-83
	1983	1974-83		1988	1980-88[vi]
	1988	1980-88[vi]		1993	1985-93
	1993	1985-93	- by locality size-classes and sex	1948	Latest
- by level of education, age and sex	1956	1946-55		1952	Latest
	1963	1955-63		1955	1945-54
	1964	1955-64[vi]		1962	1955-62
	1971	1962-71		1963	1955-63[vi]
	1973	1965-73[vi]		1971	1962-71
	1979	1970-79[vi]		1973	1965-73[vi]
	1983	1974-83		1979	1970-79[vi]
	1988	1980-88[vi]		1983	1974-83
	1993	1985-93		1988	1980-88[vi]
- by literacy, age and sex (see also: illiteracy, below)	1948	Latest		1993	1985-93
	1955	1945-54	- by major civil divisions	1952	Latest
	1963	1955-63		1955	1945-54
	1964	1955-64[vi]		1962	1955-62
	1971	1962-71		1963	1955-63[vi]
- by literacy, age and sex and urban/rural residence	1973	1965-73[vi]		1971	1962-71
	1979	1970-79[vi]		1973	1965-73[vi]
	1983	1974-83		1979	1970-79[vi]
	1988	1980-88[vi]		1983	1974-83
	1993	1985-93		1988	1980-88[vi]
- by localities of: 100000+ inhabitants	1948	Latest		1993	1985-93
	1952	Latest	- by marital status, age and sex (see also: married and single, below)	1948	Latest
	1955	1945-54		1940/50	1926-48
	1960	1920-61		1955	1945-54
	1962	1955-62		1958	1945-57
	1963	1955-63[vi]		1962	1955-62[vi]
	1970	1950-70		1963	1955-63[vi]
	1971	1962-71		1965	1955-65
	1973	1965-73[vi]		1968	1955-67
	1979	1970-79[vi]		1971	1962-71
	1983	1974-83		1973	1965-73[vi]
	1988	1980-88[vi]		1976	1966-75
	1993	1985-93		1978HS[ii]	1948-77
20000+ inhabitants	1948	Latest		1982	1972-81
	1952	Latest		1987	1975-86
	1955	1945-54		1990	1980-89
				1997HS[iii]	1948-96
			- for persons 60+ and urban/rural	1991PA[vii]	Latest

Subject-matter		Year of issue	Time coverage	Subject-matter		Year of issue	Time coverage
	percentage distribution	1948	Latest			1974-1997	Latest
						1997HS[iii]	1948-97
	- by religion and sex	1956	1945-55			1998-1999	Latest
		1963	1955-63			2000	1991-2000
		1964	1955-64[vi]			2001	1992-2001
		1971	1962-71			2002	1993-2002
		1973	1965-73[vi]			2003	1994-2003
		1979	1970-79[vi]		- by single years of age and sex	1955	1945-54
		1983	1974-83			1962	1955-62
		1988	1980-88[vi]			1963	1955-63[vi]
		1993	1985-93			1971	1962-71
	- by school attendance, age and sex	1956	1945-55			1973	1965-73[vi]
		1963	1955-63			1979	1970-79[vi]
		1964	1955-64[vi]			1983	1974-83
		1971	1962-71			1988	1980-88[vi]
		1973	1965-73[vi]			1993	1985-93
		1979	1970-79		- cities (see: of cities, below)		
		1983	1974-83				
		1988	1980-88[vi]		- civil division (see: by major civil divisions, above)		
		1993	1985-93				
	- by sex:						
	enumerated	1948-1952	Latest		- density (see: Density)		
		1953	1950-52				
		1954-1959	Latest		- Disabled	1991PA[vii]	Latest
		1960	1900-61		- economically active:		
		1961	Latest		by age and sex	1945	1945-54
		1962	1900-62			1956	1945-55
		1963	1955-63			1964	1955-64
		1964	1955-64			1972	1962-72
		1965-1969	Latest		by age and sex and urban/rural residence	1973	1965-73[vi]
		1970	1950-70			1979	1970-79[vi]
		1971	1962-71			1984	1974-84
		1972	Latest			1988	1980-88[vi]
		1973	1965-73			1994	1985-94
		1974-1978	Latest		by age and sex, per cent	1949/50	1930-48
		1978HS[ii]	1948-78			1954	Latest
		1979-1982	Latest			1955	1945-54
		1983	1974-83			1956	1945-55
		1984-1997	Latest			1964	1955-64
		1997HS[iii]	1948-97			1972	1962-72
		1998-2003	Latest		by age and sex, per cent and urban/rural residence		
	estimated	1948-	1945			1973	1965-73[vi]
		1949/50	and latest			1979	1970-79[vi]
		1951-1954	Latest			1984	1974-84
		1955-1959	Latest				
		1960	1940-60				
		1961-1969	Latest				
		1970	1950-70				
		1971	1962-71				
		1972	Latest				
		1973	1965-73				

Subject-matter	Year of issue	Time coverage	Subject-matter	Year of issue	Time coverage
	1988	1980-88[vi]	by occupation, status and sex and urban/rural residence		
	1994	1985-94			
by industry, age and sex	1956	1945-55		1973	1965-73[vi]
	1964	1955-64		1979	1970-7vi[vi]
	1972	1962-72		1984	1974-84
by industry, age, sex and urban/rural residence				1988	1980-88[vi]
	1973	1965-74[vi]		1994	1985-94
	1979	1970-79[vi]	by sex	1948	Latest
	1984	1974-84		1949/50	1926-48
	1988	1980-88[vi]		1955	1945-54
	1994	1985-94		1956	1945-55
by industry, status and sex				1960	1920-60
	1948	Latest		1963	1955-63
	1949/50	Latest		1964	1955-64
	1955	1945-54		1970	1950-70
	1964	1955-64		1972	1962-72
	1972	1962-72		1973	1965-73[vi]
by industry, status and sex and urban/rural residence				1979	1970-79[vi]
				1984	1974-84
	1973	1965-73[vi]		1994	1985-94
	1979	1970-79[vi]	by status, age and sex		
	1984	1974-84		1956	1945-55
	1988	1980-88[vi]		1964	1955-64
	1994	1985-94		1972	1962-72
by living arrangements, age, sex and urban/rural residence			by status, age and sex and urban/rural residence		
	1987	1975-86		1973	1965-73[vi]
	1995	1985-95		1979	1970-79[vi]
by occupation, age and sex				1984	1974-84
				1988	1980-88[vi]
	1956	1945-55		1994	1985-94
	1964	1955-64	by status, industry and sex	1948	Latest
	1972	1962-72		1949/50	Latest
by occupation, age and sex and urban/rural residence				1955	1945-54
				1964	1955-64
				1972	1962-72
	1973	1965-73[vi]	by status, industry, and sex and urban/rural residence		
	1979	1970-79[vi]			
	1984	1974-84			
	1988	1980-88[vi]		1973	1965-73[vi]
	1994	1985-94		1979	1970-79[vi]
by occupation, status and sex				1984	1974-84
				1988	1980-88[vi]
	1956	1945-55		1994	1985-94
	1964	1955-64	by status, occupation and sex	1956	1945-55
	1972	1962-72			

Subject-matter	Year of issue	Time coverage	Subject-matter	Year of issue	Time coverage
	1964	1955-64	- by economic, socio-demographic and urban/rural	1991PA[vii]	1950-90
	1972	1962-72	-female:		
by status, occupation and sex and urban/rural residence			by age and duration of marriage	1968	Latest
	1973	1965-73[vi]	by number of children born alive and age	1949/50	Latest
	1979	1970-79[vi]		1954	1930-53
	1984	1974-84		1955	1945-54
	1988	1980-88[vi]		1959	1949-58
	1994	1985-94		1963	1955-63
female, by marital status and age				1965	1955-65
	1956	1945-55		1969	Latest
	1964	1955-64		1971	1962-71
	1968	Latest		1973	1965-73[vi]
	1972	1962-72		1975	1965-74
female, by marital status and age and urban/rural residence				1978HS[ii]	1948-77
				1981	1972-80
				1986	1977-85
	1973	1965-73[vi]		1997HS[iii]	1948-96
	1979	1970-79[vi]	by number of children living and age		
	1984	1974-84		1949/50	Latest
	1988	1980-88[vi]		1954	1930-53
	1994	1985-94		1955	1945-54
foreign-born by occupation, age and sex (see also: country of birth above)				1959	1949-58
				1963	1955-63
	1984	1974-84		1965	1955-65
		1980-88		1968-1969	Latest
	1994	1985-94		1971	1962-71
foreign-born by occupation and sex (see also: country of birth above)				1973	1965-73[vi]
				1975	1965-74
	1977	Latest		1978HS[ii]	1948-77
unemployed, by age and sex	1949/50	1946-49		1981	1972-80
- economically inactive by sub-groups and sex				1986	1977-85
				1997HS[iii]	1948-96
	1956	1945-54	in households by age, sex of householder, size and relationship to householder and urban/rural residence		
	1964	1955-64			
	1972	1962-72			
	1973	1965-73[vi]			
	1979	1970-79[vi]			
	1984	1974-84[vi]			
	1988	1980-88[vi]			
	1994	1985-94		1987	1975-86
- Elderly				1995	1991-95

Subject-matter	Year of issue	Time coverage	Subject-matter	Year of issue	Time coverage
institutional, by age, sex and urban/rural residence			average annual for the world, macro-regions (continents) and regions		
	1987	1875-86			
	1995	1991-95			
-growth rates:				1957	1950-56
average annual for countries or areas				1958	1950-57
				1959	1950-58
				1960	1950-59
	1957	1953-56		1961	1950-60
	1958	1953-57		1962	1950-61
	1959	1953-58		1963	1958-62
	1960	1953-59			1960-62
	1961	1953-60		1964	1958-63
	1962	1958-61			1960-63
	1963	1958-62		1965	1958-64
	1964	1958-63			1960-64
	1965	1958-64		1966	1958-66
	1966	1958-66			1960-66
	1967	1963-67		1967	1960-67
	1968	1963-68			1963-67
	1969	1963-69		1968	1960-68
	1970	1963-70			1963-68
	1971	1963-71		1969	1960-69
	1972	1963-72			1963-69
	1973	1970-73		1970	1963-70
	1974	1970-74			1965-70
	1975	1970-75		1971	1963-71
	1976	1970-76			1965-71
	1977	1970-77		1972	1963-72
	1978	1975-78			1965-72
	1979	1975-79		1973	1965-73
	1980	1975-80			1970-73
	1981	1975-81		1974	1965-74
	1982	1975-82			1970-74
	1983	1980-83		1975	1965-75
	1984	1980-84			1970-75
	1985	1980-85		1976	1965-76
	1986	1980-86			1970-76
	1987	1980-87		1977	1965-77
	1988	1985-88			1970-77
	1989	1985-89		1978-1979	1970-75
	1990	1985-90		1980-1983	1975-80
	1991	1985-91		1984-1986	1980-85
	1992	1985-92		1987-1992	1985-90
	1993	1990-93		1993-1997	1990-95
	1994	1990-94		1998-2000	1995-00
	1995	1990-95		2001-2003	2000-05
	1996	1990-96	- Homeless by age and sex		
	1997	1990-97		1991PA[vii]	Latest
	1998	1993-98	- illiteracy rates by sex		
	1999	1995-99		1948	Latest
	2000	1995-00		1955	1945-54
	2001-2003	2000-05		1960	1920-60

Subject-matter	Year of issue	Time coverage
	1963	1955-63[vi]
	1964	1955-64[vi]
	1970	1950-70
- illiteracy rates by sex and urban/rural residence		
	1973	1965-73
	1979	1970-79[vi]
	1983	1974-83
	1988	1980-88[vi]
	1993	1985-93
- illiterate, by sex	1948	Latest
	1955	1945-54
	1960	1920-60
	1963	1955-63
	1964	1955-64
	1970	1950-70
- illiterate, by sex and age	1948	Latest
	1955	1945-54
	1963	1955-63
	1964	1955-64[vi]
	1970	1950-70
- illiterate, by sex and age and urban/rural residence	1973	1965-73
	1979	1970-79[vi]
	1983	1974-83
	1988	1980-88[vi]
	1993	1985-93
- illiterate, by sex and urban/rural residence	1973	1965-73
	1979	1970-79[vi]
	1983	1974-83
	1988	1980-88[vi]
	1993	1985-93
- in collective living quarters and homeless	1991PA[vii]	Latest
- in households (see: by household type, above, also: Households)		
- in localities (see: by localities and by locality size-classes, above)		
- increase rates (see: growth rates, above)		

Subject-matter	Year of issue	Time coverage
- literacy rates: by sex (see also: illiteracy rates, above)	1955	1945-54
- literacy rates, by sex and age	1955	1945-54
- literate, by sex and age (see also: illiterate, above)	1948	Latest
	1955	1945-54
	1963	1955-63
	1964	1955-64[vi]
- literate, by sex and age by urban/rural residence	1971	1962-71
	1973	1965-73[vi]
	1979	1970-74[vi]
	1983	1974-83
	1988	1980-88[vi]
	1993	1985-93
	1987	1975-86
- living arrangements	1991PA[vii]	1950-90
	1995	1985-95
- localities (see: by localities, above)		
- major civil divisions (see: by major civil divisions, above)		
- married by age and sex (see also: by marital status, above): numbers and percent	1954	1926-52
	1960	1920-60
	1970	1950-70
- married female by percentage and duration of marriage	1968	Latest
- never married proportion by sex, selected ages	1976	1966-75
	1978HS[ii]	1948-77
	1982	1972-81
	1990	1980-89
- not economically active	1972	1962-72
- not economically active by urban/rural residence	1973	1965-73[vi]
	1979	1970-79[vi]

Subject-matter	Year of issue	Time coverage	Subject-matter	Year of issue	Time coverage
	1984	1974-84		1953	1920-53
	1988	1980-88[vi]		1954	1920-54
	1994	1985-94		1955	1920-55
- of cities:				1956	1920-56
capital city	1952	Latest		1957	1940-57
	1955	1945-54		1958	1939-58
	1957	Latest		1959	1940-59
	1960	1939-61		1960	1920-60
	1962	1955-62		1961	1941-61
	1963	1955-63		1962	1942-62
	1964-1969	Latest		1963	1943-63
	1970	1950-70		1964	1955-64
	1971	1962-71		1965	1946-65
	1972	Latest		1966	1947-66
	1973	1965-73		1967	1958-67
	1974-2002	Latest		1968	1959-68
of 100000+				1969	1960-69
inhabitants	1952	Latest		1970	1950-70
	1955	1945-54		1971	1962-71
	1957	Latest		1972	1963-72
	1960	1939-61		1973	1964-73
	1962	1955-62		1974	1965-74
	1963	1955-63		1975	1966-75
	1964-1969	Latest		1976	1967-76
	1970	1950-70		1977	1968-77
	1971	1962-71		1978	1969-78
	1972	Latest		1978HS[ii]	1948-78
	1973	1965-73		1979	1970-79
	1974-2003	Latest		1980	1971-80
- of continents (see: of macro regions, below)				1981	1972-81
				1982	1973-82
- of countries or areas (totals):				1983	1974-83
				1984	1975-84
enumerated	1948	1900-48		1985	1976-85
	1949/50	1900-50		1986	1977-86
	1951	1900-51		1987	1978-87
	1952	1850-1952		1988	1979-88
	1953	1850-1953		1989	1980-89
	1954	Latest		1990	1981-90
	1955	1850-1954		1991	1982-91
	1956-1961	Latest		1992	1983-92
	1962	1900-62		1993	1984-93
	1963	Latest		1994	1985-94
	1964	1955-64		1995	1986-95
	1965-1978	Latest		1996	1987-96
	1978HS[ii]	1948-78		1997	1988-97
	1979-1997	Latest		1997HS[iii]	1948-97
	1997HS[iii]	1948-97		1998	1989-98
	1998-2003	Latest		1999	1990-99
				2000	1991-00
estimated	1948	1932-47		2001	1992-01
	1949/50	1932-49		2002	1993-02
	1951	1930-50		2003	1994-03
	1952	1920-51			

Subject-matter	Year of issue	Time coverage	Subject-matter	Year of issue	Time coverage
- of major regions	1949/50	1920-49	- of regions	1949/50	1920-49
	1951	1950		1952	1920-51
	1952	1920-51		1953	1920-52
	1953	1920-52		1954	1920-53
	1954	1920-53		1955	1920-54
	1955	1920-54		1956	1920-55
	1956	1920-55		1957	1920-56
	1957	1920-56		1958	1920-57
	1958	1920-57		1959	1920-58
	1959	1920-58		1960	1920-59
	1960	1920-59		1961	1920-60
	1961	1920-60		1962	1920-61
	1962	1920-61		1963	1930-62
	1963	1930-62		1964	1930-63
	1964	1930-63		1965	1930-65
	1965	1930-65		1966	1930-66
	1966	1930-66		1967	1930-67
	1967	1930-67		1968	1930-68
	1968	1930-68		1969	1930-69
	1969	1930-69		1970	1950-70
	1970	1950-70		1971	1950-71
	1971	1950-71		1972	1950-72
	1972	1950-72		1973	1950-73
	1973	1950-73		1974	1950-74
	1974	1950-74		1975	1950-75
	1975	1950-75		1976	1950-76
	1976	1950-76		1977	1950-77
	1977	1950-77		1978	1950-78
	1978	1950-78		1979	1950-79
	1979	1950-79		1980	1950-80
	1980	1950-80		1981	1950-81
	1981	1950-81		1982	1950-82
	1982	1950-82		1983	1950-83
	1983	1950-83		1984	1950-84
	1984	1950-84		1985	1950-85
	1985	1950-85		1986	1950-86
	1986	1950-86		1987	1950-87
	1987	1950-87		1988	1950-88
	1988	1950-88		1989	1950-89
	1989	1950-89		1990	1950-90
	1990	1950-90		1991	1950-91
	1991	1950-91		1992	1950-92
	1992	1950-92		1993	1950-93
	1993	1950-93		1994	1950-94
	1994	1950-94		1995	1950-95
	1995	1950-95		1996	1950-96
	1996	1950-96		1997	1950-97
	1997	1950-97		1998-1999	1950-00
	1998-1999	1950-00		2000	1950-00
	2000	1950-00		2001	1950-01
	2001	1950-01		2002	1950-02
	2002	1950-02		2003	1950-03
	2003	1950-03			
			- of the world	1949/50	1920-49

Subject-matter	Year of issue	Time coverage	Subject-matter	Year of issue	Time coverage
	1951	1950			
	1952	1920-51	- single, by age and sex (see also: by marital status, above):		
	1953	1920-52			
	1954	1920-53			
	1955	1920-54	numbers	1960	1920-60
	1956	1920-55		1970	1950-70
	1957	1920-56	percent	1949/50	1926-48
	1958	1920-57		1960	1920-60
	1959	1920-58		1970	1950-70
	1960	1920-59			
	1961	1920-60	- urban/rural residence	1968	1964-68
	1962	1920-61		1969	1965-69
	1963	1930-62		1970	1950-70
	1964	1930-63		1971	1962-71
	1965	1930-65		1972	1968-72
	1966	1930-66		1973	1965-73
	1967	1930-67		1974	1966-74
	1968	1930-68		1975	1967-75
	1969	1930-69		1976	1967-76
	1970	1950-70		1977	1968-77
	1971	1950-71		1978	1969-78
	1972	1950-72		1979	1970-79
	1973	1950-73		1980	1971-80
	1974	1950-74		1981	1972-81
	1975	1950-75		1982	1973-82
	1976	1950-76		1983	1974-83
	1977	1950-77		1984	1975-84
	1978	1950-78		1985	1976-85
	1979	1950-79		1986	1977-86
	1980	1950-80		1987	1978-87
	1981	1950-81		1988	1979-88
	1982	1950-82		1989	1980-89
	1983	1950-83		1990	1981-90
	1984	1950-84		1991	1982-91
	1985	1950-85		1992	1983-92
	1986	1950-86		1993	1984-93
	1987	1950-87		1994	1985-94
	1988	1950-88		1995	1986-95
	1989	1950-89		1996	1987-96
	1990	1950-90		1997	1988-97
	1991	1950-91		1998	1989-98
	1992	1950-92		1999	1990-99
	1993	1950-93		2000	1991-00
	1994	1950-94		2001	1992-01
	1995	1950-95		2002	1993-02
	1996	1950-96	by age and sex:		
	1997	1950-97	enumerated	1963	1955-63
	1998-1999	1950-00		1964	1955-64[vi]
	2000	1950-00		1967	Latest
	2001	1950-01		1970	1950-70
	2002	1950-02		1971	1962-71
	2003	1950-03		1972	Latest
- rural residence (see: urban/rural residence, below)				1973	1965-73

Index
Historical index
(See notes at end of index)

Subject-matter	Year of issue	Time coverage
	1974-1978	Latest
	1978HS[ii]	1948-77
	1979-1996	Latest
	1979-1997	Latest
	1997HS[iii]	1948-96
	1998-2003	Latest
estimated	1963	Latest
	1967	Latest
	1970	1950-70
	1971-1997	Latest
	1997HS[iii]	1948-96
	1998-2003	Latest
by country or area of birth and sex	1971	1962-71
	1973	1965-73[vi]
by country or area of birth and sex and age	1977	Latest
by citizenship and sex	1971	1962-71
	1973	1965-73[vi]
by citizenship and sex and age	1977	Latest
	1983	1974-83
	1989	1980-88
by ethnic composition and sex	1971	Latest
	1973	1965-73[vi]
	1979	1970-79[vi]
	1983	1974-83
	1988	1980-88[vi]
	1993	1985-93
by households, number and size (see also: Households)	1968	Latest
	1971	1962-71
	1973	1965-73[vi]
	1976	Latest
	1982	Latest
	1987	1975-86
	1990	1980-89
	1995	1985-95
by language and sex	1971	1962-71
	1973	1965-73[vi]
	1979	1970-79[vi]
	1983	1974-83
	1988	1980-88[vi]
	1993	1985-93
by level of education,	1971	1962-71

Subject-matter	Year of issue	Time coverage
age and sex		
	1973	1965-73[vi]
	1979	1970-79[vi]
	1983	1974-83
	1988	1980-88[vi]
	1993	1985-93
by literacy, age and sex	1971	1962-71
	1973	1965-73[vi]
	1979	1970-79[vi]
	1983	1974-83
	1988	1980-88[vi]
	1993	1985-93
by major civil divisions	1971	1962-71
	1973	1965-73[vi]
	1979	1970-79[vi]
	1983	1974-83
	1988	1980-88[vi]
	1993	1985-93
by marital status, age and sex	1971	1962-71
	1973	1965-73[vi]
by religion and sex	1971	1962-71
	1973	1965-73[vi]
	1979	1970-79[vi]
	1983	1974-83
	1988	1980-88[vi]
	1993	1985-93
by school attendance, age and sex	1971	1962-71
	1973	1965-73[vi]
	1979	1970-79[vi]
	1983	1974-83
	1988	1980-88[vi]
	1993	1985-93
by sex:		
numbers	1948	Latest
	1952	1900-51
	1955	1945-54
	1960	1920-60
	1962	1955-62
	1963	1955-63
	1964	1955-64[vi]
	1967	Latest
	1970	1950-70
	1971	1962-71
	1972	Latest
	1973	1965-73
	1974	1966-74
	1975	1967-75
	1976	1967-76

Subject-matter	Year of issue	Time coverage	Subject-matter	Year of issue	Time coverage
	1977	1968-77		1992	1983-92
	1978	1969-78		1993	1984-93
	1979	1970-79		1994	1985-94
	1980	1971-80		1995	1986-95
	1981	1972-81		1996	1987-96
	1982	1973-82		1997	1988-97
	1983	1974-83		1998	1989-98
	1984	1975-84		1999	1990-99
	1985	1976-85		2000	1991-00
	1986	1977-86		2001	1992-01
	1987	1978-87		2002	1993-02
	1988	1979-88		2003	1994-03
	1989	1980-89	by single years of age and sex		
	1990	1981-90		1971	1962-71
	1991	1982-91		1973	1965-73[vi]
	1992	1983-92		1979	1970-79[vi]
	1993	1984-93		1983	1974-83
	1994	1985-94		1993	1985-93
	1995	1986-95	female: by number of children born alive and age		
	1996	1987-96		1971	1962-71
	1997	1988-97		1973	1965-73[vi]
	1998	1989-98		1975	1965-74
	1999	1990-99		1978HS[ii]	1948-77
	2000	1991-00		1981	1972-80
	2001	1992-01		1986	1977-85
	2002	1993-02		1997HS[iii]	1948-96
	2003	1994-03	female: by number of children living and age		
percent	1948	Latest		1971	1962-71
	1952	1900-51		1973	1965-73[vi]
	1955	1945-54		1975	1965-74
	1960	1920-60		1978HS[ii]	1948-77
	1962	1955-62		1981	1972-80
	1970	1950-70		1986	1977-85
	1971	1962-71		1997HS[iii]	1948-96
	1973	1965-73			
	1974	1966-74	**Post-neo-natal deaths:**		
	1975	1967-75	- by sex	1948	1936-47
	1976	1967-76		1951	1936-50
	1977	1968-77		1957	1948-56
	1978	1969-78		1961	1952-60
	1979	1970-79		1963-1965	Latest
	1980	1971-80		1966	1961-65
	1981	1972-81		1967	1962-66
	1982	1973-82		1968-1970	Latest
	1983	1974-83		2000-2003	Latest
	1984	1975-84	- by age and sex	2000-2003	Latest
	1985	1976-85	- by sex and urban/rural		
	1986	1977-86	residence	1971-1973	Latest
	1987	1978-87		1974	1965-73
	1988	1979-88			
	1989	1980-89			
	1990	1981-90			
	1991	1982-91			

Subject-matter	Year of issue	Time coverage
	1975-1979	Latest
	1980	1971-79
	1981-1984	Latest
	1985	1976-84
	1986-1991	Latest
	1992	1983-92
	1993-1995	Latest
	1996	1987-95
	1997-1999	Latest
Post-neo-natal mortality rates:		
- by sex	1948	1936-47
	1951	1936-50
	1957	1948-56
	1961	1952-60
	1966	1956-65
	1967	1962-66
	1968-1970	Latest
	2000-2003	Latest
- by age and sex	2000-2003	Latest
- by sex and urban/rural residence	1971-1973	Latest
	1974	1965-73
	1975-1979	Latest
	1980	1971-79
	1981-1984	Latest
	1985	1976-84
	1986-1991	Latest
	1992	1983-92
	1993-1995	Latest
	1996	1987-95
	1997-1999	Latest

R

Rates (see under following subject-matter headings: Annulments, Births, Deaths, Divorces, Fertility, Illiteracy, Infant Mortality, Intercensal, Life Tables, Literacy Marriages, Maternal mortality, Natural increase, Neo-natal mortality, Population growth, Post-neo-natal mortality, Reproduction)

Ratios (see under following subject matter headings: Births, Child-woman, Fertility, Foetal deaths, Perinatal mortality)

Refugees, by country or

Subject-matter	Year of issue	Time coverage
area of destination:		
- repatriated by the International Refugee Organization	1952	1947-51
- resettled by the International Refugee Organization	1952	1947-51
Religion and sex (see: Population)		
Reproduction rates, gross and net	1948	1920-47
	1949/50	1900-48
	1954	1920-53
	1965	1930-64
	1969	1963-68
	1975	1966-74
	1978HS[ii]	1948-77
	1981	1962-80
	1986	1967-85
	1997HS[iii]	1948-96
	1999CD[iv]	1980-99
Rural/urban births [see: Birth(s)]		
Rural/urban population (see: Population: urban/rural residence)		

S

Sex (see appropriate subject entry, e.g., Births, Death rates, Migration, Population, etc.)

Subject-matter	Year of issue	Time coverage
Size of (living) family:		
- female population by age (see also: Children)	1949/50	Latest
	1954	1930-53
	1955	1945-54
	1959	1949-58
	1963	1955-63
	1965	1955-65
	1968	1955-67
	1969	Latest
	1971	1962-71
	1973	1965-73[vi]
	1975	1965-74
	1978HS[ii]	1948-77
	1981	1972-80
	1986	1977-85

Subject-matter	Year of issue	Time coverage	Subject-matter	Year of issue	Time coverage
	1997HS[iii]	1948-96	- Historical Supplement	1978HS[ii]	1948-78
				1997HS[iii]	1948-97
Special text (see separate listing in Appendix to this Index)			- Marriage and Divorce	1958	1930-57
				1968	1920-68
Special topic (see: Topic of each Demographic Yearbook)				1976	1957-76
				1982	1963-82
				1990	1971-90
Still birth(s) [see: Foetal death(s), late)]			- Migration (international)	1977	1958-76
				1989	1975-88
Surface area			- Mortality	1951	1905-50
- of continents	1949/50			1957	1930-56
	1999	Latest		1961	1945-61
	2000	2000		1966	1920-66
	2001	2001		1967	1900-67
	2002	2002		1974	1965-74
	2003	2003		1980	1971-80
- of countries or areas	1948-2003	Latest		1985	1976-85
				1992	1983-92
- of macro-regions	1964-1999	Latest		1996	1987-96
	2000	2000			
	2001	2001	- Natality	1949/50	1932-40
	2002	2002		1954	1920-53
	2003	2003		1959	1920-58
- of regions	1952-1999	Latest		1965	1920-65
	2000	2000		1969	1925-69
	2001	2001		1975	1956-75
	2002	2002		1981	1962-81
	2003	2003		1986	1967-86
- of the world	1949/50			1992	1983-92
	1999	Latest		1999CD[iv]	1980-99
	2000	2000	- Nuptiality (see: Marriage and Divorce, above)		
	2001	2001			
	2002	2002			
	2003	2003	- Population Ageing and the Situation of Elderly Persons	1991PA[vii]	1950-90
Survivors (see: Life tables)					
			- Population Census: Economic characteristics	1956	1945-55
T				1964	1955-64
Text (see separate listing in Appendix to this Index)				1972	1962-72
				1973	1965-73[vi]
				1979	1970-79[vi]
Topic of each Demographic Yearbook				1984	1974-84
- Divorce (see: Marriage and Divorce, below)				1988	1980-88[vi]
				1994	1985-94
- General demography	1948	1900-48	Educational characteristics	1955	1945-54
	1953	1850-1953		1956	1945-55
				1963	1955-63

Subject-matter	Year of issue	Time coverage	Subject-matter	Year of issue	Time coverage
	1964	1955-64[vi]	Household characteristics	1955	1945-54
	1971	1962-71		1962	1955-62
	1973	1965-73[vi]		1963	1955-63[vi]
	1979	1970-79[vi]		1971	1962-71
	1983	1974-83		1973	1965-73[vi]
	1988	1980-88[vi]		1976	1966-75
	1993	1985-93		1983	1974-83
Ethnic characteristics	1956	1945-55		1987	1975-86
	1963	1955-63		1995	1985-95
	1964	1955-64[vi]	Personal characteristics	1955	1945-54
	1971	1962-71		1962	1955-62
	1973	1965-73[vi]		1971	1962-71
	1979	1970-79[vi]		1973	1965-73[vi]
	1983	1974-83		1979	1970-79[vi]
	1988	1980-88[vi]		1983	1974-83
	1993	1985-93		1988	1980-88[vi]
Fertility characteristics	1940/50	1900-50		1993	1985-93
	1954	1900-53	-Population trends	1960	1920-60
	1955	1945-54		1970	1950-70
	1959	1935-59			
	1963	1955-63			
	1965	1955-65			
	1969	Latest			
	1971	1962-71			
	1973	1965-73[vi]			
	1975	1965-75			
	1981	1972-81			
	1986	1977-86			
	1992	1983-92			
Geographic characteristics	1952	1900-51			
	1955	1945-54			
	1962	1955-62			
	1964	1955-64[vi]			
	1971	1962-71			
	1973	1965-73[vi]			
	1979	1970-79[vi]			
	1983	1974-83			
	1988	1980-88[vi]			
	1993	1985-93			

U

Urban/rural births
(see: Births)

Urban/rural deaths
(see: Deaths)

Urban/rural infant deaths
(see: Infant deaths)

Urban/rural population
(see: Population:
urban/rural residence)

**Urban/rural population
by average size of
households** (see:
Households)

APPENDIX

Special text of each Demographic Yearbook:

Divorce:
'Uses of Marriage and Divorce Statistics', 1958.

Marriage:
'Uses of Marriage and Divorce Statistics', 1958.

Households:
'Concepts and definitions of households, householder and institutional population', 1987.

Migration:
'Statistics of International Migration', 1977.

Mortality:
'Recent Mortality Trends', 1951.
'Development of Statistics of Causes of Death', 1951.
'Factors in Declining Mortality', 1957.
'Notes on Methods of Evaluating the Reliability of Conventional Mortality Statistics', 1961.
'Recent Trends of Mortality', 1966.
'Mortality Trends among Elderly Persons', 1991PA[vii].

Natality:
'Graphic Presentation of Trends in Fertility', 1959.
'Recent Trends in Birth Rates', 1965.
'Recent Changes in World Fertility', 1969.

Population
'World Population Trends, 1920-1949', 1949/50.
'Urban Trends and Characteristics', 1952.
'Background to the1950 Censuses of Population', 1955.
'The World Demographic Situation', 1956.
'How Well Do We Know the Present Size and Trend of the World's Population?', 1960.
'Notes on Availability of National Population Census Data and Methods of Estimating their Reliability', 1962.
'Availability and Adequacy of Selected Data Obtained from Population Censuses Taken 1955-1963', 1963.
'Availability of Selected Population Census Statistics: 1955-1964', 1964.
'Statistical Concepts and Definitions of Urban and Rural Population', 1967.
'Statistical Concepts and Definitions of Household', 1968.
'How Well Do We Know the Present Size and Trend of the World's Population?', 1970.
'United Nations Recommendations on Topics to be Investigated in a Population Census
Compared with Country Practice in National Censuses taken 1965-1971', 1971.
'Statistical Definitions of Urban Population and their Use in Applied Demography', 1972.
'Dates of National Population and Housing Census carried out during the decade1965-1974', 1974.
'Dates of National Population and/or Housing Censuses taken or anticipated during the decade 1975-1984', 1979.
'Dates of National Population and/or Housing Censuses taken during the decade1965-1974 and
taken or anticipated during the decade 1975-1984', 1983.
'Dates of National Population and/or Housing Censuses taken during the decade1975-1984 and taken or anticipated
during the decade 1985-1994', 1988 and 1993.
'Statistics Concerning the Economically Active Population: An Overview', 1984.
'Disability', 1991PA[vii].
'Population Ageing', 1991PA[vii].
'Special Needs for the Study of Population Ageing and Elderly Persons', 1991PA[vii].

General Notes

This cumulative index covers the contents of each of the 52 issues of the Demographic Yearbook. 'Year of issue' stands for the particular issue in which the indicated subject-matter appears. Unless otherwise specified, 'Time coverage' designates the years for which annual statistics are shown in the Demographic Yearbook referred to in 'Year of issue' column. 'Latest' or '2-Latest' indicates that data are for latest available year(s) only.

[i] Only titles not available for preceding bibliography.

[ii] Historical Supplement to the 30th DYB published in a separate volume in year 1979.

[iii] Historical Supplement to the 49th DYB published in a separate volume (CD-ROM) in year 2000.

[iv] Supplement to the 51st DYB focusing on natality published in a separate volume (CD-ROM) in year 2002.

[v] Five-year average rates.

[vi] Only data not available for preceding issue.

[vii] Population ageing published in separate volume.

Index
Index historique (suite)
(Voir notes à la fin de l'index)

Sujet	Année de l'édition	Période considérée

A

Accroissement intercensitaire de la population, taux d' ....

	1948	1900-48
	1949/50	1900-50
	1951	1900-51
	1952	1850-1952
	1953	1850-1953
	1955	1850-1954
	1960	1900-61
	1962	1900-62
	1964	1955-64
	1970	1900-70
	1978 SR [i]	1948-78
	1997 SR [ii]	1948-97

Accroissement naturel, taux d' ....

	1958-1978	Dernière
	1978 SR [i]	1948-78
	1979-1997	Dernière
	1997 SR [ii]	1948-97
	1998	1995-98
	1999	1996-99
	2000	1995-00
	2001	2000-05
	2002	2000-05
	2003	2000-05

Activité économique (voir: Population active)

Age (voir la rubrique appropriée par sujet, p.ex. Immigrants: Mortalité, taux de: Naissances: Population: etc.)

Analphabètes (voir:Population)

Alphabétisme selon le sexe, taux d' ....

	1948	Dernière
	1955	1945-54
	1960	1920-60
	1963	1955-63
	1964	1955-64 [iii]
	1970	1950-70
	1971	1962-71
	1973	1965-73[3]
	1979	1970-79 [iii]
	1983	1974-83
	1988	1980-88 [iii]
	1993	1985-93 [iii]

Alphabétisme selon le sexe et | 1948 | Dernière |

Sujet	Année de l'édition	Période considérée

l'âge, taux d' ....

	1955	1945-54
	1971	1962-71
	1973	1965-73 [iii]
	1979	1970-79 [iii]
	1983	1974-83
	1988	1980-88 [iii]

Alphabètes (voir: Population)

Annulations

	1958	1948-57
	1968	1958-67
	1976	1966-75

Annulations, taux ....

	1958	1948-57
	1968	1958-67
	1976	1966-75

Avortements, légaux ....

	1971	Dernière
	1972	1964-72
	1973	1965-73
	1974	1965-74
	1975	1965-74
	1976	1965-75
	1977	1967-76
	1978	1968-77
	1979	1969-78
	1980	1971-79
	1981	1972-80
	1982	1973-81
	1983	1974-82
	1984	1975-83
	1985	1976-84
	1986	1977-85
	1987	1978-86
	1988	1979-87
	1989	1980-88
	1990	1981-89
	1992	1983-91
	1993	1984-92
	1994	1985-93
	1995	1986-94
	1996	1987-95
	1997	1988-96
	1998	1989-97
	1999	1990-98
	2000	1991-99
	2001	1993-01
	2002	1993-02
	2003	1994-03

-selon l'âge de la mère et le nombre des naissances vivantes antérieures de la mère

	1971-1975	Dernière
	1977-1981	Dernière
	1983-2003	Dernière

Index
Index historique (suite)
(Voir notes à la fin de l'index)

Sujet	Année de l'édition	Période considérée	Sujet	Année de l'édition	Période considérée
B				1984	1980-84
				1985	1976-85
				1986	1982-86
Bibliographie..............................	1948	1930-48		1987	1983-87
	1949/50	1930-50		1988	1984-88
	1951-1952	1930-51 [iv]		1989	1985-89
	1953	1900-53		1990	1986-90
	1954	1900-54 [iv]		1991	1987-91
	1955	1900-55 [iv]		1992	1983-92
				1993	1989-93
C				1994	1990-94
				1995	1991-95
				1996	1987-96
Cause de décès (voir: Décès)				1997	1993-97
				1997SR [ii]	1948-97
Chômeurs (voir: Population)				1998	1994-98
				1999	1995-99
Composition ethnique (voir: Population)				2000	1996-00
				2001	1997-01
				2002	1998-02
Décès	1948	1932-47		2003	1999-03
	1949/50	1934-49	-d'enfants de moins d'un an (voir: Mortalité infantile)		
	1951	1935-50	-selon l'âge et le sexe	1948	1936-47
	1952	1936-51		1951	1936-50
	1953	1950-52		1955-1956	Dernière
	1954	1946-53		1957	1948-56
	1955	1946-54		1958-1960	Dernière
	1956	1947-55		1961	1955-60
	1957	1940-56		1962-1965	Dernière
	1958	1948-57		1966	1961-65
	1959	1949-58		1967-1973	Dernière
	1960	1950-59		1974	1965-73
	1961	1952-61		1975-1979	Dernière
	1962	1953-62		1978 SR [i]	1948-77
	1963	1954-63		1980	1971-79
	1964	1960-64		1981-1984	Dernière
	1965	1961-65		1985	1976-84
	1966	1947-66		1986-1991	Dernière
	1967	1963-67		1992	1983-92
	1968	1964-68		1993-1995	Dernière
	1969	1965-69		1996	1987-95
	1970	1966-70		1997	Dernière
	1971	1967-71		1997SR [ii]	1948-96
	1972	1968-72		1998-2003	Dernière
	1973	1969-73	-selon l'âge et le sexe et la résidence (urbaine/rurale)	1967-1973	Dernière
	1974	1965-74		1974	1965-73
	1975	1971-75		1975-1979	Dernière
	1976	1972-76		1980	1971-79
	1977	1973-77		1981-1984	Dernière
	1978	1974-78		1985	1976-84
	1978SR [i]	1948-78		1986-1991	Dernière
	1979	1975-79		1992	1983-92
	1980	1971-80		1993-1995	Dernière
	1981	1977-81		1996	1987-95
	1982	1978-82		1997	Dernière
	1983	1979-83			

Index
Index historique (suite)
(Voir notes à la fin de l'index)

Sujet	Année de l'édition	Période considérée
	1997SR [ii]	1948-96
	1998-2003	Dernière
-selon la cause	1951	1947-50
	1952	1947-51 [iii]
	1953	Dernière
	1954	1945-53
	1955-1956	Dernière
	1957	1952-56
	1958-1960	Dernière
	1961	1955-60
	1962-1965	Dernière
	1966	1960-65
	1967-1973	Dernière
	1974	1965-73
	1975-1979	Dernière
	1980	1971-79
	1981-1984	Dernière
	1985	1976-84
	1986-1995	Dernière
	1996	1987-95
	1997-2000	Dernière
	2002	1995-02
-selon la cause, l'âge et le sexe	1951	Dernière
	1952	Dernière [iii]
	1957	Dernière
	1961	Dernière
	1967	Dernière
	1974	Dernière
	1980	Dernière
	1985	Dernière
	1991 VP [v]	1960-90
	1996	Dernière
-selon la cause, l'âge et le sexe et la résidence (urbaine/rurale)	1967	Dernière
-selon la cause et le sexe	1967	Dernière
	1974	Dernière
	1980	Dernière
	1985	Dernière
	1991VP [v]	1960-90
	1996	Dernière
-selon la résidence (urbaine/rurale)	1967	Dernière
	1968	1964-68
	1969	1965-69
	1970	1966-70
	1971	1967-71
	1972	1968-72
	1973	1969-73
	1974	1965-74
	1975	1971-75
	1976	1972-76
	1977	1973-77
	1978	1974-78
	1979	1975-79

Sujet	Année de l'édition	Période considérée
	1980	1971-80
	1981	1977-81
	1982	1978-82
	1983	1979-83
	1984	1980-84
	1985	1976-85
	1986	1982-86
	1987	1983-87
	1988	1984-88
	1989	1985-89
	1990	1986-90
	1991	1987-91
	1992	1983-92
	1993	1989-93
	1994	1990-94
	1995	1991-95
	1996	1987-96
	1997	1993-97
	1998	1994-98
	1999	1995-99
	2001	1997-01
	2002	1998-02
	2003	1999-03
-selon l'état matrimonial, l'âge et le sexe	1958	Dernière
	1961	Dernière
	1967	Dernière
	1974	Dernière
	1980	Dernière
	1985	Dernière
	1991 VP [v]	1950-90
	1996	Dernière
	2003	Dernière
-selon le mois	1951	1946-50
	1967	1962-66
	1974	1965-73
	1980	1971-79
	1985	1976-84
	2001	1985-00
-selon la profession et l'âge (sexe masculin)	1957	Dernière
	1961	1957-60
	1967	1962-66
-selon le type de certification et la cause: nombres	1957	Dernière
	1974	1965-73
	1980	1971-79
	1985	1976-84
pourcentage	1957	Dernière
	1961	1955-60
	1966	1960-65
	1974	1965-73
	1980	1971-79
	1985	1976-84

Index
Index historique (suite)
(Voir notes à la fin de l'index)

Sujet	Année de l'édition	Période considérée	Sujet	Année de l'édition	Période considérée
Décès, taux de............	1948	1932-47		1996	1987-96
	1949/50	1932-49		1997	1993-97
	1951	1905-30 [vi]		1997SR [ii]	1948-97
		1930-50		1998	1994-98
	1952	1920-34 [vi]		1999	1995-99
		1934-51		2000	1996-00
	1953	1920-39 [vi]		2001	1997-01
		1940-52		2002	1998-02
	1954	1920-39 [vi]		2003	1999-03
		1946-53	-d'enfants de moins d'un an (voir: Mortalités infantile)		
	1955	1920-34 [vi]			
		1946-54	-estimatifs:		
	1956	1947-55	pour les continents	1949/50	1947
	1957	1930-56		1956-1977	Dernière
	1958	1948-57		1978-1979	1970-75
	1959	1949-58		1980-1983	1975-80
	1960	1950-59		1984-1986	1980-85
	1961	1945-59 [vi]		1987-1992	1985-90
		1952-61		1993-1997	1990-95
	1962	1945-54 [vi]		1998-2000	1995-00
		1952-62		2001-2003	2000-05
	1963	1945-59 [vi]	pour les grandes régions (continentales)	1964-1977	Dernière
		1954-63			
	1964	1960-64		1978-1979	1970-75
	1965	1961-65		1980-1983	1975-80
	1966	1920-64 [vi]		1984-1986	1980-85
		1951-66		1987-1992	1985-90
	1967	1963-67		1993-1997	1990-95
	1968	1964-68		1998-2000	1995-00
	1969	1965-69		2001-2003	2000-05
	1970	1966-70			
	1971	1967-71	pour les régions	1949/50	1947
	1972	1968-72		1956-1977	Dernière
	1973	1969-73		1978-1979	1970-75
	1974	1965-74		1980-1983	1975-80
	1975	1971-75		1984-1986	1980-85
	1976	1972-76		1987-1992	1985-90
	1977	1973-77		1993-1997	1990-95
	1978	1974-78		1998-2000	1995-00
	1978SR [i]	1948-78		2001-2003	2000-05
	1979	1975-79			
	1980	1971-80	pour l'ensemble du monde	1949/50	1947
	1981	1977-81			
	1982	1978-82		1956-1977	Dernière
	1983	1979-83		1978-1979	1970-75
	1984	1980-84		1980-1983	1975-80
	1985	1976-85		1984-1986	1980-85
	1986	1982-86		1987-1992	1985-90
	1987	1983-87		1993-1997	1990-95
	1988	1984-88		1998-2000	1995-00
	1989	1985-89		2001-2003	2000-05
	1990	1986-90			
	1991	1987-91	-selon l'âge et le sexe	1948	1935-47
	1992	1983-92		1949/50	1936-49
	1993	1989-93		1951	1936-50
	1994	1990-94		1952	1936-51
	1995	1991-95		1953	1940-52

Index
Index historique (suite)
(Voir notes à la fin de l'index)

Sujet	Année de l'édition	Période considérée	Sujet	Année de l'édition	Période considérée
	1954	1946-53		1980	Dernière
	1955-1956	Dernière		1985	Dernière
	1957	1948-56		1996	Dernière
	1961	1952-60	-selon la profession et l'âge (sexe masculin)	1961	Dernière
	1966	1950-65		1967	Dernière
	1967	Dernière			
	1972	Dernière	-selon la résidence (urbaine/rurale)	1967	Dernière
	1974	1965-73		1968	1964-68
	1975-1978	Dernière		1969	1965-69
	1978SR [i]	1948-77		1970	1966-70
	1979	Dernière		1971	1967-71
	1980	1971-79		1972	1968-72
	1981-1984	Dernière		1973	1969-73
	1985	1976-84		1974	1965-74
	1986-1991	Dernière		1975	1971-75
	1991 VP [v]	1950-90		1976	1972-76
	1992	1983-92		1977	1973-77
	1993-1995	Dernière		1978	1974-78
	1996	1987-95		1979	1975-79
	1997	Dernière		1980	1971-80
	1997SR [ii]	1948-96		1981	1977-81
	1998-2003	Dernière		1982	1978-82
-selon la cause	1951	1947-49		1983	1979-83
	1952	1947-51		1984	1980-84
	1953	1947-52		1985	1976-85
	1954	1945-53		1986	1982-86
	1955-1956	Dernière		1987	1983-87
	1957	1952-56		1988	1984-88
	1958-1960	Dernière		1989	1985-89
	1961	1955-60		1990	1986-90
	1962-1965	Dernière		1991	1987-91
	1966	1960-65		1992	1983-92
	1967-1973	Dernière		1993	1989-93
	1974	1965-73		1994	1990-94
	1975-1979	Dernière		1995	1991-95
	1980	1971-79 [vi]		1996	1987-96
	1981-1984	Dernière		1997	1993-97
	1985	1976-84		1998	1994-98
	1986-1995	Dernière		1999	1995-99
	1996	1987-95		2000	1996-00
	1997-2000	Dernière		2001	1997-01
	2002	1985-02		2002	1998-02
-selon la cause, l'âge et le sexe	1957	Dernière		2003	1999-03
	1961	Dernière	**Densité de population:**		
	1991 VP [v]	1960-90	-des continents	1949/50	1920-49
-selon la cause et le sexe	1967	Dernière		1951-2003	Dernière
	1974	Dernière	-des grandes régions (continentales)	1964-2003	Dernière
	1980	Dernière	-des pays ou zones	1948-2003	Dernière
	1985	Dernière	-des régions	1949/50	1920-49
	1991 VP [v]	1960-90		1952-2003	Dernière
	1996	Dernière	-du monde	1949/50	1920-49
-selon l'état matrimonial, l'âge et le sexe	1961	Dernière		1952-2003	Dernière
	1967	Dernière	**Dimension de la famille vivante:**		
	1974	Dernière			

Index
Index historique (suite)
(Voir notes à la fin de l'index)

Sujet	Année de l'édition	Période considérée	Sujet	Année de l'édition	Période considérée
-selon l'âge des femmes				1975	1971-75
(voir également: Enfants)	1949-1950	Dernière		1976	1957-76
	1954	1930-53		1977	1973-77
	1955	1945-54		1978	1974-78
	1959	1949-58		1979	1975-79
	1963	1955-63		1980	1976-80
	1965	1955-65		1981	1977-81
	1968	1955-67		1982	1963-82
	1969	Dernière		1983	1979-83
	1971	1962-71		1984	1980-84
	1973	1965-73 [iii]		1985	1981-85
	1975	1965-74		1986	1982-86
	1978SR [i]	1948-77		1987	1983-87
	1981	1972-80		1988	1984-88
	1986	1977-85		1989	1985-89
	1997SR [ii]	1948-96		1990	1971-90
				1991	1987-91
Divorces.....................	1951	1935-50		1992	1988-92
	1952	1936-51		1993	1989-93
	1953	1950-52		1994	1990-94
	1954	1946-53		1995	1991-95
	1955	1946-54		1996	1992-96
	1956	1947-55		1997	1993-97
	1957	1948-56		1998	1994-98
	1958	1940-57		1999	1995-99
	1959	1949-58		2000	1996-00
	1960	1950-59		2001	1997-01
	1961	1952-61		2002	1998-02
	1962	1953-62		2003	1999-03
	1963	1954-63	-selon l'âge de l'épouse	1968	1958-67
	1964	1960-64		1976	1966-75
	1965	1961-65		1982	1972-81
	1966	1962-66		1987	1975-86
	1967	1963-67		1990	1980-89
	1968	1949-68	-selon l'âge de l'épouse,		
	1969	1965-69	classés par âge de l'époux	1958	1946-57
	1970	1966-70		1968	Dernière
	1971	1967-71		1976	Dernière
	1972	1968-72		1982	Dernière
	1973	1969-73		1990	Dernière
	1974	1970-74	-selon l'âge de l'époux	1968	1958-67
	1975	1971-75		1976	1966-75
	1976	1957-76		1982	1972-81
	1977	1973-77		1987	1975-86
	1962	1953-62		1990	1980-89
	1963	1954-63	-selon la durée du mariage	1958	1948-57
	1964	1960-64		1968	1958-67
	1965	1961-65		1976	1966-75
	1966	1962-66		1982	1972-81
	1967	1963-67		1990	1980-89
	1968	1949-68	-selon la durée du mariage,		
	1969	1965-69	classés selon l'âge de		
	1970	1966-70	l'épouse et selon l'âge de		
	1971	1967-71	l'époux	1958	1946-57
	1972	1968-72		1968	Dernière
	1973	1969-73		1976	Dernière
	1974	1970-74		1982	Dernière

Index
Index historique (suite)
(Voir notes à la fin de l'index)

Sujet	Année de l'édition	Période considérée
	1990	Dernière
-selon le nombre d'enfants	1958	1948-57
	1968	1958-67
	1976	1966-75
	1982	1972-81
Divortialité, taux de....................	1952	1935-51
	1953	1936-52
	1954	1946-53
	1955	1946-54
	1956	1947-55
	1957	1948-56
	1958	1930-57
	1959	1949-58
	1960	1950-59
	1961	1952-61
	1962	1953-62
	1963	1954-63
	1964	1960-64
	1965	1961-65
	1966	1962-66
	1967	1963-67
	1968	1920-64 [vi]
		1953-68
	1969	1965-69
	1970	1966-70
	1971	1967-71
	1972	1968-72
	1973	1969-73
	1974	1970-74
	1975	1971-75
	1976	1957-76
	1977	1973-77
	1978	1974-78
	1979	1975-79
	1980	1976-80
	1981	1977-81
	1982	1963-82
	1983	1979-83
	1984	1980-84
	1985	1981-85
	1986	1982-86
	1987	1983-87
	1988	1984-88
	1989	1985-89
	1990	1971-90
	1991	1987-91
	1992	1988-92
	1993	1989-93
	1994	1990-94
	1995	1991-95
	1996	1992-96
	1997	1993-97
	1998	1994-98
	1999	1995-99
	2000	1996-00
	2001	1997-01

Sujet	Année de l'édition	Période considérée
	2002	1998-02
	2003	1999-03
-pour la population mariée	1953	1935-52
	1954	1935-53
	1958	1935-56
	1968	1935-67
	1976	1966-75
	1978SR [i]	1948-77
	1982	1972-81
	1990	1980-89
-selon l'âge de l'épouse	1968	Dernière
	1976	Dernière
	1982	Dernière
	1987	1975-86
	1990	1980-89
-selon l'âge de l'époux	1968	Dernière
	1976	Dernière
	1982	Dernière
	1987	1975-86
	1990	1980-89

Durée du mariage (voir: Divorces)

E

Emigrants (voir: Migration internationale)

Enfants, nombre:		
-dont il est tenu compte dans les divorces	1958	1948-57
	1968	1958-67
	1976	1966-75
	1982	1972-81
	1990	1980-89
-mis au monde, selon l'âge de la mère	1949/50	Dernière
	1954	1930-53
	1955	1945-54
	1959	1949-58
	1963	1955-63
	1965	1955-65
	1969	Dernière
	1971	1962-71
	1973	1965-73 [iii]
	1975	1965-74
	1978SR [i]	1948-77
	1981	1972-80
	1986	1977-85
	1997SR [ii]	1948-96
-vivants, selon l'âge de la mère	1940/50	Dernière
	1954	1930-53
	1955	1945-54

779

Index
Index historique (suite)
(Voir notes à la fin de l'index)

Sujet	Année de l'édition	Période considérée
	1959	1949-58
	1963	1955-63
	1965	1955-65
	1968	1955-67
	1969	Dernière
	1971	1962-71
	1973	1965-73 [iii]
	1975	1965-74
	1978SR [i]	1948-77
	1981	1972-80
	1986	1977-85
	1997SR [ii]	1948-96

Espérance de vie (voir: Mortalité, tables de)

Etat matrimonial (voir la rubrique appropriée par sujet, p.ex., Décès, Population, etc.)

F

Sujet	Année de l'édition	Période considérée
Fécondité, indice synthétique de	1987-1997	Dernière
	1997SR [ii]	1948-96
	1998	1995-98
	1999	1996-99
	1999CD [vii]	1980-99
Fécondité proportionnelle	1949/50	1900-50
	1954	1900-52
	1955	1945-54
	1959	1935-59
	1963	1955-63
	1965	1955-65
	1969	Dernière
	1975	1966-74
	1978SR [i]	1948-77
	1981	1962-80
	1986	1967-85
	1997SR [ii]	1948-96
	1999CD [vii]	1980-99
Fécondité, taux global de	1948	1936-47
	1949/50	1936-49
	1951	1936-50
	1952	1936-50
	1953	1936-52
	1954	1936-53
	1955-1956	Dernière
	1959	1949-58
	1960-1964	Dernière
	1965	1955-64
	1966-1974	Dernière
	1975	1966-74
	1976-1978	Dernière
	1978SR [i]	1948-77

Sujet	Année de l'édition	Période considérée
	1979-1980	Dernière
	1981	1962-80
	1982-1985	Dernière
	1986	1977-85
	1987-1991	Dernière
	1992	1983-92
	1993-1997	Dernière
	1997SR [ii]	1948-96
	1998-2003	Dernière

I

Illégitime (voir également: Naissances et morts fœtales tardives):

Sujet	Année de l'édition	Période considérée
-morts fœtales tardives	1961	1952-60
	1965	5-Dernières
	1969	1963-68
	1975	1966-74
	1981	1972-80
	1986	1977-85
-morts fœtales tardives, rapports de	1961	1952-60
	1965	5-Dernières
	1969	1963-68
	1975	1966-74
	1981	1972-80
	1986	1977-85
-naissances	1959	1949-58
	1965	1955-64
	1969	1963-68
	1975	1966-74
	1981	1972-80
	1986	1977-85
	1999CD [vii]	1990-98
-naissances, rapports de	1959	1949-58
	1965	1955-64
	1969	1963-68
	1975	1966-74
	1981	1972-80
	1986	1977-85
	1999CD [vii]	1990-98

Immigrants (voir: Migration internationale)

Instruction, degré d' (voir: Population)

L

Langue et sexe (voir: Population)

Localités (voir: Population)

Index
Index historique (suite)
(Voir notes à la fin de l'index)

Sujet	Année de l'édition	Période considérée	Sujet	Année de l'édition	Période considérée
M				2002	1998-02
				2003	1999-03
			-selon l'âge de l'épouse		
Mariages	1948	1932-47		1948	1936-47
	1949/50	1934-49		1949/50	1936-49
	1951	1935-50		1958	1948-57
	1952	1936-51		1959-1967	Dernière
	1953	1950-52		1968	1958-67
	1954	1946-53		1969-1975	Dernière
	1955	1946-54		1976	1966-75
	1956	1947-55		1977-1981	Dernière
	1957	1948-56		1982	1972-81
	1958	1940-57		1983-1986	Dernière
	1959	1949-58		1987	1975-86
	1960	1950-59		1988-1989	Dernière
	1961	1952-61		1990	1980-89
	1962	1953-62		1991-1997	Dernière
	1963	1954-63		1998	1993-97
	1964	1960-64		1999	1994-98
	1965	1956-65		2000	1995-99
	1966	1962-66		2001	1997-01
	1967	1963-67		2002	1998-02
	1968	1949-68		2003	1999-03
	1969	1965-69	-selon l'âge de l'épouse et l'âge de l'époux	1958	1948-57
	1970	1966-70		1968	Dernière
	1971	1967-71		1976	Dernière
	1972	1968-72		1982	Dernière
	1973	1969-73		1990	Dernière
	1974	1970-74	-selon l'âge de l'épouse et l'état matrimonial antérieur	1958	1948-57
	1975	1971-75		1968	Dernière
	1976	1957-76		1976	Dernière
	1977	1973-77		1982	Dernière
	1978	1974-78		1990	Dernière
	1979	1975-79	-selon l'âge de l'époux	1948	1936-47
	1980	1976-80		1949/50	1936-49
	1981	1977-81		1958	1948-57
	1982	1963-82		1959-1967	Dernière
	1983	1979-83		1968	1958-67
	1984	1980-84		1969-1975	Dernière
	1985	1981-85		1976	1966-75
	1986	1982-86		1977-1981	Dernière
	1987	1983-87		1982	1972-81
	1988	1984-88		1983-1986	Dernière
	1989	1985-89		1987	1975-86
	1990	1971-90		1988-1989	Dernière
	1991	1987-91		1990	1980-89
	1992	1988-92		1991-1997	Dernière
	1993	1989-93		1998	1993-97
	1994	1990-94		1999	1994-98
	1995	1991-95		2000	1995-99
	1996	1992-96		2001	1997-01
	1997	1993-97		2002	1998-02
	1998	1994-98		2003	1999-03
	1999	1995-99	-selon l'âge de l'époux et l'âge de l'épouse	1958	1948-57
	2000	1996-00			
	2001	1997-01			

Index
Index historique (suite)
(Voir notes à la fin de l'index)

Sujet	Année de l'édition	Période considérée
	1968	Dernière
	1976	Dernière
	1982	Dernière
	1990	Dernière
-selon l'âge de l'époux et l'état matrimonial Antérieur	1958	1946-57
	1968	Dernière
	1976	Dernière
	1982	Dernière
	1990	Dernière
-selon l'état matrimonial antérieur de l'épouse: et l'âge	1958	1946-57
	1968	Dernière
	1976	Dernière
	1982	Dernière
	1990	Dernière
-selon l'état matrimonial antérieur de l'épouse (suite): et l'état matrimonial antérieur de l'époux	1949/50	Dernière
	1958	1948-57
	1968	1958-67
	1976	1966-75
	1982	1972-81
	1990	1980-89
-selon l'état matrimonial antérieur de l'époux et l'âge	1958	1946-57
	1968	Dernière
	1976	Dernière
	1982	Dernière
	1990	Dernière
et l'état matrimonial antérieur de l'épouse	1949/50	Dernière
	1958	1948-57
	1968	1958-67
	1976	1966-75
	1982	1972-81
	1990	1980-89
-selon la résidence (urbaine/rurale)	1968	Dernière
	1969	1965-69
	1970	1966-70
	1971	1967-71
	1972	1968-72
	1973	1969-73
	1974	1970-74
	1975	1971-75
	1976	1957-76
	1977	1973-77
	1978	1974-78
	1979	1975-79
	1980	1976-80
	1981	1977-81
	1982	1963-82
	1983	1979-83

Sujet	Année de l'édition	Période considérée
	1984	1980-84
	1985	1981-85
	1986	1982-86
	1987	1983-87
	1988	1984-88
	1989	1985-89
	1990	1971-90
	1991	1987-91
	1992	1988-92
	1993	1989-93
	1994	1990-94
	1995	1991-95
	1996	1992-96
	1997	1993-97
	1998	1994-98
	1999	1995-99
	2000	1996-00
	2001	1997-01
	2002	1998-02
	2003	1999-03
-selon le mois	1968	1963-67
Mariages, premiers:		
-classification détaillé selon l'âge de l'épouse et de l'époux	1976	Dernière
	1982	1972-81
	1990	1980-89
Mariages, taux de (voir: Nuptialité, taux de)		
Ménages:		
-dimension moyenne des	1962	1955-62
	1963	1955-63 [iii]
	1968	Dernière
	1971	1962-71
	1973	1965-73 [iii]
	1976	Dernière
	1982	Dernière
	1987	1975-86
	1990	1980-89
	1995	1985-95
-le lien avec le chef de ménage et la résidence urbaine/rurale	1987	1975-86
	1995	1985-95
-nombre de	1955	1945-54
	1962	1955-62
	1963	1955-63 [iii]
	1968	Dernière
	1971	1962-71
	1973	1965-73 [iii]
	1976	Dernière
	1982	Dernière
	1987	1975-86
	1990	1980-89

Index
Index historique (suite)
(Voir notes à la fin de l'index)

Sujet	Année de l'édition	Période considérée	Sujet	Année de l'édition	Période considérée
	1995	1985-95		1990	1980-89
-personnes 60+	1991 VP [v]	Dernière	-selon l'âge et le sexe du chef de ménage, la dimension et la résidence urbaine/rurale		
-nombre de noyaux familiaux, selon la dimension des	1973	1965-73		1987	1976-86
	1976	Dernière		1995	1985-95
	1982	Dernière	-selon la situation matrimoniale et la résidence urbaine/rurale		
	1987	1975-86		1987	1975-86
	1990	1980-89		1995	1985-95
-population dans chaque dimension des	1955	1945-54	-selon le lien avec le chef de ménage et la résidence urbaine/rurale		
	1962	1955-62		1991 VP [v]	Dernière
	1963	1955-63 [iii]		1987	1975-86
	1968	Dernière		1995	1985-95
-population dans chaque dimension des (suite):	1971	1962-71	-selon le type de famille et la résidence urbaine/rurale	1987	1975-86
	1973	1965-73		1995	1985-95
	1976	Dernière	-selon le type et la résidence urbaine/rurale	1987	1975-86
	1982	Dernière		1995	1985-95
	1987	1975-86			
	1990	1980-89			
	1995	1985-95			
-et personnes 60+	1991 VP [v]	Dernière	**Migration internationale:**		
-population dans chaque catégorie de	1955	1945-54	-continentale et intercontinentale	1948	1936-47
	1962	1955-62		1977	1967-76
	1963	1955-63 [iii]	-émigrants, à long terme:		
	1968	Dernière	selon l'âge et le sexe	1948	1945-47
	1971	1962-71		1949/50	1946-48
	1973	1965-73 [iii]		1951	1948-50
	1976	Dernière		1952	1949-51
	1982	Dernière		1954	1950-53
	1987	1975-86		1957	1953-56
	1990	1980-89		1959	1955-58
	1995	1985-95		1962	1958-61
-répartition des chefs, âge, sexe et résidence urbaine/rurale				1966	1960-65
				1970	1962-69
	1987	1975-86		1977	1967-76
	1995	1985-95		1989	1975-88
-selon la dimension	1955	1945-54	selon le pays ou zone de résidence projetée	1948	1945-47
	1962	1955-62		1949/50	1945-48
	1963	1955-63 [iii]		1951	1948-50
	1971	1962-71		1952	1949-51
	1973	1965-73 [iii]		1954	1950-53
	1976	Dernière		1957	1953-56
	1982	Dernière		1959	1956-58
	1987	1975-86		1977	1958-76
	1990	1980-89		1989	1975-88
	1995	1985-95			
-et personnes 60+	1991 VP [v]	Dernière	-entrées	1970	1963-69
-selon la résidence (urbaine/rurale)	1968	Dernière		1972	1965-71
	1971	1962-71		1974	1967-73
	1973	1965-73 [iii]		1976	1969-75
	1976	Dernière		1977	1967-76
	1982	Dernière		1985	1975-84
	1987	1975-86		1989	1979-88
				1996	1986-95

Index
Index historique (suite)
(Voir notes à la fin de l'index)

Sujet	Année de l'édition	Période considérée	Sujet	Année de l'édition	Période considérée
-entrées, par catégories principales	1949/50	1945-49	principales		
	1951	1946-50		1951	1946-50
	1952	1947-51		1952	1947-51
	1954	1948-53		1954	1948-53
	1957	1951-56		1957	1951-56
	1959	1953-58		1959	1953-58
	1962	1956-61		1962	1956-61
	1966	1960-65		1966	1960-65
	1968	1966-67		1968	1966-67
	1977	1967-76		1977	1967-76
	1985	1975-84		1985	1975-84
	1989	1979-88		1989	1979-88
	1996	1986-95		1996	1986-95
-immigrants, à long terme: selon l'âge et le sexe	1948	1945-47	**Mortalité** (voir: Décès; Enfants de moins d'un an, décès d';		
	1949/50	1946-48	Mortalité fœtale, rapports de;		
	1951	1948-50	Mortalité infantile, taux de;		
	1952	1949-51	Mortalité maternelle, taux de;		
	1954	1950-53	Mortalité néonatale, taux de;		
	1957	1953-56	Mortalité périnatale; Mortalité		
	1959	1955-58	post-néonatale, taux de;		
	1962	1958-61	Mortalité, tables de; Mortalité,		
	1966	1960-65	taux de Morts fœtales; Morts		
	1970	1962-69	néonatales; Morts post-		
	1977	1967-76	néonatales)		
	1989	1975-88			
selon le pays ou zone de dernière résidence	1948	1945-47	**Mortalité fœtale** (voir: Morts fœtales)		
	1949/50	1945-48			
	1951	1948-50			
	1952	1949-51	**Mortalité fœtale, rapports de**		
	1954	1950-53	-selon la période de gestation	1957	1950-56
	1957	1953-56		1959	1949-58
	1959	1956-58		1961	1952-60
	1977	1958-76		1965	5-Dernières
	1989	1975-88		1966	1956-65
-réfugiés selon le pays ou zone de destination:				1967-1968	Dernière
				1969	1963-68
rapatriés par l'Organisation internationale pour les réfugiés	1952	1947-51		1974	1965-73
				1975	1966-74
				1980	1971-79
				1981	1972-80
réinstallés par l'Organisation Internationale pour les Réfugiés	1952	1947-51		1985	1976-84
				1986	1977-85
				1996	1987-95
-sorties	1970	1963-69		1999CD [vii]	1990-98
	1972	1965-71			
	1974	1967-73	**Mortalité fœtale tardive** (voir: Morts fœtales tardives)		
	1976	1969-75			
	1977	1967-76	**Mortalité fœtale tardive, rapports de**	1951	1935-50
	1985	1975-84		1952	1935-51
	1989	1979-88		1953	1936-52
	1996	1986-95		1954	1938-53
-sorties par catégories	1949/50	1945-49		1955	1946-54

Index
Index historique (suite)
(Voir notes à la fin de l'index)

Sujet	Année de l'édition	Période considérée	Sujet	Année de l'édition	Période considérée
	1956	1947-55	-illégitimes	1961	1952-60
	1957	1948-56		1965	5-Dernières
	1958	1948-57	-légitimes	1959	1949-58
	1959	1920-54 [vi]		1965	1955-64
		1953-58		1969	1963-68
	1960	1950-59		1975	1966-74
	1961	1945-49 [vi]		1981	1972-80
		1952-60		1986	1977-85
	1962	1945-54 [vi]	-légitimes selon l'âge de la mère		
		1952-61		1959	1949-58
	1963	1945-59 [vi]		1965	1955-64
		1953-62		1969	1963-68
	1964	1959-63		1975	1966-74
	1965	1950-64 [vi]		1981	1972-80
		1955-64		1986	1977-85
	1966	1950-64 [vi]	-selon l'âge de la mère	1954	1936-53
		1956-65		1959	1949-58
	1967	1962-66		1965	1955-64
	1968	1963-67		1969	1963-68
	1969	1950-64 [vi]		1975	1966-74
	1969	1959-68		1981	1972-80
	1970	1965-69		1986	1977-85
	1971	1966-70		1999CD [vii]	1990-98
	1972	1967-71	-selon l'âge de la mère et le rang de naissance		
	1973	1968-72		1954	Dernière
	1974	1965-73		1959	1949-58
	1975	1966-74		1965	3-Dernières
	1976	1971-75		1969	1963-68
	1977	1972-76		1975	1966-74
	1978	1973-77		1981	1972-80
	1979	1974-78		1986	1977-85
	1980	1971-79		1999CD [vii]	1990-98
	1981	1972-80	-selon la période de gestation		
	1982	1977-81		1957	1950-56
	1983	1978-82		1959	1949-58
	1984	1979-83		1961	1952-60
	1985	1975-84		1965	5-Dernières
	1986	1977-85		1966	1956-65
	1987	1982-86		1967-1968	Dernière
	1988	1983-87		1969	1963-68
	1989	1984-88		1974	1965-73
	1964	1959-63		1975	1966-74
	1990	1985-89		1980	1971-79
	1991	1986-90		1981	1972-80
	1992	1987-91		1985	1976-84
	1993	1988-92		1986	1977-85
	1994	1989-93		1996	1987-95
	1995	1990-94	-selon la résidence (urbaine/rurale)		
	1996	1987-95		1971	1966-70
	1997	1992-96		1972	1967-71
	1998	1993-97		1973	1968-72
	1999	1994-98		1974	1965-73
	1999CD [vii]	1990-98		1975	1966-74
	2000	1995-99		1976	1971-75
	2001	1997-01		1977	1972-76
	2002	1998-02		1978	1973-77
	2003	1999-03		1979	1974-78

Index
Index historique (suite)
(Voir notes à la fin de l'index)

Sujet	Année de l'édition	Période considérée	Sujet	Année de l'édition	Période considérée
	1980	1971-79		1979	1975-79
	1981	1972-80		1980	1971-80
	1982	1977-81		1981	1977-81
	1983	1978-82		1982	1978-82
	1984	1979-83		1983	1979-83
	1985	1975-84		1984	1980-84
	1986	1977-85		1985	1976-85
	1987	1982-86		1986	1982-86
	1988	1983-87		1987	1983-87
	1989	1984-88		1988	1984-88
	1990	1985-89		1989	1985-89
	1991	1986-90		1990	1986-90
	1992	1987-91		1991	1987-91
	1993	1988-92		1992	1983-92
	1994	1989-93		1993	1989-93
	1995	1990-94		1994	1990-94
	1996	1987-95		1995	1991-95
	1997	1992-96		1996	1987-96
	1998	1993-97		1997	1993-97
	1999	1994-98		1997SR [ii]	1948-97
	1999CD [vii]	1990-98		1998	1994-98
	2000	1995-99		1999	1995-99
	2001	1997-01		2000	1996-00
	2002	1998-02		2001	1997-01
	2003	1999-03		2002	1998-02
				2003	1999-03
Mortalité infantile (nombres)	1948	1932-47	-selon l'âge et le sexe	1948	1936-47
	1949/50	1934-49		1951	1936-49
	1951	1935-50		1957	1948-56
	1952	1936-51		1961	1952-60
	1953	1950-52		1962-1965	Dernière
	1954	1946-53		1966	1961-65
	1955	1946-54		1967	1962-66
	1956	1947-55	-selon l'âge et le sexe et la		
	1957	1948-56	résidence (urbaine/rurale)	1968-1973	Dernière
	1958	1948-57		1974	1965-73
	1959	1949-58		1975-1979	Dernière
	1960	1950-59		1980	1971-79
	1961	1952-61		1981-1984	Dernière
	1962	1953-62		1985	1976-84
	1963	1954-63		1986-1991	Dernière
	1964	1960-64		1992	1983-92
	1965	1961-65		1993-1995	Dernière
	1966	1947-66		1996	1987-95
	1967	1963-67		1998-2003	Dernière
	1968	1964-68	-selon la résidence	1967	Dernière
	1969	1965-69	(urbaine/rurale)	1968	1964-68
	1970	1966-70		1969	1965-69
	1971	1967-71		1970	1966-70
	1972	1968-72		1971	1967-71
	1973	1969-73		1972	1968-72
	1974	1965-74		1973	1969-73
	1975	1971-75		1974	1965-74
	1976	1972-76		1975	1971-75
	1977	1973-77		1976	1972-76
	1978	1974-78		1977	1973-77
	1978SR [i]	1948-78		1978	1974-78

Index
Index historique (suite)
(Voir notes à la fin de l'index)

Sujet	Année de l'édition	Période considérée	Sujet	Année de l'édition	Période considérée
	1979	1975-79		1968	1964-68
	1980	1971-80		1969	1965-69
	1981	1977-81		1970	1966-70
	1982	1978-82		1971	1967-71
	1983	1979-83		1972	1968-72
	1984	1980-84		1973	1969-73
	1985	1976-85		1974	1965-74
	1986	1982-86		1975	1971-75
	1987	1983-87		1976	1972-76
	1988	1984-88		1977	1973-77
	1989	1985-89		1978	1974-78
	1990	1986-90		1978SR [i]	1948-78
	1991	1987-91		1979	1975-79
	1992	1983-92		1980	1971-80
	1993	1989-93		1981	1977-81
	1994	1990-94		1982	1978-82
	1995	1991-95		1983	1979-83
	1996	1987-96		1984	1980-84
	1997	1993-97		1985	1976-85
	1998	1994-98		1986	1982-86
	1999	1995-99		1987	1983-87
	2000	1996-00		1988	1984-88
	2001	1997-01		1989	1985-89
	2002	1998-02		1990	1986-90
	2003	1999-03		1991	1987-91
-selon le mois	1967	1962-66		1992	1983-92
	1974	1965-73		1993	1989-93
	1980	1971-79		1994	1990-94
	1985	1976-84		1995	1991-95
				1996	1987-96
Mortalité infantile, taux de	1948	1932-47		1997	1993-97
	1949/50	1932-49		1997SR [ii]	1948-97
	1951	1930-50		1998	1994-98
	1952	1920-34 [vi]		1999	1995-99
		1934-51		2000	1996-00
	1953	1920-39 [vi]		2001	1997-01
		1940-52		2002	1998-02
	1954	1920-39 [vi]		2003	1999-03
		1946-53	-selon l'âge et le sexe	1948	1936-47
	1955	1920-34 [vi]		1951	1936-49
		1946-54		1957	1948-56
	1956	1947-55		1961	1952-60
	1957	1948-56		1966	1956-65
	1958	1948-57	-selon l'âge et le sexe et la		
	1959	1949-58	résidence (urbaine/rurale)	1971-1973	Dernière
	1960	1950-59		1974	1965-73
	1961	1945-59 [vi]		1975-1979	Dernière
		1952-61		1980	1971-79
	1962	1945-59 [vi]		1981-1984	Dernière
		1952-62		1985	1976-84
	1963	1945-59 [vi]		1986-1991	Dernière
		1954-63		1992	1983-92
	1964	1960-64		1993-1995	Dernière
	1965	1961-65		1996	1987-95
	1966	1920-64 [vi]		1997-2003	Dernière
		1951-66	-selon la résidence		
	1967	1963-67	(urbaine/rurale)	1967	Dernière

Index
Index historique (suite)
(Voir notes à la fin de l'index)

Sujet	Année de l'édition	Période considérée	Sujet	Année de l'édition	Période considérée
	1968	1964-68		1993	1983-92
	1969	1965-69		1994	1984-93
	1970	1966-70		1995	1985-94
	1971	1967-71		1996	1986-95
	1972	1968-72		1997	1987-96
	1973	1969-73		1998	1988-97
	1974	1965-74		1999	1989-98
	1975	1971-75		1958	Dernière
	1976	1972-76		1975	1966-74
	1977	1973-77		1976	1966-75
	1978	1974-78		1977	1967-76
	1979	1975-79		1978	1968-77
	1980	1971-80		1979	1969-78
	1981	1977-81		1980	1971-79
	1982	1978-82		1981	1972-80
	1983	1979-83		1982	1972-81
	1984	1980-84			
	1985	1976-85	**Mortalité maternelle**		
	1986	1982-86	**(nombres)**........................... 1951		1947-50
	1987	1983-87		1952	1947-51
	1988	1984-88		1953	Dernière
	1989	1985-89		1954	1945-53
	1990	1986-90		1955-1956	Dernière
	1991	1987-91		1957	1952-56
	1992	1983-92		1958-1960	Dernière
	1993	1989-93		1961	1955-60
	1994	1990-94		1962-1965	Dernière
	1995	1991-95		1966	1960-65
	1996	1987-96		1967-1973	Dernière
	1997	1993-97		1974	1965-73
	1998	1994-98		1975-1979	Dernière
	1999	1995-99		1980	1971-79
	2000	1996-00		1981	1972-80
	2001	1997-01		1982	1972-81
	2002	1998-02		1983	1973-82
	2003	1999-03		1984	1974-83
				1985	1975-84
				1986	1976-85
Mortalité liée à la maternité,				1987	1977-86
taux de 1958		Dernière		1988	1978-87
	1975	1966-74		1989	1979-88
	1976	1966-75		1990	1980-89
	1977	1967-76		1991	1981-90
	1978	1968-77		1992	1982-91
	1979	1969-78		1993	1983-92
	1980	1971-79		1994	1984-93
	1981	1972-80		1995	1985-94
	1982	1972-81		1996	1986-95
	1983	1973-82		1997	1987-96
	1984	1974-83		1998	1988-97
	1985	1975-84		1999	1989-98
	1986	1976-85		2000	1991-00
	1987	1977-86		2001	1991-00
	1988	1978-87		2002	1995-02
	1989	1979-88		2003	1995-02
	1990	1980-89	-selon l'âge	1951	Dernière
	1991	1981-90		1952	Dernière
	1992	1982-91			

Index
Index historique (suite)
(Voir notes à la fin de l'index)

Sujet	Année de l'édition	Période considérée	Sujet	Année de l'édition	Période considérée
	1957	Dernière		1963-1965	Dernière
	1961	Dernière		1966	1961-65
	1967	Dernière		1967	1962-66
	1974	Dernière	-selon le sexe et la		
	1980	Dernière	résidence (urbaine/rurale)	1968-1973	Dernière
	1985	Dernière		1974	1965-73
	1996	Dernière		1975-1979	Dernière
				1980	1971-79
Mortalité maternelle, taux de	1951	1947-50		1981-1984	Dernière
	1952	1947-51		1985	1976-84
	1953	Dernière		1986-1991	Dernière
	1954	1945-53		1992	1983-92
	1955-1956	Dernière		1993-1995	Dernière
	1957	1952-56		1996	1987-95
	1958-1960	Dernière		1997	Dernière
	1961	1955-60		1997SR [ii]	1948-96
	1962-1965	Dernière		1998-2003	Dernière
	1966	1960-65			
	1967-1973	Dernière	Mortalité néonatale, taux de		
	1974	1965-73	-selon le sexe	1948	1936-47
	1975	1966-74		1951	1936-50
	1976	1966-75		1957	1948-56
	1977	1967-76		1961	1952-60
	1978	1968-77		1966	1956-65
	1979	1969-78		1967	1962-66
	1980	1971-79	-selon le sexe et la		
	1981	1972-80	résidence (urbaine/rurale)	1968	Dernière
	1982	1072-81		1971-1973	Dernière
	1983	1973-82		1974	1965-73
	1984	1974-83		1975-1979	Dernière
	1985	1975-84		1980	1971-79
	1986	1976-85		1981-1984	Dernière
	1987	1977-86		1985	1976-84
	1988	1978-87		1986-1991	Dernière
	1989	1979-88		1992	1983-92
	1990	1980-89		1993-1995	Dernière
	1991	1981-90		1996	1987-95
	1992	1982-91		1997	Dernière
	1993	1983-92		1997SR [ii]	1948-96
	1994	1984-93		1998-2003	Dernière
	1995	1985-94			
	1996	1986-95	Mortalité périnatale (nombres)..	1961	1952-60
	1997	1987-96		1966	1956-65
	1998	1988-97		1971	1966-70
	1999	1989-98		1974	1965-73
	2000	1991-00		1980	1971-79
	2001	1991-00		1985	1976-84
	2002	1995-02		1996	1987-95
	2003	1995-02	-selon la résidence		
-selon l'âge	1957	Dernière	(urbaine/rurale)	1971	1966-70
	1961	Dernière		1974	1965-73
				1980	1971-79
Mortalité néonatale:				1985	1976-84
-selon le sexe (nombres)	1948	1936-47		1996	1987-95
	1951	1936-50			
	1957	1948-56	Mortalité périnatale, rapports		
	1961	1952-60	de.	1961	1952-60

Index
Index historique (suite)
(Voir notes à la fin de l'index)

Sujet	Année de l'édition	Période considérée	Sujet	Année de l'édition	Période considérée
	1966	1956-65		1966	1956-65
	1971	1966-70		1967	1962-66
	1974	1965-73		1968-1973	Dernière
	1980	1971-79		1974	1965-73
	1985	1976-84		1975-1979	Dernière
	1996	1987-95		1980	1971-79
				1981-1984	Dernière
-selon la résidence				1985	1976-84
(urbaine/rurale)	1971	1966-70		1986-1991	Dernière
	1974	1965-73		1992	1983-92
	1980	1971-79		1993-1995	Dernière
	1985	1976-84		1996	1987-95
	1996	1987-95		1997	Dernière
				1997SR [ii]	1948-96
Mortalité post-néonatale				1998-2003	Dernière
(nombres):			-selon la résidence	1971-1973	Dernière
-selon le sexe	1948	1936-47	(urbaine/rurale)	1974	1965-73
	1951	1936-50		1975-1979	Dernière
	1957	1948-56		1980	1971-79
	1961	1952-60		1981-1984	Dernière
	1963-1965	Dernière		1985	1976-84
	1966	1961-65		1986-1991	Dernière
	1967	1962-66		1992	1983-92
	1968-1973	Dernière		1993-1995	Dernière
	1974	1965-73		1996	1987-95
	1975-1979	Dernière		1997	Dernière
	1980	1971-79		1997SR [ii]	1948-96
	1981-1984	Dernière		1998-2003	Dernière
	1985	1976-84			
	1986-1991	Dernière	**Mortalité, tables de:**		
	1992	1983-92	-espérance de vie à la		
	1993-1995	Dernière	naissance selon le sexe	1959-1973	Dernière
	1996	1987-95		1974	2-Dernière
	1997	Dernière		1975-1978	Dernière
	1997SR [ii]	1948-96		1978SR [i]	1948-77
	1998-2002	Dernière		1979	Dernière
-selon la résidence				1980	2-Dernières
(urbaine/rurale)	1971-1973	Dernière		1981-1984	Dernière
	1974	1965-73		1985	2-Dernières
	1975-1979	Dernière		1986-1991	Dernière
	1980	1971-79		1991 VP [v]	1950-90
	1981-1984	Dernière		1992-1995	Dernière
	1985	1976-84		1996	2-Dernières
	1986-1991	Dernière		1997	Dernière
	1992	1983-92		1997SR [ii]	1948-1996
	1993-1995	Dernière		1998-2003	Dernière
	1996	1987-95	-espérance de vie à un âge		
	1997	Dernière	donné selon le sexe	1948	1891-1945
	1997SR [ii]	1948-96		1951	1891-1950
	1998-2003	Dernière		1952	1891-1951 [iii]
				1953	1891-1952
Mortalité post-néonatale, taux				1954	1891-1953 [iii]
de:				1955-1956	Dernière
-selon le sexe	1948	1936-47		1957	1900-56
	1951	1936-50		1958-1960	Dernière
	1957	1948-56		1961	1940-60
	1961	1952-60		1962-64	Dernière

Index
Index historique (suite)
(Voir notes à la fin de l'index)

Sujet	Année de l'édition	Période considérée
	1966	2-Dernières
	1967	1900-66
	1968-1973	Dernière
	1974	2-Dernières
	1975-1978	Dernière
	1978HS [i]	1948-77
	1979	Dernière
	1980	2-Dernières
	1981-1984	Dernière
	1985	2-Dernières
	1986-1991	Dernière
	1991 VP [v]	1950-90
	1992-1994	Dernière
	1996	2-Dernières
	1997	Dernière
	1997SR [ii]	1948-96
	1998-2003	Dernière
-taux de mortalité à un âge donné selon le sexe	1948	1891-1945
	1951	1891-1950
	1952	1891-1951 [iii]
	1953	1891-1952
	1954	1891-1953 [iii]
	1957	1900-56
	1961	1940-60
	1966	2-Dernières
	1974	2-Dernières
	1980	2-Dernières
	1985	2 Dernières
	1996	2-Dernières
-survivants à un âge donné selon le sexe	1948	1891-1945
	1951	1891-1950
	1952	1891-1951 [iii]
	1953	1891-1952
	1954	1891-1953 [iii]
	1957	1900-56
	1961	1940-60
	1966	2-Dernières
	1974	2-Dernières
	1980	2-Dernières
	1985	2-Dernières
	1996	2-Dernières
Mortalité, taux de	1948	1932-47
	1949/50	1932-49
	1951	1905-30 [vi]
		1930-50
	1952	1920-34 [vi]
		1934-51
	1953	1920-39 [vi]
		1940-52
	1954	1920-39 [vi]
		1946-53
	1955	1920-34 [vi]
		1946-54
	1956	1947-55

Sujet	Année de l'édition	Période considérée
	1957	1930-56
	1958	1948-57
	1959	1949-58
	1960	1950-59
	1961	1945-59 [vi]
		1952-61
	1962	1945-54 [vi]
		1952-62
	1963	1945-59 [vi]
		1954-63
	1964	1960-64
	1965	1961-65
	1966	1920-64 [vi]
		1951-66
	1967	1963-67
	1968	1964-68
	1969	1965-69
	1970	1966-70
	1971	1967-71
	1972	1968-72
	1973	1969-73
	1974	1965-74
	1975	1971-75
	1976	1972-76
	1977	1973-77
	1978	1974-78
	1978SR [i]	1948-78
	1979	1975-79
	1980	1971-80
	1981	1977-81
	1982	1978-82
	1983	1979-83
	1984	1980-84
	1985	1976-85
	1986	1982-86
	1987	1983-87
	1988	1984-88
	1989	1985-89
	1990	1986-90
	1991	1987-91
	1992	1983-92
	1993	1989-93
	1994	1990-94
	1995	1991-95
	1996	1987-96
	1997	1993-97
	1997SR [ii]	1948-96
	1998	1994-98
	1999	1995-99
	2000	1996-00
	2001	1997-01
	2002	1998-02
	2003	1999-03
-estimatifs: pour les continents	1949/50	1947
	1956-1977	Dernière
	1978-1979	1970-75

Index
Index historique (suite)
(Voir notes à la fin de l'index)

Sujet	Année de l'édition	Période considérée
	1980-1983	1975-80
	1984-1986	1980-85
	1987-1992	1985-90
	1993-1997	1990-95
	1998-2000	1995-00
	2001-2003	2000-05
pour les grandes régions (continentales)	1964-1977	Dernière
	1978-1970	1970-75
	1980-1983	1975-80
	1984-1986	1980-85
	1987-1992	1985-90
	1993-1997	1990-95
	1998-2000	1995-00
	2001-2003	2000-05
pour les régions	1949/50	1947
	1956-1977	Dernière
	1978-1979	1970-75
	1980-1983	1975-80
	1984-1986	1980-85
	1987-1992	1985-90
	1993-1997	1990-95
	1998-2000	1995-00
	2001-2003	2000-05
pour l'ensemble du monde	1949/50	1947
	1956-1977	Dernière
	1978-1979	1970-75
	1980-1983	1975-80
	1984-1986	1980-85
	1987-1992	1985-90
	1993-1997	1990-95
	1998-2000	1995-00
	2001-2003	2000-05
-selon l'âge et le sexe	1948	1935-47
	1949/50	1936-49
	1951	1936-50
	1952	1936-51
	1953	1940-52
	1954	1946-53
	1955-1956	Dernière
	1957	1948-1956
	1961	1952-60
	1966	1950-65
	1978SR [i]	1948-77
	1998-2003	Dernière
-selon l'âge et le sexe et la résidence (urbaine/rurale)	1967	Dernière
	1972	Dernière
	1974	1965-73
	1975-1978	Dernière
	1979	Dernière
	1980	1971-79
	1981-1984	Dernière
	1985	1976-84
	1986-1991	Dernière

Sujet	Année de l'édition	Période considérée
	1991 VP [v]	1950-90
	1992	1983-92
	1993-1995	Dernière
	1996	1987-95
	1997	Dernière
	1997SR [ii]	1948-96
	1998-2003	Dernière
-selon la cause	1951	1947-49
	1952	1947-51 [iii]
	1953	1947-52
	1954	1945-53
	1955-1956	Dernière
	1957	1952-56
	1958-1960	Dernière
	1961	1955-60
	1962-1965	Dernière
	1966	1960-65
	1967-1973	Dernière
	1974	1965-73
	1975-1979	Dernière
	1980	1971-79
	1981-1984	Dernière
	1985	1976-84
	1986-1991	Dernière
	1991 VP [v]	1960-90
	1992-1995	Dernière
	1996	1987-95
	1997-2000	Dernière
	2002	1995-02
-selon la cause, l'âge et le sexe	1957	Dernière
	1961	Dernière
	1991 VP [v]	1960-90
-selon la cause et le sexe	1967	Dernière
	1974	Dernière
	1980	Dernière
	1985	Dernière
	1991 VP [v]	1960-90
	1996	Dernière
-selon l'état matrimonial, l'âge et le sexe	1961	Dernière
	1967	Dernière
	1974	Dernière
	1980	Dernière
	1985	Dernière
	1996	Dernière
-selon la profession, l'âge et le sexe	1957	Dernière
-selon la profession et l'âge (sexe masculin)	1961	Dernière
	1967	Dernière
-selon la résidence (urbaine/rurale)	1967	Dernière
	1968	1964-68
	1969	1965-69
	1970	1966-70

Index
Index historique (suite)
(Voir notes à la fin de l'index)

Sujet	Année de l'édition	Période considérée	Sujet	Année de l'édition	Période considérée
	1971	1967-71		1953	1936-52
	1972	1968-72		1954	1938-53
	1973	1969-73		1955	1946-54
	1974	1965-74		1956	1947-55
	1975	1971-75		1957	1948-56
	1976	1972-76		1958	1948-57
	1977	1973-77		1959	1949-58
	1978	1974-78		1960	1950-59
	1979	1975-79		1961	1952-60
	1980	1971-80		1962	1953-61
	1981	1977-81		1963	1953-62
	1982	1978-82		1964	1959-63
	1983	1979-83		1965	1955-64
	1984	1980-84		1966	1947-65
	1985	1976-85		1967	1962-66
	1986	1982-86		1968	1963-67
	1987	1983-87		1969	1959-68
	1988	1984-88		1970	1965-69
	1989	1985-89		1971	1966-70
	1990	1986-90		1972	1967-71
	1991	1987-91		1973	1968-72
	1992	1983-92		1974	1965-73
	1993	1989-93		1975	1966-74
	1994	1990-94		1976	1971-75
	1995	1991-95		1977	1972-76
	1996	1987-96		1978	1973-77
	1997	1993-97		1979	1974-78
	1998	1994-98		1980	1971-79
	1999	1995-99		1981	1972-80
	2000	1996-00		1982	1977-81
	2001	1997-01		1983	1978-82
	2002	1998-02		1984	1979-83
	2003	1999-03		1985	1975-84
				1986	1977-85
Mort-nés (voir: Morts fœtales tardives)				1987	1982-86
				1988	1983-87
				1989	1984-88
Morts fœtales:				1990	1985-89
-selon la période de gestation	1957	1950-56		1991	1986-90
	1959	1949-58		1992	1987-91
	1961	1952-60		1993	1988-92
	1965	5-Dernières		1994	1989-93
	1966	1956-65		1995	1990-94
	1967-1968	Dernière		1996	1987-95
	1969	1963-68		1997	1992-96
	1974	1965-73		1998	1993-97
	1975	1966-74		1999	1994-98
	1980	1971-79		1999CD [vii]	1990-98
	1981	1972-80		2000	1995-99
	1985	1976-84		2001	1997-01
	1986	1977-85		2002	1998-02
	1996	1987-95		2003	1999-03
	1999CD [vii]	1990-98	-illégitimes	1961	1952-60
				1965	5-Dernières
Morts fœtales tardives	1951	1935-50		1969	1963-68
	1952	1936-51		1975	1966-74
				1981	1972-80

Index
Index historique (suite)
(Voir notes à la fin de l'index)

Sujet	Année de l'édition	Période considérée	Sujet	Année de l'édition	Période considérée
	1986	1977-85		1975	1966-74
-illégitimes, en pourcentage	1961	1952-60		1976	1971-75
	1965	5-Dernières		1977	1972-76
	1969	1963-68		1978	1973-77
	1975	1966-74		1979	1974-78
	1981	1972-80		1980	1971-79
	1986	1977-85		1981	1972-80
-légitimes	1959	1949-58		1982	1977-81
	1965	1955-64		1983	1978-82
	1969	1963-68		1984	1979-83
	1975	1966-74		1985	1975-84
	1981	1972-80		1986	1977-85
	1986	1977-85		1987	1982-86
-légitimes selon l'âge de la mère				1988	1983-87
	1959	1949-58		1989	1984-88
	1965	1955-64		1990	1985-89
	1969	1963-68		1991	1986-90
	1975	1966-74		1992	1987-91
	1981	1972-80		1993	1988-92
	1986	1977-85		1994	1989-93
-selon l'âge de la mère	1954	1936-53		1995	1990-94
	1959	1949-58		1996	1987-95
	1965	1955-64		1997	1992-96
	1969	1963-68		1998	1993-97
	1975	1966-74		1999	1994-98
	1981	1972-80		1999CD [vii]	1990-98
	1986	1977-85		2000	1995-99
	1999CD [vii]	1990-98		2001	1997-01
-selon l'âge de la mère et le rang de naissance				2002	1998-02
	1954	Dernière		2003	1999-03
	1959	1949-58	-selon le sexe	1961	1952-60
	1965	3-Dernières		1965	5-Dernières
	1969	1963-68		1969	1963-68
	1975	1966-74		1975	1966-74
	1981	1972-80		1981	1972-80
	1986	1977-85		1986	1977-85
	1999CD [vii]	1990-98			
-selon la période de gestation			**Mortinatalité, rapports de** (voir: Mortalité fœtale tardive)		
	1957	1950-56			
	1959	1949-58	**Morts néonatales, selon le sexe** (voir: Mortalité post-néonatale)		
	1961	1952-60			
	1965	5-Dernières			
	1966	1956-65	**Morts post-néonatales, selon le sexe** (voir: Mortalité post-néonatale)		
	1967-1968	Dernière			
	1969	1963-68			
	1974	1965-73			
	1975	1966-74			
	1980	1971-79	**N**		
	1981	1972-80			
	1985	1976-84	**Naissances**	1948	1932-47
	1986	1977-85		1949/50	1934-49
	1996	1987-95		1951	1935-50
-selon la résidence (urbaine/rurale)				1952	1936-51
	1971	1966-70		1953	1950-52
	1972	1967-71		1954	1938-53
	1973	1968-72		1955	1946-54
	1974	1965-73			

Index
Index historique (suite)
(Voir notes à la fin de l'index)

Sujet	Année de l'édition	Période considérée	Sujet	Année de l'édition	Période considérée
	1956	1947-55		1986	1977-85
	1957	1948-56		1999CD [vii]	1990-98
	1958	1948-57	-légitimes	1948	1936-47
	1959	1949-58		1949/50	1936-49
	1960	1950-59		1954	1936-53
	1961	1952-61		1959	1949-58
	1962	1953-62		1965	1955-64
	1963	1954-63		1969	1963-68
	1964	1960-64		1975	1966-74
	1965	1946-65		1981	1972-80
	1966	1957-66		1986	1977-85
	1967	1963-67		1999CD [vii]	1990-98
	1968	1964-68	-légitimes selon l'âge de la mère		
	1969	1950-69		1954	1936-53
	1970	1966-70		1959	1949-58
	1971	1967-71		1965	1955-64
	1972	1968-72		1969	1963-68
	1973	1969-73		1975	1966-74
	1974	1970-74		1981	1972-80
	1975	1956-75		1986	1977-85
	1976	1972-76	-légitimes selon l'âge du père		
	1977	1973-77		1959	1949-58
	1978	1974-78		1965	1955-64
	1978SR [i]	1948-78		1969	1963-68
	1979	1975-79		1975	1966-74
	1980	1976-80		1981	1972-80
	1981	1962-81		1986	1977-85
	1982	1978-82	-légitimes selon la durée du mariage		
	1983	1979-83		1948	1936-47
	1984	1980-84		1949/50	1936-49
	1985	1981-85		1954	1936-53
	1986	1967-86		1959	1949-58
	1987	1983-87		1965	1955-64
	1988	1984-88		1969	1963-68
	1989	1985-89		1975	1966-74
	1990	1986-90		1981	1972-80
	1991	1987-91		1986	1977-85
	1992	1983-92		1999CD [vii]	1990-98
	1993	1989-93	-selon l'âge de la mère	1948	1936-47
	1994	1990-94		1949/50	1936-49
	1995	1991-95		1954	1936-53
	1996	1992-96		1955-1956	Dernière
	1997	1993-97		1958	Dernière
	1997SR [ii]	1948-97		1959	1949-58
	1998	1994-98		1960-1964	Dernière
	1999	1995-99		1965	1955-64
	1999CD [vii]	1980-99		1966-1968	Dernière
	2000	1996-00		1969	1963-68
	2001	1997-01		1970-1974	Dernière
	2002	1998-02		1975	1966-74
	2003	1999-03		1976-1978	Dernière
-illégitimes (voir également: légitimes)			1978SR [i]	1948-77
	1959	1949-58		1979-1980	Dernière
	1965	1955-64		1981	1972-80
	1969	1963-68		1982-1985	Dernière
	1975	1966-74		1986	1977-85
	1981	1972-80		1987-1991	Dernière

Index
Index historique (suite)
(Voir notes à la fin de l'index)

Sujet	Année de l'édition	Période considérée	Sujet	Année de l'édition	Période considérée
	1992	1983-92	-selon le mois	2002	1980-02
	1993-1997	Dernière			
	1997SR [ii]	1948-96'	-selon la profession du père	1965	Dernière
	1998-1999	Dernière		1969	Dernière
	1999CD [vii]	1990-98	-selon la résidence (urbaine/rurale)		
	2000-2003	Dernière		1965	Dernière
-selon l'âge de la mère et le rang de naissance	1949/50	1936-47		1967	Dernière
	1954	Dernière		1968	1964-68
	1959	1949-58		1969	1964-68
	1965	1955-64		1970	1966-70
	1969	1963-68		1971	1967-71
	1975	1966-74		1972	1968-72
	1981	1972-80		1973	1969-73
	1986	1977-85		1974	1970-74
	1999CD [vii]	1990-98		1975	1956-75
-selon l'âge de la mère et la résidence (urbaine/rurale) (voir: selon la résidence (urbaine/rurale), ci-dessous)				1976	1972-76
				1977	1973-77
				1978	1974-78
				1979	1975-79
				1980	1976-80
-selon l'âge de la mère et le sexe	1965-1968	Dernière		1981	1962-81
	1969	1963-68		1982	1978-82
	1970-1974	Dernière		1983	1979-83
	1975	1966-74		1984	1980-84
	1976-1978	Dernière		1985	1981-85
	1978SR [i]	1948-77		1986	1967-86
	1979-1980	Dernière		1987	1983-87
	1981	1972-80		1988	1984-88
	1982-1985	Dernière		1989	1985-89
	1986	1977-85		1990	1986-90
	1987-1991	Dernière		1991	1987-91
	1992	1983-92		1992	1983-92
	1993-1997	Dernière		1993	1989-93
	1997SR [ii]	1948-96		1994	1990-94
	1998-1999	Dernière		1995	1991-95
	1999CD [vii]	1990-98		1996	1992-96
-selon l'âge du père	1949/50	1942-49		1997	1993-97
	1954	1936-53		1998	1994-98
	1959	1949-58		1999	1995-99
	1965	1955-64		1999CD [vii]	1980-99
	1969	1963-68		2000	1996-00
	1975	1966-74		2001	1997-01
	1981	1972-80		2002	1998-02
	1986	1977-85		2003	1999-03
	1999CD [vii]	1990-98	-selon la résidence (urbaine/rurale) et l'âge de la mère	1965	Dernière
-selon la durée de gestation	1975	Dernière		1969-1974	Dernière
	1981	1972-80		1975	1966-74
	1986	1977-85		1976-1980	Dernière
	1999CD [vii]	1990-98		1981	1972-80
-selon la durée du mariage (voir: légitimes selon la durée du mariage)				1982-1985	Dernière
				1986	1977-85
				1987-1991	Dernière
				1992	1983-92
				1993-1997	Dernière
				1997SR [ii]	1948-96

Index
Index historique (suite)
(Voir notes à la fin de l'index)

Sujet	Année de l'édition	Période considérée
	1998-1999	Dernière
	1999CD [vii]	1990-98
	2000-2003	Dernière
-selon le poids à la naissance	1975	Dernière
	1981	1972-80
	1986	1977-85
	1999CD [vii]	1990-98
-selon le rang de naissance	1948	1936-47
	1949/50	1936-49
	1954	1936-53
	1955	Dernière
	1959	1949-58
	1965	1955-64
	1969	1963-68
	1975	1966-74
	1981	1972-80
	1986	1977-85
	1999CD [vii]	1990-98
-selon le sexe	1959	1949-58
	1965	1955-64
	1967-1968	Dernière
	1969	1963-68
	1970-1974	Dernière
	1975	1956-75
	1976-1980	Dernière
	1981	1962-81
	1982-1985	Dernière
	1986	1967-86
	1987-1991	Dernière
	1992	1983-92
	1993-1997	Dernière
	1997SR [ii]	1948-96
	1998-1999	Dernière
	1999CD [vii]	1980-1999
	2000-2003	Dernière
-selon les naissances multiples	1965	Dernière
	1969	Dernière
	1975	Dernière
	1981	1972-80
	1986	1977-85
	1999CD [vii]	1990-98
Naissances des femmes de moins de 20 ans selon l'âge de la mère: -et la résidence (urbaine/rurale)	1986	1970-85
Natalité proportionnelle:		
-fécondité	1949/50	Dernière
	1954	Dernière
	1959	1949-58
	1965	1955-65
	1969	1963-68
	1975	1965-74
	1978SR [i]	1948-77

Sujet	Année de l'édition	Période considérée
	1981	1972-80
	1986	1977-85
	1997SR [ii]	1948-1996
	1999CD [vii]	1980-99
-illégitime	1959	1949-58
	1965	1955-65
	1969	1963-68
	1975	1965-74
	1981	1972-80
	1986	1977-85
Natalité, taux de	1948	1932-47
	1949/50	1932-49
	1951	1905-30 [vi]
		1930-50
	1952	1920-34 [vi]
		1934-51
	1953	1920-39 [vi]
		1940-52
	1954	1920-39 [vi]
		1939-53
	1955	1920-34 [vi]
		1946-54
	1956	1947-55
	1957	1948-56
	1958	1948-57
	1959	1920-54 [vi]
		1963-58
	1960	1950-59
	1961	1945-59 [vi]
		1952-61
	1962	1945-54 [vi]
		1952-62
	1963	1945-59 [vi]
		1954-63
	1964	1960-64
	1965	1920-64 [vi]
		1950-65
	1966	1950-64 [vi]
		1957-66
	1967	1963-67
	1968	1964-68
	1969	1925-69 [vi]
		1954-69
	1970	1966-70
	1971	1967-71
	1972	1968-72
	1973	1969-73
	1974	1970-74
	1975	1956-75
	1976	1972-76
	1977	1973-77
	1978	1974-78
	1978SR [i]	1948-78
	1979	1975-79
	1980	1976-80
	1981	1962-81

Index
Index historique (suite)
(Voir notes à la fin de l'index)

Sujet	Année de l'édition	Période considérée	Sujet	Année de l'édition	Période considérée
	1982	1978-82		1998-2000	1995-00
	1983	1979-83		2001-2003	2000-05
	1984	1980-84	-illégitimes (voir également légitimes)		
	1985	1981-85		1959	1949-58
	1986	1967-86	-légitimes	1954	1936-53
	1987	1983-87		1959	1949-58
	1988	1984-88		1965	Dernière
	1989	1985-89		1969	Dernière
	1990	1986-90		1975	Dernière
	1991	1987-91		1981	Dernière
	1992	1983-92		1986	Dernière
	1993	1989-93	-légitimes selon l'âge de la mère		
	1994	1990-94		1954	1936-53
	1995	1991-95		1959	1949-58
	1996	1992-96		1965	Dernière
	1997	1993-97		1969	Dernière
	1997SR [ii]	1948-97		1975	Dernière
	1998	1994-98		1981	Dernière
	1999	1995-99		1986	Dernière
	1999CD [vii]	1985-99	-légitimes selon l'âge du père		
	2000	1996-00		1959	1949-58
	2001	1997-01		1965	Dernière
	2002	1998-02		1969	Dernière
	2003	1999-03		1975	Dernière
-estimatifs:				1981	Dernière
pour les continents	1949/50	1947		1986	Dernière
	1956-1977	Dernière	-légitimes selon la durée du mariage		
	1978-1979	1970-75		1959	1950-57
	1980-1986	1975-80		1965	Dernière
	1987-1992	1985-90		1969	Dernière
	1993-1997	1990-95		1975	Dernière
	1998-2000	1995-00	-selon l'âge de la mère	1948	1936-47
	2001-2003	2000-05		1949/50	1936-49
pour les grandes régions	1964-1977	Dernière		1951	1936-50
	1978-1979	1970-75		1952	1936-50
	1980-1983	1975-80		1953	1936-52
	1984-1986	1980-85		1954	1936-53
	1987-1992	1985-90		1955-1956	Dernière
	1993-1997	1990-95		1959	1949-58
	1998-2000	1995-00		1965	1955-64
	2001-2003	2000-05		1969	1963-68
pour les régions	1949/50	1947		1975	1966-74
	1956-1977	Dernière		1976-1978	Dernière
	1978-1979	1970-75		1978SR [i]	1948-77
	1980-1983	1975-80		1979-1980	Dernière
	1984-1986	1980-85		1981	1972-80
	1987-1992	1985-90		1982-1985	Dernière
	1993-1997	1990-95		1986	1977-85
	1998-2000	1995-00		1987-1991	Dernière
	2001-2003	2000-05		1992	1983-92
pour le monde	1949/50	1947		1993-1997	Dernière
	1956-1977	Dernière		1975SR [ii]	1948-96
	1978-1979	1970-75		1998-1999	Dernière
	1980-1983	1975-80		1999CD [vii]	1990-98
	1984-1986	1980-85		2000-2003	Dernière
	1987-1992	1985-90	-selon l'âge de la mère et le rang de naissance		
	1993-1997	1990-95		1954	1948 et 1951

Index
Index historique (suite)
(Voir notes à la fin de l'index)

Sujet	Année de l'édition	Période considérée		Sujet	Année de l'édition	Période considérée
	1959	1949-58			1987	1983-87
	1965	1955-64			1988	1984-88
	1969	1963-68			1989	1985-89
	1975	1966-74			1990	1986-90
	1981	1972-80			1991	1987-91
	1986	1977-85			1992	1983-92
	1999CD [vii]	1990-98			1993	1989-93
-selon l'âge de la mère et la résidence (urbaine/rurale) (voir: (urbaine/rurale), ci-dessous)					1994	1990-94
					1995	1991-95
					1996	1992-96
					1997	1993-97
-selon l'âge du père	1949/50	1942-49			1998	1994-98
	1954	1936-53			1999	1995-99
	1959	1949-58			1999CD [vii]	1985-99
	1965	1955-64			2000	1996-00
	1969	1963-68			2001	1997-01
	1975	1966-74			2002	1998-02
	1981	1972-80			2003	1999-03
	1986	1977-85		-selon la résidence (urbaine/rurale) et l'âge de la mère		
	1999CD [vii]	1990-98				
-selon la durée du mariage (voir: légitimes selon la duré du mariage)					1965	Dernière
					1969	Dernière
					1975	1966-74
-selon le rang de naissance	1951	1936-49			1976-1980	Dernière
	1952	1936-50			1981	1972-80
	1953	1936-52			1982-1985	Dernière
	1954	1936-53			1986	1977-85
	1955	Dernière			1987-1991	Dernière
	1959	1949-58			1992	1983-92
	1965	1955-64			1993-1997	Dernière
	1969	1963-68			1997SR [ii]	1948-96
	1975	1966-74			1998-1999	Dernière
	1981	1972-80			1999CD [vii]	1990-98
	1986	1977-85			2000-2003	Dernière
	1999CD [vii]	1990-98				
-selon la résidence(urbaine/rurale)	1965	Dernière		**Nationalité** (voir: Population)		
	1967	Dernière				
	1968	1964-68		**Nuptialité** (voir: Mariages)		
	1969	1964-68				
	1970	1966-70		**Nuptialité, taux de**	1948	1932-47
	1971	1967-71			1949/50	1932-49
	1972	1968-72			1951	1930-50
	1973	1969-73			1952	1920-34 [vi]
	1974	1970-74				1934-51
	1975	1956-75			1953	1920-39 [vi]
	1976	1972-76				1940-52
	1977	1973-77			1954	1920-39 [vi]
	1978	1974-78				1946-53
	1979	1975-79			1955	1920-34 [vi]
	1980	1976-80				1946-54
	1981	1962-81			1956	1947-55
	1982	1978-82			1957	1948-56
	1983	1979-83			1958	1930-57
	1984	1980-84			1959	1949-58
	1985	1981-85			1960	1950-59
	1986	1967-86			1961	1952-61
					1962	1953-62

Index
Index historique (suite)
(Voir notes à la fin de l'index)

Sujet	Année de l'édition	Période considérée	Sujet	Année de l'édition	Période considérée
	1963	1954-63		1991	1987-91
	1964	1960-64		1992	1988-92
	1965	1956-65		1993	1989-93
	1966	1962-66		1994	1990-94
	1967	1963-67		1995	1991-95
	1968	1920-646		1996	1992-96
		1953-68		1997	1993-97
	1969	1965-69		1998	1994-98
	1970	1966-70		1999	1995-99
	1971	1967-71		2000	1996-00
	1972	1968-72		2001	1997-01
	1973	1969-73		2002	1998-02
	1974	1970-74		2003	1999-03
	1975	1971-75	-selon l'âge et le sexe	1948	1936-46
	1976	1957-76		1949/50	1936-49
	1977	1973-77		1953	1936-51
	1978	1974-78		1954	1936-52
	1979	1975-79		1958	1935-56
	1980	1976-80		1968	1955-67
	1981	1977-81		1976	1966-75
	1982	1963-82		1982	1972-81
	1983	1979-83		1987	1975-86
	1984	1980-84		1990	1980-89
	1985	1981-85	-selon la résidence		
	1986	1982-86	(urbaine/rurale)	1968	Dernière
	1987	1983-87		1969	1965-69
	1988	1984-88		1970	1966-70
	1989	1985-89		1971	1967-71
	1990	1971-90		1972	1968-72
	1991	1987-91		1973	1969-73
	1992	1988-92		1974	1970-74
	1993	1989-93		1975	1971-75
	1994	1990-94		1976	1957-76
	1995	1991-95		1977	1973-77
	1996	1992-96		1978	1974-78
	1997	1993-97		1979	1975-79
	1998	1994-98		1980	1976-80
	1999	1995-99		1981	1977-81
	1972	1968-72		1982	1963-82
	1973	1969-73		1983	1979-83
	1974	1970-74		1984	1980-84
	1975	1971-75		1985	1981-85
	1976	1957-76		1986	1982-86
	1977	1973-77		1987	1983-87
	1978	1974-78		1988	1984-88
	1979	1975-79		1989	1985-89
	1980	1976-80		1990	1971-90
	1981	1977-81		1991	1987-91
	1982	1963-82		1992	1988-92
	1983	1979-83		1993	1989-93
	1984	1980-84		1994	1990-94
	1985	1981-85		1995	1991-95
	1986	1982-86		1996	1992-96
	1987	1983-87		1997	1993-97
	1988	1984-88		1998	1994-98
	1989	1985-89		1999	1995-99
	1990	1971-90		2000	1996-00

Index
Index historique (suite)
(Voir notes à la fin de l'index)

Sujet	Année de l'édition	Période considérée
	2001	1997-01
	2002	1998-02
	2003	1999-03
-selon le sexe et la population mariable	1958	1935-56
	1968	1935-67
	1976	1966-75
	1982	1972-81
	1990	1980-89
Nuptialité au premier mariage, taux de, classification détaillée selon l'âge de l'épouse et de l'époux	1982	1972-81
	1990	1980-89

P

Sujet	Année de l'édition	Période considérée
Population:		
-accroissement, taux d'......: annuels moyens pour les pays ou zones	1957	1953-56
	1958	1953-57
	1959	1953-58
	1960	1953-59
	1961	1953-60
	1962	1958-61
	1963	1958-62
	1964	1958-63
	1965	1958-64
	1966	1958-66
	1967	1963-67
	1968	1963-68
	1969	1963-69
	1970	1963-70
	1971	1963-71
	1972	1963-72
	1973	1970-73
	1974	1970-74
	1975	1970-75
	1976	1970-76
	1977	1970-77
	1978	1975-78
	1979	1975-79
	1980	1975-80
	1981	1975-81
	1982	1975-82
	1983	1980-83
	1984	1980-84
	1985	1980-85
	1986	1980-86
	1987	1980-87
	1988	1985-88
	1989	1985-89
	1990	1985-90
	1991	1985-91

Sujet	Année de l'édition	Période considérée
	1992	1985-92
	1993	1990-93
	1994	1990-94
	1995	1990-95
	1996	1990-96
	1997	1990-97
	1998	1993-98
	1999	1995-99
	2000	1996-00
	2001	1997-01
	2002	1998-02
	2003	1999-03
annuels moyens pour le monde, les grandes régions (continentes) et les régions géographiques	1957	1950-56
	1958	1950-57
	1959	1950-58
	1960	1950-59
	1961	1950-60
	1962	1950-61
	1963	1958-62
		1960-62
	1964	1958-63
		1960-63
	1965	1958-64
		1960-64
	1966	1958-66
		1960-66
	1967	1960-67
		1963-67
	1968	1960-68
		1963-68
	1969	1960-69
		1963-69
	1970	1963-70
		1965-70
	1971	1963-71
		1965-71
	1972	1963-72
		1965-72
	1973	1965-73
		1970-73
	1974	1965-74
		1970-74
	1975	1965-75
		1970-75
	1976	1965-76
		1970-76
	1977	1965-77
		1970-77
	1978-1979	1970-75
	1980-1983	1975-80
	1984-1986	1980-85
	1987-1992	1985-90

Index
Index historique (suite)
(Voir notes à la fin de l'index)

Sujet	Année de l'édition	Période considérée
	1993-1997	1990-95
	1998-2000	1995-00
	2001-2003	2000-05
-active:		
féminin, selon l'état matrimonial et l'âge	1956	1945-55
	1967	1955-64
	1968	Dernière
	1972	1962-77
féminin, selon l'état matrimonial et l'âge et la résidence (urbaine/rurale)	1973	1965-73
	1979	1970-79
	1984	1974-84
	1988	1980-88 [iii]
née à l'étranger selon la profession, l'âge et le sexe	1984	1974-84
	1989	1980-88
née à l'étranger selon la profession, l'âge et le sexe	1977	Dernière
selon l'âge et le sexe	1955	1945-54
	1956	1945-55
	1964	1955-64
	1972	1962-72
selon l'âge et le sexe et la résidence (urbaine/rurale)	1973	1965-73 [iii]
	1979	1970-79 [iii]
	1984	1974-84
	1988	1980-88 [iii]
	1994	1985-94
selon l'âge et le sexe en pourcentage	1948	Dernière
	1949/50	1930-48
	1955	1945-54
	1956	1945-55
	1964	1955-64
	1972	1962-72
selon l'âge et le sexe en pourcentage et la résidence (urbaine/rurale)	1973	1965-73 [iii]
	1979	1970-79 [iii]
	1984	1974-84
	1988	1980-88 [iii]
	1994	1985-94
selon la branche d'activité économique, le sexe, et l'âge	1956	1945-55
	1964	1955-64
	1972	1962-72
selon la branche d'activité économique, le sexe, et l'âge et la résidence (urbaine/rurale)	1973	1965-73 [iii]
	1979	1970-79 [iii]
	1984	1974-84

Sujet	Année de l'édition	Période considérée
	1988	1980-88 [iii]
selon la branche d'activité économique la situation dans la profession et le sexe	1948	Dernière
	1949/50	Dernière
	1955	1945-54
	1964	1955-64
	1972	1962-72
selon la branche d'activité économique la situation dans la profession et le sexe et la résidence (urbaine/rurale)	1973	1965-73 [iii]
	1979	1970-79
	1984	1974-84
	1988	1980-88 [iii]
	1994	1985-94
selon l'état matrimonial et l'âge (sexe féminin)	1956	1945-55
	1964	1955-64
	1968	Dernière
	1972	1962-72
selon l'état matrimonial et l'âge (sexe féminin) et la résidence (urbaine/rurale)	1973	1965-73 [iii]
	1979	1970-79 [iii]
	1984	1974-84
	1988	1980-88 [iii]
	1994	1985-94
selon la profession, la l'âge et le sexe	1956	1945-55
	1964	1955-64
	1972	1962-72
selon la profession, l'âge et le sexe et la résidence (urbaine/rurale)	1973	1965-73 [iii]
	1979	1970-79 [iii]
	1984	1974-84
	1988	1980-88 [iii]
selon la profession, la situation dans la profession et le sexe	1956	1945-55
	1964	1955-64
	1972	1962-72
selon la profession, la situation dans la profession et le sexe et la résidence (urbaine/rurale)	1973	1965-73 [iii]
	1979	1970-79 [iii]
	1984	1974-84
	1988	1980-88 [iii]
	1994	1985-94
selon la situation dans la profession, la branche d'activité économique et	1948	Dernière

Index
Index historique (suite)
(Voir notes à la fin de l'index)

Sujet	Année de l'édition	Période considérée
le sexe		
	1949/50	Dernière
	1955	1945-54
	1964	1955-64
	1972	1962-72
selon la situation dans la profession, la branche d'activité économique et le sexe et la résidence (urbaine/rurale)	1973	1965-73 [iii]
	1979	1970-79 [iii]
	1984	1974-84
	1988	1980-88 [iii]
	1994	1985-94
selon la situation dans la profession et le sexe et l'âge	1956	1945-55
	1964	1955-64
	1972	1962-72
selon la situation dans la profession et le sexe et l'âge et la résidence (urbaine/rurale)	1973	1965-73 [iii]
	1979	1970-79 [iii]
	1984	1974-84
	1988	1980-88 [iii]
	1994	1985-94
selon la situation dans la profession, la profession et le sexe	1956	1945-55
	1964	1955-64
	1972	1962-72
selon la situation dans la profession, la profession et le sexe et la résidence (urbaine/rurale)	1973	1965-73 [iii]
	1979	1970-79 [iii]
	1984	1974-84
	1988	1980-88 [iii]
	1994	1985-94
selon le sexe	1948	Dernière
	1949/50	1926-48
	1955	1945-54
	1956	1945-55
	1960	1920-60
	1963	1955-63
	1964	1955-64
	1970	1950-70
	1972	1962-72
	1973	1965-73 [iii]
	1979	1970-79 [iii]
	1984	1974-84
	1988	1980-88 [iii]
	1994	1985-94
-alphabète selon l'âge et le sexe (voir également: analphabète, ci-dessous)	1948	Dernière

Sujet	Année de l'édition	Période considérée
	1955	1945-54
	1963	1955-63
	1964	1955-64 [iii]
	1971	1962-71
-alphabète selon l'âge et le sexe et la résidence (urbaine/rurale)	1973	1965-73 [iii]
	1979	1970-79 [iii]
	1984	1974-84
	1988	1980-88 [iii]
	1993	1985-93
-alphabétisme selon le sexe, taux d'...... (voir également: analphabétisme, taux d', ci-dessous)	1955	1945-54
-alphabétisme selon le sexe et l'âge, taux d'......	1955	1945-54
-analphabète selon le sexe	1948	Dernière
	1955	1945-54
	1960	1920-60
	1963	1955-63
	1964	1955-64 [iii]
	1970	1950-70
-analphabète selon le sexe et la résidence (urbaine/rurale)	1973	1965-73
	1979	1970-79 [iii]
	1983	1974-83
	1988	1980-88 [iii]
-analphabète selon le sexe et l'âge	1948	Dernière
	1955	1945-54
	1963	1955-63
	1964	1955-64 [iii]
	1970	1950-70
-analphabète selon le sexe et l'âge et la résidence (urbaine/rurale)	1973	1965-73
	1979	1970-79 [iii]
	1983	1974-83
	1988	1980-88 [iii]
	1993	1985-93 [iii]
-analphabète selon le sexe, taux d'......	1948	Dernière
	1955	1945-54
	1960	1920-60
	1963	1955-63
	1964	1955-64 [iii]
	1970	1950-70
-analphabète selon le sexe, taux d'...... et la résidence (urbaine/rurale)	1973	1965-73
	1979	1970-79 [iii]
	1983	1974-83
	1988	1980-88 [iii]
	1993	1985-93 [iii]
-analphabète selon le sexe	1948	Dernière

Index
Index historique (suite)
(Voir notes à la fin de l'index)

Sujet	Année de l'édition	Période considérée	Sujet	Année de l'édition	Période considérée
et l'âge, taux d'......				1962	1920-61
	1955	1945-54		1963	1930-62
	1960	1920-60		1964	1930-63
	1963	1955-63 [iii]		1965	1930-65
	1964	1955-64 [iii]		1966	1930-66
	1970	1950-70		1967	1930-67
-analphabète selon le sexe				1968	1930-68
et l'âge, taux d'...... et la				1969	1930-69
résidence (urbaine/rurale)	1973	1965-73		1970	1950-70
	1979	1970-79 [iii]		1971	1950-71
	1983	1974-83		1972	1950-72
	1988	1980-88 [iii]		1973	1950-73
	1993	1985-93 [iii]		1974	1950-74
-célibataire selon l'âge et le				1975	1950-75
sexe (voir également: selon				1976	1950-76
l'état matrimonial, ci-				1977	1950-77
dessous):				1978	1950-78
nombres	1960	1920-60		1979	1950-79
	1970	1950-70		1980	1950-80
pourcentages	1949/50	1926-48		1981	1950-81
	1960	1920-60		1982	1950-82
	1970	1950-70		1983	1950-83
-chômeurs selon l'âge et le				1984	1950-84
sexe	1949/50	1946-49		1985	1950-85
-dans les localités (voir:				1986	1950-86
selon l'importance des				1987	1950-87
localités, ci-dessous)				1988	1950-88
des collectivités, âge et				1989	1950-89
sexe et résidence				1990	1950-90
urbaine/rurale	1987	1975-86		1991	1950-91
	1995	1985-95		1992	1950-92
-dans les ménages selon le				1993	1950-93
type et la dimension des				1994	1950-94
ménages privés (voir				1995	1950-95
également: Ménages)	1955	1945-54		1996	1950-96
	1962	1955-62		1997	1950-97
	1963	1955-63 [iii]		1998-2000	1950-00
-dans les logements				2001	1950-01
collectifs et sans abri	1991VP [v]	Dernière		2002	1950-02
-dans les villes (voir: des				2003	1950-03
grandes régions)			-des pays ou zones (total):		
-des continents (voir: des			dénombrée	1948	1900-48
grandes régions				1949/50	1900-50
(continentales))				1951	1900-51
-des grandes régions				1952	1850-1952
(continentales)	1949/50	1920-49		1953	1850-1953
	1951	1950		1954	Dernière
	1952	1920-51		1955	1850-1954
	1953	1920-52		1956-1961	Dernière
	1954	1920-53		1962	1900-62
	1955	1920-54		1963	Dernière
	1956	1920-55		1964	1955-64
	1957	1920-56		1965-1978	Dernière
	1958	1920-57		1978SR [i]	1948-78
	1959	1920-58		1979-1997	Dernière
	1960	1920-59		1979SR [ii]	1948-78
	1961	1920-60		1998-2003	Dernière

Index
Index historique (suite)
(Voir notes à la fin de l'index)

Sujet	Année de l'édition	Période considérée	Sujet	Année de l'édition	Période considérée
estimée	1948	1932-47	-des principales divisions administratives		
	1949/50	1932-49		1952	Dernière
	1951	1930-50		1955	1945-54
	1952	1920-51		1962	1955-62
	1953	1920-53		1963	1955-63 [iii]
	1954	1920-54		1971	1962-71
	1955	1920-55		1973	1965-73 [iii]
	1956	1920-56		1979	1970-79 [iii]
	1957	1940-57		1983	1974-83
	1958	1939-58		1988	1980-88 [iii]
	1959	1940-59		1993	1985-93
	1960	1920-60	-des régions	1949/50	1920-49
	1961	1941-61		1952	1920-51
	1962	1942-62		1953	1920-52
	1963	1943-63		1954	1920-53
	1964	1955-64		1955	1920-54
	1965	1946-65		1956	1920-55
	1966	1947-66		1957	1920-56
	1967	1958-67		1958	1920-57
	1968	1959-68		1959	1920-58
	1969	1960-69		1960	1920-59
	1970	1950-70		1961	1920-60
	1971	1962-71		1962	1920-61
	1972	1963-72		1963	1930-62
	1973	1964-73		1964	1930-63
	1974	1965-74		1965	1930-65
	1975	1966-75		1966	1930-66
	1976	1967-76		1967	1930-67
	1977	1968-77		1968	1930-68
	1978	1969-78		1969	1930-69
	1978SR [i]	1948-78		1970	1950-70
	1979	1970-79		1971	1950-71
	1980	1971-80		1972	1950-72
	1981	1972-81		1973	1950-73
	1982	1973-82		1974	1950-74
	1983	1974-83		1975	1950-75
	1984	1975-84		1976	1950-76
	1985	1976-85		1977	1950-77
	1986	1977-86		1978	1950-78
	1987	1978-87		1979	1950-79
	1988	1979-88		1980	1950-80
	1989	1980-89		1981	1950-81
	1990	1981-90		1982	1950-82
	1991	1982-91		1983	1950-83
	1992	1983-92		1984	1950-84
	1993	1984-93		1985	1950-85
	1994	1985-94		1986	1950-86
	1995	1986-95		1987	1950-87
	1996	1987-96		1988	1950-88
	1997	1988-97		1989	1950-89
	1997SR [ii]	1948-97		1990	1950-90
	1998	1989-98		1991	1950-91
	1999	1990-99		1992	1950-92
	2000	1991-00		1993	1950-93
	2001	1992-01		1994	1950-94
	2002	1993-02		1995	1950-95
	2003	1994-03		1996	1950-96

Index
Index historique (suite)
(Voir notes à la fin de l'index)

Sujet	Année de l'édition	Période considérée	Sujet	Année de l'édition	Période considérée
	1997	1950-97		1976	1950-76
	1998-2000	1950-00		1977	1950-77
	2001	1950-01		1978	1950-78
	2002	1950-02		1979	1950-79
	2003	1950-03		1980	1950-80
-des villes:				1981	1950-81
capitale	1952	Dernière		1982	1950-82
	1955	1945-54		1983	1950-83
	1957	Dernière		1984	1950-84
	1960	1939-61		1985	1950-85
	1962	1955-62		1986	1950-86
	1963	1955-63		1987	1950-87
	1964-1969	Dernière		1988	1950-88
	1970	1950-70		1989	1950-89
	1971	1962-71		1990	1950-90
	1972	Dernière		1991	1950-91
	1973	1965-73		1992	1950-92
	1974-2003	Dernière		1993	1950-93
de 100 000 habitants et				1994	1950-94
plus	1952	Dernière		1995	1950-95
	1955	1945-54		1996	1950-96
	1957	Dernière		1997	1950-97
	1960	1939-61		1998-2000	1950-00
	1962	1955-62		2001	1950-01
	1963	1955-63		2002	1950-02
	1964-1969	Dernière		2003	1950-03
	1970	1950-70	-effectifs des ménages, âge,		
	1971	1962-71	sexe et résidence		
	1972	Dernière	urbaine/rurale	1987	1975-86
	1973	1965-73		1995	1950-95
	1974-2003	Dernière	-féminine:		
-du monde	1949/50	1920-49	selon l'âge et selon l'âge		
	1951	1950	et la durée du mariage	1968	Dernière
	1952	1920-51	selon le nombre total		
	1953	1920-52	d'enfants nés vivants et		
	1954	1920-53	l'âge	1949/50	Dernière
	1955	1920-54		1954	1930-53
	1956	1920-55		1955	1945-54
	1957	1920-56		1959	1949-58
	1958	1920-57		1963	1955-63
	1959	1920-58		1965	1955-65
	1960	1920-59		1969	Dernière
	1961	1920-60		1971	1962-71
	1962	1920-61		1973	1965-73 [iii]
	1963	1930-62		1975	1965-74
	1964	1930-63		1978SR [i]	1948-77
	1965	1930-65		1981	1972-80
	1966	1930-66		1986	1977-85
	1967	1930-67		1997SR [ii]	1948-96
	1968	1930-68	selon le nombre total		
	1969	1930-69	d'enfants vivants et l'âge	1949/50	Dernière
	1970	1950-70		1954	1930-53
	1971	1950-71		1955	1945-54
	1972	1950-72		1959	1949-58
	1973	1950-73		1963	1955-63
	1974	1950-74		1965	1955-65
	1975	1950-75		1968-1969	Dernière

Index
Index historique (suite)
(Voir notes à la fin de l'index)

Sujet	Année de l'édition	Période considérée
	1971	1962-71
	1973	1965-73 [iii]
	1975	1965-74
	1978SR [i]	1948-77
	1981	1972-80
	1986	1977-85
	1997SR [ii]	1948-96
-féminine mariée: selon l'âge actuel et la durée du présent mariage	1968	Dernière
-fréquentant l'école selon l'âge et le sexe	1956	1945-55
	1963	1955-63
	1964	1955-64 [iii]
	1971	1962-71
	1973	1965-73 [iii]
	1979	1970-79
	1983	1974-83
	1988	1980-88 [iii]
	1993	1985-93 [iii]
-indicateurs divers de conditions d'habitation	1991 VP [v]	Dernière
-inactive par sous-groupes, âge et sexe	1956	1945-55
	1964	1955-64
	1972	1962-72
	1973	1965-73 [iii]
	1979	1970-79 [iii]
	1984	1974-84
	1988	1980-88 [iii]
	1994	1985-94
-mariée selon l'âge et le sexe (voir également: Population selon l'état matrimonial) nombres et pourcentages	1954	1926-52
	1960	1920-60
	1970	1950-70
-par année d'âge et par sexe	1955	1945-54
	1962	1955-62
	1963	1955-63 [iii]
	1971	1962-71
	1973	1965-73 [iii]
	1979	1970-79 [iii]
	1983	1974-83
	1988	1980-88 [iii]
	1993	1985-93
-par groupes d'âge et par sexe:		
dénombrée	1948-1952	Dernière
	1953	1950-52
	1954-1959	Dernière
	1960	1940-60
	1961	Dernière
	1962	1955-62
	1963	1955-63

Sujet	Année de l'édition	Période considérée
	1964	1955-64 [iii]
	1965-1969	Dernière
	1970	1950-70
	1971	1962-71
	1972	Dernière
	1973	1965-73
	1974-1978	Dernière
	1978SR [i]	1948-77
	1979-1991	Dernière
	1991 VP [v]	1950-90
	1992-1997	Dernière
	1997SR [ii]	1948-97
	1998-2003	Dernière
estimée	1948-	
	1949/50	1945 et Dernière
	1951-1954	Dernière
	1955-1959	Dernière
	1960	1940-60
	1961-1969	Dernière
	1970	1950-70
	1971-1997	Dernière
	1997SR [ii]	1948-97
	1998-2003	Dernière
pourcentage	1948-	
	1949/50	1945 et Dernière
	1951-1952	Dernière
-par ménages, nombres et dimension moyenne selon la résidence (urbaine/rurale)(voir aussi: Ménages)	1955	1945-54
	1962	1955-62
	1963	1955-63 [iii]
	1968	Dernière
	1971	1962-71
	1973	1965-72 [iii]
	1976	1ernière
	1982	Dernière
	1987	1975-86
	1990	1980-89
	1995	1985-95
-personnes âgées selon caractéristique socio-démographique	1991VP [v]	1950-90
selon caractéristique économique	1991VP [v]	1950-90
personnes atteintes d'incapacités	1991VP [v]	Dernière
-rurale (voir: urbaine/rurale (résidence), ci-dessous)		
-selon l'âge et le sexe (voir: par groupes d'âge et par sexe, ci-dessous)		
-selon la composition ethnique et le sexe	1956	1945-55

Index
Index historique (suite)
(Voir notes à la fin de l'index)

Sujet	Année de l'édition	Période considérée	Sujet	Année de l'édition	Période considérée
	1963	1955-63		1979	1970-79 [iii]
	1964	1955-64 [iii]		1983	1974-83
	1971	1962-71		1988	1980-88 [iii]
	1973	1965-73 [iii]		1993	1985-93
	1979	1970-79 [iii]	-selon l'importance des localités et le sexe	1948	Dernière
	1983	1974-83		1952	Dernière
	1988	1980-88 [iii]		1955	1945-54
	1993	1985-93		1962	1955-62
-selon l'état matrimonial, l'âge et le sexe (voir également: Population mariée et célibataire)	1948	Dernière		1963	1955-63 [iii]
	1949/50	1926-48		1971	1962-71
	1955	1945-54		1973	1965-73 [iii]
	1958	1945-57		1979	1970-79 [iii]
	1962	1955-62		1983	1974-83
	1963	1955-63 [iii]		1988	1980-88 [iii]
	1965	1955-65		1993	1985-93
	1968	1955-67	-selon la langue et le sexe	1956	1945-55
	1971	1962-71		1963	1955-63
	1973	1965-73 [iii]		1964	1955-64 [iii]
	1976	1966-75		1971	1962-71
	1978 SR [i]	1948-77		1973	1965-73 [iii]
	1982	1972-81		1979	1970-79 [iii]
	1987	1975-86		1983	1974-83
	1990	1980-89		1988	1980-88 [iii]
	1997SR [ii]	1948-96		1993	1985-93
répartition en pourcentage	1948	Dernière	-selon le niveau d'instruction, l'âge et le sexe	1956	1945-55
-selon le type de ménage et la résidence urbaine/rurale	1987	1975-86		1963	1955-63
	1995	1985-95		1964	1955-64 [iii]
-selon l'importance des localités:				1971	1962-71
de 100 000 habitants et plus	1948	Dernière		1973	1965-73 [iii]
	1952	Dernière		1979	1970-79 [iii]
	1955	1945-54		1983	1974-83
	1960	1920-61		1988	1980-88 [iii]
	1962	1955-62		1993	1985-93
	1963	1955-63 [iii]	-selon le pays ou zone de naissance et le sexe	1956	1945-55
	1970	1950-70		1963	1955-63
	1971	1962-71		1964	1955-64 [iii]
	1973	1965-73 [iii]		1971	1962-71
	1979	1970-79 [iii]		1973	1965-73 [iii]
	1983	1974-83	-selon le pays ou zone de naissance et le sexe et l'âge	1977	Dernière
	1988	1980-88 [iii]		1983	1974-83
	1993	1985-93		1989	1980-88
de 20 000 habitants et plus	1948	Dernière	-selon la nationalité juridique et le sexe	1956	1945-55
	1952	Dernière		1963	1955-63
	1955	1945-54		1964	1955-64 [iii]
	1960	1920-61		1971	1962-71
	1962	1955-62		1973	1965-73 [iii]
	1963	1955-63 [iii]	-selon la nationalité juridique et le sexe et l'âge	1977	Dernière
	1970	1950-70		1983	1974-83
	1971	1962-71		1989	1980-88
	1973	1965-73 [iii]	-selon les principales divisions administratives		

Index
Index historique (suite)
(Voir notes à la fin de l'index)

Sujet	Année de l'édition	Période considérée	Sujet	Année de l'édition	Période considérée
(voir: des principales divisions administratives, ci-dessus)			-urbaine/rurale (résidence)	1968	1964-68
				1969	1965-69
-selon la religion et le sexe	1956	1945-55		1970	1950-70
	1963	1955-63		1971	1962-71
	1964	1955-64 [iii]		1972	1968-72
	1971	1962-71		1973	1965-73
	1973	1965-73 [iii]		1974	1966-74
	1979	1970-79 [iii]		1975	1967-75
	1983	1974-83		1976	1967-76
	1988	1980-88 [iii]		1977	1968-77
	1993	1985-93		1978	1969-78
-selon la résidence (urbaine/rurale) (voir: urbaine/rurale (résidence), ci-dessous)				1979	1970-79
				1980	1971-80
				1981	1972-81
-selon le sexe (voir: également: par année d'âge et par sexe, et aussi par groupes d'âge et par sexe, ci-dessus):				1982	1973-82
				1983	1974-83
				1984	1975-84
				1985	1976-85
				1986	1977-86
				1987	1978-87
dénombrée	1948-1952	Dernière		1988	1979-88
	1953	1950-52		1989	1980-89
	1954-1959	Dernière		1990	1981-90
	1960	1900-61		1991	1982-91
	1961	Dernière		1992	1983-92
	1962	1900-62		1993	1984-93
	1963	1955-63		1994	1985-94
	1964	1955-64		1995	1986-95
	1965-1969	Dernière		1996	1987-96
	1970	1950-70		1997	1988-97
	1971	1962-71		1998	1989-98
	1972	Dernière		1999	1990-99
	1973	1965-73		2000	1991-00
	1974-1978	Dernière		2001	1992-01
	1978SR [i]	1948-78		2002	1993-02
	1979-1982	Dernière		2003	1994-03
	1983	1974-83	féminine: selon le nombre total d'enfants nés vivants et l'âge		
	1984-1991	Dernière		1971	1962-71
	1991 VP [v]	1950-90		1973	1965-73 [iii]
	1992-1997	Dernière		1975	1965-74
	1997SR [ii]	1948-97		1978SR [i]	1948-77
	1998-2003	Dernière		1981	1972-80
estimée	1948-			1986	1977-85
	1949/50	1945 et Dernière		1997SR [ii]	1948-96
	1951-1954	Dernière [iii]	féminine: selon le nombre total d'enfants vivants et l'âge		
	1955-1959	Dernière		1971	1962-71
	1960	1940-60		1973	1965-73 [iii]
	1961-1969	Dernière		1975	1965-74
	1970	1950-70		1978SR [i]	1948-77
	1971	1962-71		1981	1972-80
	1972	Dernière		1986	1977-85
	1973	1965-73		1997SR [ii]	1948-96
	1974-1997	Dernière	fréquentant l'école selon l'âge et le sexe		
	1997SR [ii]	1948-97		1971	1962-71
	1998-2003	Dernière		1973	1965-73 [iii]

809

Index
Index historique (suite)
(Voir notes à la fin de l'index)

Sujet	Année de l'édition	Période considérée	Sujet	Année de l'édition	Période considérée
	1979	1970-79 [iii]		1993	1985-93
	1983	1974-83	selon la nationalité juridique et le sexe	1971	1962-71
	1988	1980-88 [iii]		1973	1965-73 [iii]
	1988	1980-88 [iii]	selon la nationalité juridique et le sexe et l'âge	1977	Dernière
	1993	1985-93		1983	1974-83
par année d'âge et par sexe	1971	1962-71		1989	1980-88
	1973	1965-73 [iii]	selon le niveau d'instruction, l'âge et le sexe	1971	1962-71
	1979	1970-79 [iii]		1973	1965-73 [iii]
	1983	1974-83		1979	1970-79 [iii]
	1993	1985-93		1983	1974-83
selon la situation familiale	1991 VP [v]	Dernière		1988	1980-88 [iii]
selon l'âge et le sexe: dénombrée	1963	1955-63		1993	1985-93
	1964	1955-64 [iii]	selon le pays ou zone de naissance et le sexe	1971	1962-71
	1967	Dernière		1973	1965-73 [iii]
	1970	1950-70	selon le pays ou zone de naissance et le sexe et l'âge	1977	Dernière
	1971	1962-71		1983	1974-83
	1972	Dernière		1989	1980-88
	1973	1965-73	selon les principales divisions administratives	1971	1962-71
	1974-1978	Dernière		1973	1965-73 [iii]
	1978SR [i]	1948-77		1979	1970-79 [iii]
	1979-1991	Dernière		1983	1974-83
	1991VP [v]	1950-90		1988	1980-88 [iii]
	1992-1997	Dernière		1993	1985-93
	1997SR [ii]	1948-97	selon la religion et le sexe	1971	1962-71
	1998-2003	Dernière		1973	1965-73 [iii]
selon l'âge et le sexe: estimée	1963	Dernière		1979	1970-79 [iii]
	1967	Dernière		1983	1974-83
	1970	1950-70		1988	1980-88 [iii]
	1971-1997	Dernière		1993	1985-93
	1997SR [ii]	1948-97	selon le sexe: nombres	1948	Dernière
	1998-1999	Dernière		1952	1900-51
selon l'alphabétisme, l'âge et le sexe	1971	1962-71		1955	1945-54
	1973	1965-73 [iii]		1960	1920-60
	1979	1970-79 [iii]		1962	1955-62
	1983	1974-83		1963	1955-63
	1988	1980-88 [iii]		1964	1955-64 [iii]
	1993	1985-93		1967	Dernière
selon la composition ethnique et le sexe	1971	1962-71		1970	1950-70
	1973	1965-73 [iii]		1971	1962-71
	1979	1970-79 [iii]		1972	Dernière
	1983	1974-83		1973	1965-73
	1988	1980-88 [iii]		1974	1966-74
	1993	1985-93		1975	1967-75
	1971	1962-71		1976	1967-76
selon l'état matrimonial, l'âge et le sexe	1971	1962-71		1977	1968-77
	1973	1965-73 [iii]		1978	1969-78
selon la langue et le sexe	1971	1962-71			
	1973	1965-73 [iii]			
	1979	1970-79 [iii]			
	1983	1974-83			
	1988	1980-88 [iii]			

Index
Index historique (suite)
(Voir notes à la fin de l'index)

Sujet	Année de l'édition	Période considérée	Sujet	Année de l'édition	Période considérée
	1979	1970-79		1998	1989-98
	1980	1971-80		1999	1990-99
	1981	1972-81		2000	1991-00
	1982	1973-82		2001	1992-01
	1983	1974-83		2002	1993-02
	1984	1975-84		2003	1994-03
	1985	1976-85			
	1986	1977-86	-Vieillissement indicateurs divers	1991 VP [v]	1950-90
	1987	1978-87	-Villes (voir: des villes, ci-dessus)		
	1988	1979-88			
	1989	1980-89	**R**		
	1990	1981-90			
	1991	1982-91	**Rapports** (voir: Fécondité proportionnelle; Mortalité fœtale (tardive), rapports de; Mortalité périnatale, rapports de; Natalité proportionnelle; Rapports enfants-femmes)		
	1992	1983-92			
	1993	1984-93			
	1994	1985-94			
	1995	1986-95			
	1996	1987-96			
	1997	1988-97			
	1998	1989-98	**Rapports enfants-femmes**	1949/50	1900-50
	1999	1990-99		1954	1900-52
	2000	1991-00		1955	1945-54
	2001	1992-01		1959	1935-59
	2002	1993-02		1963	1955-63
	2003	1994-03		1965	1945-65
pourcentage	1948	Dernière		1969	Dernière
	1952	1900-51		1975	1966-74
	1955	1945-54		1978SR [i]	1948-77
	1960	1920-60		1981	1962-80
	1962	1955-62		1986	1967-85
	1970	1950-70		1997SR [ii]	1948-96
	1971	1962-71		1999CD [vii]	1980-1999
	1973	1965-73	-dans les zones (urbaines/rurales)	1965	Dernière
	1974	1966-74		1969	Dernière
	1975	1967-75			
	1976	1967-76	**Réfugiés selon le pays ou zone de destination:**		
	1977	1968-77	-rapatriés par l'Organisation Internationale pour les réfugiés	1952	1947-51
	1978	1969-78			
	1979	1970-79	-réinstallés par l'Organisation Internationale pour les réfugiés	1952	1947-51
	1980	1971-80			
	1981	1972-81			
	1982	1973-82			
	1983	1974-83			
	1984	1975-84			
	1985	1976-85	**Religion** (voir: Population)		
	1986	1977-86			
	1987	1978-87			
	1988	1979-88	**Reproduction, taux bruts et nets de**	1948	1920-47
	1989	1980-89		1949/50	1900-48
	1990	1981-90		1954	1920-53
	1991	1982-91		1965	1930-64
	1992	1983-92		1969	1963-68
	1993	1984-93		1975	1966-74
	1994	1985-94			
	1995	1986-95			
	1996	1987-96			
	1997	1988-97			

Index
Index historique (suite)
(Voir notes à la fin de l'index)

Sujet	Année de l'édition	Période considérée
	1978SR [i]	1948-77
	1981	1962-80
	1986	1967-85
	1997SR [ii]	1948-96
	1999CD [vii]	1980-99

S

Sans abri (voir : Population)

Sexe (voir: la rubrique appropriée par sujet, p. ex., Immigrants; Mortalité, taux de; Naissance; Population, etc.)

Situation dans la profession (voir: Population active)

Sujet spécial des divers Annuaires démographiques:

Sujet	Année de l'édition	Période considérée
-Démographie générale	1948	1900-48
	1953	1850-1953
-Divorce (voir: Mariage et divorce, ci-dessous)		
-Mariage et Divorce	1958	1930-57
	1968	1920-68
	1976	1957-76
	1982	1963-82
	1990	1971-90
-Migration (Internationale)	1977	1958-76
	1989	1975-88
-Mortalité	1951	1905-50
	1957	1930-56
	1961	1945-61
	1966	1920-66
-Mortalité (suite):	1967	1900-67
	1974	1965-74
	1980	1971-80
	1985	1976-85
	1992	1983-92
	1996	1987-96
-Natalité	1949/50	1932-49
	1954	1920-53
	1959	1920-58
	1965	1920-65
	1969	1925-69
	1975	1956-75
	1981	1962-81
	1986	1967-86
	1992	1983-92
	1999CD [vii]	1980-99
-Nuptialité (voir: Mariage et Divorce, ci-dessus)		
-Recensements de population:		
Caractéristiques	1956	1945-55

Sujet	Année de l'édition	Période considérée
économiques		
	1964	1955-64
	1972	1962-72
	1973	1965-73 [iii]
	1979	1970-79 [iii]
	1984	1974-84
	1988	1980-88 [iii]
	1994	1985-94
Caractéristiques ethniques	1956	1945-55
	1963	1955-63
	1964	1955-64 [iii]
	1971	1962-71
	1973	1965-73 [iii]
	1979	1970-79 [iii]
	1983	1974-83
	1988	1980-88 [iii]
	1993	1985-93
Caractéristiques géographiques	1952	1900-51
	1955	1945-54
	1962	1955-62
	1964	1955-64 [iii]
	1971	1962-71
	1973	1965-73 [iii]
	1979	1970-79 [iii]
	1983	1974-83
	1988	1980-88 [iii]
	1993	1985-93
Caractéristiques individuelles	1955	1945-54
	1962	1955-62
	1971	1962-71
	1973	1965-73 [iii]
	1979	1970-79 [iii]
	1983	1974-83
	1988	1980-88 [iii]
	1993	1985-93
Caractéristiques relatives à l'éducation	1955	1945-54
	1956	1945-55
	1963	1955-63 [iii]
	1964	1955-64
	1971	1962-71
	1973	1965-73 [iii]
	1979	1970-79
	1983	1974-83
	1988	1980-88
	1993	1985-93
Caractéristiques relatives aux ménages	1955	1945-54
	1962	1955-62
	1963	1955-63 [iii]
	1971	1962-71
	1973	1965-73 [iii]
	1976	1966-75
	1983	1974-83

Index
Index historique (suite)
(Voir notes à la fin de l'index)

Sujet	Année de l'édition	Période considérée	Sujet	Année de l'édition	Période considérée
	1987	1975-86	**Taux** (voir: Accroissement intercensitaire de la population; Accroissement naturel; Alphabétisme; Analphabétisme; Annulation; Divortialité; Fécondité Intercensitaire; Mortalité Infantile, Mortalité maternelle; Mortalité néonatale; Mortalité post-néonatale; Mortalité, tables de; Mortalité; Natalité; Nuptialité; Reproduction; taux bruts et nets de)		
	1995	1985-95			
Caractéristiques relatives à la fécondité	1949/50	1900-50			
	1954	1900-53			
	1955	1945-54			
	1959	1935-59			
	1963	1955-63			
	1965	1955-65			
	1969	Dernière			
	1971	1962-71			
	1973	1965-73 [iii]			
	1975	1965-75			
	1981	1972-81			
	1986	1977-86			
	1992	1983-92			
	1999CD [vii]	1980-99	**Taux bruts de reproduction** (voir: Reproduction)		
-Evolution de la population	1960	1920-60			
	1970	1950-70			
-Supplément historique	1978SR [i]	1948-78	**Taux nets de reproduction** (voir: Reproduction)		
	1997SR [ii]	1948-97			
Superficie			**Texte spécial** (voir liste détaillée dans l'Appendice de cet index)		
-des continents	1949/50-1992-2003	Dernière			
-des grandes régions(continentales)	1964-2003	Dernière			
-des pays ou zones	1948-2003	Dernière			
-des régions	1952-2003	Dernière	**Urbaine/rurale (décès)** (voir: Décès)		
-du monde	1949/50-2003	Dernière			
-Vieillissement de la population et situation des personnes âgées	1991VP [v]	1950-90	**Urbaine/rurale (ménages: dimension moyenne des)** (voir: Ménages)		

Survivants (voir: Mortalité, tables de)

Tables de mortalité (voir: Mortalité, tables de)

U

Urbaine/rurale (décès) (voir: Décès)

Urbaine/rurale (ménages: dimension moyenne des) (voir: Ménages)

Urbaine/rurale (mortalité infantile) (voir: Mortalité infantile)

Urbaine/rurale(naissances) (voir: Naissances)

Urbaine/rurale(population) (voir: Population selon la résidence (urbaine/rurale))

V

Vieillissement (voir: Population)

Villes (voir: Population)

Index
Index historique (suite)
(Voir notes à la fin de l'index)

APPENDICE

Texte spécial de chaque Annuaire démographique

Divorce:

"Application des statistiques de la nuptialité et de la divortialité", 1958.

Mariage:

"Application des statistiques de la nuptialité et de la divortialité", 1958.

Ménages:

"Concepts et définitions des ménages, du chef de ménage et de la population des collectivités", 1987.

Migration:

"'Statistiques des migrations internationales",1977.

Mortalité:

"Tendances récentes de la mortalité", 1951.
"Développement des statistiques des causes de décès",1951.
"Les facteurs du fléchissement de la mortalité",1957.
"Notes sur les méthodes d'évaluation de la fiabilité des statistiques classiques de la mortalité",1961.
"Mortalité: Tendances récentes",1966.
"Tendances de la mortalité chez les personnes âgées",1991VP [v].

Natalité:

"Présentation graphiques des tendances de la fécondité",1959.

"Taux de natalité: Tendances récentes",1965.

Population:

"Tendances démo-graphiques mondiales,1920-1949",1949/50.
"Mouvements d'urbanisation et ses caractéristiques",1952.
"Les recensements de population de 1950",1955.
"Situation démographique mondiale",1956.
"Ce que nous savons de l'état et de l'évolution de la population mondiale",1960.
"Notes sur les statistiques disponibles des recensements nationaux de population et méthodes d'évaluation de leur exactitude",1962.
"Disponibilité et qualité de certaines données statistiques fondées sur les recensements de population effectués entre 1955 et 1963",1963.
"Disponibilité de certaines statistiques fondées sur les recensements de population: 1955-1964",1964.
"Définitions et concepts statistiques de la population urbaine et de la population rurale",1967.
"Application des statistiques de la nuptialité et de la divortialité",1958.
"Ce que nous savons de l'état et de l'évolution de la population mondiale",1970.
"Recommandations de l'Organisation des Nations Unies quant aux sujets sur lesquels doit porter un recensement de population, en regard de la pratique adoptée par les différents pays dans les recensements nationaux effectués de 1965 à 1971",1971.
"Les définitions statistiques de la population urbaine et leurs usages en démographie appliquée",1972.
"Evolution récente de la fécondité dans le monde",1969.
"Dates des recensements nationaux de la population et de l'habitation effectués au cours de la décennie 1965-1974", 1974.
"Dates des recensements nationaux de la population et de l'habitation effectués ou prévus, au cours de la décennie 1975-1984",1979.
"Dates des recensements nationaux de la population et/ou de l'habitation effectués au cours de la décennie 1965-1974 et effectués ou prévus au cours de la décennie1975-1984",1983.
"Définitions et concepts statistiques du ménage",1968.
"Dates des recensements nationaux de la population et/ou de l'habitation effectués au cours de la décennie 1975-1984 et effectués ou prévus au cours de la décennie1985-1994", 1988, 1993.
"Statistiques concernant la population active: un aperçu",1984.

Index
Index historique (suite)
(Voir notes à la fin de l'index)

'"Etude du vieillissement et de la situation des personnes âgées: Besoins particuliers",1991VP [v].
"Les incapacités", 1991VP [v].
"Le vieillissement", 1991VP [v].

Notes générales

Cet index alphabétique donne la liste des sujets traités dans chacune de 51 éditions de l'Annuaire démographique. La colonne "Année de l'édition" indique l'édition spécifique dans laquelle le sujet a été traité. Sauf indication contraire, la colonne "Période considérée" désigne les années pour lesquelles les statistiques annuelles apparaissent dans l'Annuaire démographique sont indiquées sous la colonne "Année de l'édition". La rubrique "Dernière" ou " 2-Dernières" indique que les données représentent la ou les dernières années disponibles seulement.

---

[i] Le Supplément rétrospectif du 30ème Annuaire Démographique fait l'objet d'un tirage spécial publié en 1979.

[ii] Le Supplément rétrospectif du 49ème Annuaire Démographique fait l'objet d'un tirage spécial (CD-ROM) publié en 2000

[iii] Données non disponibles dans l'édition précédente seulement.

[iv] Titres non disponibles dans la bibliographie précédente seulement.

[v] Taux moyens pour 5 ans.

[vi] Vieillissement de la population.

[vii] Le Supplément du 51 Annuaire Démographique, ayant comme suject la natalité, fait l'objet d'un tirage spécial (CD-ROM) publié en 2002.

Litho in United Nations, New York   ISSN 0082-8041   United Nations publication
05-66371—June 2006—3,740   Sales No. E/F.06.XIII.1
ISBN 92-1-051097-6   ST/ESA/STAT/SER.R/34